# The
# Interlinear

## HEBREW/GREEK
## ENGLISH

## Bible

*Four Volume Edition*

*Volume Four*

**(The New Testament)**

# The
# Interlinear
## HEBREW/GREEK
## ENGLISH
# Bible

*Four Volume Edition*

*Volume Four*

(The New Testament)

**Jay Green,**

**general editor and translator**

ASSOCIATED PUBLISHERS AND AUTHORS
LAFAYETTE, INDIANA 47903

## 1979

The King James II Version,
Fourth Edition
Copyright © 1979,
by Jay P. Green, Sr.

The Interlinear-Hebrew Greek-English Bible,
Volume Four (The New Testament)
Copyright © 1979 by Jay P. Green, Sr.
All Rights Reserved

*Four-volume set*
*ISBN: 0934-774-01-3*

*The Interlinear New Testament*
*(Volume IV only)*
*ISBN: 0934-774-06-4*

*The King James II Version*
*ISBN: 0934-774-35-8*

Published by Associated Publishers & Authors, Inc.
Lafayette, Indiana 47903

The Greek Text in this volume used by
permission of the copyright holder
© Copyright 1976, by
THE TRINITARIAN BIBLE SOCIETY
London, England

Printed in the United States of America

# CONTENTS

# ACKNOWLEDGMENTS

With thanksgiving, we acknowledge the immeasurable value of the work performed by our fellow-laborer, Rev. Maurice Robinson, who perused and offered suggestions on more than half these pages. We also are thankful to all the others who worked on various portions, giving many good suggestions for the improvement of the translations.

*"Every Scripture (is) God-breathed, and (is) profitable for teaching, for reproof, for correction, for instruction in righteousness; so that the man of God may be fitted out, having been fully furnished for every good work."—2 Timothy 3:16.*

You now have in your hand the fourth and final volume of *The Interlinear Hebrew-Greek-English Bible*, which is presented to you and to all the Christian community with much exultation, tempered by fear and trembling and awe toward our almighty God and Savior, Jesus Christ.

It is hoped that you will discern that we have fully believed all the words of this holy Book, handling it with reverence, knowing that *"Man shall not live by bread alone, but by every word that proceeds out of the mouth of God"*—Matt. 4:4; also recognizing that these words did not come *"by the will of man, but men spoke from God, being borne along by (the) Holy Spirit."*—2 Peter 1:21. It also has been written that each of the sons of men shall be judged by the words of this Book, *"And if anyone hears My words, and does not believe, I do not judge him . . . the word which I spoke is that which will judge him in the last day."*—John 12:47,48. And the words of this Book being the ones that will judge every person having lived in all the ages, how important it must be that the very words of God, and no other, shall be contained in a portable book, to be distributed far and wide, in a form and in a commonly understood language easily and immediately taken into the heart and into the consciousness of all who have the privilege to read them. With these considerations in mind, and in holy fear inculcated by our God, we have sought to provide in *The Interlinear Hebrew-Greek-English Bible* all the original God-breathed Hebrew, Aramaic, and Greek words. And after much prayer and laborious study, it was concluded that this could best be done by providing you with the two attested texts that alone have been uniquely preserved whole, and accepted in all generations, in all lands, by the vast majority of God's people as their 'received texts.' Other texts have been put forth from time to time, usually by those scholars yearning to be the magi of their age, but none have been powerful enough to displace these two texts: The Masoretic Text of the Old Testament, and the Received Text of the New Testament. These remain in the hearts of the majority of God's people.

## WHY ANOTHER INTERLINEAR IS NEEDED IN OUR PRESENT AGE

The market-place is being glutted with 'new' books which are being represented as 'versions' of the Bible. Each one claims that this is the very word of God, yet there are literally thousands of differences between them — and such differences that one must conclude there is much disagreement as which Greek words are to be translated, or paraphrased. But in one way new 'versions' seem to agree: they all leave out dozens of references to the deity of Jesus Christ, and they insert words which call into question His virgin birth, His substitutionary, fully satisfying atonement. This is due to their dependence on an Alexandrian textbase, instead of that body of God's words which has been universally received and believed for nineteen centuries, known to us as the Received Text. And, admittedly, the words they virtually all leave out of their 'versions' of the Bible comprise at least four whole pages of words, phrases, sentences, and verses that have been attested as God's words by overwhelming evidence contained in all the Greek manuscripts, in the ancient versions, in the writings of the early fathers. And these from every inhabited land on the earth where Christianity has been.

Therefore we conclude that another interlineary New Testament is needed, that those who love every word of God, and who live by every word of God, may be able to compare the versions to the original Greek, and to know if any of the words of God are being withheld from their hearts. Then they will know that it is important to their spiritual life to be reading the right 'version' of the Bible.

Therefore, again, the question should be posed: Has Satan, like a sleight-of-hand shell-game artist, finally brought us to the point where we are searching desperately for the true Word of God? Are we to believe that it cannot now be intact, having been run through the shredder of unholy hands and heads? Let it not be said! Let your answer be a resounding, crashing NO!

For it is written, *"For I say to you, Until the heavens and the earth pass away, in no way shall pass away one iota or one point from the Law, until all things come to pass."*—Matt. 5:18. The Lord Jesus said it here, and in Matt. 24:35, in Mark 13:31, and in Luke 21:33. Who then will you believe? If our almighty God assures us that not even an iota, or a point, of His word shall pass away, then an important word, or phrase, or sentence, or verse surely cannot be lost! But still, version after version after version is pouring off the presses without page after page of those words which have always been held to be the words of God. Who then are these men who tell us these are not God's words? And what company do they keep? And what evidence do they present to you to persuade you to give up these historically accepted, venerable words that have stood the test of time, and this despite the onslaughts of emperors, heathen hordes, philosophers, popes, and fleshly inducements? And what is the nature of the words they are so determined to leave out of your Bible? Lastly, how did these words come to be questioned in the first place? What is behind these omissions?

A cardinal rule for the Bible reader should be: *"Let God be true, and every man a liar"*—Romans 3:4. The Lord Jesus did not trust Himself to men, and not a one of us should do so. Instead, let the reader put his faith in God, for it is only by faith that the Word of God can be apprehended. If one puts on the whole armor of God, then he may *"stand against the wiliness of the Devil,"* and *"be able to resist in the evil day, and having worked out all things, to stand,"* by girding the loins with truth, by putting on the breastplace of righteousness, and shoeing the feet with the preparation of the gospel; and above all, taking up the shield of faith, by which one is able to quench the darts of the Evil One. (See Ephesians 6:11-18).

Being thus armed with faith toward God, depending on Him to verify the words which are truly His words, and at the same time armed with a healthy suspicion of men, one can then ask, Who are these men who are saying to us, This or that word, or phrase, or verse does not belong in our Bible? Are they learned men, scholars? Should we not allow their scholarly minds to guide us as to what words we are to believe? No! For several reasons: (1) God tells us that the Holy Spirit is the Author of the Scriptures, and that this same God the Spirit will be our guide, *"And we have not received the spirit of the world, but the Spirit from God, that we may know the things freely given to us by God; which things we also speak, not in words taught of human wisdom, but in (words) taught of (the) Holy Spirit."*—1 Cor. 2:12,13. *"But the Paraclete, the Holy Spirit which the Father will send in My name, that One will teach you all things, and remind you (of) all things which I said to you."*—John 14:26. *"But when that One, the Spirit of truth comes, He will guide you into all the truth."*—John 16:13. (2) These men associate with, and accommodate themselves to, unbelievers, *"Do not become unequally yoked (with) unbelievers; for what partnership (have) righteousness and lawlessness? Or what part a believer with an unbeliever?"*—2 Cor. 6:14,15. Look through the list of translators of your modern versions. Are they all men trusting to Christ Jesus as their God and Savior? Not at all. There will be a Jew usually. A Jew does not trust in Christ, nor does He believe that the New Testament is true Scripture. Can a Jew be trusted to handle the words of Christ, when he believes Christ to be a false Messiah? There will be one or more Unitarians. A Unitarian is committed to prove that Jesus Christ is not God. Will you allow such a one to tell us that when he deletes *"Son of God"* from Mark 1:1, and when he adds *"only-begotten God"* to John 1:18, he is not following his purpose to make Jesus to be a begotten creature, and not an equal Person eternally in the Godhead? Some will not believe in the virgin birth. Prof. Grant of the RSV translation committee stood before an audience and said that not a single one of those translators believed in the virgin birth of Christ. Most will not believe that the Scriptures are without error. This allows them to take out, or to thrust in, words that suit their purposes. In the new NIV 'version' there are more than eight pages of Scriptures which they have done away with. (3) What is the evidence they give to persuade you to give up these precious words? They cite two manuscripts, admittedly old, but also admittedly carelessly executed. The Sinaiticus has up to seven different 'textual critics' who have changed it again, and again, and again, twisting it like a nose of wax to meet their purposes. It is no wonder it was discarded, found in a wastebasket fourteen centuries after it was executed. The Vaticanus lay on a shelf in the Vatican library at Rome until 1431, so corrupt that no one had any use for it. It has errors so absurd that the books on textual 'science' carefully avoid mentioning them to students. They add to these a handful of other manuscripts from the Alexandrian textbase, all of them very loose in their handling of the Scriptures. Then they give you their theories, their hypotheses, their glosses. Every year dozens of these are destroyed.

(4) But let them be known by their fruits. What are these words which they have so freely removed from the Scriptures as they are represented in thousands of Greek manuscripts and lectionaries? Here are a few examples: (a) They have made Joseph to be the father of Jesus (check Luke 2:33); (b) they have made Jesus to be but a begotten creature (John 1:18); (c) they have deleted *"Son of God"* from Mark 1:1; preferring to call Jesus the Son of man; (d) in fact, they have removed from their 'versions' Christ, or Jesus, or Christ Jesus, or Christ as God, twenty-five or more times; then, (e) in 1 Cor. 5:7, they have Christ suffering, but not *"for us;"* (f) in 1 Peter 4:1, they have Christ sacrificed, but not *"for us;"* (g) in Luke 24:3,6,12,36,40,51,52, they have systematically removed Luke's witness to the ascension of Christ—and, of course, they have done away entirely with Mark's witness to the ascension, simply because these twelve verses do not appear in those two corrupt manuscripts, the Vaticanus and the Sinaiticus (yet the Vaticanus has a space where these twelve verses belong, exactly big enough to accommodate them—how did the scribe know how much space to leave, if the older manuscript from which he copied did not have these twelve verses?)

You can see that the words they are taking away from us are very important words. Why then should we give them up without overwhelming evidence?

The fact is, history is repeating itself again. In the beginning, it was the old Serpent, Satan, who tried his hand at textual criticism. Successfully, he insinuated into the itching ear of Eve, *"You shall not surely die . . , you shall be as God"* (Gen. 3:1-5) From that point on, men have preferred to believe the lie, if the lie suited their fancy better than the Scripture. Like Origen, an early textual critic, many men believe that "The Scriptures are of little use to those who understand them as they are written" (quoted by McClintock & Strong Cyclopedia, article on Origen). And given the opportunity, many like Origen will actually alter the manuscripts to make them say what they understand them to mean.

Such things were done as soon as the Word of God was complete. Remember, the apostles, Paul, Peter, and John all warned that corrupters of the word were already plying their trade within the churches. For example, God warned His children through Paul, *"I am amazed that you are quickly being transported away from Him who has called you by (the) grace of Christ, to a different gospel, which is not another, except there are some troubling you and desiring to pervert the gospel of Christ."*—Gal. 1:6,7. And through John, He tells us, *"For many false prophets have gone out into the world."*—1 John 4:1. And through Peter, we learn that perverters of Scripture were already rampant in Christian circles, *"even as our beloved brother Paul wrote to you, according to the wisdom given to him . . . among which things are some things hard to understand, which the ignorant and unsettled ones pervert, as also the other Scriptures, to their own destruction."*—2 Peter 3:15,16.

By these Scriptures and others, we see that the apostles were not yet in the bosom of Abraham before the Bible-tinkerers began to distort and adulterate the word of God. By the time John died, gnosticism had gotten a toehold in many Christian churches. And quickly thereafter they expanded their poisonous influence at a rapid pace. Justin Martyr, Valentinus, Clement of Alexandria, Marcion, Tatian, and a horde of other 'textual critics' operated on manuscripts, or wrote their own. To this we have many testimonies, such as this one, "The worst corruptions to which the New Testament has ever been subjected originated within a hundred years after it was composed; that Ireneus (A.D. 150), and the African Fathers, and the whole Western, . . . used far inferior manuscripts to those employed by Stunica, or Erasmus, or Stephens thirteen centuries later, when moulding the Textus Receptus."—Scrivener, Introduction to N.T. third edition, p.511. And Eusebius quotes a second century father as writing : "Wherefore, they have not feared to lay hands on the divine Scriptures under pretence of correcting them . . . As for their denying their guilt, the thing is impossible, since the copies were written in their own hand; and they did not receive the Scriptures in this condition from their teachers, nor can they show the originals from which they made their copies."—Eusebius, H.E., LCS, vol. 1, pp. 522-524. And even Origen condemned Marcion and Lucian for altering the Scriptures, though he himself can be shown to have quoted the same verse of Scripture in two contradictory wordings in many places. He molded the Scriptures according to his Platonian philosophy, or the allegory of the day, or his fancy, having no twinge of conscience for doing so. It is to this Origen, considered by his pupils Jerome and Eusebius to be the master textual critic, that we owe so many of the invidious deletions from our modern 'versions.' Do we see the Godhood of Jesus being quietly removed from these modern 'versions'? Origen believed that Jesus Christ was a created being, and by his reputation and his influence on his pupils, the Latin Vulgate, the ornate manuscripts made for the libraries of his day, and our latter-day attackers of the Majority Text, we who love every word that proceeded from the mouth of God are asked to do without a host of testimonies to the Godhead of our Lord and Savior, Jesus Christ. For example, in the current Nestle Greek Text, as presented in Marshall's Interlinear New Testament, in Matthew 24:36, the Godhead of Jesus is flatly denied, by adding these words, *"nor the Son"* thereby making the holy Scriptures say that the Son did not know the day and the hour of the demise of the earth. Also, in Mark 1:1, the Son of God is omitted; in Luke 23:42, Lord is changed to read Jesus; in John 3:13, *"who is in Heaven"* is omitted, because it makes the Son to be in Heaven at the same time that He is on earth—in other words, that God the Son was omnipresent at the same time He was in the body on earth. Since this stumbled some early 'textual critic,' he simply erased those four words of testimony to the omnipresence of God the Son. And to this day, all the later 'versions' continue to deny this attribute of omnipresence to God the Son, either by omitting *"who is in Heaven,"* or by putting down "whose home is in Heaven," a reading that does not appear in any Greek manuscript—it is a fraud to cover up the theft of those four words testifying that Jesus was omnipresent God even while He was here in the body. Of the twenty best-selling New Testaments of our age, only the KJV, the KJV II, and the New KJB retain this most important testimony to the co-equal Godhood of our Lord Jesus. In John 9:35, the Son of God is changed to read "Son of man." In the first centuries it was Satan's shrewd strategy to deny Godhood to Jesus Christ, and he employed his minions as 'textual critics,' as a means of deleting from the Scriptures their testimony to it. This is recognized by many of our modern critics, one (Colwell) stating flatly that most of the variations in the various manuscripts were introduced during the first two centuries, and that words were deliberately added or deleted in order to make the Scriptures conform to the beliefs of those doing this dastardly work. The amazing thing, though, is this, that though the vast majority of existing manuscripts, and the witness of ancient versions and fathers, too, give a massive testimony to the authenticity of those omitted Scriptures, yet our 'textual critics' today continue to pretend that there is not sufficient reason to print these doctrinally important words of God in their 'versions' of God's Word.

## THE PROVIDENTIAL PRESERVATION OF THE TEXT

We believe wholeheartedly that God has preserved His word, that He guided His true followers to carefully copy, and to use the whole Bible, as is represented in the majority of the extant manuscripts. We believe that He did this in the same way He guarded the Canon of the New Testament, using the Greek Orthodox Church and the Greek manuscripts used by the churches in all the outlying lands, to safeguard the deposit which He had given to us. It took the churches two centuries to form and defend the Canon, the sixty-six books of the Bible as we now have them, and it took them another century and a half to finally discard those manuscripts with spurious additions, and with serious omissions. All modern-day critics will admit that the text as essentially displayed in the majority of the extant manuscripts has been virtually identical in copy after copy for the period from the fourth century until the invention of the printing press. In other words, the Received Text was so widely and so completely accepted in all countries, and in all denominations except the Roman Catholic, that Westcott and Hort had to invent a mythical council of church fathers, who supposedly met and fixed the text as we now know it—an event completely unknown to historians, and otherwise totally undemonstrable.

The fact is, God in His mercy did not leave His people to grope after the true New Testament text. Through the leading of the Holy Spirit, He guided them to preserve it during the manuscript period. God brought this to pass through the working of His preserving and governing providence. First, many trustworthy copies were produced by faithful scribes. Second, these were read, used, and re-copied by true believers through the centuries. Third, untrustworthy copies (such as the Vaticanus and the Sinaiticus) were laid aside and consigned to oblivion. There are 5,000+ manuscripts and lectionaries as Greek witnesses to the New Testament text, and 95% of them witness to the Received Text readings.

So it is evident that all the trustworthy manuscripts were being worn out by use, and were discarded when a faithful copy had been made from them. But the untrustworthy ones were not used, and thus were preserved to this day. In the dry regions, such as in Egypt, these were better preserved, not rotting away —thus we have these Alexandrian manuscripts appearing, bearing the aberrations of the Alexandrian school of textual criticism—and the careless, sleepy-eyed, blatant errors in all of them should cause a recognition of their spurious value.

For centuries now, some have pretended the Received Text is not ancient. Now that manuscripts from the second century are being unearthed, and many of those readings of the Received Text which had been tagged scornfully as 'late readings' by unanimous consent of those same textual 'scientists' that are now a self-appointed jury to abolish from our Bible pages and pages—those same readings before called 'late,' and 'spurious,' are being found in all these early-date manuscripts (e.g. the Chester Beatty Papyri contained 65 readings which had been before rejected by our critics; and Papyrus Bodmer II, of the second century, actually contains 13% of all the so-called 'late readings' of the despised Majority Text.) Day by day we see the conjectures of these so-called experts being swept away in a moment, along with their hypotheses and their 'versions.' Should we then allow them to succeed in stealing away the words of God from us, on a pretence that they know which are and which are not the words of God? They are blind leaders of the blind, and those putting their trust in them will wind up in the ditch, being chastised by God for not putting trust in God the Spirit. Remember that it is written, *"You shall not add to the word which I (am) commanding you, and not take away from it"*—Deut. 4:2; and, *"Do not add to His words, lest He reprove you, and you be found a liar"*—Prov. 30:6; and, *"If anyone take away from the words of (the) Book of this Prophecy, God will take away his part from (the) Book of Life."*—Rev. 22:19. Do not be misled by an appeal to your logic. Try the spirits, whether they are of God.

## THE GREEK TEXT IN THIS VOLUME

The Greek text herein is purportedly that which directly underlies the KJV, as reconstructed by F. H. A. Scrivener in 1894. It thus differs to a degree from all previously printed editions of the Received Text (e.g. there are over 250 differences—most of them quite minor— between this text and the Stephens 1550 "standard" *Textus Receptus*.) The present text was typeset in England for the Trinitarian Bible Society by Stephen Austin and Sons, and corresponds to "The New Testament in the Original Greek according to the text followed in the Authorized Version," edited by F. H. A. Scrivener, and originally published by Cambridge University Press in 1894 and 1902. The present Trinitarian Bible Society edition was first printed in 1976.

Careful study, however, will show that this present text does not agree 100% with the text used by the KJV translators (though it virtually always does so do). In places it has a differing reading than that found in the KJV (e.g. Mt. 12:24,27, Gk. *Beelzeboul,* KJV "Beelzebub;" John 8:21, Gk. sin, KJV "sins;" John 10:16, Gk. "one flock," KJV "one fold;" 1 Cor. 14:10, KJV "of these" omitted in Gk.; 1 Cor. 16:1, KJV "churches," Gk. "church::–this with no MSS support at all!) In other places, the present text gives Greek words where the KJV translators indicate they had none, using italic type (e.g. the following KJV italicised words are actually given in the Greek of this TBS edition: Mk. 8:14, *the disciples;* Mk. 9:42, *these;* John 8:6, *as though he heard them not*; Acts 1:4, *them;* 1 Jn. 3:16, *of God.* Some of these readings do have minority MSS support, but it seems clear that these readings were not in the text chosen to underlie the KJV. Nevertheless, to all intents and purposes the TBS edition faithfully reproduces the KJV Greek text, as nearly as could be done at this date.

Although we admit to the knowledge that Erasmus has added to this Text a handful of readings from the Latin Vulgate, two or three without Greek manuscript authority (e.g. Acts 9:5,6), and one from the Complutension Bible (e.g. 1 John 5:7), we have not deleted these from the Greek text as supplied by the Trinitarian Bible Society—though we do not accept them as true Scripture. See the Majority Text Notes in the Appendix as a corrective to such additions.

## THE TRANSLATIONS IN THIS INTERLINEAR NEW TESTAMENT

There are two translations in this volume, one appearing as the literal translation of the Greek words, with English equivalents directly under each of the Greek words, and the other, *The King James II Version*, on the side of the page, in order to provide a straight-forward translation for the purpose of making it easy for the reader to see the proper word order in English, and to assimilate the message given in God's words on that page. Both these translations are accomplished in a word-for-word translation. We have rejected, and thus have studiously avoided, the conceptual idea form of 'translating' the word of God, believing firmly that no person has the right, nor the inspiration, to rewrite God's Word using his own concepts as a guide to what should be written in a 'Bible,' and pass these off as if they originated with God. This can only be a dodge to permit the paraphraser to "be as God," as Satan promised Eve.

We hope that our accomplishment of these literal word-for-word translations will demonstrate that a true word-for-word translation can also be a readable and easily understood representation of God's Word. This has been denied in the past, perhaps as an excuse to vary the word by the paraphrasing in of personal illusions regarding what the word of God ought to say.

## INTERPRETATIONS

In the matter of interpretation, or as some would call it, bias, there is no hesitation on our part to admit to the fact that there are many interpretative decisions that must be made in any translation of the Bible. It has been our determination, backed by constant prayer, to let the text say what it says. And it is our hope, and belief, that we have not inserted a peculiar set of beliefs into the text by way of our translation. Nevertheless, by the very fact that a true translation must take into consideration the entire context of a word, or phrase, or sentence, or verse, interpretation must be present in making that translation—especially in those places where a Greek word may bear several different English words supplied as a true translation of the word itself (not considering the context). It does make a difference whether a person is "cured," or "saved." And conceivably there could be differences of opinion in the choice of an English word to express a Greek word in such cases. If a list of interpretative renditions were to be compiled, we would list these, at least, as present in this volume: (1) We have added punctuation, and, of course, the original manuscripts have none; (2) We also have used capitals and small letters, whereas the originals had only capitals. Especially we have attempted to aid the reader by capitalizing pronouns whenever the pronoun, or a name, is connected to a Person of the Godhead. Here there is undoubtedly room for differences of opinion. And in those places quoted from the Old Testament, the New Testament writers nearly always fix the deity of the persons quoted, therefore these are not so interpretative. But in another class of places, we have endeavored to capitalize, or not to capitalize the pronouns, according to whether or not the persons addressing Jesus acknowledged Him as God. Of course this is highly interpretative. (3) Wherever we added a word or words to inform the reader of the sense, we have been careful in all those places to put the supplied words within parentheses. Therefore, any word within () is not an expression of the actual Greek word.

## PRESUPPOSITIONS

Being a willing slave of our God and Savior, Jesus Christ, and joyfully submitting to His higher thoughts, we gladly admit to a number of presuppositions: (1) We have acted upon the premise that *"the Scriptures cannot be broken,"* meaning that not an iota or a point of them has been lost; with the firm conviction in our minds that each word was God-breathed—therefore, we dared not change a word, or supply a word, or change the word-order, so as to persuade the reader. If God used an ambiguous word, we tried to leave it that way, etc; (2) We have presupposed that Jesus Christ is not only our personal Savior and Lord, but that the Scriptures clearly reveal Him as equal with the Father and the Holy Spirit, one of the three Persons in the Godhead; (3) that He came to earth to give Himself a ransom for many; (4) that He both lived and died as a substitute for the sins of all those who shall come to a saving knowledge and belief in Him;(5) Also that He has risen to sit at the right of God the Father, ruling the world from there, interceding for and providentially guarding and guiding His own, until He destroys the earth by fire, coming to receive all of them at His right hand; (6) And lastly, that He will sit as supreme Judge of all men of all ages, and will use the words of the Bible to judge the deeds of each and every person that inhabited the earth, casting all unbelievers into the Lake of Fire with the Devil.

## SOME TRANSLATIONS THAT ARE DIFFERENT

For easy apprehension, and continuity with the Old Testament, we have translated the Greek representing the names of Old Testament characters and places by the same English names that we have used in the Old Testament translation.

In the application of our principle, to translate each Greek word literally, a number of translations have emerged which are quite different from the usual.

The Greek word designating the mother of Jesus has always been translated as "Mary," but the Greek word actually stands for Mariam (or Miriam); therefore we have so given it. Not that we think we can at this late date change her name in the mind of others from Mary to Mariam; we simply translated literally. It answers to the objection raised, as to whether two Marys were in her family.

In translating the Greek words for "I am" in certain places, we have capitalized these words, viz. I AM (see John 8:59, other places)—because it is our firm conviction that in those cases Jesus is identifying Himself as Jehovah (Jehovah properly translated meaning, I AM THAT I AM.) Jesus is of course the English name assigned to a word which means, Jehovah is salvation; and this same word in Greek would translate the Hebrew word for Joshua. Under the Greek we have translated literally, *"to the ages,"* although we surely believe that the words are a clearcut idiomatic expression for "forever." In the marginal translation, we have reversed this. Likewise, we have translated "clean" heart, and also in other places, where we firmly believe that "pure" could idiomatically be used. There is another difference in this translation, in that we have tried to translate various places in a way that would not be misleading as to sex. Many times other translators have put "any man" where "anyone" was literally the correct translation. Male pronouns abound, and male references abound, in the Bible. There is no good reason that we can see for supplying additional male references.

This is now the only interlineary New Testament in current, proper English—all others continuing to use Elizabethan English. In the past we tried to defend the use of Elizabethan English in the Bible, but a four-year-old girl confounded us with two simple questions: (a) What means that? and, (b) Why? Our studies soon revealed to us that the Bible was written in simple Hebrew and Greek, and there was no special language used when addressing God. The Bible was not intended to be encased in a stilted language of another age, whether it be Latin or Elizabethan English. As Tyndale said, every plowboy should be able to understand it. Otherwise, we may as well leave it in the original languages.

Our constant aim in translation has been to represent the meaning of the Greek words in English as precisely, as accurately, and as exegetically as the English language will allow. This has included an attempt to display the meaning of compound words so that the parts of them are expressed. For example, in John 8:7, Jesus did not merely rise, or stand up; He had bent down, and now He was bending back up — by which words we can visualize exactly what He was doing. We confess that this has been imperfectly accomplished, but in succeeding editions more of this type of accuracy can be achieved.

We have striven for consistency, having noted so much inconsistency in our previous translations (this being our eighth), and in other translations. And we believe that we have achieved more consistency than in others now available. Of course, we were greatly aided by having others before us.

## PROBLEMS AND CHALLENGES TO THE TRANSLATOR

Just as there are difficult places to understand, so there are difficult places to translate. And sometimes the difficulty is not so much in assigning meanings to the Greek words, so much as to punctuate them so as to catch the apostle's meaning. For example, in 1 Cor. 12:2, understanding how the words set up in the Greek-minded apostle is difficult—therefore the expression in English, with the punctuation of it, is difficult. Marshall here dodges the question by suggesting that some scribe made an error in transmitting the text. Since the manuscripts on which he places so much reliance (the Vaticanus and Sinaiticus MSS), are blotched throughout by careless, sloppy errors, he may think nothing of ascribing a difficulty to a 'scribal error;' (see page 689 of his Interlinear NT). But no such errors appear in the Majority Text with regularity, and none can be proven to have been copied from one manuscript to another (The eminent textual critic, Kirsopp Lake, labored long and hard in order to prove that the variations of the Received/Majority Text were due to scribal errors copied from one manuscript to another—yet in the end admitted that not a single instance could be found). As for us, we must insist that the Scriptures teach that they are totally without error. We do not believe that God has allowed His pure, innerrant Deposit to be systematically and progressively adulterated with 'scribal errors.'

As to other problems, we have made many decisions; some, if not all, of which may be challenged. We have in places left a Greek word untranslated, usually a particle or an article, where it was redundant, or otherwise not suitable to English transmission. Where the Greek order of words is difficult, we have not used superior figures, but have depended on the translation in the margin to give the English order. We have for the most part chosen to express each word of an idiomatic phrase where that would be more explanatory than the idiom. This is not consistently done, however. In some places where the present tense in Greek takes an English past for proper English, we have changed to a past tense. In a great many cases we have not done so, depending on the reader to realize that a difference in the two languages exists. This is also true of the aorist. In fact, we believe that the New Testament writers themselves did not use the aorist in the strict (or restricted) way that Greek grammarians interpret it.

Due to space problems, we have not always been able to translate the participle where the English words "having been" are proper, but have many times merely used "being." Also in other places where a Greek word is short, and its English equivalent is long, we have had to substitute (e.g. "by" instead of "through"). In the case of double-negative construction in the Greek, usually we have let it lie as it appears (rather than to change one negative to a positive and thus to make good English out of it). In some cases, we have attempted to show the added strength of the negative, as intended in the Greek, by the use of punctuation.

There are of course many other problems encountered in rendering Greek into English. We respectfully refer the reader to other introductions to the Greek New Testament, especially to those in the other interlineary New Testaments.

## THE APPENDIX: THE MAJORITY TEXT NOTES

Happily, a very live debate is beginning to rage between the adherents to the Alexandrian textbase which underlies most of the modern 'versions,' and those who believe that the Byzantine/Majority textbase is the only true text of the New Testament. Mr. William G. Pierpont, of Wichita, Kansas, has prepared The Majority Text Notes, so that there may be a direct comparison between the Received Text as represented in this volume, and the text as it appears in the majority of the Greek manuscripts. These notes represent years of research, and we are all privileged to be able to share in them in this volume.

By the use of the Majority Text Notes, one can with little difficulty convert the Greek text presented in this volume into that Greek text which appears in the majority of the Greek manuscripts. They clearly show to what small extent the Greek text underlying the KJV varies from the Majority Text of the Greek New Testament. Of the New Testament versions today, only the *King James Version, the King James II Version,* and *the New King James Bible* agree in near total certainty with the text of the majority of the Greek New Testament manuscripts. In the texts underlying all the other versions, there are well over 5,000 differences between this Majority Text and the Alexandrian textbase that they are using in the United Bible Society, Nestle, etc. editions. And a host of these are very serious differences affecting the message God has given to us. But only some 1,500 differences can be shown between the Majority Text and the text underlying the KJV and KJV II versions (these quite minor, too, such as spelling, word order, etc.).

Instructions for using the appendix have been prepared by Mr. Pierpont, and appear at the beginning of the Majority Text Notes in the appendix.

## RESPONSIBILITY FOR THE TRANSLATION

The English translations in this volume, both the literal translations under each Greek word and the translation named, *The King James II Version,* are the work of Jay P. Green, Sr., improved and corrected by the suggestions of others who have reviewed the manuscript pages. Therefore the responsibility for the assignment of English equivalents belongs to Jay P. Green, Sr., since he was the sole judge of what would, or would not, be allowed in either of the English translations. As regards *The King James II Version,* this is the fourth edition of this very well received translation. Each edition has incorporated a host of helpful improvements which have been submitted by men and women from all walks of life. In each edition, an invitation for such suggestions for improvement has been issued. And the results have been very gratifying indeed, with full proof that there are astute students of the Bible in all streams of English-reading Christians, both those who are disciplined scholars, and those who could do no more than to question whether a certain translation could not be improved in a particular way. Many of this second group based their suggestions on what they had gleaned from the study of an interlineary New Testament, or from the study of either *The New Englishman's Greek Concordance,* or, *New Thayer's Greek-English Lexicon to the New Testament,* both of which are from A P & A's very helpful BREAK-THROUGH-THE-LANGUAGE-BARRIER SERIES (in which each volume has been coded with the numbering system from *Strong's Exhaustive Concordance,* thereby enabling those who do not read the original Biblical languages to use the Hebrew and Greek concordances and lexicons).

## An Invitation

An open invitation is hereby issued to the reader to participate in the next edition of *The Interlinear New Testament.* The publishers and the editor recognize that God gives gifts of time, talents, and specialized knowledge to many different individuals. Some of you may very well be able to suggest to us improved renderings of certain portions of the Bible, and your suggestions will be gladly received.

In order to prevent a state of confusion from developing, please follow these rules in submitting your suggestions: (1) Suggestions must be brief. There is no staff to read and to consider long dissertations on the reasoning behind your suggestions; (2) Give relative evidence. Particularly, cite Biblical usage, because we consider that to be more important than etymology alone; also cite authorities, periodicals, or significant monographs; (3) Your suggestion must be on the basis of a word-on-word translation, rather than 'conceptual idea-on-word.' It is not our purpose to re-express, or to restructure, God's word according to our personal concepts, but merely to render each word according to its Biblical meaning; (4) All suggestions must be based on the Received/Majority textbase; (5) Place all suggestions on a separate page—do not include suggestions in the body of a letter dealing with other matters.

Please recognize that there can be no correspondence in regards to these suggestions. Each suggestion will be carefully considered by our review board, but no staff will be set up for the purpose of carrying on correspondence with those interested enough in an accurate rendering of God's Word to make suggestions for an improved edition of *The Interlinear New Testament.*

Please send all suggestions to: The Editor, A P & A, Inc., P. O. Box 4998, Lafayette, Indiana, U.S.A. 47903. Thank you.

JAY P. GREEN, SR.
General Editor

# THE GREEK ALPHABET

The Greek alphabet has twenty-four letters : —

| Form. | | Equivalent. | | Name. |
|---|---|---|---|---|
| Α | α | a | ἄλφα | Alpha |
| Β | β | b | βῆτα | Beta |
| Γ | γ | g | γάμμα | Gamma |
| Δ | δ | d | δέλτα | Delta |
| Ε | ε | e (short) | εἶ, ἒ ψῑλόν | Epsĭlon |
| Ζ | ζ | z | ζῆτα | Zeta |
| Η | η | e (long) | ἦτα | Eta |
| Θ | θ ϑ | th | θῆτα | Theta |
| Ι | ι | i | ἰῶτα | Iota |
| Κ | κ | k or hard c | κάππα | Kappa |
| Λ | λ | l | λά(μ)βδα | Lambda |
| Μ | μ | m | μῦ | Mu |
| Ν | ν | n | νῦ | Nu |
| Ξ | ξ | x | ξεῖ, ξῖ | Xi |
| Ο | ο | o (short) | οὖ, ὂ μῑκρόν | Omĭcron |
| Π | π | p | πεῖ, πῖ | Pi |
| Ρ | ρ | r | ῥῶ | Rho |
| Σ | σ ς | s | σίγμα | Sigma |
| Τ | τ | t | ταῦ | Tau |
| Υ | υ | (u) y | ὖ, ὖ ψῑλόν | Upsĭlon |
| Φ | φ | ph | φεῖ, φῖ | Phi |
| Χ | χ | kh | χεῖ, χῖ | Chi |
| Ψ | ψ | ps | ψεῖ, ψῖ | Psi |
| Ω | ω | o (long) | ὦ, ὦ μέγα | Omĕga |

N. At the end of a word the form ς is used, elsewhere, the form σ; thus, σύστασις.

# ΕΥΑΓΓΕΛΙΟΝ
## GOSPEL
# ΤΟ ΚΑΤΑ ΜΑΤΘΑΙΟΝ
### THE ACCORDING TO MATTHEW

THE
GOSPEL ACCORDING TO
MATTHEW

### CHAPTER 1

CHAPTER 1

[1] (The) Book of (the) generation of Jesus Christ, (the) son of David, (the) son of Abraham. [2] Abraham fathered Isaac, and Isaac fathered Jacob, and Jacob fathered Judah and his brothers. [3] And Judah fathered Pharez and Zarah out of Tamar; And Pharez fathered Hezron; and Hezron fathered Aram; [4] and Aram fathered Amminadab; and Amminadab fathered Nahshon; and Nahshon fathered Salmon; [5] and Salmon fathered Boaz out of Rahab; and Boaz fathered Obed out of Ruth; and Obed fathered Jesse; [6] and Jesse fathered David the king.

[6] And David the king fathered Solomon out of the (wife) of Uriah; [7] and Solomon fathered Rehoboam; and Rehoboam fathered Abijah; and Abijah fathered Asa; [8] And Asa fathered Jehoshaphat; and Jehoshaphat fathered Jehoram; and Jehoram fathered Uzziah. [9] And Uzziah fathered Jotham; and Jotham fathered Ahaz; and Ahaz fathered Hezekiah. [10] And Hezekiah fathered Manasseh; and Manasseh fathered Amon; and Amon fathered Josiah. [11] And Josiah fathered Jehoiachin and his brothers, at the carrying away of Babylon. [12] And after the carrying away of Babylon, Jehoiachin fathered Shealtiel; and Shealtiel fathered Zerubbabel. [13] And Zerubbabel fathered Abiud; and Abiud fathered Eliakim; and Eliakim fathered Azor. [14] And Azor fathered

**1** Βίβλος γενέσεως Ἰησοῦ Χριστοῦ, υἱοῦ Δαβίδ, υἱοῦ
(The) Book of generation of Jesus Christ, son of David, son
Ἀβραάμ.
of Abraham.

**2** Ἀβραάμ ἐγέννησε τὸν Ἰσαάκ· Ἰσαὰκ δὲ ἐγέννησε τὸν
Abraham fathered Isaac, Isaac and fathered
Ἰακώβ· Ἰακὼβ δὲ ἐγέννησε τὸν Ἰούδαν καὶ τοὺς ἀδελφοὺς
Jacob, Jacob and fathered Judah and the brothers
**3** αὐτοῦ· Ἰούδας δὲ ἐγέννησε τὸν Φαρὲς καὶ τὸν Ζαρὰ ἐκ τῆς
of him. Judah And fathered Pharez and Zarah out of
Θάμαρ· Φαρὲς δὲ ἐγέννησε τὸν Ἐσρώμ· Ἐσρὼμ δὲ ἐγέννησε
Tamar; Pharez and fathered Hezron; Hezron and fathered
**4** τὸν Ἀράμ· Ἀρὰμ δὲ ἐγέννησε τὸν Ἀμιναδάβ· Ἀμιναδὰβ
Aram; Aram and fathered Amminadab; Amminadab
δὲ ἐγέννησε τὸν Ναασσών· Ναασσὼν δὲ ἐγέννησε τὸν
and fathered Nahshon; Nahshon and fathered
**5** Σαλμών· Σαλμὼν δὲ ἐγέννησε τὸν Βοὸζ ἐκ τῆς Ῥαχάβ·
Salmon; Salmon and fathered Boaz out of Rahab;
Βοὸζ δὲ ἐγέννησε τὸν Ὠβὴδ ἐκ τῆς Ῥούθ· Ὠβὴδ δὲ
Boaz and fathered Obed out of Ruth; Obed and
**6** ἐγέννησε τὸν Ἰεσσαί· Ἰεσσαὶ δὲ ἐγέννησε τὸν Δαβίδ τὸν
fathered Jesse; Jesse and fathered David the
βασιλέα.
king.

Δαβὶδ δὲ ὁ βασιλεὺς ἐγέννησε τὸν Σολομῶντα ἐκ τῆς
David And the king fathered Solomon out of the
**7** τοῦ Οὐρίου· Σολομὼν δὲ ἐγέννησε τὸν Ῥοβοάμ· Ῥοβοὰμ
(wife) of Uriah; Solomon and fathered Rehoboam; Rehoboam
**8** δὲ ἐγέννησε τὸν Ἀβιά· Ἀβιὰ δὲ ἐγέννησε τὸν Ἀσά· Ἀσὰ
and fathered Abijah; Abijah and fathered Asa; Asa
δὲ ἐγέννησε τὸν Ἰωσαφάτ· Ἰωσαφὰτ δὲ ἐγέννησε τὸν
and fathered Jehoshaphat; Jehoshaphat and fathered
**9** Ἰωράμ· Ἰωρὰμ δὲ ἐγέννησε τὸν Ὀζίαν· Ὀζίας δὲ ἐγέννησε
Jehoram; Jehoram and fathered Uzziah; Uzziah and fathered
τὸν Ἰωάθαμ· Ἰωάθαμ δὲ ἐγέννησε τὸν Ἄχαζ· Ἄχαζ δὲ
Jotham; Jotham and fathered Ahaz; Ahaz and
**10** ἐγέννησε τὸν Ἐζεκίαν· Ἐζεκίας δὲ ἐγέννησε τὸν Μανασσῆ·
fathered Hezekiah; Hezekiah and fathered Manasseh;
Μανασσῆς δὲ ἐγέννησε τὸν Ἀμών· Ἀμὼν δὲ ἐγέννησε τὸν
Manasseh and fathered Amon; Amon and fathered
**11** Ἰωσίαν· Ἰωσίας δὲ ἐγέννησε τὸν Ἰεχονίαν καὶ τοὺς
Josiah; Josiah and fathered Jehoiachin and the
ἀδελφοὺς αὐτοῦ, ἐπὶ τῆς μετοικεσίας Βαβυλῶνος.
brothers of him, at the deportation of Babylon.

**12** Μετὰ δὲ τὴν μετοικεσίαν Βαβυλῶνος, Ἰεχονίας ἐγέννησε
after And the deportation of Babylon, Jehoiachin fathered
τὸν Σαλαθιήλ· Σαλαθιὴλ δὲ ἐγέννησε τὸν Ζοροβάβελ·
Shealtiel; Shealtiel and fathered Zerubbabel;
**13** Ζοροβάβελ δὲ ἐγέννησε τὸν Ἀβιούδ· Ἀβιοὺδ δὲ ἐγέννησε
Zerubbabel and fathered Abiud; Abiud and fathered
**14** τὸν Ἐλιακείμ· Ἐλιακεὶμ δὲ ἐγέννησε τὸν Ἀζώρ· Ἀζὼρ δὲ
Eliakim; Eliakim and fathered Azor; Azor and

Sadoc, and Sadoc fathered Achim, and Achim fathered Eliud, [15] and Eliud fathered Eleazar, and Eleazar fathered Matthan, and Matthan fathered Jacob. [16] And Jacob fathered Joseph, the husband of Mary, of whom Jesus was born, who is called Christ. [17] So all the generations from Abraham to David were fourteen generations; and from David to the carrying away into Babylon, fourteen generations; and from the carrying away into Babylon until Christ, fourteen generations.

[18] Now the birth of Jesus Christ happened this way — for his mother Mary had been betrothed to Joseph — before they came together she was discovered to be with child of the Holy Spirit. [19] But Joseph, her husband, being righteous and not willing to make her a public example intending to put her away secretly. [20] And as he thought about these things, behold, an angel of the Lord appeared to him in a dream; and said, Joseph, son of David, do not be afraid to take Mary as your wife. For that which is in her is conceived of the Holy Spirit. [21] And she shall give birth to a son; and you shall call His name Jesus, for He shall save His people from their sins. [22] Now all this happened so that it might be fulfilled which was spoken by the Lord through the prophet, saying, [23] "Behold! The virgin shall be with child and shall give birth to a son, and they shall call His name Immanuel" — which translated means, "God with us." [24] And having been aroused from the sleep, Joseph did as the angel of the Lord commanded him, and took his wife; [25] and did not know her until she had brought forth her firstborn son; and he called His name Jesus.

ἐγέννησε τὸν Σαδώκ· Σαδὼκ δὲ ἐγέννησε τὸν Ἀχείμ· Ἀχεὶμ
fathered　　　Sadoc;　　Sadoc and fathered　　　　Achim; Achim

15 δὲ ἐγέννησε τὸν Ἐλιούδ· Ἐλιοὺδ δὲ ἐγέννησε τὸν Ἐλεάζαρ·
and fathered　　　Eliud;　Eliud and fathered　　　　Eleazer;

Ἐλεάζαρ δὲ ἐγέννησε τὸν Ματθάν· Ματθὰν δὲ ἐγέννησε τὸν
Eleazer and fathered　　　Matthan;　Matthan and fathered

16 Ἰακώβ· Ἰακὼβ δὲ ἐγέννησε τὸν Ἰωσὴφ τὸν ἄνδρα Μαρίας,
Jacob;　Jacob and fathered　　　Joseph the husband of Mariam,

ἐξ ἧς ἐγεννήθη Ἰησοῦς ὁ λεγόμενος Χριστός.
out of who was born Jesus, He called Christ.

17 Πᾶσαι οὖν αἱ γενεαὶ ἀπὸ Ἀβραὰμ ἕως Δαβὶδ γενεαὶ
all Then the generations from Abraham until David, generations

δεκατέσσαρες· καὶ ἀπὸ Δαβὶδ ἕως τῆς μετοικεσίας Βαβυλῶνος
fourteen;　and from David until the deportation to Babylon,

γενεαὶ δεκατέσσαρες· καὶ ἀπὸ τῆς μετοικεσίας Βαβυλῶνος
generations fourteen;　and from the deportation to Babylon

ἕως τοῦ Χριστοῦ γενεαὶ δεκατέσσαρες.
until the Christ, generations fourteen.

18 Τοῦ δὲ Ἰησοῦ Χριστοῦ ἡ γέννησις οὕτως ἦν. μνηστευθεί-
Now of Jesus Christ the birth thus was: being betrothed

σης γὰρ τῆς μητρὸς αὐτοῦ Μαρίας τῷ Ἰωσήφ, πρὶν ἢ
for the mother of Him, Mariam, to Joseph, before

συνελθεῖν αὐτούς, εὑρέθη ἐν γαστρὶ ἔχουσα ἐκ Πνεύματος
joining of them, she was found in womb, pregnant by Spirit

19 Ἁγίου. Ἰωσὴφ δὲ ὁ ἀνὴρ αὐτῆς, δίκαιος ὤν, καὶ μὴ θέλων
Holy. Joseph And the husband of her, just being, and not willing

αὐτὴν παραδειγματίσαι, ἐβουλήθη λάθρα ἀπολῦσαι αὐτήν.
her to expose publicly, purposed secretly to put away her.

20 ταῦτα δὲ αὐτοῦ ἐνθυμηθέντος, ἰδού, ἄγγελος Κυρίου κατ'
these things And he meditating on, behold, an angel of (the) Lord by

ὄναρ ἐφάνη αὐτῷ, λέγων, Ἰωσήφ, υἱὸς Δαβίδ, μὴ φοβηθῇς
a dream was seen by him, saying, Joseph, son of David, not do fear

παραλαβεῖν Μαριὰμ τὴν γυναῖκά σου· τὸ γὰρ ἐν αὐτῇ
to take Mariam (as) the wife of you. that For in her

21 γεννηθὲν ἐκ Πνεύματός ἐστιν Ἁγίου. τέξεται δὲ υἱόν, καὶ
begotten by (the) Spirit is Holy. she will bear And a son, and

καλέσεις τὸ ὄνομα αὐτοῦ Ἰησοῦν· αὐτὸς γὰρ σώσει τὸν λαὸν
you shall call the name of Him Jesus. He For will save the people

22 αὐτοῦ ἀπὸ τῶν ἁμαρτιῶν αὐτῶν. τοῦτο δὲ ὅλον γέγονεν,
of Him from the sins of them. this Now all happened,

ἵνα πληρωθῇ τὸ ῥηθὲν ὑπὸ τοῦ Κυρίου διὰ τοῦ προφήτου,
that be fulfilled that spoken by the Lord through the prophet,

23 λέγοντος, Ἰδού, ἡ παρθένος ἐν γαστρὶ ἕξει καὶ τέξεται υἱόν,
saying, Behold, the virgin in womb will conceive and will bear a son,

καὶ καλέσουσι τὸ ὄνομα αὐτοῦ Ἐμμανουήλ, ὅ ἐστι μεθερμη-
and they will call the name of Him Emmanuel, which is, translated,

24 νευόμενον, Μεθ' ἡμῶν ὁ Θεός. διεγερθεὶς δὲ ὁ Ἰωσὴφ ἀπὸ
with us God. being aroused And Joseph from

τοῦ ὕπνου ἐποίησεν ὡς προσέταξεν αὐτῷ ὁ ἄγγελος Κυρίου·
the sleep, he did as commanded him the angel of (the) Lord,

καὶ παρέλαβε τὴν γυναῖκα αὐτοῦ, καὶ οὐκ ἐγίνωσκεν αὐτὴν
and took (as) the wife of him, and not did know her

25 ἕως οὗ ἔτεκε τὸν υἱὸν αὐτῆς τὸν πρωτότοκον· καὶ ἐκάλεσε
until she bore the son of her, the firstborn. And he called

τὸ ὄνομα αὐτοῦ ἸΗΣΟΥΝ.
the name of Him, JESUS.

## CHAPTER 2

CHAPTER 2

[1] Now when Jesus had been born in Bethlehem of Judea in the days of Herod the king, behold, wise men arrived from the east to Jerusalem, [2] saying, Where is He who has been born king of the Jews? For we saw His star in the east and have come to worship him. [3] But Herod the king having heard this, he was troubled, and all Jerusalem with him. [4] And having gathered all the chief priests and scribes of the people together, he asked of them where the Christ should be born. [5] And they said to him, in Bethlehem of Judea, for thus it has been written by the prophet, [6] "And you, Bethlehem in the land of Judea, in no way are the least among the governors of Judah, for out of you shall come a Governor who shall shepherd My people Israel."

[7] Then Herod secretly called the wise men and asked exactly of them the time of the star appearing. [8] And having sent them to Bethlehem, he said, Having gone, search carefully for the little child. And when you shall have found him, bring me word again so that having come, I may worship him also. [9] And having heard the king, they departed. And, behold! The star which they saw in the east went before them until having come it stood over the little child. [10] And having seen the star, they rejoiced with great, overwhelming joy. [11] And having come into the house, they found the little child with His mother, Mary. And having fallen down, worshiped Him. And having opened their treasures, they presented gifts to Him: gold and frankincense and myrrh. [12] Then having been warned of God in a dream not to return to Herod, they went away into their own country by another way.

1 Τοῦ δὲ ᾽Ιησοῦ γεννηθέντος ἐν Βηθλεὲμ τῆς ᾽Ιουδαίας, ἐν
And Jesus having been born in Bethlehem of Judea, in
ἡμέραις ῾Ηρώδου τοῦ βασιλέως, ἰδού, μάγοι ἀπὸ ἀνατολῶν
(the) days of Herod the king, behold, Magi from (the) east
2 παρεγένοντο εἰς ᾽Ιεροσόλυμα, λέγοντες, Ποῦ ἐστιν ὁ τεχθεὶς
arrived into Jerusalem, saying, where is he born
βασιλεὺς τῶν ᾽Ιουδαίων; εἴδομεν γὰρ αὐτοῦ τὸν ἀστέρα ἐν
king of the Jews? we saw For of him the star in
3 τῇ ἀνατολῇ, καὶ ἤλθομεν προσκυνῆσαι αὐτῷ. ἀκούσας δὲ
the east, and came to worship him. hearing And
῾Ηρώδης ὁ βασιλεὺς ἐταράχθη, καὶ πᾶσα ᾽Ιεροσόλυμα μετ᾽
Herod the king was troubled, and all Jerusalem with
αὐτοῦ. καὶ συναγαγὼν πάντας τοὺς ἀρχιερεῖς καὶ γραμ-
4 him. And gathering all the chief priests and scribes
ματεῖς τοῦ λαοῦ, ἐπυνθάνετο παρ᾽ αὐτῶν ποῦ ὁ Χριστὸς
of the people, he inquired from them where the Christ
5 γεννᾶται. οἱ δὲ εἶπον αὐτῷ, ᾽Εν Βηθλεὲμ τῆς ᾽Ιουδαίας·
was to be born. they And said to him, In Bethlehem of Judea.
6 οὕτω γὰρ γέγραπται διὰ τοῦ προφήτου, Καὶ σὺ Βηθλεέμ,
thus For it has been written by the prophet, And you, Bethlehem,
γῆ ᾽Ιούδα, οὐδαμῶς ἐλαχίστη εἶ ἐν τοῖς ἡγεμόσιν ᾽Ιούδα· ἐκ
land of Judah, not at all least are you among the governors of Judah, out of
σοῦ γὰρ ἐξελεύσεται ἡγούμενος, ὅστις ποιμανεῖ τὸν λαόν
of you For will come out a Governor who will shepherd the people
7 μου τὸν ᾽Ισραήλ. τότε ῾Ηρώδης, λάθρα καλέσας τοὺς
of Me, (even) Israel. Then Herod, secretly calling the
μάγους, ἠκρίβωσε παρ᾽ αὐτῶν τὸν χρόνον τοῦ φαινο-
Magi, asked exactly from them the time of the appearing
8 μένου ἀστέρος. καὶ πέμψας αὐτοὺς εἰς Βηθλεὲμ εἶπε, Πορευ-
star. And sending them to Bethlehem, he said, Having
θέντες ἀκριβῶς ἐξετάσατε περὶ τοῦ παιδίου· ἐπὰν δὲ εὕρητε,
gone, exactly inquire about the child. when And you find,
ἀπαγγείλατέ μοι, ὅπως κἀγὼ ἐλθὼν προσκυνήσω αὐτῷ.
report to me, so that I also coming may worship him.
9 οἱ δὲ ἀκούσαντες τοῦ βασιλέως ἐπορεύθησαν· καὶ ἰδού, ὁ
they And having heard the king departed. And, behold, the
ἀστήρ, ὃν εἶδον ἐν τῇ ἀνατολῇ, προῆγεν αὐτούς, ἕως ἐλθὼν
star which they saw in the east went before them until coming
10 ἔστη ἐπάνω οὗ ἦν τὸ παιδίον. ᾽Ιδόντες δὲ τὸν ἀστέρα,
it stood over where was the child. seeing And the star,
11 ἐχάρησαν χαρὰν μεγάλην σφόδρα. καὶ ἐλθόντες εἰς τὴν
they rejoiced a joy great, exceedingly. And coming into the
οἰκίαν, εἶδον τὸ παιδίον μετὰ Μαρίας τῆς μητρὸς αὐτοῦ,
house, they saw the child with Mariam the mother of Him.
καὶ πεσόντες προσεκύνησαν αὐτῷ, καὶ ἀνοίξαντες τοὺς
And falling down, they worshiped Him. And opening the
θησαυροὺς αὐτῶν προσήνεγκαν αὐτῷ δῶρα, χρυσὸν καὶ
treasures of them, they offered to Him gifts: gold and
12 λίβανον καὶ σμύρναν. καὶ χρηματισθέντες κατ᾽ ὄναρ μὴ
frankincense and myrrh. And having been warned by a dream not
ἀνακάμψαι πρὸς ῾Ηρώδην, δι᾽ ἄλλης ὁδοῦ ἀνεχώρησαν εἰς
to return to Herod, by another way they departed into
τὴν χώραν αὐτῶν.
the country of them.

[13] And they having departed, lo, an angel of the Lord appears to Joseph in a dream, saying, Having arisen, take the little child and His mother with you and escape into Egypt. And be there until I tell you. For Herod is about to look for the little child in order to destroy Him. [14] And he having risen took the little child and His mother by night, and withdrew into Egypt; [15] and was there until the death of Herod; that might be fulfilled that which was spoken by the Lord through the prophet, saying, "Out of Egypt I have called My Son." [16] Then Herod, having seen that he was fooled by the wise men, was greatly enraged, and having sent he killed all the boys that (were) in Bethlehem and in all its borders, from two years old and under, according to the time which he had accurately inquired from the wise men. [17] Then that was fulfilled which was spoken by Jeremiah the prophet, saying, [18] "A voice was heard in Ramah, wailing and bitter weeping, and great mourning, Rachel weeping (for) her children, and would not be comforted, because they are (not)."

[19] But Herod having died, behold, an angel of (the) Lord appears to Joseph in a dream in Egypt, [20] saying, Rising up, take the child and His mother and pass over into (the) land of Israel; for those seeking the soul of the child have died. [21] And rising up, he took the child and His mother and came into (the) land of Israel. [22] But hearing that Archelaus reigns over Judea in place of Herod his father, he feared to go there. And having been warned in a dream, he departed into the parts of Galilee. [23] And having come, he dwelt in a city called Nazareth; so as to fulfill tha spoken by the prophet: "He shall be called a Nazarene."

13 Ἀναχωρησάντων δὲ αὐτῶν, ἰδού, ἄγγελος Κυρίου
   having departed    Now  they,   behold,  an angel  of (the) Lord
φαίνεται κατ' ὄναρ τῷ Ἰωσήφ, λέγων, Ἐγερθεὶς παράλαβε
appears   by a dream  to Joseph,  saying,   Rise up;  take with (you)
τὸ παιδίον καὶ τὴν μητέρα αὐτοῦ, καὶ φεῦγε εἰς Αἴγυπτον,
the child  and the  mother  of Him,  and  flee  into  Egypt
καὶ ἴσθι ἐκεῖ ἕως ἂν εἴπω σοί· μέλλει γὰρ Ἡρώδης ζητεῖν τὸ
and be  there until I shall say to you. is about For  Herod   to seek  the

14 παιδίον, τοῦ ἀπολέσαι αὐτό. ὁ δὲ ἐγερθεὶς παρέλαβε τὸ
child,    to destroy    Him. he And rising up  took along  the
παιδίον καὶ τὴν μητέρα αὐτοῦ νυκτός, καὶ ἀνεχώρησεν εἰς
child  and the   mother  of Him by night,  and  departed    into

15 Αἴγυπτον, καὶ ἦν ἐκεῖ ἕως τῆς τελευτῆς Ἡρώδου· ἵνα
Egypt.    And he was there until the  end    of Herod; that
πληρωθῇ τὸ ῥηθὲν ὑπὸ τοῦ Κυρίου διὰ τοῦ προφήτου,
be fulfilled that spoken by   the  Lord   through the  prophet,

16 λέγοντος, Ἐξ Αἰγύπτου ἐκάλεσα τὸν υἱόν μου. τότε
saying,   Out of  Egypt   I have called  the  Son of Me. Then
Ἡρώδης, ἰδὼν ὅτι ἐνεπαίχθη ὑπὸ τῶν μάγων, ἐθυμώθη
Herod,   seeing that he was mocked by  the  Magi,   was enraged
λίαν, καὶ ἀποστείλας ἀνεῖλε πάντας τοὺς παῖδας τοὺς ἐν
greatly, and sending,   he killed  all    the  male-children  in
Βηθλεὲμ καὶ ἐν πᾶσι τοῖς ὁρίοις αὐτῆς, ἀπὸ διετοῦς καὶ
Bethlehem and in  all   the  districts of it,  from two years and
κατωτέρω, κατὰ τὸν χρόνον ὃν ἠκρίβωσε παρὰ τῶν μάγων.
under,  according to the  time  which he exactly asked from the  Magi.

17 τότε ἐπληρώθη τὸ ῥηθὲν ὑπὸ Ἱερεμίου τοῦ προφήτου,
Then was fulfilled that spoken  by  Jeremiah the   prophet,

18 λέγοντος, Φωνὴ ἐν Ῥαμᾶ ἠκούσθη, θρῆνος καὶ κλαυθμὸς
saying,   A voice in  Rama  was heard, lamenting and  weeping
καὶ ὀδυρμὸς πολύς, Ῥαχὴλ κλαίουσα τὰ τέκνα αὐτῆς, καὶ
and mourning much;   Rachel  weeping for the children of her,  and

19 οὐκ ἤθελε παρακληθῆναι, ὅτι οὐκ εἰσί. τελευτήσαντος δὲ
not willing to be comforted, because not they were. having expired But
τοῦ Ἡρώδου, ἰδού, ἄγγελος Κυρίου κατ' ὄναρ φαίνεται τῷ
Herod,    behold, an angel of (the) Lord by a dream appears

20 Ἰωσὴφ ἐν Αἰγύπτῳ, λέγων, Ἐγερθεὶς παράλαβε τὸ παιδίον
to Joseph in  Egypt,  saying,  Rising up, take along  the  child
καὶ τὴν μητέρα αὐτοῦ, καὶ πορεύου εἰς γῆν Ἰσραήλ· τεθνή-
and the mother  of Him, and pass over into (the) land of Israel;  have

21 κασι γὰρ οἱ ζητοῦντες τὴν ψυχὴν τοῦ παιδίου. ὁ δὲ ἐγερθεὶς
expired for those seeking   the  soul   of the child.  he And rising up
παρέλαβε τὸ παιδίον καὶ τὴν μητέρα αὐτοῦ, καὶ ἦλθεν εἰς
took along the child  and  the   mother  of Him,  and came into

22 γῆν Ἰσραήλ. ἀκούσας δὲ ὅτι Ἀρχέλαος βασιλεύει ἐπὶ τῆς
(the) land of Israel. hearing But that Archelaus   reigns    over
Ἰουδαίας ἀντὶ Ἡρώδου τοῦ πατρὸς αὐτοῦ, ἐφοβήθη ἐκεῖ
Judea in place of Herod  tne  father  of him,  he feared  there
ἀπελθεῖν· χρηματισθεὶς δὲ κατ' ὄναρ, ἀνεχώρησεν εἰς τὰ μέρη
to go.    being warned And by a dream,  he departed  into the parts

23 τῆς Γαλιλαίας, καὶ ἐλθὼν κατῴκησεν εἰς πόλιν λεγομένην
of Galilee.   And having come, he dwelt  in  a city   called
Ναζαρέθ· ὅπως πληρωθῇ τὸ ῥηθὲν διὰ τῶν προφητῶν ὅτι
Nazareth;  thus  to fulfill  that spoken through the   prophet:
Ναζωραῖος κληθήσεται.
A Nazarene He shall be called.

## CHAPTER 3

CHAPTER 3

[1] Now in those days John the Baptist comes preaching in the wilderness of Judea, [2] and saying, Repent, for the kingdom of Heaven has drawn near. [3] For this is He who was spoken of by Isaiah the prophet, saying, "The voice of one crying in the wilderness! Prepare the way of the Lord! Make His paths straight!" [4] And John himself had his clothing of camel's hair, and a girdle of leather about his loins, and his food was locusts and wild honey.

[5] Then Jerusalem went out to him, and all Judea, and all the country around the Jordan; [6] and were baptized in the Jordan by him, confessing their sins. [7] But having seen many of the Pharisees and Sadducees coming to his baptism, he said to them, Children of vipers! Who warned you to flee from the coming wrath? [8] Therefore bring forth fruits worthy of repentance; [9] and do not think to say within yourselves, We have Abraham (as) father; for I say to you that God is able to raise up children to Abraham from these stones. [10] But already the axe is laid to the root of the trees; therefore every tree not bearing good fruit is cut down and is thrown into fire. [11] I indeed baptize you in water to repentance; but He who (is) coming after me is mightier than I, whose sandals I am not fit to carry. He will baptize you in (the) Holy Spirit and fire. [12] Of whom the fan (is) in His hand, and He will cleanse His floor, and will gather His wheat into the storehouse; but He will burn up the chaff with fire that cannot be put out.

[13] Then Jesus comes from Galilee to the Jordan,

---

**1** Ἐν δὲ ταῖς ἡμέραις ἐκείναις παραγίνεται Ἰωάννης ὁ
in Now days those comes John the

βαπτιστής, κηρύσσων ἐν τῇ ἐρήμῳ τῆς Ἰουδαίας, καὶ λέγων,
Baptist proclaiming in the wilderness of Judea, and saying,

**2** Μετανοεῖτε· ἤγγικε γὰρ ἡ βασιλεία τῶν οὐρανῶν. οὗτος
Repent! has come near For the kingdom of the heavens. this

γάρ ἐστιν ὁ ῥηθεὶς ὑπὸ Ἠσαΐου τοῦ προφήτου, λέγοντος,
For is he spoken of by Isaiah the prophet, saying,

**3** Φωνὴ βοῶντος ἐν τῇ ἐρήμῳ, Ἑτοιμάσατε τὴν ὁδὸν Κυρίου·
A voice of (one) crying in the wilderness: Prepare the way of (the) Lord;

**4** εὐθείας ποιεῖτε τὰς τρίβους αὐτοῦ. αὐτὸς δὲ ὁ Ἰωάννης εἶχε
straight make the paths of Him. he Now, John, had

τὸ ἔνδυμα αὐτοῦ ἀπὸ τριχῶν καμήλου, καὶ ζώνην δερ-
the clothing of him from hairs of a camel, and a belt of

ματίνην περὶ τὴν ὀσφὺν αὐτοῦ· ἡ δὲ τροφὴ αὐτοῦ ἦν
leather around the loin of him. the And food of him was

**5** ἀκρίδες καὶ μέλι ἄγριον. τότε ἐξεπορεύετο πρὸς αὐτὸν
locusts and honey wild. Then went out to him

Ἱεροσόλυμα καὶ πᾶσα ἡ Ἰουδαία καὶ πᾶσα ἡ περίχωρος τοῦ
Jerusalem and all Judea, and all the neighborhood of the

**6** Ἰορδάνου· καὶ ἐβαπτίζοντο ἐν τῷ Ἰορδάνῃ ὑπ' αὐτοῦ,
Jordan; and were baptized in the Jordan by him,

**7** ἐξομολογούμενοι τὰς ἁμαρτίας αὐτῶν. Ἰδὼν δὲ πολλοὺς τῶν
confessing the sins of them. seeing And many of the

Φαρισαίων καὶ Σαδδουκαίων ἐρχομένους ἐπὶ τὸ βάπτισμα
Pharisees and Sadducees coming on the baptism

αὐτοῦ, εἶπεν αὐτοῖς, Γεννήματα ἐχιδνῶν, τίς ὑπέδειξεν ὑμῖν
of him, he said to them, Offspring of vipers! Who warned you

**8** φυγεῖν ἀπὸ τῆς μελλούσης ὀργῆς; ποιήσατε οὖν καρποὺς
to flee from the coming wrath? Produce, then, fruits

**9** ἀξίους τῆς μετανοίας· καὶ μὴ δόξητε λέγειν ἐν ἑαυτοῖς,
worthy of repentance; and not do think to say in yourselves,

Πατέρα ἔχομεν τὸν Ἀβραάμ. λέγω γὰρ ὑμῖν ὅτι δύναται ὁ
A father we have Abraham. I say For to you that is able

**10** Θεὸς ἐκ τῶν λίθων τούτων ἐγεῖραι τέκνα τῷ Ἀβραάμ. ἤδη
God out of stones these to raise up children to Abraham. already

δὲ καὶ ἡ ἀξίνη πρὸς τὴν ῥίζαν τῶν δένδρων κεῖται· πᾶν οὖν
And even the axe at the root of the trees is laid. any Then

δένδρον μὴ ποιοῦν καρπὸν καλὸν ἐκκόπτεται καὶ εἰς πῦρ
tree not producing fruit good is cut off, and into fire

**11** βάλλεται. ἐγὼ μὲν βαπτίζω ὑμᾶς ἐν ὕδατι εἰς μετάνοιαν· ὁ
is thrown. I indeed baptize you in water to repentance. He

δὲ ὀπίσω μου ἐρχόμενος ἰσχυρότερός μου ἐστίν, οὗ οὐκ εἰμὶ
But after me coming stronger than me is, of whom not I am

ἱκανὸς τὰ ὑποδήματα βαστάσαι· αὐτὸς ὑμᾶς βαπτίσει ἐν
worthy the sandals to bear. He you will baptize in

**12** Πνεύματι Ἁγίῳ καὶ πυρί. οὗ τὸ πτύον ἐν τῇ χειρὶ αὐτοῦ,
(the) Spirit Holy and fire; of whom the fan (is) in the hand of Him.

καὶ διακαθαριεῖ τὴν ἅλωνα αὐτοῦ, καὶ συνάξει τὸν σῖτον
And He will cleanse the floor of Him, and will gather the wheat

αὐτοῦ εἰς τὴν ἀποθήκην, τὸ δὲ ἄχυρον κατακαύσει πυρὶ
of Him into the barn. the But chaff He will burn with fire

**13** ἀσβέστῳ. Τότε παραγίνεται ὁ Ἰησοῦς ἀπὸ τῆς Γαλιλαίας
unquenchable. Then arrives Jesus from Galilee

to John, to be baptized by him. [14] But John was restraining him, saying, I have need to be baptized by You, and do You come to me? [15] But Jesus answering said to him, Allow (it) now, for it is becoming to us this way to fulfill all righteousness. Then he allows Him. [16] And having been baptized, Jesus went up immediately from the water; and, behold, the heavens were opened to Him, and He saw the Spirit of God descending as a dove, and coming upon Him. [17] And behold, a voice out of Heaven, saying, This is My Son, the beloved, in whom I have found delight.

ἐπὶ τὸν Ἰορδάνην πρὸς τὸν Ἰωάννην, τοῦ βαπτισθῆναι ὑπ'
at the Jordan to John, to be baptized by

14 αὐτοῦ. ὁ δὲ Ἰωάννης διεκώλυεν αὐτόν, λέγων, Ἐγὼ χρε-
him. But John restrained Him, saying, I need

ίαν ἔχω ὑπὸ σοῦ βαπτισθῆναι, καὶ σὺ ἔρχῃ πρός με; ἀποκ-
have by You to be baptized; and You come to me? an-

15 ριθεὶς δὲ ὁ Ἰησοῦς εἶπε πρὸς αὐτόν, Ἄφες ἄρτι· οὕτω γὰρ
swering But, Jesus said to him, Allow (it) now; thus for

πρέπον ἐστὶν ἡμῖν πληρῶσαι πᾶσαν δικαιοσύνην. τότε
fitting it is to us to fulfill all righteousness. Then

16 ἀφίησιν αὐτόν. καὶ βαπτισθεὶς ὁ Ἰησοῦς ἀνέβη εὐθὺς ἀπὸ τοῦ
he allows Him. And being baptized, Jesus went up at once from the

ὕδατος· καὶ ἰδού, ἀνεῴχθησαν αὐτῷ οἱ οὐρανοί, καὶ εἶδε τὸ
water. And, behold, were opened to Him the heavens; and He saw the

Πνεῦμα τοῦ Θεοῦ καταβαῖνον ὡσεὶ περιστερὰν καὶ ἐρχόμε
Spirit of God descending as a dove, and coming

17 νον ἐπ' αὐτόν. καὶ ἰδού, φωνὴ ἐκ τῶν οὐρανῶν, λέγουσα,
upon Him. And, behold, a voice out of the heavens, saying,

Οὗτός ἐστιν ὁ υἱός μου ὁ ἀγαπητός, ἐν ᾧ εὐδόκησα.
This is the Son of Me, the Beloved, in whom I have found delight.

## CHAPTER 4

[1] Then Jesus was led up into the wilderness by the Spirit, to be tempted by the devil. [2] And having fasted forty days and forty nights, afterwards He hungered. [3] And having come to Him the Tempter said, If You are (the) Son of God, speak that these stones may become loaves. [4] But answering He said, It has been written, "Man shall not live by bread alone, but by every word going out of (the) mouth of God." [5] Then the devil takes Him to the holy city, and sets Him on the edge of the Temple, [6] and says to Him, If You are (the) Son of God, throw Yourself down; for it has been written, "He shall give His angels charge concerning You, and they shall bear You in (their) hands, lest You strike Your foot against a stone." [7] Jesus said to him, Again it has been written, "You shall not tempt (the) Lord your God." [8] Again the devil takes Him to a very high mountain, and shows to Him all the kingdoms of the world and their glory. [9] And (he) says to Him, I will give all these things to You if You falling down will worship

## CHAPTER 4

1 Τότε ὁ Ἰησοῦς ἀνήχθη εἰς τὴν ἔρημον ὑπὸ τοῦ Πνεύ-
Then Jesus was led up into the wilderness by the Spirit.

2 ματος, πειρασθῆναι ὑπὸ τοῦ διαβόλου. καὶ νηστεύσας
to be tested by the Devil. And having fasted

ἡμέρας τεσσαράκοντα καὶ νύκτας τεσσαράκοντα, ὕστερον
days forty and nights forty, afterward

3 ἐπείνασε. καὶ προσελθὼν αὐτῷ ὁ πειράζων εἶπεν, Εἰ υἱὸς
He hungered. And coming near Him, the Tempter said, If Son

4 εἶ τοῦ Θεοῦ, εἰπὲ ἵνα οἱ λίθοι οὗτοι ἄρτοι γένωνται. ὁ δὲ
You are of God, say that stones these loaves may become. He But

ἀποκριθεὶς εἶπε, Γέγραπται, Οὐκ ἐπ' ἄρτῳ μόνῳ ζήσεται
answering said, It has been written: Not on bread alone shall live

ἄνθρωπος, ἀλλ' ἐπὶ παντὶ ῥήματι ἐκπορευομένῳ διὰ στό-
man, but on every word proceeding through (the)

5 ματος Θεοῦ. τότε παραλαμβάνει αὐτὸν ὁ διάβολος εἰς τὴν
mouth of God. Then takes Him the Devil into the

ἁγίαν πόλιν, καὶ ἵστησιν αὐτὸν ἐπὶ τὸ πτερύγιον τοῦ ἱεροῦ,
holy city, and sets Him on the wing of the Temple,

6 καὶ λέγει αὐτῷ, Εἰ υἱὸς εἶ τοῦ Θεοῦ, βάλε σεαυτὸν κάτω·
and says to Him, If Son You are of God, Throw Yourself down;

γέγραπται γὰρ ὅτι Τοῖς ἀγγέλοις αὐτοῦ ἐντελεῖται περὶ
it has been written for: To the angels of Him He will give charge about

σοῦ, καὶ ἐπὶ χειρῶν ἀροῦσί σε, μήποτε προσκόψῃς πρὸς
You; and on hands they will bear You, lest You strike against

7 λίθον τὸν πόδα σοῦ. ἔφη αὐτῷ ὁ Ἰησοῦς, Πάλιν γέγραπται,
a stone the foot of You. said to him Jesus, Again, it has been written,

8 Οὐκ ἐκπειράσεις Κύριον τὸν Θεόν σου. πάλιν παραλαμβάνει
Not you shall tempt (the) Lord God of you. Again takes

αὐτὸν ὁ διάβολος εἰς ὄρος ὑψηλὸν λίαν, καὶ δείκνυσιν αὐτῷ
Him the Devil to a mount high exceeding, and shows Him

9 πάσας τὰς βασιλείας τοῦ κόσμου καὶ τὴν δόξαν αὐτῶν, καὶ
all the kingdoms of the world, and the glory of them; and

λέγει αὐτῷ, Ταῦτα πάντα σοι δώσω, ἐὰν πεσὼν προσ-
says to Him, These things all to You I will give, if falling down You

me. [10] Then Jesus says to him, Go, Satan! For it has been written: "(The) Lord God of you, you shall worship, and Him only you shall serve." [11] Then the Devil leaves Him. And, behold, angels came near and ministered to Him.

[12] But Jesus having heard that John was betrayed, He withdrew into Galilee. [13] And having left Nazareth, having come he lived at Capernaum, which (is) on the seacoast, in (the) borders of Zebulun and Naphtali; [14] so that might be fulfilled that which was spoken by Isaiah the prophet, saying, [15] "Land of Zebulun and land of Naphtali, by way of (the) sea, beyond the Jordan, Galilee of the nations; [16] the people which were sitting in the darkness have seen a Great Light, and to those who were sitting in (the) region and shadow of death, light sprang up to them."

[17] From that time Jesus began to preach and to say, Repent! For the kingdom of Heaven has drawn near.

[18] And Jesus walking beside the sea of Galilee saw two brothers, Simon called Peter, and his brother Andrew, casting a net into the sea, for they were fishers. [19] And He says to them, Come after Me, and I will make you fishers of men. [20] And they immediately followed Him, having left the nets. [21] And having gone on from there, He saw two other brothers, James the (son) of Zebedee, and his brother John, in the boat with their father Zebedee, mending their nets; and He called them. [22] And they immediately having left the boat and their father followed Him.

[23] And Jesus went around all Galilee teaching in their synagogues, and preaching the gospel of the kingdom, and healing every disease and every bodily

10 κυνήσῃς μοι. τότε λέγει αὐτῷ ὁ Ἰησοῦς, Ὕπαγε, Σατανᾶ
will worship me. Then says to him Jesus, Go, Satan
γέγραπται γάρ, Κύριον τὸν Θεόν σου προσκυνήσεις, καὶ
it has been written for: (The) Lord God of you you shall worship, and
11 αὐτῷ μόνῳ λατρεύσεις. τότε ἀφίησιν αὐτὸν ὁ διάβολος· καὶ
Him only you shall serve. Then leaves Him the Devil, and
12 ἰδού, ἄγγελοι προσῆλθον καὶ διηκόνουν αὐτῷ. Ἀκούσας δὲ
behold, angels came near and ministered to Him. having heard But
ὁ Ἰησοῦς ὅτι Ἰωάννης παρεδόθη, ἀνεχώρησεν εἰς τὴν
Jesus that John was delivered up, He withdrew into
13 Γαλιλαίαν· καὶ καταλιπὼν τὴν Ναζαρὲθ ἐλθὼν κατῴκησεν
Galilee. And having left Nazareth, coming He dwelt
εἰς Καπερναοὺμ τὴν παραθαλασσίαν, ἐν ὁρίοις Ζαβουλὼν
in Capernaum beside the sea, in districts of Zebulun
14 καὶ Νεφθαλείμ. ἵνα πληρωθῇ τὸ ῥηθὲν διὰ Ἡσαΐου τοῦ προ-
and Naphthali, that may be fulfilled that spoken by Isaiah the
15 φήτου, λέγοντος, Γῆ Ζαβουλὼν καὶ γῆ Νεφθαλείμ, ὁδὸν
prophet, saying, Land of Zebulun and land of Naphthali, way
16 θαλάσσης, πέραν τοῦ Ἰορδάνου, Γαλιλαία τῶν ἐθνῶν, ὁ λαὸς
of (the) sea beyond the Jordan, Galilee of the nations; the people
ὁ καθήμενος ἐν σκότει εἶδε φῶς μέγα, καὶ τοῖς καθημένοις ἐν
sitting in darkness saw a light great, and to those sitting in
χώρᾳ καὶ σκιᾷ θανάτου, φῶς ἀνέτειλεν αὐτοῖς.
a region and shadow of death, light sprang up to them.
17 Ἀπὸ τότε ἤρξατο ὁ Ἰησοῦς κηρύσσειν καὶ λέγειν,
From then began Jesus to proclaim and to say,
Μετανοεῖτε· ἤγγικε γὰρ ἡ βασιλεία τῶν οὐρανῶν.
Repent! has come near For the kingdom of the heavens.
18 Περιπατῶν δὲ ὁ Ἰησοῦς παρὰ τὴν θάλασσαν τῆς
walking And Jesus beside the sea
Γαλιλαίας εἶδε δύο ἀδελφούς, Σίμωνα τὸν λεγόμενον Πέτρον,
of Galilee, He saw two brothers, Simon called Peter,
καὶ Ἀνδρέαν τὸν ἀδελφὸν αὐτοῦ, βάλλοντας ἀμφίβληστρον
and Andrew the brother of him, casting a net
19 εἰς τὴν θάλασσαν· ἦσαν γὰρ ἁλιεῖς. καὶ λέγει αὐτοῖς, Δεῦτε
into the sea. they were For fishers. And He says to them, Come
20 ὀπίσω μου, καὶ ποιήσω ὑμᾶς ἁλιεῖς ἀνθρώπων. οἱ δὲ εὐθέως
after Me, and I will make you fishers of men. they And at once
21 ἀφέντες τὰ δίκτυα ἠκολούθησαν αὐτῷ. καὶ προβὰς ἐκεῖθεν,
forsaking the nets followed Him. And going on from there,
εἶδεν ἄλλους δύο ἀδελφούς, Ἰάκωβον τὸν τοῦ Ζεβεδαίου καὶ
He saw other two brothers, James the (son) of Zebedee, and
Ἰωάννην τὸν ἀδελφὸν αὐτοῦ, ἐν τῷ πλοίῳ μετὰ Ζεβεδαίου
John the brother of him, in the boat with Zebedee
τοῦ πατρὸς αὐτῶν, καταρτίζοντας τὰ δίκτυα αὐτῶν·
the father of them, mending the nets of them.
22 καὶ ἐκάλεσεν αὐτούς. οἱ δὲ εὐθέως ἀφέντες τὸ πλοῖον καὶ τὸν
And He called them. they And at once forsaking the boat and the
πατέρα αὐτῶν ἠκολούθησαν αὐτῷ.
father of them followed Him.
23 Καὶ περιῆγεν ὅλην τὴν Γαλιλαίαν ὁ Ἰησοῦς, διδάσκων
And went about all Galilee Jesus, teaching
ἐν ταῖς συναγωγαῖς αὐτῶν, καὶ κηρύσσων τὸ εὐαγγέλιον
in the synagogues of them, and proclaiming the gospel
τῆς βασιλείας, καὶ θεραπεύων πᾶσαν νόσον καὶ πᾶσαν
of the kingdom, and healing every disease and every

weakness among the people. [24] And His fame went out into all Syria. And they brought to Him all those having illness, suffering from various diseases and torments, and possessed by demons, and lunatics, and paralytics; and He healed them. [25] And great crowds followed Him from Galilee, and Decapolis, and Jerusalem, and Judea, and beyond the Jordan.

**CHAPTER 5**

[1] But seeing the crowds, He went up into the mountain; and He having sat down, His disciples came to Him. [2] And having opened His mouth He taught them, saying, [3] Blessed (are) the poor in spirit! For theirs is the kingdom of Heaven. [4] Blessed (are) they who mourn! For they shall be comforted. [5] Blessed (are) the meek! For they shall inherit the earth. [6] Blessed (are) they who hunger and thirst after righteousness! For they shall be filled. [7] Blessed (are) the merciful! For they shall obtain mercy. [8] Blessed (are) the pure in heart! For they shall see God. [9] Blessed (are) the peacemakers! For they shall be called sons of God. [10] Blessed (are) they who have been persecuted for righteousness' sake! For theirs is the kingdom of Heaven. [11] Blessed are you when they shall reproach you and shall persecute, and shall say every evil word against you, lying, on account of Me. [12] Rejoice and leap for joy, for your reward (is) great in Heaven; for in this way they persecute the prophets who (were) before you. [13] You are the salt of the earth; but if the salt becomes tasteless, with

**24** μαλακίαν ἐν τῷ λαῷ. καὶ ἀπῆλθεν ἡ ἀκοὴ αὐτοῦ εἰς ὅλην
sicknesses among the people. And went the report of Him into all
τὴν Συρίαν· καὶ προσήνεγκαν αὐτῷ πάντας τοὺς κακῶς
Syria. And they brought to Him all those illness
ἔχοντας, ποικίλαις νόσοις καὶ βασάνοις συνεχομένους, καὶ
having, various diseases and torments suffering, and
δαιμονιζομένους, καὶ σεληνιαζομένους, καὶ παραλυτικούς·
demon-possessed, and lunatics, and paralytics.
**25** καὶ ἐθεράπευσεν αὐτούς. καὶ ἠκολούθησαν αὐτῷ ὄχλοι
And He healed them. And followed Him crowds
πολλοὶ ἀπὸ τῆς Γαλιλαίας καὶ Δεκαπόλεως καὶ Ἱεροσολύμων
many from Galilee and Decapolis and Jerusalem
καὶ Ἰουδαίας καὶ πέραν τοῦ Ἰορδάνου.
and Judea, and beyond the Jordan.

**CHAPTER 5**

**1** Ἰδὼν δὲ τοὺς ὄχλους ἀνέβη εἰς τὸ ὄρος καὶ καθίσαντος
seeing And the crowds, He went into the mount and sitting down
**2** αὐτοῦ, προσῆλθον αὐτῷ οἱ μαθηταὶ αὐτοῦ· καὶ ἀνοίξας
Himself, came near to Him the disciples of Him. And opening
τὸ στόμα αὐτοῦ, ἐδίδασκεν αὐτούς, λέγων,
the mouth of Him, He taught them, saying,
**3** Μακάριοι οἱ πτωχοὶ τῷ πνεύματι· ὅτι αὐτῶν ἐστιν ἡ
Blessed (are) the poor in spirit, because of them is the
βασιλεία τῶν οὐρανῶν.
kingdom of the heavens.
**4** Μακάριοι οἱ πενθοῦντες· ὅτι αὐτοὶ παρακληθήσονται.
Blessed (are) the (ones) mourning, because they shall be comforted.
**5** Μακάριοι οἱ πραεῖς· ὅτι αὐτοὶ κληρονομήσουσι τὴν γῆν.
Blessed (are) the meek, because they shall inherit the earth.
**6** Μακάριοι οἱ πεινῶντες καὶ διψῶντες τὴν δικαιοσύνην·
Blessed (are) the (ones) hungering and thirsting (after) righteousness,
ὅτι αὐτοὶ χορτασθήσονται.
because they shall be filled.
**7** Μακάριοι οἱ ἐλεήμονες· ὅτι αὐτοὶ ἐλεηθήσονται.
Blessed (are) the merciful, because they shall receive mercy.
**8** Μακάριοι οἱ καθαροὶ τῇ καρδίᾳ· ὅτι αὐτοὶ τὸν Θεὸν
Blessed (are) the pure in heart, because they God
ὄψονται.
shall see.
**9** Μακάριοι οἱ εἰρηνοποιοί· ὅτι αὐτοὶ υἱοὶ Θεοῦ κληθήσονται.
Blessed (are) the peacemakers, because they sons of God shall be called.
**10** Μακάριοι οἱ δεδιωγμένοι ἕνεκεν δικαιοσύνης· ὅτι αὐτῶν
Blessed (are) those being persecuted because of righteousness, for of them
**11** ἐστιν ἡ βασιλεία τῶν οὐρανῶν. Μακάριοί ἐστε, ὅταν ὀνειδί-
is the kingdom of the heavens. Blessed are you when they will
σωσιν ὑμᾶς καὶ διώξωσι, καὶ εἴπωσι πᾶν πονηρὸν ῥῆμα
reproach you and persecute, and shall say every evil word
**12** καθ' ὑμῶν ψευδόμενοι, ἕνεκεν ἐμοῦ. χαίρετε καὶ ἀγαλλιᾶσθε,
against you, lying, for the sake of Me; rejoice and be glad,
ὅτι ὁ μισθὸς ὑμῶν πολὺς ἐν τοῖς οὐρανοῖς· οὕτω γὰρ ἐδίω-
because the reward of you (is) great in the heavens. thus For they per-
ξαν τοὺς προφήτας τοὺς πρὸ ὑμῶν.
secuted the prophets before you.
**13** Ὑμεῖς ἐστε τὸ ἅλας τῆς γῆς· ἐὰν δὲ τὸ ἅλας μωρανθῇ, ἐν
You are the salt of the earth. if But the salt be tasteless, by

what shall it be salted? For it has strength for nothing anymore, but to be thrown out, and the be trampled upon by men. [14] You are the light of the world, a city on a mountain cannot be hidden. [15] Nor do they light a lamp and put it under the grain measure, but on the lampstand; and it shines for all who (are) in the house. [16] So let your light shine before men, so that they may see your good works, and may glorify your Father who (is) in Heaven.

[17] Do not think that I came to abolish the Law or the Prophets; I did not come to do away, but to fulfill. [18] For truly I say to you, Until the sky and the earth pass away, in no way shall one iota or one tittle pass away from the Law until all come to pass. [19] Whoever then shall break one of these commandments, the least, and shall teach men so, shall be called least in the kingdom of Heaven; but whoever shall practice and shall teach (them), this (one) shall be called great in the kingdom of Heaven. [20] But I say to you, that unless your righteousness shall abound and be above (that) of the scribes and Pharisees, you in no way shall enter into the kingdom of Heaven.

[21] You have heard that it was said to the ancient ones, "You shall not commit murder, but whoever shall commit murder shall be liable to the Judgment. [22] But I say to you, that everyone who is angry with his brother without cause, shall be liable to the Judgme.it. But whoever shall say, Fool! (he) shall be liable to the fire of hell. [23] If you therefore shall offer your gift at the altar, and there shall remember that your brother has something against you, [24] leave your gift there before the altar, and depart to be first reconciled to

τίνι ἀλισθήσεται ; εἰς οὐδὲν ἰσχύει ἔτι, εἰ μὴ βληθῆναι ἔξω
what shall it be salted? for nothing It is strong still, except to be thrown out,

14 καὶ καταπατεῖσθαι ὑπὸ τῶν ἀνθρώπων. ὑμεῖς ἐστε τὸ φῶς
and to be trampled under by   men.   You are the light

τοῦ κόσμου· οὐ δύναται πόλις κρυβῆναι ἐπάνω ὄρους
of the world; not is able a city to be hidden on a mount

15 κειμένη· οὐδὲ καίουσι λύχνον καὶ τιθέασιν αὐτὸν ὑπὸ τὸν
situated. Nor do they light a lamp and place it under the

μόδιον, ἀλλ᾽ ἐπὶ τὴν λυχνίαν, καὶ λάμπει πᾶσι τοῖς ἐν τῇ
grain-measure, but on the lampstand, and it lightens all those in the

16 οἰκίᾳ. οὕτω λαμψάτω τὸ φῶς ὑμῶν ἔμπροσθεν τῶν ἀνθρώ-
house. Thus let shine the light of you before men,

πων, ὅπως ἴδωσιν ὑμῶν τὰ καλὰ ἔργα, καὶ δοξάσωσι τὸν
so that they may see of you the good works, and may glorify the

πατέρα ὑμῶν τὸν ἐν τοῖς οὐρανοῖς.
Father of you in the heavens.

17 Μὴ νομίσητε ὅτι ἦλθον καταλῦσαι τὸν νόμον ἢ τοὺς
Not do think that I came to annul the law or the

18 προφήτας· οὐκ ἦλθον καταλῦσαι ἀλλὰ πληρῶσαι. ἀμὴν
prophets. Not I came to annul, but to fulfill. truly

γὰρ λέγω ὑμῖν, ἕως ἂν παρέλθῃ ὁ οὐρανὸς καὶ ἡ γῆ, ἰῶτα
For I say to you, Until pass away the heavens and the earth, iota

ἓν ἢ μία κεραία οὐ μὴ παρέλθῃ ἀπὸ τοῦ νόμου, ἕως ἂν
one or one point in no way shall pass away from the law, until

19 πάντα γένηται. ὃς ἐὰν οὖν λύσῃ μίαν τῶν ἐντολῶν τούτων
all things occur. Whoever, then, relaxes one of commandments these

τῶν ἐλαχίστων,· καὶ διδάξῃ οὕτω τοὺς ἀνθρώπους, ἐλά-
the least, and teaches so men, least

χιστος κληθήσεται ἐν τῇ βασιλείᾳ τῶν οὐρανῶν· ὃς δ᾽ ἂν
he shall be called in the kingdom of the heavens. who But ever

ποιήσῃ καὶ διδάξῃ, οὗτος μέγας κληθήσεται ἐν τῇ βασιλείᾳ
does (them) and teaches, this one great shall be called in the kingdom

20 τῶν οὐρανῶν. λέγω γὰρ ὑμῖν ὅτι ἐὰν μὴ περισσεύσῃ ἡ
of the heavens. I say For to you that if not shall exceed the

δικαιοσύνη ὑμῶν πλεῖον τῶν γραμματέων καὶ Φαρισαίων,
righteousness of you more than the scribes and Pharisees,

οὐ μὴ εἰσέλθητε εἰς τὴν βασιλείαν τῶν οὐρανῶν.
in no way shall you go into the kingdom of the heavens.

21 Ἠκούσατε ὅτι ἐρρέθη τοῖς ἀρχαίοις, Οὐ φονεύσεις· ὃς
You heard that it was said to the ancients: Not do murder; who

22 δ᾽ ἂν φονεύσῃ, ἔνοχος ἔσται τῇ κρίσει· ἐγὼ δὲ λέγω ὑμῖν
and ever murders, liable shall be to the Judgment. I But say to you

ὅτι πᾶς ὁ ὀργιζόμενος τῷ ἀδελφῷ αὐτοῦ εἰκῆ ἔνοχος ἔσται
that each who is angry with the brother of him without cause liable shall be

τῇ κρίσει· ὃς δ᾽ ἂν εἴπῃ τῷ ἀδελφῷ αὐτοῦ, Ρακά, ἔνοχος
to the Judgment. who And ever says to the brother of him, Raca, liable

ἔσται τῷ συνεδρίῳ· ὃς δ᾽ ἂν εἴπῃ, Μωρέ, ἔνοχος ἔσται εἰς
shall be to the sanhedrin; who and ever says, Fool, liable shall be into

23 τὴν γέενναν τοῦ πυρός. ἐὰν οὖν προσφέρῃς τὸ δῶρόν σου
the Gehenna of fire. If, then, you offer the gift of you

ἐπὶ τὸ θυσιαστήριον, κἀκεῖ μνησθῇς ὅτι ὁ ἀδελφός σου ἔχει
on the altar, and there remember that the brother of you has

24 τι κατὰ σοῦ, ἄφες ἐκεῖ τὸ δῶρόν σου ἔμπροσθεν τοῦ θυσια-
some-thing against you, leave there the gift of you before the altar,

στηρίου, καὶ ὕπαγε, πρῶτον διαλλάγηθι τῷ ἀδελφῷ σου,
and go; first be reconciled to the brother of you,

your brother, and then having come, offer your gift. [25] Be agreeable with your opponent quickly, while you are in the way with him, lest the opponent deliver you to the judge, and the judge deliver you to the officer, and you be thrown into prison. [26] Truly, I say to you, In no way shall you leave there until you pay the last bit of money.

[27] You have heard that it was said to the ancients, Do not commit adultery. [28] But I say to you that everyone looking at a woman to lust after her has already committed adultery in his heart. [29] But if your right eye offends you, take it out and throw (it) from you—for it is profitable to you that one of your members should perish, and not all your body be thrown into hell. [30] And if your right hand causes you to offend, cut it off and throw it from you—for it is profitable to you that one of your members should perish, and not your whole body be thrown into hell.

[31] It was also said, Whoever puts away his wife, let him give her a bill of divorce. [32] But I say to you that whoever puts away his wife, apart from a matter of fornication, makes him commit adultery; and whoever shall marry the one put away commits adultery.

[33] Again, you have heard that it was said to the ancients, You shall not swear falsely, but shall give your oaths to the Lord. [34] But I say to you, Do not swear (at) all, neither by Heaven, because it is God's throne; [35] nor by the earth, because it is the footstool of His feet; nor by Jerusalem, because it is (the) city of the great King. [36] Nor shall you swear by your head, because you are not able to make one hair white or black. [37] But let your word by Yes, yes; No, no. For whatever is more than these is from evil.

[38] You have heard that it was said, Eye for eye, and tooth for tooth; [39] but I say to you, Do

25 καὶ τότε ἐλθὼν πρόσφερε τὸ δῶρόν σου. ἴσθι εὐνοῶν τῷ
and then coming offer the gift of you. Be well-minded with the
ἀντιδίκῳ σου ταχύ, ἕως ὅτου εἶ ἐν τῇ ὁδῷ μετ' αὐτοῦ,
opponent of you quickly, until that you are in the way with him,
μήποτέ σε παραδῷ ὁ ἀντίδικος τῷ κριτῇ, καὶ ὁ κριτής σε
lest you deliver the opponent to the judge, and the judge you

26 παραδῷ τῷ ὑπηρέτῃ, καὶ εἰς φυλακὴν βληθήσῃ. ἀμὴν λέγω
deliver to the officer, and into prison you be thrown. Truly, I say
σοι, οὐ μὴ ἐξέλθῃς ἐκεῖθεν, ἕως ἂν ἀποδῷς τὸν ἔσχατον
to you, in no way shall you exit from there until you pay the last

27 κοδράντην. Ἠκούσατε ὅτι ἐρρέθη τοῖς ἀρχαίοις, Οὐ μοιχεύ

28 kodrantes. You heard that it was said to the ancients, Not commit
σεις· ἐγὼ δὲ λέγω ὑμῖν, ὅτι πᾶς ὁ βλέπων γυναῖκα πρὸς τὸ
adultery. I But I say to you that each one looking at a woman to
ἐπιθυμῆσαι αὐτῆς ἤδη ἐμοίχευσεν αὐτὴν ἐν τῇ καρδίᾳ αὐτοῦ.
lust after her already has committed adultery with her in the heart of him.

29 εἰ δὲ ὁ ὀφθαλμός σου ὁ δεξιὸς σκανδαλίζει σε, ἔξελε αὐτὸν
if But the eye of you right offends you, take out it
καὶ βάλε ἀπὸ σοῦ· συμφέρει γάρ σοι ἵνα ἀπόληται ἓν τῶν
and throw(it) from you. profitable For to you that should perish one of the

30 μελῶν σου, καὶ μὴ ὅλον τὸ σῶμά σου βληθῇ εἰς γέενναν. καὶ
parts of you, and not all the body of you be cast into Gehenna. And
εἰ ἡ δεξιά σου χεὶρ σκανδαλίζει σε, ἔκκοψον αὐτὴν καὶ βάλε
if the right of you hand causes to offend you, cut off it and throw
ἀπὸ σοῦ συμφέρει γάρ σοι ἵνα ἀπόληται ἓν τῶν μελῶν σου,
from you. profitable For you that should perish one of the parts of you,

31 καὶ μὴ ὅλον τὸ σῶμά σου βληθῇ εἰς γέενναν. ἐρρέθη δὲ ὅτι
and not all the body of you be cast into Gehenna. it was said And,
Ὃς ἂν ἀπολύσῃ τὴν γυναῖκα αὐτοῦ, δότω αὐτῇ ἀποσ
Whoever puts away the wife of him, let him give her a bill

32 τάσιον· ἐγὼ δὲ λέγω ὑμῖν, ὅτι ὃς ἂν ἀπολύσῃ τὴν γυναῖκα
of divorce. I But say to you that whoever puts away the wife
αὐτοῦ, παρεκτὸς λόγου πορνείας, ποιεῖ αὐτὴν μοιχᾶσθαι·
of him, apart from a matter of fornication, makes her commit adultery;
καὶ ὃς ἐὰν ἀπολελυμένην γαμήσῃ μοιχᾶται.
and whoever the put away one shall marry commits adultery.

33 Πάλιν ἠκούσατε ὅτι ἐρρέθη τοῖς ἀρχαίοις, Οὐκ ἐπιορκή
Again, you heard that it was said to the ancients, Not you shall per-

34 σεις, ἀποδώσεις δὲ τῷ Κυρίῳ τοὺς ὅρκους σου· ἐγὼ δὲ λέγω
jure, shall deliver but to the Lord the oaths of you. I But say
ὑμῖν μὴ ὀμόσαι ὅλως· μήτε ἐν τῷ οὐρανῷ, ὅτι θρόνος ἐστὶ
to you, Not do swear (at) all, neither by Heaven, because throne it is

35 τοῦ Θεοῦ· μήτε ἐν τῇ γῇ, ὅτι ὑποπόδιόν ἐστι τῶν ποδῶν
of God; neither by the earth, because footstool it is of the feet
αὐτοῦ· μήτε εἰς Ἱεροσόλυμα, ὅτι πόλις ἐστὶ τοῦ μεγάλου
of Him; neither to Jerusalem, because city it is of the great

36 βασιλέως· μήτε ἐν τῇ κεφαλῇ σου ὀμόσῃς, ὅτι οὐ δύνασαι
King; neither by the head of you swear, because not you are able

37 μίαν τρίχα λευκὴν ἢ μέλαιναν ποιῆσαι. ἔστω δὲ ὁ λόγος
one hair white or black to make. let be But the word
ὑμῶν, ναὶ ναί, οὒ οὔ· τὸ δὲ περισσὸν τούτων ἐκ τοῦ πονηροῦ
of you, Yes, yes, no, no. the And excess of these out of the evil one

38 ἐστιν. Ἠκούσατε ὅτι ἐρρέθη, Ὀφθαλμὸν ἀντὶ ὀφθαλμοῦ, καὶ
is. You heard that it was said, An eye instead of an eye, and

39 ὀδόντα ἀντὶ ὀδόντος· ἐγὼ δὲ λέγω ὑμῖν μὴ ἀντιστῆναι τῷ
a tooth instead of a tooth. I But say to you, Not do resist the

not resist evil; but whoever shall strike you on your right cheek, turn the other to him also; [40] and to him who would go to law with you and take your tunic, give (your) coat to him also; [41] and whoever will compel you to go one mile, go two with him. [42] He asking you to give, and he asking you to borrow, do not turn away.

[43] You have heard that it was said, You shall love your neighbor and hate your enemy. [44] But I say to you, Love your enemies, bless those who curse you, do well to those who hate you, and pray for those who despitefully use you and persecute you; [45] so that you may be sons of your Father who (is) in Heaven; for He causes His sun to rise on evil and good, and sends rain on (the) just and unjust. [46] For if you love those who love you, what reward do you have? Do not the tax-collectors do the same? [47] And if you greet your brothers only, what more do you do? Do not the tax-collectors do so? [48] Therefore, you shall be perfect, even as your Father who is in Heaven is perfect.

πονηρῷ· ἀλλ' ὅστις σε ῥαπίσει ἐπὶ τὴν δεξιάν σου σιαγόνα,
evil,　　but　　who you strikes　　on　the right of you　cheek

40 στρέψον αὐτῷ καὶ τὴν ἄλλην· καὶ τῷ θέλοντί σοι κριθῆναι
turn　　to him also the　other; and he wishing　you to sue,

41 καὶ τὸν χιτῶνά σου λαβεῖν, ἄφες αὐτῷ καὶ τὸ ἱμάτιον· καὶ
and the　tunic of you to take, allow him also the coat.　And

42 ὅστις σε ἀγγαρεύσει μίλιον ἕν, ὕπαγε μετ' αὐτοῦ δύο. τῷ
who you shall compel to go mile one, go　with　him　two. He
αἰτοῦντί σε δίδου· καὶ τὸν θέλοντα ἀπὸ σοῦ δανείσασθαι μὴ
asking you to give, and he wishing　from you to borrow,　not
ἀποστραφῇς.
do turn away.

43 Ἠκούσατε ὅτι ἐρρέθη, Ἀγαπήσεις τὸν πλησίον σου, καὶ
You heard that it was said, You shall love the　neighbor of you, and

44 μισήσεις τὸν ἐχθρόν σου· ἐγὼ δὲ λέγω ὑμῖν, ἀγαπᾶτε τοὺς
you shall hate the enemy of you. I But I say to you,　Love　the
ἐχθροὺς ὑμῶν, εὐλογεῖτε τοὺς καταρωμένους ὑμᾶς, καλῶς
enemies of you, bless　those　cursing　you, well
ποιεῖτε. τοὺς μισοῦντας ὑμᾶς, καὶ προσεύχεσθε ὑπὲρ τῶν
do　to those hating　you, and　pray　on behalf of those

45 ἐπηρεαζόντων ὑμᾶς, καὶ διωκόντων ὑμᾶς· ὅπως γένησθε
abusing　　you　and persecuting　you; so that you may be
υἱοὶ τοῦ πατρὸς ὑμῶν τοῦ ἐν οὐρανοῖς, ὅτι τὸν ἥλιον αὐτοῦ
sons of the Father of you in (the) heavens. Because the sun of Him
ἀνατέλλει ἐπὶ πονηροὺς καὶ ἀγαθούς, καὶ βρέχει ἐπὶ
He makes rise on (the) evil　and (the) good,　and　sends rain on

46 δικαίους καὶ ἀδίκους. ἐὰν γὰρ ἀγαπήσητε τοὺς ἀγαπῶντας
(the) just and (the) unjust. if For　you love　those　loving
ὑμᾶς, τίνα μισθὸν ἔχετε; οὐχὶ καὶ οἱ τελῶναι τὸ αὐτὸ
you,　what reward　have you? Not even do the tax-collectors the same

47 ποιοῦσι; καὶ ἐὰν ἀσπάσησθε τοὺς ἀδελφοὺς ὑμῶν μόνον,
practice? And if you greet　the　brothers of you　only,
τί περισσὸν ποιεῖτε; οὐχὶ καὶ οἱ τελῶναι οὕτω ποιοῦσιν;
what exceptional do you? Not do even the tax-collectors so　do?

48 Ἔσεσθε οὖν ὑμεῖς τέλειοι, ὥσπερ ὁ πατὴρ ὑμῶν ὁ ἐν τοῖς
be　then You perfect. even as the Father of you　in　the
οὐρανοῖς τέλειός ἐστι.
heavens　perfect is.

## CHAPTER 6

### CHAPTER 6

[1] Be careful not to do your good deeds before men, in order to be seen by them; otherwise you have no reward with your Father who is in Heaven [2] Therefore when you do good deeds, do not sound a trumpet before you, as the hypocrites do in the synagogues and in the streets, that they may have glory from men. Truly I say to you, they have their reward. [3] But you (in) doing good deeds, do not let your left hand know what your right hand

1 Προσέχετε τὴν ἐλεημοσύνην ὑμῶν μὴ ποιεῖν ἔμπροσθεν
Take care　the merciful deeds　of you　not to do　before
τῶν ἀνθρώπων, πρὸς τὸ θεαθῆναι αὐτοῖς· εἰ δὲ μήγε,
men,　in order to　be seen of them. if But not,
μισθὸν οὐκ ἔχετε παρὰ τῷ πατρὶ ὑμῶν τῷ ἐν τοῖς οὐρανοῖς.
reward not you have from the Father of you　in the　heavens

2 Ὅταν οὖν ποιῇς ἐλεημοσύνην, μὴ σαλπίσῃς ἔμπροσθέν
when Then you do merciful deeds, not do trumpet　before
σου, ὥσπερ οἱ ὑποκριταὶ ποιοῦσιν ἐν ταῖς συναγωγαῖς καὶ
you, as　the hypocrites　do　in the　synagogues　and
ἐν ταῖς ῥύμαις, ὅπως δοξασθῶσιν ὑπὸ τῶν ἀνθρώπων·
in the　streets,　so that they may be glorified by　men.

3 ἀμὴν λέγω ὑμῖν, ἀπέχουσι τὸν μισθὸν αὐτῶν. σοῦ δὲ ποιοῦν-
Truly, I say to you, they have the reward of them. you But doing
τος ἐλεημοσύνην, μὴ γνώτω ἡ ἀριστερά σου τί ποιεῖ ἡ
merciful deeds,　not do let know the left　of you what does the

does, [4] so that your good deeds may be in secret; and your Father who sees in secret shall Himself give to you openly.

[5] And when you pray, you shall not be as the hypocrites, for they love to pray standing in the synagogues and in the corners of the streets, so that they may be seen by men. Truly I say to you, that they have their reward. [6] But you, when you pray, enter into your room, and having shut your door, pray to your Father who (is) in secret; and your Father who sees in secret will give to you openly. [7] But when you pray do not babble vain words, as the heathen, for they think that they shall be heard in their many words.

[8] Therefore do not be like them, for your Father knows what things you have need of before you ask Him. [9] Therefore you (should) pray this way: Our Father who (is) in Heaven, Hallowed be Your name; [10] let Your kingdom come; let Your will be done, on earth as it is in Heaven. [11] Give us today our daily bread, [12] and forgive us our debts as we also forgive our debtors; [13] and do not lead us into temptation, but deliver us from evil, for Yours is the kingdom and the power and the glory, forever. Amen. [14] For if you forgive men their offenses, your heavenly Father will forgive your offenses [15] But if you will not forgive men their offenses, neither will your Father forgive your offenses.

[16] And when you fast, do not be as the hypocrites, sad of face; for they disfigure their faces so

**4** δεξιά σου, ὅπως ᾖ σου ἡ ἐλεημοσύνη ἐν τῷ κρυπτῷ· καὶ ὁ
right of you, so that of you the merciful deeds in secret, and the
πατήρ σου ὁ βλέπων ἐν τῷ κρυπτῷ αὐτὸς ἀποδώσει σοι ἐν
Father of you seeing in secret Him(self) will repay you in
τῷ φανερῷ.
the open

**5** Καὶ ὅταν προσεύχῃ, οὐκ ἔσῃ ὥσπερ οἱ ὑποκριταί, ὅτι
And when you pray, not you shall be as the hypocrites, because
φιλοῦσιν ἐν ταῖς συναγωγαῖς καὶ ἐν ταῖς γωνίαις τῶν
they love in the synagogues and in the corners of the
πλατειῶν ἑστῶτες προσεύχεσθαι, ὅπως ἂν φανῶσι τοῖς
open streets standing to pray, so that may they appear
ἀνθρώποις· ἀμὴν λέγω ὑμῖν ὅτι ἀπέχουσι τὸν μισθὸν
to men. Truly, I say to you that they have the reward

**6** αὐτῶν. σὺ δέ, ὅταν προσεύχῃ, εἴσελθε εἰς τὸ ταμιεῖόν σου,
of them. you But, when you pray, enter into the room of you
καὶ κλείσας τὴν θύραν σου, πρόσευξαι τῷ πατρί σου τῷ
and shutting the door of you, pray to the Father of you
ἐν τῷ κρυπτῷ· καὶ ὁ πατήρ σου ὁ βλέπων ἐν τῷ κρυπτῷ
in secret; and the Father of you seeing in secret

**7** ἀποδώσει σοι ἐν τῷ φανερῷ. προσευχόμενοι δὲ μὴ βαττο-
will repay you in the open. when praying But, not do use
λογήσητε, ὥσπερ οἱ ἐθνικοί· δοκοῦσι γὰρ ὅτι ἐν τῇ πολυ-
vain repetition, as the nations; they think for that in much

**8** λογίᾳ αὐτῶν εἰσακουσθήσονται. μὴ οὖν ὁμοιωθῆτε αὐτοῖς·
speaking of them they will be heard. not Then do be like them,
οἶδε γὰρ ὁ πατὴρ ὑμῶν ὧν χρείαν ἔχετε, πρὸ τοῦ ὑμᾶς
knows for the Father of you what things need you have before you

**9** αἰτῆσαι αὐτόν. οὕτως οὖν προσεύχεσθε ὑμεῖς· Πάτερ ἡμῶν
ask Him. So then pray you, Father of us

**10** ὁ ἐν τοῖς οὐρανοῖς, ἁγιασθήτω τὸ ὄνομά σου· ἐλθέτω ἡ
in the heavens, let be sanctified the name of You. Let come the
βασιλεία σου· γενηθήτω τὸ θέλημά σου, ὡς ἐν οὐρανῷ, καὶ
kingdom of You; let be done the will of You, as in Heaven, also

**11** ἐπὶ τῆς γῆς· τὸν ἄρτον ἡμῶν τὸν ἐπιούσιον δὸς ἡμῖν
on the earth. The bread of us daily, give to us

**12** σήμερον· καὶ ἄφες ἡμῖν τὰ ὀφειλήματα ἡμῶν, ὡς καὶ ἡμεῖς
today, and forgive us the debts of us, as also we

**13** ἀφίεμεν τοῖς ὀφειλέταις ἡμῶν· καὶ μὴ εἰσενέγκῃς ἡμᾶς εἰς
forgive the debtors of us. And not lead us into
πειρασμόν, ἀλλὰ ῥῦσαι ἡμᾶς ἀπὸ τοῦ πονηροῦ. ὅτι σοῦ
temptation, but deliver us from evil; because of You
ἐστιν ἡ βασιλεία καὶ ἡ δύναμις καὶ ἡ δόξα εἰς τοὺς αἰῶνας.
is the kingdom, and the power, and the glory to the ages.

**14** ἀμήν. ἐὰν γὰρ ἀφῆτε τοῖς ἀνθρώποις τὰ παραπτώματα
Amen. if For you forgive men the trespasses

**15** αὐτῶν, ἀφήσει καὶ ὑμῖν ὁ πατὴρ ὑμῶν ὁ οὐράνιος· ἐὰν δὲ
of them, will forgive also you the Father of you heavenly. if But
μὴ ἀφῆτε τοῖς ἀνθρώποις τὰ παραπτώματα αὐτῶν, οὐδὲ ὁ
not you forgive men the trespasses of them, neither the
πατὴρ ὑμῶν ἀφήσει τὰ παραπτώματα ὑμῶν.
Father of you will forgive the trespasses of you.

**16** Ὅταν δὲ νηστεύητε, μὴ γίνεσθε ὥσπερ οἱ ὑποκριταὶ
when And you fast, not do be as the hypocrites
σκυθρωποί· ἀφανίζουσι γὰρ τὰ πρόσωπα αὐτῶν, ὅπως
darkening the they disfigure for the faces of them so as
face;

that they may appear to be fasting to men. Truly I say to you, that they have their reward. [17] But you (in) fasting, anoint your head and wash your face, [18] so that you may not appear to be fasting to men, but to your Father who (is) in secret; and your Father who sees in secret will give to you openly.

[19] Do not treasure up for you treasures on the earth, where moth and rust make vanish, and where thieves dig through and steal. [20] But treasure up for you treasures in Heaven, where neither moth nor rust make vanish, and where thieves do not dig through nor steal. [21] For where your treasure is, there will be also your heart. [22] The lamp of the body is the eye. If, then, your eye be sound, all your body is light. [23] But if your eye be evil, all your body is dark. If, then, the light in you is darkness, how great the darkness!

[24] No one is able to serve two lords; for either he will hate the one, and he will love the other, or he will hold to one, and he will despise the other. You are not able to serve God and mammon. [25] Because of this I say to you, Do not be anxious as to your life, what you should eat and what you should drink; nor as to your body, what you should put on. Is not the life more than the food, and the body than the clothing? [26] Look at the birds of the heaven, that they do not sow, nor reap, nor gather into barns; yet your heavenly Father feeds them. Do not you more excel than them? [27] But who of you being anxious is able to add to the stature of him one cubit? [28] And why are you anxious about clothing? Consider the lilies of the field, how they grow. They do not labor nor do

φανῶσι τοῖς ἀνθρώποις νηστεύοντες· ἀμὴν λέγω ὑμῖν ὅτι
they appear     to men        fasting.     Truly,  I say to you that

17 ἀπέχουσι τὸν μισθὸν αὐτῶν. σὺ δὲ νηστεύων ἄλειψαί σου
they have    the reward  of them. you But (in) fasting,  anoint  of you

18 τὴν κεφαλήν, καὶ τὸ πρόσωπόν σου νίψαι, ὅπως μὴ φανῇς
the head,    and the  face     of you  wash, so as not to appear

τοῖς ἀνθρώποις νηστεύων, ἀλλὰ τῷ πατρί σου τῷ ἐν τῷ
to men          fasting,    but  to the Father of you   in

κρυπτῷ· καὶ ὁ πατήρ σου ὁ βλέπων ἐν τῷ κρυπτῷ ἀποδώ-
secret; and the Father of you seeing   in      secret  will repay

σει σοι ἐν τῷ φανερῷ.
you  in the  open.

19 Μὴ θησαυρίζετε ὑμῖν θησαυροὺς ἐπὶ τῆς γῆς, ὅπου σὴς
Not do treasure up for you treasures on the earth, where moth

καὶ βρῶσις ἀφανίζει, καὶ ὅπου κλέπται διορύσσουσι καὶ
and rust cause to vanish, and where thieves    dig through    and

20 κλέπτουσι· θησαυρίζετε δὲ ὑμῖν θησαυροὺς ἐν οὐρανῷ,
steal.      treasure up  But for you treasures    in   Heaven,

ὅπου οὔτε σὴς οὔτε βρῶσις ἀφανίζει, καὶ ὅπου κλέπται οὐ
where neither moth nor rust cause to vanish, and where thieves   not

21 διορύσσουσιν οὐδὲ κλέπτουσιν. ὅπου γάρ ἐστιν ὁ θησαυρὸς
dig through   nor   steal.    where For   is   the treasure

22 ὑμῶν, ἐκεῖ ἔσται καὶ ἡ καρδία ὑμῶν. ὁ λύχνος τοῦ σώματός
of you, there will be also the heart of you. The lamp of the  body

ἐστιν ὁ ὀφθαλμός· ἐὰν οὖν ὁ ὀφθαλμός σου ἁπλοῦς ᾖ, ὅλον
is the eye.      If, then, the eye    of you sound be,  all

23 τὸ σῶμά σου φωτεινὸν ἔσται· ἐὰν δὲ ὁ ὀφθαλμός σου πονη-
the body of you light    is.    if But  the  eye    of you  evil

ρὸς ᾖ, ὅλον τὸ σῶμά σου σκοτεινὸν ἔσται. εἰ οὖν τὸ φῶς τὸ
be,  all the body of you dark      is.   If, then, the light

24 ἐν σοὶ σκότος ἐστί, τὸ σκότος πόσον; οὐδεὶς δύναται δυσὶ
in you darkness is,  the darkness how great! No one  is able   two

κυρίοις δουλεύειν· ἢ γὰρ τὸν ἕνα μισήσει, καὶ τὸν ἕτερον
lords   to serve. either For  the one he will hate, and  the  other

ἀγαπήσει· ἢ ἑνὸς ἀνθέξεται, καὶ τοῦ ἑτέρου καταφρονήσει.
he will love, or one he will cleave to, and the  other  he will despise.

25 οὐ δύνασθε Θεῷ δουλεύειν καὶ μαμμωνᾷ. διὰ τοῦτο λέγω
not you are able God  to serve   and    wealth. Because of this, I say

ὑμῖν, μὴ μεριμνᾶτε τῇ ψυχῇ ὑμῶν, τί φάγητε καὶ τί πίητε·
to you, not do be anxious for the soul of you, what you eat, and what drink;

μηδὲ τῷ σώματι ὑμῶν, τί ἐνδύσησθε. οὐχὶ ἡ ψυχὴ πλεῖόν
nor for the body of you, what you put on.   not the soul   more

26 ἐστι τῆς τροφῆς, καὶ τὸ σῶμα τοῦ ἐνδύματος; ἐμβλέψατε
Is than the food,  and the body  of the clothing?      Look

εἰς τὰ πετεινὰ τοῦ οὐρανοῦ, ὅτι οὐ σπείρουσιν, οὐδὲ θερί-
at the birds   of the heaven, that not they sow,   nor do they

ζουσιν, οὐδὲ συνάγουσιν εἰς ἀποθήκας, καὶ ὁ πατὴρ ὑμῶν ὁ
reap,   nor do gather   into  barns;   yet the Father of you

οὐράνιος τρέφει αὐτά· οὐχ ὑμεῖς μᾶλλον διαφέρετε αὐτῶν;
heavenly feeds them. Not do you  rather  excel    them?

27 τίς δὲ ἐξ ὑμῶν μεριμνῶν δύναται προσθεῖναι ἐπὶ τὴν
who But of  you being anxious is able  to add      onto  the

28 ἡλικίαν αὐτοῦ πῆχυν ἕνα; καὶ περὶ ἐνδύματος τί μεριμνᾶτε;
stature of him cubit one? And concerning clothing, why are you anxious?

καταμάθετε τὰ κρίνα τοῦ ἀγροῦ, πῶς αὐξάνει· οὐ κοπιᾷ,
Consider   the lilies of the field,   how they grow; not they labor,

they spin; [29] but I say to you that not even Solomon in all his glory was clothed as one of these. [30] But if God so enrobes the grass of the field — which is today and is thrown into the oven tomorrow — (will He) not much rather you? O (you) of little faith! [31] Therefore, do not be anxious, saying, What shall we eat, or, what shall we drink; or, with what shall we be clothed? [32] For all these things the nations seek after. For your heavenly Father knows that you have need of all these things. [33] But seek first the kingdom of God and His righteousness, and all these things shall be added to you. [34] Therefore, do not be anxious for tomorrow; for tomorrow shall be anxious for its own (things). (Each) day (has) enough evil of itself.

29 οὐδὲ νήθει· λέγω δὲ ὑμῖν ὅτι οὐδὲ Σολομὼν ἐν πάσῃ τῇ
   nor spin.   I say  But to you that not even Solomon  in   all   the
30 δόξῃ αὐτοῦ περιεβάλετο ὡς ἐν τούτων. εἰ δὲ τὸν χόρτον τοῦ
   glory of him was clothed   as one of these. if But  the  grass  of the
   ἀγροῦ, σήμερον ὄντα, καὶ αὔριον εἰς κλίβανον βαλλόμενον,
   field,  today    being, and tomorrow into a furnace  being thrown,
   ὁ Θεὸς οὕτως ἀμφιέννυσιν, οὐ πολλῷ μᾶλλον ὑμᾶς, ὀλιγό-
   God  thus   enrobes;    not much   more (are) you, little-
31 πιστοι ; μὴ οὖν μεριμνήσητε, λέγοντες, Τί φάγωμεν, ἢ τί
   faiths?  not Then be anxious,   saying,   What may we eat? Or, what
32 πίωμεν, ἢ τί περιβαλώμεθα ; πάντα γὰρ ταῦτα τὰ ἔθνη
   may we drink? Or, what may we clothe us?  all   For these things the nations
   ἐπιζητεῖ· οἶδε γὰρ ὁ πατὴρ ὑμῶν ὁ οὐράνιος ὅτι χρῄζετε
   seek.   knows For the Father of you  heavenly  that you need
33 τούτων ἁπάντων. ζητεῖτε δὲ πρῶτον τὴν βασιλείαν τοῦ
   these  of all.    seek But first    the  kingdom
   Θεοῦ καὶ τὴν δικαιοσύνην αὐτοῦ, καὶ ταῦτα πάντα προσ-
   of God and the  righteousness of Him, and these things all   will be
34 τεθήσεται ὑμῖν. μὴ οὖν μεριμνήσητε εἰς τὴν αὔριον· ἡ γὰρ
   added  to you. not Then do be anxious  for the  morrow; the for
   αὔριον μεριμνήσει τὰ ἑαυτῆς. ἀρκετὸν τῇ ἡμέρᾳ ἡ κακία
   morrow will be anxious of itself. Sufficient to the  day (is) the badness
   αὑτῆς.
   of it.

## CHAPTER 7

[1] Do not judge, that you may not be judged; [2] for with whatever judgment you judge, you shall be judged; and with whatever measure you measure, it shall be measured again to you. [3] But why do you look on the twig that (is) in the eye of your brother, but do not see the log in your eye? [4] Or how will you say to your brother, Allow me to cast out the twig from your eye; and, behold, the log (is) in your eye! [5] Hypocrite, first cast the log out of your eye, and then you will see clearly to cast the twig out of the eye of your brother.

[6] Do not give that which (is) holy to the dogs, nor throw your pearls before the swine, lest they should trample on them with their feet, and they having turned may tear you.

[7] Ask, and it shall be given to you; seek, and you shall find; knock, and it shall be opened to you. [8] For everyone that asks receives, and he that seeks find, and to him that knocks it shall be opened.

## CHAPTER 7

1  Μὴ κρίνετε, ἵνα μὴ κριθητε· εν ᾧ γὰρ κρίματι κρίνετε,
2  Not do judge, that not you be judged. in what For judgment you judge,
   κριθήσεσθε· καὶ ἐν ᾧ μέτρῳ μετρεῖτε, ἀντιμετρηθησεται
   you will be judged. and in what measure you measure, it will be measured
3  ὑμῖν. τί δὲ βλέπεις τὸ κάρφος τὸ ἐν τῷ ὀφθαλμῷ τοῦ ἀδελφοῦ
   to you. why But do you see the twig  in the eye  of the brother
4  σου, τὴν δὲ ἐν τῷ σῷ ὀφθαλμῷ δοκὸν οὐ κατανοεῖς ; ἢ πῶς
   of you, the but in the of you eye  log  not you perceive? Or how
   ἐρεῖς τῷ ἀδελφῷ σου, Ἄφες ἐκβάλω τὸ κάρφος ἀπὸ τοῦ
   will you say to the brother of you, Permit (me) to take out the twig from the
   ὀφθαλμοῦ σου· καὶ ἰδού, ἡ δοκὸς ἐν τῷ ὀφθαλμῷ σου ;
   the eye  of you, and behold, the log (is) in the eye  of you?
5  ὑποκριτά, ἔκβαλε πρῶτον τὴν δοκὸν ἐκ τοῦ ὀφθαλμοῦ σου,
   Hypocrite! take out First the  log out of the eye  of you,
   καὶ τότε διαβλέψεις ἐκβαλεῖν τὸ κάρφος ἐκ τοῦ ὀφθαλμοῦ
   and then you will see clearly to take out the twig out of the eye
   τοῦ ἀδελφοῦ σου.
   of the brother of you.
6  Μὴ δῶτε τὸ ἅγιον τοῖς κυσί· μηδὲ βάλητε τοὺς μαργαρί-
   Not do give the holy to the dogs,  nor throw  the pearls
   τας ὑμῶν ἔμπροσθεν τῶν χοίρων, μήποτε καταπατήσωσιν
   of you before    the  pigs,    lest  they trample
   αὐτοὺς ἐν τοῖς ποσὶν αὐτῶν, καὶ στραφέντες ῥήξωσιν ὑμᾶς.
   them with the feet  of them, and turning  they charge you.
7  Αἰτεῖτε, καὶ δοθήσεται ὑμῖν· ζητεῖτε, καὶ εὑρήσετε·
   Ask,   and it will be given to you;  seek,   and you will find;
8  κρούετε, καὶ ἀνοιγήσεται ὑμῖν. πᾶς γὰρ ὁ αἰτῶν λαμβάνει·
   knock,  and it will be opened to you. each For  asking,  receives;
9  καὶ ὁ ζητῶν εὑρίσκει, καὶ τῷ κρούοντι ἀνοιγήσεται. ἢ τίς
   and he seeking,  finds; and to the (one) knocking, it will be opened. Or who

[9] Or what man of you is there who will give a stone if his son shall ask bread (of) him? [10] And if he should ask a fish, will he give him a snake? [11] If therefore you, being evil, know to give good gifts to your children, how much more your father who (is) in Heaven will give good things to those that ask Him?

[12] Therefore all things whatever you desire that men should do to you, so also you should do to them; for this is the Law and the Prophets.

ἐστιν ἐξ ὑμῶν ἄνθρωπος, ὃν ἐὰν αἰτήσῃ ὁ υἱὸς αὐτοῦ ἄρτον,
is    of you    a man,    who if should ask the son of him a loaf,
10 μὴ λίθον ἐπιδώσει αὐτῷ; καὶ ἐὰν ἰχθὺν αἰτήσῃ, μὴ ὄφιν
a stone he will give him?  And if a fish he should ask,    a snake
11 ἐπιδώσει αὐτῷ; εἰ οὖν ὑμεῖς, πονηροὶ ὄντες, οἴδατε δόματα
he will give him?  If, then, you,    evil  being,  know  gifts
ἀγαθὰ διδόναι τοῖς τέκνοις ὑμῶν, πόσῳ μᾶλλον ὁ πατὴρ
good  to give  to the children of you, how much more the Father
ὑμῶν ὁ ἐν τοῖς οὐρανοῖς δώσει ἀγαθὰ τοῖς αἰτοῦσιν αὐτόν;
of you in the    heavens will give good things to those asking  Him!
12 πάντα οὖν ὅσα ἂν θέλητε ἵνα ποιῶσιν ὑμῖν οἱ ἄνθρωποι,
all things Then, what ever you desire that may do to you    men,
οὕτω καὶ ὑμεῖς ποιεῖτε αὐτοῖς· οὗτος γάρ ἐστιν ὁ νόμος καὶ
so    also you    do  to them. this For is  the Law and
οἱ προφῆται.
the Prophets.

[13] Go in through the narrow gate; for wide is the gate and broad is the way that leads to death, and many are they who go through it; [14] For narrow is the gate and tight the way that leads to life and few are they who find it. [15] But beware of the false prophets who come to you in sheep's clothing, but inside are plundering wolves. [16] By their fruits you shall know them. Do they gather grapes from thorns, or figs from thistles? [17] So every good tree produces good fruits; but the corrupt tree produces evil fruits. [18] A good tree cannot produce evil fruits, nor a corrupt tree produce good fruits. [19] Every tree not producing good fruit is cut down and is thrown into fire. [20] Then surely, by their fruits you shall know them.

13 Εἰσέλθετε διὰ τῆς στενῆς πύλης· ὅτι πλατεῖα ἡ πύλη, καὶ
Enter in through the narrow gate; because wide (is) the gate and
εὐρύχωρος ἡ ὁδὸς ἡ ἀπάγουσα εἰς τὴν ἀπώλειαν, καὶ πολλοί
broad (is) the way    leading away into    destruction; and many
14 εἰσιν οἱ εἰσερχόμενοι δι' αὐτῆς· ὅτι στενὴ ἡ πύλη, καὶ
are those entering in through it; because narrow the gate,  and
τεθλιμμένη ἡ ὁδὸς ἡ ἀπάγουσα εἰς τὴν ζωήν, καὶ ὀλίγοι
constricted (is) the way    leading away into    Life; and few
εἰσὶν οἱ εὑρίσκοντες αὐτήν.
are those finding    it.
15 Προσέχετε δὲ ἀπὸ τῶν ψευδοπροφητῶν, οἵτινες ἔρχονται
take care But from the    false prophets,    who  come
πρὸς ὑμᾶς ἐν ἐνδύμασι προβάτων, ἔσωθεν δέ εἰσι λύκοι
to you in clothing  of sheep;  within but they are wolves
16 ἅρπαγες. ἀπὸ τῶν καρπῶν αὐτῶν ἐπιγνώσεσθε αὐτούς·
plundering. From the    fruits    of them, you shall know them.
μήτι συλλέγουσιν ἀπὸ ἀκανθῶν σταφυλήν, ἢ ἀπὸ τριβόλων
Neither do they gather from thorns    grapes,  or from thistles
17 σῦκα; οὕτω πᾶν δένδρον ἀγαθὸν καρποὺς καλοὺς ποιεῖ·
figs?  So  every tree    good    fruits    good    produces.
18 τὸ δὲ σαπρὸν δένδρον καρποὺς πονηροὺς ποιεῖ. οὐ δύναται
the But corrupt tree    fruits    evil    produces. Not is able
δένδρον ἀγαθὸν καρποὺς πονηροὺς ποιεῖν, οὐδὲ δένδρον
a tree  good    fruits    evil    to produce; nor  a tree
19 σαπρὸν καρποὺς καλοὺς ποιεῖν. πᾶν δένδρον μὴ ποιοῦν
corrupt fruits    good to produce. Every tree    not producing
20 καρπὸν καλὸν ἐκκόπτεται καὶ εἰς πῦρ βάλλεται. ἆραγε ἀπὸ
fruits  good  is cut out,  and into fire is thrown.  Surely, from

[21] Not everyone who says to Me, Lord, Lord, shall enter into the kingdom of Heaven, but he who does the will of My Father who (is) in Heaven. [22] Many will say to Me in that day, Lord, Lord, did we not prophesy through Your name, and through Your name throw out demons, and through Your name do many

21 τῶν καρπῶν αὐτῶν ἐπιγνώσεσθε αὐτούς. οὐ πᾶς ὁ λέγων
the  fruits    of them you will know  them. Not everyone saying
μοι, Κύριε, Κύριε, εἰσελεύσεται εἰς τὴν βασιλείαν τῶν
to Me, Lord,  Lord,    will enter  into the    kingdom of the
οὐρανῶν· ἀλλ' ὁ ποιῶν τὸ θέλημα τοῦ πατρός μου τοῦ ἐν
heavens,  but those doing the will of the Father of Me    in
22 οὐρανοῖς. πολλοὶ ἐροῦσί μοι ἐν ἐκείνῃ τῇ ἡμέρᾳ, Κύριε, Κύριε,
(the) heavens. Many will say to Me in that    day.  Lord,  Lord,
οὐ τῷ σῷ ὀνόματι προεφητεύσαμεν, καὶ τῷ σῷ ὀνόματι
not in Your name  did we prophesy,    and in Your  name
δαιμόνια ἐξεβάλομεν, καὶ τῷ σῷ ὀνόματι δυνάμεις πολλὰς
demons  cast out, and    in Your name works of power many

mighty works? [23] And then I will confess to them, I never knew you; depart from Me, you who work lawlessness!

[24] Therefore everyone who hears these words of Mine, and does them, I will compare him to a wise man who built his house on the rock; [25] and the rain came down, and the floods came, and the winds blew, and fell upon that house, but it did not fall; for it had been founded on the rock. [26] And everyone who hears these words, and does not do them, he shall be compared to a foolish man who built his house on the sand; [27] and the rain came down, and the floods came, and the winds blew, and beat upon that house; and it fell, and great was its fall.

[28] And it came to pass, when Jesus had finished these words, the crowds were astonished at His teaching. [29] For He was teaching them as having authority, and not as the scribes.

CHAPTER 8

[1] And when He had come down from the mountain, great crowds followed Him. [2] And, behold, a leper having come fell down before Him, saying, Lord, if You cleanse me. [3] And having stretched (his) hand, Jesus touched him, saying, I desire (it). Be cleansed! And instantly his leprosy was cleansed. [4] And Jesus said to him, See (that) you tell no one; but go show yourself to the priest, and offer the gift which Moses commanded, for a testimony to them.

[5] And Jesus having entered into Capernaum, a centurion came near Him, beseeching Him, [6] and saying, Lord, my child is

---

**23** ἐποιήσαμεν ; καὶ τότε ὁμολογήσω αὐτοῖς, ὅτι οὐδέποτε
we performed? And then I will declare to them, Never

ἔγνων ὑμᾶς· ἀποχωρεῖτε ἀπ᾽ ἐμοῦ οἱ ἐργαζόμενοι τὴν
I knew you; depart from Me, those working

**24** ἀνομίαν. πᾶς οὖν ὅστις ἀκούει μου τοὺς λόγους τούτους καὶ
lawlessness. Every-one then who hears from Me words these, and

ποιεῖ αὐτούς, ὁμοιώσω αὐτὸν ἀνδρὶ φρονίμῳ, ὅστις ᾠκοδό-
does them, I will compare him to a man prudent, who built

**25** μησε τὴν οἰκίαν αὐτοῦ ἐπὶ τὴν πέτραν· καὶ κατέβη ἡ βροχὴ
the house of him on the rock. And came down the rain,

καὶ ἦλθον οἱ ποταμοὶ καὶ ἔπνευσαν οἱ ἄνεμοι, καὶ προσ-
and came up the rivers, and blew the winds, and fell

ἔπεσον τῇ οἰκίᾳ ἐκείνῃ, καὶ οὐκ ἔπεσε· τεθεμελίωτο γὰρ ἐπὶ
against house that; yet not it fell; it had been founded for on

**26** τὴν πέτραν. καὶ πᾶς ὁ ἀκούων μου τοὺς λόγους τούτους
the rock. And everyone hearing of Me words these,

καὶ μὴ ποιῶν αὐτούς, ὁμοιωθήσεται ἀνδρὶ μωρῷ, ὅστις
and not doing them, will be compared to a man foolish, who

**27** ᾠκοδόμησε τὴν οἰκίαν αὐτοῦ ἐπὶ τὴν ἄμμον· καὶ κατέβη ἡ
built the house of him on the sand; and came down the

βροχὴ καὶ ἦλθον οἱ ποταμοὶ καὶ ἔπνευσαν οἱ ἄνεμοι, καὶ
rain, and came up the rivers, and blew the winds, and

προσέκοψαν τῇ οἰκίᾳ ἐκείνῃ, καὶ ἔπεσε· καὶ ἦν ἡ πτῶσις
beat against house that; and it fell, and was the collapse

αὐτῆς μεγάλη.
of it great.

**28** Καὶ ἐγένετο ὅτε συνετέλεσεν ὁ Ἰησοῦς τοὺς λόγους τού-
And happened, when had finished Jesus sayings these,

**29** τους, ἐξεπλήσσοντο οἱ ὄχλοι ἐπὶ τῇ διδαχῇ αὐτοῦ· ἦν γὰρ
were astonished the crowds at the teaching of him. He was For

διδάσκων αὐτοὺς ὡς ἐξουσίαν ἔχων, καὶ οὐχ ὡς οἱ γραμ-
teaching them as authority having, and not as the

ματεῖς.
scribes.

## CHAPTER 8

**1** Καταβάντι δὲ αὐτῷ ἀπὸ τοῦ ὄρους, ἠκολούθησαν αὐτῷ
having come down And He from the mount, followed Him

**2** ὄχλοι πολλοί· καὶ ἰδού, λεπρὸς ἐλθὼν προσεκύνει αὐτῷ,
crowds great. And behold, a leper having come worshiped Him,

**3** λέγων, Κύριε, ἐὰν θέλῃς, δύνασαί με καθαρίσαι. καὶ ἐκτείνας
saying, Lord, if You will, You are able me to cleanse. And stretching

τὴν χεῖρα, ἥψατο αὐτοῦ ὁ Ἰησοῦς, λέγων, Θέλω, καθαρί-
the hand, touched him Jesus, saying, I will, be

**4** σθητι. καὶ εὐθέως ἐκαθαρίσθη αὐτοῦ ἡ λέπρα. καὶ λέγει
cleansed! And instantly was cleansed of Him the leprosy. And says

αὐτῷ ὁ Ἰησοῦς, Ὅρα μηδενὶ εἴπῃς· ἀλλ᾽ ὕπαγε, σεαυτὸν
to him Jesus, See (that) no one you tell, but go, yourself

δεῖξον τῷ ἱερεῖ, καὶ προσένεγκε τὸ δῶρον ὃ προσέταξε
show to the priest, and offer the gift which ordered

Μωσῆς, εἰς μαρτύριον αὐτοῖς.
Moses, for a testimony to them.

**5** Εἰσελθόντι δὲ τῷ Ἰησοῦ εἰς Καπερναούμ, προσῆλθεν
having entered And Jesus into Capernaum, came near

**6** αὐτῷ ἑκατόνταρχος παρακαλῶν αὐτόν, καὶ λέγων, Κύριε,
to Him a centurion beseeching Him, and saying, Lord,

laid in the house a paralytic, grievously afflicted. [7] And Jesus said to him, I will come and heal him. [8] And answering the centurian said, Lord, I am not worthy that You should come under my roof; but only speak a word, and my servant shall be healed. [9] For I also am a man under authority, having soldiers under myself; and I say to this one, Go, and he goes; and to another, Come, and he comes; and to my slave, Do this, and he does. [10] And Jesus having heard marveled, and said to those following, Truly I say to you, Not even in Israel have I found such great faith. [11] But I say to you, that many shall come from east and west, and shall recline with Abraham and Isaac and Jacob in the kingdom of Heaven; [12] but the sons of the kingdom shall be thrown out into the outer darkness; there shall be weeping and gnashing of teeth. [13] And Jesus said to the centurion, Go, and as you have believed, so let it be to you. And his servant was healed in that hour. [14] And having come to the house of Peter, Jesus saw his wife's mother laid out and in a fever; [15] and He touched her hand, and her fever left her; and she arose and served them. [16] And evening having come, they brought to Him many possessed with demons; and He cast out the spirits by a word, and all who were ill He healed; [17] so that it might be fulfilled that which was spoken by Isaiah the prophet, saying, "He took upon Himself our weaknesses and bore (our) sicknesses." [18] And seeing great crowds around him, Jesus gave orders to go over to the other side. [19] And one having come, a scribe, said to Him, Teacher, I will follow You wherever You may go. [20] And Jesus said to him, The foxes have holes,

ὁ παῖς μου βέβληται ἐν τῇ οἰκίᾳ παραλυτικός, δεινῶς βασανι-
the child of me has been laid in the house a paralytic, grievously being

7 ζόμενος. καὶ λέγει αὐτῷ ὁ Ἰησοῦς, Ἐγὼ ἐλθὼν θεραπεύσω
tormented. And says to him Jesus, I having come will heal

8 αὐτόν. καὶ ἀποκριθεὶς ὁ ἑκατόνταρχος ἔφη, Κύριε, οὐκ εἰμὶ
him. And answering the centurion said, Lord, not I am
ἱκανὸς ἵνα μου ὑπὸ τὴν στέγην εἰσέλθῃς· ἀλλὰ μόνον εἰπὲ
worthy that of me under the roof You may enter, but only say

9 λόγον, καὶ ἰαθήσεται ὁ παῖς μου. καὶ γὰρ ἐγὼ ἄνθρωπός
a word, and will be healed the child of me. also For I a man
εἰμι ὑπὸ ἐξουσίαν, ἔχων ὑπ' ἐμαυτὸν στρατιώτας· καὶ λέγω
am under authority, having under myself soldiers; and I way
τούτῳ, Πορεύθητι, καὶ πορεύεται· καὶ ἄλλῳ, Ἔρχου, καὶ
to this (one), Go And he goes. And to another, Come! And
ἔρχεται· καὶ τῷ δούλῳ μου, Ποίησον τοῦτο, καὶ ποιεῖ.
he comes. And to the slave of me, Do this! And he does.

10 ἀκούσας δὲ ὁ Ἰησοῦς ἐθαύμασε, καὶ εἶπε τοῖς ἀκολουθοῦσιν,
hearing And, Jesus marveled, and said to those following,
Ἀμὴν λέγω ὑμῖν, οὐδὲ ἐν τῷ Ἰσραὴλ τοσαύτην πίστιν
Truly, I say to you, Not even in Israel such faith

11 εὗρον. λέγω δὲ ὑμῖν, ὅτι πολλοὶ ἀπὸ ἀνατολῶν καὶ δυσμῶν
I found. I say And to you that many from east and vest
ἥξουσι, καὶ ἀνακλιθήσονται μετὰ Ἀβραὰμ καὶ Ἰσαὰκ καὶ
will come, and will recline with Abraham and Isaac and

12 Ἰακὼβ ἐν τῇ βασιλείᾳ τῶν οὐρανῶν· οἱ δὲ υἱοὶ ~ βασιλείας
Jacob in the kingdom of the heavens. the But sor .ne kingdom
ἐκβληθήσονται εἰς τὸ σκότος τὸ ἐξώτερον· ἐκεῖ ἔσται ὁ
shall be cast out into the darkness outer; there shall be

13 κλαυθμὸς καὶ ὁ βρυγμὸς τῶν ὀδόντων. καὶ εἶπεν ὁ Ἰησοῦς
weeping and gnashing of the teeth. And said Jesus
τῷ ἑκατοντάρχῳ, Ὕπαγε, καὶ ὡς ἐπίστευσας γενηθήτω σοι.
to the centurion, Go! And as you believed, let it be to you.
καὶ ἰάθη ὁ παῖς αὐτοῦ ἐν τῇ ὥρᾳ ἐκείνῃ.
And was healed the child of him in hour that.

14 Καὶ ἐλθὼν ὁ Ἰησοῦς εἰς τὴν οἰκίαν Πέτρου, εἶδε τὴν
And having come, Jesus into the house of Peter, He saw the

15 πενθερὰν αὐτοῦ βεβλημένην καὶ πυρέσσουσαν, καὶ ἥψατο
mother-in-law of him having been laid and fever-stricken. And He touched
τῆς χειρὸς αὐτῆς, καὶ ἀφῆκεν αὐτὴν ὁ πυρετός· καὶ ἠγέρθη,
the hand of her, and left her the fever. And she arose

16 καὶ διηκόνει αὐτοῖς. ὀψίας δὲ γενομένης προσήνεγκαν αὐτῷ
and ministered to them. evening And having come, they brought to Him
δαιμονιζομένους πολλούς· καὶ ἐξέβαλε τὰ πνεύματα λόγῳ,
demon-possessed many. And He cast out the spirits by a word;

17 καὶ πάντας τοὺς κακῶς ἔχοντας ἐθεράπευσεν· ὅπως πληρωθῇ
and all those illness having, He healed; so as may be fulfilled
τὸ ῥηθὲν διὰ Ἡσαΐου τοῦ προφήτου. λέγοντος, Αὐτὸς τὰς
that spoken through Isaiah the prophet, saying, He the
Ἰδὼν δὲ ὁ Ἰησοῦς πολλοὺς ὄχλους περ αὐτόν, ἐκέλευσεν
seeing And Jesus great crowds around Him, He ordered

18 ἀπελθεῖν εἰς τὸ πέραν. καὶ προσελθὼν εἷς γραμματεὺς εἶπεν
to go away to the other side. And coming near one scribe said

19 αὐτῷ, Διδάσκαλε, ἀκολουθήσω σοι ὅπου ἐὰν ἀπέρχῃ. καὶ
to Him, Teacher, I will follow you whereever you go. And

20 λέγει αὐτῷ ὁ Ἰησοῦς, Αἱ ἀλώπεκες φωλεοὺς ἔχουσι, καὶ τὰ
says to him Jesus, The foxes holes have, and the

and the birds of the sky nests., but the Son of man has nowhere He may lay the head. [21] And another of His disciples said to Him, Lord, allow me first to go and bury my father. [22] But Jesus said to him, Follow Me, and leave the dead to bury their own dead.

[23] And He having entered into the boat, His disciples followed Him. [24] And behold, a great storm rose up in the sea, so that the boat was covered by the waves; but He was sleeping. [25] And His disciples having come awoke Him, saying, Lord, save us· we are perishing. [26] And He said to them, Why are you afraid, O (you) of little faith? Then rising up He rebuked the winds and the sea, and there was a great calm [27] And the men marveled, saying, What kind (of man) is this, that even the winds and the sea obey Him?

[28] And when He had come to the other side, to the country of the Gergesenes, two demon-possessed ones met Him, coming out of the tombs, very violent, so that no one was able to pass by that way [29] And, behold, they cried out, saying, What to us and to you, Jesus, Son of God! Have You come here before time to torment us? [30] Now there was far off from them a herd of many swine feeding; [31] and the demons begged Him, saying, If You throw us out, allow us to go away into the herd of the swine. [32] And He said to them, Go! And having gone they went away into the herd of the swine; and, behold, all the herd of the swine rushed down the cliff into the sea and died in the waters! [33] But those who fed (them) fled, and having gone into the city told

πετεινὰ τοῦ οὐρανοῦ κατασκηνώσεις· ὁ δὲ υἱὸς τοῦ ἀνθρώ-
birds of the heaven nests, the but Son of

21 που οὐκ ἔχει ποῦ τὴν κεφαλὴν κλίνη. ἕτερος δὲ τῶν μαθητῶν
man not has where the head He may lay. another And of the disciples

αὐτοῦ εἶπεν αὐτῷ, Κύριε, ἐπίτρεψόν μοι πρῶτον ἀπελθεῖν
of Him said to Him, Lord, allow me first to go away

22 καὶ θάψαι τὸν πατέρα μου. ὁ δὲ Ἰησοῦς εἶπεν αὐτῷ, Ἀκολού-
and to buy the father of me. And Jesus said to him, Follow

θει μοι, καὶ ἄφες τοὺς νεκροὺς θάψαι τοὺς ἑαυτῶν νεκρούς.
Me, and allow the dead to bury the of themselves dead.

23 Καὶ ἐμβάντι αὐτῷ εἰς τὸ πλοῖον, ἠκολούθησαν αὐτῷ οἱ
And having entered He into the boat, followed Him the

24 μαθηταὶ αὐτοῦ. καὶ ἰδού, σεισμὸς μέγας ἐγένετο ἐν τῇ θα-
disciples of Him. And behold, a shaking great occurred in the

λάσσῃ, ὥστε τὸ πλοῖον καλύπτεσθαι ὑπὸ τῶν κυμάτων·
sea, so that the boat was covered by the waves.

25 αὐτὸς δὲ ἐκάθευδε. καὶ προσελθόντες οἱ μαθηταὶ αὐτοῦ
He But was sleeping. And having come near, the disciples of Him

ἤγειραν αὐτόν, λέγοντες, Κύριε, σῶσον ἡμᾶς, ἀπολλύμεθα.
aroused Him, saying, Lord, save us; we are perishing.

26 καὶ λέγει αὐτοῖς, Τί δειλοί ἐστε, ὀλιγόπιστοι; τότε ἐγερθεὶς
And He says to them, Why afraid are you, little-faiths? Then arising,

ἐπετίμησε τοῖς ἀνέμοις καὶ τῇ θαλάσσῃ, καὶ ἐγένετο γαλήνη
He rebuked the wind and the sea, and there was a calm

27 μεγάλη. οἱ δὲ ἄνθρωποι ἐθαύμασαν, λέγοντες, Ποταπός
great. the And men marveled, saying, Of what kind

ἐστιν οὗτος, ὅτι καὶ οἱ ἄνεμοι καὶ ἡ θάλασσα ὑπακούουσιν
is this, that even the winds and the sea obey

αὐτῷ;
Him?

28 Καὶ ἐλθόντι αὐτῷ εἰς τὸ πέραν εἰς τὴν χώραν τῶν
And having come He to the other side, into the country of the

Γεργεσηνῶν, ὑπήντησαν αὐτῷ δύο δαιμονιζόμενοι ἐκ τῶν
Gergesenes, met Him two demon-possessed out of the

μνημείων ἐξερχόμενοι, χαλεποὶ λίαν, ὥστε μὴ ἰσχύειν τινὰ
tombs coming out, violent exceedingly, so as not was able any

29 παρελθεῖν διὰ τῆς ὁδοῦ ἐκείνης· καὶ ἰδού, ἔκραξαν λέγοντες,
to pass through way that. And behold, they cried out, saying,

Τί ἡμῖν καὶ σοί, Ἰησοῦ, υἱὲ τοῦ Θεοῦ; ἦλθες ὧδε πρὸ καιροῦ
What to us and to You, Jesus, Son of God? Come You here before time

30 βασανίσαι ἡμᾶς; ἦν δὲ μακρὰν ἀπ᾽ αὐτῶν ἀγέλη χοίρων
to torment us? was And at a distance from them a herd of pigs

31 πολλῶν βοσκομένη. οἱ δὲ δαίμονες παρεκάλουν αὐτόν,
many feeding. the And demons begged Him,

λέγοντες, Εἰ ἐκβάλλεις ἡμᾶς, ἐπίτρεψον ἡμῖν ἀπελθεῖν εἰς τὴν
saying, If You expel us, allow us to go away into the

32 ἀγέλην τῶν χοίρων. καὶ εἶπεν αὐτοῖς, Ὑπάγετε. οἱ δὲ
herd. of the pigs. And He said to them, Go! those And

ἐξελθόντες ἀπῆλθον εἰς τὴν ἀγέλην τῶν χοίρων· καὶ ἰδού,
coming out went away into the herd of the pigs. And behold,

ὥρμησε πᾶσα ἡ ἀγέλη τῶν χοίρων κατὰ τοῦ κρημνοῦ εἰς
rushed all the herd of the pigs down the cliff into

33 τὴν θάλασσαν, καὶ ἀπέθανον ἐν τοῖς ὕδασιν. οἱ δὲ βόσκοντες
the sea, and died in the waters. those But feeding

ἔφυγον, καὶ ἀπελθόντες εἰς τὴν πόλιν ἀπήγγειλαν πάντα,
fled, and having gone into the city told all things,

everything, and about those possessed by demons. [34] And, behold, all the city went out to meet Jesus; and seeing Him, they begged that He would depart from their borders.

34 καὶ τὰ τῶν δαιμονιζομένων. καὶ ἰδού, πᾶσα ἡ πόλις ἐξῆλ-
and the (things) of the demon-possessed. And behold, all the city went
θεν εἰς συνάντησιν τῷ 'Ιησοῦ· καὶ ἰδόντες αὐτόν, παρεκα-
out to    meet with    Jesus;    and  seeing    Him,    they
λεσαν ὅπως μεταβῇ ἀπὸ τῶν ὁρίων αὐτῶν.
begged    that He move from the    borders of them.

## CHAPTER 9

[1] And having entered into the boat, He passed over and came to His own city. [2] And, behold, they brought a paralytic lying on a bed to Him, and Jesus seeing their face, said to the paralytic, Be comforted, child; your sins have been forgiven you! [3] And, behold, some of the scribes said to themselves, This one blasphemes. [4] And Jesus knowing their thoughts said, Why do you think evil in your hearts? [15] For which is easier, to say, Your sins have been forgiven you, or to say, Arise and walk? [6] But that you may know that the Son of man has authority on earth to forgive sins; then He said to the paralytic, Having risen up, take up your bed and go to your house. [7] And having risen up, he went away to his house. [8] And the crowds having seen wondered, and glorified God who gave such authority to men.

1 Καὶ ἐμβὰς εἰς τὸ πλοῖον διεπέρασε καὶ ἦλθεν εἰς τὴν ἰδίαν
And entering into the boat,    He passed over and came into the own
2 πόλιν. καὶ ἰδού, προσέφερον αὐτῷ παραλυτικὸν ἐπὶ κλίνης
city.    And behold, they brought  to Him    a paralytic    on   a cot
βεβλημένον· καὶ ἰδὼν ὁ 'Ιησοῦς τὴν πίστιν αὐτῶν εἶπε τῷ
laid out.    And seeing    Jesus    the    faith    of them, He said to the
παραλυτικῷ, Θάρσει, τέκνον· ἀφέωνταί σοι αἱ ἁμαρτίαι
paralytic,    Be comforted, child; have been forgiven you  the    sins
3 σου. καὶ ἰδού, τινὲς τῶν γραμματέων εἶπον ἐν ἑαυτοῖς,
of you. And behold, some of the    scribes    said within themselves,
4 Οὗτος βλασφημεῖ. καὶ ἰδὼν ὁ 'Ιησοῦς τὰς ἐνθυμήσεις αὐτῶν
This (one) blasphemes. And seeing    Jesus    the    thoughts    of them
εἶπεν, 'Ινατί ὑμεῖς ἐνθυμεῖσθε πονηρὰ ἐν ταῖς καρδίαις ὑμῶν ;
He said, Why do you    think    evil    in  the   hearts  of you?
5 τί γάρ ἐστιν εὐκοπώτερον, εἰπεῖν, 'Αφέωνταί σοι αἱ
what For  is    easier,    to say, Have been forgiven you the
6 ἁμαρτίαι· ἢ εἰπεῖν, "Εγειραι καὶ περιπάτει ; ἵνα δὲ εἰδῆτε,
sins;    or to say,    Rise up and    walk?    that But you may know
ὅτι ἐξουσίαν ἔχει ὁ υἱὸς τοῦ ἀνθρώπου ἐπὶ τῆς γῆς ἀφιέναι
that authority  has the Son    of man    on the  earth to forgive
ἁμαρτίας (τότε λέγει τῷ παραλυτικῷ), 'Εγερθεὶς ἆρόν σου
sins —    then He says to the  paralytic,    Having risen, lift your
7 τὴν κλίνην, καὶ ὕπαγε εἰς τὸν οἶκόν σου. καὶ ἐγερθεὶς ἀπῆλ-
cot,    and go    to the house of you. And rising up, he went
8 θεν εἰς τὸν οἶκον αὐτοῦ. ἰδόντες δὲ οἱ ὄχλοι ἐθαύμασαν, καὶ
away to the house of him. having seen And the crowds marveled,  and
ἐδόξασαν τὸν Θεόν, τὸν δόντα ἐξουσίαν τοιαύτην τοῖς
glorified    God, the (One) giving    authority    such
ἀνθρώποις.
to men.

[9] And Jesus passing from there saw a man named Matthew sitting at the tax office, and said to him, Follow Me. And having risen up he followed Him. [10] And it came to pass, He reclining in the house, that behold, many tax-collectors and sinners having come were reclining with Jesus and His disciples. [11] And the Pharisees having seen said to His disciples, Why does your teacher eat with tax-collectors and sinners? [12] But Jesus having heard, He said to them, They who are strong have no need of a physician, but

9 Καὶ παράγων ὁ 'Ιησοῦς ἐκεῖθεν εἶδεν ἄνθρωπον καθήμενον
And passing by    Jesus from there    saw    a man    sitting
ἐπὶ τὸ τελώνιον, Ματθαῖον λεγόμενον, καὶ λέγει αὐτῷ,
at the tax-office,    Matthew    called;    and  says to him,
'Ακολούθει μοι. καὶ ἀναστὰς ἠκολούθησεν αὐτῷ.
Follow    me. And rising up,    he followed    Him.
10 Καὶ ἐγένετο αὐτοῦ ἀνακειμένου ἐν τῇ οἰκίᾳ, καὶ ἰδού,
And it happened,    He  reclining    in the  house, and, behold,
πολλοὶ τελῶναι καὶ ἁμαρτωλοὶ ἐλθόντες συνανέκειντο τῷ
many tax-collectors and  sinners    having come  were reclining
11 'Ιησοῦ καὶ τοῖς μαθηταῖς αὐτοῦ. καὶ ἰδόντες οἱ Φαρισαῖοι
with Jesus and the  disciples    of Him.   And having seen, the Pharisees
εἶπον τοῖς μαθηταῖς αὐτοῦ, Διατί μετὰ τῶν τελωνῶν καὶ
said    to the disciples of Him,    Why with  the tax-collectors and
12 ἁμαρτωλῶν ἐσθίει ὁ διδάσκαλος ὑμῶν ; ὁ δὲ 'Ιησοῦς ἀκούσας
sinners    eats    the teacher    of you?    But Jesus having heard,
εἶπεν αὐτοῖς, Οὐ χρείαν ἔχουσιν οἱ ἰσχύοντες ἰατροῦ, ἀλλ'
He said to them, Not    need    have    those being strong of a healer, but

they who are sick. [13] But having gone, learn what this (is), "I desire mercy and not sacrifice." For I did not come to call the righteous to repentance, but sinners.

[14] Then the disciples of John came to Him, saying, Why do we and the Pharisees fast much, and Your disciples do not fast? [15] And Jesus said to them, Can the sons of the bridechamber mourn as long as the bridegroom is with them? But the days will come when the bridegroom will have been taken away from them, and then they will fast. [16] But no one puts a piece of new cloth onto an old garment; for its filling up takes away from the garment, and a worse tear takes (its) place. [17] Nor do they put new wine into old skins, otherwise the skins are burst, and the wine is spilled out, and the skins will be ruined; but they put new wine into new skins, and both are preserved together.

[18] As He spoke these things to them, behold, a ruler having come bowed down to Him, saying, My daughter has just now died; but having come, lay Your hand on her, and she shall live. [19] And having risen up, Jesus followed him, His disciples also.

[20] And, behold, a woman who had a flow of blood for twelve years came up behind and touched the hem of his robe. [21] For she said within herself, If only I shall touch His robe I shall be cured. [22] But Jesus having turned and having seen her, He said, Be comforted, daughter; your faith has cured you. And the woman was cured from that hour.

[23] And Jesus having come into the house of the ruler, and having seen the flute-players and the crowd making a tumult, [24] (He) said to them, Go back, for the little girl is not dead but sleeps; and they laughed at Him.

13 οἱ κακῶς ἔχοντες. πορευθέντες δὲ μάθετε τί ἐστιν, Ἐλεον
those illness having. having gone But, learn what it is: mercy
θέλω, καὶ οὐ θυσίαν· οὐ γὰρ ἦλθον καλέσαι δικαίους, ἀλλ'
I desire, and not sacrifice; not for I came to call righteous but (ones)
ἁμαρτωλοὺς εἰς μετάνοιαν.
sinners to repentance.

14 Τότε προσέρχονται αὐτῷ οἱ μαθηταὶ Ἰωάννου, λέγοντες,
Then came near to Him the disciples of John, saying,
Διατί ἡμεῖς καὶ οἱ Φαρισαῖοι νηστεύομεν πολλά, οἱ δὲ
Why we and the Pharisees do fast much, the but

15 μαθηταί σου οὐ νηστεύουσι; καὶ εἶπεν αὐτοῖς ὁ Ἰησοῦς, Μὴ
disciples of You not do fast? And said to them Jesus, not
δύνανται οἱ υἱοὶ τοῦ νυμφῶνος πενθεῖν, ἐφ' ὅσον μετ' αὐτῶν
Are able the sons of the bridechamber to mourn as long as with them

16 ἐστιν ὁ νυμφίος; ἐλεύσονται δὲ ἡμέραι ὅταν ἀπαρθῇ ἀπ'
is the bridegroom? will come But days when will have been taken from
αὐτῶν ὁ νυμφίος, καὶ τότε νηστεύσουσιν. οὐδεὶς δὲ ἐπιβάλ-
them the bridegroom, and then they will fast. no one But puts
λει ἐπίβλημα ῥάκους ἀγνάφου ἐπὶ ἱματίῳ παλαιῷ· αἴρει
a piece of cloth unfulled on a garment old; takes away
γὰρ τὸ πλήρωμα αὐτοῦ ἀπὸ τοῦ ἱματίου, καὶ χεῖρον
for the fullness of it from the garment, and a worse

17 σχίσμα γίνεται. οὐδὲ βάλλουσιν οἶνον νέον εἰς ἀσκοὺς
tear occurs. Neither do they put wine new into wineskins
παλαιούς· εἰ δὲ μήγε, ῥήγνυνται οἱ ἀσκοί, καὶ ὁ οἶνος
old; otherwise are burst the wineskins, and the wine
ἐκχεῖται, καὶ οἱ ἀσκοὶ ἀπολοῦνται· ἀλλὰ βάλλουσιν οἶνον
pours out, and the wineskins will be ruined; but they put wine
νέον εἰς ἀσκοὺς καινούς, καὶ ἀμφότερα συντηροῦνται.
new into wineskins fresh, and both are preserved together.

18 Ταῦτα αὐτοῦ λαλοῦντος αὐτοῖς, ἰδού, ἄρχων εἷς ἐλθὼν
(As) these things He is speaking to them, behold, a ruler one coming
προσεκύνει αὐτῷ, λέγων ὅτι Ἡ θυγάτηρ μου ἄρτι ἐτελεύ-
worshiped Him, saying, — The daughter of me just now has
τησεν· ἀλλὰ ἐλθὼν ἐπίθες τὴν χεῖρά σου ἐπ' αὐτήν, καὶ
died, but coming lay the hand of You on her, and

19 ζήσεται. καὶ ἐγερθεὶς ὁ Ἰησοῦς ἠκολούθησεν αὐτῷ καὶ οἱ
she will live. And rising up, — Jesus followed him, and the

20 μαθηταὶ αὐτοῦ. καὶ ἰδού, γυνὴ αἱμορροοῦσα δώδεκα ἔτη,
disciples of Him. And, behold, a woman having flow of blood twelve years
προσελθοῦσα ὄπισθεν, ἥψατο τοῦ κρασπέδου τοῦ ἱματίου
coming near behind, touched the fringe of the garment

21 αὐτοῦ. ἔλεγε γὰρ ἐν ἑαυτῇ, Ἐὰν μόνον ἅψωμαι τοῦ ἱματίου
of Him. she said For within herself, If only I shall touch the garment

22 αὐτοῦ, σωθήσομαι. ὁ δὲ Ἰησοῦς ἐπιστραφεὶς καὶ ἰδὼν αὐτὴν
of Him, I shall be cured.— But Jesus having turned and seeing her
εἶπε, Θάρσει, θύγατερ· ἡ πίστις σου σέσωκέ σε. καὶ ἐσώθη
said, Be comforted, daughter; the faith of you has saved you.. And was saved

23 ἡ γυνὴ ἀπὸ τῆς ὥρας ἐκείνης. καὶ ἐλθὼν ὁ Ἰησοῦς εἰς τὴν
the woman from — hour that. And coming Jesus into the
οἰκίαν τοῦ ἄρχοντος, καὶ ἰδὼν τοὺς αὐλητὰς καὶ τὸν ὄχλον
house of the ruler, and seeing the flute-players and the crowd

24 θορυβούμενον, λέγει αὐτοῖς, Ἀναχωρεῖτε· οὐ γὰρ ἀπέθανε
causing a tumult, said to them, Go back not for has died

25 τὸ κοράσιον, ἀλλὰ καθεύδει. καὶ κατεγέλων αὐτοῦ. ὅτε δὲ
the girl, but she sleeps. And they laughed at Him. when But

[25] But when the crowd had been put out, He having entered took hold of her hand, and the little girl arose. [26] And this report went out into all that land.

[27] And Jesus passing on from there, two blind ones followed Him, crying and saying, Have pity on us, Son of David. [28] And having come into the house, the blind ones came and Jesus said to them, Do you believe that I am able to do this? And they said to Him, Yes Lord. [29] Then He touched their eyes, saying, According to your faith, let it be to you. [30] And their eyes were opened; and Jesus strictly commanded them, saying, Let no one know. [31] But they having gone out made Him known in all that land. [32] And as they were going out, behold, they brought a dumb man to Him, possessed by a demon. [33] And the demon having been cast out, the dumb one spoke. And the crowds marveled, saying, Never was it seen this way in Israel. [34] But the Pharisees said, He casts out the demons by the prince of the demons.

[35] And Jesus went about all the cities and the villages, teaching in their synagogues, and preaching the gospel of the kingdom, and healing every sickness and weakness of body among the people. [36] And having seen the crowds, He was moved with compassion for them, because they were tired and scattered as sheep having no shepherd. [37] Then He said to His disciples, The harvest truly (is) great, but the workers few. [38] Pray then that the Lord of the harvest may send out workers into His harvest.

ἐξεβλήθη ὁ ὄχλος, εἰσελθὼν ἐκράτησε τῆς χειρὸς αὐτῆς, καὶ
had been put out the crowd, entering He took hold of the hand of her,  and

26 ἠγέρθη τὸ κοράσιον. καὶ ἐξῆλθεν ἡ φήμη αὕτη εἰς ὅλην τὴν
arose   the girl.      And went out the report  this into all     –

γῆν ἐκείνην.
land  that.

27 Καὶ παράγοντι ἐκεῖθεν τῷ Ἰησοῦ, ἠκολούθησαν αὐτῷ δύο
And passing on   from there – Jesus,   followed     Him   two
τυφλοί, κράζοντες καὶ λέγοντες, Ἐλέησον ἡμᾶς, υἱὲ Δαβίδ.
blind ones, crying   and  saying,    Have pity on  us, Son of David.

28 ἐλθόντι δὲ εἰς τὴν οἰκίαν, προσῆλθον αὐτῷ οἱ τυφλοί, καὶ
coming And into the   house,   came near  to Him the blind ones and
λέγει αὐτοῖς ὁ Ἰησοῦς, Πιστεύετε ὅτι δύναμαι τοῦτο ποιῆ-
said to them  –  Jesus,  Do you believe that I am able  this   to do?

29 σαι; λέγουσιν αὐτῷ, Ναί, Κύριε. τότε ἥψατο τῶν ὀφθαλμῶν
They say to Him, Yes, Lord.   Then He touched the   eyes

30 αὐτῶν, λέγων, Κατὰ τὴν πίστιν ὑμῶν γενηθήτω ὑμῖν. καὶ
of them,  saying, According to the faith  of you   let it be    to you. And
ἀνεῴχθησαν αὐτῶν οἱ ὀφθαλμοί· καὶ ἐνεβριμήσατο αὐτοῖς ὁ
were opened    their   –   eyes;  and strictly ordered   them   –

31 Ἰησοῦς, λέγων, Ὁρᾶτε μηδεὶς γινωσκέτω. οἱ δὲ ἐξελθόντες
Jesus,  saying,  See,  no one  let know.  they But going out
διεφήμισαν αὐτὸν ἐν ὅλῃ τῇ γῇ ἐκείνῃ.
declared    Him  in all  – land that.

32 Αὐτῶν δὲ ἐξερχομένων, ἰδού, προσήνεγκαν αὐτῷ ἄνθρω-
(as) they And were going out, behold, they brought   to Him a man

33 πον κωφὸν δαιμονιζόμενον. καὶ ἐκβληθέντος τοῦ δαιμονίου,
dumb  demon-possessed.  And having been cast out the demon,
ἐλάλησεν ὁ κωφός· καὶ ἐθαύμασαν οἱ ὄχλοι, λέγοντες·
spoke    the dumb. And  marveled    the crowds,  saying,

34 Οὐδέποτε ἐφάνη οὕτως ἐν τῷ Ἰσραήλ. οἱ δὲ Φαρισαῖοι
Never   was it seen thus  in  –  Israel.  the But Pharisees
ἔλεγον, Ἐν τῷ ἄρχοντι τῶν δαιμονίων ἐκβάλλει τὰ
said,   By the  prince   of the  demons   He casts out the
δαιμόνια.
demons.

35 Καὶ περιῆγεν ὁ Ἰησοῦς τὰς πόλεις πάσας καὶ τὰς κώμας,
And went about – Jesus  the cities   all   and the villages,
διδάσκων ἐν ταῖς συναγωγαῖς αὐτῶν, καὶ κηρύσσων τὸ
teaching  in  the  synagogues   of them, and  proclaiming the
εὐαγγέλιον τῆς βασιλείας, καὶ θεραπεύων πᾶσαν νόσον καὶ
gospel     of the kingdom,  and  healing   every sickness and

36 πᾶσαν μαλακίαν ἐν τῷ λαῷ. ἰδὼν δὲ τοὺς ὄχλους, ἐσπλαγ-
every weakness  in the people. seeing And the crowds He was moved
χνίσθη περὶ αὐτῶν, ὅτι ἦσαν ἐκλελυμένοι καὶ ἐρριμμένοι
with pity for  them, because they were tired   and  scattered

37 ὡσεὶ πρόβατα μὴ ἔχοντα ποιμένα. τότε λέγει τοῖς μαθηταῖς
as   sheep   not having a shepherd. Then He says to the disciples
αὐτοῦ, Ὁ μὲν θερισμὸς πολύς, οἱ δὲ ἐργάται ὀλίγοι·
of Him, the Indeed harvest (is) great, the but workmen few;

38 δεήθητε οὖν τοῦ Κυρίου τοῦ θερισμοῦ, ὅπως ἐκβάλῃ ἐργάτας
pray   then the Lord  of the harvest, that He may send workmen
εἰς τὸν θερισμὸν αὐτοῦ.
into the  harvest   of Him.

## CHAPTER 10

## CHAPTER 10

[1] And having called His twelve disciples, He gave them authority over unclean spirits, so as to tnrow them out, and to heal every disease and every weakness of body. [2] Now the names of the twelve apostles are these: First, Simon who is called Peter, and his brother Andrew; James the (son) of Zebedee, and his brother John; [3] Philip, and Bartholomew, Thomas and Matthew the tax-collector; James the (son) of Alpheus, and Lebbeus whose last name (was) Thaddeus; [4] Simon the Canaanite, and Judah Iscariot, who also betrayed Him.

[5] Jesus sent these twelve out, having commanded them, saying, Do not go into (the) way of the nations, and do not go into a city of (the) Samaritans; [6] but rather go to the sheep, the lost of (the) house of Israel. [7] And going on preach, saying, The kingdom of Heaven has drawn near. [8] Heal sick ones, cleanse lepers, raise dead ones, throw out demons; you have freely received, freely give. [9] Do not provide gold, nor silver, nor money in your belt, [10] nor provision-bag for (the) road, nor two tunics, nor sandals, nor a staff; for the worker is worthy of his food. [11] And into whatever city or village you enter, ask who in it is worthy, and remain there until you go out. [12] But entering into the house, greet it; [13] and if the house truly is worthy, let your peace come upon it; but if it is not worthy, let your peace return to you. [14] And whoever will not receive you, nor will hear your words, going out of that house or city, shake off the dust from your feet. [15] Truly I say to you that it shall be more bearable for the land of Sodom and Gomorrah in

**1** καὶ προσκαλεσάμενος᾿ τοὺς δώδεκα μαθητὰς αὐτοῦ, ἔδωκεν
And having called near  the  twelve  disciples  of Him,  He gave

αὐτοῖς ἐξουσίαν πνευμάτων ἀκαθάρ των, ὥστε ἐκβάλλειν
to them  authority  over spirits  unclean  the  so as  to cast out

αὐτά, καὶ θεραπεύειν πᾶσαν νόσον καὶ πᾶσαν μαλακίαν.
them, and  to heal  every  disease and every  weakness.

**2** Τῶν δὲ δώδεκα ἀποστόλων τὰ ὀνόματά ἐστι ταῦτα·
the And twelve  apostles  the  names  are  these:

πρῶτος Σίμων ὁ λεγόμενος Πέτρος, καὶ ᾿Ανδρέας ὁ ἀδελφὸς
first  Simon who is called  Peter,  and  Andrew  the brother

αὐτοῦ· ᾿Ιάκωβος ὁ τοῦ Ζεβεδαίου, καὶ ᾿Ιωάννης ὁ ἀδελφὸς
of him;  James  the (son of) Zebedee, and  John  the brother

**3** αὐτοῦ· Φίλιππος, καὶ Βαρθολομαῖος· Θωμᾶς, καὶ Ματθαῖος
of him;  Philip,  and  Bartholomew ,  Thomas, and Matthew

ὁ τελώνης· ᾿Ιάκωβος ὁ τοῦ ᾿Αλφαίου, καὶ Λεββαῖος ὁ
the tax-collector; James  the (son) of Alpheus,  and  Lebbeus who

**4** ἐπικληθεὶς Θαδδαῖος· Σίμων ὁ Κανανίτης, καὶ ᾿Ιούδας
was surnamed Thaddeus;  Simon the Canaanite,  and  Judas

**5** ᾿Ισκαριώτης ὁ καὶ παραδοὺς αὐτόν. τούτους τοὺς δώδεκα
Iscariot  who also betrayed  Him.  These  —  twelve

ἀπέστειλεν ὁ ᾿Ιησοῦς, παραγγείλας αὐτοῖς, λέγων,
sent out  Jesus,  having charged  them,  saying,

Εἰς ὁδὸν ἐθνῶν μὴ ἀπέλθητε, καὶ εἰς πόλιν Σαμαρειτῶν
Into the way of nations do not  go,  and into  a city of (the) Samaritans

**6** μὴ εἰσέλθητε· πορεύεσθε δὲ μᾶλλον πρὸς τὰ πρόβατα τὰ
not do enter,  go  but rather  tc  the  sheep,  the

**7** ἀπολωλότα οἴκου ᾿Ισραήλ. πορευόμενοι δὲ κηρύσσετε, λέγον-
lost  of (the) house of Israel. going on.  And proclaim,  saying,

**8** τες ὅτι ῎Ηγγικεν ἡ βασιλεία τῶν οὐρανῶν. ἀσθενοῦντας
— Has drawn near the kingdom of the heavens.  Sick ones

θεραπεύετε, λεπροὺς καθαρίζετε, νεκροὺς ἐγείρετε, δαιμόνια
heal,  lepers  cleanse,  dead ones raise,  demons

**9** ἐκβάλλετε. δωρεὰν ἐλάβετε, δωρεὰν δότε. μὴ κτήσησθε
cast out.  Freely  you received, freely  give.  Not provide

χρυσόν, μηδὲ ἄργυρον, μηδὲ χαλκὸν εἰς τὰς ζώνας ὑμῶν,
gold,  nor  silver,  nor  copper  in the belts  of you,

**10** μὴ πήραν εἰς ὁδόν, μηδὲ δύο χιτῶνας, μηδὲ ὑποδήματα,
nor a bag  for (the) way, nor  two  tunics,  nor  sandals,

μηδὲ ῥάβδους· ἄξιος γὰρ ὁ ἐργάτης τῆς τροφῆς αὐτοῦ ἐστιν.
nor staves,  worthy for  the worker of the food  of him is.

**11** εἰς ἣν δ᾿ ἂν πόλιν ἢ κώμην εἰσέλθητε, ἐξετάσατε τίς ἐν αὐτῇ
into what And ever city village  you enter,  ask  who in  it

**12** ἄξιός ἐστι· κἀκεῖ μείνατε, ἕως ἂν ἐξέλθητε. εἰσερχόμενοι δὲ
worthy is, and there remain  until you go out .  entering  But

**13** εἰς τὴν οἰκίαν, ἀσπάσασθε αὐτήν. καὶ ἐὰν μὲν ᾖ ἡ οἰκία ἀξία,
into the house,  greet  it;  and if indeed be the house worthy,

ἐλθέτω ἡ εἰρήνη ὑμῶν ἐπ᾿ αὐτήν· ἐὰν δὲ μη η ἀξία, ἡ εἰρήνη
let come the peace of you on  it;  if But not it is worthy, the peace

**14** ὑμῶν πρὸς ὑμᾶς ἐπιστραφήτω. καὶ ὃς ἐὰν μὴ δέξηται ὑμᾶς
of you to  you  let return.  And whoever not will receive you

μηδὲ ἀκούσῃ τοὺς λόγους ὑμῶν, ἐξερχόμενοι τῆς οἰκίας ἢ τῆς
nor will hear the words  of you, going out (of) the house or the –

πόλεως ἐκείνης, ἐκτινάξατε τὸν κονιορτὸν τῶν ποδῶν ὑμῶν.
city  that  shake off  the  dust  of the feet  of you.

**15** ἀμὴν λέγω ὑμῖν, ἀνεκτότερον ἔσται γῆ Σοδόμων καὶ Γομόρ-
Truly I say to you, More bearable it will be to the of Sodom and Gomor-
land

the day of judgment than for that city. [16] Behold, I send you out as sheep in (the) middle of wolves; therefore be wise as serpents and harmless as doves. [17] But beware of men; for they will deliver you to sanhedrins, and they will beat you in their synagogues. [18] And you shall be brought before governors and kings for My sake, for a witness to them and to the nations. [19] But when they deliver you up, do not be anxious how or what you should speak, for it shall be given you in that hour what you shall speak; [20] for you are not they who speak, but the Spirit of your Father which speaks in you. [21] But brother will deliver up brother to death; and father (his) child; and children will rise up against parents, and will put them to death. [22] And you will be hated by all on account of My name; but he that endures to (the) end, he shall be saved. [23] But when they persecute you in this city, flee to another; for truly I say to you, In no way will you have finished the cities of Israel until the Son of man comes. [24] A disciple is not above the teacher, nor a slave above his lord. [25] (It is) enough for the disciple that he be as his teacher, and the slave as his lord. If they call the Master of the house Beelzebub, how much more those of H i s    h o u s e h o l d? [26] Therefore you should not fear them, for nothing is covered which shall not be uncovered, and hidden which shall not be known. [27] What I tell you in the darkness, speak in the light; and what you hear in the ear, preach on the housetops. [28] And you should not fear because of those who kill the body, but are not able to kill the soul; but you should rather fear Him who is able to destroy both soul and body in hell. [29] Are not two sparrows sold for an

ρων ἐν ἡμέρᾳ κρίσεως, ἢ τῇ πόλει ἐκείνη.
rah  in (the) day of judgment than   city   that.

**16** Ἰδού, ἐγὼ ἀποστέλλω ὑμᾶς ὡς πρόβατα ἐν μέσῳ λύκων·
Behold,  I    send out     you   as   sheep in (the) midst of wolves;

γίνεσθε οὖν φρόνιμοι ὡς οἱ ὄφεις, καὶ ἀκέραιοι ὡς αἱ περιστε-
you be  then   wise    as  — serpents and harmless as  —  doves.

**17** ραί. προσέχετε δὲ ἀπὸ τῶν ἀνθρώπων· παραδώσουσι γὰρ
beware  And from  —    men;       they will betray For

ὑμᾶς εἰς συνέδρια, καὶ ἐν ταῖς συναγωγαῖς αὐτῶν μαστιγώ-
you  to  sanhedrins and in the  synagogues   of them  they will

**18** σουσιν ὑμᾶς· καὶ ἐπὶ ἡγεμόνας δὲ καὶ βασιλεῖς ἀχθήσεσθε
scourge  you;  and before governors also and  kings  you will be brought

**19** ἕνεκεν ἐμοῦ, εἰς μαρτύριον αὐτοῖς καὶ ταῖς ἔθνεσιν. ὅταν δὲ
for My sake,  for a testimony  to them  and  to the nations. when But

παραδιδῶσιν ὑμᾶς, μὴ μεριμνήσητε πῶς ἢ τί λαλήσητε·
they deliver up  you,  not  be anxious  how  or what you may say;

**20** δοθήσεται γὰρ ὑμῖν ἐν ἐκείνῃ τῇ ὥρᾳ τί λαλήσετε· οὐ γὰρ
it is given  for  to you in that  — hour what you may say; not For

ὑμεῖς ἐστε οἱ λαλοῦντες, ἀλλὰ τὸ Πνεῦμα τοῦ πατρὸς υμων
you  are the (ones) speaking, but  the Spirit  of the Father of you

**21** τὸ λαλοῦν ἐν ὑμῖν. παραδώσει δὲ ἀδελφὸς ἀδελφὸν εἰς
which speaks in  you.  will deliver up But brother    brother  to

θάνατον, καὶ πατὴρ τέκνον· καὶ ἐπαναστήσονται τέκνα ἐπὶ
death,   and  Father (the) child;  and  will rise up    children against

**22** γονεῖς, καὶ θανατώσουσιν αὐτούς. καὶ ἔσεσθε μισούμενοι ὑπὸ
parents, and put to death     them.  And you will be hated    by

πάντων διὰ τὸ ὄνομά μου· ὁ δὲ ὑπομείνας εἰς τέλος, οὗτος
all  because of the name of Me. he But  enduring  to (the) end, this (one)

**23** σωθήσεται. ὅταν δὲ διώκωσιν ὑμᾶς ἐν τῇ πόλει ταύτῃ,
shall be saved.  when But they persecute you in    city    this,

φεύγετε εἰς τὴν ἄλλην· ἀμὴν γὰρ λέγω ὑμῖν, οὐ μὴ τελέσητε
flee   to  another;  truly  for I say to you, In no way will you
                                                              finish

τὰς πόλεις τοῦ Ἰσραήλ, ἕως ἂν ἔλθῃ ὁ υἱὸς τοῦ ἀνθρώπου.
the cities  of  Israel,  until may  come the Son  of man.

**24** Οὐκ ἔστι μαθητὴς ὑπὲρ τὸν διδάσκαλον, οὐδὲ δοῦλος
Not  is  a disciple  above  the  teacher,   nor a slave

**25** ὑπὲρ τὸν κύριον αὐτοῦ. ἀρκετὸν τῷ μαθητῇ ἵνα γένηται ὡς
above  the  Lord  of him. (It is) enough for the disciple that he become as

ὁ διδάσκαλος αὐτοῦ· καὶ ὁ δοῦλος ὡς ὁ κύριος αὐτοῦ. εἰ τὸν
the teacher  of him,  and the slave  as the the lord of him. If  the

οἰκοδεσπότην Βεελζεβοὺβ ἐκάλεσαν, πόσῳ μᾶλλον τοὺς·
master of the house Beelzebub  they called,  how much more  those

**26** οἰκιακοὺς αὐτοῦ ; μὴ οὖν φοβηθῆτε αὐτούς· οὐδὲν γάρ ἐστι
of his household?  Not, then, you should fear them,  nothing for  is

κεκαλυμμένον ὃ οὐκ ἀποκαλυφθήσεται· καὶ κρυπτὸν ὃ οὐ
covered     which  will not be uncovered,  and  hidden  which not

**27** γνωσθήσεται. ὃ λέγω ὑμῖν ἐν τῇ σκοτίᾳ, εἴπατε ἐν τῷ φωτί·
will be made known. What I say to you in the dark, you say  in  the light;

**28** καὶ ὃ εἰς τὸ οὖς ἀκούετε, κηρύξατε ἐπὶ τῶν δωμάτων. καὶ μὴ
and what in the ear you hear, proclaim  on the housetops. And not

φοβηθῆτε ἀπὸ τῶν ἀποκτεινόντων τὸ σῶμα, τὴν δὲ ψυχὴν
you should fear — the (ones) killing  the body,  the but  soul

μὴ δυναμένων ἀποκτεῖναι· φοβήθητε δὲ μᾶλλον τὸν δυνά-
not being able  to kill;     fear   but  rather  the (one)

**29** μενον καὶ ψυχὴν καὶ σῶμα ἀπολέσαι ἐν γεέννῃ. οὐχὶ δύο
being able both the soul and the body to destroy in Gehenna. Are not two

assarion? Yet not one of them shall fall to the ground without your Father. [30] But even the hairs of your head are all numbered. [31] Therefore you should not fear; you are better than many sparrows. [32] Therefore everyone whoever shall confess Me before men, I will confess him also before My Father who (is) in Heaven. [33] But whoever shall deny Me before men, I also will deny him before My Father who (is) in Heaven. [34] Do not think that I came to bring peace on earth; I did not come to bring peace, but a sword. [35] I came to set a man against his father, and a daughter against her mother, and a daughter-in-law against her mother-in-law. [36] And a man's enemies (shall be) his own household. [37] He that loves father or mother above Me is not worthy of Me; and he that loves son or daughter above Me is not worthy of Me. [38] And he that does not take up his cross and follow after Me is not worthy of Me. [39] He that has found his life shall lose it; and he that has lost his life on account of Me shall find it. [40] He that receives you receives Me; and he that received Me receives Him who sent Me. [41] He that receives a prophet in (the) name of a prophet shall receive (the) reward of a prophet; and he that receives a righteous one in (the) name of a righteous one shall receive the reward of a righteous one. [42] And whoever shall give drink to one of the these little ones, only a cup of cold (water) in the name of a disciple, truly I say to you, in no way shall he lose his reward.

30 στρουθία ἀσσαρίου πωλεῖται ; καὶ ἓν ἐξ αὐτῶν οὐ πεσεῖται
sparrows for an assarion sold? And one of them not shall fall

ἐπὶ τὴν γῆν ἄνευ τοῦ πατρὸς ὑμῶν· ὑμῶν δὲ καὶ αἱ τρίχες τῆς
on the earth without the Father of you. of you But even the hairs of the

31 κεφαλῆς πᾶσαι ἠριθμημέναι εἰσί. μὴ οὖν φοβηθῆτε· πολλῶν
head all numbered are. not Then fear; many

32 στρουθίων διαφέρετε ὑμεῖς. πᾶς οὖν ὅστις ὁμολογήσει ἐν
sparrows excel you. Everyone then who shall confess —

ἐμοὶ ἔμπροσθεν τῶν ἀνθρώπων, ὁμολογήσω κἀγὼ ἐν αὐτῷ
Me before — men, will confess I also — him

33 ἔμπροσθεν τοῦ πατρός μου τοῦ ἐν οὐρανοῖς. ὅστις δ᾽ ἂν
before the Father of Me — in Heaven whoever and —

ἀρνήσηταί με ἔμπροσθεν τῶν ἀνθρώπων, ἀρνήσομαι αὐτὸν
denies Me before — men, will deny him

κἀγὼ ἔμπροσθεν τοῦ πατρός μου τοῦ ἐν οὐρανοῖς.
I also before the Father of Me who (is) in Heaven.

34 Μὴ νομίσητε ὅτι ἦλθον βαλεῖν εἰρήνην ἐπὶ τὴν γῆν· οὐκ
Not think that I came to cast peace on the earth; not

35 ἦλθον βαλεῖν εἰρήνην, ἀλλὰ μάχαιραν. ἦλθον γὰρ διχάσαι
I came to cast peace, but a sword. I came For to dissever

ἄνθρωπον κατὰ τοῦ πατρὸς αὐτοῦ, καὶ θυγατέρα κατὰ τῆς
a man with the father of him, and a daughter with the

36 μητρὸς αὐτῆς, καὶ νύμφην κατὰ τῆς πενθερᾶς αὐτῆς· καὶ
mother of her, and a bride with the mother-in-law of her, and

37 ἐχθροὶ τοῦ ἀνθρώπου οἱ οἰκιακοὶ αὐτοῦ. ὁ φιλῶν πατέρα ἢ
enemies of the man those of the house of him He loving father or

μητέρα ὑπὲρ ἐμέ, οὐκ ἔστι μου ἄξιος· καὶ ὁ φιλῶν υἱὸν ἢ
mother above Me not is of Me worthy; and he loving son or

38 θυγατέρα ὑπὲρ ἐμέ, οὐκ ἔστι μου ἄξιος· καὶ ὃς οὐ λαμβάνει
daughter above Me not is of Me worthy. And who not does take

τὸν σταυρὸν αὐτοῦ καὶ ἀκολουθεῖ ὀπίσω μου, οὐκ ἔστι μου
the cross of him and follow after Me not is of Me

39 ἄξιος. ὁ εὑρὼν τὴν ψυχὴν αὐτοῦ ἀπολέσει αὐτήν· καὶ ὁ
worthy. He finding the soul of him will lose it, and he

ἀπολέσας τὴν ψυχὴν αὐτοῦ ἕνεκεν ἐμοῦ εὑρήσει αὐτήν.
losing the soul of him for sake My will find it.

40 Ὁ δεχόμενος ὑμᾶς ἐμὲ δέχεται· καὶ ὁ ἐμὲ δεχόμενος δέχεται
He receiving you Me receives, and he Me receiving receives

41 τὸν ἀποστείλαντά με. ὁ δεχόμενος προφήτην εἰς ὄνομα
the (one) sending Me. He receiving a prophet in (the) name

προφήτου μισθὸν προφήτου λήψεται· καὶ ὁ δεχόμενος
of a prophet (the) reward of a prophet will receive; and he receiving

42 δίκαιον εἰς ὄνομα δικαίου μισθὸν δικαίου λήψεται. καὶ ὃς ἐὰν
(one) just in the name of a just (one), reward a just will receive. And whoever

ποτίσῃ ἕνα τῶν μικρῶν τούτων ποτήριον ψυχροῦ μόνον
gives drink to one little ones of these a cup of cold (water) only

εἰς ὄνομα μαθητοῦ, ἀμὴν λέγω ὑμῖν, οὐ μὴ ἀπολέσῃ τὸν
in (the) name of a disciple, truly I say to you, in no way will he lose the

μισθὸν αὐτοῦ.
reward of him.

## CHAPTER 11

[1] And it happened, when Jesus had finished commanding his twelve disciples, that He left there to

## CHAPTER 11

1 Καὶ ἐγένετο ὅτε ἐτέλεσεν ὁ Ἰησοῦς διατάσσων τοῖς
And it was, when finished — Jesus giving command to the

δώδεκα μαθηταῖς αὐτοῦ, μετέβη ἐκεῖθεν τοῦ διδάσκειν καὶ
disciples of Him, He moved from there — to teach and

teach and to preach in their cities.

[2] Now John having heard in the prison the works of Christ, having sent two of his disciples, [3] said to Him, Are You the One coming, or are we to look for another? [4] And answering Jesus said to them, Having returned tell John what you hear and see: [5] The blind receive sight, and the lame walk, lepers are cleansed, and the deaf hear; the dead are raised, and the poor are evangelized. [6] And blessed is (he), whoever shall not be offended in Me.

[7] But as these were going Jesus began to say to the crowds about John, What did you go out into the wilderness to see? A reed shaken with the wind? [8] But what did you go out to see? A man clothed in soft clothing? Behold, those who wear soft things are in the houses of kings. [9] But what did you go out to see? A prophet? Yes, I say to you, and (one) more excellent than a prophet. [10] For this is (he) about whom it has been written, "Behold, I send My messenger before Your face, who shall prepare Your way before You." [11] Truly, I tell you, Not has arisen in (those) born of a woman a greater (than) John the Baptist; but the lesser in the kingdom of Heaven is greater (than) he. [12] But from the days of John the Baptist until now, the kingdom of Heaven suffers violence, and the violent seize it. [13] For all the Prophets and the Law prophesied until John. [14] And if you are willing to receive, he is Elijah, he about to come. [15] He having ears to hear, let him hear. [16] But to what shall I compare this generation? It is like little children sitting in (the) markets, and calling to their mates, [17] and saying, We piped to you and you did not dance; we

κηρύσσειν ἐν ταῖς πόλεσιν αὐτῶν.
to proclaim in the cities of them.

**2** Ὁ δὲ Ἰωάννης ἀκούσας ἐν τῷ δεσμωτηρίῳ τὰ ἔργα τοῦ
— But John having heard in the prison the works —

**3** Χριστοῦ, πέμψας δύο τῶν μαθητῶν αὐτοῦ, εἶπεν αὐτῷ, Σὺ
of Christ, sending two of the disciples of him, said to Him, You

**4** εἶ ὁ ἐρχόμενος, ἢ ἕτερον προσδοκῶμεν; καὶ ἀποκριθεὶς ὁ
are the coming (One), or another may we expect? And answering, —

Ἰησοῦς εἶπεν αὐτοῖς, Πορευθέντες ἀπαγγείλατε Ἰωάννῃ ἃ
Jesus said to them, Going relate to John what

**5** ἀκούετε καὶ βλέπετε· τυφλοὶ ἀναβλέπουσι, καὶ χωλοὶ περι-
you hear and see: blind ones receive sight, and lame ones walk

πατοῦσι, λεπροὶ καθαρίζονται, καὶ κωφοὶ ἀκούουσι, νεκροὶ
about; lepers are cleansed, and deaf ones hear; dead ones

**6** ἐγείρονται, καὶ πτωχοὶ εὐαγγελίζονται· καὶ μακάριός ἐστιν,
are raised, and poor ones are evangelized; and blessed he is,

**7** ὃς ἐὰν μὴ σκανδαλισθῇ ἐν ἐμοί. τούτων δὲ πορευομένων,
whoever not shall be offended in Me. (as) these But were going,

ἤρξατο ὁ Ἰησοῦς λέγειν τοῖς ὄχλοις περὶ Ἰωάννου, Τί
began — Jesus to say to the crowds concerning John, What

ἐξήλθετε εἰς τὴν ἔρημον θεάσασθαι; κάλαμον ὑπὸ ἀνέμου
went you out to the wilderness to view? A reed by wind

**8** σαλευόμενον; ἀλλὰ τί ἐξήλθετε ἰδεῖν; ἄνθρωπον ἐν μαλακοῖς
being shaken? But what went ye out to see? A man in soft

ἱματίοις ἠμφιεσμένον; ἰδού, οἱ τὰ μαλακὰ φοροῦντες ἐν τοῖς
garments clothed? Behold, those the soft wearing (are) in the

**9** οἴκοις τῶν βασιλέων εἰσίν. ἀλλὰ τί ἐξήλθετε ἰδεῖν; προφήτην;
houses — of kings. are. But what went you out to see? A prophet?

**10** ναί, λέγω ὑμῖν, καὶ περισσότερον προφήτου· οὗτος γὰρ
Yea, I say to you, and (one) more excellent than a prophet. this For

ἔστι περὶ οὗ γέγραπται, Ἰδού, ἐγὼ ἀποστέλλω τὸν
is (he) about whom it has been written, Behold, I send forth the

ἄγγελόν μου πρὸ προσώπου σου, ὃς κατασκευάσει τὴν
messenger of Me before your face, who shall prepare the

**11** ὁδόν σου ἔμπροσθέν σου. ἀμὴν λέγω ὑμῖν, οὐκ ἐγήγερται ἐν
way of you before you. Truly I say to you not has arisen in

γεννητοῖς γυναικῶν μείζων Ἰωάννου τοῦ βαπτιστοῦ· ὁ δὲ
(those) born of a woman a greater (than) John the Baptist; the but

μικρότερος ἐν τῇ βασιλείᾳ τῶν οὐρανῶν μείζων αὐτοῦ ἐστιν.
lesser in the kingdom of the heavens greater (than) he is.

**12** ἀπὸ δὲ τῶν ἡμερῶν Ἰωάννου τοῦ βαπτιστοῦ ἕως ἄρτι ἡ
from And the days of John the Baptist until now the

βασιλεία τῶν οὐρανῶν βιάζεται, καὶ βιασταὶ ἁρπάζουσιν
kingdom of the heavens suffers violence, and the violent seize

**13** αὐτήν. πάντες γὰρ οἱ προφῆται καὶ ὁ νόμος ἕως Ἰωάννου
it. all For the prophets and the law until John

**14** προεφήτευσαν· καὶ εἰ θέλετε δέξασθαι, αὐτός ἐστιν Ἠλίας ὁ
prophesied; and if you are willing to receive, he is Elijah, he

**15** **16** μέλλων ἔρχεσθαι. ὁ ἔχων ὦτα ἀκούειν ἀκουέτω. τίνι δὲ
about to come. He having ears to hear, let him hear. to what But

ὁμοιώσω τὴν γενεὰν ταύτην; ὁμοία ἐστὶ παιδαρίοις ἐν
shall I liken — generation this? like It is to little children in

ἀγοραῖς καθημένοις, καὶ προσφωνοῦσι τοῖς ἑταίροις αὐτῶν,
markets sitting, and calling to the mates of them,

**17** καὶ λέγουσιν, Ηὐλήσαμεν ὑμῖν, καὶ οὐκ ὠρχήσασθε· ἐθρηνή-
and saying, We piped to you and not you did dance; we

mourned to you, and you did not wail. [18] For John came neither eating nor drinking, and they say, Behold, he has a demon. [19] The Son of man came eating and drinking, and they say, Behold, a gluttonous man, and a winedrinker, and a friend of tax-men, and of sinners. And wisdom was justified by her children.

[20] Then He began to reproach the cities in which had occurred His most powerful (acts), for they had not repented. [21] Woe to you, Chorazin! Woe to you, Bethsaida! For if the mighty works which have taken place in you had happened in Tyre and Sidon, they would have repented long ago in sackcloth and ashes. [22] But I say to you, It shall be more bearable for Tyre and Sidon in the day of judgment than for you. [23] And you, Capernaum, who have been lifted up to Heaven, shall be brought down into hell; for if the mighty works which have taken place in you had happened in Sodom, it would have remained until this day. [24] But I say to you, that it shall be more bearable for the land of Sodom in the day of judgment than for you.

[25] Answering at that time, Jesus said, I praise You, Father, Lord of Heaven and of earth, because You hid these things from (the) sophisticated and cunning, and revealed them to babes. [26] Yes, Father, for so it was pleasing before You. [27] All things were yielded up to Me by My Father; and no one knows the Son except the Father; nor does any know the Father, except the Son, and to whomever the Son wills to reveal (Him). [28] Come to Me, all those laboring and being burdened, and I will give you rest. [29] Take My yoke upon you, and learn from Me, because I am meek and lowly in heart; and you will find rest to your souls. [30] For My yoke is easy, and My burden is light.

18 σαμεν ὑμῖν, καὶ οὐκ ἐκόψασθε. ἦλθε γὰρ Ἰωάννης μήτε ἐσθίων
mourned to you and not you did wail. came For John neither eating

19 μήτε πίνων, καὶ λέγουσι, Δαιμόνιον ἔχει. ἦλθεν ὁ υἱὸς τοῦ
nor drinking, and they say, A demon he has. Came the Son —

ἀνθρώπου ἐσθίων καὶ πίνων, καὶ λέγουσιν, Ἰδού, ἄνθρωπος
of man eating and drinking, and they say, Behold, a man

φάγος καὶ οἰνοπότης, τελωνῶν φίλος καὶ ἁμαρτωλῶν. καὶ
gluttonous, and a winedrinker, of tax-collectors a friend and of sinners. And

ἐδικαιώθη ἡ σοφία ἀπὸ τῶν τέκνων αὐτῆς.
was justified — wisdom by the children of her.

20 Τότε ἤρξατο ὀνειδίζειν τὰς πόλεις ἐν αἷς ἐγένοντο αἱ
Then He began to reproach the cities in which had occurred the

21 πλεῖσται δυνάμεις αὐτοῦ, ὅτι οὐ μετενόησαν. Οὐαί σοι,
most powerful (acts) of His; because not they repented. Woe to you,

Χοραζίν, οὐαί σοι, Βηθσαϊδά, ὅτι εἰ ἐν Τύρῳ καὶ Σιδῶνι
Chorazin; woe to you, Bethsaida! Because if in Tyre and Sidon

ἐγένοντο αἱ δυνάμεις αἱ γενόμεναι ἐν ὑμῖν, πάλαι ἂν ἐν σάκκῳ
occurred the powerful (acts) happening in you, long ago — in sackcloth

22 καὶ σποδῷ μετενόησαν. πλὴν λέγω ὑμῖν, Τύρῳ καὶ Σιδῶνι
and ashes they had repented. However, say to you, For Tyre and for Sidon

23 ἀνεκτότερον ἔσται ἐν ἡμέρᾳ κρίσεως, ἢ ὑμῖν. καὶ σύ, Καπερ-
more tolerable it will be in (the) day of judgment than for you; and you, Ca-

ναούμ, ἡ ἕως τοῦ οὐρανοῦ ὑψωθεῖσα, ἕως ᾅδου καταβιβα-
pernaum, who to the heaven have been exalted, to Hades will be cast

σθήσῃ· ὅτι εἰ ἐν Σοδόμοις ἐγένοντο αἱ δυνάμεις αἱ γενόμεναι ἐν
down, because if in Sodom occurred the powerful (acts) happening in

24 σοί, ἔμειναν ἂν μέχρι τῆς σήμερον. πλὴν λέγω ὑμῖν, ὅτι γῇ
you, it would last until today. However, I tell you that for land

Σοδόμων ἀνεκτότερον ἔσται ἐν ἡμέρᾳ κρίσεως, ἢ σοί.
of Sodom more tolerable it will be in (the) day of judgment than for you.

25 Ἐν ἐκείνῳ τῷ καιρῷ ἀποκριθεὶς ὁ Ἰησοῦς εἶπεν, Ἐξομολο-
At that — time answering — Jesus said, I give praise

γοῦμαί σοι, πάτερ, Κύριε τοῦ οὐρανοῦ καὶ τῆς γῆς, ὅτι
to You, Father, Lord of the heaven and of the earth, for

ἀπέκρυψας ταῦτα ἀπὸ σοφῶν καὶ συνετῶν, καὶ ἀπεκάλυψας
You hid these things from sophisti- and cunning, and revealed
cated

26 αὐτὰ νηπίοις. ναὶ ὁ πατήρ, ὅτι οὕτως ἐγένετο εὐδοκία
them to babes. Yea, — Father, because thus it was well-pleasing

27 ἔμπροσθέν σου. πάντα μοι παρεδόθη ὑπὸ τοῦ πατρός μου·
before You. All things to Me are yielded by the Father of Me;

καὶ οὐδεὶς ἐπιγινώσκει τὸν υἱόν, εἰ μὴ ὁ πατήρ· οὐδὲ τὸν
and no one knows the Son except the Father, nor the

πατέρα τις ἐπιγινώσκει, εἰ μὴ ὁ υἱός, καὶ ᾧ ἐὰν βούληται ὁ
Father anyone does know, except the Son, and to whomever wills the

28 υἱὸς ἀποκαλύψαι. δεῦτε πρός με πάντες οἱ κοπιῶντες καὶ
Son to reveal. Come to Me, all the (ones) laboring and

29 πεφορτισμένοι, κἀγὼ ἀναπαύσω ὑμᾶς. ἄρατε τὸν ζυγόν
being burdened, and I will give rest you. Take the yoke

μου ἐφ᾽ ὑμᾶς καὶ μάθετε ἀπ᾽ ἐμοῦ, ὅτι πρᾷός εἰμι καὶ ταπεινὸς
of Me on you and learn from Me, because meek I am and lowly

30 τῇ καρδίᾳ· καὶ εὑρήσετε ἀνάπαυσιν ταῖς ψυχαῖς ὑμῶν. ὁ
— in heart; and you will find rest to the souls of you; the

γὰρ ζυγός μου χρηστός, καὶ τὸ φορτίον μου ἐλαφρόν ἐστιν.
for yoke of Me pleasant and the burden of me light is.

**CHAPTER 12**

[1] At that time on the Sabbath Jesus went through the grain fields; and His disciples were hungry and began to pluck ears and to eat. [2] But the Pharisees having seen said to Him, Behold, Your disciples are doing what it is not lawful to do on the Sabbath. [3] But He said to them, Have you not read what David did, when he and those with him hungered? [4] How he entered into the house of God, and he ate the showbread, which it was not lawful for him to eat, nor for those with him, but for the priests only? [5] Or have you not read in the Law, that on the Sabbaths the priests ,in the Temple profane the Sabbath, and are not guilty? [6] But I say to you, One greater than the Temple is here. [7] But if you had known what (this) is, "I desire mercy and not sacrifice," you would not have condemned those who are not guilty. [8] For the Son of man is also Lord of the Sabbath.

[9] And having left there, He went into their synagogue. [10] And, behold, a man was there, having (a) withered hand. And they asked Him, saying, Is it lawful to heal on the sabbaths?—that they might accuse Him. [11] But He said, to them, What man of you will be who will have one sheep, and if (it) fall into a pit on the sabbaths, he will seize it and raise (it)? [12] How much, then, surpasses a man a sheep! So that it is lawful to do well on the sabbaths. [13] Then He says to the man, Stretch out your hand! And he stretched out and it was restored sound as the other.

[14] But having left, the Pharisees took up a council against Him, how they may destroy Him. [15] But having known, Jesus withdrew from there, and many crowds followed Him; and He healed them all, [16] and warned them that they not make Him manifest. [17] So that might be ful-

**CHAPTER 12**

1 Ἐν ἐκείνῳ τῷ καιρῷ ἐπορεύθη ὁ Ἰησοῦς τοῖς σάββασι διὰ
At that — time went — Jesus on the Sabbath through
τῶν σπορίμων· οἱ δὲ μαθηταὶ αὐτοῦ ἐπείνασαν, καὶ ἤρξαντο
the grainfields; the and disciples of Him hungered, and began
2 τίλλειν στάχυας καὶ ἐσθίειν. οἱ δὲ Φαρισαῖοι ἰδόντες εἶπον
to pluck ears and to eat. the But Pharisees seeing said
αὐτῷ, Ἰδού, οἱ μαθηταί σου ποιοῦσιν ὃ οὐκ ἔξεστι ποιεῖν
to Him, Behold, the disciples of You are doing what not it is lawful to do
3 ἐν σαββάτῳ. ὁ δὲ εἶπεν αὐτοῖς, Οὐκ ἀνέγνωτε τί ἐποίησε
on a Sabbath. He And said to them, Not did you read what did
4 Δαβίδ, ὅτε ἐπείνασεν αὐτὸς καὶ οἱ μετ' αὐτοῦ· πῶς εἰσῆλθεν
David, when he hungered Himself and those with him? How he went in
εἰς τὸν οἶκον τοῦ Θεοῦ, καὶ τοὺς ἄρτους τῆς προθέσεως
into the house — of God, and the loaves of the presentation
ἔφαγεν, οὓς οὐκ ἐξὸν ἦν αὐτῷ φαγεῖν, οὐδὲ τοῖς μετ' αὐτοῦ,
he ate, which not lawful it was for him to eat, nor for those with him,
5 εἰ μὴ τοῖς ἱερεῦσι μόνοις; ἢ οὐκ ἀνέγνωτε ἐν τῷ νόμῳ, ὅτι
except for the priests only? Or not did you read in the law that
τοῖς σάββασιν οἱ ἱερεῖς ἐν τῷ ἱερῷ τὸ σάββατον βεβηλοῦσι,
on the Sabbaths the priests in the Temple the Sabbath profane,
6 καὶ ἀναίτιοί εἰσι; λέγω δὲ ὑμῖν ὅτι τοῦ ἱεροῦ μείζων ἐστὶν
and guiltless are? I say But to you that the Temple a greater than is
7 ὧδε. εἰ δὲ ἐγνώκειτε τί ἐστιν, Ἔλεον θέλω καὶ οὐ θυσίαν,
here. if But you had known what it is, Mercy I desire, and not sacrifice,
8 οὐκ ἂν κατεδικάσατε τοὺς ἀναιτίους. κύριος γάρ ἐστι καὶ τοῦ
not would you have judged the guiltless. Lord For is also of the
σαββάτου ὁ υἱὸς τοῦ ἀνθρώπου.
Sabbath the Son — of man.
9
10 Καὶ μεταβὰς ἐκεῖθεν ἦλθεν εἰς τὴν συναγωγὴν αὐτῶν. καὶ
And moving from there He came into the synagogue of them. And
ἰδού, ἄνθρωπος ἦν τὴν χεῖρα ἔχων ξηράν· καὶ ἐπηρώτησαν
behold, a man was, the hand having withered, and they questioned
αὐτόν, λέγοντες, Εἰ ἔξεστι τοῖς σάββασι θεραπεύειν; ἵνα
Him, saying, If it is lawful on the Sabbaths to heal? That
11 κατηγορήσωσιν αὐτοῦ. ὁ δὲ εἶπεν αὐτοῖς, Τίς ἔσται ἐξ
they might accuse Him. He But said to them, What will be of
ὑμῶν ἄνθρωπος, ὃς ἕξει πρόβατον ἕν, καὶ ἐὰν ἐμπέσῃ τοῦτο
you a man who will have sheep one, and if fall (in) this
τοῖς σάββασιν εἰς βόθυνον, οὐχὶ κρατήσει αὐτὸ καὶ ἐγερεῖ;
on the Sabbaths into a pit, not will he lay hold of it and raise (it)?
12 πόσῳ οὖν διαφέρει ἄνθρωπος προβάτου. ὥστε ἔξεστι τοῖς
How much then surpasses a man a sheep! So that it is lawful on the
13 σάββασι καλῶς ποιεῖν. τότε λέγει τῷ ἀνθρώπῳ, Ἔκτεινον
Sabbaths well to do. Then He says to the man, Stretch out
τὴν χεῖρά σου. καὶ ἐξέτεινε, καὶ ἀποκατεστάθη ὑγιὴς ὡς ἡ
the hand of you, and he stretched, and it was restored sound as the
14 ἄλλη. οἱ δὲ Φαρισαῖοι συμβούλιον ἔλαβον κατ' αὐτοῦ
other. the But Pharisees a council took against Him,
15 ἐξελθόντες, ὅπως αὐτὸν ἀπολέσωσιν. ὁ δὲ Ἰησοῦς γνοὺς
they having left, how Him they might destroy. But Jesus knowing
ἀνεχώρησεν ἐκεῖθεν· καὶ ἠκολούθησαν αὐτῷ ὄχλοι πολλοί,
withdrew from there. And followed Him crowds many,
16 καὶ ἐθεράπευσεν αὐτοὺς πάντας, καὶ ἐπετίμησεν αὐτοῖς,
and He healed them all, and warned them
17 ἵνα μὴ φανερὸν αὐτὸν ποιήσωσιν· ὅπως πληρωθῇ τὸ
that not manifest Him they should make; so that may be that fulfilled

filled that spoken by Isaiah the prophet, saying, [18] Behold, My child whom I chose; My Beloved, in whom My soul has found delight! I will put My Spirit on Him, and He shall declare judgment to the nations. [19] He shall not strive nor cry out, nor shall anyone hear His voice in the streets. [20] A bruised reed He will not break, and a smoking wick He will not quench, until He brings forth judgment to victory. [21] And the nations shall hope in His name."

[22] Then one possessed by a demon was brought to Him, blind and dumb, and He healed him so that the blind and dumb both spoke and saw. [23] And all the crowds were amazed and said, Is this the son of David? [24] But having heard the Pharisees said, This one does not cast out demons except by Beelzebub prince of the demons. [25] But Jesus knowing their thoughts, He said to them, Every kingdom divided against itself is brought to ruin, and every city or house divided against itself will not stand. [26] And if Satan throw out Satan, he was divided against himself. How then will his kingdom stand? [27] And if I by Beelzebub throw out the demons, by whom do your sons throw them out? Because of this they shall be your judges. [28] But if I cast out the demons by the Spirit of God, then the kingdom of God has come upon you. [29] Or how is anyone able to enter into the house of the strong one and plunder his goods, unless first he tie up the strong one, and then his house he will plunder? [30] He who is not with Me is against Me; and he who does not gather with Me scatters. [31] Because of this I say to you, Every sin and blasphemy shall be forgiven to men; but the blasphemy concerning the Spirit shall not be forgiven to men. [32] And whoever speaks a word against the

**18** ῥηθὲν διὰ Ἠσαΐου τοῦ προφήτου, λέγοντος, Ἰδού, ὁ παῖς
spoken through Isaiah the prophet, saying, Behold, the child

μου ὃν ἡρέτισα· ὁ ἀγαπητός μου εἰς ὃν εὐδόκησεν ἡ ψυχή
of Me whom I chose, the beloved of Me in whom has delighted the soul

μου ὃν ἡρέτισα· ὁ ἀγαπητός μου εἰς ὃν εὐδόκησεν ἡ ψυχή
of Me. I will put the Spirit of Me on Him, and judgment to the nations

**19** ἀπαγγελεῖ. οὐκ ἐρίσει, οὐδὲ κραυγάσει· οὐδὲ ἀκούσει τις ἐν
He will declare. Not He will strive, nor cry out, nor will hear any in

**20** ταῖς πλατείαις τὴν φωνὴν αὐτοῦ. κάλαμον συντετριμμένον
the streets the voice of Him. A reed bruised

οὐ κατεάξει, καὶ λίνον τυφόμενον οὐ σβέσει· ἕως ἂν ἐκβάλη
not He will break, and flax smoking not He will quench, until He expel

**21** εἰς νῖκος τὴν κρίσιν. καὶ ἐν τῷ ὀνόματι αὐτοῦ ἔθνη ἐλπιοῦσι.
to victory the judgment. And in the name of Him nations will hope.

**22** Τότε προσηνέχθη αὐτῷ δαιμονιζόμενος, τυφλὸς· καὶ
Then was brought to Him a demon-possessed one blind and

κωφός· καὶ ἐθεράπευσεν αὐτόν, ὥστε τὸν τυφλὸν καὶ κωφὸν
dumb; and He healed him, so that the blind and dumb

**23** καὶ λαλεῖν καὶ βλέπειν. καὶ ἐξίσταντο πάντες οἱ ὄχλοι καὶ
both could speak and see. And were amazed all the crowds, and

**24** ἔλεγον, Μήτι οὗτός ἐστιν ὁ υἱὸς Δαβίδ; οἱ δὲ Φαρισαῖοι
said, Not this is the son of David? the But Pharisees

ἀκούσαντες εἶπον, Οὗτος οὐκ ἐκβάλλει τὰ δαιμόνια, εἰ μὴ
having heard said, This (one) not casts out the demons except

**25** ἐν τῷ Βεελζεβοὺλ ἄρχοντι τῶν δαιμονίων. εἰδὼς δὲ ὁ
by — Beelzebub, ruler of the demons. knowing But

Ἰησοῦς τὰς ἐνθυμήσεις αὐτῶν εἶπεν αὐτοῖς, Πᾶσα βασιλεία
Jesus the thoughts of them, He said to them, Every kingdom

μερισθεῖσα καθ᾽ ἑαυτῆς ἐρημοῦται· καὶ πᾶσα πόλις ἢ οἰκία
divided against itself is brought to ruin, and every city or house

**26** μερισθεῖσα καθ᾽ ἑαυτῆς οὐ σταθήσεται. καὶ εἰ ὁ Σατανᾶς τὸν
divided against itself not will stand. and if — Satan —

Σατανᾶν ἐκβάλλει, ἐφ᾽ ἑαυτὸν ἐμερίσθη· πῶς οὖν σταθήσεται
Satan casts out, against himself he was divided. How then will stand

**27** ἡ βασιλεία αὐτοῦ; καὶ εἰ ἐγὼ ἐν Βεελζεβοὺλ ἐκβάλλω τὰ
the kingdom of him? And if I by Beelzebub cast out the

δαιμόνια, οἱ υἱοὶ ὑμῶν ἐν τίνι ἐκβάλλουσι; διὰ τοῦτο αὐτοὶ
demons, the sons of you by whom do they cast out? Therefore they

**28** ὑμῶν ἔσονται κριταί. εἰ δὲ ἐγὼ ἐν Πνεύματι Θεοῦ ἐκβάλλω
of you shall be judges. if But I by (the) Spirit of God cast out

**29** τὰ δαιμόνια, ἄρα ἔφθασεν ἐφ᾽ ὑμᾶς ἡ βασιλεία τοῦ Θεοῦ. ἢ
the demons, then has come upon you the kingdom — of God. Or

πῶς δύναταί τις εἰσελθεῖν εἰς τὴν οἰκίαν τοῦ ἰσχυροῦ καὶ τὰ
how can anyone enter into the house of the strong one and the

σκεύη αὐτοῦ διαρπάσαι, ἐὰν μὴ πρῶτον δήσῃ τὸν ἰσχυρόν;
vessels of him to plunder, if not first he binds the strong one?

**30** καὶ τότε τὴν οἰκίαν αὐτοῦ διαρπάσει. ὁ μὴ ὢν μετ᾽ ἐμοῦ,
And then the house of him he will plunder. He not being with Me

**31** κατ᾽ ἐμοῦ ἐστι, καὶ ὁ μὴ συνάγων μετ᾽ ἐμοῦ, σκορπίζει. διὰ
against Me is; and he not gathering with Me scatters. Because

τοῦτο λέγω ὑμῖν, Πᾶσα ἁμαρτία καὶ βλασφημία ἀφεθήσεται
of this I say to you, Every sin and blasphemy shall be forgiven

τοῖς ἀνθρώποις· ἡ δὲ τοῦ Πνεύματος βλασφημία οὐκ ἀφεθή-
— to men; the but of the Spirit blasphemy not will be

**32** σεται τοῖς ἀνθρώποις. καὶ ὃς ἂν εἴπῃ λόγον κατὰ τοῦ υἱοῦ
forgiven — to men. And whoever speaks a word against the Son

Son of man, it shall be forgiven him. But whoever speaks against the Holy Spirit, it shall not be forgiven him, not in this age nor in the coming one. [33] Either make the tree good and its fruit good, or make the tree corrupt and its fruit corrupt; for the tree is known by the fruit. [34] Offspring of vipers! How can you being evil speak good things? For out of the abundance of the heart the mouth speaks. [35] The good man out of the good treasure of the heart brings forth good things; and the wicked man out of the wicked treasure brings forth wicked things. [36] But I say to you, that every idle word, whatever men may speak, they shall give an account of it in (the) day of judgment. [37] For by your words you shall be justified, and by your words you shall be condemned.

[38] Then some of the scribes and Pharisees answered, saying, Teacher, we desire to see a sign from you. [39] But answering He said to them, A wicked and adulterous generation seeks a sign, and a sign shall not be given to it, except the sign of Jonah the prophet. [40] And even as Jonah was in the belly of the great fish three days and three nights, so shall the Son of man be in the heart of the earth three days and three nights. [41] (The) men of Nineveh shall stand up in the Judgment with this generation, and shall condemn it, for they repented at the preaching of Jonah; and, behold, a greater than Jonah (is) here. [42] The queen of (the) south shall rise up in the Judgment with this generation, and shall condemn it; for she came from the ends of the earth to hear the wisdom of Solomon; and, behold, a greater than Solomon (is) here. [43] But when the unclean spirit goes out

τοῦ ἀνθρώπου, ἀφεθήσεται αὐτῷ· ὃς δ' ἂν εἴπῃ κατὰ τοῦ
— of man,    it will be forgiven him; but whoever speaks against the

Πνεύματος τοῦ Ἁγίου, οὐκ ἀφεθήσεται αὐτῷ, οὔτε ἐν τούτῳ
Spirit    the   Holy,   not it shall be forgiven him,  neither in   this

33 τῷ αἰῶνι οὔτε ἐν τῷ μέλλοντι. ἢ ποιήσατε τὸ δένδρον
— age   nor  in  the  coming (one). Either make   the   tree

καλόν, καὶ τὸν καρπὸν αὐτοῦ καλόν, ἢ ποιήσατε τὸ δένδρον
good,  and the fruit   of it  good,  or  make   the  tree

σαπρόν, καὶ τὸν καρπὸν αὐτοῦ σαπρόν· ἐκ γὰρ τοῦ καρποῦ
corrupt  and the fruit    of it  corrupt;  of  for  the  fruit

34 τὸ δένδρον γινώσκεται. γεννήματα ἐχιδνῶν, πῶς δύνασθε
the  tree   is known.   Offspring   of vipers!  How  can you

ἀγαθὰ λαλεῖν, πονηροὶ ὄντες; ἐκ γὰρ τοῦ περισσεύματος
good things speak,  evil  being? out of For  the  abundance

35 τῆς καρδίας τὸ στόμα λαλεῖ. ὁ ἀγαθὸς ἄνθρωπος ἐκ τοῦ
of the heart  the mouth  speaks. The good   man   out of the

ἀγαθοῦ θησαυροῦ τῆς καρδίας ἐκβάλλει τὰ ἀγαθά· καὶ ὁ
good   treasure   of the heart  puts forth  the good things, and the

πονηρὸς ἄνθρωπος ἐκ τοῦ πονηροῦ θησαυροῦ ἐκβάλλει
evil    man    out of the evil   treasure    puts forth

36 πονηρά. λέγω δὲ ὑμῖν, ὅτι πᾶν ῥῆμα ἀργόν, ὃ ἐὰν λαλή-
evil things. I say  But to you, that every word  idle   whatever may speak

σωσιν οἱ ἄνθρωποι, ἀποδώσουσι περὶ αὐτοῦ λόγον ἐν
— men,   they will give  concerning it   account  in

37 ἡμέρᾳ κρίσεως. ἐκ γὰρ τῶν λόγων σου δικαιωθήσῃ, καὶ ἐκ
(the) day of judgment, by For  the words of you you will be justified, and by

τῶν λόγων σου καταδικασθήσῃ.
the  words of you you will be condemned.

38 Τότε ἀπεκρίθησάν τινες τῶν γραμματέων καὶ Φαρισαίων,
Then answered   some of the scribes   and Pharisees,

39 λέγοντες, Διδάσκαλε, θέλομεν ἀπὸ σοῦ σημεῖον ἰδεῖν. ὁ δὲ
saying,   Teacher,   we wish from You  a sign  to see. He But

ἀποκριθεὶς εἶπεν αὐτοῖς, Γενεὰ πονηρὰ καὶ μοιχαλὶς σημεῖον
answering  said  to them,  generation An evil and adulterous a sign

ἐπιζητεῖ· καὶ σημεῖον οὐ δοθήσεται αὐτῇ, εἰ μὴ τὸ σημεῖον
seeks,   and a sign  not shall be given to it except  the  sign

40 Ἰωνᾶ τοῦ προφήτου. ὥσπερ γὰρ ἦν Ἰωνᾶς ἐν τῇ κοιλίᾳ
of Jonah the prophet.   even as  For was Jonah  in the belly

τοῦ κήτους τρεῖς ἡμέρας καὶ τρεῖς νύκτας, οὕτως ἔσται ὁ υἱὸς
of the huge fish three days  and three nights,  so  will be the Son

τοῦ ἀνθρώπου ἐν τῇ καρδίᾳ τῆς γῆς τρεῖς ἡμέρας καὶ τρεῖς
— of man  in the heart of the earth three days   and three

41 νύκτας. ἄνδρες Νινευῖται ἀναστήσονται ἐν τῇ κρίσει μετὰ
nights.  Men, Ninevites  will stand up  in the judgment with

τῆς γενεᾶς ταύτης καὶ κατακρινοῦσιν αὐτήν· ὅτι μετενόησαν
— generation this and will condemn  it; because they repented

42 εἰς τὸ κήρυγμα Ἰωνᾶ· καὶ ἰδού, πλεῖον Ἰωνᾶ ὧδε. βασίλισσα
at the preaching of Jonah, and behold, a greater than Jonah (is) here. (The) queen

νότου ἐγερθήσεται ἐν τῇ κρίσει μετὰ τῆς γενεᾶς ταύτης καὶ
of (the) south will be raised in the judgment with — generation this and

κατακρινεῖ αὐτήν· ὅτι ἦλθεν ἐκ τῶν περάτων τῆς γῆς
will condemn  it; because she came out of the limits   of the earth

ἀκοῦσαι τὴν σοφίαν Σολομῶντος· καὶ ἰδού, πλεῖον Σολο-
to hear  the  wisdom of Solomon,   and, behold, a greater than Solomon

43 μῶντος ὧδε. ὅταν δὲ τὸ ἀκάθαρτον πνεῦμα ἐξέλθῃ ἀπὸ τοῦ
(is) here. when Now the unclean   spirit  goes out from  —

from a man, he goes through desert places seeking rest, and does not find (it). [44] Then he says, I will return to my house from which I came out. And having come, he finds (it) empty, swept and decorated. [45] Then he goes and takes with himself seven other spirits more wicked than himself; and entering in, they live there; and the last of that man becomes worse than the first. So it shall be also to this wicked generation.

[46] But while He yet was speaking to the crowds, behold, (His) mother and brothers were standing outside, seeking to speak to Him. [47] Then one said to Him, Behold, Your mother and Your brothers are standing outside, seeking to speak to You. [48] But answering He said to him who spoke to Him, Who is My mother? And who are My brothers? [49] And stretching out His hand to His disciples, He said, Behold, My mother and My brothers. [50] For whoever shall do the will of My Father who is in Heaven, he is My brother and sister and mother.

### CHAPTER 13

[1] And in that day, having gone forth from the house, Jesus sat down by the sea. [2] And great crowds were gathered to Him, so that He having entered into a boat sat down, and all the crowd on the shore stood. [3] And He spoke to them many things in parables, saying, Behold, the sower went out to sow. [4] And as he sowed some fell by the wayside, and the birds came and ate them. [5] And some fell on the stony places, where they did not have much earth; and immediately sprang up through not having deepness of earth; [6] and (the) sun having risen, they were scorched; and through not having root were dried up.

44 ἀνθρώπου, διέρχεται δι᾽ ἀνύδρων τόπων, ζητοῦν ἀνάπαυσιν,
a man,          he goes through dry     places     seeking     rest,
καὶ οὐχ εὑρίσκει. τότε λέγει, Ἐπιστρέψω εἰς τὸν οἶκόν μου
and not does find.    Then he says, I will return   to the house of me,
ὅθεν ἐξῆλθον· καὶ ἐλθὸν εὑρίσκει σχολάζοντα, σεσαρωμένον,
from where I came, and coming he finds (it) standing empty,     swept

45 καὶ κεκοσμημένον. τότε πορεύεται καὶ παραλαμβάνει μεθ᾽
and  decorated.        Then  he goes      and      takes along     with
ἑαυτοῦ ἑπτὰ ἕτερα πνεύματα πονηρότερα ἑαυτοῦ, καὶ
him     seven  other   spirits      more evil  (than) him,   and
εἰσελθόντα κατοικεῖ ἐκεῖ· καὶ γίνεται τὰ ἔσχατα τοῦ ἀνθρώ-
entering       dwells    there; and becomes the last things  — of man
που ἐκείνου χείρονα τῶν πρώτων. οὕτως ἔσται καὶ τῇ γενεᾷ
that worse than the   first.       Thus  it will be also to gene-
ταύτῃ τῇ πονηρᾷ.
ration this —   evil.

46 Ἔτι δὲ αὐτοῦ λαλοῦντος τοῖς ὄχλοις, ἰδού, ἡ μήτηρ καὶ
while But He is speaking   to the crowds, behold, the mother and
οἱ ἀδελφοὶ αὐτοῦ εἱστήκεισαν ἔξω, ζητοῦντες αὐτῷ λαλῆσαι.
the brothers of Him    stood        outside, seeking     to Him to speak.

47 εἶπε δέ τις αὐτῷ, Ἰδού, ἡ μήτηρ σου καὶ οἱ ἀδελφοί σου ἔξω
said And one to Him, Behold, the mother of You and the brothers of You out

48 ἑστήκασι, ζητοῦντές σοι λαλῆσαι. ὁ δὲ ἀποκριθεὶς εἶπε τῷ
are standing,  seeking   to You to speak.  He And answering  said to the
εἰπόντι αὐτῷ, Τίς ἐστιν ἡ μήτηρ μου; καὶ τίνες εἰσὶν οἱ
(one) saying to Him, Who is  the mother of Me, and  who    are  the

49 ἀδελφοί μου; καὶ ἐκτείνας τὴν χεῖρα αὐτοῦ ἐπὶ τοὺς
brothers of Me? And stretching out the hand  of Him on   the
μαθητὰς αὐτοῦ εἶπεν, Ἰδού, ἡ μήτηρ μου καὶ οἱ ἀδελφοί μου.
disciples of Him He said, Behold, the mother of Me and the brothers of Me.

50 ὅστις γὰρ ἂν ποιήσῃ τὸ θέλημα τοῦ πατρός μου τοῦ ἐν
who  for ever   does   the   will    of the Father of Me
οὐρανοῖς, αὐτός μου ἀδελφὸς καὶ ἀδελφὴ καὶ μήτηρ ἐστίν.
heavens,    he of Me brother  and   sister  and  mother is.

### CHAPTER 13

1 Ἐν δὲ τῇ ἡμέρᾳ ἐκείνῃ ἐξελθὼν ὁ Ἰησοῦς ἀπὸ τῆς οἰκίας
in And —    day   that  going forth — Jesus   from the house

2 ἐκάθητο παρὰ τὴν θάλασσαν. καὶ συνήχθησαν πρὸς αὐτὸν
He sat down by   the   sea.       And were assembled  to   Him
ὄχλοι πολλοί, ὥστε αὐτὸν εἰς τὸ πλοῖον ἐμβάντα καθῆσθαι·
crowds great,  so that He  into the boat having entered sat down,

3 καὶ πᾶς ὁ ὄχλος ἐπὶ τὸν αἰγιαλὸν εἱστήκει. καὶ ἐλάλησεν
and all the crowd on the    shore   stood.    And He spoke
αὐτοῖς πολλὰ ἐν παραβολαῖς, λέγων, Ἰδού, ἐξῆλθεν ὁ
to them  many things in parables,   saying, Behold, went out the

4 σπείρων τοῦ σπείρειν. καὶ ἐν τῷ σπείρειν αὐτόν, ἃ μὲν ἔπεσε
(one) sowing — to sow,    and in the  sowing  of him, some truly fell
παρὰ τὴν ὁδόν· καὶ ἦλθε τὰ πετεινὰ καὶ κατέφαγεν αὐτά.
by   the  wayside, and came the  birds   and   ate        them.

5 ἄλλα δὲ ἔπεσεν ἐπὶ τὰ πετρώδη, ὅπου οὐκ εἶχε γῆν πολλήν·
other and fell  upon the rocky places, where not they had earth much

6 καὶ εὐθέως ἐξανέτειλε, διὰ τὸ μὴ ἔχειν βάθος γῆς· ἡλίου δὲ
and immediately it sprang up because not having depth of earth; sun and
ἀνατείλαντος ἐκαυματίσθη, καὶ διὰ τὸ μὴ ἔχειν ῥίζαν,
rising,       it was scorched, and because of — not having    root,

[7] And some fell on the thorns, and the thorns grew up and choked them. [8] And some fell on the good ground, and yielded fruit, one a hundred, another sixty, another thirty. [9] He that has ears to hear, let him hear.

[10] And having come, the disciples said to Him, Why do You speak to them in parables? [11] And answering He said to them, Because it has been given to you to know the mysteries of the kingdom of Heaven, but it has not been given to them. [12] For whoever has, to him shall be given, and he shall have over-abundance; but whoever has not, even what he has shall be taken away from him. [13] Because of this, I speak to them in parables, because seeing they do not see, and hearing they do not hear, nor do they understand. [14] And the prophecy of Isaiah is fulfilled in them, which says, "In hearing you shall hear, and in no way understand; and seeing, you shall see, yet in no way know. [15] For the heart of this people has grown fat, and they have heard with the ears sluggishly, and they have closed their eyes lest they see with the eyes, and they hear with the ears, and with the heart understand, and be converted, and I heal them." [16] But your eyes (are) blessed, because they see, and your ears, because they hear. [17] For truly I tell you that many prophets and righteous (ones) desired to see what you see, and did not see; and to hear what you hear, and did not hear.

[18] Therefore hear the parable of the sower: [19] Everyone hearing the word of the kingdom, and does not understand, the evil one comes and catches away that which was sown in his heart. This is he who was seeded by the roadside. [20] And he who was seeded on the stony places is he who hears the word and immediately receives it with joy; [21] but has no root in himself, but is temporary; and tribulation

---

**7** ἐξηράνθη. ἄλλα δὲ ἔπεσεν ἐπὶ τὰς ἀκάνθας, καὶ ἀνέβησαν αἱ
it was dried.　　And fell　upon the thorns,　and grew up　the

**8** ἄκανθαι καὶ ἀπέπνιξαν αὐτά. ἄλλα δὲ ἔπεσεν ἐπὶ τὴν γῆν
thorns　and choked　them.　other And fell　upon the earth

τὴν καλήν, καὶ ἐδίδου καρπόν, ὃ μὲν ἑκατόν, ὃ δὲ ἑξήκοντα,
– good,　and yielded　fruit,　one　in-deed hundred, one and sixty,

**9** ὃ δὲ τριάκοντα. ὁ ἔχων ὦτα ἀκούειν ἀκουέτω.
one and thirty. The (one) having ears to hear, let him hear.

**10** Καὶ προσελθόντες οἱ μαθηταὶ εἶπον αὐτῷ, Διατί ἐν
And having come,　the disciples　said　to Him,　Why in

**11** παραβολαῖς λαλεῖς αὐτοῖς; ὁ δὲ ἀποκριθεὶς εἶπεν αὐτοῖς ὅτι
parables　do You speak to them? He And answering said to them, Because

Ὑμῖν δέδοται γνῶναι τὰ μυστήρια τῆς βασιλείας τῶν
to you it has been given to know the mysteries of the kingdom　of the

**12** οὐρανῶν, ἐκείνοις δὲ οὐ δέδοται. ὅστις γὰρ ἔχει, δοθήσεται
heavens,　to those but not it has been given. who　for has,　will be given

αὐτῷ καὶ περισσευθήσεται· ὅστις δὲ οὐκ ἔχει, καὶ ὃ ἔχει,
to him, and he will have abundance; who but not has, even what he has

**13** ἀρθήσεται ἀπ' αὐτοῦ. διὰ τοῦτο ἐν παραβολαῖς αὐτοῖς λαλῶ,
will be taken from him. Because of this, in parables　to them I speak,

ὅτι βλέποντες οὐ βλέπουσι, καὶ ἀκούοντες οὐκ ἀκούουσιν,
because seeing　not they see,　and hearing　not they hear.

**14** οὐδὲ συνιοῦσι. καὶ ἀναπληροῦται ἐπ' αὐτοῖς ἡ προφητεία
neither understand. And is fulfilled　upon them the prophecy

Ἡσαΐου, ἡ λέγουσα, Ἀκοῇ ἀκούσετε καὶ οὐ μὴ συνῆτε· καὶ
of Isaiah, which says,　In hearing you will hear and in no way know, and

**15** βλέποντες βλέψετε, καὶ οὐ μὴ ἴδητε. ἐπαχύνθη γὰρ ἡ καρδία
seeing　you will see and by no way perceive; has grown for the heart

τοῦ λαοῦ τούτου, καὶ τοῖς ὠσὶ βαρέως ἤκουσαν, καὶ τοὺς
– of people this　and with the ears heavily they heard,　and the

ὀφθαλμοὺς αὐτῶν ἐκάμμυσαν· μήποτε ἴδωσι τοῖς ὀφθαλμοῖς,
eyes　of them they closed,　lest　they see with the eyes,

καὶ τοῖς ὠσὶν ἀκούσωσι, καὶ τῇ καρδίᾳ συνῶσι, καὶ ἐπι-
and with the ears they hear,　and with the heart understand,　and be

**16** στρέψωσι, καὶ ἰάσωμαι αὐτούς. ὑμῶν δὲ μακάριοι οἱ ὀφθαλ-
converted,　and I heal　them.　of you But blessed (are) the eyes,

**17** μοί, ὅτι βλέπουσι· καὶ τὰ ὦτα ὑμῶν, ὅτι ἀκούει. ἀμὴν γὰρ
because they see,　and the ears of you, because they hear. truly For

λέγω ὑμῖν ὅτι πολλοὶ προφῆται καὶ δίκαιοι ἐπεθύμησαν
I say to you, that many　prophets and righteous (ones) desired

ἰδεῖν ἃ βλέπετε, καὶ οὐκ εἶδον· καὶ ἀκοῦσαι ἃ ἀκούετε, καὶ
to see what you see, and　not did see; and to hear what you hear, and

**18** οὐκ ἤκουσαν. ὑμεῖς οὖν ἀκούσατε τὴν παραβολὴν τοῦ
not did hear.　You therefore hear　the　parable　of the

**19** σπείροντος. παντὸς ἀκούοντος τὸν λόγον τῆς βασιλείας καὶ
sower:　Everyone hearing　the　word of the kingdom　and

μὴ συνιέντος, ἔρχεται ὁ πονηρος, καὶ ἁρπάζει τὸ ἐσπαρ-
not understands, comes　the evil one　and catches away that which was

μένον ἐν τῇ καρδίᾳ αὐτοῦ· οὗτός ἐστιν ὁ παρὰ τὴν ὁδὸν
sown　in the heart of him. This　is the (word) by the wayside

**20** σπαρείς. ὁ δὲ ἐπὶ τὰ πετρώδη σπαρείς, οὗτός ἐστιν ὁ τὸν
sown. the (word) and on the rocky places was sown, this　is the (one) the

**21** λόγον ἀκούων, καὶ εὐθὺς μετὰ χαρᾶς λαμβάνων αὐτόν· οὐκ
word　hearing, and at once with　joy　receiving　it;　no

ἔχει δὲ ῥίζαν ἐν ἑαυτῷ, ἀλλὰ πρόσκαιρός ἐστι· γενομένης δὲ
has but root　in himself, but　temporary　is;　occurring but

having risen, or persecution because of the word, he is at once offended. [22] And he who was seeded among the thorns, this is he who hears the word, and the care of this life and the deceitfulness of riches choke the word, and it becomes unfruitful. [23] But he who was seeded on the good ground, this is he who hears the word and understands; who truly brings forth fruit and produces, one a hundred times, another sixty, another thirty.

[24] He presented another parable before them, saying, The kingdom of heaven has become like a man sowing good seed in his field; [25] but while the men slept, his enemy came and sowed darnel in (the) midst of the wheat, and went away. [26] And when the blade sprouted and fruit came forth, then the darnel also appeared. [27] And having come, the servants of the master of the house said to him, Sir, did you not sow good seed in your field? Where then has it (gotten) the darnel? [28] And he said to them, A man, an enemy has done this. And the servants said to him, Do you desire that we having gone out should gather them? [29] But he said, No, lest gathering the darnel, you should uproot the wheat with them. [30] Allow both to grow together until the harvest; and in the time of the harvest I will say to the reapers, First gather the darnel, and bind them into bundles to burn them; but gather the wheat into my granary.

[31] He presented another parable before them, saying, The kingdom of Heaven is like a grain of mustard seed which a man having taken sowed in his field; [32] which indeed is less than all the seeds, but when it is grown it is greater than the plants, and becomes a tree, so that the

**22** θλίψεως ἢ διωγμοῦ διὰ τὸν λόγον, εὐθὺς σκανδαλίζεται. ὁ
tribulation or persecution through the word, at once he is offended.　he who
δὲ εἰς τὰς ἀκάνθας σπαρείς, οὗτός ἐστιν ὁ τὸν λόγον ἀκούων,
And in the thorns　　sown, this　　is the (one) the word hearing,
καὶ ἡ μέριμνα τοῦ αἰῶνος τούτου καὶ ἡ ἀπάτη τοῦ πλούτου
and the anxiety of the age　　this　and the deceit　　of riches
**23** συμπνίγει τὸν λόγον, καὶ ἄκαρπος γίνεται. ὁ δὲ ἐπὶ τὴν γῆν
choke　　the　　word, and unfruitful it becomes. he But on the earth
τὴν καλὴν σπαρείς, οὗτός ἐστιν ὁ τὸν λόγον ἀκούων καὶ
　　good　　was sown, this　　is the (one) the word　　hearing and
συνιών· ὃς δὴ καρποφορεῖ, καὶ ποιεῖ ὁ μὲν ἑκατόν, ὁ δὲ
understands; who indeed bears fruit and produces one truly a hundred, one and
ἑξήκοντα, ὁ δὲ τριάκοντα.
sixty,　　one and　　thirty.
**24** Ἄλλην παραβολὴν παρέθηκεν αὐτοῖς, λέγων, Ὡμοιώθη
　　Another　parable　　He put before them, saying,　is likened
ἡ βασιλεία τῶν οὐρανῶν ἀνθρώπῳ σπείραντι καλὸν
the kingdom　of the heavens　to a man　　sowing　　good
**25** σπέρμα ἐν τῷ ἀγρῷ αὐτοῦ· ἐν δὲ τῷ καθεύδειν τοὺς ἀνθρώ-
seed　　in the fields　of him: in but the sleeping of the men
πους, ἦλθεν αὐτοῦ ὁ ἐχθρὸς καὶ ἔσπειρε ζιζάνια ἀνὰ μέσον
　　came his　　enemy and sowed　darnel　amidst
**26** τοῦ σίτου, καὶ ἀπῆλθεν. ὅτε δὲ ἐβλάστησεν ὁ χόρτος καὶ
the　wheat, and went away. when And sprouted　the blade, and
**27** καρπὸν ἐποίησε, τότε ἐφάνη καὶ τὰ ζιζάνια. προσελθόντες
fruit　　produced, then appeared also the　darnel.　coming near
δὲ οἱ δοῦλοι τοῦ οἰκοδεσπότου εἶπον αὐτῷ, Κύριε, οὐχὶ
And the slaves　of the master of the house said to him, Lord　not
καλὸν σπέρμα ἔσπειρας ἐν τῷ σῷ ἀγρῷ; πόθεν οὖν ἔχει τὰ
good　seed did you sow in the of you field? Whence then has it the
**28** ζιζάνια; ὁ δὲ ἔφη αὐτοῖς, Ἐχθρὸς ἄνθρωπος τοῦτο ἐποίησεν.
darnel? he And said to them, An enemy, a man,　this　did.
οἱ δὲ δοῦλοι εἶπον αὐτῷ, Θέλεις οὖν ἀπελθόντες συλλέξωμεν
the And slaves　said to him, Will you then having gone out we may collect
**29** αὐτά; ὁ δὲ ἔφη, Οὔ· μήποτε, συλλέγοντες τὰ ζιζάνια,
them? he But said, No,　lest　collecting　the　darnel
**30** ἐκριζώσητε ἅμα αὐτοῖς τὸν σῖτον. ἄφετε συναυξάνεσθαι
you may uproot with them　the wheat. Allow　to grow together
ἀμφότερα μέχρι τοῦ θερισμοῦ· καὶ ἐν τῷ καιρῷ τοῦ θερισμοῦ
both　until the harvest; and in the time of the harvest
ἐρῶ τοῖς θερισταῖς, Συλλέξατε πρῶτον τὰ ζιζάνια, καὶ
I will say to the reapers,　Collect　first　the darnel, and
δήσατε αὐτὰ εἰς δέσμας πρὸς τὸ κατακαῦσαι αὐτά· τὸν δὲ
bind　them into bundles in order　to burn　them; the but
σῖτον συναγάγετε εἰς τὴν ἀποθήκην μου.
wheat bring together into the　granary　of me.
**31** Ἄλλην παραβολὴν παρέθηκεν αὐτοῖς, λέγων, Ὁμοία
　Another parable　He presented to them, saying,　Like
ἐστὶν ἡ βασιλεία τῶν οὐρανῶν κόκκῳ σινάπεως, ὃν λαβὼν
is the　kingdom of the heavens to a grain of mustard, which taking
**32** ἄνθρωπος ἔσπειρεν ἐν τῷ ἀγρῷ αὐτοῦ· ὃ μικρότερον μέν
a man　　sowed　in the field　of him, which lesser　truly
ἐστι πάντων τῶν σπερμάτων· ὅταν δὲ αὐξηθῇ, μεῖζον τῶν
is　than all　the seeds,　when but it is grown, greater the
　　　　　　　　　　　　　　　　　　　　　　　　　than
λαχάνων ἐστί, καὶ γίνεται δένδρον, ὥστε ἐλθεῖν τὰ πετεινὰ
plants　is, and becomes　a tree,　so that come　the birds

birds of the sky come and roost in its branches.

[33] He spoke another parable to them: The kingdom of Heaven is like leaven, which having taken, a women hid in three measures of meal, until all was leavened.

[34] Jesus spoke of all these things in parables to the crowds, and He did not speak to them without a párable; [35] so that it might be fulfilled that which was spoken by the prophet, saying, "I will open My mouth in parables; I will say things hidden from (the) foundation of (the) world."

[36] Then having sent the crowds away, Jesus went into the house; and His disciples came to Him, saying, Explain to us the parable of the darnel of the field. [37] And answering He said to them, He who sows the good seed is the Son of man; [38] and the field is the world; and the good seed, these are the sons of the kingdom; but the darnel are the sons of the evil; [39] and the enemy who sowed them is the devil; and the harvest is the end of the age; and angels are the reapers. [40] Therefore, as the darnel is gathered and is burned in the fire, so it shall be in the end of this age. [41] The Son of man shall send forth His angels, and they shall gather out of His kingdom all the offenses and those who practice lawlessness, [42] and they shall throw them into the furnace of fire; there shall be weeping and gnashing of the teeth. [43] Then the righteous shall shine like the sun in the kingdom of their Father. He that has ears to hear, let him hear.

[44] Again, the kingdom of Heaven is like treasure hidden in the field, which a man having found hid, and for the joy

**33** τοῦ οὐρανοῦ καὶ κατασκηνοῦν ἐν τοῖς κλάδοις αὐτοῦ.
of the heaven   and   roost           in   the branches   of it.

"Ἄλλην παραβολὴν ἐλάλησεν αὐτοῖς, Ὁμοία ἐστὶν ἡ
Another   parable   He spoke   to them:   Like   is   the

βασιλεία τῶν οὐρανῶν ζύμῃ, ἣν λαβοῦσα γυνὴ ἐνέκρυψεν
kingdom   of the heavens   to leaven, which taking   a woman   hid

εἰς ἀλεύρου σάτα τρία, ἕως οὗ ἐζυμώθη ὅλον.
in   meal   measures three,   until   was leavened   the whole.

**34** Ταῦτα πάντα ἐλάλησεν ὁ Ἰησοῦς ἐν παραβολαῖς τοῖς
These things all   spoke   —   Jesus   in   parables   to the

**35** ὄχλοις, καὶ χωρὶς παραβολῆς οὐκ ἐλάλει αὐτοῖς· ὅπως
crowds,   and   without   a parable   not He spoke to them; so that

πληρωθῇ τὸ ῥηθὲν διὰ τοῦ προφήτου, λέγοντος, Ἀνοίξω
was fulfilled that spoken through the   prophet,   saying,   I will open

ἐν παραβολαῖς τὸ στόμα μου, ἐρεύξομαι κεκρυμμένα ἀπὸ
in   parables   the mouth of Me; I will utter   things hidden   from

καταβολῆς κόσμου.
(the) foundation of (the) world.

**36** Τότε ἀφεὶς τοὺς ὄχλους ἦλθεν εἰς τὴν οἰκίαν ὁ Ἰησοῦς· καὶ
Then sending away the crowds,came into the house   —   Jesus;   and

προσῆλθον αὐτῷ οἱ μαθηταὶ αὐτοῦ, λέγοντες, Φράσον ἡμῖν
came   to Him   the disciples of Him,   saying,   Explain   to us

**37** τὴν παραβολὴν τῶν ζιζανίων τοῦ ἀγροῦ. ὁ δὲ ἀποκριθεὶς
the   parable   of the   darnel   of the field.   He And answering

εἶπεν αὐτοῖς, Ὁ σπείρων τὸ καλὸν σπέρμα ἐστὶν ὁ υἱὸς τοῦ
said   to them, The (one) sowing the   good seed   is   the Son   —

**38** ἀνθρώπου· ὁ δὲ ἀγρός ἐστιν ὁ κόσμος· τὸ δὲ καλὸν σπέρμα,
of man;   the and field   is   the   world; the and good   seed,

οὗτοί εἰσιν οἱ υἱοὶ τῆς βασιλείας· τὰ δὲ ζιζάνιά εἰσιν οἱ υἱοὶ
these   are the sons of the kingdom; the but darnel   are the sons

**39** τοῦ πονηροῦ· ὁ δὲ ἐχθρὸς ὁ σπείρας αὐτά ἐστιν ὁ διάβολος·
of the evil one; the and enemy who sowed   them   is   the   Devil;

ὁ δὲ θερισμὸς συντέλεια τοῦ αἰῶνός ἐστιν· οἱ δὲ θερισταὶ
the and harvest (the) completion of the age   is,   the and reapers

**40** ἄγγελοί εἰσιν. ὥσπερ οὖν συλλέγεται τὰ ζιζάνια καὶ πυρὶ
angels   are.   As therefore is collected   the   darnel,   and in fire

κατακαίεται, οὕτως ἔσται ἐν τῇ συντελείᾳ τοῦ αἰῶνος
is consumed,   thus   it shall be in the   completion of the   age

**41** τούτου. ἀποστελεῖ ὁ υἱὸς τοῦ ἀνθρώπου τοὺς ἀγγέλους
this.   Shall send out the Son   —   of man   the   angels

αὐτοῦ, καὶ συλλέξουσιν ἐκ τῆς βασιλείας αὐτοῦ πάντα τὰ
of Him, and they will collect out of the kingdom   of Him   all   the

**42** σκάνδαλα καὶ τοὺς ποιοῦντας τὴν ἀνομίαν, καὶ βαλοῦσιν
offenses   and   those who practice   —   lawlessness, and they will cast

αὐτοὺς εἰς τὴν κάμινον τοῦ πυρός· ἐκεῖ ἔσται ὁ κλαυθμὸς καὶ
them   into the furnace of the fire:   there shall be the weeping   and

**43** ὁ βρυγμὸς τῶν ὀδόντων. τότε οἱ δίκαιοι ἐκλάμψουσιν ὡς ὁ
the gnashing of the teeth.   Then the righteous will shine forth as the

ἥλιος ἐν τῇ βασιλείᾳ τοῦ πατρὸς αὐτῶν. ὁ ἔχων ὦτα ἀκούειν
sun   in the kingdom of the Father of them. He having ears to hear,

ἀκουέτω.
let him hear.

**44** Πάλιν ὁμοία ἐστὶν ἡ βασιλεία τῶν οὐρανῶν θησαυρῷ
Again   like   is   the kingdom   of the heavens   to treasure

κεκρυμμένῳ ἐν τῷ ἀγρῷ, ὃν εὑρὼν ἄνθρωπος ἔκρυψε· καὶ ἀπὸ
hid   in the field,   which having found a man   hid,   and from

of it goes and he sells all things, as many as he has, and buys that field.

[45] Again, the kingdom of Heaven is like a man, a merchant seeking beautiful pearls; [46] who having found one very precious pearl, having gone away has sold all things, as many as he had, and bought it.

[47] Again, the kingdom of Heaven is like a drag net thrown into the sea, and gathering together of every kind; [48] which when it was filled, drawing it up on the shore, and having sat down, they gathered the good into containers, and they threw out the bad. [49] So it shall be in the end of the age: the angels shall go out and shall separate the wicked from (the) midst of the righteous, [50] and shall throw them into the furnace of fire; there shall be wailing and gnashing of the teeth.

[51] Jesus said to them, Have you understood all these things? They said to Him, Yes, Lord. [52] And He said to them, Because of this every scribe schooled to the kingdom of Heaven is like a man, a master of a house, who puts forth out of his treasure new and old.

[53] And it came to pass, when Jesus had finished these parables, He left there; [54] and having come into His own country, He taught them in their synagogue, so that they were astonished and said, Where did this one (get) this wisdom and the mighty works? [55] Is this not the son of the carpenter? (Is) not his mother called Mary, and his brothers, James, and Joseph, and Simon, and Judas? [56] And are not his sisters all with us? From where then did this one (get) all these things? [57] And they were offended in Him. But Jesus said to them, A prophet is

---

τῆς χαρᾶς αὐτοῦ ὑπάγει, καὶ πάντα ὅσα ἔχει πωλεῖ, καὶ
the  joy  of it he goes,  and all things what- he has, he sells, and
                                                    ever
ἀγοράζει τὸν ἀγρὸν ἐκεῖνον.
buys   —   field   that.

45 Πάλιν ὁμοία ἐστὶν ἡ βασιλεία τῶν οὐρανῶν ἀνθρώπῳ
   Again  like  is  the  kingdom  of the heavens  to a man

46 ἐμπόρῳ ζητοῦντι καλοὺς μαργαρίτας· ὃς εὑρὼν ἕνα πολύ-
   a merchant seeking  excellent  pearls;  who finding  one very
τιμον μαργαρίτην, ἀπελθὼν πέπρακε πάντα ὅσα εἶχε, καὶ
precious pearl,   going away  has sold all things  that he has, and
ἠγόρασεν αὐτόν.
bought  it.

47 Πάλιν ὁμοία ἐστὶν ἡ βασιλεία τῶν οὐρανῶν σαγήνῃ
   Again  like  is  the  kingdom of the  heavens  to a net
βληθείσῃ εἰς τὴν θάλασσαν, καὶ ἐκ παντὸς γένους συναγα-
thrown  into  the  sea.   and of every  kind  gathering

48 γούσῃ· ἥν, ὅτε ἐπληρώθη, ἀναβιβάσαντες ἐπὶ τὸν αἰγιαλόν,
   together; which when it was filled, drawing up  onto the  shore,
καὶ καθίσαντες, συνέλεξαν τὰ καλὰ εἰς ἀγγεῖα, τὰ δὲ σαπρὰ
and sitting down,(men)collected the good into vessels,  the and corrupt

49 ἔξω ἔβαλον. οὕτως ἔσται ἐν τῇ συντελείᾳ τοῦ αἰῶνος· ἐξελεύ-
   out they threw. Thus it will be in the completion of the age:  will go
σονται οἱ ἄγγελοι, καὶ ἀφοριοῦσι τοὺς πονηροὺς ἐκ μέσου
out   the  angels,   and will separate  the  evil  from (the) midst

50 τῶν δικαίων, καὶ βαλοῦσιν αὐτοὺς εἰς τὴν κάμινον τοῦ πυρός·
   of the righteous, and will throw  them  into the  furnace of the fire;
ἐκεῖ ἔσται ὁ κλαυθμὸς καὶ ὁ βρυγμὸς τῶν ὀδόντων.
there will be the weeping and the gnashing of the  teeth.

51 Λέγει αὐτοῖς ὁ Ἰησοῦς, Συνήκατε ταῦτα πάντα ; λέγουσιν
   says to them — Jesus, Did you discern these things all?  They say

52 αὐτῷ, Ναί, Κύριε. ὁ δὲ εἶπεν αὐτοῖς, Διὰ τοῦτο πᾶς γραμ-
   to Him. Yes,  Lord. He And said  to them, Because of this every  scribe
ματεὺς μαθητευθεὶς εἰς τὴν βασιλείαν τῶν οὐρανῶν ὅμοιός
discipled  into  the  kingdom  of the heavens  like
ἐστιν ἀνθρώπῳ οἰκοδεσπότῃ, ὅστις ἐκβάλλει ἐκ τοῦ θησαυ-
is  to a man,  a master of a house, who  puts forth out of the treasure
ροῦ αὐτοῦ καινὰ καὶ παλαιά.
of him  new and old.

53 Καὶ ἐγένετο ὅτε ἐτέλεσεν ὁ Ἰησοῦς τὰς παραβολὰς ταύτας,
   And it was, when had ended — Jesus  —  parables  these,

54 μετῆρεν ἐκεῖθεν· καὶ ἐλθὼν εἰς τὴν πατρίδα αὐτοῦ ἐδίδασκεν
   He moved from there;and coming into the country  of Him,  He taught
αὐτοὺς ἐν τῇ συναγωγῇ αὐτῶν, ὥστε ἐκπλήττεσθαι αὐτοὺς
them  in the  synagogue of them,  so that were astounded  they,

55 καὶ λέγειν, Πόθεν τούτῳ ἡ σοφία αὕτη καὶ αἱ δυνάμεις ; οὐχ
   even to say, Whence to this one  wisdom this, and the works of power? Not
οὗτός ἐστιν ὁ τοῦ τέκτονος υἱός ; οὐχὶ ἡ μήτηρ αὐτοῦ
this   is   the  of the carpenter son? (Is) not the mother  of him
λέγεται Μαριάμ, καὶ οἱ ἀδελφοὶ αὐτοῦ Ἰάκωβος καὶ Ἰωσῆς
called  Mary,  and the brothers of him,  James  and Joseph

56 καὶ Σίμων καὶ Ἰούδας ; καὶ αἱ ἀδελφαὶ αὐτοῦ οὐχὶ πᾶσαι
   and Simon and  Judas ?  And the sisters  of him not  all

57 πρὸς ἡμᾶς εἰσί ; πόθεν οὖν τούτῳ ταῦτα πάντα ; καὶ
   with  us   are ? Whence then to this (one) these things all ?  And
ἐσκανδαλίζοντο ἐν αὐτῷ ὁ δὲ Ἰησοῦς εἶπεν αὐτοῖς, Οὐκ
they were offended in  Him.  But Jesus  said  to them,  Not

not without honor except in his own country and in his own house. [58] And He did not do many mighty works there because of their unbelief.

ἔστι προφήτης ἄτιμος, εἰ μὴ ἐν τῇ πατρίδι αὐτοῦ καὶ ἐν τῇ
is    a prophet honorless, except in  the homeland of him, and in the

58 οἰκίᾳ αὐτοῦ. καὶ οὐκ ἐποίησεν ἐκεῖ δυνάμεις πολλάς, διὰ
house of him. And not He did    there power-works many, because

τὴν ἀπιστίαν αὐτῶν.
of the unbelief of them.

## CHAPTER 14

### CHAPTER 14

[1] At that time Herod the tetrarch heard the fame of Jesus, [2] and said to his servants, This is John the Baptist; he has risen from the dead, and because of this mighty works are working in him. [3] For having seized John, Herod bound him and put (him) in prison, because of Herodias, the wife of his brother Philip. [4] For John said to him, It is not lawful you to have her. [5] And desiring to kill him, he feared the multitude, because they held him as a prophet. [6] But a birthday of Herod being celebrated, the daughter of Herodias danced in the midst, and pleased Herod; [7] at which he promised with an oath to give her whatever she should ask. [8] But she being urged on by her mother, she says, Give me here on a platter the head of John the Baptist. [9] And the king was grieved; but because of the oath and those who reclined with (him), he commanded (it) to be given. [10] And having sent, he beheaded John in the prison. [11] And his head was brought on a platter and was given to the girl, and she brought (it) to her mother. [12] And having come, his disciples took the body and buried; and having come reported to Jesus. [13] And having heard Jesus withdrew from there by boat, to a deserted place apart. [14] And the crowds having heard followed Him on foot from the cities. and having gone out, Jesus saw a great crowd, and was moved with compassion toward them; and He

1 Ἐν ἐκείνῳ τῷ καιρῷ ἤκουσεν Ἡρώδης ὁ τετράρχης τὴν
At that    time    heard Herod    the tetrarch the

2 ἀκοὴν Ἰησοῦ, καὶ εἶπε τοῖς παισὶν αὐτοῦ, Οὗτός ἐστιν
fame of Jesus, and said to the servants of him, This    is

Ἰωάννης ὁ Βαπτιστής· αὐτὸς ἠγέρθη ἀπὸ τῶν νεκρῶν, καὶ
John the Baptist;    he is risen from the dead, and

3 διὰ τοῦτο αἱ δυνάμεις ἐνεργοῦσιν ἐν αὐτῷ. ὁ γὰρ Ἡρώδης
because of this the power works operate in him. For    Herod

κρατήσας τὸν Ἰωάννην ἔδησεν αὐτὸν καὶ ἔθετο ἐν φυλακῇ,
having seized — John bound him and put in prison,

διὰ Ἡρωδιάδα τὴν γυναῖκα Φιλίππου τοῦ ἀδελφοῦ αὐτοῦ.
because of Herodias the wife    of Philip, the brother of him.

4 ἔλεγε γὰρ αὐτῷ ὁ Ἰωάννης, Οὐκ ἔξεστί σοι ἔχειν αὐτήν.
said For to him — John,    Not it is lawful for you to have her.

5 καὶ θέλων αὐτὸν ἀποκτεῖναι, ἐφοβήθη τὸν ὄχλον, ὅτι ὡς
And wishing him to kill,    he feared the crowd, because as

6 προφήτην αὐτὸν εἶχον. γενεσίων δὲ ἀγομένων τοῦ Ἡρώδου,
a prophet him they held. a birthday But being held — of Herod,

ὠρχήσατο ἡ θυγάτηρ τῆς Ἡρωδιάδος ἐν τῷ μέσῳ, καὶ
danced    the daughter — of Herodias in the midst, and

7 ἤρεσε τῷ Ἡρώδη. ὅθεν μεθ᾽ ὅρκου ὡμολόγησεν αὐτῇ δοῦναι
pleased — Herod. Whence with an oath he acknowledged to her to give

8 ὃ ἐὰν αἰτήσηται. ἡ δέ, προβιβασθεῖσα ὑπὸ τῆς μητρὸς
whatever she might ask. she So being urged on    by the mother

αὐτῆς, Δός μοι, φησίν, ὧδε ἐπὶ πίνακι τὴν κεφαλὴν Ἰωάννου
of her, Give me, she says, here on a platter the head of John

9 τοῦ Βαπτιστοῦ. καὶ ἐλυπήθη ὁ βασιλεύς, διὰ δὲ τοὺς ὅρκους
the Baptist.    And was grieved the king, because of but the oaths

10 καὶ τοὺς συνανακειμένους ἐκέλευσε δοθῆναι· καὶ πέμψας
and those who reclined with (him), he ordered (it) be given. And sending

11 ἀπεκεφάλισε τὸν Ἰωάννην ἐν τῇ φυλακῇ. καὶ ἠνέχθη ἡ
he beheaded — John in the prison. And was brought the

κεφαλὴ αὐτοῦ ἐπὶ πίνακι, καὶ ἐδόθη τῷ κορασίῳ· καὶ ἤνεγκε
head of him on a platter, and was given to the girl,    and she brought

12 τῇ μητρὶ αὐτῆς. καὶ προσελθόντες οἱ μαθηταὶ αὐτοῦ ἦραν
to the mother of her. And having come the disciples of him took

τὸ σῶμα, καὶ ἔθαψαν αὐτό καὶ ἐλθόντες ἀπήγγειλαν τῷ
the body, and buried it; and coming told —

Ἰησοῦ.
to Jesus.

13 Καὶ ἀκούσας ὁ Ἰησοῦς ἀνεχώρησεν ἐκεῖθεν ἐν πλοίῳ εἰς
And having heard Jesus withdrew from there in a boat into

ἔρημον τόπον κατ᾽ ἰδίαν· καὶ ἀκούσαντες οἱ ὄχλοι ἠκολού-
a desert place privately.    And having heard the crowds followed

14 θησαν αὐτῷ πεζῇ ἀπὸ τῶν πόλεων. καὶ ἐξελθὼν ὁ Ἰησοῦς
Him on foot from the cities.    And going out, — Jesus

εἶδε πολὺν ὄχλον, καὶ ἐσπλαγχνίσθη ἐπ᾽ αὐτούς, καὶ
saw great a crowd, and was filled with pity toward them, and

healed their infirm ones. [15] And evening having come, His disciples came to Him, saying, The place is deserted,· and the time is already gone; dismiss the crowds, that having gone into the villages they may buy food for themselves. [16] But Jesus said to them, They have no need to go away; you give them (food) to eat. [17] But they said to Him, We have nothing here except five loaves and two fish. [18] And He said, Bring them to Me here. [19] And having commanded the crowds to recline on the grass, and having taken the five loaves and the two fish, having looked up to Heaven, He blessed; and having broken He gave the loaves to the disciples, and the disciples to the crowds. [20] And all ate and were satisfied; and they took up that which was in excess of the pieces, twelve baskets full. [21] And those who ate were about five thousand men, besides women and children.

[22] And immediately Jesus made His disciples get into a boat and to go before Him to the other side, until He should have sent away the crowds. [23] And having sent away the crowds, He went up into the mountain alone to pray. And evening coming on, He was there alone. [24] But the ship was now in (the) middle of the sea, tossed by the waves, for the wind was contrary. [25] But in (the) fourth watch of the night, Jesus went out to them, walking on the sea. [26] And seeing Him walking on the sea, the disciples were troubled, saying, It is a ghost! And they cried out from the fear. [27] But immediately Jesus spoke to them, saying, Be comforted, I AM! Do not fear. [28] And answering Him, Peter said, Lord, if it is You, tell me to come to You on the waters. [29] And He said, Come.

---

**15** ἐθεράπευσε τοὺς ἀρρώστους αὐτῶν. ὀψίας δὲ γενομένης,
He healed the infirm of them. evening And coming,

προσῆλθον αὐτῷ οἱ μαθηταὶ αὐτοῦ, λέγοντες, Ἔρημός
came near to Him the disciples of Him, saying, Desert

ἐστιν ὁ τόπος, καὶ ἡ ὥρα ἤδη παρῆλθεν· ἀπόλυσον τοὺς
is the place, and the hour already is gone by. Dismiss the

ὄχλους, ἵνα ἀπελθόντες εἰς τὰς κώμας ἀγοράσωσιν ἑαυτοῖς
crowds, that going away into the villages they may buy for themselves

**16** βρώματα. ὁ δὲ Ἰησοῦς εἶπεν αὐτοῖς, Οὐ χρείαν ἔχουσιν
foods. – But Jesus said to them, Not need they have

**17** ἀπελθεῖν· δότε αὐτοῖς ὑμεῖς φαγεῖν. οἱ δὲ λέγουσιν αὐτῷ,
to go away; give to them you to eat. they But say to Him,

**18** Οὐκ ἔχομεν ὧδε εἰ μὴ πέντε ἄρτους καὶ δύο ἰχθύας. ὁ δὲ εἶπε,
Not we have here except five loaves and two fish. he And said,

**19** Φέρετέ μοι αὐτοὺς ὧδε. καὶ κελεύσας τοὺς ὄχλους ἀνακλιθῆ-
Bear to Me them here. And commanding the crowds to recline

ναι ἐπὶ τοὺς χόρτους, καὶ λαβὼν τοὺς πέντε ἄρτους καὶ τοὺς
on the grass, and taking the five loaves and the

δύο ἰχθύας, ἀναβλέψας εἰς τὸν οὐρανόν, εὐλόγησε, καὶ
two fish, looking up to the Heaven, He blessed, and

κλάσας ἔδωκε τοῖς μαθηταῖς τοὺς ἄρτους, οἱ δὲ μαθηταὶ τοῖς
breaking He gave to the disciples the loaves, the and disciples to the

**20** ὄχλοις. καὶ ἔφαγον πάντες, καὶ ἐχορτάσθησαν· καὶ ἦραν τὸ
crowds. And ate all and were satisfied; and they took the

**21** περισσεῦον τῶν κλασμάτων, δώδεκα κοφίνους πλήρεις. οἱ
excess of the fragments, twelve handbaskets full. the (ones)

δὲ ἐσθίοντες ἦσαν ἄνδρες ὡσεὶ πεντακισχίλιοι, χωρὶς γυναι-
And eating were men about five thousand, apart from women

κῶν καὶ παιδίων.
and children.

**22** Καὶ εὐθέως ἠνάγκασεν ὁ Ἰησοῦς τοὺς μαθητὰς αὐτοῦ
And instantly constrained Jesus the disciples of Him

ἐμβῆναι εἰς τὸ πλοῖον, καὶ προάγειν αὐτὸν εἰς τὸ πέραν,
to enter into the boat and to go before Him to the other side,

**23** ἕως οὗ ἀπολύσῃ τοὺς ὄχλους. καὶ ἀπολύσας τοὺς ὄχλους,
until He should dismiss the crowds. And having dismissed the crowds,

ἀνέβη εἰς τὸ ὄρος κατ' ἰδίαν προσεύξασθαι· ὀψίας δὲ γενο-
He went into the mountain apart in order to pray: evening And com-

**24** μένης, μόνος ἦν ἐκεῖ. τὸ δὲ πλοῖον ἤδη μέσον τῆς θαλάσσης
ing, alone He was there. the And boat now amidst the sea

ἦν, βασανιζόμενον ὑπὸ τῶν κυμάτων· ἦν γὰρ ἐναντίος ὁ
was, tossed by the waves; was for contrary the

**25** ἄνεμος. τετάρτῃ δὲ φυλακῇ τῆς νυκτὸς ἀπῆλθε πρὸς αὐτοὺς
wind. in fourth But watch of the night went toward them

**26** ὁ Ἰησοῦς, περιπατῶν ἐπὶ τῆς θαλάσσης. καὶ ἰδόντες αὐτὸν
Jesus, walking on the sea. And seeing Him

οἱ μαθηταὶ ἐπὶ τὴν θάλασσαν περιπατοῦντα ἐταράχθησαν,
the disciples on the sea walking they were troubled,

λέγοντες ὅτι Φάντασμά ἐστι· καὶ ἀπὸ τοῦ φόβου ἔκραξαν.
saying, A phantom it is, and out of — fear they cried out.

**27** εὐθέως δὲ ἐλάλησεν αὐτοῖς ὁ Ἰησοῦς, λέγων, Θαρσεῖτε· ἐγώ
at once But spoke to them — Jesus, saying, Be comforted, I

**28** εἰμι· μὴ φοβεῖσθε. ἀποκριθεὶς δὲ αὐτῷ ὁ Πέτρος εἶπε, Κύριε,
AM! not Do fear. answering And Him — Peter said, Lord,

**29** εἰ σὺ εἶ, κέλευσόν με πρός σε ἐλθεῖν ἐπὶ τὰ ὕδατα. ὁ δὲ εἶπε,
if You are, command me to You to come on the waters. He And said,

And having come down from the ship, Peter walked on the waters to go to Jesus. [30] But seeing the violent wind, he was afraid, and beginning to sink, he cried out, saying, Lord, save me! [31] And immediately Jesus, having stretched out the hand, took hold of him, and said to him, O (you) of little faith, why did you doubt? [32] And having come into the boat, the wind stopped. [33] And those in the boat came and worshiped Him, saying, Truly You are the Son of God.

[34] And having passed over, they came to the land of Gennesaret. [35] And having recognized him, the men of that place sent to all the surrounding country, and brought to Him all those who were diseased; [36] and begged Him that they might only touch the hem of His robe; and as many as touched were made perfectly well.

## CHAPTER 15

[1] Then the scribes and Pharisees came to Jesus from Jerusalem, saying, [2] Why do Your disciples violate the tradition of the elders? For they did not wash their hands when they eat bread. [3] But He answering said to them, Why do you also violate the commandment of God on account of your tradition? [4] For God commanded, saying, "Honor your father and mother;" and, "He who speaks evil of father or mother, by death let him die." [5] But you say, Whoever shall say to father or mother, A gift, whatever you might be profited by me; and in no way honor his father or his mother. [6] And you voided the commandment of God on account of your tradition. [7] Hypocrites! Well did Isaiah prophesy concerning you, saying, [8] "This people draws near to Me

**30** Ἐλθέ. καὶ καταβὰς ἀπὸ τοῦ πλοίου ὁ Πέτρος περιεπάτησεν
Come! And descending from the boat,   — Peter   walked
ἐπὶ τὰ ὕδατα, ἐλθεῖν πρὸς τὸν Ἰησοῦν. βλέπων δὲ τὸν
on   the   waters, to come toward   —   Jesus.   seeing But the
ἄνεμον ἰσχυρὸν ἐφοβήθη· καὶ ἀρξάμενος καταποντίζεσθαι
wind   strong,   he was frightened, and beginning   to sink

**31** ἔκραξε, λέγων, Κύριε, σῶσόν με. εὐθέως δὲ ὁ Ἰησοῦς ἐκτείνας
he cried out, saying, Lord,   save   me! instantly And —   Jesus extending
τὴν χεῖρα ἐπελάβετο αυτοῦ, καὶ λέγει αὐτῷ, Ὀλιγόπιστε,
the   hand   took hold   of him, and says to him,   Little-faith,

**32** εἰς τί ἐδίστασας; καὶ ἐμβάντων αὐτῶν εἰς τὸ πλοῖον,
why   did you doubt? And   going up   they   into   the   boat,

**33** ἐκόπασεν ὁ ἄνεμος· οἱ δὲ ἐν τῷ πλοίῳ ἐλθόντες προσεκύνησαν
ceased   the   wind. the (ones) And in the boat coming   worshiped
αὐτῷ, λέγοντες, Ἀληθῶς Θεοῦ υἱὸς εἶ.
Him,   saying,   Truly   of God Son You are!

**34**
**35** Καὶ διαπεράσαντες ἦλθον εἰς τὴν γῆν Γεννησαρέτ. καὶ
And   passing over   they came into the   land of Gennessaret. And
ἐπιγνόντες αὐτὸν οἱ ἄνδρες τοῦ τόπου ἐκείνου ἀπέστειλαν
recognizing   Him   the men   of place   that   sent
εἰς ὅλην τὴν περίχωρον ἐκείνην, καὶ προσήνεγκαν αὐτῷ
into all   — neighborhood   that,   and   brought   to Him

**36** πάντας τοὺς κακῶς ἔχοντας· καὶ παρεκάλουν αὐτόν, ἵνα
all   those illness   having,   and   begged   Him   that
μόνον ἅψωνται τοῦ κρασπέδου τοῦ ἱματίου αὐτοῦ· καὶ
only   they might touch the   fringe   of the   garment   of Him. And
ὅσοι ἥψαντο διεσώθησαν.
as many as touched were made perfectly well.

## CHAPTER 15

**1** Τότε προσέρχονται τῷ Ἰησοῦ οἱ ἀπὸ Ἱεροσολύμων
Then   approach   — to Jesus the (ones) from   Jerusalem,

**2** γραμματεῖς καὶ Φαρισαῖοι, λέγοντες, Διατί οἱ μαθηταί σου
scribes   and Pharisees,   saying,   Why the disciples of you
παραβαίνουσι τὴν παράδοσιν τῶν πρεσβυτέρων; οὐ γὰρ
transgress   the   tradition   of the   elders?   not for

**3** νίπτονται τὰς χεῖρας αὐτῶν, ὅταν ἄρτον ἐσθίωσιν. ὁ δὲ
they wash   the   hands   of them,   when   bread   they eat. He But
ἀποκριθεὶς εἶπεν αὐτοῖς, Διατί καὶ ὑμεῖς παραβαίνετε τὴν
answering   said   to them, Why   also do you   transgress   the

**4** ἐντολὴν τοῦ Θεοῦ διὰ τὴν παράδοσιν ὑμῶν; ὁ γὰρ Θεὸς
command — of God on account of the tradition of you? — For God
ἐνετείλατο, λέγων, Τίμα τὸν πατέρα σοῦ, καὶ τὴν μητέρα·
commanded, saying, Honor the   father of you, and   the mother;
καί, Ὁ κακολογῶν πατέρα ἢ μητέρα θανάτῳ τελευτάτω·
and, The (one) speaking evil of father or mother   by death   let him end.

**5** ὑμεῖς δὲ λέγετε, Ὃς ἂν εἴπῃ τῷ πατρὶ ἢ τῇ μητρί, Δῶρον,
you But   say,   Whoever says to the   father or the mother, A gift,
ὃ ἐὰν ἐξ ἐμοῦ ὠφεληθῇς, καὶ οὐ μὴ τιμήσῃ τὸν πατέρα
whatever by me you would gain,   and in no way he honors the   father

**6** αὐτοῦ ἢ τὴν μητέρα αὐτοῦ· καὶ ἠκυρώσατε τὴν ἐντολὴν τοῦ
of him or the mother of him; and you annulled   the command —

**7** Θεοῦ διὰ τὴν παράδοσιν ὑμῶν. ὑποκριταί, καλῶς προεφή-
of God on account of tradition   your. Hypocrites!   Well   proph-

**8** τευσε περὶ ὑμῶν Ἠσαΐας, λέγων, Ἐγγίζει μοι ὁ λαὸς οὗτος
esied concerning you Isaiah,   saying,   Draws near to Me people this

with their mouth, and with their lips honor Me, but their heart is far from Me; [9] but in vain they worship Me teaching for doctrines the commandments of men." [10] And having called the crowd, He said to them, Hear and understand. [11] Not that which enters into the mouth defiles the man, but that which goes forth out of the mouth, this defiles the man.

[12] Then the disciples having come said to Him, You know that the Pharisees having heard the word were offended? [13] But answering He said, Every plant which My heavenly Father has not planted shall be rooted up. [14] Leave them alone; they are blind leaders of the blind; if the blind lead the blind, both will fall into a pit. [15] And answering Peter said to Him, Explain this parable to us. [16] But Jesus said, Are you also still without understanding? [17] Do you not yet understand that everything which enters into the mouth goes into the belly, and is thrown out into (the) wastebowl? [18] But the things which go forth out of the mouth come out from the heart, and these defile the man. [19] For out of the heart comes forth evil thoughts, murders, adulteries, fornications, thefts, lies, blasphemies. [20] These things are they which defile the man; but eating with unwashed hands do not defile the man.

[21] And going out from there, Jesus withdrew to the parts of Tyre and Sidon. [22] And, behold, a woman of Canaan having come out from those borders cried to him, saying, Have pity on me, Lord, Son of David; my daughter is miserably possessed by a demon. [23] But He did not answer her a word. And having come, His disciples asked Him, saying, Send her away, for she cries after us. [24] But answering He said, I was

τῷ στόματι αὐτῶν, καὶ τοῖς χείλεσί με τιμᾷ· ἡ δὲ καρδία
with the mouth of them, and with the lips Me it honors; the but heart

9 αὐτῶν πόρρω ἀπέχει ἀπ' ἐμοῦ. μάτην δὲ σέβονταί με,
of them far is away from Me. in vain But they adore Me,

10 διδάσκοντες διδασκαλίας ἐντάλματα ἀνθρώπων. καὶ προσκα-
teaching (as) teachings ordinances of men. And calling

11 λεσάμενος τὸν ὄχλον, εἶπεν αὐτοῖς, Ἀκούετε καὶ συνίετε. οὐ
near the crowd, He said to them, Hear and understand, not

τὸ εἰσερχόμενον εἰς τὸ στόμα κοινοῖ τὸν ἄνθρωπον· ἀλλὰ τὸ
the (thing) entering into the mouth defiles the man, but the (thing)

ἐκπορευόμενον ἐκ τοῦ στόματος, τοῦτο κοινοῖ τὸν ἄνθρωπον.
coming forth from the mouth, this defiles the man.

12 τότε προσελθόντες οἱ μαθηταὶ αὐτοῦ εἶπον αὐτῷ, Οἶδας ὅτι
Then having come the disciples to Him, they said to Him, Know You that

13 οἱ Φαρισαῖοι ἀκούσαντες τὸν λόγον ἐσκανδαλίσθησαν; ὁ
the Pharisees having heard the saying were offended? He

δὲ ἀποκριθεὶς εἶπε, Πᾶσα φυτεία, ἣν οὐκ ἐφύτευσεν ὁ πατὴρ
But answering said, Every plant which not has planted the Father

14 μου ὁ οὐράνιος, ἐκριζωθήσεται. ἄφετε αὐτούς· ὁδηγοί εἰσι
of Me the heavenly shall be rooted up. Leave them; leaders they are

τυφλοὶ τυφλῶν· τυφλὸς δὲ τυφλὸν ἐὰν ὁδηγῇ, ἀμφότεροι εἰς
blind of blind; blind and blind if lead, both into

15 βόθυνον πεσοῦνται. ἀποκριθεὶς δὲ ὁ Πέτρος εἶπεν αὐτῷ,
a pit will fall. answering And — Peter said to Him,

16 Φράσον ἡμῖν τὴν παραβολὴν ταύτην. ὁ δὲ Ἰησοῦς εἶπεν,
Explain to us — parable this. — But Jesus said,

17 Ἀκμὴν καὶ ὑμεῖς ἀσύνετοί ἐστε; οὔπω νοεῖτε, ὅτι πᾶν τὸ
Yet also you unintelligent are? Not yet you perceive that everything

εἰσπορευόμενον εἰς τὸ στόμα εἰς τὴν κοιλίαν χωρεῖ, καὶ εἰς
entering into the mouth into the stomach goes, and into

18 ἀφεδρῶνα ἐκβάλλεται; τὰ δὲ ἐκπορευόμενα ἐκ τοῦ στόματος
(the) wastebowl is thrown out; the but (things) coming forth from the mouth

19 ἐκ τῆς καρδίας ἐξέρχεται, κἀκεῖνα κοινοῖ τὸν ἄνθρωπον. ἐκ
from the heart come forth, and those defile the man. from

γὰρ τῆς καρδίας ἐξέρχονται διαλογισμοὶ πονηροί, φόνοι,
For the heart come forth thoughts evil, murders,

μοιχεῖαι, πορνεῖαι, κλοπαί, ψευδομαρτυρίαι, βλασφημίαι·
adulteries, fornications, thefts, false witnessing, blasphemies;

20 ταῦτά ἐστι τὰ κοινοῦντα τὸν ἄνθρωπον· τὸ δὲ ἀνίπτοις
these things are the (ones) defiling the man; but with unwashed

χερσὶ φαγεῖν οὐ κοινοῖ τὸν ἄνθρωπον.
hands to eat not defiles the man.

21 Καὶ ἐξελθὼν ἐκεῖθεν ὁ Ἰησοῦς ἀνεχώρησεν εἰς τὰ μέρη
And going out from there — Jesus withdrew into the parts

22 Τύρου καὶ Σιδῶνος. καὶ ἰδού, γυνὴ Χαναναία ἀπὸ τῶν ὁρίων
of Tyre and Sidon. And behold, a woman Canaanite from — borders

ἐκείνων ἐξελθοῦσα ἐκραύγασεν αὐτῷ, λέγουσα, Ἐλέησόν
those coming forth cried out to Him, saying, Have pity on

23 με, Κύριε, υἱὲ Δαβίδ· ἡ θυγάτηρ μου κακῶς δαιμονίζεται. ὁ
me, Lord, Son of David; the daughter of me badly is demon-possessed. He

δὲ οὐκ ἀπεκρίθη αὐτῇ λόγον. καὶ προσελθόντες οἱ μαθηταὶ
But not answered her a word. And having come near the disciples

αὐτοῦ ἠρώτων αὐτόν, λέγοντες, Ἀπόλυσον αὐτήν, ὅτι
of Him asked Him. saying, Send away her, because

24 κράζει ὄπισθεν ἡμῶν. ὁ δὲ ἀποκριθεὶς εἶπεν, Οὐκ ἀπεστάλην
she cries out after us. He But answering said, not I was sent

not sent except to the lost sheep of (the) house of Israel. [25] But having come she bowed down to Him, saying, Lord, help me! [26] But answering He said, It is not good to take the bread of the children and to throw (it) to the little dogs. [27] But she said, Yes, Lord; for even the little dogs eat of the crumbs which fall from the table of their masters. [28] Then answering Jesus said to her; O woman, your faith (is) great; let it be to you as you desire. And her daughter was healed from that hour.

[29] And having left from there, Jesus came toward the sea of Galilee; and having gone up into the mountain, He was sitting there. [30] And great crowds came to Him, having with them lame, blind, dumb, maimed, and many others; and they flung them down at the feet of Jesus, and He healed them; [31] so that the crowds wondered, seeing the dumb speaking, the maimed sound, the lame walking, and the blind seeing; and they glorified the God of Israel. [32] But having called His disciples, Jesus said, I am moved with compassion toward the crowd, because they continue with Me three days already, and have nothing which they may eat; and I am not willing to send them away fasting, lest they faint in the way. [33] And His disciples said to Him, From where in a desert (will come) to us so many loaves as to satisfy so great a crowd? [34] And Jesus said to them, How many loaves do you have? And they said, Seven, and a few small fish. [35] And He commanded the crowds to recline on the ground; [36] and having taken the seven loaves and the fish, having given thanks, He broke and gave to His disciples, and the disciples to the crowd. [37] And all ate and were satisfied; and

25  εἰ μὴ εἰς τὰ πρόβατα τὰ ἀπολωλότα οἴκου ᾿Ισραήλ. ἡ δὲ
     except to the sheep    —    lost   of (the) house of Israel, she but

26  ἐλθοῦσα προσεκύνει αὐτῷ λέγουσα, Κύριε, βοήθει μοι. ὁ δὲ
     coming   worshiped  Him,  saying,   Lord,   help  me! He But
     ἀποκριθεὶς εἶπεν, Οὐκ ἐστι καλὸν λαβεῖν τὸν ἄρτον τῶν
     answering   said,    not It is  good to take  the  bread of the

27  τέκνων, καὶ βαλεῖν τοῖς κυναρίοις. ἡ δὲ εἶπε, Ναί, Κύριε· καὶ
     children and to throw to the dogs.   she And said, Yes, Lord, even
     γὰρ τὰ κυνάρια ἐσθίει ἀπὸ τῶν ψιχίων τῶν πιπτόντων
     For the dogs   eat  from  the crumbs   —   falling

28  ἀπὸ τῆς τραπέζης τῶν κυρίων αὐτῶν. τότε ἀποκριθεὶς ὁ
     from  the  table  of the lords of them. Then  answering  —
     ᾿Ιησοῦς εἶπεν αὐτῇ, ῏Ω γύναι, μεγάλη σου ἡ πίστις·
     Jesus    said to her,  O  woman, great (is) of you the  faith;
     γενηθήτω σοι ὡς θέλεις. καὶ ἰάθη ἡ θυγάτηρ αὐτῆς ἀπὸ τῆς
     let it be  to you as you will. And was healed the daughter of her from  —
     ὥρας ἐκείνης.
     hour  that.

29  Καὶ μεταβὰς ἐκεῖθεν ὁ ᾿Ιησοῦς ἦλθε παρὰ τὴν θάλασσαν
     And moving from there — Jesus came beside the  Sea

30  τῆς Γαλιλαίας· καὶ ἀναβὰς εἰς τὸ ὄρος ἐκάθητο ἐκεῖ. καὶ
     — of Galilee;  and going up into the mountain He sat there. And
     προσῆλθον αὐτῷ ὄχλοι πολλοί, ἔχοντες μεθ᾿ ἑαυτῶν χωλούς,
     came      to Him crowds great,  having with themselves (the) lame,
     τυφλούς, κωφούς, κυλλούς, καὶ ἑτέρους πολλούς, καὶ ἔρριψαν
     blind,   dumb,   maimed,  and others    many;   and they flung
     αὐτοὺς παρὰ τοὺς πόδας τοῦ ᾿Ιησοῦ καὶ ἐθεράπευσεν αὐτούς·
     them     at  the   feet   — of Jesus; and He healed     them;

31  ὥστε τοὺς ὄχλους θαυμάσαι, βλέποντας κωφοὺς λαλοῦντας,
     so that the crowds (had) to marvel,  seeing   dumb ones speaking,
     κυλλοὺς ὑγιεῖς, χωλοὺς περιπατοῦντας, καὶ τυφλοὺς
     maimed ones sound, lame ones walking,      and blind ones
     βλέποντας· καὶ ἐδόξασαν τὸν Θεὸν ᾿Ισραήλ.
     seeing;    and they glorified the  God of Israel.

32  ῾Ο δὲ ᾿Ιησοῦς προσκαλεσάμενος τοὺς μαθητὰς αὐτοῦ εἶπε,
     And Jesus    having called near   the disciples  of Him said,
     Σπλαγχνίζομαι ἐπὶ τὸν ὄχλον, ὅτι ἤδη ἡμέρας τρεῖς προσ-
     I am filled with pity upon the crowd, because now days three  they
     μένουσί μοι, καὶ οὐκ ἔχουσι τί φάγωσι· καὶ ἀπολῦσαι
     remain with Me, and·  not have anything they may eat; and to send away

33  αὐτοὺς νήστεις οὐ θέλω, μήποτε ἐκλυθῶσιν ἐν τῇ ὁδῷ. καὶ
     them    fasting  not I desire, lest  they be weary in the way. And
     λέγουσιν αὐτῷ οἱ μαθηταὶ αὐτοῦ, Πόθεν ἡμῖν ἐν· ἐρημίᾳ
     say       to Him the disciples of Him,  From where to us in  a desert

34  ἄρτοι τοσοῦτοι, ὥστε χορτάσαι ὄχλον τοσοῦτον; καὶ
     loaves so many,   as  to satisfy a crowd  so great?  And
     λέγει αὐτοῖς ὁ ᾿Ιησοῦς, Πόσους ἄρτους ἔχετε; οἱ δὲ εἶπον,
     said  to them — Jesus,  How many loaves have you? they and said,

35  ῾Επτά, καὶ ὀλίγα ἰχθύδια. καὶ ἐκέλευσε τοῖς ὄχλοις ἀναπε-
     Seven,  and a few small fish. And He ordered the crowd  to recline

36  σεῖν ἐπὶ τὴν γῆν· καὶ λαβὼν τοὺς ἑπτὰ ἄρτους καὶ τοὺς
      on  the ground; and taking the   seven  loaves  and the
     ἰχθύας, εὐχαριστήσας ἔκλασε, καὶ ἔδωκε τοῖς μαθηταῖς αὐτοῦ,
     fish,    giving thanks  He broke, and gave  to the disciples of Him,

37  οἱ δὲ μαθηταὶ τῷ ὄχλῳ. καὶ ἔφαγον πάντες καὶ ἐχορτά-
     the and disciples to the crowd. And ate   all,   and   were

they took up that which was in excess of the pieces, seven baskets full. [38] And they who ate were four thousand men, besides women and children. [39] And having sent away the crowds, He entered into the boat, and came to the borders of Magdala.

## CHAPTER 16

[1] And the Pharisees and Sadducees having come tempting asked Him to show them a sign out of Heaven. [2] But answering He said to them, Evening having come, you say, Fine weather; for the sky is red. [3] And at morning, Today a storm; for the sky is red (and) gloomy; hypocrites! You indeed know how to tell the face of the sky, but you cannot the signs of the times. [4] A wicked and adulterous generation seeks a sign, and a sign shall not be given to it, except the sign of Jonah the prophet. And leaving them, He went away.

[5] And His disciples having come to the other side, they forgot to take loaves. [6] And Jesus said to them, Watch! And beware of the leaven of the Pharisees and Sadducees. [7] And they reasoned among themselves, saying Because we did not take loaves. [8] And having known, Jesus said to them, Why do you reason among yourselves, little-faiths, because you took no loaves? [9] Do you not perceive nor recall the five loaves of the five thousand, and how many baskets you took up? [10] Nor the seven loaves of the four thousand, and how many lunch-baskets you took up? [11] How do you not perceive that not about loaves I said to you to take heed from the leaven of the Pharisees and Sadducees? [12] Then they knew that He did not say to take heed from the leaven of bread, but from the teaching of the Pharisees and Sadducees.

σθησαν· καὶ ἦραν τὸ περισσεῦον τῶν κλασμάτων, ἑπτὰ
**filled; and they took up the excess of the fragments, seven**

38 σπυρίδας πλήρεις. οἱ δὲ ἐσθίοντες ἦσαν τετρακισχίλιοι
**lunch-baskets full. the And (ones) eating were four thousand**

39 ἄνδρες, χωρὶς γυναικῶν καὶ παιδίων. καὶ ἀπολύσας τοὺς
**men apart from women and children. And sending away the**

ὄχλους ἐνέβη εἰς τὸ πλοῖον, καὶ ἦλθεν εἰς τὰ ὅρια Μαγδαλά.
**crowds He went into the boat, and came into the borders of Magdala.**

## CHAPTER 16

1 Καὶ προσελθόντες οἱ Φαρισαῖοι καὶ Σαδδουκαῖοι πειρά-
**And having come the Pharisees and Sadducees tempting**

ζοντες ἐπηρώτησαν αὐτὸν σημεῖον ἐκ τοῦ οὐρανοῦ ἐπιδεῖξαι
**asked Him a sign from — Heaven to show**

2 αὐτοῖς. ὁ δὲ ἀποκριθεὶς εἶπεν αὐτοῖς, Ὀψίας γενομένης
**them. He But answering said to them, Evening coming on**

3 λέγετε, Εὐδία· πυρράζει γὰρ ὁ οὐρανός. καὶ πρωΐ, Σήμερον
**you say, Clear sky; is red for the heaven. And at morning, Today**

χειμών· πυρράζει γὰρ στυγνάζων ὁ οὐρανός. ὑποκριταί,
**a storm; is red for being overcast the heaven. Hypocrites!**

τὸ μὲν πρόσωπον τοῦ οὐρανοῦ γινώσκετε διακρίνειν, τὰ
**the Indeed face of the heaven you know to discern, the**

4 δὲ σημεῖα τῶν καιρῶν οὐ δύνασθε ; γενεὰ πονηρὰ καὶ
**but signs of the times not you are able. A generation evil and**

μοιχαλὶς σημεῖον ἐπιζητεῖ· καὶ σημεῖον οὐ δοθήσεται αὐτῇ,
**adulterous a sign seeks; and a sign not shall be given to it,**

εἰ μὴ τὸ σημεῖον Ἰωνᾶ τοῦ προφήτου. καὶ καταλιπὼν
**except the sign of Jonah. the prophet. And forsaking**

αὐτούς, ἀπῆλθε.
**them He went away.**

5 Καὶ ἐλθόντες οἱ μαθηταὶ αὐτοῦ εἰς τὸ πέραν ἐπελάθοντο
**And coming the disciples of Him to the other side they forgot**

6 ἄρτους λαβεῖν. ὁ δὲ Ἰησοῦς εἶπεν αὐτοῖς, Ὁρᾶτε καὶ προσ-
**loaves to take. — And Jesus said to them, Beware and take**

7 έχετε ἀπὸ τῆς ζύμης τῶν Φαρισαίων καὶ Σαδδουκαίων. οἱ
**heed from the leaven of the Pharisees and the Sadducees. they**

δὲ διελογίζοντο ἐν ἑαυτοῖς, λέγοντες ὅτι Ἄρτους οὐκ
**But reasoned among themselves, saying, Because loaves not**

8 ἐλάβομεν. γνοὺς δὲ ὁ Ἰησοῦς εἶπεν αὐτοῖς, Τί διαλογίζεσθε
**we took. knowing And Jesus said to them, Why do you reason**

9 ἐν ἑαυτοῖς, ὀλιγόπιστοι, ὅτι ἄρτους οὐκ ἐλάβετε ; οὔπω
**among yourselves, little-faiths, because loaves not you took? not**

νοεῖτε, οὐδὲ μνημονεύετε τοὺς πέντε ἄρτους τῶν πεντακι-
**you perceive nor remember the five loaves of the five**

10 σχιλίων, καὶ πόσους κοφίνους ἐλάβετε ; οὐδὲ τοὺς ἑπτὰ
**thousand, and how many baskets you took? Neither the seven**

ἄρτους τῶν τετρακισχιλίων, καὶ πόσας σπυρίδας ἐλάβετε ;
**loaves of the four thousand, and how many lunch-baskets you took?**

11 πῶς οὐ νοεῖτε, ὅτι οὐ περὶ ἄρτου εἶπον ὑμῖν προσέχειν ἀπὸ
**How not perceive that not about loaves I said to you to take heed from**

12 τῆς ζύμης τῶν Φαρισαίων καὶ Σαδδουκαίων ; τότε συνῆκαν
**the leaven of the Pharisees and Sadducees. Then they knew**

ὅτι οὐκ εἶπε προσέχειν ἀπὸ τῆς ζύμης τοῦ ἄρτου, ἀλλ' ἀπὸ
**that not He said to take heed from the leaven — of bread, but from**

τῆς διδαχῆς τῶν Φαρισαίων καὶ Σαδδουκαίων.
**the teaching of the Pharisees and Sadducees.**

[13] And Jesus having come into the parts of Caesarea Philippi, He queried His disciples, saying, Whom do men say to be the Son of man? [14] And they said, Some (say) John the Baptist; and others Elijah; and and others Jeremiah, or one of the prophets. [15] He says to them, But you, whom do you say Me to be? [16] And answering Simon Peter said, You are the Christ, the Son of the living God. [17] And answering Jesus said to him, Blessed are you, Simon, son of Jonah, for flesh and blood did not reveal (it) to you, but My Father who (is) in Heaven. [18] And I also say to you, that you are Peter, and on this rock I will build My church, and (the) gates of hades shall not prevail against it. [19] And I will give to you the keys of the kingdom of Heaven; and whatever you may bind on the earth shall occur, having already been bound in Heaven; and whatever you may loose on the earth shall occur, having been already loosed in Heaven. [20] Then He charged His disciples that they should not say to anyone that He is Jesus the Christ.

[21] From that time Jesus began to show to His disciples that it was necessary for Him to go away to Jerusalem, and to suffer many things from the elders and chief priests and scribes, and to be raised the third day. [22] And having taken Him, Peter began to rebuke Him, saying, (God be) gracious to You, Lord, this shall never be to You. [23] But having turned, He said to Peter, Go behind Me, Satan! You are an offense to Me, for your thoughts are not of the things of God, but the things of men. [24] Then Jesus said to His disciples, If anyone desires to come after Me, let him deny himself, and let him take up his cross and let him follow Me. [25] For whoever may desire to save His

**13** Ἐλθὼν δὲ ὁ Ἰησοῦς εἰς τὰ μέρη Καισαρείας τῆς Φιλίππου
coming And — Jesus into the parts of Caesarea — of Philip

ἠρώτα τοὺς μαθητὰς αὐτοῦ, λέγων, Τίνα με λέγουσιν οἱ
He queried the disciples of Him, saying, Whom Me do say —

**14** ἄνθρωποι εἶναι, τὸν υἱὸν τοῦ ἀνθρώπου ; οἱ δὲ εἶπον, Οἱ μὲν
men to be, the Son — of man? they And said, Some

Ἰωάννην τὸν Βαπτιστήν· ἄλλοι δὲ Ἠλίαν· ἕτεροι δὲ
John the Baptist; others and Elijah; others and

**15** Ἰερεμίαν, ἢ ἕνα τῶν προφητῶν. λέγει αὐτοῖς, Ὑμεῖς δὲ τίνα
Jeremiah, or one of the prophets. He says to them, you But, whom

**16** με λέγετε εἶναι ; ἀποκριθεὶς δὲ Σίμων Πέτρος εἶπε, Σὺ εἶ ὁ
Me do you say to be? answering And Simon Peter said, You are the

**17** Χριστός, ὁ υἱὸς τοῦ Θεοῦ τοῦ ζῶντος. καὶ ἀποκριθεὶς ὁ
Christ, the Son — of God the living. And answering —

Ἰησοῦς εἶπεν αὐτῷ, Μακάριος εἶ, Σίμων Βὰρ Ἰωνᾶ, ὅτι σὰρξ
Jesus said to him, Blessed are you, Simon Bar-jonah because flesh

καὶ αἷμα οὐκ ἀπεκάλυψέ σοι, ἀλλ᾽ ὁ πατήρ μου ὁ ἐν τοῖς
and blood not did reveal to you, but the Father of Me — in the

**18** οὐρανοῖς. κἀγὼ δέ σοι λέγω, ὅτι σὺ εἶ Πέτρος, καὶ ἐπὶ ταύτῃ
heavens. I also And to you say, — You are Peter, and on this

τῇ πέτρᾳ οἰκοδομήσω μου τὴν ἐκκλησίαν, καὶ πύλαι ᾅδου
— rock I will build of Me the church, and (the) gates of Hades

**19** οὐ κατισχύσουσιν αὐτῆς. καὶ δώσω σοὶ τὰς κλεῖς τῆς
not will prevail against her. And I will give to you the keys of the

βασιλείας τῶν οὐρανῶν· καὶ ὃ ἐὰν δήσῃς ἐπὶ τῆς γῆς, ἔσται
kingdom of the heavens, and whatever you bind on the earth shall be

δεδεμένον ἐν τοῖς οὐρανοῖς· καὶ ὃ ἐὰν λύσῃς ἐπὶ τῆς γῆς,
having been bound in the heavens, and whatever you loose on the earth

**20** ἔσται λελυμένον ἐν τοῖς οὐρανοῖς. τότε διεστείλατο τοῖς
shall be, having been loosed in the heavens. Then He warned the

μαθηταῖς αὐτοῦ ἵνα μηδενὶ εἴπωσιν ὅτι αὐτός ἐστιν Ἰησοῦς
disciples of Him that to no one they may tell that He is Jesus

ὁ Χριστός.
the Christ.

**21** Ἀπὸ τότε ἤρξατο ὁ Ἰησοῦς δεικνύειν τοῖς μαθηταῖς
From then began — Jesus to show to the disciples

αὐτοῦ ὅτι δεῖ αὐτὸν ἀπελθεῖν εἰς Ἱεροσόλυμα, καὶ πολλὰ
of Him that it behoves Him to go away to Jerusalem, and many things

παθεῖν ἀπὸ τῶν πρεσβυτέρων καὶ ἀρχιερέων καὶ γραμ-
to suffer from the elders and chief priests and scribes,

ματέων, καὶ ἀποκτανθῆναι, καὶ τῇ τρίτῃ ἡμέρᾳ ἐγερθῆναι.
and to be killed, and on the third day to be raised.

**22** καὶ προσλαβόμενος αὐτὸν ὁ Πέτρος ἤρξατο ἐπιτιμᾶν αὐτῷ
And taking near Him, — Peter began to rebuke Him,

**23** λέγων, Ἵλεώς σοι, Κύριε· οὐ μὴ ἔσται σοι τοῦτο. ὁ δὲ στραφεὶς
saying, Gracious to You, Lord, in no way shall be to You this. He But turning

εἶπε τῷ Πέτρῳ, Ὕπαγε ὀπίσω μου, Σατανᾶ, σκάνδαλόν μου
said — to Peter, Go behind Me, Satan, an offense to Me

εἶ· ὅτι οὐ φρονεῖς τὰ τοῦ Θεοῦ, ἀλλὰ τὰ τῶν ἀνθρώπων.
you are, for not you think the things of God, but the things — of men.

**24** τότε ὁ Ἰησοῦς εἶπε τοῖς μαθηταῖς αὐτοῦ, Εἴ τις θέλει ὀπίσω
Then — Jesus said to the disciples of Him, If anyone desires after

μου ἐλθεῖν, ἀπαρνησάσθω ἑαυτόν, καὶ ἀράτω τὸν σταυρὸν
Me to come, let him deny himself, and let him bear the cross

**25** αὐτοῦ, καὶ ἀκολουθείτω μοι. ὃς γὰρ ἂν θέλῃ τὴν ψυχὴν
of him, and let him follow Me. whoever For may desire the soul

αὐτοῦ σῶσαι ἀπολέσει αὐτήν· ὃς δ᾽ ἂν ἀπολέσῃ τὴν ψυχὴν
of him  to save  he will lose    it ; and whoever may lose   the   soul

live shall lose it; but
whoever may lose his life    **26**  αὐτοῦ ἕνεκεν ἐμοῦ εὑρήσει αὐτήν· τί γὰρ ὠφελεῖται ἄνθρω-
for My sake shall find it.         of him for the sake of Me, he will find  it.  what  For will be benefited a
[26] For what is a man
profited, if he gain the          πος ἐὰν τὸν κόσμον ὅλον κερδήσῃ, τὴν δὲ ψυχὴν αὐτοῦ
whole world and lose his          man if  the  world  whole he should gain,  the but  soul  of him
own soul? On what will a    **27**  ζημιωθῇ ; ἢ τί δώσει ἄνθρωπος ἀντάλλαγμα τῆς ψυχῆς
man give in exchange for          forfeits?  Or what will give  a man    (as) an exchange (for) the soul
his soul? [27] For the Son
of man is about to come in        αὐτοῦ ; μέλλει γὰρ ὁ υἱὸς τοῦ ἀνθρώπου ἔρχεσθαι ἐν τῇ
the glory of His Father           of him?  is about For  the Son  —  of man  to come  in the
with His angels; and then
He will give to each accord-      δόξῃ τοῦ πατρὸς αὐτοῦ μετὰ τῶν ἀγγέλων αὐτοῦ, καὶ
ing to his works. [28] Tru-       glory  of the Father  of Him with  the  angels  of Him, and
ly I say to you, There are    **28**  τότε ἀποδώσει ἑκάστῳ κατὰ τὴν πρᾶξιν αὐτοῦ. ἀμὴν λέγω
some of those standing            then he will reward to each according to the works of him.  Truly  I say
here who in no way shall
taste of death until they         ὑμῖν, εἰσί τινες τῶν ὧδε ἑστηκότων, οἵτινες οὐ μὴ γεύ-
have seen the Son of man          to you, there are some — here standing  who  not at all will
coming in His kingdom.
                                  σωνται θανάτου, ἕως ἂν ἴδωσι τὸν υἱὸν τοῦ ἀνθρώπου
                                  taste  of death  until they see the Son — of man

                                  ἐρχόμενον ἐν τῇ βασιλείᾳ αὐτοῦ.
                                  coming  in  the  kingdom of Him.

## CHAPTER 17                          ## CHAPTER 17

[1] And after six days,    **1**  Καὶ μεθ᾽ ἡμέρας ἓξ παραλαμβάνει ὁ Ἰησοῦς τὸν Πέτρον καὶ
Jesus took Peter and             And after  days  six  takes  — Jesus —  Peter and
James, and his brother
John, and brought them up         Ἰάκωβον καὶ Ἰωάννην τὸν ἀδελφὸν αὐτοῦ, καὶ ἀναφέρει
into a high mountain apart.       James  and  John  the  brother  of him,  and  leads up
[2] And He was transfigur-  **2**  αὐτοὺς εἰς ὄρος ὑψηλὸν κατ᾽ ἰδίαν. καὶ μετεμορφώθη
ed before them, and His          them  into mountain a high  privately.  And He was transfigured
face shone like the sun,
and His clothing became           ἔμπροσθεν αὐτῶν, καὶ ἔλαμψε τὸ πρόσωπον αὐτοῦ ὡς ὁ
white  as  the  light!           before  them,  and shone  the  face  of Him like the
[3] And, behold, Moses     **3**  ἥλιος, τὰ δὲ ἱμάτια αὐτοῦ ἐγένετο λευκὰ ὡς τὸ φῶς. καὶ ἰδού,
and Elijah appeared to           sun,  the and garments of Him became  white  as  the light, and behold,
them, talking with Him.
[4] And answering, Peter          ὤφθησαν αὐτοῖς Μωσῆς καὶ Ἠλίας, μετ᾽ αὐτοῦ συλλαλοῦν-
said to Jesus, Lord, it is       appeared  to them  Moses  and Elijah  with  Him  talking to-
good for us to be here. If  **4**  τες. ἀποκριθεὶς δὲ ὁ Πέτρος εἶπε τῷ Ἰησοῦ, Κύριε, καλόν
You will, let us make here        gether answering  And — Peter  said  — to Jesus,  Lord,  good
three tabernacles, one for
You, one for Moses, and           ἐστιν ἡμᾶς ὧδε εἶναι· εἰ θέλεις, ποιήσωμεν ὧδε τρεῖς σκηνάς,
for Elijah. [5] While he          it is  for us  here to be.  If You desire, let us make here  three  tents,
was yet speaking, behold, a  **5**  σοὶ μίαν, καὶ Μωσῇ μίαν, καὶ μίαν Ἠλίᾳ. ἔτι αὐτοῦ λαλοῦν-
bright cloud overshadowed         for You one, and for Moses one, and one  for Elijah. While he (was) speaking,
them; and lo, a voice out
of the cloud saying, This is      τος, ἰδού, νεφέλη φωτεινὴ ἐπεσκίασεν αὐτούς· καὶ ἰδού,
My beloved Son, in whom           behold, a cloud  radiant  overshadowed  them,  and behold,
I have found delight; hear
Him. [6] And hearing the          φωνὴ ἐκ τῆς νεφέλης, λέγουσα, Οὗτός ἐστιν ὁ υἱός μου
disciples fell on their face      a voice out of the  cloud,  saying,  This  is  the Son of Me,
and were greatly terrified.  **6**  ὁ ἀγαπητός, ἐν ᾧ εὐδόκησα· αὐτοῦ ἀκούετε. καὶ ἀκούσαντες
[7] And having come,             the beloved,  in whom I delight;  of Him hear.  And hearing,
Jesus touched them and
said, Rise up, and do not         οἱ μαθηταὶ ἔπεσον ἐπὶ πρόσωπον αὐτῶν, καὶ ἐφοβήθησαν
be terrified. [8] And hav-        the disciples fell  on the face  of them,  and were terrified
ing lifted up their eyes,    **7**  σφόδρα. καὶ προσελθὼν ὁ Ἰησοῦς ἥψατο αὐτῶν καὶ εἶπεν,
they saw no one except           greatly.  And coming near,—  Jesus  touched them,  and  said,
Jesus, alone.
[9] And as they were    **8**  Ἐγέρθητε καὶ μὴ φοβεῖσθε. ἐπάραντες δὲ τοὺς ὀφθαλμοὺς
descending from the moun-         Arise,  and not  fear.  lifting up  And the  eyes
tain, Jesus commanded        **9**  αὐτῶν, οὐδένα εἶδον, εἰ μὴ τὸν Ἰησοῦν μόνον.
                                  of them, no one  they saw except — Jesus  alone.

                                  Καὶ καταβαινόντων αὐτῶν ἀπὸ τοῦ ὄρους, ἐνετείλατο
                                  And coming down  they  from  the mountain,  enjoined

αὐτοῖς ὁ Ἰησοῦς, λέγων, Μηδενὶ εἴπητε τὸ ὅραμα, ἕως οὗ ὁ
them  —  Jesus,  saying, To no one  tell   the vision,    until the

10 υἱὸς τοῦ ἀνθρώπου ἐκ νεκρῶν ἀναστῇ. καὶ ἐπηρώτησαν
Son  —  of man    from the dead  is raised.  And  questioned

αὐτὸν οἱ μαθηταὶ αὐτοῦ λέγοντες, Τί οὖν οἱ γραμματεῖς
Him  the  disciples of Him  saying,   Why then  the   scribes

11 λέγουσιν ὅτι Ἠλίαν δεῖ ἐλθεῖν πρῶτον ; ὁ δὲ Ἰησοῦς ἀποκρι-
say     that Elijah it behoves to come first?   And Jesus, answering

θεὶς εἶπεν αὐτοῖς, Ἠλίας μὲν ἔρχεται πρῶτον, καὶ ἀποκατα-
said  to them,  Elijah indeed comes    first    and shall restore

12 στήσει πάντα· λέγω δὲ ὑμῖν ὅτι Ἠλίας ἤδη ἦλθε, καὶ οὐκ
all things; I tell but   you that Elijah already is come, and not

ἐπέγνωσαν αὐτόν, ἀλλ᾽ ἐποίησαν ἐν αὐτῷ ὅσα ἠθέλησαν·
they knew   him,  but    did    to  him whatever they wished;

οὕτω καὶ ὁ υἱὸς τοῦ ἀνθρώπου μέλλει πάσχειν ὑπ᾽ αὐτῶν.
thus  also the Son  —   of man   is about to suffer   by   them.

13 τότε συνῆκαν οἱ μαθηταὶ ὅτι περὶ Ἰωάννου τοῦ Βαπτιστοῦ
Then  understood the disciples that concerning John  the  Baptist

εἶπεν αὐτοῖς.
He spoke to them.

14 Καὶ ἐλθόντων αὐτῶν πρὸς τὸν ὄχλον, προσῆλθεν αὐτῷ
And having come  they  toward the crowd,   came near to Him

15 ἄνθρωπος γονυπετῶν αὐτῷ καὶ λέγων, Κύριε, ἐλέησόν μου
a man      kneeling down to Him and saying, Lord,  pity  of me

τὸν υἱόν, ὅτι σεληνιάζεται καὶ κακῶς πάσχει· πολλάκις γὰρ
the son,  because he is moonstruck and illness suffers;  often   for

16 πίπτει εἰς τὸ πῦρ, καὶ πολλάκις εἰς τὸ ὕδωρ. καὶ προσήνεγκα
he falls into the fire, and   often   into the water. And I brought

αὐτὸν τοῖς μαθηταῖς σου, καὶ οὐκ ἠδυνήθησαν αὐτὸν
him   to the  disciples of You,  and  not they were able    him

17 θεραπεῦσαι. ἀποκριθεὶς δὲ ὁ Ἰησοῦς εἶπεν, Ὦ γενεὰ ἄπιστος
to heal.     answering And  —  Jesus  said,  O generation faithless

καὶ διεστραμμένη, ἕως πότε ἔσομαι μεθ᾽ ὑμῶν ; ἕως πότε
and   perverted,   until when shall I be  with  you?  Until when

18 ἀνέξομαι ὑμῶν ; φέρετέ μοι αὐτὸν ὧδε. καὶ ἐπετίμησεν αὐτῷ
shall I endure you? Bring to Me  him  here. And rebuked    it

ὁ Ἰησοῦς, καὶ ἐξῆλθεν ἀπ᾽ αὐτοῦ τὸ δαιμόνιον, καὶ ἐθεραπεύ-
—  Jesus, and came out from  him   the   demon,   and  was healed

19 θη ὁ παῖς ἀπὸ τῆς ὥρας ἐκείνης. τότε προσελθόντες οἱ
the boy from  —  hour   that.   Then  coming up   the

μαθηταὶ τῷ Ἰησοῦ κατ᾽ ἰδίαν εἶπον, Διατί ἡμεῖς οὐκ ἠδυνή-
disciples  — to Jesus  privately said,  Why we   not were

20 θημεν ἐκβαλεῖν αὐτό ; ὁ δὲ Ἰησοῦς εἶπεν αὐτοῖς, Διὰ τὴν
able   to cast out him?  — And Jesus  said   to them, Through the

ἀπιστίαν ὑμῶν. ἀμὴν γὰρ λέγω ὑμῖν, ἐὰν ἔχητε πίστιν ὡς
unbelief of you.  truly For I say to you, if you have  faith   as

κόκκον σινάπεως, ἐρεῖτε τῷ ὄρει τούτῳ, Μετάβηθι ἐντεῦθεν
a grain of mustard, you will say to mountain this,   Move    from here

21 ἐκεῖ, καὶ μεταβήσεται· καὶ οὐδὲν ἀδυνατήσει ὑμῖν. τοῦτο δὲ
to there and it will move, and nothing shall be impossible to you. this But

τὸ γένος οὐκ ἐκπορεύεται εἰ μὴ ἐν προσευχῇ καὶ νηστείᾳ.
kind not  does go out    except by prayer    and  fasting.

22 Ἀναστρεφομένων δὲ αὐτῶν ἐν τῇ Γαλιλαίᾳ, εἶπεν αὐτοῖς
while were remaining And they  in   the   Galilee,   said  to them

ὁ Ἰησοῦς, Μέλλει ὁ υἱὸς τοῦ ἀνθρώπου παραδίδοσθαι εἰς
—  Jesus,  is about the Son  —  of man      to be delivered into

---

them, saying, Tell the vision to no one until the Son of man is risen from among (the) dead. [10] And His disciples asked Him, saying, Why then do the scribes say that Elijah must come first? [11] And answering Jesus said to them, Elijah indeed comes first, and shall restore all things. [12] But I say to you that Elijah already has come, and they did not know him, but did to him whatever they desired. So also the Son of man is about to suffer from them. [13] Then the disciples understood that He spoke to them about John the Baptist.

[14] And they having come to the crowd, a man came to Him, kneeling down to Him, and saying, [15] Lord, have pity on my son, for he is (a) lunatic and suffers miserably; for he often falls into the fire, and often into the water. [16] And I brought him to your disciples, and they were not able to heal him. [17] And answering Jesus said, O faithless and perverted generation! How long will I be with you? How long will I bear with you? Bring him here to Me. [18] And Jesus rebuked him, and the demon went out from him, and the boy was healed from that hour. [19] Then having come to Jesus apart, the disciples said, Why were we not able to throw him out? [20] And Jesus said to them, Because of your unbelief. For truly I say to you, If you have faith as a grain of mustard, you shall say to this mountain, Move from here to there! And it will move; and nothing shall be impossible to you. [21] But this kind does not go out except by prayer and fasting.

[22] And while they were staying in Galilee, Jesus said to them, The Son of man is about to be delivered into (the) hands

of men; [23] and they will kill Him; and the third day He shall be raised up. And they were greatly grieved.

[24] And they having come to Capernaum, those who received the didrachmas came to Peter and said, Does your Teacher pay the didrachmas?

[25] He said, Yes. And when he entered into the house, Jesus anticipated him, saying, What do you think, Simon? The kings of the earth, from whom do they receive custom or tribute? From their sons, or from strangers? [26] Peter said to him, From strangers. Jesus said to him, Then indeed the sons are free. [27] But that we may not offend them, having gone to the sea throw in a hook, and take the first fish coming up, and having opened its mouth, you shall find a piece of money; having taken that, give to them for Me and you.

23 χεῖρας ἀνθρώπων, καὶ ἀποκτενοῦσιν αὐτόν, καὶ τῇ τρίτῃ
(the) hands of men, and they will kill Him, and on the third
ἡμέρᾳ ἐγερθήσεται. καὶ ἐλυπήθησαν σφόδρα.
day He will be raised. And they grieved exceedingly.

24 Ἐλθόντων δὲ αὐτῶν εἰς Καπερναούμ, προσῆλθον οἱ τὰ
coming And they into Capernaum came up those the
δίδραχμα λαμβάνοντες τῷ Πέτρῳ καὶ εἶπον, Ὁ διδάσκαλος
didrachmas receiving — to Peter, and said, The teacher

25 ὑμῶν οὐ τελεῖ τὰ δίδραχμα ; λέγει, Ναί. καὶ ὅτε εἰσῆλθεν εἰς
of you not pays the didrachma ? He says, Yes. And when he entered into
τὴν οἰκίαν, προέφθασεν αὐτὸν ὁ Ἰησοῦς, λέγων, Τί σοι
the house, anticipated him — Jesus, saying, What you
δοκεῖ, Σίμων ; οἱ βασιλεῖς τῆς γῆς ἀπὸ τίνων λαμβάνουσι
think, Simon? The kings of the earth, from whom do they receive
τέλη ἢ κῆνσον ; ἀπὸ τῶν υἱῶν αὐτῶν, ἢ ἀπὸ τῶν
custom or poll-tax? From the sons of them, or from the

26 ἀλλοτρίων ; λέγει αὐτῷ ὁ Πέτρος, Ἀπὸ τῶν ἀλλοτρίων.
strangers? says to Him — Peter, From the strangers.

27 ἔφη αὐτῷ ὁ Ἰησοῦς, Ἄραγε ἐλεύθεροί εἰσιν οἱ υἱοί. ἵνα δὲ μὴ
said to him — Jesus, Then indeed free are the sons. that But not
σκανδαλίσωμεν αὐτούς, πορευθεὶς εἰς τὴν θάλασσαν βάλε
we may offend them, having gone to the sea, throw
ἄγκιστρον, καὶ τὸν ἀναβάντα πρῶτον ἰχθὺν ἆρον· καὶ
a hook, and the coming up first fish take, and
ἀνοίξας τὸ στόμα αὐτοῦ, εὑρήσεις στατῆρα· ἐκεῖνον λαβὼν
opening the mouth of it, you will find a stater; that taking
δὸς αὐτοῖς ἀντὶ ἐμοῦ καὶ σοῦ.
give them for Me and you.

## CHAPTER 18

[1] In that hour the disciples came to Jesus, saying, Who then is greatest in the kingdom of Heaven? [2] And Jesus having called a little child, He set it in their midst, [3] and said, Truly I say to you, unless you be converted and become as the little children, in no way shall you enter into the kingdom of Heaven. [4] Whoever therefore will humble himself as this little child he is the greatest in the kingdom of Heaven. [5] And whoever will receive one such little child in My name, receives Me. [6] But whoever shall cause one of these little ones who believe in Me to offend, it is profitable for him that a millstone turned by an ass should be hung on his neck, and he be sunk in the depth of the sea. [7] Woe to the world because of offenses! It is necessary for offenses to

## CHAPTER 18

1 Ἐν ἐκείνῃ τῇ ὥρᾳ προσῆλθον οἱ μαθηταὶ τῷ Ἰησοῦ,
In that — hour, came up the disciples — to Jesus,
λέγοντες Τίς ἄρα μείζων ἐστὶν ἐν τῇ βασιλείᾳ τῶν οὐρα-
saying, Who then greater is in the kingdom of the heavens?

2 νῶν ; καὶ προσκαλεσάμενος ὁ Ἰησοῦς παιδίον ἔστησεν
And calling forward — Jesus a child, He set

3 αὐτὸ ἐν μέσῳ αὐτῶν, καὶ εἶπεν, Ἀμὴν λέγω ὑμῖν, ἐὰν μὴ
him in the midst of them, and said, Truly I say to you, except
στραφῆτε καὶ γένησθε ὡς τὰ παιδία, οὐ μὴ εἰσέλθητε εἰς τὴν
you convert and become as the children, cannot you enter into the

4 βασιλείαν τῶν οὐρανῶν. ὅστις οὖν ταπεινώσῃ ἑαυτὸν ὡς τὸ
kingdom of the heavens. Whoever then will humble himself as —
παιδίον τοῦτο, οὗτός ἐστιν ὁ μείζων ἐν τῇ βασιλείᾳ τῶν
child this, this (one) is the greater in the kingdom of the

5 οὐρανῶν. καὶ ὃς ἐὰν δέξηται παιδίον τοιοῦτον ἓν ἐπὶ τῷ
heavens. And whoever receives child such one on the

6 ὀνόματί μου, ἐμὲ δέχεται· ὃς δ᾽ ἂν σκανδαλίσῃ ἕνα τῶν
name of Me, Me receives. who But ever causes to offend one of the
μικρῶν τούτων τῶν πιστευόντων εἰς ἐμέ, συμφέρει αὐτῷ ἵνα
little (ones) these — believing in Me, it is gain for him that
κρεμασθῇ μύλος ὀνικὸς ἐπὶ τὸν τράχηλον αὐτοῦ, καὶ κατα-
be hung a millstone an ass's on the neck of him, and he be

7 ποντισθῇ ἐν τῷ πελάγει τῆς θαλάσσης. οὐαὶ τῷ κόσμῳ
sunk in the depth of the sea. Woe to the world
ἀπὸ τῶν σκανδάλων· ἀνάγκη γάρ ἐστιν ἐλθεῖν τὰ σκάνδαλα·
from — offenses; necessity for it is to come the offenses,

come, yet woe to that man by whom the offense comes! [8] And if your hand or your foot cause you to offend, cut them off and throw (them) from you; it is good for you to enter into life lame or maimed than having two hands or two feet to be thrown into the everlasting fire. [9] And if your eye cause you to offend, pluck it out and throw (it) from you; it is good for you to enter into life one eyed than having two eyes to be thrown into the hell of fire. [10] See that you do not despise one of these little ones, for I say to you, that their angels in Heaven continually look upon the face of My Father who is in Heaven. [11] For the Son of man is come to save that which has been lost. [12] What do you think? If there should belong to any man a hundred sheep, and one of them be gone astray, (does he) not, having left the ninety-nine on the mountains, having gone, seek that which is gone astray? [13] And if it should be that he find it, truly I say to you, that he rejoices over it more than over the ninety-nine which have not gone astray. [14] So it is not (the) will before your Father who is in Heaven, that one of these little ones should perish.

[15] But if your brother sin against you, go and reprove him between you and him alone. If he will hear you, you have gained your brother. [16] But if he will not hear, take one or two more with you, that upon (the) mouth of two witnesses or of three every word may stand. [17] But if he fails to listen to them, tell (it) to the church. And also if he fails to listen to the church, let him be to you as the nations and the tax-collectors. [18] Truly I say to you, Whatever you shall bind on the earth shall occur, having been already bound in Heaven. And whatever you shall loose on earth shall occur, having been already loosed

---

**8** πλὴν οὐαὶ τῷ ἀνθρώπῳ ἐκείνῳ, δι' οὗ τὸ σκάνδαλον
yet woe to man that through whom the offense
ἔρχεται. εἰ δὲ ἡ χείρ σου ἢ ὁ πούς σου σκανδαλίζει σε,
comes! if And the hand of you or the foot of you offends you,
ἔκκοψον αὐτὰ καὶ βάλε ἀπὸ σοῦ· καλόν σοι ἐστὶν εἰσελθεῖν
cut off it and throw from you; good for you it is to enter
εἰς τὴν ζωὴν χωλὸν ἢ κυλλόν, ἢ δύο χεῖρας ἢ δύο πόδας
into — life lame or maimed than two hands or two feet

**9** ἔχοντα βληθῆναι εἰς τὸ πῦρ τὸ αἰώνιον. καὶ εἰ ὁ ὀφθαλμός
having to be thrown into the fire — everlasting. And if the eye
σου σκανδαλίζει σε, ἔξελε αὐτὸν καὶ βάλε ἀπὸ σοῦ· καλὸν
of you offends you, pluck out it and throw from you; good
σοι ἐστὶ μονόφθαλμον εἰς τὴν ζωὴν εἰσελθεῖν, ἢ δύο ὀφθαλ-
for you it is one-eyed into — life to enter, than two eyes

**10** μοὺς ἔχοντα βληθῆναι εἰς τὴν γέενναν τοῦ πυρός. ὁρᾶτε μὴ
having to be thrown into Gehenna — of fire. See (that) not
καταφρονήσητε ἑνὸς τῶν μικρῶν τούτων, λέγω γὰρ ὑμῖν
you despise one of little (ones) these; I for you
ὅτι οἱ ἄγγελοι αὐτῶν ἐν οὐρανοῖς διὰ παντὸς βλέπουσι τὸ
that the angels of them in heavens always behold the

**11** πρόσωπον τοῦ πατρός μου τοῦ ἐν οὐρανοῖς. ἦλθε γὰρ ὁ
face of the Father of Me — in heavens. is come For the

**12** υἱὸς τοῦ ἀνθρώπου σῶσαι τὸ ἀπολωλός. τί ὑμῖν δοκεῖ; ἐὰν
Son — of man to save that which was lost. What to you seems; if
γένηταί τινι ἀνθρώπῳ ἑκατὸν πρόβατα, καὶ πλανηθῇ ἓν ἐξ
there be to any' man a hundred sheep, and strays one of
αὐτῶν· οὐχὶ ἀφεὶς τὰ ἐννενηκονταεννέα, ἐπὶ τὰ ὄρη πορευθεὶς
them, not will he leave the ninety-nine on the mounts, going

**13** ζητεῖ τὸ πλανώμενον; καὶ ἐὰν γένηται εὑρεῖν αὐτό, ἀμὴν
he seeks the straying (one)? And if he happens to find it, truly
λέγω ὑμῖν ὅτι χαίρει ἐπ' αὐτῷ μᾶλλον, ἢ ἐπὶ τοῖς ἐννενη-
I say to you that he rejoices over it more than over the ninety-

**14** κονταεννέα τοῖς μὴ πεπλανημένοις. οὕτως οὐκ ἔστι θέλημα
nine — not going astray. So not it is the will
ἔμπροσθεν τοῦ πατρὸς ὑμῶν τοῦ ἐν οὐρανοῖς, ἵνα ἀπόληται
before the Father of you — in that should perish
εἰς τῶν μικρῶν τούτων.
one of little (ones) these.

**15** Ἐὰν δὲ ἁμαρτήσῃ εἰς σὲ ὁ ἀδελφός σου, ὕπαγε καὶ
if But sins against you the brother of you, go and
ἔλεγξον αὐτὸν μεταξὺ σοῦ καὶ αὐτοῦ μόνου. ἐάν σου
reprove him between you and him alone. If you

**16** ἀκούσῃ, ἐκέρδησας τὸν ἀδελφόν σου· ἐὰν δὲ μὴ ἀκούσῃ,
he hear, you have gained the brother of you; if but not he hear,
παράλαβε μετὰ σοῦ ἔτι ἕνα ἢ δύο, ἵνα ἐπὶ στόματος δύο
take along with you besides one or two, that upon (the) mouth of two

**17** μαρτύρων ἢ τριῶν σταθῇ πᾶν ῥῆμα. ἐὰν δὲ παρακούσῃ
witnesses or three may stand every word. if But he fails to hear
αὐτῶν, εἰπὲ τῇ ἐκκλησίᾳ· ἐὰν δὲ καὶ τῆς ἐκκλησίας
them, tell to the church; if and even the church

**18** παρακούσῃ, ἔστω σοι ὥσπερ ὁ ἐθνικὸς καὶ ὁ τελώνης. ἀμὴν
he fails to hear, let him be to you as the nations and the tax-collector. Truly
λέγω ὑμῖν, ὅσα ἐὰν δήσητε ἐπὶ τῆς γῆς, ἔσται δεδεμένα ἐν
I say to you, whatever you bind on the earth shall occur, being bound in
τῷ οὐρανῷ· καὶ ὅσα ἐὰν λύσητε ἐπὶ τῆς γῆς, ἔσται λελυμένα
— Heaven; and whatever you loose on the earth shall occur, being loosed

in Heaven. [19] Again I say to you, that if two of you may agree on earth as to anything, whatever they shall ask, it shall be done to them from My Father who (is) in Heaven. [20] For where two or three are gathered together in My name, there I am in (the) midst of them.

[21] Then having come to Him, Peter said, Lord, how often shall my brother sin against me and I forgive him? Until seven times? [22] Jesus said to him, I say not to you until seven times, but until seventy times seven. [23] Because of this the kingdom of Heaven has been compared to a man, a king who decided on an accounting with his servants. [24] And having begun to count, one debtor was brought to him (owing) ten thousand talents. [25] But he not having (any) to pay, his lord commanded him to be sold, and his wife and children, and all, as much as he had, and payment to be made. [26] Then having fallen down, the servant bowed down to him, saying, Lord, have patience with me, and I will pay all to you. [27] And having been moved with compassion, the lord of that servant released him, and forgave him the loan. [28] But having gone out, that servant found one of his fellow servants who owed him a hundred coins, and having seized him, he choked (him), saying, Pay me what you owe. [29] Then having fallen down at his feet, the fellow slave of him begged him, saying, Have patience on me, and I will pay you all. [30] But he would not, but having gone out, he threw him into prison, until he should pay that which was owing. [31] But his fellow-servants having seen what things had taken place greatly grieved, and having gone, reported all that had taken place to their lord. [32] Then having called him, his lord said to him, Wicked servant! I

19 ἐν τῷ οὐρανῷ. πάλιν λέγω ὑμῖν, ὅτι ἐὰν δύο ὑμῶν συμφωνή-
in — Heaven. Again, I say to you that if two of you may agree
σωσιν ἐπὶ τῆς γῆς περὶ παντὸς πράγματος οὗ ἐὰν αἰτή-
on the earth concerning every matter, whatever they
σωνται, γενήσεται αὐτοῖς παρὰ τοῦ πατρός μου τοῦ ἐν
may ask it shall occur to them from the Father of Me — in

20 οὐρανοῖς. οὗ γάρ εἰσι δύο ἢ τρεῖς συνηγμένοι εἰς τὸ ἐμὸν
heavens. where For are two or three gathered together in — my
ὄνομα, ἐκεῖ εἰμι ἐν μέσῳ αὐτῶν.
name, there I am in midst of them.

21 Τότε προσελθὼν αὐτῷ ὁ Πέτρος εἶπε, Κύριε, ποσάκις
Then coming up to Him — Peter said, Lord, how often
ἁμαρτήσει εἰς ἐμὲ ὁ ἀδελφός μου, καὶ ἀφήσω αὐτῷ ; ἕως
shall sin against me the brother of me, and I forgive him? Until

22 ἑπτάκις ; λέγει αὐτῷ ὁ Ἰησοῦς, Οὐ λέγω σοι ἕως ἑπτάκις,
seven times? Says to him — Jesus, not I say to you until seven times,

23 ἀλλ' ἕως ἑβδομηκοντάκις ἑπτά. διὰ τοῦτο ὡμοιώθη ἡ
but until seventy times seven. For this reason, was likened the
βασιλεία τῶν οὐρανῶν ἀνθρώπῳ βασιλεῖ, ὃς ἠθέλησε
kingdom of the heavens to a man, a king, who decided

24 συνᾶραι λόγον μετὰ τῶν δούλων αὐτοῦ. ἀρξαμένου δὲ
to take account with the slaves of him. beginning And
αὐτοῦ συναίρειν, προσηνέχθη αὐτῷ εἷς ὀφειλέτης μυρίων
him to reckon, was brought near to him one debtor of ten thousand

25 ταλάντων. μὴ ἔχοντος δὲ αὐτοῦ ἀποδοῦναι, ἐκέλευσεν αὐτὸν
talents. not having. And he to repay, commanded him
ὁ κύριος αὐτοῦ πραθῆναι, καὶ τὴν γυναῖκα αὐτοῦ καὶ τὰ
the lord of him to be sold, and the wife of him and the

26 τέκνα, καὶ πάντα ὅσα εἶχε, καὶ ἀποδοθῆναι. πεσὼν οὖν ὁ
children, and all as much as he had, and to pay back. Falling then the
δοῦλος προσεκύνει αὐτῷ, λέγων, Κύριε, μακροθύμησον ἐπ'
slave bowed the knee to him, saying, Lord, have patience over

27 ἐμοί, καὶ πάντα σοι ἀποδώσω. σπλαγχνισθεὶς δὲ ὁ κύριος
me, and all to you I will repay. filled with pity And, the lord
τοῦ δούλου ἐκείνου ἀπέλυσεν αὐτόν, καὶ τὸ δάνειον ἀφῆκεν
slave of that released him, and the loan forgave

28 αὐτῷ. ἐξελθὼν δὲ ὁ δοῦλος ἐκεῖνος εὗρεν ἕνα τῶν συνδούλων
him. going out But slave that found one of the fellow-slaves
αὐτοῦ, ὃς ὤφειλεν αὐτῷ ἑκατὸν δηνάρια, καὶ κρατήσας
of him, who owed him a hundred denarii, and seizing

29 αὐτὸν ἔπνιγε, λέγων, Ἀπόδος μοι ὅ τι ὀφείλεις. πεσὼν οὖν
him he throttled, saying, Pay back to me whatever you owed. Falling then
ὁ σύνδουλος αὐτοῦ εἰς τοὺς πόδας αὐτοῦ παρεκάλει αὐτόν,
the fellow-slave of him to the feet of him begged him,
λέγων, Μακροθύμησον ἐπ' ἐμοί, καὶ πάντα ἀποδώσω σοι.
saying, Have patience over me and all I will repay to you.

30 ὁ δὲ οὐκ ἤθελεν, ἀλλ' ἀπελθὼν ἔβαλεν αὐτὸν εἰς φυλακήν,
he But not willed (it), but going away threw him into prison

31 ἕως οὗ ἀποδῷ τὸ ὀφειλόμενον. ἰδόντες δὲ οἱ σύνδουλοι αὐτοῦ
until he pay back that owing. seeing And the fellow-slaves of him
τὰ γενόμενα ἐλυπήθησαν σφόδρα· καὶ ἐλθόντες διεσάφησαν
that occurring, they were grieved greatly, and coming reported

32 τῷ κυρίῳ αὐτῶν πάντα τὰ γενόμενα. τότε προσκαλεσά-
to the lord of them all the (things) occurring. Then calling near
μενος αὐτὸν ὁ κύριος αὐτοῦ λέγει αὐτῷ, Δοῦλε πονηρέ,
him, the lord of him says to him, slave Wicked,

his wife, it
to marry.
d to them,
this word,
whom it has
2] for there
no were born
eir) mother's
there are
o were made
men; and there
s who made
themselves for
the kingdom of
e who is able to
et Him receive

Then little child-
brought to Him,
might lay hands on
nd might pray; but
iples-rebuked them.
ut Jesus said, Allow
tle children, and do
rbid them to come
e; for of. such is the
dom of Heaven.
And having laid
s on them, He went
y from there.
[16] And, behold, hav-
come, one said to Him,
od Teacher, what good
ing shall I do that I may
ave eternal life? [17] And
e said to him, Why do
ou call Me good? No one
(is) good except One, God!
But if you desire to enter
into life, keep the com-
mandments. [18] He said
to Him, Which? And Jesus
said, You shall not commit
murder; you shall not commit adultery; you shall not
steal; you shall not bear
false witness; [19] honor
your father and your
mother; and, you shall love
your neighbor as yourself.
[20] The young man said
to him, All these things I
have kept from my mouth;
what do I still lack?
[21] Jesus said to him, If
you desire to be perfect, go
sell your property and give
to (the) poor, and you
shall have treasure in
Heaven; and come follow
Me. [22] But having heard
the word, the young man
went away sorrowful, for
he had many possessions.
[23] And Jesus said to
His disciples, Truly I say to
you that a rich man shall
with great difficulty enter
into the kingdom of
Heaven. [24] And again I
say to you, It is easier for a

11 ἀνθρώπου μετὰ τῆς γυναικός, οὐ συμφέρει γαμῆσαι. ὁ δὲ εἶπεν
man with the wife, not it is gain to marry. He But said
αὐτοῖς, Οὐ πάντες χωροῦσι τὸν λόγον τοῦτον, ἀλλ' οἷς
to them, Not all make room for— word this. only to whom
12 δέδοται. εἰσὶ γὰρ εὐνοῦχοι, οἵτινες ἐκ κοιλίας μητρὸς
it is given, there are For eunuchs who from (the) womb of a mother
ἐγεννήθησαν οὕτω· καὶ εἰσιν εὐνοῦχοι, οἵτινες εὐνουχίσθησαν
were born so; and there are eunuchs who were made eunuchs
ὑπὸ τῶν ἀνθρώπων· καὶ εἰσιν εὐνοῦχοι, οἵτινες εὐνούχισαν
by — men; and there are eunuchs who made eunuchs
ἑαυτοὺς διὰ τὴν βασιλείαν τῶν οὐρανῶν. ὁ δυνάμενος
(of) themselves due to the kingdom of the heavens. The (one) able
χωρεῖν χωρείτω.
to receive, let him receive (it).

13 Τότε προσηνέχθη αὐτῷ παιδία, ἵνα τὰς χεῖρας ἐπιθῇ
Then were brought to Him children, that — hands He might lay
αὐτοῖς, καὶ προσεύξηται· οἱ δὲ μαθηταὶ ἐπετίμησαν αὐτοῖς.
on them and to pray; the but disciples rebuked them.
14 ὁ δὲ Ἰησοῦς εἶπεν, Ἄφετε τὰ παιδία, καὶ μὴ κωλύετε αὐτὰ
— But Jesus said, Permit the children, and not do prevent them
ἐλθεῖν πρός με· τῶν γὰρ τοιούτων ἐστὶν ἡ βασιλεία τῶν
to come to Me; — for of such is the kingdom of the
15 οὐρανῶν. καὶ ἐπιθεὶς αὐτοῖς τὰς χεῖρας, ἐπορεύθη ἐκεῖθεν.
heavens. And laying on them — hands, He went away from there.
16 Καὶ ἰδού, εἰς προσελθὼν εἶπεν αὐτῷ, Διδάσκαλε ἀγαθέ,
And behold! One coming near said to Him, teacher Good
17 τί ἀγαθὸν ποιήσω, ἵνα ἔχω ζωὴν αἰώνιον ; ὁ δὲ εἶπεν αὐτῷ,
what good shall I do that I may have life eternal? He And said to him,
Τί με λέγεις ἀγαθόν ; οὐδεὶς ἀγαθός, εἰ μὴ εἷς, ὁ Θεός. εἰ δὲ
Why Me you call good? No one (is) good except One — God. if But
18 θέλεις εἰσελθεῖν εἰς τὴν ζωήν, τήρησον τὰς ἐντολάς. λέγει
you desire to enter into — life, keep the commands. He says
αὐτῷ, Ποίας ; ὁ δὲ Ἰησοῦς εἶπε, Τὸ οὐ φονεύσεις· οὐ μοιχεύ-
to Him, Which? — And Jesus said, not You shall murder;not commit
19 σεις· οὐ κλέψεις· οὐ ψευδομαρτυρήσεις· τίμα τὸν πατέρα
adultery; not steal; not bear false witness; honor — father
σου καὶ τὴν μητέρα· καὶ, ἀγαπήσεις τὸν πλησίον σου ὡς
your and — mother; and, you shall love the neighbor of you as
20 σεαυτόν. λέγει αὐτῷ ὁ νεανίσκος, Πάντα ταῦτα ἐφυλαξάμην
yourself. says to Him The young man, All these things I have kept
21 ἐκ νεότητός μου· τί ἔτι ὑστερῶ ; ἔφη αὐτῷ ὁ Ἰησοῦς, Εἰ θέλεις
from my youth; What yet do I lack? said to him — Jesus, If you wish
τέλειος εἶναι, ὕπαγε, πώλησόν σου τὰ ὑπάρχοντα καὶ δὸς
perfect to be, go sell your — property and give
πτωχοῖς, καὶ ἕξεις θησαυρὸν ἐν οὐρανῷ· καὶ δεῦρο, ἀκολούθει
to (the) poor, and you will have treasure in Heaven; and come, follow
22 μοι. ἀκούσας δὲ ὁ νεανίσκος τὸν λόγον ἀπῆλθε λυπούμενος·
Me. hearing But the young man the word went away grieving,
ἦν γὰρ ἔχων κτήματα πολλά.
he was for having possessions many.
23 Ὁ δὲ Ἰησοῦς εἶπε τοῖς μαθηταῖς αὐτοῦ, Ἀμὴν λέγω ὑμῖν,
— And Jesus said to the disciples of Him, Truly I say to you,
ὅτι δυσκόλως πλούσιος εἰσελεύσεται εἰς τὴν βασιλείαν τῶν
that with difficulty a rich man will enter into the kingdom of the
24 οὐρανῶν. πάλιν δὲ λέγω ὑμῖν, εὐκοπώτερόν ἐστι κάμηλον
heavens. again And I tell you, easier It is a camel

πᾶσαν τὴν ὀφειλὴν ἐκείν
all — debt that

48

man be so with
is not good
[11] But He sa
Not all receive
but (those) to
been given; [
are eunuchs w
thus from (th
womb, and
eunuchs wh
eunuchs by
are eunuc
eunuchs o
the sake o
Heaven. H
receive,
(it).
[13]
ren wer
that He
them,
the disc
[14] B
the li
not f
to M
king
[15]
han
aw
in
G
th
h

forgave you all that debt
because you begged me;
[33] Must not even you
have shown mercy to your
fellow-slave, as I also had
shown mercy to you? [34]
And being angry, his lord
delivered him up to the tormentors, until he pay, back
all the debt to him. [35] So
also My heavenly Father
will do to you unless each
of you from your hearts
forgive his brother their
offenses.

33 οὐκ ἔδει καὶ σὲ ἐλεῆσαι τὸ
not must be even you to favor th

34 ἠλέησα ; καὶ ὀργισθεὶς ὁ κ
had favored. And being angry, the l
τοῖς βασανισταῖς, ἕως οὗ ἀπο
to the tormentors, until that he rep

35 οὕτω καὶ ὁ πατήρ μου ὁ ἐπουρ
So also the Father of Me- heavenl
ἀφῆτε ἕκαστος τῷ ἀδελφῷ αὐτοῦ
you forgive each one the brother of him fr
παραπτώματα αὐτῶν.
offenses of them.

## CHAPTER 19

[1] And it came to
pass, when Jesus had
finished these words, He
departed from Galilee and
came to the borders of
Judah beyond the Jordan.
[2] And great crowds fol-
lowed Him, and He healed
them there.

[3] And the Pharisees
came to Him, tempting
Him, and saying to Him, Is
it lawful for a man to put
away his wife for every
reason? [4] But answering
He said to them, Have you
not read that He who
created from the beginning
made them male and fe-
male. [5] And (He) said,
"For this reason a man
shall leave father and
mother and shall be joined
to his wife, and the two
shall become one flesh.
[6] So that they are no
longer two, but one flesh.
Therefore, what God has
joined together, let not
man separate. [7] They
said to Him, Why then did
Moses command to give a
bill of divorce, and to put
her away? [8] He said to
them, In view of your hard
heartedness, Moses allowed
you to put away your
wives, but from the be-
ginning it was not so.
[9] And I say to you, that
whoever shall put away his
wife, if not for fornication,
and shall marry another,
commits adultery; and he
who marries her (who was)
put away commits adult-
ery. [10] His disciples said
to Him, If the case of the

## CHAPTER 19

1 Καὶ ἐγένετο ὅτε ἐτέλεσεν ὁ Ἰησοῦς τ
And it was, when ended — Jesus
μετῆρεν ἀπὸ τῆς Γαλιλαίας, καὶ ἦλθεν
He moved from — Galilee and came

2 Ἰουδαίας πέραν τοῦ Ἰορδάνου. καὶ ἠκο
of Judea, across the Jordan. And fo
ὄχλοι πολλοί, καὶ ἐθεράπευσεν αὐτοὺς ἐκεῖ.
crowds much, and He healed them there.

3 Καὶ προσῆλθον αὐτῷ οἱ Φαρισαῖοι πειρά
And approached him the Pharisees, temptin
καὶ λέγοντες αὐτῷ, Εἰ ἔξεστιν ἀνθρώπῳ ἀπ
and saying to Him, If it is lawful for a man to pu

4 γυναῖκα αὐτοῦ κατὰ πᾶσαν αἰτίαν ; ὁ δὲ ἀποκρ
wife of him for every reason? He And answerin
αὐτοῖς, Οὐκ ἀνέγνωτε ὅτι ὁ ποιήσας ἀπ' ἀρχῆς ἄ
to them, not Did you read that He making from beginning

5 θῆλυ ἐποίησεν αὐτούς, καὶ εἶπεν, Ἕνεκεν τούτου κατα
female made them? And He said, For the sake of this shall l
ἄνθρωπος τὸν πατέρα καὶ τὴν μητέρα, καὶ προσκολλ
a man — father and — mother, and shall be joined
σεται τῇ γυναικὶ αὐτοῦ, καὶ ἔσονται οἱ δύο εἰς σάρκα μία
the wife of him; and shall be the two for flesh one;

6 ὥστε οὐκέτι εἰσὶ δύο, ἀλλὰ σὰρξ μία· ὁ οὖν ὁ Θεὸς συνέζευξεν,
so that no longer are they two, but flesh one. What then God yoked together

7 ἄνθρωπος μὴ χωριζέτω. λέγουσιν αὐτῷ, Τί οὖν Μωσῆς
man do not let separate. They say to Him, Why then Moses
ἐνετείλατο δοῦναι βιβλίον ἀποστασίου, καὶ ἀπολῦσαι
did command to give a bill of divorce, and to put away

8 αὐτήν ; λέγει αὐτοῖς ὅτι Μωσῆς πρὸς τὴν σκληροκαρδίαν
her? He says to them, — Moses in view of the obduracy
ὑμῶν ἐπέτρεψεν ὑμῖν ἀπολῦσαι τὰς γυναῖκας ὑμῶν· ἀπ'
of you allowed you to put away the wives of you. from

9 ἀρχῆς δὲ οὐ γέγονεν οὕτω. λέγω δὲ ὑμῖν ὅτι ὃς ἂν ἀπολύσῃ
the beginning but not it was so. I say And to you that whoever puts away
τὴν γυναῖκα αὐτοῦ, εἰ μὴ ἐπὶ πορνείᾳ, καὶ γαμήσῃ ἄλλην,
the wife of him, if not for fornication, and shall marry another,

10 μοιχᾶται· καὶ ὁ ἀπολελυμένην γαμήσας μοιχᾶται. λέγουσιν
commits adultery and he her put away marrying commits adultery. Say
αὐτῷ οἱ μαθηταὶ αὐτοῦ, Εἰ οὕτως ἐστὶν ἡ αἰτία τοῦ
to Him the disciples of Him, If thus is the case of the

camel to go through (the) eye of a needle than for for a rich man to enter the kingdom of God. [25] And His disciples were amazed when they heard this, saying, Who then can be saved? [26] But looking on (them), Jesus said to them, With men this is impossible, but with God all things are possible.

[27] Then answering Peter said to Him, Behold, we left all things and followed You; what then shall happen to us? [28] And Jesus said to them, Truly I say to you, that you who have followed Me, in the regeneration, when the Son of man shall sit on the throne of glory, you also shall sit on twelve thrones, judging the twelve tribes of Israel. [29] And everyone who has left houses, or brothers, or sisters, or father, or mother, or wife, or children, or lands, for My name's sake shall receive a hundredfold, and shall inherit everlasting life. [30] But many first (ones) shall be last, and last (ones) first

CHAPTER 20

[1] For the kingdom of Heaven is like a man, who went out with (the) morning to hire workers for his vineyard. [2] And having agreed with the workers for a denarius (for) the day, he sent them into his vineyard. [3] And having gone out about the third hour, he saw others standing in the marketplace idle; [4] and he said to them, You also go into the vineyard, and whatever may be right I will give you; and they went. [5] Again, having gone out about (the) sixth and ninth hour, he did likewise. [6] And having gone out about the eleventh hour, he found others standing idle, and said to them, Why do you stand here idle all this day? [7] They said to him, Because no one has

---

διὰ τρυπήματος ῥαφίδος διελθεῖν, ἢ πλούσιον εἰς τὴν βασι-
through (the) eye    of a needle to pass,    than a rich man   into the king-

25 λείαν τοῦ Θεοῦ εἰσελθεῖν. ἀκούσαντες δὲ οἱ μαθηταὶ αὐτοῦ
dom   — of God to enter.   having heard  And the disciples of Him

ἐξεπλήσσοντο σφόδρα, λέγοντες, Τίς ἄρα δύναται σωθῆναι ;
were astonished exceedingly, saying,   Who then is able     to be saved?

26 ἐμβλέψας δὲ ὁ Ἰησοῦς εἶπεν αὐτοῖς, Παρὰ ἀνθρώποις τοῦτο
looking But  — Jesus    said to them, With   men    this

27 ἀδύνατόν ἐστι, παρὰ δὲ Θεῷ πάντα δυνατά ἐστι. τότε
impossible  is,   with But  God all things possible  are.   Then

ἀποκριθεὶς ὁ Πέτρος εἶπεν αὐτῷ, Ἰδού, ἡμεῖς ἀφήκαμεν
answering   — Peter  said  to Him, Behold,  we     left

28 πάντα καὶ ἠκολουθήσαμέν σοι· τί ἄρα ἔσται ἡμῖν; ὁ δὲ Ἰη-
all things and  followed       You. What then shall be to us? — And

σοῦς εἶπεν αὐτοῖς, Ἀμὴν λέγω ὑμῖν ὅτι ὑμεῖς οἱ ἀκολουθή-
Jesus said  to them, Truly  I tell you  that you the (ones) having

σαντές μοι, ἐν τῇ παλιγγενεσίᾳ ὅταν καθίσῃ ὁ υἱὸς τοῦ
followed Me, in the  regeneration,  when  sits   the Son  —

ἀνθρώπου ἐπὶ θρόνου δόξης αὐτοῦ, καθίσεσθε καὶ ὑμεῖς ἐπὶ
of man    on (the) throne of glory of Him, You will sit even you   on

δώδεκα θρόνους, κρίνοντες τὰς δώδεκα φυλὰς τοῦ Ἰσραήλ.
twelve   thrones,  judging   the  twelve  tribes  — of Israel.

29 καὶ πᾶς ὃς ἀφῆκεν οἰκίας, ἢ ἀδελφοὺς, ἢ ἀδελφάς, ἢ πατέρα,
And everyone who left  houses,  or brothers,  or sisters,   or father,

ἢ μητέρα, ἢ γυναῖκα, ἢ τέκνα, ἢ ἀγρούς, ἕνεκεν τοῦ ὀνόματός
or mother, or wife,    or children, or lands, for the sake of  the name

μου, ἑκατονταπλασίονα λήψεται, καὶ ζωὴν αἰώνιον κλη-
of Me,  a hundredfold     shall receive, and  life    eternal  shall

30 ρονομήσει. πολλοὶ δὲ ἔσονται πρῶτοι ἔσχατοι, καὶ ἔσχατοι
inherit.   many But shall be   first    last,    and   last

πρῶτοι.
first.

CHAPTER 20

1 ὁμοία γάρ ἐστιν ἡ βασιλεία τῶν οὐρανῶν ἀνθρώπῳ
like  For  is   the kingdom of the heavens   to a man,

οἰκοδεσπότῃ, ὅστις ἐξῆλθεν ἅμα πρωῒ μισθώσασθαι ἐργάτας
a housemaster,  who  went out when early   to hire    workmen

2 εἰς τὸν ἀμπελῶνα αὐτοῦ. συμφωνήσας δὲ μετὰ τῶν ἐργατῶν
into the vineyard    of him. agreeing   And with the workmen

ἐκ δηναρίου τὴν ἡμέραν, ἀπέστειλεν αὐτοὺς εἰς τὸν ἀμπελῶνα
for a denarius the day,    he sent       them   into the vineyard

3 αὐτοῦ. καὶ ἐξελθὼν περὶ τὴν τρίτην ὥραν, εἶδεν ἄλλους
of him. And going out about the third   hour, he saw others

4 ἑστῶτας ἐν τῇ ἀγορᾷ ἀργούς· κἀκείνοις εἶπεν, Ὑπάγετε καὶ
standing  in the market idle,    and to them said,    Go     also

5 ὑμεῖς εἰς τὸν ἀμπελῶνα, καὶ ὃ ἐὰν ᾖ δίκαιον δώσω ὑμῖν. οἱ
you  into the vineyard,   and whatever is just   I will give you. they

δὲ ἀπῆλθον. πάλιν ἐξελθὼν περὶ ἕκτην καὶ ἐννάτην ὥραν,
And went.    Again going out about (the) sixth and  ninth    hour,

6 ἐποίησεν ὡσαύτως. περὶ δὲ τὴν ἑνδεκάτην ὥραν ἐξελθών,
he did   likewise.  about And the eleventh   hour,  going out.

εὖρεν ἄλλους ἑστῶτας ἀργούς, καὶ λέγει αὐτοῖς, Τί ὧδε
he found others  standing   idle,   and says to them,  Why here

7 ἑστήκατε ὅλην τὴν ἡμέραν ἀργοί ; λέγουσιν αὐτῷ, Ὅτι
do you stand all   the   day    idle?  They say   to him, Because

hired us. He said to them, You also go into the vineyard, and whatever may be right you shall receive. [8] But evening having come, the lord of the vineyard said to his steward, Call the workers and pay them (their) wages, beginning from the last to the first. [9] And those (hired) about the eleventh hour having come, they each received a denarius. [10] And the first having come, they thought that they would receive more, and they themselves also received each a denarius. [11] And having received (it), they murmured against the master of the house, [12] saying, These last have worked one hour, and you have made them equal to us who have borne the burden and the heat of the day. [13] But answering he said to one of them, Friend, I do no wrong to you. Did you not agree with me for a denarius? [14] Take yours and go. But I want to give to this last as also to you. [15] Or is it not lawful for me to do what I will with my things? Or is your eye evil because I am good? [16] So the last shall be first, and the first last; for many are called, but few chosen.

[17] And going up to Jerusalem, Jesus took the twelve disciples apart in the way, and said to them, [18] Behold, we go up to Jerusalem, and the Son of man will be delivered up to the chief priests and scribes; and they will condemn Him to death. [19] And they will deliver Him up to the nations to mock and to scourge and to crucify; and the third day He will rise again.

[20] Then the mother of the sons of Zebedee came to Him with her sons, bowing down and asking something from Him. [21] And He said to her, What do you desire? She said to Him, Say that these my two sons may sit one on Your right hand and one on (Your) left in Your

---

**8** οὐδεὶς ἡμᾶς ἐμισθώσατο. λέγει αὐτοῖς, Ὑπάγετε καὶ ὑμεῖς εἰς
no one us has hired. He says to them, Go also you into

τὸν ἀμπελῶνα, καὶ ὃ ἐὰν ᾖ δίκαιον λήψεσθε. ὀψίας δὲ γενο-
the vineyard, and whatever is just you will receive. eve But com-

μένης λέγει ὁ κύριος τοῦ ἀμπελῶνος τῷ ἐπιτρόπῳ αὐτοῦ,
ing, says the lord of the vineyard to the manager of him,

Κάλεσον τοὺς ἐργάτας, καὶ ἀπόδος αὐτοῖς τὸν μισθόν,
Call the workmen, and pay them the wage,

**9** ἀρξάμενος ἀπὸ τῶν ἐσχάτων ἕως τῶν πρώτων. καὶ ἐλθόντες,
beginning from the last ones until the first. And coming,

**10** οἱ περὶ τὴν ἐνδεκάτην ὥραν ἔλαβον ἀνὰ δηνάριον. ἐλθόντες
those about the eleventh hour received each a denarius. coming

δὲ οἱ πρῶτοι ἐνόμισαν ὅτι πλείονα λήψονται· καὶ ἔλαβον καὶ
And the first supposed that more they will get; and they got also

**11** αὐτοὶ ἀνὰ δηνάριον. λαβόντες δὲ ἐγόγγυζον κατὰ τοῦ
themselves each a denarius. receiving And they murmured against the

**12** οἰκοδεσπότου, λέγοντες ὅτι Οὗτοι οἱ ἔσχατοι μίαν ὥραν
housemaster, saying, These — last one hour

ἐποίησαν, καὶ ἴσους ἡμῖν αὐτοὺς ἐποίησας, τοῖς βαστάσασι
performed and equal to us them you have made, who have borne

**13** τὸ βάρος τῆς ἡμέρας καὶ τὸν καύσωνα. ὁ δὲ ἀποκριθεὶς
the burden of the day and the heat. he But answering

εἶπεν ἑνὶ αὐτῶν, Ἑταῖρε, οὐκ ἀδικῶ σε· οὐχὶ δηναρίῳ
said to one of them, Friend, not I am unjust to you; not of a denarius

**14** συνεφώνησάς μοι ; ἆρον τὸ σὸν καὶ ὕπαγε· θέλω δὲ τούτῳ
you agreed with me? Take — yours and go; I desire But to this

**15** τῷ ἐσχάτῳ δοῦναι ὡς καὶ σοί. ἢ οὐκ ἔξεστί μοι ποιῆσαι ὃ
last to give as also to you. Or not is it lawful for me to do what

θέλω ἐν τοῖς ἐμοῖς ; εἰ ὁ ὀφθαλμός σου πονηρός ἐστιν, ὅτι
I desire in the things of me; or the eye of you evil is, because

**16** ἐγὼ ἀγαθός εἰμι ; οὕτως ἔσονται οἱ ἔσχατοι πρῶτοι, καὶ οἱ
I good am? So shall be the last first, and the

πρῶτοι ἔσχατοι· πολλοὶ γάρ εἰσι κλητοί, ὀλίγοι δὲ ἐκλεκτοί.
first last; many for are called, few but chosen.

**17** Καὶ ἀναβαίνων ὁ Ἰησοῦς εἰς Ἱεροσόλυμα παρέλαβε τοὺς
And going up — Jesus to Jerusalem He took the

**18** δώδεκα μαθητὰς κατ' ἰδίαν ἐν τῇ ὁδῷ, καὶ εἶπεν αὐτοῖς, ἰδού,
twelve disciples privately, in the way and said to them, Behold,

ἀναβαίνομεν εἰς Ἱεροσόλυμα, καὶ ὁ υἱὸς τοῦ ἀνθρώπου
we are going up to Jerusalem, and the Son — of man

παραδοθήσεται τοῖς ἀρχιερεῦσι καὶ γραμματεῦσι· καὶ κατα-
will be delivered up to the chief priests and scribes. And they

**19** κρινοῦσιν αὐτὸν θανάτῳ, καὶ παραδώσουσιν αὐτὸν τοῖς
will condemn Him to death. And they will deliver up Him to the

ἔθνεσιν εἰς τὸ ἐμπαῖξαι καὶ μαστιγῶσαι καὶ σταυρῶσαι·
nations to — mock and to scourge and to crucify.

καὶ τῇ τρίτῃ ἡμέρᾳ ἀναστήσεται.
And the third day He will rise again.

**20** Τότε προσῆλθεν αὐτῷ ἡ μήτηρ τῶν υἱῶν Ζεβεδαίου μετὰ
Then came near to Him the mother of the sons of Zebedee with

τῶν υἱῶν αὐτῆς, προσκυνοῦσα καὶ αἰτοῦσά τι παρ' αὐτοῦ.
the sons of her, bowing the knee and asking something from Him.

**21** ὁ δὲ εἶπεν αὐτῇ, Τί θέλεις ; λέγει αὐτῷ, Εἰπὲ ἵνα καθίσωσιν
He And said to her, What desire you? She says to Him, Say that may sit

οὗτοι οἱ δύο υἱοί μου, εἷς ἐκ δεξιῶν σου, καὶ εἷς ἐξ εὐωνύμων,
these the two sons of me one on the right of You and one on the left

kingdom. [22] But answering Jesus said, You do not know what you ask for. Are you able to drink the cup which I am about to drink, and to be baptized with the baptism I am baptized with? They said to Him, We are able. [23] And He said to them, Indeed you shall drink My cup, and you shall be baptized with the baptism which I am baptized with; but to sit on My right hand and on My left is not Mine to give, but (to those) for whom it has been prepared by My Father. [24] And having heard, the ten were indignant about the two brothers. [25] But having called them, Jesus said, You know that the rulers of the nations excise lordship over them, and the great ones exercise authority over them. [26] However it shall not be so among you; but whoever would become great among you, let him be your servant; [27] and whoever would be first, let him be your slave; [28] even as the Son of man did not come to be served, but to serve, and to give His life a ransom for many.

[29] And as they were going out from Jericho, a great crowd followed Him. [30] And, behold, two blind ones sitting beside the way, having heard that Jesus was passing by, cried out, sáying, Have pity on us Lord, Son of David! [31] But the crowd rebuked them that they should be silent. But they more cried out, saying, Have pity on us, Lord, Son of David! [32] And having stopped, Jesus called them and said, What do you desire I should do to you? [33] They said to Him, Lord, that our eyes may be opened. [34] And moved with compassion, Jesus touched their eyes; and immediately their eyes received sight, and they followed Him.

**22** ἐν τῇ βασιλείᾳ σου. ἀποκριθεὶς δὲ ὁ Ἰησοῦς εἶπεν, Οὐκ
in the kingdom of You. answering But — Jesus said, not
οἴδατε τί αἰτεῖσθε. δύνασθε πιεῖν τὸ ποτήριον ὃ ἐγὼ μέλλω
You know what you ask. Can you drink the cup which I am about
πίνειν, καὶ τὸ βάπτισμα ὃ ἐγὼ βαπτίζομαι βαπτισθῆναι;
to drink, and the baptism which I am baptised to be baptised?

**23** λέγουσιν αὐτῷ, Δυνάμεθα. καὶ λέγει αὐτοῖς, Τὸ μὲν
They say to Him, We can. And He says to them, the indeed
ποτήριόν μου πίεσθε, καὶ τὸ βάπτισμα ὃ ἐγὼ βαπτίζομαι
cup of Me you will drink, and the baptism which I am baptized
βαπτισθήσεσθε· τὸ δὲ καθίσαι ἐκ δεξιῶν μου καὶ ἐξ εὐωνύμων
you will be baptized (with), but to sit off the right of Me and off the left
μου, οὐκ ἔστιν ἐμὸν δοῦναι, ἀλλ' οἷς ἡτοίμασται ὑπὸ τοῦ
of Me, not is Mine to give, but for whom it was prepared by the

**24** πατρός μου. καὶ ἀκούσαντες οἱ δέκα ἠγανάκτησαν περὶ τῶν
Father of Me. And having heard the ten were indignant about the

**25** δύο ἀδελφῶν. ὁ δὲ Ἰησοῦς προσκαλεσάμενος αὐτοὺς εἶπεν,
two brothers. — But Jesus having called near them said,
Οἴδατε ὅτι οἱ ἄρχοντες τῶν ἐθνῶν κατακυριεύουσιν αὐτῶν,
You know that the rulers of the nations exercise lordship over them;

**26** καὶ οἱ μεγάλοι κατεξουσιάζουσιν αὐτῶν. οὐχ οὕτως δὲ ἔσται
and the great ones exercise authority over them. not so But it will be
ἐν ὑμῖν· ἀλλ' ὃς ἐὰν θέλῃ ἐν ὑμῖν μέγας γενέσθαι ἔστω ὑμῶν
among you; but whoever would among you great become, let him be of you

**27** διάκονος· καὶ ὃς ἐὰν θέλῃ ἐν ὑμῖν εἶναι πρῶτος ἔστω ὑμῶν
a servant. And whoever desires among you to be first, he shall be of you

**28** δοῦλος· ὥσπερ ὁ υἱὸς τοῦ ἀνθρώπου οὐκ ἦλθε διακονηθῆναι,
a slave. even as the Son — of man not did come to be served,
ἀλλὰ διακονῆσαι, καὶ δοῦναι τὴν ψυχὴν αὐτοῦ λύτρον ἀντὶ
but to serve, and to give the life of Him a ransom for
πολλῶν.
many.

**29** Καὶ ἐκπορευομένων αὐτῶν ἀπὸ Ἰεριχώ, ἠκολούθησεν
And going out they from Jericho, followed

**30** αὐτῷ ὄχλος πολύς. καὶ ἰδού, δύο τυφλοὶ καθήμενοι παρὰ
Him a crowd great. And behold, two blind (ones) sitting beside
τὴν ὁδόν, ἀκούσαντες ὅτι Ἰησοῦς παράγει, ἔκραξαν,
the way, hearing that Jesus is passing by, cried out,

**31** λέγοντες, Ἐλέησον ἡμᾶς, Κύριε, υἱὸς Δαβίδ. ὁ δὲ ὄχλος
saying, Have pity on us, Lord, Son of David. the But crowd
ἐπετίμησεν αὐτοῖς ἵνα σιωπήσωσιν. οἱ δὲ μεῖζον ἔκραζον,
rebuked them, that they be silent. they But more cried out,

**32** λέγοντες, Ἐλέησον ἡμᾶς, Κύριε, υἱὸς Δαβίδ. καὶ στὰς ὁ
saying, Have mercy on us, Lord, Son of David. And stopping —
Ἰησοῦς ἐφώνησεν αὐτούς, καὶ εἶπε, Τί θέλετε ποιήσω ὑμῖν;
Jesus called them, and said, What do you desire I do to you?

**33** λέγουσιν αὐτῷ, Κύριε, ἵνα ἀνοιχθῶσιν ἡμῶν οἱ ὀφθαλμοί.
They say to Him, Lord, that may be opened of us the eyes.

**34** σπλαγχνισθεὶς δὲ ὁ Ἰησοῦς ἥψατο τῶν ὀφθαλμῶν αὐτῶν·
moved with pity And — Jesus touched the eyes of them,
καὶ εὐθέως ἀνέβλεψαν αὐτῶν οἱ ὀφθαλμοί, καὶ ἠκολούθησαν
and instantly received sight of them the eyes, and they followed
αὐτῷ.
Him.

## CHAPTER 21

[1] And when they drew near to Jerusalem, and came to Bethphage toward the Mount of Olives, then Jesus sent two disciples, [2] saying to them, Go into the village opposite you, and immediately you will find an ass tied, and a colt with her; having loosed (them) bring to Me. [3] And if anyone says anything to you, you shall say, The Lord has need of them; and he will send them at once. [4] But all this happened that might be fulfilled that which was spoken by the prophet, saying, [5] "Tell the daughter of Zion, Behold, your King comes to you, meek and mounted on an ass, even a colt, the foal of a beast of burden." [6] And the disciples having gone, and having done as Jesus ordered them, [7] they brought the ass and the colt, and put on them their garments, and He sat on them. [8] And most (of the) crowd spread their coats on the road; and others were cutting down branches from the trees and were spreading on the road. [9] And the crowd, those going before and those following, were crying out, saying, Hosanna to the Son of David! Blessed (is) He who comes in (the) name of (the) Lord! Hosanna in the highest! [10] And as He entered into Jerusalem, all the city was moved, saying, Who is this? [11] And the multitudes said, This is Jesus the Prophet, He who is from Nazareth of Galilee.

[12] And Jesus entered into the temple of God, and threw out all those selling and buying in the Temple; and He overthrew the tables of the money-changers, and the seats of those selling the doves. [13] And He said to them, It has been written, "My house shall be called a house of prayer," but you have made it a den of thieves. [14] And blind

## CHAPTER 21

**1** Καὶ ὅτε ἤγγισαν εἰς Ἱεροσόλυμα, καὶ ἦλθον εἰς Βηθφαγῆ
And when they drew near to Jerusalem, and came into Bethphage,

πρὸς τὸ ὄρος τῶν ἐλαιῶν, τότε ὁ Ἰησοῦς ἀπέστειλε δύο
towards the mount of the olives, then — Jesus sent two

**2** μαθητάς, λέγων αὐτοῖς, Πορεύθητε εἰς τὴν κώμην τὴν ἀπέ-
disciples, telling them, You go into the village, that

ναντι ὑμῶν, καὶ εὐθέως εὑρήσετε ὄνον δεδεμένην, καὶ πῶλον
opposite you, and at once you will find an ass tied, and a colt

**3** μετ' αὐτῆς· λύσαντες ἀγάγετέ μοι. καὶ ἐάν τις ὑμῖν εἴπῃ τι,
with her. Loosen (and) lead to Me. And if any to you says any-thing,

ἐρεῖτε ὅτι Ὁ Κύριος αὐτῶν χρείαν ἔχει· εὐθέως δὲ ἀποστελεῖ
you shall say, The Lord of them need has; at once and he will send

**4** αὐτούς. τοῦτο δὲ ὅλον γέγονεν, ἵνα πληρωθῇ τὸ ῥηθὲν διὰ
them. this But all came to pass that may be fulfilled that spoken by

**5** τοῦ προφήτου, λέγοντος, Εἴπατε τῇ θυγατρὶ Σιών, Ἰδού,
the prophet, saying, Tell the daughter of Zion, Behold,

ὁ βασιλεύς σου ἔρχεταί σοι, πραῢς καὶ ἐπιβεβηκὼς ἐπὶ ὄνον
the king of you comes to you, meek and mounted on an ass,

**6** καὶ πῶλον υἱὸν ὑποζυγίου. πορευθέντες δὲ οἱ μαθηταί, καὶ
even a colt (the) son of an ass. having gone And the disciples, and

**7** ποιήσαντες καθὼς προσέταξεν αὐτοῖς ὁ Ἰησοῦς, ἤγαγον
having done as ordered them — Jesus, they led

τὴν ὄνον καὶ τὸν πῶλον, καὶ ἐπέθηκαν ἐπάνω αὐτῶν τὰ
the ass and the colt, and put upon them the

**8** ἱμάτια αὐτῶν, καὶ ἐπεκάθισαν ἐπάνω αὐτῶν. ὁ δὲ πλεῖστος
garments of them; and He sat on them. the And most of

ὄχλος ἔστρωσαν ἑαυτῶν τὰ ἱμάτια ἐν τῇ ὁδῷ· ἄλλοι δὲ
(the) crowd strewed of themselves the garments on the way. others And

ἔκοπτον κλάδους ἀπὸ τῶν δένδρων, καὶ ἐστρώννυον ἐν τῇ
were cutting branches from the trees and were spreading in the

**9** ὁδῷ. οἱ δὲ ὄχλοι οἱ προάγοντες καὶ οἱ ἀκολουθοῦντες
way. the And crowds, the (ones) going before and the (ones) following,

ἔκραζον, λέγοντες, Ὡσαννὰ τῷ υἱῷ Δαβίδ· εὐλογημένος ὁ
were crying out, saying, Hosanna to the Son of David! Blessed (is) He

ἐρχόμενος ἐν ὀνόματι Κυρίου· Ὡσαννὰ ἐν τοῖς ὑψίστοις.
coming in (the) name of the Lord; Hosanna in the highest!

**10** καὶ εἰσελθόντος αὐτοῦ εἰς Ἱεροσόλυμα, ἐσείσθη πᾶσα ἡ
And entering He into Jerusalem, was shaken all the

**11** πόλις, λέγουσα, Τίς ἐστιν οὗτος; οἱ δὲ ὄχλοι ἔλεγον,
city, saying, Who is this? the And crowds said,

Οὗτός ἐστιν Ἰησοῦς ὁ προφήτης, ὁ ἀπὸ Ναζαρὲθ τῆς
This is Jesus the prophet, the (one) from Nazareth —

Γαλιλαίας.
of Galilee.

**12** Καὶ εἰσῆλθεν ὁ Ἰησοῦς εἰς τὸ ἱερὸν τοῦ Θεοῦ, καὶ ἐξέβαλε
And went in — Jesus into the Temple — of God, and threw out

πάντας τοὺς πωλοῦντας καὶ ἀγοράζοντας ἐν τῷ ἱερῷ, καὶ
all the (ones) selling and buying in the Temple. And

τὰς τραπέζας τῶν κολλυβιστῶν κατέστρεψε, καὶ τὰς
the tables of the moneychangers He overthrew, and the

**13** καθέδρας τῶν πωλούντων τὰς περιστεράς. καὶ λέγει αὐτοῖς,
seats of the (ones) selling the doves. And He says to them,

Γέγραπται, Ὁ οἶκός μου οἶκος προσευχῆς κληθήσεται·
It has been written, The house of Me a house of prayer shall be called;

**14** ὑμεῖς δὲ αὐτὸν ἐποιήσατε σπήλαιον λῃστῶν. καὶ προσῆλθον
you but it have made a den of robbers. And came near

and lame ones came to
Him in the Temple, and He
healed them. [15] But the
chief priests and the scribes
seeing the wonders which
He worked, and the chil-
dren crying in the Temple,
and saying, Hosanna to the
son of David, they were
indignant; [16] and said to
Him, Do you hear what
these say? And Jesus said
to them, Yes; have you
never read, "Out of the
mouth of babes and suck-
lings You have perfected
praise"? [17] And having
left them, He went out of
the city to Bethany, and
spent the night there.

[18] Now early in the
morning, coming back into
the city, He hungered;
[19] and seeing one fig-
tree by the roadside, He
came to it, and found
nothing on it except leaves
only. And He said to it,
Let there be no more fruit
from you forever. And the
fig-tree immediately dried
up. [20] And seeing (it),
the disciples wondered,
saying, How quickly the
fig-tree is dried up!
[21] And answering Jesus
said to them, Truly, I say
to you, If you have faith
and do not doubt, not only
shall you do the (miracle)
of the fig-tree, but even if
you should say to this
mountain, Be moved and
be thrown into the sea, it
shall happen. [22] And all
things, whatever you may
ask in prayer, believing,
you shall receive.

[23] And on coming
into the Temple (and)
teaching, the chief priests
and the elders of the
people came up to Him,
saying, By what authority
do You do these things?
And who gave You this
authority? [24] And an-
swering Jesus said to them,
I will also ask you one
thing, which if you tell Me,
I also will tell you by what
authority I do these things.
[25] The baptism of John,
where was it from? From
Heaven, or from men?
[26] And they reasoned
with themselves, saying, If
we should say, From
Heaven, He will say to us,
Then why did you not
believe him? But if we
should say, From men, we

αὐτῷ τυφλοὶ καὶ χωλοὶ ἐν τῷ ἱερῷ· καὶ ἐθεράπευσεν αὐτούς.
to Him blind and lame in the Temple. and He healed them.
15 ἰδόντες δὲ οἱ ἀρχιερεῖς καὶ οἱ γραμματεῖς τὰ θαυμάσια ἃ
seeing But the chief priests and the scribes the wonders which
ἐποίησε, καὶ τοὺς παῖδας κράζοντας ἐν τῷ ἱερῷ, καὶ λέγον-
He did and the children crying out in the Temple, and saying,
16 τας, Ὡσαννὰ τῷ υἱῷ Δαβὶδ, ἠγανάκτησαν, καὶ εἶπον αὐτῷ,
Hosanna to the Son of David, they were incensed, and said to Him,
Ἀκούεις τί οὗτοι λέγουσιν; ὁ δὲ Ἰησοῦς λέγει αὐτοῖς, Ναί·
Do you hear what these say? And Jesus says to them, Yes.
οὐδέποτε ἀνέγνωτε ὅτι Ἐκ στόματος νηπίων καὶ θηλα-
never Did you read, — Out of (the) mouth of babes and sucking
17 ζόντων κατηρτίσω αἶνον; καὶ καταλιπὼν αὐτοὺς ἐξῆλθεν
(ones) You have perfected praise? And leaving them He went
ἔξω τῆς πόλεως εἰς Βηθανίαν, καὶ ηὐλίσθη ἐκεῖ.
out of the city to Bethany, and lodged there.
18 Πρωΐας δὲ ἐπανάγων εἰς τὴν πόλιν, ἐπείνασε· καὶ ἰδὼν
19 early And returning to the city, He hungered.And seeing
συκῆν μίαν ἐπὶ τῆς ὁδοῦ, ἦλθεν ἐπ' αὐτήν, καὶ οὐδὲν εὗρεν
fig-tree one on the way, He went up (to) it, and nothing found
ἐν αὐτῇ εἰ μὴ φύλλα μόνον· καὶ λέγει αὐτῇ, Μηκέτι ἐκ σοῦ
in it, except leaves only, and He says to it, No longer of you
καρπὸς γένηται εἰς τὸν αἰῶνα. καὶ ἐξηράνθη παραχρῆμα ἡ
fruit may be to the age. And was dried up instantly the
20 συκῆ. καὶ ἰδόντες οἱ μαθηταὶ ἐθαύμασαν, λέγοντες, Πῶς
fig-tree. And seeing, the disciples marveled, saying, How
21 παραχρῆμα ἐξηράνθη ἡ συκῆ; ἀποκριθεὶς δὲ ὁ Ἰησοῦς
instantly was withered the fig-tree! answering And — Jesus
εἶπεν αὐτοῖς, Ἀμὴν λέγω ὑμῖν, ἐὰν ἔχητε πίστιν, καὶ μὴ
said to them, Truly I say to you, If you have faith and not
διακριθῆτε, οὐ μόνον τὸ τῆς συκῆς ποιήσετε, ἀλλὰ κἂν τῷ
do doubt, not only that of the fig-tree you will do, but also if to
ὄρει τούτῳ εἴπητε, Ἄρθητι καὶ βλήθητι εἰς τὴν θάλασσαν,
mountain this you say, Be taken and thrown into the sea,
22 γενήσεται. καὶ πάντα ὅσα ἂν αἰτήσητε ἐν τῇ προσευχῇ,
it will be. And all things, whatever you ask in — prayer,
πιστεύοντες, λήψεσθε.
believing, you will receive.
23 Καὶ ἐλθόντι αὐτῷ εἰς τὸ ἱερόν, προσῆλθον αὐτῷ διδά-
And coming He into the Temple, approached to Him teach-
σκοντι οἱ ἀρχιερεῖς καὶ οἱ πρεσβύτεροι τοῦ λαοῦ, λέγοντες,
ing the chief priests and the elders of the people, saying,
Ἐν ποίᾳ ἐξουσίᾳ ταῦτα ποιεῖς; καὶ τίς σοι ἔδωκε τὴν
By what authority these things do you? And who to you gave —
24 ἐξουσίαν ταύτην; ἀποκριθεὶς δὲ ὁ Ἰησοῦς εἶπεν αὐτοῖς,
authority this? answering And — Jesus said to them,
Ἐρωτήσω ὑμᾶς κἀγὼ λόγον ἕνα, ὃν ἐὰν εἴπητέ μοι, κἀγὼ
will question you I also word one, which if you tell Me, I also
25 ὑμῖν ἐρῶ ἐν ποίᾳ ἐξουσίᾳ ταῦτα ποιῶ. τὸ βάπτισμα Ἰωάννου
you I will tell by what authority these I do: The baptism of John,
πόθεν ἦν; ἐξ οὐρανοῦ ἢ ἐξ ἀνθρώπων; οἱ δὲ διελογίζοντο
whence was it? From Heaven or from men? they And reasoned
παρ' ἑαυτοῖς, λέγοντες, Ἐὰν εἴπωμεν, Ἐξ οὐρανοῦ, ἐρεῖ ἡμῖν,
by themselves, saying, If we say from Heaven, He will say to us
26 Διατί οὖν οὐκ ἐπιστεύσατε αὐτῷ; ἐὰν δὲ εἴπωμεν, Ἐξ ἀνθρώ-
Why then not you did believe him? if But we say from men,

πων, φοβούμεθα τὸν ὄχλον· πάντες γὰρ ἔχουσι τὸν Ἰωάννην
we fear   the crowd.   all    For   hold   —   John

fear the people. For all hold John to be a prophet. [27] And answering Jesus they said, We do not know. He also said to them, Neither do I tell you by what authority I do these things. [28] But what do you think? A man had two children, and having come to the first he said, Child, go today, work in my vineyard. [29] And answering he said, I will not; but afterward having repented he went. [30] And having come to the second, he said likewise. And answering he said, I (go), sir; and did not go. [31] Which of the two did the will of the father? They said to him, The first. Jesus said to them, Truly I say to you, that the tax-collectors and the harlots go before you into the kingdom of God. [32] For John came to you in (the) way of righteousness, and you did not believe him; but the tax-collectors and the harlots believed him; but having seen you did not repent afterwards to believe him.

**27** ὡς προφήτην. καὶ ἀποκριθέντες τῷ Ἰησοῦ εἶπον, Οὐκ
as   a prophet.   And   answering   —   Jesus they said,   not

οἴδαμεν. ἔφη αὐτοῖς καὶ αὐτός, Οὐδὲ ἐγὼ λέγω ὑμῖν ἐν ποίᾳ
we do know. said to them And He,   Neither   I   tell you by what

**28** ἐξουσίᾳ ταῦτα ποιῶ. τί δὲ ὑμῖν δοκεῖ; ἄνθρωπος εἶχε
authority these things I do.   what But to you seems it?    A man    had

τέκνα δύο, καὶ προσελθὼν τῷ πρώτῳ εἶπε, Τέκνον, ὕπαγε,
children two, and having come to the first he said, Child,   go,

**29** σήμερον ἐργάζου ἐν τῷ ἀμπελῶνί μου. ὁ δὲ ἀποκριθεὶς εἶπεν,
today    work   in the   vineyard of me. he And answering said,

**30** Οὐ θέλω· ὕστερον δὲ μεταμεληθείς, ἀπῆλθε. καὶ προσελθὼν
not I will. afterwards But   feeling sorry   he went. And having come

τῷ δευτέρῳ εἶπεν ὡσαύτως. ὁ δὲ ἀποκριθεὶς εἶπεν, Ἐγώ,
to the second, he said likewise.   he And answering   said,   I (go),

**31** κύριε· καὶ οὐκ ἀπῆλθε. τίς ἐκ τῶν δύο ἐποίησε τὸ θέλημα
lord,   and not did leave. Who of the two   did    the    will

τοῦ πατρός; λέγουσιν αὐτῷ, Ὁ πρῶτος. λέγει αὐτοῖς ὁ
of the father? They say to Him, The first.    says to them —

Ἰησοῦς, Ἀμὴν λέγω ὑμῖν, ὅτι οἱ τελῶναι καὶ αἱ πόρναι
Jesus,   Truly   I say to you, that the tax-collectors and the harlots

**32** προάγουσιν ὑμᾶς εἰς τὴν βασιλείαν τοῦ Θεοῦ. ἦλθε γὰρ
go before    you into the kingdom    — of God. came For

πρὸς ὑμᾶς Ἰωάννης ἐν ὁδῷ δικαιοσύνης, καὶ οὐκ ἐπιστεύ-
to   you    John   in (the) way of righteousness, and not you did

σατε αὐτῷ· οἱ δὲ τελῶναι καὶ αἱ πόρναι ἐπίστευσαν αὐτῷ·
believe him; the but tax-collectors and the harlots believed    him.

ὑμεῖς δὲ ἰδόντες οὐ μετεμελήθητε ὕστερον τοῦ πιστεῦσαι
you And seeing,   not felt sorry    afterwards — to believe

αὐτῷ.
him.

[33] Hear another parable: There was a certain man, a master of a house, who planted a vineyard and placed a hedge around it, and dug a winepress in it, and built a tower, and rented it to vinedressers, and left the country. [34] And when the season of the fruits came, he sent his servants to the vinedressers to receive his fruits. [35] And the husbandmen having taken his servants, they beat one, and they killed another, and they stoned another. [36] Again he sent other servants, more than the first, and they did to them in like manner. [37] And at last he sent his son to them, saying, They will have respect for my son. [38] But seeing the son, the vinedressers said among themselves, This is the heir;

**33** Ἄλλην παραβολὴν ἀκούσατε. ἄνθρωπός τις ἦν οἰκοδε-
Another    parable    hear:     A man   certain was a house-

σπότης, ὅστις ἐφύτευσεν ἀμπελῶνα, καὶ φραγμὸν αὐτῷ
master,   who   planted    a vineyard,    and a hedge   it

περιέθηκε, καὶ ὤρυξεν ἐν αὐτῷ ληνόν, καὶ ᾠκοδόμησε πύργον,
put around, and dug in   it a winepress, and built    a tower,

**34** καὶ ἐξέδοτο αὐτὸν γεωργοῖς, καὶ ἀπεδήμησεν. ὅτε δὲ
and rented    it   to vinedressers, and departed.    when And

ἤγγισεν ὁ καιρὸς τῶν καρπῶν, ἀπέστειλε τοὺς δούλους
drew near the time of the fruits,   he sent    the    slaves

αὐτοῦ πρὸς τοὺς γεωργούς, λαβεῖν τοὺς καρποὺς αὐτοῦ·
of him to the vinedressers, to receive the fruits    of it.

**35** καὶ λαβόντες οἱ γεωργοὶ τοὺς δούλους αὐτοῦ, ὃν μὲν ἔδειραν,
And taking the vinedressers the slaves   of him, this one they beat,

**36** ὃν δὲ ἀπέκτειναν, ὃν δὲ ἐλιθοβόλησαν. πάλιν ἀπέστειλεν
one and they killed;   one and they stoned.    Again   he sent

ἄλλους δούλους πλείονας τῶν πρώτων· καὶ ἐποίησαν αὐτοῖς
other   slaves,   more (than) the   first,   and they did   to them

**37** ὡσαύτως. ὕστερον δὲ ἀπέστειλε πρὸς αὐτοὺς τὸν υἱὸν
likewise.   later   But he sent    to    them    the son

**38** αὐτοῦ, λέγων, Ἐντραπήσονται τὸν υἱόν μου. οἱ δὲ γεωργοὶ
of him, saying, They will respect    the son of me. the But vinedressers

ἰδόντες τὸν υἱὸν εἶπον ἐν ἑαυτοῖς, Οὗτός ἐστιν ὁ κληρονόμος·
seeing    the   son   said among themselves, This   is   the   heir;

come, let us kill him, and get hold of his inheritance. [39] And having taken him, they threw (him) out of the vineyard and killed (him). [40] Therefore, when the lord of the vineyard shall come, what will he do to these vine-dressers? [41] They said to Him, Evil ones! He will miserably destroy them, and he will rent out the vineyard to other vinedres-sers who will give to him the fruits in their seasons. [42] Jesus said to them, Did you never read in the Scriptures, "(The) Stone which the builders rejected is the one that has become the head of the corner: this was from the Lord, and it is wonderful in our eyes"? [43] Because of this I say to you, The kingdom of God shall be taken from you, and it shall be given to a nation bringing forth the fruits of it. [44] And he who falls on this Stone shall be broken; but on whomever it shall fall, it will grind him to powder. [45] And hearing His para-bles, the chief priests and the Pharisees knew that He was speaking about them. [46] And seeking to lay hold of Him, they feared the multitude, because they held Him as a prophet.

### CHAPTER 22

[1] And answering Jesus again spoke to them in parables, saying, [2] The kingdom of Heaven has been compared to a man, a king, who made a wedding feast for his son; [3] and sent his servants to call those who had been invited to the wedding feasts; but they would not come. [4] A-gain he sent other servants, saying, Say to those who have been invited, Behold, I prepared my dinner, my oxen, and the fatlings are killed, and all things ready; come to the wedding feast. [5] But they not listening went away, one to his own field, and another to his

δεῦτε, ἀποκτείνωμεν αὐτόν, καὶ κατάσχωμεν τὴν κληρονο-
come, let us kill      him,      and let us possess  the inheritance

39 μίαν αὐτοῦ. καὶ λαβόντες αὐτὸν ἐξέβαλον ἔξω τοῦ ἀμπε-
of him.     And taking     him,   they threw out   the vine-

40 λῶνος καὶ ἀπέκτειναν. ὅταν οὖν ἔλθη ὁ κύριος τοῦ
yard   and killed         When therefore comes the lord   of the

41 ἀμπελῶνος, τί ποιήσει τοῖς γεωργοῖς ἐκείνοις; λέγουσιν
vineyard,    what will he do  to vinedressers  those?   They say

αὐτῷ, Κακοὺς κακῶς ἀπολέσει αὐτούς, καὶ τὸν ἀμπελῶνα
to Him, Bad men, badly  he will destroy them,   and the   vineyard

ἐκδόσεται ἄλλοις γεωργοῖς, οἵτινες ἀποδώσουσιν αὐτῷ
he will give out to other vinedressers,  who   will render   to him

42 τοὺς καρποὺς ἐν τοῖς καιροῖς αὐτῶν. λέγει αὐτοῖς ὁ Ἰησοῦς,
the  fruits   in the seasons of them.  says  to them —  Jesus,

Οὐδέποτε ἀνέγνωτε ἐν ταῖς γραφαῖς, Λίθον ὃν ἀπεδοκί-
never    Did you read  in the Scriptures: A stone which rejected

μασαν οἱ οἰκοδομοῦντες, οὗτος ἐγενήθη εἰς κεφαλὴν
the builders,      this (one) became  —  head

γωνίας· παρὰ Κυρίου ἐγένετο αὕτη, καὶ ἔστι θαυμαστὴ ἐν
of corner; from (the) Lord happened  this,  and it is  a wonder  in

43 ὀφθαλμοῖς ἡμῶν; διὰ τοῦτο λέγω ὑμῖν ὅτι ἀρθήσεται ἀφ'
(the) eyes  of us?  Because of this I tell  you,  that will be taken from

ὑμῶν ἡ βασιλεία τοῦ Θεοῦ, καὶ δοθήσεται ἔθνει ποιοῦντι
you  the kingdom  —  of God, and will be given to a nation producing

44 τοὺς καρποὺς ἐν τοῖς καιροῖς αὐτῶν. λέγει αὐτοῖς ὁ Ἰησοῦς,
the  fruits   of it.  And the (one) falling on  —  stone  this

45 συνθλασθήσεται· ἐφ' ὃν δ' ἂν πέση, λικμήσει αὐτόν. καὶ
will be broken up; upon whom but ever it fall,  it will pulverize him. And

ἀκούσαντες οἱ ἀρχιερεῖς καὶ οἱ Φαρισαῖοι τὰς παραβολὰς
hearing    the chief priests and the Pharisees  the  parables

46 αὐτοῦ ἔγνωσαν ὅτι περὶ αὐτῶν λέγει. καὶ ζητοῦντες αὐτὸν
of Him,  they knew that about them He says; and seeking  Him

κρατῆσαι, ἐφοβήθησαν τοὺς ὄχλους, ἐπειδὴ ὡς προφήτην
to seize,  they feared  the crowds,   because as  a prophet

αὐτὸν εἶχον.
Him  they held.

### CHAPTER 22

1 Καὶ ἀποκριθεὶς ὁ Ἰησοῦς πάλιν εἶπεν αὐτοῖς ἐν παρα-
And answering  —  Jesus  again spoke to them in parables,

2 βολαῖς, λέγων, Ὡμοιώθη ἡ βασιλεία τῶν οὐρανῶν ἀνθρώπῳ
saying,    Is likened the kingdom of the heavens  to a man,

3 βασιλεῖ, ὅστις ἐποίησε γάμους τῷ υἱῷ αὐτοῦ· καὶ ἀπέστειλε
a king,  who  made  a wedding feast to the son of him. And  he sent

τοὺς δούλους αὐτοῦ καλέσαι τοὺς κεκλημένους εἰς τοὺς
the  slaves  of him  to call the (ones) being called  to  the

4 γάμους, καὶ οὐκ ἤθελον ἐλθεῖν. πάλιν ἀπέστειλεν ἄλλους
wedding.  And not they desired to come. Again  he sent     other

δούλους, λέγων, Εἴπατε τοῖς κεκλημένοις. Ἰδού, τὸ ἄριστόν
slaves, saying,   Tell the (ones) called,   Behold, the supper

μου ἡτοίμασα, οἱ ταῦροί μου καὶ τὰ σιτιστὰ τεθυμένα, καὶ
of me I have readied; the oxen of me and the fatted beasts are killed, and

5 πάντα ἕτοιμα· δεῦτε εἰς τοὺς γάμους. οἱ δὲ ἀμελήσαντες
all things ready.  Come  to the wedding feast they But not caring

ἀπῆλθον, ὁ μὲν εἰς τὸν ἴδιον ἀγρόν, ὁ δὲ εἰς τὴν ἐμπορίαν
went off,   one  to the  own   field,  one and to the  trading

business. [6] And the rest, having laid hold of his servants, insulted and killed. [7] And having heard, the king was angry; and having sent his army he destroyed those murderers and he burned their city. [8] Then he said to his servants, Indeed the wedding feast is ready, but those who had been invited were not worthy; [9] therefore go into the exits of the highway and invite as many as you shall find to the wedding feast. [10] And those servants having gone out into the highways brought together all, as many as they found, both good and evil; and the wedding feast became full of guests. [11] And coming in to see the guests, the king saw there a man not clothed with a wedding garment; [12] and he said to him, Friend, how did you get in here, not having a wedding garment? But he was speechless. [13] Then the king said to the servants, Having bound his feet and hands, take him away and throw (him) into the outer darkness; there shall be weeping and gnashing of the teeth. [14] For many are called, but few chosen.

[15] Then having gone, the Pharisees took counsel how they might trap Him in words. [16] And they sent to Him their disciples with the Herodians, saying, Teacher, we know that you are true, and teach the way of God in truth; and you do not care about anyone, for you do not look upon the face of men. [17] Then tell us, what do you think? Is it lawful to give tribute to Caesar or not? [18] But knowing their wickedness, Jesus said, Why do you tempt Me, hypocrites? [19] Show Me the tribute coin. And they presented to Him a danarius. [20] And He said to them, Whose image and writing is this? [21] And they said to Him, Caesar's. Then He

6 αὐτοῦ· οἱ δὲ λοιποὶ κρατήσαντες τοὺς δούλους αὐτοῦ
of him; the and rest seizing the slaves of him

7 ὕβρισαν καὶ ἀπέκτειναν. ἀκούσας δὲ ὁ βασιλεὺς ὠργίσθη,
insulted and killed. hearing And the king became angry,
καὶ πέμψας τὰ στρατεύματα αὐτοῦ ἀπώλεσε τοὺς φονεῖς
and sending the armies of him destroyed murderers

8 ἐκείνους, καὶ τὴν πόλιν αὐτῶν ἐνέπρησε. τότε λέγει τοῖς
those, also the city of them burned. Then he says to the
δούλοις αὐτοῦ, Ὁ μὲν γάμος ἕτοιμός ἐστιν, οἱ δὲ κεκλημένοι
slaves of him, the Indeed wedding ready is, those but called

9 οὐκ ἦσαν ἄξιοι. πορεύεσθε οὖν ἐπὶ τὰς διεξόδους τῶν ὁδῶν,
not were worthy. You go therefore onto the exits of the ways,

10 καὶ ὅσους ἂν εὕρητε, καλέσατε εἰς τοὺς γάμους. καὶ ἐξελ-
and as many as you find call to the feast. And going
θόντες οἱ δοῦλοι ἐκεῖνοι εἰς τὰς ὁδοὺς συνήγαγον πάντας
forth — slaves those into the ways gathered all
ὅσους εὗρον, πονηρούς τε καὶ ἀγαθούς· καὶ ἐπλήσθη ὁ
as many as they found, evil both and good; and was filled the

11 γάμος ἀνακειμένων. εἰσελθὼν δὲ ὁ βασιλεὺς θεάσασθαι τοὺς
wedding with recliners. coming in And the king to view those
ἀνακειμένους εἶδεν ἐκεῖ ἄνθρωπον οὐκ ἐνδεδυμένον ἔνδυμα
reclining he saw there a man not being dressed (in) a dress

12 γάμου· καὶ λέγει αὐτῷ, Ἑταῖρε, πῶς εἰσῆλθες ὧδε μὴ ἔχων
of wedding. And he to him, Friend, how did you enter here not having

13 ἔνδυμα γάμου ; ὁ δὲ ἐφιμώθη. τότε εἶπεν ὁ βασιλεὺς τοῖς
a dress of wedding? he But was silent. Then said the king to the
διακόνοις, Δήσαντες αὐτοῦ πόδας καὶ χεῖρας, ἄρατε αὐτὸν
servants, Binding of him (the) feet and hands, take away him
καὶ ἐκβάλετε εἰς τὸ σκότος τὸ ἐξώτερον· ἐκεῖ ἔσται ὁ κλαυθμὸς
and throw out into the darkness outer, there shall be the weeping

14 καὶ ὁ βρυγμὸς τῶν ὀδόντων. πολλοὶ γάρ εἰσι κλητοί, ὀλίγοι
and the gnashing of the teeth. many For are called, few
δὲ ἐκλεκτοί.
but chosen.

15 Τότε πορευθέντες οἱ Φαρισαῖοι συμβούλιον ἔλαβον ὅπως
Then going the Pharisees counsel took so as

16 αὐτὸν παγιδεύσωσιν ἐν λόγῳ. καὶ ἀποστέλλουσιν αὐτῷ
Him they might trap in discourse. And they send forth to Him
τοὺς μαθητὰς αὐτῶν μετὰ τῶν Ἡρωδιανῶν, λέγοντες,
the disciples of them with the Herodians, saying,
Διδάσκαλε, οἴδαμεν ὅτι ἀληθὴς εἶ, καὶ τὴν ὁδὸν τοῦ Θεοῦ
Teacher, we know that truthful you are, and the way — of God
ἐν ἀληθείᾳ διδάσκεις, καὶ οὐ μέλει σοι περὶ οὐδενός, οὐ γὰρ
in truth you teach, and not it concerns you about no one; not for

17 βλέπεις εἰς πρόσωπον ἀνθρώπων. εἰπὲ οὖν ἡμῖν, τί σοι
you look to face of men. Tell therefore us, what you

18 δοκεῖ· ἔξεστι δοῦναι κῆνσον Καίσαρι, ἢ οὔ; γνοὺς δὲ ὁ
think: Is it lawful to give tribute to Caesar, or not? knowing But
Ἰησοῦς τὴν πονηρίαν αὐτῶν εἶπε, Τί με πειράζετε, ὑπο-
Jesus the wickedness of them, said, Why Me you tempt, hypo-

19 κριταί ; ἐπιδείξατέ μοι τὸ νόμισμα τοῦ κήνσου. οἱ δὲ προσ-
crites? Show Me the coin of the tribute. they And brought

20 ἤνεγκαν αὐτῷ δηνάριον. καὶ λέγει αὐτοῖς, Τίνος ἡ εἰκὼν
to Him a denarius. And He says to them, Of whom — image

21 αὕτη καὶ ἡ ἐπιγραφή ; λέγουσιν αὐτῷ, Καίσαρος. τότε λέγει
this and — superscription? They say to Him, Of Caesar. Then He says

said to them, Then give to Caesar the things of Caesar, and to God the things of God. [22] And having heard, they wondered; and leaving him went away.

αὐτοῖς, Ἀπόδοτε οὖν τὰ Καίσαρος Καίσαρι· καὶ τὰ τοῦ
to them,   Render   then the things of Caesar to Caesar, and the things of

**22** Θεοῦ τῷ Θεῷ. καὶ ἀκούσαντες ἐθαύμασαν· καὶ ἀφέντες αὐτὸν
of God – to God. And hearing      they marveled, and leaving   Him

ἀπῆλθον.
they went away.

[23] On that day Sadducees came to him, who say there is no resurrection; and they questioned Him, [24] saying, Teacher, Moses, said, If anyone should die not having children, his brother shall marry his wife and shall raise up seed to his brother. [25] Now there were seven brothers with us; and having married the first died, and not having seed left his wife to his brother. [26] In like manner also the second, and the third, to the seven. [27] And last of all the woman also died. [28] Therefore, in the resurrection, of which of the seven shall she be wife? For all had her. [29] And answering Jesus said to them, You err, not knowing the Scriptures nor the power of God. [30] For in the resurrection they neither marry nor are given in marriage, but they are as the angels of God in Heaven. [31] But concerning the resurrection of the dead, have you not read that which was spoken to you by God, saying, [32] "I am the God of Abraham and the God of Isaac and the God of Jacob"? God is not God of the dead, but of the living. [33] And having heard, the crowds were astonished at His teaching.

[34] But the Pharisees, having heard that He had silenced the Sadducees, were gathered together. [35] And one of them, a doctor of the Law, tempting Him and saying, [36] Teacher, which (is the) great commandment in the Law? [37] And Jesus said to him, You shall love (the) Lord your God with all your heart, and with all your soul, and with all your mind. [38] This is (the) first and great commandment. [39] And (the) second (is)

**23** Ἐν ἐκείνῃ τῇ ἡμέρᾳ προσῆλθον αὐτῷ Σαδδουκαῖοι, οἱ
On  that  –  day   approaching  to Him  Sadducees,  who

λέγοντες μὴ εἶναι ἀνάστασιν, καὶ ἐπηρώτησαν αὐτόν,
are saying not  to be  a resurrection. And they questioned  Him,

**24** λέγοντες, Διδάσκαλε, Μωσῆς εἶπεν, Ἐάν τις ἀποθάνῃ μὴ
saying,    Teacher,    Moses said,  If any (man) die  not

ἔχων τέκνα, ἐπιγαμβρεύσει ὁ ἀδελφὸς αὐτοῦ τὴν γυναῖκα
having children, shall take to wife the brother  of him  the  wife

**25** αὐτοῦ, καὶ ἀναστήσει σπέρμα τῷ ἀδελφῷ αὐτοῦ. ἦσαν δὲ
of him, and shall raise up  seed to the brother  of him. were And

παρ' ἡμῖν ἑπτὰ ἀδελφοί· καὶ ὁ πρῶτος γαμήσας ἐτελεύτησε·
with  us  seven brothers; and the first  having married ended (his life)

καὶ μὴ ἔχων σπέρμα, ἀφῆκε τὴν γυναῖκα αὐτοῦ τῷ ἀδελφῷ
and not having seed   left  the  wife  of him to the brother

**26** αὐτοῦ. ὁμοίως καὶ ὁ δεύτερος, καὶ ὁ τρίτος, ἕως τῶν ἑπτά.
of him; likewise also the second,  and the third,  until the  seven.

**27** ὕστερον δὲ πάντων ἀπέθανε καὶ ἡ γυνή. ἐν τῇ οὖν ἀναστάσει,
**28** last   And of all   died  also the woman. in. the Then resurrection,

τίνος τῶν ἑπτὰ ἔσται γυνή; πάντες γὰρ ἔσχον αὐτήν.
of which of the seven will she be wife?  all  For  had  her.

**29** ἀποκριθεὶς δὲ ὁ Ἰησοῦς εἶπεν αὐτοῖς, Πλανᾶσθε, μὴ εἰδότες
answering And – Jesus  said to them, You err,  not knowing

**30** τὰς γραφάς, μηδὲ τὴν δύναμιν τοῦ Θεοῦ. ἐν γὰρ τῇ ἀναστά-
the Scriptures, nor  the  power  – of God. in For the resurrection

σει οὔτε γαμοῦσιν, οὔτε ἐκγαμίζονται, ἀλλ' ὡς ἄγγελοι τοῦ
neither they marry,  nor are given in marriage; but as  angels  –

**31** Θεοῦ ἐν οὐρανῷ εἰσι. περὶ δὲ τῆς ἀναστάσεως τῶν νεκρῶν,
of God. in Heaven they are. about But the resurrection  of the  dead,

**32** οὐκ ἀνέγνωτε τὸ ῥηθὲν ὑμῖν ὑπὸ τοῦ Θεοῦ, λέγοντος, Ἐγώ
not have you read that spoken to you by  –  God,  saying,  I

εἰμι ὁ Θεὸς Ἀβραάμ, καὶ ὁ Θεὸς Ἰσαάκ, καὶ ὁ Θεὸς Ἰακώβ;
am the God of Abraham, and the God of Isaac, and the God of Jacob?

**33** οὐκ ἔστιν ὁ Θεὸς Θεὸς νεκρῶν, ἀλλὰ ζώντων. καὶ ἀκού-
not  is  God  God of the dead, but  of (the) living. And having

σαντες οἱ ὄχλοι ἐξεπλήσσοντο ἐπὶ τῇ διδαχῇ αὐτοῦ.
heard,  the crowds were astounded at  the teaching of Him.

**34** Οἱ δὲ Φαρισαῖοι, ἀκούσαντες ὅτι ἐφίμωσε τοὺς Σαδδου-
the But Pharisees   hearing   that He silenced the Sadducees,

**35** καίους, συνήχθησαν ἐπὶ τὸ αὐτό. καὶ ἐπηρώτησεν εἷς ἐξ
were assembled   together,   and  questioned  one of

**36** αὐτῶν νομικός, πειράζων αὐτόν, καὶ λέγων, Διδάσκαλε,
them, a lawyer,  tempting  Him; and  saying,  Teacher,

**37** ποία ἐντολὴ μεγάλη ἐν τῷ νόμῳ; ὁ δὲ Ἰησοῦς εἶπεν αὐτῷ,
which command (is) great in the Law?  And Jesus said to him,

Ἀγαπήσεις Κύριον τὸν Θεόν σου, ἐν ὅλῃ τῇ καρδίᾳ σου,
You shall love the Lord the God of you, with all the  heart of you,

**38** καὶ ἐν ὅλῃ τῇ ψυχῇ σου, καὶ ἐν ὅλῃ τῇ διανοίᾳ σου. αὕτη
and with all the soul of you, and with all  the mind of you. This

**39** ἐστὶ πρώτη καὶ μεγάλη ἐντολή. δευτέρα δὲ ὁμοία αὐτῇ,
is   the first and  great commandment; second and like  to it,

**40**

like it, you shall love your
neighbor as yourself.
[40] On these two com-
mandments all the Law
and the Prophets hang.

[41] Put the Pharisees
having been assembled
together, Jesus questioned
them, [42] saying, What
do you think about the
Christ? Whose son is He?
They said to Him, of
David. [43] He said to
them, How then does
David in Spirit call Him
Lord, saying, [44] "The
Lord said to my Lord, Sit
on My right hand until I
place Your enemies as a
footstool for Your feet"?
[45] Therefore if David
calls Him Lord, how is He
his son? [46] And no one
was able to answer a word,
nor did anyone dare from
that day to question Him
any more.

### CHAPTER 23

[1] Then Jesus spoke
to the crowds and to His
disciples, [2] saying, The
scribes and the Pharisees
have sat down on Moses'
seat; [3] therefore all
things, whatever they may
tell you to keep, keep and
do. But do not according
to their work, for they say
and do not. [4] For they
bind heavy burdens and
hard (ones) to bear, and
lay (them) on the should-
ers of men; but they will
not move them with their
own finger. [5] And they
do all their works to be
seen by men; and they
make their phylacteries
broad, and enlarge the
borders of their robes;
[6] and love the first place
in the suppers, and the first
seats in the synagogues,
[7] and the greetings in
the market-places, and to
be called by men Rabbi,
Rabbi. [8] But you, be
not called Rabbi; for one is
your Instructor, the Christ;
and you are all brothers.
[9] And do not call (any-
one) father on earth, for
one is your Father, who is
in Heaven. [10] Nor be

Ἀγαπήσεις τὸν πλησίον σου ὡς σεαυτόν. ἐν ταύταις ταῖς
You shall love the neighbor of you as yourself. In these —
δυσὶν ἐντολαῖς ὅλος ὁ νόμος καὶ οἱ προφῆται κρέμανται.
two commandments all the Law and the prophets hang.

41 Συνηγμένων δὲ τῶν Φαρισαίων, ἐπηρώτησεν αὐτοὺς ὁ
having been assembled But the Pharisees, questioned them

42 Ἰησοῦς, λέγων, Τί ὑμῖν δοκεῖ περὶ τοῦ Χριστοῦ; τίνος υἱός
Jesus, saying, What to you seems about the Christ? Of whom son

43 ἐστι; λέγουσιν αὐτῷ, Τοῦ Δαβίδ. λέγει αὐτοῖς, Πῶς οὖν
is He? They say to Him, Of David. He says to them, How then

44 Δαβὶδ ἐν πνεύματι Κύριον αὐτὸν καλεῖ, λέγων, Εἶπεν ὁ
David by (the) Spirit Lord Him does call, saying, Said the
Κύριος τῷ Κυρίῳ μου, Κάθου ἐκ δεξιῶν μου, ἕως ἂν θῶ τοὺς
Lord to the Lord of Me, Sit on the right of Me until I put the

45 ἐχθρούς σου ὑποπόδιον τῶν ποδῶν σου; εἰ οὖν Δαβὶδ
enemies of You (as) a footstool of the feet of You? If, then, David

46 καλεῖ αὐτὸν Κύριον, πῶς υἱὸς αὐτοῦ ἐστι; καὶ οὐδεὶς ἐδύνατο
calls Him Lord, how a son of him is He? And no one was able
αὐτῷ ἀποκριθῆναι λόγον· οὐδὲ ἐτόλμησέ τις ἀπ' ἐκείνης τῆς
Him to answer a word, nor dared anyone from that —
ἡμέρας ἐπερωτῆσαι αὐτὸν οὐκέτι.
day to question Him .no longer.

### CHAPTER 23

1 Τότε ὁ Ἰησοῦς ἐλάλησε τοῖς ὄχλοις καὶ τοῖς μαθηταῖς
Then — Jesus spoke to the crowd and to the disciples

2 αὐτοῦ, λέγων, Ἐπὶ τῆς Μωσέως καθέδρας ἐκάθισαν οἱ
of Him, saying, On the of Moses seat sat the

3 γραμματεῖς καὶ οἱ Φαρισαῖοι· πάντα οὖν ὅσα ἂν εἴπωσιν
scribes and the Pharisees. All things, then, whatever they tell
ὑμῖν τηρεῖν, τηρεῖτε καὶ ποιεῖτε· κατὰ δὲ τὰ ἔργα αὐτῶν μὴ
you to keep, keep and do. after But the works of them not

4 ποιεῖτε, λέγουσι γὰρ καὶ οὐ ποιοῦσι. δεσμεύουσι γὰρ φορτία
do you. they say For and not do. they bind For burdens
βαρέα καὶ δυσβάστακτα, καὶ ἐπιτιθέασιν ἐπὶ τοὺς ὤμους
heavy, and hard to bear, and lay (them) on the shoulders
τῶν ἀνθρώπων, τῷ δὲ δακτύλῳ αὐτῶν οὐ θέλουσι κινῆσαι
— of men; with the but finger of them not they wish to move

5 αὐτά. πάντα δὲ τὰ ἔργα αὐτῶν ποιοῦσι πρὸς τὸ θεαθῆναι
them. all But the works of them they do in order to be seen
τοῖς ἀνθρώποις· πλατύνουσι δὲ τὰ φυλακτήρια αὐτῶν, καὶ
— by men; they broaden And the phylacteries of them, and

6 μεγαλύνουσι τὰ κράσπεδα τῶν ἱματίων αὐτῶν· φιλοῦσί τε
enlarge the fringes of the garments of them; they love and
τὴν πρωτοκλισίαν ἐν τοῖς δείπνοις, καὶ τὰς πρωτοκαθεδρίας
the first couch in the suppers, and the first seats

7 ἐν ταῖς συναγωγαῖς, καὶ τοὺς ἀσπασμοὺς ἐν ταῖς ἀγοραῖς,
in the synagogues, and the greetings in the markets,

8 καὶ καλεῖσθαι ὑπὸ τῶν ἀνθρώπων, ῥαββί, ῥαββί· ὑμεῖς δὲ μὴ
and to be called by — men, Rabbi, Rabbi! you But not
κληθῆτε ῥαββί· εἷς γάρ ἐστιν ὑμῶν ὁ καθηγητής, ὁ Χριστός·
be called Rabbi; one for is of you the leader, the Christ,

9 πάντες δὲ ὑμεῖς ἀδελφοί ἐστε. καὶ πατέρα μὴ καλέσητε ὑμῶν
all and you brothers are. And Father not call of you
ἐπὶ τῆς γῆς· εἷς γάρ ἐστιν ὁ πατὴρ ὑμῶν, ὁ ἐν τοῖς οὐρανοῖς·
on the earth; one for is the Father of you, the (One) in the heavens

called instructors; for one is your Instructor, the Christ. [11] But the greater of you shall be your servant. [12] And whoever will exalt himself shall be humbled; and whoever will humble himself shall be exalted.

[13] But woe to you, scribes and Pharisees, hypocrites, for you devour the houses of widows, and as a pretext praying at great length. Because of this you shall receive more abundant judgment. [14] Woe to you, scribes and Pharisees, for you shut up the kingdom of Heaven before men; for you do not enter, nor do you allow even those who are entering to go in. [15] Woe to you, scribes and Pharisees, hypocrites, for you go about the sea and the dry (land) to make one proselyte; and when he has become (so), you make him twofold more a son of hell than yourselves. [16] Woe to you, blind guides, who say, Whoever shall swear by the Temple, it is nothing; but whoever shall swear by the gold of the Temple, is a debtor. [17] Fools and blind, for which is greater, the gold, or the Temple which sanctifies the gold? [18] And, whoever shall swear by the altar, it is nothing; but whoever shall swear by the gift that (is) on it, is a debtor. [19] Fools and blind, for which (is) greater, the gift, or the altar which sanctifies the gift? [20] He therefore that swears by the altar swears by it and by all things on it. [21] And he that swears by the Temple swears by it and by Him who dwells in it. [22] And he that swears by Heaven swears by the throne of God, and by Him who sits upon it. [23] Woe to you, scribes and Pharisees, hypocrites, for you pay tithes of mint and anise and cummin, and you

**10** μηδὲ κληθῆτε καθηγηταί· εἷς γὰρ ὑμῶν ἐστιν ὁ καθηγητής,
Neither be called leaders; One for of you is the Leader,

**11** ὁ Χριστός. ὁ δὲ μείζων ὑμῶν ἔσται ὑμῶν διάκονος. ὅστις δὲ
**12** the Christ. the And greater of you shall be of you a servant, whoever And

ὑψώσει ἑαυτόν, ταπεινωθήσεται· καὶ ὅστις ταπεινώσει
will exalt himself shall be humbled, and whoever will humble

ἑαυτόν, ὑψωθήσεται.
himself shall be exalted.

**13** Οὐαὶ δὲ ὑμῖν, γραμματεῖς καὶ Φαρισαῖοι, ὑποκριταί, ὅτι
woe But to you, scribes and Pharisees, hypocrites! Because

κλείετε τὴν βασιλείαν τῶν οὐρανῶν ἔμπροσθεν τῶν ἀνθρώ-
you shut the kingdom of the heavens before — men;

πων· ὑμεῖς γὰρ οὐκ εἰσέρχεσθε, οὐδὲ τοὺς εἰσερχομένους
you for not do enter, nor the (ones) entering

ἀφίετε εἰσελθεῖν.
do you allow to enter.

**14** Οὐαὶ ὑμῖν, γραμματεῖς καὶ Φαρισαῖοι, ὑποκριταί, ὅτι
Woe to you, scribes and Pharisees, hypocrites! Because

κατεσθίετε τὰς οἰκίας τῶν χηρῶν, καὶ προφάσει μακρὰ
you devour the houses of the widows, and as a pretext (are) long

προσευχόμενοι· διὰ τοῦτο λήψεσθε περισσότερον κρίμα.
praying. Because of this you will receive more abundant judgment.

**15** Οὐαὶ ὑμῖν, γραμματεῖς καὶ Φαρισαῖοι, ὑποκριταί, ὅτι
Woe to you, scribes and Pharisees, hypocrites! Because

περιάγετε τὴν θάλασσαν καὶ τὴν ξηρὰν ποιῆσαι ἕνα προσή-
you go about the sea and the dry (land) to make one prose-

λυτον, καὶ ὅταν γένηται, ποιεῖτε αὐτὸν υἱὸν γεέννης διπλό-
lyte, and when he becomes, you make him a son of Gehenna twofold

τερον ὑμῶν.
more than you.

**16** Οὐαὶ ὑμῖν, ὁδηγοὶ τυφλοί, οἱ λέγοντες, Ὃς ἂν ὀμόσῃ ἐν
Woe to you, leaders blind, the (ones) saying, Whoever swears by

τῷ ναῷ, οὐδέν ἐστιν· ὃς δ᾽ ἂν ὀμόσῃ ἐν τῷ χρυσῷ τοῦ ναοῦ,
the Temple, nothing it is; who but ever swears by the gold of the Temple,

**17** ὀφείλει. μωροὶ καὶ τυφλοί· τίς γὰρ μείζων ἐστίν, ὁ χρυσός, ἢ
is a debtor. Fools and blind! what For greater is, the gold, or

**18** ὁ ναὸς ὁ ἁγιάζων τὸν χρυσόν; καί, Ὃς ἐὰν ὀμόσῃ ἐν τῷ
the Temple sanctifying the gold? And, whoever swears by the

θυσιαστηρίῳ, οὐδέν ἐστιν· ὃς δ᾽ ἂν ὀμόσῃ ἐν τῷ δώρῳ τῷ
altar, nothing it is; who but ever swears by the gift

**19** ἐπάνω αὐτοῦ, ὀφείλει. μωροὶ καὶ τυφλοί· τί γὰρ μεῖζον,
upon it, is a debtor. Fools and blind! what For is greater

**20** τὸ δῶρον, ἢ τὸ θυσιαστήριον τὸ ἁγιάζον τὸ δῶρον; ὁ οὖν
the gift or the altar — sanctifying the gift? he Then

ὀμόσας ἐν τῷ θυσιαστηρίῳ ὀμνύει ἐν αὐτῷ καὶ ἐν πᾶσι τοῖς
swearing by the altar swears by it and by all the things

**21** ἐπάνω αὐτοῦ· καὶ ὁ ὀμόσας ἐν τῷ ναῷ ὀμνύει ἐν αὐτῷ καὶ ἐν
upon it; and he swearing by the Temple swears by it and by

**22** τῷ κατοικοῦντι αὐτόν· καὶ ὁ ὀμόσας ἐν τῷ οὐρανῷ ὀμνύει
the (One) inhabiting it. And the (one) swearing by Heaven swears

ἐν τῷ θρόνῳ τοῦ Θεοῦ καὶ ἐν τῷ καθημένῳ ἐπάνω αὐτοῦ.
by the throne — of God and by the (One) sitting upon it.

**23** Οὐαὶ ὑμῖν, γραμματεῖς καὶ Φαρισαῖοι, ὑποκριταί, ὅτι
Woe to you, scribes and Pharisees, hypocrites! Because

ἀποδεκατοῦτε τὸ ἡδύοσμον καὶ τὸ ἄνηθον καὶ τὸ κύμινον,
you tithe the mint and the dill and the cummin,

have left aside the weightier (matters) of the Law, judgment, and mercy, and faith; it was right to do these, and not to have left those aside. [24] Blind guides, who strain out the gnat, but swallow the camel!

καὶ ἀφήκατε τὰ βαρύτερα τοῦ νόμου, τὴν κρίσιν καὶ τὸν
and you have left the weightier matters of the law, — judgment and —
ἔλεον καὶ τὴν πίστιν· ταῦτα ἔδει ποιῆσαι, κἀκεῖνα μὴ ἀφιέναι.
mercy and — faith; these things one needs to do, and those not to leave.

**24** ὁδηγοὶ τυφλοί, οἱ διϋλίζοντες τὸν κώνωπα, τὴν δὲ κάμηλον
leaders Blind, the (ones) straining out the gnat, the but camel
καταπίνοντες.
swallowing.

[25] Woe to you, scribes and Pharisees, hypocrites, for you cleanse the outside of the cup and of the dish, but within they are full of robbery and excess. [26] Blind Pharisee! First cleanse the inside of the cup and of the dish, that the outside of them may become clean also. [27] Woe to you, scribes and Pharisees, hypocrites, for you are like whitened graves which outwardly indeed appear beautiful, but within are full of bones of (the) dead and of all uncleanness. [28] So you also indeed outwardly appear righteous to men, but within are full of hypocrisy and lawlessness. [29] Woe to you, scribes and Pharisees, hypocrites, for you build the tombs of the prophets, and adorn the tombs of the righteous, [30] and you say, If we had been in the days of our fathers, we would not have been partakers with them in the blood of the prophets. [31] So you bear witness to yourselves, that you are the sons of those who murdered the prophets; [32] and you fill up the measure of your fathers. [33] Serpents, offspring of vipers, how shall you escape the judgment of hell? [34] Because of this, behold, I send to you prophets and wise ones and scribes; and (some) of them you will kill and crucify, and (some) of them you will scourge in your synagogues, and will persecute from city to city; [35] so that should come on you all (the) righteous blood poured out on the earth from the blood of righteous Abel to the

**25** Οὐαὶ ὑμῖν, γραμματεῖς καὶ Φαρισαῖοι, ὑποκριταί, ὅτι
Woe to you, scribes and Pharisees, hypocrites! Because
καθαρίζετε τὸ ἔξωθεν τοῦ ποτηρίου καὶ τῆς παροψίδος,
you cleanse the outside of the cup and the dish,

**26** ἔσωθεν δὲ γέμουσιν ἐξ ἁρπαγῆς καὶ ἀκρασίας. Φαρισαῖε τυφλέ,
within but they are full of robbery and excess. Pharisee Blind,
καθάρισον πρῶτον τὸ ἐντὸς τοῦ ποτηρίου καὶ τῆς παροψί-
cleanse first the inside of the cup and of the dish,
δος, ἵνα γένηται καὶ τὸ ἐκτὸς αὐτῶν καθαρόν.
that may become also the outside of them clean.

**27** Οὐαὶ ὑμῖν, γραμματεῖς καὶ Φαρισαῖοι, ὑποκριταί, ὅτι
Woe to you, scribes and Pharisees, hypocrites! Because
παρομοιάζετε τάφοις κεκονιαμένοις, οἵτινες ἔξωθεν μὲν
you are like graves whitewashed, who outwardly indeed
φαίνονται ὡραῖοι, ἔσωθεν δὲ γέμουσιν ὀστέων νεκρῶν καὶ
appear beautiful, within but are full of bones of the dead and

**28** πάσης ἀκαθαρσίας. οὕτω καὶ ὑμεῖς ἔξωθεν μὲν φαίνεσθε τοῖς
of all uncleanness. So also you outwardly indeed appear —
ἀνθρώποις δίκαιοι, ἔσωθεν δὲ μεστοί ἐστε ὑποκρίσεως καὶ
to men righteous, within but full are of hypocrisy and
ἀνομίας.
lawlessness.

**29** Οὐαὶ ὑμῖν, γραμματεῖς καὶ Φαρισαῖοι, ὑποκριταί, ὅτι
Woe to you, scribes and Pharisees, hypocrites! Because
οἰκοδομεῖτε τοὺς τάφους τῶν προφητῶν, καὶ κοσμεῖτε τὰ
you build the graves of the prophets, and decorate the

**30** μνημεῖα τῶν δικαίων, καὶ λέγετε, Εἰ ἦμεν ἐν ταῖς ἡμέραις
monuments of the righteous, and say, If we had been in the days
τῶν πατέρων ἡμῶν, οὐκ ἂν ἦμεν κοινωνοὶ αὐτῶν ἐν τῷ
of the fathers of us, not would we have been sharers of them in the

**31** αἵματι τῶν προφητῶν. ὥστε μαρτυρεῖτε ἑαυτοῖς ὅτι υἱοί
blood of the prophets. So you witness to yourselves that sons

**32** ἐστε τῶν φονευσάντων τοὺς προφήτας· καὶ ὑμεῖς πληρώσατε
you are of those murdering the prophets and you fill up

**33** τὸ μέτρον τῶν πατέρων ὑμῶν. ὄφεις, γεννήματα ἐχιδνῶν,
the measure of the fathers of you. Serpents! Offspring of vipers!

**34** πῶς φύγητε ἀπὸ τῆς κρίσεως τῆς γεέννης; διὰ τοῦτο, ἰδού,
How do you escape from the judgment — of Gehenna? Therefore, behold,
ἐγὼ ἀποστέλλω πρὸς ὑμᾶς προφήτας καὶ σοφοὺς καὶ γραμ-
I send to you prophets and wise ones and scribes;
ματεῖς· καὶ ἐξ αὐτῶν ἀποκτενεῖτε καὶ σταυρώσετε, καὶ ἐξ
and of them you will kill and crucify; and of
αὐτῶν μαστιγώσετε ἐν ταῖς συναγωγαῖς ὑμῶν καὶ διώξετε
them you will scourge in the synagogues of you, and persecute

**35** ἀπὸ πόλεως εἰς πόλιν· ὅπως ἔλθῃ ἐφ' ὑμᾶς πᾶν αἷμα δίκαιον
from city to city; so comes upon you all blood righteous
ἐκχυνόμενον ἐπὶ τῆς γῆς, ἀπὸ τοῦ αἵματος Ἄβελ τοῦ
being poured out on the earth, from the blood of Abel the

blood of Zechariah the son of Berechiah, whom you murdered between the Temple and the altar. [36] Truly I say to you, All these things shall come upon this generation. [37] Jerusalem, Jerusalem, who killed the prophets and stoned those who have been sent to her, how often I would have gathered your children together, in the way a hen gathers her chicks from under (her) wings, and you would not! [38] Behold, your house is left to you desolate. [39] For I say to you, In no way shall you see Me from now on until you say, "Blessed is He who comes in (the) name of (the) Lord."

δικαίου, ἕως τοῦ αἵματος Ζαχαρίου υἱοῦ Βαραχίου, ἐν
righteous, to the blood of Zachariah (the) son of Barachiah, whom

36 ἐφονεύσατε μεταξὺ τοῦ ναοῦ καὶ τοῦ θυσιαστηρίου. ἀμὴν
you murdered between the Temple and the altar. Truly

λέγω ὑμῖν, ἥξει ταῦτα πάντα ἐπὶ τὴν γενεὰν ταύτην.
I say to you, will come all these things on — generation this.

37 Ἰερουσαλήμ, Ἰερουσαλήμ, ἡ ἀποκτείνουσα τοὺς προφή-
Jerusalem, Jerusalem, the (one) killing the prophets

τας καὶ λιθοβολοῦσα τοὺς ἀπεσταλμένους πρὸς αὐτήν,
and stoning the (ones) sent to her,

ποσάκις ἠθέλησα ἐπισυναγαγεῖν τὰ τέκνα σου, ὃν τρόπον
how often I desired to gather together the children of you, in the way

ἐπισυνάγει ὄρνις τὰ νοσσία ἑαυτῆς ὑπὸ τὰς πτέρυγας, καὶ
gathers together a bird the young of her under the wings, and

38 οὐκ ἠθελήσατε. ἰδού, ἀφίεται ὑμῖν ὁ οἶκος ὑμῶν ἔρημος.
not you desired. Behold, is left to you the house of you desolate;

39 λέγω γὰρ ὑμῖν, Οὐ μή με ἴδητε ἀπ' ἄρτι, ἕως ἂν εἴπητε,
I say For to you, Not at all Me shall you see from now until you say,

Εὐλογημένος ὁ ἐρχόμενος ἐν ὀνόματι Κυρίου.
Blessed the (one) coming in (the) name of (the) Lord.

## CHAPTER 24

[1] And going out, Jesus left the Temple. And His disciples came to point out to Him the buildings of the Temple. [2] But Jesus said to them, Do you not see all these things? Truly I say to you, There shall not be left here (one) stone on (a) stone which shall not be thrown down. [3] And as He was sitting on the Mount of Olives, the disciples came to Him apart, saying, Tell us, when shall these things be? And, what (is) the sign of Your coming and of the end of the age? [4] And answering Jesus said to them, Be careful, lest anyone mislead you. [5] For many will come in My name, saying, I am the Christ; and they will mislead many. [6] But you shall begin to hear of wars and rumors of wars. See, do not be disturbed; for all these things must take place, but the end is not yet. [7] For nation shall rise up against nation, and kingdom against kingdom; and there shall be famines and plagues and earthquakes in (many) places. [8] But all these (are) a beginning of sorrows. [9] Then they will deliver you up to trouble, and will kill you:

## CHAPTER 24

1 Καὶ ἐξελθὼν ὁ Ἰησοῦς ἐπορεύετο ἀπὸ τοῦ ἱεροῦ· καὶ
And going forth — Jesus went away from the Temple, and

προσῆλθον οἱ μαθηταὶ αὐτοῦ ἐπιδεῖξαι αὐτῷ τὰς οἰκοδομὰς
came up the disciples of Him to show Him the buildings

2 τοῦ ἱεροῦ. ὁ δὲ Ἰησοῦς εἶπεν αὐτοῖς, Οὐ βλέπετε πάντα
of the Temple. And Jesus said to them, Not you see all

ταῦτα; ἀμὴν λέγω ὑμῖν, οὐ μὴ ἀφεθῇ ὧδε λίθος ἐπὶ λίθον, ὃς
these? Truly I say to you, Not at all will be left here stone on stone which

οὐ μὴ καταλυθήσεται.
not at all shall be thrown down.

3 Καθημένου δὲ αὐτοῦ ἐπὶ τοῦ ὄρους τῶν ἐλαιῶν, προσῆλ-
sitting And He on the mount of the olives, came

θον αὐτῷ οἱ μαθηταὶ κατ' ἰδίαν, λέγοντες, Εἰπὲ ἡμῖν, πότε
up to Him the disciples privately, saying, Tell us, when

ταῦτα ἔσται; καὶ τί τὸ σημεῖον τῆς σῆς παρουσίας, καὶ τῆς
these things will be; and what the sign of Your presence, and of the

4 συντελείας τοῦ αἰῶνος; καὶ ἀποκριθεὶς ὁ Ἰησοῦς εἶπεν αὐτοῖς,
termination of the age? And answering — Jesus said to them,

5 Βλέπετε, μή τις ὑμᾶς πλανήσῃ. πολλοὶ γὰρ ἐλεύσονται ἐπὶ
See, not any you misleads. many For will come on

τῷ ὀνόματί μου, λέγοντες, Ἐγώ εἰμι ὁ Χριστός· καὶ πολλοὺς
the name of Me, saying, I am the Christ; and many

6 πλανήσουσι. μελλήσετε δὲ ἀκούειν πολέμους καὶ ἀκοὰς
will cause to err. you will be about But to hear of wars and rumors

πολέμων· ὁρᾶτε, μὴ θροεῖσθε· δεῖ γὰρ πάντα γενέσθαι· ἀλλ'
of wars. See, do not be upset; it is right for all things to happen, but

7 οὔπω ἐστὶ τὸ τέλος. ἐγερθήσεται γὰρ ἔθνος ἐπὶ ἔθνος, καὶ
not yet is the end. will be raised For nation against nation, and

βασιλεία ἐπὶ βασιλείαν· καὶ ἔσονται λιμοὶ καὶ λοιμοὶ καὶ
kingdom against kingdom; and there will be famines and plagues and

8
9 σεισμοὶ κατὰ τόπους. πάντα δὲ ταῦτα ἀρχὴ ὠδίνων. τότε
earthquakes against places all but these things beginning of throes. Then

παραδώσουσιν ὑμᾶς εἰς θλῖψιν, καὶ ἀποκτενοῦσιν ὑμᾶς· καὶ
they will deliver up you to affliction, and will kill you, and

and you will be hated by all nations for My name's sake. [10] And then many will be offended, and they will deliver up one another, and will hate one another; [11] and many false prophets will arise and will mislead many; [12] and because lawlessness shall have been multiplied, the love of many will grow cold; [13] but he who endures to (the) end, he shall be saved. [14] And this gospel of the kingdom shall be preached in all the earth, for a testimony to all the nations; and then shall come the end. [15] Therefore, when you shall see the abomination of desolation, which was spoken of by Daniel the prophet, standing in (the) holy place — he who reads let him understand — [16] then let those in Judea flee to the mountains; [17] he on the housetop, let him not come down to take anything out of his house; [18] and he in the field, let him not turn back to take his clothes. [19] But woe to those that are with child, and to those suckling in those days. [20] And pray that your flight may not be in winter, nor on the sabbath; [21] for there shall be great trouble, such as has not happened from (the) beginning of (the) world until now; no, nor ever shall be. [22] And unless those days had been shortened, not any flesh would have been saved; but on account of the elect, those days shall be shortened. [23] Then if anyone say to you, Behold, here (is) the Christ; or, Here, do not believe. [24] For the false christs will arise, and false prophets, and give great signs and wonders, so as to mislead, if possible, even the elect. [25] Behold, I have told you beforehand. [26] Then if they say to you, Behold, He is in the wilderness; do not go out. Behold, in the inner rooms, do not believe. [27] For as the lightning comes from

ἔσεσθε μισούμενοι ὑπὸ πάντων τῶν ἐθνῶν διὰ τὸ ὄνομά μου.
you will be hated by all the nations for the name of Me.

10 καὶ τότε σκανδαλισθήσονται πολλοί, καὶ ἀλλήλους παραδώ-
And then will be offended many, and one another will

11 σουσι, καὶ μισήσουσιν ἀλλήλους. καὶ πολλοὶ ψευδοπρο-
deliver, and they will hate one another. And many false

12 φῆται ἐγερθήσονται, καὶ πλανήσουσι πολλούς. καὶ διὰ τὸ
prophets will be raised up, and will cause to err many; and because of

πληθυνθῆναι τὴν ἀνομίαν, ψυγήσεται ἡ ἀγάπη τῶν
shall have been multiplied lawlessness, will grow cold the love of the

13
14 πολλῶν· ὁ δὲ ὑπομείνας εἰς τέλος, οὗτος σωθήσεται. καὶ
many. the (one) But enduring to (the) end, this one will be saved. And

κηρυχθήσεται τοῦτο τὸ εὐαγγέλιον τῆς βασιλείας ἐν ὅλη
will be proclaimed this — gospel of the kingdom in all

τῇ οἰκουμένη εἰς μαρτύριον πᾶσι τοῖς ἔθνεσι· καὶ τότε ἥξει
the inhabited earth for a testimony to all the nations, and then will come

τὸ τέλος.
the end.

15 Ὅταν οὖν ἴδητε τὸ βδέλυγμα τῆς ἐρημώσεως, τὸ ῥηθὲν διὰ
When therefore you see the abomination of desolation — spoken via

Δανιὴλ τοῦ προφήτου, ἑστὼς ἐν τόπῳ ἁγίῳ (ὁ ἀναγινώ-
Daniel the prophet, standing in place holy [the one reading

16 σκων νοείτω), τότε οἱ ἐν τῇ Ἰουδαίᾳ φευγέτωσαν ἐπὶ τὰ
let him understand] then the(se) in Judea, let them flee upon the

17 ὄρη· ὁ ἐπὶ τοῦ δώματος μὴ καταβαινέτω ἆραί τι ἐκ τῆς
mounts, he on the housetop not let him descend to take things from the

18 οἰκίας αὐτοῦ· καὶ ὁ ἐν τῷ ἀγρῷ μὴ ἐπιστρεψάτω ὀπίσω
house of him; and the (one) in the field, not let him return behind

19 ἆραι τὰ ἱμάτια αὐτοῦ. οὐαὶ δὲ ταῖς ἐν γαστρὶ ἐχούσαις καὶ
to take the garment of him. Woe And to the(se) in womb having and

20 ταῖς θηλαζούσαις ἐν ἐκείναις ταῖς ἡμέραις. προσεύχεσθε δὲ
to those suckling in those — days. pray And

ἵνα μὴ γένηται ἡ φυγὴ ὑμῶν χειμῶνος, μηδὲ ἐν σαββάτῳ·
that will not occur the flight of you of winter, nor on a sabbath;

21 ἔσται γὰρ τότε θλῖψις μεγάλη, οἵα οὐ γέγονεν ἀπ' ἀρχῆς
will be for then affliction great, such as not has occurred from origin

22 κόσμου ἕως τοῦ νῦν, οὐδ' οὐ μὴ γένηται. καὶ εἰ μὴ ἐκολοβώ-
of world until now; neither by no means occur. And except were cut

θησαν αἱ ἡμέραι ἐκεῖναι, οὐκ ἂν ἐσώθη πᾶσα σάρξ· διὰ δὲ
short — days those, not would be saved any flesh; because of the

23 τοὺς ἐκλεκτοὺς κολοβωθήσονται αἱ ἡμέραι ἐκεῖναι. τότε ἐὰν
the elect will be cut short — days those. Then if

τις ὑμῖν εἴπη, Ἰδού, ὧδε ὁ Χριστός, ἢ ὧδε, μὴ πιστεύσητε.
anyone to you says, Behold, here the Christ; or, Here; not believe;

24 ἐγερθήσονται γὰρ ψευδόχριστοι καὶ ψευδοπροφῆται, καὶ
will arise for false Christs and false prophets, and

δώσουσι σημεῖα μεγάλα καὶ τέρατα, ὥστε πλανῆσαι, εἰ
they will give signs great and wonders, so as to cause to err, if

25
26 δυνατόν, καὶ τοὺς ἐκλεκτούς. ἰδού, προείρηκα ὑμῖν. ἐὰν οὖν
possible, even the elect. Behold, I tell before to you. If then

εἴπωσιν ὑμῖν, Ἰδού, ἐν τῇ ἐρήμῳ ἐστί, μὴ ἐξέλθητε· Ἰδού,
they say to you, Behold, in the desert He is, not go forth; Behold,

27 ἐν τοῖς ταμείοις, μὴ πιστεύσητε. ὥσπερ γὰρ ἡ ἀστραπὴ
in the private rooms, not believe. as For the lightning

ἐξέρχεται ἀπὸ ἀνατολῶν καὶ φαίνεται ἕως δυσμῶν, οὕτως
comes forth from (the) east and shines as far as (the) west, so

the coming of the Son of man also. [28] For wherever the dead body may be, there the eagles will be gathered together. [29] But immediately after the trouble of those days, the sun shall be darkened, and the moon shall give her light, and the stars shall fall from the sky, and the powers of the heavens shall be shaken. [30] And then shall appear the sign of the Son of man in the sky; and then all the tribes of the land shall wail, and they shall see the Son of man coming on the clouds of the sky with power and great .glory. [31] And He shall send His angels with a great sound of a trumpet, and they shall gather together His elect from the four winds, from (the) extremities of (the) heavens to (the) extremities of them. [32] But learn the parable from the fig-tree: when its branch already is become tender, and it puts forth the leaves, you know that the summer (is) near. [33] So also you, when you see all these things, know that it is near, at the doors. [34] Truly I say to you, In no way will this generation have passed away until all these things shall have taken place. [35] The sky and the earth shall pass away, but My words in no way shall pass away. [36] But as to that day and the hour, no one knows, not even the angels of Heaven, but My Father only. [37] But as the days of Noah, so also shall be the coming of the Son of man. [38] For as they were in the days before the flood, eating and drinking, marrying and giving in marriage, until the day that Noah entered into the ark — [39] and they did not know until the flood came and took away — so shall be also the coming of the Son of man. [40] Then two will be in the field, the

**28** ἔσται καὶ ἡ παρουσία τοῦ υἱοῦ τοῦ ἀνθρώπου. ὅπου γὰρ
will be also the coming of the Son — of man. Wherever For
ἐὰν ᾖ τὸ πτῶμα, ἐκεῖ συναχθήσονται οἱ ἀετοί.
if may be the carcase, there will be gathered the eagles.

**29** Εὐθέως δὲ μετὰ τὴν θλίψιν τῶν ἡμερῶν ἐκείνων, ὁ ἥλιος
immediately And after the affliction — of days those, the sun
σκοτισθήσεται, καὶ ἡ σελήνη οὐ δώσει τὸ φέγγος αὐτῆς,
will be darkened, and the moon not will give the light of her,
καὶ οἱ ἀστέρες πεσοῦνται ἀπὸ τοῦ οὐρανοῦ, καὶ αἱ δυνάμεις
and the stars will fall from — heaven, and the powers

**30** τῶν οὐρανῶν σαλευθήσονται. καὶ τότε φανήσεται τὸ
of the heavens will be shaken. And then will appear the
σημεῖον τοῦ υἱοῦ τοῦ ἀνθρώπου ἐν τῷ οὐρανῷ· καὶ τότε
sign of the Son — of man in the heaven; and then
κόψονται πᾶσαι αἱ φυλαὶ τῆς γῆς, καὶ ὄψονται τὸν υἱὸν τοῦ
will wail all the tribes of the land, and they will see the Son —
ἀνθρώπου ἐρχόμενον ἐπὶ τῶν νεφελῶν τοῦ οὐρανοῦ μετὰ
of man coming on the clouds of heaven with

**31** δυνάμεως καὶ δόξης πολλῆς. καὶ ἀποστελεῖ τοὺς ἀγγέλους
power and glory much; and He will send the angels
αὐτοῦ μετὰ σάλπιγγος φωνῆς μεγάλης, καὶ ἐπισυνάξουσι
of Him with a trumpet sound great, and they will gather
τοὺς ἐκλεκτοὺς αὐτοῦ ἐκ τῶν τεσσάρων ἀνέμων, ἀπ' ἄκρων
the elect of Him out of the four winds from (the) ends
οὐρανῶν ἕως ἄκρων αὐτῶν.
of (the) heavens to (the) ends of them.

**32** Ἀπὸ δὲ τῆς συκῆς μάθετε τὴν παραβολήν· ὅταν ἤδη ὁ
from And the fig-tree learn the parable: When now the
κλάδος αὐτῆς γένηται ἁπαλός, καὶ τὰ φύλλα ἐκφύῃ, γινώ-
branch of it becomes tender, and the leaves it puts out, you

**33** σκετε ὅτι ἐγγὺς τὸ θέρος· οὕτω καὶ ὑμεῖς, ὅταν ἴδητε πάντα
know that near (is) the summer: so also you when you see all

**34** ταῦτα, γινώσκετε ὅτι ἐγγύς ἐστιν ἐπὶ θύραις. ἀμὴν λέγω
these things know that near it is on (the) doors. Truly I say
ὑμῖν, οὐ μὴ παρέλθῃ ἡ γενεὰ αὕτη, ἕως ἂν πάντα ταῦτα
to you, In no way passes away generation this until all these things

**35** γένηται. ὁ οὐρανὸς καὶ ἡ γῆ παρελεύσονται, οἱ δὲ λόγοι
have occurred. The heavens and the earth will pass away, the but words

**36** μου οὐ μὴ παρέλθωσι. περὶ δὲ τῆς ἡμέρας ἐκείνης καὶ τῆς
of Me in no way may pass away. about But — day that and the
ὥρας οὐδεὶς οἶδεν, οὐδὲ οἱ ἄγγελοι τῶν οὐρανῶν, εἰ μὴ ὁ
hour no one knows, neither the angels of the heavens, except the

**37** πατήρ μου μόνος. ὥσπερ δὲ αἱ ἡμέραι τοῦ Νῶε, οὕτως
Father of Me only. as But the days — of Noah, so

**38** ἔσται καὶ ἡ παρουσία τοῦ υἱοῦ τοῦ ἀνθρώπου. ὥσπερ γὰρ
will be also the coming of the Son — of man. as For
ἦσαν ἐν ταῖς ἡμέραις ταῖς πρὸ τοῦ κατακλυσμοῦ τρώγοντες
they were in the days before the flood, eating
καὶ πίνοντες, γαμοῦντες καὶ ἐκγαμίζοντες, ἄχρι ἧς ἡμέρας
and drinking, marrying and giving in marriage, until which day

**39** εἰσῆλθε Νῶε εἰς τὴν κιβωτόν, καὶ οὐκ ἔγνωσαν, ἕως ἦλθεν
entered Noah into the ark, and not did know until came
ὁ κατακλυσμὸς καὶ ἦρεν ἅπαντας, οὕτως ἔσται καὶ ἡ παρου-
the flood and took all, so will be the coming

**40** σία τοῦ υἱοῦ τοῦ ἀνθρώπου. τότε δύο ἔσονται ἐν τῷ ἀγρῷ·
of the Son — of man. Then two will be in the field,

one is taken, and the one is left; [41] two grinding at the mill, one is taken, and one is left. [42] Watch, then, for you do not know in what hour your Lord comes. [43] But know this, that if the master of the house had known in what watch the thief comes, he would have watched, and not have allowed his house to be broken into. [44] Because of this, you also be ready for in that hour you think not, the Son of man comes. [45] Who then is the faithful and wise servant, whom his lord has set over his household, to give to them the food in season? [46] That servant whom his lord shall find so doing when he comes will be blessed. [47] Truly I say to you, that he will set him over all his substance. [48] But if that evil servant should say in his heart, My lord delays to come, [49] and should begin to beat (his) fellow-servants, and to eat and to drink with the drunkards, [50] the lord of that servant will come in a day in which he does not expect, and in an hour which he does not know, [51] and will cut him in two, and will appoint his portion with the hypocrites; there will be weeping and gnashing of the teeth.

**CHAPTER 25**

[1] Then the kingdom of Heaven shall be compared to ten virgins, who took their lamps and went out to meet the bridegroom. [2] And five of them were wise, and five foolish. [3] They who (were) foolish, having taken their lamps, did not take oil with themselves. [4] But the wise took oil in their vessels with their lamps. [5] But the bridegroom delaying, they all nodded and slept. [6] But in (the) middle of (the) night there was a cry, Behold, the bridegroom

**41** ὁ εἷς παραλαμβάνεται, καὶ ὁ εἷς ἀφίεται. δύο ἀλήθουσαι ἐν
the one is taken away    and the one is left.   Two       grinding in

**42** τῷ μύλωνι· μία παραλαμβάνεται, καὶ μία ἀφίεται. γρηγο-
the mill,   one     is taken away    and one is left.    Watch

ρεῖτε οὖν, ὅτι οὐκ οἴδατε ποίᾳ ὥρᾳ ὁ Κύριος ὑμῶν ἔρχεται.
therefore that not you know on what hour the Lord of you is coming.

**43** ἐκεῖνο δὲ γινώσκετε, ὅτι εἰ ᾔδει ὁ οἰκοδεσπότης ποίᾳ φυλακῇ
this     And   know,    that if knew the housemaster in what watch

ὁ κλέπτης ἔρχεται, ἐγρηγόρησεν ἄν, καὶ οὐκ ἂν εἴασε διο-
the thief    is coming, he would have watched and not might allow to be

**44** ρυγῆναι τὴν οἰκίαν αὐτοῦ. διὰ τοῦτο καὶ ὑμεῖς γίνεσθε
dug through the   house   of him.    Therefore   also   you     be

ἕτοιμοι· ὅτι ᾗ ὥρᾳ οὐ δοκεῖτε, ὁ υἱὸς τοῦ ἀνθρώπου ἔρχεται.
ready, because that hour not you think the Son   —   of man   comes.

**45** τίς ἄρα ἐστὶν ὁ πιστὸς δοῦλος καὶ φρόνιμος, ὃν κατέστησεν ὁ
Who then is   the faithful slave   and   prudent   whom appointed the

κύριος αὐτοῦ ἐπὶ τῆς θεραπείας αὐτοῦ, τοῦ διδόναι αὐτοῖς
lord    of him over the   service    of him   —   to give to them

**46** τὴν τροφὴν ἐν καιρῷ ; μακάριος ὁ δοῦλος ἐκεῖνος, ὃν ἐλθὼν
the   food    in season? Blessed (is) —   slave    that whom coming

**47** ὁ κύριος αὐτοῦ εὑρήσει ποιοῦντα οὕτως. ἀμὴν λέγω ὑμῖν,
the lord   of him will find   doing     so.    Truly   I say to you,

ὅτι ἐπὶ πᾶσι τοῖς ὑπάρχουσιν αὐτου καταστήσει αὐτόν.
that over   all    the   goods    of him he will appoint   him.

**48** ἐὰν δὲ εἴπῃ ὁ κακὸς δοῦλος. ἐκεῖνος ἐν τῇ καρδίᾳ αὐτοῦ,
if But says — wicked   slave    that   in   the   heart    of him,

**49** Χρονίζει ὁ κύριός μου ἐλθεῖν, καὶ ἄρξηται τύπτειν τοὺς συν-
delays    the   lord of me to come, and should begin to beat   the fellow-

**50** δούλους, ἐσθίειν δὲ καὶ πίνειν μετὰ τῶν μεθυόντων, ἥξει ὁ
slaves,     to eat and, and, to drink with   the (ones) drunk, comes the

κύριος τοῦ δούλου ἐκείνου ἐν ἡμέρᾳ ᾗ οὐ προσδοκᾷ, καὶ ἐν
lord     of slave    that on a day which not he expects, and in

**51** ὥρᾳ ᾗ οὐ γινώσκει, καὶ διχοτομήσει αὐτόν, καὶ τὸ μέρος
an hour which not he knows, and will cut in two   him, and the portion

αὐτοῦ μετὰ τῶν ὑποκριτῶν θήσει· ἐκεῖ ἔσται ὁ κλαυθμὸς καὶ
of him with   the   hypocrites will put; there will be the   weeping and

ὁ βρυγμος τῶν ὀδόντων.
the gnashing of the   teeth.

**CHAPTER 25**

**1** Τότε ὁμοιωθήσεται ἡ βασιλεία τῶν οὐρανῶν δέκα παρθέ-
   Then shall be compared the kingdom of the heavens to ten virgins,

νοις, αἵτινες λαβοῦσαι τὰς λαμπάδας αὐτῶν ἐξῆλθον εἰς
    who    taking    the   lamps    of them went out to

**2** ἀπάντησιν τοῦ νυμφίου. πέντε δὲ ἦσαν ἐξ αὐτῶν φρόνιμοι,
a meeting   of the bridegroom. five And were of   them    prudent

**3** καὶ αἱ πέντε μωραί. αἵτινες μωραί, λαβοῦσαι τὰς λαμπάδας
and — five fools   those (being) fools, having taken the    lamps

**4** ἑαυτῶν, οὐκ ἔλαβον μεθ' ἑαυτῶν ἔλαιον· αἱ δὲ φρόνιμοι
of them, not did take with themselves oil;    the but prudent

ἔλαβον ἔλαιον ἐν τοῖς ἀγγείοις αὐτῶν μετὰ τῶν λαμπάδων
took     oil    in the the vessels of them with   the    lamps

**5** αὐτῶν. χρονίζοντος δὲ τοῦ νυμφίου, ἐνύσταξαν πᾶσαι καὶ
of them. delaying    But the bridegroom,   nodded    all   and

**6** ἐκάθευδον. μέσης δὲ νυκτὸς κραυγὴ γέγονεν, Ἰδού, ὁ
slept.    (at) mid- And night,   a cry   occurred:   Behold, the

comes! Go out to meet him. [7] Then all those virgins rose up and trimmed their lamps. [8] And the foolish said to the wise, Give us of your oil, for our lamps are going out. [9] But the wise answered saying, (No) lest there should not be enough for us and for you; but rather go to those who sell, and buy for yourselves. [10] But as they went away to buy, the bridegroom came, and those ready went in with him to the wedding feast, and the door was shut. [11] And afterwards the other virgins also came, saying, Lord, Lord, open to us. [12] But answering he said, Truly I say to you, I do not know you. [13] Watch, therefore, for you do not know the day nor the hour in which the Son of man comes.

[14] For (it is) as (if) a man leaving the country called his own servants and delivered his substance to them. [15] And to one he gave five talents, and to another two, and to another one, to each according to (his) own ability; and went abroad at once. [16] And going, he receiving five talents worked with them, and made another five talents. [17] In the same way, he with the two also; he also gained another two. [18] But the one receiving one, going away dug in the earth, and hid the silver of his lord. [19] And after much time, the lord of those slaves comes, and takes account with them. [20] And coming up, he receiving five talents brought near another five talents, saying, Lord, you delivered to me five talents. Behold, another five talents I gained over them. [21] And his lord said to him, Well (done), good and faithful slave; you were faithful over a few. I will set you over many. Enter into the joy of your lord.

**7** νυμφίος ἔρχεται, ἐξέρχεσθε εἰς ἀπάντησιν αὐτοῦ. τότε
bridegroom comes!    Go forth    to a meeting    of him.    Then
ἠγέρθησαν πᾶσαι αἱ παρθένοι ἐκεῖναι, καὶ ἐκόσμησαν τὰς
arose    all  —  virgins  those,  and prepared    the

**8** λαμπάδας αὐτῶν. αἱ δὲ μωραὶ ταῖς φρονίμοις εἶπον, Δότε
lamps    of them. the And fools to the prudent  said,  Give
ἡμῖν ἐκ τοῦ ἐλαίου ὑμῶν, ὅτι αἱ λαμπάδες ἡμῶν σβέννυνται.
us   the   oil  of you, for the  lamps  of us are going out.

**9** ἀπεκρίθησαν δὲ αἱ φρόνιμοι, λέγουσαι, Μήποτε οὐκ
answered    But the  prudent,  saying,  (No,) lest  not
ἀρκέσῃ ἡμῖν καὶ ὑμῖν· πορεύεσθε δὲ μᾶλλον πρὸς τοὺς
it suffices to us and to you.  go  But  rather  to the (ones)

**10** πωλοῦντας καὶ ἀγοράσατε ἑαυταῖς. ἀπερχομένων δὲ αὐτῶν
selling    and  buy  for yourselves.  going away And they
ἀγοράσαι, ἦλθεν ὁ νυμφίος· καὶ αἱ ἕτοιμοι εἰσῆλθον μετ'
to buy,  came  the bridegroom and the ready (ones) went in  with

**11** αὐτοῦ εἰς τοὺς γάμους, καὶ ἐκλείσθη ἡ θύρα. ὕστερον δὲ
him  to  the wedding feast, and was shut the door.  later  δὲ
ἔρχονται καὶ αἱ λοιπαὶ παρθένοι, λέγουσαι, Κύριε, κύριε,
come  also the remaining virgins,  saying,  Lord, Lord,

**12** ἄνοιξον ἡμῖν. ὁ δὲ ἀποκριθεὶς εἶπεν, Ἀμὴν λέγω ὑμῖν, οὐκ
open  to us. he But answering  said,  Truly  I say to you, not

**13** οἶδα ὑμᾶς. γρηγορεῖτε οὖν, ὅτι οὐκ οἴδατε τὴν ἡμέραν οὐδὲ
I know you.  Watch,  therefore, for not you know the day  nor
τὴν ὥραν, ἐν ᾗ ὁ υἱὸς τοῦ ἀνθρώπου ἔρχεται.
the  hour in which the Son — of man  comes.

**14** Ὥσπερ γὰρ ἄνθρωπος ἀποδημῶν ἐκάλεσε τοὺς ἰδίους
(it is) as if For  a man  going abroad  called  the  own

**15** δούλους, καὶ παρέδωκεν αὐτοῖς τὰ ὑπάρχοντα αὐτοῦ· καὶ
slaves,  and  delivered  to them the  goods  of him, and
ᾧ μὲν ἔδωκε πέντε τάλαντα, ᾧ δὲ δύο, ᾧ δὲ ἕν, ἑκάστῳ κατὰ
to one he gave five  talents; to one and two; to and one; to each  by
indeed                                              one

**16** τὴν ἰδίαν δύναμιν· καὶ ἀπεδήμησεν εὐθέως. πορευθεὶς δὲ ὁ
the own  ability,  and went abroad Immediately. going  And he
τὰ πέντε τάλαντα λαβὼν εἰργάσατο ἐν αὐτοῖς, καὶ ἐποίησεν
the five  talents receiving worked  with  them  and made

**17** ἄλλα πέντε τάλαντα. ὡσαύτως καὶ ὁ τὰ δύο ἐκέρδησε καὶ
other five  talents.  Likewise, also the (one) the two ; gained also

**18** αὐτὸς ἄλλα δύο. ὁ δὲ τὸ ἓν λαβὼν ἀπελθὼν ὤρυξεν ἐν τῇ
he  other two. he But the one receiving , going away dug  in the

**19** γῇ, καὶ ἀπέκρυψε τὸ ἀργύριον τοῦ κυρίου αὐτοῦ. μετὰ δὲ
earth, and hid  the  silver  of the lord  of him. after And
χρόνον πολὺν ἔρχεται ὁ κύριος τῶν δούλων ἐκείνων, καὶ
time  much  comes the lord  — of slaves  those, and

**20** συναίρει μετ' αὐτῶν λόγον. καὶ προσελθὼν ὁ τὰ πέντε
takes  with  them account. And coming up, the (one) the five
τάλαντα λαβὼν προσήνεγκεν ἄλλα πέντε τάλαντα, λέγων,
talents receiving brought near other five talents,  saying,
Κύριε, πέντε τάλαντά μοι παρέδωκας· ἴδε, ἄλλα πέντε
Lord,  five  talents to me you delivered. Behold, other  five

**21** τάλαντα ἐκέρδησα ἐπ' αὐτοῖς. ἔφη δὲ αὐτῷ ὁ κύριος αὐτοῦ,
talents  I gained  over  them.  said And to him the lord  of him,
Εὖ, δοῦλε ἀγαθὲ καὶ πιστέ, ἐπὶ ὀλίγα ἧς πιστός, ἐπὶ πολλῶν
Well, slave  good and faithful, over a few you were faithful, over many
σε καταστήσω· εἴσελθε εἰς τὴν χαρὰν τοῦ κυρίου σου.
you I will set.  Enter into the  joy  of the lord of you.

[22] And he receiving two talents coming up also said, Lord, you delivered two talents to me; behold I have gained two other talents over them. [23] His lord said to him, Well (done), good and faithful slave; you were faithful over a few, I will set you over many. Enter into the joy of your lord. [24] And coming also he receiving the one talent said, Lord, I knew you, that you are a hard man, reaping where you did not sow, and gathering where you did not scatter; [25] and fearing, going away I hid your talent in the earth. Behold, you have yours. [26] And answering his lord said to him, Wicked and slothful servant, you knew that I reaped where I did not sow, and gathered from where I did not scatter; [27] therefore you ought to (have) put my money to the money-lenders, and coming I should have received my own with interest. [28] Therefore take the talent from him, and give (it) to him who has the ten talents. [29] For to everyone who has shall be given, and (he) shall be in abundance; but from him who has not, even that which he has will be taken from him. [30] And throw the worthless slave out into the outer darkness; there will be weeping and gnashing of the teeth.

[31] But when the Son of man comes in His glory, and all the holy angels with Him, then He will sit on the throne of His glory. [32] And before Him shall be gathered all the nations, and He will separate them from one another, as the shepherd separates the sheep from the goats. [33] And He will set the sheep on His right hand, but the goats on (His) left. [34] Then the King will say to those on His right hand, Come, the blessed of My Father; inherit the kingdom prepared for you from (the) foundation of (the) world. [35] For I was hungry, and you gave

22 προσελθὼν δὲ καὶ ὁ τὰ δύο τάλαντα λαβὼν εἶπε, Κύριε,
coming up And also the (one) the two talents receiving said, Lord,
δύο τάλαντά μοι παρέδωκας· ἴδε, ἄλλα δύο τάλαντα
two talents to me you delivered. Behold, other two talents

23 ἐκέρδησα ἐπ᾽ αὐτοῖς. ἔφη αὐτῷ ὁ κύριος αὐτοῦ, Εὖ, δοῦλε
I gained over them. said to him The lord of him, Well, slave
ἀγαθὲ καὶ πιστέ, ἐπὶ ὀλίγα ἧς πιστός, ἐπὶ πολλῶν σε
good and faithful, over a few you were faithful; over many you

24 καταστήσω· εἴσελθε εἰς τὴν χαρὰν τοῦ κυρίου σου. προσ-
I will set. Enter into the joy of the lord of you. coming
ελθὼν δὲ καὶ ὁ τὸ ἓν τάλαντον εἰληφὼς εἶπε, Κύριε, ἔγνων
up And also the (one) the one talent having received, said, Lord, I knew
σε ὅτι σκληρὸς εἶ ἄνθρωπος, θερίζων ὅπου οὐκ ἔσπειρας, καὶ
you, that hard you are a man, reaping where not you sowed, and

25 συνάγων ὅθεν οὐ διεσκόρπισας· καὶ φοβηθείς, ἀπελθὼν
gathering from where not you scattered; and fearing, going away
ἔκρυψα τὸ τάλαντόν σου ἐν τῇ γῇ· ἴδε, ἔχεις τὸ σόν.
I hid the talent of you in the earth. Behold, you have yours.

26 ἀποκριθεὶς δὲ ὁ κύριος αὐτοῦ εἶπεν αὐτῷ, Πονηρὲ δοῦλε καὶ
answering And, the lord of him said to him, Evil slave and
ὀκνηρέ, ᾔδεις ὅτι θερίζω ὅπου οὐκ ἔσπειρα, καὶ συνάγω ὅθεν
slothful, you knew that I reap where not I sowed, and I gather where

27 οὐ διεσκόρπισα· ἔδει οὖν σε βαλεῖν τὸ ἀργύριόν μου τοῖς
not I scattered. It behoved then you to put the silver of me to the
τραπεζίταις, καὶ ἐλθὼν ἐγὼ ἐκομισάμην ἂν τὸ ἐμὸν σὺν
bankers, and coming I would have received again mine with

28 τόκῳ. ἄρατε οὖν ἀπ᾽ αὐτοῦ τὸ τάλαντον, καὶ δότε τῷ
interest. Take, therefore, from him the talent, and give to him

29 ἔχοντι τὰ δέκα τάλαντα. τῷ γὰρ ἔχοντι παντὶ δοθήσεται,
having the ten talents. to him For having, each will be given
καὶ περισσευθήσεται· ἀπὸ δὲ τοῦ μὴ ἔχοντος, καὶ ὃ ἔχει,
and he will abound; from but the (one) not having ever what he has

30 ἀρθήσεται ἀπ᾽ αὐτοῦ. καὶ τὸν ἀχρεῖον δοῦλον ἐκβάλλετε
will be taken from him. And the worthless slave throw out
εἰς τὸ σκότος τὸ ἐξώτερον. ἐκεῖ ἔσται ὁ κλαυθμὸς καὶ ὁ
into the darkness — outer; there will be the weeping and the
βρυγμὸς τῶν ὀδόντων.
gnashing of the teeth.

31 Ὅταν δὲ ἔλθῃ ὁ υἱὸς τοῦ ἀνθρώπου ἐν τῇ δόξῃ αὐτοῦ,
when And comes the Son — of man in the glory of Him,
καὶ πάντες οἱ ἅγιοι ἄγγελοι μετ᾽ αὐτοῦ, τότε καθίσει ἐπὶ
and all the holy angels with Him, then He will sit on

32 θρόνου δόξης αὐτοῦ, καὶ συναχθήσεται ἔμπροσθεν αὐτοῦ
a throne of glory of Him, and will be assembled before Him
πάντα τὰ ἔθνη, καὶ ἀφοριεῖ αὐτούς ἀπ᾽ ἀλλήλων, ὥσπερ ὁ
all the nations, and He will part them from one another, as the

33 ποιμὴν ἀφορίζει τὰ πρόβατα ἀπὸ τῶν ἐρίφων· καὶ στήσει
shepherd parts the sheep from the goats, and will set
τὰ μὲν πρόβατα ἐκ δεξιῶν αὐτοῦ, τὰ δὲ ἐρίφια ἐξ εὐωνύμων.
the even sheep off right his, the but goats off (the) left.

34 τότε ἐρεῖ ὁ βασιλεὺς τοῖς ἐκ δεξιῶν αὐτοῦ, Δεῦτε, οἱ εὐλογη-
Then will say the King to those off His right, Come, the blessed
μένοι τοῦ πατρός μου, κληρονομήσατε τὴν ἡτοιμασμένην
of the Father of Me; inherit the prepared

35 ὑμῖν βασιλείαν ἀπὸ καταβολῆς κόσμου. ἐπείνασα γάρ, καὶ
for you kingdom from foundation of (the) world. I hungered For, and

Me (food) to eat; I was thirsty, and you gave Me drink; I was a stranger, and you took Me in; [36] naked, and you clothed Me; I was sick, and you visited Me; I was in prison, and you came to Me. [37] Then the righteous will answer, saying, Lord, when did we see You hungry and nourished; or thirsty, and gave drink; [38] and when did we see You a stranger, and gathered (in) You? or naked, and clothed (You)? [39] And when did we see You sick, or in prison, and came to You? [40] And answering the King will say to them, Truly I say to you, As long as you did (it) to one of these the least of My brothers, you did (it) to Me. [41] Then He will also say to those on (the) left, Go away from Me cursed ones, into the everlasting fire which has been prepared for the Devil and his angels. [42] For I was hungry, and you gave nothing to Me to eat; I was thirsty, and you gave nothing to Me to drink; [43] I was a stranger, and you did not take Me in; naked, and you did not clothe Me; sick, and in prison, and you did not visit Me. [44] Then they also will answer Him, saying, Lord, when did we see You hungry, or thirsty, or a stranger, or naked, or sick, or in prison, and did not minister to You? [45] Then He will answer them, saying, Truly I say to you, As long as you did not do (it) to one of these, the least, you did (it) not to Me. [46] And these shall go away into everlasting punishment; but the righteous into everlasting life.

## CHAPTER 26

[1] And it happened, when Jesus had finished all these sayings, that He said to His disciples, [2] You know that after two days the Passover takes place, and the Son of man is yielded up to be crucified. [3] Then the chief priests and scribes and the elders of the people were gather-

**36** ἐδώκατέ μοι φαγεῖν· ἐδίψησα, καὶ ἐποτίσατέ με· ξένος ἤμην,
you gave Me to eat; I thirsted, and you gave drink Me; an alien I was
καὶ συνηγάγετέ με· γυμνός, καὶ περιεβάλετέ με· ἠσθένησα,
and you took in Me; naked, and you clothed Me; I was sick,
καὶ ἐπεσκέψασθέ με· ἐν φυλακῇ ἤμην, καὶ ἤλθετε πρός με.
and you visited Me in prison I was, and you came to Me.

**37** τότε ἀποκριθήσονται αὐτῷ οἱ δίκαιοι, λέγοντες, Κύριε,
Then will answer Him the righteous, saying, Lord,
πότε σὲ εἴδομεν πεινῶντα, καὶ ἐθρέψαμεν ; ἢ διψῶντα, καὶ
when You did we see hungering, and fed, or thirsting, and

**38** ἐποτίσαμεν ; πότε δέ σε εἴδομεν ξένον, καὶ συνηγάγομεν ;
gave drink; when and You did we see an alien,, and gathered (You) in;

**39** ἢ γυμνόν, καὶ περιεβάλομεν ; πότε δέ σε εἴδομεν ἀσθενῆ, ἢ ἐν
or naked, and clothed? when And You did we see sick, or in

**40** φυλακῇ, καὶ ἤλθομεν πρός σε ; καὶ ἀποκριθεὶς ὁ βασιλεὺς ἐρεῖ
prison, and came to You? And answering the King will say
αὐτοῖς, Ἀμὴν λέγω ὑμῖν, ἐφ᾽ ὅσον ἐποιήσατε ἑνὶ τούτων τῶν
to them, Truly I say to you, inasmuch as you did to one of these the

**41** ἀδελφῶν μου τῶν ἐλαχίστων, ἐμοὶ ἐποιήσατε. τότε ἐρεῖ καὶ
brothers of Me the least, to Me you did. Then He says also
τοῖς ἐξ εὐωνύμων, Πορεύεσθε ἀπ᾽ ἐμοῦ, οἱ κατηραμένοι, εἰς
to those off (the) left, Go from Me, those cursed into
τὸ πῦρ τὸ αἰώνιον, τὸ ἡτοιμασμένον τῷ διαβόλῳ καὶ τοῖς
the fire — everlasting — having been prepared for the Devil and the

**42** ἀγγέλοις αὐτοῦ. ἐπείνασα γάρ, καὶ οὐκ ἐδώκατέ μοι φαγεῖν·
angels of him. I hungered For, and not you gave Me to eat;

**43** ἐδίψησα, καὶ οὐκ ἐποτίσατέ με· ξένος ἤμην, καὶ οὐ συνηγά-
I thirsted, and not you gave drink to Me; an alien I was, and not you gathered
γετέ με· γυμνός, καὶ οὐ περιεβάλετέ με· ἀσθενής, καὶ ἐν
in Me; naked, and not you clothed Me; sick, and in

**44** φυλακῇ, καὶ οὐκ ἐπεσκέψασθέ με. τότε ἀποκριθήσονται
prison, and not you visited Me. Then will answer
αὐτῷ καὶ αὐτοί, λέγοντες, Κύριε, πότε σὲ εἴδομεν πεινῶντα,
Him also they, saying, Lord, when You did we see hungering,
ἢ διψῶντα, ἢ ξένον, ἢ γυμνόν, ἢ ἀσθενῆ, ἢ ἐν φυλακῇ, καὶ
or thirsting, or an alien, or naked, or sick, or in prison, and

**45** οὐ διηκονήσαμέν σοι ; τότε ἀποκριθήσεται αὐτοῖς, λέγων,
not did minister to You? Then He will answer them, saying,
Ἀμὴν λέγω ὑμῖν, ἐφ᾽ ὅσον οὐκ ἐποιήσατε ἑνὶ τούτων τῶν
Truly I say to you; Inasmuch as not you did to one of these, the

**46** ἐλαχίστων, οὐδὲ ἐμοὶ ἐποιήσατε. καὶ ἀπελεύσονται οὗτοι
least (ones), neither to Me you did. And will go away these
εἰς κόλασιν αἰώνιον· οἱ δὲ δίκαιοι εἰς ζωὴν αἰώνιον.
into punishment eternal, the but righteous into life eternal.

## CHAPTER 26

**1** Καὶ ἐγένετο ὅτε ἐτέλεσεν ὁ Ἰησοῦς πάντας τοὺς λόγους
And it was, when ended — Jesus all sayings

**2** τούτους, εἶπε τοῖς μαθηταῖς αὐτοῦ, Οἴδατε ὅτι μετὰ δύο
these, He said to the disciples of Him, You know that after two
ἡμέρας τὸ πάσχα γίνεται, καὶ ὁ υἱὸς τοῦ ἀνθρώπου παραδί-
days the Passover comes, and the Son — of man is be-

**3** δοται εἰς τὸ σταυρωθῆναι. τότε συνήχθησαν οἱ ἀρχιερεῖς
trayed to be crucified. Then were assembled the chief priests
καὶ οἱ γραμματεῖς καὶ οἱ πρεσβύτεροι τοῦ λαοῦ εἰς τὴν
and the scribes and the elders of the people to the

ed together to the court of the high priest, who was called Caiaphas; [4] and plotted in order that they might seize Jesus by guile, and kill (Him). [5] But they said, Not during the feast, that there be no uproar among the people.

[6] Now Jesus being in Bethany, in (the) house of Simon the leper, [7] a woman came to Him having an alabaster vial of ointment, very precious, and poured (it) on His head as He reclined. [8] But seeing (this) His disciples became indignant, saying, For what (is) this waste? [9] For this ointment could have been sold for much and have been given to (the) poor. [10] But knowing (this) Jesus said to them, Why do you cause trouble to the woman? For she has worked a good work toward Me. [11] For you always have the poor with you, but you do not always have Me. [12] For this (woman) in pouring this ointment on My body, she did it for My burying. [13] Truly I say to you, Wherever this gospel shall be preached in all the world, that which this one did shall be spoken of also for a memorial of her.

[14] Then one of the twelve who was called Judas Iscariot having gone to the chief priests, [15] said, What are you willing to give, and I will deliver Him up to you? And they appointed to him thirty pieces of silver. [16] And from then he sought opportunity that he might deliver Him up.

[17] Now on the first (day) of unleavened bread the disciples came to Jesus, saying to Him, Where do You desire we should prepare for You to eat the Passover? [18] And He said, Go into the city to a certain one and say to him, The Teacher says, My time is near; I will keep the Passover with My disciples with you. [19] And the disciples did as Jesus commanded them, and pre-

**4** αὐλὴν τοῦ ἀρχιερέως τοῦ λεγομένου Καϊάφα, καὶ συνεβου-
court of the high priest — named Caiaphas, and consulted
λεύσαντο ἵνα τὸν Ἰησοῦν κρατήσωσι δόλῳ καὶ ἀπο-
together that — Jesus they might seize by guile, and
**5** κτείνωσιν. ἔλεγον δέ, Μὴ ἐν τῇ ἑορτῇ, ἵνα μὴ θόρυβος
kill (Him). they said But, Not at the feast, lest a turmoil
γένηται ἐν τῷ λαῷ.
occur among the people.

**6** Τοῦ δὲ Ἰησοῦ γενομένου ἐν Βηθανίᾳ ἐν οἰκίᾳ Σίμωνος τοῦ
— And Jesus being in Bethany in (the) house of Simon the
**7** λεπροῦ, προσῆλθεν αὐτῷ γυνὴ ἀλάβαστρον μύρου ἔχουσα
leper, came up to Him a woman an alabaster vial of ointment having
βαρυτίμου, καὶ κατέχεεν ἐπὶ τὴν κεφαλὴν αὐτοῦ ἀνακει-
very precious, and poured (it) on the head of Him reclining.
**8** μένου. ἰδόντες δὲ οἱ μαθηταὶ αὐτοῦ ἠγανάκτησαν, λέγοντες,
seeing And the disciples of Him were indignant, saying,
**9** Εἰς τί ἡ ἀπώλεια αὕτη; ἠδύνατο γὰρ τοῦτο τὸ μύρον
To what — waste this? could For this the ointment
**10** πραθῆναι πολλοῦ, καὶ δοθῆναι πτωχοῖς. γνοὺς δὲ ὁ Ἰησοῦς
have been sold of much, and to be given to (the) poor? knowing And Jesus
εἶπεν αὐτοῖς, Τί κόπους παρέχετε τῇ γυναικί; ἔργον γὰρ
said to them, Why trouble do you cause to the woman? work For
**11** καλὸν εἰργάσατο εἰς ἐμέ. πάντοτε γὰρ τοὺς πτωχοὺς ἔχετε
a good she worked toward Me, always for the poor you have
**12** μεθ' ἑαυτῶν, ἐμὲ δὲ οὐ πάντοτε ἔχετε. βαλοῦσα γὰρ αὕτη
with yourselves, Me but not always you have. putting For she
τὸ μύρον τοῦτο ἐπὶ τοῦ σώματός μου, πρὸς τὸ ἐνταφιάσαι
ointment this on the body of Me, in order to bury
**13** με ἐποίησεν. ἀμὴν λέγω ὑμῖν, ὅπου ἐὰν κηρυχθῇ τὸ εὐαγ-
Me she did (it). Truly I say to you, wherever is proclaimed gospel
γέλιον τοῦτο ἐν ὅλῳ τῷ κόσμῳ, λαληθήσεται καὶ ὃ ἐποίησεν
this in all the world, will be spoken also what did
αὕτη, εἰς μνημόσυνον αὐτῆς.
she for a memorial of her.

**14** Τότε πορευθεὶς εἷς τῶν δώδεκα, ὁ λεγόμενος Ἰούδας
Then going one of the twelve, the (one) named Judas
**15** Ἰσκαριώτης, πρὸς τοὺς ἀρχιερεῖς, εἶπε, Τί θέλετέ μοι δοῦναι,
Iscariot, to the chief priests, said, What will You Me to give,
κἀγὼ ὑμῖν παραδώσω αὐτόν; οἱ δὲ ἔστησαν αὐτῷ τριά-
and I to you will deliver up Him? they And weighed him thirty
**16** κοντα ἀργύρια. καὶ ἀπὸ τότε ἐζήτει εὐκαιρίαν ἵνα αὐτὸν
silver pieces. And from then he sought opportunity that Him
παραδῷ.
he might deliver.

**17** Τῇ δὲ πρώτῃ τῶν ἀζύμων προσῆλθον οἱ μαθηταὶ τῷ
on the And first unleavened came the disciples to
Ἰησοῦ, λέγοντες αὐτῷ, Ποῦ θέλεις ἑτοιμάσωμέν σοι φαγεῖν
Jesus, saying to Him, Where will You we may prepare for You to eat
**18** τὸ πάσχα; ὁ δὲ εἶπεν, Ὑπάγετε εἰς τὴν πόλιν πρὸς τὸν
the Passover? He And said, Go into the city to such
δεῖνα, καὶ εἴπατε αὐτῷ, Ὁ διδάσκαλος λέγει, Ὁ καιρός μου
a one, and say to him, The Teacher says, The time of Me
ἐγγύς ἐστι· πρὸς σὲ ποιῶ τὸ πάσχα μετὰ τῶν μαθητῶν μου.
near is; toward you I make the Passover, with the disciples of Me.
**19** καὶ ἐποίησαν οἱ μαθηταὶ ὡς συνέταξεν αὐτοῖς ὁ Ἰησοῦς, καὶ
And did the disciples as ordered them — Jesus, and

pared the Passover.

[20] And evening being come, He reclined with the twelve. [21] And as they were eating He said, Truly I say to you, that one of you will deliver Me up. [22] And being grieved exceedingly they began to say to Him, each of them, Lord, not I am (he)? [23] But answering He said, He dipping the hand with Me in the dish will betray Me. [24] Indeed (the) Son of man goes, as it has been written about Him, but woe to that man by whom the Son of man is betrayed. It were good for him if that man was not born. [25] And answering Judas, who was betraying Him, said, Not I am (he), Rabbi? He said to him, You said (it).

[26] And (as) they ate, Jesus taking the bread, and blessing (it), broke and gave to the disciples; and said, Take, eat; this is My body. [27] And taking the cup, and giving thanks, He gave to them, saying, Drink all of it. [28] For this is My blood of the New Covenant which concerning many is poured out for remission of sins

[29] But I say to you, that I will not at all drink of this fruit of the vine after this, until that day when I drink it new with you in the kingdom of My Father. [30] And having sung a hymn, they went out to the Mount of Olives. [31] Then Jesus said to them, You all will be offended in Me during this night. For it has been written, "I will smite the shepherd, and the sheep of the flock will be scattered abroad." [32] But after My resurrection I will go before you into Galilee. [33] And answering Peter said to Him, Even if all will be offended in You, I will never be offended. [34] Jesus said to him, Truly I say to you, that during this night, before cock-crowing, you will deny Me three times.

20 ἡτοίμασαν τὸ πάσχα. ὀψίας δὲ γενομένης ἀνέκειτο μετὰ τῶν
prepared    the Passover. evening And coming,    He reclined with   the

21 δώδεκα. καὶ ἐσθιόντων αὐτῶν εἶπεν, Ἀμὴν λέγω ὑμῖν ὅτι
twelve.    And    eating    they, He said,  Truly  I say to you that

22 εἷς ἐξ ὑμῶν παραδώσει με. καὶ λυπούμενοι σφόδρα ἤρξαντο
one of you  will betray  Me. And grieving  exceedingly they began

23 λέγειν αὐτῷ ἕκαστος αὐτῶν, Μήτι ἐγώ εἰμι, Κύριε; ὁ δὲ
to say  to Him,  each  of them,  Not   I am (he),  Lord? He But
ἀποκριθεὶς εἶπεν, Ὁ ἐμβάψας μετ' ἐμοῦ ἐν τῷ τρυβλίῳ τὴν
answering  said, The (one) dipping with Me in  the   dish   the

24 χεῖρα, οὗτός με παραδώσει. ὁ μὲν υἱὸς τοῦ ἀνθρώπου ὑπάγει,
hand,   Me will betray.   the Indeed Son  of man   goes,
καθὼς γέγραπται περὶ αὐτοῦ· οὐαὶ δὲ τῷ ἀνθρώπῳ ἐκείνῳ,
as   it has been written about Him, woe but  to   man   that
δι' οὗ ὁ υἱὸς τοῦ ἀνθρώπου παραδίδοται· καλὸν ἦν αὐτῷ εἰ
by whom the Son  of man   is betrayed;  good were it for him if

25 οὐκ ἐγεννήθη ὁ ἄνθρωπος ἐκεῖνος. ἀποκριθεὶς δὲ Ἰούδας ὁ
not was born   man   that. answering And Judas who
παραδιδοὺς αὐτὸν εἶπε, Μήτι ἐγώ εἰμι, ῥαββί; λέγει αὐτῷ,
was betraying Him  said, Not  I  am,  Rabbi? He says to him,

26 Σὺ εἶπας. ἐσθιόντων δὲ αὐτῶν, λαβὼν ὁ Ἰησοῦς τὸν ἄρτον,
You said (it). eating  And they, taking  — Jesus  the bread,
καὶ εὐλογήσας, ἔκλασε καὶ ἐδίδου τοῖς μαθηταῖς, καὶ εἶπε,
and blessing,  He broke  and gave to the disciples, and said,

27 Λάβετε, φάγετε· τοῦτό ἐστι τὸ σῶμά μου. καὶ λαβὼν τὸ
Take,   eat·   this  is the body of Me. And taking the
ποτήριον, καὶ εὐχαριστήσας, ἔδωκεν αὐτοῖς, λέγων, Πίετε
cup,   and giving thanks, He gave to them, saying, Drink

28 ἐξ αὐτοῦ πάντες· τοῦτο γάρ ἐστι τὸ αἷμά μου, τὸ τῆς καινῆς
of it  all; this for is the blood of Me — of the New
διαθήκης, τὸ περὶ πολλῶν ἐκχυνόμενον εἰς ἄφεσιν ἁμαρτιῶν.
Covenant, which concern many  s being   for forgiveness of sins.
                            ing    poured out

29 λέγω δὲ ὑμῖν ὅτι οὐ μὴ πίω ἀπ' ἄρτι ἐκ τούτου τοῦ γεννή-
I say And to you that never will I drink from now of this   fruit
ματος τῆς ἀμπέλου, ἕως τῆς ἡμέρας ἐκείνης ὅταν αὐτὸ πίνω
of the vine   until  —  day  that   when it  I drink
μεθ' ὑμῶν καινὸν ἐν τῇ βασιλείᾳ τοῦ πατρός μου.
with you new  in the kingdom of the Father of Me.

30 Καὶ ὑμνήσαντες ἐξῆλθον εἰς τὸ ὄρος τῶν ἐλαιῶν.
And  having sung a hymn they went into the mount of the  olives.

31 Τότε λέγει αὐτοῖς ὁ Ἰησοῦς, Πάντες ὑμεῖς σκανδαλισθη-
Then  says to them Jesus,  All  you   will be offended
σεσθε ἐν ἐμοὶ ἐν τῇ νυκτὶ ταύτῃ· γέγραπται γάρ, Πατάξω
in Me during  night  this; it has been written for, I will strike
τὸν ποιμένα, καὶ διασκορπισθήσεται τὰ πρόβατα τῆς
the shepherd, and will be scattered   the sheep  of the

32 ποίμνης. μετὰ δὲ τὸ ἐγερθῆναί με, προάξω ὑμᾶς εἰς τὴν
flock;  after but the rising (of) Me, I will go before you to  —

33 Γαλιλαίαν. ἀποκριθεὶς δὲ ὁ Πέτρος εἶπεν αὐτῷ, Εἰ καὶ πάντες
Galilee.  answering And Peter  said to Him, If even  all
σκανδαλισθήσονται ἐν σοί, ἐγὼ οὐδέποτε σκανδαλισθή-
be offended   in You, I  never   will be offended.

34 σομαι. ἔφη αὐτῷ ὁ Ἰησοῦς, Ἀμὴν λέγω σοι ὅτι ἐν ταύτῃ τῇ
said to him Jesus, Truly  I say to you that in this  —

35 νυκτί, πρὶν ἀλέκτορα φωνῆσαι, τρὶς ἀπαρνήσῃ με. λέγει
night, before (the) cock  crows,  thrice you will deny Me. Says

[35] Peter said to Him, Even if it were necessary for me to die with You, I will in no way deny You. Also all the disciples said the same.

[36] Then Jesus came with them to a place called Gethsemane, and he said to the disciples, Sit here until having gone away I shall pray over there. [37] And having taken Peter and the two sons of Zebedee, He began to be sorrowful and deeply troubled. [38] Then He said to them, My soul is very sorrowful, even to death; stay here and watch with Me. [39] And having gone forward a little, He fell on His face praying and saying, My Father, if it is possible, let this cup pass from Me; nevertheless, not as I desire, but as You. [40] And He came to the disciples and found them sleeping, and said to Peter, So! Were you not able to watch one hour with Me? [41] Watch and pray that you do not enter into temptation; the spirit indeed (is) willing, but the flesh is weak. [42] Again, a second time having gone away, He prayed, saying, My Father, if this cup cannot pass away from Me without My drinking it, let Your will be done. [43] And having come He found them sleeping again, for their eyes were heavy. [44] And leaving them, having gone away again, He prayed a third time, saying the same things. [45] Then He came to His disciples and said to them, Sleep on now, and take your rest; behold, the hour has come near, and the Son of man is delivered up into (the) hands of sinners. [46] Rise up, let us go; behold, he who is delivering me has come near. [47] And as He was still speaking, behold, Judas came, one of the twelve, and with him a great crowd with swords

αὐτῷ ὁ Πέτρος, Κἂν δέῃ με σὺν σοὶ ἀποθανεῖν, οὐ μή σε
to Him — Peter, Even if need I with You to die, in no way You
ἀπαρνήσομαι. ὁμοίως καὶ πάντες οἱ μαθηταὶ εἶπον.
I will deny. Likewise also all the disciples said.

36 Τότε ἔρχεται μετ' αὐτῶν ὁ Ἰησοῦς εἰς χωρίον λεγόμενον
Then comes with them — Jesus to a place called
Γεθσημανῆ, καὶ λέγει τοῖς μαθηταῖς, Καθίσατε αὐτοῦ, ἕως οὗ
Gethsemane, and says to the disciples, Sit on this until

37 ἀπελθὼν προσεύξωμαι ἐκεῖ. καὶ παραλαβὼν τὸν Πέτρον καὶ
going away I shall pray there. And taking along — Peter and
τοὺς δύο υἱοὺς Ζεβεδαίου, ἤρξατο λυπεῖσθαι καὶ ἀδημονεῖν.
the two sons of Zebedee, He began to grieve and be distressed.

38 τότε λέγει αὐτοῖς, Περίλυπός ἐστιν ἡ ψυχή μου ἕως θανάτου·
Then He says to them, deeply grieved is the soul of Me unto death;

39 μείνατε ὧδε καὶ γρηγορεῖτε μετ' ἐμοῦ. καὶ προελθὼν μικρόν,
remain here and watch with Me. And going forward a little,
ἔπεσεν ἐπὶ πρόσωπον αὐτοῦ προσευχόμενος καὶ λέγων,
He fell on (the) face of Him, praying and saying,
Πάτερ μου, εἰ δυνατόν ἐστι, παρελθέτω ἀπ' ἐμοῦ τὸ ποτή-
Father of Me, if possible it is, let pass from Me — cup

40 ριον τοῦτο· πλὴν οὐχ ὡς ἐγὼ θέλω, ἀλλ' ὡς σύ. καὶ ἔρχεται
this; yet not as I will, but as You. And He comes
πρὸς τοὺς μαθητάς, καὶ εὑρίσκει αὐτοὺς καθεύδοντας, καὶ
toward the disciples and finds them sleeping, and
λέγει τῷ Πέτρῳ, Οὕτως οὐκ ἰσχύσατε μίαν ὥραν γρηγορῆ-
says — to Peter, So, not were you able one hour to watch

41 σαι μετ' ἐμοῦ; γρηγορεῖτε καὶ προσεύχεσθε, ἵνα μὴ
with Me? Watch and pray, lest
εἰσέλθητε εἰς πειρασμόν· τὸ μὲν πνεῦμα πρόθυμον, ἡ δὲ
you enter into temptation; the indeed spirit (is) eager, the but

42 σὰρξ ἀσθενής. πάλιν ἐκ δευτέρου ἀπελθὼν προσηύξατο,
flesh (is) weak. Again, for a second (time) going away He prayed,
λέγων, Πάτερ μου, εἰ οὐ δύναται τοῦτο τὸ ποτήριον
saying, Father of Me, if not can this — cup
παρελθεῖν ἀπ' ἐμοῦ, ἐὰν μὴ αὐτὸ πίω, γενηθήτω τὸ θέλημά
pass away from Me unless it I drink, let be done the will

43 σου. καὶ ἐλθὼν εὑρίσκει αὐτοὺς πάλιν καθεύδοντας, ἦσαν
of You. And coming He finds them again sleeping, were

44 γὰρ αὐτῶν οἱ ὀφθαλμοὶ βεβαρημένοι. καὶ ἀφεὶς αὐτοὺς
for of them the eyes heavy. And leaving them
ἀπελθὼν πάλιν προσηύξατο ἐκ τρίτου, τὸν αὐτὸν λόγον
going away again, He prayed a third (time), the same word

45 εἰπών. τότε ἔρχεται πρὸς τοὺς μαθητὰς αὐτοῦ, καὶ λέγει
saying. Then He comes to the disciples of Him, and says
αὐτοῖς, Καθεύδετε τὸ λοιπὸν καὶ ἀναπαύεσθε· ἰδού, ἤγγικεν
to them, Sleep (for) what remains and rest; behold, draws near
ἡ ὥρα, καὶ ὁ υἱὸς τοῦ ἀνθρώπου παραδίδοται εἰς χεῖρας
the hour and the Son — of man is betrayed into hands

46 ἁμαρτωλῶν. ἐγείρεσθε, ἄγωμεν. ἰδού, ἤγγικεν ὁ παραδι-
of sinners. Rise, let us go, Behold, draws near the (one)
δούς με.
betraying Me.

47 Καὶ ἔτι αὐτοῦ λαλοῦντος, ἰδού, Ἰούδας εἷς τῶν δώδεκα
And while He was speaking, behold Judas, one of the twelve,
ἦλθε, καὶ μετ' αὐτοῦ ὄχλος πολὺς μετὰ μαχαιρῶν καὶ
came, and with him a crowd numerous with swords and

and staves, from the chief priests and elders of the people. [48] And he who was delivering Him up gave them a sign, saying, Whomever I shall kiss, it is He; seize Him. [49] And having come up immediately to Jesus, he said, Greetings, Master, and ardently kissed Him. [50] But Jesus said to him, Friend, why are you here? Then having come they laid hands on Jesus and seized Him. [51] And behold, one of those with Jesus, having stretched out (his) hand drew his sword; and striking the servant of the high priest, took off his ear. [52] Then Jesus said to him, Return your sword to its place; for all who take (the) sword shall perish by (the) sword. [53] Or do you think that I am not able now to call upon My Father, and He will place beside Me more than twelve legions of angels? [54] How then should the Scriptures be fulfilled, that it must happen this way?

[55] In that hour Jesus said to the crowds, Have you come out to take Me with swords and staves, as against a robber? I sat daily with you, teaching in the Temple, and you did not lay hands on Me. [56] But all this is happening that the Scriptures of the prophets may be fulfilled. Then all the disciples ran away, forsaking Him.

[57] And they who had seized Jesus led (Him) away to Caiaphas the high priest, where the scribes and the elders were gathered together. [58] And Peter followed Him from a distance, even to the court of the high priest; and having entered inside, he sat with the officers to see the end. [59] And the chief priests and the elders and the whole Sanhedrin looked for false evidence against Jesus, so that they might put Him to death. [60] And none (were) found; even though many false witnesses having come

**48** ξύλων, ἀπὸ τῶν ἀρχιερέων καὶ πρεσβυτέρων τοῦ λαοῦ. ὁ
clubs,  from  the chief priests  and  elders  of the people. he
δὲ παραδιδοὺς αὐτὸν ἔδωκεν αὐτοῖς σημεῖον, λέγων, "Ον
And betraying  Him  gave to them  a sign,  saying, Whom-
**49** ἂν φιλήσω, αὐτός ἐστι· κρατήσατε αὐτόν. καὶ εὐθέως
ever I may kiss, He  it is;  seize  Him.  And at once
προσελθὼν τῷ Ἰησοῦ εἶπε, Χαῖρε, ῥαββί· καὶ κατεφίλησεν
coming up  — to Jesus he said, Hail,  Rabbi, and ardently kissed
**50** αὐτόν. ὁ δὲ Ἰησοῦς εἶπεν αὐτῷ, Ἑταῖρε, ἐφ' ᾧ πάρει ; τότε
Him.  — But Jesus  said  to him, Friend,  why are you here? Then
προσελθόντες ἐπέβαλον τὰς χεῖρας ἐπὶ τὸν Ἰησοῦν, καὶ
coming up,  they laid on the hands,  on  —  Jesus,  and
**51** ἐκράτησαν αὐτόν. καὶ ἰδού, εἷς τῶν μετὰ Ἰησοῦ, ἐκτείνας
seized  Him.  And behold, one of those with Jesus, stretching
τὴν χεῖρα, ἀπέσπασε τὴν μάχαιραν αὐτοῦ, καὶ πατάξας τὸν
the hand,  drew  the  sword  of him, and  striking the
**52** δοῦλον τοῦ ἀρχιερέως ἀφεῖλεν αὐτοῦ τὸ ὠτίον. τότε λέγει
slave  of the high priest took off  of him the ear.  Then says
αὐτῷ ὁ Ἰησοῦς, Ἀπόστρεψόν σου τὴν μάχαιραν εἰς τὸν
to him — Jesus,  Put back  of you the  sword  to the
τόπον αὐτῆς· πάντες γὰρ οἱ λαβόντες μάχαιραν ἐν μαχαίρᾳ
place  of it;  all  for those taking (the) sword by a sword
**53** ἀπολοῦνται. ἢ δοκεῖς ὅτι οὐ δύναμαι ἄρτι παρακαλέσαι τὸν
shall perish.  Or think you that not  I can now  call upon  the
πατέρα μου, καὶ παραστήσει μοι πλείους ἢ δώδεκα λεγεῶνας
Father of Me, and He will place near Me more than twelve  legions
**54** ἀγγέλων ; πῶς οὖν πληρωθῶσιν αἱ γραφαί, ὅτι οὕτω δεῖ
of angels?  How, then, should be fulfilled the Scriptures that so it must
**55** γενέσθαι ; ἐν ἐκείνῃ τῇ ὥρᾳ εἶπεν ὁ Ἰησοῦς τοῖς ὄχλοις, Ὡς
be?  In that  — hour said — Jesus  to the crowds, As
ἐπὶ λῃστὴν ἐξήλθετε μετὰ μαχαιρῶν καὶ ξύλων συλλαβεῖν
on  a robber came you with  swords  and clubs together to take
με ; καθ' ἡμέραν πρὸς ὑμᾶς ἐκαθεζόμην διδάσκων ἐν τῷ ἱερῷ,
Me? Daily  with you I sat  teaching  in the Temple,
**56** καὶ οὐκ ἐκρατήσατέ με. τοῦτο δὲ ὅλον γέγονεν, ἵνα πληρωθῶ-
and not you seized Me. this But all has happened that may be ful-
σιν αἱ γραφαὶ τῶν προφητῶν. τότε οἱ μαθηταὶ πάντες
filled the Scriptures of the  prophets. Then the  disciples  all
ἀφέντες αὐτὸν ἔφυγον.
leaving  Him  fled.
**57** Οἱ δὲ κρατήσαντες τὸν Ἰησοῦν ἀπήγαγον πρὸς Καιάφαν
the (ones) But seizing  —  Jesus led away  to  Caiaphas
τὸν ἀρχιερέα, ὅπου οἱ γραμματεῖς καὶ οἱ πρεσβύτεροι
the high priest, where the scribes  and the  elders
**58** συνήχθησαν. ὁ δὲ Πέτρος ἠκολούθει αὐτῷ ἀπὸ μακρόθεν
were assembled. — And Peter  followed  Him  from afar
ἕως τῆς αὐλῆς τοῦ ἀρχιερέως, καὶ εἰσελθὼν ἔσω ἐκάθητο
up to the  court of the high priest, and  entering within  sat
**59** μετὰ τῶν ὑπηρετῶν, ἰδεῖν τὸ τέλος. οἱ δὲ ἀρχιερεῖς καὶ οἱ
with the under-officers to see the end. the And chief priests and the
πρεσβύτεροι καὶ τὸ συνέδριον ὅλον ἐζήτουν ψευδομαρτυ-
elders  and the sanhedrin whole sought  false testimony
**60** ρίαν κατὰ τοῦ Ἰησοῦ, ὅπως αὐτὸν θανατώσωσι. καὶ οὐχ
against — Jesus so as  Him they might execute, but not
εὗρον· καὶ πολλῶν ψευδομαρτύρων προσελθόντων, οὐχ
did find, even many  false witnesses  coming forward  not

forward, they did not find (any). But at last two false witnesses came up, [61] saying, This one said, I am able to destroy Temple of God, and in three days to build it. [62] And having stood up the high priest said to Him, Do you answer nothing? What do these witness against you? [63] But Jesus was silent, and answering the high priest said to Him, I adjure you by the living God that you tell us if you are the Christ, the Son of God. [64] Jesus said to him, You have said (it)! I say more to you, From this time you shall see the Son of man sitting at (the) right (hand) of power, and coming on the clouds of Heaven. [65] Then the high priest tore his garments, saying, He has blasphemed! Why do we have any more need of witnesses? Behold, now you have heard his blasphemy. [66] What do you think? And answering they said, He is deserving of death. [67] Then they spat in His face, and beat Him, and some slapped (Him), [68] saying, Prophesy to us, Christ; Who is he that struck you?

[69] And Peter sat outside in the court; and one girl came near to him, saying, And you were with Jesus the Galilean. [70] But he denied before all, saying, I do not know what you say. [71] And he going out into the porch, another saw him, and says to those there, And this one was with Jesus the Nazarene. [72] And again he denied with an oath, I do not know the man. [73] And after a little, those standing by coming near said to Peter, Truly you also are of them, for even your speech makes you manifest. [74] Then he began to curse and to swear, I do not know the man. And immediately a cock sounded. [75] And Peter recalled the word of Jesus, saying to him, Before a cock sounds, you will deny Me three times. And

εὗρον. ὕστερον δὲ προσελθόντες δύο ψευδομάρτυρες εἶπον,
did find. at last But coming up two false witnesses said,

61 Οὗτος ἔφη, Δύναμαι καταλῦσαι τὸν ναὸν τοῦ Θεοῦ, καὶ διὰ
This one said, I am able to destroy the temple — of God, and via

62 τριῶν ἡμερῶν οἰκοδομῆσαι αὐτόν. καὶ ἀναστὰς ὁ ἀρχιερεὺς
three days to build it. And standing up the high priest

εἶπεν αὐτῷ, Οὐδὲν ἀποκρίνῃ; τί οὗτοί σου καταμαρτυροῦ-
said to Him, Nothing do you reply? of what these of you do witness

63 σιν; ὁ δὲ Ἰησοῦς ἐσιώπα. καὶ ἀποκριθεὶς ὁ ἀρχιερεὺς εἶπεν
against? But Jesus kept silent. And answering, the high priest said

αὐτῷ, Ἐξορκίζω σε κατὰ τοῦ Θεοῦ τοῦ ζῶντος, ἵνα ἡμῖν
to Him, I adjure you by God the living that us

εἴπῃς εἰ σὺ εἶ ὁ Χριστός, ὁ υἱὸς τοῦ Θεοῦ. λέγει αὐτῷ ὁ
you tell if you are the Christ, the Son of God! Says to him —

64 Ἰησοῦς, Σὺ εἶπας. πλὴν λέγω ὑμῖν, ἀπ’ ἄρτι ὄψεσθε τὸν
Jesus, You said (it). Yet I tell you, from now you will see the

υἱὸν τοῦ ἀνθρώπου καθήμενον ἐκ δεξιῶν τῆς δυνάμεως καὶ
Son — of man sitting off (the) right (hand) of power and

65 ἐρχόμενον ἐπὶ τῶν νεφελῶν τοῦ οὐρανοῦ. τότε ὁ ἀρχιερεὺς
coming on the clouds — of Heaven. Then the high priest

διέρρηξε τὰ ἱμάτια αὐτοῦ, λέγων ὅτι Ἐβλασφήμησε· τί ἔτι
tore the garments of him, saying, — He blasphemed; Why yet

χρείαν ἔχομεν μαρτύρων; ἴδε, νῦν ἠκούσατε τὴν βλασφημίαν
need have we of witnesses? Behold, now, you heard the blasphemy.

66 αὐτοῦ. τί ὑμῖν δοκεῖ; οἱ δὲ ἀποκριθέντες εἶπον, Ἔνοχος
of him. What to you seems it? they And answering said, Liable

67 θανάτου ἐστί. τότε ἐνέπτυσαν εἰς τὸ πρόσωπον αὐτοῦ καὶ
of death he is. Then they spat in the face of Him, and

68 ἐκολάφισαν αὐτόν· οἱ δὲ ἐρράπισαν, λέγοντες, Προφή-
beat with the fist Him, they and slapped (Him), saying, Prophesy

τευσον ἡμῖν, Χριστέ, τίς ἐστιν ὁ παίσας σε;
to us, Christ, who is it, the (one) having struck you?

69 Ὁ δὲ Πέτρος ἔξω ἐκάθητο ἐν τῇ αὐλῇ· καὶ προσῆλθεν
— And Peter outside sat in the court; and came near

αὐτῷ μία παιδίσκη, λέγουσα, Καὶ σὺ ἦσθα μετὰ Ἰησοῦ τοῦ
to him one maid, saying, And you were with Jesus the

70 Γαλιλαίου. ὁ δὲ ἠρνήσατο ἔμπροσθεν πάντων, λέγων, Οὐκ
Galilean. he But denied before all, saying, not

71 οἶδα τί λέγεις. ἐξελθόντα δὲ αὐτὸν εἰς τὸν πυλῶνα, εἶδεν
I know what you say. going out And he into the porch, saw

αὐτὸν ἄλλη, καὶ λέγει τοῖς ἐκεῖ, Καὶ οὗτος ἦν μετὰ Ἰησοῦ
him another, and says to those there, And this one was with Jesus

72 τοῦ Ναζωραίου. καὶ πάλιν ἠρνήσατο μεθ’ ὅρκου ὅτι Οὐκ
the Nazarene. And again he denied, with an oath, — not

73 οἶδα τὸν ἄνθρωπον. μετὰ μικρὸν δὲ προσελθόντες οἱ ἑστῶτες
I know the man. after a little And coming near those standing

εἶπον τῷ Πέτρῳ, Ἀληθῶς καὶ σὺ ἐξ αὐτῶν εἶ· καὶ γὰρ ἡ
said — to Peter, Truly also you of them are, even for the

74 λαλιά σου δῆλόν σε ποιεῖ. τότε ἤρξατο καταναθεματίζειν καὶ
speech of you manifest you makes. Then he began to curse and

ὀμνύειν ὅτι Οὐκ οἶδα τὸν ἄνθρωπον. καὶ εὐθέως ἀλέκτωρ
to swear, — not I know the man. And immediately a cock

75 ἐφώνησε. καὶ ἐμνήσθη ὁ Πέτρος τοῦ ῥήματος τοῦ Ἰησοῦ
crowed. And remembered — Peter the word — of Jesus,

εἰρηκότος αὐτῷ ὅτι Πρὶν ἀλέκτορα φωνῆσαι, τρὶς ἀπαρνήσῃ
having said to him, — Before a cock crows, thrice you will deny

going out, he wept bitterly.

με. καὶ ἐξελθὼν ἔξω ἔκλαυσε πικρῶς.
Me. And going forth outside he wept bitterly.

## CHAPTER 27

[1] And early morning occurring, all the chief priests and the elders of the people took counsel together against Jesus, so as to execute Him. [2] And having bound Him, they led away and delivered Him to Pontius Pilate the governor.

[3] Then Judas, he betraying Him, seeing that He was condemned, sorrowing, returned the thirty pieces of silver to the chief priests and elders, [4] saying, I sinned, betraying innocent blood. But they said, What (is it) to us? You see (to it). [5] And tossing the silver pieces into the Temple, he left; and going away hanged himself. [6] And the chief priests taking the pieces of silver said, It is not lawful to put them into the treasury, since it is (the) price of blood. [7] And taking counsel, they bought of them the potter's field, for burial for the strangers. [8] Therefore that Field was called, Field of Blood, until today. [9] Then was fulfilled that (which was) spoken by Jeremiah the prophet, saying, "And I took the thirty pieces of silver, the price of Him who was priced, on whom they of the sons of Israel set a price, [10] and gave them for the potter's field, as the Lord commanded me."

[11] But Jesus stood before the governor; and the governor questioned Him, saying, Are you the king of the Jews? And Jesus said to him, You say (it). [12] And when He was accused by the chief priests and the elders, He answered nothing. [13] Then Pilate says to Him, Do you not hear how many things they testify against you? [14] And He did not answer him, even to one word, so that the governor greatly marveled.

[15] And at a feast, the governor customarily released one prisoner to the

## CHAPTER 27

1 Πρωΐας δὲ γενομένης, συμβούλιον ἔλαβον πάντες οἱ
early morning And occurring, counsel together took all the
ἀρχιερεῖς καὶ οἱ πρεσβύτεροι τοῦ λαοῦ κατὰ τοῦ Ἰησοῦ,
chief priests and the elders of the people against — Jesus.

2 ὥστε θανατῶσαι αὐτόν· καὶ δήσαντες αὐτὸν ἀπήγαγον καὶ
so as to execute Him. And having bound Him, they led away and
παρέδωκαν αὐτὸν Ποντίῳ Πιλάτῳ τῷ ἡγεμόνι.
delivered Him to Pontius Pilate the governor.

3 Τότε ἰδὼν Ἰούδας ὁ παραδιδοὺς αὐτὸν ὅτι κατεκρίθη,
Then seeing Judas, the (one) betraying Him, that He was condemned,
μεταμεληθεὶς ἀπέστρεψε τὰ τριάκοντα ἀργύρια τοῖς ἀρχιε-
sorrowing returned the thirty pieces of silver to the chief

4 ρεῦσι καὶ τοῖς πρεσβυτέροις, λέγων, Ἥμαρτον παραδοὺς
priests and the elders, saying, I sinned, betraying

5 αἷμα ἀθῶον. οἱ δὲ εἶπον, Τί πρὸς ἡμᾶς; σὺ ὄψει. καὶ ῥίψας
blood innocent. they But said, What to us? You see (to it) And tossing
τὰ ἀργύρια ἐν τῷ ναῷ, ἀνεχώρησε· καὶ ἀπελθὼν ἀπήγξατο.
the silver pieces into the temple, he left, and going away hanged himself.

6 οἱ δὲ ἀρχιερεῖς λαβόντες τὰ ἀργύρια εἶπον, Οὐκ ἔξεστι
the But chief priests taking the silver pieces said, not It is lawful
βαλεῖν αὐτὰ εἰς τὸν κορβανᾶν, ἐπεὶ τιμὴ αἵματός ἐστι. συμ-
to put them into the treasury, since price of blood it is.

7 βούλιον δὲ λαβόντες ἠγόρασαν ἐξ αὐτῶν τὸν ἀγρὸν τοῦ
counsel And taking, they bought of them the field of the

8 κεραμέως, εἰς ταφὴν τοῖς ξένοις. διὸ ἐκλήθη ὁ ἀγρὸς ἐκεῖνος
potter, for burial for the strangers. Thus was called field that,

9 ἀγρὸς αἵματος, ἕως τῆς σήμερον. τότε ἐπληρώθη τὸ ῥηθὲν
Field of Blood, until — today. Then was fulfilled that spoken
διὰ Ἰερεμίου τοῦ προφήτου, λέγοντος, Καὶ ἔλαβον τὰ
through Jeremiah the prophet, saying, And I took the
τριάκοντα ἀργύρια, τὴν τιμὴν τοῦ τετιμημένου, ὃν ἐτιμή-
thirty silver pieces, the price of the (one) priced, whom they

10 σαντο ἀπὸ υἱῶν Ἰσραήλ· καὶ ἔδωκαν αὐτὰ εἰς τὸν ἀγρὸν
priced from sons of Israel, and gave them for the field
τοῦ κεραμέως, καθὰ συνέταξέ μοι Κύριος.
of the potter, as directed me the Lord.

11 Ὁ δὲ Ἰησοῦς ἔστη ἔμπροσθεν τοῦ ἡγεμόνος· καὶ ἐπηρώ-
—And Jesus stood before the governor, and questioned
τησεν αὐτὸν ὁ ἡγεμών, λέγων, Σὺ εἶ ὁ βασιλεὺς τῶν
Him the governor, saying, You are the king of the

12 Ἰουδαίων; ὁ δὲ Ἰησοῦς ἔφη αὐτῷ, Σὺ λέγεις. καὶ ἐν τῷ
Jews? — And Jesus said to him, You say (it). And in the
κατηγορεῖσθαι αὐτὸν ὑπὸ τῶν ἀρχιερέων καὶ τῶν πρε-
accusing (of) Him by the chief priests and the

13 σβυτέρων, οὐδὲν ἀπεκρίνατο. τότε λέγει αὐτῷ ὁ Πιλάτος,
elders, nothing He answered. Then says to Him — Pilate,

14 Οὐκ ἀκούεις πόσα σοῦ καταμαρτυροῦσι; καὶ οὐκ ἀπεκρίθη
do not you hear what you they witness against? And not He answered
αὐτῷ πρὸς οὐδὲ ἓν ῥῆμα, ὥστε θαυμάζειν τὸν ἡγεμόνα λίαν.
him, to not even one word, so as to marvel the governor much.

15 κατὰ δὲ ἑορτὴν εἰώθει ὁ ἡγεμὼν ἀπολύειν ἕνα τῷ ὄχλῳ
at And a feast used the governor to release one to the crowd

crowd, whom they wished. [16] And they had then a notable prisoner called Barabbas. [17] Then they being assembled, Pilate said to them, Whom do you wish I may release to you, Barabbas, or Jesus called Christ? [18] For he knew they delivered Him up through envy. [19] But as he was sitting on the tribunal seat, his wife sent to him, saying, Let nothing (be) to you and that just one; for I have suffered many things today by a dream because of him. [20] But the chief priests and the elders persuaded the crowds, that they should ask (for) Barabbas; and to destroy Jesus. [21] And the governor said to them, Which do you wish from the two I may release to you? And they said, Barrabbas. [22] Pilate says to them, What then should I do (to) Jesus called Christ? [23] They all say to him, Let him be crucified. But the governor said, For what wrong did he do? But they more so cried out, saying, Let him be crucified. [24] And seeing that nothing (is) gained, but rather an uproar occurs, taking water he washed (his) hands before the crowd, saying, I am innocent of the blood of this righteous 'one; you will see. [25] And answering all the people said, His blood (be) on us and on our children. [26] Then he released Barabbas to them; but having Jesus whipped, he delivered (Him) up that He might be crucified. [27] Then the soldiers of the governor, having taken Jesus to the praetorium, gathered all the band against Him; [28] and having stripped Him, they put a scarlet cloak around Him; [29] and having plaited a crown of thorns and put it on His head, and a reed in His right hand; and bowing down before Him, they mocked Him, saying, Hail, king of the Jews! [30] And having spit upon

**16** δέσμιον, ὃν ἤθελον. εἶχον δὲ τότε δέσμιον ἐπίσημον, λεγό-
prisoner, whom they wished. they had And then a prisoner notable called

**17** μενον Βαραββᾶν. συνηγμένων οὖν αυτῶν, εἶπεν αὐτοῖς ὁ
Barabbas. having assembled then they said to them —
Πιλᾶτος, Τίνα θέλετε ἀπολύσω ὑμῖν; Βαραββᾶν, ἢ Ἰησοῦν
Pilate, Whom wish you I may release to you, Barabbas, or Jesus

**18** τὸν λεγόμενον Χριστόν; ᾔδει γὰρ ὅτι διὰ φθόνον παρέδωκαν
— called Christ? he knew For that through envy they delivered

**19** αὐτόν. καθημένου δὲ αὐτοῦ ἐπὶ τοῦ βήματος, ἀπέστειλε
Him. sitting And he on the tribunal sent
πρὸς αὐτὸν ἡ γυνὴ αὐτοῦ, λέγουσα, Μηδέν σοι καὶ τῷ
to him the wife of him, saying, Nothing to you and to
δικαίῳ ἐκείνῳ· πολλὰ γὰρ ἔπαθον σήμερον κατ' ὄναρ δι'
just one that; many things for I suffered today by a dream via

**20** αὐτόν. οἱ δὲ ἀρχιερεῖς καὶ οἱ πρεσβύτεροι ἔπεισαν τοὺς
him. the But chief priests and the elders persuaded the
ὄχλους ἵνα αἰτήσωνται τὸν Βαραββᾶν, τὸν δὲ Ἰησοῦν
crowds that they should ask — Barabbas, — and Jesus

**21** ἀπολέσωσιν. ἀποκριθεὶς δὲ ὁ ἡγεμὼν εἶπεν αὐτοῖς, Τίνα
to destroy. answering And the governor said to them, Which
θέλετε ἀπὸ τῶν δύο ἀπολύσω ὑμῖν; οἱ δὲ εἶπον, Βαραββᾶν.
wish you from the two I may release to you? they And said, Barabbas.

**22** λέγει αὐτοῖς ὁ Πιλᾶτος, Τί οὖν ποιήσω Ἰησοῦν τὸν λεγό-
Says to them, — Pilate, What then may I do (to) Jesus — called

**23** μενον Χριστόν; λέγουσιν αὐτῷ πάντες, Σταυρωθήτω. ὁ
Christ? They say to him all, Let him be crucified. the
δὲ ἡγεμὼν ἔφη, Τί γὰρ κακὸν ἐποίησεν; οἱ δὲ περισσῶς
But governor said, what For badness did he? they But more

**24** ἔκραζον, λέγοντες, Σταυρωθήτω. ἰδὼν δὲ ὁ Πιλᾶτος ὅτι
cried out, saying, Let him be crucified. seeing And — Pilate that
οὐδὲν ὠφελεῖ, ἀλλὰ μᾶλλον θόρυβος γίνεται, λαβὼν ὕδωρ,
nothing is gained, but rather an uproar occurs, taking water
ἀπενίψατο τὰς χεῖρας ἀπέναντι τοῦ ὄχλου, λέγων, Ἀθῷός

he washed the hands before the crowd, saying, Innocent

**25** εἰμι ἀπὸ τοῦ αἵματος τοῦ δικαίου τούτου· ὑμεῖς ὄψεσθε. καὶ
I am from the blood of righteous one this, you will see. And
ἀποκριθεὶς πᾶς ὁ λαὸς εἶπε, Τὸ αἷμα αὐτοῦ ἐφ' ἡμᾶς καὶ ἐπὶ
answering, all the people said, The blood of him on us and on

**26** τὰ τέκνα ἡμῶν. τότε ἀπέλυσεν αὐτοῖς τὸν Βαραββᾶν· τὸν
the children of us. Then he released to them — Barabbas —
δὲ Ἰησοῦν φραγελλώσας παρέδωκεν ἵνα σταυρωθῇ.
But Jesus having whipped, he delivered that he might be crucified.

**27** Τότε οἱ στρατιῶται τοῦ ἡγεμόνος, παραλαβόντες τὸν
Then the soldiers of the governor, having taken —
Ἰησοῦν εἰς τὸ πραιτώριον, συνήγαγον ἐπ' αὐτὸν ὅλην τὴν
Jesus into the praetorium, gathered against Him all the

**28** σπεῖραν· καὶ ἐκδύσαντες αὐτόν, περιέθηκαν αὐτῷ χλαμύδα
cohort. And stripping Him, they put around Him a cloak

**29** κοκκίνην. καὶ πλέξαντες στέφανον ἐξ ἀκανθῶν, ἐπέθηκαν
scarlet. and having plaited a crown of thorns, they placed
ἐπὶ τὴν κεφαλὴν αὐτοῦ, καὶ κάλαμον ἐπὶ τὴν δεξιὰν αὐτοῦ·
on the head of Him, and a reed upon the right of Him.
καὶ γονυπετήσαντες ἔμπροσθεν αὐτοῦ ἐνέπαιζον αὐτῷ,
And bowing the knee in front of Him they mocked at Him,

**30** λέγοντες, Χαῖρε, ὁ βασιλεὺς τῶν Ἰουδαίων· καὶ ἐμπτύσαντες
saying, Hail, king of the Jews; and spitting

Him, they took the reed and struck (Him) on His head. [31] And when they had mocked Him, they took the robe off of Him, and they put His own clothes on Him; and led Him away to crucify.

[32] And going out they found a man, a Cyrenean by the name of Simon; they forced Him that He might carry His cross. [33] And having come to a place called Golgotha, which is called Place of a Skull, [34] they gave Him vinegar mingled with gall to drink; and having tasted it He would not drink. [35] And having crucified Him, they divided His garments, casting a lot — that might be fulfilled that which was spoken by the prophet, "They divided My garments among themselves, and they cast a lot for My clothing." [36] And sitting down they watched Him there. [37] And they put up over His head His accusation written, THIS IS JESUS THE KING OF THE JEWS. [38] Then two thieves were crucified with Him, one at (the) right hand, and one at (the) left.

[39] But those passing by blasphemed Him, shaking their heads, [40] and saying, You who destroy the Temple and build it in three days, save Yourself. If You are the Son of God, come down from the cross. [41] And in the same way the chief priests, mocking with the scribes and elders, said, [42] He saved others, he is not able to save himself. If he is the king of Israel, let him come down now from the cross, and we will believe him. [43] He trusted on God, let Him deliver him now, if He will (have) him. For He said, I am the Son of God. [44] And also the robbers who were crucified together with Him reviled Him, (saying) the same.

[45] Now from (the) sixth hour, the darkness was over all the land until

---

**31** εἰς αὐτόν, ἔλαβον τὸν κάλαμον, καὶ ἔτυπτον εἰς τὴν κεφαλὴν
at   Him   took   the   reed   and   struck   at   the   head
αὐτοῦ. καὶ ὅτε ἐνέπαιξαν αὐτῷ, ἐξέδυσαν αὐτὸν τὴν
of Him.   And when they mocked at Him, they stripped off Him   the
χλαμύδα, καὶ ἐνέδυσαν αὐτὸν τὰ ἱμάτια αὐτοῦ, καὶ ἀπή-
cloak   and put on   Him   the garments of Him, and led
γαγον αὐτὸν εἰς τὸ σταυρῶσαι.
away   Him   —   — to crucify.

**32** Ἐξερχόμενοι δὲ εὗρον ἄνθρωπον Κυρηναῖον, ὀνόματι
going forth   And they found   a man,   a Cyrenian,   by name
Σίμωνα· τοῦτον ἠγγάρευσαν ἵνα ἄρῃ τὸν σταυρὸν αὐτοῦ.
Simon.   This one they compelled, that he bear the   cross   of Him.

**33** καὶ ἐλθόντες εἰς τόπον λεγόμενον Γολγοθᾶ, ὅς ἐστι λεγόμενος
And coming   to a place   called   Golgotha, which is   saying,

**34** κρανίου τόπος, ἔδωκαν αὐτῷ πιεῖν ὄξος μετὰ χολῆς μεμιγ-
Of a skull place,   they gave   Him   to drink vinegar with   gall   mixed;

**35** μένον· καὶ γευσάμενος οὐκ ἤθελε πιεῖν. σταυρώσαντες δὲ
and having tasted (it), not He would drink. having crucified And
αὐτόν, διεμερίσαντο τὰ ἱμάτια αὐτοῦ, βάλλοντες κλῆρον·
Him,   they divided   the garments of Him,   casting   a lot,
ἵνα πληρωθῇ τὸ ῥηθὲν ὑπὸ τοῦ προφήτου, Διεμερίσαντο τὰ
that may be fulfilled the spoken by the prophet,   They divided   the
ἱμάτιά μου ἑαυτοῖς, καὶ ἐπὶ τὸν ἱματισμόν μου ἔβαλον κλῆρον.
garments of Me themselves and on the clothing   of Me they cast a lot.

**36**
**37** καὶ καθήμενοι ἐτήρουν αὐτὸν ἐκεῖ. καὶ ἐπέθηκαν ἐπάνω τῆς
and sitting down they guarded Him there. And they placed above   the
κεφαλῆς αὐτοῦ τὴν αἰτίαν αὐτοῦ γεγραμμένην, Οὗτός ἐστιν
the head of Him the charge of Him, having been written, THIS IS

**38** Ἰησοῦς ὁ βασιλεὺς τῶν Ἰουδαίων. τότε σταυροῦνται σὺν
JESUS THE KING   OF THE JEWS.   Then are crucified   with

**39** αὐτῷ δύο λῃσταί, εἰς ἐκ δεξιῶν καὶ εἰς ἐξ εὐωνύμων. οἱ δὲ
Him two   robbers,   one off (the) right and one off (the) left.   And
παραπορευόμενοι ἐβλασφήμουν αὐτόν, κινοῦντες τὰς κεφα-
passing by   blasphemed   Him,   shaking   the heads

**40** λὰς αὐτῶν, καὶ λέγοντες, Ὁ καταλύων τὸν ναὸν καὶ ἐν
of them, and saying,   The (one) destroying the temple and in
τρισὶν ἡμέραις οἰκοδομῶν, σῶσον σεαυτόν· εἰ υἱὸς εἶ τοῦ
three   days building (it),   save   yourself,   if Son You are

**41** Θεοῦ, κατάβηθι ἀπὸ τοῦ σταυροῦ. ὁμοίως δὲ καὶ οἱ
of God, come down from   the   cross.   likewise And also the
ἀρχιερεῖς ἐμπαίζοντες μετὰ τῶν γραμματέων καὶ πρεσ-
chief priests   mocking   with   the   scribes   and elders

**42** βυτέρων ἔλεγον, Ἄλλους ἔσωσεν, ἑαυτὸν οὐ δύναται σῶσαι.
said,   Others He saved, Himself not He is able to save.
εἰ βασιλεὺς Ἰσραήλ ἐστι, καταβάτω νῦν ἀπὸ τοῦ σταυροῦ,
if   king   of Israel He is, let Him descend now from the   cross,

**43** καὶ πιστεύσομεν αὐτῷ. πέποιθεν ἐπὶ τὸν Θεόν· ῥυσάσθω
and we will believe   Him.   He trusted on   —   God, let Him rescue
νῦν αὐτόν, εἰ θέλει αὐτόν. εἶπε γὰρ ὅτι Θεοῦ εἰμι υἱός. τὸ
now Him, if He desires Him. He said For, — of God I am Son. the

**44** δ᾽ αὐτὸ καὶ οἱ λῃσταὶ οἱ συσταυρωθέντες αὐτῷ ὠνείδιζον
And same also the robbers   —   crucified together with Him reproached
αὐτῷ.
Him.

**45** Ἀπὸ δὲ ἕκτης ὥρας σκότος ἐγένετο ἐπὶ πᾶσαν τὴν γῆν
from And sixth   hour   darkness occurred over   all   the land

(the) ninth hour. [46] And about the ninth hour, Jesus cried out with a loud voice, saying, Eli, Eli, lama sabachthani — that is, My God, My God, why have You forsaken Me? [47] And some of those who were standing, having heard, said, This one calls Elijah. [48] And immediately one of them having run and taken a sponge, and filled with vinegar, and put (it) on a reed, gave drink to Him. [49] But the rest said, Let be; let us see if Elijah comes to save him.

[50] And Jesus again having cried with a loud voice yielded up (His) spirit. [51] And, behold, the veil of the Temple was torn in two from top to bottom; and the earth quaked, and the rocks were sheared! [52] And the tombs were opened, and many bodies of the saints who had fallen asleep arose, [53] and having gone out of the tombs after His resurrection, entered into the holy city and appeared to many.

[54] But the centurion, and they who watched over Jesus with him, having seen the earth quake and the things that took place, feared greatly, saying, Truly this was God's Son! [55] And many women were there, watching from a distance, who followed Jesus from Galilee, ministering to Him, [56] among whom was Mary Magdalene, and Mary the mother of James and Joses, and the mother of the sons of Zebedee.

[57] And evening being come a rich man from Arimathea, named Joseph, who also himself was discipled to Jesus. [58] Having gone to Pilate, he begged the body of Jesus. Then Pilate commanded the body to be given up. [59] And having taken the body, Joseph wrapped it in a clean linen cloth, [60] and laid it in his new tomb which he had cut out in the rock; and having rolled a great stone to the

---

**46** ἕως ὥρας ἐννάτης· περὶ δὲ τὴν ἐννάτην ὥραν ἀνεβόησεν ὁ
until hour (the) ninth. about And the ninth hour cried out —

Ἰησοῦς φωνῇ μεγάλῃ, λέγων, Ἠλί, Ἠλί, λαμὰ σαβαχθανί ;
Jesus a voice great, saying, Eli, Eli, lama sabachthani?

τοῦτ' ἔστι, Θεέ μου, Θεέ μου, ἱνατί με ἐγκατέλιπες ; τινὲς
this is, God of Me, God of Me, why Me did You forsake? some

**47** δὲ τῶν ἐκεῖ ἑστώτων ἀκούσαντες ἔλεγον ὅτι Ἠλίαν φωνεῖ
And of those there standing hearing said, — Elijah calls

**48** οὗτος. καὶ εὐθέως δραμὼν εἷς ἐξ αὐτῶν, καὶ λαβὼν σπόγγον,
this one. And at once running one of them and taking a sponge,

**49** πλήσας τε ὄξους, καὶ περιθεὶς καλάμῳ, ἐπότιζεν αὐτόν. οἱ δὲ
filling and with vinegar, and put on a reed, gave to drink Him. the But

λοιποὶ ἔλεγον, Ἄφες, ἴδωμεν εἰ ἔρχεται Ἠλίας σώσων αὐτόν.
rest said, Leave! Let us see if comes Elijah to save Him.

**50** ὁ δὲ Ἰησοῦς πάλιν κράξας φωνῇ μεγάλῃ ἀφῆκε τὸ πνεῦμα.
—And Jesus again crying with a voice great released the spirit.

**51** καὶ ἰδού, τὸ καταπέτασμα τοῦ ναοῦ ἐσχίσθη εἰς δύο ἀπὸ
And behold, the veil of the Temple was torn into two, from

ἄνωθεν ἕως κάτω· καὶ ἡ γῆ ἐσείσθη καὶ αἱ πέτραι ἐσχίσθη-
above until below and the earth was shaken, and the rocks were

**52** σαν· καὶ τὰ μνημεῖα ἀνεῴχθησαν· καὶ πολλὰ σώματα τῶν
torn, and the tombs were opened, and many bodies of the

**53** κεκοιμημένων ἁγίων ἠγέρθη· καὶ ἐξελθόντες ἐκ τῶν μνημείων
having fallen asleep saints were raised; and coming forth out of the tombs

μετὰ τὴν ἔγερσιν αὐτοῦ εἰσῆλθον εἰς τὴν ἁγίαν πόλιν, καὶ
after the rising of Him entered into the holy city and

**54** ἐνεφανίσθησαν πολλοῖς. ὁ δὲ ἑκατόνταρχος καὶ οἱ μετ' αὐτοῦ
were manifested to many. the And centurion and those with him

τηροῦντες τὸν Ἰησοῦν, ἰδόντες τὸν σεισμὸν καὶ τὰ γενόμενα,
guarding — Jesus, seeing the earthquake and the happenings,

ἐφοβήθησαν σφόδρα, λέγοντες, Ἀληθῶς Θεοῦ υἱὸς ἦν
feared exceedingly, saying, Truly of God Son was

**55** οὗτος. ἦσαν δὲ ἐκεῖ γυναῖκες πολλαὶ ἀπὸ μακρόθεν θεωροῦ-
this One. were And there women many from afar beholding

σαι, αἵτινες ἠκολούθησαν τῷ Ἰησοῦ ἀπὸ τῆς Γαλιλαίας,
who followed — Jesus from the Galilee,

**56** διακονοῦσαι αὐτῷ· ἐν αἷς ἦν Μαρία ἡ Μαγδαληνή, καὶ
ministering to Him; among whom was Mary the Magdalene, and

Μαρία ἡ τοῦ Ἰακώβου καὶ Ἰωσῆ μήτηρ, καὶ ἡ μήτηρ τῶν
Mary the — of James and Joses mother, and the mother of the

υἱῶν Ζεβεδαίου.
sons of Zebedee.

**57** Ὀψίας δὲ γενομένης, ἦλθεν ἄνθρωπος πλούσιος ἀπὸ
evening And having come, came a man rich from

Ἀριμαθαίας, τοὔνομα Ἰωσήφ, ὃς καὶ αὐτὸς ἐμαθήτευσε τῷ
Arimathea, by name Joseph, who also himself was discipled —

**58** Ἰησοῦ· οὗτος προσελθὼν τῷ Πιλάτῳ, ᾐτήσατο τὸ σῶμα
to Jesus; this one coming up — to Pilate asked the body

τοῦ Ἰησοῦ. τότε ὁ Πιλᾶτος ἐκέλευσεν ἀποδοθῆναι τὸ σῶμα.
— of Jesus. Then — Pilate commanded to be given the body.

**59** καὶ λαβὼν τὸ σῶμα ὁ Ἰωσὴφ ἐνετύλιξεν αὐτὸ σινδόνι
And taking the body, — Joseph wrapped it in linen

**60** καθαρᾷ, καὶ ἔθηκεν αὐτὸ ἐν τῷ καινῷ αὐτοῦ μνημείῳ, ὃ
clean, and placed it in the new of him tomb, which

ἐλατόμησεν ἐν τῇ πέτρα· καὶ προσκυλίσας λίθον μέγαν τῇ
he had hewed in the rock, and having rolled a stone great to the

door of the tomb, (he) departed. [61] And there was Mary Magdalene and the other Mary sitting there across from the grave.

**61** θύρα τοῦ μνημείου, ἀπῆλθεν. ἦν δὲ ἐκεῖ Μαρία ἡ Μαγδαληνή,
door of the tomb,　he went away. was And there Mary the Magdalene,

καὶ ἡ ἄλλη Μαρία, καθήμεναι ἀπέναντι τοῦ τάφου.
and the other Mary,　sitting　opposite　the　grave.

[62] Now on the next day, which is after the preparation, the chief priests and the Pharisees were gathered to Pilate, [63] saying, Sir, that that deceiver said while living, After three days I will rise.

**62** Τῇ δὲ ἐπαύριον, ἥτις ἐστὶ μετὰ τὴν Παρασκευήν, συνή-
on the And morrow, which　is　after　the Preparation,　were

**63** χθησαν οἱ ἀρχιερεῖς καὶ οἱ Φαρισαῖοι πρὸς Πιλάτον, λέγοντες,
assembled the chief priests and the Pharisees to　Pilate,　saying,

Κύριε, ἐμνήσθημεν ὅτι ἐκεῖνος ὁ πλάνος εἶπεν ἔτι ζῶν, Μετὰ
Sir, we have recalled　that that　— deceiver said yet living, After

[64] Therefore command that the grave be secured until the third day, lest his disciples coming by night steal him away, and say to the people, He has risen from the dead; and the last deception shall be worse than the first. [65] And Pilate said to them, You have a guard; go away; make (it as) secure as you know (how). [66] And they having gone made the grave secure, sealing the stone, together with the guard.

**64** τρεῖς ἡμέρας ἐγείρομαι. κέλευσον οὖν ἀσφαλισθῆναι τὸν
three days I arise.　Command then to be made secure the

τάφον ἕως τῆς τρίτης ἡμέρας· μήποτε ἐλθόντες οἱ μαθηταὶ
grave until the third　day,　lest　coming the disciples

αὐτοῦ νυκτὸς κλέψωσιν αὐτόν, καὶ εἴπωσι τῷ λαῷ, Ἠγέρ-
of him by night may steal　him　and may say to the people, He is

θη ἀπὸ τῶν νεκρῶν· καὶ ἔσται ἡ ἐσχάτη πλάνη χείρων τῆς
raised from the dead,　and will be the last　deceit worse than the

**65** πρώτης. ἔφη δὲ αὐτοῖς ὁ Πιλάτος, Ἔχετε κουστωδίαν·
first.　Said and to them　—　Pilate, You have　a guard;

**66** ὑπάγετε, ἀσφαλίσασθε ὡς οἴδατε. οἱ δὲ πορευθέντες ἠσφαλί-
go,　make secure　as you know. they And going　made

σαντο τὸν τάφον, σφραγίσαντες τὸν λίθον, μετὰ τῆς
secure　the grave,　sealing　the stone,　with the

κουστωδίας.
guard.

## CHAPTER 28

[1] Now late on the Sabbath, as it was dawning toward the first day of the week, Mary Magdalene and the other Mary came to see the grave.

## CHAPTER 28

**1** Ὀψὲ δὲ σαββάτων, τῇ ἐπιφωσκούσῃ εἰς μίαν σαββάτων,
late in But the week, at the dawning　into the first of (the) week,

ἦλθε Μαρία ἡ Μαγδαληνή, καὶ ἡ ἄλλη Μαρία, θεωρῆσαι
came Mary the Magdalene　and the other　Mary　to view

[2] And, behold, there was a great earthquake! For an angel of (the) Lord having come down out of Heaven, having come (and) rolled away the stone from the door, was even sitting on it. [3] And his face was as lightning, and his clothing white as snow. [4] And those keeping guard trembled from fear of him, and became as dead (men).

**2** τὸν τάφον. καὶ ἰδού, σεισμὸς ἐγένετο μέγας· ἄγγελος γὰρ
the grave. And, behold, an earthquake occurred great; an angel for

Κυρίου καταβὰς ἐξ οὐρανοῦ, προσελθὼν ἀπεκύλισε τὸν
of (the) Lord descending from Heaven,　and coming up　rolled away the

**3** λίθον ἀπὸ τῆς θύρας, καὶ ἐκάθητο ἐπάνω αὐτοῦ. ἦν δὲ ἡ
stone　from the door, and sitting　on　it.　was And the

ἰδέα αὐτοῦ ὡς ἀστραπή, καὶ τὸ ἔνδυμα αὐτοῦ λευκὸν ὡσεὶ
look of him as lightning, and the dress　of him white as

**4** χιών. ἀπὸ δὲ τοῦ φόβου αὐτοῦ ἐσείσθησαν οἱ τηροῦντες
snow. from And the　fear　of him　were shaken those guarding

[5] But answering, the angel said to the women, You must not fear, for I know that you seek Jesus who has been crucified. [6] He is not here, for He is risen, as He said. Come see the place where the Lord was lying. [7] And going quickly say to His disciples, that He is risen from the dead; and behold, He goes before you into Galilee; you shall see Him there. See, I have told you.

**5** καὶ ἐγένοντο ὡσεὶ νεκροί. ἀποκριθεὶς δὲ ὁ ἄγγελος εἶπε ταῖς
and they became as　dead.　answering And the angel　said to the

γυναιξί, Μὴ φοβεῖσθε ὑμεῖς· οἶδα γὰρ ὅτι Ἰησοῦν τὸν
women, Do not　fear　you;　I know for that　Jesus the (One)

**6** ἐσταυρωμένον ζητεῖτε. οὐκ ἔστιν ὧδε· ἠγέρθη γάρ, καθὼς
having been crucified you seek. not He is here; He was raised for,　as

**7** εἶπε. δεῦτε, ἴδετε τὸν τόπον ὅπου ἔκειτο ὁ Κύριος. καὶ ταχὺ
He said; come, see　the place where　lay the Lord.　And quickly

πορευθεῖσαι εἴπατε τοῖς μαθηταῖς αὐτοῦ ὅτι Ἠγέρθη ἀπὸ
going tell to　the　disciples　of Him that He was raised from

τῶν νεκρῶν· καὶ ἰδού, προάγει ὑμᾶς εἰς τὴν Γαλιλαίαν· ἐκεῖ
the dead, and, behold, He goes before you into　—　Galilee.　There

[8] And having gone out

**8** αὐτὸν ὄψεσθε· ἰδού, εἶπον ὑμῖν. καὶ ἐξελθοῦσαι ταχὺ ἀπὸ
Him you will see. Behold, I told you. And going away　quickly from

τοῦ μνημείου μετὰ φόβου καὶ χαρᾶς μεγάλης, ἔδραμον
the  tomb,     with  fear  and  joy    great,     they ran

**9** quickly from the tomb with great joy and fear, they ran to tell His disciples. [9] But as they were going to tell His disciples, behold also, Jesus met them, saying, Greetings. And having come to (Him) they seized His feet and worshiped Him. [10] Then Jesus said to them, Do not fear; go tell My brothers that they go to Galilee, and they shall see Me there.

ἀπαγγεῖλαι τοῖς μαθηταῖς αὐτοῦ. ὡς δὲ ἐπορεύοντο ἀπαγ-
to announce  to the disciples  of Him.    as But they were going to

γεῖλαι τοῖς μαθηταις αὐτοῦ, καὶ ἰδού, ὁ ᾽Ιησοῦς ἀπήντησεν
tell (it) to the disciples  of Him, also behold, —  Jesus    met

αὐταῖς, λέγων, Χαίρετε. αἱ δὲ προσελθοῦσαι ἐκράτησαν
them,   saying,  Hail!   they And coming near    seized

**10** αὐτοῦ τοὺς πόδας, καὶ προσεκύνησαν αὐτῷ. τότε λέγει
of Him  the  feet,   and  worshiped     Him.  Then says

αὐταῖς ὁ ᾽Ιησοῦς· Μὴ φοβεῖσθε· ὑπάγετε, ἀπαγγείλατε τοῖς
to them — Jesus,   Do not fear.   Go,       announce    to the

ἀδελφοῖς μου ἵνα ἀπέλθωσιν εἰς τὴν Γαλιλαίαν, κἀκεῖ με
brothers  of Me that they may go  into  —  Galilee,   and there Me

ὄψονται.
they will see.

[11] And as they were going, behold, some of the guard having gone into the city reported to the chief priest all things that were done. [12] And having been gathered together with the elders, and having taken counsel, they gave much money to the soldiers, [13] saying, Say that his disciples having come stole him by night, we being asleep. [14] And if this be heard by the governor, we will persuade him, and will make you free from care. [15] And having taken the money they did as they were taught. And this report is spread abroad among (the) Jews until the present.
[16] But the eleven disciples went into Galilee, to the Mountain where Jesus commanded them. [17] And seeing Him, they worshiped Him. But they doubted. [18] And having come, Jesus spoke to them, saying, All authority in Heaven and on earth has been given to Me. [19] Go therefore, disciple all the nations, baptizing them into the name of the Father and of the Son and of the Holy Spirit; [20] teaching them to observe all things whatever I commanded you. And lo, I am with you all the days until the end of the age. Amen.

**11** Πορευομένων δὲ αὐτῶν, ἰδού, τινὲς τῆς κουστωδίας
going     And they,  behold, some of the   guard

ἐλθόντες εἰς τὴν πόλιν ἀπήγγειλαν τοῖς ἀρχιερεῦσιν ἅπαντα
coming  into the  city   announced   to the chief priests all things

**12** τὰ γενόμενα. καὶ συναχθέντες μετὰ τῶν πρεσβυτέρων, συμ-
that occurred.  And being assembled with  the  elders,

βούλιόν τε λαβόντες, ἀργύρια ἱκανὰ ἔδωκαν τοῖς στρατιώ-
counsel and taking,    silver  enough  gave  to the soldiers,

**13** ταις, λέγοντες, Εἴπατε ὅτι Οἱ μαθηταὶ αὐτοῦ νυκτὸς
       saying,  Say,      The disciples of Him by night

**14** ἐλθόντες ἔκλεψαν αὐτὸν ἡμῶν κοιμωμένων. καὶ ἐὰν ἀκουσθῇ
coming  stole    Him,  we   being asleep.  And if is heard

τοῦτο ἐπὶ τοῦ ἡγεμόνος, ἡμεῖς πείσομεν αὐτόν, καὶ ὑμᾶς
this  before the  governor,   we   will persuade him,  and  you

**15** ἀμερίμνους ποιήσομεν. οἱ δὲ λαβόντες τὰ ἀργύρια ἐποίη-
free from anxiety we will make. they And taking  the  silver      did

σαν ὡς ἐδιδάχθησαν. καὶ διεφημίσθη ὁ λόγος οὗτος παρὰ
    as they were taught. And was spread  — saying  this    by

᾽Ιουδαίοις μέχρι τῆς σήμερον.
Jews      until  —   today.

**16** Οἱ δὲ ἕνδεκα μαθηταὶ ἐπορεύθησαν εἰς τὴν Γαλιλαίαν, εἰς
the And eleven  disciples  went       to  —   Galilee,    to

**17** τὸ ὄρος οὗ ἐτάξατο αὐτοῖς ὁ ᾽Ιησοῦς. καὶ ἰδόντες αὐτὸν
the mount where appointed them  —  Jesus. And   seeing   Him,

**18** προσεκύνησαν αὐτῷ· οἱ δὲ ἐδίστασαν. καὶ προσελθὼν ὁ
they worshiped    Him, they but doubted.    And coming up   —

᾽Ιησοῦς ἐλάλησεν αὐτοῖς, λέγων, ᾽Εδόθη μοι πᾶσα ἐξουσία
Jesus   talked    with them, saying,  was given Me All  authority

**19** ἐν οὐρανῷ καὶ ἐπὶ γῆς. πορευθέντες οὖν μαθητεύσατε πάντα
in  Heaven and upon earth. Having gone, then,  disciple     all

τὰ ἔθνη, βαπτίζοντες αὐτοὺς εἰς τὸ ὄνομα τοῦ Πατρὸς καὶ
the nations, baptizing   them  into the name  of the Father  and

**20** τοῦ Υἱοῦ καὶ τοῦ ᾽Αγίου Πνεύματος· διδάσκοντες αὐτοὺς
of the Son and of the Holy   Spirit,    teaching      them

τηρεῖν πάντα ὅσα ἐνετειλάμην ὑμῖν· καὶ ἰδού, ἐγὼ μεθ᾽
to observe all things whatever I commanded you; and, behold,  I  with

ὑμῶν εἰμι πάσας τὰς ἡμέρας ἕως τῆς συντελείας τοῦ αἰῶνος.
you  am  all   the  days  until the  completion  of the  age.

᾽Αμήν.
Amen.

## CHAPTER 1

[1] The beginning of the gospel of Jesus Christ, the Son of God, [2] as it has been written in the prophets, "Behold! I send My messenger before Your face, who shall prepare Your way before You, [3] (the) voice of one crying in the wilderness, Prepare the way of the Lord; make His paths straight." [4] John came baptizing in the wilderness, and preaching the baptism of repentance for remission of sins. [5] And all the country of Judea, and they of Jerusalem, went out to him, and were all baptized by him in the Jordan River, confessing their sins. [6] And John was clothed in hair of a camel, and a girdle of leather about his loins, and eating locusts and wild honey. [7] And he preached, saying, He who comes after me is mightier than I, of whom I am not fit having stooped down to loose the latchet of His sandals. [8] I indeed baptize you with water, but He will baptize you with the Holy Spirit.

[9] And it came to pass in those days, (that) Jesus came from Nazareth of Galilee, and was baptized by John in the Jordan. [10] And immediately going up from the water, He saw the heavens opening, and the Spirit as a

# ΕΥΑΓΓΕΛΙΟΝ
### GOSPEL
# ΤΟ ΚΑΤΑ ΜΑΡΚΟΝ
### THE ACCORDING TO MARK

## CHAPTER 1

1 Ἀρχὴ τοῦ εὐαγγελίου Ἰησοῦ Χριστοῦ, υἱοῦ τοῦ Θεοῦ·
(The) beginning of the gospel of Jesus Christ, Son — of God,

2 Ὡς γέγραπται ἐν τοῖς προφήταις, Ἰδού, ἐγὼ ἀποστέλλω
As it has been written in the prophets. Behold, I send

τὸν ἄγγελόν μου πρὸ προσώπου σου, ὃς κατασκευάσει τὴν
the messenger of Me before (the) face of you, who will prepare the

3 ὁδόν σου ἔμπροσθέν σου. φωνὴ βοῶντος ἐν τῇ ἐρήμῳ,
way of You before You. (The) voice of one crying in the wilderness.

Ἑτοιμάσατε τὴν ὁδὸν Κυρίου· εὐθείας ποιεῖτε τὰς τρίβους
Prepare the way of (the) Lord; straight make the paths

4 αὐτοῦ. ἐγένετο Ἰωάννης βαπτίζων ἐν τῇ ἐρήμῳ, καὶ κηρύσ-
of Him. came John baptizing in the desert, and proclaim-

5 σων βάπτισμα μετανοίας εἰς ἄφεσιν ἁμαρτιῶν. καὶ ἐξεπορεύ-
ing a baptism of repentance for forgiveness of sins. And went out

ετο πρὸς αὐτὸν πᾶσα ἡ Ἰουδαία χώρα, καὶ οἱ Ἱεροσολυμῖται,
to him all the Judean country, and the Jerusalemites,

καὶ ἐβαπτίζοντο πάντες ἐν τῷ Ἰορδάνῃ ποταμῷ ὑπ' αὐτοῦ,
and were baptised all in the Jordan River by him,

6 ἐξομολογούμενοι τὰς ἁμαρτίας αὐτῶν. ἦν δὲ Ἰωάννης
confessing the sins of them. was And John

ἐνδεδυμένος τρίχας καμήλου, καὶ ζώνην δερματίνην περὶ
clothed in hair of a camel, and a girdle leather about

τὴν ὀσφὺν αὐτοῦ, καὶ ἐσθίων ἀκρίδας καὶ μέλι ἄγριον.
the loin of him, and eating locusts and honey wild.

7 καὶ ἐκήρυσσε, λέγων, Ἔρχεται ὁ ἰσχυρότερός μου ὀπίσω
And he proclaimed, saying, Comes He stronger than me after

μου, οὗ οὐκ εἰμὶ ἱκανὸς κύψας λῦσαι τὸν ἱμάντα τῶν
me, of whom not I am fit stooping down to loosen the thong of the

8 ὑποδημάτων αὐτοῦ. ἐγὼ μὲν ἐβάπτισα ὑμᾶς ἐν ὕδατι· αὐτὸς
sandals of Him. I indeed baptised you in water, He

δὲ βαπτίσει ὑμᾶς ἐν Πνεύματι Ἁγίῳ.
but will baptize you in (the) Spirit Holy.

9 Καὶ ἐγένετο ἐν ἐκείναις ταῖς ἡμέραις, ἦλθεν Ἰησοῦς ἀπὸ
And it was, in those — days, came Jesus from

Ναζαρὲθ τῆς Γαλιλαίας, καὶ ἐβαπτίσθη ὑπὸ Ἰωάννου εἰς τὸν
Nazareth of Galilee and was baptised by John in the

10 Ἰορδάνην. καὶ εὐθέως ἀναβαίνων ἀπὸ τοῦ ὕδατος, εἶδε
Jordan. And immediately going up from the water, he saw

σχιζομένους τοὺς οὐρανούς, καὶ τὸ Πνεῦμα ὡσεὶ περιστερὰν
being torn the heavens, and the Spirit as a dove

dove coming down upon Him. [11] And a voice came out of the heavens, You are My Son, the Beloved, in whom I have found delight.

[12] And immediately the Spirit drove Him out into the wilderness. [13] And He was there in the wilderness forty days, tempted by Satan, and was with the beasts; and the angels ministered to Him.

[14] And after John was delivered up, Jesus came into Galilee, preaching the gospel of the kingdom of God, [15] and saying, The time has been fulfilled, and the kingdom of God has drawn near; repent and believe in the gospel. [16] And walking by the sea of Galilee, He saw Simon and his brother Andrew throwing a large net in the sea, for they were fishers. [17] And Jesus said to them, Come after Me and I will make you become fishers of men. [18] And immediately having left their nets they followed Him. [19] And having gone on from there a little, He saw James the (son) of Zebedee, and his brother John, and these in the ship mending the nets. [20] And immediately He called them; and having left their father Zebedee in the ship with the hired servants, they went away after Him.

[21] And they went into Capernaum; and immediately He taught on the sabbaths, having entered into the synagogue. [22] And they were astonished at His teaching; for He was teaching them as having authority, and not as the scribes. [23] And there was a man in their synagogue with an unclean spirit; and he cried out, [24] saying, Ha! What have we to do with You, Jesus, Nazarene? Have You

**11** καταβαῖνον ἐπ' αὐτόν· καὶ φωνὴ ἐγένετο ἐκ τῶν οὐρανῶν,
coming down upon Him. And a voice there was out of the heavens:
Σὺ εἶ ὁ υἱός μου ὁ ἀγαπητός, ἐν ᾧ εὐδόκησα.
You are the Son of Me the Beloved, in whom I take delight.

**12** Καὶ εὐθὺς τὸ Πνεῦμα αὐτὸν ἐκβάλλει εἰς τὴν ἔρημον. καὶ
**13** And instantly the Spirit Him thrusts into the desert. And
ἦν ἐκεῖ ἐν τῇ ἐρήμῳ ἡμέρας τεσσαράκοντα πειραζόμενος ὑπὸ
He was there in the desert days forty being tempted by
τοῦ Σατανᾶ, καὶ ἦν μετὰ τῶν θηρίων, καὶ οἱ ἄγγελοι διη-
Satan, and was with the wild beasts, and the angels
κόνουν αὐτῷ.
ministered to Him.

**14** Μετὰ δὲ τὸ παραδοθῆναι τὸν Ἰωάννην, ἦλθεν ὁ Ἰησοῦς
after And — was delivered up — John, came — Jesus
εἰς τὴν Γαλιλαίαν, κηρύσσων τὸ εὐαγγέλιον τῆς βασιλείας
into - Galilee, proclaiming the gospel of the kingdom
**15** τοῦ Θεοῦ, καὶ λέγων ὅτι Πεπλήρωται ὁ καιρός, καὶ ἤγγικεν
— of God, and saying, — Has been fulfilled the time, and draw near
ἡ βασιλεία τοῦ Θεοῦ· μετανοεῖτε, καὶ πιστεύετε ἐν τῷ
the kingdom — of God; repent and believe in the
εὐαγγελίῳ.
gospel.

**16** Περιπατῶν δὲ παρὰ τὴν θάλασσαν τῆς Γαλιλαίας εἶδε
walking along And beside the Sea — of Galilee, He saw
Σίμωνα καὶ Ἀνδρέαν τὸν ἀδελφὸν αὐτοῦ, βάλλοντας
Simon and Andrew the brother of him, casting
**17** ἀμφίβληστρον ἐν τῇ θαλάσσῃ· ἦσαν γὰρ ἁλιεῖς. καὶ εἶπεν
a small net in the sea; they were for fishers. And said
αὐτοῖς ὁ Ἰησοῦς. Δεῦτε ὀπίσω μου, καὶ ποιήσω ὑμᾶς
to them — Jesus, Come after Me, and I will make you
**18** γενέσθαι ἁλιεῖς ἀνθρώπων. καὶ εὐθέως ἀφέντες τὰ δίκτυα
to become fishers of men. And at once leaving the nets.
**19** αὐτῶν, ἠκολούθησαν αὐτῷ. καὶ προβὰς ἐκεῖθεν ὀλίγον,
of them, they followed Him. And going forward from there a bit,
εἶδεν Ἰάκωβον τὸν τοῦ Ζεβεδαίου, καὶ Ἰωάννην τὸν
He saw James the (son) — of Zebedee and John the
ἀδελφὸν αὐτοῦ, καὶ αὐτοὺς ἐν τῷ πλοίῳ καταρτίζοντας τὰ
brother of him, and they in the boat mending the
**20** δίκτυα. καὶ εὐθέως ἐκάλεσεν αὐτούς· καὶ ἀφέντες τὸν πατέρα
nets. And at once He called them. And leaving the father
αὐτῶν Ζεβεδαῖον ἐν τῷ πλοίῳ μετὰ τῶν μισθωτῶν ἀπῆλθον
of them, Zebedee, in the boat with the hired servants, they went
ὀπίσω αὐτοῦ.
after Him.

**21** Καὶ εἰσπορεύονται εἰς Καπερναούμ· καὶ εὐθέως τοῖς
And they passed along into Capernaum, and at once on the
**22** σάββασιν εἰσελθὼν εἰς τὴν συναγωγήν, ἐδίδασκε. καὶ
sabbaths entering into the synagogue. He taught. And
ἐξεπλήσσοντο ἐπὶ τῇ διδαχῇ αὐτοῦ· ἦν γὰρ διδάσκων
they were astounded at the teaching of Him, He was for teaching
**23** αὐτοὺς ὡς ἐξουσίαν ἔχων, καὶ οὐχ ὡς οἱ γραμματεῖς. καὶ
them as authority having, and not as the scribes. And
ἦν ἐν τῇ συναγωγῇ αὐτῶν ἄνθρωπος ἐν πνεύματι ἀκαθάρτῳ,
was in the synagogue of them a man with a spirit unclean;
**24** καὶ ἀνέκραξε, λέγων, Ἔα, τί ἡμῖν καὶ σοί, Ἰησοῦ Ναζαρηνέ;
and he cried out, saying, Ah! What to us and to You, Jesus, Nazarene?

come to destroy us? I know You, You are the Holy One of God! [25] And Jesus rebuked Him, saying, Be quiet, and come out of him. [26] And the unclean spirit having thrown him into convulsions, and having cried with a loud voice, came out of him. [27] And all were astonished, so that they questioned together among themselves, saying, What is this? What (is) this new teaching, that with authority He commands even the unclean spirits, and they obey Him? [28] And His fame went out immediately in all the country around Galilee.

[29] And having gone out of the synagogue, they at once came to the house of Simon and Andrew, with James and John. [30] And the mother-in-law of Simon was lying in a fever. And immediately they spoke to Him about her. [31] And having come, He raised her up, having taken her hand. And the fever left her instantly, and she served them. [32] And evening being come, when the sun went down, they brought to Him all who were ill and those possessed by demons; [33] and the whole city was gathered together at the door. [34] And He healed many that were sick of various diseases, and He cast out many demons, and did not allow the demons to speak, because they knew Him.

[35] And very early, while night continued, having risen up He went out and went into a deserted place; and was praying there. [36] And Simon and those with Him went after Him; [37] and having found Him, they said to Him, All seek after You. [38] And He said to them, Let us go into the next towns, that I may preach there also; because for this I have come. [39 And He was preaching in their synagogues in all Galilee, and casting out the demons.

25 ἦλθες ἀπολέσαι ἡμᾶς ; οἶδά σε τίς εἶ, ὁ ἅγιος τοῦ Θεοῦ. καὶ
Came You to destroy us? I know You who You are, the Holy of God. And
ἐπετίμησεν αὐτῷ ὁ Ἰησοῦς, λέγων, Φιμώθητι, καὶ ἔξελθε
rebuked him — Jesus, saying, Be quiet, and come

26 ἐξ αὐτοῦ. καὶ σπαράξαν αὐτὸν τὸ πνεῦμα τὸ ἀκάθαρτον καὶ
out of him. And convulsing him the spirit — unclean, and

27 κράξαν φωνῇ μεγάλῃ, ἐξῆλθεν ἐξ αὐτοῦ. καὶ ἐθαμβήθησαν
crying out with a voice great, he came out of him. And were astounded
πάντες, ὥστε συζητεῖν πρὸς αὐτούς, λέγοντας, Τί ἐστι
all, so as to discuss to themselves, saying What is
τοῦτο ; τίς ἡ διδαχὴ ἡ καινὴ αὕτη, ὅτι κατ' ἐξουσίαν καὶ
this? What teaching new (is) this, that with authority even
τοῖς πνεύμασι τοῖς ἀκαθάρτοις ἐπιτάσσει, καὶ ὑπακούουσιν
the spirits — unclean he commands, and they obey

28 αὐτῷ ; ἐξῆλθε δὲ ἡ ἀκοὴ αὐτοῦ εὐθὺς εἰς ὅλην τὴν περίχωρον
Him. went out And the fame of Him at once in all the neighborhood
τῆς Γαλιλαίας.
— of Galilee.

29 Καὶ εὐθέως ἐκ τῆς συναγωγῆς ἐξελθόντες, ἦλθον εἰς τὴν
And at once out of the synagogue going forth, they came into the
οἰκίαν Σίμωνος καὶ Ἀνδρέου, μετὰ Ἰακώβου καὶ Ἰωάννου.
house of Simon and Andrew, with James and John.

30 ἡ δὲ πενθερὰ Σίμωνος κατέκειτο πυρέσσουσα, καὶ εὐθέως
the And mother-in-law of Simon was laid fever-stricken. And immediately

31 λέγουσιν αὐτῷ περὶ αὐτῆς· καὶ προσελθὼν ἤγειρεν αὐτήν,
they say to Him about her. And coming near He raised her,
κρατήσας τῆς χειρὸς αὐτῆς· καὶ ἀφῆκεν αὐτὴν ὁ πυρετὸς
holding the hand of her, and left her the fever.
εὐθέως, καὶ διηκόνει αὐτοῖς.
at once. And she served them.

32 Ὀψίας δὲ γενομένης, ὅτε ἔδυ ὁ ἥλιος, ἔφερον πρὸς αὐτὸν
evening And coming, when set the sun, they brought to Him

33 πάντας τοὺς κακῶς ἔχοντας καὶ τοὺς δαιμονιζομένους· καὶ
all the (ones) illness having, and the (ones) demon-possessed. And

34 ἡ πόλις ὅλη ἐπισυνηγμένη ἦν πρὸς τὴν θύραν. καὶ ἐθεράπευσε
the city whole gathered was at the door. And He healed
πολλοὺς κακῶς ἔχοντας ποικίλαις νόσοις, καὶ δαιμόνια
many illness having of various diseases, and demons
πολλὰ ἐξέβαλε, καὶ οὐκ ἤφιε λαλεῖν τὰ δαιμόνια, ὅτι ᾔδεισαν
many He cast out, and not allowed to speak the demons, because they knew
αὐτόν.
Him.

35 Καὶ πρωῒ ἔννυχον λίαν ἀναστὰς ἐξῆλθε, καὶ ἀπῆλθεν εἰς
And early in night quite rising up He went out, and went away to

36 ἔρημον τόπον, κἀκεῖ προσηύχετο. καὶ κατεδίωξαν αὐτὸν ὁ
a desert place, and there was praying. And searched for Him —

37 Σίμων καὶ οἱ μετ' αὐτοῦ· καὶ εὑρόντες αὐτόν λέγουσιν αὐτῷ
Simon and those with him, and finding Him they say to Him,

38 ὅτι Πάντες ζητοῦσί σε. καὶ λέγει αὐτοῖς, Ἄγωμεν εἰς τὰς
— All are seeking You. And He says to them, Let us go into the
ἐχομένας κωμοπόλεις, ἵνα κἀκεῖ κηρύξω· εἰς τοῦτο γὰρ
neighboring towns, that there also I may proclaim. for this For

39 ἐξελήλυθα. καὶ ἦν κηρύσσων ἐν ταῖς συναγωγαῖς αὐτῶν εἰς
I came forth. And He was proclaiming in the synagogues of them in
ὅλην τὴν Γαλιλαίαν, καὶ τὰ δαιμόνια ἐκβάλλων.
all — Galilee, and the demons casting out.

[40] And a leper comes to Him, begging Him, and kneeling down to Him, and saying to Him, If You choose, You can cleanse me. [41] And being moved with pity, Jesus reaching out the hand touched him, and says to him, I choose: be cleansed! [42] And He having spoken, the leprosy instantly departed from him, and he was cleansed. [43] And having strictly warned him, He at once put him out,[44] and says to him, See, say nothing to anyone, but go show yourself to the priest and offer concerning your cleansing what Moses directed for a testimony to them. [45] But going out he began to publicize the matter, so as He no longer could openly enter into a city; but He was outside in desert places. And they came to Him from every quarter.

**40** Καὶ ἔρχεται πρὸς αὐτὸν λειπρός, παρακαλῶν αὐτὸν καὶ
And comes to Him a leper, begging Him and
γονευπετῶν αὐτόν, καὶ λέγων αὐτῷ ὅτι Ἐὰν θέλῃς, δύνασαί
falling on knees to Him, and saying to Him, — If You will, You are able

**41** με καθαρίσαι. ὁ δὲ Ἰησοῦς σπλαγχνισθείς, ἐκτείνας τὴν
me to make clean. —And Jesus being filled with pity, reaching out the
χεῖρα, ἥψατο αὐτοῦ, καὶ λέγει αὐτῷ, Θέλω, καθαρίσθητι.
hand, He touched him, and says to him, I am willing, be made clean.

**42** καὶ εἰπόντος αὐτοῦ εὐθέως ἀπῆλθεν ἀπ' αὐτοῦ ἡ λέπρα,
And having spoken He instantly departed from him the leprosy,

**43** καὶ ἐκαθαρίσθη. καὶ ἐμβριμησάμενος αὐτῷ, εὐθέως ἐξέβαλεν
and he was cleansed. And strictly warning him, immediately he put out

**44** αὐτόν, καὶ λέγει αὐτῷ, Ὅρα, μηδενὶ μηδὲν εἴπῃς· ἀλλ'
him, and says to him, See, no one nothing tell, but
ὕπαγε, σεαυτὸν δεῖξόν τῷ ἱερεῖ, καὶ προσένεγκε περὶ τοῦ
go yourself show to the priest and offer concerning the
καθαρισμοῦ σου ἃ προσέταξε Μωσῆς, εἰς μαρτύριον αὐτοῖς.
cleansing of you, what ordered Moses, for a testimony to them.

**45** ὁ δὲ ἐξελθὼν ἤρξατο κηρύσσειν πολλὰ καὶ διαφημίζειν τὸν
he But going out began to proclaim much, and to spread about the
λόγον, ὥστε μηκέτι αὐτὸν δύνασθαι φανερῶς εἰς πόλιν
matter, so as no longer He to be able openly into a city
εἰσελθεῖν, ἀλλ' ἔξω ἐν ἐρήμοις τόποις ἦν· καὶ ἤρχοντο πρὸς
to enter, but outside on desert places He was, and they came to
αὐτὸν πανταχόθεν.
Him from every quarter.

## CHAPTER 2

[1] And again He entered into Capernaum after (some) days, and it was heard that He was in (the) house; [2] and at once many were gathered together, so that there was no longer any room, not even at the door; and He spoke the word to them. [3] And they came to Him, bringing a paralytic, carried by four. [4] And not being able to come near to Him, because of the crowd, they uncovered the roof where He was, and having broken through, they let down the bed on which the paralytic was lying. [5] And seeing their faith, Jesus said to the paralytic, Child, your sins have been forgiven you. [6] But some of the scribes were sitting there, and reasoning in their hearts, [7] Why does this one speak blasphemies this way? Who is able to forgive sins, except One, God? [8] And Jesus, instantly knowing in His spirit that they were reasoning within themselves this way, said to them, Why do you

## CHAPTER 2

**1** Καὶ πάλιν εἰσῆλθεν εἰς Καπερναοὺμ δι' ἡμερῶν· καὶ
And again He entered into Capernaum through days. And

**2** ἠκούσθη ὅτι εἰς οἶκόν ἐστι. καὶ εὐθέως συνήχθησαν πολλοί,
it was heard that in (a) house He is. And at once were assembled many,
ὥστε μηκέτι χωρεῖν μηδὲ τὰ πρὸς τὴν θύραν· καὶ ἐλάλει
so as no longer to have room not even to the door, and He spoke

**3** αὐτοῖς τὸν λόγον καὶ ἔρχονται πρὸς αὐτόν, παραλυτικὸν
to them the word. And they come to Him a paralytic

**4** φέροντες, αἰρόμενον ὑπὸ τεσσάρων. καὶ μὴ δυνάμενοι
carrying, being borne by four. And not being able
προσεγγίσαι αὐτῷ διὰ τὸν ὄχλον, ἀπεστέγασαν τὴν στέγην
to draw near to Him due to the crowd, they unroofed the roof
ὅπου ἦν, καὶ ἐξορύξαντες χαλῶσι τὸν κράββατον ἐφ' ᾧ ὁ
where He was, and digging through they lower the cot on which the

**5** παραλυτικὸς κατέκειτο. Ἰδὼν δὲ ὁ Ἰησοῦς τὴν πίστιν αὐτῶν
paralytic was lying. seeing And — Jesus the faith of them,
λέγει τῷ παραλυτικῷ, Τέκνον, ἀφέωνταί σοι αἱ ἁμαρτίαι
He says to the paralytic, Child, are forgiven to you the sins

**6** σου. ἦσαν δέ τινες τῶν γραμματέων ἐκεῖ καθήμενοι, καὶ
of you. were But some of the scribes there sitting, and

**7** διαλογιζόμενοι ἐν ταῖς καρδίαις αὐτῶν, Τί οὗτος οὕτω
reasoning in the hearts of them, Why this one thus
λαλεῖ βλασφημίας ; τίς δύναται ἀφιέναι ἁμαρτίας εἰ μὴ εἷς,
speaks blasphemies? Who is able to forgive sins except one,

**8** ὁ Θεός ; καὶ εὐθέως ἐπιγνοὺς ὁ Ἰησοῦς τῷ πνεύματι αὐτοῦ
— God? And instantly knowing — Jesus in the spirit of Him
ὅτι οὕτως διαλογίζονται ἐν ἑαυτοῖς, εἶπεν αὐτοῖς, Τί ταῦτα
that so they reason among themselves, He says to them, Why these

question these things in your hearts? [9] Which is easier, to say to the paralytic, Sins have been forgiven you, or to say, Arise and take up your bed and walk? [10] But that you may know that the Son of man has authority to forgive sins on the earth, He said to the paralytic, [11] I say to you, Arise, and take up your bed and go to your house. [12] And he arose immediately, and having taken up the bed, went out before all; so that all were amazed, and glorified God, saying, Never did we see (it) this way.

[13] And He went out by the sea again, and all the crowds came to Him, and He taught them. [14] And passing on He saw Levi the (son) of Alpheus, sitting at the tax-office, and said to him, Follow Me. And having arisen, he followed Him.

[15] And it came to pass as He reclined in his house, that many tax-collectors and sinners were reclining with Jesus and His disciples; for they were many, and they followed Him. [16] And the scribes and the Pharisees, having seen Him eating with the tax-collectors and sinners, said to His disciples, Why (is it) that He eats and drinks with the tax-collectors and sinners? [17] And having heard Jesus said to them, They who are strong have no need of a physician, but they who are sick. I did not come to call the righteous to repentance, but sinners.

[18] And the disciples of John, and those of the Pharisees, were fasting; and they came and said to Him, Why do the disciples of John and those of the Pharisees fast, but Your disciples do not fast? [19] And Jesus said to them, Can the sons of the bridechamber fast while the bridegroom is with

**9** διαλογίζεσθε ἐν ταῖς καρδίαις ὑμῶν ; τί ἐστιν εὐκοπώτερον,
do you reason in the hearts of you? What is easier,

εἰπεῖν τῷ παραλυτικῷ, Ἀφέωνταί σοι αἱ ἁμαρτίαι, ἢ εἰπεῖν,
to say to the paralytic, are forgiven to you the sins, or to say,

**10** Ἔγειραι, καὶ ἆρόν σου τὸν κράββατον, καὶ περιπάτει ; ἵνα
Rise, and take up of you the cot and walk? that

δὲ εἰδῆτε ὅτι ἐξουσίαν ἔχει ὁ υἱὸς τοῦ ἀνθρώπου ἀφιέναι ἐπὶ
But you know that authority has the Son — of man to forgive on

**11** τῆς γῆς ἁμαρτίας (λέγει τῷ παραλυτικῷ), Σοὶ λέγω,
the earth sins, He says to the paralytic, To you I say,

ἔγειραι, καὶ ἆρον τὸν κράββατόν σου, καὶ ὕπαγε εἰς τὸν
Rise, and take up the cot of you, and go to the

**12** οἶκόν σου. καὶ ἠγέρθη εὐθέως, καὶ ἄρας τὸν κράββατον,
house of you. And he arose at once, and taking up the cot

ἐξῆλθεν ἐναντίον πάντων· ὥστε ἐξίστασθαι πάντας, καὶ
he went out before all, so as to be astounded all, and

δοξάζειν τὸν Θεόν, λέγοντας ὅτι Οὐδέποτε οὕτως εἴδομεν.
to glorify — God, saying, — Never thus we saw.

**13** Καὶ ἐξῆλθε πάλιν παρὰ τὴν θάλασσαν· καὶ πᾶς ὁ ὄχλος
And He went out again by the sea. And all the crowd

**14** ἤρχετο πρὸς αὐτόν, καὶ ἐδίδασκεν αὐτούς. καὶ παράγων
came to Him, and He taught them. And passing along

εἶδε Λευῒν τὸν τοῦ Ἀλφαίου καθήμενον ἐπὶ τὸ τελώνιον, καὶ
He saw Levi the (son) of Alpheus sitting at the tax-office, and

λέγει αὐτῷ, Ἀκολούθει μοι. καὶ ἀναστὰς ἠκολούθησεν
says to him, Follow Me. And rising up, he followed

**15** αὐτῷ. καὶ ἐγένετο ἐν τῷ κατακεῖσθαι αὐτὸν ἐν τῇ οἰκίᾳ
Him. And it was, while reclined He in the house

αὐτοῦ, καὶ πολλοὶ τελῶναι καὶ ἁμαρτωλοὶ συνανέκειντο τῷ
of him, and many tax-collectors and sinners reclined with —

Ἰησοῦ καὶ τοῖς μαθηταῖς αὐτοῦ· ἦσαν γὰρ πολλοί, καὶ
Jesus and the disciples of Him. they were For many, and

**16** ἠκολούθησαν αὐτῷ. καὶ οἱ γραμματεῖς καὶ οἱ Φαρισαῖοι,
they followed Him. And the scribes and the Pharisees

ἰδόντες αὐτὸν ἐσθίοντα μετὰ τῶν τελωνῶν καὶ ἁμαρτωλῶν,
seeing Him eating with — tax-collectors and sinners,

ἔλεγον τοῖς μαθηταῖς αὐτοῦ, Τί ὅτι μετὰ τῶν τελωνῶν καὶ
said to the disciples of Him, Why that with the tax-collectors and

**17** ἁμαρτωλῶν ἐσθίει καὶ πίνει ; καὶ ἀκούσας ὁ Ἰησοῦς λέγει
sinners does He eat and drink? And hearing — Jesus says

αὐτοῖς, Οὐ χρείαν ἔχουσιν οἱ ἰσχύοντες ἰατροῦ, ἀλλ' οἱ
to them, Not need have those being strong of a physician, but those

κακῶς ἔχοντες. οὐκ ἦλθον καλέσαι δικαίους, ἀλλὰ ἁμαρ-
illness having. not I came to call righteous ones, but sin-

τωλοὺς εἰς μετάνοιαν.
ners to repentance.

**18** Καὶ ἦσαν οἱ μαθηταὶ Ἰωάννου καὶ οἱ τῶν Φαρισαίων
And were the disciples of John and those of the Pharisees

νηστεύοντες· καὶ ἔρχονται καὶ λέγουσιν αὐτῷ, Διατί οἱ
fasting. And they come and say to Him, Why do the

μαθηταὶ Ἰωάννου καὶ οἱ τῶν Φαρισαίων νηστεύουσιν, οἱ
disciples of John and those of the Pharisees fast, —

**19** δὲ σοὶ μαθηταὶ οὐ νηστεύουσι ; καὶ εἶπεν αὐτοῖς ὁ Ἰησοῦς,
but Your disciples not do fast? And said to them — Jesus,

Μὴ δύνανται οἱ υἱοὶ τοῦ νυμφῶνος, ἐν ᾧ ὁ νυμφίος μετ'
Not are able the sons of the bridechamber, while the groom with

them? As long as they have the bridegroom with them, they are not able to fast. [20] But the days will come when the bridegroom will have been taken away from them, and then they will fast in those days. [21] And no one sews a piece of unmilled cloth on an old garment; else the new filling up of it takes away from the old, and a worse takes place. [22] And no one puts new wine into old wineskins; else the new wine bursts the wineskins, and the wine is poured out, and the wineskins will be ruined; but new wine is to be put into new wineskins.

[23] And it came to pass that He went on the Sabbath through the grain fields, and His disciples began to make way, plucking the ears. [24] And the Pharisees said to Him, Behold, why do they do that which is not lawful on the Sabbath? [25] And He said to them, Did you never read what David did, when he had need and hungered, he and those with him? [26] How he entered into the house of God in (the days of) Abiathar the high priest, and ate the showbread, which it is not lawful to eat except for the priests, and even gave to those who were with him? [27] And He said to them, The sabbath was made for man, not man for the sabbath; [28] so then the Son of man is Lord also of the sabbath.

## CHAPTER 3

[1] And He again went into the synagogue, and a man was there having (his) hand withered. [2] And they were watching Him, whether He would heal him on the Sabbath; in order that they might accuse Him. [3] And He said to the man who had the withered hand, Rise up into the middle. [4] And He said to them, Is it lawful to do good on the

αὐτῶν ἐστι, νηστεύειν ; ὅσον χρόνον μεθ' ἑαυτῶν ἔχουσι τὸν
them is. to fast? What time with them they have the

20 νυμφίον, οὐ δύνανται νηστεύειν· ἐλεύσονται δὲ ἡμέραι ὅταν
bridegroom, not they are able to fast. will come But days when

ἀπαρθῇ ἀπ' αὐτῶν ὁ νυμφίος, καὶ τότε νηστεύσουσιν ἐν
will be taken away from them the bridegroom, and then they will fast in

21 ἐκείναις ταῖς ἡμέραις. καὶ οὐδεὶς ἐπίβλημα ῥάκους ἀγνάφου
those days. And no one a patch of cloth unfulled

ἐπιρράπτει ἐπὶ ἱματίῳ παλαιῷ· εἰ δὲ μή, αἴρει τὸ πλήρωμα
sews on a garment old; else takes away the fullness

αὐτοῦ τὸ καινὸν τοῦ παλαιοῦ, καὶ χεῖρον σχίσμα γίνεται.
of it the new (from) the old, and a worse tear occurs.

22 καὶ οὐδεὶς βάλλει οἶνον νέον εἰς ἀσκοὺς παλαιούς· εἰ δὲ μή,
And no one puts wine new into wineskins old; if But not,

ῥήσσει ὁ οἶνος ὁ νέος τοὺς ἀσκούς, καὶ ὁ οἶνος ἐκχεῖται καὶ οἱ
will burst the wine new the wineskins, and the wine pours out, and the

ἀσκοὶ ἀπολοῦνται· ἀλλὰ οἶνον νέον εἰς ἀσκοὺς καινοὺς
skins will be destroyed; but wine new into wineskins fresh

βλητέον.
is to be put.

23 Καὶ ἐγένετο παραπορεύεσθαι αὐτὸν ἐν τοῖς σάββασι διὰ
And it was, went along He in the sabbaths through

τῶν σπορίμων, καὶ ἤρξαντο οἱ μαθηταὶ αὐτοῦ ὁδὸν ποιεῖν
the grainfields, and began the disciples of Him (a) way to make

24 τίλλοντες τοὺς στάχυας. καὶ οἱ Φαρισαῖοι ἔλεγον αὐτῷ,
plucking the ears (of grain). And the Pharisees said to Him,

25 Ἴδε, τί ποιοῦσιν ἐν τοῖς σάββασιν ὃ οὐκ ἔξεστι ; καὶ αὐτὸς
Behold, why do they in the sabbaths what not is lawful? And He

ἔλεγεν αὐτοῖς, Οὐδέποτε ἀνέγνωτε τί ἐποίησε Δαβίδ, ὅτε
said to them, never Did you read what did David when

26 χρείαν ἔσχε καὶ ἐπείνασεν αὐτὸς καὶ οἱ μετ' αὐτοῦ ; πῶς
need he had, and hungered. he and the (ones) with him; how

εἰσῆλθεν εἰς τὸν οἶκον τοῦ Θεοῦ ἐπὶ Ἀβιάθαρ τοῦ ἀρχιερέως,
he entered into the house - of God on Abiathar the high priest,

καὶ τοὺς ἄρτους τῆς προθέσεως ἔφαγεν, οὓς οὐκ ἔξεστι
and the loaves of the presentation ate, which not is lawful

φαγεῖν εἰ μὴ τοῖς ἱερεῦσι, καὶ ἔδωκε καὶ τοῖς σὺν αὐτῷ οὖσι ;
to eat except the priests, and gave also to those with him; being?

27 καὶ ἔλεγεν αὐτοῖς, Τὸ σάββατον διὰ τὸν ἄνθρωπον ἐγένετο,
And He said to them, The sabbath for the sake of man came into being,

28 οὐχ ὁ ἄνθρωπος διὰ τὸ σάββατον· ὥστε Κύριός ἐστιν ὁ υἱὸς
not man for the sake of the sabbath; so then Lord is the Son

τοῦ ἀνθρώπου καὶ τοῦ σαββάτου.
- of man also of the sabbath.

## CHAPTER 3

1 Καὶ εἰσῆλθε πάλιν εἰς τὴν συναγωγήν, καὶ ἦν ἐκεῖ ἄνθρω-
And He entered again into the synagogue, and was there a

2 πος ἐξηραμμένην ἔχων τὴν χεῖρα. καὶ παρετήρουν αὐτὸν εἰ
man a withering having (of) the hand. And they watched Him, if

τοῖς σάββασι θεραπεύσει αὐτόν, ἵνα κατηγορήσωσιν αὐτοῦ.
on the sabbaths He will heal him, that they might accuse Him.

3 καὶ λέγει τῷ ἀνθρώπῳ τῷ ἐξηραμμένην ἔχοντι τὴν χεῖρα,
And He says to the man - a withering having (of) the hand,

4 Ἔγειραι εἰς τὸ μέσον. καὶ λέγει αὐτοῖς, Ἔξεστι τοῖς σάββασιν
Rise into the midst. And he says to them, Lawful on the sabbaths

sabbaths or to do evil? to save life, or to kill? But they were silent. [5] And having looked around on them with anger, being grieved with the hardness of their heart, He said to the man, Stretch out your hand! And he stretched out, and his hand was restored sound as the other. [6] And having gone out the Pharisees immediately took counsel with the Herodians against Him, how they might destroy Him.

[7] And Jesus withdrew to the sea with His disciples; and a great multitude from Galilee followed Him, and from Judea, [8] and (also they were) from Jerusalem and beyond the Jordan; and they around Tyre and Sidon, a great multitude, having heard how much He was doing, came to Him. [9] And He spoke to His disciples, that a small boat might wait on Him, because of the crowd, that they might not press upon Him. [10] For He healed many, so that they threw themselves on Him, that they might touch Him, as many as had afflictions. [11] And the unclean spirits, when they saw Him, fell down before Him and cried out, saying, You are the Son of God! [12] And He very much rebuked them, so that they should not reveal Him.

[13] And He went up into the mountain, and called whom He desired; and they went to Him. [14] And He appointed twelve, that they might be with Him, and that He might send them to preach, [15] and to have authority to heal diseases and to cast out demons. [16] And He added (the) name Peter to Simon; [17] and James the (son) of Zebedee, and John the brother of James; and He added to them (the) name Boanerges, which is, Sons of Thunder. [18] Also Andrew, and Philip, and Bartholomew, and Matthew, and Thomas, and James the (son) of Al-

ἀγαθοποιῆσαι, ἢ κακοποιῆσαι; ψυχὴν σῶσαι, ἢ ἀπο-
to do good, or to do evil; a soul to save, or to

5 κτεῖναι; οἱ δὲ ἐσιώπων. καὶ περιβλεψάμενος αὐτοὺς μετ᾽
kill? they But were silent. And looking around (on) them with

ὀργῆς, συλλυπούμενος ἐπὶ τῇ πωρώσει τῆς καρδίας αὐτῶν,
anger, being greatly grieved on the hardness of the heart of them,

λέγει τῷ ἀνθρώπῳ, Ἔκτεινον τὴν χεῖρά σου. καὶ ἐξέτεινε,
He says to the man, Stretch out the hand of you. And he stretched,

6 καὶ ἀποκατεστάθη ἡ χεὶρ αὐτοῦ ὑγιὴς ὡς ἡ ἄλλη. καὶ
and was restored the hand of him sound as the other. And

ἐξελθόντες οἱ Φαρισαῖοι εὐθέως μετὰ τῶν Ἡρωδιανῶν
having gone out the Pharisees immediately with the Herodians

συμβούλιον ἐποίουν κατ᾽ αὐτοῦ, ὅπως αὐτὸν ἀπολέσωσι.
counsel made against Him, how that Him they might destroy.

7 Καὶ ὁ Ἰησοῦς ἀνεχώρησε μετὰ τῶν μαθητῶν αὐτοῦ πρὸς
And — Jesus withdrew with the disciples of Him to

τὴν θάλασσαν· καὶ πολὺ πλῆθος ἀπὸ τῆς Γαλιλαίας ἠκολού-
the sea; and a great multitude from — Galilee followed

8 θησαν αὐτῷ, καὶ ἀπὸ τῆς Ἰουδαίας, καὶ ἀπὸ Ἱεροσολύμων,
Him; and from — Judea, and from Jerusalem,

καὶ ἀπὸ τῆς Ἰδουμαίας, καὶ πέραν τοῦ Ἰορδάνου, καὶ οἱ
and from — Idumea, and beyond the Jordan, and those

περὶ Τύρον καὶ Σιδῶνα, πλῆθος πολύ, ἀκούσαντες ὅσα
around Tyre and Sidon; a multitude great, hearing what

9 ἐποίει, ἦλθον πρὸς αὐτόν. καὶ εἶπε τοῖς μαθηταῖς αὐτοῦ
He was doing came to Him. And He told the disciples of Him

ἵνα πλοιάριον προσκαρτερῇ αὐτῷ διὰ τὸν ὄχλον, ἵνα μὴ
that a small boat should stay near Him because of the crowd, lest

10 θλίβωσιν αὐτόν. πολλοὺς γὰρ ἐθεράπευσεν, ὥστε ἐπιπί-
they press on Him. many For He healed, so that (they) fell

11 πτειν αὐτῷ, ἵνα αὐτοῦ ἅψωνται, ὅσοι εἶχον μάστιγας. καὶ τὰ
upon Him, that Him they might touch, as many as had plagues; and the

πνεύματα τὰ ἀκάθαρτα, ὅταν αὐτὸν ἐθεώρει, προσέπιπτεν
spirits — unclean when Him they saw fell before

12 αὐτῷ, καὶ ἔκραζε, λέγοντα ὅτι Σὺ εἶ ὁ υἱὸς τοῦ Θεοῦ. καὶ
Him and cried out, saying, — You are the Son — of God. And

πολλὰ ἐπετίμα αὐτοῖς ἵνα μὴ αὐτὸν φανερὸν ποιήσωσι.
much He warned them that not Him manifest they should make.

13 Καὶ ἀναβαίνει εἰς τὸ ὄρος, καὶ προσκαλεῖται οὓς ἤθελεν
And He goes up into the mountain, and called near whom wished

14 αὐτός· καὶ ἀπῆλθον πρὸς αὐτόν. καὶ ἐποίησε δώδεκα, ἵνα
He, and they went to Him. And He made twelve, that

15 ὦσι μετ᾽ αὐτοῦ, καὶ ἵνα ἀποστέλλῃ αὐτοὺς κηρύσσειν καὶ
they might be with Him, and that He might send them to proclaim, and

ἔχειν ἐξουσίαν θεραπεύειν τὰς νόσους, καὶ ἐκβάλλειν τὰ
to have authority to heal the diseases, and to cast out the

16 δαιμόνια· καὶ ἐπέθηκε τῷ Σίμωνι ὄνομα Πέτρον· καὶ Ἰάκωβον
demons. And He put upon Simon a name, Peter; and James

17 τὸν τοῦ Ζεβεδαίου, καὶ Ἰωάννην τὸν ἀδελφὸν τοῦ Ἰακώβου·
the (son) of Zebedee, and John the brother — of James,

καὶ ἐπέθηκεν αὐτοῖς ὀνόματα Βοανεργές, ὅ ἐστιν, Υἱοὶ
and He put upon them (the) names Boanerges, which is, Sons

18 βροντῆς· καὶ Ἀνδρέαν, καὶ Φίλιππον, καὶ Βαρθολομαῖον,
of Thunder; and Andrew and Philip; and Bartholomew;

καὶ Ματθαῖον, καὶ Θωμᾶν, καὶ Ἰάκωβον τὸν τοῦ Ἀλφαίου,
and Matthew; and Thomas; and James the (son) of Alpheus,

pheus and Thaddeus, and Simon the Canaanite. [19] and Judas Iscariot, who also betrayed Him. And they come into a house; [20] and a crowd gathers, so as they could not even eat bread. [21] And hearing, those with Him went out to seize Him, for they said, He is out of wits. [22] And the scribes from Jerusalem coming down said, He has Beelzebub; and, He evicts demons by the ruler of the demons. [23] And having called near them, He spoke in parables to them, How can Satan evict Satan? [24] And if a kingdom is divided against itself, that kingdom cannot stand; [25] and if a house is divided against itself, that house cannot stand; [26] and if Satan rises upon himself, and has been divided, he cannot stand, but he has

an end. [27] No one in any way is able to plunder the goods of the strong man, having entered into his house, unless he first ties up the strong man, and then he will plunder his house. [28] Truly I say to you that all the sins shall be forgiven to the sons o' men, and whatever blasphemies they shall have blasphemed; [29] but whoever shall blaspheme against the Holy Spirit has no forgiveness to eternity, but is liable to everlasting judgment; [30] because they said, He has an unclean spirit.

[31] Then came His mother and brothers, and standing outside sent to Him, calling Him. [32] And a crowd sat around Him; and they said to Him, Behold, Your mother and Your brothers outside seek You. [33] And He answered them, saying, Who is My mother or My brothers? [34] And having looked around on those who were sitting in a circle around Him, He said, Behold, My mother and My brothers! [35] For whoever shall do

**19** καὶ Θαδδαῖον, καὶ Σίμωνα τὸν Κανανίτην, καὶ Ἰούδαν
and Thaddeus, and Simon the Canaanite, and Judas
Ἰσκαριώτην, ὃς καὶ παρέδωκεν αὐτόν.
Iscariot. who also betrayed Him.

**20** Καὶ ἔρχονται εἰς οἶκον· καὶ συνέρχεται πάλιν ὄχλος, ὥστε
And He comes into a house; and comes together again a crowd, so as
**21** μὴ δύνασθαι αὐτοὺς μήτε ἄρτον φαγεῖν. καὶ ἀκούσαντες οἱ
not are able they not even bread to eat. And having heard those
παρ' αὐτοῦ ἐξῆλθον κρατῆσαι αὐτόν· ἔλεγον γὰρ ὅτι
with Him went forth to take hold (of) Him, they said for, —
**22** Ἐξέστη. καὶ οἱ γραμματεῖς οἱ ἀπὸ Ἱεροσολύμων καταβάντες
He is insane. And the scribes — from Jerusalem coming down
ἔλεγον ὅτι Βεελζεβοὺλ ἔχει, καὶ ὅτι Ἐν τῷ ἄρχοντι τῶν
said, — Beelzebub He has, and, — By the ruler of the
**23** δαιμονίων ἐκβάλλει τὰ δαιμόνια. καὶ προσκαλεσάμενος
demons he casts out the demons. And calling near
αὐτούς, ἐν παραβολαῖς ἔλεγεν αὐτοῖς, Πῶς δύναται Σατανᾶς
them, in parables He spoke to them, How is able Satan
**24** Σατανᾶν ἐκβάλλειν ; καὶ ἐὰν βασιλεία ἐφ' ἑαυτὴν μερισθῇ, οὐ
Satan to cast out? And if a kingdom against itself is divided, not
**25** δύναται σταθῆναι ἡ βασιλεία ἐκείνη. καὶ ἐὰν οἰκία ἐφ'
is able to stand — kingdom that. And if a house against
**26** ἑαυτὴν μερισθῇ, οὐ δύναται σταθῆναι ἡ οἰκία ἐκείνη. καὶ εἰ
itself is divided, not is able to stand — house that. And if
ὁ Σατανᾶς ἀνέστη ἐφ' ἑαυτὸν καὶ μεμέρισται, οὐ δύναται
— Satan rises upon himself and has been divided, not he is able
**27** σταθῆναι, ἀλλὰ τέλος ἔχει. οὐ δύναται οὐδεὶς τὰ σκεύη τοῦ
to stand, but an end he has. not is able No one the goods of the
ἰσχυροῦ, εἰσελθὼν εἰς τὴν οἰκίαν αὐτοῦ, διαρπάσαι, ἐὰν μὴ
strong one having entered into the house of him, to plunder, unless
πρῶτον τὸν ἰσχυρὸν δήσῃ, καὶ τότε τὴν οἰκίαν αὐτοῦ διαρ-
first the strong one he bind, and then the house of him he will
**28** πάσει. ἀμὴν λέγω ὑμῖν, ὅτι πάντα ἀφεθήσεται τὰ ἁμαρτή-
plunder. Truly I say to you, that all will be forgiven the sins
ματα τοῖς υἱοῖς τῶν ἀνθρώπων, καὶ βλασφημίαι ὅσας ἂν
of the sons — of men, and blasphemies whatever
**29** βλασφημήσωσιν· ὃς δ' ἂν βλασφημήσῃ εἰς τὸ Πνεῦμα τὸ
they have blasphemed; who but ever blasphemes against the Spirit —
Ἅγιον, οὐκ ἔχει ἄφεσιν εἰς τὸν αἰῶνα, ἀλλ' ἔνοχός ἐστιν
Holy, not has forgiveness unto the age, but liable is
**30** αἰωνίου κρίσεως. ὅτι ἔλεγον, Πνεῦμα ἀκάθαρτον ἔχει.
of an eternal judgment; for they said, A spirit unclean He has.
**31** Ἔρχονται οὖν οἱ ἀδελφοὶ καὶ ἡ μήτηρ αὐτοῦ, καὶ ἔξω
come Then the brothers and the mother of Him, and outside
**32** ἑστῶτες ἀπέστειλαν πρὸς αὐτόν, φωνοῦντες αὐτόν. καὶ
standing sent to Him, calling Him. And
ἐκάθητο ὄχλος περὶ αὐτόν· εἶπον δὲ αὐτῷ, Ἰδού, ἡ μήτηρ
sat a crowd around Him. they said And to Him, Behold, the mother
**33** σου καὶ οἱ ἀδελφοί σου ἔξω ζητοῦσί σε. καὶ ἀπεκρίθη αὐτοῖς
of you and the brothers of you outside seek You. And He answered them,
**34** λέγων, Τίς ἐστιν ἡ μήτηρ μου ἢ οἱ ἀδελφοί μου ; καὶ
saying, Who is the mother of Me or the brothers of Me? And
περιβλεψάμενος κύκλῳ τοὺς περὶ αὐτὸν καθημένους, λέγει,
looking around In a circle (at) those around Him sitting, He says
**35** Ἴδε, ἡ μήτηρ μου καὶ οἱ ἀδελφοί μου. ὃς γὰρ ἂν ποιήσῃ τὸ
Behold, the mother of Me and the brothers of Me! who For ever does the

the will of God, he is My brother and My sister and mother.

## CHAPTER 4

[1] And again He began to teach by the sea. And a great crowd was gathered to Him, so that He having entered into the boat sat in the sea, and all the crowd was close to the sea on the land. [2] And He taught them many things in parables, and said to them in His teaching, [3] Listen, behold, the sower went out to sow. [4] And it came to pass as he sowed, one fell by the wayside; and the birds of the sky came and ate it up. [5] And another fell on the rocky place, where it had not much earth. And it sprang up at once, through not having deepness of earth; [6] and (the) sun having arisen, it was scorched; and through having no root, it withered away. [7] And another fell among the thorns, and the thorns grew up and choked it, and it yielded no fruit. [8] And another fell into the good ground, and yielded fruit, going up and increasing, and one bore thirty, and one sixty, and one a hundred. [9] And He said to them, He that has ears to hear, let him hear. [10] And when He was alone, those about Him, with the twelve, asked Him (as to) the parable. [11] And He said to them, To you has been given to know the mystery of the kingdom of God; but to those who are outside, all things are done in parables, [12] that seeing they may see, and not perceive; and hearing they may hear, and not understanding, lest they should be converted, and sins should be forgiven them. [13] And He said to them, Do you not understand this parable? And how will you know all the parables? [14] The sower sows the word. [15] And these are

## CHAPTER 4

1 Καὶ πάλιν ἤρξατο διδάσκειν παρὰ τὴν θάλασσαν. καὶ
And again He began to teach by the sea. And
συνήχθη πρὸς αὐτὸν ὄχλος πολύς, ὥστε αὐτὸν ἐμβάντα εἰς
is assembled to Him a crowd large, so that He entering into
τὸ πλοῖον καθῆσθαι ἐν τῇ θαλάσσῃ· καὶ πᾶς ὁ ὄχλος πρὸς
the boat (had) to sit in the sea., and all the crowd toward

2 τὴν θάλασσαν ἐπὶ τῆς γῆς ἦν. καὶ ἐδίδασκεν αὐτοὺς ἐν
the sea on the land were. And He taught them in
παραβολαῖς πολλά, καὶ ἔλεγεν αὐτοῖς ἐν τῇ διδαχῇ αὐτοῦ,
parables many things, and said to them in the teaching of Him,

3 Ἀκούετε· ἰδού, ἐξῆλθεν ὁ σπείρων·τοῦ σπεῖραι· καὶ ἐγένετο
4 Hear! Behold, went out the (one) sowing to sow. And it was,
ἐν τῷ σπείρειν, ὃ μὲν ἔπεσε παρὰ τὴν ὁδόν, καὶ ἦλθε τὰ
while sowing one indeed fell by the way, and came the

5 πετεινὰ τοῦ οὐρανοῦ καὶ κατέφαγεν αὐτό. ἄλλο δὲ ἔπεσεν
birds of the heaven and devoured it. other And fell
ἐπὶ τὸ πετρῶδες, ὅπου οὐκ εἶχε γῆν πολλήν· καὶ εὐθέως
on the rocky place where not it had earth much, and at once

6 ἐξανέτειλε, διὰ τὸ μὴ ἔχειν βάθος γῆς· ἡλίου δὲ ἀνατείλαντος
it sprang up, due to not having depth of earth; sun And arising

7 ἐκαυματίσθη, καὶ διὰ τὸ μὴ ἔχειν ῥίζαν ἐξηράνθη. καὶ ἄλλο
it was scorched, and through not to have root it was dried up. And other
ἔπεσεν εἰς τὰς ἀκάνθας, καὶ ἀνέβησαν αἱ ἄκανθαι, καὶ συνέ-
fell into the thorns, and grew the thorns and choked

8 πνιξαν αὐτό, καὶ καρπὸν οὐκ ἔδωκε. καὶ ἄλλο ἔπεσεν εἰς τὴν
it, and fruit not it did give. And other fell into the
γῆν τὴν καλήν· καὶ ἐδίδου καρπὸν ἀναβαίνοντα καὶ
earth — good, and gave fruit going up and
αὐξάνοντα, καὶ ἔφερεν ἓν τριάκοντα, καὶ ἓν ἑξήκοντα, καὶ
increasing, and bore one thirty, and one sixty, and

9 ἓν ἑκατόν. καὶ ἔλεγεν αὐτοῖς, Ὁ ἔχων ὦτα ἀκούειν ἀκουέτω.
one a hundred. And He said to them, He having ears to hear, let him hear.

10 Ὅτε δὲ ἐγένετο καταμόνας, ἠρώτησαν αὐτὸν οἱ περὶ
when And He became alone, asked Him those around

11 αὐτὸν σὺν τοῖς δώδεκα τὴν παραβολήν. καὶ ἔλεγεν αὐτοῖς,
Him with the twelve the parable. And He said to them,
Ὑμῖν δέδοται γνῶναι τὸ μυστήριον τῆς βασιλείας τοῦ
To you has been given to know the mystery of the kingdom —
Θεοῦ· ἐκείνοις δὲ τοῖς ἔξω, ἐν παραβολαῖς τὰ πάντα γίνεται·
of God; to these but those outside in parables — all things became

12 ἵνα βλέποντες βλέπωσι, καὶ μὴ ἴδωσι· καὶ ἀκούοντες
that seeing they may see, and not perceive; and hearing
ἀκούωσι, καὶ μὴ συνιῶσι· μήποτε ἐπιστρέψωσι, καὶ
they may hear, and not understand, lest they should convert, and

13 ἀφεθῇ αὐτοῖς τὰ ἁμαρτήματα. καὶ λέγει αὐτοῖς, Οὐκ οἴδατε
be forgiven them the sins. And He says to them, not Know you
τὴν παραβολὴν ταύτην ; καὶ πῶς πάσας τὰς παραβολὰς
— parable this ? And how all the parables

14 γνώσεσθε ; ὁ σπείρων τὸν λόγον σπείρει. οὗτοι δέ εἰσιν οἱ
15 will you know? He sowing the word sows. these And are those

they by the way, where the word is sown; and when they hear, Satan comes at once and takes the word having been sown in their hearts. [16] And likewise, these are the ones who are sown on the rock places, who, when they hear the word, immediately receive it with joy, [17] and have no root in themselves, but are temporary; then trouble or persecution having arisen on account of the word, they are immediately offended. [18] These are those being sown into the thorns, those hearing the word, [19] and the cares of this age, and the deceitfulness of riches, and the lusts about other things, entering in choke the word, and it becomes unfruitful. [20] And these are those being sown on the good earth, who hear and welcome the word, and bring forth fruit —one thirty, and one sixty, and one a hundred. [21] And He said to them, Does the lamp come that it may be put under the grain measure or under the bed? (Is it) not that it may be put on the lampstand? [22] For not anything is hidden except it shall be made manifest; nor has a secret thing taken place but that it shall come to light. [23] If anyone has ears to hear, let him hear. [24] And He said to them, Be careful what you hear; with what measure you measure, it shall be measured to you, and more shall be added to you who hear; [25] for whoever may have, more shall be given to him; and he who has not, even that which he has shall be taken from him.

[26] And He said, So is the kingdom of God, as if a man should cast seed on the earth, [27] and should sleep and rise night and day, and the seed sprout and lengthen of itself, as he not knows; [28] for of itself the earth bears fruit: first greenery, then an ear, then full grain in the ear. [29] And when the fruit yields, immediately he sends forth the

παρὰ τὴν ὁδόν, ὅπου σπείρεται ὁ λόγος, καὶ ὅταν ἀκούσω-
by the way, where is sown the word; and when they hear,

σιν, εὐθέως ἔρχεται ὁ Σατανᾶς καὶ αἴρει τὸν λόγον τὸν
immediately comes — Satan and takes the word —

**16** ἐσπαρμένον ἐν ταῖς καρδίαις αὐτῶν. καὶ οὗτοί εἰσιν ὁμοίως
having been sown in the hearts of them. And these are likewise

οἱ ἐπὶ τὰ πετρώδη σπειρόμενοι, οἵ, ὅταν ἀκούσωσι τὸν
these on the rocky places being sown, who when they hear the

**17** λόγον, εὐθέως μετὰ χαρᾶς λαμβάνουσιν αὐτόν, καὶ οὐκ
word, immediately with joy they receive it, and not

ἔχουσι ῥίζαν ἐν ἑαυτοῖς, ἀλλὰ πρόσκαιροί εἰσιν· εἶτα γενο-
they have root in themselves, but temporary they are; then having

μένης θλίψεως ἢ διωγμοῦ διὰ τὸν λόγον, εὐθέως σκανδαλί-
become trouble or persecution through the word, immediately they are

**18** ζονται. καὶ οὗτοί εἰσιν οἱ εἰς τὰς ἀκάνθας σπειρόμενοι, οἱ τὸν
offended. And these are those into the thorns being sown; those the

**19** λόγον ἀκούοντες, καὶ αἱ μέριμναι τοῦ αἰῶνος τούτου, καὶ ἡ
word hearing, and the cares of — age this, and the

ἀπάτη τοῦ πλούτου, καὶ. αἱ περὶ τὰ λοιπὰ ἐπιθυμίαι
deceitfulness — of riches, and the about the other things desires

εἰσπορευόμεναι συμπνίγουσι τὸν λόγον, καὶ ἄκαρπος
entering in choke the word, and unfruitful

**20** γίνεται. καὶ οὗτοί εἰσιν οἱ ἐπὶ τὴν γῆν τὴν καλὴν σπαρέντες,
it becomes. And these are the (ones) on the earth — good being sown,

οἵτινες ἀκούουσι τὸν λόγον, καὶ παραδέχονται, καὶ καρ-
who hear the word, and welcome (it), and bring

ποφοροῦσιν, ἐν τριάκοντα, καὶ ἐν ἑξήκοντα, καὶ ἐν ἑκατόν.
forth fruit, one thirty, and one sixty, and one a hundred.

**21** Καὶ ἔλεγεν αὐτοῖς, Μήτι ὁ λύχνος ἔρχεται ἵνα ὑπὸ τὸν
And He said to them, Not (is) the lamp come that under the

μόδιον τεθῇ ἢ ὑπὸ τὴν κλίνην; οὐχ ἵνα ἐπὶ τὴν λυχνίαν
bushel it be placed, or under the couch? (is it) not that on the lampstand

**22** ἐπιτεθῇ; οὐ γάρ ἐστί τι κρυπτόν, ὃ ἐὰν μὴ φανερωθῇ· οὐδὲ
it be placed? not For is a thing hidden, which if not it may be revealed, nor

**23** ἐγένετο ἀπόκρυφον, ἀλλ' ἵνα εἰς φανερὸν ἔλθη. εἴ τις ἔχει
became covered, but that to light it may come. If any have

**24** ὦτα ἀκούειν ἀκουέτω. καὶ ἔλεγεν αὐτοῖς, Βλέπετε τί ἀκούετε.
ears to hear, let him hear. And He said to them, Be careful what you hear.

ἐν ᾧ μέτρῳ μετρεῖτε μετρηθήσεται ὑμῖν, καὶ προστεθήσεται
In what measure you measure it will be measured to you. And it will be added

**25** ὑμῖν τοῖς ἀκούουσιν. ὃς γὰρ ἂν ἔχῃ, δοθήσεται αὐτῷ· καὶ
to you, the (ones) hearing. who For ever may have, it will be given to him; and

ὃς οὐκ ἔχει, καὶ ὃ ἔχει ἀρθήσεται ἀπ' αὐτοῦ.
who not has, even what he has will be taken from him.

**26** Καὶ ἔλεγεν, Οὕτως ἐστὶν ἡ βασιλεία τοῦ Θεοῦ, ὡς ἐὰν
And He said, Thus is the kingdom — of God, as if

**27** ἄνθρωπος βάλῃ τὸν σπόρον ἐπὶ τῆς γῆς, καὶ καθεύδῃ καὶ
a man should cast the seed on the earth, and should sleep and

ἐγείρηται νύκτα καὶ ἡμέραν, καὶ ὁ σπόρος βλαστάνῃ καὶ
rise night and day, and the seed should sprout and

**28** μηκύνηται ὡς οὐκ οἶδεν αὐτός. αὐτομάτη γὰρ ἡ γῆ καρπο-
lengthen as not knows he of itself. For the earth bears

φορεῖ, πρῶτον χόρτον, εἶτα στάχυν, εἶτα πλήρη σῖτον ἐν
fruit, first greenery, then an ear, then full grain in

**29** τῷ στάχυϊ. ὅταν δὲ παραδῷ ὁ καρπός, εὐθέως ἀποστέλλει
the ear. when But yields the fruit, immediately he sends forth

sickle, for the harvest has come.

τὸ δρέπανον, ὅτι παρέστηκεν ὁ θερισμός.
the sickle,     because stands ready   the harvest.

[30] And He said, To what shall we compare the kingdom of God? Or with what parable shall we compare it? [31] Like a grain of mustard, which, when it has been sown on the earth (is) less than all the seeds which are on the earth; [32] and when it has been sown, it grows up and becomes greater than all the plants, and produces great branches, so that the birds of the sky are able to roost under its shadow. [33] And with many parables He spoke the word to them, as they were able to hear; [34] but He did not speak to them without a parable; and He explained all things to His disciples alone.

30 Καὶ ἔλεγε, Τίνι ὁμοιώσωμεν τὴν βασιλείαν τοῦ Θεοῦ;
   And He said,  How may we compare the  kingdom   – of God;

31 ἢ ἐν ποίᾳ παραβολῇ παραβάλωμεν αὐτήν; ὡς κόκκῳ
   or by what  parable  may we compare  it?  As to a grain

σινάπεως, ὅς, ὅταν σπαρῇ ἐπὶ τῆς γῆς, μικρότερος πάντων
of mustard, which, when it is sown on the earth,  lesser      than all

32 τῶν σπερμάτων ἐστὶ τῶν ἐπὶ τῆς γῆς· καὶ ὅταν σπαρῇ,
   the  seeds     It is of those on  the earth.  And when  it is sown,

ἀναβαίνει, καὶ γίνεται πάντων τῶν λαχάνων μείζων, καὶ
comes up,    and becomes  than all  the  plants  greater, and

ποιεῖ κλάδους μεγάλους, ὥστε δύνασθαι ὑπὸ τὴν σκιὰν
makes branches  great,   so as to be able  under  the  shade

αὐτοῦ τὰ πετεινὰ τοῦ οὐρανοῦ κατασκηνοῦν.
of it  the  birds of the heaven   to roost.

33 Καὶ τοιαύταις παραβολαῖς πολλαῖς ἐλάλει αὐτοῖς τὸν
   And  such   parables   many  He spoke to them the

34 λόγον, καθὼς ἠδύναντο ἀκούειν· χωρὶς δὲ παραβολῆς ·οὐκ
   word,  even as they were able to hear; without and a parable   not

ἐλάλει αὐτοῖς· κατ᾽ ἰδίαν δὲ τοῖς μαθηταῖς αὐτοῦ ἐπέλυε
He spoke to them,     privately but to the disciples  of Him, He explained

πάντα.
all things.

[35] And He said to them on that day, evening being come, Let us pass over to the other side. [36] And having dismissed the crowd, they took Him, as He was in the boat; but also other small boats were with Him. [37] And a violent storm of wind came, and the waves beat into the boat, so that it was already filled. [38] And He was on the stern, sleeping on the pillow. And they wakened Him, and said to Him, Master, is it no concern to You that we perish? [39] And having been a-wakened, He rebuked the wind, and said to the sea, Peace! Be still! And the wind ceased, and there was a great calm. [40] And He said to them, Why are you afraid this way? How do you not have faith? [41] And they feared (with) great fear, and said to one another, Who then is this, that even the wind and the sea obey Him?

35 Καὶ λέγει αὐτοῖς ἐν ἐκείνῃ τῇ ἡμέρᾳ, ὀψίας γενομένης,
   And He says  to them on that   – day,    evening having come,

36 Διέλθωμεν εἰς τὸ πέραν. καὶ ἀφέντες τὸν ὄχλον, παραλαμ-
   Let us pass over to the other side. And dismissing the crowd,  they take

βάνουσιν αὐτὸν ὡς ἦν ἐν τῷ πλοίῳ. καὶ ἄλλα δὲ πλοιάρια
along    Him  as He was in the boat.  also  other And small boats

37 ἦν μετ᾽ αὐτοῦ. καὶ γίνεται λαῖλαψ ἀνέμου μεγάλη· τὰ δὲ
   were with Him.  And occurs a storm  of wind great    the and

κύματα ἐπέβαλλεν εἰς τὸ πλοῖον, ὥστε αὐτὸ ἤδη γεμίζεσθαι.
waves   beat    into the boat,  so as it  already was filled.

38 καὶ ἦν αὐτὸς ἐπὶ τῇ πρύμνῃ ἐπὶ τὸ προσκεφάλαιον καθεύδων·
   And was He  on the stern,  on the headrest   sleeping.

καὶ διεγείρουσιν αὐτόν, καὶ λέγουσιν αὐτῷ, Διδάσκαλε, οὐ
And they awaken Him,   and say   to Him, Teacher,  not

39 μέλει σοι ὅτι ἀπολλύμεθα; καὶ διεγερθεὶς ἐπετίμησε τῷ
   it matters to You that we are perishing?  And being awakened He rebuked the

ἀνέμῳ, καὶ εἶπε τῇ θαλάσσῃ, Σιώπα, πεφίμωσο. καὶ ἐκόπα-
wind,   and said to the sea,  Silence! Be still!  And cut off

40 σεν ὁ ἄνεμος, καὶ ἐγένετο γαλήνη μεγάλη. καὶ εἶπεν αὐτοῖς,
   the wind,  and there was a calm  great.  And He said to them,

41 Τί δειλοί ἐστε οὕτω; πῶς οὐκ ἔχετε πίστιν; καὶ ἐφοβήθησαν
   Why fearful are you so? How not have you faith?  And they feared

φόβον μέγαν, καὶ ἔλεγον πρὸς ἀλλήλους, Τίς ἄρα οὗτός
a fear  great,  and said   to one another, Who then this One

ἐστιν, ὅτι καὶ ὁ ἄνεμος ·καὶ ἡ θάλασσα ὑπακούουσιν αὐτῷ;
is,   that even the wind and the  sea   obey     Him?

## CHAPTER 5

[1] And they came to the other side of the sea, to the country of the Gadarenes. [2] And on His having gone forth out of the ship,

## CHAPTER 5

1 Καὶ ἦλθον εἰς τὸ πέραν τῆς θαλάσσης, εἰς τὴν χώραν τῶν
  And they came to the other side of the sea,   into the country of the

2 Γαδαρηνῶν. καὶ ἐξελθόντι αὐτῷ ἐκ τοῦ πλοίου, εὐθέως
  Gaderenes.    And coming out He  from the  boat, immediately

immediately a man with an unclean spirit met Him out of the tombs, [3] who had (his) dwelling in the tombs; and no one was able to tie him up, not even with chains, [4] because he had often been bound with fetters and chains, and the chains had been torn in two by him, and the fetters had been shattered, and no one was able to subdue him. [5] And continually night and day in the mountains and in the tombs, he was crying and cutting himself with stones. [6] And having seen Jesus from a distance, he ran and bowed down to Him, [7] and crying with a loud voice he said, What to me and to You, Jesus, Son of God the most high? I adjure You by God, not (to) torment me. [8] For He was saying to him, Unclean spirit, come out of the man! [9] And He asked him, What (is) your name? And he answered, saying, My name (is) Legion, because we are many. [10] And he begged Him very much that He would not send them out of the country, [11] now a great herd of pigs were feeding there near the mountain; [12] and all the demons begged Him, saying, Send us into the pigs, that we may enter into them. [13] And Jesus immediately allowed them. And having gone out, the unclean spirits entered into the pigs, and the herd rushed down the steep place to the sea — and they were about two thousand — and they were choked in the sea. [14] And those who fed the pigs fled, and told it to the city and to the country. And they went out to see what it was that had been done. [15] And they came to Jesus, and the demon-possessed one sitting and clothed and of sound mind, him who had the legion; and they were afraid. [16] And those who had seen related to them how it happened to him possessed by demons, and about the pigs. [17] And they began to

ἀπήντησεν αὐτῷ ἐκ τῶν μνημείων ἄνθρωπος ἐν πνεύματι
met    Him   out of the   tombs     a man    in a spirit

3 ἀκαθάρτῳ, ὃς τὴν κατοίκησιν εἶχεν ἐν τοῖς μνημείοις· καὶ
unclean, who the   dwelling    had among the   tombs,    and

4 οὔτε ἁλύσεσιν οὐδεὶς ἠδύνατο αὐτὸν δῆσαι, διὰ τὸ αὐτὸν
not with a chain no one   was able   him to bind, because that he

πολλάκις πέδαις καὶ ἁλύσεσι δεδέσθαι, καὶ διεσπᾶσθαι ὑπ'
often    with fetters and chains   had been bound, and had been torn by

αὐτοῦ τὰς ἁλύσεις, καὶ τὰς πέδας συντετρίφθαι· καὶ οὐδεὶς
him    the chains,    and the fetters had been broken, and no one

5 αὐτὸν ἴσχυε δαμάσαι· καὶ διὰ παντός, νυκτὸς καὶ ἡμέρας,
him   was able to subdue; and through all,    night and    day,

ἐν τοῖς ὄρεσι καὶ ἐν τοῖς μνήμασιν ἦν κράζων καὶ κατακόπτων
among the hills and in   the tombs he was crying and   cutting

6 ἑαυτὸν λίθοις. ἰδὼν δὲ τὸν Ἰησοῦν ἀπὸ μακρόθεν, ἔδραμε
himself with stones. seeing And    Jesus    from afar,    he ran

7 καὶ προσεκύνησεν αὐτῷ, καὶ κράξας φωνῇ μεγάλῃ εἶπε. Τί
and bowed the knee to Him,   and crying with a voice great   said, What

ἐμοὶ καὶ σοί, Ἰησοῦ, υἱὲ τοῦ Θεοῦ τοῦ ὑψίστου; ὁρκίζω σε
to me and to You, Jesus, Son — of God the Most High? I adjure You

8 τὸν Θεόν, μή με βασανίσῃς. ἔλεγε γὰρ αὐτῷ, Ἔξελθε, τὸ
(by) God   not me     torment. He said For to him,   Come out, the

9 πνεῦμα τὸ ἀκάθαρτον, ἐκ τοῦ ἀνθρώπου. καὶ ἐπηρώτα
spirit    —    unclean,   out of the   man!     And He questioned

αὐτόν, Τί σοι ὄνομα; καὶ ἀπεκρίθη, λέγων, Λεγεὼν ὄνομά
him, What (is) to you name? And he answered, saying, Legion (the) name

10 μοι, ὅτι πολλοί ἐσμεν. καὶ παρεκάλει αὐτὸν πολλά, ἵνα μὴ
of me, for many   we are. And he begged    Him   much, that not

11 αὐτοὺς ἀποστείλῃ ἔξω τῆς χώρας. ἦν δὲ ἐκεῖ πρὸς τὰ ὄρη
them   He would send outside the country. was And there near the mount

12 ἀγέλη χοίρων μεγάλη βοσκομένη· καὶ παρεκάλεσαν αὐτὸν
herd    of pigs a great   feeding;   and    begged    Him,

πάντες οἱ δαίμονες, λέγοντες, Πέμψον ἡμᾶς εἰς τοὺς χοίρους,
all    the demons,   saying,   Send    us into the    pigs.

13 ἵνα εἰς αὐτοὺς εἰσέλθωμεν. καὶ ἐπέτρεψεν αὐτοῖς εὐθέως ὁ
that into them   we may enter. And   allowed    them immediately—

Ἰησοῦς. καὶ ἐξελθόντα τὰ πνεύματα τὰ ἀκάθαρτα εἰσῆλθον
Jesus.    And coming out, the   spirits    —    unclean   entered

εἰς τοὺς χοίρους· καὶ ὥρμησεν ἡ ἀγέλη κατὰ τοῦ κρημνοῦ
into the pigs,   and rushed the herd   down the precipice

εἰς τὴν θάλασσαν· ἦσαν δὲ ὡς δισχίλιοι· καὶ ἐπνίγοντο ἐν τῇ
into the sea,    they were And about two thousand and were choked in the

14 θαλάσσῃ. οἱ δὲ βόσκοντες τοὺς χοίρους ἔφυγον, καὶ ἀνήγ-
sea. those And feeding   the   pigs    fled,    and told

γειλαν εἰς τὴν πόλιν καὶ εἰς τοὺς ἀγρούς. καὶ ἐξῆλθον ἰδεῖν
(it)    to the city, and to the    fields. And they came out to see

15 τί ἐστι τὸ γεγονός· καὶ ἔρχονται πρὸς τὸν Ἰησοῦν, καὶ
what is that having occurred, and they come to    — Jesus,   and

θεωροῦσι τὸν δαιμονιζόμενον καθήμενον καὶ ἱματισμένον
gaze upon the   demon-possed one    sitting    and having been robed

καὶ σωφρονοῦντα, τὸν ἐσχηκότα τὸν λεγεῶνα· καὶ ἐφοβήθη-
and being in his senses, the one having had the    legion,    and they feared.

16 σαν. καὶ διηγήσαντο αὐτοῖς οἱ ἰδόντες πῶς ἐγένετο τῷ
    And related       to them the (ones) seeing how it occurred to the

17 δαιμονιζομένῳ, καὶ περὶ τῶν χοίρων. καὶ ἤρξαντο παρα-
demon-possessed one, and about the   pigs.    And they began to beg

beg Him to depart from their borders. [18] And He having entered into the boat, he who had been demon-possessed begged Him, that he might be with Him. [19] But Jesus did not allow him, but said to him, Go to your house, to your own, and tell them how much the Lord did for you, and pitied you. [20] And he left and began to preach in Decapolis, how much Jesus had done for him; and all wondered.

[21] And Jesus having passed over in the boat again to the other side, a great crowd was gathered to Him; and He was by the sea. [22] And behold, one of the rulers of the synagogue came, Jairus by name, and seeing Him fell at His feet; [23] and he begged Him greatly, saying, My little daughter is at the end; (I pray) that having come You would lay hands on her, so that she may be cured, and she shall live. [24] And He went with him, and a great crowd followed Him, and pressed on Him. [25] And a certain woman being with a flow of blood for twelve years, [26] and having suffered much under many physicians, and having spent all her means, and having in no way benefited, but rather having come to worse, [27] having heard about Jesus, having come in the crowd behind, touched His garment; [28] for she said, If I but touch His garments, I shall be cured. [29] And immediately the fountain of her blood was dried up, and she knew in (her) body that she was healed from the affliction. [30] And immediately Jesus, knowing in Himself (that) the power had gone out of Him, having turned in the crowd, said, Who touched My garments? [31] And His disciples said to Him, You see the crowd pressing on You, and do You say, Who touched Me? [32] And He looked around to see her who had done this. [33] But the woman, being afraid and

**18** καλεῖν αὐτὸν ἀπελθεῖν ἀπὸ τῶν ὁρίων αὐτῶν. καὶ ἐμβάντος
Him to depart from the territory of them. And entering

αὐτοῦ εἰς τὸ πλοῖον, παρεκάλει αὐτὸν ὁ δαιμονισθείς, ἵνα ᾖ
He into the boat, begged Him the demoniac, that he be

**19** μετ᾽ αὐτοῦ. ὁ δὲ Ἰησοῦς οὐκ ἀφῆκεν αὐτόν. ἀλλὰ λέγει αὐτῷ,
with Him. — But Jesus not did allow him, but says to him

"Υπαγε εἰς τὸν οἶκόν σου πρὸς τοὺς σούς, καὶ ἀνάγγειλον
Go to the house of you to those of you, and announce

**20** αὐτοῖς ὅσα σοι ὁ Κύριος ἐποίησε, καὶ ἠλέησέ σε. καὶ ἀπῆλθε
to them how to you the Lord has done, and favored you. And he left

καὶ ἤρξατο κηρύσσειν ἐν τῇ Δεκαπόλει ὅσα ἐποίησεν αὐτῷ ὁ
and began to proclaim in — Decapolis how much did to him —

Ἰησοῦς· καὶ πάντες ἐθαύμαζον.
Jesus. And all marvelled.

**21** Καὶ διαπεράσαντος τοῦ Ἰησοῦ ἐν τῷ πλοίῳ πάλιν εἰς τὸ
And crossing over — Jesus in the boat again to the

πέραν, συνήχθη ὄχλος πολὺς ἐπ᾽ αὐτόν, καὶ ἦν παρὰ τὴν
other side, was collected a crowd big upon Him, and He was by the

**22** θάλασσαν. καὶ ἰδού, ἔρχεται εἷς τῶν ἀρχισυναγώγων,
sea. And behold, comes one of the synagogue chiefs,

ὀνόματι Ἰάειρος, καὶ ἰδὼν αὐτόν, πίπτει πρὸς τοὺς πόδας
by name Jairus, and seeing Him he falls at the feet

**23** αὐτοῦ, καὶ παρεκάλει αὐτὸν πολλά, λέγων ὅτι Τὸ θυγάτριόν
of Him, and begs Him much, saying, — The daughter

μου ἐσχάτως ἔχει· ἵνα ἐλθὼν ἐπιθῇς αὐτῇ τὰς χεῖρας, ὅπως
of me is at the last end, that coming You may lay on her the hands, that (she)

**24** σωθῇ καὶ ζήσεται. καὶ ἀπῆλθε μετ᾽ αὐτοῦ· καὶ ἠκολούθει
be cured and may live. And He went with him. And followed

αὐτῷ ὄχλος πολύς, καὶ συνέθλιβον αὐτόν.
Him a crowd great, and pressed upon Him.

**25 26** Καὶ γυνή τις οὖσα ἐν ῥύσει αἵματος ἔτη δώδεκα, καὶ
And a woman certain being in a flow of blood years twelve, and

πολλὰ παθοῦσα ὑπὸ πολλῶν ἰατρῶν, καὶ δαπανήσασα τὰ
many things suffering by many physicians, and having spent that

παρ᾽ ἑαυτῆς πάντα, καὶ μηδὲν ὠφεληθεῖσα, ἀλλὰ μᾶλλον
by her all things, and nothing having been gained, but rather

**27** εἰς τὸ χεῖρον ἐλθοῦσα, ἀκούσασα περὶ τοῦ Ἰησοῦ, ἐλθοῦσα
to the worse having come, hearing about — Jesus, coming

**28** ἐν τῷ ὄχλῳ ὄπισθεν, ἥψατο τοῦ ἱματίου αὐτοῦ· ἔλεγε γὰρ
in the crowd behind she touched the garment of Him. she said For

**29** ὅτι Κἂν τῶν ἱματίων αὐτοῦ ἅψωμαι, σωθήσομαι. καὶ
— If but the garments of Him I may touch, I will be cured. And

εὐθέως ἐξηράνθη ἡ πηγὴ τοῦ αἵματος αὐτῆς, καὶ ἔγνω τῷ
instantly was dried up the fountain of the blood of her, and she knew in

**30** σώματι ὅτι ἴαται ἀπὸ τῆς μάστιγος. καὶ εὐθέως ὁ Ἰησοῦς
(her) body that she is healed of the plague And instantly — Jesus

ἐπιγνοὺς ἐν ἑαυτῷ τὴν ἐξ αὐτοῦ δύναμιν ἐξελθοῦσαν,
knowing within Himself that out of Him power had gone forth,

ἐπιστραφεὶς ἐν τῷ ὄχλῳ, ἔλεγε, Τίς μου ἥψατο τῶν ἱματίων;
turning in the crowd said, Who of Me touched the garments?

**31** καὶ ἔλεγον αὐτῷ οἱ μαθηταὶ αὐτοῦ, Βλέπεις τὸν ὄχλον
And said to Him the disciples of Him, You see the crowd

**32** συνθλίβοντά σε, καὶ λέγεις, Τίς μου ἥψατο; καὶ περιεβλέ-
pressing upon You, and You say, Who of Me touched? And He looked

**33** πετο ἰδεῖν τὴν τοῦτο ποιήσασαν. ἡ δὲ γυνὴ φοβηθεῖσα καὶ
around to see the (one) this having done. the And woman fearing and

trembling, knowing what had been done upon her, came and fell down before Him, and told Him all the 34 truth. [34] And He said to her, Daughter, your faith has cured you; go in peace, and be well from your affliction. [35] (While) He was yet speaking, they came from the ruler of the 35 synagogue's (house), saying, Your daughter has died; Why do you still trouble the Master? [36] But Jesus 36 having heard the word spoken immediately said to the ruler of the synagogue, Do not fear; only believe. [37] And He did not allow 37 anyone to go with Him, except Peter and James and John, the brother of James. [38] And they come into 38 the house of the ruler of the synagogue; and He sees a 39 tumult, even much weeping and wailing. [39] And entering He says to them, Why do you make a tumult and weep? The child is not dead but 40 sleeps. [40] And they laughed at Him. But He having put out all takes along the father of the child, and the mother, and those with Him, and goes into where the child is lying. [41] And taking hold of the 41 child's hand, He says to her, Talitha, koumi! Which is, being translated, Little girl, I say to you, Arise! [42] And 42 instantly the little girl rose up and walked. For she was twelve years of (age). And they were amazed with a great amazement. [43] And 43 He ordered them fully that no one should know this, and said to give her (something) to eat.

τρέμουσα, εἰδυῖα ὃ γέγονεν ἐπ' αὐτῇ, ἦλθε καὶ προσέπεσεν
trembling, knowing what happened upon her, came and fell before
αὐτῷ, καὶ εἶπεν αὐτῷ πᾶσαν τὴν ἀλήθειαν. ὁ δὲ εἶπεν αὐτῇ,
Him, and told Him all the truth. He And said to her,
Θύγατερ, ἡ πίστις σου σέσωκέ σε· ὕπαγε εἰς εἰρήνην, καὶ
Daughter, the faith of you has healed you; go in peace, and
ἴσθι ὑγιὴς ἀπὸ τῆς μάστιγός σου.
be whole from the plague of you.
Ἔτι αὐτοῦ λαλοῦντος, ἔρχονται ἀπὸ τοῦ ἀρχισυναγώ-
While He was speaking, they come from the synagogue
γου, λέγοντες ὅτι Ἡ θυγάτηρ σου ἀπέθανε· τί ἔτι σκύλλεις
chief, saying, — The daughter of you has died: why still trouble
τὸν διδάσκαλον; ὁ δὲ Ἰησοῦς εὐθέως ἀκούσας τὸν λόγον
the Teacher? — But Jesus immediately, hearing the word
λαλούμενον λέγει τῷ ἀρχισυναγώγῳ, Μὴ φοβοῦ, μόνον
spoken, says to the synagogue chief, Do not fear; only
πίστευε. καὶ οὐκ ἀφῆκεν οὐδένα αὐτῷ συνακολουθῆσαι, εἰ
believe. And not He did allow no one Him to accompany, ex-
μὴ Πέτρον καὶ Ἰάκωβον καὶ Ἰωάννην τὸν ἀδελφὸν Ἰακώβου.
cept Peter and James and John the brother of James.
καὶ ἔρχεται εἰς τὸν οἶκον τοῦ ἀρχισυναγώγου, καὶ θεωρεῖ
And they come into the house of the synagogue-chief, and He sees
θόρυβον, καὶ κλαίοντας καὶ ἀλαλάζοντας πολλά. καὶ
a tumult, and weeping and wailing much. And
εἰσελθὼν λέγει αὐτοῖς, Τί θορυβεῖσθε καὶ · κλαίετε; τὸ
entering He says to them, Why do you make a tumult and weep? The
παιδίον οὐκ ἀπέθανεν, ἀλλὰ καθεύδει. καὶ κατεγέλων αὐτοῦ.
child not has died, but sleeps. And they laughed at Him.
ὁ δέ, ἐκβαλὼν ἅπαντας, παραλαμβάνει τὸν πατέρα τοῦ
He But having put out all takes along the father of the
παιδίου καὶ τὴν μητέρα καὶ τοὺς μετ' αὐτοῦ, καὶ εἰσπορεύε-
child and the mother and those with Him, and passes into
ται ὅπου ἦν τὸ παιδίον ἀνακείμενον. καὶ κρατήσας τῆς
where was the child lying. And taking hold of the
χειρὸς τοῦ παιδίου, λέγει αὐτῇ, Ταλιθά, κοῦμι· ὅ ἐστι
hand of the child, He says to her, Talitha koumi; which is,
μεθερμηνευόμενον, Τὸ κοράσιον, σοὶ λέγω, ἔγειραι. καὶ
being translated, — Little girl, to you I say, Arise! And
εὐθέως ἀνέστη τὸ κοράσιον καὶ περιεπάτει, ἦν γὰρ ἐτῶν
instantly rose up the little girl and walked. she was For of years
δώδεκα· καὶ ἐξέστησαν ἐκστάσει μεγάλῃ. καὶ διεστείλατο
twelve. And they were amazed with amazement great. And He ordered
αὐτοῖς πολλὰ ἵνα μηδεὶς γνῷ τοῦτο· καὶ εἶπε δοθῆναι
them much that no one should know this, and said to give
αὐτῇ φαγεῖν.
to her to eat.

## CHAPTER 6

[1] And He went out 1 from there, and comes to His native-place; and the disciples follow Him. [2] And a sab- 2 bath occurring, He began to teach in the synagogue. And many hearing were astonished, saying, From where (come) these things to this one? And

## CHAPTER 6

Καὶ ἐξῆλθεν ἐκεῖθεν, καὶ ἦλθεν εἰς τὴν πατρίδα αὐτοῦ·
And He went out from there, and comes to the native-place of Him.
καὶ ἀκολουθοῦσιν αὐτῷ οἱ μαθηταὶ αὐτοῦ. καὶ γενομένου
and follow Him the disciples of Him. And occurring
σαββάτου, ἤρξατο ἐν τῇ συναγωγῇ διδάσκειν· καὶ πολλοὶ
a sabbath, He began in the synagogue to teach, and many
ἀκούοντες ἐξεπλήσσοντο, λέγοντες, Πόθεν τούτῳ ταῦτα;
hearing were astonished, saying, From where to this one these things?

what (is) the wisdom given to Him, that even such works of power come about through His hands? [3] Is this one not the carpenter, the son of Mary, and brother of James and Joseph and Judas and Simon? And are the His sisters here with us? And they were offended in Him. [4] And Jesus said to them, A prophet is not without honor, except in his native place, and among the relatives, and in his (own) house. [5] And He could not do any work of power there, except He healed a few infirm ones, laying on (His) hands. [6] And He marveled because of the unbelief of them. And He went around the villages in circuit, teaching.

[7] And He calls near the twelve, and began to send them out two by two, and gave to them authority (over) the unclean spirits, [8] and charged them that they take nothing in (the) way, except a staff only— no bag, no bread, nor copper in the belt; [9] but tying on sandals, and not putting on two tunics. [10] And He said to them, Wherever you enter into a house, remain there until you go out from there. [11] And as many as will not receive you, nor hear from you, going out from there, shake off the dust under your feet for a testimony to them. Truly I say to you, it will be more tolerable for Sodom or Gomorrah in (the) Day of judgment than for that city. [12] And having gone out, they preached that (men) should repent. [13] And they cast out many demons; and anointed with oil and healed many sick ones. [14] And the king, Herod, heard; for His name became publicly known. And he said, John the Baptist has been raised from the dead, and because of this the works of power operate in him. [15]

καὶ τίς ἡ σοφία ἡ δοθεῖσα αὐτῷ. ὅτι καὶ δυνάμεις τοιαῦται
and what the wisdom given to Him that even works of power such

3 διὰ τῶν χειρῶν αὐτοῦ γίνονται; οὐχ οὗτός ἐστιν ὁ τέκτων,
through the hands of Him coming about? Not this one is the carpenter,

ὁ υἱὸς Μαρίας, ἀδελφὸς δὲ Ἰακώβου καὶ Ἰωσῆ καὶ Ἰούδα
the son of Mary, brother and of James and Joseph and Judas

καὶ Σίμωνος; καὶ οὐκ εἰσὶν αἱ ἀδελφαὶ αὐτοῦ ὧδε πρὸς ἡμᾶς;
and Simon? And not are the sisters of Him here with us?

4 καὶ ἐσκανδαλίζοντο ἐν αὐτῷ. ἔλεγε δὲ αὐτοῖς ὁ Ἰησοῦς ὅτι
And they were offended in Him. said And to them — Jesus, —

Οὐκ ἔστι προφήτης ἄτιμος, εἰ μὴ ἐν τῇ πατρίδι αὐτοῦ, καὶ
Not is a prophet unhonored, except in the native place of him, and

5 ἐν τοῖς συγγενέσι καὶ ἐν τῇ οἰκίᾳ αὐτοῦ. καὶ οὐκ ἠδύνατο
among the relatives, and in the house of him. And not He could

ἐκεῖ οὐδεμίαν δύναμιν ποιῆσαι, εἰ μὴ ὀλίγοις ἀρρώστοις
there no work of power do, except on a few infirm ones

6 ἐπιθεὶς τὰς χεῖρας, ἐθεράπευσε. καὶ ἐθαύμαζε διὰ τὴν ἀπι-
laying on the hands He healed. And He marveled through the un-

στίαν αὐτῶν.
belief of them.

Καὶ περιῆγε τὰς κώμας κύκλῳ διδάσκων.
And He went around the villages in circuit teaching.

7 Καὶ προσκαλεῖται τοὺς δώδεκα, καὶ ἤρξατο αὐτοὺς
And He calls near the twelve, and began them

ἀποστέλλειν δύο δύο, καὶ ἐδίδου αὐτοῖς ἐξουσίαν τῶν
to send out two by two, and gave to them authority (over) the

8 πνευμάτων τῶν ἀκαθάρτων. καὶ παρήγγειλεν αὐτοῖς ἵνα
spirits — unclean, and charged them that

μηδὲν αἴρωσιν εἰς ὁδόν, εἰ μὴ ῥάβδον μόνον· μὴ πήραν, μὴ
nothing they take in (the) way, except a staff only, not a bag, nor

9 ἄρτον, μὴ εἰς τὴν ζώνην χαλκόν· ἀλλ' ὑποδεδεμένους
bread, nor in the belt copper; but having tied under

10 σανδάλια· καὶ μὴ ἐνδύσασθαι δύο χιτῶνας. καὶ ἔλεγεν
sandals; and not put on two tunics. And He said

αὐτοῖς, Ὅπου ἐὰν εἰσέλθητε εἰς οἰκίαν, ἐκεῖ μένετε ἕως ἂν
to them, Wherever you enter into a house, there remain until

11 ἐξέλθητε ἐκεῖθεν. καὶ ὅσοι ἂν μὴ δέξωνται ὑμᾶς, μηδὲ
you go out from there. And as many as not will receive you, nor

ἀκούσωσιν ὑμῶν, ἐκπορευόμενοι ἐκεῖθεν, ἐκτινάξατε τὸν
hear from you, going out from there shake off the

χοῦν τὸν ὑποκάτω τῶν ποδῶν ὑμῶν εἰς μαρτύριον αὐτοῖς.
dust — under the feet of you for a testimony to them.

ἀμὴν λέγω ὑμῖν, ἀνεκτότερον ἔσται Σοδόμοις ἢ Γομόρροις ἐν
Truly I say to you, more tolerable it will be for Sodom or Gomorrah in

12 ἡμέρᾳ κρίσεως, ἢ τῇ πόλει ἐκείνῃ. καὶ ἐξελθόντες ἐκήρυσσον
day of judgment, than for city that. And having gone out they preached

13 ἵνα μετανοήσωσι· καὶ δαιμόνια πολλὰ ἐξέβαλλον, καὶ
that (men) should repent. And demons many they cast out; and

ἤλειφον ἐλαίῳ πολλοὺς ἀρρώστους καὶ ἐθεράπευον.
anointed with oil many sick ones, and healed.

14 Καὶ ἤκουσεν ὁ βασιλεὺς Ἡρώδης, φανερὸν γὰρ ἐγένετο τὸ
And heard the king, Herod, manifest for became the

ὄνομα αὐτοῦ, καὶ ἔλεγεν ὅτι Ἰωάννης ὁ βαπτίζων ἐκ νεκρῶν
name of Him. And he said, — John the Baptist from the dead

ἠγέρθη, καὶ διὰ τοῦτο ἐνεργοῦσιν αἱ δυνάμεις ἐν αὐτῷ.
has been raised, and therefore operate the works of power in him.

Others said, He is Elijah; and others said, He is a prophet, or as one of the prophets. [16] But Herod hearing, (he) said This one is John, whom I beheaded. He is risen from the dead. [17] For Herod himself sending had seized John, and had bound him in prison, because of Herodias, the wife of his brother Philip, because he had married her. [18] For John had said to Herod, It is not lawful for you to have your brother's wife. [19] And Herodias held it against him, and desired to kill him, but was not able; [20] for Herod feared John, knowing him (to be) a holy and just man, and kept him safe; and hearing him, he did many things, and gladly heard from him. [21] And a suitable day coming, when (as) a birth-feast Herod made a supper for his great ones, and the chief captains, and the first ones of Galilee. [22] And entering her daughter, the (daughter) of Herodias, and dancing, she also pleased Herod and those reclining with (him). The king said to the girl, Ask me whatever you wish, and I will give to you. [23] And he swore to her Whatever you ask me, I will give to you, up to half of my kingdom. [24] And she going out said to her mother, What shall I ask? And she said, The head of John the Baptist. [25] And entering immediately, with haste to the king she asked, saying, I desire that you give to me at once the head of John the Baptist on a dish. [26] And becoming deeply grieved the king did not wish to reject her because of the oaths, and those reclining together. [27] And the king at once sending a guardsman, he ordered the head of him to be brought. [28] And having gone out,

15 ἄλλοι ἔλεγον ὅτι Ἠλίας ἐστίν· ἄλλοι δὲ ἔλεγον ὅτι Προφή
   Others  said,      Elijah    he is  others and said,          a proph
16 ἐστίν, ἢ ὡς εἷς τῶν προφητῶν. ἀκούσας δὲ ὁ Ἡρώδης εἶ
   he is  or as one of the prophets.   hearing But, — Herod  sai
   ὅτι "Ὃν ἐγὼ ἀπεκεφάλισα Ἰωάννην, οὗτός ἐστιν· αὐ
   — whom I    beheaded,         John,       this one  he is. He
17 ἠγέρθη ἐκ νεκρῶν. αὐτὸς γὰρ ὁ Ἡρώδης ἀποστείλ
   is risen from the dead.  himself For — Herod      sending
   ἐκράτησε τὸν Ἰωάννην, καὶ ἔδησεν αὐτὸν ἐν τῇ φυλα
   had seized — John,    and bound   him  in the prison,
   διὰ Ἡρωδιάδα τὴν γυναῖκα Φιλίππου τοῦ ἀδελφοῦ αὐτ
   because of Herodias the wife  of Philip,  the brother  of hi
18 ὅτι αὐτὴν ἐγάμησεν. ἔλεγε γὰρ ὁ Ἰωάννης τῷ Ἡρώ
   because her he had married, had said For — John    —    to He
   ὅτι Οὐκ ἔξεστί σοι ἔχειν τὴν γυναῖκα τοῦ ἀδελφοῦ σα
   — not it is lawful for you to have the wife  of the brother of yo
19 ἡ δὲ Ἡρωδιὰς ἐνεῖχεν αὐτῷ, καὶ ἤθελεν αὐτὸν ἀποκτεῖν
   — And Herodias  held it  against him, and wished him  to kill,
20 καὶ οὐκ ἠδύνατο· ὁ γὰρ Ἡρώδης ἐφοβεῖτο τὸν Ἰωάννt
   and not was able; — for  Herod    feared     John
   εἰδὼς αὐτὸν ἄνδρα δίκαιον καὶ ἅγιον, καὶ συνετήρει αὐτ
   knowing him  a man   just  and holy,  and kept safe   him
   καὶ ἀκούσας αὐτοῦ, πολλὰ ἐποίει, καὶ ἡδέως αὐτοῦ ἤκου
   and hearing  him, many things he did, and gladly from him heard.
21 καὶ γενομένης ἡμέρας εὐκαίρου, ὅτε Ἡρώδης τοῖς γενεσίc
   And coming   a day    suitable   when Herod on the birth-fea
   αὐτοῦ δεῖπνον ἐποίει τοῖς μεγιστᾶσιν αὐτοῦ καὶ τc
   of him a supper  made  for the great ones of him, and th
22 χιλιάρχοις καὶ τοῖς πρώτοις τῆς Γαλιλαίας, καὶ εἰσελθούc
   chiliarchs, and the first ones — of Galilee.  And entering
   τῆς θυγατρὸς αὐτῆς τῆς Ἡρωδιάδος καὶ ὀρχησαμένης, κ
   the daughter of her, — of Herodias,   and dancing,    and
   ἀρεσάσης τῷ Ἡρώδῃ καὶ τοῖς συνανακειμένοις, εἶπεν
   she pleased — Herod  and those reclining with (him). said
   βασιλεὺς τῷ κορασίῳ, Αἴτησόν με ὃ ἐὰν θέλῃς, καὶ δώ
   king   to the girl,  Ask  me whatever you wish, and I will g
23 σοί· καὶ ὤμοσεν αὐτῇ ὅτι "Ὃ ἐάν με αἰτήσῃς, δώσω σc
   to you. And he swore to her, — Whatever me you ask, I will give to y
24 ἕως ἡμίσους τῆς βασιλείας μου. ἡ δὲ ἐξελθοῦσα εἶπε
   up to half of the  kingdom of me. she and going out   said t
   μητρὶ αὐτῆς, Τί αἰτήσομαι; ἡ δὲ εἶπε, Τὴν κεφαλ
   mother of her, What shall I ask? she And said, The head
25 Ἰωάννου τοῦ Βαπτιστοῦ. καὶ εἰσελθοῦσα εὐθέως μετ
   of John  the Baptist.     And entering immediately  wi
   σπουδῆς πρὸς τὸν βασιλέα, ᾐτήσατο, λέγουσα, Θέλω ἵ
   haste    to the  king,    she asked,  saying,  I desire th
   μοι δῷς ἐξαυτῆς ἐπὶ πίνακι τὴν κεφαλὴν Ἰωάννου τc
   to me you give at once on a dish the head  of John  t
26 Βαπτιστοῦ. καὶ περίλυπος γενόμενος ὁ βασιλεύς, διὰ το
   Baptist.       And deeply grieved becoming the king, because of t
   ὅρκους καὶ τοὺς συνανακειμένους οὐκ ἠθέλησεν αὐτὴν ἀθ
   oaths,  and those reclining together  not did wish  her  to
27 τῆσαι. καὶ εὐθέως ἀποστείλας ὁ βασιλεὺς σπεκουλάτοc
   reject.  And at once sending   the king    a guardsman
28 ἐπέταξεν ἐνεχθῆναι τὴν κεφαλὴν αὐτοῦ. ὁ δὲ ἀπελθὼ
   he ordered to be brought the head   of him. he And having gon

ἀπεκεφάλισεν αὐτὸν ἐν τῇ φυλακῇ, καὶ ἤνεγκε τὴν κεφαλὴν
beheaded     him     in the   prison,   and brought    the    head

αὐτοῦ ἐπὶ πίνακι, καὶ ἔδωκεν αὐτὴν τῷ κορασίῳ· καὶ τὸ
of him   on a dish,    and    gave    it    to the    girl;    and the

**29** κοράσιον ἔδωκεν αὐτὴν τῇ μητρὶ αὐτῆς. καὶ ἀκούσαντες
girl     gave     it   to the mother of her. And   having heard.

οἱ μαθηταὶ αὐτοῦ ἦλθον, καὶ ἦραν τὸ πτῶμα αὐτοῦ, καὶ
the disciples of him    went    and   took the corpse of him,   and

ἔθηκαν αὐτὸ ἐν μνημείῳ.
placed it    in   a tomb.

**30**    Καὶ συνάγονται οἱ ἀπόστολοι πρὸς τὸν Ἰησοῦν, καὶ
And are assembled    the    apostles    to    —    Jesus,    and

ἀπήγγειλαν αὐτῷ πάντα, καὶ ὅσα ἐποίησαν καὶ ὅσα ἐδί-
told     Him all things, even what they did    and what they

**31** δαξαν. καὶ εἶπεν αὐτοῖς, Δεῦτε ὑμεῖς αὐτοὶ κατ' ἰδίαν εἰς
taught. And He said to them, Come   yourselves    privately     to

ἔρημον τόπον, καὶ ἀναπαύεσθε ὀλίγον. ἦσαν γὰρ οἱ
a desert   place,    and    rest    a little.    were For those

ἐρχόμενοι καὶ οἱ ὑπάγοντες πολλοί, καὶ οὐδὲ φαγεῖν ηὐκαί-
coming and the (ones) going    many, and not even to eat they had

**32** ρουν. καὶ ἀπῆλθον εἰς ἔρημον τόπον τῷ πλοίῳ κατ' ἰδίαν.
opportunity. And they left into a desert place, by the boat,   privately.

**33** καὶ εἶδον αὐτοὺς ὑπάγοντας οἱ ὄχλοι, καὶ ἐπέγνωσαν αὐτὸν
And saw   them    going    the crowds, and recognized    Him

πολλοί, καὶ πεζῇ ἀπὸ πασῶν τῶν πόλεων συνέδραμον ἐκεῖ,
many,    and on foot from   all    the    cities    ran together there,

**34** καὶ προῆλθον αὐτούς, καὶ συνῆλθον πρὸς αὐτόν. καὶ
and came before them,    and came together to    Him.   And

ἐξελθὼν εἶδεν ὁ Ἰησοῦς πολὺν ὄχλον, καὶ ἐσπλαγχνίσθη
going out saw   ὁ Jesus a much crowd,   and   had compassion

ἐπ' αὐτοῖς, ὅτι ἦσαν ὡς πρόβατα μὴ ἔχοντα ποιμένα· καὶ
on    them, because they were as   sheep   not having a shepherd. And

**35** ἤρξατο διδάσκειν αὐτοὺς πολλά. καὶ ἤδη ὥρας πολλῆς
He began to teach    them   many things. And now an hour a much

γενομένης, προσελθόντες αὐτῷ οἱ μαθηταὶ αὐτοῦ λέγουσιν
occurring    drawing near   to Him the disciples of Him    said,

**36** ὅτι Ἔρημός ἐστιν ὁ τόπος, καὶ ἤδη ὥρα πολλή· ἀπόλυσον
—    desert   is The place,   and now a hour   much. Send away

αὐτούς, ἵνα ἀπελθόντες εἰς τοὺς κύκλῳ ἀγροὺς καὶ κώμας
them,   that going away    to the    surrounding fields and villages

ἀγοράσωσιν ἑαυτοῖς ἄρτους. τί γὰρ φάγωσιν οὐκ ἔχουσιν.
they may buy for themselves bread. what For they may eat not they have.

**37** ὁ δὲ ἀποκριθεὶς εἶπεν αὐτοῖς, Δότε αὐτοῖς ὑμεῖς φαγεῖν. καὶ
He But answering   said to them, Give    them    you to eat.   And

λέγουσιν αὐτῷ, Ἀπελθόντες ἀγοράσωμεν διακοσίων δηνα-
they say to Him, Having gone, should we buy    two hundred   de-

**38** ρίων ἄρτους, καὶ δῶμεν αὐτοῖς φαγεῖν ; ὁ δὲ λέγει αὐτοῖς,
narii of bread,   and give    them   to eat? He And says to them,

Πόσους ἄρτους ἔχετε ; ὑπάγετε καὶ ἴδετε. καὶ γνόντες
How many loaves do you have? Go    and see. And knowing

**39** λέγουσι, Πέντε, καὶ δύο ἰχθύας. καὶ ἐπέταξεν αὐτοῖς ἀνα-
they say, Five,   and two fish.    And He ordered   them to

κλῖναι πάντας συμπόσια συμπόσια ἐπὶ τῷ χλωρῷ χόρτῳ.
recline all,    companies (by) companies on   the green    grass.

**40** καὶ ἀνέπεσον πρασιαὶ πρασιαί, ἀνὰ ἑκατὸν καὶ ἀνὰ πεντή-
And they sat    group (by) group    by hundred   and by fifty.

---

he beheaded him in the prison, and brought his head on a dish, and gave it to the girl; and the girl gave it to her mother. [29] And having heard, his disciples went out and took his corpse, and placed it in a tomb. [30] And the apostles assembled to Jesus, and told Him all things, even what they did, and what they taught. [31] And He said to them, Come you, yourselves, privately to a desert place, and rest a little. For those coming and those going (were) many, and they did not even have opportunity to eat. [32] And they departed into a desert place, by boat, privately. [33] And the crowds saw them going, and many recognized Him; and (they) ran together there on foot, from all the cities; and came before them, and came together to Him. [34] And having gone out, Jesus saw a great crowd, and had compassion on them, because they were as sheep not having a shepherd. And He began to teach them many things. [35] And now a late hour occurring, the disciples drawing near to Him said, The place is desert, and (it is) a late hour. [36] Send them away, that going away to the surrounding fields and villages, they may buy for themselves bread. For they do not have what they may eat. [37] And He answering said to them, You give them (food) to eat. And they say to Him, Going, should we buy two hundred denarii of bread, and give (it to) them to eat? [38] And He says to them, How many loaves do you have? Go and see. And having known, they said, Five, and two fish. [39] And He ordered them all to recline, companies (by) companies on the green grass. [40] And they sat, group (by) group, by hundred and by fifty. [41] And taking the five loaves and the two fish, looking up to Heaven, He blessed, and broke the loaves, and gave to His disciples, that they may set before them. And He divided the two fish to all. [42] And all ate, and were satisfied. [43] And they took up fragments, twelve handbaskets full; also from the fish. [44] And those eating the loaves were about five thousand men. [45] And at once He constrained His disciples to enter into the boat, and to go before to the other side, to Bethsaida, unti He should dismiss the crowd. [46] And taking leave (of) them, He went away to the mountain to pray. [47] And evening occurring, the boat was in (the) midst of the sea, and He alone on the land. [48] And He saw them being distressed in the rowing, for the wind was contrary to them, and (it was) about (the) fourth watch of the night (when) He comes toward them, walking on the sea, and willed to go by them. [49] But they, seeing Him walking on the sea, thought (it) to be a ghost, and cried out. [50] For all saw Him, and were troubled. And immediately He spoke to them, and says to them, Have courage, I AM! Do not fear. [51] And He went up to them into the boat, and the wind was cut off. And they were amazed exceedingly beyond measure within themselves, and marveled. [52] For they did not understand (the miracle) on the loaves, for their hearts were hardened.

[53] And crossing over, they came onto the land of Gennesaret, and drew to shore. [54] And they coming out of the boat, at once knowing Him, [55] running around all that neighborhood, they began to carry about on the cots those having illness, where they heard that He is there. [56] And

**41** κοντα. καὶ λαβὼν τοὺς πέντε ἄρτους καὶ τοὺς δύο ἰχθύας,
And taking the five loaves and the two fish,

ἀναβλέψας εἰς τὸν οὐρανόν, εὐλόγησε, καὶ κατέκλασε τοὺς
looking up to — Heaven, He blessed, and broke the

ἄρτους, καὶ ἐδίδου τοῖς μαθηταῖς αὐτοῦ ἵνα παραθῶσιν
loaves, and gave to the disciples of Him, that they may set before

**42** αὐτοῖς· καὶ τοὺς δύο ἰχθύας ἐμέρισε πᾶσι. καὶ ἔφαγον πάντες,
them. And the two fish He divided to all. And ate all,

**43** καὶ ἐχορτάσθησαν· καὶ ἦραν κλασμάτων δώδεκα κοφίνους
and were satisfied. And they took fragments, twelve handbaskets

**44** πλήρεις, καὶ ἀπὸ τῶν ἰχθύων. καὶ ἦσαν οἱ φαγόντες τοὺς
full, and from the fish. And were the (ones) eating the

ἄρτους ὡσεὶ πεντακισχίλιοι ἄνδρες.
loaves about five thousand men.

**45** Καὶ εὐθέως ἠνάγκασε τοὺς μαθητὰς αὐτοῦ ἐμβῆναι εἰς τὸ
And at once He constrained the disciples of Him to enter into the

πλοῖον, καὶ προάγειν εἰς τὸ πέραν πρὸς Βηθσαϊδά, ἕως
boat, and to go before to the other side, to Bethsaida, until

**46** αὐτὸς ἀπολύσῃ τὸν ὄχλον. καὶ ἀποταξάμενος αὐτοῖς,
He should dismiss the crowd. And taking leave (of) them,

**47** ἀπῆλθεν εἰς τὸ ὄρος προσεύξασθαι. καὶ ὀψίας γενομένης,
He went away to the mountain to pray. And evening occurring,

ἦν τὸ πλοῖον ἐν μέσῳ τῆς θαλάσσης, καὶ αὐτὸς μόνος ἐπὶ τῆς
was the boat in (the) midst of the sea, and He alone on the

**48** γῆς. καὶ εἶδεν αὐτοὺς βασανιζομένους ἐν τῷ ἐλαύνειν, ἦν
land. And He saw them being distressed in the row(ing), was

γὰρ ὁ ἄνεμος ἐναντίος αὐτοῖς, καὶ περὶ τετάρτην φυλακὴν
for the wind contrary to them, and about (the) fourth watch

τῆς νυκτὸς ἔρχεται πρὸς αὐτούς, περιπατῶν ἐπὶ τῆς
of the night He comes toward them, walking on the

**49** θαλάσσης· καὶ ἤθελε παρελθεῖν αὐτούς. οἱ δέ, ἰδόντες αὐτὸν
sea; and willed to go by them. they But, seeing Him

περιπατοῦντα ἐπὶ τῆς θαλάσσης, ἔδοξαν φάντασμα εἶναι,
walking on the sea, thought a ghost (it) to be,

**50** καὶ ἀνέκραξαν· πάντες γὰρ αὐτὸν εἶδον, καὶ ἐταράχθησαν.
and cried out. all For Him saw, and were troubled.

καὶ εὐθέως ἐλάλησε μετ᾽ αὐτῶν, καὶ λέγει αὐτοῖς, Θαρσεῖτε·
And immediately He spoke with them, and says to them, Have courage,

**51** ἐγώ εἰμι, μὴ φοβεῖσθε. καὶ ἀνέβη πρὸς αὐτοὺς εἰς τὸ πλοῖον,
I AM! Do not fear. And He went up to them into the boat,

καὶ ἐκόπασεν ὁ ἄνεμος· καὶ λίαν ἐκ περισσοῦ ἐν ἑαυτοῖς
and was cut the wind. And exceedingly beyond measure in themselves

**52** ἐξίσταντο, καὶ ἐθαύμαζον. οὐ γὰρ συνῆκαν ἐπὶ τοῖς ἄρτοις·
they were amazed, and marveled. not For they understood by the loaves.

ἦν γὰρ ἡ καρδία αὐτῶν πεπωρωμένη.
was for the hearts of them hardened.

**53** Καὶ διαπεράσαντες ἦλθον ἐπὶ τὴν γῆν Γεννησαρέτ, καὶ
And crossing over they came onto the land of Gennesaret, and

**54** προσωρμίσθησαν. καὶ ἐξελθόντων αὐτῶν ἐκ τοῦ πλοίου,
drew to shore. And coming out they out of the boat,

**55** εὐθέως ἐπιγνόντες αὐτόν, περιδραμόντες ὅλην τὴν περίχω-
at once knowing Him they ran around all — neighborhood

ρον ἐκείνην, ἤρξαντο ἐπὶ τοῖς κραββάτοις τοὺς κακῶς
that, they began on the cots those illness

**56** ἔχοντας περιφέρειν, ὅπου ἤκουον ὅτι ἐκεῖ ἐστι. καὶ ὅπου ἂν
having to carry about, where they heard that there He is. And wherever

wherever He entered into villages or cities or fields, they laid the ailing (ones) in the markets, and begged Him that if even they may touch the fringe of His garment. And as many as touched Him, (they) were healed.

εἰσεπορεύετο εἰς κώμας ἢ πόλεις ἢ ἀγρούς, ἐν ταῖς ἀγοραῖς
He entered      into villages or cities   or   fields,   in  the  markets
ἐτίθουν τοὺς ἀσθενοῦντας, καὶ παρεκάλουν αὐτόν ἵνα κἂν
they laid the    ailing (ones),  and   begged      Him   that if even
τοῦ κρασπέδου τοῦ ἱματίου αὐτοῦ ἅψωνται· καὶ ὅσοι ἂν
the    fringe       of the garment of Him they may touch; and as many as
ἥπτοντο αὐτοῦ ἐσώζοντο.
touched    Him    were healed.

## CHAPTER 7

## CHAPTER 7

[1] And the Pharisees were gathered together to Him, and some of the scribes, coming from Jerusalem. [2] And seeing some of His disciples eating bread with unclean hands, that is, unwashed, they found fault. [3] For the Pharisees and all the Jews do not eat, unless they wash the hands with (the) fist, holding the tradition of the elders. [4] And (coming) from the market, they do not eat unless they wash themselves. And there are many other things which they received to hold, washings of cups and of utensils, and of bronze vessels and couches. [5] Then the Pharisees and the scribes questioned Him, Why do your disciples not walk according to the tradition of the elders, but eat bread with unwashed hands? [6] And answering He said to them, Well did Isaiah prophesy concerning you, hypocrites; as it has been written, "This people honors Me with the lips, but their heart is far away from Me; [7] and in vain they worship Me, teaching (as) teachings (the) commandments of men. [8] For forsaking the commandment of God, you hold the tradition of men: washings of utensils and cups, and other many such like things you do. [9] And He said to them, Nobly you set aside the commandment of God, that you may keep your tradition. [10] For Moses said, Honor your father and your mother; and, He speaking evil of father or mother, let him expire by death. [11] But you say, If a

1 Καὶ συνάγονται πρὸς αὐτὸν οἱ Φαρισαῖοι, καί τινες τῶν
And were assembled   to     Him  the   Pharisees,  and  some of the
2 γραμματέων, ἐλθόντες ἀπὸ Ἱεροσολύμων· καὶ ἰδόντες τινὰς
scribes,     coming    from     Jerusalem.      And seeing   some
τῶν μαθητῶν αὐτοῦ κοιναῖς χερσί, τοῦτ' ἔστιν ἀνίπτοις,
of the disciples  of Him with unclean hands, that   is     unwashed,
3 ἐσθίοντας ἄρτους ἐμέμψαντο. οἱ γὰρ Φαρισαῖοι καὶ πάντες
eating     bread,  they found fault. the For Pharisees    and   all
οἱ Ἰουδαῖοι, ἐὰν μὴ πυγμῇ νίψωνται τὰς χεῖρας, οὐκ
the  Jews       unless with (the) fist they wash  the   hands,   not
ἐσθίουσι, κρατοῦντες τὴν παράδοσιν τῶν πρεσβυτέρων·
do they eat,  holding      the    tradition   of the    elders.
4 καὶ ἀπὸ ἀγορᾶς, ἐὰν μὴ βαπτίσωνται, οὐκ ἐσθίουσι· καὶ
And from market.  unless   they wash themselves, not they eat,  and
ἄλλα πολλά ἐστιν ἃ παρέλαβον κρατεῖν, βαπτισμοὺς
other things many there are which they received to hold,   washings
5 ποτηρίων καὶ ξεστῶν καὶ χαλκίων καὶ κλινῶν. ἔπειτα
of cups      and of utensils and of bronze vessels and couches.  Then
ἐπερωτῶσιν αὐτὸν οἱ Φαρισαῖοι καὶ οἱ γραμματεῖς, Διατί οἱ
question      Him  the Pharisees   and the scribes,    Why the
μαθηταί σου οὐ περιπατοῦσι κατὰ τὴν παράδοσιν τῶν
disciples of you not   walk      according to the  tradition  of the
πρεσβυτέρων, ἀλλὰ ἀνίπτοις χερσὶν ἐσθίουσι τὸν ἄρτον;
elders,          but with unwashed hands   eat     the  bread?
6 ὁ δὲ ἀποκριθεὶς εἶπεν αὐτοῖς ὅτι Καλῶς προεφήτευσεν
He And answering   said to them,  —   Well     prophesied
Ἡσαΐας περὶ ὑμῶν τῶν ὑποκριτῶν, ὡς γέγραπται, Οὗτος ὁ
Isaiah concerning you,  —  hypocrites,  as it has been written, This
λαὸς τοῖς χείλεσί με τιμᾷ, ἡ δὲ καρδία αὐτῶν πόρρω ἀπέχει
people with the  lips Me honors, the but heart of them  far   is away
7 ἀπ' ἐμοῦ. μάτην δὲ σέβονταί με, διδάσκοντες διδασκαλίας
from Me;   in vain and they worship Me, teaching (as)   teachings
8 ἐντάλματα ἀνθρώπων. ἀφέντες γὰρ τὴν ἐντολὴν τοῦ Θεοῦ,
commandments of men. forsaking  For the commandment — of God,
κρατεῖτε τὴν παράδοσιν τῶν ἀνθρώπων, βαπτισμοὺς
you hold   the  tradition    —    of men       washings
ξεστῶν καὶ ποτηρίων· καὶ ἄλλα παρόμοια τοιαῦτα πολλὰ
of utensils and  cups      and other  like things   such    many
9 ποιεῖτε. καὶ ἔλεγεν αὐτοῖς, Καλῶς ἀθετεῖτε τὴν ἐντολὴν τοῦ
you do. And He said to them,  Well do you set aside the commandment
10 Θεοῦ, ἵνα τὴν παράδοσιν ὑμῶν τηρήσητε. Μωσῆς γὰρ εἶπε,
of God, that the   tradition    of you you may keep. Moses  For said,
Τίμα τὸν πατέρα σου καὶ τὴν μητέρα σου· καί, Ὁ κακολογῶν
Honor the father of you and the  mother of you, and, He speaking evil
11 πατέρα ἢ μητέρα θανάτῳ τελευτάτω· ὑμεῖς δὲ λέγετε, Ἐὰν
of father or mother by death let him end.   you But   say,      If

man says to (his) father or to (his) mother Corban—which is, A gift; whatever you might profit by me! [12] and you no longer allow him anything to do for his father and his mother, [13] making of no effect the word of God by your tradition which you delivered. And many such like things you do. [14] And calling near all the crowd, He said to them, All hear Me, and understand, [15] There is nothing from outside the man entering into him which is able to defile him; but the things going out from him, those are the things defiling the man. [16] If anyone has ears to hear, let him hear. [17] And when He entered into a house from the crowd, His disciples questioned Him about the parable. [18] And He says to them, Are you also so undiscerning? Do you not perceive that all that enters from outside into the man is not able to defile him, [19] because it does not enter into his heart, but into the belly; and (it) goes out into the waste-bowl, purging all the foods? [20] And He said, That passing out of the man, that (is it) that defiles the man. [21] For from within, out of the heart of men, pass out the evil thoughts, adulteries, fornications, murders, [22] thefts, greedy desires, iniquities, deceit, lustful desires, a wicked eye, blasphemy, pride, foolishness; [23] all these evil things pass out from within and defile the man.

[24] And rising up from there, He went away into the borders of Tyre and Sidon. And entering into the house, He desired no one to know; but He could not be hidden. [25] For hearing about Him, a woman whose daughter had an unclean spirit coming up fell down at His feet [26] —and the woman was a Greek, a

εἴπῃ ἄνθρωπος τῷ πατρὶ ἢ τῇ μητρί, Κορβᾶν, ὅ ἐστι,
says   a man  to the father  or to the mother, Corban,—which is,

12 δῶρον, ὃ ἐὰν ἐξ ἐμοῦ ὠφεληθῆς· καὶ οὐκέτι ἀφίετε αὐτὸν
A gift — whatever by  me you might profit; and no longer you allow him

13 οὐδὲν ποιῆσαι τῷ πατρὶ αὐτοῦ ἢ τῇ μητρὶ αὐτοῦ, ἀκυ-
nothing to do  for the father  of him or the mother  of him, making

ροῦντες τὸν λόγον τοῦ Θεοῦ τῇ παραδόσει ὑμῶν ᾗ· παρεδώ-
void    the word  — of God by the tradition  of you which you

14 κατε· καὶ παρόμοια τοιαῦτα πολλὰ ποιεῖτε. καὶ προσκαλε-
delivered. And like things such   many  you do. And calling near

σάμενος πάντα τὸν ὄχλον, ἔλεγεν αὐτοῖς, Ἀκούετέ μου
(Him)   all   the  crowd, He said  to them,   Hear  Me

15 πάντες, καὶ συνίετε. οὐδέν ἐστιν ἔξωθεν τοῦ ἀνθρώπου
all,  and understand. nothing There is from outside the  man

εἰσπορευόμενον εἰς αὐτόν, ὃ δύναται αὐτὸν κοινῶσαι· ἀλλὰ
entering   into him which is able  him to profane; but

τὰ ἐκπορευόμενα ἀπ' αὐτοῦ, ἐκεῖνά ἐστι τὰ κοινοῦντα τὸν
the things going out from  him,  those are the things profaning the

16 ἄνθρωπον. εἴ τις ἔχει ὦτα ἀκούειν ἀκουέτω. καὶ ὅτε εἰσῆλθεν
17 man.   If anyone has ear.  to hear, let him hear. And when He entered

εἰς οἶκον ἀπὸ τοῦ ὄχλου, ἐπηρώτων αὐτὸν οἱ μαθηταὶ
into a house from  the crowd,  questioned  Him the disciples

18 αὐτοῦ περὶ τῆς παραβολῆς. καὶ λέγει αὐτοῖς, Οὕτω καὶ
of Him about the  parable.  And He says to them, Thus also

ὑμεῖς ἀσύνετοί ἐστε ; οὐ νοεῖτε ὅτι πᾶν τὸ ἔξωθεν εἰσπορευό-
you undiscerning are? Not perceive you that all that from outside enter-

19 μενον εἰς τὸν ἄνθρωπον οὐ δύναται αὐτὸν κοινῶσαι, ὅτι
ing  into   man  not is able   him to profane because

οὐκ εἰσπορεύεται αὐτοῦ εἰς τὴν καρδίαν, ἀλλ' εἰς τὴν
not it does enter  of him into the  heart,  but into the

κοιλίαν· καὶ εἰς τὸν ἀφεδρῶνα ἐκπορεύεται, καθαρίζον
belly,  and into the  waste-bowl  goes out,  purging

20 πάντα τὰ βρώματα. ἔλεγε δὲ ὅτι Τὸ ἐκ τοῦ ἀνθρώπου
all   the  foods?   He said And — That out of the   man

21 ἐκπορευόμενον, ἐκεῖνο κοινοῖ τὸν ἄνθρωπον. ἔσωθεν γάρ,
passing out,   that profanes the   man.  from within For,

ἐκ τῆς καρδίας τῶν ἀνθρώπων, οἱ διαλογισμοὶ οἱ κακοὶ
out of the heart  — of men  the thoughts  — evil

22 ἐκπορεύονται, μοιχεῖαι, πορνεῖαι, φόνοι, κλοπαί, πλεονεξίαι,
pass out,  adulteries, fornications, murders, thefts,  greedy desires,

πονηρίαι, δόλος, ἀσέλγεια, ὀφθαλμὸς πονηρός, βλασφημία,
iniquities,  deceit, lustful desires, an eye   wicked, blasphemy,

23 ὑπερηφανία, ἀφροσύνη· πάντα ταῦτα τὰ πονηρὰ ἔσωθεν
pride,   foolishness— all   these  — evil things from within

ἐκπορεύεται, καὶ κοινοῖ τὸν ἄνθρωπον.
pass out  and profane the   man.

24 Καὶ ἐκεῖθεν ἀναστὰς ἀπῆλθεν εἰς τὰ μεθόρια Τύρου καὶ
And from there rising up He went away into the borders of Tyre and

Σιδῶνος. καὶ εἰσελθὼν εἰς τὴν οἰκίαν, οὐδένα ἤθελε γνῶναι,
Sidon.  And entering  into the house,  no one He desired to know,

25 καὶ οὐκ ἠδυνήθη λαθεῖν. ἀκούσασα γὰρ γυνὴ περὶ αὐτοῦ,
But not He could be hidden. hearing  For a woman about  Him,

ἧς εἶχε τὸ θυγάτριον αὐτῆς πνεῦμα ἀκάθαρτον, ἐλθοῦσα
of whom had the daughter  of her a spirit  unclean,  coming

26 προσέπεσε πρὸς τοὺς πόδας αὐτοῦ· ἦν δὲ ἡ γυνὴ Ἑλληνίς,
fell down  to   the  feet of Him; was and the woman a Greek,

Syrophenician by race—and she asked that He would expel the demon from her daughter. [27] And Jesus said to her, First, allow the children to be satisfied; for it is not good to take the bread of the children and to throw (it) to the dogs. [28] But she answered and says to Him, Yes, Lord; for even the dogs under the table eat from the crumbs of the children. [29] And He said to her, Because of this word, go. The demon has gone out from your daughter. [30] And going away to her house, she found the demon had gone out, and (her) daughter was laid on the couch.

27 Συροφοίνισσα τῷ γένει· καὶ ἠρώτα αὐτὸν ἵνα τὸ δαιμόνιον
a Syrophoenician — by race. And she asked Him that the demon
ἐκβάλλῃ ἐκ τῆς θυγατρὸς αὐτῆς. ὁ δὲ Ἰησοῦς εἶπεν αὐτῇ,
He would expel from the daughter of her. — And Jesus said to her,
Ἀφες πρῶτον χορτασθῆναι τὰ τέκνα· οὐ γὰρ καλόν ἐστι
Allow first to be satisfied the children; not for good is
28 λαβεῖν τὸν ἄρτον τῶν τέκνων καὶ βαλεῖν τοις κυναρίοις. ἡ
to take the bread of the children and to throw to the dogs. she
δὲ ἀπεκρίθη καὶ λέγει αὐτῷ, Ναί. Κύριε· καὶ γὰρ τὰ κυνάρια
And answered and says to Him, Yes, Lord; even for the dogs
ὑποκάτω τῆς τραπέζης ἐσθίει ἀπὸ τῶν ψιχίων τῶν παιδίων.
under the table eat from the crumbs of the children.
29 καὶ εἶπεν αὐτῇ, Διὰ τοῦτον τὸν λόγον ὕπαγε· ἐξελήλυθε τὸ
And He said to her, Because of this — word, go; has gone out the
30 δαιμόνιον ἐκ τῆς θυγατρός σου. καὶ ἀπελθοῦσα εἰς τὸν οἶκον
demon from the daughter of you. And going away to the house
αὐτῆς, εὗρε τὸ δαιμόνιον ἐξεληλυθός, καὶ τὴν θυγατέρα
of her, she found the demon had gone out, and the daughter
βεβλημένην ἐπὶ τῆς κλίνης.
was laid on the couch.

[31] And again going out from the borders of Tyre and Sidon, He came to the sea of Galilee, in the midst of the borders of (the) Decapolis. [32] And they bring to Him a deaf one, hardly speaking; and they begged Him, that He put (His) hand on him. [33] And taking him away from the crowd, privately, He put His fingers into his ears, and spitting, He touched his tongue; [34] and having looked up into Heaven, He groaned, and says to him, Ephphatha! Which is, Be opened! [35] And instantly his hearing was opened, and the bond of his tongue was loosened; and he spoke rightly. [36] And he ordered them that they should tell no one; but as much as He ordered them, much more abundantly they proclaimed [37] And they were most exceedingly amazed, saying, He has done all things excellently: He makes even the deaf to hear, and the dumb to speak.

31 Καὶ πάλιν ἐξελθὼν ἐκ τῶν ὁρίων Τύρου καὶ Σιδῶνος, ἦλθε
And again going out from the borders of Tyre and Sidon, He came
πρὸς τὴν θάλασσαν τῆς Γαλιλαίας, ἀνὰ μέσον τῶν ὁρίων
to the sea — of Galilee in the midst of the borders
32 Δεκαπόλεως. καὶ φέρουσιν αὐτῷ κωφὸν μογιλάλον, καὶ
of (the) Decapolis. And they bring to Him a deaf one, hardly speaking, and
33 παρακαλοῦσιν αὐτὸν ἵνα ἐπιθῇ αὐτῷ τὴν χεῖρα. καὶ ἀπολα-
they begged Him that He put on him the hand. And taking
βόμενος αὐτὸν ἀπὸ τοῦ ὄχλου κατ' ἰδίαν, ἔβαλε τοὺς δα-
away him from the crowd, privately He put the
κτύλους αὐτοῦ εἰς τὰ ὦτα αὐτοῦ, καὶ πτύσας ἥψατο τῆς
fingers of Him into the ears of him, and spitting He touched the
34 γλώσσης αὐτοῦ, καὶ ἀναβλέψας εἰς τὸν οὐρανόν, ἐστέναξε,
tongue of him, and looking up into — Heaven, He groaned,
35 καὶ λέγει αὐτῷ, Ἐφφαθά, ὅ ἐστι, Διανοίχθητι. καὶ εὐθέως
and says to him, Ephphatha, which is, Be opened! And instantly
διηνοίχθησαν αὐτοῦ αἱ ἀκοαί· καὶ ἐλύθη ὁ δεσμὸς τῆς γλώσ-
were opened of him the hearing, and was loosened the bond of the tongue
36 σης αὐτοῦ, καὶ ἐλάλει ὀρθῶς. καὶ διεστείλατο αὐτοῖς ἵνα
of him, and He spoke correctly. And He ordered them that
μηδενὶ εἴπωσιν· ὅσον δὲ αὐτὸς αὐτοῖς διεστέλλετο, μᾶλλον
no one they should tell; as much as but He them ordered, much
37 περισσότερον ἐκήρυσσον. καὶ ὑπερπερισσῶς ἐξεπλήσσοντο,
more abundantly they proclaimed. And most exceedingly they were amazed,
λέγοντες, Καλῶς πάντα πεποίηκε· καὶ τοὺς κωφοὺς ποιεῖ
saying, Well all things He has done, even the deaf He makes
ἀκούειν, καὶ τοὺς ἀλάλους λαλεῖν.
to hear, and the dumb to speak.

## CHAPTER 8

CHAPTER 8

[1] The crowd being very great in those days, and not having anything they may eat, Jesus calling near His disciples, He says to them, [2] I have pity on the crowd,

1 Ἐν ἐκείναις ταῖς ἡμέραις, παμπόλλου ὄχλου ὄντος, καὶ
In those — days very great the crowd being, and
μὴ ἐχόντων τί φάγωσι, προσκαλεσάμενος ὁ Ἰησοῦς τοὺς
not having anything they may eat, calling near — Jesus the
2 μαθητὰς αὐτοῦ λέγει αὐτοῖς, Σπλαγχνίζομαι ἐπὶ τὸν ὄχλον·
disciples of Him, He says to them, I have pity on the crowd

because now three days they continue with Me, and they do not have what they may eat; [3] and if I send them away fasting to their house, they will faint in the way; for some of them come from afar. [4] And His disciples answered Him, From where will anyone be able here to satisfy these (with) bread on a desert? [5] And He asked them, How many loaves do you have? And they said, Seven. [6] And He ordered the crowd to recline on the ground, And taking the seven loaves, giving thanks, He broke and gave to His disciples, that they may serve. And they served the crowd. [7] And they had a few fish. And blessing, He said (for) these also to be served. [8] And they ate, and were satisfied; and (they) took up over and above fragments, seven baskets. [9] And those eating were about four thousand. And He sent them away. [10] And at once entering into the boat with His disciples, He came into the region of Dalmanutha.

[11] And the Pharisees went out and began to argue with Him, seeking from Him a sign from Heaven, tempting Him. [12] And groaning in His spirit, He says, Why does this generation seek a sign? Truly, I say to you, (As) if this generation will be given a sign! [13] And leaving them, again entering into the boat, He went away to the other side. [14] And the disciples forgot to take loaves, and they did not have with them (any), except one loaf in the boat. [15] And He charged them, saying, See! Beware from the leaven of the Pharisees, and of the leaven of Herod. [16] And they reasoned with one another, saying, We have no loaves. [17] And knowing Jesus says to them, Why do you reason because you do not have loaves? Do you not yet perceive, nor realize? Have you still hardened your heart?

ὅτι ἤδη ἡμέρας τρεῖς προσμένουσί μοι, καὶ οὐκ ἔχουσι τί
because now days three they continue with Me, and not have what

3 φάγωσι· καὶ ἐὰν ἀπολύσω αὐτοὺς νήστεις εἰς οἶκον αὐτῶν,
they may eat; and if I send away them fasting to (the) house of them,

ἐκλυθήσονται ἐν τῇ ὁδῷ· τινὲς γὰρ αὐτῶν μακρόθεν ἥκασι.
they will faint in the way; some for of them from afar ` are come.

4 καὶ ἀπεκρίθησαν αὐτῷ οἱ μαθηταὶ αὐτοῦ, Πόθεν τούτους
And answered Him the disciples of Him, From where these

5 δυνήσεταί τις ὧδε χορτάσαι ἄρτων ἐπ' ἐρημίας; καὶ
will be able anyone here to satisfy (with) bread on a desert? And

ἐπηρώτα αὐτούς, Πόσους ἔχετε ἄρτους; οἱ δὲ εἶπον, Ἑπτά.
He asked them, How many have you loaves? they And said, Seven.

6 καὶ παρήγγειλε τῷ ὄχλῳ ἀναπεσεῖν ἐπὶ τῆς γῆς· καὶ λαβὼν
And He ordered the crowd to recline on the ground. And taking

τοὺς ἑπτὰ ἄρτους, εὐχαριστήσας ἔκλασε καὶ ἐδίδου τοῖς
the seven loaves, giving thanks, He broke and gave to the

μαθηταῖς αὐτοῦ, ἵνα παραθῶσι· καὶ παρέθηκαν τῷ ὄχλῳ.
disciples of Him, that they may serve. And they served the crowd

7 καὶ εἶχον ἰχθύδια ὀλίγα· καὶ εὐλογήσας εἶπε παραθεῖναι καὶ
And they had fish a few. And blessing He said to be served also

8 αὐτά. ἔφαγον δέ, καὶ ἐχορτάσθησαν· καὶ ἦραν περισσεύματα
these. they ate And, and were satisfied, and took up over and above

9 κλασμάτων ἑπτὰ σπυρίδας. ἦσαν δὲ οἱ φαγόντες ὡς
fragments, seven baskets. were And those eating about

10 τετρακισχίλιοι· καὶ ἀπέλυσεν αὐτούς. καὶ εὐθέως ἐμβὰς εἰς
four thousand. And He sent away them. And at once entering into

τὸ πλοῖον μετὰ τῶν μαθητῶν αὐτοῦ, ἦλθεν εἰς τὰ μέρη
the boat with the disciples of Him, He came into the region

Δαλμανουθά.
ot Dalmanutha.

11 Καὶ ἐξῆλθον οἱ Φαρισαῖοι, καὶ ἤρξαντο συζητεῖν αὐτῷ,
And went out the Pharisees and began to argue with Him,

ζητοῦντες παρ' αὐτοῦ σημεῖον ἀπὸ τοῦ οὐρανοῦ, πειρά-
seeking from Him a sign from — Heaven, tempting

12 ζοντες αὐτόν. καὶ ἀναστενάξας τῷ πνεύματι αὐτοῦ λέγει,
Him. And groaning in the spirit of Him, He says,

Τί ἡ γενεὰ αὕτη σημεῖον ἐπιζητεῖ; ἀμὴν λέγω ὑμῖν, εἰ
Why — generation this a sign seeks? Truly, I say to you, (As) if

13 δοθήσεται τῇ γενεᾷ ταύτῃ σημεῖον. καὶ ἀφεὶς αὐτούς, ἐμβὰς
will be given — generation this a sign! And leaving them, entering

πάλιν εἰς τὸ πλοῖον, ἀπῆλθεν εἰς τὸ πέραν.
again into the boat, He went away to the other side.

14 Καὶ ἐπελάθοντο οἱ μαθηταὶ λαβεῖν ἄρτους, καὶ εἰ μὴ ἕνα
And forgot the disciples to take loaves, and except one

15 ἄρτον οὐκ εἶχον μεθ' ἑαυτῶν ἐν τῷ πλοίῳ. καὶ διεστέλλετο
loaf not they had with them in the boat. And He charged

αὐτοῖς, λέγων, Ὁρᾶτε, βλέπετε ἀπὸ τῆς ζύμης τῶν
them, saying, See, Look out! From the leaven of the

16 Φαρισαίων καὶ τῆς ζύμης Ἡρώδου. καὶ διελογίζοντο πρὸς
Pharisees, and of the leaven of Herod. And they reasoned with

17 ἀλλήλους, λέγοντες ὅτι Ἄρτους οὐκ ἔχομεν. καὶ γνοὺς ὁ
one another, saying, Loaves not we have. And knowing —

Ἰησοῦς λέγει αὐτοῖς, Τί δ:αλογίζεσθε ὅτι ἄρτους οὐκ ἔχετε;
Jesus says to them, Why do you reason because loaves not you have?

οὔπω νοεῖτε, οὐδὲ συνίετε; ἔτι πεπωρωμένην ἔχετε τὴν
not yet Do you perceive nor realize? yet hardened have you the

[18] Having eyes, do you not see? And having ears, do you not hear? And do you not remember [19] when I broke the five loaves to the five thousand, how many handbaskets full of fragments you took up? They say to Him, Twelve. [20] And when the seven to the four thousand, how many baskets full (of) fragments you took up? And they said, Seven. [21] And He said to them, How do you not understand? [22] And He comes to Bethsaida. And they carry to Him a blind one, and beg Him that He would touch him. [23] And laying hold of the hand of the blind one, He led him forth outside the village. And having spit into his eyes, laying (His) hands on him, He asked him if he sees anything. [24] And having looked he said, I see men, as trees walking. [25] Then again He placed (His) hands on his eyes, and made him look up. And he was restored, and saw all clearly. [26] And He sent him to his house, saying, Do not go into the village, nor tell anyone in the village

18 καρδίαν ὑμῶν; ὀφθαλμοὺς ἔχοντες οὐ βλέπετε; καὶ ὦτα
heart　　of you?　eyes　　having,　　not do you see? And ears

19 ἔχοντες οὐκ ἀκούετε; καὶ οὐ μνημονεύετε; ὅτε τοὺς πέντε
having,　not do you hear? And not do you remember when the five

ἄρτους ἔκλασα εἰς τοὺς πεντακισχιλίους, πόσους κοφίνους
loaves　I broke to the　five thousand,　how many handbaskets

20 πλήρεις κλασμάτων ἤρατε; λέγουσιν αὐτῷ, Δώδεκα. Ὅτε
full　of fragments you took? They say　to Him, Twelve.　when

δὲ τοὺς ἑπτὰ εἰς τοὺς τετρακισχιλίους, πόσων σπυρίδων
And the seven to the　four thousand,　of how many baskets

21 πληρώματα κλασμάτων ἤρατε; οἱ δὲ εἶπον, Ἑπτά. καὶ
(the) fillings of fragments you took? they And said,　Seven. And

ἔλεγεν αὐτοῖς, Πῶς οὐ συνίετε;
He said to them, How not do you understand?

22 Καὶ ἔρχεται εἰς Βηθσαϊδά. καὶ φέρουσιν αὐτῷ τυφλόν,
And He comes to Bethsaida.　And they bear　to Him a blind one,

23 καὶ παρακαλοῦσιν αὐτὸν ἵνα αὐτοῦ ἅψηται. καὶ ἐπιλαβό-
and beg　　Him　that　him He would touch.And　laying

μενος τῆς χειρὸς τοῦ τυφλοῦ, ἐξήγαγεν αὐτὸν ἔξω τῆς
hold of the hand　of the blind one, He led forth　him outside the

κώμης· καὶ πτύσας εἰς τὰ ὄμματα αὐτοῦ, ἐπιθεὶς τὰς χεῖρας
village. And having spit into the eyes　of him, having laid the hands

24 αὐτῷ, ἐπηρώτα αὐτὸν εἴ τι βλέπει. καὶ ἀναβλέψας ἔλεγε,
on him, He asked　him　if anything he sees. And having looked he said,

25 Βλέπω τοὺς ἀνθρώπους ὡς δένδρα περιπατοῦντας. εἶτα
I see　—　men,　　as trees　　walking.　Then

πάλιν ἐπέθηκε τὰς χεῖρας ἐπὶ τοὺς ὀφθαλμοὺς αὐτοῦ, καὶ
again He placed　the hands upon　the　eyes　　of him, and

ἐποίησεν αὐτὸν ἀναβλέψαι. καὶ ἀποκατεστάθη, καὶ ἐνέβλεψε
made　him　look up.　And he was restored,　and saw

26 τηλαυγῶς ἅπαντας. καὶ ἀπέστειλεν αὐτὸν εἰς τὸν οἶκον
clearly　all　And He sent　him　to the house

αὐτοῦ, λέγων, Μηδὲ εἰς τὴν κώμην εἰσέλθῃς, μηδὲ εἴπῃς
of him, saying,　Not into　the village you may go in, nor may tell

τινὶ ἐν τῇ κώμῃ.
anyone in the village.

[27] And Jesus and His disciples went out to the villages of Caesarea of Philip. And in the way He questioned His disciples, saying to them, Whom do men say Me to be? [28] And they answered, John the Baptist; and others, Elijah; but others, one of the prophets. [29] And He says to them, And you, whom do you say Me to be? And answering, Peter says to Him, You are the Christ. [30] And He warned them, that they may tell no one about Him. [31] And He began to teach them that it behoves the Son of man to suffer many things, and to be rejected from the elders and chief priests and

27 Καὶ ἐξῆλθεν ὁ Ἰησοῦς καὶ οἱ μαθηταὶ αὐτοῦ εἰς τὰς
And went out —　Jesus　and the disciples of Him to　the

κώμας Καισαρείας τῆς Φιλίππου· καὶ ἐν τῇ ὁδῷ ἐπηρώτα
villages of Caesarea　—　of Philip. And in the way He questioned

τοὺς μαθητὰς αὐτοῦ, λέγων αὐτοῖς, Τίνα με λέγουσιν οἱ
the disciples of Him,　saying to them, Whom Me say　the

28 ἄνθρωποι εἶναι; οἱ δὲ ἀπεκρίθησαν, Ἰωάννην τὸν Βαπτι-
men　to be? they And answered　　John　the Baptist;

29 στήν· καὶ ἄλλοι Ἡλίαν, ἄλλοι δὲ ἕνα τῶν προφητῶν. καὶ
and others Elijah;　others but, one of the prophets　And

αὐτὸς λέγει αὐτοῖς, Ὑμεῖς δὲ τίνα με λέγετε εἶναι; ἀποκριθεὶς
He　says to them. you And, whom Me say you to be? answering

30 δὲ ὁ Πέτρος λέγει αὐτῷ, Σὺ εἶ ὁ Χριστός. καὶ ἐπετίμησεν
And— Peter　says　to Him, You are the Christ!　And He warned

31 αὐτοῖς. ἵνα μηδενὶ λέγωσι περὶ αὐτοῦ. καὶ ἤρξατο διδάσκειν
them, that no one they may tell about Him. And He began to teach

αὐτούς, ὅτι δεῖ τὸν υἱὸν τοῦ ἀνθρώπου πολλὰ παθεῖν, καὶ
them　that it behoves the Son　—　of man　many things to suffer, and

ἀποδοκιμασθῆναι ἀπὸ τῶν πρεσβυτέρων καὶ ἀρχιερέων καὶ
to be rejected　of　the　elders　and chief priests　and

scribes, and to be killed, and after three days to rise again. [32] And He spoke the word openly. And taking Him aside, Peter began to rebuke Him. [33] But He turning around and seeing His disciples rebuked Peter, saying, Get behind Me, Satan; because you do not mind the things of God, but the things of men. [34] And calling near the crowd with His disciples, He said to them, Whoever desires to come after Me, let him deny himself and take his cross, and let him follow Me. [35] For whoever desires to save his soul, (he) shall lose it; but whoever may lose his soul for My sake and the gospel, this one will save it. [36] For what shall it profit a man if he gain the whole world, yet damage his soul? [37] Or what shall a man give (as) an exchange (for) his soul? [38] For whoever may be ashamed of Me and My words in this adulterous and sinful generation, the Son of man also will be ashamed of him when He comes in the glory of His Father, along with the holy angels.

γραμματέων, καὶ ἀποκτανθῆναι, καὶ μετὰ τρεῖς ἡμέρας
scribes,         and    to be killed,    and    after three    days

32 ἀναστῆναι· καὶ παρρησίᾳ τὸν λόγον ἐλάλει. καὶ προσλαβό-
to rise again. And openly    the word He spoke. And taking aside

33 μενος αὐτὸν ὁ Πέτρος ἤρξατο ἐπιτιμᾶν αὐτῷ. ὁ δὲ ἐπιστρα-
Him, — Peter    began    to rebuke Him. He But turning

φείς, καὶ ἰδὼν τοὺς μαθητὰς αὐτοῦ, ἐπετίμησε τῷ Πέτρῳ,
around and seeing the disciples of Him, rebuked    — Peter,

λέγων, Ὕπαγε ὀπίσω μου, Σατανᾶ· ὅτι οὐ φρονεῖς τὰ τοῦ
saying,   Get behind Me,    Satan,   because not you mind the things

34 Θεοῦ, ἀλλὰ τὰ τῶν ἀνθρώπων. καὶ προσκαλεσάμενος τὸν
of God, but the things   of men.    And    calling near    the

ὄχλον σὺν τοῖς μαθηταῖς αὐτοῦ, εἶπεν αὐτοῖς, Ὅστις θέλει
crowd with the disciples   of Him, He said to them, Whoever desires

ὀπίσω μου ἐλθεῖν, ἀπαρνησάσθω ἑαυτόν, καὶ ἀράτω τὸν
after   Me to come, let him deny    himself    and take    the

35 σταυρὸν αὐτοῦ, καὶ ἀκολουθείτω μοί. ὃς γὰρ ἂν θέλη τὴν
cross    of him,   and let him follow   Me. who For ever desires the

ψυχὴν αὐτοῦ σῶσαι, ἀπολέσει αὐτήν· ὃς δ᾽ ἂν ἀπολέσῃ τὴν
soul    of him to save, shall lose    it:   who but ever may lose   the

ψυχὴν αὐτοῦ ἕνεκεν ἐμοῦ καὶ τοῦ εὐαγγελίου, οὗτος σώσει
soul    of him for the sake of Me and the    gospel,    this one will save

36 αὐτήν. τί γὰρ ὠφελήσει ἄνθρωπον, ἐὰν κερδήσῃ τὸν
it.    what For shall it profit    a man    if    he gain    the

37 κόσμον ὅλον, καὶ ζημιωθῇ τὴν ψυχὴν αὐτοῦ; ἢ τί δώσει
world    whole, yet    damage the    soul    of him. Or what shall give

38 ἄνθρωπος ἀντάλλαγμα τῆς ψυχῆς αὐτοῦ; ὃς γὰρ ἂν ἐπαι-
a man (as)    an exchange (for) the soul   of him? who For ever    may be

σχυνθῇ με καὶ τοὺς ἐμοὺς λόγους ἐν τῇ γενεᾷ ταύτῃ τῇ
ashamed of Me and    —    My    words in — generation this    —

μοιχαλίδι καὶ ἁμαρτωλῷ, καὶ ὁ υἱὸς τοῦ ἀνθρώπου ἐπαι-
adulterous and    sinful,    also the Son    —    of man    will be

σχυνθήσεται αὐτόν, ὅταν ἔλθῃ ἐν τῇ δόξῃ τοῦ πατρὸς
ashamed of    him,    when He comes in the glory of the Father

αὐτοῦ μετὰ τῶν ἀγγέλων τῶν ἁγίων.
of him, with    the    angels    —    holy.

## CHAPTER 9

### CHAPTER 9

[1] And He said to them, Truly I say to you, that there are some of those standing here who in no way shall taste of death until they see the kingdom of God coming in power. [2] And after six days, Jesus takes along Peter and James and John, and carries them into a high mount, privately, alone. And He was transfigured before them. [3] And His garments became shining, very white, like snow, such as no fuller on earth is able to whiten. [4] And they saw Elijah with Moses, and they were

1 καὶ ἔλεγεν αὐτοῖς, Ἀμὴν λέγω ὑμῖν, ὅτι εἰσί τινες τῶν
And He said to them, Truly I say to you, that are some of those

ὧδε ἑστηκότων, οἵτινες οὐ μὴ γεύσωνται θανάτου, ἕως ἂν
here    standing who    in no way shall taste of death    until

ἴδωσι τὴν βασιλείαν τοῦ Θεοῦ ἐληλυθυῖαν ἐν δυνάμει.
they see the kingdom    —    of God having come in power,

2 Καὶ μεθ᾽ ἡμέρας ἓξ παραλαμβάνει ὁ Ἰησοῦς τὸν Πέτρον
And after    days    six takes along   — Jesus   —   Peter

καὶ τὸν Ἰάκωβον καὶ τὸν Ἰωάννην, καὶ ἀναφέρει αὐτοὺς
and   —   James    and   —   John,    and carries    them

εἰς ὄρος ὑψηλὸν κατ᾽ ἰδίαν μόνους· καὶ μετεμορφώθη ἔμπρο-
into a mount high,    privately,    alone. And He was transfigured before

3 σθεν αὐτῶν· καὶ τὰ ἱμάτια αὐτοῦ ἐγένετο στίλβοντα, λευκὰ
them. And the garments of Him became    shining,    white

λίαν ὡς χιών, οἷα γναφεὺς ἐπὶ τῆς γῆς οὐ δύναται λευκᾶναι.
very, as snow, such as a fuller on the earth not is able    to whiten.

4 καὶ ὤφθη αὐτοῖς Ἡλίας σὺν Μωσεῖ, καὶ ἦσαν συλλαλοῦντε
And was seen by them Elijah with Moses,   and they were speaking with

speaking with Jesus. [5] And answering Peter says to Jesus, Rabbi. it is good (for) us to be here; and let us make three tabernacles, one for You, and one for Moses, and one for Elijah. [6] For he did not know what to say, for they were very fearful. [7] And a cloud was overshadowing them, and a voice came out of the cloud, saying, This is My Son, the Beloved; hear Him. [8] And suddenly, looking around, they no longer saw anyone, but only Jesus with themselves. [9] And as they were coming down from the mountain, He commanded them that they should tell no one what they saw, except when the Son of man may rise from (the) dead. [10] And the word they held to themselves, debating what (it) is, to rise from (the) dead.

[11] And they asked Him, saying, Do (not) the scribes say that Elijah must come first? [12] And answering He said to then., Indeed, Elijah coming first restores all things. And how has it been written on the Son of man, that He suffer many things, and be despised? [13] But I say to you that even Elijah has come, and they did to him whatever they desired, even as it has been written of him. [14] And coming to the disciples, He saw a great crowd around them, and scribes arguing with them. [15] And at once all the crowd seeing Him, (they, were greatly amazed, and running up greeted Him. [16] And He questioned the scribes, What are you disputing with them? [17] And one answered out of the crowd, saying, Teacher, I broug my son to You, having a dumb spirit;

[18] and wherever it seizes him, it dashes him, and he foams and gnashes his teeth, and he wastes away. And I told your disciples, that they

5 τῷ Ἰησοῦ. καὶ ἀποκριθεὶς ὁ Πέτρος λέγει τῷ Ἰησοῦ, Ῥαββί,
— Jesus. And answering — Peter says — to Jesus, Rabbi,
καλόν ἐστιν ἡμᾶς ὧδε εἶναι· καὶ ποιήσωμεν σκηνὰς τρεῖς,
good it is us here to be, and let us make tents three,
6 σοὶ μίαν, καὶ Μωσεῖ μίαν, καὶ Ἠλία μίαν. οὐ γὰρ ᾔδει τί
for You one, and for Moses one , and for Elijah one. not For he knew what
7 λαλήσῃ· ἦσαν γὰρ ἔκφοβοι. καὶ ἐγένετο νεφέλη ἐπισκιάζουσα
to say, they were for very fearful. And was a cloud overshadowing
αὐτοῖς· καὶ ἦλθε φωνὴ ἐκ τῆς νεφέλης, λέγουσα, Οὗτός ἐστιν
them, and came a voice out of the cloud, saying, This is
8 ὁ υἱός μου ὁ ἀγαπητός· αὐτοῦ ἀκούετε. καὶ ἐξάπινα
the Son of Me, the Beloved; Him hear. And suddenly,
περιβλεψάμενοι, οὐκέτι οὐδένα εἶδον, ἀλλὰ τὸν Ἰησοῦν
looking around, no longer no one they saw, but — Jesus
μόνον μεθ' ἑαυτῶν.
alone with themselves.

9 Καταβαινόντων δὲ αὐτῶν ἀπὸ τοῦ ὄρους, διεστείλατο
as were descending And they from the mountain, He commanded
αὐτοῖς ἵνα μηδενὶ διηγήσωνται ἃ εἶδον, εἰ μὴ ὅταν ὁ υἱὸς
them that to no one they should tell what they saw, except when the Son
10 τοῦ ἀνθρώπου ἐκ νεκρῶν ἀναστῇ. καὶ τὸν λόγον ἐκράτησαν
— of man from (the) dead may rise. And the word they held
πρὸς ἑαυτούς, συζητοῦντες τί ἐστι τὸ ἐκ νεκρῶν ἀναστῆναι.
to themselves, debating what is (it) from (the) dead to rise.

11 καὶ ἐπηρώτων αὐτόν, λέγοντες ὅτι Λέγουσιν οἱ γραμματεῖς
And they asked Him, saying, Do (not) say the scribes
12 ὅτι Ἠλίαν δεῖ ἐλθεῖν πρῶτον ; ὁ δὲ ἀποκριθείς, εἶπεν αὐτοῖς,
that Elijah it behoves to come first? He And answering said to them,
Ἠλίας μὲν ἐλθὼν πρῶτον, ἀποκαθιστᾷ πάντα· καὶ πῶς
Elijah indeed having come first restores all things. And how
γέγραπται ἐπὶ τὸν υἱὸν τοῦ ἀνθρώπου, ἵνα πολλὰ πάθη
has it been written on the Son — of man, that many things He suffer
13 καὶ ἐξουδενωθῇ. ἀλλὰ λέγω ὑμῖν ὅτι καὶ Ἠλίας ἐλήλυθε,
and be despised. But I say to you, that also Elijah has come,
καὶ ἐποίησαν αὐτῷ ὅσα ἠθέλησαν, καθὼς γέγραπται ἐπ'
and they did to him what- they desired, even as it has been written of
ever
αὐτόν.
him.

14 Καὶ ἐλθὼν πρὸς τοὺς μαθητάς, εἶδεν ὄχλον πολὺν περὶ
And coming to the disciples, He saw a crowd great around
15 αὐτούς, καὶ γραμματεῖς συζητοῦντας αὐτοῖς. καὶ εὐθέως
them, and scribes arguing with them. And at once
πᾶς ὁ ὄχλος ἰδὼν αὐτὸν ἐξεθαμβήθη, καὶ προστρέχοντες
all the crowd seeing Him were greatly amazed, and running up
16 ἠσπάζοντο αὐτόν. καὶ ἐπηρώτησε τοὺς γραμματεῖς, Τί
greeted Him. And He questioned the scribes, What
17 συζητεῖτε πρὸς αὐτούς ; καὶ ἀποκριθεὶς εἷς ἐκ τοῦ ὄχλου
are you arguing with them? And answered, one out of the crowd,
εἶπε, Διδάσκαλε, ἤνεγκα τὸν υἱόν μου πρός σε, ἔχοντα
said, Teacher, I brought the son of me to You, having
18 πνεῦμα ἄλαλον. καὶ ὅπου ἂν αὐτὸν καταλάβῃ, ῥήσσει
a spirit dumb; and wherever him it seizes, it dashes
αὐτόν· καὶ ἀφρίζει, καὶ τρίζει τοὺς ὀδόντας αὐτοῦ, καὶ
him, and he foams, and gnashes the teeth of him and
ξηραίνεται· καὶ εἶπον τοῖς μαθηταῖς σου ἵνα αὐτὸ ἐκβάλωσι,
he wastes away. And I told the disciples of You that it they might expel,

might expel it, and they were not able. [19] And answering them, He says, O unbelieving generation, how long will I be with you? How long shall I endure you? Bring him to Me. [20] And they brought him to Him. And seeing Him, the spirit immediately convulsed him. And falling on the ground, he wallowed, foaming. [21] And He questioned his father, How long a time is it since this has happened to him? And he said, From childhood. [22] And often it threw him both into fire and into water, that it might destroy him. But if You can do anything, help us, having pity on us. [23] And Jesus said to him, If you are able to believe, all things are possible to the believing. [24] And immediately crying out, the father of the child with tears said, Lord, I believe! Help my unbelief! [25] And Jesus seeing that a crowd is running together, (He) rebuked the unclean spirit, saying, Dumb and deaf spirit, I command you, Come out from him, and you no more may go into him! [26] And crying out, and convulsing him very much, it came out. And he became as if dead, so as many to say that he died. [27] But having taken hold of his hand, Jesus raised him up, and he stood up. [28] And He entering into a house, His disciples questioned Him privately, (Why) were we not able to cast it out. [29] And He said to them, This kind can go out by nothing except by prayer and fasting.

[30] And going forth from there, they passed by through Galilee. And He desired that not anyone know; [31] for He taught His disciples, and said to them, The Son of man is betrayed into (the) hands of men, and they will kill Him; and having been killed, He will rise up the third day. [32] But they did not know the word, and feared to ques

**19** καὶ οὐκ ἴσχυσαν. ὁ δὲ ἀποκριθεὶς αὐτῷ λέγει, Ὦ γενεὰ
and not they were able. He And answering them says, O generation

ἄπιστος, ἕως πότε πρὸς ὑμᾶς ἔσομαι ; ἕως πότε ἀνέξομαι
unbelieving, until when with you will I be? Until when shall I endure

**20** ὑμῶν ; φέρετε αὐτὸν πρός με. καὶ ἤνεγκαν αὐτὸν πρὸς αὐτόν·
you? Bring him to Me. And they brought him to Him.

καὶ ἰδὼν αὐτόν, εὐθέως τὸ πνεῦμα ἐσπάραξεν αὐτόν· καὶ
And seeing Him, instantly the spirit convulsed him; and

**21** πεσὼν ἐπὶ τῆς γῆς, ἐκυλίετο ἀφρίζων. καὶ ἐπηρώτησε τὸν
falling on the ground, he wallowed, foaming. And He questioned the

πατέρα αὐτοῦ, Πόσος χρόνος ἐστίν, ὡς τοῦτο γέγονεν αὐτῷ ;
father of him, How long a time is it while this has happened to him?

**22** ὁ δὲ εἶπε, Παιδιόθεν. καὶ πολλάκις αὐτὸν καὶ εἰς πῦρ ἔβαλε
he And said, From childhood. And often him both into fire it threw

καὶ εἰς ὕδατα, ἵνα ἀπολέσῃ αὐτόν· ἀλλ' εἴ τι δύνασαι,
and into water, that it might destroy him. But if anything You can do,

**23** βοήθησον ἡμῖν, σπλαγχνισθεὶς ἐφ' ἡμᾶς. ὁ δὲ Ἰησοῦς εἶπεν
help us, having pity on us. — And Jesus said

αὐτῷ τό, Εἰ δύνασαι πιστεῦσαι, πάντα δυνατὰ τῷ
to him, — If you are able to believe, all things possible to the

**24** πιστεύοντι. καὶ εὐθέως κράξας ὁ πατὴρ τοῦ παιδίου, μετὰ
believing. And immediately crying out the father of the child, with

δακρύων ἔλεγε, Πιστεύω, Κύριε, βοήθει μου τῇ ἀπιστίᾳ.
tears, said, I believe! Lord, help of me the unbelief!

**25** Ἰδὼν δὲ ὁ Ἰησοῦς ὅτι ἐπισυντρέχει ὄχλος, ἐπετίμησε τῷ
seeing And — Jesus that is running together a crowd, rebuked the

πνεύματι τῷ ἀκαθάρτῳ, λέγων αὐτῷ, Τὸ πνεῦμα τὸ ἄλαλον
spirit unclean, saying to it, — Spirit — dumb

καὶ κωφόν, ἐγὼ σοι ἐπιτάσσω, ἔξελθε ἐξ αὐτοῦ, καὶ μηκέτι
and deaf, I you command, Come forth from him, and no more

**26** εἰσέλθῃς εἰς αὐτόν. καὶ κράξαν, καὶ πολλὰ σπαράξαν αὐτόν,
may you go into him. And crying out, and much convulsing him,

ἐξῆλθε· καὶ ἐγένετο ὡσεὶ νεκρός, ὥστε πολλοὺς λέγειν ὅτι
it came out. And he became as if dead, so as many to say that

**27** ἀπέθανεν. ὁ δὲ Ἰησοῦς κρατήσας αὐτὸν τῆς χειρός, ἤγειρεν
he died. — But Jesus having taken hold of him the hand, raised

**28** αὐτόν· καὶ ἀνέστη. καὶ εἰσελθόντα αὐτὸν εἰς οἶκον, οἱ
him, and he stood up. And entering He into a house, the

μαθηταὶ αὐτοῦ ἐπηρώτων αὐτὸν κατ' ἰδίαν ὅτι Ἡμεῖς οὐκ
disciples of Him questioned Him privately, (Why) we not

**29** ἠδυνήθημεν ἐκβαλεῖν αὐτό ; καὶ εἶπεν αὐτοῖς, Τοῦτο τὸ
were able to cast out it? And He said to them, This —

γένος ἐν οὐδενὶ δύναται ἐξελθεῖν, εἰ μὴ ἐν προσευχῇ καὶ
kind by nothing can go out, except by prayer and

νηστείᾳ.
fasting.

**30** Καὶ ἐκεῖθεν ἐξελθόντες παρεπορεύοντο διὰ τῆς Γαλιλαίας·
And from there going forth, they passed by through — Galilee,

**31** καὶ οὐκ ἤθελεν ἵνα τις γνῷ. ἐδίδασκε γὰρ τοὺς μαθητὰς
And not He desired that anyone know; He taught for the disciples

αὐτοῦ, καὶ ἔλεγεν αὐτοῖς ὅτι Ὁ υἱὸς τοῦ ἀνθρώπου παραδί-
of Him, and said to them, — The Son — of man is

δοται εἰς χεῖρας ἀνθρώπων, καὶ ἀποκτενοῦσιν αὐτόν· καὶ
betrayed into hands of men, and they will kill Him; and

**32** ἀποκτανθείς, τῇ τρίτῃ ἡμέρᾳ ἀναστήσεται. οἱ δὲ ἠγνόουν
having been killed, the third day He will rise up. they But knew not

tion Him. [33] And they
came to Capernaum. And
having come into the house,
He questioned them, What
were you disputing to your
selves in the way? [34] And
they were silent, for they
argued with one another in
the way who (was) greater.
[35] And sitting, He called
the twelve and says to them,
If anyone desires to be first,
he shall be last of all; and
servant of all. [36] And taking a child, He set it in their
midst, and having embraced
it, He said to them, [37]
Whoever receives one of such
children on My name, receives
Me; and whoever receives Me,
not (only) does receive Me,
but the (One) having sent
Me. [38] And John answered
Him, saying, Teacher, we saw
someone casting out demons
in Your name, who does not
follow us; and we forbade
him, because he does not
follow us. [39] But Jesus
said, Do not forbid him; for
there is no one who shall do
a work of power on My
name, yet be able to quickly
speak evil of Me. [40] For
who not is against us, is for
us. [41] For whoever gives
you a cup of water to drink
in My name, because you are
of Christ, truly I say to you,
in no way he will lose his
reward. [42] And whoever
causes one of these little ones
believing in Me to offend, it
is good for him if rather a
mill stone be laid about his
neck, and he be thrown into
the sea.



[43] And if your
hand offend you, cut it off;
for it is well for you to enter
into life maimed, than having
two hands to go away into
Hell, into the unquenchable
fire, [44] where there worm
has no end, and the fire is
not quenched. [45] And if
your foot causes you to
offend, cut it off; for it is

τὸ ῥῆμα, καὶ ἐφοβοῦντο αὐτὸν ἐπερωτῆσαι.
the word,   and   feared        Him     to question.

**33** Καὶ ἦλθεν εἰς Καπερναούμ· καὶ ἐν τῇ οἰκίᾳ γενόμενος
And they came to Capernaum.    And in  the house having come,
ἐπηρώτα αὐτούς, Τί ἐν τῇ ὁδῷ πρὸς ἑαυτοὺς διελογίζεσθε ;
He questioned them, What in the way  toward  yourselves were you arguing?

**34** οἱ δὲ ἐσιώπων· πρὸς ἀλλήλους γὰρ διελέχθησαν ἐν τῇ ὁδῷ,
they And were quiet with one another, for they argued   in  the  way

**35** τίς μείζων. καὶ καθίσας ἐφώνησε τοὺς δώδεκα, καὶ λέγει
who (was) greater. And sitting  He called   the  twelve   and says
αὐτοῖς, Εἴ τις θέλει πρῶτος εἶναι, ἔσται πάντων ἔσχατος,
to them, If any one desires first  to be, he shall be of all    last,

**36** καὶ πάντων διάκονος. καὶ λαβὼν παιδίον, ἔστησεν αὐτὸ
and    of all    servant.  And having taken a child,  He set  it
ἐν μέσῳ αὐτῶν· καὶ ἐναγκαλισάμενος αὐτό, εἶπεν αὐτοῖς·
in (the) midst of them, and having embraced   it,   He said  to them,

**37** Ὃς ἐὰν ἓν τῶν τοιούτων παιδίων δέξηται ἐπὶ τῷ ὀνόματί
Whoever one  — of such   children receives  on  the   name
μου, ἐμὲ δέχεται· καὶ ὃς ἐὰν ἐμὲ δέξηται, οὐκ ἐμὲ δέχεται,
of Me, Me receives; and whoever Me receives, not  Me receives,
ἀλλὰ τὸν ἀποστείλαντά με.
but the (One) having sent   Me.

**38** Ἀπεκρίθη δὲ αὐτῷ ὁ Ἰωάννης, λέγων, Διδάσκαλε,
answered And  Him  —  John,    saying,    Teacher,
εἴδομέν τινα ἐν τῷ ὀνόματί σου ἐκβάλλοντα δαιμόνια, ὃς
we saw someone in the  name of You casting out  demons, who
οὐκ ἀκολουθεῖ ἡμῖν· καὶ ἐκωλύσαμεν αὐτόν, ὅτι οὐκ
not does follow  us;   and   we forbade    him, because not

**39** ἀκολουθεῖ ἡμῖν. ὁ δὲ Ἰησοῦς εἶπε, Μὴ κωλύετε αὐτόν·
he follows  us. — But  Jesus   said,  not Do forbid   him;
οὐδεὶς γάρ ἐστιν ὃς ποιήσει δύναμιν ἐπὶ τῷ ὀνόματί μου,
no one  for  is   who shall do a work of power on the name  of Me,

**40** καὶ δυνήσεται ταχὺ κακολογῆσαί με. ὃς γὰρ οὐκ ἔστι καθ'
yet be able   quickly to speak evil of  Me. who For not   is against

**41** ἡμῶν, ὑπὲρ ἡμῶν ἐστιν. ὃς γὰρ ἂν ποτίσῃ ὑμᾶς ποτήριον
us,   for   us  is.  who For ever gives drink  you   a cup
ὕδατος ἐν τῷ ὀνόματί μου, ὅτι Χριστοῦ ἐστέ, ἀμὴν λέγω
of water in the  name of Me, because of Christ you are,  truly I say

**42** ὑμῖν, οὐ μὴ ἀπολέσῃ τὸν μισθὸν αὐτοῦ. καὶ ὃς ἂν σκαν-
to you, in no way he will lose the   reward  of him. And whoever causes to
δαλίσῃ ἕνα τῶν μικρῶν τούτων τῶν πιστευόντων εἰς ἐμέ,
offend   one — little (ones) of these   —   believing     in Me,
καλόν ἐστιν αὐτῷ μᾶλλον εἰ περίκειται λίθος μυλικὸς περὶ
good   is it  for him  rather  if be laid about a stone of a mill around

**43** τὸν τράχηλον αὐτοῦ, καὶ βέβληται εἰς τὴν θάλασσαν. καὶ
the  neck       of him, and he be thrown into the   sea.       And
ἐὰν σκανδαλίζῃ σε ἡ χείρ σου, ἀπόκοψον αὐτήν· καλόν σοι
if  offend       you the hand of you, cut off   it;  well for you
ἐστί κυλλὸν εἰς τὴν ζωὴν εἰσελθεῖν, ἢ τὰς δύο χεῖρας ἔχοντα
is it maimed into — life  to enter,  than the two  hands  having

**44** ἀπελθεῖν εἰς τὴν γέενναν, εἰς τὸ πῦρ τὸ ἄσβεστον. ὅπου ὁ
to go away into —  Gehenna, into the fire  — unquenchable, where the

**45** σκώληξ αὐτῶν οὐ τελευτᾷ, καὶ τὸ πῦρ οὐ σβέννυται. καὶ
worm   of them  not has an end, and the fire not  is quenched. And
ἐὰν ὁ πούς σου σκανδαλίζῃ σε, ἀπόκοψον αὐτόν· καλόν ἐστί
if  the foot of you causes to offend you, cut off    it;  well   is it

well for you to enter into
life lame, than having two
feet to be thrown into Hell
into the unquenchable fire.
[46] where their worm has
no end, and the fire is not
quenched. [47] And if your
eye offends you, cast it out;
for it is well for you to enter
into the kingdom of God
one-eyed, than having two
eyes to be thrown into the
Hell of fire, [48] where their
work has no end, and the
fire is not quenched. [49]
For everyone will be salted
with fire, and every sacrifice
will be salted with salt. [50]
Salt (is) good, but if the salt
becomes saltless, by what will
you season it? Have salt in
yourselves, and be at peace
among one another.

σοι εἰσελθεῖν εἰς τὴν ζωὴν χωλόν, ἢ τοὺς δύο πόδας ἔχοντα
you to enter into — life lame, than the two feet having
46 βληθῆναι εἰς τὴν γέενναν, εἰς τὸ πῦρ τὸ ἄσβεστον, ὅπου
to be thrown into — Gehenna into the fire unquenchable, where
47 ὁ σκώληξ αὐτῶν οὐ τελευτᾷ, καὶ τὸ πῦρ οὐ σβέννυται. καὶ
the worm of them not has an end, and the fire not is quenched. And
ἐὰν ὁ ὀφθαλμός σου σκανδαλίζῃ σε, ἔκβαλε αὐτόν· καλόν
if the eye of you offends you, cast out it; well
σοι ἐστὶ μονόφθαλμον εἰσελθεῖν εἰς τὴν βασιλείαν τοῦ Θεοῦ,
for you it is one eyed to enter into the kingdom — of God,
ἢ δύο ὀφθαλμοὺς ἔχοντα βληθῆναι εἰς τὴν γέενναν τοῦ
than two eyes having to be thrown into the Gehenna —
48 πυρός, ὅπου ὁ σκώληξ αὐτῶν οὐ τελευτᾷ, καὶ τὸ πῦρ οὐ
of fire, where the worm of them not has an end, and the fire not
49 σβέννυται. πᾶς γὰρ πυρὶ ἁλισθήσεται, καὶ πᾶσα θυσία ἁλὶ
is quenched. everyone For with fire will be salted, and every sacrifice with salt
50 ἁλισθήσεται. καλὸν τὸ ἅλας· ἐὰν δὲ τὸ ἅλας ἄναλον γένηται,
will be salted. Good (is) the salt, if but the salt saltless becomes,
ἐν τίνι αὐτὸ ἀρτύσετε ; ἔχετε ἐν ἑαυτοῖς ἅλας, καὶ εἰρηνεύετε
by what it will you season? Have in yourselves salt, and be at peace
ἐν ἀλλήλοις.
among one another.

## CHAPTER 10

[1] And rising up from
there He came into the
borders of Judea, by the
other side of the Jordan
And again a crowd came
together to Him, and as He
had been accustomed, He
again taught them.
[2] And the Pharisees
coming to (Him) asked
Him if it is lawful for a
husband to put away a
wife, tempting Him.
[3] But answering He said
to them, What did Moses
command you? [4] And
they said, Moses allowed to
write a bill of divorce, and
to put away. [5] And
answering Jesus said to
them, In view of your
hard-heartedness he wrote
this commandment for
you; [6] but from (the)
beginning of creation God
made them male and
female. [7] Because of this
a man shall leave his father
and mother and shall be
joined to his wife, [8] and
the two shall be one flesh;
so that they no longer are
two, but one flesh.
[9] What therefore God
united together, let not
man separate. [10] And
again in the house His
disciples asked Him about
the same thing. [11] And
He said to them, Whoever

## CHAPTER 10

1 Κἀκεῖθεν ἀναστὰς ἔρχεται εἰς τὰ ὅρια τῆς Ἰουδαίας διὰ
And from there arising, He comes into the borders — of Judea by
τοῦ πέραν τοῦ Ἰορδάνου· καὶ συμπορεύονται πάλιν ὄχλοι
the other side of the Jordan. And came together again crowds
2 πρὸς αὐτόν· καί, ὡς εἰώθει, πάλιν ἐδίδασκεν αὐτούς. καὶ
with Him, and as He did usually, again He taught them. And
προσελθόντες οἱ Φαρισαῖοι ἐπηρώτησαν αὐτόν, Εἰ ἔξεστιν
coming up the Pharisees questioned Him Is it lawful
3 ἀνδρὶ γυναῖκα ἀπολῦσαι, πειράζοντες αὐτόν. ὁ δὲ ἀποκρι-
for a man a wife to dismiss, testing Him. He And answering
4 θεὶς εἶπεν αὐτοῖς, Τί ὑμῖν ἐνετείλατο Μωσῆς ; οἱ δὲ εἶπον,
said to them, What you did command Moses? they And said,
Μωσῆς ἐπέτρεψε βιβλίον ἀποστασίου γράψαι, καὶ ἀπολῦ-
Moses allowed a roll of divorce to write, and to dismiss.
5 σαι. καὶ ἀποκριθεὶς ὁ Ἰησοῦς εἶπεν αὐτοῖς, Πρὸς τὴν
And answering, — Jesus said to them, For the
σκληροκαρδίαν ὑμῶν ἔγραψεν ὑμῖν τὴν ἐντολὴν ταύτην·
hardheartedness of you he wrote to you — commandment this.
6 ἀπὸ δὲ ἀρχῆς κτίσεως, ἄρσεν καὶ θῆλυ ἐποίησεν αὐτοὺς ὁ
from But beginning of creation male and female made them, —
7 Θεός. ἕνεκεν τούτου καταλείψει ἄνθρωπος τὸν πατέρα αὐτοῦ
God. On account of this shall leave a man the father of him
καὶ τὴν μητέρα· καὶ προσκολληθήσεται πρὸς τὴν γυναῖκα
and the mother, and shall be joined to the wife
8 αὐτοῦ, καὶ ἔσονται οἱ δύο εἰς σάρκα μίαν. ὥστε οὐκέτι εἰσὶ
of him, and shall become the two into flesh one ; so as no longer are they
9 δύο, ἀλλὰ μία σάρξ. ὃ οὖν ὁ Θεὸς συνέζευξεν, ἄνθρωπος μὴ
two, but one flesh. What then God yoked together, man not
10 χωριζέτω. καὶ ἐν τῇ οἰκίᾳ πάλιν οἱ μαθηταὶ αὐτοῦ περὶ τοῦ
let put apart. And in the house again the disciples of Him about the
11 αὐτοῦ ἐπηρώτησαν αὐτόν. καὶ λέγει αὐτοῖς, Ὃς ἐὰν ἀπο-
same questioned Him. And He says to them, Whoever may

should put away his wife and should marry another commits adultery against her. [12] And if a woman should put away her husband and be married to another, she commits adultery.

[13] And they brought little children to Him that He might touch them. But the disciples rebuked those who brought them. [14] But having seen, Jesus was indignant, and said to them, Allow the little children to come to Me, and do not hinder them; for of such is the kingdom of God. [15] Truly I say to you, Whoever shall not receive the kingdom of God as a little child, in no way shall enter into it. [16] And having taken them in (His) arms, having laid hands on them, He blessed them.

[17] And He going forth into (the) highway, one running up and kneeling down to Him asked Him, Good teacher, what shall I do that I may inherit eternal life? [18] But Jesus said to him, Why do you call Me good? No one (is) good, except One, God. [19] You know the commandments: Do not commit adultery; do not commit murder; do not steal; do not bear false witness; do not defraud; honor your father and mother. [20] And answering he said to Him, Teacher, all these I observed from my youth. [21] And looking on him Jesus loved him and said to him, One thing is lacking to you; go, as much as you have, sell and give to the poor, and you shall have treasure in Heaven, and come, follow Me, taking up the cross. [22] But he, being saddened at the word, went away grieved, for he had many possessions. [23] And looking around Jesus said to His disciples, How hardly shall those having riches enter into the kingdom of God! [24] And the disciples were astonished at His words. And answering

λύσῃ τὴν γυναῖκα αὐτοῦ καὶ γαμήσῃ ἄλλην, μοιχᾶται ἐπ᾽
dismiss the　wife　of him and　marry　another is in adultery with

12 αὐτήν· καὶ ἐὰν γυνὴ ἀπολύσῃ τὸν ἄνδρα αὐτῆς καὶ γαμηθῇ
her;　and　if a woman may dismiss　husband　her　and marries
ἄλλῳ, μοιχᾶται.
another　she commits adultery.

13 Καὶ προσέφερον αὐτῷ παιδία ἵνα ἅψηται αὐτῶν· οἱ δὲ
And　they carried　to Him children, that He might touch them. the But

14 μαθηταὶ ἐπετίμων τοῖς προσφέρουσιν. ἰδὼν δὲ ὁ Ἰησοῦς
disciples　rebuked the (ones) carrying (them) seeing But　—　Jesus
ἠγανάκτησε, καὶ εἶπεν αὐτοῖς, Ἄφετε τὰ παιδία ἔρχεσθαι
was indignant, and He said to them, Allow　the children　to come
πρός με, καὶ μὴ κωλύετε αὐτά· τῶν γὰρ τοιούτων ἐστὶν ἡ
to Me; and not forbid　them; of these for　such　is　the

15 βασιλεία τοῦ Θεοῦ. ἀμὴν λέγω ὑμῖν, ὃς ἐὰν μὴ δέξηται τὴν
kingdom　— of God. Truly I say to you, Whoever not receives　the
βασιλείαν τοῦ Θεοῦ ὡς παιδίον, οὐ μὴ εἰσέλθῃ εἰς αὐτήν.
kingdom　— of God as　a child, in no way may enter into　it.

16 καὶ ἐναγκαλισάμενος αὐτά, τιθεὶς τὰς χεῖρας ἐπ᾽ αὐτά,
And having taken in arms　them, having laid the　hands　on them,
ηὐλόγει αὐτά.
He blessed them .

17 Καὶ ἐκπορευομένου αὐτοῦ εἰς ὁδόν, προσδραμὼν εἷς καὶ
And　going forth　Him　into (the) way, running up　one and
γονυπετήσας αὐτὸν ἐπηρώτα αὐτόν, Διδάσκαλε ἀγαθέ, τί
kneeling down to Him questioned　Him,　teacher　Good, What

18 ποιήσω ἵνα ζωὴν αἰώνιον κληρονομήσω; ὁ δὲ Ἰησοῦς
shall I do that　life　eternal　I may inherit?　— And Jesus
εἶπεν αὐτῷ, Τί με λέγεις ἀγαθόν; οὐδεὶς ἀγαθός, εἰ μὴ εἷς, ὁ
said to him,　Why Me call you　good? No one (is) good,　except one, —

19 Θεός. τὰς ἐντολὰς οἶδας, Μὴ μοιχεύσῃς, μὴ φονεύσῃς, μὴ
God. The commandments you know:Do not adultery; do not murder; do not
κλέψῃς, μὴ ψευδομαρτυρήσῃς, μὴ ἀποστερήσῃς, τίμα τὸν
steal, do not bear false witness;　do not defraud;　honor　the

20 πατέρα σου καὶ τὴν μητέρα. ὁ δὲ ἀποκριθεὶς εἶπεν αὐτῷ,
father of you and　the　mother. he And answering　said　to Him,

21 Διδάσκαλε, ταῦτα πάντα ἐφυλαξάμην ἐκ νεότητός μου. ὁ δὲ
Teacher,　these　All　I observed　from youth　of me. But
Ἰησοῦς ἐμβλέψας αὐτῷ ἠγάπησεν αὐτόν, καὶ εἶπεν αὐτῷ,
Jesus,　looking at　him,　loved　him, and said to him,
Ἕν σοι ὑστερεῖ· ὕπαγε, ὅσα ἔχεις πώλησον, καὶ δὸς τοῖς
One to you is lacking; go, what things you have sell,　and give to the
πτωχοῖς, καὶ ἕξεις θησαυρὸν ἐν οὐρανῷ· καὶ δεῦρο, ἀκολούθει
poor:　and you will have treasure in Heaven; and come,　follow

22 μοι, ἄρας τὸν σταυρόν. ὁ δὲ στυγνάσας ἐπὶ τῷ λόγῳ ἀπῆλθε
Me, taking up the cross.　he But being sad　at the　word went away
λυπούμενος· ἦν γὰρ ἔχων κτήματα πολλά.
grieving;　he was for having possessions many.

23 Καὶ περιβλεψάμενος ὁ Ἰησοῦς λέγει τοῖς μαθηταῖς αὐτοῦ,
And　looking around,　— Jesus　says to the disciples of Him,
Πῶς δυσκόλως οἱ τὰ χρήματα ἔχοντες εἰς τὴν βασιλείαν τοῦ
How hardly　the (ones) the riches　having　into the　kingdom　—

24 Θεοῦ εἰσελεύσονται. οἱ δὲ μαθηταὶ ἐθαμβοῦντο ἐπὶ τοῖς
of God will enter.　the And　disciples　were amazed　at　the
λόγοις αὐτοῦ. ὁ δὲ Ἰησοῦς πάλιν ἀποκριθεὶς λέγει αὐτοῖς,
words　of Him. — And Jesus　again　answering　says　to them,

Jesus again said to them, Children, how difficult it is (for) those who trust in riches to enter into the kingdom of God! [25] It is easier (for) a camel to pass through the eye of the needle, than (for) a rich man to enter into the kingdom of God. [26] And they were exceedingly astonished, saying among themselves, And who is able to be saved? [27] But looking on them Jesus said, With men (it is) impossible, but not with God; for all things are possible with God. [28] And Peter began to say to Him, Behold, we left all and followed you. [29] But answering Jesus said, Truly I say to you, There is no one who has left house, or brothers, or sisters, or father, or mother, or wife, or children, or land, for the gospel and My sake, [30] that shall not receive a hundredfold now in this time; houses and brothers and sisters and mothers and children and lands, with persecutions, and in the age that is coming, everlasting life. [31] But many first shall be last, and the last first.

[32] And they were in the highway, going up to Jerusalem, and Jesus was going on before them; and they were filled with holy fear, and were following, afraid. And having taken the twelve to (Him) again, He began to tell the things which were about to happen to Him: [33] Behold, we go up to Jerusalem, and the Son of man will be delivered up to the chief priests and to the scribes, and they will condemn Him to death, and will deliver Him up to the nations. [34] And they will mock Him and will whip Him, and will spit on Him, and will kill Him; and on the third day He will rise again.

[35] And James and John came up to Him, the

---

Τέκνα, πῶς δύσκολόν ἐστι τοὺς πεποιθότας ἐπὶ τοῖς
Children, how hard it is for those trusting on the

25 χρήμασιν εἰς τὴν βασιλείαν τοῦ Θεοῦ εἰσελθεῖν. εὐκοπώ-
riches into the kingdom — of God to enter! Easier

τερόν ἐστι κάμηλον διὰ τῆς τρυμαλιᾶς τῆς ῥαφίδος
it is (for) a camel through the eye of the needle

διελθεῖν, ἢ πλούσιον εἰς τὴν βασιλείαν τοῦ Θεοῦ εἰσελθεῖν.
to pass, than (for) a rich one into the kingdom — of God to enter.

26 οἱ δὲ περισσῶς ἐξεπλήσσοντο, λέγοντες πρὸς ἑαυτούς, Καὶ
they But exceedingly were astonished, saying to themselves, And

27 τίς δύναται σωθῆναι; ἐμβλέψας δὲ αὐτοῖς ὁ Ἰησοῦς λέγει,
who is able to be saved? looking at And them, — Jesus says,

Παρὰ ἀνθρώποις ἀδύνατον, ἀλλ᾽ οὐ παρὰ τῷ Θεῷ· πάντα
From men (it is) impossible; but not from — God; all things

28 γὰρ δυνατά ἐστι παρὰ τῷ Θεῷ. καὶ ἤρξατο ὁ Πέτρος
for possible are from — God. And began — Peter

λέγειν αὐτῷ, Ἰδού, ἡμεῖς ἀφήκαμεν πάντα, καὶ ἠκολουθή-
to say to Him, Behold, we forsook all, and have followed

29 σαμέν σοι. ἀποκριθεὶς δὲ ὁ Ἰησοῦς εἶπεν, Ἀμὴν λέγω ὑμῖν,
You. answering But — Jesus said, Truly I say to you,

οὐδείς ἐστιν ὃς ἀφῆκεν οἰκίαν, ἢ ἀδελφούς, ἢ ἀδελφάς, ἢ
no one there is who forsook house, or brothers, or sisters, or

πατέρα, ἢ μητέρα, ἢ γυναῖκα, ἢ τέκνα, ἢ ἀγρούς, ἕνεκεν
father, or mother, or wife, or children, or fields, for the sake

30 ἐμοῦ καὶ τοῦ εὐαγγελίου, ἐὰν μὴ λάβῃ ἑκατονταπλασίονα
of Me and the gospel, except he receives a hundredfold

νῦν ἐν τῷ καιρῷ τούτῳ, οἰκίας καὶ ἀδελφοὺς καὶ ἀδελφὰς
now in — time this, houses, and brothers, and sisters,

καὶ μητέρας καὶ τέκνα καὶ ἀγρούς, μετὰ διωγμῶν, καὶ ἐν τῷ
and mothers, and children, and fields, with persecutions: and in the

31 αἰῶνι τῷ ἐρχομένῳ ζωὴν αἰώνιον. πολλοὶ δὲ ἔσονται
age — coming, life eternal. many And will be

πρῶτοι ἔσχατοι, καὶ οἱ ἔσχατοι πρῶτοι.
first last; and the last, first.

32 Ἦσαν δὲ ἐν τῇ ὁδῷ ἀναβαίνοντες εἰς Ἱεροσόλυμα· καὶ
they were And in the way, going up to Jerusalem. And

ἦν προάγων αὐτοὺς ὁ Ἰησοῦς, καὶ ἐθαμβοῦντο, καὶ
was going before them — Jesus, and they were astonished and

ἀκολουθοῦντες ἐφοβοῦντο. καὶ παραλαβὼν πάλιν τοὺς
following were afraid. And having taken again the

δώδεκα, ἤρξατο αὐτοῖς λέγειν τὰ μέλλοντα αὐτῷ συμβαίνειν
twelve, He began them to tell the things about to Him to happen,

33 ὅτι Ἰδού, ἀναβαίνομεν εἰς Ἱεροσόλυμα, καὶ ὁ υἱὸς τοῦ
— Behold, we are going up to Jerusalem, and the Son —

ἀνθρώπου παραδοθήσεται τοῖς ἀρχιερεῦσι καὶ τοῖς γραμ-
of man will be betrayed to the chief priests and to the

ματεῦσι, καὶ κατακρινοῦσιν αὐτὸν θανάτῳ, καὶ παραδώ-
scribes, and they will condemn Him to death, and will deliver

34 σουσιν αὐτὸν τοῖς ἔθνεσι, καὶ ἐμπαίξουσιν αὐτῷ, καὶ
up Him to the nations. And they will mock Him, and

μαστιγώσουσιν αὐτόν, καὶ ἐμπτύσουσιν αὐτῷ, καὶ ἀπο-
will scourge Him, and will spit at Him, and will

κτενοῦσιν αὐτόν· καὶ τῇ τρίτῃ ἡμέρᾳ ἀναστήσεται.
kill Him; and on the third day He will rise again.

35 Καὶ προσπορεύονται αὐτῷ Ἰάκωβος καὶ Ἰωάννης οἱ
And come up to Him James and John, the

υἱοὶ Ζεβεδαίου, λέγοντες, Διδάσκαλε, θέλομεν ἵνα ὃ ἐὰν
sons of Zebedee,　saying,　　Teacher,　we desire　that whatever

**36** αἰτήσωμεν, ποιήσῃς ἡμῖν. ὁ δὲ εἶπεν αὐτοῖς, Τί θέλετε
we may ask　You would do for us.　He And said　to them,　What desire

**37** ποιῆσαί με ὑμῖν; οἱ δὲ εἶπον αὐτῷ, Δὸς ἡμῖν, ἵνα εἷς ἐκ
to do　Me for you? they And said to Him,　Give　us　that one off

δεξιῶν σου καὶ εἷς ἐξ εὐωνύμων σου καθίσωμεν ἐν τῇ δόξῃ
(the) right of You and one off (the) left of You we may sit in the glory

**38** σου. ὁ δὲ Ἰησοῦς εἶπεν αὐτοῖς, Οὐκ οἴδατε τί αἰτεῖσθε.
of You. And Jesus　said　to them,　not You know what you ask.

δύνασθε πιεῖν τὸ ποτήριον ὃ ἐγὼ πίνω, καὶ τὸ βάπτισμα ὃ
Can you　drink the　cup　which I　drink,　and the　baptism which

**39** ἐγὼ βαπτίζομαι βαπτισθῆναι; οἱ δὲ εἶπον αὐτῷ, Δυνάμεθα.
I　am baptized to be baptized (with)? they And said to Him,　We can.

ὁ δὲ Ἰησοῦς εἶπεν αὐτοῖς, Τὰ μὲν ποτήριον ὃ ἐγὼ πίνω
-- And Jesus　said　to them, the Indeed　cup　which I　drink

πίεσθε· καὶ τὸ βάπτισμα ὃ ἐγὼ βαπτίζομαι βαπτισθήσεσθε·
you will drink, and the baptism which I am baptized (with) you will be baptized;

**40** τὸ δὲ καθίσαι ἐκ δεξιῶν μου καὶ ἐξ εὐωνύμων μου οὐκ ἔστιν
but　to sit off (the) right of Me and off (the) left of Me　not　is.

**41** ἐμὸν δοῦναι, ἀλλ᾽ οἷς ἡτοίμασται. καὶ ἀκούσαντες οἱ δέκα
Mine to give,　but for whom it has been prepared. And　hearing　the ten

**42** ἤρξαντο ἀγανακτεῖν περὶ Ἰακώβου καὶ Ἰωάννου. ὁ δὲ Ἰησοῦς
began　to be indignant about　James and　John.　-- But　Jesus

προσκαλεσάμενος αὐτοὺς λέγει αὐτοῖς, Οἴδατε ὅτι οἱ δοκοῦν-
having called near　them　says to them, You know that those seem-

τες ἄρχειν τῶν ἐθνῶν κατακυριεύουσιν αὐτῶν· καὶ οἱ μεγάλοι
ing to rule　the　nations lord it over　them, and　the great (ones)

**43** αὐτῶν κατεξουσιάζουσιν αὐτῶν. οὐχ οὕτω δὲ ἔσται ἐν ὑμῖν·
of them exercise authority over them.　not　so But to be among you;

ἀλλ᾽ ὃς ἐὰν θέλῃ γενέσθαι μέγας ἐν ὑμῖν, ἔσται διάκονος ὑμῶν·
but whoever desires to become great among you, shall be servant of you;

**44** καὶ ὃς ἂν θέλῃ ὑμῶν γενέσθαι πρῶτος, ἔσται πάντων δοῦλος.
and whoever desires of you to become first,　shall be of all　slave.

**45** καὶ γὰρ ὁ υἱὸς τοῦ ἀνθρώπου οὐκ ἦλθε διακονηθῆναι,
even For the Son　--　of man　not did come to be served,

ἀλλὰ διακονῆσαι, καὶ δοῦναι τὴν ψυχὴν αὐτοῦ λύτρον ἀντὶ
but　to serve　and to give the　soul　of Him a ransom for

πολλῶν.
many.

**46** Καὶ ἔρχονται εἰς Ἰεριχώ· καὶ ἐκπορευομένου αὐτοῦ ἀπὸ
And they come to Jericho. And　going out　He　from

Ἰεριχώ, καὶ τῶν μαθητῶν αὐτοῦ, καὶ ὄχλου ἱκανοῦ, υἱὸς
Jericho,　and the　disciples　of Him, and a crowd　large,　son

Τιμαίου Βαρτίμαιος ὁ τυφλὸς ἐκάθητο παρὰ τὴν ὁδὸν
of Timaeus Bartimaeus　the　blind　sat　by　the　way,

**47** προσαιτῶν. καὶ ἀκούσας ὅτι Ἰησοῦς ὁ Ναζωραῖός ἐστιν,
begging.　And having heard that　Jesus the Nazarene　it is,

ἤρξατο κράζειν καὶ λέγειν, Ὁ υἱὸς Δαβίδ, Ἰησοῦ, ἐλέησόν
he began to cry out and to say,　-- Son of David,　Jesus, have mercy on

**48** με. καὶ ἐπετίμων αὐτῷ πολλοί, ἵνα σιωπήσῃ· ὁ δὲ πολλῷ
me And warned　him　many,　that he be quiet. he But　much

**49** μᾶλλον ἔκραζεν, Υἱὲ Δαβίδ, ἐλέησόν με. καὶ στὰς ὁ Ἰησοῦς
more　cried out, Son of David, have mercy on me! And standing　Jesus

εἶπεν αὐτὸν φωνηθῆναι· καὶ φωνοῦσι τὸν τυφλὸν, λέγοντες
said for him　to be called.　And they call　the blind (one),　saying

sons of Zebedee, saying, Teacher, we desire that whatever we may ask You would do for us. [36] And He said to them, What do you desire Me to do for you? [37] And they said to Him, Give us that one off Your right, and one off Your left we may sit in Your glory. [38] But Jesus said to them, You know not what you ask — Can you drink the cup which I drink, and be baptized (with) the baptism I am baptized (with)? [39] And they said to Him, We can. But Jesus said to them, Indeed you will drink the cup which I drink, and you will be baptized (with) the baptism (with) which I am baptized; [40] but to sit off My right and off My left is not Mine to give, but whom it has been prepared. [41] And having heard, the ten began to be indignant about James and John. [42] But Jesus having called them near, says to them, You know that those seeming to rule the nations lord it over them; and their great (ones) exercise authority over them; [43] but not so it is among you; but whoever desires to become great among you shall be your servant; [44] and whoever of you desires to become first, (he) shall be servant of all. [45] For even the Son of man did not come to be served, but to serve, and to give His soul a ransome for many. [46] And they come to Jericho. And He having gone out from Jericho, and His disciples, and a large crowd, a son of Timeus, Bartimeus the blind, was sitting beside the highway, begging. [47] And having heard that it was Jesus the Nazarene, he began to cry out and to say, Son of David, Jesus, have pity on me! [48] And many rebuked him that he should be quiet; but he much more cried out, Son of David, have pity on me! [49] And having stopped Jesus asked for him to be called. And they called the

blind one, saying to him,
Be of good courage, rise
up, he calls you. [50] And
he throwing away his
garment, having risen up,
he came to Jesus.
[51] And answering Jesus
said to him, What do you
desire I should do to
Him, Master, that I may
receive sight. [52] And
Jesus said to him, Go, your
faith has healed you. And
immediately he received
sight, and followed Jesus in
the highway.

CHAPTER 11
[1] And when they
drew near to Jerusalem, to
Bethphage and Bethany,
toward the Mount of
Olives, He sent two of His
disciples, [2] and said to
them, Go into the village,
that opposite you, and
immediately entering into
it you will find a colt tied,
upon which no one of men
has sat; having loosened it,
lead (it). [3] And if
anyone says to you, Why
do you do this, say, The
Lord has need of it, and
immediately he will send it
here. [4] And they
departed, and found the
colt tied at the door
outside, by the crossway,
and they untied it.
[5] And some of those
standing there said to
them, What are you doing
untying the colt? [6] And
they said to them as Jesus
commanded. And they
allowed them. [7] And
they led the colt to Jesus.
And they threw their
garments on it, and He sat
on it; [8] and many
scattered their garments on
the highway, and others
were cutting branches from
the trees and were
scattering on the way.
[9] And those going
before and those following
were crying out, saying,
Hosanna! Blessed (is) He
who comes in (the) name
of (the) Lord!
[10] Blessed (is) the
coming kingdom of our
father David in (the) name
of (the) Lord! Hosanna in
the highest! [11] And
Jesus entered into

50 αὐτῷ, Θάρσει· ἔγειραι, φωνεῖ σε. ὁ δὲ ἀποβαλὼν τὸ ἱμάτιον
to him, Be comforted, arise, He calls you. he And casting away the garment

51 αὐτοῦ ἀναστὰς ἦλθε πρὸς τὸν Ἰησοῦν. καὶ ἀποκριθεὶς λέγει
of him, rising up, came to — Jesus. And answering says
αὐτῷ ὁ Ἰησοῦς, Τί θέλεις ποιήσω σοί; ὁ δὲ τυφλὸς εἶπεν
to him — Jesus, What desire you I do for you? the And blind one said

52 αὐτῷ, Ῥαββονί, ἵνα ἀναβλέψω. ὁ δὲ Ἰησοῦς εἶπεν αὐτῷ,
to Him, My Lord, that I may see again. And Jesus said to him,
Ὕπαγε· ἡ πίστις σου σέσωκέ σε. καὶ εὐθέως ἀνέβλεψε, καὶ
Go, the faith of you has healed you. And instantly he saw again, and
ἠκολούθει τῷ Ἰησοῦ ἐν τῇ ὁδῷ.
followed — Jesus in the way.

## CHAPTER 11

1 Καὶ ὅτε ἐγγίζουσιν εἰς Ἱερουσαλήμ, εἰς Βηθφαγὴ καὶ
And when they draw near to Jerusalem, to Bethphage and
Βηθανίαν, πρὸς τὸ ὄρος τῶν ἐλαιῶν, ἀποστέλλει δύο τῶν
Bethany, towards the mount — of olives, He sends two of the

2 μαθητῶν αὐτοῦ, καὶ λέγει αὐτοῖς, Ὑπάγετε εἰς τὴν κώμην
disciples of Him and says to them, Go into the village
τὴν κατέναντι ὑμῶν· καὶ εὐθέως εἰσπορευόμενοι εἰς αὐτὴν
— opposite you, and at once entering into it
εὑρήσετε πῶλον δεδεμένον, ἐφ' ὃν οὐδεὶς ἀνθρώπων κεκάθικε·
you will find a colt having been tied, on which no one of men has sat.

3 λύσαντες αὐτὸν ἀγάγετε. καὶ ἐάν τις ὑμῖν εἴπῃ, Τί ποιεῖτε
Loosing it, lead. And if anyone to you says, Why do you do
τοῦτο; εἴπατε ὅτι Ὁ Κύριος αὐτοῦ χρείαν ἔχει· καὶ εὐθέως
this? Say, The Lord of it need has, and at once

4 αὐτὸν ἀποστελεῖ ὧδε. ἀπῆλθον δὲ καὶ εὗρον τὸν πῶλον
it he will send here. they departed And and found the colt
δεδεμένον πρὸς τὴν θύραν ἔξω ἐπὶ τοῦ ἀμφόδου, καὶ
having been tied to the door outside on the crossway, and

5 λύουσιν αὐτόν. καί τινες τῶν ἐκεῖ ἑστηκότων ἔλεγον αὐτοῖς,
they loosen it. And some of those there standing said to them,

6 Τί ποιεῖτε λύοντες τὸν πῶλον; οἱ δὲ εἶπον αὐτοῖς καθὼς
What do you do loosening the colt? they And said to them as

7 ἐνετείλατο ὁ Ἰησοῦς· καὶ ἀφῆκαν αὐτούς. καὶ ἤγαγον τὸν
commanded — Jesus, and they let go them. And they led the
πῶλον πρὸς τὸν Ἰησοῦν, καὶ ἐπέβαλον αὐτῷ τὰ ἱμάτια
colt to — Jesus; and they throw on it the garments

8 αὐτῶν, καὶ ἐκάθισεν ἐπ' αὐτῷ. πολλοὶ δὲ τὰ ἱμάτια αὐτῶν
of them and He sat on it. many And the garments of them
ἔστρωσαν εἰς τὴν ὁδόν. ἄλλοι δὲ στοιβάδας ἔκοπτον ἐκ
scattered into the way, others and branches were cutting from

9 τῶν δένδρων, καὶ ἐστρώννυον εἰς τὴν ὁδόν. καὶ οἱ προάγον-
the trees, and were scattering into the way. And those going be-
τες καὶ οἱ ἀκολουθοῦντες ἔκραζον, λέγοντες, Ὡσαννά·
fore, and those following cried out, saying, Hosanna!

10 εὐλογημένος ὁ ἐρχόμενος ἐν ὀνόματι Κυρίου· εὐλογημένη
Blessed (be) the (One) coming in (the) name of (the) Lord! Blessed
ἡ ἐρχομένη βασιλεία ἐν ὀνόματι Κυρίου τοῦ πατρὸς ἡμῶν
the coming kingdom in (the) name of (the) Lord, of the father of us
Δαβίδ· Ὡσαννὰ ἐν τοῖς ὑψίστοις.
David! Hosanna in the highest!

11 Καὶ εἰσῆλθεν εἰς Ἱεροσόλυμα ὁ Ἰησοῦς, καὶ εἰς τὸ ἱερόν·
And entered into Jerusalem — Jesus, and into the Temple,

Jerusalem and into the Temple; and having looked around on all things, the hour being already late, He went out to Bethany with the twelve.

[12] And on the next day, they having gone out from Bethany, He hungered. [13] And seeing a fig-tree afar off having leaves, He went, if perhaps He would find anything on it. And having come to it, He found nothing but leaves, for it was not (the) time of figs. [14] And answering Jesus said to it, Let no one eat fruit of you any more forever. And His disciples heard. [15] And they came to Jerusalem; and Jesus, having entered into the Temple, He began to throw out those selling and buying in the Temple, and He overthrew the tables of the money-changers and the seats of those selling doves; [16] and did not allow that anyone should carry a vessel through the Temple. [17] And He taught, saying to them, Has it not been written, My house shall be called a house of prayer for all the nations? But you made it a den of robbers. [18] And the scribes and the chief priests heard, and they sought how they shall destroy Him; for they feared Him, because all the people were astonished at His teaching. [19] And when evening came, He went out of the city.

[20] And in the morning passing along, they saw the fig-tree dried up from (the) roots. [21] And having remembered, Peter says to Him, Rabbi, behold the fig-tree which You cursed is dried up. [22] And answering, Jesus says to them, Have faith (in) God. [23] For truly I say to you that whoever says to this mountain, Be taken away, and be thrown into the sea; and does not doubt in his heart, but believes that what he says occurs; whatever he says, it will be to him. [24] For this reason I say to you, All things

καὶ περιβλεψάμενος πάντα, ὀψίας ἤδη οὔσης τῆς ὥρας,
and looking around at all things, late already being the hour,
ἐξῆλθεν εἰς Βηθανίαν μετὰ τῶν δώδεκα.
He went out to Bethany with the twelve.

12 Καὶ τῇ ἐπαύριον ἐξελθόντων αὐτῶν ἀπὸ Βηθανίας,
And on the morrow having gone out they from Bethany,
13 ἐπείνασε. καὶ ἰδὼν συκῆν μακρόθεν, ἔχουσαν φύλλα, ἦλθεν
He hungered. And seeing a fig-tree afar off having leaves, He came
εἰ ἄρα εὑρήσει τι ἐν αὐτῇ· καὶ ἐλθὼν ἐπ' αὐτήν, οὐδὲν
if perhaps He will find any in it. And coming upon it, nothing
14 εὗρεν εἰ μὴ φύλλα· οὐ γὰρ ἦν καιρὸς σύκων. καὶ ἀποκριθεὶς
He found except leaves; not for it was time of figs. And answering
ὁ Ἰησοῦς εἶπεν αὐτῇ, Μηκέτι ἐκ σοῦ εἰς τὸν αἰῶνα μηδεὶς
– Jesus said to it, No more from you to the age no one
καρπὸν φάγοι. καὶ ἤκουον οἱ μαθηταὶ αὐτοῦ.
fruit may eat. And heard the disciples of Him.
15 Καὶ ἔρχονται εἰς Ἱεροσόλυμα· καὶ εἰσελθὼν ὁ Ἰησοῦς εἰς
And they come to Jerusalem. And entering Jesus into
τὸ ἱερὸν ἤρξατο ἐκβάλλειν τοὺς πωλοῦντας καὶ ἀγοράζοντας
the Temple, He began to cast out those selling, and buying
ἐν τῷ ἱερῷ· καὶ τὰς τραπέζας τῶν κολλυβιστῶν, καὶ τὰς
in the Temple, and the tables of the moneychangers, and the
16 καθέδρας τῶν πωλούντων τὰς περιστερὰς κατέστρεψε· καὶ
seats of those selling the doves He overturned, and
17 οὐκ ἤφιεν ἵνα τις διενέγκῃ σκεῦος διὰ τοῦ ἱεροῦ. καὶ ἐδίδασκε,
not did allow that any may carry a vessel through the Temple, and taught,
λέγων αὐτοῖς, Οὐ γέγραπται ὅτι Ὁ οἶκός μου οἶκος
saying to them, not Has it been written that the house of Me a house
προσευχῆς κληθήσεται πᾶσι τοῖς ἔθνεσιν; ὑμεῖς δὲ ἐποιή-
of prayer shall be called for all the nations? you But have
18 σατε αὐτὸν σπήλαιον λῃστῶν. καὶ ἤκουσαν οἱ γραμματεῖς
made it a den of robbers. And heard the scribes
καὶ οἱ ἀρχιερεῖς, καὶ ἐζήτουν πῶς αὐτὸν ἀπολέσουσιν·
and the chief priests, and they sought how Him they might destroy;
ἐφοβοῦντο γὰρ αὐτόν, ὅτι πᾶς ὁ ὄχλος ἐξεπλήσσετο ἐπὶ
they feared for Him; because all the crowd was astounded at
τῇ διδαχῇ αὐτοῦ.
the teaching of Him.
19 Καὶ ὅτε ὀψὲ ἐγένετο, ἐξεπορεύετο ἔξω τῆς πόλεως.
And when evening came, He went forth out of the city.
20 Καὶ πρωῒ παραπορευόμενοι, εἶδον τὴν συκῆν ἐξηραμ-
And in the morning passing along they saw the fig-tree withered
21 μένην ἐκ ῥιζῶν. καὶ ἀναμνησθεὶς ὁ Πέτρος λέγει αὐτῷ,
from (the) roots. And remembering – Peter says to Him,
22 Ῥαββί, ἴδε, ἡ συκῆ ἣν κατηράσω ἐξήρανται. καὶ ἀποκριθεὶς
Rabbi, behold, the fig-tree which You cursed has withered. And answering
23 Ἰησοῦς λέγει αὐτοῖς, Ἔχετε πίστιν Θεοῦ. ἀμὴν γὰρ λέγω
Jesus says to them, Have faith (in) God. truly For I say
ὑμῖν ὅτι ὃς ἂν εἴπῃ τῷ ὄρει τούτῳ, Ἄρθητι, καὶ βλήθητι εἰς
to you that whoever says – mountain to this, Be taken, and be thrown into
τὴν θάλασσαν, καὶ μὴ διακριθῇ ἐν τῇ καρδίᾳ αὐτοῦ, ἀλλὰ
the sea, and not does doubt in the heart of him, but
24 πιστεύσῃ ὅτι ἃ λέγει γίνεται· ἔσται αὐτῷ ὃ ἐὰν εἴπῃ. διὰ
believes that what he says occurs, it will be to him, whatever he says. There-
τοῦτο λέγω ὑμῖν, Πάντα ὅσα ἂν προσευχόμενοι αἰτεῖσθε,
fore, I say to you, All things whatever praying you ask,

whatever you ask praying, believe that you receive, and (they) shall occur to you. [25] And when you may stand praying, if you have anything against anyone, forgive so that your Father who is in Heaven may also forgive you your sins. [26] But if you do not forgive, your Father who is in Heaven will not forgive your sins. [27] And they came again to Jerusalem. And as He was walking in the Temple, the chief priests and the scribes and the elders came to Him, [28] and they said to Him, By what authority do you do these things? And who gave this authority to you, that you should do these things? [29] And Jesus answering said to them, I also will ask you one thing, and answer Me, and I will tell you by what authority I do these things: [30] The baptism of John, was it out of Heaven, or out of men? Answer Me. [31] And they argued with themselves, saying, If we say, Out of Heaven, He will say, Why then did you not believe him? [32] But if we say, Out of men — they feared the people; for all held that John really was a prophet. [33] And answering, they say to Jesus, We do not know. And answering, Jesus says to them, Neither do I tell you by what authority I do these things.

**25** πιστεύετε ὅτι λαμβάνετε, καὶ ἔσται ὑμῖν. καὶ ὅταν στήκητε
believe　　that you receive,　and it will be to you. And when you stand
προσευχόμενοι, ἀφίετε εἴ τι ἔχετε κατά τινος· ἵνα καὶ ὁ
praying,　　forgive if anything you have against any, that also the
πατὴρ ὑμῶν ὁ ἐν τοῖς οὐρανοῖς ἀφῇ ὑμῖν τὰ παραπτώματα
Father of you — in the heavens may forgive you the transgressions
**26** ὑμῶν. εἰ δὲ ὑμεῖς οὐκ ἀφίετε, οὐδὲ ὁ πατὴρ ὑμῶν ὁ ἐν τοῖς
of you. if But you not do forgive, neither the Father of you — in the
οὐρανοῖς ἀφήσει τὰ παραπτώματα ὑμῶν.
heavens will forgive the transgressions of you.
**27** Καὶ ἔρχονται πάλιν εἰς Ἱεροσόλυμα· καὶ ἐν τῷ ἱερῷ
And they come again to Jerusalem. And in the Temple
περιπατοῦντος αὐτοῦ, ἔρχονται πρὸς αὐτὸν οἱ ἀρχιερεῖς
walking Him, come to Him the chief priests
**28** καὶ οἱ γραμματεῖς καὶ οἱ πρεσβύτεροι, καὶ λέγουσιν αὐτῷ,
and the scribes and the elders, and they say to Him,
Ἐν ποίᾳ ἐξουσίᾳ ταῦτα ποιεῖς; καὶ τίς σοι τὴν ἐξουσίαν
By what authority these things do You? And who You authority
**29** ταύτην ἔδωκεν ἵνα ταῦτα ποιῇς; ὁ δὲ Ἰησοῦς ἀποκριθεὶς
this gave that these things You do? But Jesus answering
εἶπεν αὐτοῖς, Ἐπερωτήσω ὑμᾶς κἀγὼ ἕνα λόγον, καὶ
said to them, I will ask you, I also, one thing, and
ἀποκρίθητέ μοι, καὶ ἐρῶ ὑμῖν ἐν ποίᾳ ἐξουσίᾳ ταῦτα ποιῶ.
answer to Me, and I will tell you by what authority these things I do.
**30** τὸ βάπτισμα Ἰωάννου. ἐξ οὐρανοῦ ἦν, ἢ ἐξ ἀνθρώπων;
The baptism of John, out of Heaven was it, or out of men?
**31** ἀποκρίθητέ μοι. καὶ ἐλογίζοντο πρὸς ἑαυτούς, λέγοντες,
Answer Me. And they argued with themselves, saying,
Ἐὰν εἴπωμεν, Ἐξ οὐρανοῦ, ἐρεῖ, Διατί οὖν οὐκ ἐπιστεύσατε
if we say, Out of Heaven, He will say, Why then not did you believe
**32** αὐτῷ; ἀλλ' ἐὰν εἴπωμεν, Ἐξ ἀνθρώπων, ἐφοβοῦντο τὸν
him? But if we say. Out of men — they feared the
λαόν· ἅπαντες γὰρ εἶχον τὸν Ἰωάννην, ὅτι ὄντως προφήτης
people, all for held — John, that really a prophet
**33** ἦν. καὶ ἀποκριθέντες λέγουσι τῷ Ἰησοῦ, Οὐκ οἴδαμεν. καὶ ὁ
he was. And answering they say — to Jesus, not We do know. And
Ἰησοῦς ἀποκριθεὶς λέγει αὐτοῖς, Οὐδὲ ἐγὼ λέγω ὑμῖν ἐν ποίᾳ
Jesus answering says to them, Neither I tell you by what
ἐξουσίᾳ ταῦτα ποιῶ.
authority these things I do.

## CHAPTER 12

[1] And He began to say to them in parables, A man planted a vineyard, and set a fence around (it), and dug a winevat, and built a tower, and let it out to vinedressers, and left the country. [2] And he sent a servant to the vinedressers at the season, that he might receive from the vinedressers the fruit of the vineyard. [3] But having taken him they beat (him) and sent (him) away empty. [4] And again he sent to them another

## CHAPTER 12

**1** Καὶ ἤρξατο αὐτοῖς ἐν παραβολαῖς λέγειν, Ἀμπελῶνα
And He began to them in parables to speak, a vineyard
ἐφύτευσεν ἄνθρωπος, καὶ περιέθηκε φραγμόν, καὶ ὤρυξεν
planted A man, and put around (it) a fence, and dug
ὑπολήνιον, καὶ ᾠκοδόμησε πύργον, καὶ ἐξέδοτο αὐτὸν
a winevat, and built a tower, and gave out it
**2** γεωργοῖς, καὶ ἀπεδήμησε. καὶ ἀπέστειλε πρὸς τοὺς γεωργοὺς
to vinedressers, and went away. And he sent to the vinedressers
τῷ καιρῷ δοῦλον, ἵνα παρὰ τῶν γεωργῶν λάβῃ ἀπὸ τοῦ
at the time a slave, that from the vinedressers he receive from the
**3** καρποῦ τοῦ ἀμπελῶνος. οἱ δὲ λαβόντες αὐτὸν ἔδειραν, καὶ
fruit of the vineyard. they But having taken, him beat, and
**4** ἀπέστειλαν κενόν. καὶ πάλιν ἀπέστειλε πρὸς αὐτοὺς ἄλλον
sent (him) away empty. And again he sent to them another

servant, and having stoned him, they struck (him) on the head and sent (him) away, having insulted (him). [5] And again he sent another, and they killed him; also many others, beating some, and killing others. [6] Yet, then, having one beloved, his own son, he sent him also to them last, saying, They will have respect for my son. [7] But these vinedressers said among themselves, This is the heir, come, let us kill him, and the inheritance will be ours. [8] And having taken him, they killed (him) and threw (him) outside the vineyard. [9] Therefore what will the lord of the vineyard do? He will come and will destroy the vinedressers, and will give the vineyard to others. [10] Have you not read even this Scripture, "(The) Stone which the builders rejected, this one is become head of (the) corner; [11] this was from (the) Lord, and it is marvelous in our eyes"? [12] And they sought to seize Him, yet feared the people; for they knew that He said the parable against them. And leaving Him, they went away.

[13] And they sent some of the Pharisees and of the Herodians to Him, that they might catch Him in a word. [14] And having come, they say to Him, Teacher, we know that you are true, and there is not a care to you about anyone, for you do not look to (the) face of men, but teach on the way of God (in) truth : Is it lawful to give tribute to Caesar, or not? [15] Should we give, or should we not give? But knowing their hypocrisy, He said to them, Why do you tempt Me? Bring Me a denarius, that I may see. [16] And they brought. And He says to them, Whose image and inscription (is) this? And they said to Him, Caesar's. [17] And answering, Jesus said to them, Render to Caesar the things of Caesar, and to God the

δοῦλον· κἀκεῖνον λιθοβολήσαντες ἐκεφαλαίωσαν, καὶ ἀπέ-
slave;   that one   having stoned   they struck in the head, and sent

5 στειλαν ἠτιμωμένον. καὶ πάλιν ἄλλον ἀπέστειλε· κἀκεῖνον
(him) away, insulting him. And again another   he sent,   that one

ἀπέκτειναν· καὶ πολλοὺς ἄλλους, τοὺς μὲν δέροντες, τοὺς
they killed;   and many   others,   these indeed beating,   these

6 δὲ ἀποκτείνοντες. ἔτι οὖν ἕνα υἱὸν ἔχων ἀγαπητὸν αὐτοῦ,
and   killing.   Still, then, one son having   beloved   his own,

ἀπέστειλε καὶ αὐτὸν πρὸς αὐτοὺς ἔσχατον, λέγων ὅτι
he sent   also   him   to   them   last,   saying, —

7 Ἐντραπήσονται τὸν υἱόν μου. ἐκεῖνοι δὲ οἱ γεωργοὶ εἶπον
They will respect   the son of me. those But — vinedressers said

πρὸς ἑαυτοὺς ὅτι Οὗτός ἐστιν ὁ κληρονόμος· δεῦτε, ἀπο-
to themselves, — This   is   the heir,   come,   let us

8 κτείνωμεν αὐτόν, καὶ ἡμῶν ἔσται ἡ κληρονομία. καὶ λαβόντες
kill   him,   and of us will be the inheritance. And taking

9 αὐτὸν ἀπέκτειναν, καὶ ἐξέβαλον ἔξω τοῦ ἀμπελῶνος. τί οὖν
him   they killed,   and cast (him) outside the vineyard.   What then

ποιήσει ὁ κύριος τοῦ ἀμπελῶνος ; ἐλεύσεται καὶ ἀπολέσει
will do   the lord   of the vineyard?   He will come and   will destroy

10 τοὺς γεωργούς, καὶ δώσει τὸν ἀμπελῶνα ἄλλοις. οὐδὲ τὴν
the vinedressers, and will give the vineyard to others. not even —

γραφὴν ταύτην ἀνέγνωτε, Λίθον ὃν ἀπεδοκίμασαν οἱ
scripture this   Did you read? (The) Stone which rejected   those

11 οἰκοδομοῦντες, οὗτος ἐγενήθη εἰς κεφαλὴν γωνίας· παρὰ
building,   this one became for   head   of (the) corner; from

Κυρίου ἐγένετο αὕτη, καὶ ἔστι θαυμαστὴ ἐν ὀφθαλμοῖς
(the) Lord occurred this,   and it is marvelous   in   eyes

12 ἡμῶν ; καὶ ἐζήτουν αὐτὸν κρατῆσαι, καὶ ἐφοβήθησαν τὸν
of us? And they sought Him   to seize,   and   feared   the

ὄχλον· ἔγνωσαν γὰρ ὅτι πρὸς αὐτοὺς τὴν παραβολὴν
crowd;   they knew for that to   them   the   parable

εἶπε· καὶ ἀφέντες αὐτὸν ἀπῆλθον.
He told. And leaving   Him,   they went away.

13 Καὶ ἀποστέλλουσι πρὸς αὐτόν τινας τῶν Φαρισαίων καὶ
And they send   to   Him some of the Pharisees and

14 τῶν Ἡρωδιανῶν, ἵνα αὐτὸν ἀγρεύσωσι λόγῳ. οἱ δὲ
the Herodians,   that   Him they might catch in a word. they And

ἐλθόντες λέγουσιν αὐτῷ, Διδάσκαλε, οἴδαμεν ὅτι ἀληθὴς
having come say   to Him,   Teacher,   we know that true

εἶ, καὶ οὐ μέλει σοι περὶ οὐδενός· οὐ γὰρ βλέπεις εἰς πρό-
you are, and not a care to you about no one; not for you look to (the)

σωπον ἀνθρώπων, ἀλλ' ἐπ' ἀληθείας τὴν ὁδὸν τοῦ Θεοῦ
face   of men,   but   on truth   the way — of God

15 διδάσκεις· ἔξεστι κῆνσον Καίσαρι δοῦναι ἢ οὔ ; δῶμεν, ἢ
teach: Is it lawful tribute to Caesar to give, or not? Should we or give

μὴ δῶμεν ; ὁ δὲ εἰδὼς αὐτῶν τὴν ὑπόκρισιν εἶπεν αὐτοῖς,
not should we He But knowing their hypocrisy   said to them, give?

16 Τί με πειράζετε ; φέρετέ μοι δηνάριον, ἵνα ἴδω. οἱ δὲ ἤνεγκαν.
Why Me tempt you? Bring Me a denarius, that I may see. they And brought.

καὶ λέγει αὐτοῖς, Τίνος ἡ εἰκὼν αὕτη καὶ ἡ ἐπιγραφή ; οἱ
And He says to them, Whose (is) image this and — superscription? they

17 δὲ εἶπον αὐτῷ, Καίσαρος. καὶ ἀποκριθεὶς ὁ Ἰησοῦς εἶπεν
And said to Him, Caesar's. And answering, — Jesus said

αὐτοῖς, Ἀπόδοτε τὰ Καίσαρος Καίσαρι, καὶ τὰ τοῦ Θεοῦ
to them, Render the things of Caesar to Caesar, and the things of God

things of God. And they marveled at Him.

[18] And Sadducees came to Him, who say there is no resurrection. And they questioned Him, saying, [19] Teacher, Moses wrote for us, that if a brother of anyone should die and leave behind a wife, and leave no children, that his brother should take his wife and raise up seed to his brother. [20] There were seven brothers; and the first took a wife, and dying left no seed; [21] and the second took her, and died, and neither did he leave seed; and the third likewise. [22] And the seven took her, and left no seed. Last of all the woman also died. [23] Therefore in the resurrection, when they shall arise; and the first took a wife, of which of them shall she be wife? For the seven had her as wife. [24] And answering Jesus said to them, Do you not err because of this, not knowing the Scriptures nor the power of God? [25] For when they rise from among (the) dead, they neither marry nor are given in marriage, but are as angels in Heaven. [26] But concerning the dead, that they rise, have you not read in the book of Moses, upon the Bush, how God spoke to him, saying, I (am) the God of Abraham and the God of Isaac and the God of Jacob? [27] He is not the God of (the) dead, but God of (the) living. Therefore you greatly err. [28] And one of the scribes having come up, having heard them reasoning together, seeing that He answered them well, questioned Him, Which is (the) first commandment of all? [29] And Jesus answered him, (The) first of all the commandments (is), Hear, Israel; (the) Lord our God is one Lord. [30] and you shall love (the) Lord your God with all your heart,

---

τῷ Θεῷ. καὶ ἐθαύμασαν ἐπ᾽ αὐτῷ.
— to God. And they marveled at Him.

**18** Καὶ ἔρχονται Σαδδουκαῖοι πρὸς αὐτόν, οἵτινες λέγουσιν
And come Sadducees to Him, who say
ἀνάστασιν μὴ εἶναι· καὶ ἐπηρώτησαν αὐτόν, λέγοντες,
a resurrection not to be, and questioned Him, saying,

**19** Διδάσκαλε, Μωσῆς ἔγραψεν ἡμῖν, ὅτι ἐὰν τινος ἀδελφὸς
Teacher, Moses wrote to us that if of anyone a brother
ἀποθάνῃ, καὶ καταλίπῃ γυναῖκα, καὶ τέκνα μὴ ἀφῇ, ἵνα
should die and leave behind a wife, and children not leave, that
λάβῃ ὁ ἀδελφὸς αὐτοῦ τὴν γυναῖκα αὐτοῦ, καὶ ἐξαναστήσῃ
should take the brother of him the wife of him and should raise up

**20** σπέρμα τῷ ἀδελφῷ αὐτοῦ· ἑπτὰ οὖν ἀδελφοὶ ἦσαν· καὶ ὁ
seed to the brother of him. Seven then brothers were; and the
πρῶτος ἔλαβε γυναῖκα, καὶ ἀποθνήσκων οὐκ ἀφῆκε σπέρμα·
first took a wife, and dying not did leave seed.

**21** καὶ ὁ δεύτερος ἔλαβεν αὐτήν, καὶ ἀπέθανε, καὶ οὐδὲ αὐτὸς
And the second took her, and died, and neither he

**22** ἀφῆκε σπέρμα· καὶ ὁ τρίτος ὡσαύτως. καὶ ἔλαβον αὐτὴν
left behind seed. And the third likewise. And took her
οἱ ἑπτά, καὶ οὐκ ἀφῆκαν σπέρμα. ἐσχάτη πάντων ἀπέθανε
the seven, and not did leave seed. Last of all died

**23** καὶ ἡ γυνή. ἐν τῇ οὖν ἀναστάσει, ὅταν ἀναστῶσι, τίνος
also the wife. In the then resurrection, when they rise again, of which
αὐτῶν ἔσται γυνή ; οἱ γὰρ ἑπτὰ ἔσχον αὐτὴν γυναῖκα.
of them will she be wife? the For seven had her (as) wife.

**24** καὶ ἀποκριθεὶς ὁ Ἰησοῦς εἶπεν αὐτοῖς, Οὐ διὰ τοῦτο
And answering — Jesus said to them, Not therefore
πλανᾶσθε, μὴ εἰδότες τὰς γραφάς, μηδὲ τὴν δύναμιν τοῦ
do you err, not knowing the Scriptures, nor the power of

**25** Θεοῦ ; ὅταν γὰρ ἐκ νεκρῶν ἀναστῶσιν, οὔτε γαμοῦσιν,
of God? when For from (the) dead they rise again, neither they marry,
οὔτε γαμίσκονται, ἀλλ᾽ εἰσὶν ὡς ἄγγελοι οἱ ἐν τοῖς οὐρανοῖς.
nor are given in marriage, but are as angels — in the heavens.

**26** περὶ δὲ τῶν νεκρῶν, ὅτι ἐγείρονται, οὐκ ἀνέγνωτε ἐν τῇ
about But the dead, that they are raised, not did you read in the
βίβλῳ Μωσέως, ἐπὶ τῆς βάτου, ὡς εἶπεν αὐτῷ ὁ Θεός, λέγων,
roll of Moses at the Bush, as spoke to him God, saying,
Ἐγὼ ὁ Θεὸς Ἀβραάμ, καὶ ὁ Θεὸς Ἰσσάκ, καὶ ὁ Θεὸς Ἰακώβ ;
I (am) the God of Abraham, and the God of Isaac, and the God of Jacob?

**27** οὐκ ἔστιν ὁ Θεὸς νεκρῶν, ἀλλὰ Θεὸς ζώντων· ὑμεῖς οὖν πολὺ
not He is the God of (the) dead, but God of (the) living You then much
πλανᾶσθε.
err.

**28** Καὶ προσελθὼν εἷς τῶν γραμματέων, ἀκούσας αὐτῶν
And coming up one of the scribes, hearing them
συζητούντων, εἰδὼς ὅτι καλῶς αὐτοῖς ἀπεκρίθη, ἐπηρώ-
arguing, knowing that well to them He answered, asked

**29** τησεν αὐτόν, Ποία ἐστὶ πρώτη πασῶν ἐντολή ; ὁ δὲ
Him, What is (the) first of all commandments? — And
Ἰησοῦς ἀπεκρίθη αὐτῷ ὅτι Πρώτη πασῶν τῶν ἐντολῶν,
Jesus answered him, — The first of all the commandments (is)

**30** Ἄκουε, Ἰσραήλ· Κύριος ὁ Θεὸς ἡμῶν, Κύριος εἷς ἐστί· καὶ
Hear, Israel, Lord the God of us Lord one is, and
ἀγαπήσεις Κύριον τὸν Θεόν σου ἐξ ὅλης τῆς καρδίας σου,
you shall love the Lord the God of you from all the heart of you,

and with all your soul, and with all your mind, and with all your strength. This (is the) first commandment. [31] And (the) second (is) like this, You shall love your neighbor as yourself. There is not another commandment greater than these. [32] And the scribe said to Him, Right, teacher, you have spoken according to truth, that God is one, and there is no other besides Him; [33] and to love Him with all the heart and with all the understanding, and with all the soul and with all the strength, and to love (one's) neighbor as oneself, is more than all the burnt offerings and the sacrifices. [34] And seeing him, that he answered intelligently, Jesus said to him, You are not far from the kingdom of God. And no one dared any more to question Him.

[35] And answering Jesus said, teaching in the Temple, How do the scribes say that Christ is the son of David? [36] For David himself said by the Holy Spirit, "The Lord said to my Lord, Sit at My right hand until I place Your enemies as a footstool for Your feet." [37] Then David himself calls Him Lord; and from where is He his son? And the large crowd heard Him gladly.

[38] And He said to them in His teaching, Be careful of the scribes, those desiring to walk about in robes, and greetings in the markets, [39] and first seats in the synagogues, and first couches in the dinners [40] those devouring the houses of widows, and for a pretense praying at length these shall receive more abundant judgment.

[41] And Jesus having sat down opposite the treasury, He saw how the crowd threw money into the treasury; and many rich ones were throwing (in) much. [42] And having come one poor

καὶ ἐξ ὅλης τῆς ψυχῆς σου, καὶ ἐξ ὅλης τῆς διανοίας σου,
and from all    the    soul    of you, and from all    the    mind    of you,

31 καὶ ἐξ ὅλης τῆς ἰσχύος σου. αὕτη πρώτη ἐντολή. καὶ δευτέρα
and from all    the    strength of you. This the first commandment; and second
ὁμοία αὕτη, Ἀγαπήσεις τὸν πλησίον σου ὡς σεαυτόν. μείζων
like    this,    You shall love    the    neighbor of you as yourself.    Greater

32 τούτων ἄλλη ἐντολή οὐκ ἔστι. καὶ εἶπεν αὐτῷ ὁ γραμματεύς,
(than) these other command not is.    And said to Him the    scribe,
Καλῶς, διδάσκαλε, ἐπ᾿ ἀληθείας εἶπας ὅτι εἷς ἐστι Θεός, καὶ
Well,    Teacher,    by    truth    you say that one is    God, and

33 οὐκ ἔστιν ἄλλος πλὴν αὐτοῦ. καὶ τὸ ἀγαπᾶν αὐτὸν ἐξ
not there is    another besides    Him;    and — to love    Him out of
ὅλης τῆς καρδίας, καὶ ἐξ ὅλης τῆς συνέσεως, καὶ ἐξ ὅλης τῆς
all    the heart,    and out of all    the understanding, and out of all    the
ψυχῆς, καὶ ἐξ ὅλης τῆς ἰσχύος, καὶ τὸ ἀγαπᾶν τὸν πλησίον
soul,    and from all    the strength;    and — to love    the neighbor
ὡς ἑαυτόν, πλεῖόν ἐστι πάντων τῶν ὁλοκαυτωμάτων καὶ
as    oneself,    more    is    than all    the    burnt offerings    and

34 τῶν θυσιῶν. καὶ ὁ Ἰησοῦς ἰδὼν αὐτὸν ὅτι νουνεχῶς
the    sacrifices.    And — Jesus    seeing    him,    that intelligently
ἀπεκρίθη, εἶπεν αὐτῷ, Οὐ μακρὰν εἶ ἀπὸ τῆς βασιλείας τοῦ
he answered, said to him,    Not far are you from the    kingdom —
Θεοῦ. καὶ οὐδεὶς οὐκέτι ἐτόλμα αὐτὸν ἐπερωτῆσαι.
of God. And no one no more dared    Him    to question.

35 Καὶ ἀποκριθεὶς ὁ Ἰησοῦς ἔλεγε, διδάσκων ἐν τῷ ἱερῷ, Πῶς
And answering, — Jesus    said,    teaching    in the Temple, How
λέγουσιν οἱ γραμματεῖς ὅτι ὁ Χριστὸς υἱός ἐστι Δαβίδ;
say    the    scribes    that the Christ    son    is    of David?

36 αὐτὸς γὰρ Δαβίδ εἶπεν ἐν τῷ Πνεύματι τῷ Ἁγίῳ, Εἶπεν ὁ
himself For    David    said in the Spirit    the    Holy, Said the
Κύριος τῷ Κυρίῳ μου, Κάθου ἐκ δεξιῶν μου, ἕως ἂν θῶ τοὺς
Lord    to the Lord of me, Sit    off (the) right of Me until    I put the

37 ἐχθρούς σου ὑποπόδιον τῶν ποδῶν σου. Αὐτὸς οὖν Δαβὶδ
enemies of You (as) a footstool for the    feet    of You. Himself, Then, David
λέγει αὐτὸν Κύριον· καὶ πόθεν υἱός αὐτοῦ ἐστι ; καὶ ὁ πολὺς
says    Him (to be) Lord, and from where son of him is He? And the large
ὄχλος ἤκουεν αὐτοῦ ἡδέως.
crowd    heard    Him    gladly.

38 Καὶ ἔλεγεν αὐτοῖς ἐν τῇ διδαχῇ αὐτοῦ, Βλέπετε ἀπὸ τῶν
And He said to them in the    teaching of Him, Be careful from the
γραμματέων, τῶν θελόντων ἐν στολαῖς περιπατεῖν, καὶ
scribes,    the (ones) desiring    in    robes    to walk about, and

39 ἀσπασμοὺς ἐν ταῖς ἀγοραῖς, καὶ πρωτοκαθεδρίας ἐν ταῖς
greetings    in the markets,    and chief seats    in    the

40 συναγωγαῖς, καὶ πρωτοκλισίας ἐν τοῖς δείπνοις· οἱ κατε-
synagogues,    and chief couches    in the    dinners; the (ones)
σθίοντες τὰς οἰκίας τῶν χηρῶν, καὶ προφάσει μακρὰ
devouring the    houses    of the widows,    and for a pretence lengthily
προσευχόμενοι· οὗτοι λήψονται περισσότερον κρίμα.
praying;    these will receive more abundant    judgment.

41 Καὶ καθίσας ὁ Ἰησοῦς κατέναντι τοῦ γαζοφυλακίου
And    sitting    — Jesus    opposite    the    treasury,
ἐθεώρει πῶς ὁ ὄχλος βάλλει χαλκὸν εἰς τὸ γαζοφυλάκιον·
He watched how the crowd cast copper coins into the    treasury.

42 καὶ πολλοὶ πλούσιοι ἔβαλλον πολλά. καὶ ἐλθοῦσα μία
And    many    rich ones    cast in    much;    and    coming    one

widow threw (in) two lepta, which is a kodrantes. [43] And having called His disciples, He said to them, Truly I say to you, that this poor widow has thrown (in) more than all of those casting into the treasury. [44] For all threw (in) out of what was abounding to them, but she out of her poverty threw (in) all, as much as she had, her whole livelihood.

**CHAPTER 13**

[1] And as He was going out of the Temple, one of His disciples said to Him, Teacher, see, what stones and what buildings! [2] And answering Jesus said to him, Do you see these great buildings? Not one stone shall be left on (a) stone which shall not be thrown down. [3] And as He was sitting on the Mount of Olives opposite the Temple, Peter and James and John and Andrew asked Him privately, [4] Tell us when these things shall be? And what the sign when all these things should be about to be accomplished? [5] And Jesus answering to them began to say, Be careful lest anyone mislead you. [6] For many will come in My name, saying, I AM! And they will mislead many. [7] But when you hear of wars and rumors of wars, do not be disturbed; for it must come to pass, but the end (is) not yet. [8] For nations shall rise up against nation, and kingdom against kingdom; and there shall be earthquakes in different places, and there shall be famines and troubles. These (are) beginnings of anguishes. [9] But you take heed to yourselves; for they will deliver you up to sanhedrins and to synagogues. You will be beaten, and you will be brought before governors and kings for My sake, for a witness to them.

---

**43** χήρα πτωχὴ ἔβαλε λεπτὰ δύο, ὅ ἐστι κοδράντης. καὶ
widow poor cast lepta two, which is a quadrans. And
προσκαλεσάμενος τοὺς μαθητὰς αὐτοῦ, λέγει αὐτοῖς, 'Αμὴν
calling near the disciples of Him, He says to them, Truly
λέγω ὑμῖν ὅτι ἡ χήρα αὕτη ἡ πτωχὴ πλεῖον πάντων
I say to you that — widow, this — poor more than all

**44** βέβληκε τῶν βαλόντων εἰς τὸ γαζοφυλάκιον· πάντες γὰρ
has cast the (ones) casting into the treasury; all for
ἐκ τοῦ περισσεύοντος αὐτοῖς ἔβαλον· αὕτη δὲ ἐκ τῆς
out of that abounding to them cast, she but out of the
ὑστερήσεως αὐτῆς πάντα ὅσα εἶχεν ἔβαλεν. ὅλον τὸν βίον
poverty of her all, as much as she had cast all the living
αὐτῆς.
of her.

**CHAPTER 13**

**1** Καὶ ἐκπορευομένου αὐτοῦ ἐκ τοῦ ἱεροῦ, λέγει αὐτῷ εἷς
And going forth He out of the Temple, says to Him one
τῶν μαθητῶν αὐτοῦ, Διδάσκαλε, ἴδε, ποταποὶ λίθοι καὶ
of the disciples of Him, Teacher, Behold, what kind of stones and

**2** ποταπαὶ οἰκοδομαί. καὶ ὁ 'Ιησοῦς ἀποκριθεὶς εἶπεν αὐτῷ,
what kind of buildings! And — Jesus answering said to him,
Βλέπεις ταύτας τὰς μεγάλας οἰκοδομάς ; οὐ μὴ ἀφεθῇ λίθος
Do you see these — great buildings? In no way will be left stone
ἐπὶ λίθῳ, ὃς οὐ μὴ καταλυθῇ.
upon stone that not at all (will) be thrown down.

**3** Καὶ καθημένου αὐτοῦ εἰς τὸ ὄρος τῶν ἐλαιῶν κατέναντι
And sitting He in the mount of the olives opposite
τοῦ ἱεροῦ, ἐπηρώτων αὐτὸν κατ' ἰδίαν Πέτρος καὶ 'Ιάκωβος
the Temple, questioned Him privately Peter and James

**4** καὶ 'Ιωάννης καὶ 'Ανδρέας, Εἰπὲ ἡμῖν, πότε ταῦτα ἔσται ;
and John and Andrew, Tell us, when these things will be?
καὶ τί τὸ σημεῖον ὅταν μέλλῃ πάντα ταῦτα συντελεῖσθαι ;
And what the sign when are about all these things to be accomplished?

**5** ὁ δὲ 'Ιησοῦς ἀποκριθεὶς αὐτοῖς ἤρξατο λέγειν, Βλέπετε μη τις
And Jesus answering to them began to say, Be careful not any

**6** ὑμᾶς πλανήσῃ. πολλοὶ γὰρ ἐλεύσονται ἐπὶ τῷ ὀνόματί μου,
you lead astray many For will come on the name of Me,

**7** λέγοντες ὅτι 'Εγώ εἰμι· καὶ πολλοὺς πλανήσουσιν. ὅταν δὲ
saying, — I AM! And many they will lead astray. when But
ἀκούσητε πολέμους καὶ ἀκοὰς πολέμων, μὴ θροεῖσθε· δεῖ
you hear (of) wars and rumors of wars, do not be alarmed. it must

**8** γὰρ γενέσθαι· ἀλλ' οὔπω τὸ τέλος. ἐγερθήσεται γὰρ ἔθνος
For happen, but not yet the end. will be raised For nation
ἐπὶ ἔθνος, καὶ βασιλεία ἐπὶ βασιλείαν· καὶ ἔσονται σεισμοὶ
against nation, and kingdom against kingdom; and shall be earthquakes
κατὰ τόπους, καὶ ἔσονται λιμοὶ καὶ ταραχαί· ἀρχαὶ ὠδίνων
in many places; and shall be famines and troubles. Beginnings of travails
ταῦτα.
these things (are).

**9** Βλέπετε δὲ ὑμεῖς ἑαυτούς· παραδώσουσι γὰρ ὑμᾶς εἰς
be careful But you yourselves; they will deliver for you to
συνέδρια, καὶ εἰς συναγωγὰς δαρήσεσθε, καὶ ἐπὶ ἡγεμόνων
sanhedrins, and to synagogues—you will be beaten; and before rulers
καὶ βασιλέων ἀχθήσεσθε ἕνεκεν ἐμοῦ, εἰς μαρτύριον αὐτοῖς.
and kings you will be led for the sake of Me, for a testimony to them.

[15] And he will show you a large upper room, ready prepared. There prepare for us. [16] And His disciples went away and came into the city, and found as He has said to them; and they prepared the passover. [17] And evening being come, He came with the twelve. [18] And as they were reclining and were eating, Jesus said, Truly I say to you, that one of you who is eating with Me will betray Me. [19] And they began to be sorrowful, and to say to Him, one by one, (Is it) I? And another, (Is it) I? [20] But answering He said to them, (It is) one of the Twelve, he who is dipping with Me in the dish. [21] Truly the Son of man goes as it has been written concerning Him; but woe to that man by whom the Son of man is betrayed; it were good for him if that man had not been born.

[22] And as they were eating, Jesus having taken a loaf, having blessed, He broke and gave to them, and said, Take, eat; this is My body. [23] And having taken the cup, having given thanks, He gave to them, and they drank all of it. [24] And He said to them, This is My blood, that of the new Covenant, which is poured out for many. [25] Truly I say to you that I will at all drink of the fruit of the vine any more until the day when I drink it new in the kingdom of God. [26] And having sung a hymn, they went out to Mount of Olives. And Jesus said to All of you will be offended in Me in this for it has been "I will strike the ...rd and the sheep be scattered." But after My ...tion, I will go you into Galilee. Peter said to him, all should be ..., yet not I.

16 αὐτὸς ὑμῖν δείξει ἀνώγεον μέγα ἐστρωμένον ἕτοιμον· ἐκεῖ
he you will show an upper room large being spread, ready. There
ἑτοιμάσατε ἡμῖν. καὶ ἐξῆλθον οἱ μαθηταὶ αὐτοῦ, καὶ ἦλθον
you prepare for us. And went forth the disciples of Him. and came
εἰς τὴν πόλιν, καὶ εὗρον καθὼς εἶπεν αὐτοῖς, καὶ ἡτοίμασαν
into the city, and found as He told them, and they prepared
τὸ πάσχα.
the Passover.

17 Καὶ ὀψίας γενομένης ἔρχεται μετὰ τῶν δώδεκα. καὶ ἀνακει-
18 And evening occurring, He comes with the twelve. And reclining
μένων αὐτῶν καὶ ἐσθιόντων, εἶπεν ὁ Ἰησοῦς, Ἀμὴν λέγω
they, and eating, said - Jesus, Truly I say
19 ὑμῖν, ὅτι εἷς ἐξ ὑμῶν παραδώσει με, ὁ ἐσθίων μετ' ἐμοῦ. οἱ
to you that one from you will betray Me, the (one) eating with Me, they
δὲ ἤρξαντο λυπεῖσθαι, καὶ λέγειν αὐτῷ εἷς καθ' εἷς, Μή τι
And began to be grieved, and to say to Him one by one, Not at all
20 ἐγώ; καὶ ἄλλος, Μή τι ἐγώ; ὁ δὲ ἀποκριθεὶς εἶπεν αὐτοῖς,
I? And another, Not at all I? He And answering said to them,
Εἷς ἐκ τῶν δώδεκα, ὁ ἐμβαπτόμενος μετ' ἐμοῦ εἰς τὸ τρυβλίον.
One from the twelve, the (one) dipping in with Me in the dish.
21 ὁ μὲν υἱὸς τοῦ ἀνθρώπου ὑπάγει, καθὼς γέγραπται περὶ
the Indeed Son - of man is going as it has been written about
αὐτοῦ· οὐαὶ δὲ τῷ ἀνθρώπῳ ἐκείνῳ δι' οὗ ὁ υἱὸς τοῦ
Him. woe But to man that through whom the Son -
ἀνθρώπου παραδίδοται· καλὸν ἦν αὐτῷ εἰ οὐκ ἐγεννήθη ὁ
of man is betrayed; good were it for him if not was born -
ἄνθρωπος ἐκεῖνος.
man that.
22 Καὶ ἐσθιόντων αὐτῶν, λαβὼν ὁ Ἰησοῦς ἄρτον εὐλογήσας
And eating they, taking Jesus a loaf, blessing
ἔκλασε, καὶ ἔδωκεν αὐτοῖς, καὶ εἶπε, Λάβετε, φάγετε· τοῦτό
He broke and gave to them, and said, Take, eat; this
23 ἐστι τὸ σῶμά μου. καὶ λαβὼν τὸ ποτήριον εὐχαριστήσας
is the body of Me. And taking the cup, giving thanks,
24 ἔδωκεν αὐτοῖς· καὶ ἔπιον ἐξ αὐτοῦ πάντες. καὶ εἶπεν αὐτοῖς,
He gave to them, and drank from it all. And He said to them,
Τοῦτό ἐστι τὸ αἷμά μου, τὸ τῆς καινῆς διαθήκης, τὸ περὶ
This is the blood of Me, that of the New Covenant concerning
25 πολλῶν ἐκχυνόμενον. ἀμὴν λέγω ὑμῖν ὅτι οὐκέτι οὐ μὴ πίω
many being poured out. Truly I say to you that no more in no way I may drink
ἐκ τοῦ γεννήματος τῆς ἀμπέλου, ἕως τῆς ἡμέρας ἐκείνης ὅταν
of the offspring of the vine until - day that when
αὐτὸ πίνω καινὸν ἐν τῇ βασιλείᾳ τοῦ Θεοῦ.
it I drink new in the kingdom - of God.
26 Καὶ ὑμνήσαντες ἐξῆλθον εἰς τὸ ὄρος τῶν ἐλαιῶν.
And having sung a hymn they went into the mount of the olives.
27 Καὶ λέγει αὐτοῖς ὁ Ἰησοῦς ὅτι Πάντες σκανδαλισθήσεσθε
And says to them - Jesus, - All you will be offended
ἐν ἐμοὶ ἐν τῇ νυκτὶ ταύτῃ· ὅτι γέγραπται, Πατάξω τὸν
in Me in - night this, because it has been written: I will strike the
28 ποιμένα, καὶ διασκορπισθήσεται τὰ πρόβατα. ἀλλὰ μετὰ
Shepherd, and will be scattered the sheep. But after
29 τὸ ἐγερθῆναί με, προάξω ὑμᾶς εἰς τὴν Γαλιλαίαν. ὁ δὲ
the arising of Me, I will go before you into - Galilee. - And
Πέτρος ἔφη αὐτῷ, Καὶ εἰ πάντες σκανδαλισθήσονται, ἀλλ'
Peter said to Him, Even if all shall be offended, yet

---

[10] And the gospel must be preached to all the nations first. [11] But whenever they may lead you away, delivering up, do not be anxious beforehand what you should say ot think; but whatever may be given to you in that hour, speak that; for you are not they who speak, but the Holy Spirit. [12] And brother will deliver up brother to death, and a father ...child; and children will rise up on parents, and will put them to death; [13] and you will be hated by all on account of My name. But he enduring to the end will be saved. [14] But when you see the abomination of desolation, the (one) spoken of by Daniel the prophet, standing where it ought not—he reading, let him understand—then let those in Judea flee into the mountains [15] And he on the housetop, let him not go down into the house, nor go in to take anything out of his house. [16] And he being in the field, let him not return to the things behind, to take his garment. [17] But woe to those that are with child, and to those giving suck in those days! [18] And pray that your flight may not be in winter; [19] for tribulation shall be (in) those days, such as has not been the like from (the) beginning of creation which God created until now, and never shall be; [20] and if (the) Lord had not shortened the days, there would not any flesh have been saved; but because of the elect whom He chose, He has shortened the days. [21] And then if anyone say to you, Behold, here (is) the Christ; or, Behold, there; you shall not believe. [22] For there will arise false christs and false prophets, and will give signs and wonders, to if possible deceive even the elect. [23] But you be careful; behold, I have foretold all things to you. [24] But in those days,

10 καὶ εἰς πάντα τὰ ἔθνη δεῖ πρῶτον κηρυχθῆναι τὸ εὐαγγέλιον
And to all the nations must first be proclaimed the gospel.
11 ὅταν δὲ ἀγάγωσιν ὑμᾶς παραδιδόντες, μὴ προμεριμνᾶτε τί
when And they lead away you, delivering (you), not be anxious before what
λαλήσητε, μηδὲ μελετᾶτε· ἀλλ' ὃ ἐὰν δοθῇ ὑμῖν ἐν ἐκείνῃ τῇ
you may say, nor meditate; but whatever is given you in that -
ὥρᾳ, τοῦτο λαλεῖτε· οὐ γὰρ ἐστε ὑμεῖς οἱ λαλοῦντες, ἀλλὰ
hour, this speak; not for are you the (ones) speaking, but
12 τὸ Πνεῦμα τὸ Ἅγιον. παραδώσει δὲ ἀδελφὸς ἀδελφὸν εἰς
the Spirit - Holy. will deliver And a brother a brother to
θάνατον, καὶ πατὴρ τέκνον· καὶ ἐπαναστήσονται τέκνα ἐπὶ
to death, and a father a child; and will rise up children upon
13 γονεῖς, καὶ θανατώσουσιν αὐτούς· καὶ ἔσεσθε μισούμενοι
parents, and will put to death them; and you will be hated
ὑπὸ πάντων διὰ τὸ ὄνομά μου· ὁ δὲ ὑπομείνας εἰς τέλος,
by all on account of the name of Me. he But enduring to the end,
οὗτος σωθήσεται.
this (one) will be saved.
14 Ὅταν δὲ ἴδητε τὸ βδέλυγμα τῆς ἐρημώσεως, τὸ ῥηθὲν
when But you see the abomination - of desolation, the (one) spoken
ὑπὸ Δανιὴλ τοῦ προφήτου, ἑστὸς ὅπου οὐ δεῖ (ὁ ἀναγινώ-
by Daniel the prophet, standing where not it ought, he reading
σκων νοείτω), τότε οἱ ἐν τῇ Ἰουδαίᾳ φευγέτωσαν εἰς τὰ
let him understand, then those in Judea, let them flee into the
15 ὄρη· ὁ δὲ ἐπὶ τοῦ δώματος μὴ καταβάτω εἰς τὴν οἰκίαν,
mounts. he And on the housetop, not let him descend into the house,
16 μηδὲ εἰσελθέτω ἆραί τι ἐκ τῆς οἰκίας αὐτοῦ· καὶ ὁ εἰς τὸν
nor enter to take anything out of the house of him; and he in the
ἀγρὸν ὢν μὴ ἐπιστρεψάτω εἰς τὰ ὀπίσω, ἆραι τὸ ἱμάτιον
field, being, not let him return to the things behind to take the garment
17 αὐτοῦ. οὐαὶ δὲ ταῖς ἐν γαστρὶ ἐχούσαις καὶ ταῖς θηλαζού-
of him. woe But to those in womb holding, and to those giving
18 σαις ἐν ἐκείναις ταῖς ἡμέραις. προσεύχεσθε δὲ ἵνα μὴ γένηται
suck in those - days. pray But that not may occur
19 ἡ φυγὴ ὑμῶν χειμῶνος. ἔσονται γὰρ αἱ ἡμέραι ἐκεῖναι θλίψις,
the flight of you in winter, will be for - days those affliction
οἷα οὐ γέγονε τοιαύτη ἀπ' ἀρχῆς κτίσεως ἧς ἔκτισεν ὁ
such as not has been the like from beginning of creation which created -
20 Θεὸς ἕως τοῦ νῦν, καὶ οὐ μὴ γένηται. καὶ εἰ μὴ Κύριος
God until - now, and in no way may be. And unless (the) Lord
ἐκολόβωσε τὰς ἡμέρας, οὐκ ἂν ἐσώθη πᾶσα σάρξ· ἀλλὰ διὰ
had shortened the days, not would be saved any flesh; but because of
21 τοὺς ἐκλεκτοὺς, οὓς ἐξελέξατο, ἐκολόβωσε τὰς ἡμέρας. καὶ
the elect, whom He elected, He shortened the days. And
τότε ἐάν τις ὑμῖν εἴπῃ, Ἰδού, ὧδε ὁ Χριστός, ἢ Ἰδού, ἐκεῖ,
then if anyone to you says, Behold, here the Christ, or behold, there, not
22 πιστεύσητε. ἐγερθήσονται γαρ ψευδόχριστοι καὶ ψευδο-
believe. will be raised For false Christs and false
προφῆται, καὶ δώσουσι σημεῖα καὶ τέρατα, πρὸς τὸ ἀπο-
prophets, and they will give signs and wonders in order to - lead
23 πλανᾶν, εἰ δυνατόν, καὶ τοὺς ἐκλεκτούς. ὑμεῖς δὲ βλέπετε·
astray, if possible, even the elect. you But be careful.
ἰδού, προείρηκα ὑμῖν πάντα.
Behold, I have told before you all things.
24 Ἀλλ' ἐν ἐκείναις ταῖς ἡμέραις, μετὰ τὴν θλίψιν ἐκείνην, ὁ
But in those - days, after - affliction that, the

after that tribulation, the sun shall be darkened, and the moon shall not give her light; [25] and the stars of the sky shall be falling, and the powers which (are) in the heavens shall be shaken; [26] and then they shall see the Son of man coming in clouds with great power and glory; [27] and then He will send His angels and will gather together His elect from the four winds, from the furthest part of the earth to the furthest part of Heaven. [28] And from the fig-tree learn the parable: When its branch is already become tender, and it puts forth leaves, you know that the summer is near. [29] So you also, when you see these things happening, know that it is near, at (the) doors. [30] Truly I say to you, that in no way will this generation have passed away until all these things shall have taken place. [31] The heaven and the earth shall pass away, but My word shall never pass away. [32] But concerning that day and the hour, no one knows, not even the angels, those in Heaven, nor the Son, but the Father. [33] Be careful, watch and pray; for you do not know when the time is: [34] As a man going abroad (and) leaving his house, and giving the authority to his slaves, and to each his work; and he directed his door-keeper, that he should watch; [35] then you watch for you do not know when the lord of the house comes, at evening, or at midnight, or at cock-crowing, or early; [36] lest coming suddenly, he find you sleeping. [37] And what I say to you, I say to all: Watch!

CHAPTER 14

[1] Now it was the Passover and the (feast of) unleavened bread after two days. And the chief priests and the scribes were seeking how they might get hold of Him by guile (and) and they might kill (Him). [2] But they said, Not in

25 ἥλιος σκοτισθήσεται, καὶ ἡ σελήνη οὐ δώσει τὸ φέγγος
sun will be darkened, and the moon not will give the light

αὐτῆς, καὶ οἱ ἀστέρες τοῦ οὐρανοῦ ἔσονται ἐκπίπτοντες,
of her. And the stars of the heaven will be falling,

26 καὶ αἱ δυνάμεις αἱ ἐν τοῖς οὐρανοῖς σαλευθήσονται. καὶ τότε
and the powers – in the heavens will be shaken. And then

ὄψονται τὸν υἱὸν τοῦ ἀνθρώπου ἐρχόμενον ἐν νεφέλαις
they will see the Son – of man coming in clouds

27 μετὰ δυνάμεως πολλῆς καὶ δόξης. καὶ τότε ἀποστελεῖ τοὺς
with power much and glory. And then He will send the

ἀγγέλους αὐτοῦ, καὶ ἐπισυνάξει τοὺς ἐκλεκτοὺς αὐτοῦ ἐκ
angels of Him, and they will gather the elect of Him out o

τῶν τεσσάρων ἀνέμων, ἀπ' ἄκρου γῆς ἕως ἄκρου οὐρανοῦ.
the four winds, from (the) end of earth to (the) end of heaven.

28 Ἀπὸ δὲ τῆς συκῆς μάθετε τὴν παραβολήν· ὅταν αὐτῆς
from And the fig-tree learn the parable: when of it

ἤδη ὁ κλάδος ἁπαλὸς γένηται καὶ ἐκφύῃ τὰ φύλλα, γινώ-
now the branch tender becomes and puts out the leaves, you

29 σκετε ὅτι ἐγγὺς τὸ θέρος ἐστίν· οὕτω καὶ ὑμεῖς, ὅταν ταῦτα
know that near the summer is. So also you, when these things

30 ἴδητε γινόμενα, γινώσκετε ὅτι ἐγγύς ἐστιν ἐπὶ θύραις. ἀμὴν
you see happening, know that near is it, at (the) doors. Truly

λέγω ὑμῖν ὅτι οὐ μὴ παρέλθῃ ἡ γενεὰ αὕτη, μέχρις οὗ
I say to you that in no way will pass away generation this until

31 πάντα ταῦτα γένηται. ὁ οὐρανὸς καὶ ἡ γῆ παρελεύσονται·
all these things happen. The heaven and the earth will pass away,

32 οἱ δὲ λόγοι μου οὐ μὴ παρέλθωσι. περὶ δὲ τῆς ἡμέρας
the but words of Me in no way will pass away. concerning But day

ἐκείνης καὶ τῆς ὥρας οὐδεὶς οἶδεν, οὐδὲ οἱ ἄγγελοι οἱ ἐν
that and the hour no one knows, not the angels – in

33 οὐρανῷ, οὐδὲ ὁ υἱός, εἰ μὴ ὁ πατήρ. βλέπετε, ἀγρυπνεῖτε καὶ
Heaven, nor the Son, except the Father. Be careful, be wakeful, and

34 προσεύχεσθε· οὐκ οἴδατε γὰρ πότε ὁ καιρός ἐστιν. ὡς
pray. you know when the time is. As

ἄνθρωπος ἀπόδημος ἀφεὶς τὴν οἰκίαν αὐτοῦ, καὶ δοὺς τοῖς
a man going abroad, leaving the house of him, and giving to the

δούλοις αὐτοῦ τὴν ἐξουσίαν, καὶ ἑκάστῳ τὸ ἔργον αὐτοῦ,
slaves of him the authority, and to each the work of him,

35 καὶ τῷ θυρωρῷ ἐνετείλατο ἵνα γρηγορῇ. γρηγορεῖτε οὖν·
and the doorkeeper He ordered that he should watch. You watch, then,

οὐκ οἴδατε γὰρ πότε ὁ κύριος τῆς οἰκίας ἔρχεται, ὀψέ, ἢ
not you know for when the lord of the house comes, evening, or

36 μεσονυκτίου, ἢ ἀλεκτοροφωνίας, ἢ πρωΐ· μὴ ἐλθὼν ἐξαίφνης
at midnight, or at cock-crowing, or early; lest coming suddenly

37 εὕρῃ ὑμᾶς καθεύδοντας. ἃ δὲ ὑμῖν πᾶσι λέγω,
he find you sleeping. what And to you I say, to all I say,

Γρηγορεῖτε.
Watch!

CHAPTER 14

1 Ἦν δὲ τὸ πάσχα καὶ τὰ ἄζυμα μετὰ δύο ἡμέρας· καὶ
it was And the Passover and the unleavened bread after two days. And

ἐζήτουν οἱ ἀρχιερεῖς καὶ οἱ γραμματεῖς πῶς αὐτὸν ἐν δόλῳ
sought the chief priests and the scribes how Him by guile

2 κρατήσαντες ἀποκτείνωσιν· ἔλεγον δέ, Μὴ ἐν τῇ ἑορτῇ,
seizing they might kill. they said And, Not at the feast,

the feast, lest there shall be a tumult of the people. [3] And He being in Bethany, in the house of Simon the leper, as He reclined, a woman came having an alabaster vial of pure ointment, of spikenard of great price; and having broken the alabaster vial, she poured on His head. [4] And some were indignant within themselves, and saying, For what has this waste of the ointment occurred? [5] For this could be sold (for) over three hundred denarii, and to be given to the poor. And they were incensed with her. [6] But Jesus said, Let her alone. Why do you cause her trouble? She worked a good work toward Me. [7] For you always have the poor with you, and when you desire, you are able to do well toward them. But you do not always have Me. [8] What this one held, she did; she took beforehand to anoint My body for the burial. [9] Truly I say to you, wherever this gospel is proclaimed in all the world, also what this (one) did will be spoken of for her memorial. [10] And Judas Iscariot, one of the twelve, went away to the chief priests, that he might deliver Him up to them. [11] And having heard they rejoiced and promised to give him money. And he sought how he might betray Him conveniently. [12] And on the first day of unleavened (bread), when they killed the passover, his disciples say to Him, Where do You desire (that) going we may prepare that You may eat the passover? [13] And He sends two of His disciples, and says to them, Go into the city, and a man carrying a pitcher of water will meet you; follow him; [14] and wherever he goes in, say to the housemaster, The Teacher says, Where is the guest room where I may eat the passover with My disciples? [15]

μήποτε θόρυβος ἔσται τοῦ λαοῦ.
lest a tumult will be of the people.

3 Καὶ ὄντος αὐτοῦ ἐν Βηθανίᾳ, ἐν τῇ οἰκίᾳ Σίμωνος τοῦ
And being He in Bethany in the house of Simon the

λεπροῦ, κατακειμένου αὐτοῦ, ἦλθε γυνὴ ἔχουσα ἀλάβαστρον
leper, reclining He came a woman having an alabaster vial

μύρου νάρδου πιστικῆς πολυτελοῦς· καὶ συντρίψασα τὸ
of ointment of nard pure costly. And breaking the

ἀλάβαστρον, κατέχεεν αὐτοῦ κατὰ τῆς κεφαλῆς. ἦσαν δὲ
alabaster vial she poured (it) of Him down the head. were And

4 τινες ἀγανακτοῦντες πρὸς ἑαυτούς, καὶ λέγοντες, Εἰς τί ἡ
some being indignant to themselves, and saying. To what –

5 ἀπώλεια αὕτη τοῦ μύρου γέγονεν; ἠδύνατο γὰρ τοῦτο
waste this of the ointment has occurred? could For this

πραθῆναι ἐπάνω τριακοσίων δηναρίων, καὶ δοθῆναι τοῖς
be sold (for) over three hundred denarii, and to be given to the

6 πτωχοῖς. καὶ ἐνεβριμῶντο αὐτῇ. ὁ δὲ Ἰησοῦς εἶπεν, Ἄφετε
poor. And they were incensed with her. But Jesus said, Let alone

αὐτήν· τί αὐτῇ κόπους παρέχετε; καλὸν ἔργον εἰργάσατο
her. Why to her troubles do you cause? a good work she worked

7 εἰς ἐμέ. πάντοτε γὰρ τοὺς πτωχοὺς ἔχετε μεθ' ἑαυτῶν, καὶ
to Me. always For the poor you have with yourselves, and

ὅταν θέλητε δύνασθε αὐτοὺς εὖ ποιῆσαι· ἐμὲ δὲ οὐ πάντοτε
when you wish you are able (to) them well to do, Me but not always

8 ἔχετε. ὃ εἶχεν αὕτη ἐποίησε· προέλαβε μυρίσαι μου τὸ
you have. What held this one, she did; she took beforehand to anoint Me th

9 σῶμα εἰς τὸν ἐνταφιασμόν. ἀμὴν λέγω ὑμῖν, ὅπου
body for the burial. Truly I say to you, where e

κηρυχθῇ τὸ εὐαγγέλιον τοῦτο εἰς ὅλον τὸν κόσμον, κα
is proclaimed gospel this in all the world, also

ἐποίησεν αὕτη λαληθήσεται εἰς μνημόσυνον αὐτῆς.
did this (one) will be spoken for a memorial of her.

10 Καὶ ὁ Ἰούδας ὁ Ἰσκαριώτης, εἷς τῶν δώδεκα,
And – Judas Iscariot, one of the twelve, w

11 πρὸς τοὺς ἀρχιερεῖς, ἵνα παραδῷ αὐτὸν αὐτοῖς. οἱ
to the chief priests, that he might betray Him to them. the

σαντες ἐχάρησαν, καὶ ἐπηγγείλαντο αὐτῷ ἀργύριο
hearing rejoiced and promised him silver

καὶ ἐζήτει πῶς εὐκαίρως αὐτὸν παραδῷ.
And he sought how opportunely Him he might betray.

12 Καὶ τῇ πρώτῃ ἡμέρᾳ τῶν ἀζύμων, ὅτε τὸ π
And on the first day of the unleavened, when the Pa

λέγουσιν αὐτῷ οἱ μαθηταὶ αὐτοῦ, Ποῦ θέλε
say to Him the disciples of Him, Where do Y

13 ἑτοιμάσωμεν ἵνα φάγῃς τὸ πάσχα; καὶ ἀπο
we may prepare that You eat the Passover? And He se

μαθητῶν αὐτοῦ, καὶ λέγει αὐτοῖς, Ὑπάγετ
disciples of Him, and says to them, Go

καὶ ἀπαντήσει ὑμῖν ἄνθρωπος κεράμιον ὕ
and will meet you a man a pitcher

14 ἀκολουθήσατε αὐτῷ, καὶ ὅπου ἐὰν εἰ
follow him. And where ever h

οἰκοδεσπότῃ ὅτι Ὁ διδάσκαλος λέγει,
housemaster, – The Teacher says,

15 λυμα, ὅπου τὸ πάσχα μετὰ τῶν μαθ
room where the Passover with the dis

[30] And Jesus said to him, Truly I say to you, that today, in this night, before (the) cock crows thrice, you will deny Me three times. [31] But he spoke more strongly, If it were needful for me to die with You, in no way will I deny You. And in the same way they all also spoke.

[32] And they came to a place of which the name (was) Gethsemane; and He said to His disciples. Sit here while I pray. [33] And He takes along Peter and James and John with Him. And He began to be greatly amazed, and to be distressed, and says to them, My soul is deeply grieved, unto death; stay here and watch. [35] And having gone forward a little, He fell on the earth, and prayed that if it were possible, the hour might pass from Him. [36] And He said, Abba, Father, all things (are) possible to You; take away this cup from me; but not what I will, but what You (will). [37] And He came and found them sleeping. And He said to Peter, Simon, do you sleep? Were you not able to watch one hour? [38] Watch and pray, that you may not enter into temptation. The spirit (is) truly willing, but the flesh (is) weak. [39] And having gone away again He prayed, saying the same thing. [40] And having returned He found them sleeping again, for their eyes were heavy; and they did not know what they should answer Him. [41] And He came the third time, and said to them, Sleep on now, and take your rest. It is enough; the hour has come; behold, the Son of man has been betrayed into the hands of sinners. [42] Rise up, let us go. Behold, the (one) betraying Me has drawn near.

[43] And immediately as He was yet speaking, Judas came up, being one of the twelve, and with him a great crowd with sword and staves, from the

30 οὐκ ἐγώ. καὶ λέγει αὐτῷ ὁ Ἰησοῦς, Ἀμὴν λέγω σοι, ὅτι
not I. And says to him — Jesus, Truly I say to you, —
σήμερον ἐν τῇ νυκτὶ ταύτῃ, πρὶν ἢ δὶς ἀλέκτορα φωνῆσαι,
Today, in — night this, before — twice (the) cock sounds,

31 τρὶς ἀπαρνήσῃ με. ὁ δὲ ἐκ περισσοῦ ἔλεγε μᾶλλον, Ἐάν με
thrice you will deny Me. he But exceedingly said more, If me
δέῃ συναποθανεῖν σοι, οὐ μή σε ἀπαρνήσομαι. ὡσαύτως
must die with You, in no way You will I deny. likewise
δὲ καὶ πάντες ἔλεγον.
And also all said.

32 Καὶ ἔρχονται εἰς χωρίον οὗ τὸ ὄνομα Γεθσημανῆ· καὶ
And they come to a place of which the name (was) Gethsemane. And
λέγει τοῖς μαθηταῖς αὐτοῦ, Καθίσατε ὧδε, ἕως προσεύξω-
He says to the disciples of Him, Sit here while I pray.

33 μαι. καὶ παραλαμβάνει τὸν Πέτρον καὶ τὸν Ἰάκωβον καὶ
And He takes along — Peter and — James and
Ἰωάννην μεθ' ἑαυτοῦ, καὶ ἤρξατο ἐκθαμβεῖσθαι καὶ ἀδη-
John with Him. And He began to be much amazed, and to be

34 μονεῖν. καὶ λέγει αὐτοῖς, Περίλυπός ἐστιν ἡ ψυχή μου ἕως
distressed, and says to them, Deeply grieved is the soul of Me unto

35 θανάτου· μείνατε ὧδε καὶ γρηγορεῖτε. καὶ προελθὼν μικρόν,
death. Remain here and watch. And going forward a little,
ἔπεσεν ἐπὶ τῆς γῆς, καὶ προσηύχετο ἵνα, εἰ δυνατόν ἐστι,
He fell on the ground, and prayed that if possible it is

36 παρέλθῃ ἀπ' αὐτοῦ ἡ ὥρα. καὶ ἔλεγεν, Ἀββᾶ, ὁ πατήρ,
might pass from Him the hour. And He said, Abba, — Father,
πάντα δυνατά σοι. παρένεγκε τὸ ποτήριον ἀπ' ἐμοῦ τοῦτο·
all things possible to You. Remove — cup from Me this;

37 ἀλλ' οὐ τί ἐγὼ θέλω, ἀλλὰ τί σύ. καὶ ἔρχεται καὶ εὑρίσκει
but not what I desire but what You. And He comes and finds
αὐτοὺς καθεύδοντας, καὶ λέγει τῷ Πέτρῳ, Σίμων, καθεύδεις;
them sleeping, and says to Peter, Simon, do you sleep?

38 οὐκ ἴσχυσας μίαν ὥραν γρηγορῆσαι; γρηγορεῖτε καὶ
not were you strong one hour to watch? Watch and
προσεύχεσθε, ἵνα μὴ εἰσέλθητε εἰς πειρασμόν. τὸ μὲν πνεῦμα
pray, that not you enter into temptation; the indeed spirit

39 πρόθυμον, ἡ δὲ σὰρξ ἀσθενής. καὶ πάλιν ἀπελθὼν προσηύ-
(is) eager, the but flesh (is) weak. And again going away He prayed,

40 ξατο, τὸν αὐτὸν λόγον εἰπών. καὶ ὑποστρέψας εὗρεν αὐτοὺς
the same word saying. And having returned He found them
πάλιν καθεύδοντας· ἦσαν γὰρ οἱ ὀφθαλμοὶ αὐτῶν βεβαρη-
again sleeping; were for the eyes of them heavy.

41 μένοι, καὶ οὐκ ᾔδεισαν τί αὐτῷ ἀποκριθῶσι. καὶ ἔρχεται τὸ
And not they knew what Him to answer. And He comes the
τρίτον, καὶ λέγει αὐτοῖς, Καθεύδετε τὸ λοιπὸν καὶ ἀναπαύε-
third, and says to them, Sleep now and rest;
σθε. ἀπέχει· ἦλθεν ἡ ὥρα· ἰδού, παραδίδοται ὁ υἱὸς τοῦ
it is enough; has come the hour; behold, is betrayed the Son —

42 ἀνθρώπου εἰς τὰς χεῖρας τῶν ἁμαρτωλῶν. ἐγείρεσθε, ἄγωμεν·
of man into the hands of the sinners. Arise, let us go;
ἰδού, ὁ παραδιδούς με ἤγγικε.
behold, the (one) betraying Me has drawn near.

43 Καὶ εὐθέως, ἔτι αὐτοῦ λαλοῦντος, παραγίνεται Ἰούδας,
And at once, yet He speaking, comes up Judas,
εἷς ὢν τῶν δώδεκα, καὶ μετ' αὐτοῦ ὄχλος πολὺς μετὰ μαχαι-
one being of the twelve, and with him a crowd large with swords

chief priests and the scribes and the elders. [44] Now he who was betraying Him had given them a sign, saying, Whomever I shall kiss, (it) is He; seize Him and lead away safely. [45] And being come, immediately coming up to Him, he said, Master! Master! And he ardently kissed Him. [46] And they laid their hands on Him and seized Him. [47] But a certain one of those standing by, having drawn the sword, struck the servant of the high priest and took off his ear. [48] And answering Jesus said to them, Have you come out with sword and staves to take Me, as against a robber? [49] I was daily with you in the Temple teaching, and you did not seize Me; but (it is) that the Scriptures may be fulfilled. [50] And leaving Him, all fled. [51] And one, a certain young man was following Him, having thrown a linen cloth around (his) naked (body); and the young men caught him; [52] but he, leaving behind the linen cloth, fled from them naked.

[53] And they led away Jesus to the high priest. And they came together to him, all the chief priests and the elders and the scribes. [54] And Peter followed Him from a distance, to the inside of the hall of the chief priest, and he was sitting with the officers, and warming himself near the fire. [55] And the chief priests and the whole sanhedrin sought testimony against Jesus, to put Him to death, and did not find (any). [56] For many bore false witness against Him, and their testimonies were not alike. [57] And some, having risen up, bore false witness against Him, saying, [58] We heard him saying, I will destroy this Temple made with hands, and in three days I will build another not made with hands. [59] And

ρῶν καὶ ξύλων, παρὰ τῶν ἀρχιερέων καὶ τῶν γραμματέων
and   clubs   from the chief priests and   the   scribes

44 καὶ τῶν πρεσβυτέρων. δεδώκει δὲ ὁ παραδιδοὺς αὐτὸν
and the   elders.       had given And the (one) betraying   Him

σύσσημον αὐτοῖς, λέγων, "Ον ἂν φιλήσω, αὐτός ἐστι κρατή-
a signal   them,   saying, Whomever I kiss,  He it is;   seize

45 σατε αὐτόν, καὶ ἀπαγάγετε ἀσφαλῶς. καὶ ἐλθὼν, εὐθέως
Him,   and lead away   securely.   And coming, at once

προσελθὼν αὐτῷ λέγει, 'Ραββί, ῥαββί· καὶ κατεφίλησεν
coming near to Him, he says,  Rabbi,   Rabbi;  and fervently kissed

46 αὐτόν. οἱ δὲ ἐπέβαλον ἐπ' αὐτὸν τὰς χεῖρας αὐτῶν, καὶ
Him.   they And laid   on   Him   the hands of them   and

47 ἐκράτησαν αὐτόν. εἷς δέ τις τῶν παρεστηκότων σπασά-
seized   Him.   one But certain of the (ones) standing by, drawing

μενος τὴν μάχαιραν ἔπαισε τὸν δοῦλον τοῦ ἀρχιερέως, καὶ
the sword   struck   the slave  of the high priest, and

48 ἀφεῖλεν αὐτοῦ τὸ ὠτίον. καὶ ἀποκριθεὶς ὁ Ἰησοῦς εἶπεν
took off of him   the ear.   And answering — Jesus   said

αὐτοῖς, Ὡς ἐπὶ λῃστὴν ἐξήλθετε μετὰ μαχαιρῶν καὶ ξύλων
to them, As against a robber come you out with   swords   and clubs

49 συλλαβεῖν με; καθ' ἡμέραν ἤμην πρὸς ὑμᾶς ἐν τῷ ἱερῷ
to take   Me? Daily   I was   with you in the Temple

διδάσκων, καὶ οὐκ ἐκρατήσατέ με· ἀλλ' ἵνα πληρωθῶσιν αἱ
teaching,   and not you did seize Me; but that may be fulfilled the

50 γραφαί. καὶ ἀφέντες αὐτὸν πάντες ἔφυγον.
Scriptures. And forsaking Him,   all   fled.

51 Καὶ εἷς τις νεανίσκος ἠκολούθει αὐτῷ, περιβεβλημένος
And one certain young man was following Him,   having thrown about

52 σινδόνα ἐπὶ γυμνοῦ. καὶ κρατοῦσιν αὐτὸν οἱ νεανίσκοι· ὁ
a linen cloth upon (his) naked (body) And seized   him the young men. he

δὲ καταλιπὼν τὴν σινδόνα γυμνὸς ἔφυγεν ἀπ' αὐτῶν.
But forsaking   the linen cloth   naked   fled from them.

53 Καὶ ἀπήγαγον τὸν Ἰησοῦν πρὸς τὸν ἀρχιερέα· καὶ συνέρ-
And they led away — Jesus   to   the high priest,   and come

χονται αὐτῷ πάντες οἱ ἀρχιερεῖς καὶ οἱ πρεσβύτεροι καὶ οἱ
together to him   all   the chief priests and the   elders   and the

54 γραμματεῖς. καὶ ὁ Πέτρος ἀπὸ μακρόθεν ἠκολούθησεν αὐτῷ
scribes.   And — Peter from   afar   followed   Him,

ἕως ἔσω εἰς τὴν αὐλὴν τοῦ ἀρχιερέως· καὶ ἦν συγκαθήμενος
until within, in the court of the high priest; and was   sitting together

55 μετὰ τῶν ὑπηρετῶν, καὶ θερμαινόμενος πρὸς τὸ φῶς. οἱ δὲ
with the   attendants, and warming himself toward the light. the And

ἀρχιερεῖς καὶ ὅλον τὸ συνέδριον ἐζήτουν κατὰ τοῦ Ἰησοῦ
chief priests and all   the sanhedrin   sought   against — Jesus

μαρτυρίαν, εἰς τὸ θανατῶσαι αὐτόν· καὶ οὐχ εὕρισκον.
witness,   for the putting to death Him,   and not   did find.

56 πολλοὶ γὰρ ἐψευδομαρτύρουν κατ' αὐτοῦ, καὶ ἴσαι αἱ
Many   falsely testified   against   Him, and identical the

57 μαρτυρίαι οὐκ ἦσαν. καί τινες ἀναστάντες ἐψευδομαρτύρουν
testimonies not were. And some   standing up   falsely testified

58 κατ' αὐτοῦ, λέγοντες ὅτι Ἡμεῖς ἠκούσαμεν αὐτοῦ λέγοντος
against Him,   saying, — We   heard   Him saying,

ὅτι Ἐγὼ καταλύσω τὸν ναὸν τοῦτον τὸν χειροποίητον, καὶ
— I   will throw down Temple this   — made with hands, and

59 διὰ τριῶν ἡμερῶν ἄλλον ἀχειροποίητον οἰκοδομήσω. καὶ
through three   days   another not made with hands I will build.   And

neither in this was their testimony alike. [60] And the high priest having stood up in the midst questioned Jesus, saying, Do you answer nothing? What do these testify against you? [61] But He was silent and answered nothing. Again the high priest was questioning Him, and said to Him, Are you the Christ, the Son of the Blessed? [62] And Jesus said, i AM! And you shall see the Son of man sitting at (the) right hand of power and coming with the clouds of the heavens. [63] And the high priest having torn his garments said, What need have we of witnesses any more? [64] You heard the blasphemy. What appears to you? And they all condemned Him to be deserving of death. [65] And some began to spit upon Him, and to cover His face, and strike Him, and to say to Him, Prophesy. And the officers struck Him with slaps.

[66] And Peter being in the court below, one of the maids of the high priest came, [67] and seeing Peter warming himself, having looked at him, said, And you were with Jesus the Nazarean. [68] But he denied, saying, I do not know nor understand what you say. And He went out into the forecourt. And a cock crowed. [69] And the maid seeing him again began to say to those standing by, This one is of them. [70] And again he denied. And after a little, those standing by again said to Peter, Truly you are from them, for you are both a Galilean and your speech agrees. [71] But he began to curse and to swear, I do not know this man whom you speak of. [72] And a second time a cock crowed. And Peter remembered the word Jesus said to him, Before a cock crows twice, you will deny Me thrice. And thinking on (it), he wept.

**60** οὐδὲ οὕτως ἴση ἦν ἡ μαρτυρία αὐτῶν. καὶ ἀναστὰς ὁ ἀρχιε-
neither thus identical was the witness of them. And standing up the high

ρεὺς εἰς τὸ μέσον ἐπηρώτησε τὸν Ἰησοῦν, λέγων, Οὐκ ἀπο-
priest in the midst, he questioned — Jesus, saying, Do not you

**61** κρίνῃ οὐδέν ; τί οὗτοί σου καταμαρτυροῦσιν ; ὁ δὲ ἐσιώπα,
answer nothing; what these you testify against? He But was silent,

καὶ οὐδὲν ἀπεκρίνατο. πάλιν ὁ ἀρχιερεὺς ἐπηρώτα αὐτόν, καὶ
and nothing answered. Again the high priest questioned Him, and

**62** λέγει αὐτῷ, Σὺ εἶ ὁ Χριστός, ὁ υἱὸς τοῦ εὐλογητοῦ ; ὁ δὲ
says to Him, You are the Christ, the Son of the Blessed (One)? — And

Ἰησοῦς εἶπεν, Ἐγώ εἰμι. καὶ ὄψεσθε τὸν υἱὸν τοῦ ἀνθρώπου
Jesus said, I AM! And you will see the Son — of man

καθήμενον ἐκ δεξιῶν τῆς δυνάμεως, καὶ ἐρχόμενον μετὰ τῶν
sitting off (the) right of the Power, and coming with the

**63** νεφελῶν τοῦ οὐρανοῦ. ὁ δὲ ἀρχιερεὺς διαρρήξας τοὺς
clouds of Heaven. the And high priest, tearing the

χιτῶνας αὐτοῦ λέγει, Τί ἔτι χρείαν ἔχομεν μαρτύρων ;
garments of him, says, Why still need do we have of witnesses?

**64** ἠκούσατε τῆς βλασφημίας· τί ὑμῖν φαίνεται ; οἱ δὲ πάντες
You heard the blasphemy. What to you appears it? they And all

**65** κατέκριναν αὐτὸν εἶναι ἔνοχον θανάτου. καὶ ἤρξαντό τινες
condemned Him to be liable of death. And began some

ἐμπτύειν αὐτῷ, καὶ περικαλύπτειν τὸ πρόσωπον αὐτοῦ,
to spit at Him, and to cover the face of Him,

καὶ κολαφίζειν αὐτόν, καὶ λέγειν αὐτῷ, Προφήτευσον· καὶ
and to beat with a fist Him, and to say to Him, Prophesy! And

οἱ ὑπηρέται ῥαπίσμασιν αὐτὸν ἔβαλλον.
the attendants with slaps Him struck.

**66** Καὶ ὄντος τοῦ Πέτρου ἐν τῇ αὐλῇ κάτω, ἔρχεται μία τῶν
And being — Peter in the court below, comes one of the

**67** παιδισκῶν τοῦ ἀρχιερέως, καὶ ἰδοῦσα τὸν Πέτρον θερμαινό-
maids of the high priest, and seeing — Peter warming

μενον, ἐμβλέψασα αὐτῷ λέγει, Καὶ σὺ μετὰ τοῦ Ναζαρηνοῦ
himself, looking at him says, And you with the Nazarene

**68** Ἰησοῦ ἦσθα. ὁ δὲ ἠρνήσατο, λέγων, Οὐκ οἶδα, οὐδὲ
Jesus were. he But denied, saying, not I know, nor

ἐπίσταμαι τί σὺ λέγεις. καὶ ἐξῆλθεν ἔξω εἰς τὸ προαύλιον·
understand what you say. And he went outside into the forecourt;

**69** καὶ ἀλέκτωρ ἐφώνησε. καὶ ἡ παιδίσκη ἰδοῦσα αὐτὸν πάλιν
and a cock crowed. And the maid seeing him again

ἤρξατο λέγειν τοῖς παρεστηκόσιν ὅτι Οὗτος ἐξ αὐτῶν ἐστίν.
began to say to the (ones) standing by, This one of them is.

**70** ὁ δὲ πάλιν ἠρνεῖτο. καὶ μετὰ μικρὸν πάλιν οἱ παρεστῶτες
he But again denied. And after a little again the (ones) standing by

ἔλεγον τῷ Πέτρῳ, Ἀληθῶς ἐξ αὐτῶν εἶ· καὶ γὰρ Γαλιλαῖος
said — to Peter, Truly of them you are; even for a Galilean

**71** εἶ, καὶ ἡ λαλιά σου ὁμοιάζει. ὁ δὲ ἤρξατο ἀναθεματίζειν καὶ
you and the speech of you agrees. he And began to curse and
are,

**72** ὀμνύειν ὅτι Οὐκ οἶδα τὸν ἄνθρωπον τοῦτον ὃν λέγετε. καὶ
to swear, — not I know — man this whom you say. And

ἐκ δευτέρου ἀλέκτωρ ἐφώνησε. καὶ ἀνεμνήσθη ὁ Πέτρος τοῦ
for a second time a cock crowed. And remembered — Peter the

ῥήματος οὗ εἶπεν αὐτῷ ὁ Ἰησοῦς, ὅτι Πρὶν ἀλέκτορα
word said to him — Jesus, Before a cock

φωνῆσαι δίς, ἀπαρνήσῃ με τρίς. καὶ ἐπιβαλὼν ἔκλαιε.
crows twice, you will deny Me thrice. And thinking on (it) he wept.

## CHAPTER 15

CHAPTER 15
[1] And immediately in the morning, the chief priests with the elders and scribes having formed a counsel, and the whole sandedrin having bound Jesus, (they) carried (Him) away and delivered (Him) up to Pilate. [2] And Pilate questioned Him, Are you the king of the Jews? And He answering said to him, You say it.

[3] And the chief priests urgently accused Him (of) many things; but He answered nothing. [4] But Pilate again questioned Him, saying, Do you answer nothing? Behold, how many things they testify against you. [5] But Jesus answered nothing any more; so as (for) Pilate to marvel. [6] And at a feast he released to them one prisoner, whom they asked. [7] And there was one called Barabbas, being bound with the insurgents, who in the insurrection had committed murder. [8] And crying aloud, the crowd began to beg (him to do) as he always did to them. [9] But Pilate answered them, saying, Do you desire I should release to you the king of the Jews? [10] For he knew that the chief priests had delivered Him up through envy. [11] But the chief priests stirred up the crowd that he might rather release Barabbas to them. [12] And Pilate answering again said to them, What then desire you I do (to him) whom you call king of the Jews? [13] And again they cried out, Crucify him! [14] But Pilate said to them, For what evil did he do? But they much more cried out, Crucify him! [15] And Pilate deciding to do the easiest to the crowd, he released Barabbas to them, and having whipped (Him), delivered up Jesus that He be crucified.

[16] And the soldiers led Him away inside the court, which is (the) praetorium; and they called together the entire band. [17] And they put

1 Καὶ εὐθέως ἐπὶ τὸ πρωῒ συμβούλιον ποιήσαντες οἱ
And immediately on (morn) early, a council having made the
ἀρχιερεῖς μετὰ τῶν πρεσβυτέρων καὶ γραμματέων, καὶ ὅλον
chief priests with the elders and scribes, and all
τὸ συνέδριον, δήσαντες τὸν Ἰησοῦν ἀπήνεγκαν καὶ παρέδω-
the sanhedrin, having bound — Jesus led (Him) away and delivered

2 καν τῷ Πιλάτῳ. καὶ ἐπηρώτησεν αὐτὸν ὁ Πιλάτος, Σὺ εἶ ὁ
(Him) — to Pilate. And questioned Him — Pilate, You are the
βασιλεὺς τῶν Ἰουδαίων; ὁ δὲ ἀποκριθεὶς εἶπεν αὐτῷ, Σὺ
king of the Jews? He And answering said to him, You

3 λέγεις. καὶ κατηγόρουν αὐτοῦ οἱ ἀρχιερεῖς πολλά· αὐτὸς δὲ
say (it). And accused Him the chief priests many things, He but

4 οὐδὲν ἀπεκρίνατο. ὁ δὲ Πιλάτος πάλιν ἐπηρώτησεν αὐτόν,
nothing answered. — But Pilate again questioned Him,
λέγων, Οὐκ ἀποκρίνῃ οὐδέν; ἴδε, πόσα σου καταμαρτυ-
saying, not Do you answer nothing? Behold, how many things you they testify

5 ροῦσιν. ὁ δὲ Ἰησοῦς οὐκέτι οὐδὲν ἀπεκρίθη, ὥστε θαυμάζειν
against. — But Jesus no more nothing answered, so as to marvel
τὸν Πιλάτον.
Pilate.

6 Κατὰ δὲ ἑορτὴν ἀπέλυεν αὐτοῖς ἕνα δέσμιον, ὅνπερ
at And a feast he released to them one prisoner, whomever

7 ᾐτοῦντο. ἦν δὲ ὁ λεγόμενος Βαραββᾶς μετὰ τῶν συστασια-
they asked. was And one called Barabbas with the insurgents

8 στῶν δεδεμένος, οἵτινες ἐν τῇ στάσει φόνον πεποιήκεισαν. καὶ
having been bound, who in the insurrection murder had committed. And
ἀναβοήσας ὁ ὄχλος ἤρξατο αἰτεῖσθαι καθὼς ἀεὶ ἐποίει αὐτοῖς.
crying aloud the crowd began to beg as always he did for them.

9 ὁ δὲ Πιλάτος ἀπεκρίθη αὐτοῖς, λέγων, Θέλετε ἀπολύσω ὑμῖν
—But Pilate answered them, saying, Desire you I may release to you

10 τὸν βασιλέα τῶν Ἰουδαίων; ἐγίνωσκε γὰρ ὅτι διὰ φθόνον
the king of the Jews? he knew For that for envy

11 παραδεδώκεισαν αὐτὸν οἱ ἀρχιερεῖς. οἱ δὲ ἀρχιερεῖς ἀνέσει-
had delivered over Him the chief priests. the But chief priests stirred
σαν τὸν ὄχλον, ἵνα μᾶλλον τὸν Βαραββᾶν ἀπολύσῃ αὐτοῖς.
up the crowd, that rather — Barabbas he should release to them.

12 ὁ δὲ Πιλάτος ἀποκριθεὶς πάλιν εἶπεν αὐτοῖς, Τί οὖν θέλετε
— But Pilate answering again said to them, What then wish you

13 ποιήσω ὃν λέγετε βασιλέα τῶν Ἰουδαίων; οἱ δὲ πάλιν
I do (with) whom you call king of the Jews? they And again

14 ἔκραξαν, Σταύρωσον αὐτόν. ὁ δὲ Πιλάτος ἔλεγεν αὐτοῖς, Τί
cried out, Crucify Him! — But Pilate said to them, what
γὰρ κακὸν ἐποίησεν; οἱ δὲ περισσοτέρως ἔκραξαν, Σταύ-
For evil did he do? they And much more cried out, Crucify

15 ρωσον αὐτόν. ὁ δὲ Πιλάτος βουλόμενος τῷ ὄχλῳ τὸ ἱκανὸν
Him! — But Pilate deciding the crowd the easiest
ποιῆσαι, ἀπέλυσεν αὐτοῖς τὸν Βαραββᾶν· καὶ παρέδωκε τὸν
to do, released to them Barabbas, and delivered up —
Ἰησοῦν, φραγελλώσας, ἵνα σταυρωθῇ.
Jesus, having whipped (Him) that He might be crucified.

16 Οἱ δὲ στρατιῶται ἀπήγαγον αὐτὸν ἔσω τῆς αὐλῆς, ὅ ἐστι
the And soldiers led away Him inside the court, which is

17 πραιτώριον, καὶ συγκαλοῦσιν ὅλην τὴν σπεῖραν. καὶ
praetorium, and they call together all the cohort. And

purple on Him, and they plaited and placed a crown of thorns on Him. [18] And they began to salute Him, Hail, King of the Jews! [19] And they struck His head with a reed, and spat on Him, and bending the knees bowed down to Him. [20] And when they had mocked Him, they took the purple off Him, and put His own garments on Him; and they led Him out that they might crucify Him. [21] And they compelled one passing by, Simon a Cyrenian coming from a field, the father of Alexander and Rufus, that he might carry His cross.

[22] And they brought Him to a place, Golgotha, which translated is, place of a skull. [23] And they gave Him wine medicated with myrrh to drink; but He did not take (it). [24] And having crucified Him, they divided His garments, casting a lot on them, who (and) what (each) should take. [25] And it was (the) third hour, and they crucified Him. [26] And the title of His accusation was written above: THE KING OF THE JEWS. [27] And they crucified two robbers with Him, one at (the) right (hand), and one at (the) left of Him.

[28] And the Scripture was fulfilled which says, "And He was numbered with (the) lawless," [29] And those passing by blasphemed Him, shaking their heads and saying, Aha, (you) razing the temple, and in three days building (it)! [30] Save yourself and come down from the cross. [31] And likewise the chief priests and the scribes mocking to one another said, He saved others; himself he cannot save. [32] The Christ, the King of Israel? Let him now come down from the cross, that we may see and believe. And they who were crucified with Him insulted Him. [33] And (the) sixth hour being

**18** ἐνδύουσιν αὐτὸν πορφύραν, καὶ περιτιθέασιν αὐτῷ πλέ-
they put on   Him   purple,     and placed around    Him   having
ξαντες ἀκάνθινον στέφανον, καὶ ἤρξαντο ἀσπάζεσθαι αὐτόν,
plaited a thorny     crown.     And they began to salute     Him,

**19** Χαῖρε, βασιλεῦ τῶν Ἰουδαίων· καὶ ἔτυπτον αὐτοῦ τὴν
Hail,     King of the    Jews!     And they struck of Him    the
κεφαλὴν καλάμῳ, καὶ ἐνέπτυον αὐτῷ, καὶ τιθέντες τὰ γόνατα
head   with a reed, and   spit    at Him; and placing the    knees

**20** προσεκύνουν αὐτῷ. καὶ ὅτε ἐνέπαιξαν αὐτῷ, ἐξέδυσαν
did homage to    Him.     And when they had mocked Him, they took off
αὐτὸν τὴν πορφύραν, καὶ ἐνέδυσαν αὐτὸν τὰ ἱμάτια τὰ ἴδια.
Him    the    purple,     and put on     Him the garments, his own.

**21** Καὶ ἐξάγουσιν αὐτον ἵνα σταυρώσωσιν αὐτόν. καὶ
And they lead forth   Him,    that they might crucify   Him.    And
ἀγγαρεύουσι παράγοντά τινα Σίμωνα Κυρηναῖον, ἐρχόμενον
they compel     passing by   a certain Simon, a Cyrenian    coming
ἀπ᾽ ἀγροῦ, τὸν πατέρα Ἀλεξάνδρου καὶ Ῥούφου, ἵνα ἄρῃ
from a field,   the    father   of Alexander and   of Rufus, that he bear

**22** τὸν σταυρὸν αὐτοῦ. καὶ φέρουσιν αὐτὸν ἐπὶ Γολγοθᾶ τόπον,
the   cross    of Him. And they bring Him to   Golgotha    place,

**23** ὅ ἐστι μεθερμηνευόμενον, κρανίου τόπος καὶ ἐδίδουν αὐτῷ
which is,   being translated,   of a Skull Place.   And they gave    Him

**24** πιεῖν ἐσμυρνισμένον οἶνον· ὁ δὲ οὐκ ἔλαβε. καὶ σταυρώσαντες
to
drink   spiced with myrrh wine, He but not did take. And having crucified
αὐτόν, διεμέριζον τὰ ἱμάτια αὐτοῦ, βάλλοντες κλῆρον ἐπ᾽
Him,     they divided the garments of Him,   casting     a lot     on

**25** αὐτά, τίς τί ἄρῃ. ἦν δὲ ὥρα τρίτη, καὶ ἐσταύρωσαν αὐτόν.
them, who what may take. was And hour third,   and they crucified Him.

**26** καὶ ἦν ἡ ἐπιγραφὴ τῆς αἰτίας αὐτοῦ ἐπιγεγραμμένη, Ὁ
And was the superscription of the accusa-tion of Him   written over (Him), THE

**27** βασιλεὺς τῶν Ἰουδαίων. καὶ σὺν αὐτῷ σταυροῦσι δύο
KING    OF THE    JEWS.    And with   Him they crucify   two

**28** λῃστάς, ἕνα ἐκ δεξιῶν καὶ ἕνα ἐξ εὐωνύμων αὐτοῦ. καὶ
robbers, one off (the) right, and one off   (the) left   of Him.     And
ἐπληρώθη ἡ γραφὴ ἡ λέγουσα, Καὶ μετὰ ἀνόμων ἐλογίσθη.
was fulfilled the scripture which says, And with (the) lawless He was counted.

**29** καὶ οἱ παραπορευόμενοι ἐβλασφήμουν αὐτόν, κινοῦντες τὰς
And those passing by     blasphemed    Him, shaking     the
κεφαλὰς αὐτῶν, καὶ λέγοντες, Οὐά, ὁ καταλύων τὸν ναόν,
heads of them, and   saying,    Aha, the (one) razing   the temple

**30** καὶ ἐν τρισὶν ἡμέραις οἰκοδομῶν, σῶσον σεαυτόν. καὶ κατάβα
and in three    days    building,    save    yourself,   and come down

**31** ἀπὸ τοῦ σταυροῦ. ὁμοίως δὲ καὶ οἱ ἀρχιερεῖς ἐμπαίζοντες
from the    cross.     likewise And also the chief priests mocking
πρὸς ἀλλήλους μετὰ τῶν γραμματέων ἔλεγον, Ἄλλους
to one another, with   the     scribes,     said,     Others

**32** ἔσωσεν, ἑαυτὸν οὐ δύναται σῶσαι. ὁ Χριστὸς ὁ βασιλεὺς
he saved, himself   not he is able   to save; the Christ, the   king
τοῦ Ἰσραὴλ καταβάτω νῦν ἀπὸ τοῦ σταυροῦ, ἵνα ἴδωμεν
— of Israel, let Him descend now from   the    cross,    that we may see
καὶ πιστεύσωμεν. καὶ οἱ συνεσταυρωμένοι αὐτῷ ὠνείδιζον
and   believe.     And the (ones) crucified with    Him    insulted
αὐτόν.
Him.

**33** Γενομένης δὲ ὥρας ἕκτης, σκότος ἐγένετο ἐφ᾽ ὅλην τὴν γῆν
occurring   And hour sixth,    darkness   came    over    all   the   land

come, darkness came over all the land until (the) ninth hour; [34] and at the ninth hour Jesus cried with a loud voice, saying, Eloi, Eloi, lama, sabachthani? which being translated is, My God, My God, why did You forsake Me? [35] And hearing, some of those standing by said, Behold, he calls Elijah. [36] And one running up, and having filled a sponge with vinegar, and putting it on a reed, gave Him to drink saying, Leave. Let us see if Elijah comes to lower Him.

[37] And having let out a loud cry, Jesus expired. [38] And the veil of the Temple was torn into two from top to bottom. [39] And the centurion standing off opposite Him seeing that having cried out so, He expired, (he) said, Truly, this Man was Son of God. [40] And women from a distance were watching, in whom also was Mary the Magdalene; and Mary the mother of James the less and Joses; and Salome, [41] who also followed Him and ministered to Him when He was in Galilee; and many other who came up with Him to Jerusalem.

[42] And evening already being come, since it was (the) preparation, that is (the) day before sabbath, [43] Joseph of Arimathea came, (an) honorable councillor, who himself was also waiting for the kingdom of God, having boldness he went into Pilate and begged the body of Jesus. [44] And Pilate wondered if He were already dead; and having called to the centurion, he questioned him if He had been dead long. [45] And having known from the centurion, he granted the body to Joseph. [46] And having bought a linen cloth, and having taken Him down, he wrapped (Him) in the linen cloth, and laid Him in a tomb which was cut out of a rock, and rolled a stone to the mouth of the tomb. [47] And Mary Magdalene,

**34** ἕως ὥρας ἐννάτης. καὶ τῇ ὥρᾳ τῇ ἐννάτῃ ἐβόησεν ὁ Ἰησοῦς
until hour ninth. And at the hour — ninth cried — Jesus
φωνῇ μεγάλῃ, λέγων, Ἐλωΐ, Ἐλωΐ, λαμμᾶ σαβαχθανί;
with a voice great, saying, Eloi, Eloi, Lama sabachthani?
ὅ ἐστι μεθερμηνευόμενον, Ὁ Θεός μου, ὁ Θεός μου, εἰς τί με
which is, being translated, The God of Me, the God of Me, why Me

**35** ἐγκατέλιπες; καί τινες τῶν παρεστηκότων ἀκούσαντες
did You forsake? And some of the (ones) standing by having heard

**36** ἔλεγον, Ἰδού, Ἠλίαν φωνεῖ. δραμὼν δὲ εἷς, καὶ γεμίσας
said, Behold, Elijah he calls. running And one, and having filled
σπόγγον ὄξους, περιθείς τε καλάμῳ, ἐπότιζεν αὐτόν, λέγων,
a sponge of vinegar, putting it and on a reed, gave to drink Him, saying,

**37** Ἄφετε, ἴδωμεν εἰ ἔρχεται Ἠλίας καθελεῖν αὐτόν. ὁ δὲ
Leave, let us see if comes Elijah to take down Him. — But

**38** Ἰησοῦς ἀφεὶς φωνὴν μεγάλην ἐξέπνευσε. καὶ τὸ καταπέτασμα
Jesus letting out a voice great expired. And the veil

**39** τοῦ ναοῦ ἐσχίσθη εἰς δύο ἀπὸ ἄνωθεν ἕως κάτω. ἰδὼν δὲ ὁ
of the temple was torn into two, from top to bottom. seeing And the
κεντυρίων ὁ παρεστηκὼς ἐξ ἐναντίας αὐτοῦ ὅτι οὕτω
centurion — standing near off the opposite of Him, that thus
κράξας ἐξέπνευσεν, εἶπεν, Ἀληθῶς ὁ ἄνθρωπος οὗτος υἱὸς
having cried out He expired, said, Truly, — man this Son

**40** ἦν Θεοῦ. ἦσαν δὲ καὶ γυναῖκες ἀπὸ μακρόθεν θεωροῦσαι,
was of God. were And also women from afar watching,
ἐν αἷς ἦν καὶ Μαρία ἡ Μαγδαληνή, καὶ Μαρία ἡ τοῦ
among whom was also Mary the Magdalene, and Mary the —

**41** Ἰακώβου τοῦ μικροῦ καὶ Ἰωσῆ μήτηρ καὶ Σαλώμη, αἳ καί,
of James the less, and of Joses (the) mother and Salome, who also
ὅτε ἦν ἐν τῇ Γαλιλαίᾳ, ἠκολούθουν αὐτῷ, καὶ διηκόνουν
when He was in — Galilee had followed Him, and ministered
αὐτῷ, καὶ ἄλλαι πολλαὶ αἱ συναναβᾶσαι αὐτῷ εἰς
to Him, and other (women) many who came up with Him to
Ἱεροσόλυμα.
Jerusalem.

**42** Καὶ ἤδη ὀψίας γενομένης, ἐπεὶ ἦν Παρασκευή, ὅ ἐστι
And now evening occurring, since it was (the) preparation which is

**43** προσάββατον, ἦλθεν Ἰωσὴφ ὁ ἀπὸ Ἀριμαθαίας, εὐσχήμων
(the) day before sabbath, coming Joseph from Arimathea, an honorable
βουλευτής, ὃς καὶ αὐτὸς ἦν προσδεχόμενος τὴν βασιλείαν
councillor, who also (him)self was expecting the kingdom
τοῦ Θεοῦ· τολμήσας εἰσῆλθε πρὸς Πιλάτον, καὶ ἠτήσατο
— of God, taking courage went in to Pilate, and asked

**44** τὸ σῶμα τοῦ Ἰησοῦ. ὁ δὲ Πιλάτος ἐθαύμασεν εἰ ἤδη
the body — of Jesus. — And Pilate marveled if already
τέθνηκε· καὶ προσκαλεσάμενος τὸν κεντυρίωνα, ἐπηρώτησεν
He had died, and calling near the centurion, he questioned

**45** αὐτὸν εἰ πάλαι ἀπέθανε. καὶ γνοὺς ἀπὸ τοῦ κεντυρίωνος,
him if long ago He died. And knowing from the centurion,

**46** ἐδωρήσατο τὸ σῶμα τῷ Ἰωσήφ. καὶ ἀγοράσας σινδόνα,
he granted the body to Joseph. And having bought a linen cloth
καὶ καθελὼν αὐτόν, ἐνείλησε τῇ σινδόνι, καὶ κατέθηκεν αὐτὸν
and having taken Him, he wrapped in the linen, and laid Him
ἐν μνημείῳ, ὃ ἦν λελατομημένον ἐκ πέτρας· καὶ προσεκύλισε
in a tomb, which was cut out of rock, and rolled

**47** λίθον ἐπὶ τὴν θύραν τοῦ μνημείου. ἡ δὲ Μαρία ἡ Μαγδαληνή
a stone against the door of the tomb. — And Mary the Magdalene

and Mary of Joseph, saw where He was laid.

καὶ Μαρία ᾿Ιωσῆ ἐθεώρουν ποῦ τίθεται.
and　Mary of Joses　beheld　where He had been laid.

## CHAPTER 16

[1] And the sabbath being past, Mary Magdalene and Mary (the mother) of James, and Salome brought spices that having come they might anoint Him. [2] And very early on the first of the week they came to the tomb, the sun having risen. [3] And they said among themselves, Who will roll away for us the stone from the mouth of the tomb? [4] And having looked up, they see that the stone has been rolled away; for it was very large. [5] And having entered into the tomb, they saw a young man sitting on the right, clothed with a white robe, and they were greatly amazed. [6] But He said to them, Do not be amazed. You seek Jesus the Nazarene, who has been crucified. He has risen, He is not here; see the place where they laid Him? [7] But go, say to His disciples and to Peter, that He goes before you into Galilee; you shall see Him there as He said to you. [8] And having gone out quickly, they fled from the tomb. And trembling and ecstasy took hold of them. And neither did they say anything to anyone, for they were afraid.

[9] Now having risen early (the) first of the week, He first appeared to Mary Magdalene, from whom He had cast out seven demons. [10] Having gone she told those who had been with Him, (who were) grieving and weeping. [11] And they having heard that He was alive and had been seen by her did not believe. [12] And after these things He was revealed in another form to two of them as they walked going into (the) country. [13] And having gone they told (it) to the rest; neither did they believe them. [14] Afterward as they

## CHAPTER 16

1　Καὶ διαγενομένου τοῦ σαββάτου, Μαρία ἡ Μαγδαληνὴ
　　And　passing　　the sabbath,　　Mary the Magdalene,
　　καὶ Μαρία ἡ τοῦ ᾿Ιακώβου καὶ Σαλώμη ἠγόρασαν ἀρώματα,
　　and　Mary the (mother) of James and Salome　bought　　spices
2　ἵνα ἐλθοῦσαι ἀλείψωσιν αὐτόν. καὶ λίαν πρωῒ τῆς μιᾶς
　　that　coming they might anoint Him.　And　very　early　on the first
　　σαββάτων ἔρχονται ἐπὶ τὸ μνημεῖον, ἀνατείλαντος τοῦ
　　of the week　they come　upon the　tomb,　　having risen　　the
3　ἡλίου. καὶ ἔλεγον πρὸς ἑαυτάς, Τίς ἀποκυλίσει ἡμῖν τὸν
　　sun.　And they said to themselves, Who will roll away for us the
4　λίθον ἐκ τῆς θύρας τοῦ μνημείου; καὶ ἀναβλέψασαι
　　stone from the　door of the　　tomb?　　And　looking up
　　θεωροῦσιν ὅτι ἀποκεκύλισται ὁ λίθος· ἦν γὰρ μέγας
　　they see　　that has been rolled back the stone. it was For　great
5　σφόδρα. καὶ εἰσελθοῦσαι εἰς τὸ μνημεῖον, εἶδον νεανίσκον
　　exceedingly. And having entered into the　tomb,　　they saw a young man
　　καθήμενον ἐν τοῖς δεξιοῖς, περιβεβλημένον στολὴν λευκήν·
　　sitting　　on the　right,　having been clothed (in) a robe　white.
6　καὶ ἐξεθαμβήθησαν. ὁ δὲ λέγει αὐταῖς, Μὴ ἐκθαμβεῖσθε·
　　and they were much amazed. he But says　to them,　not Be much amazed;
　　᾿Ιησοῦν ζητεῖτε τὸν Ναζαρηνὸν τὸν ἐσταυρωμένον· ἠγέρθη,
　　Jesus　you seek,　the Nazarene;　　– having been crucified, He was raised
7　οὐκ ἔστιν ὧδε· ἴδε, ὁ τόπος ὅπου ἔθηκαν αὐτόν. ἀλλ᾿
　　not He is　here; behold, the place　where they put Him.　But
　　ὑπάγετε, εἴπατε τοῖς μαθηταῖς αὐτοῦ καὶ τῷ Πέτρῳ ὅτι
　　go　　tell　the　disciples　of Him, and　–　Peter,　–
　　Προάγει ὑμᾶς εἰς τὴν Γαλιλαίαν· ἐκεῖ αὐτὸν ὄψεσθε, καθὼς
　　He goes before you into –　　Galilee;　there Him you will see, even as
8　εἶπεν ὑμῖν. καὶ ἐξελθοῦσαι ταχὺ ἔφυγον ἀπὸ τοῦ μνημείου·
　　He told you. And　going out　quickly, they fled from　the　tomb.
　　εἶχε δὲ αὐτὰς τρόμος καὶ ἔκστασις· καὶ οὐδενὶ οὐδὲν εἶπον,
　　held And them　trembling and ecstasy;　　and no one nothing they told;
　　ἐφοβοῦντο γάρ.
　　they were afraid for.
9　᾿Αναστὰς δὲ πρωῒ πρώτῃ σαββάτου ἐφάνη πρῶτον
　　having risen And early on the first of the week, He appeared first
　　Μαρίᾳ τῇ Μαγδαληνῇ, ἀφ᾿ ἧς ἐκβεβλήκει ἑπτὰ δαιμόνια.
　　to Mary the Magdalene,　from whom He had cast seven　demons.
10　ἐκείνη πορευθεῖσα ἀπήγγειλε τοῖς μετ᾿ αὐτοῦ γενομένοις,
　　That (one) having gone reported to the (ones) with Him　having been,
11　πενθοῦσι καὶ κλαίουσι. κἀκεῖνοι ἀκούσαντες ὅτι ζῇ καὶ
　　mourning　and weeping.　And those　hearing　　that He lives and
　　ἐθεάθη ὑπ᾿ αὐτῆς ἠπίστησαν.
　　was seen by　her they disbelieved.
12　Μετὰ δὲ ταῦτα δυσὶν ἐξ αὐτῶν περιπατοῦσιν ἐφανερώθη
　　after　And these to two of　them　walking　　He was revealed
　　　　things
13　ἐν ἑτέρᾳ μορφῇ, πορευομένοις εἰς ἀγρόν. κἀκεῖνοι ἀπελθόντες
　　in a different form,　going　　into the country. And those going
　　ἀπήγγειλαν τοῖς λοιποῖς· οὐδὲ ἐκείνοις ἐπίστευσαν.
　　reported　　to the rest;　neither those　they believed.
14　῞Υστερον ἀνακειμένοις αὐτοῖς τοῖς ἕνδεκα ἐφανερώθη, καὶ
　　Later　as reclined　　they　to the eleven He was revealed, and

reclined, He was revealed to the Eleven, and reproached their unbelief and hardness of heart, because they did not believe those who had seen Him arisen. [15] And He said to them, Having gone into the world, preach the gospel to all the creation. [16] He that believes and is baptized shall be saved, and he that does not believe shall be condemned. [17] And these signs shall follow those that believe: they shall cast out demons in My name; they shall speak new languages; [18] they shall take up snakes; and if they drink anything deadly it shall in no way hurt them; they shall lay hands on (the) sick, and they shall be well.

[19] Then indeed, after speaking to them, the Lord was taken up into Heaven, and sat at (the) right hand of God. [20] And having gone forth they preached everywhere, the Lord working with (them), and confirming the word by the signs following. Amen.

ὠνείδισε τὴν ἀπιστίαν αὐτῶν καὶ σκληροκαρδίαν, ὅτι τοῖς
reproached the  unbelief   of them and hardness of heart, because those

**15** θεασαμένοις αὐτὸν ἐγηγερμένον οὐκ ἐπίστευσαν. καὶ εἶπεν
having seen   Him. having been raised, not they believed.   And He said

αὐτοῖς, Πορευθέντες εἰς τὸν κόσμον ἅπαντα, κηρύξατε τὸ
to them, Going        into the  world    all,    preach    the

**16** εὐαγγέλιον πάσῃ τῇ κτίσει. ὁ πιστεύσας καὶ βαπτισθεὶς
gospel       to all   the creation. The (one) believing and being baptized

**17** σωθήσεται· ὁ δὲ ἀπιστήσας κατακριθήσεται. σημεῖα δὲ τοῖς
will be saved; he but not believing will be condemned.   signs And to those

πιστεύσασι ταῦτα παρακολουθήσει· ἐν τῷ ὀνόματί μου
believing    these    will follow,    in the    name   of Me

**18** δαιμόνια ἐκβαλοῦσι· γλώσσαις λαλήσουσι καιναῖς· ὄφεις
demons they will cast out; languages   they shall speak  new;    snakes.

ἀροῦσι· κἂν θανάσιμόν τι πίωσιν, οὐ μὴ αὐτοὺς βλάψει· ἐπὶ
they will take; and if deadly anything they drink, in no way them it will hurt; on

ἀρρώστους χεῖρας ἐπιθήσουσι, καὶ καλῶς ἕξουσιν.
infirm ones   hands  they will place, and wellness they will have.

**19** Ὁ μὲν οὖν Κύριος, μετὰ τὸ λαλῆσαι αὐτοῖς, ἀνελήφθη εἰς
The indeed then Lord,  after the  speaking   to them, was taken up into

**20** τὸν οὐρανόν, καὶ ἐκάθισεν ἐκ δεξιῶν τοῦ Θεοῦ. ἐκεῖνοι δὲ
—  Heaven,   and  sat    off (the) right   —  of God. they   But

ἐξελθόντες ἐκήρυξαν πανταχοῦ, τοῦ Κυρίου συνεργοῦντος,
having gone out preached everywhere,  the   Lord   working with (them),

καὶ τὸν λόγον βεβαιοῦντος διὰ τῶν ἐπακολουθούντων
and  the   word   confirming  through the   accompanying

σημείων. Ἀμήν.
signs.    Amen.

# ΕΥΑΓΓΕΛΙΟΝ
## GOSPEL
# ΤΟ ΚΑΤΑ ΛΟΥΚΑΝ
### THE ACCORDING TO LUKE

## THE
## GOSPEL ACCORDING TO
## LUKE

### CHAPTER 1

[1] Since many took in hand to draw up an account concerning the matters having been borne out among us, [2] as those from (the) beginning delivered to us, becoming eyewitnesses and ministers of the word. [3] it seemed good also to me, having traced out all things accurately from the first, in order to write to you, most excellent Theophilus, [4] that you may know the certainty concerning (all that) which you were taught (in) words.

[5] There was in the days of Herod the king of Judea a certain priest, Zacharias by name, of (the) course of Abijah, and his wife of the daughters of Aaron, and her name Elizabeth. [6] And they were both righteous before God, walking blameless in all the commandments and ordinances of the Lord. [7] And a child was not (born) to them, since Elizabeth was barren, and both were advanced in their days. [8] And it came to pass in fulfilling his priestly service in the order of his course before God, [9] according to the custom of the priestly service, it fell to him by lot to burn incense, having entered into the Temple of the Lord. [10] And all the multitude of the people were praying outside at the hour of incense. [11] And an angel of (the) Lord

### CHAPTER 1

**1** Ἐπειδήπερ πολλοὶ ἐπεχείρησαν ἀνατάξασθαι διήγησιν
Since many took in hand to draw up an account
**2** περὶ τῶν πεπληροφορημένων ἐν ἡμῖν πραγμάτων, καθὼς
concerning the having been fully borne out among us matters. as
παρέδοσαν ἡμῖν οἱ ἀπ' ἀρχῆς αὐτόπται καὶ ὑπηρέται
delivered to us the (ones) from beginning, eyewitnesses and ministers
**3** γενόμενοι τοῦ λόγου, ἔδοξε κἀμοί, παρηκολουθηκότι ἄνωθεν
becoming of the word, it seemed good also to me, following from the first
**4** πᾶσιν ἀκριβῶς, καθεξῆς σοι γράψαι, κράτιστε Θεόφιλε, ἵνα
all things accurately, in order to you to write, most excellent Theophilus, that
ἐπιγνῷς περὶ ὧν κατηχήθης λόγων τὴν ἀσφάλειαν.
you may know about which you were taught (in) words the certainty.
**5** Ἐγένετο ἐν ταῖς ἡμέραις Ἡρώδου τοῦ βασιλέως τῆς
There was in the days of Herod the king of the
Ἰουδαίας ἱερεύς τις ὀνόματι Ζαχαρίας, ἐξ ἐφημερίας Ἀβιά·
of Judea a priest a certain by name Zacharias, of (the) daily course of Abia,
καὶ ἡ γυνὴ αὐτοῦ ἐκ τῶν θυγατέρων Ἀαρών, καὶ τὸ ὄνομα
and the wife of him of the daughters of Aaron, and the name
**6** αὐτῆς Ἐλισάβετ. ἦσαν δὲ δίκαιοι ἀμφότεροι ἐνώπιον τοῦ
of her Elizabeth. they were And righteous both in (the) sight of —
Θεοῦ, πορευόμενοι ἐν πάσαις ταῖς ἐντολαῖς καὶ δικαιώμασι
God, walking in all the commandments and ordinances
**7** τοῦ Κυρίου ἄμεμπτοι. καὶ οὐκ ἦν αὐτοῖς τέκνον, καθότι
of the Lord blameless. And not was to them a child, because
ἡ Ἐλισάβετ ἦν στεῖρα, καὶ ἀμφότεροι προβεβηκότες ἐν ταῖς
— Elizabeth was barren, and both advanced in the
ἡμέραις αὐτῶν ἦσαν.
days of them were.
**8** Ἐγένετο δὲ ἐν τῷ ἱερατεύειν αὐτὸν ἐν τῇ τάξει τῆς ἐφη-
it was And, in the serving as priest of him in the order of the
**9** μερίας αὐτοῦ ἔναντι τοῦ Θεοῦ, κατὰ τὸ ἔθος τῆς ἱερατείας,
course of nim before — God, according to the custom of the priests,
**10** ἔλαχε τοῦ θυμιάσαι εἰσελθὼν εἰς τὸν ναὸν τοῦ Κυρίου. καὶ
(his) lot to burn incense entering into the temple of the Lord. And
πᾶν τὸ πλῆθος τοῦ λαοῦ ἦν προσευχόμενον ἔξω τῇ ὥρᾳ
all the multitude of the people was praying outside at the hour
**11** τοῦ θυμιάματος. ὤφθη δὲ αὐτῷ ἄγγελος Κυρίου, ἑστὼς ἐκ
— of incense. appeared And to him an angel of (the) Lord. standing on

appeared to him, standing at (the) right of the altar of incense. [12] And seeing Zacharias was troubled, and fear fell on him. [13] But the angel said to him, Do not fear, Zacharias, because your prayer has been heard, and your wife Elizabeth shall bear a son to you, and you shall call his name John. [14] And he shall be joy and exaltation to you, and many shall rejoice at his birth. [15] For he shall be great before the Lord; and he shall in no way drink wine and strong drink, and he shall be filled with (the) Holy Spirit even from (the) womb of his mother. [16] And many of the sons of Israel shall he turn to (the) Lord their God. [17] And he shall go out before Him in the spirit and power of Elijah, to turn hearts of fathers to children, and (the) disobedient to (the) wisdom of the righteous, to make ready a people prepared for (the) Lord. [18] And Zacharias said to the angel, By what shall I know this? For I am an old man, and my wife advanced in her days. [19] And answering the angel said to him, I am Gabriel, who stands before God, and I was sent to speak to you and to announce to you these glad tidings. [20] And behold, you shall be silent and not able to speak until the day in which these things take place, because you did not believe my words, which shall be fulfilled in their season. [21] And the people were expecting Zacharias, and they wondered at his delaying in the Temple. [22] But having come out he was not able to speak to them, and they recognized that he had seen a vision in the Temple. And he was making signs to them, and continued dumb. [23] And it came to pass when the days of his service were fulfilled, he departed to his house. [24] Now after these days his wife Elizabeth

---

**12** δεξιῶν τοῦ θυσιαστηρίου τοῦ θυμιάματος. καὶ ἐταράχθη
(the) right of the altar     — of incense.    And was troubled
Ζαχαρίας ἰδών, καὶ φόβος ἐπέπεσεν ἐπ' αὐτόν. εἶπε δὲ πρὸς
Zacharias seeing, and fear fell upon him. said But to

**13** αὐτὸν ὁ ἄγγελος, Μὴ φοβοῦ, Ζαχαρία· διότι εἰσηκούσθη ἡ
him the angel, Do not fear, Zacharias because was heard the
δέησίς σου, καὶ ἡ γυνή σου Ἐλισάβετ γεννήσει υἱόν σοι, καὶ
request of you, and the wife of you, Elizabeth, will bear a son to you, and

**14** καλέσεις τὸ ὄνομα αὐτοῦ Ἰωάννην. καὶ ἔσται χαρά σοι καὶ
you shall call the name of him John. And he shall be joy to you and
ἀγαλλίασις, καὶ πολλοὶ ἐπὶ τῇ γεννήσει αὐτοῦ χαρήσονται.
exultation and many over the birth of him will rejoice.

**15** ἔσται γὰρ μέγας ἐνώπιον τοῦ Κυρίου, καὶ οἶνον καὶ σίκερα
he will be For great in the eyes of the Lord, and wine and strong drink
οὐ μὴ πίῃ, καὶ Πνεύματος Ἁγίου πλησθήσεται ἔτι ἐκ κοιλίας
not at all he may drink, and of (the)Spirit Holy he will be filled even from womb

**16** μητρὸς αὐτοῦ. καὶ πολλοὺς ιῶν υἱῶν Ἰσραὴλ ἐπιστρέψει
of mother of him. And many of the sons of Israel he will turn

**17** ἐπὶ Κύριον τὸν Θεὸν αὐτῶν· καὶ αὐτὸς προελεύσεται
to (the) Lord the God of them; and he will go ahead
ἐνώπιον αὐτοῦ ἐν πνεύματι καὶ δυνάμει Ἠλίου, ἐπιστρέψαι
before Him in (the) spirit and power of Elijah, to turn
καρδίας πατέρων ἐπὶ τέκνα, καὶ ἀπειθεῖς ἐν φρονήσει
(the) hearts of fathers to children, and disobedient to (the) wisdom

**18** δικαίων, ἑτοιμάσαι Κυρίῳ λαὸν κατεσκευασμένον. καὶ εἶπε
of (the) just, to prepare for (the) Lord a people having been prepared. And said
Ζαχαρίας πρὸς τὸν ἄγγελον, Κατὰ τί γνώσομαι τοῦτο ;
Zacharias to the angel, By what shall I know this?
ἐγὼ γὰρ εἰμι πρεσβύτης, καὶ ἡ γυνή μου προβεβηκυῖα ἐν
I For am old, and the wife of me is advanced in

**19** ταῖς ἡμέραις αὐτῆς. καὶ ἀποκριθεὶς ὁ ἄγγελος εἶπεν αὐτῷ,
the days of her And answering the angel said to him,
Ἐγώ εἰμι Γαβριὴλ ὁ παρεστηκὼς ἐνώπιον τοῦ Θεοῦ· καὶ
I am Gabriel the(one) standing by before — God, and
ἀπεστάλην λαλῆσαι πρός σε, καὶ εὐαγγελίσασθαί σοι
I was sent to speak to you, and to give good news to you

**20** ταῦτα. καὶ ἰδού, ἔσῃ σιωπῶν καὶ μὴ δυνάμενος λαλῆσαι,
of these. And behold,you will be silent and not able to speak
ἄχρι ἧς ἡμέρας γένηται ταῦτα, ἀνθ' ὧν οὐκ ἐπίστευσας
until which day occurs these things, because not you believed
τοῖς λόγοις μου, οἵτινες πληρωθήσονται εἰς τὸν καιρὸν
the words of me, which will be fulfilled in the time

**21** αὐτῶν. καὶ ἦν ὁ λαὸς προσδοκῶν τὸν Ζαχαρίαν· καὶ
of them. And the people expecting — Zacharias, and

**22** ἐθαύμαζον ἐν τῷ χρονίζειν αὐτὸν ἐν τῷ ναῷ. ἐξελθὼν δὲ οὐκ
they marveled in the delay of him in the temple coming out.And not
ηουνατο λαλῆσαι αὐτοῖς· καὶ ἐπέγνωσαν ὅτι ὀπτασίαν
he was able to speak to them, and they knew that a vision
ἑώρακεν ἐν τῷ ναῷ· καὶ αὐτὸς ἦν διανεύων αὐτοῖς, καὶ

he had seen in the Temple and he was signaling to them, and

**23** διέμενε κωφός. καὶ ἐγένετο, ὡς ἐπλήσθησαν αἱ ἡμέραι τῆς
remained dumb. And it was, as were fulfilled the days of the
λειτουργίας αὐτοῦ, ἀπῆλθεν εἰς τὸν οἶκον αὐτοῦ.
service of him, he went away to the house of him.

**24** Μετὰ δὲ ταύτας τὰς ἡμέρας συνέλαβεν Ἐλισάβετ ἡ γυνὴ
after And these — days, conceived Elizabeth the wife

conceived, and hid herself five months, saying, [25] So has the Lord done to me in (the) days in which He looked on (me) to take away my reproach among men.

[26] And in the sixth month the angel Gabriel was sent by God to a city of Galilee named Nazareth,

[27] to a virgin betrothed to a man whose name (was) Joseph, of (the) house of David; and the name of the virgin (was) Mary. [28] And entering, the angel said to her, Hail, (one) receiving grace! The Lord (is) with you. You (are) blessed among women. [29] And seeing, she was disturbed at his word, and considered of what kind may be this greeting. [30] And the angel said to her, Do not fear, Mary, for you found favor with God; [31] and behold, you will conceive in womb and bear a son; and you will call His name Jesus. [32] He shall be great, and will be called Son of (the) most High. And the Lord God will give Him the throne of David His father; [33] and He will reign over the house of Jacob forever; and of His kingdom there will be no end. [34] But Mary said to the angel, How shall this be since I know not a man? [35] And answering the angel said to her, (The) Holy Spirit shall come upon you, and power of (the) Highest shall overshadow you; for this reason also the holy thing born of you shall be called Son of God. [36] And behold, your kinswoman Elizabeth, she also has conceived a son in her old age, and this is (the) sixth month to her who (was) called barren; [37] for nothing shall be impossible with God. [38] And Mary said, Behold, The bondslave of (the) Lord! May it be to me according to your word. And the angel departed from her.

[39] And rising up in those days Mary went into the hill-country with haste, to a city of Judah,

25 αὐτοῦ, καὶ περιέκρυβεν ἑαυτὴν μῆνας πέντε, λέγουσα ὅτι
of him, and hid herself months five, saying,
οὕτω μοι πεποίηκεν ὁ Κύριος ἐν ἡμέραις αἷς ἐπεῖδεν ἀφελεῖν
Thus to me has done the Lord in days in which He saw to remove
τὸ ὄνειδός μου ἐν ἀνθρώποις.
the reproach of me among men.

26 Ἐν δὲ τῷ μηνὶ τῷ ἕκτῳ ἀπεστάλη ὁ ἄγγελος Γαβριὴλ
in And the month sixth was sent the angel Gabriel
ὑπὸ τοῦ Θεοῦ εἰς πόλιν τῆς Γαλιλαίας, ᾗ ὄνομα Ναζαρέθ,
by — God to a city — of Galilee, to (the) which name was Nazareth,

27 πρὸς παρθένον μεμνηστευμένην ἀνδρί, ᾧ ὄνομα Ἰωσήφ,
to a virgin having been betrothed to a man to (the) whom name (was) Joseph,
ἐξ οἴκου Δαβίδ· καὶ τὸ ὄνομα τῆς παρθένου Μαριαμ. καὶ
of house of David, and the name of the virgin (was) Mariam. And
εἰσελθὼν ὁ ἄγγελος πρὸς αὐτὴν εἶπε, Χαῖρε, κεχαριτωμένη·
entering the angel to her said, Hail, (one) receiving grace,
ὁ Κύριος μετὰ σου, εὐλογημένη σὺ ἐν γυναιξίν. ἡ δὲ ἰδοῦσα
the Lord (is) with you. Blessed (are) you among women. she And seeing,
διεταράχθη ἐπὶ τῷ λόγῳ αὐτοῦ, καὶ διελογίζετο ποταπὸς
was disturbed at the word of him, and considered of what kind
εἴη ὁ ἀσπασμὸς οὗτος. καὶ εἶπεν ὁ ἄγγελος αὐτῇ, Μὴ φοβοῦ,
may be greeting this. And said the angel to her, Do not fear,

31 Μαριάμ· εὗρες γὰρ χάριν παρὰ τῷ Θεῷ. καὶ ἰδού, συλλήψῃ
Mariam, you found for favor with — God. And, lo, you will conceive
ἐν γαστρί, καὶ τέξῃ υἱόν, καὶ καλέσεις τὸ ὄνομα αὐτοῦ
in womb and bear a son, and you will call the name of Him

32 Ἰησοῦν. οὗτος ἔσται μέγας, καὶ υἱὸς ὑψίστου κληθήσεται·
Jesus. This One will be great, and Son of Most High will be called,
καὶ δώσει αὐτῷ Κύριος ὁ Θεὸς τὸν θρόνον Δαβὶδ τοῦ πατρὸς
and will give Him (the) Lord — God the throne of David the father

33 αὐτοῦ, καὶ βασιλεύσει ἐπὶ τὸν οἶκον Ἰακὼβ εἰς τοὺς αἰῶνας,
of Him; and He will reign over the house of Jacob to the ages,

34 καὶ τῆς βασιλείας αὐτοῦ οὐκ ἔσται τέλος. εἶπε δὲ Μαριὰμ πρὸς
and of the kingdom of Him not will be an end. said And Mariam to

35 τὸν ἄγγελον, Πῶς ἔσται τοῦτο, ἐπεὶ ἄνδρα οὐ γινώσκω; καὶ
the angel, How will be this, since a man not I know? And
ἀποκριθεὶς ὁ ἄγγελος εἶπεν αὐτῇ, Πνεῦμα Ἅγιον ἐπελεύσεται
answering the angel said to her, (The) Spirit Holy will come up
ἐπὶ σέ, καὶ δύναμις ὑψίστου ἐπισκιάσει σοι· διὸ καὶ τὸ γεννώ-
upon you, and power of Most High will overshadow you, so also that being

36 μενον ἐκ σοῦ ἅγιον κληθήσεται υἱὸς Θεοῦ. καὶ ἰδού, Ἐλισάβετ
born of you holy will be called Son of God. And, behold, Elizabeth
ἡ συγγενής σου, καὶ αὐτὴ συνειληφυῖα υἱὸν ἐν γήρᾳ αὐτῆς·
the relative of you, also she conceived a son in old age of her,

37 καὶ οὗτος μὴν ἕκτος ἐστὶν αὐτῇ τῇ καλουμένῃ στείρα. ὅτι
and this month sixth is with her, the (one) called barren; because

38 οὐκ ἀδυνατήσει παρὰ τῷ Θεῷ πᾶν ῥῆμα. εἶπε δὲ Μαριάμ,
not will be impossible with — God every word. said And Mariam,
Ἰδού, ἡ δούλη Κυρίου· γένοιτό μοι κατὰ τὸ ῥῆμά σου. καὶ
Behold, the slave of (the) Lord; may it be to me as the word of you. And
ἀπῆλθεν ἀπ᾽ αὐτῆς ὁ ἄγγελος.
went away from her the angel.

39 Ἀναστᾶσα δὲ Μαριὰμ ἐν ταῖς ἡμέραις ταύταις ἐπορεύθη
rising up And Mariam in days these, she went
εἰς τὴν ὀρεινὴν μετὰ σπουδῆς, εἰς πόλιν Ἰούδα, καὶ εἰσῆλθεν
to the hill-country with haste, to a city of Judah and entered

[40] and entered into the house of Zacharias and greeted Elizabeth. [41] And it happened, as Elizabeth heard the greeting of Mary, the babe in her womb leaped, and Elizabeth was filled of (the) Holy Spirit, [42] and cried out with a loud voice and said, Blessed (are) you among women, and blessed (is) the fruit of your womb. [43] And why this to me, that the mother of My Lord comes to me? [44] For behold, as the sound of your greeting came to my ears, the babe in my womb leaped in exultation. [45] And blessed (is) she believing, for there will be a completion to the things spoken to her from (the) Lord.

[46] And Mary said, My soul magnifies the Lord, [47] and my spirit rejoiced in God my Savior. [48] For He looked upon the humiliation of His bondmaid; for behold, from now on all generations will count me blessed. [49] For the Mighty One has done great things to me, and holy (is) His name; [50] and His mercy (is) to generations of generations to those fearing Him. [51] He worked power with His arm; He scattered (the) proud in (the) thought of their hearts. [52] He put down rulers from thrones, and exalted (the) lowly; [53] He filled (the) hungry with good things, and He sent away empty (the) rich. [54] He helped His servant Israel, in order to remember mercy, [55] according as He spoke to our fathers, to Abraham and to his seed forever. [56] And Mary stayed with her about three months, and returned to her house.

[57] Now the time was fulfilled to Elizabeth that she should bring forth, and she bore a son. [58] And the neighbors and her relatives heard that (the) Lord was magnifying His mercy with her, and they

40 εἰς τὸν οἶκον Ζαχαρίου, καὶ ἠσπάσατο τὴν Ἐλισάβετ καὶ
into the house of Zacharias, and greeted — Elizabeth. And

41 ἐγένετο ὡς ἤκουσεν ἡ Ἐλισάβετ τὸν ἀσπασμὸν τῆς Μαρίας,
it was, as heard — Elizabeth the greeting — of Mariam,
ἐσκίρτησε τὸ βρέφος ἐν τῇ κοιλίᾳ αὐτῆς· καὶ ἐπλήσθη Πνεύ-
leaped the babe in the womb of her, and was filled of (the)

42 ματος Ἁγίου ἡ Ἐλισάβετ, καὶ ἀνεφώνησε φωνῇ μεγάλη
Spirit Holy — Elizabeth, and she called out with a voice great,
καὶ εἶπεν, Εὐλογημένη σὺ ἐν γυναιξί, καὶ εὐλογημένος ὁ
and said, Blessed (are) you among women, and blessed (is) the

43 καρπὸς τῆς κοιλίας σου. καὶ πόθεν μοι τοῦτο, ἵνα ἔλθη ἡ
fruit of the womb of you. And whence to me this, that comes the

44 μήτηρ τοῦ Κυρίου μου πρός με ; ἰδοὺ γάρ, ὡς ἐγένετο ἡ φωνὴ
mother of the Lord of me to me? behold For, as came the sound
τοῦ ἀσπασμοῦ σου εἰς τὰ ὦτά μου, ἐσκίρτησεν ἐν ἀγαλλιάσει
of the greeting of you to the ears of me, leaped in exultation

45 τὸ βρέφος ἐν τῇ κοιλίᾳ μου. καὶ μακαρία ἡ πιστεύσασα, ὅτι
the babe in the womb of me. And blessed the (one) believing, because
ἔσται τελείωσις τοῖς λελαλημένοις αὐτῇ παρὰ Κυρίου. καὶ
will be a completion to the things spoken to her from (the) Lord. And

46 εἶπε Μαριάμ, Μεγαλύνει ἡ ψυχή μου τὸν Κύριον, καὶ
said Mariam, magnifies The soul of me the Lord, and

47 ἠγαλλίασε τὸ πνεῦμά μου ἐπὶ τῷ Θεῷ τῷ σωτῆρί μου. ὅτι
exulted the spirit of me on — God the Savior of me; because

48 ἐπέβλεψεν ἐπὶ τὴν ταπείνωσιν τῆς δούλης αὐτοῦ. ἰδοὺ γάρ,
He looked upon the humiliation of the bondslave of Him. behold For,
ἀπὸ τοῦ νῦν μακαριοῦσί με πᾶσαι αἱ γενεαί. ὅτι ἐποίησέ μοι
from — now will count blessed me all the generations; for did to me

49 μεγαλεῖα ὁ δυνατός, καὶ ἅγιον τὸ ὄνομα αὐτοῦ. καὶ τὸ
great things the Mighty One. And holy the name of Him, and the

50 ἔλεος αὐτοῦ εἰς γενεὰς γενεῶν τοῖς φοβουμένοις αὐτόν.
mercy of Him to generations of generations to those fearing Him.

51 ἐποίησε κράτος ἐν βραχίονι αὐτοῦ· διεσκόρπισεν ὑπερη-
He did might(ily) with (the) arm of Him; He scattered proud

52 φάνους διανοίᾳ καρδίας αὐτῶν. καθεῖλε δυνάστας ἀπὸ
ones in (the) thought of the heart of them; He pulled down potentates from

53 θρόνων, καὶ ὕψωσε ταπεινούς. πεινῶντας ἐνέπλησεν
thrones, and exalted humble ones. hungering ones He filled

54 ἀγαθῶν, καὶ πλουτοῦντας ἐξαπέστειλε κενούς. ἀντελάβετο
of good things, and rich ones He sent away empty. He succored

55 Ἰσραὴλ παιδὸς αυτου, μνησθῆναι ἐλέους (καθὼς ἐλάλησε
Israel (the) servant of Him, to remember mercy, even as He spoke
πρὸς τοὺς πατέρας ἡμῶν) τῷ Ἀβραὰμ καὶ τῷ σπέρματι
to the fathers of us, — to Abraham and to the seed
αὐτοῦ εἰς τὸν αἰῶνα.
of him to the age.

56 Ἔμεινε δὲ Μαριὰμ σὺν αὐτῇ ὡσεὶ μῆνας τρεῖς, καὶ ὑπέ-
remained And Mariam with her about months three, and
στρεψεν εἰς τὸν οἶκον αὐτῆς.
returned to the house of her.

57 Τῇ δὲ Ἐλισάβετ ἐπλήσθη ὁ χρόνος τοῦ τεκεῖν αὐτήν,
- And to Elizabeth was fulfilled the time — to bear her,

58 καὶ ἐγέννησεν υἱόν. καὶ ἤκουσαν οἱ περίοικοι καὶ οἱ συγ-
and she bore a son. And heard the neighbors and the
γενεῖς αὐτῆς ὅτι ἐμεγάλυνε Κύριος τὸ ἔλεος αὐτοῦ μετ'
relatives of her that magnified (the) Lord the mercy of Him with

rejoiced with her.
[59] And it came to pass
on the eighth day they
came to circumcise the
little child, and were
calling it after the name of
his father Zacharias.
[60] And answering his
mother said, No; but he
shall be called John.
[61] And they said to her,
No one is among your
relatives who is called by
this name. [62] And they
made signs to his father (as
to) what he might wish
him to be called. [63] And
having asked for a writing
tablet, he wrote, saying,
John is his name. And they
all wondered. [64] And
immediately his mouth and
his tongue were opened,
and he spoke, blessing
God. [65] And fear came
on all those who lived
around them; and in the
whole hill-country of
Judea these things were
told. [66] And all who
heard laid (them) up in
their hearts, saying, What
then will this little child
be? And (the) hand of
(the) Lord was with him.

[67] And his father
Zacharias was filled with
(the) Holy Spirit, and
prophesied, saying,
[68] Blessed be (the)
Lord, the God of Israel,
because He looked on and
worked redemption for His
people, [69] and raised up
a Horn of salvation for us
in the house of His servant
David; [70] according as
He spoke by (the) mouth
of His holy prophets since
time began; [71] salvation
from our enemies, and
from (the) hand of all
those who hate us; [72] to
fulfill mercy with our
fathers, and to remember
His holy covenant,
[73] (the) oath which He
swore to our father
Abraham, [74] to grant to
us (that) we, being
delivered out of the hand
of our enemies, should
serve Him without fear,
[75] in holiness and
righteousness before Him
all the days of our life.
[76] And you, little child,
shall be called prophet of

59 αὐτῆς, καὶ συνέχαιρον αὐτῇ. καὶ ἐγένετο ἐν τῇ ὀγδόῃ ἡμέρᾳ,
   her,    and they rejoiced with her. And it was,    on the   eighth   day,
   ἦλθον περιτεμεῖν τὸ παιδίον· καὶ ἐκάλουν αὐτὸ ἐπὶ τῷ
   they came to circumcise the child,    and were calling   it   by   the
60 ὀνόματι τοῦ πατρὸς αὐτοῦ Ζαχαρίαν. καὶ ἀποκριθεῖσα, ἡ
   name   of the   father  of him, Zacharias.   And   answering   the
61 μήτηρ αὐτοῦ εἶπεν, Οὐχί, ἀλλὰ κληθήσεται Ἰωάννης. καὶ
   mother of him   said,   Not so, but he shall be called   John.   And
   εἶπον πρὸς αὐτὴν ὅτι Οὐδείς ἐστιν ἐν τῇ συγγενείᾳ σου
   they said to   her,   —   No one there is   in the   kindred   of you
62 ὃς καλεῖται τῷ ὀνόματι τούτῳ. ἐνένευον δὲ τῷ πατρὶ αὐτοῦ,
   who is called by   name   this.   they signaled And to the father of him,
63 τὸ τί ἂν θέλοι καλεῖσθαι αὐτόν. καὶ αἰτήσας πινακίδιον
   —  what he may desire to be called   him.   And asking for   a tablet,
64 ἔγραψε, λέγων, Ἰωάννης ἐστὶ τὸ ὄνομα αὐτοῦ· καὶ ἐθαύ-
   he wrote,   saying,   John   is   the   name   of him. And   mar-
   μασαν πάντες. ἀνεῴχθη δὲ τὸ στόμα αὐτοῦ παραχρῆμα
   veled   all.   was opened And the   mouth of him   instantly,
65 καὶ ἡ γλῶσσα αὐτοῦ, καὶ ἐλάλει εὐλογῶν τὸν Θεόν. καὶ
   and the tongue   of him, and he spoke blessing   —   God. And
   ἐγένετο ἐπὶ πάντας φόβος τοὺς περιοικοῦντας αὐτούς· καὶ
   came   upon all   fear the (ones) living around   them,   and
   ἐν ὅλῃ τῇ ὀρεινῇ τῆς Ἰουδαίας διελαλεῖτο πάντα τὰ ῥήματα
   in all   the hill-country  — of Judea were talked   all   — facts
66 ταῦτα. καὶ ἔθεντο πάντες οἱ ἀκούσαντες ἐν τῇ καρδίᾳ αὐτῶν,
   these.   And laid up   all the (ones) hearing   in the heart   of them,
   λέγοντες, Τί ἄρα τὸ παιδίον τοῦτο ἔσται; καὶ χεὶρ Κυρίου
   saying,   What then   —   child   this will be? And (the) hand of Lord
   ἦν μετ' αὐτοῦ.
   was with   him.
67 Καὶ Ζαχαρίας ὁ πατὴρ αὐτοῦ ἐπλήσθη Πνεύματος
   And Zacharias the   father   of him   was filled of (the) Spirit
68 Ἁγίου, καὶ προεφήτευσε, λέγων, Εὐλογητὸς Κύριος ὁ
   Holy, and prophesied,   saying,   Blessed (be) (the) Lord the
   Θεὸς τοῦ Ἰσραήλ, ὅτι ἐπεσκέψατο καὶ ἐποίησε λύτρωσιν
   God  — of Israel, because He visited   and   worked   redemption
69 τῷ λαῷ αὐτοῦ, καὶ ἤγειρε κέρας σωτηρίας ἡμῖν ἐν τῷ οἴκῳ
   for the people of Him, and raised a horn   of salvation for us in the house
70 Δαβὶδ τοῦ παιδὸς αὐτοῦ (καθὼς ἐλάλησε διὰ στόματος τῶν
   of David the servant of Him; even as He spoke through (the) mouth of the
71 ἁγίων τῶν ἀπ' αἰῶνος προφητῶν αὐτοῦ), σωτηρίαν ἐξ
   holy   — from (the) age   prophets   of Him. salvation out of
   ἐχθρῶν ἡμῶν, καὶ ἐκ χειρὸς πάντων τῶν μισούντων ἡμᾶς·
   (the) enemies of us, and out of hand of all   the (ones) hating   us,
72 ποιῆσαι ἔλεος μετὰ τῶν πατέρων ἡμῶν, καὶ μνησθῆναι
   to execute mercy with   the   fathers   of us,   and to remember
73 διαθήκης ἁγίας αὐτοῦ, ὅρκον ὃν ὤμοσε πρὸς Ἀβραὰμ τὸν
   (the) covenant holy of Him, (the) oath which He swore to Abraham the
74 πατέρα ἡμῶν, τοῦ δοῦναι ἡμῖν, ἀφόβως, ἐκ χειρὸς τῶν
   father   of us,  — to give   to us without fear of (the) hand of the
75 ἐχθρῶν ἡμῶν ῥυσθέντας, λατρεύειν αὐτῷ ἐν ὁσιότητι καὶ
   enemies of us   being delivered   to serve   Him   in consecration and
   δικαιοσύνῃ ἐνώπιον αὐτοῦ πάσας τὰς ἡμέρας τῆς ζωῆς
   righteousness   before   Him   all   the   days of the life
76 ἡμῶν. καὶ σύ, παιδίον, προφήτης ὑψίστου κληθήσῃ·
   of us.   And you,   child,   a prophet of (the) Most High will be called

(the) Highest; for you shall go before (the) face of (the) Lord to prepare His way; [77] to give knowledge of salvation to His people in remission of their sins, [78] through the tender mercies of compassion of our God, in which (the) Dayspring from on high has visited us, [79] to shine on those sitting in darkness and in (the) shadow of death; to direct our feet into (the) way of peace.

[80] And the child grew and became strong in spirit; and (he) was in the desert until (the) days of his showing to Israel.

CHAPTER 2

[1] And it happened in those days, a decree went out from Caesar Augustus (for) all the habitable world to be registered. [2] This registration first occurred (under) the governing of Syria (by) Cyrenius. [3] And all went to be registered, each to his own city; [4] and Joseph also went from Galilee, out of Nazareth city to Judea, to a city of David which is called Bethlehem, because of his being of (the) house and family of David; [5] to be registered with Mary, she being betrothed to him as wife, being pregnant. [6] And it happened (as) they were there, the days were fulfilled (for) her to bear; [7] and she bore the first-born son of her; and she wrapped Him, and laid Him in the manger, for no place was for them in the inn.

[8] And shepherds were in the same country, staying in the fields and keeping watch by night over their flock. [9] And behold, an angel of (the) Lord stood by them, and (the) glory of (the) Lord shown around them, and they feared (with) great fear. [10] And the angel said to them, Do not fear; for behold, I announce good news of great joy, which shall be to all people; [11] for to you

77 προπορεύσῃ γὰρ πρὸ προσώπου Κυρίου ἑτοιμάσαι ὁδοὺς
you will go   for before (the) face of (the) Lord to prepare (the) ways
αὐτοῦ· τοῦ δοῦναι γνῶσιν σωτηρίας τῷ λαῷ αὐτοῦ ἐν
of Him,   –   to give a knowledge of salvation to the people of Him by

78 ἀφέσει ἁμαρτιῶν αὐτῶν, διὰ σπλάγχνα ἐλέους Θεοῦ ἡμῶν,
forgiveness of sins   of them, through (the) bowels of mercy of God of us,

79 ἐν οἷς ἐπεσκέψατο ἡμᾶς ἀνατολὴ ἐξ ὕψους, ἐπιφᾶναι τοῖς ἐν
in which (will) visit   us (the) Dayspring from on high, to appear to those in
σκότει καὶ σκιᾷ θανάτου καθημένοις, τοῦ κατευθῦναι τοὺς
darkness and in shadow of death   sitting,   – to direct   the
πόδας ἡμῶν εἰς ὁδὸν εἰρήνης.
feet   of us into a way of peace.

80 Τὸ δὲ παιδίον ηὔξανε καὶ ἐκραταιοῦτο πνεύματι, καὶ ἦν ἐν
  the And child   grew and   became strong in spirit,   and was in
ταῖς ἐρήμοις ἕως ἡμέρας ἀναδείξεως αὐτοῦ πρὸς τὸν Ἰσραήλ.
the desert until (the) days of showing of him to   –   Israel.

CHAPTER 2

1 Ἐγένετο δὲ ἐν ταῖς ἡμέραις ἐκείναις, ἐξῆλθε δόγμα παρὰ
  it was And, in   days   those, went out a decree from
Καίσαρος Αὐγούστου, ἀπογράφεσθαι πᾶσαν τὴν οἰκου-
Caesar   Augustus   to be registered   all   the inhabited

2 μένην. αὕτη ἡ ἀπογραφὴ πρώτη ἐγένετο ἡγεμονεύοντος τῆς
earth. This   registration first   was (during the) governing of

3 Συρίας Κυρηνίου. καὶ ἐπορεύοντο πάντες ἀπογράφεσθαι,
Syria (by) Cyrenius. And   went   all   to be registered,

4 ἕκαστος εἰς τὴν ἰδίαν πόλιν. ἀνέβη δὲ καὶ Ἰωσὴφ ἀπὸ τῆς
each one into (his) own   city. went up And also Joseph from –
Γαλιλαίας, ἐκ πόλεως Ναζαρέθ, εἰς τὴν Ἰουδαίαν, εἰς πόλιν
Galilee   out of (the) city Nazareth to   –   Judea, into (the) city
Δαβίδ, ἥτις καλεῖται Βηθλεέμ, διὰ τὸ εἶναι αὐτὸν ἐξ οἴκου καὶ
of David which is called Bethlehem, because of being   him of (the) house and

5 πατριᾶς Δαβίδ, ἀπογράψασθαι σὺν Μαριὰμ τῇ μεμνηστευ-
family   of David; to be registered   with Mariam the (one) being be-

6 μένῃ αὐτῷ γυναικί, οὔσῃ ἐγκύῳ. ἐγένετο δὲ ἐν τῷ εἶναι
trothed to him (as) wife, being pregnant. it was And, in   being

7 αὐτοὺς ἐκεῖ, ἐπλήσθησαν αἱ ἡμέραι τοῦ τεκεῖν αὐτήν. καὶ
they   there, were fulfilled   the days (for) the bearing (of) her; and
ἔτεκε τὸν υἱὸν αὐτῆς τὸν πρωτότοκον, καὶ ἐσπαργάνωσεν
she bore the son of her,   the first-born,   and she wrapped
αὐτόν, καὶ ἀνέκλινεν αὐτὸν ἐν τῇ φάτνῃ, διότι οὐκ ἦν αὐτοῖς
Him   and laid   Him in the manger, because not was for them
τόπος ἐν τῷ καταλύματι.
a place in the   inn.

8 Καὶ ποιμένες ἦσαν ἐν τῇ χώρᾳ τῇ αὐτῇ ἀγραυλοῦντες καὶ
  And shepherds were in the country   same living in the fields and
φυλάσσοντες φυλακὰς τῆς νυκτὸς ἐπὶ τὴν ποίμνην αὐτῶν.
keeping   guard of the night over   the   flock of them.

9 καὶ ἰδού, ἄγγελος Κυρίου ἐπέστη αὐτοῖς, καὶ δόξα Κυρίου
And behold, an angel of (the) Lord came on them,   and (the) glory of Lord

10 περιέλαμψεν αὐτούς· καὶ ἐφοβήθησαν φόβον μέγαν. καὶ εἶπεν
shone around them,   and they feared (with) a fear great.   And said
αὐτοῖς ὁ ἄγγελος, Μὴ φοβεῖσθε· ἰδοὺ γάρ, εὐαγγελίζομαι
to them the angel, Do not   fear;   behold for,   I give good news

11 ὑμῖν χαρὰν μεγάλην, ἥτις ἔσται παντὶ τῷ λαῷ· ὅτι ἐτέχθη
to you, a joy   great,   which will be to all the people, because was born

today was born a Savior, who is Christ (the) Lord, in (the) city of David. [12] And this (is) the sign to you: You shall find a babe wrapped in a navel-band, lying in the manger. [13] And suddenly there was with the angel a multitude of (the) heavenly host, praising God and saying, [14] Glory to God in the highest, and peace on earth, good will in men. [15] And it came to pass as the angels departed from them into Heaven, that the shepherd men said to one another, Indeed, let us go over to Bethlehem, and let us see this thing which has happened, which the Lord made known to us. [16] And they came, having hurried, and found both Mary and Joseph, and the babe lying in the manger. [17] And having seen, they publicly told about the thing which had been told them concerning this little child. [18] And all who heard wondered concerning the things which had been spoken by the shepherds to them. [19] But Mary kept all these sayings, meditating in her heart. [20] And the shepherds returned, glorifying and praising God for all things which they had heard and seen, as it was said to them.

[21] And when eight days were fulfilled for circumcising the little child, His name was called Jesus, which (He) was called by the angel before He was conceived in the womb.

[22] And when the days for their purifcation were fulfilled according to the law of Moses, they brought Him to Jerusalem to present to the Lord, [23] as it has been written in the Law of (the) Lord, that "every male opening a womb shall be called holy to the Lord," [24] and to offer a sacrifice according to that which has been said in (the) Law of (the) Lord, a pair of turtledoves or two young pigeons.

ὑμῖν σήμερον Σωτήρ, ὅς ἐστι Χριστὸς Κύριος, ἐν πόλει Δαβίδ.
to you today a Savior, who is Christ (the) Lord, into the city of David.

12 καὶ τοῦτο ὑμῖν τὸ σημεῖον· εὑρήσετε βρέφος ἐσπαργανω-
And this to you a sign· you will find a babe having been

13 μένον, κείμενον ἐν τῇ φάτνη. καὶ ἐξαίφνης ἐγένετο σὺν τῷ
wrapped, lying in manger. And suddenly there was with the

ἀγγέλῳ πλῆθος στρατιᾶς οὐρανίου, αἰνούντων τὸν Θεόν,
angel a multitude of (the) host heavenly, praising — God

14 καὶ λεγόντων, Δόξα ἐν ὑψίστοις Θεῷ, καὶ ἐπὶ γῆς εἰρήνη·
and saying, Glory in the highest to God, and on earth peace,

ἐν ἀνθρώποις εὐδοκία.
in men, good will.

15 Καὶ ἐγένετο, ὡς ἀπῆλθον ἀπ᾽ αὐτῶν εἰς τὸν οὐρανὸν οἱ
And it was, as departed from them into — Heaven the

ἄγγελοι, καὶ οἱ ἄνθρωποι οἱ ποιμένες εἶπον πρὸς ἀλλήλους,
angels, even the men. the shepherds, said to one another,

Διέλθωμεν δὴ ἕως Βηθλεέμ, καὶ ἴδωμεν τὸ ῥῆμα τοῦτο τὸ
Let us go indeed unto Bethlehem, and let us see — thing this —

16 γεγονός, ὃ ὁ Κύριος ἐγνώρισεν ἡμῖν. καὶ ἦλθον σπεύσαντες,
having occurred, which the Lord made known to us. And they came, hurrying,

καὶ ἀνεῦρον τήν τε Μαριὰμ καὶ τὸν Ἰωσήφ, καὶ τὸ βρέφος
and sought out — both Mariam and — Joseph, and the babe

17 κείμενον ἐν τῇ φάτνη. ἰδόντες δὲ διεγνώρισαν περὶ τοῦ
lying in the manger. seeing And, they publicly told about the

ῥήματος τοῦ λαληθέντος αὐτοῖς περὶ τοῦ παιδίου τούτου.
saying spoken to them about — child this.

18 καὶ πάντες οἱ ἀκούσαντες ἐθαύμασαν περὶ τῶν λαληθέντων
And all those hearing marveled concerning the things spoken

19 ὑπὸ τῶν ποιμένων πρὸς αὐτούς. ἡ δὲ Μαριὰμ πάντα
by the shepherds to them. — And Mariam all

συνετήρει τὰ ῥήματα ταῦτα, συμβάλλουσα ἐν τῇ καρδίᾳ
kept — sayings these, meditating in the heart

20 αὐτῆς. καὶ ἐπέστρεψαν οἱ ποιμένες, δοξάζοντες καὶ αἰνοῦντες
of her. And returned the shepherds, glorifying and praising

τὸν Θεὸν ἐπὶ πᾶσιν οἷς ἤκουσαν καὶ εἶδον, καθὼς ἐλαλήθη
— God at all things which they heard and saw, even as was spoken

πρὸς αὐτούς.
to them.

21 Καὶ ὅτε ἐπλήσθησαν ἡμέραι ὀκτὼ τοῦ περιτεμεῖν τὸ
And when were fulfilled days eight — to circumcise the

παιδίον, καὶ ἐκλήθη τὸ ὄνομα αὐτοῦ Ἰησοῦς, τὸ κληθὲν ὑπὸ
child, and was called the name of Him Jesus, that called by

τοῦ ἀγγέλου πρὸ τοῦ συλληφθῆναι αὐτὸν ἐν τῇ κοιλίᾳ.
the angel before — was conceived Him in the womb.

22 Καὶ ὅτε ἐπλήσθησαν αἱ ἡμέραι τοῦ καθαρισμοῦ αὐτῆς
And when were fulfilled the days of the cleansing of her,

κατὰ τὸν νόμον Μωσέως, ἀνήγαγον αὐτὸν εἰς Ἱεροσόλυμα,
according to the law of Moses, they took up Him to Jerusalem

23 παραστῆσαι τῷ Κυρίῳ (καθὼς γέγραπται ἐν νόμῳ Κυρίου
to present to the Lord, as it has been written in (the) law of the Lord,

ὅτι Πᾶν ἄρσεν διανοῖγον μήτραν ἅγιον τῷ Κυρίῳ κληθήσε-
— Every male opening a womb holy to the Lord shall be

24 ται ), καὶ τοῦ δοῦναι θυσίαν κατὰ τὸ εἰρημένον ἐν νόμῳ
called; and — to give a sacrifice according to that said in the Law

Κυρίου, Ζεῦγος τρυγόνων ἢ δύο νεοσσοὺς περιστερῶν. καὶ
of (the) Lord: a pair of turtledoves, or two nestlings of doves. And

[25] And behold, there was a man in Jerusalem whose name (was) Simeon; and this man (was) just and pious, waiting for (the) Comfort of Israel, and (the) Holy Spirit was upon him. [26] And it was divinely revealed to him by the Holy Spirit that he should not see death before he should see the Christ of (the) Lord. [27] And he came in the Spirit into the Temple; and in the parents bringing in the child Jesus (for) them to do according to the custom of the law concerning Him, [28] even he received Him into his arms, and blessed God and said, [29] Now You will let Your servant go, O Master, according to Your word, in peace; [30] for my eyes have seen Your salvation, [31] which You have prepared before (the) face of all the peoples; [32] light for enlightening the nations, and (the) glory of Your people Israel. [33] And Joseph and His mother were wondering at the things which were said about Him. [34] And Simeon blessed them, and said to His mother Mary, Behold, this One is set for (the) fall and rising up of many in Israel, and for a sign spoken against; [35] yea, a sword also shall pierce your own soul; so that the thoughts of many hearts may be revealed.

[36] And was Anna, a prophetess, a daughter of Phanuel, of (the) tribe of Asher—she advanced in many days, having lived seven years with a husband from her virginity. [37] and she a widow eighty-four years — who not departed from the Temple, serving night and day with fastings and prayers. [38] And she coming on at the very hour gave thanks to the Lord, and spoke concerning Him to all those eagerly expecting redemption in Jerusalem. [39] And when they had finished all things according to the law of (the) Lord, they returned

25 ἰδού, ἦν ἄνθρωπος ἐν Ἰερουσαλήμ, ᾧ ὄνομα Σιμεών, καὶ ὁ
behold was a man in Jerusalem, to whom name Simeon. And —
ἄνθρωπος οὗτος δίκαιος καὶ εὐλαβής, προσδεχόμενος
man this (was) righteous and devout, expecting eagerly
παράκλησιν τοῦ Ἰσραήλ, καὶ Πνεῦμα Ἅγιον ἦν ἐπ᾽ αὐτόν.
(the) consolation — of Israel; and (the) Spirit Holy was upon him.

26 καὶ ἦν αὐτῷ κεχρηματισμένον ὑπὸ τοῦ Πνεύματος τοῦ
And was to him, having been instructed by the Spirit
Ἁγίου, μὴ ἰδεῖν θάνατον πρὶν ἢ ἴδῃ τὸν Χριστὸν Κυρίου.
Holy, not to see death before that he sees the Christ of (the) Lord.

27 καὶ ἦλθεν ἐν τῷ Πνεύματι εἰς τὸ ἱερόν· καὶ ἐν τῷ εἰσαγαγεῖν
And he came by the Spirit into the Temple; and in the bringing in
τοὺς γονεῖς τὸ παιδίον Ἰησοῦν, τοῦ ποιῆσαι αὐτοὺς κατὰ
the parents the child Jesus — to do them according to

28 τὸ εἰθισμένον τοῦ νόμου περὶ αὐτοῦ, καὶ αὐτὸς ἐδέξατο αὐτὸ
to the custom of the law concerning Him; and he received Him
εἰς τὰς ἀγκάλας αὐτοῦ, καὶ εὐλόγησε τὸν Θεόν, καὶ εἶπε,
in the arms of him, and blessed — God and said,

29 Νῦν ἀπολύεις τὸν δοῦλόν σου, δέσποτα, κατὰ τὸ ῥῆμά σου,
Now let go the slave of You, Master, according to the word of You

30 ἐν εἰρήνη· ὅτι εἶδον οἱ ὀφθαλμοί μου τὸ σωτήριόν σου, ὃ
in peace; because saw the eyes of me the salvation of You which

31 ἡτοίμασας κατὰ πρόσωπον πάντων τῶν λαῶν· φῶς εἰς
You prepared before (the) face of all the peoples; a light for

32 ἀποκάλυψιν ἐθνῶν. καὶ δόξαν λαοῦ σου ἰσραήλ. καὶ ἦν
revelation (to the) nations, and a glory of people of You Israel. And was

33 Ἰωσήφ καὶ ἡ μήτηρ αὐτοῦ θαυμάζοντες ἐπὶ τοῖς λαλου-
Joseph and the mother of Him marveling at the things being

34 μένοις περὶ αὐτοῦ. καὶ εὐλόγησεν αὐτοὺς Σιμεών, καὶ εἶπε
said about Him. And blessed them Simeon, and said
πρὸς Μαριὰμ τὴν μητέρα αὐτοῦ, Ἰδού, οὗτος κεῖται εἰς
to Mariam the mother of Him, Behold, this (One) is set for
πτῶσιν καὶ ἀνάστασιν πολλῶν ἐν τῷ Ἰσραήλ, καὶ εἰς σημεῖον
fall and rising of many in — Israel, and for a sign

35 ἀντιλεγόμενον· καὶ σοῦ δὲ αὐτῆς τὴν ψυχὴν διελεύσεται
spoken against, and of you also of her soul will pierce
ῥομφαία· ὅπως ἂν ἀποκαλυφθῶσιν ἐκ πολλῶν καρδιῶν
a sword. so as — may be revealed of many hearts

36 διαλογισμοί. καὶ ἦν Ἄννα προφῆτις, θυγάτηρ Φανουήλ,
(the) thoughts. And was Anna a prophetess, a daughter of Phanuel,
ἐκ φυλῆς Ἀσήρ (αὕτη προβεβηκυῖα ἐν ἡμέραις πολλαῖς,
of (the) tribe of Asher; she advanced in days many,
ζήσασα ἔτη μετὰ ἀνδρὸς ἑπτὰ ἀπὸ τῆς παρθενίας αὐτῆς,
having lived years with a husband seven from the virginity of her,

37 καὶ αὕτη χήρα ὡς ἐτῶν ὀγδοηκοντατεσσάρων ), ἢ οὐκ ἀφί-
and she a widow years eighty-four, who not
στατο ἀπὸ τοῦ ἱεροῦ, νηστείαις καὶ δεήσεσι λατρεύουσα
departed from the Temple, with fastings and petitionings serving

38 νύκτα καὶ ἡμέραν. καὶ αὕτη αὐτῇ τῇ ὥρᾳ ἐπιστᾶσα ἀνθω-
night and day. And she at the very hour coming on, she
μολογεῖτο τῷ Κυρίῳ, καὶ ἐλάλει περὶ αὐτοῦ πᾶσι τοῖς
gave thanks to the Lord, and spoke concerning Him to all, those

39 προσδεχομένοις λύτρωσιν ἐν Ἰερουσαλήμ. καὶ ὡς ἐτέλεσαν
expecting eagerly redemption in Jerusalem. And as they finished
ἅπαντα τὰ κατὰ τὸν νόμον Κυρίου, ὑπέστρεψαν εἰς τὴν
all things — according to the law of (the) Lord, they returned to —

to Galilee, to their city
Nazareth. [40] And the
little child grew and
became strong in spirit, **40**
being filled with wisdom,
and God's grace was upon
Him.

[41] And His parents **41**
went yearly to Jerusalem
at the Feast of the
Passover. [42] And when **42**
He was twelve years old,
they having gone up to **43**
Jerusalem according to the
custom of the Feast,
[43] and having completed
the days, as they returned
the child Jesus remained
behind in Jerusalem, and
Joseph and His mother did **44**
not know. [44] But
supposing Him to be in the
company, they went a
day's journey, and looked
for Him among the **45**
relatives and among the
acquaintances. [45] And **46**
not having found Him,
they returned to
Jerusalem, looking for
Him. [46] And it came to
pass after three days they **47**
found Him in the Temple,
sitting in (the) midst of the
teachers, both hearing
them and questioning
them. [47] And all those **48**
hearing Him were amazed
at (His) understanding and
His answers. [48] And
seeing Him they were
astonished. And His
mother said to Him, Child,
why have You done this to **49**
us? Behold, Your father
and I were full of sorrow
seeking You. [49] And He **50**
said to them, Why were
you seeking Me? Did you **51**
not know that it behooves
Me to be in the (business)
of My Father? [50] And
they did not understand
the word which He spoke
to them. [51] And He
went down with them and
came to Nazareth, and He
was subject to them. And
His mother kept all these **52**
things in her heart.
[52] And Jesus advanced
in wisdom and stature, and
in favor with God and
men.

[1] Now in the
fifteenth year of the
government of Tiberias

---

Γαλιλαίαν, εἰς τὴν πόλιν αὐτῶν Ναζαρέθ.
Galilee,   to the city  of them, Nazareth.

Τὸ δὲ παιδίον ηὔξανε, καὶ ἐκραταιοῦτο πνεύματι, πληρού- **40**
the And child    grew,   and became strong in spirit   being

μενον σοφίας· καὶ χάρις Θεου ην επ αὐτό.
filled with wisdom, and the grace of God was upon Him.

Καὶ ἐπορεύοντο οἱ γονεῖς αὐτοῦ κατ᾽ ἔτος εἰς Ἱερουσαλὴμ **41**
And  went   the parents of Him year by year into Jerusalem

τῇ ἑορτῇ τοῦ πάσχα. καὶ ὅτε ἐγένετο ἐτῶν δώδεκα, ἀναβάν- **42**
at the feast of the Passover. And when He was years twelve,  going up

των αὐτῶν εἰς Ἱεροσόλυμα κατὰ τὸ ἔθος τῆς ἑορτῆς, καὶ **43**
them  to   Jerusalem according to the custom of the feast, and

τελειωσάντων τὰς ἡμέρας, ἐν τῷ ὑποστρέφειν αὐτούς, ὑπέ-
fulfilling   the days,  in the  returning   of them,

μεινεν Ἰησοῦς ὁ παῖς ἐν Ἱερουσαλὴμ καὶ οὐκ ἔγνω Ἰωσὴφ
stayed  Jesus the boy in  Jerusalem;  and not did know Joseph

καὶ ἡ μήτηρ αὐτοῦ· νομίσαντες δὲ αὐτὸν ἐν τῇ συνοδίᾳ εἶναι, **44**
and the mother of Him. supposing But Him in the company to be,

ἦλθον ἡμέρας ὁδὸν καὶ ἀνεζήτουν αὐτὸν ἐν τοῖς συγγενέσι
they a day on the and looked for  Him among the relatives
went   way,

καὶ ἐν τοῖς γνωστοῖς· καὶ μὴ εὑρόντες αὐτόν, ὑπέστρεψαν εἰς **45**
and among the friends, and not finding  Him, they returned into

Ἱερουσαλήμ, ζητοῦντες αὐτόν. καὶ ἐγένετο, μεθ᾽ ἡμέρας **46**
Jerusalem,  seeking  Him.  And it was,  after  days

τρεῖς εὗρον αὐτὸν ἐν τῷ ἱερῷ, καθεζόμενον ἐν μέσῳ τῶν
three they found Him in the Temple, sitting  in (the) midst of the

διδασκάλων, καὶ ἀκούοντα αὐτῶν, καὶ ἐπερωτῶντα αὐτούς. **47**
teachers,  even hearing them and questioning them

ἐξίσταντο δὲ πάντες οἱ ἀκούοντες αὐτοῦ ἐπὶ τῇ συνέσει καὶ
were amazed And all those hearing  Him at the intelligence and

ταῖς ἀποκρίσεσιν αὐτοῦ. καὶ ἰδόντες αὐτὸν ἐξεπλάγησαν· **48**
the   answers   of Him. And seeing  Him, they were astounded,

καὶ πρὸς αὐτὸν ἡ μήτηρ αὐτοῦ εἶπε, Τέκνον, τί ἐποίησας
and to  Him the mother of Him said,  Child, why did You do

ἡμῖν οὕτως; ἰδού, ὁ πατήρ σου κἀγὼ ὀδυνώμενοι ἐζητοῦμέν
to us thus? Behold, the father of You and I greatly distressed are seeking

σε. καὶ εἶπε πρὸς αὐτούς, Τί ὅτι ἐζητεῖτέ με; οὐκ ἤδειτε ὅτι ἐν **49**
You. And He said to them, Why that You sought Me? not know that in

τοῖς τοῦ πατρός μου δεῖ εἶναί με; καὶ αὐτοὶ οὐ συνῆκαν τὸ **50**
the (affairs) of My Father must be Me? And they not understood the

ῥῆμα ὃ ἐλάλησεν αὐτοῖς. καὶ κατέβη μετ᾽ αὐτῶν, καὶ ἦλθεν **51**
word which He spoke to them. And He went with them, and came

εἰς Ναζαρέθ· καὶ ἦν ὑποτασσόμενος αὐτοῖς· καὶ ἡ μήτηρ
to Nazareth, and was being subject  to them.  And the mother

αὐτοῦ διετήρει πάντα τὰ ῥήματα ταῦτα ἐν τῇ καρδίᾳ
of Him carefully kept all  —  sayings  these  in the heart

αὐτῆς.
of her.

Καὶ Ἰησοῦς προέκοπτε σοφίᾳ καὶ ἡλικίᾳ, καὶ χάριτι παρὰ **52**
And  Jesus progressed (in) wisdom and stature and favor before

Θεῷ καὶ ἀνθρώποις.
God and  men.

## CHAPTER 3

Ἐν ἔτει δὲ πεντεκαιδεκάτῳ τῆς ἡγεμονίας Τιβερίου
in (the) year And  fifteenth  of the government of Tiberius

Caesar, Pontius Pilate being governor of Judea, and Herod being tetrarch of Galilee, and his brother Philip being tetrarch of Iturea and of (the) region of Trachonitis, and Lysanias being tetrarch of Abilene, [2] in (the) high-priesthood of Annas and Caiaphas, came (the) word of God upon John the son of Zacharias in the wilderness. [3] And he went into all the country around the Jordan preaching the baptism of repentance for remission of sins; [4] as it has been written in (the) book of (the) words of Isaiah the prophet, saying, "The voice of one crying in the wilderness. Prepare the way of (the) Lord; make His paths straight — [5] every valley shall be filled and every mountain and hill shall be made low; and the crooked places shall become straight, and the rough roads smooth; [6] and all flesh shall see the salvation of God." [7] Then he said to the crowd coming out to be baptized by him, Offspring of vipers, who forewarned you to flee from the coming wrath? [8] Therefore bring forth fruits worthy of repentance; and do not begin to say in yourselves, We have Abraham (as) father, for I say to you that God is able to raise up children to Abraham from these stones. [9] And also the axe is already laid to the root of the trees; therefore every tree not producing good fruit is cut down and is thrown into (the) fire. [10] And the crowd asked him, saying, What then shall we do? [11] And answering he said to them, He that has two coats, let him give to him that has not; and he that has food, let him do likewise. [12] And tax-collectors also came to be baptized, and they said to him, Teacher, what shall we do? [13] And he said to them, Exact no more beyond that which is appointed to you.

Καίσαρος, ἡγεμονεύοντος Ποντίου Πιλάτου τῆς Ἰουδαίας,
Caesar, (in the)governing   of Pontius   Pilate   of Judea

καὶ τετραρχοῦντος τῆς Γαλιλαίας Ἡρώδου, Φιλίππου δὲ
and ruling as tetrarch   — of Galilee   Herod,   Philip   and

τοῦ ἀδελφοῦ αὐτοῦ τετραρχοῦντος τῆς Ἰτουραίας καὶ
the brother   of him ruling as tetrarch   — of Iturea and

**2** Τραχωνίτιδος χώρας, καὶ Λυσανίου τῆς Ἀβιληνῆς τετραρ-
of Trachonitis country,   and Lysanias   — of Abilene ruling as

χοῦντος, ἐπ᾽ ἀρχιερέων Ἄννα καὶ Καϊάφα, ἐγένετο ῥῆμα
tetrarch,   at   high priesthood of Anna and Caiaphas,   came a word

Θεοῦ ἐπὶ Ἰωάννην τὸν τοῦ Ζαχαρίου υἱὸν ἐν τῇ ἐρήμῳ. κα᾽
of God upon John   the — of Zachariah son   in the desert. And

**3** ἦλθεν εἰς πᾶσαν τὴν περίχωρον τοῦ Ἰορδάνου, κηρύσσων
he came into all   the neighborhood of the Jordan,   proclaiming

**4** βάπτισμα μετανοίας εἰς ἄφεσιν ἁμαρτιῶν· ὡς γέγραπται ἐν
a baptism of repentance for forgiveness of sins,   as it has been written in

βίβλῳ λόγων Ἡσαΐου τοῦ προφήτου, λέγοντος, Φωνή
(the) roll of (the) words of Isaiah   the   prophet,   saying, (The) voice

βοῶντος ἐν τῇ ἐρήμῳ, Ἑτοιμάσατε τὴν ὁδὸν Κυρίου· εὐθείας
of (one) crying in the wilderness, prepare   the   way of (the) Lord, straight

**5** ποιεῖτε τὰς τρίβους αὐτοῦ. πᾶσα φάραγξ πληρωθήσεται,
make   the paths   of Him;   every   valley   shall be filled up,

καὶ πᾶν ὄρος καὶ βουνὸς ταπεινωθήσεται· καὶ ἔσται τὰ
and every mountain and hill   shall be laid low;   and shall be the

**6** σκολιὰ εἰς εὐθείαν, καὶ αἱ τραχεῖαι εἰς ὁδοὺς λείας· καὶ
crooked into straight,   and the rough (places) into ways smooth; and

ὄψεται πᾶσα σάρξ τὸ σωτήριον τοῦ Θεοῦ.
shall see all   flesh the   salvation   — of God.

**7** Ἔλεγεν οὖν τοῖς ἐκπορευομένοις ὄχλοις βαπτισθῆναι ὑπ᾽
He said therefore to the   going out   crowds to be baptized   by

αὐτοῦ, Γεννήματα ἐχιδνῶν, τίς ὑπέδειξεν ὑμῖν φυγεῖν ἀπὸ
him,   Offspring   of vipers! Who warned   you to flee   from

**8** τῆς μελλούσης ὀργῆς; ποιήσατε οὖν καρποὺς ἀξίους τῆς
the coming   wrath? Produce therefore fruits   worthy   —

μετανοίας· καὶ μὴ ἄρξησθε λέγειν ἐν ἑαυτοῖς, Πατέρα ἔχομεν
of repentance; and not do begin to say among yourselves, Father we have

τὸν Ἀβραάμ. λέγω γὰρ ὑμῖν ὅτι δύναται ὁ Θεὸς ἐκ τῶν
Abraham. I say For to you that is able   — God out of —

**9** λίθων τούτων ἐγεῖραι τέκνα τῷ Ἀβραάμ. ἤδη δὲ καὶ ἡ ἀξίνη
stones these   to raise up children — to Abraham. And even the axe

πρὸς τὴν ῥίζαν τῶν δένδρων κεῖται· πᾶν οὖν δένδρον μὴ
to   the root of the trees   is laid; every therefore tree   not

ποιοῦν καρπὸν καλὸν ἐκκόπτεται καὶ εἰς πῦρ βάλλεται. καὶ
producing fruit good is being cut down and into fire being cast. And

**10** ἐπηρώτων αὐτὸν οἱ ὄχλοι λέγοντες, Τί οὖν ποιήσομεν;
asked   him the crowd, saying, What, then, may we do?

**11** ἀποκριθεὶς δὲ λέγει αὐτοῖς, Ὁ ἔχων δύο χιτῶνας μεταδότω
answering And he says to them, He having, two tunics let him impart

τῷ μὴ ἔχοντι· καὶ ὁ ἔχων βρώματα ὁμοίως ποιείτω. ἦλθον
to (the) not having; and the (one) having foods   likewise let him do. came

**12** δὲ καὶ τελῶναι βαπτισθῆναι, καὶ εἶπον πρὸς αὐτόν,
And also tax-collectors to be baptized,   and said   to   him,

**13** Διδάσκαλε, τί ποιήσομεν; ὁ δὲ εἶπε πρὸς αὐτούς, Μηδὲν
Teacher,   what may we do? he And said to   them, Nothing

πλέον παρὰ τὸ διατεταγμένον ὑμῖν πράσσετε. ἐπηρώ-
more besides that commanded   to you keep doing.   asked

[14] And also those who were soldiers asked him, saying, And what shall we do? And he said to them, Oppress no one, nor accuse falsely, and be satisfied with your wages.

[15] But as the people were in expectation, and were reasoning in their hearts about John, whether or not he might be the Christ, [16] John answered all, saying, I indeed baptize you with water, but He comes who (is) mightier than I, of whom I am not fit to loose the latchet of His sandals; He will baptize you with (the) Holy Spirit and with fire; [17] of whom the sifting fan (is) in His hand, and He will thoroughly purge His floor, and will gather the wheat into His barn, but He will burn the chaff with unquenchable fire. [18] And then exhorting many different things, he preached the gospel to the people. [19] But Herod the tetrarch, being reproved by him concerning Herodias the wife of his brother Philip, and concerning all (the) evil things Herod did, [20] he also added this above all, he even locked up John in the prison.

[21] Now it came to pass, all the people having been baptized, and Jesus having been baptized and praying, Heaven was opened, [22] and the Holy Spirit descended in a bodily form as a dove upon Him, and a voice out of Heaven came, saying, You are My beloved Son; in You I have found delight!

[23] And Jesus Himself was beginning to be about thirty years old, being, as was supposed, the son of Joseph, the (son) of Heli, [24] the (son) of Matthat, the (son) of Levi, the (son) of Melchi, the (son) of Janna, the (son) of Joseph, [25] the (son) of Mattathias, the (son) of Amos, the (son) of Nahum, the (son) of Esli, the (son) of Naggai, [26] the (son)

---

14 τῶν δὲ αὐτὸν καὶ στρατευόμενοι, λέγοντες, Καὶ ἡμεῖς τί
— And him   also ones serving as soldiers, saying,   And  we, what
ποιήσωμεν; καὶ εἶπε πρὸς αὐτούς, Μηδένα διασείσητε,
may we do?  And he said  to   them,   No one   oppress,
μηδὲ συκοφαντήσητε· καὶ ἀρκεῖσθε τοῖς ὀψωνίοις ὑμῶν.
nor  accuse falsely;   and be satisfied with the pay   of you.

15 Προσδοκῶντος δὲ τοῦ λαοῦ, καὶ διαλογιζομένων πάντων
expecting    And the people, and  reasoning    all
ἐν ταῖς καρδίαις αὐτῶν περὶ τοῦ Ἰωάννου, μήποτε αὐτὸς
in the  hearts  of them about —  John,   lest perhaps he

16 εἴη ὁ Χριστός, ἀπεκρίνατο ὁ Ἰωάννης, ἅπασι λέγων, Ἐγὼ
is the Christ,   answered   —  John   to all, saying, I
μὲν ὕδατι βαπτίζω ὑμᾶς· ἔρχεται δὲ ὁ ἰσχυρότερός μου, οὖ
indeed with water baptize you;  comes  but (He) stronger than me, of whom
οὐκ εἰμὶ ἱκανὸς λῦσαι τὸν ἱμάντα τῶν ὑποδημάτων αὐτοῦ·
not I am fit  to loose the latchet of the sandals   of Him;

17 αὐτὸς ὑμᾶς βαπτίσει ἐν Πνεύματι Ἁγίῳ καὶ πυρί· οὖ τὸ
He   you  will baptize in (the) Spirit Holy  and fire; of whom the
πτύον ἐν τῇ χειρὶ αὐτοῦ, καὶ διακαθαριεῖ τὴν ἅλωνα αὐτοῦ,
fan (is) in the hand of Him, and He will fully purge the threshing-floor of Him,
καὶ συνάξει τὸν σῖτον εἰς τὴν ἀποθήκην αὐτοῦ, τὸ δὲ ἄχυρον
and will gather the wheat into the  barn   of Him; the but chaff
κατακαύσει πυρὶ ἀσβέστῳ.
He will burn up with fire unquenchable.

18 Πολλὰ μὲν οὖν καὶ ἕτερα παρακαλῶν εὐηγγελίζετο τὸν
Many things indeed then and different exhorting, he preached the gospel to the

19 λαόν· ὁ δὲ Ἡρώδης ὁ τετράρχης, ἐλεγχόμενος ὑπ' αὐτοῦ
people. — But Herod  the tetrarch,   being reproved  by   him
περὶ Ἡρωδιάδος τῆς γυναικὸς Φιλίππου τοῦ ἀδελφοῦ αὐτοῦ,
concerning Herodias the  wife  of Philip  the  brother  of him,
καὶ περὶ πάντων ὧν ἐποίησε πονηρῶν ὁ Ἡρώδης, προσέ-
and concerning all things which did  evil  —  Herod,  he

20 θηκε καὶ τοῦτο ἐπὶ πᾶσι, καὶ κατέκλεισε τὸν Ἰωάννην ἐν τῇ
added also this above all,  even he shut up  —  John  in the
φυλακῇ.
prison.

21 Ἐγένετο δὲ ἐν τῷ βαπτισθῆναι ἅπαντα τὸν λαόν, καὶ
it was  And in the baptizing  (of) all  the people, also
Ἰησοῦ βαπτισθέντος καὶ προσευχομένου, ἀνεῳχθῆναι τὸν
Jesus  being baptized and praying,     was opened  the

22 οὐρανόν, καὶ καταβῆναι τὸ Πνεῦμα τὸ Ἅγιον σωματικῷ
heaven   and came down the Spirit  — Holy in a bodily
εἴδει ὡσεὶ περιστερὰν ἐπ' αὐτόν, καὶ φωνὴν ἐξ οὐρανοῦ
form  as  a dove    upon Him,  and a voice out of Heaven
γενέσθαι, λέγουσαν, Σὺ εἶ ὁ υἱός μου ὁ ἀγαπητός· ἐν σοὶ
occurred, saying,   You are the Son of Me, the Beloved;  in You
ηὐδόκησα.
I am delighted.

23 Καὶ αὐτὸς ἦν ὁ Ἰησοῦς ὡσεὶ ἐτῶν τριάκοντα ἀρχόμενος,
And Himself was — Jesus about years (old) thirty  beginning,

24 ὢν (ὡς ἐνομίζετο) υἱὸς Ἰωσήφ, τοῦ Ἡλί, τοῦ Ματθάτ, τοῦ
being, as was supposed, son of Joseph. — of Heli — of Matthat.

25 Λευΐ, τοῦ Μελχί, τοῦ Ἰαννά, τοῦ Ἰωσήφ, τοῦ Ματταθίου
of Levi, — of Melchi, — of Janna, — of Joseph, — of Mattathias,

26 τοῦ Ἀμώς, τοῦ Ναούμ, τοῦ Ἐσλί, τοῦ Ναγγαί, τοῦ Μαάθ,
— of Amos, — of Nahum, — of Esli, — of Naggai, — of Maath,

of Maath, of Mattathias, of
Semei, of Joseph, of Juda,
[27] of Joannes, of Rhesa,
of Zerubbabei, of Shealtiel,
of Neri, [28] of Melchi, of
Addi, of Cosam, of Elmo-
dam, of Er, [29] of Joses,
of Eliezer, of Jorim, of Matthat, of Levi, [30] of Simeon, of Juda, of Joseph, of
Jonan, of Eliakim,[31] of
Melea, of Menna, of Mattatha, of Nathan, of David,
[32] of Jesse, of Obed, of
Boaz, of Salmon, of Nah-
shon, [33] of Amminadab,
of Aram, of Hezron, of Pharez, of Judah, [34] of Jacob, of Isaac, of Abraham,
of Terah, of Nahor, [35]
of Serug, of Reu, of Peleg,
of Eber, of Salah, [36] of
Cainan, of Arphaxad, of
Shem, of Noah, of Lamech,
[37] of Methuselah, of E-
noch, of Jared, of Mahalaleel, of Cainan, [38] of E-
nos, of Seth, of Adam, the
(son) of God.

τοῦ Ματταθίου, τοῦ Σεμεΐ, τοῦ Ἰωσήφ, τοῦ Ἰούδα, τοῦ
— of Mattathias, — of Semei, — of Joseph,   — of Judah, —

27 Ἰωαννᾶ, τοῦ Ῥησά, τοῦ Ζοροβάβελ, τοῦ Σαλαθιήλ, τοῦ
of Joannes,   — of Rhesa,   — of Zerubbabel,   — of Salathiel,  —

28 Νηρί, τοῦ Μελχί, τοῦ Ἀδδί, τοῦ Κωσάμ, τοῦ Ἐλμωδάμ,
of Neri,   — of Melchi,   — of Addi,   — of Cosain,   — of Elmodam,

29 τοῦ Ἤρ, τοῦ Ἰωσή, τοῦ Ἐλιέζερ, τοῦ Ἰωρείμ, τοῦ Ματθάτ,
of Er,        of Joseph,   — of Eliezer,   — of Joreim,   — of Matthai,

30 τοῦ Λευΐ, τοῦ Σιμεών, τοῦ Ἰούδα, τοῦ Ἰωσήφ, τοῦ Ἰωνάν,
— of Levi,   — of Simeon,   — of Judah,   — of Joseph,   — of Jonan,

31 τοῦ Ἐλιακείμ, τοῦ Μελεᾶ, τοῦ Μενάμ, τοῦ Ματταθά, τοῦ
— of Eliakim,   — of Melea,   — of Menam,   — of Mattatha,   —

32 Ναθάν, τοῦ Δαβίδ, τοῦ Ἰεσσαί, τοῦ Ὠβήδ, τοῦ Βοόζ, τοῦ
of Nathan, — of David.   — of Jesse,   — of Obed,   — of Boaz,   —

33 Σαλμών, τοῦ Ναασσών, τοῦ Ἀμιναδάβ, τοῦ Ἀράμ, τοῦ
of Salmon,   — of Nahshon,   — of Amminadab,   — of Ram,   —

34 Ἐσρώμ, τοῦ Φαρές, τοῦ Ἰούδα, τοῦ Ἰακώβ, τοῦ Ἰσαάκ,
of Hezron,   — of Pharez,   — of Judah,   — of Jacob,   — of Isaac,

35 τοῦ Ἀβραάμ, τοῦ Θάρα, τοῦ Ναχώρ, τοῦ Σαρούχ, τοῦ
— of Abraham, of   Terah,   — of Nahor,   — of Serug,   —

Ῥαγαῦ, τοῦ Φαλέκ, τοῦ Ἐβέρ, τοῦ Σαλά, τοῦ Καϊνάν, τοῦ
of Reu,   — of Peleg,   — of Eber. — of Salah,   — of Cainan,   —

36 Ἀρφαξάδ, τοῦ Σήμ, τοῦ Νῶε, τοῦ Λάμεχ, τοῦ Μαθουσάλα,
of Arphaxad, — of Shem, — of Noah, — of Lamech,   — of Methuselah,

37 τοῦ Ἐνώχ, τοῦ Ἰαρέδ, τοῦ Μαλελεήλ, τοῦ Καϊνάν, τοῦ
— of Enoch,   — of Jared,   — of Mahalaleel,   — of Cainan,   —

38 Ἐνώς, τοῦ Σήθ, τοῦ Ἀδάμ, τοῦ Θεοῦ.
of Enos, — of Seth,   — of Adam,   — of God.

## CHAPTER 4

CHAPTER 4
[1] And Jesus, full of
(the) Holy Spirit, returned
from the Jordan, and was
led by the Spirit into the
wilderness [2] forty days,
being tempted by the devil;
and He ate nothing in
those days, and   being
ended, He afterwards
hungered. [3] And the
devil said to Him. If you
are Son of God, speak to
this stone that it become
bread. [4] And Jesus
answered to him, saying, It
has been written, "Man
shall not live by bread
alone, but by every word
of God." [5] And leading
Him up into a high
mountain the devil showed
Him all the kingdoms of
the world in a moment of
time. [6] And the devil
said to Him, I will give all
this authority and their
glory to you, for it has
been delivered to me, and I
give to whomever I wish;

1 Ἰησοῦς δὲ Πνεύματος Ἁγίου πλήρης ὑπέστρεψεν ἀπὸ τοῦ
Jesus And of (the) Spirit Holy   full   returned   from   the

2 Ἰορδάνου, καὶ ἤγετο ἐν τῷ Πνεύματι εἰς τὴν ἔρημον, ἡμέρας
Jordan,   and was led by the   Spirit   into the wilderness, days

τεσσαράκοντα πειραζόμενος ὑπὸ τοῦ διαβόλου. καὶ οὐκ
forty         being tempted by   the   Devil.   And not

ἔφαγεν οὐδὲν ἐν ταῖς ἡμέραις ἐκείναις· καὶ συντελεσθεισῶν
He ate, nothing in   —   days   those;   and being ended

3 αὐτῶν, ὕστερον ἐπείνασε. καὶ εἶπεν αὐτῷ ὁ διάβολος, Εἰ
them, afterwards He hungered. And said   to Him the Devil,   if

υἱὸς εἶ τοῦ Θεοῦ, εἰπὲ τῷ λίθῳ τούτῳ ἵνα γένηται ἄρτος.
Son you are — of God say to   stone   this   that it become   a loaf.

4 καὶ ἀπεκρίθη Ἰησοῦς πρὸς αὐτόν, λέγων, Γέγραπται ὅτι
And made answer   Jesus   to   him,   saying. It has been written, —

Οὐκ ἐπ' ἄρτῳ μόνῳ ζήσεται ὁ ἄνθρωπος, ἀλλ' ἐπὶ παντὶ
Not on   bread only   shall live — man.   but on every

5 ῥήματι Θεοῦ. καὶ ἀναγαγὼν αὐτὸν ὁ διάβολος εἰς ὄρος
word   of God. And leading up   Him   the   Devil   into a mount

ὑψηλὸν ἔδειξεν αὐτῷ πάσας τὰς βασιλείας τῆς οἰκουμένης
high, he showed Him   all   the   kingdoms of the habitable world

6 ἐν στιγμῇ χρόνου. καὶ εἶπεν αὐτῷ ὁ διάβολος, Σοὶ δώσω τὴν
in a moment of time. And said   to Him the Devil, To you I will give   —

ἐξουσίαν ταύτην ἅπασαν καὶ τὴν δόξαν αὐτῶν· ὅτι ἐμοὶ
authority   this   all   and   the glory of them, because to me

7 παραδέδοται, καὶ ᾧ ἐὰν θέλω δίδωμι αὐτήν. σὺ οὖν ἐὰν
it has been delivered, and to whomever I wish I give   it;   you, then,   if

[7] then if you worship before me, all things will be yours. [8] And answering to him, Jesus said, Get behind Me, Satan! For it has been written, You shall worship (the) Lord your God, and Him only you shall serve. [9] And he led Him to Jerusalem, and stood Him on the pinnacle of the Temple, and said to Him, If you are the Son of God, throw yourself down from here; [10] for it has been written, He will command His angels about You, and to preserve You; [11] that on (their) hands they shall bear You, lest You strike Your foot against a stone. [12] And answering, Jesus said to him, It has been said, You shall not tempt (the) Lord your God. [13] And having finished every temptation the devil departed from Him until a time.

[14] And Jesus returned in the power of the Spirit to Galilee. And a rumor went out through all the neighborhood about Him. [15] And He taught in their synagogue, being glorified by all. [16] And He came to Nazareth, where He was brought up, and He went in, as was His custom, on the day of the sabbaths, into the synagogue, and stood up to read. [17] And (the) book of Isaiah the prophet was handed to Him. And having unrolled the book, He found the place where it was written, [18] "The Spirit of the Lord is upon Me, because He has anointed Me to preach the gospel to the poor; He has sent Me to heal the brokenhearted, to announce deliverance to the captives and recovery of sight to the blind, to send forth the bruised with deliverance; [19] to proclaim the acceptable year of the Lord." [20] And having rolled up the book, having delivered (it) to the attendant, He sat down, and the eyes of all in the synagogue were fixed on Him. [21] And He began to say to them,

8 προσκυνήσης ἐνώπιόν μου, ἔσται σου πάντα. καὶ ἀποκρι-
you worship     before    me,    will be of you  all.    And answering

θεὶς αὐτῷ εἶπεν ὁ Ἰησοῦς, Ὕπαγε ὀπίσω μου, Σατανᾶ·
to him   said  —  Jesus,   Get behind   Me,   Satan!

γέγραπται γάρ, Προσκυνήσεις Κύριον τὸν Θεόν σου, καὶ
it has been written For, You shall worship (the) Lord the  God of you, and

9 αὐτῷ μόνῳ λατρεύσεις. καὶ ἤγαγεν αὐτὸν εἰς Ἰερουσαλήμ,
Him only you shall serve.  And he led   Him   to   Jerusalem,

καὶ ἔστησεν αὐτὸν ἐπὶ τὸ πτερύγιον τοῦ ἱεροῦ, καὶ εἶπεν
and    stood   Him  on  the  pinnacle of the Temple, and  said

αὐτῷ, Εἰ ὁ υἱὸς εἶ τοῦ Θεοῦ, βάλε σεαυτὸν ἐντεῦθεν κάτω·
to Him, If the Son you are — of God, throw yourself from here  down;

10 γέγραπται γάρ ὅτι Τοῖς ἀγγέλοις αὐτοῦ ἐντελεῖται περὶ
it has been written For,   To the  angels   of Him He will command about

11 σοῦ, τοῦ διαφυλάξαι σέ καὶ ὅτι Ἐπὶ χειρῶν ἀροῦσί σε,
You,  —  to preserve  You and,    In (their) hands they will bear You,

12 μήποτε προσκόψῃς πρὸς λίθον τὸν πόδα σου. καὶ ἀπο-
lest     You strike  against a stone  the  foot of You And answering

κριθεὶς εἶπεν αὐτῷ ὁ Ἰησοῦς ὅτι Εἴρηται, Οὐκ ἐκπειράσεις
said to him    Jesus,  — It has been said, not You shall tempt

13 Κύριον τὸν Θεόν σου. καὶ συντελέσας πάντα πειρασμὸν ὁ
(the) Lord the  God of you. And having finished every  temptation, the

διάβολος ἀπέστη ἀπ' αὐτοῦ ἄχρι καιροῦ.
Devil     departed from Him  until  a season.

14 Καὶ ὑπέστρεψεν ὁ Ἰησοῦς ἐν τῇ δυνάμει τοῦ Πνεύματος
And returned   —  Jesus  in the  power  of the Spirit

εἰς τὴν Γαλιλαίαν· καὶ φήμη ἐξῆλθε καθ' ὅλης τῆς περιχώρου
to  —  Galilee;    and a rumor went out through all the neighborhood

15 περὶ αὐτοῦ. καὶ αὐτὸς ἐδίδασκεν ἐν ταῖς συναγωγαῖς
concerning Him. And He  taught   in  the  synagogues

αὐτῶν, δοξαζόμενος ὑπὸ πάντων.
of them, being glorified by   all.

16 Καὶ ἦλθεν εἰς τὴν Ναζαρέθ, οὗ ἦν τεθραμμένος· καὶ
And He came to  —  Nazareth, where He was brought up,  and

εἰσῆλθε, κατὰ τὸ εἰωθὸς αὐτῷ, ἐν τῇ ἡμέρᾳ τῶν σαββάτων
He went in as (was) the custom to Him, on the day of the sabbaths,

17 εἰς τὴν συναγωγήν, καὶ ἀνέστη ἀναγνῶναι. καὶ ἐπεδόθη
into the synagogue, and  stood up to read.    And was handed

αὐτῷ βιβλίον Ἡσαΐου τοῦ προφήτου. καὶ ἀναπτύξας τὸ
to Him a roll  of Isaiah the  prophet.   And having unrolled the

18 βιβλίον, εὗρε τὸν τόπον οὗ ἦν γεγραμμένον, Πνεῦμα Κυρίου
roll,   He found the place where it was written, (the) Spirit of (the) Lord

ἐπ' ἐμέ, οὗ ἕνεκεν ἔχρισέ με εὐαγγελίζεσθαι πτωχοῖς· ἀπέ-
(is) on Me; therefore He anointed Me to preach the gospel to (the) poor; He

σταλκέ με ἰάσασθαι τοὺς συντετριμμένους τὴν καρδίαν·
has sent  Me to heal    the   broken    —  (in) heart,

κηρύξαι αἰχμαλώτοις ἄφεσιν, καὶ τυφλοῖς ἀνάβλεψιν,
to preach  to captives  deliverance, and to (the) blind new sight,

19 ἀποστεῖλαι τεθραυσμένους ἐν ἀφέσει, κηρύξαι ἐνιαυτὸν
to send away  crushed ones   in  deliverance, to preach  a year

20 Κυρίου δεκτόν. καὶ πτύξας τὸ βιβλίον, ἀποδοὺς τῷ ὑπηρέτῃ,
(the) acceptable. And closing the roll,  returning (it) to the attendant,
Lord

ἐκάθισε· καὶ πάντων ἐν τῇ συναγωγῇ οἱ ὀφθαλμοὶ ἦσαν
He sat.  And of all  in the  synagogue  the   eyes   were

21 ἀτενίζοντες αὐτῷ. ἤρξατο δὲ λέγειν πρὸς αὐτοὺς ὅτι
fixed       on Him. He began And to say   to    them,

Today this Scripture is fulfilled in your ears. [22] And all bore witness to Him, and wondered at the words of grace which proceeded out of His mouth; and they said, Is this not the son of Joseph? [23] And He said to them, Surely you will say to Me this parable, Physician, heal yourself; whatever we have heard being done in Capernaum, do also here in your country. [24] But He said, Truly I say to you, that no prophet is acceptable in his own country. [25] But truly I say to you, many widows were in the days of Elijah in Israel, when the sky was shut up for three years and six months, when there was a great famine on all the land; [26] and to none of them was Elijah sent, except to Zarephath of Sidon, to a woman, a widow. [27] And many lepers were in Israel in the time of Elisha the prophet, and none of them was cleansed except Naaman the Syrian. [28] And all were filled with indignation in the synagogue, hearing these things; [29] and having risen up they threw him out of (the) city, and led Him to the brow of the mountain on which their city had been built, in order to throw Him down headlong; [30] but He went away, passing through (the) midst of them.

[31] And He went down to Capernaum, a city of Galilee, and was teaching them on the sabbaths. [32] And they were astonished at His teaching, for His word was with authority. [33] And in the synagogue was a man having a spirit of an unclean demon; and he cried out with a loud voice, [34] saying, Ha! What do we have to do with You, Jesus, Nazarene? Have you come to destroy us? I know You; You are the Holy One of God. [35] And Jesus rebuked him, saying, Be silent, and come out of him! And the

**22** Σήμερον πεπλήρωται ἡ γραφὴ αὕτη ἐν τοῖς ὠσὶν ὑμῶν.
Today has been fulfilled — scripture this in the ears of you.
καὶ πάντες ἐμαρτύρουν αὐτῷ, καὶ ἐθαύμαζον ἐπὶ τοῖς λόγοις
And all bore witness to Him and marveled at the words
τῆς χάριτος τοῖς ἐκπορευομένοις ἐκ τοῦ στόματος αὐτοῦ, καὶ
— of grace — proceeding from the mouth of Him. And

**23** ἔλεγον, Οὐχ οὗτός ἐστιν ὁ υἱὸς Ἰωσήφ; καὶ εἶπε πρὸς αὐτούς,
they said, Not this Is the son of Joseph? And He said to them,
Πάντως ἐρεῖτέ μοι τὴν παραβολὴν ταύτην, Ἰατρέ, θερά-
Surely you will say to Me — parable this, Physician, heal
πευσον σεαυτόν· ὅσα ἠκούσαμεν γενόμενα ἐν τῇ Καπερναουμ,
yourself! What things we heard happening in — Capernaum,

**24** ποίησον καὶ ὧδε ἐν τῇ πατρίδι σου. εἶπε δέ, Ἀμὴν λέγω
do also here in the native-place of you. He said And, Truly, I say
ὑμῖν ὅτι οὐδεὶς προφήτης δεκτός ἐστιν ἐν τῇ πατρίδι αὐτοῦ.
to you that no prophet acceptable is in the native-place of him.

**25** ἐπ' ἀληθείας δὲ λέγω ὑμῖν, πολλαὶ χῆραι ἦσαν ἐν ταῖς
on a truth But I say to you, Many widows were in the
ἡμέραις Ἠλίου ἐν τῷ Ἰσραήλ, ὅτε ἐκλείσθη ὁ οὐρανὸς ἐπὶ
days of Elijah in — Israel, when was shut up the heaven over
ἔτη τρία καὶ μῆνας ἕξ, ὡς ἐγένετο λιμὸς μέγας ἐπὶ πᾶσαν τὴν
years three and months six, when came a famine great upon all the

**26** γῆν· καὶ πρὸς οὐδεμίαν αὐτῶν ἐπέμφθη Ἠλίας, εἰ μὴ εἰς
land; and to no one of them was sent Elijah except to

**27** Σάρεπτα τῆς Σιδῶνος πρὸς γυναῖκα χήραν. καὶ πολλοὶ
Sarepta — of Sidon, to a woman, a widow. And many
λεπροὶ ἦσαν ἐπὶ Ἐλισσαίου τοῦ προφήτου ἐν τῷ Ἰσραήλ·
lepers were during Elisha the prophet in — Israel,

**28** καὶ οὐδεὶς αὐτῶν ἐκαθαρίσθη, εἰ μὴ Νεεμὰν ὁ Σύρος. καὶ
and none of them was cleansed except Naaman the Syrian. And
ἐπλήσθησαν πάντες θυμοῦ ἐν τῇ συναγωγῇ, ἀκούοντες
were filled all (with) anger in the synagogue hearing

**29** ταῦτα, καὶ ἀναστάντες ἐξέβαλον αὐτὸν ἔξω τῆς πόλεως, καὶ
these things, and rising up they threw Him outside the city. and
ἤγαγον αὐτὸν ἕως τῆς ὀφρύος τοῦ ὄρους ἐφ' οὗ ἡ πόλις
led Him up to the brow of the hill on which the city

**30** αὐτῶν ᾠκοδόμητο, εἰς τὸ κατακρημνίσαι αὐτόν. αὐτὸς δὲ
of them was built, in order to — throw down Him. He But
διελθὼν διὰ μέσου αὐτῶν ἐπορεύετο.
passing through (the) midst of them went away.

**31** Καὶ κατῆλθεν εἰς Καπερναοὺμ πόλιν τῆς Γαλιλαίας· καὶ
And He went down to Capernaum, a city — of Galilee. And

**32** ἦν διδάσκων αὐτοὺς ἐν τοῖς σάββασι. καὶ ἐξεπλήσσοντο
He was teaching them in the sabbaths. And they were astounded

**33** ἐπὶ τῇ διδαχῇ αὐτοῦ, ὅτι ἐν ἐξουσίᾳ ἦν ὁ λόγος αὐτοῦ. καὶ
at the teaching of Him, for with authority was the word of Him. And
ἐν τῇ συναγωγῇ ἦν ἄνθρωπος ἔχων πνεῦμα δαιμονίου
in the synagogue there was a man having a spirit of a demon

**34** ἀκαθάρτου, καὶ ἀνέκραξε φωνῇ μεγάλῃ, λέγων, Ἔα, τί ἡμῖν
unclean, and cried out with a voice great, saying, Aha! What to us
καὶ σοί, Ἰησοῦ Ναζαρηνέ; ἦλθες ἀπολέσαι ἡμᾶς; οἶδά
and to You, Jesus, Nazarene? Did You come to destroy us? I know

**35** σε τίς εἶ, ὁ ἅγιος τοῦ Θεοῦ. καὶ ἐπετίμησεν αὐτῷ ὁ Ἰησοῦς,
You, who you are, the holy of God. And rebuked him — Jesus,
λέγων, Φιμώθητι, καὶ ἔξελθε ἐξ αὐτοῦ. καὶ ρίψαν αὐτὸν τὸ
saying, Be silent, and come out from him. And throwing him the

demon having thrown him into the midst came out from him, and nothing having hurt him. [36] And astonishment came upon all, and they spoke to one another, saying, What word (is) this, that with authority and power he commands the unclean spirits, and they come out. [37] And a report about Him went out into every place of the country around.

[38] And rising up out of the synagogue, He entered into the house of Simon. And the mother-in-law of Simon was oppressed with a great fever; and they asked Him concerning her. [39] And standing over her, He rebuked the fever, and it left her; and instantly arising, she served them.

[40] And at sundown all, as many as had sick ones with various diseases, brought them to Him, and He having laid hands on each one of them healed them; [41] and also demons went out from many, crying out ,and saying, You are the Christ the Son of God! And rebuking them He did not allow them to speak, because they knew Him to be the Christ.

[42] And day being come, having gone out, He went into a deserted place; and the crowd sought Him, and came up to Him, and were keeping Him, that He might not leave them. [43] But He said to them, It behooves Me to preach the gospel to the other cities, the kingdom of God; because for this I have been sent out. [44] And He was praching in the synagogues of Galilee.

CHAPTER 5
[1] And it came to pass in the (time) the crowd pressed on Him to hear the word of God, that He was standing by the lake of Gennesaret. [2] And He saw two boats standing by the lake, but the fishermen having gone out from them

**36** δαιμόνιον εἰς τὸ μέσον ἐξῆλθεν ἀπ᾽ αὐτοῦ, μηδὲν βλάψαν
demon       in the midst  came out  from  him,   nothing  injuring
αὐτόν. καὶ ἐγένετο θάμβος ἐπὶ πάντας, καὶ συνελάλουν πρὸς
him.    And came astonishment on all,   and they spoke with
ἀλλήλους, λέγοντες, Τίς ὁ λόγος οὗτος, ὅτι ἐν ἐξουσίᾳ καὶ
one another,  saying,  What (is) word this,  that with authority and
δυνάμει ἐπιτάσσει τοῖς ἀκαθάρτοις πνεύμασι, καὶ ἐξέρχον-
power  He commands  the  unclean      spirits,    and they come
**37** ται; καὶ ἐξεπορεύετο ἦχος περὶ αὐτοῦ εἰς πάντα τόπον τῆς
out?  And went forth  a rumor concerning Him into every  place of the
περιχώρου.
neighborhood.

**38** Ἀναστὰς δὲ ἐκ τῆς συναγωγῆς, εἰσῆλθεν εἰς τὴν οἰκίαν
rising up And from the synagogue,  He went  into  the  house
Σίμωνος· ἡ πενθερὰ δὲ τοῦ Σίμωνος ἦν συνεχομένη πυρετῷ
of Simon. the mother-in-law And of Simon was being seized with a fever
**39** μεγάλῳ· καὶ ἠρώτησαν αὐτὸν περὶ αὐτῆς. καὶ ἐπιστὰς
great,    and they ask   Him concerning her.   And standing
ἐπάνω αὐτῆς, ἐπετίμησε τῷ πυρετῷ, καὶ ἀφῆκεν αὐτήν·
over   her,   He rebuked   the fever;   and it left  her.
παραχρῆμα δὲ ἀναστᾶσα διηκόνει αὐτοῖς.
at once   And  rising up  she served  them.

**40** Δύνοντος δὲ τοῦ ἡλίου, πάντες ὅσοι εἶχον ἀσθενοῦντας
sinking  And the  sun,   all, as many as had   sick ones
νόσοις ποικίλαις ἤγαγον αὐτοὺς πρὸς αὐτόν· ὁ δὲ ἑνὶ
with various diseases, brought  them    to  Him. He And one
ἑκάστῳ αὐτῶν τὰς χεῖρας ἐπιθεὶς ἐθεράπευσεν αὐτούς.
each   of them the hands  laying on  healed      them.
**41** ἐξήρχετο δὲ καὶ δαιμόνια ἀπὸ πολλῶν, κράζοντα καὶ
came out  And also demons  from  many,   crying out and
λέγοντα ὅτι Σὺ εἶ ὁ Χριστὸς ὁ υἱὸς τοῦ Θεοῦ. καὶ ἐπιτιμῶν
saying,  — You are the Christ, the Son — of God. And rebuking
οὐκ εἴα αὐτὰ λαλεῖν, ὅτι ᾔδεισαν τὸν Χριστὸν αὐτὸν εἶναι.
not He allowed them to speak, for they knew the Christ Him to be.
**42** Γενομένης δὲ ἡμέρας, ἐξελθὼν ἐπορεύθη εἰς ἔρημον τόπον,
coming  And day,  going out He went  to a desert  place.
καὶ οἱ ὄχλοι ἐζήτουν αὐτόν, καὶ ἦλθον ἕως αὐτοῦ, καὶ
And the crowds looked for  Him,  and came up to  Him,  and
**43** κατεῖχον αὐτὸν τοῦ μὴ πορεύεσθαι ἀπ᾽ αὐτῶν. ὁ δὲ εἶπε
held fast Him,    not  to pass   from  them. He But said
πρὸς αὐτοὺς ὅτι Καὶ ταῖς ἑτέραις πόλεσιν εὐαγγελίσασθαί
to  them,  — Also to the  other  cities to preach the gospel
με δεῖ τὴν βασιλείαν τοῦ Θεοῦ· ὅτι εἰς τοῦτο ἀπέσταλμαι.
Me it behoves, the kingdom — of God, for on this  I was sent.
**44** Καὶ ἦν κηρύσσων ἐν ταῖς συναγωγαῖς τῆς Γαλιλαίας.
And He was proclaiming in the  synagogues    of Judea.

CHAPTER 5

**1** Ἐγένετο δὲ ἐν τῷ τὸν ὄχλον ἐπικεῖσθαι αὐτῷ τοῦ ἀκούειν
it was And in — the crowd pressing on Him — to hear
τὸν λόγον τοῦ Θεοῦ, καὶ αὐτὸς ἦν ἑστὼς παρὰ τὴν λίμνην
the word — of God, even He  was standing by  the lake
**2** Γεννησαρέτ· καὶ εἶδε δύο πλοῖα ἑστῶτα παρὰ τὴν λίμνην·
Gennesaret.  And He saw two boats standing by  the lake;
οἱ δὲ ἁλιεῖς ἀποβάντες ἀπ᾽ αὐτῶν ἀπέπλυναν τὰ δίκτυα.
the but fishermen having gone from  them  were washing the nets.

washed the nets. [3] And having entered into one of the boats, which was Simon's, He asked him to put off a little from the land; and having sat down He taught the crowd from the boat. [4] And when He quit speaking, He said to Simon, Put off into the deep and let down your nets for a haul. [5] And answering Simon said to Him, Master, laboring all through the night, we have taken nothing; but at Your word I will let down the net. [6] And having done this they netted a great number of fish; and their net was breaking. [7] And they signaled to the partners, those in the other ship, that coming they should help them. And they came, and filled both the boats, so that they were sinking. [8] And having seen Simon Peter fell at the knees of Jesus, saying, Depart from me, for I am a man, a sinner, Lord. [9] For astonishment laid hold on him, and all with him, at the haul of the fish which they had taken; [10] and in the same way also James and John, sons of Zebedee, who were partners with Simon. And Jesus said to Simon, Do not fear; from now on you shall be catching men. [11] And having brought the boats to the land, leaving all they followed Him.

[12] And it came to pass as He was in one of the cities, that behold, a man full of leprosy! And seeing Jesus, falling on (his) face, he begged Him, saying, Lord, if You choose, You are able to cleanse me. [13] And having stretched out the hand, He touched him, saying, I choose: be cleansed! And immediately the leprosy departed from him. [14] And He commanded him to tell no one; but having gone show yourself to the priest, and offer for your cleansing, as Moses commanded, for a testimony to them.

---

**3** ἐμβὰς δὲ εἰς ἓν τῶν πλοίων, ὃ ἦν τοῦ Σίμωνος, ἠρώτησεν
entering And into one of the boats, which was — Simon's, He asked

αὐτὸν ἀπὸ τῆς γῆς ἐπαναγαγεῖν ὀλίγον. καὶ καθίσας
him from the land to put out a little. And sitting

**4** ἐδίδασκεν ἐκ τοῦ πλοίου τοὺς ὄχλους. ὡς δὲ ἐπαύσατο
He taught from the boat the crowd. as And He quit

λαλῶν, εἶπε πρὸς τὸν Σίμωνα, Ἐπανάγαγε εἰς τὸ βάθος,
speaking, He said to — Simon, Put out into the deep,

**5** καὶ χαλάσατε τὰ δίκτυα ὑμῶν εἰς ἄγραν. καὶ ἀποκριθεὶς ὁ
and let down the nets of you for a haul. And answering —

Σίμων εἶπεν αὐτῷ, Ἐπιστάτα, δι' ὅλης τῆς νυκτὸς κοπιά-
Simon said to Him, Master, through all the night laboring

σαντες οὐδὲν ἐλάβομεν· ἐπὶ δὲ τῷ ῥήματί σου χαλάσω τὸ
nothing we took, at but the word of You I will let down the

**6** δίκτυον. καὶ τοῦτο ποιήσαντες, συνέκλεισαν ἰχθύων πλῆθος
net. And this doing, they enclosed of fish a multitude

**7** πολύ· διερρήγνυτο δὲ τὸ δίκτυον αὐτῶν· καὶ κατένευσαν
much was being torn and the nets of them. And they signaled

τοῖς μετόχοις τοῖς ἐν τῷ ἑτέρῳ πλοίῳ, τοῦ ἐλθόντας συλ-
the partners, those in the other boat,. coming to

λαβέσθαι αὐτοῖς· καὶ ἦλθον καὶ ἔπλησαν ἀμφότερα τὰ
help them; and they came and filled both the

**8** πλοῖα, ὥστε βυθίζεσθαι αὐτά. Ἰδὼν δὲ Σίμων Πέτρος
boats, so as were sinking they. having seen And Simon Peter

προσέπεσε τοῖς γόνασι τοῦ Ἰησοῦ, λέγων, Ἔξελθε ἀπ' ἐμοῦ,
fell at the knees — of Jesus, saying, Depart from me,

**9** ὅτι ἀνὴρ ἁμαρτωλός εἰμι, Κύριε. θάμβος γὰρ περιέσχεν
because a man sinful I am, Lord. astonishment For seized

αὐτὸν καὶ πάντας τοὺς σὺν αὐτῷ, ἐπὶ τῇ ἄγρᾳ τῶν ἰχθύων
him and all the (ones) with him at the haul — of fish

**10** ᾗ συνέλαβον· ὁμοίως δὲ καὶ Ἰάκωβον καὶ Ἰωάννην, υἱοὺς
which they took; likewise and both James and John, sons

Ζεβεδαίου, οἳ ἦσαν κοινωνοὶ τῷ Σίμωνι. καὶ εἶπε πρὸς τὸν
of Zabedee, who were sharers — with Simon. And said to —

Σίμωνα ὁ Ἰησοῦς, Μὴ φοβοῦ· ἀπὸ τοῦ νῦν ἀνθρώπους ἔσῃ
Simon — Jesus, Not do fear; from — now men you will be

**11** ζωγρῶν. καὶ καταγαγόντες τὰ πλοῖα ἐπὶ τὴν γῆν, ἀφέντες
taking alive. And bringing down the boats onto the land, forsaking

ἅπαντα, ἠκολούθησαν αὐτῷ.
all things, they followed Him.

**12** Καὶ ἐγένετο, ἐν τῷ εἶναι αὐτὸν ἐν μιᾷ τῶν πόλεων, καὶ
And it was, in the being of Him in one of the cities, and

ἰδού, ἀνὴρ πλήρης λέπρας· καὶ ἰδὼν τὸν Ἰησοῦν, πεσὼν
behold, a man full of leprosy; and seeing — Jesus, having fallen

ἐπὶ πρόσωπον, ἐδεήθη αὐτοῦ, λέγων, Κύριε, ἐὰν θέλης,
on (his) face, he begged Him, saying, Lord, if You choose,

**13** δύνασαί με καθαρίσαι. καὶ ἐκτείνας τὴν χεῖρα ἥψατο αὐτοῦ,
You are able Me to cleanse. And stretching the hand He touched him,

εἰπών, Θέλω, καθαρίσθητι. καὶ εὐθέως ἡ λέπρα ἀπῆλθεν ἀπ'
saying, I choose, be cleansed! And instantly the leprosy departed from

**14** αὐτοῦ. καὶ αὐτὸς παρήγγειλεν αὐτῷ μηδενὶ εἰπεῖν· ἀλλὰ
him. And He charged him no one to tell, but

ἀπελθὼν δεῖξον σεαυτὸν τῷ ἱερεῖ, καὶ προσένεγκε περὶ τοῦ
going away show yourself to the priest, and offer concerning the

καθαρισμοῦ σου, καθὼς προσέταξε Μωσῆς, εἰς μαρτύριον
cleansing of you, as commanded Moses, for a testimony

[15] But the report concerning Him was spread abroad still more; and great crowds were coming to hear, and to be healed by Him from their sicknesses. [16] But He was drawing back into the deserted places and praying.

[17] And it came to pass on one of the days that He was teaching, and Pharisees and teachers of the Law were sitting by, who were come out of every village of Galilee and of Judea and of Jerusalem; and power of (the) Lord was (present) in order to heal them. [18] And behold, Men carrying a man who was paralyzed on a cot; and they sought to bring him in and to place (him) before Him. [19] And not having found by what way they should bring him in, because of the crowd, going up on the housetop, they let him down through the tiles with the little cot into the midst before Jesus. [20] And seeing their faith, He said to him, Man, your sins have been forgiven you. [21] And the scribes and the Pharisees began to reason, saying, Who is this who speaks blasphemies? Who is able to forgive sins, except God alone? [22] But Jesus knowing their thoughts answering said to them, Why do you reason in your hearts? [23] Which is easier, to say, Your sins have been forgiven you, or to say, Arise and walk? [24] But that you may know that the Son of man has authority on the earth to forgive sins, He said to the paralyzed one, To you I say, Arise, and having taken up your cot go to your house. [25] And immediately, having stood up before them, having taken up (that) on which he was lying, he departed to his house, glorifying God. [26] And amazement seized all, and they glorified God, and were filled with fear, saying, We have seen strange things

15 αὐτοῖς. διήρχετο δὲ μᾶλλον ὁ λόγος περὶ αὐτοῦ· καὶ συν-
to them. spread But even more the word concerning Him, and were

ήρχοντο ὄχλοι πολλοὶ ἀκούειν, καὶ θεραπεύεσθαι ὑπ᾽ αὐτοῦ
coming crowds great to hear, and to be healed by Him

16 ἀπὸ τῶν ἀσθενειῶν αὐτῶν. αὐτὸς δὲ ἦν ὑποχωρῶν ἐν ταῖς
from the infirmities of them. He But was withdrawing in the

ἐρήμοις καὶ προσευχόμενος.
desert and praying.

17 Καὶ ἐγένετο ἐν μιᾷ τῶν ἡμερῶν, καὶ αὐτὸς ἦν διδάσκων·
And it was, on one of the days, and He was teaching,

καὶ ἦσαν καθήμενοι Φαρισαῖοι καὶ νομοδιδάσκαλοι, οἳ ἦσαν
and were sitting Pharisees and teachers of law, who were

ἐληλυθότες ἐκ πάσης κώμης τῆς Γαλιλαίας καὶ Ἰουδαίας καὶ
coming out of every village — of Galilee and Judea and

Ἱερουσαλήμ· καὶ δύναμις Κυρίου ἦν εἰς τὸ ἰᾶσθαι αὐτούς.
Jerusalem. And power of (the) Lord was, to the curing (of) them.

18 καὶ ἰδού, ἄνδρες φέροντες ἐπὶ κλίνης ἄνθρωπον ὃς ἦν παρα-
And behold, men carrying on a cot a man who was

λελυμένος, καὶ ἐζήτουν αὐτὸν εἰσενεγκεῖν καὶ θεῖναι ἐνώπιον
paralyzed; and they sought him to bring in and to lay before

19 αὐτοῦ· καὶ μὴ εὑρόντες διὰ ποίας εἰσενέγκωσιν αὐτὸν διὰ
Him. And not finding by what way they may bring in him through

τὸν ὄχλον, ἀναβάντες ἐπὶ τὸ δῶμα, διὰ τῶν κεράμων
the crowd, going up on the housetop, through the tiles

καθῆκαν αὐτὸν σὺν τῷ κλινιδίῳ εἰς τὸ μέσον ἔμπροσθεν τοῦ
they let down him with the cot into the midst in front of —

20 Ἰησοῦ· καὶ ἰδὼν τὴν πίστιν αὐτῶν, εἶπεν αὐτῷ, Ἄνθρωπε,
Jesus. And seeing the faith of them, He said to him, Man,

21 ἀφέωνταί σοι αἱ ἁμαρτίαι σου. καὶ ἤρξαντο διαλογίζεσθαι
have been forgiven you the sins of you. And began to reason

οἱ γραμματεῖς καὶ οἱ Φαρισαῖοι, λέγοντες, Τίς ἐστιν οὗτος
the scribes and the Pharisees, saying, Who is this one

ὃς λαλεῖ βλασφημίας; τίς δύναται ἀφιέναι ἁμαρτίας, εἰ μὴ
who speaks blasphemies? Who is able to forgive sins, except

22 μόνος ὁ Θεός; ἐπιγνοὺς δὲ ὁ Ἰησοῦς τοὺς διαλογισμοὺς
only — God? knowing But — Jesus the reasonings

αὐτῶν ἀποκριθεὶς εἶπε πρὸς αὐτούς, Τί διαλογίζεσθε ἐν ταῖς
of them, answering said to them, Why do you reason in the

23 καρδίαις ὑμῶν; τί ἐστιν εὐκοπώτερον, εἰπεῖν, Ἀφέωνταί
hearts of you? What is easier, to say, Have been forgiven

σοι αἱ ἁμαρτίαι σου, ἢ εἰπεῖν, Ἔγειραι καὶ περιπάτει; ἵνα
you the sins of you, or to say, Rise up and walk? that

24 δὲ εἰδῆτε ὅτι ἐξουσίαν ἔχει ὁ υἱὸς τοῦ ἀνθρώπου ἐπὶ τῆς γῆς
But you may know authority has the Son — of man on the earth

ἀφιέναι ἁμαρτίας εἶπε τῷ παραλελυμένῳ Σοὶ λέγω,
to forgive sins, He said to the paralytic, To you I say,

ἔγειραι, καὶ ἄρας τὸ κλινίδιόν σου, πορεύου εἰς τὸν οἶκόν
Rise up, and taking the cot of you, go to the house

25 σου. καὶ παραχρῆμα ἀναστὰς ἐνώπιον αὐτῶν, ἄρας ἐφ᾽ ᾧ
of you. And at once rising up before them, taking on which

κατέκειτο, ἀπῆλθεν εἰς τὸν οἶκον αὐτοῦ, δοξάζων τὸν Θεόν.
he was lying, he went to the house of him, glorifying — God.

26 καὶ ἔκστασις ἔλαβεν ἅπαντας, καὶ ἐδόξαζον τὸν Θεον, καὶ
And amazement seized all, and they glorified — God, and

ἐπλήσθησαν φόβου, λέγοντες ὅτι Εἴδομεν παράδοξα
were filled (with) fear, saying, — We saw wonderful things

today.

[27] And after these things He went out and saw a tax-collector by the name of Levi, sitting at the tax office, and said to him, Follow Me. [28] And having left all, having arisen, he followed Him. [29] And Levi made a great banquet for Him in his house, and there was a great many tax-collectors and others who were reclining with them. [30] And their scribes and the Pharisees murmured at His disciples, saying, Why do you eat and drink with tax-collectors and sinners? [31] And answering Jesus said to them, They who are well have no need of a physician, but they who are sick. [32] I did not come to call the righteous to repentance, but sinners. [33] And they said to Him, Why do the disciples of John fast often and make supplications; and the same way also those of the Pharisees; but those of you eat and drink? [34] And He said to them, Are you able to make the sons of the bride-chamber fast while the bridegroom is with them? [35] But the days will come when the bridegroom also shall be taken away from them, then they will fast in those days. [36] And He also spoke a parable to them: No one puts a piece of a new garment on an old garment, otherwise he both tears the new and the old does not match the piece which is from the new. [37] And no one puts new wine into wineskins, otherwise the new wine will burst the wineskins, and it will be spilled out, and the wineskins will be ruined; [38] but new wine is to be put into new wineskins, and both are preserved together [39] And no one having drunk old (wine) immediately desires new; for he says, The old is better.

σήμερον.
**today.**

**27** Καὶ μετὰ ταῦτα ἐξῆλθε, καὶ ἐθεάσατο τελώνην, ὀνόματι
And after these things He went, and saw a tax-collector, by name

Λευΐν, καθήμενον ἐπὶ τὸ τελώνιον, καὶ εἶπεν αὐτῷ, Ἀκολού-
Levi, sitting at the custom-house, and said to him, Follow

**28** θει μοι. καὶ καταλιπὼν ἅπαντα, ἀναστὰς ἠκολούθησεν αὐτῷ.
Me! And having left all things, rising up he followed Him.

**29** καὶ ἐποίησε δοχὴν μεγάλην ὁ Λευῒς αὐτῷ ἐν τῇ οἰκίᾳ αὐτοῦ·
And made a feast great — Levi for Him in the house of him;

καὶ ἦν ὄχλος τελωνῶν πολύς, καὶ ἄλλων οἳ ἦσαν μετ'
and was a crowd of tax-collectors, much, and of others who were with

**30** αὐτῶν κατακείμενοι καὶ ἐγόγγυζον οἱ γραμματεῖς αὐτῶν
them reclining And murmured the scribes of them

καὶ οἱ Φαρισαῖοι πρὸς τοὺς μαθητὰς αὐτοῦ, λέγοντες, Διατί
and the Pharisees at the disciples of Him, saying, Why

μετὰ τελωνῶν καὶ ἁμαρτωλῶν ἐσθίετε καὶ πίνετε; καὶ
with tax-collectors and sinners do you eat and drink? And

**31** ἀποκριθεὶς ὁ Ἰησοῦς εἶπε πρὸς αὐτούς, Οὐ χρείαν ἔχουσιν
answering — Jesus said to them, Not need have

**32** οἱ ὑγιαίνοντες ἰατροῦ, ἀλλ' οἱ κακῶς ἔχοντες. οὐκ ἐλήλυθα
those being sound of a physician, but those illness having. not I have come

καλέσαι δικαίους, ἀλλὰ ἁμαρτωλοὺς εἰς μετάνοιαν. οἱ δὲ
to call righteous ones, but sinners to repentance. they But

**33** εἶπον πρὸς αὐτόν, Διατί οἱ μαθηταὶ Ἰωάννου νηστεύουσι
said to Him, Why the disciples of John fast

πυκνά, καὶ δεήσεις ποιοῦνται, ὁμοίως καὶ οἱ τῶν Φαρισαίων·
often, and prayers make, likewise also those of the Pharisees;

**34** οἱ δὲ σοὶ ἐσθίουσι καὶ πίνουσιν; ὁ δὲ εἶπε πρὸς αὐτούς, Μὴ
those but to you eat and drink? He But said to them, Not

δύνασθε τοὺς υἱοὺς τοῦ νυμφῶνος, ἐν ᾧ ὁ νυμφίος μετ' αὐτῶν
are able the sons of the bride-chamber, while the groom with them

**35** ἐστι, ποιῆσαι νηστεύειν; ἐλεύσονται δὲ ἡμέραι, καὶ ὅταν
is, to make to fast, will come but days, and when

ἀπαρθῇ ἀπ' αὐτῶν ὁ νυμφίος, τότε νηστεύσουσιν ἐν
is taken away from them the bridegroom, then they will fast in

**36** ἐκείναις ταῖς ἡμέραις. ἔλεγε δὲ καὶ παραβολὴν πρὸς αὐτούς
those — days. He told And also a parable to them,

ὅτι Οὐδεὶς ἐπίβλημα ἱματίου καινοῦ ἐπιβάλλει ἐπὶ ἱμάτιον
— No one a piece of a garment new puts on a garment

παλαιόν· εἰ δὲ μήγε, καὶ τὸ καινὸν σχίζει, καὶ τῷ παλαιῷ
old, otherwise, both the new will tear, and with the old

**37** οὐ συμφωνεῖ ἐπίβλημα τὸ ἀπὸ τοῦ καινοῦ. καὶ οὐδεὶς βάλλει
not does agree (the) piece — from the new. And no one puts

οἶνον νέον εἰς ἀσκοὺς παλαιούς· εἰ δὲ μήγε, ῥήξει ὁ νέος οἶνος
wine new into wineskins old; otherwise, will burst the new wine

τοὺς ἀσκούς, καὶ αὐτὸς ἐκχυθήσεται, καὶ οἱ ἀσκοὶ ἀπολοῦν-
the wineskins, and it will be poured out, and the wineskins will

**38** ται ἀλλὰ οἶνον νέον εἰς ἀσκοὺς καινοὺς βλητέον, καὶ ἀμφό-
perish. But wine new into wineskins new is to be put, and both

τεροι συντηροῦνται. καὶ οὐδεὶς πιὼν παλαιὸν εὐθέως θέλει
are preserved together. And no one drinking old at once desires

νέον· λέγει γάρ, Ὁ παλαιὸς χρηστότερός ἐστιν
new; he says for, The old better is.

## CHAPTER 6

**CHAPTER 6**

[1] And it came to pass on the second sabbath (after the) first, He passed along through the grain fields; and His disciples were plucking the ears, and were eating, rubbing in the hands. [2] But some of the Pharisees said to them, Why do you do that which is not lawful to do on the sabbaths? [3] And answered to them Jesus said, Did you never read this, that which David did, when he hungered, himself and those who were with him? [4] How he entered into the house of God and took the showbread, and ate, and gave also to those with him, which it is not lawful to eat except only the priests? [5] And He said to them, The Son of man is Lord also of the sabbath.

[6] And also it came to pass on another sabbath He entered into the synagogue and taught; and a man was there, and his right hand was withered. [7] And the scribes and the Pharisees were watching Him, whether He would heal on the Sabbath, that they might find a charge against Him. [8] But He knew their thoughts and said to the man who had the withered hand, Arise, and stand in the midst. And having risen up, he stood. [9] Then Jesus said to them, I will ask of you whether it is lawful on the sabbath to do good or to do evil; to save life or to destroy? [10] And having looked around on all them He said to the man, Stretch out your hand! And he did so, and his hand was restored sound as the other. [11] But they were filled with madness, and plotted with one another (as to) what they should do to Jesus.

[12] And it happened in those days He went out into the mountain to pray, and He was spending the night in prayer to God.

1 Ἐγένετο δὲ ἐν σαββάτῳ δευτεροπρώτῳ διαπορεύεσθαι
it was   And on a sabbath,   the second chief   passed along

αὐτὸν διὰ τῶν σπορίμων· καὶ ἔτιλλον οἱ μαθηταὶ αὐτοῦ
He   through the sown fields,   and plucked the disciples   of Him

2 τοὺς στάχυας, καὶ ἤσθιον, ψώχοντες ταῖς χερσί. τινὲς δὲ τῶν
the   heads,   and were eating, rubbing with the hands. some And of the

Φαρισαίων εἶπον αὐτοῖς, Τί ποιεῖτε ὃ οὐκ ἔξεστι ποιεῖν ἐν
Pharisees   said   to them, Why do you what not is lawful to do   on

3 τοῖς σάββασι ; καὶ ἀποκριθεὶς πρὸς αὐτοὺς εἶπεν ὁ Ἰησοῦς,
the   sabbaths? And answering   to   them   said — Jesus,

Οὐδὲ τοῦτο ἀνέγνωτε, ὃ ἐποίησε Δαβίδ, ὁπότε ἐπείνασεν
Not this   you read, what   did David   when he hungered,

4 αὐτὸς καὶ οἱ μετ᾽ αὐτοῦ ὄντες ; ὡς εἰσῆλθεν εἰς τὸν οἶκον τοῦ
he   and those with him   being? As he entered into the house —

Θεοῦ, καὶ τοὺς ἄρτους τῆς προθέσεως ἔλαβε, καὶ ἔφαγε, καὶ
of God, and the   loaves of the presentation he took   and ate,   and

ἔδωκε καὶ τοῖς μετ᾽ αὐτοῦ, οὓς οὐκ ἔξεστι φαγεῖν εἰ μὴ μόνους
gave even to those with him, which not it is lawful to eat except only

5 τοὺς ἱερεῖς ; καὶ ἔλεγεν αὐτοῖς ὅτι Κύριός ἐστιν ὁ υἱὸς τοῦ
the priests? And He said   to them,   — Lord   is   The Son —

ἀνθρώπου καὶ τοῦ σαββάτου.
of man even of the   sabbath.

6 Ἐγένετο δὲ καὶ ἐν ἑτέρῳ σαββάτῳ εἰσελθεῖν αὐτὸν εἰς τὴν
it was And also on another sabbath,   entering   He into the

συναγωγὴν καὶ διδάσκειν· καὶ ἦν ἐκεῖ ἄνθρωπος, καὶ ἡ χεὶρ
synagogue   and teaching; and was there a man,   and the hand

7 αὐτοῦ ἡ δεξιὰ ἦν ξηρά. παρετήρουν δὲ αὐτὸν οἱ γραμματεῖς
of him, the right, was withered.   kept close by And Him the scribes

καὶ οἱ Φαρισαῖοι, εἰ ἐν τῷ σαββάτῳ θεραπεύσει· ἵνα εὕρωσι
and the Pharisees, if on the   sabbath   He will heal; that they might find

8 κατηγορίαν αὐτοῦ. αὐτὸς δὲ ᾔδει τοὺς διαλογισμοὺς αὐτῶν,
an accusation of Him.   He But knew the   reasonings   of them,

καὶ εἶπε τῷ ἀνθρώπῳ τῷ ξηρὰν ἔχοντι τὴν χεῖρα, Ἔγειραι,
and said to the   man   — withered having   the hand, Rise up

9 καὶ στῆθι εἰς τὸ μέσον. ὁ δὲ ἀναστὰς ἔστη. εἶπεν οὖν ὁ Ἰησοῦς
and stand in the middle! he And rising up stood. said Then — Jesus

πρὸς αὐτούς, Ἐπερωτήσω ὑμᾶς τί, Ἔξεστι τοῖς σάββασιν,
to   them,   I will ask   you one: Is it lawful on the sabbaths

ἀγαθοποιῆσαι ἢ κακοποιῆσαι ; ψυχὴν σῶσαι ἢ ἀπολέσαι ;
to do good,   or   to do ill?   A soul   to save, or to destroy?

10 καὶ περιβλεψάμενος πάντας αὐτούς, εἶπε τῷ ἀνθρώπῳ,
And   looking around at   all (of) them,   He said to the   man,

Ἔκτεινον τὴν χεῖρά σου. ὁ δὲ ἐποίησεν οὕτω. καὶ ἀποκατε-
Stretch out the hand of you. he And did   so,   and was

11 στάθη ἡ χεὶρ αὐτοῦ ὑγιὴς ὡς ἡ ἄλλη. αὐτοὶ δὲ ἐπλήσθησαν
restored the hand of him sound as the other. they But were filled

ἀνοίας· καὶ διελάλουν πρὸς ἀλλήλους, τί ἂν ποιήσειαν τῷ
(with) madness and talked   to   one another, what they might do —

Ἰησοῦ.
to Jesus.

12 Ἐγένετο δὲ ἐν ταῖς ἡμέραις ταύταις ἐξῆλθεν εἰς τὸ ὄρος
it was   And in — days   these, He went out into the mount

προσεύξασθαι· καὶ ἦν διανυκτερεύων ἐν τῇ προσευχῇ τοῦ
to pray,   and He was spending the night in — prayer

[13] And when day came, He called His disciples and chose out twelve from them, whom also He named apostles: [14] Simon whom He also named Peter, and his brother Andrew, James and John, Philip and Bartholomew, [15] Matthew and Thomas, James the (son) of Alpheus, and Simon, the (one) being called Zealot; [16] Judas (brother) of James, and Judas Iscariot, who also became (the) betrayer. [17] And going down with them, He stood on a level place, and a crowd of His disciples and a great multitude of the people from all Judea, and Jerusalem and the sea coast of Tyre and Sidon, who came to hear Him, and to be healed of their diseases, [18] and those beset by unclean spirits — and they were healed. [19] And all the crowd sought to touch Him, for power went out from Him and healed all.

[20] And lifting up His eyes upon His disciples He said, Blessed (are) the poor, for yours is the kingdom of God. [21] Blessed (are you) who hunger now, for you shall be filled. Blessed (are you) who weep now, for you shall laugh. [22] Blessed (are you) when men shall hate you, and when they shall cut you off, and shall reproach, and cast out your name as wicked, on account of the Son of man; [23] rejoice in that day and leap for joy, for, lo, your reward (is) great in Heaven; for their fathers did to the prophets according to these things. [24] But woe to you rich ones, for you are receiving your comfort! [25] Woe to you who have been filled, for you shall hunger! Woe to you who laugh now, for you shall mourn and weep! [26] Woe to you when all men speak well of you, for their

---

**13** Θεοῦ. καὶ ὅτε ἐγένετο ἡμέρα, προσεφώνησε τοὺς μαθητὰς
of God. And when it became day, He called to the disciples

αὐτοῦ· καὶ ἐκλεξάμενος ἀπ' αὐτῶν δώδεκα, οὓς καὶ ἀποστό-
of Him, and elected from them twelve, whom also apostles

**14** λους ὠνόμασε, Σίμωνα ὃν καὶ ὠνόμασε Πέτρον, καὶ Ἀνδρέαν
He named: Simon, whom also He named Peter; and Andrew

τὸν ἀδελφὸν αὐτοῦ, Ἰάκωβον καὶ Ἰωάννην, Φίλιππον καὶ
the brother of him; James and John; Philip and

**15** Βαρθολομαῖον, Ματθαῖον καὶ Θωμᾶν, Ἰάκωβον τὸν τοῦ
Bartholomew; Matthew and Thomas; James the (son) —

**16** Ἀλφαίου, καὶ Σίμωνα τὸν καλούμενον Ζηλωτήν, Ἰούδαν
of Alpheus; and Simon the (one) being called Zealot; Judas

Ἰακώβου, καὶ Ἰούδαν Ἰσκαριώτην, ὃς καὶ ἐγένετο προδό-
of James; and Judas Iscariot, who also became betrayer.

**17** της, καὶ καταβὰς μετ' αὐτῶν, ἔστη ἐπὶ τόπου πεδινοῦ, καὶ
And coming down with them, He stood on a place level, and

ὄχλος μαθητῶν αὐτοῦ, καὶ πλῆθος πολὺ τοῦ λαοῦ ἀπὸ
crowd of disciples of Him, and a multitude much of the people from

πάσης τῆς Ἰουδαίας καὶ Ἱερουσαλήμ, καὶ τῆς παραλίου
all — Judea and Jerusalem, and the coast country

Τύρου καὶ Σιδῶνος, οἳ ἦλθον ἀκοῦσαι αὐτοῦ, καὶ ἰαθῆναι
of Tyre and Sidon, who came to hear Him, and to be healed

**18** ἀπὸ τῶν νόσων αὐτῶν· καὶ οἱ ὀχλούμενοι ὑπὸ πνευμάτων
from the diseases of them, and those being tormented by spirits

**19** ἀκαθάρτων, καὶ ἐθεραπεύοντο. καὶ πᾶς ὁ ὄχλος ἐζήτει
unclean, and they were healed. And all the crowd sought

ἅπτεσθαι αὐτοῦ· ὅτι δύναμις παρ' αὐτοῦ ἐξήρχετο καὶ ἰᾶτο
to touch Him, because power from Him went out and healed

πάντας.
all.

**20** Καὶ αὐτὸς ἐπάρας τοὺς ὀφθαλμοὺς αὐτοῦ εἰς τοὺς μαθητὰς
And He lifting up the eyes of Him to the disciples

αὐτοῦ ἔλεγε, Μακάριοι οἱ πτωχοί, ὅτι ὑμετέρα ἐστὶν ἡ
of Him said, Blessed (are) the poor, because yours is the

**21** βασιλεία τοῦ Θεοῦ. μακάριοι οἱ πεινῶντες νῦν, ὅτι χορτασθή-
kingdom of God. Blessed (are) those hungering now, for you will be

σεσθε. μακάριοι οἱ κλαίοντες νῦν, ὅτι γελάσετε. μακάριοί
filled. Blessed (are) those weeping now, because you will laugh. Blessed

**22** ἐστε, ὅταν μισήσωσιν ὑμᾶς οἱ ἄνθρωποι, καὶ ὅταν ἀφο-
are you when hate you — men, and when they

ρίσωσιν ὑμᾶς, καὶ ὀνειδίσωσι, καὶ ἐκβάλωσι τὸ ὄνομα ὑμῶν
separate you, and will reproach, and will cast out the name of you

**23** ὡς πονηρόν, ἕνεκα τοῦ υἱοῦ τοῦ ἀνθρώπου. χαίρετε ἐν
as evil, for the sake of the Son — of man. Rejoice in

ἐκείνῃ τῇ ἡμέρᾳ καὶ σκιρτήσατε· ἰδοὺ γάρ, ὁ μισθὸς ὑμῶν
that day and leap for joy. behold For, the reward of you

πολὺς ἐν τῷ οὐρανῷ· κατὰ ταῦτα γὰρ ἐποίουν τοῖς προφή-
much in — Heaven! according to these For did to the prophets

**24** ταις οἱ πατέρες αὐτῶν. πλὴν οὐαὶ ὑμῖν τοῖς πλουσίοις,
the fathers of them. But woe to you the rich ones,

**25** ὅτι ἀπέχετε τὴν παράκλησιν ὑμῶν. οὐαὶ ὑμῖν, οἱ ἐμπεπλη-
because you have the comfort of you! Woe to you, those having

σμένοι, ὅτι πεινάσετε. οὐαὶ ὑμῖν, οἱ γελῶντες νῦν, ὅτι
been filled, for you will hunger! Woe to you, those laughing now because

**26** πενθήσετε καὶ κλαύσετε. οὐαὶ ὑμῖν, ὅταν καλῶς ὑμᾶς εἴπωσι
you will mourn and lament! Woe to you, when well (of) you speak

πάντες οἱ ἄνθρωποι· κατὰ ταῦτα γὰρ ἐποίουν τοῖς ψευδο-
all — men according to these For did to the false

προφήταις οἱ πατέρες αὐτῶν.
prophets the fathers of them.

fathers did according to these things to the false prophets! [27] But I say to you who hear, Love your enemies; do good to those who hate you; [28] bless those who curse you, and pray for those who despitefully use you. [29] To him who strikes you on the cheek, offer the other also; and from him who takes away your cloak, do not forbid the coat also. [30] And to everyone who asks you, give; and from him who takes away what is yours, do not ask (it) back. [31] And according as you desire that men should do to you, you also do to them in the same way. [32] And if you love those who love you, what thanks is it to you, for even sinners love those who love them? [33] And if you do good to those who do good to you, what thanks is it to you, for even sinners do the same? [34] And if you lend (to those) from whom you hope to receive, what thanks is it to you, for even sinners lend to sinners in order that they may receive the like? [35] But love your enemies, and do good, and lend, hoping for nothing again; and your reward shall be great, and you shall be sons of the Highest; for He is good to the unthankful and evil ones. [36] Therefore be merciful, as your Father is also merciful. [37] And judge not, that you may in no way be judged; condemn not, that you in no way be condemned. Forgive, and you shall be forgiven. [38] Give, and it shall be given to you, good measure pressed down and shaken together and running over they shall give into your bosom; for with the same measure with which you measure, it shall be measured again to you. [39] And He spoke a parable to them: Is a blind one able to lead a blind

**27** Ἀλλ' ὑμῖν λέγω τοῖς ἀκούουσιν, Ἀγαπᾶτε τοὺς ἐχθροὺς
But to you I say, those hearing, Love the enemies

**28** ὑμῶν, καλῶς ποιεῖτε τοῖς μισοῦσιν ὑμᾶς, εὐλογεῖτε τοὺς
of you; well do to those hating you; bless those

καταρωμένους ὑμῖν, καὶ προσεύχεσθε ὑπὲρ τῶν ἐπηρεαζόν-
cursing you; and pray for those insulting

**29** των ὑμᾶς. τῷ τύπτοντί σε ἐπὶ τὴν σιαγόνα, πάρεχε καὶ τὴν
you. To those striking you on the cheek, turn also the

ἄλλην· καὶ ἀπὸ τοῦ αἴροντός σου τὸ ἱμάτιον, καὶ τὸν
other; and from those taking of you the garment, also the

**30** χιτῶνα μὴ κωλύσῃς. παντὶ δὲ τῷ αἰτοῦντί σε δίδου· καὶ
tunic not do keep back. To everyone And asking you, give; and

**31** ἀπὸ τοῦ αἴροντος τὰ σὰ μὴ ἀπαίτει. καὶ καθὼς θέλετε ἵνα
from those taking your things, not do ask back. And as you desire that

ποιῶσιν ὑμῖν οἱ ἄνθρωποι, καὶ ὑμεῖς ποιεῖτε αὐτοῖς ὁμοίως.
may do to you men, also you do to them likewise.

**32** καὶ εἰ ἀγαπᾶτε τοὺς ἀγαπῶντας ὑμᾶς, ποία ὑμῖν χάρις
And if you love those loving you, what to you thanks

ἐστί ; καὶ γὰρ οἱ ἁμαρτωλοὶ τοὺς ἀγαπῶντας αὐτοὺς ἀγα-
is there? even For the sinners those loving them love.

**33** πῶσι. καὶ ἐὰν ἀγαθοποιῆτε τοὺς ἀγαθοποιοῦντας ὑμᾶς,
And if you do good to those doing good to you,

ποία ὑμῖν χάρις ἐστί ; καὶ γὰρ οἱ ἁμαρτωλοὶ τὸ αὐτὸ
what to you thanks is there? even For the sinners the same

**34** ποιοῦσι. καὶ ἐὰν δανείζητε παρ' ὧν ἐλπίζητε ἀπολαβεῖν,
do. And if you lend from whom you hope to receive,

ποία ὑμῖν χάρις ἐστί ; καὶ γὰρ οἱ ἁμαρτωλοὶ ἁμαρτωλοῖς
what to you thanks is there? even For the sinners to sinners

**35** δανείζουσιν, ἵνα ἀπολάβωσι τὰ ἴσα. πλὴν ἀγαπᾶτε τοὺς
lend, that they may receive the same. But love the

ἐχθροὺς ὑμῶν, καὶ ἀγαθοποιεῖτε, καὶ δανείζετε, μηδὲν ἀπελ-
enemies of you, and do good and lend, nothing

πίζοντες· καὶ ἔσται ὁ μισθὸς ὑμῶν πολύς, καὶ ἔσεσθε υἱοὶ τοῦ
despairing, and will be the reward of you much; and you will be sons of the

ὑψίστου· ὅτι αὐτὸς χρηστός ἐστιν ἐπὶ τοὺς ἀχαρίστους καὶ
most High because He kind is to the unthankful and

**36** πονηρούς. γίνεσθε οὖν οἰκτίρμονες, καθὼς καὶ ὁ πατὴρ
evil ones. Be then merciful, even as also the Father

ὑμῶν οἰκτίρμων ἐστί. μὴ κρίνετε, καὶ οὐ μὴ κριθῆτε. μὴ κατα-
of you merciful is. not Judge, and in no way be judged; do not

**37** δικάζετε, καὶ οὐ μὴ καταδικασθῆτε· ἀπολύετε, καὶ ἀπολυθή-
condemn, and in no way you will be condemned; forgive, and you will be

**38** σεσθε· δίδοτε, καὶ δοθήσεται ὑμῖν· μέτρον καλόν, πεπιε-
forgiven; give, and will be given to you measure good, pressed

σμένον καὶ σεσαλευμένον καὶ ὑπερεκχυνόμενον δώσουσιν εἰς
down and shaken together and running over shall they give into

τὸν κόλπον ὑμῶν. τῷ γὰρ αὐτῷ μέτρῳ ᾧ μετρεῖτε ἀντι-
the bosom of you. the For same measure which you mete it will

μετρηθήσεται ὑμῖν.
be measured back to you.

**39** Εἶπε δὲ παραβολὴν αὐτοῖς, Μήτι δύναται τυφλὸς τυφλὸν
He spoke And a parable to them, Not is able a blind one a blind one

one? Will not both fall into a ditch? [40] A disciple is not above his teacher; but everyone perfected shall be like his teacher. [41] But why do you look on the twig that is in the eye of your brother, but do not see the log that is in your own eye? [42] Or how can you say to your brother, Brother, let me pull out the twig that is in your eye, not seeing the log in your own eye? Hypocrite, first throw the log out of your own eye, and then you will see clearly to throw out the twig that (is) in the eye of your brother. [43] For there is not a good tree that produces bad fruit,

nor a bad tree that produces good fruit. [44] For each tree is known by its own fruit, for they do not gather figs from thorns, nor do they gather a bunch of grapes from a bramble. [45] A good man out of the good treasure of his heart brings forth that which (is) good; and the wicked man out of the wicked treasure of his heart brings forth that which (is) wicked; for out of the abundance of the heart his mouth speaks. [46] And why do you call Me Lord, Lord, and do not do what I say? [47] Everyone who is coming to Me and hearing My words, and doing them, I will show you to whom he is like. [48] He is like a man building a house, who dug and deepened, and laid a foundation on the rock; and a flood occurring, the stream burst against that house, and could not shake it, for it had been founded on the rock. [49] But he who heard and did not is like a man having built a house on the earth without a foundation; on which the stream burst, and it immediately fell, and the ruin of that house was

ὁδηγεῖν ; οὐχὶ ἀμφότεροι εἰς βόθυνον πεσοῦνται ; οὐκ ἔστι
guide.      not Will they    into the ditch    fall in?      Not   is

40 μαθητὴς ὑπὲρ τὸν διδάσκαλον αὐτοῦ· κατηρτισμένος δὲ
a disciple above    the    teacher    of him, having been perfected but

41 πᾶς ἔσται ὡς ὁ διδάσκαλος αὐτοῦ. τί δὲ βλέπεις τὸ κάρφος
everyone will be as the   teacher    of him. why And do you see the twig

τὸ ἐν τῷ ὀφθαλμῷ τοῦ ἀδελφοῦ σου, τὴν δὲ δοκὸν τὴν ἐν
— in the eye    of the brother of you, the   but    log    —   in

42 τῷ ἰδίῳ ὀφθαλμῷ οὐ κατανοεῖς ; ἢ πῶς δύνασαι λέγειν τῷ
(your) own    eye    not you consider? Or how are you able to say to the

ἀδελφῷ σου, Ἀδελφέ, ἄφες ἐκβάλω τὸ κάρφος τὸ ἐν τῷ
brother of you, Brother,    allow I may take out the twig    — in the

ὀφθαλμῷ σου, αὐτὸς τὴν ἐν τῷ ὀφθαλμῷ σου δοκὸν οὐ
eye    of you, yourself the  in the    eye   of you log not

βλέπων ; ὑποκριτά, ἔκβαλε πρῶτον τὴν δοκὸν ἐκ τοῦ
seeing?    Hypocrite, take out   first    the    log   out of the

ὀφθαλμοῦ σου, καὶ τότε διαβλέψεις ἐκβαλεῖν τὸ κάρφος τὸ
eye    of you, and then you will see clearly to take out the twig

43 ἐν τῷ ὀφθαλμῷ τοῦ ἀδελφοῦ σου. οὐ γάρ ἐστι δένδρον
in the    eye    of the brother of you. not For is    a tree

καλὸν ποιοῦν καρπὸν σαπρόν· οὐδὲ δένδρον σαπρὸν ποιοῦν
good producing fruit    bad,    nor    tree    a bad    producing

44 καρπὸν καλόν. ἕκαστον γὰρ δένδρον ἐκ τοῦ ἰδίου καρποῦ
fruit   good.    each   For   tree   out of the own   fruit

γινώσκεται. οὐ γὰρ ἐξ ἀκανθῶν συλλέγουσι σῦκα, οὐδὲ ἐκ
is known.   not For out of thorns  do they gather  figs,  nor out of

45 βάτου τρυγῶσι σταφυλήν. ὁ ἀγαθὸς ἄνθρωπος ἐκ τοῦ
a bramble a grape  do they gather. The  good    man    out of the

ἀγαθοῦ θησαυροῦ τῆς καρδίας αὐτοῦ προφέρει τὸ ἀγαθόν·
good    treasure of the  heart  of him brings forth the  good;

καὶ ὁ πονηρὸς ἄνθρωπος ἐκ τοῦ πονηροῦ θησαυροῦ τῆς
and the evil    man    out of the    evil    treasure of the

καρδίας αὐτοῦ προφέρει τὸ πονηρόν· ἐκ γὰρ τοῦ περισσεύ-
heart   of him brings forth the evil;   out of for  the abundance

ματος τῆς καρδίας λαλεῖ τὸ στόμα αὐτοῦ.
of the   heart speaks the mouth of him.

46 Τί δέ με καλεῖτε, Κύριε, Κύριε, καὶ οὐ ποιεῖτε ἃ λέγω ;
why And Me do you call, Lord,  Lord,  and not do    what I say?

47 πᾶς ὁ ἐρχόμενος πρός με καὶ ἀκούων μου τῶν λόγων καὶ
Everyone coming    to Me and hearing of Me the   words, and

48 ποιῶν αὐτούς, ὑποδείξω ὑμῖν τίνι ἐστὶν ὅμοιος· ὅμοιός ἐστιν
doing    them, I will show you to whom he is like.   like   He is

ἀνθρώπῳ οἰκοδομοῦντι οἰκίαν, ὃς ἔσκαψε καὶ ἐβάθυνε, καὶ
a man    building    a house, who dug  and deepened, and

ἔθηκε θεμέλιον ἐπὶ τὴν πέτραν· πλημμύρας δὲ γενομένης,
laid a foundation on the   rock;    a flood    and happening,

προσέρρηξεν ὁ ποταμὸς τῇ οἰκίᾳ ἐκείνῃ καὶ οὐκ ἴσχυσε
burst against  the  stream   — house   that,  and not could

49 σαλεῦσαι αὐτήν· τεθεμελίωτο γὰρ ἐπὶ τὴν πέτραν. ὁ δὲ
shake    it,    it had been founded for on the  rock.  he But

ἀκούσας καὶ μὴ ποιήσας ὅμοιός ἐστιν ἀνθρώπῳ οἰκοδομή-
heard    and not performed like  is    to a man    having

σαντι οἰκίαν ἐπὶ τὴν γῆν χωρὶς θεμελίου· ᾗ προσέρρηξεν ὁ
built   a house on the earth without a foundation, on which burst the

ποταμός, καὶ εὐθέως ἔπεσε, καὶ ἐγένετο τὸ ῥῆγμα τῆς
stream,   and immediately it fell, and was    the    ruin    —

οἰκίας ἐκείνης μέγα.
house of that great.

great.

## CHAPTER 7

[1] And when He had completed all His words in the ears of the people, He went into Capernaum. [2] And a certain slave of a centurion being ill was about to die, who was respected by him. [3] And having heard about Jesus, he sent elders of the Jews to Him, begging Him that having come He might cure his slave. [4] And having come to Jesus they begged Him earnestly, saying, that he to whom He shall grant this is worthy, [5] for he loves our nation, and he built the synagogue for us. [6] And Jesus went out with them; but He already being not far distant from the house, the centurion sent friends to Him, saying to Him, Lord, trouble not, for I am not worthy that You should come under my roof. [7] Therefore I did not count myself worthy to come to You; but say by a word, and my servant shall be healed. [8] For I also am a man appointed under authority, having soldiers under myself; and I say to this one, Go, and he goes; and to another, Come, and he comes; and to my slave, Do this, and he does. [9] And having heard these things Jesus marveled at him; and turning to the crowd following Him, He said, I say to you not even in Israel did I find so great faith. [10] And those sent having returned to the house found the sick slave in good health.

[11] And it came to pass on the next (day) He went into a city called Nain, and His disciples and a great crowd went with Him. [12] And, behold, as He drew near to the gate of the city, (one) who had

## CHAPTER 7

**1** Ἐπεὶ δὲ ἐπλήρωσε πάντα τὰ ῥήματα αὐτοῦ εἰς τὰς ἀκοὰς
when And He completed all the words of Him in the ears

τοῦ λαοῦ, εἰσῆλθεν εἰς Καπερναούμ.
of the people, He went into Capernaum.

**2** Ἑκατοντάρχου δέ τινος δοῦλος κακῶς ἔχων ἤμελλε
of a centurion And a certain slave illness having was about

**3** τελευτᾶν, ὃς ἦν αὐτῷ ἔντιμος. ἀκούσας δὲ περὶ τοῦ Ἰησοῦ,
to expire, who was to him dear. hearing And about — Jesus,

ἀπέστειλε πρὸς αὐτὸν πρεσβυτέρους τῶν Ἰουδαίων,
he sent to Him elders of the Jews

ἐρωτῶν αὐτόν, ὅπως ἐλθὼν διασώσῃ τὸν δοῦλον αὐτοῦ. οἱ
asking Him that coming He might restore the slave of him. they

**4** δὲ, παραγενόμενοι πρὸς τὸν Ἰησοῦν, παρεκάλουν αὐτὸν
And coming to — Jesus, begged Him

σπουδαίως, λέγοντες ὅτι ἄξιός ἐστιν ᾧ παρέξει τοῦτο·
earnestly, saying, — worthy He is for whom You give this.

**5** ἀγαπᾷ γὰρ τὸ ἔθνος ἡμῶν, καὶ τὴν συναγωγὴν αὐτὸς
he loves For the nation of us, and the synagogue he

**6** ᾠκοδόμησεν ἡμῖν. ὁ δὲ Ἰησοῦς ἐπορεύετο σὺν αὐτοῖς. ἤδη
built for us. — And Jesus went with them. yet

δὲ αὐτοῦ οὐ μακρὰν ἀπέχοντος ἀπὸ τῆς οἰκίας, ἔπεμψε πρὸς
And Him not far being away from the house, sent to

αὐτὸν ὁ ἑκατόνταρχος φίλους, λέγων αὐτῷ, Κύριε, μὴ
Him the centurion friends, saying to Him, Lord not

σκύλλου· οὐ γὰρ εἰμι ἱκανὸς ἵνα ὑπὸ τὴν στέγην μου
do trouble. not For I am worthy that under the roof of me

**7** εἰσέλθῃς· διὸ οὐδὲ ἐμαυτὸν ἠξίωσα πρός σε ἐλθεῖν· ἀλλὰ
You enter. Therefore not myself I counted worthy to You to come, but

**8** εἰπὲ λόγῳ, καὶ ἰαθήσεται ὁ παῖς μου. καὶ γὰρ ἐγὼ ἄνθρωπός
say in a word, and let be cured the servant of me. even For I a man

εἰμι ὑπὸ ἐξουσίαν τασσόμενος, ἔχων ὑπ᾽ ἐμαυτὸν στρατιώ-
am under authority being set, having under myself soldiers,

τας, καὶ λέγω τούτῳ, Πορεύθητι, καὶ πορεύεται· καὶ ἄλλῳ,
and I tell this one, Go, and he goes; and another,

Ἔρχου, καὶ ἔρχεται· καὶ τῷ δούλῳ μου, Ποίησον τοῦτο, καὶ
Come, and he comes; and the slave of me, Do this, and

**9** ποιεῖ. ἀκούσας δὲ ταῦτα ὁ Ἰησοῦς ἐθαύμασεν αὐτόν, καὶ
he does. hearing And these, — Jesus marveled at him, and

στραφεὶς τῷ ἀκολουθοῦντι αὐτῷ ὄχλῳ εἶπε, Λέγω ὑμῖν, οὐδὲ
turning to the following Him crowd said, I say to you, not

**10** ἐν τῷ Ἰσραὴλ τοσαύτην πίστιν εὗρον. καὶ ὑποστρέψαντες οἱ
in — Israel such faith I found. And returning those

πεμφθέντες εἰς τὸν οἶκον εὗρον τὸν ἀσθενοῦντα δοῦλον
sent to the house found the sick slave

ὑγιαίνοντα.
well.

**11** Καὶ ἐγένετο ἐν τῇ ἑξῆς, ἐπορεύετο εἰς πόλιν καλουμένην
And it was on the next (day), He went into a city being called

Ναΐν καὶ συνεπορεύοντο αὐτῷ οἱ μαθηταὶ αὐτοῦ ἱκανοί,
Nain, and went with Him the disciples of Him many,

**12** καὶ ὄχλος πολύς. ὡς δὲ ἤγγισε τῇ πύλῃ τῆς πόλεως, καὶ ἰδού,
and a crowd much. as And He drew to the gate of the city, even behold,
near

died was being carried out, an only son to his mother; and she was a widow, and a large crowd of the city (was) with her. [13] And seeing her the Lord was moved with pity on her and said to her, Do not weep. [14] And coming up He touched the bier, and those carrying (it) stopped. And He said, Young man, I say to you, Arise! [15] And the dead sat up and began to speak, and He gave him to his mother. [16] And fear seized all, and they glorified God, saying, A great prophet has risen up amongst us; and, God has visited His people. [17] And this report went out in all of Judea concerning Him, and in all the country around.

[18] And His disciples brought word to John about all these things. [19] And having called to certain ones of his disciples, John sent to Jesus, saying, Are You the (One) coming, or are we to look for another? [20] And the men having come to Him said, John the Baptist has sent us to You, saying, Are You the (One) coming, are are we to look for another? [21] And in the same hour He healed many of diseases and affliction and evil spirits, and He granted sight to many blind ones. [22] And answering Jesus said to them, Having returned tell John what you have seen and heard: that the blind receive sight, the lame walk, the lepers are cleansed, the deaf hear, the dead are raised, the poor are evangelized; [23] and blessed is he who shall not be offended in Me.
[24] And the messengers of John having departed, He began to speak to the crowd concerning John: What have you gone out into the wilderness to see? a reed shaken by the wind?

ἐξεκομίζετο τεθνηκώς, υἱὸς μονογενὴς τῇ μητρὶ αὐτοῦ, καὶ
was being borne, having died, son an only born to the mother of him; and

αὕτη ἦν χήρα· καὶ ὄχλος τῆς πόλεως ἱκανὸς ἦν σὺν αὐτῇ.
this was a widow. And a crowd of the city considerable was with her.

13 καὶ ἰδὼν αὐτὴν ὁ Κύριος ἐσπλαγχνίσθη ἐπ᾽ αὐτῇ, καὶ εἶπεν
And seeing her the Lord felt pity over her, and said

14 αὐτῇ, Μὴ κλαῖε. καὶ προσελθὼν ἥψατο τῆς σοροῦ· οἱ δὲ
to her, Stop weeping. And coming up He touched the coffin, those and

βαστάζοντες ἔστησαν. καὶ εἶπε, Νεανίσκε, σοὶ λέγω,
bearing stood still. And He said, Young man, to you I say,

15 ἐγέρθητι. καὶ ἀνεκάθισεν ὁ νεκρός, καὶ ἤρξατο λαλεῖν. καὶ
Arise! And sat up the dead one, and began to speak; and

16 ἔδωκεν αὐτὸν τῇ μητρὶ αὐτοῦ. ἔλαβε δὲ φόβος ἅπαντας, καὶ
He gave him to the mother of him. took And fear all, and

ἐδόξαζον τὸν Θεόν, λέγοντες ὅτι Προφήτης μέγας ἐγήγερται
they glorified — God, saying, — A prophet great has risen up

17 ἐν ἡμῖν, καὶ ὅτι Ἐπεσκέψατο ὁ Θεὸς τὸν λαὸν αὐτοῦ. καὶ
among us, and, — has visited — God the people of Him. And

ἐξῆλθεν ὁ λόγος οὗτος ἐν ὅλῃ τῇ Ἰουδαίᾳ περὶ αὐτοῦ, καὶ
went out — word this in all — Judea concerning Him, and

ἐν πάσῃ τῇ περιχώρῳ.
in all the neighborhood.

18 Καὶ ἀπήγγειλαν Ἰωάννῃ οἱ μαθηταὶ αὐτοῦ περὶ πάντων
And reported to John the disciples of him about all

19 τούτων. καὶ προσκαλεσάμενος δύο τινὰς τῶν μαθητῶν
these things. And calling near two a certain of the disciples

αὐτοῦ ὁ Ἰωάννης ἔπεμψε πρὸς τὸν Ἰησοῦν, λέγων, Σὺ εἶ ὁ
of him, — John sent to — Jesus, saying, you Are the

20 ἐρχόμενος, ἢ ἄλλον προσδοκῶμεν; παραγενόμενοι δὲ πρὸς
coming One? Or another should we expect? coming And to

αὐτὸν οἱ ἄνδρες εἶπον, Ἰωάννης ὁ Βαπτιστὴς ἀπέσταλκεν
Him the men said, John the Baptist sent

ἡμᾶς πρός σε, λέγων, Σὺ εἶ ὁ ἐρχόμενος, ἢ ἄλλον προσδοκῶ-
us to You, saying, you Are the coming One, or another should we

21 μεν; ἐν αὐτῇ δὲ τῇ ὥρᾳ ἐθεράπευσε πολλοὺς ἀπὸ νόσων καὶ
expect? In the same And hour He healed many from diseases and

μαστίγων καὶ πνευμάτων πονηρῶν, καὶ τυφλοῖς πολλοῖς
plagues and spirits evil; and blind ones to many

22 ἐχαρίσατο τὸ βλέπειν. καὶ ἀποκριθεὶς ὁ Ἰησοῦς εἶπεν αὐτοῖς,
He gave to see. And answering — Jesus said to them,

Πορευθέντες ἀπαγγείλατε Ἰωάννῃ ἃ εἴδετε καὶ ἠκούσατε·
Going report to John what you saw and heard:

ὅτι τυφλοὶ ἀναβλέπουσι, χωλοὶ περιπατοῦσι, λεπροὶ
— Blind ones see again; lame ones walk about; lepers

καθαρίζονται, κωφοὶ ἀκούουσι, νεκροὶ ἐγείρονται, πτωχοὶ
are being cleansed; deaf ones hear; dead ones are raised; poor ones

23 εὐαγγελίζονται· καὶ μακάριός ἐστιν, ὃς ἐὰν μὴ σκανδαλισθῇ
are given the gospel; and blessed is whoever not is offended

ἐν ἐμοί.
in Me.

24 Ἀπελθόντων δὲ τῶν ἀγγέλων Ἰωάννου, ἤρξατο λέγειν
going away And the messengers of John, He began to say

πρὸς τοὺς ὄχλους περὶ Ἰωάννου, Τί ἐξεληλύθατε εἰς τὴν
to the crowds about John, What did you go out to the

ἔρημον θεάσασθαι; κάλαμον ὑπὸ ἀνέμου σαλευόμενον; ἀλλὰ
wilderness to see? A reed by wind being shaken? But

[25] But what have you gone out to see? a man dressed in soft clothing? Behold, those being in luxury and in splendid clothing are in king's palaces. [26] But what did you go out to see? A prophet? Yes, I say to you, even more than a prophet! [27] This is he about whom it has been written, Behold, I send My messenger before Your face, who will prepare Your way before You. [28] For I say to you, no one among those born of women is greater than John the Baptist. But the least (one) in the kingdom of God is greater than he is. [29] And all the tax-collectors and the people having heard, they justified God, being baptized (with) the baptism of John. [30] But the Pharisees and the lawyers set aside the counsel of God as to themselves, not having been baptized by him. [31] And the Lord said, To what, then, shall I compare the men of this generation? And to what are they like? [32] They are like little children sitting in a market place, and calling to one another and saying, We piped to you, and you did not dance; we mourned to you, and you did not weep. [33] For John the Baptist has come neither eating bread nor drinking wine, and you say, He has a demon. [34] The Son of man has come eating and drinking, and you say, Behold, a man, a glutton and a drunkard, a friend of tax-collectors and of sinners. [35] Yet wisdom was justified by all her children.

[36] And one of the Pharisees asked Him, that He should eat with him. And having entered into the house of the Pharisee, He reclined. [37] And behold, a woman who was a sinner in the city, having known that He had reclined in the house of the Pharisee, having taken an alabaster vial of ointment, [38] and standing at His feet,

25 τί ἐξεληλύθατε ἰδεῖν; ἄνθρωπον ἐν μαλακοῖς ἱματίοις
what did you go out to see? A man in soft clothing
ἠμφιεσμένον; ἰδού, οἱ ἐν ἱματισμῷ ἐνδόξῳ καὶ τρυφῇ
dressed? Behold, those in clothing splendid and in luxury
26 ὑπάρχοντες ἐν τοῖς βασιλείοις εἰσίν. ἀλλὰ τί ἐξεληλύθατε
being in — king's palaces are. But what did you go out
ἰδεῖν; προφήτην; ναί, λέγω ὑμῖν, καὶ περισσότερον προ-
to see? A prophet? Yes, I say to you, Even more than a
27 φήτου. οὗτος ἐστι περὶ οὗ γέγραπται, Ἰδοὺ, ἐγὼ ἀπο-
prophet! This is he about whom it has been written, Behold, I
στέλλω τὸν ἄγγελόν μου πρὸ προσώπου σου, ὃς κατα-
send the messenger of Me before (the) face of You, who will
28 σκευάσει τὴν ὁδόν σου ἔμπροσθέν σου. λέγω γὰρ ὑμῖν, μείζων
prepare the way of You before You. I say For to you, greater
ἐν γεννητοῖς γυναικῶν προφήτης Ἰωάννου τοῦ Βαπτιστοῦ
among (those) born of women prophet than John the Baptist
οὐδεὶς ἐστιν· ὁ δὲ μικρότερος ἐν τῇ βασιλείᾳ τοῦ Θεοῦ
no one is. the But least (one) in the kingdom — of God
29 μείζων αὐτοῦ ἐστι. καὶ πᾶς ὁ λαὸς ἀκούσας καὶ οἱ τελῶναι
greater than he is. And all the people hearing, and the tax-collectors,
ἐδικαίωσαν τὸν Θεόν, βαπτισθέντες τὸ βάπτισμα Ἰωάννου·
justified — God, being baptized (with) the baptism of John.
30 οἱ δὲ Φαρισαῖοι καὶ οἱ νομικοὶ τὴν βουλὴν τοῦ Θεοῦ
the But Pharisees and the lawyers the counsel — of God
ἠθέτησαν εἰς ἑαυτούς, μὴ βαπτισθέντες ὑπ' αὐτοῦ. εἶπε δὲ
set aside, for themselves not had been baptized by him. said And
31 ὁ Κύριος, Τίνι οὖν ὁμοιώσω τοὺς ἀνθρώπους τῆς γενεᾶς
the Lord, To what then shall I liken the men generation
32 ταύτης, καὶ τίνι εἰσὶν ὅμοιοι; ὅμοιοί εἰσι παιδίοις τοῖς ἐν
of this, and to what are they like? like They are children — in
ἀγορᾷ καθημένοις, καὶ προσφωνοῦσιν ἀλλήλοις, καὶ
a market sitting and calling to one another, and
λέγουσιν, Ηὐλήσαμεν ὑμῖν, καὶ οὐκ ὠρχήσασθε· ἐθρηνή-
saying, We piped to you, and not you danced; we
33 σαμεν ὑμῖν, καὶ οὐκ ἐκλαύσατε. ἐλήλυθε γὰρ Ἰωάννης ὁ
mourned to you, and not you wept. has come For John the
Βαπτιστὴς μήτε ἄρτον ἐσθίων μήτε οἶνον πίνων, καὶ λέγετε,
Baptist not bread eating, nor wine drinking, and you say,
34 Δαιμόνιον ἔχει. ἐλήλυθεν ὁ υἱὸς τοῦ ἀνθρώπου ἐσθίων καὶ
A demon he has. has come The Son — of man eating and
πίνων, καὶ λέγετε, Ἰδού, ἄνθρωπος φάγος καὶ οἰνοπότης,
drinking, and you say, Behold, a man, a glutton and a winebibber,
35 τελωνῶν φίλος καὶ ἁμαρτωλῶν. καὶ ἐδικαιώθη ἡ σοφία ἀπὸ
of tax-collectors friend and sinners. And was justified — wisdom from
τῶν τέκνων αὐτῆς πάντων.
the children of her all.
36 Ἠρώτα δὲ τις αὐτὸν τῶν Φαρισαίων ἵνα φάγῃ μετ'
asked And a certain Him of the Pharisees, that He eat with
αὐτοῦ· καὶ εἰσελθὼν εἰς τὴν οἰκίαν τοῦ Φαρισαίου ἀνεκλίθη.
him. And going into the house of the Pharisee He reclined
37 καὶ ἰδού, γυνὴ ἐν τῇ πόλει, ἥτις ἦν ἁμαρτωλός, ἐπιγνοῦσα
And behold, a woman in the city who was a sinner, having known
ὅτι ἀνάκειται ἐν τῇ οἰκίᾳ τοῦ Φαρισαίου, κομίσασα ἀλά-
that He had reclined in the house of the Pharisee, having taken an
38 βαστρον μύρου, καὶ στᾶσα παρὰ τοὺς πόδας αὐτοῦ ὀπίσω
alabaster vial of ointment, and standing at the feet of Him behind

weeping behind (Him), began to wash His feet with tears, and she was wiping with the hairs of her head, and was ardently kissing His feet, and was anointing (them) with the ointment. [39] But having seen the Pharisee who invited Him spoke within himself, saying, This one, if he were a prophet, would have known who and what the woman who touches him (is), for she is a sinner. [40] And answering Jesus said to the man, Simon, I have something to say to you. And he said, Teacher, say (on). [41] There were two debtors to a certain creditor; the one owed five hundred denarii, and the other fifty. [42] But they not having (anything) to pay, he forgave both. Therefore which of them, say (you), will love him most? [43] And answering Simon said, I take it (to be he) to whom he forgave the most. And he said to him, You have judged rightly. [44] And having turned to the woman, He said to Simon, Do you see this woman? I came into your house, you did not give water for my feet, but she washed my feet with tears, and dried with the hairs of her head. [45] You gave Me no kiss, but she from which (time) I came in did not cease kissing My feet. [46] You did not anoint My head with oil, but she anointed My feet with ointment. [47] For which reason I say to you, her many sins have been forgiven; for she loved much; but to whom little is forgiven, he loves little. [48] And He said to her, Your sins have been forgiven. [49] And those reclining began to say within themselves, Who is this who even forgives sins? [50] But He said to the woman, Your faith has saved you; go in peace.

CHAPTER 8

[1] And it happened afterwards, even He traveled in every city and village, preaching and announcing the gospel of the kingdom

κλαίουσα, ἤρξατο βρέχειν τοὺς πόδας αὐτοῦ τοῖς δάκρυσι,
weeping,   began   to wet   the   feet   of Him with the tears,

καὶ ταῖς θριξὶ τῆς κεφαλῆς αὐτῆς ἐξέμασσε, καὶ κατεφίλει
and with the hairs of the head   of her   she was wiping, and   kissing

39 τοὺς πόδας αὐτοῦ, καὶ ἤλειφε τῷ μύρῳ. ἰδὼν δὲ ὁ Φαρισαῖος
the   feet   of Him, and anointing with the ointment, seeing And the Pharisee

ὁ καλέσας αὐτὸν εἶπεν ἐν ἑαυτῷ λέγων, Οὗτος, εἰ ἦν
having invited   Him, he spoke in himself,   saying,   This one, if he was

προφήτης, ἐγίνωσκεν ἂν τίς καὶ ποταπὴ ἡ γυνὴ ἥτις
a prophet would have known   who and   what   the woman (is) who

40 ἅπτεται αὐτοῦ, ὅτι ἁμαρτωλός ἐστι. καὶ ἀποκριθεὶς ὁ
touches   him, because a sinner   she is. And   answering   —

Ἰησοῦς εἶπε πρὸς αὐτόν, Σίμων, ἔχω σοί τι εἰπεῖν. ὁ δέ φησι,
Jesus   said   to   him,   Simon, I have to you a thing to say. he And says,

41 Διδάσκαλε, εἰπέ. Δύο χρεωφειλέται ἦσαν δανειστῇ τινί·
Teacher,   say.   Two   debtors   were   to a creditor certain.

42 ὁ εἷς ὤφειλε δηνάρια πεντακόσια, ὁ δὲ ἕτερος πεντήκοντα. μὴ
The one owed   denarii   five hundred, the and (the) other   fifty.   not

ἐχόντων δὲ αὐτῶν ἀποδοῦναι, ἀμφοτέροις ἐχαρίσατο. τίς
having   And them (a thing) to repay,   both   he freely forgave. Who

43 οὖν αὐτῶν, εἰπέ, πλεῖον αὐτὸν ἀγαπήσει; ἀποκριθεὶς δὲ ὁ
then of them say (you) more   him   will love?   answering   And   —

Σίμων εἶπεν, Ὑπολαμβάνω ὅτι ᾧ τὸ πλεῖον ἐχαρίσατο. ὁ
Simon   said,   I suppose,   —to whom the more he freely forgave. He

44 δὲ εἶπεν αὐτῷ, Ὀρθῶς ἔκρινας. καὶ στραφεὶς πρὸς τὴν
And   said to him,   Rightly you judged. And   turning   to   the

γυναῖκα, τῷ Σίμωνι ἔφη, Βλέπεις ταύτην τὴν γυναῖκα;
woman,   — to Simon He said, Do you see this   —   woman?

εἰσῆλθόν σου εἰς τὴν οἰκίαν, ὕδωρ ἐπὶ τοὺς πόδας μου οὐκ
I went   of you into the house, water   on   the   feet   of Me not

ἔδωκας· αὕτη δὲ τοῖς δάκρυσιν ἔβρεξέ μου τοὺς πόδας, καὶ
you gave.   she But with the tears   wet   of Me the   feet,   and

45 ταῖς θριξὶ τῆς κεφαλῆς αὐτῆς ἐξέμαξε. φίλημά μοι οὐκ ἔδωκας·
with the hairs — head   of her wiped off. A kiss to Me not you gave,

αὕτη δέ, ἀφ' ἧς εἰσῆλθον, οὐ διέλιπε καταφιλοῦσά μου τοὺς
she   but from (when) I entered not did stop fervently kissing of Me the

46 πόδας. ἐλαίῳ τὴν κεφαλήν μου οὐκ ἤλειψας· αὕτη δὲ μύρῳ
feet.   With oil the   head   of Me not you anointed, she but with ointment

47 ἤλειψέ μου τοὺς πόδας. οὗ χάριν, λέγω σοι, ἀφέωνται αἱ
anointed of Me the   feet.   For this reason I say to you, are forgiven the

ἁμαρτίαι αὐτῆς αἱ πολλαί, ὅτι ἠγάπησε πολύ· ᾧ δὲ ὀλίγον
sins   of her   many, because she loved much, to whom but little

48 ἀφίεται, ὀλίγον ἀγαπᾷ. εἶπε δὲ αὐτῇ, Ἀφέωνταί σου αἱ
is forgiven, little   he loves. He said And to her, are forgiven of you The

49 ἁμαρτίαι. καὶ ἤρξαντο οἱ συνανακείμενοι λέγειν ἐν ἑαυτοῖς,
sins.   And   began   those reclining with (Him) to say in themselves,

50 Τίς οὗτός ἐστιν ὃς καὶ ἁμαρτίας ἀφίησιν; εἶπε δὲ πρὸς τὴν
Who this   is,   who even   sins   forgives? He said But to   the

γυναῖκα, Ἡ πίστις σου σέσωκέ σε· πορεύου εἰς εἰρήνην.
woman,   The faith of you has saved you; Go   in   peace.

CHAPTER 8

1 Καὶ ἐγένετο ἐν τῷ καθεξῆς, καὶ αὐτὸς διώδευε κατὰ πόλιν
And it was.   afterwards,   and   He   traveled through every city

καὶ κώμην, κηρύσσων, καὶ εὐαγγελιζόμενος τὴν βασιλείαν
and village,   preaching   and announcing the gospel of the   kingdom

of God; and the twelve with him. [2] And certain women who had been cured from evil spirits and infirmities, Mary who is called Magdalene, from whom seven demons had gone out; [3] and Joanna wife of Chuza, a steward of Herod; and Susanna, and many others, who were ministering to Him of their property.

[4] And a great crowd assembling, and those who were coming from each city to Him, He spoke by a parable. [5] The sower went out to sow his seed; and as he sowed some fell by the wayside, and it was trampled upon, and the birds of the sky ate it. [6] And other fell on the rock, and having sprouted it withered, because it had no moisture. [7] And other fell in (the) midst of the thorns, and having sprung up together the thorns choked it. [8] And others fell on the good ground, and having sprung up produced fruit a hundredfold. Saying these things he cried, He that has ears to hear let him hear.

[9] And His disciples asked Him, saying, What may this parable be? [10] And He said, To you it has been given to know the mysteries of the kingdom of God, but to the rest in parables, that seeing they may not see, and hearing they may not understand. [11] Now this is the parable: The seed is the word of God; [12] and those by the wayside are those who hear; then the Devil comes and takes away the word from their heart, lest having believed they should be saved. [13] And those on the rock (are) those who, when they hear, receive the word with joy; but these who believe for a time but in time of temptation fall away have no root. [14] And that which fell into the thorns,

2 τοῦ Θεοῦ· καὶ οἱ δώδεκα σὺν αὐτῷ, καὶ γυναῖκές τινες αἳ
— of God, and the twelve with Him. also women certain who
ἦσαν τεθεραπευμέναι ἀπὸ πνευμάτων πονηρῶν καὶ
were healed from spirits evil and
ἀσθενειῶν, Μαρία ἡ καλουμένη Μαγδαληνή, ἀφ᾽ ἧς δαιμόνια
infirmities; Mary being called Magdalene, from whom demons

3 ἑπτὰ ἐξεληλύθει, καὶ Ἰωάννα γυνὴ Χουζᾶ ἐπιτρόπου Ἡρώ-
seven had gone out; and Joanna wife of Chuza, steward of
δου, καὶ Σουσάννα, καὶ ἕτεραι πολλαί, αἵτινες διηκόνουν
Herod; and Susanna; and others many; who ministered
αὐτῷ ἀπὸ τῶν ὑπαρχόντων αὐταῖς.
to them from the possessions of them.

4 Συνιόντος δὲ ὄχλου πολλοῦ, καὶ τῶν κατὰ πόλιν ἐπιπο-
coming together And crowd a much, and those in each city coming
ρευομένων πρὸς αὐτόν, εἶπε διὰ παραβολῆς, Ἐξῆλθεν ὁ
to Him, He said through a parable: Went out those

5 σπείρων τοῦ σπεῖραι τὸν σπόρον αὐτοῦ καὶ ἐν τῷ σπείρειν
sowing — to sow the seed of him. And in the sowing
αὐτόν, ὃ μὲν ἔπεσε παρὰ τὴν ὁδόν, καὶ κατεπατήθη, καὶ τὰ
of him, the one fell by the way, and was trampled; and the

6 πετεινὰ τοῦ οὐρανοῦ κατέφαγεν αὐτό. καὶ ἕτερον ἔπεσεν
birds of the heaven ate it. And other fell
ἐπὶ τὴν πέτραν, καὶ φυὲν ἐξηράνθη, διὰ τὸ μὴ ἔχειν ἰκμάδα.
on the rock, and growing it dried up, because of not having moisture.

7 καὶ ἕτερον ἔπεσεν ἐν μέσῳ τῶν ἀκανθῶν, καὶ συμφυεῖσαι αἱ
And other fell amidst the thorns, and growing up with the

8 ἄκανθαι ἀπέπνιξαν αὐτό. καὶ ἕτερον ἔπεσεν ἐπὶ τὴν
thorns choked it. And other fell on the
γῆν τὴν ἀγαθήν, καὶ φυὲν ἐποίησε καρπὸν ἑκατοντα-
earth — good. and growing it produced fruit a hundred-
πλασίονα. ταῦτα λέγων ἐφώνει, Ὁ ἔχων ὦτα ἀκούειν
fold. these things saying He called, Those having ears to hear,
ἀκουέτω.
let him hear.

9 Ἐπηρώτων δὲ αὐτὸν οἱ μαθηταὶ αὐτοῦ, λέγοντες, Τίς
questioned And Him the disciples of Him, saying, What

10 εἴη ἡ παραβολὴ αὕτη; ὁ δὲ εἶπεν, Ὑμῖν δέδοται γνῶναι τὰ
might be parable this? He And said, To you it was given to know the
μυστήρια τῆς βασιλείας τοῦ Θεοῦ· τοῖς δὲ λοιποῖς ἐν
mysteries of the kingdom — of God, to the but rest in
παραβολαῖς, ἵνα βλέποντες μὴ βλέπωσι, καὶ ἀκούοντες μὴ
parables, that seeing not they might see, and hearing not

11 συνιῶσιν. ἔστι δὲ αὕτη ἡ παραβολή· ὁ σπόρος ἐστὶν ὁ
they might know. is And this the parable: The seed is the

12 λόγος τοῦ Θεοῦ. οἱ δὲ παρὰ τὴν ὁδόν εἰσιν οἱ ἀκούοντες,
word — of God. the And (ones) by the way are those hearing;
εἶτα ἔρχεται ὁ διάβολος καὶ αἴρει τὸν λόγον ἀπὸ τῆς καρδίας
then comes the devil and takes the word from the heart

13 αὐτῶν, ἵνα μὴ πιστεύσαντες σωθῶσιν. οἱ δὲ ἐπὶ τῆς
of them, lest believing they may be saved. those And on the
πέτρας οἵ, ὅταν ἀκούσωσι, μετὰ χαρᾶς δέχονται τὸν λόγον,
rock who when they hear with joy receive the word,
καὶ οὗτοι ῥίζαν οὐκ ἔχουσιν, οἳ πρὸς καιρὸν πιστεύουσι,
and these root not do have, who for a time believe,

14 καὶ ἐν καιρῷ πειρασμοῦ ἀφίστανται. τὸ δὲ εἰς τὰς ἀκάνθας
and in time of trial draw back. those And in the thorns

these are those having heard, and under cares and riches and pleasures of life moving along they are choked, and do not bear to maturity. [15] And those in the good earth, these are (those) who in a right and good heart, having heard the word, they hold (it) and bear fruit with patience. [16] And no one having lighted a lamp covers it with a vessel, or puts (it) under a bed, but puts (it) on a lampstand, that they who come in may see the light. [17] For nothing is hidden which shall not be uncovered, nor secret which shall not be known and come to light. [18] Therefore be careful how you hear; for whoever may have, more shall be given to him; and whoever may not have, even what he seems to have shall be taken from him.

[19] And His brothers and mother came to Him, and were not able to get to Him because of the crowd. [20] And it was told Him, saying, Your mother and your brothers are standing outside, wishing to see you. [21] And He answering said to them, My mother and My brothers are those who are hearing the word of God and doing it.

[22] And it happened on one of the days that He and His disciples entered into a boat, and He said to them, Let us pass over to the other side of the lake; and they cast off. [23] And as they sailed He fell asleep; and a storm of wind came on the lake; and they were flooded and were in danger. [24] And having come they aroused Him, saying, Master, Master, we are perishing. And having arisen He rebuked the wind and the raging of the water; and they ceased, and there was a calm. [25] And He said to them, Where is your faith? And being afraid they wondered, saying to one another, Who then is this, that He commands even the winds and the

---

15 πεσόν, οὗτοί εἰσιν οἱ ἀκούσαντες, καὶ ὑπὸ μεριμνῶν καὶ
falling, these are those hearing, and under cares and
πλούτου καὶ ἡδονῶν τοῦ βίου πορευόμενοι συμπνίγονται,
riches and pleasures — of life moving along, they are choked
καὶ οὐ τελεσφοροῦσι. τὸ δὲ ἐν τῇ καλῇ γῇ, οὗτοί εἰσιν
and not do bear to maturity. those And in the good earth, these are
οἵτινες ἐν καρδίᾳ καλῇ καὶ ἀγαθῇ, ἀκούσαντες τὸν λόγον
(those) who in a heart right and good hearing the word,
κατέχουσι, καὶ καρποφοροῦσιν ἐν ὑπομονῇ.
they hold (it), and bear fruit in patience.

16 Οὐδεὶς δὲ λύχνον ἅψας καλύπτει αὐτὸν σκεύει, ἢ ὑποκάτω
no one But a lamp having lit covers it with a vessel, or underneath
κλίνης τίθησιν, ἀλλ’ ἐπὶ λυχνίας ἐπιτίθησιν, ἵνα οἱ εἰσπορευό-
a couch puts (it), but on a lampstand puts (it), that those coming in

17 μενοι βλέπωσι τὸ φῶς. οὐ γάρ ἐστι κρυπτόν, ὃ οὐ φανερὸν
may see the light. not For is hidden which not revealed
γενήσεται· οὐδὲ ἀπόκρυφον, ὃ οὐ γνωσθήσεται καὶ εἰς
will be, nor secret which not will be known and to (be)

18 φανερὸν ἔλθῃ. βλέπετε οὖν πῶς ἀκούετε· ὃς γὰρ ἂν ἔχῃ,
revealed come. see Therefore how you hear; whoever for has,
δοθήσεται αὐτῷ· καὶ ὃς ἂν μὴ ἔχῃ, καὶ ὃ δοκεῖ ἔχειν ἀρθή-
it will be given to him, and whoever not has, even what he seems to have will
σεται ἀπ’ αὐτοῦ.
be taken from him.

19 Παρεγένοντο δὲ πρὸς αὐτὸν ἡ μήτηρ καὶ οἱ ἀδελφοὶ
came And to Him the mother and the brothers
αὐτοῦ, καὶ οὐκ ἠδύναντο συντυχεῖν αὐτῷ διὰ τὸν ὄχλον.
of Him, and not were able to come up with Him through the crowd.

20 καὶ ἀπηγγέλη αὐτῷ, λεγόντων, Ἡ μήτηρ σου καὶ οἱ
And it was told to Him, saying, The mother of You and the
ἀδελφοί σου ἑστήκασιν ἔξω, ἰδεῖν σε θέλοντες. ὁ δὲ ἀποκριθεὶς
brothers of You are standing outside to see You desiring. He And answering

21 εἶπε πρὸς αὐτούς, Μήτηρ μου καὶ ἀδελφοί μου οὗτοί εἰσιν
said to them, Mother of Me and brothers of Me these are,
οἱ τὸν λόγον τοῦ Θεοῦ ἀκούοντες καὶ ποιοῦντες αὐτόν.
those the word — of God hearing and doing it.

22 Καὶ ἐγένετο ἐν μιᾷ τῶν ἡμερῶν, καὶ αὐτὸς ἐνέβη εἰς πλοῖον
And it was on one of the days, and He entered into a boat,
καὶ οἱ μαθηταὶ αὐτοῦ, καὶ εἶπε πρὸς αὐτούς, Διέλθωμεν εἰς
also the disciples of Him; and He said to them, Let us go over to

23 τὸ πέραν τῆς λίμνης· καὶ ἀνήχθησαν. πλεόντων δὲ αὐτῶν
the other side of the lake; and they put out to sea. sailing And them,
ἀφύπνωσε· καὶ κατέβη λαῖλαψ ἀνέμου εἰς τὴν λίμνην, καὶ
He fell asleep. And came down a storm of wind onto the lake, and

24 συνεπληροῦντο, καὶ ἐκινδύνευον. προσελθόντες δὲ διήγειραν
they were being filled, and were in danger. coming up And they awoke
αὐτόν, λέγοντες, Ἐπιστάτα, ἐπιστάτα, ἀπολλύμεθα. ὁ δὲ
Him, saying, Master! Master! We are perishing. He And
ἐγερθεὶς ἐπετίμησε τῷ ἀνέμῳ καὶ τῷ κλύδωνι τοῦ ὕδατος·
being aroused rebuked the wind and the roughness of the water,

25 καὶ ἐπαύσαντο, καὶ ἐγένετο γαλήνη. εἶπε δὲ αὐτοῖς, Ποῦ
and they ceased; and there was a calm. He said And to them, Where
ἐστιν ἡ πίστις ὑμῶν; φοβηθέντες δὲ ἐθαύμασαν, λέγοντες
is the faith of you? fearing And, they marveled, saying,
πρὸς ἀλλήλους, Τίς ἄρα οὗτός ἐστιν, ὅτι καὶ τοῖς ἀνέμοις
to one another, Who then this One is, that even the wind

water, and they obey Him?

[26] And they sailed down to the country of the Gadarenes, which is opposite Galilee. [27] And He going out onto the land, a certain man met him out of the city, who had demons for a long time, and he put no garment on, and he did not stay in a house, but among the tombs. [28] And seeing Jesus, and crying out, he fell down before Him, and with a loud voice said, What to me and to You, Jesus, Son of God the most High? I beg You, do not torment me. [29] For He charged the unclean spirit to come out of the man. For many times it had seized him, and he was bound with fetters and with chains, being guarded; and tearing apart the bonds, he was driven by the demons into the deserts. [30] And Jesus questioned him, saying, What is your name? And he said, Legion, because many demons had entered into him. [31] And he begged Him that He would not command them to go away into the bottomless pit. [32] Now there was a herd of many pigs feeding there in the mountain, and they begged Him that He would allow them to go into those; and He allowed them. [33] And the demons having gone out from the man, they entered into the pigs, and the herd rushed down the steep into the lake, and were choked. [34] And those who fed (them), having seen what had taken place, fled, and having gone away reported to the city and to the country. [35] And they went out to see what had taken place, and came to Jesus, and found seated the man from whom the demons had gone out, clothed and of sound mind, at the feet of Jesus. And they were afraid. [36] And also those who had seen (it) told them how he who had been possessed by demons was healed. [37] And all the multitude of the country around of the

ἐπιτάσσει καὶ τῷ ὕδατι, καὶ ὑπακούουσιν αὐτῷ ;
He commands and the water, and they obey Him?

26 Καὶ κατέπλευσαν εἰς τὴν χώραν τῶν Γαδαρηνῶν, ἥτις
And they sailed down to the country of the Gadarenes, which

27 ἐστὶν ἀντιπέραν τῆς Γαλιλαίας. ἐξελθόντι δὲ αὐτῷ ἐπὶ τὴν
is opposite — Galilee. going out And Him onto the
γῆν, ὑπήντησεν αὐτῷ ἀνήρ τις ἐκ τῆς πόλεως, ὃς εἶχε δαι-
land, met Him a man certain out of the city, who had
μόνια ἐκ χρόνων ἱκανῶν, καὶ ἱμάτιον οὐκ ἐνεδιδύσκετο, καὶ
demons from a time long, and a garment not he put on, and

28 ἐν οἰκίᾳ οὐκ ἔμενεν, αλλ' ἐν τοῖς μνήμασιν. ἰδὼν δὲ τὸν
in a house not he stayed, but among the tombs. seeing And —
'Ἰησοῦν, καὶ ἀνακράξας, προσέπεσεν αὐτῷ, καὶ φωνῇ μεγάλῃ
Jesus, and crying out, he fell down before Him, and with a voice great
εἶπε, Τί ἐμοὶ καὶ σοί, 'Ἰησοῦ, υἱὲ τοῦ Θεοῦ τοῦ ὑψίστου ;
said, What to me and to You, Jesus, Son — of God the Most High?

29 δέομαί σου, μή με βασανίσῃς. παρήγγειλε γὰρ τῷ πνεύματι
I beg You, not me do torment. He charged For the spirit
τῷ ἀκαθάρτῳ ἐξελθεῖν ἀπὸ τοῦ ἀνθρώπου· πολλοῖς γὰρ
— unclean to come out from the man. many For
χρόνοις συνηρπάκει αὐτόν, καὶ ἐδεσμεῖτο ἁλύσεσι καὶ πέδαις
times it had seized him, and he was bound with chains and fetters,
φυλασσόμενος, καὶ διαρρήσσων τὰ δεσμὰ ἡλαύνετο ὑπὸ τοῦ
being guarded, and tearing apart the bonds, he was driven by the

30 δαίμονος εἰς τὰς ἐρήμους. ἐπηρώτησε δὲ αὐτὸν ὁ 'Ἰησους,
demons into the deserts. questioned And Him — Jesus,
λέγων, Τί σοι ἐστιν ὄνομα ; ὁ δὲ εἶπε, Λεγεών· ὅτι δαιμόνια
saying, What to you is (the) name? he And said, Legion, because demons

31 πολλὰ εἰσῆλθεν εἰς αὐτόν. καὶ παρεκάλουν αὐτὸν ἵνα μὴ
many entered into him. And they begged Him that not

32 ἐπιτάξῃ αὐτοῖς εἰς τὴν ἄβυσσον ἀπελθεῖν. ἦν δὲ ἐκεῖ ἀγέλη
He order them into the abyss to go away. was And there a herd
χοίρων ἱκανῶν βοσκομένων ἐν τῷ ὄρει· καὶ παρεκάλουν
pigs of many feeding in the mountain; and they begged
αὐτὸν ἵνα ἐπιτρέψῃ αὐτοῖς εἰς ἐκείνους εἰσελθεῖν. καὶ ἐπέτρε-
Him that He would let them into those to enter. And He let

33 ψεν αὐτοῖς. ἐξελθόντα δὲ τὰ δαιμόνια ἀπὸ τοῦ ἀνθρώπου
them. coming out And the demons from the man
εἰσῆλθεν εἰς τοὺς χοίρους· καὶ ὥρμησεν ἡ ἀγέλη κατὰ τοῦ
entered into the pigs, and rushed the herd down the

34 κρημνοῦ εἰς τὴν λίμνην, καὶ ἀπεπνίγη. ἰδόντες δὲ οἱ
precipice into the lake, and was choked. seeing And those
βόσκοντες τὸ γεγενημένον ἔφυγον, καὶ ἀπελθόντες ἀπήγ-
feeding the thing happening, they fled and having left

35 γειλαν εἰς τὴν πόλιν καὶ εἰς τοὺς ἀγρούς. ἐξῆλθον δὲ ἰδεῖν
reported to the city and to the farms. they went And to see
τὸ γεγονός· καὶ ἦλθον πρὸς τὸν 'Ἰησοῦν, καὶ ευρον καθή-
the thing happening and came to — Jesus, and found sitting
μενον τὸν ἄνθρωπον ἀφ' οὗ τὰ δαιμόνια ἐξεληλύθει, ἱματι-
the man from whom the demons had gone out, clothed
σμένον καὶ σωφρονοῦντα, παρὰ τοὺς πόδας τοῦ 'Ἰησοῦ· καὶ
and of sound mind, at the feet — of Jesus. And

36 ἐφοβήθησαν. ἀπήγγειλαν δὲ αὐτοῖς καὶ οἱ ἰδόντες πῶς ἐσώθη
they were afraid. related And to them also those seeing how was healed

37 ὁ δαιμονισθείς. καὶ ἠρώτησαν αὐτὸν ἅπαν τὸ πλῆθος τῆς
the demon-possessed. And asked Him all the multitude of the

Gadarenes asked Him to depart from them, for they were possessed with great fear. And having entered into the boat He returned. [38] And the man from whom had gone the demons was begging Him to be (taken) with Him. But Jesus sent him away, saying, [39] Return to your house and tell all that God has done for you. And he went, telling all that Jesus had done for him throughout the whole city.

[40] And it came to pass on Jesus' returning, the crowd gladly received Him, for they were all looking for Him. [41] And behold, a man named Jairus came, and he was a ruler of the synagogue. And having fallen at the feet of Jesus, he begged Him to come to his house, [42] because an only daughter was his, about twelve years old, and she was dying. And as He went, the crowd thronged Him. [43] And a woman being with a flow of blood since twelve years, having spent (her) whole living on physicians could be cured by no one, [44] having come behind touched the border of His garment, and immediately the flow of her blood stopped. [45] And Jesus said, Who was that touching Me? And all denied, Peter and those with Him said, Master, the crowds throng You and press, and do You say, Who was that touching Me? [46] And Jesus said, Someone touched Me, for I know power went out from Me. [47] And the woman seeing that she was not hidden, she came trembling, and having fallen down before Him, she told Him before all the people for what cause she touched Him, and how she was healed immediately. [48] And He said to her, Be comforted, daughter, your faith has cured you; go in peace. [49] As He

περιχώρου τῶν Γαδαρηνῶν ἀπελθεῖν ἀπ' αὐτῶν, ὅτι φόβῳ
**neighborhood of the Gadarenes to depart from them, for with a fear**
μεγάλῳ συνείχοντο· αὐτὸς δὲ ἐμβὰς εἰς τὸ πλοῖον ὑπέ-
**great they were seized; He and entering into the boat**
**38** στρεψεν. ἐδέετο δὲ αὐτοῦ ὁ ἀνὴρ ἀφ' οὗ ἐξεληλύθει τὰ
**returned. begged And Him the man from whom had gone out the**
δαιμόνια εἶναι σὺν αὐτῷ. ἀπέλυσε δὲ αὐτὸν ὁ Ἰησοῦς λέγων,
**demons to be with Him; dismissed But him — Jesus, saying,**
**39** Ὑπόστρεφε εἰς τὸν οἶκόν σου, καὶ διηγοῦ ὅσα ἐποίησέ σοι
**Go back to the house of you, and relate what did to you**
ὁ Θεός. καὶ ἀπῆλθε, καθ' ὅλην τὴν πόλιν κηρύσσων ὅσα
**— God. And he went away through all the city proclaiming what things**
ἐποίησεν αὐτῷ ὁ Ἰησοῦς.
**did to him — Jesus.**
**40** Ἐγένετο δὲ ἐν τῷ ὑποστρέψαι τὸν Ἰησοῦν, ἀπεδέξατο
**it was And, in the returning — Jesus, gladly received**
**41** αὐτὸν ὁ ὄχλος· ἦσαν γὰρ πάντες προσδοκῶντες αὐτόν. καὶ
**Him the crowd; they were for all expecting Him. And**
ἰδού, ἦλθεν ἀνὴρ ᾧ ὄνομα Ἰάειρος, καὶ αὐτὸς ἄρχων τῆς
**behold, came a man to whom name Jairus, and this one a ruler of the**
συναγωγῆς ὑπῆρχε, καὶ πεσὼν παρὰ τοὺς πόδας τοῦ Ἰησοῦ
**synagogue was. And falling at the feet — of Jesus,**
**42** παρεκάλει αὐτὸν εἰσελθεῖν εἰς τὸν οἶκον αὐτοῦ· ὅτι θυγάτηρ
**he begged Him to come into the house of him, because daughter**
μονογενὴς ἦν αὐτῷ ὡς ἐτῶν δώδεκα, καὶ αὕτη ἀπέθνη-
**an only born was to him, about years twelve, and she was dying.**
σκεν. ἐν δὲ τῷ ὑπάγειν αὐτὸν οἱ ὄχλοι συνέπνιγον αὐτόν.
**in And the going (of) Him, the crowd pressed upon Him.**
**43** Καὶ γυνὴ οὖσα ἐν ρύσει αἵματος ἀπὸ ἐτῶν δώδεκα, ἥτις
**And a woman being in a flow of blood from years twelve, who**
εἰς ἰατροὺς προσαναλώσασα ὅλον τὸν βίον οὐκ ἴσχυσεν
**to physicians had spent whole — (her) living, not could**
**44** ὑπ' οὐδενὸς θεραπευθῆναι, προσελθοῦσα ὄπισθεν, ἥψατο
**by no one be cured, having come up behind she touched**
τοῦ κρασπέδου τοῦ ἱματίου αὐτοῦ· καὶ παραχρῆμα ἔστη
**the border of the garment of Him, and immediately stopped**
ἡ ρύσις τοῦ αἵματος αὐτῆς. καὶ εἶπεν ὁ Ἰησοῦς, Τίς ὁ
**the flow of the blood of her. And said — Jesus, Who**
**45** ἁψάμενός μου; ἀρνουμένων δὲ πάντων, εἶπεν ὁ Πέτρος καὶ
**(was) touching Me? denying And all, said — Peter and**
οἱ μετ' αὐτοῦ, Ἐπιστάτα, οἱ ὄχλοι συνέχουσί σε, καὶ
**those with Him, Master, the crowds press upon You and**
**46** ἀποθλίβουσι, καὶ λέγεις, Τίς ὁ ἁψάμενός μου; ὁ δὲ Ἰησοῦς
**jostle. And do You say, Who was touching Me? — But Jesus**
εἶπεν, Ἥψατό μού τις· ἐγὼ γὰρ ἔγνων δύναμιν ἐξελθοῦσαν
**said, touched Me Someone; I for knew power having gone forth**
**47** ἀπ' ἐμοῦ. ἰδοῦσα δὲ ἡ γυνὴ ὅτι οὐκ ἔλαθε, τρέμουσα ἦλθε,
**from Me. seeing And the woman that not she was hid, trembling came**
καὶ προσπεσοῦσα αὐτῷ, δι' ἣν αἰτίαν ἥψατο αὐτοῦ
**and kneeled down before Him, for what cause she touched Him**
ἀπήγγειλεν αὐτῷ ἐνώπιον παντὸς τοῦ λαοῦ, καὶ ὡς ἰάθη
**she declared to Him before all the people, and how was cured**
**48** παραχρῆμα. ὁ δὲ εἶπεν αὐτῇ, Θάρσει, θύγατερ, ἡ πίστις
**immediately. He And said to her, Be comforted, daughter, the faith**
**49** σου σέσωκέ σε· πορεύου εἰς εἰρήνην.
**of you has healed you; go in peace.**

was yet speaking one came from the ruler of the synagogue saying to Him, Your daughter has died; do not trouble the Teacher. [50] But Jesus having heard answered him, saying, Do not fear; only believe, and she shall be restored. [51] And having gone into the house, He did not allow anyone to go in except Peter and James and John, and the father and the mother of the child. [52] And they were all weeping and bewailing her. But He said, Do not weep; she is not dead, but sleeps. [53] And they laughed at Him, knowing that she was dead. [54] But having put out all, and having taken hold of her hand, He cried, saying, Child, arise! [55] And her spirit returned, and she rose up immediately; and He ordered (something) to be given her to eat. [56] And her parents were amazed; and He commanded them to tell no one what had happened.

CHAPTER 9

[1] And having called His twelve disciples, He gave to them power and authority over all the demons, and to heal diseases, [2] and sent them to preach the kingdom of God, and to heal those being sick. [3] And He said to them, Take nothing for the wayside; not staves, nor bags, nor bread, nor money, nor each to have two coats. [4] And into whatever house you may enter, remain there, and go forth from there. [5] And as many as may not receive you, going out from that city shake off even the dust from your feet for a testimony against them. [6] And going out they passed through the villages, preaching the gospel and healing everywhere.

[7] And Herod the tetrarch heard of all the things being done by Him,

---

Ἔτι αὐτοῦ λαλοῦντος, ἔρχεταί τις παρὰ τοῦ ἀρχισυναγώ
Yet Him   speaking,   comes someone from the synagogue ruler

50  γου, λέγων αὐτῷ ὅτι Τέθνηκεν ἡ θυγάτηρ σου· μὴ σκύλλε
saying to Him,   —   has expired The daughter of you; not trouble

τὸν διδάσκαλον. ὁ δὲ Ἰησοῦς ἀκούσας ἀπεκρίθη αὐτῷ,
the   Teacher.   — But Jesus   hearing   answered   him,

λέγων, Μὴ φοβοῦ· μόνον πίστευε, καὶ σωθήσεται. εἰσελθὼν
saying,  Do not fear;   only   believe,   and she will be healed. coming

51  δὲ εἰς τὴν οἰκίαν, οὐκ ἀφῆκεν εἰσελθεῖν οὐδένα, εἰ μὴ Πέτρον
And to the house,  not He allowed  to enter   anyone   except Peter

καὶ Ἰάκωβον καὶ Ἰωάννην, καὶ τὸν πατέρα τῆς παιδὸς καὶ
and  James   and  John,   and the  father of  the  child.   and

52  τὴν μητέρα. ἔκλαιον δὲ πάντες, καὶ ἐκόπτοντο αὐτήν. ὁ δὲ
the  mother. were weeping And all   and  bewailing   her.  He But

53  εἶπε, Μὴ κλαίετε· οὐκ ἀπέθανεν, ἀλλὰ καθεύδει. καὶ κατε-
said, Stop weeping!  not  she died,   but   sleeps.   And they

γέλων αὐτοῦ, εἰδότες ὅτι ἀπέθανεν. αὐτὸς δὲ ἐκβαλὼν ἔξω
ridiculed Him,   knowing that she died.   He But having put outside

54  πάντας, καὶ κρατήσας τῆς χειρὸς αὐτῆς, ἐφώνησε λέγων,
all,   and having taken hold of the hand  of her,  He called,  saying,

55  Ἡ παῖς ἐγείρου. καὶ ἐπέστρεψε τὸ πνεῦμα αὐτῆς, καὶ ἀνέστη
Child,  arise!   And returned   the   spirit   of her, and she arose

56  παραχρῆμα· καὶ διέταξεν αὐτῇ δοθῆναι φαγεῖν. καὶ ἐξέστη-
immediately.   And He ordered  her  to be given to eat. And were

σαν οἱ γονεῖς αὐτῆς. ὁ δὲ παρήγγειλεν αὐτοῖς μηδενὶ εἰπεῖν
amazed the parents of her. He But  charged   them  to no one to tell

τὸ γεγονός.
the thing having happened.

CHAPTER 9

1  Συγκαλεσάμενος δὲ τοὺς δώδεκα μαθητὰς αὐτοῦ, ἔδωκεν
having called together And the   twelve   disciples  of Him,  He gave

αὐτοῖς δύναμιν καὶ ἐξουσίαν ἐπὶ πάντα τὰ δαιμόνια, καὶ
them  power  and  authority over   all   the  demons,   and

2  νόσους θεραπεύειν. καὶ ἀπέστειλεν αὐτοὺς κηρύσσειν τὴν
diseases  to heal.   And He sent   them   to proclaim   the

3  βασιλείαν τοῦ Θεοῦ, καὶ ἰᾶσθαι τοὺς ἀσθενοῦντας. καὶ εἶπε
kingdom   — of God, and to cure those   being sick.   And He said

πρὸς αὐτούς, Μηδὲν αἴρετε εἰς τὴν ὁδόν· μήτε ῥάβδους,
to   them,  Nothing take  for the   way,  neither staffs,

μήτε πήραν, μήτε ἄρτον, μήτε ἀργύριον, μήτε ἀνὰ δύο
nor money bags,  nor   bread,  nor   silver,   nor  each two

4  χιτῶνας ἔχειν. καὶ εἰς ἣν ἂν οἰκίαν εἰσέλθητε, ἐκεῖ μένετε, καὶ
tunics  to have. And into whatever house you go in,  there remain, and

5  ἐκεῖθεν ἐξέρχεσθε. καὶ ὅσοι ἂν μὴ δέξωνται ὑμᾶς, ἐξερχό-
from there go out.   And as many as not may receive you,   going

μενοι ἀπὸ τῆς πόλεως ἐκείνης καὶ τὸν κονιορτὸν ἀπὸ τῶν
out from   —   city   that  even the  dust   from the

6  ποδῶν ὑμῶν ἀποτινάξατε εἰς μαρτύριον ἐπ' αὐτούς. ἐξερχό-
feet  of you shake off,   for a testimony against them.  going

μενοι δὲ διήρχοντο κατὰ τὰς κώμας, εὐαγγελιζόμενοι καὶ
out And they passed  through the villages preaching the gospel   and

θεραπεύοντες πανταχοῦ.
healing   everywhere.

7  Ἤκουσε δὲ Ἡρώδης ὁ τετράρχης τὰ γινόμενα ὑπ' αὐτοῦ
heard  And  Herod the  tetrarch   the things happening by  Him

and was puzzled, because it was said by some John has been raised from among (the) dead; [8] by some also, that Elijah had appeared; by others also that a prophet, one of the ancients, had arisen. [9] Ad Herod said, I beheaded John, but who is this about whom I hear such things? And he sought to see Him.

[10] And the apostles having returned told Him whatever they had done. And having taken them He drew them aside into a deserted place, of a city called Bethsaida. [11] But the crowds having known followed Him; and having received them He spoke to them about the kingdom of God; and those having need of healing He cured. [12] But the day began to wane, and the twelve having come said to Him, Turn the crowd loose, that having gone into the villages and the country around they may lodge, and may find food; for here we are in a deserted place. [13] But He said to them, You give them to eat. But they said, There are not to us more than five loaves and two fishes, unless indeed having gone we should buy food for all this people; [14] for they were about five thousand men. But He said to His disciples, Make them recline in companies by fifties. [15] And they did so, and made all recline. [16] And having taken the five loaves and the two fishes, having looked up to Heaven, He blessed them and broke, and gave to the disciples to set before the crowd. [17] And they ate and were all satisfied; and twelve baskets of fragments were taken up, that which was left over to them.

[18] And it happened, as He was praying alone, the disciples were with Him, and He questioned them, saying, Whom do the

---

πάντα· καὶ διηπόρει, διὰ τὸ λέγεσθαι ὑπό τινων ὅτι
all,    and    was puzzled, because of the saying   by    some    that

8 Ἰωάννης ἐγήγερται ἐκ νεκρῶν· ὑπό τινων δὲ ὅτι Ἠλίας
John     has been raised from the dead, by    some and that Elijah

ἐφάνη ἄλλων δὲ ὅτι Προφήτης εἷς τῶν ἀρχαίων ἀνέστη
had appeared; others and that a   prophet of    the    ancients rose again.

9 καὶ εἶπεν ὁ Ἡρώδης, Ἰωάννην ἐγὼ ἀπεκεφάλισα· τίς δέ
And said   —   Herod,    John    I     beheaded,    who but

ἐστιν οὗτος, περὶ οὗ ἐγὼ ἀκούω τοιαῦτα ; καὶ ἐζήτει ἰδεῖν
is    this about whom I     hear   such things? And he tried to see

αὐτόν.
Him.

10 Καὶ ὑποστρέψαντες οἱ ἀπόστολοι διηγήσαντο αὐτῷ ὅσα
And   having returned   the   apostles     told     Him   what

ἐποίησαν. καὶ παραλαβὼν αὐτούς, ὑπεχώρησε κατ' ἰδίαν
they did. And taking     them,    He departed   privately

11 εἰς τόπον ἔρημον πόλεως καλουμένης Βηθσαϊδά. οἱ δὲ ὄχλοι
to   a place desert of a city    called     Bethsaida. the But crowds

γνόντες ἠκολούθησαν αὐτῷ· καὶ δεξάμενος αὐτούς, ἐλάλει
having known followed    Him. And having received them, He spoke

αὐτοῖς περὶ τῆς βασιλείας τοῦ Θεοῦ, καὶ τοὺς χρείαν
to them about the   kingdom    —   of God, and those   need

12 ἔχοντας θεραπείας ἰᾶτο. ἡ δὲ ἡμέρα ἤρξατο κλίνειν· προσ-
having    of healing He cured. the But day   began   to decline; coming

ελθόντες δὲ οἱ δώδεκα εἶπον αὐτῷ. Ἀπόλυσον τὸν ὄχλον,
up     and the twelve   said to Him, Let go     the crowd,

ἵνα ἀπελθόντες εἰς τὰς κύκλω κώμας καὶ τοὺς ἀγροὺς κατα-
that going    to the around villages and the   farms   they

λύσωσι, καὶ εὕρωσιν ἐπισιτισμόν· ὅτι ὧδε ἐν ἐρήμῳ τόπῳ
may lodge, and may find food supplies, because here in a desert   place

13 ἐσμέν. εἶπε δὲ πρὸς αὐτούς, Δότε αὐτοῖς ὑμεῖς φαγεῖν. οἱ δὲ
we are. He said And to   them,   give    them    You to eat. they But

εἶπον, Οὐκ εἰσὶν ἡμῖν πλεῖον ἢ πέντε ἄρτοι καὶ δύο ἰχθύες,
said, Not   is   to us more than five    loaves and two fish,

εἰ μήτι πορευθέντες ἡμεῖς ἀγοράσωμεν εἰς πάντα τὸν λαὸν
unless    going     we   may buy    for   all     people

14 τοῦτον βρώματα. ἦσαν γὰρ ὡσεὶ ἄνδρες πεντακισχίλιοι.
this    foods. there were For about    men    five thousand.

εἶπε δὲ πρὸς τοὺς μαθητὰς αὐτοῦ, Κατακλίνατε αὐτοὺς
He said And to   the   disciples of Him, Cause to recline    them

15 κλισίας ἀνὰ πεντήκοντα. καὶ ἐποίησαν οὕτω, καὶ ἀνέκλιναν
in groups by   fifties.     And they did    so,   and caused to recline

16 ἅπαντας. λαβὼν δὲ τοὺς πέντε ἄρτους καὶ τοὺς δύο ἰχθύας,
all.     taking And the five   loaves   and the   two fish,

ἀναβλέψας εἰς τὸν οὐρανόν, εὐλόγησεν αὐτούς, καὶ κατέ-
looking up to   —   Heaven.   He blessed    them, and broke

17 κλασε, καὶ ἐδίδου τοῖς μαθηταῖς παρατιθέναι τῷ ὄχλῳ. καὶ
    and gave to the disciples   to set before    the crowd. And

ἔφαγον καὶ ἐχορτάσθησαν πάντες· καὶ ἤρθη τὸ περισσεῦσαν
they ate and   were filled     all;    and were taken the excess

αὐτοῖς κλασμάτων, κόφινοι δώδεκα.
to them of fragments, baskets twelve.

18 Καὶ ἐγένετο ἐν τῷ εἶναι αὐτὸν προσευχόμενον καταμόνας,
And it was (as)    was    Him    praying      alone,

συνῆσαν αὐτῷ οἱ μαθηταί· καὶ ἐπηρώτησεν αὐτούς, λέγων,
were with Him the disciples, and He questioned    them,    saying,

crowds say Me to be?
[19] And they answering said, John the Baptist; and others, Elijah; and others, that some prophet of the ancients has risen. [20] And He said to them, But you, whom do you say Me to be? And answering Peter said, The Christ of God. [21] And strictly warning them, He commanded to tell no one this, [22] saying, The Son of man must suffer many things, and be rejected by the elders and chief priests and scribes, and be killed, and be raised the third day. [23] And He said to all, If anyone desires to come after Me, let him deny himself, and let him take up his cross daily, and let him follow Me; [24] for whoever may desire to save his life, shall lose it; but whoever may lose his life for My sake, he shall save it. [25] For what is a man profited, having gained the whole world, but having destroyed or suffered the loss of himself? [26] For whoever may have been ashamed of Me and My words, the Son of man will be ashamed of him when he shall come in the glory of Himself and of the Father and of the holy angels. [27] But truly I say to you, there are some of those standing here who in no way shall taste of death until they shall have seen the kingdom of God.

[28] And about eight days after these words, it happened that having taken Peter and John and James, He went up into the mountain to pray. [29] And it happened as He prayed, the appearance of His face changed, and His clothing (became) dazzling white. [30] And behold, two men talked with Him, who were Moses and Elijah; [31] who appearing in glory spoke of His exodus which He was about to accomplish in Jerusalem. [32] But Peter and those with him were

**19** Τίνα με λέγουσιν οἱ ὄχλοι εἶναι ; οἱ δὲ ἀποκριθέντες εἶπον,
Whom Me say        the crowds to be?  they And answering        said,

Ἰωάννην τὸν Βαπτιστήν· ἄλλοι δὲ Ἠλίαν· ἄλλοι δέ, ὅτι
John     the  Baptist;       others but  Elijah;  others and that

**20** προφήτης τις τῶν ἀρχαίων ἀνέστη. εἶπε δὲ αὐτοῖς, Ὑμεῖς
prophet a certain of the  ancients rose again. He said And to them,   you

δὲ τίνα με λέγετε εἶναι ; ἀποκριθεὶς δὲ ὁ Πέτρος εἶπε, Τὸν
And, whom Me say  to be?    answering  And —  Peter   said, The

**21** Χριστὸν τοῦ Θεοῦ. ὁ δὲ ἐπιτιμήσας αὐτοῖς παρήγγειλε
Christ   — of God. He But warning     them       ordered

**22** μηδενὶ εἰπεῖν τοῦτο, εἰπὼν ὅτι Δεῖ τὸν υἱὸν τοῦ ἀνθρώπου
no one to tell this,   saying that it behoves the Son —  of man

πολλὰ παθεῖν, καὶ ἀποδοκιμασθῆναι ἀπὸ τῶν πρεσβυτέ-
many things to suffer, and to be rejected    from  the    elders

ρων καὶ ἀρχιερέων καὶ γραμματέων, καὶ ἀποκτανθῆναι,
and chief priests and  scribes,      and  to be killed,

**23** καὶ τῇ τρίτῃ ἡμέρᾳ ἐγερθῆναι. ἔλεγε δὲ πρὸς πάντας, Εἴ τις
and the third  day  to be raised. He said And  to   all,   If anyone

θέλει ὀπίσω μου ἐλθεῖν, ἀπαρνησάσθω ἑαυτόν, καὶ ἀράτω
desires after Me to come, let him deny   himself   and take up

**24** τὸν σταυρὸν αὐτοῦ καθ' ἡμέραν, καὶ ἀκολουθείτω μοι. ὃς
the  cross   of Him  daily.       And let him follow Me. whoever

γὰρ ἂν θέλῃ τὴν ψυχὴν αὐτοῦ σῶσαι, ἀπολέσει αὐτήν· ὃς
For  desires the life  of him to save, he will lose  it; whoever

δ' ἂν ἀπολέσῃ τὴν ψυχὴν αὐτοῦ ἕνεκεν ἐμοῦ, οὗτος σώσει
But loses    the  life  of him for My sake, this one will save

**25** αὐτήν. τί γὰρ ὠφελεῖται ἄνθρωπος, κερδήσας τὸν κόσμον
it.    what For is profited  a man    gaining    the  world

**26** ὅλον, ἑαυτὸν δὲ ἀπολέσας ἢ ζημιωθείς ; ὃς γὰρ ἂν ἐπαισχυνθῇ
whole, himself but destroying or suffering loss? whoever For is ashamed of

με καὶ τοὺς ἐμοὺς λόγους, τοῦτον ὁ υἱὸς τοῦ ἀνθρώπου
Me and  —  My    words,  this one the Son  —  of man

ἐπαισχυνθήσεται, ὅταν ἔλθῃ ἐν τῇ δόξῃ αὐτοῦ καὶ τοῦ
will be ashamed of  when He comes in the glory of Him, and of the

**27** πατρὸς καὶ τῶν ἁγίων ἀγγέλων. λέγω δὲ ὑμῖν ἀληθῶς,
Father, and  the  holy  angels.   I say But to you truly,

εἰσί τινες τῶν ὧδε ἑστηκότων, οἳ οὐ μὴ γεύσονται θανάτου,
are some of those here standing who in no way shall taste  of death

ἕως ἂν ἴδωσι τὴν βασιλείαν τοῦ Θεοῦ.
until they see the kingdom  — of God.

**28** Ἐγένετο δὲ μετὰ τοὺς λόγους τούτους ὡσεὶ ἡμέραι ὀκτώ,
it was And, after  the sayings  these, about days   eight,

καὶ παραλαβὼν τὸν Πέτρον καὶ Ἰωάννην καὶ Ἰάκωβον,
and taking    —  Peter   and John     and James,

**29** ἀνέβη εἰς τὸ ὄρος προσεύξασθαι. καὶ ἐγένετο, ἐν τῷ
He went into the mountain to pray.    And became    in the

προσεύχεσθαι αὐτόν, τὸ εἶδος τοῦ προσώπου αὐτοῦ ἕτερον,
praying    (of) Him the appearance of the face   of Him different,

**30** καὶ ὁ ἱματισμὸς αὐτοῦ λευκὸς ἐξαστράπτων. καὶ ἰδού,
and the clothing  of Him white  dazzling       And, behold,

ἄνδρες δύο συνελάλουν αὐτῷ, οἵτινες ἦσαν Μωσῆς καὶ
men  two talked    with Him,  who    were Moses and

**31** Ἠλίας, οἳ ὀφθέντες ἐν δόξῃ ἔλεγον τὴν ἔξοδον αὐτοῦ ἣν
Elijah, who appearing in glory spoke of the exodus of Him, which

**32** ἔμελλε πληροῦν ἐν Ἱερουσαλήμ. ὁ δὲ Πέτρος καὶ οἱ σὺν αὐτῷ
He was about to finish in Jerusalem.  -- And Peter and those with him

pressed down with sleep, and having awakened fully they saw His glory, and the two men who stood with Him. [33] And it happened as these departed from Him, Peter said to Jesus, Master, it is good for us to be here; and let us make three tabernacles, one for You, and one for Moses, and one for Elijah — not knowing what he was saying. [34] But as he was saying these things, a cloud came and overshadowed them, and they were afraid as those entered into the cloud; [35] and a voice came out of the cloud, saying, This is My beloved Son; hear Him. [36] And as the voice happened, Jesus was found alone; and they were quiet, and they told no one in those days anything of what they had seen.

[37] And it happened on the next day, they having come down from the mountain met a great crowd. [38] And behold, a man cried out from the crowd, saying, Teacher, I beg you look upon my son, for he is an only-born to me. [39] And behold, a spirit takes him and he suddenly cries out, and it throws him into convulsions with foaming, and departs from him with pain, bruising him. [40] And I begged Your disciples that they might cast it out, and they were not able. [41] And answering Jesus said, O unbelieving and perverted generation, how long shall I be with you and bear with you? Bring your son here. [42] But as he was yet coming near, the demon dashed him down and threw (him) into convulsions. And Jesus rebuked the unclean spirit and healed the child, and gave him back to his father. [43] And all were astonished at the majesty of God.

---

33 ἦσαν βεβαρημένοι ὕπνῳ· διαγρηγορήσαντες δὲ εἶδον τὴν
were pressed down with sleep. awakening fully    But they saw the
δόξαν αὐτοῦ, καὶ τοὺς δύο ἄνδρας τοὺς συνεστῶτας αὐτῷ.
glory of Him, and the two men — standing with Him.
καὶ ἐγένετο, ἐν τῷ διαχωρίζεσθαι αὐτούς ἀπ' αὐτοῦ, εἶπεν
And it was, in the parting (of) them from Him, said
ὁ Πέτρος πρὸς τὸν Ἰησοῦν, Ἐπιστάτα, καλόν ἐστιν ἡμᾶς
— Peter to — Jesus, Master, good it is (for) us

34 ὧδε εἶναι· καὶ ποιήσωμεν σκηνὰς τρεῖς, μίαν σοί, καὶ
here to be, and let us make tents three, one for You, and
Μωσεῖ μίαν, καὶ μίαν Ἡλίᾳ· μὴ εἰδὼς ὃ λέγει. ταῦτα δὲ
Moses one, and one for Elijah, not knowing what he says. these And
αὐτοῦ λέγοντος, ἐγένετο νεφέλη καὶ ἐπεσκίασεν αὐτούς·
him saying, came a cloud and overshadowed them;

35 ἐφοβήθησαν δὲ ἐν τῷ ἐκείνους εἰσελθεῖν εἰς τὴν νεφέλην. καὶ
they feared and in the of those entering into the cloud. And
φωνὴ ἐγένετο ἐκ τῆς νεφέλης, λέγουσα, Οὗτός ἐστιν ὁ υἱός
a voice came out of the cloud, saying, This is the Son

36 μου ὁ ἀγαπητός· αὐτοῦ ἀκούετε. καὶ ἐν τῷ γενέσθαι τὴν
of Me, the Beloved; Him hear. And in the occurring of the
φωνήν, εὑρέθη ὁ Ἰησοῦς μόνος. καὶ αὐτοὶ ἐσίγησαν, καὶ
voice, was found — Jesus alone. And they were quiet; and
οὐδενὶ ἀπήγγειλαν ἐν ἐκείναις ταῖς ἡμέραις οὐδὲν ὧν
to no one reported in those days, nothing which
ἑωράκασιν.
they had seen.

37 Ἐγένετο δὲ ἐν τῇ ἑξῆς ἡμέρᾳ, κατελθόντων αὐτῶν ἀπὸ
it was And on the next day, coming down them from

38 τοῦ ὄρους, συνήντησεν αὐτῷ ὄχλος πολύς. καὶ ἰδού, ἀνὴρ
the mountain, met Him a crowd much. And behold, a man
ἀπὸ τοῦ ὄχλου ἀνεβόησε, λέγων, Διδάσκαλε, δέομαί σου,
from the crowd called aloud, saying, Teacher, I beg You,

39 ἐπίβλεψον ἐπὶ τὸν υἱόν μου, ὅτι μονογενής ἐστί μοι· καὶ
to look at the son of me, because only born he is to me, and
ἰδού, πνεῦμα λαμβάνει αὐτόν, καὶ ἐξαίφνης κράζει, καὶ
behold, a spirit takes him, and suddenly cries out, and
σπαράσσει αὐτὸν μετὰ ἀφροῦ, καὶ μόγις ἀποχωρεῖ ἀπ'
convulses him with foam, and with pain departs from

40 αὐτοῦ, συντρίβον αὐτόν. καὶ ἐδεήθην τῶν μαθητῶν σου
him, bruising him. And I begged the disciples of You

41 ἵνα ἐκβάλλωσιν αὐτό, καὶ οὐκ ἠδυνήθησαν. ἀποκριθεὶς δὲ
that they cast out it, and not they were able. answering And
ὁ Ἰησοῦς εἶπεν, Ὦ γενεὰ ἄπιστος καὶ διεστραμμένη, ἕως
— Jesus said, O generation unbelieving and having been perverted, until
πότε ἔσομαι πρὸς ὑμᾶς, καὶ ἀνέξομαι ὑμῶν; προσάγαγε
when shall I be with you, and endure you? Bring

42 ὧδε τὸν υἱόν σου. ἔτι δὲ προσερχομένου αὐτοῦ, ἔρρηξεν
here the son of you. yet But (as was) coming up him, tore
αὐτὸν τὸ δαιμόνιον καὶ συνεσπάραξεν· ἐπετίμησε δὲ ὁ
him the demon, and violently convulsed. rebuked But —
Ἰησοῦς τῷ πνεύματι τῷ ἀκαθάρτῳ, καὶ ἰάσατο τὸν παῖδα,
Jesus the spirit — unclean, and healed the child,

43 καὶ ἀπέδωκεν αὐτὸν τῷ πατρὶ αὐτοῦ. ἐξεπλήσσοντο δὲ
and restored him to the father of him. were astounded And
πάντες ἐπὶ τῇ μεγαλειότητι τοῦ Θεοῦ.
all at the majesty — of God.

Πάντων δὲ θαυμαζόντων ἐπὶ πᾶσιν οἶς ἐποίησεν ὁ
all    And    marveling    at    all things    which    He did    —

And (as) all were
wondering at all which
Jesus did, He said to His
disciples, [44] You lay into
your ears these sayings
for the Son of man is
about to be delivered up
into (the) hands of men.
[45] But they did not
understand this saying, and
it was veiled from them
that they should not
perceive it. And they
feared to ask Him about
this thing. [46] But an
argument came up among
them, this, who might be
greatest of them. [47] And
Jesus having seen the
thoughts of their heart,
having taken hold of a
little child, He set it by
Him, [48] and said to
them, Whoever shall
receive this little child in
My name, receives Me; and
whoever shall receive Me,
receives Him who sent Me.
For he who is least among
you all is he who shall be
great. [49] And answering
John said, Master, we saw
someone casting out
demons in Your name, and
we forbade him, because
he does not follow with us.
[50] And Jesus said to
him, Do not forbid; for
whoever is not against us is
for us.

[51] And when the
days of His taking up were
being fulfilled, that He set
His face steadfastly to go
to Jerusalem. [52] And He
sent messengers before His
face. And having gone they
entered into a village of
Samaritans, so as to make
ready for Him. [53] And
they did not receive Him,
because His face was going
toward Jerusalem.
[54] And seeing (it) His
disciples, James and John,
said, Lord, desire You we
should call fire to come
down from Heaven and
consume them, and as
Elijah also did? [55] But
turning He rebuked them,

44 Ἰησοῦς, εἶπε πρὸς τοὺς μαθητὰς αὐτοῦ, Θέσθε ὑμεῖς εἰς τὰ
Jesus    said    to    the    disciples    of Him,    Lay    you into the

ὦτα ὑμῶν τοὺς λόγους τούτους· ὁ γὰρ υἱὸς τοῦ ἀνθρώπου
ears of you    —    sayings    these; the    for    Son    —    of man

45 μέλλει παραδίδοσθαι εἰς χεῖρας ἀνθρώπων. οἱ δὲ ἠγνόουν
is about to be betrayed    into the hands of men.    they But knew not

τὸ ῥῆμα τοῦτο, καὶ ἦν παρακεκαλυμμένον ἀπ' αὐτῶν, ἵνα
— word    this,    and it was    veiled    from    them, lest

μὴ αἴσθωνται αὐτό· καὶ ἐφοβοῦντο ἐρωτῆσαι αὐτὸν περὶ
they perceive it.    And they feared    to ask    Him    about

τοῦ ῥήματος τούτου.
word    this.

46 Εἰσῆλθε δὲ διαλογισμὸς ἐν αὐτοῖς, τὸ τίς ἂν εἴη μείζων
came in But an argument among    them,    — who might be greater

47 αὐτῶν. ὁ δὲ Ἰησοῦς ἰδὼν τὸν διαλογισμὸν τῆς καρδίας
of them.    — And Jesus having seen    the argument    of the    heart

αὐτῶν, ἐπιλαβόμενος παιδίου, ἔστησεν αὐτὸ παρ' ἑαυτῷ,
of them,    taking    a child    stood    it    beside Himself,

48 καὶ εἶπεν αὐτοῖς, "Ὃς ἐὰν δέξηται τοῦτο τὸ παιδίον ἐπὶ τῷ
and said to them, Whoever    receives    this    — child    upon the

ὀνόματί μου ἐμὲ δέχεται· καὶ ὃς ἐὰν ἐμὲ δέξηται δέχεται τὸν
name    of Me, Me receives. And whoever Me receives receives the (One)

ἀποστείλαντά με· ὁ γὰρ μικρότερος ἐν πᾶσιν ὑμῖν ὑπάρχων
having sent    Me. the For    lesser    among    all    you    being,

οὗτος ἔσται μέγας.
this one is    great.

49 Ἀποκριθεὶς δὲ ὁ Ἰωάννης εἶπεν, Ἐπιστάτα, εἴδομέν τινα
answering And —    John said,    Master,    we saw someone

ἐπὶ τῷ ὀνόματί σου ἐκβάλλοντα τὰ δαιμόνια· καὶ ἐκωλύ-
on the    name    of You casting out    — demons,    and we pre-

50 σαμεν αὐτόν, ὅτι οὐκ ἀκολουθεῖ μεθ' ἡμῶν. καὶ εἶπε πρὸς
vented    him, because not he follows    with us.    And said to

αὐτὸν ὁ Ἰησοῦς, Μὴ κωλύετε· ὃς γὰρ οὐκ ἔστι καθ' ἡμῶν
them —    Jesus,    Do not prevent; whoever for    not is    against us,

ὑπὲρ ἡμῶν ἐστιν.
for    us    is.

51 Ἐγένετο δὲ ἐν τῷ συμπληροῦσθαι τὰς ἡμέρας τῆς
it was    And in    the fulfilling (of)    the    days    of the

ἀναλήψεως αὐτοῦ, καὶ αὐτὸς τὸ πρόσωπον αὐτοῦ ἐστήριξε
taking up    of Him, even He    the    face    of Him set

52 τοῦ πορεύεσθαι εἰς Ἱερουσαλήμ, καὶ ἀπέστειλεν ἀγγέλους
—    to go    to    Jerusalem,    and    sent    messengers

πρὸ προσώπου αὐτοῦ· καὶ πορευθέντες εἰσῆλθον εἰς κώμην
before    the face    of Him. And    going    they went into a village

53 Σαμαρειτῶν, ὥστε ἑτοιμάσαι αὐτῷ. καὶ οὐκ ἐδέξαντο αὐτόν,
of Samaritans, so as    to prepare    for Him. And not they received    Him,

ὅτι τὸ πρόσωπον αὐτοῦ ἦν πορευόμενον εἰς Ἱερουσαλήμ.
because the face    of Him was    going    to    Jerusalem.

54 ἰδόντες δὲ οἱ μαθηταὶ αὐτοῦ Ἰάκωβος καὶ Ἰωάννης εἶπον,
seeing And the disciples of Him, James    and    John    said,

Κύριε, θέλεις εἴπωμεν πῦρ καταβῆναι ἀπὸ τοῦ οὐρανοῦ, καὶ
Lord, desire You (that) we tell fire to come down from —    Heaven    and

55 ἀναλῶσαι αὐτούς, ὡς καὶ Ἡλίας ἐποίησε; στραφεὶς δὲ
to destroy    them,    as also Elijah    did?    turning But

and said, You know not of
what spirit you are.
[56] For the Son of man
did not come to destroy
men's lives, but to save.
And they went to another
village.

[57] And it happened,
as they were going in the
way, someone said to Him,
I will follow You wherever
You may go, Lord.
[58] And Jesus said to
him, The foxes have holes,
and the birds of the sky
nests; but the Son of man
has no where He may lay
the head. [59] And He
said to another, Follow
Me. But he said, Lord,
allow me going away first
to bury my father.
[60] But Jesus said to him,
Leave the dead to bury
their own dead; but you
going out declare the
kingdom of God.
[61] And also another
said, I will follow You,
Lord, but first allow me to
take leave of those of my
house. [62] But Jesus said
to him, No one having laid
his hand on (the) plow,
and looking on the things
behind, is fit for the
kingdom of God.

---

CHAPTER 10
[1] Now after these
things the Lord also
appointed seventy others,
and sent them two and two
before His face, into every
city and place where He
was about to come
Himself. [2] He therefore
said to them, Truly the
harvest (is) great, but the
laborers few. Therefore
pray the Lord of the
harvest, that He may send
out laborers into His
harvest. [3] Go; behold, I
send you out as lambs in
(the) midst of wolves.
[4] Do not carry purse, or
bag, or sandals, and greet
no one on the way.
[5] And into whatever
house you may enter, first

---

56 ἐπετίμησεν αὐτοῖς, καὶ εἶπεν, Οὐκ οἴδατε οἵου πνεύματός
He rebuked them, and said, Not you know of what spirit

ἐστε ὑμεῖς· ὁ γὰρ υἱὸς τοῦ ἀνθρώπου οὐκ ἦλθε ψυχὰς
are you. the For Son — of man not did come the lives

ἀνθρώπων ἀπολέσαι, ἀλλὰ σῶσαι. καὶ ἐπορεύθησαν εἰς
of men to destroy, but to save. And they went to

ἑτέραν κώμην.
another village.

57 Ἐγένετο δὲ πορευομένων αὐτῶν ἐν τῇ ὁδῷ, εἶπέ τις πρὸς
it was And, going them in the way, said one to

αὐτόν, Ἀκολουθήσω σοι ὅπου ἂν ἀπέρχῃ, Κύριε. καὶ εἶπεν
Him, I will follow You wherever You go, Lord. And said

58 αὐτῷ ὁ Ἰησοῦς, Αἱ ἀλώπεκες φωλεοὺς ἔχουσι, καὶ τὰ
to him — Jesus, The foxes holes have, and the

πετεινὰ τοῦ οὐρανοῦ κατασκηνώσεις· ὁ δὲ υἱὸς τοῦ ἀνθρώ-
birds of the heaven nests; the but Son — of man

59 που οὐκ ἔχει ποῦ τὴν κεφαλὴν κλίνῃ. εἶπε δὲ πρὸς ἕτερον,
not has where the head He may lay. He said And to another,

Ἀκολούθει μοι. ὁ δὲ εἶπε, Κύριε, ἐπίτρεψόν μοι ἀπελθόντι
Follow Me. he But said, Lord, allow me having gone

60 πρῶτον θάψαι τὸν πατέρα μου. εἶπε δὲ αὐτῷ ὁ Ἰησοῦς,
first to bury the father of me. said But to him — Jesus,

Ἄφες τοὺς νεκροὺς θάψαι τοὺς ἑαυτῶν νεκρούς· σὺ δὲ
Leave the dead to bury the of themselves dead, you but

61 ἀπελθὼν διάγγελλε τὴν βασιλείαν τοῦ Θεοῦ. εἶπε δὲ καὶ
going out announce the kingdom — of God. said And also

ἕτερος, Ἀκολουθήσω σοι, Κύριε· πρῶτον δὲ ἐπίτρεψόν μοι
another, I will follow You, Lord; first but allow me

62 ἀποτάξασθαι τοῖς εἰς τὸν οἶκόν μου. εἶπε δὲ πρὸς αὐτὸν ὁ
to take leave of those in the house of me. said But to him —

Ἰησοῦς, Οὐδείς, ἐπιβαλὼν τὴν χεῖρα αὐτοῦ ἐπ’ ἄροτρον,
Jesus, No one putting the hand of him on the plow

καὶ βλέπων εἰς τὰ ὀπίσω, εὔθετός ἐστιν εἰς τὴν βασιλείαν
and looking at the things behind fit is for the kingdom

τοῦ Θεοῦ.
— of God.

CHAPTER 10

1 Μετὰ δὲ ταῦτα ἀνέδειξεν ὁ Κύριος καὶ ἑτέρους ἑβδομή-
after And these things appointed the Lord and others seventy

κοντα, καὶ ἀπέστειλεν αὐτοὺς ἀνὰ δύο πρὸ προσώπου
and sent them two by two before (the) face

αὐτοῦ εἰς πᾶσαν πόλιν καὶ τόπον οὗ ἔμελλεν αὐτὸς ἔρχεσθαι.
of Him into every city and place where was about He to come.

2 ἔλεγεν οὖν πρὸς αὐτούς, Ὁ μὲν θερισμὸς πολύς, οἱ δὲ ἐργάται
He said Then to them, the Indeed harvest (is) much, the but workers

ὀλίγοι· δεήθητε οὖν τοῦ Κυρίου τοῦ θερισμοῦ, ὅπως ἐκβάλλῃ
few; pray therefore of the Lord of the harvest, that He send out

3 ἐργάτας εἰς τὸν θερισμὸν αὐτοῦ. ὑπάγετε· ἰδού, ἐγὼ ἀπο-
workers into the harvest of Him. Go! Behold, I send

4 στέλλω ὑμᾶς ὡς ἄρνας ἐν μέσῳ λύκων. μὴ βαστάζετε βαλάν-
out you as lambs in (the) midst of wolves. Do not carry a

τιον, μὴ πήραν, μηδὲ ὑποδήματα· καὶ μηδένα κατὰ τὴν
purse, nor a moneybag, nor sandals; and no one by the

5 ὁδὸν ἀσπάσησθε. εἰς ἣν δ’ ἂν οἰκίαν εἰσέρχησθε, πρῶτον
way greet. into whatever And house you may enter, first

say, Peace to this house. [6] And if a son of peace truly be there, your peace shall rest upon it; but if not so, it shall return to you. [7] And remain in the same house, eating and drinking the things (provided) by them; for the laborer is worthy of his hire. Do not move from house to house. [8] And into whatever city you may go, and they receive you, eat the things set before you, [9] and heal the sick in it, and say to them, The kingdom of God has drawn near to you. [10] But into whatever city you may go, and they do not receive you, having gone out into its streets, say, [11] Even the dust which clung to us out of your city, we wipe off against you; yet know this, that the kingdom of God has drawn near to you. [12] And I say to you that it shall be more tolerable for Sodom in that day than for that city. [13] Woe to you, Chorazin! Woe to you, Bethsaida! For if the works of power which have been taking place in you had taken place in Tyre and Sidom, they would have repented sitting in sackcloth and ashes. [14] But it will be more tolerable for Tyre and Sidon in the Judgment than for you. [15] And you, Capernaum, who has been lifted up to Heaven, you shall be brought down to Hades. [16] Those hearing you hears Me, and he despising you despises Me, and he despising Me despises Him who sent Me. [17] And the seventy returned with joy, saying, Lord, even the demons are subject to us through Your name. [18] And He said to them, I saw Satan as lightning falling out of Heaven. [19] Behold, I give to you the authority to tread upon snakes and scorpions, and on the power of the enemy, and nothing shall hurt you in any way. [20] Yet do not rejoice in this, that the spirits are subjected to

**6** λέγετε, Εἰρήνη τῷ οἴκῳ τούτῳ. καὶ ἐὰν μὲν ᾖ ἐκεῖ ὁ υἱὸς
say,    Peace    –  house  to this.  And if indeed is there  – a son

εἰρήνης, ἐπαναπαύσεται ἐπ' αὐτὸν ἡ εἰρήνη ὑμῶν· εἰ δὲ
of peace,  shall rest    upon   it   the peace   of you; if but

**7** μήγε, ἐφ' ὑμᾶς ἀνακάμψει. ἐν αὐτῇ δὲ τῇ οἰκίᾳ μένετε, ἐσθίον-
not so, on  you it shall return. In same And the house remain,  eating

τες καὶ πίνοντες τὰ παρ' αὐτῶν· ἄξιος γὰρ ὁ ἐργάτης τοῦ
and drinking the things with them; worthy for  the   worker of the

**8** μισθοῦ αὐτοῦ ἐστι. μὴ μεταβαίνετε ἐξ οἰκίας εἰς οἰκίαν. καὶ
pay   of him  is.   Do not move   from house to house. And

εἰς ἣν δ' ἂν πόλιν εἰσέρχησθε, καὶ δέχωνται ὑμᾶς, ἐσθίετε τὰ
into whatever city  you enter,  and they receive you,  eat  the things

**9** παρατιθέμενα ὑμῖν, καὶ θεραπεύετε τοὺς ἐν αὐτῇ ἀσθενεῖς,
being set before you, and heal      the  in it   sick,

καὶ λέγετε αὐτοῖς, Ἤγγικεν ἐφ' ὑμᾶς ἡ βασιλεία τοῦ Θεοῦ.
and say   to them, has drawn near on you the kingdom  – of God.

**10** εἰς ἣν δ' ἂν πόλιν εἰσέρχησθε, καὶ μὴ δέχωνται ὑμᾶς, ἐξελ-
And into whatever city you enter,  and not they receive you,  going

**11** θόντες εἰς τὰς πλατείας αὐτῆς εἴπατε, Καὶ τὸν κονιορτὸν τὸν
out   into the  streets    of it  say,   Even the  dust    –

κολληθέντα ἡμῖν ἐκ τῆς πόλεως ὑμῶν ἀπομασσόμεθα ὑμῖν·
clinging   to us out of the city  of you  we shake off     to you

πλὴν τοῦτο γινώσκετε, ὅτι ἤγγικεν ἐφ' ὑμᾶς ἡ βασιλεία τοῦ
yet  this   know,    that has drawn near on you the kingdom

**12** Θεοῦ. λέγω δὲ ὑμῖν, ὅτι Σοδόμοις ἐν τῇ ἡμέρᾳ ἐκείνῃ ἀνε-
of God. I say And to you that for Sodom in – day   that   more

**13** κτότερον ἔσται, ἢ τῇ πόλει ἐκείνῃ. οὐαί σοι, Χωραζίν, οὐαί
tolerable it will be than – city for that. Woe to you, Chorazin! Woe

σοι, Βηθσαϊδά· ὅτι εἰ ἐν Τύρῳ καὶ Σιδῶνι ἐγένοντο αἱ δυνά-
to you, Bethsaida! For if in  Tyre and Sidon  happened the works

μεις αἱ γενόμεναι ἐν ὑμῖν, πάλαι ἂν ἐν σάκκῳ καὶ σποδῷ
of power happening in you, long ago – in sackcloth and ashes

**14** καθημεναι μετενόησαν. πλὴν Τύρῳ καὶ Σιδῶνι ἀνεκτότερον
sitting they would have repented. But for Tyre and Sidon more tolerable

**15** ἔσται ἐν τῇ κρίσει, ἢ ὑμῖν. καὶ σύ, Καπερναούμ, ἡ ἕως τοῦ
it will be in the Judgment than for you. And you, Capernaum, not to –

**16** οὐρανοῦ ὑψωθεῖσα, ἕως ᾅδου καταβιβασθήσῃ. ὁ ἀκούων
Heaven were you lifted? To Hades you will come down. Those hearing

ὑμῶν ἐμοῦ ἀκούει· καὶ ὁ ἀθετῶν ὑμᾶς ἐμὲ ἀθετεῖ· ὁ δὲ ἐμὲ
you  Me  hears, and those rejecting you  Me rejects; those and Me

ἀθετῶν ἀθετεῖ τὸν ἀποστείλαντά με.
rejecting rejects the (One) having sent  Me.

**17** Ὑπέστρεψαν δὲ οἱ ἑβδομήκοντα μετὰ χαρᾶς, λέγοντες,
returned    And the seventy     with joy,   saying,

Κύριε, καὶ τὰ δαιμόνια ὑποτάσσεται ἡμῖν ἐν τῷ ὀνόματί
Lord, even the demons    submit      to us  in the  name

**18** σου. εἶπε δὲ αὐτοῖς, Ἐθεώρουν τὸν Σατανᾶν ὡς ἀστραπὴν
of You. He said But to them, I saw  –   Satan   as  lightning

**19** ἐκ τοῦ οὐρανοῦ πεσόντα. ἰδού, δίδωμι ὑμῖν τὴν ἐξουσίαν
out of – Heaven  fall.  Behold, I have given you the authority

τοῦ πατεῖν ἐπάνω ὄφεων καὶ σκορπίων, καὶ ἐπὶ πᾶσαν τὴν
– to tread  on  snakes and scorpions,  and on all   the

**20** δύναμιν τοῦ ἐχθροῦ· καὶ οὐδὲν ὑμᾶς οὐ μὴ ἀδικήσει. πλὴν
power of the enemy, and nothing you in no way shall hurt. But

ἐν τούτῳ μὴ χαίρετε ὅτι τὰ πνεύματα ὑμῖν ὑποτάσσεται·
in this   stop rejoicing that the spirits   to you  submit,

you, but rejoice rather that your names are written in Heaven. [21] In the same hour Jesus rejoiced in the Spirit, and said, I praise You, O Father, Lord of the Heaven and of the earth, that You hid these things from the sophisticated and cunning, and have revealed them to babes; yes, Father, for so it was pleasing in Your sight. [22] And having turned to the disciples He said, All things were delivered to Me by My Father, and no one knows who the Son is except the Father, and who the Father, except the Son, and he to whomever the Son may desire to reveal (Him). [23] And having turned to the disciples alone He said, Blessed (are) the eyes which see what you see. [24] For I say to you that many prophets and kings desire to see what you see, and did not see; and to hear what you hear, and did not hear.

[25] And behold, a certain doctor of the law stood up, tempting Him, and saying, Teacher, what shall I do to inherit eternal life? [26] And He said to him, What has been written in the Law? How do you read? [27] And answering he said, You shall love (the) Lord your God with all your heart and with all your soul and with all your strength and with all your mind; and your neighbor as yourself. [28] And He said to him, You have answered rightly; do this, and you shall live. [29] But desiring to justify himself he said to Jesus, And who is my neighbor? [30] And taking (it) up Jesus said, A certain man was going down from Jerusalem to Jericho, and fell among robbers, who both stripped him and having inflicted wounds went away (and) left, (he) being half-dead. [31] But by a coincidence a certain priest went down on that road, and having seen him

χαίρετε δὲ μᾶλλον ὅτι τὰ ὀνόματα ὑμῶν ἐγράφη ἐν τοῖς
rejoice but rather that the names of you are written in the
οὐρανοις.
heavens.

**21** Ἐν αὐτῇ τῇ ὥρᾳ ἠγαλλιάσατο τῷ πνεύματι ὁ Ἰησοῦς
In same the hour exulted in the Spirit — Jesus
καὶ εἶπεν, Ἐξομολογοῦμαί σοι, πάτερ, Κύριε τοῦ οὐρανοῦ
and said, I praise You, Father, Lord — of Heaven
καὶ τῆς γῆς, ὅτι ἀπέκρυψας ταῦτα ἀπὸ σοφῶν καὶ συνετῶν,
and — of earth, for You hid these things from sophisticated and cunning
καὶ ἀπεκάλυψας αὐτὰ νηπίοις· ναί, ὁ πατήρ, ὅτι οὕτως
and revealed them to babes; yes, — Father, because thus
ἐγένετο εὐδοκία ἔμπροσθέν σου. πάντα παρεδόθη μοι ὑπὸ
it was well pleasing before You. All things were delivered to Me by
**22** τοῦ πατρός μου· καὶ οὐδεὶς γινώσκει τίς ἐστιν ὁ υἱός, εἰ μὴ
the Father of Me, and no one knows who is the Son, except
ὁ πατήρ, καὶ τίς ἐστιν ὁ πατήρ, εἰ μὴ ὁ υἱός, καὶ ᾧ ἐὰν
the Father, and who is the Father, except the Son, and whoever
βούληται ὁ υἱὸς ἀποκαλύψαι. καὶ στραφεὶς πρὸς τοὺς
may desire the Son to reveal (Him). And having turned to the
**23** μαθητὰς κατ᾽ ἰδίαν εἶπε, Μακάριοι οἱ ὀφθαλμοὶ οἱ βλέποντες
disciples, privately He said, Blessed the eyes — seeing
ἃ βλέπετε. λέγω γὰρ ὑμῖν, ὅτι πολλοὶ προφῆται καὶ
what you see. I say For to you that many prophets and
**24** βασιλεῖς ἠθέλησαν ἰδεῖν ἃ ὑμεῖς βλέπετε, καὶ οὐκ εἶδον· καὶ
kings desired to see what you see, and not did see; and
ἀκοῦσαι ἃ ἀκούετε, καὶ οὐκ ἤκουσαν.
to hear what you hear, and not did hear.

**25** Καὶ ἰδού, νομικός τις ἀνέστη, ἐκπειράζων αὐτόν, καὶ
And behold, lawyer a certain stood up, tempting Him, and
λέγων, Διδάσκαλε, τί ποιήσας ζωὴν αἰώνιον κληρονομήσω;
said, Teacher, what doing life eternal I may inherit?
**26** ὁ δὲ εἶπε πρὸς αὐτόν, Ἐν τῷ νόμῳ τί γέγραπται; πῶς
He And said to him, In the law what is written? How
**27** ἀναγινώσκεις; ὁ δὲ ἀποκριθεὶς εἶπεν, Ἀγαπήσεις Κύριον
do you read? he And answering said, You shall love (the) Lord
τὸν Θεόν σου, ἐξ ὅλης τῆς καρδίας σου, καὶ ἐξ ὅλης τῆς
the God of you from all the heart of you, and from all the
ψυχῆς σου, καὶ ἐξ ὅλης τῆς ἰσχύος σου, καὶ ἐξ ὅλης τῆς
soul of you, and from all the strength of you, and from all the
**28** διανοίας σου· καὶ τὸν πλησίον σου ὡς σεαυτόν. εἶπε δὲ
mind of you; and the neighbor of you as yourself. He said And
αὐτῷ, Ὀρθῶς ἀπεκρίθης· τοῦτο ποίει, καὶ ζήσῃ. ὁ δὲ θέλων
to him, Rightly you answered; this do, and you will live. he But willing
**29** δικαιοῦν ἑαυτὸν εἶπε πρὸς τὸν Ἰησοῦν, Καὶ τίς ἐστί μου
to justify himself said to — Jesus, And who is of me
πλησίον; ὑπολαβὼν δὲ ὁ Ἰησοῦς εἶπεν, Ἄνθρωπός τις
neighbor? Taking (it) up And, — Jesus said, man A certain
**30** κατέβαινεν ἀπὸ Ἰερουσαλὴμ εἰς Ἰεριχώ, καὶ λῃσταῖς
was going down from Jerusalem to Jericho, and robbers
περιέπεσεν, οἳ καὶ ἐκδύσαντες αὐτὸν καὶ πληγὰς ἐπιθέντες
fell in with, who both stripping him and blows laying on,
**31** ἀπῆλθον, ἀφέντες ἡμιθανῆ τυγχάνοντα. κατὰ συγκυρίαν
went away, leaving (him) half dead being. by a coincidence
δὲ ἱερεύς τις κατέβαινεν ἐν τῇ ὁδῷ ἐκείνῃ· καὶ ἰδὼν αὐτὸν
And priest a certain was going in — way that and seeing him

he passed by on the opposite side. [32] And in the same way a Levite also, being at the spot, having come and having seen, passed by on the opposite side. [33] But a certain Samaritan traveling came to him, and having seen him was moved with pity, [34] and having come up bound up his wounds, pouring on oil and wine; and having put him on his own animal brought him to an inn, and took care of him. [35] And on the morrow going forth, taking out two denarii he gave to the innkeeper, and said to him, Take care of him, and whatever you may expend more, I on my return will repay you. [36] Therefore which of these three seems to you to have been neighbor of him who fell among the robbers? [37] And he said, He who showed pity toward him. Therefore Jesus said to him, Go and you do likewise.

[38] And as they went on, it happened that He entered into a certain village; and a certain woman named Martha received Him into her house. [39] And she had a sister called Mary, who also having sat down at the feet of Jesus was listening to His word. [40] But Martha was troubled about much service; and coming up she said, Lord, is it no concern to You that my sister left me alone to serve? Therefore speak to her that she may help me. [41] But answering Jesus said to her, Martha, Martha, you are anxious and troubled about many things. [42] But one thing is needful; and Mary chose the good part, which shall not be taken from her.

CHAPTER 11
[1] And it came to pass as He was in a certain place praying, when He stopped, one of His disciples said to Him, Lord, teach us to pray, as John also taught

32　ἀντιπαρῆλθεν. ὁμοίως δὲ καὶ Λευίτης γενόμενος κατὰ τὸν
　　passed opposite. likewise And also a Levite being at the

33　τόπον ἐλθὼν καὶ ἰδὼν ἀντιπαρῆλθε. Σαμαρείτης δέ τις
　　place, coming and seeing, passed opposite. Samaritan But a certain

　　ὁδεύων ἦλθε κατ’ αὐτόν, καὶ ἰδὼν αὐτὸν ἐσπλαγχνίσθη,
　　traveling came upon him, and' seeing him was filled with pity;

34　καὶ προσελθὼν κατέδησε τὰ τραύματα αὐτοῦ, ἐπιχέων
　　and coming up bound up the wounds of him, pouring

　　ἔλαιον καὶ οἶνον· ἐπιβιβάσας δὲ αὐτὸν ἐπὶ τὸ ἴδιον κτῆνος,
　　oil and wine; placing and him on the own beast

35　ἤγαγεν αὐτὸν εἰς πανδοχεῖον, καὶ ἐπεμελήθη αὐτοῦ. καὶ ἐπὶ
　　brought him to an inn, and cared for him. And on

　　τὴν αὔριον ἐξελθών, ἐκβαλὼν δύο δηνάρια ἔδωκε τῷ παν-
　　the morrow going out, taking out two denarii he gave to the inn-

　　δοχεῖ, καὶ εἶπεν αὐτῷ, ’Επιμελήθητι αὐτοῦ· καὶ ὅ τι ἂν
　　keeper, and said to him, care for him, and whatever

　　προσδαπανήσης, ἐγὼ ἐν τῷ ἐπανέρχεσθαί με ἀποδώσω σοι.
　　you spend more, I in the returnıng (of) me will repay you.

36　τίς οὖν τούτων τῶν· τριῶν δοκεῖ σοι πλησίον γεγονέναι
　　Who, then, of these — three seems it to you neighbor to have become

37　τοῦ ἐμπεσόντος εἰς τοὺς λῃστάς ; ὁ δὲ εἶπεν, ῾Ο ποιήσας τὸ
　　of those falling among the robbers? he And said, The (one) doing the

　　ἔλεος μετ’ αὐτοῦ. εἶπεν οὖν αὐτῷ ὁ ’Ιησοῦς, Πορεύου, καὶ
　　mercy with him. said Then to him — Jesus, Go, and

　　σὺ ποίει ὁμοίως.
　　you do likewise.

38　’Εγένετο δὲ ἐν τῷ πορεύεσθαι αὐτούς, καὶ αὐτὸς εἰσῆλθεν
　　it occurred And ın the going (of) them, also He entered

　　εἰς κώμην τινά· γυνὴ δέ τις ὀνόματι . Μάρθα ὑπεδέξατο
　　into village a certain. woman And a certain by name Martha received

39　αὐτὸν εἰς τὸν οἶκον αὐτῆς. καὶ τῇδε ἦν ἀδελφὴ καλουμένη
　　Him into the house of her. And to this was a sister being called

　　Μαρία, ἥ καὶ παρακαθίσασα παρὰ τοὺς πόδας τοῦ ’Ιησοῦ
　　Mary, who also sitting beside at the feet of Jesus

40　ἤκουε τὸν λογον αὐτοῦ. ἡ δὲ Μάρθα περιεσπᾶτο περὶ
　　heard the word of Him. — But Martha was distracted about

　　πολλὴν διακονίαν· ἐπιστᾶσα δὲ εἶπε, Κύριε, οὐ μέλει σοι ὅτι
　　much serving; coming on And she said, Lord, not a care to You that

　　ἡ ἀδελφή μου μονην με κατέλιπε διακονεῖν ; εἰπὲ οὖν αὐτῇ
　　the sister of me alone me left to serve? tell Then her

41　ἵνα μοι συναντιλάβηται. ἀποκριθεὶς δὲ εἶπεν αὐτῇ ὁ ’Ιησοῦς,
　　that me she should help. answering And said to her — Jesus,

　　Μάρθα, Μάρθα, μεριμνᾷς καὶ τυρβάζῃ περὶ πολλά· ἑνὸς
　　Martha, Martha, you are anxious and troubled about many things of one

42　δέ ἐστι χρεία· Μαρία δὲ τὴν ἀγαθὴν μερίδα ἐξελέξατο, ἥτις
　　but is need; Mary and the good part chose, which

　　οὐκ ἀφαιρεθήσεται ἀπ’ αὐτῆς.
　　not shall be taken from her.

## CHAPTER 11

1　Καὶ ἐγένετο ἐν τῷ εἶναι αὐτὸν ἐν τόπῳ τινὶ προσευχό-
　　And it was in the being (of) Him in place a certain praying,

　　μενον, ὡς ἐπαύσατο, εἶπέ τις τῶν μαθητῶν αὐτοῦ πρὸς
　　as He ceased, said a certain one of the disciples of Him to

　　αὐτόν, Κύριε, δίδαξον ἡμᾶς προσεύχεσθαι, καθὼς καὶ
　　Him, Lord, teach us to pray, even as also

his disciples. [2] And He said to them, When you pray, say, Our Father who is in Heaven, holy is Your name; may Your kingdom come; may Your will be done, on the earth as it also is in Heaven. [3] Give us our needed bread day by day; [4] and forgive us our sins, for we ourselves forgive everyone indebted to us; and lead us not into temptation, but deliver us from evil. [5] And He said to them, Who among you shall have a friend, and shall go to him at midnight and say to him, Friend, lend me three loaves, [6] since a friend of mine is come from a journey to me, and I have not what I shall set before him? [7] And he from within answering shall say, Do not cause me trouble; the door already has been shut, and my children are in bed with me; I cannot get up to give to you. [8] I say to you, Even if he will not give to him, having risen up, because of being his friend, yet because of his shameless insisting having risen he will give him as many as he needs. [9] And I say to you, Ask, and it shall be given to you; seek, and you shall find; knock, and it shall be opened to you. [10] For everyone that asks receives; and he that seeks finds; and to him that knocks it will be opened. [11] And which of you who (is) a father, if the son shall ask bread, will he give him a stone? And if a fish, will he give him a snake instead of a fish? [12] And if he should ask an egg, will he give him a scorpion? [13] Therefore if you, being evil, know (how) to give good gifts to your children, how much more the Father who (is) from Heaven will give (the) Holy Spirit to those who ask Him?

[14] And He was casting out a demon, and it was dumb; and on the demon having gone out (that) the dumb spoke. And the crowd

**2** Ἰωάννης ἐδίδαξε τοὺς μαθητὰς αὐτοῦ. εἶπε δὲ αὐτοῖς,
John      taught    the    disciples   of him. He said And to them,

Ὅταν προσεύχησθε, λέγετε, Πάτερ ἡμῶν ὁ ἐν τοῖς οὐρανοῖς
When  you pray,    say,    Father  Our, who in  the  heavens,

ἁγιασθήτω τὸ ὄνομά σου. ἐλθέτω ἡ βασιλεία σου. γενηθήτω
holy be    the name of You; let come the kingdom of You. Let be done

**3** τὸ θέλημά σου, ὡς ἐν οὐρανῷ, καὶ ἐπὶ τῆς γῆς. τὸν ἄρτον
the will  of You, as in  Heaven, also  on  the earth. The bread

**4** ἡμῶν τὸν ἐπιούσιον δίδου ἡμῖν τὸ καθ' ἡμέραν. καὶ ἄφες
of us  the  needed   give   us   —  day by day.  And forgive

ἡμῖν τὰς ἁμαρτίας ἡμῶν, καὶ γὰρ αὐτοὶ ἀφίεμεν παντὶ
us  the  sins    of us,  also for ourselves we forgive everyone

ὀφείλοντι ἡμῖν. καὶ μὴ εἰσενέγκῃς ἡμᾶς εἰς πειρασμόν, ἀλλὰ
indebted  to us. And do not lead    us  into temptation,  but

ῥῦσαι ἡμᾶς ἀπὸ τοῦ πονηροῦ.
deliver  us from  —  evil.

**5** Καὶ εἶπε πρὸς αὐτούς, Τίς ἐξ ὑμῶν ἕξει φίλον, καὶ πορεύ-
And He said to   them,  Who of you shall have a friend, and  will

σεται πρὸς αὐτὸν μεσονυκτίου, καὶ εἴπῃ αὐτῷ, Φίλε,
come  to    him  at midnight,    and  say  to him, Friend,

**6** χρῆσόν μοι τρεῖς ἄρτους, ἐπειδὴ φίλος μου παρεγένετο ἐξ
lend    me three  loaves,  since a friend of me  arrived  off

**7** ὁδοῦ πρός με, καὶ οὐκ ἔχω ὃ παραθήσω αὐτῷ· κἀκεῖνος
a journey to me, and  not I have what I may set before him; and that one

ἔσωθεν ἀποκριθεὶς εἴπῃ, Μή μοι κόπους πάρεχε· ἤδη ἡ
within  answering  may say, Not me troubles  cause; now the

θύρα κέκλεισται, καὶ τὰ παιδία μου μετ' ἐμοῦ εἰς τὴν κοίτην
door has been shut, and the children of me with me  in  the  bed

**8** εἰσίν· οὐ δύναμαι ἀναστὰς δοῦναί σοι. λέγω ὑμῖν, εἰ καὶ
are;  not I am able rising up  to give you. I say  to you, if even

οὐ δώσει αὐτῷ ἀναστάς, διὰ τὸ εἶναι αὐτοῦ φίλον, διά γε
not he will give him, rising up on account of being of him  friend, yet because of

τὴν ἀναίδειαν αὐτοῦ ἐγερθεὶς δώσει αὐτῷ ὅσων χρῄζει.
the importunity of him   rising he will give him  as many as he needs.

**9** κἀγὼ ὑμῖν λέγω, Αἰτεῖτε, καὶ δοθήσεται ὑμῖν· ζητεῖτε, καὶ
And I to you say,  Ask,    and it will be given to you;  seek,  and

**10** εὑρήσετε· κρούετε, καὶ ἀνοιγήσεται ὑμῖν. πᾶς γὰρ ὁ αἰτῶν
you will find; knock, and it will be opened to you. everyone For  asking

λαμβάνει· καὶ ὁ ζητῶν εὑρίσκει· καὶ τῷ κρούοντι ἀνοιγή-
receives,  and those seeking  finds,  and to those knocking, it will be

**11** σεται. τίνα δὲ ὑμῶν τὸν πατέρα αἰτήσει ὁ υἱὸς ἄρτον, μὴ
opened. what And of you  —  father (of whom) asks the son  bread,

λίθον ἐπιδώσει αὐτῷ; εἰ καὶ ἰχθύν, μὴ ἀντὶ ἰχθύος ὄφιν
a stone will he give him?  if And a fish,    instead of a fish, a snake

**12** ἐπιδώσει αὐτῷ; ἢ καὶ ἐὰν αἰτήσῃ ὠόν, μὴ ἐπιδώσει αὐτῷ
will he give him? Or also if he should ask an egg, will he give  to him

**13** σκορπίον; εἰ οὖν ὑμεῖς πονηροὶ ὑπάρχοντες οἴδατε ἀγαθὰ
a scorpion? If, then, you  evil    being    know  good

δόματα διδόναι τοῖς τέκνοις ὑμῶν, πόσῳ μᾶλλον ὁ πατὴρ
gifts  to give  to the children of you, how much more the Father

ὁ ἐξ οὐρανοῦ δώσει Πνεῦμα Ἅγιον τοῖς αἰτοῦσιν αὐτόν;
of  Heaven will give (the) Spirit  Holy  to those asking  Him.

**14** Καὶ ἦν ἐκβάλλων δαιμόνιον, καὶ αὐτὸ ἦν κωφόν. ἐγένετο
And He was casting out a demon,  and  it  was  dumb.  it was

δέ, τοῦ δαιμονίου ἐξελθόντος, ἐλάλησεν ὁ κωφός· καὶ
And, the  demon   going out,    spoke  the dumb one. And

wondered. [15] But some of them said, By Beelzebub the prince of the demons he casts out the demons. [16] And others tempting were seeking from Him a sign from Heaven. [17] But knowing their thoughts He said to them, Every kingdom divided against itself is brought to ruin; and a house against a house falls. [18] And also if Satan is divided against himself, how shall his kingdom stand? Because you say, I cast out the demons by Beelzebub. [19] And if I cast out the demons by Beelzebub, by whom do your sons cast out? Because of this they shall be your judges. [20] But if I cast out the demons by (the) finger of God, then the kingdom of God is come upon you. [21] When the strong one being armed may keep his own house safe, his goods are in peace; [22] but as soon as he stronger (than) he comes on, (he) overcomes him, he takes away his armor on which he relied, and divides his arms. [23] He that is not with Me is against Me, and he that does not gather with Me scatters. [24] When the unclean spirit is gone out from the man, he goes through waterless places, seeking rest; and not finding (any) he says, I will return to my house from where I came out. [25] And having come he finds (it) swept and decorated. [26] Then he goes and takes seven other spirits more wicked than himself, and having entered they live there. And the last (state) of that man becomes worse than the first. [27] And as He spoke these things it happened that a certain woman lifting up (her) voice from the crowd said to Him, Blessed the womb that bore You, and (the) breast which You sucked. [28] And He said, Yes, rather, blessed they who hear the word of God and keep it.

15 ἐθαύμασαν οἱ ὄχλοι. τινὲς δὲ ἐξ αὐτῶν εἶπον, Ἐν Βεελζεβούλ
marveled the crowds. some But of them said, By Beelzebub
16 ἄρχοντι τῶν δαιμονίων ἐκβάλλει τὰ δαιμόνια. ἕτεροι δὲ
the chief of the demons He casts out the demons. others And
17 πειράζοντες σημεῖον παρ' αὐτοῦ ἐζήτουν ἐξ οὐρανοῦ. αὐτὸς
tempting a sign from Him were seeking from Heaven. He
δὲ εἰδὼς αὐτῶν τὰ διανοήματα εἶπεν αὐτοῖς, Πᾶσα βασιλεία
But knowing of them the thoughts said to them, Every kingdom
ἐφ' ἑαυτὴν διαμερισθεῖσα ἐρημοῦται· καὶ οἶκος ἐπὶ οἶκον,
against itself divided is brought to ruin, and a house against a house
18 πίπτει. εἰ δὲ καὶ ὁ Σατανᾶς ἐφ' ἑαυτὸν διεμερίσθη, πῶς
falls. if And also — Satan against himself is divided, how
σταθήσεται ἡ βασιλεία αὐτοῦ; ὅτι λέγετε, ἐν Βεελζεβούλ
shall stand the kingdom of him? Because you say by Beelzebub
19 ἐκβάλλειν με τὰ δαιμόνια. εἰ δὲ ἐγὼ ἐν Βεελζεβούλ ἐκβάλλω
casting out I (am) the demons. if But I by Beelzebub cast out
τὰ δαιμόνια, οἱ υἱοὶ ὑμῶν ἐν τίνι ἐκβάλλουσι; διὰ τοῦτο
the demons, the sons of you, by what do they cast out? Therefore
20 κριταὶ ὑμῶν αὐτοὶ ἔσονται. εἰ δὲ ἐν δακτύλῳ Θεοῦ ἐκβάλλω
judges of you they shall be. if But by (the) finger of God I cast out
τὰ δαιμόνια, ἄρα ἔφθασεν ἐφ' ὑμᾶς ἡ βασιλεία τοῦ Θεοῦ.
the demons, then came upon you the kingdom — of God.
21 ὅταν ὁ ἰσχυρὸς καθωπλισμένος φυλάσσῃ τὴν ἑαυτοῦ αὐλήν,
When the strong one being armed guards the dwelling of him,
22 ἐν εἰρήνῃ ἐστὶ τὰ ὑπάρχοντα αὐτοῦ· ἐπὰν δὲ ὁ ἰσχυρότερος
in peace are the goods of him. when But one stronger
αὐτοῦ ἐπελθὼν νικήσῃ αὐτόν, τὴν πανοπλίαν αὐτοῦ αἴρει
(than) him coming overcomes him, the armor of him he takes,
ἐφ' ᾖ ἐπεποίθει, καὶ τὰ σκῦλα αὐτοῦ διαδίδωσιν. ὁ μὴ ὢν
on which he relied, and the arms of him distributes. Those not being
μετ' ἐμοῦ κατ' ἐμοῦ ἐστι· καὶ ὁ μὴ συνάγων μετ' ἐμοῦ σκορπί-
with Me, against Me is! And those not gathering with Me, scatters!
24 ζει. ὅταν τὸ ἀκάθαρτον πνεῦμα ἐξέλθῃ ἀπὸ τοῦ ἀνθρώπου,
When the unclean spirit goes out from the man,
διέρχεται δι' ἀνύδρων τόπων, ζητοῦν ἀνάπαυσιν· καὶ μὴ
he goes through dry places seeking rest, and not
εὑρίσκον λέγει, Ὑποστρέψω εἰς τὸν οἶκόν μου ὅθεν ἐξῆλθον.
finding says, I will return to the house of me from where I came.
25 καὶ ἐλθὸν εὑρίσκει σεσαρωμένον καὶ κεκοσμημένον. τότε
And coming he finds (it) having been swept and decorated. Then
26 πορεύεται καὶ παραλαμβάνει ἑπτὰ ἕτερα πνεύματα πονηρό-
he goes and takes seven other spirits more wicked
τερα ἑαυτοῦ, καὶ εἰσελθόντα κατοικεῖ ἐκεῖ· καὶ γίνεται τὰ
(than) himself, and entering he lives there; and becomes the
ἔσχατα τοῦ ἀνθρώπου ἐκείνου χείρονα τῶν πρώτων.
last things — man of that worse (than) the first.
27 Ἐγένετο δὲ ἐν τῷ λέγειν αὐτὸν ταῦτα, ἐπάρασά τις γυνὴ
it was And in the saying (of) Him these things, lifting a certain woman
φωνὴν ἐκ τοῦ ὄχλου εἶπεν αὐτῷ, Μακαρία ἡ κοιλία ἡ βαστά-
(her) voice out the crowd said to Him, Blessed the womb having
28 σασά σε, καὶ μαστοὶ οὓς ἐθήλασας. αὐτὸς δὲ εἶπε, Μενοῦνγε
borne You, and (the) breasts which You sucked. He But said, No, rather
μακάριοι οἱ ἀκούοντες τὸν λόγον τοῦ Θεοῦ καὶ φυλάσσοντες
blessed those hearing the word — of God and keeping
αὐτόν.
it.

[29] But the crowds being thronged together He began to say, This generation is evil; it seeks after a sign, and a sign shall not be given to it except the sign of Jonah the prophet. [30] For as Jonah was a sign to the Ninevites, so shall the Son of man also be to this generation. [31] A queen of (the) south shall rise up in the judgment with the men of this generation, and shall condemn them; for she came from the ends of the earth to hear the wisdom of Solomon, and behold, a greater than Solomon (is) here. [32] Men of Nineveh will rise up in the Judgment with this generation, and will condemn it, because they repented at the preaching of Jonah; and behold, a greater than Jonah (is) here. [33] But no one having lit a lamp places it in secret; nor under a grain measure, but on the lamp stand, that those entering may see the light. [34] The lamp of the body is the eye. Therefore when your eye is sound, also all your body is light; but when it is evil, your body (is) also dark. [35] Watch, then, lest the light in you be darkness. [36] If, then, your whole body (is) light not having any part dark, all will be light, as when the lamp with (its) shining enlightens you.

[37] Now as (He) was speaking, a certain Pharisee asked Him that He would dine with him; and having gone in He reclined Himself. [38] But the Pharisee watching wondered that He did not first wash before the dinner. [39] But the Lord said to him, Now you Pharisees cleanse the outside of the cup and of the dish, but your inside is full of robbery and wickedness. [40] Fools! Did not He who made the outside also make the inside? [41] But give alms of the things which are within, and behold, all things are clean

---

**29** Τῶν δὲ ὄχλων ἐπαθροιζομένων ἤρξατο λέγειν, Ἡ γενεὰ
the And crowds   pressing upon (Him), He began to say,   generation

αὕτη πονηρά ἐστι· σημεῖον ἐπιζητεῖ, καὶ σημεῖον οὐ δοθή-
This an evil is.   a sign It seeks,   and a sign not will

**30** σεται αὐτῇ, εἰ μὴ τὸ σημεῖον Ἰωνᾶ τοῦ προφήτου. καθὼς
be given to it, except the sign of Jonah the prophet.   even as

γὰρ ἐγένετο Ἰωνᾶς σημεῖον τοῖς Νινευΐταις οὕτως ἔσται
For became Jonah a sign to the Ninevites   so will be

**31** καὶ ὁ υἱὸς τοῦ ἀνθρώπου τῇ γενεᾷ ταύτῃ. βασίλισσα νότου
also the Son — of man —generation to this. (The) queen of south

ἐγερθήσεται ἐν τῇ κρίσει μετὰ τῶν ἀνδρῶν τῆς γενεᾶς ταύτης,
will be raised in the Judgment with the men — generation of this

καὶ κατακρινεῖ αὐτούς· ὅτι ἦλθεν ἐκ τῶν περάτων τῆς γῆς
and will condemn them; because she came from the ends of the earth

ἀκοῦσαι τὴν σοφίαν Σολομῶντος, καὶ ἰδού, πλεῖον Σολομῶν-
to hear the wisdom of Solomon, and behold, a greater than Solomon

**32** τος ὧδε. ἄνδρες Νινευῒ ἀναστήσονται ἐν τῇ κρίσει μετὰ τῆς
(is) here. Men, Ninevites, will rise up in the Judgment with —

γενεᾶς ταύτης, καὶ κατακρινοῦσιν αὐτήν· ὅτι μετενόησαν
generation this, and will condemn it, because they repented

εἰς τὸ κήρυγμα Ἰωνᾶ, καὶ ἰδού, πλεῖον Ἰωνᾶ ὧδε.
at the preaching of Jonah; and behold, a greater than Jonah (is) here.

**33** Οὐδεὶς δὲ λύχνον ἅψας εἰς κρυπτὸν τίθησιν, οὐδὲ ὑπὸ τὸν
No one But a lamp having lit in secret places (it), nor under the

μόδιον, ἀλλ' ἐπὶ τὴν λυχνίαν, ἵνα οἱ εἰσπορευόμενοι τὸ
grain-measure, but on the lampstand, that the (ones) entering the

**34** φέγγος βλέπωσιν. ὁ λύχνος τοῦ σώματός ἐστιν ὁ ὀφθαλμός·
light may see. The lamp of the body is the eye.

ὅταν οὖν ὁ ὀφθαλμός σου ἁπλοῦς ᾖ, καὶ ὅλον τὸ σῶμά σου
when Then the eye of you single is, also all the body of you

φωτεινόν ἐστιν· ἐπὰν δὲ πονηρὸς ᾖ, καὶ τὸ σῶμά σου σκο-
bright is; when but evil it is, also the body of you (is)

**35** τεινόν. σκόπει οὖν μὴ τὸ φῶς τὸ ἐν σοὶ σκότος ἐστίν. εἰ οὖν
dark. Watch, then, lest the light — in you darkness is. If, then,

**36** τὸ σῶμά σου ὅλον φωτεινόν μὴ ἔχον τι μέρος σκοτεινόν,
the body of you whole (is) bright, not having any part dark,

ἔσται φωτεινόν ὅλον, ὡς ὅταν ὁ λύχνος τῇ ἀστραπῇ
will be bright all, as when the lamp with the shining

φωτίζῃ σε.
enlightens you.

**37** Ἐν δὲ τῷ λαλῆσαι, ἠρώτα αὐτὸν Φαρισαῖός τις ὅπως
in And the speaking, asked Him Pharisee certain that

**38** ἀριστήσῃ παρ' αὐτῷ· εἰσελθὼν δὲ ἀνέπεσεν. ὁ δὲ Φαρισαῖος
He would dine with him; entering and He reclined. the But Pharisee

ἰδὼν ἐθαύμασεν ὅτι οὐ πρῶτον ἐβαπτίσθη πρὸ τοῦ ἀρίστου.
seeing marveled that not first He washed before the dinner.

**39** εἶπε δὲ ὁ Κύριος πρὸς αὐτόν, Νῦν ὑμεῖς οἱ Φαρισαῖοι τὸ
said But the Lord to him, Now you — Pharisees the

ἔξωθεν τοῦ ποτηρίου καὶ τοῦ πίνακος καθαρίζετε, τὸ δὲ
outside of the cup and of the dish cleanse, the but

**40** ἔσωθεν υμῶν γέμει ἁρπαγῆς καὶ πονηρίας. ἄφρονες, οὐχ
inside of you is full of robbery and evil. Fools! Did not

**41** ὁ ποιήσας τὸ ἔξωθεν καὶ τὸ ἔσωθεν ἐποίησε; πλὴν τὰ
the (One) making the outside also the inside make; But (of) the things

ἐνόντα δότε ἐλεημοσύνην· καὶ ἰδού, πάντα καθαρὰ ὑμῖν
being within give alms, and behold, all things clean to you

ἐστιν.
is.

to you. [42] But woe to you, Pharisees, for you pay tithes of the mint and the rue and every plant, and pass by the judgment and the love of God. It was right to do these things, but not to leave aside those. [43] Woe to you, Pharisees, for you love the first seats in the synagogues and the greetings in the marketplaces. [44] Woe to you, scribes and Pharisees, hypocrites, for you are as the unseen tomb, and the men who walk over (them) do not know (it). [45] And answering, one of the doctors of the law said to Him, Teacher, saying these things you also insult us. [46] And He said, Woe to you doctors of the law also, for you load men (with) burdens heavy to bear, and do not touch the burdens yourselves with one of your fingers. [47] Woe to you, for you build the tombs of the prophets, and your fathers killed them. [48] So you bear witness and consent to the works of your fathers; for they indeed killed them, and you build their tombs. [49] And because of this the wisdom of God said, I will send prophets and apostles to them, and (some) of them they will kill and drive out, [50] that the blood of all the prophets poured out from the foundation of the world may be required of this generation, [51] from the blood of Abel to the blood of Zechariah, who died between the altar and the House; yes, I say to you, it shall be required of this generation. [52] Woe to you, doctors of the law, for you took away the key of knowledge; you did not enter, and you kept back those who were entering! [53] And as He was saying these things to them, the scribes and the Pharisees began urgently to press

**42** 'Αλλ' οὐαὶ ὑμῖν τοῖς Φαρισαίοις, ὅτι ἀπαδεκατοῦτε τὸ
But woe to you — Pharisees, because you tithe the

ἡδύοσμον καὶ τὸ πήγανον καὶ πᾶν λάχανον, καὶ παρέρ-
mint and the rue and every plant, and pass

χεσθε τὴν κρίσιν καὶ τὴν ἀγάπην τοῦ Θεοῦ· ταῦτα ἔδει
by the judgment and the love — of God; these things must

ποιῆσαι, κἀκεῖνα μὴ ἀφιέναι. οὐαὶ ὑμῖν τοῖς Φαρισαίοις,
(you) do, and those not to leave aside. Woe to you — Pharisees,

**43** ὅτι ἀγαπᾶτε τὴν πρωτοκαθεδρίαν ἐν ταῖς συναγωγαῖς,
because you love the chief seat in the synagogues,

καὶ τοὺς ἀσπασμοὺς ἐν ταῖς ἀγοραῖς. οὐαὶ ὑμῖν, γραμματεῖς
and the greetings in the markets! Woe to you, scribes

**44** καὶ Φαρισαῖοι. ὑποκριταί, ὅτι ἐστὲ ὡς τὰ μνημεῖα τὰ ἄδηλα,
and Pharisees, hypocrites! For you are as the tombs — unseen,

καὶ οἱ ἄνθρωποι οἱ περιπατοῦντες ἐπάνω οὐκ οἴδασιν.
and the men — walking over not do know.

**45** 'Αποκριθεὶς δέ τις τῶν νομικῶν λέγει αὐτῷ, Διδάσκαλε,
answering And one of the lawyers says to Him, Teacher,

ταῦτα λέγων καὶ ἡμᾶς ὑβρίζεις. ὁ δὲ εἶπε, Καὶ ὑμῖν τοῖς
these things saying also us You insult. He And said, Also to you

**46** νομικοῖς οὐαί, ὅτι φορτίζετε τοὺς ἀνθρώπους φορτία
lawyers, woe! Because you burden — men (with) burdens

δυσβάστακτα, καὶ αὐτοὶ ἑνὶ τῶν δακτύλων ὑμων οὐ
difficult to carry, and yourselves with one of the fingers of you not

**47** προσψαύετε τοῖς φορτίοις. οὐαὶ ὑμῖν, ὅτι οἰκοδομεῖτε τὰ
you touch the burdens. Woe to you, because you build the

μνημεῖα τῶν προφητῶν, οἱ δὲ πατέρες ὑμῶν ἀπέκτειναν
tombs of the prophets, the and fathers of you killed

**48** αὐτούς. ἄρα μαρτυρεῖτε καὶ συνευδοκεῖτε τοῖς ἔργοις τῶν
them! Then witnesses and consent to the works of the

πατέρων ὑμῶν· ὅτι αὐτοὶ μὲν ἀπέκτειναν αὐτούς, ὑμεῖς δὲ
fathers of you; for they indeed killed them, you but

**49** οἰκοδομεῖτε αὐτῶν τὰ μνημεῖα. διὰ τοῦτο καὶ ἡ σοφία τοῦ
build of them the tombs. Because of this also the wisdom —

Θεοῦ εἶπεν, Ἀποστελῶ εἰς αὐτοὺς προφήτας καὶ ἀποστό-
of God said, I will send to them prophets and apostles,

**50** λους, καὶ ἐξ αὐτῶν ἀποκτενοῦσι καὶ ἐκδιώξουσιν· ἵνα
and of them they will kill and drive out, that

ἐκζητηθῇ τὸ αἷμα πάντων τῶν προφητῶν τὸ ἐκχυνόμενον
may be required the blood of all the prophets — having been shed

**51** ἀπὸ καταβολῆς κόσμου ἀπὸ τῆς γενεᾶς ταύτης, ἀπὸ τοῦ
from (the) foundation of world from — generation this, from the

αἵματος Ἄβελ ἕως τοῦ αἵματος Ζαχαρίου τοῦ ἀπολομένου
blood of Abel until the blood of Zechariah — (who) perished

μεταξὺ τοῦ θυσιαστηρίου καὶ τοῦ οἴκου· ναί, λέγω ὑμῖν,
between the altar and the house; yes, I say to you,

**52** ἐκζητηθήσεται ἀπὸ τῆς γενεᾶς ταύτης. οὐαὶ ὑμῖν τοῖς
it will be required from — generation this. Woe to you, —

νομικοῖς, ὅτι ἤρατε τὴν κλεῖδα τῆς γνώσεως· αὐτοὶ οὐκ
lawyers! Because you took the key — of knowledge; yourselves not

εἰσήλθετε, καὶ τοὺς εἰσερχομένους ἐκωλύσατε.
you entered, and those entering you kept out.

**53** Λέγοντος δὲ αὐτοῦ ταῦτα πρὸς αὐτούς, ἤρξαντο οἱ
as was saying And He these things to them, began the

upon (Him), and to make Him speak about many **54** things; [54] watching Him and seeking to catch something out of His mouth that they might accuse Him.

γραμματεῖς καὶ οἱ Φαρισαῖοι δεινῶς ἐνέχειν, καὶ ἀποστο-
scribes and the Pharisees terribly to be angry, and to draw

ματίζειν αὐτὸν περὶ πλειόνων, ἐνεδρεύοντες αὐτόν, καὶ
out Him concerning many things, lying in wait for Him, and

ζητοῦντες θηρεῦσαί τι ἐκ τοῦ στόματος αὐτοῦ, ἵνα κατηγορή-
seeking to catch something from the mouth of Him, that they might

σωσιν αὐτοῦ.
accuse Him.

## CHAPTER 12

[1] At which time the myriads of the crowd being **1** gathered together, so as to trample upon one another, He began to say to His disciples first, Take heed to yourselves of the leaven of the Pharisees, which is hypocrisy; [2] but nothing **2** is concealed which shall not be uncovered, nor hidden which shall not be known; [3] therefore **3** whatever you said in the darkness, shall be heard in the light; and what you spoke in the ear in the room, shall be proclaimed on the housetops. [4] But **4** I say to you, my friends, You should not fear because of those killing the body, and after these things are not able to do anything more. [5] But I **5** will show you whom you shall fear, fear Him who after having killed has authority to cast into hell; yes, I say to you, Fear Him. [6] Are not five **6** sparrows sold for two assaria? And not one of them is forgotten before God. [7] But even the **7** hairs of your head have all been numbered. Therefore do not fear, you are better than many sparrows. [8] But I say to you, **8** Everyone who may confess Me before men, the Son of man will also confess him before the angels of God; [9] but he that has denied **9** Me before men will be denied before the angels of God. [10] And everyone who shall say a word against the Son of man, it **10** shall be forgiven Him; but to him who has blasphemed against the Holy Spirit, it shall not be forgiven. [11] But when **11** they bring you before the

## CHAPTER 12

Ἐν οἷς ἐπισυναχθεισῶν τῶν μυριάδων τοῦ ὄχλου, ὥστε
In which things being assembled the thousands of the crowd, so as

καταπατεῖν ἀλλήλους, ἤρξατο λέγειν πρὸς τοὺς μαθητὰς
to trample on one another, He began to say to the disciples

αὐτοῦ πρῶτον, Προσέχετε ἑαυτοῖς ἀπὸ τῆς ζύμης τῶν
of Him first, Beware to yourselves from the leaven of the

Φαρισαίων, ἥτις ἐστὶν ὑπόκρισις. οὐδὲν δὲ συγκεκαλυμ-
Pharisees, which is hypocrisy. nothing And being completely

μένον ἐστίν, ὃ οὐκ ἀποκαλυφθήσεται, καὶ κρυπτόν, ὃ οὐ
concealed is, which not will be uncovered; and hidden, which not

γνωσθήσεται. ἀνθ' ὧν ὅσα ἐν τῇ σκοτίᾳ εἴπατε, ἐν τῷ φωτὶ
will be known. Therefore, what in the darkness you said, in the light

ἀκουσθήσεται· καὶ ὃ πρὸς τὸ οὖς ἐλαλήσατε ἐν τοῖς ταμείοις,
it will be heard; and what to the ear you spoke in the secret rooms,

κηρυχθήσεται ἐπὶ τῶν δωμάτων. λέγω δὲ ὑμῖν τοῖς φίλοις
will be proclaimed on the housetops. I say But to you, the friends

μου, Μὴ φοβηθῆτε ἀπὸ τῶν ἀποκτεινόντων τὸ σῶμα, καὶ
of Me, Stop being afraid from those killing the body, and

μετὰ ταῦτα μὴ ἐχόντων περισσότερόν τι ποιῆσαι. ὑποδείξω
after these things not having anything more — to do. I will warn

δὲ ὑμῖν τίνα φοβηθῆτε· φοβήθητε τὸν μετὰ τὸ ἀποκτεῖναι
But you whom you may fear, fear those after the killing

ἐξουσίαν ἔχοντα ἐμβαλεῖν εἰς τὴν γέενναν· ναί, λέγω ὑμῖν,
authority having to throw into Gehenna. Yes, I say to you,

τοῦτον φοβήθητε. οὐχὶ πέντε στρουθία πωλεῖται ἀσσαρίων
this one fear! not five sparrows Are sold (for) assaria

δύο; καὶ ἓν ἐξ αὐτῶν οὐκ ἔστιν ἐπιλελησμένον ἐνώπιον τοῦ
two? And one of them not is having been forgotten before —

Θεοῦ. ἀλλὰ καὶ αἱ τρίχες τῆς κεφαλῆς ὑμῶν πᾶσαι ἠρίθ-
God. But even the hairs of the head of you all have been

μηνται. μὴ οὖν φοβεῖσθε· πολλῶν στρουθίων διαφέρετε.
numbered. stop, Then, being afraid; from many sparrows you differ.

λέγω δὲ ὑμῖν, Πᾶς ὃς ἂν ὁμολογήσῃ ἐν ἐμοὶ ἔμπροσθεν τῶν
I say And to you, everyone who confesses — Me before —

ἀνθρώπων, καὶ ὁ υἱὸς τοῦ ἀνθρώπου ὁμολογήσει ἐν αὐτῷ
men, also the Son — of man will confess — him

ἔμπροσθεν τῶν ἀγγέλων τοῦ Θεοῦ· ὁ δὲ ἀρνησάμενός με
before the angels — of God. those And denying Me

ἐνώπιον τῶν ἀνθρώπων ἀπαρνηθήσεται ἐνώπιον τῶν
before — men will be denied before the

ἀγγέλων τοῦ Θεοῦ. καὶ πᾶς ὃς ἐρεῖ λόγον εἰς τὸν υἱὸν τοῦ
angels — of God. And everyone who says a word against the Son —

ἀνθρώπου, ἀφεθήσεται αὐτῷ· τῷ δὲ εἰς τὸ Ἅγιον Πνεῦμα
of man, it will be forgiven him, those but against the Holy Spirit

βλασφημήσαντι οὐκ ἀφεθήσεται. ὅταν δὲ προσφέρωσιν ὑμᾶς
blaspheming not will be forgiven. when And they bring in you

synagogues and the rulers and the authorities, do not be careful how or what you shall reply, or what you should say; [12] for the Holy Spirit will teach you in that same hour what you ought to say.

[13] And one from the crowd said to Him, Teacher, tell my brother to divide the inheritance with me. [14] But He said to him, Man, who appointed Me a judge or divider over you? [15] And He said to them, Beware, and keep back from covetousness; for one's life is not in the abundance of the things which are to him. [16] And He spoke a parable to them, saying, A certain rich man produced well (from) the land. [17] And he reasoned within himself, saying, What may I do, for I have no where I may gather my fruits? [18] And he said, I will do this; I will tear down my barns, and I will build larger; and I will gather there all my produce and my goods; [19] and I will say to my soul, Soul, you have many goods laid (up) for many years; take rest, eat, drink, be merry. [20] But God said to him, Fool! This night they require your soul of you; and to whom shall be that which you prepared? [21] This (is) he who treasures up for himself, and is not rich toward God. [22] And He said to His disciples, Because of this I say to you, Do not be anxious as to your life, what you should eat, nor as to the body, what you should put on. [23] The life is more than the food, and the body than the clothing. [24] Consider the ravens, for they do not sow, nor do they reap; to which there is no storehouse nor barn, and God feeds them. How much rather you differ from the birds. [25] And who of you (by) being anxious is able to add one cubit to his stature? [26] Therefore if you are not able to do even (the) least, why are you anxious about the rest?

**12** ἐπὶ τὰς συναγωγὰς καὶ τὰς ἀρχὰς καὶ τὰς ἐξουσίας, μὴ
before — synagogues and — rulers and — authorities, do not

μεριμνᾶτε πῶς ἢ τί ἀπολογήσησθε, ἢ τί εἴπητε· τὸ γὰρ
be anxious how or what you may answer, or what you may say; the for

"Ἅγιον Πνεῦμα διδάξει ὑμᾶς ἐν αὐτῇ τῇ ὥρᾳ, ἃ δεῖ εἰπεῖν.
Holy Spirit will teach you in same the hour what must you say.

**13** Εἶπε δέ τις αὐτῷ ἐκ τοῦ ὄχλου, Διδάσκαλε, εἰπὲ τῷ ἀδελφῷ
said And one to Him from the crowd, Teacher, tell the brother

**14** μου μερίσασθαι μετ' ἐμοῦ τὴν κληρονομίαν. ὁ δὲ εἶπεν αὐτῷ,
of me to divide with me the inheritance. He But said to him,

"Ἄνθρωπε, τίς με κατέστησε δικαστὴν ἢ μεριστὴν ἐφ' ὑμᾶς ;
Man, who Me appointed a judge or a divider over you?

**15** εἶπε δὲ πρὸς αὐτούς, Ὁρᾶτε καὶ φυλάσσεσθε ἀπὸ τῆς πλεονε-
He said And to them, Beware, and keep back from covetous-

ξίας· ὅτι οὐκ ἐν τῷ περισσεύειν τινὶ ἡ ζωὴ αὐτοῦ ἐστὶν ἐκ
ness; for not in the abundance to anyone the life of him is out of

**16** τῶν ὑπαρχόντων αὐτοῦ. εἶπε δὲ παραβολὴν πρὸς αὐτούς,
the things existing of him. He spoke And a parable to them,

**17** λέγων, Ἀνθρώπου τινὸς πλουσίου εὐφόρησεν ἡ χώρα· καὶ
saying, A man certain rich produced well the land. And

διελογίζετο ἐν ἑαυτῷ λέγων, Τί ποιήσω, ὅτι οὐκ ἔχω ποῦ
he reasoned within himself, saying, What may I do, because not I have where

**18** συνάξω τοὺς καρπούς μου ; καὶ εἶπε, Τοῦτο ποιήσω· καθελῶ
I may gather the fruits of me? And he said, This I will do; I will raze

μου τὰς ἀποθήκας, καὶ μείζονας οἰκοδομήσω, καὶ συνάξω
of me the barns, and larger I will build; and I will gather

**19** ἐκεῖ πάντα τὰ γενήματά μου καὶ τὰ ἀγαθά μου. καὶ ἐρῶ
there all the produce of me and the goods of me; and I will say

τῇ ψυχῇ μου, Ψυχή, ἔχεις πολλὰ ἀγαθὰ κείμενα εἰς ἔτη
to the soul of me, Soul, you have many goods laid (up) for years

**20** πολλά· ἀναπαύου, φάγε, πίε, εὐφραίνου. εἶπε δὲ αὐτῷ ὁ
many; take rest, eat, drink, be glad. said But to him —

Θεός, Ἄφρον, ταύτῃ τῇ νυκτὶ τὴν ψυχήν σου ἀπαιτοῦσιν
God, Fool! This — night the soul of you they demand

**21** ἀπὸ σοῦ· ἃ δὲ ἡτοίμασας, τίνι ἔσται ; οὕτως ὁ θησαυρίζων
from you; that and you prepared, to whom will it be? So the (one) treasuring

ἑαυτῷ, καὶ μὴ εἰς Θεὸν πλουτῶν.
for himself, and not to God, (they) being rich.

**22** Εἶπε δὲ πρὸς τοὺς μαθητὰς αὐτοῦ, Διὰ τοῦτο ὑμῖν λέγω,
He said And to the disciples of Him, For this reason to you I say,

μὴ μεριμνᾶτε τῇ ψυχῇ ὑμῶν, τί φάγητε· μηδὲ τῷ σώματι,
Stop being anxious for the life of you, what you eat, nor for the body,

**23** τί ἐνδύσησθε. ἡ ψυχὴ πλεῖόν ἐστι τῆς τροφῆς, καὶ τὸ σῶμα
what you put on. The life more is (than) the food, and the body

**24** τοῦ ἐνδύματος. κατανοήσατε τοὺς κόρακας, ὅτι οὐ σπεί-
(than) the clothing. Consider the ravens, for not they

ρουσιν, οὐδὲ θερίζουσιν, οἷς οὐκ ἔστι ταμεῖον οὐδὲ ἀποθήκη,
sow, nor do they reap, to which not is storehouse nor barn

καὶ ὁ Θεὸς τρέφει αὐτούς· πόσῳ μᾶλλον ὑμεῖς διαφέρετε τῶν
and God feeds them; by how much rather you differ from the

**25** πετεινῶν ; τίς δὲ ἐξ ὑμῶν μεριμνῶν δύναται προσθεῖναι ἐπὶ
birds; who And of you being anxious is able to add on

**26** τὴν ἡλικίαν αὐτοῦ πῆχυν ἕνα ; εἰ οὖν οὔτε ἐλάχιστον
the stature of him cubit one? If, then, not (the) least

δύνασθε, τί περὶ τῶν λοιπῶν μεριμνᾶτε ; κατανοήσατε τὰ
you are able, why about the other things are you anxious? Consider the

[27] Consider the lilies, how they grow; they do not labor, nor do they spend; but I say to you, Not even Solomon in all his glory was clothed as one of these. [28] But if God so dresses the grass, which is today in the field, and tomorrow is thrown into the oven, how much rather you, O (you) of little faith? [29] And you, do not seek what you may eat or what you drink, and be not in anxiety; [30] for these things all the nations of the world seek after; and your Father knows that you have need of these things. [31] But seek the kingdom of God, and all these things shall be added to you. [32] Do not fear, little flock, for your Father took delight in giving you the kingdom. [33] Sell your possessions, and give alms; make yourselves purses that do not grow old, and unfailing treasure in Heaven, where the thief does not come, nor the moth destroy. [34] For where your treasure is, there your heart will be also. [35] Let your loins be girded about and the lamps burning [36] and you like men awaiting their lord, whenever he shall return from the wedding feasts, that having come and having knocked, they may immediately open to him. [37] Blessed those slaves whom the lord coming shall find watching. Truly I say to you, that he will gird himself and will make them recline, and coming up will serve them. [38] And if he comes in the second watch, and in the third watch he come and find (it) so, blessed are those slaves. [39] But know this that if the householder had known the hour the thief is coming, he would have watched, and would not have allowed his house to be broken through. [40] And you, therefore you be ready; for in the hour you do not expect, the Son of man comes.

27 κρίνα πῶς αὐξάνει· οὐ κοπιᾷ, οὐδὲ νήθει· λέγω δὲ ὑμῖν, οὐδὲ
lilies, how they grow; not they labor, nor spin, I say but to you, Not
Σολομὼν ἐν πάσῃ τῇ δόξῃ αὐτοῦ περιεβάλετο ὡς ἓν τούτων.
Solomon in all the glory of him was clothed as one of these.

28 εἰ δὲ τὸν χόρτον ἐν τῷ ἀγρῷ σήμερον ὄντα, καὶ αὔριον εἰς
if And the grass in the field, today (is) which, and tomorrow into
κλίβανον βαλλόμενον, ὁ Θεὸς οὕτως ἀμφιέννυσι. πόσῳ μᾶλλον
an oven is thrown, God so clothes, by how much rather

29 ὑμᾶς, ὀλιγόπιστοι; καὶ ὑμεῖς μὴ ζητεῖτε τί φάγητε, ἢ τί
you, little-faiths? And you stop seeking what you eat, or what

30 πίητε· καὶ μὴ μετεωρίζεσθε. ταῦτα γὰρ πάντα τὰ ἔθνη τοῦ
you drink, and stop being in anxiety. these things For all the nations of the
κόσμου ἐπιζητεῖ· ὑμῶν δὲ ὁ πατὴρ οἶδεν ὅτι χρῄζετε τούτων.
world seek after; of you But the Father knows that you need these.

31 πλὴν ζητεῖτε τὴν βασιλείαν τοῦ Θεοῦ, καὶ ταῦτα πάντα
But you seek the kingdom of God, and these things all

32 προστεθήσεται ὑμῖν. μὴ φοβοῦ, τὸ μικρὸν ποίμνιον· ὅτι
will be added to you. Stop fearing, — little flock; because
εὐδόκησεν ὁ πατὴρ ὑμῶν δοῦναι ὑμῖν τὴν βασιλείαν.
was pleased the Father of you to give you the kingdom.

33 πωλήσατε τὰ ὑπάρχοντα ὑμῶν καὶ δότε ἐλεημοσύνην.
Sell the possessions of you and give alms;
ποιήσατε ἑαυτοῖς βαλάντια μὴ παλαιούμενα, θησαυρὸν
make for yourselves purses not growing old, a treasure
ἀνέκλειπτον ἐν τοῖς οὐρανοῖς, ὅπου κλέπτης οὐκ ἐγγίζει οὐδὲ
unfailing in the heavens, where a thief not can approach, nor

34 σὴς διαφθείρει· ὅπου γάρ ἐστιν ὁ θησαυρὸς ὑμῶν, ἐκεῖ καὶ
moth can corrupt; where for is the treasure of you, there also
ἡ καρδία ὑμῶν ἔσται.
the heart of you will be.

35 Ἔστωσαν ὑμῶν αἱ ὀσφύες περιεζωσμέναι, καὶ οἱ λύχνοι
Let be of you the loins having been girded, and the lamps

36 καιόμενοι· καὶ ὑμεῖς ὅμοιοι ἀνθρώποις προσδεχομένοις τὸν
burning; and you like men awaiting the
κύριον ἑαυτῶν, πότε ἀναλύσει ἐκ τῶν γάμων, ἵνα, ἐλθόντος
lord of themselves, when he returns from the feast, that, coming

37 καὶ κρούσαντος, εὐθέως ἀνοίξωσιν αὐτῷ. μακάριοι οἱ δοῦλοι
and knocking, at once they will open to him. Blessed — slaves
ἐκεῖνοι, οὓς ἐλθὼν ὁ κύριος εὑρήσει γρηγοροῦντας· ἀμὴν
those, whom coming the lord will find watching; truly
λέγω ὑμῖν ὅτι περιζώσεται καὶ ἀνακλινεῖ αὐτούς, καὶ παρ-
I say to you that he will gird himself and cause to recline them, and coming

38 ελθὼν διακονήσει αὐτοῖς. καὶ ἐὰν ἔλθῃ ἐν τῇ δευτέρᾳ φυλακῇ,
up to will serve them. And if he come in the second watch,
καὶ ἐν τῇ τρίτῃ φυλακῇ ἔλθῃ, καὶ εὕρῃ οὕτω μακάριοί εἰσιν
even in the third watch he come, and find (it) so, blessed are

39 οἱ δοῦλοι ἐκεῖνοι. τοῦτο δὲ γινώσκετε, ὅτι εἰ ᾔδει ὁ οἰκοδε-
— slaves those. this But know, that if had known the house-
σπότης ποίᾳ ὥρᾳ ὁ κλέπτης ἔρχεται, ἐγρηγόρησεν ἄν, καὶ
master in what hour the thief is coming, he would have watched, and

40 οὐκ ἂν ἀφῆκε διορυγῆναι τὸν οἶκον αὐτοῦ. καὶ ὑμεῖς οὖν
not have allowed to be dug through the house of him. And you, then,
γίνεσθε ἕτοιμοι· ὅτι ᾗ ὥρᾳ οὐ δοκεῖτε ὁ υἱὸς τοῦ ἀνθρώπου
be prepared, for the hour not you think the Son — of man
ἔρχεται.
comes.

[41] And Peter said to him, Lord do You speak this parable to us, or also to all? [42] And the Lord said, Who then is the faithful and wise steward, whom the lord will set over his household, to give the measure of grain in season? [43] Blessed that slave whom having come his lord will find doing this. [44] Truly I say to you, that he will set him over all his possessions. [45] But if that slave should say in his heart, My lord delays to come, and should begin to beat the men servants and the maid servants, and to eat and to drink and be drunk, [46] the lord of that slave will come in the day in which he expects not, and in an hour which he knows not, and will cut him apart, and will put his portion with the unbelievers. [47] But that slave knowing the will of his Lord, and did not prepare, nor did according to his will, will be beaten with many (stripes). [48] But he not knowing, and doing (things) worthy of stripes, will be beaten with few. And everyone given much, much will be demanded from him; and to whom much was deposited, more exceedingly they will ask him. [49] I came to hurl fire into the earth, and what will I if it already was lit? [50] But I have a baptism to be immersed in, and how am I pressed until it is done! [51] Do you think that I came to give peace in the earth? No, I say to you, but rather division. [52] For from now on there will be five divided in one house, three against two, and two against three. [53] Father will be divided against son, and son against father; mother against daughter, and daughter against mother; mother-in-law against her daughter-in-law, and daughter-in-law against her mother-in-law.

[54] And He also said to the crowd, When you see the cloud rising up from (the) west, you immediately say, A storm

41 Εἶπε δὲ αὐτῷ ὁ Πέτρος, Κύριε, πρὸς ἡμᾶς τὴν παραβολὴν
said And to Him — Peter, Lord, to us — parable

42 ταύτην λέγεις, ἢ καὶ πρὸς πάντας ; εἶπε δὲ ὁ Κύριος, Τίς ἄρα
this do You say, or also to all? said And the Lord, Who then
ἐστὶν ὁ πιστὸς οἰκονόμος καὶ φρόνιμος, ὃν καταστήσει ὁ
is the faithful steward and prudent, whom will appoint the
κύριος ἐπὶ τῆς θεραπείας αὐτοῦ, τοῦ διδόναι ἐν καιρῷ τὸ
lord over the houseservants of him, — to give in season the

43 σιτομέτριον ; μακάριος ὁ δοῦλος ἐκεῖνος, ὃν ἐλθὼν ὁ κύριος
portion of food? Blessed — slave that, whom coming the lord

44 αὐτοῦ εὑρήσει ποιοῦντα οὕτως. ἀληθῶς λέγω ὑμῖν ὅτι ἐπὶ
of him will find doing so. Truly I say to you that over

45 πᾶσι τοῖς ὑπάρχουσιν αὐτοῦ καταστήσει αὐτόν. ἐὰν δὲ εἴπῃ
all the possessions of him he will appoint him. if But savs
ὁ δοῦλος ἐκεῖνος ἐν τῇ καρδίᾳ αὐτοῦ, Χρονίζει ὁ κυριός μου
— slave that in the heart of him, Delays the lord of me
ἔρχεσθαι, καὶ ἄρξηται τύπτειν τοὺς παῖδας καὶ τὰς παιδί-
to come, and begins to beat the menservants and the maid-

46 σκας, ἐσθίειν τε καὶ πίνειν καὶ μεθύσκεσθαι ἥξει ὁ κύριος τοῦ
servants. to eat both and to drink and to become drunk, will come the lord of
δούλου ἐκείνου ἐν ἡμέρᾳ ᾗ οὐ προσδοκᾷ. καὶ ἐν ὥρᾳ ᾗ οὐ
slave that in a day in which not he expects, and in an hour which not
γινώσκει· καὶ διχοτομήσει αὐτόν, καὶ τὸ μέρος αὐτοῦ μετὰ
he knows, and will cut apart him, and the portion of him with

47 τῶν ἀπίστων θήσει. ἐκεῖνος δὲ ὁ δοῦλος ὁ γνοὺς τὸ θέλημα
the unbelievers will place. that But — slave — having known the will
τοῦ κυρίου ἑαυτοῦ, καὶ μὴ ἑτοιμάσας μηδὲ ποιήσας πρὸς τὸ
of the Lord of him, and not did prepare nor did according to the

48 θέλημα αὐτοῦ, δαρήσεται πολλάς· ὁ δὲ μὴ γνούς, ποιήσας
will of Him, will be beaten with many. he But not knowing, doing
δὲ ἄξια πληγῶν, δαρήσεται ὀλίγας. παντὶ δὲ ᾧ ἐδόθη πολύ,
and worthy of stripes will be beaten with few. everyone And given much,
πολὺ ζητηθήσεται παρ' αὐτοῦ· καὶ ᾧ παρέθεντο πολύ,
much will be demanded from him; and to whom was deposited much,
περισσότερον αἰτήσουσιν αὐτόν.
more exceedingly they will ask him.

49 Πῦρ ἦλθον βαλεῖν εἰς τὴν γῆν, καὶ τί θέλω εἰ ἤδη ἀνήφθη ;
Fire I came to cast into the earth, and what will I if already it was lit?

50 βάπτισμα δὲ ἔχω βαπτισθῆναι, καὶ πῶς συνέχομαι ἕως οὗ
a baptism And I have to be baptized, and how I am compressed until

51 τελεσθῇ. δοκεῖτε ὅτι εἰρήνην παρεγενόμην δοῦναι ἐν τῇ γῇ ;
it is finished! Think that peace I came to give in the earth?

52 οὐχί, λέγω ὑμῖν, ἀλλ' ἢ διαμερισμόν. ἔσονται γὰρ ἀπὸ τοῦ
No, I say to you, but rather division. will be For from —
νῦν πέντε ἐν οἴκῳ ἑνὶ διαμεμερισμένοι, τρεῖς ἐπὶ δυσί, καὶ
now five in house one having been divided; three against two, and

53 δύο ἐπὶ τρισί. διαμερισθήσεται πατὴρ ἐφ' υἱῷ, καὶ υἱὸς ἐπὶ
two against three will be divided; father against son, and son against
πατρί· μήτηρ ἐπὶ θυγατρί, καὶ θυγάτηρ ἐπὶ μητρί πενθερὰ
father; mother against daughter, and daughter against mother; mother-in-law
ἐπὶ τὴν νύμφην αὐτῆς, καὶ νύμφη ἐπὶ τὴν πενθερὰν αὐτῆς.
against the daughter-in-law of her, and daughter-in-law against the mother-in-law of her.

54 Ἔλεγε δὲ καὶ τοῖς ὄχλοις, Ὅταν ἴδητε τὴν νεφέλην
He said And also to the crowds, When you see the cloud
ἀνατέλλουσαν ἀπὸ δυσμῶν, εὐθέως λέγετε Ὄμβρος ἔρχεται·
rising up from (the) west, at once you say, A storm is coming

is coming; and it happened
so. [55] And when a south
wind (is) blowing, you say,
There will be heat; and it
happens. [56] Hypocrites,
you know to discern the
face of the earth and of the
sky, but how (is it) you do
not know this time?
[57] And why do you not
judge what (is) right of
yourselves? [58] For as
you go with your adversary
before a judge, give
diligence to be set free
from him, lest he should
drag you away to the
judge, and the judge should
deliver you to the officer,
and the officer should
throw you into prison.
[59] I say to you, In no
way shall you come out
from there until you shall
have paid even the last
lepton.

CHAPTER 13
[1] And some were pres-
ent at the same time telling
Him about the Galileans,
the blood of whom Pilate
mingled with their
sacrifices. [2] And
answering Jesus said to
them, Do you think that
these Galileans were
sinners beyond all the
Galileans, because they
suffered such things.
[3] No, I say to you; but if
you do not repent, you
shall all perish in the same
way. [4] Or those eighteen
on whom the tower in
Siloam fell and killed
them, do you think that
these were sinners beyond
all men who lived in
Jerusalem? [5] No, I say
to you; but if you do not
repent, you shall all perish
in the same way.
[6] And He spoke this
parable: A certain one had
planted a fig-tree in his
vineyard; and he came
looking for fruit on it, and
did not find (any).
[7] And he said to the
vinedresser, Behold, three
years I come looking for
fruit on this fig-tree and do
not find. Cut it down, and
why does it waste the
ground? [8] And the vine-
dresser said to him, Sir,
leave it also this year, until I

55 καὶ γίνεται οὕτω. καὶ ὅταν νότον πνέοντα, λέγετε ὅτι
and it happens   so.    And when a south wind blowing you say that

56 Καύσων ἔσται· καὶ γίνεται. ὑποκριταί, τὸ πρόσωπον τοῦ
heat     will be, and it happens. Hypocrites!  The   face        of the

οὐρανοῦ καὶ τῆς γῆς οἴδατε δοκιμάζειν· τὸν δὲ καιρὸν
heaven   and the earth you know to discern,  —  but   time

57 τοῦτον πῶς οὐ δοκιμάζετε ; τί δὲ καὶ ἀφ' ἑαυτῶν οὐ κρίνετε
this    how not do you discern? why And even from yourselves not do judge

58 τὸ δίκαιον ; ὡς γὰρ ὑπάγεις μετὰ τοῦ ἀντιδίκου σου ἐπ'
the righteous? as For you go with   the   adversary of you to

ἄρχοντα, ἐν τῇ ὁδῷ δὸς ἐργασίαν ἀπηλλάχθαι ἀπ' αὐτοῦ·
a magistrate, in the way give pains  to be freed   from   him,

μήποτε κατασύρῃ σε πρὸς τὸν κριτήν, καὶ ὁ κριτής σε
lest    he drag you to   the  judge,  and the judge you

παραδῷ τῷ πράκτορι, καὶ ὁ πράκτωρ σε βάλλῃ εἰς φυλακήν.
will deliver to the officer,  and the officer you throw into prison.

59 λέγω σοι, οὐ μὴ ἐξέλθῃς ἐκεῖθεν, ἕως οὗ καὶ τὸ ἔσχατον
I say to you, in no way may you leave there until   even the   last

λεπτὸν ἀποδῷς.
lepton you pay.

## CHAPTER 13

1 Παρῆσαν δέ τινες ἐν αὐτῷ τῷ καιρῷ ἀπαγγέλλοντες
were present And some at same the  time    reporting

αὐτῷ περὶ τῶν Γαλιλαίων, ὧν τὸ αἷμα Πιλάτος ἔμιξε μετὰ
to Him about the Galileans, of whom the blood Pilate mixed with

2 τῶν θυσιῶν αὐτῶν. καὶ ἀποκριθεὶς ὁ Ἰησοῦς εἶπεν αὐτοῖς,
the sacrifices of them. And answering  —  Jesus  said to them,

Δοκεῖτε ὅτι οἱ Γαλιλαῖοι οὗτοι ἁμαρτωλοὶ παρὰ πάντας
Do you think that Galileans those sinners  above   all

3 τοὺς Γαλιλαίους ἐγένοντο, ὅτι τοιαῦτα πεπόνθασιν ; οὐχί,
the Galileans  were, because these things they have suffered? No,

λέγω ὑμῖν· ἀλλ' ἐὰν μὴ μετανοῆτε, πάντες ὡσαύτως
I say to you, but except you repent,   all    likewise

4 ἀπολεῖσθε. ἢ ἐκεῖνοι οἱ δέκα καὶ ὀκτώ, ἐφ' οὓς ἔπεσεν ὁ
you will perish. Or those — eighteen   on whom fell  the

πύργος ἐν τῷ Σιλωὰμ καὶ ἀπέκτεινεν αὐτούς, δοκεῖτε ὅτι
tower in  — Siloam, and killed      them, do you think that

οὗτοι ὀφειλέται ἐγένοντο παρὰ πάντας ἀνθρώπους τοὺς
they debtors    were    above   all      men,      those

5 κατοικοῦντας ἐν Ἱερουσαλήμ ; οὐχί, λέγω ὑμῖν· ἀλλ' ἐὰν
dwelling     in Jerusalem?    No, I say to you, but ex-

6 μὴ μετανοῆτε, πάντες ὁμοίως ἀπολεῖσθε. ἔλεγε δὲ ταύτην
cept you repent,  all likewise you will perish. He told And this

τὴν παραβολήν· Συκῆν εἶχέ τις ἐν τῷ ἀμπελῶνι αὐτοῦ
—   parable:  A fig-tree had a certain in the vineyard of him

πεφυτευμένην· καὶ ἦλθε καρπὸν ζητῶν ἐν αὐτῇ, καὶ οὐχ
planted,     and came fruit  seeking in it,  and not

7 εὗρεν. εἶπε δὲ πρὸς τὸν ἀμπελουργόν, Ἰδού, τρία ἔτη
he found. he said And to the  vinedresser,   Behold, three years

ἔρχομαι ζητῶν καρπὸν ἐν τῇ συκῇ ταύτῃ, καὶ οὐχ εὑρίσκω·
I come  seeking fruit  on — fig-tree this,  and not do find;

8 ἔκκοψον αὐτήν· ἱνατί καὶ τὴν γῆν καταργεῖ ; ὁ δὲ ἀποκριθεὶς
cut down  it;   why even the  ground it spoils? the And vinedresser

λέγει αὐτῷ, Κύριε, ἄφες αὐτὴν καὶ τοῦτο τὸ ἔτος, ἕως ὅτου
said to him,  Lord, leave  it   also  this  — year,   until

shall dig around it and cast manure, and if indeed it makes fruit; but if not, in the future you cut it down.

[10] And He was teaching in one of the synagogues on the sabbaths. [11] And behold, there was a woman having infirmity eighteen years, and was bent together, and was not able to be completely erect. [12] And seeing her, Jesus called (her) near and said to her, Woman you have been freed from your infirmity. [13] And He laid hands on her, and instantly she was made erect, and glorified God. [14] But answering, the synagogue ruler, being angry that Jesus healed on the sabbath, said to the crowd, There are six days in which it is right to work; therefore coming in these be healed, and not on the sabbath day. [15] Therefore the Lord answered him and said, Hypocrite, each one of you on the sabbath, does he not loosen his ox or ass from the manger, and having led away give (it) drink? [16] And this one, being a daughter of Abraham, whom Satan has bound, lo, eighteen years, ought (she) not to be loosened from this bond on the sabbath day? [17] And on His saying these things all who were opposed to Him were ashamed; and all the crowd were rejoicing at all the glorious things which were being done by Him.

[18] And He said, What is the kingdom of God like? And to what shall I compare it? [19] It is like a grain of mustard, which a man having taken threw into his garden; and it grew and came into a great tree, and the birds of the sky roosted in its branches. [20] And again He said, To what shall I compare the kingdom of God? [21] It is like leaven, which a woman having taken hid in three seahs of meal, until all was leavened.

[22] And He went through by cities and villages teaching, and

9 σκάψω περὶ αὐτήν, καὶ βάλω κοπρίαν· κἂν μὲν ποιήσῃ
I may dig around   it,   and throw  manure;  and if indeed it makes
καρπόν· εἰ δὲ μήγε, εἰς τὸ μέλλον ἐκκόψεις αὐτήν.
fruit;   if but   not,   in the future you may cut down it.

10 Ἦν δὲ διδάσκων ἐν μιᾷ τῶν συναγωγῶν ἐν τοῖς σάββασι·
He was And teaching in one of the  synagogues  on the  sabbaths.

11 καὶ ἰδού, γυνὴ ἦν πνεῦμα ἔχουσα ἀσθενείας ἔτη δέκα καὶ
And behold, a woman was a spirit having  of infirmity years eighteen
ὀκτώ, καὶ ἦν συγκύπτουσα, καὶ μὴ δυναμένη ἀνακύψαι εἰς
       and was bent together,   and not was able to be erect com-

12 τὸ παντελές. ἰδὼν δὲ αὐτὴν ὁ Ἰησοῦς προσεφώνησε, καὶ
pletely.        seeing And her, — Jesus  called near       and

13 εἶπεν αὐτῇ, Γύναι, ἀπολέλυσαι τῆς ἀσθενείας σοῦ. καὶ
said to her, Woman, you have been freed from the infirmity of you. And
ἐπέθηκεν αὐτῇ τὰς χεῖρας· καὶ παραχρῆμα ἀνωρθώθη,
He laid on  her the hands,  and  immediately she was made erect,

14 καὶ ἐδόξαζε τὸν Θεόν. ἀποκριθεὶς δὲ ὁ ἀρχισυνάγωγος,
and glorified — God. answering But the synagogue ruler,
ἀγανακτῶν ὅτι τῷ σαββάτῳ ἐθεράπευσεν ὁ Ἰησοῦς, ἔλεγε
being angry  that on the sabbath  healed   — Jesus,  said
τῷ ὄχλῳ, "Ἓξ ἡμέραι εἰσὶν ἐν αἷς δεῖ ἐργάζεσθαι· ἐν ταύταις
to the crowd, Six days there are in which it is right to work; on  these
οὖν ἐρχόμενοι θεραπεύεσθε, καὶ μὴ τῇ ἡμέρᾳ τοῦ σαββάτου.
then coming  be healed,   and not on the day of the sabbath.

15 ἀπεκρίθη οὖν αὐτῷ ὁ Κύριος, καὶ εἶπεν, Ὑποκριτά, ἕκαστος
answered Then him the Lord, and said, Hypocrites!  Each one
ὑμῶν τῷ σαββάτῳ οὐ λύει τὸν βοῦν αὐτοῦ ἢ τὸν ὄνον ἀπὸ
of you on the sabbath, not loosen the ox of him or the ass from

16 τῆς φάτνης, καὶ ἀπαγαγὼν ποτίζει ; ταύτην δέ, θυγατέρα
the manger, and leading away give drink? this one And, a daughter
Ἀβραὰμ οὖσαν, ἣν ἔδησεν ὁ Σατανᾶς, ἰδού, δέκα καὶ ὀκτὼ
of Abraham being, whom bound — Satan, behold,  eighteen
ἔτη, οὐκ ἔδει λυθῆναι ἀπὸ τοῦ δεσμοῦ τούτου τῇ ἡμέρᾳ τοῦ
years, not was it right to free from — bond  this on the day of the

17 σαββάτου ; καὶ ταῦτα λέγοντος αὐτοῦ, κατησχύνοντο
sabbath?   And these things saying  Him, were put to shame
πάντες οἱ ἀντικείμενοι αὐτῷ· καὶ πᾶς ὁ ὄχλος ἔχαιρεν ἐπὶ
all   those opposing   Him, and all the crowd rejoiced over
πᾶσι τοῖς ἐνδόξοις τοῖς γινομένοις ὑπ' αὐτοῦ.
all the glorious things — happening by Him.

18 Ἔλεγε δέ, Τίνι ὁμοία ἐστὶν ἡ βασιλεία τοῦ Θεοῦ ; καὶ τίνι
He said And, To what like is the kingdom — of God, and to what

19 ὁμοιώσω αὐτήν ; ὁμοία ἐστὶ κόκκῳ σινάπεως, ὃν λαβὼν
may I compare it?  like It is a grain of mustard, which taking
ἄνθρωπος ἔβαλεν εἰς κῆπον ἑαυτοῦ· καὶ ηὔξησε, καὶ ἐγένετο
a man   threw into a garden of himself; and it grew, and became
εἰς δένδρον μέγα, καὶ τὰ πετεινὰ τοῦ οὐρανου κατεσκήνωσεν
into a tree great, and the birds of the heaven  perched

20 ἐν τοῖς κλάδοις αὐτοῦ. καὶ πάλιν εἶπε, Τίνι ὁμοιώσω τὴν
in the branches of it.   And again He said, To what may I compare the

21 βασιλείαν τοῦ Θεοῦ ; ὁμοία ἐστὶ ζύμῃ, ἣν λαβοῦσα γυνὴ
kingdom  — of God? like It is to leaven, which taking a woman
ἐνέκρυψεν εἰς ἀλεύρου σάτα τρία, ἕως οὗ ἐζυμώθη ὅλον.
hid    in of meal measures three, until were leavened all.

22 Καὶ διεπορεύετο κατὰ πόλεις καὶ κώμας διδάσκων, καὶ
And He traveled throughout cities and villages teaching,  and

making progress toward Jerusalem. [23] And one said to Him, Lord, (are) those being saved few? But He said to them, [24] Labor to enter in through the narrow gate; for I say to you many will seek to enter in and will not be able. [25] From the time the householders shall have arisen, and shall have shut the door, and you begin to stand outside and to knock at the door, saying, Lord, Lord, open to us; and answering He will say to you, I do not know you, where you are from. [26] Then you will begin to say, We ate and drank in Your presence, and You taught in our streets. [27] And He will say, I tell you, I do not know you, from where you are; depart from Me, all the workers of unrighteousness. [28] There shall be weeping and gnashing of the teeth when you see Abraham and Isaac and Jacob and all the prophets in the kingdom of God, but yourselves being cast out. [29] And they shall come from east and west, and from north and south, and shall recline in the kingdom of God. [30] And behold, there are last who shall be first, and there are first who shall be last.

[31] In the same day certain Pharisees came saying to Him, Go out and go on from here, for Herod desires to kill you. [32] And He said to them, Going say to that fox, Behold, today and tomorrow I throw out demons and I complete cures, and the third day I am perfected. [33] But it is right for Me today and tomorrow and the (day) following to go on; for it is not possible (for) a prophet to perish outside of Jerusalem. [34] Jerusalem, Jerusalem, who kill the prophets, and stone those who have been sent to her, how often I would have gathered your children, in the way a hen (gathers) her brood under (her) wings, and you did not desire (it). [35] Behold, your house is

23 πορείαν ποιούμενος εἰς Ἱερουσαλήμ. εἶπε δέ τις αὐτῷ, Κύριε,
    progress  making   toward   Jerusalem.    said And one to Him, Lord,

24 εἰ ὀλίγοι οἱ σωζόμενοι ; ὁ δὲ εἶπε πρὸς αὐτούς, Ἀγωνίζεσθε
   If few those being saved? He And said to     them,   Strive

εἰσελθεῖν διὰ τῆς στενῆς πύλης· ὅτι πολλοί, λέγω ὑμῖν,
to enter through the narrow  gate, in that many,  I say to you,

25 ζητήσουσιν εἰσελθεῖν, καὶ οὐκ ἰσχύσουσιν. ἀφ' οὗ ἂν ἐγερθῇ ὁ
   will seek   to enter in, and not will have strength. From when is risen the

οἰκοδεσπότης καὶ ἀποκλείσῃ τὴν θύραν, καὶ ἄρξησθε ἔξω
house-master,   and  he shuts   the   door,   and you begin outside

ἑστάναι καὶ κρούειν τὴν θύραν, λέγοντες, Κύριε, Κύριε,
to stand and to knock the   door,  saying,  Lord,  Lord,

ἄνοιξον ἡμῖν· καὶ ἀποκριθεὶς ἐρεῖ ὑμῖν, Οὐκ οἶδα ὑμᾶς, πόθεν
open  to us, and  answering He say to you, not I know you, from where

26 ἐστέ· τότε ἄρξεσθε λέγειν, Ἐφάγομεν ἐνώπιόν σου καὶ
   you are. Then you will begin to say,  We ate   before   You and

27 ἐπίομεν, καὶ ἐν ταῖς πλατείαις ἡμῶν ἐδίδαξας. καὶ ἐρεῖ,
   drank,   and in the   streets   of us You taught. And He will
                                         say

Λέγω ὑμῖν, οὐκ οἶδα ὑμᾶς πόθεν ἐστέ· ἀπόστητε ἀπ' ἐμοῦ
I tell  you, not I know  you, from where you are. Stand back from Me,

28 πάντες οἱ ἐργάται τῆς ἀδικίας. ἐκεῖ ἔσται ὁ κλαυθμὸς καὶ ὁ
   all    the workers of unrighteousness. There will be the weeping and the

βρυγμὸς τῶν ὀδόντων, ὅταν ὄψησθε Ἀβραὰμ καὶ Ἰσαὰκ
gnashing of the   teeth,   when you see  Abraham and  Isaac

καὶ Ἰακὼβ καὶ πάντας τοὺς προφήτας ἐν τῇ βασιλείᾳ τοῦ
and Jacob and  all   the    prophets in the   kingdom —

29 Θεοῦ, ὑμᾶς δὲ ἐκβαλλομένους ἔξω. καὶ ἥξουσιν ἀπὸ ἀνατο-
   of God, you and being thrust    outside. And they will come from east

λῶν καὶ δυσμῶν, καὶ ἀπὸ βορρᾶ καὶ νότου, καὶ ἀνακλιθή-
and   west,   and  from north and south,  and will recline

30 σονται ἐν τῇ βασιλείᾳ τοῦ Θεοῦ. καὶ ἰδού. εἰσὶν ἔσχατοι οἳ
       in the   kingdom    of God. And behold, are  last ones who

ἔσονται πρῶτοι, καί εἰσι πρῶτοι οἳ ἔσονται ἔσχατοι.
will be   first,   and are first ones who will be   last.

31 Ἐν αὐτῇ τῇ ἡμέρᾳ προσῆλθόν τινες Φαρισαῖοι, λέγοντες
   In  same   the  day   came to (Him) certain Pharisees,  saying

αὐτῷ, Ἔξελθε καὶ πορεύου ἐντεῦθεν, ὅτι Ἡρώδης θέλει σε
to Him,  Go out and go on   from here, because Herod  desires you

32 ἀποκτεῖναι. καὶ εἶπεν αὐτοῖς, Πορευθέντες εἴπατε τῇ ἀλώπεκι
   to kill.    And He said to them,  Going    say —    fox

ταύτῃ, Ἰδού, ἐκβάλλω δαιμόνια καὶ ἰάσεις ἐπιτελῶ σήμερον
to that, Behold, I cast out  demons  and cures I finish   today,

33 καὶ αὔριον, καὶ τῇ τρίτῃ τελειοῦμαι. πλὴν δεῖ με σήμερον
   and tomorrow, and the third (day) I am perfected. But I must  today

καὶ αὔριον καὶ τῇ ἐχομένῃ πορεύεσθαι· ὅτι οὐκ ἐνδέχεται
and tomorrow and on the following  travel on, because not it is possible

34 προφήτην ἀπολέσθαι ἔξω Ἱερουσαλήμ. Ἱερουσαλήμ, Ἱερου-
   a prophet  to perish  outside  Jerusalem.   Jerusalem!   Jerus-

σαλήμ, ἡ ἀποκτείνουσα τοὺς προφήτας, καὶ λιθοβολοῦσα
alem! The (one)  killing   the   prophets,   and  stoning

τοὺς ἀπεσταλμένους πρὸς αὐτήν, ποσάκις ἠθέλησα ἐπισυνά-
those having been sent  to   her. How often I desired   to gather

ξαι τὰ τέκνα σου, ὃν τρόπον ὄρνις τὴν ἑαυτῆς νοσσιὰν ὑπὸ
   the children of you in the way a hen (gathers) her    brood   under

35 τὰς πτέρυγας, καὶ οὐκ ἠθελήσατε. Ἰδού, ἀφίεται ὑμῖν ὁ οἶκος
   —   wings,   and not you desired (it). Behold, is left to you the house

left to you desolate; and truly I say to you, that you shall not see Me at all until it come when you say, Blessed (is) He coming in (the) name of (the) Lord.

CHAPTER 14

[1] And it occurred on His going into a house of one of the Pharisee leaders on a sabbath to eat bread, and they were closely observing Him. [2] And behold, a certain man was dropsical before Him. [3] And answering Jesus said to the lawyers and Pharisees, saying, Is it lawful to heal on the sabbath? [4] And they were silent. And taking (him), He cured him, and let (him) go. [5] And answering to them He said, Of whom of you an ass or an ox should fall into a pit, and he will not at once pull it up on the sabbath day? [6] And they could not reply to Him against these things.

[7] And He spoke a parable to those who were invited, remarking how they were choosing out the first places, saying to them, [8] When you are invited by anyone to wedding feasts, do not recline in the first place, lest the more honorable than you may have been invited by him, [9] and he who invited you having come, (he) will say to you, Give this one place; and then you begin with shame to take the last place. [10] But when you are invited, having gone recline in the last place, that when he may come who has invited you, he may say to you, Friend, come up higher. Then glory shall be to you before those who recline with you; [11] For everyone that exalts himself shall be humbled, and he that humbles himself shall be exalted.

[12] And He also said to him who had invited Him, When you make a dinner or supper, do not call your friends, nor your brothers, nor your relatives, nor rich neighbors, lest they also should invite you in return.

ὑμῶν ἔρημος· ἀμὴν δὲ λέγω ὑμῖν ὅτι Οὐ μή με ἴδητε ἕως ἂν
of you desolate. truly And I say  to you that in no way Me shall you see until

ἥξῃ, ὅτε εἴπητε, Εὐλογημένος ὁ ἐρχόμενος ἐν ὀνόματι Κυρίου.
it come when you say,  Blessed  the (One) coming in (the) name of (the) Lord.

CHAPTER 14

1  Καὶ ἐγένετο ἐν τῷ ἐλθεῖν αὐτὸν εἰς οἶκόν τινος τῶν
And  it was  in the going (of) Him into a house of one of the

ἀρχόντων τῶν Φαρισαίων σαββάτῳ φαγεῖν ἄρτον, καὶ
leaders  of the  Pharisees on a sabbath to eat  bread, and

2  αὐτοὶ ἦσαν παρατηρούμενοι αὐτόν. καὶ ἰδού, ἄνθρωπός τις
they were carefully watching  Him. And, behold,  man a certain

3  ἦν ὑδρωπικὸς ἔμπροσθεν αὐτοῦ. καὶ ἀποκριθεὶς ὁ Ἰησοῦς
was dropsical  before  Him. And answering  —  Jesus

εἶπε πρὸς τοὺς νομικοὺς καὶ Φαρισαίους, λέγων, Εἰ ἔξεστι
said to  the  lawyers  and  Pharisees,  saying, If it is lawful

4  τῷ σαββάτῳ θεραπεύειν; οἱ δὲ ἡσύχασαν. καὶ ἐπιλαβόμενος
on the sabbath  to heal,  they and were silent. And  taking (him),

5  ἰάσατο αὐτόν, καὶ ἀπέλυσε. καὶ ἀποκριθεὶς πρὸς αὐτοὺς
He cured him,  and dismissed (him). And answering  to  them

εἶπε, Τίνος ὑμῶν ὄνος ἢ βοῦς εἰς φρέαρ ἐμπεσεῖται, καὶ οὐκ
He said, Of whom of you an ass or ox into  a pit should fall,  and not

6  εὐθέως ἀνασπάσει αὐτὸν ἐν τῇ ἡμέρᾳ τοῦ σαββάτου; καὶ
at once he will pull up  it on the day of the  sabbath? And

οὐκ ἴσχυσαν ἀνταποκριθῆναι αὐτῷ πρὸς ταῦτα.
not they were able to reply  to Him against these things.

7  Ἔλεγε δὲ πρὸς τοὺς κεκλημένους παραβολήν, ἐπέχων πῶς
He told And to  those having been invited a parable  noting how

8  τὰς πρωτοκλισίας ἐξελέγοντο, λέγων πρὸς αὐτούς, Ὅταν
the chief seats  they were choosing, saying to  them,  When

κληθῇς ὑπό τινος εἰς γάμους, μὴ κατακλιθῇς εἰς τὴν πρωτοκλι-
you are invited by one to  feasts, do not recline  at the chief seat,

9  σίαν· μήποτε ἐντιμότερός σου ᾖ κεκλημένος ὑπ' αὐτοῦ, καὶ
lest (one) more honorable (than) you be invited by  him, and

ἐλθὼν ὁ σὲ καὶ αὐτὸν καλέσας ἐρεῖ σοι, Δὸς τούτῳ τόπον· καὶ
coming he to you and him inviting will say to you, Give this one place. And

10  τότε ἄρξῃ μετ' αἰσχύνης τὸν ἔσχατον τόπον κατέχειν. ἀλλ'
then you begin with shame  the  last  place  to take. But

ὅταν κληθῇς, πορευθεὶς ἀνάπεσον εἰς τὸν ἔσχατον τόπον·
when you are invited, going  recline  in  the  last  place,

ἵνα, ὅταν ἔλθῃ ὁ κεκληκώς σε, εἴπῃ σοι, Φίλε, προσανάβηθι
that when comes he inviting  you, he say to you, Friend, go up

ἀνώτερον· τότε ἔσται σοι δόξα ἐνώπιον τῶν συνανακειμένων
higher.  Then will be to you glory before  those  reclining with

11  σοι. ὅτι πᾶς ὁ ὑψῶν ἑαυτὸν ταπεινωθήσεται, καὶ ὁ ταπεινῶν
you. For everyone exalting himself will be humbled; and he humbling

ἑαυτὸν ὑψωθήσεται.
himself will be exalted.

12  Ἔλεγε δὲ καὶ τῷ κεκληκότι αὐτόν, Ὅταν ποιῇς ἄριστον ἢ
He said And also to those inviting Him,  When you make a dinner or

δεῖπνον, μὴ φώνει τοὺς φίλους σου, μηδὲ τοὺς ἀδελφούς σου,
a supper, do not call the  friends of you, nor the  brothers of you,

μηδὲ τοὺς συγγενεῖς σου, μηδὲ γείτονας πλουσίους· μήποτε
nor  the relatives of you, nor  neighbors  rich,  lest

καὶ αὐτοί σε ἀντικαλέσωσι, καὶ γένηταί σοι ἀνταπόδομα.
also they you invite in return,  and it becomes to you a repayment.

and you be repaid. [13] But when you make a feast, call the poor, the crippled, the lame, the blind; [14] and then you shall be blessed; for they have nothing to repay you; it shall be repaid to you in the resurrection of the just.

[15] And one of those reclining with (Him) having heard these things said to Him, Blessed (is he) who shall eat bread in the kingdom of God. [16] But He said to him, A certain man made a great supper and invited many. [17] And he sent his slave at the supper hour to say to those who had been invited, Come, for now all is ready. [18] And all with one (mind) began to excuse themselves. The first said to him, I have bought a field, and I must go out and see it; I beg you hold me excused. [19] And another said, I have bought five pairs of oxen, and I go to try them; I beg you hold me excused. [20] And another said, I have married a wife, and because of this I am unable to come. [21] And having come that slave reported these things to his lord. Then being angry the householder said to his slave, Go out quickly into the streets and lanes of the city, and bring in here the poor and crippled and lame and blind. [22] And the slave said, Sir, it has been done as you commanded, and still there is room. [23] And the lord said to the slave, Go out into the highways and hedges and compel to come in, that my house may be filled. [24] For I say to you that not one of those men who have been invited shall taste of my supper.

[25] And great crowds were going with Him; and having turned He said to them, [26] If anyone comes to Me and does not hate his father and mother and wife and children and

---

**13** ἀλλ' ὅταν ποιῇς δοχήν, κάλει πτωχούς, ἀναπήρους, χωλούς,
But when a party you make, invite poor ones, maimed ones, lame ones,

**14** τυφλούς· καὶ μακάριος ἔσῃ, ὅτι οὐκ ἔχουσιν ἀνταποδοῦναί
blind ones, and blessed you will be, for not they have (with which) to repay

σοι· ἀνταποδοθήσεται γάρ σοι ἐν τῇ ἀναστάσει τῶν
you. it will be repaid For to you in the resurrection of the

δικαίων.
just.

**15** Ἀκούσας δέ τις τῶν συνανακειμένων ταῦτα εἶπεν αὐτῷ,
hearing And one of those reclining with these things said to Him,

**16** Μακάριος, ὃς φάγεται ἄρτον ἐν τῇ βασιλείᾳ τοῦ Θεοῦ. ὁ δὲ
Blessed those eating bread in the kingdom — of God. He But

εἶπεν αὐτῷ, Ἄνθρωπός τις ἐποίησε δεῖπνον μέγα, καὶ
said to him, man A certain made a supper great, and

**17** ἐκάλεσε πολλούς· καὶ ἀπέστειλε τὸν δοῦλον αὐτοῦ τῇ ὥρᾳ
invited many, and sent the slave of him at the hour

τοῦ δείπνου εἰπεῖν τοῖς κεκλημένοις, Ἔρχεσθε, ὅτι ἤδη
of the supper to say to those having been invited, Come, because now

**18** ἕτοιμά ἐστι πάντα. καὶ ἤρξαντο ἀπὸ μιᾶς παραιτεῖσθαι
ready it is all. And they began with one (mind) to beg off

πάντες. ὁ πρῶτος εἶπεν αὐτῷ, Ἀγρὸν ἠγόρασα, καὶ ἔχω
all. The first said to him, A field I have bought, and I have

ἀνάγκην ἐξελθεῖν καὶ ἰδεῖν αὐτόν· ἐρωτῶ σε, ἔχε με παρῃτη-
need to go out and to see it; I ask you, have me excused.

**19** μένον. καὶ ἕτερος εἶπε, Ζεύγη βοῶν ἠγόρασα πέντε, καὶ
And another said, yoke of oxen I bought five, and

πορεύομαι δοκιμάσαι αὐτά· ἐρωτῶ σε, ἔχε με παρῃτημένον.
I am going to try out them; I ask you, have me excused.

**20** καὶ ἕτερος εἶπε, Γυναῖκα ἔγημα, καὶ διὰ τοῦτο οὐ δύναμαι
And another said, a wife I married, and therefore not I am able

**21** ἐλθεῖν. καὶ παραγενόμενος ὁ δοῦλος ἐκεῖνος ἀπήγγειλε τῷ
to come. And coming up slave that reported to the

κυρίῳ αὐτοῦ ταῦτα. τότε ὀργισθεὶς ὁ οἰκοδεσπότης εἶπε τῷ
lord of him these things. Then being angry the house-master said to the

δούλῳ αὐτοῦ, Ἔξελθε ταχέως εἰς τὰς πλατείας καὶ ῥύμας τῆς
slave of him, Go out quickly into the streets and lanes of the

πόλεως, καὶ τοὺς πτωχοὺς καὶ ἀναπήρους καὶ χωλοὺς καὶ
city, and the poor and maimed and lame and

**22** τυφλοὺς εἰσάγαγε ὧδε. καὶ εἶπεν ὁ δοῦλος, Κύριε, γέγονεν ὡς
blind bring in here. And said the slave, Lord, has occurred as

**23** ἐπέταξας, καὶ ἔτι τόπος ἐστί. καὶ εἶπεν ὁ κύριος πρὸς τὸν
you ordered, and yet room there is. And said the lord to the

δοῦλον, Ἔξελθε εἰς τὰς ὁδοὺς καὶ φραγμούς, καὶ ἀνάγκασον
slave, Go out into the ways and hedges, and compel (them)

**24** εἰσελθεῖν, ἵνα γεμισθῇ ὁ οἶκός μου. λέγω γὰρ ὑμῖν ὅτι οὐδεὶς
to come in, that may be filled the house of me. I say For to you that not one

τῶν ἀνδρῶν ἐκείνων τῶν κεκλημένων γεύσεταί μου τοῦ
— men of those — having been invited shall taste of me the

δείπνου.
supper.

**25** Συνεπορεύοντο δὲ αὐτῷ ὄχλοι πολλοί· καὶ στραφεὶς εἶπε
came together And to Him crowds many; and turning He said

**26** πρὸς αὐτούς, Εἴ τις ἔρχεται πρός με, καὶ οὐ μισεῖ τὸν πατέρα
to them, If anyone comes to Me, and not hates the father

ἑαυτοῦ, καὶ τὴν μητέρα, καὶ τὴν γυναῖκα, καὶ τὰ τέκνα, καὶ
of him and the mother, and the wife, and the children, and

τοὺς ἀδελφούς, καὶ τὰς ἀδελφάς, ἔτι δὲ καὶ τὴν ἑαυτοῦ ψυχήν,
the  brothers,  and the  sisters, besides and even the of himself life,

brothers and sisters, and
his own life too, he cannot
be My disciple. [27] And
27 οὐ δύναταί μου μαθητὴς εἶναι. καὶ ὅστις οὐ βαστάζει τὸν
not he is able of Me a disciple to be.   And who  not does bear  the

whoever does not bear his
cross and come after Me
cannot be My disciple.
σταυρὸν αὐτοῦ καὶ ἔρχεται ὀπίσω μου, οὐ δύναταί μου
cross   of him and comes  after  Me, not he is able of Me

[28] For which of you
desiring to build a tower
28 εἶναι μαθητής. τίς γὰρ ἐξ ὑμῶν, θέλων πύργον οἰκοδομῆσαι,
to be a disciple. who For of  you desiring a tower  to build,

does not first sit down and
count the cost, whether he
οὐχὶ πρῶτον καθίσας ψηφίζει τὴν δαπάνην, εἰ ἔχει τὰ πρὸς
does not first  sitting  count  the cost,  if he has that to

has (enough) to finish?
[29] Lest having laid its
29 ἀπαρτισμόν; ἵνα μήποτε, θέντος αὐτοῦ θεμέλιον καὶ μὴ
bring to completion; lest  laying  him a foundation, and not

foundation and not being
able to finish, all who
watch should begin to
ἰσχύοντος ἐκτελέσαι, πάντες οἱ θεωροῦντες ἄρξωνται ἐμπαί-
having strength to finish  all,  those seeing  begin  to mock

mock at him, [30] saying,
This man began to build
30 ζειν αὐτῷ, λέγον ἐς ὅτι Οὗτος ὁ ἄνθρωπος ἤρξατο οἰκοδο-
him, saying, — This  man  began to build,

and was not able to finish.
[31] Or what king going
31 μεῖν, καὶ οὐκ ἴσχυσεν ἐκτελέσαι. ἢ τίς βασιλεὺς πορευόμενος
and not had strengh to finish. Or what  king  going

out to engage another king
in war having sat down
συμβαλεῖν ἑτέρῳ βασιλεῖ εἰς πόλεμον οὐχὶ καθίσας πρῶτον
to attack another  king  in  war does not sitting  first

does not first take counsel
whether he is able with ten
βουλεύεται εἰ δυνατός ἐστιν ἐν δέκα χιλιάσιν ἀπαντῆσαι
take counsel whether able  he is with ten  thousands  to meet

thousand to meet him who
comes against him with
twenty thousand?
32 τῷ μετὰ εἴκοσι χιλιάδων ἐρχομένῳ ἐπ' αὐτόν; εἰ δὲ μήγε,
those with twenty thousands coming  upon  him? Otherwise,

[32] But if not, he being
still far off, having sent an
embassy he asks the
ἔτι αὐτοῦ πόρρω ὄντος, πρεσβείαν ἀποστείλας ἐρωτᾷ τὰ
yet him  afar  being, a delegation  sending  he asks the

(terms) for peace. [33] So
in the same way everyone
33 πρὸς εἰρήνην. οὕτως οὖν πᾶς ἐξ ὑμῶν ὃς οὐκ ἀποτάσσεται
for  peace.  So, then everyone of you  who not does abandon

of you who does not
abandon all that he himself
πᾶσι τοῖς ἑαυτοῦ ὑπάρχουσιν, οὐ δύναταί μου εἶναι
to all  the of himself possessions  not  is able of Me to be

possesses cannot be My
disciple. [34] The salt (is)
34 μαθητής. καλὸν τὸ ἅλας· ἐὰν δὲ τὸ ἅλας μωρανθῇ, ἐν τίνι
a disciple. Good (is) the salt;  if but  the salt becomes useless, with what

good, but if the salt
becomes tasteless, with
what shall it be seasoned?
35 ἀρτυθήσετε; οὔτε εἰς γῆν οὔτε εἰς κοπρίαν εὔθετόν ἐστιν·
will it be seasoned? Not for soil  nor  for  manure  fit  it is.

[35] It is neither fit for
land nor for fertilizer; they
throw it out. He that has
ἔξω βάλλουσιν αὐτό. ὁ ἔχων ὦτα ἀκούειν ἀκουέτω.
out  They throw  it. The (one) having ears to hear, let him hear.

ears to hear, let him hear.

## CHAPTER 15

[1] And all the
tax-collectors and sinners
1 Ἦσαν δὲ ἐγγίζοντες αὐτῷ πάντες οἱ τελῶναι καὶ οἱ
were  And drawing near to Him all  the tax-collectors and the

were coming near to Him
to hear Him; [2] and the
2 ἁμαρτωλοί, ἀκούειν αὐτοῦ. καὶ διεγόγγυζον οἱ Φαρισαῖοι
sinners,  to hear  Him. And murmured  the Pharisees

Pharisees and the scribes
murmured, saying, This
one receives sinners and
καὶ οἱ γραμματεῖς λέγοντες ὅτι Οὗτος ἁμαρτωλοὺς προσδέ-
and the scribes,  saying  — This one  sinners  receives,

eats with them. [3] And
He spoke to them this
χεται, καὶ συνεσθίει αὐτοῖς.
and eats with  them.

parable, saying, [4] What
man of you having a
3 Εἶπε δὲ πρὸς αὐτοὺς τὴν παραβολὴν ταύτην, λέγων, Τίς
He spoke and to  them  —  parable  this,  saying, What

hundred sheep, and having
lost one of them, does not
4 ἄνθρωπος ἐξ ὑμῶν ἔχων ἑκατὸν πρόβατα, καὶ ἀπολέσας ἐν
man  of  you having a hundred  sheep,  and losing  one

leave the ninety-nine in the
wilderness and goes after
ἐξ αὐτῶν, οὐ καταλείπει τὰ ἐννενηκονταεννέα ἐν τῇ ἐρήμῳ,
of them, not does leave  the  ninety-nine  in the desert

that which has been lost,
until it finds it? [5] And
5 καὶ πορεύεται ἐπὶ τὸ ἀπολωλός, ἕως εὕρῃ αὐτό; καὶ εὑρὼν
and goes  after the lost (one) until he finds it?  And finding

having found (it), he lays
(it) on his shoulders
rejoicing, [6] and having
6 ἐπιτίθησιν ἐπὶ τοὺς ὤμους ἑαυτοῦ χαίρων. καὶ ἐλθὼν εἰς τὸν
puts (it)  on  the shoulders of himself, rejoicing. And coming to the

come to the house he calls

together friends and neighbors, saying to them, Rejoice with me, for I have found my sheep that was lost. [7] I say to you that in the same way joy shall be in Heaven over one sinner repenting, (more) than over ninety-nine righteous ones who have no need of repentance. [8] Or what woman having ten drachmas, if she should lose one drachma does not light a lamp and sweep the house and look carefully until she finds (it)? [9] And having found (it), she calls together friends and neighbors, saying, Rejoice with me, for I have found the drachma which I lost. [10] I say to you in the same way there is joy in the presence of the angels of God. over one sinner repenting.

[11] And He said, A certain man had two sons; [12] and the younger of them said to (his) father, Father, give me that portion of the property falling (to me). And he divided the living to them. [13] And not many days after, having gathered together all, the younger son went away into a distant country, and there wasted his property, living dissolutely. [14] But he having spent all, a severe famine arose throughout that country, and he began to be in need. [15] And having gone he joined himself to one of the citizens of that country, and he sent him into his fields to feed pigs. [16] And he was longing to fill his belly from the husks which the pigs were eating; but no one gave to him. [17] But having come to himself, he said, How many hired servants of my father have plenty of bread, and I am perishing with famine. [18] Having risen up I will go to my father, and I will say to him, Father, I have sinned against Heaven and before you; [19] and no longer am I worthy to be called your son. Make me as one of your hired servants.

οἶκον, συγκαλεῖ τοὺς φίλους καὶ τοὺς γείτονας, λέγων αὐτοῖς,
house, he calls together the friends and the neighbors, saying to them,

Συγχάρητέ μοι, ὅτι εὗρον τὸ πρόβατόν μου τὸ ἀπολωλός.
Rejoice with me, for I have found the sheep of me — having been lost.

7 λέγω ὑμῖν ὅτι οὕτω χαρὰ ἔσται ἐν τῷ οὐρανῷ ἐπὶ ἑνὶ ἁμαρ-
I say to you that thus joy is in — Heaven over one sinner

τωλῷ μετανοοῦντι, ἢ ἐπὶ ἐννενηκονταεννέα δικαίοις, οἵτινες
repenting, than over ninety-nine just ones who

οὐ χρείαν ἔχουσι μετανοίας.
no need have of repentance.

8 Ἢ τίς γυνὴ δραχμὰς ἔχουσα δέκα, ἐὰν ἀπολέσῃ δραχμὴν
Or what woman drachmas having ten, if she loses drachma

μίαν, οὐχὶ ἅπτει λύχνον, καὶ σαροῖ τὴν οἰκίαν, καὶ ζητεῖ
one, does not light a lamp and sweep the house, and seek

9 ἐπιμελῶς ἕως ὅτου εὕρῃ; καὶ εὑροῦσα συγκαλεῖται τὰς
carefully until she finds? And finding she calls together the

φίλας καὶ τὰς γείτονας, λέγουσα, Συγχάρητέ μοι, ὅτι εὗρον
friends and the neighbors, saying, Rejoice with me, for I have found

10 τὴν δραχμὴν ἣν ἀπώλεσα. οὕτω, λέγω ὑμῖν, χαρὰ γίνεται
the drachma which I lost. So, I say to you, joy there is

ἐνώπιον τῶν ἀγγέλων τοῦ Θεοῦ ἐπὶ ἑνὶ ἁμαρτωλῷ
before the angels — of God over one sinner

11 μετανοοῦντι.
repenting.

12 Εἶπε δέ, Ἄνθρωπός τις εἶχε δύο υἱούς· καὶ εἶπεν ὁ νεώτερος
He said And, man a certain had two sons. And said the younger

αὐτῶν τῷ πατρί, Πάτερ, δός μοι τὸ ἐπιβάλλον μέρος τῆς
of them to the father, Father, give me the falling (to me) share of the

13 οὐσίας. καὶ διεῖλεν αὐτοῖς τὸν βίον. καὶ μετ' οὐ πολλὰς
property. And he divided to them the living. And after not many

ἡμέρας συναγαγὼν ἅπαντα ὁ νεώτερος υἱὸς ἀπεδήμησεν εἰς
days, having gathered all things, the younger son went away to

χώραν μακράν, καὶ ἐκεῖ διεσκόρπισε τὴν οὐσίαν αὐτοῦ, ζῶν
a country distant, and there scattered the property of him, living

14 ἀσώτως. δαπανήσαντος δὲ αὐτοῦ πάντα, ἐγένετο λιμὸς
dissolutely. having spent But him all things, came famine

ἰσχυρὸς κατὰ τὴν χώραν ἐκείνην, καὶ αὐτὸς ἤρξατο ὑστερεῖ-
a severe throughout country that; and he began to be in

15 σθαι. καὶ πορευθεὶς ἐκολλήθη ἑνὶ τῶν πολιτῶν τῆς χώρας
need. And going he was joined to one of the citizens country

ἐκείνης· καὶ ἔπεμψεν αὐτὸν εἰς τοὺς ἀγροὺς αὐτοῦ βόσκειν
of that, and he sent him into the fields of him to feed

16 χοίρους. καὶ ἐπεθύμει γεμίσαι τὴν κοιλίαν αὐτοῦ ἀπὸ τῶν
pigs. And he longed to fill the stomach of him from the

κερατίων ὧν ἤσθιον οἱ χοῖροι· καὶ οὐδεὶς ἐδίδου αὐτῷ. εἰς
husks which ate the pigs; and no one gave to him. to

17 ἑαυτὸν δὲ ἐλθὼν εἶπε, Πόσοι μίσθιοι τοῦ πατρός μου περισ-
himself But coming, he said, How many servants of the father of me

18 σεύουσιν ἄρτων, ἐγὼ δὲ λιμῷ ἀπόλλυμαι· ἀναστὰς πορεύ-
abound in loaves, I but with famine am perishing. Rising up I will

σομαι πρὸς τὸν πατέρα μου, καὶ ἐρῶ αὐτῷ, Πάτερ, ἥμαρτον
go to the father of Me, and I will say to him, Father, I sinned

19 εἰς τὸν οὐρανὸν καὶ ἐνώπιόν σου· καὶ οὐκέτι εἰμὶ ἄξιος κληθῆ-
against Heaven, and before you; and no longer am I worthy to be

ναι υἱός σου· ποίησόν με ὡς ἕνα τῶν μισθίων σου. καὶ
called son of you. Make me as one of the servants of you. And

[20] And having risen up he went to his father. But he yet being a long distance away, his father saw him and was moved with pity, and running fell on his neck and kissed him. [21] And the son said to him, Father, I have sinned against Heaven and before you, and no longer am I worthy to be called your son. [22] But the father said to his slaves, Bring out the best robe and clothe him, and give a ring for his hand, and sandals for the feet; [23] and having brought the fattened calf, kill (it), and eating let us be merry; [24] for this my son was dead, and is alive again; and was lost, and is found. And they began to be merry. [25] And his elder. son was in a field; and as he (was) coming, he drew near to the house (and) he heard music and dancing. [26] And having called one of his servants, he inquired what these things might be. [27] And he said to him, Your brother is come, and your father killed the fattened calf, because he received him safe and well. [28] But he was angry and was not willing to go in. Therefore his father having gone out begged him. [29] But answering he said to (his) father, Lo, I serve you so many years and I never transgressed your commandment, and you never gave a kid to me that I might make merry with my friends; [30] but when this your son who devoured your living with harlots came, you killed the fattened calf for him. [31] But he said to him, Child, you are always with me, and all that (is) mine is yours. [32] But it was right to make merry and rejoice, because this your brother was dead, and is alive again; and was lost, and is found.

CHAPTER 16

[1] And He also said to His disciples, A certain man was rich, who had a

---

**20** ἀναστὰς ἦλθε πρὸς τὸν πατέρα ἑαυτοῦ. ἔτι δὲ αὐτοῦ μακρὰν
rising up he came to the father of himself. yet But him afar

ἀπέχοντος, εἶδεν αὐτὸν ὁ πατὴρ αὐτοῦ, καὶ ἐσπλαγχνίσθη,
being away, saw him the father of him, and was moved with pity;

καὶ δραμὼν ἐπέπεσεν ἐπὶ τὸν τράχηλον αὐτοῦ, καὶ κατε-
and running fell upon the neck of him, and fervently

**21** φίλησεν αὐτόν. εἶπε δὲ αὐτῷ ὁ υἱός, Πάτερ, ἥμαρτον εἰς τὸν
kissed him. said And to him the son, Father, I sinned against —

οὐρανὸν καὶ ἐνώπιόν σου, καὶ οὐκέτι εἰμὶ ἄξιος κληθῆναι
Heaven and before you; and no longer am I worthy to be called

**22** υἱός σου. εἶπε δὲ ὁ πατὴρ πρὸς τοὺς δούλους αὐτοῦ, Ἐξε-
son of you. said But the father to the slaves of him, Bring

νέγκατε τὴν στολὴν τὴν πρώτην καὶ ἐνδύσατε αὐτόν, καὶ
out robe the first, and clothe him, and

δότε δακτύλιον εἰς τὴν χεῖρα αὐτοῦ, καὶ ὑποδήματα εἰς τοὺς
give a ring to the hand of him, and sandals to the

**23** πόδας· καὶ ἐνέγκαντες τὸν μόσχον τὸν σιτευτὸν θύσατε, καὶ
feet; and bring the calf — fattened, kill, and

**24** φαγόντες εὐφρανθῶμεν· ὅτι οὗτος ὁ υἱός μου νεκρὸς ἦν, καὶ
eating let us be merry; because this — son of me dead was, and

ἀνέζησε· καὶ ἀπολωλὼς ἦν, καὶ εὑρέθη. καὶ ἤρξαντο
lived again; and lost was, and was found. And they began

**25** εὐφραίνεσθαι. ἦν δὲ ὁ υἱὸς αὐτοῦ ὁ πρεσβύτερος ἐν ἀγρῷ·
to be merry. was But the son of him — older in a field;

καὶ ὡς ἐρχόμενος ἤγγισε τῇ οἰκίᾳ, ἤκουσε συμφωνίας καὶ
and as coming he drew near to the house, he heard music and

**26** χορῶν. καὶ προσκαλεσάμενος ἕνα τῶν παίδων, ἐπυνθάνετο
dances. And calling to (him) one of the children, he inquired

**27** τί εἴη ταῦτα. ὁ δὲ εἶπεν αὐτῷ ὅτι Ὁ ἀδελφός σου ἥκει· καὶ
what may be this. he And said to him, — The brother of you came, and

ἔθυσεν ὁ πατήρ σου τὸν μόσχον τὸν σιτευτόν, ὅτι
killed the father of you the calf — fattened, because

**28** ὑγιαίνοντα αὐτὸν ἀπέλαβεν. ὠργίσθη δέ, καὶ οὐκ ἤθελεν
being in health him he received back. he was angry But, and not desired

**29** εἰσελθεῖν· ὁ οὖν πατὴρ αὐτοῦ ἐξελθὼν παρεκάλει αὐτόν. ὁ δὲ
to go in. the Then father of him coming out begged him. he But

ἀποκριθεὶς εἶπε τῷ πατρί, Ἰδού, τοσαῦτα ἔτη δουλεύω σοι,
answering said to the father, Behold, so many years I serve you,

καὶ οὐδέποτε ἐντολήν σου παρῆλθον, καὶ ἐμοὶ οὐδέποτε
and never a command of you I transgressed; and to me never

**30** ἔδωκας ἔριφον, ἵνα μετὰ τῶν φίλων μου εὐφρανθῶ. ὅτε δὲ ὁ
you gave a goat that with the friends of me I might be merry. when But

υἱός σου οὗτος ὁ καταφαγών σου τὸν βίον μετὰ πορνῶν
son of you this, having devoured of you the living with harlots,

ἦλθεν, ἔθυσας αὐτῷ τὸν μόσχον τὸν σιτευτόν. ὁ δὲ εἶπεν
came, you killed for him the calf — fattened. he And said

**31** αὐτῷ, Τέκνον, σὺ πάντοτε μετ᾽ ἐμοῦ εἶ, καὶ πάντα τὰ ἐμὰ σά
to him, Child, you always with me are, and all things (of) mine yours

**32** ἐστιν. εὐφρανθῆναι δὲ καὶ χαρῆναι ἔδει· ὅτι ὁ ἀδελφός σου
are. to be merry And, and to rejoice must be, for the brother of you

οὗτος νεκρὸς ἦν, καὶ ἀνέζησε· καὶ ἀπολωλὼς ἦν, καὶ εὑρέθη.
this dead was, and lived again, and having been lost also was found.

CHAPTER 16

**1** Ἔλεγε δὲ καὶ πρὸς τοὺς μαθητὰς αὐτοῦ, Ἄνθρωπός τις ἦν
He said And also to the disciples of Him, man A certain was

steward, and he was accused to him as wasting his goods. [2] And having called him, he said to him, What (is) this I hear about you? Give the account of your stewardship; for you can no longer be steward. [3] And the steward said within himself, What shall I do, for my lord is taking away the stewardship from me? I am unable to dig, I am ashamed to beg. [4] I know what I will do, that when I shall have been removed (from) the stewardship, they may receive me into their houses. [5] And calling to (him) each one of the debtors of his lord, he said to the first, How much do you owe to my lord? [6] And he said, A hundred baths of oil. And he said to him, Take your statements, and sitting down quickly write fifty. [7] Then to another he said, And you, how much do you owe? And he said, a hundred cors of wheat. And he said to him, Take your statement and write eighty. [8] And the lord praised the unrighteous steward, because he acted prudently. For the sons of this age are more prudent than the sons of light in their generation. [9] And I say to you, Make to yourselves friends by the mammon of unrighteousness, that when you fail they may receive you into the everlasting dwellings. [10] He that (is) faithful in (the) least is also faithful in much; and he that in (the) least (is) unrighteous also is unrighteous in much. [11] If therefore you have not been faithful in the unrighteous mammon, who will entrust the true to you? [12] And if you have not been faithful in that which (is) another's, who will give your own to you? [13] No servant is able to serve two lords, for either he will hate the one, and he will love the other; or he will hold to one, and the other he will despise. You are unable to serve God and mammon.

πλούσιος, ὃς εἶχεν οἰκονόμον· καὶ οὗτος διεβλήθη αὐτῷ ὡς
rich,       who had    a steward,   and this one was accused to him as

2 διασκορπίζων τὰ ὑπαρχοντα αὐτοῦ. καὶ φωνήσας αὐτὸν
wasting          the possessions of him.   And calling      him,

εἶπεν αὐτῷ, Τί τοῦτο ἀκούω περὶ σοῦ ; ἀπόδος τὸν λόγον
he said to him, What (is) this I hear  about you?  Render the account

3 τῆς οἰκονομίας σου· οὐ γὰρ δυνήσῃ ἔτι οἰκονομεῖν. εἶπε δὲ
of the stewardship of you; not for you can longer  be steward.   said And

ἐν ἑαυτῷ ὁ οἰκονόμος, Τί ποιήσω, ὅτι ὁ κύριός μου ἀφαι-
within himself the steward, What may I do, because the lord of me takes

ρεῖται τὴν οἰκονομίαν ἀπ' ἐμοῦ ; σκάπτειν οὐκ ἰσχύω, ἐπαι-
away  the stewardship  from me?  to dig      not I am able; to

4 τεῖν αἰσχύνομαι. ἔγνων τί ποιήσω, ἵνα, ὅταν μετασταθῶ
beg  I am ashamed.  I know what I may do, that  when  I am removed

5 τῆς οἰκονομίας, δέξωνταί με εἰς τοὺς οἴκους αὐτων. καὶ
(from) the stewardship, they receive me into the  houses  of them.  And

προσκαλεσάμενος ἕνα ἕκαστον τῶν χρεωφειλετῶν τοῦ κυρίου
calling to (him)       one   each  of the  debtors      of the lord

ἑαυτοῦ, ἔλεγε τῷ πρώτῳ, Πόσον ὀφείλεις τῷ κυρίῳ μου ;
of himself, he said to the  first,  How much do you owe to the lord of me?

6 ὁ δὲ εἶπεν, Ἑκατὸν βάτους ἐλαίου. καὶ εἶπεν αὐτῷ, Δέξαι σου
he And said, A hundred baths of oil.   And he said to him, Take of you

τὸ γράμμα, καὶ καθίσας ταχέως γράψον πεντήκοντα. ἔπειτα
the statements, and sitting  quickly  write     fifty.        Then

7 ἑτέρῳ εἶπε, Σὺ δὲ πόσον ὀφείλεις ; ὁ δὲ εἶπεν, Ἑκατὸν κόρους
to another he said, you And how much owe you? he And said, A hundred cors

σίτου. καὶ λέγει αὐτῷ, Δέξαι σου τὸ γράμμα, καὶ γράψον
of wheat. And he said to him, Take of you the statement,  and  write

8 ὀγδοήκοντα. καὶ ἐπήνεσεν ὁ κύριος τὸν οἰκονόμον τῆς ἀδικίας
eighty.         And praised the lord the steward    of unrigh-
                                                       teousness

ὅτι φρονίμως ἐποίησεν· ὅτι οἱ υἱοὶ τοῦ αἰῶνος τούτου
because prudently he acted.  For the sons —    age   of this

φρονιμώτεροι ὑπὲρ τοὺς υἱοὺς τοῦ φωτὸς εἰς τὴν γενεὰν
more prudent    than  the  sons of the light  in the generation

9 ἑαυτῶν εἰσί. κἀγὼ ὑμῖν λέγω, Ποιήσατε ἑαυτοῖς φίλους ἐκ
of themselves are. And I to you say,    Make to  yourselves friends by

τοῦ μαμωνᾶ τῆς ἀδικίας, ἵνα, ὅταν ἐκλίπητε, δέξωνται
the  mammon of unrighteousness, that, when it fails,   they may receive

10 ὑμᾶς εἰς τὰς αἰωνίους σκηνας. ὁ πιστὸς ἐν ἐλαχίστῳ καὶ ἐν
you   into the eternal   dwellings. He faithful in   least   also in

πολλῷ πιστός ἐστι, καὶ ὁ ἐν ἐλαχίστῳ ἄδικος καὶ ἐν πολλῷ
much  faithful  is;  and he in   least (is) unrighteous also in  much

11 ἄδικός ἐστιν. εἰ οὖν ἐν τῷ ἀδίκῳ μαμωνᾷ πιστοὶ οὐκ ἐγένεσθε,
unrighteous is.  If, then, in the unrighteous mammon faithful not you were,

12 τὸ ἀληθινὸν τίς ὑμῖν πιστεύσει ; καὶ εἰ ἐν τῷ ἀλλοτρίῳ
the  true   who to you will entrust?  And if in  that of another

13 πιστοὶ οὐκ ἐγένεσθε, τὸ ὑμέτερον τίς ὑμῖν δώσει ; οὐδεὶς
faithful not you were, that being yours (is) who to you will give? No

οἰκέτης δύναται δυσὶ κυρίοις δουλεύειν· ἢ γὰρ τὸν ἕνα
houseslave is able   two  lords   to serve; either for the  one

μισήσει, καὶ τὸν ἕτερον ἀγαπήσει· ἢ ἑνὸς ἀνθέξεται, καὶ τοῦ
he will hate, and the other he will love,  or one he will cling to, and the

ἑτέρου καταφρονήσει. οὐ δύνασθε Θεῷ δουλεύειν καὶ μαμωνᾶ.
other  he will despise.  not You are able God to serve   and mammon.

Ἤκουον δὲ ταῦτα πάντα καὶ οἱ Φαρισαῖοι φιλάργυροι
heard  And these things all   also the Pharisees,   moneylovers

[14] And being covetous, the Pharisees also heard all these things, and they derided Him. [15] And He said to them, You are those justifying yourselves before men, but God knows your hearts; for that highly esteemed among men is an abomination before God. [16] The Law and the Prophets (were) until John; from then the kingdom of God is being preached, and everyone is pressing into it. [17] But it is easier (for) the sky and the earth to pass away, than one tittle of the law to fall. [18] Everyone putting away his wife, and marrying another commits adultery; and everyone marrying her put away from a husband commits adultery.

[19] Now there was a certain rich man, and he was clothed in purple and fine linen, making merry every day in luxury. [20] And there was a certain poor man named Lazarus, who was laid at his porch, being full of sores, [21] and he desiring to be satisfied from the crumbs which fell from the rich man's table; but even the dogs coming licked his sores. [22] And it happened that the poor man died, and he was carried away by the angels into the bosom of Abraham. And the rich man also died, and was buried. [23] And being in torment in hell, having lifted up his eyes, he saw Abraham afar off, and Lazarus in his bosom. [24] And he crying out said, Father Abraham, have pity on me, and send Lazarus, that he may dip the tip of his finger in water and cool my tongue; for I am suffering in this flame. [25] But Abraham said, Child, remember that you fully received your good things in your lifetime, and Lazarus likewise evil things. But now he is comforted, and you are suffering. [26] And besides all these things, a great chasm has been fixed between us and

**14** ὑπάρχοντες, καὶ ἐξεμυκτήριζον αὐτόν. καὶ εἶπεν αὐτοῖς,
being;          and they derided          Him.    And He said  to them,

**15** Ὑμεῖς ἐστε οἱ δικαιοῦντες ἑαυτοὺς ἐνώπιον τῶν ἀνθρώπων
You  are those  justifying  yourselves before —  men,

ὁ δὲ Θεὸς γινώσκει τὰς καρδίας ὑμῶν· ὅτι τὸ ἐν ἀνθρώποις
—But God  knows  the   hearts  of you; for the thing among men

**16** ὑψηλὸν βδέλυγμα ἐνώπιον τοῦ Θεοῦ ἐστιν. ὁ νόμος καὶ οἱ
highly prized an abomination before —  God  is.  The Law and the

προφῆται ἕως Ἰωάννου· ἀπὸ τότε ἡ βασιλεία τοῦ Θεοῦ
Prophets (were) until John;  from then the kingdom —  of God

**17** εὐαγγελίζεται, καὶ πᾶς εἰς αὐτὴν βιάζεται. εὐκοπώτερον δέ
is being preached; and everyone into it  is pressing .  easier    But

ἐστι τὸν οὐρανὸν καὶ τὴν γῆν παρελθεῖν, ἢ τοῦ νόμου μίαν
it is  the  heaven  and  the earth to pass away, than of the law  one

**18** κεραίαν πεσεῖν. πᾶς ὁ ἀπολύων τὴν γυναῖκα αὐτοῦ καὶ
tittle  to fall. Everyone putting away  the  wife  of him and

γαμῶν ἑτέραν μοιχεύει· καὶ πᾶς ὁ ἀπολελυμένην ἀπὸ ἀνδρὸς
marrying another commits and everyone  having been  from a husband
                         adultery             put away her

γαμῶν μοιχεύει.
marrying, commits adultery.

**19** Ἄνθρωπος δέ τις ἦν πλούσιος, καὶ ἐνεδιδύσκετο πορφύραν
man   And a certain was rich,  and customarily donned a purple robe

**20** καὶ βύσσον, εὐφραινόμενος καθ' ἡμέραν λαμπρῶς. πτωχὸς
and fine linen,  being merry   day by day,  in luxury  poor one

δέ τις ἦν ὀνόματι Λάζαρος, ὃς ἐβέβλητο πρὸς τὸν πυλῶνα
And a was by name  Lazarus  who had been laid at  the  porch

**21** αὐτοῦ ἡλκωμένος καὶ ἐπιθυμῶν χορτασθῆναι ἀπὸ τῶν
of him, being sore-plagued and desiring  to be filled  from  the

ψιχίων τῶν πιπτόντων ἀπὸ τῆς τραπέζης τοῦ πλουσίου·
crumbs that were falling from the  table  of the  rich one.

ἀλλὰ καὶ οἱ κύνες ἐρχόμενοι ἀπέλειχον τὰ ἕλκη αὐτοῦ.
But  even the dogs  coming  licked  the sores  of him.

**22** ἐγένετο δὲ ἀποθανεῖν τὸν πτωχόν, καὶ ἀπενεχθῆναι αὐτὸν
it was And,  died  the poor one, and was carried away  him

ὑπὸ τῶν ἀγγέλων εἰς τὸν κόλπον τοῦ Ἀβραάμ· ἀπέθανε δὲ
by the angels  into  the bosom — of Abraham. died And

**23** καὶ ὁ πλούσιος, καὶ ἐτάφη. καὶ ἐν τῷ ᾅδῃ ἐπάρας τοὺς
also the rich one,  and was buried. And in — Hades lifting up the

ὀφθαλμοὺς αὐτοῦ, ὑπάρχων ἐν βασάνοις, ὁρᾷ τὸν Ἀβραὰμ
eyes  of him,  being  in torments, he sees —  Abraham

**24** ἀπὸ μακρόθεν, καὶ Λάζαρον ἐν τοῖς κόλποις αὐτοῦ. καὶ αὐτὸς
from afar,  and Lazarus in the bosoms of him. And he

φωνήσας εἶπε, Πάτερ Ἀβραάμ, ἐλέησόν με, καὶ πέμψον
calling  said, Father Abraham,  pity  me, and  send

Λάζαρον, ἵνα βάψῃ τὸ ἄκρον τοῦ δακτύλου αὐτοῦ ὕδατος,
Lazarus,  that he may dip the lip of the  finger  of him of water,

καὶ καταψύξῃ τὴν γλῶσσάν μου· ὅτι ὀδυνῶμαι ἐν τῇ
and may cool  the  tongue  of me because I am suffering in  —

**25** φλογὶ ταύτῃ. εἶπε δὲ Ἀβραάμ, Τέκνον, μνήσθητι ὅτι ἀπέ-
flame this.  said But Abraham,  Child, remember that fully re-

λαβες σὺ τὰ ἀγαθά σου ἐν τῇ ζωῇ σου, καὶ Λάζαρος ὁμοίως
ceived you things good of you in the life of you, and Lazarus  likewise

**26** τὰ κακά· νῦν δὲ ὅδε παρακαλεῖται, σὺ δὲ ὀδυνᾶσαι. καὶ ἐπὶ
the bad.  now But here he is comforted. you but are suffering. And besides

πᾶσι τούτοις, μεταξὺ ἡμῶν καὶ ὑμῶν χάσμα μέγα ἐστή-
all these things, between us and  you a chasm  great  has

you, so that they who desire to pass from here to you are not able, nor can they pass from there to us. [27] And he said, Then I beg you, father, that you would send him to the house of my father, [28] for I have five brothers, so that he may earnestly testify to them, that they may not also come to this place of torment. [29] Abraham said to him, They have Moses and the Prophets; let them hear them. [30] But he said, No, father Abraham, but if one should go from (the) dead to them, they will repent. [31] And he said to him, If they will not hear Moses and the prophets, they will not be persuaded even if one from (the) dead should rise.

ρικται, ὅπως οἱ θέλοντες διαβῆναι ἐντεῦθεν πρὸς ὑμᾶς μὴ
been fixed so that those desiring to pass from here to you not

[27] δύνωνται, μηδὲ οἱ ἐκεῖθεν πρὸς ἡμᾶς διαπερῶσιν. εἶπε δέ,
are able, nor those from there to us may cross over. he said And,

Ἐρωτῶ οὖν σε, πάτερ, ἵνα πέμψῃς αὐτὸν εἰς τὸν οἶκον τοῦ
I ask Then you, father, that you send him to the house of the

[28] πατρός μου, ἔχω γὰρ πέντε ἀδελφούς, ὅπως διαμαρτύρηται
father of me; I have for five brothers; so that he may witness

αὐτοῖς, ἵνα μὴ καὶ αὐτοὶ ἔλθωσιν εἰς τὸν τόπον τοῦτον τῆς
to them, that not also they come to — place this —

[29] βασάνου. λέγει αὐτῷ Ἀβραάμ, Ἔχουσι Μωσέα καὶ τοὺς
of torment. says to him Abraham, They have Moses and the

[30] προφήτας· ἀκουσάτωσαν αὐτῶν. ὁ δὲ εἶπεν, Οὐχί, πάτερ
prophets, let them hear them. he But said, No, father

Ἀβραάμ· ἀλλ' ἐάν τις ἀπὸ νεκρῶν πορευθῇ πρὸς αὐτούς,
Abraham, but if one from (the) dead should go to them,

[31] μετανοήσουσιν. εἶπε δὲ αὐτῷ, Εἰ Μωσέως καὶ τῶν προφη-
they will repent. he said And to him, If Moses and the prophets

τῶν οὐκ ἀκούουσιν, οὐδέ, ἐάν τις ἐκ νεκρῶν ἀναστῇ,
not they will hear, not even if one from (the) dead should rise

πεισθήσονται.
will they be persuaded.

## CHAPTER 17

[1] And He said to the disciples, It is impossible that offenses should not come, but woe (to him) by whom they come. [2] It is profitable for him if a millstone turned by an ass is put about his neck, and he be cast into the sea, than that he should cause one of these little ones to offend. [3] Take heed to yourselves; and if your brothers should sin against you, rebuke him; and if he should repent, forgive him. [4] And seven times in a day he should sin against you, and seven times in a day should return to you, saying, I repent; you shall forgive him.

[5] And the apostles said to the Lord, Give us more faith. [6] But the Lord said, If you had faith as a grain of mustard, you might say to this sycamine tree, Be rooted up, and be planted in the sea! And it would obey you. [7] But which of you having a slave plowing or feeding will say immediately (to him) who comes in out of the field, Come, recline? [8] But will he not say to him, Prepare what I may eat, and girding yourself serve

## CHAPTER 17

[1] Εἶπε δὲ πρὸς τοὺς μαθητάς, Ἀνένδεκτόν ἐστι τοῦ μὴ
He said And to the disciples, Impossible it is — not

[2] ἐλθεῖν τὰ σκάνδαλα· οὐαὶ δὲ δι' οὗ ἔρχεται. λυσιτελεῖ αὐτῷ
should come offenses, woe but through whom they come It profits him

εἰ μύλος ὀνικὸς περίκειται περὶ τὸν τράχηλον αὐτοῦ, καὶ
If a millstone of an ass is put around the neck of him, and

ἔρριπται εἰς τὴν θάλασσαν, ἢ ἵνα σκανδαλίσῃ ἕνα τῶν
he be cast into the sea, than that he should offend one —

[3] μικρῶν τούτων. προσέχετε ἑαυτοῖς. ἐὰν δὲ ἁμάρτῃ εἰς σὲ ὁ
little one of these. Take heed to yourselves. if And sins against you the

ἀδελφός σου, ἐπιτίμησον αὐτῷ· καὶ ἐὰν μετανοήσῃ, ἄφες
brother of you, rebuke him; and if he repents, forgive

[4] αὐτῷ. καὶ ἐὰν ἑπτάκις τῆς ἡμέρας ἁμάρτῃ εἰς σέ, καὶ
him. And if seven times of the day he sins against you, and

ἑπτάκις τῆς ἡμέρας ἐπιστρέψῃ ἐπί σε, λέγων, Μετανοῶ,
seven times of the day turns to you, saying, I repent;

ἀφήσεις αὐτῷ.
you shall forgive him.

[5] Καὶ εἶπον οἱ ἀπόστολοι τῷ Κυρίῳ, Πρόσθες ἡμῖν πίστιν.
And said the apostles to the Lord, Add to us faith.

[6] εἶπε δὲ ὁ Κύριος, Εἰ εἴχετε πίστιν ὡς κόκκον σινάπεως,
said And the Lord, If you have faith as a grain of mustard,

ἐλέγετε ἂν τῇ συκαμίνῳ ταύτῃ, Ἐκριζώθητι, καὶ φυτεύθητι
you may say — sycamine to this, Be rooted up, and be planted

[7] ἐν τῇ θαλάσσῃ· καὶ ὑπήκουσεν ἂν ὑμῖν. τίς δὲ ἐξ ὑμῶν δοῦλον
in the sea; even it would obey you. who But of you a slave

ἔχων ἀροτριῶντα ἢ ποιμαίνοντα, ὃς εἰσελθόντι ἐκ τοῦ
having plowing or shepherding, who (to him) come out of the

[8] ἀγροῦ ἐρεῖ εὐθέως, Παρελθὼν ἀνάπεσαι· ἀλλ' οὐχὶ ἐρεῖ
field will say immediately, Having come, recline? But not will say

αὐτῷ, Ἑτοίμασον τί δειπνήσω, καὶ περιζωσάμενος διακόνει
to him, Prepare something I may eat; and having girded yourself serve

me, while I eat and drink; and after these things you shall eat and drink? [9] Is he thankful to that slave because he did the things commanded him? I think not. [10] So also you when you may have done all things commanded you, say, We are unprofitable slaves, for we have done that which we were bound to do.

[11] And it came to pass in His going up to Jerusalem that He passed through (the) midst of Samaria and Galilee. [12] And on His entering into a certain village, ten leprous men met Him, who stood afar off. [13] And they lifted up (their) voice, saying, Jesus, Master, have pity on us. [14] And seeing (them), He said to them, Having gone show yourselves to the priests. And it came to pass in their going they were cleansed. [15] And one of them, seeing that he was healed, turned back, glorifying God with a loud voice, [16] and fell on (his) face at His feet, giving thanks to Him; and he was a Samaritan. [17] And Jesus answering said, Were not the ten cleansed? But where (are) the nine? [18] Were there not found (any) returning to give glory to God except this stranger? [19] And He said to him, Having risen up, go; your faith has cured you.

[20] And having been asked by the Pharisees when the kingdom of God is coming, He answered them and said, The kingdom of God does not come with observation; [21] nor shall they say, Lo, here! Or, Lo, there! For behold, the kingdom of God is in the midst of you. [22] And He said to the disciples, Days will come when you will desire to see one of the days of the Son of man, and shall not see. [23] And they will say to you, Lo, here! Or, lo, there! Do not go out nor follow. [24] For as the lightning flashes out

9 μοι, ἕως φάγω καὶ πίω· καὶ μετὰ ταῦτα φάγεσαι καὶ πίεσαι
me until I eat and drink; and after these things eat and drink

σύ ; μὴ χάριν ἔχει τῷ δούλῳ ἐκείνῳ ὅτι ἐποίησε τὰ δια-
you. (Does)thanks he have    slave to that because he did the things

10 ταχθέντα αὐτῷ ; οὐ δοκῶ. οὕτω καὶ ὑμεῖς, ὅταν ποιήσητε
commanded of him? not I think.   So also you,  when you have done

πάντα τὰ διαταχθέντα ὑμῖν, λέγετε ὅτι Δοῦλοι ἀχρεῖοί ἐσμεν·
all things commanded you, say, — Slaves unprofitable we are;

ὅτι ὃ ὠφείλομεν. ποιῆσαι πεποιήκαμεν.
what we ought   to do,   we have done.

11 Καὶ ἐγένετο ἐν τῷ πορεύεσθαι αὐτὸν εἰς Ἱερουσαλήμ, καὶ
And it was, in the going of Him to Jerusalem, even

12 αὐτὸς διήρχετο διὰ μέσου Σαμαρείας καὶ Γαλιλαίας. καὶ
He passed through (the) midst of Samaria and Galilee. And

εἰσερχομένου αὐτοῦ εἴς τινα κώμην, ἀπήντησαν αὐτῷ δέκα
entering him into a certain village, met Him ten

13 λεπροὶ ἄνδρες, οἳ ἔστησαν πόρρωθεν· καὶ αὐτοὶ ἦραν φωνήν,
leprous men, who stood afar off, and they lifted voice,

14 λέγοντες, Ἰησοῦ, ἐπιστάτα, ἐλέησον ἡμᾶς. καὶ ἰδὼν εἶπεν
saying, Jesus, Master, pity us. And seeing He said

αὐτοῖς, Πορευθέντες ἐπιδείξατε ἑαυτοὺς τοῖς ἱερεῦσι. καὶ
to them, Going show yourselves to the priests. And

15 ἐγένετο ἐν τῷ ὑπάγειν αὐτούς, ἐκαθαρίσθησαν. εἷς δὲ ἐξ
it was, in the going (of)them, they were cleansed. one But of

αὐτῶν, ἰδὼν ὅτι ἰάθη, ὑπέστρεψε, μετὰ φωνῆς μεγάλης
them, seeing that he was cured, returned with a voice great

16 δοξάζων τὸν Θεόν· καὶ ἔπεσεν ἐπὶ πρόσωπον παρὰ τοὺς
glorifying — God, and fell upon (his) face at the

πόδας αὐτοῦ, εὐχαριστῶν αὐτῷ· καὶ αὐτὸς ἦν Σαμαρείτης.
feet of Him, thanking Him; and he was a Samaritan.

17 ἀποκριθεὶς δὲ ὁ Ἰησοῦς εἶπεν, Οὐχὶ οἱ δέκα ἐκαθαρίσθησαν ;
answering And — Jesus said, Not the ten were cleansed?

18 οἱ δὲ ἐννέα ποῦ ; οὐχ εὑρέθησαν ὑποστρέψαντες δοῦναι δόξαν
the But nine, where? not Were found returning to give glory

19 τῷ Θεῷ, εἰ μὴ ὁ ἀλλογενὴς οὗτος, καὶ εἶπεν αὐτῷ, Ἀναστὰς
to God, except stranger this? And He said to him, Rising up

πορεύου· ἡ πίστις σου σέσωκέ σε.
go! The faith of you has healed you.

20 Ἐπερωτηθεὶς δὲ ὑπὸ τῶν Φαρισαίων, πότε ἔρχεται ἡ
being questioned And by the Pharisees, when comes the

βασιλεία τοῦ Θεοῦ, ἀπεκρίθη αὐτοῖς καὶ εἶπεν, Οὐκ ἔρχεται
kingdom — of God, He answered them and said, does not come

21 ἡ βασιλεία τοῦ Θεοῦ μετὰ παρατηρήσεως· οὐδὲ ἐροῦσιν,
The kingdom — of God with observation, nor will they say,

Ἰδοὺ ὧδε, ἤ, ἰδοὺ ἐκεῖ. ἰδοὺ γάρ, ἡ βασιλεία τοῦ Θεοῦ ἐντὸς
Behold, here; or behold, there. behold For, the kingdom — of God within

ὑμῶν ἐστίν.
you is.

22 Εἶπε δὲ πρὸς τοὺς μαθητάς, Ἐλεύσονται ἡμέραι ὅτε
He said And to the disciples, will come Days when

ἐπιθυμήσετε μίαν τῶν ἡμερῶν τοῦ υἱοῦ τοῦ ἀνθρώπου ἰδεῖν,
you will long one of the days of the Son — of man to see,

23 καὶ οὐκ ὄψεσθε. καὶ ἐροῦσιν ὑμῖν, Ἰδοὺ ὧδε, ἤ, ἰδοὺ ἐκεῖ· μὴ
and not will see. And they will say to you, Behold here; or, behold, there; not

24 ἀπέλθητε, μηδὲ διώξητε. ὥσπερ γὰρ ἡ ἀστραπὴ ἡ ἀστρά-
do go away, nor follow. as For the lightning which lights up

πτουσα ἐκ τῆς ὑπ' οὐρανὸν εἰς τὴν ὑπ' οὐρανὸν λάμπει, οὕτως
flashing out of that under heaven to that under heaven shines,　so

from the (one part) under heaven and shines to the (other part) under heaven, so will the Son of man be in His day. [25] But first He must suffer many things, and be rejected from this generation. [26] And as it was in the days of Noah, so also it will be in the days of the Son of man. [27] They were eating, drinking, marrying, being given in marriage, until (the) day Noah went into the ark, and the flood came and destroyed all. [28] And likewise, as it was in the days of Lot, they were eating, drinking, buying, selling, planting, building; [29] but on (the) day Lot went out from Sodom, it rained fire and brimstone from Heaven and destroyed all. [30] Even so it shall be in the day the Son of man is revealed.

25　ἔσται καὶ ὁ υἱὸς τοῦ ἀνθρώπου ἐν τῇ ἡμέρᾳ αὐτοῦ. πρῶτον
will be also the Son － of man in the day of Him. first

δὲ δεῖ αὐτὸν πολλὰ παθεῖν καὶ ἀποδοκιμασθῆναι ἀπὸ τῆς
But must Him many things suffer, and to be rejected from －

26　γενεᾶς ταύτης. καὶ καθὼς ἐγένετο ἐν ταῖς ἡμέραις τοῦ Νῶε,
generation this. And as it was in the days － of Noah,

οὕτως ἔσται καὶ ἐν ταῖς ἡμέραις τοῦ υἱοῦ τοῦ ἀνθρώπου.
so it will be also in the days of the Son － of man.

27　ἤσθιον, ἔπινον, ἐγάμουν, ἐξεγαμίζοντο, ἄχρι ἧς ἡμέρας
They were eating, drinking, marrying, giving in marriage, until which day

εἰσῆλθε Νῶε εἰς τὴν κιβωτόν, καὶ ἦλθεν ὁ κατακλυσμός, καὶ
went in Noah into the ark. And came the Flood and

28　ἀπώλεσεν ἅπαντας. ὁμοίως καὶ ὡς ἐγένετο ἐν ταῖς ἡμέραις
destroyed all. Likewise also, as it was in the days

Λώτ· ἤσθιον; ἔπινον, ἠγόραζον, ἐπώλουν, ἐφύτευον,
of Lot, they were eating, drinking, buying,　selling,　planting,

29　ᾠκοδόμουν· ᾗ δὲ ἡμέρᾳ ἐξῆλθε Λὼτ ἀπὸ Σοδόμων, ἔβρεξε
building; on which but day went out Lot from Sodom, it rained

30　πῦρ καὶ θεῖον ἀπ' οὐρανοῦ, καὶ ἀπώλεσεν ἅπαντας· κατὰ
fire and brimstone from heaven and destroyed all. In this

ταῦτα ἔσται ἡ ἡμέρα ὁ υἱὸς τοῦ ἀνθρώπου ἀποκαλύπτεται.
way it will be in the day the Son － of man is revealed.

[31] In that day (he) who shall be on the housetop, and his goods in the house, let him not come down to take them away; and he in the field likewise, let him not return to the things behind. [32] Remember Lot's wife. [33] Whoever may seek to save his life shall lose it; and whoever may lose it shall save it. [34] I say to you, In that night there shall be two on one bed; the one shall be taken, and the other shall be left. [35] Two shall be grinding together, one shall be taken, and the other shall be left. [36] Two shall be in the field together, one shall be taken, and the other shall be left. [37] And answering they said to Him, Where, Lord? And He said to them, Where the body (is), there the eagles will be gathered together.

31　ἐν ἐκείνῃ τῇ ἡμέρᾳ, ὃς ἔσται ἐπὶ τοῦ δώματος, καὶ τὰ
In that － day, who will be on the housetop, and the

σκεύη αὐτοῦ ἐν τῇ οἰκίᾳ, μὴ καταβάτω ἆραι αὐτά· καὶ ὁ
goods of him in the house, not let him descend to take them; and those

32　ἐν τῷ ἀγρῷ ὁμοίως μὴ ἐπιστρεψάτω εἰς τὰ ὀπίσω. μνη-
in the field likewise, not let him turn back to the things behind. Re-

33　μονεύετε τῆς γυναικὸς Λώτ. ὃς ἐὰν ζητήσῃ τὴν ψυχὴν
member the wife of Lot. Whoever seeks the life

αὐτοῦ σῶσαι ἀπολέσει αὐτήν· καὶ ὃς ἐὰν ἀπολέσῃ αὐτὴν
of him to save, he will lose it; and whoever will lose it,

34　ζωογονήσει αὐτήν. λέγω ὑμῖν, ταύτῃ τῇ νυκτὶ ἔσονται δύο
will preserve it. I say to you, in this － night will be two

ἐπὶ κλίνης μιᾶς· ὁ εἷς παραληφθήσεται, καὶ ὁ ἕτερος ἀφεθή-
on bed one; the one will be taken, and the other will

35　σεται. δύο ἔσονται ἀλήθουσαι ἐπὶ τὸ αὐτό ἡ μία παρα-
be left. Two will be grinding together; the one will

36　ληφθήσεται, καὶ ἡ ἑτέρα ἀφεθήσεται. δύο ἔσονται ἐν τῷ
be taken, and the other will be left. Two will be in the

37　ἀγρῷ ὁ εἷς παραληφθήσεται, καὶ ὁ ἕτερος ἀφεθήσεται. καὶ
field; the one will be taken, and the other will be left. And

ἀποκριθέντες λέγουσιν αὐτῷ, Ποῦ, Κύριε; ὁ δὲ εἶπεν αὐτοῖς,
answering they say to Him, Where, Lord? He And said to them,

Ὅπου τὸ σῶμα, ἐκεῖ συναχθήσονται οἱ ἀετοί.
Where the body (is), there will be gathered the eagles.

## CHAPTER 18

[1] And He also spoke a parable to them to show that it is always right to pray, and not to faint, [2] saying, A certain judge was in a certain city, not fearing God and not

1　Ἔλεγε δὲ καὶ παραβολὴν αὐτοῖς πρὸς τὸ δεῖν πάντοτε
He told And also a parable to them to (teach) it is right always

2　προσεύχεσθαι, καὶ μὴ ἐκκακεῖν, λέγων, Κριτής τις ἦν ἔν τινι
to pray, and not to faint, saying, A judge certain was in a

πόλει, τὸν Θεὸν μὴ φοβούμενος, καὶ ἄνθρωπον μὴ ἐντρεπό-
city, God not fearing, and man not respecting.

respecting man. [3] And a widow was in that city, and she was coming to him, saying, Avenge me of my adversary. [4] And he would not for a time; but afterward he said within himself, Even if I do not fear God and do not respect man, [5] yet because this widow causes me trouble, I will avenge her, lest perpetually coming she harrass me. [6] And the Lord said, Hear what the unrighteous judge says. [7] And shall not God carry out the avenging of His elect who cry to Him day and night, and (is) being patient over them? [8] I say to you, that He will carry out the avenging of them speedily. But the Son of man having come, will He truly find faith on the earth?

[9] And He also spoke this parable to some who trusted in themselves that they are righteous, and despised the rest: [10] Two men went up into the Temple to pray; the one a Pharisee and the other a tax-collector. [11] The Pharisee was standing and praying with himself this way, God, I thank You that I am not as the rest of men, robbers, unrighteous, adulterers, or even as this tax-collector. [12] I fast twice in the week, I tithe all things, as many as I gain. [13] And the tax-collector standing afar off would not even lift up the eyes to the Heaven, but was striking on his breast, saying, God, be merciful to me the sinner. [14] I say to you, This one went down to his house justified rather than that one. For everyone that exalts himself shall be humbled; and he that humbles himself shall be exalted.

[15] And they brought to Him the infants also, that He might touch them; but having seen the disciples rebuked them.

**3** μενος· χήρα δὲ ἦν ἐν τῇ πόλει ἐκείνῃ, καὶ ἤρχετο πρὸς αὐτόν
a widow And was in     city      that,  and she came to    him,

**4** λέγουσα, Ἐκδίκησόν με ἀπὸ τοῦ ἀντιδίκου μου. καὶ οὐκ
saying,      Avenge    me from the adversary of me.  And not

ἠθέλησεν ἐπὶ χρόνον· μετὰ δὲ ταῦτα εἶπεν ἐν ἑαυτῷ, Εἰ
he would    for  a time;   after but these things he said in himself,  If

καὶ τὸν Θεὸν οὐ φοβοῦμαι, καὶ ἄνθρωπον οὐκ ἐντρέπομαι·
even —    God not I fear,   and     man    not respect,

**5** διὰ γε τὸ παρέχειν μοι κόπον τὴν χήραν ταύτην, ἐκδικήσω
yet because    causes  me trouble  —  widow    this,   I will avenge

**6** αὐτήν, ἵνα μὴ εἰς τέλος ἐρχομένη ὑπωπιάζῃ με. εἶπε δὲ ὁ
her,   lest  in (the) end  coming   she subdue me. said And the

**7** Κύριος, Ἀκούσατε τί ὁ κριτὴς τῆς ἀδικίας λέγει. ὁ δὲ Θεὸς
Lord,   Hear    what the  judge of unrighteousness says; — and  God

οὐ μὴ ποιήσει τὴν ἐκδίκησιν τῶν ἐκλεκτῶν αὐτοῦ τῶν
in no way will execute the  avenging  of the   elect   of Him, those

βοώντων πρὸς αὐτὸν ἡμέρας καὶ νυκτός, καὶ μακροθυμῶν
crying     to  Him     day   and  night,   and being patient

**8** ἐπ᾽ αὐτοῖς; λέγω ὑμῖν ὅτι ποιήσει τὴν ἐκδίκησιν αὐτῶν ἐν
over  them? I say to you that He will execute the avenging  of them

τάχει. πλὴν ὁ υἱὸς τοῦ ἀνθρώπου ἐλθὼν ἄρα εὑρήσει τὴν
speedily But the Son   —  of man      coming then, will He find —

πίστιν ἐπὶ τῆς γῆς;
faith   on  the earth?

**9** Εἶπε δὲ καὶ πρός τινας τοὺς πεποιθότας ἐφ᾽ ἑαυτοῖς ὅτι
He said And also to  some (of) those relying    on themselves, that

εἰσὶ δίκαιοι, καὶ ἐξουθενοῦντας τοὺς λοιπούς, τὴν παρα-
they are righteous, also despising      the    rest;

**10** βολὴν ταύτην. Ἄνθρωποι δύο ἀνέβησαν εἰς τὸ ἱερὸν
parable   this,      men    Two went up    to the Temple

**11** προσεύξασθαι· ὁ εἷς Φαρισαῖος, καὶ ὁ ἕτερος τελώνης. ὁ
to pray,      the one a Pharisee, and the other a tax-collector. The

Φαρισαῖος σταθεὶς πρὸς ἑαυτὸν ταῦτα προσηύχετο, Ὁ
Pharisee   standing, to  himself  these things praying,

Θεός, εὐχαριστῶ σοι ὅτι οὐκ εἰμὶ ὥσπερ οἱ λοιποὶ τῶν
God,  I thank   You that not I am  as     the  rest  —

ἀνθρώπων, ἅρπαγες, ἄδικοι, μοιχοί, ἢ καὶ ὡς οὗτος ὁ
of men,   rapacious, unrighteous, adulterers, or even as  this

**12** τελώνης. νηστεύω δὶς τοῦ σαββάτου, ἀποδεκατῶ πάντα
tax-collector. I fast twice (in) the week;   I tithe   all things,

**13** ὅσα κτῶμαι. καὶ ὁ τελώνης μακρόθεν ἑστὼς οὐκ ἤθελεν οὐδὲ
as many as I get. And the tax-collector afar off standing not would not even

τοὺς ὀφθαλμοὺς εἰς τὸν οὐρανὸν ἐπᾶραι, ἀλλ᾽ ἔτυπτεν εἰς τὸ
the  eyes      to   — Heaven lift up,   but  smote    on the

στῆθος αὐτοῦ, λέγων, Ὁ Θεός, ἱλάσθητί μοι τῷ ἁμαρτωλῷ.
breast  of him,  saying,   God,  be merciful to me the   sinner.

**14** λέγω ὑμῖν, κατέβη οὗτος δεδικαιωμένος εἰς τὸν οἶκον αὐτοῦ
I say  to you, went down this one having been justified to the house of him,

ἢ ἐκεῖνος· ὅτι πᾶς ὁ ὑψῶν ἑαυτὸν ταπεινωθήσεται, ὁ δὲ τα-
than that one, for everyone exalting himself will be humbled;   he And

πεινῶν ἑαυτὸν ὑψωθήσεται.
humbling himself  will be exalted.

**15** Προσέφερον δὲ αὐτῷ καὶ τὰ βρέφη, ἵνα αὐτῶν ἅπτηται·
they brought And to Him also the babes,  that  them He might touch;

ἰδόντες δὲ οἱ μαθηταὶ ἐπετίμησαν αὐτοῖς. ὁ δὲ Ἰησοῦς
seeing but, the disciples  rebuked       them.  — But Jesus

[16] But Jesus having called them said, Allow the children to come to Me, and do not prevent them; for of such is the kingdom of God. [17] Truly I say to you, whoever receives not the kingdom of God as a child, in no way enters into it.

[18] And a certain ruler asked Him, saying, Good Teacher, what may I do (to) inherit eternal life? [19] But Jesus said to him, Why do you call Me good? No one (is) good, except One: God. [20] You know the commandments: Do not commit adultery; do not murder; do not steal; do not bear false witness; honor your father and your mother. [21] And he said, I have kept all these from my youth. [22] And hearing these things, Jesus said to him, Yet one (thing) you lack: sell all, as much as you have, and distribute to (the) poor; and you will have treasure in Heaven, and come follow Me. [23] But he hearing these things became very grieved, for he was very rich. [24] And Jesus seeing him having become very grieved, said, How hardly those having riches shall enter into the kingdom of God. [25] For it is easier for a camel to go through a needle's eye, than a rich man to enter into the kingdom. of God. [26] And those hearing said, And who is able to be saved? [27] But He said, The things impossible with men are possible with God. [28] And Peter said, Behold, we left all and followed You. [29] And He said to them, Truly I say to you, that there is no one who has left house, or parents, or brothers, or wife, or children, for the sake of the kingdom of God, [30] who shall not receive many times more in this time, and in the age that is coming everlasting life.

[31] And having taken the twelve, He said to them, Behold, We go up to Jerusalem, and all things shall be accomplished

**16** προσκαλεσάμενος αὐτὰ εἶπεν, Ἄφετε τὰ παιδία ἔρχεσθαι
called near     them saying, Allow the children to come
πρός με, καὶ μὴ κωλύετε αὐτά· τῶν γὰρ τοιούτων ἐστὶν ἡ
to Me, and not do prevent them, — for of such     is the

**17** βασιλεία τοῦ Θεοῦ. ἀμὴν λέγω ὑμῖν, ὃς ἐὰν μὴ δέξηται τὴν
kingdom — of God. Truly I say to you, whoever not receives the
βασιλείαν τοῦ Θεοῦ ὡς παιδίον, οὐ μὴ εἰσέλθη εἰς αὐτήν.
kingdom — of God as a child, in no way enters into it.

**18** Καὶ ἐπηρώτησέ τις αὐτὸν ἄρχων, λέγων, Διδάσκαλε
And questioned a certain Him ruler, saying, Teacher

**19** ἀγαθέ, τί ποιήσας ζωὴν αἰώνιον κληρονομήσω; εἶπε δὲ
good, what doing life eternal I may inherit? said And
αὐτῷ ὁ Ἰησοῦς, Τί με λέγεις ἀγαθόν; οὐδεὶς ἀγαθός, εἰ μὴ
to him — Jesus, Why Me you say (is) good? No one (is) good, except

**20** εἷς, ὁ Θεός. τὰς ἐντολὰς οἶδας, Μὴ μοιχεύσῃς, μὴ φονεύσῃς,
One, God. The commands you know, Not do adultery, not kill,
μὴ κλέψῃς, μὴ ψευδομαρτυρήσῃς, τίμα τὸν πατέρα σου καὶ
not steal, not bear false witness, honor the father of you and

**21** τὴν μητέρα σου. ὁ δὲ εἶπε, Ταῦτα πάντα ἐφυλαξάμην ἐκ
the mother of you. he And said, these things All I have kept from

**22** νεότητός μου. ἀκούσας δὲ ταῦτα ὁ Ἰησοῦς εἶπεν αὐτῷ, Ἔτι
youth my. hearing But these things, Jesus said to him, Yet
ἕν σοι λείπει· πάντα ὅσα ἔχεις πώλησον, καὶ διάδος πτωχοῖς,
one to you is lacking: all, as much as you have, sell, and distribute to (the) poor,
καὶ ἕξεις θησαυρὸν ἐν οὐρανῷ· καὶ δεῦρο, ἀκολούθει μοι. ὁ δὲ
and you will have treasure in Heaven; and come, follow Me. he But

**23** ἀκούσας ταῦτα περίλυπος ἐγένετο· ἦν γὰρ πλούσιος σφόδρα.
hearing these things very grieved became, he was for rich exceedingly.

**24** Ἰδὼν δὲ αὐτὸν ὁ Ἰησοῦς περίλυπον γενόμενον εἶπε, Πῶς
seeing And him, Jesus very grieved having become said, How
δυσκόλως οἱ τὰ χρήματα ἔχοντες εἰσελεύσονται εἰς τὴν
hardly those — riches having shall enter into the

**25** βασιλείαν τοῦ Θεοῦ. εὐκοπώτερον γάρ ἐστι κάμηλον διὰ
kingdom — of God. easier For it is (for) a camel through
τρυμαλιᾶς ῥαφίδος εἰσελθεῖν, ἢ πλούσιον εἰς τὴν βασιλείαν
(the) eye of a needle to go in, than a rich one into the kingdom

**26** τοῦ Θεοῦ εἰσελθεῖν. εἶπον δὲ οἱ ἀκούσαντες, Καὶ τίς δύναται
— of God to enter. said And those hearing, And who is able

**27** σωθῆναι; ὁ δὲ εἶπε, Τὰ ἀδύνατα παρὰ ἀνθρώποις δυνατά
to be saved? He And said, The things impossible with men possible

**28** ἐστι παρὰ τῷ Θεῷ. εἶπε δὲ ὁ Πέτρος, Ἰδού, ἡμεῖς ἀφή-
is with — God. said And — Peter, Behold, we

**29** καμεν πάντα, καὶ ἠκολουθήσαμέν σοι. ὁ δὲ εἶπεν αὐτοῖς,
left all and followed You. He And said to them,
Ἀμὴν λέγω ὑμῖν ὅτι οὐδείς ἐστιν ὃς ἀφῆκεν οἰκίαν, ἢ
Truly I say to you that no one there is who has left house, or
γονεῖς, ἢ ἀδελφούς, ἢ γυναῖκα, ἢ τέκνα, ἕνεκεν τῆς βασιλείας
parents, or brothers, or wife, or children for the sake of the kingdom

**30** τοῦ Θεοῦ, ὃς οὐ μὴ ἀπολάβη πολλαπλασίονα ἐν τῷ καιρῷ
of God, who — not shall receive many times more in — time

**31** τούτῳ, καὶ ἐν τῷ αἰῶνι τῷ ἐρχομένῳ ζωὴν αἰώνιον.
this and in the age coming life everlasting.
Παραλαβὼν δὲ τοὺς δώδεκα, εἶπε πρὸς αὐτούς, Ἰδού,
taking And the twelve, He said to them, Behold,
ἀναβαίνομεν εἰς Ἱεροσόλυμα, καὶ τελεσθήσεται πάντα τὰ
we are going up to Jerusalem, and will be completed all things —

which have been written
by the prophets about the
Son of man; [32] for He
will be delivered up to the
nations, and will be mocked, and will be insulted, and
will be spit upon. [33] And
having whipped, they will
kill Him; and on the third
day He will rise again. [34]
And they understood none
of these things, and this saying being hidden from them
they also did not know the
things being said.

[35] And it happened in
His drawing near to Jericho,
a certain blind one sat begging by the wayside. [36]
And a crowd passing by, he
asked what this might be.
[37] And they told him
that Jesus the Nazarene is
passing. [38] And he cried
out saying, Jesus, son of
David, pity me. [39] And
those going before rebuked
him, that he be quiet. But
he much more cried out,
Son of David, pity me! [40]
And Jesus standing com-
manded him to be brought
to Him. And drawing near
him, He asked him, [41]
saying, What do you desire
I do to you? And he said,
Lord, that I may see again.
[42] And Jesus said to him,
See again! Your faith has
healed you. [43] And in-
stantly he saw again, and
followed Him, glorifying
God. And all the people seeing gave praise to God.

CHAPTER 19

[1] And having gone in,
He passed through Jericho.
[2] And behold, a man
called by name Zaccheus!
And he was a chief
tax-collector, and he was
rich. [3] And he was
seeking to see Jesus, who
He was. And he was not
able because of the crowd,
because he was small in
stature. [4] And having
run on before, he went up
into a sycamore so that he
might see Him, for He was
about to pass by that
(way). [5] And as He came
to the place, looking up,
Jesus saw him and said to

γεγραμμένα διὰ τῶν προφητῶν τῷ υἱῷ τοῦ ἀνθρώπου.
having been written via the prophets to the Son — of man.
τούτῳ, καὶ ἐν τῷ αἰῶνι τῷ ἐρχομένῳ ζωὴν αἰώνιον.
this, and in the age — coming life eternal.

**32** παραδοθήσεται γὰρ τοῖς ἔθνεσι, καὶ ἐμπαιχθήσεται, καὶ
He will be delivered for to the nations, and will be mocked, and

**33** ὑβρισθήσεται, καὶ ἐμπτυσθήσεται, καὶ μαστιγώσαντες
will be insulted, and will be spat upon. And having scourged
ἀποκτενοῦσιν αὐτόν· καὶ τῇ ἡμέρᾳ τῇ τρίτῃ ἀναστήσεται.
they will kill Him; and on the day — third He will rise again.

**34** καὶ αὐτοὶ οὐδὲν τούτων συνῆκαν, καὶ ἦν τὸ ῥῆμα τοῦτο
And they none of these things understood, and was — saying this
κεκρυμμένον ἀπ᾽ αὐτῶν, καὶ οὐκ ἐγίνωσκον τα λεγόμενα.
having been hidden from them; and not they knew the things being said.

**35** Ἐγένετο δὲ ἐν τῷ ἐγγίζειν αὐτὸν εἰς Ἰεριχώ, τυφλός τις
it was And in the drawing near (of) Him to Jericho, blind one a certain

**36** ἐκάθητο παρὰ τὴν ὁδὸν προσαιτῶν· ἀκούσας δὲ ὄχλου
sat by the way begging. hearing And a crowd

**37** διαπορευομένου, ἐπυνθάνετο τί εἴη τοῦτό. ἀπήγγειλαν δὲ
passing through, he asked what might be this. they reported And

**38** αὐτῷ ὅτι Ἰησοῦς ὁ Ναζωραῖος παρέρχεται. καὶ ἐβόησε,
to him that Jesus the Nazarene is passing by. And he cried,

**39** λέγων, Ἰησοῦ, υἱὲ Δαβίδ, ἐλέησόν με. καὶ οἱ προάγοντες
saying, Jesus, son of David, pity me. And those going before
ἐπετίμων αὐτῷ ἵνα σιωπήσῃ· αὐτὸς δὲ πολλῷ μᾶλλον
rebuked him, that he be quiet. he But by much more

**40** ἔκραζεν, Υἱὲ Δαβίδ, ἐλέησόν με. σταθεὶς δὲ ὁ Ἰησοῦς ἐκέλευσεν
cried out, Son of David, pity me. standing And — Jesus commanded

**41** αὐτὸν ἀχθῆναι πρὸς αὐτόν· ἐγγίσαντος δὲ αὐτοῦ ἐπηρώ-
him to be brought to Him. drawing near And him, He asked
τησεν αὐτόν, λέγων, Τί σοι θέλεις ποιήσω ; ὁ δὲ εἶπε, Κύριε,
him, saying, What to you wish you I do? he And said, Lord,

**42** ἵνα ἀναβλέψω. καὶ ὁ Ἰησοῦς εἶπεν αὐτῷ Ἀνάβλεψον· ἡ
that I may see again. And Jesus said to him, See again! The

**43** πίστις σου σέσωκέ σε. καὶ παραχρῆμα ἀνέβλεψε, καὶ
faith of you has healed you. And at once he saw again, and
ἠκολούθει αὐτῷ, δοξάζων τὸν Θεόν· καὶ πᾶς ὁ λαὸς ἰδὼν
followed Him, glorifying — God. And all the people seeing
ἔδωκεν αἶνον τῷ Θεῷ.
gave praise — to God.

CHAPTER 19

**1**
**2** Καὶ εἰσελθὼν διήρχετο τὴν Ἰεριχώ. καὶ ἰδού, ἀνήρ
And having entered He traversed — Jericho. And behold, a man
ὀνόματι καλούμενος Ζακχαῖος, καὶ αὐτὸς ἦν ἀρχιτελώνης,
by name being called Zaccheus; and he was a chief tax-collector.

**3** καὶ οὗτος ἦν πλούσιος. καὶ ἐζήτει ἰδεῖν τὸν Ἰησοῦν τίς ἐστι,
and he was rich. And he sought to see — Jesus, who He is,
καὶ οὐκ ἠδύνατο ἀπὸ τοῦ ὄχλου, ὅτι τῇ ἡλικίᾳ μικρὸς ἦν.
And not he was able from the crowd, because — in stature little he was.

**4** καὶ προδραμὼν ἔμπροσθεν ἀνέβη ἐπὶ συκομωραίαν ἵνα ἴδη
And having run ahead before, he went up onto a sycamore-tree, that he see

**5** αὐτόν· ὅτι δι᾽ ἐκείνης ἤμελλε διέρχεσθαι. καὶ ὡς ἦλθεν ἐπὶ
Him, because via that (way) He was going to pass. And as He came upon
τὸν τόπον, ἀναβλέψας ὁ Ἰησοῦς εἶδεν αὐτόν, καὶ εἶπε πρὸς
the place, looking up — Jesus saw him, and said to

him, Zaccheus, hurry, come down, for today I must stay in your house. [6] And hastening he came down and received Him rejoicing. [7] And having seen, all murmured, saying, He has gone in to stay with a sinful man. [8] But standing Zaccheus said to the Lord, Behold, the half of my possessions, Lord, I give to the poor; and if I took anything of anyone by false accusation, I return fourfold. [9] And Jesus said to him, Today salvation is come to this house, for he also is a son of Abraham; [10] for the Son of man came to seek and to save that which has been lost.

[11] But as they were hearing these things He spoke adding a parable, because He was near Jerusalem, and they thought that the kingdom of God was immediately to be revealed. [12] He therefore said, A certain high-born man went to a distant country to receive a kingdom for himself and to return. [13] And having called ten of his slaves, he gave to them ten minas, and said to them, Trade until I come. [14] But his citizens hated him and sent an embassy after him, saying, We are not willing (for) this one to reign over us. [15] And it came to pass on his coming back again, having received the kingdom, that he commanded these slaves to be called to him, to whom he gave the money, in order that he might know what each had gained by trading. [16] And the first came up, saying, Lord, your mina has gained ten minas. [17] And he said to him, Well done, good slave! Because you were faithful in a very little, you be over ten cities having authority. [18] And the second came, saying, Lord, your mina has made five minas. [19] And he said also to this one, And you be over five cities. [20] And another came, saying, Lord, see, your mina which

**6** αὐτόν, Ζακχαῖε, σπεύσας κατάβηθι· σήμερον γὰρ ἐν τῷ
him, Zaccheus, making haste, come down; today for in the

οἴκῳ σου δεῖ με μεῖναι. καὶ σπεύσας κατέβη, καὶ ὑπεδέξατο
house of you must Me to stay. And hastening he came down, and welcomed

**7** αὐτὸν χαίρων. καὶ ἰδόντες ἅπαντες διεγόγγυζον, λέγοντες
Him, rejoicing. And seeing all murmured, saying,

**8** ὅτι Παρὰ ἁμαρτωλῷ ἀνδρὶ εἰσῆλθε καταλῦσαι. σταθεὶς δὲ
— With a sinful man He went in to lodge. standing And

Ζακχαῖος εἶπε πρὸς τὸν Κύριον, Ἰδού, τὰ ἡμίση τῶν
Zaccheus said to the Lord, Behold, the half of the

ὑπαρχόντων μου, Κύριε, δίδωμι τοῖς πτωχοῖς· καὶ εἴ τινός
possessions of me, Lord, I give to the poor; and if anyone

**9** τι ἐσυκοφάντησα, ἀποδίδωμι τετραπλοῦν. εἶπε δὲ πρὸς
anything I accused falsely, I restore fourfold said And to

αὐτὸν ὁ Ἰησοῦς ὅτι Σήμερον σωτηρία τῷ οἴκῳ τούτῳ ἐγέ-
him — Jesus, — Today salvation — house to this is

**10** νετο, καθότι καὶ αὐτὸς υἱὸς Ἀβραάμ ἐστιν. ἦλθε γὰρ ὁ υἱὸς
come, because even he a son of Abraham is. came For the Son

τοῦ ἀνθρώπου ζητῆσαι καὶ σῶσαι τὸ ἀπολωλός.
of man to seek and to save the thing having been lost.

**11** Ἀκουόντων δὲ αὐτῶν ταῦτα, προσθεὶς εἶπε παραβολήν,
hearing And them these things, adding He told a parable,

διὰ τὸ ἐγγὺς αὐτὸν εἶναι Ἱερουσαλήμ, καὶ δοκεῖν αὐτοὺς ὅτι
because near He was to Jerusalem, and thought they that

**12** παραχρῆμα μέλλει ἡ βασιλεία τοῦ Θεοῦ ἀναφαίνεσθαι.
immediately was about the kingdom — of God to be revealed.

**13** εἶπεν οὖν, Ἄνθρωπός τις εὐγενὴς ἐπορεύθη εἰς χώραν μακράν,
He said, then, man a certain well-born went to a country distant

λαβεῖν ἑαυτῷ βασιλείαν, καὶ ὑποστρέψαι. καλέσας δὲ δέκα
to receive for himself a kingdom, and to return. having called And ten

**14** δούλους ἑαυτοῦ, ἔδωκεν αὐτοῖς δέκα μνᾶς, καὶ εἶπε πρὸς
slaves of himself, He gave to them ten minas, and said to

αὐτούς, Πραγματεύσασθε ἕως ἔρχομαι. οἱ δὲ πολῖται
them, Trade until I come. the But citizens

αὐτοῦ ἐμίσουν αὐτόν, καὶ ἀπέστειλαν πρεσβείαν ὀπίσω
of him hated him, and sent a delegation after

αὐτοῦ, λέγοντες, Οὐ θέλομεν τοῦτον βασιλεῦσαι ἐφ' ἡμᾶς.
him, saying, not We desire this one to reign over us.

**15** καὶ ἐγένετο ἐν τῷ ἐπανελθεῖν αὐτὸν λαβόντα τὴν βασιλείαν,
And it was, in the returning (of) him, having received the kingdom,

καὶ εἶπε φωνηθῆναι αὐτῷ τοὺς δούλους τούτους, οἷς ἔδωκε
even he said to be called to him — slaves those to whom he gave

**16** τὸ ἀργύριον, ἵνα γνῷ τίς τί διεπραγματεύσατο. παρε-
the silver, that he know what each had gained by trading. came

γένετο δὲ ὁ πρῶτος, λέγων, Κύριε, ἡ μνᾶ σου προσειργάσατο
And the first, saying, Lord, the mina of you has gained

**17** δέκα μνᾶς. καὶ εἶπεν αὐτῷ, Εὖ, ἀγαθὲ δοῦλε· ὅτι ἐν ἐλαχίστῳ
ten minas. And he said to him, Well, good slave; for in a least thing

**18** πιστὸς ἐγένου, ἴσθι ἐξουσίαν ἔχων ἐπάνω δέκα πόλεων. καὶ
faithful you were; be authority having over ten cities. And

ἦλθεν ὁ δεύτερος, λέγων, Κύριε, ἡ μνᾶ σου ἐποίησε πέντε
came the second, saying, Lord, the mina of you has made five

**19** μνᾶς. εἶπε δὲ καὶ τούτῳ, Καὶ σὺ γίνου ἐπάνω πέντε πόλεων.
minas. he said And also to this, And you be over five cities.

**20** καὶ ἕτερος ἦλθε, λέγων, Κύριε, ἰδού, ἡ μνᾶ σου, ἢν εἶχον
And another came, saying, Lord, Behold, the mina of you which I had

I kept laid up in a handkerchief. [21] For I feared you, because you are a harsh man; you take up what you did not lay down, and you reap what you did not sow. [22] But he said to him, I will judge you out of your own mouth, wicked slave; you knew that I am a harsh man, taking up what I did not lay down and reaping what I did not sow! [23] And why did you not give my money to the bank, that I coming might have required it with interest? [24] And to those standing by he said, Take from him the mina, and give to him who has the ten minas. [25] And they said to him, Lord, he has ten minas. [26] For I say to you that to everyone who has shall be given; but from him who has not, even that which he has will be taken from him. [27] But these enemies of me, those not desiring me to reign over them, bring here and execute before me.

[28] And having said these things He went on before, going up to Jerusalem. [29] And it came to pass as He drew near to Bethphage and Bethany, toward that called Mount of Olives, He sent two of His disciples, [30] saying, Go into the village opposite (you), in which entering you will find a colt tied, on which no one of men ever yet sat; having untied it, bring (it). [31] And if anyone asks you, Why do you untie (it)? You shall say this to him, Because the Lord has need of it. [32] And having gone, those who had been sent found (it) as He had said to them. [33] And as they untied the colt, its owners said to them, Why do you untie the colt? [34] And they said, The Lord needs him. [35] And they led it to Jesus; and having thrown their coats on the colt, they placed Jesus on (it). [36] And as He went, they were spreading their coats

**21** ἀποκειμένην ἐν σουδαρίῳ· ἐφοβούμην γάρ σε, ὅτι ἄνθρωπος
reserved   in a napkin;   I feared   for you, for a man
αὐστηρὸς εἶ· αἴρεις ὃ οὐκ ἔθηκας, καὶ θερίζεις ὃ οὐκ ἔσπειρας.
exacting you are, taking what not you lay, and reaping what not you sowed.

**22** λέγει δὲ αὐτῷ, Ἐκ τοῦ στόματός σου κρινῶ σε, πονηρὲ δοῦλε.
he says And to him, From the mouth of you I will judge you, wicked slave.
ᾔδεις ὅτι ἐγὼ ἄνθρωπος αὐστηρός εἰμι, αἴρων ὃ οὐκ ἔθηκα,
You knew that I an exacting   man   am,   taking what not I laid,

**23** καὶ θερίζων ὃ οὐκ ἔσπειρα· καὶ διατί οὐκ ἔδωκας τὸ ἀργύριόν
and reaping what not I sowed. And why   not did you give the silver
μου ἐπὶ τὴν τράπεζαν, καὶ ἐγὼ ἐλθὼν σὺν τόκῳ ἂν ἔπραξα
of me on the (bank) table? And I   coming, with interest may have exacted

**24** αὐτό; καὶ τοῖς παρεστῶσιν εἶπεν, Ἄρατε ἀπ' αὐτοῦ τὴν
it.   And to those standing by he said,   Take   from him   the
**25** μνᾶν, καὶ δότε τῷ τὰς δέκα μνᾶς ἔχοντι. καὶ εἶπον αὐτῷ,
mina, and give to the (one) ten   minas having.   And they said to him,
**26** Κύριε, ἔχει δέκα μνᾶς. λέγω γὰρ ὑμῖν, ὅτι παντὶ τῷ ἔχοντι
Lord, he has ten minas. I say For to you, that to everyone having,
δοθήσεται· ἀπὸ δὲ τοῦ μὴ ἔχοντος, καὶ ὃ ἔχει ἀρθήσεται
it will be given, from and the (one) not having, even what he has will be taken
**27** ἀπ' αὐτοῦ. πλὴν τοὺς ἐχθρούς μου ἐκείνους, τοὺς μὴ θελή-
from him. But — enemies of me these,   those not
σαντάς με βασιλεῦσαι ἐπ' αὐτούς, ἀγάγετε ὧδε, καὶ
desiring me to reign   over   them,   bring   here,   and
κατασφάξατε ἔμπροσθέν μου.
execute   before   me.

**28** Καὶ εἰπὼν ταῦτα, ἐπορεύετο ἔμπροσθεν, ἀναβαίνων εἰς
And having said these things, He went   in front,   going up   to
Ἱεροσόλυμα.
Jerusalem.

**29** Καὶ ἐγένετο ὡς ἤγγισεν εἰς Βηθφαγὴ καὶ Βηθανίαν πρὸς
And it was, as He drew near to Bethphage and Bethany   toward
τὸ ὄρος τὸ καλούμενον ἐλαιῶν, ἀπέστειλε δύο τῶν μαθητῶν
the mount — being called   of olives, He sent   two of the disciples
**30** αὐτοῦ, εἰπών, Ὑπάγετε εἰς τὴν κατέναντι κώμην· ἐν ᾗ
of Him, saying, Go   into the   opposite   village, in which
εἰσπορευόμενοι εὑρήσετε πῶλον δεδεμένον, ἐφ' ὃν οὐδεὶς
entering   you will find a colt having been tied, on which no one
πώποτε ἀνθρώπων ἐκάθισε· λύσαντες αὐτὸν ἀγάγετε. καὶ
ever yet   of men   sat.   Having untied it,   bring (it) And
**31** ἐάν τις ὑμᾶς ἐρωτᾷ, Διατί λύετε; οὕτως ἐρεῖτε αὐτῷ ὅτι
if anyone you   asks,   Why do you untie, thus you shall say to them,—
**32** Ὁ Κύριος αὐτοῦ χρείαν ἔχει. ἀπελθόντες δὲ οἱ ἀπεσταλ-
The Lord   of it   need   has.   having gone And, those having been
**33** μένοι εὗρον καθὼς εἶπεν αὐτοῖς. λυόντων δὲ αὐτῶν τὸν
sent   found   as   He told   them.   untying And them the
πῶλον, εἶπον οἱ κύριοι αὐτοῦ πρὸς αὐτούς, Τί λύετε τὸν
colt,   said the owners   of it   to   them, Why do you untie the
**34** πῶλον; οἱ δὲ εἶπον, Ὁ Κύριος αὐτοῦ χρείαν ἔχει. καὶ
colt? they And said, The Lord   of it need   has. And
**35** ἤγαγον αὐτὸν πρὸς τὸν Ἰησοῦν· καὶ ἐπιρρίψαντες ἑαυτῶν
they led   it   to — Jesus,   and throwing   of themselves
τὰ ἱμάτια ἐπὶ τὸν πῶλον ἐπεβίβασαν τὸν Ἰησοῦν. πορευο-
the garments on the   colt,   they put on (it) — Jesus.   going
**36** μένου δὲ αὐτοῦ, ὑπεστρώννυον τὰ ἱμάτια αὐτῶν ἐν τῇ ὁδῷ.
And Him,   they spread out the garments of them in the way.

in the way. [37] And as He was coming near, already at the descent of the Mount of Olives, the multitude of the disciples all began rejoicing, to praise God with a loud voice for all (the) mighty works they had seen, [38] saying, Blessed (is) the King coming in (the) name of (the) Lord. Peace in Heaven and glory in (the) highest. [39] And some of the Pharisees from the crowd said to Him, Teacher, rebuke your disciples. [40] And answering He said to them, I say to you, that if these should be silent, the stones will cry out. [41] And as He came near, seeing the city, He wept over it, [42] saying, If you had known, even you, even at least in this your day, the things for your peace; but now they are hidden from your eyes; [43] for days shall come on you and your enemies shall throw a rampart against you, and shall surround you and keep you in on every side; [44] and shall level you with the ground, and your children in you, and shall not leave in you a stone on a stone, because you did not know the time of your visitation.

[45] And having entered into the Temple, He began to throw out those selling and buying in it, [46] saying to them, It has been written, "My house is a house of prayer;" but you have made it a den of robbers. [47] And He was teaching day by day in the Temple; and the chief priests and the scribes were lusting to kill Him, also the chief of the people, [48] and did not find what they might do, for the people were all hanging on Him, listening.

CHAPTER 20

[1] And it happened on one of those days, as He was teaching the people in the Temple and preaching the gospel, the chief priests

**37** ἐγγίζοντος δὲ αὐτοῦ ἤδη πρὸς τῇ καταβάσει τοῦ ὄρους τῶν
drawing near And Him now to the descent of the mount of the
ἐλαιῶν, ἤρξαντο ἄπαν τὸ πλῆθος τῶν μαθητῶν χαίροντες·
olives, began all the multitude of the disciples rejoicing
αἰνεῖν τὸν Θεὸν φωνῇ μεγάλῃ περὶ πασῶν ὧν εἶδον δυνά-
to praise — God with a voice great about all which they saw, works
**38** μεων, λέγοντες,
of power, saying,

Εὐλογημένος ὁ ἐρχόμενος βασιλεὺς ἐν ὀνόματι Κυρίου·
Blessed the coming One, the king, in the name of the Lord;
εἰρήνη ἐν οὐρανῷ, καὶ δόξα ἐν ὑψίστοις.
peace in Heaven, and glory in highest places.

**39** Καί τινες τῶν Φαρισαίων ἀπὸ τοῦ ὄχλου εἶπον πρὸς
And some of the Pharisees from the crowd said to
**40** αὐτόν, Διδάσκαλε, ἐπιτίμησον τοῖς μαθηταῖς σου. καὶ ἀπο-
Him, Teacher, rebuke the disciples of you. And
κριθεὶς εἶπεν αὐτοῖς, Λέγω ὑμῖν ὅτι, ἐὰν οὗτοι σιωπήσωσιν,
answering He said to them, I say to you, — if these shall be silent,
οἱ λίθοι κεκράξονται.
the stones will cry out.

**41** Καὶ ὡς ἤγγισεν, ἰδὼν τὴν πόλιν, ἔκλαυσεν ἐπ᾽ αὐτῇ,
And as He drew near, seeing the city, He wept over it,
**42** λέγων ὅτι Εἰ ἔγνως καὶ σύ, καί γε ἐν τῇ ἡμέρᾳ σου ταύτῃ,
saying, — If you knew, even you, even at least in day of you this,
**43** τὰ πρὸς εἰρήνην σου· νῦν δὲ ἐκρύβη ἀπὸ ὀφθαλμῶν σου. ὅτι
the things for peace of you, now but were hid from the eyes of you. For
ἥξουσιν ἡμέραι ἐπὶ σέ, καὶ περιβαλοῦσιν οἱ ἐχθροί σου
will come days on you, and will raise up the enemies of you
χάρακά σοι, καὶ περικυκλώσουσί σε, καὶ συνέξουσί σε πάντο-
a rampart to you, and will surround you, and will keep in you on all
**44** θεν, καὶ ἐδαφιοῦσί σε καὶ τὰ τέκνα σου ἐν σοί, καὶ οὐκ
sides, and raze you, and the children of you in you, and not
ἀφήσουσιν ἐν σοὶ λίθον ἐπὶ λίθῳ· ἀνθ᾽ ὧν οὐκ ἔγνως τὸν
will leave in you stone upon stone because not you knew the
καιρὸν τῆς ἐπισκοπῆς σου.
time of the visitation of you.

**45** Καὶ εἰσελθὼν εἰς τὸ ἱερόν, ἤρξατο ἐκβάλλειν τοὺς πωλοῦν-
And entering into the Temple, He began to throw out the(ones) selling
**46** τας ἐν αὐτῷ καὶ ἀγοράζοντας, λέγων αὐτοῖς, Γέγραπται,
in it, and buying, saying to them, It has been written,
Ὁ οἶκός μου οἶκος προσευχῆς ἐστιν· ὑμεῖς δὲ αὐτὸν ἐποιήσατε
The house of Me a house of prayer is; you but it made
**47** σπήλαιον λῃστῶν. καὶ ἦν διδάσκων τὸ καθ᾽ ἡμέραν ἐν τῷ
a den of robbers. And He was teaching day by day in the
ἱερῷ· οἱ δὲ ἀρχιερεῖς καὶ οἱ γραμματεῖς ἐζήτουν αὐτὸν
Temple. the But chief priests and the scribes sought Him
**48** ἀπολέσαι, καὶ οἱ πρῶτοι του λαοῦ· καὶ οὐχ εὕρισκον τὸ τί
to destroy, and the chief men of the people; and not did find — what
ποιήσωσιν, ὁ λαὸς γὰρ ἅπας ἐξεκρέματο αὐτοῦ ἀκούων.
they might do; the people for all hung upon Him, hearing.

CHAPTER 20

**1** Καὶ ἐγένετο ἐν μιᾷ τῶν ἡμερῶν ἐκείνων, διδάσκοντος αὐτοῦ
And it was, on one of — days those, teaching Him
τὸν λαὸν ἐν τῷ ἱερῷ καὶ εὐαγγελιζομένου, ἐπέστησαν οἱ
the people in the Temple, and preaching the gospel; came upon the

and scribes with the elders came up [2] and spoke to Him, saying, Tell us by what authority you do these things, or who is it who gave to you this authority? [3] And answering He said to them, I will ask me you one thing, and tell me, [4] The baptism of John, was it from Heaven or from men? [5] And they reasoned among themselves, saying, If we should say from Heaven, he will say, Why then did you not believe him? [6] But if we should say from men, All the people will stone us; for they are persuaded (that) John was a prophet. [7] And they answered that they did not know where. [8] And Jesus said to them, Neither will I tell you by what authority I do these things.

[9] And He began to speak this parable to the people: A certain man planted a vineyard, and let it out to vinedressers, and left the country for a long time. [10] And in season he sent to the vinedressers a slave, that they might give to him the fruit of the vineyard; but the vinedressers having beat him sent (him) away empty. [11] And he again sent another slave; but they also having beat and dishonored (him) sent (him) away empty. [12] And he again sent a third; and they also having wounded him threw (him) out. [13] And the lord of the vineyard said, What shall I do? I will send my beloved son; perhaps having seen him they will have respect. [14] And seeing him, the vinedressers reasoned with themselves, saying, This is the heir. Come, let us kill him, that the inheritance may become ours. [15] And casting him outside the vineyard, they killed (him). Therefore what will the lord of the vineyard do to them? [16] He will come and will destroy these vinedressers, and will give the vineyard to others.

2 ἀρχιερεῖς καὶ οἱ γραμματεῖς σὺν τοῖς πρεσβυτέροις, καὶ εἶπον
chief priests and the scribes with the elders, and spoke,
πρὸς αὐτόν, λέγοντες, Εἰπὲ ἡμῖν, ἐν ποίᾳ ἐξουσίᾳ ταῦτα
to Him, saying, Tell us, by what authority these things
ποιεῖς, ἢ τίς ἐστιν ὁ δούς σοι τὴν ἐξουσίαν ταύτην; ἀπο-
you do, or who is the (one) giving you authority this?

3 κριθεὶς δὲ εἶπε πρὸς αὐτούς, Ἐρωτήσω ὑμᾶς κἀγὼ ἕνα
answering And He said to them, will ask you I also one

4 λόγον, καὶ εἴπατέ μοι· Τὸ βάπτισμα Ἰωάννου ἐξ οὐρανοῦ
word, and you tell Me: The baptism of John, from Heaven

5 ἦν, ἢ ἐξ ἀνθρώπων; οἱ δὲ συνελογίσαντο πρὸς ἑαυτούς,
was it, or from men? they And debated with themselves,
λέγοντες ὅτι Ἐὰν εἴπωμεν, Ἐξ οὐρανοῦ, ἐρεῖ, Διατί οὖν οὐκ
saying, — If we say, From Heaven, he will say, Why, then, not

6 ἐπιστεύσατε αὐτῷ; ἐὰν δὲ εἴπωμεν, Ἐξ ἀνθρώπων, πᾶς ὁ
you believed him? if And we say From men, all the
λαὸς καταλιθάσει ἡμᾶς· πεπεισμένος γάρ ἐστιν Ἰωάννην
people will stone us, having been convinced for John

7 προφήτην εἶναι. καὶ ἀπεκρίθησαν μὴ εἰδέναι πόθεν. καὶ ὁ
a prophet was. And they answered not they knew from where. And

8 Ἰησοῦς εἶπεν αὐτοῖς, Οὐδὲ ἐγὼ λέγω ὑμῖν ἐν ποίᾳ ἐξουσίᾳ
Jesus said to them, Neither do I tell you by what authority
ταῦτα ποιῶ.
these things I do.

9 Ἤρξατο δὲ πρὸς τὸν λαὸν λέγειν τὴν παραβολὴν ταύτην·
He began And to the people to tell — parable this:
Ἄνθρωπός τις ἐφύτευσεν ἀμπελῶνα, καὶ ἐξέδοτο αὐτὸν
A man certain planted a vineyard, and let out it

10 γεωργοῖς, καὶ ἀπεδήμησε χρόνους ἱκανούς· καὶ ἐν καιρῷ
to vinedressers, and went away periods for considerable. And in time
ἀπέστειλε πρὸς τοὺς γεωργοὺς δοῦλον, ἵνα ἀπὸ τοῦ καρποῦ
he sent to the vinedressers a slave, that from the fruit
τοῦ ἀμπελῶνος δῶσιν αὐτῷ· οἱ δὲ γεωργοὶ δείραντες αὐτὸν
of the vineyard they will give him. the But vinedressers sent away him,

11 ἐξαπέστειλαν κενόν. καὶ προσέθετο πέμψαι ἕτερον δοῦλον·
beating (him) empty. And he added to send another slave·
οἱ δὲ κἀκεῖνον δείραντες καὶ ἀτιμάσαντες ἐξαπέστειλαν κενόν.
they but that one also, beating and insulting (him), sent away empty.

12 καὶ προσέθετο πέμψαι τρίτον· οἱ δὲ καὶ τοῦτον τραυματί-
And he added to send a third. they But also this one, wounding

13 σαντες ἐξέβαλον. εἶπε δὲ ὁ κύριος τοῦ ἀμπελῶνος, Τί ποιήσω;
(him) threw out. said And the lord of the vineyard, What shall I do?
πέμψω τὸν υἱόν μου τὸν ἀγαπητόν· ἴσως τοῦτον ἰδόντες
I will send the son of me, the beloved; perhaps this one having seen

14 ἐντραπήσονται. ἰδόντες δὲ αὐτὸν οἱ γεωργοὶ διελογίζοντο
they will respect. seeing And him, the vinedressers reasoned
πρὸς ἑαυτούς, λέγοντες, Οὗτός ἐστιν ὁ κληρονόμος· δεῦτε,
with themselves, saying, This is the heir; come,

15 ἀποκτείνωμεν αὐτόν, ἵνα ἡμῶν γένηται ἡ κληρονομία. καὶ
let us kill him, that of us may become the inheritance. And
ἐκβαλόντες αὐτὸν ἔξω τοῦ ἀμπελῶνος, ἀπέκτειναν. τί οὖν
throwing out him out of the vineyard, they killed. What, then,

16 ποιήσει αὐτοῖς ὁ κύριος τοῦ ἀμπελῶνος; ἐλεύσεται καὶ
will do to them the lord of the vineyard? He will come and
ἀπολέσει τοὺς γεωργοὺς τούτους, καὶ δώσει τὸν ἀμπελῶνα
will destroy vinedressers these, and will give the vineyard

And having heard they said, Let it not be! [17] And looking at them, He said, What then is this having been written, (The) Stone that the builders rejected, this One came to be (the) Head of (the) corner? [18] Everyone falling on that Stone will be shattered; but on whomever It falls, it will crush him. [19] And the chief priests, and the scribes sought to lay hands on Him in the same hour, but feared the people, for they knew that He spoke this parable against them.

[20] And having watched they sent secret agents, pretending themselves to be righteous, that they might seize upon a word of His in order to deliver Him up to the power and to the authority of the governor. [21] And they questioned Him, saying, Teacher, we know that you say and teach rightly, and accept the person of no one, but teach the way of God with truth. [22] Is it lawful for us to give tribute to Caesar, or not? [23] But perceiving their slyness, He said to them, Why do you tempt Me? [24] Show me a denarius. Whose image and inscription has it? And answering they said, Caesar's. [25] And He said to them, Therefore give the things to Caesar to Caesar, the things of God to God. [26] And they were not able to take hold of His speech before the people; and wondering at His answer, they were silent.

[27] And some of the Sadducees having come, who deny there is a resurrection, they questioned Him, [28] saying, Teacher, Moses wrote to us, If anyone's brother should die having a wife, and he should die childless, that his brother should take the wife and should raise up seed to his brother. [29] Then there were seven brothers; and the first having taken a wife died childless; [30] and the

---

**17** ἄλλοις. ἀκούσαντες δὲ εἶπον, Μὴ γένοιτο. ὁ δὲ ἐμβλέψας
to others. hearing And, they said, Not let it be! He And looking at

αὐτοῖς εἶπε, Τί οὖν ἐστι τὸ γεγραμμένον τοῦτο, Λίθον ὃν
them said, What, then, is having been written this: (The) stone that

ἀπεδοκίμασαν οἱ οἰκοδομοῦντες, οὗτος ἐγενήθη εἰς κεφαλὴν
rejected those building, this one came to be for (the) head

**18** γωνίας; πᾶς ὁ πεσὼν ἐπ᾽ ἐκεῖνον τὸν λίθον συνθλασθή-
of (the) corner? Everyone falling on that — stone will be broken in

σεται ἐφ᾽ ὃν δ᾽ ἂν πέσῃ, λικμήσει αὐτόν.
pieces; on whomever but it falls, it will crush him.

**19** Καὶ ἐζήτησαν οἱ ἀρχιερεῖς καὶ οἱ γραμματεῖς ἐπιβαλεῖν
And sought the chief priests and the scribes to lay

ἐπ᾽ αὐτὸν τὰς χεῖρας ἐν αὐτῇ τῇ ὥρᾳ, καὶ ἐφοβήθησαν τὸν
on Him the hands in same the hour; and feared the

**20** λαόν· ἔγνωσαν γὰρ ὅτι πρὸς αὐτοὺς τὴν παραβολὴν ταύτην
people; they knew for that at them — parable this

εἶπε. καὶ παρατηρήσαντες ἀπέστειλαν ἐγκαθέτους ὑπο-
He told. And watching carefully they sent spies,

κρινομένους ἑαυτοὺς δικαίους εἶναι, ἵνα ἐπιλάβωνται αὐτοῦ
pretending themselves righteous to be; that they might seize of Him

λόγου, εἰς τὸ παραδοῦναι αὐτὸν τῇ ἀρχῇ καὶ τῇ ἐξουσίᾳ
a word, in order to deliver Him to the power and to the authority

**21** τοῦ ἡγεμόνος. καὶ ἐπηρώτησαν αὐτόν, λέγοντες, Διδάσκαλε,
of the governor And they questioned Him, saying, Teacher,

οἴδαμεν ὅτι ὀρθῶς λέγεις καὶ διδάσκεις, καὶ οὐ λαμβάνεις
we know that rightly you speak, and teach, and not do receive

πρόσωπον, ἀλλ᾽ ἐπ᾽ ἀληθείας τὴν ὁδὸν τοῦ Θεοῦ διδάσκεις,
a face, but upon truth the way — of God you teach.

**22** ἔξεστιν ἡμῖν Καίσαρι φόρον δοῦναι, ἢ οὔ; κατανοήσας δὲ
**23** Is it lawful for us to Caesar tribute to give, or not? perceiving And

αὐτῶν τὴν πανουργίαν, εἶπε πρὸς αὐτούς, Τί με πειράζετε;
of them the slyness, He said to them, Why Me do you tempt;

**24** ἐπιδείξατέ μοι δηνάριον· τίνος ἔχει εἰκόνα καὶ ἐπιγραφήν;
show Me a denarius; of whom has it an image and superscription?

**25** ἀποκριθέντες δὲ εἶπον, Καίσαρος. ὁ δὲ εἶπεν αὐτοῖς, Ἀπόδοτε
answering And they said, Of Caesar. He And said to them, Render

τοίνυν τὰ Καίσαρος Καίσαρι, καὶ τὰ τοῦ Θεοῦ τῷ Θεῷ.
then the things of Caesar to Caesar, and the things — of God — to God.

**26** καὶ οὐκ ἴσχυσαν ἐπιλαβέσθαι αὐτοῦ ῥήματος ἐναντίον τοῦ
And not they were able to lay hold of Him (the) speech before the

λαοῦ· καὶ θαυμάσαντες ἐπὶ τῇ ἀποκρίσει αὐτοῦ, ἐσίγησαν.
people; and marveling at the answer of Him, they were silent.

**27** Προσελθόντες δέ τινες τῶν Σαδδουκαίων, οἱ ἀντιλέγοντες
coming up And some of the Sadducees, those speaking against

**28** ἀνάστασιν μὴ εἶναι, ἐπηρώτησαν αὐτόν, λέγοντες, Διδά-
a resurrection not to be. They questioned Him, saying, Teacher,

σκαλε, Μωσῆς ἔγραψεν ἡμῖν, ἐάν τινος ἀδελφὸς ἀποθάνῃ
Moses wrote to us, If of anyone a brother dies

ἔχων γυναῖκα, καὶ οὗτος ἄτεκνος ἀποθάνῃ, ἵνα λάβῃ ὁ
having a wife, and this one childless should die, that should take the

ἀδελφὸς αὐτοῦ τὴν γυναῖκα, καὶ ἐξαναστήσῃ σπέρμα τῷ
brother of him the wife, and raise up seed to the

**29** ἀδελφῷ αὐτοῦ. ἑπτὰ οὖν ἀδελφοὶ ἦσαν· καὶ ὁ πρῶτος
brother of him. seven Then brothers there were, and the first

**30** λαβὼν γυναῖκα ἀπέθανεν ἄτεκνος· καὶ ἔλαβεν ὁ δεύτερος
having taken a wife died childless; and took the second

second took the **woman,**
and he died **childless;**
[31] and the third took
her; and likewise also the
seven did not leave
children, and died;
[32] and last of all the
woman also died.
[33] Therefore in the
resurrection of which of
them does she become
wife? For the seven had
her as wife. [34] And
answering Jesus said to
them, The sons of this age
marry and are given in
marriage; [35] but those
counted worthy to ob-
tain of that age, and the
resurrection which (is)
from among (the) dead,
neither marry nor are given
in marriage; [36] for
neither can they die
anymore; for they are
equal to angels, and are
sons of God, being sons of
the resurrection. [37] But
that the dead are raised,
even Moses showed, on the
Bush, when he calls (the)
Lord the God of Abraham
and the God of Isaac and
the God of Jacob;
[38] but He is not God of
(the) dead, but of (the)
living; for all live for Him.
[39] And some of the
scribes answering said,
Teacher, you have spoken
well. [40] And they did
not dare any more to ask
Him anything.

[41] And He said to
them, How do you say the
Christ is son of David?
[42] And David himself
said in (the) book of
Psalms, "The Lord said to
my Lord, Sit on My right
hand [43] until I place
Your enemies (as) a foot-
stool of Your feet. [44] David, then, calls Him Lord,
and how is He his son?

[45] And as all tne
people were listening, He
said to His disciples;
[46] Beware of the scribes
who like to walk in long
robes, and love greetings in
the market-places, and first
seats in the synagogues,
and first places in the
suppers; [47] who devour
the houses of widows, and
as a pretext pray at great
length. These shall receive

τὴν γυναῖκα, καὶ οὗτος ἀπέθανεν ἄτεκνος. καὶ ὁ τρίτος
the    wife,    and this one    died    childless. And the third

**31** ἔλαβεν αὐτήν. ὡσαύτως δὲ καὶ οἱ ἑπτά· καὶ οὐ κατέλιπον
took    her,    likewise    and also the seven  even  not did leave

**32** τέκνα, καὶ ἀπέθανον. ὕστερον πάντων ἀπέθανε καὶ ἡ γυνή
children, and died.    Lastly    of all    died    also the woman.

**33** ἐν τῇ οὖν ἀναστάσει, τίνος αὐτῶν γίνεται γυνή; οἱ γὰρ
in the Then  resurrection, of which of them becomes she wife;  the  for

**34** ἑπτὰ ἔσχον αὐτὴν γυναῖκα. καὶ ἀποκριθεὶς εἶπεν αὐτοῖς ὁ
seven had    her  (for)wife? And answering    said    to them

'Ιησοῦς, Οἱ υἱοὶ τοῦ αἰῶνος τούτου γαμοῦσι καὶ ἐκγαμί-
Jesus,    The sons —    age    of this    marry    and are given

**35** σκονται· οἱ δὲ καταξιωθέντες τοῦ αἰῶνος ἐκείνου τυχεῖν καὶ
marriage, those but counted worthy —    age    of that to obtain, and

τῆς ἀναστάσεως τῆς ἐκ νεκρῶν οὔτε γαμοῦσιν οὔτε ἐκγαμί-
the  resurrection from among (the) dead, neither marry  nor are given

**36** σκονται· οὔτε γὰρ ἀποθανεῖν ἔτι δύνανται· ἰσάγγελοι γὰρ
in marriage; not even for  to die  (any) more they are able, equal to angels for

εἰσι, καὶ υἱοί εἰσι τοῦ Θεοῦ, τῆς ἀναστάσεως υἱοὶ ὄντες. ὅτι
they are; and sons are —  of God, of the resurrection  sons  being. that

**37** δὲ ἐγείρονται οἱ νεκροί, καὶ Μωσῆς ἐμήνυσεν ἐπὶ τῆς βάτου,
But are raised  the dead, even Moses  pointed out at  the  Bush,

ὡς λέγει Κύριον τὸν Θεὸν 'Αβραὰμ καὶ τὸν Θεὸν 'Ισαὰκ καὶ
as he calls (the) Lord the  God of Abraham and the  God  of Isaac and

**38** τὸν Θεὸν 'Ιακώβ. Θεὸς δὲ οὐκ ἔστι νεκρῶν, ἀλλὰ ζώντων·
the  God  of Jacob. God But  not He is of dead ones, but  of living ones;

**39** πάντες γὰρ αὐτῷ ζῶσιν. ἀποκριθέντες δέ τινες τῶν γραμ-
all    for to Him  live.    answering    And some of the

**40** ματέων εἶπον, Διδάσκαλε, καλῶς εἶπας. Οὐκέτι δὲ ἐτόλμων
scribes  said, Teacher,    Well you say. no more And they dared

ἐπερωτᾶν αὐτὸν οὐδέν.
to question  Him, nothing.

**41** Εἶπε δὲ πρὸς αὐτούς, Πῶς λέγουσι τὸν Χριστὸν υἱὸν
He said And to    them, How do they say the  Christ  son

**42** Δαβὶδ εἶναι; καὶ αὐτὸς Δαβὶδ λέγει ἐν βίβλῳ ψαλμῶν,
of David is?  Even himself David says  in (the) roll of Psalms:

**43** Εἶπεν ὁ Κύριος τῷ Κυρίῳ μου, Κάθου ἐκ δεξιῶν μου, ἕως ἂν
Said the  Lord to the Lord of me,  Sit  at (the) right of Me until

**44** θῶ τοὺς ἐχθρούς σου ὑποπόδιον τῶν ποδῶν σου. Δαβὶδ
I put the  enemies of You  a footstool of the  foot of You. David

οὖν Κύριον αὐτὸν καλεῖ, καὶ πῶς υἱὸς αὐτοῦ ἐστιν;
then Lord  Him  calls. And how son of him  is He?

**45** 'Ακούοντος δὲ παντὸς τοῦ λαοῦ, εἶπε τοῖς μαθηταῖς αὐτοῦ,
hearing  And all  the people, He said to the disciples of Him,

**46** Προσέχετε ἀπὸ τῶν γραμματέων τῶν θελόντων περιπατεῖν
Beware  of  the  scribes,  those desiring  to walk about

ἐν στολαῖς, καὶ φιλούντων ἀσπασμοὺς ἐν ταῖς ἀγοραῖς, καὶ
in robes,  and  liking  greetings  in  the  markets,  and

πρωτοκαθεδρίας ἐν ταῖς συναγωγαῖς, καὶ πρωτοκλισίας ἐν
chief seats  in  the  synagogues,  and chief couches  in

**47** τοῖς δείπνοις· οἳ κατεσθίουσι τὰς οἰκίας τῶν χηρῶν, καὶ
the  suppers; those devouring  the  houses of the widows, and

προφάσει μακρὰ προσεύχονται. οὗτοι λήψονται περισσό-
under pretence long    pray.    These  will receive  a more

a greater judgment.

τερον κρίμα.
**severe judgment.**

## CHAPTER 21

## CHAPTER 21

[1] And looking up, He saw rich ones putting their gifts into the treasury. [2] And He also saw a certain poor widow putting two lepta there. [3] And He said, Truly I say to you, This poor widow put (in) more than all; [4] for all these out of their abundance put into the gifts to God; but she out of her want put (in) all the livelihood she had.

[5] And as some were speaking about the Temple, that it was decorated with beautiful stones and gifts, He said, [6] (As to) these things that you see, days will come in which a stone not will be left on a stone which will not be thrown down.

[7] And they asked Him saying, Teacher, then when will these things be? And what the sign when these things are about to occur? [8] And He said, Watch, lest you be led astray. For many will come on My name, saying, I AM; and, The time has come. Then do not go after them. [9] And when you hear of wars and disturbances, do not be afraid; for these things must first occur—but the end (is) not at once. [10] Then He said to them, Nation will be lifted up against nation, and kingdom against kingdom; [11] also there will be great earthquakes from place to place, and famines and plagues; and will be also great signs from Heaven. [12] But before all these things, they will lay their hands on you, and will persecute, delivering (you) into the synagogues and prisons; being led away before kings and governors on account of My name; [13] but it will return to you for a testimony. [14] Therefore put into your hearts not to premeditate to make a defense, [15] for I will give you a mouth and

**1** Ἀναβλέψας δὲ εἶδε τοὺς βάλλοντας τὰ δῶρα αὐτῶν εἰς
   looking up    And He saw those   putting      the gifts   of them   into

**2** τὸ γαζοφυλάκιον πλουσίους· εἶδε δὲ καί τινα χήραν
  the     treasury       rich ones.    He saw And also a certain   widow

**3** πενιχρὰν βάλλουσαν ἐκεῖ δύο λεπτά, καὶ εἶπεν, Ἀληθῶς
  poor       putting     there   two   lepta;   and He said,   Truly

λέγω ὑμῖν, ὅτι ἡ χήρα ἡ πτωχὴ αὕτη πλεῖον πάντων ἔβαλεν·
I sav to you,      widow   poor   This   more (than) all    cast.

**4** ἅπαντες γὰρ οὗτοι ἐκ τοῦ περισσεύοντος αὐτοῖς ἔβαλον εἰς
  all       For     these out of the   abundance     to them    cast   into

τὰ δῶρα τοῦ Θεοῦ, αὕτη δὲ ἐκ τοῦ ὑστερήματος αὐτῆς
the gifts   — to God,    she   but out of the    want      of her

ἅπαντα τὸν βίον ὃν εἶχεν ἔβαλε.
all      the   living which she had put.

**5** Καὶ τινων λεγόντων περὶ τοῦ ἱεροῦ, ὅτι λίθοις καλοῖς
  And   some   speaking    about the   Temple,   that with stones beautiful

**6** καὶ ἀναθήμασι κεκόσμηται, εἶπε, Ταῦτα ἃ θεωρεῖτε, ἐλεύ-
  and    gifts     it has been decorated, He said, These things that you see, will

σονται ἡμέραι ἐν αἷς οὐκ ἀφεθήσεται λίθος ἐπὶ λίθῳ, ὃς ου
come     days   in which not   will be left    stone on   stone which not

**7** καταλυθήσεται. ἐπηρώτησαν δὲ αὐτόν, λέγοντες, Διδά-
  will be thrown over   they questioned And   Him,      saying,      Teacher,

σκαλε, πότε οὖν ταῦτα ἔσται ; καὶ τί τὸ σημεῖον, ὅταν μέλλῃ
     when, then, these things will be? And what the sign   when   are about

**8** ταῦτα γίνεσθαι ; ὁ δὲ εἶπε, Βλέπετε μὴ πλανηθῆτε· πολλοὶ
  these things to occur? He And said,   Watch,    lest you be led astray;   many

γὰρ ἐλεύσονται ἐπὶ τῷ ὀνόματί μου, λέγοντες ὅτι Ἐγώ εἰμι·
for   will come    on the   name of Me,   saying,    —    I   AM;

**9** καί, Ὁ καιρὸς ἤγγικε. μὴ οὖν πορευθῆτε ὀπίσω αὐτῶν. ὅταν
  and, The time has come. not Therefore go    after     them.    when

δὲ ἀκούσητε πολέμους καὶ ἀκαταστασίας, μὴ πτοηθῆτε·
And you hear    of wars    and    disturbances,    Do not be afraid.

δεῖ γὰρ ταῦτα γενέσθαι πρῶτον, ἀλλ' οὐκ εὐθέως τὸ τέλος.
must For these things occur    first,    but   not at once   the end.

**10** Τότε ἔλεγεν αὐτοῖς, Ἐγερθήσεται ἔθνος ἐπὶ ἔθνος, καὶ
  Then He said   to them,   will be raised   Nation against nation, and

**11** βασιλεία ἐπὶ βασιλείαν· σεισμοί τε μεγαλοι κατὰ τόπους
  kingdom against kingdom, earthquakes and great    from place to place;

καὶ λιμοὶ καὶ λοιμοὶ ἔσονται, φόβητρά τε καὶ σημεῖα ἀπ'
and famines and plagues there will be; terrors and, also signs   from

**12** οὐρανοῦ μεγάλα ἔσται. πρὸ δὲ τούτων ἁπάντων ἐπι-
  Heaven      great will be. before But these things    all     they

βαλοῦσιν ἐφ' ὑμᾶς τὰς χεῖρας αὐτῶν, καὶ διώξουσι, παραδι-
will lay    on   you   the hands of them,   and will persecute, delivering

δόντες εἰς συναγωγὰς καὶ φυλακάς, ἀγομένους ἐπὶ βασιλεῖς
      into the synagogues and   prisons, being led away before   kings

**13** καὶ ἡγεμόνας, ἕνεκεν τοῦ ὀνόματός μου. ἀποβήσεται δὲ
  and governors, on account of the     name   of Me. it will return But

**14** ὑμῖν εἰς μαρτύριον. θέσθε οὖν εἰς τὰς καρδίας ὑμῶν μὴ
  to you for a testimonv. put Therefore into the   hearts   of you   not

**15** προμελετᾶν ἀπολογηθῆναι· ἐγὼ γὰρ δώσω ὑμῖν στόμα καὶ
  to premeditate to make a defense.   I    For will give   you a mouth   and

wisdom, which all those opposing you will not be able to withstand nor to resist. [16] But you will be delivered up even by parents and brothers and relatives and friends, and they will put (some) from among you to death; [17] and you will be hated by all because of My name. [18] And a hair of your head shall in no wise perish. [19] By your patience, gain your souls. [20] But when you see Jerusalem being encircled with armies, then know that her ruin has drawn near. [21] Then those in Judea, let them flee to the mountains; and those in her midst, let them not go out; and those in the countries, let them not go into her; [22] for these are days of vengeance, (that) all things having been written may be fulfilled. [23] But woe to the pregnant women and those suckling in those days; for great distress will be on the earth, and wrath on this people. [24] And they will fall by (the) sword's mouth, and will be led captive to all the nations. And Jerusalem will be trodden down by nations, until (the) times of (the) nations are fulfilled. [25] And there shall be signs in sun and moon and stars, and strangling of nations on the earth, with bewilderment, roaring of (the) sea and roiling waves, [26] men fainting at heart from fear and expectation of that which is coming on the earth; for the powers of the heavens shall be shaken. [27] And then they shall see the Son of man coming in a cloud with power and great glory. [28] But these things beginning to come to pass, look up and lift up your head, because your redemption draws near. [29] And He spoke a parable to them: Watch the fig-tree and all the trees; [30] now when they spread out, looking yourselves you know that already the summer is near. [31] So also you, when

16 σοφίαν, ἧ οὐ δυνήσονται ἀντειπεῖν οὐδὲ ἀντιστῆναι πάντες
wisdom, which not will be able to withstand nor contradict all
οἱ ἀντικείμενοι ὑμῖν. παραδοθήσεσθε δὲ καὶ ὑπὸ γονέων
those opposing you. you will be betrayed And also by parents

17 καὶ ἀδελφῶν καὶ συγγενῶν καὶ φίλων, καὶ θανατώσουσιν
and brothers and relatives and friends, and they will execute
ἐξ ὑμῶν. καὶ ἔσεσθε μισούμενοι ὑπὸ πάντων διὰ τὸ ὄνομά
of you. And you will be hated by all because of the name

18 μου. καὶ θρὶξ ἐκ τῆς κεφαλῆς ὑμῶν οὐ μὴ ἀπόληται. ἐν τῇ
of Me. And a hair of the head of you in no way shall perish. in the

19 ὑπομονῇ ὑμῶν κτήσασθε τὰς ψυχὰς ὑμῶν.
patience of you, you will gain the souls of you.

20 Ὅταν δὲ ἴδητε κυκλουμένην ὑπὸ στρατοπέδων τὴν
when And you see being encircled by armies —
Ἰερουσαλήμ, τότε γνῶτε ὅτι ἤγγικεν ἡ ἐρήμωσις αὐτῆς.
Jerusalem, then know that has come the ruin of it.

21 τότε οἱ ἐν τῇ Ἰουδαίᾳ φευγέτωσαν εἰς τὰ ὄρη καὶ οἱ ἐν
Then those in — Judea, let them flee into the mounts, and those in
μέσῳ αὐτῆς ἐκχωρείτωσαν· καὶ οἱ ἐν ταῖς χώραις μὴ εἰσερχέ-
midst of it, let them go out, and those in the open spaces not let them

22 σθωσαν εἰς αὐτήν. ὅτι ἡμέραι ἐκδικήσεως αὗταί εἰσι, τοῦ
enter into it. For days of vengeance these are, —

23 πληρωθῆναι πάντα τὰ γεγραμμένα. οὐαὶ δὲ ταῖς ἐν γαστρὶ
to be fulfilled all the things having been written woe But to the pregnant
ἐχούσαις καὶ ταῖς θηλαζούσαις ἐν ἐκείναις ταῖς ἡμέραις·
women, and those giving suck in those — days;
ἔσται γὰρ ἀνάγκη μεγάλη ἐπὶ τῆς γῆς, καὶ ὀργὴ ἐν τῷ λαῷ
will be for distress great on the earth, and wrath on people

24 τούτῳ. καὶ πεσοῦνται στόματι μαχαίρας, καὶ αἰχμαλω-
this. And they will fall by (the) mouth of (the) sword, and will be led
τισθήσονται εἰς πάντα τὰ ἔθνη· καὶ Ἰερουσαλὴμ ἔσται
captive to all the nations. And Jerusalem will be

25 πατουμένη ὑπὸ ἐθνῶν, ἄχρι πληρωθῶσι καιροὶ ἐθνῶν. καὶ
trodden down by nations; until are fulfilled (the) times of nations. And
ἔσται σημεῖα ἐν ἡλίῳ καὶ σελήνῃ καὶ ἄστροις, καὶ ἐπὶ τῆς
will be signs in sun and moon and stars, And on the
γῆς συνοχὴ ἐθνῶν ἐν ἀπορίᾳ, ἠχούσης θαλάσσης καὶ σάλου,
earth, anxiety of nations in perplexity of sound, of sea, and of surf,

26 ἀποψυχόντων ἀνθρώπων ἀπὸ φόβου καὶ προσδοκίας τῶν
fainting men from fear and expectation of the
ἐπερχομένων τῇ οἰκουμένῃ· αἱ γὰρ δυνάμεις τῶν οὐρανῶν
things coming on the habitable earth; the for powers of the heavens

27 σαλευθήσονται. καὶ τότε ὄψονται τὸν υἱὸν τοῦ ἀνθρώπου
will be shaken. And then they will see the Son — of man

28 ἐρχόμενον ἐν νεφέλῃ μετὰ δυνάμεως καὶ δόξης πολλῆς. ἀρχο-
coming in a cloud with power and glory much. begin-
μένων δὲ τούτων γίνεσθαι, ἀνακύψατε καὶ ἐπάρατε τὰς
ning And these things to happen, stand erect and lift up the
κεφαλὰς ὑμῶν· διότι ἐγγίζει ἡ ἀπολύτρωσις ὑμῶν.
heads of you, because draws near the redemption of you.

29 Καὶ εἶπε παραβολὴν αὐτοῖς, Ἴδετε τὴν συκῆν καὶ πάντα
And He told a parable to them: You see the fig-tree and all

30 τὰ δένδρα· ὅταν προβάλωσιν ἤδη, βλέποντες ἀφ᾽ ἑαυτῶν
the trees; when they sprout leaves now, seeing from yourselves

31 γινώσκετε ὅτι ἤδη ἐγγὺς τὸ θέρος ἐστίν. οὕτω καὶ ὑμεῖς,
you know that now near the summer is. So also you,

you see these things coming to pass, know that the kingdom of God is near. [32] Truly I say to you, that in no way will this generation have passed away until all (these) things occur. [33] The heaven and the earth will pass away, but My words in no way will pass away. [34] But take heed to yourselves, lest your hearts be loaded down with headaches and drinking and anxieties of life, and suddenly that day come on you [35] as a snare, for it will come in on all those sitting on (the) face of all the earth. [36] Then be watchful at every time, begging that you be counted worthy to escape all these things being about to happen, and to stand before the Son of man.

[37] And He was teaching in the Temple in the days, and going out (in) the nights, He lodged in the Mount called Of Olives; [38] and all the people came early to Him in the Temple, to hear Him.

CHAPTER 22

[1] And the feast of unleavened (bread) drew near, which (is) called Passover; [2] and the chief priests and the scribes were seeking as to how they might put Him to death, for they feared the people. [3] And Satan entered into Judas who is surnamed Iscariot, being of the number of the twelve. [4] And having gone away he spoke with the chief priests and the captains as to how he might deliver Him up to them. [5] And they rejoiced, and agreed to give him money. [6] And he promised, and looked for opportunity to deliver Him up to them away from (the) crowd.

[7] And the day of unleavened (bread) came, in which the passover must be killed. [8] And He sent Peter and John, saying, Having gone prepare the passover for Me, that we may eat. [9] But they said to Him, Where do you desire we should prepare? [10] And He said to them, Behold, you having entered

**32** ὅταν ἴδητε ταῦτα γινόμενα, γινώσκετε ὅτι ἐγγύς ἐστιν ἡ
when you see these things occurring, know that near is the
βασιλεία τοῦ Θεοῦ. ἀμὴν λέγω ὑμῖν ὅτι οὐ μὴ παρέλθῃ ἡ
kingdom — of God. Truly I say to you that in no way will pass away the
**33** γενεὰ αὕτη, ἕως ἂν πάντα γένηται. ὁ οὐρανὸς καὶ ἡ γῆ
generation this until all things occur The heaven and the earth
παρελεύσονται, οἱ δὲ λόγοι μου οὐ μὴ παρέλθωσι.
will pass away, the but words of Me in no way will pass away.
**34** Προσέχετε δὲ ἑαυτοῖς, μήποτε βαρυνθῶσιν ὑμῶν αἱ
take heed And to yourselves, lest be loaded down of you the
καρδίαι ἐν κραιπάλῃ καὶ μέθῃ καὶ μερίμναις βιωτικαῖς. καὶ
hearts in headaches and drinking and anxieties of life. And
**35** αἰφνίδιος ἐφ' ὑμᾶς ἐπιστῇ ἡ ἡμέρα ἐκείνη· ὡς παγὶς γὰρ
come on you suddenly — day that; as a snare for
ἐπελεύσεται ἐπὶ πάντας τοὺς καθημένους ἐπὶ πρόσωπον
it will come in on all those sitting on (the) face
**36** πάσης τῆς γῆς. ἀγρυπνεῖτε οὖν ἐν παντὶ καιρῷ δεόμενοι, ἵνα
of all the earth. you be watchful Then at every time, begging that
καταξιωθῆτε ἐκφυγεῖν ταῦτα πάντα τὰ μέλλοντα γίνεσθαι,
you be counted worthy to escape these all things being about to occur,
καὶ σταθῆναι ἔμπροσθεν τοῦ υἱοῦ τοῦ ἀνθρώπου.
and to stand before the Son — of man.
**37** Ἦν δὲ τὰς ἡμέρας ἐν τῷ ἱερῷ διδάσκων· τὰς δὲ νύκτας
He was And (in) the days in the Temple teaching, (in) the and nights
**38** ἐξερχόμενος ηὐλίζετο εἰς τὸ ὄρος τὸ καλούμενον ἐλαιῶν. καὶ
going out He lodged in the mountain being called of olives. And
πᾶς ὁ λαὸς ὤρθριζε πρὸς αὐτὸν ἐν τῷ ἱερῷ ἀκούειν αὐτοῦ.
all the people came early to Him in the Temple to hear Him.

CHAPTER 22

**1** Ἤγγιζε δὲ ἡ ἑορτὴ τῶν ἀζύμων, ἡ λεγομένη πάσχα.
drew near And the feast of the unleavened (bread), being called Passover.
**2** καὶ ἐζήτουν οἱ ἀρχιερεῖς καὶ οἱ γραμματεῖς τὸ πῶς ἀνέλωσιν
And sought the chief priests and the scribes — how to destroy
αὐτόν· ἐφοβοῦντο γὰρ τὸν λαόν.
Him, they feared for the people.
**3** Εἰσῆλθε δὲ ὁ Σατανᾶς εἰς Ἰούδαν τὸν ἐπικαλούμενον
entered And — Satan into Judas the (one) being called
**4** Ἰσκαριώτην, ὄντα ἐκ τοῦ ἀριθμοῦ τῶν δώδεκα. καὶ ἀπελθὼν
Iscariot, being of the number of the twelve. And going,
συνελάλησε τοῖς ἀρχιερεῦσι καὶ τοις στρατηγοῖς τὸ πῶς
he talked with the chief priests and the captains (as to) how
**5** αὐτὸν παραδῷ αὐτοῖς. καὶ ἐχάρησαν, καὶ συνέθεντο αὐτῶ
he might betray Him. And they exulted, and they agreed him
**6** ἀργύριον δοῦναι. καὶ ἐξωμολόγησε, καὶ ἐζήτει εὐκαιρίαν
silver to give. And he fully consented, and sought opportunity
τοῦ παραδοῦναι αὐτὸν αὐτοῖς ἄτερ ὄχλου.
— to betray Him to them away from (the) crowd.
**7** Ἦλθε δὲ ἡ ἡμέρα τῶν ἀζύμων, ἐν ᾗ ἔδει θύεσθαι τὸ πάσχα.
came And the day of the unleavened, on which must be the passover. killed
**8** καὶ ἀπέστειλε Πέτρον καὶ Ἰωάννην, εἰπών, Πορευθέντες
And He sent Peter and John, saying, Going,
**9** ἑτοιμάσατε ἡμῖν τὸ πάσχα, ἵνα φάγωμεν. οἱ δὲ εἶπον αὐτῷ,
prepare for us the passover, that we may eat. they And said to Him,
**10** Ποῦ θέλεις ἑτοιμάσωμεν; ὁ δὲ εἶπεν αὐτοῖς, Ἰδού, εἰσελθόντων
Where You desire we prepare? He And told them, Behold, going in

into the city, a man will meet you carrying a pitcher of water, follow him into the house where he goes in. [11] And you will say to the house-master, The Teacher says to you, Where is the guest-room where I may eat the passover with My disciples? [12] And he will show you a large upper room having been spread; prepare there. [13] And going they found as He had told them; and they prepared the passover.

[14] And when came the hour, He reclined, and the twelve apostles with Him. [15] And He said to them, With desire I desired to eat this passover with you, before My suffering. [16] For I say to you that never in any way I will eat of it until it is fulfilled in the kingdom of God. [17] And having taken a cup, having given thanks, He said, Take this and divide (it) among yourselves. [18] For I say to you that in no way I will drink from the produce of the vine until the kingdom of God has come. [19] And taking a loaf, having given thanks, He broke, and gave to them, saying, This is My body being given for you; for this do (in) remembrance of Me. [20] In the same way also the cup after having supped, saying, This cup (is) the new covenant in My blood, which is poured out for you. [21] But, behold, the hand of him delivering Me up (is) with Me on the table; [22] and indeed the Son of Man goes according as it has been determined, but woe to that man by whom He is delivered up! [23] And they began to ask among themselves this, who then it might be of them who was about to do this.

[24] And there was also a dispute among them, this, which of them is thought to be (the) greater. [25] And He said to them, The kings of the nations rule over them, and those exercising authority over them are called

---

ὑμῶν εἰς τὴν πόλιν, συναντήσει ὑμῖν ἄνθρωπος κεράμιον
you into the city, will meet you a man a pitcher

**11** ὕδατος βαστάζων· ἀκολουθήσατε αὐτῷ εἰς τὴν οἰκίαν οὗ
of water carrying. Follow him into the house where

εἰσπορεύεται. καὶ ἐρεῖτε τῷ οἰκοδεσπότῃ τῆς οἰκίας, Λέγει
he goes in.          And you will say to the house-master of the house, Says

**12** σοι ὁ διδάσκαλος, Ποῦ ἐστι τὸ κατάλυμα, ὅπου τὸ πάσχα
to you the Teacher, Where is the guest room where the passover

μετὰ τῶν μαθητῶν μου φάγω ; κἀκεῖνος ὑμῖν δείξει ἀνώγεον
with the disciples of Me I may eat? And that one you will show an upper room

**13** μέγα ἐστρωμένον· ἐκεῖ ἑτοιμάσατε. ἀπελθόντες δὲ εὗρον
large having been spread; there prepare.        going      And they found

καθὼς εἴρηκεν αὐτοῖς· καὶ ἡτοίμασαν τὸ πάσχα.
as     He had told them,    and they prepared the passover.

**14** Καὶ ὅτε ἐγένετο ἡ ὥρα, ἀνέπεσε, καὶ οἱ δώδεκα ἀπόστολοι
And when came the hour, He reclined, and the twelve apostles

**15** σὺν αὐτῷ. καὶ εἶπε πρὸς αὐτούς, Ἐπιθυμίᾳ ἐπεθύμησα τοῦτο
with Him. And He said to them, With desire I desired this

**16** τὸ πάσχα φαγεῖν μεθ' ὑμῶν πρὸ τοῦ με παθεῖν· λέγω γὰρ
– passover to eat with you, before the Me to suffer. I say For

ὑμῖν ὅτι οὐκέτι οὐ μὴ φάγω ἐξ αὐτοῦ, ἕως ὅτου πληρωθῇ ἐν
to you that never in any way I eat of it, until when it is fulfilled in

**17** τῇ βασιλείᾳ τοῦ Θεοῦ. καὶ δεξάμενος ποτήριον, εὐχαριστή-
the kingdom – of God. And taking a cup, having given thanks,

**18** σας εἶπε, Λάβετε τοῦτο, καὶ διαμερίσατε ἑαυτοῖς· λέγω γὰρ
He said, Take this, and divide among yourselves. I say For

ὑμῖν ὅτι οὐ μὴ πίω ἀπὸ τοῦ γεννήματος τῆς ἀμπέλου, ἕως
to you that in no way I drink from the produce of the vine until

**19** ὅτου ἡ βασιλεία τοῦ Θεοῦ ἔλθη. καὶ λαβὼν ἄρτον, εὐχαριστή-
when the kingdom – of God comes. And taking a loaf, having given

σας ἔκλασε, καὶ ἔδωκεν αὐτοῖς, λέγων, Τοῦτό ἐστι τὸ σῶμά
thanks, He broke, and gave to them, saying, This is the body

μου, τὸ ὑπὲρ ὑμῶν διδόμενον· τοῦτο ποιεῖτε εἰς τὴν ἐμὴν
of Me, – for you being given; this do for – My

**20** ἀνάμνησιν. ὡσαύτως καὶ τὸ ποτήριον μετὰ τὸ δειπνῆσαι,
remembrance. in like manner And the cup after having supped,

λέγων, Τοῦτο τὸ ποτήριον ἡ καινὴ διαθήκη ἐν τῷ αἵματί
saying, This – cup (is) the new covenant in the blood

**21** μου, τὸ ὑπὲρ ὑμῶν ἐκχυνόμενον πλὴν ἰδού, ἡ χεὶρ τοῦ
of Me, – for you being poured out. But, behold, the hand of the

**22** παραδιδόντος με μετ' ἐμοῦ ἐπὶ τῆς τραπέζης. καὶ ὁ μὲν υἱὸς
betrayer of Me with Me on the table. And, indeed the Son

τοῦ ἀνθρώπου πορεύεται κατὰ τὸ ὡρισμένον· πλὴν οὐαὶ τῷ
– of man goes, according as was determined, but woe

**23** ἀνθρώπῳ ἐκείνῳ δι' οὗ παραδίδοται. καὶ αὐτοὶ ἤρξαντο
man to that through whom He is betrayed! And they began

συζητεῖν πρὸς ἑαυτοὺς τὸ τίς ἄρα εἴη ἐξ αὐτῶν ὁ τοῦτο
to argue with themselves – who then it may be of them, he this

μέλλων πράσσειν.
being about to do.

**24** Ἐγένετο δὲ καὶ φιλονεικία ἐν αὐτοῖς τὸ τίς αὐτῶν δοκεῖ
there was And also a dispute among them, – who of them seems

**25** εἶναι μείζων. ὁ δὲ εἶπεν αὐτοῖς, Οἱ βασιλεῖς τῶν ἐθνῶν
to be greater. He And said to them, The kings of the nations

κυριεύουσιν αὐτῶν, καὶ οἱ ἐξουσιάζοντες αὐτῶν εὐεργέται
lord it over them, and the authorities over them benefactors

benefactors. [26] But you shall not be this way; but the greater among you, let him be as the younger, and he who leads as he that serves. [27] For which (is) greater, he that reclines, or he that serves? (Is it) not he that reclines? But I am in your midst as he that serves. [28] But you are they who have continued with Me in My temptations. [29] And I appoint to you as My Father appointed to Me, a kingdom, [30] that you may eat and drink at My table in My kingdom, and you will sit on thrones judging the twelve tribes of Israel.

[31] And the Lord said, Simon, Simon, lo, Satan demanded to have you, for the sifting (of you) as wheat; [32] but I prayed for you, that your faith may not fail; and when you have turned again, confirm your brothers. [33] And he said to Him, Lord, I am ready to go both to prison and to death with You. [34] And He said, I tell you, Peter, (the) cock shall not crow today before you will deny knowing Me three times.

[35] And He said to them, When I sent you without purse and bag and sandals, did you lack anything? And they said, Nothing. [36] Then He said to them, However, now, he who has a purse, let him take (it), in the same way also bag; and he who has not (one) let him sell his coat and buy a sword; [37] for I say to you that this that has been written must yet be accomplished in Me, "And He was numbered with (the) lawless;" for the things concerning Me have an end also. [38] And they said, Lord, behold, here (are) two swords. And He said to them, It is enough.

[39] And going out He went according to custom to the Mount of Olives, and His disciples also followed Him. [40] and having arrived at the place He said to them, Pray not

---

26 καλοῦνται. ὑμεῖς δὲ οὐχ οὕτως· ἀλλ' ὁ μείζων ἐν ὑμῖν
are called.     you But not     so,     but     the     greater among you
γενέσθω ὡς ὁ νεώτερος· καὶ ὁ ἡγούμενος ὡς ὁ διακονῶν. τίς
let him be as the lesser,     and he governing     as he     serving. who

27 γὰρ μείζων, ὁ ἀνακείμενος ἢ ὁ διακονῶν; οὐχὶ ὁ ἀνακεί-
For (is)greater, he reclining     or he     serving? (Is it) not he reclining?

28 μενος; ἐγὼ δέ εἰμι ἐν μέσῳ ὑμῶν ὡς ὁ διακονῶν. ὑμεῖς δέ
     I But am in (the) midst of you as (one) serving.     you But
ἐστε οἱ διαμεμενηκότες μετ' ἐμοῦ ἐν τοῖς πειρασμοῖς μου·
are those having continued     with     Me in the     temptation of Me;

29 κἀγὼ διατίθεμαι ὑμῖν, καθὼς διέθετό μοι ὁ πατήρ μου,
and I     appoint     to you ,     as     appointed to Me the Father of Me

30 βασιλείαν, ἵνα ἐσθίητε καὶ πίνητε ἐπὶ τῆς τραπέζης μου
a kingdom,     that you may eat and drink     at     the     table     of Me
ἐν τῇ βασιλείᾳ μου, καὶ καθίσησθε ἐπὶ θρόνων, κρίνοντες
in the     kingdom of Me; and you will sit on     thrones     judging

31 τὰς δώδεκα φυλὰς τοῦ Ἰσραήλ. εἶπε δὲ ὁ Κύριος, Σίμων,
the     twelve     tribes     —     Of Israel. said And the Lord,     Simon,
Σίμων, ἰδού, ὁ Σατανᾶς ἐξῃτήσατο ὑμᾶς, τοῦ σινιάσαι ὡς
Simon, behold, — Satan     asked     for you —     to sift (you) as

32 τὸν σῖτον· ἐγὼ δὲ ἐδεήθην περὶ σοῦ, ἵνα μὴ ἐκλείπῃ ἡ πίστις
the wheat; I but entreated about you, that not might fail the faith
σου· καὶ σύ ποτε ἐπιστρέψας στήριξον τοὺς ἀδελφούς σου.
of you; and you when having turned confirm     the     brothers of you.

33 ὁ δὲ εἶπεν αὐτῷ, Κύριε, μετὰ σοῦ ἕτοιμός εἰμι καὶ εἰς φυλακὴν
he And said to him, Lord, with You prepared I am both to prison

34 καὶ εἰς θάνατον πορεύεσθαι. ὁ δὲ εἶπε, Λέγω σοι, Πέτρε, οὐ
and to death     to go.     He But said, I say to you, Peter, not
μὴ φωνήσει σήμερον ἀλέκτωρ, πρὶν ἢ τρὶς ἀπαρνήσῃ μὴ
     will sound     today     a cock     before     thrice you will deny     —
εἰδέναι με.
knowing Me.

35 Καὶ εἶπεν αὐτοῖς, Ὅτε ἀπέστειλα ὑμᾶς ἄτερ βαλαντίου καὶ
     And He said to them, When I sent     you     without a purse     and
πήρας καὶ ὑποδημάτων, μή τινος ὑστερήσατε; οἱ δὲ εἶπον,
a wallet and     sandals,     not anything you lacked? they And said,

36 Οὐδενός. εἶπεν οὖν αὐτοῖς, Ἀλλὰ νῦν ὁ ἔχων βαλάντιον
Nothing.     He said Then to them,     But now he having     a purse,
ἀράτω, ὁμοίως καὶ πήραν· καὶ ὁ μὴ ἔχων, πωλησάτω τὸ
let him take; likewise also a wallet; and he not having, let him sell     the

37 ἱμάτιον αὐτοῦ, καὶ ἀγορασάτω μάχαιραν. λέγω γὰρ ὑμῖν
garment of him     and     let him buy     a sword.     I say For to you
ὅτι ἔτι τοῦτο τὸ γεγραμμένον δεῖ τελεσθῆναι ἐν ἐμοί, τὸ Καὶ
that yet this that has been written must be completed in Me: — And
μετὰ ἀνόμων ἐλογίσθη· καὶ γὰρ τὰ περὶ ἐμοῦ τέλος ἔχει. οἱ
with (the) lawless He was counted; also for that about Me an end has. they

38 δὲ εἶπον, Κύριε, ἰδού, μάχαιραι ὧδε δύο. ὁ δὲ εἶπεν αὐτοῖς,
And said, Lord, behold,     swords here (are) two. He And said to them,
Ἱκανόν ἐστι.
Enough it is.

39 Καὶ ἐξελθὼν ἐπορεύθη κατὰ τὸ ἔθος εἰς τὸ ὄρος τῶν
     And going forth He went according to the custom to the mount of the
ἐλαιῶν· ἠκολούθησαν δὲ αὐτῷ καὶ οἱ μαθηταὶ αὐτοῦ. γενό-
olives;     followed     and Him also the disciples of Him.

40 μενος δὲ ἐπὶ τοῦ τόπου, εἶπεν αὐτοῖς, Προσεύχεσθε μὴ εἰσελ-
coming And on the place, He said to them,     Pray you (will) not enter

to enter into temptation. [41] And He was withdrawn from them, about a stone's throw, and falling on (His) knees He prayed, [42] saying, Father, if You are willing, remove this cup from Me; but not My will be done, but Yours. [43] And an angel from Heaven appeared to Him, strengthening Him. [44] And being in agony, He prayed more intently. And His sweat became as great drops of blood falling down to the earth. [45] And having risen up from prayer, coming to the disciples, He found them sleeping from grief. [46] And He said to them, Why do you sleep? Having risen up pray, that you may not enter into temptation.

[47] And as He was yet speaking, behold a crowd! And he who was called Judas, one of the twelve, was going before them, and drew near to Jesus to kiss Him. [48] But Jesus said to him, Judas, do you deliver up the Son of man with a kiss? [49] And those around Him seeing what was about to happen said to Him, Lord, shall we strike with (the) sword? [50] And a certain one of them struck the slave of the high priest, and took off his right ear. [51] And answering Jesus said, Allow (it) this far. And having touched the ear of him, He healed him. [52] And Jesus said to those who had come against Him, chief priests and captains of the Temple and elders, Have you come out with swords and staves as against a robber? [53] When I was with you daily in the Temple, you did not stretch out your hands against Me; but this is your hour, and the power of darkness.

[54] And having seized Him, they led away and led Him into the house of the high priest. And Peter was following at a distance. [55] And having kindled a fire in (the) midst of the court, and they having sat

**41** θεῖν εἰς πειρασμόν. καὶ αὐτὸς ἀπεσπάσθη ἀπ' αὐτῶν ὡσεὶ
into temptation. And He was withdrawn from them, about

**42** λίθου βολήν, καὶ θεὶς τὰ γόνατα προσηύχετο, λέγων, Πάτερ,
a stone's throw. And placing the knees, He prayed, saying, Father,

εἰ βούλει, παρένεγκε τὸ ποτήριον τοῦτο ἀπ' ἐμοῦ· πλὴν μὴ
if You will, take away — cup this from Me; but not

**43** τὸ θέλημά μου, ἀλλὰ τὸ σὸν γενέσθω. ὤφθη δὲ αὐτῷ ἄγγελος
the will of Me, but — of you let be. appeared And to Him an angel

**44** ἀπ' οὐρανοῦ ἐνισχύων αὐτόν. καὶ γενόμενος ἐν ἀγωνίᾳ,
from Heaven strengthening Him. And becoming in an agony,

ἐκτενέστερον προσηύχετο. ἐγένετο δὲ ὁ ἱδρὼς αὐτοῦ ὡσεὶ
more instantly He prayed. became And the sweat of Him as

**45** θρόμβοι αἵματος καταβαίνοντες ἐπὶ τὴν γῆν. καὶ ἀναστὰς
drops of blood falling down onto the earth. And rising up

ἀπὸ τῆς προσευχῆς, ἐλθὼν πρὸς τοὺς μαθητὰς αὐτοῦ,
from the prayer, coming to the disciples of Him,

**46** εὗρεν αὐτοὺς κοιμωμένους ἀπὸ τῆς λύπης, καὶ εἶπεν αὐτοῖς,
He found them sleeping from the grief, and said to them,

Τί καθεύδετε ; ἀναστάντες προσεύχεσθε, ἵνα μὴ εἰσέλθητε
Why do you sleep? Having arisen, pray, lest you enter

εἰς πειρασμόν.
into temptation.

**47** Ἔτι δὲ αὐτοῦ λαλοῦντος, ἰδού, ὄχλος, καὶ ὁ λεγόμενος
yet And Him speaking, behold, a crowd. And the (one) called

Ἰούδας, εἷς τῶν δώδεκα, προήρχετο αὐτῶν. καὶ ἤγγισε τῷ
Judas, one of the twelve, came before them, and drew near to

**48** Ἰησοῦ φιλῆσαι αὐτόν. ὁ δὲ Ἰησοῦς εἶπεν αὐτῷ, Ἰούδα,
Jesus in order to kiss Him. — But Jesus said to him, Judas,

**49** φιλήματι τὸν υἱὸν τοῦ ἀνθρώπου παραδίδως ; ἰδόντες δὲ οἱ
with a kiss the Son — of man do you betray? seeing And those

περὶ αὐτὸν τὸ ἐσόμενον εἶπον αὐτῷ, Κύριε, εἰ πατάξομεν ἐν
around him that about to occur said to Him, Lord, if we shall strike with

**50** μαχαίρᾳ ; καὶ ἐπάταξεν εἷς τις ἐξ αὐτῶν τὸν δοῦλον τοῦ
a sword? And struck a certain one of them of the slave of the

**51** ἀρχιερέως, καὶ ἀφεῖλεν αὐτοῦ τὸ οὖς τὸ δεξιόν. ἀποκριθεὶς
high priest, and cut off of him the ear, the right. answering

δὲ ὁ Ἰησοῦς εἶπεν, Ἐᾶτε ἕως τούτου. καὶ ἁψάμενος τοῦ
And Jesus said, Allow (it) until this. And touching the

**52** ὠτίου αὐτοῦ, ἰάσατο αὐτόν. εἶπε δὲ ὁ Ἰησοῦς πρὸς τοὺς
ear of him, He cured him. said And — Jesus to those

παραγενομένους ἐπ' αὐτὸν ἀρχιερεῖς καὶ στρατηγοὺς τοῦ
coming upon Him, chief priests, and captains of the

ἱεροῦ καὶ πρεσβυτέρους, Ὡς ἐπὶ λῃστὴν ἐξεληλύθατε μετὰ
Temple, and elders: As against a robber did you come out with

**53** μαχαιρῶν καὶ ξύλων : καθ' ἡμέραν ὄντος μου μεθ' ὑμῶν
swords and clubs? Day by day being Me with you

ἐν τῷ ἱερῷ, οὐκ ἐξετείνατε τὰς χεῖρας ἐπ' ἐμέ. ἀλλ' αὕτη
in the Temple, not you stretched the hand on Me. But this

ὑμῶν ἐστιν ἡ ὥρα, καὶ ἡ ἐξουσία τοῦ σκότους.
your is — hour, and the authority of the darkness.

**54** Συλλαβόντες δὲ αὐτὸν ἤγαγον, καὶ εἰσήγαγον αὐτὸν
having seized And Him, they led away, and brought Him

εἰς τὸν οἶκον τοῦ ἀρχιερέως. ὁ δὲ Πέτρος ἠκολούθει μακρόθεν.
into the house of the high priest.—And Peter followed afar off.

**55** ἁψάντων δὲ πῦρ ἐν μέσῳ τῆς αὐλῆς, καὶ συγκαθισάντων
lighting And a fire in (the) midst of the court, and sitting down

down together, Peter sat in their midst. [56] And a certain maidservant seeing him sitting near the light, and looking intently at him, said, And this one was with him. [57] But he denied Him, saying, Woman, I do not know Him. [58] And after a while, another seeing him said, And you are of them. But Peter said, Man, I am not. [59] And intervening about an hour. a certain other boldly charged, saying, Truly this one also was with Him; for he is also a Galilean. [60] And Peter said, Man, I do not know what you say. And immediately, as he was yet speaking, the cock crowed. [61] And having turned, the Lord looked at Peter; and Peter remembered the word of the Lord, how He said to him, Before cock crow you will deny Me three times. [62] And Peter having gone outside wept bitterly.

[63] And the men who were holding Jesus mocked Him, beating (Him) [64] And blindfolding Him, they were striking His face, and questioned Him, saying, Prophesy, who is he stinging you? [65] And many other things, blaspheming, they said to Him.

[66] And when it became day the elderhood of the people were gathered together, both chief priests and scribes, and they led Him into their sanhedrin, saying, [67] If you are the Christ, tell us. And He said to them, If I should tell you, you would not at all believe; [68] and also if I should ask, you would not at all answer Me, nor let (Me) go. [69] From now on the Son of man shall be sitting at the right hand of the power of God. [70] And they all said, Then are you the Son of God? And He said, You say (it), because I AM! [71] And they said, Why do we still have need of witness? For we ourselves heard (it) from His mouth.

**56** χὐτῶν, ἐκάθητο ὁ Πέτρος ἐν μέσῳ αὐτῶν. ἰδοῦσα δὲ αὐτὸν
they,　sat　—　Peter　in (the) midst of them. seeing And　him
παιδίσκη τις καθημένον πρὸς τὸ φῶς, καὶ ἀτενίσασα αὐτῷ,
maidservant a certain sitting　near the light, and looking intently at him,

**57** εἶπε, Καὶ οὗτος σὺν αὐτῷ ἦν. ὁ δὲ ἠρνήσατο αὐτόν, λέγων,
said, And this one with him was. he But denied　Him, saying,

**58** Γύναι, οὐκ οἶδα αὐτόν. καὶ μετὰ βραχὺ ἕτερος ἰδὼν αὐτὸν
Woman, not I know Him. And after a while another seeing him
ἔφη, Καὶ σὺ ἐξ αὐτῶν εἶ. ὁ δὲ Πέτρος εἶπεν, Ἄνθρωπε, οὐκ
said, And you of them are. — But Peter said, Man, not

**59** εἰμί. καὶ διαστάσης ωσεὶ ὥρας μιᾶς, ἄλλος τις διϊσχυρίζετο,
I am. And intervening about hour one, other a certain boldly charged,
λέγων, Ἐπ' ἀληθείας καὶ οὗτος μετ' αὐτοῦ ἦν· καὶ γὰρ
saying. In truth also this one with him was, also for

**60** Γαλιλαῖός ἐστιν. εἶπε δὲ ὁ Πέτρος, Ἄνθρωπε, οὐκ οἶδα ὃ
a Galilean he is. said And — Peter, Man, not I know what
λέγεις. καὶ παραχρῆμα, ἔτι λαλοῦντος αὐτοῦ, ἐφώνησεν ὁ
you say. And immediately, yet speaking him, sounded the

**61** ἀλέκτωρ. καὶ στραφεὶς ὁ Κύριος ἐνέβλεψε τῷ Πέτρῳ. καὶ
cock. And turning the Lord looked at — Peter. And
ὑπεμνήσθη ὁ Πέτρος τοῦ λόγου τοῦ Κυρίου, ὡς εἶπεν αὐτῷ
remembered — Peter the word of the Lord, as He told him

**62** ὅτι Πρὶν ἀλέκτορα φωνῆσαι, ἀπαρνήσῃ με τρίς. καὶ ἐξελθὼν
Before a cock would sound, you will deny Me thrice. And going
ἔξω ὁ Πέτρος ἔκλαυσε πικρῶς.
outside Peter wept bitterly.

**63** Καὶ οἱ ἄνδρες οἱ συνέχοντες τὸν Ἰησοῦν ἐνέπαιζον αὐτῷ,
And the men — having in charge — Jesus mocked Him,

**64** δέροντες. καὶ περικαλύψαντες αὐτόν, ἔτυπτον αὐτοῦ τὸ
beating (Him) And having blindfolded Him, striking of Him the
πρόσωπον, καὶ ἐπηρώτων αὐτόν, λέγοντες, Προφήτευσον·
face, and questioned Him, saying, Prophesy,

**65** τίς ἐστιν ὁ παίσας σε; καὶ ἕτερα πολλὰ βλασφημοῦντες
who is the (one) stinging you? And other things many, blaspheming,
ἔλεγον εἰς αὐτόν.
they said to Him.

**66** Καὶ ὡς ἐγένετο ἡμέρα, συνήχθη τὸ πρεσβυτέριον τοῦ
And when came day, was assembled the body of elders of the
λαοῦ, ἀρχιερεῖς τε καὶ γραμματεῖς, καὶ ἀνήγαγον αὐτὸν εἰς
people, chief priests and scribes, and led away Him to

**67** τὸ συνέδριον ἑαυτῶν, λέγοντες, Εἰ σὺ εἶ ὁ Χριστός, εἰπὲ
the sanhedrin of themselves, saying, If you are the Christ, tell
ἡμῖν. εἶπε δὲ αὐτοῖς, Ἐὰν ὑμῖν εἴπω, οὐ μὴ πιστεύσητε·
us. He said And to them, If you I tell, in no way will you believe.

**68** ἐὰν δὲ καὶ ἐρωτήσω, οὐ μὴ ἀποκριθῆτέ μοι, ἢ ἀπολύσητε.
if And also I ask, in no way you will answer Me, or let Me go.

**69** ἀπὸ τοῦ νῦν ἔσται ὁ υἱὸς τοῦ ἀνθρώπου καθήμενος ἐκ
From now on will be the Son — of man sitting at

**70** δεξιῶν τῆς δυνάμεως τοῦ Θεοῦ. εἶπον δὲ πάντες, Σὺ οὖν εἶ ὁ
the right of the power — of God. they said And all, You, then, are the
υἱὸς τοῦ Θεοῦ; ὁ δὲ πρὸς αὐτοὺς ἔφη, Ὑμεῖς λέγετε ὅτι ἐγώ
Son — of God? He And to them said, You say (it), because I

**71** εἰμι. οἱ δὲ εἶπον, Τί ἔτι χρείαν ἔχομεν μαρτυρίας; αὐτοὶ γὰρ
am. they And said, Why yet have we need of witness? ourselves For
ἠκούσαμεν ἀπὸ τοῦ στόματος αὐτοῦ.
we heard from the mouth of Him.

# CHAPTER 23

CHAPTER 23

[1] And all the multitude of them having risen up led Him to Pilate. [2] And they began to accuse Him, saying, We found this one perverting the nation, and forbidding to give tribute to Caesar, claiming himself to be a king, Christ. [3] And Pilate questioned Him, saying, Are you the king of the Jews? And answering him He said, You say. [4] And Pilate said to the chief priests and the crowd, I find no fault in this man. [5] And they were insisting, saying, He stirs up the people, teaching throughout the whole of Judea, beginning from Galilee to here. [6] But Pilate having heard Galilee asked if the man was a Galilean; [7] and having known that He is from the jurisdiction of Herod, he sent Him up to Herod, he also being at Jerusalem in those days. [8] And seeing Jesus Herod rejoiced greatly, for He was wishing to see Him for long, because of hearing many things about Him; and he was hoping to see some miracle done by Him. [9] And he questioned Him in many words, but He answered him nothing. [10] And the chief priests and the scribes had stood violently accusing Him. [11] And Herod having humiliated Him with his troops, and having mocked (Him), having put luxurious clothing on Him, he sent Him back to Pilate. [12] And on that same day both Pilate and Herod became friends with one another, for before they were at enmity between themselves.

[13] And having called together the chief priests and the rulers and the people, [14] Pilate said to them, You brought this man to me as turning away the people; and, behold,

1 Καὶ ἀναστὰν ἅπαν τὸ πλῆθος αὐτῶν, ἤγαγεν αὐτὸν ἐπὶ
And rising up all the multitude of them led him before

2 τὸν Πιλᾶτον. ἤρξαντο δὲ κατηγορεῖν αὐτοῦ, λέγοντες,
— Pilate. they began And to accuse Him, saying,

Τοῦτον εὕρομεν διαστρέφοντα τὸ ἔθνος, καὶ κωλύοντα Καί-
This one we found perverting the nation, and forbidding to

σαρι φόρους διδόναι, λέγοντα ἑαυτὸν Χριστὸν βασιλέα εἶναι.
Caesar tribute to give, saying himself Christ a king to be.

3 ὁ δὲ Πιλᾶτος ἐπηρώτησεν αὐτόν, λέγων, Σὺ εἶ ὁ βασιλεὺς
—And Pilate questioned Him, saying, you Are the king

4 τῶν Ἰουδαίων; ὁ δὲ ἀποκριθεὶς αὐτῷ ἔφη, Σὺ λέγεις. ὁ δὲ
of the Jews? He And answering him said, You say (it). —And

Πιλᾶτος εἶπε πρὸς τοὺς ἀρχιερεῖς καὶ τοὺς ὄχλους, Οὐδὲν
Pilate said to the chief priests and the crowds Nothing

5 εὑρίσκω αἴτιον ἐν τῷ ἀνθρώπῳ τούτῳ. οἱ δὲ ἐπίσχυον
I find blameable in — man this. they But insisted,

λέγοντες ὅτι Ἀνασείει τὸν λαόν, διδάσκων καθ' ὅλης τῆς
saying, — He stirs up the people, teaching throughout all —

6 Ἰουδαίας, ἀρξάμενος ἀπὸ τῆς Γαλιλαίας ἕως ὧδε. Πιλᾶτος δὲ
Judea, beginning from Galilee to here. Pilate And

ἀκούσας Γαλιλαίαν ἐπηρώτησεν εἰ ὁ ἄνθρωπος Γαλιλαῖός
hearing Galilee, (he) asked if the man a Galilean

7 ἐστι. καὶ ἐπιγνοὺς ὅτι ἐκ τῆς ἐξουσίας Ἡρώδου ἐστίν, ἀνέ-
is. And having known that from the jurisdiction of Herod He is, he

πεμψεν αὐτὸν πρὸς Ἡρώδην, ὄντα καὶ αὐτὸν ἐν Ἱεροσολύ-
sent up Him to Herod, being also him in Jerusalem

μοις ἐν ταύταις ταῖς ἡμέραις.
in these — days.

8 Ὁ δὲ Ἡρώδης ἰδὼν τὸν Ἰησοῦν ἐχάρη λίαν· ἦν γὰρ
— And Herod seeing — Jesus rejoiced greatly; he was for

θέλων ἐξ ἱκανοῦ ἰδεῖν αὐτόν, διὰ τὸ ἀκουειν πολλὰ περὶ
wishing of a long (time) to see Him, because of hearing many things about

αὐτοῦ· καὶ ἤλπιζέ τι σημεῖον ἰδεῖν ὑπ' αὐτοῦ γινόμενον.
Him. And he hoped some sign to see by Him brought about.

9 ἐπηρώτα δὲ αὐτὸν ἐν λόγοις ἱκανοῖς· αὐτὸς δὲ οὐδὲν ἀπεκρί-
questioned And Him in words many. He But nothing

10 νατο αὐτῷ. εἱστήκεισαν δὲ οἱ ἀρχιερεῖς καὶ οἱ γραμματεῖς,
answered him. stood And the chief priests and the scribes

εὐτόνως κατηγοροῦντες αὐτοῦ. ἐξουθενήσας δὲ αὐτὸν ὁ
vehemently accusing Him. having humiliated And Him, —

11 Ἡρώδης σὺν τοῖς στρατεύμασιν αὐτοῦ, καὶ ἐμπαίξας,
Herod with the soldiery of him, and mocking

περιβαλὼν αὐτὸν ἐσθῆτα λαμπράν, ἀνέπεμψεν αὐτὸν τῷ
putting around Him clothing luxurious, sent back Him —

12 Πιλάτῳ. ἐγένοντο δὲ φίλοι ὅ τε Πιλᾶτος καὶ ὁ Ἡρώδης ἐν
to Pilate. became And friends — both Pilate and — Herod on

αὐτῇ τῇ ἡμέρᾳ μετ' ἀλλήλων· προϋπῆρχον γὰρ ἐν ἔχθρᾳ
same the day with each other; they before for in enmity

ὄντες πρὸς ἑαυτούς.
being with themselves.

13 Πιλᾶτος δὲ συγκαλεσάμενος τοὺς ἀρχιερεῖς καὶ τοὺς ἄρχον-
Pilate And calling together the chief priests and the leaders

14 τας καὶ τὸν λαόν, εἶπε πρὸς αὐτούς, Προσηνέγκατέ μοι τὸν
and the people, said to them, You brought to me —

ἄνθρωπον τοῦτον, ὡς ἀποστρέφοντα τὸν λαόν· καὶ ἰδού,
man this, as perverting the people, and behold,

having examined (Him) before you I found no fault in this man (regarding that) which you charge against Him; [15] nor even Herod, for I sent you up to him, and lo, nothing worthy of death is done by Him. [16] Therefore having beat Him, I will release (Him). [17] Now he had need to release to them one at (the) feast. [18] But they cried out in concert, saying, Away with this one, and release to us Barabbas — [19] who was thrown into prison due to some revolt occurring in the city, and murder. [20] Then again Pilate called near, desiring to free Jesus. [21] But they shouted, saying, Crucify! Crucify him! [22] And he a third (time) said to them, For what evil did this one? I found no cause of death in him. Having chastised him, then, I will release (him). [23] But with loud voices, they insisted, asking for Him to be crucified. And their voices and of the chief priests prevailed. [24] And Pilate adjudged their request to be done. [25] And he released to them (him) thrown into prison due to revolt and murder, whom they asked. But He delivered Jesus to their will.

[26] And as they led Him away, having laid hold on Simon, a certain Cyrenian coming from a field, they put on him the cross, to bear (it) behind Jesus. [27] And a great multitude of the people and of women were following Him, who also were bewailing and lamenting Him. [28] And turning to them Jesus said, Daughters of Jerusalem, do not weep over Me, but weep over yourselves and over your children; [29] for behold, days will come in which they will say, Blessed the barren, and the wombs which did not bear, and breasts which did not suckle. [30] Then they shall begin to say to the mountains, Fall on us; and

ἐγὼ ἐνώπιον ὑμῶν ἀνακρίνας οὐδὲν εὗρον ἐν τῷ ἀνθρώπῳ
I       before    you   examining  nothing  found   in  —    man

15 τούτῳ αἴτιον ὧν κατηγορεῖτε κατ' αὐτοῦ· ἀλλ' οὐδὲ
this blameable of which you bring charge against him.   But  neither

Ἡρώδης· ἀνέπεμψα γὰρ ὑμᾶς πρὸς αὐτόν, καὶ ἰδού, οὐδὲν
Herod;    I sent up   for   you    to     him,   and, behold, nothing

16 ἄξιον θανάτου ἐστὶ πεπραγμένον αὐτῷ. παιδεύσας οὖν
worthy of death  is     done      by him. Having chastised, then,

17 αὐτὸν ἀπολύσω. ἀνάγκην δὲ εἶχεν ἀπολύειν αὐτοῖς κατὰ
him  I will release.  need   And he had  to release  to them   at

18 ἑορτὴν ἕνα. ἀνέκραξαν δὲ παμπληθεί, λέγοντες, Αἶρε τοῦτον,
(the) feast one. they shouted And, all enmass, saying,  Take this one,

ἀπόλυσον δὲ ἡμῖν τὸν Βαραββᾶν· ὅστις ἦν διὰ στάσιν τινὰ
release     and to us  —   Barabbas;   who  was due to revolt some

19 γενομένην ἐν τῇ πόλει καὶ φόνον βεβλημένος εἰς φυλακήν.
occurring   in  the  city, and murder,  thrown     into  prison.

20 πάλιν οὖν ὁ Πιλᾶτος προσεφώνησε, θέλων ἀπολῦσαι τὸν
again Then — Pilate    called (to them), desiring to release   —

21 Ἰησοῦν. οἱ δὲ ἐπεφώνουν, λέγοντες, Σταύρωσον, σταύρωσον
Jesus.   they But shouted,   saying,    Crucify!       Crucify

22 αὐτόν. ὁ δὲ τρίτον εἶπε πρὸς αὐτούς, Τί γὰρ κακὸν ἐποίησεν
him!  he But a third said  to   them, what For  evil     did

οὗτος; οὐδὲν αἴτιον θανάτου εὗρον ἐν αὐτῷ· παιδεύσας οὖν
this one? nothing cause of death  I found in  him; having chastised, then,

23 αὐτὸν ἀπολύσω. οἱ δὲ ἐπέκειντο φωναῖς μεγάλαις, αἰτού-
him   I will release. they But insisted   voices   with great,   asking

μενοι αὐτὸν σταυρωθῆναι· καὶ κατίσχυον αἱ φωναὶ αὐτῶν
for      Him   to be crucified.  And  prevailed   the voices of them

24 καὶ τῶν ἀρχιερέων. ὁ δὲ Πιλᾶτος ἐπέκρινε γενέσθαι τὸ αἴτημα
and of the chief priests. And  Pilate    adjudged  to be done the request

25 αὐτῶν ἀπέλυσε δὲ αὐτοῖς τὸν διὰ στάσιν καὶ φόνον βεβλη-
of them. he released And to them (him) due to revolt and murder had been

μένον εἰς τὴν φυλακήν, ὃν ᾐτοῦντο· τὸν δὲ Ἰησοῦν παρέδωκε
thrown into  the  prison,   whom they asked; — but  Jesus    he delivered

τῷ θελήματι αὐτῶν.
to the will      of them.

26 Καὶ ὡς ἀπήγαγον αὐτόν, ἐπιλαβόμενοι Σίμωνός τινος
And as they led away  Him,  having laid hold on  Simon a certain

Κυρηναίου τοῦ ἐρχομένου ἀπ' ἀγροῦ, ἐπέθηκαν αὐτῷ τὸν
a Cyrenian   —    coming   from a field, they put on    him   the

σταυρόν, φέρειν ὄπισθεν τοῦ Ἰησοῦ.
cross,    to bear (it) behind —   Jesus.

27 Ἠκολούθει δὲ αὐτῷ πολὺ πλῆθος τοῦ λαοῦ, καὶ γυναικῶν
were following And Him  a much multitude of the people, and of women

28 αἳ καὶ ἐκόπτοντο καὶ ἐθρήνουν αὐτόν. στραφεὶς δὲ πρὸς
who also were bewailing and lamenting  Him.   turning  And  to

αὐτὰς ὁ Ἰησοῦς εἶπε, Θυγατέρες Ἰερουσαλήμ, μὴ κλαίετε
them —  Jesus    said, Daughters  of Jerusalem,  not do weep

29 ἐπ' ἐμέ, πλὴν ἐφ' ἑαυτὰς κλαίετε καὶ ἐπὶ τὰ τέκνα ὑμῶν. ὅτι
over Me, but  over yourselves weep,  and  over the children of you. For,

ἰδού, ἔρχονται ἡμέραι ἐν αἷς ἐροῦσι, Μακάριαι αἱ στεῖραι,
behold, will come  days  in which they will say, Blessed the barren,

καὶ κοιλίαι αἲ οὐκ ἐγέννησαν, καὶ μαστοὶ οἳ οὐκ ἐθήλασαν.
and the wombs which not did bear,  and  breasts that not did give suck.

30 τότε ἄρξονται λέγειν τοῖς ὄρεσι, Πέσετε ἐφ' ἡμᾶς· καὶ τοῖς
Then they will begin to say to the mountains, Fall  on  us! And to the

to the hills, Cover us. [31] For if they do these things in the green tree, what may take place in the dry?

[32] And two other — criminals — were led with Him to be put to death. [33] And when they came to the place called A Skull, there they crucified Him, and the criminals, the one on (the) right, and one on (the) left. [34] And Jesus said, Father, forgive them, for they do not know what they do. And dividing His garments, they cast a lot. [35] And the people stood watching, and the rulers also were with them, deriding, saying, He saved others, let him save himself if this is the Christ, the chosen of God. [36] And the soldiers also ridiculed Him, coming near and offering to Him vinegar; [37] and saying, If you are the king of the Jews, save yourself. [38] And also an inscription was written over Him, in Greek and Latin and Hebrew letters: THIS IS THE KING OF THE JEWS.

[39] Now one of the criminals who had been hanged blasphemed Him, saying, If you are the Christ, save yourself and us. [40] But the other answering rebuked him, saying, Do you not even fear God, (you) that are under the same judgment? [41] And we indeed justly; for we received a due reward of what we did; but this One did nothing wrong. [42] And he said to Jesus, Remember me, Lord, when You come in Your kingdom. [43] And Jesus said to him, Truly I say to you, Today you shall be with Me in Paradise.

[44] And it was about (the) sixth hour, and darkness came over all the land until (the) ninth hour; [45] and the sun was darkened; and the veil of the Temple was torn in (the) middle. [46] And having cried with a loud

**31** βουνοῖς, Καλύψατε ἡμᾶς. ὅτι εἰ ἐν τῷ ὑγρῷ ξύλῳ ταῦτα
hills,　Cover　us, because If in　the sappy　tree these things
ποιοῦσιν, ἐν τῷ ξηρῷ τί γένηται ;
they do,　in　the dry what may occur?

**32** ῎Ηγοντο δὲ καὶ ἕτεροι δύο κακοῦργοι σὺν αὐτῷ ἀναι-
were led And also　others, two　criminals,　with Him to be
ρεθῆναι.
executed.

**33** Καὶ ὅτε ἀπῆλθον ἐπὶ τὸν τόπον τὸν καλούμενον Κρανίον,
And when they came upon the　place —— being called　Skull,
ἐκεῖ ἐσταύρωσαν αὐτόν, καὶ τοὺς κακούργους, ὃν μὲν ἐκ
there they crucified　Him,　and the　criminals,　one on

**34** δεξιῶν, ὃν δὲ ἐξ ἀριστερῶν. ὁ δὲ ᾿Ιησοῦς ἔλεγε, Πάτερ, ἄφες
(the) right, and one on (the) left.　— And Jesus said,　Father, forgive
αὐτοῖς· οὐ γὰρ οἴδασι τί ποιοῦσι. διαμεριζόμενοι δὲ τὰ
them,　not for they know what they are doing.　dividing　And the

**35** ἱμάτια αὐτοῦ, ἔβαλον κλῆρον. καὶ εἱστήκει ὁ λαὸς θεωρῶν.
garments of Him, they cast　lots.　And stood　the people watching.
ἐξεμυκτήριζον δὲ καὶ οἱ ἄρχοντες σὺν αὐτοῖς, λέγοντες,
scoffed　And also　the　rulers　with　them,　saying,
῎Αλλους ἔσωσε, σωσάτω ἑαυτόν, εἰ οὗτός ἐστιν ὁ Χριστός, ὁ
Others　he saved, let him save himself, if this one is　the Christ, the

**36** τοῦ Θεοῦ ἐκλεκτός. ἐνέπαιζον δὲ αὐτῷ καὶ οἱ στρατιῶται,
of God elect.　mocked And Him also the soldiers,

**37** προσερχόμενοι καὶ ὄξος προσφέροντες αὐτῷ, καὶ λέγοντες,
coming near　and vinegar　offering　to Him, and saying,

**38** Εἰ σὺ εἶ ὁ βασιλεὺς τῶν ᾿Ιουδαίων, σῶσον σεαυτόν. ἦν δὲ καὶ
If you are the king　of the Jews,　save　yourself. was And also
ἐπιγραφὴ γεγραμμένη ἐπ᾿ αὐτῷ γράμμασιν ῾Ελληνικοῖς καὶ
an epigraph　written　over　Him in letters　Greek.　and
῾Ρωμαϊκοῖς καὶ ῾Εβραϊκοῖς, Οὗτός ἐστιν ὁ βασιλεὺς τῶν
Latin　and　Hebrew,　THIS　IS　THE KING OF THE
᾿Ιουδαίων.
JEWS.

**39** Εἷς δὲ τῶν κρεμασθέντων κακούργων ἐβλασφήμει αὐτόν,
one And of the　hanged　criminals　blasphemed　Him,
λέγων, Εἰ σὺ εἶ ὁ Χριστός, σῶσον σεαυτὸν καὶ ἡμᾶς. ἀπο-
saying,　If you are the Christ,　save　yourself and us.

**40** κριθεὶς δὲ ὁ ἕτερος ἐπετίμα αὐτῷ, λέγων, Οὐδὲ φοβῇ σὺ τὸν
answering But the other rebuked　him,　saying, Do not fear you —

**41** Θεόν, ὅτι ἐν τῷ αὐτῷ κρίματι εἶ ; καὶ ἡμεῖς μὲν δικαίως, ἄξια
God, because in the same judgment are? And we indeed justly,　things worthy
γὰρ ὧν ἐπράξαμεν ἀπολαμβάνομεν· οὗτος δὲ οὐδὲν ἄτοπον
for of what we did　we receive.　this One But nothing amiss

**42** ἔπραξε. καὶ ἔλεγε τῷ ᾿Ιησοῦ, Μνήσθητί μου, Κύριε, ὅταν
did.　And he said — to Jesus,　Remember me, Lord,　when

**43** ἔλθῃς ἐν τῇ βασιλείᾳ σου. καὶ εἶπεν αὐτῷ ὁ ᾿Ιησοῦς, ᾿Αμὴν
You come in the kingdom of You. And said to him　Jesus, Truly
λέγω σοι, σήμερον μετ᾿ ἐμοῦ ἔσῃ ἐν τῷ παραδείσῳ.
I say to you, Today　with　Me you will be in　Paradise.

**44** ῏Ην δὲ ὡσεὶ ὥρα ἕκτη, καὶ σκότος ἐγένετο ἐφ᾿ ὅλην τὴν
it was And about hour sixth, and darkness came　over all　the

**45** γῆν ἕως ὥρας ἐννάτης. καὶ ἐσκοτίσθη ὁ ἥλιος, καὶ ἐσχίσθη τὸ
land, until hour　ninth,　and was darkened the sun,　and was torn the

**46** καταπέτασμα τοῦ ναοῦ μέσον. καὶ φωνήσας φωνῇ μεγάλῃ ὁ
veil　of the temple in two. And crying　with a voice great

voice, Jesus said, Father,
into Your hands I will
commit My spirit. And
having said these things, He **47**
breathed forth the spirit.
[47] Now the centurion
having seen that which
took place glorified God,
saying, Indeed this Man **48**
was righteous. [48] And
all the crowd who had
come together to this sight,
seeing the things which
took place, returning **49**
beating their breasts.
[49] And all those known
to Him stood at a dis-
tance, also some women
accompanying Him from
Galilee, watching these
things.                    **50**
    [50] And, behold, a
man named Joseph, being a
councillor, a good and just
man — [51] he had not
assented to the council and **51**
the deed of them — from
Arimathea, a city of the
Jews, and he who was also
himself waiting for the **52**
kingdom of God; [52] he
having gone to Pilate
begged the body of Jesus. **53**
[53] And having taken it
down he wrapped it in a
linen cloth and placed it in
a tomb cut in a rock, in
which no one ever yet had **54**
been laid. [54] And it was
Preparation Day, and **55**
sabbath was coming on.
    [55] And women
having also followed, who
had come with Him out of
Galilee, saw the tomb and **56**
how His body was laid.
[56] And having returned
they prepared spices and
ointments, and on the
sabbath remained quiet,
according to the
commandment.

### CHAPTER 24
    [1] But on the first of
the week at early dawn **1**
they came to the tomb,
bringing spices which they
had prepared, and some **2**
with them. [2] And they
found the stone rolled **3**
away from the tomb;
[3] and having entered, **4**
they did not find the body
of the Lord Jesus. [4] And
it came to pass as they
were perplexed about this,
that behold, two men
stood by them in shining

Ἰησοῦς εἶπε, Πάτερ, εἰς χεῖράς σου παραθήσομαι τὸ πνεῦμά
**Jesus    said    Father, into the hands of You I commit    the spirit**
μου· καὶ ταῦτα εἰπὼν ἐξέπνευσεν. Ἰδὼν δὲ ὁ ἑκατόνταρχος
**of Me. And this    saying, He breathed out seeing And,  the centurion**
**the Spirit**
τὸ γενόμενον ἐδόξασε τὸν Θεόν, λέγων, Ὄντως ὁ ἄνθρωπος
**the thing happening glorified —    God,   saying, Truly —   man**
οὗτος δίκαιος ἦν. καὶ πάντες οἱ συμπαραγενόμενοι ὄχλοι
**this righteous was. And   all    the arriving together    crowd**
ἐπὶ τὴν θεωρίαν ταύτην, θεωροῦντες τὰ γενόμενα, τύπτοντες
**at —  sight   this,   watching the things occurring,   beating**
ἑαυτῶν τὰ στήθη ὑπέστρεφον. εἱστήκεισαν δὲ πάντες οἱ
**of themselves the breasts, returned.    stood   And   all  those**
γνωστοὶ αὐτοῦ μακρόθεν, καὶ γυναῖκες αἱ συνακολουθήσασαι
**known   to Him afar off,  and  women, those accompanying**
αὐτῷ ἀπὸ τῆς Γαλιλαίας, ὁρῶσαι ταῦτα.
**Him from —    Galilee,    seeing these things.**
Καὶ ἰδού, ἀνὴρ ὀνόματι Ἰωσήφ, βουλευτὴς ὑπάρχων
**And behold, a man  by name Joseph, a councillor   being,**
ἀνὴρ ἀγαθὸς καὶ δίκαιος (οὗτος οὐκ ἦν συγκατατεθειμένος
**a man good   and righteous; this one not was  agreeing with**
τῇ βουλῇ καὶ τῇ πράξει αὐτῶν), ἀπὸ Ἀριμαθαίας πόλεως
**the counsel and  the action  of them; from Arimathea  a city**
τῶν Ἰουδαίων, ὃς καὶ προσεδέχετο καὶ αὐτὸς τὴν βασιλείαν
**of the   Jews,  who and was eagerly expecting also himself  kingdom**
τοῦ Θεοῦ· οὗτος προσελθὼν τῷ Πιλάτῳ ᾐτήσατο τὸ σῶμα
**—   of God; this one coming near — to Pilate  asked   the body**
τοῦ Ἰησοῦ. καὶ καθελὼν αὐτὸ ἐνετύλιξεν αὐτὸ σινδόνι, καὶ
**—  of Jesus. And taking down it,  he wrapped  it   in linen,  and**
ἔθηκεν αὐτὸ ἐν μνήματι λαξευτῷ, οὗ οὐκ ἦν οὐδέπω οὐδεὶς
**placed  it  in a tomb  hewn,  where not was no one  not yet**
κείμενος. καὶ ἡμέρα ἦν Παρασκευή, καὶ σάββατον ἐπέφωσκε.
**laid.    And day it was of preparation, and a sabbath was coming on.**
κατακολουθήσασαι δὲ καὶ γυναῖκες, αἵτινες ἦσαν συνεληλυ-
**following    And also  women,   who   were accompanying**
θυῖαι αὐτῷ ἐκ τῆς Γαλιλαίας, ἐθεάσαντο τὸ μνημεῖον, καὶ ὡς
**Him out of  Galilee,   watched  the tomb,   and how**
ἐτέθη τὸ σῶμα αὐτοῦ. ὑποστρέψασαι δὲ ἡτοίμασαν ἀρώ-
**was placed the body of Him.  returning   And prepared**
ματα καὶ μύρα.
**spices and ointment.**

### CHAPTER 24

Καὶ τὸ μὲν σάββατον ἡσύχασαν κατὰ τὴν ἐντολήν. τῇ δὲ
**And (on) the sabbath   they rested according to the command. the But**
μιᾷ τῶν σαββάτων, ὄρθρου βαθέος, ἦλθον ἐπὶ τὸ μνῆμα,
**one of the  week,  while still very early, they came on the tomb,**
φέρουσαι ἃ ἡτοίμασαν ἀρώματα, καί τινες σὺν αὐταῖς. εὗρον
**carrying which they prepared spices,  and some with  them. they found**
δὲ τὸν λίθον ἀποκεκυλισμένον ἀπὸ τοῦ μνημείου. καὶ
**And the   stone having been rolled away from the   tomb.    And**
εἰσελθοῦσαι οὐχ εὗρον τὸ σῶμα τοῦ Κυρίου Ἰησοῦ. καὶ
**going in   not they found the body of the  Lord   Jesus. And**
ἐγένετο ἐν τῷ διαπορεῖσθαι αὐτὰς περὶ τούτου, καὶ ἰδού,
**it was   in  the perplexing  (of) them about  this;  and behold,**
δύο ἄνδρες ἐπέστησαν αὐταῖς ἐν ἐσθήσεσιν ἀστραπτούσαις·
**two  men  stood by  them in clothing    shining.**

garments. [5] And they being filled with fear and bowing the face to the earth, they said to them, Why do you seek the living with the dead? [6] He is not here, but is risen. Remember how He spoke to you, while being in Galilee, [7] saying, The Son of man must be delivered up into the hands of sinful men, and to be crucified, and the third day to arise. [8] And they remembered His words. [9] And having returned from the tomb, they told all these things to the Eleven and to all the rest. [10] Now it was Mary Magdalene and Joanna and Mary of James, and the rest with them, who told these things to the apostles. [11] And their words seemed to them like idle talk, and they did not believe them. [12] But Peter having risen up ran to the tomb, and having stooped down he saw the linen clothes lying alone, and went away home wondering at that which had happened.

[13] And behold, two of them were going on the same day to a village being sixty furlongs off from Jerusalem, whose name (is) Emmaus. [14] And they were talking with one another about all these things which had taken place. [15] And it happened, as they talked and reasoned, that Jesus Himself, having drawn near, went with them; [16] but their eyes were held (so as) not to know Him. [17] And He said to them, What words (are) these which you exchange with one another as you walk, and are sad of face? [18] And the one answering, whose name (was) Cleopas, said to Him, Do you stay alone in Jerusalem, and have not known the things which happened in these days? [19] And He said to them, What things? And they said to Him, The things concerning Jesus the Nazarene, who was a man, a prophet mighty in deed

5 ἐμφόβων δὲ γενομένων αὐτῶν, καὶ κλινουσῶν το πρόσωπον
terrified And becoming them, and bending the faces

εἰς τὴν γῆν, εἶπον πρὸς αὐτάς, Τί ζητεῖτε τὸν ζῶντα μετὰ
to the earth, they said to them, Why seek you the Living One with

6 τῶν νεκρῶν; οὐκ ἔστιν ὧδε, ἀλλ' ἠγέρθη· μνήσθητε ὡς
the dead ones? not He is here, but was raised. Remember how

7 ἐλάλησεν ὑμῖν, ἔτι ὢν ἐν τῇ Γαλιλαίᾳ, λέγων ὅτι δεῖ τὸν υἱὸν
He spoke to you, yet being in — Galilee, saying, that must the Son

τοῦ ἀνθρώπου παραδοθῆναι εἰς χεῖρας ἀνθρώπων ἁμαρτω-
— of man be delivered into (the) hands men of sinful,

λῶν, καὶ σταυρωθῆναι, καὶ τῇ τρίτῃ ἡμέρᾳ ἀναστῆναι.
and to be crucified, and the third day to rise again.

8 καὶ ἐμνήσθησαν τῶν ῥημάτων αὐτοῦ, καὶ ὑποστρέψασαι
And they remembered the words of Him, and returning

9 ἀπὸ τοῦ μνημείου, ἀπήγγειλαν ταῦτα πάντα τοῖς ἔνδεκα
from the tomb reported these things all to the eleven,

10 καὶ πᾶσι τοῖς λοιποῖς. ἦσαν δὲ ἡ Μαγδαληνὴ Μαρία καὶ
and to all the rest. they were And the Magdalene Mary, and

Ἰωάννα καὶ Μαρία Ἰακώβου, καὶ αἱ λοιπαὶ σὺν αὐταῖς, αἳ
Joanna, and Mary of James, and the rest with them, who

11 ἔλεγον πρὸς τοὺς ἀποστόλους ταῦτα. καὶ ἐφάνησαν ἐνώπιον
told to the apostles these things. And seemed before

αὐτῶν ὡσεὶ λῆρος τὰ ῥήματα αὐτῶν, καὶ ἠπίστουν αὐταῖς.
them as folly the words of them, and they disbelieved them.

12 ὁ δὲ Πέτρος ἀναστὰς ἔδραμεν ἐπὶ τὸ μνημεῖον, καὶ παρα-
And Peter having arisen ran to the tomb, and stooping

κύψας βλέπει τὰ ὀθόνια κείμενα μόνα· καὶ ἀπῆλθε πρὸς
down he sees the linen lying alone, and went away to

ἑαυτὸν θαυμάζων τὸ γεγονός.
himself wondering (at what) had happened.

13 Καὶ ἰδού, δύο εξ αὐτῶν ἦσαν πορευόμενοι ἐν αὐτῇ τῇ
And behold, two of them were going on same the

ἡμέρᾳ εἰς κώμην ἀπέχουσαν σταδίους ἑξήκοντα ἀπὸ
day to a village being distant furlongs sixty from

14 Ἰερουσαλήμ, ᾗ ὄνομα Ἐμμαούς. καὶ αὐτοὶ ὡμίλουν πρὸς
Jerusalem, to which name Emmaus; and they talked to

15 ἀλλήλους περὶ πάντων τῶν συμβεβηκότων τούτων. καὶ
each other about all having happened these things. And

ἐγένετο ἐν τῷ ὁμιλεῖν αὐτοὺς καὶ συζητεῖν, καὶ αὐτὸς ὁ
it was, in the talking (of) them and discussing, even Himself,

16 Ἰησοῦς ἐγγίσας συνεπορεύετο αὐτοῖς. οἱ δὲ ὀφθαλμοὶ αὐτῶν
Jesus, coming near traveled with them. the And eyes of them

17 ἐκρατοῦντο τοῦ μὴ ἐπιγνῶναι αὐτόν. εἶπε δὲ πρὸς αὐτούς,
were held — not to recognize Him. He said And to them,

Τίνες οἱ λόγοι οὗτοι οὓς ἀντιβάλλετε πρὸς ἀλλήλους
What — words these which you exchange with each other

18 περιπατοῦντες, καί ἐστε σκυθρωποί; ἀποκριθεὶς δὲ ὁ εἷς, ᾧ
(while) walking, and are downcast? answering And one, whose

ὄνομα Κλεόπας, εἶπε πρὸς αὐτόν, Σὺ μόνος παροικεῖς ἐν
name (was) Cleopas, said to Him, (Are) you only a stranger in

Ἰερουσαλήμ, καὶ οὐκ ἔγνως τὰ γενόμενα ἐν αὐτῇ ἐν ταῖς
Jerusalem, and not know the things occurring in it in —

19 ἡμέραις ταύταις; καὶ εἶπεν αὐτοῖς, Ποῖα; οἱ δὲ εἶπον αὐτῷ,
days these? And He said to them, What? they And said to Him,

Τὰ περὶ Ἰησοῦ τοῦ Ναζωραίου, ὃς ἐγένετο ἀνὴρ προφήτης
The things about Jesus the Nazarene, who was a man, a prophet

and word, before God and all the people; [20] and how the chief priests and our rulers delivered Him up to judgment of death, and crucified Him. [21] But we were hoping it was He who is about to redeem Israel. But then with all these things, this brings today the third day since these things happened. [22] And also certain women from among us astonished us, having been early at the tomb, [23] and not having found His body, came claiming to have seen also a vision of angels, who say He is living. [24] And some of those with us went to the tomb and found (it) so, as also the women said but they did not see Him. [25] And He said to them, O fools and slow of heart to believe all that the prophets spoke! [26] Was it not needful for the Christ to suffer these things, and to enter into His glory? [27] And beginning from Moses and from all the prophets, He interpreted to them in all the Scriptures with things concerning Himself. [28] And they drew near to the village where they were going, and He seemed to be going. [29] And they constrained Him, saying, Stay with us, for it is towards evening, and the day has declined. And He went in to stay with them. [30] And it happened as He reclined with them, having taken the bread, He blessed; and having broken, He gave to them. [31] And their eyes were opened, and they knew Him. And He disappeared from them. [32] And they said to one another, Was not our heart burning in us as He was speaking to us in the highway, and He was opening to us the Scriptures? [33] And rising up that same hour they returned to Jerusalem, and they found the Eleven and those with them gathering together,

---

**20** δυνατὸς ἐν ἔργῳ καὶ λόγῳ ἐναντίον τοῦ Θεοῦ καὶ παντὸς
powerful in work and word before   —   God and all
τοῦ λαοῦ· ὅπως τε παρέδωκαν αὐτὸν οἱ ἀρχιερεῖς καὶ οἱ
the people, how both delivered   Him the chief priests and the
ἄρχοντες ἡμῶν εἰς κρίμα θανάτου, καὶ ἐσταύρωσαν αὐτόν.
rulers   of us to (the) judgment of death, and crucified   Him.

**21** ἡμεῖς δὲ ἠλπίζομεν ὅτι αὐτός ἐστιν ὁ μέλλων λυτροῦσθαι τὸν
we But were hoping that He   is the (One) going to redeem   —
Ἰσραήλ. ἀλλά γε σὺν πᾶσι τούτοις τρίτην ταύτην ἡμέραν
Israel. But   with all these things third this   day

**22** ἄγει σήμερον ἀφ᾽ οὗ ταῦτα ἐγένετο. ἀλλὰ καὶ γυναῖκές τινες
comes today since these things occurred. But also women   some
ἐξ ἡμῶν ἐξέστησαν ἡμᾶς, γενόμεναι ὄρθριαι ἐπὶ τὸ μνημεῖον·
of us astounded us, being   early at the tomb,

**23** καὶ μὴ εὑροῦσαι τὸ σῶμα αὐτοῦ, ἦλθον λέγουσαι καὶ ὀπτα-
and not finding the body of Him, came saying   also a vision

**24** σίαν ἀγγέλων ἑωρακέναι, οἳ λέγουσιν αὐτὸν ζῆν. καὶ ἀπ-
of angels to have seen, who say   Him to live. And
ἦλθόν τινες τῶν σὺν ἡμῖν ἐπὶ τὸ μνημεῖον, καὶ εὗρον οὕτω
went some of those with us to the tomb, and found so

**25** καθὼς καὶ αἱ γυναῖκες εἶπον· αὐτὸν δὲ οὐκ εἶδον. καὶ αὐτὸς
as also the women said; Him but not they saw. And He
εἶπε πρὸς αὐτούς, Ὦ ἀνόητοι καὶ βραδεῖς τῇ καρδίᾳ τοῦ
said to them, O fools and slow   — in heart   —

**26** πιστεύειν ἐπὶ πᾶσιν οἷς ἐλάλησαν οἱ προφῆται· οὐχὶ ταῦτα
to believe on all things which spoke the prophets! Not these things
ἔδει παθεῖν τὸν Χριστόν, καὶ εἰσελθεῖν εἰς τὴν δόξαν αὐτοῦ ;
must suffer the Christ, and to enter into the glory of Him?

**27** καὶ ἀρξάμενος ἀπὸ Μωσέως καὶ ἀπὸ πάντων τῶν προφητῶν,
And beginning from Moses and from all   the prophets,
διηρμήνευεν αὐτοῖς ἐν πάσαις ταῖς γραφαῖς τὰ περὶ ἑαυτοῦ.
He interpreted to them in all   the Scriptures that about Himself.

**28** καὶ ἤγγισαν εἰς τὴν κώμην οὗ ἐπορεύοντο· καὶ αὐτὸς
And they drew near to the village where they were going, and He

**29** προσεποιεῖτο πορρωτέρω πορεύεσθαι. καὶ παρεβιάσαντο
appeared further   to be going. And they constrained
αὐτόν, λέγοντες, Μεῖνον μεθ᾽ ἡμῶν, ὅτι πρὸς ἑσπέραν ἐστί,
Him, saying, Stay with us, because toward evening it is,

**30** καὶ κέκλικεν ἡ ἡμέρα. καὶ εἰσῆλθε τοῦ μεῖναι σὺν αὐτοῖς. καὶ
and has declined the day. And He went in — to stay with them. And
ἐγένετο ἐν τῷ κατακλιθῆναι αὐτὸν μετ᾽ αὐτῶν, λαβὼν τὸν
it was, in the reclining (of) Him with them, taking the

**31** ἄρτον εὐλόγησε, καὶ κλάσας ἐπεδίδου αὐτοῖς. αὐτῶν δὲ
loaf He blessed, and having broken He gave to them. of them And
διηνοίχθησαν οἱ ὀφθαλμοί, καὶ ἐπέγνωσαν αὐτόν· καὶ
was opened the eyes, and they remembered Him. And

**32** αὐτὸς ἄφαντος ἐγένετο ἀπ᾽ αὐτῶν. καὶ εἶπον πρὸς ἀλλή-
He invisible became from them. And they said to each
λους, Οὐχὶ ἡ καρδία ἡμῶν καιομένη ἦν ἐν ἡμῖν, ὡς ἐλάλει
other, Not the heart of us burning was in us as He spoke

**33** ἡμῖν ἐν τῇ ὁδῷ, καὶ ὡς διήνοιγεν ἡμῖν τὰς γραφάς ; καὶ
to us in the way, and as He opened up to us the Scriptures? And
ἀναστάντες αὐτῇ τῇ ὥρᾳ ὑπέστρεψαν εἰς Ἰερουσαλήμ, καὶ
rising up same in the hour they returned to Jerusalem, and
εὗρον συνηθροισμένους τοὺς ἕνδεκα καὶ τοὺς σὺν αὐτοῖς,
found, having been gathered, the eleven and those with them,

[34] saying, The Lord truly is risen and appeared to Simon. [35] And they told the things in the highway, and how He was known to them in the breaking of the bread.

[36] And as they were telling these things, Jesus Himself stood in their midst and said to them, Peace to you. [37] But being terrified and filled with fear, they thought they saw a ghost. [38] And He said to them, Why are you troubled? And why do thoughts come up in your heart; [39] see My hands and My feet, that I am He? Handle Me and see, for a spirit has not flesh and bones, as you see Me having. [40] And having said this, He showed to them (His) hands and feet. [41] But yet while they were not believing for joy, and were wondering, He said to them, Do you have anything edible here? [42] And they gave a part of a broiled fish to Him, and of a honeycomb. [43] And having taken (these), He ate before them. [44] And He said to them, These (are) the words which I spoke to you, yet being with you, that must be fulfilled, all things that have been written in the Law of Moses and the Prophets and the Psalms concerning Me. [45] Then He opened their understanding to understand the Scriptures, [46] and said to them, So it has been written, and so it was necessary that the Christ should suffer and rise from among the dead the third day; [47] and repentance and remission of sins should be preached in His name to all nations, beginning at Jerusalem. [48] And you are witnesses of these things. [49] And behold, I send the promise of My Father on you; but you remain in the city of Jerusalem until you are clothed with power from on high.

[50] And He led them out as far as to Bethany, and having lifted up His

---

**34** λέγοντας ὅτι Ἠγέρθη ὁ Κύριος ὄντως, καὶ ὤφθη Σίμωνι. καὶ
saying, — was raised the Lord really, and appeared to Simon. And

**35** αὐτοὶ ἐξηγοῦντο τὰ ἐν τῇ ὁδῷ, καὶ ὡς ἐγνώσθη αὐτοῖς ἐν
they related the things in the way, and how He was known to them in

τῇ κλάσει τοῦ ἄρτου.
the breaking of the loaf.

**36** Ταῦτα δὲ αὐτῶν λαλούντων, αὐτὸς ὁ Ἰησοῦς ἔστη ἐν
these things And them saying, Himself, — Jesus, stood in

**37** μέσῳ αὐτῶν, καὶ λέγει αὐτοῖς, Εἰρήνη ὑμῖν. πτοηθέντες δὲ
(the) midst of them, and says to them, Peace to you. terrified But

**38** καὶ ἔμφοβοι γενόμενοι ἐδόκουν πνεῦμα θεωρεῖν. καὶ εἶπεν
and filled with fear being, they thought a spirit they beheld. And He said

αὐτοῖς, Τί τεταραγμένοι ἐστέ; καὶ διατί διαλογισμοὶ
to them, Why troubled are you? And why do reasonings

**39** ἀναβαίνουσιν ἐν ταῖς καρδίαις ὑμῶν; ἴδετε τὰς χεῖράς μου
come up in the hearts of you? See the hands of Me

καὶ τοὺς πόδας μου, ὅτι αὐτὸς ἐγώ εἰμι· ψηλαφήσατέ με καὶ
and the feet of Me, that He I am. Feel Me and

ἴδετε, ὅτι πνεῦμα σάρκα καὶ ὀστέα οὐκ ἔχει, καθὼς ἐμὲ
see, because a spirit flesh and bones not has, as Me

**40** θεωρεῖτε ἔχοντα. καὶ τοῦτο εἰπὼν ἐπέδειξεν αὐτοῖς τὰς
you behold having. And this having said, He showed to them the

**41** χεῖρας καὶ τοὺς πόδας. ἔτι δὲ ἀπιστούντων αὐτῶν ἀπὸ τῆς
hands and the feet. yet And disbelieving them, from the

χαρᾶς καὶ θαυμαζόντων, εἶπεν αὐτοῖς, Ἔχετέ τι βρώσιμον
joy and marveling, He said to them, Have you any food

**42** ἐνθάδε, οἱ δὲ ἐπέδωκαν αὐτῷ ἰχθύος ὀπτοῦ μέρος, καὶ ἀπὸ
here? they And handed to Him of a fish broiled part, and from

**43** μελισσίου κηρίου. καὶ λαβὼν ἐνώπιον αὐτῶν ἔφαγεν.
a honey-comb. And taking before them, He ate.

**44** Εἶπε δὲ αὐτοῖς, Οὗτοι οἱ λόγοι, οὓς ἐλάλησα πρὸς ὑμᾶς
He said And to them, These — words which I spoke to you,

ἔτι ὢν σὺν ὑμῖν, ὅτι δεῖ πληρωθῆναι πάντα τὰ γεγραμμένα
yet being with you, that must be fulfilled all the things being written

ἐν τῷ νόμῳ Μωσέως καὶ προφήταις καὶ ψαλμοῖς περὶ ἐμοῦ.
in the law of Moses and (the) prophets and Psalms, about Me.

**45** τότε διήνοιξεν αὐτῶν τὸν νοῦν, τοῦ συνιέναι τὰς γραφάς·
Then He opened up of them the mind — to understand the Scriptures;

**46** καὶ εἶπεν αὐτοῖς ὅτι Οὕτω γέγραπται, καὶ οὕτως ἔδει παθεῖν
and said to them, — Thus it is written, and thus must suffer

τὸν Χριστόν, καὶ ἀναστῆναι ἐκ νεκρῶν τῇ τρίτῃ ἡμέρᾳ, καὶ
the Christ, and to rise from (the) dead the third day, and

**47** κηρυχθῆναι ἐπὶ τῷ ὀνόματι αὐτοῦ μετάνοιαν καὶ ἄφεσιν
to be preached on the name of Him repentance and forgiveness

ἁμαρτιῶν εἰς πάντα τὰ ἔθνη, ἀρξάμενον ἀπὸ Ἰερουσαλήμ.
of sins to all the nations, beginning from Jerusalem.

**48** ὑμεῖς δέ ἐστε μάρτυρες τούτων. καὶ ἰδού, ἐγὼ ἀποστέλλω
**49** You And are witnesses of these things. And behold, I send forth

τὴν ἐπαγγελίαν τοῦ πατρός μου ἐφ’ ὑμᾶς· ὑμεῖς δὲ καθίσατε
the promise of the Father of Me on you. you But sit

ἐν τῇ πόλει Ἰερουσαλήμ, ἕως οὗ ἐνδύσησθε δύναμιν ἐξ
in the city of Jerusalem, until you are clothed wi 'h power from

ὕψους.
on high.

**50** Ἐξήγαγε δὲ αὐτοὺς ἔξω ἕως εἰς Βηθανίαν· καὶ ἐπάρας τὰς
He led And them out until to Bethany, and lifting up the

hands He blessed them.
[51] And it came to pass
as He was blessing them,
He was separated from
them and was carried up
into Heaven. [52] And
they having worshiped Him
returned to Jerusalem with
great joy, [53] and were
continually in the Temple,
praising and blessing God.
Amen.

**51** χεῖρας αὐτοῦ εὐλόγησεν αὐτούς. καὶ ἐγένετο ἐν τῷ εὐλογεῖν
hands of Him, He blessed them. And it was, in the blessing
αὐτὸν αὐτούς, διέστη ἀπ' αὐτῶν, καὶ ἀνεφέρετο εἰς τὸ
(of) Him them, He withdrew from them, and was carried into —
**52** οὐρανόν. καὶ αὐτοὶ προσκυνήσαντες αὐτόν, ὑπέστρεψαν
Heaven. And they having worshiped Him returned
**53** εἰς Ἰερουσαλὴμ μετὰ χαρᾶς μεγάλης· καὶ ἦσαν διὰ παντὸς
to Jerusalem with joy great, and were continually
ἐν τῷ ἱερῷ, αἰνοῦντες καὶ εὐλογοῦντες τὸν Θεόν. Ἀμήν.
in the Temple, praising and blessing — God. Amen.

## CHAPTER 1

[1] In (the) beginning was the Word, and the Word was with God, and the Word was God. [2] He was in the beginning with God. [3] All things through Him came into being, and without Him came into being not even one (thing) that came into being. [4] In Him was life, and the life was the light of men, [5] and the light shines in the darkness, and not did overtake it the darkness.

[6] There was a man sent from God, his name, John. [7] He came for a witness, that he might witness about the light, that all might believe through Him. [8] He was not that light, but that he might witness about the light. [9] He was the true light, He enlightening every man coming into the world. [10] He was in the world, and the world came into being through Him; yet the world did not know Him. [11] He came into (His) own, and (His) own did not receive Him. [12] But as many as received Him, He gave to them authority to become children of God, to those believing into His name; [13] who were born not of bloods, nor of (the) will of (the) flesh, nor of the will of man, but of God (were born).

[14] And the Word became flesh, and tabernacled among us; and we beheld His glory, glory as of an only-begotten from (the) Father, full of grace and of truth. [15] John witnesses about Him, and has cried out, saying, This One was (He) of whom I said, He coming after me has been before me, for He preceded

# ΕΥΑΓΓΕΛΙΟΝ
## GOSPEL
# ΤΟ ΚΑΤΑ ΙΩΑΝΝΗΝ
## THE ACCORDING TO JOHN

## CHAPTER 1

1 Ἐν ἀρχῇ ἦν ὁ λόγος, καὶ ὁ λόγος ἦν πρὸς τὸν Θεόν, καὶ
In (the) beginning was the Word, and the Word was with — God, and

2 Θεὸς ἦν ὁ λόγος. οὗτος ἦν ἐν ἀρχῇ πρὸς τὸν Θεόν. πάντα
3 God was the Word. This One was in beginning with — God. All things

δι᾽ αὐτοῦ ἐγένετο, καὶ χωρὶς αὐτοῦ ἐγένετο οὐδὲ ἕν ὃ γέγονεν.
through Him came into being, and without Him came into not one that came into being even (thing) being.

4 ἐν αὐτῷ ζωὴ ἦν, καὶ ἡ ζωὴ ἦν τὸ φῶς τῶν ἀνθρώπων, καὶ
5 in Him life was, and the life was the light — of men, and

τὸ φῶς ἐν τῇ σκοτίᾳ φαίνει, καὶ ἡ σκοτία αὐτὸ οὐ κατέλαβεν.
the light in the darkness shines, and the darkness it not did overtake.

6 ἐγένετο ἄνθρωπος ἀπεσταλμένος παρὰ Θεοῦ, ὄνομα αὐτῷ
There was a man having been sent from God, (the) name to him,

7 Ἰωάννης. οὗτος ἦλθεν εἰς μαρτυρίαν, ἵνα μαρτυρήσῃ περὶ
John; this one came for a witness, that he might witness about

8 τοῦ φωτός, ἵνα πάντες πιστεύσωσι δι᾽ αὐτοῦ. οὐκ ἦν ἐκεῖνος
the light, that all might believe through him. not He was that

9 τὸ φῶς, ἀλλ᾽ ἵνα μαρτυρήσῃ περὶ τοῦ φωτός. ἦν τὸ φῶς τὸ
— light, but that he might witness about the light. He was the light —

ἀληθινόν, ὃ φωτίζει πάντα ἄνθρωπον ἐρχόμενον εἰς τὸν
true, which enlightens every man coming into the

10 κόσμον. ἐν τῷ κόσμῳ ἦν, καὶ ὁ κόσμος δι᾽ αὐτοῦ ἐγένετο, καὶ
world. In the world He was, and the world through Him became, and

11 ὁ κόσμος αὐτὸν οὐκ ἔγνω. εἰς τὰ ἴδια ἦλθε, καὶ οἱ ἴδιοι αὐτὸν
the world Him did not know. Into (His) own He came, and (His) own Him

12 οὐ παρέλαβον. ὅσοι δὲ ἔλαβον αὐτόν, ἔδωκεν αὐτοῖς ἐξουσίαν
not did receive. as many as But received Him, He gave to them authority

τέκνα Θεοῦ γενέσθαι, τοῖς πιστεύουσιν εἰς τὸ ὄνομα αὐτοῦ·
children of God to become, to those believing into the name of Him,

13 οἳ οὐκ ἐξ αἱμάτων, οὐδὲ ἐκ θελήματος σαρκός, οὐδὲ ἐκ θελή-
who not of bloods, nor of (the) will of (the) flesh, nor of (the)

14 ματος ἀνδρός, ἀλλ᾽ ἐκ Θεοῦ ἐγεννήθησαν. καὶ ὁ λόγος σὰρξ
will of man, but of God were born. And the Word flesh

ἐγένετο, καὶ ἐσκήνωσεν ἐν ἡμῖν (καὶ ἐθεασάμεθα τὴν δόξαν
became, and tabernacled among us, and we beheld the glory

αὐτοῦ, δόξαν ὡς μονογενοῦς παρὰ πατρός), πλήρης χάριτος
of Him, glory as of an only-begotten from (the) Father, full of grace

15 καὶ ἀληθείας. Ἰωάννης μαρτυρεῖ περὶ αὐτοῦ, καὶ κέκραγε
and of truth. John witnesses concerning Him, and has cried out

λέγων, Οὗτος ἦν ὃν εἶπον, Ὁ ὀπίσω μου ἐρχόμενος ἔμπρο-
saying, This One was (He) of whom I said, He after me coming before

16 σθέν μου γέγονεν· ὅτι πρῶτός μου ἦν. καὶ ἐκ τοῦ πληρώματος
me has become, for preceding me He was. And out of the fullness

213

[16] And of His fullness we all received, and grace upon grace. [17] For the Law was given through Moses; the grace and the truth came through Jesus Christ. [18] No one has seen God at any time; the only-begotten Son, who is in the bosom of the Father, He revealed (Him). [19] And this is the witness of John, when the Jews sent priests and Levites from Jerusalem, that they might ask him, Who are you? [20] And he confessed and denied not, and confessed, I am not the Christ. [21] And they asked him, What then? Are you Elijah? And he said, I am not. Are you the Prophet? And he answered, No. [22] They therefore said to him, Who are you, that we may give answer to those who sent us? What do you say about yourself? [23] He said, "I am a voice crying in the wilderness; make straight the way of the Lord," as Isaiah the prophet said. [24] And those who had been sent were from the Pharisees. [25] And they asked him and said to him, Why then do you baptize, if you are not the Christ, nor Elijah, nor the Prophet? [26] John answered them saying, I baptize with water; but (One) stands in your midst whom you do not know; [27] He it is who comes after me, who has the right to go before me, of whom I am not worthy that I should untie the latchet of (His) sandal. [28] These things took place in Bethabara across the Jordan, where John was baptizing.

[29] On the morrow John saw Jesus coming to him and said, Behold, the Lamb of God, who takes away the sins of the world! [30] It is He about whom I said, After me comes a Man who has the right to go before me, because He was before me. [31] And I did not know Him; but that He might be revealed to Israel, therefore I came in the water baptizing

---

**17** αὐτοῦ ἡμεῖς πάντες ἐλάβομεν, καὶ χάριν ἀντὶ χάριτος. ὅτι ὁ
of Him we all received, and grace on top of grace, because the

νόμος διὰ Μωσέως ἐδόθη, ἡ χάρις καὶ ἡ ἀλήθεια διὰ Ἰησοῦ
Law through Moses was given, — grace and — truth through Jesus

**18** Χριστοῦ ἐγένετο. Θεὸν οὐδεὶς ἑώρακε πώποτε· ὁ μονογενὴς
Christ came into being. God no one has seen, at any time; the only-begotten

υἱός, ὁ ὢν εἰς τὸν κόλπον τοῦ πατρός, ἐκεῖνος ἐξηγήσατο.
Son, who is in the bosom of the Father, that One explains (Him).

**19** Καὶ αὕτη ἐστὶν ἡ μαρτυρία τοῦ Ἰωάννου, ὅτε ἀπέστειλαν
And this is the witness — of John, when sent

οἱ Ἰουδαῖοι ἐξ Ἱεροσολύμων ἱερεῖς καὶ Λευΐτας ἵνα ἐρωτή-
the Jews from Jerusalem priests and Levites, that they might

**20** σωσιν αὐτόν, Σὺ τίς εἶ; καὶ ὡμολόγησε, καὶ οὐκ ἠρνήσατο·
ask him, you Who are? And he acknowledged and not denied,

**21** καὶ ὡμολόγησεν ὅτι Οὐκ εἰμὶ ἐγὼ ὁ Χριστός. καὶ ἠρώτησαν
and he acknowledged, not am I the Christ. And they asked

αὐτόν, Τί οὖν; Ἡλίας εἶ σύ; καὶ λέγει, Οὐκ εἰμί. Ὁ προφή-
him, What, then? Elijah you? And he says, not I am. The prophet

**22** της εἶ σύ; καὶ ἀπεκρίθη, Οὔ. εἶπον οὖν αὐτῷ Τίς εἶ; ἵνα
-- are you? And he answered, No. They said then to him Who are you? that

ἀπόκρισιν δῶμεν τοῖς πέμψασιν ἡμᾶς. τί λέγεις περὶ
an answer we may give to those having sent us. What do you say about

**23** σεαυτοῦ; ἔφη, Ἐγὼ φωνὴ βοῶντος ἐν τῇ ἐρήμῳ, Εὐθύνατε
yourself? He said, I (am) a voice crying in the wilderness, Make straight

**24** τὴν ὁδὸν Κυρίου, καθὼς εἶπεν Ἡσαΐας ὁ προφήτης. καὶ οἱ
the way of (the) Lord, as said Isaiah the prophet. And those

**25** ἀπεσταλμένοι ἦσαν ἐκ τῶν Φαρισαίων. καὶ ἠρώτησαν
having been sent were of the Pharisees. And they asked

αὐτον, καὶ εἶπον αὐτῷ, Τί οὖν βαπτίζεις, εἰ σὺ οὐκ εἶ ὁ
him, and said to him, Why then do you baptize, if you not are the

**26** Χριστός, οὔτε Ἡλίας, οὔτε ὁ προφήτης; ἀπεκρίθη αὐτοῖς ὁ
Christ, nor Elijah, nor the prophet? Answered them —

Ἰωάννης λέγων, Ἐγὼ βαπτίζω ἐν ὕδατι· μέσος δὲ ὑμῶν
John, saying, I baptize in water; amidst but you

**27** ἕστηκεν ὃν ὑμεῖς οὐκ οἴδατε. αὐτός ἐστιν ὁ ὀπίσω μου
stands (One) whom you not do know. This One it is who after me

ἐρχόμενος, ὃς ἔμπροσθέν μου γέγονεν· οὗ ἐγὼ οὐκ εἰμὶ ἄξιος
coming, who me before me has become, of whom I not am worthy

**28** ἵνα λύσω αὐτοῦ τὸν ἱμάντα τοῦ ὑποδήματος. ταῦτα ἐν
that I should untie of Him the latchet of the sandal. These things in

Βηθαβαρᾶ ἐγένετο πέραν τοῦ Ἰορδάνου, ὅπου ἦν Ἰωάννης
Bethabara occurred beyond the Jordan, where was John

βαπτίζων.
baptizing.

**29** Τῇ ἐπαύριον βλέπει ὁ Ἰωάννης τὸν Ἰησοῦν ἐρχόμενον
On the morrow sees — John — Jesus coming

πρὸς αὐτόν, καὶ λέγει, Ἴδε ὁ ἀμνὸς τοῦ Θεοῦ, ὁ αἴρων τὴν
toward him, and says, Behold, the Lamb — of God, taking the

**30** ἁμαρτίαν τοῦ κόσμου. οὗτός ἐστι περὶ οὗ ἐγὼ εἶπον,
sin of the world. This is He about whom I said,

Ὀπίσω μου ἔρχεται ἀνὴρ ὃς ἔμπροσθέν μου γέγονεν ὅτι
After me comes a Man who before me has become, for

**31** πρῶτός μου ἦν. κἀγὼ οὐκ ᾔδειν αὐτόν· ἀλλ' ἵνα φανερωθῇ
preceding me He was. And I not did know Him, but that He be revealed

τῷ Ἰσραήλ, διὰ τοῦτο ἦλθον ἐγὼ ἐν τῷ ὕδατι βαπτίζων.
— to Israel, therefore came I in the water baptizing.

[32] And John bore witness saying, I have seen the Spirit descending as a dove out of Heaven, and it abode on Him. [33] And I did not know Him; but He who sent me to baptize with water, He said to me, Upon whom you shall see the Spirit descending and abiding on Him, He it is who baptizes with (the) Holy Spirit. [34] And I have seen, and have borne witness that this is the Son of God.

[35] Again on the morrow, John was standing, and two of his disciples. [36] And looking at Jesus walking, he said, Behold, The Lamb of God! [37] And the two disciples heard him speaking, and followed Jesus. [38] But Jesus seeing them following, said to them, What do you seek? And they said to Him, Rabbi — which translated means teacher — where are you staying? [39] He said to them, Come and see. They went and saw where He stays; and they stayed with Him that day. Now (the) hour was about (the) tenth. [40] Andrew, the brother of Simon Peter, was one of the two who heard this from John and followed Him. [41] First he found his own brother Simon, and said to him, We have found the Messiah, which translated is The Christ. [42] And he led him to Jesus. And looking at him Jesus said, You are Simon the son of Jonah; you shall be called Cephas, which translated is stone.

[43] On the morrow Jesus desired to go out into Galilee, and He found Philip and said to him, Follow Me. [44] Now Philip was from Bethsaida, of the city of Andrew and Peter. [45] Philip found Nathanael and said to him, We have found (Him) whom Moses wrote of in the Law and the Prophets.

---

**32** καὶ ἐμαρτύρησεν Ἰωάννης λέγων ὅτι Τεθέαμαι τὸ Πνεῦμα
And witnessed John saying, — I have beheld the Spirit

καταβαῖνον ὡσεὶ περιστερὰν ἐξ οὐρανοῦ, καὶ ἔμεινεν ἐπ'
coming down as a dove out of Heaven, and He abode on

**33** αὐτόν. κἀγὼ οὐκ ᾔδειν αὐτόν· ἀλλ' ὁ πέμψας με βαπτίζειν
Him. And I did not know Him, but the (One) sending me to baptize

ἐν ὕδατι, ἐκεῖνός μοι εἶπεν, Ἐφ' ὃν ἂν ἴδῃς τὸ Πνεῦμα κατα-
in water, that One to me said, On whomever you see the Spirit coming

βαῖνον καὶ μένον ἐπ' αὐτόν, οὗτός ἐστιν ὁ βαπτίζων ἐν
down and abiding on Him, this is the (One) baptizing in

**34** Πνεύματι Ἁγίῳ. κἀγὼ ἑώρακα, καὶ μεμαρτύρηκα ὅτι οὗτός
(the) Spirit Holy. And I have seen, and have witnessed, that this One

ἐστιν ὁ υἱὸς τοῦ Θεοῦ.
is the Son — of God.

**35** Τῇ ἐπαύριον πάλιν εἱστήκει ὁ Ἰωάννης, καὶ ἐκ τῶν
On the morrow again stood — John, and out of the

**36** μαθητῶν αὐτοῦ δύο· καὶ ἐμβλέψας τῷ Ἰησοῦ περιπατοῦντι,
disciples of him two; and looking at — Jesus walking,

**37** λέγει, Ἴδε ὁ ἀμνὸς τοῦ Θεοῦ. καὶ ἤκουσαν αὐτοῦ οἱ δύο
he says, Behold, the Lamb of God. And heard him the two

**38** μαθηταὶ λαλοῦντος, καὶ ἠκολούθησαν τῷ Ἰησοῦ. στραφεὶς
disciples speaking, and they followed — Jesus. turning

δὲ ὁ Ἰησοῦς καὶ θεασάμενος αὐτοὺς ἀκολουθοῦντας, λέγει
And — Jesus, and beholding them following, He says

αὐτοῖς, Τί ζητεῖτε; οἱ δὲ εἶπον αὐτῷ, Ῥαββί (ὃ λέγεται
to them, What do you seek? they And said to Him, Rabbi, which is called,

**39** ἑρμηνευόμενον, Διδάσκαλε), ποῦ μένεις; λέγει αὐτοῖς, Ἔρχε-
being translated, Teacher, where do you stay? He says to them, Come

σθε καὶ ἴδετε. ἦλθον καὶ εἶδον ποῦ μένει· καὶ παρ' αὐτῷ
and see. They went and saw where He stayed, and with Him

**40** ἔμειναν τὴν ἡμέραν ἐκείνην· ὥρα δὲ ἦν ὡς δεκάτη. ἦν
abode. — day that; (the) hour and was about (the) tenth. was

Ἀνδρέας ὁ ἀδελφὸς Σίμωνος Πέτρου εἷς ἐκ τῶν δύο τῶν
Andrew the brother of Simon Peter, one of the two —

ἀκουσάντων παρὰ Ἰωάννου καὶ ἀκολουθησάντων αὐτῷ.
hearing from John, and following Him.

**41** εὑρίσκει οὗτος πρῶτος τὸν ἀδελφὸν τὸν ἴδιον Σίμωνα, καὶ
finds This one first brother (his) own Simon, and

λέγει αὐτῷ, Εὑρήκαμεν τὸν Μεσσίαν (ὅ ἐστι μεθερμηνευό-
tells him, We have found the Messiah — which is, being translated

**42** μενον, ὁ Χριστός). καὶ ἤγαγεν αὐτὸν πρὸς τὸν Ἰησοῦν.
the Christ — and he led him to — Jesus.

ἐμβλέψας δὲ αὐτῷ ὁ Ἰησοῦς εἶπε, Σὺ εἶ Σίμων ὁ υἱὸς Ἰωνᾶ·
looking at And him — Jesus said, You are Simon the son of Jonah;

σὺ κληθήσῃ Κηφᾶς (ὃ ἑρμηνεύεται Πέτρος).
you shall be called Cephas—which translated is Peter.

**43** Τῇ ἐπαύριον ἠθέλησεν ὁ Ἰησοῦς ἐξελθεῖν εἰς τὴν Γαλιλαίαν,
On the morrow decided — Jesus to go out into — Galilee.

**44** καὶ εὑρίσκει Φίλιππον, καὶ λέγει αὐτῷ, Ἀκολούθει μοι. ἦν δὲ
And He finds Philip, and says to him, Follow me. was And

ὁ Φίλιππος ἀπὸ Βηθσαϊδά, ἐκ τῆς πόλεως Ἀνδρέου καὶ
— Philip from Bethsaida, of the city of Andrew and

**45** Πέτρου. εὑρίσκει Φίλιππος τὸν Ναθαναήλ, καὶ λέγει αὐτῷ,
Peter. finds Philip — Nathanael, and says to him,

Ὃν ἔγραψε Μωσῆς ἐν τῷ νόμῳ καὶ οἱ προφῆται εὑρήκαμεν,
(He) whom wrote Moses in the law and the prophets, we have found

Jesus the son of Joseph who (is) from Nazareth. [46] And Nathanael said to him, Can any good thing be out of Nazareth? Philip said to him, Come and see. [47] Jesus saw Nathanael coming to Him, and said about him, Behold, truly an Israelite, in whom is no guile! [48] Nathanael said to Him, From where do you know me? Jesus answered and said to him, Before Philip called you, being under the fig-tree, I saw you. [49] Nathanael answered and says to Him, Rabbi, You are the Son of God; You are the king of Israel. [50] Jesus answered and said to him, Because I said to you I saw you underneath the fig-tree, you believe? You will see greater things than these. [51] And He says to him, Truly, truly, I say to you, From now on you will see Heaven opened and the angels of God ascending and descending on the Son of man.

CHAPTER 2

[1] And on the third day a marriage took place in Cana of Galilee, and the mother of Jesus was there. [2] And Jesus was also invited, and His disciples, to the marriage. [3] And being short of wine, the mother of Jesus said to Him, They have no wine. [4] Jesus said to her, What is that to Me and to you, woman? My hour is not yet come. [5] His mother said to the servants, Whatever He may say to you, do. [6] And there were six stone waterpots standing there, according to the purification of the Jews, each hold two or three measures. [7] Jesus said to them, Fill the waterpots with water. And they filled them to (the) brim. [8] And He said to them, Now draw out and carry to the master of the feast. And they carried (it). [9] But when the master of the feast had tasted the water that had become wine, and did not know what it was from — but the

**46** Ἰησοῦν τὸν υἱὸν τοῦ Ἰωσὴφ τὸν ἀπὸ Ναζαρέθ. καὶ εἶπεν
Jesus the son — of Joseph — from Nazareth. And said

αὐτῷ Ναθαναήλ, Ἐκ Ναζαρὲθ δύναταί τι ἀγαθὸν εἶναι ;
to him Nathanael, Out of Nazareth can anything good be?

**47** λέγει αὐτῷ Φίλιππος, Ἔρχου καὶ ἴδε. εἶδεν ὁ Ἰησοῦς τὸν
Says to him Philip, Come and see. saw — Jesus —

Ναθαναὴλ ἐρχόμενον πρὸς αὐτόν, καὶ λέγει περὶ αὐτοῦ, Ἴδε
Nathanael coming toward Him, and says about him, Behold,

**48** ἀληθῶς Ἰσραηλίτης, ἐν ᾧ δόλος οὐκ ἔστι. λέγει αὐτῷ
truly an Israelite, in whom guile not is. says to Him

Ναθαναήλ, Πόθεν με γινώσκεις ; ἀπεκρίθη ὁ Ἰησοῦς καὶ
Nathanael, From where me do You know? Answered — Jesus and

εἶπεν αὐτῷ, Πρὸ τοῦ σε Φίλιππον φωνῆσαι, ὄντα ὑπὸ τὴν
said to him, Before — you Philip called, being under the

**49** συκῆν, εἶδόν σε. ἀπεκρίθη Ναθαναὴλ καὶ λέγει αὐτῷ, Ῥαββί,
fig-tree, I saw you. answered Nathanael and says to Him, Rabbi,

**50** σὺ εἶ ὁ υἱὸς τοῦ Θεοῦ, σὺ εἶ ὁ βασιλεὺς τοῦ Ἰσραήλ. ἀπεκρίθη
You are the Son — of God; You are the king — of Israel. answered

Ἰησοῦς καὶ εἶπεν αὐτῷ, Ὅτι εἶπόν σοι, εἶδόν σε ὑποκάτω
Jesus and said to him, Because I told you I saw you underneath

**51** τῆς συκῆς, πιστεύεις ; μείζω τούτων ὄψει. καὶ λέγει αὐτῷ,
the fig-tree, you believe? Greater than these you will see; and He says to him,

Ἀμὴν αμην λέγω ὑμῖν, ἀπ᾽ ἄρτι ὄψεσθε τὸν οὐρανὸν ἀνεῳ-
Truly, truly, I say to you, from now on you will see the heaven opened

γότα, καὶ τοὺς ἀγγέλους τοῦ Θεοῦ ἀναβαίνοντας καὶ κατα-
and the angels — of God ascending and

βαίνοντας ἐπὶ τὸν υἱὸν τοῦ ἀνθρώπου.
descending on the Son — of man.

## CHAPTER 2

**1** Καὶ τῇ ἡμέρᾳ τῇ τρίτῃ γάμος ἐγένετο ἐν Κανᾷ τῆς
And on the day — third a wedding there was in Cana —

**2** Γαλιλαίας, καὶ ἦν ἡ μήτηρ τοῦ Ἰησοῦ ἐκεῖ· ἐκλήθη δὲ καὶ ὁ
of Galilee, and was the mother — of Jesus there. was invited And also

**3** Ἰησοῦς καὶ οἱ μαθηταὶ αὐτοῦ εἰς τὸν γάμον. καὶ ὑστερή-
Jesus and the disciples of Him to the wedding. And being

σαντος οἴνου, λέγει ἡ μήτηρ τοῦ Ἰησοῦ πρὸς αὐτόν, Οἶνον
short of wine, says the mother — of Jesus to Him, wine

**4** οὐκ ἔχουσι. λέγει αὐτῇ ὁ Ἰησοῦς, Τί ἐμοὶ καὶ σοί, γύναι ;
not They have. says to her — Jesus, What to Me and to you, woman?

**5** οὔπω ἥκει ἡ ὥρα μου. λέγει ἡ μήτηρ αὐτοῦ τοῖς διακόνοις,
Not yet is come the hour of Me. Says the mother of Him to the servants,

**6** Ὅ τι ἂν λέγῃ ὑμῖν, ποιήσατε. ἦσαν δὲ ἐκεῖ ὑδρίαι λίθιναι
Whatever He says to you, do. were And there waterpots stone

ἐξ κείμεναι κατὰ τὸν καθαρισμὸν τῶν Ἰουδαίων, χωροῦσαι
six standing according to the purification of the Jews. containing

**7** ἀνὰ μετρητὰς δύο ἢ τρεῖς. λέγει αὐτοῖς ὁ Ἰησοῦς, Γεμίσατε
each measures two or three. says to them — Jesus, Fill

**8** τὰς ὑδρίας ὕδατος. καὶ ἐγέμισαν αὐτὰς ἕως ἄνω. καὶ λέγει
the waterpots of water. And they filled them up to (the) top. And He says

αὐτοῖς, Ἀντλήσατε νῦν, καὶ φέρετε τῷ ἀρχιτρικλίνῳ. καὶ
to them Draw out now, and carry to the master of the feast. And

**9** ἤνεγκαν. ὡς δὲ ἐγεύσατο ὁ ἀρχιτρίκλινος τὸ ὕδωρ οἶνον
they carried. as But tasted the master of the feast the water wine

γεγενημένον, καὶ οὐκ ᾔδει πόθεν ἐστίν (οἱ δὲ διάκονοι
having become, and not knew from where it is — the but servants

servants who had drawn the water knew — the master of the feast called the bridegroom [10] and said to him, Every man first sets on the good wine, and when they have drunk freely then the inferior; you have kept the good wine until now. [11] This beginning of the miracles Jesus did in Cana of Galilee, and revealed His glory; and His disciples believed on Him.

[12] After this He went down to Capernaum, He and His mother and His brothers and His disciples, and there they stayed not many days. [13] And the Passover of the Jews was near, and Jesus went up to Jerusalem. [14] And He found in the Temple those who sold oxen and sheep and doves, and the money-changers sitting; [15] and having made a whip of cords, He drove out all from the Temple, both the sheep and the oxen, and the moneychangers, pouring out the money, and overturning the tables.

[16] And to those who sold doves He said, Take these things from here; do not make the house of My Father a house of merchandise. [17] And His disciples remembered that it was written, "The zeal of Your house has eaten Me up." [18] Then the Jews answered and said to Him, What miracle do you show to us that you do these things? [19] Jesus answered and said to them, Destroy this Temple, and in three days I will raise it up. [20] Then the Jews said, This Temple was forty-six years building, and you will raise it up in three days? [21] But He spoke about the temple of His body. [22] Therefore when He was raised up from among (the) dead, His disciples remembered that He had said this to them, and believed the Scripture and the word

ἤδεισαν οἱ ἠντληκότες τὸ ὕδωρ), φωνεῖ τὸν νυμφίον ὁ
knew, those having drawn the water — calls the bridegroom the

10 ἀρχιτρίκλινος, καὶ λέγει αὐτῷ, Πᾶς ἄνθρωπος πρῶτον τὸν
master of the feast, and says to him, Every man first the

καλὸν οἶνον τίθησι, καὶ ὅταν μεθυσθῶσι, τότε τὸν ἐλάσσω·
good wine sets on, and when they have drunk, then the worse;

11 σὺ τετήρηκας τὸν καλὸν οἶνον ἕως ἄρτι. ταύτην ἐποίησε
you have kept the good wine until now. This did

τὴν ἀρχὴν τῶν σημείων ὁ Ἰησοῦς ἐν Κανᾷ τῆς Γαλιλαίας,
the beginning of the signs — Jesus in Cana — of Galilee.

καὶ ἐφανέρωσε τὴν δόξαν αὐτοῦ· καὶ ἐπίστευσαν εἰς αὐτὸν οἱ
And (it) revealed the glory of Him, and believed in Him the

μαθηταὶ αὐτοῦ.
disciples of Him.

12 Μετὰ τοῦτο κατέβη εἰς Καπερναούμ, αὐτὸς καὶ ἡ μήτηρ
After this went down to Capernaum He, and the mother

αὐτοῦ, καὶ οἱ ἀδελφοὶ αὐτοῦ, καὶ οἱ μαθηταὶ αὐτοῦ· καὶ ἐκεῖ
of Him, and the brothers of Him, and the disciples of Him, and there

ἔμειναν οὐ πολλὰς ἡμέρας.
He abode not many days.

13 Καὶ ἐγγὺς ἦν τὸ πάσχα τῶν Ἰουδαίων, καὶ ἀνέβη εἰς
And near was the Passover of the Jews. And went up to

14 Ἱεροσόλυμα ὁ Ἰησοῦς. καὶ εὗρεν ἐν τῷ ἱερῷ τοὺς πωλοῦντας
Jerusalem — Jesus. And He found in the Temple those selling

βόας καὶ πρόβατα καὶ περιστεράς, καὶ τοὺς κερματιστὰς
oxen and sheep and doves, and the money-merchants

15 καθημένους. καὶ ποιήσας φραγέλλιον ἐκ σχοινίων πάντας
sitting. And having made a whip out of ropes, all

ἐξέβαλεν ἐκ τοῦ ἱεροῦ, τά τε πρόβατα καὶ τοὺς βόας· καὶ τῶν
He threw out of the Temple, the both sheep and the oxen and the

κολλυβιστῶν ἐξέχεε τὸ κέρμα, καὶ τὰς τραπέζας ἀνέστρεψε·
moneychangers, pouring out the money, and the tables overturning.

16 καὶ τοῖς τὰς περιστερὰς πωλοῦσιν εἶπεν, Ἄρατε ταῦτα
And to those doves He said, Take these things

ἐντεῦθεν· μὴ ποιεῖτε τὸν οἶκον τοῦ πατρός μου οἶκον
from here! Do not make the house of the Father of Me a house

17 ἐμπορίου. ἐμνήσθησαν δὲ οἱ μαθηταὶ αὐτοῦ ὅτι γεγραμ-
of merchandise. remembered And the disciples of Him that having been

μένον ἐστίν, Ὁ ζῆλος τοῦ οἴκου σου κατέφαγέ με. ἀπεκρίθη-
written is: The zeal of the house of You has devoured Me. answered

18 σαν οὖν οἱ Ἰουδαῖοι καὶ εἶπον αὐτῷ, Τί σημεῖον δεικνύεις
Then the Jews and said to Him, What sign do You show

19 ἡμῖν, ὅτι ταῦτα ποιεῖς; ἀπεκρίθη ὁ Ἰησοῦς καὶ εἶπεν αὐτοῖς,
to us, since these things You do? answered — Jesus and said to them,

Λύσατε τὸν ναὸν τοῦτον, καὶ ἐν τρισὶν ἡμέραις ἐγερῶ αὐτόν.
Destroy — temple this, and in three days I will raise it.

20 εἶπον οὖν οἱ Ἰουδαῖοι, Τεσσαράκοντα καὶ ἓξ ἔτεσιν ᾠκο-
said Then the Jews, Forty and six years is being

δομήθη ὁ ναὸς οὗτος, καὶ σὺ ἐν τρισὶν ἡμέραις ἐγερεῖς αὐτόν;
built — temple this, and you in three days will raise it?

21 ἐκεῖνος δὲ ἔλεγε περὶ τοῦ ναοῦ τοῦ σώματος αὐτοῦ. ὅτε
22 that One But spoke about the temple of the body of Him. When

οὖν ἠγέρθη ἐκ νεκρῶν, ἐμνήσθησαν οἱ μαθηταὶ αὐτοῦ ὅτι
then, He was raised from dead, recalled the disciples of Him that

τοῦτο ἔλεγεν αὐτοῖς· καὶ ἐπίστευσαν τῇ γραφῇ, καὶ τῷ λόγῳ
this He said to them; and they believed the Scripture and the word

which Jesus had spoken.

[23] But when He was in Jerusalem at the Passover, at the feast, many believed on His name, watching His miracles which He was doing. [24] But Jesus Himself did not trust Himself to them, because of His knowing all, [25] and because He did not need for any to testify about man, for He knew what was in man.

CHAPTER 3

[1] But there was a man of the Pharisees, Nicodemus his name, a ruler of the Jews; [2] he came to Jesus by night, and said to Him, Rabbi, we know that You are a teacher come from God, for no one is able to do these miracles which You do unless God is with him. [3] Jesus answered and said to him, Truly, truly, I say to you, Unless one is born again, he cannot see the kingdom of God. [4] Nicodemus said to Him, How can a man be born being old? Can he enter a second time into the womb of his mother and be born? [5] Jesus answered, Truly, truly, I say to you, Unless one is born of water and of (the) Spirit, he cannot enter into the kingdom of God. [6] That which has been born of the flesh is flesh, and that which has been born of the Spirit is spirit. [7] Do not wonder that I said to you, You must be born again. [8] The Spirit breathes where He desires, and you hear His voice, but you do not know from where He comes and where

He goes; so is everyone who has been born of the Spirit. [9] Nicodemus answered and said to him, How can these things be? [10] Jesus answered and said to Him, You are the teacher of Israel, and do you not know these

---

ᾧ εἶπεν ὁ Ἰησοῦς.
**which said —    Jesus.**

**23** Ὡς δὲ ἦν ἐν Ἱεροσολύμοις ἐν τῷ πάσχα, ἐν τῇ ἑορτῇ,
**as And He was in   Jerusalem,    at   the Passover,   at   the   feast,**

πολλοὶ ἐπίστευσαν εἰς τὸ ὄνομα αὐτοῦ, θεωροῦντες αὐτοῦ τὰ
**many   believed    in   the name   of Him,   beholding   of Him the**

**24** σημεῖα ἃ ἐποίει. αὐτὸς δὲ ὁ Ἰησοῦς οὐκ ἐπίστευεν ἑαυτὸν
**signs which He did. Himself But, —   Jesus    not did commit   Himself**

**25** αὐτοῖς, διὰ τὸ αὐτὸν γινώσκειν πάντας, καὶ ὅτι οὐ χρείαν
**to them, because (of) Him   knowing    all,    and because no   need**

εἶχεν ἵνα τις μαρτυρήσῃ περὶ τοῦ ἀνθρώπου· αὐτὸς γὰρ
**He had that any should witness concerning --   mar ;      He   for**

ἐγίνωσκε τί ἦν ἐν τῷ ἀνθρώπῳ.
**knew   what was in —    man.**

## CHAPTER 3

**1** Ἦν δὲ ἄνθρωπος ἐκ τῶν Φαρισαίων, Νικόδημος ὄνομα
**was And a man    out of the   Pharisees,     Nicodemus (the) name**

**2** αὐτῷ, ἄρχων τῶν Ἰουδαίων· οὗτος ἦλθε πρὸς τὸν Ἰησοῦν
**to him, a ruler of the    Jews.    This one came   to    —   Jesus**

νυκτός, καὶ εἶπεν αὐτῷ, Ῥαββί, οἴδαμεν ὅτι ἀπὸ Θεοῦ ἐλή-
**by night, and said to Him,   Rabbi, we know   that from   God You**

λυθας διδάσκαλος· οὐδεὶς γὰρ ταῦτα τὰ σημεῖα δύναται
**have come a teacher;   no one for    these    —   signs    is able**

**3** ποιεῖν ἃ σὺ ποιεῖς, ἐὰν μὴ ᾖ ὁ Θεὸς μετ' αὐτοῦ. ἀπεκρίθη ὁ
**to do which You do,    except be    God with   Him. answered —**

Ἰησοῦς καὶ εἶπεν αὐτῷ, Ἀμὴν ἀμὴν λέγω σοι, ἐὰν μή τις
**Jesus   and said to him,   Truly, truly,   I say to you,   Except one**

γεννηθῇ ἄνωθεν, οὐ δύναται ἰδεῖν τὴν βασιλείαν τοῦ Θεοῦ.
**receive from above, not he is able to see the    kingdom    —   of God.**
**birth**

**4** λέγει πρὸς αὐτὸν ὁ Νικόδημος, Πῶς δύναται ἄνθρωπος
**says to    Him   — Nicodemus, How is able    a man**

γεννηθῆναι γέρων ὤν; μὴ δύναται εἰς τὴν κοιλίαν τῆς
**to be born,    old being? Not he is able into the womb of the**

**5** μητρὸς αὐτοῦ δεύτερον εἰσελθεῖν καὶ γεννηθῆναι : ἀπεκρίθη
**mother of him a second (time) to enter and be born?    answered**

ὁ Ἰησοῦς, Ἀμὴν ἀμὴν λέγω σοι, ἐὰν μή τις γεννηθῇ ἐξ
**Jesus,   Truly, truly,   I say to you, Except one receive of**
**birth**

ὕδατος καὶ Πνεύματος, οὐ δύναται εἰσελθεῖν εἰς τὴν βασιλείαν
**water and    Spirit,    not he is able to enter into the    kingdom**

**6** τοῦ Θεοῦ. τὸ γεγεννημένον ἐκ τῆς σαρκὸς σάρξ ἐστι· καὶ τὸ
**— of God. That receive    from the   flesh, flesh is; and that**
**birth**

**7** γεγεννημένον ἐκ τοῦ πνεύματος πνεῦμά ἐστι. μὴ θαυμάσῃς
**receiving birth from the    Spirit,    spirit is. Do not wonder**

**8** ὅτι εἶπόν σοι, Δεῖ ὑμᾶς γεννηθῆναι ἄνωθεν. τὸ πνεῦμα ὅπου
**because I told you, must You receive birth from above. The Spirit   where**

θέλει πνεῖ, καὶ τὴν φωνὴν αὐτοῦ ἀκούεις, ἀλλ' οὐκ οἶδας
**He desires breathes, and the voice of Him you hear, but   not you know**

πόθεν ἔρχεται καὶ ποῦ ὑπάγει· οὕτως ἐστὶ πᾶς ὁ γεγεννη-
**from where He comes and where He goes; so    is everyone having received**

**9** μένος ἐκ τοῦ πνεύματος. ἀπεκρίθη Νικόδημος καὶ εἶπεν αὐτῷ,
**birth from the    Spirit.    answered Nicodemus and said to Him,**

**10** Πῶς δύναται ταῦτα γενέσθαι ; ἀπεκρίθη ὁ Ἰησοῦς καὶ εἶπεν
**How   can   these things come about? answered   —   Jesus and   said**

αὐτῷ, Σὺ εἶ ὁ διδάσκαλος τοῦ Ἰσραήλ, καὶ ταῦτα οὐ
**to him, You are the    teacher    — of Israel,   and these things not**

things? [11] Truly, truly, I say to you, that which we know we speak, and that which we have seen we testify; and you received not our witness. [12] If I tell you earthly things, and you do not believe, how will you believe if I tell you heavenly things? [13] And no one has gone up into Heaven except He who came down out of Heaven, the Son of man who is in Heaven. [14] And even as Moses lifted up the serpent in the wilderness, so must the Son of man be lifted up, [15] that everyone that believes on Him may not perish, but may have everlasting life. [16] For God so loved the world that He gave His only-begotten Son, that everyone who believes on Him may not perish, but may have everlasting life. [17] For God did not send His Son into the world that He might judge the world, but that the world might be saved through Him. [18] He that believes on Him is not judged; but he that does not believe has already been judged, because he has not believed on the name of the only-begotten Son of God [19] And this is the judgment, that the Light has come into the world, and men loved the darkness rather than the Light; for their works were evil. [20] For everyone that does evil hates the light, and does not come to the light, that his works may not be exposed; [21] but he that practices the truth comes to the Light, that his works may be revealed, that they had been worked in God.

[22] After these things Jesus and His disciples came into the land of Judea; and He stayed there with them and was baptizing. [23] And John was also baptizing in Enon, near Salim, because there were many waters there; and they were coming and being baptized. [24] For John had not yet been cast

**11** γινώσκεις ; ἀμὴν ἀμὴν λέγω σοι ὅτι ὃ οἴδαμεν λαλοῦμεν, καὶ
you do know? Truly, truly, I say to you, – what we know we speak, and
ὃ ἐωράκαμεν μαρτυροῦμεν· καὶ τὴν μαρτυρίαν ἡμῶν οὐ
what we have seen we witness, and the witness of us not

**12** λαμβάνετε. εἰ τὰ ἐπίγεια εἶπον ὑμῖν καὶ οὐ πιστεύετε, πῶς,
you receive. If earthly things I told you and not you believe, how,

**13** ἐὰν εἴπω ὑμῖν τὰ ἐπουράνια, πιστεύσετε ; καὶ οὐδεὶς ἀναβέ-
if I tell you the heavenly things, will you believe? And no one has gone
βηκεν εἰς τὸν οὐρανόν, εἰ μὴ ὁ ἐκ τοῦ οὐρανοῦ καταβάς, ὁ
up into – Heaven except He out of – Heaven having come down the

**14** υἱὸς τοῦ ἀνθρώπου ὁ ὢν ἐν τῷ οὐρανῷ. καὶ καθὼς Μωσῆς
Son – of man, who is in – Heaven. And as Moses
ὕψωσε τὸν ὄφιν ἐν τῇ ἐρήμῳ, οὕτως ὑψωθῆναι δεῖ τὸν υἱὸν
lifted up the serpent in the wilderness, so to be lifted up must the Son

**15** τοῦ ἀνθρώπου· ἵνα πᾶς ὁ πιστεύων εἰς αὐτὸν μὴ ἀπόληται,
– of man, that everyone believing in Him not may perish,
ἀλλ᾽ ἔχῃ ζωὴν αἰώνιον.
but have life everlasting.

**16** Οὕτω γὰρ ἠγάπησεν ὁ Θεὸς τὸν κόσμον, ὥστε τὸν υἱὸν
so For loved – God the world, so as the Son
αὐτοῦ τὸν μονογενῆ ἔδωκεν, ἵνα πᾶς ὁ πιστεύων εἰς αὐτὸν
of Him, the only-begotten, He gave, that everyone believing into Him

**17** μὴ ἀπόληται, ἀλλ᾽ ἔχῃ ζωὴν αἰώνιον. οὐ γὰρ ἀπέστειλεν ὁ
not may perish, but have life everlasting. not For sent
Θεὸς τὸν υἱὸν αὐτοῦ εἰς τὸν κόσμον ἵνα κρίνῃ τὸν κόσμον,
God the Son of Him into the world that He judge the world,

**18** ἀλλ᾽ ἵνα σωθῇ ὁ κόσμος δι᾽ αὐτοῦ. ὁ πιστεύων εἰς αὐτὸν οὐ
but that may be saved the world via Him. The (one) believing in Him not
κρίνεται· ὁ δὲ μὴ πιστεύων ἤδη κέκριται, ὅτι μὴ πεπί-
is judged; the (one) but not believing already has been judged, for not he has

**19** στευκεν εἰς τὸ ὄνομα τοῦ μονογενοῦς υἱοῦ τοῦ Θεοῦ. αὕτη δέ
believed into the name of the only-begotten Son – of God. this And
ἐστιν ἡ κρίσις, ὅτι τὸ φῶς ἐλήλυθεν εἰς τὸν κόσμον, καὶ
is the judgment, that the light has come into the world, and
ἠγάπησαν οἱ ἄνθρωποι μᾶλλον τὸ σκότος ἢ τὸ φῶς· ἦν
loved – men more the darkness than the light; were

**20** γὰρ πονηρὰ αὐτῶν τὰ ἔργα. πᾶς γὰρ ὁ φαῦλα πράσσων
for evil of them the works. everyone For wickedness practicing
μισεῖ τὸ φῶς, καὶ οὐκ ἔρχεται προς τὸ φῶς, ἵνα μὴ ἐλεγχθῇ
hates the light, and not does come to the light, that not be reproved

**21** τὰ ἔργα αὐτοῦ. ὁ δὲ ποιῶν τὴν ἀλήθειαν ἔρχεται πρὸς τὸ
the works of him. the (one) But doing the truth comes to the
φῶς, ἵνα φανερωθῇ αὐτοῦ τὰ ἔργα, ὅτι ἐν Θεῷ ἐστιν
light, that may be revealed of him the works, that in God they are
εἰργασμένα.
having been worked.

**22** Μετὰ ταῦτα ἦλθεν ὁ Ἰησοῦς καὶ οἱ μαθηταὶ αὐτοῦ εἰς
After these things came – Jesus and the disciples of Him into
τὴν Ἰουδαίαν γῆν· καὶ ἐκεῖ διέτριβε μετ᾽ αὐτῶν καὶ ἐβάπτι-
the Judean land, and there continued with them and baptized.

**23** ζεν. ἦν δὲ καὶ Ἰωάννης βαπτίζων ἐν Αἰνὼν ἐγγὺς τοῦ Σαλείμ,
was And also John baptizing in Aenon near – Salem,
ὅτι ὕδατα πολλὰ ἦν ἐκεῖ· καὶ παρεγίνοντο καὶ ἐβαπτίζοντο
for waters many were there; and they came and were being baptized.

**24** οὔπω γὰρ ἦν βεβλημένος εἰς τὴν φυλακὴν ὁ Ἰωάννης.
not yet For was having been cast into the prison – John.

into prison. [25] Then a question arose from the disciples of John with Jews about cleansing. [26] And they came to John and said to him, Teacher, (He) who was with you beyond the Jordan, to whom you have witnessed, behold, He baptizes, and all are coming to Him. [27] John answered and said, A man is able to receive nothing unless it is given to him from Heaven. [28] You yourselves testify to me that I said, I am not the Christ, but that I am sent before Him. [29] He that has the bride is the bridegroom; but the friend of the bridegroom, who stands and hears him, rejoices with joy because of the voice of the bridegroom; this then my joy is fulfilled. [30] It is right for Him to increase, but me to decrease. [31] He who comes from above is above all. He who is from the earth is of the earth, and speaks of the earth. He who comes from Heaven is above all. [32] And what He has seen and heard, He testifies this; and no one receives His testimony. [33] He that has received His testimony has set to his seal that God is true; [34] for He whom God sent speaks the words of God; for God does not give the Spirit by measure. [35] The Father loves the Son, and has given all things into His hand. [36] He that believes on the Son has everlasting life; but he not obeying the Son shall not see life, but the wrath of God remains on him.

CHAPTER 4
[1] Then when the Lord knew that the Pharisees heard that Jesus makes and baptizing more disciples than John — [2] although indeed Jesus Himself was not baptizing, but His disciples — [3] He left Judea and went away again into Galilee. [4] And it was necessary for Him to pass through Samaria.

25 ἐγένετο οὖν ζήτησις ἐκ τῶν μαθητῶν Ἰωάννου μετὰ
was Therefore a questioning of the disciples of John with
26 Ἰουδαίων περὶ καθαρισμοῦ. καὶ ἦλθον πρὸς τὸν Ἰωάννην
Jews concerning purifying. And they came to — John
καὶ εἶπον αὐτῷ, Ῥαββί, ὃς ἦν μετὰ σοῦ πέραν τοῦ Ἰορδάνου.
and said to him, Rabbi, (He) who was with you beyond the Jordan,
ᾧ σὺ μεμαρτύρηκας, ἴδε οὗτος βαπτίζει, καὶ πάντες ἔρχονται
to whom you have witnessed, behold, this one baptizes, and all are coming
27 πρὸς αὐτόν. ἀπεκρίθη Ἰωάννης καὶ εἶπεν, Οὐ δύναται
to Him. answered John and said, not is able
ἄνθρωπος λαμβάνειν οὐδέν, ἐὰν μὴ ᾖ δεδομένον αὐτῷ ἐκ τοῦ
A man to receive nothing unless it is having been given to him from
28 οὐρανοῦ. αὐτοὶ ὑμεῖς μοι μαρτυρεῖτε ὅτι εἶπον, Οὐκ εἰμὶ
Heaven. (your)selves You to me witness that I said, not am
ἐγὼ ὁ Χριστός, ἀλλ' ὅτι ἀπεσταλμένος εἰμὶ ἔμπροσθεν
I the Christ, but that having been sent I am preceding
29 ἐκείνου. ὁ ἔχων τὴν νύμφην νυμφίος ἐστίν· ὁ δὲ φίλος τοῦ
that One. He having the bride (the) bridegroom is, the but friend of the
νυμφίου, ὁ ἑστηκὼς καὶ ἀκούων αὐτοῦ, χαρᾷ χαίρει διὰ τὴν
bridegroom, standing and hearing him, with joy rejoices for the
φωνὴν τοῦ νυμφίου· αὕτη οὖν ἡ χαρὰ ἡ ἐμὴ πεπλήρωται.
voice of the bridegroom. this Then the joy of me has been fulfilled.
30 ἐκεῖνον δεῖ αὐξάνειν, ἐμὲ δὲ ἐλαττοῦσθαι.
That One must increase, me but to decrease.
31 Ὁ ἄνωθεν ἐρχόμενος ἐπάνω πάντων ἐστίν. ὁ ὢν ἐκ τῆς
The One from above coming above all is, the (one) being of the
γῆς, ἐκ τῆς γῆς ἐστι, καὶ ἐκ τῆς γῆς λαλεῖ· ὁ ἐκ τοῦ οὐρανοῦ
earth of the earth is, and of the earth speaks. He from Heaven
32 ἐρχόμενος ἐπάνω πάντων ἐστί. καὶ ὃ ἑώρακε καὶ ἤκουσε,
coming above all is. And what He has seen and heard,
τοῦτο μαρτυρεῖ· καὶ τὴν μαρτυρίαν αὐτοῦ οὐδεὶς λαμβάνει.
this He witnesses, and the witness of Him no one receives.
33 ὁ λαβὼν αὐτοῦ τὴν μαρτυρίαν ἐσφράγισεν ὅτι ὁ Θεὸς ἀληθής
He receiving of Him the witness has sealed that — God true.
34 ἐστιν. ὃν γὰρ ἀπέστειλεν ὁ Θεός, τὰ ῥήματα τοῦ Θεοῦ λαλεῖ·
is. (He) whom For sent — God, the words — of God speaks;
35 οὐ γὰρ ἐκ μέτρου δίδωσιν ὁ Θεὸς τὸ Πνεῦμα. ὁ πατὴρ ἀγαπᾷ
not for by measure gives — God the Spirit. the Father loves
36 τὸν υἱόν, καὶ πάντα δέδωκεν ἐν τῇ χειρὶ αὐτοῦ. ὁ πιστεύων
the Son, and all things has given into the hand of Him. The (one) believing
εἰς τὸν υἱὸν ἔχει ζωὴν αἰώνιον· ὁ δὲ ἀπειθῶν τῷ υἱῷ οὐκ
into the Son has life everlasting; the (one) but disobeying the Son not
ὄψεται ζωήν, ἀλλ' ἡ ὀργὴ τοῦ Θεοῦ μένει ἐπ' αὐτόν.
will see life, but the wrath — of God remains on him.

CHAPTER 4

1 Ὡς οὖν ἔγνω ὁ Κύριος ὅτι ἤκουσαν οἱ Φαρισαῖοι ὅτι
As therefore knew the Lord that heard the Pharisees that
Ἰησοῦς πλείονας μαθητὰς ποιεῖ καὶ βαπτίζει ἢ Ἰωάννης
Jesus more disciples makes and baptizes than John,
2 (καίτοιγε Ἰησοῦς αὐτὸς οὐκ ἐβάπτιζεν, ἀλλ' οἱ μαθηταὶ
though Jesus Himself not baptized but the disciples
3 αὐτοῦ), ἀφῆκε τὴν Ἰουδαίαν, καὶ ἀπῆλθε πάλιν εἰς τὴν
of Him; He left — Judea and went away again into —
4 Γαλιλαίαν. ἔδει δὲ αὐτὸν διέρχεσθαι διὰ τῆς Σαμαρείας. ἔρχε-
5 Galilee. it behoved And Him to pass through — Samaria. He

[5] Then He came to a city of Samaria called Sychar, near the land which Jacob gave to his son Joseph. [6] Now there was Jacob's well there; therefore Jesus being wearied from the journey sat this way at the fountain. (The) hour was about (the) sixth. [7] A woman came out of Samaria to draw water. Jesus said to her, Give Me to drink; [8] for His disciples had gone away into the city that they might buy food. [9] Then the woman said to Him, How do you, being a Jew, ask to drink from me, being a Samaritan woman? For Jews associate not with Samaritans. [10] Jesus answered and said to her, If you knew the gift of God, and He who is saying to you, Give Me to drink, you would have asked Him, and He would give you living water. [11] The woman said to Him, Sir, you have no vessel, and the well is deep. From where then have you living water? [12] Are you greater than Jacob the father of us, who gave us the well, and himself drank of it, and his sons and his cattle? [13] Jesus answered and said to her, Everyone that drinks of this water will thirst again; [14] but whoever may drink of the water which I will give him will never ever thirst; but the water which I will give to him shall become within him a well of water springing up into everlasting life. [15] The woman said to Him, Sir, give me this water, that I may not thirst nor come here to draw. [16] Jesus said to her, Go, call your husband and come here. [17] The woman answered and said, I have no husband. Jesus said to her, Well did you say, I have no husband. [18] For you have had five husbands, and now he whom you have is not your husband. You have spoken this truly. [19] The woman said to Him, Sir, I see that you are a prophet.

6 ται οὖν εἰς πόλιν τῆς Σαμαρείας λεγομένην Συχάρ, πλησίον
**comes then to a city — of Samaria called Sychar, near**
τοῦ χωρίου ὃ ἔδωκεν Ἰακὼβ Ἰωσὴφ τῷ υἱῷ αὐτοῦ· ἦν δὲ
**the piece of land that gave Jacob to Joseph the son of him. was And**
ἐκεῖ πηγὴ τοῦ Ἰακώβ. ὁ οὖν Ἰησοῦς κεκοπιακὼς ἐκ τῆς
**there a fountain — of Jacob. Therefore, Jesus having wearied from the**
ὁδοιπορίας ἐκαθέζετο οὕτως ἐπὶ τῇ πηγῇ. ὥρα ἦν ὡσεὶ
**journey sat thus on the fountain; hour was about**

7 ἕκτη. ἔρχεται γυνὴ ἐκ τῆς Σαμαρείας ἀντλῆσαι ὕδωρ· λέγει
**sixth. Comes a woman of — Samaria to draw water. says**

8 αὐτῇ ὁ Ἰησοῦς, Δός μοι πιεῖν. οἱ γὰρ μαθηταὶ αὐτοῦ ἀπελη-
**to her Jesus, Give Me to drink. the For disciples of Him had gone**

9 λύθεισαν εἰς τὴν πόλιν, ἵνα τροφὰς ἀγοράσωσι. λέγει οὖν
**away into the city, that foods they might buy. says Then**
αὐτῷ ἡ γυνὴ ἡ Σαμαρεῖτις, Πῶς σὺ Ἰουδαῖος ὢν παρ' ἐμοῦ
**to Him the woman the Samaritan, How do you, a Jew being, from me**
πιεῖν αἰτεῖς, οὔσης γυναικὸς Σαμαρείτιδος; (οὐ γὰρ συγ-
**to drink ask, (I) being woman a Samaritan? not For**

10 χρῶνται Ἰουδαῖοι Σαμαρείταις.) ἀπεκρίθη Ἰησοῦς καὶ εἶπεν
**associate Jews with Samaritans. answered Jesus and said**
αὐτῇ, Εἰ ᾔδεις τὴν δωρεὰν τοῦ Θεοῦ, καὶ τίς ἐστιν ὁ λέγων
**to her, If you knew the gift — of God, and who is the (one) saying**
σοι, Δός μοι πιεῖν, σὺ ἂν ᾔτησας αὐτόν καὶ ἔδωκεν ἄν σοι
**to you, Give Me to drink, you would have asked Him, and He would give you**

11 ὕδωρ ζῶν. λέγει αὐτῷ ἡ γυνή, Κύριε, οὔτε ἄντλημα ἔχεις, καὶ
**water living. says to Him The woman, Lord, no vessel you have, and**

12 τὸ φρέαρ ἐστὶ βαθύ· πόθεν οὖν ἔχεις τὸ ὕδωρ τὸ ζῶν; μὴ σὺ
**the well is deep; from where then have you water living? not You**
μείζων εἶ τοῦ πατρὸς ἡμῶν Ἰακώβ, ὃς ἔδωκεν ἡμῖν τὸ φρέαρ,
**greater are (than) the father of us, Jacob, who gave us the well,**
καὶ αὐτὸς ἐξ αὐτοῦ ἔπιε, καὶ οἱ υἱοὶ αὐτοῦ, καὶ τὰ θρέμματα
**and he out of it drank, and the sons of him, and the livestock**

13 αὐτοῦ; ἀπεκρίθη ὁ Ἰησοῦς καὶ εἶπεν αὐτῇ, Πᾶς ὁ πίνων ἐκ
**of him? answered — Jesus and said to her, Everyone drinking of**

14 τοῦ ὕδατος τούτου, διψήσει πάλιν· ὃς δ' ἂν πίῃ ἐκ τοῦ
**— water this will thirst again; who but ever drinks of the**
ὕδατος οὗ ἐγὼ δώσω αὐτῷ, οὐ μὴ διψήσῃ εἰς τὸν αἰῶνα·
**water which I will give him, in no way will thirst unto the age,**
ἀλλὰ τὸ ὕδωρ ὃ δώσω αὐτῷ γενήσεται ἐν αὐτῷ πηγὴ
**but the water which I will give him will become in him a fountain**

15 ὕδατος ἁλλομένου εἰς ζωὴν αἰώνιον. λέγει πρὸς αὐτὸν ἡ
**of water springing to life everlasting. says to Him The**
γυνή, Κύριε, δός μοι τοῦτο τὸ ὕδωρ, ἵνα μὴ διψῶ, μηδὲ
**woman, Lord, give me this — water, that not I thirst, nor**

16 ἔρχωμαι ἐνθάδε ἀντλεῖν. λέγει αὐτῇ ὁ Ἰησοῦς, Ὕπαγε,
**come here to draw. says to her Jesus, Go,**

17 φώνησον τὸν ἄνδρα σου, καὶ ἐλθὲ ἐνθάδε. ἀπεκρίθη ἡ γυνὴ
**call the husband of you, and come here. answered The woman**
καὶ εἶπεν, Οὐκ ἔχω ἄνδρα. λέγει αὐτῇ ὁ Ἰησοῦς, Καλῶς εἶπας
**and said, not I have a husband. says to her — Jesus, well You say,**

18 ὅτι Ἄνδρα οὐκ ἔχω· πέντε γὰρ ἄνδρας ἔσχες, καὶ νῦν ὃν
**— A husband not I have; five for husbands you had, and now whom**

19 ἔχεις οὐκ ἔστι σου ἀνήρ· τοῦτο ἀληθὲς εἴρηκας. λέγει αὐτῷ
**you have not is your husband; this truly you have said. says to Him**

20 ἡ γυνή, Κύριε, θεωρῶ ὅτι προφήτης εἶ σύ. οἱ πατέρες ἡμῶν
**The woman, Lord, I perceive that a prophet are you. The fathers of us**

[20] Our fathers worshiped in this mountain, and you say that in Jerusalem is the place where it is necessary to worship. [21] Jesus said to her, Woman, believe Me, that an hour is coming when neither in this mountain nor in Jerusalem you shall worship the Father. [22] You worship what you do not know; we worship what we know; for salvation is of the Jews. [23] But an hour is coming, and now is, when the true worshipers will worship the Father in spirit and in truth; for also the Father seeks such who worship Him. [24] God (is) a spirit, and they that worship Him must worship in spirit and truth. [25] The woman said to Him, I know that Messiah is coming, who is called Christ; when He comes, He will tell us all things. [26] Jesus said to her, I AM, whom am speaking to you. [27] And upon this His disciples came, and wondered that He was speaking with the woman; however no one said, What do You seek, or, Why do You speak with her?

[28] The woman then left her waterpot and went away into the city, and said to the men, [29] Come, see a Man who told me all things whatever I did; is this not the Christ? [30] Therefore they went out of the city and came to Him.

[31] But in the meantime the disciples were asking Him, saying, Rabbi, eat. [32] But He said to them, I have food to eat which you know not. [33] Then the disciples said to one another, Did anyone bring Him (food) to eat?. [34] Jesus said to them, My food is that I should do the will of Him who sent Me, and to finish His work. [35] You should not say, that it is yet four months and the harvest comes. Behold, I say to you, Lift up your eyes and see the

---

ἐν τούτῳ τῷ ὄρει πυοσεκύνησαν· καὶ ὑμεῖς λέγετε ὅτι ἐν
in this — mountain worshiped, and you say that in

**21** Ἱεροσολύμοις ἐστιν ὁ τόπος ὅπου δεῖ προσκυνεῖν. λέγει
Jerusalem is the place where it is right to worship. says

αὐτῇ ὁ Ἰησοῦς, Γύναι, πίστευσόν μοι, ὅτι ἔρχεται ὥρα,
to her — Jesus, Woman, believe me, that comes an hour,

ὅτε οὔτε ἐν τῷ ὄρει τούτῳ οὔτε ἐν Ἱεροσολύμοις προσκυνή-
when neither in — mountain this, nor in Jerusalem, will you worship

**22** σετε τῷ πατρί. ὑμεῖς προσκυνεῖτε ὃ οὐκ οἴδατε· ἡμεῖς
the Father You worship what not you know, we

προσκυνοῦμεν ὃ οἴδαμεν· ὅτι ἡ σωτηρία ἐκ τῶν Ἰουδαίων
worship what we know. since salvation of the Jews

**23** ἐστίν. ἀλλ᾽ ἔρχεται ὥρα καὶ νῦν ἐστιν, ὅτε οἱ ἀληθινοὶ
is. But is coming an hour, and now is, when the true

προσκυνηταὶ προσκυνήσουσι τῷ πατρὶ ἐν πνεύματι καὶ
worshipers will worship the Father in spirit and

ἀληθείᾳ· καὶ γὰρ ὁ πατηρ τοιούτους ζητεῖ τοὺς προσ-
truth; also for the Father such seeks, those

**24** κυνοῦντας αὐτόν. Πνεῦμα ὁ Θεός· καὶ τοὺς προσκυνοῦντας
worshiping Him. A spirit — God (is) and those worshiping

**25** αὐτόν, ἐν πνεύματι καὶ ἀληθείᾳ δεῖ προσκυνεῖν. λέγει αὐτῷ
Him in spirit and truth need to worship. says to Him

ἡ γυνή, Οἶδα ὅτι Μεσσίας ἔρχεται (ὁ λεγόμενος Χριστός)·
The woman, I know that Messiah is coming, the (One) called Christ;

ὅταν ἔλθῃ ἐκεῖνος, ἀναγγελεῖ ἡμῖν πάντα. λέγει αὐτῇ ὁ
when comes that One, He will announce to us all things. says to her —

Ἰησοῦς, Ἐγώ εἰμι, ὁ λαλῶν σοι.
Jesus, I AM, He speaking to you.

**27** Καὶ ἐπὶ τούτῳ ἦλθον οἱ μαθηταὶ αὐτοῦ, καὶ ἐθαύμασαν
And on this came the disciples of Him, and marveled

ὅτι μετὰ γυναικὸς ἐλάλει· οὐδεὶς μέντοι εἶπε, Τί ζητεῖς·
that with a woman He was speaking; no one, though, said, What seek you?

**28** ἤ, Τί λαλεῖς μετ᾽ αὐτῆς; ἀφῆκεν οὖν τὴν ὑδρίαν αὐτῆς ἡ
or, Why speak You with her? left, then, the waterpot of her The

γυνή, καὶ ἀπῆλθεν εἰς τὴν πόλιν, καὶ λέγει τοῖς ἀνθρώποις,
woman, and went away into the city, and says to the men,

**29** Δεῦτε, ἴδετε ἄνθρωπον, ὃς εἶπέ μοι πάντα ὅσα ἐποίησα· μήτι
Come! See a man who told me all things whatever I did. Not

**30** οὗτός ἐστιν ὁ Χριστός; ἐξῆλθον οὖν ἐκ τῆς πόλεως, καὶ
this One Is the Christ? They went out, then, from the city, and

**31** ἤρχοντο πρὸς αὐτόν. ἐν δὲ τῷ μεταξὺ ἠρώτων αὐτὸν οἱ
came to Him. In And the meantime asked Him the

**32** μαθηταί, λέγοντες, Ῥαββί, φάγε. ὁ δὲ εἶπεν αὐτοῖς, Ἐγὼ
disciples, saying, Rabbi, eat. He But said to them, I

**33** βρῶσιν ἔχω φαγεῖν ἣν ὑμεῖς οὐκ οἴδατε. ἔλεγον οὖν οἱ
food have to eat which you not do know. said Therefore the

μαθηταὶ πρὸς ἀλλήλους, Μήτις ἤνεγκεν αὐτῷ φαγεῖν;
disciples to one another, No one brought Him to eat?

**34** λέγει αὐτοῖς ὁ Ἰησοῦς, Ἐμὸν βρῶμά ἐστιν, ἵνα ποιῶ τὸ θέλημα
says to them — Jesus, My food is that I may do the will

**35** τοῦ πέμψαντός με, καὶ τελειώσω αὐτοῦ τὸ ἔργον. οὐχ ὑμεῖς
of (Him) having sent Me, and I may finish of Him the work. Not you

λέγετε ὅτι Ἔτι τετράμηνόν ἐστι, καὶ ὁ θερισμὸς ἔρχεται·
say, Yet four months it is, and the harvest comes.

ἰδού, λέγω ὑμῖν, Ἐπάρατε τοὺς ὀφθαλμοὺς ὑμῶν, καὶ
Behold, I say to you, Lift up the eyes of you, and

fields, for they are white to harvest already. [36] And he that reaps receives a reward, and gathers fruit to everlasting life, that both he that sows and he that reaps may rejoice together. [37] For in this the word is true, that another is the (one) sowing, and another the (one) reaping. [38] I sent you to reap what you have not labored over. Others have labored, and you have entered into their labor.

[39] And many of the Samaritans out of that city believed into Him, because of the word of the woman testifying, He told me all things, whatever I did. [40] Then as the Samaritans came to Him, they asked Him to stay with them; and He stayed there two days. [41] And many more believed because of His word; [42] and they said to the woman, We no longer believe because of your saying, for we ourselves have heard, and we know that this is truly the Savior of the world, the Christ.

[43] But after the two days He went out from there, and went away into Galilee; [44] for Jesus Himself testified that a prophet has no honor in his own country. [45] Therefore when He came into Galilee, the Galileans received Him, having seen all the things which He did in Jerusalem during the feast, for they also went to the feast.

[46] Then Jesus came again to Cana of Galilee, where He made the water wine. And there was a certain nobleman whose son was sick in Capernaum. [47] He having heard that Jesus had come out of Judea into Galilee went to Him, and asked Him that He would come down and heal his son; for he was about to die. [48] Therefore Jesus said to him, Unless you see signs and wonders you will in no way believe. [49] The nobleman said to him, Sir

θεάσασθε τὰς χώρας, ὅτι λευκαί εἰσι πρὸς θερισμὸν ἤδη.
behold    the    fields, because white  they are to  harvest  already.

**36** καὶ ὁ θερίζων μισθὸν λαμβάνει, καὶ συνάγει καρπὸν εἰς ζωὴν
And he reaping reward receives,    and gathers fruit  to  life
αἰώνιον· ἵνα καὶ ὁ σπείρων ὁμοῦ χαίρῃ καὶ ὁ θερίζων.
eternal,  that also  he sowing  together may rejoice and he reaping.

**37** ἐν γὰρ τούτῳ ὁ λόγος ἐστὶν· ἀληθινός, ὅτι ἄλλος ἐστὶν ὁ
in For  this the  word  is    true,   that  another  is the (one)

**38** σπείρων, καὶ ἄλλος ὁ θερίζων. ἐγὼ ἀπέστειλα ὑμᾶς θερίζειν
sowing,   and another the (one) reaping. I  sent    you  to reap
ὃ οὐχ ὑμεῖς κεκοπιάκατε· ἄλλοι κεκοπιάκασι, καὶ ὑμεῖς εἰς τὸν
what not you have labored over. Others have labored,  and you into the
κόπον αὐτῶν εἰσεληλύθατε.
labor  of them  have entered.

**39** Ἐκ δὲ τῆς πόλεως ἐκείνης πολλοὶ ἐπίστευσαν εἰς αὐτὸν
out of And  city   that   many  believed  in  Him
τῶν Σαμαρειτῶν διὰ τὸν λόγον τῆς γυναικὸς μαρτυρούσης
of the Samaritans because of the word of the woman  testifying,

**40** ὅτι Εἶπέ μοι πάντα ὅσα ἐποίησα. ὡς οὖν ἦλθον πρὸς αὐτὸν
— He told me all things whatever I did.  As therefore came to  Him
οἱ Σαμαρεῖται, ἠρώτων αὐτὸν μεῖναι παρ' αὐτοῖς· καὶ ἔμεινεν
the Samaritans, they asked  Him to stay  with them,  and He stayed

**41** ἐκεῖ δύο ἡμέρας. καὶ πολλῷ πλείους ἐπίστευσαν διὰ τὸν
there two  days.  And more  many  believed  through the

**42** λόγον αὐτοῦ, τῇ τε γυναικι ἔλεγον ὅτι Οὐκέτι διὰ τὴν σὴν
word  of Him. to the And woman they said, — No longer because of your
λαλιὰν πιστεύομεν· αὐτοὶ γὰρ ἀκηκόαμεν, καὶ οἴδαμεν ὅτι
speaking we believe; (our)selves for we have heard, and we know  that
οὗτός ἐστιν ἀληϑῶς ὁ Σωτὴρ τοῦ κόσμου, ὁ Χριστός.
this One is  truly  the Savior of the world,  the Christ.

**43** Μετὰ δὲ τὰς δυο ἡμέρας ἐξῆλθεν ἐκεῖθεν, καὶ ἀπῆλθεν εἰς
after And the two  days, He went out from there, and went  into

**44** τὴν Γαλιλαιαν. αὐτὸς γὰρ ὁ Ἰησοῦς ἐμαρτύρησεν ὅτι προφή-
—  Galilee. (Him)self For,  Jesus  testified  that a prophet

**45** της ἐν τῇ ἰδίᾳ πατρίδι τιμὴν οὐκ ἔχει. ὅτε οὖν ἦλθεν εἰς τὴν
in the own  native-place honor not has. When, then, He came into —
Γαλιλαίαν, ἐδέξαντο αὐτὸν οἱ Γαλιλαῖοι, πάντα ἑωρακότες
Galilee,   received  Him  the Galileans, all things having seen
ἃ ἐποίησεν ἐν Ἱεροσολύμοις ἐν τῇ ἑορτῇ· καὶ αὐτοὶ γὰρ ἦλθον
which He did in Jerusalem  at the feast. also they For went
εἰς τὴν ἑορτήν.
to the  feast.

**46** Ἦλθεν οὖν ὁ Ἰησοῦς πάλιν εἰς τὴν Κανᾶ τῆς Γαλιλαίας,
came then — Jesus  again to  Cana   of Galilee,
ὅπου ἐποίησε τὸ ὕδωρ οἶνον. καὶ ἦν τις βασιλικός, οὗ ὁ υἱὸς
where He made the water  wine. And was one noble  of whom the son

**47** ἠσθένει ἐν Καπερναούμ. οὗτος ἀκούσας ὅτι Ἰησοῦς ἥκει ἐκ
was ill in Capernaum.  This one hearing that Jesus comes from
τῆς Ἰουδαίας εἰς τὴν Γαλιλαίαν, ἀπῆλθε ·πρὸς αὐτόν, καὶ
—  Judea  into  —  Galilee,   went out to  Him, and
ἠρώτα αὐτὸν ἵνα καταβῇ καὶ ἰάσηται αὐτοῦ τὸν υἱόν·
asked  Him, that He would come and would cure of him the son;

**48** ἤμελλε γὰρ ἀποθνήσκειν. εἶπεν οὖν ὁ Ἰησοῦς πρὸς αὐτόν,
he was For about to die.  said Then  Jesus  to  him,

**49** Ἐὰν μὴ σημεῖα καὶ τέρατα ἴδητε, οὐ μὴ πιστεύσητε. λέγει
Except signs and wonders you see, in no way you believe. says
will

come down before my little child dies. [50] Jesus said to him, Go, your son lives. And the man believed the word which Jesus said to him, and went away. [51] But already as he was going down his slaves met him, and reported, saying, The child lives. [52] He than asked from them the hour in which he got better. And they said to him, Yesterday (at the) seventh hour the fever left him. [53] Then the father knew that (it was) at that hour in which Jesus said to him, Your son lives. And he himself believed, and his whole household. [54] This again a second miracle Jesus did, having come out of Judea into Galilee.

πρὸς αὐτὸν ὁ βασιλικός, Κύριε, κατάβηθι πρὶν ἀποθανεῖν
to   Him The   noble    Lord, come down before dies

**50** τὸ παιδίον μου. λέγει αὐτῷ ὁ Ἰησοῦς, Πορεύου· ὁ υἱός σου
the child of me. says   to him   —   Jesus,   Go,     the son of you

ζῇ. καὶ ἐπίστευσεν ὁ ἄνθρωπος τῷ λόγῳ ᾧ εἶπεν αὐτῷ
lives. And   believed   the man     the word which said to him

**51** Ἰησοῦς, καὶ ἐπορεύετο. ἤδη δὲ αὐτοῦ καταβαίνοντος, οἱ
Jesus,   and   went away. already And (as) he (was) going down   the

δοῦλοι αὐτοῦ ἀπήντησαν αὐτῷ, καὶ ἀπήγγειλαν λέγοντες
slaves of him   met     him, and   reported,     saying,

**52** ὅτι Ὁ παῖς σου ζῇ. ἐπύθετο οὖν παρ' αὐτῶν τὴν ὥραν ἐν
—   The child of you lives. He asked then from   them   the   hour   in

ᾗ κομψότερον ἔσχε. καὶ εἶπον αὐτῷ ὅτι Χθὲς ὥραν ἑβδόμην
which better    he had. And they said to him, Yesterday (at) hour seventh

**53** ἀφῆκεν αὐτὸν ὁ πυρετός. ἔγνω οὖν ὁ πατὴρ ὅτι ἐν ἐκείνῃ τῇ
left    him the fever.   Knew, then, the father that in that   —

ὥρα, ἐν ᾗ εἶπεν αὐτῷ ὁ Ἰησοῦς ὅτι Ὁ υἱός σου ζῇ· καὶ
hour in which said   to him   —   Jesus,   — The son of you lives. And

**54** ἐπίστευσεν αὐτὸς καὶ ἡ οἰκία αὐτοῦ ὅλη. τοῦτο πάλιν
he believed, himself and the house of him whole. This     again,

δεύτερον σημεῖον ἐποίησεν ὁ Ἰησοῦς, ἐλθὼν ἐκ τῆς Ἰουδαίας
a second    sign,     did    —   Jesus, having come from   Judea

εἰς τὴν Γαλιλαίαν.
into —     Galilee.

# CHAPTER 5

## CHAPTER 5

[1] After these things there was a feast of the Jews, and Jesus went up to Jerusalem. [2] And there is in Jerusalem at the Sheepgate a pool, which (is) called in Hebrew, Bethesda, having five porches. [3] In these were lying a great multitude of those who were sick, blind, lame, withered, awaiting the moving of the water. [4] For an angel from time to time descended into the pool and agitated the water; then he who entered after the agitation of the water became well, whatever disease he was held by. [5] But a certain man was there, being thirty-eight years in infirmity. [6] Jesus seeing him lying, and knowing that he had been a long time already, said to him, Do you desire to become well? [7] The infirm one answered Him, Sir, I have no man, that when the water has been agitated he may put me into the pool; but while I am coming,

**1** Μετὰ ταῦτα ἦν ἑορτὴ τῶν Ἰουδαίων, καὶ ἀνέβη ὁ
After these things was a feast of the    Jews,     and went up —

Ἰησοῦς εἰς Ἱεροσόλυμα.
Jesus to     Jerusalem.

**2** Ἔστι δὲ ἐν τοῖς Ἱεροσολύμοις ἐπὶ τῇ προβατικῇ κολυμ-
is   And in   —    Jerusalem    at   the Sheep Gate   a pool,

βήθρα, ἡ ἐπιλεγομένη Ἑβραϊστὶ Βηθεσδά, πέντε στοὰς
which (is) called    in Hebrew Bethesda,   five   porches

**3** ἔχουσα. ἐν ταύταις κατέκειτο πλῆθος πολὺ τῶν ἀσθενούν-
having. In   these    were lying a multitude   great, of the infirm,

των, τυφλῶν, χωλῶν, ξηρῶν, ἐκδεχομένων τὴν τοῦ ὕδατος
blind ones, lame ones, withered ones, awaiting    the of the water

**4** κίνησιν. ἄγγελος γὰρ κατὰ καιρὸν κατέβαινεν ἐν τῇ
stirring.   an angel For   at   a time     descended    in the

κολυμβήθρα, καὶ ἐτάρασσε τὸ ὕδωρ· ὁ οὖν πρῶτος ἐμβὰς
pool,    and agitated    the water. he Then   first   entering

μετὰ τὴν ταραχὴν τοῦ ὕδατος, ὑγιὴς ἐγίνετο, ᾧ δήποτε
after the   agitation   of the   water.   whole became, to what ever

**5** κατείχετο νοσήματι. ἦν δέ τις ἄνθρωπος ἐκεῖ τριάκοντα καὶ
he was held by   disease. was But a certain   man    there thirty     and

**6** ὀκτὼ ἔτη ἔχων ἐν τῇ ἀσθενείᾳ. τοῦτον ἰδὼν ὁ Ἰησοῦς
eight years being in — infirmity.    this one, seeing — Jesus,

κατακείμενον, καὶ γνοὺς ὅτι πολὺν ἤδη χρόνον ἔχει, λέγει
lying (there)   and knowing that   much already   time he has (spent), says

**7** αὐτῷ, Θέλεις ὑγιὴς γενέσθαι : ἀπεκρίθη αὐτῷ ὁ ἀσθενῶν,
to him. Desire you whole to become?   answered    Him The sick one,

Κύριε, ἄνθρωπον οὐκ ἔχω ἵνα, ὅταν ταραχθῇ τὸ ὕδωρ,
Lord,    a man   not I have, that   when is agitated the   water,

βάλλῃ με εἰς τὴν κολυμβήθραν· ἐν ᾧ δὲ ἔρχομαι ἐγώ, ἄλλος
he cast me into the     pool;     while but am coming I,   another

another descends before me. [8] Jesus said to him, Rise up, take up your bed and walk. [9] And immediately the man became well, and took up his bed, and walked; and it was sabbath on that day. [10] Therefore the Jews said to him who had been healed, It is sabbath, it is not lawful for you to take up the bed. [11] He answered them, He who made me well, He said to me, Take up your bed and walk. [12] Therefore they asked him, Who is the man who said to you, Take up your bed and walk? [13] But he who had been healed did not know it was, for Jesus had moved away, a crowd being in that place. [14] After these things Jesus found him in the Temple, and said to him, Behold, you have become well; sin no more, that nothing worse happens to you. [15] The man went away and told the Jews that it was Jesus who made him well. [16] And because of this the Jews persecuted Jesus, and lusted to kill Him, because He did these things on a sabbath. [17] But Jesus answered them, My Father works until now, and I work. [18] Because of this, therefore, the Jews the more lusted to kill Him, because not only did He break the sabbath, but also called God His own Father, making Himself equal to God. [19] Therefore Jesus answered and said to them, Truly, truly, I say to you, the Son is able to do nothing from Himself, except what He may see the Father doing; for whatever He does, these things the Son also does in the same way. [20] For the Father loves the Son, and shows all things to Him which He Himself does. And He will show Him greater works than these in order that you may marvel. [21] For even as the Father raises up the dead and gives life, so also the Son gives life to whomever He will;

**8** προ ἐμοῦ καταβαίνει. λέγει αὐτῷ ὁ Ἰησοῦς, Ἔγειραι, ἆρον
before me goes down. says to him Jesus, Rise, Take up

**9** τὸν κράββατόν σου, καὶ περιπάτει. καὶ εὐθέως ἐγένετο ὑγιὴς
the mattress of you, and walk! And instantly became whole

ὁ ἄνθρωπος, καὶ ἦρε τὸν κράββατον αὐτοῦ καὶ περιεπάτει.
the man, and took up the mattress of him and walked.

**10** Ἦν δὲ σάββατον ἐν ἐκείνῃ τῇ ἡμέρᾳ. ἔλεγον οὖν οἱ
it was And a sabbath on that — day. said Therefore the

Ἰουδαῖοι τῷ τεθεραπευμένῳ, Σάββατόν ἐστιν· οὐκ ἔξεστί
Jews to the (one) having been healed, A sabbath it is; not it is lawful

**11** σοι ἆραι τὸν κράββατον. ἀπεκρίθη αὐτοῖς, Ὁ ποιήσας με
for you to lift the mattress. He answered them, The (One) making me

ὑγιῆ, ἐκεῖνός μοι εἶπεν, Ἆρον τὸν κράββατόν σου καὶ
whole, that One to me said, Lift up the mattress of you, and

**12** περιπάτει. ἠρώτησαν οὖν αὐτόν, Τίς ἐστιν ὁ ἄνθρωπος ὁ
walk. they asked Therefore him, Who is the man who

**13** εἰπών σοι, Ἆρον τὸν κράββατόν σου καὶ περιπάτει; ὁ δὲ
told you, Lift up the mattress of you and walk? he But

ἰαθεὶς οὐκ ᾔδει τίς ἐστιν· ὁ γὰρ Ἰησοῦς ἐξένευσεν, ὄχλου
cured not did know who it is. — For Jesus had withdrawn, a crowd

**14** ὄντος ἐν τῷ τόπῳ. μετὰ ταῦτα εὑρίσκει αὐτὸν ὁ Ἰησοῦς
being in the place. After these things finds him — Jesus

ἐν τῷ ἱερῷ, καὶ εἶπεν αὐτῷ, Ἴδε ὑγιὴς γέγονας· μηκέτι
in the Temple, and said to him, Behold, whole you have become; no more

**15** ἁμάρτανε, ἵνα μὴ χεῖρόν τί σοι γένηται. ἀπῆλθεν ὁ ἄνθρω-
sin, lest a worse thing to you occur. went away The man

πος, καὶ ἀνήγγειλε τοῖς Ἰουδαίοις ὅτι Ἰησοῦς ἐστιν ὁ ποιή-
and told the Jews that Jesus is He

**16** σας αὐτὸν ὑγιῆ. καὶ διὰ τοῦτο ἐδίωκον τὸν Ἰησοῦν οἱ
making him whole. And therefore persecuted — Jesus the

Ἰουδαῖοι, καὶ ἐζήτουν αὐτὸν ἀποκτεῖναι, ὅτι ταῦτα ἐποίει
Jews, and sought Him to kill, because these things He did

**17** ἐν σαββάτῳ. ὁ δὲ Ἰησοῦς ἀπεκρίνατο αὐτοῖς, Ὁ πατήρ μου
on a sabbath. — But Jesus answered to them, The Father of Me

**18** ἕως ἄρτι ἐργάζεται, κἀγὼ ἐργάζομαι. διὰ τοῦτο οὖν μᾶλλον
until now works, and I work. Because of this, then, the more

ἐζήτουν αὐτὸν οἱ Ἰουδαῖοι ἀποκτεῖναι, ὅτι οὐ μόνον ἔλυε τὸ
sought him the Jews to kill, because not only He broke the

σάββατον, ἀλλὰ καὶ πατέρα ἴδιον ἔλεγε τὸν Θεόν, ἴσον
sabbath, but also Father His own called — God, equal

ἑαυτὸν ποιῶν τῷ Θεῷ.
Himself making — to God.

**19** Ἀπεκρίνατο οὖν ὁ Ἰησοῦς καὶ εἶπεν αὐτοῖς, Ἀμὴν ἀμὴν
answered Therefore Jesus and said to them, Truly, truly

λέγω ὑμῖν, οὐ δύναται ὁ υἱὸς ποιεῖν ἀφ᾽ ἑαυτοῦ οὐδέν, ἐὰν
I say to you, not is able the Son to do from Himself nothing, un-

μή τι βλέπῃ τὸν πατέρα ποιοῦντα· ἃ γὰρ ἂν ἐκεῖνος ποιῇ,
less what He may see the Father doing; what For ever that One does

**20** ταῦτα καὶ ὁ υἱὸς ὁμοίως ποιεῖ. ὁ γὰρ πατὴρ φιλεῖ τὸν υἱόν,
these things also the Son likewise does. the For Father loves the Son,

καὶ πάντα δείκνυσιν αὐτῷ ἃ αὐτὸς ποιεῖ· καὶ μείζονα τούτων
and all things shows to Him which He does; and greater (than) these

**21** δείξει αὐτῷ ἔργα, ἵνα ὑμεῖς θαυμάζητε. ὥσπερ γὰρ ὁ πατὴρ
He will show Him works, that you may marvel. even as For the Father

ἐγείρει τοὺς νεκροὺς καὶ ζωοποιεῖ, οὕτω καὶ ὁ υἱὸς οὓς θέλει
raises up the dead and makes alive so also the Son whom He wills

[22] for the Father judges no one, but has given all judgment to the Son, [23] that all may honor the Son even as they honor the Father. He that does not honor the Son does not honor the Father who sent Him. [24] Truly, truly, I say to you, that he that hears My word, and believes Him who sent Me, has everlasting life, and does not come into judgment, but has passed out of death into life. [25] Truly, truly, I say to you that an hour is coming and now is when the dead shall hear the voice of the Son of God, and those having heard shall live. [26] For even as the Father has life in Himself, so He gave also to the Son to have life in Himself, [27] and gave authority to Him also to execute judgment, because He is Son of man. [28] Do not marvel at this, for an hour is coming in which all those in the tombs shall hear His voice, [29] and shall come forth, those that have practiced good to a resurrection of life, and those that did evil to a resurrection of judgment. [30] I am not able to do anything for Myself; even as I hear I judge, and My judgment is just, because I do not seek My will, but the will of the Father who sent Me. [31] If I bear witness concerning Myself, My witness is not true; [32] it is another who bears witness about Me, and I know that the witness which He testifies concerning Me is true. [33] You have sent to John, and he has testified to the truth. [34] But I do not receive witness from man, but I say these things that you may be saved. [35] He was the burning and shining lamp, and you were willing to rejoice for an hour in his light. [36] But I have the greater witness than John's, for the works that the Father gave Me, that I should

**22** ζωοποιεῖ. οὐδὲ γὰρ ὁ πατὴρ κρίνει οὐδένα, ἀλλὰ τὴν κρίσιν
He makes alive. not For the Father judges no one, but — judgment

**23** πᾶσαν δέδωκε τῷ υἱῷ· ἵνα πάντες τιμῶσι τὸν υἱόν, καθὼς
all He has given to the Son, that all may honor the Son, even as

τιμῶσι τὸν πατέρα ὁ μὴ τιμῶν τὸν· υἱόν, οὐ τιμᾷ τὸν
they honor the Father. He not honoring the Son not does honor the

**24** πατέρα τὸν πέμψαντα αὐτόν. ἀμὴν ἀμὴν λέγω ὑμῖν ὅτι ὁ
Father, the (One) having sent Him. Truly, truly I say to you, The (one)

τὸν λόγον μου ἀκούων, καὶ πιστεύων τῷ πέμψαντί με, ἔχει
the word of Me hearing, and believing the (One) having sent Me, has

ζωὴν αἰώνιον· καὶ εἰς κρίσιν οὐκ ἔρχεται, ἀλλὰ μεταβέβηκεν
life everlasting and into judgment not comes, but has passed

**25** ἐκ τοῦ θανάτου εἰς τὴν ζωήν. ἀμὴν ἀμὴν λέγω ὑμῖν ὅτι
out of — death into — life. Truly, truly, I say to you, —

ἔρχεται ὥρα καὶ νῦν ἐστιν, ὅτε οἱ νεκροὶ ἀκούσονται τῆς
comes An hour, and now is, when the dead will hear from the

φωνῆς τοῦ υἱοῦ τοῦ Θεοῦ, καὶ οἱ ἀκούσαντες ζήσονται.
voice of the Son — of God, and those hearing will live. .

**26** ὥσπερ γὰρ ὁ πατὴρ ἔχει ζωὴν ἐν ἑαυτῷ, οὕτως ἔδωκε καὶ
even as For the Father has life in Himself, so He gave also

**27** τῷ υἱῷ ζωὴν ἔχειν ἐν ἑαυτῷ· καὶ ἐξουσίαν ἔδωκεν αὐτῷ καὶ
to the Son life to have in Himself. And authority He gave to Him, also

**28** κρίσιν ποιεῖν, ὅτι υἱὸς ἀνθρώπου ἐστί. μὴ θαυμάζετε τοῦτο·
judgment to do, because(the) Son of man He is. not Marvel (at) this

ὅτι ἔρχεται ὥρα, ἐν ᾗ πάντες οἱ ἐν τοῖς μνημείοις ἀκούσονται
for comes an hour in which all those in the tombs will hear

**29** τῆς φωνῆς αὐτοῦ, καὶ ἐκπορεύσονται, οἱ τὰ ἀγαθὰ ποιή-
the voice of Him, and will come out; those the good having

σαντες, εἰς ἀνάστασιν ζωῆς· οἱ δὲ τὰ φαῦλα πράξαντες, εἰς
done, into a resurrection of life; those and the evil having practiced into

ἀνάστασιν κρίσεως.
a resurrection of judgment.

**30** Οὐ δύναμαι ἐγὼ ποιεῖν ἀπ᾽ ἐμαυτοῦ οὐδέν· καθὼς ἀκούω,
not am able I to do from Myself nothing; just as I hear,

κρίνω· καὶ ἡ κρίσις ἡ ἐμὴ δικαία ἐστίν· ὅτι οὐ ζητῶ τὸ
I judge; and judgment — My just is, because not I seek —

θέλημα τὸ ἐμόν, ἀλλὰ τὸ θέλημα τοῦ πέμψαντός με πατρός.
will — My, but the will of the (One) sending Me, (the) Father.

**31** ἐὰν ἐγὼ μαρτυρῶ περὶ ἐμαυτοῦ, ἡ μαρτυρία μου οὐκ ἔστιν
If I witness concerning Myself, the witness of Me not is

**32** ἀληθής. ἄλλος ἐστὶν ὁ μαρτυρῶν περὶ ἐμοῦ, καὶ οἶδα ὅτι
true; another there is that witnesses concerning Me, and I know that

**33** ἀληθής ἐστιν ἡ μαρτυρία ἣν μαρτυρεῖ περὶ ἐμοῦ. ὑμεῖς
true is the witness which He witnesses concerning Me. You

ἀπεστάλκατε πρὸς Ἰωάννην, καὶ μεμαρτύρηκε τῇ ἀληθείᾳ.
have sent to John, and he has witnessed to the truth;

**34** ἐγὼ δὲ οὐ παρὰ ἀνθρώπου τὴν μαρτυρίαν λαμβάνω, ἀλλὰ
I but not from man the witness receive, but

**35** ταῦτα λέγω ἵνα ὑμεῖς σωθῆτε. ἐκεῖνος ἦν ὁ λύχνος ὁ καιό-
these things I say that you may be saved. That one was the lamp —

μενος καὶ φαίνων, ὑμεῖς δὲ ἠθελήσατε ἀγαλλιασθῆναι πρὸς
burning and shining; you and were willing to exult for

**36** ὥραν ἐν τῷ φωτὶ αὐτοῦ. ἐγὼ δὲ ἔχω τὴν μαρτυρίαν μείζω
an hour in the light of him. I But have the witness greater

τοῦ Ἰωάννου· τὰ γὰρ ἔργα ἃ ἔδωκέ μοι ὁ πατὴρ ἵνα
than of John; the for works which has given Me the Father that

finish them, the works which I do themselves witness about Me, that the Father has sent Me. [37] And the Father who sent Me has Himself borne witness concerning Me. You have neither heard His voice at any time, nor have you seen His form. [38] And you do not have His word abiding in you, for whom He sent, you do not believe Him. [39] You search the Scriptures, for you think to have everlasting life in them, and they are they which bear witness concerning Me; [40] and you are unwilling to come to Me that you may have life. [41] I do not receive glory from men; [42] but I have known you that you do not have the love of God in yourselves. [43] I have come in the name of My Father, and you do not receive Me; if another should come in his own name, you will receive him. [44] How are you able to believe, who receive glory from one another, and the glory which (is) from the only God you do not seek? [45] Do not think that I will accuse you to the Father; there is (one) accusing you, Moses, in whom you have hoped. [46] For if you were believing Moses, you then were believing Me; for that one wrote about Me. [47] But if you believe not that one's writings, how will you believe My words?

CHAPTER 6

[1] After these things Jesus went away over the Sea of Galilee, the Tiberian (Sea). [2] And a great crowd followed Him, because they saw His miracles which He worked on those who were sick. [3] And Jesus went up into the mountain, and sat there with His disciples; [4] and the Passover was near, the feast of the Jews. [5] Then Jesus lifting up the eyes, and beholding a great crowd is coming to Him, He says to Philip, From where shall we buy loaves that these may eat?

τελειώσω αὐτά, αὐτὰ τὰ ἔργα ἃ ἐγὼ ποιῶ, μαρτυρεῖ περὶ
I may finish them,   themselves the works that I do      witness   about

**37** ἐμοῦ ὅτι ὁ πατήρ με ἀπέσταλκε. καὶ ὁ πέμψας με πατήρ,
Me, that the Father  Me has sent.     And He having sent Me (the) Father,

αὐτὸς μεμαρτύρηκε περὶ ἐμοῦ. οὔτε φωνὴν αὐτοῦ ἀκηκόατε
He      has witnessed concerning Me. Neither the voice of Him have you heard

**38** πώποτε, οὔτε εἶδος αὐτοῦ ἑωράκατε. καὶ τὸν λόγον αὐτοῦ
at any time, nor  form  His have you seen. And the word  of Him

οὐκ ἔχετε μένοντα ἐν ὑμῖν, ὅτι ὃν ἀπέστειλεν ἐκεῖνος, τούτῳ
not you have abiding  in you, for whom sent    that One, this One

**39** ὑμεῖς οὐ πιστεύετε. ἐρευνᾶτε τὰς γραφάς, ὅτι ὑμεῖς δοκεῖτε
you  do not believe. You search  the Scriptures, because you think

ἐν αὐταῖς ζωὴν αἰώνιον ἔχειν, καὶ ἐκεῖναί εἰσιν αἱ μαρτυ-
in them  life everlasting you have, and those    are the (ones)

**40** ροῦσαι περὶ ἐμοῦ· καὶ οὐ θέλετε ἐλθεῖν πρός με, ἵνα ζωὴν
witnessing about Me.   And not you desire to come to  Me. that life

**41** ἔχητε. δόξαν παρὰ ἀνθρώπων οὐ λαμβάνω· ἀλλ' ἔγνωκα
**42** you may have. glory from    men    not I receive,   but I have known

ὑμᾶς, ὅτι τὴν ἀγάπην τοῦ Θεοῦ οὐκ ἔχετε ἐν ἑαυτοῖς.
you, that the love   — of God not you have in yourselves.

**43** ἐγὼ ἐλήλυθα ἐν τῷ ὀνόματι τοῦ πατρός μου, καὶ οὐ
I    have come in the  name  of the Father of Me, and not

λαμβάνετέ με· ἐὰν ἄλλος ἔλθῃ ἐν τῷ ὀνόματι τῷ ἰδίῳ, ἐκεῖνον
you receive  Me; if another comes in — name    the own, that one

**44** λήψεσθε. πῶς δύνασθε ὑμεῖς πιστεῦσαι, δόξαν παρὰ ἀλλή-
you will receive. How can  you   believe,    glory from one

λων λαμβάνοντες, καὶ τὴν δόξαν τὴν παρὰ τοῦ μόνου Θεοῦ
another receiving, and the glory   — from the only God

**45** οὐ ζητεῖτε; μὴ δοκεῖτε ὅτι ἐγὼ κατηγορήσω ὑμῶν πρὸς τὸν
not you seek? Do not think that I  will accuse  you to the

πατέρα· ἔστιν ὁ κατηγορῶν ὑμῶν, Μωσῆς, εἰς ὃν ὑμεῖς
Father; there is the (one) accusing  you,  Moses,  in whom you

**46** ἠλπίκατε. εἰ γὰρ ἐπιστεύετε Μωσῆ, ἐπιστεύετε ἂν ἐμοί·
have hoped. if For you were believing Moses, you were believing then Me;

**47** περὶ γὰρ ἐμοῦ ἐκεῖνος ἔγραψεν. εἰ δὲ τοῖς ἐκείνου γράμμασιν
about for   Me that one wrote.   if But the of that one writings

οὐ πιστεύετε, πῶς τοῖς ἐμοῖς ῥήμασι πιστεύσετε;
not you believe, how —  My  words  will you believe?

## CHAPTER 6

**1** Μετὰ ταῦτα ἀπῆλθεν ὁ Ἰησοῦς πέραν τῆς θαλάσσης τῆς
After these things went away Jesus   across   the   sea   —

**2** Γαλιλαίας, τῆς Τιβεριάδος. καὶ ἠκολούθει αὐτῷ ὄχλος πολύς,
of Galilee,  —  of Tiberias.  And followed   Him a crowd great

ὅτι ἑώρων αὐτοῦ τὰ σημεῖα ἃ ἐποίει ἐπὶ τῶν ἀσθενούντων.
for they saw  of Him the signs which He did on the  sick ones.

**3** ἀνῆλθε δὲ εἰς τὸ ὄρος ὁ Ἰησοῦς, καὶ ἐκεῖ ἐκάθητο μετὰ τῶν
went up And to the mountain Jesus,  and there sat     with the

**4** μαθητῶν αὐτοῦ. ἦν δὲ ἐγγὺς τὸ πάσχα, ἡ ἑορτὴ τῶ
disciples  of Him. was And near the Passover, the feast of the

**5** Ἰουδαίων. ἐπάρας οὖν ὁ Ἰησοῦς τοὺς ὀφθαλμούς, καὶ
Jews.  lifting up Then  Jesus  the   eyes,   and

θεασάμενος ὅτι πολὺς ὄχλος ἔρχεται πρὸς αὐτόν, λέγει πρὸς
beholding that a great  crowd is coming to   Him, He says to

τὸν Φίλιππον, Πόθεν ἀγοράσωμεν ἄρτους, ἵνα φάγωσιν
Philip.  From where may we buy    loaves   that may eat

[6] But He said this testing him, for He knew what He was about to do. [7] Philip answered Him, Loaves for two hundred denarii are not enough for them, that each of them may receive a little. [8] One of His disciples said to Him, Andrew the brother of Simon Peter, [9] A little boy is here who has five barley loaves and two small fish; for what are these for so many? [10] And Jesus said, Make the men to recline. Now much grass was in the place; therefore the men reclined, the number about five thousand. [11] And Jesus took the loaves, and having given thanks, distributed to the disciples, and the disciples to those reclining. And in the same way of the small fish as much as they wished. [12] And when they were filled, He said to His disciples, Collect the fragments over and above, that nothing may be lost. [13] Therefore they collected and filled twelve baskets of fragments from the five barley loaves which were left over to those who had eaten. [14] Then the men having seen what miracle Jesus had done said, This is truly the Prophet who is coming into the world. [15] Then Jesus knowing that they were about to come and seize Him, that they might make Him king, withdrew again to the mountain, alone (by) Himself.

[16] And when it became evening, His disciples went down to the sea, [17] And having entered into the boat, they were going over the sea to Capernaum. And it had already become dark, and Jesus had not come to them. [18] And the sea was turbulent because of a strong wind blowing. [19] Having rode then about twenty-five or thirty furlongs, they saw Jesus walking on the sea, and coming near the boat, and they were frightened. [20] But He said to them, I AM; do not fear. [21] Then they were

**6** οὗτοι ; τοῦτο δὲ ἔλεγε πειράζων αὐτόν· αὐτὸς γὰρ ᾔδει τί
these? this And He said testing him; he for knew what
**7** ἔμελλε ποιεῖν. ἀπεκρίθη αὐτῷ Φίλιππος Διακοσίων
He was going to do. answered Him Philip, Of two hundred
δηναρίων ἄρτοι οὐκ ἀρκοῦσιν αὐτοῖς, ἵνα ἕκαστος αὐτῶν
denarii loaves not are enough for them, that each of them
**8** βραχύ τι λάβῃ. λέγει αὐτῷ εἷς ἐκ τῶν μαθητῶν αὐτοῦ,
a little may receive. says to Him one of the disciples of Him,
Ἀνδρέας ὁ ἀδελφὸς Σίμωνος Πέτρου, Ἔστι παιδάριον ἓν
Andrew the brother of Simon Peter, There is little boy one
ὧδε, ὃ ἔχει πέντε ἄρτους κριθίνους καὶ δύο ὀψάρια· ἀλλὰ
here, who has five loaves (of) barley, and two fish; but
**10** ταῦτα τί ἐστιν εἰς τοσούτους ; εἶπε δὲ ὁ Ἰησοῦς, Ποιήσατε
these what are to so many? said And— Jesus, Make
τοὺς ἀνθρώπους ἀναπεσεῖν. ἦν δὲ χόρτος πολὺς ἐν τῷ τόπῳ.
the men to recline was And grass much in the place.
ἀνέπεσον οὖν οἱ ἄνδρες τὸν ἀριθμὸν ὡσεὶ πεντακισχίλιοι.
Reclined, therefore, the men, the number about five thousand.
**11** ἔλαβε δὲ τοὺς ἄρτους ὁ Ἰησοῦς, καὶ εὐχαριστήσας διέδωκε
took And the loaves — Jesus, and having given thanks dealt out
τοῖς μαθηταῖς, οἱ δὲ μαθηταὶ τοῖς ἀνακειμένοις· ὁμοίως καὶ ἐκ
to the disciples, the and disciples to those reclining; likewise and
**12** τῶν ὀψαρίων ὅσον ἤθελον. ὡς δὲ ἐνεπλήσθησαν, λέγει τοῖς
the fish, as much as they desired. as and they were filled, He says to the
μαθηταῖς αὐτοῦ, Συναγάγετε τὰ περισσεύσαντα κλάσματα,
disciples of Him, Gather together the left over fragments,
**13** ἵνα μή τι ἀπόληται. συνήγαγον οὖν, καὶ ἐγέμισαν δώδεκα
that not anything be lost. they gathered Then, and filled twelve
κοφίνους κλασμάτων ἐκ τῶν πέντε ἄρτων τῶν κριθίνων, ἃ
baskets with fragments of the five loaves — (of) barley which
**14** ἐπερίσσευσε τοῖς βεβρωκόσιν. οἱ οὖν ἄνθρωποι ἰδόντες ὃ
were left over to those having eaten. the Therefore men, seeing what
ἐποίησε σημεῖον ὁ Ἰησοῦς, ἔλεγον ὅτι Οὗτός ἐστιν ἀληθῶς ὁ
did sir — Jesus, said, — This is truly the
**15** προφήτης ὁ ἐρχόμενος εἰς τὸν κόσμον. Ἰησοῦς οὖν γνοὺς
prophet, the (one) coming into the world. Jesus Then, knowing
ὅτι μέλλουσιν ἔρχεσθαι καὶ ἁρπάζειν αὐτόν, ἵνα ποιήσωσιν
that they are about to come and seize Him, that they may make
αὐτὸν βασιλέα, ἀνεχώρησε πάλιν εἰς τὸ ὄρος αὐτὸς μόνος.
Him king, withdrew again into the mountain, Himself alone.
**16** Ὡς δὲ ὀψία ἐγένετο, κατέβησαν οἱ μαθηταὶ αὐτοῦ ἐπὶ τὴν
when And evening it was, went down the disciples of Him on the
**17** θάλασσαν, καὶ ἐμβάντες εἰς τὸ πλοῖον, ἤρχοντο πέραν τῆς
sea. And having entered into the boat, they were going across the
θαλάσσης εἰς Καπερναούμ. καὶ σκοτία ἤδη ἐγεγόνει, καὶ οὐκ
sea to Capernaum. And darkness already occurred, and not
**18** ἐληλύθει πρὸς αὐτοὺς ὁ Ἰησοῦς. ἥ τε θάλασσα ἀνέμου μεγά-
had come to them — Jesus. And the sea by a wind great
**19** λου πνέοντος διηγείρετο. ἐληλακότες οὖν ὡς σταδίους εἴκοσι-
blowing was aroused. having rowed Then about furlongs twenty-
πέντε ἢ τριάκοντα, θεωροῦσι τὸν Ἰησοῦν περιπατοῦντα ἐπὶ
five, or thirty, they behold — Jesus walking on
τῆς θαλάσσης, καὶ ἐγγὺς τοῦ πλοίου γινόμενον· καὶ ἐφοβήθη-
the sea, and near the boat becoming; and they feared.
**20** σαν. ὁ δὲ λέγει αὐτοῖς, Ἐγώ εἰμι· μὴ φοβεῖσθε. ἤθελον οὖν
**21** He But says to them, I AM! Do not fear. they desired Then

willing to receive Him into the boat, and the boat was instantly at the land to which they were going.

[22] On the morrow the crowd which stood on the other side of the sea, having seen that no other small boat was there except one, that into which His disciples entered, and that Jesus did not go with His disciples into the small boat, but that the disciples went away alone — [23] but other small boats came from Tiberias near the place where they ate the bread, the Lord having given thanks — [24] therefore ' when the crowd saw that Jesus was not there, nor His disciples, they themselves also entered into the boats and came to Capernaum seeking Jesus. [25] And having found Him on the other side of the sea, they said to Him, Teacher, when did you come here? [26] Jesus answered them and said, Truly, truly, I say to you, you seek Me not because you saw miracles, but because you ate of the loaves and were satisfied. [27] Do not labor (for) the food which perishes but for the food which endures to everlasting life, which the Son of man will give to you; for Him the Father sealed, (even) God. [28] Then they said to Him, What shall we do that we may work the works of God? [29] Jesus answered and said to Him, This is the work of God, that you should believe on Him whom He sent. [30] Then they said to Him, What miracle then do you do that we may see and may believe you? What do you work? [31] Our fathers ate the manna in the wilderness, as it is written, "He gave them bread out of Heaven to eat.'' [32] Then Jesus said to them, Truly, truly, I say to you, Moses has not given you the bread out of Heaven, but My Father gives you the bread out of the true Heaven.

λαβεῖν αὐτὸν εἰς τὸ πλοῖον· καὶ εὐθέως τὸ πλοῖον ἐγένετο
to take    Him into the    boat; and instantly the boat    became

ἐπὶ τῆς γῆς εἰς ἣν ὑπῆγον.
at the land to which they were going.

**22** Τῇ ἐπαύριον ὁ ὄχλος ὁ ἑστηκὼς πέραν τῆς θαλάσσης,
On the morrow the crowd — standing   across  the   sea

ἰδὼν ὅτι πλοιάριον ἀλλο οὐκ ἦν ἐκεῖ εἰ μὴ ἓν ἐκεῖνο εἰς ὃ
had seen  that little boat another not was there, except one, that into which

ἐνέβησαν οἱ μαθηταὶ αὐτοῦ, καὶ ὅτι οὐ συνεισῆλθε τοῖς
entered  the disciples of Him; and that not went with  the

μαθηταῖς αὐτου ὁ Ἰησοῦς εἰς το πλοιάριον, ἀλλὰ μόνοι οἱ
disciples of Him — Jesus into the little boat,  but alone the

**23** μαθηταὶ αὐτοῦ ἀπῆλθον, (ἀλλὰ δὲ ἦλθε πλοιάρια ἐκ
disciples of Him went away.  other But came little boats from

Τιβεριάδος ἐγγὺς τοῦ τόπου ὅπου ἔφαγον τὸν ἄρτον,
Tiberias  near   the place where they ate the loaves,

**24** εὐχαριστήσαντος τοῦ Κυρίου)· ὅτε οὖν εἶδεν ὁ ὄχλος ὅτι
having given thanks the Lord.  when Therefore saw the crowd that

Ἰησοῦς οὐκ ἔστιν ἐκεῖ οὐδὲ οἱ μαθηταὶ αὐτοῦ, ἐνέβησαν καὶ
Jesus  not is there,  nor the disciples of Him, they entered also

αὐτοὶ εἰς τὰ πλοῖα, καὶ ἦλθον εἰς Καπερναούμ, ζητοῦντες τὸν
themselves into the boats, and came to Capernaum  seeking —

**25** Ἰησοῦν. καὶ εὑρόντες αὐτὸν πέραν τῆς θαλάσσης, εἶπον
Jesus. And having found Him across the sea,  they said

**26** αὐτῷ, Ῥαββί, πότε ὧδε γέγονας; ἀπεκρίθη αὐτοῖς ὁ
to Him, Rabbi,  when here did you come? answered them —

Ἰησοῦς καὶ εἶπεν, Ἀμὴν ἀμὴν λέγω ὑμῖν, ζητεῖτέ με, οὐχ ὅτι
Jesus and said,  Truly, truly, I say to you, You seek Me, not because

εἴδετε σημεῖα, ἀλλ' ὅτι ἐφάγετε ἐκ τῶν ἄρτων καὶ ἐχορτά-
you saw signs, but because you ate of the loaves and were

**27** σθητε. ἐργάζεσθε μὴ τὴν βρῶσιν τὴν ἀπολλυμένην, ἀλλὰ
satisfied. Work  not (for) the food  —  perishing,  but

τὴν βρῶσιν τὴν μένουσαν εἰς ζωὴν αἰώνιον, ἣν ὁ υἱὸς τοῦ
the food  — enduring to life everlasting, which the Son —

ἀνθρώπου ὑμῖν δώσει· τοῦτον γὰρ ὁ πατὴρ ἐσφράγισεν,
of man  to you will give; this One for the Father sealed,

**28** ὁ Θεός. εἶπον οὖν πρὸς αὐτόν, Τί ποιῶμεν, ἵνα ἐργαζώμεθα
— God. they said Then to Him, What may we do that we may work

**29** τὰ ἔργα τοῦ Θεοῦ; ἀπεκρίθη ὁ Ἰησοῦς καὶ εἶπεν αὐτοῖς,
the works — of God? answered — Jesus and said to them,

Τοῦτό ἐστι τὸ ἔργον τοῦ Θεοῦ, ἵνα πιστεύσητε εἰς ὃν
This is  the work — of God, that you believe into whom

**30** ἀπέστειλεν ἐκεῖνος. εἶπον οὖν αὐτῷ, Τί οὖν ποιεῖς σὺ
sent    that One. They said, then, to Him, What then do You

**31** σημεῖον, ἵνα ἴδωμεν καὶ πιστεύσωμέν σοι; τί ἐργάζῃ; οἱ
(as) a sign, that we may see and may believe You? What do you work? The

πατέρες ἡμῶν τὸ μάννα ἔφαγον ἐν τῇ ἐρήμῳ, καθώς ἐστι
fathers  of us the manna ate  in the wilderness, as  it is

γεγραμμένον, Ἄρτον ἐκ τοῦ οὐρανοῦ ἔδωκεν αὐτοῖς φαγεῖν.
having been written, Bread out of — Heaven He gave to them to eat.

**32** εἶπεν οὖν αὐτοῖς ὁ Ἰησοῦς, Ἀμὴν ἀμὴν λέγω ὑμῖν, Οὐ
said therefore to them — Jesus. Truly, truly, I say to you, not

Μωσῆς δέδωκεν ὑμῖν τὸν ἄρτον ἐκ τοῦ οὐρανοῦ· ἀλλ' ὁ
Moses has given you the bread out of — Heaven, but the

πατὴρ μου δίδωσιν ὑμῖν τὸν ἄρτον ἐκ τοῦ οὐρανοῦ τὸν
Father of Me gives to you the bread out of — Heaven —

[33] For the bread of God is He who comes down out of Heaven, and gives life to the world. [34] Then they said to Him, Lord, always give us this bread. [35] Jesus said to them, I am the Bread of life; he that comes to Me, shall never ever hunger ; and he that believes on Me shall never thirst at any time. [36] But I said to you that you also have seen Me and believed not. [37] All that the Father gives to Me shall come to Me, and him that comes to Me I will not at all cast out. [38] For I have come down out of Heaven not that I should do My will, but the will of Him who sent Me. [39] And this is the will of the Father who sent Me, that (of) all that He has given Me, I should not lose (any) of it, but should raise it up in the last day. [40] And this is the will of Him who sent Me, that everyone who sees the Son and believes on Him should have everlasting life; and I will raise him up at the last day. [41] Therefore the Jews were murmuring about Him, because He said, I am the Bread which came down out of Heaven. [42] And (they) were saying, Is this not Jesus the son of Joseph, of whom we know the father, and the mother? How then does he say, I have come down out of Heaven? [43] Then Jesus answered and said to them, Do not murmur with one another. [44] No one is able to come to Me unless the Father who sent Me draw him, and I will raise him up at the last day. [45] It is written in the Prophets, "And they shall all be taught of God." So everyone that has heard and has learned from the Father comes to Me; [46] not that anyone has seen the Father, except He who is from God, He has seen the Father. [47] Truly, truly, I say to you, He that believes on Me has life everlasting. [48] I am the Bread of life.

**33** ἀληθινόν. ὁ γὰρ ἄρτος τοῦ Θεοῦ ἐστιν ὁ καταβαίνων ἐκ τοῦ
true.       the For bread   — of God  is the (One) coming down out of

**34** οὐρανοῦ καὶ ζωὴν διδοὺς τῷ κόσμῳ. εἶπον οὖν πρὸς αὐτόν,
Heaven   and life   giving   to the world. They said, then, to   Him,

**35** Κύριε, πάντοτε δὸς ἡμῖν τὸν ἄρτον τοῦτον. εἶπε δὲ αὐτοῖς
Lord,   always  give us   — bread   this.     said And to them

ὁ Ἰησοῦς, Ἐγώ εἰμι ὁ ἄρτος τῆς ζωῆς· ὁ ἐρχόμενος πρός με
— Jesus,   I  am the bread  — of life, the (one) coming to   Me

οὐ μὴ πεινάσῃ· καὶ ὁ πιστεύων εἰς ἐμὲ οὐ μὴ διψήσῃ
not at all will hunger, and the (one) believing in  Me  in no way will thirst,

**36** πώποτε. ἀλλ᾽ εἶπον ὑμῖν ὅτι καὶ ἑωράκατέ με, καὶ οὐ
ever!   But I told   you   that both  you have seen Me, and not

**37** πιστεύετε. πᾶν ὃ δίδωσί μοι ὁ πατὴρ πρὸς ἐμὲ ἥξει· καὶ τὸν
believe.   All that gives to Me the Father to  Me will come, and he

**38** ἐρχόμενον πρός με οὐ μὴ ἐκβάλω ἔξω. ὅτι καταβέβηκα ἐκ
coming    to  Me in no way I will cast out. For I have descended from

τοῦ οὐρανοῦ, οὐχ ἵνα ποιῶ τὸ θέλημα τὸ ἐμόν, ἀλλὰ τὸ
— Heaven    not that I may do   will   — My, but   the

**39** θέλημα τοῦ πέμψαντός με. τοῦτο δέ ἐστι τὸ θέλημα τοῦ
will  of the (One) sending Me. this  And is  the will of  the

πέμψαντός με πατρός, ἵνα πᾶν ὃ δέδωκέ μοι, μὴ ἀπολέσω
having sent  Me Father,   that all which He has given Me, not I shall lose

**40** ἐξ αὐτοῦ, ἀλλὰ ἀναστήσω αὐτὸ ἐν τῇ ἐσχάτῃ ἡμέρᾳ. τοῦτο
of  it,  but shall raise up  it  in the last   day   this

δέ ἐστι τὸ θέλημα τοῦ πέμψαντος με, ἵνα πᾶς ὁ θεωρῶν τὸν
And is  the will  of the (One) sending Me, that everyone seeing  the

υἱὸν καὶ πιστεύων εἰς αὐτόν, ἔχῃ ζωὴν αἰώνιον, καὶ ἀνα-
Son  and believing in Him should have life everlasting; and will

στήσω αὐτὸν ἐγὼ τῇ ἐσχάτῃ ἡμέρᾳ.
raise up him  I  at the last   day.

**41** Ἐγόγγυζον οὖν οἱ Ἰουδαῖοι περὶ αὐτοῦ, ὅτι εἶπεν, Ἐγώ
murmured Therefore the  Jews concerning Him, because He said,  I

**42** εἰμι ὁ ἄρτος ὁ καταβὰς ἐκ τοῦ οὐρανοῦ. καὶ ἔλεγον, Οὐχ
am the bread  — coming down out of   Heaven.  And they said, not

οὗτός ἐστιν Ἰησοῦς ὁ υἱὸς Ἰωσήφ, οὗ ἡμεῖς οἴδαμεν τὸν
this   Is   Jesus the son of Joseph, of whom we know  the

πατέρα καὶ τὴν μητέρα ; πῶς οὖν λέγει οὗτος ὅτι Ἐκ τοῦ
father  and  the  mother? How now says this one  — Out of —

**43** οὐρανοῦ καταβέβηκα ; ἀπεκρίθη οὖν ὁ Ἰησοῦς καὶ εἶπεν αὐτοῖς,
Heaven I have come down? answered Then  Jesus and said  to them,

**44** Μὴ γογγύζετε μετ᾽ ἀλλήλων. οὐδεὶς δύναται ἐλθεῖν πρός με,
Do not murmur with one another. No one is able to come to  Me

ἐὰν μὴ ὁ πατὴρ ὁ πέμψας με ἑλκύσῃ αὐτόν, καὶ ἐγὼ ἀναστή-
unless the Father who sent Me draws   him,  and I  will raise

**45** σω αὐτὸν τῇ ἐσχάτῃ ἡμέρᾳ. ἔστι γεγραμμένον ἐν τοῖς προφή-
up him in the last   day.  It is having been written in the prophets,

ταις, Καὶ ἔσονται πάντες διδακτοὶ τοῦ Θεοῦ. πᾶς οὖν ὁ
And they shall be all   taught   — of God; everyone, then,

**46** ἀκούσας παρὰ τοῦ πατρὸς καὶ μαθών, ἔρχεται πρός με. οὐχ
hearing  from  the  Father  and learning comes  to  Me. Not

ὅτι τὸν πατέρα τις ἑώρακεν, εἰ μὴ ὁ ὢν παρὰ τοῦ Θεοῦ,
that the  Father anyone has seen, except the (One) being from  God,

**47** οὗτος ἑώρακε τὸν πατέρα. ἀμὴν ἀμὴν λέγω ὑμῖν, ὁ πιστεύων
this One has seen the Father.   Truly, truly, I say to you, he believing

**48** εἰς ἐμέ, ἔχει ζωὴν αἰώνιον. ἐγώ εἰμι ὁ ἄρτος τῆς ζωῆς. οἱ
**49** in Me  has  life everlasting.  I  am the bread  — of life. The

[49] Your fathers ate the manna in the desert and died. [50] This is the Bread which comes down out of Heaven, that anyone may eat of it and not die. [51] I am the Living Bread which came down out of Heaven; if anyone shall have eaten of this Bread, he shall live forever; and also the bread which I will give is My flesh, which I will give for the life of the world. [52] Therefore the Jews were arguing with one another, saying, How is he able to give his flesh to eat? [53] Then Jesus said to them, Truly, truly, I say to you, Unless you shall have eaten the flesh of the Son of man and shall have drunk His blood, you shall have life in yourselves. [54] He that eats My flesh and drinks My blood has everlasting life, and I will raise him up in the last day. [55] For My flesh is truly food, and My blood is truly drink. [56] He that eats My flesh and drinks My blood abides in Me, and I in him. [57] As the living Father sent Me, and I live because of the Father, also he that eats Me, he also shall live because of Me. [58] This is the Bread which came down out of Heaven. Not as your fathers ate the manna and died, he that eats this Bread shall live forever. [59] He said these things in (the) synagogue, teaching in Capernaum. [60] Therefore many of His disciples having heard said, This word is hard, who is able to hear? [61] But Jesus knowing in Himself that His disciples murmured concerning this said to them, Does this offend you? [62] Then what if you should see the Son of man going up where He was before? [63] It is the Spirit who gives life, the flesh does not profit anything. The words which I speak to you are spirit

πατέρες ὑμῶν ἔφαγον τὸ μάννα ἐν τῇ ἐρήμῳ, καὶ ἀπέθανον.
fathers of you       ate      the   manna in the wilderness, and      died.

50 οὗτός ἐστιν ὁ ἄρτος ὁ ἐκ τοῦ οὐρανοῦ καταβαίνων, ἵνα τις
This      is     the   bread out of —   Heaven   coming down, that anyone

51 ἐξ αὐτοῦ φάγῃ καὶ μὴ ἀποθάνῃ. ἐγώ εἰμι ὁ ἄρτος ὁ ζῶν, ὁ ἐκ
of    it   may eat and not   die.     I   am the bread — living that from

τοῦ οὐρανοῦ καταβάς· ἐάν τις φάγῃ ἐκ τούτου τοῦ ἄρτου,
—    Heaven   came down; if anyone eats of   this   —    bread,

ζήσεται εἰς τὸν αἰῶνα. καὶ ὁ ἄρτος δὲ ὃν ἐγὼ δώσω, ἡ σάρξ
he will live to the   age. indeed the bread And which I   will give, the flesh

μου ἐστίν, ἣν ἐγὼ δώσω ὑπὲρ τῆς τοῦ κόσμου ζωῆς.
of Me is,   which I   will give  for the  of the world   life.

52 Ἐμάχοντο οὖν πρὸς ἀλλήλους οἱ Ἰουδαῖοι λέγοντες, Πῶς
Argued therefore with one another the Jews,      saying   How

53 δύναται οὗτος ἡμῖν δοῦναι τὴν σάρκα φαγεῖν; εἶπεν οὖν
can      this one  us   give   the flesh to eat?   said Then

αὐτοῖς ὁ Ἰησοῦς, Ἀμὴν ἀμὴν λέγω ὑμῖν, ἐὰν μὴ φάγητε τὴν
to them — Jesus,  Truly, truly, I say to you, Except you eat  the

σάρκα τοῦ υἱοῦ τοῦ ἀνθρώπου καὶ πίητε αὐτοῦ τὸ αἷμα,
flesh of the Son  —  of man    and drink of Him the blood

54 οὐκ ἔχετε ζωὴν ἐν ἑαυτοῖς. ὁ τρώγων μου τὴν σάρκα καὶ
not you do life  in yourselves. He partaking of Me the flesh   and
   have

πίνων μου τὸ αἷμα, ἔχει ζωὴν αἰώνιον, καὶ ἐγὼ ἀναστήσω
drinking of Me the blood has life everlasting, and I    will raise up

55 αὐτὸν τῇ ἐσχάτῃ ἡμέρᾳ. ἡ γὰρ σάρξ μου ἀληθῶς ἐστι
him at the   last     day   the For flesh of Me truly    is

56 βρῶσις, καὶ τὸ αἷμά μου ἀληθῶς ἐστι πόσις. ὁ τρώγων μου
food,   and the blood of Me truly   is   drink. He partaking of Me

τὴν σάρκα καὶ πίνων μου τὸ αἷμα, ἐν ἐμοὶ μένει, κἀγὼ ἐν
the   flesh and drinking of Me the blood in   Me abides, and I in

57 αὐτῷ. καθὼς ἀπέστειλέ με ὁ ζῶν πατήρ, κἀγὼ ζῶ διὰ τὸν
him. Even as   sent   Me the living Father, and I live via the

58 πατέρα· καὶ ὁ τρώγων με, κἀκεῖνος ζήσεται δι' ἐμέ. οὗτός
Father, also he partaking Me, even that one will live via Me. This

ἐστιν ὁ ἄρτος ὁ ἐκ τοῦ οὐρανοῦ καταβάς· οὐ καθὼς ἔφαγον
is   the bread which out of Heaven  came down, not as    ate

οἱ πατέρες ὑμῶν τὸ μάννα, καὶ ἀπέθανον· ὁ τρώγων τοῦτον
the fathers of you the manna, and    died; he partaking   this

59 τὸν ἄρτον, ζήσεται εἰς τὸν αἰῶνα. ταῦτα εἶπεν ἐν συναγωγῇ
—  bread will live   to the  age. These things He said in a synagogue

διδάσκων ἐν Καπερναούμ.
teaching  in Capernaum.

60 Πολλοὶ οὖν ἀκούσαντες ἐκ τῶν μαθητῶν αὐτοῦ εἶπον,
many Therefore hearing   of  the  disciples  of Him said,

Σκληρός ἐστιν οὗτος ὁ λόγος· τίς δύναται αὐτοῦ ἀκούειν;
Hard    is    this — word; who is able   it    to hear?

61 εἰδὼς δὲ ὁ Ἰησοῦς ἐν ἑαυτῷ ὅτι γογγύζουσι περὶ τούτου
knowing But Jesus  in Himself that are murmuring about this

οἱ μαθηταὶ αὐτοῦ, εἶπεν αὐτοῖς, Τοῦτο ὑμᾶς σκανδαλίζει;
the disciples of Him, He said to them, Does this you   offend?

62 ἐὰν οὖν θεωρῆτε τὸν υἱὸν τοῦ ἀνθρώπου ἀναβαίνοντα ὅπου
If then you behold the Son  —   of man    going up    where

63 ἦν τὸ πρότερον; τὸ πνεῦμά ἐστι τὸ ζωοποιοῦν, ἡ σάρξ οὐκ
He was at first?  The Spirit it is (that) makes alive; the flesh not

ὠφελεῖ οὐδέν· τὰ ῥήματα ἃ ἐγὼ λαλῶ ὑμῖν, πνεῦμά ἐστι
profits nothing; the words which I speak to you  spirit    is

and are life. [64] But there are some of you who do not believe. For Jesus knew from (the) beginning who they were who did not believe, and who he was who shall deliver Him up. [65] And He said, Therefore I have said to you that no one is able to come to Me unless it is given to him from My Father. [66] From that (time) many of His disciples went back, and walked no more with Him. [67] Therefore Jesus said to the Twelve, Are you also wishing to go away? [68] Then Simon Peter answered Him, Lord, to whom shall we go? You have the words of everlasting life. [69] And we have believed and have known that You are the Christ, the Son of the living God. [70] Jesus answered them, Did not I choose you as the Twelve, and one of you is a devil? [71] But He spoke of Judas Iscariot, Simon's son, for he was about to deliver Him up, being one of the Twelve.

CHAPTER 7

[1] And after these things Jesus was walking in Galilee, for He did not desire to walk in Judea, because the Jews were lusting to kill Him. [2] Now the feast of the Jews, of the tabernacles, was near. [3] Therefore His brothers said to Him, Move away from here and go to Judea so that your may also see your works which you do — [4] for no one does anything in secret and himself seeks to be in public. If you do these things, reveal yourself to he world. [5] For His brothers did not believe on Him. [6] And Jesus said to them, My time is not yet come, but your time is always ready. [7] The world cannot hate you, but it hates Me, because I bear witness concerning it, that

**64** καὶ ζωή ἐστιν. ἀλλ᾽ εἰσὶν ἐξ ὑμῶν τινες οἳ οὐ πιστεύουσιν.
and life is. But are of you some who not are believing

ἤδει γὰρ ἐξ ἀρχῆς ὁ Ἰησοῦς, τίνες εἰσὶν οἱ μὴ πιστεύοντες,
knew For from beginning Jesus who are those not believing,

**65** καὶ τίς ἐστιν ὁ παραδώσων αὐτόν. καὶ ἔλεγε, Διὰ τοῦτο
and who is the (one) betraying Him. And He said, Therefore

εἴρηκα ὑμῖν, ὅτι οὐδεὶς δύναται ἐλθεῖν πρός με, ἐὰν μὴ ᾖ
I have told you, that no one is able to come to Me unless it is

δεδομένον αὐτῷ ἐκ τοῦ πατρός μου.
given to him from the Father of Me.

**66** Ἐκ τούτου πολλοὶ ἀπῆλθον τῶν μαθητῶν αὐτοῦ εἰς
From this many went away of the disciples of Him into

**67** τὰ ὀπίσω, καὶ οὐκέτι μετ᾽ αὐτοῦ περιεπάτουν. εἶπεν οὖν ὁ
the behind, and no longer with Him walked. said Therefore
things

**68** Ἰησοῦς τοῖς δώδεκα, Μὴ καὶ ὑμεῖς θέλετε ὑπάγειν; ἀπεκρίθη
Jesus to the twelve, Not also you wish to go? answered

οὖν αὐτῷ Σίμων Πέτρος, Κύριε, πρὸς τίνα ἀπελευσόμεθα;
Then Him Simon Peter, Lord, to whom shall we go?

**69** ῥήματα ζωῆς αἰωνίου ἔχεις. καὶ ἡμεῖς πεπιστεύκαμὲν καὶ
words of life eternal You have. And we have believed and

ἐγνώκαμεν ὅτι σὺ εἶ ὁ Χριστὸς ὁ υἱὸς τοῦ Θεοῦ τοῦ ζῶντος.
have known that You are the Christ, the Son — of God the living.

**70** ἀπεκρίθη αὐτοῖς ὁ Ἰησοῦς, Οὐκ ἐγὼ ὑμᾶς τοὺς δώδεκα
answered them — Jesus, Did not I you the twelve

**71** ἐξελεξάμην, καὶ ἐξ ὑμῶν εἷς διάβολός ἐστιν; ἔλεγε δὲ τὸν
choose? And (of) you one a devil is. He spoke And —

Ἰούδαν Σίμωνος Ἰσκαριώτην· οὗτος γὰρ ἤμελλεν αὐτὸν
Judas of Simon Iscariot; this one for was about Him

παραδιδόναι, εἷς ὢν ἐκ τῶν δώδεκα.
to betray, one being of the twelve.

CHAPTER 7

**1** Καὶ περιεπάτει ὁ Ἰησοῦς μετὰ ταῦτα ἐν τῇ Γαλιλαίᾳ· οὐ
And was walking — Jesus after these things in — Galilee; not

γὰρ ἤθελεν ἐν τῇ Ἰουδαίᾳ περιπατεῖν, ὅτι ἐζήτουν αὐτὸν
For He desired in — Judea to walk, because were seeking Him

**2** οἱ Ἰουδαῖοι ἀποκτεῖναι. ἦν δὲ ἐγγὺς ἡ ἑορτὴ τῶν Ἰουδαίων
the Jews to kill. was And near the feast of the Jews,

**3** ἡ σκηνοπηγία. εἶπον οὖν προς αὐτὸν οἱ ἀδελφοὶ αὐτοῦ,
The Tabernacles. said Therefore to Him the brothers of Him,

Μετάβηθι ἐντεῦθεν, καὶ ὕπαγε εἰς τὴν Ἰουδαίαν, ἵνα καὶ οἱ
Depart from here, and go to — Judea, that also the

**4** μαθηταί σου θεωρήσωσι τὰ ἔργα σου ἃ ποιεῖς· οὐδεὶς γὰρ
disciples of you will behold the works of you which you do. no one For

ἐν κρυπτῷ τι ποιεῖ, καὶ ζητεῖ αὐτὸς ἐν παρρησίᾳ εἶναι. εἰ
in secret anything does, and seeks himself in public to be. If

**5** ταῦτα ποιεῖς, φανέρωσον σεαυτὸν τῷ κόσμῳ. οὐδὲ γὰρ οἱ
these things you do, reveal yourself to the world. not even For the

**6** ἀδελφοὶ αὐτοῦ ἐπίστευον εἰς αὐτόν. λέγει οὖν αὐτοῖς ὁ
brothers of Him believed in Him. says Then to them —

Ἰησοῦς, Ὁ καιρὸς ὁ ἐμὸς οὔπω πάρεστιν, ὁ δὲ καιρὸς ὁ
Jesus, The time — of Me not yet is present, but time —

**7** ὑμέτερος πάντοτέ ἐστιν ἕτοιμος. οὐ δύναται ὁ κόσμος
your always is ready. not is able The world

μισεῖν ὑμᾶς· ἐμὲ δὲ μισεῖ, ὅτι ἐγὼ μαρτυρῶ περὶ αὐτοῦ, ὅτι
to hate you; Me but it hates, because I witness about it, that

its works are evil. [8] You go up to the feast. I am not yet going up to the feast, for My time has not yet been fulfilled. [9] And having said these things to them, He remained in Galilee. [10] But when His brothers had gone up, then He also went up to the feast, not openly, but as in secret. [11] Therefore the Jews were seeking Him at the feast, and said, Where is he? [12] And there was much murmuring about Him among the crowd. Some said, He is good; but other said, No, but he deceives the crowd. [13] However no one spoke publicly about Him, because of the fear of the Jews.

[14] But now (it) being the middle of the feast, Jesus went up into the Temple and was teaching. [15] And the Jews were wondering, saying, How does this one know letters, not having learned? [16] Jesus answered them and said, My teaching is not Mine, but His who sent Me. [17] If anyone desire to practice His will, he shall know as to the teaching, whether it is from God, or I speak from Myself. [18] He that speaks from himself seeks his own glory; but He that seeks the glory of Him that sent Him, He is true and unrighteousness is not in Him. [19] Has not Moses given you the Law, and not one of you practices the Law? Why do you seek to kill Me? [20] The crowd answered and said, You have a demon; who seeks to kill you? [21] Jesus answered and said to them, I did one work, and you all wonder. [22] Therefore Moses has given you circumcision, not that it is of Moses, but of the fathers, and on Sabbath you circumcise a man. [23] If a man receives circumcision on Sabbath, so that the Law of Moses may not be broken, are you angry with Me because I made a man entirely

**8** τὰ ἔργα αὐτοῦ πονηρά ἐστιν. ὑμεῖς ἀνάβητε εἰς τὴν ἑορτὴν
the works of it    evil    are.    You go up    to    the    feast
ταύτην· ἐγὼ οὔπω ἀναβαίνω εἰς τὴν ἑορτὴν ταύτην, ὅτι ὁ
this;    I    not yet am going to  —  feast    this, because

**9** καιρὸς ὁ ἐμὸς οὔπω πεπλήρωται. ταῦτα δὲ εἰπὼν αὐτοῖς,
time    My    not yet has been fulfilled. these things And saying to them,
ἔμεινεν ἐν τῇ Γαλιλαίᾳ.
He stayed in  —  Galilee.

**10** Ὡς δὲ ἀνέβησαν οἱ ἀδελφοὶ αὐτοῦ, τότε καὶ αὐτὸς ἀνέβη
when But went up    the brothers of Him,    then also He    went up

**11** εἰς τὴν ἑορτήν, οὐ φανερῶς, ἀλλ' ὡς ἐν κρυπτῷ. οἱ οὖν
to the    feast,    not openly,    but as in secret.    the Then
Ἰουδαῖοι ἐζήτουν αὐτὸν ἐν τῇ ἑορτῇ, καὶ ἔλεγον, Ποῦ ἐστιν
the Jews sought    Him in the    feast,    and said,    Where is

**12** ἐκεῖνος ; καὶ γογγυσμὸς πολὺς περὶ αὐτοῦ ἦν ἐν τοῖς ὄχλοις·
that one? And murmuring    much about Him was in the    crowds;
οἱ μὲν ἔλεγον ὅτι Ἀγαθός ἐστιν· ἄλλοι δὲ ἔλεγον, Οὔ, ἀλλὰ
some said,  —  A good one He is;    others but    said,    No,    but

**13** πλανᾷ τὸν ὄχλον. οὐδεὶς μέντοι παρρησίᾳ ἐλάλει περὶ αὐτοῦ
he deceives the crowd. No one however    publicly    spoke about    Him,
διὰ τὸν φόβον τῶν Ἰουδαίων.
because of the fear of the    Jews.

**14** Ἤδη δὲ τῆς ἑορτῆς μεσούσης, ἀνέβη ὁ Ἰησοῦς εἰς τὸ ἱερόν,
now But the feast being in middle went up    Jesus    to the Temple

**15** καὶ ἐδίδασκε. καὶ ἐθαύμαζον οἱ Ἰουδαῖοι λέγοντες, Πῶς οὗτος
and taught.    And marveled the Jews,    saying,    How this one

**16** γράμματα οἶδε, μὴ μεμαθηκώς ; ἀπεκρίθη αὐτοῖς ὁ Ἰησοῦς
letters    knows, not being taught? answered    them  —  Jesus
καὶ εἶπεν, Ἡ ἐμὴ διδαχὴ οὐκ ἔστιν ἐμή, ἀλλὰ τοῦ πέμψαντός
and said,    My teaching not is    Mine, but of the (One) sending

**17** με. ἐάν τις θέλῃ τὸ θέλημα αὐτοῦ ποιεῖν, γνώσεται περὶ τῆς
Me. If anyone desires the    will    of Him    to do, he will know concerning the
διδαχῆς, πότερον ἐκ τοῦ Θεοῦ ἐστιν, ἢ ἐγὼ ἀπ' ἐμαυτοῦ
teaching, whether of  —  God it is,    or I from    Myself

**18** λαλῶ. ὁ ἀφ' ἑαυτοῦ λαλῶν, τὴν δόξαν τὴν ἰδίαν ζητεῖ· ὁ δὲ
speak. The (one) from himself speaking the glory  —  own seeks; he But
ζητῶν τὴν δόξαν τοῦ πέμψαντος αὐτόν, οὗτος ἀληθής ἐστι,.
seeking    the glory of the (One) sending    Him, this one    true    is,

**19** καὶ ἀδικία ἐν αὐτῷ οὐκ ἔστιν. οὐ Μωσῆς δέδωκεν ὑμῖν τὸν
and unrighteousness in him not    is. Did not Moses give    you    the
νόμον, καὶ οὐδεὶς ἐξ ὑμῶν ποιεῖ τὸν νόμον ; τί με ζητεῖτε
law,    and no one of you does the    law.    Why Me seek you

**20** ἀποκτεῖναι ; ἀπεκρίθη ὁ ὄχλος καὶ εἶπε, Δαιμόνιον ἔχεις· τίς
to kill?    answered the crowd and said,    A demon you have; who

**21** σε ζητεῖ ἀποκτεῖναι ; ἀπεκρίθη ὁ Ἰησοῦς καὶ εἶπεν αὐτοῖς,
you seeks to kill?    answered  —  Jesus and said to them,

**22** Ἓν ἔργον ἐποίησα, καὶ πάντες θαυμάζετε. διὰ τοῦτο Μωσῆς
One work I did,    and all you marvel. Because of this Moses
δέδωκεν ὑμῖν τὴν περιτομήν (οὐχ ὅτι ἐκ τοῦ Μωσέως ἐστίν,
has given you  —  circumcision; not that of    Moses it is,
ἀλλ' ἐκ τῶν πατέρων)· καὶ ἐν σαββάτῳ περιτέμνετε
but of the    fathers;    and on a sabbath you circumcise

**23** ἄνθρωπον. εἰ περιτομὴν λαμβάνει ἄνθρωπος ἐν σαββάτῳ,
a man.    If circumcision receives    a man    on a sabbath,
ἵνα μὴ λυθῇ ὁ νόμος Μωσέως, ἐμοὶ χολᾶτε ὅτι ὅλον ἄνθρω-
that not is broken the law of Moses, with Me are you angry that a whole man

sound on Sabbath? [24] Judge not according to sight, but judge righteous judgment. [25] Therefore some of those of Jerusalem said, Is this not he whom they seek to kill? [26] And behold, he speaks publicly, and they say nothing to him. Truly those who rule have recognized that this is really the Christ? [27] But we know this one, where he is from; but the Christ, whenever He may, no one knows from where He is. [28] Therefore Jesus cried in the Temple and saying, You both know Me, and you know from where I am; and I have not come of Myself, but He who sent Me is true, whom you do not know. [29] But I know Him, because I am from Him; and He sent Me. [30] Then they were seeking to seize Him, but no one laid (his) hand on Him, because His hour had not yet come. [31] But many of the crowd believed on Him, and said, The Christ, when He comes, will He do more miracles than these which this One did? [32] The Pharisees heard the crowd murmuring these things about Him, and the Pharisees and the chief priests sent officers that they might seize Him. [33] Therefore Jesus said to them, Yet a little while I am with you, and I go to Him who sent Me. [34] You will seek Me and shall not find (Me), and where I am, you are unable to come. [35] Then the Jews said amongst themselves, Where is he about to go that we shall not find him? Is he about to go to the Dispersion among the Greeks and teach the Greeks? [36] What is this word which he said, You will seek Me and shall not find (Me); and, Where I am, you are not able to come? [37] And in the last of the great feast Jesus stood

**24** πον ὑγιῆ ἐποίησα ἐν σαββάτῳ : μὴ κρίνετε κατ' ὄψιν, ἀλλὰ
healthy I made on a sabbath? Do not judge by sight, but
τὴν δικαίαν κρίσιν κρίνατε.
– righteous judgment judge.

**25** Ἔλεγον οὖν τινες ἐκ τῶν Ἱεροσολυμιτῶν, Οὐχ οὗτός ἐστιν
said Therefore some of the Jerusalemites, not this one Is it

**26** ὃν ζητοῦσιν ἀποκτεῖναι : καὶ ἴδε παρρησίᾳ λαλεῖ, καὶ οὐδὲν
whom they are seeking to kill? And behold, publicly He speaks, and nothing
αὐτῷ λέγουσι. μήποτε ἀληθῶς ἔγνωσαν οἱ ἄρχοντες ὅτι
to Him they say. Perhaps truly knew the rulers that

**27** οὗτός ἐστιν ἀληθῶς ὁ Χριστός ; ἀλλὰ τοῦτον οἴδαμεν πόθεν
this is indeed the Christ? But this one we know from where
ἐστίν· ὁ δὲ Χριστὸς ὅταν ἔρχηται, οὐδεὶς γινώσκει πόθεν
he is; the but Christ when comes, no one knows from where

**28** ἐστίν. ἔκραξεν οὖν ἐν τῷ ἱερῷ διδάσκων ὁ Ἰησοῦς καὶ λέγων·
He is. cried out Then in the Temple teaching – Jesus, and · saying,
Κἀμὲ οἴδατε, καὶ οἴδατε πόθεν εἰμί· καὶ ἀπ' ἐμαυτου οὐκ
And Me you know, and you know from where I am; and from Myself not
ἐλήλυθα, ἀλλ' ἔστιν ἀληθινὸς ὁ πέμψας με, ὃν ὑμεῖς οὐκ
I have come, but He is true, the (One) sending Me, whom you not

**29** οἴδατε. ἐγὼ δὲ οἶδα αὐτόν, ὅτι παρ' αὐτοῦ εἰμι, κἀκεῖνός με
know. I But do know Him, because from Him I am, and that One Me

**30** ἀπέστειλεν. ἐζήτουν οὖν αὐτὸν πιάσαι. καὶ οὐδεὶς ἐπέβαλεν
sent. they sought Then Him to seize: and no one laid
ἐπ' αὐτὸν τὴν χεῖρα, ὅτι οὔπω ἐληλύθει ἡ ὥρα αὐτοῦ.
on Him the hand, because not yet had come the hour of Him.

**31** πολλοὶ δὲ ἐκ τοῦ ὄχλου ἐπίστευσαν εἰς αὐτόν, καὶ ἔλεγον
many But of the crowd believed in Him, and said,
ὅτι Ὁ Χριστὸς ὅταν ἔλθῃ, μήτι πλείονα σημεῖα τούτων
– The Christ, when He comes, not greater signs than these

**32** ποιήσει ὧν οὗτος ἐποίησεν ; ἤκουσαν οἱ Φαρισαῖοι τοῦ
will He do which this One did? Heard the Pharisees the
ὄχλου γογγύζοντος περὶ αὐτοῦ ταῦτα· καὶ ἀπέστειλαν οἱ
crowd murmuring concerning Him these things and sent the
Φαρισαῖοι καὶ οἱ ἀρχιερεῖς ὑπηρέτας ἵνα πιάσωσιν αὐτόν.
Pharisees and the chief priests officers, that they might seize Him.

**33** εἶπεν οὖν αὐτοῖς ὁ Ἰησοῦς, Ἔτι μικρὸν χρόνον μεθ' ὑμῶν
said Therefore to them Jesus, Yet a little time with you

**34** εἰμι, καὶ ὑπάγω πρὸς τὸν πέμψαντά με. ζητήσετέ με, καὶ
I am, and I go to the (One) sending Me. You will seek Me, and
οὐχ εὑρήσετε· καὶ ὅπου εἰμὶ ἐγώ, ὑμεῖς οὐ δύνασθε ἐλθεῖν
not will find, and where am I, you not are able to come.

**35** εἶπον οὖν οἱ Ἰουδαῖοι πρὸς ἑαυτούς, Ποῦ οὗτος μέλλει
said Then the Jews to themselves, Where this one is about
πορεύεσθαι ὅτι ἡμεῖς οὐχ εὑρήσομεν αὐτόν ; μὴ εἰς τὴν
to go that we not will find Him? not to the
διασπορὰν τῶν Ἑλλήνων μέλλει πορεύεσθαι, καὶ διδάσκειν
Dispersion of the Greeks is he about to go, and to teach

**36** τοὺς Ἕλληνας ; τίς ἐστιν οὗτος ὁ λόγος ὃν εἶπε, Ζητήσετέ
the Greeks? What is this – word which He said: You will seek
με, καὶ οὐχ εὑρήσετε· καὶ ὅπου εἰμὶ ἐγώ, ὑμεῖς οὐ δύνασθε
Me, and not you will find, and where am I, you not are able
ἐλθεῖν ;
to come?

**37** Ἐν δὲ τῇ ἐσχάτῃ ἡμέρᾳ τῇ μεγάλῃ τῆς ἑορτῆς εἱστήκει
in And the last day, the great, of the feast stood

and cried, saying, If anyone thirsts, let him come to Me and drink. [38] He that believes on Me, as the Scripture said, "Out of his belly shall flow rivers of living water." [39] But He said this concerning the Spirit which those believing on Him were about to receive; for (the) Holy Spirit was yet (given) because Jesus was not yet glorified. [40] Therefore many out of the crowd, having heard the word said, This is truly the Prophet. [41] Others said, This is the Christ. And other said, Does the Christ then come out of Galilee? [42] Have not the Scriptures said that out of the seed of David, and from the village of Bethlehem where David was, the Christ comes? [43] Therefore a division occured in the crowd because of Him. [44] But some of them desired to take Him, but no one laid hands on Him. [45] Then the officers came to the chief priests and Pharisees, and they said to them, Why did you not bring him? [46] The officers answered, No man ever spoke this way, as this man. [47] Therefore the Pharisees answered them, Have you also been deceived? [48] Has anyone of the rulers believed on him, or of the Pharisees? [49] But this crowd which does not know the Law is cursed. [50] Nicodemus said to them — he who came by night to Him, being one of themselves — [51] Does our Law judge a man, unless it has heard from himself first, and has known what he does? [52] They answered and said to him, Are you also of Galilee? Search and look, that a prophet has not arisen out of Galilee. [53] And each went to his house.

CHAPTER 8
[1] But Jesus went to

ὁ Ἰησοῦς καὶ ἔκραξε, λέγων, Ἐάν τις διψᾷ, ἐρχέσθω πρός
- Jesus and cried out, saying, If anyone thirst, let him come to

**38** με καὶ πινέτω. ὁ πιστεύων εἰς ἐμέ, καθὼς εἶπεν ἡ γραφή,
Me and drink. He believing into Me, as said the Writing,

ποταμοὶ ἐκ τῆς κοιλίας αὐτοῦ ῥεύσουσιν ὕδατος ζῶντος.
rivers Out of the belly of him will flow water of living .

**39** τοῦτο δὲ εἶπε περὶ τοῦ Πνεύματος οὗ ἔμελλον λαμβάνειν οἱ
this But He said about the Spirit whom were about to receive those

πιστεύοντες εἰς αὐτόν· οὔπω γὰρ ἦν Πνεῦμα Ἅγιον, ὅτι
believing in Him; not yet for was (the) Spirit Holy, because

**40** ὁ Ἰησοῦς οὐδέπω ἐδοξάσθη. πολλοὶ οὖν ἐκ του ὄχλου
- Jesus not yet was glorified. Many therefore of the .crowd

ἀκούσαντες τὸν λόγον ἔλεγον, Οὗτός ἐστιν ἀληθῶς ὁ προφή-
hearing the word said, This· is truly the prophet.

**41** της. ἄλλοι ἔλεγον, Οὗτός ἐστιν ὁ Χριστός. ἄλλοι δὲ ἔλεγον,
Others said, This is the Christ. others But said, (No!)

**42** Μὴ γὰρ ἐκ τῆς Γαλιλαίας ὁ Χριστὸς ἔρχεται ; οὐχὶ ἡ γραφὴ
not For out of — Galilee the Christ comes? Has' not the Scripture

εἶπεν ὅτι ἐκ τοῦ σπέρματος Δαβίδ, καὶ ἀπὸ Βηθλεέμ, τῆς
said that out of the seed of David, and from Bethlehem, the

**43** κώμης ὅπου ἦν Δαβίδ, ὁ Χριστὸς ἔρχεται ; σχίσμα οὖν ἐν
village where was David, the Christ comes? a division Then in

**44** τῷ ὄχλῳ ἐγένετο δι᾽ αὐτόν. τινὲς δὲ ἤθελον ἐξ αὐτῶν
the crowd occurred. because of Him. some And desired of them

πιάσαι αὐτόν, ἀλλ᾽ οὐδεὶς ἐπέβαλεν ἐπ᾽ αὐτὸν τὰς χεῖρας.
to seize Him, but no one laid on Him the hands.

**45** Ἦλθον οὖν οἱ ὑπηρέται πρὸς τοὺς ἀρχιερεῖς καὶ Φαρι-
came Then the officers to the chief priests and

σαίους· καὶ εἶπον αὐτοῖς ἐκεῖνοι, Διατί οὐκ ἠγάγετε αὐτόν ;
Pharisees, and said to them those, Why not did you bring him?

**46** ἀπεκρίθησαν οἱ ὑπηρέται, Οὐδέποτε οὕτως ἐλάλησεν
answered The officers, Never so spoke

**47** ἄνθρωπος, ὡς οὗτος ὁ ἄνθρωπος. ἀπεκρίθησαν οὖν αὐτοῖς
a man as this man. answered Then them

**48** οἱ Φαρισαῖοι, Μὴ καὶ ὑμεῖς πεπλάνησθε ; μή τις ἐκ τῶν
the Pharisees, Not also you have been deceived? Not any from the

**49** ἀρχόντων ἐπίστευσεν εἰς αὐτόν, ἢ ἐκ τῶν Φαρισαίων ; ἀλλ᾽
rulers have believed into him, or from the Pharisees? But

ὁ ὄχλος οὗτος ὁ μὴ γινώσκων τὸν νόμον ἐπικατάρατοί εἰσι.
crowd this not knowing the Law cursed upon are.

**50** Λέγει Νικόδημος πρὸς αὐτούς (ὁ ἐλθὼν νυκτὸς πρὸς αὐτόν,
says Nicodemus to them —he having come (by) night to Him,

**51** εἷς ὢν ἐξ αὐτῶν), Μὴ ὁ νόμος ἡμῶν κρίνει τὸν ἄνθρωπον
one being of themselves—Not the Law of us does judge the man

ἐὰν μὴ ἀκούσῃ παρ᾽ αὐτοῦ πρότερον καὶ γνῷ τί ποιεῖ ;
unless it hear from him first and know what he does?

**52** ἀπεκρίθησαν καὶ εἶπον αὐτῷ, Μὴ καὶ σὺ ἐκ τῆς Γαλιλαίας εἶ ;
They answered and said to him, Not also you of — Galilee are?

**53** ἐρεύνησον καὶ ἴδε ὅτι προφήτης ἐκ τῆς Γαλιλαίας οὐκ
Search (the Scripture)and see that a prophet out of Galilee not

ἐγήγερται. Καὶ ἐπορεύθη ἕκαστος εἰς τὸν οἶκον αὐτοῦ
has been raised. And they went each one to the house of him.

**CHAPTER 8**

**1** Ἰησοῦς δὲ                    ἐπορεύθη εἰς τὸ
Jesus And                    went to the

the Mount of Olives. [2] And at dawn He came again into the Temple, and all the people came to Him; and having sat down He was teaching them. [3] And the scribes and the Pharisees brought a woman to Him, having been taken in adultery, and having set her in (the) middle, [4] they said to Him, Teacher, this woman was taken in the very act, committing adultery. [5] Now in the Law Moses commanded us that such should be stoned; you therefore, what do you say? [6] But they said this tempting Him that they might have (reason) to accuse Him. But having stooped down, Jesus wrote on the ground with (His) finger. [7] But as they continued asking Him, having lifted Himself up He said to them, He who is sinless among you, let him throw the first stone at her. [8] And having stooped down again, He wrote on the ground. [9] But having heard, and being convicted by the conscience, they went out one by one, beginning from the elder ones until the last; and Jesus was left alone, and the woman standing in (the) middle. [10] And having lifted Himself up, and seeing no one but the woman, Jesus said to her, Woman, where are those, your accusers? Did no one give judgment against you? [11] And she said, No one, Lord. And Jesus said to her, Neither do I judge you. Go, and do not sin any more.

[12] Then Jesus again spoke to them, saying, I am the Light of the world; he that follows Me shall never walk in the darkness, but shall have the light of the life. [13] Then the Pharisees said to Him, You bear witness concerning yourself; your witness is not true. [14] Jesus answered and said to them, Even if I bear witness concerning Myself, My witness is true, because I know from where I came and where I go; but you do

**2** ὄρος τῶν ἐλαιῶν ὄρθρου δὲ πάλιν παρε-
mount of the olives. at dawn And again He

γένετο εἰς τὸ ἱερόν, καὶ πᾶς ὁ λαὸς ἤρχετο πρὸς αὐτόν· καὶ
arrived in the Temple and all the people came to Him, and

**3** καθίσας ἐδίδασκεν αὐτούς. ἄγουσι δὲ οἱ γραμματεῖς καὶ οἱ·
sitting He taught them. lead And the scribes and the

Φαρισαῖοι πρὸς αὐτὸν γυναῖκα ἐν μοιχείᾳ κατειλημμένην,
Pharisees to Him a woman in adultery having been taken,

**4** καὶ στήσαντες αὐτὴν ἐν μέσῳ, λέγουσιν αὐτῷ, Διδάσκαλε,
and standing her in (the) midst they say to Him, Teacher,

**5** αὕτη ἡ γυνὴ κατείληφθη ἐπαυτοφώρῳ μοιχευομένη. ἐν δὲ τῷ
this woman has been taken in the very act committing adultery. And the

νόμῳ Μωσῆς ἡμῖν ἐνετείλατο τὰς τοιαύτας λιθοβολεῖσθαι·
Law Moses to us commanded such (women) to be stoned;

**6** σὺ οὖν τί λέγεις; τοῦτο δὲ ἔλεγον πειράζοντες αὐτόν, ἵνα
you, then, what say you? this But they said tempting Him, that

ἔχωσι κατηγορεῖν αὐτοῦ. ὁ δὲ Ἰησοῦς κάτω κύψας, τῷ
they may have to accuse Him. — But Jesus down stooping with the

δακτύλῳ ἔγραφεν εἰς τὴν γῆν, μὴ προσποιούμενος. ὡς δὲ
**7** finger wrote in the earth, not appearing (to hear). as And

ἐπέμενον ἐρωτῶντες αὐτόν. ἀνακύψας εἶπε πρὸς αὐτούς,
they continued questioning Him. bending back up He said to them,

Ὁ ἀναμάρτητος ὑμῶν, πρῶτος τὸν λίθον ἐπ' αὐτῇ βαλέτω.
The (one) sinless of you, first the stone on her let him cast.

**8 9** καὶ πάλιν κάτω κύψας ἔγραφεν εἰς τὴν γῆν. οἱ δέ, ἀκούσαν-
And again down stooping He wrote in the earth. they But, having

τες, καὶ ὑπὸ τῆς συνειδήσεως ἐλεγχόμενοι, ἐξήρχοντο εἷς καθ'
heard, and by the conscience being convicted, went out one by

εἷς, ἀρξάμενοι ἀπὸ τῶν πρεσβυτέρων ἕως τῶν ἐσχάτων· καὶ
one, beginning from the older ones, until the last. And

κατελείφθη μόνος ὁ Ἰησοῦς, καὶ ἡ γυνὴ ἐν μέσῳ ἑστῶσα.
was left alone — Jesus, and the woman in (the) midst standing.

**10** ἀνακύψας δὲ ὁ Ἰησοῦς, καὶ μηδένα θεασάμενος πλὴν τῆς
bending back up And Jesus, and no one observing but the

γυναικός, εἶπεν αὐτῇ Ἡ γυνή, ποῦ εἰσιν ἐκεῖνοι οἱ κατήγοροί
woman, He said to her, Woman, where are those, the accusers

**11** σου; οὐδείς σε κατέκρινεν; ἡ δὲ εἶπεν, Οὐδείς, Κύριε. εἶπε δὲ
of you? No one you judged? she And said, No one, Lord. said And

αὕτη ὁ Ἰησοῦς, Οὐδὲ ἐγώ σε κατακρίνω· πορεύου καὶ μηκέτι
to her Jesus, Neither I you do judge; go, and no more

ἁμάρτανε.
sin.

**12** Πάλιν οὖν ὁ Ἰησοῦς αὐτοῖς ἐλάλησε λέγων, Ἐγώ εἰμι τὸ
Again, then, Jesus to them spoke, saying, I am the

φῶς τοῦ κόσμου· ὁ ἀκολουθῶν ἐμοὶ οὐ μὴ περιπατήσει ἐν τῇ
light of the world; the (one) following Me in no way will walk in the

**13** σκοτίᾳ, ἀλλ' ἕξει τὸ φῶς τῆς ζωῆς. εἶπον οὖν αὐτῷ οἱ
darkness, but will have the light of life. said Then to Him the

Φαρισαῖοι, Σὺ περὶ σεαυτοῦ μαρτυρεῖς· ἡ μαρτυρία σου οὐκ
Pharisees, You about yourself witnessed. The witness of you not

ἔστιν ἀληθής. ἀπεκρίθη Ἰησοῦς καὶ εἶπεν αὐτοῖς, Κἂν
is true. answered Jesus and said to them, Even if

ἐγὼ μαρτυρῶ περὶ ἐμαυτοῦ, ἀληθής ἐστιν ἡ μαρτυρία μου
**14** I witness about Myself, true is the witness of Me

ὅτι οἶδα πόθεν ἦλθον, καὶ ποῦ ὑπάγω· ὑμεῖς δὲ οὐκ οἴδατε
because I know from I came, and where I go; you but not do know
where

not know from where I come and where I go. [15] You judge according to the flesh; I judge no one. [16] And if I also judge, My judgment is true, because I am not alone, but I and the Father who sent Me. [17] And in your Law also, it is been written that the witness of two men is true. [18] I am (one) who bears witness concerning Myself, and the Father who sent Me bears witness concerning Me. [19] Then they said to Him, Where is your father? Jesus answered, You do not know Me nor My Father. If you had known Me, you would have known My Father also. [20] Jesus spoke these words in the treasury, teaching in the Temple; and no one took Him, for His hour had not yet come.

[21] Then Jesus said to the them again, I go away, and you will seek Me, and you will die in your sins; where I go you cannot come. [22] Then the Jews said, Will he kill himself, that he says, Where I go you cannot come? [23] And He said to them, You are from beneath; I am from above. You are of this world; I am not of this world. [24] Therefore I said to you that you will die in your sins; for if you do not believe that I AM, you will die in your sins. [25] Then they said to Him, Who are you? And Jesus said to them, Altogether that which I also say to you. [26] I have many things to say and to judge concerning you; but He who sent Me is true, and those things I heard from Him, these I say to the world. [27] They did not know that He spoke to them of the Father. [28] Then Jesus said to them, When you shall have lifted up the Son of man, then you shall know that I AM; and from Myself I do nothing, but as

**15** πόθεν ἔρχομαι, καὶ ποῦ ὑπάγω. ὑμεῖς κατὰ τὴν σάρκα
from where I come, or where I go.       You according to the flesh

**16** κρίνετε· ἐγὼ οὐ κρίνω οὐδένα. καὶ ἐὰν κρίνω δὲ ἐγώ, ἢ
judge.   I do not judge   no one. even if   judge But I,
κρίσις ἡ ἐμὴ ἀληθής ἐστιν· ὅτι μόνος οὐκ εἰμί, ἀλλ᾽ ἐγὼ καὶ
judgment My   true   is because alone not I am, but   I and

**17** ὁ πέμψας με πατήρ. καὶ ἐν τῷ νόμῳ δὲ τῷ ὑμετέρῳ γέγρα-
He sending Me,(the) Father.Also in   Law and   your it has been

**18** πται ὅτι δύο ἀνθρώπων ἡ μαρτυρία ἀληθής ἐστιν. ἐγώ εἰμι
written that of two men   the witness   true   is.   I am
ὁ μαρτυρῶν περὶ ἐμαυτοῦ, καὶ μαρτυρεῖ περὶ ἐμοῦ ὁ πέμψας
the(one) witnessing about Myself, and witnesses about Me He sending,

**19** με πατήρ. ἔλεγον οὖν αὐτῷ, Ποῦ ἐστιν ὁ πατήρ σου
Me,(the) Father. they said Then to Him, Where   is the   father of you?
ἀπεκρίθη ὁ Ἰησοῦς, Οὔτε ἐμὲ οἴδατε, οὔτε τὸν πατέρα μου·
answered   Jesus,   Neither Me you know, nor the Father of Me;

**20** εἰ ἐμὲ ᾔδειτε, καὶ τὸν πατέρα μού ᾔδειτε ἄν. ταῦτα τὰ
if Me you knew, also the   Father of Me   you had known then. These —
ῥήματα ἐλάλησεν ὁ Ἰησοῦς ἐν τῷ γαζοφυλακίῳ, διδάσκων
words   spoke   Jesus in the treasury,   teaching
ἐν τῷ ἱερῷ· καὶ οὐδεὶς ἐπίασεν αὐτόν, ὅτι οὔπω ἐληλύθει ἡ
in the Temple. And no one seized   Him, because not yet had come the
ὥρα αὐτου.
hour of Him.

**21** Εἶπεν οὖν πάλιν αὐτοῖς ὁ Ἰησοῦς, Ἐγὼ ὑπάγω, καὶ
said therefore again to them — Jesus, I go,   and
ζητήσετέ με, καὶ ἐν τῇ ἁμαρτίᾳ ὑμῶν ἀποθανεῖσθε· ὅπου
you will seek Me; and in the   sin   of you you will die.   Where

**22** ἐγὼ ὑπάγω, ὑμεῖς οὐ δύνασθε ἐλθεῖν. ἔλεγον οὖν οἱ Ἰουδαῖοι,
I   go,   you not are able to come. said Then the   Jews,
Μήτι ἀποκτενεῖ ἑαυτόν, ὅτι λέγει, Ὅπου ἐγὼ ὑπάγω,
Not   will he kill   himself, because he says, Where I   go,

**23** ὑμεῖς οὐ δύνασθε ἐλθεῖν; καὶ εἶπεν αὐτοῖς, Ὑμεῖς ἐκ τῶν κάτω
you not are able to come? And He said to them, You from below
ἐστέ, ἐγὼ ἐκ τῶν ἄνω εἰμί· ὑμεῖς ἐκ τοῦ κόσμου τούτου ἐστέ,
are; I from above am. You from   world   this   are;

**24** ἐγὼ οὐκ εἰμὶ ἐκ τοῦ κόσμου τούτου. εἶπον οὖν ὑμῖν ὅτι
I   not am from — world   this.   I said therefore to you that
ἀποθανεῖσθε ἐν ταῖς ἁμαρτίαις ὑμῶν· ἐὰν γὰρ μὴ πιστεύσητε
you will die   in the   sins   of you; if   for not you believe

**25** ὅτι ἐγώ εἰμι, ἀποθανεῖσθε ἐν ταῖς ἁμαρτίαις ὑμῶν. ἔλεγον
that I   AM, you will die in the   sins   of you. They said
οὖν αὐτῷ, Σὺ τίς εἶ; καὶ εἶπεν αὐτοῖς ὁ Ἰησοῦς, Τὴν ἀρχὴν
then to Him, you Who are? And said to them — Jesus,   Altogether

**26** ὅ τι καὶ λαλῶ ὑμῖν. πολλὰ ἔχω περὶ ὑμῶν λαλεῖν καὶ
what even I say to you. Many things I have about you to say   and
κρίνειν· ἀλλ᾽ ὁ πέμψας με ἀληθής ἐστι, κἀγὼ ἃ ἤκουσα παρ᾽
to judge, but the(One)sending Me true   is, and I what I heard from

**27** αὐτοῦ, ταῦτα λέγω εἰς τὸν κόσμον. οὐκ ἔγνωσαν ὅτι τὸν
Him, these things I say to the   world.   not They knew that (of) the

**28** πατέρα αὐτοῖς ἔλεγεν. εἶπεν οὖν αὐτοῖς ὁ Ἰησοῦς, Ὅταν
Father   to them He spoke.   said therefore to them   Jesus,   When
ὑψώσητε τὸν υἱὸν τοῦ ἀνθρώπου, τότε γνώσεσθε ὅτι ἐγώ
you lift up the Son — of man,   then you will know that I
εἰμι, καὶ ἀπ᾽ ἐμαυτοῦ ποιῶ οὐδέν, ἀλλὰ καθὼς ἐδίδαξέ με ὁ
AM; and from Myself I do nothing, but   as   taught Me the

My Father taught Me, these things I speak. [29] And He who sent Me is with Me; the Father did not leave Me alone, because I always do the things that are pleasing to Him. [30] As He spoke these things, many believed on Him.

[31] Then Jesus said to the Jews who had believed on Him, If you abide in My word, you are truly My disciples. [32] And you shall know the truth, and the truth shall set you free. [33] They answered Him, We are Abraham's seed, and have never been under bondage to anyone; how do you say, You shall become free? [34] Jesus answered them, Indeed, I tell you truly that everyone that practices sin is the slave of sin. [35] Now the slave does not remain in the house forever; the Son remains forever. [36] Therefore if the Son shall set you free, you shall be really free. [37] I know that you are Abraham's seed, but you seek to kill Me because My word has no interest in you. [38] I speak what I have seen with My Father, and so do you always do what you have seen with your father. [39] They answered and said to Him, Abraham is our father. Jesus said to them, If you were children of Abraham, you would do the works of Abraham. [40] But now you seek to kill Me, a man who has spoken the truth to you, which I heard from God; this Abraham did not do. [41] You do the works of your father. They said then to Him, We have not been born of fornication; we have one father, God. [42] Then Jesus said to them, If God were your Father you would love Me, for I came forth and am come from God. For I have not come of Myself, but He sent Me. [43] Why do you not understand My speech? Because you are unable to hear My word.

**29** πατηρ μου, ταῦτα λαλῶ. καὶ ὁ πέμψας με μετ᾽ ἐμοῦ ἐστιν·
Father of Me, these things I say. And the (One) sending Me with Me    is.

οὐκ ἀφῆκέ με μόνον ὁ πατήρ, ὅτι ἐγὼ τὰ ἀρεστὰ αὐτῷ ποιῶ
Not left   Me alone the Father, for I the things pleasing to Him do

**30** πάντοτε. ταῦτα αὐτοῦ λαλοῦντος πολλοὶ ἐπίστευσαν εἰς
always.   These things He   saying,   many   believed   into

αὐτόν.
Him.

**31** Ἔλεγεν οὖν ὁ Ἰησοῦς πρὸς τοὺς πεπιστευκότας αὐτῷ
said Therefore  Jesus  to   the  having believed  in Him

Ἰουδαίους, Ἐὰν ὑμεῖς μείνητε ἐν τῷ λόγῳ τῷ ἐμῷ, ἀληθῶς
Jews.   If  you continue in the word  — My, truly

**32** μαθηταί μου ἐστέ· καὶ γνώσεσθε τὴν ἀλήθειαν, καὶ ἡ ἀλήθεια
disciples of Me you are; and you will know the truth,   and the truth

**33** ἐλευθερώσει ὑμᾶς. ἀπεκρίθησαν αὐτῷ, Σπέρμα Ἀβραάμ
will set free   you.  They answered to Him,  seed  of Abraham

ἐσμεν, καὶ οὐδενὶ δεδουλεύκαμεν πώποτε· πῶς σὺ λέγεις ὅτι
We are, and to no one have we been enslaved, never.  How do you say,  —

**34** Ἐλεύθεροι γενήσεσθε; ἀπεκρίθη αὐτοῖς ὁ Ἰησοῦς, Ἀμὴν
free  You will become? answered  them  —  Jesus,  Truly,

ἀμὴν λέγω ὑμῖν, ὅτι πᾶς ὁ ποιῶν τὴν ἁμαρτίαν δοῦλός ἐστι
truly,  I say to you, that everyone doing  —  sin   a slave  is

**35** τῆς ἁμαρτίας. ὁ δὲ δοῦλος οὐ μένει ἐν τῇ οἰκίᾳ εἰς τὸν αἰῶνα·
— of sin.   the But slave not remains in the house for   ever;

**36** ὁ υἱὸς μένει εἰς τὸν αἰῶνα. ἐὰν οὖν ὁ υἱὸς ὑμᾶς ἐλευθερώσῃ,
the son remains to the  age.  If, then, the Son you  sets free,

**37** ὄντως ἐλεύθεροι ἔσεσθε. οἶδα ὅτι σπέρμα Ἀβραάμ ἐστε·
really   free   you are. I know that the seed of Abraham you are,

ἀλλὰ ζητεῖτέ με ἀποκτεῖναι, ὅτι ὁ λόγος ὁ ἐμὸς οὐ χωρεῖ ἐν
but you seek Me to kill,  because word  —  My not has place in

**38** ὑμῖν. ἐγὼ ὃ ἑώρακα παρὰ τῷ πατρί μου, λαλῶ· καὶ ὑμεῖς οὖν
you.  I what I have seen with the Father of Me, I speak; and you, then,

**39** ὃ ἑωράκατε παρὰ τῷ πατρὶ ὑμῶν, ποιεῖτε. ἀπεκρίθησαν καὶ
what you have seen with the father of you, you do.  They answered and

εἶπον αὐτῷ, Ὁ πατὴρ ἡμῶν Ἀβραάμ ἐστι. λέγει αὐτοῖς ὁ
said to Him, The father of us  Abraham is.   says to them —

Ἰησοῦς, Εἰ τέκνα τοῦ Ἀβραὰμ ἦτε, τὰ ἔργα τοῦ Ἀβραὰμ
Jesus,  If children  —  of Abraham you were, the works — of Abraham

**40** ἐποιεῖτε ἄν. νῦν δὲ ζητεῖτέ με ἀποκτεῖναι, ἄνθρωπον ὃς τὴν
you would do. now And you seek Me  to kill,   a man   who the

ἀλήθειαν ὑμῖν λελάληκα, ἣν ἤκουσα παρὰ τοῦ Θεοῦ· τοῦτο
truth  to you has spoken, which I heard beside  — God; this

**41** Ἀβραὰμ οὐκ ἐποίησεν. ὑμεῖς ποιεῖτε τὰ ἔργα τοῦ πατρὸς
Abraham not did do.   You  do  the works of the  father

ὑμῶν. εἶπον οὖν αὐτῷ, Ἡμεῖς ἐκ πορνείας οὐ γεγεννήμεθα·
of you. They said, then, to Him, We  of fornication not were born;

**42** ἕνα πατέρα ἔχομεν, τὸν Θεόν. εἶπεν αὐτοῖς ὁ Ἰησοῦς, Εἰ ὁ
one father we have,  — God.  said to them — Jesus, If  —

Θεὸς πατὴρ ὑμῶν ἦν, ἠγαπᾶτε ἂν ἐμέ· ἐγὼ γὰρ ἐκ τοῦ Θεοῦ
God Father of you was, you would love Me; I  from  —  God

ἐξῆλθον καὶ ἥκω· οὐδὲ γὰρ ἀπ᾽ ἐμαυτοῦ ἐλήλυθα, ἀλλ᾽
came forth, and have come; not for  from  Myself I have come, but

**43** ἐκεῖνός με ἀπέστειλε. διατί τὴν λαλιὰν τὴν ἐμὴν οὐ γινώ-
that One Me sent.   Why  —  speech  —  My not you

**44** σκετε; ὅτι οὐ δύνασθε ἀκούειν τὸν λόγον τὸν ἐμόν. ὑμεῖς
know? Because not you are able to hear  —  word  — My. You

[44] You are of the devil (as) father, and the lusts of your father you desire to do. He was a murderer from (the) beginning, and has not stood in the truth, because there is no truth in him. Whenever he may speak the lie, he speaks from his own; for he is a liar and the father of it. [45] And because I speak the truth, you do not believe Me. [46] Which of you convicts Me concerning sin? But if I speak truth, why do you not believe Me? [47] He that is of God hears the words of God; therefore you do not hear because you are not of God. [48] Then the Jews answered and said to Him, Do we not say well that you are a Samaritan, and have a demon? [49] Jesus answered, I do not have a demon; but I honor My Father, and you dishonor Me. [50] But I do not seek My glory; there is He who seeks and judges. [51] Indeed, I tell you truly, if anyone keep My word, he shall never ever see death. [52] Then the Jews said to Him, Now we know that you have a demon. Abraham died, and the prophets, and you say If anyone keep my word, he shall never ever taste of death. [53] Are you greater than our father Abraham who died? And the prophets died! Whom do you make yourself? [54] Jesus answered, If I glorify Myself, My glory is nothing; it is My Father who glorifies Me, (of) whom you say that He is your God. [55] And you have not known Him, but I know Him; and if I say that I do not know Him, I shall be like you, a liar. But I know Him, and I keep His word. [56] Your father Abraham leaped for joy in that he should see My day, and he saw, and rejoiced. [57] Therefore the Jews said to Him, You are not yet fifty years old, and have you seen Abraham?

ἐκ πατρὸς τοῦ διαβόλου ἐστέ, καὶ τὰς ἐπιθυμίας τοῦ πατρὸς
from (your) father the Devil   are;   and the   lusts   of the father

ὑμῶν θέλετε ποιεῖν. ἐκεῖνος ἀνθρωποκτόνος ἦν ἀπ᾽ ἀρχῆς,
of you you desire to do. That one   a murderer   was   from (the) first,

45 καὶ ἐν τῇ ἀληθείᾳ οὐχ ἔστηκεν, ὅτι οὐκ ἔστιν ἀλήθεια ἐν αὐτῷ.
and in the truth   not has stood, because not is   truth   in him.

ὅταν λαλῇ τὸ ψεῦδος, ἐκ τῶν ἰδίων λαλεῖ· ὅτι ψεύστης ἐστὶ
When he speaks the lie, out of the   own he speaks, for a liar   he is,

45 καὶ ὁ πατὴρ αὐτοῦ. ἐγὼ δὲ ὅτι τὴν ἀλήθειαν λέγω, οὐ πι-
and the father   of it.   I But because the   truth   I say, not you

46 στεύετέ μοι. τίς ἐξ ὑμῶν ἐλέγχει με περὶ ἁμαρτίας; εἰ δὲ ἀλή-
believe   Me. Who of you   reproves Me concerning sin?   if And

47 θειαν λέγω, διατί ὑμεῖς οὐ πιστεύετέ μοι; ὁ ὢν ἐκ τοῦ Θεοῦ
truth I say, why   you do not believe   Me? He being of —   God

τὰ ῥήματα τοῦ Θεοῦ ἀκούει· διὰ τοῦτο ὑμεῖς οὐκ ἀκούετε,
the words   — of God   hears; therefore   you do not hear,

48 ὅτι ἐκ τοῦ Θεοῦ οὐκ ἐστέ. ἀπεκρίθησαν οὖν οἱ Ἰουδαῖοι καὶ
since from   God not you are. answered,   then, The   Jews   and

εἶπον αὐτῷ, Οὐ καλῶς λέγομεν ἡμεῖς ὅτι Σαμαρείτης εἶ σύ,
said to Him, Not well   say   we   that   a Samaritan are you,

49 καὶ δαιμόνιον ἔχεις; ἀπεκρίθη Ἰησοῦς, Ἐγὼ δαιμόνιον οὐκ
and   a demon you have? answered Jesus,   I   a demon   not

ἔχω, ἀλλὰ τιμῶ τὸν πατέρα μου, καὶ ὑμεῖς ἀτιμάζετέ με.
have, but I honor   the Father of Me, and you   dishonor   Me.

50 ἐγὼ δὲ οὐ ζητῶ τὴν δόξαν μου· ἔστιν ὁ ζητῶν καὶ κρίνων
I But not do seek   the glory of Me; One is   seeking and judging.

51 ἀμὴν ἀμὴν λέγω ὑμῖν, ἐάν τις τὸν λόγον τὸν ἐμὸν τηρήσῃ,
Truly, truly, I say to you, if anyone —   word   —   My   keeps,

52 θάνατον οὐ μὴ θεωρήσῃ εἰς τὸν αἰῶνα. εἶπον οὖν αὐτῷ
death   in no way will he behold for   ever.   said,   then, to Him

οἱ Ἰουδαῖοι, Νῦν ἐγνώκαμεν ὅτι δαιμόνιον ἔχεις. Ἀβραὰμ
The Jews,   Now   we have known that   a demon you have. Abraham

ἀπέθανε καὶ οἱ προφῆται, καὶ σὺ λέγεις, Ἐάν τις τὸν λόγον
died,   and the prophets,   and you say,   If anyone the word

53 μου τηρήσῃ, οὐ μὴ γεύσεται θανάτου εἰς τὸν αἰῶνα. μὴ σὺ
of Me keeps,   in no way will he taste of death for   ever. Not you

μείζων εἶ τοῦ πατρὸς ἡμῶν Ἀβραάμ, ὅστις ἀπέθανε; καὶ
greater are than the father   of us, Abraham,   who   died? Also

54 οἱ προφῆται ἀπέθανον· τίνα σεαυτὸν σὺ ποιεῖς; ἀπεκρίθη
the prophets   died.   Whom Yourself you do make?   answered

Ἰησοῦς, Ἐὰν ἐγὼ δοξάζω ἐμαυτόν, ἡ δόξα μου οὐδέν ἐστιν·
Jesus,   If I   glorify   Myself,   the glory of Me nothing is;

ἔστιν ὁ πατήρ μου ὁ δοξάζων με, ὃν ὑμεῖς λέγετε ὅτι Θεὸς
it is the Father of Me glorifying Me,   whom you   say   that God

55 ὑμῶν ἐστι, καὶ οὐκ ἐγνώκατε αὐτόν· ἐγὼ δὲ οἶδα αὐτόν,
of you is.   And not you have known Him;   I but know   Him,

καὶ ἐὰν εἴπω ὅτι οὐκ οἶδα αὐτόν, ἔσομαι ὅμοιος ὑμῶν,
and if   I say that not I know   Him, I shall be   like   you,

ψεύστης· ἀλλ᾽ οἶδα αὐτόν, καὶ τὸν λόγον αὐτοῦ τηρῶ.
a liar.   But I know   Him, and the   word of Him I keep.

56 Ἀβραὰμ ὁ πατὴρ ὑμῶν ἠγαλλιάσατο ἵνα ἴδῃ τὴν ἡμέραν
Abraham the father   of you leaped for joy that he may see   day

57 τὴν ἐμήν, καὶ εἶδε καὶ ἐχάρη. εἶπον οὖν οἱ Ἰουδαῖοι πρὸς
—   My,   and he saw and rejoiced. said Then the   Jews   to

αὐτόν, Πεντήκοντα ἔτη οὔπω ἔχεις, καὶ Ἀβραὰμ ἑώρακας;
Him,   Fifty   years   not yet you have, and Abraham you have seen?

[58] Jesus said to them, Indeed, I tell you truly, before Abraham was, I AM. [59] They therefore took up stones that they might throw at Him; but Jesus hid Himself and went forth out of the Temple, going through the middle of them, and so passed on.

**58** εἶπεν αὐτοῖς ὁ Ἰησοῦς, Ἀμὴν ἀμὴν λέγω ὑμῖν, πρὶν Ἀβραὰμ
said to them — Jesus, Truly, truly I say to you, before Abraham
**59** γενέσθαι, ἐγώ εἰμι. ἦραν οὖν λίθους ἵνα βάλωσιν ἐπ' αὐτόν·
came into being, I AM. they took Then stones that they might cast on Him;
Ἰησοῦς δὲ ἐκρύβη, καὶ ἐξῆλθεν ἐκ τοῦ ἱεροῦ, διελθὼν διὰ
Jesus but was hidden, and went forth out of the Temple, going through
μέσου αὐτῶν· καὶ παρῆγεν οὕτως.
(the) midst of them, and passed by thus.

## CHAPTER 9

CHAPTER 9
[1] And passing He saw a man blind from birth. [2] And His disciples asked Him saying, Teacher, who sinned, this one or his parents, that he should be born blind? [3] Jesus answered, Neither this one sinned nor his parents; but that the works of God should be revealed in him. [4] It is necessary for Me to work the works of Him who sent Me while it is day; night comes when no one is able to work. [5] While I may be in the world, I am (the) Light of the world. [6] Having said these things, He spat on (the) ground, and made clay of the spittle, and applied the clay to the eyes of the blind one. [7] And He said to him, Go, wash in the pool of Siloam, which translated is Sent. Therefore he went and washed, and came away seeing. [8] Therefore the neighbors and those who saw him before, that he was blind, said, Is this not he who was sitting and begging? [9] Some said, It is he; but others, He is like him. He said, I am (he) [10] Therefore they said to him, How were your eyes opened? [11] He answered and said, A man called Jesus made clay and spread it on my eyes and said to me, Go to the the pool of Siloam and wash. And having gone and washed, I received sight. [12] Then they said to him, Where is he? He said, I do not know.
[13] They brought him to the Pharisees, he who (was) once blind.

**1** Καὶ παράγων εἶδεν ἄνθρωπον τυφλὸν ἐκ γενετῆς. καὶ
And passing by, He saw a man blind from birth. And
**2** ἠρώτησαν αὐτὸν οἱ μαθηταὶ αὐτοῦ λέγοντες, Ῥαββί, τίς
asked Him the disciples of Him, saying, Rabbi, who
ἥμαρτεν, οὗτος ἢ οἱ γονεῖς αὐτοῦ, ἵνα τυφλὸς γεννηθῇ;
sinned, this one, or the parents of him, that blind he was born?
**3** ἀπεκρίθη ὁ Ἰησοῦς, Οὔτε οὗτος ἥμαρτεν οὔτε οἱ γονεῖς
answered — Jesus, Neither this one sinned, nor the parents
αὐτοῦ· ἀλλ' ἵνα φανερωθῇ τὰ ἔργα τοῦ Θεοῦ ἐν αὐτῷ.
of him, but that might be revealed the works — of God in Him.
**4** ἐμὲ δεῖ ἐργάζεσθαι τὰ ἔργα τοῦ πέμψαντός με ἕως ἡμέρα
Me it behoves to work the works of the (One) sending Me while day
**5** ἐστίν· ἔρχεται νύξ, ὅτε οὐδεὶς δύναται ἐργάζεσθαι. ὅταν ἐν
It is. comes Night, when no one is able to work. When in
**6** τῷ κόσμῳ ὦ, φῶς εἰμι τοῦ κόσμου. ταῦτα εἰπών, ἔπτυσε
the world I am (the) light I am of the world. These things saying, He spat
χαμαί, καὶ ἐποίησε πηλὸν ἐκ τοῦ πτύσματος, καὶ ἐπέχρισε
on earth and made clay out of the spittle, and anointed
**7** τὸν πηλὸν ἐπὶ τοὺς ὀφθαλμοὺς τοῦ τυφλοῦ, καὶ εἶπεν αὐτῷ,
the clay on the eyes of the blind one, and said to him,
Ὕπαγε νίψαι εἰς τὴν κολυμβήθραν τοῦ Σιλωάμ (ὃ ἑρμη-
Go, wash in the pool — of Siloam; which is
νεύεται, ἀπεσταλμένος). ἀπῆλθεν οὖν καὶ ἐνίψατο, καὶ ἦλθε
translated, having been sent. He went then, and washed, and came
**8** βλέπων. οἱ οὖν γείτονες καὶ οἱ θεωροῦντες αὐτὸν τὸ πρό-
seeing. the Then neighbors and those beholding him formerly,
τερον ὅτι τυφλὸς ἦν, ἔλεγον, Οὐχ οὗτός ἐστιν ὁ καθή-
that blind he was, said, Not this one is the (one)
**9** μενος καὶ προσαιτῶν; ἄλλοι ἔλεγον ὅτι Οὗτός ἐστιν· ἄλλοι
sitting and begging? Some said, — This is he; Others
δὲ ὅτι Ὅμοιος αὐτῷ ἐστιν. ἐκεῖνος ἔλεγεν ὅτι Ἐγώ εἰμι.
and, like him he is. That one said, — I am.
**10** ἔλεγον οὖν αὐτῷ, Πῶς ἀνεῴχθησάν σου οἱ ὀφθαλμοί;
they said Then to him, How were opened of you the eyes?
**11** ἀπεκρίθη ἐκεῖνος καὶ εἶπεν, Ἄνθρωπος λεγόμενος Ἰησοῦς
answered That one and said, (The) man being called Jesus
πηλὸν ἐποίησε, καὶ ἐπέχρισέ μου τοὺς ὀφθαλμούς, καὶ εἶπε
clay made and anointed of me the eyes, and told
μοι, Ὕπαγε εἰς τὴν κολυμβήθραν τοῦ Σιλωάμ, καὶ νίψαι.
me, Go to the pool — of Siloam, and wash.
**12** ἀπελθὼν δὲ καὶ νιψάμενος, ἀνέβλεψα. εἶπον οὖν αὐτῷ, Ποῦ
going And, and washing, I received sight. They said then to him, Where
ἐστιν ἐκεῖνος; λέγει, Οὐκ οἶδα.
is that one? He says, Not I do know.
**13** Ἄγουσιν αὐτὸν πρὸς τοὺς Φαρισαίους, τὸν ποτὲ τυφλόν.
They lead him to the Pharisees, the (one) once blind.

[14] Now it was Sabbath when Jesus made clay and opened his eyes. [15] Therefore the Pharisees also again asked him how he received sight. And he said to them, He put clay on my eyes, and I washed, and I see. [16] Therefore some of the Pharisees said, This man is not from God, for he does not keep Sabbath. Others said, How can a man, a sinner, do such miracles? And a division was among them. [17] They said to the blind one again, What do you say about him, for he opened your eyes? And he said, He is a prophet. [18] Therefore the Jews did not believe about him, that he was blind and received sight, until they called the parents of him who had received sight. [19] And they asked them, saying, Is this your son, of whom you say that he was born blind? How then does he now see? [20] His parents answered them and said, We know that this is our son, and that he was born blind; [21] but how he now sees we do not know, or who opened his eyes, we do not know; he is of age, ask him. He shall speak concerning himself. [22] His parents said these things because they feared the Jews; for the Jews had already agreed together that if anyone should confess Him (the) Christ, he should be put out of the synagogue. [23] Because of this his parents said, He is of age, ask him. [24] Therefore they called a second time the man who was blind, and said to him, Give glory to God; we know that this man is a sinner. [25] Then he answered and said, Whether he is a sinner, I do not know. One (thing) I do know, that being blind, now I see. [26] And they said to him again, What did he do to you? How did he open your eyes?

**14** ἦν δὲ σάββατον ὅτε τὸν πηλὸν ἐποίησεν ὁ Ἰησοῦς, καὶ
it was And a sabbath when the clay made — Jesus, and

**15** ἀνέῳξεν αὐτοῦ τοὺς ὀφθαλμούς. πάλιν οὖν ἠρώτων αὐτὸν
opened of him the eyes. Again, therefore, asked him

καὶ οἱ Φαρισαῖοι, πῶς ἀνέβλεψεν. ὁ δὲ εἶπεν αὐτοῖς, Πηλὸν
also the Pharisees how he received sight. he And said to them, Clay

ἐπέθηκεν ἐπὶ τοὺς ὀφθαλμούς μου, καὶ ἐνιψάμην, καὶ
He put on the eyes of me, and I washed, and

**16** βλέπω. ἔλεγον οὖν ἐκ τῶν Φαρισαίων τινές, Οὗτος ὁ ἄνθρω-
I see. said Then of the Pharisees some, This man-

πος οὐκ ἔστι παρὰ τοῦ Θεοῦ, ὅτι τὸ σάββατον οὐ τηρεῖ.
not is from — God, because the sabbath not He keeps.

ἄλλοι ἔλεγον, Πῶς δύναται ἄνθρωπος ἁμαρτωλὸς τοιαῦτα
Others said, How is able a man, a sinner, such

**17** σημεῖα ποιεῖν; καὶ σχίσμα ἦν ἐν αὐτοῖς. λέγουσι τῷ τυφλῷ
signs do? And a division was among them. They say to the blind one

πάλιν, Σὺ τί λέγεις περὶ αὐτοῦ, ὅτι ἤνοιξέ σου τοὺς ὀφθαλ-
again, you What say concerning him, because he opened of you the eyes?

**18** μούς; ὁ δὲ εἶπεν ὅτι Προφήτης ἐστίν. οὐκ ἐπίστευσαν οὖν οἱ
he And said, — A prophet He is. Not did believe, therefore,the

Ἰουδαῖοι περὶ αὐτοῦ, ὅτι τυφλὸς ἦν καὶ ἀνέβλεψεν, ἕως
Jews concerning Him, that blind he was and received sight, until

**19** ὅτου ἐφώνησαν τοὺς γονεῖς αὐτοῦ τοῦ ἀναβλέψαντος, καὶ
when they called the parents of him — having received sight; and

ἠρώτησαν αὐτοὺς λέγοντες, Οὗτός ἐστιν ὁ υἱὸς ὑμῶν, ὃν
they asked them, saying, this Is the son of you, whom

ὑμεῖς λέγετε ὅτι τυφλὸς ἐγεννήθη; πῶς οὖν ἄρτι βλέπει
you say that blind he was born? How, then, just now he sees?

**20** ἀπεκρίθησαν αὐτοῖς οἱ γονεῖς αὐτοῦ καὶ εἶπον, Οἴδαμεν ὅτι
answered them The parents of him and said, We know that

**21** οὗτός ἐστιν ὁ υἱὸς ἡμῶν, καὶ ὅτι τυφλὸς ἐγεννήθη· πῶς δὲ νῦν
this is the son of us, and that blind he was born. how But now

βλέπει, οὐκ οἴδαμεν· ἢ τίς ἤνοιξεν αὐτοῦ τοὺς ὀφθαλμούς,
he sees, not we know, or who opened of him the eyes,

ἡμεῖς οὐκ οἴδαμεν· αὐτὸς ἡλικίαν ἔχει· αὐτὸν ἐρωτήσατε,
we not know. He age has, him ask.

**22** αὐτὸς περὶ αὐτοῦ λαλήσει. ταῦτα εἶπον οἱ γονεῖς αὐτοῦ, ὅτι
He concerning himself will speak. These things said the parents of him, for

ἐφοβοῦντο τοὺς Ἰουδαίους· ἤδη γὰρ συνετέθειντο οἱ
they feared the Jews; already for had agreed the

Ἰουδαῖοι, ἵνα ἐάν τις αὐτὸν ὁμολογήσῃ Χριστόν, ἀποσυνά-
Jews that if anyone Him should confess (as) Christ, from synagogue

**23** γωγος γένηται. διὰ τοῦτο οἱ γονεῖς αὐτοῦ εἶπον ὅτι
expelled he would be. Because of this the parents of him said, —

**24** Ἡλικίαν ἔχει, αὐτὸν ἐρωτήσατε. ἐφώνησαν οὖν ἐκ δευτέρου
age He has, him ask. They called therefore a second time

τὸν ἄνθρωπον ὃς ἦν τυφλός, καὶ εἶπον αὐτῷ, Δὸς δόξαν τῷ
the man who was blind, and said to him, Give glory to

Θεῷ· ἡμεῖς οἴδαμεν ὅτι ὁ ἄνθρωπος οὗτος ἁμαρτωλός ἐστιν.
God; we know that man this a sinner is.

**25** ἀπεκρίθη οὖν ἐκεῖνος καὶ εἶπεν, Εἰ ἁμαρτωλός ἐστιν, οὐκ
answered Then that one and said, If a sinner He is, not

**26** οἶδα· ἓν οἶδα, ὅτι τυφλὸς ὤν, ἄρτι βλέπω. εἶπον δὲ αὐτῷ
I know; one I know, that blind being, just now I see. they said And to him

πάλιν, Τί ἐποίησέ σοι; πῶς ἤνοιξέ σου τοὺς ὀφθαλμούς;
again, What did he to you? How opened he of you the eyes?

[27] He answered them, I already told you, and you did not hear; why do you wish to hear again? Do you also wish to become his disciples? [28] They shouted at him and said, You are his disciple, but we are Moses' disciples. [29] We know that God has spoken to Moses, but we do not know where this one is from. [30] The man answered and said to them, Indeed this is a wonderful thing, that you do not know from where he is, and he opened my eyes. [31] But we know that God does not hear sinners; but if anyone is God-fearing, and does His will, He hears him. [32] Was it ever heard that anyone opened (the) eyes of (one) having been born blind. [33] If this one was not from God, he could do nothing. [34] They answered and said to him, You were born wholly in sins, and do you teach us? And they threw him out. [35] Jesus heard that they threw him out, and having found him said to him, Do you believe on the Son of God? [36] And he answered and said, Who is He, Lord, that I may believe on Him? [37] And Jesus said to him, You have both seen Him, and He who speaks with you is He. [38] And he said, I believe, Lord; and he worshiped Him. [39] And Jesus said, I came into this world for judgment, that they that do not see might see, and that they that see might become blind. [40] And those of the Pharisees who were with Him heard these things, and they said, Are we blind, too? [41] Jesus said to them, If you were blind, you would not have sinned; but now you say, We see, therefore your sin remains.

**CHAPTER 10**

[1] Indeed, I tell you truly, He that does not enter in by the door to the

**27** ἀπεκρίθη αὐτοῖς, Εἶπον ὑμῖν ἤδη, καὶ οὐκ ἠκούσατε. τί πάλιν
He answered them, I told you already, and not you heard. Why again

θέλετε ἀκούειν ; μὴ καὶ ὑμεῖς θέλετε αὐτοῦ μαθηταὶ γενέσθαι
do you wish to hear? Not also you wish of him disciples to become?

**28** ἐλοιδόρησαν οὖν αὐτόν, καὶ εἶπον, Σὺ εἶ μαθητὴς ἐκείνου·
they reviled Then him and said, You are a disciple of that one,

**29** ἡμεῖς δὲ τοῦ Μωσέως ἐσμὲν μαθηταί ἡμεῖς οἴδαμεν ὅτι Μωσῇ
we but — of Moses are disciples. We know that by Moses

λελάληκεν ὁ Θεός· τοῦτον δὲ οὐκ οἴδαμεν πόθεν ἐστίν.
has spoken God, this one but not we know from where he is.

**30** ἀπεκρίθη ὁ ἄνθρωπος καὶ εἶπεν αὐτοῖς, Ἐν γὰρ τούτῳ
answered The man and said to them, in For this

θαυμαστόν ἐστιν, ὅτι ὑμεῖς οὐκ οἴδατε πόθεν ἐστί, καὶ
a marvel is, that you do not know from where He is, and

**31** ἀνέῳξέ μου τοὺς ὀφθαλμούς. οἴδαμεν δὲ ὅτι ἁμαρτωλῶν ὁ
He opened of me the eyes. we know And that sinful ones

Θεὸς οὐκ ἀκούει· ἀλλ᾽ ἐάν τις θεοσεβὴς ᾖ, καὶ τὸ θέλημα
God not hears, but if anyone God-fearing is, and the will

**32** αὐτοῦ ποιῇ, τούτου ἀκούει. ἐκ τοῦ αἰῶνος οὐκ ἠκούσθη
of Him does, this one He hears. From the age not it was heard

**33** ὅτι ἤνοιξέ τις ὀφθαλμοὺς τυφλοῦ γεγεννημένου. εἰ μὴ ἦν
that opened anyone eyes of one blind having been born. If not was

**34** οὗτος παρὰ Θεοῦ, οὐκ ἠδύνατο ποιεῖν οὐδέν. ἀπεκρίθησαν
this One from God, not He could do nothing. They answered

καὶ εἶπον αὐτῷ, Ἐν ἁμαρτίαις σὺ ἐγεννήθης ὅλος, καὶ σὺ
and said to him, In sins you were born wholly, and you

διδάσκεις ἡμᾶς ; καὶ ἐξέβαλον αὐτὸν ἔξω.
teach us? And they threw him outside.

**35** Ἤκουσεν ὁ Ἰησοῦς ὅτι ἐξέβαλον αὐτὸν ἔξω· καὶ εὑρὼν
heard Jesus that they threw him outside, and finding

**36** αὐτόν, εἶπεν αὐτῷ, Σὺ πιστεύεις εἰς τὸν υἱὸν τοῦ Θεοῦ ; ἀπε-
him. He said to him, You do believe in the Son — of God?

κρίθη ἐκεῖνος καὶ εἶπε, Τίς ἐστι, Κύριε, ἵνα πιστεύσω εἰς
answered That one and said, Who is He. Lord, that I may believe in

**37** αὐτόν ; εἶπε δὲ αὐτῷ ὁ Ἰησοῦς, Καὶ ἑώρακας αὐτόν, καὶ ὁ
Him? said And to him — Jesus, Even you have seen him, and He

**38** λαλῶν μετὰ σοῦ ἐκεῖνός ἐστιν. ὁ δὲ ἔφη, Πιστεύω, Κύριε·
speaking with you that One is. he And said, I believe, Lord;

**39** καὶ προσεκύνησεν αὐτῷ. καὶ εἶπεν ὁ Ἰησοῦς, Εἰς κρίμα ἐγὼ
and he worshiped Him. And said — Jesus, For judgment I

εἰς τὸν κόσμον τοῦτον ἦλθον, ἵνα οἱ μὴ βλέποντες βλέπω-
to — world this came, that the (ones) not seeing may see,

**40** σι, καὶ οἱ βλέποντες τυφλοὶ γένωνται. καὶ ἤκουσαν ἐκ τῶν
and those seeing blind may become. And heard of the

Φαρισαίων ταῦτα οἱ ὄντες μετ᾽ αὐτοῦ, καὶ εἶπον αὐτῷ, Μὴ
Pharisees these things, those being with Him, and said to Him, Not

**41** καὶ ἡμεῖς τυφλοί ἐσμεν ; εἶπεν αὐτοῖς ὁ Ἰησοῦς, Εἰ τυφλοὶ
also we blind are? said to them Jesus, If blind

ἦτε, οὐκ ἂν εἴχετε ἁμαρτίαν· νῦν δὲ λέγετε ὅτι Βλέπομεν·
you were, not you would have sin; now but you say, — We see;

ἡ οὖν ἁμαρτία ὑμῶν μένει.
the then sin of you remains.

**CHAPTER 10**

**1** Ἀμὴν ἀμὴν λέγω ὑμῖν, ὁ μὴ εἰσερχόμενος διὰ τῆς θύρας
Truly, truly I say to you, he not entering through the door

sheepfold, but climbs up some other place, he is a thief and a robber; [2] but he that goes in by the door is the shepherd of the sheep. [3] The gatekeeper opens to him, and the sheep hear his voice, and he calls his own sheep by name, and leads them out. [4] And when he puts forth his own sheep, he goes before them; and the sheep follow him, because they know his voice. [5] But they would never follow a stranger, but will tlee from him, because they do not know the voice of strangers. [6] Jesus spoke this allegory to them, but they did not know what it was which He spoke to them.

[7] Then Jesus said again to them, Indeed, I tell you truly that I am the door of the sheep.·[8] All those who came before Me are thieves and robbers; but the sheep did not hear them. [9] I am the door; if anyone enter in by Me, he shall be saved and shall go in and shall go out, and shall find pasture. [10] The thief does not come except that he may steal and may kill and may destroy; I came that they might have life and might have (it) abundantly. [11] I am the Good Shepherd! The Good Shepherd lays down His life for the sheep. [12] But the hired servant, who is not (the) shepherd, who does not own the sheep, sees the wolf coming, and leaves the sheep and flees; and the wolf captures them and scatters the sheep. [13] But the hired servants flees because he is a hired servant, and is not himself concerned about the sheep. [14] I am the Good Shepherd, and I know those that are Mine; and I am known by those that are Mine. [15] Even as the Father knows Me, I also know the Father; and I lay down My life for the sheep. [16] And I have other sheep which are not

εἰς τὴν αὐλὴν τῶν προβατων, ἀλλὰ ἀναβαίνων ἀλλαχόθεν,
into the fold of the sheep, but going up by another way,

2 ἐκεῖνος κλέπτης ἐστι καὶ λῃστής. ὁ δὲ εἰσερχόμενος διὰ τῆς
that one a thief is and a robber. he But entering through the

3 θύρας ποιμήν ἐστι τῶν προβάτων. τούτῳ ὁ θυρωρὸς
door shepherd is of the sheep. To this one the doorkeeper

ἀνοίγει, καὶ τὰ πρόβατα τῆς φωνῆς αὐτοῦ ἀκούει, καὶ τὰ
opens, and the sheep the voice of him hears, and the

4 ἴδια πρόβατα καλεῖ κατ' ὄνομα, καὶ ἐξάγει αὐτά. καὶ ὅταν
own sheep he calls by name, and leads out them. And when

τὰ ἴδια πρόβατα ἐκβάλῃ, ἔμπροσθεν αὐτῶν ποοεύεται· καὶ
the own sheep he passes, in front of them he goes, and

τὰ πρόβατα αὐτῷ ἀκολουθεῖ, ὅτι οἴδασι τὴν φωνὴν αὐτοῦ.
the sheep should they follow, because they know. the voice of him.

5 ἀλλοτρίῳ δὲ οὐ μὴ ἀκολουθήσωσιν, ἀλλὰ φεύξονται ἀπ'
a stranger But in no way to him follow, but will flee from

6 αὐτοῦ· ὅτι οὐκ οἴδασι τῶν ἀλλοτρίων τὴν φωνήν. ταύτην
him, because not they know of the strangers the voice. This

τὴν παροιμίαν εἶπεν αὐτοῖς ὁ Ἰησοῦς· ἐκεῖνοι δὲ οὐκ ἔγνωσαν
— allegory said to them — Jesus, those but not knew

τίνα ἦν ἃ ἐλάλει αὐτοῖς.
what it was which He spoke to them.

7 Εἶπεν οὖν πάλιν αὐτοῖς ὁ Ἰησοῦς, Ἀμὴν ἀμὴν λέγω ὑμῖν
said Therefore again to them — Jesus, Truly, truly, I say to you

8 ὅτι Ἐγώ εἰμι ἡ θύρα τῶν προβάτων. πάντες ὅσοι πρὸ ἐμοῦ
that I am the door of the sheep. All who before Me

ἦλθον κλέπται εἰσὶ καὶ λῃσταί· ἀλλ' οὐκ ἤκουσαν αὐτῶν τὰ
came thieves are and robbers; but did not. hear them the

9 πρόβατα. ἐγώ εἰμι ἡ θύρα· δι' ἐμοῦ ἐάν τις εἰσέλθη, σωθή-
sheep. I am the door; through Me If anyone enter he will

σεται, καὶ εἰσελεύσεται καὶ ἐξελεύσεται, καὶ νομὴν εὑρήσει.
be saved, and will go in and will go out, and pasture will find.

10 ὁ κλέπτης οὐκ ἔρχεται εἰ μὴ ἵνα κλέψῃ καὶ θύσῃ καὶ ἀπολέσῃ·
The thief not comes except that he may steal and slay and destroy;

11 ἐγὼ ἦλθον ἵνα ζωὴν ἔχωσι, καὶ περισσὸν ἔχωσιν. ἐγώ εἰμι
I came that life they may have, and abundantly may have. I am

ὁ ποιμὴν ὁ καλός ὁ ποιμὴν ὁ καλὸς τὴν ψυχὴν αὐτοῦ
the Shepherd — Good. The Shepherd — Good the soul of Him

12 τίθησιν ὑπὲρ τῶν προβάτων. ὁ μισθωτὸς δέ, καὶ οὐκ ὢν
lays down for the sheep. the hireling And, even not being

ποιμήν, οὐ οὔκ εἰσὶ τὰ πρόβατα ἴδια, θεωρεῖ τὸν λύκον
a shepherd, whose not are the sheep (his) own, beholds the wolf

ἐρχόμενον, καὶ ἀφίησι τὰ πρόβατα, καὶ φεύγει· καὶ ὁ λύκος
coming, and forsakes the sheep, and flees, and the wolf

13 ἁρπάζει αὐτά, καὶ σκορπίζει τὰ πρόβατα. ὁ δὲ μισθωτὸς
seizes them and scatters the sheep. the Now hireling

φεύγει, ὅτι μισθωτός ἐστι, καὶ οὐ μέλει αὐτῷ περὶ τῶν
flees because a hireling he is, and not is care to him about

14 προβάτων. ἐγώ εἰμι ὁ ποιμὴν ὁ καλός, καὶ γινώσκω τὰ ἐμά,
sheep. I am the Shepherd Good, and I know — Mine,

15 καὶ γινώσκομαι ὑπὸ τῶν ἐμῶν. καθὼς γινώσκει με ὁ πατήρ,
and am known by — Mine. As knows Me the Father,

κἀγὼ γινώσκω τὸν πατέρα· καὶ τὴν ψυχήν μου τίθημι ὑπὲρ
I also know the Father: and the soul of Me I lay down for

16 τῶν προβάτων. καὶ ἄλλα πρόβατα ἔχω, ἃ οὔκ ἔστιν ἐκ τῆς
the sheep. And other sheep I have, which not are of —

of this fold; it is needful that I bring these also, and they shall hear My voice, and there shall be one flock, one Shepherd. [17] Because of this the Father loves Me, because I lay down My life, that I may take it again. [18] No one takes it from Me, but I lay it down of Myself. I have authority to lay it down, and I have authority to take it again. I received this commandment from My Father. [19] Therefore there was again a division among the Jews, because of these words. [20] And many of them said, He has a demon and is insane; why do you hear him? [21] Others said, These are not sayings of one possessed by a demon. Is a demon able to open eyes of (the) blind?

[22] And the Feast of Dedication took place at Jerusalem, and it was winter. [23] And Jesus was walking in the Temple, in the porch of Solomon. [24] Then the Jews encircled Him and said to Him, How long do you hold our soul in suspense? If you are the Christ, tell us plainly. [25] Jesus answered them, I told you, and you did not believe. The works which I do in the name of My Father, these bear witness concerning Me; [26] but you do not believe, for you are not of my sheep, as I said to you. [27] My sheep hear My voice, and I know them, and they follow Me; [28] and I give eternal life to them; and in no way shall they perish forever; and no one shall pluck them out of My hand. [29] My Father who has given (them) to Me is greater than all, and no one is able to pluck out of My Father's hand. [30] The Father and I are one! [31] Then again the Jews took up stones that they may stone Him. [32] Jesus answered them, I showed you many

αὐλῆς ταύτης· κἀκεῖνά με δεῖ ἀγαγεῖν, καὶ τῆς φωνῆς μου
fold   this;   those also Me it is right to lead, and of the voice of Me

17 ἀκούσουσι· καὶ γενήσεται μία ποίμνη, εἷς ποιμήν. διὰ τοῦτο
they will hear, and will become one   flock, one Shepherd. Therefore

ὁ πατήρ με ἀγαπᾷ, ὅτι ἐγὼ τίθημι τὴν ψυχήν μου, ἵνα
the Father Me loves, because I lay down the   soul   of Me, that

18 πάλιν λάβω αὐτήν. οὐδεὶς αἴρει αὐτὴν ἀπ' ἐμοῦ, ἀλλ' ἐγὼ
again I may take it.   No one   takes up   from   Me,   but   I

τίθημι αὐτὴν ἀπ' ἐμαυτοῦ. ἐξουσίαν ἔχω θεῖναι αὐτήν, καὶ
lay down it   from Myself.   authority I have to lay down it,   and

ἐξουσίαν ἔχω πάλιν λαβεῖν αὐτήν· ταύτην τὴν ἐντολὴν
authority   I have again to take   it.   This     — commandment

ἔλαβον παρὰ τοῦ πατρός μου.
I received from the   Father   of Me.

19 Σχίσμα οὖν πάλιν ἐγένετο ἐν τοῖς Ἰουδαίοις διὰ τοὺς
a division Therefore again occurred among the   Jews, because of —

20 λόγους τούτους. ἔλεγον δὲ πολλοὶ ἐξ αὐτῶν, Δαιμόνιον ἔχει
words   these.   said And many of them,   A demon he has,

21 καὶ μαίνεται· τί αὐτοῦ ἀκούετε; ἄλλοι ἔλεγον, Ταῦτα τὰ
and is insane. Why him do you hear? Others said,   These —

ῥήματα οὐκ ἔστι δαιμονιζομένου· μὴ δαιμόνιον δύναται
words   not   is of one demon-possessed; not a demon   is able

τυφλῶν ὀφθαλμοὺς ἀνοίγειν;
of blind ones eyes   to open?

22 Ἐγένετο δὲ τὰ ἐγκαίνια ἐν τοῖς Ἱεροσολύμοις, καὶ
occurred And the Dedication in   —   Jerusalem;   and

23 χειμὼν ἦν· καὶ περιεπάτει ὁ Ἰησοῦς ἐν τῷ ἱερῷ ἐν τῇ στοᾷ
winter it was. And walked   — Jesus in the Temple in the porch

24 τοῦ Σολομῶντος. ἐκύκλωσαν οὖν αὐτὸν οἱ Ἰουδαῖοι, καὶ
— of Solomon.   encircled· Then Him the Jews.   and

ἔλεγον αὐτῷ, Ἕως πότε τὴν ψυχὴν ἡμῶν αἴρεις; εἰ σὺ εἶ ὁ
said to Him, Until when the   soul of us   lift up? If you are the

25 Χριστός, εἰπὲ ἡμῖν παρρησίᾳ. ἀπεκρίθη αὐτοῖς ὁ Ἰησοῦς,
Christ, tell us   publicly.   answered   them — Jesus,

Εἶπον ὑμῖν, καὶ οὐ πιστεύετε· τὰ ἔργα ἃ ἐγὼ ποιῶ ἐν τῷ
I said to you, and not you believe; the works which I   do   in the

26 ὀνόματι τοῦ πατρός μου, ταῦτα μαρτυρεῖ περὶ ἐμοῦ· ἀλλ'
name of the Father of Me,   these   witness concerning Me; but

ὑμεῖς οὐ πιστεύετε· οὐ γάρ ἐστε ἐκ τῶν προβάτων τῶν ἐμῶν,
you not do believe   not for you are of the   sheep   — of Me.

27 καθὼς εἶπον ὑμῖν. τὰ πρόβατα τὰ ἐμὰ τῆς φωνῆς μου ἀκούει,
As   I said to you, — sheep   — My of the voice of Me   hear,

28 κἀγὼ γινώσκω αὐτά, καὶ ἀκολουθοῦσί μοι· κἀγὼ ζωὴν
and I know   them,   and they follow Me; and I   life

αἰώνιον δίδωμι αὐτοῖς· καὶ οὐ μὴ ἀπόλωνται εἰς τὸν αἰῶνα,
eternal   give to them; and in no way shall they perish for   ever,

29 καὶ οὐχ ἁρπάσει τις αὐτὰ ἐκ τῆς χειρός μου. ὁ πατήρ μου
and not shall pluck anyone them out of the hand of Me. The Father of Me

ὃς δέδωκέ μοι, μείζων πάντων ἐστί· καὶ οὐδεὶς δύναται
who has given to Me, greater than all   is,   and no one   is able

30 ἁρπάζειν ἐκ τῆς χειρὸς τοῦ πατρός μου. ἐγὼ καὶ ὁ πατὴρ
to pluck out of the hand of the Father of Me.   I   and the Father

31 ἓν ἐσμεν. ἐβάστασαν οὖν πάλιν λίθους οἱ Ἰουδαῖοι ἵνα
one are.   took up Therefore again stones the   Jews,   that

32 λιθάσωσιν αὐτόν. ἀπεκρίθη αὐτοῖς ὁ Ἰησοῦς, Πολλὰ καλὰ
they might stone Him.   answered them — Jesus,   Many   good

good works from My Father; for which work of these are you stoning Me? [33] The Jews answered Him, saying, We do not stone you for a good work, but for blasphemy, and because you, being a man, make yourself God. [34] Jesus answered them, Is it not written in your Law, "I said, you are gods"? [35] If He called them gods, to whom the word of God came — and the Scriptures cannot be broken — [36] do you say (of Him) whom the Father sanctified and sent into the world, You blaspheme, because I said, I am Son of God? [37] If I do not do the works of My Father, do not believe Me; [38] but if I do, even if you do not believe Me, believe the works, that you may perceive and may believe that the Father (is) in Me, and I in Him. [39] Therefore they sought again to take Him, and He went forth out of their hands; [40] and went again beyond the Jordan, to the place where John was first baptizing; and He stayed there. [41] And many came to Him, and said, John really did no miracle, but all things that John said about this One were true. [42] And many believed on Him there.

CHAPTER 11

[1] Now there was a certain sick one, Lazarus of Bethany, of the village of Mary and Martha her sister. [2] And it was Mary who anointed the Lord with ointment and wiped His feet with her hair, whose brother Lazarus was sick. [3] Therefore the sisters sent to Him, saying, Lord, behold, he whom You love is sick. [4] But having heard Jesus said, This sickness is not to death, but for the glory of God, that the Son of God may be glorified by it. [5] Now Jesus loved Martha and her sister and Lazarus. [6] Therefore when He

ἔργα ἔδειξα ὑμῖν ἐκ τοῦ πατρός μου· διὰ ποῖον αὐτῶν ἔργον
works I showed you from the Father of Me; for which of them work

**33** λιθάζετέ με; ἀπεκρίθησαν αὐτῷ οἱ Ἰουδαῖοι λέγοντες, Περὶ
do you stone Me? answered Him the Jews, saying, Concerning

καλοῦ ἔργου οὐ λιθάζομέν σε, ἀλλὰ περὶ βλασφημίας, καὶ
a good work not we stone you, but concerning blasphemy, and

**34** ὅτι σὺ ἄνθρωπος ὢν ποιεῖς σεαυτὸν Θεόν. ἀπεκρίθη αὐτοῖς
because you a man being make yourself God. answered them

ὁ Ἰησοῦς, Οὐκ ἔστι γεγραμμένον ἐν τῷ νόμῳ ὑμῶν, Ἐγὼ
Jesus, not Is it having been written in the law of you, I

**35** εἶπα, θεοί ἐστε; εἰ ἐκείνους εἶπε θεούς, πρὸς οὓς ὁ λόγος τοῦ
said, gods you are. If those He called gods, with whom the word —

**36** Θεοῦ ἐγένετο (καὶ οὐ δύναται λυθῆναι ἡ γραφή), ὃν ὁ
of God was — and not can be broken the Scripture — whom the

πατὴρ ἡγίασε καὶ ἀπέστειλεν εἰς τὸν κόσμον, ὑμεῖς λέγετε
Father sanctified and sent into the world, you say,

**37** ὅτι Βλασφημεῖς, ὅτι εἶπον, Υἱὸς τοῦ Θεοῦ εἰμι; εἰ οὐ ποιῶ
— You blaspheme! Because I said, Son — of God I am? If not I do

**38** τὰ ἔργα τοῦ πατρός μου, μὴ πιστεύετέ μοι· εἰ δὲ ποιῶ, κἂν
the works of the Father of Me, not do believe Me. if But I do, even if

ἐμοὶ μὴ πιστεύητε, τοῖς ἔργοις πιστεύσατε· ἵνα γνῶτε καὶ
Me not you believe, the works believe, that you may know and

**39** πιστεύσητε ὅτι ἐν ἐμοὶ ὁ πατήρ, κἀγὼ ἐν αὐτῷ. ἐζήτουν
may believe that in Me the Father (is), and I in Him. They sought

οὖν πάλιν αὐτὸν πιάσαι· καὶ ἐξῆλθεν ἐκ τῆς χειρὸς αὐτῶν.
then again Him to seize. And He went out of the hand of them.

**40** Καὶ ἀπῆλθε πάλιν πέραν τοῦ Ἰορδάνου εἰς τὸν τόπον
And He went away again across the Jordan to the place

**41** ὅπου ἦν Ἰωάννης τὸ πρῶτον βαπτίζων· καὶ ἔμεινεν ἐκεῖ. καὶ
where was John at first baptizing, and remained there. And

πολλοὶ ἦλθον πρὸς αὐτόν, καὶ ἔλεγον ὅτι Ἰωάννης μὲν
many came to Him, and said, — John indeed

σημεῖον ἐποίησεν οὐδέν· πάντα δὲ ὅσα εἶπεν Ἰωάννης περὶ
sign did none, all things but whatever said John concerning

**42** τούτου, ἀληθῆ ἦν. καὶ ἐπίστευσαν πολλοὶ ἐκεῖ εἰς αὐτόν.
this One — true were. And believed many there in Him.

CHAPTER 11

**1** Ἦν δέ τις ἀσθενῶν Λάζαρος ἀπὸ Βηθανίας, ἐκ τῆς κώμης
was And a certain sick one, Lazarus from Bethany, of the village

**2** Μαρίας καὶ Μάρθας τῆς ἀδελφῆς αὐτῆς. ἦν δὲ Μαρία ἡ
of Mary and Martha the sister of her. was And Mary the (one)

ἀλείψασα τὸν Κύριον μύρῳ, καὶ ἐκμάξασα τοὺς πόδας αὐτοῦ
rubbing the Lord with ointment, and wiping off the feet of Him

**3** ταῖς θριξὶν αὐτῆς, ἧς ὁ ἀδελφὸς Λάζαρος ἠσθένει. ἀπέστειλαν
with the hairs of her, of whom the brother Lazarus was sick. sent

οὖν αἱ ἀδελφαὶ πρὸς αὐτὸν λέγουσαι, Κύριε, ἴδε ὃν φιλεῖς
Then the sisters to Him, saying, Lord, behold, whom You love

**4** ἀσθενεῖ. ἀκούσας δὲ ὁ Ἰησοῦς εἶπεν, Αὕτη ἡ ἀσθένεια οὐκ ἔστι
is sick. hearing And, — Jesus said, This — sickness not is

πρὸς θάνατον, ἀλλ᾽ ὑπὲρ τῆς δόξης τοῦ Θεοῦ, ἵνα δοξασθῇ ὁ
to death, but for the glory — of God, that be glorified the

**5** υἱὸς τοῦ Θεοῦ δι᾽ αὐτῆς. ἠγάπα δὲ ὁ Ἰησοῦς τὴν Μάρθαν καὶ
Son — of God by it. loved Now — Jesus — Martha and

**6** τὴν ἀδελφὴν αὐτῆς καὶ τὸν Λάζαρον. ὡς οὖν ἤκουσεν ὅτι
the sister of her and — Lazarus. As, then, He heard that

heard that he was sick,
then indeed He remained
in that place He was two
days. [7] Then after this
He said to the disciples,
Let us go into Judea again.
[8] The disciples said to
Him, Teacher, just now the
Jews were seeking to stone
You, and do You go there
again? [9] Jesus answered,
Are there not twelve hours
in the day? If anyone
walks in the day, he does
not stumble; he sees
because of the light of the
world; [10] but if anyone
walks in the night, he
stumbles, because the light
is not in him. [11] He said
these things; and after this
He said to them, Our
friend Lazarus has fallen
asleep; but I go that I may
awaken him. [12] His
disciples then said, Lord, if
he has fallen asleep he will
get well. [13] But Jesus
had spoke of his death, but
they thought that He
spoke of the rest of sleep.
[14] Therefore Jesus said
to them plainly, Lazarus
died. [15] And I rejoice on
your account in order that
you may believe, that I was
not there. But let us go to
him. [16] Then said
Thomas, called Didymus,
to the fellow-disciples, Let
us go also, that we may die
with Him. [17] Then
having come, Jesus found
him having been already
four days in the tomb.
[18] Now Bethany was
near Jerusalem, about
fifteen furlongs off.
[19] And many of the
Jews had come to those
around Martha and Mary,
that they might console
them concerning their
brother. [20] Therefore
when Martha heard that
Jesus was coming, she met
him; but Mary was sitting
in the house. [21] Then
Martha said to Jesus, Lord,
if You had been here, my
brother had not died;
[22] but even now I know
that whatever You may ask
of God, God will give You
[23] Jesus said to her,
Your brother will rise
again. [24] Martha said to
Him, I know that he will
rise again in the

**7** ἀσθενεῖ, τότε μὲν ἔμεινεν ἐν ᾧ ἦν τόπῳ δύο ἡμέρας. ἔπειτα
he is sick, then, indeed, He abode in He place two days. Then
which was
μετὰ τοῦτο λέγει τοῖς μαθηταῖς, Ἄγωμεν εἰς τὴν Ἰουδαίαν
after this He says to the disciples, Let us go to — Judea

**8** πάλιν. λέγουσιν αὐτῷ οἱ μαθηταί, Ῥαββί, νῦν ἐζήτουν σε
again. Said to Him the disciples, Rabbi, now were seeking You

**9** λιθάσαι οἱ Ἰουδαῖοι, καὶ πάλιν ὑπάγεις ἐκεῖ; ἀπεκρίθη ὁ
to stone the Jews, and again do You go there? answered —
Ἰησοῦς, Οὐχὶ δώδεκά εἰσιν ὧραι τῆς ἡμέρας; ἐάν τις περι-
Jesus, Not twelve are there hours in the day? If anyone walks
πατῇ ἐν τῇ ἡμέρᾳ, οὐ προσκόπτει, ὅτι τὸ φῶς τοῦ κόσμου
in the day, not he stumbles, because the light — world

**10** τούτου βλέπει. ἐὰν δέ τις περιπατῇ ἐν τῇ νυκτί, προσκόπτει,
this he sees. if But anyone walk in the night, he stumbles,

**11** ὅτι τὸ φῶς οὐκ ἔστιν ἐν αὐτῷ. ταῦτα εἶπε, καὶ μετὰ τοῦτο
because the light not is in him. These things He said, and after this
λέγει αὐτοῖς, Λάζαρος ὁ φίλος ἡμῶν κεκοίμηται· ἀλλὰ
He says to them, Lazarus the friend of us has fallen asleep; but

**12** πορεύομαι ἵνα ἐξυπνίσω αὐτόν. εἶπον οὖν οἱ μαθηταὶ αὐτοῦ,
I am going that I may awaken him. said Then the disciples of Him.

**13** Κύριε, εἰ κεκοίμηται, σωθήσεται. εἰρήκει δὲ ὁ Ἰησοῦς περὶ τοῦ
Lord, if he has slept, he will recover. had spoken And Jesus about the
θανάτου αὐτοῦ· ἐκεῖνοι δὲ ἔδοξαν ὅτι περὶ τῆς κοιμήσεως τοῦ
death of him, those but thought that about the sleep —

**14** ὕπνου λέγει. τότε οὖν εἶπεν αὐτοῖς ὁ Ἰησοῦς παρρησίᾳ,
of slumber He says. Then therefore told them — Jesus openly,

**15** Λάζαρος ἀπέθανε. καὶ χαίρω δι' ὑμᾶς. ἵνα πιστεύσητε, ὅτι
Lazarus has died. And I rejoice because of you, that you may believe, that

**16** οὐκ ἤμην ἐκεῖ· ἀλλ' ἄγωμεν πρὸς αὐτόν. εἶπεν οὖν Θωμᾶς, ὁ
not I was there. But let us go to him. said Then Thomas —
λεγόμενος Δίδυμος, τοῖς συμμαθηταῖς, Ἄγωμεν καὶ ἡμεῖς, ἵνα
being called Twin, to the fellow-disciples, Let us go, even we, that
ἀποθάνωμεν μετ' αὐτοῦ
we may die with Him.

**17** Ἐλθὼν οὖν ὁ Ἰησοῦς εὗρεν αὐτὸν τέσσαρας ἡμέρας ἤδη
coming Then — Jesus found him four days already

**18** ἔχοντα ἐν τῷ μνημείῳ. ἦν δὲ ἡ Βηθανία ἐγγὺς τῶν Ἱεροσολύ-
being held in the tomb. was And Bethany near — Jerusalem,

**19** μων, ὡς ἀπὸ σταδίων δεκαπέντε· καὶ πολλοὶ ἐκ τῶν
as from stadia fifteen. And many of the
Ἰουδαίων ἐληλύθεισαν πρὸς τὰς περὶ Μάρθαν καὶ Μαρίαν,
Jews had come to those around Martha and Mary,

**20** ἵνα παραμυθήσωνται αὐτὰς περὶ τοῦ ἀδελφοῦ αὐτῶν. ἡ
that they might console them concerning the brother of them.
οὖν Μάρθα, ὡς ἤκουσεν ὅτι ὁ Ἰησοῦς ἔρχεται, ὑπήντησεν
Therefore Martha, when she heard that Jesus is coming, met

**21** αὐτῷ· Μαρία δὲ ἐν τῷ οἴκῳ ἐκαθέζετο. εἶπεν οὖν ἡ Μάρθα
Him; Mary but in the house was sitting. said Then Martha
πρὸς τὸν Ἰησοῦν, Κύριε, εἰ ἦς ὧδε, ὁ ἀδελφός μου οὐκ ἂν
to — Jesus, Lord, if You were here, the brother of me not would

**22** ἐτεθνήκει. ἀλλὰ καὶ νῦν οἶδα ὅτι ὅσα ἂν αἰτήσῃ τὸν Θεόν,
be dead. But also now I know that whatever you may ask — God,

**23** δώσει σοι ὁ Θεός. λέγει αὐτῇ ὁ Ἰησοῦς, Ἀναστήσεται ὁ
will give You God. says to her — Jesus, will rise again The

**24** ἀδελφός σου. λέγει αὐτῷ Μάρθα, Οἶδα ὅτι ἀναστήσεται ἐν
brother of you. says to Him Martha, I know that he will rise again in

resurrection in the last day
[25] Jesus said to her, I
am the Resurrection and
the Life; he that believes
on Me, though he die he
shall live; [26] and
everyone who lives and
believes on Me shall never
ever die. Do you believe
this? [27] She said to Him,
Yea, Lord, I have believed
that You are the Christ,
the Son of God, who
comes into the world.
[28] And having said these
things she went away and
called he sister Mary
secretly, saying, The
Teacher is come and calls
you. [29] When she heard,
she rose up quickly and
came to Him. [30] Now
Jesus had not yet come
into the village, but was in
the place where Martha
met Him. [31] Therefore
the Jews who were with
her in the house and
consoling her, having seen
Mary that she quickly rose
up and went out, followed
her, saying, She is going to
the tomb that she may
weep there. [32] Then
when she came where Jesus
was, seeing Him, Mary fell
at His feet, saying to Him,
Lord, if You had been here
my brother had not died.
[33] Then Jesus when He
saw her weeping, and the
Jews who came with her
weeping, He groaned in
spirit and troubled
Himself, [34] and said,
Where have you laid him?
They said to Him, Lord,
come and see. [35] Jesus
wept. [36] Therefore the
Jews said, Behold, how He
loved him! [37] But some
of them said, Was not this
One who opened the eyes
of the blind one able to
have caused that this one
also should not have died?
[38] Then Jesus groaning
again in Himself came to
the tomb. Now it was a
cave, and a stone was lying
on it. [39] Jesus said, Take
away the stone. Martha,
the sister of him who had
died, said, Lord, he already
stinks, for it is four days.
[40] Jesus said to her, Did
I not say to you that if you

25 τῇ ἀναστάσει ἐν τῇ ἐσχάτῃ ἡμέρᾳ. εἶπεν αὐτῇ ὁ Ἰησοῦς,
the resurrection in the last Day. said to her — Jesus.
Ἐγώ εἰμι ἡ ἀνάστασις καὶ ἡ ζωή· ὁ πιστεύων εἰς ἐμέ, κἂν
I am the resurrection and the life; the (one) believing in, Me, though

26 ἀποθάνῃ, ζήσεται· καὶ πᾶς ὁ ζῶν καὶ πιστεύων εἰς ἐμέ, οὐ
he die, he shall live; and everyone living and believing in Me, in no

27 μὴ ἀποθάνῃ εἰς τὸν αἰῶνα. πιστεύεις τοῦτο ; λέγει αὐτῷ,
way shall die for ever. Do you believe this? She says to Him
Ναί, Κύριε· ἐγὼ πεπίστευκα, ὅτι σὺ εἶ ὁ Χριστός, ὁ υἱὸς τοῦ
Yes, Lord, I have believed that You are the Christ, the Son —

28 Θεοῦ, ὁ εἰς τὸν κόσμον ἐρχόμενος. καὶ ταῦτα εἰποῦσα,
of God, who into the world comes. And these things having said,
ἀπῆλθε, καὶ ἐφώνησε Μαρίαν τὴν ἀδελφὴν αὐτῆς λάθρα,
she went away, and called Mary the sister of her secretly,

29 εἰποῦσα, Ὁ διδάσκαλος πάρεστι καὶ φωνεῖ σε. ἐκείνη ὡς
saying, The Teacher is here and calls you. That one as

30 ἤκουσεν, ἐγείρεται ταχὺ καὶ ἔρχεται πρὸς αὐτόν. (οὔπω
she heard rises up quickly and comes to Him. not yet
δὲ ἐληλύθει ὁ Ἰησοῦς εἰς τὴν κώμην, ἀλλ᾽ ἦν ἐν τῷ τόπῳ
And had come — Jesus into the village, but was in the place

31 ὅπου ὑπήντησεν αὐτῷ ἡ Μάρθα.) οἱ οὖν Ἰουδαῖοι οἱ ὄντες
where met Him Martha. the Then Jews, those being
μετ᾽ αὐτῆς ἐν τῇ οἰκίᾳ καὶ παραμυθούμενοι αὐτήν, ἰδόντες
with her in the house and consoling her, seeing
τὴν Μαρίαν ὅτι ταχέως ἀνέστη καὶ ἐξῆλθεν, ἠκολούθησαν
— Mary, that quickly she rose up and went out, followed
αὐτῇ, λέγοντες ὅτι ὑπάγει εἰς τὸ μνημεῖον, ἵνα κλαύσῃ ἐκεῖ.
her, saying that she goes to the tomb. that she may weep there.

32 ἡ οὖν Μαρία, ὡς ἦλθεν ὅπου ἦν ὁ Ἰησοῦς, ἰδοῦσα αὐτόν,
Then Mary, when she came where was — Jesus. seeing Him.
ἔπεσεν εἰς τοὺς πόδας αὐτοῦ, λέγουσα αὐτῷ, Κύριε, εἰ ἦς
fell at the feet of Him, saying to Him, Lord, if You wer

33 ὧδε, οὐκ ἂν ἀπέθανέ μου ὁ ἀδελφός. Ἰησοῦς οὖν ὡς εἶδεν
here, not would have died of me the brother. Jesus Then, as He saw
αὐτὴν κλαίουσαν, καὶ τοὺς συνελθόντας αὐτῇ Ἰουδαίους
her weeping, and the coming down with her Jews
κλαίοντας, ἐνεβριμήσατο τῷ πνεύματι, καὶ ἐτάραξεν ἑαυτόν,
weeping, groaned in the spirit, and troubled Himself,

34 καὶ εἶπε, Ποῦ τεθείκατε αὐτόν ; λέγουσιν αὐτῷ, Κύριε, ἔρχου
and said, Where have you put him? They say to Him, Lord, come

35 καὶ ἴδε. ἐδάκρυσεν ὁ Ἰησοῦς. ἔλεγον οὖν οἱ Ἰουδαῖοι, Ἴδε
and see. shed tears — Jesus. said Therefore the Jews, See

36
37 πῶς ἐφίλει αὐτόν. τινὲς δὲ ἐξ αὐτῶν εἶπον, Οὐκ ἠδύνατο
how He loved him. some And of them said, Not was able
οὗτος, ὁ ἀνοίξας τοὺς ὀφθαλμοὺς τοῦ τυφλοῦ, ποιῆσαι ἵνα
this One, He opening the eyes of the blind, to have caused that

38 καὶ οὗτος μὴ ἀποθάνῃ ; Ἰησοῦς οὖν πάλιν ἐμβριμώμενος
also this one not should die. Jesus Then again groaning
ἐν ἑαυτῷ ἔρχεται εἰς τὸ μνημεῖον. ἦν δὲ σπήλαιον, καὶ λίθος
in Himself comes to the tomb. it was And a cave, and a stone

39 ἐπέκειτο ἐπ᾽ αὐτῷ. λέγει ὁ Ἰησοῦς, Ἄρατε τὸν λίθον. λέγει
was lying on it. says — Jesus, Lift the stone. says
αὐτῷ ἡ ἀδελφὴ τοῦ τεθνηκότος Μάρθα, Κύριε, ἤδη ὄζει·
to Him the sister of the (one) having died, Martha, Lord, already he smells,

40 τεταρταῖος γάρ ἐστι. λέγει αὐτῇ ὁ Ἰησοῦς, Οὐκ εἶπόν σοι,
(the) fourth (day) for it is. says to her — Jesus, Did not I say to you

would believe, you shall see the glory of God? [41] Therefore they took away the stone where the dead was laid. And Jesus lifted the eyes upward and said, Father, I thank You that You heard Me; [42] and I know that You always hear Me; but because of the crowd who stand around I said (it), that they might believe that You sent Me. [43] And having said these things, He cried with a loud voice, Lazarus, come forth! [44] And he who had been dead came forth, bound hands and feet with gravecloths, and his face bound about with a gravecloth. Jesus said to them, Untie him and let him go. [45]· Therefore many of the Jews who came to Mary and saw what Jesus did believed on Him; [46] but some of them went to the Pharisees and told them what Jesus did. [47] Therefore the chief priests and the Pharisees gathered a council, and said, What shall we do? For this man does many miracles. [48] If we let him alone this way, all will believe on him, and the Romans will come and will take away from us both the place and the nation. [49] But a certain one of them, Caiaphas, being high priest of that year, said to them, You know nothing, [50] nor consider that it is profitable for us that one man should die for the people, and not that the whole nation should be lost. [51] But he did not say this from himself, but being high priest of that year, prophesied that Jesus was about to die for the nation; [52] and not for the nation only, but that also the children of God who had been scattered abroad He might gather into one. [53] Therefore from that day they plotted together that they might kill Him.

41 ὅτι ἐὰν πιστεύσῃς, ὄψει τὴν δόξαν τοῦ Θεοῦ ; ἦραν οὖν τὸν
that if    you believe you will see the glory    — of God? they lifted Then the
λίθον, οὗ ἦν ὁ τεθνηκὼς κείμενος. ὁ δὲ Ἰησοῦς ἦρε τοὺς
stone, where was the dead one    laid.    And Jesus lifted the
ὀφθαλμοὺς ἄνω, καὶ εἶπε, Πάτερ, εὐχαριστῶ σοι ὅτι ἤκουσάς
eyes    upward, and said,    Father,  I thank  You that You heard

42 μου. ἐγὼ δὲ ᾔδειν ὅτι πάντοτέ μου ἀκούεις· ἀλλὰ διὰ τὸν
Me. I And knew that  always  Me  You hear. But because of the
ὄχλον τὸν περιεστῶτα εἶπον, ἵνα πιστεύσωσιν ὅτι σύ με
crowd —  standing around I said, that they might believe that You Me

43 ἀπέστειλας. καὶ ταῦτα εἰπών, φωνῇ μεγάλῃ ἐκραύγασε,
did send.    And these things saying,  with a voice great  He cried out,

44 Λάζαρε, δεῦρο ἔξω. καὶ ἐξῆλθεν ὁ τεθνηκώς, δεδεμένος τοὺς
Lazarus, Here! Outside! And came out the (one) having died, being bound the
πόδας καὶ τὰς χεῖρας κειρίαις, καὶ ἡ ὄψις αὐτοῦ σουδαρίῳ
feet and the  hands with sheets, and the face of him with a cloth
περιεδέδετο. λέγει αὐτοῖς ὁ Ἰησοῦς, Λύσατε αὐτόν, καὶ ἄφετε
being bound. says to them — Jesus,  Loosen him,  and allow (him)
ὑπάγειν.
to depart.

45 Πολλοὶ οὖν ἐκ τῶν Ἰουδαίων, οἱ ἐλθόντες πρὸς τὴν Μαρίαν
Many therefore of the  Jews, those coming to — Mary
καὶ θεασάμενοι ἃ ἐποίησεν ὁ Ἰησοῦς, ἐπίστευσαν εἰς αὐτόν.
and having beheld what did  Jesus,  believed in Him.

46 τινὲς δὲ ἐξ αὐτῶν ἀπῆλθον πρὸς τοὺς Φαρισαίους, καὶ εἶπον
some But of them went away to  the  Pharisees  and told
αὐτοῖς ἃ ἐποίησεν ὁ Ἰησοῦς.
them what had done — Jesus.

47 Συνήγαγον οὖν οἱ ἀρχιερεῖς καὶ οἱ Φαρισαῖοι συνέδριον,
assembled  Then the chief priests and the  Pharisees a sanhedrin,
καὶ ἔλεγον, Τί ποιοῦμεν ; ὅτι οὗτος ὁ ἄνθρωπος πολλὰ
and said,  What are we doing, because this  man  many

48 σημεῖα ποιεῖ. ἐὰν ἀφῶμεν αὐτὸν οὕτω, πάντες πιστεύσουσιν
signs  does? If we leave  him  thus,  all  will believe
εἰς αὐτόν· καὶ ἐλεύσονται οἱ Ῥωμαῖοι καὶ ἀροῦσιν ἡμῶν καὶ
in  him, and will come the Romans  and will take of us both

49 τὸν τόπον καὶ τὸ ἔθνος. εἰς δέ τις ἐξ αὐτῶν Καϊάφας, ἀρχιερεὺς
the place and the nation. one But man of them, Caiaphas, high priest
ὢν τοῦ ἐνιαυτοῦ ἐκείνου, εἶπεν αὐτοῖς, Ὑμεῖς οὐκ οἴδατε
being of year  that,  said to them, You do not know

50 οὐδέν, οὐδὲ διαλογίζεσθε ὅτι συμφέρει ἡμῖν ἵνα εἷς ἄνθρωπος
nothing, nor  consider  that it is profitable for us that one man
ἀποθάνῃ ὑπὲρ τοῦ λαοῦ, καὶ μὴ ὅλον τὸ ἔθνος ἀπόληται.
die  for the people, and not all the nation to perish.

51 τοῦτο δὲ ἀφ' ἑαυτοῦ οὐκ εἶπεν, ἀλλὰ ἀρχιερεὺς ὢν τοῦ ἐνιαυ-
this But from himself not he said, but high priest being of year
τοῦ ἐκείνου, προεφήτευσεν ὅτι ἔμελλεν ὁ Ἰησοῦς ἀποθνή-
—  that, he prophesied that was about — Jesus to die

52 σκειν ὑπὲρ τοῦ ἔθνους, καὶ οὐχ ὑπὲρ τοῦ ἔθνους μόνον, ἀλλ
on behalf of the nation, and not on behalf of the nation only,  but
ἵνα καὶ τὰ τέκνα τοῦ Θεοῦ τὰ διεσκορπισμένα συναγάγῃ
that also the children — of God — having been scattered He might gather

53 εἰς ἕν. ἀπ' ἐκείνης οὖν τῆς ἡμέρας συνεβουλεύσαντο ἵνα
into one. from that Therefore — day, they took counsel that
ἀποκτείνωσιν αὐτόν.
they might kill  Him.

[54] Therefore Jesus no longer publicly walked among the Jews, but went away from there into the country near the desert to a city called Ephraim, and He stayed there with His disciples.

[55] Now the Passover of the Jews was near, and many went up to Jerusalem out of the country before the Passover, that they might purify themselves. [56] Then they were seeking Jesus, and were saying among one another in standing in the Temple, What does it seem to you, that He will never come to the feast? [57] Now both the chief priests and the Pharisees had given a command, that if anyone should know where He was, he should reveal (it), that they might seize Him.

CHAPTER 12

[1] Therefore six days before the Passover, Jesus came to Bethany, where Lazarus who had died was, whom He had raised from among (the) dead. [2] Then they made Him a supper there, and Martha served, but Lazarus was one of those reclining with Him. [3] Then Mary, having taken a pound of ointment of pure spikenard of great price, anointed the feet of Jesus, and wiped His feet with her hair; and the house was filled with the odor of the ointment. [4] Therefore one of His disciples, Judas, Simon's (son) Iscariot, who was about to deliver Him up, [5] Why was this ointment not sold for three hundred denarii, and given to (the) poor? [6] But he said this not that he was caring for the poor, but because he was a thief, and had the bag, and carried what was put into (it). [7] Then Jesus said, Let her alone; for she has kept it for the day of My burial. [8] For you always have the poor with you, but you do not have Me always.

[9] Then a great crowd of the Jews learned that He was there.

**54** Ἰησοῦς οὖν οὐκέτι παρρησίᾳ περιεπάτει ἐν τοῖς Ἰουδαίοις,
Jesus Therefore no longer publicly walked among the Jews

ἀλλὰ ἀπῆλθεν ἐκεῖθεν εἰς τὴν χώραν ἐγγὺς τῆς ἐρήμου, εἰς
but went away from there into the country near the desert, to

Ἐφραῒμ λεγομένην πόλιν, κἀκεῖ διέτριβε μετὰ τῶν μαθητῶν
Ephraim being called a city, and there stayed with the disciples

**55** αὐτοῦ. ἦν δὲ ἐγγὺς τὸ πάσχα τῶν Ἰουδαίων· καὶ ἀνέβησαν
of Him. was And near the Passover of the Jews, and went up

πολλοὶ εἰς Ἱεροσόλυμα ἐκ τῆς χώρας πρὸ τοῦ πάσχα, ἵνα
many to Jerusalem out of the country before the Passover, that

**56** ἁγνίσωσιν ἑαυτούς. ἐζήτουν οὖν τὸν Ἰησοῦν, καὶ ἔλεγον μετ᾽
they might purify themselves. they sought Then Jesus, and said with

ἀλλήλων ἐν τῷ ἱερῷ ἑστηκότες, Τί δοκεῖ ὑμῖν; ὅτι οὐ μὴ
one another in the Temple standing, What seems it to you? That not at all

**57** ἔλθῃ εἰς τὴν ἑορτήν; δεδώκεισαν δὲ καὶ οἱ ἀρχιερεῖς καὶ οἱ
He comes to the feast? had given And also the chief priests and the

Φαρισαῖοι ἐντολήν, ἵνα ἐάν τις γνῷ ποῦ ἐστι, μηνύσῃ, ὅπως
Pharisees commands that if anyone knew where He is, he should inform so

πιάσωσιν αὐτόν.
they might seize Him.

## CHAPTER 12

**1** Ὁ οὖν Ἰησοῦς πρὸ ἓξ ἡμερῶν τοῦ πάσχα ἦλθεν εἰς
Therefore Jesus before six days the Passover came to

Βηθανίαν, ὅπου ἦν Λάζαρος ὁ τεθνηκώς, ὃν ἤγειρεν ἐκ νε-
Bethany, where was Lazarus, who had died, whom He raised out of

**2** κρῶν. ἐποίησαν οὖν αὐτῷ δεῖπνον ἐκεῖ, καὶ ἡ Μάρθα διηκόνει·
(the) dead. they made Then for Him a supper there, and Martha served,

**3** ὁ δὲ Λάζαρος εἷς ἦν τῶν συνανακειμένων αὐτῷ. ἡ οὖν Μαρία
but Lazarus one was of those reclining with Him. Then Mary

λαβοῦσα λίτραν μύρου νάρδου πιστικῆς πολυτίμου,
taking a pound of ointment of spikenard pure costly

ἤλειψε τοὺς πόδας τοῦ Ἰησοῦ, καὶ ἐξέμαξε ταῖς θριξὶν αὐτῆς
rubbed the feet — of Jesus, and wiped off with the hairs of her

τοὺς πόδας αὐτοῦ· ἡ δὲ οἰκία ἐπληρώθη ἐκ τῆς ὀσμῆς τοῦ
the feet of Him. the And house was filled of the odor of the

**4** μύρου. λέγει οὖν εἷς ἐκ τῶν μαθητῶν αὐτοῦ, Ἰούδας Σίμωνος
ointment. says Then one of the disciples of Him, Judas of Simon

**5** Ἰσκαριώτης, ὁ μέλλων αὐτὸν παραδιδόναι, Διατί τοῦτο τὸ
Iscariot, the (one) being about Him to betray, Why this —

μύρον οὐκ ἐπράθη τριακοσίων δηναρίων, καὶ ἐδόθη πτω-
ointment not was sold (for) three hundred denarii, and given to (the)

**6** χοῖς; εἶπε δὲ τοῦτο, οὐχ ὅτι περὶ τῶν πτωχῶν ἔμελεν αὐτῷ,
poor? he said But this, not because about the poor was a care to him,

ἀλλὰ ὅτι κλέπτης ἦν, καὶ τὸ γλωσσόκομον εἶχε, καὶ τὰ
but that a thief he was, and the moneybag held and that

**7** βαλλόμενα ἐβάσταζεν. εἶπεν οὖν ὁ Ἰησοῦς, Ἄφες αὐτήν·
being put (in) carried away. said Therefore Jesus, Allow - her;

**8** εἰς τὴν ἡμέραν τοῦ ἐνταφιασμοῦ μου τετήρηκεν αὐτό. τοὺς
for the day of the burial of Me she has kept it. the

πτωχοὺς γὰρ πάντοτε ἔχετε μεθ᾽ ἑαυτῶν, ἐμὲ δὲ οὐ πάντοτε
poor For always you have with yourselves, Me but not always

ἔχετε.
you have.

**9** Ἔγνω οὖν ὄχλος πολὺς ἐκ τῶν Ἰουδαίων ὅτι ἐκεῖ ἐστι·
knew Then crowd the much of the Jews that there He is,

And they came, not because of Jesus only, but that they might see Lazarus also, whom He raised from among (the) dead. [10] But the chief priests plotted together so that they might also put Lazarus to death, [11] because many of the Jews were going away, and were believing on Jesus.

[12] On the morrow a great crowd who came to the feast, having heard that Jesus was coming into Jerusalem, [13] took palm branches and went out to meet Him, and were crying, Hosanna, blessed (is) He who comes in (the) name of (the) Lord, the King of Israel! [14] And Jesus having found a young ass sat upon it, as it is written, [15] "Do not fear, daughter of Zion. Behold! Your king comes sitting on the colt of an ass." [16] Now His disciples did not know these things at first, but when Jesus was glorified then they remembered that these things were written of Him, and they did these things to Him. [17] Then the crowd that was with His bore witness, when He called Lazarus out of the tomb, and raised him from among (the) dead. [18] Because of this also the crowd met Him, because it heard of His having done this miracle. [19] Therefore the Pharisees said among themselves, Do you see that you gain nothing? Behold, the world is gone after Him.

[20] And there were certain Greeks among those, coming up that they might worship in the feast; [21] these therefore came to Philip, who was from Bethsaida of Galilee, and they asked him, saying, Sir, we desire to see Jesus. [22] Philip came and told Andrew, and again Andrew and Philip told Jesus. [23] But Jesus answered them saying, The hour has come that the Son of man should be glorified. [24] Indeed, I tell you truly, unless the grain of wheat falling into the

καὶ ἦλθον οὐ διὰ τὸν Ἰησοῦν μόνον, ἀλλ᾽ ἵνα καὶ τὸν
and they came not because of    Jesus     alone,   but that also —

10 Λάζαρον ἴδωσιν, ὃν ἤγειρεν ἐκ νεκρῶν. ἐβουλεύσαντο δὲ οἱ
Lazarus they might see, whom He raised from dead.   took counsel But th

11 ἀρχιερεῖς ἵνα καὶ τὸν Λάζαρον ἀποκτείνωσιν· ὅτι πολλοὶ δι᾽
chief priests that also —  Lazarus they might kill, because  many throu

αὐτὸν ὑπῆγον των Ἰουδαίων, καὶ ἐπίστευον εἰς τὸν Ἰησοῦν.
him  departed of the   Jews,     and believed in  —  Jesus.

12 Τῇ ἐπαύριον ὄχλος πολὺς ὁ ἐλθὼν εἰς τὴν ἑορτήν, ἀκού-
On the morrow a crowd   much  coming to the  feast,

13 σαντες ὅτι ἔρχεται ὁ Ἰησοῦς εἰς Ἱεροσόλυμα, ἔλαβον τὰ
hearing that is coming — Jesus    to   Jerusalem,    took  the

βαΐα τῶν φοινίκων, καὶ ἐξῆλθον εἰς ὑπάντησιν αὐτῷ, καὶ
branches of the palm-trees and  went out to a meeting   with Him, and

ἔκραζον, Ὡσαννά· εὐλογημένος ὁ ἐρχόμενος ἐν ὀνόματι
cried out, Hosanna!  Blessed (is)  He   coming     in (the) nam

14 Κυρίου, ὁ βασιλεὺς τοῦ Ἰσραήλ. εὑρὼν δὲ ὁ Ἰησοῦς ὀνάριον,
of (the) Lord, the king  —  of Israel.  finding And  Jesus an ass colt,

15 ἐκάθισεν ἐπ᾽ αὐτό, καθώς ἐστι γεγραμμένον, Μὴ φοβοῦ,
He sat   upon  it,  even as  it is having been written, Do not fear

θύγατερ Σιών· ἰδού, ὁ βασιλεύς σου ἔρχεται, καθήμενος ἐπὶ
daughter of Zion. Behold, the King of you  comes,   sitting   on

16 πῶλον ὄνου. ταῦτα δὲ οὐκ ἔγνωσαν οἱ μαθηταὶ αὐτοῦ τὸ
the foal of an ass, these things But not knew  the  disciples of Him at the

πρῶτον· ἀλλ᾽ ὅτε ἐδοξάσθη ὁ Ἰησοῦς, τότε ἐμνήσθησαν ὅτι
first,   but when was glorified  Jesus,  then they remembered that

ταῦτα ἦν ἐπ᾽ αὐτῷ γεγραμμένα, καὶ ταῦτα ἐποίησαν αὐτῷ.
these things were on Him having been written, and these they did  to Him.

17 ἐμαρτύρει οὖν ὁ ὄχλος ὁ ὢν μετ᾽ αὐτοῦ ὅτε τὸν Λάζαρον
witnessed Therefore the crowd which was with Him  when — Lazarus

18 ἐφώνησεν ἐκ τοῦ μνημείου, καὶ ἤγειρεν αὐτὸν ἐκ νεκρῶν. διὰ
He called out of the  tomb,   and raised  him out of (the) dead. Ther

τοῦτο καὶ ὑπήντησεν αὐτῷ ὁ ὄχλος, ὅτι ἤκουσε τοῦτο
fore  also   met    with Him the crowd, because it heard  this

19 αὐτὸν πεποιηκέναι τὸ σημεῖον. οἱ οὖν Φαρισαῖοι εἶπον πρὸς
(which) He had done   sign.   the Then Pharisees  said to

ἑαυτούς, Θεωρεῖτε ὅτι οὐκ ὠφελεῖτε οὐδέν· ἴδε ὁ κόσμος
themselves, Observe, that not you  profit nothing. Behold, the world

ὀπίσω αὐτοῦ ἀπῆλθεν.
after  Him   has gone

20 Ἦσαν δέ τινες Ἕλληνες ἐκ τῶν ἀναβαινόντων ἵνα προσ-
were And some  Greeks   of those   going up   that they

21 κυνήσωσιν ἐν τῇ ἑορτῇ· οὗτοι οὖν προσῆλθον Φιλίππω
might worship at the feast.  these Then came toward  Philip

τῷ ἀπὸ Βηθσαϊδὰ τῆς Γαλιλαίας, καὶ ἠρώτων αὐτὸν
the (one) from Bethsaida  — of Galilee,   and asked  him

22 λέγοντες, Κύριε, θέλομεν τὸν Ἰησοῦν ἰδεῖν. ἔρχεται Φίλιππος
saying,   Sir, we desire  Jesus to see. Comes  Philip

καὶ λέγει τῷ Ἀνδρέᾳ καὶ πάλιν Ἀνδρέας καὶ Φίλιππος
and tells  —  Andrew,  and again  Andrew  and  Philip

23 λέγουσι τῷ Ἰησοῦ. ὁ δὲ Ἰησοῦς ἀπεκρίνατο αὐτοῖς λέγων,
tell   —  Jesus.  And Jesus   answers   them,  saying,

24 Ἐλήλυθεν ἡ ὥρα ἵνα δοξασθῇ ὁ υἱὸς τοῦ ἀνθρώπου. ἀμὴν
has come The hour that should be the Son  — of man.   Truly,
                         glorified

ἀμὴν λέγω ὑμῖν, ἐὰν μη ὁ κόκκος τοῦ σίτου πεσὼν εἰς τὴν
truly, I say to you, Unless the grain — of wheat falling into the

ground should die, it abides alone; but if it should die, it bears much fruit. [25] He that loves his soul shall lose it, and he that hates his soul in this world shall keep it to life everlasting. [26] If anyone serves Me, let him follow Me; and where I am there My servant shall be also. And if anyone serves Me, the Father will honor him.

[27] Now My soul has been troubled, and what shall I say? Father, save Me from this hour. But on account of this I came to this hour. [28] Father, glorify Your name. Therefore a voice came out of Heaven, I both glorified and will glorify (it) again. [29] Then the crowd which stood and heard said, There has been thunder; others said, An angel has spoken to Him. [30] Jesus answered and said, This voice has come not because of Me, but because of you. [31] Now judgment is of this world; now the prince of this world shall be cast out; [32] and I, if I be lifted up from the earth, will draw all to Myself. [33] But He said this, signifying by what death He was about to die. [34] The crowd answered Him, We heard out of the Law that the Christ lives forever. And how do You say, that the Son of man must be lifted up? Who is this Son of man? [35] Therefore Jesus said to them, Yet a little while the Light is with you. Walk while you have the Light, that darkness may not overtake you. And he who walks in the darkness does not know where he goes. [36] While you have the Light, believe in the Light, that you may become sons of light. Jesus spoke these things, and going away was hidden from them. [37] But (though) He had done so many miracles before them, they did not believe on Him, [38] that the word of Isaiah the prophet might be fulfilled, which he said, ''Lord, who believed our report? And

**25** γῆν ἀποθάνῃ, αὐτὸς μόνος μένει· ἐὰν δὲ ἀποθάνῃ, πολὺν
earth dies,    it   alone remains; if but   it die    much
καρπὸν φέρει. ὁ φιλῶν τὴν ψυχὴν αὐτοῦ ἀπολέσει αὐτήν·
fruit it bears. He loving the soul    of him   loses     it:

καὶ ὁ μισῶν τὴν ψυχὴν αὐτοῦ ἐν τῷ κόσμῳ τούτῳ εἰς ζωὴν
and he hating the    of him  in   world   this, to life

**26** αἰώνιον φυλάξει αὐτήν. ἐὰν ἐμοὶ διακονῇ τις, ἐμοὶ ἀκολου-
eternal  will keep   it.    If Me serves anyone, Me  let him
θείτω· καὶ ὅπου εἰμὶ ἐγώ, ἐκεῖ καὶ ὁ διάκονος ὁ ἐμὸς ἔσται·
follow; and where am I,   there also   servant   My will be.

**27** καὶ ἐάν τις ἐμοὶ διακονῇ, τιμήσει αὐτὸν ὁ πατήρ. νῦν ἡ ψυχή
And if anyone Me serves, will honor him  the Father. Now the soul
μου τετάρακται· καὶ τί εἴπω; πάτερ, σῶσόν με ἐκ τῆς ὥρας
of Me is agitated, and what may I say? Father, save   Me out of   hour

**28** ταύτης. ἀλλὰ διὰ τοῦτο ἦλθον εἰς τὴν ὥραν ταύτην. πάτερ,
this.  But on account of this I came to   hour   this.    Father,
δόξασόν σου τὸ ὄνομα. ἦλθεν οὖν φωνὴ ἐκ τοῦ οὐρανοῦ,
glorify of You the name.  came Then a voice out of    Heaven:

**29** Καὶ ἐδόξασα, καὶ πάλιν δοξάσω. ὁ οὖν ὄχλος ὁ ἑστὼς καὶ
Both I glorified   and again I will glorify. the Then crowd  standing and
ἀκούσας ἔλεγε βροντὴν γεγονέναι· ἄλλοι ἔλεγον, Ἄγγελος
hearing   said   thunder to have occurred. Others said,   An angel

**30** αὐτῷ λελάληκεν. ἀπεκρίθη ὁ Ἰησοῦς καὶ εἶπεν, Οὐ δι' ἐμὲ
to Him  has spoken, answered — Jesus and said, Not via Me

**31** αὕτη ἡ φωνὴ γέγονεν, ἀλλὰ δι' ὑμᾶς. νῦν κρίσις ἐστὶ τοῦ
this    voice occurred, but because of you. Now judgment is   —
κόσμου τούτου· νῦν ὁ ἄρχων τοῦ κόσμου τούτου ἐκβληθή-
of world  this;  now the ruler   of world   this shall be

**32** σεται ἔξω. κἀγὼ ἐὰν ὑψωθῶ ἐκ τῆς γῆς, πάντας ἑλκύσω
thrown out. And I  if I be lifted up from the earth,  all   I will draw

**33** πρὸς ἐμαυτόν. τοῦτο δὲ ἔλεγε, σημαίνων ποίῳ θανάτῳ
to   Myself.   this  And He said, signifying by what kind (of) death

**34** ἤμελλεν ἀποθνήσκειν. ἀπεκρίθη αὐτῷ ὁ ὄχλος, Ἡμεῖς ἠκού-
He was about to die.     answered  Him The crowd. We   heard
σαμεν ἐκ τοῦ νόμου ὅτι ὁ Χριστὸς μένει εἰς τὸν αἰῶνα· καὶ πῶς
   out of the law that the Christ abides to the  age;  and how
σὺ λέγεις ὅτι Δεῖ ὑψωθῆναι τὸν υἱὸν τοῦ ἀνθρώπου; τίς
do you say  that it behoves to be lifted up the Son — of man?  Who

**35** ἐστιν οὗτος ὁ υἱὸς τοῦ ἀνθρώπου; εἶπεν οὖν αὐτοῖς ὁ Ἰησοῦς,
is  this    Son  —  of man?  said Then to them   Jesus,
Ἔτι μικρὸν χρόνον τὸ φῶς μεθ' ὑμῶν ἐστι. περιπατεῖτε ἕως
Yet  a little   time  the light with you   is.    Walk    while
τὸ φῶς ἔχετε, ἵνα μὴ σκοτία ὑμᾶς καταλάβῃ· καὶ ὁ περιπα-
the light you have, lest darkness  you  overtake;  and the (one) walk-

**36** τῶν ἐν τῇ σκοτίᾳ οὐκ οἶδε ποῦ ὑπάγει. ἕως τὸ φῶς ἔχετε,
ing in the darkness  not knows where he is going. While the light you have,
πιστεύετε εἰς τὸ φῶς, ἵνα υἱοὶ φωτὸς γένησθε.
believe    in the light, that sons of light you may become.

Ταῦτα ἐλάλησεν ὁ Ἰησοῦς, καὶ ἀπελθὼν ἐκρύβη ἀπ'
These things spoke  —  Jesus, and   going away was hidden from

**37** αὐτῶν. τοσαῦτα δὲ αὐτοῦ σημεῖα πεποιηκότος ἔμπροσθεν
them.  so many But He   signs   having done   before

**38** αὐτῶν, οὐκ ἐπίστευον εἰς αὐτόν· ἵνα ὁ λόγος Ἡσαΐου τοῦ
them,  not they believed in  Him  that the word of Isaiah the
προφήτου πληρωθῇ, ὃν εἶπε, Κύριε, τίς ἐπίστευσε τῇ ἀκοῇ
prophet  might be fulfilled which he  Lord, who has believed the report
said,

the arm of (the) Lord, to whom was it revealed? [39] Because of this they could not believe, because Isaiah again said, [40] "He has blinded their eyes and has hardened their heart so that they should not see with their eyes and understand with their heart and be converted, and I should heal them." [41] Isaiah said these things when he saw His glory and spoke about Him. [42] Still, even among the rulers, many did believe on Him. But because of the Pharisees they did not confess, that they might not be put out of the synagogue; [43] for they loved the glory of men more than the glory of God. [44] But Jesus cried and said, He that believes on Me does not believe on Me, but on Him who sent Me; [45] and he who that sees Me sees Him who sent Me. [46] I have come a Light into the world, that everyone that believes on Me may not remain in the darkness. [47] And if anyone hear My words and not believe, I do not judge him, for I did not come that I might judge the world, but that I might save the world. [48] He that rejects Me and does not receive My words has one who judges him: the word which I spoke, that shall judge him in the last day; [49] for I did not speak from Myself, but the Father who sent Me Himself gave Me commandment what I should say and what I should speak; [50] and I know that His commandment is life everlasting. Therefore what I speak, I speak just as the Father has spoken to Me.

CHAPTER 13
[1] Now before the Feast of the Passover, Jesus knowing that His hour had come that He should depart out of this world to the Father, having loved His own which (were) in the world, He loved them to (the) end. [2] And supper taking place, the

**39** ἡμῶν ; καὶ ὁ βραχίων Κυρίου τίνι ἀπεκαλύφθη ; διὰ τοῦτο
of us? And the arm of (the) Lord, to whom was it revealed? Therefore

**40** οὐκ ἠδύναντο πιστεύειν, ὅτι πάλιν εἶπεν Ἠσαΐας, Τετύ-
not they could believe, because again said Isaiah, He has

φλωκεν αὐτῶν τοὺς ὀφθαλμούς, καὶ πεπώρωκεν αὐτῶν τὴν
blinded of them the eyes, and hardened of them the

**41** καρδίαν· ἵνα μὴ ἴδωσι τοῖς ὀφθαλμοῖς, καὶ νοήσωσι τῇ
heart; lest they might see with the eyes, and understand with the

καρδίᾳ, καὶ ἐπιστραφῶσι, καὶ ἰάσωμαι αὐτούς. ταῦτα εἶπεν
heart, and be converted, and I should heal them. These things said

Ἠσαΐας, ὅτε εἶδε τὴν δόξαν αὐτοῦ, καὶ ἐλάλησε περὶ αὐτοῦ.
Isaiah when he saw the glory of Him, and spoke about Him.

**42** ὅμως μέντοι καὶ ἐκ τῶν ἀρχόντων πολλοὶ ἐπίστευσαν εἰς
Still, however, even of the rulers many believed in

αὐτόν· ἀλλὰ διὰ τοὺς Φαρισαίους οὐχ ὡμολόγουν, ἵνα μὴ
Him, but because of the Pharisees not were confessing lest

**43** ἀποσυνάγωγοι γένωνται. ἠγάπησαν γὰρ τὴν δόξαν τῶν
put out of the synagogue they be. they loved For the glory —

ἀνθρώπων μᾶλλον ἤπερ τὴν δόξαν τοῦ Θεοῦ.
of men more than the glory — of God.

**44** Ἰησοῦς δὲ ἔκραξε καὶ εἶπεν, Ὁ πιστεύων εἰς ἐμέ, οὐ
Jesus But cried out and said, The (one) believing in Me, not

**45** πιστεύει εἰς ἐμέ, ἀλλ᾽ εἰς τὸν πέμψαντά με· καὶ ὁ θεωρῶν
believes in Me, but in the (one) sending Me; and the (One seeing

**46** ἐμέ, θεωρεῖ τὸν πέμψαντά με. ἐγὼ φῶς εἰς τὸν κόσμον
Me sees the (One) sending Me. I a light to the world

ἐλήλυθα, ἵνα πᾶς ὁ πιστεύων εἰς ἐμέ, ἐν τῇ σκοτίᾳ μὴ μείνῃ.
have come, that everyone believing in Me in the darkness not may abide.

**47** καὶ ἐάν τις μου ἀκούσῃ τῶν ῥημάτων καὶ μὴ πιστεύσῃ,
And if anyone of Me hears the words, and not believes,

ἐγὼ οὐ κρίνω αὐτόν· οὐ γὰρ ἦλθον ἵνα κρίνω τὸν κόσμον,
I do not judge him; not for I came that I might judge the world,

**48** ἀλλ᾽ ἵνα σώσω τὸν κόσμον. ὁ ἀθετῶν ἐμὲ καὶ μὴ λαμβάνων
but that I might save the world. The (one) rejecting Me and not receiving

τὰ ῥήματά μου, ἔχει τὸν κρίνοντα αὐτόν· ὁ λόγος ὃν
the words of Me has that judging him: the word which

**49** ἐλάλησα, ἐκεῖνος κρινεῖ αὐτὸν ἐν τῇ ἐσχάτῃ ἡμέρᾳ. ὅτι ἐγὼ
I spoke, that will judge him in the last Day. Because I

ἐξ ἐμαυτοῦ οὐκ ἐλάλησα· ἀλλ᾽ ὁ πέμψας με πατήρ, αὐτός μοι
from Myself not spoke, but He sending Me, (the) Father. He Me

**50** ἐντολὴν ἔδωκε, τί εἴπω καὶ τί λαλήσω. καὶ οἶδα ὅτι ἡ
command has given, what I may say and what I may speak. And I know that the

ἐντολὴ αὐτοῦ ζωὴ αἰώνιός ἐστιν· ἃ οὖν λαλῶ ἐγώ, καθὼς
command of Him life eternal is. What things then speak I, as

εἴρηκέ μοι ὁ πατήρ, οὕτω λαλῶ.
has said to Me the Father, so I speak.

## CHAPTER 13

**1** Πρὸ δὲ τῆς ἑορτῆς τοῦ πάσχα, εἰδὼς ὁ Ἰησοῦς ὅτι
before And the feast of the Passover, knowing Jesus that

ἐλήλυθεν αὐτοῦ ἡ ὥρα ἵνα μεταβῇ ἐκ τοῦ κόσμου τούτου
had come of Him the hour that He should move from world this,

πρὸς τὸν πατέρα, ἀγαπήσας τοὺς ἰδίους τοὺς ἐν τῷ κόσμῳ,
to the Father, loving the own — in the world,

**2** εἰς τέλος ἠγάπησεν αὐτούς. καὶ δείπνου γενομένου, τοῦ
to (the) end He loved them. And supper having occurred the

devil already having put into the heart of Judas, Simon's (son) Iscariot, that he should deliver Him up, [3] Jesus knowing that the Father had given Him all things into His hands, and that He came out from God, and goes to God, [4] He rose from the supper and laid aside (His) garments, and having taken a towel He girded Himself. [5] Afterwards He poured water into the washbowl, and began to wash the feet of the disciples, and to wipe with the towel with which He was girded. [6] He then came to Simon Peter, and he said to Him, Lord, do You wash my feet? [7] Jesus answered and said to him, What I do you do not know now, but you shall know hereafter. [8] Peter said to Him, You may never ever wash my feet. Jesus answered him, Unless I wash you, you have no part with Me. [9] Simon Peter said to Him, Lord, not my feet only, but also the hands and the head. [10] Jesus said to him, He that has been washed has no need (other) than to wash the feet, but is wholly clean; and you are clean, but not all. [11] For He knew him who was delivering Him up. Because of this He said, You are not all clean. [12] Then when He had washed their feet and had taken His garments, having again reclined, He said to them, Do you know what I have done to you? [13] You call Me the Teacher and the Lord, and you say well, for I am. [14] If then I washed your feet, the Lord and the Teacher, you also ought to wash the feet of one another. [15] For I gave you an example, that as I did to you, you should also do. [16] Indeed, I tell you truly, a slave is not greater than his lord, nor a messenger greater than he who sends him. [17] If you know these things, blessed are you if you do hem. [18] I do not speak

διαβόλου ἤδη βεβληκότος εἰς τὴν καρδίαν Ἰούδα Σίμωνος
devil    already having put  into·  the  heart  of Judas of Simon

**3** Ἰσκαριώτου ἵνα αὐτὸν παραδῷ, εἰδὼς ὁ Ἰησοῦς ὅτι πάντα
Iscariot,    that   Him he should betray, knowing  Jesus  that all things

δέδωκεν αὐτῷ ὁ πατὴρ εἰς τὰς χεῖρας, καὶ ὅτι ἀπὸ Θεοῦ
has given Him the Father into the  hands,  and that from God

**4** ἐξῆλθε καὶ πρὸς τὸν Θεὸν ὑπάγει, ἐγείρεται ἐκ τοῦ δείπνου,
He came, and  to    —    God departs,  He rises  from the supper

καὶ τίθησι τὰ ἱμάτια, καὶ λαβὼν λέντιον διέζωσεν ἑαυτόν.
and lays aside the garments, and taking a towel He girded ▪ Himself.

**5** εἶτα βάλλει ὕδωρ εἰς τὸν νιπτῆρα, καὶ ἤρξατο νίπτειν τοὺς
Then He puts water into the  basin,  and began  to wash  the

πόδας τῶν μαθητῶν, καὶ ἐκμάσσειν τῷ λεντίῳ ᾧ ἦν διεζω-
feet of the disciples,  and to wipe off with the towel with which He

**6** σμένος. ἔρχεται οὖν πρὸς Σίμωνα Πέτρον· καὶ λέγει αὐτῷ
was girded. He comes, then, to   Simon   Peter  and said to Him

**7** ἐκεῖνος, Κύριε, σύ μου νίπτεις τοὺς πόδας; ἀπεκρίθη Ἰησοῦς
that one, Lord, Do You of me wash  the  feet?   answered  Jesus

καὶ εἶπεν αὐτῷ, Ὃ ἐγὼ ποιῶ, σὺ οὐκ οἶδας ἄρτι, γνώσῃ
and said to him, What I am doing, you not  know  yet, you will know

**8** δὲ μετὰ ταῦτα. λέγει αὐτῷ Πέτρος, Οὐ μὴ νίψῃς τοὺς πόδας
but after these things. says to Him Peter, In no way may You the feet
                                                       wash

μου εἰς τὸν αἰῶνα. ἀπεκρίθη αὐτῷ ὁ Ἰησους, Ἐὰν μὴ νίψω
of me to  the age.  answered to him —  Jesus,  Unless I wash

**9** σε, οὐκ ἔχεις μέρος μετ᾽ ἐμοῦ. λέγει αὐτῷ Σίμων Πέτρος,
you, not you have part with  Me.  says to Him Simon  Peter,

Κύριε, μὴ τοὺς πόδας μου μόνον, ἀλλὰ καὶ τὰς χεῖρας καὶ
Lord, not the feet of Me only, but also the hands and

**10** τὴν κεφαλήν. λέγει αὐτῷ ὁ Ἰησοῦς, Ὁ λελουμένος οὐ χρείαν
the head.   says to him  Jesus,  He having bathed no need

ἔχει ἢ τοὺς πόδας νίψασθαι, ἀλλ᾽ ἔστι καθαρὸς ὅλος· καὶ
has than the  feet to wash,  but  is clean wholly; and

**11** ὑμεῖς καθαροί ἐστε ἀλλ᾽ οὐχὶ πάντες. ᾔδει γὰρ τὸν παραδι-
you  clean are,  but not all.  He knew For the (one) betray-

δόντα αὐτόν· διὰ τοῦτο εἶπεν, Οὐχὶ πάντες καθαροί ἐστε.
ing  Him; for this reason He said, Not  all  clean you are.

**12** Ὅτε οὖν ἔνιψε τοὺς πόδας αὐτῶν, καὶ ἔλαβε τὰ ἱμάτια
When, therefore, He washed the feet of them, and took  the garments

αὐτοῦ, ἀναπεσὼν πάλιν, εἶπεν αὐτοῖς, Γινώσκετε τί πεποίη-
of Him. Reclining again, He said to them, Do you know what I have

**13** κα ὑμῖν; ὑμεῖς φωνεῖτέ με, Ὁ διδάσκαλος, καὶ Ὁ κύριος· καὶ
done to you? You call Me, The Teacher, and, The Lord; and

**14** καλῶς λέγετε, εἰμὶ γάρ. εἰ οὖν ἐγὼ ἔνιψα ὑμῶν τοὺς πόδας,
well you say; I am for. If, then, I washed of you the feet,

ὁ κύριος καὶ ὁ διδάσκαλος, καὶ ὑμεῖς ὀφείλετε ἀλλήλων
the Lord and the Teacher; also you ought of one another

**15** νίπτειν τοὺς πόδας. ὑπόδειγμα γὰρ ἔδωκα ὑμῖν, ἵνα καθὼς
to wash the feet.  an example For I gave you, that as

**16** ἐγὼ ἐποίησα ὑμῖν, καὶ ὑμεῖς ποιῆτε. ἀμὴν ἀμὴν λέγω ὑμῖν,
I   did to you, also you should do. Truly, truly, I say to you,

Οὐκ ἔστι δοῦλος μείζων τοῦ κυρίου αὐτοῦ, οὐδὲ ἀπόστολος
not is A slave greater than the lord of him, nor a messenger

**17** μείζων τοῦ πέμψαντος αὐτόν. εἰ ταῦτα οἴδατε, μακάριοί
greater than the (one) sending him. If these things you know, blessed

**18** ἐστε ἐὰν ποιῆτε αὐτά. οὐ περὶ πάντων ὑμῶν λέγω· ἐγὼ
are you if you do them. Not concerning all of you I speak:

whom I chose, but that the Scripture might be fulfilled, "He that eats bread with Me lifted up his heel against Me." [19] From this time I tell you before it comes to pass, that when it comes to pass, you may believe that I AM. [20] Indeed, I tell you truly, He that receives whomever I shall send receives Me; and he that receives Me receives Him who sent Me. [21] Saying these things Jesus was troubled in spirit, and testified and said, Indeed, I tell you truly that one of you will deliver Me up. [22] Then the disciples looked upon one another, doubting of whom He spoke. [23] But there was one of His disciples reclining in the bosom of Jesus, whom Jesus loved. [24] Therefore Simon Peter signaled to him to ask who it might be of whom He spoke. [25] And he having leaned on the breast of Jesus said to Him, Lord, who is it? [26] Jesus answered, It is he to whom I having dipped the morsel shall give (it). And having dipped the morsel he gave (it) to Judas, Simon's (son) Iscariot. [27] And after the morsel, then Satan entered into him. Then Jesus said to him, What you do, do quickly. [28] But no one of those reclining knew this, why He spoke to him; [29] for some thought, since Judas had the bag, that Jesus was saying to him, Buy what things we have need (of) for the feast; or that he should give something to the poor. [30] Therefore having received the morsel, he immediately went out; and it was night.

[31] When he had gone out Jesus said, Now the Son of man has been glorified, and God has been glorified in Him. [32] If God has been glorified in Him, God also shall glorify Him in Himself, and immediately shall glorify Him. [33] Little children, yet a little while I am with you. You will seek Me; and as I said to the Jews, that

**19** οἶδα οὓς ἐξελεξάμην· ἀλλ' ἵνα ἡ γραφὴ πληρωθῇ, Ὁ τρώγων
know whom I chose out, but that the Scripture be fulfilled: The (one) eating
μετ' ἐμοῦ τὸν ἄρτον ἐπῆρεν ἐπ' ἐμὲ τὴν πτέρναν αὐτοῦ. ἀπ'
with Me the bread lifted up against Me the heel of him. From
ἄρτι λέγω ὑμῖν πρὸ τοῦ γενέσθαι, ἵνα, ὅταν γένηται,
now I tell you, before the happening, that when it happens
**20** πιστεύσητε ὅτι ἐγώ εἰμι. ἀμὴν ἀμὴν λέγω ὑμῖν, Ὁ λαμβάνων
you may believe that I AM. Truly, truly, I say to you, the (one) receiving
ἐάν τινα πέμψω, ἐμὲ λαμβάνει· ὁ δὲ ἐμὲ λαμβάνων, λαμβάνει
whomever I may send, Me receives, he and Me receiving, receives
τὸν πέμψαντά με.
the (one) sending Me.

**21** Ταῦτα εἰπὼν ὁ Ἰησοῦς ἐταράχθη τῷ πνεύματι, καὶ
These things saying — Jesus was agitated in the spirit, and
ἐμαρτύρησε καὶ εἶπεν, Ἀμὴν ἀμὴν λέγω ὑμῖν ὅτι εἷς ἐξ ὑμῶν
witnessed and said, Truly, truly, I say to you that one of you
**22** παραδώσει με. ἔβλεπον οὖν εἰς ἀλλήλους οἱ μαθηταί,
will betray Me. looked Then at one another the disciples,
**23** ἀπορούμενοι περὶ τίνος λέγει. ἦν δὲ ἀνακείμενος εἷς τῶν
being perplexed about whom He speaks. was And reclining one of the
μαθητῶν αὐτοῦ ἐν τῷ κόλπῳ τοῦ Ἰησοῦ, ὃν ἠγάπα ὁ
disciples of Him on the bosom — of Jesus, whom loved —
**24** Ἰησοῦς· νεύει οὖν τούτῳ Σίμων Πέτρος πυθέσθαι τίς ἂν εἴη
Jesus; nods then to this one Simon Peter to ask who it might be
**25** περὶ οὗ λέγει. ἐπιπεσὼν δὲ ἐκεῖνος ἐπὶ τὸ στῆθος τοῦ Ἰησοῦ,
about whom He speaks. leaning And that one on the breast — of Jesus,
**26** λέγει αὐτῷ, Κύριε, τίς ἐστιν; ἀποκρίνεται ὁ Ἰησοῦς,
he said to Him, Lord, who is it? answers — Jesus,
Ἐκεῖνός ἐστιν ᾧ ἐγὼ βάψας τὸ ψωμίον ἐπιδώσω. καὶ ἐμβά-
That one it is to whom I having dipped the morsel shall give it. And dipping
**27** ψας τὸ ψωμίον, δίδωσιν Ἰούδᾳ Σίμωνος Ἰσκαριώτῃ. καὶ
the morsel, He gave to Judas of Simon Iscariot. And
μετὰ τὸ ψωμίον, τότε εἰσῆλθεν εἰς ἐκεῖνον ὁ Σατανᾶς. λέγει
after the morsel, then entered into that one Satan. says
**28** οὖν αὐτῷ ὁ Ἰησοῦς, Ὁ ποιεῖς, ποίησον τάχιον. τοῦτο δὲ
Then to him Jesus, What you do, do quickly. this But
**29** οὐδεὶς ἔγνω τῶν ἀνακειμένων πρὸς τί εἶπεν αὐτῷ. τινὲς γὰρ
no one knew of those reclining for what He spoke to him. some For
ἐδόκουν, ἐπεὶ τὸ γλωσσόκομον εἶχεν ὁ Ἰούδας, ὅτι λέγει
thought, since the money-bag held — Judas, that tells
αὐτῷ ὁ Ἰησοῦς, Ἀγόρασον ὧν χρείαν ἔχομεν εἰς τὴν
him Jesus, Buy of what things need we have for the
**30** ἑορτήν· ἢ τοῖς πτωχοῖς ἵνα τι δῷ. λαβὼν οὖν τὸ ψωμίον
feast; or, to the poor that a thing he give. Receiving, then, the morsel
ἐκεῖνος, εὐθέως ἐξῆλθεν· ἦν δὲ νύξ.
that one, at once went out. it was And night.

**31** Ὅτε οὖν ἐξῆλθε, λέγει ὁ Ἰησοῦς, Νῦν ἐδοξάσθη ὁ υἱὸς τοῦ
when Then he went, says Jesus, Now was glorified the Son —
**32** ἀνθρώπου, καὶ ὁ Θεὸς ἐδοξάσθη ἐν αὐτῷ. εἰ ὁ Θεὸς ἐδοξάσθη
of man, and God was glorified in Him; if God was glorified
ἐν αὐτῷ, καὶ ὁ Θεὸς δοξάσει αὐτὸν ἐν ἑαυτῷ, καὶ εὐθὺς
in Him, both God will glorify Him in Himself, and at once
**33** δοξάσει αὐτόν. τεκνία, ἔτι μικρὸν μεθ' ὑμῶν εἰμι. ζητήσετέ
will glorify Him. Children, yet a little with you I am. You will seek
με, καὶ καθὼς εἶπον τοῖς Ἰουδαίοις ὅτι Ὅπου ὑπάγω ἐγώ,
Me, and as I said to the Jews, — Where go I,

where I go, you are not able to come; I also say to you now. [34] I give a new commandment to you, that you should love one another; according as I loved you, you should also love one another. [35] By this all shall know that you are My disciples, if you have love among one another. [36] Simon Peter said to Him, Lord, where do You go? Jesus answered him, Where I go you are not able to follow now, but afterwards you shall follow Me. [37] Peter said to Him, Lord, why am I not able to follow now? I will lay down my life for You. [38] Jesus answered him, Will you lay down your life for Me? Indeed, I tell you truly, in no way will (the) cock crow until you will deny Me three times.

**CHAPTER 14**

[1] Do not let your heart be troubled, you believe on God, believe also on Me. [2] In My Father's house are many places to live. If it were not so I would have told you. I am going to prepare a place for you. [3] And if I go and prepare a place for you, I am coming again and will receive you to Myself, that where I am you may be also. [4] And where I go you know, and the way you know. [5] Thomas said to Him, Lord, we do not know where You go, and how can we know the way? [6] Jesus said to him, I am the Way and the Truth and the Life. No one comes to the Father but by Me. [7] If you had known Me, you would have known My Father also; and from now on you know Him, and have seen Him. [8] And Philip said to Him, Lord, show us the Father, and it suffices us. [9] Jesus said to him, Am I so long a time with you, and you have not known me, Philip? He that has seen Me has seen the Father; and how do you say, Show us

**34** ὑμεῖς οὐ δύνασθε ἐλθεῖν, καὶ ὑμῖν λέγω ἄρτι. ἐντολὴν
you not are able to come, also to you I say now. A command
καινὴν δίδωμι ὑμῖν, ἵνα ἀγαπᾶτε ἀλλήλους· καθὼς ἠγά-
A new I give you, that you love one another as I
**35** πησα ὑμᾶς, ἵνα καὶ ὑμεῖς ἀγαπᾶτε ἀλλήλους. ἐν τούτῳ γνώ-
loved you that also you should love one another. By this will
σονται πάντες ὅτι ἐμοὶ μαθηταί ἐστε, ἐὰν ἀγάπην ἔχητε ἐν
know all that to Me disciples you are, if love you have among
ἀλλήλοις.
one another.
**36** Λέγει αὐτῷ Σίμων Πέτρος, Κύριε, ποῦ ὑπάγεις ; ἀπεκρίθη
says to Him Simon Peter, Lord, where do You go? answered
αὐτῷ ὁ Ἰησοῦς, Ὅπου ὑπάγω, οὐ δύνασαί μοι νῦν ἀκο-
him Jesus, Where I go, not you are able Me now to
**37** λουθῆσαι, ὕστερον δὲ ἀκολουθήσεις μοι. λέγει αὐτῷ ὁ
follow; later but you will follow Me. says to Him
Πέτρος, Κύριε, διατί οὐ δύναμαί σοι ἀκολουθῆσαι ἄρτι ;
Peter, Lord, why not am I able You to follow now?
**38** τὴν ψυχήν μου ὑπὲρ σοῦ θήσω. ἀπεκρίθη αὐτῷ ὁ Ἰησοῦς,
The soul of me for You I will lay down. answers him — Jesus,
Τὴν ψυχήν σου ὑπὲρ ἐμοῦ θήσεις ; ἀμὴν ἀμὴν λέγω σοι, οὐ
The soul of you for Me you will lay down? Truly, truly I say to you, in
μὴ ἀλέκτωρ φωνήσει ἕως οὗ ἀπαρνήσῃ με τρίς.
no way a cock will crow until you deny Me three times.

**CHAPTER 14**

**1** Μὴ ταρασσέσθω ὑμῶν ἡ καρδία· πιστεύετε εἰς τὸν Θεόν,
Not let be agitated of you the heart; believe in God,
**2** καὶ εἰς ἐμὲ πιστεύετε. ἐν τῇ οἰκίᾳ τοῦ πατρός μου μοναὶ
and in Me believe. In the house of the Father of Me dwellings
πολλαί εἰσιν· εἰ δὲ μή, εἶπον ἂν ὑμῖν· πορεύομαι ἑτοιμάσαι
many are. Otherwise, I would have told you. I go to prepare
**3** τόπον ὑμῖν. καὶ ἐὰν πορευθῶ καὶ ἑτοιμάσω ὑμῖν τόπον,
a place for you, and if I go and prepare for you a place,
πάλιν ἔρχομαι καὶ παραλήψομαι ὑμᾶς πρὸς ἐμαυτόν· ἵνα
again I am coming and will receive you to Myself, that
**4** ὅπου εἰμὶ ἐγώ, καὶ ὑμεῖς ἦτε. καὶ ὅπου ἐγὼ ὑπάγω οἴδατε,
where am I, also you may be. And where I go you know.
**5** καὶ τὴν ὁδὸν οἴδατε. λέγει αὐτῷ Θωμᾶς, Κύριε, οὐκ οἴδαμεν
and the way you know. says to Him Thomas, Lord, not we know
**6** ποῦ ὑπάγεις· καὶ πῶς δυνάμεθα τὴν ὁδὸν εἰδέναι ; λέγει
where You go, and how are we able the way to know? says
αὐτῷ ὁ Ἰησοῦς, Ἐγώ εἰμι ἡ ὁδὸς καὶ ἡ ἀλήθεια καὶ ἡ ζωή·
to him — Jesus, I am the way and the truth and the life;
**7** οὐδεὶς ἔρχεται πρὸς τὸν πατέρα, εἰ μὴ δι' ἐμοῦ. εἰ ἐγνώκειτέ
no one comes to the Father except through Me. If you had known
με, καὶ τὸν πατέρα μου ἐγνώκειτε ἄν· καὶ ἀπ' ἄρτι γινώ-
Me, also the Father of Me you would have known, and from now you
**8** σκετε αὐτόν, καὶ ἑωράκατε αὐτόν. λέγει αὐτῷ Φίλιππος,
know Him, and have seen Him. says to Him Philip,
**9** Κύριε. δεῖξον ἡμῖν τὸν πατέρα, καὶ ἀρκεῖ ἡμῖν. λέγει αὐτῷ
Lord, show us the Father, and it suffices us. says to him
ὁ Ἰησοῦς, Τοσοῦτον χρόνον μεθ' ὑμῶν εἰμι, καὶ οὐκ ἔγνωκάς
— Jesus, so long a time with you Am I, and not you know
με. Φίλιππε ; ὁ ἑωρακὼς ἐμέ, ἑώρακε τὸν πατέρα· καὶ πῶς σὺ
Me, Philip? The (one) seeing Me has seen the Father; and how do you

the Father? [10] Do you not believe that I (am) in the Father and the Father is in Me? The words which I speak to you, I do not speak from Myself; but the Father who lives in Me, He does the works. [11] Believe Me, that I (am) in the Father, and the Father in Me; but if not, believe Me because of the works themselves. [12] Indeed, I tell you truly, He that believes on Me, the works which I do, he shall also do, and greater than these he shall do, because I go to My Father. [13] And whatever you may ask in My name, this I will do, that the Father may be glorified in the Son. [14] If you ask anything in My name, I will do (it). [15] If you love Me, keep My commandments. [16] And I will ask the Father, and He will give you another Comforter, that He may remain with you forever, [17] the Spirit of Truth, whom the world cannot receive, because it does not see Him, nor know Him; but you know Him, for He abides with you, and shall be in you. [18] I will not leave you orphans, I am coming to you. [19] Yet a little while and the world no longer sees Me, but you see Me; because I live, you also shall live. [20] In that day you shall know that I (am) in My Father, and you in Me, and I in you. [21] He that has My commandments and keeps them, he it is that loves Me; but he that loves Me shall be loved by My Father; and I will love him and will reveal Myself to him. [22] Judas said to Him — not the Iscariot — Lord, what has happened that You are about to reveal Yourself to us, and not to the world? [23] Jesus answered and said to him, If anyone loves Me, he will keep My word, and My Father will love him, and We will come to him and will make a home with him. [24] He that does not love Me does not keep My words; and

**10** λέγεις, Δεῖξον ἡμῖν τὸν πατέρα ; οὐ πιστεύεις ὅτι ἐγὼ ἐν τῷ
say. Show us the Father? Not do you believe that I in the

πατρί, καὶ ὁ πατὴρ ἐν ἐμοί ἐστι ; τὰ ῥήματα ἃ ἐγὼ λαλῶ
Father (am), and the Father in Me is? The words which I speak

ὑμῖν, ἀπ' ἐμαυτοῦ οὐ λαλῶ· ὁ δὲ πατὴρ ὁ ἐν ἐμοὶ μένων,
to you, from Myself not I speak, the but Father who in Me abides;

**11** αὐτὸς ποιεῖ τὰ ἔργα. πιστεύετέ μοι ὅτι ἐγὼ ἐν τῷ πατρί,
He does the works. Believe Me, that I (am) in the Father,

καὶ ὁ πατὴρ ἐν ἐμοί· εἰ δὲ μή, διὰ τὰ ἔργα αὐτὰ πιστεύετέ
and the Father in Me (is). if And not, for the works themselves believe

**12** μοι. ἀμὴν ἀμὴν λέγω ὑμῖν, ὁ πιστεύων εἰς ἐμέ, τὰ ἔργα ἃ ἐγὼ
Me. Truly, truly, I say to you, the (one) believing in Me, the works that I

ποιῶ κἀκεῖνος ποιήσει, καὶ μείζονα τούτων ποιήσει· ὅτι
do, also that one will do, and greater (than) these he will do, because

**13** ἐγὼ πρὸς τὸν πατέρα μου πορεύομαι. καὶ ὅ τι ἂν αἰτήσητε
I to the Father of Me go. And whatever you may ask

ἐν τῷ ὀνόματί μου, τοῦτο ποιήσω, ἵνα δοξασθῇ ὁ πατὴρ ἐν
in the name of Me, this I will do, that may be glorified the Father in

**14** τῷ υἱῷ. ἐάν τι αἰτήσητε ἐν τῷ ὀνόματί μου, ἐγὼ ποιήσω
the Son. If anything you ask in the name of Me, I will do

**15** ἐὰν ἀγαπᾶτέ με, τὰς ἐντολὰς τὰς ἐμὰς τηρήσατε. καὶ ἐγὼ
If you love Me, commandments — My you will keep. And I

**16** ἐρωτήσω τὸν πατέρα, καὶ ἄλλον παράκλητον δώσει ὑμῖν,
will petition the Father, and another Paraclete He will give you,

**17** ἵνα μένῃ μεθ' ὑμῶν εἰς τὸν αἰῶνα, τὸ πνεῦμα τῆς ἀληθείας, ὃ
that He abide with you for ever, the Spirit — of Truth, whom

ὁ κόσμος οὐ δύναται λαβεῖν, ὅτι οὐ θεωρεῖ αὐτό, οὐδὲ γινώ-
the world not is able to receive because not it sees Him, nor knows.

σκει αὐτό· ὑμεῖς δὲ γινώσκετε αὐτό, ὅτι παρ' ὑμῖν μένει, καὶ
Him. you But know Him, because with you He abides, and

**18** ἐν ὑμῖν ἔσται. οὐκ ἀφήσω ὑμᾶς ὀρφανούς· ἔρχομαι πρὸς
in you will be. Not I will leave you orphans; I am coming to

**19** ὑμᾶς. ἔτι μικρὸν καὶ ὁ κόσμος με οὐκέτι θεωρεῖ, ὑμεῖς δὲ θεω-
you. Yet a little and the world Me no longer beholds, you But behold

**20** ρεῖτέ με· ὅτι ἐγὼ ζῶ, καὶ ὑμεῖς ζήσεσθε. ἐν ἐκείνῃ τῇ ἡμέρᾳ
Me; because I live, also you will live. In that day

γνώσεσθε ὑμεῖς ὅτι ἐγὼ ἐν τῷ πατρί μου, καὶ ὑμεῖς ἐν ἐμοί,
will know you that I (am) in the Father of Me, and you in Me,

**21** κἀγὼ ἐν ὑμῖν. ὁ ἔχων τὰς ἐντολάς μου καὶ τηρῶν αὐτάς,
and I in you. He having the commandments of Me and keeping them,

ἐκεῖνός ἐστιν ὁ ἀγαπῶν με· ὁ δὲ ἀγαπῶν με, ἀγαπηθήσεται
that one is the (one) loving Me; he And loving Me will be loved

ὑπὸ τοῦ πατρός μου· καὶ ἐγὼ ἀγαπήσω αὐτόν, καὶ ἐμφανίσω
by the Father of Me, and I will love him, and will reveal

**22** αὐτῷ ἐμαυτόν. λέγει αὐτῷ Ἰούδας, οὐχ ὁ Ἰσκαριώτης,
to him Myself. says to him Judas, not the Iscariot,

Κύριε, τί γέγονεν ὅτι ἡμῖν μέλλεις ἐμφανίζειν σεαυτόν, καὶ
Lord, what has occurred that to us you are about to reveal Yourself, and

**23** οὐχὶ τῷ κόσμῳ ; ἀπεκρίθη ὁ Ἰησοῦς καὶ εἶπεν αὐτῷ, Ἐάν
not at to the world? answered Jesus and said to him, If
all

τίς ἀγαπᾷ με, τὸν λόγον μου τηρήσει, καὶ ὁ πατήρ μου
anyone loves Me, the word of Me he will keep, and the Father of Me

ἀγαπήσει αὐτόν, καὶ πρὸς αὐτὸν ἐλευσόμεθα, καὶ μονὴν
will love him, and to him We will come, and an abode

**24** παρ' αὐτῷ ποιήσομεν. ὁ μὴ ἀγαπῶν με, τοὺς λόγους μου
with him We will make. The (one) not loving Me, the words of Me

*(handwritten margin notes: "Troubled AFRAID? FEAR" "ANOINTING Fall on me")*

the word which you hear is not Mine, but of the Father who sent Me. [25] I have spoken these things to you, abiding with you; [26] but the Comforter, the Holy Spirit whom the Father will send in My name, He will teach you all things, and will bring to your memory all things that I said to you. [27] I leave peace with you; My peace I give to you; not as the world gives, I give to you. Let not your heart be troubled, nor let it fear. [28] You heard that I said to you I am going away and I am coming to you. If you loved Me, you would have rejoiced that I said, I am going to the Father; for My Father is greater than I. [29] And now I have told you before it comes to pass, that when it shall come to pass you may believe. [30] I will not speak with you much longer, for the ruler of this world comes, and he has nothing in Me; [31] but that the world may know that I love the Father, and as the Father commanded Me, so I do. Rise up, let us go from here.

## CHAPTER 15

[1] I am the True Vine, and My Father is the Vinedresser. [2] He takes away every branch in Me bearing no fruit; and everyone that bears fruit, He prunes it so that it may bear more fruit. [3] You are already clean through the word which I have spoken to you. [4] Remain in Me and I in you. As the branch is not able to bear fruit of itself, unless it remain in the vine, so neither (can) you unless you remain in Me. [5] I am the Vine; you (are) the branches. He that remains in Me, and I in him, he bears much fruit; for apart from Me you are not able to do anything. [6] Unless anyone remain in Me, he is thrown out as the branch, and is dried up, and they gather and throw them

οὐ τηρεῖ καὶ ὁ λόγος ὃν ἀκούετε οὐκ ἔστιν ἐμός, ἀλλὰ τοῦ
not keeps; and the word which you hear not is Mine, but of Him
πέμψαντός με πατρός.
having sent Me (the) Father.

**25**
**26** Ταῦτα λελάληκα ὑμῖν παρ' ὑμῖν μένων. ὁ δὲ παράκλητος,
These things I have spoken to you with you abiding. the But Paraclete,

τὸ Πνεῦμα τὸ Ἅγιον, ὃ πέμψει ὁ πατὴρ ἐν τῷ ὀνόματί μου,
the Spirit — Holy which will send the Father in the name of Me,
ἐκεῖνος ὑμᾶς διδάξει πάντα, καὶ ὑπομνήσει ὑμᾶς πάντα ἃ
that One you will teach all things, and remind you (of) all which

**27** εἶπον ὑμῖν. εἰρήνην ἀφίημι ὑμῖν, εἰρήνην τὴν ἐμὴν δίδωμι
I told you. Peace I leave to you; peace — My I give
ὑμῖν· οὐ καθὼς ὁ κόσμος δίδωσιν, ἐγω δίδωμι ὑμῖν. μὴ
you; not as the world gives I give you. Not

**28** ταρασσέσθω ὑμῶν ἡ καρδία, μηδὲ δειλιάτω. ἠκούσατε ὅτι
let be agitated of you the heart, nor let it be fearful. You heard that
*(handwritten: "Timid shrinking")*
ἐγὼ εἶπον ὑμῖν, Ὑπάγω καὶ ἔρχομαι πρὸς ὑμᾶς. εἰ ἠγαπᾶτέ
I told you: I go, and come to you. If you loved
με, ἐχάρητε ἂν ὅτι εἶπον, Πορεύομαι πρὸς τὸν πατέρα·
Me, you would have rejoiced that I said, I am going to the Father,

**29** ὅτι ὁ πατήρ μου μείζων μού ἐστι. καὶ νῦν εἴρηκα ὑμῖν πρὶν
for the Father of Me greater than Me is. And now I have told you before

**30** γενέσθαι ἵνα, ὅταν γένηται, πιστεύσητε. οὐκέτι πολλὰ
(it) happens, that when it happens you may believe. No longer many things
λαλήσω μεθ' ὑμῶν· ἔρχεται γὰρ ὁ τοῦ κόσμου τούτου
I will speak with you, is coming for the of the world this

**31** ἄρχων, καὶ ἐν ἐμοὶ οὐκ ἔχει οὐδέν· ἀλλ' ἵνα γνῷ ὁ κόσμος
ruler, and in Me not He has nothing. But that may know the world
ὅτι ἀγαπῶ τὸν πατέρα, καὶ καθὼς ἐνετείλατό μοι ὁ πατήρ,
that I love the Father, and as commanded Me the Father,
οὕτω ποιῶ· ἐγείρεσθε, ἄγωμεν ἐντεῦθεν.
so I do. Rise, let us go from here.

## CHAPTER 15

**1** Ἐγὼ εἰμι ἡ ἄμπελος ἡ ἀληθινή, καὶ ὁ πατήρ μου ὁ
I am the vine — true, and the Father of Me the

**2** γεωργός ἐστι. πᾶν κλῆμα ἐν ἐμοὶ μὴ φέρον καρπόν, αἴρει
Vinedresser is. Every branch in Me not bearing fruit, He takes
αὐτό· καὶ πᾶν τὸ καρπὸν φέρον, καθαίρει αὐτό, ἵνα πλείονα
it. And each the fruit bearing, He prunes it so that more

**3** καρπὸν φέρῃ. ἤδη ὑμεῖς καθαροί ἐστε διὰ τὸν λόγον ὃν
fruit it may bear. Now you pruned are because of the word which

**4** λελάληκα ὑμῖν. μείνατε ἐν ἐμοί, κἀγὼ ἐν ὑμῖν. καθὼς τὸ
I have spoken to you. Remain in Me, and I in you. As the
κλῆμα οὐ δύναται καρπὸν φέρειν ἀφ' ἑαυτοῦ, ἐὰν μὴ μείνῃ

**5** branch not is able fruit to bear from itself unless it remain
ἐν τῇ ἀμπέλῳ, οὕτως οὐδὲ ὑμεῖς, ἐὰν μὴ ἐν ἐμοὶ μείνητε. ἐγώ
in the vine, so neither you unless in Me you remain. I
εἰμι ἡ ἄμπελος, ὑμεῖς τὰ κλήματα. ὁ μένων ἐν ἐμοί, κἀγω ἐν
am the vine, you (are) the branches. He remaining in Me, and I in
αὐτῷ, οὗτος φέρει καρπὸν πολύν· ὅτι χωρὶς ἐμοῦ οὐ δύνασθε
him, this one bears fruit much, because apart from Me not you can

**6** ποιεῖν οὐδέν. ἐὰν μή τις μείνῃ ἐν ἐμοί, ἐβλήθη ἔξω ὡς τὸ
do nothing. Unless anyone remains in Me, he is cast out as the
κλῆμα, καὶ ἐξηράνθη, καὶ συνάγουσιν αὐτὰ· καὶ εἰς πῦρ
branch, and is withered and they gather them and into a fire

into a fire, and it is burned.
[7] If you remain in Me,
and My words remain in
you, whatever you desire
you shall ask, and it shall
come to pass to you.
[8] In this My Father is
glorified, that you should
bear much fruit, and you
shall become disciples to
Me. [9] As the Father
loved Me, I also loved you;
continue in My love.
[10] If you keep My
commandments, you shall
continue in My love, as I
have kept the command-
ments of My Father and
continue in His love.
[11] I have spoken these
things to you that My joy
may abide in you, and
your joy may be full.
[12] This is My command-
ment, that you love one an
other as I loved you. [13]
Greater love than this has
no one, that any should lay
down his soul for his friends
—[14] you are My friends if
you do whatever I com-
mand you. [15] I no longer
call you slaves, for the slave
does not know what his lord
does. But I called you
friends, for all things which
I heard from My Father, I
made know to you. [16]
You have not chosen Me,
but I chose you, and planted you, that you should go
and bear fruit, and your
fruit remain; that whatever
you may ask the Father in
My name, He may give you.
[17] These things I com-
mand you, that you love
one another. [18] If the
world hates you, you know
that it has hated Me before
you. [19] If you were of
the world, the world would
love its own; but because
you are not of the world,
but I chose you out of the
world, because of this the
world hates you.
[20] Remember the word
which I said to you, A
slave is not greater than his
master. If they persecuted
Me, they will also
persecute you; if they kept
My word, they will also
keep yours. [21] But all
these things they will do to
you because of My name,
because they do not know
Him who sent Me. [22] If

**7** βάλλουσι, καὶ καίεται. ἐὰν μείνητε ἐν ἐμοί, καὶ τὰ ῥήματά
they throw, and they are burned. If you remain in Me, and the words
μου ἐν ὑμῖν μείνῃ, ὃ ἐὰν θέλητε αἰτήσεσθε, καὶ γενήσεται
of Me in you remain, whatever you will, ask, and it shall happen

**8** ὑμῖν. ἐν τούτῳ ἐδοξάσθη ὁ πατήρ μου, ἵνα καρπὸν πολὺν
to you. In this is glorified the Father of Me, that fruit much

**9** φέρητε· καὶ γενήσεσθε ἐμοὶ μαθηταί. καθὼς ἠγάπησέ με ὁ
you shall bear, and you will be to Me disciples. As loved Me the
πατήρ, κἀγὼ ἠγάπησα ὑμᾶς· μείνατε ἐν τῇ ἀγάπῃ τῇ ἐμῇ.
Father, I also loved you; remain in love — My.

**10** ἐὰν τὰς ἐντολάς μου τηρήσητε, μενεῖτε ἐν τῇ ἀγάπῃ μου·
If the commandments of Me you keep, you will remain in the love of Me.
καθὼς ἐγὼ τὰς ἐντολὰς τοῦ πατρός μου τετήρηκα, καὶ μένω
as I the command of the Father of Me have kept, and remain

**11** αὐτοῦ ἐν τῇ ἀγάπῃ. ταῦτα λελάληκα ὑμῖν, ἵνα ἡ χαρὰ ἡ
of Him in the love. These things I have spoken to you that joy

**12** ἐμὴ ἐν ὑμῖν μείνῃ, καὶ ἡ χαρὰ ὑμῶν πληρωθῇ. αὕτη ἐστὶν ἡ
of Me in you remain, and the joy of you may be filled. This is
ἐντολὴ ἡ ἐμή, ἵνα ἀγαπᾶτε ἀλλήλους. καθὼς ἠγάπησα
commandment My, that you love one another even as I loved

**13** ὑμᾶς. μείζονα ταύτης ἀγάπην οὐδεὶς ἔχει ἵνα τις τὴν ψυχὴν
you. Greater than this love no one has, that anyone the soul

**14** αὐτοῦ θῇ ὑπὲρ τῶν φίλων αὐτοῦ. ὑμεῖς φίλοι μου ἐστέ, ἐὰν
of him lay down for the friends of him. You friends of Me are, if

**15** ποιῆτε ὅσα ἐγὼ ἐντέλλομαι ὑμῖν. οὐκέτι ὑμᾶς λέγω δούλους,
you do whatever I command you. No longer you I call slaves,
ὅτι ὁ δοῦλος οὐκ οἶδε τί ποιεῖ αὐτοῦ ὁ κύριος· ὑμᾶς δὲ εἴρηκα
for the slave not knows what does of him the lord; you but I called
φίλους, ὅτι πάντα ἃ ἤκουσα παρὰ τοῦ πατρός μου ἐγνώ-
friends, because all things which I heard from the Father of Me I made

**16** ρισα ὑμῖν. οὐχ ὑμεῖς με ἐξελέξασθε, ἀλλ᾽ ἐγὼ ἐξελεξάμην ὑμᾶς,
known to you. not You Me have chosen, but I chose out you,
καὶ ἔθηκα ὑμᾶς, ἵνα ὑμεῖς ὑπάγητε καὶ καρπὸν φέρητε, καὶ ὁ
and planted you, that you should go and fruit should bear, and the
καρπὸς ὑμῶν μένῃ· ἵνα ὅ τι ἂν αἰτήσητε τὸν πατέρα ἐν τῷ
fruit of you remain, that whatever you may ask the Father in the

**17** ὀνόματί μου, δῷ ὑμῖν. ταῦτα ἐντέλλομαι ὑμῖν, ἵνα
name of Me, He may give you. These things I command you, that

**18** ἀγαπᾶτε ἀλλήλους. εἰ ὁ κόσμος ὑμᾶς μισεῖ, γινώσκετε ὅτι
you love one another. If the world you hates, you know that

**19** ἐμὲ πρῶτον ὑμῶν μεμίσηκεν. εἰ ἐκ τοῦ κόσμου ἦτε, ὁ κόσμος
Me before you it has hated. If of the world you were, the world
ἂν τὸ ἴδιον ἐφίλει· ὅτι δὲ ἐκ τοῦ κόσμου οὐκ ἐστέ, ἀλλ᾽ ἐγὼ
would the own have loved; that but of the world not you are, but I
ἐξελεξάμην ὑμᾶς ἐκ τοῦ κόσμου, διὰ τοῦτο μισεῖ ὑμᾶς ὁ
chose out you out of the world, therefore hates you the

**20** κόσμος. μνημονεύετε τοῦ λόγου οὗ ἐγὼ εἶπον ὑμῖν, Οὐκ ἔστι
world. Remember the word which I said to you: Not is
δοῦλος μείζων τοῦ κυρίου αὐτοῦ. εἰ ἐμὲ ἐδίωξαν, καὶ ὑμᾶς
a slave greater than the lord of him If Me they persecuted, also you
διώξουσιν·· εἰ τὸν λόγον μου ἐτήρησαν, καὶ τὸν ὑμέτερον
they will persecute; if the word of Me they kept, also — yours

**21** τηρήσουσιν. ἀλλὰ ταῦτα πάντα ποιήσουσιν ὑμῖν διὰ τὸ
they will keep. But these things all they will do to you because of

**22** ὄνομά μου, ὅτι οὐκ οἴδασι τὸν πέμψαντά με. εἰ μὴ ἦλθον καὶ
name My, for not they know the (One) sending Me. Unless I came and

not I came and spoke to them, they had no sin; but now they have no excuse as to their sin. [23] He hating Me also hates My Father. [24] If I did not do the works among them which no other did, they had no sin, but now they both have seen and have hated both Me and My Father. [25] But that may be fulfilled the word that has been written in their law, "they hated Me without a cause." [26] And when the Comforter comes, whom I will send to you from the Father, the Spirit of truth, who proceeds from the Father. That One will witness about Me; [27] And you also witness, because you are with Me from the beginning.

CHAPTER 16

[1] I have spoken these things to you so that you may not be offended. [2] They will put you out of the synagogues; but an hour is coming that everyone who kills you will think to do service to God; [3] and they will do these things to you because they do not know the Father or Me. [4] But I have said these things to you that when the hour may have come you may remember them, that I said (them) to you. But I did not say these things to you from (the) beginning because I was with you. [5] But now I go to Him who sent Me, and none of You asks Me, Where do You go? [6] But because I have said these things to you, grief has filled your heart. [7] But I say the truth to you, it is profitable for you that I should go away; for if I do not go away, the Comforter will not come to you; but if I go, I will send Him to you. [8] And that One coming, He will convict the world concerning sin, and concerning righteousness, and concerning judgment. [9] Concerning sin, because they do not believe on Me; [10] concerning righteousness, because I go away to My Father, and you no longer see Me; [11] and concerning

ἐλάλησα αὐτοῖς, ἁμαρτίαν οὐκ εἶχον· νῦν δὲ προφασιν οὐκ
**spoke       to them      sin     not they had; now but an excuse   not**

23 ἔχουσι περὶ τῆς ἁμαρτίας αὐτῶν. ὁ ἐμὲ μισῶν, καὶ τὸν
**they have concerning   sin   of them. The (one) Me hating   also   the**

24 πατέρα μου μισεῖ. εἰ τὰ ἔργα μὴ ἐποίησά ἐν αὐτοῖς ἃ οὐδεὶς
**Father  of Me hates. If the works not I did   among them which none**

ἄλλος πεποίηκεν, ἁμαρτίαν οὐκ εἶχον· νῦν δὲ καὶ ἑωράκασι
**other   did,        sin     not they had; now but both they have seen**

25 καὶ μεμισήκασι καὶ ἐμὲ καὶ τὸν πατέρα μου. ἀλλ' ἵνα πλη-
**and have hated   both Me and the   Father of Me.   But that may be**

ρωθῇ ὁ λόγος ὁ γεγραμμένος ἐν τῷ νόμῳ αὐτῶν ὅτι Ἐμίση-
**fulfilled the word that has been written in the law of them,   —   They**

σάν με δωρεάν.
**hated Me freely.**

26 Ὅταν δὲ ἔλθῃ ὁ παράκλητος, ὃν ἐγὼ πέμψω ὑμῖν παρὰ
**when And comes the Paraclete,  whom I   will send to you   from**

τοῦ πατρός, τὸ πνεῦμα τῆς ἀληθείας, ὁ παρὰ τοῦ πατρὸς
**the Father, the Spirit   —   of truth who   from   the Father**

27 ἐκπορεύεται, ἐκεῖνος μαρτυρήσει περὶ ἐμοῦ· καὶ ὑμεῖς δὲ
**proceeds,     that One   will witness concerning Me; also you and**

μαρτυρεῖτε, ὅτι ἀπ' ἀρχῆς μετ' ἐμοῦ ἐστε.
**witness,   because from (the) beginning with Me you are.**

CHAPTER 16

1 Ταῦτα λελάληκα ὑμῖν, ἵνα μὴ σκανδαλισθῆτε. ἀπο-
2 **These things I have spoken to you that not   you be offended.   Put from**

συναγώγους ποιήσουσιν ὑμᾶς· ἀλλ' ἔρχεται ὥρα, ἵνα πᾶς
**(the) synagogue they will make   you, but   comes an hour that everyone**

3 ὁ ἀποκτείνας ὑμᾶς δόξῃ λατρείαν προσφέρειν τῷ Θεῷ. καὶ
**killing       you will think a service to bear before   —   God. And**

ταῦτα ποιήσουσιν ὑμῖν, ὅτι οὐκ ἔγνωσαν τὸν πατέρα οὐδὲ
**these things they will do to you because not they knew the Father   nor**

4 ἐμέ. ἀλλὰ ταῦτα λελάληκα ὑμῖν, ἵνα ὅταν ἔλθῃ ἡ ὥρα,
**Me. But these things I have spoken to you that when comes the hour**

μνημονεύητε αὐτῶν, ὅτι ἐγὼ εἶπον ὑμῖν. ταῦτα δὲ ὑμῖν ἐξ
**you may recall   them,   that I told you. these things And to you from**

5 ἀρχῆς οὐκ εἶπον, ὅτι μεθ' ὑμῶν ἤμην. νῦν δὲ ὑπάγω πρὸς
**(the) first not I said, because with you I was.   now But I am going to**

τὸν πέμψαντά με, καὶ οὐδεὶς ἐξ ὑμῶν ἐρωτᾷ με, Ποῦ ὑπάγεις;
**the (One) sending Me, and not one of you   asks   Me, Where are you going**

6 ἀλλ' ὅτι ταῦτα λελάληκα ὑμῖν, ἡ λύπη πεπλήρωκεν ὑμῶν
**But because these things I have said to you, grief   has filled   of you**

7 τὴν καρδίαν. ἀλλ' ἐγὼ τὴν ἀλήθειαν λέγω ὑμῖν· συμφέρει
**the heart.   But   I   the   truth   tell   you, it is profitable**

ὑμῖν ἵνα ἐγὼ ἀπέλθω· ἐὰν γὰρ μὴ ἀπέλθω, ὁ παράκλητος
**for you that I should go.   if   For not I go away, the Paraclete**

οὐκ ἐλεύσεται πρὸς ὑμᾶς· ἐὰν δὲ πορευθῶ, πέμψω αὐτὸν
**not will come   to   you; if but   I go,   I will send   Him**

8 πρὸς ὑμᾶς. καὶ ἐλθὼν ἐκεῖνος ἐλέγξει τὸν κόσμον περὶ ἁμαρ-
**to   you. And coming that One will convict the world concerning sin,**

9 τίας καὶ περὶ δικαιοσύνης καὶ περὶ κρίσεως· περὶ ἁμαρτίας
**and concerning righteousness and concerning judgment; concerning sin**

10 μέν, ὅτι οὐ πιστεύουσιν εἰς ἐμέ· περὶ δικαιοσύνης δέ, ὅτι
**because not they believe   in Me; concerning righteousness and becaus**

11 πρὸς τὸν πατέρα μου ὑπάγω, καὶ οὐκέτι θεωρεῖτέ με· περὶ
**to   the   Father of Me I am going; and no longer you behold Me; con-
cerning**

judgment, because the ruler of this world has been judged. [12] Yet I have many things to say to you, but you are not able to bear now. [13] But when He comes, the Spirit of truth, He will guide you into all truth; for He will not speak from Himself, but whatever He may hear He will speak and the coming things He will announce to you. [14] He will glorify Me, for He will receive from Mine and will announce to you. [15] All things which the Father has are Mine; for this cause I said that He receives from Mine, and will announce to you. [16] A little and you do not see Me; and again a little (while) and you will see Me, because I go away to the Father. [17] Therefore they said, What is this which He says to us, A little (while) and you do not see Me, and again, A little and you will see Me? Also, because I go to the Father? [18] Therefore they said, What is this that He says, The little? We do not know what He says. [19] Then Jesus knew that they desired to ask Him, and said to them, Do you ask about this among one another, that I said, A little (while) and you do not see Me; and again a little (while) and you shall see Me? [20] Indeed, I tell you truly that you will weep and will lament, but the world will rejoice; but you will be grieved, but your grief will become joy. [21] The woman has grief when she bears, because her hour came; but when she brings forth the child, she no longer recalls the distress because of the joy that a man was born into the world. [22] And you, then, truly have grief now; but I will see you again, and your heart will rejoice, and no one takes your joy from you [23] and in that day you will ask Me nothing. Truly, truly, I say to you that whatever you may ask the Father in My name, He will give you. [24] Until now you asked nothing in My name; ask, and you will receive.

**12** δὲ κρίσεως, ὅτι ὁ ἄρχων τοῦ κόσμου τούτου κέκριται. ἔτι
and judgment, because the ruler   of world   this   has been judged. Yet
πολλὰ ἔχω λέγειν ὑμῖν, ἀλλ' οὐ δύνασθε βαστάζειν ἄρτι.
many things I have to tell you,   but   not you are able to bear   now;

**13** ὅταν δὲ ἔλθη ἐκεῖνος, τὸ πνεῦμα τῆς ἀληθείας, ὁδηγήσει
when but comes that One, the   Spirit   — of truth,   He will guide
ὑμᾶς εἰς πᾶσαν τὴν ἀλήθειαν· οὐ γὰρ λαλήσει ἀφ' ἑαυτοῦ,
you into all   the   truth;   not for will He speak from Himself,
ἀλλ' ὅσα ἂν ἀκούση λαλήσει, καὶ τὰ ἐρχόμενα ἀναγγελεῖ
but   what ever He hears He will speak, and the coming things He will announce

**14** ὑμῖν. ἐκεῖνος ἐμὲ δοξάσει, ὅτι ἐκ τοῦ ἐμοῦ λήψεται, καὶ
to you. That One Me will glorify because from   Mine He will receive and

**15** ἀναγγελεῖ ὑμῖν. πάντα ὅσα ἔχει ὁ πατὴρ ἐμά ἐστι· διὰ
will announce to you. All things which has the Father, Mine   is; for this
τοῦτο εἶπον, ὅτι ἐκ τοῦ ἐμοῦ λήψεται, καὶ ἀναγγελει υμιν.
reason   I said that from   Mine   He receives, and will announce to you.

**16** μικρὸν καὶ οὐ θεωρεῖτέ με, καὶ πάλιν μικρὸν καὶ ὄψεσθέ με,
A little and not you behold Me, and   again a little   and you will see Me.

**17** ὅτι ἐγὼ ὑπάγω πρὸς τὸν πατέρα. εἶπον οὖν ἐκ τῶν
because I   go   to   the Father. said Therefore of the
μαθητῶν αὐτοῦ πρὸς ἀλλήλους, Τί ἐστι τοῦτο ὃ λεγει ἡμῖν,
disciples of Him to one another, What is   this which He tells us:
Μικρὸν καὶ οὐ θεωρεῖτέ με, καὶ πάλιν μικρὸν καὶ ὄψεσθέ με;
A little   and not you behold Me, and   again a little and you will see Me?

**18** καὶ ὅτι Ἐγὼ ὑπάγω πρὸς τὸν πατέρα; ἔλεγον οὖν, Τοῦτο
Also, Because I   go   to   the Father? they said Therefore, this

**19** τί ἐστιν ὃ λέγει, τὸ μικρόν; οὐκ οἴδαμεν τί λαλεῖ. ἔγνω οὖν
What is that He says, The little? do not We know what He says. knew Then
ὁ Ἰησοῦς ὅτι ἤθελον αὐτὸν ἐρωτᾶν, καὶ εἶπεν αὐτοῖς, Περὶ
Jesus that they desired Him to question, and said to them, Concerning
τούτου ζητεῖτε μετ' ἀλλήλων, ὅτι εἶπον, Μικρὸν καὶ οὐ
this do you seek with one another, because I said, A little   and not

**20** θεωρεῖτέ με, καὶ πάλιν μικρον καὶ ὄψεσθέ με; ἀμὴν ἀμὴν
you behold Me, and   again a little and you will see Me? Truly, truly,
λέγω ὑμῖν ὅτι κλαύσετε καὶ θρηνήσετε ὑμεῖς, ὁ δὲ κόσμος
I say to you that will weep and will lament you, the and world
χαρήσεται· ὑμεῖς δὲ λυπηθήσεσθε, ἀλλ' ἡ λύπη ὑμῶν εἰς
will rejoice.   you And will be grieved,   but the grief of you into

**21** χαρὰν γενήσεται. ἡ γυνὴ ὅταν τίκτη λύπην ἔχει, ὅτι ἦλθεν
joy   will become. The woman when she bears grief   has, because came
ἡ ὥρα αὐτῆς· ὅταν δὲ γεννήση τὸ παιδίον, οὐκέτι μνημονεύει
the hour of her; when but she brings forth the child, no longer she remembers
τῆς θλίψεως, διὰ τὴν χαρὰν ὅτι ἐγεννήθη ἄνθρωπος εἰς
the distress, because of the joy   that was born   a man   into

**22** τὸν κόσμον. καὶ ὑμεῖς οὖν λύπην μὲν νῦν ἔχετε· πάλιν δὲ
the   world. And you, therefore, grief indeed now have;   again but
ὄψομαι ὑμᾶς, καὶ χαρήσεται ὑμῶν ἡ καρδία, καὶ τὴν χαρὰν
will see you, and will rejoice of you the heart, and the   joy

**23** ὑμῶν οὐδεὶς αἴρει ἀφ' ὑμῶν. καὶ ἐν ἐκείνη τῇ ἡμέρα ἐμὲ οὐκ
of you no one takes from you. And in that   — day Me not
ἐρωτήσετε οὐδέν. ἀμὴν ἀμὴν λέγω ὑμῖν ὅτι ὅσα ἂν αἰτή-
you will question nothing. Truly, truly, I say to you that whatever you

**24** σητε τὸν πατέρα ἐν τῷ ὀνόματί μου, δώσει ὑμῖν. ἕως ἄρτι
ask   the Father in the name of Me, He will give you. Until now
οὐκ ἠτήσατε οὐδὲν ἐν τῷ ὀνόματί μου· αἰτεῖτε, καὶ λήψεσθε,
not you asked nothing in the name of Me; ask, and you will receive

that your joy may be full.
[25] I have spoken these things to you in allegories; (but) an hour comes when I will no longer speak to you in allegories, but I will declare the Father plainly to you. [26] In that day you will ask in My name, and I do not tell you that I will petition the Father about you; [27] for the Father Himself loves you, because you have loved Me, and have believed that I came out from God. [28] I came out from the Father, and have come into the world; again, I leave the world and go to the Father. [29] His disciples said to Him, Behold, now You speak plainly and speak no allegory. [30] Now we know that You know all things, and do not need for anyone to ask You. By this we believe that You came forth from God. [31] Jesus answered them, Do you believe now? [32] Behold, an hour is coming and now has come, that you will each be scattered to his own, and you will leave Me alone; yet I am not alone, for the Father is with Me. [33] I have spoken these things to you that you may have peace in Me. You have pain in the world; but be of good courage, I have overcome the world.

ἵνα ἡ χαρὰ ὑμῶν ᾖ πεπληρωμένη.
that the joy of you may be   filled.

25  Ταῦτα ἐν παροιμίαις λελάληκα ὑμῖν· ἔρχεται ὥρα ὅτε
These things in allegories   I have spoken to you;  comes an hour when
οὐκέτι ἐν παροιμίαις λαλήσω ὑμῖν, ἀλλὰ παρρησίᾳ περὶ τοῦ
no longer in allegories I will speak to you, but   plainly concerning the

26  πατρὸς ἀναγγελῶ ὑμῖν. ἐν ἐκείνῃ τῇ ἡμέρᾳ ἐν τῷ ὀνόματί μου
Father I will declare to you. In that  — day in the  name of Me
αἰτήσεσθε· καὶ οὐ λέγω ὑμῖν ὅτι ἐγὼ ἐρωτήσω τὸν πατέρα
you will ask, and not I tell you that I   will petition the Father

27  περὶ ὑμῶν· αὐτὸς γὰρ ὁ πατὴρ φιλεῖ ὑμᾶς, ὅτι ὑμεῖς ἐμὲ
concerning you; Himself for the Father  loves  you, because you Me
πεφιλήκατε, καὶ πεπιστεύκατε ὅτι ἐγὼ παρὰ τοῦ Θεοῦ
have loved,   and  have believed that I   from  — God

28  ἐξῆλθον. ἐξῆλθον παρὰ τοῦ πατρός, καὶ ἐλήλυθα εἰς τὸν
came forth. I came forth from the  Father, and have come into the
κόσμον· πάλιν ἀφίημι τὸν κόσμον, καὶ πορεύομαι πρὸς τὸν
world;  again I leave  the  world,  and  go  to the

29  πατέρα. λέγουσιν αὐτῷ οἱ μαθηταὶ αὐτοῦ, Ἴδε, νῦν παρ-
Father.  say   to Him The disciples of Him,  Behold, now

30  ρησίᾳ λαλεῖς, καὶ παροιμίαν οὐδεμίαν λέγεις. νῦν οἴδαμεν
plainly You speak, and  allegory   not one You say.  Now we know
ὅτι οἶδας πάντα, καὶ οὐ χρείαν ἔχεις ἵνα τίς σε ἐρωτᾷ ἐν
that You know all things, and no  need  have that anyone You query; by

31  τούτῳ πιστεύομεν ὅτι ἀπὸ Θεοῦ ἐξῆλθες. ἀπεκρίθη αὐτοῖς ὁ
this  we believe  that from God You came. answered   them  —

32  Ἰησοῦς, Ἄρτι πιστεύετε; ἰδού, ἔρχεται ὥρα καὶ νῦν ἐλή-
Jesus,  Now do you believe? Behold, comes  an hour and now has
λυθεν, ἵνα σκορπισθῆτε ἕκαστος εἰς τὰ ἴδια, καὶ ἐμὲ μόνον
come, that you are scattered,  each one  to the own things, and Me alone

33  ἀφῆτε· καὶ οὐκ εἰμὶ μόνος, ὅτι ὁ πατὴρ μετ᾽ ἐμοῦ ἐστι. ταῦτα
you leave; and not I am alone, because the Father with Me  is. These things
λελάληκα ὑμῖν, ἵνα ἐν ἐμοὶ εἰρήνην ἔχητε. ἐν τῷ κόσμῳ
I have spoken to you, that in  Me  peace you may have. In the  world
θλῖψιν ἕξετε· ἀλλὰ θαρσεῖτε, ἐγὼ νενίκηκα τὸν κόσμον.
distress you have, but be encouraged, I  have overcome the world.

## CHAPTER 17

[1] Jesus said these things, and lifted up His eyes to Heaven and said, Father, the hour has come. Glorify Your Son, that Your Son also may glorify You; [2] as You gave Him authority over all flesh, that (of) all which You have given Him, He should give to them everlasting life. [3] And this is the everlasting life, that they should know You, the only true God, and Jesus Christ whom You have sent. [4] I have glorified You on the earth; I finished the work that You have given Me to do. [5] And now You glorify Me, Father, with Yourself, with the glory which I had with You before.

## CHAPTER 17

1  Ταῦτα ἐλάλησεν ὁ Ἰησοῦς, καὶ ἐπῆρε τοὺς ὀφθαλμοὺς
These things spoke  —  Jesus,  and lifting up the  eyes
αὐτοῦ εἰς τὸν οὐρανόν, καὶ εἶπε, Πάτερ, ἐλήλυθεν ἡ ὥρα·
of Him to  —  Heaven,  and said, Father, has come  the  hour

2  δόξασόν σου τὸν υἱόν, ἵνα καὶ ὁ υἱός σου δοξάσῃ σε· καθὼς
glorify   of You the Son, that also the Son of You may glorify You.  As
ἔδωκας αὐτῷ ἐξουσίαν πάσης σαρκός, ἵνα πᾶν ὃ δέδωκας
You gave Him authority  of all  flesh,  that all which You gave

3  αὐτῷ, δώσῃ αὐτοῖς ζωὴν αἰώνιον. αὕτη δέ ἐστιν ἡ αἰώνιος
to Him, He may give to them life everlasting. this And  is  everlasting
ζωή, ἵνα γινώσκωσί σε τὸν μόνον ἀληθινὸν Θεόν, καὶ ὃν
life, that they may know You the only  true  God, and whom

4  ἀπέστειλας Ἰησοῦν Χριστόν. ἐγὼ σε ἐδόξασα ἐπὶ τῆς γῆς·
You sent,  Jesus  Christ.  I  You glorified  on the earth,

5  τὸ ἔργον ἐτελείωσα ὃ δέδωκάς μοι ἵνα ποιήσω. καὶ νῦν
the work  finishing which You gave to Me that I should do. And now
δόξασόν με σύ, πάτερ, παρὰ σεαυτῷ τῇ δόξῃ ᾗ εἶχον πρὸ
glorify  Me You, Father,  with Yourself with the glory that I had before

I had with you before the existence of the world. [6] I revealed Your name to the men whom You have given Me out of the world. They were Yours, and You have given them to Me, and they have kept Your word. [7] Now they have known that all things whatever You have given Me are of You; [8] for the words which You have given Me, I have given them, and they received and knew truly that I came out from You, and they believed that You sent Me. [9] I pray for them; I do not pray for the world, but for those whom You have given Me, for they are Yours; [10] and all My things are Yours, and Yours are Mine, and I have been glorified in them. [11] And I no longer am in the world, and these are in the world, and I come to You. Holy Father, keep them in Your name, those whom You have given Me, that they may be one as We. [12] When I was with them in the world, I was keeping them in Your name; I watched over those You have given to Me, and not one of them was lost, except the son of perdition, that the Scripture might be fulfilled. [13] And now I come to You; and I speak these things in the world that they may have My joy fulfilled in them. [14] I have given them Your word, and the world hated them, because they are not of the world, as I am not of the world. [15] I do not pray for You to take them out of the world, but for You to keep them from evil. [16] They are not of the world, even as I am not of the world. [17] Sanctify them by Your truth; Your word is truth. [18] As You sent Me into the world, I also sent them into the world; [19] and I sanctify Myself for them, that they may also be sanctified in truth. [20] Neither do I pray for these alone, but also for those who will believe into Me through their words; [21] that all

**6** τοῦ τὸν κόσμον εἶναι παρὰ σοί. ἐφανέρωσά σου τὸ ὄνομα
the of the world being with You. I revealed of You the name
τοῖς ἀνθρώποις οὓς δέδωκάς μοι ἐκ τοῦ κόσμου· σοὶ ἦσαν,
to the men whom You gave to Me out of the world. To You they were,
καὶ ἐμοὶ αὐτοὺς δέδωκας· καὶ τὸν λόγον σου τετηρήκασι.
and to Me them You gave; and the word of You they have kept.

**7** νῦν ἔγνωκαν ὅτι πάντα ὅσα δέδωκάς μοι, παρὰ σοῦ ἐστιν·
Now they have known that all whatever You gave to Me from You is;

**8** ὅτι τὰ ῥήματα ἃ δέδωκάς μοι, δέδωκα αὐτοῖς· καὶ αὐτοὶ
because the words which You gave to Me I have given to them, and they
ἔλαβον, καὶ ἔγνωσαν ἀληθῶς ὅτι παρὰ σοῦ ἐξῆλθον, καὶ
received, and knew truly that from/beside You I came forth; and

**9** ἐπίστευσαν ὅτι σύ με ἀπέστειλας. ἐγὼ περὶ αὐτῶν ἐρωτῶ·
they believed that You Me sent. I concerning them petition;
οὐ περὶ τοῦ κόσμου ἐρωτῶ, ἀλλὰ περὶ ὧν δέδωκάς μοι, ὅτι
not about the world I petition, but concerning whom You gave Me, for

**10** σοί εἰσι· καὶ τὰ ἐμὰ πάντα σά ἐστι, καὶ τὰ σὰ ἐμά· καὶ
to You they are, and things My all Yours are, and Your things Mine; and

**11** δεδόξασμαι ἐν αὐτοῖς. καὶ οὐκέτι εἰμὶ ἐν τῷ κόσμῳ, καὶ
I have been glorified in them. And no longer am I in the world, and
οὗτοι ἐν τῷ κόσμῳ εἰσί, καὶ ἐγὼ πρός σε ἔρχομαι. πάτερ
these in the world are, and I to You come. Father
ἅγιε, τήρησον αὐτοὺς ἐν τῷ ὀνόματί σου, οὓς δέδωκάς μοι,
Holy. keep them in the name of You. whom You gave to Me

**12** ἵνα ὦσιν ἕν, καθὼς ἡμεῖς. ὅτε ἤμην μετ᾽ αὐτῶν ἐν τῷ κόσμῳ,
that may be one, as we. When I was with them in the world.
ἐγὼ ἐτήρουν αὐτοὺς ἐν τῷ ὀνόματί σου· οὓς δέδωκάς μοι
I was keeping them in the name of You; whom You gave to Me
ἐφύλαξα, καὶ οὐδεὶς ἐξ αὐτῶν ἀπώλετο, εἰ μὴ ὁ υἱὸς τῆς
I guarded, and not one of them perished. except the son —

**13** ἀπωλείας, ἵνα ἡ γραφὴ πληρωθῇ. νῦν δὲ πρός σε ἔρχομαι,
of perdition, that the Scripture might be fulfilled. now And to You I come.
καὶ ταῦτα λαλῶ ἐν τῷ κόσμῳ, ἵνα ἔχωσι τὴν χαρὰν τὴν
and these things I speak in the world. that they have - joy -

**14** ἐμὴν πεπληρωμένην ἐν αὐτοῖς. ἐγὼ δέδωκα αὐτοῖς τὸν
My having been fulfilled in them. I have given them the
λόγον σου, καὶ ὁ κόσμος ἐμίσησεν αὐτούς, ὅτι οὐκ εἰσὶν ἐκ
word of You, and the world hated them because not they are of

**15** τοῦ κόσμου, καθὼς ἐγὼ οὐκ εἰμὶ ἐκ τοῦ κόσμου. οὐκ ἐρωτῶ
the world, even as I not am of the world. not I petition
ἵνα ἄρῃς αὐτοὺς ἐκ τοῦ κόσμου, ἀλλ᾽ ἵνα τηρήσῃς αὐτοὺς
that You take them out of the world, but that You keep them

**16** ἐκ τοῦ πονηροῦ. ἐκ τοῦ κόσμου οὐκ εἰσί, καθὼς ἐγὼ ἐκ τοῦ
from - evil. Of the world not they are, even as I of the

**17** κόσμου· οὐκ εἰμί. ἁγίασον αὐτοὺς ἐν τῇ ἀληθείᾳ σου· ὁ
world not am. Sanctify them in the truth of You; -

**18** λόγος ὁ σὸς ἀλήθειά ἐστι. καθὼς ἐμὲ ἀπέστειλας εἰς τὸν
word - Your truth is. Even as Me You sent into the

**19** κόσμον, κἀγὼ ἀπέστειλα αὐτοὺς εἰς τὸν κόσμον. καὶ ὑπὲρ
world, I also sent them into the world. And for
αὐτῶν ἐγὼ ἁγιάζω ἐμαυτόν, ἵνα καὶ αὐτοὶ ὦσιν ἡγιασμένοι
them I sanctify Myself, that also they may be sanctified

**20** ἐν ἀληθείᾳ. οὐ περὶ τούτων δὲ ἐρωτῶ μόνον, ἀλλὰ καὶ περὶ
in truth. not concerning these And I petition only, but also concerning

**21** τῶν πιστευόντων διὰ τοῦ λόγου αὐτῶν εἰς ἐμέ· ἵνα πάντες
those who shall believe through the word of them into Me; that all

may be one, as You (are) in Me, Father, and I in You, that they also may be one in Us, that the world may believe that You sent Me. [22] And I have given them the glory that You have given Me, that they may be one, as We are one; [23] I in them, and You in Me, that they may be perfected in one, and that the world may know that You sent Me and loved them, even as You loved Me. [24] Father, I desire that whom You have given Me, that where I am, those that may be with Me also, that they may behold My glory which You gave Me because You loved Me before (the) foundation of (the) world. [25] Righteous Father, indeed the world did not know You, but I knew You, and these knew that You sent Me, [26] and I made known Your name to them, and will make known that the love (with) which You loved Me may be in them, and I in them.

CHAPTER 18

[1] Having said these things Jesus went out with His disciples beyond the torrent Kidron, where there was a garden into which He and His disciples entered. [2] And Judas who was delivering Him up also knew the place, because Jesus often was there with His disciples. [3] Therefore Judas having received the band and officers from the chief priests and Pharisees, came there with torches and lamps and weapons. [4] Then Jesus knowing all things that were coming upon Him, having gone forth said to them, Whom do you seek? [5] They answered Him, Jesus the Nazarene. Jesus said to them, I AM. And Judas who was delivering Him up was also standing with them. [6] Therefore when He said to them, I AM, they went backward and fell to (the) ground. [7] Again He asked them, Whom do you seek? And they said, Jesus the Nazarene. [8] Jesus answered, I told you that I

ἐν ὦσι· καθὼς σύ, πάτερ, ἐν ἐμοί, κἀγὼ ἐν σοί, ἵνα καὶ αὐτοὶ
one may be, as You, Father, in Me,    and I in You, that also they
ἐν ἡμῖν ἐν ὦσιν· ἵνα ὁ κόσμος πιστεύσῃ ὅτι σύ με ἀπέστειλας.
in Us one may be, that the world may believe that You Me sent.

22 καὶ ἐγὼ τὴν δόξαν ἣν δέδωκάς μοι, δέδωκα αὐτοῖς, ἵνα
And I the glory which You have given Me have given to them, that

23 ὦσιν ἕν, καθὼς ἡμεῖς ἕν ἐσμεν. ἐγὼ ἐν αὐτοῖς, καὶ σὺ ἐν ἐμοί,
they may be one, as We one are; I in them, and You in Me,
ἵνα ὦσι τετελειωμένοι εἰς ἕν, καὶ ἵνα γινώσκῃ ὁ κόσμος ὅτι
that they may be perfected into one, and that may know the world that
σύ με ἀπέστειλας, καὶ ἠγάπησας αὐτούς, καθὼς ἐμὲ ἠγάπη-
You Me sent and loved them even as Me You

24 σας. πάτερ, οὓς δέδωκάς μοι, θέλω ἵνα ὅπου εἰμὶ ἐγώ,
loved. Father, whom You have given to Me, I desire that where am I;
κἀκεῖνοι ὦσι μετ' ἐμοῦ· ἵνα θεωρῶσι τὴν δόξαν τὴν ἐμήν,
those also may be with Me, that they may behold glory — My,
ἣν ἔδωκάς μοι, ὅτι ἠγάπησάς με προ καταβολῆς κόσμου.
which You gave Me because You loved Me before foundation of (the) world.

25 πάτερ δίκαιε, καὶ ὁ κόσμος σε οὐκ ἔγνω, ἐγὼ δέ σε ἔγνων,
Father Righteous, indeed the world You not knew, I but You knew,

26 καὶ οὗτοι ἔγνωσαν ὅτι σύ με ἀπέστειλας· καὶ ἐγνώρισα
and these knew that You Me sent; and I made known
αὐτοῖς τὸ ὄνομά σου, καὶ γνωρίσω· ἵνα ἡ ἀγάπη, ἣν
to them the name of You, and will make known; that the love (with) which
ἠγάπησάς. με, ἐν αὐτοῖς ᾖ, κἀγὼ ἐν αὐτοῖς.
You loved Me, in them may be, and I in them.

CHAPTER 18

1 Ταῦτα εἰπὼν ὁ Ἰησοῦς ἐξῆλθε σὺν τοῖς μαθηταῖς αὐτοῦ
These things having said Jesus went forth with the disciples of Him
πέραν τοῦ χειμάρρου τῶν Κέδρων, ὅπου ἦν κῆπος, εἰς ὃν
across the torrent — of Kidron, where was a garden, into which

2 εἰσῆλθεν αὐτὸς καὶ οἱ μαθηταὶ αὐτοῦ. ᾔδει δὲ καὶ Ἰούδας, ὁ
entered He and the disciples of Him. knew And also Judas, he
παραδιδοὺς αὐτόν, τὸν τόπον· ὅτι πολλάκις συνήχθη ὁ
betraying Him, the place, because many times assembled

3 Ἰησοῦς ἐκεῖ μετὰ τῶν μαθητῶν αὐτοῦ. ὁ οὖν Ἰούδας, λαβὼν
Jesus there with the disciples of Him. Therefore Judas, receiving
τὴν σπεῖραν, καὶ ἐκ τῶν ἀρχιερέων καὶ Φαρισαίων ὑπηρέτας,
the band, and from the chief priests and the Pharisees officers,

4 ἔρχεται ἐκεῖ μετὰ φανῶν καὶ λαμπάδων καὶ ὅπλων. Ἰησοῦς
comes there with torches and lamps and weapons Jesus
οὖν, εἰδὼς πάντα τὰ ἐρχόμενα ἐπ' αὐτόν, ἐξελθὼν εἶπεν
Then, knowing all the things coming on Him, going forth said

5 αὐτοῖς, Τίνα ζητεῖτε; ἀπεκρίθησαν αὐτῷ, Ἰησοῦν τὸν
to them, Whom do you seek? They answered Him, Jesus the
Ναζωραῖον. λέγει αὐτοῖς ὁ Ἰησοῦς, Ἐγώ εἰμι. εἱστήκει δὲ
Nazarene. tells them — Jesus, I AM. stood And

6 καὶ Ἰούδας ὁ παραδιδοὺς αὐτὸν μετ' αὐτῶν. ὡς οὖν εἶπεν
also Judas, the (one) betraying Him, with them. when Then He told
αὐτοῖς ὅτι Ἐγώ εἰμι, ἀπῆλθον εἰς τὰ ὀπίσω, καὶ ἔπεσον
them, — I AM. they went away into the rear, and fell

7 χαμαί. πάλιν οὖν αὐτοὺς ἐπηρώτησε, Τίνα ζητεῖτε; οἱ δὲ
to earth. Again, then, He inquired, Whom do you seek? they And

8 εἶπον, Ἰησοῦν τὸν Ναζωραῖον. ἀπεκρίθη ὁ Ἰησοῦς, Εἶπον
said, Jesus the Nazarene. answered — Jesus, I told

AM. Therefore if you seek
Me, allow these to go
away; [9] that the Word
might be fulfilled which He
said, "Of those whom You
have given Me, I did not
lose one." [10] Then
Simon Peter having a
sword drew it and struck
the slave of the high priest,
and cut off his right ear.
And the slave's name was
Malchus. [11] Then Jesus
said to Peter, Put your
sword into the sheath; the
cup which the Father has
given Me, should I not
drink it? [12] Then the
band and the chief captains
and the officers of the
Jews took hold of Jesus
and bound Him. [13] And
they led Him away to
Annas first; for he was
father-in-law of Caiaphas,
who was high priest that
year. [14] And it was
Caiaphas who gave counsel
to the Jews, that it was
profitable for one man to
perish for the people.
[15] Now Simon Peter and
the other disciple followed
Jesus. And that disciple
was known to the high
priest, and went in with
Jesus into the court of the
high priest. [16] But Peter
stood at the door outside.
Therefore the other
disciple who was known to
the high priest went out
and spoke to the
doorkeeper and brought
Peter in. [17] Therefore
the maid, the doorkeeper,
said to Peter, Are you not
also of the disciples of this
man? He said, I am not.
[18] But the slaves and the
officers were standing,
having made a fire of coals,
for it was cold, and were
warming themselves; and
Peter was standing with
them and warming himself.
[19] Then the high priest
questioned Jesus about His
disciples, and about His
teaching. [20] Jesus
answered him, I openly
spoke to the world; I
always taught in the
synagogue and in the
Temple, where the Jews

9 ὑμῖν ὅτι ἐγώ εἰμι· εἰ οὖν ἐμὲ ζητεῖτε, ἄφετε τούτους ὑπάγειν·
  you that I AM. If, then, Me you seek, allow these to go;

9 ἵνα πληρωθῇ ὁ λόγος ὅν εἶπεν ὅτι Οὕς δέδωκάς μοι, οὐκ
  that might be fulfilled the word which said, — Whom You gave to Me, not

10 ἀπώλεσα ἐξ αὐτῶν οὐδένα. Σίμων οὖν Πέτρος ἔχων μάχαιραν
   I lost (any) of them, no one. Simon Then Peter having a sword,

   εἵλκυσεν αὐτήν, καὶ ἔπαισε τὸν τοῦ ἀρχιερέως δοῦλον, καὶ
   drew it, and struck the of the high priest slave, and

   ἀπέκοψεν αὐτοῦ τὸ ὠτίον τὸ δεξιόν. ἦν δὲ ὄνομα τῷ δούλῳ
   cut off of him the ear — right. was And a name to the slave,

11 Μάλχος. εἶπεν οὖν ὁ Ἰησοῦς τῷ Πέτρῳ, Βάλε τὴν μάχαιράν
   Malchus. said Then — Jesus to Peter, Put the sword

   σου εἰς τὴν θήκην· τὸ ποτήριον ὅ δέδωκέ μοι ὁ πατήρ, οὐ μὴ
   of you into the sheath; the cup which has given Me the Father, in no way

   πίω αὐτό;
   shall I drink it?

12 Ἡ οὖν σπεῖρα καὶ ὁ χιλίαρχος καὶ οἱ ὑπηρέται τῶν Ἰου-
   the Then band and the chiliarch and the officers of the

13 δαίων συνέλαβον τὸν Ἰησοῦν, καὶ ἔδησαν αὐτόν, καὶ ἀπή-
   Jews together seized Jesus, and bound Him, and led

   γαγον αὐτὸν πρὸς Ἄνναν πρῶτον· ἦν γὰρ πενθερὸς τοῦ
   away Him to Annas first; he was for father-in-law —

14 Καϊάφα, ὅς ἦν ἀρχιερεὺς τοῦ ἐνιαυτοῦ ἐκείνου. ἦν δὲ Καϊάφας
   of Caiaphas, who was high priest — of year that. was And Caiaphas

   ὁ συμβουλεύσας τοῖς Ἰουδαίοις, ὅτι συμφέρει ἕνα ἄνθρωπον
   the (one) having advised the Jews that it is profitable for one man

   ἀπολέσθαι ὑπὲρ τοῦ λαοῦ.
   to perish for the people.

15 Ἠκολούθει δὲ τῷ Ἰησοῦ Σίμων Πέτρος, καὶ ἄλλος μαθητής.
   followed And — Jesus Simon Peter and another disciple.

   ὁ δὲ μαθητὴς ἐκεῖνος ἦν γνωστὸς τῷ ἀρχιερεῖ, καὶ συνεισῆλθε
   And disciple that was known to the high priest, and went in with

16 τῷ Ἰησοῦ εἰς τὴν αὐλὴν τοῦ ἀρχιερέως· ὁ δὲ Πέτρος εἱστήκει
   Jesus into the court of the high priest; —but Peter stood

   πρὸς τῇ θύρᾳ ἔξω. ἐξῆλθεν οὖν ὁ μαθητὴς ὁ ἄλλος ὅς ἦν
   at the door outside. went out Then the disciple — other who was

   γνωστὸς τῷ ἀρχιερεῖ, καὶ εἶπε τῇ θυρωρῷ, καὶ εἰσήγαγε τὸν
   known to the high priest, and spoke to the portress, and brought in —

17 Πέτρον. λέγει οὖν ἡ παιδίσκη ἡ θυρωρὸς τῷ Πέτρῳ, Μὴ καὶ
   Peter. says Then the maidservant, the portress, — to Peter, Not also

   σὺ ἐκ τῶν μαθητῶν εἶ τοῦ ἀνθρώπου τούτου; λέγει ἐκεῖνος,
   you of the disciples are — of man this? says That one

18 Οὐκ εἰμί. εἱστήκεισαν δὲ οἱ δοῦλοι καὶ οἱ ὑπηρέται ἀνθρακιὰν
   Not I am. were standing And the slaves and the officers, a fire of coals

   πεποιηκότες, ὅτι ψῦχος ἦν, καὶ ἐθερμαίνοντο· ἦν δὲ μετ'
   having made, because cold it was, and were warming; was and with

   αὐτῶν ὁ Πέτρος ἑστὼς καὶ θερμαινόμενος.
   them — Peter standing and warming himself.

19 Ὁ οὖν ἀρχιερεὺς ἠρώτησε τὸν Ἰησοῦν περὶ τῶν μαθητῶν
   the Then high priest questioned — Jesus concerning the disciples

20 αὐτοῦ, καὶ περὶ τῆς διδαχῆς αὐτοῦ. ἀπεκρίθη αὐτῷ ὁ
   of Him, and concerning the teaching of Him. answered him —

   Ἰησοῦς, Ἐγὼ παρρησίᾳ ἐλάλησα τῷ κόσμῳ· ἐγὼ πάντοτε
   Jesus, I publicly spoke to the world; I always

   ἐδίδαξα ἐν τῇ συναγωγῇ καὶ ἐν τῷ ἱερῷ, ὅπου πάντοτε ο
   taught in the synagogue and in the Temple, where always

always come together; and I spoke nothing in secret. [21] Why do you question Me? Ask those who have heard what I spoke to them; behold, they know what I said. [22] But on His saying these things one of the officers standing by gave a blow with the palm to Jesus, saying, Do you answer the high priest this way? [23] Jesus answered him, If I spoke evil, bear witness concerning the evil but if well, why do you strike Me? [24] Annas sent Him bound to Caiaphas the high priest.

[25] Now Simon Peter was standing and warming himself. They therefore said to him, Are you not also of his disciples? He denied, and said, I am not. [26] One of the slaves of the high priest, being kinsman (of him) of whom Peter cut off the ear, said, Did I not see you in the garden with him? [27] Again then Peter denied, and immediately a cock crowed.

[28] Then they led Jesus from Caiaphas into the praetorium, and it was early. And they did not go into the praetorium, that they might not be defiled, but that they might eat the Passover. [29] Therefore Pilate went out to them, and said, What charge do you bring against this man? [30] They answered and said to him, If he were not an evil doer, we would have not delivered him up to you. [31] Then Pilate said to them, You take him and judge him according to your law. Then the Jews said to him, It is not permitted to us to put anyone to death — [32] that the word of Jesus might be fulfilled which He spoke signifying by what death He was about to die. [33] Then Pilate again went into the praetorium and called Jesus, and said to Him, Are you the king of the Jews? [34] Jesus answered him, Do you say this from yourself,

---

**21** Ἰουδαῖοι συνέρχονται, καὶ ἐν κρυπτῷ ἐλάλησα οὐδέν. τί με
Jews   come together,  and  in secret   I spoke   nothing. Why Me
ἐπερωτᾷς ; ἐπερώτησον τοὺς ἀκηκοότας, τί ἐλάλησα αὐτοῖς·
do you question? Question  those having heard  what I spoke  to them.

**22** ἴδε, οὗτοι οἴδασιν ἃ εἶπον ἐγώ· ταῦτα δὲ αὐτοῦ εἰπόντος,
Behold, these know what said   I. these things And He  saying,
εἰς τῶν ὑπηρετῶν παρεστηκὼς ἔδωκε ῥάπισμα τῷ Ἰησοῦ,
one of the officers   standing by   gave  a blow  — to Jesus,

**23** εἰπών, Οὕτως ἀποκρίνῃ τῷ ἀρχιερεῖ ; ἀπεκρίθη αὐτῷ ὁ
saying, Thus   answer you  the high priest? answered to him  —
Ἰησοῦς, Εἰ κακῶς ἐλάλησα, μαρτύρησον περὶ τοῦ κακοῦ·
Jesus, If evilly  I spoke,  bear witness concerning the  evil;

**24** εἰ δὲ καλῶς, τί με δέρεις ; ἀπέστειλεν οὖν αὐτὸν ὁ Ἄννας
if but well,  why Me do you beat? Sent  therefore  Him  — Annas
δεδεμένον πρὸς Καϊάφαν τὸν ἀρχιερέα.
being bound to   Caiaphas  the  high priest.

**25** Ἦν δὲ Σίμων Πέτρος ἑστὼς καὶ θερμαινόμενος· εἶπον οὖν
was And Simon  Peter  standing and  warming himself. they said Then
αὐτῷ, Μὴ καὶ σὺ ἐκ τῶν μαθητῶν αὐτοῦ εἶ ; ἠρνήσατο
to him, Not also you of the  disciples  of him are?   denied

**26** ἐκεῖνος, καὶ εἶπεν, Οὐκ εἰμί. λέγει εἷς ἐκ τῶν δούλων τοῦ
That one, and said,  not I am. says One of  the  slaves of the
ἀρχιερέως, συγγενὴς ὢν οὗ ἀπέκοψε Πέτρος τὸ ὠτίον,
high priest,  a relative  being of whom cut off  Peter  the  ear,

**27** Οὐκ ἐγώ σε εἶδον ἐν τῷ κήπῳ μετ' αὐτοῦ ; πάλιν οὖν
Not I  you did see in  the  garden with  Him?  again Then
ἠρνήσατο ὁ Πέτρος, καὶ εὐθέως ἀλέκτωρ ἐφώνησεν.
denied  — Peter,  and at once  a cock  sounded.

**28** Ἄγουσιν οὖν τὸν Ἰησοῦν ἀπὸ τοῦ Καϊάφα εἰς τὸ πραιτώ-
they lead Then  — Jesus from  — Caiaphas to  the  praetorium;
ριον· ἦν δὲ πρωΐα, καὶ αὐτοὶ οὐκ εἰσῆλθον εἰς τὸ πραιτώ-
it was and  early;  and  they did not  enter into the praetorium,

**29** ριον, ἵνα μὴ μιανθῶσιν, ἀλλ' ἵνα φάγωσι τὸ πάσχα. ἐξῆλθεν
lest  they be defiled, but that they may eat the Passover. went out
οὖν ὁ Πιλᾶτος πρὸς αὐτούς, καὶ εἶπε, Τίνα κατηγορίαν
Therefore Pilate  to   them,  and  said,  What accusation

**30** φέρετε κατὰ τοῦ ἀνθρώπου τούτου ; ἀπεκρίθησαν καὶ εἶπον
bring you against   man    this?  They answered  said
αὐτῷ, Εἰ μὴ ἦν οὗτος κακοποιός, οὐκ ἄν σοι παρεδώκαμεν
to him, Unless was this one an evildoer, not then to you we had delivered

**31** αὐτόν. εἶπεν οὖν αὐτοῖς ὁ Πιλᾶτος, Λάβετε αὐτὸν ὑμεῖς, καὶ
him.  said Then to them  Pilate,  take  him You,  and
κατὰ τὸν νόμον ὑμῶν κρίνατε αὐτόν. εἶπον οὖν αὐτῷ οἱ
according to the law of you judge  him.  said Then to him the

**32** Ἰουδαῖοι, Ἡμῖν οὐκ ἔξεστιν ἀποκτεῖναι οὐδένα· ἵνα ὁ λόγος
Jews,  for us Not it is lawful to put to death no one; that the word
τοῦ Ἰησοῦ πληρωθῇ, ὃν εἶπε, σημαίνων ποίῳ θανάτῳ
— of Jesus might be fulfilled, which He said, signifying by what kind (of) death
ἤμελλεν ἀποθνήσκειν.
He was about to die.

**33** Εἰσῆλθεν οὖν εἰς τὸ πραιτώριον πάλιν ὁ Πιλᾶτος, καὶ
entered  Then into the  praetorium  again  Pilate,  and
ἐφώνησε τὸν Ἰησοῦν, καὶ εἶπεν αὐτῷ, Σὺ εἶ ὁ βασιλεὺς τῶν
called  — Jesus, and  said to Him, you Are the king  of the

**34** Ἰουδαίων ; ἀπεκρίθη αὐτῷ ὁ Ἰησοῦς, Ἀφ' ἑαυτοῦ σὺ τοῦτο
Jews?  answered  him  — Jesus, From yourself  you this

35 λέγεις, ἢ ἄλλοι σοι εἶπον περὶ ἐμοῦ ; ἀπεκρίθη ὁ Πιλᾶτος,
   say,   or others you   told   about Me?   answered      Pilate,
   Μήτι ἐγὼ Ἰουδαῖός εἰμι ; τὸ ἔθνος τὸ σὸν καὶ οἱ ἀρχιερεῖς
   Not  I   a Jew    am?    nation   Your and the chief priests

36 παρέδωκάν σε ἐμοί· τί ἐποίησας ; ἀπεκρίθη ὁ Ἰησοῦς, Ἡ
   delivered up You to me; what did you do? answered   —  Jesus,
   βασιλεία ἡ ἐμὴ οὐκ ἔστιν ἐκ τοῦ κόσμου τούτου· εἰ ἐκ τοῦ
   kingdom  My  not is   of   world  this;  If of
   κόσμου τούτου ἦν ἡ βασιλεία ἡ ἐμή, οἱ ὑπηρέται ἂν οἱ ἐμοὶ
   world  this  was  kingdom   My,  servants would  My
   ἠγωνίζοντο, ἵνα μὴ παραδοθῶ τοῖς Ἰουδαίοις· νῦν δὲ ἡ
   have fought,  that not I should be delivered to the Jews.  now But

37 βασιλεία ἡ ἐμὴ οὐκ ἔστιν ἐντεῦθεν. εἶπεν οὖν αὐτῷ ὁ Πιλᾶτος,
   kingdom  My  not is  from here.  said Then to Him    Pilate,
   Οὐκοῦν βασιλεὺς εἶ σύ ; ἀπεκρίθη ὁ Ἰησοῦς, Σὺ λέγεις ὅτι
   Really not a king are you? answered   —  Jesus, You say  that
   βασιλεύς εἰμι ἐγώ. ἐγὼ εἰς τοῦτο γεγέννημαι, καὶ εἰς τοῦτο
   a king  am I  I    for this I have been born, and for this
   ἐλήλυθα εἰς τὸν κόσμον, ἵνα μαρτυρήσω τῇ ἀληθείᾳ. πᾶς ὁ
   I have come into the world, that I might witness to the truth, everyone

38 ὢν ἐκ τῆς ἀληθείας ἀκούει μου τῆς φωνῆς. λέγει αὐτῷ ὁ
   being of the truth    hears of Me the voice.  says to Him
   Πιλᾶτος, Τί ἐστιν ἀλήθεια ;
   Pilate, What is   truth?

   Καὶ τοῦτο εἰπών, πάλιν ἐξῆλθε πρὸς τοὺς Ἰουδαίους, καὶ
   And this having said, again he went out to  the  Jews,    and

39 λέγει αὐτοῖς, Ἐγὼ οὐδεμίαν αἰτίαν εὑρίσκω ἐν αὐτῷ. ἔστι
   tells them,  I   not one   crime   find   in  him.  is
   δὲ συνήθεια ὑμῖν, ἵνα ἕνα ὑμῖν ἀπολύσω ἐν τῷ πάσχα·
   But a custom  to you, that one to you I should release at the Passover;
   βούλεσθε οὖν ὑμῖν ἀπολύσω τὸν βασιλέα τῶν Ἰουδαίων ;
   decide you, then, to you I should release the king of the Jews?

40 ἐκραύγασαν οὖν πάλιν πάντες, λέγοντες, Μὴ τοῦτον, ἀλλὰ
   cried out   Then again  all,   saying,  Not this one, but
   τὸν Βαραββᾶν· ἦν δὲ ὁ Βαραββᾶς λῃστής.
   —  Barabbas.  was But   Barabbas  a robber.

CHAPTER 19

1 Τότε οὖν ἔλαβεν ὁ Πιλᾶτος τὸν Ἰησοῦν, καὶ ἐμαστίγωσε.
  Then, therefore, took  Pilate   —  Jesus  and scourged (Him).

2 καὶ οἱ στρατιῶται πλέξαντες στέφανον ἐξ ἀκανθῶν ἐπέθηκαν
  And the soldiers  having plaited a wreath out of thorns  put (it) on
  αὐτοῦ τῇ κεφαλῇ, καὶ ἱμάτιον πορφυροῦν περιέβαλον αὐτόν,
  of Him the head,  and a garment  purple   threw around  Him;

3 καὶ ἔλεγον, Χαῖρε, ὁ βασιλεὺς τῶν Ἰουδαίων· καὶ ἐδίδουν
  and said,  Hail,  king of the  Jews;  and they gave

4 αὐτῷ ῥαπίσματα. ἐξῆλθεν οὖν πάλιν ἔξω ὁ Πιλατος, καὶ
  Him  slaps.    went out Then again outside Pilate   and
  λέγει αὐτοῖς, Ἴδε, ἄγω ὑμῖν αὐτὸν ἔξω, ἵνα γνῶτε ὅτι ἐν
  said to them, Behold, I bring to you him out.  that you may know that in

5 αὐτῷ οὐδεμίαν αἰτίαν εὑρίσκω. ἐξῆλθεν οὖν ὁ Ἰησοῦς ἔξω,
  him  not one   crime  I find.  came out Then  —  Jesus out,
  φορῶν τὸν ἀκάνθινον στέφανον καὶ τὸ πορφυροῦν ἱμάτιον.
  bearing the thorny   wreath  and the  purple  garment.

6 καὶ λέγει αὐτοῖς, Ἴδε, ὁ ἄνθρωπος. ὅτε οὖν εἶδον αὐτὸν οἱ
  And he says to them, Behold, the man!  when Then  saw  Him the

or did others say· (it)
to you about Me?
[35] Pilate answered, Am I
a Jew? Your nation and
the chief priests delivered
you up to me. What did
you do? [36] Jesus
answered, My kingdom is
not of this world; if My
kingdom were of this
world, My servants would
fight, that I might not be
delivered up to the Jews;
but now My kingdom is
not from here. [37] Then
Pilate said to Him, Then
are you a king? Jesus
answered, You say (it), for
I am a king. For this I have
been born, and for this I
have come into the world,
that I may bear witness to
the truth. Everyone that is
of the truth hears My voice.
[38] Pilate said to Him,
What is truth? And having
said this, he again went out
to the Jews and said to
them, I do not find any
fault in Him. [39] But it is
a custom with you that I
should release one to you
at the Passover; therefore
do you desire I should
release the king of the
Jews? [40] Then they all
cried out again, saying, Not
this one, but Barabbas.
Now Barabbas was a
robber.

CHAPTER 19
[1] So Pilate then took
Jesus and whipped (Him).
[2] And the soldiers
having plaited a crown of
thorns, put (it) on His
head, and threw a purple
robe around Him, [3] and
said, Hail, king of the
Jews! And they gave Him
blows with the palm.
[4] Then Pilate went out
again and said to them,
Behold, I bring him out to
you that you may know
that I do not find any fault
in him. [5] Then Jesus
went out, wearing the
thorny crown and the
purple robe; and he said to
them, Behold the man!
[6] Then when the chief

priests and the officers saw Him, they cried out, saying, Crucify! Crucify! Pilate said to them, You take him and crucify (him), for I do not find a fault. in him. [7] The Jews answered him, We have a law, and according to our law he ought to die, because he made himself son of God. [8] Then when Pilate heard this word, he was more afraid, [9] and went into the praetorium again, and said to Jesus, Where are you from? But Jesus did not give him an answer. [10] So Pilate said to Him, Do you not speak to me? Do you not know that I have authority to crucify you, and I have authority to release you? [11] Jesus answered, You would have no authority against Me if were not given to you from above. Because of this he who delivers Me up to you has greater sin. [12] From this Pilate sought to release Him; but the Jews cried out, saying, If you release this one, you are not a friend of Caesar. Everyone making himself the king speaks against Caesar. [13] Then Pilate having heard this word led Jesus out and sat down on the judgment seat, at a place called Pavement, but in Hebrew, Gabbatha. [14] And it was (the) preparation of the Passover, and (the) hour about the sixth. And he said to the Jews, Behold your king! [15] But they cried out, Away, away, crucify him! Pilate said to them, Shall I crucify your king? The chief priests answered, We have no king except Caesar. [16] Therefore then he delivered Him up to them that He might be crucified. And they took Jesus and led (Him) away. [17] And He went out bearing His cross to the place called, A Skull; which is called in Hebrew, Golgotha; [18] where they crucified

ἀρχιερεῖς καὶ οἱ ὑπηρέται, ἐκραύγασαν λέγοντες, Σταύρω-
chief priests and the officers, they cried out saying Crucify!

σον, σταύρωσον. λέγει αὐτοῖς ὁ Πιλάτος, Λάβετε αὐτὸν
Crucify! says to them Pilate, Take Him

ὑμεῖς καὶ σταυρώσατε· ἐγὼ γὰρ οὐχ εὑρίσκω ἐν αὐτῷ αἰτίαν.
you, and crucify, I for not do find in him a crime.

**7** ἀπεκρίθησαν αὐτῷ οἱ Ἰουδαῖοι, Ἡμεῖς νόμον ἔχομεν, καὶ
answered him The Jews, We a law have, and

κατὰ τὸν νόμον ἡμῶν ὀφείλει ἀποθανεῖν, ὅτι ἑαυτὸν υἱὸν τοῦ
according to the law of us he ought to die, because himself Son —

**8** Θεοῦ ἐποίησεν. ὅτε οὖν ἤκουσεν ὁ Πιλάτος τοῦτον τὸν
of God he has made. when Then heard Pilate this —

**9** λόγον, μᾶλλον ἐφοβήθη, καὶ εἰσῆλθεν εἰς τὸ πραιτώριον
word, more he was afraid, and entered into the praetorium

πάλιν, καὶ λέγει τῷ Ἰησοῦ, Πόθεν εἶ σύ; ὁ δὲ Ἰησοῦς ἀπό-
again and says — to Jesus, From where are You? But Jesus an-

**10** κρισιν οὐκ ἔδωκεν αὐτῷ. λέγει οὖν αὐτῷ ὁ Πιλάτος, Ἐμοὶ
answer did not give him. says Then to Him Pilate, To me

οὐ λαλεῖς; οὐκ οἶδας ὅτι ἐξουσίαν ἔχω σταυρῶσαί σε, καὶ
not you speak? not you know that authority I have to crucify you, and

**11** ἐξουσίαν ἔχω ἀπολῦσαί σε; ἀπεκρίθη ὁ Ἰησοῦς, Οὐκ εἶχες
authority I have to release you? answered Jesus, not You had

ἐξουσίαν οὐδεμίαν κατ' ἐμοῦ, εἰ μὴ ἦν σοι δεδομένον ἄνωθεν·
authority, not any against Me, if not it was to you being given from above;

**12** διὰ τοῦτο ὁ παραδιδούς μέ σοι μείζονα ἁμαρτίαν ἔχει. ἐκ
therefore the (one) delivering Me to you a greater sin has. From

τούτου ἐζήτει ὁ Πιλάτος ἀπολῦσαι αὐτόν. οἱ δὲ Ἰουδαῖοι
this sought Pilate to release Him, the but Jews

ἔκραζον λέγοντες, Ἐὰν τοῦτον ἀπολύσῃς, οὐκ εἶ φίλος τοῦ
cried out saying, If this one you release not you are friend —

Καίσαρος· πᾶς ὁ βασιλέα αὐτὸν ποιῶν, ἀντιλέγει τῷ
of Caesar; everyone a king himself making speaks against

**13** Καίσαρι. ὁ οὖν Πιλάτος ἀκούσας τοῦτον τὸν λόγον ἤγαγεν
Caesar. Therefore Pilate hearing this word led

ἔξω τὸν Ἰησοῦν, καὶ ἐκάθισεν ἐπὶ τοῦ βήματος, εἰς τόπον
out — Jesus, and sat down on the judgment seat at a place

**14** λεγόμενον Λιθόστρωτον, Ἑβραϊστὶ δὲ Γαββαθᾶ· ἦν δὲ
called (The) Pavement, in Hebrew but, Gabbatha. it was And

Παρασκευὴ τοῦ πάσχα, ὥρα δὲ ὡσεὶ ἕκτη· καὶ λέγει τοῖς
preparation of the Passover, hour and about (the) sixth, and he says to the

**15** Ἰουδαίοις, Ἴδε, ὁ βασιλεὺς ὑμῶν. οἱ δὲ ἐκραύγασαν, Ἆρον,
Jews, Behold, the king of you. they But cried out, Away,

ἆρον, σταύρωσον αὐτόν. λέγει αὐτοῖς ὁ Πιλάτος, Τὸν
away, crucify him! says to them Pilate, The

βασιλέα ὑμῶν σταυρώσω; ἀπεκρίθησαν οἱ ἀρχιερεῖς, Οὐκ
king of you shall I crucify? answered The chief priests, not

**16** ἔχομεν βασιλέα εἰ μὴ Καίσαρα. τότε οὖν παρέδωκεν αὐτὸν
We have a king except Caesar. Then, therefore, he delivered up Him

αὐτοῖς, ἵνα σταυρωθῇ.
to them, that He might be crucified.

**17** Παρέλαβον δὲ τὸν Ἰησοῦν καὶ ἀπήγαγον· καὶ βαστάζων
they took And Jesus and led away, and bearing

τὸν σταυρὸν αὐτοῦ ἐξῆλθεν εἰς τὸν λεγόμενον Κρανίου
the cross of Him, He went out to that called Of a skull,

**18** τόπον, ὃς λέγεται Ἑβραϊστὶ Γολγοθᾶ· ὅπου αὐτὸν ἐσταύ-
(the) place, which is called in Hebrew, Golgotha; where Him they

Him, and with Him two others on this side and on that side, and Jesus in the middle. [19] And Pilate also wrote a sign and put it on the cross; and it was inscribed, JESUS THE NAZARENE, THE KING OF THE JEWS. [20] So many of the Jews read this sign, for the place was near the city, where Jesus was crucified; and it was written in Hebrew, in Greek, and Latin. [21] Then the chief priests of the Jews said to Pilate, Do not write, The king of the Jews, but that he said, I am king of the Jews. [22] Pilate answered, What I have written I have written. [23] Then when they crucified Jesus, the soldiers took His garments and made four parts, to each soldier a part, and the robe; but the robe was seamless, woven from the top throughout. [24] Therefore they said to one another, Let us not tear it, but let us throw lots for it, whose it shall be; that the Scripture might be fulfilled which says, "They divided My garments among them, and they threw lots for My garment." Therefore, the soldiers did these things. [25] And by the cross of Jesus stood His mother, and His mother's sister, Mary the (wife) of Clopas and Mary Magdalene. [26] Then Jesus seeing (His) mother, and the disciple whom He loved standing by, said to His mother, Woman, behold your son! [27] Then He said to the disciple, Behold your mother! And from that hour the disciple took her to his own (home). [28] After this Jesus knowing that all things now had been finished, that the Scripture might be fulfilled, He said, I thirst. [29] So a vessel full of vinegar was set, and they having filled a sponge with vinegar, and having put (it) on hyssop, they brought to

**19** ρωσαν, καὶ μετ' αὐτοῦ ἄλλους δύο, ἐντεῦθεν καὶ ἐντεῦθεν,
crucified, and with him others two, on this side and on that side,
μέσον δὲ τὸν 'Ιησοῦν. ἔγραψε δὲ καὶ τίτλον ὁ Πιλάτος,
in center and Jesus. wrote And also a title Pilate;
καὶ ἔθηκεν ἐπὶ τοῦ σταυροῦ· ἦν δὲ γεγραμμένον, 'Ιησοῦς ὁ
and put (it) on the cross; it was and having been written, JESUS THE

**20** Ναζωραῖος ὁ βασιλεὺς τῶν 'Ιουδαίων. τοῦτον οὖν τὸν
NAZARENE, THE KING OF THE JEWS. This, therefore —
τίτλον πολλοὶ ἀνέγνωσαν τῶν 'Ιουδαίων, ὅτι ἐγγὺς ἦν
title many read of the Jews, because near was
τῆς πόλεως ὁ τόπος ὅπου ἐσταυρώθη ὁ 'Ιησοῦς· καὶ ἦν
the city the place where was crucified Jesus; and it was

**21** γεγραμμένον 'Εβραϊστί, 'Ελληνιστί, 'Ρωμαϊστί. ἔλεγον
having been written in Hebrew, in Greek, in Latin. said.
οὖν τῷ Πιλάτῳ οἱ ἀρχιερεῖς τῶν 'Ιουδαίων, Μὴ γράφε,
Therefore to Pilate the chief priests of the Jews, Not do write,
'Ο βασιλεὺς τῶν 'Ιουδαίων ἀλλ' ὅτι ἐκεῖνος εἶπε, Βασιλεύ
The king of the Jews; but that that one said, king

**22** εἰμι τῶν 'Ιουδαίων. ἀπεκρίθη ὁ Πιλάτος, Ὁ γέγραφα,
I am of the Jews. answered Pilate, What I have written,
γέγραφα.
I have written.

**23** Οἱ οὖν στρατιῶται, ὅτε ἐσταύρωσαν τὸν 'Ιησοῦν, ἔλαβον
the Then soldiers, when they crucified — Jesus, took
τὰ ἱμάτια αὐτοῦ, καὶ ἐποίησαν τέσσαρα μέρη, ἑκάστῳ
the garments of Him, and made four parts, to each
στρατιώτῃ μέρος, καὶ τὸν χιτῶνα· ἦν δὲ ὁ χιτὼν ἄρραφος,
soldier a part; also the tunic. was And the tunic seamless,

**24** ἐκ τῶν ἄνωθεν ὑφαντὸς δι' ὅλου. εἶπον οὖν πρὸς ἀλλήλους,
from the top woven throughout. They said, then, to one another,
Μὴ σχίσωμεν αὐτόν, ἀλλὰ λάχωμεν περὶ αὐτοῦ, τίνος
Not let us tear it, but let us cast lots about it, whose
ἔσται· ἵνα ἡ γραφὴ πληρωθῇ ἡ λέγουσα, Διεμερίσαντο τὰ
it will be; that the Scripture be fulfilled which said, They divided the
ἱμάτιά μου ἑαυτοῖς, καὶ ἐπὶ τὸν ἱματισμόν μου ἔβαλον κλῆρον.
the garments of Me to themselves, and on the garment of Me cast a lot.

**25** οἱ μὲν οὖν στρατιῶται ταῦτα ἐποίησαν. εἱστήκεισαν δὲ
the Therefore soldiers these things did. there stood But
παρὰ τῷ σταυρῷ τοῦ 'Ιησοῦ ἡ μήτηρ αὐτοῦ, καὶ ἡ ἀδελφὴ
by the cross — of Jesus the mother of Him, and the sister
τῆς μητρὸς αὐτοῦ, Μαρία ἡ τοῦ Κλωπᾶ, καὶ Μαρία ἡ
of the mother of Him, Mary the (wife) of Clopas, and Mary the

**26** Μαγδαληνή. 'Ιησοῦς οὖν ἰδὼν τὴν μητέρα, καὶ τὸν μαθητὴν
Magdalene. Jesus Therefore seeing the mother, and the disciple
παρεστῶτα ὃν ἠγάπα, λέγει τῇ μητρὶ αὐτοῦ, Γύναι, ἰδοὺ ὁ
standing by, whom He loved, says to the mother of Him, Woman, behold the

**27** υἱός σου. εἶτα λέγει τῷ μαθητῇ, 'Ιδοὺ ἡ μήτηρ σου. καὶ ἀπ'
son of you. Then He says to the disciple, Behold, the mother of you. And from
ἐκείνης τῆς ὥρας ἔλαβεν αὐτὴν ὁ μαθητὴς εἰς τὰ ἴδια.
that — hour took her the disciple into the own (home).

**28** Μετὰ τοῦτο εἰδὼς ὁ 'Ιησοῦς ὅτι πάντα ἤδη τετέλεσται,
After this knowing. Jesus that all things already have been finished,

**29** ἵνα τελειωθῇ ἡ γραφή, λέγει, Διψῶ. σκεῦος οὖν ἔκειτο ὄξους
that be completed the Scripture, says, I thirst. a vessel Then was set, of vinegar
μεστόν· οἱ δέ, πλήσαντες σπόγγον ὄξους, καὶ ὑσσώπῳ
full; they and, having filled a sponge (with) vinegar, and hyssop

(His) mouth. [30] Then when Jesus took the vinegar, He cried, It has been finished! And having bowed the head, He yielded up (His) spirit. [31] Therefore the Jews asked Pilate that their legs might be broken, and that (they be) taken away — so that the bodies might not remain on the cross on the sabbath, because it was (the) preparation — for that great day was sabbath. [32] Therefore the soldiers came and broke the legs of the first and of the other who was crucified with Him; [33] but having come to Jesus, when they saw He was already dead, they did not break His legs, [34] but one of the soldiers pierced His side with a spear, and immediately blood and water came out. [35] And he who has seen has borne witness, and his witness is true, and he knows that he speaks truly, that you may believe. [36] For these things took place that the Scripture might be fulfilled, "Not a bone of Him shall be broken." [37] And again another Scripture says, "They shall look upon Him whom they pierced."

[38] And after these things Joseph — from Arimathea, being a disciples of Jesus, but hidden through fear of the Jews — asked Pilate that he might take away the body of Jesus; and Pilate gave permission. Therefore he came and took the body of Jesus. [39] And Nicodemus also came, who came to Jesus by night at first, bearing a mixture of myrrh and aloes, about a hundred pounds. [40] Then they took the body of Jesus and bound it in linen clothes with the spices, as is a custom among the Jews to prepare for burial. [41] Now there was in the place where He was crucified a garden, and in the garden a new tomb, in which no one ever was laid. [42] There, then, because of the preparation of the Jews, because the

---

**30** περιθέντες, προσήνεγκαν αὐτοῦ τῷ στόματι. ὅτε οὖν ἔλαβε
putting around, they brought to of Him the mouth, when Then took
τὸ ὄξος ὁ Ἰησοῦς, εἶπε, Τετέλεσται· καὶ κλίνας τὴν κεφαλήν,
the vinegar Jesus, He said, it has been completed, and bowing the head
παρέδωκε τὸ πνεῦμα.
delivered up the spirit.

**31** Οἱ οὖν Ἰουδαῖοι, ἐπεὶ Παρασκευὴ ἦν, ἵνα μὴ μείνῃ ἐπὶ τοῦ
the Therefore Jews, since preparation it was, that not may remain on the
σταυροῦ τὰ σώματα ἐν τῷ σαββάτῳ (ἦν γὰρ μεγάλη ἡ
cross the bodies on the sabbath, was for great the
ἡμέρα ἐκείνου τοῦ σαββάτου). ἠρώτησαν τὸν Πιλᾶτον ἵνα
day of that — sabbath; they asked Pilate that

**32** κατεαγῶσιν αὐτῶν τὰ σκέλη, καὶ ἀρθῶσιν. ἦλθον οὖν οἱ
might be broken of them the legs, and they be taken. came Then the
στρατιῶται, καὶ τοῦ μὲν πρώτου κατέαξαν τὰ σκέλη καὶ τοῦ
soldiers, and of the first broke the legs, and of the

**33** ἄλλου τοῦ συσταυρωθέντος αὐτῷ· ἐπὶ δὲ τὸν Ἰησοῦν ἐλ-
other — crucified with Him; upon but — Jesus
θόντες, ὡς εἶδον αὐτὸν ἤδη τεθνηκότα, οὐ κατέαξαν αὐτοῦ
coming, when they saw He already was dead, not they broke of Him

**34** τὰ σκέλη· ἀλλ' εἷς τῶν στρατιωτῶν λόγχῃ αὐτοῦ τὴν πλευ-
the legs, but one of the soldiers a lance of him the side

**35** ρὰν ἔνυξε, καὶ εὐθὺς ἐξῆλθεν αἷμα καὶ ὕδωρ. καὶ ὁ ἑωρακὼς
pierced, and at once came out blood and water. And the (one) seeing
μεμαρτύρηκε, καὶ ἀληθινὴ αὐτοῦ ἐστιν ἡ μαρτυρία, κἀκεῖνος
has witnessed, and true of him is the witness, and that one

**36** οἶδεν ὅτι ἀληθῆ λέγει, ἵνα ὑμεῖς πιστεύσητε. ἐγένετο γὰρ
knows that true he speaks, that you may believe. happened For
ταῦτα ἵνα ἡ γραφὴ πληρωθῇ, Ὀστοῦν οὐ συντριβήσεταί
these things that the Scripture be fulfilled: A bone not shall be splintered

**37** αὐτοῦ. καὶ πάλιν ἑτέρα γραφὴ λέγει, Ὄψονται εἰς ὃν
of Him. And again a different Scripture says, They shall look at whom
ἐξεκέντησαν.
they have pierced.

**38** Μετὰ δὲ ταῦτα ἠρώτησε τὸν Πιλᾶτον ὁ Ἰωσὴφ ὁ ἀπὸ
after And these things asked Pilate Joseph from
Ἀριμαθαίας, ὢν μαθητὴς τοῦ Ἰησοῦ, κεκρυμμένος δὲ διὰ
Arimathea, being a disciple of Jesus, concealed but through
τὸν φόβον τῶν Ἰουδαίων, ἵνα ἄρῃ τὸ σῶμα τοῦ Ἰησοῦ· καὶ
the fear of the Jews, that he take the body — of Jesus. And
ἐπέτρεψεν ὁ Πιλᾶτος. ἦλθεν οὖν καὶ ἦρε τὸ σῶμα τοῦ Ἰησοῦ.
allowed (it) Pilate. He came, then, and took the body — of Jesus.

**39** ἦλθε δὲ καὶ Νικόδημος, ὁ ἐλθὼν πρὸς τὸν Ἰησοῦν νυκτὸς τὸ
came And also Nicodemus, the (one) coming to — Jesus (by) night at
πρῶτον, φέρων μίγμα σμύρνης καὶ ἀλόης ὡσεὶ λίτρας ἑκατόν.
first, bearing a mixture of myrrh and aloes, about litrae a hundred.

**40** ἔλαβον οὖν τὸ σῶμα τοῦ Ἰησοῦ, καὶ ἔδησαν αὐτὸ ὀθονίοις
they took Then the body — of Jesus, and bound it in linens
μετὰ τῶν ἀρωμάτων, καθὼς ἔθος ἐστὶ τοῖς Ἰουδαίοις
with the spices, as custom is with the Jews

**41** ἐνταφιάζειν. ἦν δὲ ἐν τῷ τόπῳ ὅπου ἐσταυρώθη κῆπος, καὶ
to bury. was And in the place where He was crucified a garden, and

**42** ἐν τῷ κήπῳ μνημεῖον καινόν, ἐν ᾧ οὐδέπω οὐδεὶς ἐτέθη. ἐκεῖ
in the garden tomb new, in which never yet no one was put. There,
οὖν διὰ τὴν Παρασκευὴν τῶν Ἰουδαίων, ὅτι ἐγγὺς ἦν τὸ
then, because of the preparation of the Jews, because near was the

tomb was near, they laid Jesus.

μνημεῖον, ἔθηκαν τὸν Ἰησοῦν.
tomb,        they put —    Jesus.

## CHAPTER 20

[1] But on the first of the week Mary Magdalene came early to the tomb, it still being dark, and saw the stone taken away from the tomb. [2] Therefore she ran and came to Simon Peter and to the other disciple whom Jesus loved, and said to them, They took away the Lord out of the tomb, and we do not know where they laid Him. [3] Therefore Peter and the other disciple went out and came to the tomb. [4] And the two ran together, and the other disciple ran forward faster than Peter and came to the tomb, [5] and stooping down he saw the linen clothes lying; however he did not go in. [6] Then came Simon Peter following him, and went into the tomb, and saw the linen clothes lying, [7] and the gravecloth which was on His head, not lying with the linen clothes, but folded up in a place by itself. [8] So, then, the other disciple who came to the tomb first also went in, and saw and believed; [9] for they did not yet know the Scripture, that it was necessary for Him to rise again from among (the) dead. [10] Therefore the disciples went away again to their (home). [11] But Mary stood at the tomb weeping outside. Then as she wept, she stooped down into the tomb, [12] and saw two angels in white sitting, one at the head and one at the feet, where the body of Jesus was laid. [13] And they said to her, Woman, why do you weep? She said to them, Because they took away my Lord, and I do not know where they laid Him. [14] And having said these things she turned backward, and saw Jesus standing, and did not know that it was Jesus. [15] Jesus said to her,

## CHAPTER 20

**1** Τῇ δὲ μιᾷ τῶν σαββάτων Μαρία ἡ Μαγδαληνὴ ἔρχεται
on the And first of the sabbaths,    Mary the Magdalene    comes
πρωΐ, σκοτίας ἔτι οὔσης, εἰς τὸ μνημεῖον, καὶ βλέπει τὸν
early. darkness  yet  being  to the  tomb,   and sees  the
**2** λίθον ἠρμένον ἐκ τοῦ μνημείου. τρέχει οὖν καὶ ἔρχεται πρὸς
stone being removed from the tomb  she runs Then and comes   to
Σίμωνα Πέτρον καὶ πρὸς τὸν ἄλλον μαθητὴν ὃν ἐφίλει ὁ
Simon   Peter,  and to   the  other   disciples whom loved
Ἰησοῦς, καὶ λέγει αὐτοῖς, Ἦραν τὸν Κύριον ἐκ τοῦ μνημείου,
Jesus; and says to them, They took the Lord out of the  tomb,
**3** κ‧.ι οὐκ οἴδαμεν ποῦ ἔθηκαν αὐτόν. ἐξῆλθεν οὖν ὁ Πέτρος καὶ
and not we know  where they put  Him.  went out Then  Peter  and
**4** ὁ ἄλλος μαθητής, καὶ ἤρχοντο εἰς τὸ μνημεῖον. ἔτρεχον δὲ οἱ
the other disciple,  and came  to the  tomb.    ran And the
δύο ὁμοῦ· καὶ ὁ ἄλλος μαθητὴς προέδραμε τάχιον τοῦ
two together; and the other   disciple   ran in front, more quickly than
**5** Πέτρου, καὶ ἦλθε πρῶτος εἰς τὸ μνημεῖον, καὶ παρακυψας
Peter,   and came  first  to the  tomb,   and  stooping
**6** βλέπει κείμενα τὰ ὀθόνια, οὐ μέντοι εἰσῆλθεν. ἔρχεται οὖν
sees   lying  the  linens; not, however, he went in.  Comes, therefore,
Σίμων Πέτρος ἀκολουθῶν αὐτῷ, καὶ εἰσῆλθεν εἰς τὸ μνημεῖον,
Simon  Peter  following  him,  and  entered into the  tomb.
**7** καὶ θεωρεῖ τὰ ὀθόνια κείμενα, καὶ τὸ σουδάριον ὃ ἦν ἐπὶ τῆς
And he beholds the linens lying,  and the  cloth  which was on the
κεφαλῆς αὐτοῦ, οὐ μετὰ τῶν ὀθονίων κείμενον, ἀλλὰ χωρὶς
head  of Him, not with the  linens  lying,   but  apart
**8** ἐντετυλιγμένον εἰς ἕνα τόπον. τότε οὖν εἰσῆλθε καὶ ὁ ἄλλος
being wrapped up into one  place. Then, therefore entered also the other
μαθητὴς ὁ ἐλθὼν πρῶτος εἰς τὸ μνημεῖον, καὶ εἶδε, καὶ
disciple  having come first  to the  tomb,   and he saw, and
**9** ἐπίστευσεν· οὐδέπω γὰρ ᾔδεισαν τὴν γραφήν, ὅτι δεῖ
believed.   not yet For they knew  the Scripture, that it behoves
αὐτὸν ἐκ νεκρῶν ἀναστῆναι. ἀπῆλθον οὖν πάλιν πρὸς
Him from (the) dead to rise.      went away Then  again  to
ἑαυτοὺς οἱ μαθηταί.
themselves the disciples.

**11** Μαρία δὲ εἰστήκει πρὸς τὸ μνημεῖον κλαίουσα ἔξω· ὡς
Mary And stood   at the  tomb   weeping outside. As
**12** οὖν ἔκλαιε, παρέκυψεν εἰς τὸ μνημεῖον, καὶ θεωρεῖ δύο
then she wept, she stooped into the  tomb.  and beholds two
ἀγγέλους ἐν λευκοῖς καθεζομένους, ἕνα πρὸς τῇ κεφαλῇ, καὶ
angels   in white   sitting,    one at the head, . and
**13** ἕνα πρὸς τοῖς ποσίν, ὅπου ἔκειτο τὸ σῶμα τοῦ Ἰησοῦ. καὶ
one at the feet,  where had lain the body  — of Jesus. And
λέγουσιν αὐτῇ ἐκεῖνοι, Γύναι, τί κλαίεις; λέγει αὐτοῖς, Ὅτι
say   to her those, Woman, why do you weep? She says to them, For
**14** ἦραν τὸν Κύριόν μου, καὶ οὐκ οἶδα ποῦ ἔθηκαν αὐτόν. καὶ
they removed the Lord of me, and not I know where they put  Him. And
ταῦτα εἰποῦσα ἐστράφη εἰς τὰ ὀπίσω, καὶ θεωρεῖ τὸν
these things Saying, she turned  into the rear,  and beholds  —
**15** Ἰησοῦν ἑστῶτα, καὶ οὐκ ᾔδει ὅτι ὁ Ἰησοῦς ἐστι. λέγει αὐτῇ
Jesus  standing, and not knows that   Jesus it is. says to her

Woman, why do you weep? Whom do you seek? Thinking that it was the gardener, she said to Him, Sir, if you carried Him off, tell me where you laid Him, and I will take Him away. [16] Jesus said to her, Mary! Turning around she said to Him, Rabboni, that is to say, Teacher. [17] Jesus said to her, Do not touch Me, for I have not yet ascended to My Father; but go to My brothers and say to them, I am ascending to My Father and your Father, and My God and your God. [18] Mary Magdalene came bringing word to the disciples, (that) she had seen the Lord, and these things He said to her. [19] It being therefore evening on that day, the first of the week, and the doors having been shut where the disciples were assembled, through fear of the Jews, Jesus came and stood in the midst and said to them, Peace to you. [20] And having said this He showed to them the hands and His side. Therefore the disciples rejoiced, having seen the Lord. [21] Then Jesus said again to them, Peace to you; as the Father has sent Me, I also send you. [22] And having said this, He breathed into (them) and said to them, Receive (the) Holy Spirit. [23] Of whomever you may forgive the sins, they are forgiven to them; or whomever you may retain, they have been retained. [24] But Thomas, called Didymus, one of the Twelve, was not with them when Jesus came. [25] Therefore the other disciples said to him, We have seen the Lord. But he said to them, Unless I see in His hands the mark of the nails, and put my finger into the mark of the nails, and put my hand into His side, I will not at all believe. [26] And after eight days His disciples were inside again, and

ὁ Ἰησοῦς, Γύναι, τί κλαίεις; τίνα ζητεῖς; ἐκείνη, δοκοῦσα
Jesus,   Woman, why do you weep? Whom seek you?   That one   thinking
ὅτι ὁ κηπουρός ἐστι, λέγει αὐτῷ, Κύριε, εἰ σὺ ἐβάστασας
that the gardener   it is   says   to Him,   Sir,   if you carried away

16 αὐτόν, εἰπέ μοι ποῦ αὐτὸν ἔθηκας, κἀγὼ αὐτὸν ἀρῶ. λέγει
Him,   tell, me where Him you put, and I   Him will take.   says
αὐτῇ ὁ Ἰησοῦς, Μαρία. στραφεῖσα ἐκείνη λέγει αὐτῷ,
to her   Jesus,   Mary!   turning   That one   says to Him

17 Ῥαββουνί· ὃ λέγεται, Διδάσκαλε. λέγει αὐτῇ ὁ Ἰησοῦς, Μή
Rabboni, that is to say,   Teacher.   says to her   Jesus, Do not
μου ἅπτου, οὔπω γὰρ ἀναβέβηκα πρὸς τὸν πατέρα μου·
Me touch, not yet   for I have ascended   to the   Father of Me.
πορεύου δὲ πρὸς τοὺς ἀδελφούς μου, καὶ εἰπὲ αὐτοῖς,
go   But to   the   brothers of Me,   and   say to them,
Ἀναβαίνω πρὸς τὸν πατέρα μου καὶ πατέρα ὑμῶν, καὶ
I ascend   to   the   Father of Me and the Father, of you, and

18 Θεόν μου καὶ Θεὸν ὑμῶν. ἔρχεται Μαρία ἡ Μαγδαληνὴ
the God of Me and the God of you. comes   Mary   the   Magdalene
ἀπαγγέλλουσα τοῖς μαθηταῖς ὅτι ἑώρακε τὸν Κύριον, καὶ
bringing word   to the disciples, that she has seen the Lord, and
ταῦτα εἶπεν αὐτῇ.
these things He told her.

19 Οὔσης οὖν ὀψίας, τῇ ἡμέρᾳ ἐκείνῃ τῇ μιᾷ τῶν σαββάτων,
it being Then evening —   day on that, the   first of the sabbaths,
καὶ τῶν θυρῶν κεκλεισμένων ὅπου ἦσαν οἱ μαθηταὶ συνηγ-
and the doors having been locked where were the disciples gathered
μένοι, διὰ τὸν φόβον τῶν Ἰουδαίων, ἦλθεν ὁ Ἰησοῦς καὶ
together, because of the fear of the   Jews,   came   Jesus   and

20 ἔστη εἰς τὸ μέσον, καὶ λέγει αὐτοῖς, Εἰρήνη ὑμῖν. καὶ τοῦτο
stood in the midst,   and   says to them, Peace to you. And this
εἰπὼν ἔδειξεν αὐτοῖς τὰς χεῖρας καὶ τὴν πλευρὰν αὐτοῦ.
saying He showed them   the hands   and the   side   of Him.

21 ἐχάρησαν οὖν οἱ μαθηταὶ ἰδόντες τὸν Κύριον. εἶπεν οὖν
Rejoiced, therefore, the disciples   seeing   the Lord.   said Then
αὐτοῖς ὁ Ἰησοῦς πάλιν, Εἰρήνη ὑμῖν· καθὼς ἀπέσταλκέ με ὁ
to them   Jesus again,   Peace to you. As   has sent   Me the

22 πατήρ, κἀγὼ πέμπω ὑμᾶς. καὶ τοῦτο εἰπὼν ἐνεφύσησε καὶ
Father, I also   send   you. And this having said, He breathed on, and

23 λέγει αὐτοῖς, Λάβετε Πνεῦμα Ἅγιον. ἂν τινων ἀφῆτε τὰς
said to them, Receive (the) Spirit   Holy. Ever of whom you forgive the
ἁμαρτίας, ἀφίενται αὐτοῖς· ἂν τινων κρατῆτε, κεκράτηνται.
sins, they are forgiven to them; ever of whom you retain, they are retained.

24 Θωμᾶς δέ, εἷς ἐκ τῶν δώδεκα, ὁ λεγόμενος Δίδυμος, οὐκ ἦν
Thomas But, one of the twelve, the (one) called   Twin,   not was

25 μετ' αὐτῶν ὅτε ἦλθεν ὁ Ἰησοῦς. ἔλεγον οὖν αὐτῷ οἱ ἄλλοι
with   them when came   Jesus.   said Then to him the other
μαθηταί, Ἑωράκαμεν τὸν Κύριον ὁ δὲ εἶπεν αὐτοῖς, Ἐὰν μὴ
disciples, We have seen the Lord. he But said to them,   Unless
ἴδω ἐν ταῖς χερσὶν αὐτοῦ τὸν τύπον τῶν ἥλων, καὶ βάλω
I see in the hands of Him the mark of the nails, and thrust
τὸν δάκτυλόν μου εἰς τὸν τύπον τῶν ἥλων, καὶ βάλω τὴν
the finger of me into the mark of the nails, and thrust the
χεῖρά μου εἰς τὴν πλευρὰν αὐτοῦ, οὐ μὴ πιστεύσω.
hand of me into the side   of Him, in no way will I believe.

26 Καὶ μεθ' ἡμέρας ὀκτὼ πάλιν ἦσαν ἔσω οἱ μαθηταὶ αὐτοῦ,
And after days   eight,   again were inside the disciples of Him,

Thomas with them. Jesus came, the door having been shut, and stood in the midst and said, Peace to you. [27] Then He said to Thomas, Bring your finger here and see My hands; and bring your hand and put (it) into My side; and be not unbelieving, but believing. [28] And Thomas answered and said to Him, My Lord and my God! [29] Jesus said to him, Because you have seen Me, Thomas, you have believed; blessed (are) they who have not seen and have believed.

[30] Then Jesus did many other miracles in the presence of His disciples, which are not written in this book. [31] But these have been written that you may believe that Jesus is the Christ, the Son of God, and that believing you may have life in His name.

CHAPTER 21

[1] After these things Jesus revealed Himself again to the disciples at the sea of Tiberias. And He revealed (Himself) this way: [2] Simon Peter, and Thomas called Didymus, and Nathanael from Cana of Galilee, and the (sons) of Zebedee, and two others of His disciples were together. [3] Simon Peter said to them, I am going to fish. They said to him, We also are coming with you. They went out and went up into the boat immediately, and during that night they caught nothing. [4] And morning already being come, Jesus stood on the shore; however the disciples did not know that it was Jesus. [5] Then Jesus said to them, Little children, have you any food? They answered Him, No. [6] And He said to them, Throw the net to the right side of the boat, and you shall find. Therefore they threw, and they were no longer able to draw, from the multitude of the fish.

καὶ Θωμᾶς μετ᾽ αὐτῶν. ἔρχεται ὁ Ἰησοῦς, τῶν θυρῶν
and Thomas with them. comes — Jesus, the doors
κεκλεισμένων, καὶ ἔστη εἰς τὸ μέσον καὶ εἶπεν, Εἰρήνη ὑμῖν.
having been locked, and stood in the midst, and said, Peace to you.

27 εἶτα λέγει τῷ Θωμᾷ, Φέρε τὸν δάκτυλόν σου ὧδε, καὶ ἴδε τὰς
Then He says — to Thomas, Bring the finger of you here, and see the
χεῖράς μου· καὶ φέρε τὴν χεῖρά σου, καὶ βάλε εἰς τὴν πλευ-
hands of Me, and bring the hand of you, and thrust into the side

28 ράν μου· καὶ μὴ γίνου ἄπιστος, ἀλλὰ πιστός. καὶ ἀπεκρίθη
of Me, and not become unbelieving, but believing. And answered

29 ὁ Θωμᾶς, καὶ εἶπεν αὐτῷ, Ὁ Κύριός μου καὶ ὁ Θεός μου. λέγει
Thomas, and said to Him, The Lord of me, and the God of me. says
αὐτῷ ὁ Ἰησοῦς, Ὅτι ἑώρακάς με, Θωμᾶ, πεπίστευκας·
to him Jesus, Because you have seen Me, Thomas, you have believed.
μακάριοι οἱ μὴ ἰδόντες, καὶ πιστεύσαντες.
Blessed those not seeing, and believing.

30 Πολλὰ μὲν οὖν καὶ ἄλλα σημεῖα ἐποίησεν ὁ Ἰησοῦς ἐνώ-
Many, therefore, and other signs did Jesus in (the)
πιον τῶν μαθητῶν αὐτοῦ, ἃ οὐκ ἔστι γεγραμμένα ἐν τῷ
sight of the disciples of Him, which not is written in

31 βιβλίῳ τούτῳ. ταῦτα δὲ γέγραπται, ἵνα πιστεύσητε ὅτι ὁ
roll this. these things But have been written that you believe that
Ἰησοῦς ἐστιν ὁ Χριστὸς ὁ υἱὸς τοῦ Θεοῦ, καὶ ἵνα πιστεύοντες
Jesus is the Christ the Son — of God, and that believing
ζωὴν ἔχητε ἐν τῷ ὀνόματι αὐτοῦ.
life you may have in the name of Him.

CHAPTER 21

1 Μετὰ ταῦτα ἐφανέρωσεν ἑαυτὸν πάλιν ὁ Ἰησοῦς τοῖς
After these things revealed Himself again Jesus to the
μαθηταῖς ἐπὶ τῆς θαλάσσης τῆς Τιβεριάδος· ἐφανέρωσε δὲ
disciples on the sea — of Tiberias: He revealed and

2 οὕτως. ἦσαν ὁμοῦ Σίμων Πέτρος, καὶ Θωμᾶς ὁ λεγόμενος
thus: Were together Simon Peter, and Thomas being called
Δίδυμος, καὶ Ναθαναὴλ ὁ ἀπὸ Κανᾶ τῆς Γαλιλαίας, καὶ οἱ
Twin, and Nathanael from Cana, of Galilee, and those
τοῦ Ζεβεδαίου, καὶ ἄλλοι ἐκ τῶν μαθητῶν αὐτοῦ δύο.
— of Zebedee, and others of the disciples of Him two.

3 λέγει αὐτοῖς Σίμων Πέτρος, Ὑπάγω ἁλιεύειν. λέγουσιν
says to them Simon Peter, I am going out to fish. They say
αὐτῷ, Ἐρχόμεθα καὶ ἡμεῖς σὺν σοί. ἐξῆλθον καὶ ἀνέβησαν
to him, are coming also We with you. They went and entered
εἰς τὸ πλοῖον εὐθύς, καὶ ἐν ἐκείνῃ τῇ νυκτὶ ἐπίασαν οὐδέν.
into the boat at once. And in that — night, they caught nothing.

4 πρωΐας δὲ ἤδη γενομένης ἔστη ὁ Ἰησοῦς εἰς τὸν αἰγιαλόν·
early morn But now (it) becoming, stood Jesus in the shore;

5 οὐ μέντοι ᾔδεισαν οἱ μαθηταὶ ὅτι Ἰησοῦς ἐστι. λέγει οὖν
not, however, knew the disciples that Jesus it is. says Then
αὐτοῖς ὁ Ἰησοῦς, Παιδία, μή τι προσφάγιον ἔχετε; ἀπεκρί-
to them Jesus, Children, not anything for eating have you? They

6 θησαν αὐτῷ, Οὔ. ὁ δὲ εἶπεν αὐτοῖς, Βάλετε εἰς τὰ δεξιὰ
answered Him, No. He And said to them, Cast in the right
μέρη τοῦ πλοίου τὸ δίκτυον, καὶ εὑρήσετε. ἔβαλον οὖν, καὶ
parts of the boat the net, and you will find. They cast, then, and
οὐκέτι αὐτὸ ἑλκύσαι ἴσχυσαν ἀπὸ τοῦ πλήθους τῶν ἰχθύων.
no longer it to draw had they might from the multitude of the fish.

[7] Therefore that disciple whom Jesus loved says to Peter, It is the Lord. Then Simon Peter, hearing that it is the Lord, girded on the coat—for he was naked—and threw himself into the sea. [8] And the other disciples came in the little boat —for they were not far from the land, but about two hundred cubits from (it)—dragging the net of the fish. [9] Then when they went up on the land, they saw a coal fire lying, and a fish lying on (it), and bread. [10] Jesus says to them, Bring from the little fish which you caught now. [11] Simon Peter went up and dragged the net onto the land, full of big fish, a hundred and fifty three; and (though being so many, the net was not torn. [12] Jesus says to them, Come, break fast. And no one of the disciples dared to question Him (saying), Who are You, knowing that it was the Lord, [13] Then Jesus came and took the bread and gave to them, and likewise the little fish. [14] This (is) now the third time Jesus was revealed to His disciples, having been raised from (the) dead.

[15] Then when they broke fast, Jesus said to Simon Peter, Simon (son) of Jonah, do you love Me more than these? He said to Him, Yes, Lord; You know that I love You. He says to Him, Feed My lambs! [16] Again He says to him secondly, Simon (son) of Jonah, do you love Me? He says to Him, Yes, Lord; You know that I love You. He says to Him, Shepherd My sheep! [17] He says to him thirdly, Simon (son) of Jonah, do you love Me? Peter was grieved that He said to him thirdly, Do you love Me? And he said to Him, Lord, You perceive all things, You know that I love You! Jesus says to him, Feed My sheep! [18] Truly, truly, I tell you, when you were younger you dressed yourself, and you went where you chose, but when you grow old you will

**7** λέγει οὖν ὁ μαθητὴς ἐκεῖνος ὃν ἠγάπα ὁ Ἰησοῦς τῷ Πέτρῳ,
says Then disciple that whom loved Jesus — to Peter,
Ὁ Κύριός ἐστι. Σίμων οὖν Πέτρος, ἀκούσας ὅτι ὁ Κύριός
The Lord it is. Simon Then Peter, hearing that the Lord
ἐστι, τὸν ἐπενδύτην διεζώσατο (ἦν γὰρ γυμνός), καὶ
it is. the coat (having) girded on. he was For naked, and

**8** ἔβαλεν ἑαυτὸν εἰς τὴν θάλασσαν· οἱ δὲ ἄλλοι μαθηταὶ τῷ
threw himself into the sea. the And other disciples in the
πλοιαρίῳ ἦλθον (οὐ γὰρ ἦσαν μακρὰν ἀπὸ τῆς γῆς, ἀλλ'
little boat came, not for they were far from the land, but
ὡς ἀπὸ πηχῶν διακοσίων), σύροντες τὸ δίκτυον τῶν
about from cubits two hundred, dragging the net of the

**9** ἰχθύων. ὡς οὖν ἀπέβησαν εἰς τὴν γῆν, βλέπουσιν ἀνθρακιὰν
fish. when Then they went up on the land, they saw a coal fire

**10** κειμένην καὶ ὀψάριον ἐπικείμενον, καὶ ἄρτον. λέγει αὐτοῖς
lying, and a fish lying on, and bread. says to them
ὁ Ἰησοῦς, Ἐνέγκατε ἀπὸ τῶν ὀψαρίων ὧν ἐπιάσατε νῦν.
Jesus, Bring from the little fish which you caught now.

**11** ἀνέβη Σίμων Πέτρος, καὶ εἵλκυσε τὸ δίκτυον ἐπὶ τῆς γῆς,
went up Simon Peter, and dragged the net onto the land,
μεστὸν ἰχθύων μεγάλων ἑκατὸν πεντηκοντατριῶν· καὶ
full of fish of great a hundred fifty three. And

**12** τοσούτων ὄντων, οὐκ ἐσχίσθη τὸ δίκτυον. λέγει αὐτοῖς ὁ
so many being not was torn the net. says to them
Ἰησοῦς, Δεῦτε ἀριστήσατε. οὐδεὶς δὲ ἐτόλμα τῶν μαθητῶν
Jesus, Come, break fast. no one And dared of the disciples
ἐξετάσαι αὐτόν, Σὺ τίς εἶ; εἰδότες ὅτι ὁ Κύριός ἐστιν.
to question Him, You Who are, knowing that the Lord it is.

**13** ἔρχεται οὖν ὁ Ἰησοῦς, καὶ λαμβάνει τὸν ἄρτον, καὶ δίδωσιν
comes Then Jesus and takes the bread, and gives

**14** αὐτοῖς, καὶ τὸ ὀψάριον ὁμοίως. τοῦτο ἤδη τρίτον ἐφανερώθη
to them, and the little fish likewise. This already thrice was revealed
ὁ Ἰησοῦς τοῖς μαθηταῖς αὐτοῦ, ἐγερθεὶς ἐκ νεκρῶν.
Jesus to the disciples of Him, having been raised from (the) dead.

**15** Ὅτε οὖν ἠρίστησαν, λέγει τῷ Σίμωνι Πέτρῳ ὁ Ἰησοῦς,
when Then they breakfasted, says to Simon Peter Jesus,
Σίμων Ἰωνᾶ, ἀγαπᾷς με πλεῖον τούτων; λέγει αὐτῷ, Ναί
Simon of Jonah, do you love Me more (than) these? He says to Him, Yes,
Κύριε· σὺ οἶδας ὅτι φιλῶ σε. λέγει αὐτῷ, Βόσκε τὰ ἀρνία μου.
Lord, You know that I love You. He says to him, Feed the lambs of Me.

**16** λέγει αὐτῷ πάλιν δεύτερον, Σίμων Ἰωνᾶ, ἀγαπᾷς με; λέγει
He says to him again secondly, Simon of Jonah, do you love Me? He says
αὐτῷ, Ναὶ Κύριε· σὺ οἶδας ὅτι φιλῶ σε. λέγει αὐτῷ, Ποίμαινε
to Him, Yes, Lord, You know that I love You. He says to him, Shepherd

**17** τὰ πρόβατά μου. λέγει αὐτῷ τὸ τρίτον, Σίμων Ἰωνᾶ, φιλεῖς
the sheep of Me. He says to him thirdly, Simon of Jonah, do you love
με; ἐλυπήθη ὁ Πέτρος ὅτι εἶπεν αὐτῷ τὸ τρίτον, φιλεῖς με;
Me? was grieved Peter that He said to him thirdly, Do you love Me?
καὶ εἶπεν αὐτῷ, Κύριε, σὺ πάντα οἶδας· σὺ γινώσκεις ὅτι
And he said to Him, Lord You all things perceive, You know that

**18** φιλῶ σε. λέγει αὐτῷ ὁ Ἰησοῦς, Βόσκε τὰ πρόβατά μου. ἀμὴν
I love You. says to him Jesus, Feed the little sheep of Me. Truly,
ἀμὴν λέγω σοι, ὅτε ἦς νεώτερος, ἐζώννυες σεαυτόν, καὶ
truly, I say to you, when you were younger, you girded yourself, and
περιεπάτεις ὅπου ἤθελες· ὅταν δὲ γηράσῃς, ἐκτενεῖς τὰς
you walked where you desired, when but you grow old you will stretch the

stretch out your hands and another shall dress you, and bring you where you do not desire. [19] But He said this signifying by what death he should glorify God. And having said this, He said to him, Follow Me. [20] But having turned Peter saw the disciple whom Jesus loved following, who also reclined at the Supper on His breast and said, Lord, who is it who is delivering You up? [21] Seeing him Peter said to Jesus, Lord, but what of this one? [22] Jesus said to him, If I desire him to remain until I come, what (is that) to you? You follow Me. [23] Therefore this word went out among the brothers, that that disciples would not die. However Jesus did not say to him that he does not die; but, If I desire him to remain until I come, what (is that) to you?

[24] This is the disciple who bears witness about these things, and (who) wrote these things; and we know that his witness is true. [25] And there are also many other things, whatever Jesus did, which if they should be written one by one, I suppose not even the world itself would contain the books written. Amen.

χεῖράς σου, καὶ ἄλλος σε ζώσει, καὶ οἴσει ὅπου οὐ θέλεις.
hands of you, and another you will gird, and will carry where not you want

19 τοῦτο δὲ εἶπε, σημαίνων ποίῳ θανάτῳ δοξάσει τὸν Θεόν.
this And He said, signifying by what death he will glorify — God.

20 καὶ τοῦτο εἰπὼν λέγει αὐτῷ, Ἀκολούθει μοι. ἐπιστραφεὶς δὲ
And this said, He tells him, Follow Me. turning And
ὁ Πέτρος βλέπει τὸν μαθητὴν ὃν ἠγάπα ὁ Ἰησοῦς ἀκολου-
Peter sees the disciple whom loved Jesus, following,
θοῦντα, ὃς καὶ ἀνέπεσεν ἐν τῷ δείπνῳ ἐπὶ τὸ στῆθος αὐτοῦ
who also leaned at the supper on the breast of Him

21 καὶ εἶπε, Κύριε, τίς ἐστιν ὁ παραδιδούς σε; τοῦτον ἰδὼν ὁ
and said, Lord, who is the(one) betraying You? This one seeing —

22 Πέτρος λέγει τῷ Ἰησοῦ, Κύριε, οὗτος δὲ τί; λέγει αὐτῷ ὁ
Peter says — to Jesus, Lord, this one and what? says to him —
Ἰησοῦς, Ἐὰν αὐτὸν θέλω μένειν ἕως ἔρχομαι, τί πρός σε
Jesus, If him I desire to remain until I come, what to you?

23 σὺ ἀκολούθει μοι. ἐξῆλθεν οὖν ὁ λόγος οὗτος εἰς τοὺς ἀδελ-
You follow Me. went out Therefore word this to the brothers,
φούς, ὅτι ὁ μαθητὴς ἐκεῖνος οὐκ ἀποθνήσκει· καὶ οὐκ εἶπεν
that disciple that not does die; and not said
αὐτῷ ὁ Ἰησοῦς, ὅτι οὐκ ἀποθνήσκει· ἀλλ᾽, Ἐὰν αὐτὸν θέλω
to him — Jesus that not he does die; but, If him I desire
μένειν ἕως ἔρχομαι, τί πρός σε;
to remain until I come, what to you?

24 Οὗτός ἐστιν ὁ μαθητὴς ὁ μαρτυρῶν περὶ τούτων, καὶ
This is the disciple witnessing concerning these, and
γράψας ταῦτα· καὶ οἴδαμεν ὅτι ἀληθής ἐστιν ἡ μαρτυρία
writing these things, and we know that true is the witness
αὐτοῦ.
of him.

25 Ἔστι δὲ καὶ ἄλλα πολλὰ ὅσα ἐποίησεν ὁ Ἰησοῦς, ἅτινα
are And also other things many whatever did Jesus, which
ἐὰν γράφηται καθ᾽ ἕν, οὐδὲ αὐτὸν οἶμαι τὸν κόσμον χωρῆσα
if they were written singly, not itself I suppose the world to contain
τὰ γραφόμενα βιβλία. Ἀμην.
those being written rolls. Amen.

# ΠΡΑΞΕΙΣ
## ACTS
# ΤΩΝ ΑΠΟΣΤΟΛΩΝ
## OF THE APOSTLES

CHAPTER 1

CHAPTER 1

[1] Indeed, O Theophilus, I made the first report as to all the things Jesus set out both to do and to teach, [2] until the day He was taken up, having given command to the apostles whom He chose by (the) Holy Spirit; [3] to whom He also presented Himself living after He had suffered, with many proofs, being seen of them during forty days, and speaking the things concerning the kingdom of God; [4] and being gathered together, He commanded them not to leave Jerusalem, but to await the promise of the Father, "which you heard of Me. [5] For John indeed baptized with water, but You shall be baptized with (the) Holy Spirit not many days after." [6] Then, indeed, having come together they asked Him, saying, Lord, do You restore the kingdom to Israel at this time? [7] And He said to them, It is not yours to know times or seasons, which the Father placed in His own authority; [8] but you will receive power, the Holy Spirit having come upon you, and you shall be witnesses to Me both in Jerusalem and in all Judea and Samaria and to (the) uttermost parts of the earth. [9] And having said these things, they watching, He was taken up, and a cloud hid Him from their eyes.

[10] And as they were looking intently into the heavens, as He was going

1 Τὸν μὲν πρῶτον λόγον ἐποιησάμην περὶ πάντων, ὦ
The — first account I made concerning all things, O

2 Θεόφιλε, ὧν ἤρξατο ὁ Ἰησοῦς ποιεῖν τε καὶ διδάσκειν, ἄχρι
Theophilus, which began — Jesus to do both and to teach, until

ἧς ἡμέρας, ἐντειλάμενος τοῖς ἀποστόλοις διὰ Πνεύματος
which day, having given directions to the apostles through (the) Spirit

3 Ἁγίου οὓς ἐξελέξατο, ἀνελήφθη· οἷς καὶ παρέστησεν ἑαυτὸν
Holy whom He chose, He was taken up; to whom also He showed Himself

ζῶντα μετὰ τὸ παθεῖν αὐτὸν ἐν πολλοῖς τεκμηρίοις, δι'
living after the suffering (of) Him by many infallible proofs through

ἡμερῶν τεσσαράκοντα ὀπτανόμενος αὐτοῖς, καὶ λέγων τὰ
days forty being seen by them, and saying the things

4 περὶ τῆς βασιλείας τοῦ Θεοῦ. καὶ συναλιζόμενος μετ' αὐτῶν
about the kingdom — of God. And meeting with them

παρήγγειλεν αὐτοῖς ἀπὸ Ἱεροσολύμων μὴ χωρίζεσθαι,
He charged them from Jerusalem not to depart,

ἀλλὰ περιμένειν τὴν ἐπαγγελίαν τοῦ πατρός, ἣν ἠκούσατέ
but to await the promise of the Father, which you heard

5 μου· ὅτι Ἰωάννης μὲν ἐβάπτισεν ὕδατι, ὑμεῖς δὲ βαπτισθή-
of Me, because John indeed baptized in water, you but will be

σεσθε ἐν Πνεύματι Ἁγίῳ οὐ μετὰ πολλὰς ταύτας ἡμέρας.
baptized in (the) Spirit Holy not after many these days.

6 Οἱ μὲν οὖν συνελθόντες ἐπηρώτων αὐτὸν λέγοντες, Κύριε,
those So then coming together questioned Him, saying, Lord,

εἰ ἐν τῷ χρόνῳ τούτῳ ἀποκαθιστάνεις τὴν βασιλείαν τῷ
if at — time this restore You the kingdom —

7 Ἰσραήλ; εἶπε δὲ πρὸς αὐτούς, Οὐχ ὑμῶν ἐστι γνῶναι
to Israel? He said And to them, Not of you it is to know

χρόνους ἢ καιροὺς οὓς ὁ πατὴρ ἔθετο ἐν τῇ ἰδίᾳ ἐξουσίᾳ.
times or seasons which the Father placed in the own authority.

8 ἀλλὰ λήψεσθε δύναμιν, ἐπελθόντος τοῦ Ἁγίου Πνεύματος
But you will receive power, coming the Holy Spirit

ἐφ' ὑμᾶς· καὶ ἔσεσθέ μοι μάρτυρες ἔν τε Ἰερουσαλήμ, καὶ ἐν
upon you, and you will be of Me witnesses in both Jerusalem, and in

πάσῃ τῇ Ἰουδαίᾳ καὶ Σαμαρείᾳ, καὶ ἕως ἐσχάτου τῆς γῆς.
all — Judea, and Samaria, and unto (the) end of the earth.

9 καὶ ταῦτα εἰπών, βλεπόντων αὐτῶν ἐπήρθη, καὶ νεφέλη
And these things saying, looking them, He was taken up, and a cloud

10 ὑπέλαβεν αὐτὸν ἀπὸ τῶν ὀφθαλμῶν αὐτῶν. καὶ ὡς ἀτενί-
received Him from the eyes of them. And as gazing

ζοντες ἦσαν εἰς τὸν οὐρανόν, πορευομένου αὐτοῦ, καὶ ἰδοὺ
they were to Heaven, going Him, and behold,

up, two men also stood beside him in white clothing, [11] who also said, Men, Galileans, why do you stand looking into the heavens? This Jesus who was taken up from you into Heaven will come this way, in the same way you saw Him going into Heaven. [12] Then they returned to Jerusalem from that called Mount of Olives, which is near Jerusalem, being a sabbath's journey distant. [13] And when they had gone in, they went up to the upper room, where both Peter and James and John and Andrew, Philip and Thomas, Bartholomew and Matthew, James of Alpheus and Simon the Zelote, and Jude (brother) of James were staying. [14] These all were steadfastly continuing with one accord in prayer and supplication with (the) women, and Mary the mother of Jesus, and with His brothers.

[15] And in those days Peter having stood up in (the) midst of the disciples said — and (the) number of names was altogether about a hundred and twenty — [16] Men, brothers, it was necessary (for) this Scripture to have been fulfilled which the Holy Spirit spoke before by (the) mouth of David concerning Judas, who became guide to those who took Jesus; [17] for he was counted with us and was given a part in this ministry. [18] Now, then, this one got a field out of the reward of unrighteousness, and having fallen headlong burst in (the) middle, and all his bowels gushed out. [19] And it became known to all those living in Jerusalem, so that that field was called in their own language, Akeldama, that is, Field of Blood. [20] For it has been written in (the) book of Psalms, "Let his home become forsaken and let there be no one living in it," and, "let another take his office." [21] Therefore

**11** ἄνδρες δύο παρειστήκεισαν αὐτοῖς ἐν ἐσθῆτι λευκῇ, οἳ καὶ
men  two  stood by  them  in clothing  white,  who also
εἶπον, Ἄνδρες Γαλιλαῖοι, τί ἑστήκατε ἐμβλέποντες εἰς τὸν
said,  Men,  Galileans,  why do you stand  looking  to —
οὐρανόν; οὗτος ὁ Ἰησοῦς, ὁ ἀναληφθεὶς ἀφ' ὑμῶν εἰς τὸν
Heaven?  This —  Jesus, the (one) being taken from you  to —
οὐρανόν, οὕτως ἐλεύσεται ὃν τρόπον ἐθεάσασθε αὐτὸν
Heaven,  thus  will come  in the way  you beheld  Him
πορευόμενον εἰς τὸν οὐρανόν.
going  into —  Heaven.

**12** Τότε ὑπέστρεψαν εἰς Ἰερουσαλὴμ ἀπὸ ὄρους τοῦ καλου-
Then they returned to  Jerusalem  from (the) mount  being
μένου Ἐλαιῶνος, ὅ ἐστιν ἐγγὺς Ἰερουσαλήμ, σαββάτου
called Of olive grove, which is  near  Jerusalem,  a sabbath's

**13** ἔχον ὁδόν. καὶ ὅτε εἰσῆλθον, ἀνέβησαν εἰς τὸ ὑπερῷον οὗ
having a way. And when they entered, they went up to the upper room where
ἦσαν καταμένοντες, ὅ τε Πέτρος καὶ Ἰάκωβος καὶ Ἰωάννης καὶ
they were waiting,  both Peter and  James  and  John  and
Ἀνδρέας, Φίλιππος καὶ Θωμᾶς, Βαρθολομαῖος καὶ Ματθαῖος,
Andrew,  Philip  and Thomas,  Bartholomew  and  Matthew,
Ἰάκωβος Ἀλφαίου καὶ Σίμων ὁ Ζηλωτής, καὶ Ἰούδας Ἰακώ-
James  of Alpheus and Simon the Zealot,  and  Judas  of

**14** βου. οὗτοι πάντες ἦσαν προσκαρτεροῦντες ὁμοθυμαδὸν τῇ
James. These  all  were  continuing steadfastly  with one mind —
προσευχῇ καὶ τῇ δεήσει, σὺν γυναιξὶ καὶ Μαρίᾳ τῇ μητρὶ τοῦ
in prayer  and in supplication, with (the) women, and Mary the mother —
Ἰησοῦ, καὶ σὺν τοῖς ἀδελφοῖς αὐτοῦ.
of Jesus, and with the  brothers  of Him.

**15** Καὶ ἐν ταῖς ἡμέραις ταύταις ἀναστὰς Πέτρος ἐν μέσῳ τῶν
And in  days  these  standing up Peter  in (the) midst of the
μαθητῶν εἶπεν (ἦν τε ὄχλος ὀνομάτων ἐπὶ τὸ αὐτὸ ὡς ἑκατὸν
disciples  said; was and the crowd of names  together  about a hundred

**16** εἴκοσιν), Ἄνδρες ἀδελφοί, ἔδει πληρωθῆναι τὴν γραφὴν
twenty;  Men,  brothers, it behoved to be fulfilled  — Scripture
ταύτην, ἣν προεῖπε τὸ Πνεῦμα τὸ Ἅγιον διὰ στόματος
this,  which spoke the Spirit  —  Holy through (the) mouth
Δαβὶδ περὶ Ἰούδα, τοῦ γενομένου ὁδηγοῦ τοῖς συλλαβοῦσι
David concerning Judas, the (one) being  guide  to the (ones) taking

**17** τὸν Ἰησοῦν. ὅτι κατηριθμημένος ἦν σὺν ἡμῖν, καὶ ἔλαχε τὸν
—  Jesus; because being numbered he was with us,  and obtained the

**18** κλῆρον τῆς διακονίας ταύτης. (οὗτος μὲν οὖν ἐκτήσατο
portion —  of ministry this;  this one  therefore  bought
χωρίον ἐκ τοῦ μισθοῦ τῆς ἀδικίας, καὶ πρηνὴς γενόμενος
a field out of the  reward  — of unrighteousnes, and headlong becoming

**19** ἐλάκησε μέσος, καὶ ἐξεχύθη πάντα τὰ σπλάγχνα αὐτοῦ. καὶ
he burst in (the) middle, and poured out all the  bowels  of him. And
γνωστὸν ἐγένετο πᾶσι τοῖς κατοικοῦσιν Ἰερουσαλήμ, ὥστε
known  it became to all those  inhabiting  Jerusalem,  so as
κληθῆναι τὸ χωρίον ἐκεῖνο τῇ ἰδίᾳ διαλέκτῳ αὐτῶν Ἀκελ-
to be called — field  that  in the own dialect  of them  Akel-

**20** δαμά, τοῦτ' ἔστι, χωρίον αἵματος.) γέγραπται γὰρ ἐν βίβλῳ
dama, that  is,  Field of Blood.  it has been written For in (the) roll
Ψαλμῶν, Γενηθήτω ἡ ἔπαυλις αὐτοῦ ἔρημος, καὶ μὴ ἔστω ὁ
of Psalms, Let become the estate  of him forsaken,  and not  be he

**21** κατοικῶν ἐν αὐτῇ· καί, Τὴν ἐπισκοπὴν αὐτοῦ λάβοι ἕτερος.
dwelling in it;  and,  The  office  of him let take another.

it is right that one of those men who have been with us all the time in which the Lord Jesus came in and went out among us, [22] beginning from the baptism of John until the day in which He was taken up from us, one of these to become with us a witness of His resurrection. [23] And they set out two, Joseph called Barsabas, who was surnamed Justus, and Matthias. [24] And praying they said, You, Lord, knower of all hearts, show which one of these two you chose [25] to receive the share of this service and apostleship from which Judas sinning fell, to go to his own place. [26] And they gave their lots, and the lot fell on Mathias; and he was numbered with the eleven apostles.

δεῖ οὖν τῶν συνελθόντων ἡμῖν ἀνδρῶν ἐν παντὶ χρόνῳ ἐν ᾧ
must Then of the accompanying us     men     in  all (the) time in which

εἰσῆλθε καὶ ἐξῆλθεν ἐφ' ἡμᾶς ὁ Κύριος Ἰησοῦς, ἀρξάμενος ἀπὸ
went in and and went out among us the Lord  Jesus,  beginning  from

**22** τοῦ βαπτίσματος Ἰωάννου, ἕως τῆς ἡμέρας ἧς ἀνελήφθη ἀφ'
the  baptism    of John   until the day  when He was taken from

ἡμῶν, μάρτυρα τῆς ἀναστάσεως αὐτοῦ γενέσθαι σὺν ἡμῖν
us,  a witness of the  resurrection  of Him to become with  us

**23** ἕνα τούτων. καὶ ἔστησαν δύο, Ἰωσὴφ τὸν καλούμενον
one of these.  And they set  two,  Joseph the (one) being called

**24** Βαρσαβᾶν, ὃς ἐπεκλήθη Ἰοῦστος, καὶ Ματθίαν. καὶ προσ-
Barsabas,  who was surnamed Justus, and Matthias.  And

ευξάμενοι εἶπον, Σὺ Κύριε καρδιογνῶστα πάντων, ἀνά-
praying   they said, You, Lord,  Heart-knower  of all,   show

**25** δειξον ἐκ τούτων τῶν δύο ὃν ἕνα ἐξελέξω, λαβεῖν τὸν κλῆρον
out of these   — two which one You chose to take the  part

τῆς διακονίας ταύτης καὶ ἀποστολῆς, ἐξ ἧς παρέβη Ἰούδας,
of ministry   this and apostleship, from which fell  Judas,

**26** πορευθῆναι εἰς τὸν τόπον τὸν ἴδιον. καὶ ἔδωκαν κλήρους
to go    to the place  —  own.  And they gave  lots

αὐτῶν, καὶ ἔπεσεν ὁ κλῆρος ἐπὶ Ματθίαν, καὶ συγκατεψη-
for them, and  fell  the lot  on  Matthias; and he was counted

φίσθη μετὰ τῶν ἕνδεκα ἀποστόλων.
with the eleven   apostles.

## CHAPTER 2

[1] And during the fulfilling of the day of Pentecost, they were all with one accord in the same place. [2] And suddenly a sound came out of the sky, like a rushing violent wind! And it filled the whole house where they were sitting. [3] And divided tongues appeared to them, like fire, and sat on each one of them. [4] And they were all filled with (the) Holy Spirit, and began to speak with other languages, as the Spirit gave them (ability) to speak. [5] Now Jews were living in Jerusalem, pious men from every nation of those under the heavens. [6] But the rumor having arisen, the multitude came together and were confounded, because each one heard them speaking in his own dialect. [7] And all were amazed and wondered, saying to one another, Behold, are not all these who are speaking Galileans? [8] And how do we hear each one in our own dialect in which we

**1** Καὶ ἐν τῷ συμπληροῦσθαι τὴν ἡμέραν τῆς Πεντηκοστῆς,
And in the  fulfilling  of the Day  —  of Pentecost,

**2** ἦσαν ἅπαντες ὁμοθυμαδὸν ἐπὶ τὸ αὐτό. καὶ ἐγένετο ἄφνω
they were all  with one mind in the same place. And was  suddenly

ἐκ τοῦ οὐρανοῦ ἦχος ὥσπερ φερομένης πνοῆς βιαίας, καὶ
out of Heaven a sound  as  being borne of a wind violent,  and

**3** ἐπλήρωσεν ὅλον τὸν οἶκον οὗ ἦσαν καθήμενοι. καὶ ὤφθησαν
it filled   all  the house where they were sitting. And appeared

αὐτοῖς διαμεριζόμεναι γλῶσσαι ὡσεὶ πυρός, ἐκάθισέ τε ἐφ'
to them being distributed  tongues  as  of fire,  it sat and on

**4** ἕνα ἕκαστον αὐτῶν. καὶ ἐπλήσθησαν ἅπαντες Πνεύματος
one  each  of them. And they were filled all  of (the) Spirit

Ἁγίου, καὶ ἤρξαντο λαλεῖν ἑτέραις γλώσσαις, καθὼς τὸ
Holy,  and  began to speak in other  languages,  as  the

Πνεῦμα ἐδίδου αὐτοῖς ἀποφθέγγεσθαι.
Spirit  gave to them  to speak.

**5** Ἦσαν δὲ ἐν Ἰερουσαλὴμ κατοικοῦντες Ἰουδαῖοι, ἄνδρες
were And in  Jerusalem   living   Jews,  men

**6** εὐλαβεῖς, ἀπὸ παντὸς ἔθνους τῶν ὑπὸ τὸν οὐρανόν. γενο-
devout  from  every nation of those under — Heaven. happen-

μένης δὲ τῆς φωνῆς ταύτης, συνῆλθε τὸ πλῆθος καὶ συνεχύθη,
ing And — sound  this,  came together the multitude and were confounded

ὅτι ἤκουον εἷς ἕκαστος τῇ ἰδίᾳ διαλέκτῳ λαλούντων αὐτῶν.
because they heard each in the own  dialect  speaking  them.

**7** ἐξίσταντο δὲ πάντες καὶ ἐθαύμαζον, λέγοντες πρὸς ἀλλή-
were amazed And all  and marveled,  saying  to one

λους, Οὐκ ἰδοὺ πάντες οὗτοί εἰσιν οἱ λαλοῦντες Γαλιλαῖοι;
another, not, Behold, all  these  are those speaking  Galileans?

**8** καὶ πῶς ἡμεῖς ἀκούομεν ἕκαστος τῇ ἰδίᾳ διαλέκτῳ ἡμῶν ἐν
And how we  hear  each  in the own  dialect  of us  in

were born, [9] Parthians and Medes and Elamites, and those who live in Mesopotamia, and Judea and Cappadocia, Pontus and Asia, [10] both Phrygia and Pamphylia, Egypt and the parts of Libya which (is) about Cyrene, and the Romans visiting, both Jews and proselytes, [11] Cretans and Arabians, we hear them speaking in our own languages the great things of God? [12] And all were amazed and were puzzled, saying to one another, What would this be? [13] But others ridiculing said, They are full of new wine.

[14] But Peter standing up with the eleven, lifted up his voice and spoke out to them, Men, Jews, and all you who live in Jerusalem, let this be known to you, and listen to my words: [15] For these are not drunks, as you take it, for it is (the) third hour of the day; [16] But this is that which has been spoken by the prophet Joel, [17] "And it shall happen in the last days, God says, I will pour out of My Spirit on all flesh; and your sons and your daughters shall prophesy; and your young men shall see visions, and your old men shall dream dreams; [18] and also I will pour out My Spirit on My slaves and slave-girls in those days, and they shall prophesy. [19] And I will give wonders in the Heaven above, and miracles on the earth below, blood and fire and vapor of smoke. [20] The sun shall be turned into darkness and the moon into blood, before the coming of the great and glorious day of the Lord. [21] And it shall be, everyone who shall call on the name of the Lord shall be saved." [22] Men, Israelites, hear these words,

**9** ἧ ἐγεννήθημεν; Πάρθοι καὶ Μῆδοι καὶ Ἐλαμῖται, καὶ οἱ
which we were born, Parthians and Medes and Elamites, and those
κατοικοῦντες τὴν Μεσοποταμίαν, Ἰουδαίαν τε καὶ Καπ-
inhabiting — Mesopotamia, Judea both and Cappa-

**10** παδοκίαν, Πόντον καὶ τὴν Ἀσίαν, Φρυγίαν τε καὶ Παμφυ-
docia, Pontus and — Asia, Phrygia both and Pam-
λίαν, Αἴγυπτον καὶ τὰ μέρη τῆς Λιβύης τῆς κατὰ Κυρήνην,
phylia, Egypt and the regions — of Libya — over against Cyrene,
καὶ οἱ ἐπιδημοῦντες Ῥωμαῖοι, Ἰουδαῖοί τε καὶ προσήλυτοι,
and the temporarily residing Romans, Jews both and proselytes,

**11** Κρῆτες καὶ Ἄραβες, ἀκούομεν λαλούντων αὐτῶν ταῖς
Cretans and Arabians, we hear speaking them in
ἡμετέραις γλώσσαις τὰ μεγαλεῖα τοῦ Θεοῦ. ἐξίσταντο δὲ
our languages the great deeds — of God. were amazed And

**12** πάντες καὶ διηπόρουν, ἄλλος πρὸς ἄλλον λέγοντες, Τί ἂν
all and were puzzled, other to other saying, What would

**13** θέλοι τοῦτο εἶναι; ἕτεροι δὲ χλευάζοντες ἔλεγον ὅτι λεύκους
you wish this to be? others But mocking said, — Of sweet wine
μεμεστωμένοι εἰσί.
full they are.

**14** Σταθεὶς δὲ Πέτρος σὺν τοῖς ἕνδεκα, ἐπῆρε τὴν φωνὴν αὐ-
standing But Peter with the eleven lifted up the voice of
τοῦ, καὶ ἀπεφθέγξατο αὐτοῖς, Ἄνδρες Ἰουδαῖοι, καὶ οἱ κατ-
him and spoke out to them, Men, Jews, and those
οἰκοῦντες Ἰερουσαλὴμ ἅπαντες, τοῦτο ὑμῖν γνωστὸν ἔστω,
inhabiting Jerusalem all, this to you known let be,

**15** καὶ ἐνωτίσασθε τὰ ῥήματά μου. οὐ γάρ, ὡς ὑμεῖς ὑπολαμ-
and give ear to the words of me. not For, as you imagine,
βάνετε, οὗτοι μεθύουσιν· ἔστι γὰρ ὥρα τρίτη τῆς ἡμέρας·
these are drunk, it is for hour third of the day;

**16** ἀλλὰ τοῦτό ἐστι τὸ εἰρημένον διὰ τοῦ προφήτου Ἰωήλ,
but this is the thing being spoken through the prophet Joel:

**17** Καὶ ἔσται ἐν ταῖς ἐσχάταις ἡμέραις, λέγει ὁ Θεός, ἐκχεῶ ἀπὸ
And it shall be in the last days, says — God, I will pour from
τοῦ πνεύματός μου ἐπὶ πᾶσαν σάρκα· καὶ προφητεύσουσιν
the Spirit of Me on all flesh, and will prophesy
οἱ υἱοὶ ὑμῶν καὶ αἱ θυγατέρες ὑμῶν. καὶ οἱ νεανίσκοι ὑμῶν
the sons of you, and the daughters of you, and the young men of you
ὁράσεις ὄψονται, καὶ οἱ πρεσβύτεροι ὑμῶν ἐνύπνια ἐνυπνια-
visions will see, and the old men of you dreams will

**18** σθήσονται· καί γε ἐπὶ τοὺς δούλους μου καὶ ἐπὶ τὰς δούλας
dream, and — on the male slaves of Me, and on the female slaves
μου ἐν ταῖς ἡμέραις ἐκείναις ἐκχεῶ ἀπὸ τοῦ πνεύματός μου, καὶ
of Me, in — days those I will pour from the Spirit of Me, and

**19** προφητεύσουσι. καὶ δώσω τέρατα ἐν τῷ οὐρανῷ ἄνω, καὶ
they will prophesy. And I will give wonders in the heaven above, and
σημεῖα ἐπὶ τῆς γῆς κάτω, αἷμα καὶ πῦρ καὶ ἀτμίδα καπνοῦ·
signs on the earth below, blood and fire and vapor of smoke.

**20** ὁ ἥλιος μεταστραφήσεται εἰς σκότος, καὶ ἡ σελήνη εἰς
The sun will be turned into darkness and the moon into
αἷμα, πρὶν ἢ ἐλθεῖν τὴν ἡμέραν Κυρίου τὴν μεγάλην καὶ
blood, before comes the day of (the) Lord the great and

**21** ἐπιφανῆ· καὶ ἔσται, πᾶς ὃς ἂν ἐπικαλέσηται τὸ ὄνομα Κυρίου
notable. And it will be everyone whoever calls on the name of (the) Lord

**22** σωθήσεται. ἄνδρες Ἰσραηλῖται, ἀκούσατε τοὺς λόγους
will be saved. Men, Israelites, hear — words

Jesus the Nazarene, a man set forth by God to you by works of power and wonders and miracles, which God worked by Him in your midst, as yourselves also know; [23] Him, by the before-determined counsel and foreknowledge of God was delivered to you, (and) having taken by lawless hands, having crucified, you put to death. [24] Whom God raised up, having loosed the throes of death, in as much as it was not possible (for) Him to be held by it; [25] for David said as to Him, "I always foresaw the Lord before Me, because He is at My right (hand), that I may not be moved. [26] For this reason My heart rejoiced and My tongue was glad; yes, more, My flesh shall rest in hope, [27] for You will not leave My soul in Hades, nor will you give Your Holy One to see corruption. [28] You revealed to Me paths of life; You will fill Me with joy with Your face." [29] Men, brothers, it is permitted (me) to speak with freedom to you about the patriarch David, that both he died and was buried, and his tomb is among us to this day. [30] Being a prophet, then, and knowing that God swore to him with an oath, of (the) fruit of his loins as concerning flesh to raise up the Christ, to sit on his throne; [31] foreseeing he spoke about the resurrection of the Christ, that His soul was not left in Hades, nor His flesh saw corruption. [32] This Jesus God raised up of which all we are witnesses. [33] Therefore, having been exalted by the right hand of God, and having received the promise of the Holy Spirit from the Father, He poured out this which you now see and hear. [34] For David did not ascend into Heaven, but he himself said, "The Lord said to my Lord, Sit at My right hand [35] until I place Your enemies as a

τούτους· Ἰησοῦν τὸν Ναζωραῖον, ἄνδρα ἀπὸ τοῦ Θεοῦ
these:　Jesus　the Nazarene,　a man from　—　God

ἀποδεδειγμένον εἰς ὑμᾶς δυνάμεσι καὶ τέρασι καὶ σημείοις,
having been approved among you by powerful deeds and wonders and signs,

οἷς ἐποίησε δι' αὐτοῦ ὁ Θεὸς ἐν μεσω υμων, καθὼς καὶ αὐτοὶ
which did through Him　God amidst you,　as also yourselves

23 οἴδατε, τοῦτον τῇ ὡρισμένῃ βουλῇ καὶ προγνώσει τοῦ Θεοῦ
you know, this One by the before determined counsel and foreknowledge — of God

ἔκδοτον λαβόντες, διὰ χειρῶν ἀνόμων προσπήξαντες,
given up having taken by hands lawless, having crucified,

24 ἀνείλετε· ὃν ὁ Θεὸς ἀνέστησε, λύσας τὰς ὠδῖνας τοῦ θανάτου,
you killed, whom God raised up, having loosed the throes — of death,

25 καθότι οὐκ ἦν δυνατὸν κρατεῖσθαι αὐτὸν ὑπ' αὐτοῦ. Δαβίδ
because not it was possible to be held Him by it. David

γὰρ λέγει εἰς αὐτόν, Προωρώμην τὸν Κύριον ἐνώπιόν μου
For says (as) to Him, I foresaw the Lord before Me

26 διὰ παντός· ὅτι ἐκ δεξιῶν μου ἐστίν, ἵνα μὴ σαλευθῶ· διὰ
always, because on (the) right Me He is, that not I be moved. There-

τοῦτο εὐφράνθη ἡ καρδία μου, καὶ ἠγαλλιάσατο ἡ γλῶσσά
fore was glad the heart of Me and exulted the tongue

27 μου· ἔτι δὲ καὶ ἡ σάρξ μου κατασκηνώσει ἐπ' ἐλπίδι· ὅτι οὐκ
of Me; yet And also the flesh of Me will dwell on hope, because not

ἐγκαταλείψεις τὴν ψυχήν μου εἰς ᾅδου, οὐδὲ δώσεις τὸν
You will leave the soul of Me in Hades, nor will You give the

28 ὅσιόν σου ἰδεῖν διαφθοράν. ἐγνώρισάς μοι ὁδοὺς ζωῆς·
Holy One of You to see corruption. You revealed to Me paths of life.

29 πληρώσεις με εὐφροσύνης μετὰ τοῦ προσώπου σου. ἄνδρες
You will fill Me with joy with the face of You. Men,

ἀδελφοί, ἐξὸν εἰπεῖν μετὰ παρρησίας πρὸς ὑμᾶς περὶ τοῦ
brothers, it is permitted to say with plainness to you concerning the

πατριάρχου Δαβίδ, ὅτι καὶ ἐτελεύτησε καὶ ἐτάφη, καὶ τὸ
patriarch David, that both he died and was buried, and the

30 μνῆμα αὐτοῦ ἐστιν ἐν ἡμῖν ἄχρι τῆς ἡμέρας ταύτης. προφή-
tomb of him is among us until — day this. a prophet

της οὖν ὑπάρχων, καὶ εἰδὼς ὅτι ὅρκῳ ὤμοσεν αὐτῷ ὁ Θεός,
Then being, and knowing that with an oath sworn to him God

ἐκ καρποῦ τῆς ὀσφύος αὐτοῦ τὸ κατὰ σάρκα ἀναστήσειν
of (the) fruit of the loin of him as concerning flesh to raise up

31 τὸν Χριστόν, καθίσαι ἐπὶ τοῦ θρόνου αὐτοῦ, προϊδὼν
the Christ, to sit on the throne of him, foreseeing

ἐλάλησε περὶ τῆς ἀναστάσεως τοῦ Χριστοῦ, ὅτι οὐ κατελείφθη
he spoke concerning the resurrection of the Christ, that not was left

ἡ ψυχὴ αὐτοῦ εἰς ᾅδου, οὐδὲ ἡ σὰρξ αὐτοῦ εἶδε διαφθοράν.
the soul of Him in Hades, nor the flesh of Him saw corruption.

32 τοῦτον τὸν Ἰησοῦν ἀνέστησεν ὁ Θεός, οὗ πάντες ἡμεῖς ἐσμεν
This — Jesus raised up God, of which all we are

33 μάρτυρες. τῇ δεξιᾷ οὖν τοῦ Θεοῦ ὑψωθείς, τήν τε ἐπαγγελίαν
witnesses; to the right, therefore, of God being exalted, the and promise

τοῦ Ἁγίου Πνεύματος λαβὼν παρὰ τοῦ πατρός, ἐξέχεε
of the Holy Spirit receiving from the Father, He poured

34 τοῦτο ὃ νῦν ὑμεῖς βλέπετε καὶ ἀκούετε. οὐ γὰρ Δαβίδ ἀνέβη
this which now you see and hear. not For David ascended

εἰς τοὺς οὐρανούς, λέγει δὲ αὐτός, Εἶπεν ὁ Κύριος τῷ Κυρίῳ
to the heavens, says but he, said The Lord to the Lord

35 μου, Κάθου ἐκ δεξιῶν μου, ἕως ἂν θῶ τοὺς ἐχθρούς σου
of me, Sit at (the) right of Me until I place the enemies of You

footstool for Your feet."
[36] Then assuredly, let all
(the) house of Israel ac-
knowledge that God made
Him both Lord and Christ,
this same Jesus whom you
crucified.

[37] And having heard,
they were stabbed in the
heart and said to Peter and
the other apostles, What
shall we do, men, brothers?
[38] And Peter said to
them, Repent and be
baptized, each of you in
the name of Jesus Christ,
for remission of sins, and
you will receive the gift of
the Holy Spirit. [39] For
the promise is to you and
to your children, and to all
those at a distance, as
many as (the) Lord our
God may call. [40] And
with many other words he
earnestly testified and
exhorted, saying, Be saved
from this crooked
generation. [41] Then
those who gladly had
welcomed his word were
baptized; and that day
about three thousand souls
were added. [42] And
they were steadfatly
continuing in the teaching
of the apostles and in
fellowship, and the
breaking of bread and
prayers. [43] And fear
came on every soul, and
many wonders and
miracles took place
through the apostles.
[44] And all who believed
were together and had all
common, [45] and they
sold possessions and goods
and divided them to all,
according as anyone had
need. [46] And every day
steadfastly continuing with
one accord in the Temple,
and breaking bread in
(their) houses, they took
food with gladness and
simplicity of heart,
[47] praising God, and
having favor with all the
people; and the Lord
added to the church daily
those who were being
saved.

**36** ὑποπόδιον τῶν ποδῶν σου. ἀσφαλῶς οὖν γινωσκέτω πᾶς
a footstool to the      feet of You. Assuredly, therefore, let know    all
οἶκος Ἰσραήλ, ὅτι καὶ Κύριον καὶ Χριστὸν αὐτὸν ὁ Θεὸς
the house of Israel that both    Lord    and    Christ    Him     God
ἐποίησε, τοῦτον τὸν Ἰησοῦν ὃν ὑμεῖς ἐσταυρώσατε.
made,    this    —    Jesus whom you    crucified.

**37** Ἀκούσαντες δὲ κατενύγησαν τῇ καρδίᾳ, εἶπόν τε πρὸς
having heard And, they were stabbed in the heart,   said and   to
τὸν Πέτρον καὶ τοὺς λοιποὺς ἀποστόλους, Τί ποιήσομεν,
—    Peter,    and    the remaining    apostles,    What may we do,

**38** ἄνδρες ἀδελφοί; Πέτρος δὲ ἔφη πρὸς αὐτούς, Μετανοήσατε,
men.   brothers? Peter And said to    them,    Repent
καὶ βαπτισθήτω ἕκαστος ὑμῶν ἐπὶ τῷ ὀνόματι Ἰησοῦ
and be baptized    each    of you   on   the    name   of Jesus
Χριστοῦ εἰς ἄφεσιν ἁμαρτιῶι, καὶ λήψεσθε τὴν δωρεὰν
Christ    to forgiveness of sins,    and you will receive the    gift

**39** τοῦ Ἁγίου Πνεύματος. ὑμῖν γάρ ἐστιν ἡ ἐπαγγελία, καὶ
of the Holy   Spirit.    to you For   is   the   promise,    and
τοῖς τέκνοις ὑμῶν, καὶ πᾶσι τοῖς εἰς μακράν, ὅσους ἂν προσ-
to the children of you, even to all those at a distance, as many as    may

**40** καλέσηται Κύριος ὁ Θεὸς ἡμῶν. ἑτέροις τε λόγοις πλείοσι
call    (the) Lord, the God of us.    with other And words    many
διεμαρτύρετο καὶ παρεκάλει λέγων, Σώθητε ἀπὸ τῆς γενεᾶς
he earnestly testified and exhorted, saying,    Be saved from   — generation

**41** τῆς σκολιᾶς ταύτης. οἱ μὲν οὖν ἀσμένως ἀποδεξάμενοι τὸν
—   perverse this.    Those, then,    gladly    welcoming    the
λόγον αὐτοῦ ἐβαπτίσθησαν· καὶ προσετέθησαν τῇ ἡμέρᾳ
words of him   were baptized,    and there were added   —   day

**42** ἐκείνῃ ψυχαὶ ὡσεὶ τρισχίλιαι. ἦσαν δὲ προσκαρτεροῦντες
that souls,   about three thousand. they were And steadfastly continuing
τῇ διδαχῇ τῶν ἀποστόλων καὶ τῇ κοινωνίᾳ, καὶ τῇ κλάσει
in the teaching of the apostles.    and in the fellowship, and in the breaking
τοῦ ἄρτου καὶ ταῖς προσευχαῖς.
of the bread, and in the    prayers.

**43** Ἐγένετο δὲ πάσῃ ψυχῇ φόβος, πολλά τε τέρατα καὶ
came    And to every   soul    fear;   many    and wonders and

**44** σημεῖα διὰ τῶν ἀποστόλων ἐγίνετο. πάντες δὲ οἱ πιστεύ-
signs through the apostles    occurred.    all    And the believing

**45** οντες ἦσαν ἐπὶ τὸ αὐτό, καὶ εἶχον ἅπαντα κοινά, καὶ τὰ
ones were    together,    and had   all things common, and the
κτήματα καὶ τὰς ὑπάρξεις ἐπίπρασκον, καὶ διεμέριζον αὐτὰ
goods    and the possessions they sold    and distributed    them

**46** πᾶσι, καθότι ἄν τις χρείαν εἶχε. καθ' ἡμέραν τε προσκαρτε-
to all,   according as anyone need had. from day to day And continuing
ροῦντες ὁμοθυμαδὸν εν τῷ ἱερῷ, κλῶντές τε κατ' οἶκον
steadfastly with one mind in the   Temple breaking and from to house / house
ἄρτον, μετελάμβανον τροφῆς ἐν ἀγαλλιάσει καὶ ἀφελοτητι
bread,   they shared    food    in   gladness    and simplicity

**47** καρδίας, αἰνοῦντες τὸν Θεόν, καὶ ἔχοντες χάριν πρὸς ὅλον
of heart, praising    —    God, and having    favor   with all
τὸν λαόν. ὁ δὲ Κύριος προσετίθει τοὺς σωζομένους καθ'
the people. the And Lord    added    those    being saved from
ἡμέραν τῇ ἐκκλησίᾳ.
day      to the church.

## CHAPTER 3

**CHAPTER 3**

[1] And Peter and John went up together into the Temple at the hour of prayer, the ninth; [2] and a certain man, being lame from his mother's womb, was being carried, whom they placed daily at the door of the Temple called Beautiful, to ask alms from those who were going into the Temple; [3] who seeing Peter and John being about to enter into the Temple, asked to receive alms. [4] And Peter with John looking intently on him said, Look to us. [5] And he attended to them, expecting to receive something from them. [6] But Peter said, There is no silver and gold to me, but what I have, this I give to you: In the name of Jesus Christ the Nazarean rise up and walk! [7] And having taken him by the right hand, he raised (him) up, and immediately his feet and ankle-bones were strengthened. [8] And leaping up he stood and walked, and went in with them into the Temple, walking and leaping and praising God. [9] And all the people saw him walking and praising God. [10] And they recognized him, that it was he who (was) sitting at the Beautiful Gate of the Temple for alms; and they were filled with wonder and amazement at that which had happened to him. [11] And as the lame one who had been healed hugged Peter and John, all the people ran together to them in the Porch called Solomon's, greatly amazed. [12] And seeing (it) Peter answered to the people, Men, Israelites, why do you wonder at this? Or why do you look intently on us as if by (own) power or goodness (we) had made him to walk? [13] The God of Abraham and Isaac and Jacob, the God of our fathers, glorified His

1 Ἐπὶ τὸ αὐτὸ δὲ Πέτρος καὶ Ἰωάννης ἀνέβαινον εἰς τὸ
on the same (day) And Peter and John were going into the

2 ἱερὸν ἐπὶ τὴν ὥραν τῆς προσευχῆς τὴν ἐννάτην. καί τις
Temple at the hour — of prayer, the ninth, and a certain

ἀνὴρ χωλὸς ἐκ κοιλίας μητρὸς αὐτοῦ ὑπάρχων ἐβαστάζετο·
man lame from womb mother's his being, was being carried

ὃν ἐτίθουν καθ' ἡμέραν πρὸς τὴν θύραν τοῦ ἱεροῦ τὴν
whom they put from day to day at the door of the Temple —

λεγομένην Ὡραίαν, τοῦ αἰτεῖν ἐλεημοσύνην παρὰ τῶν
being called Beautiful, — to ask alms from those

3 εἰσπορευομένων εἰς τὸ ἱερόν. ὃς ἰδὼν Πέτρον καὶ Ἰωάννην
going into the Temple, who seeing Peter and John

μέλλοντας εἰσιέναι εἰς τὸ ἱερόν, ἠρώτα ἐλεημοσύνην. ἀτενίσας
being about to go into the Temple, asked alms. gazing intently

4 δὲ Πέτρος εἰς αὐτὸν σὺν τῷ Ἰωάννῃ, εἶπε, Βλέψον εἰς ἡμᾶς. ὁ
And Peter at him, with — John, he said, Look at us! he

5 δὲ ἐπεῖχεν αὐτοῖς, προσδοκῶν τι παρ' αὐτῶν λαβεῖν. εἶπε δὲ
And paid heed to them, expecting something from them to receive. said And

6 Πέτρος, Ἀργύριον καὶ χρυσίον οὐχ ὑπάρχει μοι· ὃ δὲ ἔχω,
Peter, Silver and gold not is to me, what but I have,

τοῦτό σοι δίδωμι. ἐν τῷ ὀνόματι Ἰησοῦ Χριστοῦ τοῦ Ναζω-
this to you I give, in the name of Jesus Christ the Naza--

7 ραίου, ἔγειραι καὶ περιπάτει. καὶ πιάσας αὐτὸν τῆς δεξιᾶς
rean, rise up and walk! And taking him by the right

χειρὸς ἤγειρε· παραχρῆμα δὲ ἐστερεώθησαν αὐτοῦ αἱ βάσεις
hand, he raised up, immediately and were strengthened of him the feet

8 καὶ τὰ σφυρά. καὶ ἐξαλλόμενος ἔστη καὶ περιεπάτει, καὶ
and the ankle-bones. And leaping up he stood, and walked, and

εἰσῆλθε σὺν αὐτοῖς εἰς τὸ ἱερόν, περιπατῶν καὶ ἀλλόμενος
went in with them into the Temple, walking and leaping

9 καὶ αἰνῶν τὸν Θεόν. καὶ εἶδεν αὐτὸν πᾶς ὁ λαὸς περιπα-
and praising — God. And saw him all the people walking

10 τοῦντα καὶ αἰνοῦντα τὸν Θεόν· ἐπεγίνωσκόν τε αὐτὸν ὅτι
and praising — God; they recognized and him, that

οὗτος ἦν ὁ πρὸς τὴν ἐλεημοσύνην καθήμενος ἐπὶ τῇ Ὡραίᾳ
this was he for — alms sitting at the Beautiful

πύλῃ τοῦ ἱεροῦ· καὶ ἐπλήσθησαν θάμβους καὶ ἐκστάσεως
Gate of the Temple. And they were filled of amazement and ecstasy

ἐπὶ τῷ συμβεβηκότι αὐτῷ.
at the thing having happened to him.

11 Κρατοῦντος δὲ τοῦ ἰαθέντος χωλοῦ τὸν Πέτρον καὶ
holding And the healed lame (one) Peter and

Ἰωάννην, συνέδραμε πρὸς αὐτοὺς πᾶς ὁ λαὸς ἐπὶ τῇ στοᾷ
John, ran together to them all the people on the porch

12 τῇ καλουμένῃ Σολομῶντος, ἔκθαμβοι. ἰδὼν δὲ Πέτρος ἀπε-
— called Solomon's, greatly amazed. seeing And Peter

κρίνατο πρὸς τὸν λαόν, Ἄνδρες Ἰσραηλῖται, τί θαυμάζετε
answered to the people, Men, Israelites, Why do you marvel

ἐπὶ τούτῳ, ἢ ἡμῖν τί ἀτενίζετε, ὡς ἰδίᾳ δυνάμει ἢ εὐσεβείᾳ
at this one, or at us why do you gaze, as by own power or piety

13 πεποιηκόσι τοῦ περιπατεῖν αὐτόν; ὁ Θεὸς Ἀβραὰμ καὶ
having made — to walk him? The God of Abraham and

Ἰσαὰκ καὶ Ἰακώβ, ὁ Θεὸς τῶν πατέρων ἡμῶν, ἐδόξασε τὸν
of Isaac and of Jacob, the God of the fathers of us, glorified the

Servant Jesus, whom you delivered up, and denied Him in the presence of Pilate, he having decided to let (Him) go; [14] but you denied the holy and righteous One, and demanded a man, a murderer, to be granted to you. [15] But you killed the Author of life, whom God raised up from (the) dead, of which we are witnesses. [16] And by faith in His name, this one whom you behold and know (is) made strong by His name; and the faith which (is) through Him has given to him this complete soundness before all of you. [17] And now, brothers, I know that you acted in ignorance, as did your rulers also; [18] but what God before announced by (the) mouth of all His prophets, (that) the Christ should suffer, He fulfilled this way. [19] Therefore repent and be converted, for the blotting out of your sins, so that times of refreshing may come from (the) presence of the Lord, [20] and (that) He may send Him who was before proclaimed to you, Jesus Christ, [21] whom Heaven must indeed receive till times of restoration of all things, of which God spoke by (the) mouth of all His holy prophets from the past. [22] For Moses indeed said to the fathers, (The) Lord God will raise up to you a Prophet from among your brothers, like me; you shall hear Him in all things, whatever He may say to you. [23] And it shall be (that) every soul which may not hear that Prophet shall be destroyed from among the people. [24] And indeed all the prophets from Samuel, and those following, as many as spoke, also told of these days beforehand. [25] You are sons of the prophets and of the covenant which God appointed to our fathers, saying to Abraham, "And in your Seed shall all the families of the earth be blessed." [26] To you first

**14** παῖδα αὐτοῦ Ἰησοῦν· ὃν ὑμεῖς παρεδώκατε, καὶ ἠρνήσασθε
servant of Him, Jesus, whom you delivered up, and denied

αὐτὸν κατὰ πρόσωπον Πιλάτου, κρίναντος ἐκείνου ἀπο-
Him in the presence of Pilate, having decided that one to re-

λύειν. ὑμεῖς δὲ τὸν ἅγιον καὶ δίκαιον ἠρνήσασθε, καὶ ἠτή-
lease (Him), you but the holy and righteous One denied, and

**15** σασθε ἄνδρα φονέα χαρισθῆναι ὑμῖν, τὸν δὲ ἀρχηγὸν τῆς
asked a man, a murderer, to be granted to you, the and Author —

ζωῆς ἀπεκτείνατε· ὃν ὁ Θεὸς ἤγειρεν ἐκ νεκρῶν, οὗ ἡμεῖς
of life you killed, whom God raised from (the) dead, of which we

**16** μάρτυρές ἐσμεν. καὶ ἐπὶ τῇ πίστει τοῦ ὀνόματος αὐτοῦ,
witnesses are. And on the faith of the name of Him,

τοῦτον ὃν θεωρεῖτε καὶ οἴδατε ἐστερέωσε τὸ ὄνομα αὐτοῦ·
this one whom you behold and know made strong the name of Him,

καὶ ἡ πίστις ἡ δι' αὐτοῦ ἔδωκεν αὐτῷ τὴν ὁλοκληρίαν
and the faith which through Him gave to him complete soundness

**17** ταύτην ἀπέναντι πάντων ὑμῶν. καὶ νῦν, ἀδελφοί. οἶδα ὅτι
this before all of you. And now, brothers, I know that

**18** κατὰ ἄγνοιαν ἐπράξατε, ὥσπερ καὶ οἱ ἄρχοντες ὑμῶν. ὁ δὲ
by way of ignorance you acted, as also the rulers of you, But

Θεὸς ἃ προκατήγγειλε διὰ στόματος πάντων τῶν προ-
God that He before announced through (the) mouth of all the

φητῶν αὐτοῦ, παθεῖν τὸν Χριστόν, ἐπλήρωσεν οὕτω.
prophets of Him, to suffer the Christ, He fulfilled thus.

**19** μετανοήσατε οὖν καὶ ἐπιστρέψατε, εἰς τὸ ἐξαλειφθῆναι ὑμῶν
Repent, therefore, and be converted, for the blotting out of you

τὰς ἁμαρτίας, ὅπως ἂν ἔλθωσι καιροὶ ἀναψύξεως ἀπὸ προσ-
the sins, so as may come times of refreshing from (the)

**20** ώπου τοῦ Κυρίου, καὶ ἀποστείλῃ τὸν προκεκηρυγμένον
presence of the Lord, and He may send the (One) before proclaimed

**21** ὑμῖν Ἰησοῦν Χριστόν· ὃν δεῖ οὐρανὸν μὲν δέξασθαι ἄχρι
to you, Jesus Christ, whom it is right Heaven to receive until

χρόνων ἀποκαταστάσεως πάντων, ὧν ἐλάλησεν ὁ Θεὸς
(the) times of restitution of all things, which spoke God

διὰ στόματος πάντων ἁγίων αὐτοῦ προφητῶν ἀπ' αἰῶνος.
through (the) mouth of all holy of Him prophets from (the) age.

**22** Μωσῆς μὲν γὰρ πρὸς τοὺς πατέρας εἶπεν ὅτι Προφήτην
Moses indeed For to the fathers said, — A prophet

ὑμῖν ἀναστήσει Κύριος ὁ Θεὸς ὑμῶν ἐκ τῶν ἀδελφῶν ὑμῶν
for you will raise up (the) Lord God of you from the brothers of you

ὡς ἐμέ· αὐτοῦ ἀκούσεσθε κατὰ πάντα ὅσα ἂν λαλήσῃ πρὸς
like me; Him you shall hear according to all, whatever He may speak to

**23** ὑμᾶς. ἔσται δέ, πᾶσα ψυχή, ἥτις ἂν μὴ ἀκούσῃ τοῦ προφή-
you. it shall be And, every soul, whoever may not hear — prophet

**24** του ἐκείνου, ἐξολοθρευθήσεται ἐκ τοῦ λαοῦ. καὶ πάντες δὲ
that, will be utterly destroyed from the people. also all And

οἱ προφῆται ἀπὸ Σαμουὴλ καὶ τῶν καθεξῆς, ὅσοι ἐλάλησαν,
the prophets from Samuel, and those in order, as many as spoke,

**25** καὶ προκατήγγειλαν τὰς ἡμέρας ταύτας. ὑμεῖς ἐστε υἱοὶ τῶν
also before announced — days these. You are sons of the

προφητῶν, καὶ τῆς διαθήκης ἧς διέθετο ὁ Θεὸς πρὸς τοὺς
prophets, and of the covenant which appointed God to the

πατέρας ἡμῶν, λέγων πρὸς Ἀβραάμ, Καὶ τῷ σπέρματί σου
fathers of us, saying to Abraham, And in the seed of you

**26** ἐνευλογηθήσονται πᾶσαι αἱ πατριαὶ τῆς γῆς. ὑμῖν πρῶτον
shall be blessed all the families of the earth. To you first

ὁ Θεός, ἀναστήσας τὸν παῖδα αὐτοῦ Ἰησοῦν, ἀπέστειλεν
God   having raised up the   Child   of Him,   Jesus,    sent

αὐτὸν εὐλογοῦντα ὑμᾶς, ἐν τῷ ἀποστρέφειν ἕκαστον ἀπὸ
Him    blessing    you  in the   turning away (of) each one from

τῶν πονηριῶν ὑμῶν.
the   iniquities   of you.

God, having raised up His Child Jesus, sent Him, blessing you in turning each from your sins.

## CHAPTER 4

[1] And as they were speaking to the people, the priests and the captain of the Temple, and the Sadducees, came upon them, [2] being distressed because they taught the people and preached the resurrection in Jesus which (is) from among (the) dead; [3] and they laid hands on them and put (them) in custody until the morrow; for it was already evening. [4] But many of those who had heard the word believed, and the number of the men became about five thousand. [5] And it came to pass on the morrow their rulers and elders and scribes were gathered together at Jerusalem. [6] And Annas the high priest, and Caiaphas, and John, and Alexander, and as many as were of high-priestly family (came). [7] And having placed them in the middle, they inquired, in what power or in what name did you do this? [8] Then Peter, filled with (the) Holy Spirit, said to them, Rulers of the people and elders of Israel, [9] if we today are examined as to a good work (to the) lame man, by what he has been cured, [10] be it known to all you and to all the people of Israel that in the name of Jesus Christ the Nazarean, whom you crucified, whom God raised from among (the) dead, by Him this one stands before you sound. [11] This is the Stone which has been counted worthless by you the builders, which is become Head of (the) corner. [12] And there is salvation in no other One, for neither is there' any other name

## CHAPTER 4

Λαλούντων δὲ αὐτῶν πρὸς τὸν λαόν, ἐπέστησαν αὐτοῖς
speaking   And they   to   the people, came upon    them

**1**

οἱ ἱερεῖς καὶ ὁ στρατηγὸς τοῦ ἱεροῦ καὶ οἱ Σαδδουκαῖοι,
the priests and the commander of the Temple and the   Sadducees,

διαπονούμενοι διὰ τὸ διδάσκειν αὐτοὺς τὸν λαόν, καὶ
being distressed because of the teaching   (of) them the people,  even

**2**

καταγγέλλειν ἐν τῷ Ἰησοῦ τὴν ἀνάστασιν τὴν ἐκ νεκρῶν.
to announce    by  —  Jesus the  resurrection  — from(the)dead.

καὶ ἐπέβαλον αὐτοῖς τὰς χεῖρας, καὶ ἔθεντο εἰς τήρησιν εἰς
And (they) laid on them  the  hands, and  put  into custody unto

**3**

τὴν αὔριον· ἦν γὰρ ἑσπέρα ἤδη. πολλοὶ δὲ τῶν ἀκουσάντων
the morrow; it was for evening now.   many And of those hearing

**4**

τὸν λόγον ἐπίστευσαν· καὶ ἐγενήθη ὁ ἀριθμὸς τῶν ἀνδρῶν
the   word    believed,   and became  the number of the    men

ὡσεὶ χιλιάδες πέντε.
about  thousands  five.

Ἐγένετο δὲ ἐπὶ τὴν αὔριον συναχθῆναι αὐτῶν τοὺς
it was   And, on the   morrow  to be assembled  of them   the

**5**

ἄρχοντας καὶ πρεσβυτέρους καὶ γραμματεῖς εἰς Ἰερουσαλήμ,
rulers    and   elders     and   scribes   to   Jerusalem,

καὶ Ἄνναν τὸν ἀρχιερέα, καὶ Καϊάφαν, καὶ Ἰωάννην, καὶ
and Annas the high priest, and Caiaphas,  and   John,    and

**6**

Ἀλέξανδρον, καὶ ὅσοι ἦσαν ἐκ γένους ἀρχιερατικοῦ. καὶ
Alexander,   and as many as were of (the)family high priestly.   And

**7**

στήσαντες αὐτοὺς ἐν τῷ μέσῳ ἐπυνθάνοντο, Ἐν ποίᾳ
having stood  them   in  the  midst   inquired,   By what

δυνάμει ἢ ἐν ποίῳ ὀνόματι ἐποιήσατε τοῦτο ὑμεῖς ; τότε
power   or in what   name   did do   this    you?   Then

**8**

Πέτρος πλησθεὶς Πνεύματος Ἁγίου εἶπε πρὸς αὐτούς,
Peter,   filled   of (the) Spirit  Holy   said  to   them,

Ἄρχοντες τοῦ λαοῦ καὶ πρεσβύτεροι τοῦ Ἰσραήλ, εἰ ἡμεῖς
Rulers    of the people and  elders    of Israel, if  we

**9**

σήμερον ἀνακρινόμεθα ἐπὶ εὐεργεσίᾳ ἀνθρώπου ἀσθενοῦς,
today   are being examined on a good  work  of a man    infirm

ἐν τίνι οὗτος σέσωσται· γνωστὸν ἔστω πᾶσιν ὑμῖν καὶ
by what  this one has been healed, known let it be  to all of you  and

**10**

παντὶ τῷ λαῷ Ἰσραήλ, ὅτι ἐν τῷ ὀνόματι Ἰησοῦ Χριστοῦ
to all  the people of Israel,  that in  the   name   of Jesus   Christ

τοῦ Ναζωραίου, ὃν ὑμεῖς ἐσταυρώσατε, ὃν ὁ Θεὸς ἤγειρεν
the Nazarean, whom you crucified,    whom the God raised

ἐκ νεκρῶν, ἐν τούτῳ οὗτος παρέστηκεν ἐνώπιον ὑμῶ ὑγιής.
from (the) dead, in this, this one  stands      before   you  whole.

οὗτός ἐστιν ὁ λίθος ὁ ἐξουθενηθεὶς ὑφ᾽ ὑμῶν τῶν οἰκοδο-
This   is the Stone  counted worthless by  you  the builders,

**11**

μούντων, ὁ γενόμενος εἰς κεφαλὴν γωνίας. καὶ οὐκ ἔστιν ἐν
which has become to (be head of (the) corner. And not  is   in
         the)

ἄλλῳ οὐδενὶ ἡ σωτηρία· οὔτε γὰρ ὄνομά ἐστιν ἕτερον ὑπὸ τὸν
other  none the salvation; neither for name  is   another  under —

**12**

under Heaven given among men by which we must be saved.

οὐρανὸν τὸ δεδομένον ἐν ἀνθρώποις, ἐν ᾧ δεῖ σωθῆναι ἡμᾶς.
Heaven —having been given among men   by which must be saved us.

[13] But seeing the boldness of Peter and of John, and having perceived that they are without learning and uneducated, they wondered, and they recognized them that they were with Jesus.

**13** Θεωροῦντες δὲ τὴν τοῦ Πέτρου παρρησίαν καὶ Ἰωάννου,
beholding And the — of Peter boldness and of John,
καὶ καταλαβόμενοι ὅτι ἄνθρωποι ἀγράμματοί εἰσι καὶ
and having perceived that men unlettered they are, and
ἰδιῶται, ἐθαύμαζον, ἐπεγίνωσκόν τε αὐτοὺς ὅτι σὺν τῷ
private, they marveled, recognized and them that with —

[14] But seeing the man who had been healed standing with them, they had nothing to gainsay.

**14** Ἰησοῦ ἦσαν. τὸν δὲ ἄνθρωπον βλέποντες σὺν αὐτοῖς ἑστῶτα
Jesus they were. the And man seeing with them standing
τὸν τεθεραπευμένον, οὐδὲν εἶχον ἀντειπεῖν. κελεύσαντες δὲ
the (one) having been healed, nothing they had to gainsay. commanding And

[15] But having commanded them to go outside the sanhedrin, they conferred with one another,

**15** αὐτοὺς ἔξω τοῦ συνεδρίου ἀπελθεῖν, συνέβαλον πρὸς ἀλλή-
them outside the sanhedrin to go, they conferred with one

[16] saying, What shall we do to these men? For that indeed a notable miracle has taken place through them (is) plain to all those living in Jerusalem, and we are unable to deny.

**16** λους, λέγοντες, Τί ποιήσομεν τοῖς ἀνθρώποις τούτοις ; ὅτι
another, saying, What may we do to men these; that
μὲν γὰρ γνωστὸν σημεῖον γέγονε δι᾽ αὐτῶν, πᾶσι τοῖς κατοι-
indeed for a notable sign has occurred through them, to all those inhabit-
κοῦσιν Ἱερουσαλὴμ φανερόν, καὶ οὐ δυνάμεθα ἀρνήσασθαι.
ing Jerusalem (is) manifest, and not we are able to deny;

[17] But that it may not spread further among the people, let us threaten them with a threat no longer to speak in this name to any man.

**17** ἀλλ᾽ ἵνα μὴ ἐπὶ πλεῖον διανεμηθῇ εἰς τὸν λαόν, ἀπειλῇ
but lest — more it be spread abroad to the people, let us with a threat
ἀπειλησώμεθα αὐτοῖς μηκέτι λαλεῖν ἐπὶ τῷ ὀνόματι τούτῳ
threaten them no longer to speak on name this

[18] And having called them they commanded them not to speak at all nor to teach in the name of Jesus.

**18** μηδενὶ ἀνθρώπων. καὶ καλέσαντες αὐτούς, παρήγγειλαν
to no one of men. And calling them, they ordered
αὐτοῖς τὸ καθόλου μὴ φθέγγεσθαι μηδὲ διδάσκειν ἐπὶ τῷ
them — at all not to speak nor to teach on the

[19] But Peter and John answering to them said, Whether it is right before God to listen to you rather than God, you judge;

**19** ὀνόματι τοῦ Ἰησοῦ. ὁ δὲ Πέτρος καὶ Ἰωάννης ἀποκριθέντες
name of Jesus. But Peter and John answering
πρὸς αὐτοὺς εἶπον, Εἰ δίκαιόν ἐστιν ἐνώπιον τοῦ Θεοῦ ὑμῶν
to them said, If right it is before — God you

[20] For we cannot but speak what we saw and heard.

**20** ἀκούειν μᾶλλον ἢ τοῦ Θεοῦ, κρίνατε. οὐ δυνάμεθα γὰρ ἡμεῖς,
to hear rather than — God, you judge. not are able For we
ἃ εἴδομεν καὶ ἠκούσαμεν, μὴ λαλεῖν. οἱ δὲ προσαπειλησά-
what we saw and heard, not to speak. they But having threatened

[21] But they have further threatened let them go, finding nothing as to how they might punish them, on account of the people, because all were glorifying God for that which had taken place;

**21** μενοι ἀπέλυσαν αὐτούς, μηδὲν εὑρίσκοντες τὸ πῶς κολάσων-
again released them, nothing finding — how they might
ται αὐτούς, διὰ τὸν λαόν, ὅτι πάντες ἐδόξαζον τὸν Θεὸν ἐπὶ
punish them, due to the people, because all glorified — God on

[22] for the man on whom this miracle of healing had taken place was more than forty.

**22** τῷ γεγονότι. ἐτῶν γὰρ ἦν πλειόνων τεσσαράκοντα ὁ ἄν-
the thing occurring. of years For was more (than) forty the
θρωπος ἐφ᾽ ὃν ἐγεγόνει τὸ σημεῖον τοῦτο τῆς ἰάσεως.
man on whom had happened sign this — of healing.

[23] And having been let go, they came to their own and reported to them whatever the chief priests and the elders said.

**23** Ἀπολυθέντες δὲ ἦλθον πρὸς τοὺς ἰδίους, καὶ ἀπήγγειλαν
being released And they went to the own, and reported
ὅσα πρὸς αὐτοὺς οἱ ἀρχιερεῖς καὶ οἱ πρεσβύτεροι εἶπον. οἱ
what to them the chief priests and the elders said. they

[24] And having heard they with one accord lifted up (their) voice to God and said, O Master, You (are) the God who made the sky and the earth and the sea, and all that (are) in them,

**24** δὲ ἀκούσαντες ὁμοθυμαδὸν ἦραν φωνὴν πρὸς τὸν Θεόν, καὶ
And having heard, with one passion lifted voice to — God, and
εἶπον, Δέσποτα, σὺ ὁ Θεὸς ὁ ποιήσας τὸν οὐρανὸν καὶ τὴν
said, Master, You the God who made the heaven and the
γῆν καὶ τὴν θάλασσαν καὶ πάντα τὰ ἐν αὐτοῖς· ὁ διὰ στό-
earth and the sea and all things in them, who through (the)

[25] who by (the) mouth of David Your child said, "Why did the heathen rage

**25** ματος Δαβὶδ τοῦ παιδός σου εἰπών, Ἱνατί ἐφρύαξαν ἔθνη,
mouth of David the child of You said, Why did rage the nations,

and the peoples think foolish things? [26] The kings of the earth stood up, and the rulers were gathered together against the Lord and against His Christ." [27] For indeed both Herod and Pontius Pilate, with the heathen and the peoples of Israel, were gathered together against Your holy child Jesus, whom You anointed, [28] to do whatever Your hand and counsel before determined to be done. [29] And now, Lord, look on their threatenings, and give to Your slaves boldness to speak all Your word; [30] in that You may stretch out Your hand for healing and miracles and wonders (to) take place through the name of Your holy child Jesus. [31] And they having prayed, the place in which they had gathered was shaken; and they were all filled with (the) Holy Spirit, and spoke the word of God with boldness.

[32] And of the multitude of those who believed, their hearts and their souls were one, and no one possessed anything of that which he said was his own, but all things were to them common. [33] And with great power the apostles gave testimony of the resurrection of the Lord Jesus, and great grace was upon all of them. [34] For neither was there anyone among them in need; for as many as were owners of estates or houses, selling (them) brought the values of the (things) sold [35] and laid (them) at the feet of the apostles; and it was distributed to each according as anyone had need.

[36] And Joseph who was surnamed Barnabas by the apostles, which translated is, Son of consolation, a Levite, a Cypriot by birth, [37] having sold land, having brought the money and laid (it) at the feet of the apostles.

**26** καὶ λαοὶ ἐμελέτησαν κενά ; παρέστησαν οἱ βασιλεῖς τῆς γῆς,
and peoples meditated vain things? stood up    The kings of the earth,

καὶ οἱ ἄρχοντες συνήχθησαν ἐπὶ τὸ αὐτὸ κατὰ τοῦ Κυρίου,
and the rulers    were assembled    on the same (day) against the Lord,

**27** καὶ κατὰ τοῦ Χριστοῦ αὐτοῦ· συνήχθησαν γὰρ ἐπ' ἀληθείας
and against the    Christ of Him; were assembled    for of a truth

ἐπὶ τὸν ἅγιον παῖδά σου Ἰησοῦν, ὃν ἔχρισας, Ἡρώδης τε
against the holy    child of You, Jesus,    whom You anointed, Herod both

καὶ Πόντιος Πιλάτος, σὺν ἔθνεσι καὶ λαοῖς Ἰσραήλ, ποιῆσαι
and Pontius    Pilate,    with nations and peoples of Israel, to do

**28** ὅσα ἡ χείρ σου καὶ ἡ βουλή σου προώρισε γενέσθαι. καὶ
whatever the hand of You and the counsel of You predetermined to occur. And

**29** τὰ νῦν, Κύριε, ἔπιδε ἐπὶ τὰς ἀπειλὰς αὐτῶν, καὶ δὸς τοῖς
— now, Lord, look    upon the threatenings of them, and give to the

δούλοις σου μετὰ παρρησίας πάσης λαλεῖν τὸν λόγον σου,
slaves of You with    boldness    all    to speak the word of You,

**30** ἐν τῷ τὴν χεῖρά σου ἐκτείνειν σε εἰς ἴασιν, καὶ σημεῖα καὶ
by the    hand of You stretching You for healing, and    signs    and

τέρατα γίνεσθαι διὰ τοῦ ὀνόματος τοῦ ἁγίου παιδός σου
wonders to happen through the    name    of the holy    child of You,

**31** Ἰησοῦ. καὶ δεηθέντων αὐτῶν ἐσαλεύθη ὁ τόπος ἐν ᾧ ἦσαν
Jesus. And having petitioned they, was shaken the place in which they were

συνηγμένοι, καὶ ἐπλήσθησαν ἅπαντες Πνεύματος Ἁγίου,
assembled,    and they were filled    all    with (the) Spirit Holy,

καὶ ἐλάλουν τὸν λόγον τοῦ Θεοῦ μετὰ παρρησίας.
and spoke    the word    — of God with    boldness.

**32** Τοῦ δὲ πλήθους τῶν πιστευσάντων ἦν ἡ καρδία καὶ ἡ
of the And multitude of those    believing    were the heart    and the

ψυχὴ μία· καὶ οὐδ' εἷς τι τῶν ὑπαρχόντων αὐτῷ ἔλεγεν
soul    one, and not one anything of the possessions    to him he said

**33** ἴδιον εἶναι, ἀλλ' ἦν αὐτοῖς ἅπαντα κοινά. καὶ μεγάλῃ
own    to be, but    were to them all things common. And with great

δυνάμει ἀπεδίδουν τὸ μαρτύριον οἱ ἀπόστολοι τῆς ἀναστά-
power    gave    the testimony the apostles of the resurrection

σεως τοῦ Κυρίου Ἰησοῦ, χάρις τε μεγάλη ἦν ἐπὶ πάντας
of the    Lord    Jesus,    grace and great    was upon all

**34** αὐτούς. οὐδὲ γὰρ ἐνδεής τις ὑπῆρχεν ἐν αὐτοῖς· ὅσοι γὰρ
of them. neither For needy anyone was    among them, as many as for

κτήτορες χωρίων ἢ οἰκιῶν ὑπῆρχον, πωλοῦντες ἔφερον τὰς
owners    of lands or houses were,    having sold brought    the

**35** τιμὰς τῶν πιπρασκομένων, καὶ ἐτίθουν παρὰ τοὺς πόδας
values of those being sold,    and placed    at    the    feet

τῶν ἀποστόλων· διεδίδοτο δὲ ἑκάστῳ καθότι ἄν τις χρείαν
of the    apostles; it was distributed and to each according to any need

εἶχεν.
had.

**36** Ἰωσῆς δέ, ὁ ἐπικληθεὶς Βαρνάβας ὑπὸ τῶν ἀποστόλων
Joses And, he surnamed    Barnabas    by the    apostles,

(ὅ ἐστι, μεθερμηνευόμενον, υἱὸς παρακλήσεως), Λευίτης,
which is, being translated,    Son of Consolation,    a Levite,

**37** Κύπριος τῷ γένει, ὑπάρχοντος αὐτῷ ἀγροῦ, πωλήσας
a Cypriot — by race, being    to him a field,    having sold

ἤνεγκε τὸ χρῆμα, καὶ ἔθηκε παρὰ τοὺς πόδας τῶν ἀποστόλων.
brought the proceeds and placed at    the feet of the    apostles.

## CHAPTER 5

CHAPTER 5

[1] But a certain man named Ananias, with his wife Sapphira, sold a possession [2] and kept back from the value, his wife also knowing, and having brought a certain part laid (it) at the feet of the apostles. [3] But Peter said, Ananias, why did Satan fill your heart (for) you to lie to the Holy Spirit, and to keep back from the price of the estate? [4] Remaining, did it not remain yours? And having been sold, was it in your authority? What (is it) that it was agreed together with you to tempt the lie to men, but to God. [5] And Ananias hearing these words, falling down died. And great fear came on all who heard these things. [6] And the younger ones having risen wrapped him and having carried out buried (him). [7] And it came to pass about three hours afterward his wife also came in, not knowing what had happened. [8] And Peter answered her, Tell me if you sold the estate for so much? And she said, Yes, for so much. [9] And Peter said to ner, What (is it) that you agreed together to tempt the Spirit of (the) Lord? Lo, the feet of those who buried your husband (are) at the door, and they shall carry you out. [10] And she immediately fell down at his feet and died. And the young ones having come in found her dead; and having carried out they buried (her) by her husband. [11] And great fear came on the whole assembly, and on all who heard these things. [12] And by the hands of the apostles came to pass many miracles and wonders among the people; and they were all with one accord in the Porch of Solomon, [13] and of the rest no one dared join

**1** Ἀνὴρ δέ τις Ἀνανίας ὀνόματι, σὺν Σαπφείρῃ τῇ γυναικὶ
man And a certain, Ananias by name, with Sapphira the wife

**2** αὐτοῦ, ἐπώλησε κτῆμα, καὶ ἐνοσφίσατο ἀπὸ τῆς τιμῆς,
of him, sold a property, and secretly kept back from the price,

συνειδυίας καὶ τῆς γυναικὸς αὐτοῦ, καὶ ἐνέγκας μέρος τι
aware of (it) also the wife of him, and bringing a part certain

**3** παρὰ τοὺς πόδας τῶν ἀποστόλων ἔθηκεν. εἶπε δὲ Πέτρος,
to the feet of the apostles placed (it). said But Peter,

Ἀνανία, διατί ἐπλήρωσεν ὁ Σατανᾶς τὴν καρδίαν σου,
Ananias, why filled — Satan the heart of you,

ψεύσασθαί σε τὸ Πνεῦμα τὸ Ἅγιον, καὶ νοσφίσασθαι ἀπὸ
to deceive you the Spirit — Holy, and to secretly keep back from

**4** τῆς τιμῆς τοῦ χωρίου ; οὐχὶ μένον σοὶ ἔμενε, καὶ πραθὲν ἐν
the price of the land? not Remaining to you remain, and sold in

τῇ σῇ ἐξουσία ὑπῆρχε ; τί ὅτι ἔθου ἐν τῇ καρδίᾳ σου τὸ
— your authority it was? What (is it) that was put in the heart of you —

πρᾶγμα τοῦτο ; οὐκ ἐψεύσω ἀνθρώποις, ἀλλὰ τῷ Θεῷ.
action this? not You lied to men, but — to God.

**5** ἀκούων δὲ Ἀνανίας τοὺς λόγους τούτους, πεσὼν ἐξέψυξε·
hearing And Ananias words these, falling expired.

καὶ ἐγένετο φόβος μέγας ἐπὶ πάντας τοὺς ἀκούοντας ταῦτα.
And came fear great on all those hearing these things.

**6** ἀναστάντες δὲ οἱ νεώτεροι συνέστειλαν αὐτόν, καὶ ἐξενέγ-
rising up And the young men they wrapped him, and carrying

καντες ἔθαψαν.
out, buried (him).

**7** Ἐγένετο δὲ ὡς ὡρῶν τριῶν διάστημα, καὶ ἡ γυνὴ αὐτοῦ
there was And about hours three afterwards and the wife of him

**8** μὴ εἰδυῖα τὸ γεγονὸς εἰσῆλθεν. ἀπεκρίθη δὲ αὐτῇ ὁ Πέτρος,
not knowing the happening, entered. answered And her — Peter,

Εἰπέ μοι, εἰ τοσούτου τὸ χωρίον ἀπέδοσθε. ἡ δὲ εἶπε, Ναί,
Tell me, if of so much the land you gave over? she And said, Yes,

**9** τοσούτου. ὁ δὲ Πέτρος εἶπε πρὸς αὐτήν, Τί ὅτι συνεφωνήθη
of so much. And Peter said to her, What (was that it was agreed

ὑμῖν πειράσαι τὸ Πνεῦμα Κυρίου ; ἰδού, οἱ πόδες τῶν θαψάν-
with you to tempt the Spirit of (the) Lord? Behold, the feet of those burying

**10** των τὸν ἄνδρα σου ἐπὶ τῇ θύρᾳ, καὶ ἐξοίσουσί σε. ἔπεσε δὲ
the husband of you at the door, and they will carry you. she fell And

παραχρῆμα παρὰ τοὺς πόδας αὐτοῦ, καὶ ἐξέψυξεν· εἰσελ-
immediately at the feet of him, and expired. entering

θόντες δὲ οἱ νεανίσκοι εὗρον αὐτὴν νεκράν, καὶ ἐξενέγκαντες
And, the young men found her dead, and carrying out

**11** ἔθαψαν πρὸς τὸν ἄνδρα αὐτῆς. καὶ ἐγένετο φόβος μέγας
buried her near the husband of her. And came fear great

ἐφ᾽ ὅλην τὴν ἐκκλησίαν, καὶ ἐπὶ πάντας τοὺς ἀκούοντας
on all the church, and on all those hearing

ταῦτα.
these things.

**12** Διὰ δὲ τῶν χειρῶν τῶν ἀποστόλων ἐγίνετο σημεῖα καὶ
through And the hands of the apostles happened signs and

τέρατα ἐν τῷ λαῷ πολλά· καὶ ἦσαν ὁμοθυμαδὸν ἅπαντες
wonders among the people many; and were with one passion all

**13** ἐν τῇ στοᾷ Σολομῶντος. τῶν δὲ λοιπῶν οὐδεὶς ἐτόλμα
in the porch of Solomon. of the And rest, no one dared

them, but the people greatly magnified them. [14] And more believing ones were added to (the) Lord, myriads of both men and women. [15] So as to bring out the sick in the streets, and place on beds and couches, that at least the shadow of Peter coming might overshadow some one of them. [16] And also the multitude came together (from) the cities around Jerusalem, bringing sick ones and those plagued by unclean spirits, who were all healed.

[17] And having risen up the high priest and all those with him, which is (the) sect of the Sadducees, were filled with anger, [18] and laid their hands on the apostles and put them in public custody. [19] But an angel of (the) Lord during the night opened the doors of the prison, and having brought them out said, [20] Go, and standing speak in the Temple to the people all the words of this Life. [21] And having heard they went at the dawn into the Temple and were teaching. But the high priest and those with him having come, he called together the sanhedrin and all the elderhood of the sons of Israel, and sent to the prison to have them brought. [22] But having come the officers did not find them in the prison; and having returned they reported, [23] saying, Indeed we found the prison shut with all security, and the keepers outside standing before the door; but having opened, we found no one inside. [24] And when they heard these words, both the priest and the captain of the Temple and the chief priests were puzzled concerning them, what this might be. [25] But having come a certain one reported to them, saying, Behold, the men whom you put in the prison are in the Temple standing and teaching the people.

κολλᾶσθαι αὐτοῖς, ἀλλ' ἐμεγάλυνεν αὐτοὺς ὁ λαός· μᾶλλον
to be joined to them, but magnified them the people; more

14 δὲ προσετίθεντο πιστεύοντες τῷ Κυρίῳ, πλήθη ἀνδρῶν τε
and were added believing ones to (the) Lord, multitudes of men both

15 καὶ γυναικῶν· ὥστε κατὰ τὰς πλατείας ἐκφέρειν τοὺς
and of women; so as in the streets to carry out the

ἀσθενεῖς, καὶ τιθέναι ἐπὶ κλινῶν καὶ κραββάτων, ἵνα ἐρχο-
sick, and to place on cots and mattresses, that coming

μένου Πέτρου κἂν ἡ σκιὰ ἐπισκιάσῃ τινὶ αὐτῶν. συνήρχετο
Peter. if even the shadow overshadow some of them. assembled

16 δὲ καὶ τὸ πλῆθος τῶν πέριξ πόλεων εἰς Ἰερουσαλήμ,
And also the multitude of the round about cities to Jerusalem,

φέροντες ἀσθενεῖς καὶ ὀχλουμένους ὑπὸ πνευμάτων ἀκαθάρ-
carrying sick (ones) and those being tormented by spirits unclean,

των, οἵτινες ἐθεραπεύοντο ἅπαντες.
who were healed all.

17 Ἀναστὰς δὲ ὁ ἀρχιερεὺς καὶ πάντες οἱ σὺν αὐτῷ (ἡ οὖσα
rising up And the high priest and all those with him, which is

αἵρεσις τῶν Σαδδουκαίων), ἐπλήσθησαν ζήλου, καὶ ἐπέ-
(the) sect of the Sadducees, were filled of jealousy, and

18 βαλον τὰς χεῖρας αὐτῶν ἐπὶ τοὺς ἀποστόλους, καὶ ἔθεντο
laid on the hands of them on the apostles, and put

19 αὐτοὺς ἐν τηρήσει δημοσίᾳ. ἄγγελος δὲ Κυρίου διὰ τῆς νυκτὸς
them in custody publicly. an angel But of (the) Lord by night

ἤνοιξε τὰς θύρας τῆς φυλακῆς, ἐξαγαγών τε αὐτοὺς εἶπε,
opened the doors of the prison, leading out and them said,

20 Πορεύεσθε, καὶ σταθέντες λαλεῖτε ἐν τῷ ἱερῷ τῷ λαῷ πάντα
Go, and standing speak in the Temple to the people all

21 τὰ ῥήματα τῆς ζωῆς ταύτης. ἀκούσαντες δὲ εἰσῆλθον ὑπὸ
the words of life this. having heard And, they entered about

τὸν ὄρθρον εἰς τὸ ἱερόν, καὶ ἐδίδασκον. παραγενόμενος δὲ ὁ
the dawn into the Temple, and taught. having come near And the

ἀρχιερεὺς καὶ οἱ σὺν αὐτῷ, συνεκάλεσαν τὸ συνέδριον καὶ
high priest and those with him, he called together the sanhedrin and

πᾶσαν τὴν γερουσίαν τῶν υἱῶν Ἰσραήλ, καὶ ἀπέστειλαν εἰς
all the elderhood of the sons of Israel. And they sent to

22 τὸ δεσμωτήριον, ἀχθῆναι αὐτούς. οἱ δὲ ὑπηρέται παρα-
the jail to be brought them. the But officers having

γενόμενοι οὐχ εὗρον αὐτοὺς ἐν τῇ φυλακῇ· ἀναστρέψαντες
come near not did find them in the prison; having returned

23 δὲ ἀπήγγειλαν, λέγοντες ὅτι Τὸ μὲν δεσμωτήριον εὕρομεν
and they reported, saying, — the Indeed jail we found

κεκλεισμένον ἐν πάσῃ ἀσφαλείᾳ, καὶ τοὺς φύλακας ἔξω
having been shut in all security, and the guards outside

ἑστῶτας πρὸ τῶν θυρῶν· ἀνοίξαντες δέ, ἔσω οὐδένα εὕρο-
standing at the doors; having opened but, inside no one we

24 μεν. ὡς δὲ ἤκουσαν τοὺς λόγους τούτους ὅ τε ἱερεὺς καὶ ὁ
found. as And heard words these the both priest and the

στρατηγὸς τοῦ ἱεροῦ καὶ οἱ ἀρχιερεῖς, διηπόρουν περὶ
commander of the Temple and the chief priests they were in doubt concerning

25 αὐτῶν, τί ἂν γένοιτο τοῦτο. παραγενόμενος δέ τις ἀπήγ-
them, what might become this. having come And one reported

γειλεν αὐτοῖς λέγων ὅτι Ἰδού, οἱ ἄνδρες οὓς ἔθεσθε ἐν τῇ
to them, saying, — Behold, the men whom you put in the

φυλακῇ εἰσὶν ἐν τῷ ἱερῷ ἑστῶτες καὶ διδάσκοντες τὸν λαόν.
prison are in the Temple standing and teaching the people.

[26] Then having gone the captain and the officers them, not with force, for they feared the people, that they might not be stoned. [27] And having brought them, they stood (them) in the sanhedrin. And the high priest asked them, [28] saying, Did we not command you by command (that) you not teach in this name? And behold, you have filled Jerusalem with your teaching, and purpose to bring on us the blood of this man. [29] But answering Peter and the apostles said, It is right to obey God rather than man. [30] The God of our fathers raised up Jesus, whom you killed, having hanged (Him) on a tree. [31] Him (whom) God exalted a Prince and Savior by His right hand, to give repentance to Israel and remission of sins. [32] And we are His witnesses of these things, and the Holy Spirit also, whom God gave to those that obey Him. [33] But having heard they were cut and took counsel to put them to death. [34] But having risen up a certain one in the sanhedrin, a Pharisee named Gamaliel, a teacher of the Law, honored by all the people, commanded the apostles to be put out for a short while. [35] And (he) said to them, Men, Israelites, take heed to yourselves as regards these men, what you are about to do; [36] for before these days Theudas rose up, claiming himself to be somebody, to whom were joined a number of men, about four hundred; who was put to death, and all, as many as were persuaded by him, were dispersed and came to nothing. [37] After this stood up Judas the Galilean in the days of the registration, and drew away much people after him; and that one perished, and all were scattered, as many as obeyed him. [38] And now I say to you, stand away from

**26** τότε ἀπελθὼν ὁ στρατηγὸς σὺν τοῖς ὑπηρέταις ἤγαγεν
Then going the commander with the officers brought

αὐτούς, οὐ μετὰ βίας, ἐφοβοῦντο γὰρ τὸν λαόν, ἵνα μὴ
them, not with force, they feared for the people, lest

**27** λιθασθῶσιν. ἀγαγόντες δὲ αὐτοὺς ἔστησαν ἐν τῷ συνεδρίῳ.
they be stoned. bringing And them, they stood in the sanhedrin.

**28** καὶ ἐπηρώτησεν αὐτοὺς ὁ ἀρχιερεύς, λέγων, Οὐ παραγ-
And questioned them the high priest, saying, Not by a

γελίᾳ παρηγγείλαμεν ὑμῖν μὴ διδάσκειν ἐπὶ τῷ ὀνόματι
charge did we charge to you not to teach on — name

τούτῳ; καὶ ἰδοὺ πεπληρώκατε τὴν Ἰερουσαλὴμ τῆς δι-
this? And, behold, you have filled — Jerusalem of the

δαχῆς ὑμῶν, καὶ βούλεσθε ἐπαγαγεῖν ἐφ' ἡμᾶς τὸ αἷμα τοῦ
teaching of you, and purpose to bring on us the blood —

**29** ἀνθρώπου τούτου. ἀποκριθεὶς δὲ ὁ Πέτρος καὶ οἱ ἀπόστολοι
of man this. answering But — Peter and the apostles

**30** εἶπον, Πειθαρχεῖν δεῖ Θεῷ μᾶλλον ἢ ἀνθρώποις. ὁ Θεὸς τῶν
said, to obey It is right God rather than men. The God of the

πατέρων ἡμῶν ἤγειρεν Ἰησοῦν, ὃν ὑμεῖς διεχειρίσασθε,
fathers of us raised Jesus, whom you laid hands upon,

**31** κρεμάσαντες ἐπὶ ξύλου. τοῦτον ὁ Θεὸς ἀρχηγὸν καὶ σωτῆρα
hanging (Him) on a tree. This One God a Ruler and a Savior

ὕψωσε τῇ δεξιᾷ αὐτοῦ, δοῦναι μετάνοιαν τῷ Ἰσραὴλ καὶ
exalted to the right (hand) of Him, to give repentance — to Israel and

**32** ἄφεσιν ἁμαρτιῶν. καὶ ἡμεῖς ἐσμεν αὐτοῦ μάρτυρες τῶν
forgiveness of sins. And we are of Him witnesses —

ῥημάτων τούτων, καὶ τὸ Πνεῦμα δὲ τὸ Ἅγιον, ὃ ἔδωκεν ὁ
of words these, also the Spirit and — Holy which gave

Θεὸς τοῖς πειθαρχοῦσιν αὐτῷ.
God to those obeying Him.

**33** Οἱ δὲ ἀκούσαντες διεπρίοντο, καὶ ἐβουλεύοντο ἀνελεῖν
those And hearing were cut, and took counsel to take away

**34** αὐτούς. ἀναστὰς δέ τις ἐν τῷ συνεδρίῳ Φαρισαῖος, ὀνό-
them. standing up But one in the sanhedrin, a Pharisee by

ματι Γαμαλιήλ, νομοδιδάσκαλος, τίμιος παντὶ τῷ λαῷ,
name Gamaliel, a teacher of the Law, honored by all the people,

**35** ἐκέλευσεν ἔξω βραχύ τι τοὺς ἀποστόλους ποιῆσαι. εἶπέ τε
commanded outside a little while the apostles to put. he said And

πρὸς αὐτούς, Ἄνδρες Ἰσραηλῖται, προσέχετε ἑαυτοῖς ἐπὶ
to them, Men, Israelites, take heed to yourselves on

**36** τοῖς ἀνθρώποις τούτοις, τί μέλλετε πράσσειν. πρὸ γὰρ
— men these, what you intend to do. before For

τούτων τῶν ἡμερῶν ἀνέστη Θευδᾶς, λέγων εἶναί τινα
these — days stood up Theudas, saying to be someone

ἑαυτόν, ᾧ προσεκολλήθη ἀριθμὸς ἀνδρῶν ὡσεὶ τετρακοσίων·
himself, to whom were joined a number of men, about four hundred,

ὃς ἀνηρέθη, καὶ πάντες ὅσοι ἐπείθοντο αὐτῷ διελύθησαν καὶ
who was taken away, and all as many as obeyed him were dispersed and

**37** ἐγένοντο εἰς οὐδέν. μετὰ τοῦτον ἀνέστη Ἰούδας ὁ Γαλιλαῖος
came to nothing. After this stood up Judas the Galilean

ἐν ταῖς ἡμέραις τῆς ἀπογραφῆς, καὶ ἀπέστησε λαὸν ἱκανὸν
in the days of the registration, and drew away people much

ὀπίσω αὐτοῦ· κἀκεῖνος ἀπώλετο, καὶ πάντες ὅσοι ἐπείθοντο
after him; and that one perished, and all as many as obeyed

**38** αὐτῷ διεσκορπίσθησαν. καὶ τὰ νῦν λέγω ὑμῖν, ἀπόστητε
him were scattered. And — now I say to you, draw away

these men, and allow them; because if this counsel be of men, or this work, it will be destroyed. [39] But if it is from God, you will not be **39** able to destroy them, lest you be found even fighters against God. [40] And they **40** obeyed him, and having called the apostles, beating (them), they commanded not to speak on the name of Jesus, and released them. [41] They then indeed departed rejoicing from (the) **41** presence of the sanhedrin, that for His name they were deemed worthy to be dishonored. [42] And every day, in the Temple, and **42** house to house, they did not cease teaching and preaching the gospel (of) Jesus the Christ.

CHAPTER 6
[1] But in those days, **1** the disciples multiplying, a murmuring of the Hellenists arose against the Hebrews, because their widows were overlooked in the daily serving. [2] And **2** the Twelve having called the multitude of the disciples said, It is not right for us to leave the word of God in order to wait **3** tables. [3] Therefore brothers, look for seven men from among yourselves of good report, full of (the) Holy Spirit and wisdom, whom we will appoint over this business. [4] But we will steadfastly **4** continue to prayer and the ministry of the word. **5** [5] And the saying was pleasing before all the multitude, and they chose Stephen, a man full of faith and (the) Holy Spirit, and Philip, and Prochorus, and Nicanor, and Timon, and Parmenas, and Nicolas a proselyte of Antioch, [6] whom they set before **6** the apostles; and having prayed they laid hands on them. [7] And the word of **7** God increased, and the number of the disciples in Jerusalem was multiplied exceedingly, and a great multitude of the priests

ἀπὸ τῶν ἀνθρώπων τούτων, καὶ ἐάσατε αὐτούς· ὅτι ἐὰν ᾖ
from — men these, and allow them; because if be
ἐξ ἀνθρώπων ἡ βουλὴ αὕτη ἢ τὸ ἔργον τοῦτο, καταλυθή-
of men counsel this, or — work this, it will be
σεται· εἰ δὲ ἐκ Θεοῦ ἐστιν, οὐ δύνασθε καταλῦσαι αὐτό,
destroyed. if But of God it is, not you will be able to destroy it,
μήποτε καὶ θεομάχοι εὑρεθῆτε. ἐπείσθησαν δὲ αὐτῷ· καὶ
lest even God-fighters you be found. they obeyed And him, and
προσκαλεσάμενοι τοὺς ἀποστόλους, δείραντες παρήγγειλαν
having called the apostles, beating (them) they charged
μὴ λαλεῖν ἐπὶ τῷ ὀνόματι τοῦ Ἰησοῦ, καὶ ἀπέλυσαν αὐτούς.
not to speak on the name — of Jesus, and released them.
οἱ μὲν οὖν ἐπορεύοντο χαίροντες ἀπὸ προσώπου τοῦ συνε-
They indeed then departed rejoicing from (the) presence of the san-
δρίου, ὅτι ὑπὲρ τοῦ ὀνόματος αὐτοῦ κατηξιώθησαν ἀτιμασθῆ-
hedrin, that for the name of Him they were deemed worthy to be
ναι. πᾶσάν τε ἡμέραν, ἐν τῷ ἱερῷ καὶ κατ᾽ οἶκον, οὐκ ἐπαύ-
dishonored every And day, in the Temple and house to house, not they
οντο διδάσκοντες καὶ εὐαγγελιζόμενοι Ἰησοῦν τὸν Χριστόν.
ceased teaching and preaching the gospel— Jesus the Christ.

CHAPTER 6

Ἐν δὲ ταῖς ἡμέραις ταύταις, πληθυνόντων τῶν μαθητῶν,
in And — days these, multiplying the disciples,
ἐγένετο γογγυσμὸς τῶν Ἑλληνιστῶν πρὸς τοὺς Ἑβραίους,
there was a murmuring of the Hellenists against the Hebrews,
ὅτι παρεθεωροῦντο ἐν τῇ διακονίᾳ τῇ καθημερινῇ αἱ χῆραι
because were overlooked in the service near daily the widows
αὐτῶν. προσκαλεσάμενοι δὲ οἱ δώδεκα τὸ πλῆθος τῶν
of them. having called near And the twelve the multitude of the
μαθητῶν, εἶπον, Οὐκ ἀρεστόν ἐστιν ἡμᾶς, καταλείψαντας
disciples, they said, not pleasing It is to us leaving
τὸν λόγον τοῦ Θεοῦ, διακονεῖν τραπέζαις. ἐπισκέψασθε οὖν,
the word — of God to serve tables. Look out, therefore,
ἀδελφοί, ἄνδρας ἐξ ὑμῶν μαρτυρουμένους ἑπτά, πλήρεις
brothers, men from you being witnessed to, seven, full
Πνεύματος Ἁγίου καὶ σοφίας, οὓς καταστήσομεν ἐπὶ τῆς
of (the) Spirit Holy, and of wisdom, whom we will appoint over —
χρείας ταύτης. ἡμεῖς δὲ τῇ προσευχῇ καὶ τῇ διακονίᾳ τοῦ
duty this. we But to prayer and the service of the
λόγου προσκαρτερήσομεν. καὶ ἤρεσεν ὁ λόγος ἐνώπιον
word will continue steadfast And was pleasing the word before
παντὸς τοῦ πλήθους· καὶ ἐξελέξαντο Στέφανον, ἄνδρα πλήρη
all the multitude, and they chose Stephen, a man full
πίστεως καὶ Πνεύματος Ἁγίου, καὶ Φίλιππον, καὶ Πρόχο-
of faith and (the) Spirit Holy, and Philip, and Prochorus,
ρον, καὶ Νικάνορα, καὶ Τίμωνα, καὶ Παρμενᾶν, καὶ Νικόλαον
and Nicanor, and Timon, and Parmenas, and Nicolas
προσήλυτον Ἀντιοχέα, οὓς ἔστησαν ἐνώπιον τῶν ἀποστό-
a proselyte of Antioch; whom they set before the apostles;
λων· καὶ προσευξάμενοι ἐπέθηκαν αὐτοῖς τὰς χεῖρας.
and having prayed they placed on them the hands.
Καὶ ὁ λόγος τοῦ Θεοῦ ηὔξανε, καὶ ἐπληθύνετο ὁ ἀριθμὸς
And the word — of God increased, and was multipled the number
τῶν μαθητῶν ἐν Ἱερουσαλὴμ σφόδρα, πολύς τε ὄχλος τῶν
of the disciples in Jerusalem exceedingly; a much and crowd of the

ἱερέων ὑπήκουον τῇ πίστει.
priests   obeyed   the   faith.

were obedient to the faith.

8   Στέφανος δὲ πλήρης πίστεως καὶ δυνάμεως ἐποίει τέρατα
Stephen   And full   of faith   and   power   did   wonders

[8] And Stephen, full of faith and power, worked great wonders and miracles among the people.

9   καὶ σημεῖα μεγάλα ἐν τῷ λαῷ. ἀνέστησαν δέ τινες τῶν ἐκ
and signs   great among the people. rose up   But   some of those of

[9] And certain of those of the synagogue called Libertines, and of Cyrenians, and of Alexandrians, and of those from Cilicia and Asia, rose up disputing with Stephen.

τῆς συναγωγῆς τῆς λεγομένης Λιβερτίνων, καὶ Κυρηναίων,
the   synagogue   — called of (the) Libertines,   and   of Cyrenians

καὶ Ἀλεξανδρέων, καὶ τῶν ἀπὸ Κιλικίας καὶ Ἀσίας, συζη-
and   of Alexandrians, and of those from Cilicia   and   Asia,

10   τοῦντες τῷ Στεφάνῳ. καὶ οὐκ ἴσχυον ἀντιστῆναι τῇ σοφίᾳ
disputing   — with Stephen. And not were able to stand against the wisdom

[10] And they were not able to resist the wisdom and the spirit by which he spoke.

11   καὶ τῷ πνεύματι ᾧ ἐλάλει. τότε ὑπέβαλον ἄνδρας λέγοντας
and the   spirit with which he spoke. Then they suborned men,   saying,

[11] Then they suborned men, saying, We have heard him speaking blasphemous words against Moses and God.

ὅτι Ἀκηκόαμεν αὐτοῦ λαλοῦντος ῥήματα βλάσφημα εἰς
— We have heard from him speaking   words   blasphemous against

12   Μωσῆν καὶ τὸν Θεόν. συνεκίνησάν τε τὸν λαὸν καὶ τοὺς
Moses and — God. they stirred up And the people and the

[12] And they stirred up the people and the elders and the scribes, and coming on they seized him and brought (him) to the sanhedrin.

πρεσβυτέρους καὶ τοὺς γραμματεῖς, καὶ ἐπιστάντες συν-
elders   and the   scribes,   and coming on   they

13   ἥρπασαν αὐτόν, καὶ ἤγαγον εἰς τὸ συνέδριον, ἔστησάν τε
seized   him, and led   to the sanhedrin they stood And

[13] And they set false witnesses, saying, This man does not cease speaking blasphemous words against this holy place and the Law;

μάρτυρας ψευδεῖς λέγοντας, Ὁ ἄνθρωπος οὗτος οὐ παύεται
witnesses false,   saying,   man   This   not   ceases

ῥήματα βλάσφημα λαλῶν κατὰ τοῦ τόπου τοῦ ἁγίου
words   blasphemous speaking against — place   —   holy

14   τούτου καὶ τοῦ νόμου· ἀκηκόαμεν γὰρ αὐτοῦ λέγοντος ὅτι
this,   and the   Law; we have heard for from him, saying

[14] for we have heard him saying that this Jesus the Nazarene will destroy this place, and will change the customs which Moses delivered to us.

Ἰησοῦς ὁ Ναζωραῖος οὗτος καταλύσει τὸν τόπον τοῦτον,
Jesus the Nazarene   this One, will destroy — place   this,

15   καὶ ἀλλάξει τὰ ἔθη ἃ παρέδωκεν ἡμῖν Μωϋσῆς. καὶ ἀτενί-
and will change the customs which delivered to us   Moses.   And looking

[15] And looking intently on him, all who sat in the sanhedrin saw his face as (the) face of an angel.

σαντες εἰς αὐτὸν ἅπαντες οἱ καθεζόμενοι ἐν τῷ συνεδρίῳ,
intently at him,   all   those   sitting   in the   sanhedrin

εἶδον τὸ πρόσωπον αὐτοῦ ὡσεὶ πρόσωπον ἀγγέλου.
saw   the   face   of him   as if a face   of an angel.

## CHAPTER 7

[1] And the high priest said, Do you hold these things so? [2] And he said, Men, brothers and fathers, listen: The God of glory appeared to our father Abraham, being in Mesopotamia, before he lived in Haran, [3] and said to him, Go out of your land and from your kindred and come into (a) land which I will show you. [4] Then going out from (the) land of Chaldeans, he lived in Haran, and after his father died He moved him from there into this land in which you now live. [5] And He did not give to him an inheritance in it,

1   Εἶπε δὲ ὁ ἀρχιερεύς, Εἰ ἄρα ταῦτα οὕτως ἔχει ; ὁ δὲ ἔφη,
said And the high priest, If, then, these things thus hold? he And said,

2   Ἄνδρες ἀδελφοὶ καὶ πατέρες, ἀκούσατε. ὁ Θεὸς τῆς δόξης
Men, brothers and fathers,   hear:   The God — of glory

ὤφθη τῷ πατρὶ ἡμῶν Ἀβραὰμ ὄντι ἐν τῇ Μεσοποταμίᾳ,
appeared to the father of us, Abraham, being in — Mesopotamia

3   πρὶν ἢ κατοικῆσαι αὐτὸν ἐν Χαρράν, καὶ εἶπε πρὸς αὐτόν,
before even dwelt   him in Haran; and said to   him,

Ἔξελθε ἐκ τῆς γῆς σου καὶ ἐκ τῆς συγγενείας σου, καὶ δεῦρο
Go out of the land of you and from the kindred of you, and come

4   εἰς γῆν ἣν ἄν σοι δείξω. τότε ἐξελθὼν ἐκ γῆς Χαλδαίων
into a land which to you I will show. Then going out of (the) land of Chaldea,

κατῴκησεν ἐν Χαρράν· κἀκεῖθεν, μετὰ τὸ ἀποθανεῖν τὸν
he dwelt   in Haran. And from there, after the dying of the

πατέρα αὐτοῦ, μετῴκισεν αὐτὸν εἰς τὴν γῆν ταύτην εἰς ἣν
father of him, (God) moved him into — land this, in which

5   ὑμεῖς νῦν κατοικεῖτε· καὶ οὐκ ἔδωκεν αὐτῷ κληρονομίαν ἐν
you now dwell.   And not He gave to him an inheritance in

CHAPTER 7

not even a foot-breadth; and promised to him to give it for a possession, and to his seed after him, there being no child to him. [6] And God spoke this way: That his seed shall be living in another land, and they will enslave it and oppress four hundred years; [7] and the nation to whom they may be in bondage I will judge, said God; and after these things they shall come out and serve Me in this place. [8] And He gave to him a covenant of circumcision; and so he fathered Isaac, and circumcised him the eighth day; and Isaac Jacob, and Jacob the twelve patriarchs. [9] And the patriarchs, envying Joseph, sold (him) into Egypt. [10] And God was with him, and delivered him out of all his troubles, and gave him favor and wisdom before Pharaoh king of Egypt; and he appointed him ruler over Egypt and his whole house. [11] But a famine came on all the land of Egypt and Canaan, and great trouble, and our fathers did not find food. [12] But Jacob having heard grain was in Egypt sent out our fathers first; [13] and at the second time Joseph was made known to his brothers, and the family of Joseph was made known to Pharaoh. [14] And Joseph having sent, he called for his father Jacob, and all his kindred, seventy-five souls. [15] And Jacob went down into Egypt and died, he and our fathers, [16] and were moved into Shechem, and were placed in the tomb which Abraham bought for a sum of money from the sons of Hamor of Shechem. [17] But as the time of the promise which God swore to Abraham drew near, the people increased and multiplied in Egypt,

αὐτῇ, οὐδὲ βῆμα ποδός· καὶ ἐπηγγείλατο αὐτῷ δοῦναι εἰς
it,   nor   space of a foot,   and   promised    him   to give   for
κατάσχεσιν αὐτήν, καὶ τῷ σπέρματι αὐτοῦ μετ' αὐτόν, οὐκ
a possession   it,    and to the   seed    of him   after    him,   not

6 ὄντος αὐτῷ τέκνου. ἐλάλησε δὲ οὕτως ὁ Θεός, ὅτι ἔσται τὸ
being to him a child.    spoke   And   thus   —   God,   that will be the
σπέρμα αὐτοῦ πάροικον ἐν γῇ ἀλλοτρίᾳ, καὶ δουλώσουσιν
seed    of him   a sojourner in a land   another,   and they will enslave

7 αὐτὸ καὶ κακώσουσιν, ἔτη τετρακόσια. καὶ τὸ ἔθνος, ᾧ ἐὰν
it,   and will oppress    years four hundred. And the nation whom may
δουλεύσωσι, κρινῶ ἐγώ, εἶπεν ὁ Θεός· καὶ μετὰ ταῦτα
they    serve, will judge   I;    said     God and, After these things

8 ἐξελεύσονται, καὶ λατρεύσουσί μοι ἐν τῷ τόπῳ τούτῳ. καὶ
they will come out, and will do service to Me in   —   place   this.    And
ἔδωκεν αὐτῷ διαθήκην περιτομῆς· καὶ οὕτως ἐγέννησε τὸν
He gave to him a covenant   of circumcision; and thus he fathered    —
Ἰσαάκ, καὶ περιέτεμεν αὐτὸν τῇ ἡμέρᾳ τῇ ὀγδόῃ· καὶ ὁ
Isaac,   and circumcised    him   on the day   —     eighth. And
Ἰσαὰκ τὸν Ἰακώβ, καὶ ὁ Ἰακὼβ τοὺς δώδεκα πατριάρχας.
Isaac (fathered) Jacob, and     Jacob   the   twelve   patriarchs.

9 καὶ οἱ πατριάρχαι ζηλώσαντες τὸν Ἰωσὴφ ἀπέδοντο εἰς
And the patriarchs    being jealous   —   Joseph   gave over    into

10 Αἴγυπτον· καὶ ἦν ὁ Θεὸς μετ' αὐτοῦ. καὶ ἐξείλετο αὐτὸν ἐκ
Egypt;     and was — God   with   him,    and   plucked him from
πασῶν τῶν θλίψεων αὐτοῦ, καὶ ἔδωκεν αὐτῷ χάριν καὶ
all    the   afflictions   of him; and   gave    him   favor   and
σοφίαν ἐναντίον Φαραὼ βασιλέως Αἰγύπτου, καὶ κατέστησεν
wisdom   over    Pharaoh   king    of Egypt,   and he appointed
αὐτὸν ἡγούμενον ἐπ' Αἴγυπτον καὶ ὅλον τὸν οἶκον αὐτοῦ.
him   governor   over Egypt    and   all    the   house   of him.

11 ἦλθε δὲ λιμὸς ἐφ' ὅλην τὴν γῆν Αἰγύπτου καὶ Χανάαν, καὶ
came But a famine over all    the land of Egypt    and Canaan, and
θλῖψις μεγάλη καὶ οὐχ εὕρισκον χορτάσματα οἱ πατέρες
affliction great;   and did not   find     sustenance    the fathers

12 ἡμῶν. ἀκούσας δὲ Ἰακὼβ ὄντα σῖτα ἐν Αἰγύπτῳ, ἐξαπέστειλε
of us. having heard But Jacob being grain in   Egypt,    he sent forth

13 τοὺς πατέρας ἡμῶν πρῶτον. καὶ ἐν τῷ δευτέρῳ ἀνεγνωρίσθη
the    fathers of us first.     And in the   second   was made known
Ἰωσὴφ τοῖς ἀδελφοῖς αὐτοῦ, καὶ φανερὸν ἐγένετο τῷ Φαραὼ
Joseph to the   brothers of him, and   manifest   became   — to Pharaoh

14 τὸ γένος τοῦ Ἰωσήφ. ἀποστείλας δὲ Ἰωσὴφ μετεκαλέσατο
the race   —   of Joseph.   sending    And   Joseph,    called
τὸν πατέρα αὐτοῦ Ἰακώβ, καὶ πᾶσαν τὴν συγγένειαν αὐτοῦ,
the   father   of him, Jacob,   and   all     the   kindred    of him,

15 ἐν ψυχαῖς ἑβδομήκοντα πέντε. κατέβη δὲ Ἰακὼβ εἰς Αἴγυ-
in souls    seventy    five. went down And Jacob into Egypt,
πτον, καὶ ἐτελεύτησεν αὐτὸς καὶ οἱ πατέρες ἡμῶν· καὶ μετετέ-
and    expired     he   and the fathers   of us, and they were

16 θησαν εἰς Συχέμ, καὶ ἐτέθησαν ἐν τῷ μνήματι ὃ ὠνήσατο
moved into Shechem, and were placed   in the   tomb    which bought
Ἀβραὰμ τιμῆς ἀργυρίου παρὰ τῶν υἱῶν Ἐμὸρ τοῦ Συχέμ.
Abraham (for) a price of silver    from    the   sons of Hamor — of Shechem.

17 καθὼς δὲ ἤγγιζεν ὁ χρόνος τῆς ἐπαγγελίας ἧς ὤμοσεν ὁ Θεὸς
as     And drew near the time of the   promise   which swore   — God
τῷ Ἀβραάμ, ηὔξησεν ὁ λαὸς καὶ ἐπληθύνθη ἐν Αἰγύπτῳ,
— to Abraham, grew    the people, and were multiplied in   Egypt,

[18] until another king rose up, who did not know Joseph. [19] This one having dealt slyly with our race oppressed our fathers, causing their infants (to be) exposed so that they might not live. [20] In which time Moses was born, and was beautiful to God; who was brought three months in the house of his father. [21] And he being exposed, Pharaoh's daughter took him up and reared him for a son to her. [22] And Moses was instructed in all (the) wisdom of Egyptians; and was powerful in words and works. [23] And when a period of forty years was fulfilled to him, it arose on his heart to look on his brothers, the sons of Israel; [24] and seeing one being wronged he defended (him), and he avenged him getting the worse, having struck the Egyptian. [25] For he thought his brothers to understand that God would give deliverance to them by his hand. But they did not understand. [26] And on the following day he appeared to those who were fighting, and urged them to peace, saying, Men, you are brothers, why do you wrong one another? [27] But he who was wronging the neighbor thrust him away, saying, Who appointed you a ruler and a judge over us? [28] Do not you want to kill me in the way you killed the Egyptian yesterday? [29] And Moses fled at this word. And he became a resident in Midian land, where he fathered two sons. [30] And forty years being fulfilled, appeared to him an Angel of (the) Lord in the Mount Sinai desert, in a flame of fire of a bush. [31] And seeing (it), Moses marveled at the vision. And he coming up to look, a voice of (the) Lord came to him, [32] "I am the God of your fathers, the God of Abraham, and the God of Isaac, and the God of Jacob." But Moses becoming trembly did not dare to look [33] And the Lord said to him, "Put off the

18 ἄχρις οὗ ἀνέστη βασιλεὺς ἕτερος, ὃς οὐκ ᾔδει τὸν Ἰωσήφ.
   until  rose up  king    another,  who not knew  —  Joseph.

19 οὗτος κατασοφισάμενος τὸ γένος ἡμῶν, ἐκάκωσε τοὺς πατέ-
   This one dealing slyly   with the race of us  oppressed the fathers
   ρας ἡμῶν, τοῦ ποιεῖν ἔκθετα τὰ βρέφη αὐτῶν, εἰς τὸ μὴ
   of us — to make exposed the babes of them unto — not

20 ζωογονεῖσθαι. ἐν ᾧ καιρῷ ἐγεννήθη Μωσῆς, καὶ ἦν ἀστεῖος
   being preserved alive. At which time was born Moses,  and he was beautiful
   τῷ Θεῷ· ὃς ἀνετράφη μῆνας τρεῖς ἐν τῷ οἴκῳ τοῦ πατρὸς
   — to God, who was reared months three in the house of the father

21 αὐτοῦ. ἐκτεθέντα δὲ αὐτόν, ἀνείλετο αὐτὸν ἡ θυγάτηρ
   of him. being exposed And he,  took up  him  the daughter

22 Φαραώ, καὶ ἀνεθρέψατο αὐτὸν ἑαυτῇ εἰς υἱόν. καὶ ἐπαιδεύθη
   of Pharaoh, and reared    him to herself for a son. And was instructed
   Μωσῆς πάσῃ σοφίᾳ Αἰγυπτίων· ἦν δὲ δυνατὸς ἐν λόγοις καὶ
   Moses in all (the) wisdom of Egyptians, was and powerful in words and

23 ἐν ἔργοις. ὡς δὲ ἐπληροῦτο αὐτῷ τεσσαρακονταετὴς χρόνος,
   in works. as But was fulfilled to him of forty years     a time,
   ἀνέβη ἐπὶ τὴν καρδίαν αὐτοῦ ἐπισκέψασθαι τοὺς ἀδελφοὺς
   it arose on the heart of him to look upon   the   brothers

24 αὐτοῦ τοὺς υἱοὺς Ἰσραήλ. καὶ ἰδών τινα ἀδικούμενον, ἠμύ-
   of him, the sons of Israel. And seeing one being wronged, he de-
   νατο καὶ ἐποίησεν ἐκδίκησιν τῷ καταπονουμένῳ, πατάξας
   fended, and he did    vengeance for the (one) getting the worse, striking

25 τὸν Αἰγύπτιον· ἐνόμιζε δὲ συνιέναι τοὺς ἀδελφοὺς αὐτοῦ ὅτι
   the Egyptian.   he thought And to understand the brothers of him that
   ὁ Θεὸς διὰ χειρὸς αὐτοῦ δίδωσιν αὐτοῖς σωτηρίαν· οἱ δὲ οὐ
   — God through hand of him would give to them deliverance; they but not

26 συνῆκαν. τῇ δὲ ἐπιούσῃ ἡμέρᾳ ὤφθη αὐτοῖς μαχομένοις, καὶ
   understood. the But following day he appeared to them fighting,    and
   συνήλασεν αὐτοὺς εἰς εἰρήνην, εἰπών, Ἄνδρες, ἀδελφοί ἐστε
   urged       them  to peace, saying,  Men,  brothers  are

27 ὑμεῖς· ἱνατί ἀδικεῖτε ἀλλήλους; ὁ δὲ ἀδικῶν τὸν πλησίον
   you,  why do you wrong one another? he But wronging the  neighbor
   ἀπώσατο αὐτόν, εἰπών, Τίς σε κατέστησεν ἄρχοντα καὶ
   thrust away him,  saying, Who you appointed   a ruler   and

28 δικαστὴν ἐφ᾽ ἡμᾶς; μὴ ἀνελεῖν με σὺ θέλεις, ὃν τρόπον ἀνεῖλες
   a judge    over us? Do not to take away me you desire, (in) what way you took away

29 χθὲς τὸν Αἰγύπτιον; ἔφυγε δὲ Μωσῆς ἐν τῷ λόγῳ τούτῳ,
   yesterday the Egyptian?  fled And Moses at — word this.
   καὶ ἐγένετο πάροικος ἐν γῇ Μαδιάμ, οὗ ἐγέννησεν υἱοὺς δύο.
   And he became a sojourner in land Midian, where he fathered sons two.

30 καὶ πληρωθέντων ἐτῶν τεσσαράκοντα, ὤφθη αὐτῷ ἐν τῇ
   And being fulfilled years   forty,      appeared to him in the
   ἐρήμῳ τοῦ ὄρους Σινᾶ ἄγγελος Κυρίου ἐν φλογὶ πυρὸς
   desert of the Mount Sinai, (the) angel of (the) Lord in a flame of fire

31 βάτου. ὁ δὲ Μωσῆς ἰδὼν ἐθαύμασε τὸ ὅραμα· προσερχο-
   of a bush. And Moses seeing marveled at the vision.  coming
   μένου δὲ αὐτοῦ κατανοῆσαι, ἐγένετο φωνὴ Κυρίου πρὸς
   up And he to look,         came  a voice of (the) Lord to

32 αὐτόν, Ἐγὼ ὁ Θεὸς τῶν πατέρων σου, ὁ Θεὸς Ἀβραὰμ καὶ
   him,   I the God of the  fathers of you, the God of Abraham and
   ὁ Θεὸς Ἰσαὰκ καὶ ὁ Θεὸς Ἰακώβ. ἔντρομος δὲ γενόμενος
   the God of Isaac and the God of Jacob(am). trembling But becoming

33 Μωσῆς οὐκ ἐτόλμα κατανοῆσαι. εἶπε δὲ αὐτῷ ὁ Κύριος,
   Moses not did dare to observe,      said And to him the Lord,

sandals from your feet, for the place where you stand is holy ground." [34] "I have seen the affliction of My people in Egypt, and I have heard their groan, and I came down in order to take them out. And now, come, I will send you into Egypt." [35] This Moses, whom they denied, saying, Who appointed ruler and judge — him God sent (as) ruler and deliverer by (the) hand of (the) Angel who appeared to him in the Bush. [36] This one led them out, having worked wonders and miracles in (the) land of Egypt and in (the) Red Sea, and in the wilderness forty years. [37] This is the Moses who said to the sons of Israel, "(The) Lord your God will raise up a Prophet to you from among your brothers, (One) like me, You shall hear Him." [38] This is he who was in the assembly in the wilderness with the Angel who spoke to him in Mount Sinai, and with our fathers; who received living words to give to us; [39] to whom our fathers would not be subject, but thrust (him) away and turned their hearts back to Egypt, [40] saying to Aaron, Make for us gods which will go before us; for this Moses who brought us out from (the) land of Egypt, we do not know what has happened to him. [41] And they made a calf in those days, and led up a sacrifice to the idol, and rejoiced in the works of their hands. [42] But God turned and delivered them up to serve the hosts of the heavens; as it has been written in (the) book of the Prophets, "Did you offer slain beasts and sacrifices to Me forty years in the wilderness, O house of Israel? [43] And you took up the tent of Moloch and the star of your god Remphan — the models which you made to worship them; and I will

Λῦσον τὸ ὑπόδημα τῶν ποδῶν σου· ὁ γὰρ τόπος ἐν ᾧ
Loosen the sandal of the feet of you, the for place on which

**34** ἕστηκας γῆ ἁγία ἐστίν. ἰδὼν εἶδον τὴν κάκωσιν τοῦ λαοῦ
you stand ground holy is. Seeing I saw the oppression of the people

μου τοῦ ἐν Αἰγύπτῳ, καὶ τοῦ στεναγμοῦ αὐτῶν ἤκουσα·
of Me — in Egypt, and the groan of them I heard,

καὶ κατέβην ἐξελέσθαι αὐτούς· καὶ νῦν δεῦρο, ἀποστελῶ σε
and I came down to rescue them; and now come, I will send you

**35** εἰς Αἴγυπτον. τοῦτον τὸν Μωϋσῆν ὃν ἠρνήσαντο εἰπόντες,
to Egypt. This — Moses whom they denied, saying,

Τίς σε κατέστησεν ἄρχοντα καὶ δικαστήν; τοῦτον ὁ Θεὸς
Who you appointed a ruler and a judge? This one — God

ἄρχοντα καὶ λυτρωτὴν ἀπέστειλεν ἐν χειρὶ ἀγγέλου τοῦ
a ruler and a deliverer has sent by (the) hand of (the) Angel

**36** ὀφθέντος αὐτῷ ἐν τῇ βάτῳ. οὗτος ἐξήγαγεν αὐτούς,
appearing to him in the Bush. This one led out them,

ποιήσας τέρατα καὶ σημεῖα ἐν γῇ Αἰγύπτου καὶ ἐν Ἐρυθρᾷ
doing wonders and signs in (the) land of Egypt, and in (the) Red

**37** θαλάσσῃ, καὶ ἐν τῇ ἐρήμῳ ἔτη τεσσαράκοντα. οὗτός ἐστιν
Sea, and in the desert years forty. This is

ὁ Μωϋσῆς ὁ εἰπὼν τοῖς υἱοῖς Ἰσραήλ, Προφήτην ὑμῖν
the Moses — saying to the sons of Israel, A prophet for you

ἀναστήσει Κύριος ὁ Θεὸς ὑμῶν ἐκ τῶν ἀδελφῶν ὑμῶν ὡς ἐμέ·
will raise up (the) Lord God of you from the brothers of you, like me.

**38** αὐτοῦ ἀκούσεσθε. οὗτός ἐστιν ὁ γενόμενος ἐν τῇ ἐκκλησίᾳ
Him you shall hear, This is the (one) having been in the assembly

ἐν τῇ ἐρήμῳ μετὰ τοῦ ἀγγέλου τοῦ λαλοῦντος αὐτῷ ἐν τῷ
in the desert with the Angel — speaking to him in the

ὄρει Σινᾶ καὶ τῶν πατέρων ἡμῶν· ὃς ἐδέξατο λόγια ζῶντα
Mount Sinai, and (with) the fathers of us, who received words living

**39** δοῦναι ἡμῖν· ᾧ οὐκ ἠθέλησαν ὑπήκοοι γενέσθαι οἱ πατέρες
to give to us, to whom not desired subject to be the fathers

ἡμῶν, ἀλλ' ἀπώσαντο, καὶ ἐστράφησαν ταῖς καρδίαις αὐτῶν
of us, but thrust away, and turned away the hearts of them

**40** εἰς Αἴγυπτον, εἰπόντες τῷ Ἀαρών, Ποίησον ἡμῖν θεοὺς οἳ
to Egypt, saying — to Aaron, Make for us gods which

προπορεύσονται ἡμῶν· ὁ γὰρ Μωσῆς οὗτος, ὃς ἐξήγαγεν
will go before us; — for Moses this, who led

**41** ἡμᾶς ἐκ γῆς Αἰγύπτου, οὐκ οἴδαμεν τί γέγονεν αὐτῷ. καὶ
us out of (the) land of Egypt, not we know what has occurred to him. And

ἐμοσχοποίησαν ἐν ταῖς ἡμέραις ἐκείναις, καὶ ἀνήγαγον
they made a calf in — days those, and led up

θυσίαν τῷ εἰδώλῳ, καὶ εὐφραίνοντο ἐν τοῖς ἔργοις τῶν
a sacrifice to the idol, and made merry in the works of the

**42** χειρῶν αὐτῶν. ἔστρεψε δὲ ὁ Θεός, καὶ παρέδωκεν αὐτοὺς
hands of them. turned And — God, and gave over them

λατρεύειν τῇ στρατιᾷ τοῦ οὐρανοῦ· καθὼς γέγραπται ἐν
to worship the host — of heaven, as it has been written in

βίβλῳ τῶν προφητῶν, Μὴ σφάγια καὶ θυσίας προσηνέγ-
(the) roll of the prophets, Not victims and sacrifices you brought

κατέ μοι ἔτη τεσσαράκοντα ἐν τῇ ἐρήμῳ, οἶκος Ἰσραήλ;
near to Me years forty in the desert, house of Israel;

**43** καὶ ἀνελάβετε τὴν σκηνὴν τοῦ Μολόχ, καὶ τὸ ἄστρον τοῦ
and you took up the tent — of Moloch, and the star of the

θεοῦ ὑμῶν Ῥεμφάν, τοὺς τύπους οὓς ἐποιήσατε προσκυνεῖν
god of you, Remphan, the models which you made to worship

remove you beyond Babylon. [44] The tabernacle of the testimony was among our fathers in the wilderness, as He who spoke to Moses commanded, to make it according to the pattern which he had seen; [45] which also having received (it) by succession our fathers brought in with Joshua, in the taking of possession of the nations, whom God drove out from our fathers, until the days of David; [46] who found favor before God, and asked to find a tabernacle for the God of Jacob; [47] but Solomon built Him a house. [48] But the Most High dwells not in temples made by hand; as the prophet says, [49] "Heaven is My throne, and the earth a footstool of My feet; what house will you build Me, says the Lord; or, What (the) place of My rest? [50] Did not My hands make all these things?" [51] O stiffnecked and uncircumcised in heart and ears, you always resist the Holy Spirit; as your fathers, also you. [52] Which of the prophets did your fathers not persecute? And they killed those who before told about the coming of the Just One, of whom you now have become betrayers and murderers; [53] who received the Law by (the) disposition of angels, and did not keep (it).

[54] And hearing these things they were cut to their hearts, and gnashed the teeth at him. [55] But being full of (the) Holy Spirit, having looked intently into Heaven, he saw (the) glory of God, and Jesus standing at the right (hand) of God, [56] and said, Behold, I see the heavens opened, and the Son of man standing at the right of God. [57] And crying out with a loud voice they held their ears, and rushed with one accord upon him. [58] And having thrown (him) out of the city, they

---

**44** αὐτοῖς· καὶ μετοικιῶ ὑμᾶς ἐπέκεινα Βαβυλῶνος. ἡ σκηνὴ τοῦ
them,    and I will remove you    beyond    Babylon.    The tent —
μαρτυρίου ἦν τοῖς πατράσιν ἡμῶν ἐν τῇ ἐρήμῳ, καθὼς
of witness  was to the fathers   of us  in the  desert,   as
διετάξατο ὁ λαλῶν τῷ Μωσῇ, ποιῆσαι αὐτὴν κατὰ τὸν
commanded the (One) speaking to Moses, to make  it  according to the

**45** τύπον ὃν ἑωράκει. ἦν καὶ εἰσήγαγον διαδεξάμενοι οἱ πατέρες
pattern which he had seen, which also   was led, having inherited the fathers
ἡμῶν μετὰ Ἰησοῦ ἐν τῇ κατασχέσει τῶν ἐθνῶν, ὧν ἐξῶσεν ὁ
of us  with Joshua in the  taking of   of the nations, whom put out
                                        possession
Θεὸς ἀπὸ προσώπου τῶν πατέρων ἡμῶν, ἕως τῶν ἡμερῶν
God from  the face   of the  fathers  of us,  until the  days

**46** Δαβίδ· ὃς εὗρε χάριν ἐνώπιον τοῦ Θεοῦ, καὶ ἠτήσατο εὑρεῖν
of David, who found favor before  — God,  and  asked  to find

**47** σκήνωμα τῷ Θεῷ Ἰακώβ. Σολομῶν δὲ ᾠκοδόμησεν αὐτῷ
a tent  for the God of Jacob. Solomon But built    for Him

**48** οἶκον. ἀλλ᾽ οὐχ ὁ ὕψιστος ἐν χειροποιήτοις ναοῖς κατοικεῖ,
a house. But not the Most High in  made by hand  temples dwells;

**49** καθὼς ὁ προφήτης λέγει, Ὁ οὐρανός μοι θρόνος, ἡ δὲ γῆ
as   the  prophet  says, The Heaven to Me a throne, the and earth
ὑποπόδιον τῶν ποδῶν μου· ποῖον οἶκον οἰκοδομήσετέ μοι ;
a footstool of the feet of Me; what  house  will you build for Me,
                                 sort of

**50** λέγει Κύριος· ἢ τίς τόπος τῆς καταπαύσεώς μου ; οὐχὶ ἡ
says (the) Lord, or what place of the   resting    of Me? Did not the
χείρ μου ἐποίησε ταῦτα πάντα ;
hand of Me make  these things all?

**51** Σκληροτράχηλοι καὶ ἀπερίτμητοι τῇ καρδίᾳ καὶ τοῖς ὠσίν,
Stiffnecked    and uncircumcised  in the heart and in the ears,
ὑμεῖς ἀεὶ τῷ Πνεύματι τῷ Ἁγίῳ ἀντιπίπτετε· ὡς οἱ πατέρες
you always the Spirit  — Holy  fell against,  as the fathers

**52** ὑμῶν, καὶ ὑμεῖς. τίνα τῶν προφητῶν οὐκ ἐδίωξαν οἱ πατέρες
of you, also you. Which of the prophets  not persecuted the fathers
ὑμῶν ; καὶ ἀπέκτειναν τοὺς προκαταγγείλαντας περὶ τῆς
of you ? And they killed  those before announcing concerning the
ἐλεύσεως τοῦ δικαίου, οὗ νῦν ὑμεῖς προδόται καὶ φονεῖς
coming of the Just One, of whom now you  betrayers and murderers

**53** γεγένησθε· οἵτινες ἐλάβετε τὸν νόμον εἰς διαταγὰς ἀγγέλων,
have become, who  received  the  Law by disposition of angels,
καὶ οὐκ ἐφυλάξατε.
and not kept (it).

**54** Ἀκούοντες δὲ ταῦτα, διεπρίοντο ταῖς καρδίαις αὐτῶν, καὶ
hearing And these things, they were cut to the hearts of them, and

**55** ἔβρυχον τοὺς ὀδόντας ἐπ᾽ αὐτόν. ὑπάρχων δὲ πλήρης
gnashed  the   teeth  at him.  being But full
Πνεύματος Ἁγίου, ἀτενίσας εἰς τὸν οὐρανόν, εἶδε δόξαν Θεοῦ,
of (the) Spirit Holy looking intently into Heaven, he saw (the) glory of God,

**56** καὶ Ἰησοῦν ἑστῶτα ἐκ δεξιῶν τοῦ Θεοῦ, καὶ εἶπεν, Ἰδού,
and Jesus  standing at (the) right — of God, and  said, Behold,
θεωρῶ τοὺς οὐρανοὺς ἀνεῳγμένους, καὶ τὸν υἱὸν τοῦ ἀνθρώ-
I see  the  heavens having been opened, and the Son — of

**57** που ἐκ δεξιῶν ἑστῶτα τοῦ Θεοῦ. κράξαντες δὲ φωνῇ μεγάλῃ,
man at (the) right standing — of God. crying out And with a voice great,
συνέσχον τὰ ὦτα αὐτῶν, καὶ ὥρμησαν ὁμοθυμαδὸν ἐπ᾽
they held the ears of them, and  rushed   with one passion on

**58** αὐτόν· καὶ ἐκβαλόντες ἔξω τῆς πόλεως, ἐλιθοβόλουν· καὶ οἱ
him,  and  throwing  outside the city,   they stoned (him). And the

stoned (him). And the witnesses laid aside their garments at the feet of a young man called Saul. [59] And they stoned Stephen, invoking and saying, Lord Jesus, receive my spirit. [60] And having bowed the knees, he cried with a loud voice, Lord, do not make stand this sin to them. And having said this, he fell asleep.

μάρτυρες ἀπέθεντο τὰ ἱμάτια αὐτῶν παρὰ τοὺς πόδας
witnesses    put off    the garments of them    at    the    feet

59 νεανίου καλουμένου Σαύλου. καὶ ἐλιθοβόλουν τὸν Στέφανον,
of a young man  called    Saul.   And they stoned    — Stephen

ἐπικαλούμενον καὶ λέγοντα, Κύριε ᾽Ιησοῦ, δέξαι τὸ πνεῦμά
invoking (God)  and saying,   Lord    Jesus,  receive the spirit

60 μου. θεὶς δὲ τὰ γόνατα, ἔκραξε φωνῇ μεγάλῃ, Κύριε, μὴ
of me. placing And the knees,  he cried  with a voice great,  Lord,  Not

στήσῃς αὐτοῖς τὴν ἁμαρτίαν ταύτην. καὶ τοῦτο εἰπὼν
make stand  to them  —  sin    this.    And  this having said,

ἐκοιμήθη
he fell asleep.

## CHAPTER 8

[1] And Saul was agreeing to the killing of him. And a great persecution took place on that day against the assembly which (was) in Jerusalem, and all were scattered throughout the countries of Judea and Samaria except the apostles. [2] And devoted men buried Stephen and made great weeping over him. [3] But Saul was ravaging the assembly, going in house by house and dragging men and women, (he) delivered (them) up to prison.

[4] Then they who had been scattered passed through preaching the gospel, the word. [5] And going down to a city of Samaria, Philip preached Christ to them; [6] and the crowds listened to the things spoken by Philip with one accord, when they heard and saw the miracles which he did. [7] For of many of those who had unclean spirits, crying with a loud voice they went out; and many having been paralyzed and lame were healed. [8] And great joy was in that city.

[9] But a certain man named Simon had long been conjuring in the city, and amazing the nation of Samaria, claiming himself to be some great one. [10] All were heeding to (him) from small to great, saying, This one is the power of God, which (is) great. [11] And they were giving heed to him, because for a long time (he) had

## CHAPTER 8

1 Σαῦλος δὲ ἦν συνευδοκῶν τῇ ἀναιρέσει αὐτοῦ.
Saul And was consenting    to the doing away of him.

᾽Εγένετο δὲ ἐν ἐκείνῃ τῇ ἡμέρᾳ διωγμὸς μέγας ἐπὶ τὴν
it was And in that  — day a persecution  great  on  the

ἐκκλησίαν τὴν ἐν ᾽Ιεροσολύμοις· πάντες τε διεσπάρησαν
the church  —  in   Jerusalem,   all   and were scattered

κατὰ τὰς χώρας τῆς ᾽Ιουδαίας καὶ Σαμαρείας, πλὴν τῶν
through the countries — of Judea  and  Samaria,  except  the

2 ἀποστόλων. συνεκόμισαν δὲ τὸν Στέφανον ἄνδρες εὐλαβεῖς,
apostles.   together carried And — Stephen  men  devout,

3 καὶ ἐποιήσαντο κοπετὸν μέγαν ἐπ᾽ αὐτῷ. Σαῦλος δὲ
and  made   a lamentation great  over  him.  Saul And

ἐλυμαίνετο τὴν ἐκκλησίαν, κατὰ τοὺς οἴκους εἰσπορευό-
ravaged   the  church,   house by house  entering,

μενος, σύρων τε ἄνδρας καὶ γυναῖκας παρεδίδου εἰς φυλακήν.
dragging both men  and  women he delivered  to  prison.

4 Οἱ μὲν οὖν διασπαρέντες διῆλθον, εὐαγγελιζόμενοι τὸν
Those, therefore, being scattered passed through preaching  the

5 λόγον. Φίλιππος δὲ κατελθὼν εἰς πόλιν τῆς Σαμαρείας,
word.   Philip  And going down  to a city  — of Samaria,

6 ἐκήρυσσεν αὐτοῖς τὸν Χριστόν. προσεῖχόν τε οἱ ὄχλοι τοῖς
proclaimed  to them the Christ.   heeded  And the crowds that

λεγομένοις ὑπὸ τοῦ Φιλίππου ὁμοθυμαδόν, ἐν τῷ ἀκούειν
being said   by  —  Philip   with one passion in the hearing

7 αὐτοὺς καὶ βλέπειν τὰ σημεῖα ἃ ἐποίει. πολλῶν γὰρ τῶν
(of) them and seeing  the signs which  he was doing. many For of the

ἐχόντων πνεύματα ἀκάθαρτα, βοῶντα μεγάλῃ φωνῇ
(ones) having  spirits  unclean,  crying with a great  voice

ἐξήρχετο· πολλοὶ δὲ παραλελυμένοι καὶ χωλοὶ ἐθεραπεύθη-
came out;  many  and having been paralyzed and lame  were healed.

8 σαν. καὶ ἐγένετο χαρὰ μεγάλη ἐν τῇ πόλει ἐκείνῃ.
And there was  joy  great  in  the  city  that.

9 ᾽Ανὴρ δὲ τις ὀνόματι Σίμων προϋπῆρχεν ἐν τῇ πόλει
a man And certain by name Simon had long been  in  the  city

μαγεύων καὶ ἐξιστῶν τὸ ἔθνος τῆς Σαμαρείας, λέγων εἶναί
conjuring and amazing the nation — of Samaria, saying  to be

10 τινα ἑαυτὸν μέγαν· ᾧ προσεῖχον πάντες ἀπὸ μικροῦ ἕως
someone himself great, to whom took heed all,  from small  to

μεγάλου, λέγοντες, Οὗτός ἐστιν ἡ δύναμις τοῦ Θεοῦ ἡ
great,  saying,  This one is  the  power  — of God —

11 μεγάλη. προσεῖχον δὲ αὐτῷ, διὰ τὸ ἱκανῷ χρόνῳ ταῖς
great.  they were heeding And him, because for a long  time  with the

amazed them (with his) conjuring. [12] But when they believed Philip preaching the gospel, the things about the kingdom of God and the name of Jesus Christ, they were baptized, both men and women. [13] And Simon himself also believed, and having been baptized was steadfastly continuing with Philip; and seeing miracles and works of great power being done was amazed. [14] And the apostles in Jerusalem having heard that Samaria had received the word of God, they sent Peter and John to them; [15] who having come down prayed for them, that they might receive (the) Holy Spirit; [16] for He had not yet fallen on any of them, but they were only baptized to the name of the Lord Jesus. [17] Then they laid hands on them and they received (the) Holy Spirit. [18] But Simon having seen that by the laying on of the hands of the apostles the Holy Spirit was given, he offered them money, [19] saying, Give me this authority also, that on whomever I may lay hands, he may receive (the) Holy Spirit. [20] But Peter said to him, May your money be destroyed with you, because you thought the gift of God could be gotten by money. [21] There is neither part nor lot to you in this matter, for your heart is not right in the sight of God. [22] Therefore repent of this your wickedness, and pray to God if indeed the thought of your heart may be forgiven you; [23] for I see that you are (in) the gall of bitterness and a bond of unrighteousness. [24] And answering Simon said, You pray on my behalf to the Lord, so that nothing may come upon me of which you have spoken. [25] Then they having earnestly testified and having spoken the word of the Lord returned

**12** μαγείαις ἐξεστακέναι αὐτούς. ὅτε δὲ ἐπίστευσαν τῷ Φιλίππῳ
conjuring (he) had amazed them. when But they believed — Philip

εὐαγγελιζομένῳ τὰ περὶ τῆς βασιλείας τοῦ Θεοῦ καὶ τοῦ
preaching the gospel, the things about the kingdom — of God, and the

ὀνόματος τοῦ Ἰησοῦ Χριστοῦ, ἐβαπτίζοντο ἄνδρες τε καὶ
name — of Jesus Christ, they were baptized, men both and

**13** γυναῖκες. ὁ δὲ Σίμων καὶ αὐτὸς ἐπίστευσε, καὶ βαπτισθεὶς
women. But Simon also himself believed, and being baptized

ἦν προσκαρτερῶν τῷ Φιλίππῳ· θεωρῶν τε δυνάμεις καὶ
was steadfastly continuing to Philip, beholding and works of power and

σημεῖα γινόμενα, ἐξίστατο.
signs happening, he was amazed.

**14** Ἀκούσαντες δὲ οἱ ἐν Ἱεροσολύμοις ἀπόστολοι ὅτι
hearing And the in Jerusalem apostles that

δέδεκται ἡ Σαμάρεια τὸν λόγον τοῦ Θεοῦ, ἀπέστειλαν πρὸς
has received Samaria the word — of God, they sent to

**15** αὐτοὺς τὸν Πέτρον καὶ Ἰωάννην· οἵτινες καταβάντες
them — Peter and John, who going down

προσηύξαντο περὶ αὐτῶν, ὅπως λάβωσι Πνεῦμα Ἅγιον·
prayed concerning them, so as they might receive (the) Spirit Holy

**16** οὔπω γὰρ ἦν ἐπ᾽ οὐδενὶ αὐτῶν ἐπιπεπτωκός, μόνον δὲ
not yet for He was on no one of them having fallen, only but

βεβαπτισμένοι ὑπῆρχον εἰς τὸ ὄνομα τοῦ Κυρίου Ἰησοῦ.
having been baptized they were in the name the Lord Jesus.

**17** τότε ἐπετίθουν τὰς χεῖρας ἐπ᾽ αὐτούς, καὶ ἐλάμβανον
Then they laid on the hands on them, and they received

**18** Πνεῦμα Ἅγιον. θεασάμενος δὲ ὁ Σίμων ὅτι διὰ τῆς ἐπιθέ-
(the) Spirit Holy. beholding And Simon that through the laying

σεως τῶν χειρῶν τῶν ἀποστόλων δίδοται τὸ Πνεῦμα τὸ
on of the hands of the apostles is given the Spirit —

**19** Ἅγιον, προσήνεγκεν αὐτοῖς χρήματα, λέγων, Δότε κἀμοὶ
Holy, he offered them money, saying, Give also to me

τὴν ἐξουσίαν ταύτην, ἵνα ᾧ ἐὰν ἐπιθῶ τὰς χεῖρας, λαμβάνῃ
— authority this, that to whom may I lay on the hands, he may receive

**20** Πνεῦμα Ἅγιον. Πέτρος δὲ εἶπε πρὸς αὐτόν, Τὸ ἀργύριόν σου
(the) Spirit Holy. Peter But said to him, The silver of you

σὺν σοὶ εἴη εἰς ἀπώλειαν, ὅτι τὴν δωρεὰν τοῦ Θεοῦ ἐνόμισας
with you be into perdition, because the gift — of God you thought

**21** διὰ χρημάτων κτᾶσθαι. οὐκ ἔστι σοι μερὶς οὐδὲ κλῆρος ἐν
through money to get. not There is to you part nor lot in

τῷ λόγῳ τούτῳ. ἡ γὰρ καρδία σου οὐκ ἔστιν εὐθεῖα ἐνώπιον
— matter this. the For heart of you not is right before

**22** τοῦ Θεοῦ. μετανόησον οὖν ἀπὸ τῆς κακίας σου ταύτης, καὶ
— God. Repent, therefore, from — wickedness of you this, and

δεήθητι τοῦ Θεοῦ, εἰ ἄρα ἀφεθήσεταί σοι ἡ ἐπίνοια τῆς
petition — God if perhaps will be forgiven you the thought of the

**23** καρδίας σου. εἰς γὰρ χολὴν πικρίας καὶ σύνδεσμον ἀδικίας
heart of you. in For (the) gall of bitterness and a bundle of unrighteousness

**24** ὁρῶ σε ὄντα. ἀποκριθεὶς δὲ ὁ Σίμων εἶπε, Δεήθητε ὑμεῖς ὑπὲρ
I see you being. answering And Simon said, Petition you for

ἐμοῦ πρὸς τὸν Κύριον, ὅπως μηδὲν ἐπέλθῃ ἐπ᾽ ἐμὲ ὧν εἰρή-
me to the Lord, so as not one may come on me of what you

κατε.
have spoken.

**25** Οἱ μὲν οὖν διαμαρτυράμενοι καὶ λαλήσαντες τὸν λόγον
They, therefore, having earnestly testified and having spoken the word

to Jerusalem, and preached the gospel (to) many villages of the Samaritans.

[26] But an angel of (the) Lord spoke to Philip, saying, Rise up and go toward (the) south, on the highway which goes down from Jerusalem to Gaza; this is desert. [27] And having risen up he went. And behold, an Ethiopian man, a eunuch, one in power under Candace the queen of (the) Ethiopians, who was over all her treasure, who had come down to Jerusalem to worship, [28] and was returning and sitting in his chariot. And he was reading the prophet Isaiah. [29] And the Spirit said to Philip, Go near and join yourself to this chariot. [30] And running up Philip heard him reading the prophet Isaiah, and said, Then do you know what you read? [31] But he said, For how should I be able unless someone should guide me? And he called Philip, having come up to sit with him. [32] And (the) content of the Scripture which he was reading was this, "He was led as a sheep to slaughter and as a lamb dumb before his shearer, so He does not open His mouth. [33] In His humiliation His judgment was taken away, and who shall declare his generation? For His life is taken from the earth." [34] And answering the eunuch said to Philip, I beg you, about whom does the prophet say this? (It is) about himself, or about some other? [35] And having opened his mouth and having begun from this Scripture, Philip preached the gospel — Jesus. [36] And as they were going along the way, they came upon a certain water, and the eunuch said, Behold, water! What hinders me to be baptized? [37] And Philip said If you believe from the whole heart, it is lawful. And answering he said, I believe

τοῦ Κυρίου, ὑπέστρεψαν εἰς Ἱερουσαλήμ, πολλάς τε κώμας
of the Lord,   returned    to   Jerusalem,    many   and villages
τῶν Σαμαρειτῶν εὐηγγελίσαντο.
of the Samaritans   having preached the gospel.

26 Ἄγγελος δὲ Κυρίου ἐλάλησε προς Φίλιππον, λέγων,
   an angel And of (the) Lord spoke   to   Philip,     saying,
Ἀνάστηθι καὶ πορεύου κατὰ μεσημβρίαν ἐπὶ τὴν ὁδὸν τὴν
Rise up   and   go    along   south,   on   the   highway
καταβαίνουσαν ἀπὸ Ἱερουσαλὴμ εἰς Γάζαν· αὕτη ἐστὶν
going down   from   Jerusalem   to   Gaza;  this   is

27 ἔρημος. καὶ ἀναστὰς ἐπορεύθη· καὶ ἰδού, ἀνὴρ Αἰθίοψ εὐνοῦ-
   desert. And rising up  he went. And, behold, a man Ethiopian, a eunuch,
χος δυνάστης Κανδάκης τῆς βασιλίσσης Αἰθιόπων, ὃς ἦν ἐπὶ
a power  of Candace  the   queen   of Ethiopians, who was over
πάσης τῆς γάζης αὐτῆς, ὃς ἐληλύθει προσκυνήσων εἰς
all   the   treasure of her,  who had come   to worship   to

28 Ἱερουσαλήμ, ἦν τε ὑποστρέφων καὶ καθήμενος ἐπὶ τοῦ
   Jerusalem,   was and returning   and   sitting   on   the
ἅρματος αὐτοῦ, ἀνεγίνωσκε τὸν προφήτην Ἠσαΐαν. εἶπε
chariot  of him,  he read   the   prophet   Isaiah.   said

29 δὲ τὸ Πνεῦμα τῷ Φιλίππῳ, Πρόσελθε καὶ κολλήθητι τῷ
   And the Spirit  —  to Philip,  Go near  and   come toward  —

30 ἅρματι τούτῳ. προσδραμὼν δὲ ὁ Φίλιππος ἤκουσεν αὐτοῦ
   chariot this.   running near And, Philip   heard   from him
ἀναγινώσκοντος τὸν προφήτην Ἠσαΐαν, καὶ εἶπεν, Ἆρά
reading   the   prophet   Isaiah,   and   said,   Then

31 γε γινώσκεις ἃ ἀναγινώσκεις; ὁ δὲ εἶπε, Πῶς γὰρ ἂν δυναί-
   do you know what you are reading? he And said,  how For   should I be
μην, ἐὰν μή τις ὁδηγήσῃ με; παρεκάλεσέ τε τὸν Φίλιππον
able,  unless someone shall guide me?  he called near And  —  Philip

32 ἀναβάντα καθίσαι σὺν αὐτῷ. ἡ δὲ περιοχὴ τῆς γραφῆς ἦν
   coming up   to sit   with   him. the And (the) content of the Scripture which
ἀνεγίνωσκεν ἦν αὕτη, Ὡς πρόβατον ἐπὶ σφαγὴν ἤχθη, καὶ
he was reading was this: As a sheep   to slaughter He was led, and
ὡς ἀμνὸς ἐναντίον τοῦ κείροντος αὐτὸν ἄφωνος, οὕτως οὐκ
as a lamb  before   he   shearing   it  (is) voiceless,   so   not

33 ἀνοίγει τὸ στόμα αὐτοῦ. ἐν τῇ ταπεινώσει αὐτοῦ ἡ κρίσις
   He opens the mouth of Him.  In the  humiliation  of Him, the judgment
αὐτοῦ ἤρθη, τὴν δὲ γενεὰν αὐτοῦ τίς διηγήσεται; ὅτι
of Him was taken; the but generation of Him  who  will recount? Because
αἴρεται ἀπὸ τῆς γῆς ἡ ζωὴ αὐτοῦ. ἀποκριθεὶς δὲ ὁ εὐνοῦχος

34 is taken  from the earth the life  of Him.   answering And the eunuch
τῷ Φιλίππῳ εἶπε, Δέομαί σου, περὶ τίνος ὁ προφήτης λέγει
  to Philip said,  I ask  you, about whom the prophet  says

35 τοῦτο; περὶ ἑαυτοῦ, ἢ περὶ ἑτέρου τινός; ἀνοίξας δὲ ὁ
   this? (Is it) about himself, or about  other someone? opening And  —
Φίλιππος τὸ στόμα αὐτοῦ, καὶ ἀρξάμενος ἀπὸ τῆς γραφῆς
Philip   the mouth  of him, and beginning  from  the  Scripture

36 ταύτης, εὐηγγελίσατο αὐτῷ τὸν Ἰησοῦν. ὡς δὲ ἐπορεύοντο
   this,  preached the gospel to him, — Jesus.  as And they were going
κατὰ τὴν ὁδόν, ἦλθον ἐπί τι ὕδωρ· καί φησιν ὁ εὐνοῦχος,
along the highway, they came on some water, and says  the eunuch,

37 Ἰδού, ὕδωρ· τί κωλύει με βαπτισθῆναι; εἶπε δὲ ὁ Φίλιππος,
   Behold, water. What prevents me to be baptized? said And — Philip,
Εἰ πιστεύεις ἐξ ὅλης τῆς καρδίας, ἔξεστιν. ἀποκριθεὶς δὲ εἶπε,
If you believe from all  the  heart,  it is lawful. answering And he said,

Jesus Christ to be the Son of God. [38] And he commanded the chariot to stand still. And they both went down into the water, both Philip and the eunuch, and he baptized him. [39] But when they came up out of the water, (the) Spirit of (the) Lord caught Philip away, and the eunuch saw him no more, for he went his way rejoicing. [40] But Philip was found at Azotus, and passing through he preached the gospel (to) all the cities, until he came to Caesarea.

## CHAPTER 9

[1] But Saul, still breathing out threatenings and slaughter toward the disciples of the Lord, having come to the high priest [2] asked from him letters to Damascus, to the synagogues, so that if he found any being of the Way, both men and women, having bound he might bring (them) to Jerusalem. [3] But in going it happened (as) he drew near to Damascus, and suddenly a light from Heaven shone around him, [4] and having fallen on the earth he heard a voice saying to him, Saul, Saul, why do you persecute Me? [5] And he said, Who are you, lord? And the Lord said, I am Jesus whom you persecute. (It is) hard for you to kick against (the) prods. [6] And trembling and astonished he said, Lord, what do you desire me to do? And the Lord (said) to him, Rise up and go into the city, and it shall be told to you what you should do. [7] But the men who were traveling with him stood speechless, hearing indeed the voice, but seeing no one. [8] And Saul rose up from the ground, and his eyes having been opened he saw no one. But leading him by the hand, they brought (him) to Damascus. [9] And he was three days not seeing, and did not eat or drink. [10] And there was a certain disciple in Damascus named Ananias.

---

**38** Πιστεύω τὸν υἱὸν τοῦ Θεοῦ εἶναι τὸν Ἰησοῦν Χριστόν. καὶ
I believe the Son – of God to be – Jesus Christ. And
ἐκέλευσε στῆναι τὸ ἅρμα· καὶ κατέβησαν ἀμφότεροι εἰς τὸ
he ordered to stand the chariot, and went down both into the
ὕδωρ, ὅ τε Φίλιππος καὶ ὁ εὐνοῦχος· καὶ ἐβάπτισεν αὐτόν.
water, – both Philip and the eunuch, and he baptized him.

**39** ὅτε δὲ ἀνέβησαν ἐκ τοῦ ὕδατος, Πνεῦμα Κυρίου ἥρπασε τὸν
when And they came up out of the water (the) Spirit of (the) Lord caught away
Φίλιππον· καὶ οὐκ εἶδεν αὐτὸν οὐκέτι ὁ εὐνοῦχος, ἐπορεύετο
Philip, and not did see him any more the eunuch, he went

**40** γὰρ τὴν ὁδὸν αὐτοῦ χαίρων. Φίλιππος δὲ εὑρέθη εἰς Ἄζωτον·
for the way of him rejoicing. Philip And was found at Azotus,
καὶ διερχόμενος εὐηγγελίζετο τὰς πόλεις πάσας, ἕως τοῦ
and passing through he preached the gospel to the cities all, until the
ἐλθεῖν αὐτὸν εἰς Καισάρειαν.
coming (of) him to Caesarea.

## CHAPTER 9

**1** Ὁ δὲ Σαῦλος ἔτι ἐμπνέων ἀπειλῆς καὶ φόνου εἰς τοὺς
– But Saul still breathing in threats and murder toward the
**2** μαθητὰς τοῦ Κυρίου, προσελθὼν τῷ ἀρχιερεῖ, ᾐτήσατο
disciples of the Lord, having come to the high priest, asked
παρ' αὐτοῦ ἐπιστολὰς εἰς Δαμασκὸν πρὸς τὰς συναγωγάς,
from him letters to Damascus, to the synagogues,
ὅπως ἐάν τινας εὕρῃ τῆς ὁδοῦ ὄντας ἄνδρας τε καὶ γυναῖκας,
so that if any be found of the way being, men both and women,
**3** δεδεμένους ἀγάγῃ εἰς Ἱερουσαλήμ. ἐν δὲ τῷ πορεύεσθαι
binding (them) he may bring to Jerusalem. in And the going
ἐγένετο αὐτὸν ἐγγίζειν τῇ Δαμασκῷ· καὶ ἐξαίφνης περι-
happened he drew near – to Damascus, and suddenly shone
**4** ήστραψεν αὐτὸν φῶς ἀπὸ τοῦ οὐρανοῦ· καὶ πεσὼν ἐπὶ τὴν
around him a light from – Heaven; and falling on the
γῆν, ἤκουσε φωνὴν λέγουσαν αὐτῷ, Σαούλ, Σαούλ, τί με
earth, he heard a voice saying to him, Saul, Saul! Why Me
**5** διώκεις; εἶπε δέ, Τίς εἶ, Κύριε; ὁ δὲ Κύριος εἶπεν, Ἐγώ εἰμι
you persecute? he said And, Who are you, Sir? And the Lord said, I am
Ἰησοῦς ὃν σὺ διώκεις· σκληρόν σοι πρὸς κέντρα λακτίζειν.
Jesus, whom you persecute; (It is) hard for you against prods to kick.
**6** τρέμων τε καὶ θαμβῶν εἶπε, Κύριε, τί με θέλεις ποιῆσαι; καὶ
trembling both And aston-he said, Lord, what me desire You to do? And
                                    ished
ὁ Κύριος πρὸς αὐτόν, Ἀνάστηθι καὶ εἴσελθε εἰς τὴν πόλιν,
the Lord (said) to him, Rise up and go into the city,
**7** καὶ λαληθήσεταί σοι τί σε δεῖ ποιεῖν. οἱ δὲ ἄνδρες οἱ συν-
and it shall be told you what you must do. the And men –
οδεύοντες αὐτῷ εἱστήκεισαν ἐννεοί, ἀκούοντες μὲν τῆς φω-
traveling with him been standing speechless, hearing indeed the sound,
                              had
**8** νῆς, μηδένα δὲ θεωροῦντες. ἠγέρθη δὲ ὁ Σαῦλος ἀπὸ τῆς
no one but beholding. was raised And – Saul from the
γῆς· ἀνεῳγμένων δὲ τῶν ὀφθαλμῶν αὐτοῦ, οὐδένα ἔβλεπε,
earth, having been opened the eyes of him, no one he saw.
χειραγωγοῦντες δὲ αὐτὸν εἰσήγαγον εἰς Δαμασκόν. καὶ ἦν
leading by the hand And him, they brought to Damascus. And he was
**9** ἡμέρας τρεῖς μὴ βλέπων, καὶ οὐκ ἔφαγεν οὐδὲ ἔπιεν.
days three not seeing, and did not eat nor drink.
**10** Ἦν δέ τις μαθητὴς ἐν Δαμασκῷ ὀνόματι Ἀνανίας, καὶ
was And a certain disciple in Damascus by name Ananias, and

And the Lord said to him in a vision, Ananias. And he said, Behold me, Lord. [11] And the Lord (said) to him, Having risen pass along on the street being called Straight, and seek in (the) house of Judas (one) named Saul of Tarsus; for behold, he prays, [12] and he has seen in a vision a man named Ananias coming and putting a hand on him, so that he should receive sight. [13] And Ananias answered, Lord, I have heard from many about this man, how many bad things he did to Your saints in Jerusalem; [14] and here he has authority from the chief priests to bind all Who call on Your name [15] And the Lord said to him, Go, for this one is a vessel of election to bear My name before Gentiles and kings, and (the) sons of Israel; [16] for I will show him how much it behooves him to suffer for My name. [17] And Ananias went away and entered into the house; and having laid hands on him, he said, Brother Saul, the Lord who appeared to you in the way in which you came, that you might receive sight and be filled with (the) Holy Spirit. [18] And immediately scales as it were fell from his eyes, and he received sight instantly, and having risen up was baptized; [19] and having taken food, he was strengthened. And Saul was with the disciples in Damascus some days.

[20] And immediately he proclaimed Christ in the synagogues, that He is the Son of God. [21] And all who heard were amazed, and said, Is this not he who destroyed those who called on this Name in Jerusalem, and had come here for this, (that) he might bring them to the chief priests? [22] But Saul more was filled with power, and confounded the Jews who lived in Damascus, proving

εἶπε πρὸς αὐτὸν ὁ Κύριος ἐν ὁράματι, ᾽Ανανία. ὁ· δὲ εἶπεν,
said   to   him   the Lord   in a vision,   Ananias. he And said,

**11** ᾽Ιδοὺ ἐγώ, Κύριε. ὁ δὲ Κύριος πρὸς αὐτόν, ᾽Αναστὰς
Behold,   I,   Lord. the And Lord   to   him,   Rising up
πορεύθητι ἐπὶ τὴν ῥύμην τὴν καλουμένην Εὐθεῖαν, καὶ ζητη-
pass along on the street — being called   Straight, and   seek-
σον ἐν οἰκίᾳ ᾽Ιούδα Σαῦλον ὀνόματι, Ταρσέα· ἰδοὺ γὰρ
in (the) house of Judas Saul   by name a Tarsian; behold for

**12** προσεύχεται, καὶ εἶδεν ἐν ὁράματι ἄνδρα ὀνόματι ᾽Ανανίαν
he is praying,   and seen/has in a vision a man by name   Ananias
εἰσελθόντα καὶ ἐπιθέντα αὐτῷ χεῖρα, ὅπως ἀναβλέψῃ.
coming in   and putting on   him a hand   so as   he may see again.

**13** ἀπεκρίθη δὲ ὁ ᾽Ανανίας, Κύριε, ἀκήκοα ἀπὸ πολλῶν περὶ
answered And — Ananias,   Lord, I have heard from   many   about
τοῦ ἀνδρὸς τούτου, ὅσα κακὰ ἐποίησε τοῖς ἁγίοις σου ἐν
— man   this, how many bad things he did to the saints of You in

**14** ᾽Ιερουσαλήμ καὶ ὧδε ἔχει ἐξουσίαν παρὰ τῶν ἀρχιερέων,
Jerusalem;   and here he has authority from   the chief priests

**15** δῆσαι πάντας τοὺς ἐπικαλουμένους τὸ ὄνομά σου. εἶπε δὲ
to bind all   the (ones) invoking   the name of You. said But
πρὸς αὐτὸν ὁ Κύριος, Πορεύου, ὅτι σκεῦος ἐκλογῆς μοι ἐστὶν
to   him the Lord,   Go,   because a vessel of election to Me   is
οὗτος, τοῦ βαστάσαι τὸ ὄνομά μου ἐνώπιον ἐθνῶν καὶ
this one,   — to bear   the name of Me before   nations and

**16** βασιλέων, υἱῶν τε ᾽Ισραήλ· ἐγὼ γὰρ ὑποδείξω αὐτῷ ὅσα
kings,   sons and of Israel;   I   for   will show   him how many

**17** δεῖ αὐτὸν ὑπὲρ τοῦ ὀνόματός μου παθεῖν. ἀπῆλθε δὲ
must he   on behalf of the name   of Me   suffer. went away And
᾽Ανανίας καὶ εἰσῆλθεν εἰς τὴν οἰκίαν, καὶ ἐπιθεὶς ἐπ᾽ αὐτὸν τὰς
Ananias   and entered into the house,   and putting on   him the
χεῖρας εἶπε, Σαοὺλ ἀδελφέ, ὁ Κύριος ἀπέσταλκέ με, ᾽Ιησοῦς
hands said,   Saul Brother, the Lord   has sent   me,   Jesus
ὁ ὀφθείς σοι ἐν τῇ ὁδῷ ᾗ ἤρχου, ὅπως ἀναβλέψῃς καὶ πλη-
He appearing to you in the way which you came, so as you may see and be

**18** σθῇς Πνεύματος ᾽Αγίου. καὶ εὐθέως ἀπέπεσον ἀπὸ τῶν
filled of (the) Spirit   Holy.   And at once   fell away   from   the
ὀφθαλμῶν αὐτοῦ ὡσεὶ λεπίδες, ἀνέβλεψέ τε παραχρῆμα,
eyes   of him   as if   scales,   he saw again and,   instantly

**19** καὶ ἀναστὰς ἐβαπτίσθη, καὶ λαβὼν τροφὴν ἐνίσχυσεν.
and rising up was baptized;   and taking   food was strengthened.

᾽Εγένετο δὲ ὁ Σαῦλος μετὰ τῶν ἐν Δαμασκῷ μαθητῶν
was And — Saul   with   the in Damascus   disciples

**20** ἡμέρας τινάς. καὶ εὐθέως ἐν ταῖς συναγωγαῖς ἐκήρυσσε τὸν
days   some,   and at once in   the synagogues   he proclaimed the

**21** Χριστόν, ὅτι οὗτός ἐστιν ὁ υἱὸς τοῦ Θεοῦ. ἐξίσταντο δὲ
Christ,   that this One is   the Son   — of God. were amazed And
πάντες οἱ ἀκούοντες καὶ ἔλεγον, Οὐχ οὗτός ἐστιν ὁ πορθήσας
all   those hearing,   and   said,   not this one Is the (one) destroying
ἐν ᾽Ιερουσαλήμ τοὺς ἐπικαλουμένους τὸ ὄνομα τοῦτο, καὶ
in   Jerusalem   those invoking   —   name   this,   and
ὧδε εἰς τοῦτο ἐληλύθει ἵνα δεδεμένους αὐτοὺς ἀγάγῃ ἐπὶ
here for   this he had come, that binding   them he may lead before

**22** τοὺς ἀρχιερεῖς; Σαῦλος δὲ μᾶλλον ἐνεδυναμοῦτο, καὶ συνέ-
the chief priests?   Saul And· more   was filled with power and con-
χυνε τοὺς ᾽Ιουδαίους τοὺς κατοικοῦντας ἐν Δαμασκῷ,
founded the   Jews   living   in   Damascus,

συμβιβάζων ὅτι οὗτός ἐστιν ὁ Χριστός.
proving            that this One    is    the    Christic.

| | |
|---|---|

that this is the Christ.
[23] Now when many
days were fulfilled, the
Jews plotted together to
put him to death. [24] But
their plot became known
to Saul. And they were
watching the gates both
day and night, that they
might kill him; [25] but
the disciples taking him by
night let (him) down
through the wall, lowering
(him) in a basket.

[26] And Saul having
arrived at Jerusalem, he
attempted to join himself
to the disciples, and all
were afraid of him, not
believing that he was a
disciple. [27] But having
taken him Barnabas
brought (him) to the
apostles and told them
how he saw the Lord in the
way, and that He spoke to
him, and how he spoke
boldly in Damascus in the
name of Jesus. [28] And
he was with them coming
in and going out in
Jerusalem, and speaking
boldly in the name of the
Lord Jesus. [29] And he
spoke and argued with the
Hellenists; but they seized
him to kill (him). [30] But
having known the brothers
brought him down to
Caesarea and sent him
away to Tarsus. [31] Then
indeed the assemblies
throughout the whole of
Judea and Galilee and
Samaria had peace, being
built up and going on in
the fear of the Lord, and
were increased in the
comfort of the Holy Spirit.
[32] Now it came to
pass (that) Peter, passing
through all went down also
to the saints that lived in
Lydda. [33] And he found
that a certain man named
Eneas, for eight years lying
on a couch, who was
paralyzed. [34] And Peter
said to him, Eneas, Jesus
the Christ heals you; rise
up and spread for yourself!
And instantly he rose up.
[35] And all those living in
Lydda and Saron saw him,

23  Ὡς δὲ ἐπληροῦντο ἡμέραι ἱκαναί, συνεβουλεύσαντο οἱ
    when And were fulfilled   days    many,     plotted together   the

24  Ἰουδαῖοι ἀνελεῖν αὐτόν· ἐγνώσθη δὲ τῷ Σαύλῳ ἡ ἐπιβουλὴ
    Jews      to kill    him,  was known but — to Saul the plot

    αὐτῶν. παρετήρουν τε τὰς πύλας ἡμέρας τε καὶ νυκτός,
    of them.  they carefully watched And the gates by day both and by night,

25  ὅπως αὐτὸν ἀνέλωσι· λαβόντες δὲ αὐτὸν οἱ μαθηταὶ νυκτός,
    so as  him they may do away; taking but him the disciples by night

    καθῆκαν διὰ τοῦ τείχους, χαλάσαντες ἐν σπυρίδι.
    let down through the wall,    lowering (him) in a basket.

26  Παραγενόμενος δὲ ὁ Σαῦλος εἰς Ἱερουσαλήμ, ἐπειρᾶτο
    arriving        And — Saul   in  Jerusalem,   he tried

    κολλᾶσθαι τοῖς μαθηταῖς· καὶ πάντες ἐφοβοῦντο αὐτόν, μὴ
    to be joined to the disciples; and all    feared      him, not

27  πιστεύοντες ὅτι ἐστὶ μαθητής. Βαρνάβας δὲ ἐπιλαβόμενος
    believing      that he is a disciple. Barnabas But taking hold of

    αὐτὸν ἤγαγε πρὸς τοὺς ἀποστόλους, καὶ διηγήσατο αὐτοῖς
    him    led    to   the  apostles,      and  told      them

    πῶς ἐν τῇ ὁδῷ εἶδε τὸν Κύριον, καὶ ὅτι ἐλάλησεν αὐτῷ,
    how in the way he saw the Lord,   and that He spoke  to him,

    καὶ πῶς ἐν Δαμασκῷ ἐπαρρησιάσατο ἐν τῷ ὀνόματι τοῦ
    and how in Damascus he spoke boldly    in  the   name    —

28  Ἰησοῦ. καὶ ἦν μετ᾽ αὐτῶν εἰσπορευόμενος καὶ ἐκπορευό-
    of Jesus. And he was with them   going in      and  going

    μενος ἐν Ἱερουσαλήμ, καὶ παρρησιαζόμενος ἐν τῷ ὀνόματι
    out   in  Jerusalem,   and speaking boldly     in  the  name

29  τοῦ Κυρίου Ἰησοῦ, ἐλάλει τε καὶ συνεζήτει πρὸς τοὺς
    of the Lord Jesus.  he spoke And and discussed  with  the

30  Ἑλληνιστάς· οἱ δὲ ἐπεχείρουν αὐτὸν ἀνελεῖν. ἐπιγινόντες δὲ
    Hellenists;   they and took in hand him to do away. knowing But

    οἱ ἀδελφοὶ κατήγαγον αὐτὸν εἰς Καισάρειαν, καὶ ἐξαπέ-
    the brothers  led down    him   to  Caesarea,    and  sent

31  στειλαν αὐτὸν εἰς Ταρσόν. αἱ μὲν οὖν ἐκκλησίαι καθ᾽
    forth     him   to  Tarsus.  the Therefore   churches throughout

    ὅλης τῆς Ἰουδαίας καὶ Γαλιλαίας καὶ Σαμαρείας εἶχον εἰρήνην
    all   —  Judea     and  Galilee    and  Samaria      had  peace,

    οἰκοδομούμεναι, καὶ πορευόμεναι τῷ φόβῳ τοῦ Κυρίου καὶ
    being built up,   and  going on   in the fear of the Lord, and

    τῇ παρακλήσει τοῦ Ἁγίου Πνεύματος ἐπληθύνοντο.
    in the comfort of the Holy  Spirit   were multiplied.

32  Ἐγένετο δὲ Πέτρον διερχόμενον διὰ πάντων κατελθεῖν καὶ
    it was  And, Peter   passing    through all    came down also

33  πρὸς τοὺς ἁγίους τοὺς κατοικοῦντας Λύδδαν. εὗρε δὲ ἐκεῖ
    to   the  saints   —  inhabiting     Lydda.  he found And there

    ἄνθρωπόν τινα Αἰνέαν ὀνόματι, ἐξ ἐτῶν ὀκτὼ κατακείμενον
    a man     certain, Aeneas by name, of years eighty    lying

34  ἐπὶ κραββάτῳ, ὃς ἦν παραλελυμένος. καὶ εἶπεν αὐτῷ ὁ
    on a mattress,  who was paralyzed.     And  said to him —

    Πέτρος, Αἰνέα, ἰᾶται σε Ἰησοῦς ὁ Χριστός· ἀνάστηθι καὶ
    Peter,  Aeneas, heals you Jesus the Christ;  rise up     and

    στρῶσον σεαυτῷ. καὶ εὐθέως ἀνέστη. καὶ εἶδον αὐτὸν
    spread   for yourself. And instantly he rose up. And saw   him

35  πάντες οἱ κατοικοῦντες Λύδδαν καὶ τὸν Σάρωνα, οἵτινες
    all    those inhabiting    Lydda  and  the Sharon (plain), who

who turned to the Lord.

[36] And in Joppa was a certain disciple named Tabitha, which translated is called Gazelle. She was full of good works and of alms which she did. [37] And it happened in those days having become ill she died; and having washed her, they put (her) in an upper room. [38] And Lydda being near to Joppa, the disciples having heard that Peter was in it, (they) sent two men to him, begging (him) not to delay to come to them. [39] And having risen up Peter went with them, whom, having arrived, they brought into the upper room, and all the widows stood beside him weeping and showing coats and garments which Dorcas was making, being with them. [40] But Peter having put all out, having bowed the knees, he prayed. And having turned to the body, he said, Tabitha, Arise! And she opened her eyes, and seeing Peter she sat up. [41] And having given her his hand, he raised her up; and having called the saints and the widows, he presented her living. [42] And it became known throughout all of Joppa, and many believed on the Lord. [43] And it was many days (that) he remained in Joppa with a certain Simon, a tanner.

CHAPTER 10

[1] But a certain man named Cornelius was in Caesarea, a centurion of a cohort being called Italian [2] pious and fearing God with all his house, both doing much alms to the people, and praying continually to God. [3] He saw plainly in a vision, about the ninth hour of the day, an angel of God coming to him, and saying to him, Cornelius! [4] But having looked intently on him and becoming afraid,

ἐπέστρεψαν ἐπὶ τὸν Κύριον.
turned        to    the   Lord.

**36** Ἐν Ἰόππῃ δέ τις ἦν μαθήτρια ὀνόματι Ταβιθά, ἣ διερμη-
in   Joppa And a certain was disciple, by name  Tabitha, which being
νευομένη λέγεται Δορκάς· αὕτη ἦν πλήρης ἀγαθῶν ἔργων καὶ
translated is called   Gazelle.   She was   full   of good   works and

**37** ἐλεημοσυνῶν ὧν ἐποίει. ἐγένετο δὲ ἐν ταῖς ἡμέραις ἐκείναις
of alms    which she did.  it was And, in —  days   those,
ἀσθενήσασαν αὐτὴν ἀποθανεῖν· λούσαντες δὲ αὐτὴν ἔθηκαν
having ailed,   she    died.   having washed And, her   they put

**38** ἐν ὑπερῴῳ. ἐγγὺς δὲ οὔσης Λύδδης τῇ Ἰόππῃ, οἱ μαθηταὶ
in an upper room. near And being   Lydda  — to Joppa, the disciples
ἀκούσαντες ὅτι Πέτρος ἐστὶν ἐν αὐτῇ, ἀπέστειλαν δύο
having heard  that Peter   is   in it,   they sent   two
ἄνδρας πρὸς αὐτόν, παρακαλοῦντες μὴ ὀκνῆσαι διελθεῖν
men   to  him,   begging (him)   not to delay  to come

**39** ἕως αὐτῶν. ἀναστὰς δὲ Πέτρος συνῆλθεν αὐτοῖς· ὃν παρα-
to  them.  rising  And Peter   went with   them; whom arriving
γενόμενον ἀνήγαγον εἰς τὸ ὑπερῷον, καὶ παρέστησαν αὐτῷ
they led up  to the upper room, and  stood by    him
πᾶσαι αἱ χῆραι κλαίουσαι καὶ ἐπιδεικνύμεναι χιτῶνας καὶ
all   the widows  weeping  and  showing   tunics  and
ἱμάτια ὅσα ἐποίει μετ’ αὐτῶν οὖσα ἡ Δορκάς. ἐκβαλὼν δὲ
garments such made with  them being  — Dorcas. thrusting And
as

**40** ἔξω πάντας ὁ Πέτρος θεὶς τὰ γόνατα προσηύξατο· καὶ
out   all,   Peter placing the knees  prayed;   and
ἐπιστρέψας πρὸς τὸ σῶμα, εἶπε, Ταβιθά, ἀνάστηθι. ἡ δὲ
turning   to   the body, he said, Tabitha,  Arise.   she And
ἤνοιξε τοὺς ὀφθαλμοὺς αὐτῆς· καὶ ἰδοῦσα τὸν Πέτρον,
opened  the   eyes    of her  and seeing  —  Peter,

**41** ἀνεκάθισε. δοὺς δὲ αὐτῇ χεῖρα, ἀνέστησεν αὐτήν· φωνήσας δὲ
she sat up.  giving And her a hand,  he raised up  her;  calling and
τοὺς ἁγίους καὶ τὰς χήρας, παρέστησεν αὐτὴν ζῶσαν. γνω-
the saints  and the widows, he presented  her   living.

**42** στὸν δὲ ἐγένετο καθ’ ὅλης τῆς Ἰόππης, καὶ πολλοὶ ἐπί-
known And it became through all  — Joppa,   and   many

**43** στευσαν ἐπὶ τὸν Κύριον. ἐγένετο δὲ ἡμέρας ἱκανὰς μεῖνι
believed  on   the  Lord.  it was And  days   sufficient remained
αὐτὸν ἐν Ἰόππῃ παρά τινι Σίμωνι βυρσεῖ.
he   in  Joppa  with one   Simon, a tanner.

CHAPTER 10

**1** Ἀνὴρ δέ τις ἦν ἐν Καισαρείᾳ ὀνόματι Κορνήλιος, ἑκατοντ-
a man And certain was in Caesarea,  by name Cornelius,  a centurion

**2** άρχης ἐκ σπείρης τῆς καλουμένης Ἰταλικῆς, εὐσεβὴς καὶ
of a cohort  —  being called  Italian;  devout  and
φοβούμενος τὸν Θεὸν σὺν παντὶ τῷ οἴκῳ αὐτοῦ, ποιῶν τε
fearing   —  God with all  the house of him,  doing both
ἐλεημοσύνας πολλὰς τῷ λαῷ, καὶ δεόμενος τοῦ Θεοῦ διὰ
alms    many to the people, and petitioning  —  God con-

**3** παντός. εἶδεν ἐν ὁράματι φανερῶς, ὡσεὶ ὥραν ἐννάτην τῆς
tinually. He saw in a vision  plainly,  about  hour   ninth of the
ἡμέρας, ἄγγελον τοῦ Θεοῦ εἰσελθόντα πρὸς αὐτόν, καὶ
day,   an angel  — of God  coming in   to  him,   and

**4** εἰπόντα αὐτῷ, Κορνήλιε. ὁ δὲ ἀτενίσας αὐτῷ καὶ ἔμφοβος
saying to him,  Cornelius!  he And was gazing at him  and  terrified

he said, What is it, lord? And he said to him, Your prayers and your alms have gone up for a memorial before God. [5] And now send men to Joppa, and send for Simon who is surnamed Peter. [6] This one is lodged with a certain Simon, a tanner, whose house is by (the) sea? He shall tell you what you should do. [7] And when the angel who spoke to Cornelius left, having called two of his servants, and a pious soldier of those continually waiting on him, [8] and explaining all things to them, he sent them to Joppa.

[9] And on the morrow, and as these are traveling to the city, drawing near, Peter went up on the housetop to pray, about the sixth hour. [10] And he became very hungry, and wished to eat. But as they were preparing an ecstasy fell on him, [11] and he saw Heaven open, and a certain vessel descending on him, like a huge sheet, bound by four corners, and let down on the earth; [12] in which were all four-footed animals of the earth, and the wild beasts, and the creeping things, and the birds of the sky. [13] And a voice came to him, Having risen up, Peter, slay and eat. [14] But Peter said, Never, Lord; for never did I eat anything common or unclean. [15] And a voice (came) again the second time to him, What God has cleansed, you do not make common. [16] And this took place three times, and again the vessel was taken up into Heaven. [17] And as Peter was perplexed in himself, what the vision which he saw might be, behold also, the men who were sent from Cornelius, having asked for the house of Simon, stood at the porch. [18] And having called out they asked whether Simon

γενόμενος εἶπε, Τί ἐστι, Κύριε ; εἶπε δὲ αὐτῷ, Αἱ προσευχαί
becoming he said, What is it, Sir?    he said And to him, The prayers

σου καὶ αἱ ἐλεημοσύναι σου ἀνέβησαν εἰς μνημόσυνον
of you and the    alms       of you went up    for   a memorial

5 ἐνώπιον τοῦ Θεοῦ. καὶ νῦν πέμψον εἰς Ἰόππην ἄνδρας, καὶ
before   —   God. And now  send   to  Joppa   men,   and

6 μετάπεμψαι Σίμωνα ὃς ἐπικαλεῖται Πέτρος· οὗτος ξενίζεται
call for    Simon who is surnamed   Peter; this one is lodged

παρά τινι Σίμωνι βυρσεῖ, ᾧ ἐστιν οἰκία παρὰ θάλασσαν·
with  one  Simon, a tanner, to whom is a house by  (the) sea

7 οὗτος λαλήσει σοι τί σε δεῖ ποιεῖν. ὡς δὲ ἀπῆλθεν ὁ ἄγγελος
this one will tell you what you must do.  as And went away the angel

ὁ λαλῶν τῷ Κορνηλίῳ, φωνήσας δύο τῶν οἰκετῶν αὐτοῦ,
— speaking — to Cornelius, having called two of the  servants of him,

καὶ στρατιώτην εὐσεβῆ τῶν προσκαρτερούντων αὐτῷ, καὶ
and  a soldier   devout of those continually waiting  on him, and

8 ἐξηγησάμενος αὐτοῖς ἅπαντα, ἀπέστειλεν αὐτοὺς εἰς τὴν
having explained to them all things,  he sent forth  them   to   —

Ἰόππην.
Joppa.

9 Τῇ δὲ ἐπαύριον, ὁδοιπορούντων ἐκείνων καὶ τῇ πόλει
on the And morrow,  passing along (the) road these,  and to the city

ἐγγιζόντων, ἀνέβη Πέτρος ἐπὶ τὸ δῶμα προσεύξασθαι, περὶ
drawing near, went up Peter on the roof to pray,  about

10 ὥραν ἕκτην· ἐγένετο δὲ πρόσπεινος, καὶ ἤθελε γεύσασθαι·
hour  sixth. he became And hungry,   and desired  to taste;

παρασκευαζόντων δὲ ἐκείνων, ἐπέπεσεν ἐπ' αὐτὸν ἔκστασις,
preparing      and they    fell   on  him  an ecstasy,

11 καὶ θεωρεῖ τὸν οὐρανὸν ἀνεῳγμένον, καὶ καταβαῖνον ἐπ'
And he beholds the  heaven   being opened,  and coming down  on

αὐτὸν σκεῦός τι ὡς ὀθόνην μεγάλην, τέσσαρσιν ἀρχαῖς
him  a vessel certain like a sheet   great,    by four    corners

12 δεδεμένον, καὶ καθιέμενον ἐπὶ τῆς γῆς· ἐν ᾧ ὑπῆρχε πάντα
being bound, and let down   onto the earth; in which were  all

τὰ τετράποδα τῆς γῆς καὶ τὰ θηρία καὶ τὰ ἑρπετὰ καὶ τὰ
the quadrupeds of the earth, and the beasts, and the reptiles, and the

13 πετεινὰ τοῦ οὐρανοῦ. καὶ ἐγένετο φωνὴ πρὸς αὐτόν,
birds   of the heaven.   And came   a voice  to   him,

14 Ἀναστάς, Πέτρε, θῦσον καὶ φάγε. ὁ δὲ Πέτρος εἶπε,
Rise up,  Peter,  slay  and  eat. — But Peter  said,

Μηδαμῶς, Κύριε· ὅτι οὐδέποτε ἔφαγον πᾶν κοινὸν ἢ ἀκάθαρ-
Not at all,  Lord, because never  did I eat anything common or un-

15 τον. καὶ φωνὴ πάλιν ἐκ δευτέρου πρὸς αὐτόν, Ἃ ὁ Θεὸς
clean. And a voice again from a second (time) to  him,  what things  God

16 ἐκαθάρισε, σὺ μὴ κοίνου. τοῦτο δὲ ἐγένετο ἐπὶ τρίς· καὶ
cleansed,   you not make common. this And happened on  three,  and

πάλιν ἀνελήφθη τὸ σκεῦος εἰς τὸν οὐρανόν.
again  was taken up the  vessel into the heaven.

17 Ὡς δὲ ἐν ἑαυτῷ διηπόρει ὁ Πέτρος τί ἂν εἴη τὸ ὅραμα ὃ
as And in himself was doubting Peter, what might be the vision which

εἶδε, καὶ ἰδού, οἱ ἄνδρες οἱ ἀπεσταλμένοι ἀπὸ τοῦ Κορνηλίου
he saw, and behold, the men — having been sent from  —  Cornelius

διερωτήσαντες τὴν οἰκίαν Σίμωνος, ἐπέστησαν ἐπὶ τὸν
having asked out  the  house  of Simon, stood     at  the

18 πυλῶνα, καὶ φωνήσαντες ἐπυνθάνοντο εἰ Σίμων, ὁ ἐπικαλού-
porch.   And calling     they inquired  if Simon, — being

who (is) surnamed Peter lodged here? [19] And (as) Peter was thinking over the vision, behold, the Spirit said to him, Three men seek you; [20] but having risen go down and go with them, doubting nothing, because I have sent them. [21] And Peter having gone down to the men who were sent from Cornelius to him said, Behold, I am (he) whom you seek; what (is) the cause for which you have come? [22] And they said, Cornelius, a centurion, a righteous man, and fearing God, and testified to by the whole nation of the Jews, was divinely instructed by a holy angel to send for you to his house, and to hear words from you. [23] Then having called them in, he housed (them).

And on the morrow Peter went out with them, and certain of the brothers went with him, those from Joppa. [24] And on the morrow they entered into Caesarea. And Cornelius was expecting them, having called together his relatives and intimate friends. [25] And as Peter was coming in, Cornelius having met him, having fallen at (his) feet worshiped. [26] But Peter raised him up, saying, Rise up; I also myself am a man. [27] And talking with him he went in, and found many gathered together. [28] And he said to them, You know how unlawful it is for a man, a Jew, to unite himself or come near to one of another race. And God showed me not to call any man unclean or common. [29] Therefore I came without complaint, having been sent for. I ask, therefore, for what reason did you send for me? [30] And Cornelius said, Four days ago until this hour I was fasting, praying in my house the ninth hour; and behold, a man

---

19 μενος Πέτρος, ἐνθάδε ξενίζεται. τοῦ δὲ Πέτρου ἐνθυμουμένου
surnamed Peter, here is lodged. — And Peter pondering
περὶ τοῦ ὁράματος, εἶπεν αὐτῷ τὸ Πνεῦμα, Ἰδού, ἄνδρες
about the vision, said to him the Spirit, Behold, men

20 τρεῖς ζητοῦσί σε. ἀλλὰ ἀναστὰς κατάβηθι, καὶ πορεύου σὺν
three are seeking you. But rising up, go down, and go with
αὐτοῖς, μηδὲν διακρινόμενος· διότι ἐγὼ ἀπέσταλκα αὐτούς.
them nothing discriminating, because I have sent them.

21 καταβὰς δὲ Πέτρος πρὸς τοὺς ἄνδρας τοὺς ἀπεσταλμένους ἀπὸ
going down And Peter to the men, those sent from
τοῦ Κορνηλίου πρὸς αὐτόν, εἶπεν, Ἰδού, ἐγώ εἰμι ὃν ζητεῖτε·
— Cornelius to him, said, Behold, I am whom you seek;

22 τίς ἡ αἰτία δι' ἣν πάρεστε ; οἱ δὲ εἶπον, Κορνήλιος ἑκατοντάρ-
what (is) the cause for which you are here? they And said, Cornelius, a centurion,
χης, ἀνὴρ δίκαιος καὶ φοβούμενος τὸν Θεόν, μαρτυρούμενός
a man just and fearing — God, being testified to
τε ὑπὸ ὅλου τοῦ ἔθνους τῶν Ἰουδαίων, ἐχρηματίσθη ὑπὸ
and by all of the nation of the Jews, was warned by
ἀγγέλου ἁγίου μεταπέμψασθαί σε εἰς τὸν οἶκον αὐτοῦ, καὶ
an angel holy to call you to the house of him, and

23 ἀκοῦσαι ῥήματα παρὰ σοῦ. εἰσκαλεσάμενος οὖν αὐτοὺς
to hear words from you. Calling in, therefore, them,
ἐξένισε.
he lodged.

Τῇ δὲ ἐπαύριον ὁ Πέτρος ἐξῆλθε σὺν αὐτοῖς, καί τινες τῶν
on the And morrow, Peter went out with them, and some of the

24 ἀδελφῶν τῶν ἀπὸ τῆς Ἰόππης συνῆλθον αὐτῷ. καὶ τῇ
brothers — from — Joppa accompanied him. And on the
ἐπαύριον εἰσῆλθον εἰς τὴν Καισάρειαν. ὁ δὲ Κορνήλιος ἦν
morrow they entered into — Caesarea. And Cornelius was
προσδοκῶν αὐτούς, συγκαλεσάμενος τοὺς συγγενεῖς αὐτοῦ
awaiting them, having called together the relatives of him

25 καὶ τοὺς ἀναγκαίους φίλους. ὡς δὲ ἐγένετο εἰσελθεῖν τὸν
and the intimate friends. when And was entering —
Πέτρον, συναντήσας αὐτῷ ὁ Κορνήλιος, πεσὼν ἐπὶ τοὺς
Peter, meeting him — Cornelius, falling at the

26 πόδας, προσεκύνησεν. ὁ δὲ Πέτρος αὐτὸν ἤγειρε λέγων,
feet worshiped. — But Peter him raised, saying,

27 Ἀνάστηθι· κἀγὼ αὐτὸς ἄνθρωπός εἰμι. καὶ συνομιλῶν αὐτῷ
Stand up; also I (my)self a man am. And talking with him
εἰσῆλθε, καὶ εὑρίσκει συνεληλυθότας πολλούς, ἔφη τε πρὸς
he entered, and finds having come together many, said and to

28 αὐτούς, Ὑμεῖς ἐπίστασθε ὡς ἀθέμιτόν ἐστιν ἀνδρὶ Ἰουδαίῳ
them, You understand how unlawful it is for a man, a Jew,
κολλᾶσθαι ἢ προσέρχεσθαι ἀλλοφύλῳ· καὶ ἐμοὶ ὁ Θεὸς
to unite with or to approach one of another race: and to me — God
ἔδειξε μηδένα κοινὸν ἢ ἀκάθαρτον λέγειν ἄνθρωπον· διὸ καὶ
showed not one common or unclean to call a man. Because of this, also

29 ἀναντιρρήτως ἦλθον μεταπεμφθείς. πυνθάνομαι οὖν, τίνι
without complaint I came, being sent for. I ask, therefore, for what

30 λόγῳ μετεπέμψασθέ με. καὶ ὁ Κορνήλιος ἔφη, Ἀπὸ τετάρτης
reason you sent for me. And Cornelius said, From fourth
ἡμέρας μέχρι ταύτης τῆς ὥρας ἤμην νηστεύων, καὶ τὴν
day until this — hour, I have been fasting, and the
ἐννάτην ὥραν προσευχόμενος ἐν τῷ οἴκῳ μου· καὶ ἰδού,
ninth hour was praying in the house of me, and behold,

stood before me in bright
clothing, [31] and said,
Cornelius, your prayer was
heard, and your alms were
remembered before God.
[32] Therefore send to
Joppa and call for Simon
who is surnamed Peter; he
stays in (the) house of
Simon, a tanner, by (the)
sea; who having come will
speak to you. [33] Then at
once I sent to you, and
you did well having come.
Now therefore we all are
present before God to hear
all things that have been
commanded you by God.
[34] And opening (his)
mouth Peter said, Truly I
see that God is not a
respecter of persons,
[35] but in every nation
he that fears Him and
works righteousness is
acceptable to Him.
[36] The word which He
sent to the sons of Israel
preaching the gospel, peace
by Jesus Christ — He is
Lord of all — [37] you
know; the message which
came throughout all Judea,
beginning from Galilee,
after the baptism which
John preached: [38] Jesus
who (was) from Nazareth,
how God anointed Him
with (the) Holy Spirit and
with power, who went
through doing good and
healing all that were being
oppressed by the devil,
because God was with
Him. [39] And we are
witnesses of all things
which He did, both in the
country of the Jews and in
Jerusalem; whom they put
to death, having hanged
(Him) on a tree. [40] This
One God raised up on the
third day, and caused Him
to be seen; [41] not to all
the people, but to
witnesses who had been
chosen before by God, to
us, who did eat and drink
with Him after He had
risen from among (the)
dead. [42] And He
commanded us to preach
to the people, and to
testify fully that it is He
who has been appointed by
God Judge of living and
dead. [43] To Him all the

**31** ἀνὴρ ἔστη ἐνώπιόν μου ἐν ἐσθῆτι λαμπρᾷ, καὶ φησι,
　　a man stood before　me　in clothing bright,　　and says,
Κορνήλιε, εἰσηκούσθη σου ἡ προσευχή, καὶ αἱ ἐλεημοσύναι
Cornelius, was listened (to) of you the praver,　　and the alms

**32** σου ἐμνήσθησαν ἐνώπιον τοῦ Θεοῦ. πέμψον οὖν εἰς Ἰόππην,
of you were remembered before ＋ God.　send Therefore to Joppa,
καὶ μετακάλεσαι Σίμωνα ὃς ἐπικαλεῖται Πέτρος· οὗτος ξενί-
and　call for　　Simon who is surnamed　Peter; this one is
ζεται ἐν οἰκίᾳ Σίμωνος βυρσέως παρὰ θάλασσαν· ὃς παρα-
lodged in (the) house of Simon, a tanner,　by　(the) sea,　who having

**33** γενόμενος λαλήσει σοι. Ἐξαυτῆς οὖν ἔπεμψα πρός σε· σύ τε
come　　will speak to you. At once, then, I sent　　to　you; you and
καλῶς ἐποίησας παραγενόμενος. νῦν οὖν πάντες ἡμεῖς ἐνώ-
well　　did　　having come.　　Now, then, all　we
πιον τοῦ Θεοῦ πάρεσμεν ἀκοῦσαι πάντα τὰ προστεταγμένα
before — God are present to hear　all the things being commanded

**34** σοι ὑπὸ τοῦ Θεοῦ. ἀνοίξας δὲ Πέτρος τὸ στόμα εἶπεν,
you by　— God. opening And Peter　the mouth　said,
Ἐπ' ἀληθείας καταλαμβάνομαι ὅτι οὐκ ἔστι προσωπολή-
On truth,　I perceive　　that not is　a receiver of

**35** πτης ὁ Θεός· ἀλλ' ἐν παντὶ ἔθνει ὁ φοβούμενος αὐτὸν καὶ
faces　God, but　in　every nation　he fearing　Him and

**36** ἐργαζόμενος δικαιοσύνην, δεκτὸς αὐτῷ ἐστι. τὸν λόγον ὃν
working　　righteousness acceptable to Him is.　The word which
ἀπέστειλε τοῖς υἱοῖς Ἰσραήλ, εὐαγγελιζόμενος εἰρήνην διὰ
He sent　to the sons of Israel,　preaching the gospel　peace through

**37** Ἰησοῦ Χριστοῦ (οὗτός ἐστι πάντων Κύριος)—ὑμεῖς οἴδατε,
Jesus　Christ; this One is　of all　Lord.　You　know
τὸ γενόμενον ῥῆμα καθ' ὅλης τῆς Ἰουδαίας, ἀρξάμενον ἀπὸ
that happened the thing through all — of Judea,　beginning　from
τῆς Γαλιλαίας, μετὰ τὸ βάπτισμα ὃ ἐκήρυξεν Ἰωάννης·
— Galilee　after the baptism　which proclaimed John;

**38** Ἰησοῦν τὸν ἀπὸ Ναζαρέθ, ὡς ἔχρισεν αὐτὸν ὁ Θεὸς Πνεύ-
Jesus　the (One) from Nazareth, how anointed Him　　God with (the)
ματι Ἁγίῳ καὶ δυνάμει, ὃς διῆλθεν εὐεργετῶν καὶ ἰώμενος
Spirit Holy, and　with power, who went about doing good and　healing
πάντας τοὺς καταδυναστευομένους ὑπὸ τοῦ διαβόλου, ὅτι
all　those　having been oppressed　by　the Devil,　because

**39** ὁ Θεὸς ἦν μετ' αὐτοῦ. καὶ ἡμεῖς ἐσμεν μάρτυρες πάντων ὧν
God was with Him. And we　are　witnesses of all things which
ἐποίησεν ἔν τε τῇ χώρᾳ τῶν Ἰουδαίων καὶ ἐν Ἰερουσαλήμ·
He did, in both the country of the　Jews　and in　Jerusalem;

**40** ὃν ἀνεῖλον κρεμάσαντες ἐπὶ ξύλου. τοῦτον ὁ Θεὸς ἤγειρε τῇ
whom they did hanging　on a tree. This One　God　raised the
　　away (with)

**41** τρίτῃ ἡμέρᾳ, καὶ ἔδωκεν αὐτὸν ἐμφανῆ γενέσθαι, οὐ παντὶ
third　day,　and gave　Him　visible to become, not to all
τῷ λαῷ, ἀλλὰ μάρτυσι τοῖς προκεχειροτονημένοις ὑπὸ
the people, but to witnesses, those having been before　by
　　　　　　　　　　　　　　hand-picked
τοῦ Θεοῦ, ἡμῖν, οἵτινες συνεφάγομεν καὶ συνεπίομεν αὐτῷ
— God, to us, who　ate with　and drank with　Him

**42** μετὰ τὸ ἀναστῆναι αὐτὸν ἐκ νεκρῶν. καὶ παρήγγειλεν
after the　rising again (of) Him out of (the) dead. And He commanded
ἡμῖν κηρύξαι τῷ λαῷ, καὶ διαμαρτύρασθαι ὅτι αὐτός
us to proclaim to the people, and to solemnly witness that　He

**43** ἐστιν ὁ ὡρισμένος ὑπὸ τοῦ Θεοῦ κριτὴς ζώντων καὶ νεκρῶν.
it is who has been　by　— God (as) judge of living　and of dead.
　　　marked out

τούτῳ πάντες οἱ προφῆται μαρτυροῦσιν, ἄφεσιν ἁμαρτιῶν
To this One all the prophets witness, forgiveness of sins

prophets bear witness (that) through His name everyone that believes on Him receives remission of sins.

λαβεῖν διὰ τοῦ ὀνόματος αὐτοῦ πάντα τὸν πιστεύοντα
to receive through the name of Him everyone — believing

εἰς αὐτόν.
in Him.

[44] Yet as Peter was speaking these words, the Holy Spirit fell on all those hearing the word.

**44** Ἔτι λαλοῦντος τοῦ Πέτρου τὰ ῥήματα ταῦτα, ἐπέπεσε τὸ
(As) yet speaking — Peter — words these, fell the

Πνεῦμα τὸ Ἅγιον ἐπὶ πάντας τοὺς ἀκούοντας τὸν λόγον.
Spirit — Holy on all those hearing the word.

[45] And the believers of the circumcision were amazed, as many as came with Peter, that the gift of the Holy Spirit had been poured out also on the nations. [46] For they heard them speaking with languages and magnifying God. Then Peter answered, [47] Can anyone forbid the water, that these should not be baptized, who the Holy Spirit received, even as we? [48] And he commanded them to be baptized in the name of the Lord, then they begged him to remain some days.

**45** καὶ ἐξέστησαν οἱ ἐκ περιτομῆς πιστοί, ὅσοι συνῆλθον τῷ
And were amazed those of circumcision faithful, as many as came with —

Πέτρῳ, ὅτι καὶ ἐπὶ τὰ ἔθνη ἡ δωρεὰ τοῦ Ἁγίου Πνεύματος
Peter, because also on the nations the gift of the Holy Spirit

**46** ἐκκέχυται. ἤκουον γὰρ αὐτῶν λαλούντων γλώσσαις, καὶ
was poured out. they heard For them speaking in languages, and

μεγαλυνόντων τὸν Θεόν. τότε ἀπεκρίθη ὁ Πέτρος, Μήτι
magnifying — God. Then answered — Peter, Not

**47** τὸ ὕδωρ κωλῦσαι δύναταί τις, τοῦ μὴ βαπτισθῆναι τούτους,
the water forbid can anyone, — not to be baptized these,

οἵτινες τὸ Πνεῦμα τὸ Ἅγιον ἔλαβον καθὼς καὶ ἡμεῖς ; προσ—
who the Spirit — Holy received even as also we? he com—

**48** έταξέ τε αὐτοὺς βαπτισθῆναι ἐν τῷ ὀνόματι τοῦ Κυρίου.
manded. And them to be baptized in the name of the Lord.

τότε ἠρώτησαν αὐτὸν ἐπιμεῖναι ἡμέρας τινάς.
Then they asked him to remain days some.

CHAPTER 11

[1] And the apostles and the brothers who were in Judea heard that the nations also received the word of God; [2] and when Peter went up to Jerusalem, those of (the) circumcision contended with him, [3] saying, You went in to uncircumcised men, and ate with them. [4] But Peter having begun, he set out to them in order, saying, I was being in (the) city of Joppa, praying, and I saw in a trance a vision, a certain vessel descending like a huge sheet, let down by four corners out of Heaven, and it came as far as me. [6] Having looked intently on (this), I observed and saw the four-footed animals of the earth, and the wild beasts, and the creeping things, and the birds of the sky. [7] And I heard a voice saying to me, Having risen up, Peter, kill and eat. [8] But I said, Never, Lord, for nothing unclean or common ever entered into my mouth. [9] But a voice answered

CHAPTER 11

**1** Ἤκουσαν δὲ οἱ ἀπόστολοι καὶ οἱ ἀδελφοὶ οἱ ὄντες κατὰ
heard And the apostles and the brothers — being throughout

τὴν Ἰουδαίαν ὅτι καὶ τὰ ἔθνη ἐδέξαντο τὸν λόγον τοῦ Θεοῦ.
— Judea that also the nations received the word — of God.

**2** καὶ ὅτε ἀνέβη Πέτρος εἰς Ἱεροσόλυμα, διεκρίνοντο πρὸς αὐτὸν
And when went Peter to Jerusalem, disputed with him

**3** οἱ ἐκ περιτομῆς, λέγοντες ὅτι Πρὸς ἄνδρας ἀκροβυστίαν
those of circumcision, saying, — To men uncircumcision

**4** ἔχοντας εἰσῆλθες, καὶ συνέφαγες αὐτοῖς. ἀρξάμενος δὲ ὁ
having you went in, and you ate with them. beginning And,

**5** Πέτρος ἐξετίθετο αὐτοῖς καθεξῆς λέγων, Ἐγὼ ἤμην ἐν πόλει
Peter explained to them in order, saying, I was being in (the) city

Ἰόππῃ προσευχόμενος, καὶ εἶδον ἐν ἐκστάσει ὅραμα, κατα—
of Joppa praying, and I saw in an ecstasy a vision, coming

βαῖνον σκεῦός τι, ὡς ὀθόνην μεγάλην τέσσαρσιν ἀρχαῖς
down a vessel certain, as a sheet great by four corners

**6** καθιεμένην ἐκ τοῦ οὐρανοῦ, καὶ ἦλθεν ἄχρις ἐμοῦ· εἰς ἣν
being let down out of the heaven, and it came to me; into which

ἀτενίσας κατενόουν, καὶ εἶδον τὰ τετράποδα τῆς γῆς καὶ
gazing I perceived, and I saw the quadrupeds of the earth, and

**7** τὰ θηρία καὶ τὰ ἑρπετὰ καὶ τὰ πετεινὰ τοῦ οὐρανοῦ. ἤκουσα
the beasts, and the reptiles, and the birds of the heaven. I heard

δὲ φωνῆς λεγούσης μοι, Ἀναστάς, Πέτρε, θῦσον καὶ φάγε.
And a voice saying to me, Rise up, Peter; slay and eat.

**8** εἶπον δέ, Μηδαμῶς, Κύριε· ὅτι πᾶν κοινὸν ἢ ἀκάθαρτον
I said And, Not at all, Lord, because anything common or unclean

**9** οὐδέποτε εἰσῆλθεν εἰς τὸ στόμα μου. ἀπεκρίθη δέ μοι φωνὴ
never entered into the mouth of me. answered And me a voice

me the second time out of Heaven, What God cleansed, you do not make common. [10] And this took place three times, and all were again pulled up into Heaven. [11] And behold, at once, three men stood at the house in which I was, sent from Caesarea to me. [12] And the Spirit said to me to go with them, discriminating nothing. And these six brothers also went with me, and we went into the house of the man. [13] And he told us how he saw the angel in his house standing and saying to him, Send men to Joppa, and send for Simon who is surnamed Peter, [14] who will speak words to you by which you and all your house shall be saved. [15] And in my beginning to speak, the Holy Spirit fell on them, even as also on us in (the) beginning. [16] And I remembered the word of (the) Lord, how He said, John indeed baptized with water, but you shall be baptized with (the) Holy Spirit. [17] If then God gave the same gift to them as also to us, having believed on the Lord Jesus Christ, and I, who was I (to be) able to forbid God? [18] And having heard these things, they were silent, and glorified God, saying, Then truly God has given repentance unto life to the nations also.

[19] Then, indeed, they who were scattered by the tribulation that took place on Stephen passed through to Phenicia and Cyprus and Antioch, speaking the word to no one except to Jews only. [20] But certain men of them were Cypriots and Cyreneans, who having come into Antioch, spoke to the Hellenists preaching the gospel, the Lord Jesus. [21] And (the) hand of (the) Lord was with them, and a great number having believed turned to the Lord. [22] And a report was heard in the ears of the

ἐκ δευτέρου ἐκ τοῦ οὐρανοῦ, Ἃ ὁ Θεὸς ἐκαθάρισε, σὺ μὴ
a second (time)out of — Heaven, What God has cleansed, you not

10 κοίνου. τοῦτο δὲ ἐγένετο ἐπὶ τρίς, καὶ πάλιν ἀνεσπάσθη
make common. this And happened on three, and again were pulled up

11 ἅπαντα εἰς τὸν οὐρανόν. καὶ ἰδού, ἐξαυτῆς τρεῖς ἄνδρες
all things into — Heaven. And, behold, at once three men

ἐπέστησαν ἐπὶ τὴν οἰκίαν ἐν ᾗ ἤμην, ἀπεσταλμένοι ἀπὸ
stood at the house in which I was, having been sent from

12 Καισαρείας πρός με. εἶπε δέ μοι τὸ Πνεῦμα συνελθεῖν αὐτοῖς,
Caesarea to me. said And to me the Spirit to go with them,

μηδὲν διακρινόμενον. ἦλθον δὲ σὺν ἐμοὶ καὶ οἱ ἓξ ἀδελφοὶ
nothing discriminating. came And with me also — six brothers

οὗτοι, καὶ εἰσήλθομεν εἰς τὸν οἶκον τοῦ ἀνδρός· ἀπήγγειλέ
these, and we entered into the house of the man. he reported

13 τε ἡμῖν πῶς εἶδε τὸν ἄγγελον ἐν τῷ οἴκῳ αὐτοῦ σταθέντα,
And to us how he saw the angel in the house of him standing,

καὶ εἰπόντα αὐτῷ, Ἀπόστειλον εἰς Ἰόππην ἄνδρας, καὶ
and saying to him, Send forth to Joppa men, and

14 μετάπεμψαι Σίμωνα, τὸν ἐπικαλούμενον Πέτρον, ὃς λαλήσει
send for Simon, the (one) surnamed Peter, who will speak

ῥήματα πρός σε, ἐν οἷς σωθήσῃ σὺ καὶ πᾶς ὁ οἶκός σου.
words to you, by which will be saved you and all the house of you.

15 ἐν δὲ τῷ ἄρξασθαί με λαλεῖν, ἐπέπεσε τὸ Πνεῦμα τὸ Ἅγιον
in And beginning me to speak, fell the Spirit — Holy

16 ἐπ᾽ αὐτούς, ὥσπερ καὶ ἐφ᾽ ἡμᾶς ἐν ἀρχῇ. ἐμνήσθην δὲ τοῦ
on them, as also on us at first. I remembered And the

ῥήματος Κυρίου, ὡς ἔλεγεν, Ἰωάννης μὲν ἐβάπτισεν ὕδατι,
word of (the) Lord, how He said, John indeed baptized with water,

17 ὑμεῖς δὲ βαπτισθήσεσθε ἐν Πνεύματι Ἁγίῳ. εἰ οὖν τὴν ἴσην
you but will be baptized in (the) Spirit Holy. If, then, the same

δωρεὰν ἔδωκεν αὐτοῖς ὁ Θεὸς ὡς καὶ ἡμῖν, πιστεύσασιν ἐπὶ
gift gave them God, as also to us, having believed on

τὸν Κύριον Ἰησοῦν Χριστόν, ἐγὼ δὲ τίς ἤμην δυνατὸς
the Lord Jesus Christ, I, and who was able

18 κωλῦσαι τὸν Θεόν; ἀκούσαντες δὲ ταῦτα ἡσύχασαν, καὶ
to prevent God? hearing And these things, they kept silent, and

ἐδόξαζον τὸν Θεόν, λέγοντες, Ἄραγε καὶ τοῖς ἔθνεσιν ὁ Θεὸς
glorified God, saying, Then also to the nations God

τὴν μετάνοιαν ἔδωκεν εἰς ζωήν.
— repentance has given unto life.

19 Οἱ μὲν οὖν διασπαρέντες ἀπὸ τῆς θλίψεως τῆς γενομένης
they indeed Then who were scattered from the affliction — occurring

ἐπὶ Στεφάνῳ διῆλθον ἕως Φοινίκης καὶ Κύπρου καὶ
over Stephen passed through to Phoenicia and Cyprus and

Ἀντιοχείας, μηδενὶ λαλοῦντες τὸν λόγον εἰ μὴ μόνον
Antioch, to no one speaking the word except only

20 Ἰουδαίοις. ἦσαν δέ τινες ἐξ αὐτῶν ἄνδρες Κύπριοι καὶ Κυρη-
to Jews. were But some of them men, Cypriots and Cyren-

ναῖοι, οἵτινες εἰσελθόντες εἰς Ἀντιόχειαν, ἐλάλουν πρὸς τοὺς
ians, who coming to Antioch, spoke to the

21 Ἑλληνιστάς, εὐαγγελιζόμενοι τὸν Κύριον Ἰησοῦν. καὶ ἦν
Hellenists, preaching the gospel of the Lord Jesus. And was

χεὶρ Κυρίου μετ᾽ αὐτῶν· πολύς τε ἀριθμὸς πιστεύσας ἐπέ-
hand (the) Lord's with them, a much and number, believing

22 στρεψεν ἐπὶ τὸν Κύριον. ἠκούσθη δὲ ὁ λόγος εἰς τὰ ὦτα τῆς
turned upon the Lord. was heard And the word into the ears of the

assembly which (was) in Jerusalem, concerning them; and they sent out Barnabas to go through as far as Antioch; [23] who having come and having seen the grace of God rejoiced, and exhorted all with purpose of heart to abide with the Lord; [24] for he was a good man and full of (the) Holy Spirit and of faith. And a great company was added to the Lord. [25] And Barnabas went out to Tarsus to look for Saul; [26] and having found him he brought him to Antioch. And it came to pass they were gathered in the assembly a whole year, and taught a huge crowd. And the disciples were first called Christians in Antioch.

[27] And in these days prophets came down from Jerusalem to Antioch; [28] and one having arisen up from among them, Agabus by name, he signified by the Spirit (that) a great famine was about to be over all the habitable earth; which also happened in Claudius Caesar's (time). [29] And the disciples, according as any was prospered, determined, each of them, to send to the brothers living in Judea, for (their) relief; [30] which they also did, sending to the elders by (the) hand of Barnabas and Saul.

CHAPTER 12

[1] And at that time Herod the king threw on (his) hands to oppress some of those of the assembly; [2] and he put to death James the brother of John with a sword. [3] And having seen that it was pleasing to the Jews, he went on to seize Peter also — and they were (the) days of unleavened bread — [4] whom having seized also, he put in prison, having delivered (him) to four sets of four soldiers to guard him, purposing to bring him out to the people after the Passover. [5] Then Peter, indeed, was kept in the prison; but

ἐκκλησίας τῆς ἐν Ἱεροσολύμοις περὶ αὐτῶν· καὶ ἐξαπέστειλαν
church — in Jerusalem about them; and they sent forth

23 Βαρνάβαν διελθεῖν ἕως Ἀντιοχείας· ὃς παραγενόμενος καὶ
Barnabas to go through to Antioch; who having come and

ἰδὼν τὴν χάριν τοῦ Θεοῦ ἐχάρη, καὶ παρεκάλει πάντας τῇ
seeing the grace of God rejoiced, and exhorted all —

24 προθέσει τῆς καρδίας προσμένειν τῷ Κυρίῳ· ὅτι ἦν ἀνὴρ
with purpose — of heart to remain near the Lord; for he was a man

ἀγαθὸς καὶ πλήρης Πνεύματος Ἁγίου καὶ πίστεως· καὶ
good, and full of (the) Spirit Holy and of faith. And

25 προσετέθη ὄχλος ἱκανὸς τῷ Κυρίῳ. ἐξῆλθε δὲ εἰς Ταρσὸν ὁ
was added a crowd sufficient to the Lord. went And to Tarsus

26 Βαρνάβας ἀναζητῆσαι Σαῦλον, καὶ εὑρὼν αὐτὸν ἤγαγεν
Barnabas to seek Saul, and finding him he led

αὐτὸν εἰς Ἀντιόχειαν. ἐγένετο δὲ αὐτοὺς ἐνιαυτὸν ὅλον
him to Antioch. it was And, to them a year whole

συναχθῆναι ἐν τῇ ἐκκλησίᾳ καὶ διδάξαι ὄχλον ἱκανόν, χρη-
were assembled in the church, and taught a crowd considerable,

ματίσαι τε πρῶτον ἐν Ἀντιοχείᾳ τοὺς μαθητὰς Χριστιανούς.
were called and (at) first Antioch the disciples Christians.

27 Ἐν ταύταις δὲ ταῖς ἡμέραις κατῆλθον ἀπὸ Ἱεροσολύμων
in these And — days came down from Jerusalem

28 προφῆται εἰς Ἀντιόχειαν. ἀναστὰς δὲ εἷς ἐξ αὐτῶν ὀνόματι
prophets to Antioch. having risen And one of them by name

Ἄγαβος, ἐσήμανε διὰ τοῦ Πνεύματος λιμὸν μέγαν μέλλειν
Agabus signified through the Spirit a famine great to be about

ἔσεσθαι ἐφ' ὅλην τὴν οἰκουμένην· ὅστις καὶ ἐγένετο ἐπὶ
to be over all the inhabited earth; which also happened on

29 Κλαυδίου Καίσαρος. τῶν δὲ μαθητῶν καθὼς ηὐπορεῖτό τις,
(the time) of Claudius Caesar. the And disciples, as was prospered any,

ὥρισαν ἕκαστος αὐτῶν εἰς διακονίαν πέμψαι τοῖς κατοι-
determined each of them for ministration to send to those

30 κοῦσιν ἐν τῇ Ἰουδαίᾳ ἀδελφοῖς· ὃ καὶ ἐποίησαν, ἀποστεί-
living in — Judea brothers; which also they did, sending

λαντες πρὸς τοὺς πρεσβυτέρους διὰ χειρὸς Βαρνάβα καὶ
to the elders through (the) hand of Barnabas and

Σαύλου.
of Saul.

CHAPTER 12

1 Κατ' ἐκεῖνον δὲ τὸν καιρὸν ἐπέβαλεν Ἡρώδης ὁ βασιλεὺς
at that And — time threw on Herod the king

2 τὰς χεῖρας κακῶσαί τινας τῶν ἀπὸ τῆς ἐκκλησίας. ἀνεῖλε δὲ
the hands to oppress some of those from the church. he did away And

3 Ἰάκωβον τὸν ἀδελφὸν Ἰωάννου μαχαίρᾳ. καὶ ἰδὼν ὅτι ἀρε-
James the brother of John with a sword. And seeing that

στόν ἐστι τοῖς Ἰουδαίοις, προσέθετο συλλαβεῖν καὶ Πέτρον·
pleasing is to the Jews, he added to seize also Peter;

4 ἦσαν δὲ ἡμέραι τῶν ἀζύμων· ὃν καὶ πιάσας ἔθετο εἰς φυλακήν,
were and days — of unleaven whom also capturing, he put in prison,

παραδοὺς τέσσαρσι τετραδίοις στρατιωτῶν φυλάσσειν
delivering to four quaternions of soldiers to guard

αὐτόν, βουλόμενος μετὰ τὸ πάσχα ἀναγαγεῖν αὐτὸν τῷ
him; intending after the Passover to lead up him to the

5 λαῷ. ὁ μὲν οὖν Πέτρος ἐτηρεῖτο ἐν τῇ φυλακῇ· προσευχὴ
people. Therefore Peter was kept in the prison; prayer

fervent prayer was made by the assembly to God concerning him. [6] But when Herod was about to bring him forth, in that night Peter was sleeping between two soldiers, bound with two chains; also guards kept the prison before the door. [7] And behold, an angel of (the) Lord stood by, and a light shone in the building. And having smitten Peter's side he roused him up, saying, Rise up in haste! And the chains fell off from (his) hands. [8] And the angel said to him, Gird yourself and tie your sandals on. And he did so. And he said to him, Throw your garment around (you) and follow me. [9] And going out he followed him, and did not know that it was real, that which was happening by means of the angel, but thought he saw a vision. [10] And having passed through a first guard and a second, they came to the iron gate that leads into the city, which opened of itself to them; and having gone out they went on through one street. and the angel instantly withdrew from him. [11] And having become within himself, Peter said, Now I know that truly (the) Lord sent out His angel and plucked me out of (the) hand of Herod, and all the expectation of the people of the Jews. [12] And considering (it), he came to the house of Mary the mother of John who is surnamed Mark, where many were gathered together and praying. [13] And Peter having knocked (at) the door of the porch, a girl named Rhoda came to listen; [14] and having recognized the voice of Peter, from the joy (of it) she did not open the porch, but having run in she reported Peter to be standing before the porch. [15] But they said to her, You are insane. But she insisted it was so. And they said, It is his angel. [16] But Peter continued

δὲ ἦν ἐκτενὴς γινομένη ὑπὸ τῆς ἐκκλησίας πρὸς τὸν Θεὸν
But was earnestly being made by the church to — God

6 ὑπὲρ αὐτοῦ. ὅτε δὲ ἔμελλεν αὐτὸν προάγειν ὁ Ἡρώδης, τῇ
about him. when And was about him to lead forth — Herod, —

νυκτὶ ἐκείνῃ ἦν ὁ Πέτρος κοιμώμενος μεταξὺ δύο στρατιω-
in night that was Peter sleeping between two soldiers,

τῶν, δεδεμένος ἁλύσεσι δυσί· φύλακές τε πρὸ τῆς θύρας
having been bound with chains two; guards and before the door

7 ἐτήρουν τὴν φυλακήν. καὶ ἰδού, ἄγγελος Κυρίου ἐπέστη, καὶ
were keeping the prison. And behold, an angel of (the) Lord stood by, and

φῶς ἔλαμψεν ἐν τῷ οἰκήματι· πατάξας δὲ τὴν πλευρὰν τοῦ
a light shone in the building; striking and the side —

Πέτρου, ἤγειρεν αὐτὸν λέγων, Ἀνάστα ἐν τάχει. καὶ ἐξέπεσον
of Peter, he raised him, saying, Rise up in haste. And fell off

8 αὐτοῦ αἱ ἁλύσεις ἐκ τῶν χειρῶν. εἰπέ τε ὁ ἄγγελος πρὸς
of him the chains from the hands. said And the angel to

αὐτόν, Περίζωσαι καὶ ὑπόδησαι τὰ σανδάλιά σου. ἐποίησε
him, Gird yourself, and put on the sandals of you. he did

δὲ οὕτω. καὶ λέγει αὐτῷ, Περιβαλοῦ τὸ ἱμάτιόν σου, καὶ
And so. And he says to him, Throw around the garment of you, and

9 ἀκολούθει μοι. καὶ ἐξελθὼν ἠκολούθει αὐτῷ· καὶ οὐκ ᾔδει ὅτι
follow me. And going out he followed him, and not knew that

ἀληθές ἐστι τὸ γινόμενον διὰ τοῦ ἀγγέλου, ἐδόκει δὲ ὅραμα
true was that happening through the angel; he thought but a vision

10 βλέπειν. διελθόντες δὲ πρώτην φυλακὴν καὶ δευτέραν, ἦλθον
to see. going through And (the) first guard and (the) second, they came

ἐπὶ τὴν πύλην τὴν σιδηρᾶν, τὴν φέρουσαν εἰς τὴν πόλιν,
on the gate — iron — carrying (one) to the city,

ἥτις αὐτομάτη ἠνοίχθη αὐτοῖς· καὶ ἐξελθόντες προῆλθον
which of itself was opened to them; and going out they went on

11 ῥύμην μίαν, καὶ εὐθέως ἀπέστη ὁ ἄγγελος ἀπ' αὐτοῦ. καὶ ὁ
street one; and instantly withdrew the angel from him. And

Πέτρος, γενόμενος ἐν ἑαυτῷ, εἶπε, Νῦν οἶδα ἀληθῶς ὅτι
Peter, having come in himself said, Now I know truly that

ἐξαπέστειλε Κύριος τὸν ἄγγελον αὐτοῦ, καὶ ἐξείλετό με ἐκ
sent out (the) Lord the angel of Him, and plucked me out of

χειρὸς Ἡρώδου καὶ πάσης τῆς προσδοκίας τοῦ λαοῦ τῶν
hand Herod's, and of all the expectation of the people of the

12 Ἰουδαίων. συνιδών τε ἦλθεν ἐπὶ τὴν οἰκίαν Μαρίας τῆς
Jews. considering And he came to the house of Mary the

μητρὸς Ἰωάννου τοῦ ἐπικαλουμένου Μάρκου, οὗ ἦσαν
mother of John, — surnamed Mark, where were

13 ἱκανοὶ συνηθροισμένοι καὶ προσευχόμενοι. κρούσαντος δὲ
many gathered together and praying. knocking And

τοῦ Πέτρου τὴν θύραν τοῦ πυλῶνος, προσῆλθε παιδίσκη
— Peter (at) the door of the porch, came near a maidservant

14 ὑπακοῦσαι, ὀνόματι Ῥόδη. καὶ ἐπιγνοῦσα τὴν φωνὴν τοῦ
to listen, by name Rhoda. And recognizing the voice —

Πέτρου, ἀπὸ τῆς χαρᾶς οὐκ ἤνοιξε τὸν πυλῶνα, εἰσδραμοῦσα
of Peter, from — joy not she opened the porch, running

15 δὲ ἀπήγγειλεν ἑστάναι τὸν Πέτρον πρὸ τοῦ πυλῶνος. οἱ δὲ
but reported to stand — Peter before the porch. they But

πρὸς αὐτὴν εἶπον, Μαίνῃ. ἡ δὲ διϊσχυρίζετο οὕτως ἔχειν.
to her said, You are raving. she But insisted so (it) to hold.

16 οἱ δ' ἔλεγον, Ὁ ἄγγελος αὐτοῦ ἐστιν. ὁ δὲ Πέτρος ἐπέμενε
they And said, The angel of him it is. But Peter continued

knocking, and having opened, they saw him and were amazed. [17] And having signaled to them with the hand to be silent, he told them how the Lord brought him out of the prison. And he said, Tell James and the brothers these things. And having gone out, he went to another place. [18] And day having come, there was no small disturbance among the soldiers, what then had become (of) Peter. [19] And Herod having sought after him and not having found, having examined the guards, he commanded (them) to be led away. And having gone down from Judea to Caesarea he stayed there. [20] And Herod was in bitter hostility with (the) Tyrians and Sidonians; but they came to him with one accord, and having gained Blastus, who (was) over the bedroom of the king, sought peace, because their country was nourished by the king's. [21] And on a set day Herod, having put on a regal garment, and having sat on the tribunal, was making a speech to them. [22] And the people were crying out, (The) voice of a god, and not of man! [23] And instantly an angel of (the) Lord struck him, because he did not give the glory to God, and being eaten by worms, his soul went out. [24] But the word of God grew and multiplied. [25] And Barnabas and Saul returned from Jerusalem, having fulfilled the service, having taken with (them) also John who was surnamed Mark.

CHAPTER 13

[1] Now there were certain ones in Antioch in the church which were there, prophets and teachers, both Barnabas and Simeon who was called Niger, and Lucius the Cyrenian, and Manaen, a foster-brother of Herod the tetrarch, and Saul. [2] And as they were ministering to the Lord

κρούων· ἀνοίξαντες δὲ εἶδον αὐτόν, καὶ ἐξέστησαν. κατα-
knocking; having opened and they saw him, and were amazed.

17 σείσας δὲ αὐτοῖς τῇ χειρὶ σιγᾶν, διηγήσατο αὐτοῖς πῶς ὁ
signaling And to them with the hand to be silent, he told them how the

Κύριος αὐτὸν ἐξήγαγεν ἐκ τῆς φυλακῆς. εἶπε δέ, Ἀπαγγεί-
Lord him led out from the prison. he said And, Report

λατε Ἰακώβῳ καὶ τοῖς ἀδελφοῖς ταῦτα. καὶ ἐξελθὼν ἐπορεύθη
to James and the brothers these things. And going out he went

18 εἰς ἕτερον τόπον. γενομένης δὲ ἡμέρας, ἦν τάραχος οὐκ
to another place. becoming And day, there was disturbance not

ὀλίγος ἐν τοῖς στρατιώταις, τί ἄρα ὁ Πέτρος ἐγένετο.
a little among the soldiers: what then (of) Peter became?

19 Ἡρώδης δὲ ἐπιζητήσας αὐτὸν καὶ μὴ εὑρών, ἀνακρίνας
Herod And searching for him, and not finding, examining

τοὺς φύλακας, ἐκέλευσεν ἀπαχθῆναι. καὶ κατελθὼν ἀπὸ τῆς
the guards, commanded to be led away; and going down from —

Ἰουδαίας εἰς τὴν Καισάρειαν διέτριβεν.
Judea to — Caesarea stayed.

20 Ἦν δὲ ὁ Ἡρώδης θυμομαχῶν Τυρίοις καὶ Σιδωνίοις·
was And Herod in bitter hostility with Tyrians and Sidonians;

ὁμοθυμαδὸν δὲ παρῆσαν πρὸς αὐτόν, καὶ πείσαντες Βλάστον
with one mind and they came to him, and persuading Blastus,

τὸν ἐπὶ τοῦ κοιτῶνος τοῦ βασιλέως, ἠτοῦντο εἰρήνην, διὰ τὸ
the (one) over the bedroom of the king, they asked peace, because the

21 τρέφεσθαι αὐτῶν τὴν χώραν ἀπὸ τῆς βασιλικῆς. τακτῇ δὲ
feeding of them the country from the royal (bounty). on a set And

ἡμέρᾳ ὁ Ἡρώδης ἐνδυσάμενος ἐσθῆτα βασιλικήν, καὶ καθίσας
day, Herod being clothed in a garment regal, and sitting

22 ἐπὶ τοῦ βήματος, ἐδημηγόρει πρὸς αὐτούς· ὁ δὲ δῆμος
on the tribunal, made a speech to them. the And mass

23 ἐπεφώνει, Θεοῦ φωνὴ καὶ οὐκ ἀνθρώπου. παραχρῆμα δὲ
cried out, of a god A voice, and not of a man! immediately And

ἐπάταξεν αὐτὸν ἄγγελος Κυρίου, ἀνθ᾽ ὧν οὐκ ἔδωκε τὴν
struck him an angel of (the) Lord, because not he gave the

δόξαν τῷ Θεῷ· καὶ γενόμενος σκωληκόβρωτος, ἐξέψυξεν.
glory — to God. And becoming eaten by worms, his soul went out.

24 Ὁ δὲ λόγος τοῦ Θεοῦ ηὔξανε καὶ ἐπληθύνετο.
the But word — of God grew and increased.

25 Βαρνάβας δὲ καὶ Σαῦλος ὑπέστρεψαν ἐξ Ἰερουσαλήμ,
Barnabas And and Saul returned out of Jerusalem

πληρώσαντες τὴν διακονίαν, συμπαραλαβόντες καὶ Ἰωάννην
having fulfilled the service, having taken with (them) and John,

τὸν ἐπικληθέντα Μάρκον.
— being surnamed Mark.

CHAPTER 13

1 Ἦσαν δέ τινες ἐν Ἀντιοχείᾳ κατὰ τὴν οὖσαν ἐκκλησίαν
were And some in Antioch among the existing church

προφῆται καὶ διδάσκαλοι, ὅ τε Βαρνάβας καὶ Συμεὼν ὁ
prophets and teachers. Both Barnabas and Simeon, he

καλούμενος Νίγερ, καὶ Λούκιος ὁ Κυρηναῖος, Μαναήν τε
being called Niger, and Lucius the Cyrenian, Manaen and

2 Ἡρώδου τοῦ τετράρχου σύντροφος, καὶ Σαῦλος. λειτουρ-
of Herod the tetrarch foster-brother, and Saul. (while) doing service

γούντων δὲ αὐτῶν τῷ Κυρίῳ καὶ νηστευόντων, εἶπε τὸ
And they to the Lord, and fasting, said the

and fasting, the Holy Spirit said, So then separate to Me both Barnabas and Saul for the work to which I have called them. [3] Then having fasted and prayed, and having laid hands on them, they let (them) go. [4] Then these indeed having been sent out by the Holy Spirit went down to Seleucia, and from there sailed away to Cyprus. [5] And having come into Salamis, they preached the word of God in the synagogues of the Jews. And they also had John (as) a helper. [6] And having passed through the island as far as Paphos, they found a certain magician, a false prophet, a Jew, whose name (was) Barjesus; [7] who was with the proconsul Sergius Paulus, an intelligent man, who called Barnabas and Saul, asking to hear the word of God. [8] But Elymus the magician withstood them there — for so his name is translated — seeking to turn the proconsul from the faith. [9] But Saul, who also (is) Paul, being filled with the Holy Spirit, and having looked steadfastly on him, [10] said, O son of the devil, full of all guile and all cunning, enemy of all righteousness, will you not stop perverting the right ways of (the) Lord? [11] And now, behold, (the) hand of the Lord (is) on you, and you shall be blind, not seeing the sun for a time. And instantly a mist and darkness fell on him, and going about he sought some to lead (him) by the hand. [12] Then the proconsul having seen what had happened believed, being astonished at the teaching of the Lord.

[13] And having sailed from Paphos (with) those about (him), Paul came to Perga of Pamphylia; and John having separated from them returned to Jerusalem. [14] But they having passed through from Perga came to Antioch of Pisidia, and

Πνεῦμα τὸ Ἅγιον, Ἀφορίσατε δή μοι τόν τε Βαρνάβαν καὶ
Spirit    —    Holy,     separate So then to me — both Barnabas and

3 τὸν Σαῦλον εἰς τὸ ἔργον ὃ προσκέκλημαι αὐτούς. τότε νηστεύ-
   —   Saul    for the work to which I have called   them.    Then having
σαντες καὶ προσευξάμενοι καὶ ἐπιθέντες τὰς χεῖρας αὐτοῖς,
fasted and having prayed,    and placing on    the   hands to them,
ἀπέλυσαν.
they let (them) go.

4 Οὗτοι μὲν οὖν, ἐκπεμφθέντες ὑπὸ τοῦ Πνεύματος τοῦ
   These indeed therefore sent out     by     the     Spirit    —
Ἁγίου, κατῆλθον εἰς τὴν Σελεύκειαν, ἐκεῖθέν τε ἀπέπλευσαν
Holy,    went down to — Seleucia,    from there sailed away

5 εἰς τὴν Κύπρον. καὶ γενόμενοι ἐν Σαλαμῖνι, κατήγγελλον τὸν
to — Cyprus. And being   in Salamis, they announced the
λόγον τοῦ Θεοῦ ἐν ταῖς συναγωγαῖς τῶν Ἰουδαίων· εἶχον δὲ
word — of God in the synagogues of the    Jews. they had And

5 καὶ Ἰωάννην ὑπηρέτην. διελθόντες δὲ τὴν νῆσον ἄχρι
also    John   (as) assistant.   passing through And the island as far as
Πάφου, εὗρόν τινα μάγον ψευδοπροφήτην Ἰουδαῖον, ᾧ
Paphos, they found a certain conjurer, a false prophet,    a Jew,    whose

7 ὄνομα Βαριησοῦς, ὃς ἦν σὺν τῷ ἀνθυπάτῳ Σεργίῳ Παύλῳ,
name (was) Barjesus, who was with the Proconsul,    Sergius   Paulus,
ἀνδρὶ συνετῷ. οὗτος προσκαλεσάμενος Βαρνάβαν καὶ
a man intelligent. This one calling to (him)     Barnabas    and
Σαῦλον ἐπεζήτησεν ἀκοῦσαι τὸν λόγον τοῦ Θεοῦ. ἀνθίστατο
Saul     sought    to hear    the word   — of God. withstood

8 δὲ αὐτοῖς Ἐλύμας, ὁ μάγος (οὕτω γὰρ μεθερμηνεύεται τὸ
But them Elymas, the conjurer,    so    for was translated    the
ὄνομα αὐτοῦ), ζητῶν διαστρέψαι τὸν ἀνθύπατον ἀπὸ τῆς
name of him — seeking to turn away the Proconsul   from the

9 πίστεως. Σαῦλος δέ, ὁ καὶ Παῦλος, πλησθεὶς Πνεύματος
faith.     Saul    But, who also (is) Paul, being filled with (the) Spirit

10 Ἁγίου, καὶ ἀτενίσας εἰς αὐτὸν εἶπεν, Ὦ πλήρης παντὸς
Holy,    and looking intently on him   said,    O    full    of all
δόλου καὶ πάσης ῥᾳδιουργίας, υἱὲ διαβόλου, ἐχθρὲ πάσης
deceit, and of all    cunning,   son of (the) Devil, enemy of all
δικαιοσύνης, οὐ παύσῃ διαστρέφων τὰς ὁδοὺς Κυρίου τὰς
righteousness, not will you cease turning away the ways of (the) Lord —

11 εὐθείας; καὶ νῦν ἰδού, χεὶρ τοῦ Κυρίου ἐπὶ σέ, καὶ ἔσῃ τυφλός,
right? And now behold, hand the Lord's    on you, and you will be blind,
μὴ βλέπων τὸν ἥλιον ἄχρι καιροῦ. παραχρῆμα δὲ ἐπέπεσεν
not seeing the sun until a time.     instantly And fell
ἐπ' αὐτὸν ἀχλὺς καὶ σκότος, καὶ περιάγων ἐζήτει χειραγω-
on him a mist   and darkness, and going about he sought leaders by

12 γούς. τότε ἰδὼν ὁ ἀνθύπατος τὸ γεγονὸς ἐπίστευσεν,
the hand. Then seeing the Proconsul the thing having occurred believed,
ἐκπλησσόμενος ἐπὶ τῇ διδαχῇ τοῦ Κυρίου.
being astounded at the teaching of the Lord.

13 Ἀναχθέντες δὲ ἀπὸ τῆς Πάφου οἱ περὶ τὸν Παῦλον ἦλθον
   having put out And from — Paphos those around — Paul    came
εἰς Πέργην τῆς Παμφυλίας. Ἰωάννης δὲ ἀποχωρήσας ἀπ'
to Perga    — of Pamphylia. John     And having separated from

14 αὐτῶν ὑπέστρεψεν εἰς Ἱεροσόλυμα. αὐτοὶ δὲ διελθόντες ἀπὸ
them returned    to Jerusalem.    they And going through from
τῆς Πέργης, παρεγένοντο εἰς Ἀντιόχειαν τῆς Πισιδίας, καὶ
— Perga    arrived    in    Antioch    the Pisidian. And

having gone into the synagogue on the Sabbath day, they sat down. [15] And after the reading of the Law and of the Prophets, the rulers of the synagogue sent to them, saying, Men, brothers, if there is a word of exhortation among you to the people, speak. [16] And Paul having risen up, and signaling with the hand, said, Men, Israelites, and those fearing God, listen: [17] The God of this people Israel chose our fathers, and exalted the people in the sojourning in (the) land of Egypt, and with a high arm brought them out of it; [18] and as (passed) forty years time, He endured them in the desert. [19] And having destroyed seven nations in Canaan land, He gave their land to them by lot.

[20] And after these things, as four hundred and fifty years, He gave judges until Samuel the prophet. [21] And then they asked for a king, and God gave to them Saul the son of Kish, a man of (the) tribe of Benjamin, (for) forty years. [22] And having removed him, He raised up to them David for king, to whom also He said, having borne witness, I found David the (son) of Jesse a man according to My own heart, who will do all My will. [23] Of the seed of this one God according to promise raised up to Israel a Savior, Jesus; [24] John having before preached a baptism of repentance to all the people of Israel before (the) face of His entrance. [25] And as John was fulfilled (his) course, he said, Whom do you suppose me to be? I am not (He), but behold, He comes after me, of whom I am not worthy to untie the sandal of the feet. [26] Men, brothers, sons of (the) race of Abraham, and those among you fearing God, to you the word of this salvation was sent; [27] for those living

---

εἰσελθόντες εἰς τὴν συναγωγὴν τῇ ἡμέρᾳ τῶν σαββάτων,
going   into the synagogue   on the day   of the sabbaths

**15** ἐκάθισαν. μετὰ δὲ τὴν ἀνάγνωσιν τοῦ νόμου καὶ τῶν
sat down.   after And the   reading   of the   Law   and of the

προφητῶν, ἀπέστειλαν οἱ ἀρχισυνάγωγοι πρὸς αὐτούς,
Prophets,   sent forth   the   synagogue rulers   to   them,

λέγοντες, "Ἄνδρες ἀδελφοί, εἰ ἔστι λόγος ἐν ὑμῖν παρακλή-
saying,   Men, brothers, if   is   a word among you of exhort-

**16** σεως πρὸς τὸν λαόν, λέγετε. ἀναστὰς δὲ Παῦλος, καὶ
ation to   the people, say (it). rising up And   Paul,   and

κατασείσας τῇ χειρί, εἶπεν,
signaling with the hand, he said,

"Ἄνδρες Ἰσραηλῖται, καὶ οἱ φοβούμενοι τὸν Θεόν, ἀκού-
Men,   Israelites,   and those fearing   —   God,

**17** σατε. ὁ Θεὸς τοῦ λαοῦ τούτου Ἰσραὴλ ἐξελέξατο τοὺς
hear: The God   — of people   this   Israel   chose out   the

πατέρας ἡμῶν, καὶ τὸν λαὸν ὕψωσεν ἐν τῇ παροικίᾳ ἐν γῇ
fathers   of us,   and the people   exalted   in the sojourn   in land

Αἰγύπτῳ, καὶ μετὰ βραχίονος ὑψηλοῦ ἐξήγαγεν αὐτοὺς ἐξ
(of) Egypt, and   with an arm   high   He led out   them out of

**18** αὐτῆς. καὶ ὡς τεσσαρακονταετῆ χρόνον ἐτροποφόρησεν
it.   And as (passed) forty years   time,   He endured

**19** αὐτοὺς ἐν τῇ ἐρήμῳ. καὶ καθελὼν ἔθνη ἑπτὰ ἐν γῇ Χαναάν,
them   in the desert. And   pulled down nations seven   in land Canaan,

**20** κατεκληροδότησεν αὐτοῖς τὴν γῆν αὐτῶν. καὶ μετὰ ταῦτα,
gave as an inheritance to them the land of them. And after these things,

ὡς ἔτεσι τετρακοσίοις καὶ πεντήκοντα, ἔδωκε κριτὰς ἕως
as years   four hundred   and fifty,   He gave judges, until

**21** Σαμουὴλ τοῦ προφήτου. κἀκεῖθεν ᾐτήσαντο βασιλέα, καὶ
Samuel   the   prophet. And from there they asked a king,   and

ἔδωκεν αὐτοῖς ὁ Θεὸς τὸν Σαοὺλ υἱὸν Κίς, ἄνδρα ἐκ φυλῆς
gave them   God   —   Saul   son of Kish, a man of   tribe

**22** Βενιαμίν, ἔτη τεσσαράκοντα. καὶ μεταστήσας αὐτόν. ἤγειρεν
of Benjamin, years   forty.   And removing   him, He raised

αὐτοῖς τὸν Δαβὶδ εἰς βασιλέα, ᾧ καὶ εἶπε μαρτυρήσας, Εὗρον
to them — David for a king, to whom also He said, witnessing, I found

Δαβὶδ τὸν τοῦ Ἰεσσαί, ἄνδρα κατὰ τὴν καρδίαν μου, ὃς
David   the (son) of Jesse   a man according to the heart of Me, who

**23** ποιήσει πάντα τὰ θελήματά μου. τούτου ὁ Θεὸς ἀπὸ τοῦ
will do   all   the   desires   of Me. Of this one   God from the

σπέρματος κατ' ἐπαγγελίαν ἤγειρε τῷ Ἰσραὴλ σωτῆρα
seed according to   promise   raised   —   to Israel a Savior,

**24** Ἰησοῦν, προκηρύξαντος Ἰωάννου πρὸ προσώπου τῆς
Jesus.   Previously proclaiming John,   before   (the) face of the

εἰσόδου αὐτοῦ βάπτισμα μετανοίας παντὶ τῷ λαῷ Ἰσραήλ.
coming of Him a baptism of repentance to all the people of Israel.

**25** ὡς δὲ ἐπλήρου ὁ Ἰωάννης τὸν δρόμον, ἔλεγε, Τίνα με
as And fulfilled   —   John   the course, he said, Whom me

ὑπονοεῖτε εἶναι ; οὐκ εἰμὶ ἐγώ. ἀλλ' ἰδού, ἔρχεται μετ' ἐμέ,
do you suppose to be? not   am I (He), but behold, He comes after me,

**26** οὗ οὐκ εἰμὶ ἄξιος τὸ ὑπόδημα τῶν ποδῶν λῦσαι. ἄνδρες
of whom not I am worthy the sandal   of (His) feet to loosen.   Men,

ἀδελφοί, υἱοὶ γένους Ἀβραάμ, καὶ οἱ ἐν ὑμῖν φοβούμενοι τὸν
brothers,   sons of (the) race of Abraham, and those in you   fearing   —

**27** Θεόν, ὑμῖν ὁ λόγος τῆς σωτηρίας ταύτης ἀπεστάλη. οἱ γὰρ
God. to you the word   of salvation   this was sent forth. those For

in Jerusalem and their rulers not having known him and the voices of the prophets who on every Sabbath are read, having judged they fulfilled. [28] And no one having found cause of death, they begged Pilate to destroy Him. [29] And as they fulfilled all things having been written about Him, taking (Him) down from the tree, they laid (Him) in a tomb. [30] But God raised Him from (the) dead. [31] who appeared for many days to those who came up with Him from Galilee to Jerusalem, who are His witnesses to the people. [32] And we preach the gospel to you, the promise made to the fathers, that this God has fulfilled tó us their children, having raised up Jesus; [33] as also it has been written in the Psalm, "You are My Son; today I have begotten You." [34] And that He raised Him from among (the) dead, no more going to be returned to corruption, He spoke this, "I will give to You the sure mercies of David." [35] Then also in another, he says, "You will not allow Your Holy One to see corruption." [36] For truly David having served his own generation by the counsel of God fell asleep, and was added to his fathers; and saw corruption. [37] But whom God raised up did not see corruption. [38] Be it known to you, therefore, men, brothers, that through this One remission of sin is preached to you, [39] and in Him everyone that believes is justified from all things from which you could not be justified in the law of Moses. [40] Be careful, therefore, that it may not come on you the thing spoken in the prophets: [41] "Behold, (you) despisers, and marvel, and be ruined! For I work a work in your days, a work which you would in no way believe if one should declare it to you." [42] But the Jews having left the synagogue, the

κατοικοῦντες ἐν Ἱερουσαλὴμ καὶ οἱ ἄρχοντες αὐτῶν, τοῦτον
dwelling in Jerusalem and the rulers of them, this One
ἀγνοήσαντες, καὶ τὰς φωνὰς τῶν προφητῶν τὰς κατὰ πᾶν
not knowing, and the voices of the prophets throughout every

28 σάββατον ἀναγινωσκομένας, κρίναντες ἐπλήρωσαν. καὶ
sabbath being read, having judged (Him), they fulfilled. And
μηδεμίαν αἰτίαν θανάτου εὑρόντες, ἠτήσαντο Πιλάτον
not one cause of death having found, they asked Pilate

29 ἀναιρεθῆναι αὐτόν. ὡς δὲ ἐτέλεσαν ἅπαντα τὰ περὶ αὐτοῦ
do away (with) Him. when And they finished all the things about Him
γεγραμ ἐνα, καθελόντες ἀπὸ τοῦ ξύλου, ἔθηκαν εἰς μνημεῖον.
having been w. .ten, taking down from the tree, they laid in a tomb.

30 ὁ δὲ Θεὸς ἤγειρεν αὐτὸν ἐκ νεκρῶν· ὃς ὤφθη ἐπὶ ἡμέρας
But God raised Him from (the) dead; who appeared for days
31 πλείους τοῖς συναναβᾶσιν αὐτῷ ἀπὸ τῆς Γαλιλαίας εἰς
many to those coming up with Him from — Galilee to
32 Ἱερουσαλήμ, οἵτινές εἰσι μάρτυρες αὐτοῦ πρὸς τὸν λαόν. καὶ
Jerusalem, who are witnesses of Him to the people. And
ἡμεῖς ὑμᾶς εὐαγγελιζόμεθα τὴν πρὸς τοὺς πατέρας ἐπαγ-
we (to) you preach the gospel, the to the fathers promise
γελίαν γενομένην, ὅτι ταύτην ὁ Θεὸς ἐκπεπλήρωκε τοῖς
having come, that this (promise) God has fulfilled to the

33 τέκνοις αὐτῶν ἡμῖν, ἀναστήσας Ἰησοῦν· ὡς καὶ ἐν τῷ ψαλμῷ
children of them to us, raising up Jesus, as also in the Psalm
τῷ δευτέρῳ γέγραπται, Υἱός μου εἶ σύ, ἐγὼ σήμερον
second, it has been written: Son of Me are You, I today
34 γεγέννηκά σε. ὅτι δὲ ἀνέστησεν αὐτὸν ἐκ νεκρῶν, μηκέτι
have begotten You. that And He raised up Him from (the) dead, no more
μέλλοντα ὑποστρέφειν εἰς διαφθοράν, οὕτως εἴρηκεν ὅτι
being about to return to corruption, thus He has said, —
35 Δώσω ὑμῖν τὰ ὅσια Δαβὶδ τὰ πιστά. διὸ καὶ ἐν ἑτέρῳ λέγει,
I will give You the holy things of David faithful. Thus also in another He says,
36 Οὐ δώσεις τὸν ὅσιόν σου ἰδεῖν διαφθοράν. Δαβὶδ μὲν γὰρ
Not You will give the holy one of You to see corruption. David indeed For
ἰδίᾳ γενεᾷ ὑπηρετήσας τῇ τοῦ Θεοῦ βουλῇ ἐκοιμήθη, καὶ
own generation having served by the — of God counsel fell asleep, and
37 προσετέθη πρὸς τοὺς πατέρας αὐτοῦ, καὶ εἶδε διαφθοράν· ὃν
was added to the fathers of him, and saw corruption. whom
38 δὲ ὁ Θεὸς ἤγειρεν, οὐκ εἶδε διαφθοράν. γνωστὸν οὖν ἔστω
But God raised up, not He saw corruption. Known, therefore, let it be
ὑμῖν, ἄνδρες ἀδελφοί, ὅτι διὰ τούτου ὑμῖν ἄφεσις ἁμαρτιῶν
to you, men, brothers, that through this One to you forgiveness of sins
39 καταγγέλλεται· καὶ ἀπὸ πάντων ὧν οὐκ ἠδυνήθητε ἐν τῷ
is announced; and from all things which not you could by the
νόμῳ Μωσέως δικαιωθῆναι, ἐν τούτῳ πᾶς ὁ πιστεύων
law of Moses be justified, in this One everyone — believing
40 δικαιοῦται. βλέπετε οὖν μὴ ἐπέλθῃ ἐφ' ὑμᾶς τὸ εἰρημένον ἐν
is justified. Look, then (that) come on you the thing spoken in
not
41 τοῖς προφήταις, Ἴδετε, οἱ καταφρονηταί, καὶ θαυμάσατε,
the prophets; See, the despisers, and marvel,
καὶ ἀφανίσθητε· ὅτι ἔργον ἐγὼ ἐργάζομαι ἐν ταῖς ἡμέραις
and vanish, because a work I work in the days
ὑμῶν, ἔργον ᾧ οὐ μὴ πιστεύσητε, ἐάν τις ἐκδιηγῆται ὑμῖν.
of you; a work which in no way you believe if anyone declare (it) to you.
42 Ἐξιόντων δὲ ἐκ τῆς συναγωγῆς τῶν Ἰουδαίων, παρεκά-
going out And of the synagogue, the Jews begged

Gentiles begged these words to be spoken to them on the next Sabbath. [43] And the synagogue having broken up, many of the Jews and of the worshiping proselytes followed Paul and Barnabas, who speaking to them persuaded them to continue in the grace of God.

[44] And on the coming Sabbath almost all the city was gathered to hear the word of God. [45] But having seen the crowd, the Jews were filled with envy, and contradicted the things spoken by Paul, contradicting and blaspheming. [46] But speaking boldly Paul and Barnabas said, (It was) necessary the word of God be spoken to you first; but since you thrust it away, and you judge yourselves not worthy of everlasting life, behold, we turn to the natives; [47] for so the Lord has commanded us, "I have set You for a light of the nations, that You be for a salvation to (the) ends of the earth." [48] And hearing the natives rejoiced, and glorified the word of the Lord, as many as were appointed to eternal life believed. [49] And the word of the Lord was carried through the whole country. [50] But the Jews excited the devoted and honorable women, and the chief men of the city, and stirred up a persecution against Paul and Barnabas, and threw them out from their borders. [51] But having shaken off the dust of their feet against them, they came to Iconium. [52] And the disciples were filled with joy and (the) Holy Spirit.

CHAPTER 14

[1] And it happened in Iconium, they went in together into the synagogue of the Jews, and spoke so that a great number both of Jews and Greeks believed.

43 λουν τὰ ἔθνη εἰς τὸ μεταξὺ σάββατον λαληθῆναι αὐτοῖς
the Gentiles on    the   next   sabbath   to be spoken to   them
τὰ ῥήματα ταῦτα. λυθείσης δὲ τῆς συναγωγῆς, ἠκολούθησαν
words  these.  being broken And the synagogue,     followed
πολλοὶ τῶν Ἰουδαίων καὶ τῶν σεβομένων προσηλύτων τῷ
many of the  Jews    and of the  devout    proselytes   —
Παύλῳ καὶ τῷ Βαρνάβᾳ· οἵτινες προσλαλοῦντες αὐτοῖς,
Paul   and —  Barnabas,   who    speaking to       them
ἔπειθον αὐτοὺς ἐπιμένειν τῇ χάριτι τοῦ Θεοῦ.
persuaded them  to continue in the grace   of God.

44 Τῷ δὲ ἐρχομένῳ σαββάτῳ σχεδὸν πᾶσα ἡ πόλις συνήχθη
in the And coming   sabbath  almost  all the city was gathered

45 ἀκοῦσαι τὸν λόγον τοῦ Θεοῦ. ἰδόντες δὲ οἱ Ἰουδαῖοι τοὺς
to hear    the  word  — of God. seeing And the  Jews     the
ὄχλους ἐπλήσθησαν ζήλου, καὶ ἀντέλεγον τοῖς ὑπὸ τοῦ
crowds, they were filled of jealousy, and contradicted the things by  —
Παύλου λεγομένοις, ἀντιλέγοντες καὶ βλασφημοῦντες.
Paul,    being spoken,   contradicting   and  blaspheming.

46 παρρησιασάμενοι δὲ ὁ Παῦλος καὶ ὁ Βαρνάβας εἶπον, Ὑμῖν
speaking boldly  But — Paul   and — Barnabas   said, To you
ἦν ἀναγκαῖον πρῶτον λαληθῆναι τὸν λόγον τοῦ Θεοῦ.
it was necessary  firstly   to be spoken  the  word  — of God.
ἐπειδὴ δὲ ἀπωθεῖσθε αὐτόν, καὶ οὐκ ἀξίους κρίνετε ἑαυτοὺς
since
indeed But you put away  it,   and not worthy  judge  yourselves

47 τῆς αἰωνίου ζωῆς, ἰδοὺ στρεφόμεθα εἰς τὰ ἔθνη. οὕτω γὰρ
of the eternal  life,  behold,  we turn   to the nations. so   For
ἐντέταλται ἡμῖν ὁ Κύριος, Τέθεικά σε εἰς φῶς ἐθνῶν, τοῦ
has commanded us the Lord; I have set You for a light of nations —

48 εἶναί σε εἰς σωτηρίαν ἕως ἐσχάτου τῆς γῆς. ἀκούοντα δὲ τὰ
to be You for salvation  to (the) end  of the earth. hearing And the
ἔθνη ἔχαιρον, καὶ ἐδόξαζον τὸν λόγον τοῦ Κυρίου, καὶ
nations rejoiced, and  glorified  the  word  of the Lord.  And

49 ἐπίστευσαν ὅσοι ἦσαν τεταγμένοι εἰς ζωὴν αἰώνιον. διεφέ-
believed  as many as were  appointed  to  life   eternal.   was

50 ρετο δὲ ὁ λόγος του Κυρίου δι' ὅλης τῆς χώρας. οἱ δὲ
carried And the word of the Lord through all  the  country. the But
Ἰουδαῖοι παρώτρυναν τὰς σεβομένας γυναῖκας καὶ τὰς
Jews     urged on       the  devout     women   and —
εὐσχήμονας καὶ τοὺς πρώτους τῆς πόλεως, καὶ ἐπήγειραν
hnorable,   and   the  chief ones of the city;  and  raised up
διωγμὸν ἐπὶ τὸν Παῦλον καὶ τὸν Βαρνάβαν, καὶ ἐξέβαλον·
persecution against — Paul  and — Barnabas,   and threw out

51 αὐτοὺς ἀπὸ τῶν ὁρίων αὐτῶν. οἱ δὲ ἐκτιναξάμενοι τὸν
them   from  the  borders of them.  they And shaking off  the
κονιορτὸν τῶν ποδῶν αὐτῶν ἐπ' αὐτούς, ἦλθον εἰς Ἰκόνιον.
dust    of the  feet of them on   them, they came into Iconium.

52 οἱ δὲ μαθηταὶ ἐπληροῦντο χαρᾶς καὶ Πνεύματος Ἁγίου.
the And disciples were filled from joy,  and from (the) Spirit Holy.

CHAPTER 14

1 Ἐγένετο δὲ ἐν Ἰκονίῳ, κατὰ τὸ αὐτὸ εἰσελθεῖν αὐτοὺς εἰς
it happened And in Iconium,    together    entered   them into
τὴν συναγωγὴν τῶν Ἰουδαίων, καὶ λαλῆσαι οὕτως ὥστε
the  synagogue  of the  Jews,    and to speak  so    as
πιστεῦσαι Ἰουδαίων τε καὶ Ἑλλήνων πολὺ πλῆθος. οἱ δὲ
to believe  of Jews both and of Greeks,  a much multitude. the But

[2] But the unbelieving Jews raised up and made malignant the souls of the Gentiles against the brothers. [3] Then they stayed a long time, speaking boldly in the Lord, who bore witness to the word of His grace, and giving miracles and wonders to be done through their hands. [4] And the multitude of the city was divided, and some were with the Jews and some with the apostles. [5] And when there was a rush both of the nations and Jews, with their rulers, to insult and to stone them, [6] they perceiving escaped to the cities of Lycaonia, Lystra, and Derbe, and the country around. [7] And they were preaching the gospel.

[8] And a certain man sat in Lystra, powerless in the feet, being lame from his mother's womb, who never had walked. [9] This one heard Paul speaking, who having looked intently on him, and seeing that he had faith to be healed, [10] said with a loud voice, Stand up on your feet upright! And he sprang up and walked. [11] And the crowd having seen what Paul did, lifted up their voice in Lycaonian saying, The gods having become like men are come down to us. [12] And they called Barnabas, Zeus; and Paul, Hermes, because he was the leader in speaking. [13] And the priest of Zeus who was before their city, having carried oxen and garlands to the gates, wished to sacrifice with the crowd. [14] But the apostles having heard, Barnabas and Paul, having torn their garments, rushed into the crowd, crying out, [15] and saying, Men, why do you do these things? We also are men of like feelings with you, to turn from these vanities to the living God, who made the Heaven and the earth and the sea, and all things in them; [16] who in the past

**2** ἀπειθοῦντες Ἰουδαῖοι ἐπήγειραν καὶ ἐκάκωσαν τὰς ψυχὰς
disobeying Jews raised up and embittered the souls

**3** τῶν ἐθνῶν κατὰ τῶν ἀδελφῶν. ἱκανὸν μὲν οὖν χρόνον
of the Gentiles against the brothers. A considerable therefore time
διέτριψαν παρρησιαζόμενοι ἐπὶ τῷ Κυρίῳ τῷ μαρτυροῦντι
they stayed speaking boldly on the Lord witnessing
τῷ λόγῳ τῆς χάριτος αὐτοῦ, καὶ διδόντι σημεῖα καὶ τέρατα
to the word of the grace of Him, and giving signs and wonders

**4** γίνεσθαι διὰ τῶν χειρῶν αὐτῶν. ἐσχίσθη δὲ τὸ πλῆθος τῆς
to happen through the hands of them. was divided But the multitude of the
πόλεως· καὶ οἱ μὲν ἦσαν σὺν τοῖς Ἰουδαίοις, οἱ δὲ σὺν τοῖς
city, and some were with the Jews, others but with the

**5** ἀποστόλοις. ὡς δὲ ἐγένετο ὁρμὴ τῶν ἐθνῶν τε καὶ Ἰουδαίων
apostles. when And occurred a rush of the Gentitles, even and Jews,
σὺν τοῖς ἄρχουσιν αὐτῶν, ὑβρίσαι καὶ λιθοβολῆσαι αὐτούς,
with the rulers of them, to insult and to stone them;

**6** συνιδόντες κατέφυγον εἰς τὰς πόλεις τῆς Λυκαονίας, Λύστραν
perceiving they fled to the cities — of Lycaonia, Lystra,

**7** καὶ Δέρβην, καὶ τὴν περίχωρον· κἀκεῖ ἦσαν εὐαγγελιζόμενοι.
and Derbe, and the surrounding country; and there they were evangelizing.

**8** Καί τις ἀνὴρ ἐν Λύστροις ἀδύνατος τοῖς ποσὶν ἐκάθητο,
And a certain man in Lystra powerless in the feet was sitting
χωλὸς ἐκ κοιλίας μητρὸς αὐτοῦ ὑπάρχων, ὃς οὐδέποτε
lame from (the) womb of (the) mother of him being, who never

**9** περιεπεπατήκει. οὗτος ἤκουε τοῦ Παύλου λαλοῦντος· ὃς
had walked. This one heard — Paul speaking, who

**10** ἀτενίσας αὐτῷ, καὶ ἰδὼν ὅτι πίστιν ἔχει τοῦ σωθῆναι, εἶπε
looking at him and seeing that faith he has — to be cured, said
μεγάλῃ τῇ φωνῇ, Ἀνάστηθι ἐπὶ τοὺς πόδας σου ὀρθός. καὶ
with a great voice, Stand up on the feet of you erect. And

**11** ἥλλετο καὶ περιεπάτει. οἱ δὲ ὄχλοι, ἰδόντες ὃ ἐποίησεν ὁ
he leaped and walked about. the And crowds seeing what did
Παῦλος, ἐπῆραν τὴν φωνὴν αὐτῶν Λυκαονιστὶ λέγοντες, Οἱ
Paul lifted up the voice of them in Lycaonian, saying, The

**12** θεοὶ ὁμοιωθέντες ἀνθρώποις κατέβησαν πρὸς ἡμᾶς. ἐκάλουν
gods having become like men have come down to us. they called
τε τὸν μὲν Βαρνάβαν, Δία· τὸν δὲ Παῦλον, Ἑρμῆν, ἐπειδὴ
And — Barnabas, Zeus; — and Paul, Hermes; since

**13** αὐτὸς ἦν ὁ ἡγούμενος τοῦ λόγου. ὁ δὲ ἱερεὺς τοῦ Διὸς τοῦ
he was the leader of the speaking. the But priest — of Zeus —
ὄντος πρὸ τῆς πόλεως αὐτῶν, ταύρους καὶ στέμματα ἐπὶ τοὺς
being before the city of them, bulls and garlands to the

**14** πυλῶνας ἐνέγκας, σὺν τοῖς ὄχλοις ἤθελε θύειν. ἀκούσαντες δὲ
gates carrying, with the crowds wished to sacrifice. hearing And
οἱ ἀπόστολοι Βαρνάβας καὶ Παῦλος, διαρρήξαντες τὰ ἱμάτια
the apostles Barnabas and Paul, having torn the garments
αὐτῶν, εἰσεπήδησαν εἰς τὸν ὄχλον, κράζοντες καὶ λέγοντες,
of them, sprang into the crowd, crying out and saying,

**15** Ἄνδρες, τί ταῦτα ποιεῖτε; καὶ ἡμεῖς ὁμοιοπαθεῖς ἐσμεν ὑμῖν
Men, why these things do you? Also we of like feelings are to you
ἄνθρωποι, εὐαγγελιζόμενοι ὑμᾶς ἀπὸ τούτων τῶν ματαίων
men, preaching the gospel to you from these — vanities
ἐπιστρέφειν ἐπὶ τὸν Θεὸν τὸν ζῶντα, ὃς ἐποίησε τὸν οὐρανὸν
to turn to the God living; who made the heaven

**16** καὶ τὴν γῆν καὶ τὴν θάλασσαν καὶ πάντα τὰ ἐν αὐτοῖς· ὃς ἐν
and the earth and the sea, and all things in them; who in

generations allowed all the nations to go in their (own) ways, [17] though indeed He did not leave Himself without witness, doing good, giving rains and fruiful seasons to us from Heaven, filling our hearts with food and gladness. [18] And saying these things, they hardly stopped the crowd from sacrificing to them. [19] But Jews came there from Antioch and Iconium, and having persuaded the crowd, and having stoned Paul, drew (him) outside the city, supposing him to have died. [20] But the disciples having surrounded him, having risen up, he entered into the city. And on the morrow he went away with Barnabas to Derbe. [21] And having preached the gospel to that city, and having discipled many, they returned to Lystra and Iconium and Antioch, [22] establishing the souls of the disciples, exhorting to continue in the faith, and that through many tribulations we must enter into the kingdom of God. [23] And having chosen elders for them in every church having prayed with fastings, they committed them to the Lord, on whom they had believed. [24] And having passed through Pisidia, they came to Pamphylia, [25] and having spoken the word in Perga, they came down to Attalia; [26] and from there they sailed to Antioch, from where they had been committed to the grace of God for the work which they fulfilled. [27] And having arrived and having gathered together the assembly, they told all that God did with them, and that He opened a door of faith to the nations. [28] And they stayed there not a little time with the disciples.

## CHAPTER 15

[1] And certain ones having come down from Judea were teaching the

ταῖς παρῳχημέναις γενεαῖς εἴασε πάντα τὰ ἔθνη πορεύεσθαι
the having passed by generations allowed all    the nations  to go

17 ταῖς ὁδοῖς αὐτῶν. καίτοιγε οὐκ ἀμάρτυρον ἑαυτὸν ἀφῆκεν
the  ways of them. And yet    not    without witness Himself left,

ἀγαθοποιῶν, οὐρανόθεν ἡμῖν ὑετοὺς διδοὺς καὶ καιροὺς
doing good,    from heaven to us  rain   giving  and  seasons

καρποφόρους, ἐμπιπλῶν τροφῆς καὶ εὐφροσύνης τὰς καρδίας
fruit-bearing    filling    of food and of gladness  the  hearts

18 ἡμῶν. καὶ ταῦτα λέγοντες, μόλις κατέπαυσαν τοὺς ὄχλους
of us. And these things saying,  hardly they stopped   the   crowds

τοῦ μὴ θύειν αὐτοῖς.
— not to sacrifice to them.

19 Ἐπῆλθον δὲ ἀπὸ Ἀντιοχείας καὶ Ἰκονίου Ἰουδαῖοι, καὶ
came over And from  Antioch   and  Iconium   Jews,   and

πείσαντες τοὺς ὄχλους, καὶ λιθάσαντες τὸν Παῦλον, ἔσυρον
persuading the crowds,  and  stoning    —  Paul, they dragged

ἔξω τῆς πόλεως, νομίσαντες αὐτὸν τεθνάναι. κυκλωσάντων
outside the city,  supposing  him to have died.  having surrounded

20 δὲ αὐτὸν τῶν μαθητῶν, ἀναστὰς εἰσῆλθεν εἰς τὴν πόλιν· καὶ
But him   the disciples,  rising up he entered  into the city.  And

21 τῇ ἐπαύριον ἐξῆλθε σὺν τῷ Βαρνάβᾳ εἰς Δέρβην. εὐαγγελι-
on the morrow he went  with — Barnabas  to Derbe.  preaching

σάμενοί τε τὴν πόλιν ἐκείνην, καὶ μαθητεύσαντες ἱκανούς,
the gospel And — city   to that, and having made disciples  many,

ὑπέστρεψαν εἰς τὴν Λύστραν καὶ Ἰκόνιον καὶ Ἀντιόχειαν,
they returned to  —  Lystra  and  Iconium and  Antioch,

22 ἐπιστηρίζοντες τὰς ψυχὰς τῶν μαθητῶν, παρακαλοῦντες
confirming    the  souls  of the  disciples,   exhorting

ἐμμένειν τῇ πίστει, καὶ ὅτι διὰ πολλῶν θλίψεων δεῖ ἡμᾶς
to continue in the faith, and that through many    afflictions must we

23 εἰσελθεῖν εἰς τὴν βασιλείαν τοῦ Θεοῦ. χειροτονήσαντες δὲ
enter    into the  kingdom  — of God. having hand-picked  And

αὐτοῖς πρεσβυτέρους κατ᾽ ἐκκλησίαν, προσευξάμενοι μετὰ
for them  elders     in (every) church   praying      with

νηστειῶν, παρέθεντο αὐτοὺς τῷ Κυρίῳ εἰς ὃν πεπιστεύ-
fastings,  they committed them to the  Lord  in whom they had

24 κεισαν. καὶ διελθόντες τὴν Πισιδίαν ἦλθον εἰς Παμφυλίαν.
believed. And passing through — Pisidia,  they came to Pamphylia.

25 καὶ λαλήσαντες ἐν Πέργῃ τὸν λόγον, κατέβησαν εἰς Ἀττά-
And speaking   in Perga  the word,  they came down to Attalia,

26 λειαν· κἀκεῖθεν ἀπέπλευσαν εἰς Ἀντιόχειαν, ὅθεν ἦσαν
and from there  sailed away    to   Antioch,  from where they had

παραδεδομένοι τῇ χάριτι τοῦ Θεοῦ εἰς τὸ ἔργον ὃ ἐπλή-
been committed to the grace  of God for the  work which they

27 ρωσαν. παραγενόμενοι δὲ καὶ συναγαγόντες τὴν ἐκκλησίαν,
fulfilled. having arrived And, and gathering    the   church,

ἀνήγγειλαν ὅσα ἐποίησεν ὁ Θεὸς μετ᾽ αὐτῶν, καὶ ὅτι ἤνοιξε
they reported what things did  God with  them, and that He opened

28 τοῖς ἔθνεσι θύραν πίστεως. διέτριβον δὲ ἐκεῖ χρόνον οὐκ
to the Gentiles a door  of faith.  they continued And there  a time  not

ὀλίγον σὺν τοῖς μαθηταῖς.
little  with the  disciples.

## CHAPTER 15

1 Καί τινες κατελθόντες ἀπὸ τῆς Ἰουδαίας, ἐδίδασκον τοὺς
And some  going down from  —  Judea    taught    the

brothers, Unless you are circumcised after the custom of Moses you cannot be saved. [2] Therefore a commotion having taken place, and not a little discussion by Paul and Barnabas with them, they chose Paul and Barnabas to go up and certain others from among them to the apostles and elders, to Jerusalem, about this question. [3] Then indeed having been sent forward by the church, they passed through Phoenicia and Samaria, telling about the conversion of the Gentiles. And they caused great joy to all the brothers.

[4] And having arrived into Jerusalem, they were welcomed by the church, and the apostles and the elders, and they declared all that God did with them. [5] And certain of those of the sect of the Pharisees who believed rose up, saying, It is necessary to circumcize them, and command to keep the law of Moses. [6] And the apostles and the elders were gathered together to see about this matter. [7] And much discussion having taken place, having risen up Peter said to them, Men, brothers, you know that from early days God chose among us (that) through my mouth the nations (were) to hear the word of the gospel and believe. [8] And the heart-knowing God bore witness to them, giving to them the Holy Spirit, as also to us. [9] And (He) put no difference both us and them, having purified their hearts by the faith. [10] Now, therefore, why do you tempt God to put a yoke on the neck of the disciples, which neither our fathers nor we were able to bear? [11] But by the grace of (the) Lord Jesus Christ we believe to be saved in the same way as

ἀδελφοὺς ὅτι Ἐὰν μὴ περιτέμνησθε τῷ ἔθει Μωϋσέως, οὐ
brothers     If not  are circumcised by the custom of Moses,  not

2 δύνασθε σωθῆναι. γενομένης οὖν στάσεως καὶ συζητήσεως
you can  be saved.  occurring Then discord and  discussion

οὐκ ὀλίγης τῷ Παύλῳ καὶ τῷ Βαρνάβᾳ πρὸς αὐτούς, ἔταξαν
not a little — by Paul and — Barnabas with them, they chose

ἀναβαίνειν Παῦλον καὶ Βαρνάβαν καί τινας ἄλλους ἐξ
to go up   Paul   and   Barnabas  and   some others of

αὐτῶν πρὸς τοὺς ἀποστόλους καὶ πρεσβυτέρους εἰς Ἱερου-
them  to the   apostles   and   elders   to

3 σαλὴμ περὶ τοῦ ζητήματος τούτου. οἱ μὲν οὖν, προπεμ-
Jerusalem about —  question  this.  they Therefore being set

φθέντες ὑπὸ τῆς ἐκκλησίας, διήρχοντο τὴν Φοινίκην καὶ
forward  by the church,  passed through — Phoenicia and

Σαμάρειαν, ἐκδιηγούμενοι τὴν ἐπιστροφὴν τῶν ἐθνῶν· καὶ
Samaria,  telling about  the conversion of the Gentiles and

4 ἐποίουν χαρὰν μεγάλην πᾶσι τοῖς ἀδελφοῖς. παραγενό-
they caused joy  great  to all the  brothers.  having arrived

μενοι δὲ εἰς Ἱερουσαλήμ, ἀπεδέχθησαν ὑπὸ τῆς ἐκκλησίας
And to Jerusalem,  they were welcomed by the church,

καὶ τῶν ἀποστόλων καὶ τῶν πρεσβυτέρων, ἀνήγγειλάν τε
and the  apostles  and the  elders,  reported and

5 ὅσα ὁ Θεὸς ἐποίησε μετ' αὐτῶν. ἐξανέστησαν δέ τινες τῶν
what things God did  with  them.  rise forth But some of those

ἀπὸ τῆς αἱρέσεως τῶν Φαρισαίων πεπιστευκότες, λέγοντες
from the sect  of the Pharisees  having believed, saying,

ὅτι Δεῖ περιτέμνειν αὐτούς, παραγγέλλειν τε τηρεῖν τὸν
—It is right to circumcise them,  to command and to keep the

νόμον Μωϋσέως.
law  of Moses.

6 Συνήχθησαν δὲ οἱ ἀπόστολοι καὶ οἱ πρεσβύτεροι ἰδεῖν
were assembled And the  apostles  and the  elders  to see

7 περὶ τοῦ λόγου τούτου. πολλῆς δὲ συζητήσεως γενομένης,
about — matter this.  much And discussion having occurred,

ἀναστὰς Πέτρος εἶπε πρὸς αὐτούς,
rising up  Peter  said to  them,

Ἄνδρες ἀδελφοί, ὑμεῖς ἐπίστασθε ὅτι ἀφ' ἡμερῶν ἀρχαίων
Men,  brothers, you understand that from days  ancient

ὁ Θεὸς ἐν ἡμῖν ἐξελέξατο, διὰ τοῦ στόματός μου ἀκοῦσαι
God among us  chose  through the mouth of me to hear

8 τὰ ἔθνη τὸν λόγον τοῦ εὐαγγελίου, καὶ πιστεῦσαι. καὶ ὁ
the nations the word of the  gospel,  and to believe. And the

καρδιογνώστης Θεὸς ἐμαρτύρησεν αὐτοῖς, δοὺς αὐτοῖς τὸ
heart-knowing  God witnessed  to them, giving them the

9 Πνεῦμα τὸ Ἅγιον, καθὼς καὶ ἡμῖν· καὶ οὐδὲν διέκρινε μεταξὺ
Spirit — Holy, as also to us, and nothing distinguished be-tween

ἡμῶν τε καὶ αὐτῶν, τῇ πίστει καθαρίσας τὰς καρδίας αὐτῶν.
us both and them, by faith having cleansed the hearts of them.

10 νῦν οὖν τί πειράζετε τὸν Θεόν, ἐπιθεῖναι ζυγὸν ἐπὶ τὸν
Now, then, why do you tempt — God, to put  a yoke on the

τράχηλον τῶν μαθητῶν, ὃν οὔτε οἱ πατέρες ἡμῶν οὔτε ἡμεῖς
neck  of the disciples, which neither the fathers of us nor we

11 ἰσχύσαμεν βαστάσαι ; ἀλλὰ διὰ τῆς χάριτος Κυρίου Ἰησοῦ
were able to bear?  But through the grace of (the) Lord Jesus

Χριστοῦ πιστεύομεν σωθῆναι, καθ' ὃν τρόπον κἀκεῖνοι.
Christ  we believe  to be saved by which means (as) even they.

they also. [12] And all the multitude kept silence and heard Barnabas and Paul telling what God did, the miracles and wonders among the nations by them. [13] And after the silence of them, James answered, saying, Men, brothers, hear me. [14] Simon told how God first oversaw to take a people out of the nations for His name. [15] And with this agree the words of the prophets, as it has been written, [16] "After these things I will return and will build again the tabernacle of David which is fallen; and I will build the ruins of it again, and I will set it up, [17] so that the men who are left may seek out the Lord, and all the nations on whom My name has been called, says the Lord, who is doing these things." [18] All His works are known to God from eternity. [19] Therefore I judge not to trouble those from the nations turning to God; [20] but to write to them to abstain from the pollutions of idols, and fornication, and that strangled, and blood. [21] For Moses from ancient generations has those proclaiming him, being read in the synagogues on every sabbath.

[22] Then it seemed good to the apostles and the elders with all the church to send chosen men from them to Antioch with Paul and Barnabas, Judas being called Barsabas, and Silas, leading men in the brothers, [23] having written by their hand thus: The apostles and the elders and the brothers to those throughout Antioch and Syria and Cilicia, brothers from (the) Gentiles, Greeting: [24] Since we have heard that some of us

**12** Ἐσίγησε δὲ πᾶν τὸ πλῆθος, καὶ ἤκουον Βαρνάβα καὶ
was silent And all   the multitude, and heard   Barnabas  and
Παύλου ἐξηγουμένων ὅσα ἐποίησεν ὁ Θεὸς σημεῖα καὶ
Paul recounting   what   did   — God  signs  and
**13** τέρατα ἐν τοῖς ἔθνεσι δι' αὐτῶν. μετὰ δὲ τὸ σιγῆσαι αὐτούς,
wonders among the nations through them. after And the silence  of them,
ἀπεκρίθη Ἰάκωβος λέγων,
answered  James,  saying,
**14** Ἄνδρες ἀδελφοί, ἀκούσατέ μου· Συμεὼν ἐξηγήσατο καθὼς
Men,  brothers,  hear   me.  Simeon recounted even as
πρῶτον ὁ Θεὸς ἐπεσκέψατο λαβεῖν ἐξ ἐθνῶν λαὸν ἐπὶ τῷ
first  God oversaw  to take out of nations a people for the
**15** ὀνόματι αὐτοῦ. καὶ τούτῳ συμφωνοῦσιν οἱ λόγοι τῶν προ-
name  of Him. And to this agree together  the words of the
**16** φητῶν, καθὼς γέγραπται, Μετὰ ταῦτα ἀναστρέψω, καὶ
prophets, as it has been written, After these things I will return, and
ἀνοικοδομήσω τὴν σκηνὴν Δαβὶδ τὴν πεπτωκυῖαν· καὶ τὰ
I will rebuild  the  tent of David — having fallen,  and that
κατεσκαμμένα αὐτῆς ἀνοικοδομήσω, καὶ ἀνορθώσω αὐτήν·
being demolished of it I will rebuild,  and   I will set up it,
**17** ὅπως ἂν ἐκζητήσωσιν οἱ κατάλοιποι τῶν ἀνθρώπων τὸν
so as — may seek  the rest  — of men  the
Κύριον, καὶ πάντα τὰ ἔθνη, ἐφ' οὓς ἐπικέκληται τὸ ὄνομά μου
Lord, even all  the nations on whom has been invoked the name of Me
**18** ἐπ' αὐτούς, λέγει Κύριος ὁ ποιῶν ταῦτα πάντα. γνωστὰ
upon them, says (the) Lord who is doing these things all.   known
**19** ἀπ' αἰῶνός ἐστι τῷ Θεῷ πάντα τὰ ἔργα αὐτοῦ. διὸ ἐγὼ
from eternity are  to God All ·  the works of Him Because of this, I
κρίνω μὴ παρενοχλεῖν τοῖς ἀπὸ τῶν ἐθνῶν ἐπιστρέφουσιν
judge  not to trouble  those from the nations  turning
**20** ἐπὶ τὸν Θεόν· ἀλλὰ ἐπιστεῖλαι αὐτοῖς τοῦ ἀπέχεσθαι ἀπὸ
to  God,  but  to write  to them — to hold back from
τῶν ἀλισγημάτων τῶν εἰδώλων καὶ τῆς πορνείας καὶ τοῦ
pollutions  of the idols,  and — fornication, and the
**21** πνικτοῦ καὶ τοῦ αἵματος. Μωσῆς γὰρ ἐκ γενεῶν ἀρχαίων
strangled, and — blood.  Moses  For from generations ancient
κατὰ πόλιν τοὺς κηρύσσοντας αὐτὸν ἔχει, ἐν ταῖς συναγω-
in every city  those proclaiming  him he has,  in the synagogues
γαῖς κατὰ πᾶν σάββατον ἀναγινωσκόμενος.
on every sabbath  being read.

**22** Τότε ἔδοξε τοῖς ἀποστόλοις καὶ τοῖς πρεσβυτέροις σὺν
Then it seemed to the apostles  and the  elders,  with
ὅλῃ τῇ ἐκκλησίᾳ, ἐκλεξαμένους ἄνδρας ἐξ αὐτῶν πέμψαι εἰς
all  the church,  chosen  men  of them to send  to
Ἀντιόχειαν σὺν τῷ Παύλῳ καὶ Βαρνάβᾳ, Ἰούδαν τὸν
Antioch  with — Paul  and  Barnabas,  Judas —
ἐπικαλούμενον Βαρσαβᾶν, καὶ Σίλαν, ἄνδρας ἡγουμένους ἐν
surnamed  Barsabas,  and  Silas,  men  leading  among
**23** τοῖς ἀδελφοῖς, γράψαντες διὰ χειρὸς αὐτῶν τάδε, Οἱ ἀπό-
the  brothers,  writing  through (the) hand of them these things: The
στολοι καὶ οἱ πρεσβύτεροι καὶ οἱ ἀδελφοὶ τοῖς κατὰ τὴν
apostles and the  elders  and the  brothers to those throughout
Ἀντιόχειαν καὶ Συρίαν καὶ Κιλικίαν ἀδελφοῖς τοῖς ἐξ ἐθνῶν,
Antioch  and Syria and Cilicia,  brothers  from (the) Gentiles,
**24** χαίρειν· ἐπειδὴ ἠκούσαμεν ὅτι τινὲς ἐξ ἡμῶν ἐξελθόντες ἐτά-
Greeting. Since  we heard  that some of us  having gone out

going out have troubled you with words, unsettling your souls, saying, Be circumcised and keep the Law; to whom we gave no command; [25] it seemed good to us, having become of one mind, to send chosen men to you with our beloved Paul and Barnabas, [26] men having given up their souls on behalf of the name of our Lord, Jesus Christ. [27] We have sent, therefore, Judas and Silas, they also through word announcing the same things. [28] For it seemed good to the Holy Spirit and to us to put not one greater burden on you than these necessary things: [29] To hold back from idol sacrifices, and blood, and that strangled, and fornication; from which continually keeping yourselves, you will do well. Be prospered.

[30] Therefore, they being let go, they went to Antioch. And having gathered the multitude, they delivered the letter. [31] And having read (it), they rejoiced at the comfort. [32] And Judas and Silas, they also being prophets, exhorted the brothers through much discussion, and established (them). [33] And having continued a time, they were let go in peace from the brothers to the apostles. [34] But it seemed good to Silas to remain with them. [35] And Paul and Barnabas stayed in Antioch, teaching and preaching the gospel, the word of the Lord, with many others also.

[36] And after some days Paul said to Barnabas. Indeed having turned back, let us (go) look after our brothers throughout every city in which we preached the word of the Lord, how they have (done). [37] And Barnabas purposed to take John with (them), (he) being called Mark. [38] But Paul thought (it) well not to take that one with (them), (he) having withdrawn from

ραξαν ὑμᾶς λόγοις, ἀνασκευάζοντες τὰς ψυχὰς ὑμῶν,
troubled you with words, unsettling the souls of you,
λέγοντες περιτέμνεσθαι καὶ τηρεῖν τὸν νόμον, οἷς οὐ διεστει-
saying, Be circumcised and keep the Law; to whom not we gave

25 λάμεθα· ἔδοξεν ἡμῖν γενομένοις ὁμοθυμαδόν, ἐκλεξαμένους
command; it seemed to us becoming of one passion chosen
ἄνδρας πέμψαι πρὸς ὑμᾶς, σὺν τοῖς ἀγαπητοῖς ἡμῶν
men to send to you, with the beloved of us

26 Βαρνάβᾳ καὶ Παύλῳ, ἀνθρώποις παραδεδωκόσι τὰς ψυχὰς
Barnabas and Paul, men having given up the souls
αὐτῶν ὑπὲρ τοῦ ὀνόματος τοῦ Κυρίου ἡμῶν Ἰησοῦ Χρι-
of them on behalf of the name of the Lord of us, Jesus Christ.

27 στοῦ. ἀπεστάλκαμεν οὖν Ἰούδαν καὶ Σίλαν, καὶ αὐτοὺς διὰ
    We have sent, therefore, Judas and Silas, and they through

28 λόγου ἀπαγγέλλοντας τὰ αὐτά. ἔδοξε γὰρ τῷ Ἁγίῳ
word announcing, the same things. it seemed For to the Holy
Πνεύματι, καὶ ἡμῖν, μηδὲν πλέον ἐπιτίθεσθαι ὑμῖν βάρος,
Spirit and to us not one greater to put on you burden

29 πλὴν τῶν ἐπάναγκες τούτων, ἀπέχεσθαι εἰδωλοθύτων καὶ
than — necessary things these: to abstain from idol sacrifices, and
αἵματος καὶ πνικτοῦ καὶ πορνείας· ἐξ ὧν διατηροῦντες
blood, and that strangled, and fornication; from which continually keeping
ἑαυτούς, εὖ πράξετε. ἔρρωσθε.
yourselves well you will do. Be prospered.

30 Οἱ μὲν οὖν ἀπολυθέντες ἦλθον εἰς Ἀντιόχειαν· καὶ συν-
They, therefore, being let go, they went to Antioch; and having

31 αγαγόντες τὸ πλῆθος, ἐπέδωκαν τὴν ἐπιστολήν. ἀναγνόντες
gathered the multitude, delivered the letter. having read

32 δέ, ἐχάρησαν ἐπὶ τῇ παρακλήσει. Ἰούδας δὲ καὶ Σίλας, καὶ
And, they rejoiced at the comfort. Judas And and Silas, also
αὐτοὶ προφῆται ὄντες, διὰ λόγου πολλοῦ παρεκάλεσαν
themselves prophets being, through speech much exhorted

33 τοὺς ἀδελφούς, καὶ ἐπεστήριξαν. ποιήσαντες δὲ χρόνον,
the brothers, and confirmed. having continued And a time,
ἀπελύθησαν μετ' εἰρήνης ἀπὸ τῶν ἀδελφῶν πρὸς τοὺς
they were let go with peace from the brothers to the

34 ἀποστόλους. ἔδοξε δὲ τῷ Σίλᾳ ἐπιμεῖναι αὐτοῦ. Παῦλος δὲ
apostles. it seemed (good) But to Silas to remain (there). Paul And

35 καὶ Βαρνάβας διέτριβον ἐν Ἀντιοχείᾳ, διδάσκοντες καὶ
and Barnabas stayed in Antioch, teaching and
εὐαγγελιζόμενοι, μετὰ καὶ ἑτέρων πολλῶν, τὸν λόγον τοῦ
preaching the gospel, with also others many the word of the
Κυρίου.
Lord.

36 Μετὰ δέ τινας ἡμέρας εἶπε Παῦλος πρὸς Βαρνάβαν,
after And some days said Paul to Barnabas,
Ἐπιστρέψαντες δὴ ἐπισκεψώμεθα τοὺς ἀδελφοὺς ἡμῶν
Having turned back indeed let us look after the brothers of us
κατὰ πᾶσαν πόλιν, ἐν αἷς κατηγγείλαμεν τὸν λόγον τοῦ
throughout every city in which we announced the word of the

37 Κυρίου, πῶς ἔχουσι. Βαρνάβας δὲ ἐβουλεύσατο συμπαραλα-
Lord, how they are. : Barnabas And purposed to take with

38 βεῖν τὸν Ἰωάννην, τὸν καλούμενον Μάρκον. Παῦλος δὲ
(them) — John, — being called Mark. Paul But
ἠξίου, τὸν ἀποστάντα ἀπ' αὐτῶν ἀπὸ Παμφυλίας, καὶ μὴ
thought fit (he) having withdrawn from them from Pamphilia, and not

them from Pamphylia, and not going with them to the work. [39] Then came into being sharp feeling, so as to separate them from each other. And Barnabas having taken Mark sailed away to Cyprus. [40] But having chosen Silas, Paul went out —being commanded by the grace of God, by the brothers; [41] and passed through Syria and Cilicia, making the churches strong.

## CHAPTER 16

[1] And he came down to Derbe and Lystra; and behold, a certain disciple was there named Timothy, the son of a certain Jewish believing woman, but (his) father a Greek; [2] who was witnessed to by the brothers in Lystra and Iconium. [3] Paul desired this one to go out with him, and having taken he circumcised him, because of the Jews who were in those places, for they all knew his father, that he was a Greek. [4] And as they passed through the cities they delivered to them to keep the decrees decided on by the apostles and the elders in Jerusalem. [5] Then the assemblies were strengthened in the faith, and increased in number every day.

[6] And having passed through Phrygia and the Galatian country, having been forbidden by the Holy Spirit to speak the word in Asia, [7] having come down to Mysia, they attempted to go to Bithynia; and the Spirit did not allow them. [8] And having passed by Mysia, they came down to Troas. [9] And a vision appeared during the night to Paul: a certain man of Macedonia was standing, begging him and saying, Having passed over into Macedonia, help us. [10] And when he saw the vision, we immediately sought to go to Macedonia, concluding that the Lord had called us to preach the gospel to them.

---

συνελθόντα αὐτοῖς εἰς τὸ ἔργον, μὴ συμπαραλαβεῖν τοῦτον.
going with them to the work, not to take with (them) that one.

**39** ἐγένετο οὖν παροξυσμός, ὥστε ἀποχωρισθῆναι αὐτοὺς ἀπ᾽
there was Then sharp feeling, so as to separate them from

ἀλλήλων, τόν τε Βαρνάβαν παραλαβόντα τὸν Μάρκον
each other; — and Barnabas taking — Mark

**40** ἐκπλεῦσαι εἰς Κύπρον· Παῦλος δὲ ἐπιλεξάμενος Σίλαν ἐξῆλθε,
to sail way to Cyprus. Paul But having chosen Silas went out,

**41** παραδοθεὶς τῇ χάριτι τοῦ Θεοῦ ὑπὸ τῶν ἀδελφῶν. διήρχετο
being commended to the grace of God by the brothers. went through

δὲ τὴν Συρίαν καὶ Κιλικίαν, ἐπιστηρίζων τὰς ἐκκλησίας.
And — Syria and Cilicia, making strong the churches.

## CHAPTER 16

**1** Κατήντησε δὲ εἰς Δέρβην καὶ Λύστραν· καὶ ἰδού, μαθητής
he came down And to Derbe and Lystra. And behold, a disciple

τις ἦν ἐκεῖ, ὀνόματι Τιμόθεος, υἱὸς γυναικός τινος Ἰουδαίας
certain was there by name Timothy, son of a woman certain Jewish

**2** πιστῆς, πατρὸς δὲ Ἕλληνος· ὃς ἐμαρτυρεῖτο ὑπὸ τῶν ἐν
faithful, father but (was) a Greek; who was witnessed to by the in

**3** Λύστροις καὶ Ἰκονίῳ ἀδελφῶν. τοῦτον ἠθέλησεν ὁ Παῦλος
Lystra and Iconium brothers. This one desired — Paul

σὺν αὐτῷ ἐξελθεῖν, καὶ λαβὼν περιέτεμεν αὐτόν, διὰ τοὺς
with him to go forth, and taking circumcised him because of the

Ἰουδαίους τοὺς ὄντας ἐν τοῖς τόποις ἐκείνοις· ᾔδεισαν γὰρ
Jews — being in — places those; they knew for

**4** ἅπαντες τὸν πατέρα αὐτοῦ, ὅτι Ἕλλην ὑπῆρχεν. ὡς δὲ
all the father of him, that a Greek he was. as And

διεπορεύοντο τὰς πόλεις, παρεδίδουν αὐτοῖς φυλάσσειν τὰ
they went through the cities, they delivered to them to keep the

δόγματα τὰ κεκριμένα ὑπὸ τῶν ἀποστόλων καὶ τῶν πρεσ-
decrees — being decided by the apostles and the

**5** βυτέρων τῶν ἐν Ἱερουσαλήμ. αἱ μὲν οὖν ἐκκλησίαι ἐστερεοῦν-
elders — in Jerusalem. the Therefore churches were made

το τῇ πίστει, καὶ ἐπερίσσευον τῷ ἀριθμῷ καθ᾽ ἡμέραν.
strong in the faith, and increased — in number day by day.

**6** Διελθόντες δὲ τὴν Φρυγίαν καὶ τὴν Γαλατικὴν χώραν,
having passed through And the Phrygia and the Galatian country,

κωλυθέντες ὑπὸ τοῦ Ἁγίου Πνεύματος λαλῆσαι τὸν λόγον
being prevented by the Holy Spirit to speak the word

**7** ἐν τῇ Ἀσίᾳ, ἐλθόντες κατὰ τὴν Μυσίαν ἐπείραζον κατὰ τὴν
in — Asia, coming against — Mysia, they attempted along

Βιθυνίαν πορεύεσθαι· καὶ οὐκ εἴασεν αὐτοὺς τὸ Πνεῦμα·
Bithynia to go, and not allowed them the Spirit.

**8** παρελθόντες δὲ τὴν Μυσίαν κατέβησαν εἰς Τρωάδα. καὶ
passing by And — Mysia they came down to Troas. And

**9** ὅραμα διὰ τῆς νυκτὸς ὤφθη τῷ Παύλῳ· ἀνήρ τις ἦν Μακεδὼν
a vision during the night appeared — to Paul, a man certain was of Macedonia

ἑστώς, παρακαλῶν αὐτὸν καὶ λέγων, Διαβὰς εἰς Μακεδονίαν,
standing, begging him and saying, Passing over to Macedonia,

**10** βοήθησον ἡμῖν. ὡς δὲ τὸ ὅραμα εἶδεν, εὐθέως ἐζητήσαμεν •
help us. when And the vision he saw, at once we sought

ἐξελθεῖν εἰς τὴν Μακεδονίαν, συμβιβάζοντες ὅτι προσκέκλη-
to go forth to — Macedonia, concluding that has called

ται ἡμᾶς ὁ Κύριος εὐαγγελίσασθαι αὐτούς.
us the Lord to preach the gospel to them.

**11** Ἀναχθέντες οὖν ἀπὸ τῆς Τρῳάδος, εὐθυδρομήσαμεν εἰς
setting sail   Then from  —   Troas,    we ran a straight course to

[11] Therefore having sailed from Troas, we came with a straight course to Samothrace, and on the following day to Neapolis,

**12** Σαμοθρᾴκην, τῇ τε ἐπιούσῃ εἰς Νεάπολιν, ἐκεῖθέν τε εἰς
Samothrace,  on the and next day  to   Neapolis,   from there and to

Φιλίππους, ἥτις ἐστὶ πρώτη τῆς μερίδος τῆς Μακεδονίας
Philippi,   which  is (the) first  of the part  — of Macedonia

[12] and from there to Philippi, which is (the) first city of (that) part of Macedonia, a colony. And we were staying in this city certain days.

πόλις, κολωνία· ἦμεν δὲ ἐν ταύτῃ τῇ πόλει διατρίβοντες
city,  a colony.  we were And in  this  —  city  staying

**13** ἡμέρας τινάς. τῇ τε ἡμέρᾳ τῶν σαββάτων ἐξήλθομεν ἔξω τῆς
days   some. on the And day of the  sabbaths, we went out  outside the

[13] And on the day of the Sabbath we went outside the city by a river, where (it) was customary (for) prayer to be, and having sat down we spoke to the women who came together.

πόλεως παρὰ ποταμόν, οὗ ἐνομίζετο προσευχὴ εἶναι, καὶ
city   by  a river,  where was customary  prayer  to be;  and

**14** καθίσαντες ἐλαλοῦμεν ταῖς συνελθούσαις γυναιξί. καί τις
sitting down  we spoke  to the who came together women. And a certain

γυνὴ ὀνόματι Λυδία, πορφυρόπωλις πόλεως Θυατείρων,
woman, by name Lydia,  a seller of purple, of (the) city of Thyatira,

[14] And a certain woman named Lydia, a seller of purple, of (the) city of Thyatira, who worshiped God, was listening; of whom the Lord opened the heart to hear the things spoken by Paul.

σεβομένη τὸν Θεόν, ἤκουεν· ἧς ὁ Κύριος διήνοιξε τὴν καρδίαν,
revering  —  God,  heard, of whom the Lord opened the  heart

**15** προσέχειν τοῖς λαλουμένοις ὑπὸ τοῦ Παύλου. ὡς δὲ ἐβαπτί-
to attend to the things  spoken by  — Paul.  when And she was

σθη, καὶ ὁ οἶκος αὐτῆς, παρεκάλεσε λέγουσα, Εἰ κεκρίκατέ
baptized, and the house of her, she beseeched, saying,  If you have judged

[15] And when she and her house were baptized, she begged, saying, If you have judged me to be faithful to the Lord, having entered into my house, stay. And she constrained us.

με πιστὴν τῷ Κυρίῳ εἶναι, εἰσελθόντες εἰς τὸν οἶκόν μου,
me believing in the Lord  to be,  entering  into  the  house of me,

μείνατε. καὶ παρεβιάσατο ἡμᾶς.
remain.  And  she urged  us.

**16** Ἐγένετο δὲ πορευομένων ἡμῶν εἰς προσευχήν, παιδίσκην
it was And, going  us into (a place of) prayer,  a girl

[16] And as we were going to prayer, it came to pass a certain girl having a spirit of Python met us, who brought much gain to her masters by divining.

τινὰ ἔχουσαν πνεῦμα Πύθωνος ἀπαντῆσαι ἡμῖν, ἥτις
certain having a spirit  of Python  met  us,  who

ἐργασίαν πολλὴν παρεῖχε τοῖς κυρίοις αὐτῆς, μαντευομένη.
gain  much  brought to the lords  of her  divining.

**17** αὕτη κατακολουθήσασα τῷ Παύλῳ καὶ ἡμῖν, ἔκραζε λέγουσα
She  following after  — Paul  and us, cried out saying,

[17] Having followed Paul and us, she cried, saying, These men are slaves of the Most High God, who preach to us (the) way of salvation.

Οὗτοι οἱ ἄνθρωποι δοῦλοι τοῦ Θεοῦ τοῦ ὑψίστου εἰσίν,
These —  men  slaves of the God  —  most high  are,

**18** οἵτινες καταγγέλλουσιν ἡμῖν ὁδὸν σωτηρίας. τοῦτο δὲ
who  announce  to us a way of salvation.  this And

ἐποίει ἐπὶ πολλὰς ἡμέρας. διαπονηθεὶς δὲ ὁ Παῦλος, καὶ
she did over many  days.  becoming distressed But Paul,  and

[18] And she did this for many days, but Paul being distressed, and having turned to the spirit said, I command you in the name of Jesus Christ to come out from her. And it came out the same hour.

ἐπιστρέψας, τῷ πνεύματι εἶπε, Παραγγέλλω σοι ἐν τῷ
turning  to the spirit  said,  I command  you  in  the

ὀνόματι Ἰησοῦ Χριστοῦ, ἐξελθεῖν ἀπ' αὐτῆς. καὶ ἐξῆλθεν
name  of Jesus  Christ  to come out from  her.  And it came out

αὐτῇ τῇ ὥρᾳ.
in  that hour.

**19** Ἰδόντες δὲ οἱ κύριοι αὐτῆς ὅτι ἐξῆλθεν ἡ ἐλπὶς τῆς
seeing And the lords  of her  that went out the hope of the

[19] And her master seeing that the hope of their gain was gone, having seized Paul and Silas, they dragged (them) into the market before the judges;

ἐργασίας αὐτῶν, ἐπιλαβόμενοι τὸν Παῦλον καὶ τὸν Σίλαν,
gain  of them, having seized  — Paul  and — Silas,

**20** εἵλκυσαν εἰς τὴν ἀγορὰν ἐπὶ τοὺς ἄρχοντας, καὶ προσ-
dragged  to the market  before the rulers,  and having

[20] and having brought them up to the captains, said, These men exceedingly trouble our city, being Jews, [21] and

ἀγαγόντες αὐτοὺς τοῖς στρατηγοῖς εἶπον, Οὗτοι οἱ ἄνθρω-
led near  them  to the governor  said, These  —  men

**21** ποι ἐκταράσσουσιν ἡμῶν τὴν πόλιν, Ἰουδαῖοι ὑπάρχοντες,
are exceedingly troubling of us the city,  Jews  being,

preach customs which it is not lawful for us to receive not to do, being Romans. [22] And the crowd rose up against them, and the captains having torn off their garments commanded to beat (them) with rods. [23] And having laid many stripes on them, they threw (then) into prison, commanding the jailer to keep them safely; [24] who having received such a command thrust them into the inner prison, and fastened their feet to the stocks. [25] And toward midnight Paul and Silas were praying, singing praises to God, and the prisoners listened to them. [26] And suddenly there was a great earthquake, so that the foundations of the prison were shaken, and immediately all the doors were opened, and all the bonds were loosened. [27] And the jailer being awakened, and seeing the doors of the prison opened, having drawn his sword was about to kill himself, supposing the prisoners had escaped. [28] But Paul called out with a loud voice, saying, Do no harm to yourself! For we are all here. [29] And having asked for lights, he rushed in, and trembling fell down before Paul and Silas. [30] And having brought them out, he said, Sirs, what must I do that I may be saved? [31] And they said, Believe on the Lord Jesus Christ, and you shall be saved, you and your house. [32] And they spoke to him the word of the Lord, and to all those in his house. [33] And having taken them in that hour of the night, he washed from the stripes; and he and all his were baptized immediately. [34] And having brought them into his house, he laid a table, and exulted with all his house, having believed in God. [35] And day having come, the captains sent the

καὶ καταγγέλλουσιν ἔθη ἃ οὐκ ἔξεστιν ἡμῖν παραδέχεσθαι
and they announce    customs which not it is lawful for us to receive,

22 οὐδὲ ποιεῖν, 'Ρωμαίοις οὖσι. καὶ συνεπέστη ὁ ὄχλος κατ'
nor  to do,        Romans being. And rose together the crowd against

αὐτῶν, καὶ οἱ στρατηγοὶ περιρρήξαντες αὐτῶν τὰ ἱμάτια
them,   and the governors       tearing off      of them the clothes

23 ἐκέλευον ῥαβδίζειν. πολλάς τε ἐπιθέντες αὐτοῖς πληγὰς
commanded to flog;      many and laying on   them    stripes

ἔβαλον εἰς φυλακήν, παραγγείλαντες τῷ δεσμοφύλακι
threw   into prison,    charging        the    jailer

24 ἀσφαλῶς τηρεῖν αὐτούς· ὅς, παραγγελίαν τοιαύτην εἰληφώς,
securely   to keep  them; who  a charge   such     having received,

ἔβαλεν αὐτοὺς εἰς τὴν ἐσωτέραν φυλακήν, καὶ τοὺς πόδας
threw   them    into the   inner    prison,  and  the  feet

25 αὐτῶν ἠσφαλίσατο εἰς τὸ ξύλον. κατὰ δὲ τὸ μεσονύκτιον
of them secured     in the stocks. about And — midnight,

Παῦλος καὶ Σίλας προσευχόμενοι ὕμνουν τὸν Θεόν, ἐπη-
Paul   and Silas  praying      praised in a hymn — God,

26 κροῶντο δὲ αὐτῶν οἱ δέσμιοι· ἄφνω δὲ σεισμὸς ἐγένετο
listened and to them the prisoners. suddenly And an earthquake was

μέγας, ὥστε σαλευθῆναι τὰ θεμέλια τοῦ δεσμωτηρίου·
great,  so as to be shaken the foundations of the  jail.

ἀνεῴχθησάν τε παραχρῆμα αἱ θύραι πᾶσαι, καὶ πάντων
were opened And immediately  the doors  all,    and  of all

27 τὰ δεσμὰ ἀνέθη. ἔξυπνος δὲ γενόμενος ὁ δεσμοφύλαξ, καὶ
the bonds were loosened. awake And becoming, the jailer,    and

ἰδὼν ἀνεῳγμένας τὰς θύρας τῆς φυλακῆς, σπασάμενος
seeing having been opened the doors of the  prison,   having drawn

μάχαιραν, ἔμελλεν ἑαυτὸν ἀναιρεῖν, νομίζων ἐκπεφευγέναι
a sword,  was about himself to do away, supposing to have escaped

28 τοὺς δεσμίους. ἐφώνησε δὲ φωνῇ μεγάλῃ ὁ Παῦλος λέγων,
the prisoners.  called   But with a voice great — Paul,  saying,

Μηδὲν πράξῃς σεαυτῷ κακόν· ἅπαντες γάρ ἐσμεν ἐνθάδε.
nothing Do  (to) yourself harm,  all     for  we are  here.

29 αἰτήσας δὲ φῶτα εἰσεπήδησε, καὶ ἔντρομος γενόμενος
asking  And lights, he rushed in,  and  trembling  becoming

30 προσέπεσε τῷ Παύλῳ καὶ τῷ Σίλᾳ, καὶ προαγαγὼν αὐτοὺς
he fell before — Paul and — Silas, and having led    them

31 ἔξω ἔφη, Κύριοι, τί με δεῖ ποιεῖν ἵνα σωθῶ; οἱ δὲ εἶπον,
outside said, Sirs, what me must do  that I may be saved? they And said,

Πίστευσον ἐπὶ τὸν Κύριον 'Ιησοῦν Χριστόν, καὶ σωθήσῃ
Believe   on  the  Lord   Jesus   Christ,  and you will be saved,

32 σὺ καὶ ὁ οἶκός σου. καὶ ἐλάλησαν αὐτῷ τὸν λόγον τοῦ
you and the house of you. And they spoke to him the word of the

33 Κυρίου, καὶ πᾶσι τοῖς ἐν τῇ οἰκίᾳ αὐτοῦ. καὶ παραλαβὼν
Lord,   and  all those in the house of him. And taking

αὐτοὺς ἐν ἐκείνῃ τῇ ὥρᾳ τῆς νυκτὸς ἔλουσεν ἀπὸ τῶν πλη-
them   in  that  — hour of the night, he washed from the stripes,

γῶν, καὶ ἐβαπτίσθη αὐτὸς καὶ οἱ αὐτοῦ πάντες παραχρῆμα.
and was baptized  he  and those of him all   at once.

34 ἀναγαγών τε αὐτοὺς εἰς τὸν οἶκον αὐτοῦ παρέθηκε τράπε-
bringing up and  them   to  the  house  of him, he  set before (them) a table,

ζαν, καὶ ἠγαλλιάσατο πανοικὶ πεπιστευκὼς τῷ Θεῷ.
and  exulted      with all the house, having believed — God.

35 'Ημέρας δὲ γενομένης, ἀπέστειλαν οἱ στρατηγοὶ τοὺς
day   And coming,    sent       the governors   the

floggers, saying, Let these men go. [36] And the jailer reported these words to Paul, The captains have sent that you may be let go. Now, then, having gone out, go in peace. [37] But Paul said to them, Having beaten us publicly, being Romans and not found guilty, they threw (us) into prison; and now do they thrust out us our secretly? No, indeed, but having come themselves, let them bring us out. [38] And the floggers reported these words to the captains. And they were afraid, having heard that they were Romans. [39] And having come, they begged them; and having brought out, they asked (them) to leave the city. [40] And having gone forth out of the prison, they came to Lydia; and having seen the brothers, they exhorted them and went away.

CHAPTER 17

[1] And after they had gone through Amphipolis and Apollonia, they came to Thessalonica, where the synagogue of the Jews was. [2] And according to the custom with Paul, he went in to them, and reasoned with them from the Scriptures for three sabbaths, [3] opening and setting forth that the Christ must have suffered and to have risen from among (the) dead, and that this is the Christ, Jesus whom I preach to you. [4] And some of them were believing and joined themselves to Paul and to Silas, and a great multitude of the worshiping Greeks, and not a few of the leading women. [5] But the unbelieving Jews having become envious, and having taken certain evil men of the market-loafers, and having collected a crowd, set the city into turmoil; and having assaulted the house of Jason, they sought to bring them out to the people. [6] But not having found them, they dragged Jason and certain brothers

ραβδούχους λέγοντες, Ἀπόλυσον τοὺς ἀνθρώπους ἐκείνους.
floggers, saying, Let go — men those.

36 ἀπήγγειλε δὲ ὁ δεσμοφύλαξ τοὺς λόγους τούτους πρὸς
announced And the jailer — words these to

τὸν Παῦλον ὅτι Ἀπεστάλκασιν οἱ στρατηγοί, ἵνα ἀπο-
— Paul, — have sent The governors, that you

37 λυθῆτε· νῦν οὖν ἐξελθόντες πορεύεσθε ἐν εἰρήνῃ. ὁ δὲ Παῦλος
be let go. Now, then, going out proceed in peace. But Paul

ἔφη πρὸς αὐτούς, Δείραντες ἡμᾶς δημοσίᾳ, ἀκατακρίτους,
said to them, Having beaten us publicly, uncondemned

ἀνθρώπους Ῥωμαίους ὑπάρχοντας, ἔβαλον εἰς φυλακήν, καὶ
men, Romans being, they threw into prison; and

νῦν λάθρᾳ ἡμᾶς ἐκβάλλουσιν; οὐ γάρ· ἀλλὰ ἐλθόντες αὐτοὶ
now secretly us they throw out? No indeed, but coming themselves

38 ἡμᾶς ἐξαγαγέτωσαν. ἀνήγγειλαν δὲ τοῖς στρατηγοῖς οἱ
us let them bring out. reported And to the governors the

ραβδοῦχοι τὰ ῥήματα ταῦτα· καὶ ἐφοβήθησαν ἀκούσαντες
floggers — words these. And they were afraid, hearing

39 ὅτι Ῥωμαῖοί εἰσι, καὶ ἐλθόντες παρεκάλεσαν αὐτούς, καὶ
that Romans they are; and coming begged them, and

40 ἐξαγαγόντες ἠρώτων ἐξελθεῖν τῆς πόλεως. ἐξελθόντες δὲ ἐκ
bringing out asked to go out of the city. going out And from

τῆς φυλακῆς εἰσῆλθον εἰς τὴν Λυδίαν· καὶ ἰδόντες τοὺς ἀδελ-
the prison, entered into (the house of) Lydia, and seeing the brothers,

φούς, παρεκάλεσαν αὐτούς, καὶ ἐξῆλθον.
they exhorted them, and went forth.

CHAPTER 17

1 Διοδεύσαντες δὲ τὴν Ἀμφίπολιν καὶ Ἀπολλωνίαν, ἦλθον
traveling through And — Amphipolis and Apollonia, they came

εἰς Θεσσαλονίκην, ὅπου ἦν ἡ συναγωγὴ τῶν Ἰουδαίων·
to Thessalonica, where was a synagogue of the Jews.

2 κατὰ δὲ τὸ εἰωθὸς τῷ Παύλῳ εἰσῆλθε πρὸς αὐτούς, καὶ ἐπὶ
as And the custom with Paul, he entered to them, and on

3 σάββατα τρία διελέγετο αὐτοῖς ἀπὸ τῶν γραφῶν, διανοίγων
sabbaths three reasoned with them from the Scriptures, opening

καὶ παρατιθέμενος, ὅτι τὸν Χριστὸν ἔδει παθεῖν καὶ ἀναστῆ-
and setting forth that the Christ must have suffered and to have

ναι ἐκ νεκρῶν, καὶ ὅτι οὗτός ἐστιν ὁ Χριστὸς Ἰησοῦς, ὃν ἐγὼ
risen from (the) dead, and that this is the Christ, Jesus, whom I

4 καταγγέλλω ὑμῖν. καί τινες ἐξ αὐτῶν ἐπείσθησαν, καὶ
announce to you. And some of them were persuaded, and

προσεκληρώθησαν τῷ Παύλῳ καὶ τῷ Σίλᾳ, τῶν τε σεβο-
joined themselves — to Paul and — Silas, of the both worship-

μένων Ἑλλήνων πολὺ πλῆθος, γυναικῶν τε τῶν πρώτων
ing Greeks a great multitude, of women and the chief,

5 οὐκ ὀλίγαι. ζηλώσαντες δὲ οἱ ἀπειθοῦντες Ἰουδαῖοι, καὶ
not a few. becoming jealous But the disobeying Jews, and

προσλαβόμενοι τῶν ἀγοραίων τινὰς ἄνδρας πονηρούς, καὶ
taking aside of the market-loafers some, men wicked, and

ὀχλοποιήσαντες, ἐθορύβουν τὴν πόλιν· ἐπιστάντες τε τῇ
gathering a crowd, set into turmoil the city, coming on and the

6 οἰκίᾳ Ἰάσονος, ἐζήτουν αὐτοὺς ἀγαγεῖν εἰς τὸν δῆμον. μὴ
house of Jason sought them to bring on to the mob; not

εὑρόντες δὲ αὐτούς, ἔσυρον τὸν Ἰάσονα καὶ τινας ἀδελφοὺς
finding but them, they dragged — Jason and some brothers

before the city magistrates, crying out, Those who have turned the world upside down have come here too, [7] whom Jason has received; and these all act contrary to the decrees of Caesar, saying there is another king, Jesus. [8] And they troubled the crowd and the city magistrates hearing these things. [9] And having taken security from Jason and the rest, they let them go. [10] But the brothers immediately sent away both Paul and Silas to Berea by night; who, being arrived, went into the synagogue of the Jews. [11] And these were more noble than those in Thessalonica, who received the word with all readiness, daily examining the Scriptures if these things were so. [12] Then many from among them truly believed, and not a few of the honorable Grecian women and men. [13] But when the Jews from Thessalonica knew that the word of God was preached by Paul also in Berea, they came there also stirring up the crowd. [14] And immediately then the brothers sent away Paul, to go as toward the sea; but both Silas and Timothy remained there. [15] But those conducting Paul brought him to Athens; and having received a command to Silas and Timothy, that as quickly as possible they should come to him, they departed.

[16] But Paul waiting for them in Athens, his spirit was pained within him seeing the city full of idols. [17] Therefore he indeed reasoned in the synagogue with the Jews, and those who worshiped, and in the market-place every day with those happening to be. [18] And

ἐπὶ τοὺς πολιτάρχας, βοῶντες ὅτι Οἱ τὴν οἰκουμένην
to the   the city judges,   crying,   —   Those the habitable world

7 ἀναστατώσαντες, οὗτοι καὶ ἐνθάδε πάρεισιν, οὓς ὑποδέδε-
having turned upside down, these also here   have come, whom has received

κται Ἰάσων· καὶ οὗτοι πάντες ἀπέναντι τῶν δογμάτων
Jason;   and   these   all   contrary   to the   decrees

Καίσαρος πράττουσι, βασιλέα λέγοντες ἕτερον εἶναι, Ἰησοῦν.
of Caesar   act,   king   saying   another to be,   Jesus.

8 ἐτάραξαν δὲ τὸν ὄχλον καὶ τοὺς πολιτάρχας ἀκούοντας
they troubled And the crowd and   the   city judges   hearing

9 ταῦτα. καὶ λαβόντες τὸ ἱκανὸν παρὰ τοῦ Ἰάσονος καὶ τῶν
these things. And taking the security from — Jason   and the

λοιπῶν, ἀπέλυσαν αὐτούς.
rest,   they let go   them.

10 Οἱ δὲ ἀδελφοὶ εὐθέως διὰ τῆς νυκτὸς ἐξέπεμψαν τόν τε
the But brothers at once during the   night   sent   — both

Παῦλον καὶ τὸν Σίλαν εἰς Βέροιαν· οἵτινες παραγενόμενοι
Paul   and —   Silas to   Berea,   who   having arrived

11 εἰς τὴν συναγωγὴν τῶν Ἰουδαίων ἀπῄεσαν. οὗτοι δὲ ἦσαν
into the   synagogue of the   Jews   went.   these And were

εὐγενέστεροι τῶν ἐν Θεσσαλονίκῃ, οἵτινες ἐδέξαντο τὸν
more noble (than) those in   Thessalonica,   who   received   the

λόγον μετὰ πάσης προθυμίας, τὸ καθ᾽ ἡμέραν ἀνακρίνοντες
word with   all   readiness,   daily   examining

12 τὰς γραφάς, εἰ ἔχοι ταῦτα οὕτως. πολλοὶ μὲν οὖν ἐξ αὐτῶν
the Scriptures, if have these things so.   Many, therefore of   them

ἐπίστευσαν, καὶ τῶν Ἑλληνίδων γυναικῶν τῶν εὐσχη-
believed,   and of the   Greek   women   —   honorable

13 μόνων καὶ ἀνδρῶν οὐκ ὀλίγοι. ὡς δὲ ἔγνωσαν οἱ ἀπὺ τῆς
and men not a few. when But knew   the from   —

Θεσσαλονίκης Ἰουδαῖοι ὅτι καὶ ἐν τῇ Βεροίᾳ κατηγγέλη
Thessalonica   Jews   that also in   —   Berea was announced

ὑπὸ τοῦ Παύλου ὁ λόγος τοῦ Θεοῦ, ἦλθον κἀκεῖ σαλεύοντες
by   —   Paul   the word   — of God, they came there also shaking

14 τοὺς ὄχλους. εὐθέως δὲ τότε τὸν Παῦλον ἐξαπέστειλαν οἱ
the crowd.   at once And, then,   —   Paul   sent away   the

ἀδελφοὶ πορεύεσθαι ὡς ἐπὶ τὴν θάλασσαν· ὑπέμενον δὲ ὅ
brothers to go   as to   the   sea.   remained But   —

15 τε Σίλας καὶ ὁ Τιμόθεος ἐκεῖ. οἱ δὲ καθιστῶντες τὸν Παῦλον
both Silas and — Timothy there. those And conducting —   Paul

ἤγαγον αὐτὸν ἕως Ἀθηνῶν· καὶ λαβόντες ἐντολὴν πρὸς
brought   him as far as   Athens;   and having received a command to

τὸν Σίλαν καὶ Τιμόθεον, ἵνα ὡς τάχιστα ἔλθωσι πρὸς αὐτόν,
—   Silas   and Timothy,   that as quickly they come to   him,

ἐξῄεσαν.
they departed.

16 Ἐν δὲ ταῖς Ἀθήναις ἐκδεχομένου αὐτοὺς τοῦ Παύλου,
in And — Athens   awaiting   them   —   Paul

παρωξύνετο τὸ πνεῦμα αὐτοῦ ἐν αὐτῷ, θεωροῦντι κατεί-
was pained   the spirit of him in   him,   beholding   full of

17 δωλον οὖσαν τὴν πόλιν. διελέγετο μὲν οὖν ἐν τῇ συναγωγῇ
images being the city.   He addressed, therefore, in the synagogue

τοῖς Ἰουδαίοις καὶ τοῖς σεβομένοις, καὶ ἐν τῇ ἀγορᾷ κατὰ
the   Jews   and those   worshiping; also in the   market   —

18 πᾶσαν ἡμέραν πρὸς τοὺς παρατυγχάνοντας. τινὲς δὲ τῶν
every   day   to   those happening to be (there). some And of the

some of the Epicureans and
of the Stoics, philosophers,
fell in with him. And some
said, What may this chatterer desire to say? And these,
He seems to be an announcer of foreign demons, be-
cause he preached Jesus and
the resurrection to them.
[19] And having taken hold
of him, they led (him) to
the Areopagus, saying, Are
we able to know what this
new teaching (is), being
spoken by you? [20] For
you bring startling things to
our ears. Therefore we are
minded to know what these
things wish to be. [21] And
all Athenians and all strangers living (there) have leisure
for nothing else (than) to
say and to hear something
newer. [22] 'And Paul hav-
.ng stood in (the) middle
of the Areopagus said,
Men, Athenians, I see
how you (are) very fear-
ful of gods in everything.
[23] For passing through
and looking up at the ob-
jects of your worship,
I also found an altar on
which had been written,
TO AN UNKNOWN GOD.
Not knowing then whom
you worship, I make Him
known to you: [24] the
God who made the world
and all things that (are) in
it, He being Lord of
Heaven and earth, lives not
in handmade temples,
[25] nor is served by
hands of men, as needing
anything; Himself giving to
all life and breath in every
(respect). [26] And He
made every nation of men
of one blood, to live on all
the face of the earth,
having ordained
beforehand the times and
boundaries of their
dwelling, [27] to seek the
Lord; if perhaps they
might feel after Him and
might find Him, though
indeed being not far from
each one of us. [28] For in
Him we live and move and
are; as also some of the
poets among you have said,
For we are also His
offspring. [29] Therefore,
being offspring of God, we
ought not to think that the
Godhead is like gold or
silver or stone, engraved by
art and the imagination of

'Επικουρείων καὶ τῶν Στωϊκῶν φιλοσόφων συνέβαλλον αὐτῷ.
Epicureans          and of the Stoics,      philosophers,    fell in with    him.

καί τινες ἔλεγον, Τί ἂν θέλοι ὁ σπερμολόγος οὗτος λέγειν ;
And some    said,    What may desire —   chatterer          this      to say?

οἱ δέ, Ξένων δαιμονίων δοκεῖ καταγγελεὺς εἶναι· ὅτι τὸν
these And, Of foreign demons he seems    an announcer   to be; because —

19 'Ιησοῦν καὶ τὴν ἀνάστασιν αὐτοῖς εὐηγγελίζετο. ἐπιλα-
   Jesus   and  the   resurrection  to them he announced.    taking

βόμενοί τε αὐτοῦ, ἐπὶ τὸν "Αρειον πάγον ἤγαγον λέγοντες,
hold    And of him,  to the     Areopagus      they led (him), saying,

Δυνάμεθα γνῶναι, τίς ἡ καινὴ αὕτη ἡ ὑπὸ σοῦ λαλουμένη
Are we able to know  what —  new  this —  by you being spoken

20 διδαχή ; ξενίζοντα γάρ τινα εἰσφέρεις εἰς τὰς ἀκοὰς ἡμῶν·
   teaching (is)?  startling things For some you bring  to the    ears   of us;

21 βουλόμεθα οὖν γνῶναι, τί ἂν θέλοι ταῦτα εἶναι. ('Αθηναῖοι
   we are minded, then, to know what  wishes these things to be.   Athenians

δὲ πάντες καὶ οἱ ἐπιδημοῦντες ξένοι εἰς οὐδὲν ἕτερον εὐκαί-
And all    the   living   strangers for nothing different have

ρουν, ἢ λέγειν τι καὶ ἀκούειν καινότερον.)
leisure either to say something, and to hear  newer (things).)

22 Σταθεὶς δὲ ὁ Παῦλος ἐν μέσῳ τοῦ 'Αρείου πάγου ἔφη,
   standing And —  Paul   in (the) midst of the   Areopagus     said,

"Ανδρες 'Αθηναῖοι, κατὰ πάντα ὡς δεισιδαιμονεστέρους ὑμᾶς
Men,    Athenians, in everything how very  fearful of gods    you

23 θεωρῶ. διερχόμενος γὰρ καὶ ἀναθεωρῶν τὰ σεβάσματα
   I behold.  passing through For and  looking up at   the objects of worship

ὑμῶν, εὗρον καὶ βωμὸν ἐν ᾧ ἐπεγέγραπτο, 'Αγνώστῳ Θεῷ.
of you, I found also an altar in which had been written, To an Unknown God.

ὃν οὖν ἀγνοοῦντες εὐσεβεῖτε, τοῦτον ἐγὼ καταγγέλλω ὑμῖν.
Whom, then, not knowing you reverence, this One I   announce   to you.

24 ὁ Θεὸς ὁ ποιήσας τὸν κόσμον καὶ πάντα τὰ ἐν αὐτῷ, οὗτος,
   The God, He having made the world  and all things    in it,   this One

οὐρανοῦ καὶ γῆς κύριος ὑπάρχων, οὐκ ἐν χειροποιήτοις
of Heaven and of earth Lord   being,      not in    handmade

25 ναοῖς κατοικεῖ, οὐδὲ ὑπὸ χειρῶν ἀνθρώπων θεραπεύεται,
   temples dwells,    nor   by   hands   of men      is served

προσδεόμενός τινος, αὐτὸς διδοὺς πᾶσι ζωὴν καὶ πνοὴν καὶ
having need of anything.  He is giving to all  life  and breath, and

26 τὰ πάντα· ἐποίησέ τε ἐξ ἑνὸς αἵματος πᾶν ἔθνος ἀνθρώπων,
   all things.  He made And of one  blood  every nation of men,

κατοικεῖν ἐπὶ πᾶν τὸ πρόσωπον τῆς γῆς, ὁρίσας προτεταγ-
to live     on   all  the   face    of the earth, ordaining ᵗᵒʳᵉ
                                                           appointed

27 μένους καιροὺς καὶ τὰς ὁροθεσίας τῆς κατοικίας αὐτῶν· ζητεῖν
          seasons   and the boundaries of the dwelling of them, to seek

τὸν Κύριον, εἰ ἄραγε ψηλαφήσειαν αὐτὸν καὶ εὕροιεν, καί-
the  Lord,   if perhaps they might feel after Him  and might find,

τοιγε οὐ μακρὰν ἀπὸ ἑνὸς ἑκάστου ἡμῶν ὑπάρχοντα. ἐν
though not far    from  one    each    of us   being.     in

28 αὐτῷ γὰρ ζῶμεν καὶ κινούμεθα καί ἐσμεν· ὡς καὶ τινες τῶν
   Him For  we live  and move        and  are,  as indeed some of the

29 καθ' ὑμᾶς ποιητῶν εἰρήκασι, Τοῦ γὰρ καὶ γένος ἐσμέν. γένος
   among you  poets    have said: of Him For  also offspring we are. offspring

οὖν ὑπάρχοντες τοῦ Θεοῦ, οὐκ ὀφείλομεν νομίζειν χρυσῷ ἢ
Then   being   — of God, not we ought   to suppose to gold, or

ἀργύρῳ ἢ λίθῳ, χαράγματι τέχνης καὶ ἐνθυμήσεως ἀνθρώ-
to silver,  or to stone, to an engraving of art  and of imagination of man,

man. [30] Truly, then, God having overlooked the times of ignorance, now commands all men everywhere to repent, [31] because He set a Day in which He is about to judge the world in righteousness, by a Man whom He appointed; having given proof to all (by) having raised Him from among (the) dead. [32] And having heard a resurrection of (the) dead, some ridiculed, and some said, We will hear you again about this. [33] And so Paul went out from their midst. [34¹ But some men joining themselves to him believed; among whom also (was) Dionysius the Areopagite, and a woman named Damaris, and others with them.

CHAPTER 18

[1] And after these things Paul having left Athens came to Corinth; [2] and having found a certain Jew named Aquila, of Pontus by race, late come from Italy, and his wife Priscilla — because Claudius had ordered all the Jews to depart out of Rome — he came to them. [3] And because being of the same trade, he lived and worked with them; for they were tentmakers by trade. [4] And he reasoned in the synagogue every sabbath, and persuaded Jews and Greeks. [5] And when both Silas and Timothy came down from Macedonia, Paul was pressed in spirit, earnestly testifying to the Jews (that) Jesus (is) the Christ. [6] Were opposing and blaspheming, (so) he having shaken his garments said to them, Your blood (be) on your own head; I (am) pure (from it); from now on (I) will go to the nations. [7] And having left there he came to (the) house of a certain one named Justus, who worshiped God, whose house was adjoining the synagogue. [8] But

**30** που, τὸ θεῖον εἶναι ὅμοιον. τοὺς μὲν οὖν χρόνους τῆς ἀγνοίας
the Godhead is like. the indeed Then times — of ignorance
ὑπεριδὼν ὁ Θεός, τὰ νῦν παραγγέλλει τοῖς ἀνθρώποις πᾶσι
overlooking, God now declares to men all
**31** πανταχοῦ μετανοεῖν· διότι ἔστησεν ἡμέραν, ἐν ᾗ μέλλει
everywhere to repent, because He set a day in which He is going
κρίνειν τὴν οἰκουμένην ἐν δικαιοσύνῃ, ἐν ἀνδρὶ ᾧ ὥρισε,
to judge the habitable world in righteousness, by a Man whom He ap- pointed
πίστιν παρασχὼν πᾶσιν, ἀναστήσας αὐτὸν ἐκ νεκρῶν.
proof having given to all, having raised Him from (the) dead.
**32** Ἀκούσαντες δὲ ἀνάστασιν νεκρῶν, οἱ μὲν ἐχλεύαζον· οἱ
hearing (of) And a resurrection of (the) dead, some indeed ridiculed;
**33** δὲ εἶπον, Ἀκουσόμεθά σου πάλιν περὶ τούτου. καὶ οὕτως ὁ
but said, We will hear you again concerning this. And thus
**34** Παῦλος ἐξῆλθεν ἐκ μέσου αὐτῶν. τινὲς δὲ ἄνδρες κολληθέντες
Paul went out from (the) midst of them. some But men adhering
αὐτῷ, ἐπίστευσαν· ἐν οἷς καὶ Διονύσιος ὁ Ἀρεοπαγίτης, καὶ
to him believed, among whom both Dionysius the Areopagite, and
γυνὴ ὀνόματι Δάμαρις, καὶ ἕτεροι σὺν αὐτοῖς.
a woman by name Damaris, and others with them.

CHAPTER 18

**1** Μετὰ δὲ ταῦτα χωρισθεὶς ὁ Παῦλος ἐκ τῶν Ἀθηνῶν ἦλθεν
after And these things departing Paul from — Athens came
**2** εἰς Κόρινθον. καὶ εὑρών τινα Ἰουδαῖον ὀνόματι Ἀκύλαν,
to Corinth. And finding a certain Jew by name Aquila,
Ποντικὸν τῷ γένει, προσφάτως ἐληλυθότα ἀπὸ τῆς Ἰταλίας,
of Pontus — by race, recently having come from — Italy,
καὶ Πρίσκιλλαν γυναῖκα αὐτοῦ, διὰ τὸ διατεταχέναι Κλαύ-
and Priscilla the wife of him, because had ordered Claud-
διον χωρίζεσθαι πάντας τοὺς Ἰουδαίους ἐκ τῆς Ῥώμης,
ius to depart all the Jews from — Rome,
**3** προσῆλθεν αὐτοῖς· καὶ διὰ τὸ ὁμότεχνον εἶναι, ἔμενε παρ'
he came to them. and because the same trade being, he abode with
αὐτοῖς καὶ εἰργάζετο· ἦσαν γὰρ σκηνοποιοὶ τὴν τέχνην.
them and worked; they were for tentmakers — by trade.
**4** διελέγετο δὲ ἐν τῇ συναγωγῇ κατὰ πᾶν σάββατον, ἔπειθέ τε
he reasoned And in the synagogue on every sabbath, persuading both
Ἰουδαίους καὶ Ἕλληνας.
Jews and Greeks.
**5** Ὡς δὲ κατῆλθον ἀπὸ τῆς Μακεδονίας ὅ τε Σίλας καὶ ὁ
when And came down from — Macedonia — both Silas and —
Τιμόθεος, συνείχετο τῷ πνεύματι ὁ Παῦλος, διαμαρτυρό-
Timothy, was pressed by the Spirit — Paul, earnestly testifying
μενος τοῖς Ἰουδαίοις τὸν Χριστὸν Ἰησοῦν. ἀντιτασσο-
to the Jews (that) Christ Jesus (is). having re-
**6** μένων δὲ αὐτῶν καὶ βλασφημούντων, ἐκτιναξάμενος τὰ
sisted But they, and blaspheming, he having shaken the
ἱμάτια, εἶπε πρὸς αὐτούς, Τὸ αἷμα ὑμῶν ἐπὶ τὴν κεφαλὴν
garments said to them, The blood of you on the head
ὑμῶν· καθαρὸς ἐγώ· ἀπὸ τοῦ νῦν εἰς τὰ ἔθνη πορεύσομαι.
of you (is); clean I from — now to the nations will go.
**7** καὶ μεταβὰς ἐκεῖθεν ἦλθεν εἰς οἰκίαν τινὸς ὀνόματι Ἰούστου,
And moving from there he went into house of one by name Justus,
σεβομένου τὸν Θεόν, οὗ ἡ οἰκία ἦν συνομοροῦσα τῇ
(one) worshiping God, of whom the house was being next door to the

Crispus, the ruler of the synagogue, believed in the Lord with his whole house; and many of the Corinthians hearing believed and were baptized. [9] And the Lord said by a vision in (the) night to Paul, Do not fear, but speak and do not be silent; [10] because I am with you, and no one shall set on you to ill-treat you; because there is much people to me in this city. [11] And he remained a year and six months, teaching among them the word of God.

[12] But Gallio being proconsul of Achaia, the Jews rose with one accord against Paul and led him to the judgment seat, [13] saying, This one persuades men to worship God contrary to the law. [14] But Paul being about to open (his) mouth, Gallio said to the Jews, If indeed, then, it was some unrighteousness or wicked crimnality, O Jews, according to reason I should have borne with you. [15] But if it is a question about a word and names and a law which (is) among you, you will see (to it) yourselves; for I do not wish to be a judge of these things. [16] And he drove them from the judgment seat. [17] And all the Greeks having seized Sosthenes the ruler of the synagogue, they beat (him) before the judgment seat. And nothing about these things mattered to Gallio.

[18] But Paul having remained yet many days, having taken leave of the brothers, sailed to Syria, and Priscilla and Aquila with him, having shaved (his) head in Cenchrea, for he had a vow. [19] And he came to Ephesus and left them there. But he himself having gone into the synagogue reasoned with the Jews. [20] And they asking (him) to remain with them for a longer time, he did not agree; [21] but took leave of

**8** συναγωγῇ. Κρίσπος δὲ ὁ ἀρχισυνάγωγος ἐπίστευσε τῷ
synagogue.    Crispus  And the synagogue ruler    believed    the
Κυρίῳ σὺν ὅλῳ τῷ οἴκῳ αὐτοῦ· καὶ πολλοὶ τῶν Κορινθίων
Lord  with all  the house of him, and  many  of the Corinthians
**9** ἀκούοντες ἐπίστευον καὶ ἐβαπτίζοντο. εἶπε δὲ ὁ Κύριος δι
hearing    believed   and  were baptized.  said And the Lord through
ὁράματος ἐν νυκτὶ τῷ Παύλῳ, Μὴ φοβοῦ, ἀλλὰ λάλει καὶ
a vision   in (the) night — to Paul,  Do not fear,  but  speak and
**10** μὴ σιωπήσῃς· διότι ἐγώ εἰμι μετὰ σοῦ, καὶ οὐδεὶς ἐπιθή-
do not keep silence, because I   am  with  you,  and no one  shall
σεταί σοι τοῦ κακῶσαί σε· διότι λαός ἐστί μοι πολὺς ἐν τῇ
set on you  —  to oppress you; because people  is to me  much in
**11** πόλει ταύτῃ. ἐκάθισέ τε ἐνιαυτὸν καὶ μῆνας ἕξ, διδάσκων
city  this.   he sat And a year   and  months six  teaching
ἐν αὐτοῖς τὸν λόγον τοῦ Θεοῦ.
among them  the word  —  of God.

**12** Γαλλίωνος δὲ ἀνθυπατεύοντος τῆς ᾽Αχαίας, κατεπέστησαν
Gallio (being) And  proconsul    — of Achaia,  rushed against
ὁμοθυμαδὸν οἱ ᾽Ιουδαῖοι τῷ Παύλῳ, καὶ ἤγαγον αὐτὸν
with one mind the  Jews    —   Paul,   and   led    him
**13** ἐπὶ τὸ βῆμα, λέγοντες ὅτι Παρὰ τὸν νόμον οὗτος ἀναπείθει
to the tribunal, saying,    Contrary to the law,  this one persuades
**14** τοὺς ἀνθρώπους σέβεσθαι τὸν Θεόν. μέλλοντος δὲ τοῦ
—    men     to worship  —  God.  being about  And  —
Παύλου ἀνοίγειν τὸ στόμα, εἶπεν ὁ Γαλλίων πρὸς τοὺς
Paul   to open  the mouth,  said  —  Gallio   to   the
᾽Ιουδαίους, Εἰ μὲν οὖν ἦν ἀδίκημά τι ἢ ῥαδιούργημα
Jews,    If indeed, then, it was wrong some or  criminality
πονηρόν, ὦ ᾽Ιουδαῖοι, κατὰ λόγον ἂν ἠνεσχόμην ὑμῶν·
wicked,   O   Jews,  according to reason I would endure   you;
**15** εἰ δὲ ζήτημά ἐστι περὶ λόγου καὶ ὀνομάτων καὶ νόμου τοῦ
if but a question it is about a word  and  names   and  law  the
καθ᾽ ὑμᾶς, ὄψεσθε αὐτοί· κριτὴς γὰρ ἐγὼ τούτων οὐ βού-
according to you, you will see to (it) (your)selves; a judge for I of these things not
**16** λομαι εἶναι. καὶ ἀπήλασεν αὐτοὺς ἀπὸ τοῦ βήματος.
intend to be.   And  he drove   them  from  the  tribunal.
**17** ἐπιλαβόμενοι δὲ πάντες οἱ ῞Ελληνες Σωσθένην τὸν ἀρχι-
seizing  But all  the  Greeks  Sosthenes  the  ruler
συνάγωγον ἔτυπτον ἔμπροσθεν τοῦ βήματος. καὶ οὐδὲν
of the synagogue, they struck (him) before the  tribunal;  and not one
τούτων τῷ Γαλλίωνι ἔμελεν.
of these things to Gallio  mattered.
**18** ῾Ο δὲ Παῦλος ἔτι προσμείνας ἡμέρας ἱκανάς, τοῖς ἀδελφοῖς
And Paul  yet having remained  days  many, to the brothers
ἀποταξάμενος, ἐξέπλει εἰς τὴν Συρίαν, καὶ σὺν αὐτῷ
taking leave,   he sailed to  —  Syria,  and  with  him
Πρίσκιλλα καὶ ᾽Ακύλας, κειράμενος τὴν κεφαλὴν ἐν Κεγχρεαῖς·
Priscilla  and  Aquila, having shorn  the  head  in Cenchrea;
**19** εἶχε γὰρ εὐχήν. κατήντησε δὲ εἰς ῎Εφεσον, κἀκείνους κατέ-
he had for a vow.  he came down And to Ephesus, and those  he
λιπεν αὐτοῦ· αὐτὸς δὲ εἰσελθὼν εἰς τὴν συναγωγὴν διε-
left  there.  he But entering  into  the synagogue reasoned
**20** λέχθη τοῖς ᾽Ιουδαίοις. ἐρωτώντων δὲ αὐτῶν ἐπὶ πλείονα
with the  Jews.    asking  And  they  over a longer
**21** χρόνον μεῖναι παρ᾽ αὐτοῖς, οὐκ ἐπένευσεν· ἀλλ᾽ ἀπετάξατο
time to remain with them,  not he did agree,  but  took leave

them, saying, I must by all means keep the coming feast at Jerusalem, but I will come again to you, God willing. And he sailed from Ephesus. [22] And having landed at Caesarea, having gone up and having greeted the assembly, he went down to Antioch. [23] And having stayed some time, he went forth, passing through the Galatian and Phrygian country in order, strengthening all the disciples.

[24] But a certain Jew named Apollos, an Alexandrian by birth, an eloquent man, came to Ephesus, being mighty in the Scriptures. [25] He was taught in the way of the Lord. And being fervent in spirit, he spoke and accurately taught the things of the Lord, knowing only the baptism of John. [26] And he began to speak boldly in the synagogue. And Priscilla and Aquila having heard him, they took him to (them), and more accurately expounded the way of God to him. [27] And he being minded to pass through into Achaia, the brothers to the disciples exhorting (them) to welcome him; who having arrived much helped those who believed through grace. [28] For he powerfully confuted the Jews publicly, showing by the Scriptures Jesus to be the Christ.

CHAPTER 19

[1] And it happened, in the (time) Apollos was in Corinth, Paul (was) passing through the higher parts to come to Ephesus, and finding some disciples. [2] he said to them, Did you receive (the) Holy Spirit, having believed? And they said to him, We did not even hear whether (the) Holy Spirit is. [3] And he said to them, To what then were you baptized? And they said, To the baptism of John.

αὐτοῖς εἰπών, Δεῖ με πάντως τὴν ἑορτὴν τὴν ἐρχομένην ποιῆ-
of them  saying, It behoves me by all the  feast  —  coming  to
                                    means

σαι εἰς ῾Ιεροσόλυμα· πάλιν δὲ ἀνακάμψω πρὸς ὑμᾶς, τοῦ Θεοῦ
keep at  Jerusalem,  again but I will come  to  you, —  God

22 θέλοντος. καὶ ἀνήχθη ἀπὸ τῆς ᾽Εφέσου. καὶ κατελθὼν εἰς
   willing.  And he sailed  from  —  Ephesus.  And landing  at

Καισάρειαν, ἀναβὰς καὶ ἀσπασάμενος τὴν ἐκκλησίαν,
Caesarea,  having gone up and  having greeted  the  church,

23 κατέβη εἰς ᾽Αντιόχειαν. καὶ ποιήσας χρόνον τινὰ ἐξῆλθε,
   he went down to Antioch.  And having spent time  some. he went out,

διερχόμενος καθεξῆς τὴν Γαλατικὴν χώραν καὶ Φρυγίαν,
passing through in order  the Galatian  country  and  Phrygia

ἐπιστηρίζων πάντας τοὺς μαθητάς.
strengthening  all  the  disciples.

24 ᾽Ιουδαῖος δέ τις ᾽Απολλὼς ὀνόματι, ᾽Αλεξανδρεὺς τῷ
   a Jew  And certain, Apollos  by name,  an Alexandrian  —

γένει, ἀνὴρ λόγιος, κατήντησεν εἰς ῎Εφεσον, δυνατὸς ὢν ἐν
by race, a man eloquent,  came  to  Ephesus,  powerful being in

25 ταῖς γραφαῖς. οὗτος ἦν κατηχημένος τὴν ὁδὸν τοῦ Κυρίου,
   the  Scriptures. This one was orally taught  the  way of the  Lord,

καὶ ζέων τῷ πνεύματι ἐλάλει καὶ ἐδίδασκεν ἀκριβῶς τὰ περὶ
and fervent —  in spirit  he spoke and  taught  accurately  the things about

τοῦ Κυρίου, ἐπιστάμενος μόνον· τὸ βάπτισμα ᾽Ιωάννου·
the  Lord,  understanding only  the  baptism  of John.

26 οὗτός τε ἤρξατο παρρησιάζεσθαι ·ἐν τῇ συναγωγῇ. ἀκού-
   this one And began  to speak boldly  in the  synagogue.  hearing

σαντες δὲ αὐτοῦ ᾽Ακύλας καὶ Πρίσκιλλα, προσελάβοντο
     And him.  Aquila  and  Priscilla  took

αὐτόν, καὶ ἀκριβέστερον αὐτῷ ἐξέθεντο τὴν τοῦ Θεοῦ ὁδόν.
him  and more accurately  to him expounded  the  of God way.

27 βουλομένου δὲ αὐτοῦ διελθεῖν εἰς τὴν ᾽Αχαΐαν, προτρεψά-
   intending  And him  to go through into  Achaia,  being encour-

μενοι οἱ ἀδελφοὶ ἔγραψαν τοῖς μαθηταῖς ἀποδέξασθαι αὐτόν·
aged the brothers wrote  to the disciples to welcome  him;

ὃς παραγενόμενος συνεβάλετο πολὺ τοῖς πεπιστευκόσι διὰ
who having arrived  helped  much  those having believed through

28 τῆς χάριτος· εὐτόνως γὰρ τοῖς ᾽Ιουδαίοις διακατηλέγχετο
   grace;  vehemently for  the  Jews  he confuted

δημοσίᾳ, ἐπιδεικνὺς διὰ τῶν γραφῶν εἶναι τὸν Χριστὸν
publicly,  proving  through the Scriptures to be  the  Christ

᾽Ιησοῦν.
Jesus.

CHAPTER 19

1 ᾽Εγένετο δέ, ἐν τῷ τὸν ᾽Απολλὼ εἶναι ἐν Κορίνθῳ, Παῦλον
  it was  And, in the (time) Apollos  was in Corinth,  Paul

διελθόντα τὰ ἀνωτερικὰ μέρη ἐλθεῖν εἰς ῎Εφεσον· καὶ εὑρών
passing through the higher  parts  came to Ephesus, and finding

2 τινας μαθητὰς εἶπε πρὸς αὐτούς, Εἰ Πνεῦμα ῞Αγιον ἐλάβετε
  some disciples,  said to  them, If (the) Spirit Holy you received

πιστεύσαντες ; οἱ δὲ εἶπον πρὸς αὐτόν, ᾽Αλλ᾽ οὐδὲ εἰ Πνεῦμα
believing?  they And said  to  him,  But not even if (the) Spirit

3 ῞Αγιόν ἐστιν, ἠκούσαμεν. εἶπέ τε πρὸς αὐτούς, Εἰς τί οὖν
  Holy  is  we heard.  he said And to  them,  To what, then,

ἐβαπτίσθητε ; οἱ δὲ εἶπον, Εἰς τὸ ᾽Ιωάννου βάπτισμα ; εἶπε
were you baptized? they And said.  To the  of John  baptism.  said

[4] And Paul said, John indeed baptized (with) a baptism of repentance, saying to the people that they should believe on Him coming after him, that is, on Jesus the Christ. [5] And having heard, they were baptized to the name of the Lord Jesus. [6] And Paul having laid hands on them, the Holy Spirit came upon them, and they were speaking with languages and prophesying. [7] And all the men were about twelve. [8] And having gone in to the synagogue, he spoke boldly, reasoning for three months and persuading the things concerning the kingdom of God. [9] But when some were hardened and did not believe, speaking evil of the Way before the multitude, having departed from them he separated the disciples, daily reasoning in the school of a certain Tyrannus. [10] And this was for two years, so that all those who lived in Asia heard the word of the Lord Jesus, both Jews and Greeks. [11] And not did God work uncommon works of power through Paul's hands. [12] so as even onto those sick to be brought from his skin handkerchiefs or aprons, and the diseases to be released from them, and the evil spirits to go out from them.

[13] But certain from the wandering Jews, exorcists, undertook to call the name of the Lord Jesus over those who had evil spirits, saying, We command you by Jesus, whom Paul preaches. [14] And there were a certain seven sons of Sceva, a Jew, a high priest, who were doing this. [15] But the evil spirit answering said, I know Jesus, and I am acquainted with Paul; but you, who are you? [16] And the man in whom the evil spirit was leaping on them and overcoming them he

**4** δὲ Παῦλος, Ἰωάννης μὲν ἐβάπτισε βάπτισμα μετανοίας, τῷ
And Paul,        John   indeed baptized   a baptism of repentance, to the
λαῷ λέγων εἰς τὸν ἐρχόμενον μετ' αὐτὸν ἵνα πιστεύσωσι,
people saying into the (One) coming after   him   that they should believe,

**5** τοῦτ' ἔστιν, εἰς τὸν Χριστὸν Ἰησοῦν. ἀκούσαντες δὲ ἐβαπτί-
this   is,     in   the Christ,    Jesus.   hearing     And they were

**6** σθησαν εἰς τὸ ὄνομα τοῦ Κυρίου Ἰησοῦ. καὶ ἐπιθέντος
baptized into the name of the Lord   Jesus.   And laying on
αὐτοῖς τοῦ Παύλου τὰς χεῖρας, ἦλθε τὸ Πνεῦμα τὸ Ἅγιον
them   —   Paul   the  hands, came the Spirit   —   Holy

**7** ἐπ' αὐτούς, ἐλάλουν τε γλώσσαις καὶ προεφήτευον. ἦσαν
on  them,   they spoke and in languages and prophesied.   were
δὲ οἱ πάντες ἄνδρες ὡσεὶ δεκαδύο.
And the all   men   about twelve.

**8** Εἰσελθὼν δὲ εἰς τὴν συναγωγὴν ἐπαρρησιάζετο, ἐπὶ
entering And into the synagogue,   he spoke boldly   over
μῆνας τρεῖς διαλεγόμενος καὶ πείθων τὰ περὶ τῆς βασιλείας
months three conversing and per- the con-   the kingdom
              with     suading things cerning

**9** τοῦ Θεοῦ. ὡς δέ τινες ἐσκληρύνοντο καὶ ἠπείθουν, κακολο-
of God. as But some were hardened and disobeyed, speaking
γοῦντες τὴν ὁδὸν ἐνώπιον τοῦ πλήθους, ἀποστὰς ἀπ'
evil    of the Way   before   the multitude, having departed from
αὐτῶν ἀφώρισε τοὺς μαθητάς, καθ' ἡμέραν διαλεγόμενος
them, he separated the disciples,   day by day   conversing

**10** ἐν τῇ σχολῇ Τυράννου τινός. τοῦτο δὲ ἐγένετο ἐπὶ ἔτη δύο,
in the school of Tyrannus a certain. this And happened over years two,
ὥστε πάντας τοὺς κατοικοῦντας τὴν Ἀσίαν ἀκοῦσαι τὸν
so as all    those inhabiting   —   Asia   heard  the
λόγον τοῦ Κυρίου Ἰησοῦ, Ἰουδαίους τε καὶ Ἕλληνας.
word of the Lord   Jesus,   Jews   both and Greeks.

**11** δυνάμεις τε οὐ τὰς τυχούσας ἐποίει ὁ Θεὸς διὰ τῶν χειρῶν
works of And not the common did   God through the hands
power

**12** Παύλου, ὥστε καὶ ἐπὶ τοὺς ἀσθενοῦντας ἐπιφέρεσθαι ἀπὸ
of Paul,   so as even onto those   sick   to be brought   from
τοῦ χρωτὸς αὐτοῦ σουδάρια ἢ σιμικίνθια, καὶ ἀπαλλάσσε-
the skin  of him handkerchiefs or aprons,   and to be released
σθαι ἀπ' αὐτῶν τὰς νόσους, τά τε πνεύματα τὰ πονηρὰ
from them   the diseases, the and spirits   —   evil

**13** ἐξέρχεσθαι ἀπ' αὐτῶν. ἐπεχείρησαν δέ τινες ἀπὸ τῶν περιερ-
to go out from   them.   undertook But some from the strolling
χομένων Ἰουδαίων ἐξορκιστῶν ὀνομάζειν ἐπὶ τοὺς ἔχοντας
Jews,     exorcists,   to name   over those having
τὰ πνεύματα τὰ πονηρὰ τὸ ὄνομα τοῦ Κυρίου Ἰησοῦ,
the spirits   —   evil   the name of the Lord   Jesus,
λέγοντες, Ὁρκίζομεν ὑμᾶς τὸν Ἰησοῦν ὃν ὁ Παῦλος·κηρύσ-
saying,   we exorcise you (by)   Jesus whom Paul proclaims.

**14** σει. ἦσαν δέ τινες υἱοὶ Σκευᾶ Ἰουδαίου ἀρχιερέως ἑπτὰ οἱ
were And of one sons, of Sceva, a Jewish chief priest, seven —

**15** τοῦτο ποιοῦντες. ἀποκριθὲν δὲ τὸ πνεῦμα τὸ πονηρὸν
this doing.   answering And the spirit   —   evil
εἶπε, Τὸν Ἰησοῦν γινώσκω, καὶ τὸν Παῦλον ἐπίσταμαι·
said,   —   Jesus I know,   and  —  Paul   I comprehend,

**16** ὑμεῖς δὲ τίνες ἐστέ; καὶ ἐφαλλόμενος ἐπ' αὐτοὺς ὁ ἄνθρωπος
you but, who are? And leaping   on   them the man
ἐν ᾧ ἦν τὸ πνεῦμα τὸ πονηρόν, καὶ κατακυριεύσας αὐτῶν,
in whom was the spirit   —   evil,   and overmastering   them,

prevailed against them, so that they fled out of the house naked and wounded. [17] And this became known to all, both Jews and Greeks, those living in Ephesus, and fear fell on all them, and the name of the Lord Jesus was magnified. [18] And many of those who believed came confessing and declaring their deeds. [19] And many of those who practiced the curious arts, having brought the books, burned (them) before all. And they counted up the prices of them and found (it) five thousand of silver. [20] So with might the word of the Lord increased and was strong.

[21] And when these things were ended, Paul having passed through Macedonia and Achaia purposed to go to Jerusalem, saying, After having been there, it is necessary for me also to see Rome. [22] And having sent into Macedonia two of those who ministered to him, Timothy and Erastus, he remained a time in Asia. [23] And at that time no small disturbance about the Way happened. [24] For a certain one named Demetrius, a silversmith, making silver temples of Diana, brought no little gain to the craftsman; [25] and whom having brought together, the workmen in such things, he said, Men, you know that from this trade is our wealth. [26] And you behold and hear that not only (those) of Ephesus but almost of all Asia, this Paul having persuaded turned away a great multitude, saying that they are not gods which are made by hands. [27] Now not only this is dangerous to us (lest) the business come into disrepute, but also the temple of the great goddess Diana will be counted nothing, and her majesty is also about to be destroyed, whom all Asia

---

ἴσχυσε κατ' αὐτῶν, ὥστε γυμνοὺς καὶ τετραυματισμένους
was strong against them,  so as     naked    and having been wounded

17 ἐκφυγεῖν ἐκ τοῦ οἴκου ἐκείνου. τοῦτο δὲ ἐγένετο γνωστὸν
to escape out of — house     that.      this And became     known

πᾶσιν Ἰουδαίοις τε καὶ Ἕλλησι τοῖς κατοικοῦσι τὴν Ἔφεσον,
to all, Jews     both and Greeks , those inhabiting — Ephesus;

καὶ ἐπέπεσε φόβος ἐπὶ πάντας αὐτούς, καὶ ἐμεγαλύνετο τὸ
and fell on   fear  on  all     them,   and was magnified the

18 ὄνομα τοῦ Κυρίου Ἰησοῦ. πολλοί τε τῶν πεπιστευκότων
name of the Lord   Jesus.  many And of those having believed

ἤρχοντο, ἐξομολογούμενοι, καὶ ἀναγγέλλοντες τὰς πράξεις
came     confessing        and  telling        the  doings

19 αὐτῶν. ἱκανοὶ δὲ τῶν τὰ περίεργα πραξάντων συνενέγκαντες
of them.  many And of those the curious arts practicing, bringing together

τὰς βίβλους κατέκαιον ἐνώπιον πάντων· καὶ συνεψήφισαν
the  rolls,  burned (them) before   all,    and they counted

20 τὰς τιμὰς αὐτῶν, καὶ εὗρον ἀργυρίου μυριάδας πέντε. οὕτω
the prices of them, and found of silver thousand  five.  Thus

κατὰ κράτος ὁ λόγος τοῦ Κυρίου ηὔξανε καὶ ἴσχυεν.
with might,  the word of the Lord increased and was strong.

21 Ὡς δὲ ἐπληρώθη ταῦτα, ἔθετο ὁ Παῦλος ἐν τῷ πνεύματι,
when And were fulfilled these things, purposed Paul in the Spirit

διελθὼν τὴν Μακεδονίαν καὶ Ἀχαΐαν, πορεύεσθαι εἰς
passing through Macedonia and Achaia    to go      to

Ἱερουσαλήμ, εἰπὼν ὅτι Μετὰ τὸ γενέσθαι με ἐκεῖ, δεῖ με καὶ
Jerusalem,   saying, — After  becoming me there, must me also

22 Ῥώμην ἰδεῖν. ἀποστείλας δὲ εἰς τὴν Μακεδονίαν δύο τῶν
Rome   see.  sending And into — Macedonia   two of those

διακονούντων αὐτῷ, Τιμόθεον καὶ Ἔραστον, αὐτὸς ἐπέσχε
ministering   to him, Timothy and Erastus,   he   delayed

χρόνον εἰς τὴν Ἀσίαν.
a time in  — Asia.

23 Ἐγένετο δὲ κατὰ τὸν καιρὸν ἐκεῖνον τάραχος οὐκ ὀλίγος
there was And about — time   that  disturbance not a little

24 περὶ τῆς ὁδοῦ. Δημήτριος γάρ τις ὀνόματι, ἀργυροκόπος,
about the Way.  Demetrius For one by name,  a silversmith,

ποιῶν ναοὺς ἀργυροῦς Ἀρτέμιδος, παρείχετο τοῖς τεχνίταις
making shrines silver  of Artemis  provided   the craftsmen

25 ἐργασίαν οὐκ ὀλίγην· οὓς συναθροίσας, καὶ τοὺς περὶ τὰ
trade      not a little; whom assembling   also the about

τοιαῦτα ἐργάτας, εἶπεν, Ἄνδρες, ἐπίστασθε ὅτι ἐκ ταύτης
such things workmen, he said, Men,  you understand that from this

26 τῆς ἐργασίας ἡ εὐπορία ἡμῶν ἐστι. καὶ θεωρεῖτε καὶ ἀκούετε
—   trade the gain  to us   is. And you behold and hear

ὅτι οὐ μόνον Ἐφέσου, ἀλλὰ σχεδὸν πάσης τῆς Ἀσίας, ὁ
that not only Ephesus, but   almost    all    — of Asia —

Παῦλος οὗτος πείσας μετέστησεν ἱκανὸν ὄχλον, λέγων ὅτι
Paul   this persuading perverted    a huge crowd, saying that

27 οὐκ εἰσὶ θεοὶ οἱ διὰ χειρῶν γινόμενοι. οὐ μόνον δὲ τοῦτο
not are gods those through hands being made. not only And this,

κινδυνεύει ἡμῖν τὸ μέρος εἰς ἀπελεγμὸν ἐλθεῖν, ἀλλὰ καὶ τὸ
is in danger to us the share into disrepute  to come, but also the

τῆς μεγάλης θεᾶς Ἀρτέμιδος ἱερὸν εἰς οὐδὲν λογισθῆναι,
of the great goddess Artemis   temple for nothing will be counted,

μέλλειν τε καὶ καθαιρεῖσθαι τὴν μεγαλειότητα αὐτῆς, ἣν ὅλη
is going and also to be diminished the greatness   of her, whom all

and the world worships. [28] And having heard, and having become full of anger, they cried out, saying, Great is Diana of (the) Ephesians. [29] And all the city was filled with confusion, and they rushed with one accord into the theater, holding fast Gaius and Aristarchus, Macedonians, traveling companions of Paul. [30] And Paul intending to enter into the mob, the disciples did not allow him. [31] And also some of the Asiarchs being his friends, sending to him, begged (him) not to give himself into the theater. [32] Then others indeed cried out a different thing, for the assembly was confounded, and the most did not know for what cause they came together. [33] But they dragged forward Alexander out of the crowd, the Jews thrusting him forward. And waving the hand, Alexander desired to defend himself to the mob. [34] But knowing that he is a Jew, one voice was from all, as they crying out over two hours, Great (is) Artemis of (the) Ephesians! [35] And the town clerk quieting the crowd, he says, Men, Ephesians, for what man is there who does not know the city of the Ephesians to be temple keepers of the great goddess Artemis, and of that fallen from the sky. [36] Then these things being undeniable, it is necessary for you having been calmed to be (so), and to do nothing rash. [37] For you brought these men, neither temple-robbers, nor blaspheming your goddess. [38] If truly then Demetrius and those craftsmen with him have a matter against anyone, courts are being (held), and proconsuls are; let them accuse one another. [39] But if you seek anything further, it will be settled in the lawful assembly. [40] For we are in danger to be accused of revolt concerning today; there being no cause about which we will be able to give account of

**28** ἡ 'Ασία καὶ ἡ οἰκουμένη σέβεται. ἀκούσαντες δὲ καὶ γενό-
Asia and the habitable world worships.   hearing   And, and
μενοι πλήρεις θυμοῦ, ἔκραζον λέγοντες, Μεγάλη ἡ ῎Αρτεμις
becoming full of anger, they cried out saying,   Great (is)   Artemis

**29** 'Εφεσίων. καὶ ἐπλήσθη ἡ πόλις ὅλη συγχύσεως· ὥρμησάν τε
    of (the)
Ephesians! And was filled the city   all of confusion,   they rushed and
ὁμοθυμαδὸν εἰς τὸ θέατρον, συναρπάσαντες Γάϊον καὶ
with one mind   to   the   theatre,   keeping a firm grip on Gaius and

**30** 'Αρίσταρχον Μακεδόνας, συνεκδήμους τοῦ Παύλου. τοῦ δὲ
Aristarchus,   Macedonians, traveling companions   of Paul.   —And
Παύλου βουλομένου εἰσελθεῖν εἰς τὸν δῆμον, οὐκ εἴων αὐτὸν
Paul intending   to enter   into the   mob,   not allowed him

**31** οἱ μαθηταί. τινὲς δὲ καὶ τῶν 'Ασιαρχῶν, ὄντες αὐτῷ φίλοι,
the disciples.   some And also of the   Asiarchs,   being of him friends,
πέμψαντες πρὸς αὐτόν, παρεκάλουν μὴ δοῦναι ἑαυτὸν εἰς
sending   to   him,   begged   not to give himself into

**32** τὸ θέατρον. ἄλλοι μὲν οὖν ἄλλο τι ἔκραζον· ἦν γὰρ ἡ
the theatre.   Others indeed, then, other some cried out,   was for the
ἐκκλησία συγκεχυμένη, καὶ οἱ πλείους οὐκ ᾔδεισαν τίνος
assembly   confounded,   and the majority not did know of what

**33** ἕνεκεν συνεληλύθεισαν. ἐκ δὲ τοῦ ὄχλου προεβίβασαν 'Αλέ-
on account they came together out But the crowd, they dragged forward
                                      of
ξανδρον, προβαλλόντων αὐτὸν τῶν 'Ιουδαίων. ὁ δὲ 'Αλέξαν-
Alexander,   thrusting forward him the   Jews.   And Alexander
δρος, κατασείσας τὴν χεῖρα, ἤθελεν ἀπολογεῖσθαι τῷ δήμῳ.
waving   the   hand   desired to defend himself to the   mob.

**34** ἐπιγνόντων δὲ ὅτι 'Ιουδαῖός ἐστι, φωνὴ ἐγένετο μία ἐκ
knowing   But that   a Jew   he is,   voice there was one from
πάντων ὡς ἐπὶ ὥρας δύο κραζόντων, Μεγάλη ἡ ῎Αρτεμις
all,   as over hours two crying out,   Great (is)   Artemis

**35** 'Εφεσίων. καταστείλας δὲ ὁ γραμματεὺς τὸν ὄχλον φησίν,
of (the) Ephesians! quieting And the town clerk   the crowd, he says,
῎Ανδρες 'Εφέσιοι, τίς γάρ ἐστιν ἄνθρωπος ὃς οὐ γινώσκει
Men,   Ephesians, what for is there   man   who not does know
τὴν 'Εφεσίων πόλιν νεωκόρον οὖσαν τῆς μεγάλης θεᾶς
the of (the) Ephesians city temple-keeper being of the great goddess

**36** 'Αρτέμιδος καὶ τοῦ Διοπετοῦς; ἀναντιρρήτων οὖν ὄντων
Artemis,   and of that fallen from the sky? undeniable   Then being
τούτων, δέον ἐστὶν ὑμᾶς κατεσταλμένους ὑπάρχειν, καὶ
these things, necessary it is you   having been quietened to be (so),   and

**37** μηδὲν προπετὲς πράττειν. ἠγάγετε γὰρ τοὺς ἄνδρας
nothing   rash   to do.   you brought For   —   men
τούτους, οὔτε ἱεροσύλους οὔτε βλασφημοῦντας τὴν θεᾶν
these,   neither temple-robbers nor   blaspheming   the goddess

**38** ὑμῶν. εἰ μὲν οὖν Δημήτριος καὶ οἱ σὺν αὐτῷ τεχνῖται πρός
of you. If indeed, then, Demetrius and those with him craftsmen against
τινα λόγον ἔχουσιν, ἀγοραῖοι ἄγονται, καὶ ἀνθύπατοί
anyone a matter have,   courts   are being (held), and proconsuls

**39** εἰσιν· ἐγκαλείτωσαν ἀλλήλοις. εἰ δέ τι περὶ ἑτέρων ἐπιζητεῖτε,
are; let them accuse   one another. if But any about other   you seek,
                                                          things

**40** ἐν τῇ ἐννόμῳ ἐκκλησίᾳ ἐπιλυθήσεται. καὶ γὰρ κινδυνεύομεν
in the lawful   assembly   it will be settled.   also For   we are in danger
ἐγκαλεῖσθαι στάσεως περὶ τῆς σήμερον, μηδενὸς αἰτίου
to be accused of insurrection concerning today;   nothing   cause
ὑπάρχοντος περὶ οὗ δυνησόμεθα ἀποδοῦναι λόγον τῆς
there being concerning which we shall be able to give   account —

this riotous gathering. [41]
And saying these things, he
dismissed the assembly.

**CHAPTER 20**

[1] But after the
tumult ceased, Paul having
called and greeted the
disciples, went away to go
to Macedonia. [2] And
having passed through
those parts, and having
exhorted them with many
words, he came to Greece.
[3] And having continued
three months, and a plot
having been made against
them by the Jews, being
about to sail into Syria, a
purpose arose to return
through Macedonia.
[4] And Sopater, a Berean;
and of Thessalonians,
Aristarchus and Secundus,
and Gaius of Derbe, and
Timothy, and of Asia,
Tychicus and Trophimus
a c c o m p a n i e d  h i m.
[5] These having gone
before waited for us in
Troas; [6] but we sailed
along after the days of
unleavened bread from
Philippi, and came to them
at Troas in five days, where
we stayed seven days.
[7] And on the first of the
week, the disciples having
been assembled to break
bread, being about to
depart on the morrow,
Paul talked to them; and
he continued the discouse
until midnight. [8] And
many lamps were in the
upper room where they
were assembled. [9] And a
certain youth named
Eutychus was sitting by
the window overpowered
by deep sleep. As Paul
talked for a longer time,
having been overpowered
by the sleep, he fell from
the third story down, and
was taken up dead.
[10] But having descended
Paul fell on him, and
having embraced (him)
said, Do not wail, for the
life of him is in him.
[11] And having gone and
having broken bread and
having eaten, and having
conversed a long time,
until daybreak, so he
departed. [12] And they
brought the boy alive and
were comforted not a

---

41  συστροφῆς ταύτης. καὶ ταῦτα εἰπών, ἀπέλυσε τὴν ἐκκλησίαν.
    crowding together of this. And these  saying,   he dismissed the  assembly.

**CHAPTER 20**

1  Μετὰ δὲ τὸ παύσασθαι τὸν θόρυβον, προσκαλεσάμενος
   after And the  ceasing   of the  tumult,      having called
   ὁ Παῦλος τοὺς μαθητάς, καὶ ἀσπασάμενος, ἐξῆλθε πορευθῆναι
   Paul   the disciples,  and greeting,      went away to go

2  εἰς τὴν Μακεδονίαν. διελθὼν δὲ τὰ μέρη ἐκεῖνα, καὶ παρα-
   to  —  Macedonia.  passing through And parts those,  and having
   καλέσας αὐτοὺς λόγῳ πολλῷ, ἦλθεν εἰς τὴν Ἑλλάδα. ποιή-
   exhorted  them with speech much, he came into — Greece. spending

3  σας τε μῆνας τρεῖς, γενομένης αὐτῷ ἐπιβουλῆς ὑπὸ τῶν
   And months three, there being (against) him a plot  by  the
   Ἰουδαίων μέλλοντι ἀνάγεσθαι εἰς τὴν Συρίαν, ἐγένετο
   Jews,  being about to set sail to  —  Syria,  he was

4  γνώμῃ τοῦ ὑποστρέφειν διὰ Μακεδονίας. συνείπετο δὲ
   of a mind —  to return  through Macedonia.  accompanied And
   αὐτῷ ἄχρι τῆς Ἀσίας Σώπατρος Βεροιαῖος· Θεσσαλονι-
   him as far as — Asia  Sopater,   a Berean,   of Thessalonians
   κέων δέ, Ἀρίσταρχος καὶ Σεκοῦνδος, καὶ Γάϊος Δερβαῖος,
   and,  Aristarchus  and  Secundus;  and  Gaius of Derbe,

5  καὶ Τιμόθεος· Ἀσιανοὶ δέ, Τυχικὸς καὶ Τρόφιμος. οὗτοι
   and Timothy,  of Asia and,  Tychicus and Trophimus. These

6  προελθόντες ἔμενον ἡμᾶς ἐν Τρωάδι. ἡμεῖς δὲ ἐξεπλεύσαμεν
   going forward awaited us in Troas.  we  And sailed away
   μετὰ τὰς ἡμέρας τῶν ἀζύμων ἀπὸ Φιλίππων, καὶ ἤλθομεν
   after  the days  – of unleavened from Philippi,   and  came
   πρὸς αὐτοὺς εἰς τὴν Τρωάδα ἄχρις ἡμερῶν πέντε, οὗ
   to  them  in  — Troas  until  days  five, where
   διετρίψαμεν ἡμέρας ἑπτά.
   we stayed  days  seven.

7  Ἐν δὲ τῇ μιᾷ τῶν σαββάτων, συνηγμένων τῶν μαθητῶν
   on And the one of the  sabbaths,  having been assembled the disciples
   τοῦ κλάσαι ἄρτον, ὁ Παῦλος διελέγετο αὐτοῖς, μέλλων
   – to break bread,  Paul   reasoned  to them, being about to
   ἐξιέναι τῇ ἐπαύριον, παρέτεινέ τε τὸν λόγον μέχρι μεσονυ-
   depart on the morrow; he continued and the discourse until midnight.

8  κτίου. ἦσαν δὲ λαμπάδες ἱκαναὶ ἐν τῷ ὑπερῴῳ οὗ ἦσαν
   there were And lamps  many  in the upper room where they were

9  συνηγμένοι. καθήμενος δέ τις νεανίας ὀνόματι Εὔτυχος ἐπὶ
   assembled.  sitting  And a certain young man by name Eutuchus on
   τῆς θυρίδος, καταφερόμενος ὕπνῳ βαθεῖ, διαλεγομένου τοῦ
   the window sill, being overborne by sleep deep,  reasoning  —
   Παύλου ἐπὶ πλεῖον, κατενεχθεὶς ἀπὸ τοῦ ὕπνου ἔπεσεν ἀπὸ
   Paul  for a longer time, being overborne by the sleep,  he fell from

10 τοῦ τριστέγου κάτω, καὶ ἤρθη νεκρός. καταβὰς δὲ ὁ Παῦλος
   the third floor  down, and was taken up dead. going down But Paul
   ἐπέπεσεν αὐτῷ, καὶ συμπεριλαβὼν εἶπε, Μὴ θορυβεῖσθε·
   fell on  him,  and having embraced  said, Do not be terrified;

11 ἡ γὰρ ψυχὴ αὐτοῦ ἐν αὐτῷ ἐστιν. ἀναβὰς δὲ καὶ κλάσας
   the for soul  of him in him  is.  going up And, and breaking
   ἄρτον καὶ γευσάμενος, ἐφ' ἱκανόν τε ὁμιλήσας ἄχρις αὐγῆς,
   bread, and  tasting,  over a long (time) and conversing until dawn,

12 οὕτως ἐξῆλθεν. ἤγαγον δὲ τὸν παῖδα ζῶντα, καὶ παρεκλήθη-
   thus  he went out. they brought and the boy living,  and were comforted

σαν οὐ μετρίως.
not moderately.

little.

[13] But having gone onto the ship before, we sailed to Assos, being about to take in Paul there; for so he had appointed, himself being about to go on foot. [14] And when he met us at Assos, having taken him in we came to Mitylene; [15] and from there having sailed away, on the following (day) arrived opposite Chios; and the next day we arrived at Samos; and having remained at Trogyllium the next (day) we came to Miletus. [16] For Paul had decided to sail by Ephesus, so that it might happen to him to spend time in Asia; for he hastened if it were possible for him to be in Jerusalem on the day of Pentecost.

[17] And from Miletus, having sent to Ephesus, he called for the elders of the assembly. [18] And when they had come to him, he said to them, You know, from the first day on which I arrived in Asia, how all the time I was with you, [19] serving the Lord with all humility, and many tears and temptations, which happened to me through the plots of the Jews; [20] how I kept nothing back of what is profitable, so as not to tell you, and to teach you publicly, and, from house to house, [21] earnestly testifying both to Jews and Greeks repentance toward God and faith toward our Lord Jesus Christ. [22] And now, behold, I bound in the Spirit go to Jerusalem, not knowing the things which shall happen in it to me; [23] except that the Holy Spirit in every city fully testifies, saying that bonds and tribulations await me. [24] But I do not think anything, nor do I hold my soul precious to myself, so as to finish my course with joy, and the

13 Ἡμεῖς δέ, προελθόντες ἐπὶ τὸ πλοῖον, ἀνήχθημεν εἰς τὴν
    we And, going before onto the ship, set sail for —

Ἄσσον, ἐκεῖθεν μέλλοντες ἀναλαμβάνειν τὸν Παῦλον· οὕτω
Assos, from there intending to take up — Paul; so

14 γὰρ ἦν διατεταγμένος, μέλλων αὐτὸς πεζεύειν. ὡς δὲ συνέ-
    For it was having been arranged, intending he to go afoot. when And he

βαλεν ἡμῖν εἰς τὴν Ἄσσον, ἀναλαβόντες αὐτὸν ἤλθομεν εἰς
met with us in — Assos, taking up him we came to

15 Μιτυλήνην. κἀκεῖθεν ἀποπλεύσαντες, τῇ ἐπιούσῃ κατηντή-
    Mitylene; and from there sailing away, on the next we

σαμεν ἀντικρὺ Χίου· τῇ δὲ ἑτέρᾳ παρεβάλομεν εἰς Σάμον· καὶ
arrived off Chios; on the and other we crossed to Samos; and

μείναντες ἐν Τρωγυλλίῳ, τῇ ἐχομένῃ ἤλθομεν εἰς Μίλητον.
having remained at Trogyllium, the next (day) we came to Mitylene.

16 ἔκρινε γὰρ ὁ Παῦλος παραπλεῦσαι τὴν Ἔφεσον, ὅπως μὴ
    had decided For Paul to sail past — Ephesus, so as not

γένηται αὐτῷ χρονοτριβῆσαι ἐν τῇ Ἀσίᾳ· ἔσπευδε γάρ, εἰ
be to him to spend time in — Asia; he hastened for, if

δυνατὸν ἦν αὐτῷ, τὴν ἡμέραν τῆς Πεντηκοστῆς γενέσθαι
possible it was for him, the day — of Pentecost to be

17 εἰς Ἱεροσόλυμα. Ἀπὸ δὲ τῆς Μιλήτου πέμψας εἰς Ἔφεσον
    in Jerusalem. from And — Mitylene sending to Ephesus

18 μετεκαλέσατο τοὺς πρεσβυτέρους τῆς ἐκκλησίας. ὡς δὲ παρε
    he called for the elders of the church. when And they

γένοντο πρὸς αὐτόν, εἶπεν αὐτοῖς,
came to him, he said to them,

Ὑμεῖς ἐπίστασθε, ἀπὸ πρώτης ἡμέρας ἀφ' ἧς ἐπέβην εἰς
    You understand from (the) first day from which I set foot in

τὴν Ἀσίαν, πῶς μεθ' ὑμῶν τὸν πάντα χρόνον ἐγενόμην,
— Asia, how with you the all time I was,

19 δουλεύων τῷ Κυρίῳ μετὰ πάσης ταπεινοφροσύνης καὶ
    serving the Lord with all humility and

πολλῶν δακρύων καὶ πειρασμῶν τῶν συμβάντων μοι ἐν
many tears and trials — happening to me by

20 ταῖς ἐπιβουλαῖς τῶν Ἰουδαίων· ὡς οὐδὲν ὑπεστειλάμην τῶν
    the plots of the Jews; as nothing I kept back of the

συμφερόντων, τοῦ μὴ ἀναγγεῖλαι ὑμῖν καὶ διδάξαι ὑμᾶς
profitable (things), — not to tell you, and to teach you

21 δημοσίᾳ καὶ κατ' οἴκους, διαμαρτυρόμενος Ἰουδαίοις τε καὶ
    publicly, and from house to house, earnestly testifying to Jews and also

Ἕλλησι τὴν εἰς τὸν Θεὸν μετάνοιαν, καὶ πίστιν τὴν εἰς τὸν
to Greeks — toward — God repentance, and faith — toward the

22 Κύριον ἡμῶν Ἰησοῦν Χριστόν. καὶ νῦν ἰδού, ἐγὼ δεδεμένος
    Lord of us, Jesus Christ. And now behold, I being bound

τῷ πνεύματι πορεύομαι εἰς Ἱερουσαλήμ, τὰ ἐν αὐτῇ συναντή-
by the Spirit am going to Jerusalem, the things in it going

23 σοντά μοι μὴ εἰδώς, πλὴν ὅτι τὸ Πνεῦμα τὸ Ἅγιον κατὰ
    to meet me not knowing, but that the Spirit — Holy city

πόλιν διαμαρτύρεται λέγον ὅτι δεσμά με καὶ θλίψεις μένουσιν.
by city testifies saying that bonds me and afflictions await.

24 ἀλλ' οὐδενὸς λόγον ποιοῦμαι, οὐδὲ ἔχω τὴν ψυχήν μου
    But of nothing account I make, nor hold the soul of me

τιμίαν ἐμαυτῷ, ὡς τελειῶσαι τὸν δρόμον μου μετὰ χαρᾶς,
precious to myself, so as I may finish the course of me with joy,

ministry which I received from the Lord Jesus Christ, to fully testify the gospel of the grace of God. [25] And now, behold, I know that you all will see my face no more, among whom I have gone about preaching the kingdom of God. [26] Therefore I testify to you in this day that I (am) pure from the blood of all, [27] for I did not keep back from preaching to you all the counsel of God. [28] Therefore, take heed to yourselves and to all the flock, in which the Holy Spirit made you overseers, to shepherd the assembly of God, which He purchased with His own blood. [29] For I know this, that after my departure grievous wolves will come in among you, not sparing the flock; [30] and from among your own selves will rise up men speaking perverted things, to draw away the disciples after themselves. [31] Therefore watch, remembering that I did not cease admonishing each one with tears three years, night and day. [32] And now I commit you, brothers, to God and to the word of His grace, which is able to build up and to give you an inheritance among all the sanctified. [33] I have desired silver or gold or clothing from no one. [34] But yourselves know that these hands ministered to my needs and to those who were with me. [35] I showed you all things, that working in this way we ought to help those being weak, and to remember the words of the Lord Jesus, that Himself said, It is more blessed to give than to receive. [36] And having said these things, having bowed his knees with them all, he prayed. [37] And there was much weeping of all; and falling on the neck of Paul they ardently kissed him,

καὶ τὴν διακονίαν ἣν ἔλαβον παρὰ τοῦ Κυρίου Ἰησοῦ,
and the ministry which I received from the Lord Jesus,

25 διαμαρτύρασθαι τὸ εὐαγγέλιον τῆς χάριτος τοῦ Θεοῦ. καὶ
to fully testify the gospel of the grace — of God. And

νῦν ἰδού, ἐγὼ οἶδα ὅτι οὐκέτι ὄψεσθε τὸ πρόσωπόν μου
now behold, I know that no more will see the face of me

ὑμεῖς πάντες, ἐν οἷς διῆλθον κηρύσσων τὴν βασιλείαν τοῦ
you all, among whom I went about proclaiming the kingdom —

26 Θεοῦ. διὸ μαρτύρομαι ὑμῖν ἐν τῇ σήμερον ἡμέρᾳ, ὅτι καθαρὸς
of God. Therefore I testify to you on — this day that clean

27 ἐγὼ ἀπὸ τοῦ αἵματος πάντων. οὐ γὰρ ὑπεστειλάμην τοῦ
I am from the blood of all; not for I kept back —

μὴ ἀναγγεῖλαι ὑμῖν πᾶσαν τὴν βουλὴν τοῦ Θεοῦ. προσ-
not to declare to you all the counsel — of God. take

28 έχετε οὖν ἑαυτοῖς καὶ παντὶ τῷ ποιμνίῳ, ἐν ᾧ ὑμᾶς τὸ
heed, therefore, to yourselves and to all the flock, in which you the

Πνεῦμα τὸ Ἅγιον ἔθετο ἐπισκόπους, ποιμαίνειν τὴν ἐκκλη-
Spirit — Holy placed overseers, to shepherd the church

σίαν τοῦ Θεοῦ, ἣν περιεποιήσατο διὰ τοῦ ἰδίου αἵματος.
— of God, which He purchased through the own blood.

29 ἐγὼ γὰρ οἶδα τοῦτο, ὅτι εἰσελεύσονται μετὰ τὴν ἄφιξίν
I For know this, that will come in after the departure

30 μου λύκοι βαρεῖς εἰς ὑμᾶς, μὴ φειδόμενοι τοῦ ποιμνίου· καὶ
of me wolves grievous into you, not sparing the flock, and

ἐξ ὑμῶν αὐτῶν ἀναστήσονται ἄνδρες λαλοῦντες διεστραμ-
out of you yourselves will rise up men speaking perverted

31 μένα, τοῦ ἀποσπᾶν τοὺς μαθητὰς ὀπίσω αὐτῶν. διὸ
things, — to draw away the disciples after themselves. Therefore

γρηγορεῖτε, μνημονεύοντες ὅτι τριετίαν νύκτα καὶ ἡμέραν
watch, remembering that three years night and cay

32 οὐκ ἐπαυσάμην μετὰ δακρύων νουθετῶν ἕνα ἕκαστον. καὶ
not I ceased with tears admonishing one each. And

τὰ νῦν παρατίθεμαι ὑμᾶς, ἀδελφοί, τῷ Θεῷ καὶ τῷ λόγῳ
— now I commend you, brothers, — to God and to the word

τῆς χάριτος αὐτοῦ, τῷ δυναμένῳ ἐποικοδομῆσαι, καὶ
— of grace of Him, — being able to build up and

33 δοῦναι ὑμῖν κληρονομίαν ἐν τοῖς ἡγιασμένοις πᾶσιν. ἀργυ-
to give you inheritance among those having been sanctified all. Silver

34 ρίου ἢ χρυσίου ἢ ἱματισμοῦ οὐδενὸς ἐπεθύμησα. αὐτοὶ δὲ
or gold or clothing of no one I desired. yourselves But

γινώσκετε ὅτι ταῖς χρείαις μου καὶ τοῖς οὖσι μετ' ἐμοῦ
know that to the needs of me and those being with me

35 ὑπηρέτησαν αἱ χεῖρες αὗται. πάντα ὑπέδειξα ὑμῖν, ὅτι
ministered hands these. All things I showed to you, that

οὕτω κοπιῶντας δεῖ ἀντιλαμβάνεσθαι τῶν ἀσθενούντων,
thus working it behoves to help those infirm (ones),

μνημονεύειν τε τῶν λόγων τοῦ Κυρίου Ἰησοῦ, ὅτι αὐτὸς
to remember and the word of the Lord Jesus, that He

εἶπε, Μακάριόν ἐστι διδόναι μᾶλλον ἢ λαμβάνειν.
said, Blessed it is to give rather than to receive.

36 Καὶ ταῦτα εἰπών, θεὶς τὰ γόνατα αὐτοῦ, σὺν πᾶσιν
And these things having said, placing the knees of him, with all

37 αὐτοῖς προσηύξατο. ἱκανὸς δὲ ἐγένετο κλαυθμὸς πάντων·
them he prayed. much And was weeping of all,

καὶ ἐπιπεσόντες ἐπὶ τὸν τράχηλον τοῦ Παύλου κατεφίλουν
and falling on the neck — of Paul they ardently kissed

[38] most of all distressed for the words which he had said, that they no more were going to see his face. And they went with him to the ship.

**CHAPTER 21**

[1] And it came to pass, having torn away from them, we sailed; having run direct we came to Coos, and on the next (day) to Rhodes, and from there to Patara. [2] And having found a ship passing over into Phenicia, having gone on board we sailed; [3] and having sighed Cyrus, and left it on the left, we sailed to Svria, and landed at Tyre, for the ship was discharging the cargo there. [4] And having found the disciples, we remained there seven days; who said to Paul by the Spirit not to go up to Jerusalem. [5] But it came to pass when we completed the days, having set out we traveled, all accompanying us, with wives and children, as far as outside the city. And having bowed the knees on the shore, we prayed. [6] And having greeted one another, we went up into the ship; and they returned to their own (homes). [7] And the voyage being completed from Tyre, we arrived at Ptolemais, and having greeted the brothers, we stayed one day with them. [8] And on the morrow Paul and those with him having gone out, they came to Caesarea; and having gone in to the house of Philip the evangelist, being of the seven, we stayed with him. [9] Now to this one there were four virgin daughters who prophesied. [10] And we remaining many days, a certain one from Judea, a prophet named Agabus, came down. [11] And having come to us, and having taken Paul's girdle, and having bound his hands and feet, said, The

---

**38** αὐτόν, ὀδυνώμενοι μάλιστα ἐπὶ τῷ λόγῳ ᾧ εἰρήκει, ὅτι
him, grieving most over the word which he said, that
οὐκέτι μέλλουσι τὸ πρόσωπον αὐτοῦ θεωρεῖν. προέπεμπον
no more they are the face of him to behold. they escorted
δὲ αὐτὸν εἰς τὸ πλοῖον.
And him to the ship.

**CHAPTER 21**

**1** Ὡς δὲ ἐγένετο ἀναχθῆναι ἡμᾶς ἀποσπασθέντας ἀπ'
when And it was (time) to sail, we having been withdrawn from
αὐτῶν, εὐθυδρομήσαντες ἤλθομεν εἰς τὴν Κῶν, τῇ δὲ ἑξῆς
them, having run direct, we came to — Coos; on the and next

**2** εἰς τὴν Ῥόδον, κἀκεῖθεν εἰς Πάταρα· καὶ εὑρόντες πλοῖον
to — Rhodes, and from there to Patara; and having found a ship
διαπερῶν εἰς Φοινίκην, ἐπιβάντες ἀνήχθημεν. ἀναφάναντες
crossing over to Phoenice, entering we set sail. having sighted

**3** δὲ τὴν Κύπρον, καὶ καταλιπόντες αὐτὴν εὐώνυμον, ἐπλέομεν
And — Cyprus, and leaving it on the left, we sailed
εἰς Συρίαν, καὶ κατήχθημεν εἰς Τύρον· ἐκεῖσε γὰρ ἦν τὸ
to Syria, and came down to Tyre; there for was the

**4** πλοῖον ἀποφορτιζόμενον τὸν γόμον. καὶ ἀνευρόντες
ship unloading the cargo. And having found
μαθητάς, ἐπεμείναμεν αὐτοῦ ἡμέρας ἑπτά· οἵτινες τῷ Παύλῳ
disciples, we remained there days seven; who — Paul
ἔλεγον διὰ τοῦ Πνεύματος, μὴ ἀναβαίνειν εἰς Ἱερουσαλήμ.
told through the Spirit not to go up to Jerusalem.

**5** ὅτε δὲ ἐγένετο ἡμᾶς ἐξαρτίσαι τὰς ἡμέρας, ἐξελθόντες ἐπο-
when But it was (time) us to complete the days, having gone out we
ρευόμεθα, προπεμπόντων ἡμᾶς πάντων σὺν γυναιξὶ καὶ
traveled, accompanying us all with women and
τέκνοις ἕως ἔξω τῆς πόλεως· καὶ θέντες τὰ γόνατα ἐπὶ τὸν
children as far as outside the city; and placing the knees on the

**6** αἰγιαλὸν προσηυξάμεθα. καὶ ἀσπασάμενοι ἀλλήλους, ἐπέ-
shore, praying, And giving parting greetings to one another, we
βημεν εἰς τὸ πλοῖον, ἐκεῖνοι δὲ ὑπέστρεψαν εἰς τὰ ἴδια.
went up into the ship, those and returned to the own.

**7** Ἡμεῖς δέ, τὸν πλοῦν διανύσαντες ἀπὸ Τύρου, κατηντή-
we And, the voyage completing from Tyre, arrived
σαμεν εἰς Πτολεμαΐδα, καὶ ἀσπασάμενοι τοὺς ἀδελφοὺς
at Ptolemais; and greeting the brothers,

**8** ἐμείναμεν ἡμέραν μίαν παρ' αὐτοῖς. τῇ δὲ ἐπαύριον ἐξελθόντες
we remained day one with them, on the And morrow going out
οἱ περὶ τὸν Παῦλον ἤλθομεν εἰς Καισάρειαν· καὶ εἰσελθόντες
those around (him), Paul came to Caesarea, and having gone
εἰς τὸν οἶκον Φιλίππου τοῦ εὐαγγελιστοῦ, τοῦ ὄντος ἐκ τῶν
to the house of Philip the evangelist, — being of the

**9** ἑπτά, ἐμείναμεν παρ' αὐτῷ. τούτῳ δὲ ἦσαν θυγατέρες
seven, we stayed with him. to this one And were daughters

**10** παρθένοι τέσσαρες προφητεύουσαι. ἐπιμενόντων δὲ ἡμῶν
virgin four prophesying. remaining And we
ἡμέρας πλείους, κατῆλθέ τις ἀπὸ τῆς Ἰουδαίας προφήτης
days more, came down a certain from — Judea prophet,

**11** ὀνόματι Ἄγαβος. καὶ ἐλθὼν πρὸς ἡμᾶς, καὶ ἄρας τὴν ζώνην
by name Agabus. and coming to us, and taking the girdle
τοῦ Παύλου, δήσας τε αὐτοῦ τὰς χεῖρας καὶ τοὺς πόδας εἶπε,
— of Paul, binding and of himself the hands and the feet, he said,

Jews shall bind the man whose girdle this is in Jerusalem, and deliver (him) up into (the) hands of (the) nations. [12] And when we heard these things, both we and those of (the) place begged him not to go up to Jerusalem. [13] But Paul answered, What are you doing, weeping and breaking my heart? For I not only am ready to be bound, but also to die at Jerusalem for the name of the Lord Jesus? [14] And he not being persuaded, we were silent, saying, The will of the Lord be done.

Τάδε λέγει τὸ Πνεῦμα τὸ Ἅγιον, Τὸν ἄνδρα οὗ ἐστιν ἡ ζώνη
These says the Spirit — Holy, The man of whom is girdle

αὕτη, οὕτω δήσουσιν ἐν Ἱερουσαλὴμ οἱ Ἰουδαῖοι, καὶ
this, thus will bind in Jerusalem the Jews, and

12 παραδώσουσιν εἰς χεῖρας ἐθνῶν. ὡς δὲ ἠκούσαμεν ταῦτα,
will deliver into (the) hands of nations. when And we heard these things,

παρεκαλοῦμεν ἡμεῖς τε καὶ οἱ ἐντόπιοι, τοῦ μὴ ἀναβαίνειν
begged we both and the residents — not to go up

13 αὐτὸν εἰς Ἱερουσαλήμ. ἀπεκρίθη δὲ ὁ Παῦλος, Τί ποιεῖτε
him to Jerusalem. answered And Paul, What are you doing,

κλαίοντες καὶ συνθρύπτοντές μου τὴν καρδίαν ; ἐγὼ γὰρ οὐ
weeping and crushing of me the heart? ! For not

μόνον δεθῆναι, ἀλλὰ καὶ ἀποθανεῖν εἰς Ἱερουσαλὴμ ἑτοίμως
only to be bound, but also to die in Jerusalem readiness

14 ἔχω ὑπὲρ τοῦ ὀνόματος τοῦ Κυρίου Ἰησοῦ. μὴ πειθομένου
I have for the name of the Lord Jesus. not being persuaded

δὲ αὐτοῦ, ἡσυχάσαμεν εἰπόντες, Τὸ θέλημα τοῦ Κυρίου
And him, we kept silence, having said, Of the will of the Lord

γενέσθω.
let be (done).

[15] And after these days, having packed the baggage, we went up to Jerusalem. [16] And also (some) of the disciples from Caesarea went with us, bringing a certain Cypriot, an ancient disciple, Mnason, with whom we might lodge. [17] And we being in Jerusalem, the brothers joyfully received us. [18] And on the next (day) Paul went in with us to James; and all the elders came..[19] And having greeted them, he related one by one what things God had worked among the nations by his ministry. [20] And having heard, they glorified the Lord. And they said to him, You see, brother, how many myriads of Jews there are who have believed, and all are zealous ones of the Law. [21] And they were told about you, that you teach the falling away from Moses, telling all the Jews among the nations not to circumcise their children, nor to walk in the customs. [22] What then is it? A multitude must certainly come together; for they will hear that you have come. [23] Therefore do this, what we say to you: Four men are with us having a vow on themselves; [24] having taken these be purified

15 Μετὰ δὲ τὰς ἡμέρας ταύτας ἀποσκευασάμενοι ἀνεβαίνομεν
after And — days these having made ready, we went up

16 εἰς Ἱερουσαλήμ. συνῆλθον δὲ καὶ τῶν μαθητῶν ἀπὸ Καισα-
to Jerusalem. went And also of the disciples from Caesarea

ρείας σὺν ἡμῖν, ἄγοντες παρ' ᾧ ξενισθῶμεν, Μνάσωνί τινι
with us, bringing (one) with whom we may lodge, Mnason a certain

Κυπρίῳ, ἀρχαίῳ μαθητῇ.
Cypriot, an ancient disciple.

17 Γενομένων δὲ ἡμῶν εἰς Ἱεροσόλυμα, ἀσμένως ἐδέξαντο
being And us in Jerusalem, joyfully received

ἡμᾶς οἱ ἀδελφοί. τῇ δὲ ἐπιούσῃ εἰσῄει ὁ Παῦλος σὺν ἡμῖν πρὸς
us the brothers. on the And next went in Paul with us to

18 Ἰάκωβον, πάντες τε παρεγένοντο οἱ πρεσβύτεροι. καὶ
James, all and came the elders. And

19 ἀσπασάμενος αὐτούς, ἐξηγεῖτο καθ' ἓν ἕκαστον ὧν ἐποίησεν
having greeted them, he related one by one of which did

20 ὁ Θεὸς ἐν τοῖς ἔθνεσι διὰ τῆς διακονίας αὐτοῦ. οἱ δὲ ἀκού-
God among the nations through the ministry of him. they And

σαντες ἐδόξαζον τὸν Κύριον· εἶπόν τε αὐτῷ, Θεωρεῖς, ἀδελφέ,
hearing glorified the Lord, said and to him, You see, brother,

πόσαι μυριάδες εἰσὶν Ἰουδαίων τῶν πεπιστευκότων· καὶ
how many myriads there are of Jews — having believed, and

21 πάντες ζηλωταὶ τοῦ νόμου ὑπάρχουσι· κατηχήθησαν δὲ
all zealous ones of the law are; they were informed and

περὶ σοῦ, ὅτι ἀποστασίαν διδάσκεις ἀπὸ Μωσέως τοὺς
about you, that falling away you teach from Moses —

κατὰ τὰ ἔθνη πάντας Ἰουδαίους, λέγων μὴ περιτέμνειν
throughout the nations all Jews, telling not to circumcise

22 αὐτοὺς τὰ τέκνα, μηδὲ τοῖς ἔθεσι περιπατεῖν. τί οὖν ἐστι ;
them the children, nor in the customs to walk. What, then, is it?

πάντως δεῖ πλῆθος συνελθεῖν· ἀκούσονται γὰρ ὅτι ἐλή-
At all events must a multitude come together will hear for that you

23 λυθας. τοῦτο οὖν ποίησον ὅ σοι λέγομεν· εἰσὶν ἡμῖν ἄνδρες
have come. This, then, do what you we tell. There are to us men

24 τέσσαρες εὐχὴν ἔχοντες ἐφ' ἑαυτῶν· τούτους παραλαβὼν
four having a vow upon themselves; these taking

with them, and be at expense for them, that they may shave the head; and all may know that of which they have been informed about you is nothing, but you yourself also walk orderly, keeping the Law. [25] But we wrote concerning those who had believed of the nations, judging them to observe no such thing, except to keep themselves from things offered to idols, and the blood, and what is strangled and (from) fornication. [26] Then Paul having taken the men, on the next day having been purified with them entered into the Temple, declaring the fulfillment of the days of the purification, until the offering was offered for each one of them. [27] But when the seven days were about to be completed, the Jews from Asia having seen him in the Temple, stirred up all the crowd and laid hands on him, [28] crying out, Men, Israelites, help! This is the man who teaches all everywhere against the people and the Law and this place, and further, he also brought Greeks into the Temple and defiled this holy place. [29] For they had before seen Trophimus the Ephesian in the city with him, whom they supposed that Paul brought into the Temple. [30] And the whole city was moved, and there was a gathering of the people; and having seized Paul, they drew him outside the Temple, and immediately the doors were shut. [31] But as they were seeking to kill him, a report came to the chief captain of the band, that all Jerusalem was in a tumult; [32] who at once having taken soldiers and centurions ran down on them. And they having seen the chief captain and the soldiers stopped beating Paul. [33] Then having gone near the chief captain laid hold of him

ἀγνίσθητι σὺν αὐτοῖς, καὶ δαπάνησον ἐπ’ αὐτοῖς, ἵνα
be purified with them, and be at expense on them, that

ξυρήσωνται τὴν κεφαλήν, καὶ γνῶσι πάντες ὅτι ὧν κατή-
they may shave the head, and may know all that of which they

χηνται περὶ σοῦ οὐδέν ἐστιν, ἀλλὰ στοιχεῖς καὶ αὐτὸς τὸν
have been told about you nothing is, but you walk also yourself the

25 νόμον φυλάσσων. περὶ δὲ τῶν πεπιστευκότων ἐθνῶν ἡμεῖς
Law keeping. concerning And the believing nations, we

ἐπεστείλαμεν, κρίναντες μηδὲν τοιοῦτον τηρεῖν αὐτούς, εἰ
joined in writing, judging no such thing to observe them, ex-

μὴ φυλάσσεσθαι αὐτοὺς τό τε εἰδωλόθυτον καὶ τὸ αἷμα καὶ
cept to keep from themselves the both idol sacrifice and the blood and

26 πνικτὸν καὶ πορνείαν. τότε ὁ Παῦλος παραλαβὼν τοὺς
a thing strangled and fornication, Then Paul taking the

ἄνδρας, τῇ ἐχομένῃ ἡμέρᾳ σὺν αὐτοῖς ἁγνισθεὶς εἰσήει εἰς
men, on the next day with them having been purified went into

τὸ ἱερόν, διαγγέλλων τὴν ἐκπλήρωσιν τῶν ἡμερῶν τοῦ
the Temple, declaring the fulfillment of the days of the

ἁγνισμοῦ, ἕως οὗ προσηνέχθη ὑπὲρ ἑνὸς ἑκάστου αὐτῶν
purification, until should be offered for one each of them

ἡ προσφορά.
the offering.

27 Ὡς δὲ ἔμελλον αἱ ἑπτὰ ἡμέραι συντελεῖσθαι, οἱ ἀπὸ τῆς
as But about to be the seven days completed, the from —

Ἀσίας Ἰουδαῖοι, θεασάμενοι αὐτὸν ἐν τῷ ἱερῷ, συνέχεον
Asia Jews, having seen him in the Temple, stirred up

πάντα τὸν ὄχλον, καὶ ἐπέβαλον τὰς χεῖρας ἐπ’ αὐτόν,
all the crowd, and laid the hands on him,

28 κράζοντες, Ἄνδρες Ἰσραηλῖται, βοηθεῖτε. οὗτός ἐστιν ὁ
crying out, Men, Israelites, help! This is the

ἄνθρωπος ὁ κατὰ τοῦ λαοῦ καὶ τοῦ νόμου καὶ τοῦ τόπου
man who against the people and the Law and — place

τούτου πάντας πανταχοῦ διδάσκων· ἔτι τε καὶ Ἕλληνας
this all everywhere teaching. further And also Greeks

εἰσήγαγεν εἰς τὸ ἱερόν, καὶ κεκοίνωκε τὸν ἅγιον τόπον
brought in to the Temple, and has defiled — holy place

29 τοῦτον. ἦσαν γὰρ προεωρακότες Τρόφιμον τὸν Ἐφέσιον ἐν
this. they were For previously seen Trophimus the Ephesian in

τῇ πόλει σὺν αὐτῷ, ὃν ἐνόμιζον ὅτι εἰς τὸ ἱερὸν εἰσήγαγεν
the city with him, whom they supposed that into the Temple brought in

30 ὁ Παῦλος. ἐκινήθη τε ἡ πόλις ὅλη, καὶ ἐγένετο συνδρομὴ τοῦ
Paul, was moved And the city whole, and there was running together the

λαοῦ· καὶ ἐπιλαβόμενοι τοῦ Παύλου εἷλκον αὐτὸν ἔξω τοῦ
people, and having seized — Paul, they drew him outside of the

31 ἱεροῦ· καὶ εὐθέως ἐκλείσθησαν αἱ θύραι. ζητούντων δὲ αὐτὸν
Temple, and at once were shut the doors. they seeking And him

ἀποκτεῖναι, ἀνέβη φάσις τῷ χιλιάρχῳ τῆς σπείρης, ὅτι
to kill, came up a report to the chiliarch of the cohort, that

32 ὅλη συγκέχυται Ἱερουσαλήμ· ὃς ἐξαυτῆς παραλαβὼν
all is in a tumult Jerusalem; who at once having taken

στρατιώτας καὶ ἑκατοντάρχους, κατέδραμεν ἐπ’ αὐτούς·
soldiers and centurions, ran down on them;

οἱ δέ, ἰδόντες τὸν χιλίαρχον καὶ τοὺς στρατιώτας, ἐπαύσαντο
they and seeing the chiliarch and the soldiers ceased

33 τύπτοντες τὸν Παῦλον. τότε ἐγγίσας ὁ χιλίαρχος ἐπελάβετο
beating — Paul. Then going near the chiliarch laid hold

and commanded (him) to be bound with two chains, **34** and asked who he might be, and what he had been doing. [34] But some were crying out one thing and some another in the crowd. **35** And not being able to know the certainty because of the tumult, he commanded him to be brought into the fortress. **36** [35] But when he came on the stairs, it happened to be borne by the soldiers because of the violence of the crowd. [36] For the multitude of the people **37** followed, crying out, Away with him! [37] But being about to be brought into **38** the fortress, Paul said to the chief captain, Is it permitted for me to say something to you? And he said, Do you know Greek? **39** [38] Are you not then the Egyptian who before these days caused a riot and led four thousand men of the assassins out into the desert? [39] But Paul said, **40** I am indeed a Jew of Tarsus, of Cilicia, no mean city, a citizen, and I beg you, allow me to speak to the people. [40] And he having allowed (him), Paul standing on the stairs signaled with his hand to the people; and great silence having taken place, he spoke in the Hebrew dialect, saying,

CHAPTER 22
[1] Men, brothers and fathers, hear my defense now to you. [2] And having heard that he spoke to them in the Hebrew dialect, they kept quiet the more; and he said, [3] I am indeed a man, a Jew born in Tarsus of Cilicia, but brought up in this city at the feet of Gamaliel, having been taught according to (the) exactness of the ancestral law, being a zealous one for God, even as you all are today; [4] who persecuted this Way to death, binding

αὐτοῦ, καὶ ἐκέλευσε δεθῆναι ἁλύσεσι δυσί· καὶ ἐπυνθάνετο τίς
of him. and commanded to be bound with chains two, and asked who

**34** ἂν εἴη, καὶ τί ἐστι πεποιηκώς. ἄλλοι δὲ ἄλλο τι ἐβόων ἐν τῷ
he may be, and what he is doing.        others And else something cried in the

ὄχλῳ· μὴ δυνάμενος δὲ γνῶναι τὸ ἀσφαλὲς διὰ τὸν θόρυβον,
crowd, not being able and to know the certain thing for the uproar,

**35** ἐκέλευσεν ἄγεσθαι αὐτὸν εἰς τὴν παρεμβολήν. ὅτε δὲ ἐγένετο
he commanded to bring him into the fortress.    when But he came

ἐπὶ τοὺς ἀναβαθμούς, συνέβη βαστάζεσθαι αὐτὸν ὑπὸ τῶν
on the steps,    it happened to be carried    him by the

**36** στρατιωτῶν διὰ τὴν βίαν τοῦ ὄχλου. ἠκολούθει γὰρ τὸ
soldiers    because of the violence of the crowd.    followed For the

πλῆθος τοῦ λαοῦ κρᾶζον, Αἶρε αὐτόν.
multitude of the people crying out, Take away him.

**37** Μέλλων τε εἰσάγεσθαι εἰς τὴν παρεμβολὴν ὁ Παῦλος λεγει
being about And to be brought into the fortress,    Paul    said

τῷ χιλιάρχῳ, Εἰ ἔξεστί μοι εἰπεῖν τι πρός σε; ὁ δὲ ἔφη,
to the chiliarch, If it is lawful for me to say a thing to you? he And said,

**38** Ἑλληνιστὶ γινώσκεις; οὐκ ἄρα σὺ εἶ ὁ Αἰγύπτιος ὁ πρὸ
in Greek    do you know? Not, then, you are the Egyptian, he before

τούτων τῶν ἡμερῶν ἀναστατώσας καὶ ἐξαγαγὼν εἰς τὴν
these    —    days    caused a riot and leading out into the

**39** ἔρημον τοὺς τετρακισχιλίους ἄνδρας τῶν σικαρίων; εἶπε δὲ ὁ
desert the four thousand    men of the assassins? said And

Παῦλος, Ἐγὼ ἄνθρωπος μέν εἰμι Ἰουδαῖος, Ταρσεὺς τῆς
Paul,    I    a man    indeed am,    a Jew,    a Tarsian —

Κιλικίας, οὐκ ἀσήμου πόλεως πολίτης· δέομαι δέ σου, ἐπί-
of Cilicia, not of a mean city    a citizen.    I beg And of you,

**40** τρεψόν μοι λαλῆσαι πρὸς τὸν λαόν. ἐπιτρέψαντος δὲ αὐτοῦ,
allow    me to speak    to the people. he having allowed And him,

ὁ Παῦλος ἑστὼς ἐπὶ τῶν ἀναβαθμῶν κατέσεισε τῇ χειρὶ τῷ
Paul standing on the steps    signaled with the hand to the

λαῷ· πολλῆς δὲ σιγῆς γενομένης, προσεφώνησε τῇ Ἑβραΐδι
people; much and silence occurring,    he spoke    in the Hebrew

διαλέκτῳ λέγων,
dialect, saying,

## CHAPTER 22

**1** Ἄνδρες ἀδελφοὶ καὶ πατέρες, ἀκούσατέ μου τῆς πρὸς
Men,    brothers and fathers,    hear    of me the to

ὑμᾶς νῦν ἀπολογίας.
you now defense.

**2** Ἀκούσαντες δὲ ὅτι τῇ Ἑβραΐδι διαλέκτῳ προσεφώνει
hearing    And that in the Hebrew dialect    he spoke

αὐτοῖς, μᾶλλον παρέσχον ἡσυχίαν. καί φησιν,
to them, more they showed quietness. And he says,

**3** Ἐγὼ μέν εἰμι ἀνὴρ Ἰουδαῖος, γεγεννημένος ἐν Ταρσῷ τῆς
I indeed am a man, a Jew, having been born in Tarsus

Κιλικίας, ἀνατεθραμμένος δὲ ἐν τῇ πόλει ταύτῃ παρὰ τοὺς
of Cilicia, having been brought up and in — city this at the

πόδας Γαμαλιήλ, πεπαιδευμένος κατὰ ἀκρίβειαν τοῦ πα-
feet    of Gamaliel; having been trained according to exactness of the

τρῴου νόμου, ζηλωτὴς ὑπάρχων τοῦ Θεοῦ, καθὼς πάντες
ancestral Law,    a zealous one being    — of God, even as all

**4** ὑμεῖς ἐστε σήμερον· ὃς ταύτην τὴν ὁδὸν ἐδίωξα ἄχρι θανάτου,
you are today; who this    —    Way persecuted as far as to death,

and delivering up both men and women to prison; [5] as also the high priest bears witness to me, and all the elderhood; and having received also letters to the brothers, I went to Damascus, to bring those who were also there bound to Jerusalem, in order that they might be punished. [6] And journeying and drawing near to Damascus, it also happened to me about midday, suddenly out of the Heaven a great light shone about me. [7] And I fell to the ground, and heard a voice saying to me, Saul, Saul, why do you persecute Me? [8] And I answered, Who are you, lord? And He said to me, I am Jesus the Nazarene, whom you persecute. [9] But those being with me indeed saw the light, and were alarmed, but did not hear His voice speaking to me. [10] And I said, What shall I do, Lord? And the Lord said to me, Having risen up, Go to Damascus, and there it shall be told you about all things which it has been appointed you to do. [11] And as I did not see from the glory of that light, being led by the hand of those being with me, I came to Damascus. [12] And a certain Ananias, a devout man according to the Law, testified to by all the Jews living (there) [13] coming to me and standing by said to me, Brother Saul, look up. And in the same hour I looked up on him. [14] And he said, The God of our fathers appointed you to know His will, and to see the Just One, and to hear a voice out of His mouth; [15] for you shall be a witness for Him to all men of what you have seen and heard. [16] And now why do you delay? Having arisen be baptized and wash away your sins, calling on the name of the Lord. [17] And it happened to me, having returned to Jerusalem, and on my praying in the Temple, I fell into a trance,

δεσμεύων καὶ παραδιδοὺς εἰς φυλακὰς ἄνδρας τε καὶ γυναῖκας.
binding   and  delivering  to  prisons   men  both and  women.

5 ὡς καὶ ὁ ἀρχιερεὺς μαρτυρεῖ μοι, καὶ πᾶν τὸ πρεσβυτέριον·
as Even the high priest  witnesses to me, and  all  the  elderhood;

παρ' ὧν καὶ ἐπιστολὰς δεξάμενος πρὸς τοὺς ἀδελφούς, εἰς
from whom also letters  having received to   the  brothers,  in

Δαμασκὸν ἐπορευόμην, ἄξων καὶ τοὺς ἐκεῖσε ὄντας δεδεμένους
Damascus,  I traveled     leading also those there being   bound

6 εἰς Ἰερουσαλήμ, ἵνα τιμωρηθῶσιν. ἐγένετο δέ μοι πορευο-
to   Jerusalem,  that they might be punished. it was And to me traveling

μένῳ καὶ ἐγγίζοντι τῇ Δαμασκῷ, περὶ μεσημβρίαν, ἐξαίφνης
and drawing near to Damascus, about midday,  suddenly

7 ἐκ τοῦ οὐρανοῦ περιαστράψαι φῶς ἱκανὸν περὶ ἐμέ. ἔπεσόν
out of the heaven  shone      light a great about me. I fell

τε εἰς τὸ ἔδαφος, καὶ ἤκουσα φωνῆς λεγούσης μοι, Σαούλ,
And to the ground, and  heard  a voice saying to me, Saul,

8 Σαούλ, τί με διώκεις; ἐγὼ δὲ ἀπεκρίθην, Τίς εἶ, Κύριε; εἶπέ
Saul,  why Me you persecute? I And answered,  Who are you, Sir? He said

τε πρός με, Ἐγώ εἰμι Ἰησοῦς ὁ Ναζωραῖος ὃν σὺ διώκεις.
And to me,  I   am     Jesus the Nazarene, whom you persecute.

9 οἱ δὲ σὺν ἐμοὶ ὄντες τὸ μὲν φῶς ἐθεάσαντο, καὶ ἔμφοβοι
those And with me being  the indeed light beheld,      and alarmed

ἐγένοντο· τὴν δὲ φωνὴν οὐκ ἤκουσαν τοῦ λαλοῦντός μοι.
were,     the but  voice not they heard of Him   speaking to me.

10 εἶπον δέ, Τί ποιήσω, Κύριε; ὁ δὲ Κύριος εἶπε πρός με,
I said And, What may I do,  Lord? the And Lord  said  to me,

Ἀναστὰς πορεύου εἰς Δαμασκόν· κἀκεῖ σοι λαληθήσεται
Rising up,  go   into  Damascus, and there to you it will be told

11 περὶ πάντων ὧν τέτακταί σοι ποιῆσαι. ὡς δὲ οὐκ ἐνέβλεπον
about all things which is appointed to you to do. as And not I saw

ἀπὸ τῆς δόξης τοῦ φωτὸς ἐκείνου, χειραγωγούμενος ὑπὸ
from the glory  light of that,   being led by the hand

12 τῶν συνόντων μοι, ἦλθον εἰς Δαμασκόν. Ἀνανίας δέ τις,
the (ones) being with me, I went into Damascus.  Ananias And a certain,

ἀνὴρ εὐσεβὴς κατὰ τὸν νόμον, μαρτυρούμενος ὑπὸ πάντων
a man devout according to the Law, testified  (to)  by   all

13 τῶν κατοικούντων Ἰουδαίων, ἐλθὼν πρός με καὶ ἐπιστὰς
the  living (there)  Jews,     coming  to  me and standing by

εἶπέ μοι, Σαούλ ἀδελφέ, ἀνάβλεψον. κἀγὼ αὐτῇ τῇ ὥρᾳ
said to me, Saul, brother,  look up.   And I  in that hour

14 ἀνέβλεψα εἰς αὐτόν. ὁ δὲ εἶπεν, Ὁ Θεὸς τῶν πατέρων ἡμῶν
looked up  at  him.  he And said, The God of the fathers  of us

προεχειρίσατό σε γνῶναι τὸ θέλημα αὐτοῦ, καὶ ἰδεῖν τὸν
before appointed you to know the will  of Him,  and to see the

15 δίκαιον, καὶ ἀκοῦσαι φωνὴν ἐκ τοῦ στόματος αὐτοῦ. ὅτι ἔσῃ
Just One, and to hear a voice out of the mouth  of Him, for you will be

μάρτυς αὐτῷ πρὸς πάντας ἀνθρώπους ὧν ἑώρακας καὶ
a witness to Him to  all   men   of which you have seen and

16 ἤκουσας. καὶ νῦν τί μέλλεις; ἀναστὰς βάπτισαι καὶ ἀπό-
heard.  And now what intend you? Rising up, be baptized and wash

λουσαι τὰς ἁμαρτίας σου, ἐπικαλεσάμενος τὸ ὄνομα τοῦ
away   the sins  of you,  calling on      the name of the

17 Κυρίου. ἐγένετο δέ μοι ὑποστρέψαντι εἰς Ἰερουσαλήμ, καὶ
Lord.  it was And to me, having returned to Jerusalem,   and

προσευχομένου μου ἐν τῷ ἱερῷ, γενέσθαι με ἐν ἐκστάσει, καὶ
praying     me  in the Temple, becoming me in an ecstasy, and

[18] and saw Him saying to me, Hurry and go away with speed out of Jerusalem, because they will not receive your testimony concerning Me. [19] And I said, Lord, themselves know that I was imprisoning and beating those believing on You in every synagogue; [20] and when the blood of Your witness Stephen was poured out, myself also was standing by and consenting to the execution of him, and holding the garments of those who killed him. [21] And He said to me, Go, for I will send you afar off to (the) nations. [22] And they heard him until this word, and lifted up their voice, saying, Away with such a one from the earth, for it is not fit (that) he should live! [23] And as they were crying out, and throwing off garments, and throwing dust into the air, [24] the chief captain commanded him to be brought into the fortress, ordering him to be examined by lashes, that he might know for what cause they cried out so against him. [25] But as he stretched him forward with the thongs, Paul said to the centurion standing by, Is it lawful for you to whip a Roman man, and (one) not found guilty? [26] And having heard the centurion having gone, he reported to the chief captain, saying, Watch what you are about to do. For this man is a Roman. [27] And the chief captain having come up said to him, Tell me, are you a Roman? And he said, Yes. [28] And the chief captain answered, I bought this citizenship with a great sum. And Paul said, But I also was born (free). [29] And therefore those being about to examine him immediately departed, and the chief captain also was afraid, having found out that he was a Roman, and because he had bound him. [30] And on the morrow, desiring to know the certainty why he was

18 ἰδεῖν αὐτὸν λέγοντά μοι, Σπεῦσον καὶ ἔξελθε ἐν τάχει ἐξ
saw Him saying to me, Hurry and go out quickly from
Ἰερουσαλήμ· διότι οὐ παραδέξονταί σου τὴν μαρτυρίαν
Jerusalem, because not they will receive of you the testimony

19 περὶ ἐμοῦ. κἀγὼ εἶπον, Κύριε, αὐτοὶ ἐπίστανται ὅτι ἐγὼ
concerning Me. And I said, Lord, they understand that I
ἤμην φυλακίζων καὶ δέρων κατὰ τὰς συναγωγὰς τοὺς
was imprisoning and beating throughout the synagogues those

20 πιστεύοντας ἐπὶ σέ· καὶ ὅτε ἐξεχεῖτο τὸ αἷμα Στεφάνου τοῦ
believing on You; and when was poured out the blood of Stephen the
μάρτυρός σου, καὶ αὐτὸς ἤμην ἐφεστὼς καὶ συνευδοκῶν τῇ
witness of You, also myself I was standing by and consenting to the
ἀναιρέσει αὐτοῦ, καὶ φυλάσσων τὰ ἱμάτια τῶν ἀναιρούντων
execution of him, and keeping the garments of those killing

21 αὐτόν. καὶ εἶπε πρός με, Πορεύου, ὅτι ἐγὼ εἰς ἔθνη μακρὰν
him. And He said to me, Go, because I to the nations afar off
ἐξαποστελῶ σε.
will send you.

22 Ἤκουον δὲ αὐτοῦ ἄχρι τούτου τοῦ λόγου, καὶ ἐπῆραν
they heard And him as far as to this — word, and lifted up
τὴν φωνὴν αὐτῶν λέγοντες, Αἶρε ἀπὸ τῆς γῆς τὸν τοιοῦτον·
the voice of them saying, Take from the earth — such a one;

23 οὐ γὰρ καθῆκον αὐτὸν ζῆν. κραυγαζόντων δὲ αὐτῶν, καὶ
not for it is fitting he should live. shouting And them, and
ῥιπτούντων τὰ ἱμάτια, καὶ κονιορτὸν βαλλόντων εἰς τὸν
tearing the garments, and dust throwing into the

24 ἀέρα, ἐκέλευσεν αὐτὸν ὁ χιλίαρχος ἄγεσθαι εἰς τὴν παρεμβο-
air, commanded him the chiliarch to bring into the fortress,
λήν, εἰπὼν μάστιξιν ἀνετάζεσθαι αὐτόν, ἵνα ἐπιγνῷ δι' ἣν
saying with scourges to be examined him, that he may know for what

25 αἰτίαν οὕτως ἐπεφώνουν αὐτῷ. ὡς δὲ προέτειναν αὐτὸν τοῖς
crime thus they cried against him. as But they stretched him with the
ἱμᾶσιν, εἶπε πρὸς τὸν ἑστῶτα ἑκατόνταρχον ὁ Παῦλος, Εἰ
thongs, said to the standing by centurion — Paul, If
ἄνθρωπον Ῥωμαῖον καὶ ἀκατάκριτον ἔξεστιν ὑμῖν μαστίζειν;
a man, a Roman, and (one) not found guilty it is lawful for you to whip?

26 ἀκούσας δὲ ὁ ἑκατόνταρχος, προσελθὼν ἀπήγγειλε τῷ
hearing And the centurion, coming near reported to the
χιλιάρχῳ λέγων, Ὅρα τί μέλλεις ποιεῖν· ὁ γὰρ ἄνθρωπος
chiliarch, saying, See what you are about to do, for man

27 οὗτος Ῥωμαῖός ἐστι. προσελθὼν δὲ ὁ χιλίαρχος εἶπεν αὐτῷ,
this a Roman is. having come up And the chiliarch, he said to him,

28 Λέγε μοι, εἰ σὺ Ῥωμαῖος εἶ; ὁ δὲ ἔφη. Ναί. ἀπεκρίθη τε ὁ
Tell me if you a Roman are, he And said, Yes. answered And the
χιλίαρχος, Ἐγὼ πολλοῦ κεφαλαίου τὴν πολιτείαν ταύτην
chiliarch, I of a much sum — citizenship this
ἐκτησάμην. ὁ δὲ Παῦλος ἔφη, Ἐγὼ δὲ καὶ γεγέννημαι.
bought. And Paul said, I But even have been born.

29 εὐθέως οὖν ἀπέστησαν ἀπ' αὐτοῦ οἱ μέλλοντες αὐτὸν ἀνε-
At once, then, stood away from him those being about him to
τάξειν. καὶ ὁ χιλίαρχος δὲ ἐφοβήθη, ἐπιγνοὺς ὅτι Ῥωμαῖός
examine. also the chiliarch And feared, fully knowing that a Roman
ἐστι, καὶ ὅτι ἦν αὐτὸν δεδεκώς.
he is, and that he was him having bound.

30 Τῇ δὲ ἐπαύριον βουλόμενος γνῶναι τὸ ἀσφαλές, τὸ τί
on the And morrow, being minded to know the certain thing — why

accused by the Jews, he loosed him from the bonds and commanded the chief priests and their whole sanhedrin to come; and having brought Paul down, he set (him) among them.

## CHAPTER 23

[1] And having looked on the sanhedrin intently, Paul said, Men, brothers, I in all good conscience have conducted myself toward God to this day. [2] But the high priest Ananias ordered those standing by him to strike his mouth. [3] Then Paul said to him, God is about to strike you, whitened wall! And do you sit judging me according to the Law, and contrary to Law command me to be struck? [4] And those who stood by said, Do you rail at the high priest of God? [5] And Paul said, I was not conscious, brothers, that he is a high priest; for it has been written, "You shall not speak evil of a ruler of your people." [6] But having known that the one part consisted of Sadducees and the other of Pharisees, Paul cried out in the sanhedrin, Men, brothers, I am a Pharisee, son of a Pharisee; I am judged concerning a hope and resurrection of (the) dead! [7] And he having spoken this, there was a striving of the Pharisees and the Sadducees, and the multitude was divided. [8] For Sadducees indeed say there is no resurrection, nor angel, nor spirit; but Pharisees confess both. [9] And there was a great clamor, and the scribes of the part of the Pharisees having risen up, they were contending, saying, We find nothing evil in this man; and if a spirit spoke to him, or an angel, let us not fight against God. [10] And a great striving arising, the chief captain fearing lest Paul should be torn in pieces by them, commanded the troop having gone down to take him by force from their

κατηγορεῖται παρὰ τῶν Ἰουδαίων, ἔλυσεν αὐτὸν ἀπὸ τῶν
he was accused by the Jews, he freed him from the
δεσμῶν, καὶ ἐκέλευσεν ἐλθεῖν τοὺς ἀρχιερεῖς καὶ ὅλον τὸ
bonds, and commanded to come the chief priests and all the
συνέδριον αὐτῶν, καὶ καταγαγὼν τὸν Παῦλον ἔστησεν εἰς
sanhedrin of them; and having brought down Paul set (him) among
αὐτούς.
them.

## CHAPTER 23

1 Ἀτενίσας δὲ ὁ Παῦλος τῷ συνεδρίῳ εἶπεν, Ἄνδρες ἀδελφοί,
having looked And Paul on the sanhedrin, he said, Men, brothers,
ἐγὼ πάσῃ συνειδήσει ἀγαθῇ πεπολίτευμαι τῷ Θεῷ ἄχρι
I in all conscience good have lived — to God until
2 ταύτης τῆς ἡμέρας. ὁ δὲ ἀρχιερεὺς Ἀνανίας ἐπέταξε τοῖς
this — day. the But high priest, Ananias, ordered those
3 παρεστῶσιν αὐτῷ τύπτειν αὐτοῦ τὸ στόμα. τότε ὁ Παῦλος
standing by him to strike of him the mouth. Then Paul
πρὸς αὐτὸν εἶπε, Τύπτειν σε μέλλει ὁ Θεός, τοῖχε κεκονιαμένε·
to him said, to strike you is about God, wall whitened!
καὶ σὺ κάθη κρίνων με κατὰ τὸν νόμον, καὶ παρανομῶν
And you sit judging me according to the Law, and contrary to law
4 κελεύεις με τύπτεσθαι ; οἱ δὲ παρεστῶτες εἶπον, Τὸν ἀρχιερέα
command me to be struck? those And standing by said, The high priest
5 τοῦ Θεοῦ λοιδορεῖς ; ἔφη τε ὁ Παῦλος, Οὐκ ᾔδειν, ἀδελφοί,
— of God do you revile? said And Paul, Not I knew, brothers,
ὅτι ἐστὶν ἀρχιερεύς· γέγραπται γάρ, Ἄρχοντα τοῦ λαοῦ σου
that he is high priest; it has been written for, A ruler of the people of you
6 οὐκ ἐρεῖς κακῶς. γνοὺς δὲ ὁ Παῦλος ὅτι τὸ ἓν μέρος ἐστὶ
not speak of evilly. knowing And Paul that the one part is
Σαδδουκαίων, τὸ δὲ ἕτερον Φαρισαίων, ἔκραξεν ἐν τῷ
of Sadducees, the and other of Pharisees, cried out in the
συνεδρίῳ, Ἄνδρες ἀδελφοί, ἐγὼ Φαρισαῖός εἰμι, υἱὸς Φαρι-
sanhedrin, Men, brothers, I a Pharisee am, a son of Phari-
σαίου· περὶ ἐλπίδος καὶ ἀναστάσεως νεκρῶν ἐγὼ κρίνομαι.
sees; concerning hope and resurrection of (the) dead I am being judged.
7 τοῦτο δὲ αὐτοῦ λαλήσαντος, ἐγένετο στάσις τῶν Φαρισαίων
this And him having spoken, there was a discord of the Pharisees
8 καὶ τῶν Σαδδουκαίων, καὶ ἐσχίσθη τὸ πλῆθος. Σαδδουκαῖοι
and the Sadducees, and was divided the multitude. Sadducees
μὲν γὰρ λέγουσι μὴ εἶναι ἀνάστασιν, μηδὲ ἄγγελον, μήτε
indeed For say not to be a resurrection, neither angel, nor
9 πνεῦμα· Φαρισαῖοι δὲ ὁμολογοῦσι τὰ ἀμφότερα. ἐγένετο δὲ
spirit. Pharisees But confess — both. there was And
κραυγὴ μεγάλη· καὶ ἀναστάντες οἱ γραμματεῖς τοῦ μέρους
a cry great, and having risen up the scribes of the part
τῶν Φαρισαίων διεμάχοντο λέγοντες, Οὐδὲν κακὸν εὑρί-
the Pharisees, they were contending, saying, Nothing evil we
σκομεν ἐν τῷ ἀνθρώπῳ τούτῳ· εἰ δὲ πνεῦμα ἐλάλησεν αὐτῷ
find in — man this; if and a spirit spoke to him
10 ἢ ἄγγελος, μὴ θεομαχῶμεν. πολλῆς δὲ γενομένης στάσεως,
or an angel, not let us fight against God. much And arising discord,
εὐλαβηθεὶς ὁ χιλίαρχος μὴ διασπασθῇ ὁ Παῦλος ὑπ' αὐτῶν,
fearing the chiliarch lest should be torn Paul by them,
ἐκέλευσε τὸ στράτευμα καταβὰν ἁρπάσαι αὐτὸν ἐκ μέσου
commanded the soldiery going down to seize him out of (the) midst

[11] But the following night the Lord standing by him said, Be of good courage, Paul; for as you fully testified the things about Me at Jerusalem, so you must also testify at Rome. [12] And it being day, some of the Jews having made a conspiracy put themselves under a curse, vowing neither to eat nor to drink until they should kill Paul. [13] And they who made this conspiracy were more than forty; [14] who having come to the chief priests and the elders said, With a curse we have cursed ourselves, to taste nothing until we should kill Paul. [15] Now, therefore, you make a statement to the chief captain with the sanhedrin, so that tomorrow he may bring him down to you, as being about to examine more accurately the things concerning him; and before his drawing near, we are ready to kill him. [16] But the son of the sister of Paul having heard of the ambush, having come near and entered into the fortress, he reported to Paul. [17] And having called one of the centurions, Paul said, Take this young man to the chief captain; he has something to report to him. [18] He indeed, then, having taken him, brought (him) to the chief captain, and said, The prisoner Paul having called me asked (me) to lead this young man to you, having something to say to you. [19] And the chief captain having taken his hand, and having withdrawn apart asked, What is it that you have to report to me? [20] And he said, The Jews agreed to ask you that tomorrow you may bring Paul down into the sanhedrin, as being about to inquire more accurately concerning him. [21] Therefore you be not persuaded by them, for more than forty men of

αὐτῶν, ἄγειν τε εἰς τὴν παρεμβολήν.
of them, to bring and into the fortress.

**11** Τῇ δὲ ἐπιούσῃ νυκτὶ ἐπιστὰς αὐτῷ ὁ Κύριος εἶπε, Θάρσει
in the And following night coming on to him the Lord said, Be cheered,

Παῦλε· ὡς γὰρ διεμαρτύρω τὰ περὶ ἐμοῦ εἰς Ἰερουσαλήμ,
Paul; as for you fully testified the things about Me in Jerusalem,

οὕτω σε δεῖ καὶ εἰς Ῥώμην μαρτυρῆσαι.
so you must also in Rome testify.

**12** Γενομένης δὲ ἡμέρας, ποιήσαντές τινες τῶν Ἰουδαίων
becoming And day, making some of the Jews

συστροφήν, ἀνεθεμάτισαν ἑαυτούς, λέγοντες μήτε φαγεῖν
a conspiracy, cursed themselves, saying neither to eat

**13** μήτε πιεῖν ἕως οὗ ἀποκτείνωσι τὸν Παῦλον. ἦσαν δὲ πλείους
nor to drink until they should kill — Paul. were And more (than)

τεσσαράκοντα οἱ ταύτην τὴν συνωμοσίαν πεποιηκότες·
forty those this — plot making;

**14** οἵτινες προσελθόντες τοῖς ἀρχιερεῦσι καὶ τοῖς πρεσβυτέροις
who having come near to the chief priests and to the elders

εἶπον, Ἀναθέματι ἀνεθεματίσαμεν ἑαυτούς, μηδενὸς γεύσα-
said, With a curse we cursed ourselves of nothing to taste

**15** σθαι ἕως οὗ ἀποκτείνωμεν τὸν Παῦλον. νῦν οὖν ὑμεῖς ἐμφανί-
until we may kill — Paul. Now, then, you inform

σατε τῷ χιλιάρχῳ σὺν τῷ συνεδρίῳ, ὅπως αὔριον αὐτὸν
the chiliarch with the sanhedrin, so as tomorrow him

καταγάγῃ πρὸς ὑμᾶς, ὡς μέλλοντας διαγινώσκειν ἀκριβέ-
he bring down to you as intending to ascertain more

στερον τὰ περὶ αὐτοῦ· ἡμεῖς δέ, πρὸ τοῦ ἐγγίσαι αὐτόν,
accurately that about him; we and before the drawing near of him

**16** ἕτοιμοί ἐσμεν τοῦ ἀνελεῖν αὐτόν. ἀκούσας δὲ ὁ υἱὸς τῆς
ready are — to kill him. hearing And the son of the

ἀδελφῆς Παύλου τὴν ἐνέδραν, παραγενόμενος καὶ εἰσελθὼν
sister of Paul of the ambush, having come near and entering

εἰς τὴν παρεμβολήν, ἀπήγγειλε τῷ Παύλῳ. προσκαλεσά-
into the fortress reported — to Paul. calling to (him)

**17** μενος δὲ ὁ Παῦλος ἕνα τῶν ἑκατοντάρχων ἔφη, Τὸν νεανίαν
And Paul one of the centurions said, — youth

τοῦτον ἀπάγαγε πρὸς τὸν χιλίαρχον· ἔχει γάρ τι ἀπαγγεῖ-
This bring up to the chiliarch, he has for something to

**18** λαι αὐτῷ. ὁ μὲν οὖν παραλαβὼν αὐτὸν ἤγαγε πρὸς τὸν
report to him. he Then taking him brought to the

χιλίαρχον, καί φησιν, Ὁ δέσμιος Παῦλος προσκαλεσάμενός
chiliarch, and says, The prisoner Paul calling near

με ἠρώτησε τοῦτον τὸν νεανίαν ἀγαγεῖν πρός σε, ἔχοντά τι
me asked this — youth to bring to you, having a thing

**19** λαλῆσαί σοι. ἐπιλαβόμενος δὲ τῆς χειρὸς αὐτοῦ ὁ χιλίαρχος,
to tell you. laying hold And of the hand of him the chiliarch

καὶ ἀναχωρήσας κατ᾽ ἰδίαν ἐπυνθάνετο, Τί ἐστιν ὃ ἔχεις
and having withdrawn privately asked, What is (it) which you have

**20** ἀπαγγεῖλαί μοι; εἶπε δὲ ὅτι Οἱ Ἰουδαῖοι συνέθεντο τοῦ
to report to me? he said And, — The Jews agreed the

ἐρωτῆσαί σε, ὅπως αὔριον εἰς τὸ συνέδριον καταγάγῃς τὸν
to ask you so as tomorrow to the sanhedrin you bring down —

Παῦλον, ὡς μέλλοντές τι ἀκριβέστερον πυνθάνεσθαι περὶ
Paul, as intending something more accurately to inquire concerning

**21** αὐτοῦ. σὺ οὖν μὴ πεισθῇς αὐτοῖς· ἐνεδρεύουσι γὰρ αὐτὸν
him. You, then, not be persuaded by them; lie in wait for for him

them lie in wait for him, who put themselves under a curse neither to eat nor to drink until they put him to death; and now they are ready, waiting the promise from you. [22] Then the chief captain dismissed the young man, having commanded (him) to tell no one that you reported these things to no one. [23] And having called (a) certain two of the centurions he said, Prepare two hundred soldiers, that they may go as far as Caesarea, and seventy horsemen, and two hundred spearmen, for the third hour of the night. [24] And provide beasts that having set Paul on they may carry (him) safe to Felix the governor; [25] having written a letter, having this form: [26] Claudius Lysias to the most excellent governor, Felix, greeting: [27] This man, having been seized by the Jews, and being about to be killed by them, having come up with the troop I rescued him, having learned that he is a Roman. [28] And desiring to know the charge on account of which they accused him, I brought him down to their sanhedrin; [29] whom I found to be accused concerning questions of their law, but having no accusation worthy of death or of bonds. [30] And it having been intimated to me of a plot against the man about to be (carried out) by the Jews, at once I sent (him) to you, having commanded the accusers also to say the things against him before you. Farewell. [31] Therefore the soldiers, according to the orders given to them, having taken Paul brought (him) by night to Antipatris; [32] and on the morrow having left the horsemen to go with him, they returned to the fortress. [33] Who having entered into Caesarea, and given up the letter to the governor, also presented Paul to him. [34] And the governor having read (it),

ἐξ αὐτῶν ἄνδρες πλείους τεσσαράκοντα, οἵτινες ἀνεθεμάτισαν
of them   men   more (than)   forty,   who   cursed

εαυτοὺς μήτε φαγεῖν μήτε πιεῖν ἕως οὗ ἀνέλωσιν αὐτόν· καὶ
themselves neither to eat nor drink until they kill   him,   and

νῦν ἕτοιμοί εἰσι προσδεχόμενοι τὴν ἀπὸ σοῦ ἐπαγγελίαν. ὁ
now ready they are,  awaiting   the from you   promise.   the

22 μὲν οὖν χιλίαρχος ἀπέλυσε τὸν νεανίαν, παραγγείλας μηδενὶ
   Then chiliarch   dismissed the  youth,   charging (him) no one

23 ἐκλαλῆσαι ὅτι ταῦτα ἐνεφάνισας πρός με. καὶ προσκαλεσά-
   to tell   that these things you reported to me. And calling near

μενος δύο τινὰς τῶν ἑκατοντάρχων εἶπεν, Ἑτοιμάσατε
two a certain of the   centurions   he said,   Prepare

στρατιώτας διακοσίους ὅπως πορευθῶσιν ἕως Καισαρείας,
soldiers   two hundred, so as  they may go   to Caesarea,

καὶ ἱππεῖς ἑβδομήκοντα, καὶ δεξιολάβους διακοσίους, ἀπὸ
and horsemen seventy,   and   spearmen   two hundred, from

24 τρίτης ὥρας τῆς νυκτός· κτήνη τε παραστῆσαι, ἵνα ἐπιβιβά-
   third hour of the night; beasts and to stand by,   that having

σαντες τὸν Παῦλον διασώσωσι πρὸς Φήλικα τὸν ἡγεμόνα·
set on   —   Paul they may bring to Felix   the governor;

25 γράψας ἐπιστολὴν περιέχουσαν τὸν τύπον τοῦτον·
   writing   a letter   having   —   form   this:

26 Κλαύδιος Λυσίας τῷ κρατίστῳ ἡγεμόνι Φήλικι χαίρειν.
   Claudius Lysias to the most excellent governor, Felix, greeting.

27 τὸν ἄνδρα τοῦτον συλληφθέντα ὑπὸ τῶν Ἰουδαίων, καὶ
   —   man   This   having been seized by the   Jews,   and

μέλλοντα ἀναιρεῖσθαι ὑπ' αὐτῶν, ἐπιστὰς σὺν τῷ στρατεύ-
being about to be killed   by   them,  coming on with the soldiers

28 ματι ἐξειλόμην αὐτόν, μαθὼν ὅτι Ῥωμαῖός ἐστι. βουλόμενος
   I rescued   him, having learned that a Roman he is.  being minded

δὲ γνῶναι τὴν αἰτίαν δι' ἣν ἐνεκάλουν αὐτῷ, κατήγαγον
And to know the charge for which they were accusing him, I brought down

29 αὐτὸν εἰς τὸ συνέδριον αὐτῶν· ὃν εὗρον ἐγκαλούμενον περὶ
   him to the sanhedrin of them; whom I found being accused concerning

ζητημάτων τοῦ νόμου αὐτῶν, μηδὲν δὲ ἄξιον θανάτου ἢ
questions of the law of them, nothing and worthy of death, or

30 δεσμῶν ἔγκλημα ἔχοντα. μηνυθείσης δέ μοι ἐπιβουλῆς εἰς τὸν
   of bonds charge having. being revealed And to me a plot against the

ἄνδρα μέλλειν ἔσεσθαι ὑπὸ τῶν Ἰουδαίων, ἐξαυτῆς ἔπεμψα
man being about to be by the   Jews,   at once   I sent

πρός σε, παραγγείλας καὶ τοῖς κατηγόροις λέγειν τὰ πρὸς
to you, commanding also the accusers to say   —   to

αὐτὸν ἐπὶ σοῦ. ἔρρωσο.
him before you. Farewell.

31 Οἱ μὲν οὖν στρατιῶται, κατὰ τὸ διατεταγμένον αὐτοῖς,
   the Therefore soldiers, according to the thing appointed to them,

ἀναλαβόντες τὸν Παῦλον, ἤγαγον διὰ τῆς νυκτὸς εἰς τὴν
taking up   —   Paul,   brought through the night to   —

32 Ἀντιπατρίδα. τῇ δὲ ἐπαύριον ἐάσαντες τοὺς ἱππεῖς πορεύ-
   Antipatris;   on the and morrow, allowing the horsemen to go

33 εσθαι σὺν αὐτῷ, ὑπέστρεψαν εἰς τὴν παρεμβολήν· οἵτινες
   with him,   they returned to the   fortress;   who

εἰσελθόντες εἰς τὴν Καισάρειαν, καὶ ἀναδόντες τὴν ἐπιστολὴν
having entered into — Caesarea,   and   giving over   the letter

34 τῷ ἡγεμόνι, παρέστησαν καὶ τὸν Παῦλον αὐτῷ. ἀναγνοὺς
   to the governor, presented   also   —   Paul to him. having read

and having asked of what province he was, and having learned that he (was) from Cilicia; [35] he said, I will hear you fully when your accusers also have arrived. And he commanded him to be kept in the praetorium of Herod.

δὲ ὁ ἡγεμών, καὶ ἐπερωτήσας ἐκ ποίας ἐπαρχίας ἐστί, καὶ
And the governor, and   asking        of   what   province  he is,   and

35 πυθόμενος ὅτι ἀπὸ Κιλικίας, Διακούσομαί σου, ἔφη, ὅταν καὶ
learning   that from Cilicia,    I will hear    you, he said, when also

οἱ κατήγοροί σου παραγένωνται. ἐκέλευσέ τε αὐτὸν ἐν τῷ
the accusers of you   arrive;        commanding and him   in the

πραιτωρίῳ τοῦ Ἡρώδου φυλάσσεσθαι.
praetorium  —   of Herod    to be kept.

## CHAPTER 24

### CHAPTER 24

[1] And after five days the high priest Ananias with the elders came down and a certain Tertullus, an orator, who made a statement to the governor against Paul. [2] And Tertullus having been called, he began to accuse, saying, [3] Obtaining great peace through you, and excellent measures having come to this nation due to your forethought, in everything and everywhere we accept with all thankfulness, most excellent Felix. [4] But that I not hinder you more, I beseech you to hear us briefly in your clemency. [5] But having found this man a pest and moving insurrection among all the Jews in the world, and a leader of the Nazarean sect; [6] who also attempted to profane the Temple, whom we also seized, and according to our law wished to judge; [7] but Lysias the chief captain coming up with great force took him away out of our hands, having commanded his accusers to come to you, [8] from whom you will be able yourself, having examined as to all these things of which we accuse him, to know. [9] And the Jews also agreed, saying these things to be so.

1 Μετὰ δὲ πέντε ἡμέρας κατερη ὁ ἀρχιερεὺς Ἀνανίας μετὰ
after And five   days   came down the high priest, Ananias, with

τῶν πρεσβυτέρων καὶ ῥήτορος Τερτύλλου τινός, οἵτινες
the   elders        and an orator, Tertullou     one,    who

2 ἐνεφάνισαν τῷ ἡγεμόνι κατὰ τοῦ Παύλου. κληθέντος δὲ
informed      the governor against — Paul.     being called And

αὐτοῦ, ἤρξατο κατηγορεῖν ὁ Τέρτυλλος λέγων,
him,    began   to accuse    Tertullas,  saying,

3 Πολλῆς εἰρήνης τυγχάνοντες διὰ σοῦ, καὶ κατορθωμάτων
Much    peace    obtaining   through you, and   excellent measures

γινομένων τῷ ἔθνει τούτῳ διὰ τῆς σῆς προνοίας, πάντη τε
coming to    nation this through — your forethought, in everything

καὶ πανταχοῦ ἀποδεχόμεθα, κράτιστε Φῆλιξ, μετὰ πάσης
and everywhere   we welcome,    most excellent Felix,   with   all

4 εὐχαριστίας. ἵνα δὲ μὴ ἐπὶ πλεῖόν σε ἐγκόπτω, παρακαλῶ
thankfulness. that But not   more   you I hinder,   I beseech

5 ἀκοῦσαί σε ἡμῶν συντόμως τῇ σῇ ἐπιεικείᾳ. εὑρόντες γὰρ
to hear  you  us   briefly   — in your forbearance. finding  For

τὸν ἄνδρα τοῦτον λοιμόν, καὶ κινοῦντα στάσιν πᾶσι τοῖς
—   man    this pestilent  and  moving insurrection among all the

Ἰουδαίοις τοῖς κατὰ τὴν οἰκουμένην, πρωτοστάτην τε τῆς
Jews     — throughout the habitable world, a ringleader   and of the

6 τῶν Ναζωραίων αἱρέσεως· ὃς καὶ τὸ ἱερὸν ἐπείρασε βεβηλῶ-
—    Nazarene   sect;    who also the Temple attempted to profane,

σαι· ὃν καὶ ἐκρατήσαμεν καὶ κατὰ τὸν ἡμέτερον νόμον ἠθελή-
whom also we seized,    and according to   our    law   wished

7 σαμεν κρίνειν. παρελθὼν δὲ Λυσίας ὁ χιλίαρχος μετὰ πολλῆς
to judge.   coming up But Lysias the chiliarch    with  much

βίας ἐκ τῶν χειρῶν ἡμῶν ἀπήγαγε, κελεύσας τοὺς κατηγό-
force out of the hands of us  took away, commanding the accusers

8 ρους αὐτοῦ ἔρχεσθαι ἐπὶ σέ· παρ' οὗ δυνήσῃ, αὐτὸς ἀνα-
of him  to come    to you; from whom you can yourself, having

κρίνας, περὶ πάντων τούτων ἐπιγνῶναι ὧν ἡμεῖς κατηγο-
examined about all   these things,   know fully of which we accuse

9 ροῦμεν αὐτοῦ. συνέθεντο δὲ καὶ οἱ Ἰουδαῖοι, φάσκοντες
him.    joined in And also the  Jews,    alleging

ταῦτα οὕτως ἔχειν.
these things so   to be.

[10] But Paul answered, the governor having signaled to him to speak, Knowing you as being judge to this nation many years, I more cheerfully make defense (as to) the things concerning myself.

10 Ἀπεκρίθη δὲ ὁ Παῦλος, νεύσαντος αὐτῷ τοῦ ἡγεμόνος
answered And  Paul,     having signaled to him the   governor

λέγειν,
to speak,

Ἐκ πολλῶν ἐτῶν ὄντα σε κριτὴν τῷ ἔθνει τούτῳ ἐπιστά-
Of many   years being you a judge     nation to this under-

μενος, εὐθυμότερον τὰ περὶ ἐμαυτοῦ ἀπολογοῦμαι, δυνα-
standing, cheerfully (as to) that about myself  I defend myself,  being

[11[ You being able to find that not more than twelve days are to me since I went worshiping in Jerusalem. [12] And neither in the Temple they found me reasoning, or making a gathering of a crowd; nor even in the synagogues, nor even throughout the city. [13] nor even are they able to prove about which they now accuse me. [14] But I confess this to you, that according to the Way, which they say (is) a sect, so I worship the ancestral God, believing all things according to that having been written (in) the Law and the Prophets, [15] having a hope toward God, which these themselves also admit (that) a resurrection of the dead (is) about to be, both of just and unjust. [16] And in this I exercise myself to have a blameless conscience toward God and men always. [17] And after many years I arrived doing alms to my nation, and offerings. [18] Among which they found me purified in the Temple, not with a crowd, nor with tumult, some Jews from Asia, [19] who ought to be present before you and to accuse, if they have anything against me. [20] or these themselves let them say, if they found any unrighteousness in me when I stood before the sanhedrin, [21] (other) than concerning this one voice which I cried out, standing among them, I am judged this day by you concerning a resurrection of (the) dead. [22] And Felix having heard these things, he put them off, knowing more accurately concerning the Way, saying, When Lysias the chief captain may have come down, I will examine the things as to you; [23] having ordered the centurion to keep Paul, and to (let him) have ease, to forbid none of his own to minister or to come to him. [24] And after certain days Felix having arrived with his wife Drusilla, who was a Jewess,

**11** μένου σου γνῶναι ὅτι οὐ πλείους εἰσί μοι ἡμέραι ἢ δεκαδύο,
able you to know that not more are to me days twelve,

**12** ἀφ' ἧς ἀνέβην προσκυνήσων ἐν Ἱερουσαλήμ· καὶ οὔτε ἐν τῷ
from which I went worshiping in Jerusalem and neither in the

ἱερῷ εὗρόν με πρός τινα διαλεγόμενον ἢ ἐπισύστασιν
Temple they found me with anyone reasoning, or a gathering

ποιοῦντα ὄχλου, οὔτε ἐν ταῖς συναγωγαῖς, οὔτε κατὰ τὴν
making of a crowd, neither in the synagogues, nor throughout the

**13** πόλιν. οὔτε παραστῆσαι δύνανται περὶ ὧν νῦν κατηγοροῦσί
city. nor to prove they are able about which now they accuse

**14** μου. ὁμολογῶ δὲ τοῦτό σοι, ὅτι κατὰ τὴν ὁδὸν ἣν λέγουσιν
me. I confess But this to you, that according to the Way which they say

αἵρεσιν, οὕτω λατρεύω τῷ πατρῴῳ Θεῷ, πιστεύων πᾶσι
a sect (is), thus I worship the ancestral God, believing all

τοῖς κατὰ τὸν νόμον καὶ τοῖς προφήταις γεγραμμένοις·
the things as to the Law and the Prophets having been written;

**15** ἐλπίδα ἔχων εἰς τὸν Θεόν, ἣν καὶ αὐτοὶ οὗτοι προσδέχονται,
hope having toward God, which also themselves these admit,

ἀνάστασιν μέλλειν ἔσεσθαι νεκρῶν, δικαίων τε καὶ ἀδίκων.
a resurrection being about to be of (the) dead, of just both and unjust.

**16** ἐν τούτῳ δὲ αὐτὸς ἀσκῶ, ἀπρόσκοπον συνείδησιν ἔχειν πρὸς
by this And myself I exercise a blameless conscience to have toward

**17** τὸν Θεὸν καὶ τοὺς ἀνθρώπους διὰ παντός. δι' ἐτῶν δὲ
— God and — men always. after years And

πλειόνων παρεγενόμην ἐλεημοσύνας ποιήσων εἰς τὸ ἔθνος
many I arrived alms doing to the nation

**18** μου καὶ προσφοράς· ἐν οἷς εὗρόν με ἡγνισμένον ἐν τῷ ἱερῷ,
of me and offerings, among which they found me purified in the Temple,

οὐ μετὰ ὄχλου οὐδὲ μετὰ θορύβου, τινὲς ἀπὸ τῆς Ἀσίας
not with a crowd, nor with tumult; some from — Asia

**19** Ἰουδαῖοι· οὓς ἔδει ἐπὶ σοῦ παρεῖναι καὶ κατηγορεῖν εἴ τι
Jews, whom it is right before you to be present and to accuse if a thing

**20** ἔχοιεν πρός με. ἢ αὐτοὶ οὗτοι εἰπάτωσαν, εἴ τι εὗρον ἐν ἐμοὶ
they have against me. Or them these let say if anything they found in me

**21** ἀδίκημα, στάντος μου ἐπὶ τοῦ συνεδρίου, ἢ περὶ μιᾶς ταύτης
unjust, standing me before the sanhedrin, than about one this

φωνῆς, ἧς ἔκραξα ἑστὼς ἐν αὐτοῖς, ὅτι Περὶ ἀναστάσεως
voice which I cried out standing among them, that concerning a resurrection

νεκρῶν ἐγὼ κρίνομαι σήμερον ὑφ' ὑμῶν.
of (the) dead I am being judged today before you.

**22** Ἀκούσας δὲ ταῦτα ὁ Φῆλιξ ἀνεβάλετο αὐτούς, ἀκριβέ-
having heard And these things Felix put off them, more

στερον εἰδὼς τὰ περὶ τῆς ὁδοῦ, εἰπών, Ὅταν Λυσίας ὁ χιλί-
accurately knowing about the Way, saying, When Lysias the chili-

**23** αρχος καταβῇ, διαγνώσομαι τὰ καθ' ὑμᾶς· διαταξάμενός τε
arch comes down I will examine the things as to you; having ordered and

τῷ ἑκατοντάρχῃ τηρεῖσθαι τὸν Παῦλον, ἔχειν τε ἄνεσιν, καὶ
the centurion to keep — Paul, to have and ease, and

μηδένα κωλύειν τῶν ἰδίων αὐτοῦ ὑπηρετεῖν ἢ προσέρχεσθαι
no one to forbid of the own him to minister or to come

αὐτῷ.
to him.

**24** Μετὰ δὲ ἡμέρας τινάς, παραγενόμενος ὁ Φῆλιξ σὺν
after And days some, having arrived Felix with

Δρουσίλλῃ τῇ γυναικὶ αὐτοῦ οὔσῃ Ἰουδαίᾳ, μετεπέμψατο
Drusilla the wife of him, being a Jewess, he sent for

τὸν Παῦλον, καὶ ἤκουσεν αὐτοῦ περὶ τῆς εἰς Χριστὸν πί-
Paul,     and    heard     him concerning the in    Christ

25 στεως. διαλεγομένου δὲ αὐτοῦ περὶ δικαιοσύνης καὶ ἐγκρατείας
faith.   reasoning    And   him concerning righteousness and self-control

καὶ τοῦ κρίματος τοῦ μέλλοντος ἔσεσθαι, ἔμφοβος γενόμενος
and the judgment  —  being about  to be,   afraid   becoming

ὁ Φῆλιξ ἀπεκρίθη, Τὸ νῦν ἔχον πορεύου· καιρὸν δὲ μεταλα-
Felix answered,   For the present  go,    time  but taking

26 βὼν μετακαλέσομαί σε· ἅμα δὲ καὶ ἐλπίζων ὅτι χρήματα
later I will send for  you; withal but also  hoping  that  silver

δοθήσεται αὐτῷ ὑπὸ τοῦ Παύλου, ὅπως λύσῃ αὐτόν· διὸ
will be given  him  by  —  Paul;   that he might free him.  So

καὶ πυκνότερον αὐτὸν μεταπεμπόμενος ὡμίλει αὐτῷ.
also more frequently  him    sending for,   he conversed with him.

27 διετίας δὲ πληρωθείσης, ἔλαβε διάδοχον ὁ Φῆλιξ Πόρκιον
two years And being completed, received a successor  Felix,  Porcius

Φῆστον· θέλων τε χάριτας καταθέσθαι τοῖς Ἰουδαίοις ὁ Φῆλιξ
Festus;  wishing and a favor  to show   to the   Jews,    Felix

κατέλιπε τὸν Παῦλον δεδεμένον.
left       Paul     bound.

### CHAPTER 25

1  Φῆστος οὖν ἐπιβὰς τῇ ἐπαρχίᾳ, μετὰ τρεῖς ἡμέρας ἀνέβη
Festus, therefore, entering the province  after  three   days went up

2 εἰς Ἱεροσόλυμα ἀπὸ Καισαρείας. ἐνεφάνισαν δὲ αὐτῷ ὁ
to   Jerusalem    from   Caesarea.   made a statement And to him the

ἀρχιερεὺς καὶ οἱ πρῶτοι τῶν Ἰουδαίων κατὰ τοῦ Παύλου,
chief priest and the chief  of the   Jews  against  —  Paul.

3 καὶ παρεκάλουν αὐτόν, αἰτούμενοι χάριν κατ᾽ αὐτοῦ, ὅπως
And they besought  him,   asking   a favor against him,   so as

μεταπέμψηται αὐτὸν εἰς Ἱερουσαλήμ, ἐνέδραν ποιοῦντες
he might send for  him  to   Jerusalem,   a plot   making

4 ἀνελεῖν αὐτὸν κατὰ τὴν ὁδόν. ὁ μὲν οὖν Φῆστος ἀπεκρίθη,
to kill   him  by    the  way.  Therefore Festus   answered

τηρεῖσθαι τὸν Παῦλον ἐν Καισαρείᾳ, ἑαυτὸν δὲ μέλλειν ἐν
to be kept  —  Paul  in  Caesarea,  himself and being about to

5 τάχει ἐκπορεύεσθαι. οἱ οὖν δυνατοὶ ἐν ὑμῖν, φησί, συγκατα-
quickly  go forth.     the  Then able ones among you, he says, going down

βάντες, εἴ τι ἐστὶν ἄτοπον ἐν τῷ ἀνδρὶ τούτῳ, κατηγορεί- .
with (me), if a thing is  amiss   in  —  man  this,   let them

τωσαν αὐτοῦ.
accuse  him.

6  Διατρίψας δὲ ἐν αὐτοῖς ἡμέρας πλείους ἢ δέκα, καταβὰς
having stayed And among them days  more than ten,  going down

εἰς Καισάρειαν, τῇ ἐπαύριον καθίσας ἐπὶ τοῦ βήματος ἐκέ-
to    Caesarea, on the  morrow  sitting   on  the  tribunal  he

7 λευσε τὸν Παῦλον ἀχθῆναι. παραγενομένου δὲ αὐτοῦ,
ordered  —  Paul  to be brought.  arriving       And   him,

περιέστησαν οἱ ἀπὸ Ἱεροσολύμων καταβεβηκότες Ἰουδαῖοι,
stood around the from  Jerusalem   having come down Jews,

πολλὰ καὶ βαρέα αἰτιάματα φέροντες κατὰ τοῦ Παύλου, ἃ
many and weighty  charges   bringing against  —  Paul, which

8 οὐκ ἴσχυον ἀποδεῖξαι, ἀπολογουμένου αὐτοῦ ὅτι Οὔτε εἰς
not they were able to prove.  Defending himself, he said, — Neither against

τὸν νόμον τῶν Ἰουδαίων, οὔτε εἰς τὸ ἱερόν, οὔτε εἰς Καίσαρά
the  law of the  Jews,   nor against the Temple, nor against Caesar

---

he sent for Paul, and heard him concerning the faith in Christ. [25] And as he reasoned concerning righteousness and self-control and the judgment that is coming, becoming afraid Felix answered, For the present go, and having found an opportunity I will call for you; [26] and with it all also hoping that money would be given to him by Paul, that he might release him; therefore also oftener sending for him, he conversed with him. [27] But two years being completed, Felix received a successor, Portius Festus, and wishing to show a favor to the Jews, Felix left Paul bound.

CHAPTER 25

[1] Then Festus being come into the province, after three days went up to Jerusalem to Caesarea. [2] And the high priest and the chief of the Jews made a statement before him against Paul, and they begged him, [3] asking a favor against him, so as he might send for him to Jerusalem, making a plot to kill him on the way. [4] Then Festus answered, Paul should be kept at Caesarea and himself was about to set out shortly. [5] Therefore those in power among you, says he, having gone down also, if anything is in this man, let them accuse him. [6] And having spent more than ten days among them, having gone down to Caesarea, on the morrow having sat on the judgment seat, he commanded Paul to be brought. [7] And he being come the Jews who had come down from Jerusalem stood around, bringing many and weighty charges against Paul, which they were not able to prove. [8] He said in defense, Neither against the Law of the Jews, nor against the Temple, nor against Caesar have I

sinned (in) anything
[9] But Festus, desiring to
gain favor with the Jews
for himself, answering Paul
said, Are you willing to go
up to Jerusalem to be
judged there concerning
these things before me?
[10] But Paul said, I am
standing before the
judgment seat of Caesar
where I ought to be
judged. I did nothing to
the Jews, as also you very
well know. [11] For if I
indeed do wrong and have
done anything worthy of
death, I do not refuse to
die; but if there is nothing
of which they accuse me,
no one can give me up to
them. I appeal to Caesar.
[12] Then Festus, having
conferred with the council,
answered, You have
appealed to Caesar; to
Caesar you shall go.

[13] And certain days
having passed, Agrippa the
king and Bernice came
down to Caesarea, greeting
Festus. [14] And when
they stayed there many
days, Festus laid before the
king the things relating to
Paul, saying, A certain man
is left by Felix a prisoner,
[15] concerning whom, on
my being in Jerusalem, the
chief priests and the elders
of the Jews made a
statement, asking judgment
against him; [16] to whom
I answered, It is not a
custom with Romans to
give up any man to
destruction before he being
accused may have the
accusers face to face, and
he may get the
opportunity of defense
concerning the accusation.
[17] Therefore they have
come here, having made no
delay, the next (day)
having sat on the judgment
seat I commanded the man
to be brought;
[18] concerning whom the
accusers standing up
brought no charge of
which I supposed;
[19] but they have against
him certain questions
concerning their own
demon-worship, and
concerning a certain Jesus
who is dead, whom Paul
claimed to be alive.
[20] And I being puzzled
as to the inquiry

9  τι ἥμαρτον. ὁ Φῆστος δὲ τοῖς ᾽Ιουδαίοις θέλων χάριν
    anything I sinned.    Festus  But  the  Jews  wishing a favor
    καταθέσθαι, ἀποκριθεὶς τῷ Παύλῳ εἶπε, Θέλεις εἰς ᾽Ιεροσό-
    to show,  answering  —  Paul  said, Desire you to Jerusalem
10  λυμα ἀναβάς, ἐκεῖ περὶ τούτων κρίνεσθαι ἐπ᾽ ἐμοῦ ; εἶπε δὲ
    to go up,  there about these things to be judged before me? said And
    ὁ Παῦλος, ᾽Επὶ τοῦ βήματος Καίσαρος ἑστώς εἰμι, οὗ με δεῖ
    Paul,  Before  the  tribunal  of Caesar standing  I am; where me must
    κρίνεσθαι· ᾽Ιουδαίους οὐδὲν ἠδίκησα, ὡς καὶ σὺ κάλλιον
    be judged.  Jews  nothing I have wronged, as indeed you very well
11  ἐπιγινώσκεις. εἰ μὲν γὰρ ἀδικῶ καὶ ἄξιον θανάτου πέπραχά
    know.       if indeed For I do wrong and worthy of death I have done
    τι, οὐ παραιτοῦμαι τὸ ἀποθανεῖν· εἰ δὲ οὐδέν ἐστιν ὧν οὗτοι
    a thing, not I refuse  —  to die;  if but not one is of which these
    κατηγοροῦσί μου, οὐδείς με δύναται αὐτοῖς χαρίσασθαι.
    accuse  me,  no one  me is able  to them  to grant.
12  Καίσαρα ἐπικαλοῦμαι. τότε ὁ Φῆστος συλλαλήσας μετὰ τοῦ
    Caesar  I appeal to.  Then  Festus having conferred with  the
    συμβουλίου ἀπεκρίθη, Καίσαρα ἐπικέκλησαι ; ἐπὶ Καίσαρα
    sanhedrin  answered,  Caesar  you have appealed to, before Caesar
    πορεύσῃ.
    you shall go.

13  ᾽Ημερῶν δὲ διαγενομένων τινῶν, ᾽Αγρίππας ὁ βασιλεὺς
    days And passing  some,  Agrippa the king
    καὶ Βερνίκη κατήντησαν εἰς Καισάρειαν, ἀσπασόμενοι τὸν
    and Bernice  arrived  at  Caesarea,  greeting
14  Φῆστον. ὡς δὲ πλείους ἡμέρας διέτριβον ἐκεῖ, ὁ Φῆστος τῷ
    Festus.  as And  more  days  they stayed there,  Festus to the
    βασιλεῖ ἀνέθετο τὰ κατὰ τὸν Παῦλον, λέγων, ᾽Ανήρ τίς ἐστι
    king  set out the things as to —  Paul,  saying, a man certain is
15  καταλελειμμένος ὑπὸ Φήλικος δέσμιος, περὶ οὗ, γενομένου
    having been left  by  Felix  a prisoner, about whom, being
    μου εἰς ᾽Ιεροσόλυμα, ἐνεφάνισαν οἱ ἀρχιερεῖς καὶ οἱ πρεσ-
    me in  Jerusalem,  made a statement the chief priests and the
16  βύτεροι τῶν ᾽Ιουδαίων, αἰτούμενοι κατ᾽ αὐτοῦ δίκην. πρὸς
    elders  of the Jews,  asking  against  him  sentence;  to
    οὓς ἀπεκρίθην, ὅτι οὐκ ἔστιν ἔθος ᾽Ρωμαίοις χαρίζεσθαί τινα
    whom I answered  that not  it is a custom with Romans to grant  any
    ἄνθρωπον εἰς ἀπώλειαν, πρὶν ἢ ὁ κατηγορούμενος κατὰ
    man  to destruction  before  the (one) being accused  face
    πρόσωπον ἔχοι τοὺς κατηγόρους, τόπον τε ἀπολογίας
    to face  should have the accusers,  place and of defense
17  λάβοι περὶ τοῦ ἐγκλήματος. συνελθόντων οὖν αὐτῶν ἐνθάδε,
    receive concerning the charge.  Coming together, then, they to here,
    ἀναβολὴν μηδεμίαν ποιησάμενος, τῇ ἑξῆς καθίσας ἐπὶ τοῦ
    delay  no  making,  on the next sitting  on the
18  βήματος, ἐκέλευσα ἀχθῆναι τὸν ἄνδρα· περὶ οὗ σταθέντες οἱ
    tribunal, I commanded to be brought the man; about whom standing the
    κατήγοροι οὐδεμίαν αἰτίαν ἐπέφερον ὧν ὑπενόουν ἐγώ,
    accusers  no  charge  brought of which suspected  I,
19  ζητήματα δέ τινα περὶ τῆς ἰδίας δεισιδαιμονίας εἶχον πρὸς
    questions but certain about the own  demon-worship they had with
    αὐτόν, καὶ περὶ τινος ᾽Ιησοῦ τεθνηκότος, ὃν ἔφασκεν ὁ Παῦλος
    him,  and about a certain Jesus having died, whom claimed  Paul
20  ζῆν. ἀπορούμενος δὲ ἐγὼ εἰς τὴν περὶ τούτου ζήτησιν,
    to live. being puzzled And I as to the concerning this  inquiry.

concerning this said, Will he be willing to go to Jerusalem, and to be judged there concerning these things. [21] But Paul having appealed for himself to be kept for the examination of Augustus, I commanded him to be held until I might send him to Caesar. [22] And Agrippa said to Festus, I also was myself desiring to hear the man. And he said, Tomorrow you shall hear him.

[23] Therefore on the morrow, Agrippa and Bernice having come with great pomp, and having entered into the auditorium, with both the chief captains and men of note, being of the city, and Festus having commanded, Paul was brought. [24] And Festus said, King Agrippa, and all the men being present with us, you see this one concerning whom all the multitude of the Jews pleaded with me in both Jerusalem and here, crying out that he ought no longer to live. [25] But I having seen he had done nothing worthy of death, and also this one himself having appealed to Augustus, I determined to send him; [26] (but) concerning whom I have nothing certain to write to (my) lord. Therefore I brought him before you, and especially before you, king Agrippa, so that the examination having taken place I may have something to write; [27] for it seems to me unreasonable to send a prisoner and not to state charges against him.

CHAPTER 26

[1] And Agrippa said to Paul, It is allowed for you yourself to speak. Then Paul made a defense, stretching out the hand: [2] Concerning all of which I am accused by Jews, king Agrippa, I count myself happy being about to make defense before you today, [3] you being especially acquainted of all the customs and also

---

ἔλεγον, εἰ βούλοιτο πορεύεσθαι εἰς Ἱερουσαλήμ, κἀκεῖ κρίνε-
said    if he desired   to go      to   Jerusalem and there to be

21 σθαι περὶ τούτων. τοῦ δὲ Παύλου ἐπικαλεσαμένου τηρηθῆναι
judged about these things. But  Paul   having appealed   to be kept

αὐτὸν εἰς τὴν τοῦ Σεβαστοῦ διάγνωσιν, ἐκέλευσα τηρεῖσθαι
him   to the   — of Augustus    examination, I commanded to be kept

22 αὐτόν, ἕως οὗ πέμψω αὐτὸν πρὸς Καίσαρα. Ἀγρίππας δὲ
him   until I may send him    to   Caesar.    Agrippa   And

πρὸς τὸν Φῆστον ἔφη, Ἐβουλόμην καὶ αὐτὸς τοῦ ἀνθρώπου
to   — Festus   said, I was minded also myself the   man

ἀκοῦσαι. ὁ δέ, Αὔριον, φησίν, ἀκούσῃ αὐτοῦ.
to hear.  he And, Tomorrow, said, you will hear him.

23 Τῇ οὖν ἐπαύριον, ἐλθόντος τοῦ Ἀγρίππα καὶ τῆς Βερνίκης
on the Then morrow   coming   —  Agrippa  and  —  Bernice

μετὰ πολλῆς φαντασίας, καὶ εἰσελθόντων εἰς τὸ ἀκροατήριον,
with  much   pomp,   and   entering   into the auditorium,

σύν τε τοῖς χιλιάρχοις καὶ ἀνδράσι τοῖς κατ᾽ ἐξοχὴν οὖσι τῆς
with both the chiliarchs  and men   the   chief    being of the

24 πόλεως, καὶ κελεύσαντος τοῦ Φήστου, ἤχθη ὁ Παῦλος. καὶ
city,   and having commanded Festus,  was brought Paul.  And

φησιν ὁ Φῆστος, Ἀγρίππα βασιλεῦ, καὶ πάντες οἱ συμπαρόν-
says — Festus,  Agrippa   King,   and  all   those present with

τες ἡμῖν ἄνδρες, θεωρεῖτε τοῦτον περὶ οὗ πᾶν τὸ πλῆθος τῶν
us, Men,   you behold  this one about whom all the multitude of the

Ἰουδαίων ἐνέτυχόν μοι ἔν τε Ἱεροσολύμοις καὶ ἐνθάδε, ἐπι-
Jews    petitioned me in both Jerusalem   and   here,

25 βοῶντες μὴ δεῖν ζῆν αὐτὸν μηκέτι. ἐγὼ δὲ καταλαβόμενος
crying  not ought to live him no longer. I And  having perceived

μηδὲν ἄξιον θανάτου αὐτὸν πεπραχέναι, καὶ αὐτοῦ δὲ τούτου
nothing worthy of death he   had done,   also himself but this one

26 ἐπικαλεσαμένου τὸν Σεβαστόν, ἔκρινα πέμπειν αὐτόν. περὶ
appealing to   —  Augustus, I decided to send   him. Concerning

οὗ ἀσφαλές τι γράψαι τῷ κυρίῳ οὐκ ἔχω. διὸ προήγαγον
whom certain anything to write to the lord not I have. So I brought forth

αὐτὸν ἐφ᾽ ὑμῶν, καὶ μάλιστα ἐπὶ σοῦ, βασιλεῦ Ἀγρίππα,
him before you,  and most   before you, king   Agrippa,

27 ὅπως τῆς ἀνακρίσεως γενομένης σχῶ τι γράψαι. ἄλογον
so as  the examination   being,  I may have what to write. unreasonable

γάρ μοι δοκεῖ, πέμποντα δέσμιον, μὴ καὶ τὰς κατ᾽ αὐτοῦ
For to me it seems sending  a prisoner, not also the against   him

αἰτίας σημᾶναι.
charges to signify.

CHAPTER 26

1 Ἀγρίππας δὲ πρὸς τὸν Παῦλον ἔφη, Ἐπιτρέπεταί σοι
Agrippa  And to  — Paul   said, It is allowed for you

ὑπὲρ σεαυτοῦ λέγειν. τότε ὁ Παῦλος ἀπελογεῖτο, ἐκτείνας
for yourself to speak. Then Paul   made a defense,  stretching

τὴν χεῖρα,
the hand,

2 Περὶ πάντων ὧν ἐγκαλοῦμαι ὑπὸ Ἰουδαίων, βασιλεῦ
Concerning all things of which I am accused by   Jews,   king

Ἀγρίππα, ἥγημαι ἐμαυτὸν μακάριον μέλλων ἀπολογεῖσθαι
Agrippa,  I count myself   happy  being about to make defense

3 ἐπὶ σοῦ σήμερον· μάλιστα γνώστην ὄντα σὲ εἰδὼς πάντων
before you today,  most of all an expert being you knowing of all

questions among the Jews;
therefore I beg you
patiently to hear me.
[4] Truly, then, all the
Jews know my way of life
from youth, which from
(the) beginning was among
my nation in Jerusalem;
[5] who before knew me
from the first, if they
would testify, that
according to the strictest
sect of our religion I lived a
Pharisee. [6] And how for
(the) hope of the promise
made to the fathers by
God, I stand being judged,
[7] to which hope our
twelve tribes serving
fervently night and day
(desire) to obtain;
concerning which hope I
am accused, O king
Agrippa, by the Jews.
[8] Why is it thought
unbelievable by any of you
that God raises the dead?
[9] Indeed, I then thought
within myself that I ought
to do many things contrary
to the name of Jesus the
Nazarene. [10] Which I
also did in Jerusalem; and I
shut up many of the saints
in prisons, having received
authority from the chief
priests; and they being put
to death, I gave (my) vote
against (them). [11] And
often punishing them in all
the synagogues, I
compelled (them) to
blaspheme. And being
exceedingly furious against
them I persecuted even as
far as to foreign cities.
[12] During which also
traveling to Damascus with
authority and a
commission from the chief
priests, [13] at midday in
the highway, I and those
traveling with me saw, O
king, a light brighter than
the sun shining around me.
[14] And all of us having
fallen to the ground, I
heard a voice speaking to
me and saying in the
Hebrew language, Saul,
Saul, why do you
persecute Me? (It is) hard
for you to kick against the
prods. [15] And I said,
Who are you, lord? And He
said, I am Jesus whom you
persecute; [16] but rise up
and stand on your feet;

τῶν κατὰ ᾽Ιουδαίους ἐθῶν τε καὶ ζητημάτων· διὸ δέομαί σου,
the among Jews customs both and questions; therefore I beg you,

4 μακροθύμως ἀκοῦσαί μου. τὴν μὲν οὖν βίωσίν μου τὴν ἐκ
patiently to hear me. the Indeed then way of life of me from

νεότητος, τὴν ἀπ' ἀρχῆς γενομένην ἐν τῷ ἔθνει μου ἐν
youth — from the beginning having been in the nation of me in

5 ᾽Ιεροσολύμοις, ἴσασι πάντες οἱ ᾽Ιουδαῖοι, προγινώσκοντές
Jerusalem, know all the Jews, before knowing

με ἄνωθεν, ἐὰν θέλωσι μαρτυρεῖν, ὅτι κατὰ τὴν ἀκριβεστά-
me from the first, if they will to testify, that according to the most exact

6 την αἵρεσιν τῆς ἡμετέρας θρησκείας ἔζησα Φαρισαῖος. καὶ
sect — of our religion I lived a Pharisee. And

νῦν ἐπ' ἐλπίδι τῆς πρὸς τοὺς πατέρας ἐπαγγελίας γενομένης
now on hope of the to the fathers promise having been

7 ὑπὸ τοῦ Θεοῦ ἕστηκα κρινόμενος, εἰς ἣν τὸ δωδεκάφυλον
by — God, I stand being judged, to which the twelve tribes

ἡμῶν ἐν ἐκτενείᾳ νύκτα καὶ ἡμέραν λατρεῦον ἐλπίζει καταν-
of us in earnestness night and day worshiping hopes to

τῆσαι· περὶ ἧς ἐλπίδος ἐγκαλοῦμαι, βασιλεῦ ᾽Αγρίππα, ὑπὸ
arrive; concerning which hope I am accused, king Agrippa, by

8 τῶν ᾽Ιουδαίων. τί ἄπιστον κρίνεται παρ' ὑμῖν, εἰ ὁ Θεὸς
the Jews. Why unbelievable is it judged by you if God

9 νεκροὺς ἐγείρει ; ἐγὼ μὲν οὖν ἔδοξα ἐμαυτῷ πρὸς τὸ ὄνομα
(the) dead raises? I indeed then thought to myself to the name

10 ᾽Ιησοῦ τοῦ Ναζωραίου δεῖν πολλὰ ἐναντία πρᾶξαι· ὃ καὶ
of Jesus the Nazarene ought many things contrary to do; which also

ἐποίησα ἐν ᾽Ιεροσολύμοις, καὶ πολλοὺς τῶν ἁγίων ἐγὼ
I did in Jerusalem, and many of the saints I

φυλακαῖς κατέκλεισα, τὴν παρὰ τῶν ἀρχιερέων ἐξουσίαν
in prisons shut up, the from the chief priests authority

11 λαβών, ἀναιρουμένων τε αὐτῶν κατήνεγκα ψῆφον. καὶ κατὰ
receiving, being killed and them, I cast a vote. And through

πάσας τὰς συναγωγὰς πολλάκις τιμωρῶν αὐτούς, ἠνάγ-
all the synagogues often punishing them, I

καζον βλασφημεῖν· περισσῶς τε ἐμμαινόμενος αὐτοῖς,
compelled to blaspheme, exceedingly and furious against them,

12 ἐδίωκον ἕως καὶ εἰς τὰς ἔξω πόλεις. ἐν οἷς καὶ πορευόμενος
I persecuted until even to the outside cities. In which also traveling

εἰς τὴν Δαμασκὸν μετ' ἐξουσίας καὶ ἐπιτροπῆς τῆς παρὰ τῶν
to — Damascus with authority and decision power — from the

13 ἀρχιερέων, ἡμέρας μέσης, κατὰ τὴν ὁδὸν εἶδον, βασιλεῦ,
chief priests, at day mid- along the way I saw, king,

οὐρανόθεν ὑπὲρ τὴν λαμπρότητα τοῦ ἡλίου, περιλάμψαν
from Heaven above the brightness of the sun shining around

14 με φῶς καὶ τοὺς σὺν ἐμοὶ πορευομένους. πάντων δὲ κατα-
me a light, also those with me traveling. all And having

πεσόντων ἡμῶν εἰς τὴν γῆν, ἤκουσα φωνὴν λαλοῦσαν πρός
fallen down us to the earth, I heard a voice speaking to

με καὶ λέγουσαν τῇ ῾Εβραΐδι διαλέκτῳ, Σαούλ, Σαούλ, τί
me, and saying in the Hebrew dialect, Saul, Saul, why

15 με διώκεις ; σκληρόν σοι πρὸς κέντρα λακτίζειν. ἐγὼ δὲ
Me persecute you? (It is) hard for you to kick against the prods. I And

εἶπον, Τίς εἶ, Κύριε ; ὁ δὲ εἶπεν, ᾽Εγώ εἰμι ᾽Ιησοῦς ὃν σὺ
said, Who are you, Sir? He And said, I am Jesus whom you

16 διώκεις. ἀλλὰ ἀνάστηθι, καὶ στῆθι ἐπὶ τοὺς πόδας σου· εἰς
persecute. But rise up, and stand on the feet of you. for

for, for this purpose I appear to you, to appoint you a servant and a witness both of what you saw and in what I shall appear to you, [17] taking you out from among the people and the nations, to whom I now send you, [18] to open their eyes, that (they) may turn from darkness to light, and the authority of Satan to God, that they may receive remission of sins and inheritance among those that have been sanctified by faith in Me. [19] Upon this, O king Agrippa, I was not disobedient to the heavenly vision; [20] but to those first in Damascus, and Jerusalem, and to all the region of Judea, and to the nations, exhorting (them) to repent and to turn to God, doing works worthy of repentance. [21] Because of these things the Jews having seized me in the Temple attempted to kill (me). [22] Therefore having obtained help from God, I have stood until this day bearing witness both to small and to great, saying nothing else than that both the prophets and Moses said was about to happen, [23] that Christ should suffer; that through the resurrection of the dead, He was first going to proclaim light to the people and to the nations. [24] And speaking these things in his defense, Festus with a loud voice says, You rave, Paul; your many letters turn (you) to madness. [25] But he said, I am not mad, most noble Festus, but I speak words of truth and sanity; [26] for the king is informed concerning these things, to whom I also speak using boldness. For I am persuaded none of these things (are) hidden from him; for this has not been done in a corner. [27] Do you believe the prophets, king Agrippa? I know that you believe. [28] And Agrippa said to Paul, Do you persuade me to become a Christian in

τοῦτο γὰρ ὤφθην σοι, προχειρίσασθαί σε ὑπηρέτην καὶ
this   For   I appeared to you,   to appoint   you a servant   and

17 μάρτυρα ὧν τε εἶδες ὧν τε ὀφθήσομαί σοι, ἐξαιρούμενός σε
a witness of what both you saw of what and I will appear to you, delivering you

ἐκ τοῦ λαοῦ καὶ τῶν ἐθνῶν, εἰς οὓς νῦν σε ἀποστέλλω,
from the people and the   nations, to whom now you I   send,

18 ἀνοῖξαι ὀφθαλμοὺς αὐτῶν, καὶ ἐπιστρέψαι ἀπὸ σκότους
to open   the eyes   of them, and to turn   from   darkness

εἰς φῶς καὶ τῆς ἐξουσίας τοῦ Σατανᾶ ἐπὶ τὸν Θεόν, τοῦ
to light, and the authority   of Satan   to  —  God,   the

λαβεῖν αὐτοὺς ἄφεσιν ἁμαρτιῶν, καὶ κλῆρον ἐν τοῖς ἡγια-
to receive them forgiveness of sins,   and   a lot   among those being

19 σμένοις πίστει τῇ εἰς ἐμέ. ὅθεν, βασιλεῦ Ἀγρίππα, οὐκ
sanctified by faith  —  in  Me. Upon this, king   Agrippa,   not

20 ἐγενόμην ἀπειθὴς τῇ οὐρανίῳ ὀπτασίᾳ· ἀλλὰ τοῖς ἐν
I was   disobedient to the heavenly   vision,   but to those in

Δαμασκῷ πρῶτον καὶ Ἱεροσολύμοις, εἰς πᾶσάν τε τὴν
Damascus firstly, and   (in) Jerusalem,   to   all   and the

χώραν τῆς Ἰουδαίας, καὶ τοῖς ἔθνεσιν, ἀπήγγελλον μετανοεῖν,
country  —  of Judea,   and to the nations, I announced   to repent

καὶ ἐπιστρέφειν ἐπὶ τὸν Θεόν, ἄξια τῆς μετανοίας ἔργα
and to turn   to  —  God, worthy of the repentance   works

21 πράσσοντας. ἕνεκα τούτων με οἱ Ἰουδαῖοι συλλαβόμενοι ἐν
doing.   Because of these things me the Jews   having seized   in

22 τῷ ἱερῷ ἐπειρῶντο διαχειρίσασθαι. ἐπικουρίας οὖν τυχὼν
the Temple   tried   to kill (me).   Help,   then, obtaining

τῆς παρὰ τοῦ Θεοῦ, ἄχρι τῆς ἡμέρας ταύτης ἕστηκα
—  from  —  God   until  —  day   this,   I stand

μαρτυρούμενος μικρῷ τε καὶ μεγάλῳ, οὐδὲν ἐκτὸς λέγων ὧν
witnessing   to small and also to great, nothing else than saying what

23 τε οἱ προφῆται ἐλάλησαν μελλόντων γίνεσθαι καὶ Μωσῆς, εἰ
both the prophets   said   being about to happen, and Moses, if

παθητὸς ὁ Χριστός, εἰ πρῶτος ἐξ ἀναστάσεως νεκρῶν φῶς
to suffer the Christ, if   first   by a resurrection of (the) dead a light

μέλλει καταγγέλλειν τῷ λαῷ καὶ τοῖς ἔθνεσι.
He is going to announce to the people and to the nations.

24 Ταῦτα δὲ αὐτοῦ ἀπολογουμένου, ὁ Φῆστος μεγάλῃ τῇ
these things And him   defending himself,   Festus   great with the

φωνῇ ἔφη, Μαίνῃ, Παῦλε· τὰ πολλά σε γράμματα εἰς μανίαν
voice says,   You rave, Paul;   the many of you letters   to madness

25 περιτρέπει. ὁ δέ, Οὐ μαίνομαι, φησί, κράτιστε Φῆστε, ἀλλ'
turn (you).   But, Not to madness, he says, most excellent Festus, but

ἀληθείας καὶ σωφροσύνης ῥήματα ἀποφθέγγομαι. ἐπίσταται
of truth   and   sanity   words   I speak.   understands

26 γὰρ περὶ τούτων ὁ βασιλεύς, πρὸς ὃν καὶ παρρησιαζόμενος
For about these things the king,   to whom even being bold of speech

λαλῶ· λανθάνειν γὰρ αὐτόν τι τούτων οὐ πείθομαι οὐδέν·
I speak, to be hidden for (from) him any of these not, I am persuaded noth-ing.

27 οὐ γάρ ἐστιν ἐν γωνίᾳ πεπραγμένον τοῦτο. πιστεύεις,
not For   is   in a corner   (the) doing   of this. Do you believe,

28 βασιλεῦ Ἀγρίππα, τοῖς προφήταις ; οἶδα ὅτι πιστεύεις. ὁ δὲ
king   Agrippa,   the prophets? I know that you believe. And

Ἀγρίππας πρὸς τὸν Παῦλον ἔφη, Ἐν ὀλίγῳ με πείθεις
Agrippa   to  —  Paul   said,   In a little   me you persuade

Χριστιανὸν γενέσθαι. ὁ δὲ Παῦλος εἶπεν, Εὐξαίμην ἂν τῷ
a Christian   to become? And   Paul   said, I would pray

but a little while? [29] And Paul said, I would wish to God, both in a little and in much not only you, but also all these hearing me today, should become such as I also am, except these bonds. [30] And having said these things, the king and the governor and Bernice rose up, and those who sat with them, [31] and having withdrawn they spoke to one another, saying, This man does nothing worthy of death or of bonds. [32] And Agrippa said to Festus, This man might have been let go if he had not appealed to Caesar.

CHAPTER 27

[1] And when it was decided that we should sail to Italy, they delivered up both Paul and certain other prisoners to a centurion named Julius, of the band of Augustus. [2] And having gone on board a ship of Adramyttium about to navigate the places along Asia, we set sail, Aristarchus a Macedonian of Thessalonica being with us. [3] And on the next (day) we landed at Sidon. And Julius having treated Paul kindly allowed (him) to go to (his) friends to receive care. [4] And setting sail from there, we sailed under Cyrus, because the winds were contrary. [5] And having sailed over the sea along Cilicia and Pamphylia, we came to Myra of Lycia. [6] And the centurion having found there a ship of Alexandria sailing to Italy, he caused us to go into it. [7] And for many days sailing slowly and having come across from Cnidus with difficulty, but the wind not allowing us, we sailed under Crete over against Salmone; [8] and coasting along it with difficulty, we came to a certain place called Fair Havens, near which was a city of Lasea.

29 Θεῷ, καὶ ἐν ὀλίγῳ καὶ ἐν πολλῷ οὐ μόνον σε, ἀλλὰ καὶ
    God, both in a little   and in   much, not only you,   but   also

πάντας τοὺς ἀκούοντάς μου σήμερον, γενέσθαι τοιούτους
all     those   hearing    me   today,   to become    such

ὁποῖος κἀγώ εἰμι, παρεκτὸς τῶν δεσμῶν τούτων.
as    also I   am,   except    —    bonds    these.

30 Καὶ ταῦτα εἰπόντος αὐτοῦ, ἀνέστη ὁ βασιλεὺς καὶ ὁ
    And these things having said he,   rose up   the   king    and the

ἡγεμών, ἥ τε Βερνίκη, καὶ οἱ συγκαθήμενοι αὐτοῖς· καὶ
governor,   and Bernice, and those   sitting with    them;   and

31 ἀναχωρήσαντες ἐλάλουν πρὸς ἀλλήλους, λέγοντες ὅτι
    having left    spoke    to    one another,   saying,    —

Οὐδὲν θανάτου ἄξιον ἢ δεσμῶν πράσσει ὁ ἄνθρωπος οὗτος.
Nothing of death worthy   or bonds    does    does     man     this.

32 Ἀγρίππας δὲ τῷ Φήστῳ ἔφη, Ἀπολελύσθαι ἐδύνατο ὁ
    Agrippa   And to   Festus   said,   to have been released was able

ἄνθρωπος οὗτος, εἰ μὴ ἐπεκέκλητο Καίσαρα.
man     this,   if   not he had appealed   to Caesar.

CHAPTER 27

1 Ὡς δὲ ἐκρίθη τοῦ ἀποπλεῖν ἡμᾶς εἰς τὴν Ἰταλίαν, παρεδί-
   when And it was decided to sail   us   to   —   Italy,    they de-

δουν τόν τε Παῦλον καί τινας ἑτέρους δεσμώτας ἑκατοντ-
livered — both Paul    and some   other     prisoners   to a cen-

2 άρχῃ, ὀνόματι Ἰουλίῳ, σπείρης Σεβαστῆς. ἐπιβάντες δὲ
   turion, by name   Julius,   of a cohort Augustan.   embarking And

πλοίῳ Ἀδραμυττηνῷ, μέλλοντες πλεῖν τοὺς κατὰ τὴν Ἀσίαν
a ship of Adramyttium,   being about   to sail to the alongside    Asia

τόπους, ἀνήχθημεν, ὄντος σὺν ἡμῖν Ἀριστάρχου Μακεδόνος
places.    we set sail,   being   with   us Aristarchus,   a Macedonian

3 Θεσσαλονικέως. τῇ τε ἑτέρᾳ κατήχθημεν εἰς Σιδῶνα· φιλαν-
of Thessalonica.   on the And next we were landed at Sidon,    kindly

θρώπως τε ὁ Ἰούλιος τῷ Παύλῳ χρησάμενος ἐπέτρεψε πρὸς
    And    Julius    Paul    treating   allowed    to

4 τοὺς φίλους πορευθέντα ἐπιμελείας τυχεῖν. κἀκεῖθεν ἀναχθέν-
   the   friends going     care    to receive. And from there putting

τες ὑπεπλεύσαμεν τὴν Κύπρον, διὰ τὸ τοὺς ἀνέμους εἶναι
to sea, we sailed close to    Cyprus, because of   the    winds   being

5 ἐναντίους. τό τε πέλαγος τὸ κατὰ τὴν Κιλικίαν καὶ Παμφυ-
contrary.   the And   sea    — against   —   Cilicia    and Pam-

6 λίαν διαπλεύσαντες, κατήλθομεν εἰς Μύρα τῆς Λυκίας. κἀκεῖ
phylia sailing over     we came down to Myra —   of Lycia. And there

εὑρὼν ὁ ἑκατόνταρχος πλοῖον Ἀλεξανδρῖνον πλέον εἰς τὴν
having found the centurion    ship     an Alexandrian   sailing to   —

7 Ἰταλίαν, ἐνεβίβασεν ἡμᾶς εἰς αὐτό. ἐν ἱκαναῖς δὲ ἡμέραις
Italy,    he placed    us in it.    in many And   days

βραδυπλοοῦντες, καὶ μόλις γενόμενοι κατὰ τὴν Κνίδον, μὴ
sailing slowly,    and hardly coming   against    — Cnidus, not

προσεῶντος ἡμᾶς τοῦ ἀνέμου, ὑπεπλεύσαμεν τὴν Κρήτην
allowing    us    the    wind,    we sailed close to   —    Crete

8 κατὰ Σαλμώνην· μόλις τε παραλεγόμενοι αὐτὴν ἤλθομεν
against Salmone,   hardly and sailing along    it    we came

εἰς τόπον τινὰ καλούμενον Καλοὺς Λιμένας, ᾧ ἐγγὺς ἦν
to a place   certain being called    Fair    Haven, to which near was

πόλις Λασαία.
a city,   Lasea

[9] And much time having passed, and the voyage already being dangerous, because the Fast already had past, Paul warned them, [10] saying, Men, I see that the voyage is about to be with disaster, and not only much loss of the cargo and of the ship, but also of our lives. [11] But the centurion was persuaded rather by the helmsman and the ship owner than by the things spoken by Paul. [12] And the port not being fit to winter in, the most counseled to set sail from there also, if by any means they might be able having arrived at Phoenix to winter (there), a port of Crete looking toward the southwest and toward northwest. [13] And a south wind blowing gently, thinking to have gained the purpose, having lifted (anchor) they coasted along close by Crete. [14] But not long after a stormy wind came down (on) it, called Euroclydon. [15] And the ship having been caught, and not able to bring (her) head to the wind, giving (her) up we were driven along. [16] But running under an islet called Clauda, we were hardly able to get mastery of the boat: [17] which, taking, they used helps, undergirding the ship; and fearing lest they fall into Syrtis, lowering the tackle, thus they were driven. [18] But we being exceedingly tempest-tossed, they made a casting on the next (day). [19] And on the third (day) they threw out the tackle of the ship with their hands. [20] And neither sun nor stars appearing for many days, and no small tempest lying (us), from then on was taken away all hope of for us to be saved. [21] And there being a long fast, then Paul standing up in their midst said, Truly, O men, you ought having been obedient to me not to have set sail from Crete, and to have gained this disaster and loss; [22] and

**9** Ἱκανοῦ δὲ χρόνου διαγενομένου, καὶ ὄντος ἤδη ἐπισφα-
much And time   having passed,   and being now dangerous

λοῦς τοῦ πλοός, διὰ τὸ καὶ τὴν νηστείαν ἤδη παρεληλυ-
the voyage, because also the Fast   now to have gone

**10** θέναι, παρήνει ὁ Παῦλος λέγων αὐτοῖς, Ἄνδρες, θεωρῶ ὅτι
by, advised Paul saying to them, Men, I see that

μετὰ ὕβρεως καὶ πολλῆς ζημίας, οὐ μόνον τοῦ φόρτου καὶ
with injury and much loss, not only of the cargo and

τοῦ πλοίου ἀλλὰ καὶ τῶν ψυχῶν ἡμῶν, μέλλειν ἔσεσθαι τὸν
of the ship, but also the souls of us, to be about to be the

**11** πλοῦν. ὁ δὲ ἑκατόνταρχος τῷ κυβερνήτῃ καὶ τῷ ναυκλήρῳ
voyage. the But centurion by the steersman and the shipmaster

ἐπείθετο μᾶλλον ἢ τοῖς ὑπὸ τοῦ Παύλου λεγομένοις.
was persuaded rather than the things by Paul said.

**12** ἀνευθέτου δὲ τοῦ λιμένος ὑπάρχοντος πρὸς παραχειμασίαν,
not fit And the port being for wintering,

οἱ πλείους ἔθεντο βουλὴν ἀναχθῆναι κἀκεῖθεν, εἴπως δύ-
the most gave counsel to set sail from there, if somehow they

ναιντο καταντήσαντες εἰς Φοίνικα παραχειμάσαι, λιμένα τῆς
may be able having arrived at Phoenloe to pass the winter, a port

**13** Κρήτης βλέποντα κατὰ λίβα καὶ κατὰ χῶρον. ὑποπνεύ-
of Crete looking toward southwest and toward northwest. blowing

σαντος δὲ νότου, δόξαντες τῆς προθέσεως κεκρατηκέναι,
gently And a south wind, thinking the purpose to have gained,

**14** ἄραντες ἆσσον παρελέγοντο τὴν Κρήτην. μετ' οὐ πολὺ δὲ
raising (anchor), close they sailed by — Crete. after not much And

ἔβαλε κατ' αὐτῆς ἄνεμος τυφωνικός, ὁ καλούμενος Εὐροκλύ-
beat down it wind a stormy, being called Euroclydon,

**15** δων· συναρπασθέντος δὲ τοῦ πλοίου, καὶ μὴ δυναμένου
being seized and the ship, and not being able

**16** ἀντοφθαλμεῖν τῷ ἀνέμῳ, ἐπιδόντες ἐφερόμεθα. νησίον δέ τι
to beat against the wind, giving way we were borne. islet But an

ὑποδραμόντες καλούμενον Κλαύδην μόλις ἰσχύσαμεν περι-
running under, being called Clauda, hardly we were able

**17** κρατεῖς γενέσθαι τῆς σκάφης· ἣν ἄραντες, βοηθείαις ἐχρῶντο,
mastery to get of the boat, which taking helps they used,

ὑποζωννύντες τὸ πλοῖον· φοβούμενοί τε μὴ εἰς τὴν σύρτιν
undergirding the ship; fearing and lest into — Syrtis

**18** ἐκπέσωσι, χαλάσαντες τὸ σκεῦος, οὕτως ἐφέροντο. σφοδρῶς
they fall, lowering the tackle, thus they were borne. exceedingly

**19** δὲ χειμαζομένων ἡμῶν, τῇ ἑξῆς ἐκβολὴν ἐποιοῦντο· καὶ τῇ
But being tempest-tossed we, on the next a casting out they made, and on the

τρίτῃ αὐτόχειρες τὴν σκευὴν τοῦ πλοίου ἐρρίψαμεν. μήτε
third with their hands the tackle of the ship they threw. neither

**20** δὲ ἡλίου μήτε ἄστρων ἐπιφαινόντων ἐπὶ πλείονας ἡμέρας,
And sun nor stars appearing over many days,

χειμῶνός τε οὐκ ὀλίγου ἐπικειμένου, λοιπὸν περιῃρεῖτο πᾶσα
tempest and no small pressing hard, now was taken away all

**21** ἐλπὶς τοῦ σώζεσθαι ἡμᾶς. πολλῆς δὲ ἀσιτίας ὑπαρχούσης,
hope — to be saved us. much And fasting being,

τότε σταθεὶς ὁ Παῦλος ἐν μέσῳ αὐτῶν εἶπεν, Ἔδει μέν, ὦ
then standing Paul in (the) midst of them said, (You) ought, O

ἄνδρες, πειθαρχήσαντάς μοι μὴ ἀνάγεσθαι ἀπὸ τῆς Κρήτης,
men, having been obedient to me not to have set sail from — Crete,

**22** κερδῆσαί τε τὴν ὕβριν ταύτην καὶ τὴν ζημίαν. καὶ τὰ νῦν
to come by and — injury this and — loss. And — now

now I exhort you to be of good cheer, for no loss of any life shall be from among you, only of the ship. [23] For tonight an angel of God stood by me, whose I am, and whom I serve, [24] saying, Do not fear, Paul, you must stand before Caesar; and, behold, God has granted to you all those sailing with you. [25] Therefore be of good cheer, men, for I believe God, that so it shall be according to the way it has been said to me. [26] But we must fall on a certain island. [27] And when the fourteenth night had come, we being driven about in the Adriatic, towards (the) middle of the night the sailors supposed some country neared them. [28] And having sounded, they found twenty fathoms, and having gone a little further and again having sounded, they found fifteen fathoms; [29] and fearing lest they should fall on rock places, and having cast four anchors out of (the) stern, they wished day to come. [30] But the sailors seeking to flee out of the ship, and having let down the boat into the sea, with pretext as from (the) prow being about to throw out anchors, [31] Paul said to the centurion and to the soldiers, Unless these remain in the ship, you cannot be saved. [32] Then the soldiers cut away the ropes of the boat and let her fall. [33] And until day was about to come Paul exhorted all to partake of food, saying, Today (is) the fourteenth day you continue watching without taking food, having taken nothing. [34] Therefore I exhort you to take food, for this is for your safety; for not a hair of your head shall fall. [35] And having said these things and having taken a loaf, he gave thanks to God before all, and having broken began to eat. [36] And all having become of good cheer themselves also took food.

παραινῶ ὑμᾶς εὐθυμεῖν· ἀποβολὴ γὰρ ψυχῆς οὐδεμία ἔσται
I advise     you to be cheered, casting away for of soul   no     will be

23 ἐξ ὑμῶν, πλὴν τοῦ πλοίου. παρέστη γάρ μοι τῇ νυκτὶ ταύτῃ
of you,   but of the ship.     stood by For me — night    this

24 ἄγγελος τοῦ Θεοῦ, οὗ εἰμι, ᾧ καὶ λατρεύω, λέγων, Μή
an angel   — of God, whose I am, whom also I serve,   saying, Do not

φοβοῦ, Παῦλε· Καίσαρί σε δεῖ παραστῆναι· καὶ ἰδού, κεχάρι-
fear,  Paul,   Caesar you must stand before,   and behold, has given

25 σταί σοι ὁ Θεὸς πάντας τοὺς πλέοντας μετὰ σοῦ. διὸ εὐθυμεῖτε
you  God   all   those sailing   with you. So be cheered,

ἄνδρες· πιστεύω γὰρ τῷ Θεῷ ὅτι οὕτως ἔσται καθ' ὃν
men,   I believe for — God, that  so   it will be in the way

26 τρόπον λελάληταί μοι. εἰς νῆσον δέ τινα δεῖ ἡμᾶς ἐκπεσεῖν.
of which it was spoken to me. Onto island But an  must   we   fall off.

27 Ὡς δὲ τεσσαρεσκαιδεκάτη νὺξ ἐγένετο, διαφερομένων
when And (the) fourteenth   night came,   being carried about

ἡμῶν ἐν τῷ Ἀδρίᾳ, κατὰ μέσον τῆς νυκτὸς ὑπενόουν οἱ
us  in the Adriatic, toward the middle of the night   supposed the

28 ναῦται προσάγειν τινὰ αὐτοῖς χώραν· καὶ βολίσαντες εὗρον
sailors to approach  some to them country. And sounding they found

ὀργυιὰς εἴκοσι· βραχὺ δὲ διαστήσαντες, καὶ πάλιν βολί-
fathoms twenty, a little and having moved   also again sounding,

29 σαντες, εὗρον ὀργυιὰς δεκαπέντε· φοβούμενοί τε μήπως εἰς
they found fathoms  fifteen;   fearing   and lest on

τραχεῖς τόπους ἐκπέσωμεν, ἐκ πρύμνης ῥίψαντες ἀγκύρας
rough  places they may fall off, our of (the) stern throwing   anchors

30 τέσσαρας, ηὔχοντο ἡμέραν γενέσθαι. τῶν δὲ ναυτῶν ζητούν-
four,   they wished day   to come.   the And sailors seeking

των φυγεῖν ἐκ τοῦ πλοίου, καὶ χαλασάντων τὴν σκάφην εἰς
to flee out of the ship,   and lowering   the boat into

τὴν θάλασσαν, προφάσει ὡς ἐκ πρώρας μελλόντων ἀγκύρας
the sea,   pretending as out of (the) prow being about anchors

31 ἐκτείνειν, εἶπεν ὁ Παῦλος τῷ ἑκατοντάρχῃ καὶ τοῖς στρατιώ-
to cast out, said   Paul to the centurion   and to the soldiers

ταις, Ἐὰν μὴ οὗτοι μείνωσιν ἐν τῷ πλοίῳ, ὑμεῖς σωθῆναι οὐ
If not these remain in the ship,   you to be saved not

32 δύνασθε. τότε οἱ στρατιῶται ἀπέκοψαν τὰ σχοινία τῆς
are able.   Then the soldiers   cut away   the ropes of the

33 σκάφης, καὶ εἴασαν αὐτὴν ἐκπεσεῖν. ἄχρι δὲ οὗ ἔμελλεν ἡμέρα
boat,   and let   it   fall off.   until And was about day

γίνεσθαι, παρεκάλει ὁ Παῦλος ἅπαντας μεταλαβεῖν τροφῆς,
to come,   begged   Paul   all   to partake of food,

λέγων, Τεσσαρεσκαιδεκάτην σήμερον ἡμέραν προσδοκῶντες
saying, (The) fourteenth   today (is) day   waiting

34 ἄσιτοι διατελεῖτε, μηδὲν προσλαβόμενοι. διὸ παρακαλῶ
without food you continued, nothing having taken. Therefore I beg

ὑμᾶς προσλαβεῖν τροφῆς· τοῦτο γὰρ πρὸς τῆς ὑμετέρας
you   to take   of food; this for   to — your

σωτηρίας ὑπάρχει· οὐδενὸς γὰρ ὑμῶν θρὶξ ἐκ τῆς κεφαλῆς
salvation   is;   of no one for of you a hair from the head

35 πεσεῖται. εἰπὼν δὲ ταῦτα, καὶ λαβὼν ἄρτον, εὐχαρίστησε
shall perish. saying And these things, and taking bread, he gave thanks

36 τῷ Θεῷ ἐνώπιον πάντων· καὶ κλάσας ἤρξατο ἐσθίειν. εὔθυμοι
— to God before   all,   and breaking began to eat.   cheered

δὲ γενόμενοι πάντες καὶ αὐτοὶ προσελάβοντο τροφῆς. ἦμεν
And becoming all,   also they   took   food. we were

[37] And we were in the ship all the souls two hundred (and) seventy-six.

**37** δὲ ἐν τῷ πλοίῳ αἱ πᾶσαι ψυχαί, διακόσιαι ἑβδομηκονταέξ.
And in the ship the all souls, two hundred seventy-six.

[38] And being satisfied with food, they lightened the ship, throwing the wheat out into the sea.

**38** κορεσθέντες δὲ τροφῆς ἐκούφιζον τὸ πλοῖον, ἐκβαλλόμενοι
having been filled And of food, they lightened the ship, throwing out

**39** τὸν σῖτον εἰς τὴν θάλασσαν. ὅτε δὲ ἡμέρα ἐγένετο, τὴν γῆν
the wheat into the sea. when And day came, the land

[39] And when it was day, they did not recognize the land; but they saw a certain bay having a shore, on which they purposed, if they should be able, to drive the ship;

οὐκ ἐπεγίνωσκον· κόλπον δέ τινα κατενόουν ἔχοντα αἰγια-
not did recognize, a bay but certain they noted having a shore,

**40** λόν, εἰς ὃν ἐβουλεύσαντο, εἰ δύναιντο, ἐξῶσαι τὸ πλοῖον. καὶ
into which they purposed, if they could, to drive the ship. And

[40] and having cut away the anchors, they left (them) in the sea, at the same time having loosened the bands of the rudders, and having hoisted the foresail to the wind, they made for the shore.

τὰς ἀγκύρας περιελόντες εἴων εἰς τὴν θάλασσαν, ἅμα ἀνέντες
the anchors having cast off they left in the sea, at the same time freeing

τὰς ζευκτηρίας τῶν πηδαλίων· καὶ ἐπάραντες τὸν ἀρτέμονα
the bands of the rudders, and raising the foresail

**41** τῇ πνεούσῃ κατεῖχον εἰς τὸν αἰγιαλόν. περιπεσόντες δὲ εἰς
to the breeze, they held to the shore. coming upon And —

[41] And having fallen into a place where two seas met, they ran the vessel aground, and the prow having stuck fast remained immovable, but the stern was broken by the violence of the waves.

τόπον διθάλασσον ἐπώκειλαν τὴν ναῦν· καὶ ἡ μὲν πρῶρα
a place between two seas, they drove the vessel, and the prow

ἐρείσασα ἔμεινεν ἀσάλευτος, ἡ δὲ πρύμνα ἐλύετο ὑπὸ τῆς
having stuck remained immovable, the but stern was broken by the

**42** βίας τῶν κυμάτων. τῶν δὲ στρατιωτῶν βουλὴ ἐγένετο ἵνα
violence of the waves. of the And soldiers (the) mind was that

[42] And (the) advice of the soldiers was that they should kill the prisoners, lest anyone swim out and escape.

τοὺς δεσμώτας ἀποκτείνωσι, μήτις ἐκκολυμβήσας διαφύγοι.
the prisoners they should kill, lest any swimming out should escape.

**43** ὁ δὲ ἑκατόνταρχος, βουλόμενος διασῶσαι τὸν Παῦλον,
the But centurion being minded to save — Paul,

[43] But the centurion desiring to save Paul hindered them of (their) purpose, and commanded those being able to swim, having cast (themselves) off first, to go out on the land;

ἐκώλυσεν αὐτοὺς τοῦ βουλήματος, ἐκέλευσέ τε τοὺς δυνα-
prevented them the purpose, commanded and those being

μένους κολυμβᾶν ἀπορρίψαντας πρώτους ἐπὶ τὴν γῆν
able to swim, throwing overboard first, onto the land

**44** ἐξιέναι· καὶ τοὺς λοιπούς, οὓς μὲν ἐπὶ σανίσιν, οὓς δὲ ἐπί
to go out. And the rest, some indeed on planks, others and on

[44] and the rest, some indeed on boards and others on some things from the ship; and so it came to pass all were brought safely to the land.

τινων τῶν ἀπὸ τοῦ πλοίου. καὶ οὕτως ἐγένετο πάντας
some of the things from the ship. And so it was, all

διασωθῆναι ἐπὶ τὴν γῆν.
to be saved on the land.

## CHAPTER 28

**CHAPTER 28**

[1] And then having been saved, they knew that the island was called Melita.

**1** Καὶ διασωθέντες, τότε ἐπέγνωσαν ὅτι Μελίτη ἡ νῆσος
And having been saved, then they knew that Melita the island

[2] And the barbarians showed no common kindness to us; for having kindled a fire, they received all of us, because of the rain that was present and because of the cold.

**2** καλεῖται. οἱ δὲ βάρβαροι παρεῖχον οὐ τὴν τυχοῦσαν
is called. the And foreigners showed not the common

φιλανθρωπίαν ἡμῖν· ἀνάψαντες γὰρ πυράν, προσελάβοντο
kindness us; having kindled for a fire, they welcomed

πάντας ἡμᾶς, διὰ τὸν ὑετὸν τὸν ἐφεστῶτα, καὶ διὰ τὸ ψῦχος.
all us, because of the rain — coming on, and due to the cold.

[3] And Paul having gathered a bunch of sticks, and having laid (them) on the fire, a viper having come out of the heat fastened on his hand.

**3** συστρέψαντος δὲ τοῦ Παύλου φρυγάνων πλῆθος, καὶ
having gathered And — Paul of sticks a bunch, and

ἐπιθέντος ἐπὶ τὴν πυράν, ἔχιδνα ἐκ τῆς θέρμης ἐξελθοῦσα
putting on the fire, a snake from the heat coming out

**4** καθῆψε τῆς χειρὸς αὐτοῦ. ὡς δὲ εἶδον οἱ βάρβαροι κρεμά-
fastened on the hand of him. when And saw the foreigners hanging

[4] And when the barbarians saw the beast hanging from his hand, they said to one another, By all means this man is a murderer, whom having been saved from the sea

μενον τὸ θηρίον ἐκ τῆς χειρὸς αὐτοῦ, ἔλεγον πρὸς ἀλλήλους,
the beast from the hand of him, they said to one another,

Πάντως φονεύς ἐστιν ὁ ἄνθρωπος οὗτος, ὃν διασωθέντα ἐκ
By all means a murderer is man this, whom being saved out of

Justice did not permit to live. [5] Then he indeed having shaken off the beast into the fire suffered no harm. [6] But they were expecting him to be about to become inflamed, or to fall down suddenly dead. But over much (time) they expecting and seeing nothing amiss happening to him, changing their opinion said he was a god. [7] Now in the (parts) about that place were lands belonging to the chief of the island, by name Publius, who having received us lodged (us) three days in a friendly way. [8] And it happened the father of Publius lay oppressed with fevers and dysentery, to whom Paul having entered and having prayed, having laid hands on him cured him. [9] Then, this having taken place, the rest who had infirmities in the island also came and were healed; [10] who also with many honors honored us. And on setting sail, they laid on (us) the things for (our) need.

[11] And after three months we sailed in a ship which had wintered in the island, an Alexandrian, with an ensign, (The) Twin Brothers. [12] And having been landed at Syracuse, we remained three days. [13] From where having gone around, we arrived at Rhegium; and after one day, a south wind having come on, on the second day we came to Puteoli; [14] where having found brothers we were begged to remain with them seven days. And so we came to Rome. [15] And from there the brothers having heard the things concerning us came out to meet us, as far as (the) market-place of Appias, and Three Taverns; whom Paul seeing, having given thanks to God, he took courage.

[16] And when we came to Rome the centurion delivered the prisoners to the commander of the camp, but Paul was allowed to remain by himself, with

**5** τῆς θαλάσσης ἡ Δίκη ζῆν οὐκ εἴασεν. ὁ μὲν οὖν, ἀποτινάξας
the sea — justice to live not allowed. He then, shaking off

**6** τὸ θηρίον εἰς τὸ πῦρ, ἔπαθεν οὐδὲν κακόν. οἱ δὲ προσεδόκων
the beast into the fire, suffered no harm. they But expected

αὐτὸν μέλλειν πίμπρασθαι ἢ καταπίπτειν ἄφνω νεκρόν· ἐπὶ
him to be about to swell, or to fall down suddenly dead. over

πολὺ δὲ αὐτῶν προσδοκώντων, καὶ θεωρούντων μηδὲν
much But they expecting, and beholding nothing

ἄτοπον εἰς αὐτὸν γινόμενον, μεταβαλλόμενοι ἔλεγον θεὸν
amiss to him happening, changing their minds they said a god

αὐτὸν εἶναι.
him to be.

**7** Ἐν δὲ τοῖς περὶ τὸν τόπον ἐκεῖνον ὑπῆρχε χωρία τῷ
in And the (parts) about place that, were lands to the

πρώτῳ τῆς νήσου, ὀνόματι Ποπλίῳ, ὃς ἀναδεξάμενος ἡμᾶς
chief of the island, by name Publius, who welcoming us

**8** τρεῖς ἡμέρας φιλοφρόνως ἐξένισεν. ἐγένετο δὲ τὸν πατέρα τοῦ
three days in a friendly way lodged (us). it was And, the father —

Ποπλίου πυρετοῖς καὶ δυσεντερίᾳ συνεχόμενον κατακεῖσθαι·
of Publius fevers and dysentery suffering from was lying down,

πρὸς ὃν ὁ Παῦλος εἰσελθών, καὶ προσευξάμενος, ἐπιθεὶς τὰς
to whom Paul having entered and praying, laying on the

**9** χεῖρας αὐτῷ, ἰάσατο αὐτόν. τούτου οὖν γενομένου, καὶ οἱ
hands him, cured him. this Then happening, also the

λοιποὶ οἱ ἔχοντες ἀσθενείας ἐν τῇ νήσῳ προσήρχοντο καὶ
rest of those having infirmities in the island came up and

**10** ἐθεραπεύοντο· οἱ καὶ πολλαῖς τιμαῖς ἐτίμησαν ἡμᾶς, καὶ
were healed; who also with many honors honored us, and

ἀναγομένοις ἐπέθεντο τὰ πρὸς τὴν χρείαν.
on our sailing laid on the things for the needs (of us).

**11** Μετὰ δὲ τρεῖς μῆνας ἀνήχθημεν ἐν πλοίῳ παρακεχει-
after And three months we sailed in a ship having

μακότι ἐν τῇ νήσῳ, Ἀλεξανδρίνῳ, παρασήμῳ Διοσκούροις.
wintered in the island, an Alexandrian, with an ensign, Twin Brothers.

**12** καὶ καταχθέντες εἰς Συρακούσας ἐπεμείναμεν ἡμέρας τρεῖς·
And having been landed at Syracuse, we remained days three,

**13** ὅθεν περιελθόντες κατηντήσαμεν εἰς Ῥήγιον, καὶ μετὰ μίαν
from where tacking we arrived at Rhegium. And after one

ἡμέραν ἐπιγενομένου νότου, δευτεραῖοι ἤλθομεν εἰς Ποτιό-
day, coming on a south wind, on the second we came to Puteoli,

**14** λους· οὗ εὑρόντες ἀδελφούς, παρεκλήθημεν ἐπ᾽ αὐτοῖς
where having found brothers, we were besought by them

ἐπιμεῖναι ἡμέρας ἑπτά· καὶ οὕτως εἰς τὴν Ῥώμην ἤλθομεν.
to remain days seven; and thus to — Rome we went.

**15** κἀκεῖθεν οἱ ἀδελφοὶ ἀκούσαντες τὰ περὶ ἡμῶν, ἐξῆλθον εἰς
And from there the brothers having heard about us came out to

ἀπάντησιν ἡμῖν ἄχρις Ἀππίου Φόρου καὶ Τριῶν Ταβερνῶν·
meet us as far as Appius Forum and Three Taverns,

οὓς ἰδὼν ὁ Παῦλος, εὐχαριστήσας τῷ Θεῷ, ἔλαβε θάρσος.
whom seeing Paul, thanking God, he took courage.

**16** Ὅτε δὲ ἤλθομεν εἰς Ῥώμην, ὁ ἑκατόνταρχος παρέδωκε
when And we went into Rome, the centurion delivered

τοὺς δεσμίους τῷ στρατοπεδάρχῃ· τῷ δὲ Παύλῳ ἐπετράπη
the prisoners to the camp commander; but Paul was allowed

μένειν καθ᾽ ἑαυτόν, σὺν τῷ φυλάσσοντι αὐτὸν στρατιώτῃ.
to remain by himself, with the guarding him soldier.

the soldier who kept him. [17] And it came to pass after three days Paul called together those who were chief ones of the Jews. And they having come together, he said to them, Men, brothers, I did nothing to the people, or to the ancestral customs. I was delivered a prisoner from Jerusalem to the hands of the Romans, [18] who having examined me wished to let (me) go, because there was not one cause of death in me. [19] But the Jews speaking contrary, I was compelled to appeal to Caesar, not as having anything to lay against my nation. [20] Therefore for this cause I call for you to see and to speak to (you); for on account of the hope of Israel I have this chain around (me). [21] And they said to him, We neither received letters concerning you from Judea, nor having arrived has any one of the brothers reported or said anything evil concerning you. [22] But we think (it) good to hear from you what you think, for truly as concerning this sect it is known to us that it is spoken against everywhere. [23] And having appointed him a day, many came to him to the lodging, to whom he expounded, fully testifying the kingdom of God, and persuading them the things concerning Jesus, both from the law of Moses and the Prophets, from morning to evening. [24] And some indeed were persuaded of the things spoken, but some disbelieved. [25] And disagreeing with one another, they departed; Paul having spoken one word, Well did the Holy Spirit speak by Isaiah the prophet to our fathers, [26] "Go to this people and say, By hearing you shall hear and in no way understand; and seeing you shall see and in no way perceive. [27] For the heart of this people has grown fat, and they have

**17** Ἐγένετο δὲ μετὰ ἡμέρας τρεῖς συγκαλέσασθαι τὸν Παῦλον
it was   And, after   days   three   called together   —   Paul
τοὺς ὄντας τῶν Ἰουδαίων πρώτους· συνελθόντων δὲ αὐτῶν,
those being of the   Jews   chief.   coming together And them,
ἔλεγε πρὸς αὐτούς, Ἄνδρες ἀδελφοί, ἐγὼ οὐδὲν ἐναντίον
he said to   them,   Men,   brothers,   I nothing contrary
ποιήσας τῷ λαῷ ἢ τοῖς ἔθεσι τοῖς πατρῴοις, δέσμιος ἐξ
did   to the people or to the customs   ancestral,   a prisoner from
Ἱεροσολύμων παρεδόθην εἰς τὰς χεῖρας τῶν Ῥωμαίων·
Jerusalem   I was delivered to   the   hands   of the   Romans,

**18** οἵτινες ἀνακρίναντές με ἐβούλοντο ἀπολῦσαι, διὰ τὸ μηδε-
who   having examined me were minded   to let me go, because   no

**19** μίαν αἰτίαν θανάτου ὑπάρχειν ἐν ἐμοί. ἀντιλεγόντων δὲ τῶν
cause   of death   to be   in   me.   speaking against But the
Ἰουδαίων, ἠναγκάσθην ἐπικαλέσασθαι Καίσαρα, οὐχ ὡς
Jews,   I was compelled   to appeal   to Caesar;   not as

**20** τοῦ ἔθνους μου ἔχων τι κατηγορῆσαι. διὰ ταύτην οὖν τὴν
the nation of me having anything to accuse. Because of this,   then,
αἰτίαν παρεκάλεσα ὑμᾶς ἰδεῖν καὶ προσλαλῆσαι· ἕνεκεν γὰρ
cause   I called   fo you to see and   to speak to;   for the sake of for
τῆς ἐλπίδος τοῦ Ἰσραὴλ τὴν ἅλυσιν ταύτην περίκειμαι.
the   hope   —   of Israel,   —   chain   this I have around (me).

**21** οἱ δὲ πρὸς αὐτὸν εἶπον, Ἡμεῖς οὔτε γράμματα περὶ σοῦ
they And to   him   said,   We   neither   letters   about you
ἐδεξάμεθα ἀπὸ τῆς Ἰουδαίας, οὔτε παραγενόμενός τις τῶν
received   from   the Jews,   nor   arriving   anyone of the
ἀδελφῶν ἀπήγγειλεν ἢ ἐλάλησέ τι περὶ σοῦ πονηρόν.
brothers   told   or   spoke anything about you   evil.

**22** ἀξιοῦμεν δὲ παρὰ σοῦ ἀκοῦσαι ἃ φρονεῖς· περὶ μὲν γὰρ τῆς
we think fit But from   you   to hear   what you think about indeed for
αἱρέσεως ταύτης γνωστὸν ἐστιν ἡμῖν ὅτι πανταχοῦ ἀντιλέ-
sect   this   known   is us, that everywhere it is
γεται.
spoken against.

**23** Ταξάμενοι δὲ αὐτῷ ἡμέραν, ἧκον πρὸς αὐτὸν εἰς τὴν
appointing And   him   a day,   came to   him   in the
ξενίαν πλείονες· οἷς ἐξετίθετο διαμαρτυρόμενος τὴν βασι-
lodging more,   to whom he set forth earnestly testifying   the king-
λείαν τοῦ Θεοῦ, πείθων τε αὐτοὺς τὰ περὶ τοῦ Ἰησοῦ, ἀπό
dom   — of God, persuading and them   concerning   — Jesus.   from
τε τοῦ νόμου Μωσέως καὶ τῶν προφητῶν, ἀπὸ πρωῒ ἕως
and the law   of Moses and   the   Prophets,   from morning until

**24** ἑσπέρας. καὶ οἱ μὲν ἐπείθοντο τοῖς λεγομένοις, οἱ δὲ ἠπίστουν.
evening.   And some were persuaded by that being said, others disbelieved.

**25** ἀσύμφωνοι δὲ ὄντες πρὸς ἀλλήλους ἀπελύοντο, εἰπόντος
being disagreed And being with one another, they were let go, having said
τοῦ Παύλου ῥῆμα ἕν, ὅτι Καλῶς τὸ Πνεῦμα τὸ Ἅγιον
—   Paul   word one,   —   Well   the   Spirit   —   Holy
ἐλάλησε διὰ Ἡσαΐου τοῦ προφήτου πρὸς τοὺς πατέρας
spoke through Isaiah   the prophet   to   the   fathers

**26** ἡμῶν, λέγων, Πορεύθητι πρὸς τὸν λαὸν τοῦτον καὶ εἰπέ,
of us, saying, Go   to   —   people this   and   say:
Ἀκοῇ ἀκούσετε, καὶ οὐ μὴ συνῆτε· καὶ βλέποντες βλέψετε,
In hearing you will hear, and not at all understand, and seeing you will see,

**27** καὶ οὐ μὴ ἴδητε· ἐπαχύνθη γὰρ ἡ καρδία τοῦ λαοῦ τούτου,
and not at all perceive, was fattened for the heart   —   people of this,

heard with heavy ears, and they have closed their eyes, lest they should see with the eyes, and they should hear with the ears, and they should understand with the heart, and should **28** be converted, and I should heal them." [28] Then let it be known to you, that the salvation of God is sent to the nations; and they will hear. [29] And he having said these things, **29** the Jews went away having much discussion among themselves.

[30] And Paul **30** remained two whole years in his own hired house, and welcomed all who came in to him, [31] preaching the **31** kingdom of God and teaching the things concerning the Lord Jesus Christ, with all freedom, without hindrance.

καὶ τοῖς ὠσὶ βαρέως ἤκουσαν, καὶ τοὺς ὀφθαλμοὺς αὐτῶν
and with the ears heavily they heard, and the eyes of them

ἐκάμμυσαν· μήποτε ἴδωσι τοῖς ὀφθαλμοῖς, καὶ τοῖς ὠσὶν
they closed, lest at any time they see with the eyes, and with the ears

ἀκούσωσι, καὶ τῇ καρδίᾳ συνῶσι, καὶ ἐπιστρέψωσι, καὶ
hear, and with the heart understand, and be converted, and

**28** ἰάσωμαι αὐτούς. γνωστὸν οὖν ἔστω ὑμῖν, ὅτι τοῖς ἔθνεσιν
I should heal them. Known, therefore, be it to you, that to the nations

ἀπεστάλη τὸ σωτήριον τοῦ Θεοῦ, αὐτοὶ καὶ ἀκούσονται.
was sent the salvation — of God, they and will hear.

**29** καὶ ταῦτα αὐτοῦ εἰπόντος, ἀπῆλθον οἱ Ἰουδαῖοι, πολλὴν
And these things he having said, went away the Jews much

ἔχοντες ἐν ἑαυτοῖς συζήτησιν.
having among themselves discussion.

**30** Ἔμεινε δὲ ὁ Παῦλος διετίαν ὅλην ἐν ἰδίῳ μισθώματι, καὶ
remained And Paul two years a whole in (his) own rented place, and

ἀπεδέχετο πάντας τοὺς εἰσπορευομένους πρὸς αὐτόν,
welcomed all those coming in to him,

**31** κηρύσσων τὴν βασιλείαν τοῦ Θεοῦ, καὶ διδάσκων τὰ περὶ
proclaiming the kingdom — of God, and teaching the things about

τοῦ Κυρίου Ἰησοῦ Χριστοῦ, μετὰ πάσης παρρησίας,
the Lord Jesus Christ, with all freedom,

ἀκωλύτως.
without hindrance.

# ΠΑΥΛΟΥ ΤΟΥ ΑΠΟΣΤΟΛΟΥ
### PAUL    THE    APOSTLE

## Η ΠΡΟΣ
### TO (THE)

# ΡΩΜΑΙΟΥΣ ΕΠΙΣΤΟΛΗ
### ROMANS    EPISTLE

**KING JAMES II VERSION**

**THE APOSTLE PAUL'S
EPISTLE TO (THE)
ROMANS**

### CHAPTER 1

[1] Paul, a slave of Jesus Christ, a called apostle, separated to the gospel of God, [2] which He before promised through His prophets in holy Scriptures, [3] concerning His Son, who came of the seed of David, according to flesh. [4] who was marked out Son of God in power, according to the Spirit of holiness, by resurrection of (the) dead, Jesus Christ our Lord. [5] by whom we received grace and apostleship to obedience of faith among all the nations, for His name's sake, [6] among whom are you also, the called out ones of Jesus Christ. [7] to all those who are in Rome, beloved of God, called out saints; grace and peace to you from God our Father, and (the) Lord Jesus Christ.

[8] First, I thank my God through Jesus Christ for you all, that your faith is spoken of in the whole world; [9] for God is my witness, whom I serve in my spirit in the gospel of His Son, how I make mention of you without ceasing, [10] always at my prayers beseeching if by any means now at length I shall be blessed by the will of God to come to you. [11] For I long to see you, that I may impart some spiritual gift to you, for the establishing of you, [12] that is, to be comforted together among you, through the faith in one another, both yours and mine. [13] But I do

### CHAPTER 1

**1** Παῦλος, δοῦλος Ἰησοῦ Χριστοῦ, κλητὸς ἀπόστολος,
Paul,   a slave   of Jesus   Christ,   called (to be) an apostle,

**2** ἀφωρισμένος εἰς εὐαγγέλιον Θεοῦ, ὃ προεπηγγείλατο διὰ
being separated to (the) gospel   of God, which He promised before through

**3** τῶν προφητῶν αὐτοῦ ἐν γραφαῖς ἁγίαις, περὶ τοῦ υἱοῦ
the prophets   of Him in Scriptures holy, concerning the Son

αὐτοῦ, τοῦ γενομένου ἐκ σπέρματος Δαβὶδ κατὰ σάρκα,
of Him,   —   come   of the   seed   of David according to flesh,

**4** τοῦ ὁρισθέντος υἱοῦ Θεοῦ ἐν δυνάμει, κατὰ πνεῦμα ἁγιω-
— marked out Son of God in power according to (the) Spirit of

σύνης, ἐξ ἀναστάσεως νεκρῶν, Ἰησοῦ Χριστοῦ τοῦ Κυρίου
holiness, by resurrection of (the) dead, Jesus   Christ   the   Lord

**5** ἡμῶν, δι' οὗ ἐλάβομεν χάριν καὶ ἀποστολὴν εἰς ὑπακοὴν
of us, through whom we received grace and apostleship to obedience

**6** πίστεως ἐν πᾶσι τοῖς ἔθνεσιν, ὑπὲρ τοῦ ὀνόματος αὐτοῦ, ἐν
of faith among all the nations, for the sake of the name of Him, among

**7** οἷς ἐστὲ καὶ ὑμεῖς, κλητοὶ Ἰησοῦ Χριστοῦ· πᾶσι τοῖς οὖσιν
whom are also you called out ones of Jesus Christ. To all those being

ἐν Ῥώμῃ ἀγαπητοῖς Θεοῦ, κλητοῖς ἁγίοις· χάρις ὑμῖν καὶ
in   Rome beloved   of God, called out   saints,   grace to you and

εἰρήνη ἀπὸ Θεοῦ πατρὸς ἡμῶν καὶ Κυρίου Ἰησοῦ Χριστοῦ.
peace from   God (the) Father of us, and (the) Lord Jesus   Christ.

**8** Πρῶτον μὲν εὐχαριστῶ τῷ Θεῷ μου διὰ Ἰησοῦ Χριστοῦ
Firstly, truly I thank   the   God of me through Jesus   Christ

ὑπὲρ πάντων ὑμῶν, ὅτι ἡ πίστις ὑμῶν καταγγέλλεται ἐν
for   all   of you, that the faith of you   is spoken of   in

**9** ὅλῳ τῷ κόσμῳ. μάρτυς γάρ μού ἐστιν ὁ Θεός, ᾧ λατρεύω
all the world. the witness For of me is   God, whom I serve

ἐν τῷ πνεύματί μου ἐν τῷ εὐαγγελίῳ τοῦ υἱοῦ αὐτοῦ, ὡς
in the spirit of me in the gospel of the Son of Him, how

**10** ἀδιαλείπτως μνείαν ὑμῶν ποιοῦμαι, πάντοτε ἐπὶ τῶν
without ceasing mention of you I make   always   on   the

προσευχῶν μου δεόμενος, εἴπως ἤδη ποτὲ εὐοδωθήσομαι ἐν
prayers   of me beseeching, if at all now at length I shall be blessed by

**11** τῷ θελήματι τοῦ Θεοῦ ἐλθεῖν πρὸς ὑμᾶς. ἐπιποθῶ γὰρ ἰδεῖν
the will   — of God to come to   you. I long   For   to see

ὑμᾶς, ἵνα τι μεταδῶ χάρισμα ὑμῖν πνευματικόν, εἰς τὸ
you, that some I may impart gift to you spiritual, for the

**12** στηριχθῆναι ὑμᾶς, τοῦτο δέ ἐστι, συμπαρακληθῆναι ἐν ὑμῖν
establishing of you. this And is to be comforted together among you

**13** διὰ τῆς ἐν ἀλλήλοις πίστεως ὑμῶν τε καὶ ἐμοῦ. οὐ θέλω δὲ
through the in one another faith of you both and of me. not I wish But

357

not wish you to be ignorant, brothers, that many times I purposed to come to you, and was hindered to the present, that I might **14** have some fruit also among you, even as among the other nations. [14] I am a **15** debtor both to Greeks and barbarians, both to wise and foolish, [15] so as far as in me (lies), I am eager to **16** preach the gospel to you in Rome also. [16] For I am not ashamed of the gospel of Christ; for it is power of God to everyone believing, **17** both to Jew first, and to Greek, [17] for in it the righteousness of God is revealed from faith to faith; even as it has been written, "But the just shall live by faith. [18] For God's wrath **18** is revealed from Heaven on all ungodliness and unrighteousness. [19] Because the thing known of God is clearly known within them, for **19** God revealed (it) to them; [20] for the unseen things **20** of Him from the creation of the world are clearly seen, being understood by the things made, both His eternal power and Godhead; for them to be without excuse. [21] Because having **21** known God, they glorified Him not as God, nor were thankful; but became vain in their thoughts, and their foolish heart was darkened; [22] professing to be wise, they became fools, **22** [23] and changed the glory of the incorruptible **23** God into a likeness of an image of corruptible man, and of birds, and four-footed animals, and creeping things. **24** [24] Therefore God also gave them up to uncleanness in the lust of their hearts, to the dishonor (of) their bodies **25** between themselves; [25] who changed the truth of God into the lie, and worshiped and served the created thing more than the Creator, who is blessed forever. Amen.

ὑμᾶς ἀγνοεῖν, ἀδελφοί, ὅτι πολλάκις προεθέμην ἐλθεῖν πρὸς
you to be ignorant, brothers, that often          I purposed to come to

ὑμᾶς (καὶ ἐκωλύθην ἄχρι τοῦ δεῦρο), ἵνα καρπόν τινα σχῶ
you,     and was hindered until     the   present,  that   fruit     some I have

καὶ ἐν ὑμῖν, καθὼς καὶ ἐν τοῖς λοιποῖς ἔθνεσιν. Ἕλλησί τε καὶ
also among you, even as also in the remaining  nations. to Greeks Both and

βαρβάροις, σοφοῖς τε καὶ ἀνοήτοις ὀφειλέτης εἰμί· οὕτω τὸ
to foreigners, to wise both and  foolish,    a debtor I am;   so    as

κατ' ἐμὲ πρόθυμον καὶ ὑμῖν τοῖς ἐν Ῥώμῃ εὐαγγελίσασθαι.
far as in me (lies) I am eager also to you  in  Rome to preach the gospel.

οὐ γὰρ ἐπαισχύνομαι τὸ εὐαγγέλιον τοῦ Χριστοῦ· δύναμις
not For  I am ashamed  of the  gospel       — of Christ,   power

γὰρ Θεοῦ ἐστιν εἰς σωτηρίαν παντὶ τῷ πιστεύοντι, Ἰουδαίῳ
for of God it is  to  salvation to everyone    believing,      to Jew

τε πρῶτον καὶ Ἕλληνι. δικαιοσύνη γὰρ Θεοῦ ἐν αὐτῷ
both firstly,   and to Greek.  a righteousness For of God in   it

ἀποκαλύπτεται ἐκ πίστεως εἰς πίστιν, καθὼς γέγραπται,
is revealed       from    faith     to      faith, even as it has been written,

Ὁ δὲ δίκαιος ἐκ πίστεως ζήσεται.
the But just   by    faith    shall live.

Ἀποκαλύπτεται γὰρ ὀργὴ Θεοῦ ἀπ' οὐρανοῦ ἐπὶ πᾶσαν
is revealed        For (the) wrath of God from Heaven  on     all

ἀσέβειαν καὶ ἀδικίαν ἀνθρώπων τῶν τὴν ἀλήθειαν ἐν ἀδικίᾳ
ungodliness and unrighteousness of men —  the  truth in unrighteousness

κατεχόντων· διότι τὸ γνωστὸν τοῦ Θεοῦ φανερόν ἐστιν ἐν
holding;     because the thing known  — of God clearly known is    in

αὐτοῖς· ὁ γὰρ Θεὸς αὐτοῖς ἐφανέρωσε. τὰ γὰρ ἀόρατα αὐτοῦ
them,    for God   to them   revealed (it). the For unseen things of Him

ἀπὸ κτίσεως κόσμου τοῖς ποιήμασι νοούμενα καθορᾶται.
from (the) creation of (the) world by the things made being realized is  being understood

ἥ τε ἀΐδιος αὐτοῦ δύναμις καὶ θειότης, εἰς τὸ εἶναι αὐτοὺς
the both eternal of Him power and Godhead; for    to be    them

ἀναπολογήτους· διότι γνόντες τὸν Θεόν, οὐχ ὡς Θεὸν
without excuse.    Because having known —  God,   not  as   God

ἐδόξασαν ἢ εὐχαρίστησαν, ἀλλ' ἐματαιώθησαν ἐν τοῖς
they glorified, nor were thankful;   but    became vain     in  the

διαλογισμοῖς αὐτῶν, καὶ ἐσκοτίσθη ἡ ἀσύνετος αὐτῶν
reasonings    of them,  and was darkened the undiscerning   of them

καρδία. φάσκοντες εἶναι σοφοὶ ἐμωράνθησαν, καὶ ἤλλαξαν
heart. Professing to be wise, they became foolish, and changed

τὴν δόξαν τοῦ ἀφθάρτου Θεοῦ ἐν ὁμοιώματι εἰκόνος φθαρτοῦ
the  glory of the incorruptible God into a likeness of an image of corruptible

ἀνθρώπου καὶ πετεινῶν καὶ τετραπόδων καὶ ἑρπετῶν.
man,    and   birds,    and four-footed animals, and reptiles.

Διὸ καὶ παρέδωκεν αὐτοὺς ὁ Θεὸς ἐν ταῖς ἐπιθυμίαις τῶν
Therefore also gave up    them   God  in  the   lusts      of the

καρδιῶν αὐτῶν εἰς ἀκαθαρσίαν τοῦ ἀτιμάζεσθαι τὰ σώματα
hearts  of them to uncleanness,   — to be dishonored the  bodies

αὐτῶν ἐν ἑαυτοῖς· οἵτινες μετήλλαξαν τὴν ἀλήθειαν τοῦ
of them among themselves; who changed     the   truth     —

Θεοῦ ἐν τῷ ψεύδει, καὶ ἐσεβάσθησαν καὶ ἐλάτρευσαν τῇ
of God into the lie,   and worshiped     and served      the

κτίσει παρὰ τὸν κτίσαντα, ὅς ἐστιν εὐλογητὸς εἰς τοὺς
creature rather than the Creator, who is   blessed     to the

αἰῶνας. ἀμήν.
ages.    Amen.

[26] Because of this God gave them up to dishonorable passions, for both their females changed the natural use to that contrary to nature; [27] and likewise the males having forsaken (the) natural use of the female also burned in their lust toward one another, males with males working out shamefulness, and receiving back the reward which was fitting for their error. [28] And even as they did not think fit to have God in (their) knowledge, God gave them up to a reprobate mind, to do the things not right, [29] having been filled with all unrighteousness, fornication, iniquity, covetousness, malice, (being) full of envy, murder, quarrels, deceit, evil habits; (becoming) whisperers, [30] slanderers, God-haters, insolent, proud, braggarts, devisers of evil things, disobedient to parents, [31] without discernment, perfidious, without natural affection, unforgiving, unmerciful; [32] who having known the righteous judgment of God, that those practicing such things are worthy of death, not only do them, but also applaud those practicing (so).

26 Διὰ τοῦτο παρέδωκεν αὐτοὺς ὁ Θεὸς εἰς πάθη ἀτιμίας·
Therefore     gave up     them     God   to passions of dishonor;

αἵ τε γὰρ θήλειαι αὐτῶν μετήλλαξαν τὴν φυσικὴν χρῆσιν
the even for females of them     changed     the natural     use

27 εἰς τὴν παρὰ φύσιν· ὁμοίως τε καὶ οἱ ἄρσενες, ἀφέντες τὴν
to the (use) against nature; likewise and also the males having forsaken the

φυσικὴν χρῆσιν τῆς θηλείας, ἐξεκαύθησαν ἐν τῇ ὀρέξει αὐτῶν
natural   use   of the female,   burned   in the lust of them

.εἰς ἀλλήλους, ἄρσενες ἐν ἄρσεσι τὴν ἀσχημοσύνην κατερ-
toward one another, males among males the shamefulness   working

γαζόμενοι, καὶ τὴν ἀντιμισθίαν ἣν ἔδει τῆς πλάνης αὐτῶν
out,     and the   reward   which behoved the straying of them,

ἐν ἑαυτοῖς ἀπολαμβάνοντες.
in themselves receiving back.

28 Καὶ καθὼς οὐκ ἐδοκίμασαν τὸν Θεὸν ἔχειν ἐν ἐπιγνώσει,
And even as not they thought fit —   God to have in   knowledge,

παρέδωκεν αὐτοὺς ὁ Θεὸς εἰς ἀδόκιμον νοῦν, ποιεῖν τὰ μὴ
gave up     them     God to a reprobate mind,   to do the things not

29 καθήκοντα, πεπληρωμένους πάσῃ ἀδικίᾳ, πορνείᾳ, πονηρίᾳ,
right,     having been filled   with all unrighteousness, fornication, iniquity,

πλεονεξίᾳ, κακίᾳ· μεστοὺς φθόνου, φόνου, ἔριδος, δόλου,
covetousness, malice,   full   of envy,   murder, quarrels, deceit,

30 κακοηθείας· ψιθυριστάς, καταλάλους, θεοστυγεῖς, ὑβριστάς,
evil habits,   whisperers,   slanderers,   God-haters,   insolent,

ὑπερηφάνους, ἀλαζόνας, ἐφευρετὰς κακῶν, γονεῦσιν ἀπει-
proud,     braggart:   devisers of evil things to parents diso-

31 θεῖς, ἀσυνέτους, ἀσυνθέτους, ἀστόργους, ἀσπόνδους, ἀνελεή-
bedient, undiscerning, perfidious, without affection implacable, unmerci-

32 μονας· οἵτινες τὸ δικαίωμα τοῦ Θεοῦ ἐπιγνόντες, ὅτι οἱ τὰ
ful;   who   the righteous order   of God having known, that those

τοιαῦτα πράσσοντες ἄξιοι θανάτου εἰσίν, οὐ μόνον αὐτὰ
such things practicing   worthy of death   are,   not only   them

ποιοῦσιν, ἀλλὰ καὶ συνευδοκοῦσι τοῖς πράσσουσι.
do,     but also   consent to   those practicing (them).

## CHAPTER 2

[1] Therefore, O man, you are without excuse, every one who judges, for in that in which you judge the other you condemn yourself; for you who judge do the same thing. [2] But we know that the judgment of God is according to truth on those that do such things. [3] And, O man, who judge those that do such things, and practice them (yourself), do you think that you shall escape the judgment of God? [4] Or do you despise the riches of His kindness, and the forbearance, and the long-suffering, not knowing that the kindness of God leads you to repentance? [5] But according to your hardness and stubborn heart, do you treasure up to yourself wrath in a day of wrath,

### CHAPTER 2

1 Διὸ ἀναπολόγητος εἶ, ὦ ἄνθρωπε πᾶς ὁ κρίνων· ἐν ᾧ γὰρ
Therefore without excuse are you, O man, everyone judging;in what for

κρίνεις τὸν ἕτερον, σεαυτὸν κατακρίνεις, τὰ γὰρ αὐτὰ πράσ-
you judge the other,   yourself you condemn;   the for same things you

2 σεις ὁ κρίνων. οἴδαμεν δὲ ὅτι τὸ κρίμα τοῦ Θεοῦ ἐστι κατὰ
practice those judging. we know But that the judgment of God is according to

3 ἀλήθειαν ἐπὶ τοὺς τὰ τοιαῦτα πράσσοντας. λογίζῃ δὲ τοῦτο,
truth   on those that such things   practice. do you think And this,

ὦ ἄνθρωπε ὁ κρίνων τοὺς τὰ τοιαῦτα πράσσοντας καὶ ποιῶν
O   man, he judging those such things   practicing   and doing

4 αὐτά, ὅτι σὺ ἐκφεύξῃ τὸ κρίμα τοῦ Θεοῦ; ἢ τοῦ πλούτου
them, that you will escape the judgment — of God? Or the   riches

τῆς χρηστότητος αὐτοῦ καὶ τῆς ἀνοχῆς καὶ τῆς μακροθυμίας
of the kindness   of Him, and the forbearance and the longsuffering

καταφρονεῖς, ἀγνοῶν ὅτι τὸ χρηστὸν τοῦ Θεοῦ εἰς μετάνοιάν
do you despise, not knowing that the kindness — of God to repentance

5 σε ἄγει; κατὰ δὲ τὴν σκληρότητά σου καὶ ἀμετανόητον
you leads? according to But the hardness   of you and the impenitent

καρδίαν θησαυρίζεις σεαυτῷ ὀργὴν ἐν ἡμέρᾳ ὀργῆς καὶ
heart,   do you treasure for yourself wrath in a day   of wrath, and

and revelation of righteous judgment of God, [6] who will give to each according to his works; [7] everlasting life indeed to those who with patience in good work are seeking glory and honor and incorruptibility? [8] But to those of contention, and do not obey the truth, but obey unrighteousness, indignation and wrath, [9] trouble and pain, on every soul of man that works out evil, both of Jew first, and of Greek. [10] But glory and honor and peace to everyone that works good, both to the Jew first, and to Greek. [11] For there is no respect of persons with God. [12] For as many as sinned without Law, shall perish without Law; and as many as sinned within Law, shall be judged by Law. [13] For not the hearers of the Law are just with God, but the doers of the Law shall be justified. [14] For when nations not having Law do by nature the things of the Law, not having Law, they are a law to themselves; [15] who show the work of the law written in their hearts, their conscience witnessing with (them); and the thoughts between one another accusing or even excusing, [16] in a day when God shall judge the hidden things of men, according to my gospel, through Jesus Christ.

[17] Behold, you are called a Jew, and rest in the Law, and boast in God, [18] and know the will, and approve the things that are more excellent, being instructed out of the Law; [19] and are persuaded you yourself are a guide of (the) blind, a light of those in darkness, [20] a teacher of foolish ones, a teacher of infants, having the pattern of knowledge and of truth in the Law; [21] you then who teach another, do you not teach yourself? You that preach not to steal, do you steal? [22] You that say, Do not commit adultery; do you commit adultery? You that

---

**6** ἀποκαλύψεως δικαιοκρισίας τοῦ Θεοῦ, ὃς ἀποδώσει ἑκάστῳ
revelation   of a righteous judgment   of God, who will give   to each one

**7** κατὰ τὰ ἔργα αὐτοῦ· τοῖς μὲν καθ' ὑπομονὴν ἔργου ἀγαθοῦ
according to   the works of him to those by   patience   work   good

δόξαν καὶ τιμὴν καὶ ἀφθαρσίαν ζητοῦσι, ζωὴν αἰώνιον· τοῖς
glory and honor and incorruptibility seeking,   life everlasting. to those

**8** δὲ ἐξ ἐριθείας, καὶ ἀπειθοῦσι μὲν τῇ ἀληθείᾳ, πειθομένοις δὲ
But of self-seeking and disobeying indeed the truth,   obeying   but

**9** τῇ ἀδικίᾳ, θυμὸς καὶ ὀργή, θλῖψις καὶ στενοχωρία, ἐπὶ
unrighteousness, anger and wrath,   trouble and   pain   on

πᾶσαν ψυχὴν ἀνθρώπου τοῦ κατεργαζομένου τὸ κακόν,
every   soul   of man   —   working out   the evil,

**10** Ἰουδαίου τε πρῶτον καὶ Ἕλληνος· δόξα δὲ καὶ τιμὴ καὶ
of Jew   both firstly, and of Greek.   glory But and honor and

εἰρήνη παντὶ τῷ ἐργαζομένῳ τὸ ἀγαθόν, Ἰουδαίῳ τε πρῶτον
peace to everyone working out the   good,   to Jew both firstly,

**11** καὶ Ἕλληνι· οὐ γάρ ἐστι προσωποληψία παρὰ τῷ Θεῷ.
and to Greek. not For   is   respect of persons   with   —   God.

**12** ὅσοι γὰρ ἀνόμως ἥμαρτον, ἀνόμως καὶ ἀπολοῦνται· καὶ
as many as For without law sinned, without law also will perish;   and

**13** ὅσοι ἐν νόμῳ ἥμαρτον, διὰ νόμου κριθήσονται· οὐ γὰρ οἱ
as many as in law sinned, through law   will be judged; not for   the

ἀκροαταὶ τοῦ νόμου δίκαιοι παρὰ τῷ Θεῷ, ἀλλ' οἱ ποιηταὶ
hearers   of the   law are just   with   — God, but the doers

**14** τοῦ νόμου δικαιωθήσονται. ὅταν γὰρ ἔθνη τὰ μὴ νόμον
of the law   shall be justified.   when For nations — not law

ἔχοντα φύσει τὰ τοῦ νόμου ποιῇ, οὗτοι, νόμον μὴ ἔχοντες,
having by nature the things of the law do,   these   law   not having,

**15** ἑαυτοῖς εἰσι νόμος· οἵτινες ἐνδείκνυνται τὸ ἔργον τοῦ νόμου
to themselves are a law;   who   show   the work of the   law

γραπτὸν ἐν ταῖς καρδίαις αὐτῶν, συμμαρτυρούσης αὐτῶν
written in the   hearts   of them,   witnessing with   of them

τῆς συνειδήσεως, καὶ μεταξὺ ἀλλήλων τῶν λογισμῶν
the   conscience,   and between one another   the   thoughts

**16** κατηγορούντων ἢ καὶ ἀπολογουμένων, ἐν ἡμέρᾳ ὅτε κρινεῖ
accusing   or even   excusing,   in a day when judges

ὁ Θεὸς τὰ κρυπτὰ τῶν ἀνθρώπων, κατὰ τὸ εὐαγγέλιόν μου,
God the hidden things   of men   according to the gospel   of me

διὰ Ἰησοῦ Χριστοῦ.
through Jesus Christ.

**17** Ἴδε σὺ Ἰουδαῖος ἐπονομάζῃ, καὶ ἐπαναπαύῃ τῷ νόμῳ,
Behold, you a Jew   are named,   and   rest   in the law,

**18** καὶ καυχᾶσαι ἐν Θεῷ, καὶ γινώσκεις τὸ θέλημα, καὶ δοκι-
and boast   in God, and know   the will,   and approve

**19** μάζεις τὰ διαφέροντα, κατηχούμενος ἐκ τοῦ νόμου, πέποιθάς
the things excelling,   being instructed out of the law, having persuaded

τε σεαυτὸν ὁδηγὸν εἶναι τυφλῶν, φῶς τῶν ἐν σκότει, παι-
and yourself   a guide   to be of blind ones, a light to those in darkness, an

**20** δευτὴν ἀφρόνων, διδάσκαλον νηπίων, ἔχοντα τὴν μόρφωσιν
instructor of foolish ones, a teacher of infants, having   the   form

**21** τῆς γνώσεως καὶ τῆς ἀληθείας ἐν τῷ νόμῳ· ὁ οὖν διδάσκων
of knowledge and of the truth   in   the law; he, then, teaching

ἕτερον, σεαυτὸν οὐ διδάσκεις ; ὁ κηρύσσων ·μὴ κλέπτειν,
another, yourself not do you teach? He proclaiming not   to steal,

**22** κλέπτεις ; ὁ λέγων μὴ μοιχεύειν, μοιχεύεις ; ὁ βδελυσσόμενος
do you steal? He saying not to commit do you commit He detesting
                    adultery,   adultery?

hate idols, do you commit sacrilege? [23] You who boast in the Law, do you dishonor God through the breaking of the Law? [24] For the name of God is blasphemed among the nations through you, even as it has been written. [25] For circumcision indeed profits if you practice the Law; but if you are a transgressor of Law, your circumcision becomes uncircumcision. [26] If, then, the uncircumcision keeps the demands of the Law, (will) not his uncircumcision be counted for circumcision? [27] And will (not) the uncircumcision by nature (by) keeping the Law judge you, he through letter and circumcision (being) transgressor of Law? [28] For he is not a Jew that is (one) outwardly, nor (is) circumcision that outwardly in flesh; [29] but he (is) a Jew that (is one) inwardly, and circumcision (is) of heart, in spirit, not in letter; of whom the praise (is) not from men, but from God.

CHAPTER 3

[1] What then (is) the superiority of the Jew? Or what the profit of circumcision? [2] Much by every way: For first, indeed that they were entrusted with the oracles of God. [3] For what if some disbelieved? Will their unbelief destroy the faith of God? [4] Let it not be! But let God be true and every man a liar, just as it has been written, "that You should be justified in Your words and overcome in Your being judged." [5] But if our unrighteousness commend God's righteousness, what shall we say? (Is) God unrighteous who lays on wrath? I speak according to man. [6] Let it not be! Otherwise how shall God judge the world? [7] For if in my lie the truth of God abounded to His glory, why yet am I judged as a sinner? [8] And not, as we are wrongly accused and as some report (that) we say, let us practice evil things so that good things may come? Whose judgment is just.

---

**23** τὰ εἴδωλα, ἱεροσυλεῖς; ὃς ἐν νόμῳ καυχᾶσαι διὰ τῆς
the idols, do you rob temples? Who in law boasts, through

**24** παραβάσεως τοῦ νόμου τὸν Θεὸν ἀτιμάζεις; τὸ γὰρ ὄνομα
transgression of the law — God do you dishonor? the For name

τοῦ Θεοῦ δι' ὑμᾶς βλασφημεῖται ἐν τοῖς ἔθνεσι, καθὼς
— of God through you is blasphemed among the nations; even as

**25** γέγραπται. περιτομὴ μὲν γὰρ ὠφελεῖ, ἐὰν νόμον πράσσῃς·
it has been written. circumcision For profits, if law you practice;

ἐὰν δὲ παραβάτης νόμου ᾖς, ἡ περιτομή σου ἀκροβυστία
if but a transgressor of law you are, the circumcision of you uncircumcision

**26** γέγονεν. ἐὰν οὖν ἡ ἀκροβυστία τὰ δικαιώματα τοῦ νόμου
becomes. If, then, the uncircumcision the ordinances of the law

φυλάσσῃ, οὐχὶ ἡ ἀκροβυστία αὐτοῦ εἰς περιτομὴν λογισθή-
keeps, (will) not the uncircumcision of him for circumcision be counted?

**27** σεται; καὶ κρινεῖ ἡ ἐκ φύσεως ἀκροβυστία, τὸν νόμον
And will judge the by nature uncircumcision the law

τελοῦσα, σὲ τὸν διὰ γράμματος καὶ περιτομῆς παραβάτην
keeping you the through letter and circumcision transgressor

**28** νόμου; οὐ γὰρ ὁ ἐν τῷ φανερῷ Ἰουδαῖός ἐστιν, οὐδὲ ἡ ἐν τῷ
of law? not For the (one) apparent a Jew is, nor (is) the

**29** φανερῷ ἐν σαρκὶ περιτομή· ἀλλ' ὁ ἐν τῷ κρυπτῷ Ἰουδαῖος,
apparent in flesh circumcision, but the (one) in private Jew (is),

καὶ περιτομὴ καρδίας ἐν πνεύματι. οὐ γράμματι· οὗ ὁ
and circumcision (is) of heart in spirit, not in letter; of whom the

ἔπαινος οὐκ ἐξ ἀνθρώπων, ἀλλ' ἐκ τοῦ Θεοῦ.
praise (is) not from men, but from — God.

**CHAPTER 3**

**1** Τί οὖν τὸ περισσὸν τοῦ Ἰουδαίου, ἢ τίς ἡ ὠφέλεια τῆς
What, then, the superiority of the Jew, or what the profit —

**2** περιτομῆς; πολὺ κατὰ πάντα τρόπον· πρῶτον μὲν γὰρ ὅτι
of circumcision? Much by every way. firstly, indeed, For, that

**3** ἐπιστεύθησαν τὰ λόγια τοῦ Θεοῦ. τί γὰρ εἰ ἠπίστησάν
they were entrusted with the oracles of God. what For? If disbelieved

τινες· μὴ ἡ ἀπιστία αὐτῶν τὴν πίστιν τοῦ Θεοῦ καταργή-
some, Not the unbelief of them the faith of God destroy?

**4** σει; μὴ γένοιτο· γινέσθω δὲ ὁ Θεὸς ἀληθής, πᾶς δὲ ἄνθρωπος
Not let it be! let be But God true, every and man

ψεύστης, καθὼς γέγραπται, "Ὅπως ἂν δικαιωθῇς ἐν τοῖς
a liar, even as it has been written, So as you may be justified in the

**5** λόγοις σου, καὶ νικήσῃς ἐν τῷ κρίνεσθαί σε. εἰ δὲ ἡ ἀδικία
sayings of you, and will overcome in the being judged you. if But the unrighteousness

ἡμῶν Θεοῦ δικαιοσύνην συνίστησι, τί ἐροῦμεν; μὴ ἄδικος
of us of God a righteousness commends, what shall we say? unrighteous

**6** ὁ Θεὸς ὁ ἐπιφέρων τὴν ὀργήν (κατὰ ἄνθρωπον λέγω); μὴ
(Is) God inflicting — wrath? —according to man I say — not

**7** γένοιτο· ἐπεὶ πῶς κρινεῖ ὁ Θεὸς τὸν κόσμον; εἰ γὰρ ἡ
let it be! Otherwise how will judge God the world? if For the

ἀλήθεια τοῦ Θεοῦ ἐν τῷ ἐμῷ ψεύσματι ἐπερίσσευσεν εἰς τὴν
truth of God by my lie abounded to the

**8** δόξαν αὐτοῦ, τί ἔτι κἀγὼ ὡς ἁμαρτωλὸς κρίνομαι; καὶ μὴ
glory of Him, why yet I also as a sinner am judged? And not

(καθὼς βλασφημούμεθα, καὶ καθώς φασί τινες ἡμᾶς λέγειν
— as we are wrongly accused, and as report some us to say—

ὅτι), Ποιήσωμεν τὰ κακὰ ἵνα ἔλθῃ τὰ ἀγαθά; ὧν τὸ κρίμα
Let us do bad things that may come good things. Of whom judgment

[9] What then? Are we better? Not at all! For we have before charged both Jews and Greeks all (with) being under sin; [10] according as it has been written, "There is none righteous, no, not one! [11] There is none that understands, there is not one that seeks after God. [12] All have gone out of the way; together they have become worthless; there is none that is doing good, no, not one! [13] Their throat is an opened grave; they use deceit with their tongues; the poison of asps is under their lips; [14] of whom the mouth is full of cursing and bitterness; [15] their feet swift to shed blood; [16] ruin and misery (are) in their ways; [17] and they did not know the way of peace; [18] there is no fear of God before their eyes." [19] Now we know that whatever the Law says, it speaks to those within the Law, that every mouth may be stopped, and all the world be under judgment to God. [20] Because by works of law no flesh will be justified before Him; for through law (is) full knowledge of sin.

[21] But now a righteousness of God has been revealed apart from Law, being witnessed by the Law and the Prophets. [22] even the righteousness of God through (the) faith of Jesus Christ toward all and upon all those believing; for there is no difference, [23] for all sinned and come short of the glory of God; [24] being justified as a free gift by His grace through the redemption in Christ Jesus; [25] whom God set forth (as) a propitiation through faith in His blood, for a showing forth of His righteousness through the passing by of the sins that had taken place before, in the forbearance of God — [26] for (the) revealing of His righteousness in the present time, for His being just and justifying him that (is) of (the) faith of Jesus. [27] Where then (is) the boasting? It was excluded. Through what Law? Of

ἔνδικόν ἐστι.
just     is.

9  Τί οὖν; προεχόμεθα; οὐ πάντως· προητιασάμεθα γὰρ
What, then?  Do we excel?  Not at all!  we before charged  For

10  Ἰουδαίους τε καὶ Ἕλληνας πάντας ὑφ' ἁμαρτίαν εἶναι, καθὼς
Jews  both and  Greeks  all  under  sin  to be,  even as

11  γέγραπται ὅτι Οὐκ ἔστι δίκαιος οὐδὲ εἷς· οὐκ ἔστιν ὁ συνιών.
has been written,  Not  a righteous, not one; not is (one) understanding;

12  οὐκ ἔστιν ὁ ἐκζητῶν τὸν Θεόν· πάντες ἐξέκλιναν, ἅμα ἠχρειώ-
not is (one) seeking  — God;  all  turned away, together became
θησαν· οὐκ ἔστι ποιῶν χρηστότητα, οὐκ ἔστιν ἕως ἑνός·
worthless, not is (one) doing  kindness,  not is so much as one.

13  τάφος ἀνεῳγμένος ὁ λάρυγξ αὐτῶν, ταῖς γλώσσαις αὐτῶν
A grave  opened (is)  the throat  of them, with the tongues  of them

14  ἐδολιοῦσαν· ἰὸς ἀσπίδων ὑπὸ τὰ χείλη αὐτῶν· ὧν τὸ στόμα
they used deceit, poison of asps under the lips  of them; of whom the mouth

15  ἀρᾶς καὶ πικρίας γέμει· ὀξεῖς οἱ πόδες αὐτῶν ἐκχέαι αἷμα·
of cursing and bitterness is full; swift  the  feet  of them to shed  blood;

16  σύντριμμα καὶ ταλαιπωρία ἐν ταῖς ὁδοῖς αὐτῶν, καὶ ὁδὸν
ruin  and  misery  in the way of them: and a way

17  εἰρήνης οὐκ ἔγνωσαν· οὐκ ἔστι φόβος Θεοῦ ἀπέναντι τῶν
of peace not they knew.  Not is  fear  of God before  the

18  ὀφθαλμῶν αὐτῶν.
eyes  of them.

19  Οἴδαμεν δὲ ὅτι ὅσα ὁ νόμος λέγει, τοῖς ἐν τῷ νόμῳ λαλεῖ,
we know But that what the law  says to those in the law  it speaks,
ἵνα πᾶν στόμα φραγῇ, καὶ ὑπόδικος γένηται πᾶς ὁ κόσμος
that every mouth be stopped, and under judgment may become all the world

20  τῷ Θεῷ· διότι ἐξ ἔργων νόμου οὐ δικαιωθήσεται πᾶσα σάρξ
to God; because by works of law not will be justified  all  flesh

21  ἐνώπιον αὐτοῦ· διὰ γὰρ νόμου ἐπίγνωσις ἁμαρτίας. νυνὶ δὲ
before  Him; through for law (is) full knowledge of sin.  now But

22  χωρὶς νόμου δικαιοσύνη Θεοῦ πεφανέρωται, μαρτυρουμένη
without law a righteousness of God has been revealed  being witnessed
ὑπὸ τοῦ νόμου καὶ τῶν προφητῶν· δικαιοσύνη δὲ Θεοῦ διὰ
by  the Law and the  Prophets,  a righteousness and of God via
πίστεως Ἰησοῦ Χριστοῦ εἰς πάντας καὶ ἐπὶ πάντας τοὺς
faith  of Jesus  Christ  to  all  and upon  all  those

23  πιστεύοντας· οὐ γάρ ἐστι διαστολή· πάντες γὰρ ἥμαρτον
believing;  not for there is a difference;  all  for  sinned

24  καὶ ὑστεροῦνται τῆς δόξης τοῦ Θεοῦ, δικαιούμενοι δωρεὰν
and  come short of the glory  — of God, being justified  freely
τῇ αὐτοῦ χάριτι διὰ τῆς ἀπολυτρώσεως τῆς ἐν Χριστῷ
by the of Him grace through the  redemption  — in  Christ

25  Ἰησοῦ· ὃν προέθετο ὁ Θεὸς ἱλαστήριον. διὰ τῆς πίστεως,
Jesus; whom set forth  God a propitiation through — faith,
ἐν τῷ αὐτοῦ αἵματι, εἰς ἔνδειξιν τῆς δικαιοσύνης αὐτοῦ, διὰ
by the of Him blood,  for a display of the righteousness of Him, through
τὴν πάρεσιν τῶν προγεγονότων ἁμαρτημάτων, ἐν τῇ ἀνοχῇ
the passing by of the that before had occurred  sins,  in the forbearance

26  τοῦ Θεοῦ· πρὸς ἔνδειξιν τῆς δικαιοσύνης αὐτοῦ ἐν τῷ νῦν
— of God  for the display of the righteousness of Him in the present
καιρῷ, εἰς τὸ εἶναι αὐτὸν δίκαιον καὶ δικαιοῦντα τὸν ἐκ
time,  for the being (of) Him  just  and  justifying the (one) of

27  πίστεως Ἰησοῦ. ποῦ οὖν ἡ καύχησις; ἐξεκλείσθη. διὰ ποίου
faith  of Jesus. Where, then, the boasting? It was excluded. Through what

works? No, but through a **28**
law of faith. [28] Then we
conclude a man to be justified without works of Law.
[29] Or (is He) the God
of Jews only, and not also **29**
of (the) nations? [30] Yes,
also of nations, since (it is) **30**
one God who will justify
circumcision by faith, and
uncircumcision through **31**
faith. [31] Then do we
make the Law of no effect
through faith? Let it not
be! But we establish Law.

### CHAPTER 4
[1] What then shall we **1**
say our father Abraham has
found according to flesh?
[2] For if Abraham was jus- **2**
tified by works, he has a
boast — but not with God. **3**
[3] For what says the Scripture?" And Abraham believed God, and it was counted
to him for righteousness."
[4] Now (to him) working, **4**
the reward is not counted
according to grace, but ac- **5**
cording to debt. [5] But to
(one) not working, but believing on Him justifying the
the ungodly, his faith is
counted for righteousness. **6**
[6] Even as also David says
of the blessedness of the
man to whom God counts
righteousness apart from
works. [7] Blessed (are) **7**
(those) whose lawlessnesses
are forgiven, and whose sins **8**
are covered. [8] Blessed the
man to whom the Lord will **9**
in no way charge sin."
[9] (Is) this blessedness
then on the circumcision, or
also on the uncircumcision?
For we say the faith was **10**
counted to Abraham for
righteousness. [10] How,
then, was it counted? Being
in circumcision, or in uncircumcision? Not in circum- **11**
cision, but in uncircumcision! [11] And he received
a sign of circumcision (as) a
seal of the righteousness of
faith (while) in uncircumcision, for him to be a father
of those believing through
uncircumcision, for righ-
teousness to be counted to
them also; [12] And a fa- **12**
ther of circumcision to
those not of circumcision
only, but also to those walking the steps of the in uncircumcision faith of our father

νόμου ; τῶν ἔργων ; οὐχί, ἀλλὰ διὰ νόμου πίστεως. λογιζό-
law?　　Of works? No,　but through a law　of faith.　we con-
μεθα οὖν πίστει δικαιοῦσθαι ἄνθρωπον, χωρὶς ἔργων νόμου.
clude Then by faith to be justified　a man　without works of law.
ἢ 'Ιουδαίων ὁ Θεὸς μόνον ; οὐχὶ δὲ καὶ ἐθνῶν ; ναὶ καὶ
Or of Jews (is He) the God only,　not and　also of nations? Yes, also
ἐθνῶν· ἐπείπερ εἷς ὁ Θεός, ὃς δικαιώσει περιτομὴν ἐκ πί-
of nations, since (it is) one God who will justify circumcision by
στεως, καὶ ἀκροβυστίαν διὰ τῆς πίστεως. νόμον οὖν καταρ-
faith, and uncircumcision through the faith.　law　Then do we
γοῦμεν διὰ τῆς πίστεως ; μὴ γένοιτο· ἀλλὰ νόμον ἱστῶμεν.
destroy though the faith?　　Not let it be!　But　law we establish.

### CHAPTER 4
Τί οὖν ἐροῦμεν 'Αβραὰμ τὸν πατέρα ἡμῶν εὑρηκέναι κατὰ
What then shall we say Abraham the father of us to have found according
σάρκα ; εἰ γὰρ 'Αβραὰμ ἐξ ἔργων ἐδικαιώθη, ἔχει καύχημα,
to flesh? if For　Abraham by works was justified, he has a boast;
ἀλλ' οὐ πρὸς τὸν Θεόν. τί γὰρ ἡ γραφὴ λέγει ; 'Επίστευσε
but not with　—　God. what For the Scripture says?　believed
δὲ 'Αβραὰμ τῷ Θεῷ, καὶ ἐλογίσθη αὐτῷ εἰς δικαιοσύνην. τῷ
And Abraham　God, and it was counted to him for righteousness. to the
δὲ ἐργαζομένῳ ὁ μισθὸς οὐ λογίζεται κατὰ χάριν, ἀλλὰ
Now (one) working the reward not is counted according to grace,　but
κατὰ τὸ ὀφείλημα. τῷ δὲ μὴ ἐργαζομένῳ, πιστεύοντι δὲ ἐπὶ
according to debt. to the But not working (one), believing　but on
τὸν δικαιοῦντα τὸν ἀσεβῆ, λογίζεται ἡ πίστις αὐτοῦ εἰς
the (One) justifying the ungodly, is counted the　faith　of him for
δικαιοσύνην. καθάπερ καὶ Δαβὶδ λέγει τὸν μακαρισμὸν τοῦ
righteousness, even as　also David says of the blessedness of the
ἀνθρώπου, ᾧ ὁ Θεὸς λογίζεται δικαιοσύνην χωρὶς ἔργων,
man　to whom God counts　righteousness without works,
Μακάριοι ὧν ἀφέθησαν αἱ ἀνομίαι, καὶ ὧν ἐπεκαλύφθησαν
Blessed of whom are forgiven the lawlessnesses, and of whom are covered
αἱ ἁμαρτίαι. μακάριος ἀνὴρ ᾧ οὐ μὴ λογίσηται Κύριος
the sins;　Blessed (the) man to whom in no way will charge (the) Lord
ἁμαρτίαν. ὁ μακαρισμὸς οὖν οὗτος ἐπὶ τὴν περιτομήν, ἢ καὶ
sin.　(Is) blessedness　then this on the circumcision,　or also
ἐπὶ τὴν ἀκροβυστίαν ; λέγομεν γὰρ ὅτι 'Ελογίσθη τῷ
on the uncircumcision?　we say For,　—　was counted
'Αβραὰμ ἡ πίστις εἰς δικαιοσύνην. πῶς οὖν ἐλογίσθη ; ἐν
to Abraham The faith for righteousness.　How, then, was it counted? In
περιτομῇ ὄντι, ἢ ἐν ἀκροβυστίᾳ ; οὐκ ἐν περιτομῇ, ἀλλ' ἐν
circumcision being, or in uncircumcision?　Not in circumcision, but　in
ἀκροβυστίᾳ· καὶ σημεῖον ἔλαβε περιτομῆς, σφραγῖδα τῆς
uncircumcision; and　a sign he received of circumcision, a seal　of the
δικαιοσύνης τῆς πίστεως τῆς ἐν τῇ ἀκροβυστίᾳ εἰς τὸ
righteousness of the faith　(while) in — uncircumcision, for the
εἶναι αὐτὸν πατέρα πάντων τῶν πιστευόντων δι' ἀκροβυ-
being (of) him a father　of all　the　believing ones through uncir-
στίας, εἰς τὸ λογισθῆναι καὶ αὐτοῖς τὴν δικαιοσύνην· καὶ
cumcision, for　to be counted also to them　—　righteousness, and
πατέρα περιτομῆς τοῖς οὐκ ἐκ περιτομῆς μόνον, ἀλλὰ καὶ
a father of circumcision to those not of circumcision only,　but　also
τοῖς στοιχοῦσι τοῖς ἴχνεσι τῆς ἐν τῇ ἀκροβυστίᾳ πίστεως
to those walking　in the steps of the in　—　uncircumcision　faith

Abraham.

[13] For the promise (was) not through law to Abraham, or to his seed, (for) him to be the heir of the world, but through a righteousness of faith. [14] For if the heirs (are) of Law, faith has been made of no effect, and the promise has been destroyed. [15] For the Law works out wrath; for where no law is, neither (is) transgression. [16] On account of this (it is) of faith, that (it be) according to grace, for the promise to be made sure to all the seed — not to that of the Law only, but also to that of (the) faith of Abraham, who is father of us all — [17] according as it has been written, "I have made you a father of many nations" — before God, whom he believed, who gives life to the dead, and calls the things that are not as being; [18] who against hope believed in hope, for him to become father of many nations, according to that which has been said, "So shall your seed be;" [19] and not being weak in the faith, he did not look at his own body already become dead, being about a hundred years old, and the deadening of the womb of Sarah; [20] and at the promise of God did not stagger through unbelief, but was strengthened in faith, giving glory to God, [21] and being fully persuaded that what He has promised, He is also able to do; [22] therefore it was also counted to him for righteousness. [23] But it was not written on account of him only, that it was counted to him, [24] but also on account of us, to whom it is about to be counted, to those believing on Him who raised our Lord Jesus out of (the) dead. [25] who was delivered for our sins, and was raised for our justification.

CHAPTER 5

[1] Therefore, having been justified by faith, we have peace toward God through our Lord Jesus Christ; [2] through whom

**13** τοῦ πατρὸς ἡμῶν Ἀβραάμ. οὐ γὰρ διὰ νόμου ἡ ἐπαγγελία
of the father of us, Abraham. not For through law the promise

τῷ Ἀβραὰμ ἢ τῷ σπέρματι αὐτοῦ, τὸ κληρονόμον αὐτὸν
to Abraham, or to the seed of him, the heir him

**14** εἶναι τοῦ κόσμου, ἀλλὰ διὰ δικαιοσύνης πίστεως. εἰ γὰρ οἱ
to be of the world, but through a righteousness of faith. if For the

ἐκ νόμου κληρονόμοι, κεκένωται ἡ πίστις, καὶ κατήργηται ἡ
of law (are) heirs, has been voided faith, and has been destroyed the

**15** ἐπαγγελία· ὁ γὰρ νόμος ὀργὴν κατεργάζεται· οὗ γὰρ οὐκ
promise. the For law wrath works out, where for not

**16** ἔστι νόμος, οὐδὲ παράβασις. διὰ τοῦτο ἐκ πίστεως, ἵνα κατὰ
is law, neither (is) transgression. Therefore (it is) of faith, that according to

χάριν, εἰς τὸ εἶναι βεβαίαν τὴν ἐπαγγελίαν παντὶ τῷ
grace, for the being made sure the promise to all the

σπέρματι, οὐ τῷ ἐκ τοῦ νόμου μόνον, ἀλλὰ καὶ τῷ ἐκ
seed, not to the (seed) of the law only, but also to (that) of

πίστεως Ἀβραάμ, ὅς ἐστι πατὴρ πάντων ἡμῶν (καθὼς
(the) faith of Abraham, who is father of all us — even as

**17** γέγραπται ὅτι Πατέρα πολλῶν ἐθνῶν τέθεικά σε) κατέναντι
it has been written, A father of many nations I have appointed you — before

οὗ ἐπίστευσε Θεοῦ, τοῦ ζωοποιοῦντος τοὺς νεκρούς, καὶ
whom he believed God, the (one) making live the dead and

**18** καλοῦντος τὰ μὴ ὄντα ὡς ὄντα. ὃς παρ' ἐλπίδα ἐπ' ἐλπίδι
calling the things not being as being; who beyond hope on hope

ἐπίστευσεν, εἰς τὸ γενέσθαι αὐτὸν πατέρα πολλῶν ἐθνῶν,
believed, for the becoming (of) him a father of many nations,

**19** κατὰ τὸ εἰρημένον, Οὕτως ἔσται τὸ σπέρμα σου. καὶ μὴ
according to what was said, So shall be the seed of you. And not

ἀσθενήσας τῇ πίστει, οὐ κατενόησε τὸ ἑαυτοῦ σῶμα ἤδη
weakening — in faith, not he considered the of himself body already

νενεκρωμένον (ἑκατονταέτης που ὑπάρχων), καὶ τὴν νέ-
to have died, a hundred years about being, and the

**20** κρωσιν τῆς μήτρας Σάρρας· εἰς δὲ τὴν ἐπαγγελίαν τοῦ Θεοῦ
death of the womb of Sarah; at but the promise of God

οὐ διεκρίθη τῇ ἀπιστίᾳ, ἀλλ' ἐνεδυναμώθη τῇ πίστει, δοὺς
not hesitated — by unbelief, but was empowered — by faith, giving

**21** δόξαν τῷ Θεῷ, καὶ πληροφορηθεὶς ὅτι ὃ ἐπήγγελται,
glory — to God, and being fully persuaded that what He has promised

**22** δυνατός ἐστι καὶ ποιῆσαι. διὸ καὶ ἐλογίσθη αὐτῷ εἰς δικαιο-
able He is also to do. Therefore also it was counted to him for right-

**23** σύνην. οὐκ ἐγράφη δὲ δι' αὐτὸν μόνον, ὅτι ἐλογίσθη αὐτῷ·
eousness. not it was written But for him only, that it was counted to him

**24** ἀλλὰ καὶ δι' ἡμᾶς, οἷς μέλλει λογίζεσθαι, τοῖς πιστεύουσιν
but also for us, to whom it is going to be counted, to those believing

**25** ἐπὶ τὸν ἐγείραντα Ἰησοῦν τὸν Κύριον ἡμῶν ἐκ νεκρῶν, ὃς
on the (One) having raised Jesus the Lord of us out of (the) dead, who

παρεδόθη διὰ τὰ παραπτώματα ἡμῶν, καὶ ἠγέρθη διὰ τὴν
was delivered for the offenses of us, and was raised for the

δικαίωσιν ἡμῶν.
justification of us.

## CHAPTER 5

**1** Δικαιωθέντες οὖν ἐκ πίστεως, εἰρήνην ἔχομεν πρὸς τὸν
having been justified Then by faith, peace we have with —

**2** Θεὸν διὰ τοῦ Κυρίου ἡμῶν Ἰησοῦ Χριστοῦ, δι' οὗ καὶ τὴν
God through the Lord of us, Jesus Christ, through whom also the

also we have had faith into this grace in which we stand, and we fill up with rejoicing in hope of the glory of God. [3] And not only (so), but also we rejoice in tribulations, knowing that the tribulation works out patience; [4] and patience proven character; and proven character hope. [5] And the hope does not make ashamed, because the love of God has been poured out in our hearts by the Holy Spirit which was given to us; [6] for while we were still without strength, in due time Christ died for the ungodly. [7] For one will hardly die for a just one; someone might even dare to die for a good one. [8] But God commends His own love to us in that while we were still sinners, Christ died for us. [9] Much more then, having been justified now by His blood, we shall be saved by Him from wrath. [10] For if being enemies we were reconciled to God through the death of His Son, much more, having been reconciled, we shall be saved by His life. [11] And not only (so), but also rejoicing in God through our Lord Jesus Christ, through whom we now receive the reconciliation.

[12] Because of this, just as sin entered into the world by one man, and death by sin, and so death passed to all men, because all sinned — [13] for sin was in (the) world until Law, but sin is not charged (when) there is no law; [14] but death reigned from Adam until Moses, even on those who had not sinned in the likeness of Adam's transgression, who is a type of the coming (One). [15] But the free gift (shall) not (be) also like the offense. For if by the offense of the one the many died, much more the grace of God, and the gift

προσαγωγὴν ἐσχήκαμεν τῇ πίστει εἰς τὴν χάριν ταύτην ἐν
access          we have had — by faith into —  grace   this   in

ᾗ ἐστήκαμεν, καὶ καυχώμεθα ἐπ᾽ ἐλπίδι τῆς δόξης τοῦ Θεοῦ.
which we stand, and  boast     on the hope of the glory — of God.

**3** οὐ μόνον δέ, ἀλλὰ καὶ καυχώμεθα ἐν ταῖς θλίψεσιν, εἰδότες
not only  And (so), but also  we boast    in  —  troubles,  knowing

**4** ὅτι ἡ θλίψις ὑπομονὴν κατεργάζεται, ἡ δὲ ὑπομονὴ δοκιμήν,
that trouble  patience   works out,       and patience   proof,

**5** ἡ δὲ δοκιμὴ ἐλπίδα· ἡ δὲ ἐλπὶς οὐ καταισχύνει, ὅτι ἡ ἀγάπη
and proof  hope,      and hope not does put to shame, for the love

τοῦ Θεοῦ ἐκκέχυται ἐν ταῖς καρδίαις ἡμῶν διὰ Πνεύματος
of God has been poured out in the hearts    of us through (the) Spirit

**6** Ἁγίου τοῦ δοθέντος ἡμῖν. ἔτι γὰρ Χριστός. ὄντων ἡμῶν
Holy  —    given  to us. yet For  Christ —    being  us

**7** ἀσθενῶν, κατὰ καιρὸν ὑπὲρ ἀσεβῶν ἀπέθανε. μόλις γὰρ ὑπὲρ
weak — according to time for ungodly ones  died.   hardly For   for

δικαίου τις ἀποθανεῖται· ὑπὲρ γὰρ τοῦ ἀγαθοῦ τάχα τις·
a just one anyone will die;  on behalf of for  the good one perhaps one

**8** καὶ τολμᾷ ἀποθανεῖν. συνίστησι δὲ τὴν ἑαυτοῦ ἀγάπην εἰς
even dares  to die;     commends but the of Himself  love   to

ἡμᾶς ὁ Θεός, ὅτι ἔτι ἁμαρτωλῶν ὄντων ἡμῶν Χριστὸς ὑπὲρ
us   God, that yet sinners     being us    Christ   for

**9** ἡμῶν ἀπέθανε. πολλῷ οὖν μᾶλλον, δικαιωθέντες νῦν ἐν τῷ
us   died.     much  Then  more   having been justified now by the

**10** αἵματι αὐτοῦ, σωθησόμεθα δι᾽ αὐτοῦ ἀπὸ τῆς ὀργῆς. εἰ
blood  of Him, we shall be saved through Him from the  wrath.  if

γὰρ ἐχθροὶ ὄντες κατηλλάγημεν τῷ Θεῷ διὰ τοῦ θανάτου
For enemies being we were reconciled — to God through the death

τοῦ υἱοῦ αὐτοῦ, πολλῷ μᾶλλον καταλλαγέντες σωθησό-
of the Son  of Him, by much    more  having been reconciled we shall be

**11** μεθα ἐν τῇ ζωῇ αὐτοῦ· οὐ μόνον δέ, ἀλλὰ καὶ καυχώμενοι ἐν
saved by the life of Him;  not only (so) And, but also  boasting    in

τῷ Θεῷ διὰ τοῦ Κυρίου ἡμῶν Ἰησοῦ Χριστοῦ, δι᾽ οὗ νῦν τὴν
—  God through the Lord  of us,  Jesus  Christ, through whom now the

καταλλαγὴν ἐλάβομεν.
reconciliation we received.

**12** Διὰ τοῦτο, ὥσπερ δι᾽ ἑνὸς ἀνθρώπου ἡ ἁμαρτία εἰς τὸν
Therefore  as through one   man      sin   into the

κόσμον εἰσῆλθε, καὶ διὰ τῆς ἁμαρτίας ὁ θάνατος, καὶ οὕτως
world entered,  and through sin       death,   also  so

**13** εἰς πάντας ἀνθρώπους ὁ θάνατος διῆλθεν, ἐφ᾽ ᾧ πάντες
to  all    men        death  passed, inasmuch as all

ἥμαρτον· ἄχρι γὰρ νόμου ἁμαρτία ἦν ἐν κόσμῳ· ἁμαρτία
sinned  —until for law   sin   was in (the) world, sin

**14** δὲ οὐκ ἐλλογεῖται, μὴ ὄντος νόμου. ἀλλ᾽ ἐβασίλευσεν ὁ
but not is charged there not being law;  but  reigned

θάνατος ἀπὸ Ἀδὰμ μέχρι Μωσέως καὶ ἐπὶ τοὺς μὴ ἁμαρτή-
death  from Adam until  Moses    even over those not sinning

σαντας ἐπὶ τῷ ὁμοιώματι τῆς παραβάσεως Ἀδάμ, ὅς ἐστι
on  the likeness  of the transgression of Adam, who is

**15** τύπος τοῦ μέλλοντος. ἀλλ᾽ οὐχ ὡς τὸ παράπτωμα, οὕτω
a type of the (One) coming. But not as the   offense,   so

καὶ τὸ χάρισμα. εἰ γὰρ τῷ τοῦ ἑνὸς παραπτώματι οἱ
also the free gift; if for by the of the one  offense    the

πολλοὶ ἀπέθανον, πολλῷ μᾶλλον ἡ χάρις τοῦ Θεοῦ καὶ ἡ
many  died,      much   more the grace — of God and the

in grace, which (is) of the one Man, Jesus Christ, did abound to the many. **16** [16] And the gift (shall) not (be) as by one having sinned; for indeed the judgment (was) of one to **17** condemnation, but the free gift (is) of many offenses to justification. [17] For if by the offense of the one death reigned by the one, much more those who are receiving the abundance of grace and the gift of righteousness shall rule in life by the One, Jesus **18** Christ. [18] So then, as through one offense (it was) toward all men to condemnation, so also by one accomplished righteousness toward all men to justification of life. **19** [19] For as through the one man's disobedience the many were constituted sinners, so also by the obedience of the One the many shall be constituted righteous. [20] But Law **20** came in beside, that the offense might abound; but where sin abounded, grace much more abounded, [21] that as sin ruled in **21** death, so also grace might rule through righteousness to everlasting life, through Jesus Christ our Lord.

δωρεὰ ἐν χάριτι τῇ τοῦ ἑνὸς ἀνθρώπου Ἰησοῦ Χριστοῦ εἰς
gift　in　grace　— of the one　Man,　Jesus　Christ, to

**16** τοὺς πολλοὺς ἐπερίσσευσε. καὶ οὐχ ὡς δι' ἑνὸς ἁμαρτή-
the　many　abounded.　And not as through one　sinning

σαντος, τὸ δώρημα· τὸ μὲν γὰρ κρίμα ἐξ ἑνὸς εἰς κατάκριμα,
of life,　(be) the gift; the indeed for judgment of one　to condemnation,

**17** τὸ δὲ χάρισμα ἐκ πολλῶν παραπτωμάτων εἰς δικαίωμα. εἰ
the But free gift (is) of many　offenses　to justification.　if

γὰρ τῷ τοῦ ἑνὸς παραπτώματι ὁ θάνατος ἐβασίλευσε διὰ
For by the of the one　offense　death　reigned　through

τοῦ ἑνός, πολλῷ μᾶλλον οἱ τὴν περισσείαν τῆς χάριτος καὶ
the one,　much　more　those the abundance of the grace　and

τῆς δωρεᾶς τῆς δικαιοσύνης λαμβάνοντες ἐν ζωῇ βασιλεύ-
of the gift　of righteousness　receiving　in life　will

**18** σουσι διὰ τοῦ ἑνὸς Ἰησοῦ Χριστοῦ. ἄρα οὖν ὡς δι' ἑνὸς
reign through the One,　Jesus　Christ.　So then, as through one

παραπτώματος εἰς πάντας ἀνθρώπους εἰς κατάκριμα, οὕτω
offense　to　all　men　to condemnation,　so

καὶ δι' ἑνὸς δικαιώματος εἰς πάντας ἀνθρώπους εἰς δικαίωσιν
also through one righteous act to　all　men　to justification

**19** ζωῆς. ὥσπερ γὰρ διὰ τῆς παρακοῆς τοῦ ἑνὸς ἀνθρώπου
of life.　as　For through the disobedience of the one　man

ἁμαρτωλοὶ κατεστάθησαν οἱ πολλοί, οὕτω καὶ διὰ τῆς
sinners　were constituted the many,　so　also through the

ὑπακοῆς τοῦ ἑνὸς δίκαιοι κατασταθήσονται οἱ πολλοί.
obedience of the One righteous will be constituted　the many.

**20** νόμος δὲ παρεισῆλθεν, ἵνα πλεονάσῃ τὸ παράπτωμα· οὗ
Law But　came in beside, that might abound the　offense;　where

δὲ ἐπλεόνασεν ἡ ἁμαρτία, ὑπερεπερίσσευσεν ἡ χάρις· ἵνα
but abounded the　sin,　more abounded　grace, that

**21** ὥσπερ ἐβασίλευσεν ἡ ἁμαρτία ἐν τῷ θανάτῳ, οὕτω καὶ ἡ
as　reigned　sin　in　death,　so　also

χάρις βασιλεύσῃ διὰ δικαιοσύνης εἰς ζωὴν αἰώνιον, διὰ
grace　might reign through righteousness　to　life everlasting through

Ἰησοῦ Χριστοῦ τοῦ Κυρίου ἡμῶν.
Jesus　Christ the　Lord　of us.

# CHAPTER 6

## CHAPTER 6

[1] What then shall we say? Shall we continue in **1** sin that grace may abound? [2] Let it not be! We who **2** died to sin, how shall we still live in it? [3] Or are **3** you ignorant that we, as many as were baptized into Christ Jesus, we were baptized into His death? [4] We therefore were **4** buried with him by baptism into death, that as Christ was raised up from among (the) dead by the glory of the Father, so also we should walk in newness of life. [5] For if we have **5** been joined together in the likeness of His death, so also shall we be in the resurrection; [6] knowing

**1** Τί οὖν ἐροῦμεν; ἐπιμενοῦμεν τῇ ἁμαρτίᾳ, ἵνα ἡ χάρις
What, then, shall we say? Shall we continue　in sin,　that　grace

**2** πλεονάσῃ; μὴ γένοιτο. οἵτινες ἀπεθάνομεν τῇ ἁμαρτίᾳ,
may abound? Not let it be!　who　We died　to sin,

**3** πῶς ἔτι ζήσομεν ἐν αὐτῇ; ἢ ἀγνοεῖτε ὅτι ὅσοι ἐβαπτίσθημεν
how still shall we live in it?　Or are you ignorant that all who were baptized

εἰς Χριστὸν Ἰησοῦν, εἰς τὸν θάνατον αὐτοῦ ἐβαπτίσθημεν;
into Christ　Jesus, into the　death　of Him　were baptized?

**4** συνετάφημεν οὖν αὐτῷ διὰ τοῦ βαπτίσματος εἰς τὸν
we were buried with Then Him through — baptism　into

θάνατον· ἵνα ὥσπερ ἠγέρθη Χριστὸς ἐκ νεκρῶν διὰ τῆς
death, that as　was raised　Christ from (the) dead through the

δόξης τοῦ πατρός, οὕτω καὶ ἡμεῖς ἐν καινότητι ζωῆς περι-
glory of the Father,　so　also　we in　newness　of life might

**5** πατήσωμεν. εἰ γὰρ σύμφυτοι γεγόναμεν τῷ ὁμοιώματι του
walk.　if For　united with we have become in the likeness　of the

θανάτου αὐτοῦ, ἀλλὰ καὶ τῆς ἀναστάσεως ἐσόμεθα· τοῦτο
death　of Him,　but also of the　resurrection we shall be.　this

this, that our old man was
crucified with (Him), that **6**
the body of sin might be
annulled, so that we no
longer should serve sin.
[7] For he that died has
been justified from sin. **7**
[8] Now if we died with
Christ, we believe that we
also shall live with Him, **8**
[9] knowing that Christ
having been raised up from **9**
among (the) dead dies no
more; death no longer rules **10**
over Him. [10] For in that
He died, He died to sin
once for all; but in that He
lives, He lives to God.
[11] So also you count **11**
yourselves to be truly dead
to sin, but alive to God, in
Christ Jesus our Lord.
[12] Therefore let not sin
rule in your mortal body,
in order to obey it in its
lust. [13] Do not yield **12**
your members instruments
of unrighteousness to sin,
but yield yourselves to God **13**
as living from among (the)
dead, and your members instruments of righteousness
to God. [14] for your sin
shall not lord it over (you), **14**
for you are not under Law,
but under grace.
[15] What then? Shall
we sin because we are not
under Law but under
grace? Let it not be! **15**
[16] Do you not know
that to whom you yield
yourselves slaves for obed- **16**
ience, to whom you obey,
you are slaves, whether of
sin to death, or obedience
to righteousness? [17] But
thanks to God that you **17**
were slaves of sin, but you
obeyed from (the) heart
the form of teaching to
which you were yielded.
[18] And having been set **18**
free from sin, you became
slaves to righteousness. **19**
[19] I speak as a man on
account of the weakness of
your flesh. For as you
yielded your members in
bondage to uncleanness
and to lawless act unto
lawless act, so now yield
your members in bondage
to righteousness to
sanctification. [20] For **20**
when you were slaves of
sin, you were free as to **21**
righteousness. [21] What
fruit therefore did you

γινώσκοντες, ὅτι ὁ παλαιὸς ἡμῶν ἄνθρωπος συνεσταυρώθη,
Knowing,    that the old  of us    man    was crucified with,
ἵνα καταργηθῇ τὸ σῶμα τῆς ἁμαρτίας, τοῦ μηκέτι δουλεύειν
that might be annulled the body   of sin,    no longer  to serve
ἡμᾶς τῇ ἁμαρτίᾳ· ὁ γὰρ ἀποθανὼν δεδικαίωται ἀπὸ τῆς
us    sin;  the (one) for having died  has been justified from
ἁμαρτίας. εἰ δὲ ἀπεθάνομεν σὺν Χριστῷ, πιστεύομεν ὅτι καὶ
sin.   if But  we died   with Christ,  we believe  that also
συζήσομεν αὐτῷ· εἰδότες ὅτι Χριστὸς ἐγερθεὶς ἐκ νεκρῶν
we shall live with Him, knowing that  Christ having been raised from dead
οὐκέτι ἀποθνήσκει· θάνατος αὐτοῦ οὐκέτι κυριεύει. ὃ γὰρ
no more  dies;    death   Him   no more lords it over. that For
ἀπέθανε, τῇ ἁμαρτίᾳ ἀπέθανεν ἐφάπαξ· ὃ δὲ ζῇ, ζῇ τῷ Θεῷ.
He died,    to sin   He died once for all that but lives, lives to God,
οὕτω καὶ ὑμεῖς λογίζεσθε ἑαυτοὺς νεκροὺς μὲν εἶναι τῇ
So   also  you count   yourselves    dead indeed to be  —
ἁμαρτίᾳ, ζῶντας δὲ τῷ Θεῷ ἐν Χριστῷ Ἰησοῦ τῷ Κυρίῳ
to sin,  living but   to God in Christ   Jesus  the Lord
ἡμῶν.
of us.

Μὴ οὖν βασιλευέτω ἡ ἁμαρτία ἐν τῷ θνητῷ ὑμῶν σώματι,
Do not, therefore, let reign  sin   in the mortal of you  body,
εἰς τὸ ὑπακούειν αὐτῇ ἐν ταῖς ἐπιθυμίαις αὐτοῦ· μηδὲ παρι-
to    obey     it  in  the  lusts    of it, neither
στάνετε τὰ μέλη ὑμῶν ὅπλα ἀδικίας τῇ ἁμαρτίᾳ· ἀλλὰ
yield   the members of you weapons of unrighteousness to sin,  but
παραστήσατε ἑαυτοὺς τῷ Θεῷ ὡς ἐκ νεκρῶν ζῶντας, καὶ τὰ
yield    yourselves   to God as from (the) dead living, and the
μέλη ὑμῶν ὅπλα δικαιοσύνης τῷ Θεῷ. ἁμαρτία γὰρ ὑμῶν οὐ
members of you weapons of righteousness to God;  sin    for of you not
κυριεύσει· οὐ γὰρ ἐστε ὑπὸ νόμον, ἀλλ' ὑπὸ χάριν.
shall lord it over. not for you are under law,  but  under  grace.
Τί οὖν ; ἁμαρτήσομεν, ὅτι οὐκ ἐσμὲν ὑπὸ νόμον, ἀλλ' ὑπὸ
What then? Shall we sin   because not we are under law,   but under
χάριν ; μὴ γένοιτο. οὐκ οἴδατε ὅτι ᾧ παριστάνετε ἑαυτοὺς
grace?  Not let it be!  not Know you that to whom you yield  yourselves
δούλους εἰς ὑπακοήν, δοῦλοί ἐστε ᾧ ὑπακούετε, ἤτοι ἁμαρ-
slaves   for obedience, slaves you are whom you obey, whether of
τίας εἰς θάνατον, ἢ ὑπακοῆς εἰς δικαιοσύνην ; χάρις δὲ τῷ
sin unto death,   or obedience unto righteousness?  thanks But
Θεῷ, ὅτι ἦτε δοῦλοι τῆς ἁμαρτίας, ὑπηκούσατε δὲ ἐκ καρδίας
to God that you were slaves of sin,   you obeyed  and from the heart
εἰς ὃν παρεδόθητε τύπον διδαχῆς· ἐλευθερωθέντες δὲ ἀπὸ
to which you were delivered a form of teaching; having been freed And from
τῆς ἁμαρτίας, ἐδουλώθητε τῇ δικαιοσύνῃ. ἀνθρώπινον λέγω
sin,   you were enslaved to righteousness. As a man   I speak
διὰ τὴν ἀσθένειαν τῆς σαρκὸς ὑμῶν· ὥσπερ γὰρ παρεστή-
because of the weakness of the flesh  of you.  as   For you yielded
σατε τὰ μέλη ὑμῶν δοῦλα τῇ ἀκαθαρσίᾳ καὶ τῇ ἀνομίᾳ εἰς
the members of you slaves  —  to uncleanness and to iniquity unto
τὴν ἀνομίαν, οὕτω νῦν παραστήσατε τὰ μέλη ὑμῶν δοῦλα
iniquity,    so   now   yield     the members of you slaves
τῇ δικαιοσύνῃ εἰς ἁγιασμόν. ὅτε γὰρ δοῦλοι ἦτε τῆς
to righteousness unto sanctification. when For   slaves you were
ἁμαρτίας, ἐλεύθεροι ἦτε τῇ δικαιοσύνῃ. τίνα οὖν καρπὸν
ot sin,   free   you were  to righteousness. what Therefore fruit

have then, in the (things) of which you now are ashamed? For the end of those things (is) death. [22] But now having been set free from sin, and having become slaves to God, you have your fruit to sanctification, and the end life everlasting. [23] For the wages of sin (is) death; but the free gift of God (is) eternal life in Christ Jesus our Lord.

CHAPTER 7

[1] Or are you ignorant, brothers — for I speak to those who know law — that the Law rules over the man for as long a time as he may live? [2] For the married woman is bound by law to the living husband; but if the husband should die, she is free from the law of the husband; [3] so then, (if) the husband (is) living, she shall be called an adulteress, if she becomes another man's; but if the husband should die, she is free from the law, so as for her not to be an adulteress, having become another man's. [4] So that, my brothers, you also were made dead to the Law by the body of the Christ, for you to be another's, who was raised from among (the) dead, that we should bring forth fruit to God. [5] For when we were in the flesh, the passions of sin, which (were) through the Law, worked in our members to the bringing forth of fruit to death; [6] but now we have been set free from the Law, having died (in that) in which we were held, so that we should serve in newness of spirit, and not in oldness of letter.

[7] What then shall we say? (Is) the Law sin? Let it not be! But I did not know sin, except by Law; for also I have not been conscious of lust unless the Law said, You shall not lust. [8] But sin having taken an opportunity through the commandment worked out every lust in me; for apart from Law, sin was dead. [9] And I

εἴχετε τότε ἐφ' οἷς νῦν ἐπαισχύνεσθε ; τὸ γὰρ τέλος ἐκείνων
had you then? Over which now you are ashamed; the for end of those

**22** θάνατος. νυνὶ δὲ ἐλευθερωθέντες ἀπὸ τῆς ἁμαρτίας, δουλω-
(is) death. now But having been freed from sin, having been

θέντες δὲ τῷ Θεῷ, ἔχετε τὸν καρπὸν ὑμῶν εἰς ἁγιασμόν, τὸ
enslaved and to God, you have the fruit of you to sanctification, the

**23** δὲ τέλος ζωὴν αἰώνιον. τὰ γὰρ ὀψώνια τῆς ἁμαρτίας
and end life everlasting. the For wages of sin

θάνατος, τὸ δὲ χάρισμα τοῦ Θεοῦ ζωὴ αἰώνιος ἐν Χριστῷ
(is) death, the and gift of God life everlasting in Christ

Ἰησοῦ τῷ Κυρίῳ ἡμῶν.
Jesus the Lord of us.

CHAPTER 7

**1** Ἢ ἀγνοεῖτε, ἀδελφοί (γινώσκουσι γὰρ νόμον λαλῶ),
Or are you ignorant, brothers — to those knowing for law I speak —

ὅτι ὁ νόμος κυριεύει τοῦ ἀνθρώπου ἐφ' ὅσον χρόνον ζῇ ; ἡ
that the law lords it over the man over such time (as) He lives. the

**2** γὰρ ὕπανδρος γυνὴ τῷ ζῶντι ἀνδρὶ δέδεται νόμῳ· ἐὰν δὲ
For married woman to the living husband was bound by law; if but

ἀποθάνῃ ὁ ἀνήρ, κατήργηται ἀπὸ τοῦ νόμου τοῦ ἀνδρός.
dies the husband, she is freed from the law of the husband.

**3** ἄρα οὖν ζῶντος τοῦ ἀνδρὸς μοιχαλὶς χρηματίσει, ἐὰν
Therefore living the husband, an adulteress she will be called, if

γένηται ἀνδρὶ ἑτέρῳ· ἐὰν δὲ ἀποθάνῃ ὁ ἀνήρ, ἐλευθέρα
she becomes man to another. if But dies the husband, free

ἐστὶν ἀπὸ τοῦ νόμου, τοῦ μὴ εἶναι αὐτὴν μοιχαλίδα, γενομέ-
she is from the law, not being her an adulteress becoming

**4** νην ἀνδρὶ ἑτέρῳ. ὥστε, ἀδελφοί μου, καὶ ὑμεῖς ἐθανατώθητε
(wife) man to another. So, brothers of me, also you were made dead

τῷ νόμῳ διὰ τοῦ σώματος τοῦ Χριστοῦ, εἰς τὸ γενέσθαι
to the law through the body — of Christ, to become

ὑμᾶς ἑτέρῳ, τῷ ἐκ νεκρῶν ἐγερθέντι, ἵνα καρποφορήσωμεν
you to Another, to (One) from dead raised, that we may bear fruit

**5** τῷ Θεῷ. ὅτε γὰρ ἦμεν ἐν τῇ σαρκί, τὰ παθήματα τῶν
to God. when For we were in the flesh, the passions

ἁμαρτιῶν τὰ διὰ τοῦ νόμου ἐνηργεῖτο ἐν τοῖς μέλεσιν
of sin through the law working in the members

**6** ἡμῶν εἰς τὸ καρποφορῆσαι τῷ θανάτῳ. νυνὶ δὲ κατηργήθη-
of us for the bearing of fruit to death. now But we were freed

μεν ἀπὸ τοῦ νόμου, ἀποθανόντος ἐν ᾧ κατειχόμεθα, ὥστε
from the law, having died (to that) in which we were held, so as

δουλεύειν ἡμᾶς ἐν καινότητι πνεύματος, καὶ οὐ παλαιότητι
to serve us in newness of spirit, and not (in) oldness

γράμματος.
of letter.

**7** Τί οὖν ἐροῦμεν ; ὁ νόμος ἁμαρτία ; μὴ γένοιτο· ἀλλὰ τὴν
What then shall we say? (is) the law sin? Not let it be! But

ἁμαρτίαν οὐκ ἔγνων, εἰ μὴ διὰ νόμου· τήν τε γὰρ ἐπιθυμίαν
sin not I knew, except through law· also For lust

**8** οὐκ ᾔδειν, εἰ μὴ ὁ νόμος ἔλεγεν, Οὐκ ἐπιθυμήσεις· ἀφορμὴν
not I knew, except the law said, not You shall lust. occasion

δὲ λαβοῦσα ἡ ἁμαρτία διὰ τῆς ἐντολῆς κατειργάσατο ἐν
But taking sin through the commandment worked in

ἐμοὶ πᾶσαν ἐπιθυμίαν· χωρὶς γὰρ νόμου ἁμαρτία νεκρά.
me every lust; without for law sin (is) dead.

was alive apart from Law once, but the commandment came and sin came alive, and I died. [10] And the commandment which (was) to life, this was found (to be) death to me; [11] for sin having taken an opportunity by the commandment deceived me, and by it killed (me). [12] So that the Law truly (is) holy, and the commandment holy and just and good. [13] Then that which (is) good, has it become death to me? Let it not be!. But sin, that it might appear (to be) sin, worked death in me by that which is good; that sin might become excessively sinful through the commandment. [14] For we know that the Law is spiritual, and I am fleshly, having been sold under sin. [15] For what I worked out, I do not approve; for I do not do that which I will, but I do that which I hate. [16] But if I do what I do not will, I consent to the Law that (it is) good. [17] Now, then, I no longer am working it out, but the sin living in me. [18] For I know that in me, that is in my flesh, dwells no good. For to desire is present with me, but to work out the right I do not find. [19] For the good that I desire, I do not do; but the evil I do not desire, this I do. [20] But if I do that which I do not desire, (it is) no longer I working it out, but sin living in me. [21] I find then a law, that when I desire to do the right, that evil is present with me. [22] For I delight in the law of God according to the inward man; [23] but I see another law in my members warring against the law of my mind, and leading me captive to the law of sin which is in my members. [24] O wretched man (that) I (am)! Who shall deliver me from the body of this death? [25] I thank God through Jesus Christ our Lord. So then I myself with the mind truly

9 ἐγὼ δὲ ἔζων χωρὶς νόμου ποτέ· ἐλθούσης δὲ τῆς ἐντολῆς,
And was living without law  then,  coming  but the commandment,

10 ἡ ἁμαρτία ἀνέζησεν, ἐγὼ δὲ ἀπέθανον· καὶ εὑρέθη μοι ἡ
sin  revived,  I  and  died,  and was found to me the

11 ἐντολὴ ἡ εἰς ζωήν, αὕτη εἰς θάνατον· ἡ γὰρ ἁμαρτία
command-ment  for life,  this  to  death (was).  For  sin

ἀφορμὴν λαβοῦσα διὰ τῆς ἐντολῆς ἐξηπάτησέ με, καὶ δι'
occasion  taking  through the commandment  deceived  me, and through

12 αὐτῆς ἀπέκτεινεν. ὥστε ὁ μὲν νόμος ἅγιος, καὶ ἡ ἐντολὴ
it  killed (me).  So  the indeed law  (is) holy, and the command-ment

13 ἁγία καὶ δικαία καὶ ἀγαθή. τὸ οὖν ἀγαθὸν ἐμοὶ γέγονε
holy and  just  and  good.  the Then  good  to me  become (has it)

θάνατος ; μὴ γένοιτο. ἀλλὰ ἡ ἁμαρτία, ἵνα φανῇ ἁμαρτία,
death?  Not let it be!  But  sin,  that it appear  sin,

διὰ τοῦ ἀγαθοῦ μοι κατεργαζομένη θάνατον,—ἵνα γένηται
through the good to me  working out  death,  that may become

καθ' ὑπερβολὴν ἁμαρτωλὸς ἡ ἁμαρτία διὰ τῆς ἐντολῆς.
excessively  sinful  sin  through the commandment.

14 οἴδαμεν γὰρ ὅτι ὁ νόμος πνευματικός ἐστιν· ἐγὼ δὲ σαρκικός
we know For that the law  spiritual  is;  I but  fleshly

15 εἰμι, πεπραμένος ὑπὸ τὴν ἁμαρτίαν. ὃ γὰρ κατεργάζομαι,
am, having been sold under  sin.  what For  I work,

οὐ γινώσκω· οὐ γὰρ ὃ θέλω, τοῦτο πράσσω· ἀλλ' ὃ μισῶ,
not I know; not for what I desire, this  I practice; but what I hate,

16 τοῦτο ποιῶ. εἰ δὲ ὃ οὐ θέλω, τοῦτο ποιῶ, σύμφημι τῷ
this  I do. if But what not I desire, this  I do,  I agree with the

17 νόμῳ ὅτι καλός. νυνὶ δὲ οὐκέτι ἐγὼ κατεργάζομαι αὐτό,
law  that (it is) good. now But no longer  I  work out  it,

18 ἀλλ' ἡ οἰκοῦσα ἐν ἐμοὶ ἁμαρτία. οἶδα γὰρ ὅτι οὐκ οἰκεῖ ἐν
but the indwelling in  me  sin.  I know For that not dwells in

ἐμοί, τοῦτ' ἔστιν ἐν τῇ σαρκί μου, ἀγαθόν· τὸ γὰρ θέλειν
me  this  is  in the flesh of me — the good;  for to desire

παράκειταί μοι, τὸ δὲ κατεργάζεσθαι τὸ καλὸν οὐχ εὑρίσκω.
is present to me,  but to work out  the good not  I find.

19 οὐ γὰρ ὃ θέλω, ποιῶ ἀγαθόν· ἀλλ' ὃ οὐ θέλω κακόν, τοῦτο
not For what I desire I do good,  but what not I desire, evil  this

20 πράσσω εἰ δὲ ὃ οὐ θέλω ἐγώ, τοῦτο ποιῶ, οὐκέτι ἐγὼ κατερ-
I practice. if But what not desire I,  this  I do, no longer  I  work

21 γάζομαι αὐτό, ἀλλ' ἡ οἰκοῦσα ἐν ἐμοὶ ἁμαρτία. εὑρίσκω ἄρα
out  it,  but the dwelling in  me  sin.  I find,  then.

τὸν νόμον τῷ θέλοντι ἐμοὶ ποιεῖν τὸ καλόν, ὅτι ἐμοὶ τὸ κακὸν
the law, the (one) desiring me to do  the good,  that to me the evil

22 παράκειται. συνήδομαι γὰρ τῷ νόμῳ τοῦ Θεοῦ κατὰ τὸν
is present.  I delight  For  in the law  of God according to the

23 ἔσω ἄνθρωπον· βλέπω δὲ ἕτερον νόμον ἐν τοῖς μέλεσί μου
inner  man.  I see But another  law  in  the members of me

ἀντιστρατευόμενον τῷ νόμῳ τοῦ νοός μου, καὶ αἰχμαλωτί-
warring against  the law of the mind of me, and  taking captive

ζοντά με τῷ νόμῳ τῆς ἁμαρτίας τῷ ὄντι ἐν τοῖς μέλεσί μου.
me by the law  of sin, the (one) being in the members of me.

24 ταλαίπωρος ἐγὼ ἄνθρωπος· τίς με ῥύσεται ἐκ τοῦ σώματος
Wretched  I  man!  Who me will deliver from the body

25 τοῦ θανάτου τούτου ; εὐχαριστῶ τῷ Θεῷ διὰ Ἰησοῦ Χρι-
death  of this?  I thank  God through Jesus Christ

στοῦ τοῦ Κυρίου ἡμῶν. ἄρα οὖν αὐτὸς ἐγὼ τῷ μὲν νοῒ δουλεύω
the Lord of us.  So then myself, I  with the mind  serve

serve God's law, but with
the flesh the law of sin.

νόμῳ Θεοῦ, τῇ δὲ σαρκὶ νόμῳ ἁμαρτίας.
(the) law of God, the and flesh (the) law of sin.

**CHAPTER 8**

[1] (There is) therefore now no condemnation to those in Christ Jesus, who do not walk according to flesh but according to Spirit. [2] For the law of the Spirit of life in Christ Jesus set me free from the law of sin and of death. [3] For the Law (being) powerless, in that it was weak through the flesh, God having sent His own Son in (the) likeness of sinful flesh, and for sin, condemned sin in the flesh, [4] so that the righteous demand of the Law should be fulfilled in us, who walk not according to flesh, but according to Spirit. [5] For they that are according to flesh mind the things of the flesh; and they according to Spirit (mind) the things of the Spirit. [6] For the mind of the flesh (is) death; but the mind of the Spirit (is) life and peace. [7] Because the mind of the flesh (is) enmity towards God; for it is not subject to the law of God, for neither can it (be); [8] and they that are in flesh cannot please God. [9] But you are not in flesh, but in the Spirit, if (the) Spirit of God truly dwells in you; but if anyone has not (the) Spirit of Christ, he is not His. [10] But if Christ (is) in you, the body indeed is dead because of sin, but the Spirit life because of righteousness. [11] But if the Spirit of Him having raised up Jesus out of (the) dead dwells in you, He having raised up the Christ out of the dead will also make your mortal bodies live through the indwelling of His Spirit in you. [12] So then, brothers, we are debtors not to the flesh, to live according to flesh; [13] for if you live according to flesh you are going to die, but if by (the) Spirit you put to death the deeds of the body, you will live. [14] For as many as are led by God's Spirit, these are God's sons.

**CHAPTER 8**

1 Οὐδὲν ἄρα νῦν κατάκριμα τοῖς ἐν Χριστῷ Ἰησοῦ, μὴ κατὰ
no Therefore now condemnation to those in Christ Jesus, not according to
2 σάρκα περιπατοῦσιν, ἀλλὰ κατὰ πνεῦμα. ὁ γὰρ νόμος του
flesh walking, but according to Spirit. the For law of the
πνεύματος τῆς ζωῆς ἐν Χριστῷ Ἰησοῦ ἠλευθέρωσέ με ἀπὸ
Spirit of life in Christ Jesus set free me from
3 τοῦ νόμου τῆς ἁμαρτίας καὶ τοῦ θανάτου. τὸ γὰρ ἀδύνατον
the law of sin and of death. the For powerless
τοῦ νόμου, ἐν ᾧ ἠσθένει διὰ τῆς σαρκός, ὁ Θεὸς τὸν ἑαυτοῦ
law, in which it was weak via the flesh, God the of Himself
υἱὸν πέμψας ἐν ὁμοιώματι σαρκὸς ἁμαρτίας καὶ περὶ ἁμαρ-
Son sending in likeness of flesh of sin, and concerning sin
4 τίας κατέκρινε τὴν ἁμαρτίαν ἐν τῇ σαρκί· ἵνα τὸ δικαίωμα
condemned sin in the flesh, that demand
τοῦ νόμου πληρωθῇ ἐν ἡμῖν. τοῖς μὴ κατὰ σάρκα περιπατοῦ-
of the law may be fulfilled in us, those not by flesh walking,
5 σιν, ἀλλὰ κατὰ πνεῦμα. οἱ γὰρ κατὰ σάρκα ὄντες τὰ τῆς
but according to Spirit. those For according to flesh being the things
σαρκὸς φρονοῦσιν· οἱ δὲ κατὰ πνεῦμα τὰ τοῦ πνεύματος. τὸ
of flesh mind; those but by Spirit the things of the Spirit. the
6 γὰρ φρόνημα τῆς σαρκὸς θάνατος· τὸ δὲ φρόνημα τοῦ πνεύ-
For mind of the flesh (is) death; the but mind of the Spirit
7 ματος ζωὴ καὶ εἰρήνη· διότι τὸ φρόνημα τῆς σαρκὸς ἔχθρα
(is) life and peace. Therefore the mind of the flesh (is) enmity
εἰς Θεόν, τῷ γὰρ νόμῳ τοῦ Θεοῦ οὐχ ὑποτάσσεται, οὐδὲ
against God, to the for law of God not it is subject, neither
8 γὰρ δύναται· οἱ δὲ ἐν σαρκὶ ὄντες Θεῷ ἀρέσαι οὐ δύνανται.
for can (be); those and in flesh being God to please not are able
9 ὑμεῖς δὲ οὐκ ἐστὲ ἐν σαρκί, ἀλλ' ἐν πνεύματι, εἴπερ Πνεῦμα
you But not are in flesh, but in Spirit, since (the) Spirit
Θεοῦ οἰκεῖ ἐν ὑμῖν. εἰ δέ τις Πνεῦμα Χριστοῦ οὐκ ἔχει, οὗτος
of God dwells in you. if But anyone (the) Spirit of Christ not has, this one
10 οὐκ ἔστιν αὐτοῦ. εἰ δὲ Χριστὸς ἐν ὑμῖν, τὸ μὲν σῶμα νεκρὸν
not is of Him. if But Christ (is) in you, the indeed body (is) dead
11 δι' ἁμαρτίαν, τὸ δὲ πνεῦμα ζωὴ διὰ δικαιοσύνην. εἰ δὲ τὸ
because of sin, the but Spirit (is) life because of righteousness. if But the
Πνεῦμα τοῦ ἐγείραντος Ἰησοῦν ἐκ νεκρῶν οἰκεῖ ἐν ὑμῖν, ὁ
Spirit of the (One) having raised Jesus from (the) dead dwells in you, the (One)
ἐγείρας τὸν Χριστὸν ἐκ νεκρῶν ζωοποιήσει καὶ τὰ θνητὰ
having raised the Christ from (the) dead will make live also the mortal
σώματα ὑμῶν, διὰ τοῦ ἐνοικοῦντος αὐτοῦ Πνεύματος ἐν
bodies of you, through the indwelling of Him Spirit in
ὑμῖν.
you.
12 Ἄρα οὖν, ἀδελφοί, ὀφειλέται ἐσμέν, οὐ τῇ σαρκί, τοῦ κατὰ
So then, brothers, debtors we are, not to the flesh — according to
13 σάρκα ζῆν· εἰ γὰρ κατὰ σάρκα ζῆτε, μέλλετε ἀποθνήσκειν·
flesh to live. if For according to flesh you live, you are going to die;
εἰ δὲ πνεύματι τὰς πράξεις τοῦ σώματος θανατοῦτε, ζήσεσθε.
if but by (the) Spirit the practices of the body you put to death, you will live.
14 ὅσοι γὰρ Πνεύματι Θεοῦ ἄγονται, οὗτοί εἰσιν υἱοὶ Θεοῦ.
as many as For by Spirit of God are led, these are sons of God.

[15] For you received not a spirit of slavery again to fear, but you received a Spirit of adoption by which we cry, Abba, Father! [16] The Spirit Himself witnesses with our spirit that we are children of God. [17] And if children, also heirs; truly heirs of God, and joint heirs of Christ; if indeed we suffer together, that we may also be glorified together.

[18] For I calculate that the sufferings of the present time (are) not worthy (to compare) to the coming glory to be revealed in us. [19] For the earnest expectation of the creation eagerly expects the revelation of the sons of God; [20] for the creation was subjected to vanity, not willingly, but through Him subjecting (it), on hope; [21] that also itself also will be freed from the slavery of corruption to the freedom of the glory of the children of God. [22] For we know that all the creation groans together and travails together until now. [23] And not only (so), but even we ourselves also groan within ourselves eagerly expecting adoption, the redemption of our body [24] for by hope we were saved, but hope being seen is not hope; for what any sees, why does he also hope? [25] But if we hope for what we do not see, we wait eagerly with patience. [26] And likewise the Spirit joins in to help our weakness, for we do not know what we should pray (for) as we ought, but the Spirit Himself pleads our case for us with groanings that cannot be spoken. [27] But He searching the hearts knows what (is) the mind of the Spirit, because He intercedes according to God. [28] But we know that all things work together for good to those who love God, to those who are called according to purpose; [29] because whom He foreknew, He also predestinated (to be) conformed to the image of His Son, for Him to be

**15** οὐ γὰρ ἐλάβετε πνεῦμα δουλείας πάλιν εἰς φόβον, ἀλλ᾽
not For you received a spirit of slavery again to fear, but
ἐλάβετε πνεῦμα υἱοθεσίας, ἐν ᾧ κράζομεν, ᾽Αββᾶ, ὁ πατήρ.
you received a Spirit of adoption, by which we cry. Abba, Father!

**16** αὐτὸ τὸ Πνεῦμα συμμαρτυρεῖ τῷ πνεύματι ἡμῶν, ὅτι ἐσμὲν
itself The Spirit bears witness with the spirit of us, that we are

**17** τέκνα Θεοῦ. εἰ δὲ τέκνα, καὶ κληρονόμοι· κληρονόμοι μὲν
children of God. if And children, also heirs; heirs truly
Θεοῦ, συγκληρονόμοι δὲ Χριστοῦ· εἴπερ συμπάσχομεν, ἵνα
of God, joint-heirs and of Christ; if indeed we suffer together, that
καὶ συνδοξασθῶμεν.
also we may be glorified together.

**18** Λογίζομαι γὰρ ὅτι οὐκ ἄξια τὰ παθήματα τοῦ νῦν καιροῦ
I calculate For that not worthy the sufferings of the present time

**19** πρὸς τὴν μέλλουσαν δόξαν ἀποκαλυφθῆναι εἰς ἡμᾶς. ἡ γὰρ
to the coming glory to be revealed in us. the For
ἀποκαραδοκία τῆς κτίσεως τὴν ἀποκάλυψιν τῶν υἱῶν τοῦ
earnest expectation of the creation the revelation of the sons

**20** Θεοῦ ἀπεκδέχεται. τῇ γὰρ ματαιότητι ἡ κτίσις ὑπετάγη,
of God is eagerly expecting. For to vanity the creation was subjected,

**21** οὐχ ἑκοῦσα, ἀλλὰ διὰ τὸν ὑποτάξαντα, ἐπ᾽ ἐλπίδι· ὅτι καὶ
not willingly, but through Him subjecting, on hope; that also
αὐτὴ ἡ κτίσις ἐλευθερωθήσεται ἀπὸ τῆς δουλείας τῆς
itself the creation will be freed from the slavery —
φθορᾶς εἰς τὴν ἐλευθερίαν τῆς δόξης τῶν τέκνων τοῦ Θεοῦ.
of corruption to the freedom of the glory of the children — of God.

**22** οἴδαμεν γὰρ ὅτι πᾶσα ἡ κτίσις συστενάζει καὶ συνωδίνει
we know For that all the creation groans together and travails

**23** ἄχρι τοῦ νῦν. οὐ μόνον δέ, ἀλλὰ καὶ αὐτοὶ τὴν ἀπαρχὴν
until now. not only And (so) but also ourselves the firstfruit
τοῦ Πνεύματος ἔχοντες, καὶ ἡμεῖς αὐτοὶ ἐν ἑαυτοῖς στενά-
of the Spirit having, also we ourselves in ourselves groan,
ζομεν, υἱοθεσίαν ἀπεκδεχόμενοι, τὴν ἀπολύτρωσιν τοῦ
adoption eagerly expecting, the redemption of the

**24** σώματος ἡμῶν. τῇ γὰρ ἐλπίδι ἐσώθημεν· ἐλπὶς δὲ βλεπομένη
body of us. For by hope we were saved, hope but being seen

**25** οὐκ ἔστιν ἐλπίς· ὃ γὰρ βλέπει τις, τί καὶ ἐλπίζει ; εἰ δὲ ὃ οὐ
not is hope; what for sees anyone, why also he hopes? if But what not
βλέπομεν ἐλπίζομεν, δι᾽ ὑπομονῆς ἀπεκδεχόμεθα.
we see we hope (for), through patience we eagerly expect.

**26** ῾Ωσαύτως δὲ καὶ τὸ Πνεῦμα συναντιλαμβάνεται ταῖς
likewise And also the Spirit joins in to help the
ἀσθενείαις ἡμῶν· τὸ γὰρ τί προσευξώμεθα καθὸ δεῖ, οὐκ
weaknesses of us, — for what we may pray (for) as we ought, not
οἴδαμεν, ἀλλ᾽ αὐτὸ τὸ πνεῦμα ὑπερεντυγχάνει ὑπὲρ ἡμῶν
we know, but itself the Spirit pleads our case for us

**27** στεναγμοῖς ἀλαλήτοις· ὁ δὲ ἐρευνῶν τὰς καρδίας οἶδε τί τὸ
with groanings unutterable. He But searching the hearts knows what (is)
φρόνημα τοῦ Πνεύματος, ὅτι κατὰ Θεὸν ἐντυγχάνει ὑπὲρ
(the) mind of the Spirit, because according to God He intercedes for

**28** ἁγίων. οἴδαμεν δὲ ὅτι τοῖς ἀγαπῶσι τὸν Θεὸν πάντα
saints. we know And that to the (ones) loving God, all things

**29** συνεργεῖ εἰς ἀγαθόν, τοῖς κατὰ πρόθεσιν κλητοῖς οὖσιν. ὅτι
work together for good, to those according to purpose called being. Because
οὓς προέγνω, καὶ προώρισε συμμόρφους τῆς εἰκόνος τοῦ υἱοῦ
whom He foreknew also He predestinated conformed to the image of the Son

(the) firstborn among many brothers. [30] But whom He predestinated, these He also called; and whom He called, these He also justified; but whom He justified, these He also glorified.

[31] What then shall we say to these things? If God (be) for us, who against us? [32] Truly He who did not spare His own Son, but gave Him up for us all, how will He not also freely give us all things with Him? [33] Who shall bring any charge against God's elect? (It is) God who justified! [34] Who is he that condemns? (It is) Christ who died, but rather also is raised up; who also is at (the) right hand of God; who also intercedes for us. [35] Who shall separate us from the love of Christ? (Shall) tribulation, or distress or persecution or hunger or nakedness or danger or sword? [36] As it is written, "For Your sake we are killed all the day long; we were counted as sheep of slaughter." [37] But in all these things we more than conquer through Him who loved us. [38] For I am persuaded that neither death, nor life, nor angels, nor rulers, nor powers, nor things present, nor things to come,. [39] nor height, nor depth, nor any other created thing will be able to separate us from the love of God, which (is) in Christ Jesus our Lord.

## CHAPTER 9

[1] I tell the truth in Christ, I do not lie, my conscience bearing witness with me in (the) Holy Spirit, [2] that I have great grief and pain that never ceases in my heart, [3] for I myself was wishing to be a curse from Christ for my brothers, my kinsmen according to flesh; [4] who are Israelites; whose (are) the adoption and the glory, and the covenants and the Law-giving, and the service and the promises; [5] whose (are) the fathers; and of whom (is) the Christ according to flesh, who is God-blessed over all forever. A-

αὐτοῦ, εἰς τὸ εἶναι αὐτὸν πρωτότοκον ἐν πολλοῖς ἀδελφοῖς·
of Him, for   to be   Him   firstborn   among many   brothers;
οὓς δὲ προώρισε, τούτους καὶ ἐκάλεσε· καὶ οὓς ἐκάλεσε, τού-
whom but He predestinated, these also He called, and whom He called,
τους καὶ ἐδικαίωσεν· οὓς δὲ ἐδικαίωσε, τούτους καὶ ἐδόξασε.
these also He justified;   whom but He justified, these   also He glorified.

30

Τί οὖν ἐροῦμεν πρὸς ταῦτα ; εἰ ὁ Θεὸς ὑπὲρ ἡμῶν, τίς
What then shall we say to these things? If   God (be) for   us,   who
καθ' ἡμῶν ; ὅς γε τοῦ ἰδίου υἱοῦ οὐκ ἐφείσατο, ἀλλ' ὑπὲρ
against us? (He) who truly the own Son   not   spared,   but   for
ἡμῶν πάντων παρέδωκεν αὐτόν, πῶς οὐχὶ καὶ σὺν αὐτῷ
us   all   gave up   Him,   how   not also with   Him
τὰ πάντα ἡμῖν χαρίσεται ; τίς ἐγκαλέσει κατὰ ἐκλεκτῶν
all things to us will He freely give? Who will bring charge against the elect
Θεοῦ ; Θεὸς ὁ δικαιῶν· τίς ὁ κατακρίνων ; Χριστὸς ὁ ἀπο-
of God? God (is) the (One) justifying. Who condemning? Christ (is) He having
θανών, μᾶλλον δὲ καὶ ἐγερθείς, ὃς καὶ ἔστιν ἐν δεξιᾷ τοῦ Θεοῦ,
died,   rather but also raised,   who also is at (the) right (hand) of God,
ὃς καὶ ἐντυγχάνει ὑπὲρ ἡμῶν. τίς ἡμᾶς χωρίσει ἀπὸ τῆς
who also intercedes   for us. Who shall separate us   from the
ἀγάπης τοῦ Χριστοῦ ; θλίψις, ἢ στενοχωρία, ἢ διωγμός, ἢ
love   of Christ? (Shall) tribulation, or distress,   or persecuting, or
λιμός, ἢ γυμνότης, ἢ κίνδυνος, ἢ μάχαιρα ; καθὼς γέγραπται·
famine, or nakedness, or danger,   or sword? Even as it has been written,
ὅτι "Ἕνεκά σου θανατούμεθα ὅλην τὴν ἡμέραν· ἐλογίσθημεν
— For the sake of You we are killed   all   the   day;   we are counted
ὡς πρόβατα σφαγῆς. ἀλλ' ἐν τούτοις πᾶσιν ὑπερνικῶμεν διὰ
as sheep of slaughter. But in these things all   we overconquer through
τοῦ ἀγαπήσαντος ἡμᾶς. πέπεισμαι γὰρ ὅτι οὔτε θάνατος
the (One) having loved   us.   I have been persuaded For that not   death
οὔτε ζωὴ οὔτε ἄγγελοι οὔτε ἀρχαὶ οὔτε δυνάμεις οὔτε
nor life nor angels   nor   rulers   nor   powers   nor
ἐνεστῶτα οὔτε μέλλοντα οὔτε ὕψωμα οὔτε βάθος οὔτε τις
things present nor things coming nor   height   nor depth nor any
κτίσις ἑτέρα δυνήσεται ἡμᾶς χωρίσαι ἀπὸ τῆς ἀγάπης τοῦ
creature other will be able us to separate   from the love   —
Θεοῦ τῆς ἐν Χριστῷ Ἰησοῦ τῷ Κυρίῳ ἡμῶν.
of God   in   Christ   Jesus   the   Lord   of us.

## CHAPTER 9

1

Ἀλήθειαν λέγω ἐν Χριστῷ, οὐ ψεύδομαι, συμμαρτυρούσης
(the) truth I tell in Christ, not I lie,   bearing witness with
μοι τῆς συνειδήσεώς μου ἐν Πνεύματι Ἁγίῳ, ὅτι λύπη μοι
me the conscience of me in (the) Spirit   Holy, that grief to me
ἐστὶ μεγάλη, καὶ ἀδιάλειπτος ὀδύνη τῇ καρδίᾳ μου. ηὐχόμην
is   great   and never ceasing pain in the heart of me. was wishing
γὰρ αὐτὸς ἐγὼ ἀνάθεμα εἶναι ἀπὸ τοῦ Χριστοῦ ὑπὲρ τῶν
For myself I   a curse to be from   —   Christ on behalf of the
ἀδελφῶν μου, τῶν συγγενῶν μου κατὰ σάρκα· οἵτινές εἰσιν
brothers of me, the kinsmen of me according to flesh; who are
Ἰσραηλῖται, ὧν ἡ υἱοθεσία καὶ ἡ δόξα καὶ αἱ διαθῆκαι καὶ ἡ
Israelites,   of whom the adoption and the glory, and the covenants and the
νομοθεσία καὶ ἡ λατρεία καὶ αἱ ἐπαγγελίαι, ὧν οἱ πατέρες,
law-giving,   and the service and the promises;   of whom the fathers,
καὶ ἐξ ὧν ὁ Χριστὸς τὸ κατὰ σάρκα, ὁ ὢν ἐπὶ πάντων, Θεὸς
and from whom the Christ according to flesh, He being over   all,   God

2

3

4

5

men. [6] Not, however, that God's word has failed. For not all those of Israel (are) Israel; [7] nor because they are Abraham's seed (are) all children; but in Isaac seed will be called to you. [8] This is: not the children of flesh (are) children of God, but the children of the promise (are) counted for a seed. [9] For this the word of promise: "According to this time I will come, and a son will be to Sarah." [10] And not only (so), but also Rebecca conceiving of one, our father Isaac. [11] for (the children) not yet being born, nor having done any good or evil, that the purpose according to election might stand, not of works, but of the (One) calling, [12] it was said to her, The greater shall serve the lesser; [13] even as it has been written: "Jacob I loved, and Esau I hated."

[14] What, then, shall we say? (Is there) not unrighteousness with God? Let it not be (said)! [15] For He says to Moses, "I will have mercy on whomever I have mercy, and I will pity whomever I pity." [16] So therefore (it is) not of the (one) willing, nor of the (one) running, but of the (One) showing mercy, of God. [17] For the Scripture says to Pharaoh, "For this very thing I raised you up, so as I might show forth in you My power, and so as might be publicized My name in all the earth. [18] So then, to whom He wills, He shows mercy. And to whom He wills, He hardens. [19] You will say then to me, Why does He yet find fault? For who has resisted His will? [20] Yes, rather, O man, who are you answering against God? Shall the thing formed say to the (One) forming, Why did You make me like this? [21] Or does not the potter have authority over the clay out of the one lump to make one vessel to honor, and one to dishonor? [22] But if God desiring to show forth wrath, and to make known His power, endured in much longsuffering vessels of wrath having been

**6** εὐλογητὸς εἰς τοὺς αἰῶνας, ἀμήν. οὐχ οἷον δὲ ὅτι ἐκπέπτωκεν
blessed  to  the  ages.  Amen.  Not, however, that has failed
ὁ λόγος τοῦ Θεοῦ. οὐ γὰρ πάντες οἱ ἐξ Ἰσραήλ, οὗτοι
the word  —  of God. not For  all  those of  Israel,  these

**7** Ἰσραήλ· οὐδ' ὅτι εἰσὶ σπέρμα Ἀβραάμ, πάντες τέκνα· ἀλλ'
(are of) Israel; nor because they are seed of Abraham (are they) all children, but

**8** Ἐν Ἰσαὰκ κληθήσεταί σοι σπέρμα. τοῦτ' ἔστιν, οὐ τὰ
In  Isaac  will be called to you  seed.  This  is,  not the
τέκνα τῆς σαρκός, ταῦτα τέκνα τοῦ Θεοῦ· ἀλλὰ τὰ τέκνα τῆς
children of the flesh  these children  — of God, but the children of the

**9** ἐπαγγελίας λογίζεται εἰς σπέρμα. ἐπαγγελίας γὰρ ὁ λόγος
promise  (is) counted  for a seed.  of promise  For the word
οὗτος, Κατὰ τὸν καιρὸν τοῦτον ἐλεύσομαι, καὶ ἔσται τῇ
this (is): According to  time  this  I will come,  and will be  —

**10** Σάρρᾳ υἱός. οὐ μόνον δέ, ἀλλὰ καὶ Ῥεβέκκα ἐξ ἑνὸς κοίτην
to Sarah a son.  not only (so) And, but also  Rebecca  from one  con-

**11** ἔχουσα, Ἰσαὰκ τοῦ πατρὸς ἡμῶν—μήπω γὰρ γεννηθέντων,
ceiving,  Isaac  the  father  of us; not yet  for  being born,
μηδὲ πραξάντων τι ἀγαθὸν ἢ κακόν, ἵνα ἡ κατ' ἐκλογὴν τοῦ
nor  practicing anything good  or  evil,  that the according election
to
Θεοῦ πρόθεσις μένη, οὐκ ἐξ ἔργων, ἀλλ' ἐκ τοῦ καλοῦντος,
of God purpose might stand, not of works,  but  of the (One) calling,

**12** ἐρρήθη αὐτῇ ὅτι Ὁ μείζων δουλεύσει τῷ ἐλάσσονι. καθὼς
**13** it was said to her — The greater shall serve the lesser; even as
γέγραπται, Τὸν Ἰακὼβ ἠγάπησα, τὸν δὲ Ἡσαῦ ἐμίσησα.
it has been written: Jacob  I loved,  — and Esau  I hated.

**14** Τί οὖν ἐροῦμεν ; μὴ ἀδικία παρὰ τῷ Θεῷ ; μὴ γένοιτο.
What then shall we say? Not unrighteousness with God?  Not let it be!

**15** τῷ γὰρ Μωσῇ λέγει, Ἐλεήσω ὃν ἂν ἐλεῶ, καὶ οἰκτειρήσω
— For to Moses He says: I will have mercy on whomever I have mercy and I will pity

**16** ὃν ἂν οἰκτείρω. ἄρα οὖν οὐ τοῦ θέλοντος, οὐδὲ τοῦ τρέ-
whomever I pity.  So therefore not of the (one) willing, nor of the (one)
χοντος, ἀλλὰ τοῦ ἐλεοῦντος Θεοῦ. λέγει γὰρ ἡ γραφὴ τῷ

**17** running, but of the (One) showing mercy, God says For the Scripture —
Φαραὼ ὅτι Εἰς αὐτὸ τοῦτο ἐξήγειρά σε, ὅπως ἐνδείξωμαι
to Pharaoh, — For this very thing I raised up you, so as I may show forth
ἐν σοὶ τὴν δύναμίν μου, καὶ ὅπως διαγγελῇ τὸ ὄνομά μου
in you the  power  of me, and so as might be publicized the name of Me

**18** ἐν πάσῃ τῇ γῇ. ἄρα οὖν ὃν θέλει ἐλεεῖ· ὃν δὲ θέλει σκληρύνει.
in all the earth. So, then, to He He whom and He He hardens.
whom wills has mercy wills,

**19** Ἐρεῖς οὖν μοι, Τί ἔτι μέμφεται ; τῷ γὰρ βουλήματι αὐτοῦ
You will say then to me, Why yet finds He fault? The For counsel  of Him

**20** τίς ἀνθέστηκε ; μενοῦνγε, ὦ ἄνθρωπε, σὺ τίς εἶ ὁ ἀνταπο-
who resisted?  Yes, rather, O  man,  you who are the (one)
κρινόμενος τῷ Θεῷ ; μὴ ἐρεῖ τὸ πλάσμα τῷ πλάσαντι, Τί με
answering against God; not will say, that formed to the Former: Why me

**21** ἐποίησας οὕτως ; ἢ οὐκ ἔχει ἐξουσίαν ὁ κεραμεὺς τοῦ πηλοῦ,
made You this way? Or not has  authority the potter  of the clay,
ἐκ τοῦ αὐτοῦ φυράματος ποιῆσαι ὃ μὲν εἰς τιμὴν σκεῦος, ὃ
out of the same  lump  to make  one to honor vessel,  one

**22** δὲ εἰς ἀτιμίαν ; εἰ δὲ θέλων ὁ Θεὸς ἐνδείξασθαι τὴν ὀργήν,
and one to dishonor? if But desiring  God to show forth  wrath,
καὶ γνωρίσαι τὸ δυνατὸν αὐτοῦ, ἤνεγκεν ἐν πολλῇ μα-
and to make known the power  of Him,  endured in  much long-
κροθυμίᾳ σκεύη ὀργῆς κατηρτισμένα εἰς ἀπώλειαν· καὶ ἵνα
suffering  vessels of wrath having been fitted for  destruction; and that

fitted for destruction; [23] and that He make known the riches of His glory on vessels of mercy which He before prepared for glory; [24] whom He also called, not only us, of Jews, but also of nations. [25] As also He says in Hosea, "I will call those not a people, My people! And those not beloved, Beloved! [26] And it shall be, in the place where it was said to them, You are not My people—there they will be called, Sons of (the) living God. [27] But Isaiah cries on behalf of Israel, If the number of the sons of Israel be as the sand of the sea, the remnant will be saved. [28] For (He is) bringing to an end (the) matter, and cutting short in righteousness, because (the) Lord will do a matter cut short on the earth." [29] And as Isaiah has said before, "Except (the) Lord of hosts left a seed to us, we would have become as Sodom, and we would have become as Gomorrah.

[30] What then shall we say? That (the) nations not following after righteousness have taken on righteousness, but a righteousness of faith; [31] but Israel following after a law of righteousness did not arrive at a law of righteousness? [32] Why? Because (it was) not of faith, but as of works of Law. For they stumbled at the Stone-of-stumbling, as it has been written: "Behold, I place in Zion a Stone-of-stumbling, and a Rock-of-offense; and everyone believing on Him will not be put to shame.

### CHAPTER 10

[1] Brothers, Indeed my heart's pleasure and request to God on behalf of Israel is for (it) to be saved. [2] For I testify to them that they have zeal to God, but not according to knowledge. [3] For being ignorant of the righteousness of God, and seeking to establish their own righteousness, they did not submit to the righteousness of God. [4] For Christ is the end of law for righteousness to every

**23** γνωρίσῃ τὸν πλοῦτον τῆς δόξης αὐτοῦ ἐπὶ σκεύη ἐλέους,
He make known the riches of the glory of Him on vessels of mercy,

**24** ἃ προητοίμασεν εἰς δόξαν, οὓς καὶ ἐκάλεσεν ἡμᾶς οὐ μόνον·
which He before prepared for glory, whom also He called, us not only

**25** ἐξ Ἰουδαίων, ἀλλὰ καὶ ἐξ ἐθνῶν; ὡς καὶ ἐν τῷ Ὡσηὲ λέγει,
of Jews, but also of nations. As also in Hosea He says:
Καλέσω τὸν οὐ λαόν μου λαόν μου· καὶ τὴν οὐκ ἠγαπη-
I will call the not people of Me a people of Me, and the not beloved

**26** μένην ἠγαπημένην. καὶ ἔσται, ἐν τῷ τόπῳ οὗ ἐρρήθη αὐτοῖς,
ones, Beloved; and it shall be, in the place where it was said to them,
Οὐ λαός μου ὑμεῖς, ἐκεῖ κληθήσονται υἱοὶ Θεοῦ ζῶντος.
not a people of Me you, there they will be called sons God of a living.

**27** Ἠσαΐας δὲ κράζει ὑπὲρ τοῦ Ἰσραήλ, Ἐὰν ᾖ ὁ ἀριθμὸς τῶν
Isaiah But cries on behalf of — Israel, If be the number of the
υἱῶν Ἰσραὴλ ὡς ἡ ἄμμος τῆς θαλάσσης, τὸ κατάλειμμα
sons of Israel as the sand of the sea, the remnant

**28** σωθήσεται· λόγον γὰρ συντελῶν καὶ συντέμνων ἐν δικαιο-
will be saved; the matter for bringing to an end and cutting short in righteous-
σύνη· ὅτι λόγον συντετμημένον ποιήσει Κύριος ἐπὶ τῆς
ness, because a matter cut short will do (the) Lord on the

**29** γῆς. καὶ καθὼς προείρηκεν Ἠσαΐας, Εἰ μὴ Κύριος Σαβαὼθ
earth. And as has said before, Isaiah: Except (the) Lord of hosts
ἐγκατέλιπεν ἡμῖν σπέρμα, ὡς Σόδομα ἂν ἐγενήθημεν, καὶ ὡς
left to us a seed, as Sodom we would have become, and as
Γόμορρα ἂν ὡμοιώθημεν.
Gomorrah we would have become.

**30** Τί οὖν ἐροῦμεν; ὅτι ἔθνη, τὰ μὴ διώκοντα δικαιοσύνην,
What then shall we say? That nations not following after righteousness
κατέλαβε δικαιοσύνην, δικαιοσύνην δὲ τὴν ἐκ πίστεως· Ἰσ-
have taken on righteousness, a righteousness but of faith;

**31** ραὴλ δέ, διώκων νόμον δικαιοσύνης, εἰς νόμον δικαιοσύνης
Israel but following after a law of righteousness at a law of righteousness

**32** οὐκ ἔφθασε. διατί; ὅτι οὐκ ἐκ πίστεως, ἀλλ' ὡς ἐξ ἔργων
not did arrive. Why? Because not of faith, but as of works
νόμου. προσέκοψαν γὰρ τῷ λίθῳ τοῦ προσκόμματος, καθὼς
of law. they stumbled For at the Stone of stumbling, even as
γέγραπται, Ἰδοὺ τίθημι ἐν Σιὼν λίθον προσκόμματος καὶ
it has been written: Behold, I place in Zion a Stone-of stumbling and
πέτραν σκανδάλου· καὶ πᾶς ὁ πιστεύων ἐπ' αὐτῷ οὐ καται-
a Rock-of-offense, and everyone believing on Him not will be
σχυνθήσεται.
put to shame.

### CHAPTER 10

**1** Ἀδελφοί, ἡ μὲν εὐδοκία τῆς ἐμῆς καρδίας καὶ ἡ δέησις ἡ
Brothers, the indeed pleasure of My heart and the request

**2** πρὸς τὸν Θεὸν ὑπὲρ τοῦ Ἰσραήλ ἐστιν εἰς σωτηρίαν. μαρ-
to God on behalf of Israel is for to be saved. I
τυρῶ γὰρ αὐτοῖς ὅτι ζῆλον Θεοῦ ἔχουσιν, ἀλλ' οὐ κατ'
testify For to them that zeal to God they have, but not according to

**3** ἐπίγνωσιν. ἀγνοοῦντες γὰρ τὴν τοῦ Θεοῦ δικαιοσύνην, καὶ
knowledge. being ignorant For the — of God righteousness, and
τὴν ἰδίαν δικαιοσύνην ζητοῦντες στῆσαι, τῇ δικαιοσύνῃ τοῦ
the own righteousness seeking to establish, to the righteousness —

**4** Θεοῦ οὐχ ὑπετάγησαν. τέλος γὰρ νόμου Χριστὸς εἰς δικαιο-
of God not they submitted. the end For of law Christ (is) for righteous-

one that believes. [5] For Moses writes (of) the righteousness (which is) of the law: "The man doing these things shall live by them." [6] But the righteousness of faith says thus: "Say not in your heart, Who will go up into Heaven?"—this is, to bring down Christ; or, [7] Who will go down into the abyss?—this is, to bring Christ up from (the) dead. [8] But what does it say? "The word is near you, in your mouth and in your heart"—this is, the word of faith which we proclaim. [9] Because if you confess (the) Lord Jesus with your mouth, and believe in your heart that God raised Him from (the) dead, you will be saved. [10] For with the heart (one) believes unto righteousness, and with (the) mouth (one) confesses unto salvation. [11] For the Scripture says, "Everyone believing on Him will not be put to shame." [12] For there is no difference both of Jew and of Greek, for the same Lord of all is rich toward all those calling on Him. [13] For everyone whoever calls on the name of (the) Lord will be saved. [14] How then may they call on (One) in whom they have not believed? And how may they believe (One) of whom they have not heard? And how may they hear without preaching? [15] And how may they preach if they are not sent? Even as it has been written: "How beautiful the feet of those preaching the gospel of peace, of those preaching the gospel of good things. [16] But not all obeyed the gospel. For Isaiah says, Lord, who has believed our report? [17] Then faith (is) of hearing, and hearing by God's word. [18] But I say, Did they not hear? Yes, rather, into all the earth went out their voice, and to the ends of the world their words. [19] But I say, Did not Israel know? First, Moses says, I will provoke you to jealousy by a nation; by an unwise nation

5 σύνην παντὶ τῷ πιστεύοντι. Μωσῆς γὰρ γράφει τὴν δι-
ness to everyone believing. Moses For writes: The

καιοσύνην τὴν ἐκ τοῦ νόμου, ὅτι ὁ ποιήσας αὐτὰ ἄνθρωπος
righteousness of law, the doing of these things man

6 ζήσεται ἐν αὐτοῖς. ἡ δὲ ἐκ πίστεως δικαιοσύνη οὕτω λέγει,
shall live by them. the But of faith righteousness thus says:

Μὴ εἴπῃς ἐν τῇ καρδίᾳ σου, Τίς ἀναβήσεται εἰς τὸν οὐρανόν ;
not Say in the heart of you, Who will go up into Heaven?

7 (τοῦτ᾽ ἔστι Χριστὸν καταγαγεῖν·) ἤ, Τίς καταβήσεται εἰς
— this is, Christ to bring down — or, Who will go down into

τὴν ἄβυσσον ; (τοῦτ᾽ ἔστι Χριστὸν ἐκ νεκρῶν ἀναγαγεῖν.)
the abyss — this is, Christ from (the) dead to bring up —

8 ἀλλὰ τί λέγει ; Ἐγγύς σου τὸ ῥῆμά ἐστιν, ἐν τῷ στόματί
but what says it? near you The word is, in the mouth

σου καὶ ἐν τῇ καρδίᾳ σου· τοῦτ᾽ ἔστι τὸ ῥῆμα τῆς πίστεως
of you and in the heart of you; this is the word of faith

9 ὃ κηρύσσομεν· ὅτι ἐὰν ὁμολογήσῃς ἐν τῷ στόματί σου
which we proclaim. Because if you confess with the mouth of you

Κύριον Ἰησοῦν, καὶ πιστεύσῃς ἐν τῇ καρδίᾳ σου ὅτι ὁ Θεὸς
(the) Lord Jesus, and believe in the heart of you that God

10 αὐτὸν ἤγειρεν ἐκ νεκρῶν, σωθήσῃ· καρδίᾳ γὰρ πιστεύεται
Him raised from (the) dead, you will be saved. with heart For (one) believes

11 εἰς δικαιοσύνην, στόματι δὲ ὁμολογεῖται εἰς σωτηρίαν. λέγει
to righteousness, with mouth and (one) confesses to salvation. says

γὰρ ἡ γραφή, Πᾶς ὁ πιστεύων ἐπ᾽ αὐτῷ οὐ καταισχυνθή-
For the Scripture: Everyone believing on Him not will be put to

12 σεται. οὐ γάρ ἐστι διαστολὴ Ἰουδαίου τε καὶ Ἕλληνος· ὁ
shame. not For is difference of Jew both and of Greek, the

γὰρ αὐτὸς Κύριος πάντων, πλουτῶν εἰς πάντας τοὺς ἐπι-
for same Lord of all, is rich to all those

13 καλουμένους αὐτόν. πᾶς γὰρ ὃς ἂν ἐπικαλέσηται τὸ ὄνομα
calling on Him. everyone For whoever calls on the name

14 Κυρίου σωθήσεται. πῶς οὖν ἐπικαλέσονται εἰς ὃν οὐκ ἐπί-
of (the) Lord will be saved. How then may they call on (One) in whom not

στευσαν ; πῶς δὲ πιστεύσουσιν οὗ οὐκ ἤκουσαν ; πῶς δὲ
they believed? how And may they believe of whom not they heard? how And

15 ἀκούσουσι χωρὶς κηρύσσοντος ; πῶς δὲ κηρύξουσιν ἐὰν μὴ
may they hear without preaching? how And may they preach if not

ἀποσταλῶσι ; καθὼς γέγραπται, Ὡς ὡραῖοι οἱ πόδες τῶν
they are sent? Even as it has been written: How beautiful the feet of those

εὐαγγελιζομένων εἰρήνην, τῶν εὐαγγελιζομένων τὰ ἀγαθά.
preaching the gospel of peace, of those preaching the gospel of good things.

16 Ἀλλ᾽ οὐ πάντες ὑπήκουσαν τῷ εὐαγγελίῳ. Ἡσαΐας γὰρ
But not all obeyed the gospel. Isaiah For

17 λέγει, Κύριε, τίς ἐπίστευσε τῇ ἀκοῇ ἡμῶν ; ἄρα ἡ πίστις ἐξ
says, Lord, who has believed the report of us? Then faith (is) of

18 ἀκοῆς, ἡ δὲ ἀκοὴ διὰ ῥήματος Θεοῦ. ἀλλὰ λέγω, Μὴ οὐκ
hearing, the and hearing through a word of God. But I say, Did not

ἤκουσαν ; μενοῦνγε· εἰς πᾶσαν τὴν γῆν ἐξῆλθεν ὁ φθόγγος
they hear? Yes, rather, to all the earth went out the utterance

αὐτῶν, καὶ εἰς τὰ πέρατα τῆς οἰκουμένης τὰ ῥήματα αὐτῶν.
of them, and to the ends of the habitable world the words of them.

19 ἀλλὰ λέγω, Μὴ οὐκ ἔγνω Ἰσραήλ ; πρῶτος Μωσῆς λέγει,
But I say, Did not know Israel? First, Moses says,

Ἐγὼ παραζηλώσω ὑμᾶς ἐπ᾽ οὐκ ἔθνει, ἐπὶ ἔθνει ἀσυνέτῳ
I will provoke to jealousy you by not a nation, by a nation unwise

I will anger you. [20] But Isaiah (is) very bold and says, "I was found by those not seeking Me; I became manifest to those not inquiring after Me." [21] But to Israel He says, "All the day I have stretched out My hands to a disobeying and contradicting people."

## CHAPTER 11

[1] I say, then, Did not God put away His people? Let it not be (said)! For I am an Israelite, out of (the) seed of Abraham; of (the) tribe of Benjamin. [2] God did not thrust away His people whom He foreknew. Or do you not know what the Scripture says in Elijah, how he pleads with God against Israel, saying, [3] "Lord, they killed Your prophets, and they dug down Your altars; and I alone am left, and they seek my soul." [4] But what says the divine answer?" "I reserved to Myself seven thousand men who did not bow a knee to Baal. [5] So then, also in the present time a remnant according to election of grace has come into being. [6] But if by grace, no longer (is it) of works; else grace no longer becomes grace. But if of works it is no longer grace; else work is no longer work [7] What then? What Israel seeks, this he did not obtain; but the election obtained (it), and the rest were hardened; [8] even as it has been written: "God gave to them a spirit of slumber, eyes not seeing and ears not hearing," until this day. [9] And David says, "Let their table become for a snare and a trap, and for a stumbling-block, and a re- compense to them; [10] let their eyes be darkened, not to see; and their back al- ways bowing. [11] I say, then, Did not they stumble that they fall? Let it not be (said)! But by their slipping away (came) salvation to the nations, to provoke them to jealousy.

**20** παροργιῶ ὑμᾶς. Ἡσαίας δὲ ἀποτολμᾷ καὶ λέγει, Εὑρέθην
I will anger you.   Isaiah But very bold and says, I was found

τοῖς ἐμὲ μὴ ζητοῦσιν, ἐμφανὴς ἐγενόμην τοῖς ἐμὲ μὴ ἐπερω-
by those Me not seeking, revealed I became to those Me not inquiring

**21** τῶσι. πρὸς δὲ τὸν Ἰσραὴλ λέγει, Ὅλην τὴν ἡμέραν ἐξεπέ-
after. to But — Israel He says, All the day I stretched

τασα τὰς χεῖράς μου πρὸς λαὸν ἀπειθοῦντα καὶ ἀντιλέγοντα.
out the hands of Me to a people disobeying and contradicting.

## CHAPTER 11

**1** Λέγω οὖν, Μὴ ἀπώσατο ὁ Θεὸς τὸν λαὸν αὐτοῦ; μὴ
I say, then, Did not put away God the people of Him? Not

γένοιτο. καὶ γὰρ ἐγὼ Ἰσραηλίτης εἰμί, ἐκ σπέρματος
let it be! even For I an Israelite am, out of (the) seed

**2** Ἀβραάμ, φυλῆς Βενιαμίν. οὐκ ἀπώσατο ὁ Θεὸς τὸν λαὸν
of Abraham, of tribe of Benjamin, not did thrust away God the people

αὐτοῦ ὃν προέγνω. ἢ οὐκ οἴδατε ἐν Ἠλίᾳ τί λέγει ἡ γραφή;
of Him whom He fore-knew. Or not you know in Eli-jah what says the Scripture,

**3** ὡς ἐντυγχάνει τῷ Θεῷ κατὰ τοῦ Ἰσραήλ, λέγων, Κύριε,
how he pleads with God against — Israel, saying: Lord,

τοὺς προφήτας σου ἀπέκτειναν, καὶ τὰ θυσιαστήριά σου
the prophets of You they killed, and the altars of You

κατέσκαψαν· κἀγὼ ὑπελείφθην μόνος, καὶ ζητοῦσι τὴν
they dug down, and I am left alone, and they seek the

**4** ψυχήν μου. ἀλλὰ τί λέγει αὐτῷ ὁ χρηματισμός; Κατέλιπον
soul of me. But what says to him the divine answer? I reserved

ἐμαυτῷ ἑπτακισχιλίους ἄνδρας, οἵτινες οὐκ ἔκαμψαν γόνυ
to Myself seven thousand men who not bowed (the) knee

**5** τῇ Βάαλ. οὕτως οὖν καὶ ἐν τῷ νῦν καιρῷ λεῖμμα κατ'
to Baal. So, then, also in the present time a remnant according to

**6** ἐκλογὴν χάριτος γέγονεν. εἰ δὲ χάριτι, οὐκέτι ἐξ ἔργων·
election of grace has become. if And by grace, no longer of works;

ἐπεὶ ἡ χάρις οὐκέτι γίνεται χάρις. εἰ δὲ ἐξ ἔργων, οὐκέτι ἐστὶ
else grace no longer becomes grace. if But of works, no longer is it

**7** χάρις· ἐπεὶ τὸ ἔργον οὐκέτι ἐστὶν ἔργον. τί οὖν; ὃ ἐπιζητεῖ
grace, else work no longer is work. What then? What seeks for

Ἰσραήλ, τούτου οὐκ ἐπέτυχεν, ἡ δὲ ἐκλογὴ ἐπέτυχεν, οἱ δὲ
Israel, this not he obtained; the but election obtained (it), the and

**8** λοιποὶ ἐπωρώθησαν· καθὼς γέγραπται. Ἔδωκεν αὐτοῖς ὁ
rest were hardened; as it has been written: gave to them

Θεὸς πνεῦμα κατανύξεως, ὀφθαλμοὺς τοῦ μὴ βλέπειν, καὶ
God a spirit of slumber, eyes not seeing, and

**9** ὦτα τοῦ μὴ ἀκούειν, ἕως τῆς σήμερον ἡμέρας. καὶ Δαβὶδ
ears not hearing; until the present day. And David

λέγει, Γενηθήτω ἡ τράπεζα αὐτῶν εἰς παγίδα, καὶ εἰς θήραν,
says: Let become the table of them for a snare, and for a trap,

**10** καὶ εἰς σκάνδαλον, καὶ εἰς ἀνταπόδομα αὐτοῖς· σκοτισθή-
and for a stumbling-block, and for a recompense to them; let be darkened

τωσαν οἱ ὀφθαλμοὶ αὐτῶν τοῦ μὴ βλέπειν καὶ τὸν νῶτον
the eyes of them not to see, and the back

**11** αὐτῶν διὰ παντὸς σύγκαμψον. λέγω οὖν, μὴ ἔπταισαν ἵνα
of them always bowing. I say, then, Did not they stumble that

πέσωσι; μὴ γένοιτο· ἀλλὰ τῷ αὐτῶν παραπτώματι ἡ
they fall? Not let it be! But by the of them slipping away (came)

σωτηρία τοῖς ἔθνεσιν, εἰς τὸ παραζηλῶσαι αὐτούς. εἰ δὲ τὸ
salvation to the nations, to provoke to jealousy them. if But the

[12] But if their slipping away (is the) riches of (the) world, and their default (the) riches of (the) nations, how much more their fullness? [13] For I speak to you, the nations, since I am an apostle of (the) nations; I glorify my ministry, [14] if somehow I may provoke to jealousy my flesh, and may save some of them. [15] For if their casting away (is the) reconciliation of (the) world, what the reception, except life from (the) dead? [16] Now if the firstfruit (is) holy, also the lump. And if the root, also the branches. [17] But if some of the branches were broken off, and you being a wild olive, were grafted in among them, and became a sharer of the root and the fatness of the olive-tree, [18] do not boast against the branches: but if you do boast, (it is) not you (that) bears the root, but the root bears you. [19] You will then say, The branches were broken off that I might be grafted in. [20] Well! for unbelief they were broken off. And you stand by faith. Do not (be) high-minded, but fear. [21] For if God did not spare the natural branches, lest perhaps He will not spare you either. [22] Behold, then, (the) kindness and severity of God: On those having fallen, severity; but on you, kindness— if you continue in the kindness; otherwise, you also will be cut off. [23] And those also, if they do not continue in unbelief, will be grafted in. For God is able to again graft them in. [24] For if you were cut out of the natural wild olive tree, and were against nature grafted into a good olive tree—how much more these (being) according to nature will be grafted into (their) own olive tree.

[25] For I do not want you to be ignorant of this mystery, brothers—so that you may not be wise within yourselves — that hardness, (in) part has happened to Israel, until the fullness of the nations comes in; [26] and so all Israel will be saved even as it has been written:

12 παράπτωμα αὐτῶν πλοῦτος κόσμου, καὶ τὸ ἥττημα αὐτῶν
slipping away of them (is the) riches of (the) world, and the default of them
πλοῦτος ἐθνῶν, πόσῳ μᾶλλον τὸ πλήρωμα αὐτῶν ;
(the) riches of (the) nations, how much more the fullness of them!

13 Ὑμῖν γὰρ λέγω τοῖς ἔθνεσιν. ἐφ' ὅσον μέν εἰμι ἐγὼ ἐθνῶν
to you For I speak, the nations, since indeed am I of nations

14 ἀπόστολος, τὴν διακονίαν μου δοξάζω· εἰ πως παραζηλώσω
an apostle, the ministry of me I glorify, if somehow I may provoke to jealousy

15 μου τὴν σάρκα, καὶ σώσω τινὰς ἐξ αὐτῶν. εἰ γὰρ ἡ ἀπο-
of me the flesh, and may save some of them. if For the casting
βολὴ αὐτῶν καταλλαγὴ κόσμου, τίς ἡ πρόσληψις, εἰ μὴ
away of them (the) reconciliation of world, what the reception, except

16 ζωὴ ἐκ νεκρῶν ; εἰ δὲ ἡ ἀπαρχὴ ἁγία, καὶ τὸ φύραμα· καὶ εἰ
life from (the) dead? if Now the firstfruit (is) holy, also the lump; and if

17 ἡ ῥίζα ἁγία, καὶ οἱ κλάδοι. εἰ δέ τινες τῶν κλάδων ἐξεκλάσθη-
the root, also the branches. if But some of the branches were broken
σαν, σὺ δὲ ἀγριέλαιος ὢν ἐνεκεντρίσθης ἐν αὐτοῖς, καὶ
off, you and, a wild olive being were grafted in among them, and
συγκοινωνὸς τῆς ῥίζης καὶ τῆς πιότητος τῆς ἐλαίας ἐγένου,
a partaker of the root and of the fatness of the olive-tree became,

18 μὴ κατακαυχῶ τῶν κλάδων· εἰ δὲ κατακαυχᾶσαι, οὐ σὺ τὴν
do not boast against the branches; if but you boast, not you the

19 ῥίζαν βαστάζεις, ἀλλ' ἡ ῥίζα σέ. ἐρεῖς οὖν, Ἐξεκλάσθησαν οἱ
root bears, but the root you. You will say then, were broken off

20 κλάδοι, ἵνα ἐγὼ ἐγκεντρισθῶ. καλῶς· τῇ ἀπιστίᾳ ἐξεκλά-
Branches, that I might be grafted in. Well, — for unbelief they were
σθησαν, σὺ δὲ τῇ πίστει ἔστηκας. μὴ ὑψηλοφρόνει, ἀλλὰ
broken off, you and by faith stand. not high minded (Be), but

21 φοβοῦ· εἰ γὰρ ὁ Θεὸς τῶν κατὰ φύσιν κλάδων οὐκ ἐφείσατο,
fear; if for God the according to nature branches not spared,

22 μήπως οὐδέ σου φείσεται. ἴδε οὖν χρηστότητα καὶ ἀποτο-
lest neither you He will spare. Behold, then, (the) kindness and severity
μίαν Θεοῦ· ἐπὶ μὲν τοὺς πεσόντας, ἀποτομίαν· ἐπὶ δέ σε,
of God on indeed those having fallen, severity; on but you,
χρηστότητα, ἐὰν ἐπιμείνῃς τῇ χρηστότητι· ἐπεὶ καὶ σὺ
kindness, if you continue in the kindness, otherwise also you

23 ἐκκοπήσῃ. καὶ ἐκεῖνοι δέ, ἐὰν μὴ ἐπιμείνωσι τῇ ἀπιστίᾳ,
will be cut off. also those And, if not they continue in unbelief,
ἐγκεντρισθήσονται· δυνατὸς γάρ ἐστιν ὁ Θεὸς πάλιν ἐγκεν-
will be grafted in; able for is God again to graft

24 τρίσαι αὐτούς. εἰ γὰρ σὺ ἐκ τῆς κατὰ φύσιν ἐξεκόπης ἀγρι-
in them. if For you out of the natural were cut out wild
ελαίου, καὶ παρὰ φύσιν ἐνεκεντρίσθης εἰς καλλιέλαιον, πόσῳ
olive, and against nature were grafted in into a good olive, how much
μᾶλλον οὗτοι, οἱ κατὰ φύσιν, ἐγκεντρισθήσονται τῇ ἰδίᾳ
more these, those according to nature, will be grafted in the own
ἐλαίᾳ ;
olive-tree?

25 Οὐ γὰρ θέλω ὑμᾶς ἀγνοεῖν, ἀδελφοί, τὸ μυστήριον τοῦτο,
not For I wish you to be ignorant, brothers, (of) mystery this
ἵνα μὴ ἦτε παρ' ἑαυτοῖς φρόνιμοι, ὅτι πώρωσις ἀπὸ μέρους
that not you be in yourselves wise, that hardness from (in) part
τῷ Ἰσραὴλ γέγονεν, ἄχρις οὗ τὸ πλήρωμα τῶν ἐθνῶν εἰσ-
to Israel has happened, until the fullness of the nations comes

26 έλθῃ· καὶ οὕτω πᾶς Ἰσραὴλ σωθήσεται· καθὼς γέγραπται.
in, and so all Israel will be saved, even as it has been written:

"The Deliverer will come out of Zion, and He will turn away ungodliness from Jacob. [27] And this (is) My covenant with them, when I take away their sins." [28] Indeed, as regards the gospel, enemies for you. But as regards the election, beloved for the sake of the fathers. [29] For the free gifts and calling of God (are) without repentance. [30] For as you also then disobeyed God, but now have obtained mercy through their disobedience, [31] so also these have disobeyed by your mercy, that they may also obtain mercy. [32] For God shut up all in disobedience, that He may show mercy to all.

[33] O (the) depth of (the) riches and of (the) wisdom and (the) knowledge of God! How unsearchable the judgments of Him, and His ways past finding out! [34] For who has known the mind of (the) Lord? Or who became His counselor? [35] Or who first gave to Him, and it will be repaid to him. [36] Because of Him, and through Him, and to Him (are) all things: to Him be the glory forever! Amen.

CHAPTER 12
[1] Therefore, brothers, I call on you by the mercies of God to present your bodies a living sacrifice, holy, pleasing to God, (which is) your reasonable service. [2] And be not conformed to this age, but be transformed by the renewing of your mind, in order to prove by you what (is) the good and pleasing and perfect will of God. [3] For I say through the grace which is given to me, to everyone that is among you, not to be high-minded above what you ought to think; but set your mind so as to think wisely, according as God has given to each a measure of faith. [4] For even as we have many members in one body, but all members do not have the same function; [5] so we, the

**27** Ἥξει ἐκ Σιὼν ὁ ῥυόμενος, καὶ ἀποστρέψει ἀσεβείας ἀπὸ
Will come out of Zion the Deliverer and He will turn away ungodliness from

Ἰακώβ· καὶ αὕτη αὐτοῖς ἡ παρ' ἐμοῦ διαθήκη, ὅταν ἀφέλω-
Jacob. And this (is) with them the from Me covenant, when I take away

**28** μαι τὰς ἁμαρτίας αὐτῶν. κατὰ μὲν τὸ εὐαγγέλιον, ἐχθροὶ δι'
the sins of them as regards Indeed the gospel, enemies for

ὑμᾶς· κατὰ δὲ τὴν ἐκλογήν, ἀγαπητοὶ διὰ τοὺς πατέρας.
you; as regards but the election, beloved for the sake of the fathers.

**29** ἀμεταμέλητα γὰρ τὰ χαρίσματα καὶ ἡ κλῆσις τοῦ Θεοῦ.
without repentance For the free gifts and the calling — of God.

**30** ὥσπερ γὰρ καὶ ὑμεῖς ποτε ἠπειθήσατε τῷ Θεῷ, νῦν δὲ
as For also you then disobeyed God, now but

**31** ἠλεήθητε τῇ τούτων ἀπειθείᾳ· οὕτω καὶ οὗτοι νῦν ἠπείθη-
you obtained mercy by the of these disobedience, so also these now disobeyed

**32** σαν, τῷ ὑμετέρῳ ἐλέει ἵνα καὶ αὐτοὶ ἐλεηθῶσι. συνέκλεισε
by your mercy that also they may obtain mercy. shut up

γὰρ ὁ Θεὸς τοὺς πάντας εἰς ἀπείθειαν, ἵνα τοὺς πάντας
For God — all in disobedience that — to all

ἐλεήσῃ.
He may show mercy.

**33** Ὦ βάθος πλούτου καὶ σοφίας καὶ γνώσεως Θεοῦ. ὡς
O (the) depth of (the) riches and of (the) wisdom and (the) knowledge of God; how

ἀνεξερεύνητα τὰ κρίματα αὐτοῦ, καὶ ἀνεξιχνίαστοι αἱ ὁδοὶ
unsearchable the judgments of Him, and past finding out the ways

**34** αὐτοῦ. τίς γὰρ ἔγνω νοῦν Κυρίου; ἢ τίς σύμβουλος αὐτοῦ
of Him! who For has known the mind of (the) Lord? or who His counselor

**35** ἐγένετο; ἢ τίς προέδωκεν αὐτῷ, καὶ ἀνταποδοθήσεται
became? or who first gave to Him, and it will be r repaid

**36** αὐτῷ; ὅτι ἐξ αὐτοῦ καὶ δι' αὐτοῦ καὶ εἰς αὐτὸν τὰ πάντα·
to him? Because of Him, and through Him, and to Him (are) all things;

αὐτῷ ἡ δόξα εἰς τοὺς αἰῶνας. ἀμήν.
to Him be the glory to the ages! Amen.

**CHAPTER 12**

**1** Παρακαλῶ οὖν ὑμᾶς, ἀδελφοί, διὰ τῶν οἰκτιρμῶν τοῦ
I beseech Therefore you, brothers, through the compassion

Θεοῦ, παραστῆσαι τὰ σώματα ὑμῶν θυσίαν ζῶσαν, ἁγίαν,
of God, to present the body of you sacrifice a living, holy,

**2** εὐάρεστον τῷ Θεῷ, τὴν λογικὴν λατρείαν ὑμῶν. καὶ μὴ
well-pleasing to God, the reasonable service of you. And not

συσχηματίζεσθε τῷ αἰῶνι τούτῳ, ἀλλὰ μεταμορφοῦσθε τῇ
be conformed to age this, but be transformed by the

ἀνακαινώσει τοῦ νοὸς ὑμῶν, εἰς τὸ δοκιμάζειν ὑμᾶς τί τὸ
renewing of the mind of you, to prove you what the

θέλημα τοῦ Θεοῦ τὸ ἀγαθὸν καὶ εὐάρεστον καὶ τέλειον.
will of God, the good and well-pleasing and perfect.

**3** Λέγω γάρ, διὰ τῆς χάριτος τῆς δοθείσης μοι, παντὶ τῷ
I say For, through the grace — given to me to everyone

ὄντι ἐν ὑμῖν, μὴ ὑπερφρονεῖν παρ' ὃ δεῖ φρονεῖν, ἀλλὰ
being among you, not to have high thoughts beyond what is right to think, but

φρονεῖν εἰς τὸ σωφρονεῖν, ἑκάστῳ ὡς ὁ Θεὸς ἐμέρισε μέτρον
to think to be sober-minded, to each as God divided a measure

**4** πίστεως. καθάπερ γὰρ ἐν ἑνὶ σώματι μέλη πολλὰ ἔχομεν, τὰ
of faith. as For in one body members many we have, the

**5** δὲ μέλη πάντα οὐ τὴν αὐτὴν ἔχει πρᾶξιν· οὕτως οἱ πολλοὶ
but members all not the same have function, so the many

many, are one body in Christ, and everyone members of one another. [6] But having different gifts according to the grace given to us, whether prophesy, according to the proportion of faith; [7] or ministry, in ministry; or he teaching, in the teaching; [8] or that exhorts, in exhortation; he that imparts, in simplicity; he that takes the lead, with diligence; he that shows mercy, with cheerfulness. [9] (Let) love (be) without dissimulation, shrinking from evil, cleaving to good; [10] in brotherly love, tender hearted toward one another, going before one another and giving honor; [11] as to diligence, not careless, but warm in spirit, serving the Lord; [12] in hope, rejoicing; in tribulation, enduring; in prayer, steadfastly continuing; [13] communicating to the needs of the saints; pursuing hospitality.

[14] Bless those persecuting you; bless and do not curse. [15] Rejoice with rejoicing ones, and weep with weeping ones; [16] minding the same thing toward one another, not minding high things, but going along with the lowly. Do not be wise in yourselves. [17] Repay no one evil for evil; providing right things before all men. [18] If possible, as far as is in you, be at peace with all men; [19] not avenging yourselves, beloved; but give place to wrath; for it has been written, "Vengeance is Mine, I will repay, says (the) Lord." [20] If therefore your enemy should hunger, feed him; if he should thirst, give him drink; for doing this you will heap coals of fire on his head. [21] Do not be overcome by evil, but overcome evil with good.

CHAPTER 13

[1] Let everyone be subject to higher authorities, for there is no authority except from God; but the existing authorities are by God, having

**6** ἓν σῶμά ἐσμεν ἐν Χριστῷ, ὁ δὲ καθ' εἷς ἀλλήλων μέλη.
one body we are in Christ, and each one of one another members.
ἔχοντες δὲ χαρίσματα κατὰ τὴν χάριν τὴν δοθεῖσαν ἡμῖν
having And gifts according to the grace given to us
διάφορα, εἴτε προφητείαν, κατὰ τὴν ἀναλογίαν τῆς πίστεως·
differing, whether prophecy, according to the proportion of faith;
**7** εἴτε διακονίαν, ἐν τῇ διακονίᾳ· εἴτε ὁ διδάσκων, ἐν τῇ
or ministry, in the ministry; or the (one) teaching, in the
**8** διδασκαλίᾳ· εἴτε ὁ παρακαλῶν, ἐν τῇ παρακλήσει· ὁ μεταδι-
teaching; or the (one) exhorting, in the exhortation; the (one) sharing,
δούς, ἐν ἁπλότητι· ὁ προϊστάμενος, ἐν σπουδῇ· ὁ ἐλεῶν ἐν
in simplicity; the (one) taking the lead in diligence, he showing mercy, in
**9** ἱλαρότητι. ἡ ἀγάπη ἀνυπόκριτος. ἀποστυγοῦντες τὸ
cheerfulness. (let) Love (be) without dissimulation; shrinking from
**10** πονηρόν, κολλώμενοι τῷ ἀγαθῷ. τῇ φιλαδελφίᾳ εἰς ἀλλή-
evil, cleaving to the good; in brotherly love to one
λους φιλόστοργοι· τῇ τιμῇ ἀλλήλους προηγούμενοι· τῇ
another loving fervently, in honor one another preferring;
**11** σπουδῇ μὴ ὀκνηροί· τῷ πνεύματι ζέοντες· τῷ Κυρίῳ δου-
in diligence, not slothful; in spirit burning; to the Lord
**12** λεύοντες· τῇ ἐλπίδι χαίροντες· τῇ θλίψει ὑπομένοντες· τῇ
serving; in hope, rejoicing; in trouble, enduring;
**13** προσευχῇ προσκαρτεροῦντες· ταῖς χρείαις τῶν ἁγίων
in prayer, steadfastly continuing; to the needs of the saints
**14** κοινωνοῦντες· τὴν φιλοξενίαν διώκοντες. εὐλογεῖτε τοὺς
imparting, hospitality pursuing. Bless those
**15** διώκοντας ὑμᾶς· εὐλογεῖτε, καὶ μὴ καταρᾶσθε. χαίρειν μετὰ
persecuting you; bless, and do not curse. Rejoice with
**16** χαιρόντων, καὶ κλαίειν μετὰ κλαιόντων. τὸ αὐτὸ εἰς ἀλλή-
rejoicing ones; and weep with weeping ones. The same toward one
λους φρονοῦντες. μὴ τὰ ὑψηλὰ φρονοῦντες, ἀλλὰ τοῖς
another minding; not the things high minding, but to the
ταπεινοῖς συναπαγόμενοι. μὴ γίνεσθε φρόνιμοι παρ' ἑαυτοῖς.
humble yield, do not become wise with yourselves.
**17** μηδενὶ κακὸν ἀντὶ κακοῦ ἀποδιδόντες. προνοούμενοι καλὰ
To no one evil for evil returning; providing for right things
**18** ἐνώπιον πάντων ἀνθρώπων. εἰ δυνατόν, τὸ ἐξ ὑμῶν, μετὰ
before all men; if possible, as far as in you, with
**19** πάντων ἀνθρώπων εἰρηνεύοντες. μὴ ἑαυτοὺς ἐκδικοῦντες,
all men seeking peace; not yourselves avenging,
ἀγαπητοί, ἀλλὰ δότε τόπον τῇ ὀργῇ· γέγραπται γάρ,
beloved, but give place to wrath, it has been written for,
**20** Ἐμοὶ ἐκδίκησις, ἐγὼ ἀνταποδώσω, λέγει Κύριος. ἐὰν οὖν πεινᾷ
To Me (is) vengeance, I will repay, says (the) Lord. if Then hungers
ὁ ἐχθρός σου, ψώμιζε αὐτόν· ἐὰν διψᾷ, πότιζε αὐτόν· τοῦτο
the enemy of you, feed him; if he thirsts, give drink to him; this
γὰρ ποιῶν, ἄνθρακας πυρὸς σωρεύσεις ἐπὶ τὴν κεφαλὴν αὐτοῦ.
for doing, coals of fire you will heap on the head of him.
**21** μὴ νικῶ ὑπὸ τοῦ κακοῦ. ἀλλὰ νίκα ἐν τῷ ἀγαθῷ τὸ κακόν.
Not be conquered by evil, but conquer with good the evil.

**CHAPTER 13**

**1** Πᾶσα ψυχὴ ἐξουσίαις ὑπερεχούσαις ὑποτασσέσθω· οὐ
Every soul to authorities higher be subject to. no
γάρ ἐστιν ἐξουσία εἰ μὴ ἀπὸ Θεοῦ, αἱ δὲ οὖσαι ἐξουσίαι ὑπὸ
For there is authority except from God, the but existing authorities by

been ordained. [2] So that he that sets himself against the authority resists the ordinance of God; and they that resist shall receive judgment to themselves. [3] For the rulers are not a terror to good works, but to evil. Do you desire not to be afraid of the authority? Practice the good, and you shall have praise from it; [4] for it is a servant of God to you for good. But if you practice evil, fear; for it does not wear the sword in vain; for it is a servant of God, an avenger for wrath to him that does evil. [5] Because of this (it is) necessary to be subject, not only on account of wrath, but also on account of conscience. [6] For on this account you also pay taxes; for they are ministers of God, always attending (to) this very thing. [7] Then give to all the dues: to him (due) tax, the tax; to him (due) tribute, the tribute; to him (due) honor, honor. [8] Owe no one anything, except to love one another; for the (one) loving the other has fulfilled the law. [9] For, "Do not commit adultery; do not murder; do not steal; do not bear false witness; do not lust;" and if (there is) any other commandment, it is summed up in this word: "You shall love your neighbor as yourself." [10] Love does not work ill to the neighbor. Love, then, (is) fulfillment of law. [11] Also this, knowing the time, that (it is) the hour that we should be aroused from sleep, for now our salvation is nearer than when we believed. [12] The night is far gone, and the day has drawn near; we should therefore cast off the works of darkness and should put on the armor of light. [13] We should walk honorably as in (the) day, not in carousings and drinking, not in cohabitation and lustful acts, not in fighting and envy. [14] But put on the Lord Jesus Christ and do

2 τοῦ Θεοῦ τεταγμέναι εἰσίν. ὥστε ὁ ἀντιτασσόμενος τῇ
— God having been ordained are. So the (one) resisting the
ἐξουσίᾳ, τῇ τοῦ Θεοῦ διαταγῇ ἀνθέστηκεν· οἱ δὲ ἀνθεστη-
authority the of God ordinance has opposed; those and having
3 κότες ἑαυτοῖς κρίμα λήψονται. οἱ γὰρ ἄρχοντες οὐκ εἰσὶ
opposed, to themselves judgment will receive. the For rulers not are
φόβος τῶν ἀγαθῶν ἔργων, ἀλλὰ τῶν κακῶν. θέλεις δὲ μὴ
a terror to good works, but to the bad. wish you And not
φοβεῖσθαι τὴν ἐξουσίαν ; τὸ ἀγαθὸν ποίει, καὶ ἕξεις ἔπαινον
to fear the authority? the good Do, and you will have praise
4 ἐξ αὐτῆς· Θεοῦ γὰρ διάκονός ἐστί σοι εἰς τὸ ἀγαθόν. ἐὰν δὲ
from it; of God For a servant he is to you for the good. if But
τὸ κακὸν ποιῇς, φοβοῦ· οὐ γὰρ εἰκῆ τὴν μάχαιραν φορεῖ·
the evil you do, fear; not for in vain the sword he bears;
Θεοῦ γὰρ διάκονός ἐστιν, ἔκδικος εἰς ὀργὴν τῷ τὸ κακὸν
of God for a servant he is, an avenger for wrath to the (one) evil
5 πράσσοντι. διὸ ἀνάγκη ὑποτάσσεσθαι, οὐ μόνον διὰ τὴν
practicing. Therefore it is necessary to be subject, not only because of
ὀργήν, ἀλλὰ καὶ διὰ τὴν συνείδησιν. διὰ τοῦτο γὰρ καὶ
wrath, but also because of conscience. on account of this For also
6 φόρους τελεῖτε· λειτουργοὶ γὰρ Θεοῦ εἰσιν, εἰς αὐτὸ τοῦτο
taxes you pay; ministers for of God they are, for this very thing
7 προσκαρτεροῦντες. ἀπόδοτε οὖν πᾶσι τὰς ὀφειλάς· τῷ τὸν
always giving attention. give Then to all the dues: to the (one) the
φόρον τὸν φόρον· τῷ τὸ τέλος τὸ τέλος· τῷ τὸν φόβον τὸν
tax (due) the tax; to the (one) the tribute the tribute; fear (due), the
φόβον· τῷ τὴν τιμὴν τὴν τιμήν.
fear; honor (due) the honor.
8 Μηδενὶ μηδὲν ὀφείλετε, εἰ μὴ τὸ ἀγαπᾶν ἀλλήλους· ὁ γὰρ
To no one nothing owe, except to love one another; he for
ἀγαπῶν τὸν ἕτερον, νόμον πεπλήρωκε. τὸ γάρ, Οὐ μοιχεύ-
loving the other, the law has fulfilled. — For: Do not commit
9 σεις, οὐ φονεύσεις, οὐ κλέψεις, οὐ ψευδομαρτυρήσεις, οὐκ
adultery; not do murder; not do steal; Do not bear false witness; not
ἐπιθυμήσεις, καὶ εἴ τις ἑτέρα ἐντολή, ἐν τούτῳ τῷ λόγῳ
lust; and if any other commandment, in this word
ἀνακεφαλαιοῦται, ἐν τῷ, Ἀγαπήσεις τὸν πλησίον σου ὡς
it is summed up: You shall love the neighbor of you as
10 ἑαυτόν. ἡ ἀγάπη τῷ πλησίον κακὸν οὐκ ἐργάζεται·
yourself. Love to the neighbor evil does not work ;
πλήρωμα οὖν νόμου ἡ ἀγάπη.
fulfillment then of law (is) love.
11 Καὶ τοῦτο, εἰδότες τὸν καιρόν, ὅτι ὥρα ἡμᾶς ἤδη ἐξ ὕπνου
And this, knowing the time, that an hour (is for you) now out of sleep
ἐγερθῆναι· νῦν γὰρ ἐγγύτερον ἡμῶν ἡ σωτηρία ἢ ὅτε ἐπι-
to be raised; now for nearer of us the salvation than when we
12 στεύσαμεν. ἡ νὺξ προέκοψεν, ἡ δὲ ἡμέρα ἤγγικεν· ἀποθώμεθα
believed. The night (is) far gone, the and day has drawn near. Let us cast off
οὖν τὰ ἔργα τοῦ σκότους, καὶ ἐνδυσώμεθα τὰ ὅπλα τοῦ
then the works of the darkness, and let us put on the weapons of the
13 φωτός. ὡς ἐν ἡμέρᾳ, εὐσχημόνως περιπατήσωμεν, μὴ κώμοις
light. As in (the) day, becomingly let us walk, not in carousings
14 καὶ μέθαις, μὴ κοίταις καὶ ἀσελγείαις, μὴ ἔριδι καὶ ζήλῳ. ἀλλ
and drinking, not in cohabitation and lustful acts, not in fighting and envy. But
ἐνδύσασθε τὸν Κύριον Ἰησοῦν Χριστόν, καὶ τῆς σαρκὸς
put on the Lord Jesus Christ, and of the flesh

not take thought for the
lusts of the flesh.

## CHAPTER 14

[1] And receive him
being weak in the faith,
not to judgments of
thoughts. [2] One believes
to eat all things; another
being weak eats vegetables.
[3] He that eats, let him
not despise him that does
not eat; and he that does
not eat, let him not judge
him that eats; for God
received him. [4] Who are
you judging another's
servant? To his own master
he stands or falls. And he
shall be made to stand; for
God is able to make him
stand. [5] One judges a
day (to be) above a day;
another judges every day
(to be alike). Let each in
his own mind be fully
assured. [6] He that
regards the day regards (it)
to (the) Lord; and he that
does not regard the day
does not regard (it) to
(the) Lord. He that eats, to
(the) Lord eats, for he
gives thanks to God; and
he that does not eat, to
(the) Lord he does not eat,
and gives thanks to God.
[7] For no one of us lives
to himself, and no one dies
to himself. [8] For both if
we should live, we should
live to the Lord; and if we
should die, we die to the
Lord; both, then, if we
should live and if we
should die, we are the
Lord's. [9] For this Christ
both died and rose and
lived again, that He might
rule over both (the) dead
and living. [10] But why do
you judge your brother? Or
why also do you despise
your brother? For all shall
stand before the judgment
seat of Christ. [11] For it
has been written, "I live,
says the Lord, that every
knee will bow to Me, and
every tongue will confess to
God." [12] So then, each of
us will give account to God
concerning himself. [13] No
longer, then, let us judge
one another; but rather
judge this, not to put a
stumbling-block or an of-
fense to the brother. [14] I
know and am persuaded in
Lord Jesus that nothing (is)

πρόνοιαν μὴ ποιεῖσθε, εἰς ἐπιθυμίας.
forethought do not make for (its) lusts.

## CHAPTER 14

1 Τὸν δὲ ἀσθενοῦντα τῇ πίστει προσλαμβάνεσθε, μὴ εἰς
the (one) And being weak in the faith receive, not to
2 διακρίσεις διαλογισμῶν. ὃς μὲν πιστεύει φαγεῖν πάντα, ὁ
judgments of thoughts. One indeed believes to eat all things, one
δὲ ἀσθενῶν λάχανα ἐσθίει. ὁ ἐσθίων τὸν μὴ ἐσθίοντα μὴ
but being weak vegetables eats. The (one) eating the (one) not eating do not
ἐξουθενείτω, καὶ ὁ μὴ ἐσθίων τὸν ἐσθίοντα μὴ κρινέτω· ὁ
despise; and the (one) not eating the (one) eating do not judge. —
4 Θεὸς γὰρ αὐτὸν προσελάβετο. σὺ τίς εἶ ὁ κρίνων ἀλλότριον
God For him received. You who are judging of another
οἰκέτην; τῷ ἰδίῳ κυρίῳ στήκει ἢ πίπτει. σταθήσεται δέ·
a servant, to the own lord he stands or falls; he will stand but,
5 δυνατὸς γάρ ἐστιν ὁ Θεὸς στῆσαι αὐτόν. ὃς μὲν κρίνει
able for is God to stand him. One indeed judges
ἡμέραν παρ' ἡμέραν, ὃς δὲ κρίνει πᾶσαν ἡμέραν. ἕκαστος
a day above a day; one and judges every day (alike). Each
6 ἐν τῷ ἰδίῳ νοΐ πληροφορείσθω. ὁ φρονῶν τὴν ἡμέραν,
in the own mind let him be fully assured. He minding the day,
Κυρίῳ φρονεῖ· καὶ ὁ μὴ φρονῶν τὴν ἡμέραν, Κυρίῳ οὐ
to (the) Lord he minds; and he not minding the day, to (the) Lord not
φρονεῖ. ὁ ἐσθίων Κυρίῳ ἐσθίει, εὐχαριστεῖ γὰρ τῷ Θεῷ· καὶ
he minds. He eating, to (the) Lord he eats; he gives thanks for to God; and
ὁ μὴ ἐσθίων Κυρίῳ οὐκ ἐσθίει, καὶ εὐχαριστεῖ τῷ Θεῷ.
he not eating, to (the) Lord not he eats; and gives thanks to God.
7 οὐδεὶς γὰρ ἡμῶν ἑαυτῷ ζῇ, καὶ οὐδεὶς ἑαυτῷ ἀποθνῄσκει.
no one For of us to himself lives, and no one to himself dies.
8 ἐάν τε γὰρ ζῶμεν, τῷ Κυρίῳ ζῶμεν· ἐάν τε ἀποθνῄσκωμεν,
if both For we live, to (the) Lord we live; if and we die,
τῷ Κυρίῳ ἀποθνῄσκομεν· ἐάν τε οὖν ζῶμεν, ἐάν τε ἀποθνή-
to (the) Lord we die. if And therefore we live, if and we
9 σκωμεν, τοῦ Κυρίου ἐσμέν. εἰς τοῦτο γὰρ Χριστὸς καὶ
die, of the Lord we are. for this For Christ also
ἀπέθανε καὶ ἀνέστη καὶ ἀνέζησεν, ἵνα καὶ νεκρῶν καὶ
died and rose and lived again, that both of dead and
ζώντων κυριεύσῃ. σὺ δὲ τί κρίνεις τὸν ἀδελφόν σου; ἢ καὶ
of living He might be Lord. you And why judge the brother of you? Or also
10 σὺ τί ἐξουθενεῖς τὸν ἀδελφόν σου; πάντες γὰρ παραστη-
you why despise the brother of you? all For shall stand
11 σόμεθα τῷ βήματι τοῦ Χριστοῦ. γέγραπται γάρ, Ζῶ ἐγώ,
before the judgment seat of Christ. it has been written For, live I,
λέγει Κύριος· ὅτι ἐμοὶ κάμψει πᾶν γόνυ, καὶ πᾶσα γλῶσσα
says (the) Lord, that to Me will bow every knee, and every tongue
12 ἐξομολογήσεται τῷ Θεῷ. ἄρα οὖν ἕκαστος ἡμῶν περὶ
will confess to God. So then, each one of us concerning
ἑαυτοῦ λόγον δώσει τῷ Θεῷ.
himself account will give to God.

13 Μηκέτι οὖν ἀλλήλους κρίνωμεν· ἀλλὰ τοῦτο κρίνατε
No longer, then, one another let us judge; but this judge
μᾶλλον, τὸ μὴ τιθέναι πρόσκομμα τῷ ἀδελφῷ ἢ σκάνδαλον.
rather, not to put a stumbling-block to the brother or an offense.
14 οἶδα καὶ πέπεισμαι ἐν Κυρίῳ Ἰησοῦ, ὅτι οὐδὲν κοινὸν δι'
know and am persuaded in (the) Lord Jesus, that nothing (is) common by

unclean of itself; except to him who judges anything to be unclean, to him (it is) unclean. [15] But if your brother is grieved on account of (your) food, you no longer walk according to love. Do not with your food destroy him for whom Christ died. [16] Then do not let your good be slandered. [17] For the kingdom of God is not eating and drinking; but righteousness and peace and joy in (the) Holy Spirit. [18] For he that serves Christ in these things is pleasing to God and approved to men. [19] So then we should pursue the things of peace, and the things for building one another up. [20] Do not destroy the work of God for the sake of food. All things indeed (are) pure, but (it is) evil to the man who through stumbling eats. [21] (It is) not right to eat flesh or drink wine, or in whatever (makes) your brother stumble, or be offended, or be weak. [22] Do you have faith? Have (it) to yourself before God. Blessed (is) he that does not condemn himself in what he approves. [23] But he that doubts, if he eats, has been condemned, because it is not of faith; and whatever (is) not of faith is sin.

CHAPTER 15

[1] But we who (are) strong ought to bear the infirmities of the weak, and not to please ourselves. [2] For let everyone f us please his neighbor for good for edifying. [3] For also Christ did not please Himself; but, according as it has been written, "The curses of those who were cursing You fell on Me." [4] For whatever things were written before were written for our instruction, that through patience and encouragement of the Scriptures we might have hope. [5] Now may the God of patience and encouragement give you to mind the same thing among one another according to Christ

ἑαυτοῦ· εἰ μὴ τῷ λογιζομένῳ τι κοινὸν εἶναι, ἐκείνῳ κοινόν.
itself,　except to the (one) counting anything common to be, to that common.

15 εἰ δὲ διὰ βρῶμα ὁ ἀδελφός σου λυπεῖται, οὐκέτι κατὰ ἀγάπην
if And for (your) food the brother of you is grieved, no longer according to love

περιπατεῖς. μὴ τῷ βρώματί σου ἐκεῖνον ἀπόλλυε, ὑπὲρ οὗ
do you walk. Not by the food of you that one destroy, for whom

16 Χριστὸς ἀπέθανε. μὴ βλασφημείσθω οὖν ὑμῶν τὸ ἀγαθόν·
Christ died, let not be evil spoken of Then of you the good.

17 σὺ γὰρ ἐστιν ἡ βασιλεία τοῦ Θεοῦ βρῶσις καὶ πόσις, ἀλλὰ
not For is the kingdom Of God eating and drinking, but

18 δικαιοσύνη καὶ εἰρήνη καὶ χαρὰ ἐν Πνεύματι Ἁγίῳ. ὁ γὰρ
righteousness and peace and joy in (the) Spirit Holy. the For

ἐν τούτοις δουλεύων τῷ Χριστῷ εὐάρεστος τῷ Θεῷ, καὶ
in these serving Christ (is) well-pleasing to God, and

19 δόκιμος τοῖς ἀνθρώποις. ἄρα οὖν τὰ τῆς εἰρήνης διώκωμεν,
approved by men. So then the things of peace let us pursue,

20 καὶ τὰ τῆς οἰκοδομῆς τῆς εἰς ἀλλήλους. μὴ ἕνεκεν βρώματος
and the things for building up for one another. Do not because of food

κατάλυε τὸ ἔργον τοῦ Θεοῦ. πάντα μὲν καθαρά, ἀλλὰ κακὸν
undo the work of God. All things truly (are) clean, but bad

21 τῷ ἀνθρώπῳ τῷ διὰ προσκόμματος ἐσθίοντι. καλὸν τὸ μὴ
to the man through a stumbling-block eating. (It is) good not

φαγεῖν κρέα, μηδὲ πιεῖν οἶνον, μηδὲ ἐν ᾧ ὁ ἀδελφός σου
to eat flesh, nor to drink wine, nor (any) by which the brother of you

22 προσκόπτει ἢ σκανδαλίζεται ἢ ἀσθενεῖ. σὺ πίστιν ἔχεις ;
stumbles, or be offended, or be weak. Do you faith have?

κατὰ σαυτὸν ἔχε ἐνώπιον τοῦ Θεοῦ. μακάριος ὁ μὴ κρίνων
By yourself have (it) before God. Blessed the (one) not judging

23 ἑαυτὸν ἐν ᾧ δοκιμάζει. ὁ δὲ διακρινόμενος, ἐὰν φάγῃ, κατα-
himself in what he approves; he but doubting, if he eats, has been

κέκριται, ὅτι οὐκ ἐκ πίστεως· πᾶν δὲ ὃ οὐκ ἐκ πίστεως
condemned, because not of faith; all and not of faith

ἁμαρτία ἐστίν.
sin is.

## CHAPTER 15

1 Ὀφείλομεν δὲ ἡμεῖς οἱ δυνατοὶ τὰ ἀσθενήματα τῶν ἀδυνά-
ought And we the strong the weaknesses of the not

2 των βαστάζειν, καὶ μὴ ἑαυτοῖς ἀρέσκειν. ἕκαστος γὰρ
strong to bear, and not ourselves please. let each one For

ἡμῶν τῷ πλησίον ἀρεσκέτω εἰς τὸ ἀγαθὸν πρὸς οἰκοδομήν.
of us the neighbor to please for good, to building up.

3 καὶ γὰρ ὁ Χριστὸς οὐχ ἑαυτῷ ἤρεσεν, ἀλλά, καθὼς
even For Christ not Himself pleased, but, even as

γέγραπται, Οἱ ὀνειδισμοὶ τῶν ὀνειδιζόντων σε ἐπέπεσον
it has been written: The reproaches of those reproaching You fell

4 ἐπ᾽ ἐμέ. ὅσα γὰρ προεγράφη, εἰς τὴν ἡμετέραν διδασκαλίαν
on Me. whatever For were written before. for our teaching

προεγράφη, ἵνα διὰ τῆς ὑπομονῆς καὶ τῆς παρακλήσεως
were written before. that through patience and encouragement

5 τῶν γραφῶν τὴν ἐλπίδα ἔχωμεν. ὁ δὲ Θεὸς τῆς ὑπομονῆς
of the Scriptures hope we might have. the And God of patience

καὶ τῆς παρακλήσεως δῴη ὑμῖν τὸ αὐτὸ φρονεῖν ἐν ἀλλήλοις
and of encouragement give to you the same, to mind among one another

κατὰ Χριστὸν Ἰησοῦν· ἵνα ὁμοθυμαδὸν ἐν ἑνὶ στόματι
according to Christ Jesus, that with one accord, with one mouth

Jesus, that with one accord with one mouth you glorify (the) God and Father of our Lord Jesus Christ. [7] Therefore, receive one another as Christ also received us, to (the) glory of God.

[8] But I say, Jesus Christ has become a minister of circumcision for (the) truth of God, to confirm the promises of the fathers, [9] and for the nations to glorify God for mercy, even as it has been written, "Because of this I will confess to You in the nations, and I will praise Your name." [10] And again He says, "Rejoice nations, with His people. [11] And again, "Praise the Lord all the nations, and praise Him all the peoples." [12] And again, Isaiah says, "The Root of Jesse shall be, and He rising up to rule the nations; on Him nations will hope." [13] Now may the God of hope fill you with all joy and peace in believing, for you to abound in hope, in power of (the) Holy Spirit.

[14] But, my brothers, I myself am persuaded concerning you, that you also yourselves are full of goodness, being filled with all knowledge, being able to warn one another. [15] But I did more boldly write to you, brothers, in part as reminding you, because of the grace which was given to be by God, [16] for me to be a minister of Jesus Christ to the nations, sacredly ministering the gospel of God, that the offering up of the nations might be acceptable (and) sanctified by (the) Holy Spirit. [17] Therefore I have boasting in Christ Jesus (as to) the things pertaining to God. [18] For I will not dare speak anything of what Christ has not worked out by me, for (the) obedience of the nations, by word and deed — [19] of miracles and wonders in power, in (the) power of (the) Spirit of God; so that I have fully preached the gospel of Christ from Jerusalem and in a circle as far as Illyricum. [20] And so I was eager to preach the

---

δοξάζητε τὸν Θεὸν καὶ πατέρα τοῦ Κυρίου ἡμῶν Ἰησοῦ
you may glorify   God   and   Father of the   Lord   of us   Jesus

Χριστοῦ. διὸ προσλαμβάνεσθε ἀλλήλους. καθὼς καὶ ὁ Χρι-
Christ. Therefore receive      one another,   even as also   Christ

στὸς προσελάβετο ἡμᾶς, εἰς δόξαν Θεοῦ. λέγω δέ, Ἰησοῦν
received      us,   to (the) glory of God. I say And, Jesus

Χριστὸν διάκονον γεγενῆσθαι περιτομῆς ὑπὲρ ἀληθείας
Christ   a minister   has become of circumcision for (the) truth

Θεοῦ, εἰς τὸ βεβαιῶσαι τὰς ἐπαγγελίας τῶν πατέρων· τὰ
of God, to   confirm   the   promises   of the   fathers,   the

δὲ ἔθνη ὑπὲρ ἐλέους δοξάσαι τὸν Θεόν, καθὼς γέγραπται.
and nations for mercy to glorify   God, even as it has been written,

Διὰ τοῦτο ἐξομολογήσομαί σοι ἐν ἔθνεσι, καὶ τῷ ὀνόματί σου
Therefore I will confess   to You among nations, and to Your name

ψαλῶ. καὶ πάλιν λέγει, Εὐφράνθητε, ἔθνη, μετὰ τοῦ λαοῦ
I will praise. And again he says, Rejoice,   nations, with the people

αὐτοῦ. καὶ πάλιν, Αἰνεῖτε τὸν Κύριον πάντα τὰ ἔθνη, καὶ
of Him. And again, Praise   the   Lord   all   the nations, and

ἐπαινέσατε αὐτὸν πάντες οἱ λαοί. καὶ πάλιν Ἡσαΐας λέγει,
praise   Him   all   the peoples And again,   Isaiah   says,

Ἔσται ἡ ῥίζα τοῦ Ἰεσσαί, καὶ ὁ ἀνιστάμενος ἄρχειν ἐθνῶν·
Shall be the Root   of Jesse, and the (One) rising up   to rule the nations;

ἐπ' αὐτῷ ἔθνη ἐλπιοῦσιν. ὁ δὲ Θεὸς τῆς ἐλπίδος πληρώσαι
on Him nations will hope.   the And God   of hope   fill

ὑμᾶς πάσης χαρᾶς καὶ εἰρήνης ἐν τῷ πιστεύειν, εἰς τὸ περισ-
you   of all   joy   and peace   in   believing,   for   to

σεύειν ὑμᾶς ἐν τῇ ἐλπίδι, ἐν δυνάμει Πνεύματος Ἁγίου.
abound you in   hope,   in power of (the) Spirit   Holy.

Πέπεισμαι δέ, ἀδελφοί μου, καὶ αὐτὸς ἐγὼ περὶ ὑμῶν, ὅτι
I am persuaded But, brothers of me, even myself,   I, concerning you, that

καὶ αὐτοὶ μεστοί ἐστε ἀγαθωσύνης, πεπληρωμένοι πάσης
also yourselves full you are of goodness,   having been filled   of all

γνώσεως, δυνάμενοι καὶ ἀλλήλους νουθετεῖν. τολμηρότερον
knowledge, being able   also one another   to warn.     more boldly

δὲ ἔγραψα ὑμῖν, ἀδελφοί, ἀπὸ μέρους, ὡς ἐπαναμιμνήσκων
And I wrote to you, brothers,   in   part   as   reminding

ὑμᾶς, διὰ τὴν χάριν τὴν δοθεῖσάν μοι ὑπὸ τοῦ Θεοῦ, εἰς τὸ
you, because of the grace   given   to me by   God, for

εἶναί με λειτουργὸν Ἰησοῦ Χριστοῦ εἰς τὰ ἔθνη, ἱερουρ-
to be me a minister   of Jesus   Christ to the nations, sacredly

γοῦντα τὸ εὐαγγέλιον τοῦ Θεοῦ, ἵνα γένηται ἡ προσφορὰ
ministering the gospel     of God, that may be the   offering

τῶν ἐθνῶν εὐπρόσδεκτος, ἡγιασμένη ἐν Πνεύματι Ἁγίῳ. ἔχω
of the nations acceptable,   sanctified   by (the) Spirit   Holy. I have

οὖν καύχησιν ἐν Χριστῷ Ἰησοῦ τὰ πρὸς Θεόν. οὐ γὰρ
therefore boasting in Christ   Jesus the things with God. not for

τολμήσω λαλεῖν τι ὧν οὐ κατειργάσατο Χριστὸς δι' ἐμοῦ,
I will dare to speak anything of which not did work out Christ through me,

εἰς ὑπακοὴν ἐθνῶν λόγῳ καὶ ἔργῳ, ἐν δυνάμει σημείων καὶ
for obedience of (the) nations in word and work, in power   of signs   and

τεράτων, ἐν δυνάμει Πνεύματος Θεοῦ· ὥστε με ἀπὸ Ἱερου-
wonders,   in power of (the) Spirit of God, so as me from Jerus-

σαλὴμ καὶ κύκλῳ μέχρι τοῦ Ἰλλυρικοῦ πεπληρωκέναι τὸ
alem   and around   to   —   Illyricum   to have fulfilled   the

εὐαγγέλιον τοῦ Χριστοῦ· οὕτω δὲ φιλοτιμούμενον εὐαγγελί-
gospel     of Christ.   so And eagerly striving   to preach the

gospel where Christ had not been named, so that I might not build on another's foundation; [21] but according as it has been written, "They shall see, to whom nothing was told about Him; and those that have not heard shall understand." [22] For this reason I was also hindered many times from coming to you. [23] But now, having no more place in these regions, and having a longing to come to you for many years, [24] Whenever I go into Spain, I will come to you; for I hope going through to see you, and to be sent forward by you to there, if first I should be filled of you in part. [25] But now I go to Jerusalem, doing service to the saints; [26] for Macedonia and Achaia were pleased to make a certain gift to the poor among the saints who are in Jerusalem. [27] For they were pleased and they are their debtors; for if the nations participated in their spiritual things, they ought also to minister to them in the fleshly things. [28] Having finished this, then, and having sealed this fruit to them, I will come by you into Spain. [29] And I know that coming to you I shall come in fullness of blessing of the gospel of Christ.

[30] But I exhort you, brothers, by our Lord Jesus Christ, and by the love of the Spirit, to strive together with me in prayers for me to God, [31] that I may be delivered from those disbelieving in Judea; and that my service which is for Jerusalem may be pleasing to the saints; [32] that I may come in joy to you by (the) will of God, and that I may be refreshed with you. [33] And the God of peace (be) with all of you. Amen.

---

ζεσθαι, οὐχ ὅπου ὠνομάσθη Χριστός, ἵνα μὴ ἐπ' ἀλλότριον
gospel, not where was named Christ, that not on another's

21 θεμέλιον οἰκοδομῶ· ἀλλά, καθὼς γέγραπται, Οἶς οὐκ
foundation I should build, but, even as it has been written: To whom not

ἀνηγγέλη περὶ αὐτοῦ, ὄψονται· καὶ οἳ οὐκ ἀκηκόασι,
it was announced about Him, they shall see; and those not having heard,

συνήσουσι.
they shall understand.

22 Διὸ καὶ ἐνεκοπτόμην τὰ πολλὰ τοῦ ἐλθεῖν πρὸς ὑμᾶς·
Therefore also I was hindered much to come to you;

23 νυνὶ δὲ μηκέτι τόπον ἔχων ἐν τοῖς κλίμασι τούτοις, ἐπιποθίαν
now but no longer place having in — regions these, a desire

24 δὲ ἔχων τοῦ ἐλθεῖν πρὸς ὑμᾶς ἀπὸ πολλῶν ἐτῶν, ὡς ἐὰν
and having to come to you from many years, whenever

πορεύωμαι εἰς τὴν Σπανίαν, ἐλεύσομαι πρὸς ὑμᾶς· ἐλπίζω
I may go into Spain, I will come to you; I hope

γὰρ διαπορευόμενος θεάσασθαι ὑμᾶς, καὶ ὑφ' ὑμῶν προ-
for traveling through to behold you, and by you to be

πεμφθῆναι ἐκεῖ, ἐὰν ὑμῶν πρῶτον ἀπὸ μέρους ἐμπλησθῶ.
set forward there. if of you firstly in part I may be filled.

25 νυνὶ δὲ πορεύομαι εἰς Ἰερουσαλήμ, διακονῶν τοῖς ἁγίοις.
now And I am going to Jerusalem ministering to the saints.

26 εὐδόκησαν γὰρ Μακεδονία καὶ Ἀχαΐα κοινωνίαν τινὰ
thought it good For Macedonia and Achaia gifts certain

ποιήσασθαι εἰς τοὺς πτωχοὺς τῶν ἁγίων τῶν ἐν Ἰερου-
to make to the poor of the saints — in Jeru-

27 σαλήμ. εὐδόκησαν γάρ, καὶ ὀφειλέται αὐτῶν εἰσιν. εἰ γὰρ
salem. they thought it good For, and debtors of them are. if For

τοῖς πνευματικοῖς αὐτῶν ἐκοινώνησαν τὰ ἔθνη. ὀφείλουσι
in the spiritual things of them shared the nations, they ought

28 καὶ ἐν τοῖς σαρκικοῖς λειτουργῆσαι αὐτοῖς. τοῦτο οὖν
also in the fleshly things to minister to them. this Then

ἐπιτελέσας, καὶ σφραγισάμενος αὐτοῖς τὸν καρπὸν τοῦτον,
having finished, and having sealed to them fruit this,

29 ἀπελεύσομαι δι' ὑμῶν εἰς τὴν Σπανίαν. οἶδα δὲ ὅτι ἐρχό-
I will go away through you to Spain. I know And that coming

μενος πρὸς ὑμᾶς ἐν πληρώματι εὐλογίας τοῦ εὐαγγελίου τοῦ
to you in the fullness of (the) blessing of the gospel

Χριστοῦ ἐλεύσομαι.
of Christ I will come.

30 Παρακαλῶ δὲ ὑμᾶς, ἀδελφοί, διὰ τοῦ Κυρίου ἡμῶν Ἰησοῦ
I exhort And you, brothers, by the Lord of us, Jesus

Χριστοῦ, καὶ διὰ τῆς ἀγάπης τοῦ Πνεύματος, συναγωνί-
Christ, and by the love of the Spirit, to strive

σασθαί μοι ἐν ταῖς προσευχαῖς ὑπὲρ ἐμοῦ πρὸς τὸν Θεόν·
together with me in the prayers on behalf of me to — God,

31 ἵνα ῥυσθῶ ἀπὸ τῶν ἀπειθούντων ἐν τῇ Ἰουδαίᾳ, καὶ ἵνα ἡ
that I be delivered from those disobeying in — Judea, and that the

διακονία μου ἡ εἰς Ἰερουσαλὴμ εὐπρόσδεκτος γένηται τοῖς
ministry of me which (is) to Jerusalem acceptable may be to the

32 ἁγίοις· ἵνα ἐν χαρᾷ ἔλθω πρὸς ὑμᾶς διὰ θελήματος Θεοῦ, καὶ
saints, that in joy coming to you through (the) will of God, and

33 συναναπαύσωμαι ὑμῖν. ὁ δὲ Θεὸς τῆς εἰρήνης μετὰ πάντων
I may be refreshed with you. the And God of peace with all

ὑμῶν. ἀμήν.
of you. Amen.

## CHAPTER 16

CHAPTER 16

[1] But I commend to you Phoebe our sister, being servant of the church in Cenchrea; [2] that you may receive her in (the) Lord (as is) worthy of the saints, and may assist her in whatever she may need of you. For she also became a helper of many, and of myself.

**1** Συνίστημι δὲ ὑμῖν Φοίβην τὴν ἀδελφὴν ἡμῶν, οὖσαν
I commend And to you Phoebe the sister of us, being

διάκονον τῆς ἐκκλησίας τῆς ἐν Κεγχρεαῖς· ἵνα αὐτὴν προσδέ-
a servant of the church in Cenchrea, that her you may

**2** ξησθε ἐν Κυρίῳ ἀξίως τῶν ἁγίων, καὶ παραστῆτε αὐτῇ ἐν ᾧ
receive in (the) Lord worthily of the saints, and may assist her in what-

ἂν ὑμῶν χρῄζῃ πράγματι· καὶ γὰρ αὕτη προστάτις πολλῶν
ever of you she may have need. also For she a helper of many

ἐγενήθη, καὶ αὐτοῦ ἐμοῦ.
became, and of myself.

[3] Greet Priscilla and Aquila, my fellow-workers in Christ Jesus. [4] who laid down the neck of themselves for my soul; to whom I not only give thanks, but also all the churches of the nations. [5] And greet the church at their house, and my beloved Epenetus, who is a firstfruit of Achaia for Christ. [6] Greet Mary, who did much labor for us. [7] Greet Andronicus and Junias, my kinsmen and fellow-prisoners, noted among the apostles, who also were in Christ before me. [8] Greet Amplias my beloved in the Lord. [9] Greet Urbanus, our helper in Christ, and my beloved Stachys. [10] Greet Apelles, approved in Christ (and) those of the household of Aristobulus. [11] Greet Herodion, my kinsman. Greet those of the household of Narcissus, who are in the Lord. [12] Greet Tryphena and Tryphosa, who labor in the Lord. Greet Persis, the beloved, who much labored in the Lord. [13] Greet Rufus, the chosen in the Lord, and his mother and mine. [14] Greet Asyncritus, Phlegon, Hermas, Patrobas, Hermes, and the brothers with them. [15] Greet Philologus and Julias, Nereus and his sister and Olympas, and all the saints

**3** Ἀσπάσασθε Πρίσκιλλαν καὶ Ἀκύλαν τοὺς συνεργούς μου
Greet Priscilla and Aquilla the fellow-workers of me

**4** ἐν Χριστῷ Ἰησοῦ, οἵτινες ὑπὲρ τῆς ψυχῆς μου τὸν ἑαυτῶν
In Christ Jesus, who for the soul of me the of themselves

τράχηλον ὑπέθηκαν, οἷς οὐκ ἐγὼ μόνος εὐχαριστῶ, ἀλλὰ
neck they laid down; to whom not I only give thanks, but

καὶ πᾶσαι αἱ ἐκκλησίαι τῶν ἐθνῶν· καὶ τὴν κατ' οἶκον αὐτῶν
also all the churches of the nations; and the in house of them

**5** ἐκκλησίαν. ἀσπάσασθε Ἐπαίνετον τὸν ἀγαπητόν μου, ὅς
church. Greet Epenetus the beloved of me, who

ἐστιν ἀπαρχὴ τῆς Ἀχαΐας εἰς Χριστόν. ἀσπάσασθε Μαριάμ,
is firstfruit of Achaia for Christ. Greet Mariam,

**6** ἥτις πολλὰ ἐκοπίασεν εἰς ἡμᾶς. ἀσπάσασθε Ἀνδρόνικον καὶ
who many things labored for you. Greet Andronicus and

**7** Ἰουνιαν τοὺς συγγενεῖς μου καὶ συναιχμαλώτους μου,
Junias the kinsmen of me and fellow-prisoners of me,

οἵτινές εἰσιν ἐπίσημοι ἐν τοῖς ἀποστόλοις, οἳ καὶ πρὸ ἐμοῦ
who are notable among the apostles, who and before me

**8** γεγόνασιν ἐν Χριστῷ. ἀσπάσασθε Ἀμπλίαν τὸν ἀγαπητόι
have been in Christ. Greet Amplias the beloved

**9** μου ἐν Κυρίῳ. ἀσπάσασθε Οὐρβανὸν τὸν συνεργὸν ἡμῶν ἐν
of me in (the) Lord. Greet Urbanus the fellow-worker of us in

**10** Χριστῷ, καὶ Στάχυν τὸν ἀγαπητόν μου. ἀσπάσασθε Ἀπελ-
Christ, and Stachys the beloved of me. Greet Apelles

λῆν τὸν δόκιμον ἐν Χριστῷ. ἀσπάσασθε τοὺς ἐκ τῶν Ἀριστο-
the approved in Christ. Greet those of Aristo-

**11** βούλου. ἀσπάσασθε Ἡροδίωνα τὸν συγγενῆ μου. ἀσπά-
bulus. Greet Herodian the kinsman of me. Greet

**12** σασθε τοὺς ἐκ τῶν Ναρκίσσου, τοὺς ὄντας ἐν Κυρίῳ. ἀσπά-
those of Narcissus, those being in (the) Lord. Greet

σασθε Τρύφαιναν καὶ Τρυφῶσαν τὰς κοπιώσας ἐν Κυρίῳ.
Tryphena and Tryphosa, those laboring in (the) Lord.

ἀσπάσασθε Περσίδα τὴν ἀγαπητήν, ἥτις πολλὰ ἐκοπίασεν
Greet Persis the beloved, who many things labored

**13** ἐν Κυρίῳ. ἀσπάσασθε Ῥοῦφον τὸν ἐκλεκτὸν ἐν Κυρίῳ, καὶ τὴν
in (the) Lord. Greet Rufus the chosen in (the) Lord, and the

μητέρα αὐτοῦ καὶ ἐμοῦ. ἀσπάσασθε Ἀσύγκριτον, Φλέγοντα,
mother of him and of me. Greet Asyncritus, Phlegon,

**14** Ἑρμᾶν, Πατρόβαν, Ἑρμῆν, καὶ τοὺς σὺν αὐτοῖς ἀδελφούς.
Hermas, Patrobas, Hermes, and the with them brothers.

**15** ἀσπάσασθε Φιλόλογον καὶ Ἰουλίαν, Νηρέα καὶ τὴν ἀδελφὴν
Greet Philologus and Julias, Nereus and the sister

αὐτοῦ, καὶ Ὀλυμπᾶν, καὶ τοὺς σὺν αὐτοῖς πάντας ἁγίους.
of him, and Olympas, and the with him all saints.

with them. [16] Greet one another with a holy kiss. the churches of Christ send greetings to you.

[17] Now I exhort you, brothers, to consider those who make divisions and causes of stumbling contrary to the teaching which you have learned; and turn away from them. [18] For such ones do not serve our Lord Jesus Christ, but their own belly, and by smooth speaking and praise deceive the hearts of the innocent. [19] For your obedience reached to all; therefore I rejoice concerning you; but I wish you to be wise (as) to good, and simple as to evil. [20] And the God of peace will bruise Satan under your feet shortly.

The grace of our Lord Jesus Christ be with you. [21] Timothy, my fellow-worker, and Lucius, and Jason, and Sosipater, my kindred, greet you. [22] I, Tertius, who wrote you the epistle in the Lord, greet you. [23] Gaius, the host of the whole church and me, greets you. Erastus, the steward of the city, and Quartus the brother, greet you. [24] The grace of our Lord Jesus Christ be with you all. Amen.

[25] Now to Him that is able to establish you according to my gospel, and the preaching of Jesus Christ, according to the revealing of the mystery — regarding which silence has been kept during eternal ages, [26] but now has been made plain — and by prophetic Scriptures, according to commandment of the everlasting God, made known for obedience of faith to all the nations, [27] the only wise God, through Jesus Christ, to whom (be) the glory forever. Amen.

---

**16** ἀσπάσασθε ἀλλήλους ἐν φιλήματι ἁγίῳ. ἀσπάζονται ὑμᾶς
Greet  one another with a kiss holy. greet  you
αἱ ἐκκλησίαι τοῦ Χριστοῦ.
the churches  of Christ.

**17** Παρακαλῶ δὲ ὑμᾶς, ἀδελφοί, σκοπεῖν τοὺς τὰς διχοστα-
I exhort And you, brothers, to watch those the divisions
σίας καὶ τὰ σκάνδαλα, παρὰ τὴν διδαχὴν ἣν ὑμεῖς ἐμάθετε,
and the offenses, against the teaching which you learned,

**18** ποιοῦντας· καὶ ἐκκλίνατε ἀπ᾽ αὐτῶν. οἱ γὰρ τοιοῦτοι τῷ
making,  and turn away from them. For such ones the
Κυρίῳ ἡμῶν Ἰησοῦ Χριστῷ οὐ δουλεύουσιν, ἀλλὰ τῇ
Lord of us, Jesus Christ, not do serve; but the
ἑαυτῶν κοιλίᾳ· καὶ διὰ τῆς χρηστολογίας καὶ εὐλογίας
of themselves belly; and through smooth speech and flattering

**19** ἐξαπατῶσι τὰς καρδίας τῶν ἀκάκων. ἡ γὰρ ὑμῶν ὑπακοὴ
deceive the hearts of the guileless. the For of you obedience
εἰς πάντας ἀφίκετο. χαίρω οὖν τὸ ἐφ᾽ ὑμῖν· θέλω δὲ ὑμᾶς
to all reached. I rejoice Therefore over you; I desire and you
σοφοὺς μὲν εἶναι εἰς τὸ ἀγαθόν, ἀκεραίους δὲ εἰς τὸ κακόν.
wise truly to be to the good; simple but toward the evil.

**20** ὁ δὲ Θεὸς τῆς εἰρήνης συντρίψει τὸν Σατανᾶν ὑπὸ τοὺς
the And God of peace will crush Satan under the
πόδας ὑμῶν ἐν τάχει.
feet of you shortly.

Ἡ χάρις τοῦ Κυρίου ἡμῶν Ἰησοῦ Χριστοῦ μεθ᾽ ὑμῶν.
The grace of the Lord of us, Jesus Christ, (be) with you.
ἀμήν.
Amen.

**21** Ἀσπάζονται ὑμᾶς Τιμόθεος ὁ συνεργός μου, καὶ Λούκιος
greets  you Timothy the fellow-worker of me, and Lucius
καὶ Ἰάσων καὶ Σωσίπατρος οἱ συγγενεῖς μου. ἀσπάζομαι
and Jason, and Sosipater the kinsman of me. greet

**22** ὑμᾶς ἐγω Τέρτιος, ὁ γράψας τὴν ἐπιστολήν, ἐν Κυρίῳ.
you I, Tertius, the (one) writing the epistle, in (the) Lord.

**23** ἀσπάζεται ὑμᾶς Γάϊος ὁ ξένος μου καὶ τῆς ἐκκλησίας ὅλης.
greets  you Gaius the host of me, and the church of all.
ἀσπάζεται ὑμᾶς Ἔραστος ὁ οἰκονόμος τῆς πόλεως, καὶ
greets  you Erastus the treasurer of the city, and
Κούαρτος ὁ ἀδελφός.
Quartus the brother.

**24** Ἡ χάρις τοῦ Κυρίου ἡμῶν Ἰησοῦ Χριστοῦ μετὰ πάντων
The grace of the Lord of us, Jesus Christ, with all

**25** ὑμῶν. ἀμήν. Τῷ δὲ δυναμένῳ ὑμᾶς στηρίξαι κατὰ τὸ
you. Amen. to the (One) And able you to establish according to
εὐαγγέλιόν μου καὶ τὸ κήρυγμα Ἰησοῦ Χριστοῦ, κατὰ
the gospel of me, and the proclamation of Jesus Christ, according
ἀποκάλυψιν μυστηρίου χρονοις αἰωνίοις σεσιγημένου,
to the revelation of (the) mystery in times eternal having been kept silent,

**26** φανερωθέντος δὲ νῦν, διά τε γραφῶν προφητικῶν, κατ᾽
revealed  but now, through and writings prophetic, according
ἐπιταγὴν τοῦ αἰωνίου Θεοῦ, εἰς ὑπακοὴν πίστεως εἰς
to the command of the eternal God for obedience of faith to

**27** παντα τὰ ἔθνη γνωρισθέντος, μόνῳ σοφῷ Θεῷ, διὰ
all the nations made known, only wise to God through
Ἰησοῦ Χριστοῦ, ἡ δόξα εἰς τοὺς αἰῶνας. ἀμήν.
Jesus Christ, to whom (be) glory to the ages. Amen.

# ΠΑΥΛΟΥ ΤΟΥ ΑΠΟΣΤΟΛΟΥ
### PAUL THE APOSTLE

## Η ΠΡΟΣ
### THE TO

# ΚΟΡΙΝΘΙΟΥΣ
## (THE) CORINTHIANS

### ΕΠΙΣΤΟΛΗ ΠΡΩΤΗ
### EPISTLE FIRST

## CHAPTER 1

**CHAPTER 1**

[1] Paul a called apostle of Jesus Christ, by (the) will of God, and Sosthenes the brother, [2] to the assembly of God which is in Corinth, having been sanctified in Christ Jesus, called out saints, with all the ones who call on the name of our Lord Jesus Christ in every place, both theirs and ours; [3] Grace to you, and peace from God our Father and the Lord Jesus Christ.

[4] I thank my God always concerning you, for the grace of God that was given to you in Christ Jesus, [5] and in everything you were made rich in him, in all discourse and all knowledge, [6] according as the testimony of Christ was confirmed in you, [7] so that you are behind in no gift, waiting for the revealing of our Lord Jesus Christ, [8] who also will confirm you to the end, blameless in the day of our Lord Jesus Christ. [9] God is faithful, by whom you were called into the fellowship of His Son Jesus Christ our Lord.

[10] Now I exhort you, brothers, by the name of our Lord Jesus Christ, that you all say the same thing, and there be no divisions among you; but you be united in the same mind and in the same judgment. [11] For it was revealed to me concerning you, my

**1** Παῦλος κλητὸς ἀπόστολος Ἰησοῦ Χριστοῦ διὰ θελήματος
Paul a called apostle of Jesus Christ through (the) will

**2** Θεοῦ, καὶ Σωσθένης ὁ ἀδελφός, τῇ ἐκκλησίᾳ τοῦ Θεοῦ τῇ
of God, and Sosthenes the brother, to the church of God

οὔσῃ ἐν Κορίνθῳ, ἡγιασμένοις ἐν Χριστῷ Ἰησοῦ, κλητοῖς
existing in Corinth, those having been sanctified in Christ Jesus, called out

ἁγίοις, σὺν πᾶσι τοῖς ἐπικαλουμένοις τὸ ὄνομα τοῦ Κυρίου
saints, with all those calling on the name of the Lord

ἡμῶν Ἰησοῦ Χριστοῦ ἐν παντὶ τόπῳ, αὐτῶν τε καὶ ἡμῶν·
of us, Jesus Christ, in every place, of them both and of us;

**3** χάρις ὑμῖν καὶ εἰρήνη ἀπὸ Θεοῦ πατρὸς ἡμῶν καὶ Κυρίου
grace to you, and peace, from God (the) Father of us and (the) Lord

Ἰησοῦ Χριστοῦ.
Jesus Christ.

**4** Εὐχαριστῶ τῷ Θεῷ μου πάντοτε περὶ ὑμῶν, ἐπὶ τῇ
I gave thanks to the God of me always concerning you, on the

**5** χάριτι τοῦ Θεοῦ τῇ δοθείσῃ ὑμῖν ἐν Χριστῷ Ἰησοῦ· ὅτι ἐν
grace of God given to you in Christ Jesus, that in

παντὶ ἐπλουτίσθητε ἐν αὐτῷ, ἐν παντὶ λόγῳ καὶ πάσῃ
everything you were enriched in Him, in all discourse and all

**6** γνώσει, καθὼς τὸ μαρτύριον τοῦ Χριστοῦ ἐβεβαιώθη ἐν
knowledge, even as the testimony of Christ was confirmed in

**7** ὑμῖν· ὥστε ὑμᾶς μὴ ὑστερεῖσθαι ἐν μηδενὶ χαρίσματι, ἀπεκ-
you, so as you not to be lacking in no gift,

δεχομένους τὴν ἀποκάλυψιν τοῦ Κυρίου ἡμῶν Ἰησοῦ
awaiting the revelation of the Lord of us, Jesus

**8** Χριστοῦ, ὃς καὶ βεβαιώσει ὑμᾶς ἕως τέλους, ἀνεγκλήτους ἐν
Christ, who also will confirm you until (the) end, blameless in

**9** τῇ ἡμέρᾳ τοῦ Κυρίου ἡμῶν Ἰησοῦ Χριστοῦ. πιστὸς ὁ Θεός,
the day of the Lord of us, Jesus Christ. Faithful (is) God,

δι' οὗ ἐκλήθητε εἰς κοινωνίαν τοῦ υἱοῦ αὐτοῦ Ἰησοῦ Χριστοῦ
through whom you were called into fellowship of the Son of Him, Jesus Christ

τοῦ Κυρίου ἡμῶν.
the Lord of us.

**10** Παρακαλῶ δὲ ὑμᾶς, ἀδελφοί, διὰ τοῦ ὀνόματος τοῦ
I exhort Now you, brothers, through the name of the

Κυρίου ἡμῶν Ἰησοῦ Χριστοῦ, ἵνα τὸ αὐτὸ λέγητε πάντες,
Lord of us, Jesus Christ, that the same thing you say all,

καὶ μὴ ᾖ ἐν ὑμῖν σχίσματα, ἦτε δὲ κατηρτισμένοι ἐν τῷ αὐτῷ
and not be among you divisions, you be but united in the same

**11** νοῒ καὶ ἐν τῇ αὐτῇ γνώμῃ. ἐδηλώθη γάρ μοι περὶ ὑμῶν,
mind and in the same judgment. it was shown For to me about you,

387

brothers, by those of (the house of) Chloe, that there are contentions among you. [12] But I say this, that each of you says, I am of Paul, and I of Apollos, and I of Cephas, and I of Christ. [13] Has Christ been divided? Was Paul crucified for you? Or were you baptized to the name of Paul? [14] I thank God that I baptized none of you. except Crispus and Gaius, [15] that no one would say that I baptized to my name. [16] And I also baptized the house of Stephanus; as to the rest I do not know if I baptized any others. [17] For Christ did not send me to baptize, but to preach the gospel; not in wisdom of word, that the cross of Christ might not be nullified. [18] For the word of the Cross is foolishness to those being lost; but to us being saved, (it) is (the) power of God. [19] For it has been written: "I will destroy the wisdom of the wise, and I will set aside the understanding of those perceiving." [20] Where (is the) wise one? Where (is the) scribe? Where (the) lawyer of this age? Did not God make the wisdom of the world foolish? [21] For since in the wisdom of God the world (by) wisdom did not know God, God was pleased by the foolishness of preaching to save those believing. [22] And since Jews ask signs, and Greeks seek wisdom [23] but we preach Christ crucified, to Jews indeed an offense, and to Greeks foolishness; [24] but to the called out ones, both to Jews and to Greeks, Christ (is) the power of God and the wisdom of God. [25] Because the foolishness of God is wiser than men, and the weakness of God is stronger than men. [26] For you see your calling, brothers, that (there are) not many wise according to flesh, not many powerful, not many highborn. [27] But God chose the foolish things of the world so that the wise

**12** ἀδελφοί μου, ὑπὸ τῶν Χλόης, ὅτι ἔριδες ἐν ὑμῖν εἰσι. λέγω
brothers of me, by those of Chloe, that strifes among you are. I say
δὲ τοῦτο, ὅτι ἕκαστος ὑμῶν λέγει, Ἐγὼ μέν εἰμι Παύλου,
And this, that each of you says, I indeed am of Paul,

**13** Ἐγὼ δὲ Ἀπολλώ, Ἐγὼ δὲ Κηφᾶ, Ἐγὼ δὲ Χριστοῦ. μεμέ-
I and of Apollos, I and of Cephas, I and of Christ. Has
ρισται ὁ Χριστός; μὴ Παῦλος ἐσταυρώθη ὑπὲρ ὑμῶν, ἢ εἰς
been divided Christ?' Not Paul was crucified for you? Or in

**14** τὸ ὄνομα Παύλου ἐβαπτίσθητε; εὐχαριστῶ τῷ Θεῷ ὅτι·
the name of Paul were you baptized? I give thanks to God that

**15** οὐδένα ὑμῶν ἐβάπτισα, εἰ μὴ Κρίσπον καὶ Γάϊον· ἵνα μή τις
not one of you I baptized, except Crispus and Gaius; lest anyone

**16** εἴπῃ ὅτι εἰς τὸ ἐμὸν ὄνομα ἐβάπτισα. ἐβάπτισα δὲ καὶ τὸν Στε-
should say that in my name you were baptized. I baptized And also the of

**17** φανᾶ οἶκον· λοιπὸν οὐκ οἶδα εἴ τινα ἄλλον ἐβάπτισα. οὐ γὰρ
Steph-house. For the rest not I know if any other I baptized. not For
anas
ἀπέστειλέ με Χριστὸς βαπτίζειν, ἀλλ' εὐαγγελίζεσθαι· οὐκ
sent me Christ to baptize, but to preach the gospel, not
ἐν σοφίᾳ λόγου, ἵνα μὴ κενωθῇ ὁ σταυρὸς τοῦ Χριστοῦ.
in wisdom of words, lest be nullified the cross of Christ.

**18** Ὁ λόγος γὰρ ὁ τοῦ σταυροῦ τοῖς. μὲν ἀπολλυμένοις
the word For of the cross to those truly perishing
μωρία ἐστί, τοῖς δὲ σωζομένοις ἡμῖν δύναμις Θεοῦ ἐστι.
foolishness is; to those and being saved to us (the) power of God is.

**19** γέγραπται γάρ, Ἀπολῶ τὴν σοφίαν τῶν σοφῶν, καὶ τὴν
it has been written For, I will destroy the wisdom of the wise, and the

**20** σύνεσιν τῶν συνετῶν ἀθετήσω. ποῦ σοφός; ποῦ γραμ-
understanding of the perceiving I will set aside. Where (the) wise? Where (the)
ματεύς; ποῦ συζητητὴς τοῦ αἰῶνος τούτου; οὐχὶ ἐμώ-
scribe? Where (the) disputer age of this? Did not make

**21** ρανεν ὁ Θεὸς τὴν σοφίαν του κόσμου τούτου; ἐπειδὴ γὰρ
foolish God the wisdom of world this? since For,
ἐν τῇ σοφίᾳ τοῦ Θεοῦ οὐκ ἔγνω ὁ κόσμος διὰ τῆς σοφίας τὸν
in the wisdom of God, not knew the world through the wisdom —
Θεόν, εὐδόκησεν ὁ Θεὸς διὰ τῆς μωρίας τοῦ κηρύγματος
God, was pleased God through the foolishness of preaching

**22** σῶσαι τοὺς πιστεύοντας. ἐπειδὴ καὶ Ἰουδαῖοι σημεῖον
to save those believing. since And Jews ask

**23** αἰτοῦσι, καὶ Ἕλληνες σοφίαν ζητοῦσιν· ἡμεῖς δὲ κηρύσσομεν
a sign and Greeks wisdom seek, we but preach
Χριστὸν ἐσταυρωμένον, Ἰουδαίοις μὲν σκάνδαλον, Ἕλλησι
Christ having been crucified: to Jews indeed an offense; to Greeks

**24** δὲ μωρίαν· αὐτοῖς δὲ τοῖς κλητοῖς, Ἰουδαίοις τε καὶ Ἕλλησι,
and foolishness; to them but the called ones, to Jews both and to Greeks,

**25** Χριστὸν Θεοῦ δύναμιν καὶ Θεοῦ σοφίαν. ὅτι τὸ μωρὸν τοῦ
Christ of God (the) power and of God (the) wisdom. For the foolish thing
Θεοῦ σοφώτερον τῶν ἀνθρώπων ἐστί, καὶ τὸ ἀσθενὲς τοῦ
of God wiser (than) men is; and the weak thing
Θεοῦ ἰσχυρότερον τῶν ἀνθρώπων ἐστί.
of God stronger (than) men is.

**26** Βλέπετε γὰρ τὴν κλῆσιν ὑμῶν, ἀδελφοί, ὅτι οὐ πολλοὶ
you see For the calling of you, brothers, that not many
σοφοὶ κατὰ σάρκα, οὐ πολλοὶ δυνατοί, οὐ πολλοὶ εὐγενεῖς·
wise ones as to flesh, not many powerful, not many well born;

**27** ἀλλὰ τὰ μωρὰ τοῦ κόσμου ἐξελέξατο ὁ Θεός, ἵνα τοὺς
but the foolish things of the world chose God, that the

might be put to shame; and God chose the weak things of the world so that He might put to shame the strong things; [28] and God chose the low-born of the world, and the despised, and the things that are not so that He might bring to nothing the things that are; [29] so that no flesh might glory in His presence. [30] But of Him you are in Christ Jesus, who was made to us wisdom from God, and righteousness, and sanctification, and redemption; [31] so that, even as it has been written, "He that glories, let him glory in (the) Lord."

## CHAPTER 2

[1] And when I came to you, brothers, I did not come with excellency of word or wisdom, declaring to you the testimony of God. [2] For I decided not to know anything among you except Jesus Christ and Him crucified. [3] And I was with you in weakness and in fear and in much trembling. [4] And my word and my preaching (was) not in moving words of human wisdom, but in proof of the Spirit and of power; [5] that your faith might not be in wisdom of men, but in power of God.

[6] But we speak wisdom among the perfect; but not the wisdom of this age, nor of the rulers of this age, those being brought to nothing. [7] But we speak (the) wisdom of God in a mystery having been hidden, which God predetermined before the ages for our glory; [8] which none of the rulers of this age has known; for if they had known, they had not crucified the Lord of glory. [9] but according as it has been written, "Eye has not seen and ear has not heard," nor has it entered into the heart of man, "the things which God has prepared for those that love Him." [10] But God revealed (them) to us by His Spirit; for the Spirit searches all things, even the depths of God. [11] For who among men knows the

**28** σοφοὺς καταισχύνῃ· καὶ τὰ ἀσθενῆ τοῦ κόσμου ἐξελέξατο ὁ
wise might be shamed; and the weak things of the world chose

Θεός, ἵνα καταισχύνῃ τὰ ἰσχυρά· καὶ τὰ ἀγενῆ τοῦ κόσμου
God, that He might shame the strong things; and the base things of the world

καὶ τὰ ἐξουθενημένα ἐξελέξατο ὁ Θεός, καὶ τὰ μὴ ὄντα, ἵνα
and the things despised chose God, and the things not being, that

**29** τὰ ὄντα καταργήσῃ· ὅπως μὴ καυχήσηται πᾶσα σὰρξ
the things being He nullify; so as not might boast all flesh

**30** ἐνώπιον αὐτοῦ. ἐξ αὐτοῦ δὲ ὑμεῖς ἐστε ἐν Χριστῷ Ἰησοῦ,
before Him. of Him And you are in Christ Jesus,

ὃς ἐγενήθη ἡμῖν σοφία ἀπὸ Θεοῦ, δικαιοσύνη τε καὶ
who became to us wisdom from God, righteousness both and

**31** ἁγιασμός, καὶ ἀπολύτρωσις· ἵνα, καθὼς γέγραπται, Ὁ
sanctification and redemption; that even as has been written: Those

καυχώμενος, ἐν Κυρίῳ καυχάσθω.
boasting, in (the) Lord let him boast

## CHAPTER 2

**1** Κἀγὼ ἐλθὼν πρὸς ὑμᾶς, ἀδελφοί, ἦλθον οὐ καθ᾽ ὑπεροχὴν
And I coming to you, brothers, came not according to excellence

λόγου ἢ σοφίας καταγγέλλων ὑμῖν τὸ μαρτύριον τοῦ Θεοῦ.
of word or wisdom, announcing to you the testimony of God.

**2** οὐ γὰρ ἔκρινα τοῦ εἰδέναι τι ἐν ὑμῖν, εἰ μὴ Ἰησοῦν Χριστόν,
not For I decided to know anything among you, except Jesus Christ,

**3** καὶ τοῦτον ἐσταυρωμένον. καὶ ἐγὼ ἐν ἀσθενείᾳ καὶ ἐν φόβῳ
and this (One) having been crucified. And I in weakness and in fear

**4** καὶ ἐν τρόμῳ πολλῷ ἐγενόμην πρὸς ὑμᾶς. καὶ ὁ λόγος μου
and in trembling much was with you. And the word of me

καὶ τὸ κήρυγμά μου οὐκ ἐν πειθοῖς ἀνθρωπίνης σοφίας
and the preaching of me not in persuasive of human wisdom

**5** λόγοις, ἀλλ᾽ ἐν ἀποδείξει πνεύματος καὶ δυνάμεως· ἵνα ἡ
words but in proof of (the) Spirit and of power; that the

πίστις ὑμῶν μὴ ᾖ ἐν σοφίᾳ ἀνθρώπων, ἀλλ᾽ ἐν δυνάμει Θεοῦ.
faith of you not be in wisdom of men, but in power of God.

**6** Σοφίαν δὲ λαλοῦμεν ἐν τοῖς τελείοις· σοφίαν δὲ οὐ τοῦ
wisdom But we speak among the perfect; the wisdom but not—

αἰῶνος τούτου, οὐδὲ τῶν ἀρχόντων τοῦ αἰῶνος τούτου,
age of this, neither of the rulers — age of this.

**7** τῶν καταργουμένων· ἀλλὰ λαλοῦμεν σοφίαν Θεοῦ ἐν μυστη-
those being brought to nothing; but we speak a wisdom of God in mystery,

ρίῳ, τὴν ἀποκεκρυμμένην, ἣν προώρισεν ὁ Θεὸς πρὸ τῶν
— having been hidden, which predetermined God before the

**8** αἰώνων εἰς δόξαν ἡμῶν· ἣν οὐδεὶς τῶν ἀρχόντων τοῦ αἰῶνος
ages for glory of us; which not one of the rulers — age

τούτου ἔγνωκεν· εἰ γὰρ ἔγνωσαν, οὐκ ἂν τὸν Κύριον τῆς
of this has known; if for they knew, not the Lord —

**9** δόξης ἐσταύρωσαν· ἀλλὰ καθὼς γέγραπται, Ἃ ὀφθαλμὸς
of glory they had crucified. But even as it has been written: Things that eye

οὐκ εἶδε, καὶ οὓς οὐκ ἤκουσε, καὶ ἐπὶ καρδίαν ἀνθρώπου οὐκ
did not see, and ear not did hear, and on the heart of man not

**10** ἀνέβη, ἃ ἡτοίμασεν ὁ Θεὸς τοῖς ἀγαπῶσιν αὐτόν. ἡμῖν δὲ ὁ
came up, how prepared God those loving Him. to us But

Θεὸς ἀπεκάλυψε διὰ τοῦ πνεύματος αὐτοῦ· τὸ γὰρ πνεῦμα
God revealed through the Spirit of Him, the for Spirit

**11** πάντα ἐρευνᾷ, καὶ τὰ βάθη τοῦ Θεοῦ. τίς γὰρ οἶδεν ἀνθρώ-
all things searches, even the deep things of God. who For knows of men

things of a man, except the spirit of a man within him? So also no one has known the things of God except the Spirit of God. [12] But we have not received the spirit of the world, but the Spirit from God, that we may know the things freely given to us by God; [13] which things we also speak, not in words taught in human wisdom, but in (words) taught of (the) Holy Spirit, comparing spiritual things with spiritual (things). [14] But a natural man receives not the things of (the) Spirit of God, for they are foolishness to him; and he is not able to know, because they are spiritually discerned. [15] But the spiritual one discerns all things, but he is discerned by no one. [16] For who knew (the) mind of (the) Lord? Who will teach Him? But we have (the) mind of Christ.

CHAPTER 3

[1] And, brothers, I was not able to speak to you as to spiritual ones, but as to fleshly, as to babes in Christ. [2] I gave you milk to drink and not food, for you were not then able; but neither now are you yet able; [3] for you are yet fleshly. For among you (is) jealousy and where among you (is) jealousy and strife and divisions, are you not fleshly and walk according to man? [4] For when one may say, I am of Paul, and another, I of Apollos, are you not fleshly? [5] Who then is Paul? And who Apollos? But ministers through whom you believed, and to each as the Lord gave. [6] I planted, Apollos watered; but God made to grow. [7] So as neither he planting is anything, nor he watering, but God making grow. [8] So he planting and he watering are one, and each one will receive (his) own reward according to (his) own labor. [9] For we are fellow-workers, a field of God, a building of God you are. [10] According to God's grace given to me, as

---

**12**

πων τὰ τοῦ ἀνθρώπου, εἰ μὴ τὸ πνεῦμα τοῦ ἀνθρώπου τὸ ἐν
the things   of a man,   except the spirit   of a man   in

αὐτῷ; οὕτω καὶ τὰ τοῦ Θεοῦ οὐδεὶς οἶδεν, εἰ μὴ τὸ Πνεῦμα
him?   So also the things of God no one has known except the Spirit

τοῦ Θεοῦ. ἡμεῖς δὲ οὐ τὸ πνεῦμα τοῦ κόσμου ἐλάβομεν, ἀλλὰ
of God.   we And not the spirit   of the world   received,   but

τὸ πνεῦμα τὸ ἐκ τοῦ Θεοῦ, ἵνα εἰδῶμεν τὰ ὑπὸ τοῦ Θεοῦ
the Spirit   from   God, that we may know the things by   God

**13**

χαρισθέντα ἡμῖν. ἃ καὶ λαλοῦμεν, οὐκ ἐν διδακτοῖς ἀνθρω-
freely given   to us; which things also we speak, not in   taught   of

πίνης σοφίας λόγοις, ἀλλ' ἐν διδακτοῖς Πνεύματος Ἁγίου,
human wisdom   words,   but in (words) taught of (the) Spirit   Holy,

**14**

πνευματικοῖς πνευματικὰ συγκρίνοντες. ψυχικὸς δὲ ἄνθρω-
with spiritual things spiritual things   comparing.   a natural But   man

πος οὐ δέχεται τὰ τοῦ Πνεύματος τοῦ Θεοῦ· μωρία γὰρ
not receives the things of (the) Spirit   of God; foolishness for

αὐτῷ ἐστι, καὶ οὐ δύναται γνῶναι, ὅτι πνευματικῶς ἀνακρί-
to him they are; and not he is able to know, because spiritually   they are dis-

**15**

νεται. ὁ δὲ πνευματικὸς ἀνακρίνει μὲν πάντα, αὐτὸς δὲ ὑπ'
cerned. the But spiritual one   discerns indeed all things,   he   but by

**16**

οὐδενὸς ἀνακρίνεται. τίς γὰρ ἔγνω νοῦν Κυρίου, ὃς συμβιβά-
no one   is discerned. who For knew (the) mind of Lord, who will teach

σει αὐτόν; ἡμεῖς δὲ νοῦν Χριστοῦ ἔχομεν.
Him?   we But (the) mind of Christ   have.

## CHAPTER 3

**1**

Καὶ ἐγώ, ἀδελφοί, οὐκ ἠδυνήθην λαλῆσαι ὑμῖν ὡς πνευ-
And I,   brothers,   not was able   to speak   to you as spiritual

**2**

ματικοῖς, ἀλλ' ὡς σαρκικοῖς, ὡς νηπίοις ἐν Χριστῷ. γάλα
ones,   but as to fleshly,   as to infants   in   Christ.   milk

ὑμᾶς ἐπότισα, καὶ οὐ βρῶμα· οὔπω γὰρ ἠδύνασθε, ἀλλ'
you I gave to drink, and not   food, not then for   you were able,   but

**3**

οὔτε ἔτι νῦν δύνασθε· ἔτι γὰρ σαρκικοί ἐστε· ὅπου γὰρ ἐν
neither yet now are you able; still for   fleshly   you are. where For among

ὑμῖν ζῆλος καὶ ἔρις καὶ διχοστασίαι, οὐχὶ σαρκικοί ἐστε,
you (is) jealousy and strife and   divisions,   not   fleshly   are you,

**4**

καὶ κατὰ ἄνθρωπον περιπατεῖτε; ὅταν γὰρ λέγῃ τις, Ἐγὼ
and according to man   walk?   when For may say one,   I

μέν εἰμι Παύλου, ἕτερος δέ, Ἐγὼ Ἀπολλώ, οὐχὶ σαρκικοί
truly am of Paul,   another and,   I   of Apollos, not   fleshly

**5**

ἐστε; τίς οὖν ἐστι Παῦλος, τίς δὲ Ἀπολλώς ἀλλ' ἢ διάκονοι
are you? What then is   Paul;   what and   Apollos? But   ministers

**6**

δι' ὧν ἐπιστεύσατε, καὶ ἑκάστῳ ὡς ὁ Κύριος ἔδωκεν; ἐγὼ
through whom you believed, and to each as the Lord   gave.   I

**7**

ἐφύτευσα, Ἀπολλὼς ἐπότισεν, ἀλλ' ὁ Θεὸς ηὔξανεν. ὥστε
planted,   Apollos   watered,   but   God made to grow. So as

οὔτε ὁ φυτεύων ἐστί τι, οὔτε ὁ ποτίζων, ἀλλ' ὁ αὐξάνων.
neither he planting is anything, nor he watering,   but   He making grow,

**8**

Θεός. ὁ φυτεύων δὲ καὶ ὁ ποτίζων ἕν εἰσιν· ἕκαστος δὲ τὸν
God. he planting So and he watering   one are, each one   and   the

**9**

ἴδιον μισθὸν λήψεται κατὰ τὸν ἴδιον κόπον. Θεοῦ γάρ ἐσμεν
own reward will receive according to the own labor. of God For we are

συνεργοί· Θεοῦ γεώργιον, Θεοῦ οἰκοδομή ἐστε.
fellow-workers; Of God, a field;   of God a building you are.

**10**

Κατὰ τὴν χάριν τοῦ Θεοῦ τὴν δοθεῖσάν μοι, ὡς σοφὸς
According to the grace   of God   given   to me,   as   a wise

builds; but let each be careful how be builds. [11] For no other foundation can anyone lay except that which is laid, which is Jesus the Christ. [12] Now if anyone build on this foundation gold, silver, precious stones, wood, grass, straw, [13] the work of each will be revealed; for the Day will make (it) known, because it is revealed in fire; and the fire will prove the work of each, what sort it is. [14] If the work of any one which he built remains, he shall receive a reward. [15] If the word of anyone shall be consumed, he shall suffer loss, but himself shall be saved, but so as through fire. [16] Do you not know that you are God's temple, and the Spirit of God dwells in you? [17] If anyone corrupt the temple of God, God shall bring him to corruption; for the temple of God is holy, which you are. [18] Let no one deceive himself; if anyone thinks (him) to be wise among you in this age, let him become foolish, that he may be wise. [19] For the wisdom of this world is foolishness with God; for it has been written, "He takes the wise in their own craftiness." [20] And again, "(The) Lord knows the thoughts of the wise, that they are worthless." [21] So let no man glory in men; for all things are yours, [22] whether Paul, or Apollos, or Peter, or the world, or life, or death, or things present, or things to come; all are yours, [23] and you are Christ's, and Christ is God's.

ἀρχιτέκτων θεμέλιον τέθεικα, ἄλλος δὲ ἐποικοδομεῖ. ἕκαστος
master builder a foundation I laid, another but builds on (it). each one

**11** δὲ βλεπέτω πῶς ἐποικοδομεῖ. θεμέλιον γὰρ ἄλλον οὐδεὶς
But let him look how he builds on(it). foundation For other no one
δύναται θεῖναι παρὰ τὸν κείμενον, ὅς ἐστιν Ἰησοῦς ὁ
is able to lay beside the (One) being laid, who is Jesus the

**12** Χριστός. εἰ δέ τις ἐποικοδομεῖ ἐπὶ τὸν θεμέλιον τοῦτον
Christ. if And anyone builds on foundation this
χρυσόν, ἄργυρον, λίθους τιμίους, ξύλα, χόρτον, καλάμην,
gold, silver, stones precious, woods, hay, stubble,

**13** ἐκάστου τὸ ἔργον φανερὸν γενήσεται· ἡ γὰρ ἡμέρα δηλώσει,
of each one the work manifest will be; the for day will declare,
ὅτι ἐν πυρὶ ἀποκαλύπτεται· καὶ ἑκάστου τὸ ἔργον ὁποῖόν
for by fire it is revealed, and of each one the work of what sort

**14** ἐστι τὸ πῦρ δοκιμάσει. εἴ τινος τὸ ἔργον μένει ὃ ἐπῳκοδό-
it is, the fire it will prove. If of someone the work remains, which he built

**15** μησε, μισθὸν λήψεται. εἴ τινος τὸ ἔργον κατακαήσεται,
on, a reward he will receive. If anyone the work will be consumed,
ζημιωθήσεται· αὐτὸς δὲ σωθήσεται, οὕτω δὲ ὡς διὰ πυρός.
he will suffer loss, he but will be saved, so but as through fire.

**16** Οὐκ οἴδατε ὅτι ναὸς Θεοῦ ἐστε, καὶ τὸ Πνεῦμα τοῦ Θεοῦ
Do not you know that a temple of God you are, and the Spirit of God

**17** οἰκεῖ ἐν ὑμῖν; εἴ τις τὸν ναὸν τοῦ Θεοῦ φθείρει. φθερεῖ
dwells in you? If anyone the temple of God corrupts, will corrupt
τοῦτον ὁ Θεός· ὁ γὰρ ναὸς τοῦ Θεοῦ ἅγιός ἐστιν, οἵτινές
this one God. the For temple of God holy is, who
ἐστε ὑμεῖς.
are you.

**18** Μηδεὶς ἑαυτὸν ἐξαπατάτω· εἴ τις δοκεῖ σοφὸς εἶναι ἐν
No one himself let deceive; if anyone thinks wise to be among
ὑμῖν ἐν τῷ αἰῶνι τούτῳ, μωρὸς γενέσθω, ἵνα γένηται σοφός.
you in age this, foolish let him become, that he become wise.

**19** ἡ γὰρ σοφία τοῦ κόσμου τούτου μωρία παρὰ τῷ Θεῷ ἐστι.
the For wisdom world of this foolishness with God is.
γέγραπται γάρ, Ὁ δρασσόμενος τοὺς σοφοὺς ἐν τῇ πανουρ-
it has been written For: He (is) taking the wise in the craftiness

**20** γίᾳ αὐτῶν. καὶ πάλιν, Κύριος γινώσκει τοὺς διαλογισμοὺς
of them. And again: (The) Lord knows the reasonings

**21** τῶν σοφῶν, ὅτι εἰσὶ μάταιοι. ὥστε μηδεὶς καυχάσθω ἐν
of the wise, that they are vain. So as no one let boast in

**22** ἀνθρώποις· πάντα γὰρ ὑμῶν ἐστιν, εἴτε Παῦλος, εἴτε
men; all things for of you is, whether Paul, or
Ἀπολλώς, εἴτε Κηφᾶς, εἴτε κόσμος, εἴτε ζωή, εἴτε θάνατος
Apollos, or Cephas, or (the) world, or life, or death,

**23** εἴτε ἐνεστῶτα, εἴτε μέλλοντα· πάντα ὑμῶν ἐστιν, ὑμεῖς δὲ
or things present, or things coming, all things of you are, you and
Χριστοῦ, Χριστὸς δὲ Θεοῦ.
of Christ, Christ and of God.

## CHAPTER 4

**CHAPTER 4**
[1] Let a man think of us as ministers of Christ and keepers of the mysteries of God. [2] But as to the rest, it is necessary in managers one must be found faithful. [3] But to me it is a very

**1** Οὕτως ἡμᾶς λογιζέσθω ἄνθρωπος, ὡς ὑπηρέτας Χριστοῦ
So us let count a man as ministers of Christ,
καὶ οἰκονόμους μυστηρίων Θεοῦ. ὃ δὲ λοιπόν, ζητεῖται ἐν

**2** and stewards of (the) mysteries of God. the And rest, it is sought among
τοῖς οἰκονόμοις, ἵνα πιστός τις εὑρεθῇ. ἐμοὶ δὲ εἰς ἐλάχιστόν

**3** — stewards, that faithful anyone be found. to me And for a little thing small thing that I should be judged by you, or by man's day. But neither do I judge myself. [4] For I am aware of nothing of myself; but I have not been justified by this, but He who judges me is (the) Lord. [5] Then do not judge anything before the time, until the Lord may have come, who both will bring to light the hidden things of darkness, and will reveal the thoughts of all hearts; and then shall each one have praise from God.

[6] Now these things, brothers, I transferred to myself and Apollos on account of you, that in us you may learn not to think above what has been written, that you not (be) puffed up one over the other. [7] For who makes you to differ? And what do you have that you did not receive? And if you received, why do you boast as (if) not receiving? [8] You are already satisfied; you already became rich. You reigned without us; and oh that you did reign, that we also may reign with you. [9] For I think that God set out us last, the apostles, as appointed to death. For we became a spectacle to the world, even to angels and to men, [10] We (are) fools for the sake of Christ, but you (are) prudent in Christ; we (are) weak, but you strong; you (are) honored, but we not honored. [11] Until the present hour we hunger, and thirst, and are naked, and are buffeted, and wander homeless, [12] and labor, working with our own hands. Cursed, we bless; persecuted, we bear; [13] defamed, we beg — we are become as (the) filth of the world, (the) dirt wiped off by all until now. [14] I do not write these things shaming you, but as my beloved children I warn (you). [15] For if you should have ten thousand teachers in Christ, yet not many fathers; for I fathered you in Christ Jesus through the gospel. [16] So I urge you,

ἐστιν ἵνα ὑφ' ὑμῶν ἀνακριθῶ, ἢ ὑπὸ ἀνθρωπίνης ἡμέρας·
it is  that by    you I am judged, or by    a man's     day;

4 ἀλλ' οὐδὲ ἐμαυτὸν ἀνακρίνω. οὐδὲν γὰρ ἐμαυτῷ σύνοιδα,
but   not    myself   I judge;   nothing for against myself I know,

ἀλλ' οὐκ ἐν τούτῳ δεδικαίωμαι· ὁ δὲ ἀνακρίνων με Κύριός
but  not by   this  have I been justified; He but judging   me   Lord

5 ἐστιν. ὥστε μὴ πρὸ καιροῦ τι κρίνετε, ἕως ἂν ἔλθῃ ὁ Κύριος,
is.    So as not before time anything judge, until   comes the Lord,

ὃς καὶ φωτίσει τὰ κρυπτὰ τοῦ σκότους, καὶ φανερώσει τὰς
who both will shed light on the hidden things of darkness, and will reveal the

βουλὰς τῶν καρδιῶν· καὶ τότε ὁ ἔπαινος γενήσεται ἑκάστῳ
counsels of the  hearts;  and then the praise   will be   to each one

ἀπὸ τοῦ Θεοῦ.
from    God.

6 Ταῦτα δέ, ἀδελφοί, μετεσχημάτισα εἰς ἐμαυτὸν καὶ
these things And, brothers,  I transferred    to   myself   and

Ἀπολλὼ δι' ὑμᾶς, ἵνα ἐν ἡμῖν μάθητε τὸ μὴ ὑπὲρ ὃ γέγρα-
Apollos because of you, that in us you may learn  not above what has been

πται φρονεῖν, ἵνα μὴ εἷς ὑπὲρ τοῦ ἑνὸς φυσιοῦσθε κατὰ τοῦ
written to think, that not one over    one you are puffed up against the

7 ἑτέρου. τίς γὰρ σε διακρίνει ; τί δὲ ἔχεις ὃ οὐκ ἔλαβες ; εἰ δὲ
other.  who For you makes differ? what And have you, not you received? if

8 καὶ ἔλαβες, τί καυχᾶσαι ὡς μὴ λαβών ; ἤδη κεκορεσμένοι
And you received, why boast you as not receiving? Already  being sated

ἐστέ, ἤδη ἐπλουτήσατε, χωρὶς ἡμῶν ἐβασιλεύσατε· καὶ
you are; already you became rich; without us   you reigned;   and

ὄφελόν γε ἐβασιλεύσατε, ἵνα καὶ ἡμεῖς ὑμῖν συμβασιλεύσω-
oh that really you did reign, that also we   you might reign with.

9 μεν. δοκῶ γὰρ ὅτι ὁ Θεὸς ἡμᾶς τοὺς ἀποστόλους ἐσχάτους
I think For that   God  us,   the   apostles,   last

ἀπέδειξεν ὡς ἐπιθανατίους· ὅτι θέατρον ἐγενήθημεν τῷ
set out,   as  appointed to death, because a spectacle we became to the

10 κόσμῳ, καὶ ἀγγέλοις, καὶ ἀνθρώποις. ἡμεῖς μωροὶ διὰ
world, and  to angels  and  to men.    We (are) fools because of

Χριστόν, ὑμεῖς δὲ φρόνιμοι ἐν Χριστῷ· ἡμεῖς ἀσθενεῖς, ὑμεῖς
Christ,  you but prudent  in  Christ;  we (are) weak,   you

11 δὲ ἰσχυροί ὑμεῖς ἔνδοξοι, ἡμεῖς δὲ ἄτιμοι. ἄχρι τῆς ἄρτι
but strong;  you (are) honored, we but unhonored. Until the present

ὥρας καὶ πεινῶμεν, καὶ διψῶμεν, καὶ γυμνητεύομεν, καὶ
hour both we hunger, and thirst,   and  are naked,    and

12 κολαφιζόμεθα, καὶ ἀστατοῦμεν, καὶ κοπιῶμεν ἐργαζομενοι
are buffeted, and wander homeless, and  labor,    working

ταῖς ἰδίαις χερσί· λοιδορούμενοι εὐλογοῦμεν· διωκόμενοι
with the own hands.  Cursed,    we bless;    persecuted

13 ἀνεχόμεθα· βλασφημούμενοι παρακαλοῦμεν· ὡς περικαθάρ-
we bear;   evilly spoken to,   we beg;    as   filth

ματα τοῦ κόσμου ἐγενήθημεν, πάντων περίψημα ἕως ἄρτι.
of the  world, we are become; of all   dirt wiped off until now.

Οὐκ ἐντρέπων ὑμᾶς γράφω ταῦτα, ἀλλ' ὡς τέκνα μου
not  shaming   you   I write these things, but  as  children of me

15 ἀγαπητὰ νουθετῶ. ἐὰν γὰρ μυρίους παιδαγωγοὺς ἔχητε ἐν
beloved  warning.  if For myriads   teachers    you have in

Χριστῷ, ἀλλ' οὐ πολλοὺς πατέρας· ἐν γὰρ Χριστῷ Ἰησοῦ
Christ,  yet not  many   fathers;  in for  Christ  Jesus

16 διὰ τοῦ εὐαγγελίου· ἐγὼ ὑμᾶς ἐγέννησα. παρακαλῶ οὖν
through the gospel   I   you   fathered.   I urge    then,

be imitators of me.

[17] On account of this I sent Timothy to you, who is my beloved child and faithful in (the) Lord, who will remind you of my ways that (are) in Christ, according as I everywhere teach in every church. [18] As to my not coming to you now, some were puffed up; [19] but I shall come shortly to you, if the Lord will, and I will not know the word of those who are puffed up, but the power. [20] For the kingdom of God (is) not in word, but in power. [21] What do you desire? that I should come to you with a rod, or in love and a spirit of meekness?

CHAPTER 5

[1] (It) is commonly reported (there is) fornication among you, and such fornication which not even is named in the nations, so as one to have (his) father's wife. [2] And you are puffed up, and did not rather mourn, that he who did this deed might be taken out of your midst. [3] For I as being absent in body, but being present in spirit, already have judged him who had done this thing, as though I were present. [4] In the name of our Lord Jesus Christ — you being gathered together with my spirit, with the power of our Lord Jesus Christ — [5] to deliver such a son to Satan for destruction of the flesh, that the spirit may be saved in the day of the Lord Jesus. [6] Your boasting (is) not good. Do you not know that a little leaven leavens the whole lump. [7] Therefore purge out the old leaven so that you may be a new lump, according as you are unleavened. For also Christ our Passover was sacrificed for us. [8] So that we should keep the feast, not with old leaven, nor with leaven of malice and wickedness, but with unleavened (bread) of sincerity and truth.

[9] I wrote to you in the letter not to associate

**17** ὑμᾶς, μιμηταί μου γίνεσθε. διὰ τοῦτο ἔπεμψα ὑμῖν Τιμόθεον,
you, imitators of me become. Because of this I sent to you Timothy,

ὅς ἐστι τέκνον μου ἀγαπητὸν καὶ πιστὸν ἐν Κυρίῳ, ὃς ὑμᾶς
who is a child of me, beloved and faithful in (the) Lord, who you

ἀναμνήσει τὰς ὁδούς μου τὰς ἐν Χριστῷ, καθὼς πανταχοῦ
will remind (of) the ways of me in Christ, as everywhere

**18** ἐν πάσῃ ἐκκλησίᾳ διδάσκω. ὡς μὴ ἐρχομένου δέ μου πρὸς
in every church I teach. When not coming now me to

**19** ὑμᾶς ἐφυσιώθησάν τινες. ἐλεύσομαι δὲ ταχέως πρὸς ὑμᾶς,
you were puffed up some. I will come But shortly to you,

ἐὰν ὁ Κύριος θελήσῃ, καὶ γνώσομαι οὐ τὸν λόγον τῶν
if the Lord wills, and I will know not the word of those

**20** πεφυσιωμένων, ἀλλὰ τὴν δύναμιν. οὐ γὰρ ἐν λόγῳ ἡ
having been puffed up, but the power. not For in word the

**21** βασιλεία τοῦ Θεοῦ, ἀλλ' ἐν δυνάμει. τί θέλετε ; ἐν ῥάβδῳ
kingdom of God, but in power. What desire you? With a rod

ἔλθω πρὸς ὑμᾶς, ἢ ἐν ἀγάπῃ πνεύματί τε πραότητος ;
I come to you, or in love, a spirit and of meekness?

## CHAPTER 5

**1** Ὅλως ἀκούεται ἐν ὑμῖν πορνεία, καὶ τοιαύτη πορνεία,
Everywhere (it) is heard among you fornication, and such fornication,

ἥτις οὐδὲ ἐν τοῖς ἔθνεσιν ὀνομάζεται, ὥστε γυναῖκά τινα
which (is) not among the nations named, so as (the) wife one

**2** τοῦ πατρὸς ἔχειν. καὶ ὑμεῖς πεφυσιωμένοι ἐστέ, καὶ οὐχὶ
of the father to have. And you having been puffed up are, and not

μᾶλλον ἐπενθήσατε, ἵνα ἐξαρθῇ ἐκ μέσου ὑμῶν ὁ τὸ ἔργον
rather mourned, that might be taken from your midst he deed

**3** τοῦτο ποιήσας. ἐγὼ μὲν γὰρ ὡς ἀπὼν τῷ σώματι παρὼν
this did. I indeed For as being absent in the body, but present

δὲ τῷ πνεύματι, ἤδη κέκρικα ὡς παρών, τὸν οὕτω τοῦτο
in the spirit, already have judged as being present he thus this thing

**4** κατεργασάμενον, ἐν τῷ ὀνόματι τοῦ Κυρίου ἡμῶν Ἰησοῦ
having worked out. In the name of the Lord of us, Jesus

Χριστοῦ, συναχθέντων ὑμῶν καὶ τοῦ ἐμοῦ πνεύματος, σὺν
Christ, being gathered together you and the of me spirit, with

**5** τῇ δυνάμει τοῦ Κυρίου ἡμῶν Ἰησοῦ Χριστοῦ, παραδοῦναι
the power of the Lord of us, Jesus Christ, to deliver

τὸν τοιοῦτον τῷ Σατανᾷ εἰς ὄλεθρον τῆς σαρκός, ἵνα τὸ
such a one to Satan for destruction of the flesh, that the

**6** πνεῦμα σωθῇ ἐν τῇ ἡμέρᾳ τοῦ Κυρίου Ἰησοῦ. οὐ καλὸν τὸ
spirit may be saved in the day of the Lord Jesus. Not good (is) the

καύχημα ὑμῶν. οὐκ οἴδατε ὅτι μικρὰ ζύμη ὅλον τὸ φύραμα
boast of you. Do not you know that a little leaven all the lump

**7** ζυμοῖ ; ἐκκαθάρατε οὖν τὴν παλαιὰν ζύμην, ἵνα ἦτε νέον
leavens? purge out Then the old leaven, that you be a new

φύραμα, καθὼς ἐστε ἄζυμοι. καὶ γὰρ τὸ πάσχα ἡμῶν ὑπὲρ
lump, as you are unleavened. also For the Passover of us for

**8** ἡμῶν ἐθύθη Χριστός· ὥστε ἑορτάζωμεν, μὴ ἐν ζύμῃ παλαιᾷ,
us was sacrificed, Christ, so as let us keep feast, not with leaven old,

μηδὲ ἐν ζύμῃ κακίας καὶ πονηρίας, ἀλλ' ἐν ἀζύμοις εἰλι-
not with leaven of malice and of evil : but with unleavened of

κρινείας καὶ ἀληθείας.
sincerity and truth.

**9** Ἔγραψα ὑμῖν ἐν τῇ ἐπιστολῇ μὴ συναναμίγνυσθαι
I wrote to you in the epistle not to associate intimately

with fornicators; [10] and not altogether with the fornicators of this world, or with the covetous, or with plunderers, or with idolaters, since then you must go out of the world. [11] But now I wrote to you not to associate intimately with (him) if anyone being called a brother (is) a fornicator, or a coveter, or an idolater, or a reviler, or a drunk, or a plunderer: with such a For what to me to judge the (ones) outside? Do not you judge those inside? [13] But God will judge those outside. And you shall put out the evil one from yourselves.

**10** πόρνοις· καὶ οὐ πάντως τοῖς πόρνοις τοῦ κόσμου τούτου,
with fornicators, and not altogether with the fornicators　world　　of this,

ἢ τοῖς πλεονέκταις, ἢ ἅρπαξιν, ἢ εἰδωλολάτραις· ἐπεὶ
or with the covetous,　　or with plunderers, or with idolaters,　　since

**11** ὀφείλετε ἄρα ἐκ τοῦ κόσμου ἐξελθεῖν. νυνὶ δὲ ἔγραψα ὑμῖν
you ought　then out of the world　to go out.　now But I wrote　to you

μὴ συναναμίγνυσθαι, ἐάν τις ἀδελφὸς ὀνομαζόμενος ᾖ
not to associate　intimately　if anyone　a brother　　is called (is) either

πόρνος, ἢ πλεονέκτης, ἢ εἰδωλολάτρης, ἢ λοίδορος, ἢ
a fornicator, or a covetous,　　or　an idolator,　　　or　a reviler,　or

**12** μέθυσος, ἢ ἅρπαξ· τῷ τοιούτῳ μηδὲ συνεσθίειν. τί γάρ μοι
drunkard, or a plunderer, with such a one not to eat.　　what For to me

**13** καὶ τοὺς ἔξω κρίνειν; οὐχὶ τοὺς ἔσω ὑμεῖς κρίνετε; τοὺς δὲ
also those outside to judge? Do not those inside you　judge?　those But

ἔξω ὁ Θεὸς κρίνει. καὶ ἐξαρεῖτε τὸν πονηρὸν ἐξ ὑμῶν αὐτῶν.
outside God will judge. And you shall put out the evil one from　yourselves.

## CHAPTER 6

### CHAPTER 6

[1] Dares anyone of you having a matter against another go to law before the unjust, and not before the saints? [2] Do you not know that the saints will judge the world? And if the world is judged by you, are you unworthy of small judgments? [3] Or do you not know that we shall judge angels, not to speak of this life? [4] If, then, you truly have judgments of this life, those being least esteemed in the church, these sit. [5] I speak shame to you. So, is not a wise one among you, not even one who will be able to judge his brother in your midst? But brother is judged with brother, and this before unbelievers! [7] Already, then, a failure is with you all, that you have lawsuits with yourselves. Why do you not instead be wronged? Why not instead be cheated? [8] But you do wrong and cheat; and these things (to) brothers! [9] Or do you not know that unjust ones will not inherit the kingdom of God? Be not led astray; neither fornicators, nor idolaters, nor adulterers, nor abusers, nor homosexuals, [10] nor thieves nor covetous, nor drunks, nor revilers, nor plunderers, shall inherit (the) kingdom of God. [11] And some were these things; but you were washed; but you were sanctified; but you were justified, in the name of

**1** Τολμᾷ τις ὑμῶν, πρᾶγμα ἔχων πρὸς τὸν ἕτερον, κρίνεσθαι
Dares anyone of you a matter having against　another　to be judged

**2** ἐπὶ τῶν ἀδίκων, καὶ οὐχὶ ἐπὶ τῶν ἁγίων; ουκ οἴδατε ὅτι οἱ
before the unjust, and not before the saints? Do not you know that the

ἅγιοι τὸν κόσμον κρινοῦσι; καὶ εἰ ἐν ὑμῖν κρίνεται ὁ κόσμος,
saints the world　will judge? And if by you is judged　the world,

**3** ἀνάξιοί ἐστε κριτηρίων ἐλαχίστων; οὐκ οἴδατε ὅτι ἀγγέ-
unworthy are you judgments of small?　Do not you know that angels

**4** λους κρινοῦμεν; μήτι γε βιωτικά; βιωτικὰ μὲν οὖν κριτήρια
we will judge, not to speak of this life? Of this life truly then judgments

ἐὰν ἔχητε, τοὺς ἐξουθενημένους ἐν τῇ ἐκκλησίᾳ, τούτους·
if you have,　those being least esteemed in the　church,　these

**5** καθίζετε. πρὸς ἐντροπὴν ὑμῖν λέγω. οὕτως οὐκ ἔστιν ἐν
sit you.　For　shame　to you I say.　Thus,　not　is among

ὑμῖν σοφὸς οὐδὲ εἷς, ὃς δυνήσεται διακρῖναι ἀνὰ μέσον τοῦ
you a wise one, not one who will be able to discern　in your midst the

**6** ἀδελφοῦ αὐτοῦ, ἀλλὰ ἀδελφὸς μετὰ ἀδελφοῦ κρίνεται, καὶ
brother　of him? But　brother　with　brother　is judged, and

**7** τοῦτο ἐπὶ ἀπίστων; ἤδη μὲν οὖν ὅλως ἥττημα ἐν ὑμῖν ἐστιν,
this　before unbelievers. Already indeed, then all a failure with you　is,

ὅτι κρίματα ἔχετε μεθ' ἑαυτῶν. διατί οὐχὶ μᾶλλον ἀδικεῖσθε;
that lawsuits you have with yourselves. Why　not　instead be wronged?

**8** διατί οὐχὶ μᾶλλον ἀποστερεῖσθε; ἀλλὰ ὑμεῖς ἀδικεῖτε καὶ
Why　not　instead　be despoiled?　　But　you do wrong and

**9** ἀποστερεῖτε, καὶ ταῦτα ἀδελφούς. ἢ οὐκ οἴδατε ὅτι ἄδικοι
despoil,　and these things (to) brothers. Or not you know that unjust ones

βασιλείαν Θεοῦ οὐ κληρονομήσουσι; μὴ πλανᾶσθε· οὔτε
(the) kingdom of God not will inherit?　　Be not led astray;　not

πόρνοι, οὔτε εἰδωλολάτραι, οὔτε μοιχοί, οὔτε μαλακοί, οὔτε
fornicators, nor idolaters,　　nor adulterers,　nor abusers,　nor

**10** ἀρσενοκοῖται, οὔτε κλέπται, οὔτε πλεονέκται, οὔτε μέθυσοι,
homosexuals,　nor　thieves,　nor covetous ones,　nor drunkards,

οὐ λοίδοροι, οὐχ ἅρπαγες, βασιλείαν Θεοῦ οὐ κληρονομή-
not revilers,　not plunderers　(the) kingdom of God not shall

**11** σουσι. καὶ ταῦτά τινες ἦτε· ἀλλὰ ἀπελούσασθε, ἀλλὰ
inherit. And these things some were.　But　you were washed; but

ἡγιάσθητε, ἀλλ' ἐδικαιώθητε ἐν τῷ ὀνόματι τοῦ Κυρίου
you were sanctified; but you were justified in the name　of the　Lord

the Lord Jesus, and by the Spirit of our God.

[12] All things are lawful to me, but not all things do good; all things are lawful to me, but I will not be brought under the power of any. [13] Food for the belly, and the belly for food; but God will bring both this and these to nothing. But the body is not for fornication, but for the Lord; and the Lord for the body. [14] And God also raised up the Lord; and will raise us up through His power. [15] Do you know that your bodies are members of Christ? Then taking the members of Christ, shall I make (them) members of a harlot? Let it not be! [16] Or do you not know that he being joined to a harlot is one body? For He says, "The two (shall be) into one flesh." [17] But he being joined to the Lord is one spirit. [18] Flee fornication. Every sin which a man may do is outside the body, but he doing fornication sins against (his) own body. [19] Or do you not know that your body is a temple of the Holy Spirit in you, which you have from God; and you are not of yourselves? [20] You were bought with a price; then glorify God in your body, and in your spirit, which are of God.

CHAPTER 7

[1] But concerning what things you wrote to me: (It is) good for a man not to touch a woman; [2] but because of fornication let each have his own wife, and let each have her own husband. [3] Let the husband give due kindness to the wife, and likewise also the wife to the husband. [4] The wife does not have authority over her own body, but the husband; and likewise also the husband does not have authority over his own body, but the wife. [5] Do not defraud one another, unless by consent for a season, that you may be free for fasting and prayer. But come together again,·

Ἰησοῦ, καὶ ἐν τῷ Πνεύματι τοῦ Θεοῦ ἡμῶν.
Jesus,   and  in  the   Spirit   —    God of us.

12 Πάντα μοι ἔξεστιν, ἀλλ' οὐ πάντα συμφέρει· πάντα μοι
All things to me are lawful, but   not all things  contribute. All things to me
ἔξεστιν, ἀλλ' οὐκ ἐγὼ ἐξουσιασθήσομαι ὑπό τινος. τὰ
are lawful, but   not    I    will be ruled         by anyone.  —

13 βρώματα τῇ κοιλίᾳ, καὶ ἡ κοιλία τοῖς βρώμασιν· ὁ δὲ Θεὸς
Foods   for the belly, and the belly  — for foods;  but God
καὶ ·ταύτην καὶ ταῦτα καταργήσει. τὸ δὲ σῶμα οὐ τῇ
both  this  and  these  will destroy. the But body not(is)

14 πορνείᾳ, ἀλλὰ τῷ Κυρίῳ, καὶ ὁ Κύριος τῷ σώματι· ὁ δὲ
for fornication, but for the Lord, and the Lord for the body.  And
Θεὸς καὶ τὸν Κύριον ἤγειρε, καὶ ἡμᾶς ἐξεγερεῖ διὰ της
God also  the  Lord  raised,   and  us  will raise up through the

15 δυνάμεως αὐτοῦ. οὐκ οἴδατε ὅτι τὰ σώματα ὑμῶν μέλη
power     of Him. Do not you know that the   bodies  of you members
Χριστοῦ ἐστιν ; ἄρας οὖν τὰ μέλη τοῦ Χριστοῦ ποιήσω
of Christ are? having taken Then the members  of Christ, Shall I make

16 πόρνης μέλη ; μὴ γένοιτο. ἢ οὐκ οἴδατε ὅτι ὁ κολλώμενος τῇ
of a harlot members? Not let it be! Or not you know that he being joined
πόρνῃ ἓν σῶμά ἐστιν ; Ἔσονται γάρ, φησίν, οἱ δύο εἰς σάρκα
to a harlot one body  is?       will be  For, He says, the two into flesh

17 μίαν. ὁ δὲ κολλώμενος τῷ Κυρίῳ ἓν πνεῦμά ἐστι. φεύγετε τὴν
one. he But being joined to the  Lord one  spirit  is.    Flee   —
18 πορνείαν. πᾶν ἁμάρτημα ὃ ἐὰν ποιήσῃ ἄνθρωπος ἐκτὸς τοῦ
fornication. Every  sin    which if  may do  a man   outside  the
σώματός ἐστιν· ὁ δὲ πορνεύων εἰς τὸ ἴδιον σῶμα ἁμαρτάνει.
body    is,  he but doing fornication against the own body   sins.

19 ἢ οὐκ οἴδατε ὅτι τὸ σῶμα ὑμῶν ναὸς τοῦ ἐν ὑμῖν Ἁγίου
Or not you know that the  body  of you a temple of the in you  Holy
Πνεύματός ἐστιν, οὗ ἔχετε ἀπὸ Θεοῦ ; καὶ οὐκ ἐστὲ ἑαυτῶν,
Spirit    is, which you have from God;  and not are you of yourselves?

20 ἠγοράσθητε γὰρ τιμῆς· δοξάσατε δὴ τὸν Θεὸν ἐν τῷ σώματι
you were bought For of a price;  glorify then    God in the  body
ὑμῶν, καὶ ἐν τῷ πνεύματι ὑμῶν, ἅτινά ἐστι τοῦ Θεοῦ.
of you, and in the  spirit  of you, which  are  of God.

CHAPTER 7

1 Περὶ δὲ ὧν ἐγράψατέ μοι, καλὸν ἀνθρώπῳ γυναικὸς μὴ
concerning But what you wrote to me, (it is) good for a man  a woman  not
2 ἅπτεσθαι. διὰ δὲ τὰς πορνείας ἕκαστος τὴν ἑαυτοῦ γυναῖκα
to touch; because of but the fornications each one the of himself   wife
3 ἐχέτω, καὶ ἑκάστη τὸν ἴδιον ἄνδρα ἐχέτω. τῇ γυναικὶ ὁ ἀνὴρ
have;  and each one the own husband have. To the wife the husband
τὴν ὀφειλομένην εὔνοιαν ἀποδιδότω· ὁμοίως δὲ καὶ ἡ γυνὴ
due    kindness let pay;      likewise and  also the  wife
4 τῷ ἀνδρί. ἡ γυνὴ τοῦ ἰδίου σώματος οὐκ ἐξουσιάζει, ἀλλ'
to the husband.The wife of the own body   not has authority, but
ὁ ἀνήρ· ὁμοίως δὲ καὶ ὁ ἀνὴρ τοῦ ἰδίου σώματος οὐκ ἐξου-
the husband; likewise and also the husband the own body   not has
5 σιάζει, ἀλλ' ἡ γυνή. μὴ ἀποστερεῖτε ἀλλήλους, εἰ μή τι ἂν
authority, but the wife. Do not deprive   one another,   unless
ἐκ συμφώνου πρὸς καιρόν, ἵνα σχολάζητε τῇ νηστείᾳ καὶ
by agreement for  a time, that you may be free  for fasting and
τῇ προσευχῇ, καὶ πάλιν ἐπὶ τὸ αὐτὸ συνέρχησθε, ἵνα μὴ
for prayer;  and again   on the same come together, that not
(place)

that Satan may not tempt you because of your incontinence. [6] But I say this by way of permission, not by way of command. [7] But I wish all men to be even as myself; but each has his own gift from God; one in this way and another in that. [8] But I say to the unmarried and to the widows, it is good for them if they should remain as I. [9] But if they do not have self-control, let them marry; for it is better to marry than to burn. [10] But I command the married, not I, but the Lord, (the) wife not to be separated from (the) husband; [11] but if she also is separated, let her remain unmarried, or be reconciled to the husband; and (the) husband not to leave (the) wife. [12] But to the rest I say, not the Lord, If any brother has an unbelieving wife, and she consents to live with him, let him not leave her. [13] And a woman who has an unbelieving husband, and he consents to live with her, let her not leave him. [14] For the unbelieving husband has been sanctified in the wife, and the unbelieving wife is sanctified in the husband; else then your children (are) unclean; but now they are holy. [15] But if the unbelieving separates, let (them) be separated; the brother or the sister is not in bondage in such matters; but God has called us in peace. [16] For what do you know, wife, if you will save the husband? Or what do you know, husband, if you will save the wife? [17] Only to each as has divided God: each as the Lord has called, so let him walk. So I order in the churches.

[18] Was anyone called having been circumcised? Do not be uncircumcised. Was any called in uncircumcision? Do not be circumcised. [19] Circumcision is nothing, and uncircumcision is nothing, but the keeping of God's commands. [20] Each in the calling in which he was called, in this remain. [21] Were you called (as) a slave? It matters not to you. But if you are able to also be

**6** πειράζῃ ὑμᾶς ὁ Σατανᾶς διὰ τὴν ἀκρασίαν ὑμῶν. τοῦτο δὲ
may tempt you      Satan    through the incontinence of you.   this   And

**7** λέγω κατὰ συγγνώμην, οὐ κατ᾽ ἐπιταγήν. θέλω γὰρ
I say   by    permission,    not   by   command.  I desire For
πάντας ἀνθρώπους εἶναι ὡς καὶ ἐμαυτόν· ἀλλ᾽ ἕκαστος ἴδιον
all        men        to be as also  myself;   but   each one (the) own
χάρισμα ἔχει ἐκ Θεοῦ, ὃς μὲν οὕτως, ὃς δὲ οὕτως.
gift      has from God,  one  thus,  one and  thus.

**8** Λέγω δὲ τοῖς ἀγάμοις καὶ ταῖς χήραις, καλὸν αὐτοῖς
I say  And to the bachelors and to the  widows,  good  for them

**9** ἐστιν ἐὰν μείνωσιν ὡς κἀγώ. εἰ δὲ οὐκ ἐγκρατεύονται,
it is  if  they remain as I also.  if But not   have self-control,
γαμησάτωσαν· κρεῖσσον γάρ ἐστι γαμῆσαι ἢ πυροῦσθαι.
let them marry;  better   for it is to marry  than to be inflamed.

**10** τοῖς δὲ γεγαμηκόσι παραγγέλλω, οὐκ ἐγώ, ἀλλ᾽ ὁ Κύριος,
to those But having married  I enjoin,   not  I,  but the Lord,

**11** γυναῖκα ἀπὸ ἀνδρὸς μὴ χωρισθῆναι (ἐὰν δὲ καὶ χωρισθῇ,
a woman from (her) husband not to be separated — if but indeed she is separated,
μενέτω ἄγαμος, ἢ τῷ ἀνδρὶ καταλλαγήτω)· καὶ ἄνδρα
remain unmarried, or to the husband  be reconciled   — and a husband

**12** γυναῖκα μὴ ἀφιέναι. τοῖς δὲ λοιποῖς ἐγὼ λέγω, οὐχ ὁ
(his) wife  not to leave. to the And  rest    I   say,   not the
Κύριος· εἴ τις ἀδελφὸς γυναῖκα ἔχει ἄπιστον, καὶ αὐτὴ
Lord:  If any  brother   a wife  has  unbelieving, and  she

**13** συνευδοκεῖ οἰκεῖν μετ᾽ αὐτοῦ, μὴ ἀφιέτω αὐτήν. καὶ γυνὴ
consents   to live with  him,  not let him leave her.  And a woman
ἥτις ἔχει ἄνδρα ἄπιστον, καὶ αὐτὸς συνευδοκεῖ οἰκεῖν μετ᾽
who has a husband unbelieving, and  he    consents   to live  with

**14** αὐτῆς, μὴ ἀφιέτω αὐτόν. ἡγίασται γὰρ ὁ ἀνὴρ ὁ ἄπιστος
her,  not let her leave him. has been sanctified For the husband unbelieving
ἐν τῇ γυναικί, καὶ ἡγίασται ἡ γυνὴ ἡ ἄπιστος ἐν τῷ ἀνδρί·
by the  wife;  and has been sanctified the wife unbelieving by the husband;
ἐπεὶ ἄρα τὰ τέκνα ὑμῶν ἀκάθαρτά ἐστι, νῦν δὲ ἅγιά ἐστιν.
else  then the children of you  unclean   is;  now but holy they are.

**15** εἰ δὲ ὁ ἄπιστος χωρίζεται, χωριζέσθω. οὐ δεδούλωται ὁ
if But the unbelieving separates,  let be separated; not is in bondage the
ἀδελφὸς ἢ ἡ ἀδελφὴ ἐν τοῖς τοιούτοις· ἐν δὲ εἰρήνῃ κέκληκεν
brother  or the sister in  such matters;  in but peace  has called

**16** ἡμᾶς ὁ Θεός. τί γὰρ οἶδας, γύναι, εἰ τὸν ἄνδρα σώσεις ; ἢ τί
us  God. what For know you, wife,  if  the husband you will save; or what

**17** οἶδας, ἄνερ, εἰ τὴν γυναῖκα σώσεις ; εἰ μὴ ἑκάστῳ ὡς ἐμέρισεν
know you, husband, if the wife you will save? Only to each  as has divided
ὁ Θεός, ἕκαστον ὡς κέκληκεν ὁ Κύριος, οὕτω περιπατείτω.
God,  each   as has called the Lord,  so  let him walk.

**18** καὶ οὕτως ἐν ταῖς ἐκκλησίαις πάσαις διατάσσομαι. περι-
And so  in  the  churches   all    I command.  Having
τετμημένος τις ἐκλήθη ; μὴ ἐπισπάσθω. ἐν ἀκροβυστίᾳ τις
been circumcised any was called not be uncircumcised; uncircumcision any
ἐκλήθη ; μὴ περιτεμνέσθω. ἡ περιτομὴ οὐδέν ἐστι, καὶ ἡ
was called, not be circumcised.  Circumcision nothing is,  and

**19** ἀκροβυστία οὐδέν ἐστιν, ἀλλὰ τήρησις ἐντολῶν Θεοῦ.
uncircumcision nothing is,    but  the keeping of the commands of God.

**20** ἕκαστος ἐν τῇ κλήσει ᾗ ἐκλήθη, ἐν ταύτῃ μενέτω. δοῦλος
Each one in  the calling in which he was called, in this remain.  a slave

**21** ἐκλήθης ; μή σοι μελέτω· ἀλλ᾽ εἰ καὶ δύνασαι ἐλεύθερος
Were you called? Not to you it matters. But if also you are able  free

free, rather use (it). [22] For he called a slave in (the) Lord is a freed man of (the) Lord. And likewise he called a free man is a slave of Christ. [23] You were redeemed with a price; do not become slaves of men. [24] Each in what (state) called, brothers, in this remain with God.

[25] But about virgins, I have no command of (the) Lord. But I give judgment, as having received mercy by (the) Lord to be faithful. [26] I think, then, this to be good, because of the necessity now; that (it is) good for a man to be thus. [27] Have you been bound to a wife? Do not seek to be released. Have you been released from a wife? Do not seek a wife. [28] But if you also marry, you do not sin; and if the virgin marries, she does not sin. But such will have trouble in the flesh. But I am sparing you. [29] But I say this, brothers, that the time has been cut short; for the rest is, that even the (ones) having wives should be as not having; [30] and those weeping as not weeping; and those rejoicing as not rejoicing; and the (ones) buying as not possessing; [31] and those using this world as not abusing (it); for the mode of this world is passing away. [32] But I desire you to be without care. The unmarried one cares for the things of the Lord, how to please the Lord; [33] but the (one) marrying cares for (the) world's things, how to please the wife. [34] The wife and the virgin (are) different. The unmarried cares for the things of (the) Lord, that she be holy in both body and spirit. But the married cares for the things of the world, how to please the husband. [35] But I say this for your advantage, not that I put a snare (before) you; but for the fitting thing, and waiting on the Lord without distraction. [36] But if anyone thinks (it) behaving indecently toward his virginity—if he (is) beyond (his) prime, and so it ought to be—let him do what he desires; he sins not;

**22** γενέσθαι, μᾶλλον χρῆσαι. ὁ γὰρ ἐν Κυρίῳ κληθεὶς δοῦλος,
to become, rather   use (it). the (one) For in (the) Lord called   a slave,
ἀπελεύθερος Κυρίου ἐστίν· ὁμοίως καὶ ὁ ἐλεύθερος κληθεὶς,
a freed man of (the) Lord is.   likewise And the (one) a free man called

**23** δοῦλός ἐστι Χριστοῦ. τιμῆς ἠγοράσθητε· μὴ γίνεσθε δοῦλοι
a slave   is   of Christ. Of a price you were bought; not become   slaves

**24** ἀνθρώπων. ἕκαστος ἐν ᾧ ἐκλήθη, ἀδελφοί, ἐν τούτῳ μενέτω
of men.   Each one in what (state) called, brothers, in this   remain
παρὰ τῷ Θεῷ.
with     God.

**25** Περὶ δὲ τῶν παρθένων ἐπιταγὴν Κυρίου οὐκ ἔχω· γνώμην
about And the   virgins   a command of (the) Lord not I have, judgment

**26** δὲ δίδωμι ὡς ἠλεημένος ὑπὸ Κυρίου πιστὸς εἶναι. νομίζω οὖν
but I give as having had mercy by (the) Lord faithful to be. I think, then,
τοῦτο καλὸν ὑπάρχειν διὰ τὴν ἐνεστῶσαν ἀνάγκην, ὅτι
this   good   to be because of the present   necessity; that (is)

**27** καλὸν ἀνθρώπῳ τὸ οὕτως εἶναι. δέδεσαι γυναικί; μὴ ζήτει
good   for a men   —   so to be. Have you been bound to a woman? Not seek

**28** λύσιν. λέλυσαι ἀπὸ γυναικός; μὴ ζήτει γυναῖκα. ἐὰν δὲ καὶ
to be loosed. Have you been loosed from a woman? Not seek a woman. if But indeed
γήμῃς, οὐχ ἥμαρτες· καὶ ἐὰν γήμῃ ἡ παρθένος, οὐχ ἥμαρτε.
you marry, not you sin. And if marries the virgin,   not she sinned.
θλῖψιν δὲ τῇ σαρκὶ ἕξουσιν οἱ τοιοῦτοι· ἐγὼ δὲ ὑμῶν φείδομαι.
trouble But in the flesh will have such.   I But you am sparing.

**29** τοῦτο δέ φημι, ἀδελφοί, ὅτι ὁ καιρὸς συνεσταλμένος· τὸ
this   But I say, brothers, that the time   has been shortened; for
λοιπόν ἐστιν ἵνα καὶ οἱ ἔχοντες γυναῖκας ὡς μὴ ἔχοντες ὦσι·
the rest   is, that even those having   wives   as not having be;

**30** καὶ οἱ κλαίοντες, ὡς μὴ κλαίοντες· καὶ οἱ χαίροντες, ὡς μὴ
and those weeping, as not weeping;   and those rejoicing, as not

**31** χαίροντες· καὶ οἱ ἀγοράζοντες, ὡς μὴ κατέχοντες· καὶ οἱ
rejoicing;   and those buying,   as not possessing;   and those
χρώμενοι τῷ κόσμῳ τούτῳ, ὡς μὴ καταχρώμενοι· παράγει
using   world   this, as not abusing (it);   is passing away

**32** γὰρ τὸ σχῆμα τοῦ κόσμου τούτου. θέλω δὲ ὑμᾶς ἀμερίμνους
for the mode   world   of this. I desire But you without care

**33** εἶναι. ὁ ἄγαμος μεριμνᾷ τὰ τοῦ Κυρίου, πῶς ἀρέσει τῷ
to be. The unmarried one cares for the things of (the) Lord, how to please the
Κυρίῳ· ὁ δὲ γαμήσας μεριμνᾷ τὰ τοῦ κόσμου, πῶς ἀρέσει
Lord;   he but having married cares for the things of the world, how to please

**34** τῇ γυναικί. μεμέρισται ἡ γυνὴ καὶ ἡ παρθένος. ἡ ἄγαμος
the wife,   Different (are) the wife and the virgin.   The unmarried
μεριμνᾷ τὰ τοῦ Κυρίου, ἵνα ᾖ ἁγία καὶ σώματι καὶ πνεύματι·
cares for the things of (the) Lord, that she be holy both in body and in spirit;
ἡ δὲ γαμήσασα μεριμνᾷ τὰ τοῦ κόσμου, πῶς ἀρέσει τῷ
the but married   cares for the things of (the) world, how to please the

**35** ἀνδρί. τοῦτο δὲ πρὸς τὸ ὑμῶν αὐτῶν συμφέρον λέγω· οὐχ
husband. this And for the   of yourselves advantage I say,   not
ἵνα βρόχον ὑμῖν ἐπιβάλω, ἀλλὰ πρὸς τὸ εὔσχημον καὶ
that a snare (before) you I put;   but for the thing fitting   and

**36** εὐπρόσεδρον τῷ Κυρίῳ ἀπερισπάστως. εἰ δέ τις ἀσχημονεῖν
waiting on   the   Lord without distraction. if But any to behave indecently
ἀνδρί. τοῦτο δὲ πρὸς τὸ ὑμῶν αὐτῶν συμφέρον λέγω· οὐχ
toward the virginity of him thinks — if he is beyond (his) prime, and so
ὀφείλει γίνεσθαι, ὃ θέλει ποιείτω· οὐχ ἁμαρτάνει· γαμείτω-
(it) ought to be, what he desires let him do; not   he sins;   let them

let them marry. [37] But he who stands firm in heart, not having necessity, but has authority over his own will, and has judged this in his heart, to keep his own virginity, he does well. [38] So that also he that gives in marriage does well; and he that does not give in marriage does better. [39] A wife is bound by law for as long a time as her husband may live; but if her husband may have fallen asleep, she is free to be married to whomever she desires, only in (the) Lord. [40] But she is happier if she should remain so, according to my judgment; and I think I also have God's Spirit.

**37** σαν. ὃς δὲ ἔστηκεν ἑδραῖος ἐν τῇ καρδίᾳ, μὴ ἔχων ἀνάγκην,
marry. (he) who but stands firm in the heart, not having necessity,

ἐξουσίαν δὲ ἔχει περὶ τοῦ ἰδίου θελήματος, καὶ τοῦτο
authority but has concerning the own will, and this

κέκρικεν ἐν τῇ καρδίᾳ αὐτοῦ, τοῦ τηρεῖν τὴν ἑαυτοῦ
has judged in the heart of him, to keep the of himself

**38** παρθένον, καλῶς ποιεῖ. ὥστε καὶ ὁ ἐκγαμίζων καλῶς ποιεῖ·
virginity, well he does. So as both he giving in marriage well does,

**39** ὁ δὲ μὴ ἐκγαμίζων κρεῖσσον ποιεῖ. γυνὴ δέδεται νόμῳ ἐφ'
he and not giving in marriage better does. A wife has been bound by law for

ὅσον χρόνον ζῇ ὁ ἀνὴρ αὐτῆς· ἐὰν δὲ κοιμηθῇ ὁ ἀνὴρ αὐτῆς,
as long a time as lives her husband; if but sleeps the husband of her,

ἐλευθέρα ἐστὶν ᾧ θέλει γαμηθῆναι, μόνον ἐν Κυρίῳ. μακα-
free she is to whom she desires to be married, only in (the) Lord.

**40** ριωτέρα δέ ἐστιν ἐὰν οὕτω μείνῃ, κατὰ τὴν ἐμὴν γνώμην·
happier But she is if so she remains, according to my judgment;

δοκῶ δὲ κἀγὼ Πνεῦμα Θεοῦ ἔχειν.
I think and I also (the) Spirit of God have.

## CHAPTER 8

[1] But concerning things sacrificed to idols, we know, for we have all knowledge; knowledge puffs up, but love edifies. [2] But if anyone thinks to know anything, he has known nothing as he ought to know it. [3] But if anyone loves God, he is known by Him. [4] Then, concerning the eating of things sacrificed to idols, we know that an idol (is) nothing in (the) world, and that (there is) no other God except one. [5] For even if (some) are called gods, either in Heaven, or on the earth; even as there are many gods, and many lords, [6] but to us (is) one God the Father, of whom (are) all things, and we for Him; and one Lord Jesus Christ, through whom (are) all things, and we by Him. [7] But the knowledge (is) not in all; but some being aware of the idol eat as an idolatrous sacrifice until now; and their conscience being weak is defiled. [8] But food will not commend us to God, for neither if we eat do we excel, nor if we do not eat are we behind. [9] But be careful lest this strength of yours become a cause of stumbling to those who are weak. [10] For if anyone sees you, who have knowledge, reclining in an idol-temple, will not the weak one's conscience be

## CHAPTER 8

**1** Περὶ δὲ τῶν εἰδωλοθύτων, οἴδαμεν ὅτι πάντες γνῶσιν
concerning And the idolatrous sacrifices, we know that all knowledge

**2** ἔχομεν. ἡ γνῶσις φυσιοῖ, ἡ δὲ ἀγάπη οἰκοδομεῖ. εἰ δέ τις
we have. Knowledge puffs up, but love builds up. if But any

δοκεῖ εἰδέναι τι, οὐδέπω οὐδὲν ἔγνωκε καθὼς δεῖ γνῶναι·
thinks to know anything, nothing yet he has known as ought he to know.

**3** εἰ δέ τις ἀγαπᾷ τὸν Θεόν, οὗτος ἔγνωσται ὑπ' αὐτοῦ.
if But anyone loves God, this one has been known by Him.

**4** περὶ τῆς βρώσεως οὖν τῶν εἰδωλοθύτων, οἴδαμεν ὅτι οὐδὲν
about the eating Then of the idolatrous sacrifices, we know that (is) not

εἴδωλον ἐν κόσμῳ, καὶ ὅτι οὐδεὶς Θεὸς ἕτερος εἰ μὴ εἷς.
an idol in (the) world, and that (there is) no God other except one.

**5** καὶ γὰρ εἴπερ εἰσὶ λεγόμενοι θεοί, εἴτε ἐν οὐρανῷ, εἴτε ἐπὶ
even For if there are (that) called gods, either in Heaven, or upon

**6** τῆς γῆς· ὥσπερ εἰσὶ θεοὶ πολλοί, καὶ κύριοι πολλοί· ἀλλ'
the earth; even as there are gods many, and lords many, but

ἡμῖν εἷς Θεὸς ὁ πατήρ, ἐξ οὗ τὰ πάντα, καὶ ἡμεῖς εἰς αὐτόν·
to us one God the Father, of whom all things, and we for Him;

καὶ εἷς Κύριος Ἰησοῦς Χριστός, δι' οὗ τὰ πάντα, καὶ ἡμεῖς
and one Lord Jesus Christ, through whom all things, and we

**7** δι' αὐτοῦ. ἀλλ' οὐκ ἐν πᾶσιν ἡ γνῶσις· τινὲς δὲ τῇ συνειδήσει
by Him. But not in all (is) the knowledge; some and conscious

τοῦ εἰδώλου ἕως ἄρτι ὡς εἰδωλόθυτον ἐσθίουσι, καὶ ἡ
of the idol until now as an idolatrous sacrifice eat, and the

**8** συνείδησις αὐτῶν ἀσθενὴς οὖσα μολύνεται. βρῶμα δὲ ἡμᾶς
conscience of them weak being is defiled. food But us

οὐ παρίστησι τῷ Θεῷ· οὔτε γὰρ ἐὰν φάγωμεν περισσεύο-
not will commend to God; neither for if we eat do we excel

**9** μεν, οὔτε ἐὰν μὴ φάγωμεν ὑστερούμεθα. βλέπετε δὲ μήπως
nor if not we eat are we behind. watch But lest

ἡ ἐξουσία ὑμῶν αὕτη πρόσκομμα γένηται τοῖς ἀσθενοῦσιν.
the authority of you this a stumbling-block becomes to the weak ones.

**10** ἐὰν γὰρ τις ἴδῃ σε τὸν ἔχοντα γνῶσιν ἐν εἰδωλείῳ κατακεί-
if For anyone sees you, the (one) having knowledge in an idol temple

μενον, οὐχὶ ἡ συνείδησις αὐτοῦ ἀσθενοῦς ὄντος οἰκοδομηθή-
sitting, not the conscience of him, weak being, be built up

lifted up so as to eat things sacrificed to idols? [11] And on your knowledge the weak brother will fall, for whom Christ died. [12] Now sinning in this way against the brothers, and wounding their weak conscience, you sin against Christ. [13] Therefore if food causes my brother to sin, I should not at all eat flesh forever, that I may not cause my brother to sin.

## CHAPTER 9

[1] Am I not an apostle? Am I not free? Have I not seen our Lord Jesus Christ? Are you not my work in (the) Lord? [2] If I am not an apostle to others, yet at any rate I am to you; for you are the seal of my apostleship in (the) Lord. [3] My answer to those who judge me is this: [4] Have we not authority to eat and to drink? [5] Have we not authority to lead about a sister, a wife, as also the other apostles, and the brothers of the Lord, and Peter? [6] Or (is it) only Barnabas and I (who) have not authority to quit work? [7] Who serves as a soldier at his own charge at any time? Who plants a vineyard, and does not eat of the fruit of it? Or who shepherds a flock and does not eat of the milk of the flock? [8] Do I speak these things according to man, or does not the Law also say these things? [9] For it has been written in the Law of Moses, "You shall not muzzle an ox treading out grain." Is it (that) there is a care with God for the oxen? [10] Or does He say (it) because of us all? For it was written because of us, that he that plows ought to plow in hope, and he that treads out grain in hope to share in hope. [11 If we have sown spiritual things to you, (is it) a great thing if we shall reap your fleshly things? [12] If others share authority over you, (should) not rather we? But we did not use this authority; but we endure all things that we should

**11** σεται εἰς τὸ τὰ εἰδωλόθυτα ἐσθίειν · καὶ ἀπολεῖται ὁ ἀσθε-
       — — the idolatrous sacrifices to eat? And is destroyed the weak
νῶν ἀδελφὸς ἐπὶ τῇ σῇ γνώσει, δι' ὃν Χριστὸς ἀπέθανεν ;
brother   by the of you knowledge, for whom Christ     died.

**12** οὕτω δὲ ἁμαρτάνοντες εἰς τοὺς ἀδελφούς, καὶ τύπτοντες
so  And   sinning     against the   brothers,   and wounding
αὐτῶν τὴν συνείδησιν ἀσθενοῦσαν, εἰς Χριστὸν ἁμαρτάνετε.
of them the conscience    being weak, against Christ   you sin.

**13** διόπερ εἰ βρῶμα σκανδαλίζει τὸν ἀδελφόν μου, οὐ μὴ φάγω
Therefore, if food    offends     the  brother of you, in no way I eat
κρέα εἰς τὸν αἰῶνα, ἵνα μὴ τὸν ἀδελφόν μου σκανδαλίσω.
flesh to the   age,   that not the   brother   of me  I offend.

## CHAPTER 9

**1** Οὐκ εἰμὶ ἀπόστολος ; οὐκ εἰμὶ ἐλεύθερος ; οὐχὶ Ἰησοῦν
   not Am I   an apostle?   not Am I     free? (Have) not Jesus
Χριστὸν τὸν Κύριον ἡμῶν ἑώρακα ; οὐ τὸ ἔργον μου ὑμεῖς
Christ    the   Lord   of us I have seen? not the work of me you

**2** ἐστε ἐν Κυρίῳ ; εἰ ἄλλοις οὐκ εἰμὶ ἀπόστολος, ἀλλά γε ὑμῖν
Are in (the) Lord? If to others not I am    an apostle,    yet indeed to you
εἰμι· ἡ γὰρ σφραγὶς τῆς ἐμῆς ἀποστολῆς ὑμεῖς ἐστε ἐν Κυρίῳ.
I am; the for seal    of my   apostleship   you are in (the) Lord.

**3** ἡ ἐμὴ ἀπολογία τοῖς ἐμὲ ἀνακρίνουσιν αὕτη ἐστί. μὴ οὐκ
   My  defense  to those me  examining       this    is.   not

**4** ἔχομεν ἐξουσίαν φαγεῖν καὶ πιεῖν ; μὴ οὐκ ἔχομεν ἐξουσίαν

**5** Have we authority to eat   and to drink?   not Have we authority
ἀδελφὴν γυναῖκα περιάγειν, ὡς καὶ οἱ λοιποὶ ἀπόστολοι,
a sister,   a wife,   to lead about, as also the rest   of (the) apostles,

**6** καὶ οἱ ἀδελφοὶ τοῦ Κυρίου, καὶ Κηφᾶς ; ἢ μόνος ἐγὼ καὶ
and the brothers of the Lord,   and Cephas? Or only I    and

**7** Βαρνάβας οὐκ ἔχομεν ἐξουσίαν τοῦ μὴ ἐργάζεσθαι ; τίς
Barnabas   not we have authority     not to work?   Who
στρατεύεται ἰδίοις ὀψωνίοις ποτέ ; τίς φυτεύει ἀμπελῶνα,
soldiers   at (his) own wages at any time? Who plants   a vineyard
καὶ ἐκ τοῦ καρποῦ αὐτοῦ οὐκ ἐσθίει ; ἢ τίς ποιμαίνει ποίμνην,
and from the fruit   of it   not eats? Or who shepherds   a flock,

**8** καὶ ἐκ τοῦ γάλακτος τῆς ποίμνης οὐκ ἐσθίει ; μὴ κατὰ ἄνθρω-
and of the milk   of the flock   not eats?   Not according to

**9** πον ταῦτα λαλῶ ; ἢ οὐχὶ καὶ ὁ νόμος ταῦτα λέγει ; ἐν γὰρ
man these things I speak, or not also the   law these things says? in   For

**10** τῷ Μωσέως νόμῳ γέγραπται, Οὐ φιμώσεις βοῦν ἀλοῶντα.
the of Moses   law it has ~~been~~ written: not You ~~shall~~ muzzle an ox threshing
μὴ τῶν βοῶν μέλει τῷ Θεῷ ; ἢ δι' ἡμᾶς πάντως λέγει ; δι'
Not     of oxen matters it to God, or because of us altogether He says? For
ἡμᾶς γὰρ ἐγράφη, ὅτι ἐπ' ἐλπίδι ὀφείλει ὁ ἀροτριῶν
us,   for it was written; because on hope     ought the (one) plowing
ἀροτριᾶν, καὶ ὁ ἀλοῶν τῆς ἐλπίδος αὐτοῦ μετέχειν ἐπ' ἐλπίδι.
to plow; and the (on) threshing of his hope     to partake on hope.

**11** εἰ ἡμεῖς ὑμῖν τὰ πνευματικὰ ἐσπείραμεν, μέγα εἰ ἡμεῖς ὑμῶν
If we to you   spiritual things   sowed,   (is it) a great thing if we of you

**12** τὰ σαρκικὰ θερίσομεν ; εἰ ἄλλοι τῆς ἐξουσίας ὑμῶν μετέ-
fleshly things shall reap? If others of the authority   of you have a
χουσιν, οὐ μᾶλλον ἡμεῖς ; ἀλλ' οὐκ ἐχρησάμεθα τῇ ἐξουσίᾳ
share,   not rather   we?   But not   we used     authority
ταύτῃ· ἀλλὰ πάντα στέγομεν, ἵνα μὴ ἐγκοπήν τινα δῶμεν
this,   but   all things we endured, that not an obstacle anyone we give

not hinder the gospel of Christ. [13] Do you not know that those laboring (about) holy things eat of the temple; those attending at the altar share with the altar? [14] So also the Lord ordained those preaching the gospel to live from the gospel. [15] But I have used none of these. And I did not write these things that it be so with me. For to me (it is)

good rather to die, than that anyone nullify my glorying. [16] For if I preach the gospel, no glory is to me, for necessity is laid on me, and it is woe to me if I do not preach the gospel. [17] For if I do this willingly, I have a reward; but if unwillingly, I am entrusted with a stewardship. [18] What then is my reward? That in preaching the gospel I should make the gospel of Christ free, so as not using my authority in the gospel as my own. [19] For being free from all, I myself became a slave to all, so that I might gain the more. [20] And I became as a Jew to the Jews, that I might gain Jews; to those under Law as under Law, that I might gain those under Law; [21] to those without Law as without Law—not being without law of God, but under (the) law of Christ—that I might gain (those) without Law. [22] I became to the weak as weak, that I might gain the weak. To all I have become all things, that in any case I might save some. [23] And I do this for the sake of the gospel, that I might become a fellow-partaker with it.

[24] Do you not know that those running in a stadium indeed all run, but one receives the prize? So run that you may obtain. [25] But everyone striving (in) all things controls himself; Then those truly that a corruptible crown they may receive, but we an incorruptible. [26] So I run accordingly, as not uncertainly; so I fight, as not beating air; [27] but I buffet my body and lead (it) a slave, lest (in) proclaiming to others I

**13** τῷ εὐαγγελίῳ τοῦ Χριστοῦ. οὐκ οἴδατε ὅτι οἱ τὰ ἱερὰ
to the  gospel          of Christ  Do not you know that those holy things

ἐργαζόμενοι ἐκ τοῦ ἱεροῦ ἐσθίουσιν, οἱ τῷ θυσιαστηρίῳ
laboring (about) of the temple eat,    those the  altar

**14** προσεδρεύοντες τῷ θυσιαστηρίῳ συμμερίζονται ; οὕτω καὶ
attending (on), the    altar          partake with.    So  also

ὁ Κύριος διέταξε τοῖς τὸ εὐαγγέλιον καταγγέλλουσιν ἐκ τοῦ
the Lord ordained those of the  gospel        announcing,    of the

**15** εὐαγγελίου ζῆν. ἐγὼ δὲ οὐδενὶ ἐχρησάμην τούτων· οὐκ
gospel    to live.  I  But not one  have used  of these.  not

ἔγραψα δὲ ταῦτα ἵνα οὕτω γένηται ἐν ἐμοί· καλὸν γάρ μοι
I write And these things that so it should be with me; good  For to me

μᾶλλον ἀποθανεῖν ἢ τὸ καύχημά μου ἵνα τις κενώσῃ. ἐὰν
rather  to die,   than the glorying of me that anyone void.    if

**16** γὰρ εὐαγγελίζωμαι, οὐκ ἔστι μοι καύχημα· ἀνάγκη γάρ
For I preach the gospel, not there is to me glory;    necessity  for

μοι ἐπίκειται· οὐαὶ δέ μοι ἐστίν, ἐὰν μὴ εὐαγγελίζωμαι. εἰ
me is laid on;  woe and to me is,    if not I preach the gospel.  if

**17** γὰρ ἑκὼν τοῦτο πράσσω, μισθὸν ἔχω· εἰ δὲ ἄκων, οἰκονομίαν
For willingly this  I do,    a reward I have; if but unwillingly, a stewardship

**18** πεπίστευμαι. τίς οὖν μοί ἐστιν ὁ μισθός ; ἵνα εὐαγγελιζό-
I am entrusted with. What then of me is the reward?  That preaching the

μενος ἀδάπανον θήσω τὸ εὐαγγέλιον τοῦ Χριστοῦ, εἰς τὸ μὴ
gospel without charge I place the  gospel      of Christ,  so as not

**19** καταχρήσασθαι τῇ ἐξουσίᾳ μου ἐν τῳ εὐαγγελίῳ. ἐλεύ-
to use to the full the authority of me in the  gospel.    free

θερος γὰρ ὢν ἐκ πάντων, πᾶσιν ἐμαυτὸν ἐδούλωσα, ἵνα
For being of all,    to all  myself  I enslaved,  that

**20** τοὺς πλείονας κερδήσω. καὶ ἐγενόμην τοῖς Ἰουδαίοις ὡς
the  more  I might gain. And I became to the  Jews    as

Ἰουδαῖος, ἵνα Ἰουδαίους κερδήσω· τοῖς ὑπὸ νόμον ὡς ὑπὸ
a Jew,   that Jews    I might gain; to those under law  as under

**21** νόμον, ἵνα τοὺς ὑπὸ νόμον κερδήσω· τοῖς ἀνόμοις ὡς ἄνομος,
law,  that those under law I might gain; to those without as without
                                              law      law

μὴ ὢν ἄνομος Θεῷ ἀλλ᾽ ἔννομος Χριστῷ, ἵνα κερδήσω ἀνό-
not being without law of God, but under law of Christ, that I might gain with-

**22** μους. ἐγενόμην τοῖς ἀσθενέσιν ὡς ἀσθενής, ἵνα τοὺς ἀσθενεῖς
out law. I became to the  weak    as weak,    that  the  weak

κερδήσω. τοῖς πᾶσι γέγονα τὰ πάντα, ἵνα πάντως τινὰς
I might gain.  To all I have become all things, that in any case some

**23** σώσω. τοῦτο δὲ ποιῶ διὰ τὸ εὐαγγέλιον, ἵνα συγκοινωνὸς
I might save. this And I do for  the gospel,    that a fellow-partaker

**24** αὐτοῦ γένωμαι. οὐκ οἴδατε ὅτι οἱ ἐν σταδίῳ τρέχοντες πάν-
of it I might become. Not know you that those in a stadium running  all

τες μὲν τρέχουσιν, εἷς δὲ λαμβάνει τὸ βραβεῖον ; οὕτω
indeed  run,    one but receives  the  prize?    So

**25** τρέχετε, ἵνα καταλάβητε. πᾶς δὲ ὁ ἀγωνιζόμενος πάντα
run  that you may obtain. everyone And striving    (in) all things

ἐγκρατεύεται· ἐκεῖνοι μὲν οὖν ἵνα φθαρτὸν στέφανον λάβω-
controls himself; those truly, then, that a corruptible crown they may

**26** σιν, ἡμεῖς δὲ ἄφθαρτον. ἐγὼ τοίνυν οὕτω τρέχω, ὡς οὐκ
receive, we but an incorruptible. I accordingly so  run,    as not

**27** ἀδήλως· οὕτω πυκτεύω, ὡς οὐκ ἀέρα δέρων· ἀλλ᾽ ὑπωπιάζω
uncertainly; so  I fight,    as not air beating; but I buffet

μου τὸ σῶμα καὶ δουλαγωγῶ, μήπως, ἄλλοις κηρύξας,
of me the body and lead (it) captive,  lest   to others proclaiming,

myself might be rejected.
## CHAPTER 10
[1] Now I do not want you to be ignorant, brothers, that our fathers were all under the cloud; and all passed through the sea. [2] And all were baptized into Moses in the cloud and in the sea; [3] and all ate the same spiritual food. [4] And all drank the same spiritual drink; for they drank of the spiritual rock following (them), and that Rock was Christ. [5] Yet God was not pleased with most of them; for they were scattered in the desert. [6] But these things became examples for us, so that we, may not be persons who lust after evil things, even as they also lusted. [7] Neither be idolaters, even as some of them, for it has been written, "The people sat down to eat and to drink, and got up to play." [8] Nor should we commit fornication, as some of them committed fornication, and twenty-three thousand fell in one day. [9] Nor should we tempt Christ, as some of them tempted, and perished by the serpents. [10] Nor should you murmur, as also some of them murmured, and perished by the destroyer. [11] Now all these things happened to them (as) examples, and were written for our warning, on whom the ends of the ages have come. [12] So that he that thinks to stand, let him be careful lest he fall. [13] No temptation has taken you except what is common to man, but God is faithful, who will not allow you to be tempted above what you are able. But with the temptation will also make a way of escape, so that you may be able to bear (it). [14] Therefore, my beloved, flee from idolatry. [15] I speak as to wise ones; you judge what I say. [16] The cup of blessing which we bless, is it not the partaking of the

αὐτὸς ἀδόκιμος γένωμαι.
myself rejected   I may become.

## CHAPTER 10

**1** Οὐ θέλω δὲ ὑμᾶς ἀγνοεῖν, ἀδελφοί, ὅτι οἱ πατέρες ἡμῶν
not I desire And you to be ignorant, brothers, that the fathers   of us

πάντες ὑπὸ τὴν νεφέλην ἦσαν, καὶ πάντες διὰ τῆς θαλάσσης
all     under the cloud    were,   and   all  through the   sea

**2** διῆλθον, καὶ πάντες εἰς τὸν Μωσῆν ἐβαπτίσαντο ἐν τῇ νεφέλῃ
passed   and  all    to     Moses   were baptized  in  the cloud

**3** καὶ ἐν τῇ θαλάσσῃ, καὶ πάντες τὸ αὐτὸ βρῶμα πνευματικὸν
and in the  sea,     and  all   the same  food   spiritual

**4** ἔφαγον, καὶ πάντες τὸ αὐτὸ πόμα πνευματικὸν ἔπιον·
ate,    and  all   the same drink spiritual    drank;

ἔπινον γὰρ ἐκ πνευματικῆς ἀκολουθούσης πέτρας· ἡ δὲ
they drank for of  a spiritual    following     rock,  the and

**5** πέτρα ἦν ὁ Χριστός. ἀλλ' οὐκ ἐν τοῖς πλείοσιν αὐτῶν
Rock  was    Christ.   But not in  the   most    of them

εὐδόκησεν ὁ Θεός· κατεστρώθησαν γὰρ ἐν τῇ ἐρήμῳ. ταῦτα
was well-pleased God; they were scattered for  in  the desert. these things

**6** δὲ τύποι ἡμῶν ἐγενήθησαν, εἰς τὸ μὴ εἶναι ἡμᾶς ἐπιθυμητὰς
And examples of us   were,   for not to be  us   lusters after

**7** κακῶν, καθὼς κἀκεῖνοι ἐπεθύμησαν. μηδὲ εἰδωλολάτραι
evil,  even as  those indeed lusted.   Neither  idolaters

γίνεσθε, καθὼς τινες αὐτῶν· ὡς γέγραπται, Ἐκάθισεν ὁ λαὸς
be,      even as some of them, as it has been written: Sat   the people

**8** φαγεῖν καὶ πιεῖν, καὶ ἀνέστησαν παίζειν. μηδὲ πορνεύωμεν,
to eat and  drink, and  stood up   to play. Neither do fornication,

καθώς τινες αὐτῶν ἐπόρνευσαν, καὶ ἔπεσον ἐν μιᾷ ἡμέρᾳ
even as some of them fornicated,   and   fell  in one   day

**9** εἰκοσιτρεῖς χιλιάδες. μηδὲ ἐκπειράζωμεν τὸν Χριστόν, καθὼς
twenty-three thousands. Neither overtempt    the   Christ,   even as

καί τινες αὐτῶν ἐπείρασαν, καὶ ὑπὸ τῶν ὄφεων ἀπώλοντο.
also some of them tempted,    and by    the   serpents were destroyed.

**10** μηδὲ γογγύζετε, καθὼς καί τινες αὐτῶν ἐγόγγυσαν, καὶ
Neither murmur     even as also some of them murmured,   and

**11** ἀπώλοντο ὑπὸ τοῦ ὀλοθρευτοῦ. ταῦτα δὲ πάντα τύποι
were destroyed by the  destroyer.   these things And  all (as) examples

συνέβαινον ἐκείνοις· ἐγράφη δὲ πρὸς νουθεσίαν ἡμῶν, εἰς
happened   to those, was written and for  warning    of us,,  to

**12** οὓς τὰ τέλη τῶν αἰώνων κατήντησεν. ὥστε ὁ δοκῶν
whom the ends of the  ages   has arrived.   So as the (one) thinking

**13** ἑστάναι, βλεπέτω μὴ πέσῃ. πειρασμὸς ὑμᾶς οὐκ εἴληφεν εἰ
to stand, let watch  lest he falls. Temptation you   not has taken ex-

μὴ ἀνθρώπινος· πιστὸς δὲ ὁ Θεός, ὃς οὐκ ἐάσει ὑμᾶς πει-
cept (what is) human; faithful but (is) God,  who not will allow you to be

ρασθῆναι ὑπὲρ ὃ δύνασθε, ἀλλὰ ποιήσει σὺν τῷ πειρασμῷ
tempted  beyond what you are able; but  will make with the  temptation

καὶ τὴν ἔκβασιν, τοῦ δύνασθαι ὑμᾶς ὑπενεγκεῖν.
also the way out,    to be able  you  to bear (it).

**14** Διόπερ, ἀγαπητοί μου, φεύγετε ἀπὸ τῆς εἰδωλολατρείας.
Therefore, beloved of me,  flee   from     idolatry.

**15** ὡς φρονίμοις λέγω, κρίνατε ὑμεῖς ὅ φημι. τὸ ποτήριον τῆς
As to prudent ones I say, judge  you what I say.  The  cup

**16** εὐλογίας ὃ εὐλογοῦμεν, οὐχὶ κοινωνία τοῦ αἵματος τοῦ
of blessing which we bless,   not a partaking of the   blood

blood of Christ? The bread which we break, is it not a partaking of the body of Christ? [17] Because we, the many, are one bread, one body, for we all partake of the one bread. [18] Look at Israel according to flesh; are not those eating the sacrifices partakers of the altar? [19] What then do I say, that an idol is anything, or that an idolatrous sacrifice is anything? [20] But the things the nations sacrifice, (they) sacrifice to demons, and not to God. But I do not want you to become sharers of demons; [21] you cannot drink (the) cup of the Lord and a cup of demons; you cannot partake of the table of (the) Lord, and of a table of demons. [22] Or do we provoke the Lord to jealousy? Are we stronger than He?

[23] All things are lawful to me, but not all things profit. All things are lawful to me, but not all things build up. [26] Let no one seek the things of himself, but each one that of the other. [25] Eat everything being sold in a meat market, examining nothing because of conscience, [26] for "the earth (is) the Lord's, and the fullness of it." [27] And if any of the unbelievers invite you, and you desire to go, eat everything set before you, examining nothing because of conscience. [28] But if anyone says to you, This was slain in sacrifice, do not eat, because of that one pointing (it) out, and the conscience; for "the earth (is) the Lord's and the fullness of it." [29] But conscience, I say, not that of yourself, but that of the other; for why is my freedom judged by another's conscience. [30] But if I partake with thanks, why am I evil spoken of for what I give thanks? [31] Whether therefore you eat, or you drink, or anything you do, do all things to the glory of God. [32] Be without offense both to Jews and Greeks, and to the church of God. [33] Even as I also please in all things, not pursuing my own profit, but that of the many, that

Χριστοῦ ἐστί ; τὸν ἄρτον ὃν κλῶμεν, οὐχὶ κοινωνία τοῦ
of Christ   is?    The bread which we break, not  a partaking of the

17 σώματος τοῦ Χριστοῦ ἐστίν ; ὅτι εἷς ἄρτος, ἓν σῶμα, οἱ
   body      of Christ   is it? Because one bread, one  body the

πολλοί ἐσμεν· οἱ γὰρ πάντες ἐκ τοῦ ἑνὸς ἄρτου μετέχομεν.
many  we are;  for   all   of  the  one  bread we partake.

18 βλέπετε τὸν Ἰσραὴλ κατὰ σάρκα· οὐχὶ οἱ ἐσθίοντες τὰς
   See        Israel according to flesh;  not those  eating  the

19 θυσίας κοινωνοὶ τοῦ θυσιαστηρίου εἰσί ; τί οὖν φημι ; ὅτι
   sacrifices sharers of the  altar     are? What then do I say, that

20 εἴδωλόν τί ἐστιν ; ἢ ὅτι εἰδωλόθυτόν τί ἐστιν ; ἀλλ’ ὅτι ἃ
   an idol anything is?  Or that an idolatrous sacrifice anything is? But that what

θύει τὰ ἔθνη, δαιμονίοις θύει, καὶ οὐ Θεῷ· οὐ θέλω δὲ ὑμᾶς
sacrifice the nations, to demons sacrifice, and not to God. not I want But you

21 κοινωνοὺς τῶν δαιμονίων γίνεσθαι. οὐ δύνασθε ποτήριον
   sharers      of demons   to become.  not You are able   a cup

Κυρίου πίνειν καὶ ποτήριον δαιμονίων· οὐ δύνασθε τραπέζης
of (the) Lord to drink and a cup  of demons;  not you are able of a table

22 Κυρίου μετέχειν καὶ τραπέζης δαιμονίων. ἢ παραζηλοῦμεν
   of (the) Lord to partake and a table of  demons.  Or do we make jealous

τὸν Κύριον ; μὴ ἰσχυρότεροι αὐτοῦ ἐσμέν ;
the  Lord? Not  stronger (than) He we are?

23 Πάντα μοι ἔξεστιν, ἀλλ’ οὐ πάντα συμφέρει. πάντα μοι
   All things to me are lawful, but  not all things contribute. All things to me

24 ἔξεστιν, ἀλλ’ οὐ πάντα οἰκοδομεῖ. μηδεὶς τὸ ἑαυτοῦ ζητείτω,
   are lawful, but  not all things build up.  No one the thing of himself seeks,

25 ἀλλὰ τὸ τοῦ ἑτέρου ἕκαστος. πᾶν τὸ ἐν μακέλλῳ πωλού-
   but    that of the other  each one. Everything in a meat market being

26 μενον ἐσθίετε, μηδὲν ἀνακρίνοντες διὰ τὴν συνείδησιν· τοῦ
   sold    eat,    nothing examining  because of   conscience; of the

27 γὰρ Κυρίου ἡ γῆ καὶ τὸ πλήρωμα αὐτῆς. εἰ δέ τις καλεῖ ὑμᾶς
   for  Lord  the earth and the fullness  of it. if And anyone invites you

τῶν ἀπίστων, καὶ θέλετε πορεύεσθαι. πᾶν τὸ παρατιθέ-
of the unbelievers, and you desire to go,   everything   set before

μενον ὑμῖν ἐσθίετε, μηδὲν ἀνακρίνοντες διὰ τὴν συνείδησιν.
you eat,     nothing examining because   of conscience.

28 ἐὰν δέ τις ὑμῖν εἴπῃ, Τοῦτο εἰδωλόθυτόν ἐστι, μὴ ἐσθίετε, δι
   if  But anyone you tells, This  slain in sacrifice is, do not eat, because

ἐκεῖνον τὸν μηνύσαντα καὶ τὴν συνείδησιν· τοῦ γὰρ Κυρίου
that one  pointing out, and   conscience;  the for (is the) Lord's

29 ἡ γῆ καὶ τὸ πλήρωμα αὐτῆς. συνείδησιν δὲ λέγω, οὐχὶ τὴν
   the earth and the fullness of it.  conscience But I say, not the (one)

ἑαυτοῦ, ἀλλὰ τὴν τοῦ ἑτέρου· ἱνατί γὰρ ἡ ἐλευθερία μου
of himself, but the (one) of the other.  why  For the freedom of me

30 κρίνεται ὑπὸ ἄλλης συνειδήσεως ; εἰ δὲ ἐγὼ χάριτι μετέχω, τί
   is judged by another's conscience?  if And I  by grace partake, why

31 βλασφημοῦμαι ὑπὲρ οὗ ἐγὼ εὐχαριστῶ ; εἴτε οὖν ἐσθίετε,
   am I evil spoken of because of what I give thanks (for)? Whether then you eat,

εἴτε πίνετε, εἴτε τι ποιεῖτε, πάντα εἰς δόξαν Θεοῦ ποιεῖτε.
or   drink, or what you do, all things to the glory of God  do.

32 ἀπρόσκοποι γίνεσθε καὶ Ἰουδαίοις καὶ Ἕλλησι καὶ τῇ
   without offense  be   both   to Jews   and to Greeks and to the

33 ἐκκλησίᾳ τοῦ Θεοῦ· καθὼς κἀγὼ πάντα πᾶσιν ἀρέσκω, μὴ
   church     of God, as   I also (in) all things all  please, not

ζητῶν τὸ ἐμαυτοῦ συμφέρον. ἀλλὰ τὸ τῶν πολλῶν, ἵνα
seeking the of myself advantage, but   of the  many,   that

σωθῶσι.
they may be saved.

## CHAPTER 11

they may be saved.

[1] Be imitators of me, even as I also of Christ.

1 μιμηταί μου γίνεσθε, καθὼς κἀγὼ Χριστοῦ.
imitators of me Be,       as      also I   of Christ.

[2] Now I praise you, brothers, that in all things you have remembered me; and according as I delivered to you, you hold fast the traditions. [3] But I want you to know that Christ is the Head of every man, and the man (is) head of a woman, and God (is the) head of Christ. [4] Every man praying or prophesying having (anything) down over (his) head shames the Head of him. [5] And every woman praying or prophesying with the head uncovered, shames her head; for it is the same (as) being shaved. [6] For if a woman is not covered, let her also be shorn. But if (it is) shameful for a woman to be shorn, or to be shaved, let her be covered. [7] For truly man ought not to have the head covered, being (the) image and glory of God; but woman is (the) glory of man. [8] For man is not of the woman, but woman of man. [9] For also man was not created for the sake of the woman, but woman for the sake of the man. [10] Because of this the woman ought to have authority on the head, on account of the angels. [11] However man (is) not apart from woman, nor woman apart from man, in (the) Lord. [12] For as the woman (is) of the man, so also the man by the woman; but all things of God. [13] Judge in yourselves: Is it becoming for a woman uncovered to pray to God? [14] Or does not nature itself even teach you that if a man have long hair it is a dishonor to him? [15] But if a woman have long hair, it is her glory; for she is given the long hair instead of a veil. [16] But if anyone thinks to be contentious, we have no such custom, nor the churches of God.

2 Ἐπαινῶ δὲ ὑμᾶς, ἀδελφοί, ὅτι πάντα μου μέμνησθε, καὶ
I praise But you,   brothers, because all things of me you recalled, and

3 καθὼς παρέδωκα ὑμῖν τὰς παραδόσεις κατέχετε. θέλω δὲ
as       I delivered to you, the traditions you hold fast. I wish But

ὑμᾶς εἰδέναι, ὅτι παντὸς ἀνδρὸς ἡ κεφαλὴ ὁ Χριστός ἐστι·
you to know, that of every  man  the  head    Christ    is;

4 κεφαλὴ δὲ γυναικός, ὁ ἀνήρ· κεφαλὴ δὲ Χριστοῦ, ὁ Θεός. πᾶς
head and of a woman, the man; (the) head and of Christ,   God. Every

ἀνὴρ προσευχόμενος ἢ προφητεύων, κατὰ κεφαλῆς ἔχων,
man    praying        or   prophesying down over (his) head having,

5 καταισχύνει τὴν κεφαλὴν αὐτοῦ. πᾶσα δὲ γυνὴ προσευχο-
shames       the  Head    of him.  every But woman praying

μένη ἢ προφητεύουσα ἀκατακαλύπτῳ τῇ κεφαλῇ, καται-
or   prophesying       uncovered        with the head,   shames

σχύνει τὴν κεφαλὴν ἑαυτῆς· ἐν γάρ ἐστι καὶ τὸ αὐτὸ τῇ ἐξυρη-
the    head    of herself, one for it is and the same with the being

6 μένῃ. εἰ γὰρ οὐ κατακαλύπτεται γυνή, καὶ κειράσθω· εἰ δὲ
shaved. if For not is covered       a woman, also let her be shorn. if But

αἰσχρὸν γυναικὶ τὸ κείρασθαι ἢ ξυρᾶσθαι, κατακαλυ-
shameful for a woman to be shorn  or to be shaved, let her be

7 πτέσθω. ἀνὴρ μὲν γὰρ οὐκ ὀφείλει κατακαλύπτεσθαι τὴν
covered.  a man indeed For not ought  to be covered         the

κεφαλήν, εἰκὼν καὶ δόξα Θεοῦ ὑπάρχων· γυνὴ δὲ δόξα
head,   (the) image and glory of God   being.   the woman But glory

8 ἀνδρός ἐστιν. οὐ γάρ ἐστιν ἀνὴρ ἐκ γυναικός, ἀλλὰ γυνὴ
of a man is.  not For is   man of woman,   but woman

9 ἐξ ἀνδρός· καὶ γὰρ οὐκ ἐκτίσθη ἀνὴρ διὰ τὴν γυναῖκα, ἀλλὰ
of man; also for not was created man because of the woman, but

10 γυνὴ διὰ τὸν ἄνδρα· διὰ τοῦτο ὀφείλει ἡ γυνὴ ἐξουσίαν
woman because of the man.  Therefore   ought the woman authority

11 ἔχειν ἐπὶ τῆς κεφαλῆς διὰ τοὺς ἀγγέλους. πλὴν οὔτε ἀνὴρ
to have on the head because of the angels.   But neither man

12 χωρὶς γυναικός, οὔτε γυνὴ χωρὶς ἀνδρός, ἐν Κυρίῳ. ὥσπερ
without woman,  nor woman without man,  in (the) Lord. as

γὰρ ἡ γυνὴ ἐκ τοῦ ἀνδρός, οὕτω καὶ ὁ ἀνὴρ διὰ τῆς
For the woman of the  man,   so also the man through the

13 γυναικός, τὰ δὲ πάντα ἐκ τοῦ Θεοῦ. ἐν ὑμῖν αὐτοῖς κρίνατε·
woman,   but all things of   God. Among you yourselves judge:

πρέπον ἐστὶ γυναῖκα ἀκατακάλυπτον τῷ Θεῷ προσεύχε-
fitting  Is it (for) a woman  uncovered        to God  to pray?

14 σθαι; ἢ οὐδὲ αὐτὴ ἡ φύσις διδάσκει ὑμᾶς, ὅτι ἀνὴρ μὲν ἐὰν
Does not herself  nature teaches you that a man indeed if

15 κομᾷ, ἀτιμία αὐτῷ ἐστι; γυνὴ δὲ ἐὰν κομᾷ, δόξα αὐτῇ
wears long hair, a dishonor to him it is; a woman but if wears hair long, a glory to her

16 ἐστίν. ὅτι ἡ κόμη ἀντὶ περιβολαίου δέδοται αὐτῇ. εἰ δέ τις
it is? Because the long hair instead of a veil has been given to her. But anyone

δοκεῖ φιλόνεικος εἶναι, ἡμεῖς τοιαύτην συνήθειαν οὐκ ἔχομεν,
thinks contentious to be, we     such       a custom   do not have,

οὐδὲ αἱ ἐκκλησίαι τοῦ Θεοῦ.
neither the churches  of God.

[17] But commanding this, I do not praise (you), because you come together not for the better but for the worse. [18] Indeed, first, I hear divisions to be among you when you come together in the church, and I partly believe. [19] For there must also be heresies among you, that the approved may be revealed among you. [20] Therefore you coming together into one place, it is not to eat (the) Lord's supper. [21] For each one takes his own supper first in eating, and one is hungry and another is drunken. [22] For do you not have houses for eating and drinking? Or do you despise the church of God, and shame those that have not? What do I say to you? Shall I praise you in this? I do not praise you. [23] For I received from the Lord what I also delivered to you, that the Lord Jesus in the night in which He was betrayed took bread, [24] and having given thanks, He broke and said, Take, eat; this is My body which (is) broken on behalf of you; this do in remembrance of Me. [25] In the same way also the cup, after supping, saying, This cup is the New Covenant in My blood; as often as you drink, do this for My remembrance. [26] For as often as you may eat this bread and drink this cup, you solemnly proclaim the death of the Lord until He comes. [27] So that whoever should eat this bread or should drink the cup of the Lord unworthily, shall be guilty of the body and blood of the Lord. [28] But let a man examine himself, and let him eat and let him drink of the cup in this way. [29] For he who eats and drinks unworthily eats and drinks judgment to himself, not discerning the body of the Lord. [30] Because of this many among you (are) weak and infirm, and many are fallen asleep. [31] For if we examined ourselves, we

**17** Τοῦτο δὲ παραγγέλλων οὐκ ἐπαινῶ, ὅτι οὐκ εἰς τὸ
this    But  enjoining,   not I praise (you),because not for  the

**18** ρεῖττον ἀλλ᾽ εἰς τὸ ἧττον συνέρχεσθε. πρῶτον μὲν γὰρ
better,   but   for the worse  you come together. firstly indeed For
συνερχομένων ὑμῶν ἐν τῇ ἐκκλησίᾳ, ἀκούω σχίσματα ἐν
coming together you,  in the  church,    I hear  divisions among

**19** ὑμῖν ὑπάρχειν, καὶ μέρος τι πιστεύω. δεῖ γὰρ καὶ αἱρέσεις ἐν
you  to be,    and  part some I believe.  must For also  heresies among

**20** ὑμῖν εἶναι, ἵνα οἱ δόκιμοι φανεροὶ γένωνται ἐν ὑμῖν. συνερχο-
you  be,  that the approved ones revealed may become among you. Coming
μένων οὖν ὑμῶν ἐπὶ τὸ αὐτό, οὐκ ἔστι Κυριακὸν δεῖπνον
together, then, you     together,  not it is of the Lord  a supper

**21** φαγεῖν. ἕκαστος γὰρ τὸ ἴδιον δεῖπνον προλαμβάνει ἐν τῷ
to eat.  each one For  the  own  supper  takes before

**22** φαγεῖν, καὶ ὃς μὲν πεινᾷ, ὃς δὲ μεθύει. μὴ γὰρ οἰκίας ὑκ
to eat;  and  one hungers, another drunken. not For houses  not
ἔχετε εἰς τὸ ἐσθίειν καὶ πίνειν; ἢ τῆς ἐκκλησίας τοῦ Θεοῦ κατα-
you have  to eat and to drink? Or the church     of God do you
φρονεῖτε, καὶ καταισχύνετε τοὺς μὴ ἔχοντας; τί ὑμῖν εἴπω;
despise,   and   shame     those not  having? What to you do I say?

**23** ἐπαινέσω ὑμᾶς ἐν τούτῳ; οὐκ ἐπαινῶ. ἐγὼ γὰρ παρέλαβον
Shall I praise you in  this?  not I praise.  I  For  I received
ἀπὸ τοῦ Κυρίου, ὃ καὶ παρέδωκα ὑμῖν, ὅτι ὁ Κύριος
from the  Lord  what also I delivered to you, that the Lord

**24** Ἰησοῦς ἐν τῇ νυκτὶ ᾗ παρεδίδοτο ἔλαβεν ἄρτον, καὶ
Jesus  in the night in which He was betrayed took  bread, and
εὐχαριστήσας ἔκλασε, καὶ εἶπε, Λάβετε, φάγετε, τοῦτό μού
having given thanks broke,  and said,  Take,  eat,  this of Me
ἐστι τὸ σῶμα τὸ ὑπὲρ ὑμῶν κλώμενον· τοῦτο ποιεῖτε εἰς
is  the  body on behalf of you  broken;  this  do  for

**25** τὴν ἐμὴν ἀνάμνησιν. ὡσαύτως καὶ τὸ ποτήριον, μετὰ τὸ
my  remembrance. In the same way And the cup,  after the
δειπνῆσαι, λέγων, Τοῦτο τὸ ποτήριον ἡ καινὴ διαθήκη
supping,  saying,  This  the cup   the new   covenant
ἐστὶν ἐν τῷ ἐμῷ αἵματι· τοῦτο ποιεῖτε, ὁσάκις ἂν πίνητε,
is  in  My blood;  this  do,  as often as you drink,

**26** εἰς τὴν ἐμὴν ἀνάμνησιν. ὁσάκις γὰρ ἂν ἐσθίητε τὸν ἄρτον
for  My  remembrance.  as often For (as) you may eat  bread
τοῦτον, καὶ τὸ ποτήριον τοῦτο πίνητε, τὸν θάνατον τοῦ
this,  and  the  cup  this  drink.  the death of the

**27** Κυρίου καταγγέλλετε ἄχρις οὗ ἂν ἔλθῃ. ὥστε ὃς ἂν ἐσθίῃ
Lord  you declare,  until He may come. So as whoever may eat
τὸν ἄρτον τοῦτον ἢ πίνῃ τὸ ποτήριον τοῦ Κυρίου ἀναξίως,
the bread  this, or drinks the cup  of the  Lord  unworthily,

**28** ἔνοχος ἔσται τοῦ σώματος καὶ αἵματος τοῦ Κυρίου. δοκι-
guilty  will be of the body  and of the blood of the Lord.  let
μαζέτω δὲ ἄνθρωπος ἑαυτόν, καὶ οὕτως ἐκ τοῦ ἄρτου
prove  But a man  himself,  and  so  of  the  bread

**29** ἐσθιέτω, καὶ ἐκ τοῦ ποτηρίου πινέτω. ὁ γὰρ ἐσθίων καὶ πίνων
let him eat, and of the  cup  let him drink. he For eating  and drinking
ἀναξίως, κρίμα ἑαυτῷ ἐσθίει καὶ πίνει, μὴ διακρίνων τὸ
unworthily judgment to himself eats  and  drinks, not  discerning the

**30** σῶμα τοῦ Κυρίου. διὰ τοῦτο ἐν ὑμῖν πολλοὶ ἀσθενεῖς καὶ
body of the Lord.   Therefore among you (are) many  weak  and

**31** ἄρρωστοι, καὶ κοιμῶνται ἱκανοί. εἰ γὰρ ἑαυτοὺς διεκρίνομεν,
feeble,  and  sleep  many. if For ourselves we discerned,

should not be judged. [32] But being judged, we are corrected by (the) Lord, that we should not be condemned with the world. [33] So that, my brothers, coming together to eat, wait for one another. [34] But if anyone is hungry, let him eat at home, that you may not come together for judgment; and the other things I will set in order whenever I may come.

CHAPTER 12

[1] But as to spiritual things, brothers, I do not wish you to be ignorant. [2] You know that you nations having been led away, you were led to dumb idols. [3] Because of this I make known to you that no one speaking by (the) Spirit of God says, Jesus is a curse. And no one is able to say, Jesus (is) Lord, except by (the) Holy Spirit. [4] But there are differences of gifts but the same Spirit; [5] and there are differences of ministries, yet the same Lord. [6] And there are differences of workings, but the same God is working all things in all. [7] But to each is given the showing forth of the Spirit to (our) profit. [8] For through the Spirit is given to one a word of wisdom; and to another a word of knowledge, according to the same Spirit; [9] and to another, faith by the same Spirit; and to another, gifts of healing, by the same Spirit; [10] and to another, workings of powers, and to another, prophecy; and to another, discerning of spirits; and to another, kinds of languages; and to another, interpretation of languages. [11] But the one and the same Spirit works all these things, distributing separately to each as He wills. [12] Even so the body is one and has many members, but all the members of the one body, being many, are one body; so also (is) Christ. [13] For also by one Spirit we all were baptized into one body, whether Jews or Greeks, whether slaves or free, and all into one Spirit

**32** οὐκ ἂν ἐκρινόμεθα. κρινόμενοι δέ, ὑπὸ Κυρίου παιδευόμεθα,
not we would be judged. being judged But by (the) Lord, we are chastened,

**33** ἵνα μὴ σὺν τῷ κόσμῳ κατακριθῶμεν. ὥστε, ἀδελφοί μου,
lest with the world we are condemned. So as, brothers of me,

**34** συνερχόμενοι εἰς τὸ φαγεῖν, ἀλλήλους ἐκδέχεσθε. εἰ δέ τις
coming together to eat, one another await. if And anyone

πεινᾷ, ἐν οἴκῳ ἐσθιέτω· ἵνα μὴ εἰς κρίμα συνέρχησθε. τὰ δὲ
hungers, at home let him eat, lest to judgment you come together. the And

λοιπά, ὡς ἂν ἔλθω, διατάξομαι.
rest, whenever I come, I will set in order.

## CHAPTER 12

**1** Περὶ δὲ τῶν πνευματικῶν, ἀδελφοί, οὐ θέλω ὑμᾶς ἀγνοεῖν.
about And the spiritual matters, brothers, not I wish you to be ignorant.

**2** οἴδατε ὅτι ἔθνη ἦτε πρὸς τὰ εἴδωλα τὰ ἄφωνα, ὡς ἂν
You know that nations you were to the idols dumb, as

**3** ἤγεσθε, ἀπαγόμενοι. διὸ γνωρίζω ὑμῖν, ὅτι οὐδεὶς ἐν Πνεύ-
you were led, being led away. Therefore I make known to you that no one by Spirit

ματι Θεοῦ λαλῶν λέγει ἀνάθεμα Ἰησοῦν· καὶ οὐδεὶς δύναται
(the) Spirit of God speaking says, A curse (is) Jesus; and no one is able

εἰπεῖν Κύριον Ἰησοῦν, εἰ μὴ ἐν Πνεύματι Ἁγίῳ.
to say, Lord Jesus, except by (the) Spirit Holy.

**4** Διαιρέσεις δὲ χαρισμάτων εἰσί, τὸ δὲ αὐτὸ Πνεῦμα. καὶ
differences But of gifts there are, the but same Spirit. And

**5** διαιρέσεις διακονιων εἰσί, καὶ ὁ αὐτὸς Κύριος. καὶ διαιρέσεις
**6** differences of ministries there are, yet the same Lord. And differences

ἐνεργημάτων εἰσίν, ὁ δὲ αὐτός ἐστι Θεός, ὁ ἐνεργῶν τὰ
of workings there are, the and same is God, working

**7** πάντα ἐν πᾶσιν. ἑκάστῳ δὲ δίδοται ἡ φανέρωσις τοῦ
all things in all. to each one But is given the showing forth of the

Πνεύματος πρὸς τὸ συμφέρον. ᾧ μὲν γὰρ διὰ τοῦ Πνεύματος
Spirit to the advantage. to one For through the Spirit

**8** δίδοται λόγος σοφίας, ἄλλῳ δὲ λόγος γνώσεως, κατὰ τὸ αὐτὸ
is given a word of wisdom; to another and a word of knowledge, per the same

**9** Πνεῦμα· ἑτέρῳ δὲ πίστις, ἐν τῷ αὐτῷ Πνεύματι· ἄλλῳ δὲ
Spirit; to another and faith, by the same Spirit; to another and

**10** χαρίσματα ἰαμάτων, ἐν τῷ αὐτῷ Πνεύματι· ἄλλῳ δὲ ἐνεργή-
gifts of healing, by the same Spirit, to another and workings

ματα δυνάμεων, ἄλλῳ δὲ προφητεία, ἄλλῳ δὲ διακρίσεις
of powers; to another and prophecy; to another and discerning

πνευμάτων, ἑτέρῳ δὲ γένη γλωσσῶν, ἄλλῳ δὲ ἑρμηνεία
of spirits; to another and kinds of languages; to another and interpretation

**11** γλωσσῶν· πάντα δὲ ταῦτα ἐνεργεῖ τὸ ἓν καὶ τὸ αὐτὸ Πνεῦμα,
of languages; all and these things works the one and the same Spirit,

διαιροῦν ἰδίᾳ ἑκάστῳ καθὼς βούλεται.
distributing separately to each as He purposes.

**12** Καθάπερ γὰρ τὸ σῶμα ἕν ἐστι, καὶ μέλη ἔχει πολλά,
as For the body one is, and members has many,

πάντα δὲ τὰ μέλη τοῦ σώματος τοῦ ἑνός, πολλὰ ὄντα, ἓν
all but the members of the body one, many being, one

**13** ἐστι σῶμα· οὕτω καὶ ὁ Χριστός. καὶ γὰρ ἐν ἑνὶ Πνεύματι
is body; so also the Christ. also For by one Spirit

ἡμεῖς πάντες εἰς ἓν σῶμα ἐβαπτίσθημεν, εἴτε Ἰουδαῖοι εἴτε
we all into one body were baptized, whether Jews or

Ἕλληνες, εἴτε δοῦλοι εἴτε ἐλεύθεροι· καὶ πάντες εἰς ἓν Πνεῦμα
Greeks, whether slaves or free, and all into one Spirit

were made to drink. [14] For also the body is not one member, but many. [15] If the foot should say, Because I am not a hand, I am not of the body, for this (reason) is it not of the body? [16] And if the ear says, I am not an eye; for this (reason) is it not of the body? [17] If the whole body (was) an eye, where the hearing? If all hearing, where the smelling? [18] But now God set each one of the members in the body, just as He pleased. [19] But if all were one part, where (would) the body be? [20] But now, indeed, many are the members, but one body. [21] And (the) eye is not able to say to the hand, I have no need of you; or again the head to the feet, I have no need of you. [22] But much rather the members of the body which seem to be weaker are necessary; [23] and those of the body which we consider less honorable, to these we give the more honor. And our unpresentable (members) have the greater propriety. [24] But our presentable (members) have no need. But God tempered the body together, giving more honor to that which has need, [25] so that there might be no division in the body, but that the members might have the same care for one another. [26] And if one member suffers, all the members suffer with (it); if one member is glorified, all the members rejoice with (it). [27] And you are a body of Christ, and members in part. [28] And God placed some in the church: firstly, apostles; secondly, prophets; thirdly, teachers; then works of power; then gifts of healing; helps; governings; kinds of languages. [29] (Are) all apostles? All prophets? All teachers? All mighty works? [30] Do all have gifts of healing? Do all speak with languages? Do all interpret? [31] But zealously strive for the better gifts, and yet I show

**14** ἐποτίσθημεν. καὶ γὰρ τὸ σῶμα οὐκ ἔστιν ἓν μέλος, ἀλλὰ
we were given to drink. also For the body not is one member, but

**15** πολλά. ἐὰν εἴπῃ ὁ πούς, "Ὅτι οὐκ εἰμὶ χείρ, οὐκ εἰμὶ ἐκ τοῦ
many. If says the foot: Because not I am a hand, not I am of the

**16** σώματος· οὐ παρὰ τοῦτο οὐκ ἔστιν ἐκ τοῦ σώματος ; καὶ
body; on account of this not is it of the body? And
ἐὰν εἴπῃ τὸ οὖς, "Ὅτι οὐκ εἰμὶ ὀφθαλμός, οὐκ εἰμὶ ἐκ τοῦ
if says the ear: Because not I am an eye, not I am of the

**17** σώματος· οὐ παρὰ τοῦτο οὐκ ἔστιν ἐκ τοῦ σώματος ; εἰ
body; on account of this not is it of the body; If
ὅλον τὸ σῶμα ὀφθαλμός, ποῦ ἡ ἀκοή ; εἰ ὅλον ἀκοή, ποῦ
all the body (was) an eye, where the hearing? If all hearing, where

**18** ἡ ὄσφρησις ; νυνὶ δὲ ὁ Θεὸς ἔθετο τὰ μέλη ἓν ἕκαστον αὐτῶν
the smelling. now But God set the members, one each of them

**19** ἐν τῷ σώματι, καθὼς ἠθέλησεν. εἰ δὲ ἦν τὰ πάντα ἓν μέλος,
in the body, as He desired. if And was all one member,

**20** ποῦ τὸ σῶμα ; νῦν δὲ πολλὰ μὲν μέλη, ἓν δὲ σῶμα. οὐ
where the body? now But many indeed members, one but body. not

**21** δύναται δὲ ὀφθαλμὸς εἰπεῖν τῇ χειρί, Χρείαν σου οὐκ ἔχω·
can And the eye say to the hand need of you not I have;

**22** ἢ πάλιν ἡ κεφαλὴ τοῖς ποσί, Χρείαν ὑμῶν οὐκ ἔχω. ἀλλὰ
or again the head to the feet, need of you not I have. But
πολλῷ μᾶλλον τὰ δοκοῦντα μέλη τοῦ σώματος ἀσθενέ-
by much more the seeming members of the body weaker

**23** στερα ὑπάρχειν, ἀναγκαῖά ἐστι· καὶ ἃ δοκοῦμεν 'ἀτιμότερα
to be, necessary is; and those which we think less honorable
εἶναι τοῦ σώματος, τούτοις τιμὴν περισσοτέραν περιτίθεμεν·
to be of the body, to these honor more abundant we put around;
καὶ τὰ ἀσχήμονα ἡμῶν εὐσχημοσύνην περισσοτέραν ἔχει·
and the unpresentable of us propriety more abundant has;

**24** τὰ δὲ εὐσχήμονα ἡμῶν οὐ χρείαν ἔχει· ἀλλ' ὁ Θεὸς συνε-
the but presentable (members) of us not need has. But God tempered
κέρασε τὸ σῶμα, τῷ ὑστεροῦντι περισσοτέραν δοὺς τιμήν,
together the body, to the (member) lacking, more abundant giving honor,

**25** ἵνα μὴ ᾖ σχίσμα ἐν τῷ σώματι, ἀλλὰ τὸ αὐτὸ ὑπὲρ ἀλλήλων
lest be division in the body; but the same on behalf of one another

**26** μεριμνῶσι τὰ μέλη. καὶ εἴτε πάσχει ἓν μέλος, συμπάσχει
should care the members. And whether suffers one member, suffers with (it)
πάντα τὰ μέλη· εἴτε δοξάζεται ἓν μέλος, συγχαίρει πάντα
all the members; or is glorified one member, rejoices with (it) all

**27** τὰ μέλη. ὑμεῖς δέ ἐστε σῶμα Χριστοῦ, καὶ μέλη ἐκ μέρους.
the members. you And are a body of Christ, and members in part.

**28** καὶ οὓς μὲν ἔθετο ὁ Θεὸς ἐν τῇ ἐκκλησίᾳ πρῶτον ἀποστόλους,
And some placed God in the church firstly apostles;
δεύτερον προφήτας, τρίτον διδασκάλους, ἔπειτα δυνάμεις,
secondly prophets; thirdly, teachers; then works of power;
εἶτα χαρίσματα ἰαμάτων, ἀντιλήψεις, κυβερνήσεις, γένη
then gifts of healing; helps; governings; kinds

**29** γλωσσῶν. μὴ πάντες ἀπόστολοι ; μὴ πάντες προφῆται ;
of languages. Not all (are) apostles? Not all (are) prophets?

**30** μὴ πάντες διδάσκαλοι ; μὴ πάντες δυνάμεις ; μὴ πάντες
Not all (are) teachers? Not all workers of power? Not all
χαρίσματα ἔχουσιν ἰαμάτων ; μὴ πάντες γλώσσαις λαλοῦσι ;
gifts have of healings? Not all languages speak?

**31** μὴ πάντες διερμηνεύουσι ; ζηλοῦτε δὲ τὰ χαρίσματα τὰ
Not all interpret? zealously strive But the gifts after

you a more excellent way.

κρείττονα. καὶ ἔτι καθ᾽ ὑπερβολὴν ὁδὸν ὑμῖν δείκνυμι.
better.    And yet according to excellence a way to you I show.

## CHAPTER 13

[1] If I speak with the tongues of men and of angels, but have not love, I have become as sounding brass or a clanging cymbal. [2] And if I have prophecy, and know all mysteries and all knowledge, and if I have all faith, so as to move mountains, but have not love, I am nothing. [3] And if I give out all my goods, and if I deliver my body that I be burned, and have not love. I am profited nothing. [4] Love has patience, is kind; love is not envious; love is not vain, is not puffed up; [5] does not behave indecently, does not pursue its own things, is not easily provoked, thinks no evil; [6] does not rejoice in unrighteousness, but rejoices in the truth; [7] silently bears all things, believes all things, hopes all things, endures all things; [8] love never fails. But if there are prophecies they shall be abolished; if languages, they shall stop; if knowledge, it shall cease. [9] For we know in part and we prophesy in part, [10] but when that which is perfect comes, then that in part shall cease to be. [11] When I was an infant, I spoke as an infant, I thought as an infant, I reasoned as an infant; but when I became a man, I did away with childish things. [12] For now we see through a mirror dimly, but then face to face; now I know in part, but then I shall know even as I also have been known. [13] And now faith, hope, and love remain, these three things, but the greatest of these (is) love.

## CHAPTER 14

[1] Pursue love, and desire spiritual things, but rather that you may prophesy. [2] For he that speaks with a tongue does not speak to men, but to

## CHAPTER 13

**1** Ἐὰν ταῖς γλώσσαις τῶν ἀνθρώπων λαλῶ καὶ τῶν
If  in the  languages  of men  I speak, even

ἀγγέλων, ἀγάπην δὲ μὴ ἔχω, γέγονα χαλκὸς ἠχῶν ἢ
of angels,  love  and not I have, I have become brass  sounding, or

**2** κύμβαλον ἀλαλάζον. καὶ ἐὰν ἔχω προφητείαν, καὶ εἰδῶ τὰ
a cymbal  tinkling. And if I have  prophecies,  and know the

μυστήρια πάντα καὶ πᾶσαν τὴν γνῶσιν, καὶ ἐὰν ἔχω πᾶσαν
mysteries  all,  and all  the  knowledge, and if I have  all

τὴν πίστιν, ὥστε ὄρη μεθιστάνειν, ἀγάπην δὲ μὴ ἔχω, οὐδέν
faith,  so as mountains to move,  love  but not have, nothing

**3** εἰμι. καὶ ἐὰν ψωμίσω πάντα τὰ ὑπάρχοντά μου, καὶ ἐὰν
I am. And if distribute  all  the  goods  of me, and if

παραδῶ τὸ σῶμά μου ἵνα καυθήσωμαι, ἀγάπην δὲ μὴ ἔχω,
I deliver the  body of me that I be burned,  love  but not I have,

**4** οὐδὲν ὠφελοῦμαι. ἡ ἀγάπη μακροθυμεῖ, χρηστεύεται· ἡ
nothing I am profited.  Love  suffers long,  is kind;

ἀγάπη οὐ ζηλοῖ· ἡ ἀγάπη οὐ περπερεύεται, οὐ φυσιοῦται,
love  not is envious;  love  not  vaunts itself,  not is puffed up,

**5** οὐκ ἀσχημονεῖ, οὐ ζητεῖ τὰ ἑαυτῆς, οὐ παροξύνεται, οὐ
not behaves indecently, not seeks things of itself, not is provoked,  not

**6** λογίζεται τὸ κακόν, οὐ χαίρει ἐπὶ τῇ ἀδικίᾳ, συγχαίρει δὲ τῇ
thinks  evil,  not rejoices over the  wrong,  rejoices with but the

**7** ἀληθείᾳ, πάντα στέγει, πάντα πιστεύει, πάντα ἐλπίζει,
truth;  all things covers quietly, all things believes, all things  hopes,

**8** πάντα ὑπομένει. ἡ ἀγάπη οὐδέποτε ἐκπίπτει· εἴτε δὲ προφη-
all things endures.  Love  never  fails;  whether but prophesies,

τεῖαι, καταργηθήσονται· εἴτε γλῶσσαι, παύσονται· εἴτε
they will be abolished;  if  languages, they shall cease;  if

**9** γνῶσις, καταργηθήσεται. ἐκ μέρους γὰρ γινώσκομεν, καὶ ἐκ
knowledge, it shall be abolished.  in part  For  we know,  and in

**10** μέρους προφητεύομεν· ὅταν δὲ ἔλθῃ τὸ τέλειον, τότε τὸ ἐκ
part  we prophesy;  when but comes the  perfect thing, then that in

**11** μέρους καταργηθήσεται. ὅτε ἤμην νήπιος, ὡς νήπιος
part  will be abolished.  When I was an infant,  as an infant

ἐλάλουν, ὡς νήπιος ἐφρόνουν, ὡς νήπιος ἐλογιζόμην· ὅτε δὲ
I spoke,  as an infant I thought,  as an infant I reasoned;  when but

**12** γέγονα ἀνήρ, κατήργηκα τὰ τοῦ νηπίου. βλέπομεν γὰρ
I became a man, I did away with the things of the infant.  we see  For

ἄρτι δι᾽ ἐσόπτρου ἐν αἰνίγματι, τότε δὲ πρόσωπον πρὸς
yet through a mirror  in  obscureness,  then but  face  to

πρόσωπον· ἄρτι γινώσκω ἐκ μέρους, τότε δὲ ἐπιγνώσομαι
face;  yet I know  in part,  then but I will fully know

**13** καθὼς καὶ ἐπεγνώσθην. νυνὶ δὲ μένει πίστις, ἐλπίς, ἀγάπη,
even as also I was fully known. now But remains faith,  hope,  love,

τὰ τρία ταῦτα· μείζων δὲ τούτων ἡ ἀγάπη.
three these things; (the) greater and of these (is) love.

## CHAPTER 14

**1** Διώκετε τὴν ἀγάπην· ζηλοῦτε δὲ τὰ πνευματικά, μαλλον
Pursue  love,  seek eagerly and the spiritual things; rather

**2** δὲ ἵνα προφητεύητε. ὁ γὰρ λαλῶν γλώσσῃ οὐκ ἀνθρώποις
and that you may prophesy he for speaking in a tongue not  to men

God; for no one hears, but in spirit he speaks mysteries. [3] But he prophesying to men speaks (for) building up and encouragement and comfort. [4] He speaking in a tongue builds himself up; but he prophesying builds a church up. [5] And I wish all of you to speak in languages, but rather that you may prophesy—for greater is he prophesying than he speaking in tongues, unless he interpret, that the church may receive building up. [6] But now, brothers, if I come to you speaking in tongues, what will I profit you, except I speak to you either in revelation, or in knowledge, or in prophecy, or in teaching? [7] Yet lifeless things giving a sound, whether pipe or harp, if they do not give a distinction in the sound, how will it be known the thing being piped, or being harped? [8] For also if a trumpet gives an uncertain sound, who will get himself ready for war? [9] So also you, if you do not give a clear word through the language, how will it be known the thing being said? For you will be speaking into air. [10] So it may be many kinds of sounds are in (the) world, and not one is without (distinct) sound. [11] if, then, I do not know the power of the sound, I will be a foreigner to him speaking, and he speaking in me a foreigner. [12] So also you, since you are zealots of spiritual things, seek to build up the church that you may abound. [13] So then, he speaking in a language, let him pray that he may interpret. [14] For if I pray in a tongue, my spirit prays, but my mind is unfruitful. [15] What then is it? I will pray with the spirit and I will also pray with the mind; I will sing with the spirit, and I will also sing with the mind. [16] Else if you bless in the spirit, he occupying the place of the unlearned, how will he say the amen at your giving of thanks, since, he does not know what you say? [17] For you truly give thanks well, but the other

**3** λαλεῖ, ἀλλὰ τῷ Θεῷ· οὐδεὶς γὰρ ἀκούει, πνεύματι δὲ λαλεῖ
speaks, but    to God;  no one for  hears,  in spirit  but he speaks
μυστήρια. ὁ δὲ προφητεύων ἀνθρώποις λαλεῖ οἰκοδομὴν καὶ
mysteries. the (one) but prophesying to men   speaks (for) building up and
**4** παράκλησιν καὶ παραμυθίαν. ὁ λαλῶν γλώσσῃ ἑαυτὸν οἰκο-
encouragement and comfort.    The (one) speaking in a tongue himself builds
**5** δομεῖ, ὁ δὲ προφητεύων ἐκκλησίαν οἰκοδομεῖ. θέλω δὲ πάντας
up, the (one) but prophesying  a church builds up.  I desire And all
ὑμᾶς λαλεῖν γλώσσαις, μᾶλλον δὲ ἵνα προφητεύητε· μείζων
you to speak in languages,  rather but  that you may prophesy; greater
γὰρ ὁ προφητεύων ἢ ὁ λαλῶν γλώσσαις, ἐκτὸς εἰ μὴ διερμη-
for the (one) prophesying than he speaking in tongues,  unless he interpret,
**6** νεύῃ, ἵνα ἡ ἐκκλησία οἰκοδομὴν λάβη. νυνὶ δέ, ἀδελφοί, ἐὰν
that the church   building up  may receive. now But, brothers, if
ἔλθω πρὸς ὑμᾶς γλώσσαις λαλῶν, τί ὑμᾶς ὠφελήσω, ἐὰν μὴ
I come to    you in languages speaking, what you will I profit,   except
ὑμῖν λαλήσω ἢ ἐν ἀποκαλύψει, ἢ ἐν γνώσει, ἢ ἐν προφητείᾳ,
to you I speak either in revelation,  or in knowledge, or in prophecy,
**7** ἡ ἐν διδαχῇ; ὅμως τὰ ἄψυχα φωνὴν διδόντα, εἴτε αὐλός,
or in teaching?  Yet  lifeless things a sound giving, whether pipe
εἴτε κιθάρα, ἐὰν διαστολὴν τοῖς φθόγγοις μὴ δῷ, πῶς
or harp,   if  a distinction in the  sound  not they give, how
**8** γνωσθήσεται τὸ αὐλούμενον ἢ τὸ κιθαριζόμενον; καὶ γὰρ
will it be known the thing being piped or the thing being harped? indeed For
ἐὰν ἄδηλον φωνὴν σάλπιγξ δῷ, τίς παρασκευάσεται εἰς
if an uncertain sound  a trumpet gives, who will get himself ready  for
**9** πόλεμον; οὕτω καὶ ὑμεῖς διὰ τῆς γλώσσης ἐὰν μὴ εὔσημον
war?    So  also  you through the language  if not a clear
λόγον δῶτε, πῶς γνωσθήσεται τὸ λαλούμενον; ἔσεσθε γὰρ
word  give,  how will it be known the thing being said?  you For
**10** εἰς ἀέρα λαλοῦντες. τοσαῦτα, εἰ τύχοι, γένη φωνῶν ἐστὶν
into air will be speaking. So many  it may be  kinds of sounds are
**11** ἐν κόσμῳ καὶ οὐδὲν ἄφωνον. ἐὰν οὖν μὴ εἰδῶ τὴν δύναμιν
in (the) world, and not one is voiceless. If, then, not I know the   power
τῆς φωνῆς, ἔσομαι τῷ λαλοῦντι βάρβαρος, καὶ ὁ λαλῶν ἐν
of the sound, I will be to the (one) speaking a foreigner, and he speaking in
**12** ἐμοὶ βάρβαρος. οὕτω καὶ ὑμεῖς, ἐπεὶ ζηλωταί ἐστε πνευ-
me a foreigner.  So  also  you, since  zealots you are of
μάτων, πρὸς τὴν οἰκοδομὴν τῆς ἐκκλησίας ζητεῖτε ἵνα περισ-
spiritual things, to the building up of the church    seek,  that you may
**13** σεύητε. διόπερ ὁ λαλῶν γλώσσῃ προσευχέσθω ἵνα διερμη-
abound. Therefore, he speaking in a language let him pray  that he may
**14** νεύῃ. ἐὰν γὰρ προσεύχωμαι γλώσσῃ, τὸ πνεῦμά μου
interpret. if For  I pray    in a tongue,   the spirit of me
**15** προσεύχεται, ὁ δὲ νοῦς μου ἄκαρπός ἐστι. τί οὖν ἐστί;
prays,    the but mind of me unfruitful  is.  What then is it?
προσεύξομαι τῷ πνεύματι, προσεύξομαι δὲ καὶ τῷ νοΐ· ψαλῶ
I will pray with the  spirit,   I will pray and also with the mind; I sing
**16** τῷ πνεύματι, ψαλῶ δὲ καὶ τῷ νοΐ. ἐπεὶ ἐὰν εὐλογήσῃς τῷ
with the spirit,  I sing and also with the mind. Else if you bless in the
πνεύματι, ὁ ἀναπληρῶν τὸν τόπον τοῦ ἰδιώτου πῶς ἐρεῖ
spirit,  the (one) occupying  the place of the unlearned, how will he say
τὸ ἀμὴν ἐπὶ τῇ σῇ εὐχαριστίᾳ, ἐπειδὴ τί λέγεις οὐκ οἶδε;
the amen at    your giving thanks? Since what you say not he knows;
**17** σὺ μὲν γὰρ καλῶς εὐχαριστεῖς, ἀλλ' ὁ ἕτερος οὐκ οἰκοδο-
you indeed for well  give thanks,  but the other  not  is built up

is not built up. [18] I thank my God (that) I speak more languages than all of you; [19] But in (the) church I desire to speak five words with my mind, that I may also instruct others, than myriads of words in a foreign language. [20] Do not be children in (your) minds, brothers, but in malice be as infants, and in (your) minds be mature. [21] It has been written in the Law, "By other tongues and by other lips I will speak to this people, and even so they will not hear Me, says (the) Lord." [22] So that tongues are not a sign to those believing, but to those not believing; but prophecy is not to those not believing, but to those believing. [23] If therefore the whole church comes together, and all speak in languages, and uninstructed ones, or unbelievers come in, will they not say that you rave? [24] But if all prophesy, and some unbeliever or uninstructed one comes in, he is convicted by all, he is judged by all; [25] and so the secrets of his heart become revealed; and so, falling on (his) face, he will worship God, declaring that God is truly among you.

[26] What, then, is it, brothers? When you may come together, each of you has a psalm, has a teaching, has a tongue, has a revelation, has an interpretation. Let all things be done for edification. [27] If anyone speak with a tongue, (let it be) by two or three (at) the most, and in succession, and let one interpret; [28] and if there is no interpreter, let him be silent in a church; and let him speak to himself and to God. [29] And let two or three prophets speak , and let the others discern. [30] But if a revelation should occur to another sitting by, let the first be silent. [31] For you can all prophesy one by one, that all may learn, and all may be encouraged. [32] And the spirits of prophets are subject to

**18** μεῖται. εὐχαριστῶ τῷ Θεῷ μου, πάντων ὑμῶν μᾶλλον
I thank      the God of me,   all    of you   more than

**19** γλώσσαις λαλῶν· ἀλλ' ἐν ἐκκλησίᾳ θέλω πέντε λόγους διὰ
in languages I speak,  but  in a church I desire  five    words   with
τοῦ νοός μου λαλῆσαι, ἵνα καὶ ἄλλους κατηχήσω, ἢ μυρίους
the mind of me to speak,   that also  others    I may instruct,  than myriads
λόγους ἐν γλώσσῃ.
of words in a foreign language.

**20** Ἀδελφοί, μὴ παιδία γίνεσθε ταῖς φρεσίν· ἀλλὰ τῇ κακίᾳ
Brothers, not children be  in the minds,  but    in malice

**21** νηπιάζετε, ταῖς δὲ φρεσὶ τέλειοι γίνεσθε. ἐν τῷ νόμῳ
be like infants in the and minds   mature   be.    In the   law
γέγραπται ὅτι Ἐν ἑτερογλώσσοις καὶ ἐν χείλεσιν ἑτέροις
it has been written:  In other tongues   and  in    lips    other
λαλήσω τῷ λαῷ τούτῳ, καὶ οὐδ' οὕτως εἰσακούσονταί μου,
I will speak to people this,  and not  so    will they hear    Me,

**22** λέγει Κύριος. ὥστε αἱ γλῶσσαι εἰς σημεῖόν εἰσιν, οὐ τοῖς
says (the) Lord. So as    tongues   for a sign    are, not to those
πιστεύουσιν, ἀλλὰ τοῖς ἀπίστοις· ἡ δὲ προφητεία, οὐ τοῖς
believing,   but to those not believing; and prophecy (is)  not to the

**23** ἀπίστοις, ἀλλὰ τοῖς πιστεύουσιν. ἐὰν οὖν συνέλθῃ ἡ
unbelievers, but   to those  believing.   If, therefore, comes the
ἐκκλησία ὅλη ἐπὶ τὸ αὐτό, καὶ πάντες γλώσσαις λαλῶσιν,
church    whole together,  and   all    in languages   speak,
εἰσέλθωσι δὲ ἰδιῶται ἢ ἄπιστοι, οὐκ ἐροῦσιν ὅτι μαίνεσθε;
come in   and uninstructed or unbelievers, not will they say that you rave?

**24** ἐὰν δὲ πάντες προφητεύωσιν, εἰσέλθῃ δέ τις ἄπιστος ἢ
if  But all   prophesy,        comes in  and some unbeliever or
ἰδιώτης, ἐλέγχεται ὑπὸ πάντων, ἀνακρίνεται ὑπὸ πάντων,
uninstructed, he is convicted by  all,    he is judged   by     all;

**25** καὶ οὕτω τὰ κρυπτὰ τῆς καρδίας αὐτοῦ φανερὰ γίνεται· καὶ
and so   the secrets of the heart   of him revealed become,   and
οὕτω πεσὼν ἐπὶ πρόσωπον προσκυνήσει τῷ Θεῷ ἀπαγ-
so  falling  on (his) face,  he will worship   God, declaring
γέλλων ὅτι ὁ Θεὸς ὄντως ἐν ὑμῖν ἐστί.
that   God   truly among you is.

**26** Τί οὖν ἐστίν, ἀδελφοί; ὅταν συνέρχησθε, ἕκαστος ὑμῶν
What then is it,   brothers?  When you come together, each one of you
ψαλμὸν ἔχει, διδαχὴν ἔχει, γλῶσσαν ἔχει, ἀποκάλυψιν ἔχει,
a psalm   has, a teaching he has, a language he has, a revelation he has,

**27** ἑρμηνείαν ἔχει. πάντα πρὸς οἰκοδομὴν γενέσθω. εἴτε
an interpretation he has. all things for  building up   let be.    If
γλώσσῃ τις λαλεῖ, κατὰ δύο ἢ τὸ πλεῖστον τρεῖς, καὶ ἀνὰ
in a language one speaks, by   two or the   most    three, and in

**28** μέρος, καὶ εἷς διερμηνευέτω· ἐὰν δὲ μὴ ᾖ διερμηνευτής, σιγάτω
turn,  and one let interpret;  if but  not (is) an interpreter, be silent

**29** ἐν ἐκκλησίᾳ· ἑαυτῷ δὲ λαλείτω καὶ τῷ Θεῷ. προφῆται δὲ
in  church,  to himself and let him speak, and to God.  prophets And
δύο ἢ τρεῖς λαλείτωσαν, καὶ οἱ ἄλλοι διακρινέτωσαν. ἐὰν δὲ

**30** two or three let them speak,  and the others   let discern;   if and

**31** ἄλλῳ ἀποκαλυφθῇ καθημένῳ, ὁ πρῶτος σιγάτω. δύνασθε
to another is revealed   sitting    the first  let be silent.  you can
γὰρ καθ' ἕνα πάντες προφητεύειν, ἵνα πάντες μανθάνωσι,
For one by one  all   prophesy,    that  all    may learn,

**32** καὶ πάντες παρακαλῶνται· καὶ πνεύματα προφητῶν προφή-
and  all   may be encouraged. And  the spirits  of prophets to prophets

prophets. [33] For God is not (God) of confusion, but of peace, as in all the churches of the saints.

[34] Let your women be silent in the churches, for it is not allowed to them to speak, but to be in subjection, as also the law says. [35] But if they desire to learn anything, let them question their husbands at home; for it is a shame for a woman to speak in a church. [36] Or did the word of God go out from you? Or did it reach only to you?

[37] If anyone thinks to be a prophet, or spiritual, let him recognize what I write to you, that they are a command of the Lord. [38] But if any be ignorant, let him be ignorant. [39] So as seek eagerly to prophesy, brothers, and to speak in languages. [40] And let all things be done decently and in order.

CHAPTER 15

[1] But, to you, brothers, I reveal the gospel which I preached to you, which you also received, in which you also stand, [2] by which you also are being saved, if you hold fast the word which I preached to you — unless you believed in vain. [3] For I delivered to you in the first place what I also received, that Christ died for our sins, according to the Scriptures; [4] and that He was buried; and that He was raised the third day, according to the Scriptures; [5] and that He appeared to Peter, then to the twelve. [6] Then He appeared to over five hundred brothers at once, of whom the greater part remain until now, but some also are fallen asleep. [7] Then He appeared to James; then to all the apostles· [8] and last of all, as to one born out of time, He appeared also to me. [9] For I am the least of the apostles, who am not fit to be called Apostle, because I persecuted the church of God. [10] But by God's grace I am what I am, and

**33** ταις ὑποτάσσεται. οὐ γάρ ἐστιν ἀκαταστασίας ὁ Θεός, ἀλλ'
(are) subject.    not For   is   of confusion    God,    but

εἰρήνης, ὡς ἐν πάσαις ταῖς ἐκκλησίαις τῶν ἁγίων.
of peace,  as in   all    the    churches    of the   saints.

**34** Αἱ γυναῖκες ὑμῶν ἐν ταῖς ἐκκλησίαις σιγάτωσαν· οὐ γάρ
Let the women  of you  in   the    churches     be silent,    not for

ἐπιτέτραπται αὐταῖς λαλεῖν, ἀλλ' ὑποτάσσεσθαι, καθὼς καὶ
it is allowed  to them to speak, but  let them be subject,  as   also

**35** ὁ νόμος λέγει. εἰ δέ τι μαθεῖν θέλουσιν, ἐν οἴκῳ τοὺς ἰδίους
the law  says. if But anything to learn they desire, at home the   own

ἄνδρας ἐπερωτάτωσαν· αἰσχρὸν γάρ ἐστι γυναιξὶν ἐν
husbands  let them question;    a shame   for  it is  for women   in

**36** ἐκκλησίᾳ λαλεῖν. ἢ ἀφ' ὑμῶν ὁ λόγος τοῦ Θεοῦ ἐξῆλθεν ; ἢ
a church  to speak. Or from  you the word    of God  went out, or

εἰς ὑμᾶς μόνους κατήντησεν ·
to   you   only   did it reach?

**37** Εἴ τις δοκεῖ προφήτης εἶναι ἢ πνευματικός, ἐπιγινωσκέτω
If anyone thinks a prophet  to be, or  a spiritual one, let him recognize

**38** ἃ γράφω ὑμῖν, ὅτι τοῦ Κυρίου εἰσὶν ἐντολαί. εἰ δέ τις ἀγνοεῖ,
what I write to you, that of the Lord they are a command. if But any be ignorant,

ἀγνοείτω.
let him be ignorant.

**39** Ὥστε, ἀδελφοί, ζηλοῦτε τὸ προφητεύειν, καὶ τὸ λαλεῖν
So as, brothers,   seek eagerly    to prophesy,   and to   speak

**40** γλώσσαις μὴ κωλύετε. πάντα εὐσχημονως καὶ κατὰ τάξιν
in languages not do forbid; all things decently    and according to order

γινέσθω.
let be done.

## CHAPTER 15

**1** Γνωρίζω δὲ ὑμῖν, ἀδελφοί, τὸ εὐαγγέλιον ὃ εὐηγγελισάμην
I make known And to you, brothers, the gospel    which I preached

**2** ὑμῖν, ὃ καὶ παρελάβετε, ἐν ᾧ καὶ ἑστήκατε, δι' οὖ καὶ σώζεσθε·
to you, which also you received, in which also you stand, by which also you are saved,

τίνι λόγῳ εὐηγγελισάμην ὑμῖν, εἰ κατέχετε, ἐκτὸς εἰ μὴ εἰκῆ
to what word I preached    to you if you hold fast,   unless in vain

**3** ἐπιστεύσατε. παρέδωκα γὰρ ὑμῖν ἐν πρώτοις, ὃ καὶ παρέ-
you believed.   I delivered   For to you among the first what also I

λαβον, ὅτι Χριστὸς ἀπέθανεν ὑπὲρ τῶν ἁμαρτιῶν ἡμῶν
received, that Christ    died    for the    sins    of us

**4** κατὰ τὰς γραφάς· καὶ ὅτι ἐτάφη· καὶ ὅτι ἐγήγερται τῇ τρίτῃ
according to the Scriptures, and that He was buried, and has been raised the third

**5** ἡμέρα κατὰ τὰς γραφάς· καὶ ὅτι ὤφθη Κηφᾷ, εἶτα τοῖς δώδεκα·
day according to the Scriptures, and that He was seen by Cephas, then by the twelve;

**6** ἔπειτα ὤφθη ἐπάνω πεντακοσίοις ἀδελφοῖς ἐφάπαξ, ἐξ ὧν οἱ
afterward He was seen over five hundreds brothers at one time, of whom the

**7** πλείους μένουσιν ἕως ἄρτι τινὲς δὲ καὶ ἐκοιμήθησαν· ἔπειτα
most   remain   until now, some but also fell asleep.   Afterward

**8** ὤφθη Ἰακώβῳ, εἶτα τοῖς ἀποστόλοις πᾶσιν· ἔσχατον δὲ
He was seen by James, then by the apostles    all;   lastly   and

**9** πάντων, ὡσπερεὶ τῷ ἐκτρώματι, ὤφθη κἀμοί. ἐγὼ γάρ
of all,    even as if to the untimely birth, He was seen by me also. I   For

**10** εἰμι ὁ ἐλάχιστος τῶν ἀποστόλων, ὃς οὐκ εἰμὶ ἱκανὸς καλεῖσθαι
am the least  of the   apostles,   who not am sufficient to be called

ἀπόστολος, διότι ἐδίωξα τὴν ἐκκλησίαν τοῦ Θεοῦ. χάριτι δὲ
an apostle,  because I persecuted the church    of God. by grace But

His grace which (was) toward me has not been without fruit, but I labored more abundantly than all of them; but not I, but the grace of God with me. [11] Therefore whether they or I, so we preach, and so you believed. [12] Now if Christ is preached, that He has been raised from among (the) dead, how do some among you say that there is no resurrection of (the) dead? [13] But if there is no resurrection of (the) dead, Christ has not been raised. [14] But if Christ has not been raised, then our preaching is worthless and our faith is also worthless. [15] And also we are found (to be) false witnesses of God, because we witnessed concerning God that He raised up Christ, whom He did not raise if then (the) dead are nor raised. [16] For if (the) dead are not raised, Christ has not been raised. [17] But if Christ has not been raised, your faith (is) foolish; you are still in your sins. [18] And then those that fell asleep in Christ were lost. [19] If in this life only we have hope in Christ, we are of all men most miserable.

[20] But now Christ has been raised from among (the) dead, He became the firstfruit of those fallen asleep. [21] For since death (is) by man, also resurrection of (the) dead (came) through man; [22] for as all die in Adam, so also all shall be made alive in Christ. [23] But each in his own order: Christ the firstfruit, then they who are of Christ at His coming. [24] Then the end — when He shall have given up the kingdom to Him who (is) God and Father; when He shall have put down all rule and all authority and power; [25] for He must reign until He shall have put all enemies under His feet; [26] the last enemy put down is death; [27] for He put all things in subjection under His

Θεοῦ εἰμι ὅ εἰμι, καὶ ἡ χάρις αὐτοῦ ἡ εἰς ἐμὲ οὐ κενὴ ἐγενήθη,
of God I am what I am, and  His grace      to me not empty was,

ἀλλὰ περισσότερον αὐτῶν πάντων ἐκοπίασα· οὐκ ἐγὼ δέ,
but  more abundantly (than) them  all     I labored,  not  I yet,

**11** ἀλλ' ἡ χάρις τοῦ Θεοῦ ἡ σὺν ἐμοί. εἴτε οὖν ἐγώ, εἴτε ἐκεῖνοι,
but the grace  of God  with me. Whether, then, I  or  those,

οὕτω κηρύσσομεν, καὶ οὕτως ἐπιστεύσατε.
so  we proclaim,  and  so  you believed.

**12** Εἰ δὲ Χριστὸς κηρύσσεται ὅτι ἐκ νεκρῶν ἐγήγερται, πῶς
If But  Christ  is proclaimed that from (the) dead He was raised, how

**13** λέγουσί τινες ἐν ὑμῖν ὅτι ἀνάστασις νεκρῶν οὐκ ἔστιν ; εἰ δὲ
say  some among you that a resurrection of dead not  is?  if But

ἀνάστασις νεκρῶν οὐκ ἔστιν, οὐδὲ Χριστὸς ἐγήγερται·
a resurrection of dead not  is,  neither Christ  has been raised;

**14** εἰ δὲ Χριστὸς οὐκ ἐγήγερται, κενὸν ἄρα τὸ κήρυγμα
if and  Christ  not has been raised, worthless then  the proclamation

**15** ἡμῶν, κενὴ δὲ καὶ ἡ πίστις ὑμῶν. εὑρισκόμεθα δὲ καὶ ψευδο-
of us, worthless and also the faith  of us. we are found  And also  false

μάρτυρες τοῦ Θεοῦ, ὅτι ἐμαρτυρήσαμεν κατὰ τοῦ Θεοῦ ὅτι
witnesses  of God, because we witnessed  as to  God that

**16** ἤγειρε τὸν Χριστόν, ὃν οὐκ ἤγειρεν, εἴπερ ἄρα νεκροὶ οὐκ
He raised  Christ, whom not He raised  if  then dead ones not

ἐγείρονται. εἰ γὰρ νεκροὶ οὐκ ἐγείρονται, οὐδὲ Χριστὸς
are raised.  if For dead ones not are raised,  neither  Christ

**17** ἐγήγερται· εἰ δὲ Χριστὸς οὐκ ἐγήγερται, ματαία ἡ πίστις
has been raised; if but Christ  not has been raised,  foolish the  faith

**18** ὑμῶν· ἔτι ἐστὲ ἐν ταῖς ἁμαρτίαις ὑμῶν. ἄρα καὶ οἱ κοιμη-
of you; still you are in  the  sins  of you. Then also those having

**19** θέντες ἐν Χριστῷ ἀπώλοντο. εἰ ἐν τῇ ζωῇ ταύτῃ ἠλπικότες
slept in Christ  were lost  If in  life this  having hoped

ἐσμὲν ἐν Χριστῷ μόνον, ἐλεεινότεροι πάντων ἀνθρώπων
we are in  Christ  only,  more miserable of all  men

ἐσμέν.
we are.

**20** Νυνὶ δὲ Χριστὸς ἐγήγερται ἐκ νεκρῶν, ἀπαρχὴ τῶν
now But  Christ  has been raised from (the) dead, firstfruit of those

**21** κεκοιμημένων ἐγένετο. ἐπειδὴ γὰρ δι' ἀνθρώπου ὁ θάνατος,
having fallen asleep He became. since For through man  (is)  death,

**22** καὶ δι' ἀνθρώπου ἀνάστασις νεκρῶν. ὥσπερ γὰρ ἐν τῷ
and through a Man  a resurrection of (the) dead.  as  For in

Ἀδὰμ πάντες ἀποθνήσκουσιν, οὕτω καὶ ἐν τῷ Χριστῷ
Adam  all  die,  so also in  Christ

**23** πάντες ζωοποιηθήσονται. ἕκαστος δὲ ἐν τῷ ἰδίῳ τάγματι·
all  will be made alive. each  But in the own  order:

ἀπαρχὴ Χριστός, ἔπειτα οἱ Χριστοῦ ἐν τῇ παρουσίᾳ αὐτοῦ.
the firstfruit Christ, afterward those of Christ in the coming  of Him.

**24** εἶτα τὸ τέλος, ὅταν παραδῷ τὴν βασιλείαν τῷ Θεῷ καὶ
Then the end — when He delivers the kingdom  to God, even

πατρί, ὅταν καταργήσῃ πᾶσαν ἀρχὴν καὶ πᾶσαν ἐξουσίαν
the Father; when He abolishes all  rule  and  all  authority

**25** καὶ δύναμιν. δεῖ γὰρ αὐτὸν βασιλεύειν, ἄχρις οὗ ἂν θῇ
and  power — it is right For Him  to reign  until  He puts

**26** πάντας τοὺς ἐχθροὺς ὑπὸ τοὺς πόδας αὐτοῦ. ἔσχατος
all  the enemies  under the  feet  of Him — (the) last

**27** ἐχθρὸς καταργεῖται ὁ θάνατος. Πάντα γὰρ ὑπέταξεν ὑπὸ
enemy  is abolished,  death —  all things for He subjected under

feet; but when it is said that all things are put in subjection, (it is) plain that excepts Him who put all things in subjection to Him; [28] and when all things shall have been put in subjection to Him, then the Son Himself also will be subject to Him who put all things under Him, so that God may be all in all — [29] otherwise, what shall they do who are being baptized for the dead, if the dead are not at all raised? Why are they also baptized for the dead? [30] Why also are we in danger every hour? [31] Day by day I die, by your boasting which I have in Christ Jesus our Lord. [32] If according to man I fought with beasts in Ephesus, what the profit to me if (the) dead are not raised? "Let us eat and drink, for tomorrow we die." [33] Do not be led astray; evil companionships ruin good habits. [34] Be righteously awake, and do not sin; for some have ignorance of God; I speak to your shame.

[35] But someone will say, How are the dead raised? And with what body do they come? [36] Fool! What you sow is not made alive unless it die. [37] And what you sow, that shall not be the body you sow, but a bare grain, it may be of wheat or of some one of the rest; [38] and God gives it a body according as He willed, and to each of the seeds its own body. [39] Not every flesh (is) the same flesh, but one flesh of men, and another flesh of beasts, and another of fish, and another of birds. [40] And (there are) heavenly bodies, and earthly bodies; but the glory of the heavenly (is) different, and that of the earthly different; [41] one glory of (the) sun, and another glory of (the) moon, and another glory of (the) stars; for a star differs from star in glory. [42] So also (is) the resurrection of the dead. It is sown in corruption; it is raised in incorruptibility.

· τοὺς πόδας αὐτοῦ. ὅταν δὲ εἴπῃ ὅτι Πάντα ὑποτέτακται,
the , feet     of Him.  when But He says that all things have been subjected,

28 δῆλον ὅτι ἐκτὸς τοῦ ὑποτάξαντος αὐτῷ τὰ πάντα. ὅταν δὲ
(it is) plain that excepted the (One) having subjected to Him all things. when But

ὑποταγῇ αὐτῷ τὰ πάντα, τότε καὶ αὐτὸς ὁ υἱὸς ὑποταγή-
is subjected to Him all things,  then also Himself, the Son, will be sub-

σεται τῷ ὑποτάξαντι αὐτῷ τὰ πάντα, ἵνα ᾖ ὁ Θεὸς τὰ
jected to the (One) having subjected to Him all things, that may be God

πάντα ἐν πᾶσιν.
all things in   all.

29 Ἐπεὶ τί ποιήσουσιν οἱ βαπτιζόμενοι ὑπὲρ τῶν νεκρῶν ;
Otherwise what will they do, those being baptized on behalf of the dead?

εἰ ὅλως νεκροὶ οὐκ ἐγείρονται, τί καὶ βαπτίζονται ὑπὲρ τῶν
If not at all dead ones not are raised, why indeed are they baptized for the

30 νεκρῶν ; τί καὶ ἡμεῖς κινδυνεύομεν πᾶσαν ὥραν ; καθ᾽ ἡμέραν
31 dead;  why also we  are in danger  every . hour?  Day by day

ἀποθνήσκω, νὴ τὴν ὑμετέραν καύχησιν, ἣν ἔχω ἐν Χριστῷ
I die,   by  your    boasting,  which I have in  Christ

32 Ἰησοῦ τῷ Κυρίῳ ἡμῶν. εἰ κατὰ ἄνθρωπον ἐθηριομάχησα
Jesus  the Lord  of us. If according to man  I fought with beasts

ἐν Ἐφέσῳ, τί μοι τὸ ὄφελος, εἰ νεκροὶ οὐκ ἐγείρονται ;
in Ephesus, what to me the profit? If dead ones not  are raised,

33 φάγωμεν καὶ πίωμεν, αὔριον γὰρ ἀποθνήσκομεν. μὴ πλανᾶ-
let us eat and  drink, tomorrow for  we die.     not Be led

34 σθε· Φθείρουσιν ἤθη χρήσθ᾽ ὁμιλίαι κακαί. ἐκνήψατε δικαίως,
astray, will corrupt habits good companionships bad. Be aroused righteously,

καὶ μὴ ἁμαρτάνετε· ἀγνωσίαν γὰρ Θεοῦ τινες ἔχουσι· πρὸς
and not sin;   ignorance for of God some  have;  for

ἐντροπὴν ὑμῖν λέγω.
shame   to you I speak.

35 Ἀλλ᾽ ἐρεῖ τις, Πῶς ἐγείρονται οἱ νεκροί ; ποίῳ δὲ σώματι
But will say someone, How are raised the dead? with what And body

36 ἔρχονται ; ἄφρον, σὺ ὃ σπείρεις, οὐ ζωοποιεῖται, ἐὰν μὴ
do they come? Foolish one, you what sow, not is made alive unless

37 ἀποθάνῃ· καὶ ὃ σπείρεις, οὐ τὸ σῶμα τὸ γενησόμενον σπεί-
it dies;  and what you sow, not the body  going to become  you

ρεις, ἀλλὰ γυμνὸν κόκκον, εἰ τύχοι, σίτου ἤ τινος τῶν
sow, but a naked  grain  it may be of wheat or some of the

38 λοιπῶν· ὁ δὲ Θεὸς αὐτῷ δίδωσι σῶμα καθὼς ἠθέλησε, καὶ
rest;    but God to it  gives a body as   He desired, and

39 ἑκάστῳ τῶν σπερμάτων τὸ ἴδιον σῶμα. οὐ πᾶσα σὰρξ ἡ
to each of the  seeds   the own body. (is) not All  flesh the

αὐτὴ σάρξ· ἀλλὰ ἄλλη μὲν σὰρξ ἀνθρώπων, ἄλλη δὲ σὰρξ
same flesh,  but  other indeed flesh of men,  other and flesh

40 κτηνῶν, ἄλλη δὲ ἰχθύων, ἄλλη δὲ πτηνῶν. καὶ σώματα
of animals, other and of fish  other  and of birds.  And (are) bodies

ἐπουράνια, καὶ σώματα ἐπίγεια· ἀλλ᾽ ἑτέρα μὲν ἡ τῶν ἐπου-
heavenly,  and bodies  earthly,  but other (is) truly the of the

41 ρανίων δόξα, ἑτέρα δὲ ἡ τῶν ἐπιγείων. ἄλλη δόξα ἡλίου, καὶ
heavenly glory, other and that of the earthly;  other glory of the sun, and

ἄλλη δόξα σελήνης, καὶ ἄλλη δόξα ἀστέρων· ἀστὴρ γὰρ
other glory of the moon, and other  glory of (the) stars; star  for

42 νεκρῶν. σπείρεται ἐν φθορᾷ, ἐγείρεται ἐν ἀφθαρσίᾳ· σπεί-
from star differs  in  glory.  So  also the resurrection of the

νεκρῶν. σπείρεται ἐν φθορᾷ, ἐγείρεται ἐν ἀφθαρσίᾳ· σπεί-
dead.  It is sown in corruption; it is raised in incorruption;  it is

[43] It is sown in dishonor; it is raised in glory. It is sown in weakness; it is raised in power. [44] It is sown a natural body, it is raised a spiritual body— there is a natural body, and there is a spiritual body. [45] So also it has been written, "The first man, Adam, became a living soul." the last Adam (became) a life-giving Spirit. [46] But not the spiritual first, but the natural; afterward the spiritual. [47] The first man (was) out of earth, earthy. The second Man (was) the Lord out of Heaven. [48] Such the earth, such also those earthy. And such the Heavenly (Man), such also the heavenly ones. [49] And as we bore the image of the earthy man, we shall also bear the image of the Heavenly (Man). [50] And I say this, brothers, that flesh and blood is not able to inherit (the) kingdom of God, nor does corruption inherit incorruptibility.

[51] Behold, I speak a mystery to you: we shall not all fall asleep, but we all shall be changed. [52] in a moment, in a glance of an eye, at the last trumpet— for a trumpet will sound, and the dead will be raised incorruptible, and we shall be changed. [53] For this corruptible must put on incorruption, and this mortal must put on immortality. [54] But when this corruptible shall put on incorruption, and this mortal shall put on immortality, then will occur the word having been written: "Death was swallowed up in victory. [55] O death, where is your sting? O grave, where is your victory?" . [56] Now the sting of death (is) sin, and the power of sin (is) the Law; [57] but thanks (be) to God, who gives us the victory by our Lord Jesus Christ. [58] So that, my beloved brothers, be firm, unmoveable, abounding in the work of the Lord always, knowing that your labor is not without fruit in (the) Lord.

---

**43** ρεται ἐν ἀτιμίᾳ, ἐγείρεται ἐν δόξῃ· σπείρεται ἐν ἀσθενείᾳ,
sown in dishonor; it is raised in glory; it is sown in weakness;

**44** ἐγείρεται ἐν δυνάμει· σπείρεται σῶμα ψυχικόν, ἐγείρεται
it is raised in power; it is sown a body natural; it is raised
σῶμα πνευματικόν. ἔστι σῶμα ψυχικόν, καὶ ἔστι σῶμα
body spiritual. There is a body natural, and there is a body

**45** πνευματικόν. οὕτω καὶ γέγραπται, Ἐγένετο ὁ πρῶτος
spiritual. So also it has been written: became The first
ἄνθρωπος Ἀδὰμ εἰς ψυχὴν ζῶσαν. ὁ ἔσχατος Ἀδὰμ εἰς
man Adam soul a living; the last Adam

**46** πνεῦμα ζωοποιοῦν. ἀλλ' οὐ πρῶτον τὸ πνευματικόν, ἀλλὰ
Spirit a life-giving. But not firstly the spiritual (body), but

**47** τὸ ψυχικόν, ἔπειτα τὸ πνευματικόν. ὁ πρῶτος ἄνθρωπος ἐκ
the natural; afterward the spiritual. The first man (was) out of
γῆς, χοϊκός· ὁ δεύτερος ἄνθρωπος, ὁ Κύριος ἐξ οὐρανοῦ.
earth, earthy; the second Man the Lord out of Heaven.

**48** οἷος ὁ χοϊκός, τοιοῦτοι καὶ οἱ χοϊκοί· καὶ οἷος ὁ ἐπουράνιος,
Such the earth, such also the earthy ones; and such the heavenly Man,

**49** τοιοῦτοι καὶ οἱ ἐπουράνιοι· καὶ καθὼς ἐφορέσαμεν τὴν εἰκόνα
such also the heavenly ones. And as we bore the image
τοῦ χοϊκοῦ, φορέσομεν καὶ τὴν εἰκόνα τοῦ ἐπουρανίου.
of the earthy man, we shall bear also the image of the heavenly Man.

**50** Τοῦτο δέ φημι, ἀδελφοί, ὅτι σὰρξ καὶ αἷμα βασιλείαν
this And I say, brothers, that flesh and blood (the) kingdom
Θεοῦ κληρονομῆσαι οὐ δύνανται, οὐδὲ ἡ φθορὰ τὴν ἀφθαρ-
of God inherit not is able to, nor corruption incorrup-

**51** σίαν κληρονομεῖ. ἰδού, μυστήριον ὑμῖν λέγω· Πάντες μὲν οὐ
tion inherit. Behold, a mystery to you I tell: all indeed not

**52** κοιμηθησόμεθα, πάντες δὲ ἀλλαγησόμεθα, ἐν ἀτόμῳ, ἐν ῥιπῇ
we shall fall asleep, all but we shall be changed, in a moment, in a glance
ὀφθαλμοῦ, ἐν τῇ ἐσχάτῃ σάλπιγγι· σαλπίσει γάρ, καὶ οἱ
of an eye, at the last trumpet; will trumpet for, and the
νεκροὶ ἐγερθήσονται ἄφθαρτοι, καὶ ἡμεῖς ἀλλαγησόμεθα.
dead will be raised incorruptible and we shall be changed.

**53** δεῖ γὰρ τὸ φθαρτὸν τοῦτο ἐνδύσασθαι ἀφθαρσίαν, καὶ τὸ
must For corruptible this put on incorruption, and

**54** θνητὸν τοῦτο ἐνδύσασθαι ἀθανασίαν. ὅταν δὲ τὸ φθαρτὸν
mortal this put on immortality. when And corruptible
ἀθανασίαν, τότε γενήσεται ὁ λόγος ὁ γεγραμμένος, Κατε-
this shall put on incorruption, and mortal this put on
ἀθανασίαν, τότε γενήσεται ὁ λόγος ὁ γεγραμμένος, Κατε-
immortality, then will occur the word having been written: was

**55** πόθη ὁ θάνατος εἰς νῖκος. Ποῦ σου, θάνατε, τὸ κέντρον ; ποῦ
swallowed Death in victory. Where of you, death, the sting; where

**56** σου, ᾅδη, τὸ νῖκος ; τὸ δὲ κέντρον τοῦ θανάτου ἡ ἁμαρτία· ἡ
of you Hades the victory? the And sting of death (is) sin, the

**57** δὲ δύναμις τῆς ἁμαρτίας ὁ νόμος· τῷ δὲ Θεῷ χάρις τῷ
and the power of sin (is) the law; but to God thanks, He
διδόντι ἡμῖν τὸ νῖκος διὰ τοῦ Κυρίου ἡμῶν Ἰησοῦ Χριστου.
giving to us the victory through the Lord of us, Jesus Christ.

**58** ὥστε, ἀδελφοί μου ἀγαπητοί, ἑδραῖοι γίνεσθε, ἀμετακίνητοι,
So as, brothers of me, beloved, firm be, unmoveable,
περισσεύοντες ἐν τῷ ἔργῳ τοῦ Κυρίου πάντοτε, εἰδότες ὅτι
abounding in the work of the Lord always, knowing that
ὁ κόπος ὑμῶν οὐκ ἔστι κενὸς ἐν Κυρίῳ.
the labor of you not is fruitless in (the) Lord.

CHAPTER 16

[1] Now about the collection which (is) for the saints, as I gave order to the churches of Galatia, so also you do. [2] On the first of a week, let each of you put by himself, storing up whatever he is prospered, that there not be then collections when I come [3] And when I arrive, whomever you approve, through these epistles, I will send to carry the grace of you to Jerusalem. [4] and if it is suitable for me to go also, they shall go with me. [5] But I will come to you when I have gone through Macedonia, for I do go through Macedonia. [6] And it may be I shall stay with you, or even I shall winter, that you may set me forward wherever I may go. [7] For I do not want to see you now in passing, but I hope to stay a while with you, if the Lord permit. [8] But I shall remain in Ephesus until Pentecost. [9] For a door has been opened to me, wonderful and mighty; and many (are) opposers. [10] Now if Timothy comes, see that he may be with you without fear; for he works the work of (the) Lord, even as I. [11] Therefore let no one despise him, but send him on in peace, that he may come to me; for I wait for him with the brothers. [12] And concerning Apollos the brother, I much urged him that he should go to you with the brothers; and it (was) not at all (his) will that he should come now; but he will come when he shall have opportnity. [13] Watch! Stand fast in the faith! Be men! Be strong! [14] Let all your things be done in love.

[15] But I exhort you, brothers — you know, the house of Stephenas, that it is Achaia's firstfruit, and they appointed themselves for service to the saints — [16] that also you be subject to such, and to everyone working and laboring with (us). [17] But I rejoice at the

## CHAPTER 16

**1** Περὶ δὲ τῆς λογίας τῆς εἰς τοὺς ἁγίους, ὥσπερ διέταξα ταῖς
about And the collection  for the  saints,  as  I charged the

**2** ἐκκλησίας τῆς Γαλατίας, οὕτω καὶ ὑμεῖς ποιήσατε. κατὰ
churches  of Galatia,  so also you  do.  Every

μίαν σαββάτων ἕκαστος ὑμῶν παρ' ἑαυτῷ τιθέτω, θησαυ-
one  of a week  each  of you  by  himself let him put, storing

ρίζων ὅ τι ἂν εὐοδῶται, ἵνα μή, ὅταν ἔλθω, τότε λογίαι
up  whatever he is prospered, that not when I come  then collections

**3** γίνωνται. ὅταν δὲ παραγένωμαι, οὓς ἐὰν δοκιμάσητε δι'
there be.  when But I arrive,  whomever you approve, through

ἐπιστολῶν, τούτους πέμψω ἀπενεγκεῖν τὴν χάριν ὑμῶν εἰς
epistles  these  I will send to carry  the grace of you to

**4** Ἰερουσαλήμ· ἐὰν δὲ ᾖ ἄξιον τοῦ κἀμὲ πορεύεσθαι, σὺν ἐμοὶ
Jerusalem.  if But it is suitable  me also to go,  with me

**5** πορεύσονται. ἐλεύσομαι δὲ πρὸς ὑμᾶς, ὅταν Μακεδονίαν
they shall go.  I will come And to  you  when Macedonia

**6** διέλθω· Μακεδονίαν γὰρ διέρχομαι· πρὸς ὑμᾶς δὲ τυχὸν
I go through. Macedonia  For I am going through, with you and possibly

παραμενῶ, ἢ καὶ παραχειμάσω, ἵνα ὑμεῖς με προπέμψητε οὗ
I will stay, or even spend the winter, that you  me may set forward

**7** ἐὰν πορεύωμαι. οὐ θέλω γὰρ ὑμᾶς ἄρτι ἐν παρόδῳ ἰδεῖν·
wherever I may go.  not I desire For you  yet in passage  to see;

ἐλπίζω δὲ χρόνον τινὰ ἐπιμεῖναι πρὸς ὑμᾶς, ἐὰν ὁ Κύριος
I am hoping and time  some to remain  with  you, if the Lord

**8** ἐπιτρέπῃ. ἐπιμενῶ δὲ ἐν Ἐφέσῳ ἕως τῆς Πεντηκοστῆς· θύρα
permits.  I will remain But in Ephesus until  Pentecost,  a door

**9** γάρ μοι ἀνέῳγε μεγάλη καὶ ἐνεργής, καὶ ἀντικείμενοι πολλοί.
for to me opened  great  and effective, and (are) opposing  many.

**10** Ἐὰν δὲ ἔλθῃ Τιμόθεος, βλέπετε ἵνα ἀφόβως γένηται πρὸς
if  But comes Timothy,  see  that without fear he is  with

**11** ὑμᾶς· τὸ γὰρ ἔργον Κυρίου ἐργάζεται ὡς καὶ ἐγώ. μή τις
you,  the for  work of (the) Lord he works,  as also I. Let not any

οὖν αὐτὸν ἐξουθενήσῃ· προπέμψατε δὲ αὐτὸν ἐν εἰρήνῃ, ἵνα
then him  despise;  set  forward but him in peace,  that

**12** ἔλθῃ πρός με· ἐκδέχομαι γὰρ αὐτὸν μετὰ τῶν ἀδελφῶν. περὶ
he come to me; I am awaiting for  him  with the  brothers. about

δὲ Ἀπολλὼ τοῦ ἀδελφοῦ, πολλὰ παρεκάλεσα αὐτὸν ἵνα
And Apollos the  brother,  much  I besought  him that

ἔλθῃ πρὸς ὑμᾶς μετὰ τῶν ἀδελφῶν· καὶ πάντως οὐκ ἦν
he come to  you with the  brothers,  and altogether not it was

θέλημα ἵνα νῦν ἔλθῃ, ἐλεύσεται δὲ ὅταν εὐκαιρήσῃ
(his) will that now he come; he will come but when he has opportunity.

**13** Γρηγορεῖτε, στήκετε ἐν τῇ πίστει, ἀνδρίζεσθε, κραταιοῦ-
Watch!  Stand  in the faith! Be men!  Be strong!

**14** σθε. πάντα ὑμῶν ἐν ἀγάπῃ γινέσθω.
All things of you in  love  let it be.

**15** Παρακαλῶ δὲ ὑμᾶς, ἀδελφοί (οἴδατε τὴν οἰκίαν Στεφανᾶ,
I beseech And you,  brothers, you know the house of Stephanas,

ὅτι ἐστὶν ἀπαρχὴ τῆς Ἀχαΐας, καὶ εἰς διακονίαν τοῖς ἁγίοις
that it is firstfruit  of Achaia, and to  ministry to the saints

**16** ἔταξαν ἑαυτούς), ἵνα καὶ ὑμεῖς ὑποτάσσησθε τοῖς τοιούτοις,
they appointed themselves, that also you may submit  to such ones,

**17** καὶ παντὶ τῷ συνεργοῦντι καὶ κοπιῶντι. χαίρω δὲ ἐπὶ τῇ
and to everyone  working with (me) and laboring.  I rejoice And at the

coming of Stephenas and Fortunatus and Achaicus; because these filled up your deficiency. [18] For they refreshed my spirit and yours; therefore recognize such ones.

[19] The churches of Asia greet you. Aquila and Priscilla much greet you in (the) Lord, with the church in their house. [20] The brothers all greet you. Greet each other with a holy kiss.

[21] The greeting with my hand, Paul. [22] If any-one does not love the Lord Jesus Christ let him be a curse: the Lord comes!

[23] The grace of the Lord Jesus Christ (be) with you. [24] My, love (be) with all of you in Christ Jesus. Amen.

παρουσίᾳ Στεφανᾶ καὶ Φουρτουνάτου καὶ ᾿Αχαϊκοῦ, ὅτι τὸ
presence of Stephanas, and of Fortunatus,    and oτ Achaicus, that

18 ὑμῶν ὑστέρημα οὗτοι ἀνεπλήρωσαν. ἀνέπαυσαν γὰρ τὸ ἐμὸν
your lack    these    supplied;    they refreshed for    my

πνεῦμα καὶ τὸ ὑμῶν· ἐπιγινώσκετε οὖν τοὺς τοιούτους.
spirit    and    of you.  Recognize, therefore,    such ones.

19 ᾿Ασπάζονται ὑμᾶς αἱ ἐκκλησίαι τῆς ᾿Ασίας· ἀσπάζονται
Greet    you the churches    of Asia    Greets

ὑμᾶς ἐν Κυρίῳ πολλὰ ᾿Ακύλας καὶ Πρίσκιλλα, σὺν τῇ κατ᾽
you in (the) Lord  much    Aquila  and  Priscilla,  with the in

20 οἶκον αὐτῶν ἐκκλησίᾳ. ἀσπάζονται ὑμᾶς οἱ ἀδελφοὶ πάντες.
(the) house of them church.    Greet    you the brothers all.

ἀσπάσασθε ἀλλήλους ἐν φιλήματι ἁγίῳ.
Greet    one another with  kiss    a holy.

21
22 ᾿Ο ἀσπασμὸς τῇ ἐμῇ χειρὶ Παύλου. εἴ τις οὐ φιλεῖ τὸν
The  greeting  with my hand,    Paul.  If anyone not love   the

23 Κύριον ᾿Ιησοῦν Χριστόν, ἤτω ἀνάθεμα. Μαρὰν ἀθά. ἡ χάρις
Lord    Jesus   Christ, let him be a curse.  The Lord comes. The grace

24 τοῦ Κυρίου ᾿Ιησοῦ Χριστοῦ μεθ᾽ ὑμῶν. ἡ ἀγάπη μου μετὰ
of the Lord    Jesus   Christ (be) with you. The love   of me (be) with

πάντων ὑμῶν ἐν Χριστῷ ᾿Ιησοῦ. ἀμήν.
all    of you in   Christ  Jesus.  Amen.

# ΠΑΥΛΟΥ ΤΟΥ ΑΠΟΣΤΟΛΟΥ
### PAUL    THE    APOSTLE

## Η ΠΡΟΣ
### THE    TO

# ΚΟΡΙΝΘΙΟΥΣ
### (THE) CORINTHIANS

## ΕΠΙΣΤΟΛΗ ΔΕΥΤΕΡΑ
### EPISTLE    SECOND

CHAPTER 1

[1] Paul, an apostle of Jesus Christ, through (the) will of God, and Timothy, the brother, to the church of God being in Corinth, with all the saints being in all Achaia; [2] Grace to you and peace from God (the) Father of us and (the) Lord Jesus Christ.

[3] Blessed (be) the God and Father of our Lord Jesus Christ, the Father of mercies and God of all comfort, [4] who comforts us in all our trouble, enabling us to comfort those in every tribulation, through that comfort with which we ourselves are comforted by God. [5] Because the sufferings of Christ abound to us, so also our comfort abounds through Christ. [6] But if we are troubled, (it is) for your comfort and salvation, being worked out in (the) endurance of the same sufferings which we also suffer; if we are comforted, (it is) for your encouragement and salvation — [7] and our hope for you (is) certain — knowing that even as you are sharers of the sufferings, so also of the comfort. [8] For, brothers, we do not want you to be ignorant as to our trouble which happened to us in Asia, that we were heavily pressed down beyond (our) strength, so as for us even to despair of living. [9] But we ourselves have

## CHAPTER 1

**1** Παῦλος ἀπόστολος Ἰησοῦ Χριστοῦ διὰ θελήματος Θεοῦ,
Paul    an apostle    of Jesus    Christ  through (the) will  of God,

καὶ Τιμόθεος ὁ ἀδελφός, τῇ ἐκκλησίᾳ τοῦ Θεοῦ τῇ οὔσῃ ἐν
and  Timothy  the brother, to the  church    of God    being   in

Κορίνθῳ, σὺν τοῖς ἁγίοις πᾶσι τοῖς οὖσιν ἐν ὅλῃ τῇ Ἀχαΐᾳ·
Corinth,  with the  saints  all  being   in  all  the  Achaia;

**2** χάρις ὑμῖν καὶ εἰρήνη ἀπὸ Θεοῦ πατρὸς ἡμῶν καὶ Κυρίου
Grace to you and peace   from God (the) Father of us   and (the) Lord

Ἰησοῦ Χριστοῦ.
Jesus Christ.

**3** Εὐλογητὸς ὁ Θεὸς καὶ πατὴρ τοῦ Κυρίου ἡμῶν Ἰησοῦ
Blessed (be) the God and Father of the Lord of Us,  Jesus

Χριστοῦ, ὁ πατὴρ τῶν οἰκτιρμῶν καὶ Θεὸς πάσης παρα-
Christ,  the Father  of compassions and the God of all    com-

**4** κλήσεως, ὁ παρακαλῶν ἡμᾶς ἐπὶ πάσῃ τῇ θλίψει ἡμῶν,
fort,   the (One) comforting us   on   all   the  trouble  of us,

εἰς τὸ δύνασθαι ἡμᾶς παρακαλεῖν τοὺς ἐν πάσῃ θλίψει, διὰ
for  to be able    us to comfort    those in every  trouble, through

τῆς παρακλήσεως ἧς παρακαλούμεθα αὐτοὶ ὑπὸ τοῦ Θεοῦ.
the  comfort    of which we are comforted ourselves by    God.

**5** ὅτι καθὼς περισσεύει τὰ παθήματα τοῦ Χριστοῦ εἰς ἡμᾶς,
Because as  abounds  the sufferings   of Christ  in us,

**6** οὕτω διὰ Χριστοῦ περισσεύει καὶ ἡ παράκλησις ἡμῶν. εἴτε
so through Christ   abounds  also the comfort   of us. whether

δὲ θλιβόμεθα, ὑπὲρ τῆς ὑμῶν παρακλήσεως καὶ σωτηρίας,
And we are troubled for  the  of you   comfort    and  salvation,

τῆς ἐνεργουμένης ἐν ὑπομονῇ τῶν αὐτῶν παθημάτων ὧν
being worked out in (the) endurance of the same  sufferings  which

καὶ ἡμεῖς πάσχομεν· εἴτε παρακαλούμεθα, ὑπὲρ τῆς ὑμῶν
also  we   suffer, whether we are comforted, (it is) for   your

**7** παρακλήσεως καὶ σωτηρίας· καὶ ἡ ἐλπὶς ἡμῶν βεβαία ὑπὲρ
comfort    and  salvation;  and the hope of us (is) certain for

ὑμῶν· εἰδότες ὅτι ὥσπερ κοινωνοί ἐστε τῶν παθημάτων,
you,  knowing that  as    sharers you are of the  sufferings,

**8** οὕτω καὶ τῆς παρακλήσεως. οὐ γὰρ θέλομεν ὑμᾶς ἀγνοεῖν,
so  also of the comfort.    not For we desire  you to be ignorant,

ἀδελφοί, ὑπὲρ τῆς θλίψεως ἡμῶν τῆς γενομένης ἡμῖν ἐν τῇ
brothers, as to  the  trouble  of us    having been to us in

Ἀσίᾳ, ὅτι καθ' ὑπερβολὴν ἐβαρήθημεν ὑπὲρ δύναμιν, ὥστε
Asia, that  excessively   we were burdened beyond power,  so as

**9** ἐξαπορηθῆναι ἡμᾶς καὶ τοῦ ζῆν. ἀλλὰ αὐτοὶ ἐν ἑαυτοῖς τὸ
to despair (of life)  us, even to live. But (our)selves in ourselves the

416

had the sentence of death in ourselves, that we should not trust in ourselves, but in God who raises the dead; [10] who delivered us from so great a death, and does deliver; in whom we have hope that He will still deliver us; [11] you also laboring together for us by prayer, that the gracious gift to us by many may be the cause of thanksgiving through many for us. [12] For our rejoicing is this, the testimony of our conscience, that we had our conduct in the world in simplicity and sincerity of God, not in fleshly wisdom, but in God's grace, and more abundantly toward you. [13] For we do not write other things to you but what you read, or even recognize; and I hope that you will recognize even to (the) end, [14] according as you also in part recognized us, that we are your rejoicing, even as also you (are) ours in the day of the Lord Jesus. [15] And with this confidence I purposed to come to you previously, that you might have a second benefit; [16] and to go by you through to Macedonia, and again from Macedonia to come to you, and to be set forward by you to Judea. [17] Therefore purposing this, did I indeed use lightness? Or what I planned, do I plan according to flesh, that may be with me yes, yes, no, no? [18] But God (is) faithful that our word to you was not yes and no. [19] For the Son of God, Jesus Christ, who was preached among you by us, by me and Silvanus and Timothy, was not yes and no, but has been yes in Him. [20] For whatever promises of God (there are), in Him (is) the Yes, and in Him the Amen, for glory to God by us. [21] Now He who establishes us with you in Christ and anoints us (is) God, [22] who also sealed us, and gave the earnest of the Spirit in our hearts.

ἀπόκριμα τοῦ θανάτου ἐσχήκαμεν, ἵνα μὴ πεποιθότες ὦμεν
sentence       of death    we have,      that not   should trust  we

10 ἐφ᾽ ἑαυτοῖς, ἀλλ᾽ ἐπὶ τῷ Θεῷ τῷ ἐγείροντι τοὺς νεκρούς· ὃς
on ourselves,  but   on      God, the (One) raising  the  dead;  who

ἐκ τηλικούτου θανάτου ἐρρύσατο ἡμᾶς καὶ ῥύεται, εἰς ὃν
out of so great   a death     delivered  us  and does deliver, in whom

11 ἠλπίκαμεν ὅτι καὶ ἔτι ῥύσεται· συνυπουργούντων καὶ ὑμῶν
we have hoped that even yet He will deliver,   laboring together also  you

ὑπὲρ ἡμῶν ἐν τῇ δεήσει, ἵνα ἐκ πολλῶν προσώπων τὸ εἰς ἡμᾶς
for   us       in prayer, that by many        persons        the for us

χάρισμα διὰ πολλῶν εὐχαριστηθῇ ὑπὲρ ἡμῶν.
gift     through many   thanks may be given for  us.

12 Ἡ γὰρ καύχησις ἡμῶν αὕτη ἐστί, τὸ μαρτύριον τῆς
the For  boasting  of us  this  is,  the  testimony  of the

συνειδήσεως ἡμῶν, ὅτι ἐν ἁπλότητι καὶ εἰλικρινείᾳ Θεοῦ,
conscience    of us,  that in simplicity  and  sincerity of God,

οὐκ ἐν σοφίᾳ σαρκικῇ, ἀλλ᾽ ἐν χάριτι Θεοῦ, ἀνεστράφημεν
not in wisdom fleshly,   but  in the grace of God  we behaved

13 ἐν τῷ κόσμῳ, περισσοτέρως δὲ πρὸς ὑμᾶς. οὐ γὰρ ἄλλα
in the world,   more abundantly and toward you. not For other things

γράφομεν ὑμῖν, ἀλλ᾽ ἢ ἃ ἀναγινώσκετε ἢ καὶ ἐπιγινώσκετε,
we write   to you, other than what you read,   or even  perceive,

14 ἐλπίζω δὲ ὅτι καὶ ἕως τέλους ἐπιγνώσεσθε· καθὼς καὶ ἐπέ-
I hope  and that also until the end  you will perceive·  as  also  you

γνωτε ἡμᾶς ἀπὸ μέρους, ὅτι καύχημα ὑμῶν ἐσμεν, καθάπερ
perceived us  from (in) part, because boasting of you we are,  even as

καὶ ὑμεῖς ἡμῶν, ἐν τῇ ἡμέρᾳ τοῦ Κυρίου Ἰησοῦ.
also  you of us, in the day    of the Lord    Jesus.

15 Καὶ ταύτῃ τῇ πεποιθήσει ἐβουλόμην πρὸς ὑμᾶς ἐλθεῖν
And  in this    confidence    I purposed    to  you to come

16 πρότερον, ἵνα δευτέραν χάριν ἔχητε· καὶ δι᾽ ὑμῶν διελθεῖν εἰς
previously,  that a second  benefit you have, and through you to go through to

Μακεδονίαν, καὶ πάλιν ἀπὸ Μακεδονίας ἐλθεῖν πρὸς ὑμᾶς,
Macedonia,   and  again  from  Macedonia  to come  to   you,

17 καὶ ὑφ᾽ ὑμῶν προπεμφθῆναι εἰς τὴν Ἰουδαίαν. τοῦτο οὖν
and by    you  to be set forward  to  the   Judea.     This,   then,

βουλευόμενος, μή τι ἄρα τῇ ἐλαφρίᾳ ἐχρησάμην; ἢ ἃ βου-
purposing,      not indeed lightness   I used?   Or what I

λεύομαι, κατὰ σάρκα βουλεύομαι, ἵνα ᾖ παρ᾽ ἐμοὶ τὸ ναὶ ναὶ
purposed, according to flesh do I purpose, that may be with me the Yes, Yes,

18 καὶ τὸ οὒ οὔ; πιστὸς δὲ ὁ Θεός, ὅτι ὁ λόγος ἡμῶν ὁ πρὸς
and the No, No? faithful But (is) God, that the word  of us       to

19 ὑμᾶς οὐκ ἐγένετο ναὶ καὶ οὔ. ὁ γὰρ τοῦ Θεοῦ υἱὸς Ἰησοῦς
you  not  became  Yes, and No. the For of the God Son, Jesus

Χριστὸς ὁ ἐν ὑμῖν δι᾽ ἡμῶν κηρυχθείς, δι᾽ ἐμοῦ καὶ Σιλουανοῦ
Christ, the (One) among you by us proclaimed, through me and Silvanus

καὶ Τιμοθέου, οὐκ ἐγένετο ναὶ καὶ οὔ, ἀλλὰ ναὶ ἐν αὐτῷ
and Timothy,  not  became  Yes, and No,  but   Yes in Him

20 γέγονεν. ὅσαι γὰρ ἐπαγγελίαι Θεοῦ, ἐν αὐτῷ τὸ ναί, καὶ ἐν
has been. as many as For (are) promises of God, in Him the Yes, and in

21 αὐτῷ τὸ ἀμήν, τῷ Θεῷ πρὸς δόξαν δι᾽ ἡμῶν. ὁ δὲ βεβαιῶν
Him the Amen,  to God unto  glory  through us.  He But confirming

22 ἡμᾶς σὺν ὑμῖν εἰς Χριστόν, καὶ χρίσας ἡμᾶς, Θεός· ὁ καὶ
us  with  you  in  Christ,    and anointing us (is)  God, He and

σφραγισάμενος ἡμᾶς, καὶ δοὺς τὸν ἀρραβῶνα τοῦ Πνεύ-
having sealed       us   and having given the  earnest   of the Spirit

[23] And I call God (as) witness to my soul, that to spare you I came no more to Corinth. [24] Not that we rule over your faith, but we are fellow-workers of your joy; for you stand by faith.

CHAPTER 2

[1] But I decided this with myself, not to come to you again in sorrow. [2] For if I make you sorry, who is it that will make me glad, but he who is made sorry by me? [3] And I wrote this same thing to you, lest having come I might have sorrow from (those) of whom I ought to rejoice; trusting in you all, that my joy is (that) of you all. [4] For out of much trouble and agony of heart I wrote to you through many tears; not that you might be saddened, but that you might know that I have the overflowing love which I have toward you. [5] But if anyone has grieved, he has not grieved me, but in part you all, that I may not overbear. [6] This censure by the majority (is) enough to such a one. [7] So that on the contrary you should rather forgive and encourage such a person, lest (he) should be swallowed up with overflowing sorrow. [8] So I urge you to confirm love toward him. [9] For to this end also I wrote, that I might know the proof of you, if you are obedient to everything. [10] But to whom you forgive anything, I also; for also if I have forgiven anything, I have forgiven it for you, in Christ's person; [11] so that we should not be overreached by Satan, for we are not ignorant of his devices.

[12] Now having come to Troas for the gospel of Christ, and a door having been opened to me in (the) Lord, [13] I had no ease in my spirit at my not finding my brother Titus; but

---

ματος ἐν ταῖς καρδίαις ἡμῶν.
in the hearts of us.

23 Ἐγὼ δὲ μάρτυρα τὸν Θεὸν ἐπικαλοῦμαι ἐπὶ τὴν ἐμὴν
I And (as) witness God call on my

24 ψυχήν, ὅτι φειδόμενος ὑμῶν οὐκέτι ἦλθον εἰς Κόρινθον. οὐχ
soul, that sparing you no more I came to Corinth. Not

ὅτι κυριεύομεν ὑμῶν τῆς πίστεως, ἀλλὰ συνεργοί ἐσμεν τῆς
that we rule over of you the faith, but fellow-workers we are of the

χαρᾶς ὑμῶν· τῇ γὰρ πίστει ἐστήκατε.
joy of you; for by faith you stand.

CHAPTER 2

1 ἔκρινα δὲ ἐμαυτῷ τοῦτο, τὸ μὴ πάλιν ἐλθεῖν ἐν λύπῃ
I decided And in myself this, not again to come in grief

2 πρὸς ὑμᾶς. εἰ γὰρ ἐγὼ λυπῶ ὑμᾶς, καὶ τίς ἐστιν ὁ
to you. if For I grieve you, even who is it

3 εὐφραίνων με, εἰ μὴ ὁ λυπού- μενος ἐξ ἐμοῦ; καὶ ἔγραψα
making glad me, if not the (one) being grieved by me? And I wrote

ὑμῖν τοῦτο αὐτό, ἵνα μὴ ἐλθὼν λύπην ἔχω ἀφ' ὧν ἔδει
to you this same thing, that not coming grief I should have from whom it behoved

4 με χαίρειν, πεποιθὼς ἐπὶ πάντας ὑμᾶς, ὅτι ἡ ἐμὴ χαρὰ
me to rejoice, trusting in all of you, that my joy

πάντων ὑμῶν ἐστίν. ἐκ γὰρ πολλῆς θλίψεως καὶ συνοχῆς
all of you is. out of For much trouble and anxiety

καρδίας ἔγραψα ὑμῖν διὰ πολλῶν δακρύων, οὐχ ἵνα
of heart I wrote to you through many tears, not that

λυπηθῆτε, ἀλλὰ τὴν ἀγάπην ἵνα γνῶτε ἣν ἔχω περισ
you be grieved, but the love that you know which I have more

σοτέρως εἰς ὑμᾶς.
abundantly to you.

5 Εἰ δέ τις λελύπηκεν, οὐκ ἐμὲ λελύπηκεν, ἀλλ' ἀπὸ μέρους·
if But anyone has grieved, not me he has grieved, but from part,

6 ἵνα μὴ ἐπιβαρῶ πάντας ὑμᾶς. ἱκανὸν τῷ τοιούτῳ ἡ ἐπιτιμία
lest I overbear all of you. Enough for such a one censure

7 αὕτη ἡ ὑπὸ τῶν πλειόνων· ὥστε τοὐναντίον μᾶλλον ὑμᾶς
this by the majority, so as on the contrary rather you

χαρίσασθαι καὶ παρακαλέσαι, μή πως τῇ περισσοτέρᾳ
to forgive and to comfort, lest (by) the more abundant

8 λύπῃ καταποθῇ ὁ τοιοῦτος. διὸ παρακαλῶ ὑμᾶς κυρῶσαι
grief be swallowed such a one. Therefore I beseech you to confirm

9 εἰς αὐτὸν ἀγάπην. εἰς τοῦτο γὰρ καὶ ἔγραψα, ἵνα γνῶ τὴν
to him (your) love. to this For also I wrote, that I might know the

10 δοκιμὴν ὑμῶν, εἰ εἰς πάντα ὑπήκοοί ἐστε. ᾧ δέ τι χαρίζεσθε.
proof of you, if in all things obedient you are. to But anything you forgive, whom

καὶ ἐγώ· καὶ γὰρ ἐγὼ εἴ τι κεχάρισμαι. ᾧ κεχάρισμαι δι
also I; indeed for I if anything I have forgiven of I have forgiven, for whom

11 ὑμᾶς ἐν προσώπῳ Χριστοῦ, ἵνα μὴ πλεονεκτηθῶμεν ὑπὸ
you (it is) in (the) person of Christ, that not we be overreached by

τοῦ Σατανᾶ· οὐ γὰρ αὐτοῦ τὰ νοήματα ἀγνοοῦμεν.
Satan, not for of him the devices we are ignorant.

12 Ἐλθὼν δὲ εἰς τὴν Τρωάδα εἰς τὸ εὐαγγέλιον τοῦ Χριστοῦ
having come And to Troas in the gospel of Christ,

13 καὶ θύρας μοι ἀνεῳγμένης ἐν Κυρίῳ, οὐκ ἔσχηκα ἄνεσιν τῷ
and a door to me having been opened in (the) Lord, not I had rest to the

πνεύματί μου, τῷ μὴ εὑρεῖν με Τίτον τὸν ἀδελφόν μου· ἀλλὰ
spirit of me, in the not finding me Titus the brother of me, but

I went out to Macedonia. [14] But thanks (be) to God, who always leads us in triumph in Christ, and who reveals by us in every place the sweet odor of the knowledge of Him. [15] For we are to God a sweet perfume in Christ, in those who are being saved, and in those being lost; [16] to the one, an odor of death unto death; and to the (other) an odor of life unto life; and who (is) good enough for these things? [17] For we are not as the many, peddling the word of God for gain — but as of sincerity, but as of God, in the sight of God, we speak in Christ.

14 ἀποταξάμενος αὐτοῖς ἐξῆλθον εἰς Μακεδονίαν. τῷ δὲ Θεῷ
saying farewell to them I went out to Macedonia. But to God
χάρις τῷ πάντοτε θριαμβεύοντι ἡμᾶς ἐν τῷ Χριστῷ, καὶ τὴν
thanks, He always leading in triumph us in Christ, and the
ὀσμὴν τῆς γνώσεως αὐτοῦ φανεροῦντι δι' ἡμῶν ἐν παντὶ
odor of the knowledge of Him revealing through us in every

15 τόπῳ. ὅτι Χριστοῦ εὐωδία ἐσμὲν τῷ Θεῷ ἐν τοῖς σωζομένοις
place; because of Christ a sweet smell we are to God in those being saved

16 καὶ ἐν τοῖς ἀπολλυμένοις· οἷς μὲν ὀσμὴ θανάτου εἰς θάνατον,
and in those being lost; to the one, an odor of death unto death;

17 οἷς δὲ ὀσμὴ ζωῆς εἰς ζωήν. καὶ πρὸς ταῦτα τίς ἱκανός ; οὐ
the others and an odor of life unto life. And for these things who is enough? not
γὰρ ἐσμεν ὡς οἱ πολλοί, καπηλεύοντες τὸν λόγον τοῦ Θεοῦ·
For we are as the many, hawking the word of God,
ἀλλ' ὡς ἐξ εἰλικρινείας, ἀλλ' ὡς ἐκ Θεοῦ, κατενώπιον τοῦ
but as of sincerity, but as of God, in the sight of
Θεοῦ, ἐν Χριστῷ λαλοῦμεν.
God, in Christ we speak.

## CHAPTER 3

### CHAPTER 3

[1] Do we begin again to commend ourselves? Or do we as some need commendatory letters to you, or commendatory (ones) from you? [2] You are our letter, having been inscribed in our hearts, being known and being read by all men, [3] (it) being revealed that you are Christ's letter, served by us; not having been written with ink, but with (the) Spirit of (the) living God; not on tablets of stone, but on fleshly tablets of (the) heart. [4] And we have such trust through Christ towards God; [5] not that we are able of ourselves to judge anything as of ourselves, but our ability (to judge is) of God; [6] who also made us able ministers of the new covenant; not of letter, but of Spirit; for the letter kills, but the Spirit makes alive. [7] But if the ministry of death in letters having been engraved in stone was with glory, so as the sons of Israel (were) not able to gaze into the face of Moses, because of the glory of his face — which was to cease, [8] now much rather shall the ministry of the Spirit be in glory! [9] For if the ministry of condemnation

1 Ἀρχόμεθα πάλιν ἑαυτοὺς συνιστάνειν ; ἢ μὴ χρήζομεν,
Do we begin again ourselves to commend? Or not need we
ὥς τινες, συστατικῶν ἐπιστολῶν πρὸς ὑμᾶς, ἢ ἐξ ὑμῶν
as some commendatory epistles to you, or from you

2 συστατικῶν ; ἡ ἐπιστολὴ ἡμῶν ὑμεῖς ἐστέ, ἐγγεγραμμένη
commendatory (ones)? The epistle of us you are, having been inscribed
ἐν ταῖς καρδίαις ἡμῶν, γινωσκομένη καὶ ἀναγινωσκομένη
in the hearts of us, being known and being read

3 ὑπὸ πάντων ἀνθρώπων· φανερούμενοι ὅτι ἐστὲ ἐπιστολὴ
by all men, being manifested that you are an epistle
Χριστοῦ διακονηθεῖσα ὑφ' ἡμῶν, ἐγγεγραμμένη οὐ μέλανι,
of Christ ministered by us, having been inscribed not by ink,
ἀλλὰ Πνεύματι Θεοῦ ζῶντος, οὐκ ἐν πλαξὶ λιθίναις, ἀλλ' ἐν
but by (the) Spirit of God a living, not in tables of stone, but in

4 πλαξὶ καρδίας σαρκίναις. πεποίθησιν δὲ τοιαύτην ἔχομεν
tablets (of the) heart fleshly. confidence And such we have

5 διὰ τοῦ Χριστοῦ πρὸς τὸν Θεόν· οὐχ ὅτι ἱκανοί ἐσμεν ἀφ'
through Christ toward God. Not that sufficient we are of
ἑαυτῶν λογίσασθαί τι ὡς ἐξ ἑαυτῶν, ἀλλ' ἡ ἱκανότης ἡμῶν
ourselves to reason out anything as out of ourselves, but the sufficiency of us

6 ἐκ τοῦ Θεοῦ· ὃς καὶ ἱκάνωσεν ἡμᾶς διακόνους καινῆς
(is) of God, who also made sufficient us (as) ministers of a new
διαθήκης, οὐ γράμματος, ἀλλὰ πνεύματος· τὸ γὰρ γράμμα
covenant, not of letter, but of spirit; the for letter

7 ἀποκτείνει, τὸ δὲ πνεῦμα ζωοποιεῖ. εἰ δὲ ἡ διακονία τοῦ
kills, the but Spirit makes alive. if And the ministry
θανάτου ἐν γράμμασιν, ἐντετυπωμένη ἐν λίθοις, ἐγενήθη ἐν
of death in letters having been engraved in stone was in
δόξῃ, ὥστε μὴ δύνασθαι ἀτενίσαι τοὺς υἱοὺς Ἰσραὴλ εἰς τὸ
glory, so as not to be able to gaze the sons of Israel into the
πρόσωπον Μωσέως διὰ τὴν δόξαν τοῦ προσώπου αὐτοῦ,
face of Moses because of the glory of the face of him,

8 τὴν καταργουμένην· πῶς οὐχὶ μᾶλλον ἡ διακονία τοῦ πνεύ-
being done away, how not rather the ministry of the Spirit

9 ματος ἔσται ἐν δόξῃ ; εἰ γὰρ ἡ διακονία τῆς κατακρίσεως
will be in glory? if For the ministry of condemnation

(was) glory, much rather the ministry of righteousness abounds in glory. [10] For even that which has been made glorious has not been made glorious in this respect, because of the glory which is far greater. [11] For if that which is being annulled (was) through glory, much more that which remains (is) in glory. [12] Therefore having such hope, we use much boldness. [13] And not as Moses, (who) put a veil over his face, for the sons of Israel not to gaze at the end of that being annulled. [14] But their minds were blinded; for to the present, the same veil remains on the reading of the Old Covenant, not removed, which is being annulled in Christ. [15] But to this day, when Moses is read, a veil lies on their heart. [16] But when it shall have turned to (the) Lord, the veil is taken away. [17] Now the Lord is the Spirit; and where the Spirit of (the) Lord (is), there (is) freedom! [18] But we all with unveiled face beholding the glory of the Lord, as in a mirror, are being changed into the same image from glory to glory, as from (the) Lord (the) Spirit.

CHAPTER 4

[1] Therefore, having this ministry, as we received mercy, we do not faint. [2] But we forsook the hidden things of shame, not walking in craftiness, nor falsifying the word of God, but by revelation of the truth commending ourselves to every conscience of men before God. [3] But also if our gospel is hidden, it is hidden in those being lost; [4] in whom the god of this age has blinded the thoughts of the unbelieving, so as the brightness of the gospel of

δόξα, πολλῷ μᾶλλον περισσεύει ἡ διακονία τῆς δικαιοσύνης
(was) glory, much rather abounds the ministry of righteousness

10 ἐν δόξῃ. καὶ γὰρ οὐδὲ δεδόξασται τὸ δεδοξασμένον ἐν τούτῳ
in glory. indeed For not has been glorified the thing glorified in this

11 τῷ μέρει, ἕνεκεν τῆς ὑπερβαλλούσης δόξης. εἰ γὰρ τὸ κατ-
respect, because of the excelling glory. if For the thing
αργούμενον, διὰ δόξης, πολλῷ μᾶλλον τὸ μένον, ἐν δόξῃ.
being done away (was) via glory, much rather the thing remaining in glory.

12 Ἔχοντες οὖν τοιαύτην ἐλπίδα, πολλῇ παρρησίᾳ χρώ-
having Therefore such hope, much boldness we

13 μεθα· καὶ οὐ καθάπερ Μωσῆς ἐτίθει κάλυμμα ἐπὶ τὸ πρόσω-
use, and not as Moses put a veil over the face
πον ἑαυτοῦ, πρὸς τὸ μὴ ἀτενίσαι τοὺς υἱοὺς Ἰσραὴλ εἰς τὸ
of himself, for not to gaze the sons of Israel at the

14 τέλος τοῦ καταργουμένου· ἀλλ' ἐπωρώθη τὰ νοήματα
end of the (thing) being done away. But were hardened the thoughts
αὐτῶν· ἄχρι γὰρ τῆς σήμερον τὸ αὐτὸ κάλυμμα ἐπὶ τῇ
of them. until For the present the same veil on the
ἀναγνώσει τῆς παλαιᾶς διαθήκης μένει μὴ ἀνακαλυπτόμενον,
reading of the Old Covenant remains, not being unveiled

15 ὅ τι ἐν Χριστῷ καταργεῖται. ἀλλ' ἕως σήμερον, ἡνίκα
that in Christ it is being done away. But until today, when
ἀναγινώσκεται Μωσῆς, κάλυμμα ἐπὶ τὴν καρδίαν αὐτῶν
is being read Moses, a veil on the heart of them

16 κεῖται. ἡνίκα δ' ἂν ἐπιστρέψῃ πρὸς Κύριον, περιαιρεῖται τὸ
lies; whenever But it turns to (the) Lord, is taken away the

17 κάλυμμα. ὁ δὲ Κύριος τὸ Πνεῦμά ἐστιν· οὗ δὲ τὸ Πνεῦμα
veil. the And Lord the Spirit is, where and the Spirit

18 Κυρίου, ἐκεῖ ἐλευθερία. ἡμεῖς δὲ πάντες, ἀνακεκαλυμμένῳ
of (the) Lord (is), there freedom (is). we But all, having been unveiled
προσώπῳ τὴν δόξαν Κυρίου κατοπτριζόμενοι, τὴν αὐτὴν
with face the glory of (the) Lord beholding in a mirror, the same
εἰκόνα μεταμορφούμεθα ἀπὸ δόξης εἰς δόξαν, καθάπερ ἀπὸ
image are being changed (into), from glory to glory, even as from
Κυρίου Πνεύματος.
(the) Lord Spirit.

CHAPTER 4

1 Διὰ τοῦτο ἔχοντες τὴν διακονίαν ταύτην, καθὼς ἠλεήθη-
Therefore, having ministry this, even as we obtained

2 μεν, οὐκ ἐκκακοῦμεν· ἀλλ' ἀπειπάμεθα τὰ κρυπτὰ τῆς
mercy, we faint; but we have renounced the hidden things
αἰσχύνης, μὴ περιπατοῦντες ἐν πανουργίᾳ μηδὲ δολοῦντες
of shame, not walking in craftiness, nor adulterating
τὸν λόγον τοῦ Θεοῦ, ἀλλὰ τῇ φανερώσει τῆς ἀληθείας
the word of God, but the revelation of the truth
συνιστῶντες ἑαυτοὺς πρὸς πᾶσαν συνείδησιν ἀνθρώπων
commending ourselves to every conscience of men

3 ἐνώπιον τοῦ Θεοῦ. εἰ δὲ καί ἐστι κεκαλυμμένον τὸ εὐαγγέλιον
before God. if But indeed is being hidden the gospel

4 ἡμῶν, ἐν τοῖς ἀπολλυμένοις ἐστὶ κεκαλυμμένον· ἐν οἷς ὁ Θεὸς
of us, in those being lost it is hidden, in whom the god
τοῦ αἰῶνος τούτου ἐτύφλωσε τὰ νοήματα τῶν ἀπίστων,
age of this has blinded the thoughts of the unbelieving,
εἰς τὸ μὴ αὐγάσαι αὐτοῖς τὸν φωτισμὸν τοῦ εὐαγγελίου
— — not to dawn on them the brightness of the gospel

the glory of Christ, who is the image of God, should not dawn on them. [5] For we do not preach ourselves, but Christ Jesus (the) Lord, and ourselves your slaves for the sake of Jesus. [6] Because (it is) God who commanded light to shine out of darkness, who shone in our hearts (to give the) brightness of the knowledge of the glory of God in (the) face of Jesus Christ. [7] But we have this treasure in earthen vessels, that the surpassing greatness of the power may be of God and not from us; [8] in every (way) pressed down, but not hemmed in; in doubt, but not utterly at a loss; [9] persecuted, but not forsaken; thrown down, but not destroyed; [10] always bearing about the dying of the Lord Jesus in the body, that also the life of the Lord Jesus may be revealed in our bodies; [11] for we who live are always delivered to death on account of Jesus, that also the life of Jesus may be revealed in our mortal flesh; [12] so that death indeed works in us, and life in you. [13] but having the same spirit of faith, according to what has been written, "I believed, therefore I spoke;" we also believe, therefore we also speak; [14] knowing that He who raised up the Lord Jesus, also will raise us up through Jesus and will present (us) with you. [15] For all things (are) for your sake, that the abounding grace may excel through the thanksgiving of the greatest number, to the glory of God.

[16] For this reason we do not faint. But even if our outward man is being brought to decay, yet the inward is being renewed day by day. [17] For the lightness of our affliction, (which is) but for a moment, works out for us a far more excellent eternal weight of glory; [18] we not looking upon the things seen, but the things

**5** τῆς δόξης τοῦ Χριστοῦ, ὅς ἐστιν εἰκὼν τοῦ Θεοῦ. οὐ γὰρ
of the glory　　　of Christ, who　is (the) image　　of God. not　For
ἑαυτοὺς κηρύσσομεν, ἀλλὰ Χριστὸν Ἰησοῦν Κύριον·
ourselves　we proclaim,　　but　　Christ　　Jesus (as)　Lord,

**6** ἑαυτοὺς δὲ δούλους ὑμῶν διὰ Ἰησοῦν. ὅτι ὁ Θεὸς ὁ εἰπὼν ἐκ
ourselves and　slaves　of you for the sake of Jesus. Because God saying: Out of
σκότους φῶς λάμψαι, ὅς ἔλαμψεν ἐν ταῖς καρδίαις ἡμῶν,
darkness　light shall shine, Who　shone　in　the　hearts　　of us,
πρὸς φωτισμὸν τῆς γνώσεως τῆς δόξης τοῦ Θεοῦ ἐν
to (give the) brightness of the knowledge of the glory　　　　of God　in
προσώπῳ Ἰησοῦ Χριστοῦ.
(the) face　of Jesus　　Christ.

**7** Ἔχομεν δὲ τὸν θησαυρὸν τοῦτον ἐν ὀστρακίνοις σκεύεσιν,
we have And　　treasure　this　in　earthen　vessels,
ἵνα ἡ ὑπερβολὴ τῆς δυνάμεως ᾖ τοῦ Θεοῦ, καὶ μὴ ἐξ ἡμῶν·
that the excellence of the power　may be　of God, and not of us;

**8** ἐν παντὶ θλιβόμενοι, ἀλλ᾽ οὐ στενοχωρούμενοι· ἀπορού-
in　every (way) being troubled, but not hemmed in;　　being per-

**9** μενοι, ἀλλ᾽ οὐκ ἐξαπορούμενοι· διωκόμενοι, ἀλλ᾽ οὐκ ἐγκατα-
plexed, but not utterly at a loss;　being persecuted, but　not forsaken,

**10** λειπόμενοι· καταβαλλόμενοι, ἀλλ᾽ οὐκ ἀπολλύμενοι· πάν-
being thrown down, but　not　destroyed;　always
τοτε τὴν νέκρωσιν τοῦ Κυρίου Ἰησοῦ ἐν τῷ σώματι περιφέ-
the　dying　of the　Lord　Jesus in the　body　bearing
ροντες, ἵνα καὶ ἡ ζωὴ τοῦ Ἰησοῦ ἐν τῷ σώματι ἡμῶν
about,　that also the life of　　Jesus in the　body　of us

**11** φανερωθῇ. ἀεὶ γὰρ ἡμεῖς οἱ ζῶντες εἰς θάνατον παραδιδό-
may be revealed. always For we the (ones) living to　death　are being deliv-
μεθα διὰ Ἰησοῦν, ἵνα καὶ ἡ ζωὴ τοῦ Ἰησοῦ φανερωθῇ ἐν τῇ
ered　on account Jesus, that also the life　of Jesus may be revealed in the

**12** θνητῇ σαρκὶ ἡμῶν. ὥστε ὁ μὲν θάνατος ἐν ἡμῖν ἐνεργεῖται,
mortal　flesh　of us. So as　indeed　death　in　us　works,

**13** ἡ δὲ ζωὴ ἐν ὑμῖν. ἔχοντες δὲ τὸ αὐτὸ πνεῦμα τῆς πίστεως,
and life　in you. having But the　same　spirit　of faith,
κατὰ τὸ γεγραμμένον, Ἐπίστευσα, διὸ ἐλάλησα, καὶ ἡμεῖς
according to that having been written: I believed, so I spoke;　both　we

**14** πιστεύομεν, διὸ καὶ λαλοῦμεν· εἰδότες ὅτι ὁ ἐγείρας τὸν
believe, therefore and　we speak,　knowing that He having raised the
Κύριον Ἰησοῦν καὶ ἡμᾶς διὰ Ἰησοῦ ἐγερεῖ, καὶ παραστήσει
Lord　Jesus also　us　with Jesus will raise, and will present (us)

**15** σὺν ὑμῖν. τὰ γὰρ πάντα δι᾽ ὑμᾶς, ἵνα ἡ χάρις πλεονάσασα
with you.　For all things for your sake, that　grace may superabound
διὰ τῶν πλειόνων τὴν εὐχαριστίαν περισσεύσῃ εἰς τὴν
through the greater number the thanksgiving　may make abound to the
δόξαν τοῦ Θεοῦ.
glory　　of God.

**16** Διὸ οὐκ ἐκκακοῦμεν· ἀλλ᾽ εἰ καὶ ὁ ἔξω ἡμῶν ἄνθρωπος
Therefore not　we faint,　but　if indeed the outward of us　man
διαφθείρεται, ἀλλ᾽ ὁ ἔσωθεν ἀνακαινοῦται ἡμέρα καὶ ἡμέρᾳ.
is being decayed, yet the inward (man is being renewed day　by　day

**17** τὸ γὰρ παραυτίκα ἐλαφρὸν τῆς θλίψεως ἡμῶν καθ᾽ ὑπερ-
the For　present　lightness of the affliction of us　— surpassing
βολὴν εἰς ὑπερβολὴν αἰώνιον βάρος δόξης κατεργάζεται
(moment) by surpassing (moment) an eternal weight of glory work out

**18** ἡμῖν, μὴ σκοπούντων ἡμῶν τὰ βλεπόμενα, ἀλλὰ τὰ μὴ
for us, not　considering　us　the things being seen, but the things not

not seen; for the things seen (are) not lasting, but the things not seen (are) everlasting.

## CHAPTER 5

[1] For we know that if our earthly house of (this) tabernacle is taken down, we have a building from God, a house not made with hands, eternal in Heaven. [2] For indeed in this we groan, greatly desiring to be clothed with our dwelling place out of Heaven; [3] if indeed (in) being clothed, we shall not be found naked. [4] For indeed being in the tabernacle we groan, being burdened; inasmuch as we do not wish to be unclothed, but to be clothed, that the mortal may be swallowed by the life. [5] Now He having worked in us for this same thing (is) God, who also (is) givng us the earnest of the Spirit. [6] Therefore, being always fully assured, and knowing that being at home in the body, we are away from home from the Lord, [7] — for we walk by faith, not by sight — [8] we are fully assured and are pleased rather to be away from home out of the body, and to be at home with the Lord. [9] Because of this, too, we are striving to be well-pleasing to Him, whether being at home, or being away from home. [10] For we all must appear before the judgment-seat of Christ, that each may receive the things (done) in the body, according to what we did, whether good or evil. [11] Knowing therefore the terror of the Lord, we persuade men, but we have been manifest to God, and I also hope to have been manifest in your consciences. [2] For we do not again commend ourselves to you, but are giving you occasion of boasting on our behalf, that you may have (such) toward those boasting in appearance and not in heart. [13] For if we were beside ourselves, (it was) to God; or are of sound mind, (it is) for you. [14] For the love of Christ constrains us, having

βλεπόμενα· τὰ γὰρ βλεπόμενα πρόσκαιρα· τὰ δὲ μὴ βλεπό-
being seen, the things For being seen (are) temporary, the things but not

μενα αἰώνια.
being seen (are) everlasting.

## CHAPTER 5

**1** Οἴδαμεν γὰρ ὅτι ἐὰν ἡ ἐπίγειος ἡμῶν οἰκία τοῦ σκήνους
we know For that if the earthly of us house of the tabernacle

καταλυθῇ, οἰκοδομὴν ἐκ Θεοῦ ἔχομεν, οἰκίαν ἀχειροποίητον,
is destroyed, a building of God we have, a house not made by hands,

**2** αἰώνιον ἐν τοῖς οὐρανοῖς. καὶ γὰρ ἐν τούτῳ στενάζομεν, τὸ
eternal in the heavens. indeed For in this we groan, the

οἰκητήριον ἡμῶν τὸ ἐξ οὐρανοῦ ἐπενδύσασθαι ἐπιποθοῦντες·
dwelling place of us out of Heaven to put on greatly desiring,

**3** εἴ γε καὶ ἐνδυσάμενοι οὐ γυμνοὶ εὑρεθησόμεθα. καὶ γὰρ οἱ
**4** if indeed being clothed, not naked we shall be found. indeed For

ὄντες ἐν τῷ σκήνει στενάζομεν βαρούμενοι· ἐφ' ᾧ οὐ θέλομεν
being in the tabernacle, we groan, being burdened, inasmuch as not we wish

ἐκδύσασθαι, ἀλλ' ἐπενδύσασθαι, ἵνα καταποθῇ τὸ θνητὸν
to be unclothed, but to be clothed, that may be swallowed the mortal

**5** ὑπὸ τῆς ζωῆς. ὁ δὲ κατεργασάμενος ἡμᾶς εἰς αὐτὸ τοῦτο
by the life. He Now having worked in us for this same thing

Θεός, ὁ καὶ δοὺς ἡμῖν τὸν ἀρραβῶνα τοῦ Πνεύματος.
(is) God, He also giving us the earnest of the Spirit.

**6** θαρροῦντες οὖν πάντοτε, καὶ εἰδότες ὅτι ἐνδημοῦντες ἐν τῷ
being assured Therefore always, and knowing that being at home in the

**7** σώματι ἐκδημοῦμεν ἀπὸ τοῦ Κυρίου (διὰ πίστεως γὰρ
body we are away from home from the Lord through faith For

**8** περιπατοῦμεν, οὐ διὰ εἴδους), θαρροῦμεν δέ, καὶ εὐδοκοῦμεν
we walk, not through sight ), we are assured, then, and think it good

μᾶλλον ἐκδημῆσαι ἐκ τοῦ σώματος, καὶ ἐνδημῆσαι πρὸς τὸν
rather to go away from home out of the body, and to come hone to the

**9** Κύριον. διὸ καὶ φιλοτιμούμεθα, εἴτε ἐνδημοῦντες, εἴτε ἐκδη-
Lord. Therefore also we are striving, whether being at home, or being away

**10** μοῦντες, εὐάρεστοι αὐτῷ εἶναι. τοὺς γὰρ πάντας ἡμᾶς
from home, well-pleasing to Him to be. — For all us

φανερωθῆναι δεῖ ἔμπροσθεν τοῦ βήματος τοῦ Χριστοῦ, ἵνα
to be revealed it behoves before the judgment-seat of Christ, that

κομίσηται ἕκαστος τὰ διὰ τοῦ σώματος, πρὸς ἃ ἔπραξεν,
may receive each one the things through the body, according to what we did,

εἴτε ἀγαθόν, εἴτε κακόν.
whether good or bad.

**11** Εἰδότες οὖν τὸν φόβον τοῦ Κυρίου ἀνθρώπους πείθομεν,
Knowing, then, the fear of the Lord, men we persuade,

Θεῷ δὲ πεφανερώμεθα· ἐλπίζω δὲ καὶ ἐν ταῖς συνειδήσεσιν
to God and we have been manifest; I hope and also in the conscience

**12** ὑμῶν πεφανερῶσθαι. οὐ γὰρ πάλιν ἑαυτοὺς συνιστάνομεν
of you to have been manifest, not For again ourselves we commend

ὑμῖν, ἀλλὰ ἀφορμὴν διδόντες ὑμῖν καυχήματος ὑπὲρ ἡμῶν,
to you, but an occasion giving to you of boasting on behalf of us,

ἵνα ἔχητε πρὸς τοὺς ἐν προσώπῳ καυχωμένους, καὶ οὐ
that you may have (it) toward those in appearance boasting, and not

**13** καρδίᾳ. εἴτε γὰρ ἐξέστημεν, Θεῷ· εἴτε σωφρονοῦμεν, ὑμῖν.
in heart. whether For we are insane, (it is) to God; or we are in our senses, for you.

**14** ἡ γὰρ ἀγάπη τοῦ Χριστοῦ συνέχει ἡμᾶς, κρίναντας τοῦτο,
the For love of Christ constrains us, having judged this

judged this, that if One died for all, then all died; [15] and He died for all, that they who live no longer should live to themselves, but to Him who died for them and was raised again. [16] So that we from now on know no one according to flesh; but even if we have known Christ according to flesh, yet now we no longer know (Him). [17] So that if anyone (is) in Christ, (that one is) a new creation; the old things passed away; behold, all things have become new! [18] And all things (are) of God, who reconciled us to Himself by Jesus Christ, and gave to us the service of reconciliation: [19] how that God was in Christ reconciling (the) world to Himself, not charging their offenses to them, and having put in us the word of reconciliation. [20] For therefore we are ambassadors (for) Christ as though God were exhorting by us, we beseech for Christ, be reconciled to God. [21] For He made Him who knew no sin (to be) sin for us, that we might become righteousness of God in Him.

CHAPTER 6

[1] But working together, we also call on you not to receive the grace of God in vain. [2] For He says, "In an accepted time I listened to you, and in a day of salvation I helped you;" behold, now (is) the accepted time! Behold, now (is) the day of salvation! [3] Not giving offense in anything, so that the ministry may not be blamed, [4] but in everything setting ourselves out as God's servants, in much patience, in troubles, in emergencies, in difficulties, [5] in stripes, in imprisonments, in riots, in labors, in watchings, in fastings, [6] in pureness, in knowledge, in long-suffering, in kindness, in the Holy Spirit, in true love, [7] in the word of truth, in the power of God,

ὅτι εἰ εἷς ὑπὲρ πάντων ἀπέθανεν, ἄρα οἱ πάντες ἀπέθανον·
that if One for all died, then the all died;

**15** καὶ ὑπὲρ πάντων ἀπέθανεν, ἵνα οἱ ζῶντες μηκέτι ἑαυτοῖς
and for all He died, that those living no more to themselves

**16** ζῶσιν, ἀλλὰ τῷ ὑπὲρ αὐτῶν ἀποθανόντι καὶ ἐγερθέντι. ὥστε
may live, but to the (One) for them having died, and having been raised So as

ἡμεῖς ἀπὸ τοῦ νῦν οὐδένα οἴδαμεν κατὰ σάρκα· εἰ δὲ καὶ
we from now no one know according to flesh; if but even

ἐγνώκαμεν κατὰ σάρκα Χριστόν, ἀλλὰ νῦν οὐκέτι γινώ-
we have known according to flesh Christ, but now no more we know

**17** σκομεν. ὥστε εἴ τις ἐν Χριστῷ, καινὴ κτίσις· τὰ ἀρχαῖα
(Him). So as if anyone (is) in Christ, (he is) a new creation; the old things

**18** παρῆλθεν, ἰδοὺ γέγονε καινὰ τὰ πάντα. τὰ δὲ πάντα ἐκ τοῦ
passed away behold, become nave new all things. the things and all (are) out of

Θεοῦ, τοῦ καταλλάξαντος ἡμᾶς ἑαυτῷ διὰ Ἰησοῦ Χριστοῦ,
God, the (One) having reconciled us to Himself through Jesus Christ,

**19** καὶ δόντος ἡμῖν τὴν διακονίαν τῆς καταλλαγῆς· ὡς ὅτι Θεὸς
and having given to us the ministry of reconciliation, as that God

ἦν ἐν Χριστῷ κόσμον καταλλάσσων ἑαυτῷ, μὴ λογιζό-
was in Christ (the) world reconciling to Himself, not charging

μενος αὐτοῖς τὰ παραπτώματα αὐτῶν, καὶ θέμενος ἐν ἡμῖν
to them the trespasses of them, and putting in us

τὸν λόγον τῆς καταλλαγῆς.
the word of reconciliation.

**20** Ὑπὲρ Χριστοῦ οὖν πρεσβεύομεν, ὡς τοῦ Θεοῦ παρακαλ-
On behalf of Christ, therefore, we are ambassadors as God exhorting

οῦντος δι' ἡμῶν· δεόμεθα ὑπὲρ Χριστοῦ, καταλλάγητε τῷ
through us; we beseech on behalf of Christ, be reconciled

**21** Θεῷ. τὸν γὰρ μὴ γνόντα ἁμαρτίαν, ὑπὲρ ἡμῶν ἁμαρτίαν
to God. the (One) For not knowing sin on behalf of us sin

ἐποίησεν, ἵνα ἡμεῖς γινώμεθα δικαιοσύνη Θεοῦ ἐν αὐτῷ.
He made. so that we might become (the) righteousness of God in Him.

CHAPTER 6

**1** συνεργοῦντες δὲ καὶ παρακαλοῦμεν μὴ εἰς κενὸν τὴν χάριν
working together And also we exhort not to in vain the grace

**2** τοῦ Θεοῦ δέξασθαι ὑμᾶς (λέγει γάρ, Καιρῷ δεκτῷ ἐπήκουσά
of God to receive you — He says For, In a time acceptable I heard

σου, καὶ ἐν ἡμέρᾳ σωτηρίας ἐβοήθησά σοι· ἰδού, νῦν καιρὸς
you, and in a day of salvation I helped you — behold, now a time

**3** εὐπρόσδεκτος, ἰδού, νῦν ἡμέρα σωτηρίας) μηδεμίαν ἐν
acceptable; behold, now a day of salvation — no in

**4** μηδενὶ διδόντες προσκοπήν, ἵνα μὴ μωμηθῇ ἡ διακονία· ἀλλ'
nothing giving cause of stumbling, that not be blamed the ministry, but

ἐν παντὶ συνιστῶντες ἑαυτοὺς ὡς Θεοῦ διάκονοι, ἐν ὑπομονῇ
in everything commending ourselves as of God ministers, in patience

**5** πολλῇ, ἐν θλίψεσιν, ἐν ἀνάγκαις, ἐν στενοχωρίαις, ἐν πλη-
much, in troubles, in emergencies, in difficulties, in stripes,

γαῖς, ἐν φυλακαῖς, ἐν ἀκαταστασίαις, ἐν κόποις, ἐν ἀγρυ-
in imprisonments, in riots, in labors, in watchings,

**6** πνίαις, ἐν νηστείαις, ἐν ἁγνότητι, ἐν γνώσει, ἐν μα-
in fastings, in pureness, in knowledge, in long-

κροθυμίᾳ, ἐν χρηστότητι, ἐν Πνεύματι Ἁγίῳ, ἐν ἀγάπῃ
suffering, in kindness, in spirit a holy, in love

**7** ἀνυποκρίτῳ, ἐν λόγῳ ἀληθείας, ἐν δυνάμει Θεοῦ, διὰ τῶν
unfeigned, in a word of truth, in (the) power of God, through the

through the weapons of righteousness on the right hand and the left, [8] through glory and dishonor, through evil report and good report — as deceivers, and yet true — [9] as unknown, and yet well-known — as dying, and yet, look, we live! — as flogged, and yet not put to death — [10] as sorrowful, but yet always rejoicing — as poor, but yet enriching many — as having nothing, yet possessing all things.

[11] Our mouth is opened to you, Corinthians, our heart has been enlarged. [12] You are not restrained in us; you are restrained in your (own) bowels. [13] But for the same reward— I speak as to children—you also be enlarged.

[14] Do not be unequally yoked with unbelievers. For what partnership does righteousness (have) with lawlessness? And what fellowship (has) light with darkness? [15] And what agreement does Christ (have) with Belial? Or what part does a believer (have) with an unbeliever? [16] And what agreement does a temple of God (have) with idols? For you are a temple of (the) living God, according as God said, "I will live in them and walk among (them); and I will be their God, and they shall be My people." [17] Therefore come out from among them and be separated, says (the) Lord, and touch not (the) unclean, and I will receive you. [18] And I will be a Father to you, and you shall be sons and daughters to Me, says (the) Lord Almighty.

CHAPTER 7

[1] Therefore, beloved, having these promises, we should cleanse ourselves from every defilement of flesh and spirit, perfecting holiness in the fear of God.

[2] Make room for us; we have done no one wrong; we have corrupted no one; we have overreached no one. [3] I do not speak for condemnation, for I have

**8** ὅπλων τῆς δικαιοσύνης τῶν δεξιῶν καὶ ἀριστερῶν, διὰ
weapons   of righteousness   on the   right   and   of left;   through
δόξης καὶ ἀτιμίας, διὰ δυσφημίας καὶ εὐφημίας· ὡς πλάνοι,
glory   and dishonor;   through evil report and good report,   as   deceivers
**9** καὶ ἀληθεῖς· ὡς ἀγνοούμενοι. καὶ ἐπιγινωσκόμενοι· ὡς
and (yet) true;   as   unknown,   and (yet) well-known;   as
ἀποθνήσκοντες, καὶ ἰδού, ζῶμεν· ὡς παιδευόμενοι, καὶ μὴ
dying,   and behold, we live;   as   flogged,   and not
**10** θανατούμενοι· ὡς λυπούμενοι, ἀεὶ δὲ χαίροντες· ὡς πτωχοί,
put to death;   as   grieved,   always and rejoicing;   as   poor,
πολλοὺς δὲ πλουτίζοντες· ὡς μηδὲν ἔχοντες, καὶ πάντα
many   but   enriching;   as   nothing   having,   and all things
κατέχοντες.
possessing.

**11** Τὸ στόμα ἡμῶν ἀνέῳγε πρὸς ὑμᾶς, Κορίνθιοι, ἡ καρδία
The mouth   of us   is opened to   you,   Corinthians,   the heart
**12** ἡμῶν πεπλάτυνται. οὐ στενοχωρεῖσθε ἐν ἡμῖν, στενοχω-
of us has been made larger.   not You are restrained   in   us,   you are
**13** ρεῖσθε δὲ ἐν τοῖς σπλάγχνοις ὑμῶν. τὴν δὲ αὐτὴν ἀντιμισθίαν
restrained but in the   bowels   of you. for the But same   reward
(ὡς τέκνοις λέγω), πλατύνθητε καὶ ὑμεῖς.
—as to children I speak — be enlarged   also   you.

**14** Μὴ γίνεσθε ἑτεροζυγοῦντες ἀπίστοις· τίς γὰρ μετοχὴ
Do not become   unequally yoked (with) unbelievers, what for partnership
δικαιοσύνη καὶ ἀνομία; τίς δὲ κοινωνία φωτὶ πρὸς σκότος;
(have) righteousness and lawlessness? what And fellowship light with darkness?
**15** τίς δὲ συμφώνησις Χριστῷ πρὸς Βελίαλ; ἢ τίς μερὶς πιστῷ
what And agreement (has) Christ   with   Belial?   Or what part a believer
**16** μετὰ ἀπίστου; τίς δὲ συγκατάθεσις ναῷ Θεοῦ μετὰ εἰδώλων;
with an unbeliever? what And   union   the temple of God with idols?
ὑμεῖς γὰρ ναὸς Θεοῦ ἐστε ζῶντος, καθὼς εἶπεν ὁ Θεὸς ὅτι
you For a temple of God   are of a living,   even as   said   God: —
Ἐνοικήσω ἐν αὐτοῖς, καὶ ἐμπεριπατήσω· καὶ ἔσομαι αὐτῶν
I will dwell among them,   and I will walk among (them) and I will be of them
**17** Θεός, καὶ αὐτοὶ ἔσονταί μοι λαός. διὸ Ἐξέλθετε ἐκ μέσου
God,   and they   shall be of me a people. Therefore come out from amidst
αὐτῶν καὶ ἀφορίσθητε, λέγει Κύριος, καὶ ἀκαθάρτου μὴ
them,   and   be separated,   says (the) Lord,   and an unclean thing not
**18** ἅπτεσθε· κἀγὼ εἰσδέξομαι ὑμᾶς, καὶ ἔσομαι ὑμῖν εἰς πατέρα,
touch;   and I   will receive   you,   and I will be to you for a Father,
καὶ ὑμεῖς ἔσεσθέ μοι εἰς υἱοὺς καὶ θυγατέρας, λέγει Κύριος
and you   will be to Me for sons   and   daughters,   says (the) Lord
παντοκράτωρ.
Almighty.

## CHAPTER 7

**1** ταύτας οὖν ἔχοντες τὰς ἐπαγγελίας, ἀγαπη-
these   Then   having   the   promises,   beloved,
τοί, καθαρίσωμεν ἑαυτοὺς ἀπὸ παντὸς μολυσμοῦ σαρκὸς
let us cleanse   ourselves   from   all   defilements of flesh
καὶ πνεύματος, ἐπιτελοῦντες ἁγιωσύνην ἐν φόβῳ Θεοῦ.
and   of spirit,   perfecting   holiness   in (the) fear of God.
**2** Χωρήσατε ἡμᾶς· οὐδένα ἠδικήσαμεν, οὐδένα ἐφθείραμεν,
Make room for us;   no one   we wronged,   no one we spoiled,
**3** οὐδένα ἐπλεονεκτήσαμεν. οὐ πρὸς κατάκρισιν λέγω· προεί-
no one   we overreached.   Not for condemnation I speak, I have

said before that you are in our hearts, for (us) to die together and to live together. [4] Great (is) my boldness toward you, great my glorying in regards to you; I have been filled with comfort; I overflow with joy at all our tribulation. [5] For, indeed, we having come into Macedonia, our flesh did not have any rest, but being troubled in every (way), fightings on the outside, fears on the inside. [6] But He who comforts those brought low, God comforted us by the coming of Titus; [7] and not only by his coming, but also by the comfort with which he was comforted as to you; telling us your longing, your mourning, your zeal for me; so as for me to rejoice the more. [8] For even if I grieved you in the letter, I do not regret, even if I did regret; for I see that that letter grieved you, even if for an hour. [9] Now I rejoice, not that you were grieved, but that you were grieved to repentance; for you were grieved according to God, that you might suffer loss in nothing by us. [10] For the grief according to God works repentance to salvation, not to be regretted; but the grief' of the world works out death. [11] For behold, this same thing, you having been grieved according to God, how much it worked out in you earnestness, but (also) defense, but (also) indignation, but (also) fear, but (also) eager desire, but (also) zeal, but (also) vengeance! In everything you proved yourselves to be clear in the matter. [12] Then even if I wrote to you, (it was) not for the sake of him who did wrong, nor for the sake of him who suffered wrong, but for the sake of revealing our care which (is) for you in the sight of God. [13] For this reason we have been much comforted in your comfort, and we rejoice the more abundantly rather at the joy of Titus, because his spirit has been refreshed by all of you.

ρηκα γάρ, ὅτι ἐν ταῖς καρδίαις ἡμῶν ἐστὲ εἰς τὸ συναποθα-
before said for, that in the hearts of us you are for to die with (you)

4 νεῖν καὶ συζῆν. πολλή μοι παρρησία πρὸς ὑμᾶς, πολλή μοι
and to live with (you) me boldness to you, Much to me

καύχησις ὑπὲρ ὑμῶν· πεπλήρωμαι τῇ παρακλήσει, ὑπερ-
boasting on behalf of you. I have been filled with comfort, I

περισσεύομαι τῇ χαρᾷ ἐπὶ πάσῃ τῇ θλίψει ἡμῶν.
overflow with joy on all the trouble of us.

5 Καὶ γὰρ ἐλθόντων ἡμῶν εἰς Μακεδονίαν οὐδεμίαν ἔσχηκεν
indeed For coming us into Macedonia no has had

ἄνεσιν ἡ σὰρξ ἡμῶν, ἀλλ᾽ ἐν παντὶ θλιβόμενοι· ἔξωθεν μάχαι,
rest the flesh of us, but in every way being troubled; without fightings,

6 ἔσωθεν φόβοι. ἀλλ᾽ ὁ παρακαλῶν τοὺς ταπεινοὺς παρε-
within fears. But the (One) comforting the lowly

7 κάλεσεν ἡμᾶς, ὁ Θεός, ἐν τῇ παρουσίᾳ Τίτου· οὐ μόνον δὲ ἐν
comforted us, God, by the presence of Titus; not only and by

τῇ παρουσίᾳ αὐτοῦ, ἀλλὰ καὶ ἐν τῇ παρακλήσει ᾗ παρεκλήθη
the presence of him, but also by the comfort with which he was comforted

ἐφ᾽ ὑμῖν, ἀναγγέλλων ἡμῖν τὴν ὑμῶν ἐπιπόθησιν, τὸν ὑμῶν
over you, telling us your longing, your

ὀδυρμόν, τὸν ὑμῶν ζῆλον ὑπὲρ ἐμοῦ, ὥστε με μᾶλλον
mourning, your zeal for me, so as for me more

8 χαρῆναι, ὅτι εἰ καὶ ἐλύπησα ὑμᾶς ἐν τῇ ἐπιστολῇ, οὐ μετα-
to rejoice. Because if even I grieved you by the epistle, not I

μέλομαι, εἰ καὶ μετεμελόμην· βλέπω γὰρ ὅτι ἡ ἐπιστολὴ
regret; if indeed I regretted, I see for that epistle

9 ἐκείνη, εἰ καὶ πρὸς ὥραν, ἐλύπησεν ὑμᾶς. νῦν χαίρω, οὐχ
that if indeed for an hour it grieved you, now I rejoice, not

ὅτι ἐλυπήθητε, ἀλλ᾽ ὅτι ἐλυπήθητε εἰς μετάνοιαν· ἐλυπήθητε
that you were grieved, but that you were grieved to repentance; you grieved

10 γὰρ κατὰ Θεόν, ἵνα ἐν μηδενὶ ζημιωθῆτε ἐξ ἡμῶν. ἡ γὰρ
for according to God, that in nothing you might suffer loss by us. the For

κατὰ Θεὸν λύπη μετάνοιαν εἰς σωτηρίαν ἀμεταμέλητον
according to God grief repentance to salvation unregrettable

κατεργάζεται· ἡ δὲ τοῦ κόσμου λύπη θάνατον κατεργά-
works: the but of the world grief death works

11 ζεται. ἰδοὺ γάρ, αὐτὸ τοῦτο, τὸ κατὰ Θεὸν λυπηθῆναι ὑμᾶς,
out. behold For, this same thing, according to God to be grieved you,

πόσην κατειργάσατο ὑμῖν σπουδήν, ἀλλὰ ἀπολογίαν,
how much it worked out in you earnestness, but defense,

ἀλλὰ ἀγανάκτησιν, ἀλλὰ φόβον, ἀλλὰ ἐπιπόθησιν, ἀλλὰ
but indignation, but fear, but eager desire, but

ζῆλον, ἀλλ᾽ ἐκδίκησιν. ἐν παντὶ συνεστήσατε ἑαυτοὺς ἁγνοὺς
zeal, but vengeance! In everything you commended yourselves clear

12 εἶναι ἐν τῷ πράγματι. ἄρα εἰ καὶ ἔγραψα ὑμῖν, οὐχ εἵνεκεν
to be in the affair. Then if even I wrote to you (it was) not for

τοῦ ἀδικήσαντος, οὐδὲ εἵνεκεν τοῦ ἀδικηθέντος, ἀλλ᾽ εἵνεκεν
the (one) having done wrong, nor for the (one) having been wronged, but for

τοῦ φανερωθῆναι τὴν σπουδὴν ἡμῶν τὴν ὑπὲρ ὑμῶν πρὸς
to be revealed the earnestness of you on behalf of us toward

13 ὑμᾶς ἐνώπιον τοῦ Θεοῦ. διὰ τοῦτο παρακεκλήμεθα ἐπὶ τῇ
you before God. For this reason we have been comforted as to the

παρακλήσει ὑμῶν· περισσοτέρως δὲ μᾶλλον ἐχάρημεν ἐπὶ τῇ
comfort of you, abundantly and more we rejoice over the

χαρᾷ Τίτου, ὅτι ἀναπέπαυται τὸ πνεῦμα αὐτοῦ ἀπὸ πάντων
joy of Titus, because has been rested the spirit of him from all

[14] Because if I have boasted anything to him about you, I was not put to shame; but as we spoke all things in truth to you, so also our boasting which (was) toward Titus became truth. [15] And his tender feelings are more abundantly toward you, remembering the obedience of all of you, as you received him with fear and trembling. [16] Therefore I rejoice, that in everything I am fully assured in you.

**14** ὑμῶν. ὅτι εἴ τι αὐτῷ ὑπὲρ ὑμῶν κεκαύχημαι, οὐ κατησχύν-
you, because if anything to him for you I have boasted, not I was ashamed

θην· ἀλλ᾽ ὡς πάντα ἐν ἀληθείᾳ ἐλαλήσαμεν ὑμῖν, οὕτω καὶ ἡ
but as all things in truth we spoke to you, so also the

**15** καύχησις ἡμῶν, ἡ ἐπὶ Τίτου, ἀλήθεια ἐγενήθη. καὶ τὰ σπλάγ-
boasting of us as to Titus truth became, and the bowels

χνα αὐτοῦ περισσοτέρως εἰς ὑμᾶς ἐστίν, ἀναμιμνησκομένου
of him abundantly toward you are, remembering

τὴν πάντων ὑμῶν ὑπακοήν, ὡς μετὰ φόβου καὶ τρόμου
the of all of you obedience, as with fear and trembling

**16** ἐδέξασθε αὐτόν. χαίρω οὖν ὅτι ἐν παντὶ θαρρῶ ἐν ὑμῖν.
you received him. I rejoice Then that in everything I am assured in you.

## CHAPTER 8

### CHAPTER 8

[1] But we make known to you, brothers, the grace of God which has been given to the churches of Macedonia, [2] that in much testing of trouble the overflowing of their joy and deep poverty abounded to the riches of their generosity. [3] For I testify (that) according to (their) ability, and beyond (their) ability, (they) chose (to give), [4] with much beseeching, begging us (that they might) receive of us the grace and the fellowship of the ministry to the saints. [5] And not as we had hoped, but they first gave themselves to the Lord, and to us, by (the) will of God. [6] So that we called on Titus, that according as he began before, so also he might complete this grace with you also. [7] But even as you excel in every (way), in faith, and word, and knowledge, and all eagerness, and in your love toward us, that also you should excel in this grace. [8] I do not speak according to command, but through the eagerness of others, and testing the trueness of your love. [9] For you know the grace of our Lord Jesus Christ, that being rich, He became poor for your sake, so that you might be made rich by His poverty. [10] And I give a judgment in this, for this is profitable for you, who began before not only to do, but also to be willing a year ago. [11] But now finish the work, so that

**1** Γνωρίζομεν δὲ ὑμῖν, ἀδελφοί, τὴν χάριν τοῦ Θεοῦ τὴν
we make known But to you, brothers, the grace of God the

**2** δεδομένην ἐν ταῖς ἐκκλησίαις τῆς Μακεδονίας· ὅτι ἐν πολλῇ
being given among the churches of Macedonia, that in much

δοκιμῇ θλίψεως ἡ περισσεία τῆς χαρᾶς αὐτῶν καὶ ἡ κατὰ
testing of trouble the overflowing of the joy of them, and the

βάθους πτωχεία αὐτῶν ἐπερίσσευσεν εἰς τὸν πλοῦτον τῆς
depth poverty of them abounded to the riches of the

**3** ἁπλότητος αὐτῶν. ὅτι κατὰ δύναμιν, μαρτυρῶ, καὶ ὑπὲρ
liberality of them. Because according to ability, I witness, and beyond

**4** δύναμιν αὐθαίρετοι, μετὰ πολλῆς παρακλήσεως δεόμενοι
(their) ability voluntarily with much beseeching begging

ἡμῶν, τὴν χάριν καὶ τὴν κοινωνίαν τῆς διακονίας τῆς εἰς
us the grace and the fellowship of the ministry to

**5** τοὺς ἁγίους δέξασθαι ἡμᾶς· καὶ οὐ καθὼς ἠλπίσαμεν, ἀλλ᾽
the saints to receive of us, and not as we hoped, but

ἑαυτοὺς ἔδωκαν πρῶτον τῷ Κυρίῳ, καὶ ἡμῖν διὰ θελήματος
themselves gave firstly to the Lord, and to us, through the will

**6** Θεοῦ. εἰς τὸ παρακαλέσαι ἡμᾶς Τίτον, ἵνα καθὼς προενήρ-
of God. For to call us on Titus, that as he began

ξατο, οὕτω καὶ ἐπιτελέσῃ εἰς ὑμᾶς καὶ τὴν χάριν ταύτην.
before, so also he should complete to you also grace this.

**7** ἀλλ᾽ ὥσπερ ἐν παντὶ περισσεύετε, πίστει, καὶ λόγῳ, καὶ
But as in everything you abound, in faith, and in word, and

γνώσει, καὶ πάσῃ σπουδῇ, καὶ τῇ ἐξ ὑμῶν ἐν ἡμῖν ἀγάπῃ,
in knowledge, and all earnestness, and the of you in us love,

**8** ἵνα καὶ ἐν ταύτῃ τῇ χάριτι περισσεύητε. οὐ κατ᾽ ἐπιταγὴν
that also in this grace you may abound. Not by command

λέγω, ἀλλὰ διὰ τῆς ἑτέρων σπουδῆς καὶ τὸ τῆς ὑμετέρας
I say, but through the of others earnestness also the of your

**9** ἀγάπης γνήσιον δοκιμάζων. γινώσκετε γὰρ τὴν χάριν τοῦ
love trueness testing; you know for the grace of the

Κυρίου ἡμῶν Ἰησοῦ Χριστοῦ, ὅτι δι᾽ ὑμᾶς ἐπτώχευσε,
Lord of us, Jesus Christ that because of you He became poor.

**10** πλούσιος ὤν, ἵνα ὑμεῖς τῇ ἐκείνου πτωχείᾳ πλουτήσητε. καὶ
rich being, that you by the of that One poverty might become rich. And

γνώμην ἐν τούτῳ δίδωμι· τοῦτο γὰρ ὑμῖν συμφέρει, οἵτινε
a judgment in this I give, this for to you is profitable, who

οὐ μόνον τὸ ποιῆσαι ἀλλὰ καὶ τὸ θέλειν προενήρξασθε ἀπὸ
not only the to do but also the to will you before began from

**11** πέρυσι. νυνὶ δὲ καὶ τὸ ποιῆσαι ἐπιτελέσατε, ὅπως, καθάπερ
last year. now But also the doing (of it) finish, so as, as

even as (there was) the readiness of being willing, so also the finishing (of it) out of that (you) own. [12] For if the eagerness is present, it is acceptable according to (what) one has, not according to (what) one does not have. [13] For (it is) not that others (have) ease, but you trouble, [14] but by equality: in the present time, your abundance for their need, so that their abundance may also be for their need—so that should be equality; [15] even as it has been written: "He (taking) much, he had nothing over; and he (taking) little, he did not have less."

[16] But thanks (be) to God, who gives the same earnestness for you in the heart of Titus. [17] For, indeed, he accepted the exhortation, but being more eager, of his own accord he went out to you. [18] But we sent with him the brother whose praise (is) in the gospel throughout all the churches; [19] and not only (so), but also he having been chosen by the churches (is) our traveling companion with this gift, being ministered by us to the glory of the Lord Himself, and your eagerness; [20] avoiding this, lest anyone should blame us in this bounty being ministered by us; [21] providing right things not only before (the) Lord, but also before men. [22] And we sent with them our brother whom we often proved in many things to be earnest, and not much more earnest by the great assurance which (I have) toward you. [23] If (any asks) as to Titus, (he is) my partner, and a fellow-helper for you — or our brothers, (they are) messengers of the churches, the glory of Christ. [24] Therefore show them a proof of your love and of our boastings toward you even in the sight of the churches.

CHAPTER 9

[1] For as to the ministry which (is) for the saints, it is superfluous for

ἡ προθυμία τοῦ θέλειν, οὕτω καὶ τὸ ἐπιτελέσαι ἐκ τοῦ ἔχειν.
the eagerness of the willing,    so    also   the finishing out of (what) have.
                                                                                    you

**12** εἰ γὰρ ἡ προθυμία πρόκειται, καθὸ ἐὰν ἔχῃ τις, εὐπρόσδε-
if For   the eagerness   is present, according to what one has, it is acceptable,

**13** κτος, οὐ καθὸ οὐκ ἔχει. οὐ γὰρ ἵνα ἄλλοις ἄνεσις, ὑμῖν δὲ
     not according to (what) one    not For that to others   ease,   you but
          to              not has.

**14** θλίψις· ἀλλ' ἐξ ἰσότητος, ἐν τῷ νῦν καιρῷ τὸ ὑμῶν περίσ-
trouble, but   by equality,   in the present time   the of you abun-
σευμα εἰς τὸ ἐκείνων ὑστέρημα, ἵνα καὶ τὸ ἐκείνων περίσσευμα
dance for the of those   lack,   that also the   of those abundance
γένηται εἰς τὸ ὑμῶν ὑστέρημα· ὅπως γένηται ἰσότης,
may be   for the of you   lack,    so as    may be equality,

**15** καθὼς γέγραπται, Ὁ τὸ πολύ, οὐκ ἐπλεόνασε· καὶ ὁ τὸ
even as it has been written: He (taking) much, not he had over, and he (taking)
ὀλίγον, οὐκ ἠλαττόνησε.
little,   not   had less.

**16** Χάρις δὲ τῷ Θεῷ τῷ διδόντι τὴν αὐτὴν σπουδὴν ὑπὲρ
thanks But   to God   giving   the   same earnestness   for

**17** ὑμῶν ἐν τῇ καρδίᾳ Τίτου. ὅτι τὴν μὲν παράκλησιν ἐδέξατο,
you in the   heart   of Titus, because the indeed beseeching he received,
σπουδαιότερος δὲ ὑπάρχων, αὐθαίρετος ἐξῆλθε πρὸς ὑμᾶς.
more earnest   and   being, of his own accord he went out to you.

**18** συνεπέμψαμεν δὲ μετ' αὐτοῦ τὸν ἀδελφόν, οὗ ὁ ἔπαινος ἐν τῷ
we sent    And with him   the brother, of whom the praise is in the

**19** εὐαγγελίῳ διὰ πασῶν τῶν ἐκκλησιῶν· οὐ μόνον δέ, ἀλλὰ
gospel   throughout all the   churches,   not only   and, but
καὶ χειροτονηθεὶς ὑπὸ τῶν ἐκκλησιῶν συνέκδημος ἡμῶν
also having been chosen by   the   churches a traveling companion to us
σὺν τῇ χάριτι ταύτῃ τῇ διακονουμένῃ ὑφ' ἡμῶν πρὸς τὴν
with   gift   this   being ministered by   us   to   the

**20** αὐτοῦ τοῦ Κυρίου δόξαν, καὶ προθυμίαν ὑμῶν· στελλόμενοι
Himself of the Lord   glory, and (the) eagerness of you; avoiding
τοῦτο, μή τις ἡμᾶς μωμήσηται ἐν τῇ ἁδρότητι ταύτῃ τῇ
this,   lest anyone us   should blame in   bounty   this

**21** διακονουμένῃ ὑφ' ἡμῶν· προνοούμενοι καλὰ οὐ μόνον
being ministered by   us;   providing   right things not   only

**22** ἐνώπιον Κυρίου ἀλλὰ καὶ ἐνώπιον ἀνθρώπων. συνεπέμψα-
before (the) Lord,   but also before   men.   we sent with
μεν δὲ αὐτοῖς τὸν ἀδελφὸν ἡμῶν, ὃν ἐδοκιμάσαμεν ἐν πολλοῖς
And them the brother   of us, whom we proved   in many things
πολλάκις σπουδαῖον ὄντα, νυνὶ δὲ πολὺ σπουδαιότερον,
many times   earnest   being,   now and much   more earnest,

**23** πεποιθήσει πολλῇ τῇ εἰς ὑμᾶς. εἴτε ὑπὲρ Τίτου, κοινωνὸς
in assurance   much   toward you. Whether as to Titus,   partner
ἐμὸς καὶ εἰς ὑμᾶς συνεργός· εἴτε ἀδελφοὶ ἡμῶν, ἀπόστολοι
my and for you fellow-worker,   or   brothers   of us,   apostles

**24** ἐκκλησιῶν, δόξα Χριστοῦ. τὴν οὖν ἔνδειξιν τῆς ἀγάπης
of churches, (the) glory of Christ. the Therefore   proof of the love
ὑμῶν, καὶ ἡμῶν καυχήσεως ὑπὲρ ὑμῶν, εἰς αὐτοὺς ἐνδείξασθε
of you and of us the boasting   as to   you   to them showing forth
καὶ εἰς πρόσωπον τῶν ἐκκλησιῶν.
and in the presence of the   churches.

CHAPTER 9

**1** Περὶ μὲν γὰρ τῆς διακονίας τῆς εἰς τοὺς ἁγίους περισσόν
concerning indeed For the ministry      to   the   saints, superfluous

me to write to you. [2] For I know your willingness, of which I boast to the Macedonians concerning you; that Achaia has been ready a year ago, and your zeal arouses a great many more. [3] But I sent the brothers, lest our boasting which (is) about you should be in vain in this respect, so that I said, you may be ready; [4] lest perhaps the Macedonians should come with me and find you not ready. We — that we may not say you — should be put to shame in this confidence of boasting. [5] So I judged (it) necessary to urge the brothers, that they should go forward to you and to arrange beforehand your promised blessing; this to be ready thus as a blessing, and not as greediness. [6] And this: he sowing sparingly will also reap sparingly; and he sowing on (hope of) blessing will also reap on blessing; [7] each as he purposes in the heart, not of grief or necessity, for God loves a cheerful giver. [8] And God is able to make all grace abound toward you, that in everything, always having all self-sufficiency, you may abound to every good work; [9] even as it has been written: "He scattered abroad he gave to the poor, his righteousness abides forever." [10] Now He that supplies seed to the sower, and bread for eating, may He supply and multiply your seed, and increase the fruits of your righteousness [11] in everything (you) being enriched to all liberality, which works out thanksgiving to God through us.

[12] Because the ministry of this service is not only fully supplying the needs of the saints, but also multiplying through many thanksgivings to God; [13] through the proof of this service, (they)

**2** μοί ἐστι τὸ γράφειν ὑμῖν· οἶδα γὰρ τὴν προθυμίαν ὑμῶν, ἣν
to me it is to write you; I know for the eagerness of you, which
ὑπὲρ ὑμῶν καυχῶμαι Μακεδόσιν, ὅτι 'Αχαΐα παρεσκεύασται
as to you I boast to Macedonia, that Achaia has made ready
ἀπὸ πέρυσι· καὶ ὁ ἐξ ὑμῶν ζῆλος ἠρέθισε τοὺς πλείονας.
from last year, and the of you zeal arouses the greater number.

**3** ἔπεμψα δὲ τοὺς ἀδελφούς, ἵνα μὴ τὸ καύχημα ἡμῶν τὸ ὑπὲρ
I sent And the brothers, lest the boast of us as to
ὑμῶν κενωθῇ ἐν τῷ μέρει τούτῳ· ἵνα, καθὼς ἔλεγον, παρε-
you should be in vain in respect this, that, as I said, having

**4** σκευασμένοι ἦτε· μή πως, ἐὰν ἔλθωσι σὺν ἐμοὶ Μακεδόνες καὶ
been ready you were, lest if come with me Macedonians and
εὕρωσιν ὑμᾶς ἀπαρασκευάστους, καταισχυνθῶμεν ἡμεῖς (ἵνα
find you not ready should be ashamed we — that
μὴ λέγωμεν ὑμεῖς) ἐν τῇ ὑποστάσει ταύτῃ τῆς καυχήσεως.
not we say you — in assurance this of boasting.

**5** ἀναγκαῖον οὖν ἡγησάμην παρακαλέσαι τοὺς ἀδελφούς, ἵνα
necessary Therefore I thought (it) to exhort the brothers, that
προέλθωσιν εἰς ὑμᾶς, καὶ προκαταρτίσωσι τὴν προκατηγ-
they go forward to you, and arrange beforehand the having been
γελμένην εὐλογίαν ὑμῶν, ταύτην ἑτοίμην εἶναι, οὕτως ὡς
promised blessing of you, this ready to be, thus as
εὐλογίαν, καὶ μὴ ὥσπερ πλεονεξίαν.
a blessing, and not as greediness.

**6** Τοῦτο δέ, ὁ σπείρων φειδομένως, φειδομένως καὶ θερίσει·
this And: he sowing sparingly, sparingly also will reap;
καὶ ὁ σπείρων ἐπ' εὐλογίαις, ἐπ' εὐλογίαις καὶ θερίσει.
and he sowing on (hope of) blessing, on blessing also will reap.

**7** ἕκαστος καθὼς προαιρεῖται τῇ καρδίᾳ· μὴ ἐκ λύπης ἢ ἐξ
Each one as he purposes in the heart, not of grief or of

**8** ἀνάγκης· ἱλαρὸν γὰρ δότην ἀγαπᾷ ὁ Θεός. δυνατὸς δὲ ὁ
necessity; a cheerful for giver loves God. is able And
Θεὸς πᾶσαν χάριν περισσεῦσαι εἰς ὑμᾶς, ἵνα ἐν παντὶ
God all grace to make abound toward you, that in everything
πάντοτε πᾶσαν αὐτάρκειαν ἔχοντες περισσεύητε εἰς πᾶν
always all self-sufficiency having you may abound to every

**9** ἔργον ἀγαθόν· καθὼς γέγραπται, 'Εσκόρπισεν, ἔδωκε τοῖς
work good; even as it has been written: He scattered; he gave to the

**10** πένησιν· ἡ δικαιοσύνη αὐτοῦ μένει εἰς τὸν αἰῶνα. ὁ δὲ
poor; the righteousness of him remains to the age. He Now
ἐπιχορηγῶν σπέρμα τῷ σπείροντι, καὶ ἄρτον εἰς βρῶσιν
that supplies seed to the sower, and bread for eating,
χορηγήσαι, καὶ πληθύναι τὸν σπόρον ὑμῶν, καὶ αὐξήσαι
may He supply and multiply the seed of you, and increase

**11** τὰ γεννήματα τῆς δικαιοσύνης ὑμῶν· ἐν παντὶ πλουτιζό-
the fruits of the righteousness of you in everything being en-
μενοι εἰς πᾶσαν ἁπλότητα, ἥτις κατεργάζεται δι' ἡμῶν
riched to all liberality, which works out through us

**12** εὐχαριστίαν τῷ Θεῷ. ὅτι ἡ διακονία τῆς λειτουργίας ταύτης
thanksgiving to God. Because the ministry service of this
οὐ μόνον ἐστὶ προσαναπληροῦσα τὰ ὑστερήματα τῶν
not only is making up the things lacking of the
ἁγίων, ἀλλὰ καὶ περισσεύουσα διὰ πολλῶν εὐχαριστιῶν
saints, but also abounding through many thanksgivings

**13** τῷ Θεῷ· διὰ τῆς δοκιμῆς τῆς διακονίας ταύτης δοξάζοντες
to God, through the proof ministry of this glorifying

glorifying God by your freely expressed obedience to the gospel of Christ, and generosity of the fellowship towards them and towards all; [14] and in their prayer for you, a longing for you, because of the overflowing grace of God on you. [15] Now thanks (be) to God for His unspeakable free gift.

### CHAPTER 10

[1] Now I myself, Paul, call on you by the meekness and gentleness of Christ — I, who indeed to look upon am lowly among you, but absent am bold toward you; [2] but I ask, not being present, that I may not be bold with the confidence which I think to be daring against some, those having thought (of) us as walking according to flesh. [3] For walking about in flesh, we do not war according to flesh. [4] For the weapons of our warfare (are) not fleshly, but powerful to God to the pulling down of strongholds, [5] pulling down imaginations and every high thing lifting (itself) up against the knowledge of God, and bringing into captivity every thought into the obedience of Christ [6] and having readiness to avenge all disobedience, whenever your obedience is fulfilled. [7] Do you look at things according to appearance? If anyone has persuaded himself to be of Christ, let him think this again as to himself, that as he (is) of Christ, so also we (are) of Christ. [8] For even if I also somewhat more fully should boast about our authority—which the Lord gave us for building up, and not for pulling you down— I will not be put to shame; [9] so that I may not seem to frighten you by letters; [10] because, truly the letters, he says, (are) weighty and strong, but the bodily presence (is) weak, and (his) speech being despised. [11] Let such a one think this, that such as we are in

τὸν Θεὸν ἐπὶ τῇ ὑποταγῇ τῆς ὁμολογίας ὑμῶν εἰς τὸ
God on the submission by the confession of you to the
εὐαγγέλιον τοῦ Χριστοῦ, καὶ ἁπλότητι τῆς κοινωνίας εἰς
gospel of Christ, and (the) liberality of the fellowship toward

**14** αὐτοὺς καὶ εἰς πάντας· καὶ αὐτῶν δεήσει ὑπὲρ ὑμῶν
them and toward all; and them with petition for you
ἐπιποθούντων ὑμᾶς διὰ τὴν ὑπερβάλλουσαν χάριν τοῦ
longing after you on account of the surpassing grace

**15** Θεοῦ ἐφ᾽ ὑμῖν. χάρις δὲ τῷ Θεῷ ἐπὶ τῇ ἀνεκδιηγήτῳ αὐτοῦ
of God upon you. thanks But to God for the unspeakable of Him
δωρεᾷ.
gift.

### CHAPTER 10

**1** Αὐτὸς δὲ ἐγὼ Παῦλος παρακαλῶ ὑμᾶς διὰ τῆς πραότητος
myself And I, Paul, exhort you through the meekness
καὶ ἐπιεικείας τοῦ Χριστοῦ, ὃς κατὰ πρόσωπον μὲν ταπεινὸς
and forbearance of Christ, who according to face indeed humble

**2** ἐν ὑμῖν, ἀπὼν δὲ θαρρῶ εἰς ὑμᾶς· δέομαι δέ, τὸ μὴ παρὼν
among you, being absent, but am bold toward you; I ask but, not being present,
θαρρῆσαι τῇ πεποιθήσει ᾗ λογίζομαι τολμῆσαι ἐπί τινας
to be bold in the confidence which I think to be daring toward some,
τοὺς λογιζομένους ἡμᾶς ὡς κατὰ σάρκα περιπατοῦντας.
those thinking us as according to flesh walking.

**3** ἐν σαρκὶ γὰρ περιπατοῦντες, οὐ κατὰ σάρκα στρατευόμεθα
in flesh For walking, not according to flesh we war;

**4** (τὰ γὰρ ὅπλα τῆς στρατείας ἡμῶν οὐ σαρκικά, ἀλλὰ
the for weapons of the warfare of us (are) not fleshly, but

**5** δυνατὰ τῷ Θεῷ πρὸς καθαίρεσιν ὀχυρωμάτων), λογισμοὺς
powerful to God in order to demolish strongholds, imaginations
καθαιροῦντες καὶ πᾶν ὕψωμα ἐπαιρόμενον κατὰ τῆς γνώσεως
demolishing, and every high thing lifting up (itself) against the knowledge
τοῦ Θεοῦ, καὶ αἰχμαλωτίζοντες πᾶν νόημα εἰς τὴν ὑπακοὴν
of God, and bringing into captivity every thought into the obedience

**6** τοῦ Χριστοῦ, καὶ ἐν ἑτοίμῳ ἔχοντες ἐκδικῆσαι πᾶσαν
of Christ, and readiness having to avenge all

**7** παρακοήν, ὅταν πληρωθῇ ὑμῶν ἡ ὑπακοή. τὰ κατὰ
disobedience, whenever is fulfilled of you the obedience. The things as to
πρόσωπον βλέπετε; εἴ τις πέποιθεν ἑαυτῷ Χριστοῦ εἶναι,
face you look (at)? If anyone has persuaded himself of Christ to be,
τοῦτο λογιζέσθω πάλιν ἀφ᾽ ἑαυτοῦ, ὅτι καθὼς αὐτὸς
this let him think again as to himself, that as he (is)

**8** Χριστοῦ, οὕτω καὶ ἡμεῖς Χριστοῦ. ἐάν τε γὰρ καὶ περισσό-
of Christ, so also we of Christ. if even For also more abun-
τερόν τι καυχήσωμαι περὶ τῆς ἐξουσίας ἡμῶν (ἣς ἔδωκεν ὁ
dantly some- what fully boast I should more about the authority of us; which gave the
Κύριος ἡμῖν εἰς οἰκοδομήν, καὶ οὐκ εἰς καθαίρεσιν ὑμῶν),
Lord to us for building up, and not for pulling down of you;

**9** οὐκ αἰσχυνθήσομαι· ἵνα μὴ δόξω ὡς ἂν ἐκφοβεῖν ὑμᾶς διὰ
not I will be put to shame; that not I seem as though to scare you through

**10** τῶν ἐπιστολῶν. ὅτι Αἱ μὲν ἐπιστολαί, φησί, βαρεῖαι καὶ
the epistles. Because the truly epistles, he says, (are) weighty and
ἰσχυραί· ἡ δὲ παρουσία τοῦ σώματος ἀσθενής, καὶ ὁ λόγος
strong, the but presence of the body (is) weak, and the speech

**11** ἐξουθενημένος. τοῦτο λογιζέσθω ὁ τοιοῦτος, ὅτι οἷοί ἐσμεν
being despised. this Let think such a one, that such as we are

word by letters, being absent, such (we) also being present in deed. [12] For we dare not rank or compare ourselves with some of those commending themselves—but they measuring themselves among themselves, and comparing themselves to themselves, (are) not perceptive. [13] But we will not boast beyond measure, but according to measure of the rule which the God of measure distributed to us, to reach even to you. [14] For we do not overstretch ourselves as not reaching to you; for we also came to you in the gospel of Christ; [15] not boasting beyond measure in the labors of others, having hope that the growing faith among you will be enlarged according to our rule, to overflowing. [16] in order to preach the gospel to that beyond you, not to boast in another's rule in things ready. [17] But the (one) boasting, in (the) Lord let him boast. [18] For not he commending himself is that one approved, but (the one) the Lord commends.

## CHAPTER 11

[1] I would that you were bearing with me a little in folly; but, indeed, bear with me. [2] For I am jealous over you with the jealousy of God, for I have promised you to one Man, to present (you) a pure virgin to Christ. [3] But I fear lest by any means as the serpent deceived Eve in his craftiness, so your thoughts should be corrupted from the purity which (is due) to Christ. [4] For if, indeed, he that comes preaches another Jesus, whom we have not preached, or you receive another spirit which you have not received, or another gospel which you never accepted, you might well endure (these). [5] For I judge (myself) nothing to have come behind the highest apostles. [6] But even if (I am) unskilled in speech, yet not in knowledge; but in every way have been manifest to you in all things. [7] Or did I commit sin, humbling myself that you may be

τῷ λόγῳ δι' ἐπιστολῶν ἀπόντες, τοιοῦτοι καὶ παρόντες
in word through epistles being absent, such also being present

**12** τῷ ἔργῳ. οὐ γὰρ τολμῶμεν ἐγκρῖναι ἢ συγκρῖναι ἑαυτούς
in work. not For we dare to rank with or compare ourselves

τισι τῶν, ἑαυτοὺς συνιστανόντων· ἀλλὰ αὐτοὶ ἐν ἑαυτοῖς
with some of those themselves commending—but they among themselves

ἑαυτοὺς μετροῦντες, καὶ συγκρίνοντες ἑαυτοὺς ἑαυτοῖς, οὐ
themselves measuring, and comparing themselves to themselves, not

**13** συνιοῦσιν. ἡμεῖς δὲ οὐχὶ εἰς τὰ ἄμετρα καυχησόμεθα, ἀλλὰ
(are) perceptive. we But not beyond measure will boast, but

κατὰ τὸ μέτρον τοῦ κανόνος οὗ ἐμέρισεν ἡμῖν ὁ Θεός, μέτρου
according to measure of the rule which divided to us the God of measure,

**14** ἐφικέσθαι ἄχρι καὶ ὑμῶν. οὐ γὰρ ὡς μὴ ἐφικνούμενοι εἰς ὑμᾶς
to reach as far as even you. not For as not reaching to you

ὑπερεκτείνομεν ἑαυτούς· ἄχρι γὰρ καὶ ὑμῶν ἐφθάσαμεν ἐν τῷ
do we overstretch ourselves until for even to you we came in the

**15** εὐαγγελίῳ τοῦ Χριστοῦ· οὐκ εἰς τὰ ἄμετρα καυχώμενοι, ἐν
gospel of Christ, not beyond measure boasting, in

ἀλλοτρίοις κόποις, ἐλπίδα δὲ ἔχοντες, αὐξανομένης τῆς
of others the labors, hope but having growing the

πίστεως ὑμῶν, ἐν ὑμῖν μεγαλυνθῆναι κατὰ τὸν κανόνα ἡμῶν
faith of you among you to be magnified according to the rule of us

**16** εἰς περισσείαν, εἰς τὰ ὑπερέκεινα ὑμῶν εὐαγγελίσασθαι, οὐκ
to overflowing, in order to (in) that beyond you to preach the gospel, not

**17** ἐν ἀλλοτρίῳ κανόνι εἰς τὰ ἕτοιμα καυχήσασθαι. ὁ δὲ καυχω-
in of another (the) rule in things ready to boast. those But boasting,

**18** μενος, ἐν Κυρίῳ καυχάσθω. οὐ γὰρ ὁ ἑαυτὸν συνιστων,
in (the) Lord let him boast. not For the (one) himself commending,

ἐκεῖνός ἐστι δόκιμος, ἀλλ' ὃν ὁ Κύριος συνίστησιν.
that one is approved, but whom the Lord commends.

## CHAPTER 11

**1** Ὄφελον ἀνείχεσθέ μου μικρὸν τῇ ἀφροσύνῃ· ἀλλὰ καὶ
I would that you endured me a little of foolishness, but, indeed,

**2** ἀνέχεσθέ μου. ζηλῶ γὰρ ὑμᾶς Θεοῦ ζήλῳ· ἡρμοσάμην γὰρ
bear with me. I am jealous For (of) you of God, with a jealousy I joined for

ὑμᾶς ἑνὶ ἀνδρὶ παρθένον ἁγνὴν παραστῆσαι τῷ Χριστῷ.
you to one husband a virgin pure to present to Christ.

**3** φοβοῦμαι δὲ μή πως ὡς ὁ ὄφις Εὕαν ἐξηπάτησεν ἐν τῇ πανουρ-
I fear And lest somehow as the serpent Eve deceived in the craftiness

γίᾳ αὑτοῦ, οὕτω φθαρῇ τὰ νοήματα ὑμῶν ἀπὸ τῆς ἁπλό-
of him so should be spoiled the thoughts of you from the simplic-

**4** τητος τῆς εἰς τὸν Χριστόν. εἰ μὲν γὰρ ὁ ἐρχόμενος ἄλλον
ity (due) to Christ. if indeed For those coming another

Ἰησοῦν κηρύσσει ὃν οὐκ ἐκηρύξαμεν, ἢ πνεῦμα ἕτερον λαμ-
Jesus proclaims, whom not we have not preached, or spirit another you

βάνετε ὃ οὐκ ἐλάβετε, ἢ εὐαγγέλιον ἕτερον ὃ οὐκ ἐδέξασθε,
receive which not you received, or gospel another which not you accepted,

**5** καλῶς ἡνείχεσθε. λογίζομαι γὰρ μηδὲν ὑστερηκέναι τῶν
(these) well you endure. I judge For nothing to have come behind the

**6** ὑπὲρ λίαν ἀποστόλων. εἰ δὲ καὶ ἰδιώτης τῷ λόγῳ, ἀλλ' οὐ
highest apostles. if But indeed unskilled in speech, yet not

**7** τῇ γνώσει· ἀλλ' ἐν παντὶ φανερωθέντες ἐν πᾶσιν εἰς ὑμᾶς. ἢ
in knowledge, but in every way having been revealed in all things to you. Or

ἁμαρτίαν ἐποίησα ἐμαυτὸν ταπεινῶν ἵνα ὑμεῖς ὑψωθῆτε,
sin did I commit myself humbling that you might be exalted,

exalted, because I preached the gospel of God to you without charge? [8] I stripped other churches, having received wages for the serving of you. [9] And being present with you, and lacking, I was not a burden to anyone; the brothers coming from Macedonia made up for my lack. And in every way I kept myself without burden (to you); and I will keep (myself). [10] The truth of Christ is in me, that this boasting shall not be silenced in me in the regions of Achaia. [11] Why? Because I do not love you? God knows. [12] But what I do, I also will do, that I may cut off the opportunity of those desiring an opportunity, so that in that which they boast, they be found also as we (are). [13] For such ones (are) false apostles, deceitful workers, transforming themselves into to apostles of Christ. [14] Did not even Satan marvelously transform himself into an angel of light? [15] (It is) not a great thing, then, if also his ministers transform themselves as ministers of righteousness; whose end will be according to their works. [16] Again I say, let not any think me to be foolish; but if not, even if as foolish, receive me, that I also may boast a little. [17] What I speak, I speak not according to (the) Lord, but as in foolishness, in this boldness of boasting. [18] Since many boast according to the flesh, I also will boast. [18] For you gladly endure fools, being wise. [20] For you endure if anyone enslaves you, if anyone devours, if anyone receives, if anyone exalts (himself), if anyone beats you in the face. [21] I speak according to dishonor, as (though) we have been weak. But in whatever anyone dares—I say (it) in foolishness — I also dare [22] Are they Hebrews? I also. Are they Israelites? I also. Are they seed of Abraham? I also. [23] Are they ministers of Christ?—I speak as beside myself—I beyond (them)! (I excell) in labors, more abundantly; in stripes,

ὅτι δωρεὰν τὸ τοῦ Θεοῦ εὐαγγέλιον εὐηγγελισάμην ὑμῖν;
because freely the of God gospel I preached to you?

8 ἄλλας ἐκκλησίας ἐσύλησα, λαβὼν ὀψώνιον πρὸς τὴν ὑμῶν
Other churches I stripped, having received wages for the of you

9 διακονίαν· καὶ παρὼν πρὸς ὑμᾶς καὶ ὑστερηθείς, οὐ κατενάρ-
ministry, and being present with you and lacking, not I was a

κησα οὐδενός· τὸ γὰρ ὑστέρημά μου προσανεπλήρωσαν
burden of no one; the for lack of me made up

οἱ ἀδελφοί, ἐλθόντες ἀπὸ Μακεδονίας· καὶ ἐν παντὶ ἀβαρῆ
the brothers coming from Macedonia; and in every way without burden

10 ὑμῖν ἐμαυτὸν ἐτήρησα καὶ τηρήσω. ἔστιν ἀλήθεια Χριστοῦ
to you, myself I kept and I will keep. is (The) truth of Christ

ἐν ἐμοί, ὅτι ἡ καύχησις αὕτη οὐ φραγήσεται εἰς ἐμὲ ἐν τοῖς
in me, that boasting this not shall be silenced in me in the

11 κλίμασι τῆς Ἀχαΐας. διατί; ὅτι οὐκ ἀγαπῶ ὑμᾶς; ὁ Θεὸς
regions of Achaia. Why? Because not I love you? God

12 οἶδεν. ὃ δὲ ποιῶ, καὶ ποιήσω, ἵνα ἐκκόψω τὴν ἀφορμὴν τῶν
knows. what But I do, also I will do, that I may cut off the opportunity of those

θελόντων ἀφορμήν, ἵνα ἐν ᾧ καυχῶνται, εὑρεθῶσι καθὼς
desiring an opportunity, that in that which they boast, they be found as

13 καὶ ἡμεῖς. οἱ γὰρ τοιοῦτοι ψευδαπόστολοι, ἐργάται δόλιοι,
also we (are). For such (are) false apostles, workers deceitful,

14 μετασχηματιζόμενοι εἰς ἀποστόλους Χριστοῦ. καὶ οὐ
transforming themselves into apostles of Christ. And not

θαυμαστόν· αὐτὸς γὰρ ὁ Σατανᾶς μετασχηματίζεται εἰς
marvelously himself For Satan transform himself into

15 ἄγγελον φωτός. οὐ μέγα οὖν εἰ καὶ οἱ διάκονοι αὐτοῦ
an angel of light? (It is) not a great thing, then, if also the ministers of him

μετασχηματίζονται ὡς διάκονοι δικαιοσύνης, ὧν τὸ τέλος
transform themselves as ministers of righteousness; of whom the end

ἔσται κατὰ τὰ ἔργα αὐτῶν.
will be according to the works of them.

16 Πάλιν λέγω, μή τίς με δόξῃ ἄφρονα εἶναι· εἰ δὲ μή γε, κἂν
Again I say, not anyone me think foolish to be; if but not, even if

17 ὡς ἄφρονα δέξασθέ με, ἵνα μικρόν τι κἀγὼ καυχήσωμαι. ὃ
as foolish receive me, that a little I also may boast. What

λαλῶ, οὐ λαλῶ κατὰ Κύριον, ἀλλ' ὡς ἐν ἀφροσύνῃ, ἐν ταύτῃ
I speak, not I speak according to (the) Lord, but as in foolishness, in this

18 τῇ ὑποστάσει τῆς καυχήσεως. ἐπεὶ πολλοὶ καυχῶνται κατὰ
boldness of boasting. Since many boast according to

19 τὴν σάρκα, κἀγὼ καυχήσομαι. ἡδέως γὰρ ἀνέχεσθε τῶν
the flesh, I also will boast. gladly For you endure

20 ἀφρόνων, φρόνιμοι ὄντες. ἀνέχεσθε γάρ, εἴ τις ὑμᾶς κατα-
fools, wise being. you endure For, if anyone you

δουλοῖ, εἴ τις κατεσθίει, εἴ τις λαμβάνει, εἴ τις ἐπαίρεται, εἴ
enslaves, if anyone devours, if anyone receives (you), if anyone lifts (himself) if

21 τις ὑμᾶς εἰς πρόσωπον δέρει. κατὰ ἀτιμίαν λέγω, ὡς ὅτι
anyone you in the face beats. According to dishonor I say, as that

ἡμεῖς ἠσθενήσαμεν· ἐν ᾧ δ' ἂν τις τολμᾷ (ἐν ἀφροσύνῃ
we have been weak; in what but ever any one dares — in foolishness

22 λέγω), τολμῶ κἀγώ. Ἑβραῖοί εἰσι; κἀγώ· Ἰσραηλῖταί
I say (it) — dare I also. Hebrews Are they? I also! Israelites

23 εἰσι; κἀγώ· σπέρμα Ἀβραάμ εἰσι; κἀγώ· διάκονοι Χριστοῦ
are they? I also! Seed of Abraham are they? I also! Ministers of Christ

εἰσι; (παραφρονῶν λαλῶ) ὑπὲρ ἐγώ· ἐν κόποις περισσοτέ-
are they? As beside myself I speak - beyond (them) I in labors more abun

beyond measure; in prisons, much more; in deaths, many times. [24] I received forty (stripes) minus one five times from Jews. [25] I was beaten with rods three times; I was stoned once; I was shipwrecked three times; I have spent a night and a day in the deep; [26] in travels often; in dangers of rivers, in dangers of robbers, in dangers from (my own) race, in dangers from (the) nations, in dangers in (the) city, in dangers in (the) desert, in dangers on (the) sea, in dangers among false brothers; [27] in hardship and toil, often in sleeplessness, in hunger and thirst, often in fastings, in cold and nakedness. [28] Besides the things outside, the care as to all the churches crowding in on me daily. [29] Who is weak, and I am not weak? Who is offended, and I do not burn? [30] If it is right to boast (in) the things concerning my infirmity, I will boast. [31] The God and Father of our Lord Jesus Christ knows, He who is blessed forever, that I do not lie. [32] In Damascus the governor of Aretas the king was guarding the city of the Damascenes, desiring to seize me. [33] And I was let down through a window in a basket through the wall, and escaped his hands.

CHAPTER 12

[1] Indeed, to boast is not profitable to me; for I will come to visions and revelations of (the) Lord. [2] I know a man in Christ fourteen years ago — whether in (the) body, I do not know; or out of the body, I do not know; God knows — such one (was) caught away into the third Heaven. [3] And I know such a man — whether in the body, or out of the body, I do not know; God knows — [4] that he was caught up into Paradise, and heard unspeakable words, which it is not permitted to man to speak. [5] But about such a one I

ρως, ἐν πληγαῖς ὑπερβαλλόντως, ἐν φυλακαῖς περισσοτέρως,
dantly, in stripes surpassing measure, in prisons more abundantly,

24 ἐν θανάτοις πολλάκις. ὑπὸ Ἰουδαίων πεντάκις τεσσαρά-
in deaths many times. By Jews five times forty

25 κοντα παρὰ μίαν ἔλαβον. τρὶς ἐρραβδίσθην, ἅπαξ ἐλιθάσθην,
(stripes) less one I received; thrice I was flogged; once I was stoned;
τρὶς ἐναυάγησα, νυχθήμερον ἐν τῷ βυθῷ πεποίηκα·
thrice I was shipwrecked; a night and a day in the deep I have done;

26 ὁδοιπορίαις πολλάκις, κινδύνοις ποταμῶν, κινδύνοις λη-
in travels many times; in dangers of rivers, in dangers of
στῶν, κινδύνοις ἐκ γένους, κινδύνοις ἐξ ἐθνῶν, κινδύνοις ἐν
robbers, in dangers from (my) race, in dangers from nations; in dangers in
πόλει, κινδύνοις ἐν ἐρημίᾳ, κινδύνοις ἐν θαλάσσῃ, κινδύνοις
a city; in dangers in a desert; in dangers in (the) sea; in dangers

27 ἐν ψευδαδέλφοις· ἐν κόπῳ καὶ μόχθῳ, ἐν ἀγρυπνίαις
among false brothers; in labor and hardship; in watchings
πολλάκις, ἐν λιμῷ καὶ δίψει, ἐν νηστείαις πολλάκις, ἐν ψύχει
many times; in hunger and thirst; in fastings many times; in cold

28 καὶ γυμνότητι. χωρὶς τῶν παρεκτός, ἡ ἐπισύστασίς μου
and nakedness; apart from the things outside, the conspiring against me

29 ἡ καθ᾽ ἡμέραν, ἡ μέριμνα πασῶν τῶν ἐκκλησιῶν. τίς
day by day; the care of all the churches. Who
ἀσθενεῖ, καὶ οὐκ ἀσθενῶ; τίς σκανδαλίζεται, καὶ οὐκ ἐγὼ
is weak, and not I am weak? Who is offended, and not I

30 πυροῦμαι; εἰ καυχᾶσθαι δεῖ, τὰ τῆς ἀσθενείας μου καυχήσο-
burn? If to boast it is right, the things of my weakness I will

31 μαι. ὁ Θεὸς καὶ πατὴρ τοῦ Κυρίου ἡμῶν Ἰησοῦ Χριστοῦ
boast. The God and Father of the Lord of us Jesus Christ,

32 οἶδεν, ὁ ὢν εὐλογητὸς εἰς τοὺς αἰῶνας, ὅτι οὐ ψεύδομαι. ἐν
knows, He being blessed to the ages, that not I am lying. In
Δαμασκῷ ὁ ἐθνάρχης Ἀρέτα τοῦ βασιλέως ἐφρούρει τὴν
Damascus the governor of Aretas the king guarded the

33 Δαμασκηνῶν πόλιν, πιάσαι με θέλων· καὶ διὰ θυρίδος ἐν
of (the) Damascenes city, to seize me desiring, and through a window in
σαργάνη ἐχαλάσθην διὰ τοῦ τείχους, καὶ ἐξέφυγον τὰς
a basket I was lowered through the wall and escaped the
χεῖρας αὐτοῦ.
hands of them.

## CHAPTER 12

1 Καυχᾶσθαι δὴ οὐ συμφέρει μοι· ἐλεύσομαι γὰρ εἰς ὀπτα-
To boast indeed not (is) profitable to me, I will come for to visions

2 σίας καὶ ἀποκαλύψεις Κυρίου. οἶδα ἄνθρωπον ἐν Χριστῷ
and revelations of (the) Lord. I know a man in Christ
πρὸ ἐτῶν δεκατεσσάρων (εἴτε ἐν σώματι, οὐκ οἶδα· εἴτε ἐκτὸς
before years fourteen —whether in (the) body, not I know; or outside
τοῦ σώματος, οὐκ οἶδα· ὁ Θεὸς οἶδεν), ἁρπαγέντα τὸν τοιοῦ-
the body, not I know; God knows — caught up such

3 τον ἕως τρίτου οὐρανοῦ. καὶ οἶδα τὸν τοιοῦτον ἄνθρωπον
a one to third Heaven. And I know such a man
(εἴτε ἐν σώματι, εἴτε ἐκτὸς τοῦ σώματος, οὐκ οἶδα· ὁ Θεὸς
—whether in (the) body, or outside the body, not I know; God

4 οἶδεν), ὅτι ἡρπάγη εἰς τὸν παράδεισον, καὶ ἤκουσεν ἄρρητα
knows— that he was caught into Paradise and heard unspeakable

5 ῥήματα. ἃ οὐκ ἐξὸν ἀνθρώπῳ λαλῆσαι. ὑπὲρ τοῦ τοιούτου
words, which not it is allowed a man to speak. On behalf of such a one

will boast, but concerning myself I will not boast, unless in my weaknesses. [6] For if I should desire to boast, I shall not be a fool. For I will tell the truth; but I spare, lest anyone reckons to me beyond what he sees me, or hears of me; [7] and the surpassing revelations, that I not be made haughty, a thorn in the flesh was given to me, a messenger of Satan, that he might buffet me, lest I be made haughty. [8] As to this, I besought the Lord three times, that it depart from me. [9] And He said to me, My grace is sufficient for you; for My power is perfected in weaknesses. Therefore, gladly I will rather boast in my weaknesses, that the power of Christ may rest on me. [10] Therefore, I take pleasure in weaknesses, in insults, in dire needs, in persecutions, in distresses, for the sake of Christ. For when I may be weak, then I am powerful.

[11] I have become foolish boasting; you compelled me; for I ought to be commended by you; for I lacked nothing of the highest apostles, even if I am nothing. [12] Truly the signs of the apostle were worked out among you in all patience, in miracles, and in wonders, and works of power. [13] For in what is it that you were worse than the other churches, except that I myself did not lazily burden you? Forgive me this injustice.

[14] Behold, I am ready to come to you a third time, and I will not lazily burden you, for I do not seek your things, but you. For the children ought not to lay up treasure for the parents, but the parents for the children. [15] Now I most gladly will spend and be fully spent for your souls — even if loving you more and more, I am loved the less — [16] but be it so, I did not burden you; but being crafty, I caught you with bait. [17] By any of whom I have sent to you,

καυχήσομαι· ὑπὲρ δὲ ἐμαυτοῦ οὐ καυχήσομαι, εἰ μὴ ἐν ταῖς
I will boast; on behalf of but myself not I will boast, except in the

**6** ἀσθενείαις μου· ἐὰν γὰρ θελήσω καυχήσασθαι, οὐκ ἔσομαι
weaknesses of me, if For I should desire to boast, not I shall be
ἄφρων· ἀλήθειαν γὰρ ἐρῶ· φείδομαι δέ, μή τις εἰς ἐμὲ λογίση-
foolish, truth for I will speak; I spare but, lest anyone to me reckons

**7** ται ὑπὲρ ὃ βλέπει με, ἢ ἀκούει τι ἐξ ἐμοῦ. καὶ τῇ ὑπερβολῇ
beyond what he sees me, or hears of me, and by the surpassing
τῶν ἀποκαλύψεων ἵνα μὴ ὑπεραίρωμαι, ἐδόθη μοι σκόλοψ
revelations, that not I be made haughty, was given to me a thorn
τῇ σαρκί, ἄγγελος Σατᾶν ἵνα με κολαφίζῃ, ἵνα μὴ ὑπεραί-
in the flesh, a messenger of Satan, that me he might buffet, lest I be made

**8** ρωμαι. ὑπὲρ τούτου τρὶς τὸν Κύριον παρεκάλεσα, ἵνα ἀποστῇ
haughty. As to this thrice the Lord I besought, that it depart

**9** ἀπ' ἐμοῦ. καὶ εἴρηκέ μοι, Ἀρκεῖ σοι ἡ χάρις μου· ἡ γὰρ
from me. And He said to me, Enough for you (is) the grace of Me; the for
δύναμίς μου ἐν ἀσθενείᾳ τελειοῦται. ἥδιστα οὖν μᾶλλον
power of Me in weaknesses is perfected. gladly Therefore rather
καυχήσομαι ἐν ταῖς ἀσθενείαις μου, ἵνα ἐπισκηνώσῃ ἐπ' ἐμὲ
I will boast in the weaknesses of me, that may overshadow me

**10** ἡ δύναμις τοῦ Χριστοῦ. διὸ εὐδοκῶ ἐν ἀσθενείαις, ἐν ὕβρεσιν,
the power of Christ. Therefore I am pleased in weaknesses, in insults,
ἐν ἀνάγκαις, ἐν διωγμοῖς, ἐν στενοχωρίαις, ὑπὲρ Χριστοῦ·
in dire needs, in persecutions, in distresses, for the sake of Christ.
ὅταν γὰρ ἀσθενῶ, τότε δυνατός εἰμι.
when For I may be weak, then powerful I am.

**11** Γέγονα ἄφρων καυχώμενος· ὑμεῖς με ἠναγκάσατε· ἐγὼ
I have become foolish boasting; you me compelled. I
γὰρ ὤφειλον ὑφ' ὑμῶν συνίστασθαι· οὐδὲν γὰρ ὑστέρησα
For ought by you to be commended. nothing For I lacked

**12** τῶν ὑπὲρ λίαν ἀποστόλων, εἰ καὶ οὐδέν εἰμι. τὰ μὲν σημεῖα
of the highest apostles, if even nothing I am. the Indeed signs
τοῦ ἀποστόλου κατειργάσθη ἐν ὑμῖν ἐν πάσῃ ὑπομονῇ, ἐν
of the apostles were worked out among you in all patience, by

**13** σημείοις καὶ τέρασι καὶ δυνάμεσι. τί γάρ ἐστιν ὃ ἡττήθητε
signs and wonders, and by works of power. what For is it which you were less
ὑπὲρ τὰς λοιπὰς ἐκκλησίας, εἰ μὴ ὅτι αὐτὸς ἐγὼ οὐ κατε-
than the rest of the churches, except that myself I not
νάρκησα ὑμῶν ; χαρίσασθέ μοι τὴν ἀδικίαν ταύτην.
burdened you? Forgive me the wrong this.

**14** Ἰδού, τρίτον ἑτοίμως ἔχω ἐλθεῖν πρὸς ὑμᾶς, καὶ οὐ
Behold, a third (time) I am ready to come to you, and not
καταναρκήσω ὑμῶν· οὐ γὰρ ζητῶ τὰ ὑμῶν, ἀλλ' ὑμᾶς· οὐ
I will burden you; not for I seek the things of you, but you. not
γὰρ ὀφείλει τὰ τέκνα τοῖς γονεῦσι θησαυρίζειν, ἀλλ' οἱ
For ought the children for the parents to lay up treasure, but the

**15** γονεῖς τοῖς τέκνοις. ἐγὼ δὲ ἥδιστα δαπανήσω καὶ ἐκδα-
parents for the children. I But most gladly will spend and be
πανηθήσομαι ὑπὲρ τῶν ψυχῶν ὑμῶν, εἰ καὶ περισσοτέρως
spent out on behalf of the souls of you; if even more abundantly

**16** ὑμᾶς ἀγαπῶν, ἧττον ἀγαπῶμαι. ἔστω δέ, ἐγὼ οὐ κατε-
you I love, (the) less I am loved. let it be But, I not
βάρησα ὑμᾶς· ἀλλ' ὑπάρχων πανοῦργος, δόλῳ ὑμᾶς
burdened you; but being crafty, with guile you

**17** ἔλαβον. μή τινα ὧν ἀπέσταλκα πρὸς ὑμᾶς, δι' αὐτοῦ
I took. Not anyone whom I have sent to you, through him

by him did I overreach you? [18] I begged Titus, and sent the brother with (him). Did Titus overreach you? Did we not walk in the same spirit? Did not (we walk) in the same steps?

[19] Again, do you think we are defending to you? We speak before God in Christ, but in all things, beloved, for your gain.. [20] For I fear lest having come I not find you such as I desire, and I be found by you such as you do not desire; lest somehow (be) strife, envyings, anger, rivalries, evil speakings, whisperings, pride, tumults, [21] lest again (in) my coming my God may humble me with you, and I shall mourn many of those having sinned, and not having repented over the uncleanness, and fornication, and lustfulness which they have practiced.

CHAPTER 13

[1] I am coming to you this third time. In (the) mouth of two or of three witnesses every matter shall be established. [2] I have before declared, and I say beforehand, as being present the second time, and being absent now, I write to those who have sinned before, and to all the rest, that if I come again, I will not spare. [3] Since you look for a proof of Christ speaking in me — who toward you is not weak, but is powerful in you; [4] for even if He was crucified in weakness, yet He lives by the power of God; for, indeed, we are weak in Him but we shall live with Him by the power of God toward you — [5] examine yourselves, whether you are in the faith; test your own selves. Or do you not recognize yourselves that Jesus Christ is in you, unless you are reprobates. [6] And I hope that you will know that we are not reprobates. [7] But I pray to God (for) you not to do evil, none; not that we may appear approved, but that you may do the good; and we (deemed) to be reprobates. [8] For we have

**18** ἐπλεονέκτησα ὑμᾶς; παρεκάλεσα Τίτον, καὶ συναπέστειλα
did I overreach you? I besought Titus, and sent with (him)

τὸν ἀδελφόν· μή τι ἐπλεονέκτησεν ὑμᾶς Τίτος; οὐ τῷ αὐτῷ
the brother, not overreached you Titus? Did not in the same

Πνεύματι περιεπατήσαμεν; οὐ τοῖς αὐτοῖς ἴχνεσι;
spirit we walk? Did not in the same steps (we walk)?

**19** Πάλιν δοκεῖτε ὅτι ὑμῖν ἀπολογούμεθα; κατενώπιον τοῦ
Again, do you think that to you we are defending? Before

Θεοῦ ἐν Χριστῷ λαλοῦμεν· τὰ δὲ πάντα, ἀγαπητοί, ὑπὲρ
God in Christ we speak; but in all things, beloved, on behalf of

**20** τῆς ὑμῶν οἰκοδομῆς. φοβοῦμαι γάρ, μή πως ἐλθὼν οὐχ
the of you building up. I fear For lest some-how coming not

οἵους θέλω εὕρω ὑμᾶς, κἀγὼ εὑρεθῶ ὑμῖν οἷον οὐ θέλετε· μή
such as I wish I find you, and I am found by you such as not you wish,

πως ἔρεις, ζῆλοι, θυμοί, ἐριθεῖαι, καταλαλιαί, ψιθυρισμοί,
some-how (be) strifes, envyings, anger, rivalries, evil speakings, whisperings,

**21** φυσιώσεις, ἀκαταστασίαι· μή πάλιν ἐλθόντα με ταπεινώση
proud thoughts, disturbances; lest again coming me may humble

ὁ Θεός μου πρὸς ὑμᾶς, καὶ πενθήσω πολλοὺς τῶν προη-
the God of me with you, and I shall mourn many of those having

μαρτηκότων, καὶ μή μετανοησάντων ἐπὶ τῇ ἀκαθαρσία και
previously sinned, and not repenting over the uncleanness and

πορνεία καὶ ἀσελγεία ᾗ ἔπραξαν.
fornication and lustfulness which they have practiced.

CHAPTER 13

**1** Τρίτον τοῦτο ἔρχομαι πρὸς ὑμᾶς. ἐπὶ στόματος δύο
(The) third (time) this (is) I am coming to you. At (the) mouth of two

**2** μαρτύρων καὶ τριῶν σταθήσεται πᾶν ῥῆμα. προείρηκα καὶ
witnesses and of three shall be established every matter. I said before, and

προλέγω, ὡς παρὼν τὸ δεύτερον, καὶ ἀπὼν νῦν γράφω
I say beforehand, as being present the second, and being absent now, I write

τοῖς προημαρτηκόσι καὶ τοῖς λοιποῖς πᾶσιν, ὅτι ἐὰν ἔλθω
to those having previously sinned, and the rest all, that if I come

**3** εἰς τὸ πάλιν, οὐ φείσομαι· ἐπεὶ δοκιμὴν ζητεῖτε τοῦ ἐν ἐμοὶ
– – again, not I will spare, since a proof you seek in me

λαλοῦντος Χριστοῦ, ὃς εἰς ὑμᾶς οὐκ ἀσθενεῖ, ἀλλὰ δυνατεῖ
speaking of Christ, who toward you not is weak, but is powerful

**4** ἐν ὑμῖν· καὶ γὰρ εἰ ἐσταυρώθη ἐξ ἀσθενείας, ἀλλὰ ζῇ ἐκ
in you. even For if He was crucified out of weakness, but He lives by

δυνάμεως Θεοῦ. καὶ γὰρ καὶ ἡμεῖς ἀσθενοῦμεν ἐν αὐτῷ, ἀλλὰ
(the) power of God. indeed For even we are weak in Him, but

**5** ζησόμεθα σὺν αὐτῷ ἐκ δυνάμεως Θεοῦ εἰς ὑμᾶς. ἑαυτοὺς
we shall live with Him by (the) power of God toward you. Yourselves

πειράζετε εἰ ἐστὲ ἐν τῇ πίστει, ἑαυτοὺς δοκιμάζετε. ἤ ουκ
examine, if you are in the faith, yourselves test; or do not

ἐπιγινώσκετε ἑαυτούς, ὅτι Ἰησοῦς Χριστὸς ἐν ὑμῖν ἐστίν;
you perceive yourselves that Jesus Christ in you is.

**6** εἰ μή τι ἀδόκιμοί ἐστε. ἐλπίζω δὲ ὅτι γνώσεσθε ὅτι ἡμεῖς οὐκ
unless reprobates you are. I hope And that you will know that we not

**7** ἐσμὲν ἀδόκιμοι. εὔχομαι δὲ πρὸς τὸν Θεόν, μή ποιῆσαι ὑμᾶς
are reprobates. I pray And to God not to do you

κακὸν μηδέν, οὐχ ἵνα ἡμεῖς δόκιμοι φανῶμεν, ἀλλ' ἵνα ὑμεῖς
evil, none; not that we approved may appear, but that you

**8** τὸ καλὸν ποιῆτε, ἡμεῖς δὲ ὡς ἀδόκιμοι ὦμεν. οὐ γὰρ δυνά-
the good may do; we and (deemed) reprobates to be. not For we can

no power against the truth, but for the truth. [9] For we rejoice when we are weak, and you may be powerful. But we pray for this also, your being made perfect. [10] Because of this, I write these things while absent, that being present I may not treat (you) with sharpness, according to the authority which the Lord gave me for building up, and not for pulling down.

[11] Finally, brothers, rejoice; be made perfect; be comforted; mind the same things; be at peace; and the God of love and of peace will be with you, [12] With a holy kiss, greet one another.

[13] All the saints greet you.

[14] The grace of the Lord Jesus Christ, and the love of God, and the fellowship of the Holy Spirit (be) with you all. Amen.

**9** μεθά τι κατὰ τῆς ἀληθείας, ἀλλ᾽ ὑπὲρ τῆς ἀληθείας. χαίρομεν
anything against the truth, but for the truth. we rejoice
γὰρ ὅταν ἡμεῖς ἀσθενῶμεν, ὑμεῖς δὲ δυνατοὶ ἦτε· τοῦτο δὲ
For when we are weak, you and powerful are; this also

**10** καὶ εὐχόμεθα, τὴν ὑμῶν κατάρτισιν. διὰ τοῦτο ταῦτα ἀπὼν
and we pray, the of you perfection. Therefore these things being absent
γράφω, ἵνα παρὼν μὴ ἀποτόμως χρήσωμαι, κατὰ τὴν
I write, that being present not sharply I may deal according to the
ἐξουσίαν ἣν ἔδωκέ μοι ὁ Κύριος εἰς οἰκοδομήν, καὶ οὐκ εἰς
authority which gave me the Lord for building up and not for
καθαίρεσιν.
pulling down.

**11** Λοιπόν, ἀδελφοί, χαίρετε· καταρτίζεσθε, παρακαλεῖσθε,
For the rest, brothers, rejoice; perfect yourselves, encourage yourselves,
τὸ αὐτὸ φρονεῖτε, εἰρηνεύετε· καὶ ὁ Θεὸς τῆς ἀγάπης καὶ
the same thing mind, be at peace, and the God of love and

**12** εἰρήνης ἔσται μεθ᾽ ὑμῶν. ἀσπάσασθε ἀλλήλους ἐν ἁγίῳ
of peace will be with you. Greet one another with a holy
φιλήματι.
kiss.

**13** Ἀσπάζονται ὑμᾶς οἱ ἅγιοι πάντες.
Greet you the saints all.

**14** Ἡ χάρις τοῦ Κυρίου Ἰησοῦ Χριστοῦ, καὶ ἡ ἀγάπη τοῦ
The grace of the Lord Jesus Christ, and the love
Θεοῦ, καὶ ἡ κοινωνία τοῦ Ἁγίου Πνεύματος μετὰ πάντων
of God, and the fellowship of the Holy Spirit (be) with all
ὑμῶν. ἀμήν.
you. Amen.

# ΠΑΥΛΟΥ
**PAUL**
## Η ΠΡΟΣ
**THE TO**
# ΓΑΛΑΤΑΣ ΕΠΙΣΤΟΛΗ
**(THE) GALATIANS EPISTLE**

**KING JAMES II VERSION**

**PAUL**

**THE TO**

**(THE) GALATIANS**

**EPISTLE**

## CHAPTER 1

[1] Paul, an apostle, not from men, nor through man, but through Jesus and God the Father, He raising Him from (the) dead; [2] and all the brothers with me, to the churches of Galatia. [3] Grace to you, and peace, from God (the) Father and our Lord Jesus Christ, [4] who gave Himself for our sins, so that He might deliver us out of the present evil age, according to the will of our God and Father, [5] to whom (be) the glory forever and ever, Amen.

[6] I wonder that you so quickly are being transferred from Him who called you in the grace of Christ, to a different gospel, [7] which is not another—only some are troubling you and desiring to pervert the gospel of Christ. [8] But even if we or an angel from Heaven should preach a gospel to you beside what we preached to you, let him be accursed. [9] As we have said before, and now I say again, if anyone preaches a gospel to you besides what you received, let him be accursed.

[10] For do I now persuade men, or God? Or do I seek to please men? For if I yet pleased men, I would not be a slave of Christ. [11] And I make known to you, brothers, the gospel which was preached by me, that it is not according to man. [12] For I did not

## CHAPTER 1

1 Παῦλος ἀπόστολος (οὐκ ἀπ᾽ ἀνθρώπων, οὐδὲ δι᾽
Paul   an apostle   not   from   men,   nor through
ἀνθρώπου. ἀλλὰ διὰ ᾽Ιησοῦ Χριστοῦ, καὶ Θεοῦ πατρὸς
man,   but through Jesus Christ,   and God (the) Father

2 τοῦ ἐγείραντος αὐτὸν ἐκ νεκρῶν), καὶ οἱ σὺν ἐμοὶ πάντες
He   having raised Him from (the) dead;   and those with me   all

3 ἀδελφοί, ταῖς ἐκκλησίαις τῆς Γαλατίας· χάρις ὑμῖν καὶ εἰρήνη
brothers, to the churches   of Galatia, Grace to you and peace

4 ἀπὸ Θεοῦ πατρός, καὶ Κυρίου ἡμῶν ᾽Ιησοῦ Χριστοῦ, τοῦ
from God (the) Father, and (the) Lord of us,   Jesus   Christ, the (One)
δόντος ἑαυτὸν ὑπὲρ τῶν ἁμαρτιῶν ἡμῶν, ὅπως ἐξέληται
having given Himself for   the   sins   of us,  so as He might deliver
ἡμᾶς ἐκ τοῦ ἐνεστῶτος αἰῶνος πονηροῦ, κατὰ τὸ θέλημα
us out of the   present   age   of evil,   according to the will

5 τοῦ Θεοῦ καὶ πατρὸς ἡμῶν· ᾧ ἡ δόξα εἰς τοὺς αἰῶνας τῶν
of the God and Father   of us, whose (is) the to the ages   of the
glory
αἰώνων. ἀμήν.
ages.   Amen.

6 Θαυμάζω ὅτι οὕτω ταχέως μετατίθεσθε ἀπὸ τοῦ καλέ-
I wonder   that so   quickly are being trans-   from the (One) hav-
ferred

7 σαντος ὑμᾶς ἐν χάριτι Χριστοῦ εἰς ἕτερον εὐαγγέλιον· ὃ
ing called you by (the) grace of Christ to another   gospel,   which
οὐκ ἔστιν ἄλλο, εἰ μὴ τινές εἰσιν οἱ ταράσσοντες ὑμᾶς καὶ
not is another,   only some there are   troubling   you and

8 θέλοντες μεταστρέψαι τὸ εὐαγγέλιον τοῦ Χριστοῦ. ἀλλὰ
desiring   to pervert   the   gospel   of Christ.   But
καὶ ἐὰν ἡμεῖς ἢ ἄγγελος ἐξ οὐρανοῦ εὐαγγελίζηται ὑμῖν παρ᾽
even if   we   or an angel out of Heaven preach a gospel   to you beside

9 ὃ εὐηγγελισάμεθα ὑμῖν, ἀνάθεμα ἔστω. ὡς προειρήκαμεν,
what we preached   to you, accursed let him be. As we have said before,
καὶ ἄρτι πάλιν λέγω, εἴ τις ὑμᾶς εὐαγγελίζεται παρ᾽ ὃ
and now again   I say, if anyone you   preaches a gospel beside what

10 παρελάβετε, ἀνάθεμα ἔστω. ἄρτι γὰρ ἀνθρώπους πείθω
you received, accursed let him be.   now For   men do I persuade,
ἢ τὸν Θεόν ; ἢ ζητῶ ἀνθρώποις ἀρέσκειν ; εἰ γὰρ ἔτι ἀνθρώ-
or   God? Or do I seek   men   to please? if For yet men
ποις ἤρεσκον, Χριστοῦ δοῦλος οὐκ ἂν ἤμην.
I pleased,   of Christ a slave   not would I be being.

11 Γνωρίζω δὲ ὑμῖν, ἀδελφοί, τὸ εὐαγγέλιον τὸ εὐαγγελισθὲν
I make known And to you, brothers, the gospel   preached

12 ὑπ᾽ ἐμοῦ, ὅτι οὐκ ἔστι κατὰ ἄνθρωπον. οὐδὲ γὰρ ἐγὼ παρὰ
by   me, that not it is according to man.   not For   I   from

receive it from man, nor was I taught (it), but by a revelation of Jesus Christ. [13] For you heard my way of life when (I was) in Judaism, that with surpassing (zeal) I persecuted the church of God, and ravaged it, [14] and progressed in Judaism beyond many contemporaries in my race, being much more a zealot of the traditions of my fathers. [15] But when God was pleased, He having separated me from my mother's womb, and having called through His grace, [16] to reveal His Son in me, that I might preach Him among the nations; immediately I did not confer with flesh and blood, [17] nor did I go up to Jerusalem to those apostles before me, but I went away into Arabia, and returned again to Damascus.

[18] Then after three years I went up to Jerusalem to learn from Peter, and remained with him fifteen days, [19] but (no) other of the apostles I say, except James the brother of the Lord. [20] And what I write to you, behold, before God I do not lie. [21] Then I went into the regions of Syria and of Cilicia; [22] but I was not known by face to the churches of Judea in Christ. [23] But only they were hearing that the (one) who then persecuted us, now preaches the faith which he then ravaged, [24] and they glorified God in me.

ἀνθρώπου παρέλαβον αὐτό, οὔτε ἐδιδάχθην, ἀλλὰ δι'
man          received   it,   nor was I taught (by man), but by

13 ἀποκαλύψεως Ἰησοῦ Χριστοῦ. ἠκούσατε γὰρ τὴν ἐμὴν
   a revelation   of Jesus  Christ.  you heard  For     my

ἀναστροφήν ποτε ἐν τῷ Ἰουδαϊσμῷ, ὅτι καθ' ὑπερβολὴν
way of life  when in  the  Judaism,    that with surpassing (zeal)

14 ἐδίωκον τὴν ἐκκλησίαν τοῦ Θεοῦ, καὶ ἐπόρθουν αὐτήν· καὶ
   I persecuted the church   of God, and  ravaged   it,   and

προέκοπτον ἐν τῷ Ἰουδαϊσμῷ ὑπὲρ πολλοὺς συνηλικιώτας.
progressed  in  the  Judaism   beyond  many   contemporaries

ἐν τῷ γένει μου, περισσοτέρως ζηλωτὴς ὑπάρχων τῶν
in the race of me,   much more    a zealot   being    of the

15 πατρικῶν μου παραδόσεων. ὅτε δὲ εὐδόκησεν ὁ Θεός, ὁ
   ancestral  of me  traditions.   when But was pleased  God, He

ἀφορίσας με ἐκ κοιλίας μητρός μου καὶ καλέσας διὰ τῆς
having separated me from my mother's womb, and having called through the

16 χάριτος αὐτοῦ, ἀποκαλύψαι τὸν υἱὸν αὐτοῦ ἐν ἐμοί, ἵνα
   grace   of Him   to reveal      the  Son  of Him in me,  that

εὐαγγελίζωμαι αὐτὸν ἐν τοῖς ἔθνεσιν, εὐθέως οὐ προσανε-
I might preach     Him  among the nations, immediately not I conferred

17 θέμην σαρκὶ καὶ αἵματι· οὐδὲ ἀνῆλθον εἰς Ἱεροσόλυμα πρὸς
   with flesh and blood, neither did I go up to   Jerusalem   to

τοὺς πρὸ ἐμοῦ ἀποστόλους, ἀλλ' ἀπῆλθον εἰς Ἀραβίαν, καὶ
the before me   apostles,     but  I went away into Arabia, and

πάλιν ὑπέστρεψα εἰς Δαμασκόν.
again  returned    to  Damascus.

18 Ἔπειτα μετὰ ἔτη τρία ἀνῆλθον εἰς Ἱεροσόλυμα ἱστορῆσαι
   Then after years three I went up to   Jerusalem   to learn from

19 Πέτρον, καὶ ἐπέμεινα πρὸς αὐτὸν ἡμέρας δεκαπέντε. ἕτερον
   Peter,  and remained with   him   days   fifteen,    other

δὲ τῶν ἀποστόλων οὐκ εἶδον, εἰ μὴ Ἰάκωβον τὸν ἀδελφὸν
but of the apostles  not I saw, except  James    the  brother

20 τοῦ Κυρίου. ἃ δὲ γράφω ὑμῖν, ἰδοὺ ἐνώπιον τοῦ Θεοῦ, ὅτι
   of the Lord. what And I write to you, behold before   God, that

21 οὐ ψεύδομαι. ἔπειτα ἦλθον εἰς τὰ κλίματα τῆς Συρίας καὶ τῆς
   not I lie.   Then   I went into the regions  of Syria  and

22 Κιλικίας. ἤμην δὲ ἀγνοούμενος τῷ προσώπῳ ταῖς ἐκκλησίαις
   of Cilicia. I was And unknown      by face    to the  churches

23 τῆς Ἰουδαίας ταῖς ἐν Χριστῷ· μόνον δὲ ἀκούοντες ἦσαν ὅτι
   of Judea     in  Christ.  only But  hearing   they were that

Ὁ διώκων ἡμᾶς ποτέ, νῦν εὐαγγελίζεται τὴν πίστιν ἥν ποτε
the (one) persecuting us then, now  preaches     the faith which then

24 ἐπόρθει. καὶ ἐδόξαζον ἐν ἐμοὶ τὸν Θεόν.
   he ravaged and they glorified in me   God.

## CHAPTER 2

[1] Then through fourteen years I again went up to Jerusalem with Barnabas, also taking with (me) Titus. [2] And I went up according to revelation, and I put before them the gospel which I proclaim in the nations, but privately to the (ones) seeming (pillars), lest I run, or ran, into vanity. [3] But not even Titus, the (one) with me, being a

## CHAPTER 2

1 Ἔπειτα διὰ δεκατεσσάρων ἐτῶν πάλιν ἀνέβην εἰς Ἱεροσό-
  Then through  fourteen      years  again I went up to  Jerusa-

2 λυμα μετὰ Βαρνάβα, συμπαραλαβὼν καὶ Τίτον. ἀνέβην δὲ
  lem with Barnabas,   taking with (me)  also Titus. I went up And

κατὰ ἀποκάλυψιν, καὶ ἀνεθέμην αὐτοῖς τὸ εὐαγγέλιον ὃ
according to a revelation, and I put before them the gospel  which

κηρύσσω ἐν τοῖς ἔθνεσιν, κατ' ἰδίαν δὲ τοῖς δοκοῦσιν, μή πως εἰς
I proclaim in the nations,  privately  but to those seeming, lest into

3 κενὸν τρέχω ἢ ἔδραμον. ἀλλ' οὐδὲ Τίτος ὁ σὺν ἐμοί, Ἕλλην
  vanity I run  or I ran.    But not even Titus, he with me,  a Greek

Greek was compelled to be circumcised. [4] But because of those false brothers stealing in, who stole in to spy on our freedom which we have in Christ Jesus, that they might enslave us; [5] to whom not even for an hour we yielded in subjection, that the truth of the gospel might continue with you. [6] But from those seeming to be something—what kind they were then matters not to me; God does not accept the face of man—for those seeming (important) conferred nothing to me; [7] but on the contrary, seeing that I have been entrusted (with) the gospel of the uncircumcision, even as Peter (for) the circumcision— [8] for the (One) working in Peter to an apostleship of the circumcision, also worked in me to the nations—[9] and having known the grace given to me, James and Cephas and John, those seeming to be pillars, gave right (hands) of fellowship to Barnabas and to me, that we (go) to the nations, but they to the circumcision; [10] only that we might remember the poor, which same thing I was eager to do.

[11] But when Peter came to Antioch, I withstood (him) to his face, because he was to be blamed. [12] For before some came from James, he ate with the nations; but when they had come, he drew back and separated himself, being afraid of those of the circumcision. [13] And the rest of the Jews also dissembled with him, so as even Barnabas was led away with their dissembling. [14] But when I saw that they did not walk uprightly with the truth of the gospel, I said to Peter before all, If you being a Jew live (as) a Gentile, and not (as the) Jews, why do you compel the Gentiles to (become like) Jews? [15] We Jews by nature, and not sinners of (the) Gentiles—[16] knowing that a man is not justified by works of law, except through faith (in) Jesus Christ — we also

**4** ὤν, ἠναγκάσθη περιτμηθῆναι· διὰ δὲ τοὺς παρεισάκτους
being, was compelled to be circumcised; because of but 'those stealing
ψευδαδέλφους, οἵτινες παρεισῆλθον κατασκοπῆσαι τὴν
false brothers, who stole in to spy on the
ἐλευθερίαν ἡμῶν ἣν ἔχομεν ἐν Χριστῷ ᾽Ιησοῦ, ἵνα ἡμᾶς
freedom of us which we have in Christ Jesus, that us

**5** καταδουλώσωνται· οἷς οὐδὲ πρὸς ὥραν εἴξαμεν τῇ ὑποταγῇ,
they desire to enslave; to whom not for an hour yielded we in subjection

**6** ἵνα ἡ ἀλήθεια τοῦ εὐαγγελίου διαμείνη πρὸς ὑμᾶς. ἀπὸ δὲ
that the truth of the gospel might continue with you. from But
τῶν δοκούντων εἶναί τι (ὁποῖοί ποτε ἦσαν οὐδέν μοι
those seeming to be something —of what kind then they were not to me
διαφέρει· πρόσωπον Θεὸς ἀνθρώπου οὐ λαμβάνει)—ἐμοὶ
matters; the face God of man does not accept —to me

**7** γὰρ οἱ δοκοῦντες οὐδὲν προσανέθεντο· ἀλλὰ τοὐναντίον,
for those seeming nothing conferred but on the contrary
ἰδόντες ὅτι πεπίστευμαι τὸ εὐαγγέλιον τῆς ἀκροβυστίας,
seeing that I have been entrusted (with) the gospel of the uncircumcision,

**8** καθὼς Πέτρος τῆς περιτομῆς (ὁ γὰρ ἐνεργήσας Πέτρῳ εἰς
even as Peter to the circumcision —the (One) for working in Peter to
ἀποστολὴν τῆς περιτομῆς, ἐνήργησε καὶ ἐμοὶ εἰς τὰ ἔθνη),
an apostleship of the circumcision, worked also in me to the nations—

**9** καὶ γνόντες τὴν χάριν τὴν δοθεῖσάν μοι, ᾽Ιάκωβος καὶ
and knowing the grace given to me, James and
Κηφᾶς καὶ ᾽Ιωάννης, οἱ δοκοῦντες στύλοι εἶναι, δεξιὰς
Cephas and John, those seeming pillars to be, right (hands)
ἔδωκαν ἐμοὶ καὶ Βαρνάβα κοινωνίας, ἵνα ἡμεῖς εἰς τὰ ἔθνη,
gave to me and to Barnabas of fellowship, that we to the nations,

**10** αὐτοὶ δὲ εἰς τὴν περιτομήν· μόνον τῶν πτωχῶν ἵνα μνημο-
they but to the circumcision; only the poor that we might
νεύωμεν, ὃ καὶ ἐσπούδασα αὐτὸ τοῦτο ποιῆσαι.
remember, which indeed I was eager this same thing to do.

**11** ῞Οτε δὲ ἦλθε Πέτρος εἰς ᾽Αντιόχειαν, κατὰ πρόσωπον
when But came Peter to Antioch, against face

**12** αὐτῷ ἀντέστην, ὅτι κατεγνωσμένος ἦν. πρὸ τοῦ γὰρ ἐλθεῖν
to him I opposed, because to be condemned he was. before the for coming
τινὰς ἀπὸ ᾽Ιακώβου, μετὰ τῶν ἐθνῶν συνήσθιεν· ὅτε δὲ
of some from James, with the nations he ate; when but
ἦλθον, ὑπέστελλε καὶ ἀφώριζεν ἑαυτόν, φοβούμενος τοὺς ἐκ
they came, he drew back and separated himself, being afraid of those of

**13** περιτομῆς. καὶ συνυπεκρίθησαν αὐτῷ καὶ οἱ λοιποὶ ᾽Ιουδαῖοι,
the circumcision. And dissembled with him also the rest of the Jews,

**14** ὥστε καὶ Βαρνάβας συναπήχθη αὐτῶν τῇ ὑποκρίσει. ἀλλ᾽
so as even Barnabas was led away with them the dissembling. But
ὅτε εἶδον ὅτι οὐκ ὀρθοποδοῦσι πρὸς τὴν ἀλήθειαν τοῦ
when I saw that not they walked uprightly with the truth of the
εὐαγγελίου, εἶπον τῷ Πέτρῳ ἔμπροσθεν πάντων, Εἰ σύ
gospel, I said to Peter, in front of all, If you
᾽Ιουδαῖος ὑπάρχων, ἐθνικῶς ζῇς καὶ οὐκ ᾽Ιουδαϊκῶς, τί τὰ
a Jew being, a Gentile live, and not (as the) Jews why the

**15** ἔθνη ἀναγκάζεις ᾽Ιουδαΐζειν; ἡμεῖς φύσει ᾽Ιουδαῖοι, καὶ οὐκ
Gentiles you compel to judaize? We by nature Jews, and not

**16** ἐξ ἐθνῶν ἁμαρτωλοί, εἰδότες ὅτι οὐ δικαιοῦται ἄνθρωπος
of (the) Gentiles sinners, knowing that not is justified a man
ἐξ ἔργων νόμου, ἐὰν μὴ διὰ πίστεως ᾽Ιησοῦ Χριστοῦ, καὶ
by works of law, except through faith (in) Jesus Christ, even

believed in Christ Jesus, that we may be justified by faith (in) Christ, and not by works of law, because all flesh will not be justified by works of law. [17] But if seeking to be justified in Christ, we also were found (to be) sinners, (is) Christ then a minister of sin? Let it not be (said)! [18] For if I build again these things I demolished, I establish myself a transgressor. [19] For I through the Law died to Law, that I might live to God. [20] I have been crucified with Christ; and I live, (yet) no longer I, but Christ lives in me; and that (life) I now live in flesh, I live by faith to the Son of God, who loved me and gave Himself over on behalf of me. [21] I do not set aside the grace of God; for if righteousness is through Law, then Christ died without just cause.

CHAPTER 3

[1] O foolish Galatians, who bewitched you not to obey the truth, to whom before (your) eyes Jesus Christ was written before among you crucified? [2] This only I desire to learn from you, Did you receive the Spirit by works of Law, or by hearing of faith? [3] Are you so foolish? Having begun in (the) Spirit, do you now become perfected in (the) flesh? [4] Did you suffer so much vainly? If indeed (it was) vainly? [5] Then He supplying the Spirit to you, and working powerful works in you, (is it) by works of Law, or by hearing of faith? [6] Even as Abraham believed God, and it was counted to him for righteousness. [7] Know, then, that those of faith, these are (the) sons of Abraham. [8] And the Scriptures foreseeing that God would justify the nations by faith, preached the gospel before to Abraham, (saying), "All the nations will be blessed in you." [9] So that those of faith are blessed with the faithful Abraham. [10] For as many as are out of works of Law, (these) are under a curse. For it has been written: "Cursed (is) everyone

ἡμεῖς εἰς Χριστὸν Ἰησοῦν ἐπιστεύσαμεν, ἵνα δικαιωθῶμεν ἐκ
we in Christ Jesus believed, that we may be justified by
πίστεως Χριστοῦ, καὶ οὐκ ἐξ ἔργων νόμου· διότι οὐ δικαιωθή-
faith (in) Christ, and not of works of law, because not will be just-
17 σεται ἐξ ἔργων νόμου πᾶσα σάρξ. εἰ δέ, ζητοῦντες δικαιωθῆ-
ified by works of law all flesh. if But seeking to be justified
ναι ἐν Χριστῷ, εὑρέθημεν καὶ αὐτοὶ ἁμαρτωλοί, ἆρα
in Christ we were found also ourselves sinners, then
18 Χριστὸς ἁμαρτίας διάκονος ; μὴ γένοιτο. εἰ γὰρ ἃ κατέλυσα,
(is) Christ of sin a minister? Let it not be! if For what I destroyed,
19 ταῦτα πάλιν οἰκοδομῶ, παραβάτην ἐμαυτὸν συνίστημι. ἐγὼ
these things again I build, a transgressor myself I establish. I
20 γὰρ διὰ νόμου νόμῳ ἀπέθανον, ἵνα Θεῷ ζήσω. Χριστῷ
For through law to law died, that to God I might live. With Christ
συνεσταύρωμαι· ζῶ δέ, οὐκέτι ἐγώ, ζῇ δὲ ἐν ἐμοὶ Χριστός·
I have been crucified; I live and, no longer I, lives but in me Christ;
ὃ δὲ νῦν ζῶ ἐν σαρκί, ἐν πίστει ζῶ τῇ τοῦ υἱοῦ τοῦ Θεοῦ, τοῦ
what and now I live in flesh, by faith I live to the Son of God
21 ἀγαπήσαντός με καὶ παραδόντος ἑαυτὸν ὑπὲρ ἐμοῦ. οὐκ
loving me and giving over Himself on behalf of me. not
ἀθετῶ τὴν χάριν τοῦ Θεοῦ· εἰ γὰρ διὰ νόμου δικαιοσύνη,
I set aside the grace of God; if for through law righteousness,
ἄρα Χριστὸς δωρεὰν ἀπέθανεν.
then Christ without cause died.

CHAPTER 3

1 Ὦ ἀνόητοι Γαλάται, τίς ὑμᾶς ἐβάσκανε τῇ ἀληθείᾳ μὴ
O foolish Galatians, who you bewitched the truth not
πείθεσθαι, οἷς κατ᾽ ὀφθαλμοὺς Ἰησοῦς Χριστὸς προεγράφη
to obey, to whom before the eyes Jesus Christ was written afore
2 ἐν ὑμῖν ἐσταυρωμένος ; τοῦτο μόνον θέλω μαθεῖν ἀφ᾽ ὑμῶν,
among you crucified? This only I desire to learn from you,
ἐξ ἔργων νόμου τὸ Πνεῦμα ἐλάβετε, ἢ ἐξ ἀκοῆς πίστεως ;
by works of law the Spirit did you receive, or by hearing of faith?
3 οὕτως ἀνόητοί ἐστε ; ἐναρξάμενοι Πνεύματι, νῦν σαρκὶ
so foolish Are you? Having begun in (the) Spirit, now in (the) flesh
4 ἐπιτελεῖσθε ; τοσαῦτα ἐπάθετε εἰκῇ ; εἴ γε καὶ εἰκῇ. ὁ οὖν
5 do you finish? So much suffered you vainly? If indeed even vainly? He then
ἐπιχορηγῶν ὑμῖν τὸ Πνεῦμα καὶ ἐνεργῶν δυνάμεις ἐν ὑμῖν,
supplying to you the Spirit and working works of power in you,
6 ἐξ ἔργων νόμου, ἢ ἐξ ἀκοῆς πίστεως ; καθὼς Ἀβραὰμ ἐπί-
by works of law, or by hearing of faith? As Abraham
7 στευσε τῷ Θεῷ, καὶ ἐλογίσθη αὐτῷ εἰς δικαιοσύνην. γινώ-
believed God, and it was counted to him for righteousness. Know
σκετε ἄρα ὅτι οἱ ἐκ πίστεως, οὗτοί εἰσιν υἱοὶ Ἀβραάμ.
then that those of faith, these are sons of Abraham.
8 προϊδοῦσα δὲ ἡ γραφὴ ὅτι ἐκ πίστεως δικαιοῖ τὰ ἔθνη ὁ
foreseeing And the Scripture that by faith would justify the nations
Θεός, προευηγγελίσατο τῷ Ἀβραὰμ ὅτι Εὐλογηθήσονται
God, preached the gospel before to Abraham that will be blessed
9 ἐν σοὶ πάντα τὰ ἔθνη. ὥστε οἱ ἐκ πίστεως εὐλογοῦνται σὺν
in you all the nations. So as those of faith are blessed with
10 τῷ πιστῷ Ἀβραάμ. ὅσοι γὰρ ἐξ ἔργων νόμου εἰσίν, ὑπὸ
the faithful Abraham. as many as For out of works of law are, under
κατάραν εἰσί· γέγραπται γάρ, Ἐπικατάρατος πᾶς ὃς οὐκ
a curse are; it has been written for: Cursed (is) everyone who not

who does not continue in all the things having been written in the book of the Law, to do them. [11] And that no one is justified by Law before God (is) clear, because: "The just shall live by faith." [12] But the Law is not of faith, but: "The man doing these things shall live in them." [13] Christ redeemed us from the curse of the Law, having become for us a curse; for it has been written: "Cursed (is) everyone who hangs on a tree;" [14] that the blessing of Abraham might be to the nations in Christ Jesus, that we might receive the promise of the Spirit through faith.

[15] Brothers — I speak according to man—a covenant having been ratified, even (among) mankind no one sets aside or adds to (it). [16] But the promises were spoken to Abraham, and to his Seed—it does not say, And to seeds, as of many, but as of one: "And to your Seed," which is Christ. [17] And I say this A covenant having been ratified before to Christ by God, (the) Law coming into being four hundred thirty years after does not annul the promise, so as to abolish (it). [18] For if the inheritance (is) of Law, (it is) no more of promise; but God has given (it) through promise to Abraham. [19] Why, then, the Law? It was added because of transgressions, until the Seed should come (to those) to whom it had been promised, having been ordained through angels in a mediator's hand. [20] But the Mediator is not of one, but God is one.

[21] Then (is) the Law against the promises? Let it not be (said)! For if a law had been given which was able to make alive, indeed righteousness would have been out of Law. [22] But the Scripture locked up all under sin, that the promise by faith of Jesus Christ might be given to those believing. [23] But before faith came, we were guarded under law, having been locked up to the faith being about to be revealed.

ἐμμένει ἐν πᾶσι τοῖς γεγραμμένοις ἐν τῷ βιβλίῳ τοῦ νόμου,
continues in all the things having been written in the roll of the law

**11** τοῦ ποιῆσαι αὐτά. ὅτι δὲ ἐν νόμῳ οὐδεὶς δικαιοῦται παρὰ
to do them. that And by law no one is justified before

**12** τῷ Θεῷ, δῆλον· ὅτι Ὁ δίκαιος ἐκ πίστεως ζήσεται· ὁ δὲ
God (is) clear, because the just one by faith will live; the and

νόμος οὐκ ἔστιν ἐκ πίστεως, ἀλλ᾽ Ὁ ποιήσας αὐτὰ ἄνθρωπος
law not is of faith, but: The doing these things man

**13** ζήσεται ἐν αὐτοῖς. Χριστὸς ἡμᾶς ἐξηγόρασεν ἐκ τῆς κατάρας
shall live in them. Christ us redeemed out of the curse

τοῦ νόμου, γενόμενος ὑπὲρ ἡμῶν κατάρα· γέγραπται γάρ,
of the law, having become for us a curse; it has been written for:

**14** Ἐπικατάρατος πᾶς ὁ κρεμάμενος ἐπὶ ξύλου· ἵνα εἰς τὰ ἔθνη
Cursed (is) everyone who hangs on a tree; that to the nations

ἡ εὐλογία τοῦ Ἀβραὰμ γένηται ἐν Χριστῷ Ἰησοῦ, ἵνα τὴν
the blessing of Abraham might be in Christ Jesus, that the

ἐπαγγελίαν τοῦ Πνεύματος λάβωμεν διὰ τῆς πίστεως.
promise of the Spirit we might receive through faith.

**15** Ἀδελφοί, κατὰ ἄνθρωπον λέγω· ὅμως ἀνθρώπου κεκυρω-
Brothers, according to man I say, even of man having been

**16** μένην διαθήκην οὐδεὶς ἀθετεῖ ἢ ἐπιδιατάσσεται. τῷ δὲ
ratified a covenant, no one sets aside or adds to (it). And

Ἀβραὰμ ἐρρήθησαν αἱ ἐπαγγελίαι, καὶ τῷ σπέρματι αὐτοῦ.
to Abraham were said the promises, and to the Seed of him.

οὐ λέγει, Καὶ τοῖς σπέρμασιν, ὡς ἐπὶ πολλῶν, ἀλλ᾽ ὡς ἐφ᾽
Not it says, And to the seeds, as upon many, but as of

**17** ἑνός, Καὶ τῷ σπέρματί σου, ὅς ἐστι Χριστός. τοῦτο δὲ λέγω,
One: And to the Seed of you, who is Christ. this And I say,

διαθήκην προκεκυρωμένην ὑπὸ τοῦ Θεοῦ εἰς Χριστὸν ὁ μετὰ
A covenant having been ratified before by God to Christ, the after

ἔτη τετρακόσια καὶ τριάκοντα γεγονὼς νόμος οὐκ ἀκυροῖ, εἰς
years four hundred and thirty coming into being Law not annuls, so

**18** τὸ καταργῆσαι τὴν ἐπαγγελίαν. εἰ γὰρ ἐκ νόμου ἡ κληρονο-
as to abolish the promise. if For of law the inheritance

μία, οὐκέτι ἐξ ἐπαγγελίας· τῷ δὲ Ἀβραὰμ δι᾽ ἐπαγγελίας
(is), no more (is it) of promise; but to Abraham through promise

**19** κεχάρισται ὁ Θεός. τί οὖν ὁ νόμος; τῶν παραβάσεων χάριν
has given (it) God. Why, then, the law? the transgressions because of

προσετέθη, ἄχρις οὗ ἔλθῃ τὸ σπέρμα ᾧ ἐπήγγελται, διατα-
It was added, until should come the Seed to whom it had been promised, being

**20** γεὶς δι᾽ ἀγγέλων ἐν χειρὶ μεσίτου. ὁ δὲ μεσίτης ἑνὸς οὐκ
ordained through angels in hand a mediator's. the But mediator of one not

**21** ἔστιν, ὁ δὲ Θεὸς εἷς ἐστίν. ὁ οὖν νόμος κατὰ τῶν ἐπαγγελιῶν
is, but God one is. the Then law against the promises

τοῦ Θεοῦ; μὴ γένοιτο. εἰ γὰρ ἐδόθη νόμος ὁ δυνάμενος
God (is)? Let it not be! if For had been given a law which was able

**22** ζωοποιῆσαι, ὄντως ἂν ἐκ νόμου ἦν ἡ δικαιοσύνη. ἀλλὰ
to make alive, indeed would out of law have been the righteousness. But

συνέκλεισεν ἡ γραφὴ τὰ πάντα ὑπὸ ἁμαρτίαν, ἵνα ἡ
locked up the Scripture all under sin, that the

ἐπαγγελία ἐκ πίστεως Ἰησοῦ Χριστοῦ δοθῇ τοῖς πιστεύουσι.
promise by faith of Jesus Christ might be given to those believing.

**23** Πρὸ τοῦ δὲ ἐλθεῖν τὴν πίστιν, ὑπὸ νόμον ἐφρουρούμεθα,
before the But coming faith, under law we were guarded,

συγκεκλεισμένοι εἰς τὴν μέλλουσαν πίστιν ἀποκαλυφθῆναι.
having been locked up to the being about faith to be revealed.

[24] So that the Law has become a trainer (until) Christ, that we might be justified by faith. [25] But faith having come, we are no longer under a trainer; [26] for you are sons of God through faith in Christ Jesus [27] For as many as were baptized into Christ, you put on Christ. [28] There cannot be Jew nor Greek; there cannot be slave nor freeman; there cannot be male and female; for you are all one in Christ Jesus. [29] And if you (are) of Christ, then you are a seed of Abraham, even heirs according to promise.

24 ὥστε ὁ νόμος παιδαγωγὸς ἡμῶν γέγονεν εἰς Χριστόν, ἵνα
So as the law　a trainer　of us has become (until) Christ,　that

25 ἐκ πίστεως δικαιωθῶμεν. ἐλθούσης δὲ τῆς πίστεως, οὐκέτι
by　faith　we might be justified. having come But　faith,　no more

26 ὑπὸ παιδαγωγόν ἐσμεν. πάντες γὰρ υἱοὶ Θεοῦ ἐστὲ διὰ τῆς
under　a trainer　we are.　all　For sons of God you are through

27 πίστεως ἐν Χριστῷ Ἰησοῦ. ὅσοι γὰρ εἰς Χριστὸν ἐβαπτί-
faith　in　Christ　Jesus. as many as For into　Christ　were

28 σθητε, Χριστὸν ἐνεδύσασθε. οὐκ ἔνι Ἰουδαῖος οὐδὲ Ἕλλην,
baptized, Christ　you put on.　not There is Jew　nor　Greek,

οὐκ ἔνι δοῦλος οὐδὲ ἐλεύθερος, οὐκ ἔνι ἄρσεν καὶ θῆλυ· πάντες
not is　slave　nor freeman;　not　is male and female;　all

29 γὰρ ὑμεῖς εἷς ἐστε ἐν Χριστῷ Ἰησοῦ. εἰ δὲ ὑμεῖς Χριστοῦ, ἄρα
for　you one　are in　Christ　Jesus. if And you (are) of Christ, then

τοῦ Ἀβραὰμ σπέρμα ἐστέ, καὶ κατ᾽ ἐπαγγελίαν κληρονό-
of Abraham　a seed you are, even according to promise　heirs.

μοι.

## CHAPTER 4

CHAPTER 4
[1] But I say, for as long a time as the heir is an infant, he differs not (from) a slave, being lord of all. [2] but is under guardians and housemasters until the (term) set before by the father. [3] So we also, when we were infants, we were under the elements of the world, being enslaved; [4] but when the fullness of the time came, God sent forth His Son, becoming out of a woman, becoming under Law, [5] that He might redeem those under Law, that we might receive the adoption of sons. [6] And because you are sons, God sent forth the Spirit of His Son into your hearts, crying, Abba, Father! [7] So that you no more are a slave, but a son; and if a son, also an heir of God through Christ.

[8] But then indeed, not knowing God, you served as slaves those not by nature being gods; [9] but now, having known God—but rather being known by God—how do you turn again to the weak and poor elements, (to) which you again desire to slave anew? [10] You observe days, and months, and seasons, and years. [11] I fear (for) you, lest somehow I have labored in vain among you.

1 Λέγω δέ, ἐφ᾽ ὅσον χρόνον ὁ κληρονόμος νήπιός ἐστιν,
I say　But,　over so long a time　the　heir　an infant　is,

2 οὐδὲν διαφέρει δούλου, κύριος πάντων ὤν· ἀλλὰ ὑπὸ
nothing he differs (from) a slave,　lord　of all　being,　but　under

ἐπιτρόπους ἐστὶ καὶ οἰκονόμους, ἄχρι τῆς προθεσμίας τοῦ
guardians　is, and　housemasters,　until the (term) set before by the

3 πατρός. οὕτω καὶ ἡμεῖς, ὅτε ἦμεν νήπιοι, ὑπὸ τὰ στοιχεῖα
father.　So　also　we,　when we were infants, under the elements

4 τοῦ κόσμου ἦμεν δεδουλωμένοι· ὅτε δὲ ἦλθε τὸ πλήρωμα
of the world we were,　being enslaved; when but came the　fullness

τοῦ χρόνου, ἐξαπέστειλεν ὁ Θεὸς τὸν υἱὸν αὐτοῦ, γενό-
of the time,　sent forth　God the　Son　of Him, becoming

5 μενον ἐκ γυναικός, γενόμενον ὑπὸ νόμον, ἵνα τοὺς ὑπὸ
of a woman,　becoming　under　law, that　those under

6 νόμον ἐξαγοράσῃ, ἵνα τὴν υἱοθεσίαν ἀπολάβωμεν. ὅτι δὲ
law He might redeem, that the adoption of sons we may receive.　because And

ἐστε υἱοί, ἐξαπέστειλεν ὁ Θεὸς τὸ Πνεῦμα τοῦ υἱοῦ αὐτοῦ
you are sons,　sent forth　God the　Spirit of the Son　of Him

7 εἰς τὰς καρδίας ὑμῶν, κρᾶζον, Ἀββᾶ, ὁ πατήρ. ὥστε οὐκέτι
into the hearts of you,　crying, Abba,　Father!　So as no more

εἶ δοῦλος, ἀλλ᾽ υἱός· εἰ δὲ υἱός, καὶ κληρονόμος Θεοῦ διὰ
are you a slave, but a son; if and a son, also　an heir　of God by

Χριστοῦ.
Christ.

8 Ἀλλὰ τότε μέν, οὐκ εἰδότες Θεόν, ἐδουλεύσατε τοῖς μὴ
But　then indeed　not knowing God, you served as slaves those not

9 φύσει οὖσι θεοῖς· νῦν δέ, γνόντες Θεόν, μᾶλλον δὲ γνωσθέντες
by nature being gods; now but knowing God,　rather　but being known

ὑπὸ Θεοῦ, πῶς ἐπιστρέφετε πάλιν ἐπὶ τὰ ἀσθενῆ καὶ
by　God,　how do you turn　again　upon the　weak　and

10 πτωχὰ στοιχεῖα, οἷς πάλιν ἄνωθεν δουλεύειν θέλετε ; ἡμέρας
poor　elements, which again　anew to slave for you desire?　days

11 παρατηρεῖσθε, καὶ μῆνας, καὶ καιρούς, καὶ ἐνιαυτούς. φοβοῦ-
You observe,　and months, and seasons,　and years.　I fear

μαι ὑμᾶς, μή πως εἰκῆ κεκοπίακα εἰς ὑμᾶς.
(for) you, lest some in vain I have labored among you.
how

[12] Brothers, I beg of you, be as I (am), because I (am) as you. You did not wrong me in anything. [13] But you know that because of weakness of the flesh I preached the gospel to you before, [14] and you did not despise my temptation in the flesh, nor disdained (it), but you received me as an angel of God, as Christ Jesus. [15] What then was your blessedness? For I testify to you that if you were able, you would have plucked out your eyes and given (them) to me. [16] So then have I become your enemy, speaking truth to you? [17] They are zealous for you, but not nobly; but they desire to shut you out, that you be zealous (to) them [18] but (it is) good to always be zealous in a good thing, and not only in my being present with you. [19] My children, (for) whom I again travail until Christ be formed in you, [20] even now I desired to be present with you, and to change my voice, for I am in doubt (as to) you.

[21] Tell me, you who desire to be under Law, do you not hear the Law? [22] For it has been written: "Abraham had two sons, one of the slave woman, and one of the free woman. [23] But indeed he of the slave woman has been born according to flesh; and he of the free woman through the promise; [24] which things are being allegorized, for these are two covenants: one indeed from Mount Sinai bringing forth to slavery—which is Hagar, [25] for Hagar is Mount Sinai in Arabia, and corresponds to the present Jerusalem, and she is in slavery with her children. [26] But the Jerusalem (from) above is free, who is the mother of all of us; [27] for it has been written: "Be glad, barren (one) not bearing, break forth and shout, the (one) not travailing, because more (are) the children of the desolate rather than she having the husband." [28] But, brothers, according to Isaac, we are children of promise. [29] But even as then he born according to flesh persecuted him according to

**12** Γίνεσθε ὡς ἐγώ, ὅτι κἀγὼ ὡς ὑμεῖς, ἀδελφοί, δέομαι ὑμῶν.
Be   as I    because I also as   you,   brothers, I beg   of you.

**13** οὐδέν με ἠδικήσατε· οἴδατε δὲ ὅτι δι' ἀσθένειαν τῆς σαρκὸς
Nothing me you wronged; you know and that because of weakness of the flesh

**14** εὐηγγελισάμην ὑμῖν τὸ πρότερον. καὶ τὸν πειρασμόν μου
I preached the gospel to you   before,    and    the   temptation of me

τὸν ἐν τῇ σαρκί μου οὐκ ἐξουθενήσατε οὐδὲ ἐξεπτύσατε,
in the   flesh of me not    you despised,    not   disdained,

ἀλλ' ὡς ἄγγελον Θεοῦ ἐδέξασθέ με, ὡς Χριστὸν Ἰησοῦν.
but   as    an angel   of God you received me, as   Christ    Jesus.

**15** τίς οὖν ἦν ὁ μακαρισμὸς ὑμῶν; μαρτυρῶ γὰρ ὑμῖν ὅτι, εἰ
What then was the blessedness of you? I witness    for to you that, if

δυνατόν, τοὺς ὀφθαλμοὺς ὑμῶν ἐξορύξαντες ἂν ἐδώκατέ μοι.
you could, the    eyes      of you   plucking out would have given me.

**16** ὥστε ἐχθρὸς ὑμῶν γέγονα ἀληθεύων ὑμῖν; ζηλοῦσιν ὑμᾶς
So then an enemy of you became I speaking truth to you? They are zealous for you,

**17** οὐ καλῶς, ἀλλὰ ἐκκλεῖσαι ὑμᾶς θέλουσιν, ἵνα αὐτοὺς ζηλοῦτε.
not well,    but   to shut out you they desire, that(to) them you be zealous:

**18** καλὸν δὲ τὸ ζηλοῦσθαι ἐν καλῷ πάντοτε, καὶ μὴ μόνον ἐν
(it is) good but to be zealous in a good thing always, and not   only   in

**19** τῷ παρεῖναί με πρὸς ὑμᾶς. τεκνία μου, οὓς πάλιν ὠδίνω,
being present me with you. Children of me, (for) whom again I travail,

**20** ἄχρις οὗ μορφωθῇ Χριστὸς ἐν ὑμῖν, ἤθελον δὲ παρεῖναι πρὸς
until should be formed Christ   in you,   I desired and to be present with

ὑμᾶς ἄρτι, καὶ ἀλλάξαι τὴν φωνήν μου, ὅτι ἀποροῦμαι ἐν
you now,   and to change the    voice of me because I am in doubt in

ὑμῖν.
you.

**21** Λέγετέ μοι, οἱ ὑπὸ νόμον θέλοντες εἶναι, τὸν νόμον οὐκ
Tell    me, those under law   desiring to be, the   law do not

**22** ἀκούετε; γέγραπται γάρ, ὅτι Ἀβραὰμ δύο υἱοὺς ἔσχεν· ἕνα
you hear? it has been written For: — Abraham two sons had, one

**23** ἐκ τῆς παιδίσκης, καὶ ἕνα ἐκ τῆς ἐλευθέρας. ἀλλ' ὁ μὲν ἐκ τῆς
of the slave-woman, and one of the free woman. But he indeed of the

παιδίσκης κατὰ σάρκα γεγέννηται, ὁ δὲ ἐκ τῆς ἐλευθέρας διὰ
slave-woman according to flesh has been born; he and of the free woman via

**24** τῆς ἐπαγγελίας. ἅτινά ἐστιν ἀλληγορούμενα· αὗται γάρ
the   promise.    Which things is    being allegorized;    these    for

εἰσιν αἱ δύο διαθῆκαι· μία μὲν ἀπὸ ὄρους Σινᾶ, εἰς δουλείαν
are    two    covenants: one indeed from Mount Sinai, to    slavery

**25** γεννῶσα, ἥτις ἐστὶν Ἄγαρ. τὸ γὰρ Ἄγαρ Σινᾶ ὄρος ἐστὶν ἐν
bringing forth, which is Hagar. the For Hagar Sinai Mount is    in

τῇ Ἀραβίᾳ, συστοιχεῖ δὲ τῇ νῦν Ἱερουσαλήμ, δουλεύει δὲ
Arabia,    corresponds and to the now Jerusalem,    she slaves and

**26** μετὰ τῶν τέκνων αὐτῆς. ἡ δὲ ἄνω Ἱερουσαλὴμ ἐλευθέρα ἐστίν,
with the children of her. the But above Jerusalem free    is,

**27** ἥτις ἐστὶ μήτηρ πάντων ἡμῶν. γέγραπται γάρ, Εὐφράνθητι
who is   mother of all    of us; it has been written for:    Be glad

στεῖρα ἡ οὐ τίκτουσα· ῥῆξον καὶ βόησον ἡ οὐκ ὠδίνουσα·
barren (one) not bearing,   break forth and shout, the (one) not travailing;

ὅτι πολλὰ τὰ τέκνα τῆς ἐρήμου μᾶλλον ἢ τῆς ἐχούσης τὸν
because more (are) the children of the desolate rather than she having   the

**28** ἄνδρα. ἡμεῖς δέ, ἀδελφοί, κατὰ Ἰσαάκ, ἐπαγγελίας τέκνα
husband. we But, brothers, according to Isaac, of promise children

**29** ἐσμέν. ἀλλ' ὥσπερ τότε ὁ κατὰ σάρκα γεννηθεὶς ἐδίωκε τὸν
we are. But even as   then he according to flesh born   persecuted the (one)

Spirit, so also now. [30] But
what says the Scripture?
"Cast out the slave woman
and her son, for in no way
shall the son of the slave
woman inherit with the Son
of the free. [31] Then,
brothers, we are not children of a slave woman, but of
the free woman.

CHAPTER 5

[1] Then stand firm in
the freedom with which
Christ made us free, and do
not again be held with a
yoke of slavery.

[2] Behold, I, Paul, say
to you that if you are circumcised, Christ will profit
you nothing. [3] And I testify again to every man being circumcised, that he is a
debtor to do all the law;
[4] you were severed from
Christ, (you) who are justified in Law; you fell from
grace. [5] For we through
the Spirit eagerly wait for
(the) hope of righteousness
out of faith. [6] For in
Christ Jesus neither circumcision nor uncircumcision
has any strength, but faith
working through love. [7]
You were running well; who
held you back (that) you do
not obey the truth? [8] The
persuasion (is) not from
Him calling you. [9] A little
leaven leavens all the lump.
[10] I trust as to you in
(the) Lord that nothing else
you will think; but he that
troubles you shall bear the
judgment, whoever he may
be.

[11] But I, brothers, if
I still preach circumcision,
why am I yet persecuted?
Then the stumbling-block
of the cross has ceased.
[12] I would that they
who are causing you to
doubt would even cut
themselves off. [13] For
you were called to
freedom, brothers; only do
not (use) the freedom for
an occasion to the flesh,
but by love serve one
another. [14] For the
whole Law is fulfilled in
one word, "You shall love
your neighbor as yourself."
[15] But if you bite and
devour one another, be
careful that you are not
destroyed by one another.

---

30　κατὰ Πνεῦμα, οὕτω καὶ νῦν. ἀλλὰ τί λέγει ἡ γραφή ; Ἔκβαλε
according to Spirit, so also now. But what says the Scripture? Cast out
τὴν παιδίσκην καὶ τὸν υἱὸν αὐτῆς, οὐ γὰρ μὴ κληρονομήσῃ
the slave-woman and the son of her, in no For way shall inherit

31　ὁ υἱὸς τῆς παιδίσκης μετὰ τοῦ υἱοῦ τῆς ἐλευθέρας. ἄρα, ἀδελ-
the son of the slave-woman with the Son of the free. Then, brothers,
φοί, οὐκ ἐσμὲν παιδίσκης τέκνα, ἀλλὰ τῆς ἐλευθέρας.
not we are of a slave-woman children, but of the free woman.

## CHAPTER 5

1　τῇ ἐλευθερίᾳ οὖν ᾗ Χριστὸς ἡμᾶς ἠλευθέρωσε, στήκετε, καὶ
In the freedom, then, with which Christ us made free, stand firm, and
μὴ πάλιν ζυγῷ δουλείας ἐνέχεσθε.
not again with a yoke of slavery be held.

2　Ἴδε, ἐγὼ Παῦλος λέγω ὑμῖν, ὅτι ἐὰν περιτέμνησθε, Χριστὸς
Behold, I, Paul, tell you, that if you are circumcised, Christ

3　ὑμᾶς οὐδὲν ὠφελήσει. μαρτύρομαι δὲ πάλιν παντὶ ἀνθρώπῳ
you nothing will profit. I testify And again to every man
περιτεμνομένῳ, ὅτι ὀφειλέτης ἐστὶν ὅλον τὸν νόμον ποιῆσαι.
being circumcised, that a debtor he is all the law to do.

4　κατηργήθητε ἀπὸ τοῦ Χριστοῦ, οἵτινες ἐν νόμῳ δικαιοῦσθε·
You were passed away from Christ, whoever by law are justified,

5　τῆς χάριτος ἐξεπέσατε. ἡμεῖς γὰρ Πνεύματι ἐκ πίστεως
grace you fell from. we For by (the) Spirit from faith

6　ἐλπίδα δικαιοσύνης ἀπεκδεχόμεθα. ἐν γὰρ Χριστῷ Ἰησοῦ
(the) hope of righteousness eagerly wait. in For Christ Jesus
οὔτε περιτομή τι ἰσχύει, οὔτε ἀκροβυστία, ἀλλὰ πίστις δι'
neither circumcision any strength has nor uncircumcision, but faith through

7　ἀγάπης ἐνεργουμένη. ἐτρέχετε καλῶς· τίς ὑμᾶς ἀνέκοψε τῇ
love working. You were running well, who you held back the

8　ἀληθείᾳ μὴ πείθεσθαι ; ἡ πεισμονὴ οὐκ ἐκ τοῦ καλοῦντος
truth not you obey? the persuasion (is) not from Him calling

9　ὑμᾶς. μικρὰ ζύμη ὅλον τὸ φύραμα ζυμοῖ. ἐγὼ πέποιθα εἰς
10　you. A little leaven all the lump leavens. I trust as to
ὑμᾶς ἐν Κυρίῳ, ὅτι οὐδὲν ἄλλο φρονήσετε· ὁ δὲ ταράσσων
you in (the) Lord, that nothing other you will think; the (one) but troubling

11　ὑμᾶς βαστάσει τὸ κρίμα, ὅστις ἂν ᾖ. ἐγὼ δέ, ἀδελφοί, εἰ
you shall bear the judgment, whoever he may be. I But, brothers, if
περιτομὴν ἔτι κηρύσσω, τί ἔτι διώκομαι ; ἄρα κατήργηται
circumcision still proclaim, why yet am I persecuted? Then has passed away

12　τὸ σκάνδαλον τοῦ σταυροῦ. ὄφελον καὶ ἀποκόψονται οἱ
the offense of the cross. Would that also will cut themselves off those
ἀναστατοῦντες ὑμᾶς.
causing to doubt you.

13　Ὑμεῖς γὰρ ἐπ' ἐλευθερίᾳ ἐκλήθητε, ἀδελφοί· μόνον μὴ τὴν
you For for freedom were called, brothers, only not the
ἐλευθερίαν εἰς ἀφορμὴν τῇ σαρκί, ἀλλὰ διὰ τῆς ἀγάπης
freedom for gain to the flesh, but through the love

14　δουλεύετε ἀλλήλοις. ὁ γὰρ πᾶς νόμος ἐν ἑνὶ λόγῳ πληροῦται,
serve as slaves to one another. the For whole law in one word is fulfilled

15　ἐν τῷ, Ἀγαπήσεις τὸν πλησίον σου ὡς ἑαυτόν. εἰ δὲ
in the (word): You shall love the neighbor of you as yourself. if But
ἀλλήλους δάκνετε καὶ κατεσθίετε, βλέπετε μὴ ὑπὸ ἀλλήλων
one another you bite and devour, see lest by one another
ἀναλωθῆτε.
you are consumed.

[16] But I say, Walk by (the) Spirit, and you will not fulfill the desire of the flesh. [17] For the flesh lusts against the Spirit; and the Spirit against the flesh; and these things are contrary to one another that whatever you may will those things you should not do. [18] But if you are led by (the) Spirit, you are not under Law. [19] Now the works of the flesh are clearly revealed: adultery, fornication, uncleanness, lustfulness, [20] idolatry, sorcery, hatreds, fightings, jealousies, indignations, party arguments, divisions, heresies, [21] envyings, murders, drunkennesses, wild parties and things like these; as to which I tell you beforehand, even as I also said before, that they who do such things shall not inherit the kingdom of God. [22] But the fruit of the Spirit is love, joy, peace, long-suffering, kindness, goodness, faith, [23] meekness, self-control; against such things there is no law. [24] But they that (are) Christ's crucified the flesh with (its) passions and lusts. [25] If we live by (the) Spirit, we should also walk by (the) Spirit. [26] We should not seek after self-glory, provoking one another, envying one another.

## CHAPTER 6

[1] Brothers, if a man is taken in some fault, you, the spiritual ones, restore such a one in a spirit of meekness, considering yourself, lest you also be tempted. [2] Bear one another's burdens, and so fulfill the law of Christ. [3] For if anyone thinks to be something, he deceives himself, being nothing. [4] But let each prove his own work, and then he alone will have rejoicing, and not as to another. [5] For each shall carry his own load.

[6] Let him being taught in the word share

**16** Λέγω·δέ, Πνεύματι περιπατεῖτε, καὶ ἐπιθυμίαν σαρκὸς οὐ
I say And, in (the) Spirit walk,          and (the) lust of (the) flesh not

**17** μὴ τελέσητε. ἡ γὰρ σὰρξ ἐπιθυμεῖ κατὰ τοῦ Πνεύματος, τὸ
at all you will fulfill. the For flesh lusts against the Spirit, the
δὲ Πνεῦμα κατὰ τῆς σαρκός· ταῦτα δὲ ἀντίκειται ἀλλήλοις,
and (the) Spirit against the flesh,   these and are contrary to one another.

**18** ἵνα μὴ ἃ ἂν θέλητε, ταῦτα ποιῆτε. εἰ δὲ Πνεύματι ἄγεσθε,
lest whatever you may will, these you do.  if But by (the) Spirit you are led,

**19** οὐκ ἐστὲ ὑπὸ νόμον. φανερὰ δέ ἐστι τὰ ἔργα τῆς σαρκός,
not you are under law. clearly revealed Now are the works of the flesh,

**20** ἅτινά ἐστι μοιχεία, πορνεία, ἀκαθαρσία, ἀσέλγεια, εἰδω-
which are:   adultery, fornication, uncleanness, lustfulness, idol-
λολατρεία, φαρμακεία, ἔχθραι, ἔρεις, ζῆλοι, θυμοί, ἐριθεῖαι,
service,   sorcery,  enmities, fightings, jealousies, angers, rivalries,

**21** διχοστασίαι, αἱρέσεις, φθόνοι, φόνοι, μέθαι, κῶμοι, καὶ τὰ
divisions,    heresies, envyings, murders,drunkennesses,revellings, and
ὅμοια τούτοις· ἃ προλέγω ὑμῖν, καθὼς καὶ προεῖπον, ὅτι
like things to these, which I tell before you, as also I said previously, that
οἱ τὰ τοιαῦτα πράσσοντες βασιλείαν Θεοῦ οὐ κληρονομή-
those such things practicing (the) kingdom of God not will inherit.

**22** σουσιν. ὁ δὲ καρπὸς τοῦ Πνεύματός ἐστιν ἀγάπη, χαρά,
the But fruit  of the  Spirit  is:  love,  joy,

**23** εἰρήνη, μακροθυμία, χρηστότης, ἀγαθωσύνη, πίστις, πραό-
peace, longsuffering, kindness,  goodness,  faith meek-

**24** της, ἐγκράτεια· κατὰ τῶν τοιούτων οὐκ ἔστι νόμος. οἱ δὲ τοῦ
ness, self-control; against  such things not is a law. those And
Χριστοῦ, τὴν σάρκα ἐσταύρωσαν σὺν τοῖς παθήμασι καὶ
of Christ the  flesh  crucified  with the  passions  and
ταῖς ἐπιθυμίαις.
the  lusts.

**25**
**26** Εἰ ζῶμεν Πνεύματι, Πνεύματι καὶ στοιχῶμεν. μὴ γινώ-
If we live in (the) Spirit, in (the) Spirit also let us walk.  not Let us be-
μεθα κενόδοξοι, ἀλλήλους προκαλούμενοι, ἀλλήλοις φθονοῦν-
come vainglorious, one another  provoking  one another envying.
τες.

## CHAPTER 6

**1** Ἀδελφοί, ἐὰν καὶ προληφθῇ ἄνθρωπος ἔν τινι παραπτώ-
Brothers, if indeed is overtaken a man  in some fault,
ματι, ὑμεῖς οἱ πνευματικοὶ καταρτίζετε τὸν τοιοῦτον ἐν
you the spiritual ones  restore  such a one  in
πνεύματι πραότητος, σκοπῶν σεαυτὸν μὴ καὶ σὺ πειρασθῇς.
the spirit of meekness, considering yourself, lest also you be tempted

**2** ἀλλήλων τὰ βάρη βαστάζετε, καὶ οὕτως ἀναπληρώσατε τὸν
Of one another the burdens bear,  and so  you will fulfill  the

**3** νόμον τοῦ Χριστοῦ. εἰ γὰρ δοκεῖ τις εἶναί τι, μηδὲν ὤν,
law  of Christ. if For thinks anyone to be something, nothing being,

**4** ἑαυτὸν φρεναπατᾷ. τὸ δὲ ἔργον ἑαυτοῦ δοκιμαζέτω ἕκαστος,
himself he deceives. the But work of himself let prove  each one,
καὶ τότε εἰς ἑαυτὸν μόνον τὸ καύχημα ἕξει, καὶ οὐκ εἰς τὸν
and then in himself alone  the boast he will have, and not in  the

**5** ἕτερον. ἕκαστος γὰρ τὸ ἴδιον φορτίον βαστάσει.
other one. each one For the own  load  will bear.

**6** Κοινωνείτω δὲ ὁ κατηχούμενος τὸν λόγον τῷ κατηχοῦντι
let him share And, he being taught in the  word, with the (one) teaching

with him who teaches in all good things. [7] Do not be deceived, God is not mocked; for whatever a man may sow, that he also shall reap. [8] For he that sows to his own flesh, from the flesh shall reap corruption; but he that sows to the Spirit, from the Spirit shall reap everlasting life. [9] But we should not lose heart in well-doing, for in due time we shall reap, if (we) do not faint. [10] So then as we have occasion we should work good towards all, and especially towards those of the household of faith.

[11] See in what large letters I write with my own hand. [12] As many as wish to have a show in (the) flesh, these compel you to be circumcised; only that they may not be persecuted for the cross of Christ. [13] For they themselves who are being circumcised do not keep the Law; but they desire you to be circumcised so that they might boast in your flesh. [14] But may it never be for me to boast, except in the cross of our Lord Jesus Christ, through whom the world has been crucified to me, and I to the world. [15] For in Christ Jesus neither circumcision is worth anything, or the lack of circumcision, but a new creation. [16] And as many as shall walk by this rule, peace and mercy (be) on them, and on the Israel of God.

[17] For the rest, let no one give trouble to me, for I bear in my body the brands of the Lord Jesus. [18] The grace of our Lord Jesus Christ (be) with your spirit, brothers. Amen.

**7** ἐν πᾶσιν ἀγαθοῖς. μὴ πλανᾶσθε, Θεὸς οὐ μυκτηρίζεται· ὃ γὰρ
in all good things. not Be led astray, God not is mocked; what For

**8** ἐὰν σπείρῃ ἄνθρωπος, τοῦτο καὶ θερίσει. ὅτι ὁ σπείρων εἰς
ever may sow a man, this also he will reap.;because he sowing to

τὴν σάρκα ἑαυτοῦ, ἐκ τῆς σαρκὸς θερίσει φθοράν· ὁ δὲ σπεί-
the flesh of himself, of the flesh will reap corruption; he but

ρων εἰς τὸ Πνεῦμα, ἐκ τοῦ Πνεύματος θερίσει ζωὴν αἰώνιον.
sowing to the Spirit, of the Spirit will reap life everlasting.

**9** τὸ δὲ καλὸν ποιοῦντες μὴ ἐκκακῶμεν· καιρῷ γὰρ ἰδίῳ θερίσο-
the And good doing, not let us weaken, in time For in its own we shall

**10** μεν, μὴ ἐκλυόμενοι. ἄρα οὖν ὡς καιρὸν ἔχομεν, ἐργαζώμεθα
reap, not (we) are) fainting.Then therefore as time we have, let us work

τὸ ἀγαθὸν πρὸς πάντας, μάλιστα δὲ πρὸς τοὺς οἰκείους τῆς
the good to all, most of all and to the household of the

πίστεως.
faith.

**11** Ἴδετε πηλίκοις ὑμῖν γράμμασιν ἔγραψα τῇ ἐμῇ χειρί. ὅσοι
See in how large to you letters I write with my hand. As

**12** many as
θέλουσιν εὐπροσωπῆσαι ἐν σαρκί, οὗτοι ἀναγκάζουσιν
desire to look well in (the) flesh, these compel

ὑμᾶς περιτέμνεσθαι, μόνον ἵνα μὴ τῷ σταυρῷ τοῦ Χριστοῦ
you to be circumcised, only that not for the cross of Christ

**13** διώκωνται. οὐδὲ γὰρ οἱ περιτεμνόμενοι αὐτοὶ νόμον φυλάσ-
they are persecuted; not For those having been themselves law keep.
even circumcised

σουσιν· ἀλλὰ θέλουσιν ὑμᾶς περιτέμνεσθαι, ἵνα ἐν τῇ ὑμετέρᾳ
but they desire you to be circumcised that in your

**14** σαρκὶ καυχήσωνται. ἐμοὶ δὲ μὴ γένοιτο καυχᾶσθαι εἰ μὴ ἐν
flesh they may boast. to me But not it may be to boast, except in

τῷ σταυρῷ τοῦ Κυρίου ἡμῶν Ἰησοῦ Χριστοῦ· δι' οὗ ἐμοὶ
the cross of (the) Lord of us, Jesus Christ through whom to me

**15** κόσμος ἐσταύρωται, κἀγὼ τῷ κόσμῳ. ἐν γὰρ Χριστῷ Ἰησοῦ
(the) world has been crucified, and I to the world. in For Christ Jesus

οὔτε περιτομή τι ἰσχύει, οὔτε ἀκροβυστία, ἀλλὰ καινὴ
neither circumcision any strength has, nor uncircumcision, but a new

**16** κτίσις. καὶ ὅσοι τῷ κανόνι τούτῳ στοιχήσουσιν, εἰρήνη ἐπ'
creation. And as many as by rule this shall walk, peace on

αὐτούς, καὶ ἔλεος, καὶ ἐπὶ τὸν Ἰσραὴλ τοῦ Θεοῦ.
them, and mercy, and on the Israel of God.

**17** Τοῦ λοιποῦ, κόπους μοι μηδεὶς παρεχέτω· ἐγὼ γὰρ τὰ
For the rest, troubles to me no one let cause; I for the

στίγματα τοῦ Κυρίου Ἰησοῦ ἐν τῷ σώματί μου βαστάζω.
brands of the Lord Jesus in the body of me bear.

**18** Ἡ χάρις τοῦ Κυρίου ἡμῶν Ἰησοῦ Χριστοῦ μετὰ τοῦ
The grace of the Lord of us, Jesus Christ,(be) with the

πνεύματος ὑμῶν, ἀδελφοί. ἀμήν.
spirit of you, brothers. Amen.

# ΠΑΥΛΟΥ ΤΟΥ ΑΠΟΣΤΟΛΟΥ
## PAUL THE APOSTLE
### Η ΠΡΟΣ
## TO THE
# ΕΦΕΣΙΟΥΣ ΕΠΙΣΤΟΛΗ

## EPHESIANS EPISTLE

## CHAPTER 1

### CHAPTER 1

[1] Paul, (an) apostle of Jesus Christ through (the) will of God, to the saints being at Ephesus and faithful in Christ Jesus: [2] Grace to you and peace from God our Father and the Lord Jesus Christ.

[3] Blessed (is) the God and Father of our Lord Jesus Christ, who blessed us with every spiritual blessing in the heavenlies with Christ; [4] according as He chose us in Him before (the) foundation of (the) world, for us to be holy and without blemish before Him in love; [5] having predestinated us for adoption through Jesus Christ to Himself, according to the good pleasure of His will, [6] to (the) praise of (the) glory of His grace, in which He favored us in the Beloved; [7] in whom we have redemption through His blood, the forgiveness of sins, according to the riches of His grace; [8] which He caused to abound toward us in all wisdom, and understanding. [9] having made known to us the mystery of His will, according to His good pleasure which He purposed in Himself [10] for (the) administration of the fullness of time; to head up all things in Christ, both the things in Heaven and the things on earth, in Him, [11] in whom also we have been chosen to an inheritance, being predestinated according to (the) purpose of Him working all things according to the counsel of His (own)

1 Παῦλος, ἀπόστολος Ἰησοῦ Χριστοῦ διὰ θελήματος Θεοῦ,
Paul, an apostle of Jesus Christ through (the) will of God,
τοῖς ἁγίοις τοῖς οὖσιν ἐν Ἐφέσῳ καὶ πιστοῖς ἐν Χριστῷ
to the saints being in Ephesus and faithful in Christ

2 Ἰησοῦ· χάρις ὑμῖν καὶ εἰρήνη ἀπὸ Θεοῦ πατρὸς ἡμῶν καὶ
Jesus: Grace to you and peace from God the Father of us, and
Κυρίου Ἰησοῦ Χριστοῦ.
(the) Lord Jesus Christ.

3 Εὐλογητὸς ὁ Θεὸς καὶ πατὴρ τοῦ Κυρίου ἡμῶν Ἰησοῦ
Blessed (is) the God and Father of the Lord of us, Jesus
Χριστοῦ, ὁ εὐλογήσας ἡμᾶς ἐν πάσῃ εὐλογίᾳ πνευματικῇ
Christ, who blessed us with every blessing spiritual

4 ἐν τοῖς ἐπουρανίοις ἐν Χριστῷ· καθὼς ἐξελέξατο ἡμᾶς ἐν
in the heavenlies in Christ; according as He chose us in
αὐτῷ πρὸ καταβολῆς κόσμου, εἶναι ἡμᾶς ἁγίους καὶ
Him before (the) foundation of (the) world, to be us holy and

5 ἀμώμους κατενώπιον αὐτοῦ ἐν ἀγάπῃ, προορίσας ἡμᾶς εἰς
unblemished before Him, in love predestinating us to
υἱοθεσίαν διὰ Ἰησοῦ Χριστοῦ εἰς αὐτόν, κατὰ τὴν εὐδοκίαν
adoption through Jesus Christ to Himself, according to the good pleasure

6 τοῦ θελήματος αὐτοῦ, εἰς ἔπαινον δόξης τῆς χάριτος αὐτοῦ,
of the will of Him, to (the) praise of (the) glory of the grace of Him,

7 ἐν ᾗ ἐχαρίτωσεν ἡμᾶς ἐν τῷ ἠγαπημένῳ· ἐν ᾧ ἔχομεν τὴν
with which He favored us in the (One) having been loved; in whom we have the
ἀπολύτρωσιν διὰ τοῦ αἵματος αὐτοῦ, τὴν ἄφεσιν τῶν
redemption through the blood of Him, the forgiveness
παραπτωμάτων, κατὰ τὸν πλοῦτον τῆς χάριτος αὐτοῦ,
of trespasses, according to the riches of the grace of Him,

8 ἧς ἐπερίσσευσεν εἰς ἡμᾶς ἐν πάσῃ σοφίᾳ καὶ φρονήσει,
which he caused to abound to us in all wisdom and intelligence,

9 γνωρίσας ἡμῖν τὸ μυστήριον τοῦ θελήματος αὐτοῦ, κατὰ
making known to us the mystery of the will of Him, according to

10 τὴν εὐδοκίαν αὐτοῦ, ἣν προέθετο ἐν αὐτῷ εἰς οἰκονομίαν τοῦ
the good pleasure of Him, which He purposed in Himself for stewardship of the [a]
πληρώματος τῶν καιρῶν, ἀνακεφαλαιώσασθαι τὰ πάντα
fullness of the times, to head up all things
ἐν τῷ Χριστῷ, τά τε ἐν τοῖς οὐρανοῖς καὶ τὰ ἐπὶ τῆς γῆς·
in Christ, the things both in the heavens and the things on the earth

11 ἐν αὐτῷ, ἐν ᾧ καὶ ἐκληρώθημεν, προορισθέντες κατὰ
in Him, in whom also we have been chosen to an inheritance, being predestinated according to
πρόθεσιν τοῦ τὰ πάντα ἐνεργοῦντος κατὰ τὴν βουλὴν τοῦ
(the) purpose of the (One) all things working according to the counsel of the

will, [12] for us to be to (the) praise of His glory, those having first trusted in Christ; [13] in whom also you having heard the word of truth, the gospel of your salvation, in whom also having believed you were sealed with the Holy Spirit of promise, [14] who is (the) earnest of our inheritance, to (the) redemption of the purchased possession, to (the) praise of His glory.

[15] Because of this, I also, hearing of your faith in the Lord Jesus and love toward all the saints. [16] do not cease giving thanks for you, making mention of you in my prayers, [17] that the God of our Lord Jesus Christ, the Father of glory, may give to you a spirit of wisdom and revelation in (the) knowledge of Him, [18] the eyes of your understanding being enlightened so that you may know what is the hope of His calling, and what (are) the riches of the glory of His inheritance in the saints, [19] and what is the surpassing greatness of His power toward us, who believe according to the working of His mighty strength, [20] which He worked in Christ (in) raising Him from (the) dead; and (He) seated (Him) at His right (hand) in the heavenlies, [21] far above all principality, and authority, and power, and lordship, and every name being named, not only in this age, but also in the coming (age); [22] and He put all things under His feet, and gave Him (to be) Head over all things to the church, [23] which is His body, the fullness of Him filling all things in all.

CHAPTER 2
[1] And (He made) you (live) who were once dead

**12** θελήματος αὐτοῦ, εἰς τὸ εἶναι ἡμᾶς εἰς ἔπαινον τῆς δόξης
will    of Him,    for    to be    us    to (the) praise of the glory

**13** αὐτοῦ, τοὺς προηλπικότας ἐν τῷ Χριστῷ· ἐν ᾧ καὶ ὑμεῖς,
of Him, those having previously trusted in    Christ;    in whom also    you,
ἀκούσαντες τὸν λόγον τῆς ἀληθείας, τὸ εὐαγγέλιον τῆς
hearing    the    word    of truth,    the    gospel    of the
σωτηρίας ὑμῶν,—ἐν ᾧ καὶ πιστεύσαντες ἐσφραγίσθητε τῷ
salvation    of you,    in whom also    believing    you were sealed with the

**14** Πνεύματι τῆς ἐπαγγελίας τῷ Ἁγίῳ, ὅς ἐστιν ἀρραβὼν τῆς
Spirit    of promise    the    Holy, who is    an earnest of the
κληρονομίας ἡμῶν, εἰς ἀπολύτρωσιν τῆς περιποιήσεως, εἰς
inheritance    of us, until (the) redemption of the    possession,    to
ἔπαινον τῆς δόξης αὐτοῦ.
(the) praise of the glory of Him.

**15** Διὰ τοῦτο κἀγώ, ἀκούσας τὴν καθ᾽ ὑμᾶς πίστιν ἐν τῷ
Therefore    I also,    hearing    the    among you    faith    in the
Κυρίῳ Ἰησοῦ καὶ τὴν ἀγάπην τὴν εἰς πάντας τοὺς ἁγίους,
Lord    Jesus and the    love    to    all    the    saints,

**16** οὐ παύομαι εὐχαριστῶν ὑπὲρ ὑμῶν, μνείαν ὑμῶν ποιού-
not do cease    giving thanks on behalf of you,    mention of you making

**17** μενος ἐπὶ τῶν προσευχῶν μου· ἵνα ὁ Θεὸς τοῦ Κυρίου ἡμῶν
on the    prayers    of me,    that the God of the Lord    of us,
Ἰησοῦ Χριστοῦ, ὁ πατὴρ τῆς δόξης, δώῃ ὑμῖν πνεῦμα
Jesus Christ,    the Father    of glory, may give to you a spirit

**18** σοφίας καὶ ἀποκαλύψεως, ἐν ἐπιγνώσει αὐτοῦ· πεφωτι-
of wisdom and    revelation    in (the) knowledge of Him, having been
σμένους τοὺς ὀφθαλμοὺς τῆς διανοίας ὑμῶν, εἰς τὸ εἰδέναι
enlightened the    eyes    of the    mind    of you, for    to know
ὑμᾶς τίς ἐστιν ἡ ἐλπὶς τῆς κλήσεως αὐτοῦ, καὶ τίς ὁ πλοῦτος
you what is    the hope of the calling    of Him, and what the riches

**19** τῆς δόξης τῆς κληρονομίας αὐτοῦ ἐν τοῖς ἁγίοις, καὶ τί τὸ
of the glory of the inheritance    of Him in the    saints; and what the
ὑπερβάλλον μέγεθος τῆς δυνάμεως αὐτοῦ εἰς ἡμᾶς τοὺς
surpassing    greatness of the    power    of Him toward us,    those
πιστεύοντας, κατὰ τὴν ἐνέργειαν τοῦ κράτους τῆς ἰσχύος
believing    according to the    working of the    might    of the strength

**20** αὐτοῦ ἣν ἐνήργησεν ἐν τῷ Χριστῷ, ἐγείρας αὐτὸν ἐκ νεκρῶν,
of Him, which He worked in    Christ raising    Him from (the) dead;

**21** καὶ ἐκάθισεν ἐν δεξιᾷ αὐτοῦ ἐν τοῖς ἐπουρανίοις, ὑπεράνω
and He seated (Him) at the right of Him in the heavenlies    far above
πάσης ἀρχῆς καὶ ἐξουσίας καὶ δυνάμεως καὶ κυριότητος,
all    rule    and authority and    power    and    lordship,
καὶ παντὸς ὀνόματος ὀνομαζομένου οὐ μόνον ἐν τῷ αἰῶνι
and every    name    being    named not only in    age

**22** τούτῳ, ἀλλὰ καὶ ἐν τῷ μέλλοντι· καὶ πάντα ὑπέταξεν ὑπὸ
this,    but also in the coming (age), and all things subjected under
τοὺς πόδας αὐτοῦ, καὶ αὐτὸν ἔδωκε κεφαλὴν ὑπὲρ πάντα τῇ
the feet    of Him, and    Him    gave (to be) Head over all things to the

**23** ἐκκλησίᾳ, ἥτις ἐστὶ τὸ σῶμα αὐτοῦ, τὸ πλήρωμα τοῦ πάντα
church, which is    the body of Him, the    fullness of the (One) all things
ἐν πᾶσι πληρουμένου.
with all things filling.

**CHAPTER 2**

**1** Καὶ ὑμᾶς ὄντας νεκροὺς τοῖς παραπτώμασι καὶ ταῖς
And    you    being    dead    in the    trespasses    and in the

in trespasses and sins, [2] in which you then walked according to the course of this world, according to the ruler of the authority of the air, the spirit now working in the sons of disobedience; [3] among whom we also conducted ourselves in times past in the lusts of our flesh, doing the things willed of the flesh and of the understandings, and were by nature the children of wrath, even as the rest. [4] But God, being rich in mercy, because of His great love (with) which He loved us, [5] even when we were dead in sins, (He) made us alive together with Christ— by grace you are being saved —[6] and raised (us) up together, and seated (us) together in the heavenlies in Christ Jesus, [7] that He might show in the coming ages the exceeding great riches of His grace in kindness toward us in Christ Jesus. [8] For by grace you are saved, through faith, and that not of yourselves, (it is) the gift of God; [9] not of works, that not anyone should boast. [10] For we are His workmanship, created in Christ Jesus unto good works, which God before prepared that we should walk in them.

[11] For this reason, remember that you (were) then the nations in (the) flesh, who are called Uncircumcision by those being called Circumcision in (the) flesh made by hand, [12] that at that time you were without Christ, alienated from the commonwealth of Israel, and strangers of the covenants of promise, having no hope, and without God in the world. [13] But now in Christ Jesus, you who were then afar off are made near by the blood of Christ. [14] For He is our peace, He making (us) both one, and having broken down the middle wall of partition. [15] having annulled in His flesh the enmity, the Law of commandments in decrees, that He

2 ἁμαρτίαις, ἐν αἷς ποτὲ περιεπατήσατε κατὰ τὸν αἰῶνα τοῦ
  sins,     in which then    you walked   according to the age
  κόσμου τούτου, κατὰ τὸν ἄρχοντα τῆς ἐξουσίας τοῦ ἀέρος,
  world    of this, according to the ruler  of the authority of the air,
  τοῦ πνεύματος τοῦ νῦν ἐνεργοῦντος ἐν τοῖς υἱοῖς τῆς ἀπει-
  the  spirit      now   working    in the sons   of dis-

3 θείας· ἐν οἷς καὶ ἡμεῖς πάντες ἀνεστράφημέν ποτε ἐν ταῖς
  obedience, among whom also we all  conducted ourselves then  in  the
  ἐπιθυμίαις τῆς σαρκὸς ἡμῶν, ποιοῦντες τὰ θελήματα τῆς
  lusts     of the flesh  of us,   doing   the things willed of the
  σαρκὸς καὶ τῶν διανοιῶν, καὶ ἦμεν τέκνα φύσει ὀργῆς, ὡς
  flesh  and of the understandings, and were children by nature of wrath, as

4 καὶ οἱ λοιποί·—ὁ δὲ Θεός, πλούσιος ὢν ἐν ἐλέει, διὰ τὴν
  also the rest.  — but God  rich    being in mercy, because of the

5 πολλὴν ἀγάπην αὐτοῦ ἣν ἠγάπησεν ἡμᾶς, καὶ ὄντας ἡμᾶς
  much   love   of Him (with) which He loved us,   even being   us
  νεκροὺς τοῖς παραπτώμασι συνεζωοποίησε τῷ Χριστῷ
  dead         in trespasses (He) made us alive with      Christ;

6 (χάριτί ἐστε σεσωσμένοι), καὶ συνήγειρε, καὶ συνεκάθισεν
  by grace you are being saved;  and raised (us) with, and seated (us) with

7 ἐν τοῖς ἐπουρανίοις ἐν Χριστῷ Ἰησοῦ· ἵνα ἐνδείξηται ἐν τοῖς
  in the  heavenlies   in Christ   Jesus, that He might show in  the
  αἰῶσι τοῖς ἐπερχομένοις τὸν ὑπερβάλλοντα πλοῦτον τῆς
  ages        coming on       the surpassing      riches  of the
  χάριτος αὐτοῦ ἐν χρηστότητι ἐφ᾽ ἡμᾶς ἐν Χριστῷ Ἰησοῦ·
  grace   of Him in kindness    toward us  in Christ   Jesus.

8 τῇ γὰρ χάριτί ἐστε σεσωσμένοι διὰ τῆς πίστεως, καὶ τοῦτο
  For by grace you are saved,   through    faith,   and this

9 οὐκ ἐξ ὑμῶν· Θεοῦ τὸ δῶρον· οὐκ ἐξ ἔργων, ἵνα μή τις
  not of you,  of God (is) the gift;  not of works,  lest anyone

10 καυχήσηται. αὐτοῦ γάρ ἐσμεν ποίημα, κτισθέντες ἐν Χριστῷ
   should boast.  of Him For we are (His) doing,  created   in  Christ
   Ἰησοῦ ἐπὶ ἔργοις ἀγαθοῖς, οἷς προητοίμασεν ὁ Θεός, ἵνα
   Jesus unto works   good,    which before prepared  God   that
   ἐν αὐτοῖς περιπατήσωμεν.
   in  them   we should walk.

11 Διὸ μνημονεύετε, ὅτι ὑμεῖς ποτὲ τὰ ἔθνη ἐν σαρκί, οἱ
   Therefore remember,  that you  then  the nations in (the) flesh, those
   λεγόμενοι ἀκροβυστία ὑπὸ τῆς λεγομένης περιτομῆς ἐν
   being called uncircumcision by those being called circumcision in

12 σαρκὶ χειροποιήτου, ὅτι ἦτε ἐν τῷ καιρῷ ἐκείνῳ χωρὶς
   (the) flesh made by hand, that you were at  time  that  without
   Χριστοῦ, ἀπηλλοτριωμένοι τῆς πολιτείας τοῦ Ἰσραήλ, καὶ
   Christ,  having been alienated from the commonwealth of Israel,  and
   ξένοι τῶν διαθηκῶν τῆς ἐπαγγελίας, ἐλπίδα μὴ ἔχοντες,
   strangers of the covenants  of promise,  hope  not having,

13 καὶ ἄθεοι ἐν τῷ κόσμῳ. νυνὶ δὲ ἐν Χριστῷ Ἰησοῦ ὑμεῖς οἱ
   and godless in the world.  now But in Christ  Jesus you, those
   ποτὲ ὄντες μακρὰν ἐγγὺς ἐγενήθητε ἐν τῷ αἵματι τοῦ
   then being afar off,  near   became    by the blood

14 Χριστοῦ. αὐτὸς γάρ ἐστιν ἡ εἰρήνη ἡμῶν, ὁ ποιήσας τὰ
   of Christ.  He For  is    the peace  of us, the (One) making

15 ἀμφότερα ἕν, καὶ τὸ μεσότοιχον τοῦ φραγμοῦ λύσας, τὴν
   both    one, and the middle wall   of partition having broken, the
   ἔχθραν ἐν τῇ σαρκὶ αὐτοῦ, τὸν νόμον τῶν ἐντολῶν ἐν
   enmity  in the flesh  of Him,  the  law  of the commandments in

might in Himself create the two into one new man, making peace; [16] and might reconcile both in one body to God through the cross, having slain the enmity by it. [17] And having come, He preached the gospel of peace to you, those afar off and to those near. [18] <u>For through Him we both have access by one Spirit to the Father.</u> [19] So then you are no longer strangers and strangers— but (you are) fellow-citizens of the saints and (of the) household of God, [20] being built up on the foundation of the apostles and prophets, Jesus Christ Himself being (the) cornerstone, [21] in whom all the building fitted together grows into a holy temple in (the) Lord, [22] in whom also you are being built together into a dwelling-place of God in (the) Spirit.

δόγμασι, καταργήσας· ἵνα τοὺς δύο κτίσῃ ἐν ἑαυτῷ εἰς ἕνα
decrees, having abolished, that the two He create in Himself into one

16 καινὸν ἄνθρωπον, ποιῶν εἰρήνην, καὶ ἀποκαταλλάξῃ τοὺς
new man, making peace, and might reconcile the

ἀμφοτέρους ἐν ἑνὶ σώματι τῷ Θεῷ διὰ τοῦ σταυροῦ,
both in one body to God through the cross,

17 ἀποκτείνας τὴν ἔχθραν ἐν αὐτῷ· καὶ ἐλθὼν εὐηγγελίσατο
slaying the enmity in Himself, and coming preached

18 εἰρήνην ὑμῖν τοῖς μακρὰν καὶ τοῖς ἐγγύς· ὅτι δι᾽ αὐτοῦ
peace to you, those afar off, and to the (ones) near, for through Him

ἔχομεν τὴν προσαγωγὴν οἱ ἀμφότεροι ἐν ἑνὶ Πνεύματι πρὸς
we have access both by one Spirit unto

19 τὸν πατέρα. ἄρα οὖν οὐκέτι ἐστὲ ξένοι καὶ πάροικοι, ἀλλὰ
the Father. Then therefore no more are you strangers and sojourners but

20 συμπολῖται τῶν ἁγίων καὶ οἰκεῖοι τοῦ Θεοῦ, ἐποικοδομη-
fellow-citizens of the saints and (of the) household of God, having been

θέντες ἐπὶ τῷ θεμελίῳ τῶν ἀποστόλων καὶ προφητῶν, ὄντος
built on the foundation of the apostles and prophets, being

21 ἀκρογωνιαίου αὐτοῦ Ἰησοῦ Χριστοῦ, ἐν ᾧ πᾶσα ἡ οἰκοδομὴ
(the) cornerstone (Him)self Jesus Christ, in whom all the building

22 συναρμολογουμένη αὔξει εἰς ναὸν ἅγιον ἐν Κυρίῳ, ἐν ᾧ καὶ
fitted together grows into a temple holy in (the) Lord, in whom also

ὑμεῖς συνοικοδομεῖσθε εἰς κατοικητήριον τοῦ Θεοῦ ἐν
you are being built together into a dwelling-place of God in

Πνεύματι.
(the) Spirit.

## CHAPTER 3

[1] For this reason, I, Paul, (am) prisoner of Jesus Christ for you, the nations, [2] if indeed you heard of the administration of the grace of God which was given to me for you, [3] that by revelation He revealed to me the mystery, as I wrote before in brief, [4] by the reading of which you are able to realize my understanding in the mystery of Christ; [5] which was not made known to the sons of men in other generations, as it now has been revealed to His holy apostles and prophets in (the) Spirit, [6] (for) the nations to be joint-heirs, and of the same body, and sharers of His promise in Christ, through the gospel; [7] of which I was made a minister, according to the gift of the grace of God given to me, according to the working of His power. [8] This grace was given to me, the least of all the saints, to preach

## CHAPTER 3

1 Τούτου χάριν ἐγὼ Παῦλος ὁ δέσμιος τοῦ Χριστοῦ Ἰησοῦ
of this By reason I, Paul, the prisoner of Christ Jesus

2 ὑπὲρ ὑμῶν τῶν ἐθνῶν,—εἴγε ἠκούσατε τὴν οἰκονομίαν τῆς
on behalf of you the nations — if indeed you heard the stewardship of the

3 χάριτος τοῦ Θεοῦ τῆς δοθείσης μοι εἰς ὑμᾶς, ὅτι κατὰ
grace of God given to me for you, that by way of

ἀποκάλυψιν ἐγνώρισέ μοι τὸ μυστήριον, καθὼς προέγραψα
revelation was made known to me the mystery, as I wrote before

4 ἐν ὀλίγῳ, πρὸς ὃ δύνασθε ἀναγινώσκοντες νοῆσαι τὴν
in brief, as to which you are able reading to realize the

5 σύνεσίν μου ἐν τῷ μυστηρίῳ τοῦ Χριστοῦ· ὃ ἐν ἑτέραις
understanding of me in the mystery of Christ, which in other

γενεαῖς οὐκ ἐγνωρίσθη τοῖς υἱοῖς τῶν ἀνθρώπων, ὡς νῦν
generations not was made known to the sons of men as now

ἀπεκαλύφθη τοῖς ἁγίοις ἀποστόλοις αὐτοῦ καὶ προφήταις
it was revealed to the holy apostles of Him and prophets

6 ἐν Πνεύματι· εἶναι τὰ ἔθνη συγκληρονόμα καὶ σύσσωμα καὶ
in (the) Spirit, to be the nations joint-heirs and a joint-body and

συμμέτοχα τῆς ἐπαγγελίας αὐτοῦ ἐν τῷ Χριστῷ, διὰ τοῦ
joint-sharers of the promise of Him in Christ, through the

7 εὐαγγελίου, οὗ ἐγενόμην διάκονος κατὰ τὴν δωρεὰν τῆς
gospel, of which I became a minister according to the gift of the

χάριτος τοῦ Θεοῦ, τὴν δοθεῖσάν μοι κατὰ τὴν ἐνέργειαν τῆς
grace of God, given to me according to the working of the

8 δυνάμεως αὐτοῦ. ἐμοὶ τῷ ἐλαχιστοτέρῳ πάντων τῶν
power of Him. To me, the least of all the

ἁγίων ἐδόθη ἡ χάρις αὕτη, ἐν τοῖς ἔθνεσιν εὐαγγελίσασθαι
saints, was given grace this, in the nations to preach

the gospel of the unsearchable riches of Christ among the nations.[9] and to bring to light what (is) the fellowship of the mystery which has been hidden from eternity in God, who created all things through Jesus Christ, [10] so that now to the rulers and authorities in the heavenlies might be known through the church the manifold wisdom of God [11] according to the eternal purpose which He purposed in Christ Jesus our Lord, [12] in whom we have boldness and access in confidence through His faith. [13] Therefore, I beg (you) not to faint at my troubles for you, which is your glory. [14] For this cause I bow my knees to the Father of our Lord Jesus Christ, [15] of whom every family in Heaven and on earth is named, [16] that He may give you according to the riches of His glory by (His) power to become mighty in the inward man, through His Spirit, [17] that through faith Christ may dwell in your hearts, that you being rooted and grounded in love [18] may be strengthened to firmly grasp, with all the saints, what (is) the breadth and length and depth and height [19] and to know the love of Christ going beyond knowledge, that you may be filled to all the fullness of God. [20] But to Him who is able to do exceedingly above what we ask or think, according to the power that works in us, [21] to Him (be) the glory in the church in Christ Jesus, to all the generations of the age forever. Amen.

9 τὸν ἀνεξιχνίαστον πλοῦτον τοῦ Χριστοῦ, καὶ φωτίσαι
the　　unsearchable　　　riches　　　　of Christ, and to bring to light
πάντας τίς ἡ κοινωνία τοῦ μυστηρίου τοῦ ἀποκεκρυμμένου
all,　what (is) the fellowship of the mystery　　　having been hidden
ἀπὸ τῶν αἰώνων ἐν τῷ Θεῷ τῷ τὰ πάντα κτίσαντι διὰ
from　the　ages　in　　God, the (One)　all things having created via

10 Ἰησοῦ Χριστοῦ, ἵνα γνωρισθῇ νῦν ταῖς ἀρχαῖς καὶ ταῖς
Jesus　　Christ,　that might be made known now to the rulers and to the
ἐξουσίαις ἐν τοῖς ἐπουρανίοις διὰ τῆς ἐκκλησίας ἡ πολυποί-
authorities in the　heavenlies　through the　church the manifold

11 κιλος σοφία τοῦ Θεοῦ, κατὰ πρόθεσιν τῶν αἰώνων ἣν ἐποίη-
wisdom　　of God, according to the purpose of the ages which He

12 σεν ἐν Χριστῷ Ἰησοῦ τῷ Κυρίῳ ἡμῶν· ἐν ᾧ ἔχομεν τὴν
made in　Christ　　Jesus　the Lord　of us,　in whom we have
παρρησίαν καὶ τὴν προσαγωγὴν ἐν πεποιθήσει διὰ τῆς
boldness　and　　the　access　　in　confidence through the

13 πίστεως αὐτοῦ. διὸ αἰτοῦμαι μὴ ἐκκακεῖν ἐν ταῖς θλίψεσί μου
faith　of Him. Therefore I ask (you) not to faint among the troubles of me
ὑπὲρ ὑμῶν, ἥτις ἐστὶ δόξα ὑμῶν.
on your behalf, which is glory　of you.

14 Τούτου χάριν κάμπτω τὰ γόνατά μου πρὸς τὸν πατέρα
of this By reason I bow　the knees　of me to　the　Father

15 τοῦ Κυρίου ἡμῶν Ἰησοῦ Χριστοῦ, ἐξ οὗ πᾶσα πατριὰ ἐν οὐ-
of the Lord　of us,　Jesus　Christ,　of whom every family　in

16 ρανοῖς καὶ ἐπὶ γῆς ὀνομάζεται, ἵνα δώῃ ὑμῖν, κατὰ τὸν πλοῦ-
Heaven and on earth　is named,　that He may give you per the riches
τον τῆς δόξης αὐτοῦ, δυνάμει κραταιωθῆναι διὰ τοῦ Πνεύ-
of the glory of Him　by power to become mighty through the

17 ματος αὐτοῦ εἰς τὸν ἔσω ἄνθρωπον, κατοικῆσαι τὸν Χριστὸν
Spirit of Him　in the inward　man,　to dwell　　Christ
διὰ τῆς πίστεως ἐν ταῖς καρδίαις ὑμῶν· ἐν ἀγάπῃ ἐρριζω-
through　faith　in　the　hearts　of you, in　love having been

18 μένοι καὶ τεθεμελιωμένοι ἵνα ἐξισχύσητε καταλαβέσθαι σὺν
rooted and having been founded, that you be strengthened to grasp　with
πᾶσι τοῖς ἁγίοις, τί τὸ πλάτος καὶ μῆκος καὶ βάθος καὶ ὕψος,
all　the saints, what (is) the breadth and length and depth and height,

19 γνῶναί τε τὴν ὑπερβάλλουσαν τῆς γνώσεως ἀγάπην τοῦ
to know and the　surpassing　　knowledge　love
Χριστοῦ, ἵνα πληρωθῆτε εἰς πᾶν τὸ πλήρωμα τοῦ Θεοῦ.
of Christ,　that you may be filled to all the　fullness　　of God.

20 Τῷ δὲ δυναμένῳ ὑπὲρ πάντα ποιῆσαι ὑπὲρ ἐκ περισσοῦ
the (One) Now being able beyond all things to do　exceedingly above
ὧν αἰτούμεθα ἢ νοοῦμεν, κατὰ τὴν δύναμιν τὴν ἐνεργου-
what we ask　or　think, according to the　power　　working

21 μένην ἐν ἡμῖν, αὐτῷ ἡ δόξα ἐν τῇ ἐκκλησίᾳ ἐν Χριστῷ Ἰησοῦ
in us, to Him (be) the glory in the church　in　Christ　Jesus
εἰς πάσας τὰς γενεὰς τοῦ αἰῶνος τῶν αἰώνων. ἀμήν.
to　all　the generations of the age　of the　ages.　Amen.

## CHAPTER 4

### CHAPTER 4
[1] I exhort you, then, I the prisoner in (the) Lord, to walk worthily of the calling with which you were called, [2] with all humility and meekness, with long-suffering, bearing with one

1 Παρακαλῶ οὖν ὑμᾶς ἐγώ, ὁ δέσμιος ἐν Κυρίῳ, ἀξίως
exhort　therefore you　I,　the prisoner in (the) Lord, worthily

2 περιπατῆσαι τῆς κλήσεως ἧς ἐκλήθητε, μετὰ πάσης ταπει-
to walk　　of the calling of which you were called, with　all
νοφροσύνης καὶ πραότητος, μετὰ μακροθυμίας, ἀνεχό-
humility,　and　meekness,　with　longsuffering,　bearing

with one another in love; [3] being eager to keep the unity of the Spirit in the bond of peace. [4] (There) (is) one body and one Spirit, even as you also were called in one hope of your calling; [5] one Lord, one faith, one baptism, [6] one God and Father of all, who (is) above all and through all and in you all. [7] But to each one of us grace was given according to the measure of the gift of Christ. [8] Therefore He says, "Having ascended on high, He led captivity captive, and gave gifts to men."

[9] But that He ascended, what is it but that He also descended first into the lower parts of the earth? [10] He that descended is the same who also ascended above all the heavens, that He might fill all things. [11] And He gave some, apostles; and some, prophets; and some, evangelists; and some, pastors and teachers; [12] with a view to the perfecting of the saints; for the work of (the) ministry, for building up of the body of Christ; [13] until we all may come to the unity of the faith and of the knowledge of the Son of God, to a full-grown man, to (the) measure of (the) stature of the fullness of Christ, [14] so that we may no longer be infants, being blown to and fro by every wind of doctrine, in the underhandedness of men, in craftiness, with a view to the trickery of error; [15] but speaking the truth in love, we may grow up into Him in all things, who is the Head, the Christ; [16] from whom all the body fitted together and compacted by every assisting joint, according to (the) working of each part in (its) measure producing the growth of the body to the building up of itself in love.

[17] Therefore, I say this, and testify in (the) Lord, that you no longer

**3** μενοι ἀλλήλων ἐν ἀγάπῃ, σπουδάζοντες τηρεῖν τὴν ἑνότητα
with one another in love, being eager to keep the unity

**4** τοῦ Πνεύματος ἐν τῷ συνδέσμῳ τῆς εἰρήνης. ἓν σῶμα καὶ
of the Spirit in the bond of peace. One body and
ἓν Πνεῦμα, καθὼς καὶ ἐκλήθητε ἐν μιᾷ ἐλπίδι τῆς κλήσεως
one Spirit (is), as also you were called in one hope of the calling

**5/** ὑμῶν· εἰς Κύριος, μία πίστις, ἐν βάπτισμα, εἰς Θεὸς καὶ
**6** of you, one Lord, one faith, one baptism, one God and
πατὴρ πάντων, ὁ ἐπὶ πάντων, καὶ διὰ πάντων, καὶ ἐν
Father of all, the (One) above all, and through all, and in

**7** πᾶσιν ὑμῖν. ἑνὶ δὲ ἑκάστῳ ἡμῶν ἐδόθη ἡ χάρις κατὰ τὸ
all you. to one But each of us was given grace according to the

**8** μέτρον τῆς δωρεᾶς τοῦ Χριστοῦ. διὸ λέγει, Ἀναβὰς εἰς
measure of the gift of Christ. Therefore He says, Having gone up on
ὕψος ἠχμαλώτευσεν αἰχμαλωσίαν, καὶ ἔδωκε δόματα τοῖς
high, He led captive captivity, and gave gifts

**9** ἀνθρώποις. (τὸ δέ, Ἀνέβη, τί ἐστιν εἰ μὴ ὅτι καὶ κατέβη
to men — the Now: He went up; what is it except that also He came down

**10** πρῶτον εἰς τὰ κατώτερα μέρη τῆς γῆς; ὁ καταβάς, αὐτός
first into the lower parts of the earth? The (One) coming down
ἐστι καὶ ὁ ἀναβὰς ὑπεράνω πάντων τῶν οὐρανῶν, ἵνα
is also the (One) going up far above all the heavens, that

**11** πληρώσῃ τὰ πάντα.) καὶ αὐτὸς ἔδωκε τοὺς μὲν ἀποστό-
He might fill all things — and He gave some apostles,
λους, τοὺς δὲ προφήτας, τοὺς δὲ εὐαγγελιστάς, τοὺς δὲ
some prophets, some evangelists, some

**12** ποιμένας καὶ διδασκάλους, πρὸς τὸν καταρτισμὸν τῶν
pastors, and teacher, for the perfecting of the
ἁγίων, εἰς ἔργον διακονίας, εἰς οἰκοδομὴν τοῦ σώματος τοῦ
saints; for (the) work of ministry, to building of the body

**13** Χριστοῦ· μέχρι καταντήσωμεν οἱ πάντες εἰς τὴν ἑνότητα
of Christ, until we may come all to the unity
τῆς πίστεως καὶ τῆς ἐπιγνώσεως τοῦ υἱοῦ τοῦ Θεοῦ, εἰς
of the faith and of the knowledge of the Son of God, to
ἄνδρα τέλειον, εἰς μέτρον ἡλικίας τοῦ πληρώματος τοῦ
a man full-grown, to (the) measure of (the) stature of the fullness

**14** Χριστοῦ· ἵνα μηκέτι ὦμεν νήπιοι, κλυδωνιζόμενοι καὶ
of Christ, that no longer we may be infants, being blown and
περιφερόμενοι παντὶ ἀνέμῳ τῆς διδασκαλίας, ἐν τῇ κυβείᾳ
being carried about by every wind of doctrine, in the sleight
τῶν ἀνθρώπων, ἐν πανουργίᾳ, πρὸς τὴν μεθοδείαν τῆς
of men, in craftiness to the trickery

**15** πλάνης· ἀληθεύοντες δὲ ἐν ἀγάπῃ αὐξήσωμεν εἰς αὐτὸν τὰ
of error; speaking truth but in love we may grow into Him in all

**16** πάντα, ὅς ἐστιν ἡ κεφαλή, ὁ Χριστός, ἐξ οὗ πᾶν τὸ σῶμα
respects, who is the Head, Christ, of whom all the body
συναρμολογούμενον καὶ συμβιβαζόμενον διὰ πάσης ἀφῆς
being fitted together and being brought together through every band
τῆς ἐπιχορηγίας, κατ᾽ ἐνέργειαν ἐν μέτρῳ ἑνὸς ἑκάστου
of assistance, according to (the) working in measure of one each
μέρους, τὴν αὔξησιν τοῦ σώματος ποιεῖται εἰς οἰκοδομὴν
part, the growth of the body producing, to the building up
ἑαυτοῦ ἐν ἀγάπῃ.
of itself in love.

**17** Τοῦτο οὖν λέγω καὶ μαρτύρομαι ἐν Κυρίῳ, μηκέτι ὑμᾶς
this Therefore I say, and testify in (the) Lord, no longer you

περιπατεῖν, καθὼς καὶ τὰ λοιπὰ ἔθνη περιπατεῖ ἐν ματαιό-
walk            even as also the rest (of the) nations walk, in vanity

**18** τητι τοῦ νοὸς αὐτῶν, ἐσκοτισμένοι τῇ διανοίᾳ, ὄντες
of the mind of them, having been darkened in the intellect, being

ἀπηλλοτριωμένοι τῆς ζωῆς τοῦ Θεοῦ διὰ τὴν ἄγνοιαν τὴν
alienated            (from) the life      of God through the ignorance

οὖσαν ἐν αὐτοῖς, διὰ τὴν πώρωσιν τῆς καρδίας αὐτῶν·
being in    them, on account of the hardness of the heart of them,

**19** οἵτινες ἀπηλγηκότες ἑαυτοὺς παρέδωκαν τῇ ἀσελγείᾳ, εἰς
who having cast off all feeling themselves gave up    to lust,    to

**20** ἐργασίαν ἀκαθαρσίας πάσης ἐν πλεονεξίᾳ. ὑμεῖς δὲ οὐχ
(the) working of uncleanness all with greediness.    you But not

**21** οὕτως ἐμάθετε τὸν Χριστόν, εἴγε αὐτὸν ἠκούσατε καὶ ἐν
so    learned    Christ,    if indeed Him you heard and by

αὐτῷ ἐδιδάχθητε, καθώς ἐστιν ἀλήθεια ἐν τῷ Ἰησοῦ·
Him were taught, even as is (the) truth in    Jesus,

**22** ἀποθέσθαι ὑμᾶς, κατὰ τὴν προτέραν ἀναστροφήν, τὸν
to put off    you, as regards the former behavior. of the

παλαιὸν ἄνθρωπον, τὸν φθειρόμενον κατὰ τὰς ἐπιθυμίας
old    man,    being corrupted according to the lusts

**23** τῆς ἀπάτης· ἀνανεοῦσθαι δὲ τῷ πνεύματι τοῦ νοὸς ὑμῶν,
of deceit, to be renewed and in the spirit of the mind of you,

**24** καὶ ἐνδύσασθαι τὸν καινὸν ἄνθρωπον, τὸν κατὰ Θεὸν κτι-
and to put on the new man    according to God

σθέντα ἐν δικαιοσύνῃ καὶ ὁσιότητι τῆς ἀληθείας.
created in righteousness and holiness    of truth.

**25** Διὸ ἀποθέμενοι τὸ ψεῦδος λαλεῖτε ἀλήθειαν ἕκαστος μετὰ
Therefore putting off the false,    speak    truth    each    with

**26** τοῦ πλησίον αὐτοῦ· ὅτι ἐσμὲν ἀλλήλων μέλη. ὀργίζεσθε καὶ
the neighbor of him, because we are one another's members. Be angry and

μὴ ἁμαρτάνετε· ὁ ἥλιος μὴ ἐπιδυέτω ἐπὶ τῷ παροργισμῷ
do not sin,    the sun not let set    on the provocation

**27/** ὑμῶν· μήτε δίδοτε τόπον τῷ διαβόλῳ. ὁ κλέπτων μηκέτι
**28** of you; nor give    place to the devil. The (one) stealing, no more

κλεπτέτω· μᾶλλον δὲ κοπιάτω, ἐργαζόμενος τὸ ἀγαθὸν ταῖς
let him steal, rather but let him labor, working    the good with the

**29** χερσίν, ἵνα ἔχῃ μεταδιδόναι τῷ χρείαν ἔχοντι. πᾶς λόγος
hands, that he may have to give to the (one) need having. Every word

σαπρὸς ἐκ τοῦ στόματος ὑμῶν μὴ ἐκπορευέσθω, ἀλλ' εἴ τις
corrupt out of the mouth of you not let go,    but if any

ἀγαθὸς πρὸς οἰκοδομὴν τῆς χρείας, ἵνα δῷ χάριν τοῖς ἀκού-
(is) good to building up the    need, that it may give grace to those

**30** ουσι. καὶ μὴ λυπεῖτε τὸ Πνεῦμα τὸ Ἅγιον τοῦ Θεοῦ, ἐν ᾧ
hearing. And do not grieve the Spirit    Holy    of God, by whom

**31** ἐσφραγίσθητε εἰς ἡμέραν ἀπολυτρώσεως. πᾶσα πικρία καὶ
you were sealed for a day of redemption.    All bitterness and

θυμὸς καὶ ὀργὴ καὶ κραυγὴ καὶ βλασφημία ἀρθήτω ἀφ' ὑμῶν,
anger and wrath and tumult and evil speaking put away from you,

**32** σὺν πάσῃ κακίᾳ· γίνεσθε δὲ εἰς ἀλλήλους χρηστοί, εὔσπλαγ-
with all evil things. be    And to one another kind,    tender-

χνοι, χαριζόμενοι ἑαυτοῖς, καθὼς καὶ ὁ Θεὸς ἐν Χριστῷ ἐχαρί-
hearted, forgiving yourselves, as    also    God in Christ

σατο ὑμῖν.
forgave you.

---

walk even as also the rest (of the) nations are walking, in (the) vanity of their mind, [18] being darkened in the understanding, being alienated (from) the life of God through the ignorance which is in them, because of the hardness of their heart, [19] who having cast off all feeling gave themselves up to lust, for (the) working of uncleanness with greediness [20] but you have not so learned Christ, [21] if indeed you heard Him and were taught in Him, as (the) truth is in Jesus; [22] for you have put off the old man, according to the former behavior, being corrupted according to deceitful lusts; [23] and to be renewed in the spirit of your mind; [24] and to have put on the new man, (which) according to God was created in righteousness and true holiness. [25] Because of this, having put off falsehood, speak truth each with his neighbor because we are members of one another, [26] Be angry, but do not sin; do not let the sun go down on your provocation, [27] nor give place to the Devil. [28] The (one) stealing, let him steal no more, but rather let him labor, working what (is) good with the hands, that he may have (something) to give to the (one) that has need. [29] Let not every filthy word go out of your mouth, but if anything, for good to building up in respect to need, that it may give grace to those who hear. [30] And do not grieve the Holy Spirit of God, by whom you were sealed to (the) day of redemption. [31] Let all bitterness, and indignation, and wrath, and tumult, and evil speaking be put away from you, along with all evil things. [32] and be kind to one another, tender-hearted, forgiving yourselves, even as also God forgave you in Christ.

## CHAPTER 5

[1] Then be imitators of God, as loved children. [2] and walk in love, even as Christ also loved us, and gave Himself for us, an offering and a sacrifice to God for an odor of a sweet smell.

[3] But fornication, and all uncleanness, or covetousness, let it not even be named among you, even as is becoming to saints; [4] and filthiness, and foolish talking or joking, these things (are) not becoming; but rather thanksgiving. [5] For be knowing this that every fornicator, or unclean person, or covetous one, who is an idolater, has any inheritance in the kingdom of Christ and of God. [6] Let no one deceive you with empty words; for the wrath of God comes on the sons of disobedience because of these things. [7] Then do not be partners with them, [8] for you were once darkness, but now (are) light in (the) Lord; walk as children of light. [9] For the fruit of the Spirit (is) in all goodness and righteousness and truth. [10] (Be always) proving what is well-pleasing to the Lord; [11] and have no fellowship with the unfruitful works of darkness, but rather even convict (them); [12] for the things being done in secret by them, it is shameful even to speak. [13] But all things being exposed by the light are clearly revealed, for everything being revealed (is) light. [14] Therefore He says: "Arise, sleeping one, and stand up from (the) dead, and Christ shall shine on you." [15] Then watch how carefully you walk, not as unwise, but as wise ones, [16] redeeming the time because the days are evil. [17] For this reason, do not be foolish, but understanding what the will of the Lord (is). [18] And do not be drunk with wine, in which is debauchery, but be filled with the Spirit, [19] speaking to yourselves in psalms and hymns and spiritual songs, singing and

## CHAPTER 5

1 Γίνεσθε οὖν μιμηταὶ τοῦ Θεοῦ, ὡς τέκνα ἀγαπητὰ καὶ
be   Then imitators   of God,   as children beloved,   and

2 περιπατεῖτε ἐν ἀγάπῃ, καθὼς καὶ ὁ Χριστὸς ἠγάπησεν ἡμᾶς,
walk   in love,   even as also   Christ   loved   us

καὶ παρέδωκεν ἑαυτὸν ὑπὲρ ἡμῶν προσφορὰν καὶ θυσίαν
and  gave up   Himself   for   us   an offering   and a sacrifice

3 τῷ Θεῷ εἰς ὀσμὴν εὐωδίας. πορνεία δὲ καὶ πᾶσα ἀκαθαρσία
to God for an odor of sweet smell. fornication But and all uncleanness

ἢ πλεονεξία μηδὲ ὀνομαζέσθω ἐν ὑμῖν, καθὼς πρέπει ἁγίοις·
or greediness not let it be named among you, as is fitting for saints,

4 καὶ αἰσχρότης, καὶ μωρολογία ἢ εὐτραπελία, τὰ οὐκ ἀνή-
and filthiness,   and foolish talking or joking,   the things not be-

5 κοντα· ἀλλὰ μᾶλλον εὐχαριστία. τοῦτο γὰρ ἐστε γινώ-
coming,   but   rather thanksgiving.   this   For be   know-

σκοντες, ὅτι πᾶς πόρνος, ἢ ἀκάθαρτος, ἢ πλεονέκτης, ὅς ἐστιν
ing, that every fornicator, or unclean one, or greedy, who is

εἰδωλολάτρης, οὐκ ἔχει κληρονομίαν ἐν τῇ βασιλείᾳ τοῦ
an idolater;   not has   inheritance   in the   kingdom

6 Χριστοῦ καὶ Θεοῦ. μηδεὶς ὑμᾶς ἀπατάτω κενοῖς λόγοις·
of Christ and of God. Let no one you   deceive with empty words;

διὰ ταῦτα γὰρ ἔρχεται ἡ ὀργὴ τοῦ Θεοῦ ἐπὶ τοὺς υἱοὺς
through these for   comes   the wrath   of God on the sons

7/ τῆς ἀπειθείας. μὴ οὖν γίνεσθε συμμέτοχοι αὐτῶν· ἦτε γὰρ
8 of disobedience. not Then be   partners   with them; you were for

ποτὲ σκότος, νῦν δὲ φῶς ἐν Κυρίῳ· ὡς τέκνα φωτὸς περι-
then darkness, now and light in (the) Lord, as children of light walk,

9 πατεῖτε (ὁ γὰρ καρπὸς τοῦ Πνεύματος ἐν πάσῃ ἀγαθωσύνῃ
—the for fruit of the   Spirit (is) in all   goodness

10 καὶ δικαιοσύνῃ καὶ ἀληθείᾳ), δοκιμάζοντες τί ἐστιν εὐάρε-
and righteousness and truth,   proving   what is well-

11 στον τῷ Κυρίῳ· καὶ μὴ συγκοινωνεῖτε τοῖς ἔργοις τοῖς
pleasing to the Lord; and do not have fellowship with the works

12 ἀκάρποις τοῦ σκότους, μᾶλλον δὲ καὶ ἐλέγχετε· τὰ γὰρ
unfruitful   of darkness,   rather but even reprove;   the for

13 κρυφῇ γινόμενα ὑπ’ αὐτῶν αἰσχρόν ἐστι καὶ λέγειν. τὰ δὲ
hidden things being done by them shameful it is even to speak; but

πάντα ἐλεγχόμενα ὑπὸ τοῦ φωτὸς φανεροῦται· πᾶν γὰρ
all things being reproved by the light is revealed; everything for

14 τὸ φανερούμενον φῶς ἐστί. διὸ λέγει, Ἔγειραι ὁ καθεύδων
being revealed light is. Therefore He says: Arise sleeping one

καὶ ἀνάστα ἐκ τῶν νεκρῶν, καὶ ἐπιφαύσει σοι ὁ Χριστός.
and stand up from the dead ones, and will shine on you Christ.

15 Βλέπετε οὖν πῶς ἀκριβῶς περιπατεῖτε, μὴ ὡς ἄσοφοι,
See, therefore, how carefully you walk, not as unwise,

16 ἀλλ’ ὡς σοφοί, ἐξαγοραζόμενοι τὸν καιρόν, ὅτι αἱ ἡμέραι
but   as wise ones,   redeeming   the time, because the days

17 πονηραί εἰσι. διὰ τοῦτο μὴ γίνεσθε ἄφρονες, ἀλλὰ συνιέντες
evil   are. Because of this, do not be   foolish,   but understanding

18 τί τὸ θέλημα τοῦ Κυρίου. καὶ μὴ μεθύσκεσθε οἴνῳ, ἐν ᾧ
what the will of the Lord (Is). And do not be drunk with wine, in which

19 ἐστιν ἀσωτία, ἀλλὰ πληροῦσθε ἐν Πνεύματι, λαλοῦντες
is   debauchery, but   be filled   by (the) Spirit,   speaking

ἑαυτοῖς ψαλμοῖς καὶ ὕμνοις καὶ ᾠδαῖς πνευματικαῖς, ᾄδοντες
to yourselves in psalms and hymns and songs   spiritual,   singing

and psalming in your heart
to the Lord; [20] giving
thanks at all times for all
things to Him, to God, even
(the) Father, in the name of
our Lord Jesus Christ, [21]
being subject to one another in (the) fear of God.

[22] Wives, subject
yourselves to (your) own
husbands as to the Lord,
[23] for the husband is
head of the wife, as also
Christ (is the) Head of the
church, and He is Savior of
the body. [24] But even as
the church is subject to
Christ, so also the wives to
their husbands in every-
thing. [25] Husbands, love
your own wives, even as also
Christ loved the church, and
gave Himself on behalf of it,
[26] that He might sanctify
it, having cleansed (it) by
the washing of water by
(the) word, [27] that He
might present to Himself
the glorious church, not
having spot· or wrinkle, or
any such things, but that it
might be holy and unblem-
ished. [28] So husbands
ought to love their own
wives as their own bodies;
he that loves his own wife
loves himself. [29] For no
one then hated his own
flesh, but nourishes and
cherishes it, even as also the
Lord the church. [30] For
we are members of His
body, of His flesh, and of
His bones. [31] "For this a
man shall leave his father
and his mother and shall be
joined to his wife, and the
two shall be one flesh."
[32] This mystery is great,
but I speak as to Christ and
as to the church. [33] However, you also, everyone, let
each love his wife as himself; and the wife, that she
may fear the husband.

CHAPTER 6

[1] Children, obey your
parents in (the) Lord, for

**20** καὶ ψάλλοντες ἐν τῇ καρδίᾳ ὑμῶν τῷ Κυρίῳ, εὐχαριστοῦντες
and psalming in the heart of you to the Lord, giving thanks

πάντοτε ὑπὲρ πάντων ἐν ὀνόματι τοῦ Κυρίου ἡμῶν Ἰησοῦ
always for all things in the name of the Lord of us, Jesus

**21** Χριστοῦ τῷ Θεῷ καὶ πατρί, ὑποτασσόμενοι ἀλλήλοις ἐν
Christ, to God, even (the) Father, being subject to one another in

φόβῳ Θεοῦ.
(the) fear of God.

**22** Αἱ γυναῖκες, τοῖς ἰδίοις ἀνδράσιν ὑποτάσσεσθε, ὡς τῷ
The wives to the own husbands subject yourselves, as to the

**23** Κυρίῳ. ὅτι ὁ ἀνήρ ἐστι κεφαλὴ τῆς γυναικός, ὡς καὶ ὁ
Lord, because a man is head of the woman, as also the

Χριστὸς κεφαλὴ τῆς ἐκκλησίας, καὶ αὐτός ἐστι σωτὴρ τοῦ
Christ (is) Head of the church, and He is Savior of the

**24** σώματος. ἀλλ' ὥσπερ ἡ ἐκκλησία ὑποτάσσεται τῷ Χριστῷ,
body. But as the church is subject to Christ,

**25** οὕτω καὶ αἱ γυναῖκες τοῖς ἰδίοις ἀνδράσιν ἐν παντί. οἱ
so also the wives to the own husband in everything. The

ἄνδρες, ἀγαπᾶτε τὰς γυναῖκας ἑαυτῶν, καθὼς καὶ ὁ Χριστὸς
husbands, love the wives (of) yourselves, even as also Christ

ἠγάπησε τὴν ἐκκλησίαν, καὶ ἑαυτὸν παρέδωκεν ὑπὲρ αὐτῆς·
loved the church, and Himself gave up on behalf of it,

**26** ἵνα αὐτὴν ἁγιάσῃ, καθαρίσας τῷ λουτρῷ τοῦ ὕδατος ἐν
that it He might sanctify, cleansing by the washing of the water by

**27** ῥήματι, ἵνα παραστήσῃ αὐτὴν ἑαυτῷ ἔνδοξον τὴν ἐκκλη-
(the) word, that might present it to Himself glorious the church,

σίαν, μὴ ἔχουσαν σπίλον ἢ ῥυτίδα ἤ τι τῶν τοιούτων, ἀλλ'
not having spot or wrinkle or any of the such things, but

**28** ἵνα ᾖ ἁγία καὶ ἄμωμος. οὕτως ὀφείλουσιν οἱ ἄνδρες ἀγαπᾶν
that it be holy and unblemished. So ought the husbands to love

τὰς ἑαυτῶν γυναῖκας ὡς τὰ ἑαυτῶν σώματα. ὁ ἀγαπῶν τὴν
the of themselves wives as the of themselves bodies. The (one) loving the

**29** ἑαυτοῦ γυναῖκα ἑαυτὸν ἀγαπᾷ· οὐδεὶς γάρ ποτε τὴν ἑαυτοῦ
of himself wife himself loves; no one for then the of himself

σάρκα ἐμίσησεν, ἀλλ' ἐκτρέφει καὶ θάλπει αὐτήν, καθὼς καὶ
flesh hated, but nourishes and cherishes it, even as also

**30** ὁ Κύριος τὴν ἐκκλησίαν· ὅτι μέλη ἐσμὲν τοῦ σώματος αὐτοῦ,
the Lord the church, because members we are of the body of Him,

**31** ἐκ τῆς σαρκὸς αὐτοῦ καὶ ἐκ τῶν ὀστέων αὐτοῦ. Ἀντὶ τού-
of the flesh of Him and of the bones of Him. For this

του καταλείψει ἄνθρωπος τὸν πατέρα αὐτοῦ καὶ τὴν
shall leave a man the father of him and the

μητέρα, καὶ προσκολληθήσεται πρὸς τὴν γυναῖκα αὐτοῦ,
mother and shall cleave to the wife of him,

**32** καὶ ἔσονται οἱ δύο εἰς σάρκα μίαν. τὸ μυστήριον τοῦτο μέγα
and shall be the two for flesh one. mystery This great

**33** ἐστίν· ἐγὼ δὲ λέγω εἰς Χριστόν, καὶ εἰς τὴν ἐκκλησίαν. πλὴν
is, I but say as to Christ and as to the church. But

καὶ ὑμεῖς οἱ καθ' ἕνα, ἕκαστος τὴν ἑαυτοῦ γυναῖκα οὕτως
also you one by one, each the of himself wife so

ἀγαπάτω ὡς ἑαυτόν· ἡ δὲ γυνὴ ἵνα φοβῆται τὸν ἄνδρα.
let him love as himself, the and wife that she fears the husband.

**CHAPTER 6**

**1** Τὰ τέκνα, ὑπακούετε τοῖς γονεῦσιν ὑμῶν ἐν Κυρίῳ· τοῦτο
The children: obey the parents of you in (the) Lord, this

this is right. [2] Honor your father and mother, which is the first commandment with a promise, [3] that it may be well with you, and you may be long-lived on the earth. [4] And fathers do not provoke your children, but bring them up in (the) instruction and admonition of (the) Lord.

[5] Slaves, obey (your) lords according to flesh, with fear and trembling, in singleness of your heart, as to Christ; [6] not with eye-service as men-pleasers, but as slaves of Christ, doing the will of God from (the) soul, [7] serving as slaves with good will to the Lord, and not (as to) men; [8] each one knowing that whatever good thing he has done, this he shall receive from the Lord, whether a slave or a freeman. [9] And lords, do the same things toward them, forbearing threatening, knowing that the Lord of both of you is in Heaven, and there is no respect of persons with Him.

[10] For the rest, my brothers, be empowered in (the) Lord, and in the might of His strength. [11] Put on all the armor of God, for you to be able to stand against the wiles of (the) Devil; [12] because we are not wrestling against flesh and blood, but against principalities against authorities, against the rulers of this world, of the darkness of this age, against the spiritual (powers) of wickedness in the heavenlies. [13] Because of this, take up all of God's armor, that you may be able to resist in the evil day, and having worked out all, to stand. [14] Therefore stand firm, having girded your loins about with truth, and having put on the breastplate of righteousness, [15] and having shod the feet with (the) preparation of the gospel of peace; [16] above all, having taken up the shield of faith, with

2 γάρ ἐστι δίκαιον. Τιμα τὸν πατέρα σου καὶ τὴν μητέρα
for is right. Honor the father of you and the mother

3 (ἥτις ἐστὶν ἐντολὴ πρώτη ἐν ἐπαγγελίᾳ), ἵνα εὖ σοι
—which is commandment (the) first with a promise — that well with you

4 γένηται, καὶ ἔσῃ μακροχρόνιος ἐπὶ τῆς γῆς. καὶ οἱ πατέρες,
i may be, and you may be long-lived on the earth. And the fathers:

μὴ παροργίζετε τὰ τέκνα ὑμῶν, ἀλλ᾽ ἐκτρέφετε αὐτὰ ἐν
do not provoke the children of you, but nurture them in

παιδείᾳ καὶ νουθεσίᾳ Κυρίου.
(the) discipline and admonition of (the) Lord.

5 Οἱ δοῦλοι, ὑπακούετε τοῖς κυρίοις κατὰ σάρκα μετὰ φόβου
The slaves: obey the lords according to flesh with fear

καὶ τρόμου, ἐν ἁπλότητι τῆς καρδίας ὑμῶν, ὡς τῷ Χριστῷ·
and trembling, in singleness of the heart of you, as to Christ

6 μὴ κατ᾽ ὀφθαλμοδουλείαν ὡς ἀνθρωπάρεσκοι, ἀλλ᾽ ὡς δοῦλοι
not by way of eye-service as men-pleasers, but as slaves

7 τοῦ Χριστοῦ, ποιοῦντες τὸ θέλημα τοῦ Θεοῦ ἐκ ψυχῆς, μετ᾽
of Christ doing the will of God from (the) soul, with

εὐνοίας δουλεύοντες ὡς τῷ Κυρίῳ καὶ οὐκ ἀνθρώποις·
goodwill serving as slaves as to the Lord and not (as to) men,

8 εἰδότες ὅτι ὃ ἐάν τι ἕκαστος ποιήσῃ ἀγαθόν, τοῦτο κομιεῖται
knowing that whatever each one he does good thing, this he will get

9 παρὰ τοῦ Κυρίου, εἴτε δοῦλος, εἴτε ἐλεύθερος. καὶ οἱ κύριοι,
from the Lord, whether a slave, or a freeman. And the lords:

τὰ αὐτὰ ποιεῖτε πρὸς αὐτούς, ἀνιέντες τὴν ἀπειλήν· εἰδότες
The same things do toward them, forbearing the threatening, knowing

ὅτι καὶ ὑμῶν αὐτῶν ὁ Κύριός ἐστιν ἐν οὐρανοῖς, καὶ προσω-
that also of you of them the Lord is in Heaven, and respect

ποληψία οὐκ ἔστι παρ᾽ αὐτῷ.
of persons not is with Him.

10 Τὸ λοιπόν, ἀδελφοί μου, ἐνδυναμοῦσθε ἐν Κυρίῳ, καὶ ἐν
For the rest, brothers of me, be empowered in (the) Lord, and in

11 τῷ κράτει τῆς ἰσχύος αὐτοῦ. ἐνδύσασθε τὴν πανοπλίαν τοῦ
the might of the strength of Him. Put on the whole armor

Θεοῦ, πρὸς τὸ δύνασθαι ὑμᾶς στῆναι πρὸς τὰς μεθοδείας τοῦ
of God, for to be able you to stand against the wiles of the

12 διαβόλου. ὅτι οὐκ ἔστιν ἡμῖν ἡ πάλη πρὸς αἷμα καὶ σάρκα,
Devil. Because not is to us wrestling against blood and flesh,

ἀλλὰ πρὸς τὰς ἀρχάς, πρὸς τὰς ἐξουσίας, πρὸς τοὺς κο-
but against the rulers, against the authorities, against the

σμοκράτορας τοῦ σκότους τοῦ αἰῶνος τούτου, πρὸς τὰ
world's rulers of the darkness age of this, against the

13 πνευματικὰ τῆς πονηρίας ἐν τοῖς ἐπουρανίοις. διὰ τοῦτο
spiritual (powers) of evil in the heavenlies. Because of this

ἀναλάβετε τὴν πανοπλίαν τοῦ Θεοῦ, ἵνα δυνηθῆτε ἀντιστῆ-
take up the whole armor of God, that you be able to resist

ναι ἐν τῇ ἡμέρᾳ τῇ πονηρᾷ, καὶ ἅπαντα κατεργασάμενοι
in the day evil, and all things having worked out

14 στῆναι. στῆτε οὖν περιζωσάμενοι τὴν ὀσφὺν ὑμῶν ἐν
to stand. Stand, therefore, having girded about the loins of you with

15 ἀληθείᾳ, καὶ ἐνδυσάμενοι τὸν θώρακα τῆς δικαιοσύνης, καὶ
truth, and putting on the breastplace of righteousness, and

ὑποδησάμενοι τοὺς πόδας ἐν ἑτοιμασίᾳ τοῦ εὐαγγελίου τῆς
having shod the feet with (the) preparation of the gospel

16 εἰρήνης· ἐπὶ πᾶσιν ἀναλαβόντες τὸν θυρεὸν τῆς πίστεως,
of peace; above all, having taken up the shield of faith,

ἐν ᾧ δυνήσεσθε πάντα τὰ βέλη τοῦ πονηροῦ τὰ πεπυρωμένα
by which you will be able all the darts of the evil one having been made fiery

17 σβέσαι. καὶ τὴν περικεφαλαίαν τοῦ σωτηρίου δέξασθε, καὶ
to quench. And the helmet of salvation take, and

18 τὴν μάχαιραν τοῦ Πνεύματος, ὅ ἐστι ῥῆμά Θεοῦ· διὰ πάσης
the sword of the Spirit, which is (the) word of God via all

προσευχῆς καὶ δεήσεως προσευχόμενοι ἐν παντὶ καιρῷ ἐν
prayer and petition, praying at every time in

Πνεύματι, καὶ εἰς αὐτὸ τοῦτο ἀγρυπνοῦντες ἐν πάσῃ
(the) Spirit, and to same thing this watching in all

19 προσκαρτερήσει καὶ δεήσει περὶ πάντων τῶν ἁγίων, καὶ
perseverance and petition concerning all the saints, and

ὑπὲρ ἐμοῦ, ἵνα μοι δοθείη λόγος ἐν ἀνοίξει τοῦ στόματός
for me, that to me may be given speech in opening of the mouth

μου ἐν παρρησίᾳ, γνωρίσαι τὸ μυστήριον τοῦ εὐαγγελίου,
of me in boldness, to make known the mystery of the gospel,

20 ὑπὲρ οὗ πρεσβεύω ἐν ἁλύσει, ἵνα ἐν αὐτῷ παρρησιάσωμαι,
for which I am an ambassador in a chain, that in it I may speak boldly

ὡς δεῖ με λαλῆσαι.
as it behoves me to speak.

21 Ἵνα δὲ εἰδῆτε καὶ ὑμεῖς τὰ κατ' ἐμέ, τί πράσσω, πάντα
that Now may know also you the things about me, what I am doing, all things

ὑμῖν γνωρίσει Τυχικὸς ὁ ἀγαπητὸς ἀδελφὸς καὶ πιστὸς
to you will make known Tychicus the beloved brother and faithful

22 διάκονος ἐν Κυρίῳ· ὃν ἔπεμψα πρὸς ὑμᾶς εἰς αὐτὸ τοῦτο,
minister in (the) Lord whom I sent to you for this same thing,

ἵνα γνῶτε τὰ περὶ ἡμῶν, καὶ παρακαλέσῃ τὰς καρδίας
that you may know the things about us, and may comfort the hearts

ὑμῶν.
of you.

23 Εἰρήνη τοῖς ἀδελφοῖς καὶ ἀγάπη μετὰ πίστεως ἀπὸ Θεοῦ
Peace to the brothers and love with faith from God

24 πατρὸς καὶ Κυρίου Ἰησοῦ Χριστοῦ. ἡ χάρις μετὰ πάντων
(the) Father and (the) Lord Jesus Christ. Grace (be) with all

τῶν ἀγαπώντων τὸν Κύριον ἡμῶν Ἰησοῦν Χριστὸν ἐν
those loving the Lord of us, Jesus Christ in

ἀφθαρσίᾳ.
incorruptibility.

---

which you will be able to quench all the burning darts ot the wicked one. [17] Also take the helmet of salvation, and the sword of the Spirit, which is God's word; [18] through all prayer and supplication praying in every season in (the) Spirit, and watching to this very thing with all perseverance and supplication concerning all saints; [19] and for me, that to me may be given utterance in (the) opening of my mouth with boldness to make known the mystery of the gospel, [20] for which I am an ambassador in a chain, that in it I may speak boldly as I ought to speak.

[21] But that you may know also the things concerning me, what I am doing, Tychicus the beloved brother and fellowservant, will make known all things to you, [22] whom I sent to you for this very thing, that you might know the things concerning us, and (he) might comfort your hearts.

[23] Peace to the brothers, and love with faith from God (the) Father and (the) Lord Jesus Christ. [24] Grace (be) with all those that love our Lord Jesus Christ in incorruptibility. Amen.

# ΠΑΥΛΟΥ ΤΟΥ ΑΠΟΣΤΟΛΟΥ
PAUL     THE     APOSTLE

## Η ΠΡΟΣ
THE TO (THE)

# ΦΙΛΙΠΠΗΣΙΟΥΣ ΕΠΙΣΤΟΛΗ
PHILIPPIANS     EPISTLE

**KING JAMES II VERSION**

## THE APOSTLE PAUL'S
## EPISTLE TO
## THE PHILIPPIANS
### CHAPTER 1

[1] Paul and Timothy, servants of Jesus Christ, to all the saints in Christ Jesus who are in Philippi, with the overseers and deacons: [2] grace to you and peace from God our Father and (the) Lord Jesus Christ.

[3] I thank my God on all the remembrance of you, [4] always in my every prayer for all of you, I make supplication with joy [5] for your fellowship in the gospel, from the first day until now, [6] being persuaded of this very thing, that He who began a good work in you will finish (it) until (the) day of Jesus Christ; [7] as it is righteous for me to think this as to you all, because you have me in your heart, both in my bonds and in the defense and confirmation of the gospel, you are all sharers of my grace. [8] For God is my witness how I long after you all in the tender affection of Jesus Christ. [9] And I pray that your love may yet abound more and more in full knowledge and all perception, [10] for you (to) approve the things that differ, that you may be pure and without blame for (the) day of Christ, [11] being filled with fruits of righteousness which (are) by Jesus Christ, to the glory and praise of God.

[12] But I want you to know, brothers, that the things concerning me have turned out to (the) advancement of the gospel, [13] so that inside the praetorium, and to all the

### CHAPTER 1

1 Παῦλος καὶ Τιμόθεος, δοῦλοι Ἰησοῦ Χριστοῦ, πᾶσι τοῖς
Paul and Timothy, slaves of Jesus Christ, to all the

ἁγίοις ἐν Χριστῷ Ἰησοῦ τοῖς οὖσιν ἐν Φιλίπποις, σὺν ἐπι-
saints in Christ Jesus being in Philippi with

2 σκόποις καὶ διακόνοις· χάρις ὑμῖν καὶ εἰρήνη ἀπὸ Θεοῦ
overseers and ministers: Grace to you and peace from God

πατρὸς ἡμῶν καὶ Κυρίου Ἰησοῦ Χριστοῦ.
(the) Father of us and (the) Lord Jesus Christ.

3 Εὐχαριστῶ τῷ Θεῷ μου ἐπὶ πάσῃ τῇ μνείᾳ ὑμῶν, πάντοτε
4 I thank the God of me at all the remembrance of you, always

ἐν πάσῃ δεήσει μου ὑπὲρ πάντων ὑμῶν μετὰ χαρᾶς τὴν
in every petition of me on behalf of all you with joy the

5 δέησιν ποιούμενος, ἐπὶ τῇ κοινωνίᾳ ὑμῶν εἰς τὸ εὐαγγέλιον,
petition making, over the fellowship of you in the gospel

6 ἀπὸ πρώτης ἡμέρας ἄχρι τοῦ νῦν· πεποιθὼς αὐτὸ τοῦτο,
from (the) first day until now, being persuaded very this thing,

ὅτι ὁ ἐναρξάμενος ἐν ὑμῖν ἔργον ἀγαθὸν ἐπιτελέσει ἄχρις
that the (One) having begun in you a work good will finish (it) until

7 ἡμέρας Ἰησοῦ Χριστοῦ· καθώς ἐστι δίκαιον ἐμοὶ τοῦτο
(the) day of Jesus Christ, as it is righteous for me this

φρονεῖν ὑπὲρ πάντων ὑμῶν, διὰ τὸ ἔχειν με ἐν τῇ καρδίᾳ
to think of all you, because of having me in the heart

ὑμᾶς, ἔν τε τοῖς δεσμοῖς μου καὶ τῇ ἀπολογίᾳ καὶ βεβαιώσει
you, in both the bonds of me and in the defense and confirmation

τοῦ εὐαγγελίου, συγκοινωνούς μου τῆς χάριτος πάντας
of the gospel, sharers with me of the grace all

8 ὑμᾶς ὄντας. μάρτυς γάρ μού ἐστιν ὁ Θεός, ὡς ἐπιποθῶ
you being. witness For of me is God, how I long after

9 πάντας ὑμᾶς ἐν σπλάγχνοις Ἰησοῦ Χριστοῦ. καὶ τοῦτο
all you in (the) bowels of Jesus Christ. And this

προσεύχομαι, ἵνα ἡ ἀγάπη ὑμῶν ἔτι μᾶλλον καὶ μᾶλλον
I pray, that the love of you yet more and more

10 περισσεύῃ ἐν ἐπιγνώσει καὶ πάσῃ αἰσθήσει, εἰς τὸ δοκιμάζειν
may abound in full knowledge and all perception, for the approving

ὑμᾶς τὰ διαφέροντα, ἵνα ἦτε εἰλικρινεῖς καὶ ἀπρόσκοποι εἰς
of you the things differing, that you be sincere and without blame for

11 ἡμέραν Χριστοῦ, πεπληρωμένοι καρπῶν δικαιοσύνης τῶν
(the) day of Christ, having been filled (with) fruits of righteousness

διὰ Ἰησοῦ Χριστοῦ, εἰς δόξαν καὶ ἔπαινον Θεοῦ.
through Jesus Christ, to (the) glory and praise of God.

12 Γινώσκειν δὲ ὑμᾶς βούλομαι, ἀδελφοί, ὅτι τὰ κατ᾽ ἐμὲ
to know And you I want, brothers, that the things about me

13 μᾶλλον εἰς προκοπὴν τοῦ εὐαγγελίου ἐλήλυθεν· ὥστε τοὺς
rather to (the) advance of the gospel has come, so as the

rest, my bonds have become known to be in Christ; [14] and the most of the brothers trusting in (the) Lord by my bonds more abundantly dare to fearlessly speak the word. [15] Some, indeed, are preaching Christ even from envy and strife, but some also from good will. [16] Those, indeed, out of contention are preaching Christ, not sincerely, thinking to add troubles to my bonds. [17] But these out of love, knowing that I am set for defense of the gospel. [18] What then? Nevertheless, in every way, whether in pretense or in truth, Christ is preached; and I rejoice in this; yes, I will also rejoice; [19] for I know that this shall turn out for me to salvation through your supplication, and (the) supply of the Spirit of Jesus Christ; [20] according to my earnest expectation and hope, that in nothing I shall be ashamed, but in all boldness, as always, so now Christ shall be magnified in my body, whether by life or by death. [21] For to me to live (is) Christ, and to die is gain; [22] but if I live in flesh, this (is) fruit of my labor; and what I shall choose, I do not know. [23] For I am pressed down by the two, having a desire to depart and to be with Christ (which is) much better; [24] but to remain in the flesh (is) more necessary for your sake; [25] and being persuaded of this, I know that I shall remain and continue with you all; for your advancement and joy of faith; [26] that your rejoicing may abound in Christ Jesus in me, through my being again with you. [27] Only keep yourselves acting worthily of the gospel of Christ, that whether I having come and having seen you, or being absent, might hear the things concerning you, that you stand fast in one spirit, with one soul striving together with the faith of the gospel; [28] and not being

δεσμούς μου φανερούς ἐν Χριστῷ γενέσθαι ἐν ὅλῳ τῷ πραι-
bonds of me clearly revealed in Christ become in all the prae-

14 τωρίῳ καὶ τοῖς λοιποῖς πᾶσι, καὶ τοὺς πλείονας τῶν ἀδελφῶν
torium, and to the rest all, and the most of the brothers

ἐν Κυρίῳ, πεποιθότας τοῖς δεσμοῖς μου, περισσοτέρως
in (the) Lord being confident in the bonds of me, more exceedingly

15 τολμᾶν ἀφόβως τὸν λόγον λαλεῖν. τινὲς μὲν καὶ διὰ φθόνον
to dare fearlessly the word to speak. Some indeed even for envy

καὶ ἔριν, τινὲς δὲ καὶ δι’ εὐδοκίαν τὸν Χριστὸν κηρύσσουσιν·
and strife, some but also for goodwill Christ proclaim;

16 οἱ μὲν ἐξ ἐριθείας τὸν Χριστὸν καταγγέλλουσιν, οὐχ ἁγνῶς,
These indeed of rivalry Christ announce, not sincerely,

17 οἰόμενοι θλῖψιν ἐπιφέρειν τοῖς δεσμοῖς μου· οἱ δὲ ἐξ ἀγάπης,
thinking trouble to add to the bonds of me. these But out of love,

18 εἰδότες ὅτι εἰς ἀπολογίαν τοῦ εὐαγγελίου κεῖμαι. τί γάρ;
knowing that for defense of the gospel I am set. what For?

πλὴν παντὶ τρόπῳ, εἴτε προφάσει εἴτε ἀληθείᾳ, Χριστὸς
Yet in every way, whether in pretence or in truth, Christ

καταγγέλλεται· καὶ ἐν τούτῳ χαίρω, ἀλλὰ καὶ χαρήσομαι.
is announced, and in this I rejoice; yet also I will rejoice.

19 οἶδα γὰρ ὅτι τοῦτό μοι ἀποβήσεται εἰς σωτηρίαν διὰ τῆς
I know For that this to me will result in salvation through the

ὑμῶν δεήσεως, καὶ ἐπιχορηγίας τοῦ Πνεύματος Ἰησοῦ
of you petition, and supply of the Spirit of Jesus

20 Χριστοῦ, κατὰ τὴν ἀποκαραδοκίαν καὶ ἐλπίδα μου, ὅτι ἐν
Christ, according to the earnest expectation and hope of me, that in

οὐδενὶ αἰσχυνθήσομαι, ἀλλ’ ἐν πάσῃ παρρησίᾳ, ὡς πάν-
nothing I shall be ashamed, but in all boldness, as always,

τοτε, καὶ νῦν μεγαλυνθήσεται Χριστὸς ἐν τῷ σώματί μου,
and now will be magnified Christ in the body of me,

21 εἴτε διὰ ζωῆς εἴτε διὰ θανάτου. ἐμοὶ γὰρ τὸ ζῆν, Χριστός·
whether via life or via death. to me For to live (is) Christ,

22 καὶ τὸ ἀποθανεῖν, κέρδος. εἰ δὲ τὸ ζῆν ἐν σαρκί, τοῦτό μοι
and to die is gain. if But to live in (the) flesh, this to me

23 καρπὸς ἔργου· καὶ τί αἱρήσομαι οὐ γνωρίζω. συνέχομαι
(is) fruit of (my) work, and what I shall choose not I perceive. I am constrained

γὰρ ἐκ τῶν δύο, τὴν ἐπιθυμίαν ἔχων εἰς τὸ ἀναλῦσαι καὶ σὺν
For by the two, the desire having to depart and with

24 Χριστῷ εἶναι, πολλῷ μᾶλλον κρεῖσσον· τὸ δὲ ἐπιμένειν ἐν
Christ be, much rather better; but to remain in

25 τῇ σαρκὶ ἀναγκαιότερον δι’ ὑμᾶς. καὶ τοῦτο πεποιθὼς
the flesh (is) more necessary on account of you. And this being assured

οἶδα ὅτι μενῶ, καὶ συμπαραμενῶ πᾶσιν ὑμῖν εἰς τὴν ὑμῶν
I know that I will remain, and will continue with all you for the of you

26 προκοπὴν καὶ χαρὰν τῆς πίστεως, ἵνα τὸ καύχημα ὑμῶν
advancement and joy of the faith, that the boast of you

περισσεύῃ ἐν Χριστῷ Ἰησοῦ ἐν ἐμοί, διὰ τῆς ἐμῆς παρου-
may abound in Christ Jesus in me, through my presence

27 σίας πάλιν πρὸς ὑμᾶς. μόνον ἀξίως τοῦ εὐαγγελίου τοῦ
again with you. Only worthily of the gospel

Χριστοῦ πολιτεύεσθε, ἵνα εἴτε ἐλθὼν καὶ ἰδὼν ὑμᾶς, εἴτε
of Christ conduct yourself, that whether coming and seeing you, or

ἀπών, ἀκούσω τὰ περὶ ὑμῶν, ὅτι στήκετε ἐν ἑνὶ πνεύματι,
being absent, I hear the things about you, that you stand in one spirit,

28 μιᾷ ψυχῇ συναθλοῦντες τῇ πίστει τοῦ εὐαγγελίου, καὶ μὴ
with one soul striving together in the faith of the gospel, and not

frightened in anything by those who oppose; which to them truly is a proof of destruction, but to you of salvation, and this from God; [29] because to you it was granted concerning Christ, not only to believe on Him, but also to suffer on His behalf, [30] having the same struggle which you saw in me, and now hear to be in me.

CHAPTER 2

[1] If then (there is) any consolation in Christ, if any comfort of love, if any fellowship of (the) Spirit, if any tenderness and mercies, [2] fulfill my joy, that you may be of the same mind, having the same love, one in soul, and minding the one thing, [3] (doing) nothing according to contention or self-glory, but in humility esteeming one another above themselves. [4] Let not each consider his own things, but each one the things of others, too. [5] For let this mind be in you which (was) also in Christ Jesus; [6] who, being in the form of God, thought it not robbery to be equal with God; [7] but emptied Himself, having taken the form of a slave, having been made in (the) likeness of men; [8] and having been found in fashion as a man, He humbled Himself, having become obedient to death, even (the) death of (the) cross. [9] For this reason God also highly exalted Him and gave Him a name which (is) above every name, [10] that at the name of Jesus every knee should bow, of (those) in Heaven, and on earth, and under the earth; [11] and every tongue should confess that Jesus Christ (is) Lord, to the glory of God (the) Father. [12] So that, my beloved, even as you always obeyed, not in my presence only, but now much rather in my absence, work out your own salvation with fear and trembling, [13] for it is God who works in you

πτυρόμενοι ἐν μηδενὶ ὑπὸ τῶν ἀντικειμένων· ἥτις αὐτοῖς
being terrified in nothing by those opposing, which to them

μέν ἐστιν ἔνδειξις ἀπωλείας, ὑμῖν δὲ σωτηρίας, καὶ τοῦτο
indeed is a proof of destruction, to you but of salvation, and this

29 ἀπὸ Θεοῦ· ὅτι ὑμῖν ἐχαρίσθη τὸ ὑπὲρ Χριστοῦ, οὐ μόνον τὸ
from God, because to you it was granted for Christ, not only

30 εἰς αὐτὸν πιστεύειν, ἀλλὰ καὶ τὸ ὑπὲρ αὐτοῦ πάσχειν· τὸν
in Him to believe, but also on behalf of Him to suffer, the

αὐτὸν ἀγῶνα ἔχοντες οἷον εἴδετε ἐν ἐμοί, καὶ νῦν ἀκούετε ἐν
same struggle having which you saw in me, and now hear in

ἐμοί.
me.

CHAPTER 2

1 Εἴ τις οὖν παράκλησις ἐν Χριστῷ, εἴ τι παραμύθιον
if (is) any Then comfort in Christ, if any consolation

ἀγάπης, εἴ τις κοινωνία Πνεύματος, εἴ τινα σπλάγχνα καὶ
of love, if any fellowship of spirit, if any compassions and

2 οἰκτιρμοί, πληρώσατέ μου τὴν χαράν, ἵνα τὸ αὐτὸ φρονῆτε,
pities, fulfill of me the joy, that the same you think,

τὴν αὐτὴν ἀγάπην ἔχοντες, σύμψυχοι, τὸ ἓν φρονοῦντες·
the same love having, one in soul, the one thing minding,

3 μηδὲν κατὰ ἐρίθειαν ἢ κενοδοξίαν, ἀλλὰ τῇ ταπεινοφροσύνῃ
nothing according to rivalry or self-glory, but in humility

4 ἀλλήλους ἡγούμενοι ὑπερέχοντας ἑαυτῶν· μὴ τὰ ἑαυτῶν
one another esteeming surpassing themselves; not their own things

5 ἕκαστος σκοπεῖτε, ἀλλὰ καὶ τὰ ἑτέρων ἕκαστος. τοῦτο γὰρ
each looking at, but also other's things each. this For

6 φρονείσθω ἐν ὑμῖν ὃ καὶ ἐν Χριστῷ Ἰησοῦ· ὃς ἐν μορφῇ Θεοῦ
think among you, which also (was) in Christ Jesus, who in (the) form of God

7 ὑπάρχων, οὐχ ἁρπαγμὸν ἡγήσατο τὸ εἶναι ἴσα Θεῷ, ἀλλ'
subsisting, not robbery thought (it) to be equal with God, but

ἑαυτὸν ἐκένωσε, μορφὴν δούλου λαβών, ἐν ὁμοιώματι ἀνθρώ-
Himself emptied, (the) form of a slave taking, in likeness of men

8 πων γενόμενος· καὶ σχήματι εὑρεθεὶς ὡς ἄνθρωπος, ἐταπείνω-
becoming; and in fashion being found as a man, He humbled

σεν ἑαυτόν, γενόμενος ὑπήκοος μέχρι θανάτου, θανάτου δὲ
Himself, becoming obedient until death, (the) death even

9 σταυροῦ. διὸ καὶ ὁ Θεὸς αὐτὸν ὑπερύψωσε, καὶ ἐχαρίσατο
of a cross. Therefore also God Him highly exalted, and gave

10 αὐτῷ ὄνομα τὸ ὑπὲρ πᾶν ὄνομα· ἵνα ἐν τῷ ὀνόματι Ἰησοῦ
to Him a name above every name, that in the name of Jesus

πᾶν γόνυ κάμψῃ ἐπουρανίων καὶ ἐπιγείων καὶ καταχθονίων,
every knee should bow, of heavenly and of earthly and those under earth,

11 καὶ πᾶσα γλῶσσα ἐξομολογήσηται ὅτι Κύριος Ἰησοῦς
and every tongue should confess that Lord Jesus

Χριστός, εἰς δόξαν Θεοῦ πατρός.
Christ (is), to (the) glory of God (the) Father.

12 Ὥστε, ἀγαπητοί μου, καθὼς πάντοτε ὑπηκούσατε, μὴ ὡς
So as, beloved of me, as always you obeyed, not as

ἐν τῇ παρουσίᾳ μου μόνον, ἀλλὰ νῦν πολλῷ μᾶλλον ἐν τῇ
in the presence of me only, but now by more rather in the

ἀπουσίᾳ μου, μετὰ φόβου καὶ τρόμου τὴν ἑαυτῶν σωτηρίαν
absence of me, with fear and trembling the of yourselves salvation

13 κατεργάζεσθε· ὁ Θεὸς γάρ ἐστιν ὁ ἐνεργῶν ἐν ὑμῖν καὶ τὸ
work out; God for is the (One) working in you both

both to will and to work for (His) good pleasure. [14] Do all things without murmurings and disputings [15] that you may be blameless and harmless, children of God without spot in the midst of a crooked and perverted generation, among whom you shine as luminaries in (the) world. [16] holding up (the) word of life, to my glory(ing) in (the) day of Christ, that I did not run in vain, nor labored in vain. [17] But if I also am poured out on the sacrifice and service of your faith, I rejoice; and I rejoice together with you all; [18] and you also take joy (in) the same, and rejoice with me. [19] But I hope in (the) Lord Jesus to send Timothy to you soon, so that I may also be of good cheer knowing the things about you. [20] For I have no one likeminded who genuinely will care for the things concerning you. [21] For all seek their own things, not the things of Christ Jesus. [22] But you know the proof of him, that as a child to a father, he served with me for the gospel. [23] Therefore I hope to send him at once, whenever I shall see the things about me. [24] But I trust in (the) Lord that I also myself will come soon. [25] But I thought it necessary to send to you Epaphroditus, my brother and fellow-worker and fellow-soldier, and your messenger and minister of my need; [26] since he was longing after you all, and being troubled, because you heard that he was sick. [27] For indeed he was sick, coming near to death, but God had mercy on him, and not on him only, but also me, that I should not have grief on grief. [28] Therefore I sent him more eagerly, that seeing him again you may rejoice, and I less grieved may be. [29] Then receive him in (the) Lord with all joy, and hold such in honor; [30] that through the work of Christ he drew near to death, exposing (his) soul, that he may fill up your

**14** θέλειν καὶ τὸ ἐνεργεῖν ὑπὲρ τῆς εὐδοκίας. πάντα ποιεῖτε
to will    and       to work on behalf of (His) good pleasure. All things do

**15** χωρὶς γογγυσμῶν καὶ διαλογισμῶν, ἵνα γένησθε ἄμεμπτοι
without murmurings   and   disputings,      that you may be blameless
καὶ ἀκέραιοι, τέκνα Θεοῦ ἀμώμητα ἐν μέσῳ γενεᾶς σκολιᾶς
and harmless,   children of God faultless     amidst a generation crooked
καὶ διεστραμμένης, ἐν οἷς φαίνεσθε ὡς φωστῆρες ἐν κόσμῳ,
and having been perverted, among whom you shine as luminaries in (the) world,

**16** λόγον ζωῆς ἐπέχοντες, εἰς καύχημα ἐμοὶ εἰς ἡμέραν Χριστοῦ,
a word of life holding up, for a boast   to me in (the) day of Christ,

**17** ὅτι οὐκ εἰς κενὸν ἔδραμον, οὐδὲ εἰς κενὸν ἐκοπίασα. ἀλλ' εἰ
that not in vain I ran,     nor in vain labored.     But if
καὶ σπένδομαι ἐπὶ τῇ θυσίᾳ καὶ λειτουργίᾳ τῆς πίστεως
indeed I am poured out on the sacrifice and service    of the   faith

**18** ὑμῶν, χαίρω καὶ συγχαίρω πᾶσιν ὑμῖν· τὸ δ' αὐτὸ καὶ ὑμεῖς
of you, I rejoice, and I rejoice with all    you; the and same also you
χαίρετε καὶ συγχαίρετέ μοι.
rejoice, and rejoice with   me.

**19** Ἐλπίζω δὲ ἐν Κυρίῳ Ἰησοῦ, Τιμόθεον ταχέως πέμψαι
I hope   But in (the) Lord Jesus   Timothy   shortly    to send

**20** ὑμῖν, ἵνα κἀγὼ εὐψυχῶ, γνοὺς τὰ περὶ ὑμῶν. οὐδένα γὰρ ἔχω
to you, that I also may be of good cheer, knowing the things about you. no one For I have

**21** ἰσόψυχον, ὅστις γνησίως τὰ περὶ ὑμῶν μεριμνήσει. οἱ πάντες
likeminded, who   genuinely the things about you will care for    all

**22** γὰρ τὰ ἑαυτῶν ζητοῦσιν, οὐ τὰ τοῦ Χριστοῦ Ἰησοῦ. τὴν δὲ
For the things of themselves seek, not the things of Christ   Jesus.   the But
δοκιμὴν αὐτοῦ γινώσκετε, ὅτι ὡς πατρὶ τέκνον, σὺν ἐμοὶ
proof   of him   you know,   that as to a father a child,   with me

**23** ἐδούλευσεν εἰς τὸ εὐαγγέλιον. τοῦτον μὲν οὖν ἐλπίζω πέμψαι,
he served   for the   gospel.     This one, therefore, I hope to send,

**24** ὡς ἂν ἀπίδω τὰ περὶ ἐμέ, ἐξαυτῆς· πέποιθα δὲ ἐν Κυρίῳ, ὅτι
whenever I shall see the things about me at once;   I trust but in (the) Lord that

**25** καὶ αὐτὸς ταχέως ἐλεύσομαι. ἀναγκαῖον δὲ ἡγησάμην
also myself shortly I will come.   necessary   But I thought (it)
Ἐπαφρόδιτον τὸν ἀδελφὸν καὶ συνεργὸν καὶ συστρατιώτην
Epaphroditus     the brother   and fellow-worker and fellow-soldier
μου, ὑμῶν δὲ ἀπόστολον, καὶ λειτουργὸν τῆς χρείας μου,
of me, of you and, apostle     and minister    of the need of me,

**26** πέμψαι πρὸς ὑμᾶς· ἐπειδὴ ἐπιποθῶν ἦν πάντας ὑμᾶς, καὶ
to send to    you    since   longing after he was all    you, and

**27** ἀδημονῶν, διότι ἠκούσατε ὅτι ἠσθένησε· καὶ γὰρ ἠσθένησε
being troubled, because you heard that he was sick. indeed For he was sick,
παραπλήσιον θανάτῳ· ἀλλ' ὁ Θεὸς αὐτὸν ἠλέησεν, οὐκ αὐτὸν
coming near   to death, but    God   him had mercy on, not on him

**28** δὲ μόνον, ἀλλὰ καὶ ἐμέ, ἵνα μὴ λύπην ἐπὶ λύπῃ σχῶ. σπου-
and only,   but also me, lest   grief    on grief I should have. More
δαιοτέρως οὖν ἔπεμψα αὐτόν, ἵνα, ἰδόντες αὐτὸν πάλιν,
eagerly,    therefore, I sent   him,    that seeing   him   again

**29** χαρῆτε, κἀγὼ ἀλυπότερος ὦ. προσδέχεσθε οὖν αὐτον ἐν
you may rejoice, and I less grieved may be. receive    Therefore him   in
Κυρίῳ μετὰ πάσης χαρᾶς, καὶ τοὺς τοιούτους ἐντίμους ἔχετε·
(the) Lord with all    joy,   and    such ones honored hold,

**30** ὅτι διὰ τὸ ἔργον τοῦ Χριστοῦ μέχρι θανάτου ἤγγισε,
that through the work      of Christ as far as   death   he drew near,
παραβουλευσάμενος τῇ ψυχῇ, ἵνα ἀναπληρώσῃ τὸ ὑμῶν
exposing       the soul, that he might fill up   the   of you

lack of service toward me.

CHAPTER 3

[1] For the rest, my brothers, rejoice in (the) Lord. To write the same things to you (is) not truly tiresome to me, but safe for you. [2] Look out for dogs; look out for evil workers; look out for the concision (party). [3] For we are the circumcision who serve God in spirit and rejoice in Christ Jesus, and do not trust in the flesh. [4] Though I, too, might have trust in flesh; if any other thinks to trust in flesh, I more: [5] in circumcision, (the) eighth day; of (the) race of Israel, (the) tribe of Benjamin; a Hebrew of the Hebrews; according to the Law, a Pharisee; [6] according to zeal, persecuting the church; according to righteousness in (the) Law, having become blameless. [7] But what things were gain to me, these I have counted loss because of Christ. [8] But, nay, rather I also count all things to be loss because of the excellency of the knowledge of Christ Jesus, my Lord, for whose sake I have suffered the loss of all things, and count (them) to be refuse, that I might gain Christ, [9] and be found in Him; not having my own righteousness, that of Law; but through (the) faith of Christ the righteousness of God (based) on faith, [10] to know Him and the power of His resurrection, and the fellowship of His sufferings, having been conformed to His death; [11] if somehow I may attain to the resurrection of the dead. [12] Not that I already have received, or already have been perfected, but I press on, if indeed I may lay hold, since I also was laid hold of by Christ Jesus. [13] Brothers, I do not count myself to have laid hold, but one thing (I do), forgetting the things behind, and reaching out to those things before, [14] I press on after a mark for the prize of the high calling of God in Christ Jesus. [15] Then as many as (are) perfect, let be of this

ὑστέρημα τῆς πρός με λειτουργίας.
lack    toward   me of service.

CHAPTER 3
CHAPTER 3

1 Τὸ λοιπόν, ἀδελφοί μου, χαίρετε ἐν Κυρίῳ. τὰ αὐτὰ
For the rest,   brothers of me,   rejoice   in (the) Lord. The same things

2 γράφειν ὑμῖν, ἐμοὶ μὲν οὐκ ὀκνηρόν, ὑμῖν δὲ ἀσφαλές. βλέπετε
to write to you for me indeed not is tiresome, for you but safe.   Look (to)

τοὺς κύνας, βλέπετε τοὺς κακοὺς ἐργάτας, βλέπετε τὴν
the   dogs,   Look (to) the evil   workers,   look (to) the

3 κατατομήν· ἡμεῖς γάρ ἐσμεν ἡ περιτομή, οἱ πνεύματι Θεῷ
concision.   we For are the circumcision, those by Spirit of God

λατρεύοντες, καὶ καυχώμενοι ἐν Χριστῷ Ἰησοῦ, καὶ οὐκ ἐν
worshiping,   and boasting   in Christ   Jesus, and not in

4 σαρκὶ πεποιθότες· καίπερ ἐγὼ ἔχων πεποίθησιν καὶ ἐν σαρκί·
(the) flesh trusting; even though I having   trust   also in (the) flesh

5 εἴ τις δοκεῖ ἄλλος πεποιθέναι ἐν σαρκί, ἐγὼ μᾶλλον· περιτομὴ
—if any thinks other to trust in (the) flesh, I   more: in circumcision

ὀκταήμερος, ἐκ γένους Ἰσραήλ, φυλῆς Βενιαμίν, Ἑβραῖος ἐξ
(the) eighth day; of (the) race of Israel; (the) tribe of Benjamin; a Hebrew of

6 Ἑβραίων, κατὰ νόμον Φαρισαῖος, κατα ζῆλον διώκων τὴν
Hebrews; according to law, a Pharisee; according to zeal, persecuting the

ἐκκλησίαν, κατὰ δικαιοσύνην τὴν ἐν νόμῳ γενόμενος ἄμεμ-
church; according to righteousness   in (the) law,   being   blame-

7 πτος. ἀλλ' ἅτινα ἦν μοι κέρδη, ταῦτα ἥγημαι διὰ τὸν Χριστὸν
less. But what things were to me gain, these I have counted because of Christ

8 ζημίαν. ἀλλὰ μενοῦνγε καὶ ἡγοῦμαι πάντα ζημίαν εἶναι διὰ
loss.   But nay, rather also I count   all things   loss to be because of

τὸ ὑπερέχον τῆς γνώσεως Χριστοῦ Ἰησοῦ τοῦ Κυρίου μου·
the excellency of the knowledge of Christ   Jesus the Lord of me,

δι' ὃν τὰ πάντα ἐζημιώθην, καὶ ἡγοῦμαι σκύβαλα εἶναι, ἵνα
for whose sake all things I suffered loss, and count   refuse   to be, that

9 Χριστὸν κερδήσω, καὶ εὑρεθῶ ἐν αὐτῷ, μὴ ἔχων ἐμὴν δικαιο-
Christ   I might gain, and be found in Him, not having my right-

σύνην τὴν ἐκ νόμου, ἀλλὰ τὴν διὰ πίστεως Χριστοῦ, τὴν ἐκ
eousness   of law.   But   through   faith   of Christ, the of

10 Θεοῦ δικαιοσύνην ἐπὶ τῇ πίστει· τοῦ γνῶναι αὐτόν, καὶ
God righteousness (based) on faith,   to know   Him   and

τὴν δύναμιν τῆς ἀναστάσεως αὐτοῦ, καὶ τὴν κοινωνίαν τῶν
the power of the resurrection of Him, and the fellowship of the

11 παθημάτων αὐτοῦ, συμμορφούμενος τῷ θανάτῳ αὐτοῦ, εἴ
sufferings of Him, being conformed to the death of Him; if

12 πως καταντήσω εἰς τὴν ἐξανάστασιν τῶν νεκρῶν. οὐχ ὅτι
somehow I may attain to the resurrection out of the dead. Not that

ἤδη ἔλαβον, ἢ ἤδη τετελείωμαι· διώκω δέ, εἰ καὶ καταλάβω
already I received, or already perfected. I follow but. if also I may lay hold,

13 ἐφ' ᾧ καὶ κατελήφθην ὑπὸ τοῦ Χριστοῦ Ἰησοῦ. ἀδελφοί,
inasmuch as also I was laid hold of bv   Christ   Jesus. Brothers,

ἐγὼ ἐμαυτὸν οὐ λογίζομαι κατειληφέναι· ἐν δέ, τὰ μὲν ὀπίσω
I   myself not reckon to have laid hold, one but, the things behind

14 ἐπιλανθανόμενος, τοῖς δὲ ἔμπροσθεν ἐπεκτεινόμενος, κατὰ
forgetting,   the things and   before   stretching forward to, after

σκοπὸν διώκω ἐπὶ τὸ βραβεῖον τῆς ἄνω κλήσεως τοῦ Θεοῦ
a mark I pursue, for the prize of the high calling   of God

15 ἐν Χριστῷ Ἰησοῦ. ὅσοι οὖν τέλειοι, τοῦτο φρονῶμεν· καὶ εἴ
in Christ   Jesus. as many as Then (are) perfect, this let us think; and if

mind; and if you think anything differently, God will also reveal this to you. [16] But as to that we have attained, let us walk by the same rule, to be of the same mind. [17] Be imitators of me, brothers, and consider those walking this way, for you have us (for) a pattern; [18] for many are walking — of whom I often told you, and now even weeping I tell (you) — (as) the enemies of the cross of Christ; [19] whose end (is) destruction, whose god (is) the belly, and glory in their shame, who mind earthly things. [20] For our citizenship is in Heaven, from which we also are looking for (the) Lord Jesus Christ (as) Savior, [21] who will transform our body of humiliation, for it to be conformed to His body of glory, according to the working of His mighty power, even to put all things under Himself.

CHAPTER 4

[1] So that, my brothers, ones loved and longed for, my crown and joy, stand firm in this way in (the) Lord, dearly beloved. [2] I call on Euodia and Syntyche to be of the same mind in (the) Lord. [3] And I also ask you, true yoke-fellow, help these who labored together with me in the gospel; also with Clement, and the rest of my fellow-workers, whose names (are) in (the) Book of Life.

[4] Rejoice in (the) Lord always; Again I say, Rejoice! [5] Let your moderation be known to all men. The Lord (is) near. [6] Do not be anxious about anything, but in everything, by prayer and by supplication, with thanksgiving, let your desires be known to God; [7] and the peace of God which passes all understanding shall keep your hearts and minds in Christ Jesus. [8] Finally, brothers, whatever (things) are true, whatever

**16** τι ἑτέρως φρονεῖτε, καὶ τοῦτο ὁ Θεὸς ὑμῖν ἀποκαλύψει· πλὴν
anything other you think, even this    God to you will reveal.    Yet
εἰς ὃ ἐφθάσαμεν, τῷ αὐτῷ στοιχεῖν κανόνι, τὸ αὐτὸ φρονεῖν.
to what we arrived, by the same   to walk rule,   of the same mind.

**17** Συμμιμηταί μου γίνεσθε, ἀδελφοί, καὶ σκοπεῖτε τοὺς οὕτω
fellow-imitators of me Be,   brothers, and mark   those   thus

**18** περιπατοῦντας, καθὼς ἔχετε τύπον ἡμᾶς. πολλοὶ γὰρ περι-
walking,    as you have an example us. many For   walking,
πατοῦσιν, οὓς πολλάκις ἔλεγον ὑμῖν, νῦν δὲ καὶ κλαίων λέγω —
walk   —of whom often I told   you, now and also weeping I say —

**19** τοὺς ἐχθροὺς τοῦ σταυροῦ τοῦ Χριστοῦ· ὧν τὸ τέλος ἀπώ-
(as) the enemies of the cross    of Christ, of whom the end (is) destruc-
λεια, ὧν ὁ θεὸς ἡ κοιλία, καὶ ἡ δόξα ἐν τῇ αἰσχύνῃ αὐτῶν, οἱ
tion, of whom the god the belly (is) and the glory in the shame   of them, those

**20** τὰ ἐπίγεια φρονοῦντες. ἡμῶν γὰρ τὸ πολίτευμα ἐν οὐρανοῖς
the earthly things thinking. of us For the citizenship in Heaven
ὑπάρχει, ἐξ οὗ καὶ Σωτῆρα ἀπεκδεχόμεθα, Κύριον Ἰησοῦν
is,   from where also a Savior we wait for, (the) Lord Jesus

**21** Χριστόν· ὃς μετασχηματίσει τὸ σῶμα τῆς ταπεινώσεως
Christ, who will change    the body of the humiliation
ἡμῶν, εἰς τὸ γενέσθαι αὐτὸ σύμμορφον τῷ σώματι τῆς δόξης
of us for   to be   it conformed   to the body of the glory
αὐτοῦ, κατὰ τὴν ἐνέργειαν τοῦ δύνασθαι αὐτὸν καὶ ὑποτάξαι
of Him, according to the working of the ability (of) Him, even to subject
ἑαυτῷ τὰ πάντα.
to Himself all things.

CHAPTER 4

**1** Ὥστε, ἀδελφοί μου ἀγαπητοὶ καὶ ἐπιπόθητοι, χαρὰ καὶ
So as, brothers of me, beloved   and longed for,   joy and
στέφανός μου, οὕτω στήκετε ἐν Κυρίῳ, ἀγαπητοί.
crown of me, so   stand in (the) Lord, beloved.

**2** Εὐοδίαν παρακαλῶ, καὶ Συντύχην παρακαλῶ, τὸ αὐτὸ
Euodia I beseech,   and Syntyche   I beseech, the same thing

**3** φρονεῖν ἐν Κυρίῳ. καὶ ἐρωτῶ καί σε, σύζυγε γνήσιε, συλλαμ-
to think in (the) Lord. And I ask also you, yoke-fellow true, help
βάνου αὐταῖς, αἵτινες ἐν τῷ εὐαγγελίῳ συνήθλησάν μοι,
them,   who   in the gospel   struggled   with me,
μετὰ καὶ Κλήμεντος, καὶ τῶν λοιπῶν συνεργῶν μου, ὧν τὰ
with and Clement,   and the rest, fellow-workers with me of the whom
ὀνόματα ἐν βίβλῳ ζωῆς.
names (are) in (the) Scroll of Life.

**4** Χαίρετε ἐν Κυρίῳ πάντοτε· πάλιν ἐρῶ, χαίρετε. τὸ ἐπιεικὲς
**5** Rejoice in (the) Lord always;   again I will say, Rejoice. The mildness
**6** ὑμῶν γνωσθήτω πᾶσιν ἀνθρώποις. ὁ Κύριος ἐγγύς. μηδὲν
of you let it be known to all   men.    The Lord (is) near.   Nothing
μεριμνᾶτε, ἀλλ᾽ ἐν παντὶ τῇ προσευχῇ καὶ τῇ δεήσει μετὰ
be anxious about, but in everything, by prayer   and by petition with
εὐχαριστίας τὰ αἰτήματα ὑμῶν γνωριζέσθω πρὸς τὸν Θεόν.
thanksgivings, the requests of you let be made known to    God.
καὶ ἡ εἰρήνη τοῦ Θεοῦ, ἡ ὑπερέχουσα πάντα νοῦν, φρουρήσει
And the peace of God which surpasses   all understanding will keep
τὰς καρδίας ὑμῶν καὶ τὰ νοήματα ὑμῶν ἐν Χριστῷ Ἰησοῦ.
the hearts of you and the minds of you in Christ   Jesus.

**8** Τὸ λοιπόν, ἀδελφοί, ὅσα ἐστὶν ἀληθῆ, ὅσα σεμνά, ὅσα
For the rest, brothers, whatever is    true, whatever honorable, whatever

honorable, whatever right, whatever pure, whatever lovely, whatever of good report; if (of) any virtue and if any praise, think on these things. [9] And what you learned and received and heard and saw in me, do these things; and the God of peace shall be with you. [10] But I rejoiced in (the) Lord greatly, that now at last you revived (your) thinking of me: although also you were thinking, but you were lacking opportunity. [11] Not that I speak as to great need; for I have learned to be content in whatever state I am. [12] But I know (how) to be humbled, and I know to abound. In everything and in all things, I am taught both to be full, and to hunger, both to abound, and to have too little. [13] I can do all things through Christ who strengthens me. [14] But you did well having fellowship with me in my troubles. [15] And you know, too, O Philippians, that in the beginning of the gospel, when I went out from Macedonia, not one church shared with me as to giving and receiving, but you only. [16] Because even in Thessalonica you sent both once and twice to my need. [17] Not that I seek the gift, but I seek the fruit multiplying to (the) account of you. [18] But I have all things, and more than enough; I am full, receiving from Epaphroditus the things from you, an odor of sweet smell, an acceptable sacrifice, well-pleasing to God. [19] But my God will fill ups all your need according to His riches in glory in Christ Jesus. [20] Now may glory be to our God and Father forever and ever. Amen. [21] Greet every saint in Christ Jesus. The brothers with me greet you. [22] All the saints greet you, and especially those of the household of Caesar. [23] The grace of our Lord Jesus Christ be with you all. Amen.

δίκαια, ὅσα ἁγνά, ὅσα προσφιλῆ, ὅσα εὔφημα, εἴ τις ἀρετὴ
just, whatever pure, whatever loveable, whatever of good report, if any virtue

9 καὶ εἴ τις ἔπαινος, ταῦτα λογίζεσθε. ἃ καὶ ἐμάθετε καὶ παρε-
and if any praise, these things consider. What things you learned and re-

λάβετε καὶ ἠκούσατε καὶ εἴδετε ἐν ἐμοί, ταῦτα πράσσετε· καὶ
ceived, and heard and saw, in me, these things practice; and

ὁ Θεὸς τῆς εἰρήνης ἔσται μεθ' ὑμῶν.
the God of peace will be with you.

10 Ἐχάρην δὲ ἐν Κυρίῳ μεγάλως, ὅτι ἤδη ποτὲ ἀνεθάλετε τὸ
I rejoiced Now in (the) Lord greatly, that now at last you revived

11 ὑπὲρ ἐμοῦ φρονεῖν· ἐφ' ᾧ καὶ ἐφρονεῖτε, ἠκαιρεῖσθε δέ. οὐχ
of me thinking, as to which indeed you thought, lacked but opportunity. Not

ὅτι καθ' ὑστέρησιν λέγω· ἐγὼ γὰρ ἔμαθον, ἐν οἷς εἰμί,
that by way of lack I say; I for learned in what state I am,

12 αὐτάρκης εἶναι. οἶδα καὶ ταπεινοῦσθαι, οἶδα καὶ περισ-
self-sufficient to be. I know both to be humbled, I know and to

σεύειν· ἐν παντὶ καὶ ἐν πᾶσι μεμύημαι· καὶ χορτάζεσθαι καὶ
abound; in everything and in all things I am taught both to be filled and

13 πεινᾶν, καὶ περισσεύειν καὶ ὑστερεῖσθαι. πάντα ἰσχύω ἐν
to hunger, both to abound and to lack. All things I can do in

14 τῷ ἐνδυναμοῦντί με Χριστῷ. πλὴν καλῶς ἐποιήσατε
the (One) empowering me, Christ. Yet well you did

15 συγκοινωνήσαντές μου τῇ θλίψει. οἴδατε δὲ καὶ ὑμεῖς,
sharing in of me the troubles. know And also you,

Φιλιππήσιοι, ὅτι ἐν ἀρχῇ τοῦ εὐαγγελίου, ὅτε ἐξῆλθον
Philippians, that in (the) beginning of the gospel, when I went out

ἀπὸ Μακεδονίας, οὐδεμία μοι ἐκκλησία ἐκοινώνησεν εἰς
from Macedonia, not one me church shared with in

16 λόγον δόσεως καὶ λήψεως, εἰ μὴ ὑμεῖς μόνοι· ὅτι καὶ ἐν
(the) matter of giving and receiving, except you only, because truly in

Θεσσαλονίκῃ καὶ ἅπαξ καὶ δὶς εἰς τὴν χρείαν μοι ἐπέμψατε.
Thessalonica both once and twice to the need of me you sent.

17 οὐχ ὅτι ἐπιζητῶ τὸ δόμα, ἀλλ' ἐπιζητῶ τὸν καρπὸν τὸν
Not that I seek the gift, but I seek the fruit

18 πλεονάζοντα εἰς λόγον ὑμῶν. ἀπέχω δὲ πάντα καὶ περισ-
multiplying to (the) account of you. I have But all things and abound;

σεύω· πεπλήρωμαι, δεξάμενος παρὰ Ἐπαφροδίτου τὰ παρ'
I have been filled, receiving from Epaphroditus the things from

ὑμῶν, ὀσμὴν εὐωδίας, θυσίαν δεκτήν, εὐάρεστον τῷ Θεῷ.
you, an odor of sweet smell, a sacrifice acceptable, well-pleasing to God.

19 ὁ δὲ Θεός μου πληρώσει πᾶσαν χρείαν ὑμῶν κατὰ τὸν
the And God of me will fill every need of you according to the

20 πλοῦτον αὐτοῦ ἐν δόξῃ, ἐν Χριστῷ Ἰησοῦ. τῷ δὲ Θεῷ καὶ
riches of Him in glory, in Christ Jesus. to the Now God and

πατρὶ ἡμῶν ἡ δόξα εἰς τοὺς αἰῶνας τῶν αἰώνων. ἀμήν.
Father of us (be) the glory to the ages of the ages. Amen.

21 Ἀσπάσασθε πάντα ἅγιον ἐν Χριστῷ Ἰησοῦ. ἀσπά-
Greet every saint in Christ Jesus. Greet

22 ζονται ὑμᾶς οἱ σὺν ἐμοὶ ἀδελφοί. ἀσπάζονται ὑμᾶς πάντες
you the with me brothers. Greet you all

οἱ ἅγιοι, μάλιστα δὲ οἱ ἐκ τῆς Καίσαρος οἰκίας.
the saints, most of all but those of the of Caesar house.

23 Ἡ χάρις τοῦ Κυρίου ἡμῶν Ἰησοῦ Χριστοῦ μετὰ πάντων
The grace of the Lord of us, Jesus Christ (be) with all

ὑμῶν. ἀμήν.
of you. Amen.

# ΠΑΥΛΟΥ ΤΟΥ ΑΠΟΣΤΟΛΟΥ
PAUL  THE  APOSTLE

## Η ΠΡΟΣ
THE TO

# ΚΟΛΟΣΣΑΕΙΣ ΕΠΙΣΤΟΛΗ
(THE) COLOSSIANS  EPISTLE

## CHAPTER 1

**CHAPTER 1**

[1] Paul, (an) apostle of Jesus Christ through the will of God, and Timothy the brother, [2] to the saints and faithful brothers in Christ in Colosse: Grace and peace to you from God our Father and (the) Lord Jesus Christ.

[3] We give thanks to God and (the) Father of our Lord Jesus Christ, praying continually about you, [4] hearing of your faith in Christ Jesus, and the love which (you have) towards all the saints, [5] through the hope having been laid up for you in Heaven; which you heard before in the word of the truth of the gospel, [6] having come to you, even as also in all the world, and is bearing fruit, even also among you, from the day in which you heard and knew the grace of God in truth; [7] even as you also learned from Epaphras our beloved fellow-slave, who is a faithful minister of Christ for you, [8] he also having shown to us your love in (the) Spirit.

[9] For this cause also, from the day in which we heard, we do not cease praying for you and asking that you may be filled (with) the knowledge of His will in all wisdom and spiritual understanding, [10] (for) you to walk worthily of the Lord to all pleasing, bearing fruit in every good work, and growing into the full knowledge of God; [11] being empowered with all power

**1** Παῦλος ἀπόστολος Ἰησοῦ Χριστοῦ διὰ θελήματος Θεοῦ,
Paul  an apostle  of Jesus  Christ  through (the) will of God,

**2** καὶ Τιμόθεος ὁ ἀδελφός, τοῖς ἐν Κολοσσαῖς ἁγίοις καὶ πιστοῖς
and Timothy the brother,  to the in  Colosse  saints  and  faithful
ἀδελφοῖς ἐν Χριστῷ· χάρις ὑμῖν καὶ εἰρήνη ἀπὸ Θεοῦ πατρὸς
brothers  in  Christ:  Grace to you and peace from  God (the) Father
ἡμῶν καὶ Κυρίου Ἰησοῦ Χριστοῦ.
of us  and (the) Lord Jesus  Christ.

**3** Εὐχαριστοῦμεν τῷ Θεῷ καὶ πατρὶ τοῦ Κυρίου ἡμῶν
We give thanks  to  God  and Father of the  Lord  of us,

**4** Ἰησοῦ Χριστοῦ, πάντοτε περὶ ὑμῶν προσευχόμενοι, ἀκού-
Jesus  Christ,  always concerning you  praying,  having
σαντες τὴν πίστιν ὑμῶν ἐν Χριστῷ Ἰησοῦ, καὶ τὴν ἀγάπην
heard  the  faith of you in Christ  Jesus, and the  love

**5** τὴν εἰς πάντας τοὺς ἁγίους, διὰ τὴν ἐλπίδα τὴν ἀποκειμένην
of all  the  saints, through the hope  being laid up
ὑμῖν ἐν τοῖς οὐρανοῖς, ἣν προηκούσατε ἐν τῷ λόγῳ τῆς
for you in the  heavens, which you heard before in the  word of the

**6** ἀληθείας τοῦ εὐαγγελίου, τοῦ παρόντος εἰς ὑμᾶς, καθὼς καὶ
truth  of the  gospel,  coming to you,  as  also
ἐν παντὶ τῷ κόσμῳ, καὶ ἔστι καρποφορούμενον, καθὼς καὶ
in all  the  world, and it is  bearing fruit,  even also
ἐν ὑμῖν, ἀφ' ἧς ἡμέρας ἠκούσατε καὶ ἐπέγνωτε τὴν χάριν τοῦ
among you, from which day you heard and fully knew  the  grace

**7** Θεοῦ ἐν ἀληθείᾳ· καθὼς καὶ ἐμάθετε ἀπὸ Ἐπαφρᾶ τοῦ
of God in  truth,  as  also you learned from Epaphras the
ἀγαπητοῦ συνδούλου ἡμῶν, ὅς ἐστι πιστὸς ὑπὲρ ὑμῶν
beloved  fellow-slave of us, who is  a faithful  for  you

**8** διάκονος τοῦ Χριστοῦ, ὁ καὶ δηλώσας ἡμῖν τὴν ὑμῶν ἀγάπην
minister  of Christ, he also having shown to us the of you  love
ἐν Πνεύματι.
in (the) Spirit.

**9** Διὰ τοῦτο καὶ ἡμεῖς, ἀφ' ἧς ἡμέρας ἠκούσαμεν, οὐ παυό-
Therefore also we,  from which day  we heard, do not cease
μεθα ὑπὲρ ὑμῶν προσευχόμενοι, καὶ αἰτούμενοι ἵνα πλη-
on behalf of you  praying,  and  asking  that you
ρωθῆτε τὴν ἐπίγνωσιν τοῦ θελήματος αὐτοῦ ἐν πάσῃ σοφίᾳ
may be filled (with) the knowledge of the  will  of Him in all  wisdom

**10** καὶ συνέσει πνευματικῇ, περιπατῆσαι ὑμᾶς ἀξίως τοῦ Κυρίου
and understanding spiritual,  to walk  you worthily of the Lord
εἰς πᾶσαν ἀρέσκειαν, ἐν παντὶ ἔργῳ ἀγαθῷ καρποφοροῦντες
to all  pleasing,  in every  work  good  bearing fruit

**11** καὶ αὐξανόμενοι εἰς τὴν ἐπίγνωσιν τοῦ Θεοῦ· ἐν πάσῃ δυνάμει
and  growing  into the full knowledge of God, with all  power

according to the might of
His glory, to all patience
and longsuffering with joy;
[12] giving thanks to the
Father, who has made us fit
for a share of the inheritance of the saints in light,
[13] who delivered us out
of the power of darkness,
and translated (us) into the
kingdom of the Son of His
love; [14] in whom we have
redemption through His
blood, the remission of sins;
[15] who is (the) image of
the invisible God, (the) firstborn of all creation; [16]
because all things were
created in Him, the things
in the heavens and the
things on the earth, the visible and the invisible,
whether thrones, or lord-
ships, or principalities, or
authorities; all things have
been created through Him,
and for Him. [17] And He
is before all things, and all
things consist in Him. [18]
And He is the Head of the
body, the church; who is
(the) beginning, (the) firstborn from (the) dead, that
He be pre-eminent in all
things; [19] because all the
fullness was pleased to
dwell in Him, [20] and
through Him making peace
by the blood of His cross,
to reconcile all things to
Himself through Him,
whether the things on the
the earth, or the things in
the heavens. [21] And you
being once alienated and
enemies in (your) mind by
wicked works, but now He
reconciled [22] in the body
of His flesh, through death,
to present you holy and
without blame and without
charge before Him. [23] if
you continue in the faith
grounded and settled and
not being moved away from
the hope of the gospel
which you heard proclaim-
ed in all the creation under
Heaven, of which I, Paul,
became a minister.
[24] Now (I am) rejoic-
ing in my sufferings for you,

δυναμούμενοι, κατὰ τὸ κράτος τῆς δόξης αὐτοῦ, εἰς πᾶσαν
being empowered, according to the might of the glory of Him,  to    all

**12** ὑπομονὴν καὶ μακροθυμίαν μετὰ χαρᾶς· εὐχαριστοῦντες τῷ
patience   and long-suffering,  with   joy,   giving thanks   to the

πατρὶ τῷ ἱκανώσαντι ἡμᾶς εἰς τὴν μερίδα τοῦ κλήρου τῶν
Father   having made fit us   for   the   share of the lot   of the

**13** ἁγίων ἐν τῷ φωτί, ὃς ἐρρύσατο ἡμᾶς ἐκ τῆς ἐξουσίας τοῦ
saints   in   light, who delivered   us out of the authority

σκότους, καὶ μετέστησεν εἰς τὴν βασιλείαν τοῦ υἱοῦ τῆς
of darkness, and translated (us) into the   kingdom of the   Son of the

**14** ἀγάπης αὐτοῦ, ἐν ᾧ ἔχομεν τὴν ἀπολύτρωσιν διὰ τοῦ
love   of Him, in whom we have   redemption   through   the

**15** αἵματος αὐτοῦ, τὴν ἄφεσιν τῶν ἁμαρτιῶν· ὅς ἐστιν εἰκὼν
blood   of Him, the forgiveness   of sins;   who   is (the) image

**16** τοῦ Θεοῦ τοῦ ἀοράτου, πρωτότοκος πάσης κτίσεως· ὅτι
of God the   invisible, (the) firstborn   of all   creation, because

ἐν αὐτῷ ἐκτίσθη τὰ πάντα, τὰ ἐν τοῖς οὐρανοῖς καὶ τὰ ἐπὶ
in   Him were created all things, the things in the heavens, and the things on

τῆς γῆς, τὰ ὁρατὰ καὶ τὰ ἀόρατα, εἴτε θρόνοι, εἴτε κυριό-
the earth, the visible and the invisible, whether thrones, or lordships

τητες, εἴτε ἀρχαί, εἴτε ἐξουσίαι· τὰ πάντα δι’ αὐτοῦ καὶ εἰς
or rulers,   or authorities; all things through   Him and for

**17** αὐτὸν ἔκτισται· καὶ αὐτός ἐστι πρὸ πάντων, καὶ τὰ πάντα
Him have been created, and He is before all things, and   all things

**18** ἐν αὐτῷ συνέστηκε. καὶ αὐτός ἐστιν ἡ κεφαλὴ τοῦ σώματος,
in Him consisted; and He is the Head of the body,

τῆς ἐκκλησίας· ὅς ἐστιν ἀρχή, πρωτότοκος ἐκ τῶν νεκρῶν,
the church, who is (the) beginning, firstborn from the   dead.

**19** ἵνα γένηται ἐν πᾶσιν αὐτὸς πρωτεύων· ὅτι ἐν αὐτῷ εὐδόκησε
that may be   in all things He   pre-eminent, because in Him was pleased

**20** πᾶν τὸ πλήρωμα κατοικῆσαι, καὶ δι’ αὐτοῦ ἀποκαταλλάξαι
all   the fullness   to dwell,   and through Him   to reconcile

τὰ πάντα εἰς αὐτόν, εἰρηνοποιήσας διὰ τοῦ αἵματος τοῦ
all things   to Himself,   making peace   through the   blood of the

σταυροῦ αὐτοῦ, δι’ αὐτοῦ, εἴτε τὰ ἐπὶ τῆς γῆς, εἴτε τὰ ἐν
cross   of Him, through Him, whether the things on the earth, or those in

**21** τοῖς οὐρανοῖς. καὶ ὑμᾶς ποτὲ ὄντας ἀπηλλοτριωμένους καὶ
the heavens. And you, then, being   alienated   and

ἐχθροὺς τῇ διανοίᾳ ἐν τοῖς ἔργοις τοῖς πονηροῖς, νυνὶ δὲ
enemies in the mind   by (your) works   evil.   now But

**22** ἀποκατήλλαξεν ἐν τῷ σώματι τῆς σαρκὸς αὐτοῦ διὰ τοῦ
He reconciled   in the body   of the flesh   of Him through the

θανάτου, παραστῆσαι ὑμᾶς ἁγίους καὶ ἀμώμους καὶ
death (of Him), to present   you   holy   and   blameless and

**23** ἀνεγκλήτους κατενώπιον αὐτοῦ· εἴγε ἐπιμένετε τῇ πίστει
without charge   before   Him, if indeed you continue in the faith

τεθεμελιωμένοι καὶ ἑδραῖοι, καὶ μὴ μετακινούμενοι ἀπὸ τῆς
having been founded and steadfast, and not being moved away from the

ἐλπίδος τοῦ εὐαγγελίου οὗ ἠκούσατε, τοῦ κηρυχθέντος ἐν
hope   of the   gospel   which you heard   proclaimed   in

πάσῃ τῇ κτίσει τῇ ὑπὸ τὸν οὐρανόν, οὗ ἐγενόμην ἐγὼ
all   the creation   under   Heaven, of which became   I,

Παῦλος διάκονος.
Paul,   a minister.

**24** Ὃς νῦν χαίρω ἐν τοῖς παθήμασί μου ὑπὲρ ὑμῶν, καὶ
Who now rejoice in   the sufferings of me   on   you, and
behalf of

and I am filling up that which is behind of the tribulations of Christ in my flesh on behalf of His body, which is the church. [25] Of which I became a minister, according to the administration of God given to me to fulfill the word of God. [26] the mystery having been hidden from the ages, and from generations, but now has been revealed to His saints; [27] to whom God desired to make known what (are) the riches of the glory of this mystery in the nations, which is Christ in you, the hope of glory; [28] whom we preach, warning every man and teaching every man in all wisdom, that we may present every man perfect in Christ Jesus. [29] For which I labor, working according to the working of Him who works in me in power.

ἀνταναπληρῶ τὰ ὑστερήματα τῶν θλίψεων τοῦ Χριστοῦ
fill up    the   things lacking of the afflictions     of Christ

ἐν τῇ σαρκί μου ὑπὲρ τοῦ σώματος αὐτοῦ, ὅ ἐστιν ἡ
in the   flesh   of me on behalf of the   body    of Him, which   is   the

25 ἐκκλησία· ἧς ἐγενόμην ἐγὼ διάκονος, κατὰ τὴν οἰκονομίαν
church, of which became I     a minister as regards the stewardship

τοῦ Θεοῦ τὴν δοθεῖσάν μοι εἰς ὑμᾶς, πληρῶσαι τὸν λόγον
of God    the   given to me for you,   to fulfill   the    word

26 τοῦ Θεοῦ, τὸ μυστήριον τὸ ἀποκεκρυμμένον ἀπὸ τῶν
of God,   the   mystery.      having been hidden    from   the

αἰώνων καὶ ἀπὸ τῶν γενεῶν· νυνὶ δὲ ἐφανερώθη τοῖς ἁγίοις
ages    and from    the generations, now but was revealed to the saints

27 αὐτοῦ, οἷς ἠθέλησεν ὁ Θεὸς γνωρίσαι τίς ὁ πλοῦτος τῆς
of Him, to whom desired     God to make known what (is) the riches of the

δόξης τοῦ μυστηρίου τούτου ἐν τοῖς ἔθνεσιν, ὅς ἐστι Χριστὸς
glory      mystery   of this among the nations, who is    Christ

28 ἐν ὑμῖν, ἡ ἐλπὶς τῆς δόξης· ὃν ἡμεῖς καταγγέλλομεν, νου-
in you, the hope of the glory, whom   we    announce,

θετοῦντες πάντα ἄνθρωπον, καὶ διδάσκοντες πάντα ἄνθρω-
warning    every    man,      and   teaching    every     man

πον ἐν πάσῃ σοφίᾳ, ἵνα παραστήσωμεν πάντα ἄνθρωπον
in    all    wisdom, that   we may present   every     man

29 τέλειον ἐν Χριστῷ Ἰησοῦ· εἰς ὃ καὶ κοπιῶ, ἀγωνιζόμενος
full-grown in   Christ     Jesus, for which also I labor,    struggling

κατὰ τὴν ἐνέργειαν αὐτοῦ, τὴν ἐνεργουμένην ἐν ἐμοὶ ἐν
according to the working   of Him, the (One) working     in   me   in

δυνάμει.
power.

## CHAPTER 2

[1] For I want you to know how great a struggle I have for you, and those in Laodicea, and as many as have not seen my face in (the) flesh; [2] that their hearts may be comforted, being knit together in love, and to all riches of the full assurance of understanding; to (the) full knowledge of the mystery of God and of Christ, [3] in whom are hidden all the treasures of wisdom and of knowledge. [4] And I say this, that no one may beguile you with winning words. [5] For though I am indeed absent in the flesh, yet I am with you in spirit, rejoicing and seeing your order and the firmness of your faith in Christ. [6] Therefore, as you received Christ Jesus the Lord, walk in Him, [7] having been rooted and built up in Him, and being established in the faith, even as you were taught, abounding in it with

1 Θέλω γὰρ ὑμᾶς εἰδέναι ἡλίκον ἀγῶνα ἔχω περὶ ὑμῶν καὶ
I want For   you to know how great a struggle I have as to   you and

τῶν ἐν Λαοδικείᾳ, καὶ ὅσοι οὐχ ἑωράκασι τὸ πρόσωπόν μου
those in Laodicea,   and as many as not have seen   the    face    of me

2 ἐν σαρκί, ἵνα παρακληθῶσιν αἱ καρδίαι αὐτῶν, συμβιβασθέν-
in (the) flesh, that may be comforted the hearts   of them, being joined to-

των ἐν ἀγάπῃ, καὶ εἰς πάντα πλοῦτον τῆς πληροφορίας τῆς
gether in love,    and for    all     riches   of the full assurance of the

συνέσεως, εἰς ἐπίγνωσιν τοῦ μυστηρίου τοῦ Θεοῦ καὶ πατρός
understanding, for full knowledge of the mystery     of God, and of Father,

3 καὶ τοῦ Χριστοῦ, ἐν ᾧ εἰσι πάντες οἱ θησαυροὶ τῆς σοφίας
and   of Christ, in whom are   all    the   treasures    of wisdom

4 καὶ τῆς γνώσεως ἀπόκρυφοι. τοῦτο δὲ λέγω, ἵνα μή τις ὑμᾶς
and    knowledge    hidden.    this And I say,   that not anyone you

5 παραλογίζηται ἐν πιθανολογίᾳ. εἰ γὰρ καὶ τῇ σαρκὶ ἄπειμι,
beguile     by persuasive words. if For indeed in the flesh    I am absent,

ἀλλὰ τῷ πνεύματι σὺν ὑμῖν εἰμί, χαίρων καὶ βλέπων ὑμῶν
yet    in the spirit   with you I am, rejoicing and seeing   of you

τὴν τάξιν, καὶ τὸ στερέωμα τῆς εἰς Χριστὸν πίστεως ὑμῶν.
the order,   and   the firmness   of the in    Christ   faith   of you.

6 Ὡς οὖν παρελάβετε τὸν Χριστὸν Ἰησοῦν τὸν Κύριον, ἐν
As, therefore, you received     Christ     Jesus    the Lord,   in

7 αὐτῷ περιπατεῖτε, ἐρριζωμένοι καὶ ἐποικοδομούμενοι ἐν
Him   walk,     having been rooted and having been built up   in

αὐτῷ, καὶ βεβαιούμενοι ἐν τῇ πίστει, καθὼς ἐδιδάχθητε,
Him,   and being confirmed in   the   faith,    as    you were taught,

thanksgiving.

[8] Watch lest there may be one who plunders you through philosophy and empty deceit, according to the tradition of men, according to the elements of the world, and not according to Christ. [9] For in Him dwells all the fullness of the Godhead bodily; [10] and having been filled, you are in Him; who is the Head of all principality and authority, [11] in whom also you were circumcised with a circumcision not made by hand, in the putting off of the body of the sins of the flesh, in the circumcision of Christ; [12] having been buried with Him in baptism, in whom also you were raised through the faith of the working of God, who raised Him from (the) dead. [13] And you, being dead in sins and the circumcision of your flesh, He made alive together with Him, having forgiven us all the offenses; [14] having blotted out the handwriting in the ordinances against us, which were contrary to us; and He has taken it out of the midst, nailing it to the cross; [15] having stripped the principalities and the authorities, He made a show of them publicly, triumphing (over) them in it.

[16] Therefore, do not let anyone judge you in eating or in drinking, or in respect of a feast, or the new moon, or sabbaths, [17] which are a shadow of things to come; but the body (is) of Christ. [18] Let no one cheat you of the prize, doing (his own) will in humility and worship of angels, pushing into things which he has not seen, without a cause puffed up by his fleshly mind, [19] and not holding fast the Head, from whom all the body by the joints and bands having been supplied and knitted together will grow (with) the growth (which comes) of God.

[20] If, then, you died with Christ from the elements of the world, why are you under (its) decrees, as if alive in (the) world?

περισσεύοντες ἐν αὐτῇ ἐν εὐχαριστίᾳ.
abounding      in it   in thanksgiving.

**8** Βλέπετε μή τις ὑμᾶς ἔσται ὁ συλαγωγῶν διὰ τῆς φιλοσο-
Watch, lest anyone you shall be robbing through philoso-
φίας καὶ κενῆς ἀπάτης, κατὰ τὴν παράδοσιν τῶν ἀνθρώπων,
phy and vain deceit, according to the tradition   of men,

**9** κατὰ τὰ στοιχεῖα τοῦ κόσμου, καὶ οὐ κατὰ Χριστόν· ὅτι ἐν
according to the elements of the world, and not according to Christ; for in
αὐτῷ κατοικεῖ πᾶν τὸ πλήρωμα τῆς θεότητος σωματικῶς,
Him dwells   all the fullness of the Godhead bodily,

**10** καὶ ἐστε ἐν αὐτῷ πεπληρωμένοι, ὅς ἐστιν ἡ κεφαλὴ πασης
and you are in Him having been filled. who is the Head of all

**11** ἀρχῆς καὶ ἐξουσίας· ἐν ᾧ καὶ περιετμήθητε περιτομῇ ἀχει-
rule and authority, in whom also circumcised circumcision not
                              you were          with a
ροποιήτῳ, ἐν τῇ ἀπεκδύσει του σώματος τῶν ἁμαρτιῶν
made by hand, by the putting off of the body   of the sins

**12** τῆς σαρκός, ἐν τῇ περιτομῇ τοῦ Χριστοῦ, συνταφέντες αὐτῷ
of the flesh, by the circumcision  of Christ, co-buried with Him
ἐν τῷ βαπτίσματι, ἐν ᾧ καὶ συνηγέρθητε διὰ τῆς πίστεως τῆς
in the baptism, in whom also you were raised through the faith of the
ἐνεργείας τοῦ Θεοῦ, τοῦ ἐγείραντος αὐτὸν ἐκ τῶν νεκρῶν.
working   of God, raising    Him  from the dead;

**13** καὶ ὑμᾶς, νεκροὺς ὄντας ἐν τοῖς παραπτώμασι καὶ τῇ ἀκρο-
and you dead being in the offenses and the uncir-
βυστίᾳ τῆς σαρκὸς ὑμῶν, συνεζωοποίησε σὺν αὐτῷ, χαρισά-
cumcision of the flesh of you, He made alive you with Him, having for-

**14** μενος ὑμῖν πάντα τὰ παραπτώματα, ἐξαλείψας τὸ καθ' ἡμῶν
given you all the offenses; blotting out the against us
χειρόγραφον τοῖς δόγμασιν, ὃ ἦν ὑπεναντίον ἡμῖν· καὶ αὐτὸ
handwriting in ordinances which were contrary to us, and it

**15** ἦρκεν ἐκ τοῦ μέσου, προσηλώσας αὐτὸ τῷ σταυρῷ· ἀπεκδυ-
has taken out of the midst, nailing it to the cross; having
σάμενος τὰς ἀρχὰς καὶ τὰς ἐξουσίας, ἐδειγμάτισεν ἐν παρ-
stripped the rulers and the authorities, He displayed (them) in
ρησίᾳ, θριαμβεύσας αὐτοὺς ἐν αὐτῷ.
public, triumphing (over) them in it.

**16** Μὴ οὖν τις ὑμᾶς κρινέτω ἐν βρώσει ἢ ἐν πόσει, ἢ ἐν μέρει
Not, therefore, anyone you let judge in eating or in drinking, or in respect

**17** ἑορτῆς ἢ νουμηνίας ἢ σαββάτων· ἅ ἐστι σκιὰ τῶν μελλόν-
of a feast, or of a new moon, or of sabbaths, which is a shadow of things

**18** των, τὸ δὲ σῶμα τοῦ Χριστοῦ. μηδεὶς ὑμᾶς καταβραβευέτω
coming, the but body (is) of Christ. No one you let give judgment
θέλων ἐν ταπεινοφροσύνη καὶ θρησκείᾳ τῶν ἀγγέλων, ἃ
wishing in humility   and worship of the angels, which
                                                        things
μὴ ἑώρακεν ἐμβατεύων, εἰκῇ φυσιούμενος ὑπὸ τοῦ νοὸς
not he has seen pushing into, without a cause puffed up by the mind

**19** τῆς σαρκὸς αὐτοῦ, καὶ οὐ κρατῶν τὴν κεφαλήν, ἐξ οὗ πᾶν
of the flesh of him, and not holding the Head, from whom all
τὸ σῶμα, διὰ τῶν ἁφῶν καὶ συνδέσμων ἐπιχορηγούμενον
the body, through the joints and bands having been supplied
καὶ συμβιβαζόμενον, αὔξει τὴν αὔξησιν τοῦ Θεοῦ.
and having been joined together will grow with the growth of God.

**20** Εἰ οὖν ἀπεθάνετε σὺν τῷ Χριστῷ ἀπὸ τῶν στοιχείων
If, then, you died with Christ from the elements

**21** τοῦ κόσμου, τί, ὡς ζῶντες ἐν κόσμῳ, δογματίζεσθε, Μὴ
of the world, why as living in (the) world, are you under decrees: Not

[21] Do not handle; do not taste; do not touch; [22] which things are all to rot away in the using, according to the injunctions and teachings of men. [23] which things indeed have a reputation of wisdom in will-worship and humility and harsh treatment of the body, not in any honor for satisfaction of the flesh.

## CHAPTER 3

[1] If, then, you were raised with Christ, seek the things above, where Christ is sitting at (the) right of God; [2] minding the things above, not the things on earth; [3] for you died, and your life has been hidden with Christ in God. [4] When Christ our life is revealed, then also you will be revealed in glory with Him. [5] Therefore, put to death your members which (are) on the earth: fornication, uncleanness, passion, evil lust, and covetousness, which is idolatry; [6] on account of which things the wrath of God is coming on the sons of disobedience; [7] among whom you also walked at one time, when you were living in these things. [8] But now, also put off all (these) things: wrath, indignation, malice, blasphemy, filthy language out of your mouth. [9] Do not lie to one another, having put off the old man with his works, [10] and having put on the new that (is) being renewed in full knowledge according to (the) image of Him who created him; [11] where there is not Greek and Jew, circumcision and uncircumcision, barbarian, Scythian, slave (or) freeman—but Christ (is) all things in all.

[12] Then put on as the elect of God, holy and beloved, tender feelings of mercy, kindness, humility, meekness, longsuffering, [13] bearing with one another, and forgiving yourselves, if any has a complaint against any; even as

---

**22** ἅψῃ, μηδὲ γεύσῃ, μηδὲ θίγῃς (ἅ ἐστι πάντα εἰς φθορὰν τῇ
touch, nor taste, nor handle- which are all for corruption in the
things
ἀποχρήσει), κατὰ τὰ ἐντάλματα καὶ διδασκαλίας τῶν
using — according to the injunctions and teachings

**23** ἀνθρώπων; ἅτινά ἐστι λόγον μὲν ἔχοντα σοφίας ἐν ἐθε-
of men? Which things is a repute indeed having of wisdom in self-
λοθρησκείᾳ καὶ ταπεινοφροσύνῃ καὶ ἀφειδίᾳ σώματος, οὐκ
imposed worship and humility and unsparing of (the) body, not
(abuse)
ἐν τιμῇ τινὶ πρὸς πλησμονὴν τῆς σαρκός.
in honor any for satisfaction of the flesh.

## CHAPTER 3

**1** Εἰ οὖν συνηγέρθητε τῷ Χριστῷ, τὰ ἄνω ζητεῖτε, οὗ ὁ
If, then, you were raised with Christ, the things above seek, where

**2** Χριστός ἐστιν ἐν δεξιᾷ τοῦ Θεοῦ καθήμενος. τὰ ἄνω φρονεῖτε,
Christ is at (the) right of God sitting; the things above mind,

**3** μὴ τὰ ἐπὶ τῆς γῆς. ἀπεθάνετε γάρ, καὶ ἡ ζωὴ ὑμῶν κέκρυ-
not the things on the earth. you died For, and the life of you has been

**4** πται σὺν τῷ Χριστῷ ἐν τῷ Θεῷ. ὅταν ὁ Χριστὸς φανερωθῇ,
hidden with Christ in God. Whenever Christ is revealed,
ἡ ζωὴ ἡμῶν, τότε καὶ ὑμεῖς σὺν αὐτῷ φανερωθήσεσθε ἐν
the life of us, then also you with Him will be revealed in
δόξῃ.
glory.

**5** Νεκρώσατε οὖν τὰ μέλη ὑμῶν τὰ ἐπὶ τῆς γῆς, πορνείαν,
put to death Therefore the members of you on the earth, fornication,
ἀκαθαρσίαν, πάθος, ἐπιθυμίαν κακήν, καὶ τὴν πλεονεξίαν,
uncleanness, passion, lust evil, and covetousness,

**6** ἥτις ἐστὶν εἰδωλολατρεία, δι' ἃ ἔρχεται ἡ ὀργὴ τοῦ Θεοῦ
which is idolatry; for which things is coming the wrath of God

**7** ἐπὶ τοὺς υἱοὺς τῆς ἀπειθείας· ἐν οἷς καὶ ὑμεῖς περιεπατήσατέ
on the sons of disobedience, among whom also you walked

**8** ποτε, ὅτε ἐζῆτε ἐν αὐτοῖς. νυνὶ δὲ ἀπόθεσθε καὶ ὑμεῖς τὰ
then, when you were living in these. now But, put off also you
πάντα, ὀργήν, θυμόν, κακίαν, βλασφημίαν, αἰσχρολογίαν
all things: wrath, anger, malice, evil speaking, shameful words

**9** ἐκ τοῦ στόματος ὑμῶν· μὴ ψεύδεσθε εἰς ἀλλήλους, ἀπεκδυσά-
out of the mouth of you. Do not lie to one another, having put
μενοι τὸν παλαιὸν ἄνθρωπον σὺν ταῖς πράξεσιν αὐτοῦ,
off the old man with the practices of him,

**10** καὶ ἐνδυσάμενοι τὸν νέον, τὸν ἀνακαινούμενον εἰς ἐπίγνωσιν
and having put on the new (man) being renewed in full knowledge

**11** κατ' εἰκόνα τοῦ κτίσαντος αὐτόν· ὅπου οὐκ ἔνι Ἕλλην καὶ
according to (the) image of Him creating him, where not there is Greek and
Ἰουδαῖος, περιτομὴ καὶ ἀκροβυστία, βάρβαρος, Σκύθης,
Jew, circumcision and uncircumcision, foreigner, Scythian,
δοῦλος, ἐλεύθερος· ἀλλὰ τὰ πάντα καὶ ἐν πᾶσι Χριστός.
slave, freeman, but all things and in all Christ (is).

**12** Ἐνδύσασθε οὖν. ὡς ἐκλεκτοὶ τοῦ Θεοῦ, ἅγιοι καὶ
put on Therefore, as elect ones of God, holy and
ἠγαπημένοι, σπλάγχνα οἰκτιρμῶν, χρηστότητα, ταπεινο-
having been loved, bowels of compassions, kindness, humility,

**13** φροσύνην, πραότητα, μακροθυμίαν· ἀνεχόμενοι ἀλλήλων,
meekness, long-suffering, forbearing one another,
καὶ χαριζόμενοι ἑαυτοῖς, ἐάν τις πρός τινα ἔχῃ μομφήν· καθὼς
and forgiving yourselves, if anyone against any has a complaint; as

14 καὶ ὁ Χριστὸς ἐχαρίσατο ὑμῖν, οὕτω καὶ ὑμεῖς· ἐπὶ πᾶσι δὲ
**indeed Christ   forgave   you,   so   also   you; above all and**
τούτοις τὴν ἀγάπην, ἥτις ἐστὶ σύνδεσμος τῆς τελειότητος.
**these things   love,   which is ( the ) bond   of perfectness.**

15 καὶ ἡ εἰρήνη τοῦ Θεοῦ βραβευέτω ἐν ταῖς καρδίαις ὑμῶν,
**And the peace   of God   let rule   in   the   hearts of you,**

16 εἰς ἣν καὶ ἐκλήθητε ἐν ἑνὶ σώματι· καὶ εὐχάριστοι γίνεσθε. ὁ
**to which indeed you were called in one body, and thankful   be.   The**
λόγος τοῦ Χριστοῦ ἐνοικείτω ἐν ὑμῖν πλουσίως ἐν πάσῃ
**word   of Christ   let dwell   in   you   richly,   in   all**
σοφίᾳ· διδάσκοντες καὶ νουθετοῦντες ἑαυτούς, ψαλμοῖς, καὶ
**wisdom   teaching   and   exhorting   yourselves, in psalms   and**

17 ὕμνοις, καὶ ᾠδαῖς πνευματικαῖς, ἐν χάριτι ᾄδοντες ἐν τῇ
**hymns and   songs   spiritual,   with grace   singing   in the**
καρδίᾳ ὑμῶν τῷ Κυρίῳ. καὶ πᾶν ὅ τι ἂν ποιῆτε, ἐν λόγῳ ἢ
**hearts   of you to the Lord. And everything, what-ever you do   in word   or**
ἐν ἔργῳ, πάντα ἐν ὀνόματι Κυρίου Ἰησοῦ, εὐχαριστοῦντες
**in work, all things (do) in the name of (the) Lord Jesus,   giving thanks**
τῷ Θεῷ καὶ πατρὶ δι᾽ αὐτοῦ.
**to God and (the) Father through Him.**

18 Αἱ γυναῖκες, ὑποτάσσεσθε τοῖς ἰδίοις ἀνδράσιν, ὡς ἀνῆκεν
**The wives:   be subject   to the own   husbands,   as is befitting**

19 ἐν Κυρίῳ. οἱ ἄνδρες, ἀγαπᾶτε τὰς γυναῖκας, καὶ μὴ πικραί-
**in (the) Lord. The husbands: love   the   wives,   and not be**

20 νεσθε πρὸς αὐτάς. τὰ τέκνα, ὑπακούετε τοῖς γονεῦσι κατὰ
**bitter toward them. The children:   obey   the   parents all in**

21 πάντα· τοῦτο γάρ ἐστιν εὐάρεστον τῷ Κυρίῳ. οἱ πατέρες,
**all,   this   for   is   well-pleasing   to the Lord. The fathers:**

22 μὴ ἐρεθίζετε τὰ τέκνα ὑμῶν, ἵνα μὴ ἀθυμῶσιν. οἱ δοῦλοι,
**do not provoke the children of you, that not   they be disheartened. The slaves:**
ὑπακούετε κατὰ πάντα τοῖς κατὰ σάρκα κυρίοις, μὴ ἐν
**obey   all in all   those according to flesh lords,   not with**
ὀφθαλμοδουλείαις ὡς ἀνθρωπάρεσκοι, ἀλλ᾽ ἐν ἁπλότητι
**eye-services   as   men-pleasers,   but in   singleness**

23 καρδίας, φοβούμενοι τὸν Θεόν· καὶ πᾶν ὅ τι ἐὰν ποιῆτε, ἐκ
**of heart,   fearing   God. And everything whatever you do, from**

24 ψυχῆς ἐργάζεσθε, ὡς τῷ Κυρίῳ καὶ οὐκ ἀνθρώποις· εἰδότες
**the soul work   as to the Lord and not   to men,   knowing**
ὅτι ἀπὸ Κυρίου ἀπολήψεσθε τὴν ἀνταπόδοσιν τῆς κληρονο-
**that from (the) Lord you will receive the   reward   of the inheritance.**

25 μίας· τῷ γὰρ Κυρίῳ Χριστῷ δουλεύετε. ὁ δὲ ἀδικῶν
**the For   Lord   Christ   you serve; the (one) and doing wrong**
κομιεῖται ὃ ἠδίκησε·
**will receive what he did wrong.**

## CHAPTER 4

Christ forgave you, so you also (do). [14] And above all these, (add) love, which is the bond of perfectness. [15] And let the peace of God rule in your hearts, to which you also were called in one body, and be thankful. [16] Let the word of Christ live in you richly, in all wisdom, teaching and exhorting yourselves in psalms and hymns and spiritual songs, singing with grace in your hearts to the Lord. [17] And everything, whatever you may do in word or in deed, (do) all in (the) name of (the) Lord Jesus, giving thanks to God and the Father by Him.

[18] Wives, subject yourselves to (your) own husband, as is becoming in (the) Lord. [19] Husbands, love the wives, and do not be bitter against them. [20] Children, obey the parents in all things; for this is well-pleasing to the Lord. [21] Fathers, do not provoke your children, that they may not be disheartened. [22] Slaves, obey the lords according to flesh in all respects, not with eye-service as men-pleasers, but in singleness of heart, fearing God [23] And whatever you may do, work from the soul, as to the Lord and not to men, [24] knowing that from (the) Lord you shall receive the reward of the inheritance, for you serve the Lord Christ. [25] But he doing wrong shall receive (for) what he did wrong, and there is no respect of persons.

### CHAPTER 4

[1] Lords, give that which (is) just and that which (is) equal to slaves, knowing that you have a Lord in Heaven.

[2] Steadfastly continue in prayer, watching in it with thanksgiving. [3] praying at the same time also for us, that God may open to

1 καὶ οὐκ ἔστι προσωποληψία. οἱ κύριοι, τὸ δίκαιον καὶ τὴν
**and not   is (any) respect of persons. The lords: the just thing and the**
ἰσότητα τοῖς δούλοις παρέχεσθε, εἰδότες ὅτι καὶ ὑμεῖς ἔχετε
**equality to the slaves   supply,   knowing that also you   have**
Κύριον ἐν οὐρανοῖς.
**a Lord in   Heaven.**

2 Τῇ προσευχῇ προσκαρτερεῖτε, γρηγοροῦντες ἐν αὐτῇ ἐν
**In the prayer   steadfastly continue, watching   in   it with**

3 εὐχαριστίᾳ· προσευχόμενοι ἅμα καὶ περὶ ἡμῶν, ἵνα ὁ Θεὸς
**thanksgiving,   praying   together also about us,   that   God**

us a door of the word to speak the mystery of Christ, on account of which I also have been bound, [4] that I may make it clear, as I ought to speak. [5] Walk in wisdom toward those outside, redeeming the time. [6] (Let) your word (be) always with grace, seasoned with salt, to know how you ought to answer each one. [7] Tychicus the beloved brother and faithful minister and fellow-slave in (the) Lord will make known to you the things about me, [8] whom I sent to you for this very thing, that you might know about us, and might comfort your hearts; [9] with Onesimus, the faithful and beloved brother, who is of you. They will make known to you all things here.

[10] Aristarchus my fellow-prisoner greets you, and Mark the cousin of Barnabas, concerning whom you received orders — if he comes to you, receive him — [11] and Jesus called Justus, who are of the circumcision. These (are) the only fellow-workers for the kingdom of God who were a comfort to me. [12] Epaphras greets you, who (is) of you, a slave of Christ, always striving for you in prayers, that you may stand perfect and complete in every will of God. [13] For I bear witness to him that he has much zeal for you and those in Laodicea, and those in Hierapolis. [14] Luke the beloved physician greets you, and Demas. [15] Greet the brothers in Laodicea, and Nymphas, and the church in his house. [16] And when this letter is read before you, cause that it be read also in the Laodicean church; and the one of Laodicea, that you also read. [17] And say to Archippus, Look (to) the ministry which you received in (the) Lord, that you may fulfill it.

ἀνοίξῃ ἡμῖν θύραν τοῦ λόγου, λαλῆσαι τὸ μυστήριον τοῦ
may open to us a door of the word, to speak the mystery

4 Χριστοῦ, δι᾽ ὃ καὶ δέδεμαι· ἵνα φανερώσω αὐτό, ὡς δεῖ με
of Christ, for which also I have been bound, that I may reveal it as it behoves me

5 λαλῆσαι. ἐν σοφίᾳ περιπατεῖτε πρὸς τοὺς ἔξω, τὸν καιρὸν
to speak. In wisdom walk toward those outside, the time

6 ἐξαγοραζόμενοι. ὁ λόγος ὑμῶν πάντοτε ἐν χάριτι, ἅλατι
redeeming. The speech of you (let be) always with grace, with salt
ἠρτυμένος, εἰδέναι πῶς δεῖ ὑμᾶς ἑνὶ ἑκάστῳ ἀποκρίνεσθαι.
being seasoned, to know how it behoves you one each to answer.

7 Τὰ κατ᾽ ἐμὲ πάντα γνωρίσει ὑμῖν Τυχικός, ὁ ἀγαπητὸς
The things about me all will make known to you Tychicus the beloved

8 ἀδελφὸς καὶ πιστὸς διάκονος καὶ σύνδουλος ἐν Κυρίῳ ὃν
brother and faithful minister, and fellow-slave in (the) Lord, whom
ἔπεμψα πρὸς ὑμᾶς εἰς αὐτὸ τοῦτο, ἵνα γνῷ τὰ περὶ ὑμῶν καὶ
I sent to you for this same thing, that he know the about us, and

9 παρακαλέσῃ τὰς καρδίας ὑμῶν· σὺν Ὀνησίμῳ τῷ πιστῷ
he might comfort the hearts of you, with Onesimus the faithful
καὶ ἀγαπητῷ ἀδελφῷ, ὅς ἐστιν ἐξ ὑμῶν. πάντα ὑμῖν
and beloved brother, who is of you; all to you
γνωριοῦσι τὰ ὧδε.
they will make known the things here.

10 Ἀσπάζεται ὑμᾶς Ἀρίσταρχος ὁ συναιχμάλωτός μου,
Greets you Aristarchus the fellow-captive of me,
καὶ Μᾶρκος ὁ ἀνεψιὸς Βαρνάβα (περὶ οὗ ἐλάβετε ἐντολάς·
and Mark the cousin of Barnabas about whom you received orders;

11 ἐὰν ἔλθῃ πρὸς ὑμᾶς, δέξασθε αὐτόν), καὶ Ἰησοῦς ὁ λεγό-
if he comes to you, receive him — and Jesus, the (one)
μενος Ἰοῦστος, οἱ ὄντες ἐκ περιτομῆς· οὗτοι μόνοι συνεργοὶ
named Justus, those being of the circumcision, these only fellow-workers
εἰς τὴν βασιλείαν τοῦ Θεοῦ, οἵτινες ἐγενήθησάν μοι
for the kingdom of God, who became to me

12 παρηγορία. ἀσπάζεται ὑμᾶς Ἐπαφρᾶς ὁ ἐξ ὑμῶν, δοῦλος
a comfort. Greets you Epaphras the (one) of you, a slave
Χριστοῦ, πάντοτε ἀγωνιζόμενος ὑπὲρ ὑμῶν ἐν ταῖς προσ-
of Christ, always struggling on behalf of you in the
ευχαῖς, ἵνα στῆτε τέλειοι καὶ πεπληρωμένοι ἐν παντὶ
prayers, that you may stand full-grown and being complete in all

13 θελήματι τοῦ Θεοῦ. μαρτυρῶ γὰρ αὐτῷ ὅτι ἔχει ζῆλον
(the) will of God. I bear witness For to him that he has zeal
πολὺν ὑπὲρ ὑμῶν καὶ τῶν ἐν Λαοδικείᾳ καὶ τῶν ἐν Ἱεραπό-
much on behalf of you, and those in Laodicea, and those in Hierapolis.

14 λει. ἀσπάζεται ὑμᾶς Λουκᾶς ὁ ἰατρὸς ὁ ἀγαπητός, καὶ
Greets you Luke the physician beloved, and

15 Δημᾶς. ἀσπάσασθε τοὺς ἐν Λαοδικείᾳ ἀδελφούς, καὶ Νυμφᾶν,
Demas. Greet the in Laodicea brothers, and Nymphas,

16 καὶ τὴν κατ᾽ οἶκον αὐτοῦ ἐκκλησίαν. καὶ ὅταν ἀναγνωσθῇ
and the at (the) house of him church. And whenever is read
παρ᾽ ὑμῖν ἡ ἐπιστολή, ποιήσατε ἵνα καὶ ἐν τῇ Λαοδικέων
before you the epistle, cause that also in the Laodicean
ἐκκλησίᾳ ἀναγνωσθῇ, καὶ τὴν ἐκ Λαοδικείας ἵνα καὶ ὑμεῖς
church it is read, and the (one) of Laodicea, that also you

17 ἀναγνῶτε. καὶ εἴπατε Ἀρχίππῳ, Βλέπε τὴν διακονίαν ἣν
read. And tell Archippus: Look (to) the ministry which
παρέλαβες ἐν Κυρίῳ, ἵνα αὐτὴν πληροῖς.
you received in (the) Lord, that it you may fulfill.

[18] The signature of
Paul by my own hand.
Reınember my bonds.
Grace (be) with you.
Amen.

**18**  Ὁ ἀσπασμὸς τῇ ἐμῇ χειρὶ Παύλου. μνημονεύετέ μου τῶν
The greeting      by my hand, of Paul.     Remember of me the

δεσμῶν. ἡ χάρις μεθ᾽ ὑμῶν. ἀμήν.
bonds.      Grace (be) with you.   Amen.

# ΠΑΥΛΟΥ ΤΟΥ ΑΠΟΣΤΟΛΟΥ

### PAUL THE APOSTLE

## Η ΠΡΟΣ

### TO THE

# ΘΕΣΣΑΛΟΝΙΚΕΙΣ

### THESSALONIANS

## ΕΠΙΣΤΟΛΗ ΠΡΩΤΗ

### EPISTLE FIRST

KING JAMES II VERSION

THE APOSTLE PAUL'S

FIRST EPISTLE TO

THE THESSALONIANS

## CHAPTER 1

CHAPTER 1

[1] Paul and Silvanius and Timothy to the church of Thessalonians in God (the) Father and (the) Lord Jesus Christ: Grace to you and peace from God our Father and (the) Lord Jesus Christ.

[2] We give thanks to God always concerning you all, making mention of you at our prayers, [3] remembering without ceasing your work of faith and labor of love and patience of hope of our Lord Jesus Christ before our God and Father; [4] knowing, brothers beloved by God, your election. [5] For our gospel did not come to you in word only, but also in power and in (the) Holy Spirit, and in very much assurance, even as you know what we were among you for your sake; [6] and you became imitators of us and of the Lord, having accepted the word in much affliction with joy of (the) Holy Spirit, [7] so that you became examples to all those who lived in Macedonia and Achaia; [8] for from you the word of the Lord has sounded out, not only in Macedonia and Achaia, but also in every place your faith which (is) towards God has gone abroad, so that there is no need for us to have to say anything; [9] for they themselves witness concerning us, what entrance we have to you,

1 Παῦλος καὶ Σιλουανὸς καὶ Τιμόθεος, τῇ ἐκκλησίᾳ Θεσ-
Paul and Silvanus and Timothy to the church of
σαλονικέων ἐν Θεῷ πατρί, καὶ Κυρίῳ Ἰησοῦ Χριστῷ· χάρις
Thessalonians in God (the) Father, and (the) Lord Jesus Christ: Grace
ὑμῖν καὶ εἰρήνη ἀπὸ Θεοῦ πατρὸς ἡμῶν καὶ Κυρίου Ἰησοῦ
to you and peace from God (the) Father of us and (the) Lord Jesus
Χριστοῦ.
Christ.

2 Εὐχαριστοῦμεν τῷ Θεῷ πάντοτε περὶ πάντων ὑμῶν,
We give thanks to God always concerning all you,
3 μνείαν ὑμῶν ποιούμενοι ἐπὶ τῶν προσευχῶν ἡμῶν, ἀδια-
mention of you making on the prayers of us, un-
λείπτως μνημονεύοντες ὑμῶν τοῦ ἔργου τῆς πίστεως, καὶ
ceasingly remembering of you the work of faith, and
τοῦ κόπου τῆς ἀγάπης, καὶ τῆς ὑπομονῆς τῆς ἐλπίδος τοῦ
the labor of love, and the patience of hope of the
Κυρίου ἡμῶν Ἰησοῦ Χριστοῦ, ἔμπροσθεν τοῦ Θεοῦ καὶ
Lord of us, Jesus Christ, before the God and
4 πατρὸς ἡμῶν· εἰδότες, ἀδελφοὶ ἠγαπημένοι, ὑπὸ Θεοῦ τὴν
Father of us, knowing, brothers, having been loved by God the
5 ἐκλογὴν ὑμῶν· ὅτι τὸ εὐαγγέλιον ἡμῶν οὐκ ἐγενήθη εἰς ὑμᾶς
election of you; because the gospel of us not came to you
ἐν λόγῳ μόνον, ἀλλὰ καὶ ἐν δυνάμει καὶ ἐν Πνεύματι Ἁγίῳ,
in word only, but also in power, and in (the) Spirit Holy,
καὶ ἐν πληροφορίᾳ πολλῇ, καθὼς οἴδατε οἷοι ἐγενήθημεν ἐν
and in assurance much, as you know what sort we were among
6 ὑμῖν δι᾽ ὑμᾶς. καὶ ὑμεῖς μιμηταὶ ἡμῶν ἐγενήθητε καὶ τοῦ
you because of you. And you imitators of us became and of the
Κυρίου, δεξάμενοι τὸν λόγον ἐν θλίψει πολλῇ μετὰ χαρᾶς
Lord, welcoming the word in affliction much with joy
7 Πνεύματος Ἁγίου, ὥστε γενέσθαι ὑμᾶς τύπους πᾶσι τοῖς
of (the) Spirit Holy, so as to become you patterns to all those
8 πιστεύουσιν ἐν τῇ Μακεδονίᾳ καὶ τῇ Ἀχαίᾳ. ἀφ᾽ ὑμῶν γὰρ
believing in Macedonia and Achaia. from you For
ἐξήχηται ὁ λόγος τοῦ Κυρίου οὐ μόνον ἐν τῇ Μακεδονίᾳ
sounded the word of the Lord not only in Macedonia
καὶ Ἀχαίᾳ, ἀλλὰ καὶ ἐν παντὶ τόπῳ ἡ πίστις ὑμῶν ἡ πρὸς
and Achaia, but also in every place the faith of you toward
τὸν Θεὸν ἐξελήλυθεν, ὥστε μὴ χρείαν ἡμᾶς ἔχειν λαλεῖν τι.
God has gone out, so as not need for us to have to speak anything.
9 αὐτοὶ γὰρ περὶ ἡμῶν ἀπαγγέλλουσιν ὁποίαν εἴσοδον ἔσχο-
themselves for about us announce what kind of entrance we

472

and how you had turned to God from the idols, to serve (the) living and true God, [10] and to eagerly expect His Son from Heaven, whom He raised from (the) dead, Jesus, He delivering us from the coming wrath.

μεν πρὸς ὑμᾶς, καὶ πῶς ἐπεστρέψατε πρὸς τὸν Θεὸν ἀπὸ τῶν
have to    you,   and how   you had turned to   the God  from  the

10 εἰδώλων, δουλεύειν Θεῷ ζῶντι καὶ ἀληθινῷ καὶ ἀναμένειν
idols,    to serve   God living and true     and to await

τὸν υἱὸν αὐτοῦ ἐκ τῶν οὐρανῶν, ὃν ἤγειρεν ἐκ νεκρῶν,
the Son of Him from the heavens, whom He raised from (the) dead,

Ἰησοῦν. τὸν ῥυόμενον ἡμᾶς ἀπὸ τῆς ὀργῆς τῆς ἐρχομένης.
Jesus.  He delivering us   from  the   wrath   coming.

## CHAPTER 2

[1] For, brothers, you yourselves know our coming in to you, that it was not fruitless; [2] but also having before suffered and having been insulted, even as you know, at Philippi, we were bold in our God to speak the gospel of God to you in much agony. [3] For our exhortation (was) not of error, nor of uncleanness, nor in guile; [4] but even as we have been approved by God to be entrusted with the gospel, so we speak; not as pleasing men, but God, who tests our hearts. [5] For at no time were we (found) with flattering words, even as you know, nor with a pretense of covetousness; God (is) witness; [6] nor seeking glory from men, neither from you nor from others, (though) being able to be burdensome as apostles of Christ. [7] But we were gentle in your midst, even as a nurse warmly loves her own children. [8] Longing over you in this way, we were pleased to have imparted to you not only the gospel of God, but also our own lives, because you have become beloved to us. [9] For you remember, brothers, our labor and hard work, for working night and day, in order not to burden anyone of you, we preached the Gospel of God to you. [10] You (are) witnesses, and God, how holily and righteously and blamelessly we were to you who believe; [11] even as you know how (to) each one of you, as a father (to) his children, exhorting and consoling you and

## CHAPTER 2

1 Αὐτοὶ γὰρ οἴδατε, ἀδελφοί, τὴν εἴσοδον ἡμῶν τὴν πρὸς
yourselves For, you know, brothers   the entrance  of us   the  to

2 ὑμᾶς, ὅτι οὐ κενὴ γέγονεν· ἀλλὰ καὶ προπαθόντες καὶ
you,   that not in vain it has been,  but  also having suffered before and

ὑβρισθέντες, καθὼς οἴδατε, ἐν Φιλίπποις, ἐπαρρησιασάμεθα
having been insulted, as you know. in Philippi     we were bold

ἐν τῷ Θεῷ ἡμῶν λαλῆσαι πρὸς ὑμᾶς τὸ εὐαγγέλιον τοῦ
in the God of us  to speak  to   you  the  gospel

3 Θεοῦ ἐν πολλῷ ἀγῶνι. ἡ γὰρ παράκλησις ἡμῶν οὐκ ἐκ
of God ,in much  struggle. the For exhortation of us    not of

4 πλάνης, οὐδὲ ἐξ ἀκαθαρσίας, οὔτε ἐν δόλῳ· ἀλλὰ καθὼς
error,   nor  of  uncleanness.  nor  in guile,  but   as

δεδοκιμάσμεθα ὑπὸ τοῦ Θεοῦ πιστευθῆναι τὸ εὐαγγέλιον,
we have been approved by   God  to be entrusted (with) the gospel,

οὕτω λαλοῦμεν, οὐχ ὡς ἀνθρώποις ἀρέσκοντες, ἀλλὰ τῷ Θεῷ
so   we speak,  not as   men      pleasing,     but   God

5 τῷ δοκιμάζοντι τὰς καρδίας ἡμῶν. οὔτε γάρ ποτε ἐν λόγῳ
the (one) testing  the  hearts  of us. neither For then in word

κολακείας ἐγενήθημεν, καθὼς οἴδατε, οὔτε ἐν προφάσει
of flattery  were we,    as   you know, not with pretext

6 πλεονεξίας· Θεὸς μάρτυς· οὔτε ζητοῦντες ἐξ ἀνθρώπων
of covetousness—God (is) witness— nor  seeking   from  men

δόξαν, οὔτε ἀφ' ὑμῶν οὔτε ἀπ' ἄλλων, δυνάμενοι ἐν βάρει
glory, neither from you, nor from others, being able with heaviness

7 εἶναι, ὡς Χριστοῦ ἀπόστολοι, ἀλλ' ἐγενήθημεν ἤπιοι ἐν
to be,  as of Christ  apostles;  but   we were   gentle in

8 μέσῳ ὑμῶν, ὡς ἂν τροφὸς θάλπη τὰ ἑαυτῆς τέκνα· οὕτως,
(the) midst of you, as if a nurse should cherish the of herself children, so

ἱμειρόμενοι ὑμῶν, εὐδοκοῦμεν μεταδοῦναι ὑμῖν οὐ μόνον τὸ
longing    for you, we were well-pleased to impart to you not only the

εὐαγγέλιον τοῦ Θεοῦ, ἀλλὰ καὶ τὰς ἑαυτῶν ψυχάς, διότι
gospel    of God,  but  also  the of ourselves souls, because

9 ἀγαπητοὶ ἡμῖν γεγένησθε. μνημονεύετε γάρ, ἀδελφοί, τὸν
beloved to us you have become. you remember For, brothers,  the

κόπον ἡμῶν καὶ τὸν μόχθον· νυκτὸς γὰρ καὶ ἡμέρας ἐργαζό-
labor of us and the  toil,   night  for and  day   working

μενοι, πρὸς τὸ μὴ ἐπιβαρῆσαί τινα ὑμῶν, ἐκηρύξαμεν εἰς
in order to   not put a burden on anyone of you, we proclaimed to

10 ὑμᾶς τὸ εὐαγγέλιον τοῦ Θεοῦ. ὑμεῖς μάρτυρες καὶ ὁ Θεός,
you  the  gospel    of God. You (are) witnesses, and   God,

ὡς ὁσίως καὶ δικαίως καὶ ἀμέμπτως ὑμῖν τοῖς πιστεύουσιν
how holily and righteously and blamelessly to you, those believing,

11 ἐγενήθημεν· καθάπερ οἴδατε ὡς ἕνα ἕκαστον ὑμῶν, ὡς πατὴρ
we were,    even as you know how one each  of you, as a father

τέκνα ἑαυτοῦ, παρακαλοῦντες ὑμᾶς καὶ παραμυθούμενοι καὶ
children of himself, exhorting     you and   consoling,      and

[12] testifying, for you to walk worthily of God, He calling you to the kingdom and glory of Himself. [13] And because of this we give thanks to God without ceasing, that having received (the) word of hearing from us, you welcomed (it as) of God, and not (as) a word of men, but even as it is truly, (the) word of God, which also works in you, those believing. [14] For brothers, you became imitators of the churches of God which are in Judea in Christ Jesus; because you also suffered the same things from your own countrymen as they also from the Jews, [15] who both killed the Lord Jesus and (their) own prophets, and driving us out, and not pleasing God, and (being) contrary to all men; [16] forbidding us to speak to the nations that they may be saved, in order to fill up their sins always; but the wrath of God has come upon them to the uttermost.

[17] But, brothers, we having been taken away from you for an hour's time — in presence, not in heart — we were much more eagerly trying to see your face with much longing. [18] Therefore, we desired to come to you, I indeed, Paul, both once and twice; and Satan hindered us. [19] For what (is) our hope or joy, or crown of boasting? (Are) you not even (to be) before the Lord of us, Jesus Christ, at His coming? [20] For you are our glory and joy.

CHAPTER 3

[1] So no longer enduring, we thought (it) good to be left in Athens alone, [2] and sent our brother and servant of God, Timothy, and our fellow-worker in the gospel of Christ, in order to establish you and to encourage you concerning

**12** μαρτυρούμενοι, εἰς τὸ περιπατῆσαι ὑμᾶς ἀξίως τοῦ Θεοῦ
testifying for to have walked you worthily of God,
τοῦ καλοῦντος ὑμᾶς εἰς τὴν ἑαυτοῦ βασιλείαν καὶ δόξαν.
the (One) calling you to the of Himself kingdom and glory.

**13** Διὰ τοῦτο καὶ ἡμεῖς εὐχαριστοῦμεν τῷ Θεῷ ἀδιαλείπτως,
therefore And we give thanks to God without ceasing,
ὅτι παραλαβόντες λόγον ἀκοῆς παρ' ἡμῶν τοῦ Θεοῦ,
that having received (the) word of hearing from us, of God,
ἐδέξασθε οὐ λόγον ἀνθρώπων, ἀλλὰ καθώς ἐστιν ἀληθῶς,
you welcomed, not (as) a word of men, but as it is truly,
λόγον Θεοῦ, ὃς καὶ ἐνεργεῖται ἐν ὑμῖν τοῖς πιστεύουσιν.
a word of God, which also works in you, those believing.

**14** ὑμεῖς γὰρ μιμηταὶ ἐγενήθητε, ἀδελφοί, τῶν ἐκκλησιῶν τοῦ
you For imitators became, brothers, of the churches
Θεοῦ τῶν οὐσῶν ἐν τῇ Ἰουδαίᾳ ἐν Χριστῷ Ἰησοῦ· ὅτι ταυτὰ
of God being in Judea in Christ Jesus, because these things
ἐπάθετε καὶ ὑμεῖς ὑπὸ τῶν ἰδίων συμφυλετῶν, καθὼς καὶ
suffered also you by the own fellow-countrymen, as also

**15** αὐτοὶ ὑπὸ τῶν Ἰουδαίων, τῶν καὶ τὸν Κύριον ἀποκτεινάν-
they by the Jews, those both the Lord killing,
των Ἰησοῦν καὶ τοὺς ἰδίους προφήτας, καὶ ἡμᾶς ἐκδιωξάν-
Jesus, and the own prophets, and us driving out
των, καὶ Θεῷ μὴ ἀρεσκόντων, καὶ πᾶσιν ἀνθρώποις
and God not pleasing, and to all men

**16** ἐναντίων, κωλυόντων ἡμᾶς τοῖς ἔθνεσι λαλῆσαι ἵνα σωθῶσιν,
contrary, hindering us to the nations to speak, that they be saved,
εἰς τὸ ἀναπληρῶσαι αὐτῶν τὰς ἁμαρτίας πάντοτε· ἔφθασε
to fill up of them the sins always. has come
δὲ ἐπ' αὐτοὺς ἡ ὀργὴ εἰς τέλος.
But on them the wrath to (the) end.

**17** Ἡμεῖς δέ, ἀδελφοί, ἀπορφανισθέντες ἀφ' ὑμῶν πρὸς καιρὸν
we But, brothers being taken away from you for time
ὥρας, προσώπῳ οὐ καρδίᾳ, περισσοτέρως ἐσπουδάσαμεν
of an hour, in face, not in heart, more abundantly were eager

**18** τὸ πρόσωπον ὑμῶν ἰδεῖν ἐν πολλῇ ἐπιθυμίᾳ· διὸ ἠθελήσαμεν
the face of you to see with much desire. Therefore we desired
ἐλθεῖν πρὸς ὑμᾶς, ἐγὼ μὲν Παῦλος καὶ ἅπαξ καὶ δίς, καὶ ἐνέ-
to come to you, I indeed Paul, both once and twice, and

**19** κοψεν ἡμᾶς ὁ Σατανᾶς. τίς γὰρ ἡμῶν ἐλπὶς ἢ χαρὰ ἢ στέ-
hindered us Satan. what For of us hope or joy or
φανος καυχήσεως ; ἢ οὐχὶ καὶ ὑμεῖς, ἔμπροσθεν τοῦ Κυρίου
crown of boasting? Not even you before the Lord

**20** ἡμῶν Ἰησοῦ Χριστοῦ ἐν τῇ αὐτοῦ παρουσίᾳ ; ὑμεῖς γάρ
of us, Jesus Christ at the of Him coming? you For
ἐστε ἡ δόξα ἡμῶν καὶ ἡ χαρά.
you are the glory of us and the joy.

CHAPTER 3

**1** Διὸ μηκέτι στέγοντες, εὐδοκήσαμεν καταλειφθῆναι ἐν
So no longer enduring, we were pleased to be left in

**2** Ἀθήναις μόνοι, καὶ ἐπέμψαμεν Τιμόθεον τὸν ἀδελφὸν ἡμῶν
Athens alone, and sent Timothy the brother of us
καὶ διάκονον τοῦ Θεοῦ καὶ συνεργὸν ἡμῶν ἐν τῷ εὐαγγελίῳ
and minister of God, and fellow-worker of us in the gospel
τοῦ Χριστοῦ, εἰς τὸ στηρίξαι ὑμᾶς καὶ παρακαλέσαι ὑμᾶς περὶ
of Christ, to establish you and to encourage you about

3 τῆς πίστεως ὑμῶν, τῷ μηδένα σαίνεσθαι ἐν ταῖς θλίψεσι
the faith    of you      no one to be drawn aside by    afflictions

4 ταύταις· αὐτοὶ γὰρ οἴδατε ὅτι εἰς τοῦτο κείμεθα. καὶ γὰρ
these.    yourselves For you know that to this we are appointed. even For

ὅτε πρὸς ὑμᾶς ἦμεν, προελέγομεν ὑμῖν ὅτι μέλλομεν θλί-
when with you we were, we said before to you that we are about to be

5 βεσθαι, καθὼς καὶ ἐγένετο καὶ οἴδατε. διὰ τοῦτο κἀγώ,
afflicted,   as    also it happened, and you know. Therefore I also

μηκέτι στέγων, ἔπεμψα εἰς τὸ γνῶναι τὴν πίστιν ὑμῶν, μή
no longer enduring sent  to    know    the faith of you, lest

πως ἐπείρασεν ὑμᾶς ὁ πειράζων, καὶ εἰς κενὸν γένηται ὁ
somehow tempted you the tempting (one), and in vain became the

6 κόπος ἡμῶν. ἄρτι δὲ ἐλθόντος Τιμοθέου πρὸς ἡμᾶς ἀφ᾽
labor of us.  now But coming  Timothy   to  us from

ὑμῶν, καὶ εὐαγγελισαμένου ἡμῖν τὴν πίστιν καὶ τὴν ἀγάπην
you, and announcing good news to us (of) the faith and the love

ὑμῶν, καὶ ὅτι ἔχετε μνείαν ἡμῶν ἀγαθὴν πάντοτε, ἐπιπο-
of you, and that you have remembrance of us good always, longing

7 θοῦντες ἡμᾶς ἰδεῖν, καθάπερ καὶ ἡμεῖς ὑμᾶς· διὰ τοῦτο
us to see,   even as   also we  you, for this reason

παρεκλήθημεν, ἀδελφοί, ἐφ᾽ ὑμῖν ἐπὶ πάσῃ τῇ θλίψει καὶ
we were comforted, brothers, over you on all the affliction and

8 ἀνάγκῃ ἡμῶν διὰ τῆς ὑμῶν πίστεως· ὅτι νῦν ζῶμεν, ἐὰν
distress of us through the of you faith, because now we live if

9 ὑμεῖς στήκητε ἐν Κυρίῳ. τίνα γὰρ εὐχαριστίαν δυνάμεθα τῷ
you  stand in (the) Lord. what For thanks   are we able

Θεῷ ἀνταποδοῦναι περὶ ὑμῶν, ἐπὶ πάσῃ τῇ χαρᾷ ᾗ χαί-
to God to return concerning you, over all the joy (with) which

10 ρομεν δι᾽ ὑμᾶς ἔμπροσθεν τοῦ Θεοῦ ἡμῶν, νυκτὸς καὶ ἡμέρας
we rejoice by you before the God of us, night and day

ὑπὲρ ἐκ περισσοῦ δεόμενοι εἰς τὸ ἰδεῖν ὑμῶν τὸ πρόσωπον,
superabundantly petitioning for to see of you the face,

καὶ καταρτίσαι τὰ ὑστερήματα τῆς πίστεως ὑμῶν ;
and to complete the things lacking in the faith of you?

11 Αὐτὸς δὲ ὁ Θεὸς καὶ πατὴρ ἡμῶν, καὶ ὁ Κύριος ἡμῶν
Himself And, the God and Father of us, and the Lord of us,

12 Ἰησοῦς Χριστός, κατευθύναι τὴν ὁδὸν ἡμῶν πρὸς ὑμᾶς· ὑμᾶς
Jesus  Christ, may He direct the way of us to you, you

δὲ ὁ Κύριος πλεονάσαι καὶ περισσεύσαι τῇ ἀγάπῃ εἰς ἀλλή-
and the Lord make to abound and to exceed in love toward one

13 λους καὶ εἰς πάντας, καθάπερ καὶ ἡμεῖς εἰς ὑμᾶς, εἰς τὸ
another and toward all,   even as   also we toward you, to

στηρίξαι ὑμῶν τὰς καρδίας ἀμέμπτους ἐν ἁγιωσύνῃ,
establish of you the hearts blameless in holiness,

ἔμπροσθεν τοῦ Θεοῦ καὶ πατρὸς ἡμῶν, ἐν τῇ παρουσίᾳ τοῦ
before  the God and Father of us, in the presence of the

Κυρίου ἡμῶν Ἰησοῦ Χριστοῦ μετὰ πάντων τῶν ἁγίων
Lord of us, Jesus Christ, with all the saints

αὐτοῦ.
of Him.

## CHAPTER 4

1 Τὸ λοιπὸν οὖν, ἀδελφοί, ἐρωτῶμεν ὑμᾶς καὶ παρακαλοῦ-
For the rest, then, brothers, we beseech you and we exhort

μεν ἐν Κυρίῳ Ἰησοῦ καθὼς παρελάβετε παρ᾽ ἡμῶν τὸ πῶς
in (the) Lord Jesus, even as you received from us how

---

your faith, [3] that no one be moved by these trials — for you yourselves know that we are appointed for this — [4] for also, when we were with you, we told you beforehand we are about to suffer trial, even as also it came to pass, and you know. [5] Because of this, I also no longer waiting, sent in order to know your faith, lest perhaps the tempter should tempt you and make our labor to no avail. [6] But now, Timothy having come to us from you, and having told us good news (of) your love and faith, and that you always have good remembrance of us, longing to see us, even as also we you; [7] because of this, we were comforted, brothers, as to you, in all our trial and need, [8] because we now live, if you should stand fast in (the) Lord. [9] For what thanks can we return to God as to you, for all the joy with which we rejoice on account of you before our God, [10] night and day praying to see your face, and to perfect the things lacking in your faith? [11] But may our God and Father Himself and our Lord Jesus Christ direct our way to you. [12] But may the Lord make you to increase and to abound in love toward one another and toward all, even as we also toward you, [13] in order to establish your hearts blameless in holiness before our God and Father at the coming of our Lord Jesus Christ with all His saints.

CHAPTER 4
[1] For the rest, then, brothers, we beg you and we exhort in (the) Lord Jesus, even as you received

from us how you ought to walk and to please God, that you abound more. [2] For you know what injunctions we gave you through the Lord Jesus. [3] For this is God's will, your sanctification, you to abstain from fornication, [4] each one of you to know to possess his vessel in purity and honor, [5] not in passion of lust, even as also the nations not knowing God; [6] not to go beyond and to overreach in the matter of his brother; because (the) avenger concerning all these (is) the Lord, even as we told you before and solemnly testified. [7] For God did not call us to uncleanness, but in purity. [8] Therefore, he that despises does not despise man, but God, even He giving His Holy Spirit to us.

[9] Now as to brotherly love, you have no need (for me) to write to you, for you yourselves are taught by God to love one another. [10] For you also do it to the brothers in all Macedonia; but, brothers, we exhort you to abound more, [11] and to try earnestly to be quiet, and to do (your) own things, and to work with your own hands, as we enjoined you, [12] that you may walk becomingly toward those outside, and you may have need of nothing.

[13] But I do not want you to be ignorant, brothers, concerning those who have fallen asleep, that you may not be grieved, even as also the rest who have no hope. [14] For if we believe that Jesus died and rose again, even so God will also bring with Him all those who are fallen asleep through Jesus. [15] For we say this to you in (the) word of (the) Lord, that we the living who remain in the coming of the Lord, in no way go before those who are fallen asleep; [16] because the Lord Himself shall descend from Heaven with a shout, with the voice of the archangel and with the trumpet of God; and the

δεῖ ὑμᾶς περιπατεῖν καὶ ἀρέσκειν Θεῷ, ἵνα περισσεύητε
it behoves you to walk and to please God, that you abound

2 μᾶλλον. οἴδατε γὰρ τίνας παραγγελίας ἐδώκαμεν ὑμῖν διὰ
more. you know For what injunctions we gave you through

3 τοῦ Κυρίου Ἰησοῦ. τοῦτο γάρ ἐστι θέλημα τοῦ Θεοῦ, ὁ
the Lord Jesus. this For is (the) will of God, the

4 ἁγιασμὸς ὑμῶν, ἀπέχεσθαι ὑμᾶς ἀπὸ τῆς πορνείας· εἰδέναι
sanctification of you, to abstain you from fornication, to know

ἕκαστον ὑμῶν τὸ ἑαυτοῦ σκεῦος κτᾶσθαι ἐν ἁγιασμῷ καὶ τιμῇ,
each one of you the of himself vessel to possess in purity and honor,

5 μὴ ἐν πάθει ἐπιθυμίας, καθάπερ καὶ τὰ ἔθνη τὰ μὴ εἰδότα τὸν
not in passion of lust, even as also the nations not knowing

6 Θεόν· τὸ μὴ ὑπερβαίνειν καὶ πλεονεκτεῖν ἐν τῷ πράγματι
God, not to go beyond and to overreach in the matter

τὸν ἀδελφὸν αὐτοῦ· διότι ἔκδικος ὁ Κύριος περὶ πάντων
the brother of him, because (the) avenger the Lord (is) concerning all

τούτων, καθὼς καὶ προείπαμεν ὑμῖν καὶ διεμαρτυράμεθα.
these, as indeed we before told you and solemnly witnessed.

7 οὐ γὰρ ἐκάλεσεν ἡμᾶς ὁ Θεὸς ἐπὶ ἀκαθαρσίᾳ, ἀλλ' ἐν
not For called us God to uncleanness, but in

8 ἁγιασμῷ. τοιγαροῦν ὁ ἀθετῶν οὐκ ἄνθρωπον ἀθετεῖ, ἀλλὰ
purity. Therefore those despising not man despises, but

τὸν Θεὸν τὸν καὶ δόντα τὸ Πνεῦμα αὐτοῦ τὸ Ἅγιον εἰς ἡμᾶς.
God, the (One) also giving the Spirit of him the Holy to you.

9 Περὶ δὲ τῆς φιλαδελφίας οὐ χρείαν ἔχετε γράφειν ὑμῖν·
concerning And brotherly love, no need you have to write to you,

αὐτοὶ γὰρ ὑμεῖς θεοδίδακτοί ἐστε εἰς τὸ ἀγαπᾶν ἀλλήλους·
yourselves for you taught by God are to love one another;

10 καὶ γὰρ ποιεῖτε αὐτὸ εἰς πάντας τοὺς ἀδελφοὺς τοὺς ἐν ὅλῃ
indeed for you do it toward all the brothers in all

τῇ Μακεδονίᾳ. παρακαλοῦμεν δὲ ὑμᾶς, ἀδελφοί, περισσεύειν
Macedonia. we exhort But you, brothers, to abound

11 μᾶλλον, καὶ φιλοτιμεῖσθαι ἡσυχάζειν, καὶ πράσσειν τὰ ἴδια,
more, and to try earnestly to be quiet, and to practice the own,

καὶ ἐργάζεσθαι ταῖς ἰδίαις χερσὶν ὑμῶν, καθὼς ὑμῖν παρηγ-
and to work with the own hands of you, as you we

12 γείλαμεν· ἵνα περιπατῆτε εὐσχημόνως πρὸς τοὺς ἔξω, καὶ
enjoined, that you may walk becomingly toward those outside, and

μηδενὸς χρείαν ἔχητε.
of nothing need you may have.

13 Οὐ θέλω δὲ ὑμᾶς ἀγνοεῖν, ἀδελφοί, περὶ τῶν κεκοιμη-
not I do desire And you to be ignorant, brothers, about those sleeping,

μένων, ἵνα μὴ λυπῆσθε, καθὼς καὶ οἱ λοιποὶ οἱ μὴ ἔχοντες
lest you grieve as also the rest not having

14 ἐλπίδα. εἰ γὰρ πιστεύομεν ὅτι Ἰησοῦς ἀπέθανε καὶ ἀνέστη,
hope. if For we believe that Jesus died and rose again,

οὕτω καὶ ὁ Θεὸς τοὺς κοιμηθέντας διὰ τοῦ Ἰησοῦ ἄξει σὺν
so also God those having slept through Jesus will bring with

15 αὐτῷ. τοῦτο γὰρ ὑμῖν λέγομεν ἐν λόγῳ Κυρίου, ὅτι ἡμεῖς οἱ
Him. this For to you we say by a word of (the) Lord, that we the

ζῶντες οἱ περιλειπόμενοι εἰς τὴν παρουσίαν τοῦ Κυρίου, οὐ
living remaining to the coming of the Lord, not

16 μὴ φθάσωμεν τοὺς κοιμηθέντας. ὅτι αὐτὸς ὁ Κύριος ἐν κελεύ-
at all may go before those having slept; because Himself the Lord with a word

σματι, ἐν φωνῇ ἀρχαγγέλου, καὶ ἐν σάλπιγγι Θεοῦ καταβή-
of command by a voice of an archangel, and with a trumpet of God, will

σεται ἀπ᾽ οὐρανοῦ, καὶ οἱ νεκροὶ ἐν Χριστῷ ἀναστήσονται
descend from Heaven,   and the   dead   in   Christ   will rise again

17 πρῶτον· ἔπειτα ἡμεῖς οἱ ζῶντες, οἱ περιλειπόμενοι, ἅμα σὺν
firstly,   then   we the living·   remaining   together with
αὐτοῖς ἁρπαγησόμεθα ἐν νεφέλαις εἰς ἀπάντησιν τοῦ Κυρίου
them   will be caught up   in  clouds   to a meeting   of the Lord

18 εἰς ἀέρα· καὶ οὕτω πάντοτε σὺν Κυρίῳ ἐσόμεθα. ὥστε παρα-
in (the) air, and so   always   with (the) Lord we will be. So then
καλεῖτε ἀλλήλους ἐν τοῖς λόγοις τούτοις.
comfort one another with   words   these.

CHAPTER 5

1 Περὶ δὲ τῶν χρόνων καὶ τῶν καιρῶν, ἀδελφοί, οὐ χρείαν
concerning And the times   and the   seasons, brothers,  not need
2 ἔχετε ὑμῖν γράφεσθαι. αὐτοὶ γὰρ ἀκριβῶς οἴδατε ὅτι ἡ ἡμέρα
have  you  to be written, yourselves for accurately you know that (the) day
3 Κυρίου ὡς κλέπτης ἐν νυκτὶ οὕτως ἔρχεται· ὅταν γὰρ
of (the) Lord as a thief   at  night   so   it comes. when For
λέγωσιν, Εἰρήνη καὶ ἀσφάλεια, τότε αἰφνίδιος αὐτοῖς
they say,  Peace   and   safety!   Then   sudden   them
ἐφίσταται ὄλεθρος, ὥσπερ ἡ ὠδὶν τῇ ἐν γαστρὶ ἐχούσῃ, καὶ
comes on destruction, as   the travail to the pregnant woman, and
4 οὐ μὴ ἐκφύγωσιν. ὑμεῖς δέ, ἀδελφοί, οὐκ ἐστὲ ἐν σκότει, ἵνα
not at all may they escape. you But, brothers,  not  are  in darkness, that
5 ἡ ἡμέρα ὑμᾶς ὡς κλέπτης καταλάβῃ· πάντες ὑμεῖς υἱοὶ φωτός
the day   you   as   a thief should overtake;  all   you sons of light
6 ἐστε καὶ υἱοὶ ἡμέρας· οὐκ ἐσμὲν νυκτὸς οὐδὲ σκότους· ἄρα οὖν
are, and sons of day. not We are of night,  nor of darkness; therefore
μὴ καθεύδωμεν ὡς καὶ οἱ λοιποί, ἀλλὰ γρηγορῶμεν καὶ
not let us sleep   as also the   rest,   but  let us watch   and
7 νήφωμεν. οἱ γὰρ καθεύδοντες νυκτὸς καθεύδουσι· καὶ οἱ
be sober.  those For  sleeping,   by night   sleep,   and those
8 μεθυσκόμενοι νυκτὸς μεθύουσιν. ἡμεῖς δέ, ἡμέρας ὄντες, νήφω-
being drunk   by night   are drunk; we but, of day   being, let us be
μεν, ἐνδυσάμενοι θώρακα πίστεως καὶ ἀγάπης, καὶ περικεφα-
sober, putting on a breastplate of faith and of love,   and a helmet
9 λαίαν, ἐλπίδα σωτηρίας. ὅτι οὐκ ἔθετο ἡμᾶς ὁ Θεὸς εἰς
of hope  of salvation; because not appointed us   God  to
ὀργήν, ἀλλ᾽ εἰς περιποίησιν σωτηρίας διὰ τοῦ Κυρίου ἡμῶν
wrath,   but  for obtainment  of salvation through the Lord  of us,
10 Ἰησοῦ Χριστοῦ, τοῦ ἀποθανόντος ὑπὲρ ἡμῶν, ἵνα, εἴτε
Jesus   Christ,  the (One) having died  on behalf of us,  that whether
11 γρηγορῶμεν εἴτε καθεύδωμεν, ἅμα σὺν αὐτῷ ζήσωμεν. διὸ
we watch   or  we sleep,   together with  Him we may live. So
παρακαλεῖτε ἀλλήλους, καὶ οἰκοδομεῖτε εἰς τὸν ἕνα, καθὼς
comfort   one another,   and  build up   one the other,  as
καὶ ποιεῖτε.
indeed you do.

12 Ἐρωτῶμεν δὲ ὑμᾶς, ἀδελφοί, εἰδέναι τοὺς κοπιῶντας ἐν
we ask   And  you,  brothers, to know those  laboring among
ὑμῖν, καὶ προϊσταμένους ὑμῶν ἐν Κυρίῳ, καὶ νουθετοῦντας
you, and  taking the lead  of you in (the) Lord, and  warning
13 ὑμᾶς, καὶ ἡγεῖσθαι αὐτοὺς ὑπὲρ ἐκ περισσοῦ ἐν ἀγάπῃ διὰ
you, and  esteem   them   most exceedingly  in love because of
14 τὸ ἔργον αὐτῶν. εἰρηνεύετε ἐν ἑαυτοῖς. παρακαλοῦμεν δὲ
the work  of them. Be at peace among yourselves. we exhort  And

---

dead in Christ shall rise first [17] then we who (are) left alive shall be caught away together with those in (the) clouds for (the) meeting of the Lord in (the) air; and so we shall always be with the Lord. [18] So comfort each other with these words.

CHAPTER 5

[1] But as to the times and the seasons, brothers, you have no need for you to be written (to), [2] for you yourselves know accurately that the day of (the) Lord comes as a thief in the night. [3] For when they say, Peace and safety! then suddenly destruction comes upon them, like travail to her that is with child; and in no way shall they escape. [4] But you, brothers, are not in darkness, that the Day should overtake you as a thief; [5] you are all sons of light and sons of day; we are not of night nor of darkness. [6] So then we should not sleep as also the rest, but we should watch, and we should be sober; [7] for they that sleep sleep by night and they that are drunken get drunk by night; [8] but we being of day should be sensible, having put on (the) breastplate of faith and love, and the hope of salvation (as) a helmet; [9] because God has not appointed us for wrath, but for obtaining salvation through our Lord Jesus Christ, [10] who died for us, that whether we may watch or we may sleep, we may live together with Him. [11] Therefore encourage one another, and build up one another, even as you are also doing.

[12] But, brothers, we beg you to know those who labor among you, and take the lead of you in (the) Lord, and warn you, [13] and to esteem them exceedingly in love because of their work. Be at peace among yourselves. [14] But we exhort you,

ὑμᾶς, ἀδελφοί, νουθετεῖτε τοὺς ἀτάκτους, παραμυθεῖσθε τοὺς
you, brothers,    warn       the insubordinate,  comfort    the

ὀλιγοψύχους, ἀντέχεσθε τῶν ἀσθενῶν, μακροθυμεῖτε πρὸς
faint-hearted,     care for  those being weak, be long-suffering toward

15 πάντας. ὁρᾶτε μή τις κακὸν ἀντὶ κακοῦ τινι ἀποδῷ· ἀλλὰ
all.      See (that) not anyone evil for  evil to anyone returns,  but

πάντοτε τὸ ἀγαθὸν διώκετε καὶ εἰς ἀλλήλους καὶ εἰς πάντας.
always    the  good      follow even toward one another and toward all.

16 πάντοτε χαίρετε· ἀδιαλείπτως προσεύχεσθε· ἐν παντὶ
17 always   Rejoice.   without ceasing  Pray.        In everything
18 εὐχαριστεῖτε· τοῦτο γὰρ θέλημα Θεοῦ ἐν Χριστῷ Ἰησοῦ εἰς
give thanks,    this  for (is) (the) will of God in Christ   Jesus as to

19 ὑμᾶς. τὸ Πνεῦμα μὴ σβέννυτε· προφητείας μὴ ἐξουθενεῖτε·
20 you.  The Spirit   not do quench.  Prophecies  not    despise.

21 πάντα δοκιμάζετε· τὸ καλὸν κατέχετε· ἀπὸ παντὸς εἴδους
22 All things test,       the good hold fast.  From every    form
πονηροῦ ἀπέχεσθε.
of evil    keep back.

23      Αὐτὸς δὲ ὁ Θεὸς τῆς εἰρήνης ἁγιάσαι ὑμᾶς ὁλοτελεῖς· καὶ
       Himself And, the God  of peace, may He sanctify you fully,   and
ὁλόκληρον ὑμῶν τὸ πνεῦμα καὶ ἡ ψυχὴ καὶ τὸ σῶμα
whole      of you  the   spirit,  and the soul,  and the body,
ἀμέμπτως ἐν τῇ παρουσίᾳ τοῦ Κυρίου ἡμῶν Ἰησοῦ Χριστοῦ
blamelessly at the coming of the  Lord    of us, Jesus    Christ

24 τηρηθείη. πιστὸς ὁ καλῶν ὑμᾶς, ὃς καὶ ποιήσει.
may be kept. Faithful (is) He calling you, who also will do (it).

25 Ἀδελφοί, προσεύχεσθε περὶ ἡμῶν.
Brothers,  pray       concerning us.

26 Ἀσπάσασθε τοὺς ἀδελφοὺς πάντας ἐν φιλήματι ἁγίῳ.
Greet         the  brothers    all    with  kiss  a holy.

27 ὁρκίζω ὑμᾶς τὸν Κύριον, ἀναγνωσθῆναι τὴν ἐπιστολὴν
I charge  you by the Lord      to be read          the   epistle
πᾶσι τοῖς ἁγίοις ἀδελφοῖς.
to all   the holy brothers.

28 Ἡ χάρις τοῦ Κυρίου ἡμῶν Ἰησοῦ Χριστοῦ μεθ᾽ ὑμῶν.
The grace of the Lord    of us,    Jesus   Christ, (be) with you.
ἀμήν.
Amen.

brothers, to warn the unruly ones, comfort the faint-hearted, sustain the weak, be patient towards all. [15] See that no one renders evil for evil, but always pursue the good, both towards one another and towards all. [16] Rejoice evermore. [17] Pray without ceasing. [18] In everything give thanks, for this (is the) will of God in Christ Jesus towards you. [19] Do not quench the Spirit. [20] Do not despise prophecies. [21] Test all things, hold to the right. [22] Keep back from every form of evil. [23] And may the God of Peace Himself fully sanctify you, and may your whole spirit and soul and body be kept blameless at the coming of our Lord Jesus Christ. [24] (He) who calls you (is) faithful, who also will perform (it). [25] Brothers, pray for us. [26] Greet all the brothers with a holy kiss. [27] I charge you by the Lord that this letter be read to all the holy brothers. [28] The grace of our Lord Jesus Christ (be) with you. Amen.

ΠΑΥΛΟΥ ΤΟΥ ΑΠΟΣΤΟΛΟΥ
PAUL    THE    APOSTLE

Η ΠΡΟΣ
THE TO

ΘΕΣΣΑΛΟΝΙΚΕΙΣ
(THE) THESSALONIANS
ΕΠΙΣΤΟΛΗ ΔΕΥΤΕΡΑ
EPISTLE   SECOND

## KING JAMES II VERSION
## THE APOSTLE PAUL'S
## SECOND EPISTLE TO
## THE THESSALONIANS

CHAPTER 1

[1] Paul and Silvanus and Timothy to the assembly of the Thessalonians in God our Father and (the) Lord Jesus Christ: [2] Grace to you and peace from God our Father and (the) Lord Jesus Christ.

[3] We are bound to thank God always concerning you, brothers, even as it is right to do so, because your faith grows more and more, and the love of each one of you all abounds toward one another; [4] so as for us to boast ourselves in you in the churches of God for your patience and faith in all your persecutions, and the trials which you are bearing; [5] a clear token of the righteous judgment of God, in order for you to be accounted worthy of the kingdom of God, for which you also suffer; [6] since (it is) a just thing with God to repay those afflicting you (with) affliction; and to you, those being afflicted, rest with us at the revelation of the Lord Jesus from Heaven with angels of His power. [8] in flaming fire taking vengeance on those that do not know God, and those that do not obey the gospel of our Lord Jesus Christ, [9] who shall suffer (the) penalty: everlasting death from the presence of the Lord and from the glory of His strength, [10] when He comes to be glorified in His saints, and to be admired in all those that believe in that Day — because our testimony to you was

## CHAPTER 1

1 Παῦλος καὶ Σιλουανὸς καὶ Τιμόθεος τῇ ἐκκλησίᾳ Θεσσα-
Paul and Silvanus and Timothy to the church of Thess-
λονικέων ἐν Θεῷ πατρὶ ἡμῶν καὶ Κυρίῳ Ἰησοῦ Χριστῷ·
alonians in God (the) Father of us and (the) Lord Jesus Christ :

2 χάρις ὑμῖν καὶ εἰρήνη ἀπὸ Θεοῦ πατρὸς ἡμῶν καὶ Κυρίου
Grace to you and peace from God (the) Father of us and (the) Lord
Ἰησοῦ Χριστοῦ.
Jesus Christ.

3 Εὐχαριστεῖν ὀφείλομεν τῷ Θεῷ πάντοτε περὶ ὑμῶν,
to give thanks We ought to God always concerning you,
ἀδελφοί, καθὼς ἄξιόν ἐστιν, ὅτι ὑπεραυξάνει ἡ πίστις ὑμῶν,
brothers, even as right it is; because grows exceedingly the faith of you,
καὶ πλεονάζει ἡ ἀγάπη ἑνὸς ἑκάστου πάντων ὑμῶν εἰς ἀλλή-
and multiplies the love one of each all of you to one

4 λους· ὥστε ἡμᾶς αὐτοὺς ἐν ὑμῖν καυχᾶσθαι ἐν ταῖς ἐκκλησίαις
another, so as us ourselves in you to boast among the churches
τοῦ Θεοῦ ὑπὲρ τῆς ὑπομονῆς ὑμῶν καὶ πίστεως ἐν πᾶσι
of God for the patience of you and faith in all

5 τοῖς διωγμοῖς ὑμῶν καὶ ταῖς θλίψεσιν αἷς ἀνέχεσθε· ἔνδειγμα
the persecutions of you and the afflictions which you endure, a clear token
τῆς δικαίας κρίσεως τοῦ Θεοῦ, εἰς τὸ καταξιωθῆναι ὑμᾶς τῆς
of the just judgment of God for to be counted worthy you of the

6 βασιλείας τοῦ Θεοῦ, ὑπὲρ ἧς καὶ πάσχετε· εἴπερ δίκαιον παρὰ
kingdom of God, for which indeed you suffer, since a just thing with

7 Θεῷ ἀνταποδοῦναι τοῖς θλίβουσιν ὑμᾶς θλῖψιν, καὶ ὑμῖν τοῖς
God to repay to those afflicting you affliction, and to you those
θλιβομένοις ἄνεσιν μεθ’ ἡμῶν, ἐν τῇ ἀποκαλύψει τοῦ Κυρίου
being afflicted rest with us, at the revelation of the Lord

8 Ἰησοῦ ἀπ’ οὐρανοῦ μετ’ ἀγγέλων δυνάμεως αὐτοῦ, ἐν πυρὶ
Jesus from Heaven with angels of power of Him, in fire
φλογός, διδόντος ἐκδίκησιν τοῖς μὴ εἰδόσι Θεόν, καὶ τοῖς
of flame, giving full vengeance to those not knowing God, and to those
μὴ ὑπακούουσι τῷ εὐαγγελίῳ τοῦ Κυρίου ἡμῶν Ἰησ

9 not obeying the gospel of the Lord of us, Jesus
Χριστοῦ· οἵτινες δίκην τίσουσιν, ὄλεθρον αἰώνιον ἀπὸ προσ-
Christ, who (the) penalty will pay, destruction eternal from (the)
ώπου τοῦ Κυρίου καὶ ἀπὸ τῆς δόξης τῆς ἰσχύος αὐτοῦ,
face of the Lord and from the glory of the strength of Him,

10 ὅταν ἔλθη ἐνδοξασθῆναι ἐν τοῖς ἁγίοις αὐτοῦ, καὶ θαυμασθῆ-
when He comes to be glorified in the saints of Him, and to be admired
ναι ἐν πᾶσι τοῖς πιστεύουσιν (ὅτι ἐπιστεύθη τὸ μαρτύριον
in all those having believed, because was believed the testimony

believed. [11] For which also we always pray for you, that our God may count you worthy of the calling and may fulfill every good pleasure of goodness and work of faith with power (in you), [12] so that the name of our Lord Jesus Christ may be glorified in you, and you in Him, according to the grace of our God and of (the) Lord Jesus Christ.

CHAPTER 2

[1] Now we beg you, brothers, by the coming of our Lord Jesus Christ and our gathering together to Him, [2] for you not to be quickly shaken in mind or troubled, either by spirit or by word or by letter, as if by us, as if the day of Christ is at hand. [3] Let no one deceive you in any way, because (that Day will not come) unless the falling away comes first, and is revealed the man of sin, the son of perdition, [4] he opposing and exalting himself over everything being called God, or object of worship, so as (for) him to sit in the temple of God as God, showing himself that he is a god. [5] Do you not remember that I told you these things, yet being with you? [6] And now the thing holding back you know, for him to be revealed in his time. [7] For the mystery of lawlessness already works —only he holding back now until it comes out of (the) midst. [8] And then the Lawless One will be revealed, whom the Lord will consume by the spirit of His mouth; and (He) will bring to nothing by the brightness of His coming; [9] whose coming is according to the working of Satan in every power and miracle and lying wonders, [10] and in every deceit of unrighteousness in those that perish, because they did not receive the love of truth in order for them to be saved. [11] And because of this God will

11 ἡμῶν ἐφ᾽ ὑμᾶς) ἐν τῇ ἡμέρᾳ ἐκείνῃ. εἰς ὃ καὶ προσευχόμεθ
of us to you in day that. For which indeed we pray
πάντοτε περὶ ὑμῶν, ἵνα ὑμᾶς ἀξιώσῃ τῆς κλήσεως ὁ Θεὸς
always concerning you, that you may count worthy of the calling the God
ἡμῶν, καὶ πληρώσῃ πᾶσαν εὐδοκίαν ἀγαθωσύνης καὶ ἔργον
of us, and may fulfill every good pleasure of goodness and work

12 πίστεως ἐν δυνάμει· ὅπως ἐνδοξασθῇ τὸ ὄνομα τοῦ Κυρίου
of faith in power, so as may be glorified the name of the Lord
ἡμῶν Ἰησοῦ Χριστοῦ ἐν ὑμῖν, καὶ ὑμεῖς ἐν αὐτῷ, κατὰ τὴν
of us. Jesus Christ in you, and you in Him, according to the
χάριν τοῦ Θεοῦ ἡμῶν καὶ Κυρίου Ἰησοῦ Χριστοῦ.
grace of the God of us and (the) Lord Jesus Christ.

CHAPTER 2

1 Ἐρωτῶμεν δὲ ὑμᾶς, ἀδελφοί, ὑπὲρ τῆς παρουσίας τοῦ
we ask And you, brothers, by the presence of the
Κυρίου ἡμῶν Ἰησοῦ Χριστοῦ, καὶ ἡμῶν ἐπισυναγωγῆς ἐπ᾽
Lord of us, Jesus Christ, and of us gathering together to

2 αὐτόν, εἰς τὸ μὴ ταχέως σαλευθῆναι ὑμᾶς ἀπὸ τοῦ νοός,
Him, for not quickly to be shaken you from the mind,
μήτε θροεῖσθαι, μήτε διὰ πνεύματος, μήτε διὰ λόγου, μήτε
nor to be troubled, neither through a spirit, nor through speech, nor
δι᾽ ἐπιστολῆς ὡς δι᾽ ἡμῶν, ὡς ὅτι ἐνέστηκεν ἡ ἡμέρα τοῦ
through epistle, as through us, as that is come the day of the

3 Χριστοῦ· μή τις ὑμᾶς ἐξαπατήσῃ κατὰ μηδένα τρόπον· ὅτι
Christ. Let not anyone you deceive, by no way, because
ἐὰν μὴ ἔλθῃ ἡ ἀποστασία πρῶτον, καὶ ἀποκαλυφθῇ ὁ ἄνθρω-
unless comes the falling away first, and is revealed the man

4 πος τῆς ἁμαρτίας, ὁ υἱὸς τῆς ἀπωλείας, ὁ ἀντικείμενος καὶ
of sin, the son of perdition, he opposing and
ὑπεραιρόμενος ἐπὶ πᾶν τὸ λεγόμενον Θεὸν ἢ σέβασμα, ὥστε
exalting himself over everything being called God, or object of worship, so as
αὐτὸν εἰς τὸν ναὸν τοῦ Θεοῦ ὡς Θεὸν καθίσαι, ἀποδεικνύντα
him in the temple of God as God to sit, showing

5 ἑαυτὸν ὅτι ἐστὶ Θεός. οὐ μνημονεύετε ὅτι ἔτι ὢν πρὸς ὑμᾶς
himself that he is a God. Do not you remember that yet being with you,

6 ταῦτα ἔλεγον ὑμῖν ; καὶ νῦν τὸ κατέχον οἴδατε, εἰς τὸ ἀπο-
these things I told you? And now the thing restraining you know, for to be

7 καλυφθῆναι αὐτὸν ἐν τῷ ἑαυτοῦ καιρῷ. τὸ γὰρ μυστήριον
revealed him in the of him time. the For mystery
ἤδη ἐνεργεῖται τῆς ἀνομίας· μόνον ὁ κατέχων ἄρτι, ἕως ἐκ
already works of lawlessness, only he restraining now, until out of

8 μέσου γένηται. καὶ τότε ἀποκαλυφθήσεται ὁ ἄνομος, ὃν ὁ
(the) midst it comes. And then will be revealed the lawless one, whom the
Κύριος ἀναλώσει τῷ πνεύματι τοῦ στόματος αὐτοῦ, καὶ
Lord will consume by the spirit of the mouth of Him, and

9 καταργήσει τῇ ἐπιφανείᾳ τῆς παρουσίας αὐτοῦ· οὗ ἐστιν
bring to nothing by the brightness of the coming of Him; of whom is
ἡ παρουσία κατ᾽ ἐνέργειαν τοῦ Σατανᾶ ἐν πάσῃ δυνάμει καὶ
the coming according to the working of Satan in all power and

10 σημείοις καὶ τέρασι ψεύδους, καὶ ἐν πάσῃ ἀπάτῃ τῆς ἀδικίας
signs and wonders of a lie, and with all deceit of unrighteousness
ἐν τοῖς ἀπολλυμένοις, ἀνθ᾽ ὧν τὴν ἀγάπην τῆς ἀληθείας
in those being lost; because the love of the truth

11 οὐκ ἐδέξαντο εἰς τὸ σωθῆναι αὐτούς. καὶ διὰ τοῦτο πέμψει
not they received for to be saved them. And because of this will send

send to them a working of error, for them to believe what (is) false, [12] that all may be judged who did not believe the truth, but delighted in unrighteousness.

[13] But we ought to give thanks to God always concerning you, brothers beloved by (the) Lord, that God chose you from (the) beginning to salvation in sanctification of (the) Spirit and belief of (the) truth; [14] to which He called you by our gospel, to gain (the) glory of our Lord Jesus Christ. [15] So then, brothers, stand firm and strongly hold to the teachings which you were taught, whether by word or by our letter. [16] But may our Lord Jesus Christ Himself, and our God and Father, who loved us and gave (us) everlasting encouragement and good hope by grace, [17] may He encourage your hearts, and may He establish you in every good word and work.

CHAPTER 3

[1] For the rest, brothers, pray for us, that the word of the Lord may run and may be glorified, even as also with you; [2] and that we may be delivered from perverse and wicked men, for faith (is) not of all. [3] But faithful is the Lord, who will establish you and will keep (you) from evil. [4] But we trust in (the) Lord as to you, that you are both doing and will do the things which we command you. [5] And may the Lord direct your hearts into the love of God, and into the patience of Christ.

[6] Now we command you, brothers, in (the) name of our Lord Jesus Christ, (that) you withdraw from every brother walking in an unruly way, and not according to the teaching which he received from us. [7] For you yourselves know how it is right to act

αὐτοῖς ὁ Θεὸς ἐνέργειαν πλάνης, εἰς τὸ πιστεῦσαι αὐτοὺς
to them    God   a working   of error   for      to believe     them

12 τῷ ψεύδει· ἵνα κριθῶσι πάντες οἱ μὴ πιστεύσαντες τῇ
the  lie,   that may be judged  all    those not    having believed the

ἀληθείᾳ, ἀλλ' εὐδοκήσαντες ἐν τῇ ἀδικίᾳ.
truth,    but  having had pleasure in    unrighteousness.

13 Ἡμεῖς δὲ ὀφείλομεν εὐχαριστεῖν τῷ Θεῷ πάντοτε περὶ
we   But   ought    to thank    God   always concerning

ὑμῶν, ἀδελφοὶ ἠγαπημένοι ὑπὸ Κυρίου, ὅτι εἵλετο ὑμᾶς
you,   brothers, having been loved by (the) Lord, because chose   you

ὁ Θεὸς ἀπ' ἀρχῆς εἰς σωτηρίαν ἐν ἁγιασμῷ Πνεύματος καὶ
God from (the) beginning to salvation in sanctification of (the) Spirit and

14 πίστει ἀληθείας· εἰς ὃ ἐκάλεσεν ὑμᾶς διὰ τοῦ εὐαγγελίου
belief of (the) truth, to which He called you through the   gospel

ἡμῶν, εἰς περιποίησιν δόξης τοῦ Κυρίου ἡμῶν Ἰησοῦ
of us,   to   obtainment of (the) glory of the Lord   of us,   Jesus

15 Χριστοῦ. ἄρα οὖν, ἀδελφοί, στήκετε, καὶ κρατεῖτε τὰς παρα-
Christ.   So then, brothers,  stand,    and  hold    the tra-

δόσεις ἃς ἐδιδάχθητε, εἴτε διὰ λόγου εἴτε δι' ἐπιστολῆς ἡμῶν.
ditions which you were taught either by word or   by an epistle    of us.

16 Αὐτὸς δὲ ὁ Κύριος ἡμῶν Ἰησοῦς Χριστός, καὶ ὁ Θεὸς καὶ
Himself And the Lord of us,   Jesus   Christ,   and the God and

πατὴρ ἡμῶν ὁ ἀγαπήσας ἡμᾶς καὶ δοὺς παράκλησιν αἰωνίαν
Father of us, the (One) loving   us and giving comfort     eternal

17 καὶ ἐλπίδα ἀγαθὴν ἐν χάριτι, παρακαλέσαι ὑμῶν τὰς
and a hope   good   by grace, may He comfort of you the

καρδίας καὶ στηρίξαι ὑμᾶς ἐν παντὶ λόγῳ καὶ ἔργῳ ἀγαθῷ.
hearts  and establish  you in every   word and work    good.

CHAPTER 3

1 Τὸ λοιπόν, προσεύχεσθε, ἀδελφοί, περὶ ἡμῶν, ἵνα ὁ λόγος
For the rest,   pray,     brothers, about us,   that the word

2 τοῦ Κυρίου τρέχῃ καὶ δοξάζηται, καθὼς καὶ πρὸς ὑμᾶς, καὶ
of the Lord may run and be glorified,   as   indeed with you, and

ἵνα ῥυσθῶμεν ἀπὸ τῶν ἀτόπων καὶ πονηρῶν ἀνθρώπων·
that we be delivered from    perverse  and   evil       men;

3 οὐ γὰρ πάντων ἡ πίστις. πιστὸς δέ ἐστιν ὁ Κύριος, ὃς
(is) not For of all    the faith.    faithful But is    the Lord, who

4 στηρίξει ὑμᾶς καὶ φυλάξει ἀπὸ τοῦ πονηροῦ. πεποίθαμεν
will establish you and will guard from the evil one.    we are persuaded

δὲ ἐν Κυρίῳ ἐφ' ὑμᾶς, ὅτι ἃ παραγγέλλομεν ὑμῖν καὶ
And in (the) Lord as to you,  that what things we enjoin    you both

5 ποιεῖτε καὶ ποιήσετε. ὁ δὲ Κύριος κατευθύναι ὑμῶν τὰς
you do  and will do.    the And Lord   direct     of you the

καρδίας εἰς τὴν ἀγάπην τοῦ Θεοῦ, καὶ εἰς τὴν ὑπομονὴν τοῦ
hearts into the   love    of God, and into the   patience

Χριστοῦ.
of Christ.

6 Παραγγέλλομεν δὲ ὑμῖν, ἀδελφοί, ἐν ὀνόματι τοῦ Κυρίου
we enjoin     And you,  brothers, in the name of the Lord

ἡμῶν Ἰησοῦ Χριστοῦ, στέλλεσθαι ὑμᾶς ἀπὸ παντὸς ἀδελφοῦ
of us, Jesus   Christ,  to draw back you from every   brother

ἀτάκτως περιπατοῦντος, καὶ μὴ κατὰ τὴν παράδοσιν ἣν
insubordinately walking,     and not according to the tradition which

7 παρέλαβε παρ' ἡμῶν. αὐτοὶ γὰρ οἴδατε πῶς δεῖ μιμεῖσθαι
you received from   us. yourselves For, you know how it is right to imitate

like us, because we did not behave in an unruly way among you; [8] nor did we eat bread from anyone (as) a gift; but by labor and toil working by night and by day in order not to burden anyone of you. [9] not that we do not have authority, but that we give ourselves an example to you, for (you) to imitate us. [10] For even when we were with you, we enjoined you, that if anyone desires not to work, let him not eat. [11] For we hear some are walking in an unruly way among you, not working at all, but being busybodies. [12] Now we command such and exhort by our Lord Jesus Christ that working with quietness they may eat their own bread. [13] But you, brothers, do not lose heart (in) well-doing. [14] But if anyone does not obey our word by the letter, mark that one and do not associate with him, that he may be ashamed; [15] and do not esteem (him) as an enemy, but warn (him) as a brother. [16] And may the Lord of peace give you peace continually in every way. The Lord (be) with all of you.

[17] The signature of Paul by my (own) hand is (the) sign in every epistle; so I write. [18] The grace of our Lord Jesus Christ (be) with you all. Amen.

**8** ἡμᾶς· ὅτι οὐκ ἠτακτήσαμεν ἐν ὑμῖν, οὐδὲ δωρεὰν ἄρτον
us, because not we were disorderly among you, nor (as) a gift bread

ἐφάγομεν παρά τινος, ἀλλ᾽ ἐν κόπῳ καὶ μόχθῳ, νύκτα καὶ
ate from anyone, but by labor and toil night and

ἡμέραν ἐργαζόμενοι, πρὸς τὸ μὴ ἐπιβαρῆσαί τινα ὑμῶν·
day working for not to burden anyone of you;

**9** οὐχ ὅτι οὐκ ἔχομεν ἐξουσίαν, ἀλλ᾽ ἵνα ἑαυτοὺς τύπον δῶμεν
not that not we have authority, but that ourselves an example we give

**10** ὑμῖν εἰς τὸ μιμεῖσθαι ἡμᾶς. καὶ γὰρ ὅτε ἦμεν πρὸς ὑμᾶς, τοῦτο
to you for to imitate us, even For when we were with you, this

παρηγγέλλομεν ὑμῖν ὅτι Εἴ τις οὐ θέλει ἐργάζεσθαι, μηδὲ
we enjoined you, — If anyone not desires to work, not

**11** ἐσθιέτω. ἀκούομεν γάρ τινας περιπατοῦντας ἐν ὑμῖν
let him eat. we hear (of) For some walking among you

**12** ἀτάκτως, μηδὲν ἐργαζομένους, ἀλλὰ περιεργαζομένους. τοῖς
disorderly, nothing working, but working all about,

δὲ τοιούτοις παραγγέλλομεν, καὶ παρακαλοῦμεν διὰ τοῦ
and such we enjoin and exhort through the

Κυρίου ἡμῶν Ἰησοῦ Χριστοῦ, ἵνα μετὰ ἡσυχίας ἐργαζόμενοι
Lord of us, Jesus Christ, that with quietness working

**13** τὸν ἑαυτῶν ἄρτον ἐσθίωσιν. ὑμεῖς δέ, ἀδελφοί, μὴ ἐκκακήσητε
the of themselves bread they may eat. you And, brothers, do not lose heart

**14** καλοποιοῦντες. εἰ δέ τις οὐχ ὑπακούει τῷ λόγῳ ἡμῶν διὰ τῆς
(in) welldoing. if And any not obeys the word of us via the

ἐπιστολῆς, τοῦτον σημειοῦσθε, καὶ μὴ συναναμίγνυσθε αὐτῷ,
epistle, this one mark, and do not associate with him,

**15** ἵνα ἐντραπῇ· καὶ μὴ ὡς ἐχθρὸν ἡγεῖσθε, ἀλλὰ νουθετεῖτε ὡς
that he be shamed; and not as an enemy esteem (him), but warn as

ἀδελφόν.
a brother.

**16** Αὐτὸς δὲ ὁ Κύριος τῆς εἰρήνης δώῃ ὑμῖν τὴν εἰρήνην διὰ
Himself And, the Lord of peace give to you the peace con-

παντὸς ἐν παντὶ τρόπῳ. ὁ Κύριος μετὰ πάντων ὑμῶν.
tinually in every way. The Lord (be) with all you.

**17** Ὁ ἀσπασμὸς τῇ ἐμῇ χειρὶ Παύλου, ὅ ἐστι σημεῖον ἐν πάσῃ
The greeting by my hand, of Paul, which is a sign in every

**18** ἐπιστολῇ· οὕτω γράφω. ἡ χάρις τοῦ Κυρίου ἡμῶν Ἰησοῦ
epistle; thus I write. The grace of the Lord of us, Jesus

Χριστοῦ μετὰ πάντων ὑμῶν. ἀμήν.
Christ (be) with all you. Amen.

THE FIRST EPISTLE OF

PAUL TO

TIMOTHY

# ΠΑΥΛΟΥ ΤΟΥ ΑΠΟΣΤΟΛΟΥ
### PAUL  THE  APOSTLE

## Η ΠΡΟΣ
### THE TO

# ΤΙΜΟΘΕΟΝ
### TIMOTHY

## ΕΠΙΣΤΟΛΗ ΠΡΩΤΗ
### EPISTLE  FIRST

## CHAPTER 1

### CHAPTER 1

[1] Paul, (an) apostle of Jesus Christ according to (the) command of God our Savior, and of (the) Lord Jesus Christ, our Hope, [2] to Timothy, (my) true child in faith: Grace, mercy, peace, from God our Father and Christ Jesus our Lord.

[3] Even as I begged you to remain in Ephesus, (I) going to Macedonia, that you might charge some not to teach other doctrines, [4] nor to give heed to fables and endless genealogies — which bring doubts rather than God's administration, which is in faith — [5] but the end of the commandment is love out of a pure heart and a good conscience, and an unpretended faith; [6] from which some, having missed the mark, turned aside to empty talking, [7] wishing to be teachers of Law, neither understanding what they say nor about that which they strongly affirm. [8] Now we know that the Law (is) good, if anyone use it lawfully; [9] knowing this, that law is not enacted for a righteous one, but for lawless and insubordinate ones, for ungodly and sinful ones, for unholy and profane ones, for beaters of fathers and beaters of mothers, for murderers, [10] homosexuals, abusers of themselves with men, slave-traders, liars, perjurers, and any other thing opposed to sound teaching, [11] according to the gospel of the glory of the blessed God, with which I was entrusted.

1 Παῦλος ἀπόστολος Ἰησοῦ Χριστοῦ κατ᾿ ἐπιταγὴν Θεοῦ
Paul  an apostle  of Jesus  Christ according to a com- mand  of God
σωτῆρος ἡμῶν, καὶ Κυρίου Ἰησοῦ Χριστοῦ τῆς ἐλπίδος
the Savior  of us,  and (the) Lord  Jesus  Christ  the  hope

2 ἡμῶν, Τιμοθέῳ γνησίῳ τέκνῳ ἐν πίστει· χάρις, ἔλεος, εἰρήνη
of us,  to Timothy, a true  child  in (the) faith: Grace, mercy, peace
ἀπὸ Θεοῦ πατρὸς ἡμῶν καὶ Ἰησοῦ Χριστοῦ τοῦ Κυρίου
from God (the) Father of us, and  Jesus  Christ  the  Lord
ἡμῶν.
of us.

3 Καθὼς παρεκάλεσά σε προσμεῖναι ἐν Ἐφέσῳ, πορευό-
As  I besought you to remain  in Ephesus, (I) going
μενος εἰς Μακεδονίαν, ἵνα παραγγείλῃς τισὶ μὴ ἑτεροδιδα-
into Macedonia,  that you might enjoin certain ones not to teach

4 σκαλεῖν, μηδὲ προσέχειν μύθοις καὶ γενεαλογίαις ἀπεράντοις,
other (doctrines), nor  to attend to tales and to genealogies  endless,
αἵτινες ζητήσεις παρέχουσι μᾶλλον ἢ οἰκοδομίαν Θεοῦ τὴν
which  doubts  provide  rather than a stewardship of God

5 ἐν πίστει—.τὸ δὲ τέλος τῆς παραγγελίας ἐστὶν ἀγάπη ἐκ
in faith.  the Now end of the commandment is  love out of
καθαρᾶς καρδίας καὶ συνειδήσεως ἀγαθῆς καὶ πίστεως
a clean  heart  and a conscience  good  and  faith

6 ἀνυποκρίτου· ὧν τινες ἀστοχήσαντες ἐξετρ  ησαν εἰς
unpretended,  which some  missing the mark  turned aside  to

7 ματαιολογίαν, θέλοντες εἶναι νομοδιδάσκαλοι, μὴ νοοῦντες
empty talking,  wishing  to be  teachers of law,  not understanding
μήτε ἃ λέγουσι, μήτε περὶ τίνων διαβεβαιοῦνται. οἴδαμεν
either what they say,  or  about what things they strongly affirm. we know

9 δὲ ὅτι καλὸς ὁ νόμος, ἐάν τις αὐτῷ νομίμως χρῆται, εἰδὼς
And that (is) good the law, if anyone it  lawfully  uses,  knowing
τοῦτο, ὅτι δικαίῳ νόμος οὐ κεῖται, ἀνόμοις δὲ καὶ ἀνυπο-
this,  that for a just one law not is laid down, for lawless but and for in-
τάκτοις, ἀσεβέσι καὶ ἁμαρτωλοῖς, ἀνοσίοις καὶ βεβήλοις,
subordinate, for ungodly and sinful ones,  for unholy  and profane ones,

10 πατραλῴαις καὶ μητραλῴαις, ἀνδροφόνοις, πόρνοις, ἀρσενο-
for father-slayers and mother-slayers, for men-slayers, for fornicators, for
κοίταις, ἀνδραποδισταῖς, ψεύσταις, ἐπιόρκοις, καὶ εἴ τι
homosexuals, for slave-traders,  for liars,  for perjurers,  and if any

11 ἕτερον τῇ ὑγιαινούσῃ διδασκαλίᾳ ἀντίκειται, κατὰ τὸ
other thing the  sound  teaching  opposes,  according to the
εὐαγγέλιον τῆς δόξης τοῦ μακαρίου Θεοῦ, ὃ ἐπιστεύθην
gospel  of the glory of the  blessed  God, which was entrusted
(with)

[12] And I have thanks to Him empowering me, our Lord Jesus Christ, because He counted me faithful, putting (me) into the ministry, [13] (I) being before a blasphemer, and persecutor, and insolent; but I was shown mercy, because being ignorant I did (it) in unbelief. [14] But the grace of our Lord abounded exceedingly with faith and love, which (is) in Christ Jesus. [15] Faithful (is) the word, and worthy of all acceptation, that Christ Jesus came into the world to save sinners, of whom I am chief. [16] But for this reason I was shown mercy, that in me first Jesus Christ might show forth all long-suffering, for an example to those being about to believe on Him to everlasting life. [17] Now to the King eternal, invisible, incorruptible, (the) only wise God, (be) honor and glory forever and ever. Amen.

ἐγώ.
I

**12** Καὶ χάριν ἔχω τῷ ἐνδυναμώσαντί με Χριστῷ Ἰησοῦ τῷ
And thanks I have to the (One) empowering me, Christ Jesus the
Κυρίῳ ἡμῶν, ὅτι πιστόν με ἡγήσατο, θέμενος εἰς διακονίαν,
Lord of us, because faithful me He counted, putting (me) into ministry,

**13** τὸν πρότερον ὄντα βλάσφημον καὶ διώκτην καὶ ὑβριστήν·
the (one) before being a blasphemer and a persecutor and insolent;

**14** ἀλλ᾽ ἠλεήθην, ὅτι ἀγνοῶν ἐποίησα ἐν ἀπιστίᾳ· ὑπερ-
but I obtained mercy, because being ignorant I did (it) in unbelief, super-
επλεόνασε δὲ ἡ χάρις τοῦ Κυρίου ἡμῶν μετὰ πίστεως καὶ
abounded the grace of the Lord, of us with faith and

**15** ἀγάπης τῆς ἐν Χριστῷ Ἰησοῦ. πιστὸς ὁ λόγος καὶ πάσης
love in Christ Jesus. Faithful (is) the word and of all
ἀποδοχῆς ἄξιος, ὅτι Χριστὸς Ἰησοῦς ἦλθεν εἰς τὸν κόσμον
acceptance worthy, that Christ Jesus came into the world

**16** ἁμαρτωλοὺς σῶσαι, ὧν πρῶτός εἰμι ἐγώ· ἀλλὰ διὰ τοῦτο
sinners to save, of whom chief am I; but because of this
ἠλεήθην, ἵνα ἐν ἐμοὶ πρώτῳ ἐνδείξηται Ἰησοῦς Χριστὸς τὴν
I obtained mercy, that in me first might show forth Jesus Christ
πᾶσαν μακροθυμίαν, πρὸς ὑποτύπωσιν τῶν μελλόντων
all long-suffering, for a pattern to those being about

**17** πιστεύειν ἐπ᾽ αὐτῷ εἰς ζωὴν αἰώνιον. τῷ δὲ βασιλεῖ τῶν
to believe on Him for life everlasting. to the Now King of the
αἰώνων, ἀφθάρτῳ, ἀοράτῳ, μόνῳ σοφῷ Θεῷ, τιμὴ καὶ δόξα
ages, invisible, incorruptible, (the) only wise God, (be) honor and glory
εἰς τοὺς αἰῶνας τῶν αἰώνων. ἀμήν.
to the ages of the ages. Amen.

[18] This charge I commit to you, (my) child Timothy, according to the prophecies going before as to you, that you might war a good warfare by them, [19] hold faith and a good conscience; which some having cast away made shipwreck as to faith; [20] of whom are Hymeneus and Alexander, whom I delivered up to Satan, that they may be taught not to blaspheme.

**18** Ταύτην τὴν παραγγελίαν παρατίθεμαί σοι, τέκνον
This charge I commit to you, child,
Τιμόθεε, κατὰ τὰς προαγούσας ἐπί σε προφητείας, ἵνα
Timothy, according to the going before as to you prophecies that

**19** στρατεύῃ ἐν αὐταῖς τὴν καλὴν στρατείαν, ἔχων πίστιν καὶ
you might war by them the good warfare, having faith and
ἀγαθὴν συνείδησιν, ἥν τινες ἀπωσάμενοι περὶ τὴν πίστιν
a good conscience, which some having thrust away concerning the faith

**20** ἐναυάγησαν· ὧν ἐστιν Ὑμέναιος καὶ Ἀλέξανδρος, οὓς
made shipwreck; of whom is Hymeneus and Alexander, whom
παρέδωκα τῷ Σατανᾷ, ἵνα παιδευθῶσι μὴ βλασφημεῖν.
I delivered to Satan, that they may be taught not to blaspheme.

CHAPTER 2

[1] First of all, then, I exhort (that) supplications prayers, intercessions, (and) thanksgivings be made on behalf of all men; [2] for kings and all those being in high position, that a peaceful and quiet existence we may lead in all godliness and reverence. [3] For this (is) good and acceptable before our deliverer, God, [4] who desires all men to be delivered and to come to knowledge of truth. [5] For God

CHAPTER 2

**1** Παρακαλῶ οὖν πρῶτον πάντων ποιεῖσθαι δεήσεις, προσ-
I exhort Therefore firstly of all to be made petitions, prayers,
ευχάς, ἐντεύξεις, εὐχαριστίας, ὑπὲρ πάντων ἀνθρώπων·
intercessions, thanksgivings on behalf of all men;

**2** ὑπὲρ βασιλέων καὶ πάντων τῶν ἐν ὑπεροχῇ ὄντων, ἵνα
for kings and all those in high position being, that
ἤρεμον καὶ ἡσύχιον βίον διάγωμεν ἐν πάσῃ εὐσεβείᾳ καὶ
a tranquil and quiet existence we may lead in all godliness and

**3** σεμνότητι. τοῦτο γὰρ καλὸν καὶ ἀπόδεκτον ἐνώπιον τοῦ
reverence. this (is) For good and acceptable before the

**4** σωτῆρος ἡμῶν Θεοῦ, ὃς πάντας ἀνθρώπους θέλει σωθῆναι
deliverer of us, God, who all men desires to be delivered

**5** καὶ εἰς ἐπίγνωσιν ἀληθείας ἐλθεῖν. εἷς γὰρ Θεός, εἷς καὶ
and to a full knowledge of truth to come. one For God (is), one also

(is) one, and one mediator between God and men, (the) man Christ Jesus, [6] who gave Himself a ransom for all, the witness (to be given) in its own times, [7] to which I was appointed a herald and apostle — I speak the truth in Christ and do not lie — a teacher of (the) nations, in faith and truth.

[8] Therefore, I desire the men in every place to pray, lifting up holy hands without wrath and doubting. [9] In the same way also, that the women adorn themselves in decent clothes, with modesty and sensibleness, not with braided (hair), or gold, or pearls, or expensive garments, [10] But what becomes women professing (the) fear of God: through good works. [11] Let a woman learn in silence, in all subjection. [12] But I do not allow a woman to teach, nor to exercise authority (over) a man, but to be in silence. [13] For Adam was formed first, then Eve; [14] And Adam was not deceived; but the woman having been deceived has become in transgression; [15] but she will be delivered through the bearing of children, if they remain in faith and love and holiness with sensibleness.

CHAPTER 3

[1] Faithful (is) the word: If any reaches out to overseership, he is desirous of a good work. [2] The overseer must, then, be blameless, husband of one wife, temperate, discreet, modest, hospitable, apt to teach; [3] not given to wine, not quarrelsome, not greedy of ill gain, but gentle, not full of strife, not loving money; [4] ruling his own house well, having children in subjection with all honor — [5] but if one does not know to rule his own house, how shall he take care of (the) church of God? [6] Not a novice, lest being puffed up he may fall into the judgment of the Devil. [7] But he must also have a good witness from those outside, lest

μεσίτης Θεοῦ καὶ ἀνθρώπων, ἄνθρωπος Χριστὸς Ἰησοῦς,
Mediator of God and   of men,    (the) man   Christ   Jesus,

6 ὁ δοὺς ἑαυτὸν ἀντίλυτρον ὑπὲρ πάντων, τὸ μαρτύριον
He having given Himself a ransom on behalf of all,   the testimony

7 καιροῖς ἰδίοις, εἰς ὃ ἐτέθην ἐγὼ κήρυξ καὶ ἀπόστολος (ἀλή-
in its own times; to which was appointed I a herald and apostle   — truth
θειαν λέγω ἐν Χριστῷ, οὐ ψεύδομαι), διδάσκαλος ἐθνῶν ἐν
I say   in Christ,   do not I lie   — a teacher   of nations in
πίστει καὶ ἀληθείᾳ.
faith and   truth.

8 Βούλομαι οὖν προσεύχεσθαι τοὺς ἄνδρας ἐν παντὶ τόπῳ,
I desire Therefore to pray    the men   in every   place,
ἐπαίροντας ὁσίους χεῖρας, χωρὶς ὀργῆς καὶ διαλογισμοῦ.
lifting up   holy   hands, without wrath and   doubting.

9 ὡσαύτως καὶ τὰς γυναῖκας ἐν καταστολῇ κοσμίῳ, μετὰ αἰδοῦς
Likewise also the women   in clothing    decent, with modesty
καὶ σωφροσύνης, κοσμεῖν ἑαυτάς, μὴ ἐν πλέγμασιν, ἢ χρυσῷ,
and sensibleness, to adorn themselves, not with plaiting,   or gold,

10 ἢ μαργαρίταις, ἢ ἱματισμῷ πολυτελεῖ, ἀλλ᾽ (ὃ πρέπει
or pearls,    or garments   expensive, but   what becomes
γυναιξὶν ἐπαγγελλομέναις θεοσέβειαν) δι᾽ ἔργων ἀγαθῶν.
women    professing     fear of God, by means of works good.

11 γυνὴ ἐν ἡσυχίᾳ μανθανέτω ἐν πάσῃ ὑποταγῇ. γυναικὶ δὲ
A woman in silence let learn    in   all    subjection. a woman But

12 διδάσκειν οὐκ ἐπιτρέπω, οὐδὲ αὐθεντεῖν ἀνδρός, ἀλλ᾽ εἶναι
to teach    not I allow,    nor to exercise authority of a man, but to be

13 ἐν ἡσυχίᾳ. Ἀδὰμ γὰρ πρῶτος ἐπλάσθη, εἶτα Εὔα· καὶ
in silence.    Adam For   first   was formed,   then Eve. And

14 Ἀδὰμ οὐκ ἠπατήθη, ἡ δὲ γυνὴ ἀπατηθεῖσα ἐν παραβάσει
Adam not was deceived, the but woman being deceived in transgression

15 γέγονε· σωθήσεται δὲ διὰ τῆς τεκνογονίας, ἐὰν μείνωσιν ἐν
has become; she will be saved but through the childbearing, if they remain in
πίστει καὶ ἀγάπῃ καὶ ἁγιασμῷ μετὰ σωφροσύνης.
faith   and love   and holiness   with   sensibleness.

CHAPTER 3

1 Πιστὸς ὁ λόγος· Εἴ τις ἐπισκοπῆς ὀρέγεται, καλοῦ ἔργου
Faithful (is) the word: If anyone overseership aspires to, a good   work

2 ἐπιθυμεῖ. δεῖ οὖν τὸν ἐπίσκοπον ἀνεπίληπτον εἶναι, μιᾶς
he desires. It behoves, then, the overseer   without reproach to be, of one
γυναικὸς ἄνδρα, νηφάλιον, σώφρονα, κόσμιον, φιλόξενον,
wife    husband, temperate,   sensible,   modest,    hospitable,

3 διδακτικόν· μὴ πάροινον, μὴ πλήκτην, μὴ αἰσχροκερδῆ,
apt at teaching, not a drinker,   not a striker,   not greedy of ill gain,

4 ἀλλ᾽ ἐπιεικῆ, ἄμαχον, ἀφιλάργυρον· τοῦ ἰδίου οἴκου καλῶς
but   gentle, not quarrelsome, not avaricious,   the own house    well
προϊστάμενον, τέκνα ἔχοντα ἐν ὑποταγῇ μετὰ πάσης
ruling,     children having in subjection with   all

5 σεμνότητος (εἰ δέ τις τοῦ ἰδίου οἴκου προστῆναι οὐκ οἶδε,
reverence   — if but anyone the own house   to rule    not knows,

6 πῶς ἐκκλησίας Θεοῦ ἐπιμελήσεται ;)· μὴ νεόφυτον, ἵνα μὴ
how a church of God will he care for? — not a novice,    lest

7 τυφωθεὶς εἰς κρίμα ἐμπέσῃ τοῦ διαβόλου. δεῖ δὲ αὐτὸν καὶ
being puffed up into judgment he fall of the Devil. it behoves And him   also
μαρτυρίαν καλὴν ἔχειν ἀπὸ τῶν ἔξωθεν, ἵνα μὴ εἰς ὀνειδισμὸν
a witness   good to have from those outside,   lest   into reproach

he may fall into shame, and (into) a snare of the Devil. [8] Likewise, deacons (to be) reverent, not double-tongued, not addicted to much wine, not greedy of ill gain [9] having the mystery of the faith with a pure conscience. [10] And also let these be tested first, then let them minister, being without reproach. [11] Likewise, (their) wives (to be) reverent, not slanderers, temperate, faithful in all things. [12] Let deacons be husbands of one wife, ruling (their) own households and children well. [13] For the (ones) having ministered well gain for themselves a good degree and much boldness in faith, those in Christ Jesus.

[14] I write these things to you, hoping to come to you shortly; [15] but if I delay, that you may know how to behave in God's house, which is (the) church of (the) living God, (the) pillar and foundation of the truth. [16] And confessedly, great is the mystery of godliness; God was manifested in flesh, was justified in Spirit, was seen by angels, was proclaimed among nations, was believed on in (the) world, was taken up in glory.

CHAPTER 4

[1] But the Spirit expressly says that in the latter times some shall depart from the faith, adhering to deceiving spirits and teachings of demons, [2] in hypocrisy, liars, being seared in their own conscience, [3] forbidding to marry, (saying) to abstain from foods, which God created for reception with thanksgiving for the faithful and those who know the truth. [4] Because every creature of God (is) good, and nothing to be thrust away, but received with thanksgiving; [5] for through God's word and prayerful intercourse it is sanctified. [6] Having suggested these things to the brothers, you will be a

**8** ἐμπέσῃ καὶ παγίδα τοῦ διαβόλου. διακόνους ὡσαύτως
he fall, and (into) a snare of the Devil.        deacons      Likewise
σεμνούς, μὴ διλόγους, μὴ οἴνῳ πολλῷ προσέχοντας, μὴ
reverent (to be), not double-tongued, not wine to much addicted,      not

**9** αἰσχροκερδεῖς, ἔχοντας τὸ μυστήριον τῆς πίστεως ἐν καθαρᾷ
greedy of ill gain, having the mystery   of the faith  with a clean

**10** συνειδήσει. καὶ οὗτοι δὲ δοκιμαζέσθωσαν πρῶτον, εἶτα
conscience. also these And let be tested       first,       then

**11** διακονείτωσαν, ἀνέγκλητοι ὄντες. γυναῖκας ὡσαύτως
let them minister, without reproach being.   wives      Likewise

**12** σεμνάς, μὴ διαβόλους, νηφαλίους, πιστὰς ἐν πᾶσι. διάκονοι
reverent (to be), not slanderers, temperate, faithful in all things. deacons
ἔστωσαν μιᾶς γυναικὸς ἄνδρες, τέκνων καλῶς προϊστάμενοι
Let be  of one  wife   husbands children well    ruling

**13** καὶ τῶν ἰδίων οἴκων. οἱ γὰρ καλῶς διακονήσαντες βαθμὸν
and the own households. those For well  having ministered a grade
ἑαυτοῖς καλὸν περιποιοῦνται, καὶ πολλὴν παρρησίαν ἐν
for themselves good gain,        and  much   boldness  in
πίστει τῇ ἐν Χριστῷ Ἰησοῦ.
faith, those in  Christ   Jesus.

**14** Ταῦτά σοι γράφω, ἐλπίζων ἐλθεῖν πρός σε τάχιον· ἐὰν δὲ
These things to you I write, hoping to come to you shortly; if but

**15** βραδύνω, ἵνα εἰδῇς πῶς δεῖ ἐν οἴκῳ Θεοῦ ἀναστρέφεσθαι,
I delay,  that you may know how must in (the) house of God to behave,
ἥτις ἐστὶν ἐκκλησία Θεοῦ ζῶντος, στύλος καὶ ἑδραίωμα τῆς
which is (the) church of God (the) living, pillar and foundation of the

**16** ἀληθείας. καὶ ὁμολογουμένως μέγα ἐστὶ τὸ τῆς εὐσεβείας
truth. And confessedly,     great is  the  of godliness
μυστήριον· Θεὸς ἐφανερώθη ἐν σαρκί, ἐδικαιώθη ἐν πνεύματι,
mystery, God was manifested in flesh, was justified in  spirit,
ὤφθη ἀγγέλοις, ἐκηρύχθη ἐν ἔθνεσιν, ἐπιστεύθη ἐν κόσμῳ,
was seen by angels, was proclaimed among nations, was believed in (the) world,
ἀνελήφθη ἐν δόξῃ.
was taken up in glory.

CHAPTER 4

**1** Τὸ δὲ Πνεῦμα ῥητῶς λέγει, ὅτι ἐν ὑστέροις καιροῖς ἀποστή-
the But Spirit in words says that in latter times will
σονταί τινες τῆς πίστεως, προσέχοντες πνεύμασι πλάνοις
depart from some the faith,    adhering to spirits  deceiving

**2** καὶ διδασκαλίαις δαιμονίων, ἐν ὑποκρίσει ψευδολόγων,
and teachings of demons, in hypocrisy    of liars,

**3** κεκαυτηριασμένων τὴν ἰδίαν συνείδησιν, κωλυόντων γαμεῖν,
having been seared on the own conscience, forbidding to marry,
ἀπέχεσθαι βρωμάτων, ἃ ὁ Θεὸς ἔκτισεν εἰς μετάληψιν μετὰ
(saying) to abstain from foods which God created for partaking with

**4** εὐχαριστίας τοῖς πιστοῖς καὶ ἐπεγνωκόσι τὴν ἀλήθειαν. ὅτι
thanksgiving by the believers and (those) knowing the truth.  Because
πᾶν κτίσμα Θεοῦ καλόν, καὶ οὐδὲν ἀπόβλητον, μετὰ εὐχαρι-
every creature of God (is) good, and nothing to be put away, with thanks-

**5** στίας λαμβανόμενον· ἁγιάζεται γὰρ διὰ λόγου Θεοῦ καὶ
giving having been received; it is sanctified for through a word of God and
ἐντεύξεως.
prayerful intercourse.

**6** Ταῦτα ὑποτιθέμενος τοῖς ἀδελφοῖς καλὸς ἔσῃ διάκονος
These things having suggested to the brothers, good you will be minister

good servant of Jesus Christ, being nourished by the words of faith, and by the good teaching which you have followed. [7] But refuse the profane and old-womanish tales; and exercise yourself to godliness. [8] For bodily exercise is profitable for a little, but godliness is profitable to all things, having promise of the present life, and of that coming. [9] Faithful (is) the word, and worthy of all acceptance; [10] for to this we labor and (are) reproached, because we hope on (the) living God, who is deliverer of all men, especially of believers. [11] Enjoin and teach these things. [12] Let no one despise your youth, but become an example of the believers, in word, in conduct, in love, in spirit, in faith, in purity. [13] Until I come, attend to reading to exhortation, to teaching. [14] Do not be neglectful of the gift in you, which was given to you through prophecy, with laying on of the hands of the elderhood. [15] Meditate on these things; be in these things in order that your progress may be plain in all. [16] Hold on to yourself, and to the teaching; continue in them; for doing this, you will both deliver yourself, and those hearing you.

CHAPTER 5

[1] Do not sharply rebuke an elder, but exhort as a father; younger (men) as brothers; [2] elder (women) as mothers; younger as sisters, with all purity. [3] Honor widows that (are) truly widows; [4] but if any widow have children or grandchildren, let them learn first to be godly (as to) their own house, and to give a return to (their) parents; for this is good and pleasing before God. [5] Now she who (is) truly a widow, and left alone, has (her) hope in God, and continues in supplications and prayers night and day. [6] But the (one) living in self-pleasure has died (while) living. [7] And (you) enjoin these

'Ιησοῦ Χριστοῦ, ἐντρεφόμενος τοῖς λόγοις τῆς πίστεως, καὶ
of Jesus Christ, being nourished by the words of the faith, and

7 τῆς καλῆς διδασκαλίας ἧ παρηκολούθηκας. τοὺς δὲ βεβήλους
by the good teaching which you have followed. the But profane

καὶ γραώδεις μύθους παραιτοῦ. γύμναζε δὲ σεαυτὸν πρὸς
and old-womanish tales refuse. exercise And yourself to

8 εὐσέβειαν· ἡ γὰρ σωματικὴ γυμνασία πρὸς ὀλίγον ἐστὶν
godliness. For bodily exercise for a little is

ὠφέλιμος· ἡ δὲ εὐσέβεια πρὸς πάντα ὠφέλιμός ἐστιν, ἐπαγ-
profitable, but godliness to all things profitable is,

9 γελίαν ἔχουσα ζωῆς τῆς νῦν καὶ τῆς μελλούσης. πιστὸς ὁ
promise having life of the now and of the coming. Faithful (is) the

10 λόγος καὶ πάσης ἀποδοχῆς ἄξιος. εἰς τοῦτο γὰρ καὶ κοπιῶ-
word and of all acceptance worthy. to this For also we labor

μεν καὶ ὀνειδιζόμεθα, ὅτι ἠλπίκαμεν ἐπὶ Θεῷ ζῶντι, ὅς ἐστι
and (are) reproached because we have set hope on God (the) living, who is

11 σωτὴρ πάντων ἀνθρώπων, μάλιστα πιστῶν. παράγγελλε
deliverer of all men, especially of believers. Enjoin

12 ταῦτα καὶ δίδασκε. μηδείς σου τῆς νεότητος καταφρονείτω,
these things and teach. no one of you the youth Let despise,

ἀλλὰ τύπος γίνου τῶν πιστῶν ἐν λόγῳ, ἐν ἀναστροφῇ, ἐν
but an example become of the believers in word, in conduct, in

13 ἀγάπῃ, ἐν πνεύματι, ἐν πίστει, ἐν ἁγνείᾳ. ἕως ἔρχομαι,
love, in spirit, in faith, in purity. Until I come,

14 πρόσεχε τῇ ἀναγνώσει, τῇ παρακλήσει, τῇ διδασκαλίᾳ. μὴ
attend to the reading, to the exhortation, to the teaching. Do not

ἀμέλει τοῦ ἐν σοὶ χαρίσματος, ὃ ἐδόθη σοι διὰ προφητείας
be neglectful of the in you gift, which was given you via prophecy

15 μετὰ ἐπιθέσεως τῶν χειρῶν τοῦ πρεσβυτερίου. ταῦτα μελέτα,
with laying on of the hands of the elderhood. these things Give care to

16 ἐν τούτοις ἴσθι, ἵνα σου ἡ προκοπὴ φανερὰ ᾖ ἐν πᾶσιν. ἔπεχε
in these things be, that of you the progress plain may be to all. Hold on

σεαυτῷ καὶ τῇ διδασκαλίᾳ. ἐπίμενε αὐτοῖς· τοῦτο γὰρ ποιῶν
to yourself and to the teaching; continue in them; this for doing

καὶ σεαυτὸν σώσεις καὶ τοὺς ἀκούοντάς σου.
both yourself you will deliver, and those hearing you.

CHAPTER 5

1 Πρεσβυτέρῳ μὴ ἐπιπλήξῃς, ἀλλὰ παρακάλει ὡς πατέρα·
an older man Do not rebuke, but exhort as a father;

2 νεωτέρους, ὡς ἀδελφούς· πρεσβυτέρας, ὡς μητέρας· νεωτέρας,
younger ones as brothers; older women as mothers; younger women

3 ὡς ἀδελφάς, ἐν πάσῃ ἁγνείᾳ. χήρας τίμα τὰς ὄντως χήρας.
as sisters, in all purity. widows Honor, those being really widows.

4 εἰ δέ τις χήρα τέκνα ἢ ἔκγονα ἔχει, μανθανέτωσαν πρῶτον
if But any widow children or grandchildren has, let them learn firstly

τὸν ἴδιον οἶκον εὐσεβεῖν, καὶ ἀμοιβὰς ἀποδιδόναι τοῖς προγό-
the own house to be godly to, and repayments return to the fore-

νοις· τοῦτο γάρ ἐστι καλὸν καὶ ἀπόδεκτον ἐνώπιον τοῦ Θεοῦ.
bears; this for is good and acceptable before God.

5 ἡ δὲ ὄντως χήρα καὶ μεμονωμένη ἤλπικεν ἐπὶ τὸν Θεόν,
the But being really widow even having been left has set hope on God,

καὶ προσμένει ταῖς δεήσεσι καὶ ταῖς προσευχαῖς νυκτὸς καὶ
and continues in the petitions and the prayers night and

6 ἡμέρας. ἡ δὲ σπαταλῶσα, ζῶσα τέθνηκε. καὶ ταῦτα παράγ-
day. the But (one) living in self-pleasure living (while) has died. And these things enjoin

things that they may be blameless. [8] But if anyone does not provide for (his) own, and especially (his) family, he has denied the faith, and is worse than an unbeliever. [9] Let a widow be enrolled having become not less than sixty years, wife of one man. [10] being witnessed by good works: if she brought up children, if she hosted strangers, if she washed the feet of saints, if she relieved afflicted ones, if she followed after every good work. [11] But refuse younger widows; for whenever they grow lustful against Christ, they desire to marry, [12] having guilt because they set aside the first faith; [13] and with it all, they also learn (to be) idle, going around the houses; and not only idle, but also gossips and busy bodies, saving the things not proper. [14] Therefore, I will (the) younger women to marry, to bear children, to rule the house, giving no occasion to the adversary on account of reproach. [15] For some already have turned aside behind Satan. [16] If any believing man or believing woman have widows, let them relieve (them); and do not burden the church, that it may relieve those being really widows.

[17] Let the elders who take the lead be counted worthy of double honor, especially those laboring in word and teaching; [18] for the Scripture says, "You shall not muzzle an ox treading out corn," and, "The laborer (is) worthy of his hire." [19] Do not receive an accusation against an elder except on (the testimony of) two or three witnesses. [20] Those that sin before all, convict, so that the rest may have fear. [21] I earnestly testify before God and (the) Lord Jesus Christ, and the elect angels, that you should keep these things, without prejudice, doing nothing by partiality. [22] Lay hands quickly on no one, nor share in (the) sins of others. Keep yourself pure. [23] No

**8** γελλε, ἵνα ἀνεπίληπτοι ὦσιν. εἰ δέ τις τῶν ἰδίων καὶ
that   without reproach they may be.   if But anyone the own,   and
μάλιστα τῶν οἰκείων οὐ προνοεῖ, τὴν πίστιν ἤρνηται, καὶ
especially the family, not provides for, the   faith he has denied, and

**9** ἔστιν ἀπίστου χείρων. χήρα καταλεγέσθω μὴ ἔλαττον ἐτῶν
is an unbeliever worse than.   A widow let be enrolled not less (than) years

**10** ἑξήκοντα, γεγονυῖα ἑνὸς ἀνδρὸς γυνή, ἐν ἔργοις καλοῖς
sixty   having become, of one man   wife,   by works   good
μαρτυρουμένη, εἰ ἐτεκνοτρόφησεν, εἰ ἐξενοδόχησεν, εἰ ἁγίων
being witnessed, if she brought up children, if she hosted strangers, if of saints
πόδας ἔνιψεν, εἰ θλιβομένοις ἐπήρκεσεν, εἰ παντὶ ἔργῳ
feet she washed, if   afflicted ones   she relieved, if every   work

**11** ἀγαθῷ ἐπηκολούθησε. νεωτέρας δὲ χήρας παραιτοῦ· ὅταν
good she followed after.   younger But widows   refuse; whenever
γὰρ καταστρηνιάσωσι τοῦ Χριστοῦ, γαμεῖν θέλουσιν,
for they grow lustful against   Christ,   to marry they desire,

**12** ἔχουσαι κρίμα, ὅτι τὴν πρώτην πίστιν ἠθέτησαν. ἅμα δὲ
having (a) judgment, because the first   faith   they set aside; withal and

**13** καὶ ἀργαὶ μανθάνουσι, περιερχόμεναι τὰς οἰκίας, οὐ μόνον
also idle they learn (to be), going around   the houses, not only
δὲ ἀργαί, ἀλλὰ καὶ φλύαροι καὶ περίεργοι, λαλοῦσαι τὰ
and idle, but also gossips   and busybodies,   speaking the things

**14** μὴ δέοντα. βούλομαι οὖν νεωτέρας γαμεῖν, τεκνογονεῖν,
not proper.   I will, therefore, younger women to marry, to bear children,
οἰκοδεσποτεῖν, μηδεμίαν ἀφορμὴν διδόναι τῷ ἀντικειμένῳ
to rule the house,   no   occasion   to give to the (one) opposing

**15** λοιδορίας χάριν. ἤδη γάρ τινες ἐξετράπησαν ὀπίσω τοῦ
reproach on account of. already For some turned aside   behind

**16** Σατανᾶ. εἴ τις πιστὸς ἢ πιστὴ ἔχει χήρας, ἐπαρκείτω αὐταῖς,
Satan. If any believing man or believing woman has widows, relieve   them,
καὶ μὴ βαρείσθω ἡ ἐκκλησία, ἵνα ταῖς ὄντως χήραις ἐπαρ-
and not burden   the church, that those being really widows it may
κέσῃ.
relieve.

**17** Οἱ καλῶς προεστῶτες πρεσβύτεροι διπλῆς τιμῆς ἀξιού-
The well ruling   elders   of double honor count
σθωσαν, μάλιστα οἱ κοπιῶντες ἐν λόγῳ καὶ διδασκαλίᾳ.
worthy,   expecially those laboring in word and   teaching.

**18** λέγει γὰρ ἡ γραφή, Βοῦν ἀλοῶντα οὐ φιμώσεις. καί, Ἄξιος
says For the Scripture: An ox threshing not you shall muzzle, and, Worthy

**19** ὁ ἐργάτης τοῦ μισθοῦ αὐτοῦ. κατὰ πρεσβυτέρου κατη-
the workman of the pay of him. Against an elder
γορίαν μὴ παραδέχου, ἐκτὸς εἰ μὴ ἐπὶ δύο ἢ τριῶν μαρτύ-
accusation not receive,   unless on two or three wit-

**20** ρων. τοὺς ἁμαρτάνοντας ἐνώπιον πάντων ἔλεγχε, ἵνα καὶ
nesses. Those sinning   before   all,   reprove; that also

**21** οἱ λοιποὶ φόβον ἔχωσι. διαμαρτύρομαι ἐνώπιον τοῦ Θεοῦ
the rest fear may have. I solemnly witness before   God
καὶ Κυρίου Ἰησοῦ Χριστοῦ καὶ τῶν ἐκλεκτῶν ἀγγελων, ἵνα
and (the) Lord Jesus Christ, and the elect   angels, that
ταῦτα φυλάξῃς χωρὶς προκρίματος, μηδὲν ποιῶν κατὰ
these things you guard without prejudice,   nothing doing by way of

**22** πρόσκλισιν. χεῖρας ταχέως μηδενὶ ἐπιτίθει, μηδὲ κοινώνει
partiality.   hands quickly no one Lay on,   nor   share in

**23** ἁμαρτίαις ἀλλοτρίαις· σεαυτὸν ἁγνὸν τήρει. μηκέτι ὑδροπό-
sins   of others; yourself pure   keep. No longer drink

longer drink water, but use a little wine on account of your stomach and your frequent infirmities. [24] The sins of some men are plain, going before to judgment; and (of) some, also, they follow after. [25] Likewise, also the good works are plain before (all), and those otherwise cannot be hidden.

CHAPTER 6

[1] Let as many slaves as are under the yoke count their own masters worthy of all honor, that the name and teaching of God may not be blasphemed. [2] And they that have believing masters, let them not despise (them), because they are brothers; but rather let them serve (them), because they are believing ones and beloved ones who are being helped by the good service. Teach and exhort these things. [3] If anyone teaches another doctrine, and does not approve of sound words, those of our Lord Jesus Christ, and the teaching according to godliness, [4] he is puffed up, knowing nothing, but (is) sick about questions and arguments, out of which come envy, quarrels, evil-speaking, filthy suspicions, [5] worthless arguments of men ruined in mind and destitute of the truth, holding gain to be godliness — withdraw from such. [6] But godliness with contentment is great gain. [7] For we did not bring anything into the world; (it is) clear that neither are we able to carry anything out. [8] But having food and clothing, we shall be satisfied with these. [9] But those lusting to be rich fall into temptation and a snare, and many unwise and hurtful lusts which plunge men into death and everlasting ruin. [10] For the love of money is a root of all evil; which some reaching out after were seduced from the faith, and themselves pierced through with many

τει, ἀλλ' οἴνῳ ὀλίγῳ χρῶ, διὰ τὸν στόμαχόν σου καὶ τὰς
water, but wine a little use, because of the stomach of you and the

24 πυκνάς σου ἀσθενείας. τινῶν ἀνθρώπων αἱ ἁμαρτίαι
frequent of you weaknesses. of some men The sins

προδηλοί εἰσι, προάγουσαι εἰς κρίσιν· τισὶ δὲ καὶ ἐπακο-
plain before are, going before to judgment; some but indeed they

25 λουθοῦσιν. ὡσαύτως καὶ τὰ καλὰ ἔργα πρόδηλά ἐστι· καὶ
follow on; likewise also the good works plain before are, and

τὰ ἄλλως ἔχοντα κρυβῆναι οὐ δύναται.
those otherwise (being) be hidden not can.

CHAPTER 6

1 Ὅσοι εἰσὶν ὑπὸ ζυγὸν δοῦλοι, τοὺς ἰδίους δεσπότας πάσης
As many as are under a yoke, slaves, the own masters of all

τιμῆς ἀξίους ἡγείσθωσαν, ἵνα μὴ τὸ ὄνομα τοῦ Θεοῦ καὶ ἡ
honor worthy esteem, that not the name of God and the

2 διδασκαλία βλασφημῆται. οἱ δὲ πιστοὺς ἔχοντες δεσπότας
teaching be blasphemed, those And believing having masters,

μὴ καταφρονείτωσαν, ὅτι ἀδελφοί εἰσιν· ἀλλὰ μᾶλλον δου-
not let them despise because brothers they are, but rather let them

λευέτωσαν, ὅτι πιστοί εἰσι καὶ ἀγαπητοὶ οἱ τῆς εὐεργεσίας
serve as slaves, because believing are and beloved those of the good service

ἀντιλαμβανόμενοι. ταῦτα δίδασκε καὶ παρακάλει.
receiving in return. these things Teach and exhort.

3 Εἴ τις ἑτεροδιδασκαλεῖ, καὶ μὴ προσέρχεται ὑγιαίνουσι
If anyone teaches differently, and not consents to sound

λόγοις, τοῖς τοῦ Κυρίου ἡμῶν Ἰησοῦ Χριστοῦ, καὶ τῇ κατ'
words, those of the Lord of us, Jesus Christ, and to the according to

4 εὐσέβειαν διδασκαλίᾳ, τετύφωται, μηδὲν ἐπιστάμενος, ἀλλὰ
godliness teaching, he has been puffed up, nothing understanding, but

νοσῶν περὶ ζητήσεις καὶ λογομαχίας, ἐξ ὧν γίνεται φθόνος,
is sick concerning doubts and arguments, out of which comes envy,

5 ἔρις, βλασφημίαι, ὑπόνοιαι πονηραί, παραδιατριβαὶ διε-
strife, evil-speakings, suspicions evil, wearing disputes, having

φθαρμένων ἀνθρώπων τὸν νοῦν, καὶ ἀπεστερημένων τῆς
been corrupted of men · the mind, and deprived of the

ἀληθείας, νομιζόντων πορισμὸν εἶναι τὴν εὐσέβειαν. ἀφί-
truth, supposing gain to be godliness; with-

6 στασο ἀπὸ τῶν τοιούτων. ἔστι δὲ πορισμὸς μέγας ἡ εὐσέβεια
draw from such. is But gain great godliness

7 μετὰ αὐταρκείας· οὐδὲν γὰρ εἰσηνέγκαμεν εἰς τὸν κόσμον,
with contentment; nothing for we have brought into the world,

8 δῆλον ὅτι οὐδὲ ἐξενεγκεῖν τι δυνάμεθα· ἔχοντες δὲ διατροφὰς
(it is) plain that neither carry out anything can we; having but foods

9 καὶ σκεπάσματα τούτοις ἀρκεσθησόμεθα. οἱ δὲ βουλόμενοι
and clothings, with these things we will be satisfied. those but resolving

πλουτεῖν ἐμπίπτουσιν εἰς πειρασμὸν καὶ παγίδα καὶ ἐπιθυ-
to be rich fall into temptation and a snare, and lusts

μίας πολλὰς ἀνοήτους καὶ βλαβεράς, αἵτινες βυθίζουσι τοὺς
many foolish and hurtful, which cause to sink

10 ἀνθρώπους εἰς ὄλεθρον καὶ ἀπώλειαν. ῥίζα γὰρ πάντων τῶν
men into ruin and destruction. a root For of all

κακῶν ἐστιν ἡ φιλαργυρία· ἧς τινες ὀρεγόμενοι ἀπεπλανήθη-
evils is the love of money, of which some lusting after were seduced

σαν ἀπὸ τῆς πίστεως, καὶ ἑαυτοὺς περιέπειραν ὀδύναις
from the faith, and themselves pierced around pains

πολλαῖς.
by many.

sorrows. [11] But you, O man of God, flee these things, and pursue righteousness, godliness, faith, love, patience and meekness. [12] Fight the good fight of faith. Lay hold of eternal life, to which you were also called, and confessed the good confession before many witnesses. [13] I charge you in the sight of God, who makes all things live, and Christ Jesus, who witnessed a good confession before Pontius Pilate, [14] that you keep the commandment spotless, without blame, until the appearing of our Lord Jesus Christ; [15] who in His own times will show who is the blessed and only Ruler, the King of kings and Lord of lords, [16] who alone has immortality, living in light which is unapproachable, whom no one has seen nor is able to see, to whom be honor and power everlasting. Amen.

[17] (Give) charge to the rich in the present age not to be high-minded, nor to have hope in (the) uncertainty of riches, but in the living God, who gives us richly all things for enjoyment; [18] to do good, to be rich in good works, to be liberal in giving, ready to communicate, [19] treasuring up for themselves a good foundation for the future, that they may lay hold of everlasting life.

[20] O Timothy, keep the deposit committed (to you,, avoiding profane, empty babblings, and oppositions of falsely named science, [21] which some professing missed the mark in reference to the faith. Grace (be) with you. Amen.

**11** Σὺ δέ, ὦ ἄνθρωπε τοῦ Θεοῦ, ταῦτα φεῦγε· δίωκε δὲ δικαιο-
you But, O man   of God, these things flee, pursue and after
σύνην, εὐσέβειαν, πίστιν, ἀγάπην, ὑπομονήν, πραότητα.
righteousness, godliness, faith,   love,   patience,   meekness.

**12** ἀγωνίζου τὸν καλὸν ἀγῶνα τῆς πίστεως, ἐπιλαβοῦ τῆς
Fight   the   good   fight   of faith.   Lay hold on
αἰωνίου ζωῆς, εἰς ἣν καὶ ἐκλήθης, καὶ ὡμολόγησας τὴν καλὴν
everlasting life, to which also you were called, and confessed   the   good

**13** ὁμολογίαν ἐνώπιον πολλῶν μαρτύρων. παραγγέλλω σοι
confession   before   many   witnesses.   I enjoin   you
ἐνώπιον τοῦ Θεοῦ τοῦ ζωοποιοῦντος τὰ πάντα, καὶ Χριστοῦ
before   God, the (One) making alive   all things,   and   Christ
Ἰησοῦ τοῦ μαρτυρήσαντος ἐπὶ Ποντίου Πιλάτου τὴν καλὴν
Jesus, the (One) having witnessed on   Pontius   Pilate   the   good

**14** ὁμολογίαν, τηρῆσαί σε τὴν ἐντολὴν ἄσπιλον, ἀνεπίληπτον,
confession,   to keep   you the commandment unspotted, irreproachable,

**15** μέχρι τῆς ἐπιφανείας τοῦ Κυρίου ἡμῶν Ἰησοῦ Χριστοῦ, ἣν
until   the   appearing of the Lord   of us,   Jesus   Christ,   which
καιροῖς ἰδίοις δείξει ὁ μακάριος καὶ μόνος δυνάστης, ὁ Βασι-
in its own time will reveal the blessed and   only   Potentate, the King

**16** λεὺς τῶν βασιλευόντων, καὶ Κύριος τῶν κυριευόντων, ὁ
of kings,   and   Lord   of lords,   the
μόνος ἔχων ἀθανασίαν, φῶς οἰκῶν ἀπρόσιτον, ὃν εἶδεν οὐδεὶς
only (One) having immortality, light living in unapproachable, whom saw no one
ἀνθρώπων, οὐδὲ ἰδεῖν δύναται· ᾧ τιμὴ καὶ κράτος αἰώνιον.
of men,   nor   see en   can; to whom honor and might everlasting.
ἀμήν.
Amen.

**17** Τοῖς πλουσίοις ἐν τῷ νῦν αἰῶνι παράγγελλε, μὴ ὑψη-
The   rich   in   the present age   enjoin   not to be
λοφρονεῖν, μηδὲ ἠλπικέναι ἐπὶ πλούτου ἀδηλότητι, ἀλλ' ἐν
highminded, nor   to set hope   on of riches (the) uncertainty, but   on
τῷ Θεῷ τῷ ζῶντι, τῷ παρέχοντι ἡμῖν πλουσίως πάντα
God the living, the (One) offering   to us   richly   all things

**18** εἰς ἀπόλαυσιν· ἀγαθοεργεῖν, πλουτεῖν ἐν ἔργοις καλοῖς,
for enjoyment,   to work good,   to be rich   in   works   good,

**19** εὐμεταδότους εἶναι, κοινωνικούς, ἀποθησαυρίζοντας ἑαυτοῖς
ready to impart to be, generous,       treasuring away    for themselves
θεμέλιον καλὸν εἰς τὸ μέλλον, ἵνα ἐπιλάβωνται τῆς αἰωνίου
foundation a good for the coming (age), that they lay hold on   everlasting
ζωῆς.
life.

**20** Ὦ Τιμόθεε, τὴν παρακαταθήκην φύλαξον, ἐκτρεπόμενος
O Timothy,   the   deposit      guard,   having turned from
τὰς βεβήλους κενοφωνίας καὶ ἀντιθέσεις τῆς ψευδωνύμου
the   profane,   empty babblings and opposing of the falsely named
                                  theories

**21** γνώσεως· ἣν τινες ἐπαγγελλόμενοι περὶ τὴν πίστιν
knowledge, which some   asserting     concerning the   faith
ἠστόχησαν.
have missed the mark.

Ἡ χάρις μετὰ σοῦ. ἀμήν.
Grace (be) with you.   Amen.

THE APOSTLE PAUL'S
SECOND EPISTLE TO
TIMOTHY

# ΠΑΥΛΟΥ ΤΟΥ ΑΠΟΣΤΟΛΟΥ
PAUL    THE    APOSTLE

Η ΠΡΟΣ
THE TO

# ΤΙΜΟΘΕΟΝ
TIMOTHY

ΕΠΙΣΤΟΛΗ ΔΕΥΤΕΡΑ
EPISTLE   SECOND

## CHAPTER 1

CHAPTER 1

[1] Paul, (an) apostle of Jesus Christ by (the) will of God, according to the promise of life which (is) in Christ Jesus, [2] to (my) beloved child Timothy: Grace, mercy, peace from God (the) Father and Christ Jesus our Lord.

[3] I am thankful to God, whom I serve from (my) forefathers with pure conscience, how unceasingly I have the remembrance of you in my supplications night and day, [4] longing to see you, remembering your tears, that I may be filled with joy; [5] taking remembrance of the unpretended faith in you, which first dwelt in your grandmother Lois, and in your mother Eunice, and I am persuaded that (it is) also in you. [6] For which cause I remind you to kindle the gift of God which is in you by the laying on of my hands. [7] For God has not given us a spirit of fearfulness, but of power, and of love, and of a sound mind. [8] Therefore you should not be ashamed of the testimony of our Lord, nor me, His prisoner; but suffer hardship along with the gospel according to God's power; [9] who saved us and called (us) with a holy calling, not according to our works, but according to His own purpose and grace, which (was) given us in Christ Jesus before the beginning of time, [10] but now revealed by the appearing of our Savior Jesus Christ, who made death of no effect, and

**1** Παῦλος, ἀπόστολος Ἰησοῦ Χριστοῦ διὰ θελήματος Θεοῦ,
Paul    an apostle   of Jesus   Christ through (the) will of God,

**2** κατ' ἐπαγγελίαν ζωῆς τῆς ἐν Χριστῷ Ἰησοῦ, Τιμοθέῳ
by way of a promise of life    in   Christ   Jesus, to Timothy
ἀγαπητῷ τέκνῳ· χάρις, ἔλεος, εἰρήνη ἀπὸ Θεοῦ πατρὸς καὶ
beloved    child,   Grace,  hope,  peace from   God (the) Father and
Χριστοῦ Ἰησοῦ τοῦ Κυρίου ἡμῶν.
Christ    Jesus   the   Lord   of us.

**3** Χάριν ἔχω τῷ Θεῷ, ᾧ λατρεύω ἀπὸ προγόνων ἐν καθαρᾷ
Thanks I have    to God, whom I worship from (my) forebears in a clean
συνειδήσει, ὡς ἀδιάλειπτον ἔχω τὴν περὶ σοῦ μνείαν ἐν ταῖς
conscience,   as without ceasing I have the concerning you remembrance in the

**4** δεήσεσί μου νυκτὸς καὶ ἡμέρας, ἐπιποθῶν σε ἰδεῖν, μεμνημένος
petitions of me night  and   day,   longing  you to see, being reminded

**5** σου τῶν δακρύων, ἵνα χαρᾶς πληρωθῶ, ὑπόμνησιν λαμ-
of you the  tears,    that with joy I may be filled, recollection  taking
βάνων τῆς ἐν σοὶ ἀνυποκρίτου πίστεως, ἥτις ἐνῴκησε
of the in you    unpretended   faith,   which   indwelt
πρῶτον ἐν τῇ μάμμῃ σου Λωΐδι καὶ τῇ μητρί σου Εὐνίκη,
firstly  in   your grandmother Lois,  and (in) the mother of you Eunice,

**6** πέπεισμαι δὲ ὅτι καὶ ἐν σοί. δι' ἣν αἰτίαν ἀναμιμνήσκω σε
I am assured and that also in you (is). For which cause I remind    you
ἀναζωπυρεῖν τὸ χάρισμα τοῦ Θεοῦ, ὅ ἐστιν ἐν σοὶ διὰ τῆς
to fan the flame of the gift    of God, which is in you through the

**7** ἐπιθέσεως τῶν χειρῶν μου. οὐ γὰρ ἔδωκεν ἡμῖν ὁ Θεὸς
laying on of the  hands of me. not For  gave  to us   God
πνεῦμα δειλίας, ἀλλὰ δυνάμεως καὶ ἀγάπης καὶ σωφρονι-
a spirit of cowardice, but  of power  and of love  and of self-

**8** σμοῦ. μὴ οὖν ἐπαισχυνθῇς τὸ μαρτύριον τοῦ Κυρίου ἡμῶν,
control. not Therefore be ashamed of the testimony of the Lord   of us,
μηδὲ ἐμὲ τὸν δέσμιον αὐτοῦ· ἀλλὰ συγκακοπάθησον τῷ
nor (of) me, the prisoner of Him,  but   suffer hardship with  the

**9** εὐαγγελίῳ κατὰ δύναμιν Θεοῦ, τοῦ σώσαντος ἡμᾶς καὶ
gospel   according to (the) power of God, the (One) having saved us  and
καλέσαντος κλήσει ἁγίᾳ, οὐ κατὰ τὰ ἔργα ἡμῶν, ἀλλὰ κατ'
having called calling with a holy, not according to the works of us, but by
ἰδίαν πρόθεσιν καὶ χάριν τὴν δοθεῖσαν ἡμῖν ἐν Χριστῷ Ἰησοῦ
(His) own purpose and grace   given   to us in  Christ  Jesus

**10** πρὸ χρόνων αἰωνίων, φανερωθεῖσαν δὲ νῦν διὰ τῆς ἐπι-
before  times  eternal;    revealed   but now through the
φανείας τοῦ σωτῆρος ἡμῶν Ἰησοῦ Χριστοῦ, καταργήσαντος
appearance of the Savior  of us,   Jesus   Christ, making of no effect

brought life and incorruption to light through the gospel; [11] for which I was appointed a herald and an apostle, and a teacher of nations. [12] For which cause also I suffer these things; but I am not ashamed, for I know whom I have believed, and I am persuaded that He is able to keep my deposit unto that Day. [13] Have a pattern of sound words which you heard from me, in faith and love in Christ Jesus. [14] The good deposit committed (to you), guard through (the) Holy Spirit indwelling in us. [15] You know this, that all those in Asia turned away from me, of whom is Phygellus and Hermogenes. [16] May the Lord give mercy to the house of Onesiphorus, because he often refreshed me, and he was not ashamed of my chain; [17] but having come to Rome, he diligently sought and found me; [18] may the Lord give to him to find mercy from (the) Lord in that Day. And what things he served in Ephesus, you very well know.

CHAPTER 2

[1] Therefore, my son, you be strong in the grace which (is) in Christ Jesus. [2] And the things which you heard of me with many witnesses, these commit to faithful men, such as shall be able also to teach others. [3] Therefore, you suffer hardship as a good soldier of Jesus Christ. [4] No one serving as a soldier entangles himself with the affairs of life, that he may please the (one) having enlisted (him). [5] And also if anyone competes, he is not crowned unless he competes lawfully. [6] The farmer must labor before partaking of the fruits.

[7] Consider the things I say, for the Lord may give you understanding in all things. [8] Remember Jesus Christ raised from among (the) dead, of (the) seed of David, according to my gospel, [9] in which I

μὲν τὸν θάνατον, φωτίσαντος δὲ ζωὴν καὶ ἀφθαρσίαν διὰ τοῦ
death,   bringing to light and life and incorruption through the

11 εὐαγγελίου, εἰς ὃ ἐτέθην ἐγὼ κήρυξ καὶ ἀπόστολος καὶ
gospel,   for which was appointed I a herald and   apostle   and

12 διδάσκαλος ἐθνῶν. δι' ἣν αἰτίαν καὶ ταῦτα πάσχω, ἀλλ' οὐκ
a teacher of nations; for which cause also these things I suffer, but   not

ἐπαισχύνομαι· οἶδα γὰρ ᾧ πεπίστευκα, καὶ πέπεισμαι ὅτι
I am ashamed,   I know for whom I have believed, and I am persuaded that

δυνατός ἐστι τὴν παραθήκην μου φυλάξαι εἰς ἐκείνην τὴν
able   He is   the   deposit   of me to guard unto   that

13 ἡμέραν. ὑποτύπωσιν ἔχε ὑγιαινόντων λόγων ὧν παρ' ἐμοῦ
Day.   a pattern   Have   of sound   words which from me

14 ἤκουσας, ἐν πίστει καὶ ἀγάπῃ τῇ ἐν Χριστῷ Ἰησοῦ. τὴν
you heard, in faith and   love   in Christ   Jesus. The

καλὴν παρακαταθήκην φύλαξον διὰ Πνεύματος Ἁγίου τοῦ
good   deposit   guard through (the) Spirit   Holy

ἐνοικοῦντος ἐν ἡμῖν.
indwelling   in   us.

15 Οἶδας τοῦτο, ὅτι ἀπεστράφησάν με πάντες οἱ ἐν τῇ Ἀσίᾳ,
You know this,   that turned away from me all   those in   Asia,

16 ὧν ἐστὶ Φύγελλος καὶ Ἑρμογένης. δῴη ἔλεος ὁ Κύριος τῷ
of whom is Phygelus   and Hermogenes. May give mercy the Lord to the

Ὀνησιφόρου οἴκῳ· ὅτι πολλάκις με ἀνέψυξε, καὶ τὴν ἅλυσίν
of Onesiphorus house because often   me he refreshed, and the   chain

17 μου οὐκ ἐπῃσχύνθη, ἀλλὰ γενόμενος ἐν Ῥώμῃ, σπουδαιό-
of me not he was ashamed (of); but coming   to Rome,   diligently more

18 τερον ἐζήτησέ με καὶ εὗρε (δῴη αὐτῷ ὁ Κύριος εὑρεῖν ἔλεος
   he sought me and found —may give to him the Lord to find mercy

παρὰ Κυρίου ἐν ἐκείνῃ τῇ ἡμέρᾳ)· καὶ ὅσα ἐν Ἐφέσῳ
from (the) Lord in that   Day —   and what things in Ephesus

διηκόνησε, βέλτιον σὺ γινώσκεις.
he served,   very well you   know.

CHAPTER 2

1 Σὺ οὖν, τέκνον μου, ἐνδυναμοῦ ἐν τῇ χάριτι τῇ ἐν Χριστῷ
You, therefore, child of me, be empowered by   grace   in Christ

2 Ἰησοῦ. καὶ ἃ ἤκουσας παρ' ἐμοῦ διὰ πολλῶν μαρτύρων,
Jesus. And what things you heard from me through many   witnesses,

ταῦτα παράθου πιστοῖς ἀνθρώποις, οἵτινες ἱκανοὶ ἔσονται
these things commit to faithful   men,   who competent will be

3 καὶ ἑτέρους διδάξαι. σὺ οὖν κακοπάθησον ὡς καλὸς στρατιώ-
also others   to teach. You, then, suffer hardship as a good   soldier

4 της Ἰησοῦ Χριστοῦ. οὐδεὶς στρατευόμενος ἐμπλέκεται ταῖς
of Jesus Christ.   No one serving as a soldier tangles   with the

τοῦ βίου πραγματείαις, ἵνα τῷ στρατολογήσαντι ἀρέσῃ.
of life affairs,   that the (One) having enlisted (him) he please.

5 ἐὰν δὲ καὶ ἀθλῇ τις, οὐ στεφανοῦται ἐὰν μὴ νομίμως ἀθλήσῃ.
if And also competes any, not he is crowned unless lawfully he competes.

6 τὸν κοπιῶντα γεωργὸν δεῖ πρῶτον τῶν καρπῶν μετα-
The   laboring   farmer it behoves firstly of the   fruits   to

7 λαμβάνειν. νόει ἃ λέγω· δῴη γάρ σοι ὁ Κύριος σύνεσιν ἐν
partake.   Consider what I say, will give for you the Lord understanding in

8 πᾶσι. μνημόνευε Ἰησοῦν Χριστὸν ἐγηγερμένον ἐκ νεκρῶν,
all.   Remember   Jesus   Christ having been raised from (the) dead,

9 ἐκ σπέρματος Δαβίδ, κατὰ τὸ εὐαγγέλιόν μου· ἐν ᾧ κακο-
of (the) seed   of David, according to the gospel   of me; in which I

suffer hardship to bonds as an evildoer; but the word of God has not been bound. [10] Because of this, I endure all things on account of the elect, that they also may obtain salvation in Christ Jesus, with everlasting glory. [11] Faithful (is) the word; for if we died with (Him), we also shall live with (Him). [12] If we endure, we shall also reign with (Him); if we deny (Him), that One will deny us. [13] If we are unfaithful, that One continues (to be) faithful; He is not able to deny Himself.

[14] Remind (them of) these things, solemnly testifying before the Lord not to dispute about words for no profit, to (the) throwing down (of) those hearing. [15] Study to show yourself a workman unashamed, rightly dividing the word of truth. [16] But shun profane, empty babblings, for they will go on to more ungodliness, [17] and their word will have growth like gangrene; of whom is Hymeneus and Philetus; [18] who missed the mark concerning the truth, saying the resurrection already has come, and overturn the faith of some. [19] Nevertheless, the foundation of God stands firm, having this seal: "The Lord knew those being His;" and, "Let everyone naming the name of Christ depart from unrighteousness." [20] But in a great house there is not only vessels of gold and silver, but also of wood and of earth; and some to honor, and some to dishonor. [21] Therefore, if anyone cleanses himself from these, he will be a vessel to honor, having been sanctified and made useful to the Master, having been prepared to every good work. [22] But flee from youthful lusts, and pursue righteousness, faith, love, peace, with the (ones) calling on the Lord with a pure heart. [23] But refuse foolish and undisciplined questionings, knowing that they generate quarrels; [24] and a slave of the Lord ought not to quarrel, but to be gentle

πάθῶ μέχρι δεσμῶν, ὡς κακοῦργος· ἀλλ' ὁ λόγος τοῦ Θεοῦ
suffer ill unto bonds as an evildoer; but the word of God

10 οὐ δέδεται. διὰ τοῦτο πάντα ὑπομένω διὰ τοὺς ἐκλεκτούς,
not has been bound Therefore all things I endure on account of the elect
ἵνα καὶ αὐτοὶ σωτηρίας τύχωσι τῆς ἐν Χριστῷ 'Ιησοῦ, μετὰ
that also they salvation may obtain in Christ Jesus, with

11 δόξης αἰωνίου. πιστὸς ὁ λόγος· Εἰ γὰρ συναπεθάνομεν, καὶ
glory everlasting. Faithful (is) the word; if for we died with (Him), also

12 συζήσομεν· εἰ ὑπομένομεν, καὶ συμβασιλεύσομεν· εἰ ἀρνού-
we shall live with (Him); if we endure, also we shall reign with (Him); if we de-

13 μεθα, κἀκεῖνος ἀρνήσεται ἡμᾶς· εἰ ἀπιστοῦμεν, ἐκεῖνος πιστὸς
ny (Him), that One will deny us; if we are unfaithful, that One faithful
μένει· ἀρνήσασθαι ἑαυτὸν οὐ δύναται.
remains; to deny Himself not He is able.

14 Ταῦτα ὑπομίμνησκε, διαμαρτυρόμενος ἐνώπιον τοῦ
These things remind (them), solemnly testifying before the
Κυρίου μὴ λογομαχεῖν εἰς οὐδὲν χρήσιμον, ἐπὶ καταστροφῇ
Lord not to dispute for nothing useful, to throwing down
about words.

15 τῶν ἀκουόντων. σπούδασον σεαυτὸν δόκιμον παραστῆσαι
those hearing. Earnestly (study) yourself approved to show
τῷ Θεῷ, ἐργάτην ἀνεπαίσχυντον, ὀρθοτομοῦντα τὸν λόγον
to God a workman unashamed, rightly dividing the word

16 τῆς ἀληθείας. τὰς δὲ βεβήλους κενοφωνίας περιΐστασο· ἐπὶ
of truth. the But profane, empty babblings shun; to

17 πλεῖον γὰρ προκόψουσιν ἀσεβείας, καὶ ὁ λόγος αὐτῶν ὡς
more for they will advance ungodliness, and the word of them as

18 γάγγραινα νομὴν ἕξει· ὧν ἐστιν 'Υμέναιος καὶ Φιλητός· οἵτινες
gangrene feeding will have; of whom is Hymeneus and Philetus, who
περὶ τὴν ἀλήθειαν ἠστόχησαν, λέγοντες τὴν ἀνάστασιν
concerning the truth missed the mark, saying the resurrection

19 ἤδη γεγονέναι, καὶ ἀνατρέπουσι τήν τινων πίστιν. ὁ μέντοι
already to have come, and overturn the of some faith. the However,
στερεὸς θεμέλιος τοῦ Θεοῦ ἕστηκεν, ἔχων τὴν σφραγίδα
firm foundation of God stands, having the seal
ταύτην, Ἔγνω Κύριος τοὺς ὄντας αὐτοῦ, καί, 'Αποστήτω
this, knew (the) Lord those being His, and, Let depart

20 ἀπὸ ἀδικίας πᾶς ὁ ὀνομάζων τὸ ὄνομα Χριστοῦ. ἐν μεγάλη
from iniquity everyone naming the name of Christ. in a great
δὲ οἰκίᾳ οὐκ ἔστι μόνον σκεύη χρυσᾶ καὶ ἀργυρᾶ, ἀλλὰ καὶ
Now house, not is there only vessels golden and silver, but also
ξύλινα καὶ ὀστράκινα, καὶ ἃ μὲν εἰς τιμήν, ἃ δὲ εἰς ἀτιμίαν.
wooden and earthen; and some to honor, and some to dishonor.

21 ἐὰν οὖν τις ἐκκαθάρη ἑαυτὸν ἀπὸ τούτων, ἔσται σκεῦος εἰς
If, therefore anyone cleanses himself from these, he will be a vessel to
τιμήν, ἡγιασμένον, καὶ εὔχρηστον τῷ δεσπότῃ, εἰς πᾶν
honor, having been sanctified, and useful to the master, to every

22 ἔργον ἀγαθὸν ἡτοιμασμένον. τὰς δὲ νεωτερικὰς ἐπιθυμίας
work good having been prepared. the And youthful lusts
φεῦγε· δίωκε δὲ δικαιοσύνην, πίστιν, ἀγάπην, εἰρήνην, μετὰ
flee; pursue but righteousness, faith, love, peace, with

23 τῶν ἐπικαλουμένων τὸν Κύριον ἐκ καθαρᾶς καρδίας. τὰς δὲ
those calling on the Lord out of a clean heart. But
μωρὰς καὶ ἀπαιδεύτους ζητήσεις παραιτοῦ, εἰδὼς ὅτι
foolish and uninstructed questionings refuse, knowing that

24 γεννῶσι μάχας. δοῦλον δὲ Κυρίου οὐ δεῖ μάχεσθαι, ἀλλ'
they generate quarrels; a slave and of (the) Lord not it behoves to quarrel, but

towards all, apt to teach, forbearing; [25] in meekness teaching those who oppose, if perhaps God may give them repentance to acknowledgement of (the) truth, [26] and they may wake up out of the snare of the Devil, having been taken captive by him, in order to (do) his will.

CHAPTER 3

[1] But you know this, that in the last days difficult times will come; [2] for men will be lovers of themselves, lovers of money, braggarts, proud, blasphemers, disobedient to parents, unthankful, unholy, [3] without natural feeling, unyielding, slanderers, without self-control, savage, not lovers of good, [4] traitors, reckless, puffed up, lovers of pleasure rather than lovers of God, [5] having a form of godliness, but denying the power of it. And (you) turn away from these. [6] For of these are those who (are) entering into houses and leading captive silly women loaded with sins, led away by various lusts, [7] always learning and never able to come to (the) knowledge of (the) truth. [8] Now as Jannes and Jambres withstood Moses, so also these withstand the truth, men utterly corrupted in mind, found worthless as to the faith. [9] But they shall not go on further, for their foolishness shall be very clear to all, as also that of those became. [10] But you have closely followed my teaching, behavior, purpose, faith, patience, love, endurance, [11] persecutions, sufferings; such as happened to me in Antioch, in Iconium, in Lystra; what persecutions I endured; and the Lord delivered me out of all. [12] And, indeed, all who desire to live godly in Christ Jesus will be persecuted. [13] But wicked men and pretenders

25 ἤπιον εἶναι πρὸς πάντας, διδακτικόν, ἀνεξίκακον, ἐν πραό-
gentle to be  toward  all,   apt to teach,  forbearing,  in meek-
τητι παιδεύοντα τοὺς ἀντιδιατιθεμένους· μήποτε δῷ αὐτοῖς
ness teaching   those    opposing,     (if) perhaps may give them
26 ὁ Θεὸς μετάνοιαν εἰς ἐπίγνωσιν ἀληθείας, καὶ ἀνανήψωσιν
   God repentance for a full, knowledge of truth,  and they regain senses
ἐκ τῆς τοῦ διαβόλου παγίδος, ἐζωγρημένοι ὑπ' αὐτοῦ εἰς τὸ
out of the   devil    snare, having been captured by  him to (do) the
ἐκείνου θέλημα.
of that one will.

## CHAPTER 3

1 Τοῦτο δὲ γίνωσκε, ὅτι ἐν ἐσχάταις ἡμέραις ἐνστήσονται
  this And know,  that in (the) last  days  will be at hand
2 καιροὶ χαλεποί. ἔσονται γὰρ οἱ ἄνθρωποι φίλαυτοι, . φιλ-
  times grievous.  will be For  men  self-lovers, money-
ἄργυροι, ἀλαζόνες, ὑπερήφανοι, βλάσφημοι, γονεῦσιν ἀπει-
lovers,  braggarts, arrogant,  blasphemers,  to parents diso-
3 θεῖς, ἀχάριστοι, ἀνόσιοι, ἄστοργοι, ἄσπονδοι. διάβολοι,
  bedient, unthankful,  unholy, without natural feeling, implacable, slanderers,
4 ἀκρατεῖς, ἀνήμεροι, ἀφιλάγαθοι, προδόται, προπετεῖς, τετυ-
  without self-control, savage, haters of good, betrayers, reckless,  puffed
5 φωμένοι, φιλήδονοι μᾶλλον ἢ φιλόθεοι, ἔχοντες μόρφωσιν
  up,  pleasure-lovers rather than God-lovers, having  a form
εὐσεβείας, τὴν δὲ δύναμιν αὐτῆς ἠρνημένοι· καὶ τούτους
of godliness, the but  power  of it  having denied—even  these
6 ἀποτρέπου. ἐκ τούτων γάρ εἰσιν οἱ ἐνδύνοντες εἰς τὰς οἰκίας,
  turn away from. of these For are those creeping into  houses,
καὶ αἰχμαλωτεύοντες τὰ γυναικάρια σεσωρευμένα ἁμαρ-
and  leading captive    silly women  having been heaped with
7 τίαις, ἀγόμενα ἐπιθυμίαις ποικίλαις, πάντοτε μανθάνοντα
  sins,  being led  lusts  by various,  always  learning
8 καὶ μηδέποτε εἰς ἐπίγνωσιν ἀληθείας ἐλθεῖν δυνάμενα. ὃν
  and never  to a full knowledge of truth  to come  being able. by
τρόπον δὲ Ἰαννῆς καὶ Ἰαμβρῆς ἀντέστησαν Μωϋσεῖ, οὕτω
what way And Jannes and  Jambres  opposed  Moses,  so
καὶ οὗτοι ἀνθίστανται τῇ ἀληθείᾳ, ἄνθρωποι κατεφθαρ-
also these  oppose  the truth,  men  having been
9 μένοι τὸν νοῦν, ἀδόκιμοι περὶ τὴν πίστιν. ἀλλ' οὐ προκό-
  corrupted the mind, reprobate concerning the faith.  But not they will
ψουσιν ἐπὶ πλεῖον· ἡ γὰρ ἄνοια αὐτῶν ἔκδηλος ἔσται πᾶσιν,
advance to  more; the for folly  of them plain  will be  to all,
10 ὡς καὶ ἡ ἐκείνων ἐγένετο. σὺ δὲ παρηκολούθηκάς μου τῇ
   as also the (folly) of those became. you But have closely followed of me the
διδασκαλίᾳ, τῇ ἀγωγῇ, τῇ προθέσει, τῇ πίστει, τῇ μα-
teaching,  the conduct,  the purpose, the faith,  the long-
11 κροθυμίᾳ, τῇ ἀγάπῃ, τῇ ὑπομονῇ, τοῖς διωγμοῖς, τοῖς παθή-
   suffering, the love,  the patience,  the persecutions, the sufferings
μασιν, οἷά μοι ἐγένετο ἐν Ἀντιοχείᾳ, ἐν Ἰκονίῳ, ἐν Λύστροις,
which to me happened in Antioch,  in Iconium,  in Lystra;
οἵους διωγμοὺς ὑπήνεγκα· καὶ ἐκ πάντων με ἐρρύσατο ὁ
what persecutions  I bore;  yet out of all  me delivered the
12 Κύριος. καὶ πάντες δὲ οἱ θέλοντες εὐσεβῶς ζῆν ἐν Χριστῷ
   Lord.  indeed all  And those desiring godly to live in  Christ
13 Ἰησοῦ διωχθήσονται. πονηροὶ δὲ ἄνθρωποι καὶ γόητες
   Jesus will be persecuted.  evil  But  men  and pretenders

shall go on to worse, leading astray and being led astray. [14] But you keep on in the things you learned, and were assured of, having known from whom you learned (them); [15] and that from a babe you have known the Holy Scriptures, which (are) able to make you wise to salvation, through faith which is in Christ Jesus. [16] All Scripture is God-breathed and profitable for teaching, for reproof, for correction, for instruction in righteousness; [17] so that the man of God may be perfect, fully fitted to every good work.

CHAPTER 4

[1] I then call on you in the sight of God and the Lord Jesus Christ, who is about to judge living and dead according to His appearing and His kingdom, [2] preach the word; be urgent in season, out of season, convict, correct, encourage with all patience and teaching. [3] For a time will come when they will not endure sound doctrine; but according to their own lusts, having itching ears, they will heap up to themselves teachers; [4] and they will turn away their ear from the truth and will be turned aside to myths. [5] But you be clear-minded in all things, suffer hardships, do (the) work of an evangelist, fully carry out your ministry. [6] For I already am being poured out, and the time of my release is here. [7] I have fought a good fight; I have finished the course; I have kept the faith. [8] Now the crown of righteousness is laid up for me, which the Lord, the righteous Judge, will give to me in that Day; and not only to me, but also to all who love His appearing.

[9] Try to come to me quickly. [10] For Demas deserted me, having loved the present age, and is gone to Thessalonica; Crescens

προκόψουσιν ἐπὶ τὸ χεῖρον, πλανῶντες καὶ πλανώμενοι.
will go forward to worse, deceiving and being deceived.

14 σὺ δὲ μένε ἐν οἷς ἔμαθες καὶ ἐπιστώθης, εἰδὼς παρὰ τίνος
you But continue in what you learned and were assured of, knowing from whom

15 ἔμαθες, καὶ ὅτι ἀπὸ βρέφους τὰ ἱερὰ γράμματα οἶδας, τὰ
you learned, and that from a babe the holy scriptures you know, those

δυνάμενά σε σοφίσαι εἰς σωτηρίαν διὰ πίστεως τῆς ἐν
being able you to make wise to salvation through belief in

16 Χριστῷ Ἰησοῦ. πᾶσα γραφὴ θεόπνευστος καὶ ὠφέλιμος
Christ Jesus. Every Scripture (is) God-breathed and profitable

πρὸς διδασκαλίαν, πρὸς ἔλεγχον, πρὸς ἐπανόρθωσιν, πρὸς
for teaching, for reproof, for correction, for

17 παιδείαν τὴν ἐν δικαιοσύνῃ· ἵνα ἄρτιος ᾖ ὁ τοῦ Θεοῦ
instruction in righteousness, that fitted may be the of God

ἄνθρωπος, πρὸς πᾶν ἔργον ἀγαθὸν ἐξηρτισμένος.
man, for every work good having been furnished.

CHAPTER 4

1 Διαμαρτύρομαι οὖν ἐγὼ ἐνώπιον τοῦ Θεοῦ, καὶ τοῦ
solemnly witness Then I before God, and the

Κυρίου Ἰησοῦ Χριστοῦ, τοῦ μέλλοντος κρίνειν ζῶντας καὶ
Lord Jesus Christ, the (One) being about to judge living ones and

νεκροὺς κατὰ τὴν ἐπιφάνειαν αὐτοῦ καὶ τὴν βασιλείαν
dead, according to the appearance of Him and the kingdom

2 αὐτοῦ, κήρυξον τὸν λόγον, ἐπίστηθι εὐκαίρως, ἀκαίρως,
of Him, proclaim the word, be urgent in season, out of season,

ἔλεγξον, ἐπιτίμησον, παρακάλεσον, ἐν πάσῃ μακροθυμίᾳ
reprove, warn, encourage with all long-suffering

3 καὶ διδαχῇ. ἔσται γὰρ καιρὸς ὅτε τῆς ὑγιαινούσης διδα-
and teaching. there will For a time when the sound

σκαλίας οὐκ ἀνέξονται, ἀλλὰ κατὰ τὰς ἐπιθυμίας τὰς ἰδίας
doctrine not they will bear, but according to the lusts the own

ἑαυτοῖς ἐπισωρεύσουσι διδασκάλους, κνηθόμενοι τὴν ἀκοήν·
to themselves they will heap up teachers tickling the ear,

4 καὶ ἀπὸ μὲν τῆς ἀληθείας τὴν ἀκοὴν ἀποστρέψουσιν, ἐπὶ
and from indeed the truth the ear will turn away, to

5 δὲ τοὺς μύθους ἐκτραπήσονται. σὺ δὲ νῆφε ἐν πᾶσι, κακοπά-
and myths will be turned. you But be sober in all, suffer

θησον, ἔργον ποίησον εὐαγγελιστοῦ, τὴν διακονίαν σου
evil, (the) work do of an evangelist, the ministry of you

6 πληροφόρησον. ἐγὼ γὰρ ἤδη σπένδομαι, καὶ ὁ καιρὸς τῆς
fulfill. I For already am being poured out, and the time of the

7 ἐμῆς ἀναλύσεως ἐφέστηκε. τὸν ἀγῶνα τὸν καλὸν ἠγώνισμαι,
of me departure has arrived. The fight good I have fought,

8 τὸν δρόμον τετέλεκα, τὴν πίστιν τετήρηκα· λοιπόν, ἀπό-
the course I have finished, the faith I have kept; for the rest, is laid

κειταί μοι ὁ τῆς δικαιοσύνης στέφανος, ὃν ἀποδώσει μοι ὁ
up for me the of righteousness crown, which will give to me the

Κύριος ἐν ἐκείνῃ τῇ ἡμέρᾳ, ὁ δίκαιος κριτής· οὐ μόνον δὲ
Lord in that Day, the righteous Judge; not only and

ἐμοί, ἀλλὰ καὶ πασι τοῖς ἠγαπηκόσι τὴν ἐπιφάνειαν αὐτοῦ.
to me, but also all those having loved the appearance of Him.

9
10 Σπούδασον ἐλθεῖν πρός με ταχέως· Δημᾶς γάρ με ἐγκατέ-
Make haste to come to me shortly. Demas For me deserted,

λιπεν, ἀγαπήσας τὸν νῦν αἰῶνα, καὶ ἐπορεύθη εἰς Θεσ-
loving the present age, and went to Thessa-

to Galatia; Titus to
Dalmatia. [11] Luke alone
is with me. Having taken
Mark bring (him) with you,
for he is useful to me for
ministry. [12] But I sent
Tychicus to Ephesus.
[13] Bring the cloak which
I left in Troas with Carpus
(when) coming, and the
books, especially the
p a r c h m e n t s .
[14] Alexander the smith
did many evil things
against me. May the Lord
render to him according to
his works. [15] You also
beware, for he has greatly
resisted our words. [16] In
my first defense, no one
stood with me, but all
deserted me. May it not be
r e c k o n e d   t o   t h e m .
[17] But the Lord stood
by me and empowered
me, that through me the
preaching might be made
known, and all the nations
should hear; and I was
delivered out of (the)
m o u t h  o f  t h e  l i o n .
[18] And the Lord will
deliver me from every evil
work, and will preserve
(me) for His heavenly
kingdom; to whom (be)
glory forever and ever.
Amen.

[19] Greet Priscilla and
Aquila, and the house of
Onesiphorus. [20] Erastus
remained in Corinth, but I
left Trophimus sick in
Miletus. [21] Try to come
before winter. Eubulus
greets you, and Pudens,
and Linus, and Claudia,
and all the brothers.
[22] The Lord Jesus Christ
(be) with your spirit. Grace
(be) with you. Amen.

σαλονίκην· Κρήσκης εἰς Γαλατίαν, Τίτος εἰς Δαλματίαν.
Ionica,        Crescens    to   Galatia;      Titus  to   Dalmatia.

**11** Λουκᾶς ἐστι μόνος μετ' ἐμοῦ. Μᾶρκον ἀναλαβὼν ἄγε μετὰ
Luke  is   only   with  me.   Mark   having taken, bring with

**12** σεαυτοῦ· ἐστι γάρ μοι εὔχρηστος εἰς διακονίαν. Τυχικὸν δὲ
yourself,he is   for  to me useful    for ministry.

**13** ἀπέστειλα εἰς Ἔφεσον. τὸν φελόνην ὃν ἀπέλιπον ἐν Τρωάδι
I sent      to Ephesus. The cloak   which  I left   in  Troas

παρὰ Κάρπῳ, ἐρχόμενος φέρε, καὶ τὰ βιβλία, μάλιστα τὰς
with  Carpus,   coming bring, and the scrolls, especially the

**14** μεμβράνας. Ἀλέξανδρος ὁ χαλκεὺς πολλά μοι κακὰ ἐνεδεί-
parchments.  Alexander  the coppersmith much to me  evils showed;

**15** ξατο· ἀποδῴη αὐτῷ ὁ Κύριος κατὰ τὰ ἔργα αὐτοῦ· ὃν καὶ
will give to him the Lord according to the works of him;whom also

σὺ φυλάσσου, λίαν γὰρ ἀνθέστηκε τοῖς ἡμετέροις λόγοις.
you guard (against),greatly for he opposed        our   words.

**16** ἐν τῇ πρώτῃ μου ἀπολογίᾳ οὐδείς μοι συμπαρεγένετο, ἀλλὰ
At the first of me defense   no one me was beside,     but

**17** πάντες με ἐγκατέλιπον· μὴ αὐτοῖς λογισθείη. ὁ δὲ Κύριός
all   me   deserted.May it not to them be reckoned. the But Lord

μοι παρέστη, καὶ ἐνεδυνάμωσέ με, ἵνα δι' ἐμοῦ τὸ κήρυγμα
me stood with, and empowered   me, that through me the preaching

πληροφορηθῇ, καὶ ἀκούσῃ πάντα τὰ ἔθνη· καὶ ἐρρύσθην ἐκ
might be fulfilled, and might hear all the nations. And I was
                                                         delivered out of

**18** στόματος λέοντος. καὶ ῥύσεταί με ὁ Κύριος ἀπὸ παντος εργου
(the) mouth of (the) lion. And will deliver me The Lord from every work

πονηροῦ. καὶ σώσει εἰς τὴν βασιλείαν αὐτοῦ τὴν ἐπουράνιον·
wicked,     and will save for the kingdom of Him      heavenly;

ᾧ ἡ δόξα εἰς τοὺς αἰῶνας τῶν αἰώνων. ἀμήν.
to whom (be) the glory to the ages of the ages. Amen.

**19** Ἄσπασαι Πρίσκαν καὶ Ἀκύλαν, καὶ τὸν Ὀνησιφόρου
Greet   Priscilla  and  Aquila,   and the of Onesiphorus

**20** οἶκον. Ἔραστος ἔμεινεν ἐν Κορίνθῳ· Τρόφιμον δὲ ἀπέλιπον
house.  Erastus  remained in Corinth,  Trophimus But I left

**21** ἐν Μιλήτῳ ἀσθενοῦντα. σπούδασον πρὸ χειμῶνος ἐλθεῖν.
in  Miletus   sick.       Make haste  before  winter  to come.

ἀσπάζεταί σε Εὔβουλος, καὶ Πούδης, καὶ Λῖνος, καὶ Κλαυδία,
Greets     you Eubulus   and Pudens   and Linus   and Claudia,

καὶ οἱ ἀδελφοὶ πάντες.
and the brothers   all.

**22** Ὁ Κύριος Ἰησοῦς Χριστὸς μετὰ τοῦ πνεύματός σου. ἡ
The  Lord   Jesus Christ (be) with  the   spirit   of you.

χάρις μεθ' ὑμῶν. ἀμήν.
Grace (be) with you. Amen.

## PAUL'S EPISTLE TO
## TITUS

### CHAPTER 1

[1] Paul, a slave of God, and an apostle of Jesus Christ, according to (the) faith of (the) elect of God, and full knowledge of (the) truth, that according to godliness, [2] on hope of eternal life which the God that does not lie promised before eternal times, [3] but revealed in its own times in (the) proclamation of His word, which was entrusted to me by (the) command of our Savior God; [4] to Titus (my) true child according to (our) common faith: Grace, mercy, peace from God (the) Father, and (the) Lord Jesus Christ, our Savior.

[5] For this cause I left you in Crete, so that you might set in order the things lacking, and might appoint elders in every city, as I ordered you; [6] if anyone is blameless, husband of one wife, having believing children, (that are) not under accusation of loose behavior (or being unruly—[7] for the overseer must be blameless as a steward of God, not self-pleasing, not full of passion, not given to wine, not a quarreler, not greedy of ill gain; [8] but hospitable, a lover of good, discreet, just, holy, temperate, [9] clinging to the faithful word according to the teaching, that he may be able both to encourage with sound teaching and to convict those who speak against — [10] for there are many unruly, empty talkers, and mind-deluders, especially those of (the) circumcision, [11] of whom it is necessary to stop the mouths, who overthrow whole houses, teaching things which

## ΠΑΥΛΟΥ
### PAUL
## Η ΠΡΟΣ
### THE TO
# ΤΙΤΟΝ ΕΠΙΣΤΟΛΗ
### TITUS   EPISTLE

### CHAPTER 1

1 Παῦλος, δοῦλος Θεοῦ, ἀπόστολος δὲ Ἰησοῦ Χριστοῦ, κατὰ
Paul,   a slave of God, an apostle and of Jesus   Christ, according to
πίστιν ἐκλεκτῶν Θεοῦ καὶ ἐπίγνωσιν ἀληθείας τῆς και
(the) faith of (the) elect of God and full knowledge of (the) truth according

2 εὐσέβειαν, ἐπ' ἐλπίδι ζωῆς αἰωνίου, ἣν ἐπηγγείλατο ὁ
godliness,   on   hope   life of eternal which promised   the

3 ἀψευδὴς Θεὸς πρὸ χρόνων αἰωνίων, ἐφανέρωσε δὲ καιροῖς
not lying God before   times   eternal,   revealed   but times
ἰδίοις τὸν λόγον αὐτοῦ ἐν κηρύγματι ὃ ἐπιστεύθην ἐγὼ κατ'
in its own the word of Him in a proclamation which was entrusted I   by

4 ἐπιταγὴν τοῦ σωτῆρος ἡμῶν Θεοῦ, Τίτῳ γνησίῳ τέκνῳ
(the) command of the Savior   of us,   God, to Titus a true   child
κατὰ κοινὴν πίστιν· χάρις, ἔλεος, εἰρήνη ἀπὸ Θεοῦ πατρός,
according to a common faith: Grace, mercy, peace from God (the) Father
καὶ Κυρίου Ἰησοῦ Χριστοῦ τοῦ σωτῆρος ἡμῶν.
and (the) Lord Jesus   Christ, the   Savior   of us.

5 Τούτου χάριν κατέλιπόν σε ἐν Κρήτῃ, ἵνα τὰ λείποντα
For this cause   I left   you in   Crete, that the things lacking
ἐπιδιορθώσῃ, καὶ καταστήσῃς κατὰ πόλιν πρεσβυτέρους,
you set in order, and appoint   in every city   elders,

6 ὡς ἐγώ σοι διεταξάμην· εἴ τίς ἐστιν ἀνέγκλητος, μιᾶς
as I   you   ordered;   if anyone is   blameless,   of one
γυναικὸς ἀνήρ, τέκνα ἔχων πιστά, μὴ ἐν κατηγορίᾳ ἀσωτίας
wife   husband, children having believing, not in accusation of looseness

7 ἢ ἀνυπότακτα. δεῖ γὰρ τὸν ἐπίσκοπον ἀνέγκλητον εἶναι,
or   unruly. it behoves For the   overseer   blameless   to be,
ὡς Θεοῦ οἰκονόμον· μὴ αὐθάδη, μὴ ὀργίλον, μὴ πάροινον,
as of God a steward,   not self-pleasing, not passionate, not given to wine,

8 μὴ πλήκτην, μὴ αἰσχροκερδῆ, ἀλλὰ φιλόξενον, φιλάγαθον,
not a quarreler, not greedy of ill gain, but   hospitable, a lover of good,

9 σώφρονα, δίκαιον, ὅσιον, ἐγκρατῆ, ἀντεχόμενον τοῦ κατὰ
discreet,   just,   holy, temperate,   clinging   to the according to
τὴν διδαχὴν πιστοῦ λόγου, ἵνα δυνατὸς ᾖ καὶ παρακαλεῖν
the teaching faithful   word, that   able he may be both to exhort
ἐν τῇ διδασκαλίᾳ τῇ ὑγιαινούσῃ, καὶ τοὺς ἀντιλέγοντας
by the   teaching   sound,   and those contradicting
ἐλέγχειν.
to convict.

10 Εἰσὶ γὰρ πολλοὶ καὶ ἀνυπότακτοι, ματαιολόγοι καὶ
there are For   many   indeed unruly men,   empty talkers, and

11 φρεναπάται, μάλιστα οἱ ἐκ περιτομῆς, οὓς δεῖ ἐπιστομίζειν·
mind-deluders, especially those circum- of (you)stop the mouth
                           of cision whom must
οἵτινες ὅλους οἴκους ἀνατρέπουσι, διδάσκοντες ἃ μὴ δεῖ,
who   whole houses   overturn,   teaching   things not right,

(they) ought not, for the sake of ill gain. [12] One of them, a prophet of their own, said, Cretans (are) always liars, evil beasts, lazy gluttons. [13] This testimony is true; for which cause convict them severely, that they may be sound in the faith, [14] not listening to Jewish myths and commandments of men, having turned away from the truth. [15] Truly, all things (are) pure to the pure; but to those having been defiled and unbelieving, nothing is pure, but even their mind and conscience has been defiled. [16] They profess to know God, but by (their) works they deny (Him), being abominable and disobedient; and to every good work reprobate.

CHAPTER 2

[1] But you speak things which become sound doctrine: [2] aged men to be temperate, sensible, discreet, sound in faith, in love, in patience; [3] aged women likewise in reverent behavior, not slanderers, not having been enslaved by much wine, teachers of good, [4] that they might train the young women to be lovers of husbands, lovers of children, [5] discreet, chaste, keepers at home, good, subject to their own husbands, that the word of God may not be blasphemed; [6] the younger (men) in the same way exhort to be discreet; [7] in all things holding yourself out as a pattern of good works; in doctrine, in purity, sensibleness, incorruption, [8] sound speech, not to be condemned; that he who is opposed may be ashamed, having nothing evil to say about you. [9] Let slaves be subject to their own masters, in everything to be well pleasing, not contradicting; [10] not stealing, but showing all good faith, that they may adorn the teaching of our Savior God in all things. [11] For the grace of God, which brings salvation, has appeared for all men, [12] teaching us that,

---

**12** αἰσχροῦ κέρδους χάριν. εἶπέ τις ἐξ αὐτῶν, ἴδιος αὐτῶν
  ill     gain for the sake of. said One of   them,   an own of them
προφήτης, Κρῆτες ἀεὶ ψεῦσται, κακὰ θηρία, γαστέρες ἀργαί.
prophet,   Cretans (are) always liars,   evil beasts, gluttons   idle.

**13** ἡ μαρτυρία αὕτη ἐστὶν ἀληθής. δι' ἣν αἰτίαν ἔλεγχε αὐτούς
  witness This   is     true; for which cause convict them

**14** ἀποτόμως, ἵνα ὑγιαίνωσιν ἐν τῇ πίστει, μὴ προσέχοντες
  severely,   that they may be sound in the   faith,   not   listening
Ἰουδαϊκοῖς μύθοις καὶ ἐντολαῖς ἀνθρώπων ἀποστρεφομένων
to Jewish   myths and commandments of men   having perverted

**15** τὴν ἀλήθειαν· πάντα μὲν καθαρὰ τοῖς καθαροῖς· τοῖς δὲ
  the   truth.     All things indeed (are) clean to the clean,   to those but
μεμιασμένοις καὶ ἀπίστοις οὐδὲν καθαρόν· ἀλλὰ μεμίανται
having been defiled and unbelieving nothing (is) clean, but has been defiled

**16** αὐτῶν καὶ ὁ νοῦς καὶ ἡ συνείδησις. Θεὸν ὁμολογοῦσιν
  of them even the mind and the conscience.   God They profess
εἰδέναι, τοῖς δὲ ἔργοις ἀρνοῦνται, βδελυκτοὶ ὄντες καὶ
to know, by the but works they deny (Him), abominable being   and
ἀπειθεῖς καὶ πρὸς πᾶν ἔργον ἀγαθὸν ἀδόκιμοι.
disobedient and to every   work   good     reprobate.

CHAPTER 2

**1** Σὺ δὲ λάλει ἃ πρέπει τῇ ὑγιαινούσῃ διδασκαλίᾳ· πρεσ-
  you But speak things which becomes the sound     teaching.   Aged

**2** βύτας νηφαλίους εἶναι, σεμνούς, σώφρονας, ὑγιαίνοντας τῇ
  men temperate to be, sensible,   discreet,   sound     in the

**3** πίστει, τῇ ἀγάπῃ, τῇ ὑπομονῇ· πρεσβύτιδας ὡσαύτως ἐν
  faith;   in love,   in patience;   aged women   likewise in
καταστήματι ἱεροπρεπεῖς, μὴ διαβόλους, μὴ οἴνῳ πολλῷ
behavior     reverent,     not slanderers, not wine by much

**4** δεδουλωμένας, καλοδιδασκάλους, ἵνα σωφρονίζωσι τὰς νέας
  having been enslaved, teachers of good,   that they may train the   young women

**5** φιλάνδρους εἶναι, φιλοτέκνους, σώφρονας, ἁγνάς, οἰκουρούς,
  lovers of husbands to be, child-lovers, discreet,   chaste, homeworkers,
ἀγαθάς, ὑποτασσομένας τοῖς ἰδίοις ἀνδράσιν, ἵνα μὴ ὁ λόγος
good,   being subject   to the   own husbands, that not the word

**6** τοῦ Θεοῦ βλασφημῆται· τοὺς νεωτέρους ὡσαύτως παρακάλει
  of God be blasphemed.   The younger men likewise   exhort
σωφρονεῖν· περὶ πάντα σεαυτὸν παρεχόμενος τύπον καλῶν
to be discreet;about all things yourself   showing     a pattern of good
ἔργων, ἐν τῇ διδασκαλίᾳ ἀδιαφθορίαν, σεμνότητα, ἀφθ-
works,   in the   teaching,   in purity,   sensibleness,   incor-

**8** αρσίαν, λόγον ὑγιῆ, ἀκατάγνωστον, ἵνα ὁ ἐξ ἐναντίας
  ruption,   speech sound, irreprehensible,   that he of opposition

**9** ἐντραπῇ, μηδὲν ἔχων περὶ ὑμῶν λέγειν φαῦλον. δούλους ἰδίοις
  be ashamed, nothing having about us to say   bad.   Slaves to own
δεσπόταις ὑποτάσσεσθαι, ἐν πᾶσιν εὐαρέστους εἶναι, μὴ
masters   to be subject   in all things well-pleasing   to be, not

**10** ἀντιλέγοντας, μὴ νοσφιζομένους, ἀλλὰ πίστιν πᾶσαν ἐνδει-
  contradicting,   not stealing,     but   faith   all
κνυμένους ἀγαθήν, ἵνα τὴν διδασκαλίαν τοῦ σωτῆρος ἡμῶν
showing   good,     that the   teaching   of the Savior   of us,

**11** Θεοῦ κοσμῶσιν ἐν πᾶσιν. ἐπεφάνη γὰρ ἡ χάρις τοῦ Θεοῦ ἡ
  God, they may adorn in all things. appeared For the grace   of God

**12** σωτήριος πᾶσιν ἀνθρώποις, παιδεύουσα ἡμᾶς ἵνα, ἀρνησά-
  saving     to all   men,     instructing   us   that   having

having denied ungodliness and worldly lusts, we should live wisely and righteously and godly in this present world, [13] looking for the blessed hope and appearing of the glory of our great God and Savior, Jesus Christ; [14] who gave Himself for us, that He might redeem us from all iniquity, and might purify to Himself a peculiar people, zealous of good works. [15] These things speak, and exhort, and convict with all authority. Let no one despise you.

μενοι τὴν ἀσέβειαν καὶ τὰς κοσμικὰς ἐπιθυμίας, σωφρόνως καὶ
denied ungodliness     and     worldly    lusts,     discreetly   and

13 δικαίως καὶ εὐσεβῶς ζήσωμεν ἐν τῷ νῦν αἰῶνι, προσδεχό-
righteously and godly  we might live in the present age,      expecting
μενοι τὴν μακαρίαν ἐλπίδα καὶ ἐπιφάνειαν τῆς δόξης τοῦ
the blessed     hope    ,and   appearance of the glory of the

14 μεγάλου Θεοῦ καὶ σωτῆρος ἡμῶν Ἰησοῦ Χριστοῦ, ὃς ἔδωκεν
great     God and Savior   of us,    Jesus     Christ, who gave
ἑαυτὸν ὑπὲρ ἡμῶν, ἵνα λυτρώσηται ἡμᾶς ἀπὸ πάσης
Himself on behalf of us,   that He might redeem  us   from   all
ἀνομίας, καὶ καθαρίσῃ ἑαυτῷ λαὸν περιούσιον, ζηλωτὴν
iniquity  and cleanse  for Himself a people special,    zealous
καλῶν ἔργων.
of good works.

15 Ταῦτα λάλει, καὶ παρακάλει, καὶ ἔλεγχε μετὰ πάσης
These things speak,  and  exhort,     and  convict with   all
ἐπιταγῆς. μηδείς σου περιφρονείτω.
authority.  no one  you  Let despise.

## CHAPTER 3

[1] Put them in remembrance to be subject to rulers and to authorities, to be obedient, to be ready to every good work; [2] to speak evil of no one, not to be quarrelsome, gentle, showing all meekness toward all men. [3] For we also were once foolish, disobedient, led astray, serving various lusts and pleasures, living in malice and envy, hateful, hating one another. [4] But when the kindness and love of God our Savior toward man appeared, [5] not by works which we had done in righteousness, but according to His mercy He saved us, through (the) washing of regeneration and renewal of (the) Holy Spirit, [6] which he poured out on us richly through Jesus Christ our Savior; [7] that having been justified by His grace, we should become heirs according to (the) hope of eternal life. [8] Faithful (is) the word, and concerning these things I desire you to strongly affirm that they who have believed may be careful to maintain good works. These things are good and profitable to men. [9] But keep back from foolish questions and genealogies, and arguments, and quarrels about (the) Law; for they are unprofitable and vain.

## CHAPTER 3

1 Ὑπομίμνησκε αὐτοὺς ἀρχαῖς καὶ ἐξουσίαις ὑποτάσσεσθαι,
Remind        them  to rulers and  authorities to be subject,

2 πειθαρχεῖν, πρὸς πᾶν ἔργον ἀγαθὸν ἑτοίμους εἶναι, μηδένα
to be obedient, in every  work    good     ready   to be    no one
βλασφημεῖν, ἀμάχους εἶναι, ἐπιεικεῖς, πᾶσαν ἐνδεικνυμένους
to speak evil of, uncontentious to be, forbearing,  all    showing forth

3 πραότητα πρὸς πάντας ἀνθρώπους. ἦμεν γάρ ποτε καὶ
meekness    to    all      men.      were For   then also
ἡμεῖς ἀνόητοι, ἀπειθεῖς, πλανώμενοι, δουλεύοντες ἐπιθυμίαις
we  senseless, disobedient,  led astray,   slaving for     lusts
καὶ ἡδοναῖς ποικίλαις, ἐν κακίᾳ καὶ φθόνῳ διάγοντες,
and pleasures  various,    in evil  and  envy    living;

4 στυγητοί, μισοῦντες ἀλλήλους. ὅτε δὲ ἡ χρηστότης καὶ ἡ
hateful,    hating    one another. when But the kindness   and

5 φιλανθρωπία ἐπεφάνη τοῦ σωτῆρος ἡμῶν Θεοῦ, οὐκ ἐξ
love toward man appeared  of the  Savior   of us   God, not by
ἔργων τῶν ἐν δικαιοσύνῃ ὧν ἐποιήσαμεν ἡμεῖς, ἀλλὰ κατὰ
works    in righteousness which had done   we, but according to
τὸν αὐτοῦ ἔλεον ἔσωσεν ἡμᾶς, διὰ λουτροῦ παλιγγενεσίας
the of Him mercy He saved us,  through (the) washing of regeneration

6 καὶ ἀνακαινώσεως Πνεύματος Ἁγίου, οὗ ἐξέχεεν ἐφ' ἡμᾶς
and  renewal    of (the) Spirit Holy, which He poured out on us

7 πλουσίως, διὰ Ἰησοῦ Χριστοῦ τοῦ σωτῆρος ἡμῶν, ἵνα
richly     through Jesus  Christ    the  Savior   of us, that
δικαιωθέντες τῇ ἐκείνου χάριτι, κληρονόμοι γενώμεθα κατ'
being justified by the of that One grace,  heirs   we might become according to

8 ἐλπίδα ζωῆς αἰωνίου. πιστὸς ὁ λόγος, καὶ περὶ τούτων
(the) hope of life eternal.    Faithful (is) the word, and as to these things
βούλομαί σε διαβεβαιοῦσθαι, ἵνα φροντίζωσι καλῶν ἔργων
I desire  you to strongly affirm that may take thought of good works
προΐστασθαι οἱ πεπιστευκότες τῷ Θεῷ. ταῦτά ἐστι τὰ
to maintain   those having believed   God. These things are

9 καλὰ καὶ ὠφέλιμα τοῖς ἀνθρώποις· μωρὰς δὲ ζητήσεις καὶ
good and profitable   to men.      foolish But questionings and
γενεαλογίας καὶ ἔρεις καὶ μάχας νομικὰς περιΐστασο· εἰσὶ
genealogies,  and arguments, and quarrels of law keep back from; they are

[10] After the first and second warning reject a man of heresy, [11] knowing that such a one is perverted, and sins, being self-condemned.

[12] When I shall send Artemas to you, or Tychicus, try to come to me to Nicopolis; for I have decided to winter there. [13] Diligently set forward Zenas the lawyer and Apollos, that nothing may be lacking to them; [14] and let ours also learn to be forward in good works for necessary uses, that they may not be without fruit. [15] All those with me greet you. Greet those who love us in (the) faith. Grace (be) with you all. Amen.

**10** γὰρ ἀνωφελεῖς καὶ μάταιοι. αἱρετικὸν ἄνθρωπον μετὰ μίαν
for unprofitable and vain.    A heretic   man    after   one

**11** καὶ δευτέραν νουθεσίαν παραιτοῦ, εἰδὼς ὅτι ἐξέστραπται ὁ
and a second   warning    avoid,    knowing that has been perverted

τοιοῦτος, καὶ ἁμαρτάνει, ὢν αὐτοκατάκριτος.
such a one and    sins,     being self-condemned.

**12** Ὅταν πέμψω Ἀρτεμᾶν πρός σε ἢ Τυχικόν, σπούδασον
When I shall send Artemas to     you, or Tychicus,     hasten

ἐλθεῖν πρός με εἰς Νικόπολιν· ἐκεῖ γὰρ κέκρικα παραχειμάσαι.
to come to me at   Nicopolis;   there for I have decided to winter.

**13** Ζηνᾶν τὸν νομικὸν καὶ Ἀπολλὼ σπουδαίως πρόπεμψον,
Zenas the   lawyer    and   Apollos    urgently     set forward,

**14** ἵνα μηδὲν αὐτοῖς λείπῃ. μανθανέτωσαν δὲ καὶ οἱ ἡμέτεροι
that nothing to them be lacking.   let learn    And also     our (own)

καλῶν ἔργων προΐστασθαι εἰς τὰς ἀναγκαίας χρείας, ἵνα μὴ
of good works to maintain   for      necessary   uses,   that not

ὦσιν ἄκαρποι.
they be without fruit.

**15** Ἀσπάζονταί σε οἱ μετ' ἐμοῦ πάντες. ἄσπασαι τοὺς
Greet     you those with   me    all.     Greet    those

φιλοῦντας ἡμᾶς ἐν πίστει.
loving      us   in   faith.

Ἡ χάρις μετὰ πάντων ὑμῶν. ἀμήν.
Grace (be) with all      you.    Amen.

# ΠΑΥΛΟΥ
## PAUL
### Η ΠΡΟΣ
### THE TO
# ΦΙΛΗΜΟΝΑ ΕΠΙΣΤΟΛΗ
## PHILEMON  EPISTLE

## PAUL'S EPISTLE TO
## PHILEMON

[1] Paul, (a) prisoner of Christ Jesus, and Timothy the brother, to Philemon the beloved and our fellow-worker, [2] and to Apphia the beloved, and to Archippus our fellow-soldier, and to the church in your house: [3] Grace to you and peace from God our Father and (the) Lord Jesus Christ.

[4] I thank my God, always making mention of you in my prayers, [5] hearing of your love and faith which you have toward the Lord Jesus, and toward all the saints, [6] so that the fellowship of your faith may be operative in a full knowledge of every good thing in you for Jesus Christ. [7] For we have much joy and encouragement over your love, because the hearts of the saints have been refreshed through you, brother.

[8] For this reason, having much boldness in Christ to command you (to do) what (is) becoming, [9] rather because of love, I beseech, being such a one as Paul (the) aged, and now also a prisoner of Jesus Christ. [10] I beseech you concerning my child Onesimus, whom I fathered in my bonds, [11] the (one) once unprofitable to you, but now profitable to you and to me; whom I sent back— [12] even him receive, that is, my heart; [13] whom I resolved to hold with myself, that for you he might minister to me in the bonds of the gospel. [14] But I was willing to do nothing

**1** Παῦλος δέσμιος Χριστοῦ Ἰησοῦ, καὶ Τιμόθεος ὁ ἀδελφός,
Paul, a prisoner of Christ Jesus, and Timothy the brother,

**2** Φιλήμονι τῷ ἀγαπητῷ καὶ συνεργῷ ἡμῶν, καὶ Ἀπφίᾳ τῇ
to Philemon the beloved and fellow-worker to us, and to Apphia the

ἀγαπητῇ, καὶ Ἀρχίππῳ τῷ συστρατιώτῃ ἡμῶν, καὶ τῇ
beloved, and to Archippus the fellow-soldier of us, and to the

**3** κατ᾽ οἶκόν σου ἐκκλησίᾳ· χάρις ὑμῖν καὶ εἰρήνη ἀπὸ Θεοῦ
at house of you church: Grace to you and peace from God

πατρὸς ἡμῶν καὶ Κυρίου Ἰησοῦ Χριστοῦ.
(the) Father of us and (the) Lord Jesus Christ.

**4** Εὐχαριστῶ τῷ Θεῷ μου, πάντοτε μνείαν σου ποιούμενος
I thank the God of me, always mention of you making

**5** ἐπὶ τῶν προσευχῶν μου, ἀκούων σου τὴν ἀγάπην, καὶ τὴν
at the prayers of me, hearing of you the love and the

πίστιν ἣν ἔχεις πρὸς τὸν Κύριον Ἰησοῦν καὶ εἰς πάντας τοὺς
faith which you have to the Lord Jesus, and to all the

**6** ἁγίους, ὅπως ἡ κοινωνία τῆς πίστεώς σου ἐνεργὴς γένηται
saints, so as the fellowship of the faith of you operative may be

ἐν ἐπιγνώσει παντὸς ἀγαθοῦ τοῦ ἐν ὑμῖν εἰς Χριστὸν Ἰησοῦν.
in a full knowledge of every good thing in you for Christ Jesus.

**7** χαρὰν γὰρ ἔχομεν πολλὴν καὶ παράκλησιν ἐπὶ τῇ ἀγάπῃ
joy For we have much, and encouragement over the love

σου, ὅτι τὰ σπλάγχνα τῶν ἁγίων ἀναπέπαυται διὰ σοῦ,
of you, that the bowels of the saints have been refreshed through you,

ἀδελφέ.
brother.

**8** Διὸ πολλὴν ἐν Χριστῷ παρρησίαν ἔχων ἐπιτάσσειν σοι
Therefore, much in Christ boldness having to enjoin you

**9** τὸ ἀνῆκον, διὰ τὴν ἀγάπην μᾶλλον παρακαλῶ, τοιοῦτος
the thing fitting, because of love rather I beseech; such a one

ὢν ὡς Παῦλος πρεσβύτης, νυνὶ δὲ καὶ δέσμιος Ἰησοῦ
being as Paul (the) aged one, now and also a prisoner of Jesus

**10** Χριστοῦ. παρακαλῶ σε περὶ τοῦ ἐμοῦ τέκνου, ὃν ἐγέννησα ἐν
Christ. I beseech you concerning the of me child, whom I fathered in

**11** τοῖς δεσμοῖς μου, Ὀνήσιμον, τόν ποτέ σοι ἄχρηστον, νυνὶ δὲ
the bonds of me, Onesimus, the (one) then to you useless, now but

**12** σοὶ καὶ ἐμοὶ εὔχρηστον, ὃν ἀνέπεμψα· σὺ δὲ αὐτόν, τοῦτ᾽ ἔστι
to you and to me useful, whom I sent back to you, even him, this is,

**13** τὰ ἐμὰ σπλάγχνα, προσλαβοῦ· ὃν ἐγὼ ἐβουλόμην πρὸς
the of me bowels, receive (him), whom I resolved with

ἐμαυτὸν κατέχειν, ἵνα ὑπὲρ σοῦ διακονῇ μοι ἐν τοῖς δεσμοῖς
myself to hold, that for you he minister to me in the bonds

**14** τοῦ εὐαγγελίου· χωρὶς δὲ τῆς σῆς γνώμης οὐδὲν ἠθέλησα
of the gospel. without But your consent nothing I was willing

501

without your consent, that your good might not be by way of necessity, but by way of willingness. [15] For perhaps for this he was separated for an hour, that you might receive him eternally; [16] no longer as a slave, but beyond a slave, a beloved brother; especially to me, and how much more to you, both in (the) flesh and in the Lord. [17] If, then, you have me (as) a partner, receive him as me; [18] And if he wronged you (in) anything, or owes, put this to my account. [19] I, Paul, wrote with my own hand; I will repay; that I may not say to you that even yourself you owe to me also. [20] Yes, brother, may I have joy of you in (the) Lord? Refresh my heart in (the) Lord. [21] Being persuaded of your obedience, I wrote to you, knowing that you will do even beyond what I may say. [22] But with it all also prepare me a lodging; for I hope that through your prayers I shall be granted to you.

[23] Epaphras my fellow-prisoner in Christ Jesus greets you; [24] (also) Mark, Aristarchus, Demas, Luke, my fellow-workers. [25] The grace of our Lord Jesus Christ (be) with your spirit. Amen.

ποιῆσαι, ἵνα μὴ ὡς κατὰ ἀνάγκην τὸ ἀγαθόν σου ᾖ, ἀλλὰ
to do,        that not as by way of necessity the good of you be, but

15 κατὰ ἑκούσιον. τάχα γὰρ διὰ τοῦτο ἐχωρίσθη πρὸς ὥραν,
by way of willingness. perhaps For for  this he was separated for an hour,

16 ἵνα αἰώνιον αὐτὸν ἀπέχῃς· οὐκέτι ὡς δοῦλον, ἀλλ' ὑπὲρ
that eternally   him you might receive; no longer as a slave, but beyond

δοῦλον, ἀδελφὸν ἀγαπητόν, μάλιστα ἐμοί, πόσῳ δὲ μᾶλλον
a slave,   a brother beloved,      especially to me, how much and more

17 σοὶ καὶ ἐν σαρκὶ καὶ ἐν Κυρίῳ. εἰ οὖν ἐμὲ ἔχεις κοινωνόν,
to you both in flesh  and in (the) Lord. if Then me you have a partner,

18 προσλαβοῦ αὐτὸν ὡς ἐμέ. εἰ δέ τι ἠδίκησέ σε ἢ ὀφείλει, τοῦτο
receive         him   as  me. if And anything he wronged you, or owes, this

19 ἐμοὶ ἐλλόγει· ἐγὼ Παῦλος ἔγραψα τῇ ἐμῇ χειρί, ἐγὼ ἀπο-
to me reckon:    I    Paul   wrote   with my hand, I    will

20 τίσω· ἵνα μὴ λέγω σοι ὅτι καὶ σεαυτόν μοι προσοφείλεις. ναί,
repay, that not I say to you that indeed yourself to me you owe also. Yes,

ἀδελφέ, ἐγώ σου ὀναίμην ἐν Κυρίῳ· ἀνάπαυσόν μου τὰ
brother,  I of you may have help in (the) Lord, refresh      of me the

21 σπλάγχνα ἐν Κυρίῳ. πεποιθὼς τῇ ὑπακοῇ σου ἔγραψά
bowels      in (the) Lord. Having trusted to the obedience of you, I wrote

22 σοι, εἰδὼς ὅτι καὶ ὑπὲρ ὃ λέγω ποιήσεις. ἅμα δὲ καὶ ἑτοίμαζέ
to                                you      at
you, knowing that even beyond what I say will do. once And prepare

μοι ξενίαν· ἐλπίζω γὰρ ὅτι διὰ τῶν προσευχῶν ὑμῶν
for me lodging, I hope   for that through the prayers     of you

χαρισθήσομαι ὑμῖν.
I shall be given to you.

23 Ἀσπάζονται σε Ἐπαφρᾶς ὁ συναιχμάλωτός μου ἐν
Greet           you Epaphras   the fellow-captive of me   in

24 Χριστῷ Ἰησοῦ, Μάρκος, Ἀρίσταρχος, Δημᾶς, Λουκᾶς, οἱ
Christ  Jesus,     Mark,   Aristarchus,  Demas,    Luke, the

συνεργοί μου.
fellowworkers of me.

25 Ἡ χάρις τοῦ Κυρίου ἡμῶν Ἰησοῦ Χριστοῦ μετὰ τοῦ
The grace of the  Lord   of us,  Jesus   Christ,  with the

πνεύματος ὑμῶν. ἀμήν.
spirit      of you (be). Amen.

# ΠΑΥΛΟΥ ΤΟΥ ΑΠΟΣΤΟΛΟΥ
### PAUL    THE    APOSTLE

## Η ΠΡΟΣ
### THE TO

# ΕΒΡΑΙΟΥΣ ΕΠΙΣΤΟΛΗ
### (THE) HEBREWS   EPISTLE

**KING JAMES II VERSION**

**THE APOSTLE PAUL'S
EPISTLE TO THE HEBREWS**

## CHAPTER 1

[1] In many times and in many ways of old, God having spoken to the fathers in the prophets, [2] in these last days (He) spoke to us in whom He appointed heir of all things, by whom He also made the worlds; [3] who being (the) shining splendor of (His) glory and (the) express image of His essence, and upholding all things by the word of His power, having made purification of our sins by Himself, sat down on (the) right hand of the Majesty on high, [4] having become so much better than the angels, He has inherited a name more excellent beyond them. [5] For to which of the angels did He ever say, "You are My Son; today I have begotten You?" And again, "I will be a Father to Him and He shall be a Son to Me?" [6] And again, when He brought the Firstborn into the world, He said, "And let all (the) angels of God worship Him." [7] And as to the angels, He said, "Who makes His angels spirits, and His ministers a flame of fire;" [8] but as to the Son, "Your throne, O God, (is) forever and ever. A sceptre of righteousness (is) the sceptre of Your kingdom. [9] You have loved righteousness and hated lawlessness; because of this, God, Your God, has anointed You with the oil of gladness above Your companions." [10] And, "You, O Lord, in the beginning founded the

## CHAPTER 1

**1** Πολυμερῶς καὶ πολυτρόπως πάλαι ὁ Θεὸς λαλήσας τοῖς
In many times and in many ways of old   God   spoke   to the

**2** πατράσιν ἐν τοῖς προφήταις, ἐπ' ἐσχάτων τῶν ἡμερῶν τού·
fathers   by  the   prophets,  in (the) last    days   of

των ἐλάλησεν ἡμῖν ἐν υἱῷ, ὃν ἔθηκε κληρονόμον πάντων, δι'
these spoke  to us in (the) Son, whom He appointed heir of all, through

**3** οὖ καὶ τοὺς αἰῶνας ἐποίησεν, ὃς ὢν ἀπαύγασμα τῆς δόξης
whom indeed the ages  He made;  who being (the) radiance of the glory

καὶ χαρακτὴρ τῆς ὑποστάσεως αὐτοῦ, φέρων τε τὰ πάντα
and the express image of the essence  of Him, upholding and all things

τῷ ῥήματι τῆς δυνάμεως αὐτοῦ, δι' ἑαυτοῦ καθαρισμὸν
by the word of the   power   of Him, through Himself cleansing

ποιησάμενος τῶν ἁμαρτιῶν ἡμῶν, ἐκάθισεν ἐν δεξιᾷ τῆς
having made of the  sins   of us,  sat down on (the) right  the

**4** μεγαλωσύνης ἐν ὑψηλοῖς, τοσούτῳ κρείττων γενόμενος τῶν
Majesty   on  high; by so much  better  becoming (than) the

ἀγγέλων, ὅσῳ διαφορώτερον παρ' αὐτοὺς κεκληρονόμηκεν
angels,  as  a more excellent   than   them He has inherited

**5** ὄνομα. τίνι γὰρ εἶπέ ποτε τῶν ἀγγέλων, Υἱός μου εἶ σύ, ἐγὼ
name. to which For said He ever of the angels,  Son of Me are you, I

σήμερον γεγέννηκά σε; καὶ πάλιν, Ἐγὼ ἔσομαι αὐτῷ εἰς
today  have begotten You? And again,   I  will be to Him for

**6** πατέρα, καὶ αὐτὸς ἔσται μοι εἰς υἱόν; ὅταν δὲ πάλιν εἰσα-
a Father, and  He shall be to me for a Son? when And again   He

γάγῃ τὸν πρωτότοκον εἰς τὴν οἰκουμένην λέγει, Καὶ προσ-
brings  the  Firstborn   into the habitable world He says, And let

**7** κυνησάτωσαν αὐτῷ πάντες ἄγγελοι Θεοῦ. καὶ πρὸς μὲν τοὺς
worship      Him  all   angels  of God. And as to    the

ἀγγέλους λέγει, Ὁ ποιῶν τοὺς ἀγγέλους αὐτοῦ πνεύματα,
angels,  He says, The (One) making the angels   of Him  spirits,

**8** καὶ τοὺς λειτουργοὺς αὐτοῦ πυρὸς φλόγα· πρὸς δὲ τὸν υἱόν,
and the   ministers   of Him of fire a flame as to but the Son,

Ὁ θρόνος σου, ὁ Θεός, εἰς τὸν αἰῶνα τοῦ αἰῶνος· ῥάβδος
The throne of You,  God, (is) to the ages   of the ages, (the) rod

**9** εὐθύτητος ἡ ῥάβδος τῆς βασιλείας σου. ἠγάπησας δικαιο-
of uprightness (is the) rod of the kingdom of You. You loved  righteous-

σύνην, καὶ ἐμίσησας ἀνομίαν· διὰ τοῦτο ἔχρισέ σε ὁ Θεός, ὁ
ness,  and  hated  lawlessness;  therefore anointed You   God, the

**10** Θεός σου, ἔλαιον ἀγαλλιάσεως παρὰ τοὺς μετόχους σου. καί,
God of You, (with) oil of gladness  above  the  partners of You. And:

Σὺ κατ' ἀρχάς, Κύριε, τὴν γῆν ἐθεμελίωσας, καὶ ἔργα τῶν
You at (the) beginning Lord, the earth   founded,   and works of the

earth, and the heavens are works of Your hands. [11] They shall vanish away, but You shall continue; and (they) shall grow old, [12] and as a covering You shall fold them up, and they shall be changed; but You are the same, and Your years shall not fail. [13] But to which of the angels did He ever say, "Sit at My right hand until I place Your enemies (as) a footstool for Your feet?" [14] Are they not all ministering spirits, being sent out for service on account of those being about to inherit salvation?

CHAPTER 2

[1] Because of this we ought to give the more earnest attention to the things heard, lest at any time we should slip away. [2] For if the word spoken by angels was confirmed, and every transgression and disobedience received the just recompense, [3] how shall we escape (if we) neglect so great a salvation? Which having received a beginning to be spoken (of) by the Lord, was confirmed to us by those that heard; [4] God bearing witness with (them) by both miracles and wonders, and various acts of power, and distributions of (the) Holy Spirit, according to His will.

[5] For He did not put the world which is to come under angels, of which we speak; [6] but one fully testified somewhere, saying, "What is man, that You are mindful of him, or (the) son of man, that You visit him? [7] For a little You made him lower than (the) angels; You crowned him with glory and honor, and set him over the works of your hands; [8] you put all things under his feet." For in putting all things under him, He left nothing not subject to him. But now we do not yet see all things subjected to him; [9] but we do see Jesus crowned with glory and honor, who, on account of

**11** χειρῶν σού εἰσιν οἱ οὐρανοί· αὐτοὶ ἀπολοῦνται, σὺ δὲ δια-
hands of You are the heavens; they will perish, You but will

**12** μένεις· καὶ πάντες ὡς ἱμάτιον παλαιωθήσονται, καὶ ὡσεὶ
remain and all as a garment shall become old, and as

περιβόλαιον ἑλίξεις αὐτοὺς καὶ ἀλλαγήσονται· σὺ δὲ ὁ αὐτὸς
a covering You shall roll them, and shall be changed. You but the same

**13** εἶ, καὶ τὰ ἔτη σου οὐκ ἐκλείψουσι. πρὸς τίνα δὲ τῶν
are, and the years of You not shall fail. to which But of the

ἀγγέλων εἴρηκέ ποτε, Κάθου ἐκ δεξιῶν μου, ἕως ἂν θῶ τοὺς
angels has He said at any time, Sit on (the) right of Me, until I put the

**14** ἐχθρούς σου ὑποπόδιον τῶν ποδῶν σου ; οὐχὶ πάντες εἰσὶ
enemies of You a footstool of the feet of You. not all Are they

λειτουργικὰ πνεύματα, εἰς διακονίαν ἀποστελλόμενα διὰ
ministering spirits for service being sent out because of

τοὺς μέλλοντας κληρονομεῖν σωτηρίαν ;
those being about to inherit salvation?

CHAPTER 2

**1** Διὰ τοῦτο δεῖ περισσοτέρως ἡμᾶς προσέχειν τοῖς ἀκου-
For this reason ought more abundantly us to give heed to the things

**2** σθεῖσι, μή ποτε παραρρυῶμεν. εἰ γὰρ ὁ δι' ἀγγέλων
heard, lest at any time we should slip away. if For the through angels

λαληθεὶς λόγος ἐγένετο βέβαιος. καὶ πᾶσα παράβασις καὶ
spoken word was confirmed, and every transgression and

**3** παρακοὴ ἔλαβεν ἔνδικον μισθαποδοσίαν, πῶς ἡμεῖς ἐκφευ-
disobedience received a just recompense, how we shall escape

ξόμεθα τηλικαύτης ἀμελήσαντες σωτηρίας ; ἥτις, ἀρχὴν
so great neglecting a salvation? Which a beginning

λαβοῦσα λαλεῖσθαι διὰ τοῦ Κυρίου, ὑπὸ τῶν ἀκουσάντων
having received to be spoken via the Lord, by the (ones) hearing

**4** εἰς ἡμᾶς ἐβεβαιώθη, συνεπιμαρτυροῦντος τοῦ Θεοῦ σημείοις
to us was confirmed, bearing witness with God by signs

τε καὶ τέρασι, καὶ ποικίλαις δυνάμεσι, καὶ Πνεύματος Ἁγίου
both and wonders, and by various works of power, and (the) Spirit Holy

μερισμοῖς, κατὰ τὴν αὐτοῦ θέλησιν.
by distribution, according to the of Him will.

**5** Οὐ γὰρ ἀγγέλοις ὑπέταξε τὴν οἰκουμένην τὴν μέλλουσαν,
not For to angels subjected He the habitable world coming,

**6** περὶ ἧς λαλοῦμεν. διεμαρτύρατο δέ πού τις λέγων, Τί
about which we speak. solemnly witnessed But somewhere one, saying, What

ἐστιν ἄνθρωπος, ὅτι μιμνήσκῃ αὐτοῦ ; ἢ υἱὸς ἀνθρώπου,
is man that You remember him? Or the son of man

**7** ὅτι ἐπισκέπτῃ αὐτόν ; ἠλάττωσας αὐτὸν βραχύ τι παρ'
that You observed him? You made less him a little than

ἀγγέλους· δόξῃ καὶ τιμῇ ἐστεφάνωσας αὐτόν, καὶ κατέ-
the angels with glory and with honor You crowned him; and,

**8** στησας αὐτὸν ἐπὶ τὰ ἔργα τῶν χειρῶν σου· πάντα ὑπέταξας
You set him over the works of the hands of You; all things You subjected

ὑποκάτω τῶν ποδῶν αὐτοῦ. ἐν γὰρ τῷ ὑποτάξαι αὐτῷ
under the feet of him. in order For to subject to him

τὰ πάντα, οὐδὲν ἀφῆκεν αὐτῷ ἀνυπότακτον. νῦν δὲ οὔπω
all things, nothing He left to him not subjected. now But not yet

**9** ὁρῶμεν αὐτῷ τὰ πάντα ὑποτεταγμένα. τὸν δὲ βραχύ τι
do we see to him all things having been subjected. the (One) But a little

παρ' ἀγγέλους ἠλαττωμένον βλέπομεν Ἰησοῦν, διὰ τὸ
than the angels having been made less we see, Jesus, because of the

the suffering of death (was) for a little while made lower than (the) angels, so that by (the) grace of God he might taste death for every (son). [10] For it was becoming to Him, for whom (are) all things, and by whom (are) all things, bringing many sons to glory, to make perfect the Author of their salvation through sufferings. [11] For both He sanctifying and the (one) being sanctified (are) all of one; for which cause He is not ashamed to call them brothers, [12] saying, I will announce Your name to My brothers; I will sing to You in (the) midst of (the) church. [13] And again, "I will be trusting on Him." And again, "Behold, I and the children whom God gave to Me." [14] Since, then, the children have partaken of flesh and blood, in like manner also He Himself shared the same things, that through death He might cause to cease to operate the (one) having the power of death, that is, the Devil; [15] and might set these free, as many as by fear of death were subject to slavery through all the (time) to live. [16] For indeed He does not take hold of angels, but of (the) seed of Abraham, He takes hold. [17] Therefore, He ought by all means to become like (His) brothers, that He might become a merciful and faithful High Priest (in) the things respecting God, in order to make propitiation for the sins of (His) people. [18] For in what He has suffered, having been tried, He is able to help those being tried.

CHAPTER 3

[1] Therefore, holy brothers, partakers of (the) heavenly calling, consider the Apostle and High Priest of our confession, Christ Jesus, [2] being faithful to Him who appointed Him, as also Moses in all his house. [3] For He was counted worthy of more glory than Moses, by as much as He who built it has more honor than the house, [4] For every house is built by someone;

10 πάθημα τοῦ θανάτου δόξῃ καὶ τιμῇ ἐστεφανωμένον, ὅπως
suffering of death with glory and with honor having been crowned so as

χάριτι Θεοῦ ὑπὲρ παντὸς γεύσηται θανάτου. ἔπρεπε γὰρ
by grace God's for every (son) He might taste of death. it was fitting For

αὐτῷ, δι' ὃν τὰ πάντα, καὶ δι' οὗ τὰ πάντα, πολλοὺς υἱοὺς
for Him, because of whom, and through whom all things many sons

εἰς δόξαν ἀγαγόντα, τὸν ἀρχηγὸν τῆς σωτηρίας αὐτῶν
to glory bringing, the Author of the salvation of them

11 διὰ παθημάτων τελειῶσαι. ὅ τε γὰρ ἁγιάζων καὶ οἱ ἁγιαζό-
through sufferings to perfect. He both For sanctifying and the (one) being

μενοι, ἐξ ἑνὸς πάντες· δι' ἣν αἰτίαν οὐκ ἐπαισχύνεται
sanctified of one all (are); for which cause not He is ashamed

12 ἀδελφοὺς αὐτοὺς καλεῖν, λέγων, Ἀπαγγελῶ τὸ ὄνομά σου
brothers them to call, saying, I will announce the name of You

13 τοῖς ἀδελφοῖς μου, ἐν μέσῳ ἐκκλησίας ὑμνήσω σε. καὶ πάλιν,
to the brothers of Me; in (the) midst of (the) church I will hymn You. And again,

Ἐγὼ ἔσομαι πεποιθὼς ἐπ' αὐτῷ. καὶ πάλιν, Ἰδοὺ ἐγὼ καὶ
I will be trusting on Him. And again, Behold, I and

14 τὰ παιδία ἅ μοι ἔδωκεν ὁ Θεός. ἐπεὶ οὖν τὰ παιδία κεκοινώ-
the children whom to Me gave God. Since, then, the children have partaken

νηκε σαρκὸς καὶ αἵματος, καὶ αὐτὸς παραπλησίως μετέσχε
of flesh and blood, also Himself, in like manner He shared

τῶν αὐτῶν, ἵνα διὰ τοῦ θανάτου καταργήσῃ τὸν τὸ κράτος
the same things, that through the death He might annul the (one) the power

15 ἔχοντα τοῦ θανάτου, τοῦτ' ἔστι τὸν διάβολον, καὶ ἀπαλ-
having of death, this is the Devil, and might set

λάξῃ τούτους, ὅσοι φόβῳ θανάτου διὰ παντὸς τοῦ ζῆν
free these, as many as by fear of death through all the (time) to live

16 ἔνοχοι ἦσαν δουλείας. οὐ γὰρ δήπου ἀγγέλων ἐπιλαμβά-
subject were to slavery. not For indeed of angels He takes hold,

17 νεται, ἀλλὰ σπέρματος Ἀβραὰμ ἐπιλαμβάνεται. ὅθεν ὤφειλε
but of (the) seed of Abraham He takes hold. Therefore He ought

κατὰ πάντα τοῖς ἀδελφοῖς ὁμοιωθῆναι, ἵνα ἐλεήμων γένηται
by all means to the brothers to become like, that a merciful He might be

καὶ πιστὸς ἀρχιερεὺς τὰ πρὸς τὸν Θεόν, εἰς τὸ ἱλάσκεσθαι
and faithful High Priest (in) the things as to God, in order to propitiation for
make

18 τὰς ἁμαρτίας τοῦ λαοῦ. ἐν ᾧ γὰρ πέπονθεν αὐτὸς πειρα-
the sins of the people. in what For has suffered He, having been

σθείς, δύναται τοῖς πειραζομένοις βοηθῆσαι.
tempted, He is able those being tempted to help.

CHAPTER 3

1 Ὅθεν, ἀδελφοὶ ἅγιοι, κλήσεως ἐπουρανίου μέτοχοι,
Therefore, brothers holy, called (to be) of a heavenly sharers,

κατανοήσατε τὸν ἀπόστολον καὶ ἀρχιερέα τῆς ὁμολογίας
consider the Apostle and High Priest of the confession

2 ἡμῶν Χριστὸν Ἰησοῦν, πιστὸν ὄντα τῷ ποιήσαντι αὐτόν,
of us, Christ Jesus, faithful being to the (One) making Him (these),

3 ὡς καὶ Μωσῆς ἐν ὅλῳ τῷ οἴκῳ αὐτοῦ. πλείονος γὰρ δόξης
as also Moses in all the house of him. of more For glory

οὗτος παρὰ Μωσῆν ἠξίωται, καθ' ὅσον πλείονα τιμὴν ἔχει
this (One) than Moses has been by so much as more honor has (than)
counted worthy,

4 τοῦ οἴκου ὁ κατασκευάσας αὐτόν. πᾶς γὰρ οἶκος κατασκευά-
the house the (one) having built it. every For house is prepared

5 ζεται ὑπό τινος· ὁ δὲ τὰ πάντα κατασκευάσας, Θεός. καὶ
by someone, He but all things having prepared (is) God. And

but He who built all things (is) God. [5] And Moses truly (was) faithful in all his house as a ministering servant, for a testimony of the things going to be spoken; [6] but Christ as Son over His house, whose house we are, if we should hold fast the boldness and rejoicing of the hope firm to the end.

[7] For this reason, even as the Holy Spirit says, "Today, if you will hear His voice, [8] do not harden your hearts, as in the provocation, in the day of temptation, in the wilderness, [9] where your fathers tempted Me (and) proved Me, and saw My works forty years." [10] For this reason, "I was indignant with that generation, and said, They always go astray in heart; and they did not know my ways. [11] So I swore in My wrath, They shall not enter into My rest." [12] Be careful, brothers, lest perhaps shall be in any one of you an evil heart of unbelief in falling away from (the) living God. [13] But exhort yourselves each day, as long as it is being called today, that not any of you be hardened by (the) deceit of sin. [14] For we have become sharers of Christ, if truly we hold the beginning of the assurance firm to (the) end; [15] (as) in the saying, "Today, if you hear His voice, do not harden your hearts, as in the provocation." [16] For some having heard, provoked; but not all those coming out of Egypt through Moses. [17] But with whom was He angry forty years? (Was it) not with those sinning, of whom the corpses fell in the wilderness? [18] And to whom did He swear (they would) not enter into His rest, except to those not obeying?, [19] And we see that they were not able to enter in because of unbelief.

CHAPTER 4

[1] Therefore, let us fear lest perhaps a promise

**6** Μωσῆς μὲν πιστὸς ἐν ὅλῳ τῷ οἴκῳ αὐτοῦ ὡς θεράπων, εἰς
Moses indeed (was) faithful in all the house of him as a servant, for
μαρτύριον τῶν λαληθησομένων· Χριστὸς δὲ ὡς υἱὸς ἐπὶ τὸν
a testimony of the things being spoken; Christ but as a Son over the
οἶκον αὐτοῦ· οὗ οἶκός ἐσμεν ἡμεῖς, ἐάνπερ τὴν παρρησίαν καὶ
house of Him, of whom a house are we, if truly the confidence and
τὸ καύχημα τῆς ἐλπίδος μέχρι τέλους βεβαίαν κατάσχωμεν.
the boast of the hope until (the) end firm we hold fast.

**7** διό, καθὼς λέγει τὸ Πνεῦμα τὸ Ἅγιον, Σήμερον ἐὰν τῆς
Therefore, as says the Spirit — Holy, Today, if the
**8** φωνῆς αὐτοῦ ἀκούσητε, μὴ σκληρύνητε τὰς καρδίας ὑμῶν,
voice of Him you hear, do not harden the hearts of you,
ὡς ἐν τῷ παραπικρασμῷ, κατὰ τὴν ἡμέραν τοῦ πειρασμοῦ
as in the provocation in the day of the temptation
**9** ἐν τῇ ἐρήμῳ, οὗ ἐπείρασάν με οἱ πατέρες ὑμῶν, ἐδοκίμασάν
in the wilderness, when tempted Me the fathers of you, testing
**10** με, καὶ εἶδον τὰ ἔργα μου τεσσαράκοντα ἔτη. διὸ προσ-
Me, and saw the works of Me forty years. Therefore I was
ὤχθισα τῇ γενεᾷ ἐκείνῃ, καὶ εἶπον, Ἀεὶ πλανῶνται τῇ καρδίᾳ·
angry with generation that, and I said, Always they err in the heart,
**11** αὐτοὶ δὲ οὐκ ἔγνωσαν τὰς ὁδούς μου· ὡς ὤμοσα ἐν τῇ ὀργῇ
they and not did know the ways of Me; as I swore in the wrath
**12** μου, Εἰ εἰσελεύσονται εἰς τὴν κατάπαυσίν μου. βλέπετε,
of Me, If they shall enter into the rest of Me. Watch,
ἀδελφοί, μή ποτε ἔσται ἔν τινι ὑμῶν καρδία πονηρὰ ἀπιστίας
brothers, lest perhaps shall be in anyone of you a heart evil of unbelief
**13** ἐν τῷ ἀποστῆναι ἀπὸ Θεοῦ ζῶντος· ἀλλὰ παρακαλεῖτε
in departing from God a living; but exhort
ἑαυτοὺς καθ᾽ ἑκάστην ἡμέραν, ἄχρις οὗ τὸ σήμερον καλεῖται,
yourselves each day, while today it is being called,
**14** ἵνα μὴ σκληρυνθῇ τις ἐξ ὑμῶν ἀπάτῃ τῆς ἁμαρτίας· μέτοχοι
that not be hardened anyone of you by (the) deceit of sin. sharers
γὰρ γεγόναμεν τοῦ Χριστοῦ, ἐάνπερ τὴν ἀρχὴν τῆς ὑπο-
For we have become of Christ, if truly the beginning of the
**15** στάσεως μέχρι τέλους βεβαίαν κατάσχωμεν· ἐν τῷ λέγεσθαι,
assurance until (the) end firm we hold fast. In the saying,
Σήμερον ἐὰν τῆς φωνῆς αὐτοῦ ἀκούσητε, μὴ σκληρύνητε τὰς
Today, if the voice of Him you hear, do not harden the
**16** καρδίας ὑμῶν, ὡς ἐν τῷ παραπικρασμῷ. τινὲς γὰρ ἀκού-
hearts of you, as in the provocation. some For
σαντες παρεπίκραναν, ἀλλ᾽ οὐ πάντες οἱ ἐξελθόντες ἐξ
hearing provoked, but not all those coming out of
**17** Αἰγύπτου διὰ Μωσέως. τίσι δὲ προσώχθισε τεσσαράκοντα
Egypt through Moses. with whom But was He angry forty
ἔτη ; οὐχὶ τοῖς ἁμαρτήσασιν, ὧν τὰ κῶλα ἔπεσεν ἐν τῇ
years? Not with those sinning, of whom the corpses fell in the
**18** ἐρήμῳ ; τίσι δὲ ὤμοσε μὴ εἰσελεύσεσθαι εἰς τὴν κατάπαυσιν
wilderness? to whom And swore He not to enter into the rest
**19** αὐτοῦ, εἰ μὴ τοῖς ἀπειθήσασι ; καὶ βλέπομεν ὅτι οὐκ ἠδυνή-
of Him, except to those not obeying? And we see that not they were
θησαν εἰσελθεῖν δι᾽ ἀπιστίαν.
able to enter in because of unbelief.

**CHAPTER 4**

**1** Φοβηθῶμεν οὖν μή ποτε καταλειπομένης ἐπαγγελίας
let us fear Therefore, lest perhaps being left a promise

being left to enter into His rest, any of you might seem to come short. [2] For indeed we have had the gospel preached (to us) even as they also; the word of the message did not comfort them, not having been mixed with faith in those who heard. [3] For we who believed enter into the rest; as he has said, "As I swore in My wrath, they shall not enter into My rest." Though truly the works were done from (the) foundation of (the) world; [4] for He has spoken somewhere about the seventh (day) this way, "And God rested on the seventh day from all His works." [5] And in this (place) again, "They shall not enter into My rest." [6] Since, then, it remains (for) some to enter into it, and those who formerly heard the gospel did not enter in on account of unbelief, [7] He again marks out a certain day, saying in David, "Today" — after so long a time, according as it has been said — "Today, if you will hear His voice, do not harden your hearts." [8] For if Joshua gave them rest, then He would not have afterwards spoken about another day. [9] So then, there remains a rest to the people of God. [10] For He that entered into His rest, He also rested from His works, as God (did) from His own. [11] Let us therefore labor to enter into that rest, lest anyone may fall according to the same example of unbelief. [12] For the word of God (is) living and powerful, and sharper than every two-edged sword, even piercing to (the) dividing apart of both soul and spirit, of both joints and marrows, and able to discern thoughts and intents of a heart; [13] and there is no creature unrevealed before Him; but all things (are) naked and laid open to His eyes, with whom (is) our account.

[14] Therefore, having a great High Priest (who) has passed through the

εἰσελθεῖν εἰς τὴν κατάπαυσιν αὐτοῦ, δοκῇ τις ἐξ ὑμῶν
to enter into the rest of Him, seems anyone of you

2 ὑστερηκέναι. καὶ γὰρ ἐσμεν εὐηγγελισμένοι, καθάπερ
to come short. indeed For we are having had the gospel preached, even as

κἀκεῖνοι· ἀλλ' οὐκ ὠφέλησεν ὁ λόγος τῆς ἀκοῆς ἐκείνους, μὴ
those also; but did not profit the word of hearing those, not

3 συγκεκραμένος τῇ πίστει τοῖς ἀκούσασιν. εἰσερχόμεθα γὰρ
having been mixed with faith in those hearing. we enter For

εἰς τὴν κατάπαυσιν οἱ πιστεύσαντες, καθὼς εἴρηκεν, Ὡς
into the rest, those believing, even as He said, As

ὤμοσα ἐν τῇ ὀργῇ μου, Εἰ εἰσελεύσονται εἰς τὴν κατά-
I swore in the wrath of Me, If they shall enter into the rest

παυσίν μου· καίτοι τῶν ἔργων ἀπὸ καταβολῆς κόσμου
of Me; through the works from (the) foundation of world

4 γενηθέντων. εἴρηκε γὰρ που περὶ τῆς ἑβδόμης οὕτω, Καὶ
having come into He has being said, For somewhere about the seventh (day) thus: And

κατέπαυσεν ὁ Θεὸς ἐν τῇ ἡμέρᾳ τῇ ἑβδόμῃ ἀπὸ πάντων
rested God in the day seventh from all

5 τῶν ἔργων αὐτοῦ· καὶ ἐν τούτῳ πάλιν, Εἰ εἰσελεύσονται εἰς
the works of Him; and in this (place) again, If they shall enter into

6 τὴν κατάπαυσίν μου. ἐπεὶ οὖν ἀπολείπεται τινὰς εἰσελθεῖν
the rest of Me. Since therefore it remains (for) some to enter

εἰς αὐτήν, καὶ οἱ πρότερον εὐαγγελισθέντες οὐκ εἰσῆλθον δι'
into it, and those before having had the gospel preached not entered for

7 ἀπείθειαν, πάλιν τινὰ ὁρίζει ἡμέραν, Σήμερον, ἐν Δαβὶδ
disobedience, again a certain marks out day: Today; in David

λέγων, μετὰ τοσοῦτον χρόνον, καθὼς εἴρηται, Σήμερον ἐὰν
saying after such a time, as he has said, Today, if

τῆς φωνῆς αὐτοῦ ἀκούσητε, μὴ σκληρύνητε τὰς καρδίας
the voice of Him you hear, do not harden the hearts

8 ὑμῶν. εἰ γὰρ αὐτοὺς Ἰησοῦς κατέπαυσεν, οὐκ ἂν περὶ ἄλλης
of you. if For them (Joshua) rested, not concerning another

9 ἐλάλει μετὰ ταῦτα ἡμέρας. ἄρα ἀπολείπεται σαββατισμὸς
he would have spoken after these things day Then remains a sabbath rest

10 τῷ λαῷ τοῦ Θεοῦ. ὁ γὰρ εἰσελθὼν εἰς τὴν κατάπαυσιν αὐτοῦ
to the people of God. He For having entered into the rest of Him

καὶ αὐτὸς κατέπαυσεν ἀπὸ τῶν ἔργων αὐτοῦ, ὥσπερ ἀπὸ
also Himself rested from the works of Him, as from

11 τῶν ἰδίων ὁ Θεός. σπουδάσωμεν οὖν εἰσελθεῖν εἰς ἐκείνην τὴν
the own (did) God. Let us be eager, therefore, to enter into that

κατάπαυσιν, ἵνα μὴ ἐν τῷ αὐτῷ τις ὑποδείγματι πέσῃ τῆς
rest, that not in the same anyone example falls

12 ἀπειθείας. ζῶν γὰρ ὁ λόγος τοῦ Θεοῦ, καὶ ἐνεργής, καὶ
of disobedience. living For the word of God, and working, and

τομώτερος ὑπὲρ πᾶσαν μάχαιραν δίστομον, καὶ διϊκνού-
sharper than every sword two-mouthed, and piercing

μενος ἄχρι μερισμοῦ ψυχῆς τε καὶ πνεύματος, ἁρμῶν τε καὶ
as far as (the) division of soul both and spirit, of joints both and

13 μυελῶν, καὶ κριτικὸς ἐνθυμήσεων καὶ ἐννοιῶν καρδίας. καὶ
of marrows, and able to judge of thoughts and intentions of a heart; and

οὐκ ἔστι κτίσις ἀφανὴς ἐνώπιον αὐτοῦ· πάντα δὲ γυμνὰ καὶ
not is (a) creature not revealed before Him, all things but (are) naked and

τετραχηλισμένα τοῖς ὀφθαλμοῖς αὐτοῦ πρὸς ὃν ἡμῖν ὁ λόγος.
laid open to the eyes of Him with whom (is) our account.

14 Ἔχοντες οὖν ἀρχιερέα μέγαν, διεληλυθότα τοὺς οὐρανούς,
Having therefore a high priest great, having gone through the heavens,

heavens, Jesus the Son of God, let us hold fast the confession. [15] For we do not have a High Priest not being able to sympathize with our infirmities, but (One) having been tried in all respects according to (our) likeness, apart from sin. [16] Therefore, let us draw near with confidence to the throne of grace, that we may receive mercy, and we may find grace for timely help.

**15** Ἰησοῦν τὸν υἱὸν τοῦ Θεοῦ, κρατῶμεν τῆς ὁμολογίας. οὐ γὰρ
Jesus, the Son of God, let us hold fast the confession. not For

ἔχομεν ἀρχιερέα μὴ δυνάμενον συμπαθῆσαι ταῖς ἀσθενείαις
we have a high priest not being able to sympathize with the infirmities

ἡμῶν, πεπειρασμένον δὲ κατὰ πάντα καθ᾽ ὁμοιότητα, χωρὶς
of us, having been tempted but (One) in all according (our) apart
respects to likeness from

**16** ἁμαρτίας. προσερχώμεθα οὖν μετὰ παρρησίας τῷ θρόνῳ τῆς
sin. let us draw near Therefore with confidence to the throne —

χάριτος, ἵνα λάβωμεν ἔλεον, καὶ χάριν εὕρωμεν εἰς εὔκαιρον
of grace, that we may receive mercy, and grace we may find for timely

βοήθειαν.
help.

## CHAPTER 5

[1] For every high priest out of men being taken on behalf of men is appointed (in) the things respecting God, that he may offer both gifts and sacrifices for sins; [2] being able to feel in due measure for those not knowing and having been led astray, since he also is encompassed (with) weakness. [3] And because of this he ought, as concerning the people, also concerning himself to offer for sins. [4] And no one takes the honor to himself, but he being called by God, even as Aaron also. [5] So also Christ glorified not Himself to become a high priest, but He speaking to Him, "You are My Son; today I have begotten You." [6] As He also says in another, "You (are) a priest forever according to the order of Melchizedek;" [7] who in the days of his flesh offering both petitions and entreaties to Him being able to save Him from death, with strong crying and tears, and being heard from (His) godly fear; [8] though being a Son, He learned obedience from what He suffered; [9] and having been perfected, He became (the) Author of eternal salvation to all those obeying Him, [10] having been called out by God (as) a High priest according to the order of Melchizedek. [11] About whom we (have) much to say and hard to interpret, since you have become dull in hearing. [12] For indeed because of the time (you are) due to be teachers, you need one to

## CHAPTER 5

**1** Πᾶς γὰρ ἀρχιερεύς, ἐξ ἀνθρώπων λαμβανόμενος, ὑπὲρ
every For high priest out of men having been taken on
behalf of

ἀνθρώπων καθίσταται τὰ πρὸς τὸν Θεόν, ἵνα προσφέρῃ
men is appointed (in) the things as to God, that he may offer

**2** δῶρά τε καὶ θυσίας ὑπὲρ ἁμαρτιῶν· μετριοπαθεῖν δυνάμενος
gifts both and sacrifices on behalf of sins, to feel due being able
in measure

τοῖς ἀγνοοῦσι καὶ πλανωμένοις, ἐπεὶ καὶ αὐτὸς περίκειται
for those not knowing and being led astray, since also he is encompassed

**3** ἀσθένειαν· καὶ διὰ ταύτην ὀφείλει, καθὼς περὶ τοῦ λαοῦ, οὕτω
(with) weakness and for this he ought, as concerning the people, so

**4** καὶ περὶ ἑαυτοῦ, προσφέρειν ὑπὲρ ἁμαρτιῶν. καὶ οὐχ ἑαυτῷ
also concerning himself to offer on behalf of sins. And not to himself

τις λαμβάνει τὴν τιμήν, ἀλλὰ ὁ καλούμενος ὑπὸ τοῦ Θεοῦ,
anyone takes the honor, but the (one) being called by God,

**5** καθάπερ καὶ ὁ Ἀαρών. οὕτω καὶ ὁ Χριστὸς οὐχ ἑαυτὸν
even as indeed Aaron. So also Christ not Himself

ἐδόξασε γενηθῆναι ἀρχιερέα, ἀλλ᾽ ὁ λαλήσας πρὸς αὐτόν,
glorified to become a high priest, but the (One) speaking to Him:

**6** Υἱός μου εἶ σύ, ἐγὼ σήμερον γεγέννηκά σε. καθὼς καὶ ἐν ἑτέρῳ
Son of Me are You, I today have begotten You; as also in another

λέγει, Σὺ ἱερεὺς εἰς τὸν αἰῶνα κατὰ τὴν τάξιν Μελχισεδέκ.
He says, You (are) a priest to the age according to the order of Melchizedek;

**7** ὃς ἐν ταῖς ἡμέραις τῆς σαρκὸς αὐτοῦ, δεήσεις τε καὶ ἱκετηρίας
who in the days of the flesh of Him petitions both and entreaties

πρὸς τὸν δυνάμενον σώζειν αὐτὸν ἐκ θανάτου μετὰ κραυγῆς
to the (One) being able to save Him out of death. with crying

ἰσχυρᾶς καὶ δακρύων προσενέγκας, καὶ εἰσακουσθεὶς ἀπὸ τῆς
strong and tears, offering and being heard from the

**8** εὐλαβείας, καίπερ ὢν υἱός, ἔμαθεν ἀφ᾽ ὧν ἔπαθε τὴν ὑπακοήν,
godly fear, though being a Son, He learned from (that) He obedience,
which suffered

**9** καὶ τελειωθεὶς ἐγένετο τοῖς ὑπακούουσιν αὐτῷ πᾶσιν αἴτιος
and having perfected He became those obeying Him to all (the) cause

**10** σωτηρίας αἰωνίου· προσαγορευθεὶς ὑπὸ τοῦ Θεοῦ ἀρχιερεὺς
of salvation eternal having been called out by God a High Priest

κατὰ τὴν τάξιν Μελχισεδέκ.
according to the order of Melchizedek.

**11** Περὶ οὗ πολὺς ἡμῖν ὁ λόγος καὶ δυσερμήνευτος λέγειν,
Concerning whom much to us the word, and hard to interpret to say,

**12** ἐπεὶ νωθροὶ γεγόνατε ταῖς ἀκοαῖς. καὶ γὰρ ὀφείλοντες εἶναι
since dull you have become in the hearing For being due to be

διδάσκαλοι διὰ τὸν χρόνον, πάλιν χρείαν ἔχετε τοῦ διδά-
teachers because of the time, again need you have to

teach you again the rudiments of the beginning of the oracles of God, and you having become (in) need of milk, and not of solid food; [13] for everyone partaking of milk (is) not skilled (in) (the) word of righteousness, for he is an infant. [14] But solid food is for (the) full-grown ones, who through habit have exercised the senses for distinguishing both good and evil.

σκειν ὑμᾶς, τίνα τὰ στοιχεῖα τῆς ἀρχῆς τῶν λογίων τοῦ Θεοῦ·
teach you someone the rudiments of the beginning of the oracles of God,

καὶ γεγόνατε χρείαν ἔχοντες γάλακτος, καὶ οὐ στερεᾶς
and you become (in) need having of milk, and not of solid

13 τροφῆς. πᾶς γὰρ ὁ μετέχων γάλακτος ἄπειρος λόγου δι-
food. everyone For partaking of milk (is) not skilled of (the) word

14 καιοσύνης· νήπιος γάρ ἐστι. τελείων δέ ἐστιν ἡ στερεὰ
of righteouesness, an infant for he is; of full-grown but is solid

τροφή, τῶν διὰ τὴν ἕξιν τὰ αἰσθητήρια γεγυμνασμένα
food, of those through habit the faculties exercised

ἐχόντων πρὸς διάκρισιν καλοῦ τε καὶ κακοῦ.
having, for distinguishing good both and bad.

## CHAPTER 6

[1] For this reason, having left the discourse of the beginning of Christ, we should go on to full growth, not laying again a foundation of repentance from dead works, and faith in God, [2] of (the) teaching of baptisms, and of laying on of hands, and of resurrection of (the) dead, and of everlasting judgment; [3] and this we will do, if God permits. [4] For (it is) impossible (that) those once enlightened, and (who) tasted of the heavenly gift and became sharers of (the) Holy Spirit, [5] and tasted (the) good word of God, and (the) works of power of (the) age to come, [6] and (who) fell away, again to renew to repentance, crucifying for themselves again the Son of God, and shaming (Him) publicly. [7] For earth drinking the rain often coming upon it, and producing plants fit for those for whom it is also worked, receives blessing from God; [8] but bearing thorns and thistles, (it is) disapproved and near a curse, of which the end (is) for burning.

[9] But, loved ones, even if we indeed speak so, we have been persuaded better things concerning you, even holding fast salvation. [10] For God (is) not unrighteous, to forget your work and the labor of love which you showed to His name, having ministered to the saints, and (now) ministering. [11] But we

## CHAPTER 6

1 Διό, ἀφέντες τὸν τῆς ἀρχῆς τοῦ Χριστοῦ λόγον, ἐπὶ τὴν
Therefore, leaving the of the beginning of Christ discourse, on to

τελειότητα φερώμεθα, μὴ πάλιν θεμέλιον καταβαλλόμενοι
full growth let us be borne, not again a foundation laying down

2 μετανοίας ἀπὸ νεκρῶν ἔργων, καὶ πίστεως ἐπὶ Θεόν, βαπτι-
of repentance from dead works, and of faith toward God, of baptisms,

σμῶν διδαχῆς, ἐπιθέσεώς τε χειρῶν, ἀναστάσεώς τε νεκρῶν,
of teaching, of laying on and of hands, of resurrection and of dead ones

3 καὶ κρίματος αἰωνίου. καὶ τοῦτο ποιήσομεν, ἐάνπερ ἐπι-
and judgment of eternal. And this we will do if indeed

4 τρέπῃ ὁ Θεός. ἀδύνατον γὰρ τοὺς ἅπαξ φωτισθέντας,
permits God. (it is) impossible For (for) those once being enlightened,

γευσαμένους τε τῆς δωρεᾶς τῆς ἐπουρανίου, καὶ μετόχους
tasting and of the gift heavenly, and sharers

5 γενηθέντας Πνεύματος Ἁγίου, καὶ καλὸν γευσαμένους Θεοῦ
becoming Spirit of (the) Holy, and (the) good tasting of God

6 ῥῆμα, δυνάμεις τε μέλλοντος αἰῶνος, καὶ παραπεσόντας,
word, works of power and of a coming age. and falling away

πάλιν ἀνακαινίζειν εἰς μετάνοιαν, ἀνασταυροῦντας ἑαυτοῖς
again to renew to repentance, crucifying again for themselves

7 τὸν υἱὸν τοῦ Θεοῦ καὶ παραδειγματίζοντας. γῆ γὰρ ἡ
the Son of God. and putting (Him) to open shame. earth For

πιοῦσα τὸν ἐπ' αὐτῆς πολλάκις ἐρχόμενον ὑετόν, καὶ
drinking the upon it often coming rain, and

τίκτουσα βοτάνην εὔθετον ἐκείνοις δι' οὓς καὶ γεωργεῖται,
producing plants fit for those for whom indeed it is worked,

8 μεταλαμβάνει εὐλογίας ἀπὸ τοῦ Θεοῦ· ἐκφέρουσα δὲ ἀκάνθας
receives blessing from God; bringing forth but thorns

καὶ τριβόλους, ἀδόκιμος καὶ κατάρας ἐγγύς, ἧς τὸ τέλος εἰς
and thistles (it is) disapproved and a curse near, of which the end (is) for

καῦσιν.
burning.

9 Πεπείσμεθα δὲ περὶ ὑμῶν, ἀγαπητοί, τὰ κρείττονα καὶ
we have been persuaded But about you, loved ones, the things better even

10 ἐχόμενα σωτηρίας, εἰ καὶ οὕτω λαλοῦμεν· οὐ γὰρ ἄδικος ὁ
holding fast salvation, if indeed so we speak. not For unjust

Θεὸς ἐπιλαθέσθαι τοῦ ἔργου ὑμῶν, καὶ τοῦ κόπου τῆς
God (is) to be forgetful of the work of you, and of the labor

ἀγάπης ἧς ἐνεδείξασθε εἰς τὸ ὄνομα αὐτοῦ, διακονήσαντες
of love which you showed to the name of Him, having ministered

11 τοῖς ἁγίοις καὶ διακονοῦντες. ἐπιθυμοῦμεν δὲ ἕκαστον ὑμῶν
to the saints, and (now) ministering. we desire But each one of you

desire each of you to show the same eagerness, to the full assurance of the hope to (the) end; [12] that you be not dull, but imitators of those who through faith and long patience inherit the promises. [13] For God having promised Abraham, since He had no one greater to swear by, swore by Himself, [14] saying, "Surely blessing I will bless you, and multiplying I will multiply you." [15] And so, having had long patience, he obtained the promise. [16] For men indeed swear by the greater, and an oath to make things sure (is) to them the end of all gainsaying. [17] In which way, desiring to more fully declare to the heirs of promise the unchangeableness of His counsel, interposed by an oath, [18] that by two unchangeable things, in which (it was) impossible (for) God to lie, we might have strong comfort, (we) who fled for refuge to lay hold on the hope set before (us), [19] which we have as an anchor of the soul, both certain and sure, and entering into that inside the veil; [20] where Jesus has entered (as) forerunner for us, having become a High Priest forever according to the order of Melchizadek.

CHAPTER 7

[1] For this Melchizedek, king of Salem, priest of the most high God, who met Abraham returning from the smiting of the kings, and having blessed him; [2] to whom also Abraham divided a tenth of all; first being interpreted king of righteousness, and then also king of Salem, which is, king of peace, [3] without father, without mother, without pedigree, having neither beginning of days nor end of life, having been made even like the Son of God, (he) remains a priest in perpetuity. [4] Now how

τὴν αὐτὴν ἐνδείκνυσθαι σπουδὴν πρὸς τὴν πληροφορίαν τῆς
the same       to show       eagerness to    the full assurance of the

12 ἐλπίδος ἄχρι τέλους· ἵνα μὴ νωθροὶ γένησθε, μιμηταὶ δὲ
hope     unto (the)end, lest    you become; imitators but

τῶν διὰ πίστεως καὶ μακροθυμίας κληρονομούντων τὰς
of those through faith and    long-suffering      inheriting       the

ἐπαγγελίας.
promises.

13 Τῷ γὰρ ᾿Αβραὰμ ἐπαγγειλάμενος ὁ Θεός, ἐπεὶ κατ᾿
For to Abraham having made promise    God,   since  by

14 οὐδενὸς εἶχε μείζονος ὀμόσαι, ὤμοσε καθ᾿ ἑαυτοῦ, λέγων,
no one he had greater to swear, swore  by  Himself, saying,

᾿Η μὴν εὐλογῶν εὐλογήσω σε, καὶ πληθύνων πληθυνῶ σε.
If surely blessing   I will bless you, and multiplying I will multiply you.

15 καὶ οὕτω μακροθυμήσας ἐπέτυχε τῆς ἐπαγγελίας. ἄνθρωποι
16 And so   being long-suffering, he obtained the promise.      men

μὲν γὰρ κατὰ τοῦ μείζονος ὀμνύουσι, καὶ πάσης αὐτοῖς
indeed For by    the greater    swear,    and   of all (is) to them

17 ἀντιλογίας πέρας εἰς βεβαίωσιν ὁ ὅρκος. ἐν ᾧ περισσότερον
contradiction an end for confirmation the oath. In which more abundantly

βουλόμενος ὁ Θεὸς ἐπιδεῖξαι τοῖς κληρονόμοις τῆς ἐπαγ-
resolving     God   to show    to the   heirs     of the promise

γελίας τὸ ἀμετάθετον τῆς βουλῆς αὐτοῦ, ἐμεσίτευσεν ὅρκῳ
the unchangeableness of the counsel of Him, He interposed by an oath,

18 ἵνα διὰ δύο πραγμάτων ἀμεταθέτων, ἐν οἷς ἀδύνατον
that through two   things      unchangeable, in which (it was) impossible

ψεύσασθαι Θεόν, ἰσχυρὰν παράκλησιν ἔχωμεν οἱ κατα-
to lie      God, a strong    consolation  we might have, those

19 φυγόντες κρατῆσαι τῆς προκειμένης ἐλπίδος· ἣν ὡς ἄγκυραν
having fled to lay hold of the set before (us)  hope; which as an anchor

ἔχομεν τῆς ψυχῆς ἀσφαλῆ τε καὶ βεβαίαν, καὶ εἰσερχομένην
we have of the soul,  secure both and firm,   and entering

20 εἰς τὸ ἐσώτερον τοῦ καταπετάσματος· ὅπου πρόδρομος ὑπὲρ
into the inner (side) of the veil,             where a forerunner for

ἡμῶν εἰσῆλθεν ᾿Ιησοῦς, κατὰ τὴν τάξιν Μελχισεδὲκ ἀρχιερεὺς
us    entered,   Jesus, according to the order of Melchizedek a high priest

γενόμενος εἰς τὸν αἰῶνα.
becoming   to the   age.

CHAPTER 7

1 Οὗτος γὰρ ὁ Μελχισεδέκ, βασιλεὺς Σαλήμ, ἱερεὺς τοῦ Θεοῦ
this For   Melchizedek,    king of Salem,  priest of God

τοῦ ὑψίστου, ὁ συναντήσας ᾿Αβραὰμ ὑποστρέφοντι ἀπὸ τῆς
the most high, the (one) meeting Abraham returning    from the

2 κοπῆς τῶν βασιλέων καὶ εὐλογήσας αὐτόν, ᾧ καὶ δεκάτην
slaughter of the kings   and blessing    him, to whom indeed a tenth

ἀπὸ πάντων ἐμέρισεν ᾿Αβραάμ (πρῶτον μὲν ἑρμηνευόμενος
from all     divided   Abraham → firstly       being interpreted,

βασιλεὺς δικαιοσύνης, ἔπειτα δὲ καὶ βασιλεὺς Σαλήμ, ὅ ἐστι
king    of righteousness, then and also   king    of Salem, which is,

3 βασιλεὺς εἰρήνης· ἀπάτωρ, ἀμήτωρ, ἀγενεαλόγητος, μήτε
king    of peace, without father, without mother, without pedigree, nor

ἀρχὴν ἡμερῶν μήτε ζωῆς τέλος ἔχων, ἀφωμοιωμένος δὲ τῷ
beginning of days, nor of life  end having, having been made like but the

υἱῷ τοῦ Θεοῦ), μένει ἱερεὺς εἰς τὸ διηνεκές.
Son  of God — remains a priest in  perpetuity.

great this (one was), to whom even Abraham the patriarch gave a tenth of the spoils. [5] And they indeed of the sons of Levi receiving the priesthood have a command to tithe the people according to the law; that is, from their brothers, though having come out of the loins of Abraham. [6] But he not counting (his) pedigree from them has tithed Abraham, and has blessed the (one) having the promises. [7] But without all contradiction, the lesser is blessed by the better. [8] And here dying men indeed receive tithes, but there having been witnessed that he lives; [9] and as a word to say, through Abraham Levi also, he receiving tithes, has also been tithed. [10] For he was yet in the loins of his father when Melchizedek met him. [11] Truly, then, if perfection was through the Levitical priestly office —for the people has been given Law under it—why yet need (for) another priest to arise according to the order of Melchizedek, and not to be called according to the order of Aaron? [12] For the priestly office having been changed, of necessity a change of law also occurs. [13] For (He) of whom these things are said has partaken of another tribe, from which no one has given devotion at the altar. [14] For it is clear that our Lord has risen out of Judah, as to which tribe Moses spoke nothing concerning priests. [15] and it is still more abundantly clear (that) if another priest arises according to the likeness of Melchizedek, [16] who has become (so) not according to a law of a fleshly command, but according to (the) power of an indissoluble life; [17] for it is testified: "You (are) a priest forever according to the order of Melchizedek." [18] For an annulment of (the) preceding command comes about because of its weakness and unprofitableness; [19] for the Law perfected nothing, but (it was by) a bringing in of a better hope, through which we draw near to God. [20] And by how much (it was) not apart from (the)

**4** Θεωρεῖτε δὲ πηλίκος οὗτος, ᾧ καὶ δεκάτην Ἀβραὰμ ἔδωκεν
behold Now how great (one was) this whom a tenth Abraham to even gave

**5** ἐκ τῶν ἀκροθινίων ὁ πατριαρχης. καὶ οἱ μὲν ἐκ τῶν υἱῶν
of the spoils the patriarch. And those of the sons

Λευῒ τὴν ἱερατείαν λαμβάνοντες ἐντολὴν ἔχουσιν ἀποδεκα-
of Levi the priesthood receiving a commandment have to tithe

τοῦν τὸν λαὸν κατὰ τὸν νόμον, τοῦτ᾽ ἔστι τοὺς ἀδελφοὺς
the people according to the law, this is the brothers

**6** αὐτῶν, καίπερ ἐξεληλυθότας ἐκ τῆς ὀσφύος Ἀβραάμ· ὁ δὲ
of them, though having come forth out of the loins of Abraham; he but

μὴ γενεαλογούμενος ἐξ αὐτῶν δεδεκάτωκε τὸν Ἀβραάμ, καὶ
not counting (his) pedigree from them has tithed Abraham, and

**7** τὸν ἔχοντα τὰς ἐπαγγελίας εὐλόγηκε. χωρὶς δὲ πάσης ἀντι-
the (one) having the promises (he) has blessed. without And all con-

**8** λογίας, τὸ ἔλαττον ὑπὸ τοῦ κρείττονος εὐλογεῖται. καὶ ὧδε
tradiction, the lesser by the better is blessed. And here

μὲν δεκάτας ἀποθνήσκοντες ἄνθρωποι λαμβάνουσιν· ἐκεῖ δέ,
indeed tithes dying men receive, there but

**9** μαρτυρούμενος ὅτι ζῇ. καί, ὡς ἔπος εἰπεῖν, διὰ Ἀβραὰμ καὶ
being witnessed that he lives. And as a word to say, through Abraham also

**10** Λευῒ ὁ δεκάτας λαμβάνων δεδεκάτωται· ἔτι γὰρ ἐν τῇ ὀσφύϊ
Levi, the (one) tithes receiving, has been tithed. yet For in the loins

τοῦ πατρὸς ἦν, ὅτε συνήντησεν αὐτῷ ὁ Μελχισεδέκ.
of the father he was when met him Melchizedek.

**11** Εἰ μὲν οὖν τελείωσις διὰ τῆς Λευϊτικῆς ἱερωσύνης ἦν (ὁ
If therefore perfection through the Levitical priestly office was, the

λαὸς γὰρ ἐπ᾽ αὐτῇ νενομοθέτητο), τίς ἔτι χρεία, κατὰ τὴν
people for under it has been given law, why yet need according to the

τάξιν Μελχισεδὲκ ἕτερον ἀνίστασθαι ἱερέα, καὶ οὐ κατὰ τὴν
order of Melchizedek another to arise priest, and not according to the

**12** τάξιν Ἀαρὼν λέγεσθαι; μετατιθεμένης γὰρ τῆς ἱερωσύνης,
order of Aaron to be said? being changed For the priestly office,

**13** ἐξ ἀνάγκης καὶ νόμου μετάθεσις γίνεται. ἐφ᾽ ὃν γὰρ λέγεται
of necessity also of law a change occurs. of whom For are said

ταῦτα, φυλῆς ἑτέρας μετέσχηκεν, ἀφ᾽ ἧς οὐδεὶς προσέσχηκε
these things, tribe of another has partaken, from which no one has given devotion

**14** τῷ θυσιαστηρίῳ. πρόδηλον γὰρ ὅτι ἐξ Ἰούδα ἀνατέταλκεν
at the altar. it is clear For that out of Judah has risen

ὁ Κύριος ἡμῶν, εἰς ἣν φυλὴν οὐδὲν περὶ ἱερωσύνης Μωσῆς
the Lord of us, as to which tribe nothing concerning priesthood Moses

**15** ἐλάλησε. καὶ περισσότερον ἔτι κατάδηλόν ἐστιν, εἰ κατὰ τὴν
spoke. And more abundantly still quite clear is it, if according to the

**16** ὁμοιότητα Μελχισεδὲκ ἀνίσταται ἱερεὺς ἕτερος, ὃς οὐ κατὰ
likeness of Melchizedek arises priest another, who not according to

νόμον ἐντολῆς σαρκικῆς γέγονεν, ἀλλὰ κατὰ δύναμιν ζωῆς
(the) law of a command fleshly has become, but according to (the) power life

**17** ἀκαταλύτου· μαρτυρεῖ γὰρ ὅτι Σὺ ἱερεὺς εἰς τὸν αἰῶνα κατὰ
of an indissoluble. it is testified for:— You (are) a priest to the age according to

**18** τὴν τάξιν Μελχισεδέκ. ἀθέτησις μὲν γὰρ γίνεται προαγούσης
the order of Melchizedek. an annulment For comes about of (the) preceding

**19** ἐντολῆς, διὰ τὸ αὐτῆς ἀσθενὲς καὶ ἀνωφελές· οὐδὲν γὰρ
command, because of the of it weak(ness) and unprofitable(ness), nothing for

ἐτελείωσεν ὁ νόμος, ἐπεισαγωγὴ δὲ κρείττονος ἐλπίδος, δι᾽
perfected the law, a bringing in but of a better hope, through

**20** ἧς ἐγγίζομεν τῷ Θεῷ. καὶ καθ᾽ ὅσον οὐ χωρὶς ὁρκωμοσίας
which we draw near to God. And by how much (it was) not without oath-taking

swearing of an oath — for they have become priests without (the) swearing of an oath, [21] but He with (the) swearing by Him who says as to Him, "(The) Lord swore, and will not repent, You (are) a Priest forever according to the order of Melchizedek" — [22] by so much Jesus has become surety of a better covenant. [23] And they truly are many priests, being hindered from continuing because of death; [24] but He, because of His living forever, has the priesthood that cannot be changed. [25] From this also He is able to save to the uttermost those who come to God by Him, ever living to intercede for them. [26] For such a High Priest was fitting for us, holy, harmless, undefiled, and separated from sinners, and made higher than the heavens; [27] who has no need, as the high priests, to offer sacrifices day by day, first for His own sins, then for those of the people; for He did this once for all having offered up Himself. [28] For the Law makes men high priests who have infirmity; but the word of the swearing of the oath, which (is) after the Law, has perfected the Son forever.

CHAPTER 8

[1] Now a summary of the things being spoken of (is): we have such a High Priest, who sat down on (the) right hand of the throne of the Majesty in Heaven, [2] Minister of the holies and of the true tabernacle which the Lord pitched, and not man. [3] For every high priest is set in place to offer both gifts and sacrifices; from where (it is) necessary (for) this One also to have something which He may offer. [4] For if indeed He were on earth, He would not even be a priest, there being those priests offering the gifts according to the Law, [5] who serve

**21** (οἱ μὲν γὰρ χωρὶς ὀρκωμοσίας εἰσὶν ἱερεῖς γεγονότες, ὁ δὲ
—those   for without oath-taking   are   priests having become He but
μετὰ ὀρκωμοσίας, διὰ τοῦ λέγοντος πρὸς αὐτόν, Ὤμοσε
with oath-taking, through those saying to Him, Swore
Κύριος καὶ οὐ μεταμεληθήσεται, Σὺ ἱερεὺς εἰς τὸν αἰῶνα κατὰ
(the) Lord, and not will change (His) mind, You a priest to the   age;   by

**22** τὴν τάξιν Μελχισεδέκ)· κατὰ τοσοῦτον κρείττονος διαθήκης
the order of Melchizedek— by   so much of a better   covenant

**23** γέγονεν ἔγγυος Ἰησοῦς. καὶ οἱ μὲν πλείονές εἰσι γεγονότες
has become surety   Jesus. And those indeed many are, having become

**24** ἱερεῖς, διὰ τὸ θανάτῳ κωλύεσθαι παραμένειν· ὁ δέ, διὰ τὸ
priests because of by death being prevented to continue; He but, because of
μένειν αὐτὸν εἰς τὸν αἰῶνα, ἀπαράβατον ἔχει τὴν ἱερωσύνην.
remaining Him to the   age, not to be passed on has   the priestly office

**25** ὅθεν καὶ σώζειν εἰς τὸ παντελὲς δύναται τοὺς προσερχο-
from which truly to save to   perfection He is able   those drawing near
μένους δι᾽ αὐτοῦ τῷ Θεῷ, πάντοτε ζῶν εἰς τὸ ἐντυγχανειν
through Him to God,   ever living to   intercede
ὑπὲρ αὐτῶν.
on behalf of them.

**26** Τοιοῦτος γὰρ ἡμῖν ἔπρεπεν ἀρχιερεύς, ὅσιος, ἄκακος,
such For to us was fitting a High Priest, holy, harmless,
ἀμίαντος, κεχωρισμένος ἀπὸ τῶν ἁμαρτωλῶν, καὶ ὑψηλό-
undefiled, having been separated from   sinners, and higher

**27** τερος τῶν οὐρανῶν γενόμενος· ὃς οὐκ ἔχει καθ᾽ ἡμέραν
than the heavens becoming; who not has day by day
ἀνάγκην, ὥσπερ οἱ ἀρχιερεῖς, πρότερον ὑπὲρ τῶν ἰδίων
need, as do the high priests, firstly for the own
ἁμαρτιῶν θυσίας ἀναφέρειν, ἔπειτα τῶν τοῦ λαοῦ· τοῦτο
sins sacrifices to offer up, then (for) those of the people; this

**28** γὰρ ἐποίησεν ἐφάπαξ, ἑαυτὸν ἀνενέγκας. ὁ νόμος γὰρ
for He did once for all, Himself offering up. the law For
ἀνθρώπους καθίστησιν ἀρχιερεῖς, ἔχοντας ἀσθένειαν· ὁ
men appoints high priests having infirmity; the
λόγος δὲ τῆς ὀρκωμοσίας τῆς μετὰ τὸν νόμον, υἱὸν εἰς τὸν
word but of the oath-taking after the law (appoints) a Son to the
αἰῶνα τετελειωμένον.
age, having been perfected.

CHAPTER 8

**1** Κεφάλαιον δὲ ἐπὶ τοῖς λεγομένοις· τοιοῦτον ἔχομεν
a summary Now over the things being said, such we have
ἀρχιερέα, ὃς ἐκάθισεν ἐν δεξιᾷ τοῦ θρόνου τῆς μεγαλωσύνης
a High Priest, who sat at (the) right of the throne of the Majesty

**2** ἐν τοῖς οὐρανοῖς, τῶν ἁγίων λειτουργός, καὶ τῆς σκηνῆς τῆς
in Heaven, of the holy things a minister, and of the tabernacle

**3** ἀληθινῆς, ἣν ἔπηξεν ὁ Κύριος, καὶ οὐκ ἄνθρωπος. πᾶς γὰρ
true, which raised up the Lord, and not man. every For
ἀρχιερεὺς εἰς τὸ προσφέρειν δῶρά τε καὶ θυσίας καθίσταται·
high priest to offer gifts both and sacrifices is appointed;

**4** ὅθεν ἀναγκαῖον ἔχειν τι καὶ τοῦτον ὃ προσενέγκη. εἰ μὲν γὰρ
from (it is) to some- this One which He may offer. if truly For
which needful have thing also
ἦν ἐπὶ γῆς, οὐδ᾽ ἂν ἦν ἱερεύς, ὄντων τῶν ἱερέων τῶν
He were on earth, He would not be a priest, being those priests

**5** προσφερόντων κατὰ τὸν νόμον τὰ δῶρα, οἵτινες ὑποδείγματι
offering according to the law the gifts; who an example

(the) pattern and shadow of the heavenlies, even as Moses was divinely instructed, being about to make the tabernacle; for He says, "See (that) you make all things according to the pattern shown to you in the mountain." [6] But now He has gotten a more excellent ministry, by so much He is a Mediator of a better covenant, which has been enacted on better promises. [7] For if that first were faultless, place would not be sought for a second. [8] For finding fault, He said to them, "Behold, days are coming, says (the) Lord, and I will ratify a new covenant as regards the house of Israel and as regards the house of Judah: [9] not according to the covenant which I made with their fathers, in (the) day of My taking hold of their hand to lead them out of (the) land of Egypt; because they did not continue in My covenant, and I did not regard them, says (the) Lord. [10] "Because this (is) the covenant which I will make with the house of Israel: after those days, says (the) Lord, giving My laws into their mind, and I will write them on their hearts, and I will be their God, and they shall be My people. [11] And they shall no more teach each one his neighbor, and each his brother, saying, Know the Lord; because all shall know Me, from the least of them to the greatest of them. [12] For I will be merciful to their unrighteousness, and I will no more remember their lawless deeds." [13] In the saying, "New," He has made the first old; but that which grows old and aged (is) near disappearing.

καὶ σκιᾷ λατρεύουσι τῶν ἐπουρανίων, καθὼς κεχρημάτισται
and a shadow serve of the heavenly things, as has been warned
Μωσῆς μέλλων ἐπιτελεῖν τὴν σκηνήν, Ὅρα, γάρ φησι,
Moses being about to make the tabernacle,: see For, He says,
ποιήσῃς πάντα κατὰ τὸν τύπον τὸν δειχθέντα σοι ἐν τῷ ὄρει.
you make all things according to the pattern shown to you in the mount.

6 ·νυνὶ δὲ διαφορωτέρας τέτευχε λειτουργίας, ὅσῳ καὶ κρείτ-
now And a more excellent He has gotten ministry, by so much of a
τονός ἐστι διαθήκης μεσίτης, ἥτις ἐπὶ κρείττοσιν ἐπαγγελίαις
better He is covenant Mediator, which on better promises

7 νενομοθέτηται. εἰ γὰρ ἡ πρώτη ἐκείνη ἦν ἄμεμπτος, οὐκ ἂν
has been enacted. if For first that was faultless, not would

8 δευτέρας ἐζητεῖτο τόπος. μεμφόμενος γὰρ αὐτοῖς λέγει, Ἰδού,
of a second have been sought place. finding fault For them He says, Behold,
ἡμέραι ἔρχονται, λέγει Κύριος, καὶ συντελέσω ἐπὶ τὸν οἶκον
days are coming, says (the) Lord, and I will make an end upon the house

9 Ἰσραὴλ καὶ ἐπὶ τὸν οἶκον Ἰούδα διαθήκην καινήν· οὐ κατὰ
of Israel, and upon the house of Judah, covenant a new, not according to
τὴν διαθήκην ἣν ἐποίησα τοῖς πατράσιν αὐτῶν ἐν ἡμέρα
the covenant which I made with the fathers of them, in (the) day
ἐπιλαβομένου μου τῆς χειρὸς αὐτῶν ἐξαγαγεῖν αὐτούς ἐκ
taking hold Me the hand of them to lead forth them out of
γῆς Αἰγύπτου· ὅτι αὐτοὶ οὐκ ἐνέμειναν ἐν τῇ διαθήκῃ μου,
(the) land of Egypt, because they not continued in the covenant of Me,

10 κἀγὼ ἠμέλησα αὐτῶν, λέγει Κύριος. ὅτι αὕτη ἡ διαθήκη ἣν
and I not regarded them, says (the) Lord. Because this the covenant which
διαθήσομαι τῷ οἴκῳ Ἰσραὴλ μετὰ τὰς ἡμέρας ἐκείνας, λέγει
I will covenant with the house of Israel after days those, says
Κύριος, διδοὺς νόμους μου εἰς τὴν διάνοιαν αὐτῶν, καὶ ἐπὶ
(the) Lord, giving laws of Me into the mind of them, and on
καρδίας αὐτῶν ἐπιγράψω αὐτούς· καὶ ἔσομαι αὐτοῖς εἰς Θεόν,
hearts of them I will write them, and I will be to them for God,

11 καὶ αὐτοὶ ἔσονταί μοι εἰς λαόν. καὶ οὐ μὴ διδάξωσιν ἕκαστος
and they will be to Me for a people; and not at all may they teach each one
τὸν πλησίον αὐτοῦ, καὶ ἕκαστος τὸν ἀδελφὸν αὐτοῦ, λέγων,
the neighbor of him, and each one the brother of him, saying,
Γνῶθι τὸν Κύριον· ὅτι πάντες εἰδήσουσί με, ἀπὸ μικροῦ
Know the Lord; because all will know Me, from little

12 αὐτῶν ἕως μεγάλου αὐτῶν. ὅτι ἵλεως ἔσομαι ταῖς ἀδικίαις
of them unto (the) great of them. Because merciful I will be to the righteous-nesses
αὐτῶν, καὶ τῶν ἁμαρτιῶν αὐτῶν καὶ τῶν ἀνομιῶν αὐτῶν
of them; and the sins of them, and the lawlessnesses of them,

13 οὐ μὴ μνησθῶ ἔτι. ἐν τῷ λέγειν, Καινήν, πεπαλαίωκε τὴν
not at all I may remember still. In the saying, New, He has made old the
πρώτην. τὸ δὲ παλαιούμενον καὶ γηράσκον, ἐγγὺς ἀφανι-
first; the thing and being made old and growing aged (is) near dis-
σμοῦ.
appearing.

## CHAPTER 9

[1] Truly, then, the first tabernacle also had ordinances of service, and the worldly sanctuary. [2] For the first tabernacle was prepared, in which (was) both the lampstand and the table, and the showbread which is called

## CHAPTER 9

1 Εἶχε μὲν οὖν καὶ ἡ πρώτη δικαιώματα λατρείας, τό τε
had So then also the first (covenant) ordinances of service, the and

2 ἅγιον κοσμικόν. σκηνὴ γὰρ κατεσκευάσθη ἡ πρώτη, ἐν ᾗ ἥ
holy place worldly. a tabernacle For was prepared, the first, in which the
τε λυχνία καὶ ἡ τράπεζα καὶ ἡ πρόθεσις τῶν ἄρτων, ἥτις
both lampstand and the table, and the setting out of the loaves, which

holy; [3] but behind the second veil a tabernacle which (is) called Holy of Holies, [4] Having a golden censer, and the ark of the covenant covered around on all sides with gold, in which (were) a golden pot (with) the manna, and the rod of Aaron (that) budded, and the tablets of the covenant; [5] and above it (the) cherubim of glory overshadowing the mercy-seat; about which now is not (time) to speak piece by piece. [6] And these having been prepared thus, the priests go into the first tabernacle at all times completing the services. [7] But into the second the high priest (goes) alone once (in) the year, not without 'blood, which he offers for himself and the ignorances of the people; [8] the Holy Spirit signifying (by) this (that) the way of the Holies has not yet been made made manifest, the first tabernacle still having a standing; [9] which (is) a parable for the present time, in which both gifts and sacrifices are offered, (that) as regards conscience not being able to perfect the (ones) serving, [10] (being) only on food and drinks, and various washings and fleshly ordinances, until (the) time of setting things right (is) imposed.

[11] But Christ having come (as) High Priest of the coming good things, through the greater and more perfect tabernacle not made by hands, that is, not of this creation, [12] nor by blood of goats and calves but through (His) own blood, entered in once for all into the Holies, having procured everlasting redemption. [13] For if the blood of bulls and of goats, and ashes of a heifer sprinkling the defiled ones, sanctifies for the purity of the flesh, [14] how much rather the blood of Christ, who through (the) eternal Spirit offered Himself without spot to God, shall purify your conscience from dead

3  λέγεται ἅγια. μετὰ δὲ τὸ δεύτερον καταπέτασμα σκηνὴ ἡ
   is called  Holy;  after  and  the  second  veil  a tabernacle, that

4  λεγομένη ἅγια ἁγίων, χρυσοῦν ἔχουσα θυμιατήριον, καὶ
   called  Holy of Holies,  golden  having  an altar,  and
   τὴν κιβωτὸν τῆς διαθήκης περικεκαλυμμένην πάντοθεν
   the  ark  of the  covenant  having been covered around on all sides
   χρυσίῳ, ἐν ᾗ στάμνος χρυσῆ ἔχουσα τὸ μάννα, καὶ ἡ ῥάβδος
   with gold, in which a pot  golden having  the  manna,  and the rod

5  Ἀαρὼν ἡ βλαστήσασα, καὶ αἱ πλάκες τῆς διαθήκης· ὑπερ-
   of Aaron  budded,  and  the tablets  of the covenant·  above
   ἄνω δὲ αὐτῆς Χερουβὶμ δόξης κατασκιάζοντα τὸ ἱλαστή-
   and  it  cherubim of glory  overshadowing  the  mercy-

6  ριον· περὶ ὧν οὐκ ἔστι νῦν λέγειν κατὰ μέρος. τούτων δὲ οὕτω
   seat, about which not  is  now to speak piece by piece. these And thus
   κατεσκευασμένων, εἰς μὲν τὴν πρώτην σκηνὴν διὰ παντὸς
   having been prepared,  into  the  first  tabernacle  through all

7  εἰσίασιν οἱ ἱερεῖς, τὰς λατρείας ἐπιτελοῦντες· εἰς δὲ τὴν
   go  the priests,  the  services  completing,  into but the
   δευτέραν ἅπαξ τοῦ ἐνιαυτοῦ μόνος ὁ ἀρχιερεύς, οὐ χωρὶς
   second  once (in) the year  (goes) alone the high priest, not without
   αἵματος, ὃ προσφέρει ὑπὲρ ἑαυτοῦ καὶ τῶν τοῦ λαοῦ ἀγνοη-
   blood,, which he offers  for  himself and  the of the people ignorances;

8  μάτων· τοῦτο δηλοῦντος τοῦ Πνεύματος τοῦ Ἁγίου, μήπω
   this  showing  the Spirit  Holy,  not yet
   πεφανερῶσθαι τὴν τῶν ἁγίων ὁδόν, ἔτι τῆς πρώτης σκηνῆς
   having been revealed the of the Holies way, yet the  first tabernacle

9  ἐχούσης στάσιν· ἥτις παραβολὴ εἰς τὸν καιρὸν τὸν ἐνεστη-
   having  standing, which (was) a parable for  the  time  present,
   κότα, καθ' ὃν δῶρά τε καὶ θυσίαι προσφέρονται, μὴ δυνά-
   according to which gifts both and sacrifices are being offered, not being

10  μεναι κατὰ συνείδησιν τελειῶσαι τὸν λατρεύοντα, μόνον
    able as to  conscience  to perfect the (one)  serving,  only
    ἐπὶ βρώμασι καὶ πόμασι καὶ διαφόροις βαπτισμοῖς καὶ
    on  foods  and  drinks  and  various  washings, even
    δικαιώμασι σαρκός, μέχρι καιροῦ διορθώσεως ἐπικείμενα.
    ordinances of flesh  until  a time of setting things right being imposed.

11  Χριστὸς δὲ παραγενόμενος ἀρχιερεὺς τῶν μελλόντων
    Christ  But  having appeared (as) a Hight Priest of the  coming
    ἀγαθῶν, διὰ τῆς μείζονος καὶ τελειοτέρας σκηνῆς, οὐ
    good things, through the greater  and  more perfect tabernacle not

12  χειροποιήτου, τοῦτ' ἔστιν, οὐ ταύτης τῆς κτίσεως, οὐδὲ δι'
    made with hands, this  is  not of this  creation; nor through
    αἵματος τράγων καὶ μόσχων, διὰ δὲ τοῦ ἰδίου αἵματος
    blood  of goats  and of calves, through but the  own  blood
    εἰσῆλθεν ἐφάπαξ εἰς τὰ ἅγια, αἰωνίαν λύτρωσιν εὑράμενος.
    entered once for all into the Holies,  eternal  redemption having found.

13  εἰ γὰρ τὸ αἷμα ταύρων καὶ τράγων, καὶ σποδὸς δαμάλεως
    if For the blood of bulls  and  goats,  and  ashes  of a heifer
    ῥαντίζουσα τοὺς κεκοινωμένους, ἁγιάζει πρὸς τὴν τῆς
    sprinkling  those having been polluted  sanctifies to  the of the

14  σαρκὸς καθαρότητα, πόσῳ μᾶλλον τὸ αἷμα τοῦ Χριστοῦ,
    flesh  cleanness,  by how much more the blood  of Christ,
    ὃς διὰ Πνεύματος αἰωνίου ἑαυτὸν προσήνεγκεν ἄμωμον τῷ
    who through (the) Spirit Eternal Himself  offered  without spot
    Θεῷ, καθαριεῖ τὴν συνείδησιν ὑμῶν ἀπὸ νεκρῶν ἔργων, εἰς
    to God, will cleanse the conscience  of you from dead  works, for

works for (the) serving of (the) living God! [15] And because of this He is Mediator of a new covenant, so that, death having occurred for redemption of the transgressions under the first covenant, those having been called out might receive the promise of the eternal inheritance. [16] For where a covenant (is), (the) death of him covenanting must be offered; [17] for a covenant is affirmed over (those) dead, since it never has force when he covenanting (is) living. [18] From which: Neither the first was dedicated without blood. [19] For every command according to Law having been spoken by Moses to all the people, having taken the blood of the calves and goats, with water and scarlet wool and hyssop, he sprinkled both the book and all the people, [20] saying, This (is) the blood of the covenant which God enjoined to you. [21] And he likewise sprinkled both the tabernacle and the service vessels with the blood. [22] And almost all things are cleansed by blood according to the Law; and apart from shedding of blood no remission occurs. [23] (It was) needful, then, the figures of the things in the heavens to be cleansed (with) these; but the heavenly things by better sacrifices than these. [24] For Christ did not enter into (the) Holies made by hand, types of the true things, but into Heaven itself, now to appear in the presence of God on our behalf; [25] not that He often should offer Himself, even as the high priest enters into the Holies year by year with blood of others; [26] since He must often have suffered from foundation of (the) world. But now once, at the completion of the ages, He has been manifested for putting away of sin through the sacrifice of Himself. [27] And as it is reserved to men once to die, and after this, Judgment; [28] so Christ, having been once offered to bear (the) sins of many, shall appear a second time without sin to

15 τὸ λατρεύειν Θεῷ ζῶντι ; καὶ διὰ τοῦτο διαθήκης καινῆς
serving      God of (the) living. And therefore    covenant of a new
μεσίτης ἐστίν, ὅπως, θανάτου γενομένου εἰς ἀπολύτρωσιν
Mediator He is,   so as   death   having occurred for redemption
τῶν ἐπὶ τῇ πρώτῃ διαθήκῃ παραβάσεων, τὴν ἐπαγγελίαν
of the under the first   covenant   transgressions, , the   promise

16 λάβωσιν οἱ κεκλημένοι τῆς αἰωνίου κληρονομίας. ὅπου γὰρ
may receive those being called of the eternal   inheritance.  where (is) For

17 διαθήκη, θάνατον ἀνάγκη φέρεσθαι τοῦ διαθεμένου. διαθήκη
a covenant (the) death (is) needful to be offered of him covenanting a covenant
γὰρ ἐπὶ νεκροῖς βεβαία, ἐπεὶ μή ποτε ἰσχύει ὅτε ζῇ ὁ διαθέ-
for over(those) dead (is) firm, since not ever has it strength when living he cove-

18 μενος. ὅθεν οὐδ' ἡ πρώτη χωρὶς αἱματος ἐγκεκαίνισται.
nanting. From which neither the first without blood   was dedicated.
λαληθείσης γὰρ πάσης ἐντολῆς κατὰ νόμον ὑπὸ Μωϋσέως
having been spoken For every command according to law by   Moses

19 παντὶ τῷ λαῷ, λαβὼν τὸ αἷμα τῶν μόσχων καὶ τράγων,
to all the people, taking the blood of the calves   and of goats,
μετὰ ὕδατος καὶ ἐρίου κοκκίνου καὶ ὑσσώπου, αὐτό τε τὸ
with water   and wool scarlet   and hyssop,   it(self) both the

20 βιβλίον καὶ πάντα τὸν λαὸν ἐρράντισε, λέγων, Τοῦτο τὸ
scroll and   all   the people he sprinkled, saying, This (is) the

21 αἷμα τῆς διαθήκης ἧς ἐνετείλατο πρὸς ὑμᾶς ὁ Θεός. καὶ τὴν
blood of the covenant which enjoined   to   you   God. both the
σκηνὴν δὲ καὶ πάντα τὰ σκεύη τῆς λειτουργίας τῷ αἵματι
tabernacle And and all   the vessels of the service   with the blood

22 ὁμοίως ἐρράντισε. καὶ σχεδὸν ἐν αἵματι πάντα καθαρίζεται
likewise he sprinkled. And almost   by blood all things are cleansed
κατὰ τὸν νόμον, καὶ χωρὶς αἱματεκχυσίας οὐ γίνεται ἄφεσις.
according to the law, and without bloodshedding   no there comes remission.

23 Ἀνάγκη οὖν τὰ μὲν ὑποδείγματα τῶν ἐν τοῖς οὐρανοῖς,
(It was) needful, then, the   examples   of the things in the heavens
τούτοις καθαρίζεσθαι, αὐτὰ δὲ τὰ ἐπουράνια κρείττοσι
these   to be cleansed; them(selves) But the heavenly things by better

24 θυσίαις παρὰ ταύτας. οὐ γὰρ εἰς χειροποίητα ἅγια εἰσῆλθεν
sacrifices than   these. not For into made by hand Holies   entered
ὁ Χριστός, ἀντίτυπα τῶν ἀληθινῶν, ἀλλ' εἰς αὐτὸν τὸν
Christ,   figures of the true things, but into it(self)
οὐρανόν, νῦν ἐμφανισθῆναι τῷ προσώπῳ τοῦ Θεοῦ ὑπὲρ
Heaven,   now to appear in the presence   of God for

25 ἡμῶν· οὐδ' ἵνα πολλάκις προσφέρῃ ἑαυτόν, ὥσπερ ὁ
us;   not that often He should offer Himself, even as the
ἀρχιερεὺς εἰσέρχεται εἰς τὰ ἅγια κατ' ἐνιαυτὸν ἐν αἵματι
high priest enters   into the Holies year by year with blood

26 ἀλλοτρίῳ· ἐπεὶ ἔδει αὐτὸν πολλάκις παθεῖν ἀπὸ καταβολῆς
of others—since must He often have suffered from foundation
κόσμου· νῦν δὲ ἅπαξ ἐπὶ συντελείᾳ τῶν αἰώνων εἰς ἀθέτησιν
of (the) world—now but once at the completion of the ages for putting away

27 ἁμαρτίας διὰ τῆς θυσίας αὐτοῦ πεφανέρωται. καὶ καθ' ὅσον
of sin through the sacrifice of Him He has been revealed. And as
ἀπόκειται τοῖς ἀνθρώποις ἅπαξ ἀποθανεῖν, μετὰ δὲ τοῦτο
it is reserved   to men   once to die,   after and this

28 κρίσις· οὕτως ὁ Χριστός, ἅπαξ προσενεχθεὶς εἰς τὸ πολλῶν
judgment, so   Christ,   once having been offered   of many
ἀνενεγκεῖν ἁμαρτίας, ἐκ δευτέρου χωρὶς ἁμαρτίας ὀφθήσεται
to bear   sins,   a second (time) without sin   will appear

those that look to Him for salvation.

## CHAPTER 10

[1] For the Law having a shadow of the coming good things, not the image itself of (those) things, year by year with the same sacrifices which they offer continually never is able to perfect the (one) drawing near. [2] Otherwise, would they not have ceased to be offered because of (this, that) those who served once purged having no longer any conscience of sins? [3] But in these (there is) a remembrance of sins year by year. [4] For (it is) not possible (for the) blood of bulls and of goats to take away sins. [5] For this reason, coming into the world, He says, Sacrifice and offering You did not desire, but You prepared Me a body. [6] You did not delight in burnt offerings and (sacrifices) for sin. [7] Then I said, Lo, in a heading of the Book it is written of Me, I come to do Your will, O God. [8] Above, saying, You did not desire sacrifice and offering, and did not delight in burnt offerings and (sacrifices) for sin — which are offered according to the Law — [9] then He said, Lo, I come to do Your will, O God. He takes away the first in order that He may establish the second; [10] by which will we are sanctified through the offering of the body of Jesus Christ once for all. [11] And every priest stands day by day ministering, and often offering the same sacrifices, which can never take away sins. [12] But He, having offered one sacrifice for sins, in perpetuity sat down at (the) right hand of God, [13] from then on expecting until His enemies are placed (as) a footstool for His feet. [14] For by one offering He has perfected in perpetuity the sanctified (ones).
[15] And the Holy Spirit

τοῖς αὐτὸν ἀπεκδεχομένοις, εἰς σωτηρίαν.
to those Him    expecting       for    salvation.

## CHAPTER 10

**1** Σκιὰν γὰρ ἔχων ὁ νόμος τῶν μελλόντων ἀγαθῶν, οὐκ
a shadow For having the law of the   coming     good things, not
αὐτὴν τὴν εἰκόνα τῶν πραγμάτων, κατ᾽ ἐνιαυτὸν ταῖς
it(self) the image of those    things,     year by year with the
αὐταῖς θυσίαις ἃς προσφέρουσιν εἰς τὸ διηνεκές, οὐδέποτε
same sacrifices which they offer     continually     never

**2** δύναται τοὺς προσερχομένους τελειῶσαι. ἐπεὶ οὐκ ἂν
are able those    drawing near    to perfect. ; since not would
ἐπαύσαντο προσφερόμεναι, διὰ τὸ μηδεμίαν ἔχειν ἔτι συνείδη-
they have ceased being offered because of not   having still conscience

**3** σιν ἁμαρτιῶν τοὺς λατρεύοντας, ἅπαξ κεκαθαρμένους ; ἀλλ᾽
of sins those    serving,    once having been cleansed; but

**4** ἐν αὐταῖς ἀνάμνησις ἁμαρτιῶν κατ᾽ ἐνιαυτόν· ἀδύνατον γὰρ
in them a remembrance of sins    year by year; it is impossible for

**5** αἷμα ταύρων καὶ τράγων ἀφαιρεῖν ἁμαρτίας. διὸ εἰσερχό-
blood of bulls   and   of goats to take away sins. Therefore entering
μενος εἰς τὸν κόσμον λέγει, Θυσίαν καὶ προσφορὰν οὐκ
into the world, He says, Sacrifice and   offering    not

**6** ἠθέλησας, σῶμα δὲ κατηρτίσω μοι· ὁλοκαυτώματα καὶ περὶ
You desired, a body but You prepared for Me; burnt offerings (and sacrifices) as to

**7** ἁμαρτίας οὐκ εὐδόκησας· τότε εἶπον, Ἰδού, ἥκω (ἐν κεφαλίδι
sins   not You were pleased. Then I said, Behold, I come—in a heading
βιβλίου γέγραπται περὶ ἐμοῦ) τοῦ ποιῆσαι, ὁ Θεός, τὸ
of (the) Book it was written about Me —    to do     God the

**8** θέλημά σου. ἀνώτερον λέγων ὅτι Θυσίαν καὶ προσφορὰν
will of You. Above    saying that sacrifice   and   offerings
καὶ ὁλοκαυτώματα καὶ περὶ ἁμαρτίας οὐκ ἠθέλησας, οὐδὲ
and burnt offerings and (sacrifices) as to sins   not You desired, nor

**9** εὐδόκησας (αἵτινες κατὰ τὸν νόμον προσφέρονται), τότε
were pleased — which according to the law    are offered —    then
εἴρηκεν, Ἰδού, ἥκω τοῦ ποιῆσαι, ὁ Θεός, τὸ θέλημά σου.
He said, Behold, I come    to do    God   the   will of You.

**10** ἀναιρεῖ τὸ πρῶτον, ἵνα τὸ δεύτερον στήσῃ. ἐν ᾧ θελήματι
He takes away the first,   that the   second He may set up, by which will
ἡγιασμένοι ἐσμὲν διὰ τῆς προσφορᾶς τοῦ σώματος τοῦ
sanctified    we are through the offering   of the   body

**11** Ἰησοῦ Χριστοῦ ἐφάπαξ. καὶ πᾶς μὲν ἱερεὺς ἕστηκε καθ᾽
of Jesus Christ once for all. And every indeed priest stands   day
ἡμέραν λειτουργῶν, καὶ τὰς αὐτὰς πολλάκις προσφέρων
by day    ministering,    and the   same    often    offering

**12** θυσίας, αἵτινες οὐδέποτε δύνανται περιελεῖν ἁμαρτίας· αὐτὸς
sacrifices, which    never    can    take away sins;    He
δὲ μίαν ὑπὲρ ἁμαρτιῶν προσενέγκας θυσίαν εἰς τὸ διηνεκές,
but one on behalf of sins   having offered sacrifice, , in   perpetuity,

**13** ἐκάθισεν ἐν δεξιᾷ τοῦ Θεοῦ, τὸ λοιπὸν ἐκδεχομενος ἕως
sat down at (the) right   of God, from then on   expecting   until

**14** τεθῶσιν οἱ ἐχθροὶ αὐτοῦ ὑποπόδιον τῶν ποδῶν αὐτοῦ. μιᾷ
are put the enemies of Him (as) a footstool of the feet   of Him. by one
γὰρ προσφορᾷ τετελείωκεν εἰς τὸ διηνεκὲς τοὺς ἁγιαζο-
For    offering   He has perfected in    perpetuity those being sanct-

**15** μένους. μαρτυρεῖ δὲ ἡμῖν καὶ τὸ Πνεῦμα τὸ Ἅγιον· μετὰ γὰρ
ified.    witnesses And to us also the    Spirit    Holy; after   for

bears witness to us also; for after having said before, [16] This (is) the covenant which I will covenant to them after those days, says (the) Lord: Giving My laws on their hearts, and I will write them on their minds; [17] and I will not at all remember their sins and their lawlessnesses longer. [18] Now where forgiveness of these (is), there (is) no longer offering concerning sins.

[19] Therefore, brothers, having confidence for the entering of the Holies by the blood of Jesus, [20] which He consecrated for us, a new and living way through the veil; that is, His flesh; [21] and (having) a great priest over the house of God, [22] let us draw near with a true heart in full assurance of faith, (our) hearts having been sprinkled from an evil conscience, and (our) body having been washed in pure water; [23] let us hold fast the confession of the hope without yielding, for He (is) faithful having promised. [24] And let us consider one another to incitement of love and of good works; [25] not forsaking the assembling of ourselves, as (is the) custom of some, but exhorting; and so much more as you see the Day drawing near. [26] For (if) we (are) willfully sinning after receiving the knowledge of the truth, there remains no more a sacrifice concerning sins, [27] but a certain fearful expectation of judgment and zealous fire being about to consume the adversaries. [28] Anyone disregarding the Law of Moses dies without pities on (the word of) two or three witnesses; [29] how much worse punishment do you think he will be thought worthy (to receive) having trampled on the Son of God, and having deemed the blood of the covenant common in which he was sanctified, and having insulted the Spirit of grace? [30] For we know Him having said: Vengeance (belongs) to Me; I will repay, says (the) Lord; and again, (The)

---

**16** τὸ προειρηκέναι, Αὕτη ἡ διαθήκη ἣν διαθήσομαι πρὸς
having said before. This (is) the covenant which I will covenant to

αὐτοὺς μετὰ τὰς ἡμέρας ἐκείνας, λέγει Κύριος, διδοὺς νόμους
them after days those, says (the) Lord: Giving laws

μου ἐπὶ καρδίας αὐτῶν, καὶ ἐπὶ τῶν διανοιῶν αὐτῶν
of Me on hearts of them, also on the minds of them

**17** ἐπιγράψω αὐτούς· καὶ τῶν ἁμαρτιῶν αὐτῶν καὶ τῶν
I will write them, and the sins of them and the

**18** ἀνομιῶν αὐτῶν οὐ μὴ μνησθῶ ἔτι. ὅπου δὲ ἄφεσις τούτων,
lawlessnesses of them not at all I will remember still. where Now forgiveness of these (is),

οὐκέτι προσφορὰ περὶ ἁμαρτίας.
no longer (is) offering concerning sins.

**19** Ἔχοντες οὖν, ἀδελφοί, παρρησίαν εἰς τὴν εἴσοδον τῶν
Having, therefore, brothers, confidence for the entering of the

**20** ἁγίων ἐν τῷ αἵματι Ἰησοῦ, ἣν ἐνεκαίνισεν ἡμῖν ὁδὸν
Holies by the blood of Jesus, which He consecrated for us, a way

πρόσφατον καὶ ζῶσαν, διὰ τοῦ καταπετάσματος, τοῦτ'
new and living through the veil, this

**21** ἔστι, τῆς σαρκὸς αὐτοῦ, καὶ ἱερέα μέγαν ἐπὶ τὸν οἶκον τοῦ
is, the flesh of Him; and (having) a priest great over the house

**22** Θεοῦ, προσερχώμεθα μετὰ ἀληθινῆς καρδίας ἐν πληρο-
of God, let us draw near with a true heart in full

φορίᾳ πίστεως, ἐρραντισμένοι τὰς καρδίας ἀπὸ συνειδήσεως
assurance of faith, having been sprinkled the hearts from a conscience

**23** πονηρᾶς, καὶ λελουμένοι τὸ σῶμα ὕδατι καθαρῷ· κατέχω-
evil, and having been washed the body water in clean; let us hold

μεν τὴν ὁμολογίαν τῆς ἐλπίδος ἀκλινῆ, πιστὸς γὰρ ὁ
fast the confession of the hope unyieldingly, faithful for (is) He

**24** ἐπαγγειλάμενος· καὶ κατανοῶμεν ἀλλήλους εἰς παροξυσμὸν
having promised; and let us consider one another to incitement

**25** ἀγάπης καὶ καλῶν ἔργων, μὴ ἐγκαταλείποντες τὴν ἐπισυν-
of love and of good works, not forsaking the assembling

αγωγὴν ἑαυτῶν, καθὼς ἔθος τισίν, ἀλλὰ παρακαλοῦντες,
of ourselves as (the) custom of some (is), but exhorting,

καὶ τοσούτῳ μᾶλλον, ὅσῳ βλέπετε ἐγγίζουσαν τὴν ἡμέραν.
and by so much more as you see drawing near the Day.

**26** Ἑκουσίως γὰρ ἁμαρτανόντων ἡμῶν μετὰ τὸ λαβεῖν τὴν
willfully For sinning us after receiving the

ἐπίγνωσιν τῆς ἀληθείας, οὐκέτι περὶ ἁμαρτιῶν ἀπολείπεται
full knowledge of the truth, no more concerning sins remains

**27** θυσία, φοβερὰ δέ τις ἐκδοχὴ κρίσεως, καὶ πυρὸς ζῆλος
a sacrifice, fearful but some expectation of judgment, and of fire zeal

**28** ἐσθίειν μέλλοντος τοὺς ὑπεναντίους. ἀθετήσας τις νόμον
to consume being about the adversaries. disregarding Anyone law

Μωσέως χωρὶς οἰκτιρμῶν ἐπὶ δυσὶν ἢ τρισὶ μάρτυσιν
of Moses without pities on (the word of) two or three witnesses

**29** ἀποθνήσκει· πόσῳ, δοκεῖτε, χείρονος ἀξιωθήσεται τιμωρίας
dies; by how much think you of worse will be thought worthy (to receive) punishment

ὁ τὸν υἱὸν τοῦ Θεοῦ καταπατήσας, καὶ τὸ αἷμα τῆς διαθή-
he the Son of God having trampled, and the blood of the cove-

κης κοινὸν ἡγησάμενος ἐν ᾧ ἡγιάσθη, καὶ τὸ Πνεῦμα τῆς
nant common having deemed by which he was sanctified, and the Spirit

**30** χάριτος ἐνυβρίσας; οἴδαμεν γὰρ τὸν εἰπόντα, Ἐμοὶ ἐκδίκη-
of grace having insulted; we know for the (One) having said, To Me (is) ven-

σις, ἐγὼ ἀνταποδώσω, λέγει Κύριος· καὶ πάλιν, Κύριος
geance, I will repay, says (the) Lord; and again, (The) Lord

Lord will judge His people. [31] (It is) a fearful thing to fall into (the) hands of (the) living God.

[32] But call to mind the former days in which, having been enlightened, you endured much conflict of sufferings; [33] partly, being exposed both to reproaches and to afflictions; and partly, sharers of those so having conducted themselves. [34] For also you suffered together in my bonds, and (in) the seizure of your possessions you accepted with joy, knowing yourselves to have a better and abiding possession in Heaven. [35] Therefore, do not throw away your confidence, which has great reward. [36] For you have need of patience, that the will of God having done, you may obtain the promise. [37] For yet a very little (and) He coming will come, and not delay. [38] But the just shall live by faith, and if he draws back, My soul is not pleased in him. [39] But we are not of (those) drawing back to destruction, but of faith, to (the) preservation of (the) soul.

CHAPTER 11

[1] Now faith is the substance of things hoped for, (the) evidence of things not seen. [2] For by this the elders obtained witness. [3] By faith we understand the worlds to have been framed by (the) word of God, so that the things seen do not have being from (the things) appearing. [4] By faith Abel offered a more excellent sacrifice to God than Cain, by which he was borne witness as being righteous, God testifying over his gifts; and through it, having died, yet speaks. [5] By faith Enoch was translated (so as) not to see death, and was not found because God translated him. For before his translation he had obtained witness to have pleased God well. [6] But without faith it is impossible to please (God). For it is right

31 κρινεῖ τὸν λαὸν αὐτοῦ. φοβερὸν τὸ ἐμπεσεῖν εἰς χεῖρας Θεοῦ
   will judge the people of Him. A fearful thing (it is) to fall into (the) hands God
   ζῶντος.
   of (the) living.

32 Ἀναμιμνήσκεσθε δὲ τὰς πρότερον ἡμέρας, ἐν αἷς φωτι-
   call to mind      But the   former   days  in which having

33 σθέντες πολλὴν ἄθλησιν ὑπεμείνατε παθημάτων· τοῦτο μέν,
   been
   enlightened much   struggle you endured of sufferings;   this
   ὀνειδισμοῖς τε καὶ θλίψεσι θεατριζόμενοι· τοῦτο δέ, κοινωνοὶ
   to reproaches both and to afflictions being exposed; this and,   sharers

34 τῶν οὕτως ἀναστρεφομένων γενηθέντες. καὶ γὰρ τοῖς
   ot those so   living   having become. indeed For   in the
   δεσμοῖς μου συνεπαθήσατε, καὶ τὴν ἁρπαγὴν τῶν ὑπαρχόν-
   bonds of me you suffered together, and the   seizure   of the possessions
   των ὑμῶν μετὰ χαρᾶς προσεδέξασθε, γινώσκοντες ἔχειν ἐν
   of you   with   joy   you accepted,   knowing   to have in

35 ἑαυτοῖς κρείττονα ὕπαρξιν ἐν οὐρανοῖς καὶ μένουσαν. μὴ
   yourselves a better   possession in   Heaven and   abiding. do not
   ἀποβάλητε οὖν τὴν παρρησίαν ὑμῶν, ἥτις ἔχει μισθαποδο-
   cast away Therefore the confidence   of you, which has   reward

36 σίαν μεγάλην. ὑπομονῆς γὰρ ἔχετε χρείαν, ἵνα τὸ θέλημα
   great.   of patience For you have need,   that   the   will

37 τοῦ Θεοῦ ποιήσαντες κομίσησθε τὴν ἐπαγγελίαν. ἔτι γὰρ
   of God having done, you may obtain the   promise.   yet For

38 μικρὸν ὅσον ὅσον, Ὁ ἐρχόμενος ἥξει, καὶ οὐ χρονιεῖ. ὁ δὲ
   little   a very,   the coming (One) will come, and not delay; the but
   δίκαιος ἐκ πίστεως ζήσεται· καὶ ἐὰν ὑποστείληται, οὐκ
   just   by   faith   will live,   and if he draws back,   not

39 εὐδοκεῖ ἡ ψυχή μου ἐν αὐτῷ. ἡμεῖς δὲ οὐκ ἐσμὲν ὑποστολῆς·
   is pleased the soul of Me in   him.   we But not are   of (those) drawing
   εἰς ἀπώλειαν, ἀλλὰ πίστεως εἰς περιποίησιν ψυχῆς.
   to destruction,   but   of faith   to possession   of (the) soul.

CHAPTER 11

1 Ἔστι δὲ πίστις ἐλπιζομένων ὑπόστασις, πραγμάτων
   is   Now   faith of things being hoped (the) substance,   of things

2 ἔλεγχος οὐ βλεπομένων. ἐν ταύτῃ γὰρ ἐμαρτυρήθησαν οἱ
   (the) evidence not being seen. by   this   For   obtained witness   the

3 πρεσβύτεροι. πίστει νοοῦμεν κατηρτίσθαι τοὺς αἰῶνας
   elders.   By faith we understand to have been framed the worlds
   ῥήματι Θεοῦ, εἰς τὸ μὴ ἐκ φαινομένων τὰ βλεπόμενα γεγονέ-
   by a word of God,   so as not put things   the   seen   to have
                              of appearing things         come

4 ναι. πίστει πλείονα θυσίαν Ἄβελ παρὰ Κάϊν προσήνεγκε τῷ
   into
   being. By faith a greater sacrifice Abel than   Cain offered
   Θεῷ, δι᾽ ἧς ἐμαρτυρήθη εἶναι δίκαιος, μαρτυροῦντος ἐπὶ τοῖς
   to God, by which he obtained to be righteous,   testifying   over   the
                       witness
   δώροις αὐτοῦ τοῦ Θεοῦ· καὶ δι᾽ αὐτῆς ἀποθανὼν ἔτι λαλεῖ.
   gifts   of him   God, and through it   having died   yet he speaks.

5 πίστει Ἐνὼχ μετετέθη τοῦ μὴ ἰδεῖν θάνατον, καὶ οὐχ
   By faith Enoch was translated   not to see   death,   and not
   εὑρίσκετο, διότι μετέθηκεν αὐτὸν ὁ Θεός· πρὸ γὰρ τῆς μεταθέ-
   was found, because translated   him   God. before For the   trans-

6 σεως αὐτοῦ μεμαρτύρηται εὐηρεστηκέναι τῷ Θεῷ· χωρὶς δὲ
   lating of him he obtained witness to have been pleasing to God; without but
   πίστεως ἀδύνατον εὐαρεστῆσαι· πιστεῦσαι γὰρ δεῖ τὸν
   faith   it is impossible to please (God);   to believe   for   it is the
                                                                  right (one)

(for) him approaching God to believe that He is, and (that) He becomes a rewarder to those seeking Him out. [7] having been warned by God about the things not yet being seen, moved with fear, Noah by faith prepared an ark for (the) salvation of his house; through which he condemned the world, and became the heir of the righteousness according to faith. [8] Having been called out by faith, Abraham obeyed to go to a place which he was about to receive for an inheritance, and went out not understanding where he went. [9] By faith he sojourned in a land of promise as a foreigner, dwelling in tents with Isaac and Jacob, the co-heirs of the same promise; [10] for he was looking forward to the city having foundations, of which the builder and maker (is) God. [11] Also by faith Sarah herself received power for conception of seed even beyond time of age, (and) gave birth; since she deemed the (One) having promised (to be) faithful. [12] Because of this came into being from one even as the stars of the heaven in multitude, and as sand by the seaside, countless; and that (of one) having been dead.

[13] These all died by way of faith, not having ob-

tained the promises, but they seeing from afar, and being persuaded and embracing, and having confessed that they are aliens and sojourners on the earth. [14] For they saying such things make clear that they seek a fatherland. [15] And truly if they remembered that from which they came out, they had time to return —[16] But now they stretch forth to a better; that is, a heavenly (land). Therefore, God is not ashamed (of) them, to be called their God; for He prepared a city for them. [17] Being tested, Abraham by faith offered up Isaac; and he receiving the promises was offering up (his) only-begotten,

προσερχόμενον τῷ Θεῷ, ὅτι ἔστι, καὶ τοῖς ἐκζητοῦσιν αὐτὸν
approaching        God   that He is, and to those seeking out   Him

**7** μισθαποδότης γίνεται. πίστει χρηματισθεὶς Νῶε περὶ τῶν
a rewarder    He becomes. By faith having been warned by God Noah about the things

μηδέπω βλεπομένων, εὐλαβηθεὶς κατεσκεύασε κιβωτὸν εἰς
not yet   being seen, , moved with fear  prepared        an ark    for

σωτηρίαν τοῦ οἴκου αὐτοῦ· δι᾽ ἧς κατέκρινε τὸν κόσμον, καὶ
(the) salvation of the house of him, by which he condemned the world,  and

**8** τῆς κατὰ πίστιν δικαιοσύνης ἐγένετο κληρονόμος. πίστει
of the according to faith righteousness became    heir.      By faith

καλούμενος ᾽Αβραὰμ ὑπήκουσεν ἐξελθεῖν εἰς τὸν τόπον ὃν
having been called, Abraham obeyed   to go forth to  a place which

ἤμελλε λαμβάνειν εἰς κληρονομίαν, καὶ ἐξῆλθε μὴ ἐπιστά-
he was about to receive for an inheritance,  and went forth not under-

**9** μενος ποῦ ἔρχεται. πίστει παρῴκησεν εἰς τὴν γῆν τῆς ἐπαγ-
standing where he went. By faith he sojourned in  a land   of

γελίας, ὡς ἀλλοτρίαν, ἐν σκηναῖς κατοικήσας μετὰ ᾽Ισαὰκ
promise, as a foreigner, in tents   dwelling        with  Isaac

καὶ ᾽Ιακώβ, τῶν συγκληρονόμων τῆς ἐπαγγελίας τῆς αὐτῆς·
and Jacob,  the  co-heirs       of the   promise     same;

**10** ἐξεδέχετο γὰρ τὴν τοὺς θεμελίους ἔχουσαν πόλιν, ἧς τεχνίτης
looked forward for to the  the foundation having    city, of which builder

**11** καὶ δημιουργὸς ὁ Θεός. πίστει καὶ αὐτὴ Σάρρα δύναμιν εἰς
and maker      (was) God. By faith also her(self) Sarah  power   for

καταβολὴν σπέρματος ἔλαβε, καὶ παρὰ καιρὸν ἡλικίας
conception  of seed  received even beyond time   of age,

**12** ἔτεκεν, ἐπεὶ πιστὸν ἡγήσατο τὸν ἐπαγγειλάμενον. διὸ καὶ
gave birth, since faithful she deemed the (One) having promised. Therefore

ἀφ᾽ ἑνὸς ἐγεννήθησαν, καὶ ταῦτα νενεκρωμένου, καθὼς τὰ
from one  came into being —and that (of) one having died — even as the

ἄστρα τοῦ οὐρανοῦ τῷ πλήθει, καὶ ὡσεὶ ἄμμος ἡ παρὰ τὸ
stars of the heaven   in multitude, and as   sand    by the

χεῖλος τῆς θαλάσσης ἡ ἀναρίθμητος.
lip   of the  sea       countless.

**13** Κατὰ πίστιν ἀπέθανον οὗτοι πάντες, μὴ λαβόντες τὰς
By way of faith  died   these  all,    not having received the

ἐπαγγελίας, ἀλλὰ πόρρωθεν αὐτὰς ἰδόντες, καὶ πεισθέντες,
promises,    but  from afar  them   seeing, and being persuaded

καὶ ἀσπασάμενοι, καὶ ὁμολογήσαντες ὅτι ξένοι καὶ παρ-
and having embraced, and having confessed that aliens and so-

**14** επίδημοί εἰσιν ἐπὶ τῆς γῆς. οἱ γὰρ τοιαῦτα λέγοντες ἐμφανί-
journers they are on the earth. those For such things saying    make

**15** ζουσιν ὅτι πατρίδα ἐπιζητοῦσι. καὶ εἰ μὲν ἐκείνης ἐμνη-
clear   that a fatherland they seek.   And if indeed that  they remem-

**16** μόνευον ἀφ᾽ ἧς ἐξῆλθον, εἶχον ἂν καιρὸν ἀνακάμψαι. νυνὶ δὲ
bered  from which they came out, they had time to return.   now But

κρείττονος ὀρέγονται, τοῦτ᾽ ἔστιν, ἐπουρανίου· διὸ οὐκ
a better  stretch forth to, this  is,   a heavenly. Therefore not

ἐπαισχύνεται αὐτοὺς ὁ Θεός, Θεὸς ἐπικαλεῖσθαι αὐτῶν
is ashamed (of)   them   God,  God   to be called   of them;

ἡτοίμασε γὰρ αὐτοῖς πόλιν.
He prepared for  them  a city.

**17** Πίστει προσενήνοχεν ᾽Αβραὰμ τὸν ᾽Ισαὰκ πειραζόμενος,
By faith offered up      Abraham    Isaac,    being tested,

καὶ τὸν μονογενῆ προσέφερεν ὁ τὰς ἐπαγγελίας ἀναδεξά-
and the only-begotten was offering up the (one) the promises   having

[18] as to whom it was said, "In Isaac your seed shall be called;" [19] reckoning that God (was) able to raise even from (the) dead; from where indeed he obtained him in a parable. [20] Concerning coming things, Isaac by faith blessed Jacob and Esau. [21] Dying Jacob by faith blessed each of the sons of Joseph, and worshiped on the top of his staff. [22] Dying Joseph by faith remembered concerning the exodus of the sons of Israel, and gave orders concerning his bones. [23] Moses having been born was by faith hidden by his parents three months, because they saw the child (was) beautiful; and they did not fear the king's decree. [24] Having become great, Moses by faith refused to be called son of Pharaoh's daughter, [25] having chosen rather to suffer affliction with the people of God than for a time to have enjoyment of sin; [26] having deemed the reproach of Christ greater than the riches of Egypt, for he was looking to the reward.

[27] By faith he left Egypt, not fearing the anger of the king, for he kept on as seeing the invisible (One). [28] By faith he made the Passover and the sprinkling of blood, lest the destroyer of the firstborn might touch them. [29] By faith they passed through the Red Sea as through dry (land); (by) which the Egyptian having made trial were swallowed up. [30] By faith the walls of Jericho fell down, having been encircled for seven days. [31] By faith Rahab the harlot did not perish with those who were unbelieving, having received the spies with peace.

[32] And what more may I say? For the time will fail me telling of Gideon, Barak, and also Samson and Jephthah, and also David and Samuel, and of the prophets, [33] who through faith overcame kingdoms, worked out righteousness, obtained

---

18 μενος, πρὸς ὃν ἐλαλήθη ὅτι Ἐν Ἰσαὰκ κληθήσεταί σοι
accepted, as to whom it was spoken —: In Isaac shall be called of you

19 σπέρμα· λογισάμενος ὅτι καὶ ἐκ νεκρῶν ἐγείρειν δυνατὸς ὁ
the seed, reckoning that even from (the) dead to raise (was) able

20 Θεός· ὅθεν αὐτὸν καὶ ἐν παραβολῇ ἐκομίσατο. πίστει περὶ
God, from where him truly in a parable he obtained. By faith concerning

μελλόντων εὐλόγησεν Ἰσαὰκ τὸν Ἰακὼβ καὶ τὸν Ἡσαῦ.
coming things blessed Isaac the Jacob and the Esau.

21 πίστει Ἰακὼβ ἀποθνήσκων ἕκαστον τῶν υἱῶν Ἰωσὴφ
By faith Jacob dying each of the sons of Joseph

εὐλόγησε, καὶ προσεκύνησεν ἐπὶ τὸ ἄκρον τῆς ῥάβδου αὐτοῦ.
blessed, and worshipped on the top of the staff of him.

22 πίστει Ἰωσὴφ τελευτῶν περὶ τῆς ἐξόδου τῶν υἱῶν Ἰσραὴλ
By faith Joseph dying concerning the exodus of the sons of Israel

ἐμνημόνευσε, καὶ περὶ τῶν ὀστέων αὐτοῦ ἐνετείλατο.
remembered, and concerning the bones of him gave orders.

23 πίστει Μωσῆς γεννηθεὶς ἐκρύβη τρίμηνον ὑπὸ τῶν πατέρων
By faith Moses having been born was hidden three months by the parents

αὐτοῦ, διότι εἶδον ἀστεῖον τὸ παιδίον· καὶ οὐκ ἐφοβήθησαν
of him, because they saw (was) fair the child, and not they feared

24 τὸ διάταγμα τοῦ βασιλέως. πίστει Μωσῆς μέγας γενόμενος
the decree of the king. By faith Moses great having become

25 ἠρνήσατο λέγεσθαι υἱὸς θυγατρὸς Φαραω, μᾶλλον ἑλόμενος
refused to be called son of (the) daughter of Pharaoh, rather choosing

συγκακουχεῖσθαι τῷ λαῷ τοῦ Θεοῦ ἢ πρόσκαιρον ἔχειν
to suffer affliction with the people of God, than for a time to have

26 ἁμαρτίας ἀπόλαυσιν· μείζονα πλοῦτον ἡγησάμενος τῶν
of sin enjoyment, greater riches deeming (than) the

ἐν Αἰγύπτῳ θησαυρῶν τὸν ὀνειδισμὸν τοῦ Χριστοῦ· ἀπέ-
of Egypt treasures the reproach of Christ; he was

27 βλεπε γὰρ εἰς τὴν μισθαποδοσίαν. πίστει κατέλιπεν
looking for to the reward. By faith he left

Αἴγυπτον, μὴ φοβηθεὶς τὸν θυμὸν τοῦ βασιλέως· τὸν γὰρ
Egypt, not fearing the anger of the king; the for

28 ἀόρατον ὡς ὁρῶν ἐκαρτέρησε. πίστει πεποίηκε τὸ πάσχα
invisible (One) as seeing he kept on. By faith he made the Passover

καὶ τὴν πρόσχυσιν τοῦ αἵματος, ἵνα μὴ ὁ ὀλοθρεύων τὰ
and the sprinkling of blood, that not He destroying the

29 πρωτότοκα θίγη αὐτῶν. πίστει διέβησαν τὴν ἐρυθρὰν
firstborns should touch them. By faith they went through the Red

θάλασσαν ὡς διὰ ξηρᾶς· ἧς πεῖραν λαβόντες οἱ Αἰγύπτιοι
Sea as through dry, which trial taking the Egyptians

30 κατεπόθησαν. πίστει τὰ τείχη Ἰεριχὼ ἔπεσε, κυκλωθέντα
were swallowed. By faith the walls of Jericho fell, having been circled

31 ἐπὶ ἑπτὰ ἡμέρας. πίστει Ῥαὰβ ἡ πόρνη οὐ συναπώλετο
during seven days. By faith Rahab the harlot did not perish

τοῖς ἀπειθήσασι, δεξαμένη τοὺς κατασκόπους μετ' εἰρήνης.
with those disobeying, receiving the spies with peace.

32 καὶ τί ἔτι λέγω; ἐπιλείψει γάρ με διηγούμενον ὁ χρόνος περὶ
And what still may I say? will fail For me telling the times concerning

Γεδεών, Βαράκ τε καὶ Σαμψὼν καὶ Ἰεφθάε, Δαβίδ τε καὶ
Gideon, Barak, both and Samson and Jephthah, David both and

33 Σαμουὴλ καὶ τῶν προφητῶν· οἳ διὰ πίστεως κατηγωνίσαντο
Samuel, and the prophets, who through faith overcame

βασιλείας, εἰργάσαντο δικαιοσύνην, ἐπέτυχον ἐπαγγελιῶν,
kingdoms, worked out righteousness, obtained promises,

promises, stopped (the) mouths of lions, [34] quenched (the) power of fire, escaped (the) mouths of swords, were empowered from weakness, became strong in war, having made (the) armies of foreigners to yield. [35] Women received their dead by resurrection; and others were tortured, not having accepted deliverance, that they might obtain a better resurrectiȯn; [36] and others received trial of mockings and of scourgings; yea, more, of bonds and of prison. [32] They were stoned; they were tried; they were sawn in two; they died by murder of sword; they went about in sheepskins, in goatskins, being in need, being afflicted, being ill-treated; [38] of whom the world was not worthy: wandering in deserts and mountains and caves and holes of the the earth. [39] And these all, having obtained witness through the faith, did not obtain the promise, [40] God having foreseen something better concerning us, that they should not be perfected apart from us.

CHAPTER 12

[1] Therefore, we having so great a cloud of witnesses encircling us, having laid aside every weight and the easily-surrounding sin, we should run with patience the race lying before us, [2] looking away to the Author and Finisher of our faith, who in view of the joy set before Him endured (the) cross, having despised the shame, sat down at (the) right of the throne of God. [3] For consider well Him who having endured such a contradiction of sinners against Himself, that you do not grow weary, fainting in your souls. [4] You have not yet resisted unto blood, wrestling against sin. [5] And you have forgotten the exhortation which (He) speaks with you, as with sons: "My son, do not despise (the) chastening of

**34** ἔφραξαν στόματα λεόντων, ἔσβεσαν δύναμιν πυρός, ἔφυγον
stopped    mouths   of lions,    quenched (the) power of fire,   escaped

στόματα μαχαίρας, ἐνεδυναμώθησαν ἀπὸ ἀσθενείας, ἐγενή-
mouths of (the) sword,  acquired power       from weakness,  became

θησαν ἰσχυροὶ ἐν πολέμῳ, παρεμβολὰς ἔκλιναν· ἀλλοτρίων.
    strong  in   war,    armies    made to yield of foreigners,

**35** ἔλαβον γυναῖκες ἐξ ἀναστάσεως τοὺς νεκροὺς αὐτῶν· ἄλλοι
received  women   by  resurrection  the   dead   of them; others

δὲ ἐτυμπανίσθησαν, οὐ προσδεξάμενοι τὴν ἀπολύτρωσιν,
but were beaten to death, not   accepting        deliverance,

**36** ἵνα κρείττονος ἀναστάσεως τύχωσιν· ἕτεροι δὲ ἐμπαιγμῶν
that a better   resurrection they might obtain; others and of mockings

καὶ μαστίγων πεῖραν ἔλαβον, ἔτι δὲ δεσμῶν καὶ φυλακῆς·
and of floggings  trial  received, more and, bonds  and  of prison;

**37** ἐλιθάσθησαν, ἐπρίσθησαν, ἐπειράσθησαν, ἐν φόνῳ μαχαίρας
they were stoned, they were tried, they were sawn apart, by murder of sword

ἀπέθανον· περιῆλθον ἐν μηλωταῖς, ἐν αἰγείοις δέρμασιν,
they died, they went about in  sheepskins,   in    goatskins,

**38** ὑστερούμενοι, θλιβόμενοι, κακουχούμενοι (ὦν οὐκ ἦν ἄξιος
being in need,   being afflicted, being ill-treated, of whom not was worthy

ὁ κόσμος), ἐν ἐρημίαις πλανώμενοι καὶ ὄρεσι καὶ σπηλαίοις
the world,  over deserts   wandering   and mountains and  caves

**39** καὶ ταῖς ὀπαῖς τῆς γῆς. καὶ οὗτοι πάντες, μαρτυρηθέντες
and the   holes  of the earth. And these   all    having obtained witness

**40** διὰ τῆς πίστεως, οὐκ ἐκομίσαντο τὴν ἐπαγγελίαν, τοῦ
through the faith   did not obtain    the    promise,

Θεοῦ περὶ ἡμῶν κρεῖττόν τι προβλεψαμένου, ἵνα μὴ χωρὶς
God concerning us  better something having foreseen,  that not without

ἡμῶν τελειωθῶσι.
us they should be perfected.

CHAPTER 12

**1** Τοιγαροῦν καὶ ἡμεῖς, τοσοῦτον ἔχοντες περικείμενον ἡμῖν
So therefore also we,    such      having    encircling    us

νέφος μαρτύρων, ὄγκον ἀποθέμενοι πάντα καὶ τὴν εὐπερί-
a cloud of witnesses, weight  laying aside  every  and the easily sur-

στατον ἁμαρτίαν, δι' ὑπομονῆς τρέχωμεν τὸν προκείμενον
rounding   sin,   through patience let us run  the set before

**2** ἡμῖν ἀγῶνα, ἀφορῶντες εἰς τὸν τῆς πίστεως ἀρχηγὸν καὶ
us   race,   looking   to the of the  faith    Author   and

τελειωτὴν Ἰησοῦν, ὅς, ἀντὶ τῆς προκειμένης αὐτῷ χαρᾶς,
Finisher,  Jesus, who against the  set before   Him   joy

ὑπέμεινε σταυρόν, αἰσχύνης καταφρονήσας, ἐν δεξιᾷ τε τοῦ
endured (the) cross,  (the) shame   despising,    at (the) right and of the

**3** θρόνου τοῦ Θεοῦ ἐκάθισεν. ἀναλογίσασθε γὰρ τὸν τοιαυτην
throne   of God  sat down.   consider      For the (One) such

ὑπομεμενηκότα ὑπὸ τῶν ἁμαρτωλῶν εἰς αὐτὸν ἀντιλογίαν,
having endured   by   of sinners   against Himself contradiction,

**4** ἵνα μὴ κάμητε ταῖς ψυχαῖς ὑμῶν ἐκλυόμενοι. οὔπω μέχρις
lest you grow weary in the souls of you  fainting   Not yet  unto

αἵματος ἀντικατέστητε πρὸς τὴν ἁμαρτίαν ἀνταγωνιζόμε-
blood   you resisted   against the   sin     wrestling,

**5** νοι· καὶ ἐκλέλησθε τῆς παρακλήσεως, ἥτις ὑμῖν ὡς υἱοῖς
and you have forgotten the exhortation,   which with you as with sons

διαλέγεται, Υἱέ μου, μὴ ὀλιγώρει παιδείας Κυρίου, μηδὲ
(He) speaks:  Son of Me, do not despise (the) chastening of (the) Lord, nor

the Lord, nor faint being corrected by Him. [6] For whom (the) Lord loves, He disciplines, and whips every son He receives." [7] If you endure discipline, God is dealing with you as with sons—for who is (the) son whom a father does not discipline? [8] But if you are without discipline, of which all have become partakers, then you are bastards, and not sons. [9] Furthermore, we have had fathers of our flesh (as) correctors, and we respected (them); shall we not much more be subject to the Father of spirits, and we shall live? [10] For they truly disciplined (us) for a few days according to that seeming good to them; but He for (our) profit, in order (for us) to partake of His holiness. [11] And all discipline for the present does not seem to be joyous, but grievous; but afterwards it gives back righteousness to those having been exercised through it.

[12] For this reason, straighten up the hands hanging alongside, and the enfeebled knees; [13] and make straight tracks for your feet, that the lame not be turned aside, but rather healed. [14] Eagerly pursue peace and holiness with all, without which no one will see the Lord; [15] watching diligently lest any root of bitterness growing up trouble (you), and through this many be defiled; [16] lest any fornicator, or profane one, as Esau, who for one feeding gave up his birthright; [17] for you know also that afterwards desiring to inherit the blessing, he was rejected, for he found no place of repentance, although seeking it with tears.

[18] For you have not drawn near to (the) mountain being touched, and having been lit with fire; and to gloom and darkness and tempest, [19] and of a trumpet's sound, and to a voice of words; which those hearing begged that not a word be added to them; [20] for they could not bear that (which) was

---

6 ἐκλύου ὑπ' αὐτοῦ ἐλεγχόμενος· ὃν γὰρ ἀγαπᾷ Κύριος
faint by Him being corrected, whom for loves (the) Lord

7 παιδεύει· μαστιγοῖ δὲ πάντα υἱὸν ὃν παραδέχεται. εἰ
He disciplines, whips and every son whom He receives. If

παιδείαν ὑπομένετε, ὡς υἱοῖς ὑμῖν προσφέρεται ὁ Θεός· τίς
discipline you endure, as with sons with you is dealing God, who

8 γάρ ἐστιν υἱὸς ὃν οὐ παιδεύει πατήρ; εἰ δὲ χωρίς ἐστε
for is son, whom not disciplines a father? if But without you are

παιδείας, ἧς μέτοχοι γεγόνασι πάντες, ἄρα νόθοι ἐστὲ καὶ
discipline, of which sharers have become all, then bastards you are and

9 οὐχ υἱοί. εἶτα τοὺς μὲν τῆς σαρκὸς ἡμῶν πατέρας εἴχομεν
not sons. Moreover the of the flesh of us fathers we had

παιδευτάς, καὶ ἐνετρεπόμεθα· οὐ πολλῷ μᾶλλον ὑποταγησό-
(as) correctors, and we respected (them); not much more shall we be subject

10 μεθα τῷ πατρὶ τῶν πνευμάτων, καὶ ζήσομεν; οἱ μὲν γὰρ
to the Father of spirits, and we shall live? they truly For

πρὸς ὀλίγας ἡμέρας κατὰ τὸ δοκοῦν αὐτοῖς ἐπαίδευον· ὁ δὲ
for a few days according to the seeming good thing to them disciplined (us). He But

ἐπὶ τὸ συμφέρον, εἰς τὸ μεταλαβεῖν τῆς ἁγιότητος αὐτοῦ.
for the profit, to partake of the holiness of Him.

11 πᾶσα δὲ παιδεία πρὸς μὲν τὸ παρὸν οὐ δοκεῖ χαρᾶς εἶναι,
all And discipline for indeed the present does not seem of joy to be,

ἀλλὰ λύπης· ὕστερον δὲ καρπὸν εἰρηνικὸν τοῖς δι' αὐτῆς
but of grief; later but fruit peaceable to those through it

12 γεγυμνασμένοις ἀποδίδωσι δικαιοσύνης. διὸ τὰς παρειμένας
having been exercised it gives back of righteousness. Therefore the alongside

13 χεῖρας καὶ τὰ παραλελυμένα γόνατα ἀνορθώσατε· καὶ
hands and the enfeebled knees straighten up, and

τροχιὰς ὀρθὰς ποιήσατε τοῖς ποσὶν ὑμῶν, ἵνα μὴ τὸ χωλὸν
tracks straight make for the feet of you, that not the lame

ἐκτραπῇ, ἰαθῇ δὲ μᾶλλον.
be turned aside, be healed but rather.

14 Εἰρήνην διώκετε μετὰ πάντων, καὶ τὸν ἁγιασμόν, οὗ
peace Follow with all, and holiness, which

15 χωρὶς οὐδεὶς ὄψεται τὸν Κύριον· ἐπισκοποῦντες μή τις
without no one will see the Lord, watching diligently lest any

ὑστερῶν ἀπὸ τῆς χάριτος τοῦ Θεοῦ· μή τις ῥίζα πικρίας
lack from the grace of God, lest any root of bitterness

16 ἄνω φύουσα ἐνοχλῇ, καὶ διὰ ταύτης μιανθῶσι πολλοί· μή
up growing disturb, and through this be defiled many; lest

τις πόρνος, ἢ βέβηλος, ὡς Ἠσαῦ, ὃς ἀντὶ βρώσεως μιᾶς
any fornicator, or profane one, as Esau, who for feeding one

17 ἀπέδοτο τὰ πρωτοτόκια αὐτοῦ. ἴστε γὰρ ὅτι καὶ μετέπειτα,
gave up the birthright of him. you know for that indeed afterwards

θέλων κληρονομῆσαι τὴν εὐλογίαν, ἀπεδοκιμάσθη· μετανοίας
desiring to inherit the blessing, he was rejected, of repentance

γὰρ τόπον οὐχ εὗρε, καίπερ μετὰ δακρύων ἐκζητήσας αὐτήν.
for place not he found, though with tears seeking it.

18 Οὐ γὰρ προσεληλύθατε ψηλαφωμένῳ ὄρει, καὶ κεκαυ-
not For you have drawn near being touched (the) mountain, and having

19 μένῳ πυρί, καὶ γνόφῳ, καὶ σκότῳ, καὶ θυέλλῃ, καὶ σάλπιγ-
been lit with fire, and to gloom and darkness and tempest, and of trumpet,

γος ἤχῳ, καὶ φωνῇ ῥημάτων, ἧς οἱ ἀκούσαντες παρῃτή-
to a sound, and to a voice of words, which those hearing begged

20 σαντο μὴ προστεθῆναι αὐτοῖς λόγον· οὐκ ἔφερον γὰρ τὸ
not to be added to them a word; not they bore for that

enjoined: "Even if a beast touches the mountain, it will be stoned, or shot through with a dart." [21] And, so fearful was the thing appearing, Moses said, "I am terrified and trembling." [22] But you have drawn near to Mount Zion, even the city of (the) living God, to a heavenly Jerusalem, and to myriads of angels, [23] and to an assembly, a church of firstborn ones having been enrolled in Heaven; and to God (the) judge of all, and to spirits of just ones who have been perfected; [24] and to Jesus (the) Mediator of a new covenant; and to blood of sprinkling, speaking better things than (that) of Abel. [25] Watch (that) you do not refuse the (One) speaking; for if these did not escape who refused (the One) divinely warning (them) on earth, much rather we, those turning away from Heaven; [26] whose voice shook the earth then, but now He has promised, saying, "Yet once I will shake not only the earth, but also the heaven." [27] Now the (words), Yet once, makes clear the removal of the (things) being shaken, as having been made, that may remain the things not shaken. [28] Therefore, receiving an unshakeable kingdom, let us have grace, through which, we may serve God pleasingly, with reverence and awe; [29] for also, "Our God (is) a consuming fire."

CHAPTER 13

[1] Let brotherly love continue. [2] Do not forget hospitality, for by this some unknowingly took in angels as guests. [3] Be mindful of the prisoners, as having been bound with (them); of those ill-treated, as also being in the body yourselves. [4] Marriage (is) honorable in all, and the bed undefiled; but God will judge fornicators and adulterers. [5] (Set your) way of life without money-loving, being satisfied with present things; for He has said, "I will not at all leave you nor will I forsake you at all." [6] So that we may boldly say, (The) Lord (is) my helper, and I will not

---

διαστελλόμενον, Κἄν θηρίον θίγῃ τοῦ ὄρους, λιθοβοληθή-
being enjoined:     If even a beast touches the  mountain, it will be stoned;

21 σεται ἢ βολίδι κατατοξευθήσεται· καί, οὕτω φοβερὸν ἦν τὸ
or with a dart  shot through;    and,  so   fearful was the thing

φανταζόμενον, Μωσῆς εἶπεν, Ἔκφοβός εἰμι καὶ ἔντρομος.
appearing,    Moses   said:   terrified I am, and   trembling.

22 ἀλλὰ προσεληλύθατε Σιὼν ὄρει, καὶ πόλει Θεοῦ ζῶντος,
But   you have drawn near Zion Mount, and a city   God of (the) living.

23 Ἱερουσαλὴμ ἐπουρανίῳ, καὶ μυριάσιν ἀγγέλων, πανηγύρει
Jerusalem    to a heavenly, and to myriads of angels, to an assembly

καὶ ἐκκλησίᾳ πρωτοτόκων ἐν οὐρανοῖς ἀπογεγραμμένων,
and, a church  of firstborn ones in   Heaven having been enrolled,

καὶ κριτῇ Θεῷ πάντων, καὶ πνεύμασι δικαίων τετελειω-
and (the) judge God of all,   and  to spirits  of just ones having been

24 μένων, καὶ διαθήκης νέας μεσίτῃ Ἰησοῦ, καὶ αἵματι ῥαντι-
perfected, and covenant of a new Mediator to Jesus, and to blood  of

25 σμοῦ κρείττονα λαλοῦντι παρὰ τὸ Ἄβελ. βλέπετε μὴ
sprinkling a better things speaking  than (that)  of Abel. Watch (that) not

παραιτήσησθε τὸν λαλοῦντα. εἰ γὰρ ἐκεῖνοι οὐκ ἔφυγον, τὸν
you refuse    the (One) speaking; if for   these did not escape

ἐπὶ τῆς γῆς παραιτησάμενοι χρηματίζοντα, πολλῷ μᾶλλον
on the earth  refusing    (the One) divinely warning,   much   rather

26 ἡμεῖς οἱ τὸν ἀπ᾽ οὐρανῶν ἀποστρεφόμενοι· οὗ ἡ φωνὴ τὴν
we, those    from Heaven     turning away;  of whom the voice the

γῆν ἐσάλευσε τότε, νῦν δὲ ἐπήγγελται, λέγων, Ἔτι ἅπαξ
earth shook    then, now but He has promised, saying, Yet   once

27 ἐγὼ σείω οὐ μόνον τὴν γῆν, ἀλλὰ καὶ τὸν οὐρανόν. τὸ δέ,
I  shake not only the  earth, but also  the  Heaven. the (words) Now,

Ἔτι ἅπαξ, δηλοῖ τῶν σαλευομένων τὴν μετάθεσιν, ὡς
Yet   once, makes clear of the (things) being shaken the  removal,   as

28 πεποιημένων, ἵνα μείνῃ τὰ μὴ σαλευόμενα. διὸ βασιλείαν
having been made, that may remain the things not shaken. Therefore kingdom

ἀσάλευτον παραλαμβάνοντες, ἔχωμεν χάριν, δι᾽ ἧς λα-
an unshakeable receiving,      let us have  grace, through which we

29 τρεύωμεν εὐαρέστως τῷ Θεῷ μετὰ αἰδοῦς καὶ εὐλαβείας· καὶ
may serve well-pleasingly   God with reverence and   fear;  truly

γὰρ ὁ Θεὸς ἡμῶν πῦρ καταναλίσκον.
for the God of us  fire a consuming (is).

CHAPTER 13

1 Ἡ φιλαδελφία μενέτω. τῆς φιλοξενίας μὴ ἐπιλανθάνεσθε·
brotherly love Let remain.   of hospitality Be not forgetful,

2 διὰ ταύτης γὰρ ἔλαθόν τινες ξενίσαντες ἀγγέλους. μιμνή-
through this  for unknowingly some entertained  angels.   Be

3 σκεσθε τῶν δεσμίων, ὡς συνδεδεμένοι· τῶν κακουχουμένων,
mindful of the prisoners,  as being bound with (them), of those ill-treated,

4 ὡς καὶ αὐτοὶ ὄντες ἐν σώματι. τίμιος ὁ γάμος ἐν πᾶσι, καὶ ἡ
as also yourselves, being in the body. honorable marriage (is) in  all, and the

5 κοίτη ἀμίαντος· πόρνους δὲ καὶ μοιχοὺς κρινεῖ ὁ Θεός. ἀφιλ-
bed     undefiled; fornicators but and adulterers will judge God. (Let be)

άργυρος ὁ τρόπος, ἀρκούμενοι τοῖς παροῦσιν· αὐτὸς γὰρ
without  the way of life, being satisfied with the  present things; He   for
money-loving

6 εἴρηκεν, Οὐ μή σε ἀνῶ, οὐδ᾽ οὐ μή σε ἐγκαταλίπω. ὥστε
has said,   Not at all you leave, nor in any way you will I forsake. So that
will I

θαρροῦντας ἡμᾶς λέγειν, Κύριος ἐμοὶ βοηθός, καὶ οὐ φοβηθή-
may confidently we   say, (The) Lord to me (is) a helper, and not I will be

be afraid; what shall man do to me?

[7] Remember your leaders, who have spoken the word of God to you; of whom considering the result of the conduct, imitate (their) faith: [8] Jesus Christ, the same yesterday and today and forever. [9] Do not be carried away with various and strange teaching; for (it is) good (that) the heart be confirmed by grace, not by foods; in which those who walked (in them) were not profited. [10] We have an altar of which they who serve the tabernacle have no right to eat. [11] For of those animals whose blood is brought for sin into the Holies by the high priest, of these the bodies are burned outside the camp. [12] Because of this Jesus also, that He might sanctify the people by His own blood, suffered outside the gate. [13] Therefore let us go out to Him outside the camp, bearing His reproach. [14] For we do not have here a lasting city, but we are seeking the coming one. [15] By Him, then, we should offer (the) sacrifice of praise to God continually, that is, (the) fruit of the lips, confessing to His name. [16] But do not be forgetful of doing good and of sharing, for with such sacrifices God is well-pleased. [17] Obey your leaders, and be submissive; for they watch for your souls as (ones) about to give account; that they may do this with joy, and not groaning, for this (would be) unprofitable for you. [18] Pray for us; for we trust that we have a good conscience, in all things wishing to conduct ourselves well. [19] But I much more exhort (you) to do this, that I may more quickly be restored to you.

[20] Now the God of peace, who brought again from among (the) dead the

σομαι τί ποιήσει μοι ἄνθρωπος.
afraid; what shall do to me       man?

**7** Μνημονεύετε τῶν ἡγουμένων ὑμῶν, οἵτινες ἐλάλησαν ὑμῖν
Remember   the   leaders   of you,   who   spoke   to you
τὸν λόγον τοῦ Θεοῦ· ὧν ἀναθεωροῦντες τὴν ἔκβασιν τῆς
the   word   of God, of whom considering   the   issue   of the

**8** ἀναστροφῆς, μιμεῖσθε τὴν πίστιν. Ἰησοῦς Χριστὸς χθὲς καὶ
conduct,   imitate (their) faith.   Jesus   Christ yesterday and

**9** σήμερον ὁ αὐτός, καὶ εἰς τοὺς αἰῶνας. διδαχαῖς ποικίλαις καὶ
today (is) the same, even to the   ages.   teaching By various   and
ξέναις μὴ περιφέρεσθε· καλὸν γὰρ χάριτι βεβαιοῦσθαι τὴν
strange not do be carried away; good (it is) for by grace to be confirmed the
καρδίαν, οὐ βρώμασιν, ἐν οἷς οὐκ ὠφελήθησαν οἱ περιπατή-
heart,   not by foods,   by which not were profited those walking.

**10** σαντες. ἔχομεν θυσιαστήριον, ἐξ οὗ φαγεῖν οὐκ ἔχουσιν
We have   an altar   of which to eat   not   have

**11** ἐξουσίαν οἱ τῇ σκηνῇ λατρεύοντες. ὧν γὰρ εἰσφέρεται ζώων
authority those the tabernacle serving.   of what For is brought   animals
τὸ αἷμα περὶ ἁμαρτίας εἰς τὰ ἅγια διὰ τοῦ ἀρχιερέως, τούτων
the blood concerning sins into the Holies via the high priest,   of these

**12** τὰ σώματα κατακαίεται ἔξω τῆς παρεμβολῆς. διὸ καὶ
the   bodies   are burned   outside the   camp.   Therefore indeed
Ἰησοῦς, ἵνα ἁγιάσῃ διὰ τοῦ ἰδίου αἵματος τὸν λαόν, ἔξω τῆς
Jesus,   that He might sanctify through the own blood   the people, outside the

**13** πύλης ἔπαθε. τοίνυν ἐξερχώμεθα πρὸς αὐτὸν ἔξω τῆς παρ-
gate suffered.   So   let us go forth   to   Him outside the

**14** εμβολῆς, τὸν ὀνειδισμὸν αὐτοῦ φέροντες. οὐ γὰρ ἔχομεν ὧδε
camp,   the reproach   of Him   bearing. not For we have here

**15** μένουσαν πόλιν, ἀλλὰ τὴν μέλλουσαν ἐπιζητοῦμεν. δι'
a continuing city,   but the (one) coming   we seek. Through
αὐτοῦ οὖν ἀναφέρωμεν θυσίαν αἰνέσεως διὰ παντὸς τῷ Θεῷ,
Him, therefore, let us offer up a sacrifice of praise   always   to God,
τοῦτ' ἔστι, καρπὸν χειλέων ὁμολογούντων τῷ ὀνόματι
this   is, (the) fruit   of the lips,   confessing   to the   name

**16** αὐτοῦ. τῆς δὲ εὐποιΐας καὶ κοινωνίας μὴ ἐπιλανθάνεσθε·
of Him. of the But doing good   and   sharing, do not be forgetful;

**17** τοιαύταις γὰρ θυσίαις εὐαρεστεῖται ὁ Θεός. πείθεσθε τοῖς
with such   for sacrifices is well-pleased   God.   Obey   those
ἡγουμένοις ὑμῶν, καὶ ὑπείκετε· αὐτοὶ γὰρ ἀγρυπνοῦσιν
leading   of you, and submit to (them),   they   for   watch
ὑπὲρ τῶν ψυχῶν ὑμῶν, ὡς λόγον ἀποδώσοντες· ἵνα μετὰ
for   the   souls   of you, an account   giving,   that with
χαρᾶς τοῦτο ποιῶσι, καὶ μὴ στενάζοντες· ἀλυσιτελὲς γὰρ
joy   this they may do,   and not (with) groaning.; profitless   for
ὑμῖν τοῦτο.
to you this (would be).

**18** Προσεύχεσθε περὶ ἡμῶν· πεποίθαμεν γὰρ ὅτι καλὴν
Pray   concerning us,   we are persuaded for that a good
συνείδησιν ἔχομεν, ἐν πᾶσι καλῶς θέλοντες ἀναστρέφεσθαι.
conscience we have, in all   well   desiring to conduct (ourselves).

**19** περισσοτέρως δὲ παρακαλῶ τοῦτο ποιῆσαι, ἵνα τάχιον
more abundantly But I exhort (you)   this   to do,   that sooner
ἀποκατασταθῶ ὑμῖν.
I may be restored   to you.

**20** Ὁ δὲ Θεὸς τῆς εἰρήνης, ὁ ἀναγαγὼν ἐκ νεκρῶν τὸν
the Now   God   of peace, He having led up out of (the) dead, the

ποιμένα τῶν προβάτων τὸν μέγαν ἐν αἵματι διαθήκης
Shepherd of the      sheep         great, in (the) blood of a covenant

great Shepherd of the sheep, **21** αἰωνίου, τὸν Κύριον ἡμῶν Ἰησοῦν, καταρτίσαι ὑμᾶς ἐν
in (the) blood of (the) eter- eternal,    the Lord    of us,   Jesus,   perfect    you    in
nal covenant, our Lord Jesus
[21] perfect you in every παντὶ ἔργῳ ἀγαθῷ εἰς τὸ ποιῆσαι τὸ θέλημα αὐτοῦ, ποιῶν
good work, in order to do every  work   good, in order to do    the  will  of Him, doing
His will, working in you
that which (is) ἐν ὑμῖν τὸ εὐάρεστον ἐνώπιον αὐτοῦ, διὰ Ἰησοῦ Χριστοῦ·
well-pleasing in His sight, in you the thing pleasing  before   Him, through  Jesus  Christ,
through Jesus Christ — to
whom (be) glory forever ᾧ ἡ δόξα εἰς τοὺς αἰῶνας τῶν αἰώνων. ἀμήν.
and ever. Amen. [22] And to whom (be) the glory to the ages of the  ages.    Amen.
I exhort you, brothers,
bear the word of **22** Παρακαλῶ δὲ ὑμᾶς, ἀδελφοί, ἀνέχεσθε τοῦ λόγου τῆς
exhortation, for also in few      I exhort   And you,   brothers,  endure   the    word
words I wrote to you.
**23** παρακλήσεως· καὶ γὰρ διὰ βραχέων ἐπέστειλα ὑμῖν. γινώ-
[23] You know (that) of exhortation; indeed for through few (words) I wrote   to you. Know
the brother Timothy has
been released; with whom, σκετε τὸν ἀδελφὸν Τιμόθεον ἀπολελυμένον, μεθ᾽ οὗ, ἐὰν τάχιον
if he should come sooner, I       the   brother,   Timothy, having been freed, with whom, if sooner
will see you. [24] Greet all
your leaders, and all the ἔρχηται, ὄψομαι ὑμᾶς.
saints. They from Italy I come,    I will see  you.
greet you. [25] Grace (be)
with you all. Amen. **24** Ἀσπάσασθε πάντας τοὺς ἡγουμένους ὑμῶν, καὶ πάντας
Greet       all      those   leading    of you,  and   all

τοὺς ἁγίους. ἀσπάζονται ὑμᾶς οἱ ἀπὸ τῆς Ἰταλίας.
the   saints.    greet        you Those from      Italy.

**25** Ἡ χάρις μετὰ πάντων ὑμῶν. ἀμήν.
Grace (be) with all    of you.   Amen.

# ΙΑΚΩΒΟΥ
## OF JAMES
# ΕΠΙΣΤΟΛΗ ΚΑΘΟΛΙΚΗ
### EPISTLE    GENERAL

KING JAMES II VERSION

THE

GENERAL EPISTLE OF

JAMES

## CHAPTER 1

[1] James, a slave of God and of (the) Lord Jesus Christ, to the twelve tribes which (are) in the Dispersion, greeting: [2] My brothers, count (it) all joy when you fall into different kinds of temptations, [3] knowing that the proving of your faith works patience. [4] But let patience have (its) perfect work, that you may be perfect and complete, lacking nothing. [5] But if any of you lack wisdom, let him ask from God who gives to all freely, and does not reproach, and it shall be given to him. [6] But let him ask in faith, doubting nothing. For he who doubts is like a wave of (the) sea, being driven by the wind and being tossed; [7] for do not let that man think that he shall receive anything from the Lord; [8] (he is) a double-minded man, not dependable in all his ways. [9] But let (the) brother (who is) low rejoice in his lifting up; [10] and the rich in his humiliation, because he will pass away like (the) flower of (the) grass. [11] For the sun rose with burning heat, and dried up the grass, and the flower of it fell, and the beauty of its appearance perished; so also the rich will fade away in his ways. [12] Blessed (is the) man who endures temptation, for having been tried he will receive the crown of life which the Lord promised to those who (are) loving Him. [13] Let no one being tempted say, I am tempted

## CHAPTER 1

**1** Ἰάκωβος, Θεοῦ καὶ Κυρίου Ἰησοῦ Χριστοῦ δοῦλος, ταῖς
James,  of God and of (the) Lord Jesus Christ    a slave,  to the
δώδεκα φυλαῖς ταῖς ἐν τῇ διασπορᾷ, χαίρειν.
twelve  tribes    in the    dispersion, greeting.

**2** Πᾶσαν χαρὰν ἡγήσασθε, ἀδελφοί μου, ὅταν πειρασμοῖς
all    joy    Count (it),    brothers of me, when  you fall

**3** περιπέσητε ποικίλοις, γινώσκοντες ὅτι τὸ δοκίμιον ὑμῶν τῆς
into various  temptations,   knowing    that the proving  of you the

**4** πίστεως κατεργάζεται ὑπομονήν· ἡ δὲ ὑπομονὴ ἔργον
faith    works    patience.   And patience  work
τέλειον ἐχέτω, ἵνα ἦτε τέλειοι καὶ ὁλόκληροι, ἐν μηδενὶ λειπό-
perfect let it have, that you may be perfect and entire,  in  nothing lacking.
μενοι.

**5** Εἰ δέ τις ὑμῶν λείπεται σοφίας, αἰτείτω παρὰ τοῦ διδόντος
if But any of you  lacks  wisdom, let him ask from  giving
Θεοῦ πᾶσιν ἁπλῶς, καὶ μὴ ὀνειδίζοντος, καὶ δοθήσεται αὐτῷ.
God to all  freely, and not  reproaching,  and it will be given to him.

**6** αἰτείτω δὲ ἐν πίστει, μηδὲν διακρινόμενος· ὁ γὰρ διακρινό-
let him ask But in faith, nothing  doubting,   the (one) for doubting
μενος ἔοικε κλύδωνι θαλάσσης ἀνεμιζομένῳ καὶ ῥιπιζομένῳ.
(is) like  a wave  of (the) sea, being driven by wind and tossed.

**7** μὴ γὰρ οἰέσθω ὁ ἄνθρωπος ἐκεῖνος ὅτι λήψεταί τι παρὰ τοῦ
not For let suppose   man    that that he will receive anything from the

**8** Κυρίου. ἀνὴρ δίψυχος ἀκατάστατος ἐν πάσαις ταῖς ὁδοῖς
Lord,   a man two-souled undependable  in  all   the  ways
αὐτοῦ.
of him.

**9**
**10** Καυχάσθω δὲ ὁ ἀδελφὸς ὁ ταπεινὸς ἐν τῷ ὕψει αὐτοῦ· ὁ
let boast  But the brother  humble  in the height of him; the
δὲ πλούσιος ἐν τῇ ταπεινώσει αὐτοῦ· ὅτι ὡς ἄνθος χόρτου
and the rich one in the  humiliation  of him, because as a flower of grass

**11** παρελεύσεται. ἀνέτειλε γὰρ ὁ ἥλιος σὺν τῷ καύσωνι, καὶ
he will pass away.  rose  For the sun  with  the hot wind and
ἐξήρανε τὸν χόρτον, καὶ τὸ ἄνθος αὐτοῦ ἐξέπεσε, καὶ ἡ εὐπρέ-
dried  the  grass,  and the flower of it  fell out, and the beauty
πεια τοῦ προσώπου αὐτοῦ ἀπώλετο· οὕτω καὶ ὁ πλούσιος
of the appearance  of it  perished;  so also  the rich one
ἐν ταῖς πορείαις αὐτοῦ μαρανθήσεται.
in the  goings  of him will fade away.

**12** Μακάριος ἀνὴρ ὃς ὑπομένει πειρασμόν· ὅτι δόκιμος γενό-
Blessed (the) man who endures temptation, because approved having
μενος λήψεται τὸν στέφανον τῆς ζωῆς, ὃν ἐπηγγείλατο ὁ
become he will receive the crown   of life, which  promised  the

**13** Κύριος τοῖς ἀγαπῶσιν αὐτόν. μηδεὶς πειραζόμενος λεγέτω
Lord to those  loving    Him.  no one  being tempted Let say,

526

from God. For God is not to be tempted by evils, and Himself tempts no one. [14] But each one is tempted by his own lust, being drawn away and being seduced. [15] Then lust having conceived gives birth to sin. And sin having been finished brings forth death. [16] Do not be led astray, my beloved brothers, [17] every act of giving good and every perfect gift is from above, coming down from the Father of lights, with whom there is no change, nor shadow of turning. [18] Having willed (it), He brought us forth by (the) word of truth, for us to be a kind of firstfruits of His creatures.

[19] So that, my beloved brothers, let every man be swift to hear, slow to speak, slow to anger. [20] For man's anger does not work out (the) righteousness of God. [21] For this reason, having laid aside all filthiness and overflowing of wickedness, in meekness receive the implanted word which (is) able to save your souls. [22] But be doers of (the) word, and not hearers only, deceiving yourselves. [23] Because if anyone is a hearer of (the) word and not a doer, this one is like a man studying his natural face in a mirror; [24] for he studied himself, and has gone away, and immediately forgot what he was like. [25] But he that looked into the perfect law of liberty, and (is) continuing in (it), this one not having been a forgetful hearer, but a doer of (the) work, this one shall be blessed in his doing. [26] If anyone thinks to be religious among you, not bridling his tongue, but deceiving his heart, this one's religion (is) vain. [27] Pure and undefiled religion before God and (the) Father is this, to visit orphans and widows in their afflictions, to keep oneself unspotted from the world.

ὅτι ᾿Απὸ τοῦ Θεοῦ πειράζομαι· ὁ γὰρ Θεὸς ἀπείραστός ἐστι
From God I am tempted. For God not tempted is

14 κακῶν, πειράζει δὲ αὐτὸς οὐδένα· ἕκαστος δὲ πειράζεται,
by evils, tempts and He no one. each one But is tempted

15 ὑπὸ τῆς ἰδίας ἐπιθυμίας ἐξελκόμενος καὶ δελεαζόμενος. εἶτα
by the own lusts being drawn out and being seduced; then

ἡ ἐπιθυμία συλλαβοῦσα τίκτει ἁμαρτίαν· ἡ δὲ ἁμαρτία
lust having conceived produces sin; and sin

16 ἀποτελεσθεῖσα ἀποκύει θάνατον. μὴ πλανᾶσθε, ἀδελφοί
being fully formed brings forth death. Do not go astray, brothers

17 μου ἀγαπητοί. πᾶσα δόσις ἀγαθὴ καὶ πᾶν δώρημα τέλειον
of me beloved. Every giving good and every gift perfect

ἄνωθέν ἐστι, καταβαῖνον ἀπὸ τοῦ πατρὸς τῶν φώτων, παρ'
from above is, coming down from the Father of lights, with

18 ᾧ οὐκ ἔνι παραλλαγή, ἢ τροπῆς ἀποσκίασμα. βουληθεὶς
whom not there is variation or of turning shadow. Having purposed

ἀπεκύησεν ἡμᾶς λόγῳ ἀληθείας, εἰς τὸ εἶναι ἡμᾶς ἀπαρχήν
He brought forth us by a word of truth, for to be us firstfruit

τινα τῶν αὐτοῦ κτισμάτων.
a certain of the of Him creatures.

19 ῞Ωστε, ἀδελφοί μου ἀγαπητοί, ἔστω πᾶς ἄνθρωπος ταχὺς
So that, , brothers of me beloved, let be every man swift

εἰς τὸ ἀκοῦσαι, βραδὺς εἰς τὸ λαλῆσαι, βραδὺς εἰς ὀργήν·
to hear, slow to speak, slow to wrath;

20 ὀργὴ γὰρ ἀνδρὸς δικαιοσύνην Θεοῦ οὐ κατεργάζεται. διὸ
(the) wrath for of man (the) righteousness of God not works. Therefore,

21 ἀποθέμενοι πᾶσαν ῥυπαρίαν καὶ περισσείαν κακίας, ἐν πραΰ-
putting away all filthiness and overflowing of evil, in meek-

τητι, δέξασθε τὸν ἔμφυτον λόγον, τὸν δυνάμενον σῶσαι τὰς
ness receive the implanted word being able to save the

22 ψυχὰς ὑμῶν. γίνεσθε δὲ ποιηταὶ λόγου, καὶ μὴ μόνον
soul of you. become And doers of the word, and not only

23 ἀκροαταί, παραλογιζόμενοι ἑαυτούς. ὅτι εἴ τις ἀκροατὴς
hearers, deceiving yourselves. Because if anyone a hearer

λόγου ἐστὶ καὶ οὐ ποιητής, οὗτος ἔοικεν ἀνδρὶ κατανοοῦντι
of (the) word is, and not a doer, this one is like a man perceiving

24 τὸ πρόσωπον τῆς γενέσεως αὐτοῦ ἐν ἐσόπτρῳ· κατενόησε
the face of the birth of him in a mirror; he perceived

γὰρ ἑαυτὸν καὶ ἀπελήλυθε, καὶ εὐθέως ἐπελάθετο ὁποῖος ἦν.
for himself and has gone away, and immediately forgot what sort he was.

25 ὁ δὲ παρακύψας εἰς νόμον τέλειον τὸν τῆς ἐλευθερίας καὶ
he But having looked into law perfect the of freedom, and

παραμείνας, οὗτος οὐκ ἀκροατὴς ἐπιλησμονῆς γενόμενος,
continuing, this one not a hearer of forgetfulness becoming,

ἀλλὰ ποιητὴς ἔργου, οὗτος μακάριος ἐν τῇ ποιήσει αὐτοῦ
but a doer of (the) work, this one blessed in the doing of him

26 ἔσται. εἴ τις δοκεῖ θρῆσκος εἶναι ἐν ὑμῖν, μὴ χαλιναγωγῶν
will be. If anyone thinks religious to be among you, not bridling

γλῶσσαν αὐτοῦ, ἀλλ' ἀπατῶν καρδίαν αὐτοῦ, τούτου
the tongue of him, but deceiving (the) heart of himself, this one's

27 μάταιος ἡ θρησκεία. θρησκεία καθαρὰ καὶ ἀμίαντος παρὰ
vain the religion (is). religion Clean and undefiled before

τῷ Θεῷ καὶ πατρὶ αὕτη ἐστίν, ἐπισκέπτεσθαι ὀρφανοὺς καὶ
God and Father this is, to visit orphans and

χήρας ἐν τῇ θλίψει αὐτῶν, ἄσπιλον ἑαυτὸν τηρεῖν ἀπὸ τοῦ
widows in the affliction of them, unspotted himself to keep from the

## CHAPTER 2

[1] My brothers, do not with partiality to persons have the faith of our Lord Jesus Christ, (the Lord) of glory. [2] For if a man comes into your synagogue with gold rings, and splendid clothing, and (if) a poor one also comes in dirty clothing; [3] and you look on him who wears the splendid clothing, and say to him, You sit here well, and say to the poor one, You stand there, or, You sit here under my footstool: [4] did you not also discriminate among yourselves, and became judges (with) thoughts of evil? [5] Hear, my beloved brothers: Did not God choose the poor of this world, rich in faith, and heirs of the kingdom which He promised to those that love Him? [6] But you despised the poor one. Do not the rich oppress you? And do they drag you to tribunals? [7] Do they not blaspheme the good name which was called on you? [8] If you truly keep (the) royal law according to the Scripture, "You shall love your neighbor as yourself," you do well. [9] But if you have partiality to persons, you work sin, being found guilty by the Law as lawbreakers. [10] For whoever shall keep all the Law, but shall stumble in one thing, he has become guilty of all. [11] For He who said, "You shall not commit adultery," said also, "You shall not commit murder." But if you shall not commit adultery, but shall commit murder, you have became a transgressor of (the) Law. [12] So speak and so do, as being about to be judged by (the) law of liberty. [13] For judgment (will be) without mercy to him who did not do mercy. And mercy rejoices over judgment.

[14] My brothers, What gain (is it) if anyone say (he) has faith, but does not have works? Is faith able to save him? [15] Now if a

κόσμου.
**world.**

## CHAPTER 2

**1** Ἀδελφοί μου, μὴ ἐν προσωποληψίαις ἔχετε τὴν πίστιν
Brothers of me, not in respects of persons _ have the faith

**2** τοῦ Κυρίου ἡμῶν Ἰησοῦ Χριστοῦ τῆς δόξης. ἐὰν γὰρ εἰσ-
the Lord of us, Jesus Christ, of the(Lord) glory. of if For

ἔλθῃ εἰς τὴν συναγωγὴν ὑμῶν ἀνὴρ χρυσοδακτύλιος ἐν
comes into the synagogue of you a man gold-fingered, in

ἐσθῆτι λαμπρᾷ, εἰσέλθῃ δὲ καὶ πτωχὸς ἐν ῥυπαρᾷ ἐσθῆτι,
clothing fancy, comes in and also a poor one in shabby clothing,

**3** καὶ ἐπιβλέψητε ἐπὶ τὸν φοροῦντα τὴν ἐσθῆτα τὴν λαμπράν,
and you look on the (one) wearing the clothing fancy,

καὶ εἴπητε αὐτῷ, Σὺ κάθου ὧδε καλῶς, καὶ τῷ πτωχῷ
and say to him, You sit here well, and to the poor one

εἴπητε, Σὺ στῆθι ἐκεῖ, ἢ κάθου ὧδε ὑπὸ τὸ ὑποπόδιόν μου·
you say, You stand there, or sit here under the footstool of me,

**4** καὶ οὐ διεκρίθητε ἐν ἑαυτοῖς, καὶ ἐγένεσθε κριταὶ διαλογισμῶν
did make a
even not difference among yourselves, and became judges thoughts

**5** πονηρῶν ; ἀκούσατε, ἀδελφοί μου ἀγαπητοί. οὐχ ὁ Θεὸς
of evil? Hear, brothers of me beloved, Did not God

ἐξελέξατο τοὺς πτωχοὺς τοῦ κόσμου τούτου, πλουσίους
choose the poor world of this rich

ἐν πίστει, καὶ κληρονόμους τῆς βασιλείας ἧς ἐπηγγείλατο
in faith, and heirs of the kingdom which He promised

**6** τοῖς ἀγαπῶσιν αὐτόν ; ὑμεῖς δὲ ἠτιμάσατε τὸν πτωχόν. οὐχ
to those loving Him. you But dishonored the poor one. Do not

οἱ πλούσιοι καταδυναστεύουσιν ὑμῶν, καὶ αὐτοὶ ἕλκουσιν
the rich ones oppress you, and they drag

**7** ὑμᾶς εἰς κριτήρια ; οὐκ αὐτοὶ βλασφημοῦσι τὸ καλὸν ὄνομα
you to judgment seats? Do not they blaspheme the good name

**8** τὸ ἐπικληθὲν ἐφ' ὑμᾶς ; εἰ μέντοι νόμον τελεῖτε βασιλικόν,
called upon you? If indeed law you fulfill a royal,

κατὰ τὴν γραφήν, Ἀγαπήσεις τὸν πλησίον σου ὡς σεαυ-
according to the Scripture: You shall love the neighbor of you as your-

**9** τόν, καλῶς ποιεῖτε· εἰ δὲ προσωποληπτεῖτε, ἁμαρτίαν ἐργά-
self, well you do; if but you respect persons, sin you work,

**10** ζεσθε, ἐλεγχόμενοι ὑπὸ τοῦ νόμου ὡς παραβάται. ὅστις γὰρ
being reproved by the law as transgressors.(he) who For

ὅλον τὸν νόμον τηρήσει, πταίσει δὲ ἐν ἑνί, γέγονε πάντων
all the law keeps, stumbles but in one, he has become of all

**11** ἔνοχος. ὁ γὰρ εἰπών, Μὴ μοιχεύσῃς, εἶπε καί, Μὴ φονεύσῃς·
guilty. he For saying, Do not do adultery, said also, Do not murder;

εἰ δὲ οὐ μοιχεύσεις, φονεύσεις δέ, γέγονας παραβάτης νόμου.
if but not you do adultery, murder but, you have become a transgressor of law.

**12** οὕτω λαλεῖτε καὶ οὕτω ποιεῖτε, ὡς διὰ νόμου ἐλευθερίας
So speak and so do, as through a law of freedom

**13** μέλλοντες κρίνεσθαι. ἡ γὰρ κρίσις ἀνίλεως τῷ μὴ ποιήσαντι
will be
being about to be judged. the For Judgment unmerciful to those not doing

ἔλεος· καὶ κατακαυχᾶται ἔλεος κρίσεως.
mercy; and exults over mercy judgment.

**14** Τί τὸ ὄφελος, ἀδελφοί μου, ἐὰν πίστιν λέγῃ τις ἔχειν, ἔργα
What (is) the profit, brothers of me, if faith says anyone to have, works

**15** δὲ μὴ ἔχῃ ; μὴ δύναται ἡ πίστις σῶσαι αὐτόν ; ἐὰν δὲ
but not he has? Is able the faith to save him? if But

brother or a sister is naked, and may be destitute of daily food, [16] and anyone say to them from among you, Go in peace; be warmed and be filled; but does not give to them the things needful for the body, what gain (is it)? [17] So also faith, if it does not have works, is dead by itself. [18] But someone will say, You have faith, and I have works. Show me your faith from your works, and I will show you from my works my faith. [19] You believe that God is one. You do well; even the demons believe, and shudder. [20] But will you know, O vain man, that faith apart from works is dead? [21] Was not our father Abraham justified by works, having offered his son Isaac on the altar? [22] You see that faith is working with his works, and by works faith was perfected. [23] And the Scripture was fulfilled which says, "And Abraham believed God, and it was counted to him for righteousness, and he was called, Friend of God." [24] You see, then, that a man is justified by works, and not by faith alone. [25] But in the same way, was not Rahab the harlot justified by works, having received the messengers, and having sent (them) out by another way? [26] For as the body apart from the spirit is dead, so also faith apart from works is dead.

## CHAPTER 3

[1] My brothers, do not be many teachers, knowing that we shall receive greater judgment. [2] For we all often stumble. If anyone does not stumble in word, this one (is) a perfect man, able to bridle the whole body. [3] Behold, we put the bits in the mouths of the horses, for them to obey us, and we turn about their body. [4] Behold, the

ἀδελφὸς ἢ ἀδελφὴ γυμνοὶ ὑπάρχωσι καὶ λειπόμενοι ὦσι
a brother or a sister　　naked　are,　and　lacking may be

16 τῆς ἐφημέρου τροφῆς, εἴπῃ δέ τις αὐτοῖς ἐξ ὑμῶν, Ὑπάγετε
of daily　food,　says and anyone to them of you,　Go

ἐν εἰρήνῃ, θερμαίνεσθε καὶ χορτάζεσθε, μὴ δῶτε δὲ αὐτοῖς
in　peace, be warmed　and　filled,　not you give but them

17 τὰ ἐπιτήδεια τοῦ σώματος, τί τὸ ὄφελος ; οὕτω καὶ ἡ πίστις,
the necessities of the　body,　what (is) the profit? So indeed　faith,

18 ἐὰν μὴ ἔργα ἔχῃ, νεκρά ἐστι καθ' ἑαυτήν. ἀλλ' ἐρεῖ τις, Σὺ
if　not works it has, dead　is　by　itself.　But will say one, You

πίστιν ἔχεις, κἀγὼ ἔργα ἔχω· δεῖξόν μοι τὴν πίστιν σου
faith　have, and I　works have: show　me　the　faith of you

χωρὶς τῶν ἔργων σου, κἀγὼ δείξω σοι ἐκ τῶν ἔργων μου
without the　works of you, and I　will show you by　the　works of me

19 τὴν πίστιν μου. σὺ πιστεύεις ὅτι ὁ Θεὸς εἷς ἐστι· καλῶς
the　faith of me.　You　believe　that　God one　is?　well

20 ποιεῖς· καὶ τὰ δαιμόνια πιστεύουσι, καὶ φρίσσουσι. θέλεις
You do; also the　demons　believe　and tremble. are you willing

δὲ γνῶναι, ὦ ἄνθρωπε κενέ, ὅτι ἡ πίστις χωρὶς τῶν ἔργων
But to know, O　man　vain, that　faith　without　works

21 νεκρά ἐστιν ; Ἀβραὰμ ὁ πατὴρ ἡμῶν οὐκ ἐξ ἔργων ἐδικαιώθη,
dead is?　Abraham the father　of us　not by　works Was justified,

ἀνενέγκας Ἰσαὰκ τὸν υἱὸν αὐτοῦ ἐπὶ τὸ θυσιαστήριον ;
offering up　Isaac　the son of him　on　the　altar?

22 βλέπεις ὅτι ἡ πίστις συνήργει τοῖς ἔργοις αὐτοῦ, καὶ ἐκ τῶν
You see that　faith　worked with the　works of him, and by the

23 ἔργων ἡ πίστις ἐτελειώθη ; καὶ ἐπληρώθη ἡ γραφὴ ἡ
works　the faith was perfected, and was fulfilled　the Scripture,

λέγουσα, Ἐπίστευσε δὲ Ἀβραὰμ τῷ Θεῷ, καὶ ἐλογίσθη
saying,　believed And Abraham　God, and it was counted

24 αὐτῷ εἰς δικαιοσύνην, καὶ φίλος Θεοῦ ἐκλήθη. ὁρᾶτε τοίνυν
to him for righteousness, and　friend of God he was called. You see then

ὅτι ἐξ ἔργων δικαιοῦται ἄνθρωπος, καὶ οὐκ ἐκ πίστεως μόνον.
that by works is justified　a man,　and not by　faith　only.

25 ὁμοίως δὲ καὶ Ῥαὰβ ἡ πόρνη οὐκ ἐξ ἔργων ἐδικαιώθη, ὑποδε-
likewise And also Rahab the harlot not by works was justified, enter-

ξαμένη τοὺς ἀγγέλους, καὶ ἑτέρᾳ ὁδῷ ἐκβαλοῦσα ; ὥσπερ
taining the　messengers, and by another way sending out?　as

26 γὰρ τὸ σῶμα χωρὶς πνεύματος νεκρόν ἐστιν, οὕτω καὶ ἡ
For the body　without spirit　dead　is,　so　also

πίστις χωρὶς τῶν ἔργων νεκρά ἐστι.
faith　without　works　dead　is.

## CHAPTER 3

1 Μὴ πολλοὶ διδάσκαλοι γίνεσθε, ἀδελφοί μου, εἰδότες ὅτι
not many　teachers　Become, brothers of me, knowing that

2 μεῖζον κρίμα ληψόμεθα. πολλὰ γὰρ πταίομεν ἅπαντες. εἰ
greater judgment we will receive. (in) many For (ways) we stumble all.　If

τις ἐν λόγῳ οὐ πταίει, οὗτος τέλειος ἀνήρ, δυνατὸς χαλιν-
anyone in word not stumbles, this (is) a mature man,　able　to

3 αγωγῆσαι καὶ ὅλον τὸ σῶμα. ἰδού, τῶν ἵππων τοὺς χαλι-
bridle　also the whole body. Behold, of the horses　the　bits

νοὺς εἰς τὰ στόματα βάλλομεν πρὸς τὸ πείθεσθαι αὐτοὺς
in the　mouths　we put,　for　to obey　them

4 ἡμῖν, καὶ ὅλον τὸ σῶμα αὐτῶν μετάγομεν. ἰδού, καὶ τὰ
us,　and whole the　body of them we turn about. Behold, also the

ships also, being so great, and being driven by violent winds, are turned about by a very small rudder, wherever the pleasure of him who steers may will. [5] So also the tongue is a little member, and boasts great things. Behold, a little fire, how large a forest it kindles! [6] And the tongue (is) a fire, the world of unrighteousness. So the tongue is set among our members, spotting all the body, and inflaming the course of nature, and being inflamed by Hell. [7] For every species of beasts, both of animals and of birds, both of creeping things and things of the sea, is tamed, and has been tamed by the human species; [8] but the tongue no one of men is able to tame; it is an unrestrainable evil, full of death-dealing poison. [9] By this we bless God and (the) Father; and by this we curse men who have come into being according to (the) image of God. [10] Out of the same mouth comes forth blessing and cursing. My brothers, it is not fitting (for) these things to be so. [11] (Does) the fountain out of the same hole send forth the sweet and the bitter? [12] My brothers, is a fig-tree able to produce olives, or a vine, figs? So neither (can) a fountain produce (both) salt and sweet water.

[13] Who (is) wise and understanding among you; let him out of good behavior show his works in meekness of wisdom; [14] but if you have bitter jealousy and fighting in your heart, do not boast against and lie against the truth. [15] This is not the wisdom coming down from above, but (is) earthly, beastly, devilish. [16] For where jealousy and fighting (are), there (is) confusion and every evil thing. [17] But the wisdom from above is first pure, then peaceful, gentle, yielding, full of mercy and of good fruits, impartial, and unpretended. [18] But (the) fruit of righteousness

πλοῖα, τηλικαῦτα ὄντα, καὶ ὑπὸ σκληρῶν ἀνέμων ἐλαυνό-
ships       so great      being, and    by       hard       winds      being

μενα, μετάγεται ὑπὸ ἐλαχίστου πηδαλίου, ὅπου ἂν ἡ ὁρμὴ
driven, is directed     by     a very little      helm,        where      the impulse

5  τοῦ εὐθύνοντος βούληται. οὕτω καὶ ἡ γλῶσσα μικρὸν μέλος
of the (one) steering purposes.       So also  the tongue    a little member

ἐστί, καὶ μεγαλαυχεῖ. ἰδού, ὀλίγον πῦρ ἡλίκην ὕλην
is,     and  great things boasts. Behold, how little a fire  how great   wood

6  ἀνάπτει. καὶ ἡ γλῶσσα πῦρ, ὁ κόσμος τῆς ἀδικίας· οὕτως
kindles;    and  the  tongue (is) a fire,  the world      of iniquity;   so

ἡ γλῶσσα καθίσταται ἐν τοῖς μέλεσιν ἡμῶν, ἡ σπιλοῦσα
the tongue      is set       among the members    of us,     the  spotting

ὅλον τὸ σῶμα, καὶ φλογίζουσα τὸν τροχὸν τῆς γενέσεως,
all    the   body,  and    inflaming        the    course    of nature,

7  καὶ φλογιζομένη ὑπὸ τῆς γεέννης. πᾶσα γὰρ φύσις θηρίων
and  being inflamed     by           Gehenna.   every For nature  of beasts

τε καὶ πετεινῶν, ἑρπετῶν τε καὶ ἐναλίων, δαμάζεται καὶ
both and of birds   of reptiles both and of sea animals,  is tamed    and

8  δεδάμασται τῇ φύσει τῇ ἀνθρωπίνῃ· τὴν δὲ γλῶσσαν
has been tamed by the nature         human;        the  but   tongue

οὐδεὶς δύναται ἀνθρώπων δαμάσαι· ἀκατάσχετον κακόν,
no one   is able       of men       to tame; (it is) an  an unrestrain-  evil,
                                                              able

9  μεστὴ ἰοῦ θανατηφόρου. ἐν αὐτῇ εὐλογοῦμεν τὸν Θεὸν καὶ
full of poison death-dealing.   By this    we bless            God  and

πατέρα, καὶ ἐν αὐτῇ καταρώμεθα τοὺς ἀνθρώπους τοὺς καθ᾽
(the) Father, and by this      we curse               men        according to

10  ὁμοίωσιν Θεοῦ γεγονότας· ἐκ τοῦ αὐτοῦ στόματος ἐξέρχεται
(the) image of God having come into out   the same    mouth    comes forth
                                    being, of

εὐλογία καὶ κατάρα. οὐ χρή, ἀδελφοί μου, ταῦτα οὕτω
blessing and   cursing. not It is fitting, brothers of me, these things  so

11  γίνεσθαι. μήτι ἡ πηγὴ ἐκ τῆς αὐτῆς ὀπῆς βρύει τὸ γλυκὺ
to be.       (Does) the fountain out of the same  hole  send forth the sweet

12  καὶ τὸ πικρόν; μὴ δύναται, ἀδελφοί μου, συκῆ ἐλαίας
and the  bitter?        Is able,   brothers  of me, a fig-tree  olives

ποιῆσαι, ἢ ἄμπελος σῦκα; οὕτως οὐδεμία πηγὴ ἁλυκὸν καὶ
to produce, or a vine   figs?       So    neither  a fountain  salt    and

γλυκὺ ποιῆσαι ὕδωρ.
sweet  to produce water.

13  Τίς σοφὸς καὶ ἐπιστήμων ἐν ὑμῖν; δειξάτω ἐκ τῆς καλῆς
Who (is) wise  and   knowing    among you? Let him show by the  good

14  ἀναστροφῆς τὰ ἔργα αὐτοῦ ἐν πραΰτητι σοφίας. εἰ δὲ ζῆλον
behavior       the works of him  in  meekness of wisdom. if But jealousy

πικρὸν ἔχετε καὶ ἐρίθειαν ἐν τῇ καρδίᾳ ὑμῶν, μὴ κατα-
bitter you have, and contention in the   heart   of you, do not exult

15  καυχᾶσθε καὶ ψεύδεσθε κατὰ τῆς ἀληθείας. οὐκ ἔστιν αὕτη ἡ
over         and  lie          against the     truth.     not is       This the

σοφία ἄνωθεν κατερχομένη, ἀλλ᾽ ἐπίγειος, ψυχική, δαι-
wisdom from above coming down,   but (is) earthly,  beastly

16  μονιώδης. ὅπου γὰρ ζῆλος καὶ ἐρίθεια, ἐκεῖ ἀκαταστασία καὶ
devilish.   where For  jealousy and contention, there (is)  confusion  and

17  πᾶν φαῦλον πρᾶγμα. ἡ δὲ ἄνωθεν σοφία πρῶτον μὲν ἁγνή
every  foul      deed.   the But from above wisdom firstly  truly   pure

ἐστιν, ἔπειτα εἰρηνική, ἐπιεικής, εὐπειθής, μεστὴ ἐλέους καὶ
is,       then   peaceable, forbearing, yielding,    full  of mercy and

18  καρπῶν ἀγαθῶν, ἀδιάκριτος καὶ ἀνυπόκριτος. καρπὸς δὲ τῆς
fruits    of good,   not partial    and not pretended. (the) fruit And

is sown in peace for those that make peace.

## CHAPTER 4

[1] Where do wars and fightings among you (come) from? (Is it) not (from) this, from your lust which war in your members? [2] You desire and do not have. You kill and are jealous and are not able to obtain. You fight and war, but you do not have (what you want) because you do not ask God. [3] You ask, and do not receive, because you ask evilly, that you may waste (it) on your lust. [4] Adulterers and adulteresses, do you not know that the friendship of the world is enmity (with) God? Whoever, then, purposes to be a friend of the world is shown to be an enemy of God. [5] Or do you think that the Scripture vainly says: "The spirit which has dwelt in us yearns with envy"? [6] But He gives greater grace. Because of this it says, "God sets (Himself) against proud ones; but He gives grace to humble ones." [7] Then be subject to God. Resist the Devil, and he will flee from you. ⌐8⌐ Draw near to God, and He will draw near to you. Cleanse your hands, sinners, and purify (your) hearts, you double-minded. [9] Be sorrowful and mourn and weep. Let your laughter be turned to mourning, and (your) joy to heaviness. [10] Humble yourselves before the Lord, and He will exalt you.

[11] Do not speak evil against one another, brothers. He that speaks against (his) brother, and judges his brother, speaks against (the) Law, and judges (the) Law. But if you judge (the) Law, you are not a doer of (the) Law, but a judge. [12] One is the Lawgiver, who is able to save and to destroy. Who are you that judges the other?

[13] Come now, you who say, Today and tomorrow we may go into such a city, and may spend one year there, and may do business, and may make a profit; [14] you who do

δικαιοσύνης ἐν εἰρήνῃ σπείρεται τοῖς ποιοῦσιν εἰρήνην.
of righteousness in   peace   is sown for those  making   peace.

## CHAPTER 4

1  Πόθεν πόλεμοι καὶ μάχαι ἐν ὑμῖν; οὐκ ἐντεῦθεν, ἐκ τῶν
From where (come) wars and fights among you? Not from this,  from  the
ἡδονῶν ὑμῶν τῶν στρατευομένων ἐν τοῖς μέλεσιν υμῶν;
lusts  of you        warring          in  the members of you?

2  ἐπιθυμεῖτε, καὶ οὐκ ἔχετε· φονεύετε καὶ ζηλοῦτε, καὶ οὐ δύνα-
You desire,  and not  have; you murder and are jealous, and not are
σθε ἐπιτυχεῖν· μάχεσθε καὶ πολεμεῖτε, οὐκ ἔχετε δέ, διὰ τὸ μὴ
able to obtain; you fight  and  you war. do not you have and, because not

3  αἰτεῖσθαι ὑμᾶς· αἰτεῖτε, καὶ οὐ λαμβάνετε, διότι κακῶς
ask       you;  you ask,  and not you receive,  because wrongly

4  αἰτεῖσθε, ἵνα ἐν ταῖς ἡδοναῖς ὑμῶν δαπανήσητε. μοιχοὶ καὶ
you ask,  that on the  lusts  of you you may spend. Adulterers
μοιχαλίδες, οὐκ οἴδατε ὅτι ἡ φιλία τοῦ κόσμου ἔχθρα τοῦ
adulteresses, do not you know that the friendship of the world enmity
Θεοῦ ἐστιν; ὃς ἂν οὖν βουληθῇ φίλος εἶναι τοῦ κόσμου,
of God  is? Whoever, therefore, purposes a friend to be of the  world,

5  ἐχθρὸς τοῦ Θεοῦ καθίσταται. ἢ δοκεῖτε ὅτι κενῶς ἡ γραφὴ
an enemy  of God is shown to be. Or do you think that vainly the Scripture
λέγει, Πρὸς φθόνον ἐπιποθεῖ τὸ πνεῦμα ὃ κατῴκησεν ἐν ἡμῖν
says:  to  envy  yearns  The spirit which has dwelt  in  us?

6  μείζονα δὲ δίδωσι χάριν· διὸ λέγει, Ὁ Θεὸς ὑπερηφάνοις
greater But He gives grace, therefore it says:  God   proud ones

7  ἀντιτάσσεται, ταπεινοῖς δὲ δίδωσι χάριν. ὑποτάγητε οὖν
sets (Himself) against, to humble ones but He gives grace.  Be subject, therefore,
τῷ Θεῷ· ἀντίστητε τῷ διαβόλῳ, καὶ φεύξεται ἀφ' ὑμῶν.
to God;  oppose  the  devil,  and he will flee from  you.

8  ἐγγίσατε τῷ Θεῷ, καὶ ἐγγιεῖ ὑμῖν· καθαρίσατε χεῖρας,
Draw near  to God, and He will draw near to you. Cleanse (the) hands,

9  ἁμαρτωλοί, καὶ ἁγνίσατε καρδίας, δίψυχοι. ταλαιπωρή-
sinners,    and  purify (your) hearts, two-souled ones. Be distressed
σατε καὶ πενθήσατε καὶ κλαύσατε· ὁ γέλως ὑμῶν εἰς πένθος
and  mourn    and   weep,  the laughter of you to mourning

10 μεταστραφήτω, καὶ ἡ χαρὰ εἰς κατήφειαν. ταπεινώθητε
let it be turned,  and the  joy  to shame.  Be humbled
ἐνώπιον τοῦ Κυρίου, καὶ ὑψώσει ὑμᾶς.
before  the  Lord,  and He will exalt you.

11 Μὴ καταλαλεῖτε ἀλλήλων, ἀδελφοί. ὁ καταλαλῶν
Do not speak against one another, brothers. He speaking against
ἀδελφοῦ, καὶ κρίνων τὸν ἀδελφὸν αὐτοῦ, καταλαλεῖ νόμου,
a brother, and judging the brother  of him, speaks against law,
καὶ κρίνει νόμον· εἰ δὲ νόμον κρίνεις, οὐκ εἶ ποιητὴς νόμου,
and judges law; if and  law you judge, not  you are a doer of law,

12 ἀλλὰ κριτής. εἷς ἐστιν ὁ νομοθέτης, ὁ δυνάμενος σῶσαι καὶ
but  a judge. One is  the Lawgiver, who is able  to save  and
ἀπολέσαι· σὺ τίς εἶ ὃς κρίνεις τὸν ἕτερον;
to destroy; you who are who judges the  other?

13 Ἄγε νῦν οἱ λέγοντες, Σήμερον ἢ αὔριον πορευσόμεθα εἰς
Come now those saying,  Today or tomorrow we will go  into
τήνδε τὴν πόλιν, καὶ ποιήσομεν ἐκεῖ ἐνιαυτὸν ἕνα, καὶ
this    city,  and  we will spend there  year   one, and

14 ἐμπορευσόμεθα, καὶ κερδήσομεν· οἵτινες οὐκ ἐπίστασθε τὸ
we will trade  and will make a profit; who  not  know  of the

not know of the morrow; for what (is) your life? For it is a mist, which for a little (while) appears, and then disappears. [15] Instead of you saying, If the Lord wills, even we will live, and we will do this or that. [16] But now you rejoice in your boastings. All such boasting is evil. [17] Therefore, to (him) knowing to do good, and not doing (it), it is sin to him.

CHAPTER 5

[1] Come now, rich ones, weep, howling over your hardships coming on (you). [2] Your riches have rotted, and your garments have become moth-eaten. [3] Your gold and silver have rusted over, and their poison will be for a testimony against you, and will eat your flesh as fire. You have heaped up treasure in (the) last days. [4] Behold, the wages of the workmen having reaped your fields cries out, being kept back by you. And the cries of those having reaped have entered the ears of (the) Lord of hosts. [5] You lived luxuriously on the earth, and lived in self-gratification; you nourished your hearts as in a day of slaughter; [6] you condemned, you killed the just — he does not resist you.

[7] Therefore, brothers, be patient until the coming of the Lord. Behold, the farmer waits for the precious fruit of the earth, being patient for it until it receives (the) early and later rain. [8] You also be patient; strengthen your hearts, because the coming of the Lord has drawn near. [9] Do not grumble against one another, brothers, that you may not be condemned. Behold, (the) Judge stands before the door. [10] My brothers, (as) an example of suffering evils, and of patience, take the prophets who spoke in the name of (the) Lord. [11] Behold, we call those blessed who

τῆς αὔριον. ποία γὰρ ἡ ζωὴ ὑμῶν ; ἀτμὶς γάρ ἐστιν ἡ πρὸς
morrow;   what   for   the   life   of you; a mist   for   it is, which for

15 ὀλίγον φαινομένη, ἔπειτα δὲ ἀφανιζομένη. ἀντὶ τοῦ λέγειν
a little (while) appears,   then   and   disappears.   Instead of   saying
ὑμᾶς, Ἐὰν ὁ Κύριος θελήσῃ, καὶ ζήσομεν, καὶ ποιήσομεν
you,   If   the   Lord   wills,   even we will live, and we will do

16 τοῦτο ἢ ἐκεῖνο. νῦν δὲ καυχᾶσθε ἐν ταῖς ἀλαζονείαις ὑμῶν·
this   or   that.   now But you boast   in   the   vauntings   of you;

17 πᾶσα καύχησις τοιαύτη πονηρά ἐστιν. εἰδότι οὖν καλὸν
all   boastings   such   evil   is.   to (one) knowing Then good
ποιεῖν καὶ μὴ ποιοῦντι, ἁμαρτία αὐτῷ ἐστίν.
to do,   and not   doing (it),   sin   to him   it is.

CHAPTER 5

1 Ἄγε νῦν οἱ πλούσιοι, κλαύσατε ὀλολύζοντες ἐπὶ ταῖς
Come now   rich ones,   weep,   crying aloud   over   the

2 ταλαιπωρίαις ὑμῶν ταῖς ἐπερχομέναις. ὁ πλοῦτος ὑμῶν
hardships   of you   coming upon.   The riches   of you

3 σέσηπε, καὶ τὰ ἱμάτια ὑμῶν σητόβρωτα γέγονεν· ὁ χρυσὸς
have rotted, and the garments of you moth-eaten have become; the gold
ὑμῶν καὶ ὁ ἄργυρος κατίωται, καὶ ὁ ἰὸς αὐτῶν εἰς μαρτύ-
of you and the silver   have rusted over, and the poison of them for a test-
ριον ὑμῖν ἔσται, καὶ φάγεται τὰς σάρκας ὑμῶν ὡς πῦρ.
imony to you will be, and   will eat   the   flesh   of you as   fire.

4 ἐθησαυρίσατε ἐν ἐσχάταις ἡμέραις. ἰδού, ὁ μισθὸς τῶν
You heaped treasure in (the) last   days.   Behold, the wages   of the
ἐργατῶν τῶν ἀμησάντων τὰς χώρας ὑμῶν, ὁ ἀπεστερη-
workmen   having reaped   the   fields of you   being kept
μένος ἀφ᾽ ὑμῶν, κράζει· καὶ αἱ βοαὶ τῶν θερισάντων εἰς τὰ
back from   you cries out, and the cries   of those having reaped into the

5 ὦτα Κυρίου Σαβαὼθ εἰσεληλύθασιν. ἐτρυφήσατε ἐπὶ τῆς
ears of (the) Lord of Hosts   have entered.   You lived luxuriously on the
γῆς καὶ ἐσπαταλήσατε· ἐθρέψατε τὰς καρδίας ὑμῶν ὡς ἐν
earth, and lived riotously,   you nourished the hearts   of you as   in

6 ἡμέρᾳ σφαγῆς. κατεδικάσατε, ἐφονεύσατε τὸν δίκαιον· οὐκ
a day   of slaughter. You condemned, you murdered the righteous;   not
ἀντιτάσσεται ὑμῖν.
he resists   you.

7 Μακροθυμήσατε οὖν, ἀδελφοί, ἕως τῆς παρουσίας τοῦ
Be longsuffering, therefore, brothers, until the   presence   of the
Κυρίου. ἰδού, ὁ γεωργὸς ἐκδέχεται τὸν τίμιον καρπὸν τῆς
Lord.   Behold, the farmer   awaits   the   precious fruit   of the
γῆς, μακροθυμῶν ἐπ᾽ αὐτῷ, ἕως ἂν λάβῃ ὑετὸν πρώϊμον
earth, being longsuffering over it   until it may receive rain (the) early

8 καὶ ὄψιμον. μακροθυμήσατε καὶ ὑμεῖς, στηρίξατε τὰς καρδίας
and latter.   Be longsuffering also you,   establish   the   hearts

9 ὑμῶν, ὅτι ἡ παρουσία τοῦ Κυρίου ἤγγικε. μὴ στενάζετε κατ᾽
of you, because the coming of the   Lord has drawn near. not Murmur against
ἀλλήλων, ἀδελφοί, ἵνα μὴ κατακριθῆτε· ἰδού, ὁ κριτὴς πρὸ
one another, brothers, that not you be judged; behold, the Judge before

10 τῶν θυρῶν ἕστηκεν. ὑπόδειγμα λάβετε τῆς κακοπαθείας,
the   door   stands.   an example   Take   of suffering ill,
ἀδελφοί μου, καὶ τῆς μακροθυμίας, τοὺς προφήτας οἳ
brothers of me,   and   of longsuffering:   the   prophets who

11 ἐλάλησαν τῷ ὀνόματι Κυρίου. ἰδού, μακαρίζομεν τοὺς
spoke   in the   name of (the) Lord. Behold, we count blessed those

endure. You have heard of the patience of Job, and you saw the end of (the) Lord; that the Lord is full of tender mercy and pity. [12] But before all things, my brothers, do not swear, neither (by) Heaven, nor the earth, nor any other oath. But let your yes be yes, and the no, no, that you may not fall into hypocrisy. [13] Does anyone among you suffer hardships? Let him pray. Is anyone cheerful? Let him praise. [14] Is anyone sick among you? Let him call the elders of the church, and let them pray over him, having anointed him with oil in the name of the Lord; [15] And the prayer of faith shall heal the (one) being sick, and the Lord will raise him up; and if he is (one who) has committed sins, it shall be forgiven him. [16] Confess faults to one another, and pray for one another, that you may be healed. (The) fervent, prayer of a righteous one prevails. [17] Elijah was a man of like feelings to us, and he prayed with prayer (for it) not to rain; and it did not rain on the earth three years and six months; [18] And he prayed again, and the sky gave rain, and the earth caused its fruit to sprout.

[19] Brothers, if anyone among you goes astray from the truth, and any one brings him back, [20] let him know that he who brings back a sinner from (the) error of his way shall save a soul from death, and shall cover a multitude of sins.

ὑπομένοντας· τὴν ὑπομονὴν Ἰὼβ ἠκούσατε, καὶ τὸ τέλος
*enduring.    the    patience  of Job You heard (of), and the   end*

Κυρίου εἴδετε, ὅτι πολύσπλαγχνός ἐστιν ὁ Κύριος καὶ
*of (the) Lord you saw, that  very compassionate  is    the   Lord  and*

οἰκτίρμων.
*pitying.*

**12** Πρὸ πάντων δέ, ἀδελφοί μου, μὴ ὀμνύετε, μήτε τὸν
*before  all things But,  brothers  of me, do not  swear,    neither by the*

οὐρανόν, μήτε τὴν γῆν, μήτε ἄλλον τινὰ ὅρκον· ἤτω δὲ
*heaven,  nor  by the earth, nor   other    any   oath; let be but*

ὑμῶν τὸ ναί, ναί, καὶ τὸ οὔ, οὔ· ἵνα μὴ ὑπὸ κρίσιν πέσητε.
*of you the yes, yes, and the no, no, that not under judgment you fall.*

**13** Κακοπαθεῖ τις ἐν ὑμῖν; προσευχέσθω. εὐθυμεῖ τις;
*Suffers ill   any among you? Let him pray.    Is cheerful any?*

**14** ψαλλέτω. ἀσθενεῖ τις ἐν ὑμῖν; προσκαλεσάσθω τοὺς πρεσ-
*Let him sing. Is infirm any among you? Let him summon    the*

βυτέρους τῆς ἐκκλησίας, καὶ προσευξάσθωσαν ἐπ' αὐτόν,
*elders  of the  church,   and let them pray    over   him,*

**15** ἀλείψαντες αὐτὸν ἐλαίῳ ἐν τῷ ὀνόματι τοῦ Κυρίου· καὶ ἡ
*having anointed him with oil  in the   name  of the  Lord. And the*

εὐχὴ τῆς πίστεως σώσει τὸν κάμνοντα, καὶ ἐγερεῖ αὐτὸν ὁ
*prayer  of faith  will cure those being sick, and will raise  him  the*

Κύριος· κἂν ἁμαρτίας ᾖ πεποιηκώς, ἀφεθήσεται αὐτῷ.
*Lord; and if  sin  he may be having done  it will be forgiven him.*

**16** ἐξομολογεῖσθε ἀλλήλοις τὰ παραπτώματα, καὶ εὔχεσθε
*Confess    to one another the   offenses,    and   pray*

ὑπὲρ ἀλλήλων, ὅπως ἰαθῆτε. πολὺ ἰσχύει δέησις δικαίου
*for  one another, so as you may be healed. Much<sup>is a of one</sup> strong petition righteous*

**17** ἐνεργουμένη. Ἡλίας ἄνθρωπος ἦν ὁμοιοπαθὴς ἡμῖν, καὶ
*being made effective. Elijah  a man   was  of like feeling  to us, and*

προσευχῇ προσηύξατο τοῦ μὴ βρέξαι· καὶ οὐκ ἔβρεξεν ἐπὶ
*in prayer   he prayed    not  to rain, and not it rained on*

**18** τῆς γῆς ἐνιαυτοὺς τρεῖς καὶ μῆνας ἕξ. καὶ πάλιν προσηύξατο,
*the earth    years  three and months six. And again  he prayed,*

καὶ ὁ οὐρανὸς ὑετὸν ἔδωκε, καὶ ἡ γῆ ἐβλάστησε τὸν καρπὸν
*and the heaven  rain  gave,   and the earth produced   the   fruit*

αὐτῆς.
*of it.*

**19** Ἀδελφοί, ἐάν τις ἐν ὑμῖν πλανηθῇ ἀπὸ τῆς ἀληθείας, καὶ
*Brothers, if anyone among you errs    from the   truth,   and*

**20** ἐπιστρέψῃ τις αὐτόν, γινωσκέτω ὅτι ὁ ἐπιστρέψας ἁμαρ-
*turns   anyone him,   know    that the (one) turning   a*

τωλὸν ἐκ πλάνης ὁδοῦ αὐτοῦ σώσει ψυχὴν ἐκ θανάτου, καὶ
*sinner from (the) error of way of him will save (the) soul from death,  and*

καλύψει πλῆθος ἁμαρτιῶν.
*will hide a multitude of sins.*

THE FIRST GENERAL
EPISTLE OF
PETER

# ΠΕΤΡΟΥ
## OF PETER
ΕΠΙΣΤΟΛΗ ΚΑΘΟΛΙΚΗ ΠΡΩΤΗ

EPISTLE     GENERAL     FIRST

## CHAPTER 1

### CHAPTER 1

[1] Peter, an apostle of Jesus Christ, to (the) elect sojourners of (the) dispersion of Pontus, of Galatia, of Cappadocia, of Asia, and of Bithynia, [2] according to the foreknowledge of God the Father, in sanctification of (the) Spirit to obedience and sprinkling of (the) blood of Jesus Christ: Grace and peace be multiplied to you.

[3] Blessed (be) the God and Father of our Lord Jesus Christ, He according to His great mercy having regenerated us to a living hope through (the) resurrection of Jesus Christ from (the) dead, [4] to an inheritance incorruptible and undefiled and unfading, having been kept in Heaven for you [5] by (the) power of God, having been guarded through faith to a salvation ready to be revealed in (the) last time; [6] in which you exult; yet a little (while), if need be, grieving in manifold trials, [7] that the proving of your faith, much more precious than perishing gold, but having been proved through fire, may be found to praise and honor and glory at (the) revelation of Jesus Christ; [8] whom you love, not having seen (Him); in whom you exult with unspeakable joy, and have glorified; yet not seeing, but believing, [9] obtaining the end of your faith, the salvation of (your) souls. [10] About which salvation the prophets sought out and searched out, prophesying concerning the grace for you, [11] searching for what, or what sort of time, the Spirit of Christ signified within them; testifying beforehand of the sufferings (belonging) to Christ, and the glories after these.

1 Πέτρος, ἀπόστολος Ἰησοῦ Χριστοῦ, ἐκλεκτοῖς παρεπιδή-
Peter,     an apostle   of Jesus   Christ,   to (the) elect sojourners
μοις διασπορᾶς Πόντου, Γαλατίας, Καππαδοκίας, Ἀσίας,
of (the) dispersion of Pontus, of Galatia, of Cappadocia,     of Asia,
2 καὶ Βιθυνίας, κατὰ πρόγνωσιν Θεοῦ πατρός, ἐν ἁγιασμῷ
and of Bithynia, according to foreknowledge God's, the   in sanctification
                                                    Father,
Πνεύματος, εἰς ὑπακοὴν καὶ ῥαντισμὸν αἵματος Ἰησοῦ
of (the) Spirit, to   obedience   and   sprinkling of (the) blood of Jesus
Χριστοῦ· χάρις ὑμῖν καὶ εἰρήνη πληθυνθείη.
Christ:     Grace to you, and   peace,   be multiplied.
3 Εὐλογητὸς ὁ Θεὸς καὶ πατὴρ τοῦ Κυρίου ἡμῶν Ἰησοῦ
Blessed (be)   the God and   Father of the   Lord   of us,   Jesus
Χριστοῦ, ὁ κατὰ τὸ πολὺ αὐτοῦ ἔλεος ἀναγεννήσας ἡμᾶς
Christ,   the (One) according to much of Him mercy, having regenerated us
εἰς ἐλπίδα ζῶσαν δι’ ἀναστάσεως Ἰησοῦ Χριστοῦ ἐκ νεκρῶν,
to a hope   living through (the) resurrection of Jesus Christ from (the) dead,
4 εἰς κληρονομίαν ἄφθαρτον καὶ ἀμίαντον καὶ ἀμάραντον,
to an inheritance   incorruptible and   undefiled   and   unfading,
5 τετηρημένην ἐν οὐρανοῖς εἰς ὑμᾶς, τοὺς ἐν δυνάμει Θεοῦ
having been kept in   Heaven   for you   by (the) power of God,
φρουρουμένους διὰ πίστεως εἰς σωτηρίαν ἑτοίμην ἀποκαλυ-
being guarded   through faith to a salvation   ready   to be reveal-
6 φθῆναι ἐν καιρῷ ἐσχάτῳ. ἐν ᾧ ἀγαλλιᾶσθε, ὀλίγον ἄρτι,
ed   in   time (the) last. In which you exult,   a little   yet
7 εἰ δέον ἐστί, λυπηθέντες ἐν ποικίλοις πειρασμοῖς, ἵνα τὸ
if needful it is   grieving   by   manifold   trials,   that the
δοκίμιον ὑμῶν τῆς πίστεως πολὺ τιμιώτερον χρυσίου τοῦ
proving   of you of the faith,   much more precious than gold
ἀπολλυμένου, διὰ πυρὸς δὲ δοκιμαζομένου, εὑρεθῇ εἰς
of perishing,   through   fire   yet   being proved,   may be found to
ἔπαινον καὶ τιμὴν καὶ δόξαν ἐν ἀποκαλύψει Ἰησοῦ Χριστοῦ·
praise   and honor and   glory at (the) revelation of Jesus   Christ:
8 ὃν οὐκ ἰδόντες ἀγαπᾶτε, εἰς ὃν ἄρτι μὴ ὁρῶντες, πιστεύοντες
whom not having seen, you love, in whom yet not seeing,     believing
9 δέ, ἀγαλλιᾶσθε χαρᾷ ἀνεκλαλήτῳ καὶ δεδοξασμένῃ, κομιζό-
but; you exult   with joy unspeakable and   glorified,   obtaining
μενοι τὸ τέλος τῆς πίστεως ὑμῶν, σωτηρίαν ψυχῶν.
   the   end   of the faith   of you, (the) salvation of (your) souls.
10 περὶ ἧς σωτηρίας ἐξεζήτησαν καὶ ἐξηρεύνησαν προφῆται οἱ
About which salvation sought out   and   searched out   prophets the
11 περὶ τῆς εἰς ὑμᾶς χάριτος προφητεύσαντες· ἐρευνῶντες εἰς
concerning the for you   grace   prophesying,   searching   for
τίνα ἢ ποῖον καιρὸν ἐδήλου τὸ ἐν αὐτοῖς Πνεῦμα Χριστοῦ,
what or what sort of time made clear the in them   Spirit of Christ,
προμαρτυρόμενον τὰ εἰς Χριστὸν παθήματα, καὶ τὰς μετὰ
testifying beforehand of (belonging) Christ sufferings, and the after
   the   to

534

[12] To whom it was revealed that not to themselves, but to you they ministered the same things, which now were announced to you by those having preached the gospel to you in (the) Holy Spirit sent from Heaven—into which things angels long to look into.

[13] Therefore, girding up the loins of your mind, being sober, perfectly hope on the grace being brought to you at (the) revelation of Jesus Christ, [14] as obedient children, not fashioning yourselves in ignorance to your former lusts, [15] but according to the Holy One who has called you, you also become holy in all conduct; [16] because it has been written: Be holy, because I am holy." [17] And if you call on (Him as) Father, He who judges without respect to persons, according to the work of each one, pass the time of your sojourning in fear, [18] knowing that not with corruptible things, silver or gold, you were redeemed from your worthless way of life handed down by (your) fathers, [19] but with precious blood of Christ, as of an unblemished and unspotted lamb, [20] indeed having been foreknown before (the) foundation of (the) world, but manifested in (the) last times because of you, [21] those believing in God through Him, the (One) raising Him up from (the) dead, and having given glory to Him so that your faith and hope may be in God. [22] Having purified your souls in the obedience of the truth through (the) Spirit to unpretended brotherly love, love one another fervently out of a pure heart, [23] having been born again, not by corruptible seed, but incorruptible, through (the) living word of God, and remaining forever. [24] Because all flesh (is) as grass, and all (the) glory of man as (the) flower of grass—the grass was dried, and the flower of it fell out—[25] but (the) word of (the) Lord remains forever. And this is the word preached as gospel to you.

12 ταῦτα δόξας. οἷς ἀπεκαλύφθη ὅτι οὐχ ἑαυτοῖς, ἡμῖν δὲ
these glories. To whom it was revealed that not to themselves to you but

διηκόνουν αὐτά, ἃ νῦν ἀνηγγέλη ὑμῖν διὰ τῶν εὐαγγελισα-
they ministered the same, which now announced through were to you those having preached

μένων ὑμᾶς ἐν Πνεύματι Ἁγίῳ ἀποσταλέντι ἀπ᾽ οὐρανοῦ,
the gospel to you in (the) Spirit Holy sent from Heaven,

εἰς ἃ ἐπιθυμοῦσιν ἄγγελοι παρακύψαι.
into which things long angels to look into.

13 Διὸ ἀναζωσάμενοι τὰς ὀσφύας τῆς διανοίας ὑμῶν,
Therefore, girding up the loins of the mind of you,

νήφοντες, τελείως ἐλπίσατε ἐπὶ τὴν φερομένην ὑμῖν χάριν
being sober, perfectly hope on the being brought to you grace

14 ἐν ἀποκαλύψει Ἰησοῦ Χριστοῦ· ὡς τέκνα ὑπακοῆς, μὴ
at (the) revelation of Jesus Christ. As children of obedience, not

συσχηματιζόμενοι ταῖς πρότερον ἐν τῇ ἀγνοίᾳ ὑμῶν ἐπιθυ-
fashioning yourselves to the formerly in the ignorance of you lusts,

15 μίαις, ἀλλὰ κατὰ τὸν καλέσαντα ὑμᾶς ἅγιον καὶ αὐτοὶ ἅγιοι
but according to the having called you Holy one, also yourselves holy

16 ἐν πάσῃ ἀναστροφῇ γενήθητε· διότι γέγραπται, Ἅγιοι
in all conduct become. Because it has been written: holy

17 γένεσθε, ὅτι ἐγὼ ἅγιός εἰμι. καὶ εἰ πατέρα ἐπικαλεῖσθε τὸν
Be, because I holy am. And if (as) Father you call on (Him), the (One)

ἀπροσωπολήπτως κρίνοντα κατὰ τὸ ἑκάστου ἔργον, ἐν
without respect to persons judging according to the of each one work, in

18 φόβῳ τὸν τῆς παροικίας ὑμῶν χρόνον ἀναστράφητε· εἰδότες
fear the of the sojourning of you time pass, knowing

ὅτι οὐ φθαρτοῖς, ἀργυρίῳ ἢ χρυσίῳ, ἐλυτρώθητε ἐκ τῆς
that not with corruptible things, silver or gold, you were redeemed from the

19 ματαίας ὑμῶν ἀναστροφῆς πατροπαραδότου, ἀλλὰ τιμίῳ
worthless of you living handed down from fathers, but with precious

20 αἵματι ὡς ἀμνοῦ ἀμώμου καὶ ἀσπίλου Χριστοῦ, προεγνω-
blood, as of a lamb unblemished and unspotted, of Christ, having been

σμένου μὲν πρὸ καταβολῆς κόσμου, φανερωθέντος δὲ ἐπ᾽
foreknown before (the) foundation of (the) world, revealed but in

21 ἐσχάτων τῶν χρόνων δι᾽ ὑμᾶς, τοὺς δι᾽ αὐτοῦ πιστεύοντας
(the) last of the times because of you, those through Him believing

εἰς Θεόν, τὸν ἐγείραντα αὐτὸν ἐκ νεκρῶν, καὶ δόξαν αὐτῷ
in God, the (One) raising Him from (the) dead, and glory to Him

22 δόντα, ὥστε τὴν πίστιν ὑμῶν καὶ ἐλπίδα εἶναι εἰς Θεόν. τὰς
having given, so as the faith of you and hope to be in God. The

ψυχὰς ὑμῶν ἡγνικότες ἐν τῇ ὑπακοῇ τῆς ἀληθείας διὰ Πνεύ-
souls of you having purified in the obedience of the truth, through (the)

ματος εἰς φιλαδελφίαν ἀνυπόκριτον, ἐκ καθαρᾶς καρδίας
Spirit to brotherly love unpretended, from (the) pure heart

23 ἀλλήλους ἀγαπήσατε ἐκτενῶς· ἀναγεγεννημένοι οὐκ ἐκ
one another love fervently, having been regenerated not by

σπορᾶς φθαρτῆς, ἀλλὰ ἀφθάρτου, διὰ λόγου ζῶντος Θεοῦ
seed corruptible, but incorruptible, through word (the) living of God

24 καὶ μένοντος εἰς τὸν αἰῶνα. διότι πᾶσα σὰρξ ὡς χόρτος,
and remaining to the age. Because all flesh (is) as grass,

καὶ πᾶσα δόξα ἀνθρώπου ὡς ἄνθος χόρτου. ἐξηράνθη ὁ
and all (the) glory of man as (the) flower of grass; was dried the

25 χόρτος, καὶ τὸ ἄνθος αὐτοῦ ἐξέπεσε· τὸ δὲ ῥῆμα Κυρίου
grass, and the flower of it fell out, the but word of (the) Lord

μένει εἰς τὸν αἰῶνα. τοῦτο δέ ἐστι τὸ ῥῆμα τὸ εὐαγγελισθὲν
remains to the age. this And is the word preached as gospel

εἰς ὑμᾶς.

to you.

## CHAPTER 2

### CHAPTER 2

[1] Then laying aside all malice, and all guile, and hypocrisies, and envies, and all evil words. [2] as newborn babes, desire the pure spiritual milk, that you may grow by it; [3] if indeed you tasted that the Lord (is) good. [4] Having drawn near to (Him), a living Stone, indeed having been rejected by men, but elect, precious with God; [5] you also as living stones are being built a spiritual house, a holy priesthood, to offer spiritual sacrifices acceptable to God through Jesus Christ. [6] Because of this, it is also contained in the Scripture "Behold, I lay in Zion a Stone, an elect, precious Corner-foundation; and the (one) believing on Him shall not ever be shamed." [7] Then to you who believe, (belongs) the honor ; but to disobeying ones, (He is the) Stone which those building rejected—This One became (the) Head-of (the) corner; [8] and a Stone-of-stumbling, and a Rock-of-offense to those stumbling at the word, disobeying, to which also they were appointed. [9] But you are a chosen race, a royal priesthood, a holy nation, a people for a possession, so that you may openly speak of the virtues of the (One) who has called you out of darkness into His marvelous light—[10] (you) who then were not a people, but now God's people; those (then) not pitied, but now pitied. [11] Beloved, I exhort (you) as sojourners and aliens to abstain from fleshly lusts, which war against the soul; [12] having your behavior good among the nations, in that which they speak against you as evildoers, by observing (your) good works, they may glorify God in a day of visitation.

**1** Ἀποθέμενοι οὖν πᾶσαν κακίαν καὶ πάντα δόλον καὶ
laying aside  Then  all  malice  and  all  guile,  and

**2** ὑποκρίσεις καὶ φθόνους καὶ πάσας καταλαλιάς, ὡς ἀρτιγέν-
hypocrisies, and envies,  and  all  evil words,  as  newborn

νητα βρέφη, τὸ λογικὸν ἄδολον γάλα ἐπιποθήσατε, ἵνα ἐν
babes,  the spiritual  pure  milk  desire,  that by

**3**
**4** αὐτῷ αὐξηθῆτε, εἴπερ ἐγεύσασθε ὅτι χρηστός ὁ Κύριος· πρὸς
it you may grow, if indeed you tasted that good  the Lord (is), to

ὃν προσερχόμενοι, λίθον ζῶντα, ὑπὸ ἀνθρώπων μὲν ἀποδε-
whom drawing near, a stone  living,  by  men  indeed having

**5** δοκιμασμένον, παρὰ δὲ Θεῷ ἐκλεκτόν, ἔντιμον, καὶ αὐτοὶ
been rejected  by but God  elect,  precious, also yourselves

ὡς λίθοι ζῶντες οἰκοδομεῖσθε οἶκος πνευματικός, ἱεράτευμα
as stones living are being built a house  spiritual,  a priesthood

ἅγιον, ἀνενέγκαι πνευματικὰς θυσίας εὐπροσδέκτους τῷ
holy,  to offer  spiritual  sacrifices  acceptable

**6** Θεῷ διὰ Ἰησοῦ Χριστοῦ. διὸ καὶ περιέχει ἐν τῇ γραφῇ,
to God through Jesus Christ. Because indeed it is contained in the Scripture:

Ἰδού, τίθημι ἐν Σιὼν λίθον ἀκρογωνιαῖον, ἐκλεκτόν, ἔντιμον·
Behold, I lay in Zion a stone corner foundation  elect,  precious,

**7** καὶ ὁ πιστεύων ἐπ᾽ αὐτῷ οὐ μὴ καταισχυνθῇ. ὑμῖν οὖν ἡ
and the (one) believing on  Him not at all shall be shamed. To you, then, the

τιμὴ τοῖς πιστεύουσιν· ἀπειθοῦσι δέ, Λίθον ὃν ἀπεδοκί-
honor,  those believing.  to disobeying ones, But a stone which rejected

μασαν οἱ οἰκοδομοῦντες, οὗτος ἐγενήθη εἰς κεφαλὴν γωνίας,
those  building.  This (One) came to be for Head of (the) corner,

**8** καί, Λίθος προσκόμματος καὶ πέτρα σκανδάλου· οἳ προσ-
and, a Stone - of-stumbling,  and a Rock-  of-offense to those

**9** κόπτουσι τῷ λόγῳ ἀπειθοῦντες· εἰς ὃ καὶ ἐτέθησαν. ὑμεῖς
stumbling at the word  disobeying,  to which indeed they were appointed.  you

δὲ γένος ἐκλεκτόν, βασίλειον ἱεράτευμα, ἔθνος ἅγιον, λαὸς
But a race  elect,  a royal  priesthood, a nation  holy, a people

εἰς περιποίησιν, ὅπως τὰς ἀρετὰς ἐξαγγείλητε τοῦ ἐκ
for possession,  so as  the virtues you may tell out of the (One) from

σκότους ὑμᾶς καλέσαντος εἰς τὸ θαυμαστὸν αὐτοῦ φῶς·
darkness  you having called into the marvelous  of Him light;

**10** οἱ ποτὲ οὐ λαός, νῦν δὲ λαὸς Θεοῦ· οἱ οὐκ ἠλεημένοι, νῦν δὲ
who then not a people, now but people God's, those not pitied,  now but

ἐλεηθέντες.
pitied.

**11** Ἀγαπητοί, παρακαλῶ ὡς παροίκους καὶ παρεπιδή-
Beloved,  I exhort (you) as sojourners  and  aliens

μους, ἀπέχεσθαι τῶν σαρκικῶν ἐπιθυμιῶν, αἵτινες στρατεύον-
to abstain from  fleshly  lusts,  which  war

**12** ται κατὰ τῆς ψυχῆς· τὴν ἀναστροφὴν ὑμῶν ἐν τοῖς ἔθνεσιν
against the soul,  the behavior  of you among the nations

ἔχοντες καλήν, ἵνα, ἐν ᾧ καταλαλοῦσιν ὑμῶν ὡς κακοποιῶν
having  good, that in which they speak against you  as  evildoers,

ἐκ τῶν καλῶν ἔργων, ἐποπτεύσαντες, δοξάσωσι τὸν Θεὸν
by the  good  works having witnessed,  they may glorify  God

ἐν ἡμέρᾳ ἐπισκοπῆς.
in a day  of visitation.

[13] Then be in obedience to every ordinance of men because of the Lord; whether to a king, as being supreme, [14] or to governors, as through Him having indeed been sent for vengeance (on) evildoers; but praise (on) welldoers; [15] because so is the will of God —doing good to silence the ignorance of foolish men; [16] as free, and not as a cover of evil having freedom, but as slaves of God. [17] Honor all, love the brotherhood, fear God, honor the king.

[18] Servants, be obedient to (your) masters in all fear, not only to those good and forbearing, but also to the perverse (ones). [19] For this (is) a grace, if because of conscience (to) God anyone bears grief, suffering unjustly. [20] For what glory (is it) if you patiently endure (while) sinning and being buffeted? [21] For you were called to this, for even Christ suffered on our behalf, leaving behind an example to us, that you should follow His steps; [22] who did no sin, nor was guile found in His mouth; [23] who, being reviled, did not revile in return; suffering, He did not threaten, but gave up (Himself) to Him judging righteously; [24] who Himself bore in His body our sins onto the tree, that dying to sins, we might live to righteousness; of whom, by His wound, you were healed. [25] For you were straying sheep, but now you (are) turned to the Shepherd and Overseer of your souls.

**13** Ὑποτάγητε οὖν πάσῃ ἀνθρωπίνῃ κτίσει διὰ τὸν Κύριον·
Be obedient, then, to every of men ordinance because of the Lord;

**14** εἴτε βασιλεῖ, ὡς ὑπερέχοντι· εἴτε ἡγεμόσιν, ὡς δι' αὐτοῦ
whether to a king as being supreme, or to governors, as through Him
πεμπομένοις εἰς ἐκδίκησιν μὲν κακοποιῶν, ἔπαινον δὲ
having been sent for vengeance indeed (on) evildoers, praise but

**15** ἀγαθοποιῶν. ὅτι οὕτως ἐστὶ τὸ θέλημα τοῦ Θεοῦ, ἀγαθο-
of welldoers; because so is the will of God, doing
ποιοῦντας φιμοῦν τὴν τῶν ἀφρόνων ἀνθρώπων ἀγνωσίαν·
good to silence the of foolish men ignorance;

**16** ὡς ἐλεύθεροι, καὶ μὴ ὡς ἐπικάλυμμα ἔχοντες τῆς κακίας τὴν
as free, and not as a cover having of evil

**17** ἐλευθερίαν, ἀλλ' ὡς δοῦλοι Θεοῦ. πάντας τιμήσατε. τὴν
freedom, but as slaves of God. all Honor,
ἀδελφότητα ἀγαπᾶτε. τὸν Θεὸν φοβεῖσθε. τὸν βασιλέα
the brotherhood love, God fear, the king
τιμᾶτε.
honor.

**18** Οἱ οἰκέται, ὑποτασσόμενοι ἐν παντὶ φόβῳ τοῖς δεσπόταις,
Servants, be obedient in all fear to the masters (of you),
οὐ μόνον τοῖς ἀγαθοῖς καὶ ἐπιεικέσιν, ἀλλὰ καὶ τοῖς σκολιοῖς.
not only to the good and forbearing but also to the perverse.

**19** τοῦτο γὰρ χάρις, εἰ διὰ συνείδησιν Θεοῦ ὑποφέρει τις
this For (is) a grace, if because of conscience of God bears anyone

**20** λύπας, πάσχων ἀδίκως. ποῖον γὰρ κλέος, εἰ ἁμαρτάνοντες
grief, suffering unjustly. what For glory (is it) if sinning
καὶ κολαφιζόμενοι ὑπομενεῖτε; ἀλλ' εἰ ἀγαθοποιοῦντες καὶ
and being buffeted you patiently endure? But if doing good and

**21** πάσχοντες ὑπομενεῖτε, τοῦτο χάρις παρὰ Θεῷ. εἰς τοῦτο
suffering you patiently endure, this (is) a grace from God. to this
γὰρ ἐκλήθητε, ὅτι καὶ Χριστὸς ἔπαθεν ὑπὲρ ἡμων, ἡμῖν
For you were called, be- cause even Christ suffered on behalf of us, for us
ὑπολιμπάνων ὑπογραμμόν, ἵνα ἐπακολουθήσητε τοῖς
leaving behind an example that you should follow the

**22** ἴχνεσιν αὐτοῦ· ὃς ἁμαρτίαν οὐκ ἐποίησεν, οὐδὲ εὑρέθη δόλος
steps of Him; who sin did not do, nor was found guile

**23** ἐν τῷ στόματι αὐτοῦ· ὃς λοιδορούμενος οὐκ ἀντελοιδόρει,
in the mouth of Him; who being reviled did not revile in return;

**24** πάσχων οὐκ ἠπείλει, παρεδίδου δὲ τῷ κρίνοντι δικαίως· ὃς
suffering, not He threatened, gave (Himself) but to the (one) judging righ- teously, who
τὰς ἁμαρτίας ἡμῶν αὐτὸς ἀνήνεγκεν ἐν τῷ σώματι αὐτοῦ
the sins of us Himself carried up in the body of Him
ἐπὶ τὸ ξύλον, ἵνα, ταῖς ἁμαρτίαις ἀπογενόμενοι, τῇ δικαιο-
onto the tree, that to sins dying, to righteous-

**25** σύνῃ ζήσωμεν· οὗ τῷ μώλωπι αὐτοῦ ἰάθητε. ἦτε γὰρ ὡς
ness we might live; of whom by the wound of Him you were you healed. were For as
πρόβατα πλανώμενα· ἀλλ' ἐπεστράφητε νῦν ἐπὶ τὸν ποι-
sheep wandering but you turned now to the
μένα καὶ ἐπίσκοπον τῶν ψυχῶν ὑμῶν.
Shepherd and Overseer of the souls of you.

CHAPTER 3

[1] Likewise, wives, submit yourselves to (your) own husbands, that even if any disobey the Word, by

**CHAPTER 3**

**1** Ὁμοίως, αἱ γυναῖκες, ὑποτασσόμεναι τοῖς ἰδίοις ἀν-
Likewise, wives, submitting yourselves to the own
δράσιν, ἵνα, καὶ εἴ τινες ἀπειθοῦσι τῷ λόγῳ, διὰ τῆς τῶν
husbands, that even if any disobey the word, through the of the

the behavior of the wives, they will without a word be won, [2] observing your pure behavior in fear. [3] Of whom let it not be the outward (act) of braiding of hairs, and of putting gold around, or of clothing, (the) adorning of garments, [4] but the hidden man of the heart, in the incorruptible (adornment) of the meek and quiet spirit, which is of great value before God. [5] For so once indeed the holy women hoping on God adorned themselves, submitting themselves to (their) own husbands, [6] as Sarah obeyed Abraham, calling him lord; of whom you became children, doing good and fearing no terror. [7] Likewise, husbands, dwelling together according to knowledge, as with a weaker vessel, the female, bestowing honor, as (being) truly co-heirs of (the) grace of life, not cutting off your prayers.

[8] And finally, all (being) of one mind, sympathetic, loving (the) brothers, tenderhearted, friendly, [9] not giving back evil for evil, or reviling against reviling; but; on the contrary, (give) blessing; knowing that you were called to this in order that you might inherit blessing. [10] For the (one) desiring to love life, and to see good days, let him restrain his tongue from evil, even his lips not to speak guile. [11] Let him turn aside from evil, and let him do good; let him seek peace and pursue it; [12] because the eyes of (the) Lord (are) on the righteous, and His ears (open) to their petition; but the face of (the) Lord (is) against (any) doing evil things.

[13] And who (is) the (one) harming you, if you become imitators of the good? [14] But if you truly suffer because of righteousness, (you are) blessed; [15] but sanctify the Lord God in your hearts, and always

**2** γυναικῶν ἀναστροφῆς ἄνευ λόγου κερδηθήσονται, ἐπο-
wives    behavior    without a word   they will be won   having

**3** πτεύσαντες τὴν ἐν φόβῳ αγνὴν ἀναστροφὴν ὑμῶν. ὧν ἔστω
witnessed   the  in  fear  pure   behavior   of you. Of whom let it be

οὐχ ὁ ἔξωθεν ἐμπλοκῆς τριχῶν, καὶ περιθέσεως χρυσίων,
not the outward of braiding  of hairs,  and of putting around  gold (jewelry)

**4** ἢ ἐνδύσεως ἱματίων κόσμος· ἀλλ' ὁ κρυπτὸς τῆς καρδίας
or of clothing of garments adorning;  but  the hidden of the  heart

ἄνθρωπος, ἐν τῷ ἀφθάρτῳ τοῦ πραέος καὶ ἡσυχίου πνεύ-
man,      in the incorruptible of the meek  and  quiet  spirit

**5** ματος, ὅ ἐστιν ἐνώπιον τοῦ Θεοῦ πολυτελές. οὕτω γάρ ποτε
which is   before   God of great value.  so  For  then

καὶ αἱ ἅγιαι γυναῖκες αἱ ἐλπίζουσαι ἐπὶ τὸν Θεὸν ἐκόσμουν
also the holy  women    hoping    on   God adorned

**6** ἑαυτάς, ὑποτασσόμεναι τοῖς ἰδίοις ἀνδράσιν· ὡς Σάρρα
themselves, submitting themselves to the own husbands·  as  Sarah

ὑπήκουσε τῷ Ἀβραάμ, κύριον αὐτὸν καλοῦσα, ἧς ἐγενήθητε
obeyed     Abraham,  lord   him   calling, of whom you became

τέκνα, ἀγαθοποιοῦσαι καὶ μὴ φοβούμεναι μηδεμίαν πτόησιν.
children, doing good    and  fearing      no         terror.

**7** Οἱ ἄνδρες ὁμοίως, συνοικοῦντες κατὰ γνῶσιν, ὡς ἀσθενε-
Husbands likewise, dwelling together according to knowledge, as with a

στέρῳ σκεύει τῷ γυναικείῳ ἀπονέμοντες τιμήν, ὡς καὶ
weaker vessel the female    bestowing    honor,  as  truly

συγκληρονόμοι χάριτος ζωῆς, εἰς τὸ μὴ ἐκκόπτεσθαι τὰς
co-heirs      of (the) grace of life, unto  not cutting off   the

προσευχὰς ὑμῶν.
prayers    of you.

**8** Τὸ δὲ τέλος, πάντες ὁμόφρονες, συμπαθεῖς, φιλάδελφοι,
And finally,   all   of one mind,  sympathetic, loving (the) brothers,

**9** εὔσπλαγχνοι, φιλόφρονες· μὴ ἀποδιδόντες κακὸν ἀντὶ κακοῦ,
tenderhearted,  friendly,  not  giving back   evil against evil,

ἢ λοιδορίαν ἀντὶ λοιδορίας· τοὐναντίον δὲ εὐλογοῦντες,
or reviling   against reviling·  on the contrary but,  blessing,

εἰδότες ὅτι εἰς τοῦτο ἐκλήθητε, ἵνα εὐλογίαν κληρονομήσητε.
knowing that to this  you were called that blessing you might inherit.

**10** Ὁ γὰρ θέλων ζωὴν ἀγαπᾶν, καὶ ἰδεῖν ἡμέρας ἀγαθάς,
the (one) For desiring life to love,  and  to see  days   good,

παυσάτω τὴν γλῶσσαν αὐτοῦ ἀπὸ κακοῦ, καὶ χείλη αὐτοῦ
let him hold back the tongue of him from evil, even (the) lips of him

**11** τοῦ μὴ λαλῆσαι δόλον· ἐκκλινάτω ἀπὸ κακοῦ, καὶ ποιησάτω
not to speak  guile;  let him turn away from evil,  and let him do

**12** ἀγαθόν· ζητησάτω εἰρήνην, καὶ διωξάτω αὐτήν. ὅτι οἱ
good;   let him seek  peace,   and  pursue   it.  because the

ὀφθαλμοὶ Κυρίου ἐπὶ δικαίους, καὶ ὦτα αὐτοῦ εἰς δέησιν
eyes      of (the) Lord (are) on the righteous, and His ears (open) to petition

αὐτῶν· πρόσωπον δὲ Κυρίου ἐπὶ ποιοῦντας κακά.
of them;  (the) face but of (the) Lord against (any) doing evil things.

**13** Καὶ τίς ὁ κακώσων ὑμᾶς, ἐὰν τοῦ ἀγαθοῦ μιμηταὶ γένησθε;
And who (is) he harming you,  if of the  good  imitators you become?

**14** ἀλλ' εἰ καὶ πάσχοιτε διὰ δικαιοσύνην, μακάριοι· τὸν δὲ
But if truly you suffer because of righteousness, blessed (are you). the But

**15** φόβον αὐτῶν μὴ φοβηθῆτε, μηδὲ ταραχθῆτε· Κύριον δὲ τὸν
feat  of them do not fear,     nor  be troubled,  Lord but the

Θεὸν ἁγιάσατε ἐν ταῖς καρδίαις ὑμῶν· ἕτοιμοι δὲ ἀεὶ πρὸς
God sanctify  in  the  hearts  of you; ready  and always to

(be) ready to give an answer to everyone asking you a reason concerning the hope in you, with meekness and fear, [16] having a good conscience, that while they speak against you as evildoers, they may be shamed. those falsely accusing your good behavior in Christ. [17] For (it is) better, if the will of God wills (it), to suffer (for) doing good than (for) doing evil. [18] Because even Christ once suffered concerning sins, the just for the unjust, that He might bring you to God; indeed being put to death in (the) flesh, but made alive in the Spirit; [19] in which also, going in to the spirits in prison, He then proclaimed [20] to disobeying ones, when the longsuffering of God waited in (the) days of Noah, an ark having been prepared in which a few, that is, eight souls, were saved through water. [21] Which figure now also saves us, baptism: not a putting away of (the) filth of (the) flesh; but (the) answer of a good conscience toward God through (the) resurrection of Jesus Christ; [22] who is at (the) right (hand) of God, having gone into Heaven; angels and authorities and powers having been subjected to Him.

CHAPTER 4
[1] Therefore, Christ having suffered for us in (the) flesh, you also arm yourselves (with) the same mind, because he suffering in (the) flesh has ceased sin; [2] to the end (that he) no longer (will) live the remaining time in (the) flesh in (the) lusts of men, but in the will of God. [3] For (the) time of life having passed away (is) sufficient to us to have worked out the will of the nations, having gone on in wantonness, lusts, drunkennesses, parties, carousings, and unlawful idolatries; [4] in which they are surprised, your not running with (them) into the same overflow of unsavedness, blaspheming; [5] who will give account to Him having readiness to judge (the) living and dead.

ἀπολογίαν παντὶ τῷ αἰτοῦντι ὑμᾶς λόγον περὶ τῆς ἐν ὑμῖν
give an answer to everyone asking    you a word concerning the in you

16 ἐλπίδος, μετὰ πραΰτητος καὶ φόβου· συνείδησιν ἔχοντες
hope;      with  meekness   and  fear,   conscience   having

ἀγαθήν, ἵνα, ἐν ᾧ καταλαλῶσιν ὑμῶν ὡς κακοποιῶν,
a good,  that  while they speak against you   as  evildoers,

καταισχυνθῶσιν οἱ ἐπηρεάζοντες ὑμῶν τὴν ἀγαθὴν ἐν
they may be shamed , those abusing    of you  the  good   in

17 Χριστῷ ἀναστροφήν. κρεῖττον γὰρ ἀγαθοποιοῦντας, εἰ
Christ  behavior.  (it is) better For   doing good     if

18 θέλει τὸ θέλημα τοῦ Θεοῦ, πάσχειν, ἢ κακοποιοῦντας. ὅτι
wills the will      of God, to suffer, than (for) doing evil. Because

καὶ Χριστὸς ἅπαξ περὶ ἁμαρτιῶν ἔπαθε, δίκαιος ὑπὲρ
even Christ  once concerning sins  suffered,  the just  for

ἀδίκων, ἵνα ἡμᾶς προσαγάγῃ τῷ Θεῷ, θανατωθεὶς μὲν
the unjust, that you He might bring  to God, being put to death truly

19 σαρκί, ζωοποιηθεὶς δὲ τῷ πνεύματι, ἐν ᾧ καὶ τοῖς ἐν φυλακῇ
in (the) flesh, made alive but in the Spirit;  in which also to the in prison

20 πνεύμασι πορευθεὶς ἐκήρυξεν, ἀπειθήσασί ποτε, ὅτε ἅπαξ
spirits     going   He proclaimed to disobeying ones then, when once

ἐξεδέχετο ἡ τοῦ Θεοῦ μακροθυμία ἐν ἡμέραις Νῶε, κατα-
waited    the   of God longsuffering in (the) days of Noah, having

σκευαζομένης κιβωτοῦ, εἰς ἣν ὀλίγαι, τοῦτ' ἔστιν ὀκτὼ
been prepared   an ark,   in which a few,  this  is,  eight

21 ψυχαί, διεσώθησαν δι' ὕδατος· ᾧ καὶ ἡμᾶς ἀντίτυπον νῦν
souls,   were saved  through water. Which also us  figure   now

σώζει βάπτισμα, οὐ σαρκὸς ἀπόθεσις ῥύπου, ἀλλὰ συνειδή-
saves, baptism,  not of (the) flesh a putting of (the) but of a conscience
                                away filth,

σεως ἀγαθῆς ἐπερώτημα εἰς Θεόν, δι' ἀναστάσεως Ἰησοῦ
good   an answer toward God, through (the) resurrection of Jesus

22 Χριστοῦ, ὅς ἐστιν ἐν δεξιᾷ τοῦ Θεοῦ, πορευθεὶς εἰς οὐρανόν,
Christ,  who  is at (the) right   of God, having gone into Heaven,

ὑποταγέντων αὐτῷ ἀγγέλων καὶ ἐξουσιῶν καὶ δυνάμεων.
being subjected  to Him  angels  and authorities and  powers.

CHAPTER 4

1 Χριστοῦ οὖν παθόντος ὑπὲρ ἡμῶν σαρκί, καὶ ὑμεῖς τὴν
Christ Therefore having suffering for us in (the) flesh, also you  the

αὐτὴν ἔννοιαν ὁπλίσασθε· ὅτι ὁ παθὼν ἐν σαρκί, πέπαυται
same  mind arm yourselves, because. he suffering in (the) flesh has ceased

2 ἁμαρτίας· εἰς τὸ μηκέτι ἀνθρώπων ἐπιθυμίαις, ἀλλὰ θελή-
from sin;  for the no longer  of men   in (the) lusts, but in (the) will

3 ματι Θεοῦ τὸν ἐπίλοιπον ἐν σαρκὶ βιῶσαι χρόνον. ἀρκετὸς
of God the remaining  in (the) flesh to live  time.  sufficient

γὰρ ἡμῖν ὁ παρεληλυθὼς χρόνος τοῦ βίου τὸ θέλημα τῶν
For to us  the having passed away time   of life of the  will of the

ἐθνῶν κατεργάσασθαι, πεπορευμένους ἐν ἀσελγείαις, ἐπιθυ-
nations having worked out, having gone (on) in wantonness,   lusts,

μίαις, οἰνοφλυγίαις, κώμοις, πότοις, καὶ ἀθεμίτοις εἰδωλο-
drunkennesses,  parties, carousings, and  unlawful  idol-

4 λατρείαις· ἐν ᾧ ξενίζονται, μὴ συντρεχόντων ὑμῶν εἰς τὴν
atries.    While they are surprised not running with  you into the

αὐτὴν τῆς ἀσωτίας ἀνάχυσιν, βλασφημοῦντες· οἳ ἀποδώ-
same  of dissoluteness overflow,  blaspheming;   who will give

5 σουσι λόγον τῷ ἑτοίμως ἔχοντι κρῖναι ζῶντας καὶ νεκρούς.
account to the (One)  having to judge  living  and dead.
                     ready

[6] For to this (end) also the gospel was preached to (the) dead, that they might be judged according to men in (the) flesh, but might live according to God in (the) Spirit.

[7] But the end of all things has drawn near. Be of sound mind, then, and be sensible to prayers; [8] and above all things having fervent love to yourselves, because love covers a multitude of sins. [9] Be hospitable to one another without murmuring; [10] each one as he received a gift, ministering it to yourselves as good stewards of (the) manifold grace of God. [11] If anyone speaks, (let it be) as the words of God; if anyone ministers, as by strength which God supplies, that in all things God may be glorified through Jesus Christ; to whom is the glory and the might forever and ever. Amen.

[12] Beloved, do not be astonished (at) the fiery trial happening among you for your testing, as (if) a surprise (were) occurring; [13] but according as you share the sufferings of Christ, rejoice; so that you may rejoice exultingly at the revelation of His glory. [14] If you are reviled in (the) name of Christ, (you are) blessed, because the Spirit of God and of glory rests on you. Indeed, according to them He is blasphemed; but according to you, He is glorified. [15] For do not let any of you suffer as a murderer, or a thief, or an evildoer, or as a meddler. [16] But if (he suffers) as a Christian, do not let him be ashamed, but to glorify God in this respect. [17] Because the time (has come) to begin the judgment from the house of God; and if firstly from us, what (will be) the end of those disobeying the gospel? [18] And if the righteous one is scarcely saved, where will the ungodly and sinner appear? [19] So as indeed those suffering according to God's will, as to a faithful Creator, let them commit their souls in welldoing.

---

**6** εἰς τοῦτο γὰρ καὶ νεκροῖς εὐηγγελίσθη, ἵνα κριθῶσι μὲν κατὰ
for this   For indeed to dead was preached   that they might in- accord-
                        ones the gospel        be judged deed ing to
ἀνθρώπους σαρκί, ζῶσι δὲ κατὰ Θεὸν πνεύματι.
men   in (the) flesh; might live but according to God in (the) Spirit.

**7** Πάντων δὲ τὸ τέλος ἤγγικε· σωφρονήσατε οὖν καὶ
of all things But the end has drawn near. Be disciplined, then, and

**8** νήψατε εἰς τὰς προσευχάς· πρὸ πάντων δὲ τὴν εἰς ἑαυτοὺς
be sensible to prayers;   before all things and   to yourselves
ἀγάπην ἐκτενῆ ἔχοντες, ὅτι ἡ ἀγάπη καλύψει πλῆθος
love   fervent   having, because   love   will cover a multitude

**9** ἁμαρτιῶν· φιλόξενοι εἰς ἀλλήλους ἄνευ γογγυσμῶν·
of sins.   Be hospitable to one another without murmurings;

**10** ἕκαστος καθὼς ἔλαβε χάρισμα, εἰς ἑαυτοὺς αὐτὸ διακονοῦν-
each one   as he received a gift,   to yourselves it   ministering

**11** τες, ὡς καλοὶ οἰκονόμοι ποικίλης χάριτος Θεοῦ· εἴ τις λαλεῖ,
as good   stewards of (the) manifold grace of God; If any speaks,
ὡς λόγια Θεοῦ· εἴ τις διακονεῖ, ὡς ἐξ ἰσχύος ἧς χορηγεῖ ὁ
as (the) words of God; if any ministers.   as by strength which supplies
Θεός· ἵνα ἐν πᾶσι δοξάζηται ὁ Θεὸς διὰ Ἰησοῦ Χριστοῦ,
God,   that in all things may be glorified God through Jesus Christ,
ᾧ ἐστὶν ἡ δόξα καὶ τὸ κράτος εἰς τοὺς αἰῶνας τῶν αἰώνων.
to whom is the glory and the might to the ages of the ages.
ἀμήν.
Amen.

**12** Ἀγαπητοί, μὴ ξενίζεσθε τῇ ἐν ὑμῖν πυρώσει πρὸς πειρα-
Beloved, do not be astonished (at) among you fiery trial for   trial
                                  the

**13** σμὸν ὑμῖν γινομένη, ὡς ξένου ὑμῖν συμβαίνοντος· ἀλλὰ καθὸ
of you happening, as a surprise to you occurring,   but as
κοινωνεῖτε τοῖς τοῦ Χριστοῦ παθήμασι, χαίρετε, ἵνα καὶ ἐν
you share   the   of Christ sufferings,   rejoice, that also at

**14** τῇ ἀποκαλύψει τῆς δόξης αὐτοῦ χαρῆτε ἀγαλλιώμενοι. εἰ
the revelation of the glory of Him you may rejoice exultingly If
ὀνειδίζεσθε ἐν ὀνόματι Χριστοῦ, μακάριοι ὅτι τὸ τῆς δόξης
you are reviled in (the) name of Christ, blessed (are you), for the of glory
καὶ τὸ τοῦ Θεοῦ Πνεῦμα ἐφ᾽ ὑμᾶς ἀναπαύεται· κατὰ μὲν
and   the of God Spirit   on you   rests; according to truly

**15** αὐτοὺς βλασφημεῖται, κατὰ δὲ ὑμᾶς δοξάζεται. μὴ γάρ τις
them,   He is blasphemed; according to but you, He is glorified. not For any
ὑμῶν πασχέτω ὡς φονεύς, ἢ κλέπτης, ἢ κακοποιός, ἢ ὡς
of you let suffer as a murderer, or a thief,   or an evildoer,   or as

**16** ἀλλοτριοεπίσκοπος· εἰ δὲ ὡς Χριστιανός, μὴ αἰσχυνέσθω,
a meddler;   if but as   a Christian,   not let him be ashamed,

**17** δοξαζέτω δὲ τὸν Θεὸν ἐν τῷ μέρει τούτῳ. ὅτι ὁ καιρὸς τοῦ
to glorify but   God in   respect this. Because the time
ἄρξασθαι τὸ κρίμα ἀπὸ τοῦ οἴκου τοῦ Θεοῦ· εἰ δὲ πρῶτον
to begin   the judgment from the house   of God; if and firstly
ἀφ᾽ ἡμῶν, τί τὸ τέλος τῶν ἀπειθούντων τῷ τοῦ Θεοῦ
from   us, what (will be) the end those disobeying   the   of God

**18** εὐαγγελίῳ; καὶ εἰ ὁ δίκαιος μόλις σώζεται, ὁ ἀσεβὴς καὶ
gospel?   And if the righteous one scarcely is saved, the ungodly and

**19** ἁμαρτωλὸς ποῦ φανεῖται ; ὥστε καὶ οἱ πάσχοντες κατὰ τὸ
sinner   where will appear? So as indeed those suffering according to
θέλημα τοῦ Θεοῦ, ὡς πιστῷ κτίστῃ παρατιθέσθωσαν τὰς
will   God's, as to a faithful Creator, let them commit   the
ψυχὰς ἑαυτῶν ἐν ἀγαθοποιΐα.
souls   of themselves in welldoing.

CHAPTER 5

CHAPTER 5

**[1]** I, a fellow-elder, exhort the elders among you, (I being) also witness of the sufferings of Christ, and being sharer of the about to be revealed glory: **[2]** Shepherd the flock of God among you, exercising oversight, not by compulsion, but willingly; not for base gain, but readily; **[3]** nor as exercising lordship over the allotments but becoming examples of the flock. **[4]** And (at) the appearing of the chief Shepherd, you will receive the never-fading crown of glory. **[5]** Likewise, younger ones be subject to older ones; and all to one another being subject. Put on humility, because God sets (Himself) against proud ones; but he gives grace to humble ones. **[6]**

Be humbled then, under the mighty hand of God, that He may exalt you in time; **[7]** having all your anxiety cast onto Him, because it matters to Him concerning you. **[8]** Be sensible, watch, because your adversary the Devil walks about seeking someone he may devour; **[9]** whom resist firm in the faith, knowing the same sufferings (that are) in (the) world are being completed in your brotherhood. **[10]** Now the God of all grace, He calling you to His eternal glory in Christ Jesus, (you) having suffered a little, (He) Himself will perfect, confirm, strengthen, establish you. **[11]** To Him (be) the glory and the might forever and ever. Amen.

**[12]** I wrote to you through a few (words) by way of Silvanus the faithful brother, as I reckon, exhorting and witnessing this to be (the) true grace of God, in which you stand. **[13]** The fellow-elected in Babylon greets you; also Mark my son. **[14]** Greet one another with a kiss of love.

1 Πρεσβυτέρους τοὺς ἐν ὑμῖν παρακαλῶ ὁ συμπρεσβύτερος
elders          The among you  I exhort, the (one) a fellow-elder (being),
καὶ μάρτυς τῶν τοῦ Χριστοῦ παθημάτων, ὁ καὶ τῆς μελλού-
and  witness of the   of Christ   sufferings,  the also of the being

2 σης ἀποκαλύπτεσθαι δόξης κοινωνός· ποιμάνατε τὸ ἐν ὑμῖν
about to be revealed   glory  sharer;    shepherd  the among you
ποίμνιον τοῦ Θεοῦ, ἐπισκοποῦντες μὴ ἀναγκαστῶς, ἀλλ'
flock       of God, exercising oversight not by compulsion,    but

3 ἑκουσίως· μηδὲ αἰσχροκερδῶς, ἀλλὰ προθύμως· μηδ' ὡς
willingly,   nor eagerly for base gain,  but    readily;    nor  as
κατακυριεύοντες τῶν κλήρων, ἀλλὰ τύποι γινόμενοι τοῦ
as exercising lordship over the allotments, but   examples becoming of the

4 ποιμνίου. καὶ φανερωθέντος τοῦ ἀρχιποίμενος, κομιεῖσθε τὸν
flock;      and (at) the appearing of the chief Shepherd, you will receive the

5 ἀμαράντινον τῆς δόξης στέφανον. ὁμοίως, νεώτεροι, ὑποτά-
unfading         of glory    crown.   Likewise, younger ones be sub-
γητε πρεσβυτέροις· πάντες δὲ ἀλλήλοις ὑποτασσόμενοι, τὴν
ject  to older ones;   all   and to one another being subject,
ταπεινοφροσύνην ἐγκομβώσασθε· ὅτι ὁ Θεὸς ὑπερηφάνοις
humility           put on,         because  God   proud ones

6 ἀντιτάσσεται, ταπεινοῖς δὲ δίδωσι χάριν. ταπεινώθητε
sets (Himself) against, to humble ones but He gives grace.   Be humbled,
οὖν ὑπὸ τὴν κραταιὰν χεῖρα τοῦ Θεοῦ, ἵνα ὑμᾶς ὑψώσῃ ἐν
then, under the mighty   hand   of God, that you He may exalt in

7 καιρῷ, πᾶσαν τὴν μέριμναν ὑμῶν ἐπιρρίψαντες ἐπ' αὐτόν,
time;   all     the  anxiety   of you   casting     onto Him,

8 ὅτι αὐτῷ μέλει περὶ ὑμῶν. νήψατε, γρηγορήσατε, ὅτι ὁ
because to Him it concerning you. Be sensible,  watch,    because the
           matters
ἀντίδικος ὑμῶν διάβολος, ὡς λέων ὠρυόμενος, περιπατεῖ
adversary of you, (the) devil,  as a lion  roaring    walks about

9 ζητῶν τίνα καταπίῃ· ᾧ ἀντίστητε στερεοὶ τῇ πίστει,
seeking someone he may devour; whom resist  firm  in the  faith,
εἰδότες τὰ αὐτὰ τῶν παθημάτων τῇ ἐν κόσμῳ ὑμῶν ἀδελ-
knowing the same     sufferings  in the in (the) world of you brother-

10 φότητι ἐπιτελεῖσθαι. ὁ δὲ Θεὸς πάσης χάριτος, ὁ καλέσας
hood are being completed. the Now God of all   grace, the (One) calling
ἡμᾶς εἰς τὴν αἰώνιον αὐτοῦ δόξαν ἐν Χριστῷ Ἰησοῦ, ὀλίγον
us  to the  eternal  of Him  glory in Christ  Jesus, a little
παθόντας αὐτὸς καταρτίσαι ὑμᾶς, στηρίξαι, σθενώσαι,
having suffered Himself perfect   you,   confirm,   strengthen,

11 θεμελιῶσαι. αὐτῷ ἡ δόξα καὶ τὸ κράτος εἰς τοὺς αἰῶνας τῶν
establish (you). To Him the glory and the might  to   the   ages   of the
αἰώνων. ἀμήν.
ages.    Amen.

12 Διὰ Σιλουανοῦ ὑμῖν τοῦ πιστοῦ ἀδελφοῦ, ὡς λογίζομαι,
Through Silvanus  to you the  faithful  brother,   as  I reckon,
δι' ὀλίγων ἔγραψα, παρακαλῶν καὶ ἐπιμαρτυρῶν ταύτην
via a few (words) I wrote,  exhorting  and  witnessing   this

13 εἶναι ἀληθῆ χάριν τοῦ Θεοῦ εἰς ἣν ἐστήκατε. ἀσπάζεται
to be (the) true grace  of God, in which you stand.  Greets
ὑμᾶς ἡ ἐν Βαβυλῶνι συνεκλεκτή, καὶ Μάρκος ὁ υἱός μου.
you the in  Babylon   fellow-elected, and  Mark  the son of me.

14 ἀσπάσασθε ἀλλήλους ἐν φιλήματι ἀγάπης.
Greet        one another with  a kiss    of love.

Εἰρήνη ὑμῖν πᾶσι τοῖς ἐν Χριστῷ Ἰησοῦ. ἀμήν.

Peace (be) to you, all those          **Peace  to you,  all   those in   Christ   Jesus.   Amen.**
in Christ Jesus, Amen.

KING JAMES II VERSION

THE SECOND GENERAL
EPISTLE OF
PETER

ΕΠΙΣΤΟΛΗ ΚΑΘΟΛΙΚΗ ΔΕΥΤΕΡΑ
EPISTLE GENERAL SECOND

## CHAPTER 1

[1] Simon Peter, a slave of Jesus Christ, to those equally precious with us, having obtained faith in (the) righteousness of our God, and of our Savior, Jesus Christ: [2] Grace to you, and peace be multiplied by a full knowledge of God, and of Jesus, our Lord.

[3] As His divine power has given to us all things pertaining to life and godliness, through the full knowledge of Him calling us through glory and virtue; [4] by means of which He has given to us the very great and precious promises, that by means of these you might be partakers of (the) divine nature, having escaped from the corruption (that is) in (the) world by lust. [5] But also in this very thing, bringing in all diligence, supply virtue in your faith; and with virtue, knowledge; [6] and with knowledge, self-control; and with self-control, patience; and with patience, godliness; [7] and with godliness, brotherly love; and with brotherly love, love. [8] For these things being in you, and abounding, make (you to be) neither barren nor unfruitful in the knowledge of the Lord Jesus Christ. [9] For (he) in whom these things are not present is blind, being short-sighted, taking on forgetfulness of the purging of his sins in time past. [10] For this reason, brothers, rather be diligent to make sure of your calling and election; for doing these things, you will not ever fall. [11] For so will be richly furnished to you the entrance into the everlasting kingdom of our Lord and Savior, Jesus

## CHAPTER 1

**1** Σίμων Πέτρος, δοῦλος καὶ ἀπόστολος Ἰησοῦ Χριστοῦ,
Simon Peter, a slave and apostle of Jesus Christ,
τοῖς ἰσότιμον ἡμῖν λαχοῦσι πίστιν ἐν δικαιοσύνῃ τοῦ Θεοῦ
to those equally with precious us having obtained faith in (the) righteousness of the God

**2** ἡμῶν καὶ σωτῆρος ἡμῶν Ἰησοῦ Χριστοῦ· χάρις ὑμῖν καὶ
of us and Savior of us, Jesus Christ: Grace to you and
εἰρήνη πληθυνθείη ἐν ἐπιγνώσει τοῦ Θεοῦ, καὶ Ἰησοῦ τοῦ
peace be multiplied by a full knowledge of God, and of Jesus the

**3** Κυρίου ἡμῶν· ὡς πάντα ἡμῖν τῆς θείας δυνάμεως αὐτοῦ τὰ
Lord of us. As all things to us the divine power of Him
πρὸς ζωὴν καὶ εὐσέβειαν δεδωρημένης, διὰ τῆς ἐπιγνώσεως
as to life and godliness having been given, through the full knowledge

**4** τοῦ καλέσαντος ἡμᾶς διὰ δόξης καὶ ἀρετῆς· δι' ὧν τὰ μέγιστα
of the (One) calling us via glory and virtue, through which the very great
ἡμῖν καὶ τίμια ἐπαγγέλματα δεδώρηται, ἵνα διὰ τούτων
to us and precious promises He has given, that through these
γένησθε θείας κοινωνοὶ φύσεως, ἀποφυγόντες τῆς ἐν κόσμῳ
you might be of a divine partakers nature, escaping from the in (the) world

**5** ἐν ἐπιθυμίᾳ φθορᾶς. καὶ αὐτὸ τοῦτο δέ, σπουδὴν πᾶσαν
by lust corruption. also in this very thing But, diligence all
παρεισενέγκαντες, ἐπιχορηγήσατε ἐν τῇ πίστει ὑμῶν τὴν
bringing in, fill out in the faith of you

**6** ἀρετήν, ἐν δὲ τῇ ἀρετῇ τὴν γνῶσιν, ἐν δὲ τῇ γνώσει τὴν
virtue; with and virtue, knowledge; with and knowledge,
ἐγκράτειαν, ἐν δὲ τῇ ἐγκρατείᾳ τὴν ὑπομονήν, ἐν δὲ τῇ
self-control; with and self-control, patience; with and

**7** ὑπομονῇ τὴν εὐσέβειαν, ἐν δὲ τῇ εὐσεβείᾳ τὴν φιλαδελφίαν,
patience, godliness, with and godliness, brotherly love;

**8** ἐν δὲ τῇ φιλαδελφίᾳ τὴν ἀγάπην. ταῦτα γὰρ υμῖν ὑπάρ-
with and brotherly love, love. these things For in you being
χοντα καὶ πλεονάζοντα, οὐκ ἀργοὺς οὐδὲ ἀκάρπους καθί-
and abounding, not barren not unfruitful
στησιν εἰς τὴν τοῦ Κυρίου ἡμῶν Ἰησοῦ Χριστοῦ ἐπίγνωσιν.
makes (you) in the of the Lord of us Jesus Christ full knowledge.

**9** ᾧ γὰρ μὴ πάρεστι ταῦτα, τυφλός ἐστι, μυωπάζων, λήθην
(he) For in whom not is present these things, blind is, being short-sighted, forgetful

**10** λαβὼν τοῦ καθαρισμοῦ τῶν πάλαι αὐτοῦ ἁμαρτιῶν. διὸ
taking of the cleansing of the in time past of him sins. Therefore
μᾶλλον, ἀδελφοί, σπουδάσατε βεβαίαν ὑμῶν τὴν κλῆσιν
rather, brothers, be diligent sure of you the calling
καὶ ἐκλογὴν ποιεῖσθαι· ταῦτα γὰρ ποιοῦντες οὐ μὴ πταίσητέ
and election to make; these things for doing not at all you will fall

**11** ποτε· ουτω γὰρ πλουσίως ἐπιχορηγηθήσεται ὑμῖν ἡ εἴσοδος
ever. so For richly will be furnished to you the entrance
εἰς τὴν αἰώνιον βασιλείαν τοῦ Κυρίου ἡμῶν καὶ σωτῆρος
into the eternal kingdom of the Lord of us and Savior,

Christ.

[12] Therefore, I will not neglect to cause you to remember always concerning these things, though (you are) knowing, and have been confirmed in the present truth. [13] But I think (it) right, so long as I am in this tabernacle, to stir you up by a reminder, [14] knowing that the putting off of my tabernacle is soon, as indeed our Lord Jesus made clear to me. [15] And I will be diligent also, to cause you always to have the memory of these things after my departure. [16] for not following fables having been cleverly devised we made known to you the power and coming of our Lord Jesus Christ, but having become eyewitnesses of the majesty of that (One). [17] For having received honor and glory from God

(the) Father—such a voice being borne to Him from the magnificent glory: "This is My Son, the Beloved, in whom I was well-pleased." —[18] and we heard this voice being borne out of Heaven, being with Him in the holy mountain. [19] And we have the more confirmed word of the prophets —(to) which you do well to take heed, as to a lamp shining in a murky place, until day dawns and the Daystar rises in your hearts; [20] knowing this first, that every prophecy of Scripture did not come into being of (its) own interpretation; [21] for prophecy was not at any time borne by (the) will of man, but being borne along by (the) Holy Spirit, holy men of God spoke.

## CHAPTER 2

[1] But there were also false prophets among the people, as also among you will be false teachers, who will secretly bring in destructive heresies, and denying the Master who had bought them, bringing swift destruction on themselves. [2] And many will follow

'Ιησοῦ Χριστοῦ.
Jesus    Christ.

12 Διὸ οὐκ ἀμελήσω ὑμᾶς ἀεὶ ὑπομιμνήσκειν περὶ τούτων,
Therefore not I will neglect  you always to cause to remember about these,
καίπερ εἰδότας, καὶ ἐστηριγμένους ἐν τῇ παρούσῃ ἀληθείᾳ.
though knowing  and having been confirmed in the present   truth.

13 δίκαιον δὲ ἡγοῦμαι, ἐφ' ὅσον εἰμὶ ἐν τούτῳ τῷ σκηνώματι,
right  And I deem (it), so long as I am in this      tabernacle,

14 διεγείρειν ὑμᾶς ἐν ὑπομνήσει· εἰδὼς ὅτι ταχινή ἐστιν ἡ
to arouse   you  by a reminder, knowing that soon   is  the
ἀπόθεσις τοῦ σκηνώματός μου, καθὼς καὶ ὁ Κύριος ἡμῶν
putting off of the tabernacle  of me, as indeed  the Lord  of us,

15 'Ιησοῦς Χριστὸς ἐδήλωσέ μοι. σπουδάσω δὲ καὶ ἑκάστοτε
Jesus    Christ,  made clear to me. I will be diligent And also always
ἔχειν ὑμᾶς μετὰ τὴν ἐμὴν ἔξοδον τὴν τούτων μνήμην
to have you  after   my    departure  the of these things memory

16 ποιεῖσθαι. οὐ γὰρ σεσοφισμένοις μύθοις ἐξακολουθήσαντες
to cause.   not For  having been cleverly devised fables following,
ἐγνωρίσαμεν ὑμῖν τὴν τοῦ Κυρίου ἡμῶν 'Ιησοῦ Χριστοῦ
we made known to you the of the Lord  of us, Jesus   Christ,
δύναμιν καὶ παρουσίαν, ἀλλ' ἐπόπται γενηθέντες τῆς
power   and coming,    but  eyewitnesses having become of the

17 ἐκείνου μεγαλειότητος. λαβὼν γὰρ παρὰ Θεοῦ πατρὸς
of that (One) majesty.   receiving For from   God (the) Father
τιμὴν καὶ δόξαν, φωνῆς ἐνεχθείσης αὐτῷ τοιᾶσδε ὑπὸ τῆς
honor and glory,  a voice being borne to Him  such   from the
μεγαλοπρεποῦς δόξης, Οὗτός ἐστιν ὁ υἱός μου ὁ ἀγαπητός,
magnificent    glory:  This  is   the Son of Me, the Beloved,

18 εἰς ὃν ἐγὼ εὐδόκησα· καὶ ταύτην τὴν φωνὴν ἡμεῖς ἠκού-
in whom I was well-pleased. And this        voice    we    heard
σαμεν ἐξ οὐρανοῦ ἐνεχθεῖσαν, σὺν αὐτῷ ὄντες ἐν τῷ ὄρει τῷ
out of Heaven being borne,   with Him  being in the mountain

19 ἁγίῳ. καὶ ἔχομεν βεβαιότερον τὸν προφητικὸν λόγον, ᾧ
holy. And we have more firm    the  prophetic    word, in which
καλῶς ποιεῖτε προσέχοντες, ὡς λύχνῳ φαίνοντι ἐν αὐχμηρῷ
well  you do  taking heed,  as to a lamp shining in murky
τόπῳ, ἕως οὗ ἡμέρα διαυγάσῃ, καὶ φωσφόρος ἀνατείλῃ ἐν
place, until  day  dawns,    and the Daystar   rises   in

20 ταῖς καρδίαις ὑμῶν· τοῦτο πρῶτον γινώσκοντες, ὅτι πᾶσα
the  hearts   of you; this  firstly knowing,     that every

21 προφητεία γραφῆς ἰδίας ἐπιλύσεως οὐ γίνεται. οὐ γὰρ
prophecy  of Scripture of (its) own unloosing did come into not For
                                                  not being.
θελήματι ἀνθρώπου ἠνέχθη ποτὲ προφητεία, ἀλλ' ὑπὸ
by (the) will of man   was borne at any prophecy,  but  by
                                  time
Πνεύματος 'Αγίου φερόμενοι ἐλάλησαν ἅγιοι Θεοῦ ἄνθρωποι.
(the) Spirit Holy being borne spoke (the) holy of God men.
                      along

## CHAPTER 2

1 'Εγένοντο δὲ καὶ ψευδοπροφῆται ἐν τῷ λαῷ, ὡς καὶ ἐν
there were But also false prophets  among the people, as also among
ὑμῖν ἔσονται ψευδοδιδάσκαλοι, οἵτινες παρεισάξουσιν
you  will be  false teachers,   who    will secretly bring in
αἱρέσεις ἀπωλείας, καὶ τὸν ἀγοράσαντα αὐτοὺς δεσπότην
heresies of destruction, and the having bought them    Master

2 ἀρνούμενοι, ἐπάγοντες ἑαυτοῖς ταχινὴν ἀπώλειαν. καὶ
denying,    bringing on themselves swift   destruction. And

their destructive ways by whom the way of truth will be evil spoken of. [3] And by covetousness, with well-turned words, they will use you for gain; for whom judgment of old does not linger, and their destruction does not slumber. [4] For if God did not spare sinning angels, but delivered (them) to chains of darkness, thrust down into Tartarus, having been kept to judgment; [5] and did not spare (the) ancient world, but preserved (the) eighth, Noah, a herald of righteousness, having brought (the) Flood on (the) world of ungodly ones; [6] and having reduced to ashes the cities (of) Sodom and Gomorrah, (He) condemned (them) with an overthrow, setting an example to men intending to live ungodly; [7] and he delivered righteous Lot, having been oppressed by the behavior of the lawless in lustfulness. [8] For that righteous one dwelling among them day by day, in seeing and hearing, (his) righteous soul (was) tormented with (their) lawless works. [9] (But the) Lord knows to deliver the godly out of temptation, and (how) to keep the unjust for a day of judgment, being punished. [10] and most of all those going after flesh in (the) lust of defilement, even despising dominion, darers, self-satisfied; they do not tremble, speaking evil (of) glories; [11] where angels being greater in strength and power do not bring against them a reproaching charge before (the) Lord. [12] But these like unreasoning natural beasts, having been born for capture and corruption, speaking evil in that which they are ignorant (of); in their corruption, they shall utterly perish, [13] being about to receive (the) wages of unrighteousness, deeming indulgence in the day (to be) pleasure; spots and blemishes, revelling in their deceits, feasting along with you; [14] having eyes full of an adulteress, and never ceasing from sin; alluring unsettled souls; having a heart exercis-

**3** πολλοὶ ἐξακολουθήσουσιν αὐτῶν ταῖς ἀπωλείαις, δι' οὓς
many will follow of them the destructive ways, by whom
ἡ ὁδὸς τῆς ἀληθείας βλασφημηθήσεται. καὶ ἐν πλεονεξίᾳ
the way of the truth will be evil spoken of, And by covetousness
πλαστοῖς λόγοις ὑμᾶς ἐμπορεύσονται· οἷς τὸ κρίμα ἔκπαλαι
with well-turned words you they will use for gain; for the whom judgment of old

**4** οὐκ ἀργεῖ, καὶ ἡ ἀπώλεια αὐτῶν οὐ νυστάζει. εἰ γὰρ ὁ
not lingers, and the destruction of them not slumbers. if For
Θεὸς ἀγγέλων ἁμαρτησάντων οὐκ ἐφείσατο, ἀλλὰ σειραῖς
God angels sinning did not spare, but to chains

**5** ζόφου ταρταρώσας παρέδωκεν εἰς κρίσιν τετηρημένους· καὶ
of darkness thrust down into Tartarus delivered (them) to judgment having been kept; and
ἀρχαίου κόσμου οὐκ ἐφείσατο, ἀλλ' ὄγδοον Νῶε δικαιοσύνης
(the) ancient world not spared, but (the) eighth, Noah, of righteousness

**6** κήρυκα ἐφύλαξε, κατακλυσμὸν κόσμῳ ἀσεβῶν ἐπάξας· καὶ
a herald preserved, a flood a world of ungodly bringing ones on; and
πόλεις Σοδόμων καὶ Γομόρρας τεφρώσας καταστροφῇ
the cities, Sodom and Gomorrah, covering with ashes by an overthrow

**7** κατέκρινεν, ὑπόδειγμα μελλόντων ἀσεβεῖν τεθεικώς· καὶ
condemned, an example of men intending to live ungodly setting; and
δίκαιον Λώτ, καταπονούμενον ὑπὸ τῆς τῶν ἀθέσμων ἐν
righteous Lot, having been oppressed by the of the lawless in

**8** ἀσελγείᾳ ἀναστροφῆς, ἐρρύσατο (βλέμματι γὰρ καὶ ἀκοῇ ὁ
lustfulness conduct delivered — in seeing for and hearing, the
δίκαιος, ἐγκατοικῶν ἐν αὐτοῖς, ἡμέραν ἐξ ἡμέρας ψυχὴν
righteous one dwelling among them day after day (his) soul

**9** δικαίαν ἀνόμοις ἔργοις ἐβασάνιζεν)· οἶδε Κύριος εὐσεβεῖς
righteous with (the) lawless works tormented — knows (the) Lord the godly
ἐκ πειρασμῶν ῥύεσθαι, ἀδίκους δὲ εἰς ἡμέραν κρίσεως κολαζο-
out of temptation to deliver, the unjust but for a day of judgment being

**10** μένους τηρεῖν· μάλιστα δὲ τοὺς ὀπίσω σαρκὸς ἐν ἐπιθυμίᾳ
punished to keep; most of all and the after flesh in lust
μιασμοῦ πορευομένους, καὶ κυριότητος καταφρονοῦντας.
of defilement (ones) going, and dominion despising,
τολμηταί, αὐθάδεις, δόξας οὐ τρέμουσι βλασφημοῦντες·
darers, self-satisfied, glories not they tremble (at), speaking evil,

**11** ὅπου ἄγγελοι, ἰσχύϊ καὶ δυνάμει μείζονες ὄντες, οὐ φέρουσι
where angels in strength and in power greater being do not bring

**12** κατ' αὐτῶν παρὰ Κυρίῳ βλάσφημον κρίσιν. οὗτοι δέ, ὡς
against them before (the) Lord a reproaching charge. these But, as
ἄλογα ζῶα φυσικὰ γεγενημένα εἰς ἅλωσιν καὶ φθοράν, ἐν
unreason- beasts natural having been born for capture and corruption, in
ing
οἷς ἀγνοοῦσι βλασφημοῦντες, ἐν τῇ φθορᾷ αὐτῶν καταφθαρή-
which they are (of) speaking evil; in the corruption of them, they shall
ignorant utterly

**13** σονται, κομιούμενοι μισθὸν ἀδικίας, ἡδονὴν ἡγούμενοι τὴν
perish; being about to receive wages of wrong, (as) pleasure deeming the
ἐν ἡμέρᾳ τρυφήν, σπῖλοι καὶ μῶμοι, ἐντρυφῶντες ἐν ταῖς
in (the) day indulgence, spots and blemishes, revelling (in); in the

**14** ἀπάταις αὐτῶν συνευωχούμενοι ὑμῖν, ὀφθαλμοὺς ἔχοντες
deceits of them feasting along with you; eyes having
μεστοὺς μοιχαλίδος καὶ ἀκαταπαύστους ἁμαρτίας, δελεά-
full of an adulteress, and not ceasing from sin, alluring
ζοντες ψυχὰς ἀστηρίκτους, καρδίαν γεγυμνασμένην πλεονε-
souls unsettled; a heart having been busied covet-

**15** ξίαις ἔχοντες, κατάρας τέκνα· καταλιπόντες τὴν εὐθεῖαν ὁδὸν
ousness having; of curse children; forsaking a straight way,

ing (itself in) covetousness; cursed children; [15] forsaking a straight way, they went astray, having followed the way of Balaam the (son) of Beor, who loved the wages of unrighteousness, [16] but had reproof of (his) own transgression — (the) dumb ass speaking in (the) voice of a man restrained the madness of the prophet. [17] These are springs without water, clouds being driven by tempest, for whom the blackness of darkness is kept forever. [18] For speaking great swelling (words) of vanity, by (the) lusts of the flesh, by unbridled lusts, they allure those who (were) escaping those living in error, [19] promising them freedom, though themselves being slaves of corruption— for by whom anyone has been overcome, even to this one he has been enslaved. [20] For if by a full knowledge of the Lord and Savior Jesus Christ (they) have escaped the defilements of the world, and again being entangled, (they) have been overcome by these—(their) last (state is) worse than the first. [21] For it were better for them not to have fully known the way of righteousness, than fully knowing to turn from the holy commandment delivered to them. [22] But the (word) of the true proverb has happened to them: (the) dog turning to (his) own vomit; and, (the) washed sow to wallowing (in) mud.

CHAPTER 3

[1] Beloved, I now write this second epistle to you, in which by reminder I stir up your sincere mind to remember [2] the words having been spoken before by the holy prophets, and those of the apostles, by us, (by) the Lord and Savior; [3] First, knowing this, that during (the) last of the days scoffers will come, walking according to their own lusts, [4] and saying, Where is the promise of His coming? For since the fathers fell asleep,

**16** ἐπλανήθησαν, ἐξακολουθήσαντες τῇ ὁδῷ τοῦ Βαλαὰμ τοῦ
they erred,      following      the way   of Balaam the (son)

Βοσόρ, ὃς μισθὸν ἀδικίας ἠγάπησεν, ἔλεγξιν δὲ ἔσχεν ἰδίας
of Beor, who (the) wages of wrong loved,    reproof and had of own

παρανομίας· ὑποζύγιον ἄφωνον, ἐν ἀνθρώπου φωνῇ φθεγξά-
transgression;   ass    a dumb   with  of a man   voice speaking

**17** μενον, ἐκώλυσε τὴν τοῦ προφήτου παραφρονίαν. οὗτοί εἰσι
restrained the of the  prophet    madness.    These are

πηγαὶ ἄνυδροι, νεφέλαι ὑπὸ λαίλαπος ἐλαυνόμεναι, οἷς ὁ
springs without water, clouds  by   tempest  being driven, for whom the

**18** ζόφος τοῦ σκότους εἰς αἰῶνα τετήρηται. ὑπέρογκα γὰρ
blackness of darkness  to  ages   is kept. overswollen (words) For

ματαιότητος φθεγγόμενοι, δελεάζουσιν ἐν ἐπιθυμίαις σαρκός,
of vanity     speaking,    they allure  by (the) lusts of (the) flesh,

ἐν ἀσελγείαις, τοὺς ὄντως ἀποφυγόντας τοὺς ἐν πλάνῃ
in unbridled lusts, those indeed  escaping   the (ones) in  error

**19** ἀναστρεφομένους, ἐλευθερίαν αὐτοῖς ἐπαγγελλόμενοι, αὐτοὶ
living,        freedom   to them  promising,    themselves

δοῦλοι ὑπάρχοντες τῆς φθορᾶς· ᾧ γάρ τις ἥττηται, τούτῳ
slaves  being    of corruption; by for any- has been to this one
                               whom one defeated

**20** καὶ δεδούλωται. εἰ γὰρ ἀποφυγόντες τὰ μιάσματα τοῦ
also he has been enslaved. if For having escaped the defilements of the

κόσμου ἐν ἐπιγνώσει τοῦ Κυρίου καὶ σωτῆρος Ἰησοῦ Χρι-
world  by a full knowledge of the Lord and Savior   Jesus Christ,

**21** στοῦ, τούτοις δὲ πάλιν ἐμπλακέντες ἡττῶνται, γέγονεν αὐτοῖς
by these and again being entangled have been have become to them
                                       defeated,

τὰ ἔσχατα χείρονα τῶν πρώτων. κρεῖττον γὰρ ἦν αὐτοῖς
the last things worse (than) the first.   better  For it was for them

μὴ ἐπεγνωκέναι τὴν ὁδὸν τῆς δικαιοσύνης, ἢ ἐπιγνοῦσιν
not to have fully known the way  of righteousness, than fully knowing

ἐπιστρέψαι ἐκ τῆς παραδοθείσης αὐτοῖς ἁγίας ἐντολῆς.
to turn  from the - delivered    to them  holy commandment.

**22** συμβέβηκε δὲ αὐτοῖς τὸ τῆς ἀληθοῦς παροιμίας, Κύων
has happened But to them the (word) of the true   proverb: (the) dog

ἐπιστρέψας ἐπὶ τὸ ἴδιον ἐξέραμα, καὶ ὗς λουσαμένη εἰς
turning   to the  own  vomit; and, (The) sow washed,  to

κύλισμα βορβόρου.
wallowing of mud.

CHAPTER 3

**1** Ταύτην ἤδη, ἀγαπητοί, δευτέραν ὑμῖν γράφω ἐπιστολήν,
This now,  beloved,  second to you I write  epistle,

ἐν αἷς διεγείρω ὑμῶν ἐν ὑπομνήσει τὴν εἰλικρινῆ διάνοιαν,
in which I arouse  you  by  reminder  the sincere   mind,

**2** μνησθῆναι τῶν προειρημένων ῥημάτων ὑπὸ τῶν ἁγίων
to remember the having been before spoken words by  the  holy

προφητῶν, καὶ τῆς τῶν ἀποστόλων ἡμῶν ἐντολῆς τοῦ
prophets,  and the of the  apostles  by us command of the

**3** Κυρίου καὶ σωτῆρος· τοῦτο πρῶτον γινώσκοντες, ὅτι
Lord  and Savior;   this  firstly  knowing,   that

ἐλεύσονται ἐπ᾽ ἐσχάτου τῶν ἡμερῶν ἐμπαῖκται, κατὰ τὰς
will come  during (the) last of the  days  scoffers, according to the

**4** ἰδίας αὐτῶν ἐπιθυμίας πορευόμενοι, καὶ λέγοντες, Ποῦ
own  of them  lusts    walking,   and  saying,  Where

ἐστιν ἡ ἐπαγγελία τῆς παρουσίας αὐτοῦ; ἀφ᾽ ἧς γὰρ οἱ
is  the promise  of the  coming  of Him? from which for the

all things continue this way from (the) beginning of creation. [5] For desiring (it) this is hidden (from) them —that heavens were of old, and earth out of water, and through water, having been held together by the word of God; [6] through which the world at that time, being flooded by water, perished. [7] But the heavens and the earth now, having been stored up by the same word, are being kept for fire to a day of judgment and destruction of ungodly men.

[8] But let not be hidden (from) you this one thing, beloved, that one day with (the) Lord (is) as a thousand years, and a thousand years as one day. [9] The Lord is not slow (as to) the promise, as some deem slowness, but is longsuffering toward us, not having purposed any (of us) to perish, but all (of us) to come to repentance. [10] But the day of (the) Lord will come as a thief in (the) night, in which the heavens will pass away with rushing sound; and (the) elements burning will be dissolved, and earth and the works in it will be burned up. [11] Then all these things being dissolved, what sort ought you to be in holy behavior and godliness, [12] looking for and hastening the coming of the Day of God, through which (the) heavens being set afire will be dissolved, and (the) elements burning will melt. [13] But according to His promise, we look for new heavens and a new earth, in which righteousness dwells. [14] Therefore, beloved, looking for these things, be diligent, spotless, and without blemish, to be found in peace by Him; [15] and think of the longsuffering of our Lord (as) salvation, as also our beloved brother Paul wrote to you, according to the wisdom given to him; [16] as also in all (his) epistles, speaking in them concerning these things, in which are some things hard to understand, which the unlearned and unsettled pervert—as

5 πατέρες ἐκοιμήθησαν, πάντα οὕτω διαμένει ἀπ’ ἀρχῆς
fathers    fell asleep,    all things    so    remain from (the) beginning
κτίσεως. λανθάνει γὰρ αὐτοὺς τοῦτο θέλοντας, ὅτι οὐρανοὶ
of creation. is hidden (from) For them  this (by their) willing, that heavens
ἦσαν ἔκπαλαι, καὶ γῆ ἐξ ὕδατος καὶ δι’ ὕδατος συνεστῶσα,
were  of old,  and earth by water, and through water having been held together

6 τῷ τοῦ Θεοῦ λόγῳ, δι’ ὧν ὁ τότε κόσμος ὕδατι κατακλυ-
by the  of God  word, by which the then  world by water being

7 σθεὶς ἀπώλετο· οἱ δὲ νῦν οὐρανοὶ καὶ ἡ γῆ τῷ αὐτῷ λόγῳ
flooded  perished; the But now  heavens and the earth by the same word
τεθησαυρισμένοι εἰσί, πυρὶ τηρούμενοι εἰς ἡμέραν κρίσεως
having been stored up are for fire  being kept  unto a day of judgment
καὶ ἀπωλείας τῶν ἀσεβῶν ἀνθρώπων.
and destruction  of ungodly  men.

8 Ἓν δὲ τοῦτο μὴ λανθανέτω ὑμᾶς, ἀγαπητοί, ὅτι μία
one But this thing not let be hidden (from) you, beloved,  that one
ἡμέρα παρὰ Κυρίῳ ὡς χίλια ἔτη, καὶ χίλια ἔτη ὡς ἡμέρα
day    with (the) Lord (is) as a thousand years, and a thousand years as day

9 μία. οὐ βραδύνει ὁ Κύριος τῆς ἐπαγγελίας, ὡς τινες βραδυ-
one. not is slow The Lord of the  promise,  as some slowness
τῆτα ἡγοῦνται· ἀλλὰ μακροθυμεῖ εἰς ἡμᾶς, μὴ βουλόμενός
deem,    but  is longsuffering toward us, not purposing
τινας ἀπολέσθαι, ἀλλὰ πάντας εἰς μετάνοιαν χωρῆσαι.
any    to perish,  but  all    to repentance to come.

10 ἥξει δὲ ἡ ἡμέρα Κυρίου ὡς κλέπτης ἐν νυκτί, ἐν ᾗ οἱ οὐρανοὶ
will come But the day of (the) Lord as a thief in (the) night, in which the heavens
ῥοιζηδὸν παρελεύσονται, στοιχεῖα δὲ καυσούμενα λυθή-
with rushing sound will pass away, (the) elements and burning    will be

11 σονται, καὶ γῆ καὶ τὰ ἐν αὐτῇ ἔργα κατακαήσεται. τούτων
dissolved, and earth and the in it  works will be burned up. these things
οὖν πάντων λυομένων, ποταπούς δεῖ ὑπάρχειν ὑμᾶς ἐν
Then all  being dissolved, what sort ought to be  you in

12 ἁγίαις ἀναστροφαῖς καὶ εὐσεβείαις, προσδοκῶντας καὶ
holy  behavior  and godliness,  looking for  and
σπεύδοντας τὴν παρουσίαν τῆς τοῦ Θεοῦ ἡμέρας, δι’ ἣν
rushing  the  coming  of the of God  day, for which
οὐρανοὶ πυρούμενοι λυθήσονται, καὶ στοιχεῖα καυσούμενα
(the) heavens being set afire will be dissolved, and (the) elements burning

13 τήκεται; καινοὺς δὲ οὐρανοὺς καὶ γῆν καινὴν κατὰ τὸ
will melt.  new  But  heavens  and an earth new according to the
ἐπάγγελμα αὐτοῦ προσδοκῶμεν, ἐν οἷς δικαιοσύνη κατοικεῖ.
promise  of Him  we look for,  in which righteousness dwells.

14 Διό, ἀγαπητοί, ταῦτα προσδοκῶντες, σπουδάσατε
Therefore, beloved, these things  looking for,  be diligent,

15 ἄσπιλοι καὶ ἀμώμητοι αὐτῷ εὑρεθῆναι ἐν εἰρήνῃ. καὶ τὴν
spotless  and without blemish, by Him to be found in peace,  and the
τοῦ Κυρίου ἡμῶν μακροθυμίαν σωτηρίαν ἡγεῖσθε, καθὼς
of the Lord  of us  longsuffering salvation  deem,  as
καὶ ὁ ἀγαπητὸς ἡμῶν ἀδελφὸς Παῦλος κατὰ τὴν αὐτῷ
also the beloved  of us  brother,  Paul, according to the to him

16 δοθεῖσαν σοφίαν ἔγραψεν ὑμῖν· ὡς καὶ ἐν πάσαις ταῖς
given  wisdom,  wrote to you, as also  in  all (his)
ἐπιστολαῖς, λαλῶν ἐν αὐταῖς περὶ τούτων· ἐν οἷς ἔστι δυσνόη-
epistles,  speaking in them concerning these, in which are hard to understand
τά τινα, ἃ οἱ ἀμαθεῖς καὶ ἀστήρικτοι στρεβλοῦσιν, ὡς καὶ τὰς
some things, which the and unlearned  unsettled  pervert,  as also the

also (they do) the rest of Scriptures, to (their) own destruction. [17] You, then, beloved, knowing beforehand, watch lest being led away by the error of the lawless, you fall from (your) own. steadfastness.

[18] But grow in grace and knowledge of our Lord and Savior, Jesus Christ. To Him (be) the glory, both now and to (the) day of eternity. Amen.

**17** λοιπὰς γραφάς, πρὸς τὴν ἰδίαν αὐτῶν ἀπώλειαν. ὑμεῖς οὖν,
remaining Scriptures, to the own of them destruction. You, then,

ἀγαπητοί, προγινώσκοντες φυλάσσεσθε, ἵνα μή, τῇ τῶν
beloved, knowing beforehand, watch lest by the of the

ἀθέσμων πλάνῃ συναπαχθέντες, ἐκπέσητε τοῦ ἰδίου στηριγ-
lawless error being led away you fall from the own steadfast-

**18** μοῦ. αὐξάνετε δὲ ἐν χάριτι καὶ γνώσει τοῦ Κυρίου ἡμῶν καὶ
ness; grow but in grace and knowledge of the Lord of us and

σωτῆρος Ἰησοῦ Χριστοῦ. αὐτῷ ἡ δόξα καὶ νῦν καὶ εἰς
Savior, Jesus Christ. To Him (be) the glory both now and to

ἡμέραν αἰῶνος. ἀμήν.
a day of age. Amen.

# ΙΩΑΝΝΟΥ
## JOHN

### ΕΠΙΣΤΟΛΗ ΚΑΘΟΛΙΚΗ ΠΡΩΤΗ
### EPISTLE GENERAL FIRST

CHAPTER 1

CHAPTER 1

[1] (We announce to you) what was from (the) beginning, what we have heard, what we have seen with our eyes, what we beheld, and (what) our hands touched, as regards the Word of life. [2] And the Life was revealed, and we have seen, and we bear witness, and we announce to you the everlasting Life which was with the Father, and was revealed to us. [3] We announce to you what we have seen and (what) we have heard, that you also may have fellowship with us. And truly our fellowship (is) with the Father and His Son, Jesus Christ. [4] And we write these things to you, that your joy may be full.

[5] And this is the message which we have heard from Him, and we announce to you: God is light, and no darkness is in Him—none. [6] If we say that we have fellowship with Him, and we walk in the darkness, we lie and are not practicing the truth. [7] But if we walk in the light, as He is in the light, we have fellowship with one another, and the blood of Jesus Christ, His Son, cleanses us from all sin. [8] If we say that we have no sin, we deceive ourselves, and the truth is not in us. [9] If we confess our sins He is faithful and righteous, that He may forgive us the sins, and may cleanse us from all unrighteousness. [10] If we say that we have not sinned, we make Him a liar, and His word is not in us.

**1** "Ο ἦν ἀπ' ἀρχῆς, ὃ ἀκηκόαμεν, ὃ ἑωράκαμεν τοῖς ὀφθαλ-
What was from (the) beginning, what we have heard, what we have seen the with eyes
μοῖς ἡμῶν, ὃ ἐθεασάμεθα, καὶ αἱ χεῖρες ἡμῶν ἐψηλάφησαν
of us, what we beheld, and the hands of us touched,

**2** περὶ τοῦ λόγου τῆς ζωῆς (καὶ ἡ ζωὴ ἐφανερώθη, καὶ
concerning the Word of life —and the Life was revealed, and
ἑωράκαμεν, καὶ μαρτυροῦμεν, καὶ ἀπαγγέλλομεν ὑμῖν τὴν
we have seen, and we bear witness, and we announce to you the
ζωὴν τὴν αἰώνιον, ἥτις ἦν πρὸς τὸν πατέρα, καὶ ἐφανερώθη
Life everlasting, which was with the Father. and was revealed

**3** ἡμῖν)· ὃ ἑωράκαμεν καὶ ἀκηκόαμεν, ἀπαγγέλλομεν ὑμῖν,
to us— what we have seen, and we have heard, we announce to you,
ἵνα καὶ ὑμεῖς κοινωνίαν ἔχητε μεθ' ἡμῶν· καὶ ἡ κοινωνία δὲ
that also you fellowship may have with us, truly fellowship And
ἡ ἡμετέρα μετὰ τοῦ πατρὸς καὶ μετὰ τοῦ υἱοῦ αὐτοῦ Ἰησοῦ
our (is) with the Father and with the Son of Him, Jesus

**4** Χριστοῦ· καὶ ταῦτα γράφομεν ὑμῖν, ἵνα ἡ χαρὰ ὑμῶν ᾖ
Christ. And these things write to you, that the joy of you be
πεπληρωμένη.
fulfilled.

**5** Καὶ αὕτη ἐστὶν ἡ ἀγγελία ἣν ἀκηκόαμεν ἀπ' αὐτοῦ καὶ
And this is the message which we have heard from Him, and
ἀναγγέλλομεν ὑμῖν, ὅτι ὁ Θεὸς φῶς ἐστί, καὶ σκοτία ἐν αὐτῷ
we announce to you, that God light is, and darkness in Him

**6** οὐκ ἔστιν οὐδεμία. ἐὰν εἴπωμεν ὅτι κοινωνίαν ἔχομεν μετ'
not is, none. If we say that fellowship we have with
αὐτοῦ, καὶ ἐν τῷ σκότει περιπατῶμεν, ψευδόμεθα, καὶ οὐ
Him, and in the darkness we walk, we lie, and not

**7** ποιοῦμεν τὴν ἀλήθειαν· ἐὰν δὲ ἐν τῷ φωτὶ περιπατῶμεν,
are doing the truth. if But in the light we walk,
ὡς αὐτός ἐστιν ἐν τῷ φωτί, κοινωνίαν ἔχομεν μετ' ἀλλήλων,
as He is in the light, fellowship we have with one another,
καὶ τὸ αἷμα Ἰησοῦ Χριστοῦ τοῦ υἱοῦ αὐτοῦ καθαρίζει ἡμᾶς
and the blood of Jesus Christ the Son of Him cleanses us

**8** ἀπὸ πάσης ἁμαρτίας. ἐὰν εἴπωμεν ὅτι ἁμαρτίαν οὐκ ἔχομεν,
from all sin. If we say that sin not we have,

**9** ἑαυτοὺς πλανῶμεν, καὶ ἡ ἀλήθεια οὐκ ἔστιν ἐν ἡμῖν. ἐὰν
ourselves we deceive, and the truth not is in us. If
ὁμολογῶμεν τὰς ἁμαρτίας ἡμῶν, πιστός ἐστι καὶ δίκαιος
we confess the sins of us, faithful He is and righteous,
ἵνα ἀφῇ ἡμῖν τὰς ἁμαρτίας, καὶ καθαρίσῃ ἡμᾶς ἀπὸ πάσης
that He may forgive us the sins, and may cleanse us from all

**10** ἀδικίας. ἐὰν εἴπωμεν ὅτι οὐχ ἡμαρτήκαμεν, ψεύστην ποιοῦ-
unrighteousness. If we say that not we have sinned, a liar we
μεν αὐτόν, καὶ ὁ λόγος αὐτοῦ οὐκ ἔστιν ἐν ἡμῖν.
make Him, and the word of Him not is in us.

## CHAPTER 2

[1] My little children, I write these things to you so that you do not sin. And if anyone sins, we have an advocate with the Father, Jesus Christ (the) righteous; [2] and He is (the) propitiation relating to our sins, and not relating to ours only, but also relating to all the world. [3] And by this we know that we have known Him, if we keep His commands. [4] The (one) saying, I have known Him, and not keeping His commands, is a liar, and the truth is not in this one. [5] But whoever keeps His word, truly in this one the love of God has been perfected. By this we know that we are in Him. [6] The (one) saying to rest in Him ought so to walk himself as that (One) walked. [7] Not a new commandment I write to you, brothers, but an old commandment which you had from (the) beginning. The old commandment is the word which you heard from (the) beginning. [8] Again I write a new commandment to you, which is true in Him and in us, because the darkness is passing away, and the true light already shines. [9] He saying to be in the light, and hating his brother, is in the darkness until now. [10] The (one) loving his brother rests in the light, and no offense is in him. [11] But the (one) hating his brother is in the darkness, and walks in the darkness, and knows not where he is going—for the darkness blinded his eyes.

[12] Little children, I write to you, for you have been forgiven the sins because of His name. [13] I write to you, fathers, because you have known Him from (the) beginning. I write to you, young men, because you have overcome the evil one. I write to you young ones, because you have known the Father. [14] I write to you, young men, because you are strong

## CHAPTER 2

1 Τεκνία μου, ταῦτα γράφω ὑμῖν, ἵνα μὴ ἁμάρτητε. καὶ ἐάν
Little children of me, these I write to you, that not you sin.      And if
τις ἁμάρτῃ, παράκλητον ἔχομεν πρὸς τὸν πατέρα, Ἰησοῦν
anyone sins,    an advocate    we have   with   the   Father,   Jesus

2 Χριστὸν δίκαιον· καὶ αὐτὸς ἱλασμός ἐστι περὶ τῶν ἁμαρτιῶν
Christ (the) righteous; and He a propitiation is concerning the   sins
ἡμῶν· οὐ περὶ τῶν ἡμετέρων δὲ μόνον, ἀλλὰ καὶ περὶ ὅλου
of us; not concerning   ours       and only,    but also concerning all

3 τοῦ κόσμου. καὶ ἐν τούτῳ γινώσκομεν ὅτι ἐγνώκαμεν αὐτόν,
the world.   And by this   we know    that we have known Him,

4 ἐὰν τὰς ἐντολὰς αὐτοῦ τηρῶμεν. ὁ λέγων, Ἔγνωκα αὐτόν,
if the commands   of Him we keep. The (one) saying, I have known Him,
καὶ τὰς ἐντολὰς αὐτοῦ μὴ τηρῶν, ψεύστης ἐστί, καὶ ἐν τούτῳ
and the commands of Him not   keeping a liar    is,   and in   this one

5 ἡ ἀλήθεια οὐκ ἔστιν· ὃς δ᾽ ἂν τηρῇ αὐτοῦ τὸν λόγον, ἀληθῶς
the truth   not   is. whoever But keeps of Him the word,   truly
ἐν τούτῳ ἡ ἀγάπη τοῦ Θεοῦ τετελείωται. ἐν τούτῳ γινώ-
in this one the   love   of God has been perfected. By this we know

6 σκομεν ὅτι ἐν αὐτῷ ἐσμέν· ὁ λέγων ἐν αὐτῷ μένειν ὀφείλει,
that in   Him we are. The (one) saying in Him to remain   ought
καθὼς ἐκεῖνος περιεπάτησε, καὶ αὐτὸς οὕτω περιπατεῖν.
as that (One)   walked,      also himself so   to walk.

7 Ἀδελφοί, οὐκ ἐντολὴν καινὴν γράφω ὑμῖν, ἀλλ᾽ ἐντολὴν
Brothers, not a commandment new I write to you, but a commandment
παλαιάν, ἣν εἴχετε ἀπ᾽ ἀρχῆς· ἡ ἐντολὴ ἡ παλαιά ἐστιν ὁ
old,   which you had from (the) beginning the commandment old   is   the

8 λόγος ὃν ἠκούσατε ἀπ᾽ ἀρχῆς. πάλιν ἐντολὴν καινὴν γράφω
word which you have heard from (the) beginning. Again commandment new I write
ὑμῖν, ὅ ἐστιν ἀληθὲς ἐν αὐτῷ καὶ ἐν ὑμῖν· ὅτι ἡ σκοτία παρ-
to you, what is   true   in Him and in us, because the darkness is

9 άγεται, καὶ τὸ φῶς τὸ ἀληθινὸν ἤδη φαίνει. ὁ λέγων ἐν τῷ φωτὶ
passing away, and the light true     already shines. He saying in the light
εἶναι καὶ τὸν ἀδελφὸν αὐτοῦ μισῶν, ἐν τῇ σκοτίᾳ ἐστὶν ἕως
to be and the brother   of him hating   in the darkness is   until

10 ἄρτι. ὁ ἀγαπῶν τὸν ἀδελφὸν αὐτοῦ ἐν τῷ φωτὶ μένει, καὶ
now. He loving   the brother of him, in the light rests, and

11 σκάνδαλον ἐν αὐτῷ οὐκ ἔστιν. ὁ δὲ μισῶν τὸν ἀδελφὸν
offense   in him not is. the (one) But hating the brother
αὐτοῦ ἐν τῇ σκοτίᾳ ἐστί, καὶ ἐν τῇ σκοτίᾳ περιπατεῖ, καὶ οὐκ
of him, in the darkness is,   and in the darkness   walks,   and not
οἶδε ποῦ ὑπάγει, ὅτι ἡ σκοτία ἐτύφλωσε τοὺς ὀφθαλμοὺς
knows where he is going; for the darkness blinded   the   eyes
αὐτοῦ.
of him.

12 Γράφω ὑμῖν, τεκνία, ὅτι ἀφέωνται ὑμῖν αἱ ἁμαρτίαι διὰ
I write to you, little children, for have been forgiven   you the sins because of

13 τὸ ὄνομα αὐτοῦ. γράφω ὑμῖν, πατέρες, ὅτι ἐγνώκατε τὸν
the name of Him. I write to you, fathers, because you have known the (One)
ἀπ᾽ ἀρχῆς. γράφω ὑμῖν, νεανίσκοι, ὅτι νενικήκατε τὸν πονη-
from beginning. I write to you, young men, because you have overcome the evil

14 ρόν. γράφω ὑμῖν, παιδία, ὅτι ἐγνώκατε τὸν πατέρα. ἔγραψα
one. I wrote to you, young ones, for you have known the Father. I wrote
ὑμῖν, πατέρες, ὅτι ἐγνώκατε τὸν ἀπ᾽ ἀρχῆς. ἔγραψα ὑμῖν,
to you, fathers, because you have known the from beginning. I wrote to you,
known   (One)

and the word of God remains in you, and you have overcome the evil one. [15] Do not love the world, nor the things in the world. If anyone loves the world, the love of the Father is not in him; [16] because all that which (is) in the world: the lust of the flesh, and the lust of the eye, and the pride of life, is not of the Father, but is of the world. [17] And the world is passing away, and the lust of it; but he doing the will of God remains forever.

[18] Young ones, it is a last hour, and as you heard that the antichrist is coming, even now many antichrists have arisen; from which you know that it is a last hour. [19] They went out from us, but they were not of us; for if they were of us, they would have remained with us; but (they left) that it might be revealed that they are not all of us. [20] And you have an anointing from the Holy One, and you know all things. [21] I did not write to you because you do not know the truth, but because you know it, and because every lie is not of the truth. [22] Who is the liar, except the (one) denying that Jesus is not the Christ? This is the antichrist, the (one) denying the Father and the Son. [23] Everyone denying the Son neither has the Father; the (one) confessing the Son also has the Father. [24] You, then, what you heard from (the) beginning, let it remain in you. If what you heard from (the) beginning remains in you, you will remain in both the Father and in the Son. [25] And this is the promise which He promised us, life everlasting. [26] I wrote these things to you concerning those leading you astray. [27] And the anointing which you received from Him remains in you, and you have no need that anyone teach you; but as the anointing of Him teaches you concerning all things, and is true, and is not a lie, and as He taught

νεανίσκοι, ὅτι ἰσχυροί ἐστε, καὶ ὁ λόγος τοῦ Θεοῦ ἐν ὑμῖν
young men, that strong you are, and the word of God in you

15 μένει, καὶ νενικήκατε τὸν πονηρόν. μὴ ἀγαπᾶτε τὸν κόσμον,
remains, and you have overcome the evil one. Do not love the world,

μηδὲ τὰ ἐν τῷ κόσμῳ. ἐάν τις ἀγαπᾷ τὸν κόσμον, οὐκ ἔστιν
nor the things in the world. If anyone loves the world, not is

16 ἡ ἀγάπη τοῦ πατρὸς ἐν αὐτῷ. ὅτι πᾶν τὸ ἐν τῷ κόσμῳ, ἡ
the love of the Father in him; because all that in which (is) the world, the

ἐπιθυμία τῆς σαρκός, καὶ ἡ ἐπιθυμία των ὀφθαλμῶν, καὶ ἡ
lust of the flesh, and the lust of the eye, and the

ἀλαζονεία τοῦ βίου, οὐκ ἔστιν ἐκ τοῦ πατρός, ἀλλ' ἐκ τοῦ
pride of life, not is of the Father, but of the

17 κόσμου ἐστί. καὶ ὁ κόσμος παράγεται, καὶ ἡ ἐπιθυμία αὐτοῦ·
world is. And the world is passing away, and the lust of it;

ὁ δὲ ποιῶν τὸ θέλημα τοῦ Θεοῦ μένει εἰς τὸν αἰῶνα.
he but doing the will of God remains to the age.

18 Παιδία, ἐσχάτη ὥρα ἐστί· καὶ καθὼς ἠκούσατε ὅτι ὁ
Young ones, a last hour it is, and as you heard that the

ἀντίχριστος ἔρχεται, καὶ νῦν ἀντίχριστοι πολλοὶ γεγόνασιν·
antichrist is coming, even now antichrists many have arisen;

19 ὅθεν γινώσκομεν ὅτι ἐσχάτη ὥρα ἐστίν. ἐξ ἡμῶν ἐξῆλθον,
from which you know that a last hour it is. From us they went out,

ἀλλ' οὐκ ἦσαν ἐξ ἡμῶν· εἰ γὰρ ἦσαν ἐξ ἡμῶν, μεμενήκεισαν
but not they were of us; if for they were of us, they would have remained

ἂν μεθ' ἡμῶν· ἀλλ' ἵνα φανερωθῶσιν ὅτι οὐκ εἰσὶ πάντες
with us; but that it might be revealed that not they are all

20 ἐξ ἡμῶν. καὶ ὑμεῖς χρίσμα ἔχετε ἀπὸ τοῦ ἁγίου, καὶ οἴδατε
of us. And you an anointing have from the Holy One, and you know

21 πάντα. οὐκ ἔγραψα ὑμῖν, ὅτι οὐκ οἴδατε τὴν ἀλήθειαν, ἀλλ'
all. Not I wrote to you because not you know the truth, but

ὅτι οἴδατε αὐτήν, καὶ ὅτι πᾶν ψεῦδος ἐκ τῆς ἀληθείας οὐκ
because you know it, and because every lie of the truth not

22 ἔστι. τίς ἐστιν ὁ ψεύστης, εἰ μὴ ὁ ἀρνούμενος ὅτι Ἰησοῦς οὐκ
is. Who is the liar, except the (one) denying that Jesus not

ἔστιν ὁ Χριστός; οὗτός ἐστιν ὁ ἀντίχριστος, ὁ ἀρνούμενος
is the Christ? This is the antichrist, the (one) denying

23 τὸν πατέρα καὶ τὸν υἱόν. πᾶς ὁ ἀρνούμενος τὸν υἱὸν οὐδὲ
the Father and the Son. Everyone denying the Son neither

τὸν πατέρα ἔχει· ὁ ὁμολογῶν τὸν υἱὸν καὶ τὸν πατέρα ἔχει.
the Father has; the (one) confessing the Son also the Father has.

24 ὑμεῖς οὖν ὁ ἠκούσατε ἀπ' ἀρχῆς, ἐν ὑμῖν μενέτω. ἐὰν ἐν
you then What you heard from (the) beginning, in you let it remain. If in

ὑμῖν μείνῃ ὃ ἀπ' ἀρχῆς ἠκούσατε, καὶ ὑμεῖς ἐν τῷ υἱῷ καὶ
you remains what from (the) beginning you heard, both you in the Son and

25 ἐν τῷ πατρὶ μενεῖτε. καὶ αὕτη ἐστὶν ἡ ἐπαγγελία ἣν αὐτὸς
in the Father will remain. And this is the promise which He

26 ἐπηγγείλατο ἡμῖν, τὴν ζωὴν τὴν αἰώνιον. ταῦτα ἔγραψα
promised us, the life everlasting. These things I wrote

27 ὑμῖν περὶ τῶν πλανώντων ὑμᾶς. καὶ ὑμεῖς, τὸ χρίσμα ὃ
to you concerning those leading astray you. And you, the anointing which

ἐλάβετε ἀπ' αὐτοῦ ἐν ὑμῖν μένει, καὶ οὐ χρείαν ἔχετε ἵνα τις
received from Him in you remains, and no need you have that anyone

διδάσκῃ ὑμᾶς· ἀλλ' ὡς τὸ αὐτὸ χρίσμα διδάσκει ὑμᾶς περὶ
teach you; but as the of Him anointing teaches you concerning

πάντων, καὶ ἀληθές ἐστι, καὶ οὐκ ἔστι ψεῦδος, καὶ καθὼς
all things, and true is, and not is a lie, and as

you, remain in Him. [28] And now, little children, remain in Him, that when He is revealed we may have confidence, and not be shamed from Him in His coming. [29] If you know that He is righteous, know that everyone doing righteousness has been born of Him.

### CHAPTER 3

[1] See what manner of love the Father has given us, that we may be called children of God. For this reason, the world does not know us, because it did not know Him. [2] Beloved, now we are the children of God, and it was not yet revealed what we shall be; but we know that if He is revealed, we shall be like Him, because we shall see Him as He is. [3] And everyone having this hope on Him purifies himself, even as that (One) is pure. [4] Everyone doing sin also does lawlessness, and sin is lawlessness. [5] And you know that that (One) was revealed that our

sins He might bear; and sin is not in Him. [6] Everyone remaining in Him does not sin. Everyone sinning has not seen Him, nor known Him. [7] Little children, let no one lead you astray; the (one) doing righteousness is righteous, even as that (One) is righteous. [8] The (one) doing sin is of the Devil, because the Devil sins from (the) beginning. For this the Son of God was revealed, that He undo the works of the Devil. [9] Everyone having been begotten of God does not sin, because His seed remains in him, and he is not able to sin, because he has been born of God. [10] By this the children of God and the children of the Devil are revealed: Everyone not doing righteousness is not of God; also the (one) not loving his brother. [11] Because this is the message which you heard from (the) beginning, that we should love one another; [12] not

**28** ἐδίδαξεν ὑμᾶς, μενεῖτε ἐν αὐτῷ. καὶ νῦν, τεκνία, μένετε ἐν
He taught you, remain in Him. And now, little children, remain in
αὐτῷ· ἵνα ὅταν φανερωθῇ, ἔχωμεν παρρησίαν, καὶ μὴ
in Him, that when He is revealed we may have confidence, and not

**29** αἰσχυνθῶμεν ἀπ᾽ αὐτοῦ ἐν τῇ παρουσίᾳ αὐτοῦ. ἐὰν εἰδῆτε
be shamed from Him in the coming of Him. If you know
ὅτι δίκαιός ἐστι, γινώσκετε ὅτι πᾶς ὁ ποιῶν τὴν δικαιοσύνην
that righteous He is, know that everyone doing the righteousness,
ἐξ αὐτοῦ γεγέννηται.
of Him has been born.

### CHAPTER 3

**1** ῎Ιδετε ποταπὴν ἀγάπην δέδωκεν ἡμῖν ὁ πατήρ, ἵνα τέκνα
See what manner of love has given us the Father, that children
Θεοῦ κληθῶμεν. διὰ τοῦτο ὁ κόσμος οὐ γινώσκει ἡμᾶς, ὅτι
of God we may be called. Therefore the world not knows us, because

**2** οὐκ ἔγνω αὐτόν. ἀγαπητοί, νῦν τέκνα Θεοῦ ἐσμέν, καὶ οὔπω
not it knew Him. Beloved, now children of God we are, and not yet
ἐφανερώθη τί ἐσόμεθα· οἴδαμεν δὲ ὅτι ἐὰν φανερωθῇ, ὅμοιοι
was it revealed what we shall be we know but that if He is revealed, like

**3** αὐτῷ ἐσόμεθα, ὅτι ὀψόμεθα αὐτὸν καθώς ἐστι. καὶ πᾶς ὁ
Him we shall be, because we shall see Him as He is. And everyone
ἔχων τὴν ἐλπίδα ταύτην ἐπ᾽ αὐτῷ ἁγνίζει ἑαυτόν, καθὼς·
having hope this on him purifies himself, as

**4** ἐκεῖνος ἁγνός ἐστι. πᾶς ὁ ποιῶν τὴν ἁμαρτίαν, καὶ τὴν
that (One) pure is. Everyone doing sin, also

**5** ἀνομίαν ποιεῖ· καὶ ἡ ἁμαρτία ἐστὶν ἡ ἀνομία. καὶ οἴδατε ὅτι
lawlessness does; and sin is lawlessness. And you know that
ἐκεῖνος ἐφανερώθη, ἵνα τὰς ἁμαρτίας ἡμῶν ἄρῃ· καὶ ἁμαρτία
that (One) was revealed that the sins of us He might bear, and sin

**6** ἐν αὐτῷ οὐκ ἔστι. πᾶς ὁ ἐν αὐτῷ μένων οὐχ ἁμαρτάνει· πᾶς
in Him not is. Everyone in Him remaining not sins; everyone
ὁ ἁμαρτάνων οὐχ ἑώρακεν αὐτόν, οὐδὲ ἔγνωκεν αὐτόν.
sinning not has seen Him, nor known Him.

**7** τεκνία, μηδεὶς πλανάτω ὑμᾶς· ὁ ποιῶν τὴν δικαιοσύνην
Little children, no one let lead astray you; he doing righteousness

**8** δίκαιός ἐστι, καθὼς ἐκεῖνος δίκαιός ἐστιν· ὁ ποιῶν τὴν
righteous is, even as that One righteous is. The (one) doing
ἁμαρτίαν ἐκ τοῦ διαβόλου ἐστίν, ὅτι ἀπ᾽ ἀρχῆς ὁ διάβολος
sin of the Devil is, because from (the) beginning the devil
ἁμαρτάνει. εἰς τοῦτο ἐφανερώθη ὁ υἱὸς τοῦ Θεοῦ, ἵνα λύσῃ
sins. For this was revealed the Son of God, that He undo

**9** τὰ ἔργα τοῦ διαβόλου. πᾶς ὁ γεγεννημένος ἐκ τοῦ Θεοῦ
the works of the devil. Everyone having been begotten of God
ἁμαρτίαν οὐ ποιεῖ, ὅτι σπέρμα αὐτοῦ ἐν αὐτῷ μένει· καὶ οὐ
sin not does, because seed of Him in him remains; and not

**10** δύναται ἁμαρτάνειν, ὅτι ἐκ τοῦ Θεοῦ γεγέννηται. ἐν τούτῳ
he is able to sin, because of God he has been born. By this
φανερά ἐστι τὰ τέκνα τοῦ Θεοῦ καὶ τὰ τέκνα τοῦ διαβόλου·
revealed are the children of God and the children of the devil:
πᾶς ὁ μὴ ποιῶν δικαιοσύνην οὐκ ἔστιν ἐκ τοῦ Θεοῦ, καὶ ὁ μὴ
everyone not doing righteousness not is of God; also he not

**11** ἀγαπῶν τὸν ἀδελφὸν αὐτοῦ. ὅτι αὕτη ἐστὶν ἡ ἀγγελία ἣν
loving the brother of him. Because this is the message which

**12** ἠκούσατε ἀπ᾽ ἀρχῆς, ἵνα ἀγαπῶμεν ἀλλήλους· οὐ καθὼς
you heard from (the) beginning, that we should love one another; not as

Κάϊν ἐκ τοῦ πονηροῦ ἦν, καὶ ἔσφαξε τὸν ἀδελφὸν αὐτοῦ. καὶ
Cain of the evil one was, and killed the brother of him; and

χάριν τίνος ἔσφαξεν αὐτόν ; ὅτι τὰ ἔργα αὐτοῦ πονηρα ἦν,
for what did he kill him? Because the works of him evil were;

τὰ δὲ τοῦ ἀδελφοῦ αὐτοῦ δίκαια.
the things but of the brother of him righteous.

Cain was of the evil one, and killed his brother. And for what did he kill him? Because his works were evil, but the things of his brother (were) righteous.

[13] Do not marvel, my brothers, if the world hates you. [14] We know that we have passed from death to life, because we love the brothers. The (one) not loving the brother remains in death. [15] Everyone hating the brother is a murderer, and you know that every murderer does not have everlasting life remaining in him. [16] By this we have known the love of God, because that (One) laid down His soul for us; and on behalf of the brothers, we ought to lay down (our) souls. [17] Whoever has the means of life of the world, and beholds his brother having need, and shuts up his bowels from him, how does the love of God remain in him? [18] My little children, let us not love in word, or in tongue, but in work and truth. [19] And in this we shall know that we are of the truth, and shall persuade our hearts, [20] that if our heart accuses us, (we know) that God is greater than our heart and knows all things. [21] Beloved, if our heart does not accuse us, we have confidence with God. [22] And whatever we ask, we receive from Him, because we keep His commandments, and we do the things pleasing before Him. [23] And this is His commandment, that we should believe the name of His Son, Jesus Christ, and love one another, even as He gave command to us. [24] And the (one) keeping His commandments remains in Him, and He in him. And by this we know that He remains in us, by the Spirit which He gave to us.

13
14
Μὴ θαυμάζετε, ἀδελφοί μου, εἰ μισεῖ ὑμᾶς ὁ κόσμος· ἡμεῖς
Do not marvel, brothers of me, if hates you the world. We

οἴδαμεν ὅτι μεταβεβήκαμεν ἐκ τοῦ θανάτου εἰς τὴν ζωήν, ὅτι
know that we have passed from death to life, because

ἀγαπῶμεν τοὺς ἀδελφούς. ὁ μὴ ἀγαπῶν τὸν ἀδελφόν,
we love the brothers. The (one) not loving the brother

15 μένει ἐν τῷ θανάτῳ. πᾶς ὁ μισῶν τὸν ἀδελφὸν αὐτοῦ ἀνθρω-
remains in death. Everyone hating the brother of him a murderer

ποκτόνος ἐστί· καὶ οἴδατε ὅτι πᾶς ἀνθρωποκτόνος οὐκ ἔχει
is, and you know that every murderer not has

16 ζωὴν αἰώνιον ἐν αὐτῷ μένουσαν. ἐν τούτῳ ἐγνώκαμεν τὴν
life everlasting in him remaining. By this we have known the

ἀγάπην τοῦ Θεοῦ, ὅτι ἐκεῖνος ὑπὲρ ἡμῶν τὴν ψυχὴν αὐτοῦ
love of God, because that (One) for us the soul of Him

ἔθηκε· καὶ ἡμεῖς ὀφείλομεν ὑπὲρ τῶν ἀδελφῶν τὰς ψυχὰς
laid down; and we ought on behalf of the brothers the souls

17 τιθέναι. ὃς δ᾽ ἂν ἔχῃ τὸν βίον τοῦ κόσμου, καὶ θεωρῇ τὸν
to lay down. Whoever has the means of life of the world, and beholds the

ἀδελφὸν αὐτοῦ χρείαν ἔχοντα, καὶ κλείσῃ τὰ σπλάγχνα
brother of him need having, and shuts up the bowels

αὐτοῦ ἀπ᾽ αὐτοῦ, πῶς ἡ ἀγάπη τοῦ Θεοῦ μένει ἐν αὐτῷ ;
of him from him, how the love of God remains in him?

18 τεκνία μου, μὴ ἀγαπῶμεν λόγῳ μηδὲ γλώσσῃ ἀλλ᾽ ἔργῳ
Little children of me, not let us love in word, nor in tongue, but in work

19 καὶ ἀληθείᾳ. καὶ ἐν τούτῳ γινώσκομεν ὅτι ἐκ τῆς ἀληθείας
and truth. And in this we shall know that of the truth

ἐσμέν, καὶ ἔμπροσθεν αὐτοῦ πείσομεν τὰς καρδίας ἡμῶν,
we are, and before Him shall persuade the heart of us,

20 ὅτι ἐὰν καταγινώσκῃ ἡμῶν ἡ καρδία, ὅτι μείζων ἐστὶν ὁ
that if accuses of us the heart, that greater is

21 Θεὸς τῆς καρδίας ἡμῶν, καὶ γινώσκει πάντα. ἀγαπητοί,
God (than) the heart of us and knows all things. Beloved,

ἐὰν ἡ καρδία ἡμῶν μὴ καταγινώσκῃ ἡμῶν, παρρησίαν
if the heart of us not accuses us, confidence

22 ἔχομεν πρὸς τὸν Θεόν, καὶ ὃ ἐὰν αἰτῶμεν, λαμβάνομεν παρ᾽
we have with God, and whatever we ask we receive from

αὐτοῦ, ὅτι τὰς ἐντολὰς αὐτοῦ τηροῦμεν, καὶ τὰ ἀρεστὰ
Him, because the commandments of Him we keep, and the things pleasing

23 ἐνώπιον αὐτοῦ ποιοῦμεν. καὶ αὕτη ἐστὶν ἡ ἐντολὴ αὐτοῦ,
before Him we do. And this is the commandment of Him,

ἵνα πιστεύσωμεν τῷ ὀνόματι τοῦ υἱοῦ αὐτοῦ Ἰησοῦ Χρι-
that we should believe the name of the Son of Him, Jesus Christ,

στοῦ, καὶ ἀγαπῶμεν ἀλλήλους, καθὼς ἔδωκεν ἐντολὴν ἡμῖν.
and love one another, even as He gave command to us.

24 καὶ ὁ τηρῶν τὰς ἐντολὰς αὐτοῦ ἐν αὐτῷ μένει, καὶ αὐτὸς ἐν
And he keeping the commandments of Him in Him remains, and He in

αὐτῷ. καὶ ἐν τούτῳ γινώσκομεν ὅτι μένει ἐν ἡμῖν, ἐκ τοῦ
him. And by this we know that He remains in us, by the

Πνεύματος οὗ ἡμῖν ἔδωκεν.
Spirit which to us He gave.

CHAPTER 4

[1] Beloved, do not believe every spirit, but test the spirits, if they are of God; because many false prophets have gone forth into the world. [2] By this know the Spirit of God: every spirit which confesses that Jesus Christ has come in (the) flesh is of God. [3] And every spirit which does not confess that Jesus Christ has come in (the) flesh is not of God; and this is the antichrist which you heard is coming, and now is already in the world. [4] You are of God, little children, and have overcome them, because He in you is greater than the (one) in the world. [5] They are of the world; therefore they speak of the world, and the world hears them. [6] We are of God; the (one) who knows God hears us. Who(ever) is not of God does not hear us. From this we know the spirit of truth and the spirit of error.

[7] Beloved let us love one another, because love is of God, and everyone loving has been born of God, and knows God. [8] The (one) not loving has not known God, because God is love. [9] By this was revealed the love of God in us, because His Son, the Only-begotten, God has sent into the world, that we might live through Him. [10] In this is love, not that we loved God, but that he loved us, and sent His Son (to be) a propitiation relating to our sins. [11] Beloved, if God so loved us, we also ought to love one another. [12] No one has beheld God at any time. If we love one another God remains in us, and His love having been perfected

CHAPTER 4

**1** Ἀγαπητοί, μὴ παντὶ πνεύματι πιστεύετε, ἀλλὰ δοκι-
Beloved    not every    spirit    believe,    but    test

μάζετε τὰ πνεύματα, εἰ ἐκ τοῦ Θεοῦ ἐστίν· ὅτι πολλοὶ
the    spirits,    if    of    God they are, because many

**2** ψευδοπροφῆται ἐξεληλύθασιν εἰς τὸν κόσμον. ἐν τούτῳ
false prophets    have gone forth into the    world.    By    this

γινώσκετε τὸ Πνεῦμα τοῦ Θεοῦ· πᾶν πνεῦμα ὃ ὁμολογεῖ
know    the    Spirit    of God: every    spirit which confesses

Ἰησοῦν Χριστὸν ἐν σαρκὶ ἐληλυθότα ἐκ τοῦ Θεοῦ ἐστί·
Jesus    Christ    in (the) flesh having come,    of    God    is.

**3** καὶ πᾶν πνεῦμα ὃ μὴ ὁμολογεῖ τὸν Ἰησοῦν Χριστὸν ἐν
and every    spirit which not confesses    Jesus    Christ    in

σαρκὶ ἐληλυθότα, ἐκ τοῦ Θεοῦ οὐκ ἔστι· καὶ τοῦτό ἐστι τὸ
(the) flesh having come, of    God    not    is; and this    is    the

τοῦ ἀντιχρίστου, ὃ ἀκηκόατε ὅτι ἔρχεται, καὶ νῦν ἐν τῷ
antichrist    which you heard that it is coming, and now in    the

**4** κόσμῳ ἐστὶν ἤδη. ὑμεῖς ἐκ τοῦ Θεοῦ ἐστέ, τεκνία, καὶ
world    is already. You    of    God    are, little children, and

νενικήκατε αὐτούς· ὅτι μείζων ἐστὶν ὁ ἐν ὑμῖν ἢ ὁ ἐν τῷ
have overcome them, because greater    is the (One) in you than the in the
                                                                          (one)

**5** κόσμῳ. αὐτοὶ ἐκ τοῦ κόσμου εἰσί· διὰ τοῦτο ἐκ τοῦ κόσμου
world.    They of    the    world    are; therefore    of    the world

**6** λαλοῦσι, καὶ ὁ κόσμος αὐτῶν ἀκούει. ἡμεῖς ἐκ τοῦ Θεοῦ
they speak, and the    world    them    hears.    We of    God

ἐσμέν· ὁ γινώσκων τὸν Θεόν, ἀκούει ἡμῶν· ὃς οὐκ ἔστιν ἐκ
are; the (one) knowing    God    hears    us; (he) who not is    of

τοῦ Θεοῦ, οὐκ ἀκούει ἡμῶν. ἐκ τούτου γινώσκομεν τὸ
God    not hears    us. From this    we know    the

πνεῦμα τῆς ἀληθείας καὶ τὸ πνεῦμα τῆς πλάνης.
spirit    of truth,    and the    spirit    of error.

**7** Ἀγαπητοί, ἀγαπῶμεν ἀλλήλους· ὅτι ἡ ἀγάπη ἐκ τοῦ
Beloved,    let us love    one another, because    love    of

Θεοῦ ἐστί, καὶ πᾶς ὁ ἀγαπῶν ἐκ τοῦ Θεοῦ γεγέννηται, καὶ
God    is,    and everyone loving,    of    God has been born, and

**8** γινώσκει τὸν Θεόν. ὁ μὴ ἀγαπῶν οὐκ ἔγνω τὸν Θεόν· ὅτι
knows    God. The (one) not loving    not knew    God, because

**9** ὁ Θεὸς ἀγάπη ἐστίν. ἐν τούτῳ ἐφανερώθη ἡ ἀγάπη τοῦ
God    love    is.    By this    was revealed    the love

Θεοῦ ἐν ἡμῖν, ὅτι τὸν υἱὸν αὐτοῦ τὸν μονογενῆ ἀπέσταλκεν
of God in    us, because the Son    of Him the only-begotten has sent

**10** ὁ Θεὸς εἰς τὸν κόσμον, ἵνα ζήσωμεν δι' αὐτοῦ. ἐν τούτῳ
God into the    world,    that we might live through Him. In    this

ἐστὶν ἡ ἀγάπη, οὐχ ὅτι ἡμεῖς ἠγαπήσαμεν τὸν Θεόν, ἀλλ'
is    love,    not that we    loved    God, but

ὅτι αὐτὸς ἠγάπησεν ἡμᾶς, καὶ ἀπέστειλε τὸν υἱὸν αὐτοῦ
that He    loved    us, and    sent    the Son of Him

**11** ἱλασμὸν περὶ τῶν ἁμαρτιῶν ἡμῶν. ἀγαπητοί, εἰ οὕτως ὁ
a propitiation con-    the    sins    of us. Beloved,    if    so
cerning

Θεὸς ἠγάπησεν ἡμᾶς, καὶ ἡμεῖς ὀφείλομεν ἀλλήλους ἀγαπᾶν.
God    loved    us,    also we    ought    one another to love.

**12** Θεὸν οὐδεὶς πώποτε τεθέαται· ἐὰν ἀγαπῶμεν ἀλλήλους,
God    No one ever    has beheld; if    we love    one another,

ὁ Θεὸς ἐν ἡμῖν μένει, καὶ ἡ ἀγάπη αὐτοῦ τετελειωμένη
God in    us remains, and the    love    of Him having been per-
                                                                      fected

is in us. [13] By this we know that we remain in Him, and He in us, because of His Spirit He has given to us. [14] And we have beheld and bear witness that the Father has sent the Son (as) Savior of the world. [15] Whoever confesses that Jesus is the Son of God, God remains in him, and he in God. [16] And we have known and have believed the love which God has in us. God is love, and he remaining in love remains in God, and God in him. [17] By this love has been perfected with us, that we have confidence in the day of judgment: that as that (One) is, also we are in this world. [18] There is no fear in love, but perfect love casts out fear, because fear has punishment; and the (one) fearing has not been perfected in love. [19] We love Him because He first loved us. [20] If anyone says, I love God, and hates his brother, he is a liar. For the (one) not loving his brother whom he has seen, how is he able to love God whom he has not seen? [21] And we have this commandment from Him, that the (one) loving God also loves his brother.

**CHAPTER 5**

[1] Everyone believing that Jesus is the Christ has been born of God; and everyone loving the (One) begetting also loves the (one) having been born of Him. [2] By this we know that we love the children of God: when we love God and keep His commandments. [3] For this is the love of God, that we keep His commandments; and His commandments are not burdensome. [4] Because everything having been born of God overcomes the world, and this is the victory overcoming

13 ἐστὶν ἐν ἡμῖν. ἐν τούτῳ γινώσκομεν ὅτι ἐν αὐτῷ μένομεν καὶ
is in us. By this we know that in Him we remain, and
αὐτὸς ἐν ἡμῖν, ὅτι ἐκ τοῦ Πνεύματος αὐτοῦ δέδωκεν ἡμῖν.
He in us, because of the Spirit of Him He has given us.

14 καὶ ἡμεῖς τεθεάμεθα καὶ μαρτυροῦμεν ὅτι ὁ πατὴρ ἀπέσταλκε
And we we have beheld and bear witness that the Father has sent

15 τὸν υἱὸν σωτῆρα τοῦ κόσμου. ὃς ἂν ὁμολογήσῃ ὅτι Ἰησοῦς
the Son (as) Savior of the world. Whoever confesses that Jesus
ἐστὶν ὁ υἱὸς τοῦ Θεοῦ, ὁ Θεὸς ἐν αὐτῷ μένει, καὶ αὐτὸς ἐν
is the Son of God, God in him remains, and he in

16 τῷ Θεῷ. καὶ ἡμεῖς ἐγνώκαμεν καὶ πεπιστεύκαμεν τὴν ἀγάπην
God. And we have known and have believed the love
ἣν ἔχει ὁ Θεὸς ἐν ἡμῖν. ὁ Θεὸς ἀγάπη ἐστί, καὶ ὁ μένων ἐν τῇ
which has God in us. God love is, and he remaining in the

17 ἀγάπῃ, ἐν τῷ Θεῷ μένει, καὶ ὁ Θεὸς ἐν αὐτῷ. ἐν τούτῳ τετε-
love, in God remains, and God in him. By this has
λείωται ἡ ἀγάπη μεθ' ἡμῶν, ἵνα παρρησίαν ἔχωμεν ἐν τῇ
been perfected love with us, that confidence we have in the
ἡμέρᾳ τῆς κρίσεως, ὅτι καθὼς ἐκεῖνός ἐστι, καὶ ἡμεῖς ἐσμὲν ἐν
day of judgment, that as that (One) is, also we are in

18 τῷ κόσμῳ τούτῳ. φόβος οὐκ ἔστιν ἐν τῇ ἀγάπῃ, ἀλλ' ἡ
world this. Fear not is in love, but
τελεία ἀγάπη ἔξω βάλλει τὸν φόβον, ὅτι ὁ φόβος κόλασιν
perfect love out casts fear, because fear punishment

19 ἔχει ὁ δὲ φοβούμενος οὐ τετελείωται ἐν τῇ ἀγάπῃ. ἡμεῖς
has, the (one) and fearing not has been perfected in love. We

20 ἀγαπῶμεν αὐτόν, ὅτι αὐτὸς πρῶτος ἠγάπησεν ἡμᾶς. ἐάν
love Him, because He first loved us. If
τις εἴπῃ ὅτι Ἀγαπῶ τὸν Θεόν, καὶ τὸν ἀδελφὸν αὐτοῦ μισῇ,
anyone says, I love God, and the brother of him hates,
ψεύστης ἐστίν· ὁ γὰρ μὴ ἀγαπῶν τὸν ἀδελφὸν αὐτοῦ ὃν
a liar he is; the (one) for not loving the brother of him whom

21 ἑώρακε, τὸν Θεὸν ὃν οὐχ ἑώρακε πῶς δύναται ἀγαπᾶν ; καὶ
he has seen, God whom not he has seen, how is he able to love? And
ταύτην τὴν ἐντολὴν ἔχομεν ἀπ' αὐτοῦ, ἵνα ὁ ἀγαπῶν τὸν
this commandment we have from Him, that the (one) loving
Θεόν, ἀγαπᾷ καὶ τὸν ἀδελφὸν αὐτοῦ.
God, loves also the brother of him.

**CHAPTER 5**

1 Πᾶς ὁ πιστεύων ὅτι Ἰησοῦς ἐστὶν ὁ Χριστός, ἐκ τοῦ Θεοῦ
Everyone believing that Jesus is the Christ, of God
γεγέννηται· καὶ πᾶς ὁ ἀγαπῶν τὸν γεννήσαντα ἀγαπᾷ καὶ
has been born; and everyone loving the (One) begetting, loves also

2 τὸν γεγεννημένον ἐξ αὐτοῦ. ἐν τούτῳ γινώσκομεν ὅτι
the (one) having been born of Him. By this we know that
ἀγαπῶμεν τὰ τέκνα τοῦ Θεοῦ, ὅταν τὸν Θεὸν ἀγαπῶμεν,
we love the children of God, whenever God we love,

3 καὶ τὰς ἐντολὰς αὐτοῦ τηρῶμεν. αὕτη γάρ ἐστιν ἡ ἀγάπη
and the commandments of Him we keep. this For is the love
τοῦ Θεοῦ, ἵνα τὰς ἐντολὰς αὐτοῦ τηρῶμεν· καὶ αἱ ἐντολαὶ
of God, that the commandments of Him we keep; and the commands

4 αὐτοῦ βαρεῖαι οὐκ εἰσίν. ὅτι πᾶν τὸ γεγεννημένον ἐκ τοῦ
of Him heavy not are, because everything having been born of
Θεοῦ νικᾷ τὸν κόσμον· καὶ αὕτη ἐστὶν ἡ νίκη ἡ νικήσασα τὸν
God overcomes the world, and this is the victory overcoming the

the world, our faith. [5]
Who is the (one) overcoming the world except the (one) believing that Jesus is the Son of God? [6] This is He coming through water and blood, Jesus Christ; not by the water only, but by the water and the blood. And the Spirit is the (One) witnessing, because the Spirit is the truth. [7] (For there are three bearing witness in Heaven, the Father, the Word, and the Holy Spirit; and these three are one.) [8] And there are three who bear witness on the earth, The Spirit, and the water, and the blood; and the three are to the one. [9] If we receive the witness of men, the witness of God is greater; because this is the witness of God which He has witnessed about His Son: [10] The (one) believing in the Son of God has the witness in himself. The (one) not believing God has made Him a liar, because he has not believed in the witness which God has witnessed concerning His Son. [11] And this is the witness, that God gave us everlasting life, and this life is in His Son. [12] The (one) having the Son has life. He not having the Son of God does not have life.

[13] I wrote these things to you, those believing in the name of the Son of God, that you may know that you have everlasting life, and that you may believe in the name of the Son of God. [14] And this is the confidence we have toward Him, that if we ask anything according to His will, He hears us. [15] And if we know that He hears us, whatever we ask, we know that we have the requests which we have asked from Him. [16] If anyone sees his brother sinning a sin not unto death, he shall ask, and He shall give to him life, to those not sinning unto death. There is a sin unto death; I do not say that he should ask about

**5** κόσμον, ἡ πίστις ἡμῶν. τίς ἐστιν ὁ νικῶν τὸν κόσμον, εἰ μὴ ὁ
world,   the faith of us.  Who   is  the over- the  world, except  the
                                        (one) coming                (one)

**6** πιστεύων ὅτι Ἰησοῦς ἐστιν ὁ υἱὸς τοῦ Θεοῦ ; οὗτός ἐστιν ὁ
believing that  Jesus  is  the Son  of God?  This   is the (One)
ἐλθὼν δι' ὕδατος καὶ αἵματος, Ἰησοῦς ὁ Χριστός· οὐκ ἐν τῷ
coming through water and blood,   Jesus    Christ;  not by the
ὕδατι μόνον, ἀλλ' ἐν τῷ ὕδατι καὶ τῷ αἵματι. καὶ τὸ Πνεῦμά
water  only,  but  by the water and the  blood. And the Spirit

**7** ἐστι τὸ μαρτυροῦν, ὅτι τὸ Πνεῦμά ἐστιν ἡ ἀλήθεια. ὅτι τρεῖς
is the (One) witnessing, because the Spirit  is  the  truth. Because three
εἰσὶν οἱ μαρτυροῦντες ἐν τῷ οὐρανῷ, ὁ πατήρ, ὁ λόγος, καὶ
there are  bearing witness in      Heaven, the Father, the Word,  and

**8** τὸ Ἅγιον Πνεῦμα· καὶ οὗτοι οἱ τρεῖς ἕν εἰσι. καὶ τρεῖς εἰσιν
the Holy   Spirit,  and these  the three One is, And three there are
οἱ μαρτυροῦντες ἐν τῇ γῇ, τὸ Πνεῦμα, καὶ τὸ ὕδωρ, καὶ τὸ
who bear witness  on the earth, the Spirit,  and the water,  and the

**9** αἷμα· καὶ οἱ τρεῖς εἰς τὸ ἕν εἰσιν. εἰ τὴν μαρτυρίαν τῶν
blood; and the three  to the one are.  If  the   witness
ἀνθρώπων λαμβάνομεν, ἡ μαρτυρία τοῦ Θεοῦ μείζων ἐστίν·
of men   we receive,   the  witness  of God greater is,
ὅτι αὕτη ἐστὶν ἡ μαρτυρία τοῦ Θεοῦ, ἣν μεμαρτύρηκε περὶ
because this is  the  witness  of God, which He has witnessed about

**10** τοῦ υἱοῦ αὐτοῦ. ὁ πιστεύων εἰς τὸν υἱὸν τοῦ Θεοῦ ἔχει τὴν
the   Son of Him. The (one) believing in  the Son   of God  has  the
μαρτυρίαν ἐν ἑαυτῷ· ὁ μὴ πιστεύων τῷ Θεῷ ψεύστην πεποί-
witness   in himself. The (one) not believing God  a liar  has
ηκεν αὐτόν, ὅτι οὐ πεπίστευκεν εἰς τὴν μαρτυρίαν, ἣν
made  Him, because not he has believed  in  the  witness   which

**11** μεμαρτύρηκεν ὁ Θεὸς περὶ τοῦ υἱοῦ αὐτοῦ. καὶ αὕτη ἐστὶν
has witnessed   God concerning the Son of Him. And this   is
ἡ μαρτυρία, ὅτι ζωὴν αἰώνιον ἔδωκεν ἡμῖν ὁ Θεός, καὶ αὕτη
the  witness, that life everlasting gave  us   God,  and this

**12** ἡ ζωὴ ἐν τῷ υἱῷ αὐτοῦ ἐστιν. ὁ ἔχων τὸν υἱὸν ἔχει τὴν ζωήν·
life in  the Son of Him  is. The (one) having the Son has    life,
ὁ μὴ ἔχων τὸν υἱὸν τοῦ Θεοῦ τὴν ζωὴν οὐκ ἔχει.
he not having the Son   of God   life   not  has.

**13** Ταῦτα ἔγραψα ὑμῖν τοῖς πιστεύουσιν εἰς τὸ ὄνομα τοῦ
These things I wrote to you, those believing  in  the name of the
υἱοῦ τοῦ Θεοῦ, ἵνα εἰδῆτε ὅτι ζωὴν ἔχετε αἰώνιον, καὶ ἵνα
Son   of God, that you may know that life you have eternal,  and that

**14** πιστεύητε εἰς τὸ ὄνομα τοῦ υἱοῦ τοῦ Θεοῦ. καὶ αὕτη ἐστὶν
you may believe in the  name of the Son   of God. And this   is
ἡ παρρησία ἣν ἔχομεν πρὸς αὐτόν, ὅτι ἐάν τι αἰτώμεθα
the confidence which we have toward Him,  that if anything we ask

**15** κατὰ τὸ θέλημα αὐτοῦ, ἀκούει ἡμῶν· καὶ ἐὰν οἴδαμεν ὅτι
according to the will of Him, He hears  us.  And if  we know  that
ἀκούει ἡμῶν, ὃ ἂν αἰτώμεθα, οἴδαμεν ὅτι ἔχομεν τὰ
He hears  us, whatever we ask,  we know that we have  the

**16** αἰτήματα ἃ ᾐτήκαμεν παρ' αὐτοῦ. ἐάν τις ἴδῃ τὸν ἀδελφὸν
requests which we have asked from Him. If anyone sees the brother
αὐτοῦ ἁμαρτάνοντα ἁμαρτίαν μὴ πρὸς θάνατον, αἰτήσει,
of him   sinning      a sin    not unto  death,  he shall ask,
καὶ δώσει αὐτῷ ζωὴν τοῖς ἁμαρτάνουσι μὴ πρὸς θάνατον.
and He will give to him life to those sinning    not unto  death.
ἔστιν ἁμαρτία πρὸς θάνατον· οὐ περὶ ἐκείνης λέγω ἵνα
There is a sin   unto  death;  not concerning that  I say  that

that. [17] All unrighteousness is sin, and there is a sin not unto death.

[18] We know that everyone having been born of God does not sin, but the (one) born of God keeps himself, and the evil one does not touch him. [19] We know that we are of God and the whole world lies in evil. [20] And we know that the Son of God is come, and has given to us an understanding that we might know the true (One), and we are in the true (One), in His Son, Jesus Christ. This is the true God, and the life everlasting.

[21] Little children, guard yourself from idols. Amen.

**17** ἐρωτήσῃ. πᾶσα ἀδικία ἁμαρτία ἐστί· καὶ ἔστιν ἁμαρτία οὐ
he should ask.   All unrighteousness sin    is,  and there is   a sin   not

πρὸς θάνατον.
unto   death.

**18** Οἴδαμεν ὅτι πᾶς ὁ γεγεννημένος ἐκ τοῦ Θεοῦ οὐχ ἁμαρ-
We know  that everyone having been born of      God  not  sins,

τάνει· ἀλλ᾽ ὁ γεννηθεὶς ἐκ τοῦ Θεοῦ τηρεῖ ἑαυτόν, καὶ ὁ
but the (one) born  of       God    keeps himself, and the

**19** πονηρὸς οὐχ ἅπτεται αὐτοῦ. οἴδαμεν ὅτι ἐκ τοῦ Θεοῦ
evil one does not  touch     him.   We know that of       God

**20** ἐσμέν, καὶ ὁ κόσμος ὅλος ἐν τῷ πονηρῷ κεῖται. οἴδαμεν δὲ
we are, and the world  whole  in    evil      lies.  we know And

ὅτι ὁ υἱὸς τοῦ Θεοῦ ἥκει, καὶ δέδωκεν ἡμῖν διάνοιαν ἵνα
that the Son    of God is come, and has given to us an understanding that

γινώσκωμεν τὸν ἀληθινόν· καί ἐσμεν ἐν τῷ ἀληθινῷ, ἐν τῷ
we might know the  true (One),  and we are in the true (One),  in the

υἱῷ αὐτοῦ Ἰησοῦ Χριστῷ. οὗτός ἐστιν ὁ ἀληθινὸς Θεός,
Son of Him,  Jesus  Christ.  This  is   the   true    God,

**21** καὶ ἡ ζωὴ αἰώνιος. Τεκνία, φυλάξατε ἑαυτοὺς ἀπὸ τῶν
and the life everlasting. Little children, guard  yourselves from

εἰδώλων. ἀμήν.
idols.    Amen.

# ΙΩΑΝΝΟΥ
## JOHN
## ΕΠΙΣΤΟΛΗ ΔΕΥΤΕΡΑ
### EPISTLE SECOND

## THE SECOND EPISTLE
## OF JOHN

[1] The elder to (the) elect lady and her children, whom I love in truth; and not I only, but also all those who have known the truth [2] for the sake of the truth remaining among us, and will be with us forever. [3] Grace, mercy, peace, from God (the) Father and from (the) Lord Jesus Christ, the Son of the Father, in truth and love.

[4] I rejoiced greatly because I found your children walking in truth, as we received command from the Father. [5] And now I request you, lady, not writing as a new commandment, but (one) which we had from (the) beginning, that we should love one another. [6] And this is love, that we should walk according to His commandments. This is the commandment, even as you heard from (the) beginning, that you should walk in it. [7] Because many deceivers went out into the world, those not confessing Jesus Christ to have come in (the) flesh—this is the deceiver and the antichrist. [8] Watch yourselves, that we may not lose the things we worked out, but a full reward we may receive. [9] Everyone transgressing and not abiding in the teaching of Christ does not have God. The (one) abiding in the teaching of Christ, this one indeed has the Father and the Son. [10] If anyone comes to you and does not bear this teaching, do not receive him into (the) house, and do not speak a greeting to him. [11] For the (one) speaking a greeting shares in

1 'Ο πρεσβύτερος ἐκλεκτῇ κυρίᾳ καὶ τοῖς τέκνοις αὐτῆς,
The elder to (the) elect lady and the children of her,
οὓς ἐγὼ ἀγαπῶ ἐν ἀληθείᾳ, καὶ οὐκ ἐγὼ μόνος, ἀλλὰ καὶ
whom I love in truth, and not I only, but also
2 πάντες οἱ ἐγνωκότες τὴν ἀλήθειαν, διὰ τὴν ἀλήθειαν τὴν
all those who have known the truth. because of the truth
3 μένουσαν ἐν ἡμῖν, καὶ μεθ' ἡμῶν ἔσται εἰς τὸν αἰῶνα· ἔσται
remaining among us, and with us will be unto the age. will be
μεθ' ὑμῶν χάρις, ἔλεος, εἰρήνη παρὰ Θεοῦ πατρός, καὶ παρὰ
with you Grace, mercy, peace, from God (the) Father, and from
Κυρίου Ἰησοῦ Χριστοῦ τοῦ υἱοῦ τοῦ πατρός, ἐν ἀληθείᾳ καὶ
(the) Lord Jesus Christ the Son of the Father, in truth and
ἀγάπῃ.
love.

4 Ἐχάρην λίαν ὅτι εὕρηκα ἐκ τῶν τέκνων σου περιπατοῦν-
I rejoiced greatly because I found of the children of you walking
τας ἐν ἀληθείᾳ, καθὼς ἐντολὴν ἐλάβομεν παρὰ τοῦ πατρός.
in truth, as commandment we received from the Father.
5 καὶ νῦν ἐρωτῶ σε, κυρία, οὐχ ὡς ἐντολὴν γράφων σοι καινήν,
And now I request you, lady, not as a command writing to you new,
6 ἀλλὰ ἣν εἴχομεν ἀπ' ἀρχῆς, ἵνα ἀγαπῶμεν ἀλλήλους. καὶ
but which we had from (the) beginning, that we should love one another. And
αὕτη ἐστὶν ἡ ἀγάπη, ἵνα περιπατῶμεν κατὰ τὰς ἐντολας
this is love, that we should walk according to the commands
αὐτοῦ. αὕτη ἐστὶν ἡ ἐντολή, καθὼς ἠκούσατε ἀπ' ἀρχῆς,
of Him. This is the command, as you heard from (the) beginning,
7 ἵνα ἐν αὐτῇ περιπατῆτε. ὅτι πολλοὶ πλάνοι εἰσῆλθον εἰς τὸν
that in it you should walk. Because many deceivers went out into the
κόσμον, οἱ μὴ ὁμολογοῦντες Ἰησοῦν Χριστὸν ἐρχόμενον ἐν
world, those not confessing Jesus Christ coming in
8 σαρκί. οὗτός ἐστιν ὁ πλάνος καὶ ὁ ἀντίχριστος. βλέπετε
(the) flesh. This is the deceiver and the antichrist. Watch
ἑαυτούς, ἵνα μὴ ἀπολέσωμεν ἃ εἰργασάμεθα, ἀλλὰ μισθὸν
yourselves, lest we may lose the things we worked out, but a reward
9 πλήρη ἀπολάβωμεν. πᾶς ὁ παραβαίνων καὶ μὴ μένων ἐν
full we may receive. Everyone transgressing and not abiding in
τῇ διδαχῇ τοῦ Χριστοῦ, Θεὸν οὐκ ἔχει· ὁ μένων ἐν τῇ
the teaching of Christ, God not has The (one) abiding in the
διδαχῇ τοῦ Χριστοῦ, οὗτος καὶ τὸν πατέρα καὶ τὸν υἱὸν
teaching of Christ, this one even the Father and the Son
10 ἔχει. εἴ τις ἔρχεται πρὸς ὑμᾶς, καὶ ταύτην τὴν διδαχὴν οὐ
has. If anyone comes to you, and this teaching not
φέρει, μὴ λαμβάνετε αὐτὸν εἰς οἰκίαν, καὶ χαίρειν αὐτῷ μὴ
bears, not do receive him into (the) house, and a greeting to him not
11 λέγετε· ὁ γὰρ λέγων αὐτῷ χαίρειν κοινωνεῖ τοῖς ἔργοις
do speak. he For speaking to him a greeting shares in the works

the evil works of him.

[12] Many things having to write to you, I do not intend (to speak) by means of paper and ink, but I am hoping to come to you, and to speak mouth to mouth, that our joy may be full.

[13] The children of your elect sister greet you. Amen.

αὐτοῦ τοῖς πονηροῖς.
of him         evil.

**12** Πολλὰ ἔχων ὑμῖν γράφειν οὐκ ἠβουλήθην διὰ χάρτου
Many things having to you to write not I intend by means of paper
καὶ μέλανος· ἀλλὰ ἐλπίζω ἐλθεῖν πρὸς ὑμᾶς, καὶ στόμα πρὸς
and ink.     but I am hoping to come to you, and mouth to

**13** στόμα λαλῆσαι, ἵνα ἡ χαρὰ ἡμῶν ᾖ πεπληρωμένη. ἀσπά-
mouth to speak, that the joy of us may be fulfilled. greet
ζεταί σε τὰ τέκνα τῆς ἀδελφῆς σου τῆς ἐκλεκτῆς. ἀμήν.
you The children of the sister of you    elect.    Amen.

## IΩANNOY
### OF JOHN
### ΕΠΙΣΤΟΛΗ ΤΡΙΤΗ
### EPISTLE THIRD

THE THIRD EPISTLE

OF JOHN

[1] The elder to Gaius the beloved, whom I love in truth.

[2] Beloved, in regard to all things, I pray (for) you to do well, and to be in health, as your soul does well. [3] For I rejoiced greatly (at the) coming of (the) brothers even bearing witness of you in the truth, as you walk in truth. [4] I have no greater joy than these things, that I hear my children are walking in (the) truth.

[5] Beloved, faithfully you do whatever you do for the brothers and for the strangers, [6] who bore witness of you before (the) church, whom you will do well to send forward worthily of God. [7] For on behalf of His name they went out, taking nothing from the Gentiles. [8] Therefore, we ought to entertain such (men), that we may become co-workers in the truth.

[9] I wrote to the church, but he loving to be first of them, Diotrephes, does not receive us. [10] Because of this, if I come, I will recall his works which he does, ranting against us with evil words. And not being satisfied on these, neither receives he the brothers; and those willing (to do so), he prevents, and thrusts them out from the church.

[11] Beloved, do not imitate the bad, but the good. The (one) doing good is of God; but the (one) doing ill has not seen God.

[12] Witness has been borne to Demetrius by all, and by the truth itself; and we also bear witness, and

1 Ὁ πρεσβύτερος Γαΐῳ τῷ ἀγαπητῷ, ὃν ἐγὼ ἀγαπῶ ἐν
The    elder    to Gaius the    beloved,    whom I    love    in
ἀληθείᾳ.
truth.

2 Ἀγαπητέ, περὶ πάντων εὔχομαί σε εὐοδοῦσθαι καὶ
Beloved, concerning all things I pray    you    to do well,    and
3 ὑγιαίνειν, καθὼς εὐοδοῦταί σου ἡ ψυχή. ἐχάρην γὰρ λίαν,
to be in health,  as    does well of you the soul. I rejoiced For greatly,
ἐρχομένων ἀδελφῶν καὶ μαρτυρούντων σου τῇ ἀληθείᾳ,
coming    (the) brothers and bearing witness of you in the truth
4 καθὼς σὺ ἐν ἀληθείᾳ περιπατεῖς. μειζοτέραν τούτων οὐκ
as    you in truth    walk.    greater (than) these things not
ἔχω χαράν, ἵνα ἀκούω τὰ ἐμὰ τέκνα ἐν ἀληθείᾳ περι-
I have joy,    that I hear    my children in (the) truth    are
πατοῦντα.
walking.

5 Ἀγαπητέ, πιστὸν ποιεῖς ὃ ἐὰν ἐργάσῃ εἰς τοὺς ἀδελφοὺς
Beloved,    faithfully you do whatever you work for the    brothers
6 καὶ εἰς τοὺς ξένους, οἳ ἐμαρτύρησάν σου τῇ ἀγάπῃ ἐνώπιον
and for the strangers, who bore witness of you in the love in sight of
ἐκκλησίας· οὓς καλῶς ποιήσεις προπέμψας ἀξίως τοῦ Θεοῦ.
(the) church, whom well  you will do sending forward worthily    of God.
7 ὑπὲρ γὰρ τοῦ ὀνόματος αὐτοῦ ἐξῆλθον μηδὲν λαμβάνοντες
on
behalf of For the name    of Him they went out, nothing taking
8 ἀπὸ τῶν ἐθνῶν. ἡμεῖς οὖν ὀφείλομεν ἀπολαμβάνειν τοὺς
from    the Gentiles. We therefore ought    to entertain
τοιούτους, ἵνα συνεργοὶ γινώμεθα τῇ ἀληθείᾳ.
such (men)    that co-workers we may become in the truth.

9 Ἔγραψα τῇ ἐκκλησίᾳ· ἀλλ' ὁ φιλοπρωτεύων αὐτῶν
I wrote  to the    church,    but the (one) loving to be first of them,
10 Διοτρεφὴς οὐκ ἐπιδέχεται ἡμᾶς. διὰ τοῦτο, ἐὰν ἔλθω,
Diotrephes, not does receive    us.    Therefore,  If I come,
ὑπομνήσω αὐτοῦ τὰ ἔργα ἃ ποιεῖ, λόγοις πονηροῖς φλυαρῶν
I will recall of him the works which he does, with words evil prating against
ἡμᾶς· καὶ μὴ ἀρκούμενος ἐπὶ τούτοις, οὔτε αὐτὸς ἐπιδέχεται
us, and not being satisfied on    these,    neither he    receives
τοὺς ἀδελφούς, καὶ τοὺς βουλομένους κωλύει, καὶ ἐκ τῆς
the brothers,  and  those intending (to do so), he prevents, and from the
11 ἐκκλησίας ἐκβάλλει. ἀγαπητέ, μὴ μιμοῦ τὸ κακόν, ἀλλὰ τὸ
church  thrusts out. Beloved, not do imitate the bad,  but the
ἀγαθόν. ὁ ἀγαθοποιῶν ἐκ τοῦ Θεοῦ ἐστίν· ὁ δὲ κακοποιῶν
good. The (one) doing good of    God    is; the (one) but doing ill
12 οὐχ ἑώρακε τὸν Θεόν. Δημητρίῳ μεμαρτύρηται ὑπὸ
not    has seen    God. To Demetrius witness has been borne by
πάντων, καὶ ὑπ' αὐτῆς τῆς ἀληθείας· καὶ ἡμεῖς δὲ μαρτυροῦ-
all,    and by its (own) the    truth;    also  we and bear witness
self

you know that our witness
is true.

[13] I had many things
to write, but I do not desire
to write by means of pen
and ink; [14] but I am hoping to see you at once, and
we will speak mouth to
mouth.

[15] Peace to you. The
friends greet you. Greet the
friends by name.

μεν, καὶ οἴδατε ὅτι ἡ μαρτυρία ἡμῶν ἀληθής ἐστι.
and you know that the witness    of us       true      is.

13  Πολλὰ εἶχον γράφειν, ἀλλ' οὐ θέλω διὰ μέλανος καὶ
    Many things I had to write,    but not I desire via    ink      and

14  καλάμου σοι γράψαι· ἐλπίζω δὲ εὐθέως ἰδεῖν σε, καὶ στόμα
    pen    to you to write; I am hoping but at once to see you, and mouth

15  πρὸς στόμα λαλήσομεν. εἰρήνη σοι. ἀσπάζονταί σε οἱ
    to    mouth we will speak.    Peace to you.    Greet      you The

    φίλοι. ἀσπάζου τοὺς φίλους κατ' ὄνομα.
    friends.  Greet    the    friends by    name.

# ΙΟΥΔΑ
## JUDE
# ΕΠΙΣΤΟΛΗ ΚΑΘΟΛΙΚΗ
### EPISTLE GENERAL

[1] Jude, a slave of Jesus Christ, and brother of James, to those called out ones in God (the) Father, having been loved and hav-been kept for Jesus Christ: [2] Mercy and peace and love be multiplied to you.

[3] Beloved, having made all haste to write to you about the common salvation, I had need to write to you (to) exhort you to earnestly contend for the faith once delivered to the saints. [4] For certain men crept in secretly, the (ones) before of old having been marked out to this condemnation, ungodly ones perverting the grace of our God for unbridled lust ,and denying the only Master, God, and our Lord Jesus Christ.

[5] But I intend to remind you, you once knowing these things, that the Lord having saved a people out of (the) land of Egypt, in the second place He destroyed the (ones) not believing. [6] And those angels not having kept their first place, but having deserted (their) own dwelling-place, He has kept in everlasting chains under darkness for the judgment of a great Day; [7] as Sodom and Gomorrah, and the cities around them, in like manner to these, committing fornication and going away after other flesh, laid down an example beforetimes, undergoing vengeance of everlasting fire. [8] Likewise, indeed, also these dreaming ones even defile flesh, and despise lordship, and speak evil of glories. [9] But Michael the archangel, when contending with the Devil, he argued about the body of Moses, (but) he dared not bring a judgment of blasphemy, but said, Let (the)

1 Ἰούδας Ἰησοῦ Χριστοῦ δοῦλος, ἀδελφὸς δὲ Ἰακώβου,
Jude, of Jesus Christ a slave, brother and of James,
τοῖς ἐν Θεῷ πατρὶ ἡγίασμένοις, καὶ Ἰησοῦ Χριστῷ τετηρη-
to those in God Father (the) loved, having been and by Jesus Christ having been
2 μένοις, κλητοῖς· ἔλεος ὑμῖν καὶ εἰρήνη καὶ ἀγάπη πληθυνθείη.
kept, called: Mercy to you and peace and love be multiplied.
3 Ἀγαπητοί, πᾶσαν σπουδὴν ποιούμενος γράφειν ὑμῖν περὶ
Beloved, all haste making to write to you about
τῆς κοινῆς σωτηρίας, ἀνάγκην ἔσχον γράψαι ὑμῖν, παρα-
the common salvation, necessity I had to write to you, ex-
καλῶν ἐπαγωνίζεσθαι τῇ ἅπαξ παραδοθείσῃ τοῖς ἁγίοις
horting to earnestly contend for the once delivered to the saints
4 πίστει. παρεισέδυσαν γάρ τινες ἄνθρωποι, οἱ πάλαι προγε-
faith, crept in For certain men, those of old having been
γραμμένοι εἰς τοῦτο τὸ κρίμα, ἀσεβεῖς, τὴν τοῦ Θεοῦ ἡμῶν
previously written into this judgment, ungodly ones, the of the God of us
χάριν μετατιθέντες εἰς ἀσέλγειαν, καὶ τὸν μόνον δεσπότην
grace, perverting for unbridled lust, and the only Master
Θεόν, καὶ Κύριον ἡμῶν Ἰησοῦν Χριστὸν ἀρνούμενοι.
God, and Lord of us, Jesus Christ denying.
5 Ὑπομνῆσαι δὲ ὑμᾶς βούλομαι, εἰδότας ὑμᾶς ἅπαξ τοῦτο,
to remind But you I intend. knowing you once these things,
ὅτι ὁ Κύριος, λαὸν ἐκ γῆς Αἰγύπτου σώσας, τὸ δεύτερον
that the Lord people out of land of Egypt having saved, in the second place
6 τοὺς μὴ πιστεύσαντας ἀπώλεσεν. ἀγγέλους τε τοὺς μὴ
those not believing He destroyed; angels and those not
τηρήσαντας τὴν ἑαυτῶν ἀρχήν, ἀλλὰ ἀπολιπόντας τὸ
having kept the of themselves first place, but having deserted the
ἴδιον οἰκητήριον, εἰς κρίσιν μεγάλης ἡμέρας δεσμοῖς ἀϊδίοις
own dwelling-place, for (the) Judgment of a great Day in chains eternal
7 ὑπὸ ζόφον τετήρηκεν. ὡς Σόδομα καὶ Γόμορρα, καὶ αἱ περὶ
under blackness He has kept.; as Sodom and Gomorrah and the around
αὐτὰς πόλεις, τὸν ὅμοιον τούτοις τρόπον ἐκπορνευσασαι,
them cities, in the similar to these manner committing fornication
καὶ ἀπελθοῦσαι ὀπίσω σαρκὸς ἑτέρας, πρόκεινται δεῖγμα,
and going away after flesh other. laid beforetimes an example
8 πυρὸς αἰωνίου δίκην ὑπέχουσαι. ὁμοίως μέντοι καὶ ουτοι
of fire everlasting vengeance undergoing. Likewise indeed also these
ἐνυπνιαζόμενοι σάρκα μὲν μιαίνουσι, κυριότητα δὲ ἀθετοῦσι,
dreaming (ones) flesh even defile, lordship and despise,
9 δόξας δὲ βλασφημοῦσιν. ὁ δὲ Μιχαὴλ ὁ ἀρχάγγελος, ὅτε τῷ
glories and speak evil of. But Michael the archangel, when with the
διαβόλῳ διακρινόμενος διελέγετο περὶ τοῦ Μωσέως σώ-
Devil contending, he argued about the of Moses
ματος, οὐκ ἐτόλμησε κρίσιν ἐπενεγκεῖν βλασφημίας, ἀλλ᾽
body, not he dared a judgment to bring of blasphemy, but

Lord rebuke you. [10] But what things they do not know, these they speak evil of; and what things they naturally understand, like the animals without reason, they are corrupted by these. [11] Woe to them, because they went in the way of Cain, and gave themselves to the error of Balaam (for) reward, and perished in the gainsaying of Korah! [12] These are sunken rocks in your love feasts, feasting together with you, feeding themselves without fear, waterless clouds being carried about by winds, fruitless autumn trees, having died twice, having been plucked up by the roots; [13] wild waves of (the) sea foaming up shames of themselves, wandering stars for whom blackness of darkness has been kept forever. [14] And Enoch, (the) seventh from Adam also prophesied to these, saying, Behold, (the) Lord came with myriads of His holy ones to do judgment against all, and to rebuke all the ungodly of them concerning all their ungodly works which they ungodly did, and concerning all the hard things ungodly sinners spoke against Him. [16] These are murmurers, complainers, leading lives according to their lusts, and their mouth speaks proud things, admiring faces for the sake of gain. [17] But you, beloved, remember the words spoken before by the apostles of our Lord Jesus Christ, [18] because they told you that at (the) last time there will be mockers according to their lusts, leading ungodly lives. [19] These are the (ones) separating themselves, animal-like ones, not having (the) Spirit. [20] But you, beloved, building yourselves up by your most holy faith, praying in (the) Holy Spirit, [21] keep yourselves in (the) love of God, eagerly awaiting the mercy of our Lord Jesus Christ to life

10  εἶπεν, Ἐπιτιμήσαι σοι Κύριος. οὗτοι δὲ ὅσα μὲν οὐκ οἴδασι
said, Let rebuke you (the) Lord. these But what things not they know,
βλασφημοῦσιν· ὅσα δὲ φυσικῶς, ὡς τὰ ἄλογα ζῷα, ἐπί-
they speak evil of; what things and naturally—as the without reason animals—they

11  στανται, ἐν τούτοις φθείρονται. οὐαὶ αὐτοῖς ὅτι τῇ ὁδῷ τοῦ
understand, by these they are corrupted. Woe to them, because in the way of the
Κάϊν ἐπορεύθησαν, καὶ τῇ πλάνῃ τοῦ Βαλαὰμ μισθοῦ
of Cain they went, and to the error of Balaam (for) reward

12  ἐξεχύθησαν, καὶ τῇ ἀντιλογίᾳ τοῦ Κορὲ ἀπώλοντο. οὗτοί
gave themselves, and in the gainsaying of Korah perished! These
εἰσιν ἐν ταῖς ἀγάπαις ὑμῶν σπιλάδες, συνευωχούμενοι ὑμῖν,
are in the love feasts of you rocky reefs feasting together with you,
ἀφόβως ἑαυτοὺς ποιμαίνοντες· νεφέλαι ἄνυδροι, ὑπὸ
without fear themselves feeding, clouds waterless by
ἀνέμων περιφερόμεναι· δένδρα φθινοπωρινά, ἄκαρπα, δὶς
winds having been carried about trees autumn without fruit, twice

13  ἀποθανόντα, ἐκριζωθέντα· κύματα ἄγρια θαλάσσης, ἐπ-
having died, having been uprooted, waves wild of (the) sea
ἀφρίζοντα τὰς ἑαυτῶν αἰσχύνας· ἀστέρες πλανῆται, οἷς ὁ
foaming up the of themselves shames, stars wandering, for whom

14  ζόφος τοῦ σκότους εἰς τὸν αἰῶνα τετήρηται. προεφήτευσε
blackness of darkness to the age has been kept. prophesied
δὲ καὶ τούτοις ἕβδομος ἀπὸ Ἀδὰμ Ἐνώχ, λέγων, Ἰδού,
And also to these (the) seventh from Adam, Enoch, saying, Behold,

15  ἦλθε Κύριος ἐν μυριάσιν ἁγίαις αὐτοῦ, ποιῆσαι κρίσιν κατὰ
came (the) Lord with myriads saints of Him, to do judgment against
πάντων, καὶ ἐξελέγξαι πάντας τοὺς ἀσεβεῖς αὐτῶν περὶ
all, and to rebuke all the ungodly of them concerning
πάντων τῶν ἔργων ἀσεβείας αὐτῶν ὧν ἠσέβησαν, καὶ περὶ
all the works ungodly of them which they ungodly did, and about
πάντων τῶν σκληρῶν ὧν ἐλάλησαν κατ' αὐτοῦ ἁμαρτωλοὶ
all the hard things which spoke against Him sinners

16  ἀσεβεῖς. οὗτοί εἰσι γογγυσταί, μεμψίμοιροι, κατὰ τὰς
ungodly. These are murmurers, complainers, according to the
ἐπιθυμίας αὐτῶν πορευόμενοι, καὶ τὸ στόμα αὐτῶν λαλεῖ
lusts of them following and the mouth of them speaks
ὑπέρογκα, θαυμάζοντες πρόσωπα ὠφελείας χάριν.
proud things, admiring faces gain for the sake of

17  Ὑμεῖς δέ, ἀγαπητοί, μνήσθητε τῶν ῥημάτων τῶν
you But, beloved, remember the words
προειρημένων ὑπὸ τῶν ἀποστόλων τοῦ Κυρίου ἡμῶν
spoken before by the apostles of the Lord of us,

18  Ἰησοῦ Χριστοῦ· ὅτι ἔλεγον ὑμῖν, ὅτι ἐν ἐσχάτῳ χρόνῳ
Jesus Christ, because they told you that at (the) last time
ἔσονται ἐμπαῖκται, κατὰ τὰς ἑαυτῶν ἐπιθυμίας πορευό-
will be mockers according to the of themselves lusts following

19  μενοι τῶν ἀσεβειῶν. οὗτοί εἰσιν οἱ ἀποδιορίζοντες ἑαυτούς,
the ungodly. These are they dividing apart themselves,

20  ψυχικοί, Πνεῦμα μὴ ἔχοντες. ὑμεῖς δέ, ἀγαπητοί, τῇ ἁγιω-
animal-like, (the) Spirit not having. you But, beloved by the most
τάτῃ ὑμῶν πίστει ἐποικοδομοῦντες ἑαυτούς, ἐν Πνεύματι
holy of you faith building up yourselves, in (the) Spirit

21  Ἁγίῳ προσευχόμενοι, ἑαυτοὺς ἐν ἀγάπῃ Θεοῦ τηρήσατε,
Holy praying, yourselves in (the) love of God keep,
προσδεχόμενοι τὸ ἔλεος τοῦ Κυρίου ἡμῶν Ἰησοῦ Χριστοῦ
eagerly awaiting the mercy of the Lord of us, Jesus Christ

everlasting. [22] And pity some, making distinction. [23] But others save with fear, snatching (them) out of the fire, hating even the garment having been stained from the flesh.

[24] Now to Him being able to keep you without stumbling, and to set (you) before His glory without blemish, with unspeakable joy, [25] to the only wise God, our Savior, (be) glory and majesty and might and authority, even now and forever. Amen.

22/ εἰς ζωὴν αἰώνιον. καὶ οὓς μὲν ἐλεεῖτε διακρινόμενοι· οὓς δὲ
to life everlasting. And some pity, making distinction, others But

23 ἐν φόβῳ σώζετε, ἐκ τοῦ πυρὸς ἁρπάζοντες, μισοῦντες καὶ
with fear save, out of the fire snatching (them), hating even

τὸν ἀπὸ τῆς σαρκὸς ἐσπιλωμένον χιτῶνα.
the from the flesh stained garment.

24 Τῷ δὲ δυναμένῳ φυλάξαι ὑμᾶς ἀπταίστους, καὶ στῆσαι
to Him Now being able to keep you without stumbling, and to set

κατενώπιον τῆς δόξης αὐτοῦ ἀμώμους ἐν ἀγαλλιάσει,
(you) before the glory of Him without blemish with exultation,

25 μόνῳ σοφῷ Θεῷ σωτῆρι ἡμῶν, δόξα καὶ μεγαλωσύνη,
to (the) only wise God Savior of us, (be) glory and

κράτος καὶ ἐξουσία, καὶ νῦν καὶ εἰς πάντας τοὺς αἰῶνας.
might and majesty, even now and to all the ages.

ἀμήν.
Amen.

CHAPTER 1

[1] A revelation of Jesus Christ, which God gave to Him to show to His slaves things which must occur quickly. And He signified (by) sending through His angel to His slave, John, [2] who testified of the word of God and the witness of Jesus Christ; even as many as he saw. [3] Blessed (is) the (one) reading, and those hearing, the words of this prophecy, and keeping the things having been written in it; for the time (is) near.

[4] John to the seven churches in Asia: Grace to you, and peace, from He who is, and who was, and who (is) coming, and from the seven spirits which are before His throne; [5] and from Jesus Christ the faithful witness, the First-born out of the dead, and the ruler of kings of the earth. To Him loving us, and having loosed us from our sins by His blood, [6] and made us kings and priests to the God and Father of Him: To Him (is) the glory and the might forever and ever; Amen. [7] Behold, He comes with the clouds, and and every eye will see Him, and those who pierced Him, and all the tribes of the earth will wail due to Him. Yes, Amen.

[8] I am the Alpha and the Omega, the Beginning and the End, says the Lord, the (One being, and who was, and who (is) coming —the Almighty.

[9] I, John, even your brother, and co-sharer in the

# ΑΠΟΚΑΛΥΨΙΣ
## REVELATION
## ΤΟΥ ΑΓΙΟΥ
## THE HOLY
# ΙΩΑΝΝΟΥ ΤΟΥ ΘΕΟΛΟΓΟΥ
## OF JOHN    THE    DIVINE

## CHAPTER 1

**1** Ἀποκάλυψις Ἰησοῦ Χριστοῦ, ἣν ἔδωκεν αὐτῷ ὁ Θεὸς
A revelation of Jesus Christ, which gave to Him God,
δεῖξαι τοῖς δούλοις αὐτοῦ, ἃ δεῖ γενέσθαι ἐν τάχει, καὶ ἐσή-
to show to the slaves of Him things which must occur with speed; and He
μανεν ἀποστείλας διὰ τοῦ ἀγγέλου αὐτοῦ τῷ δούλῳ αὐτοῦ,
signified sending through the angel of Him to the slave of Him,

**2** Ἰωάννη, ὃς ἐμαρτύρησε τὸν λόγον τοῦ Θεοῦ καὶ τὴν μαρτυ-
John, who testified of the word of God and the witness

**3** ρίαν Ἰησοῦ Χριστοῦ, ὅσα τε εἶδε. μακάριος ὁ ἀναγινώσκων,
of Jesus Christ, as many as even he saw. Blessed the (one) reading
καὶ οἱ ἀκούοντες τοὺς λόγους τῆς προφητείας καὶ τηροῦντες·
and those hearing the words of the prophecy, and keeping
τὰ ἐν αὐτῇ γεγραμμένα· ὁ γὰρ καιρὸς ἐγγύς.
the things in it having been written, the for time (is) near.

**4** Ἰωάννης ταῖς ἑπτὰ ἐκκλησίαις ταῖς ἐν τῇ Ἀσίᾳ· χάρις ὑμῖν
John to the seven churches in Asia: Grace to you

**5** καὶ εἰρήνη ἀπὸ τοῦ ὁ ὢν καὶ ὁ ἦν καὶ ὁ ἐρχόμενος· καὶ ἀπὸ
and peace from He being who and was and who (is) coming, the Almighty.
τῶν ἑπτὰ πνευμάτων ἅ ἐστιν ἐνώπιον τοῦ θρόνου αὐτοῦ·
the seven spirits which are before the throne of Him,
καὶ ἀπὸ Ἰησοῦ Χριστοῦ, ὁ μάρτυς ὁ πιστός, ὁ πρωτότοκος
and from Jesus Christ the witness faithful, the firstborn
ἐκ τῶν νεκρῶν, καὶ ὁ ἄρχων τῶν βασιλέων τῆς γῆς. τῷ
out of the dead, and the ruler of the kings of the earth. To the (One)
ἀγαπήσαντι ἡμᾶς, καὶ λούσαντι ἡμᾶς ἀπὸ τῶν ἁμαρτιῶν
loving us, and having loosed us from the sins

**6** ἡμῶν ἐν τῷ αἵματι αὐτοῦ· καὶ ἐποίησεν ἡμᾶς βασιλεῖς καὶ
of us by the blood of Him, and made us kings, and
ἱερεῖς τῷ Θεῷ καὶ πατρὶ αὐτοῦ· αὐτῷ ἡ δόξα καὶ τὸ κράτος
priests to the God and Father of Him, to Him (is) the glory and the might

**7** εἰς τοὺς αἰῶνας τῶν αἰώνων. ἀμήν. ἰδού, ἔρχεται μετὰ τῶν
to the ages of the ages. Amen. Behold, He comes with the
νεφελῶν, καὶ ὄψεται αὐτὸν πᾶς ὀφθαλμός, καὶ οἵτινες αὐτὸν
clouds, and will see Him every eye and those who Him
ἐξεκέντησαν· καὶ κόψονται ἐπ᾽ αὐτὸν πᾶσαι αἱ φυλαὶ τῆς
pierced, and will wail due to Him all the tribes of the
γῆς. ναί, ἀμήν.
earth. Yes, Amen.

**8** Ἐγώ εἰμι τὸ Α καὶ τὸ Ω, ἀρχὴ καὶ τέλος, λέγει ὁ Κύριος,
I am the Alpha and the Omega, beginning and ending, says the Lord,
ὁ ὢν καὶ ὁ ἦν καὶ ὁ ἐρχόμενος, ὁ παντοκράτωρ.
the being (One) and was and (is) coming, the Almighty.

**9** Ἐγὼ Ἰωάννης, ὁ καὶ ἀδελφὸς ὑμῶν καὶ συγκοινωνὸς ἐν
I, John, the even brother of you, and co-sharer in

affliction, and in the kingdom and patience of Jesus Christ, came to be in the island of Patmos, because of the word of God, and because of the witness of Jesus Christ. [10] I came to be in (the) Spirit on the day (of) the Lord, and I heard behind me a great voice, as of a trumpet, [11] saying, I am the Alpha and the Omega, the First and the Last; and, What you see, write in a roll, and send to the seven churches of Asia: to Ephesus, and to Smyrna, and to Pergamos, and to Thyatira, and to Sardis, and to Philadelphia, and to Laodicea. [12] And I turned to see the voice which spoke with me. [13] And having turned, I saw seven golden lampstands, and in (the) midst of the seven lampstands (One) like (the) Son of man, having been clothed to (the) feet, and having been girded with a golden girdle at the breasts. [14] And His head and hairs (were) white as white wool, as snow, and His eyes as a flame of fire; [15] and His feet like burnished metal having been fired as in a furnace; and His voice as a sound of many waters; [16] and having in His right hand seven stars, and out of His mouth a sharp, two-mouthed sword proceeding; and His face shines as the sun in its power. [17] And when I saw Him, I fell at His feet, as dead; and He put His right hand on me, saying to me, Do not fear; I am the First and the Last, [18] and the living One; and I became dead; and, behold, I am living forever and ever. Amen. And I have the keys of Hades and of death. [19] Write what you saw, and what things are, and what things will occur after these things. [20] The mystery of the seven stars which you saw on My right, and the seven golden lampstands: the

---

τῇ θλίψει καὶ ἐν τῇ βασιλείᾳ καὶ ὑπομονῇ Ἰησοῦ Χριστοῦ,
the affliction and in the kingdom and patience of Jesus Christ,

ἐγενόμην ἐν τῇ νήσῳ τῇ καλουμένῃ Πάτμῳ, διὰ τὸν λόγον
came to be in the island being called Patmos, for the word

10 τοῦ Θεοῦ καὶ διὰ τὴν μαρτυρίαν Ἰησοῦ Χριστοῦ. ἐγενόμην
of God and because of the witness of Jesus Christ. I came to be

ἐν Πνεύματι ἐν τῇ Κυριακῇ ἡμέρᾳ· καὶ ἤκουσα ὀπίσω μου
in (the) Spirit on the (of) the Lord day, and I heard behind me

11 φωνὴν μεγάλην ὡς σάλπιγγος, λεγούσης. Ἐγώ εἰμι τὸ Α καὶ
a voice great, as of a trumpet, saying, I am the Alpha and

τὸ Ω, ὁ πρῶτος καὶ ὁ ἔσχατος· καί, Ὃ βλέπεις γράψον εἰς
the Omega, the First and the Last; and, What you see write in

βιβλίον, καὶ πέμψον ταῖς ἑπτὰ ἐκκλησίαις ταῖς ἐν Ἀσίᾳ, εἰς
a roll, and send to the seven churches in Asia, to

Ἔφεσον, καὶ εἰς Σμύρναν, καὶ εἰς Πέργαμον, καὶ εἰς Θυάτειρα,
Ephesus, and to Smyrna, and to Pergamos, and to Thyatira,

καὶ εἰς Σάρδεις, καὶ εἰς Φιλαδέλφειαν, καὶ εἰς Λαοδίκειαν.
and to Sardis, and to Philadelphia, and to Laodicea.

12 καὶ ἐπέστρεψα βλέπειν τὴν φωνὴν ἥτις ἐλάλησε μετ' ἐμοῦ.
And I turned to see the voice which spoke with me.

13 καὶ ἐπιστρέψας εἶδον ἑπτὰ λυχνίας χρυσᾶς, καὶ ἐν μέσῳ
And having turned I saw seven lampstands of gold, and in (the) midst

τῶν ἑπτὰ λυχνιῶν ὅμοιον υἱῷ ἀνθρώπου, ἐνδεδυμένον
of the seven lampstands (One) like (the) Son of man, having been clothed

ποδήρη, καὶ περιεζωσμένον πρὸς τοῖς μαστοῖς ζώνην
to (the) feet, and having been girded with at the breasts a girdle

14 χρυσῆν. ἡ δὲ κεφαλὴ αὐτοῦ καὶ αἱ τρίχες λευκαὶ ὡσεὶ ἔριον
of gold. the And head of Him, and the hairs white as wool

λευκόν, ὡς χιών· καὶ οἱ ὀφθαλμοὶ αὐτοῦ ὡς φλὸξ πυρός·
white, as snow, and the eyes of Him as a flame of fire,

15 καὶ οἱ πόδες αὐτοῦ ὅμοιοι χαλκολιβάνῳ, ὡς ἐν καμίνῳ
and the feet of Him like burnished metal as in a furnace

πεπυρωμένοι· καὶ ἡ φωνὴ αὐτοῦ ὡς φωνὴ ὑδάτων πολλῶν.
having been fired, and the voice of Him as a sound of waters many,

16 καὶ ἔχων ἐν τῇ δεξιᾷ αὐτοῦ χειρὶ ἀστέρας ἑπτά· καὶ ἐκ τοῦ
and having in the right of Him hand stars seven, and out of the

στόματος αὐτοῦ ῥομφαία δίστομος ὀξεῖα ἐκπορευομένη· καὶ
mouth of Him a sword two-mouthed sharp proceeding, and

17 ἡ ὄψις αὐτοῦ, ὡς ὁ ἥλιος φαίνει ἐν τῇ δυνάμει αὐτοῦ. καὶ ὅτε
the face of Him as the sun shines in the power of it. And when

εἶδον αὐτόν, ἔπεσα πρὸς τοὺς πόδας αὐτοῦ ὡς νεκρός· καὶ
I saw Him, I fell at the feet of Him as dead; and

ἐπέθηκε τὴν δεξιὰν αὐτοῦ χεῖρα ἐπ' ἐμέ, λέγων μοι, Μὴ
He placed the right of Him hand on me, saying to me, Not

18 φοβοῦ· ἐγὼ εἰμι ὁ πρῶτος καὶ ὁ ἔσχατος, καὶ ὁ ζῶν, καὶ
fear; I am the First and the Last, and the living One, and

ἐγενόμην νεκρός, καὶ ἰδού, ζῶν εἰμι εἰς τοὺς αἰῶνας τῶν
I became dead, and, behold, living I am to the ages of the

αἰώνων, ἀμήν· καὶ ἔχω τὰς κλεῖς τοῦ ᾅδου καὶ τοῦ θανάτου.
ages, Amen. And I have the keys of Hades and of death.

19 γράψον ἃ εἶδες, καὶ ἃ εἰσι, καὶ ἃ μέλλει γίνεσθαι μετὰ ταῦτα·
Write what you saw, and what is about occur after these things.

20 τὸ μυστήριον τῶν ἑπτὰ ἀστέρων ὧν εἶδες ἐπὶ τῆς δεξιᾶς
The mystery of the seven stars which you saw on the right

μου. καὶ τὰς ἑπτὰ λυχνίας τὰς χρυσᾶς. οἱ ἑπτὰ ἀστέρες
of Me, and the seven lampstands of gold the seven stars

seven stars are angels of the seven churches, and the seven lampstands you saw are seven churches.

## CHAPTER 2

[1] To the angel of the Ephesian church, write:

[2] These things says the (One) holding the seven stars in His right (hand), He walking in (the) midst of the seven golden lampstands: I know your works, and your labor, and your patience, and that you cannot bear evil ones; and (you) tried those pretending to be apostles, and are not, and found them (to be) liars. [3] And (I know) you bore up and have patience, and for My name's sake you have labored and have not become weary. [4] But I have against you that you left your first love. [5] Remember, then, from where you have fallen, and repent and do the first works. And if not, I am coming to you quickly, and will remove your lampstand from its place, unless you repent. [6] But this you have, that you hate the works of the Nicolaitans, which I also hate. [7] The (one) having an ear, hear what the Spirit says to the churches. To the (one) overcoming, I will give to him to eat of the tree of life, which is in (the) midst of the Paradise of God.

[8] And to the angel of Smyrna, write:

[9] These things says the First and the Last, who became dead, and lived, I know your works, and the affliction, and the poverty. but you are rich. And (I know) the evil speaking of those saying themselves to be Jews, and they are not, but (are) a synagogue of Satan. [10] Do not at all fear what you are about to suffer. Behold, the Devil is about to throw you into prison, so that you may be tried; and you will have affliction ten days. Be faithful until death, and I will give you the crown of life.

[11] The (one) having an ear, hear what the Spirit

ἄγγελοι τῶν ἑπτὰ ἐκκλησιῶν εἰσί· καὶ αἱ ἑπτὰ λυχνίαι ἃς
angels  ȯf the seven churches     are, and the  seven lampstands
εἶδες ἑπτὰ ἐκκλησίαι εἰσί.
you saw seven  churches   are.

## CHAPTER 2

1 Τῷ ἀγγέλῳ τῆς Ἐφεσίνης ἐκκλησίας γράψον,
To the angel  of the Ephesian   church    write:
Τάδε λέγει ὁ κρατῶν τοὺς ἑπτὰ ἀστέρας ἐν τῇ δεξιᾷ
These things says the (One) holding the seven  stars   in the  right
αὐτοῦ, ὁ περιπατῶν ἐν μέσῳ τῶν ἑπτὰ λυχνιῶν τῶν
of Him, the (One) walking  in (the) midst of the seven lampstands

2 χρυσῶν· Οἶδα τὰ ἔργα σου, καὶ τὸν κόπον σου, καὶ τὴν
of gold: I know the works of you, and the  labor  of you, and the
ὑπομονήν σου, καὶ ὅτι οὐ δύνῃ βαστάσαι κακούς, καὶ
patience of you, and that you cannot  bear      evil ones; and
ἐπείρασω τοὺς φάσκοντας εἶναι ἀποστόλους καὶ οὐκ εἰσί,
(you) tried those  pretending to be   apostles,     and not are,

3 καὶ εὖρες αὐτοὺς ψευδεῖς, καὶ ἐβάστασας καὶ ὑπομονὴν ἔχεις,
and found them  liars;   and you bore up and  patience  have,

4 καὶ διὰ τὸ ὄνομά μου κεκοπίακας καὶ οὐ κέκμηκας. ἀλλ' ἔχω
even due to the name of Me  you have  and not have wearied. But I have
                            labored

5 κατὰ σοῦ, ὅτι τὴν ἀγάπην σου τὴν πρώτην ἀφῆκας. μνημό-
against you that the   love   of you the first   you left. Remember
νευε οὖν πόθεν ἐκπέπτωκας, καὶ μετανόησον, καὶ τὰ πρῶτα
therefore whence you have fallen, and  repent,   and the  first
ἔργα ποίησον· εἰ δὲ μή, ἔρχομαί σοι ταχύ, καὶ κινήσω τὴν
works  do;   if and not, I am coming to you quickly, and will move the

6 λυχνίαν σου ἐκ τοῦ τόπου αὐτῆς, ἐὰν μὴ μετανοήσῃς. ἀλλὰ
lampstand of you from the place of it,   unless  you repent.   But
τοῦτο ἔχεις, ὅτι μισεῖς τὰ ἔργα τῶν Νικολαϊτῶν, ἃ κἀγὼ
this you have, that you hate the works of the Nicolaitans, which I also

7 μισῶ. ὁ ἔχων οὖς ἀκουσάτω τί τὸ Πνεῦμα λέγει ταῖς ἐκκλη-
hate. The (one) having an ear, hear what the Spirit  says to the churches.
σίαις. τῷ νικῶντι δώσω αὐτῷ φαγεῖν ἐκ τοῦ ξύλου τῆς ζωῆς,
   To the (one) over-  I will  to him to eat  of the  tree   of life,
              coming give
ὅ ἐστιν ἐν μέσῳ τοῦ παραδείσου τοῦ Θεοῦ.
which is  in (the) midst of the Paradise  of God.

8 Καὶ τῷ ἀγγέλῳ τῆς ἐκκλησίας Σμυρναίων γράψον,
And to the angel  of the church   of Smyrna   write:
Τάδε λέγει ὁ πρῶτος καὶ ὁ ἔσχατος, ὃς ἐγένετο νεκρὸς καὶ
These things says the First  and the Last,  who became  dead  and

9 ἔζησεν· Οἶδά σου τὰ ἔργα καὶ τὴν θλῖψιν καὶ τὴν πτωχείαν
lived:   I know of you the works and the affliction and the  poverty,
(πλούσιος δὲ εἶ), καὶ τὴν βλασφημίαν τῶν λεγόντων Ἰου-
rich    but you are, and the evil speaking of those  saying   Jews
δαίους εἶναι ἑαυτούς, καὶ οὐκ εἰσίν, ἀλλὰ συναγωγὴ τοῦ
to be  themselves,   and not they are, but a synagogue  of

10 Σατανᾶ. μηδὲν φοβοῦ ἃ μέλλεις πάσχειν· ἰδού, μέλλει βαλεῖν
Satan. Not at all do fear what you are about to suffer. Behold, is about to cast
ἐξ ὑμῶν ὁ διάβολος εἰς φυλακήν, ἵνα πειρασθῆτε· καὶ ἔξετε
of you  the Devil   into prison,  that you may be tried, and you will
                                                                    have
θλῖψιν ἡμερῶν δέκα. γίνου πιστὸς ἄχρι θανάτου, καὶ δώσω
affliction days  ten.  Be faithful until  death, and I will give

11 σοι τὸν στέφανον τῆς ζωῆς. ὁ ἔχων οὖς ἀκουσάτω τί τὸ
you the crown    of life. The (one) having an ear, hear what the

says to the churches. The (one) overcoming will not at all be hurt by the second death.

[12] And to the angel of the church in Pergamos, write:

[13] These things says the (One) having the sharp two-mouthed sword: I know your works, and where you dwell, where the throne of Satan is. And you hold My name, and did not deny My faith even in the days in which Antipas (was) My faithful witness — who was killed alongside you, where Satan dwells. [14] But I have a few things against you, that you have there those holding the teachings of Balaam, who taught Balak to throw a stumbling-block before the sons of Israel, to eat idol-sacrifices, and to commit fornication. [15] So you also have those holding the teachings of the Nicolaitans, which thing I hate. [16] Repent! But if not, I will come to you quickly, and I will make war with them by the sword of My mouth. [17] The (one) having an ear, hear what the Spirit says to the churches. To the (one) overcoming, I will give him to eat from the hidden manna. And I will give to him a white stone, and on the stone a new name having been written, which no one knows except the (one) receiving (it).

[18] And to the angel of the church in Thyatira, write: These things says the Son of God, the (One) having His eyes as a flame of fire, and His feet like burnished metal: [19] I know your works, and the love, and the ministry, and the faith, and the patience of you; and your works, and the last more than the first. [20] But I have a few things against you, that you allow the woman Jezebel, she say-herself (to be) a prophetess, to teach, and to cause My slaves to go astray, and to commit fornication, and to eat idol-sacrifices. [21] And I gave time to her, that she

Πνεῦμα λέγει ταῖς ἐκκλησίαις. ὁ νικῶν οὐ μὴ ἀδικηθῇ ἐκ τοῦ
Spirit says to the churches. The over-(one) coming not at all will be hurt by the

θανάτου τοῦ δευτέρου.
death. second.

**12** Καὶ τῷ ἀγγέλῳ τῆς ἐν Περγάμῳ ἐκκλησίας γράψον,
And to the angel of the in Pergamos church write:

Τάδε· λέγει ὁ ἔχων τὴν ῥομφαίαν τὴν δίστομον τὴν
These things says the (One) having the sword two-mouthed

**13** ὀξεῖαν· Οἶδα τὰ ἔργα σου καὶ ποῦ κατοικεῖς, ὅπου ὁ θρόνος
sharp: I know the works of you and where you dwell, where the throne

τοῦ Σατανᾶ· καὶ κρατεῖς τὸ ὄνομά μου, καὶ οὐκ ἠρνήσω τὴν
(is) of Satan; and you hold the name of Me, and not did deny the

πίστιν μου καὶ ἐν ταῖς ἡμέραις ἐν αἷς Ἀντίπας ὁ μάρτυς μου,
faith of Me even in the days in which (was) Antipas the witness of Me,

ὁ πιστός, ὃς ἀπεκτάνθη παρ' ὑμῖν, ὅπου κατοικεῖ ὁ Σατανᾶς.
faithful, who was killed alongside you, where dwells Satan.

**14** ἀλλ' ἔχω κατὰ σοῦ ὀλίγα, ὅτι ἔχεις ἐκεῖ κρατοῦντας τὴν
But I have against you a few things, for you have there those holding the

διδαχὴν Βαλαάμ, ὃς ἐδίδασκε τὸν Βαλὰκ βαλεῖν σκάνδαλον
teachings of Balaam, who taught Balak to throw a stumbling-block

ἐνώπιον τῶν υἱῶν Ἰσραήλ, φαγεῖν εἰδωλόθυτα καὶ πορνεῦ-
before the sons of Israel, to eat idol sacrifices and to commit

**15** σαι. οὕτως ἔχεις καὶ σὺ κρατοῦντας τὴν διδαχὴν τῶν
forni-cation. So have also you those holding the teaching of the

**16** Νικολαϊτῶν· ὃ μισῶ. μετανόησον· εἰ δὲ μή, ἔρχομαί σοι
Nicolaitans which thing I hate. Repent! if But not, I will come to you

ταχύ, καὶ πολεμήσω μετ' αὐτῶν ἐν τῇ ῥομφαίᾳ τοῦ στό-
quickly, and I will make war with them by the sword of the mouth

**17** ματός μου. ὁ ἔχων οὖς ἀκουσάτω τί τὸ Πνεῦμα λέγει ταῖς
of Me. The (one) having an ear, hear what the Spirit says to the

ἐκκλησίαις. τῷ νικῶντι δώσω αὐτῷ φαγεῖν ἀπὸ τοῦ μάννα
churches. To the (one) over-coming, I will give him to eat from the manna

τοῦ κεκρυμμένου, καὶ δώσω αὐτῷ ψῆφον λευκήν, καὶ ἐπὶ
hidden. And I will give to him a stone white, and on

τὴν ψῆφον ὄνομα καινὸν γεγραμμένον, ὃ οὐδεὶς ἔγνω εἰ μὴ
the stone a name new being written, which no one knows except

ὁ λαμβάνων.
the (one) receiving (it).

**18** Καὶ τῷ ἀγγέλῳ τῆς ἐν Θυατείροις ἐκκλησίας γράψον,
And to the angel of the in Thyatira church write:

Τάδε λέγει ὁ υἱὸς τοῦ Θεοῦ, ὁ ἔχων τοὺς ὀφθαλμοὺς αὐτοῦ
These things says the Son of God, the (One) having the eyes of Him

ὡς φλόγα πυρός, καὶ οἱ πόδες αὐτοῦ ὅμοιοι χαλκολιβάνῳ·
as a flame of fire, and the feet of Him like burnished metal:

**19** Οἶδά σου τὰ ἔργα, καὶ τὴν ἀγάπην καὶ τὴν διακονίαν, καὶ
I know of you the works, and the love and the ministry, and

τὴν πίστιν καὶ τὴν ὑπομονήν σου, καὶ τὰ ἔργα σου, καὶ τὰ
the faith and the patience of you, and the works of you, and the

**20** ἔσχατα πλείονα τῶν πρώτων. ἀλλ' ἔχω κατὰ σοῦ ὀλίγα
last more than the first. But I have against you a few things,

ὅτι ἐᾷς τὴν γυναῖκα Ἰεζαβήλ, τὴν λέγουσαν ἑαυτὴν προφῆ-
that you allow the woman Jezebel, the (one) saying herself a prophet-

τιν, διδάσκειν καὶ πλανᾶσθαι ἐμοὺς δούλους πορνεῦσαι καὶ
tess, to teach and to cause to err My slaves to commit forni-cation and

**21** εἰδωλόθυτα φαγεῖν. καὶ ἔδωκα αὐτῇ χρόνον ἵνα μετανοήσῃ
idol sacrifices to eat. And I gave to her time that she might repent

might repent of her fornication, and she did not repent. [22] Behold, I am throwing her into a bed, and those committing adultery with her into great affliction, except they repent of their works. [23] And I will kill their children with death; and all the churches will know that I am the (One) searching the inner parts and hearts; and I will give to each of you according to your works. [24] But I say to the rest in Thyatira, as many as do not have this teaching, and who did not know the deep things of Satan, as they say,—I am not casting on you another burden. [25] But what you have, hold until I shall come. [26] And the (one) overcoming, and the (one) keeping until (the) end of My works, I will give to him authority over the nations, [27] and he will shepherd them with an iron staff—as clay vessels, they are broken up—as I also have received from My Father; [28] and I will give to him the morning star. [29] The (one) having an ear, hear what the Spirit says to the churches.

CHAPTER 3

[1] And to the angel of the church in Sardis, write: These things says He having the seven spirits of God and the seven stars: I know your works, that you have the name that you live, and are dead. [2] Be watching, and establish the things left, which are about to die. For I have not found your works being fulfilled before God. [3] Then remember how you received and heard; and keep, and repent. If, then, you do not watch, I will come upon you like a thief, and you will not at all know what hour I come upon you. [4] You also have a few names in Sardis which did not defile their robes; and they shall walk with Me in white, because they are worthy. [5] The (one) overcoming, this (one) shall be clothed in white garments, and I will not at all blot out his name

22 ἐκ τῆς πορνείας αὐτῆς, καὶ οὐ μετενόησεν. ἰδού, ἐγὼ βάλλω
   of the fornication of her, and not she repented. Behold, I am casting
   αὐτὴν εἰς κλίνην, καὶ τοὺς μοιχεύοντας μετ' αὐτῆς εἰς θλίψιν
   her into a bed, and those committing adultery with her into affliction
23 μεγάλην, ἐὰν μὴ μετανοήσωσιν ἐκ τῶν ἔργων αὐτῶν. καὶ τὰ
   great, unless they may repent of the works of them. And the
   τέκνα αὐτῆς ἀποκτενῶ ἐν θανάτῳ· καὶ γνώσονται πᾶσαι
   children of her I will kill with death; and will know all
   αἱ ἐκκλησίαι ὅτι ἐγώ εἰμι ὁ ἐρευνῶν νεφροὺς καὶ καρδίας·
   the churches that I am the (One) searching kidneys and hearts,
24 καὶ δώσω ὑμῖν ἑκάστῳ κατὰ τὰ ἔργα ὑμῶν. ὑμῖν δὲ
   and I will give to you each according to the works of you. to you But
   λέγω καὶ λοιποῖς τοῖς ἐν Θυατείροις, ὅσοι οὐκ ἔχουσι τὴν
   I say and to the rest in Thyatira, as many as not have
   διδαχὴν ταύτην, καὶ οἵτινες οὐκ ἔγνωσαν τὰ βάθη τοῦ
   teaching this, and who not did know the deep things
25 Σατανᾶ, ὡς λέγουσιν, Οὐ βαλῶ ἐφ' ὑμᾶς ἄλλο βάρος. πλὴν
   of Satan, as they say, not I am casting on you another load, but
26 ὃ ἔχετε κρατήσατε, ἄχρις οὗ ἂν ἥξω. καὶ ὁ νικῶν καὶ ὁ
   what you have hold until I shall come. And the over-(one) coming and the (one)
   τηρῶν ἄχρι τέλους τὰ ἔργα μου, δώσω αὐτῷ ἐξουσίαν ἐπὶ
   keeping until (the) end the works of Me, I will give him authority over
27 τῶν ἐθνῶν· καὶ ποιμανεῖ αὐτοὺς ἐν ῥάβδῳ σιδηρᾷ· ὡς τὰ
   the nations, and he will shepherd them with a staff iron, as
   σκεύη τὰ κεραμικά, συντρίβεται· ὡς κἀγὼ εἴληφα παρὰ τοῦ
   vessels clay, they are broken· as I also have received from the
28 πατρός μου· καὶ δώσω αὐτῷ τὸν ἀστέρα τὸν πρωϊνόν.
   Father of Me, and I will give him the star morning.
29 ὁ ἔχων οὖς ἀκουσάτω τί τὸ Πνεῦμα λέγει ταῖς ἐκκλησίαις.
   he having an ear, hear what the Spirit says to the churches.

CHAPTER 3

1 Καὶ τῷ ἀγγέλῳ τῆς ἐν Σάρδεσιν ἐκκλησίας γράψον,
   And to the angel of the in Sardis church write:
   Τάδε λέγει ὁ ἔχων τὰ ἑπτὰ πνεύματα τοῦ Θεοῦ καὶ τοὺς
   These things says He having the seven spirits of God, and the
   ἑπτὰ ἀστέρας· Οἶδά σου τὰ ἔργα, ὅτι τὸ ὄνομα ἔχεις ὅτι
   seven stars: I know of you the works, that the name you have that
2 ζῆς, καὶ νεκρὸς εἶ. γίνου γρηγορῶν, καὶ στήριξον τὰ λοιπὰ
   you live, and dead are. Be watching, and establish the things left
   ἃ μέλλει ἀποθανεῖν· οὐ γὰρ εὕρηκά σου τὰ ἔργα πεπληρω-
   which are about to die; not for I have found of you the works being ful-
3 μένα ἐνώπιον τοῦ Θεοῦ. μνημόνευε οὖν πῶς εἴληφας καὶ
   filled before God. Remember, then, how you received and
   ἤκουσας, καὶ τήρει, καὶ μετανόησον. ἐὰν οὖν μὴ γρηγορή-
   heard, and keep, and repent. If, then, not you watch,
4 σῃς, ἥξω ἐπί σε ὡς κλέπτης, καὶ οὐ μὴ γνῷς ποίαν ὥραν
   I will come on you as a thief, and not at all you know what hour
   ἥξω ἐπί σε. ἔχεις ὀλίγα ὀνόματα καὶ ἐν Σάρδεσιν, ἃ οὐκ
   I come on you. You have a few names also in Sardis which not
   ἐμόλυναν τὰ ἱμάτια αὐτῶν· καὶ περιπατήσουσι μετ' ἐμοῦ ἐν
   defile the robes of them, and they shall walk with Me in
5 λευκοῖς, ὅτι ἄξιοί εἰσιν. ὁ νικῶν, οὗτος περιβαλεῖται ἐν
   white, because worthy they are. he overcoming, he shall be clothed in
   ἱματίοις λευκοῖς· καὶ οὐ μὴ ἐξαλείψω τὸ ὄνομα αὐτοῦ ἐκ τῆς
   garments white, and not at all will I blot the name of him out of the

our of the Book of Life, and I will acknowledge His name before My Father, and before His angels. [6] The (one) having an ear, hear what the Spirit says to the churches.

[7] And to the angel of the church in Philadelphia, write:

These things says the Holy One, the True One, the (One) having the key of David, the (One) opening, and no one shuts; and shuts, and no one opens: [8] I know your works. Behold, I have given before you a door being opened, and no one is able to shut it; because you have a little power, and have kept My word, and have not denied My name. [9] Behold, I give out of the synagogue of Satan those saying themselves to be Jews, and they are not, but they lie. Behold, I will make them come and bow down before your feet, and they shall know that I loved you. [10] Because you kept the word of My patience, I also will keep you out of the hour of trial which is going to come upon all the habitable world in order to try those dwelling on the earth. [11] Behold, I am coming quickly. Hold what you have that no one take your crown. [12] The (one) overcoming, I will make him a pillar in the temple of My God, and he shall not go out any more. And I will write the name of My God on him, and the name of the city of My God, the new Jerusalem which is coming down out of Heaven from My God, and My new name. [13] The (one) having an ear, hear what the Spirit says to the churches.

[14] And to the angel of the church in Laodicea, write:

These things says the Amen, the faithful and true Witness, the Head of the creation of God: [15] I know your works, that you are neither hot or cold. I would that you were cold or hot. [16] So, because you

6 βίβλου τῆς ζωῆς, καὶ ἐξομολογήσομαι τὸ ὄνομα αὐτοῦ
Scroll of Life, and I will acknowledge the name of him
ἐνώπιον τοῦ πατρός μου, καὶ ἐνώπιον τῶν ἀγγέλων αὐτοῦ.
before the Father of Me, and before the angels of Him.
ὁ ἔχων οὖς ἀκουσάτω τί τὸ Πνεῦμα λέγει ταῖς ἐκκλησίαις.
The (one) having an ear, hear what the Spirit says to the churches.

7 Καὶ τῷ ἀγγέλῳ τῆς ἐν Φιλαδελφείᾳ ἐκκλησίας γράφον·
And to the angel of the in Philadelphia church write:
Τάδε λέγει ὁ ἅγιος, ὁ ἀληθινός, ὁ ἔχων τὴν κλεῖδα τοῦ
These things says the Holy One, the True One, the (One) having the key
Δαβίδ, ὁ ἀνοίγων καὶ οὐδεὶς κλείει, καὶ κλείει καὶ οὐδεὶς
of David, the (One) opening and no one shuts, and shuts, and no one

8 ἀνοίγει· Οἶδά σου τὰ ἔργα (ἰδού, δέδωκα ἐνώπιόν σου θύραν
opens: I know of you the works. Behold, I have given before you a door
ἀνεῳγμένην, καὶ οὐδεὶς δύναται κλεῖσαι αὐτήν), ὅτι μικρὰν
being opened, and no one is able to shut it, because a little
ἔχεις δύναμιν, καὶ ἐτήρησάς μου τὸν λόγον, καὶ οὐκ ἠρνήσω
you have power, and have kept of Me the word, and not denied

9 τὸ ὄνομά μου. ἰδού, δίδωμι ἐκ τῆς συναγωγῆς τοῦ Σατανᾶ,
the name of Me. Behold, I give out of the synagogue of Satan,
τῶν λεγόντων ἑαυτοὺς Ἰουδαίους εἶναι, καὶ οὐκ εἰσίν, ἀλλὰ
those saying themselves Jews to be, and not they are, but
ψεύδονται· ἰδού, ποιήσω αὐτοὺς ἵνα ἥξωσι καὶ προσκυνή-
they lie; behold, I will make them that they shall come and shall
σωσιν ἐνώπιον τῶν ποδῶν σου, καὶ γνῶσιν ὅτι ἐγὼ
bow before the feet of you, and they shall know that I

10 ἠγάπησά σε. ὅτι ἐτήρησας τὸν λόγον τῆς ὑπομονῆς μου,
loved you. Because you kept the word of the patience of Me,
κἀγώ σε τηρήσω ἐκ τῆς ὥρας τοῦ πειρασμοῦ, τῆς μελλούσης
I also you will keep out of the hour of trial being about
ἔρχεσθαι ἐπὶ τῆς οἰκουμένης ὅλης, πειράσαι τοὺς κατοι-
to come upon the habitable world all, to try those dwelling

11 κοῦντας ἐπὶ τῆς γῆς. ἰδού, ἔρχομαι ταχύ· κράτει ὃ ἔχεις, ἵνα
on the earth. Behold, I am coming quickly; hold what you have that

12 μηδεὶς λάβῃ τὸν στέφανόν σου. ὁ νικῶν, ποιήσω αὐτὸν
no one take the crown of you. The over-coming I will make him
στύλον ἐν τῷ ναῷ τοῦ Θεοῦ μου, καὶ ἔξω οὐ μὴ ἐξέλθῃ ἔτι,
a pillar in the temple of the God of Me, and out not at all he will go yet,
καὶ γράψω ἐπ' αὐτὸν τὸ ὄνομα τοῦ Θεοῦ μου, καὶ τὸ ὄνομα
and I will write on him the name of the God of Me, and the name
τῆς πόλεως τοῦ Θεοῦ μου, τῆς καινῆς Ἱερουσαλήμ, ἣ κατα-
of the city of the God of Me, the new Jerusalem which comes
βαίνει ἐκ τοῦ οὐρανοῦ ἀπὸ τοῦ Θεοῦ μου, καὶ τὸ ὄνομά μου
down out of Heaven from the God of Me, and the name of Me

13 τὸ καινόν. ὁ ἔχων οὖς ἀκουσάτω τί τὸ Πνεῦμα λέγει ταῖς
new. The (one) having an ear, hear what the Spirit says to the
ἐκκλησίαις.
churches.

14 Καὶ τῷ ἀγγέλῳ τῆς ἐκκλησίας Λαοδικέων γράφον,
And to the angel of the church in Laodicea write:
Τάδε λέγει ὁ Ἀμήν, ὁ μάρτυς ὁ πιστὸς καὶ ἀληθινός, ἡ
These things says the Amen, the Witness faithful and true, the

15 ἀρχὴ τῆς κτίσεως τοῦ Θεοῦ· Οἶδά σου τὰ ἔργα, ὅτι οὔτε
Head of the creation of God: I know of you the works, that neither

16 ψυχρὸς εἶ οὔτε ζεστός· ὄφελον ψυχρὸς εἴης ἢ ζεστός. οὕτως
cold are you, nor hot; I would that cold you were, or hot. So

are lukewarm, and neither cold nor hot, I am about to vomit you out of My mouth. [17] Because you say, I am rich, and, I am made rich and I have need of nothing, and do not know that you are wretched and miserable and poor and blind and naked, [18] I advise you to buy from Me gold having been fired by fire, that you may be rich; and white garments, that you may be clothed, and may not be revealed your shame and nakedness. And anoint your eyes with eyesalve, that you may see. [19] I, as many as I love, I rebuke and I chasten. Be zealous, then, and repent. [20] Behold, I stand at the door and knock: If anyone hears My voice and opens the door, I will go in to him, and I will dine with him, and he with Me. [21] The (one) overcoming, I will give to him to sit with Me in My throne, as I also overcame and sat with My Father in His throne. [22] The (one) having an ear, hear what the Spirit says to the churches.

ὅτι χλιαρὸς εἶ, καὶ οὔτε ψυχρὸς οὔτε ζεστός, μέλλω σε ἐμέσαι
because warm are, luke- you and neither cold nor hot, I am about you to vomit

17 ἐκ τοῦ στόματός μου. ὅτι λέγεις ὅτι Πλούσιός εἰμι, καὶ
out of the mouth of Me. Because you say, — rich I am, and

πεπλούτηκα, καὶ οὐδενὸς χρείαν ἔχω, καὶ οὐκ οἶδας ὅτι σὺ
I am made rich, and of nothing need I have, and not know that you

εἶ ὁ ταλαίπωρος καὶ ἐλεεινὸς καὶ πτωχὸς καὶ τυφλὸς καὶ
are the wretched (one) and miserable and poor and blind and

18 γυμνός· συμβουλεύω σοι ἀγοράσαι παρ' ἐμοῦ χρυσίον
naked I advise you to buy from Me gold

πεπυρωμένον ἐκ πυρός, ἵνα πλουτήσῃς, καὶ ἱμάτια λευκά,
having been fired by fire, that you may be rich; and garments white,

ἵνα περιβάλῃ, καὶ μὴ φανερωθῇ ἡ αἰσχύνη τῆς γυμνότητός
that you be clothed, and not may be revealed the shame and the nakedness

σου· καὶ κολλούριον ἔγχρισον τοὺς ὀφθαλμούς σου, ἵνα
of you, and with eyesalve anoint the eyes of you, that

19 βλέπῃς. ἐγὼ ὅσους ἐὰν φιλῶ, ἐλέγχω καὶ παιδεύω· ζήλωσον
you may see. I as many if I love, I rebuke, and I chasten; be zealous,

20 οὖν καὶ μετανόησον. ἰδού, ἕστηκα ἐπὶ τὴν θύραν καὶ κρούω·
then. and repent. Behold, I stand at the door and knock;

ἐάν τις ἀκούσῃ τῆς φωνῆς μου, καὶ ἀνοίξῃ τὴν θύραν,
If anyone hear the voice of Me, and opens the door,

εἰσελεύσομαι πρὸς αὐτόν. καὶ δειπνήσω μετ' αὐτοῦ, καὶ
I will enter to him, and I will dine with him, and

21 αὐτὸς μετ' ἐμοῦ. ὁ νικῶν, δώσω αὐτῷ καθίσαι μετ' ἐμοῦ
he with Me. The (one) overcoming I will give to him to sit with Me

ἐν τῷ θρόνῳ μου, ὡς κἀγὼ ἐνίκησα. καὶ ἐκάθισα μετὰ τοῦ
in the throne of Me, as I also overcame and sat with the

22 πατρός μου ἐν τῷ θρόνῳ αὐτοῦ. ὁ ἔχων οὖς ἀκουσάτω τί
Father of Me in the throne of Him. The (one) having an ear, hear what

τὸ Πνεῦμα λέγει ταῖς ἐκκλησίαις.
the Spirit says to the churches.

## CHAPTER 4

[1] After these things, I saw, and behold. a door being opened in Heaven; and I heard the first voice as a trumpet speaking with me, saying, Come up here, and I will show you what needs to happen after these things. [2] And at once I became in spirit; and behold, a throne was set in Heaven, and (One) sitting on the throne. [3] And the (One) sitting was in appearance, like a jasper stone, and a sardius; and a rainbow (was) around the throne, in appearance like an emerald. [4] And around the throne (I saw) twenty-four thrones, and on the thrones I saw twenty-four elders sitting, having been clothed in white garments. And they had on their heads golden

## CHAPTER 4

1 Μετὰ ταῦτα εἶδον, καὶ ἰδού, θύρα ἠνεῳγμένη ἐν τῷ
After these things I saw, and behold, a door having been opened in

οὐρανῷ, καὶ ἡ φωνὴ ἡ πρώτη ἣν ἤκουσα ὡς σάλπιγγος
Heaven, and the voice first which I heard as a trumpet

λαλούσης μετ' ἐμοῦ, λέγουσα, Ἀνάβα ὧδε, καὶ δείξω σοι
speaking with me, saying, Come up here, and I will show you

2 ἃ δεῖ γενέσθαι μετὰ ταῦτα. καὶ εὐθέως ἐγενόμην ἐν πνεύματι·
what needs to occur after these things. And at once I became in spirit,

καὶ ἰδου, θρονος ἔκειτο ἐν τῷ οὐρανῷ, καὶ ἐπὶ τοῦ θρόνου
and behold. a throne was set in Heaven, and on the throne

3 καθήμενος· καὶ ὁ καθήμενος ἦν ὅμοιος ὁράσει λίθῳ ἰάσπιδι
(One) sitting, and the (One) sitting was like in appearance a stone jasper;

καὶ σαρδίνῳ· καὶ Ἰρις κυκλόθεν τοῦ θρόνου ὁμοία ὁράσει
and a sardius, and a rainbow (was) around the throne like in appearance

4 σμαραγδίνῳ. καὶ κυκλόθεν τοῦ θρόνου θρόνοι εἴκοσι καὶ
to an emerald And around the throne (I saw) thrones twenty and

τέσσαρες· καὶ ἐπὶ τοὺς θρόνους εἶδον τοὺς εἴκοσι καὶ τέσσαρας
four, and on the thrones I saw twenty and four

πρεσβυτέρους καθημένους, περιβεβλημένους ἐν ἱματίοις
elders sitting, having been clothed in garments

λευκοῖς, καὶ ἔσχον ἐπὶ τὰς κεφαλὰς αὐτῶν στεφάνους
white, and they had on the heads of them crowns

crowns. [5] And out of the throne come forth lightnings and thunders and voices. And seven lamps of fire (are) burning before the throne, which are the seven Spirits of God; [6] and a glassy sea before the throne, like crystal; and in (the) midst of the throne and around the throne (were) four living creatures full of eyes before and behind.

[7] And the first living creature (was) like a lion; and the second living creature like a calf; and the third living creature having a face like a man; and the fourth living creature like an eagle flying. [8] And (the) four living creatures each one had six wings around, and within was full of eyes. And they had no respite day and night, saying, Holy, holy, holy, Lord God Almighty, who is, and who was, and who (is) coming. [9] And whenever the living creatures shall give glory and honor and thanks to Him sitting on the throne, to the (One) living forever and ever, [10] the twenty-four elders fall down before Him sitting on the throne; and they will worship the (One) living forever and ever, and will throw their crowns before the throne, saying, [11] Lord, You are worthy to receive the glory and the honor and the power, because You created all things, and because by Your will they exist and were created.

5 χρυσοῦς. καὶ ἐκ τοῦ θρόνου ἐκπορεύονται ἀστραπαὶ καὶ
of gold. And out of the throne come forth lightnings and
βρονταὶ καὶ φωναί. καὶ ἑπτὰ λαμπάδες πυρὸς καιόμεναι
thunders and voices. And seven lamps of fire (are) burning
ἐνώπιον τοῦ θρόνου, αἵ εἰσι τὰ ἑπτὰ πνεύματα τοῦ Θεοῦ·
before the throne, which are the seven Spirits of God;
6 καὶ ἐνώπιον τοῦ θρόνου θάλασσα ὑαλίνη, ὁμοία κρυστάλλῳ.
and before the throne sea a glassy like to crystal;
καὶ ἐν μέσῳ τοῦ θρόνου καὶ κύκλῳ τοῦ θρόνου τέσσαρα ζῶα
and in (the) midst of the throne and around the throne four living creatures
7 γέμοντα ὀφθαλμῶν ἔμπροσθεν καὶ ὄπισθεν. καὶ τὸ ζῶον
full of eyes before and behind, and the living creature
τὸ πρῶτον ὅμοιον λέοντι, καὶ τὸ δεύτερον ζῶον ὅμοιον
first (was) like a lion, and the second living creature like
μόσχῳ, καὶ τὸ τρίτον ζῶον ἔχον τὸ πρόσωπον ὡς ἄνθρωπος,
a calf, and the third living creature having the face as of a man,
8 καὶ τὸ τέταρτον ζῶον ὅμοιον ἀετῷ πετωμένῳ. καὶ τέσσαρα
and the fourth living creature like an eagle flying. And (the) four
ζῶα, ἐν καθ’ ἑαυτὸ εἶχον ἀνὰ πτέρυγας ἓξ κυκλόθεν, καὶ
living creatures one by one having each wings six around, and
ἔσωθεν γέμοντα ὀφθαλμῶν, καὶ ἀνάπαυσιν οὐκ ἔχουσιν
within being full of eyes; and respite not they have
ἡμέρας καὶ νυκτός, λέγοντα, Ἅγιος, ἅγιος, ἅγιος Κύριος ὁ
day and night, saying, Holy, holy, holy, Lord
9 Θεὸς ὁ παντοκράτωρ, ὁ ἦν καὶ ὁ ὢν καὶ ὁ ἐρχόμενος. καὶ
God, the Almighty, the (One who) was and is and (is) coming. And
ὅταν δώσουσι τὰ ζῶα δόξαν καὶ τιμὴν καὶ εὐχαριστίαν τῷ
when shall give the living creatures glory and honor and thanks to the (One)
καθημένῳ ἐπὶ τοῦ θρόνου, τῷ ζῶντι εἰς τοὺς αἰῶνας τῶν
sitting on the throne, to the (One) living to the ages of the
10 αἰώνων, πεσοῦνται οἱ εἴκοσι καὶ τέσσαρες πρεσβύτεροι
ages, will fall down the twenty and four elders
ἐνώπιον τοῦ καθημένου ἐπὶ τοῦ θρόνου, καὶ προσκυνοῦσι τῷ
before the (One) sitting on the throne, and they will worship the (One)
ζῶντι εἰς τοὺς αἰῶνας τῶν αἰώνων, καὶ βάλλουσι τοὺς
living to the ages of the ages, and will cast the
11 στεφάνους αὐτῶν ἐνώπιον τοῦ θρόνου, λέγοντες, Ἄξιος εἶ,
crowns of them before the throne, saying, worthy are You
Κύριε, λαβεῖν τὴν δόξαν καὶ τὴν τιμὴν καὶ τὴν δύναμιν· ὅτι σὺ
Lord, to receive the glory and the honor and the power, because You
ἔκτισας τὰ πάντα, καὶ διὰ τὸ θέλημά σου εἰσὶ καὶ ἐκτίσθησαν.
created all things, and because of the will of You they exist and were created.

## CHAPTER 5

[1] And I saw on the right of Him sitting on the throne a book having been written within and on the back, having been sealed with seven seals. [2] And I saw a mighty angel proclaiming with a great voice, Who is worthy to open the book, and to loosen its seals? [3] And no one in Heaven was able, nor on the earth, nor underneath the earth, to open the book,

## CHAPTER 5

1 Καὶ εἶδον ἐπὶ τὴν δεξιὰν τοῦ καθημένου ἐπὶ τοῦ θρόνου
And I saw on the right of the (One) sitting on the throne
βιβλίον γεγραμμένον ἔσωθεν καὶ ὄπισθεν, κατεσφραγισμένον
a scroll having been written within and on the back, having been sealed
2 σφραγῖσιν ἑπτά. καὶ εἶδον ἄγγελον ἰσχυρὸν κηρύσσοντα
with seals seven,. And I saw an angel strong proclaiming
φωνῇ μεγάλῃ, Τίς ἐστιν ἄξιος ἀνοῖξαι τὸ βιβλίον, καὶ λῦσαι
with a voice great, Who is worthy to open the scroll, and to loosen
3 τὰς σφραγῖδας αὐτοῦ ; καὶ οὐδεὶς ἠδύνατο ἐν τῷ οὐρανῷ,
the seals of it? And no one was able in Heaven,
οὐδὲ ἐπὶ τῆς γῆς, οὐδὲ ὑποκάτω τῆς γῆς, ἀνοῖξαι τὸ βιβλίον,
nor on the earth, nor underneath the earth, to open the scroll

nor to see it. [4] And I wept very much, because no one worthy was found to open and to read the book, nor to see it. [5] And one of the elders said to me, Do not weep. Behold, The Lion being of the tribe of Judah, the Root of David, overcame (so as) to open the book and to loose its seven seals. [6] And I saw, and behold, in (the) midst of the throne, and of the four living creatures, and in (the) midst of the elders, (was) a Lamb standing, as having been slain, having seven horns and seven eyes, which are the seven Spirits of God, having been sent out into all the earth. [7] And He came and took the book out of the right (hand) of Him sitting on the throne. [8] And when He took the book, the four living creatures and the twenty-four elders fell down before the Lamb, each one having harps, and golden bowls full of incenses, which are the prayers of the saints. [9] And they sing a new song, saying, Worhty are You to receive the book, and to open its seals, because You were slain, and purchased us to God by Your blood out of every tribe and tongue and people and nation, [10] and made us kings and priests to our God, and we shall reign over the earth. [11] And I saw, and I heard a sound of many angels around the throne, and the living creatures, and the elders; and their number was myriads of myriads, and thousands of thousands, [12] saying with a great voice, Worthy is the Lamb having been slain to receive the power and riches and wisdom and strength and honor and glory and blessing. [13] And every creature which is in Heaven, and in the earth, and underneath the earth, and the things that are on the sea, and the things in them all, I heard saying: To Him sitting on the throne, and to the

**4** οὐδὲ βλέπειν αὐτό. καὶ ἐγὼ ἔκλαιον πολλά, ὅτι οὐδεὶς ἄξιος
nor to see     it.     And I     wept     much, because no one worthy
εὑρέθη ἀνοῖξαι καὶ ἀναγνῶναι τὸ βιβλίον, οὔτε βλέπειν αὐτό.
was found to open and to read     the scroll,     nor to     see     it.

**5** καὶ εἷς ἐκ τῶν πρεσβυτέρων λέγει μοι, Μὴ κλαῖε· ἰδού,
And one of the     elders     says to me, Not do weep; behold,
ἐνίκησεν ὁ λέων ὁ ὢν ἐκ τῆς φυλῆς Ἰούδα, ἡ ῥίζα Δαβίδ,
overcame the Lion being of the tribe     of Judah, the Root of David,
ἀνοῖξαι τὸ βιβλίον καὶ λῦσαι τὰς ἑπτὰ σφραγῖδας αὐτοῦ.
to open the scroll     and to loose the seven     seals     of it.

**6** καὶ εἶδον, καὶ ἰδού, ἐν μέσῳ τοῦ θρόνου καὶ τῶν τεσσάρων
And I saw and behold, in (the) midst of the throne and of the     four
ζώων, καὶ ἐν μέσῳ τῶν πρεσβυτέρων, ἀρνίον ἑστηκὸς ὡς
living creatures, and amidst the     elders,     a Lamb standing as
ἐσφαγμένον, ἔχον κέρατα ἑπτὰ καὶ ὀφθαλμοὺς ἑπτά, οἵ εἰσι
having been slain, having horns seven and     eyes     seven, which are
τὰ ἑπτὰ τοῦ Θεοῦ πνεύματα τὰ ἀπεσταλμένα εἰς πᾶσαν τὴν
the seven     of God Spirits,     having been sent out into all     the

**7** γῆν. καὶ ἦλθε, καὶ εἴληφε τὸ βιβλίον ἐκ τῆς δεξιᾶς τοῦ
earth. And He came, and     took     the scroll out of the right of the

**8** καθημένου ἐπὶ τοῦ θρόνου. καὶ ὅτε ἔλαβε τὸ βιβλίον, τὰ
(One) sitting on the     throne.     And when He took the scroll,     the
τέσσαρα ζῶα καὶ οἱ εἰκοσιτέσσαρες πρεσβύτεροι ἔπεσον
four living creatures and the twenty-four     elders     fell down
ἐνώπιον τοῦ ἀρνίου, ἔχοντες ἕκαστος κιθάρας, καὶ φιάλας
before     the Lamb, having each one harps,     and bowls
χρυσᾶς γεμούσας θυμιαμάτων, αἵ εἰσιν αἱ προσευχαὶ τῶν
of gold     full     of incenses, which are the prayers of the

**9** ἁγίων. καὶ ᾄδουσιν ᾠδὴν καινήν, λέγοντες, Ἄξιος εἶ λαβεῖν
saints. And they sing a song     new,     saying,     Worthy are You to receive
τὸ βιβλίον, καὶ ἀνοῖξαι τὰς σφραγῖδας αὐτοῦ· ὅτι ἐσφάγης,
the scroll,     and to open the     seals     of it, because You were slain
καὶ ἠγόρασας τῷ Θεῷ ἡμᾶς ἐν τῷ αἵματί σου ἐκ πάσης φυλῆς
and purchased the God of us by the blood of You out of every tribe

**10** καὶ γλώσσης καὶ λαοῦ καὶ ἔθνους, καὶ ἐποίησας ἡμᾶς τῷ Θεῷ
and tongue and people and nation, and     made     us to the God

**11** ἡμῶν βασιλεῖς καὶ ἱερεῖς, καὶ βασιλεύσομεν ἐπὶ τῆς γῆς. καὶ
of us kings     and priests, and we shall reign over the earth. And
εἶδον, καὶ ἤκουσα φωνὴν ἀγγέλων πολλῶν κυκλόθεν τοῦ
I saw, and     I heard a sound of angels     many     around     the
θρόνου καὶ τῶν ζώων καὶ τῶν πρεσβυτέρων· καὶ ἦν ὁ
throne, and the living creatures and of the elders,     and was the
ἀριθμὸς αὐτῶν μυριάδες μυριάδων, καὶ χιλιάδες χιλιάδων,
number of them myriads of myriads, and thousands of thousands,

**12** λέγοντες φωνῇ μεγάλῃ, Ἄξιόν ἐστι τὸ ἀρνίον τὸ ἐσφαγ-
saying with a voice     great, Worthy     is     the Lamb     having been
μένον λαβεῖν τὴν δύναμιν καὶ πλοῦτον καὶ σοφίαν καὶ
slain to receive     the power     and riches     and wisdom and

**13** ἰσχὺν καὶ τιμὴν καὶ δόξαν καὶ εὐλογίαν. καὶ πᾶν κτίσμα ὅ
strength and honor and glory and blessing.     And every creature which
ἔστιν ἐν τῷ οὐρανῷ, καὶ ἐν τῇ γῇ, καὶ ὑποκάτω τῆς γῆς, καὶ
is in     Heaven, add in the earth, and underneath the earth, and
ἐπὶ τῆς θαλάσσης ἅ ἐστι, καὶ τὰ ἐν αὐτοῖς πάντα, ἤκουσα
on the     sea the things that are, and the things in them all,     I heard
λέγοντας, Τῷ καθημένῳ ἐπὶ τοῦ θρόνου καὶ τῷ ἀρνίῳ ἡ
saying, To the (one) sitting on the     throne and to the Lamb the

Lamb (be) the blessing and the honor and the glory and the might forever and ever. [14] And the four living creatures said, Amen. And the twenty-four elders fell down and worshiped (the) Living One forever and ever.

εὐλογία καὶ ἡ τιμὴ καὶ ἡ δόξα καὶ τὸ κράτος εἰς τοὺς αἰῶνας
blessing    and the honor and the glory and the might   to   the    ages
**14** τῶν αἰώνων. καὶ τὰ τέσσαρα ζῷα ἔλεγον, Ἀμήν. καὶ οἱ
of the   ages.    And the four living creatures said,    Amen; and the
εἰκοσιτέσσαρες πρεσβύτεροι ἔπεσαν καὶ προσεκύνησαν
twenty-four          elders         fell down  and    worshiped
ζῶντι εἰς τοὺς αἰῶνας τῶν αἰώνων.
(the) Living One to the ages of the  ages.

## CHAPTER 6

[1] And I saw when the Lamb opened one of the seals. And I heard one of the four living creatures, like a sound of thunder, saying, Come and see. [2] And I saw, and behold, a white horse; and the (one) sitting on it having a bow. And a crown was given to him, and he went out overcoming, and that he might overcome.

[3] And when He opened the second seal, I heard the second living creature saying, Come and see. [4] And another horse went out, (being) red. And it was given to the (one) sitting on (it) to take peace from the earth; and that they should slay one another. And a great sword was given to him.

[5] And when He opened the third seal, I heard the third living creature saying, Come and see. And I saw, and behold, a black horse; and the (one) sitting on it having a balance in his hand. [6] And I heard a voice in (the) midst of the four living creatures, saying, A choenix of wheat (for) a denarius, and three choenixes of barley (for) a denarius; and do not harm the oil and the wine.

[7] And when He opened the fourth seal, I heard a voice of the fourth living creature, saying. Come and see. [8] And I saw, and behold, a pale green horse, and the name (of) him sitting on it (was) Death; and Hades followed with him; and was given to them to kill over the fourth of the earth with sword and with famine and with death, and by the wild beasts of the earth.

## CHAPTER 6

**1** Καὶ εἶδον ὅτε ἤνοιξε τὸ ἀρνίον μίαν ἐκ τῶν σφραγίδων,
And I saw  when opened the Lamb  one of   the      seals
καὶ ἤκουσα ἑνὸς ἐκ τῶν τεσσάρων ζώων λέγοντος, ὡς φωνῆς
and I heard  one of the  four living creatures saying,  as of a sound
**2** βροντῆς, Ἔρχου καὶ βλέπε. καὶ εἶδον, καὶ ἰδού, ἵππος
of thunder, Come   and   see; and   I saw.   And behold, a horse
λευκός, καὶ ὁ καθήμενος ἐπ' αὐτῷ ἔχων τόξον· καὶ ἐδόθη
white, and the (one) sitting   on   it   having  a bow, and was given
αὐτῷ στέφανος, καὶ ἐξῆλθε νικῶν, καὶ ἵνα νικήσῃ.
to him a crown,   and he went out overcoming, and that he might overcome.
**3** Καὶ ὅτε ἤνοιξε τὴν δευτέραν σφραγίδα, ἤκουσα τοῦ
And when He opened the  second    seal,      I heard  the
**4** δευτέρου ζώου λέγοντος, Ἔρχου καὶ βλέπε. καὶ ἐξῆλθεν
second living creature saying,  Come and  see.  And went out
ἄλλος ἵππος πυρρός· καὶ τῷ καθημένῳ ἐπ' αὐτῷ ἐδόθη
another horse,  red;   and to the (one) sitting   on  it  was given
αὐτῷ λαβεῖν τὴν εἰρήνην ἀπὸ τῆς γῆς, καὶ ἵνα ἀλλήλους
to him to take     peace    from the earth, and that one another
σφάξωσι· καὶ ἐδόθη αὐτῷ μάχαιρα μεγάλη.
they shall slay; and was given to him a sword   great.
**5** Καὶ ὅτε ἤνοιξε τὴν τρίτην σφραγίδα, ἤκουσα τοῦ τρίτου
And when He opened the third    seal,     I heard  the  third
ζώου λέγοντος, Ἔρχου καὶ βλέπε. καὶ εἶδον, καὶ ἰδού, ἵππος
living creature saying, Come  and  see  And I saw, and behold, a horse
μέλας, καὶ ὁ καθήμενος ἐπ' αὐτῷ ἔχων ζυγὸν ἐν τῇ χειρὶ
black, and the (one) sitting   on  it  having a balance in the  hand
**6** αὐτοῦ. καὶ ἤκουσα φωνὴν ἐν μέσῳ τῶν τεσσάρων ζώων
of him.  And  I heard  a voice in (the) midst of the  four living creatures
λέγουσαν, Χοῖνιξ σίτου δηναρίου, καὶ τρεῖς χοίνικες κριθῆς
saying,    A choenix of wheat (for) a denarius, and three choenixes of barley
δηναρίου· καὶ τὸ ἔλαιον καὶ τὸν οἶνον μὴ ἀδικήσῃς.
(for) a denarius; and the oil   and the wine   not  harm.
**7** Καὶ ὅτε ἤνοιξε τὴν σφραγῖδα τὴν τετάρτην, ἤκουσα
And when He opened the   seal            fourth,     I heard
**8** φωνὴν τοῦ τετάρτου ζώου λέγουσαν, Ἔρχου καὶ βλέπε. καὶ
(the) voice of the fourth living creature saying, Come  and  see.  And
εἶδον, καὶ ἰδού, ἵππος χλωρός, καὶ ὁ καθήμενος ἐπάνω
I saw.  And behold, a horse  pale green, and the (one) sitting  upon
αὐτοῦ, ὄνομα αὐτῷ ὁ θάνατος, καὶ ὁ ᾅδης ἀκολουθεῖ μετ'
it,     name to him   death,    and  Hades    followed   with
αὐτοῦ. καὶ ἐδόθη αὐτοῖς ἐξουσία ἀποκτεῖναι ἐπὶ τὸ τέταρτον
him.  and was given to them authority  to kill      over  the fourth
τῆς γῆς ἐν ρομφαίᾳ καὶ ἐν λιμῷ καὶ ἐν θανάτῳ, καὶ ὑπὸ τῶν
of the earth with sword  and with famine and with death,  and  by   the
θηρίων τῆς γῆς.
wild beasts of the earth.

[9] And when He opened the fifth seal, I saw under the altar the souls of those having been slain for the word of God, and for the witness which they had. [10] And they cried with a great voice, saying, Until when, holy and true Master, do You not judge and take vengeance (for) the blood of us, from those dwelling on the earth? [11] And there was given to each one a white robe; and it was said to them that they should rest a little time, until might be fulfilled also (the number) of their fellow-slaves and their brothers, those being about to be killed, even as they.

[12] And I saw when He opened the sixth seal, and behold, a great earthquake occurred; and the sun became black as sackcloth made of hair. And the moon became as blood; [13] and the stars of the heaven fell to the earth, as a fig-tree casts its unripe figs, having been shaken by a great wind. [14] And (the) heaven departed like a scroll being rolled up; and every mountain and island were moved out of their places; [15] and the kings of the earth, and the great ones, and the rich ones, and the chiliarchs, and the powerful ones, and every slave, and every freeman, hid themselves in the caves and in the rocks of the mountains. [16] And they say to the mountains and to the rocks, Fall on us, and hide us from (the) face of Him sitting on the throne, and from the wrath of the Lamb, [17] because the great day of His wrath is come; and who is able to stand?

CHAPTER 7

[1] And after these things I saw four angels standing on the four corners of the earth, holding the four winds of the earth, that not should blow wind on the earth, nor on the sea, nor on every tree. [2] And I saw another

---

9 Καὶ ὅτε ἤνοιξε τὴν πέμπτην σφραγῖδα, εἶδον ὑποκάτω
And when He opened the fifth seal I saw underneath
τοῦ θυσιαστηρίου τὰς ψυχὰς τῶν ἐσφαγμένων διὰ τὸν λόγον
the altar the souls of those having been slain for the word
10 τοῦ Θεοῦ, καὶ διὰ τὴν μαρτυρίαν ἣν εἶχον, καὶ ἔκραζον φωνῇ
of God, and for the witness which they had. And they cried with a voice
μεγάλῃ, λέγοντες, Ἕως πότε, ὁ δεσπότης, ὁ ἅγιος καὶ ὁ ἀλη-
great saying, Until when, Master holy and true,
θινός, οὐ κρίνεις καὶ ἐκδικεῖς τὸ αἷμα ἡμῶν ἀπὸ τῶν κατοι-
not do You judge and avenge the blood of us from those dwelling
11 κούντων ἐπὶ τῆς γῆς; καὶ ἐδόθησαν ἑκάστοις στολαὶ λευκαί,
on the earth? And was given to each one a robe white,
καὶ ἐρρέθη αὐτοῖς ἵνα ἀναπαύσωνται ἔτι χρόνον μικρόν, ἕως
and it was said to them that they should rest yet a time little, until
οὗ πληρώσονται καὶ οἱ σύνδουλοι αὐτῶν καὶ οἱ ἀδελφοὶ
should be fulfilled also the fellow-slaves of them and the brothers
αὐτῶν, οἱ μέλλοντες ἀποκτείνεσθαι ὡς καὶ αὐτοί.
of them, those being about to be killed as also they.
12 Καὶ εἶδον ὅτε ἤνοιξε τὴν σφραγῖδα τὴν ἕκτην, καὶ ἰδού,
And I saw when He opened the seal sixth, and behold,
σεισμὸς μέγας ἐγένετο, καὶ ὁ ἥλιος ἐγένετο μέλας ὡς σάκκος
an earthquake great occurred, and the sun became black as sackcloth
13 τρίχινος, καὶ ἡ σελήνη ἐγένετο ὡς αἷμα, καὶ οἱ ἀστέρες τοῦ
made of hair, and the moon became as blood, and the stars of the
οὐρανοῦ ἔπεσαν εἰς τὴν γῆν, ὡς συκῆ βάλλει τοὺς ὀλύνθους
heaven fell to the earth, as a fig-tree casts the unripe figs
14 αὐτῆς, ὑπὸ μεγάλου ἀνέμου σειομένη. καὶ οὐρανὸς ἀπεχω-
of it, by a great wind being shaken. And (the) heaven departed
ρίσθη ὡς βιβλίον εἰλισσόμενον, καὶ πᾶν ὄρος καὶ νῆσος ἐκ
as a scroll being rolled up, and every mountain and island out
15 τῶν τόπων αὐτῶν ἐκινήθησαν. καὶ οἱ βασιλεῖς τῆς γῆς, καὶ
of the places of them were moved. And the kings of the earth, and
οἱ μεγιστᾶνες, καὶ οἱ πλούσιοι, καὶ οἱ χιλίαρχοι, καὶ οἱ
the great ones, and the rich, and the chiliarchs, and the
δυνατοί, καὶ πᾶς δοῦλος καὶ πᾶς ἐλεύθερος, ἔκρυψαν ἑαυτοὺς
powerful, and every slave, and every freeman, hid themselves
16 εἰς τὰ σπήλαια καὶ εἰς τὰς πέτρας τῶν ὀρέων, καὶ λέγουσι
in the caves and in the rocks of the mountains; and they say
τοῖς ὄρεσι καὶ ταῖς πέτραις, Πέσετε ἐφ' ἡμᾶς, καὶ κρύψατε
to the mountains and to the rocks, Fall on us and hide
ἡμᾶς ἀπὸ προσώπου τοῦ καθημένου ἐπὶ τοῦ θρόνου, καὶ
us from (the) face of Him sitting on the throne, and
17 ἀπὸ τῆς ὀργῆς τοῦ ἀρνίου· ὅτι ἦλθεν ἡ ἡμέρα ἡ μεγάλη
from the wrath of the Lamb, because came the day great
τῆς ὀργῆς αὐτοῦ, καὶ τίς δύναται σταθῆναι;
of the wrath of Him, and who is able to stand?

## CHAPTER 7

1 Καὶ μετὰ ταῦτα εἶδον τέσσαρας ἀγγέλους ἑστῶτας ἐπὶ τὰς
And after these things I saw four angels standing on the
τέσσαρας γωνίας τῆς γῆς, κρατοῦντας τοὺς τέσσαρας
four corners of the earth,, holding the four
ἀνέμους τῆς γῆς, ἵνα μὴ πνέῃ ἄνεμος ἐπὶ τῆς γῆς, μήτε ἐπὶ
winds of the earth, that not should blow wind on the earth, nor on
2 τῆς θαλάσσης, μήτε ἐπὶ πᾶν δένδρον. καὶ εἶδον ἄλλον
the sea, nor on every tree. And I saw another

angel coming up from (the) rising of (the) sun, having a seal of (the) living God. And he cried with a great voice to the four angels to whom it was given to them to harm the earth and the sea, saying, [3] Do not harm the earth nor the sea, nor the trees, until we seal the slaves of our God on their foreheads. [4] And I heard the number of those having been sealed, one hundred and forty-four thousands, sealed out of every tribe of the sons of Israel: [5] Out of (the) tribe of Judah, twelve thousand having been sealed. Out of (the) tribe of Reuben, twelve thousand having been sealed. Out of (the) tribe of Gad, twelve thousand having been sealed. [6] Out of (the) tribe of Asher, twelve thousand having been sealed. Out of (the) tribe of Napthali, twelve thousand having been sealed. Out of (the) tribe of Manasseh, twelve thousand having been sealed. [7] Out of (the) tribe of Simeon, twelve thousand having been sealed. Out of (the) tribe of Levi, twelve thousand having been sealed. Out of (the) tribe of Issachar, twelve thousand having been sealed. [8] Out of the tribe of Zebulun, twelve thousand having been sealed. Out of (the) tribe of Joseph, twelve thousand having been sealed. Out of (the) tribe of Benjamin, twelve thousand having been sealed. [9] After these things I saw, and behold, a, great crowd, which no one was able to number them, out of every nation and tribes and peoples and tongues; standing in front of the throne and before the Lamb, having been clothed (with) white robes, and palms in their hands. [10] And they cry with a great voice, saying, Salvation to our God sitting on the throne, and to the Lamb. [11] And all the angels stood around the throne, and the elders, and

ἄγγελον ἀναβαίνοντα ἀπὸ ἀνατολῆς ἡλίου, ἔχοντα σφρα-
angel       coming up      from (the) rising of (the) sun, having a seal

γῖδα Θεοῦ ζῶντος· καὶ ἔκραξε φωνῇ μεγάλῃ τοῖς τέσσαρσιν
of God    (the) living, and he cried with a voice great to the   four

ἀγγέλοις, οἷς ἐδόθη αὐτοῖς ἀδικῆσαι τὴν γῆν καὶ τὴν
angels   to whom it was given to them to harm   the earth  and the

3 θάλασσαν, λέγων, Μὴ ἀδικήσητε τὴν γῆν, μήτε τὴν θάλασ-
sea,       saying,   Not do harm     the earth,  nor  the  sea

σαν, μήτε τὰ δένδρα, ἄχρις οὗ σφραγίσωμεν τοὺς δούλους
     nor  the trees,   until    we may seal   the  slaves

4 τοῦ Θεοῦ ἡμῶν ἐπὶ τῶν μετώπων αὐτῶν. καὶ ἤκουσα τὸν
of the God of us   on  the  foreheads   of them. And I heard  the

ἀριθμὸν τῶν ἐσφραγισμένων, ρμδ' χιλιάδες, ἐσφραγισμένοι
number of those having been sealed,  144  thousands, having been sealed

ἐκ πάσης φυλῆς υἱῶν Ἰσραήλ.
out of every tribe of (the) sons of Israel:

5 Ἐκ φυλῆς Ἰούδα, ιβ' χιλιάδες ἐσφραγισμένοι·
Of (the) tribe of Judah, twelve thousands having been sealed.

Ἐκ φυλῆς Ῥουβήν, ιβ' χιλιάδες ἐσφραγισμένοι·
Of (the) tribe of Reuben, twelve thousands having been sealed.

Ἐκ φυλῆς Γάδ, ιβ' χιλιάδες ἐσφραγισμένοι·
Of (the) tribe of Gad, twelve thousands having been sealed.

6 Ἐκ φυλῆς Ἀσήρ, ιβ' χιλιάδες ἐσφραγισμένοι·
Of (the) tribe of Asher, twelve thousands having been sealed.

Ἐκ φυλῆς Νεφθαλείμ, ιβ' χιλιάδες ἐσφραγισμένοι·
Of (the) tribe of Napthali,  twelve thousands having been sealed.

Ἐκ φυλῆς Μανασσῆ, ιβ' χιλιάδες ἐσφραγισμένοι·
Of (the) tribe of Manasseh, twelve thousands having been sealed.

7 Ἐκ φυλῆς Συμεών, ιβ' χιλιάδες ἐσφραγισμένοι·
Of (the) tribe of Simeon, twelve thousands having been sealed.

Ἐκ φυλῆς Λευΐ, ιβ' χιλιάδες ἐσφραγισμένοι·
Of (the) tribe of Levi, twelve thousands having been sealed.

Ἐκ φυλῆς Ἰσαχάρ, ιβ' χιλιάδες ἐσφραγισμένοι·
Of (the) tribe of Issachar, twelve thousands having been sealed.

8 Ἐκ φυλῆς Ζαβουλών, ιβ' χιλιάδες ἐσφραγισμένοι·
Of (the) tribe of Zebulun, twelve thousands having been sealed.

Ἐκ φυλῆς Ἰωσήφ, ιβ' χιλιάδες ἐσφραγισμένοι·
Of (the) tribe of Joseph, twelve thousands having been sealed.

Ἐκ φυλῆς Βενιαμίν, ιβ' χιλιάδες ἐσφραγισμένοι.
Of (the) tribe of Benjamin, twelve thousands having been sealed.

9 Μετὰ ταῦτα εἶδον, καὶ ἰδού, ὄχλος πολύς, ὃν ἀριθμῆσαι
After these things I saw, and behold, a crowd   much,  which to number

αὐτὸν οὐδεὶς ἠδύνατο, ἐκ παντὸς ἔθνους καὶ φυλῶν καὶ
them no one  was able,  out of  every  nation,  even  tribes  and

λαῶν καὶ γλωσσῶν, ἑστῶτες ἐνώπιον τοῦ θρόνου καὶ
peoples and  tongues,   standing   before    the  throne   and

ἐνώπιον τοῦ ἀρνίου, περιβεβλημένοι στολὰς λευκάς, καὶ
before   the  Lamb, having been clothed (with) robes  white,   and

10 φοίνικες ἐν ταῖς χερσὶν αὐτῶν· καὶ κράζοντες φωνῇ μεγάλῃ,
palms in  the   hands  of them. And they cry with a voice  great,

λέγοντες, Ἡ σωτηρία τῷ Θεῷ ἡμῶν τῷ καθημένῳ ἐπὶ τοῦ
saying,       Salvation to the God  of us    sitting     on  the

11 θρόνου, καὶ τῷ ἀρνίῳ. καὶ πάντες οἱ ἄγγελοι ἐστήκεσαν
throne, and to the Lamb.  And  all   the  angels    stood

κύκλῳ τοῦ θρόνου καὶ τῶν πρεσβυτέρων καὶ τῶν τεσ-
around  the  throne,  and of the    elders,    and of the  four

σάρων ζώων, καὶ ἔπεσον ἐνώπιον τοῦ ϑρόνου ἐπὶ πρόσ-
living creatures, and they fell before the throne on (the)

**12** ωπον αὐτῶν, καὶ προσεκύνησαν τῷ Θεῷ, λέγοντες, Ἀμήν·
face of them, and worshiped God, saying, Amen,

ἡ εὐλογία καὶ ἡ δόξα καὶ ἡ σοφία καὶ ἡ εὐχαριστία καὶ ἡ
blessing and glory and wisdom and thanksgiving and

τιμὴ καὶ ἡ.δύναμις καὶ ἡ ἰσχὺς τῷ Θεῷ ἡμῶν εἰς τοὺς αἰῶνας
honor and power and strength to the God of us to the ages

τῶν αἰώνων. ἀμήν.
of the ages. Amen.

**13** Καὶ ἀπεκρίθη εἷς ἐκ τῶν πρεσβυτέρων, λέγων μοι, Οὗτοι
And answered one of the elders, saying to me, These,

οἱ περιβεβλημένοι τὰς στολὰς τὰς λευκάς, τίνες εἰσί, καὶ πόθεν
having been clothed (in) the robes white, who are they, and from where

**14** ἦλθον ; καὶ εἴρηκα αὐτῷ, Κύριε, σὺ οἶδας. καὶ εἶπέ μοι, Οὗτοί
came they? And I said to him, Sir, you know. And he told me, These

εἰσιν οἱ ἐρχόμενοι ἐκ τῆς θλίψεως τῆς μεγάλης, καὶ ἔπλυναν
are those coming out of the affliction great, and they washed

τὰς στολὰς αὐτῶν, καὶ ἐλεύκαναν αὐτὰς ἐν τῷ αἵματι τοῦ
the robes of them, and whitened them in the blood of the

**15** ἀρνίου. διὰ τοῦτό εἰσιν ἐνώπιον τοῦ θρόνου τοῦ Θεοῦ,
Lamb. Therefore are they before the throne of God,

καὶ λατρεύουσιν αὐτῷ ἡμέρας καὶ νυκτὸς ἐν τῷ ναῷ αὐτοῦ·
and serve Him day and night in the temple of Him,

**16** καὶ ὁ καθήμενος ἐπὶ τοῦ θρόνου σκηνώσει ἐπ' αὐτούς. οὐ
and the(One) sitting on the throne tabernacled over them. not

πεινάσουσιν ἔτι, οὐδὲ διψήσουσιν ἔτι, οὐδὲ μὴ πέσῃ ἐπ'
they will hunger longer, nor will they thirst longer, nor not shall fall on

**17** αὐτοὺς ὁ ἥλιος, οὐδὲ πᾶν καῦμα· ὅτι τὸ ἀρνίον τὸ ἀνὰ
them the sun, nor every (kind of) heat, because the Lamb in the

μέσον τοῦ θρόνου ποιμανεῖ αὐτούς, καὶ ὁδηγήσει αὐτοὺς ἐπὶ
midst of the throne will shepherd them, and will lead them upon

ζώσας πηγὰς ὑδάτων, καὶ ἐξαλείψει ὁ Θεὸς πᾶν δάκρυον
living fountains of waters, and will wipe off God every tear

ἀπὸ τῶν ὀφθαλμῶν αὐτῶν.
from the eyes of them.

## CHAPTER 8

**1** Καὶ ὅτε ἤνοιξε τὴν σφραγῖδα τὴν ἑβδόμην, ἐγένετο σιγὴ
And when He opened the seal seventh, occurred a silence

**2** ἐν τῷ οὐρανῷ ὡς ἡμιώριον. καὶ εἶδον τοὺς ἑπτὰ ἀγγέλους οἳ
in Heaven about a half-hour. And I saw the seven angels who

ἐνώπιον τοῦ Θεοῦ ἑστήκασι, καὶ ἐδόθησαν αὐτοῖς ἑπτὰ
before God stood, and were given to them seven

σάλπιγγες.
trumpets.

**3** Καὶ ἄλλος ἄγγελος ἦλθε, καὶ ἐστάθη ἐπὶ τὸ θυσιαστήριον,
And another angel came and stood on the altar

ἔχων λιβανωτὸν χρυσοῦν· καὶ ἐδόθη αὐτῷ θυμιάματα πολλά,
having a censer of gold, and was given to him incenses many,

ἵνα δώσῃ ταῖς προσευχαῖς τῶν ἁγίων πάντων ἐπὶ τὸ θυσια-
that he give with the prayers of the saints all on the altar

**4** στήριον τὸ χρυσοῦν τὸ ἐνώπιον τοῦ θρόνου. καὶ ἀνέβη ὁ
of gold before the throne. And went up the

καπνὸς τῶν θυμιαμάτων ταῖς προσευχαῖς τῶν ἁγίων ἐκ
smoke of the incenses with the prayers of the saints out of

---

the four living creatures. And
(they) fell before the throne
on their faces, and worshiped
God, [12] saying, Amen.
Blessing and glory and wisdom
and thanksgiving and honor
and power· and strength to
our God forever and ever.
Amen. [13] And one of the
elders answered, saying to me,
These, those having been
clothed (in) the white robes,
who are they, and from
where did they come? [14]
And I said to him, Sir, you
know. And he said to me,
These are those coming out
of the great tribulation; and
(they) washed their robes and
whitened them in the blood
of the Lamb. [15] Because
of this they are before the
throne of God, and serve
Him day and night in His
temple. And He sitting on
the throne will spread (His
skirt) over them. [16] And
they will not hunger still,
nor will they thirst still, nor
at all shall fall on them the
sun, nor any (kind of) heat.
[17] Because the Lamb in
the midst of the throne will
shepherd them, and will lead
them on (the) fountains of
waters, and God will
wipe off every tear from their
eyes.

CHAPTER 8

[1] And when He opened
the seventh seal, a silence
occurred in Heaven, about a
half-hour. [2] And I saw the
seven angels who stood before
God, and seven trumpets were
given to them. [3] And
another angel came and stood
on the altar, having a golden
censer. And many incenses
were given to him, that he
give (them) with the prayers
of all the saints on the gold-
en altar before the throne.
[4] And the smoke of the
incenses went up with the
prayers of the saints out of

(the) hand of the angel before God. [5] And the angel has taken the censer, and has filled it from the fire of the altar, and cast (it) into the earth. And sounds and thunders and lightnings and earthquakes occurred. [6] And the seven angels having the seven trumpets prepared themselves, that they might trumpet. [7] And the first angel trumpeted. And hail and fire mixed with blood occurred; and it was cast onto the earth, and the third (part) of the trees was burned; and all green grass was burned down. [8] And the second angel trumpeted. And a great mountain burning with fire was thrown into the sea. And the third (part) of the sea became blood; [9] and the third of the creatures having souls died in the sea; and the third (part) of the ships was destroyed. [10] And the third angel trumpeted. And a great burning star, like a lamp, fell out of the heaven; and it fell onto the third (part) of the rivers, and onto the fountain of waters. [11] And the name of the star is said (to be) Wormwood. And the third (part) of the waters became (changed) into wormwood; and many of the men died from the waters, because they were bitter. [12] And the fourth angel trumpeted. And the third (part) of the sun and the third (part) of the moon, and the third (part) of the stars was struck, that might be darkened the third of them, and the third of the day might not appear; and likewise the night. [13] And I saw, and I heard one angel flying in mid-heaven, saying with a great voice, Woe! Woe! to those dwelling on the earth, from the rest of (the) voices of the trumpet of the three angels who (are) about to trumpet.

**5** χειρὸς τοῦ ἀγγέλου ἐνώπιον τοῦ Θεοῦ. καὶ εἴληφεν ὁ
(the) hand of the angel before God. And has taken the
ἄγγελος τὸ λιβανωτόν, καὶ ἐγέμισεν αὐτὸ ἐκ τοῦ πυρὸς τοῦ
angel the censer, and filled it from the fire of the
θυσιαστηρίου, καὶ ἔβαλεν εἰς τὴν γῆν· καὶ ἐγένοντο φωναὶ καὶ
altar, and cast it into the earth, and occurred sounds and
βρονταὶ καὶ ἀστραπαὶ καὶ σεισμός.
thunders and lightnings and an earthquake.

**6** Καὶ οἱ ἑπτὰ ἄγγελοι οἱ ἔχοντες τὰς ἑπτὰ σάλπιγγας
And the seven angels having the seven trumpets
ἡτοίμασαν ἑαυτοὺς ἵνα σαλπίσωσι.
prepared themselves that they might trumpet.

**7** Καὶ ὁ πρῶτος ἄγγελος ἐσάλπισε, καὶ ἐγένετο χάλαζα καὶ
And the first angel trumpeted, and occurred hail and
πῦρ μεμιγμένα αἵματι, καὶ ἐβλήθη εἰς τὴν γῆν· καὶ τὸ τρίτον
fire being mixed with blood, and it was cast to the earth, and the third (part)
τῶν δένδρων κατεκάη, καὶ πᾶς χόρτος χλωρὸς κατεκάη.
of the trees was burned down and all grass green was burned down.

**8** Καὶ ὁ δεύτερος ἄγγελος ἐσάλπισε, καὶ ὡς ὄρος μέγα πυρὶ
And the second angel trumpeted, and as a mountain great with fire
καιόμενον ἐβλήθη εἰς τὴν θάλασσαν· καὶ ἐγένετο τὸ τρίτον
burning it was cast into the sea; and became the third (part)
**9** τῆς θαλάσσης αἷμα· καὶ ἀπέθανε τὸ τρίτον τῶν κτισμάτων
of the sea blood, and died the third (part) of the creatures
τῶν ἐν τῇ θαλάσσῃ, τὰ ἔχοντα ψυχάς, καὶ τὸ τρίτον τῶν
in the sea those having souls; and the third (part) of the
πλοίων διεφθάρη.
ships was destroyed.

**10** Καὶ ὁ τρίτος ἄγγελος ἐσάλπισε, καὶ ἔπεσεν ἐκ τοῦ οὐρανοῦ
And the third angel trumpeted, and fell out of the heaven
ἀστὴρ μέγας καιόμενος ὡς λαμπάς, καὶ ἔπεσεν ἐπὶ τὸ τρίτον
a star great burning as a lamp, and it fell onto the third (part)
**11** τῶν ποταμῶν, καὶ ἐπὶ τὰς πηγὰς ὑδάτων. καὶ τὸ ὄνομα τοῦ
of the rivers, and onto the fountains of waters. And the name of the
ἀστέρος λέγεται Ἄψινθος· καὶ γίνεται τὸ τρίτον τῶν ὑδάτων
star is said (to be) Wormwood. And became the third (part) of the waters
εἰς ἄψινθον, καὶ πολλοὶ ἀνθρώπων ἀπέθανον ἐκ τῶν ὑδάτων,
into wormwood, and many of men died from the waters,
ὅτι ἐπικράνθησαν.
because they were bitter.

**12** Καὶ ὁ τέταρτος ἄγγελος ἐσάλπισε, καὶ ἐπλήγη τὸ τρίτον
And the fourth angel trumpeted, and was struck the third (part)
τοῦ ἡλίου καὶ τὸ τρίτον τῆς σελήνης καὶ τὸ τρίτον τῶν
of the sun and the third (part) of the moon and the third (part) of the
ἀστέρων, ἵνα σκοτισθῇ το τρίτον αὐτῶν, καὶ ἡ ἡμέρα μὴ
stars, that might be darkened the third of them, and the day not
φαίνῃ τὸ τρίτον αὐτῆς, καὶ ἡ νὺξ ὁμοίως.
might appear the third of it, and the night likewise.

**13** Καὶ εἶδον, καὶ ἤκουσα ἑνὸς ἀγγέλου πετωμένου ἐν μεσου-
And I saw, and I heard one angel flying in mid-
ρανήματι, λέγοντος φωνῇ μεγάλῃ, Οὐαί, οὐαί, οὐαί τοῖς
heaven, saying, with a voice great, Woe! Woe! Woe to those
κατοικοῦσιν ἐπὶ τῆς γῆς, ἐκ τῶν λοιπῶν φωνῶν τῆς σάλ-
dwelling on the earth, from the rest of (the) voices of the
πιγγος τῶν τ..ων ἀγγέλων τῶν μελλόντων σαλπίζειν.
trumpet of the three angels being about to trumpet.

## CHAPTER 9

CHAPTER 9

[1] And the fifth angel trumpeted. And I saw a star out of heaven falling onto the earth. And the key to the pit of the abyss was given to it. [2] And he opened the pit of the abyss; and smoke went up out of the pit, as smoke of a great furnace. And the sun was darkened, and the air, by the smoke of the pit. [3] And out of the smoke came forth locusts to the earth; and was given to them authority, and have the scorpions authority of the earth. [4] And it was said to them that they shall not harm the grass of the earth, nor every green thing, nor every tree, except only the men who do not have the seal of God on their foreheads. [5] And it was given to them that they should not kill them, but that they be tormented five months. And the torment of them (is) as (the) torment of a scorpion when it stings a man. [6] And in those days men will seek death, and they will not find it; and they will long to die, and death flees from them. [7] And the likenesses of the locusts like horses having been prepared for war; and on their heads crowns like gold. And their faces (were) as the faces of men; [8] and they had hairs as the hairs of women; and their teeth were as (those) of lions. [9] And they had breastplates as iron breastplates; and the sound of their wings (was) as the sound of many horses of chariots running to war. [10] And they have tails like scorpions, and stings were in their tails; and they (have) authority to harm men five months. [11] And they have a king over them, the angel of the abyss, his name in Hebrew (being)

1 Καὶ ὁ πέμπτος ἄγγελος ἐσάλπισε, καὶ εἶδον ἀστέρα ἐκ τοῦ
And the fifth angel trumpeted, and I saw a star out of
οὐρανοῦ πεπτωκότα εἰς τὴν γῆν, καὶ ἐδόθη αὐτῷ ἡ κλεὶς
heaven having fallen onto the earth. And was given to it the key

2 τοῦ φρέατος τῆς ἀβύσσου. καὶ ἤνοιξε τὸ φρέαρ τῆς ἀβύσσου,
to the pit of the abyss. and he opened the pit of the abyss;
καὶ ἀνέβη καπνὸς ἐκ τοῦ φρέατος ὡς καπνὸς καμίνου
and went up a smoke out of the pit as smoke of a furnace
μεγάλης, καὶ ἐσκοτίσθη ὁ ἥλιος καὶ ὁ ἀὴρ ἐκ τοῦ καπνοῦ
great. And was darkened the sun and the air the smoke

3 τοῦ φρέατος. καὶ ἐκ τοῦ καπνοῦ ἐξῆλθον ἀκρίδες εἰς τὴν γῆν,
of the pit. And out of the smoke came forth locusts to the earth,
καὶ ἐδόθη αὐταῖς ἐξουσία, ὡς ἔχουσιν ἐξουσίαν οἱ σκορπίοι
and was given to them authority, as have authority the scorpions

4 τῆς γῆς. καὶ ἐρρέθη αὐταῖς ἵνα μὴ ἀδικήσωσι τὸν χόρτον
of the earth. And it was said to them that not they should harm the grass
τῆς γῆς, οὐδὲ πᾶν χλωρόν, οὐδὲ πᾶν δένδρον, εἰ μὴ τοὺς
of the earth, nor every green thing, nor every tree, except the
ἀνθρώπους μόνους οἵτινες οὐκ ἔχουσι τὴν σφραγῖδα τοῦ
men only who not have the seal

5 Θεοῦ ἐπὶ τῶν μετώπων αὐτῶν. καὶ ἐδόθη αὐταῖς ἵνα μὴ
of God on the foreheads of them. And it was given to them that not
ἀποκτείνωσιν αὐτούς, ἀλλ᾽ ἵνα βασανισθῶσι μῆνας πέντε·
they should kill them, but that they be tormented months five;
καὶ ὁ βασανισμὸς αὐτῶν ὡς βασανισμὸς σκορπίου, ὅταν
and the torment of them (is) as (the) torment of a scorpion when

6 παίσῃ ἄνθρωπον. καὶ ἐν ταῖς ἡμέραις ἐκείναις ζητήσουσιν
it stings a man. And in days those will seek
οἱ ἄνθρωποι τὸν θάνατον, καὶ οὐχ εὑρήσουσιν αὐτόν·
men death, and not they will find it,
καὶ ἐπιθυμήσουσιν ἀποθανεῖν, καὶ φεύξεται ὁ θάνατος ἀπ᾽
and they will long to die, and will flee death from

7 αὐτῶν. καὶ τὰ ὁμοιώματα τῶν ἀκρίδων ὅμοια ἵπποις ἡτοι-
them. And the likenesses of the locusts like horses having
μασμένοις εἰς πόλεμον, καὶ ἐπὶ τὰς κεφαλὰς αὐτῶν ὡς
been prepared for war, and on the heads of them as
στέφανοι ὅμοιοι χρυσῷ, καὶ τὰ πρόσωπα αὐτῶν ὡς
crowns like gold; and the faces of them as

8 πρόσωπα ἀνθρώπων. καὶ εἶχον τρίχας ὡς τρίχας γυναικῶν,
the faces of men; and they had hairs as hairs of women;

9 καὶ οἱ ὀδόντες αὐτῶν ὡς λεόντων ἦσαν. καὶ εἶχον θώρακας
and the teeth of them as of lions were; and they had breastplates
ὡς θώρακας σιδηροῦς, καὶ ἡ φωνὴ τῶν πτερύγων αὐτῶν
as breastplates iron; and the sound of the wings of them
ὡς φωνὴ ἁρμάτων ἵππων πολλῶν τρεχόντων εἰς πόλεμον.
as sound chariots of horses many running to war.

10 καὶ ἔχουσιν οὐρὰς ὁμοίας σκορπίοις, καὶ κέντρα ἦν ἐν ταῖς
And they have tails like scorpions, and stings were in the
οὐραῖς αὐτῶν· καὶ ἡ ἐξουσία αὐτῶν ἀδικῆσαι τοὺς ἀνθρώ-
tails of them and the authority of them (is) to harm men

11 πους μῆνας πέντε. καὶ ἔχουσιν ἐπ᾽ αὐτῶν βασιλέα τὸν
months five. And they have over them a king, the
ἄγγελον τῆς ἀβύσσου· ὄνομα αὐτῷ Ἑβραϊστὶ Ἀβαδδών,
angel of the abyss; name to him in Hebrew, Abaddon,

**12** καὶ ἐν τῇ Ἑλληνικῇ ὄνομα ἔχει ᾿Απολλύων. ἡ οὐαὶ ἡ μία
and in the    Greek (the) name he has (is) Apollyon. The woe    one
ἀπῆλθεν· ἰδού, ἔρχονται ἔτι δύο οὐαὶ μετὰ ταῦτα.
has departed; behold, comes    yet two woes after these things.

Abaddon; and in the Greek he has (the) name Apollyon. [12] The first woe is past; behold, after these things yet comes two woes. [13] And the sixth angel trumpeted. And I heard one voice out of the four horns of the golden altar before God, [14] saying to the sixth angel who had the trumpet, Release the four angels, those having been bound at the great river Euphrates. [15] And the four angels were released, those having been prepared for the hour and day and month and year, that they should kill the third (part) of men. [16] And the number of the armies of the horsemen (was) two myriads of myriads. And I heard the number of them. [17] And so I saw the horses in the vision, and those sitting on them, having breastplates fire-colored, and dusky red and brimstone-like; and the heads of the horses as heads of lions. And out of their mouths comes fire and smoke and brimstone. [18] The third (part) of men was killed by these three, by the fire and by the smoke and by the brimstone coming out of their mouths. [19] For the authority of them is in their mouth, and in their tails; for their tails (are) like snakes, having heads, and with them they do harm. [20] And the rest of men, those not killed by these plagues, did not repent of the works of their hands, that they will not worship demons and golden idols, and silver and bronze and stone and wooden (idols), which neither are able to see, nor hear, nor walk. [21] And they did not repent of their murders, nor of their sorceries, nor of their fornications, nor of their thefts.

**13** Καὶ ὁ ἕκτος ἄγγελος ἐσάλπισε, καὶ ἤκουσα φωνὴν μίαν ἐκ
And the sixth angel trumpeted. And I heard a voice one out of
τῶν τεσσάρων κεράτων τοῦ θυσιαστηρίου τοῦ χρυσοῦ
the four horns of the altar of gold

**14** τοῦ ἐνώπιον τοῦ Θεοῦ, λέγουσαν τῷ ἕκτῳ ἀγγέλῳ ὃς εἶχε
before God, saying to the sixth angel who had
τὴν σάλπιγγα, Λῦσον τοὺς τέσσαρας ἀγγέλους τοὺς δεδε-
the trumpet, Loose the four angels, those having

**15** μένους ἐπὶ τῷ ποταμῷ τῷ μεγάλῳ Εὐφράτῃ. καὶ ἐλύθησαν
been bound at the river great Euphrates. And were loosed
οἱ τέσσαρες ἄγγελοι οἱ ἡτοιμασμένοι εἰς τὴν ὥραν καὶ
the four angels, those having been prepared for the hour and
ἡμέραν καὶ μῆνα καὶ ἐνιαυτόν, ἵνα ἀποκτείνωσι τὸ τρίτον
day and month and year, that they should kill the third (part)

**16** τῶν ἀνθρώπων. καὶ ὁ ἀριθμὸς στρατευμάτων τοῦ ἱππικοῦ
of men. And the number of the armies of the cavalry

**17** δύο μυριάδες μυριάδων· καὶ ἤκουσα τὸν ἀριθμὸν αὐτῶν. καὶ
two myriads of myriads; and I heard the number of them. And
οὕτως εἶδον τοὺς ἵππους ἐν τῇ ὁράσει, καὶ τοὺς καθημένους
thus I saw the horses in the vision, and those sitting
ἐπ᾿ αὐτῶν, ἔχοντας θώρακας πυρίνους καὶ ὑακινθίνους·
on them, having breastplates fire-colored and dusky red
καὶ θειώδεις· καὶ αἱ κεφαλαὶ τῶν ἵππων ὡς κεφαλαὶ λεόντων,
and brimstone-like; and the heads of the horses as heads of lions;
καὶ ἐκ τῶν στομάτων αὐτῶν ἐκπορεύεται πῦρ καὶ καπνὸς
and out of the mouths of them proceeds fire and smoke

**18** καὶ θεῖον. ὑπὸ τῶν τριῶν τούτων ἀπεκτάνθησαν τὸ τρίτον
and brimstone. By three these were killed the third (part)
τῶν ἀνθρώπων, ἐκ τοῦ πυρὸς καὶ ἐκ τοῦ καπνοῦ καὶ ἐκ τοῦ
of men, from the fire and from smoke and from the

**19** θείου τοῦ ἐκπορευομένου ἐκ τῶν στομάτων αὐτῶν. ἡ γὰρ
brimstone coming out from the mouths of them. the For
ἐξουσία αὐτῶν ἐν τῷ στόματι αὐτῶν ἐστί, καὶ ἐν ταῖς οὐραῖς
authority of them in the mouth of them is, and in the tails
αὐτῶν· αἱ γὰρ οὐραὶ αὐτῶν ὅμοιαι ὄφεσιν, ἔχουσαι κεφαλάς,
of them; the for tails of them (are) like snakes, having heads

**20** καὶ ἐν αὐταῖς ἀδικοῦσι. καὶ οἱ λοιποὶ τῶν ἀνθρώπων, οἳ οὐκ
and with them they do harm. And the rest of men, who not
ἀπεκτάνθησαν ἐν ταῖς πληγαῖς ταύταις, οὐ μετενόησαν ἐκ
were killed by plagues these, not repented of
τῶν ἔργων τῶν χειρῶν αὐτῶν, ἵνα μὴ προσκυνήσωσι τὰ
the works of the hands of them, that not they will worship
δαιμόνια, καὶ εἴδωλα τὰ χρυσᾶ καὶ τὰ ἀργυρᾶ καὶ τὰ
demons and idols gold and silver and
χαλκᾶ καὶ τὰ λίθινα καὶ τὰ ξύλινα, ἃ οὔτε βλέπειν δύναται,
bronze and stone and wood which neither to see are able,

**21** οὔτε ἀκούειν, οὔτε περιπατεῖν· καὶ οὐ μετενόησαν ἐκ τῶν
nor to hear, nor to walk; and not they repented of the
φόνων αὐτῶν, οὔτε ἐκ τῶν φαρμακειῶν αὐτῶν, οὔτε ἐκ τῆς
murders of them, nor of the sorceries of them, nor of the
πορνείας αὐτῶν, οὔτε ἐκ τῶν κλεμμάτων αὐτῶν.
fornications of them nor of the thefts of them.

# CHAPTER 10

CHAPTER 10

[1] And I saw another strong angel coming down out of Heaven, having been clothed (with) a cloud, and a rainbow on the head; and his face as the sun, and his feet as pillars of fire; [2] and having in his hand a little book having been opened. And he placed his right foot on the sea, and the left on the land, [3] and cried with a great voice, as a lion roars. And when he cried, the seven thunders spoke (with) their sounds. [4] And when the seven thunders spoke their sounds, I was about to write. And I heard a voice out of Heaven saying to me, Seal what things the seven thunders spoke, and do not write these things. [5] And the angel whom I saw standing on the sea and on the land lifted his hand to Heaven, [6] and swore by Him living forever and ever, who created the heaven and the things in it, and the earth and the things in it, and the sea and the things in it, that time not shall be any longer; [7] but in the days of the voice of the seventh angel, whenever he is about to trumpet, was even finished the mystery of God, as He preached to His slaves, the prophets. [8] And the voice which I heard out of Heaven again speaking with me, and saying, Go, take the little book having been opened in the hand of the angel standing on the sea and on the land. [9] And I went away toward the angel, saying to him, Give to me the little book. And he said to me, take and eat it up, and it will make your belly bitter, but in your mouth it will be sweet as honey. [10] And I took the little book out of the hand of the angel, and ate it up; and it was like

**1** Καὶ εἶδον ἄλλον ἄγγελον ἰσχυρὸν καταβαίνοντα ἐκ τοῦ
And I saw another strong coming down out of

οὐρανοῦ, περιβεβλημένον νεφέλην, καὶ ἶοις ἐπὶ τῆς κεφαλῆς,
Heaven, having been clothed (with) a cloud, and a rainbow on the head

καὶ τὸ πρόσωπον αὐτοῦ ὡς ὁ ἥλιος, καὶ οἱ πόδες αὐτοῦ ὡς
and the face of him as the sun, and the feet of him as

**2** στύλοι πυρός· καὶ εἶχεν ἐν τῇ χειρὶ αὐτοῦ βιβλαρίδιον
pillars of fire, and he had in the hand of him a little scroll

ἀνεῳγμένον· καὶ ἔθηκε τὸν πόδα αὐτοῦ τὸν δεξιὸν ἐπὶ τὴν
having been opened. And he placed the foot of him the right on the

**3** θάλασσαν, τὸν δὲ εὐώνυμον ἐπὶ τὴν γῆν, καὶ ἔκραξε φωνῇ
sea, the and left on the land, and cried with a voice

μεγάλῃ ὥσπερ λέων μυκᾶται· καὶ ὅτε ἔκραξεν, ἐλάλησαν αἱ
great as a lion roars. And when he cried, spoke the

**4** ἑπτὰ βρονταὶ τὰς ἑαυτῶν φωνάς. καὶ ὅτε ἐλάλησαν αἱ ἑπτὰ
seven thunders the of themselves voices. And when spoke the seven

βρονταὶ τὰς φωνὰς ἑαυτῶν, ἔμελλον γράφειν· καὶ ἤκουσα
thunders the voices of themselves, I was about to write; and I heard

φωνὴν ἐκ τοῦ οὐρανοῦ, λέγουσάν μοι, Σφράγισον ἃ ἐλά-
a voice out of Heaven, saying to me, Seal what things

**5** λησαν αἱ ἑπτὰ βρονταί, καὶ μὴ ταῦτα γράψῃς. καὶ ὁ
spoke the seven thunders, and not these things write. And the

ἄγγελος ὃν εἶδον ἑστῶτα ἐπὶ τῆς θαλάσσης καὶ ἐπὶ τῆς γῆς
angel whom I saw standing on the sea and on the land

**6** ἦρε τὴν χεῖρα αὐτοῦ εἰς τὸν οὐρανόν, καὶ ὤμοσεν ἐν τῷ
lifted the hand of him to Heaven, and swore by Him

ζῶντι εἰς τοὺς αἰῶνας τῶν αἰώνων, ὃς ἔκτισε τὸν οὐρανὸν
living to the ages of the ages, who created the heaven

καὶ τὰ ἐν αὐτῷ, καὶ τὴν γῆν καὶ τὰ ἐν αὐτῇ, καὶ τὴν θάλασ-
and the things in it, and the earth and the things in it, and the sea

**7** σαν καὶ τὰ ἐν αὐτῇ, ὅτι χρόνος οὐκ ἔσται ἔτι· ἀλλὰ ἐν ταῖς
and the things in it, that time not shall be longer, but in the

ἡμέραις τῆς φωνῆς τοῦ ἑβδόμου ἀγγέλου, ὅταν μέλλη
days of the voice of the seventh angel, whenever he is about

σαλπίζειν, καὶ τελεσθῇ τὸ μυστήριον τοῦ Θεοῦ, ὡς εὐηγ-
to trumpet, even may be ended the mystery of God, as He

**8** γέλισε τοῖς ἑαυτοῦ δούλοις τοῖς προφήταις. καὶ ἡ φωνὴ ἣν
preached to the of Himself slaves the prophets. And the voice which

ἤκουσα ἐκ τοῦ οὐρανοῦ, πάλιν λαλοῦσα μετ᾽ ἐμοῦ, καὶ
I heard out of Heaven, again speaking with me, and

λέγουσα, Ὕπαγε, λάβε τὸ βιβλαρίδιον τὸ ἠνεῳγμένον ἐν
saying, Go, take the little scroll having been opened in

τῇ χειρὶ ἀγγέλου τοῦ ἑστῶτος ἐπὶ τῆς θαλάσσης καὶ ἐπὶ
the hand of the angel standing on the sea and on

**9** τῆς γῆς. καὶ ἀπῆλθον πρὸς τὸν ἄγγελον, λέγων αὐτῷ, Δός
the land. And I went away toward the angel, saying to him, Give

μοι τὸ βιβλαρίδιον. καὶ λέγει μοι, Λάβε καὶ κατάφαγε αὐτό·
to me the little scroll. And he said to me, Take and eat up it,

καὶ πικρανεῖ σου τὴν κοιλίαν, ἀλλ᾽ ἐν τῷ στόματί σου ἔσται
and it will embitter of you the belly, but in the mouth of you it will be

**10** γλυκὺ ὡς μέλι. καὶ ἔλαβον τὸ βιβλαρίδιον ἐκ τῆς χειρὸς τοῦ
sweet as honey. And I took the little scroll out of the hand of the

ἀγγέλου, καὶ κατέφαγον αὐτό, καὶ ἦν ἐν τῷ στόματί μου
angel, and devoured it, and it was in the mouth of me

ὡς μέλι, γλυκύ· καὶ ὅτε ἔφαγον αὐτό, ἐπικράνθη ἡ κοιλία
as honey,   sweet;   and when I ate   it, was made bitter the belly

**11** μου. καὶ λέγει μοι, Δεῖ σε πάλιν προφητεῦσαι ἐπὶ λαοῖς καὶ
of me. And he says to me,  must You again  prophesy   before peoples and

ἔθνεσι καὶ γλώσσαις καὶ βασιλεῦσι πολλοῖς.
nations and  tongues   and  kings      many.

sweet honey in my mouth; and when I ate it, my belly was made bitter. [11] And he says to me, You must again prophesy before peoples and and nations and tongues and many kings:

# CHAPTER 11

**1** Καὶ ἐδόθη μοι κάλαμος ὅμοιος ῥάβδῳ, καὶ ὁ ἄγγελος
And was given to me a reed    like    a staff,   and the angel

εἰστήκει, λέγων, Ἔγειραι, καὶ μέτρησον τὸν ναὸν τοῦ Θεοῦ,
stood,   saying,   Rise   and measure the temple   of God,

**2** καὶ τὸ θυσιαστήριον, καὶ τοὺς προσκυνοῦντας ἐν αὐτῷ. καὶ
and the   altar,     and those worshiping   in  it.  And

τὴν αὐλὴν τὴν ἔξωθεν τοῦ ναοῦ ἔκβαλε ἔξω, καὶ μὴ αὐτὴν
the court     outside of the temple cast outside, and not  it

μετρήσῃς, ὅτι ἐδόθη τοῖς ἔθνεσι· καὶ τὴν πόλιν τὴν ἁγίαν
do measure, for it was given to the nations, and the  city    holy

**3** πατήσουσι μῆνας τεσσαράκοντα δύο. καὶ δώσω τοῖς δυσὶ
they will trample months     forty-two.   And I will give to the two

μάρτυσί μου, καὶ προφητεύσουσιν ἡμέρας χιλίας διακοσίας
witnesses of Me, and they will prophesy  days a thousand, two hundred

**4** ἐξήκοντα περιβεβλημένοι σάκκους. οὗτοί εἰσιν αἱ δύο ἐλαῖαι,
sixty,   having been clothed (in) sackcloth. These are  the two olive-trees,

καὶ αἱ δύο λυχνίαι αἱ ἐνώπιον τοῦ Θεοῦ τῆς γῆς ἑστῶσαι.
and the two lampstands  before   the God of the earth standing.

**5** καὶ εἴ τις αὐτοὺς θέλῃ ἀδικῆσαι, πῦρ ἐκπορεύεται ἐκ τοῦ
And if anyone them desires to harm,   fire  proceeds   out of the

στόματος αὐτῶν, καὶ κατεσθίει τοὺς ἐχθροὺς αὐτῶν· καὶ εἴ
mouth   of them and devours   the   enemies of them; and if

τις αὐτοὺς θέλῃ ἀδικῆσαι, οὕτω δεῖ αὐτὸν ἀποκτανθῆναι.
anyone them desires to harm,    thus it behoves him   to be killed.

**6** οὗτοι ἔχουσιν ἐξουσίαν κλεῖσαι τὸν οὐρανόν, ἵνα μὴ βρέχῃ
These have   authority to shut the heaven,   that not may rain

ὑετὸς ἐν ἡμέραις αὐτῶν τῆς προφητείας· καὶ ἐξουσίαν ἔχου-
rain in  days   of them of the   prophecy,   and authority they

σιν ἐπὶ τῶν ὑδάτων, στρέφειν αὐτὰ εἰς αἷμα, καὶ πατάξαι
have over the waters,  to turn  them into blood, and to strike

**7** τὴν γῆν πάσῃ πληγῇ, ὁσάκις ἐὰν θελήσωσι. καὶ ὅταν
the earth (with) every plague, as often as if they desire. And whenever

τελέσωσι τὴν μαρτυρίαν αὐτῶν, τὸ θηρίον τὸ ἀναβαῖνον ἐκ
they finish the  witness   of them, the beast     coming up out of

τῆς ἀβύσσου ποιήσει πόλεμον μετ' αὐτῶν, καὶ νικήσει
the abyss   will make   war   with  them,  and will overcome

**8** αὐτούς, καὶ ἀποκτενεῖ αὐτούς. καὶ τὰ πτώματα αὐτῶν ἐπὶ
them,   and  will kill  them.  And the bodies   of them on

τῆς πλατείας πόλεως τῆς μεγάλης, ἥτις καλεῖται πνευ-
the  street of city  the  great,   which is called spirit-

ματικῶς Σόδομα καὶ Αἴγυπτος, ὅπου καὶ ὁ Κύριος ἡμῶν
ually    Sodom, and,  Egypt,    where indeed the Lord of us

**9** ἐσταυρώθη. καὶ βλέψουσιν ἐκ τῶν λαῶν καὶ φυλῶν καὶ
was crucified. And will see (some) from the peoples and  tribes  and

γλωσσῶν καὶ ἐθνῶν τὰ πτώματα αὐτῶν ἡμέρας τρεῖς καὶ
tongues   and nations the bodies   of them   days  three and

ἥμισυ, καὶ τὰ πτώματα αὐτῶν οὐκ ἀφήσουσι τεθῆναι εἰς
a half;  and the bodies   of them   not they allow to be placed in

CHAPTER 11

[1] And was given to me a reed like a staff, and the angel saying, Rise and measure the temple of God, and the altar, and those worshiping in it. [2] And cast outside the court outside of the temple, and do not measure it; for it was given to the nations, and they will trample the holy city forty-two months. [3] And I will give to My two witnesses, and they will prophesy a thousand two hundred and sixty days, dressed (in) sackcloth. [4] These are the two olive-trees, and the two lampstands standing before the God of the earth. [5] And if anyone desires to harm them, fire proceeds out of their mouth and devours their enemies, and if anyone desires to harm them, so it behoves him to be killed. [6] These have the authority to shut the heaven, that no rain may rain in (the) days of their prophecy; and they have authority over the waters, to turn them into blood, and to strike the earth (with) every plague, as often as they desire. [7] And when they finish their witness, the beast coming up out of the abyss will make war with them, and will overcome them, and will kill them. [8] And their bodies (will be) on the open street of the great city, which is spiritually called Sodom, and, Egypt— where indeed our Lord was crucified. [9] And (some) of the peoples and tribes and tongues and nations see the bodies of them three days and a half; and the bodies of them they do not allow to

be placed in a tomb. [10] And those dwelling on the earth rejoice over them and are glad. And they will send gifts to one another, because these two prophets tormented those dwelling on the earth. [11] And after the three days and a half, a spirit of life from God entered into them, and they stood on their feet; and great fear fell on those beholding them. [12] And they heard a great voice out of Heaven saying to them, Come up here. And they went up into Heaven in the cloud; and their enemies beheld them.

[13] And in that hour occurred a great earthquake, and the tenth (part) of the city fell; and were seven thousand names of men killed in the earthquake; and the rest became terrified, and gave glory to the God of Heaven. [14] The second woe is passed away; and behold, the third woe is coming quickly. [15] And the seventh angel trumpeted. And there were great voices in Heaven, saying, The kingdoms of the world have become our Lord's, and of His Christ; and He shall reign forever (and) ever. [16] And the twenty-four elders sitting before God on their thrones fell on their faces, and worshiped God, [17] saying, We thank You, Lord God Almighty, He who is, and was, and is coming, because You took Your great power and reigned. [18] And the nations were wrathful, and Your wrath came, and the time of the judging of the dead, and to give the reward to Your slaves the prophets, and to the saints, and to those fearing Your name, to the small and to the great, and to destroy those destroy-

**10** μνήματα. καὶ οἱ κατοικοῦντες ἐπὶ τῆς γῆς χαροῦσιν ἐπ'
a tomb.    And those dwelling    on    the earth will rejoice  over
αὐτοῖς, καὶ εὐφρανθήσονται, καὶ δῶρα πέμψουσιν ἀλλήλοις,
them    and will make merry.    And gifts they will send one another
ὅτι οὗτοι οἱ δύο προφῆται ἐβασάνισαν τοὺς κατοικοῦντας
because these two    prophets    tormented    those    dwelling

**11** ἐπὶ τῆς γῆς. καὶ μετὰ τὰς τρεῖς ἡμέρας καὶ ἥμισυ, πνεῦμα
on the earth. And after the three    days    and a half,    a spirit
ζωῆς ἐκ τοῦ Θεοῦ εἰσῆλθεν ἐπ' αὐτούς καὶ ἔστησαν ἐπὶ
of life out of    God    entered into    them,    and they stood on
τοὺς πόδας αὐτῶν, καὶ φόβος μέγας ἔπεσεν ἐπὶ τοὺς θεωροῦν-
the    feet    of them, and fear    great  fell    on    those beholding

**12** τας αὐτούς. καὶ ἤκουσαν φωνὴν μεγάλην ἐκ τοῦ οὐρανοῦ,
them.  And they heard a voice    great  out of    Heaven
λέγουσαν αὐτοῖς, Ἀνάβητε ὧδε. καὶ ἀνέβησαν εἰς τὸν
saying    to them,   Come up  here.  And they went up into
οὐρανὸν ἐν τῇ νεφέλῃ, καὶ ἐθεώρησαν αὐτοὺς οἱ ἐχθροὶ
Heaven   in the  cloud; and  beheld    them    the enemies

**13** αὐτῶν. καὶ ἐν ἐκείνῃ τῇ ὥρᾳ ἐγένετο σεισμὸς μέγας, καὶ τὸ
of them. And in that    hour occurred an earthquake great, and  the
δέκατον τῆς πόλεως ἔπεσε, καὶ ἀπεκτάνθησαν ἐν τῷ σεισμῷ
tenth (part) of the city  fell,    and were killed    in the earthquake
ὀνόματα ἀνθρώπων, χιλιάδες ἑπτά· καὶ οἱ λοιποὶ ἔμφοβοι
names    of men,    thousands seven,  and the  rest  terrified
ἐγένοντο, καὶ ἔδωκαν δόξαν τῷ Θεῷ τοῦ οὐρανοῦ.
became,    and gave   glory to the God  of Heaven.

**14** Ἡ οὐαὶ ἡ δευτέρα ἀπῆλθεν· καὶ ἰδού, ἡ οὐαὶ ἡ τρίτη
The  woe    second  passed away; and behold, the woe    third
ἔρχεται ταχύ.
is coming quickly.

**15** Καὶ ὁ ἕβδομος ἄγγελος ἐσάλπισε, καὶ ἐγένοντο φωναὶ
And the  seventh    angel    trumpeted. And    there were voices
μεγάλαι ἐν τῷ οὐρανῷ, λέγουσαι, Ἐγένοντο αἱ βασιλεῖαι
great    in   Heaven,    saying,    became  The kingdoms
τοῦ κόσμου, τοῦ Κυρίου ἡμῶν, καὶ τοῦ Χριστοῦ αὐτοῦ,
of the world  of the Lord  of us, and of the    Christ of Him,

**16** καὶ βασιλεύσει εἰς τοὺς αἰῶνας τῶν αἰώνων. καὶ οἱ εἴκοσι καὶ
and He shall reign to the  ages  of the  ages.  And the twenty and
τέσσαρες πρεσβύτεροι οἱ ἐνώπιον τοῦ Θεοῦ καθήμενοι ἐπὶ
four    elders    before    God    sitting    on
τοὺς θρόνους αὐτῶν, ἔπεσαν ἐπὶ τὰ πρόσωπα αὐτῶν, καὶ
the  thrones of them,  fell    on  the  faces    of them, and

**17** προσεκύνησαν τῷ Θεῷ, λέγοντες, Εὐχαριστοῦμέν σοι, Κύριε
worshiped    God, saying,    We thank    You, Lord
ὁ Θεὸς ὁ παντοκράτωρ, ὁ ὢν καὶ ὁ ἦν καὶ ὁ ἐρχόμενος,
God    Almighty, the (One) being, and who was, and who (is) coming,
ὅτι εἴληφας τὴν δύναμίν σου τὴν μεγάλην, καὶ ἐβασίλευσας.
because You took the power of You    great,    and reigned.

**18** καὶ τὰ ἔθνη ὠργίσθησαν, καὶ ἦλθεν ἡ ὀργή σου, καὶ ὁ
And the nations were wrathful, and came the wrath of You, and the
καιρὸς τῶν νεκρῶν κριθῆναι, καὶ δοῦναι τὸν μισθὸν τοῖς
time  of the  dead  to be judged and to give  the  reward  to the
δούλοις σου τοῖς προφήταις καὶ τοῖς ἁγίοις καὶ τοῖς φοβου-
slaves of You, to the prophets  and to the  saints, and to those fearing
μένοις τὸ ὄνομά σου, τοῖς μικροῖς καὶ τοῖς μεγάλοις, καὶ
the  name of You,  to the  small  and to the    great,    and

ing the earth. [19] And the temple of God in Heaven was opened; and the ark of His covenant was seen in His temple; and lightnings and voices and thunders and earthquake and a great hail occurred.

διαφθεῖραι τοὺς διαφθείροντας τὴν γῆν.
to destroy those destroying the earth.

**19** Καὶ ἠνοίγη ὁ ναὸς τοῦ Θεοῦ ἐν τῷ οὐρανῷ, καὶ ὤφθη ἡ
And was opened the temple of God in Heaven, and was seen the

κιβωτὸς τῆς διαθήκης αὐτοῦ ἐν τῷ ναῷ αὐτοῦ· καὶ ἐγένοντο
ark of the covenant of Him in the temple of Him, and occurred

ἀστραπαὶ καὶ φωναὶ καὶ βρονταὶ καὶ σεισμὸς καὶ χάλαζα
lightnings and voices and thunders and an earthquake and a hail

μεγάλη.
great.

## CHAPTER 12

[1] And a great sign was seen in the heaven, a woman having been clothed (with) the sun, and the moon (was) underneath her feet; and on her head (was) a crown of twelve stars, [2] and having (a babe) in womb. She cries, being in travail, and being distressed to bear. [3] And was seen another sign in the heaven; and behold, a great red dragon having seven heads and ten horns; and on his heads seven diadems, [4] and his tail draws the third (part) of the stars of the heaven. And (he) throws them to the earth. And the dragon stood before the woman being about to bear, that when she bears, he might devour her child. [5] And she bore a son, a male, who is about to shepherd all the nations with an iron staff. And her child was caught away to God, and to His throne. [6] And the woman fled into the wilderness, where she has a place, (it) having been prepared from God, that there they might nourish her a thousand two hundred (and) sixty days. [7] And war occurred in Heaven, Michael and his angels making war with the dragon. And the dragon warred, and his angels, [8] and did not prevail, neither was place found (for) them still in Heaven. [9] And the great dragon, the old serpent being called Devil, and, Satan, he deceiving the whole habitable world, was cast onto

## CHAPTER 12

**1** Καὶ σημεῖον μέγα ὤφθη ἐν τῷ οὐρανῷ, γυνὴ περιβεβλη-
And a sign great was seen in Heaven a woman having been

μένη τὸν ἥλιον, καὶ ἡ σελήνη ὑποκάτω τῶν ποδῶν αὐτῆς,
clothed (with) the sun, and the moon underneath the feet of her,

**2** καὶ ἐπὶ τῆς κεφαλῆς αὐτῆς στέφανος ἀστέρων δώδεκα· καὶ
and on the head of her a crown of stars twelve, and

ἐν γαστρὶ ἔχουσα, κράζει ὠδίνουσα, καὶ βασανιζομένη
in womb having; she cries, being in travail, and having been distressed

**3** τεκεῖν. καὶ ὤφθη ἄλλο σημεῖον ἐν τῷ οὐρανῷ, καὶ ἰδού,
to bear. And was seen another sign in Heaven, and behold,

δράκων μέγας πυρρός, ἔχων κεφαλὰς ἑπτὰ καὶ κέρατα δέκα,
a dragon great red, having heads seven and horns ten,

**4** καὶ ἐπὶ τὰς κεφαλὰς αὐτοῦ διαδήματα ἑπτά. καὶ ἡ οὐρὰ
and on the heads of him diadems seven. and the tail

αὐτοῦ σύρει τὸ τρίτον τῶν ἀστέρων τοῦ οὐρανοῦ, καὶ
of him draws the third (part) of the stars of heaven, and

ἔβαλεν αὐτοὺς εἰς τὴν γῆν· καὶ ὁ δράκων ἔστηκεν ἐνώπιον
throws them to the earth. And the dragon stood before

τῆς γυναικὸς τῆς μελλούσης τεκεῖν, ἵνα, ὅταν τέκῃ, τὸ τέκνον
the woman being about to bear, that, when she bears, the child

**5** αὐτῆς καταφάγῃ. καὶ ἔτεκεν υἱὸν ἄρρενα, ὃς μέλλει ποι-
of her he may devour. And she bore a son, a male, who is about to

μαίνειν πάντα τὰ ἔθνη ἐν ῥάβδῳ σιδηρᾷ· καὶ ἡρπάσθη τὸ
shepherd all the nations with a staff iron. And was seized the

**6** τέκνον αὐτῆς πρὸς τὸν Θεὸν καὶ τὸν θρόνον αὐτοῦ. καὶ ἡ
child of her to God and the throne of Him. And the

γυνὴ ἔφυγεν εἰς τὴν ἔρημον, ὅπου ἔχει τόπον ἡτοιμασμένον
woman fled into the wilderness, where she has a place having been prepared

ἀπὸ τοῦ Θεοῦ, ἵνα ἐκεῖ τρέφωσιν αὐτὴν ἡμέρας χιλίας
from God, that there they might nourish her days a thousand

διακοσίας ἑξήκοντα.
two hundred (and) sixty.

**7** Καὶ ἐγένετο πόλεμος ἐν τῷ οὐρανῷ· ὁ Μιχαὴλ καὶ οἱ
And occurred war in Heaven, Michael and the

ἄγγελοι αὐτοῦ ἐπολέμησαν κατὰ τοῦ δράκοντος· καὶ ὁ
angels of him made war against the dragon. And the

**8** δράκων ἐπολέμησε, καὶ οἱ ἄγγελοι αὐτου, καὶ οὐκ ἴσχυσαν,
dragon warred, and the angels of him, and not they had strength,

**9** οὔτε τόπος εὑρέθη αὐτῶν ἔτι ἐν τῷ οὐρανῷ. καὶ ἐβλήθη
not even place was found of them still in Heaven. And was cast

ὁ δράκων ὁ μέγας, ὁ ὄφις ὁ ἀρχαῖος, ὁ καλούμενος διάβολος
the dragon great, the serpent old, being called Devil

καὶ ὁ Σατανᾶς, ὁ πλανῶν τὴν οἰκουμένην ὅλην· ἐβλήθη
and Satan the (one) deceiving the habitable world whole; was cast

the earth, and his angels were cast with him. [10] And I heard a great voice saying in Heaven, Now has come the salvation and the power and the kingdom of our God, and the authority of His Christ, because the accuser of our brothers is cast down, he accusing them before our God day and night. [11] And they overcame him because of the blood of the Lamb, and because of the word of their testimony. And they did not love their soul (even) until death. [12] Because of this, be glad, the heavens and those tabernacling in them. Woe (to) those dwelling on the earth and (in) the sea, because the devil came down to you having great anger, knowing that he has a little time. [13] And when the dragon saw that he was cast onto the earth, he pursued the woman who bore the male. [14] And two wings of the great eagle were given to the woman, that she may fly into the wilderness, to her place, where she is nourished there a time, and times, and half a time, from the serpent's face. [15] And the serpent threw water out of his mouth after the woman, that he might cause her (to be) carried off (by the) river. [16] And the earth helped the woman, and the earth opened its mouth and swallowed the river which the dragon threw out of his mouth. [17] And the dragon was enraged over the woman, and went away to make war with the rest of her seed, those keeping the commandments of God, and having the testimony of Jesus Christ.

εἰς τὴν γῆν, καὶ οἱ ἄγγελοι αὐτοῦ μετ' αὐτοῦ ἐβλήθησαν.
onto the earth, and the angels    of him    with    him    were cast.

10 καὶ ἤκουσα φωνὴν μεγάλην λέγουσαν ἐν τῷ οὐρανῷ, Ἄρτι
And I heard a voice    great    saying    in    Heaven,    Now
ἐγένετο ἡ σωτηρία καὶ ἡ δύναμις καὶ ἡ βασιλεία τοῦ Θεοῦ
has come into being the salvation and the power and the kingdom of the God
ἡμῶν, καὶ ἡ ἐξουσία τοῦ Χριστοῦ αὐτοῦ· ὅτι κατεβλήθη
of us, and the authority of the    Christ    of Him, because is thrown down
ὁ κατήγορος τῶν ἀδελφῶν ἡμῶν, ὁ κατηγορῶν αὐτῶν
the accuser    of the    brothers    of us, the (one) accusing    them

11 ἐνώπιον τοῦ Θεοῦ ἡμῶν ἡμέρας καὶ νυκτός. καὶ αὐτοὶ
before    the    God    of us    day    and    night. And they
ἐνίκησαν αὐτὸν διὰ τὸ αἷμα τοῦ ἀρνίου, καὶ διὰ τὸν λόγον
overcame    him, because of the blood of the Lamb, and because of the word
τῆς μαρτυρίας αὐτῶν, καὶ οὐκ ἠγάπησαν τὴν ψυχὴν αὐτῶν
of the witness    of them; and not they loved    the soul    of them

12 ἄχρι θανάτου. διὰ τοῦτο εὐφραίνεσθε, οἱ οὐρανοὶ καὶ οἱ ἐν
until    death. Therefore,    be glad,    the heavens and those in
αὐτοῖς σκηνοῦντες· οὐαὶ τοῖς κατοικοῦσι τὴν γῆν καὶ τὴν
them    tabernacling. Woe (to) those inhabiting    the    earth and the
θάλασσαν, ὅτι κατέβη ὁ διάβολος πρὸς ὑμᾶς ἔχων θυμὸν
sea,    because came down the Devil    to    you having    anger
μέγαν, εἰδὼς ὅτι ὀλίγον καιρὸν ἔχει.
great, knowing that a little    time    he has.

13 Καὶ ὅτε εἶδεν ὁ δράκων ὅτι ἐβλήθη εἰς τὴν γῆν, ἐδίωξε τὴν
And when saw the dragon that he was cast onto the earth, he pursued the

14 γυναῖκα ἥτις ἔτεκε τὸν ἄρρενα. καὶ ἐδόθησαν τῇ γυναικὶ
woman who bore    the    male.    And were given to the    woman
δύο πτέρυγες τοῦ ἀετοῦ τοῦ μεγάλου, ἵνα πέτηται εἰς τὴν
two wings    of the eagle    great,    that she may fly into the

15 ἔρημον εἰς τὸν τόπον αὐτῆς, ὅπου τρέφεται ἐκεῖ καιρόν, καὶ
wilderness, to the place    of her,    where she is nourished there a time, and
καιρούς, καὶ ἥμισυ καιροῦ, ἀπὸ προσώπου τοῦ ὄφεως. καὶ
times,    and half    a time, from (the) face    of the serpent. And
ἔβαλεν ὁ ὄφις ὀπίσω τῆς γυναικὸς ἐκ τοῦ στόματος αὐτοῦ
cast the serpent after    the    woman out of the    mouth    of him
ὕδωρ ὡς ποταμόν, ἵνα ταύτην ποταμοφόρητον ποιήσῃ.
water as    a river,    that she carried off (a) river he might make.

16 καὶ ἐβοήθησεν ἡ γῆ τῇ γυναικί, καὶ ἤνοιξεν ἡ γῆ τὸ στόμα
And helped    the earth the woman,    and opened the earth the mouth
αὐτῆς, καὶ κατέπιε τὸν ποταμὸν ὃν ἔβαλεν ὁ δράκων ἐκ τοῦ
of it    and swallowed the    river    which cast the dragon out of the

17 στόματος αὐτοῦ. καὶ ὠργίσθη ὁ δράκων ἐπὶ τῇ γυναικί, καὶ
mouth    of him. And was enraged the dragon over the woman, and
ἀπῆλθε ποιῆσαι πόλεμον μετὰ τῶν λοιπῶν τοῦ σπέρματος
went away to make    war    with    the    rest of the seed
αὐτῆς, τῶν τηρούντων τὰς ἐντολὰς τοῦ Θεοῦ καὶ ἐχόντων
of her, those    keeping    the commandments of God, and having
τὴν μαρτυρίαν τοῦ Ἰησοῦ Χριστοῦ
the witness    of Jesus    Christ.

## CHAPTER 13

CHAPTER 13

[1] And I stood on the sand of the sea. And I saw a beast coming up out of the sea, having seven heads and

1 καὶ ἐστάθην ἐπὶ τὴν ἄμμον τῆς θαλάσσης.
And I stood    on    the sand of the    sea.
Καὶ εἶδον ἐκ τῆς θαλάσσης θηρίον ἀναβαῖνον, ἔχον κεφαλὰς
And I saw out of the    sea    a beast coming up, having    heads

ten horns; and on his horns ten diadems, and on its heads a name blasphemy. [2] And the beast which I saw was like a leopard, and its feet as of a bear, and its mouth as (the) mouth of a lion. And the dragon gave to it its power, and its throne, and great authority. [3] And I saw one of its heads, as having been slain to death; and its deadly wound was healed. And the whole earth wondered after the beast.

[4] And they worshiped the dragon who gave authority to the beast; and they worshiped the beast, saying, Who (is) like the beast; who is able to make war with it? [5] And was given to it a mouth speaking great things and blasphemies; and was given to it authority to act forty-two months. [6] And it opened its mouth in blasphemies against God, to blaspheme His name, and His tabernacle, and those tabernacling in Heaven. [7] And it was given to it to make war with the saints, and to overcome them. And was given to it authority over every tribe and tongue and nation. [8] And all those dwelling on the earth will worship it, (those) of whom the names not have been written in the Book of Life of the Lamb having been slain, from (the) foundation of (the) world. [9] If anyone has an ear, let him hear. [10] If anyone brings into captivity, into captivity he goes. If anyone by a sword will kill he must by a sword be killed. Here is the patience and the faith of the saints. [11] And I saw another beast coming up out of the earth, and it had two horns like a lamb, but spoke as a dragon. [12] And all the authority of the first beast it does be-

ἑπτὰ καὶ κέρατα δέκα, καὶ ἐπὶ τῶν κεράτων αὐτοῦ δέκα
seven and horns ten, and on the horns of it ten

διαδήματα, καὶ ἐπὶ τὰς κεφαλὰς αὐτοῦ ὄνομα βλασφημίας.
diadems, and on the heads of it names of blasphemy.

**2** καὶ τὸ θηρίον, ὃ εἶδον, ἦν ὅμοιον παρδάλει, καὶ οἱ πόδες
And the beast which I saw was like a leopard, and the feet

αὐτοῦ ὡς ἄρκτου, καὶ τὸ στόμα αὐτοῦ ὡς στόμα λέοντος·
of it as of a bear, and the mouth of it as (the) mouth of a lion.

καὶ ἔδωκεν αὐτῷ ὁ δράκων τὴν δύναμιν αὐτοῦ, καὶ τὸν
And gave to it the dragon the power of it and the

**3** θρόνον αὐτοῦ, καὶ ἐξουσίαν μεγάλην. καὶ εἶδον μίαν τῶν
throne of it and authority great. And I saw one of the

κεφαλῶν αὐτοῦ ὡς ἐσφαγμένην εἰς θάνατον· καὶ ἡ πληγὴ τοῦ
heads of it as having been slain to death, and the wound of the

θανάτου αὐτοῦ ἐθεραπεύθη· καὶ ἐθαύμασεν ὅλη ἡ γῆ ὀπίσω
death of it was healed. And marveled all the earth after

**4** τοῦ θηρίου· καὶ προσεκύνησαν τὸν δράκοντα ὃς ἔδωκεν
the beast; and they worshiped the dragon who gave

ἐξουσίαν τῷ θηρίῳ, καὶ προσεκύνησαν τὸ θηρίον, λέγοντες,
authority to the beast, and they worshiped the beast, saying,

Τίς ὅμοιος τῷ θηρίῳ; τίς δύναται πολεμῆσαι μετ᾽ αὐτοῦ;
Who (is) like the beast, who is able to make war with it?

**5** καὶ ἐδόθη αὐτῷ στόμα λαλοῦν μεγάλα καὶ βλασφημίας· καὶ
And was given to it a mouth speaking great things and blasphemies; and

**6** ἐδόθη αὐτῷ ἐξουσία ποιῆσαι μῆνας τεσσαράκοντα δύο. καὶ
was given to it authority to act months forty- two. And

ἤνοιξε τὸ στόμα αὐτοῦ εἰς βλασφημίαν πρὸς τὸν Θεόν,
it opened the mouth of it in blasphemy toward God,

βλασφημῆσαι τὸ ὄνομα αὐτοῦ, καὶ τὴν σκηνὴν αὐτοῦ, καὶ
to blaspheme the name of Him, and the tabernacle of Him, and

**7** τοὺς ἐν τῷ οὐρανῷ σκηνοῦντας. καὶ ἐδόθη αὐτῷ πόλεμον
those in Heaven tabernacling. And was given to it war

ποιῆσαι μετὰ τῶν ἁγίων, καὶ νικῆσαι αὐτούς· καὶ ἐδόθη
to make with the saints, and to overcome them. And was given

αὐτῷ ἐξουσία ἐπὶ πᾶσαν φυλὴν καὶ γλῶσσαν καὶ ἔθνος.
to it authority over every tribe and tongue and nation

**8** καὶ προσκυνήσουσιν αὐτῷ πάντες οἱ κατοικοῦντες ἐπὶ τῆς
And will worship it all those dwelling on the

γῆς, ὧν οὐ γέγραπται τὰ ὀνόματα ἐν τῇ βίβλῳ τῆς ζωῆς
earth, of whom not was written the names in the Scroll of Life

**9** τοῦ ἀρνίου ἐσφαγμένου ἀπὸ καταβολῆς κόσμου. εἴ τις ἔχει
of the Lamb having been slain from (the) foundation of world. If any- one have

**10** οὖς, ἀκουσάτω. εἴ τις αἰχμαλωσίαν συνάγει, εἰς αἰχμαλω-
an ear, let him hear. If anyone captivity gathers into captivity

σίαν ὑπάγει· εἴ τις ἐν μαχαίρᾳ ἀποκτενεῖ, δεῖ αὐτὸν ἐν
he goes. If anyone by a sword will kill, must he by

μαχαίρᾳ ἀποκτανθῆναι. ὧδέ ἐστιν ἡ ὑπομονὴ καὶ ἡ πίστις
a sword be killed. Here is the patience and the faith

τῶν ἁγίων.
of the saints.

**11** Καὶ εἶδον ἄλλο θηρίον ἀναβαῖνον ἐκ τῆς γῆς, καὶ εἶχε
And I saw another beast coming up out of the earth, and it had

**12** κέρατα δύο ὅμοια ἀρνίῳ, καὶ ἐλάλει ὡς δράκων. καὶ τὴν
horns two like a lamb, and spoke as a dragon. And the

ἐξουσίαν τοῦ πρώτου θηρίου πᾶσαν ποιεῖ ἐνώπιον αὐτοῦ.
authority of the first beast all it does before it.

fore it. And the earth and those dwelling in it it causes that they shall worship the first beast, of which was healed the deadly wound of it. [13] And it does great signs, that even fire it makes to come down out of the heaven onto the earth before men. [14] And it deceives those dwelling on the earth, because of the signs which were given to it to do before the beast, saying to those dwelling on the earth to make an image to the beast who has the wound of the sword, and lived. [15] And was given to it to give spirit to the image of the beast, that even the image of the beast might speak, and might cause as many as would not worship the image of the beast that (they) should be killed. [16] And the small and the great, and the rich and the poor, and the freemen and the slaves, it causes that they give to them a mark on their right hand, or on their foreheads, [17] even that not any could buy or sell, except those having the mark, or the name of the beast, or the number of its name. [18] Here is wisdom: Let him having reason count the number of the beast; for it is (the) number of a man; and its number (is) six hundred and sixty-six.

καὶ ποιεῖ τὴν γῆν καὶ τοὺς κατοικοῦντας ἐν αὐτῇ ἵνα
And it makes the earth and those dwelling in it that

προσκυνήσωσι τὸ θηρίον τὸ πρῶτον, οὗ ἐθεραπεύθη ἡ
they should worship the beast the first, of which was healed the

13 πληγὴ τοῦ θανάτου αὐτοῦ. καὶ ποιεῖ σημεῖα μεγάλα, ἵνα
wound of death of it. And it does signs great, that

καὶ πῦρ ποιῇ καταβαίνειν ἐκ τοῦ οὐρανοῦ εἰς τὴν γῆν
even fire it makes to come down out of the heaven onto the earth

14 ἐνώπιον τῶν ἀνθρώπων. καὶ πλανᾷ τοὺς κατοικοῦντας
before men. And it deceives those dwelling

ἐπὶ τῆς γῆς διὰ τὰ σημεῖα ἃ ἐδόθη αὐτῷ ποιῆσαι ἐνώπιον
on the earth, because of the signs which were given to it to do before

τοῦ θηρίου, λέγων τοῖς κατοικουσιν ἐπὶ τῆς γῆς ποιῆσαι
the beast, saying to those dwelling on the earth to make

εἰκόνα τῷ θηρίῳ ὃ ἔχει τὴν πληγὴν τῆς μαχαίρας καὶ ἔζησε.
an image to the beast who has the wound of the sword, and lived.

15 καὶ ἐδόθη αὐτῷ δοῦναι πνεῦμα τῇ εἰκόνι τοῦ θηρίου, ἵνα καὶ
And was given to it to give a spirit to the image of the beast, that even

λαλήσῃ ἡ εἰκὼν τοῦ θηρίου, καὶ ποιήσῃ, ὅσοι ἂν μὴ
might speak the image of the beast, and might make as many as not

προσκυνήσωσι τὴν εἰκόνα τοῦ θηρίου, ἵνα ἀποκτανθῶσι.
would worship the image of the beast, that (they) be killed.

16 καὶ ποιεῖ πάντας, τοὺς μικροὺς καὶ τοὺς μεγάλους, καὶ τοὺς
And it makes all, the small and the great, and the

πλουσίους καὶ τοὺς πτωχούς, καὶ τοὺς ἐλευθέρους καὶ τοὺς
rich and the poor, and the freemen and the

δούλους, ἵνα δώσῃ αὐτοῖς χάραγμα ἐπὶ τῆς χειρὸς αὐτῶν
slaves, that it may give to them a mark on the hand of them

17 τῆς δεξιᾶς, ἢ ἐπὶ τῶν μετώπων αὐτῶν, καὶ ἵνα μή τις
right, or on the foreheads of them, even that not any

δύνηται ἀγοράσαι ἢ πωλῆσαι, εἰ μὴ ὁ ἔχων τὸ χάραγμα ἢ
could buy or sell, except he having the mark, or

18 τὸ ὄνομα τοῦ θηρίου ἢ τὸν ἀριθμὸν τοῦ ὀνόματος αὐτοῦ. ὧδε
the name of the beast, or the number of the name of it. Here

ἡ σοφία ἐστίν. ὁ ἔχων τὸν νοῦν ψηφισάτω τὸν ἀριθμὸν τοῦ
wisdom is. The (one) having reason let him count the number of the

θηρίου· ἀριθμὸς γὰρ ἀνθρώπου ἐστί, καὶ ὁ ἀριθμὸς αὐτοῦ χξϛ'.
beast; (the) number for of a man it is. And the number of it (is) 666.

## CHAPTER 14

CHAPTER 14

[1] And I saw, and behold, (the) Lamb standing on Mount Zion! And with Him (were) a hundred (and) forty-four thousands, having the name of His Father written on their foreheads. [2] And I heard a sound out of Heaven, as a sound of many waters, and as a sound of great thunder; and I heard a sound, (as) harpers harping on their harps. [3] And they sing a new song before the throne, and before the four living creatures and the elders. And no one was able

1 Καὶ εἶδον, καὶ ἰδού, ἀρνίον ἑστηκὸς ἐπὶ τὸ ὄρος Σιών, καὶ
And I saw, and behold, (the) Lamb standing on the mount Zion, and

μετ' αὐτοῦ ἑκατὸν τεσσαρακοντατέσσαρες χιλιάδες, ἔχουσαι
with Him a hundred (and) forty-four thousands, having

τὸ ὄνομα τοῦ πατρὸς αὐτοῦ γεγραμμένον ἐπὶ τῶν μετώπων
the name of the Father of Him having been written on the foreheads

2 αὐτῶν. καὶ ἤκουσα φωνὴν ἐκ τοῦ οὐρανοῦ, ὡς φωνὴν ὑδάτων
of them. And I heard a sound out of Heaven, as a sound of waters

πολλῶν, καὶ ὡς φωνὴν βροντῆς μεγάλης· καὶ φωνὴν ἤκουσα
many, and as a sound of thunder great; and a sound I heard

3 κιθαρῳδῶν κιθαριζόντων ἐν ταῖς κιθάραις αὐτῶν. καὶ
of harpers harping on the harps of them. And

ᾄδουσιν ὡς ᾠδὴν καινὴν ἐνώπιον τοῦ θρόνου, καὶ ἐνώπιον
they sing as a song new before the throne, and before

τῶν τεσσάρων ζώων καὶ τῶν πρεσβυτέρων· καὶ οὐδεὶς ἠδύ-
the four living creatures and the elders; and no one could

to learn the song, except the hundred (and) forty-four thousands, those being redeemed from the earth. [4] These are those not being defiled with women, for they are virgins. These are those following the Lamb wherever He may go. These were redeemed from men (as) firstfruit to God and to the Lamb. [5] And in their mouth was found no guile, for they are without blemish before the throne of God. [6] And I saw another angel flying in mid-heaven, having an everlasting gospel to preach to those dwelling on the earth, even (to) every nation and tribe and tongue and people, [7] saying in a great voice, Fear God, and give glory to Him, because the hour of His judgment has come. And, Worship those having made the heaven and the earth and the sea and the fountains of waters. [8] And another angel followed, saying, The great city, Babylon, has fallen, has fallen, because of the wine of the anger of her fornication (she) has made to drink all nations.

[9] And a third angel followed them, saying in a great voice, If anyone worships the beast and its image, and receives a mark on his forehead, or on his hand, [10] he also shall drink of the wine of the anger of God, being mixed undiluted in the cup of His wrath; and will be tormented by fire and brimstone before the holy angels, and before the Lamb. [11] And the smoke of the torment of them goes up forever (and) ever; and they have no rest night and day, those worshiping the beast and its image, and if anyone receives the mark of its name. [12] Here is the patience of the

 νατο μαθεῖν τὴν ὠδήν, εἰ μὴ αἱ ἑκατὸν τεσσαρακοντατέσ-
to learn the song, except the hundred (and) forty-four

**4** σαρες χιλιάδες, οἱ ἠγορασμένοι ἀπὸ τῆς γῆς. οὗτοί εἰσιν οἱ
thousands, those being redeemed from the earth. These are who

μετὰ γυναικῶν οὐκ ἐμολύνθησαν· παρθένοι γάρ εἰσιν. οὗτοί
with women not were defiled, virgins for they are. These

εἰσιν οἱ ἀκολουθοῦντες τῷ ἀρνίῳ ὅπου ἂν ὑπάγῃ. οὗτοι
are those following the Lamb wherever He may go. These

ἠγοράσθησαν ἀπὸ τῶν ἀνθρώπων, ἀπαρχὴ τῷ Θεῷ καὶ τῷ
were from men firstfruit to God and to the

**5** ἀρνίῳ. καὶ ἐν τῷ στόματι αὐτῶν οὐχ εὑρέθη δόλος· ἄμωμοι
Lamb. And in the mouth of them not was found guile; unmarked

γάρ εἰσιν ἐνώπιον τοῦ θρόνου τοῦ Θεοῦ.
for they are before the throne of God.

**6** Καὶ εἶδον ἄλλον ἄγγελον πετώμενον ἐν μεσουρανήματι,
And I saw another angel flying in mid-heaven,

ἔχοντα εὐαγγέλιον αἰώνιον, εὐαγγελίσαι τοὺς κατοικοῦντας
having a gospel everlasting to preach to those dwelling

ἐπὶ τῆς γῆς, καὶ πᾶν ἔθνος καὶ φυλὴν καὶ γλῶσσαν καὶ λαόν,
on the earth, even every nation and tribe and tongue and people,

**7** λέγοντα ἐν φωνῇ μεγάλῃ, Φοβήθητε τὸν Θεόν, καὶ δότε αὐτῷ
saying in a voice great, Fear God, and give to Him

δόξαν, ὅτι ἦλθεν ἡ ὥρα τῆς κρίσεως αὐτοῦ, καὶ προσκυνή-
glory, because came the hour of the judgment of Him; and, Worship

σατε τῷ ποιήσαντι τὸν οὐρανὸν καὶ τὴν γῆν καὶ τὴν θάλασ-
Him having made the heaven and the earth and the sea

σαν καὶ πηγὰς ὑδάτων.
and fountains of waters.

**8** Καὶ ἄλλος ἄγγελος ἠκολούθησε, λέγων, Ἔπεσεν ἔπεσε
And another angel followed, saying, Fell, fell

Βαβυλὼν ἡ πόλις ἡ μεγάλη, ὅτι ἐκ τοῦ οἴνου τοῦ θυμοῦ τῆς
Babylon the city great, because of the wine of the anger of the

πορνείας αὐτῆς πεπότικε πάντα ἔθνη.
fornication of her she made to drink all nations.

**9** Καὶ τρίτος ἄγγελος ἠκολούθησεν αὐτοῖς, λέγων ἐν φωνῇ
And a third angel followed them, saying in a voice

μεγάλῃ, Εἴ τις τὸ θηρίον προσκυνεῖ καὶ τὴν εἰκόνα αὐτοῦ,
great, If anyone the beast worships and the image of it,

καὶ λαμβάνει χάραγμα ἐπὶ τοῦ μετώπου αὐτοῦ, ἢ ἐπὶ τὴν
and receives a mark on the forehead of him, or on the

**10** χεῖρα αὐτοῦ, καὶ αὐτὸς πίεται ἐκ τοῦ οἴνου τοῦ θυμοῦ τοῦ
hand of him, even he shall drink of the wine of the anger of the

Θεοῦ, τοῦ κεκερασμένου ἀκράτου ἐν τῷ ποτηρίῳ τῆς ὀργῆς
God, having been mixed undiluted in the cup of the wrath

αὐτοῦ, καὶ βασανισθήσεται ἐν πυρὶ καὶ θείῳ ἐνώπιον τῶν
of Him, and will be tormented by fire and brimstone before the

**11** ἁγίων ἀγγέλων, καὶ ἐνώπιον τοῦ ἀρνίου· καὶ ὁ καπνὸς τοῦ
holy angels, and before the Lamb. And the smoke of the

βασανισμοῦ αὐτῶν ἀναβαίνει εἰς αἰῶνας αἰώνων· καὶ οὐκ
torment of them goes up to ages of ages; and not

ἔχουσιν ἀνάπαυσιν ἡμέρας καὶ νυκτὸς οἱ προσκυνοῦντες τὸ
have rest day and night those worshiping the

θηρίον καὶ τὴν εἰκόνα αὐτοῦ, καὶ εἴ τις λαμβάνει τὸ χάραγμα
beast and the image of it; even if anyone receives the mark

**12** τοῦ ὀνόματος αὐτοῦ. ὧδε ὑπομονὴ τῶν ἁγίων ἐστίν· ὧδε
of the name of it. Here (the) patience of the saints is. Here

out of the mouth of the beast, and out of the mouth of the false prophet, three unclean spirits (coming forth) as frogs. [14] For they are spirits of demons doing signs, which goes forth to the kings of the whole habitable world, to gather them together to the war of that great day of God Almighty. [15] Behold, I am coming as a thief, blessed (is) he watching and keeping his garments, that he does not walk naked and they see his shame. [16] And he gathered them in the place being called in Hebrew, Armageddon. [17] And the seventh angel poured out his bowl into the air, and a great voice came from the temple of Heaven, from the throne, saying, It has happened. [18] And there were voices and thunders and lightnings, and a great earthquake occurred, such as did not occur since man came into being on the earth, such an earthquake, so great. [19] And the great city came to be into three parts, and the cities of the nations fell. And Babylon the great was remembered before God, to give to her the cup of the wine of the anger of the wrath of Him. [20] And every island fled away, and mountains were not found. [21] And a great hail, as the size of a talent, comes down out of the heaven upon men; and men blasphemed God from the plague of the hail, because exceeding great is the plague of it.

καὶ ἐκ τοῦ στόματος τοῦ θηρίου, καὶ ἐκ τοῦ
and out of the mouth of the beast, and out of the

ψευδοπροφήτου, πνεύματα τρία ἀκάθαρτα ὅμ...
false prophet, spirits three unclean lik...

**14** χοις· εἰσὶ γὰρ πνεύματα δαιμόνων ποιοῦντα σ...
they are for spirits of demons doing sig...

ἐκπορεύεται ἐπὶ τοὺς βασιλεῖς τῆς γῆς καὶ τῆς οἰκου...
go forth to the kings of the earth, even of habitable...

ὅλης, συναγαγεῖν αὐτοὺς εἰς τὸν πόλεμον τῆς ἡμέρας ἐκεί...
whole, to assemble them to the war of day that

**15** τῆς μεγάλης τοῦ Θεοῦ τοῦ παντοκράτορος. (Ἰδού,
the great (day) of God Almighty. Behold,

ἔρχομαι ὡς κλέπτης. μακάριος ὁ γρηγορῶν καὶ τηρῶν τὰ
I am coming as a thief, blessed the (one) watching and keeping the

ἱμάτια αὐτοῦ, ἵνα μὴ γυμνὸς περιπατῇ, καὶ βλέπωσι τὴν
garments of him, that not naked he may walk, and they may see the

**16** ἀσχημοσύνην αὐτοῦ.) καὶ συνήγαγεν αὐτοὺς εἰς τὸν τόπον
shame of him. And he assembled them in the place

τὸν καλούμενον Ἑβραϊστὶ Ἁρμαγεδδών.
having been called in Hebrew, Armageddon.

**17** Καὶ ὁ ἕβδομος ἄγγελος ἐξέχεε τὴν φιάλην αὐτοῦ εἰς τὸν
And the seventh angel poured out the bowl of him into the

ἀέρα· καὶ ἐξῆλθε φωνὴ μεγάλη ἀπὸ τοῦ ναοῦ τοῦ οὐρανοῦ,
air, and came a voice great from the temple of Heaven,

**18** ἀπὸ τοῦ θρόνου, λέγουσα, Γέγονε. καὶ ἐγένοντο φωναὶ καὶ
from the throne, saying, It has happened. And occurred voices and

βρονταὶ καὶ ἀστραπαί, καὶ σεισμὸς ἐγένετο μέγας, οἷος οὐκ
thunders and lightnings, and an earthquake occurred great such as not

ἐγένετο ἀφ' οὗ οἱ ἄνθρωποι ἐγένοντο ἐπὶ τῆς γῆς, τηλι-
occurred from when men came into being on the earth, such a

**19** κοῦτος σεισμός, οὕτω μέγας. καὶ ἐγένετο ἡ πόλις ἡ μεγάλη
huge earthquake, so great. And came to be the city great

εἰς τρία μέρη, καὶ αἱ πόλεις τῶν ἐθνῶν ἔπεσον· καὶ Βαβυλὼν
into three parts, and the cities of the nations fell. And Babylon

ἡ μεγάλη ἐμνήσθη ἐνώπιον τοῦ Θεοῦ, δοῦναι αὐτῇ τὸ ποτή-
the great was remembered before God, to give to her the cup

**20** ριον τοῦ οἴνου τοῦ θυμοῦ τῆς ὀργῆς αὐτοῦ. καὶ πᾶσα νῆσος
of the wine of the anger of the wrath of Him. And every island

ἔφυγε, καὶ ὄρη οὐχ εὑρέθησαν. καὶ χάλαζα μεγάλη, ὡς ταλαν-
**21** fled, and mountains not were found. And a hail great, as talent-

τιαία, καταβαίνει ἐκ τοῦ οὐρανοῦ ἐπὶ τοὺς ἀνθρώπους· καὶ
sized, comes down out of the heaven on men, and

ἐβλασφήμησαν οἱ ἄνθρωποι τὸν Θεὸν ἐκ τῆς πληγῆς
blasphemed men God from the plague

τῆς χαλάζης· ὅτι μεγάλη ἐστὶν ἡ πληγὴ αὐτῆς σφόδρα.
of the hail, because great is the plague of it exceedingly.

## CHAPTER 17

[1] And one of the seven angels came, having the seven bowls, and spoke with me, saying to me, Come, I will show you the judgment of the great harlot sitting on many waters, [2] with whom committed fornication the kings

## CHAPTER 17

**1** Καὶ ἦλθεν εἷς ἐκ τῶν ἑπτὰ ἀγγέλων τῶν ἐχόντων τὰς
And came one of the seven angels having the

ἑπτὰ φιάλας, καὶ ἐλάλησε μετ' ἐμοῦ, λέγων μοι, Δεῦρο, δείξω
seven bowls, and spoke with me, saying to me, Come, I will show

σοι τὸ κρίμα τῆς πόρνης τῆς μεγάλης, τῆς καθημένης ἐπὶ τῶν
you the judgment of the harlot great sitting on the

**2** ὑδάτων τῶν πολλῶν· μεθ' ἧς ἐπόρνευσαν οἱ βασιλεῖς τῆς
waters many, with whom committed fornication the kings of the

---

saints; here (are) those keeping the commands of God and the faith of Jesus. [13] And I heard a voice out of Heaven saying to me, Write. Blessed (are) the dead, those dying in (the) Lord from now. Yes, says the Spirit, they shall rest from their labors; and their works follow with them. [14] And I saw, and behold, a white cloud, and on the cloud (One) sitting like (the) Son of man, having on His head a golden crown, and in His hand a sharp sickle. [15] And another angel went forth out of the temple, crying in a great voice to the (One) sitting on the cloud, Send Your sickle and reap, because Your hour to reap has come, because is dried the harvest of the earth. [16] And the (One) sitting on the cloud thrust His sickle upon the earth, and the earth was reaped. [17] And another angel went forth out of the temple in Heaven, he also having a sharp sickle. [18] And another angel went forth out of the altar, having authority over the fire. And he spoke with a great cry to the (one) having the sharp sickle, saying, Send your sharp sickle and gather the clusters of the vine of the earth, because the grapes of it are ripened. [19] And the angel thrust his sickle into the earth, and gathered the vine of the earth, and threw into the winepress of the great anger of God. [20] And the winepress was trodden outside the city, and blood went out of the winepress up to the bridles of the horses, from a thousand, six hundred stadia.

οἱ τηροῦντες τὰς ἐντολὰς τοῦ Θεοῦ καὶ τὴν πίστιν Ἰησοῦ.
those keeping the commandments of God and the faith of Jesus.

**13** Καὶ ἤκουσα φωνῆς ἐκ τοῦ οὐρανοῦ λεγούσης μοι, Γράψον,
And I heard a voice out of Heaven saying to me, Write,

Μακάριοι οἱ νεκροὶ οἱ ἐν Κυρίῳ ἀποθνήσκοντες ἀπ' ἄρτι·
Blessed (are) the dead, those in (the) Lord dying from now.

ναί, λέγει τὸ Πνεῦμα, ἵνα ἀναπαύσωνται ἐκ τῶν κόπων
Yes, says the Spirit, that they shall rest from the labors

αὐτῶν· τὰ δὲ ἔργα αὐτῶν ἀκολουθεῖ μετ' αὐτῶν.
of them; the and works of them follow with them.

**14** Καὶ εἶδον, καὶ ἰδού, νεφέλη λευκή, καὶ ἐπὶ τὴν νεφέλην
And I saw, and behold, a cloud white, and on the cloud

καθήμενος ὅμοιος υἱῷ ἀνθρώπου, ἔχων ἐπὶ τῆς κεφαλῆς
(One) sitting like (the) Son of man, having on the head

αὐτοῦ στέφανον χρυσοῦν, καὶ ἐν τῇ χειρὶ αὐτοῦ δρέπανον
of Him a crown of gold and in the hand of Him a sickle

ὀξύ. καὶ ἄλλος ἄγγελος ἐξῆλθεν ἐκ τοῦ ναοῦ, κράζων ἐν
sharp. And another angel went forth out of the temple, crying in

**15** μεγάλῃ φωνῇ τῷ καθημένῳ ἐπὶ τῆς νεφέλης, Πέμψον τὸ
a great voice to the (One) sitting on the cloud, Send the

δρέπανόν σου καὶ θέρισον· ὅτι ἦλθέ σοι ἡ ὥρα τοῦ θερίσαι,
sickle of You and reap because came You the hour to reap,

**16** ὅτι ἐξηράνθη ὁ θερισμὸς τῆς γῆς. καὶ ἔβαλεν ὁ καθήμενος
because was dried the harvest of the earth. And thrust the (One) sitting

ἐπὶ τὴν νεφέλην τὸ δρέπανον αὐτοῦ ἐπὶ τὴν γῆν. καὶ
on the cloud the sickle of Him on the earth, and

ἐθερίσθη ἡ γῆ.
was reaped the earth.

**17** Καὶ ἄλλος ἄγγελος ἐξῆλθεν ἐκ τοῦ ναοῦ τοῦ ἐν τῷ
And another angel went forth out of the temple in

**18** οὐρανῷ, ἔχων καὶ αὐτὸς δρέπανον ὀξύ. καὶ ἄλλος ἄγγελος
Heaven, having also he a sickle sharp. And another angel

ἐξῆλθεν ἐκ τοῦ θυσιαστηρίου, ἔχων ἐξουσίαν ἐπὶ τοῦ πυρός·
went forth out of the altar, having authority over the fire,

καὶ ἐφώνησε κραυγῇ μεγάλῃ τῷ ἔχοντι τὸ δρέπανον τὸ ὀξύ,
and he spoke with a cry great to the (one) having the sickle sharp,

λέγων, Πέμψον σου τὸ δρέπανον τὸ ὀξὺ καὶ τρύγησον τοὺς
saying, Send of you the sickle sharp and gather the

βότρυας τῆς ἀμπέλου τῆς γῆς, ὅτι ἤκμασαν αἱ σταφυλαὶ
clusters of the vine of the earth, because are ripened the grapes

**19** αὐτῆς. καὶ ἔβαλεν ὁ ἄγγελος τὸ δρέπανον αὐτοῦ εἰς τὴν γῆν,
of it. And thrust the angel the sickle of him into the earth,

καὶ ἐτρύγησε τὴν ἄμπελον τῆς γῆς, καὶ ἔβαλεν εἰς τὴν ληνὸν
and gathered the vine of the earth, and threw into the winepress

**20** τοῦ θυμοῦ τοῦ Θεοῦ τὴν μεγάλην. καὶ ἐπατήθη ἡ ληνὸς
of the anger of God great. And was trodden the winepress

ἔξω τῆς πόλεως, καὶ ἐξῆλθεν αἷμα ἐκ τῆς ληνοῦ ἄχρι τῶν
outside the city, blood out of the winepress until the

χαλινῶν τῶν ἵππων, ἀπὸ σταδίων χιλίων ἑξακοσίων.
bridles of the horses, a thousand six hundred.

## CHAPTER 15

[1] And I saw another sign in Heaven, great and wonderful seven angels having the last seven plagues, because in them was com-

## CHAPTER 15

**1** Καὶ εἶδον ἄλλο σημεῖον ἐν τῷ οὐρανῷ μέγα καὶ θαυμα-
And I saw another sign in Heaven, great and marvelous

στόν, ἀγγέλους ἑπτὰ ἔχοντας πληγὰς ἑπτὰ τὰς ἐσχάτας,
angels seven having plagues seven the last,

pleted the anger of God. [2] And I saw as a glassy having been mixed with fire, and those overcoming the beast, and its image, and its mark, of the number of its name, standing on the glassy sea, having harps of God; [3] and they sing the song of Moses the slave of God, and the song of the Lamb, saying, Great and wonderful (are) Your works, Lord God Almighty, righteous and true (are) Your ways, the King of the nations. [4] Who will not fear You, Lord, and glorify Your name? For (You) only are holy; for all the nations will come and will worship before You, because Your righteousnesses were revealed. [5] And after these things I saw, and behold, the temple of the tabernacle of the testimony in Heaven was opened; [6] and the seven angels having the seven plagues came forth out of the temple, having been clothed (in) clean and bright linen, and having been girded around the breasts (with) golden bands. [7] And one of the four living creatures gave to the seven angels seven golden bowls filled with the anger of the living God, forever (and) ever. [8] And the temple was filled with (the) glory of God, and with His power. And no one was able to enter into the temple, until should be completed the seven plagues of the seven angels.

ὅτι ἐν αὐταῖς ἐτελέσθη ὁ θυμὸς τοῦ Θεοῦ.
**because in them was completed the anger of God.**

2 Καὶ εἶδον ὡς θάλασσαν ὑαλίνην μεμιγμένην πυρί, καὶ
**And I saw as a sea glassy having been mixed with fire, and**
τοὺς νικῶντας ἐκ τοῦ θηρίου καὶ ἐκ τῆς εἰκόνος αὐτοῦ καὶ
**those overcoming of the beast and of the image of it, and**
ἐκ τοῦ χαράγματος αὐτοῦ, ἐκ τοῦ ἀριθμοῦ τοῦ ὀνόματος
**of the mark of it, of the number of the name**
αὐτοῦ, ἑστῶτας ἐπὶ τὴν θάλασσαν τὴν ὑαλίνην, ἔχοντας
**of it, standing on the sea glassy, having**

3 κιθάρας τοῦ Θεοῦ. καὶ ᾄδουσι τὴν ᾠδὴν Μωσέως τοῦ δούλου
**harps of God. And they sing the song of Moses the slave**
τοῦ Θεοῦ, καὶ τὴν ᾠδὴν τοῦ ἀρνίου, λέγοντες, Μεγάλα
**of God, and the song of the Lamb, saying, Great**
καὶ θαυμαστὰ τὰ ἔργα σου, Κύριε ὁ Θεὸς ὁ παντοκράτωρ·
**and marvelous the works of You, Lord God Almighty,**

4 δίκαιαι καὶ ἀληθιναὶ αἱ ὁδοί σου, ὁ βασιλεὺς τῶν ἁγίων. τίς
**righteous and true the ways of You, the King of the saints Who**
οὐ μὴ φοβηθῇ σε, Κύριε, καὶ δοξάσῃ τὸ ὄνομά σου; ὅτι
**in no way fear You, Lord, and glorify the name of You? For**
μόνος ὅσιος· ὅτι πάντα τὰ ἔθνη ἥξουσι καὶ προσκυνή-
**(You) only (are) holy, for all the nations will come and will worship**
σουσιν ἐνώπιόν σου, ὅτι τὰ δικαιώματά σου ἐφανερώθησαν.
**before You, because the righteousnesses of You were revealed.**

5 Καὶ μετὰ ταῦτα εἶδον, καὶ ἰδού, ἠνοίγη ὁ ναὸς τῆς σκηνῆς
**And after these things I saw, and behold, was opened the temple of the tent**

6 τοῦ μαρτυρίου ἐν τῷ οὐρανῷ· καὶ ἐξῆλθον οἱ ἑπτὰ ἄγγελοι
**of the testimony in Heaven; and came forth the seven angels**
ἔχοντες τὰς ἑπτὰ πληγὰς ἐκ τοῦ ναοῦ, ἐνδεδυμένοι λίνον
**having the seven plagues out of the temple, being clothed (with) linen**
καθαρὸν καὶ λαμπρόν, καὶ περιεζωσμένοι περὶ τὰ στήθη
**clean and bright, and having been girded around the breasts**

7 ζώνας χρυσᾶς. καὶ ἓν ἐκ τῶν τεσσάρων ζώων ἔδωκε τοῖς
**(with) girdles of gold And one of the four living creatures gave to the**
ἑπτὰ ἀγγέλοις ἑπτὰ φιάλας χρυσᾶς γεμούσας τοῦ θυμοῦ
**seven angels seven bowls of gold filled of the anger**

8 τοῦ Θεοῦ τοῦ ζῶντος εἰς τοὺς αἰῶνας τῶν αἰώνων. καὶ
**of God the living, to the ages of the ages. And**
ἐγεμίσθη ὁ ναὸς καπνοῦ ἐκ τῆς δόξης τοῦ Θεοῦ, καὶ ἐκ τῆς
**was filled the temple of smoke of the glory of God, and of the**
δυνάμεως αὐτοῦ· καὶ οὐδεὶς ἠδύνατο εἰσελθεῖν εἰς τὸν ναόν,
**power of Him. And no one could enter into the temple,**
ἄχρι τελεσθῶσιν αἱ ἑπτὰ πληγαὶ τῶν ἑπτὰ ἀγγέλων.
**until should be finished the seven plagues of the seven angels.**

## CHAPTER 16

CHAPTER 16

[1] And I heard a great voice out of the temple, saying to the seven angels, Go, and pour out the bowls of the anger of God onto the earth. [2] And the first went away, and poured out his bowl onto the earth. And a bad and evil sore came upon

1 Καὶ ἤκουσα φωνῆς μεγάλης ἐκ τοῦ ναοῦ, λεγούσης τοῖς
**And I heard a voice great out of the temple, saying to the**
ἑπτὰ ἀγγέλοις, Ὑπάγετε, καὶ ἐκχέατε τὰς φιαλας τοῦ θυμοῦ
**seven angels, Go, and pour out the bowls of the anger**
τοῦ Θεοῦ εἰς τὴν γῆν.
**of God onto the earth.**

2 Καὶ ἀπῆλθεν ὁ πρῶτος, καὶ ἐξέχεε τὴν φιάλην αὐτοῦ ἐπὶ
**And went away the first, and poured out the bowl of him onto**
τὴν γῆν· καὶ ἐγένετο ἕλκος κακὸν καὶ πονηρὸν εἰς τοὺς
**the earth; and it became a sore bad and evil into the**

---

...en, those having the ...of the beast, and those ...hiping its image. [3] And ... second angel poured out ...bowl onto the sea. And it ...came blood, as of a dead ...e, and every soul of life ...died in the sea. [4] And the third angel poured out his bowl onto the rivers, and onto the fountains of the waters; and it became blood. [5] And I heard the angel of the waters saying, Righteous is (the) Lord, He being, and who was, and who will be, because these things You judge. [6] Because they poured out (the) blood of saints and of prophets; and You gave them blood to drink, for they are deserving. [7] And I heard another in the altar saying, Yes Lord God Almighty, Your judgments (are) true and righteous. [8] And the fourth angel poured out his bowl onto the sun; and it was given to him to burn men with fire. [9] And men were burned (with) great heat, and they blasphemed the name of God, He having authority over these plagues; and they did not repent to give Him glory. [10] And the fifth angel poured out his bowl onto the throne of the beast; and its kingdom became darkened; and they gnawed their tongues from the pain. [11] And they blasphemed the God of Heaven from their pains and from their sores. And they did not repent of their works.

[12] And the sixth angel poured out his bowl onto the great river Euphrates, and its water was dried up, that might be prepared the way of the kings from (the) rising of (the) sun. [13] And I saw out of the mouth of the dragon, and

ἀνθρώπους τοὺς ἔχοντας τὸ χάραγμα τοῦ θηρίου, κα...
**men having the mark of the beast, and**
τῇ εἰκόνι αὐτοῦ προσκυνοῦντας.
**the image of it worshiping.**

3 Καὶ ὁ δεύτερος ἄγγελος ἐξέχεε τὴν φιάλην αὐτοῦ εἰς...
**And the second angel poured out the bowl of him onto...**
θάλασσαν· καὶ ἐγένετο αἷμα ὡς νεκροῦ, καὶ πᾶσα ψ...
**sea; and it became blood, as of a dead one, and every so...**
ζῶσα ἀπέθανεν ἐν τῇ θαλάσσῃ.
**living died in the sea.**

4 Καὶ ὁ τρίτος ἄγγελος ἐξέχεε τὴν φιάλην αὐτοῦ εἰς τ...
**And the third angel poured out the bowl of him onto...**
ποταμοὺς καὶ εἰς τὰς πηγὰς τῶν ὑδάτων· καὶ ἐγένετο αἷ...
**rivers and onto the fountains of the waters; and it became bloo...**

5 καὶ ἤκουσα τοῦ ἀγγέλου τῶν ὑδάτων λέγοντος, Δίκαι...
**And I heard the angel of the waters saying, Righteo...**
Κύριε, εἰ, ὁ ὢν καὶ ὁ ἦν καὶ ὁ ἐσόμενος, ὅτι ταῦτα ἔκρινα...
**Lord You are: He being, who was and who will be, because these You judge...**

6 ὅτι αἷμα ἁγίων καὶ προφητῶν ἐξέχεαν, καὶ αἷμα αὐτο...
**since (the) blood of saints and of prophets they poured out; and blood to them...**

7 ἔδωκας πιεῖν· ἄξιοι γάρ εἰσι. καὶ ἤκουσα ἄλλου ἐκ το...
**You gave to drink; deserving for they are. And I heard another out of the...**
θυσιαστηρίου λέγοντος, Ναί, Κύριε ὁ Θεὸς ὁ παντοκράτωρ,
**altar saying, Yes, Lord God Almighty,**
ἀληθιναὶ καὶ δίκαιαι αἱ κρίσεις σου.
**true and righteous the judgments of You.**

8 Καὶ ὁ τέταρτος ἄγγελος ἐξέχεε τὴν φιάλην αὐτοῦ ἐπὶ τὸν
**And the fourth angel poured out the bowl of him onto the**
ἥλιον· καὶ ἐδόθη αὐτῷ καυματίσαι τοὺς ἀνθρώπους ἐν πυρί.
**sun; and it was given to it to burn the men with fire.**

9 καὶ ἐκαυματίσθησαν οἱ ἄνθρωποι καῦμα μέγα, καὶ ἐβλασφή-
**And were burned men (with) heat great, and they blas-**
μησαν τὸ ὄνομα τοῦ Θεοῦ τοῦ ἔχοντος ἐξουσίαν ἐπὶ τὰς
**phemed the name of God, the (One) having authority over**
πληγὰς ταύτας, καὶ οὐ μετενόησαν δοῦναι αὐτῷ δόξαν.
**plagues these; and not they repented to give Him glory.**

10 Καὶ ὁ πέμπτος ἄγγελος ἐξέχεε τὴν φιάλην αὐτοῦ ἐπὶ τὸν
**And the fifth angel poured out the bowl of him onto the**
θρόνον τοῦ θηρίου· καὶ ἐγένετο ἡ βασιλεία αὐτοῦ ἐσκοτω-
**throne of the beast; and became the kingdom of it darkened,**
μένη· καὶ ἐμασσῶντο τὰς γλώσσας αὐτῶν ἐκ τοῦ πόνου,
**and they gnawed the tongues of them from the pain;**

11 καὶ ἐβλασφήμησαν τὸν Θεὸν τοῦ οὐρανοῦ ἐκ τῶν πόνων
**and they blasphemed the God of Heaven from the pains**
αὐτῶν καὶ ἐκ τῶν ἑλκῶν αὐτῶν, καὶ οὐ μετενόησαν ἐκ τῶν
**of them and from the sores of them; and not they repented of the**
ἔργων αὐτῶν.
**works of them.**

12 Καὶ ὁ ἕκτος ἄγγελος ἐξέχεε τὴν φιάλην αὐτοῦ ἐπὶ τὸν
**And the sixth angel poured out the bowl of him onto the**
ποταμὸν τὸν μέγαν τὸν Εὐφράτην· καὶ ἐξηράνθη τὸ ὕδωρ
**river great Euphrates, and was dried up the water**
αὐτοῦ, ἵνα ἑτοιμασθῇ ἡ ὁδὸς τῶν βασιλέων τῶν ἀπὸ
**of it, that might be prepared the way of the kings from**

13 ἀνατολῶν ἡλίου. καὶ εἶδον ἐκ τοῦ στόματος τοῦ δράκοντος,
**(the) rising of (the) sun. And I saw out of the mouth of the dragon,**

of the earth, and became drunk from the wine of the fornication of her, those dwelling on the earth. [3] And he carried me away into a desert in Spirit. And I saw a woman sitting on a scarlet beast, filled (with) names of blasphemy, having seven heads and ten horns. [4] And the woman was clothed (in) purple and scarlet, and being gilded with gold and precious stone and pearls, having a golden cup in her hand, filled (with) abominations and unclean things of her fornication. [5] And on her forehead a name having been written: MYSTERY, BABYLON THE GREAT, The Mother of the Harlots and of the Abominations of the Earth. [6] And I saw the woman being drunk from the blood of the saints, and from the blood of the witnesses of Jesus. And I wondered, seeing her (with) a great wonder. [7] And the angel said to me, Why did you wonder? I will tell you the mystery of the woman, and of the beast carrying her, he having the seven heads and the ten horns. [8] The beast which you saw was, and not is, and is about to come up out of the abyss, and goes to perdition. And those dwelling on the earth will wonder, (those) of whom the names has not been written on the Book of Life from (the) foundation of (the) world, seeing the beast, that it was, and not is, and now is. [9] Here is the mind having wisdom. The seven heads are seven mountains, where the woman sits on them. [10] And (the) kings are seven: the five fell, and the one is, and the other not yet has come; and when he comes, he must remain a little. [11] And the beast which was, and not is, even he is (the) eighth, and is of the seven, and to perdition goes. [12] And the ten horns which you saw are ten kings, who not yet have received a kingdom, but will receive au-

---

γῆς, καὶ ἐμεθύσθησαν ἐκ τοῦ οἴνου τῆς πορνείας αὐτῆς οἱ
earth, and became drunk from the wine of the fornication of her, those

**3** κατοικοῦντες τὴν γῆν. καὶ ἀπήνεγκέ με εἰς ἔρημον ἐν
inhabiting the earth. And he carried away me into a desert by

Πνεύματι· καὶ εἶδον γυναῖκα καθημένην ἐπὶ θηρίον κόκκινον,
(the) Spirit. And I saw a woman ,sitting on beast scarlet,

γέμον ὀνομάτων βλασφημίας, ἔχον κεφαλὰς ἑπτὰ καὶ κέρατα
full of names of blasphemy, having heads seven and horns

**4** δέκα. καὶ ἡ γυνὴ ἦν περιβεβλημένη πορφύρα καὶ κοκκίνῳ,
ten. And the woman was clothed (in) purple and scarlet,

καὶ κεχρυσωμένη χρυσῷ καὶ λίθῳ τιμίῳ καὶ μαργαρίταις,
and being gilded with gold and stone precious and pearls,

ἔχουσα χρυσοῦν ποτήριον ἐν τῇ χειρὶ αὐτῆς, γέμον βδε-
having a golden cup in the hand of her, full of

**5** λυγμάτων καὶ ἀκαθάρτητος πορνείας αὐτῆς, καὶ ἐπὶ τὸ
abominations and uncleanness of (the) fornication of her. And on the

μέτωπον αὐτῆς ὄνομα γεγραμμένον, Μυστήριον, Βαβυλὼν
forehead of her a name having been written: MYSTERY, BABYLON

ἡ μεγάλη, ἡ μήτηρ τῶν πορνῶν καὶ τῶν βδελυγμάτων τῆς
THE GREAT, The Mother of the Harlots and of the Abominations of the

**6** γῆς. καὶ εἶδον τὴν γυναῖκα μεθύουσαν ἐκ τοῦ αἵματος τῶν
Earth. And I saw the woman being drunk from the blood of the

ἁγίων, καὶ ἐκ τοῦ αἵματος τῶν μαρτύρων Ἰησοῦ. καὶ
saints, and from the blood of the witnesses of Jesus. And

**7** ἐθαύμασα, ἰδὼν αὐτήν, θαῦμα μέγα. καὶ εἶπέ μοι ὁ
I marveled seeing her (with) a marvel great. And said to me the

ἄγγελος, Διατί ἐθαύμασας; ἐγώ σοι ἐρῶ τὸ μυστήριον τῆς
angel, Why did you wonder? I you will tell the mystery of the

γυναικός, καὶ τοῦ θηρίου τοῦ βαστάζοντος αὐτήν, τοῦ
woman, and of the beast supporting her, the (one)

**8** ἔχοντος τὰς ἑπτὰ κεφαλὰς καὶ τὰ δέκα κέρατα. τὸ θηρίον, ὃ
having the seven heads and the ten horns. The beast which

εἶδες, ἦν, καὶ οὐκ ἔστι, καὶ μέλλει ἀναβαίνειν ἐκ τῆς ἀβύσσου,
you saw was, and not is, and is about to come up out of the abyss,

καὶ εἰς ἀπώλειαν ὑπάγειν. καὶ θαυμάσονται οἱ κατοικοῦντες
and to perdition goes; and will marvel those dwelling

ἐπὶ τῆς γῆς, ὧν οὐ γέγραπται τὰ ὀνόματα ἐπὶ τὸ βιβλίον
on the earth, of whom not has been written the names on the Scroll

τῆς ζωῆς ἀπὸ καταβολῆς κόσμου, βλέποντες τὸ θηρίον ὅ, τι
of Life from (the) foundation of (the) world, seeing the beast, that a thing

**9** ἦν, καὶ οὐκ ἔστι, καίπερ ἔστιν. ὧδε ὁ νοῦς ὁ ἔχων σοφίαν. αἱ
it was, and not is, although it is. Here (is) the mind having wisdom. The

ἑπτὰ κεφαλαὶ ὄρη εἰσὶν ἑπτά, ὅπου ἡ γυνὴ κάθηται ἐπ'
seven heads mountains are seven, where the woman sits on

**10** αὐτῶν. καὶ βασιλεῖς ἑπτά εἰσιν· οἱ πέντε ἔπεσαν, καὶ ὁ εἷς
them; and kings seven are: the five fell, and the one

ἔστιν, ὁ ἄλλος οὔπω ἦλθε· καί, ὅταν ἔλθῃ, ὀλίγον αὐτὸν δεῖ
is, the other not yet came; and when he comes, a little he must

**11** μεῖναι. καὶ τὸ θηρίον ὃ ἦν, καὶ οὐκ ἔστι, καὶ αὐτὸς ὄγδοός
remain. And the beast which was, and not is, even he eighth

**12** ἔστι, καὶ ἐκ τῶν ἑπτά ἐστι, καὶ εἰς ἀπώλειαν ὑπάγει. καὶ τὰ
is, and of the seven it is, and to perdition goes. And the

δέκα κέρατα, ἃ εἶδες, δέκα βασιλεῖς εἰσιν, οἵτινες βασιλείαν
ten horns which you saw, ten kings are, who a kingdom

οὔπω ἔλαβον, ἀλλ' ἐξουσίαν ὡς βασιλεῖς μίαν ὥραν λαμβά-
not yet received, but authority as kings one hour receive

thority as kings one hour with the beast. [13] These have one mind, and their power and authority they shall give up to the beast. [14] These with the Lamb will make war, and the Lamb will overcome them, because He is Lord of lords and King of kings; and those with Him (are the) called and elect and faithful ones. [15] And he says to me, The waters which you saw, where the harlot sits, are peoples and crowds, and nations and tongues. [16] And the ten horns which you saw on the beast, these will hate the harlot, and will make her desolated and naked; and will eat her flesh, and will consume her with fire. [17] For God gave into their hearts to do His mind, and to act (in) one mind, and to give their kingdom to the beast, until the words of God shall be fulfilled. [18] And the woman whom you saw is the great city, having a kingdom over the kings of the earth.

**13** νουσι μετὰ τοῦ θηρίου. οὗτοι μίαν γνώμην ἔχουσι, καὶ τὴν
with the beast. These one mind have, and the
δύναμιν καὶ τὴν ἐξουσίαν ἑαυτῶν τῷ θηρίῳ διαδιδώσουσιν.
power and the authority of themselves to the beast they shall give up.

**14** οὗτοι μετὰ τοῦ ἀρνίου πολεμήσουσι, καὶ τὸ ἀρνίον νικήσει
These with the Lamb will make war, and the Lamb will overcome
αὐτούς, ὅτι Κύριος κυρίων ἐστὶ καὶ Βασιλεὺς βασιλέων, καὶ
them, because Lord of lords He is and King of kings, and

**15** οἱ μετ' αὐτοῦ, κλητοὶ καὶ ἐκλεκτοὶ καὶ πιστοί. καὶ λέγει μοι,
those with Him (the) called and elect and faithful ones. And he says to me,
Τὰ ὕδατα, ἃ εἶδες, οὗ ἡ πόρνη κάθηται, λαοὶ καὶ ὄχλοι εἰσί,
The waters which you saw, where the harlot sits, peoples and crowds are,

**16** καὶ ἔθνη καὶ γλῶσσαι. καὶ τὰ δέκα κέρατα, ἃ εἶδες, ἐπὶ τὸ
even nations and tongues, And the ten horns which you saw on the
θηρίον, οὗτοι μισήσουσι τὴν πόρνην, καὶ ἠρημωμένην
beast, these will hate the harlot, and desolated
ποιήσουσιν αὐτὴν καὶ γυμνήν, καὶ τὰς σάρκας αὐτῆς
will make her and naked, and the flesh of her

**17** φάγονται, καὶ αὐτὴν κατακαύσουσιν ἐν πυρί. ὁ γὰρ Θεὸς
they will eat, and her will burn down with fire. For God
ἔδωκεν εἰς τὰς καρδίας αὐτῶν ποιῆσαι τὴν γνώμην αὐτοῦ,
gave into the hearts of them to do the mind of Him,
καὶ ποιῆσαι μίαν γνώμην, καὶ δοῦναι τὴν βασιλείαν αὐτῶν
and to do one mind, and to give the kingdom of them

**18** τῷ θηρίῳ, ἄχρι τελεσθῇ τὰ ῥήματα τοῦ Θεοῦ. καὶ ἡ γυνὴ
to the beast, until shall be completed the words of God. And the woman
ἣν εἶδες, ἐστὶν ἡ πόλις ἡ μεγάλη, ἡ ἔχουσα βασιλείαν ἐπὶ
whom you saw is the city great, having a kingdom over
τῶν βασιλέων τῆς γῆς.
the kings of the earth.

## CHAPTER 18

### CHAPTER 18

[1] And after these things I saw another angel coming down out of Heaven, having great authority, and the earth was lighted up from his glory. [2] And he cried in a strong, a great voice, saying, Babylon the great has fallen, has fallen, and has become a dwelling-place of demons, and a prison of every unclean spirit, and a prison of every unclean and hated bird; [3] because of the wine of the anger of her fornication all the nations have drunk, and the kings of the earth committed fornication with her; and the merchants of the earth became rich from the power of her luxury. [4] And I heard another voice out of Heaven saying, Come out of her, My people, that you may not share in her sins, and that you

**1** Καὶ μετὰ ταῦτα εἶδον ἄλλον ἄγγελον καταβαίνοντα ἐκ
And after these things I saw another angel coming down out of
τοῦ οὐρανοῦ, ἔχοντα ἐξουσίαν μεγάλην· καὶ ἡ γῆ ἐφωτίσθη
Heaven, having authority great, and the earth was lighted up

**2** ἐκ τῆς δόξης αὐτοῦ. καὶ ἔκραξεν ἐν ἰσχύϊ, φωνῇ μεγάλῃ,
from the glory of him. And he cried in a strong, with a voice great,
λέγων, Ἔπεσεν ἔπεσε Βαβυλὼν ἡ μεγάλη, καὶ ἐγένετο
saying, Fell, fell Babylon the great, and has become
κατοικητήριον δαιμόνων, καὶ φυλακὴ παντὸς πνεύματος
a dwelling-place of demons, and a prison of every spirit
ἀκαθάρτου, καὶ φυλακὴ παντὸς ὀρνέου ἀκαθάρτου καὶ
unclean, and a prison of every bird unclean and

**3** μεμισημένου. ὅτι ἐκ τοῦ οἴνου τοῦ θυμοῦ τῆς πορνείας αὐτῆς
being hated, because of the wine of the anger of the fornication of her
πέπωκε πάντα τὰ ἔθνη, καὶ οἱ βασιλεῖς τῆς γῆς μετ' αὐτῆς
have drunk all the nations, and the kings of the earth with her
ἐπόρνευσαν, καὶ οἱ ἔμποροι τῆς γῆς ἐκ τῆς δυνάμεως τοῦ
committed fornication, and the merchants of the earth from the power of the
στρήνους αὐτῆς ἐπλούτησαν.
luxury of her became rich.

**4** Καὶ ἤκουσα ἄλλην φωνὴν ἐκ τοῦ οὐρανοῦ, λέγουσαν,
And I heard another voice out of Heaven, saying,
Ἐξέλθετε ἐξ αὐτῆς ὁ λαός μου, ἵνα μὴ συγκοινωνήσητε ταῖς
Come out of her, people of Me, that not you share in the

not receive of her plagues;
[5] because her sins joined
together up to Heaven, and
God remembered her wicked
deeds. [6] Give back to her
as also she gave back to you,
and double to her double,
according to her works; in
the cup which she mixed,
mix to her double. [7] By
what things she glorified herself, and luxuriated, by so
much give back to her torment and sorrow. Because
she says in her heart, I sit
(as) a queen, and I am not a
widow, and I do not see
sorrow at all. [8] Because of
this, in one day shall come
her plagues: death and sorrow
and famine, and she will be
consumed with fire. Because
(the) Lord God judging her
(is) strong. [9] And the kings
of the earth will weep for
her, and will wail over her,
those having fornicated with
her, and having luxuriated,
when they see the smoke of
her burning; [10] standing
from afar, because of the fear
of her torment, saying, Woe!
Woe, the great city, Babylon
the strong city, for in one
hour your judgment came.
[11] And the merchants of
the earth weep and sorrow
over her, because no one buys
their cargo any more, [12]
cargo of gold, and silver, and
of precious stone, and pearls,
and of fine linen, and of
purple, and of silk, and of
scarlet, and all thyine wood,
and every ivory vessel, and
every vessel of very precious
wood, and of bronze, and of
iron, and of marble, [13] and
cinnamon, and incenses, and
ointment, and frankincense,
and wine, and oil, and fine
meal, and wheat, and beasts,
and sheep, and horses, and of
carriages, and of bodies, and
souls of men. [14] And the
ripe fruits of the lust of your
soul went away from you,
and all the fat things, and the
bright things perished from
you, and you will not at all

ἁμαρτίαις αὐτῆς, καὶ ἵνα μὴ λάβητε ἐκ τῶν πληγῶν αὐτῆς·
sins       of her,   and that not you receive of the  plagues  of her;

5  ὅτι ἐκολλήθησαν αὐτῆς αἱ ἁμαρτίαι ἄχρι τοῦ οὐρανοῦ, καὶ
   because joined together of her the sins    up to   Heaven,   and

6  ἐμνημόνευσεν ὁ Θεὸς τὰ ἀδικήματα αὐτῆς. ἀπόδοτε αὐτῇ
   remembered   God   the unjust deeds of her. Return to her

   ὡς καὶ αὐτὴ ἀπέδωκεν ὑμῖν, καὶ διπλώσατε αὐτῇ διπλᾶ
   as also she   returned to you, and double    to her double

   κατὰ τὰ ἔργα αὐτῆς· ἐν τῷ ποτηρίῳ ᾧ ἐκέρασε κεράσατε
   according to the works of her; in the cup in which she mixed, mix

7  αὐτῇ διπλοῦν. ὅσα ἐδόξασεν ἑαυτὴν καὶ ἐστρηνίασε,
   to her double  By what things she glorified herself and luxuriated,

   τοσοῦτον δότε αὐτῇ βασανισμὸν καὶ πένθος· ὅτι ἐν τῇ
   by so much give to her  torment    and mourning. Because in the

   καρδίᾳ αὐτῆς λέγει, Κάθημαι βασίλισσα, καὶ χήρα οὐκ εἰμί,
   heart  of her she says, I sit   a queen,   and a widow not I am,

8  καὶ πένθος οὐ μὴ ἴδω. διὰ τοῦτο ἐν μιᾷ ἡμέρᾳ ἥξουσιν αἱ
   and mourning not at all I see. Therefore in one day  shall come the

   πληγαὶ αὐτῆς, θάνατος καὶ πένθος καὶ λιμός, καὶ ἐν πυρὶ
   plagues of her,  death   and mourning and famine,  and with fire

   κατακαυθήσεται, ὅτι ἰσχυρὸς Κύριος ὁ Θεὸς ὁ κρίνων αὐτήν.
   she will be consumed, because strong (is the) Lord God judging her.

9  καὶ κλαύσονται αὐτήν, καὶ κόψονται ἐπ᾽ αὐτῇ οἱ βασιλεῖς τῆς
   And will weep for her,  and  will wail over  her  the kings of the

   γῆς οἱ μετ᾽ αὐτῆς πορνεύσαντες καὶ στρηνιάσαντες, ὅταν
   earth, those with her having fornicated and having luxuriated, when

10  βλέπωσι τὸν καπνὸν τῆς πυρώσεως αὐτῆς, ἀπὸ μακρόθεν
   they see the smoke of the burning   of her,  from  afar

   ἑστηκότες διὰ τὸν φόβον τοῦ βασανισμοῦ αὐτῆς, λέγοντες,
   standing because of the fear of the  torment  of her, saying,

   Οὐαί, οὐαί, ἡ πόλις ἡ μεγάλη Βαβυλών, ἡ πόλις ἡ ἰσχυρά,
   Woe!  Woe, to the city great,  Babylon,  the city   strong,

11  ὅτι ἐν μιᾷ ὥρᾳ ἦλθεν ἡ κρίσις σου. καὶ οἱ ἔμποροι τῆς γῆς
   for in one hour came the judgment of you. And the merchants of the earth

   κλαίουσι καὶ πενθοῦσιν ἐπ᾽ αὐτῇ, ὅτι τὸν γόμον αὐτῶν
   weep   and  mourn over her, because the cargo  of them

12  οὐδεὶς ἀγοράζει οὐκέτι· γόμον χρυσοῦ, καὶ ἀργύρου, καὶ
   no one buys  no more,  cargo of gold,  and of silver,  and

   λίθου τιμίου, καὶ μαργαρίτου, καὶ βύσσου, καὶ πορφύρας,
   of stone precious, and of pearls,  and of fine linen, and of purple,

   καὶ σηρικοῦ, καὶ κοκκίνου· καὶ πᾶν ξύλον θύϊνον, καὶ πᾶν
   and of silk,  and of scarlet,  and all wood sandarac, and every

   σκεῦος ἐλεφάντινον, καὶ πᾶν σκεῦος ἐκ ξύλου τιμιωτάτου,
   vessel  ivory,      and every vessel of wood very precious,

13  καὶ χαλκοῦ, καὶ σιδήρου, καὶ μαρμάρου· καὶ κινάμωμον, καὶ
   and of bronze, and of iron,  and of marble,  and cinnamon,  and

   θυμιάματα, καὶ μύρον, καὶ λίβανον, καὶ οἶνον, καὶ ἔλαιον,
   incenses,   and ointment, and frankincense, and wine, and oil,

   καὶ σεμίδαλιν, καὶ σῖτον, καὶ κτήνη, καὶ πρόβατα· καὶ ἵππων,
   and fine meal, and wheat, and beasts, and sheep,   and horses,

14  καὶ ῥεδῶν, καὶ σωμάτων· καὶ ψυχὰς ἀνθρώπων. καὶ ἡ
   and chariots, and of bodies,  and souls   of men.   And the

   ὀπώρα τῆς ἐπιθυμίας τῆς ψυχῆς σου ἀπῆλθεν ἀπὸ σοῦ, καὶ
   ripe fruits of the lust of the soul of you went away from you, and

   πάντα τὰ λιπαρὰ καὶ τὰ λαμπρὰ ἀπῆλθεν ἀπὸ σοῦ, καὶ
   all  the fat things, and the bright things went away from you, and

find them any more. [15] The merchants of these, those having been rich from her, from afar will stand because of the fear of her torment, weeping and sorrowing; [16] and saying, Woe! Woe, the great city, having been clothed (with) linen and purple and scarlet, and having been gilded with gold and precious stone and pearls. [17] For in one hour such great wealth was desolated. And every ship-pilot, and all company on the ships, and the sailors, and as many as work by sea, stood from afar, [18] and cried out, seeing the smoke of the burning of her, saying, What (city is) like the great city! [19] And they threw dust on their heads, and cried out weeping and sorrowing, saying, Woe! Woe (to) the great city, by which were rich all those having ships in the sea, from her costliness, because in one hour she was ruined. [20] Rejoice over her, Heaven and the holy apostles and the prophets, because God judged your judgment upon her. [21] And one strong angel lifted a stone like a great millstone, and threw (it) into the sea, saying, Thus Babylon the great city will with violence be thrown down, and not at all will be found still. [22] And the sound of harpers, and of musicians, and flutists, and of trumpeters, not at all will be heard in you longer, and every craftsman of every craft not at all will be found in you longer; and the sound of a mill not at all will be heard in you longer; [23] and the light of a lamp not at all (will) shine in you longer; and the voice of the bridegroom and of the bride not at all will be heard in you longer. For your merchants were the great ones of the earth, for by your sorcery all nations were misled; [24] and in her was found (the) blood of prophets and of saints, and of all those having been slain on the earth.

---

**15** οὐκέτι οὐ μὴ εὑρήσῃς αὐτά. οἱ ἔμποροι τούτων, οἱ πλουτή-
no more, not at all, they will find them. The merchants of these, those being

σαντες ἀπ᾽ αὐτῆς, ἀπὸ μακρόθεν στήσονται διὰ τὸν φόβον
enriched from her, from afar will stand because of the fear

**16** τοῦ βασανισμοῦ αὐτῆς, κλαίοντες καὶ πενθοῦντες, καὶ
of the torment of her, weeping and mourning and

λέγοντες, Οὐαί, οὐαί, ἡ πόλις ἡ μεγάλη, ἡ περιβεβλημένη
saying, Woe, woe, the city great, having been clothed in

βύσσινον καὶ πορφυροῦν καὶ κόκκινον, καὶ κεχρυσωμένη ἐν
linen and purple and scarlet, and having been gilded with

**17** χρυσῷ καὶ λίθῳ τιμίῳ καὶ μαργαρίταις· ὅτι μιᾷ ὥρᾳ ἠρη-
gold and stone precious, and pearls; because in one hour was

μώθη ὁ τοσοῦτος πλοῦτος. καὶ πᾶς κυβερνήτης, καὶ πᾶς ἐπὶ
desolated such great wealth. And every helmsman and all on

τῶν πλοίων ὁ ὅμιλος, καὶ ναῦται, καὶ ὅσοι τὴν θάλασσαν
the ships the company, and sailors, and as many as the sea

**18** ἐργάζονται, ἀπὸ μακρόθεν ἔστησαν, καὶ ἔκραζον, ὁρῶντες
work, from afar stood, and cried out seeing

τὸν καπνὸν τῆς πυρώσεως αὐτῆς, λέγοντες, Τίς ὁμοία τῇ
the smoke of the burning of her, saying, What (is) like the

**19** πόλει τῇ μεγάλῃ; καὶ ἔβαλον χοῦν ἐπὶ τὰς κεφαλὰς αὐτῶν,
city great? And they threw dust on the heads of them,

καὶ ἔκραζον κλαίοντες καὶ πενθοῦντες, λέγοντες, Οὐαί, οὐαί,
and cried out weeping and mourning, saying, Woe! Woe,

ἡ πόλις ἡ μεγάλη, ἐν ᾗ ἐπλούτησαν πάντες οἱ ἔχοντες πλοῖα
(to) the city great, by which were rich all those having ships

ἐν τῇ θαλάσσῃ ἐκ τῆς τιμιότητος αὐτῆς, ὅτι μιᾷ ὥρᾳ ἠρη-
in the sea, from the costliness of her, because in one hour was

**20** μώθη. εὐφραίνου ἐπ᾽ αὐτήν, οὐρανέ, καὶ οἱ ἅγιοι ἀπόστολοι,
she ruined. Be glad over her, Heaven and the holy apostles

καὶ οἱ προφῆται, ὅτι ἔκρινεν ὁ Θεὸς τὸ κρίμα ὑμῶν ἐξ αὐτῆς.
and the prophets, because judged God the judgment of you upon her.

**21** Καὶ ἦρεν εἷς ἄγγελος ἰσχυρὸς λίθον ὡς μύλον μέγαν, καὶ
And lifted one angel strong a stone as a millstone great, and

ἔβαλεν εἰς τὴν θάλασσαν, λέγων, Οὕτως ὁρμήματι βληθή-
threw (it) into the sea, saying, Thus on an impulse will be

**22** σεται Βαβυλὼν ἡ μεγάλη πόλις, καὶ οὐ μὴ εὑρεθῇ ἔτι. καὶ
thrown Babylon the great city, and not at all will be found yet. And

φωνὴ κιθαρῳδῶν καὶ μουσικῶν καὶ αὐλητῶν καὶ σαλπιστῶν
sound of harpers, and of musicians, and flutists, and of trumpeters,

οὐ μὴ ἀκουσθῇ ἐν σοὶ ἔτι. καὶ πᾶς τεχνίτης πάσης τέχνης
not at all will be heard in you longer, and every craftsman of every craft

οὐ μὴ εὑρεθῇ ἐν σοὶ ἔτι, καὶ φωνὴ μύλου οὐ μὴ ἀκουσθῇ ἐν
not at all will be found in you longer; and sound of a mill not at all be heard in

**23** σοὶ ἔτι, καὶ φῶς λύχνου οὐ μὴ φανῇ ἐν σοὶ ἔτι, καὶ φωνὴ
you longer; and light of a lamp not at all (will) shine in you still; and voice

νυμφίου καὶ νύμφης οὐ μὴ ἀκουσθῇ ἐν σοὶ ἔτι· ὅτι οἱ ἔμποροί
of groom and bride not at all will be heard in you still. For the merchants

σου ἦσαν οἱ μεγιστᾶνες τῆς γῆς· ὅτι ἐν τῇ φαρμακείᾳ σου
of you were the great ones of the earth, for by the sorcery of you

**24** ἐπλανήθησαν πάντα τὰ ἔθνη. καὶ ἐν αὐτῇ αἷμα προφητῶν
were misled all the nations, and in her (the) blood of prophets

καὶ ἁγίων εὑρέθη, καὶ πάντων τῶν ἐσφαγμένων ἐπὶ τῆς γῆς.
and saints was found, and of all those having been slain on the earth.

CHAPTER 19

[1] And after these things I heard a great voice of a great crowd in Heaven, saying, Hallelujah! The salvation and the glory and the honor and the power of (the) Lord our God! [2] For true and righteous (are) His judgments, because He judged the great harlot, who defiled the earth with her fornication. And He avenged the blood of His slaves out of her hand. [3] And secondly they said, Hallelujah! And her smoke goes up forever (and) ever. [4] And the twenty-four elders, and the four living creatures, fell down and worshiped God sitting on the throne, saying, Amen! Hallelujah! [5] And a voice from the throne came out, saying, Praise our God, all His slaves, and those fearing Him, the small and the great. [6] And I heard as a sound of a great crowd, and as a sound of many waters, and as a sound of strong thunders, saying, Hallelujah! Because (the) Lord God Almighty reigned. [7] Let us rejoice, and let us exult, and we will give glory to Him, because the marriage of the Lamb came, and His wife prepared herself. [8] And it was given to her that she be clothed (with) fine linen, clean and bright; for the fine linen is the righteous acts of the saints. [9] And he says to me, Write: Blessed (are) those having been called to the supper of the marriage of the Lamb. And he says to me, These words of God are true. [10] And I fell before the feet of him to worship him. And he says to me, See, do not. I am a fellow-slave of you, and of your brothers, having the testimony of Jesus. Worship God. For the testimony of Jesus is the spirit of prophecy.

# CHAPTER 19

**1** Καὶ μετὰ ταῦτα ἤκουσα φωνὴν ὄχλου πολλοῦ μεγάλην
And after these things I heard a voice of a crowd much great
ἐν τῷ οὐρανῷ, λέγοντος, Ἀλληλούϊα· ἡ σωτηρία καὶ ἡ
in Heaven, saying, Hallelujah! The salvation and the
**2** δόξα καὶ ἡ τιμὴ καὶ ἡ δύναμις Κυρίῳ τῷ Θεῷ ἡμῶν· ὅτι
glory and the honor and the power of (the) Lord God of us, because
ἀληθιναὶ καὶ δίκαιαι αἱ κρίσεις αὐτοῦ· ὅτι ἔκρινε τὴν πόρνην
true and righteous the judgments of Him, for He judged the harlot
τὴν μεγάλην, ἥτις ἔφθειρε τὴν γῆν ἐν τῇ πορνείᾳ αὐτῆς,
great, who defiled the earth with the fornication of her,
καὶ ἐξεδίκησε τὸ αἷμα τῶν δούλων αὐτοῦ ἐκ τῆς χειρὸς αὐτῆς.
and He avenged the blood of the slaves of Him out of the hand of her.
**3** καὶ δεύτερον εἴρηκαν, Ἀλληλούϊα· καὶ ὁ καπνὸς αὐτῆς
And secondly, they said, Hallelujah! And the smoke of her
**4** ἀναβαίνει εἰς τοὺς αἰῶνας τῶν αἰώνων. καὶ ἔπεσαν οἱ
goes up to the ages of the ages. And fell down the
πρεσβύτεροι οἱ εἴκοσι καὶ τέσσαρες, καὶ τὰ τέσσαρα ζῶα,
elders twenty and four, and the four living creatures,
καὶ προσεκύνησαν τῷ Θεῷ τῷ καθημένῳ ἐπὶ τοῦ θρόνου,
and worshiped God sitting on the throne
**5** λέγοντες, Ἀμήν· Ἀλληλούϊα. καὶ φωνὴ ἐκ τοῦ θρόνου
saying, Amen! Hallelujah! And a voice from the throne
ἐξῆλθε, λέγουσα, Αἰνεῖτε τὸν Θεὸν ἡμῶν πάντες οἱ δοῦλοι
came out, saying, Praise the God of us, all the slaves
αὐτοῦ, καὶ οἱ φοβούμενοι αὐτόν, καὶ οἱ μικροὶ καὶ οἱ μεγάλοι.
of Him, and those fearing Him, even the small and the great.
**6** καὶ ἤκουσα ὡς φωνὴν ὄχλου πολλοῦ, καὶ ὡς φωνὴν ὑδάτων
And I heard as a sound of a crowd much, and as a sound of waters
πολλῶν, καὶ ὡς φωνὴν βροντῶν ἰσχυρῶν, λέγοντας,
many, and as a sound thunders of strong, saying,
Ἀλληλούϊα· ὅτι ἐβασίλευσε Κύριος ὁ Θεὸς ὁ παντοκράτωρ.
Hallelujah! because reigned (the) Lord God Almighty.
**7** χαίρωμεν καὶ ἀγαλλιώμεθα, καὶ δῶμεν τὴν δόξαν αὐτῷ·
Let us rejoice and let us exult, and we will give the glory to Him,
ὅτι ἦλθεν ὁ γάμος τοῦ ἀρνίου, καὶ ἡ γυνὴ αὐτοῦ ἡτοίμασεν
because came the marriage of the Lamb, and the wife of Him prepared
**8** ἑαυτήν. καὶ ἐδόθη αὐτῇ ἵνα περιβάληται βύσσινον καθαρὸν
herself, and it was given to her that she be clothed (with) fine linen clean
καὶ λαμπρόν· τὸ γὰρ βύσσινον τὰ δικαιώματά ἐστι τῶν
and bright; the for fine linen the righteousnesses is of the
**9** ἁγίων. καὶ λέγει μοι, Γράψον, Μακάριοι οἱ εἰς τὸ δεῖπνον
saints. And he says to me, Write: Blessed those to the supper
τοῦ γάμου τοῦ ἀρνίου κεκλημένοι. καὶ λέγει μοι, Οὗτοι οἱ
of the marriage of the Lamb having been called. And he says to me, These
**10** λόγοι ἀληθινοί εἰσι τοῦ Θεοῦ. καὶ ἔπεσον ἔμπροσθεν τῶν
words true are of God, And I fell before the
ποδῶν αὐτοῦ προσκυνῆσαι αὐτῷ· καὶ λέγει μοι, Ὅρα μή·
feet of him to worship him; and he says to me, See, do not.
σύνδουλός σου εἰμὶ καὶ τῶν ἀδελφῶν σου τῶν ἐχόντων τὴν
A fellow-slave of you I am, and of the brothers of you, having the
μαρτυρίαν τοῦ Ἰησοῦ· τῷ Θεῷ προσκύνησον· ἡ γὰρ
witness of Jesus; To God, give worship. the For
μαρτυρία τοῦ Ἰησοῦ ἐστὶ τὸ πνεῦμα τῆς προφητείας.
witness of Jesus is the spirit of prophecy.

[11] And I saw Heaven being opened, and behold, a white horse, and the (One) sitting on it being called Faithful and True. And He judges and makes wars in righteousness. [12] And His eyes (were) as a flame of fire, and on His head many diadems, having a name having been written which no one knows except Himself; [13] and having been clothed (in) a garment having been dipped in blood, and His name has been called, The Word of God. [14] And the armies in Heaven were following Him on white horses, having been dressed (in) fine linen, white and clean. [15] And out of His mouth goes forth a sharp sword, that with it He may smite the nations; and He will shepherd them with an iron rod. And He treads the winepress of the wine of the anger and of the wrath of God Almighty. [16] And He has on His garment and on His thigh a name having been written: KING OF KINGS, AND LORD OF LORDS. [17] And I saw one angel standing in the sun, and he cried with a great voice, saying to all the birds flying in mid-heaven, Come and gather together to the supper of (the) great God, [18] that you may eat (the) flesh of kings, and (the) flesh of chilliarchs, and (the) flesh of strong ones, and (the) flesh of horses, and of those sitting on them, and (the) flesh of all, both freeman and slaves, even small and great. [19] And I saw the beast, and the kings of the earth, and their armies being assembled to make war with the (One) sitting on the horse, and with His army. [20] And was seized the beast, and with this one the false prophet, those doing the signs before it, by which he deceived those having received the mark of the beast, and those worshiping its im-

**11** Καὶ εἶδον τὸν οὐρανὸν ἀνεῳγμένον, καὶ ἰδού, ἵππος
And I saw         Heaven   having been opened, and behold, a horse
λευκός, καὶ ὁ καθήμενος ἐπ' αὐτόν, καλούμενος πιστὸς καὶ
white, and the (One) sitting   on   it   being called   faithful and

**12** ἀληθινός, καὶ ἐν δικαιοσύνῃ κρίνει καὶ πολεμεῖ. οἱ δὲ ὀφθαλμοὶ
true.    And in   righteousness He judges and  wars.   the And eyes
αὐτοῦ ὡς φλὸξ πυρός, καὶ ἐπὶ τὴν κεφαλὴν αὐτοῦ διαδήματα
of Him  as a flame of fire, and on   the   head    of Him    diadems
πολλά· ἔχων ὄνομα γεγραμμένον ὃ οὐδεὶς οἶδεν εἰ μὴ αὐτός,
many, having a name having been written which no one knows except Him;

**13** καὶ περιβεβλημένος ἱμάτιον βεβαμμένον αἵματι· καὶ καλεῖται
and being clothed (in) a garment having been dipped in blood, and is called

**14** τὸ ὄνομα αὐτοῦ, Ὁ λόγος τοῦ Θεοῦ. καὶ τὰ στρατεύματα·
the name   of Him, The Word    of God. And the armies
ἐν τῷ οὐρανῷ ἠκολούθει αὐτῷ ἐφ' ἵπποις λευκοῖς, ἐνδεδυ-
in   Heaven    followed   Him  on horses   white, having been

**15** μένοι βύσσινον λευκὸν καὶ καθαρόν. καὶ ἐκ τοῦ στόματος
dressed (in) fine linen, white and   clean.   And out of the  mouth
αὐτοῦ ἐκπορεύεται ρομφαία ὀξεῖα, ἵνα ἐν αὐτῇ πατάσσῃ τὰ
of Him  goes forth   a sword   sharp, that with it   He may smite the
ἔθνη· καὶ αὐτὸς ποιμανεῖ αὐτοὺς ἐν ῥάβδῳ σιδηρᾷ· καὶ αὐτὸς
nations; and  He will shepherd them with a rod   iron. And   He
πατεῖ τὴν ληνὸν τοῦ οἴνου τοῦ θυμοῦ καὶ τῆς ὀργῆς τοῦ
treads the    press of the wine of the  anger and of the wrath

**16** Θεοῦ τοῦ παντοκράτορος. καὶ ἔχει ἐπὶ τὸ ἱμάτιον καὶ ἐπὶ τὸν
of God    Almighty.     And He has on the garment and on   the
μηρὸν αὐτοῦ ὄνομα γεγραμμένον, Βασιλεὺς βασιλέων καὶ
thigh  of Him  a name having been written:  KING    OF KINGS, AND
Κύριος κυρίων.
LORD OF LORDS.

**17** Καὶ εἶδον ἕνα ἄγγελον ἑστῶτα ἐν τῷ ἡλίῳ· καὶ ἔκραξε
And I saw one  angel    standing  in  the   sun  and he cried
φωνῇ μεγάλῃ, λέγων πᾶσι τοῖς ὀρνέοις τοῖς πετωμένοις ἐν
with a voice great,  saying to all   the   birds     flying     in
μεσουρανήματι, Δεῦτε καὶ συνάγεσθε εἰς τὸ δεῖπνον τοῦ
mid-heaven,     Come and gather together to  the   supper of the

**18** μεγάλου Θεοῦ, ἵνα φάγητε σάρκας βασιλέων, καὶ σάρκας
great     God, that you may eat (the) flesh of kings,   and (the) flesh
χιλιάρχων, καὶ σάρκας ἰσχυρῶν, καὶ σάρκας ἵππων καὶ τῶν
of chiliarchs, and (the) flesh of strong ones, and (the) flesh of horses, and of those
καθημένων ἐπ' αὐτῶν, καὶ σάρκας πάντων, ἐλευθέρων τε καὶ
sitting    on  them, and (the) flesh of all,    freemen both and
δούλων, καὶ μικρῶν καὶ μεγάλων.
slaves,  even of (the) small and   great.

**19** Καὶ εἶδον τὸ θηρίον, καὶ τοὺς βασιλεῖς τῆς γῆς, καὶ τὰ
And I saw the beast,   and the   kings   of the earth, and the
στρατεύματα αὐτῶν συνηγμένα ποιῆσαι πόλεμον μετὰ τοῦ
armies       of them being assembled to make  war  with the (One)
καθημένου ἐπὶ τοῦ ἵππου, καὶ μετὰ τοῦ στρατεύματος αὐτοῦ.
sitting    on the horse, and with the   army    of Him.

**20** καὶ ἐπιάσθη τὸ θηρίον, καὶ μετὰ τούτου ὁ ψευδοπροφήτης
And was seized the beast,  and with     the false prophet
ὁ ποιήσας τὰ σημεῖα ἐνώπιον αὐτοῦ, ἐν οἷς ἐπλάνησε τοὺς
doing  the signs   before   it,  by which he  misled those
λαβόντας τὸ χάραγμα τοῦ θηρίου, καὶ τοὺς προσκυνοῦντας
having received the mark   of the beast,  and those   worshiping

age. The two were thrown alive into the Lake of Fire burning with brimstone. [21] And the rest were killed with the sword of Him sitting on the horse, having gone forth out of His mouth. And all the birds were filled by their flesh.

τῇ εἰκόνι αὐτοῦ ζῶντες ἐβλήθησαν οἱ δύο εἰς τὴν λίμνην τοῦ
the image. of it.        living were thrown. the two into the Lake

**21** πυρὸς τὴν καιομένην ἐν τῷ θείῳ· καὶ οἱ λοιποὶ ἀπεκτάνθησαν
of Fire      burning      with brimstone. And the rest    were killed

ἐν τῇ ῥομφαίᾳ τοῦ καθημένου ἐπὶ τοῦ ἵππου, τῇ ἐκπορευο-
with the sword of the (One) sitting    on    the horse,    having gone

μένῃ ἐκ τοῦ στόματος αὐτοῦ· καὶ πάντα τὰ ὄρνεα ἐχορτάσθη-
forth out of the mouth  of Him,  and  all  the  birds  were filled

σαν ἐκ τῶν σαρκῶν αὐτῶν.
from the  flesh    of them.

## CHAPTER 20

**1** Καὶ εἶδον ἄγγελον καταβαίνοντα ἐκ τοῦ οὐρανοῦ,
And  I saw  an angel    coming down  out of    Heaven,

ἔχοντα τὴν κλεῖδα τῆς ἀβύσσου, καὶ ἄλυσιν μεγάλην ἐπὶ
having  the  key  of the abyss,  and a chain    great    on

**2** τὴν χεῖρα αὐτοῦ. καὶ ἐκράτησε τὸν δράκοντα, τὸν ὄφιν τὸν
the hand  of him. And he laid hold of the dragon,    the serpent

ἀρχαῖον, ὅς ἐστι διάβολος καὶ Σατανᾶς, καὶ ἔδησεν αὐτὸν
old,  who is  Devil    and  Satan,  and  bound  him

**3** χίλια ἔτη, καὶ ἔβαλεν αὐτὸν εἰς τὴν ἄβυσσον, καὶ ἔκλεισεν
a thousand years, and threw  him  into the  abyss,    and  shut up

αὐτόν, καὶ ἐσφράγισεν ἐπάνω αὐτοῦ, ἵνα μὴ πλανήσῃ τὰ
him,  and  sealed    over  him,  that not he should mislead the

ἔθνη ἔτι, ἄχρι τελεσθῇ τὰ χίλια ἔτη· καὶ μετὰ ταῦτα δεῖ
nations still, until are ended the thousand years; and after these things must

αὐτὸν λυθῆναι μικρὸν χρόνον.
he  be loosed a little  time.

**4** Καὶ εἶδον θρόνους, καὶ ἐκάθισαν ἐπ᾽ αὐτούς, καὶ κρίμα
And I saw thrones,  and they sat  on  them,  and judgment

ἐδόθη αὐτοῖς· καὶ τὰς ψυχὰς τῶν πεπελεκισμένων διὰ τὴν
was given to them, and the souls of those having been beheaded due to the

μαρτυρίαν Ἰησοῦ, καὶ διὰ τὸν λόγον τοῦ Θεοῦ, καὶ οἵτινες
witness  of Jesus, and because of the word  of God, and  who

οὐ προσεκύνησαν τῷ θηρίῳ, οὔτε τὴν εἰκόνα αὐτοῦ, καὶ
not had worshiped the  beast  nor  the  image of it,  and

οὐκ ἔλαβον τὸ χάραγμα ἐπὶ τὸ μέτωπον αὐτῶν, καὶ ἐπὶ
not received the  mark  on  the forehead of them,  and on

τὴν χεῖρα αὐτῶν· καὶ ἔζησαν, καὶ ἐβασίλευσαν μετὰ
the  hand  of them; and they lived  and  reigned  with

**5** Χριστοῦ χίλια ἔτη. οἱ δὲ λοιποὶ τῶν νεκρῶν οὐκ ἀνέζησαν
Christ a thousand years. the But rest of the  dead  not did live again

ἕως τελεσθῇ τὰ χίλια ἔτη. αὕτη ἡ ἀνάστασις ἡ πρώτη.
until, were ended the thousand years. This (is) the resurrection  first.

**6** μακάριος καὶ ἅγιος ὁ ἔχων μέρος ἐν τῇ ἀναστάσει τῇ πρώτῃ·
Blessed  and  holy the (one) having part in the resurrection  first;

ἐπὶ τούτων ὁ θάνατος ὁ δεύτερος οὐκ ἔχει ἐξουσίαν, ἀλλ᾽
over  these  the death  second  not has authority,  but

ἔσονται ἱερεῖς τοῦ Θεοῦ καὶ τοῦ Χριστοῦ, καὶ βασιλεύσουσι
they will be priests of God and  of Christ,  and  will reign

μετ᾽ αὐτοῦ χίλια ἔτη.
with  Him a thousand years.

**7** Καὶ ὅταν τελεσθῇ τὰ χίλια ἔτη, λυθήσεται ὁ Σατανᾶς ἐκ
And whenever are ended the thousand years  will be loosed Satan out of

**8** τῆς φυλακῆς αὐτοῦ, καὶ ἐξελεύσεται πλανῆσαι τὰ ἔθνη τὰ
the  prison  of him,  and he will go out  to mislead the nations

### CHAPTER 20

[1] And I saw an angel coming down out of Heaven, having the key of the abyss, and a great chain on his hand. [2] And he laid hold of the dragon, the old serpent, who is (the) Devil, and, Satan, and bound him a thousand years, [3] and threw him into the abyss, and shut him up, and sealed over him, that he should not deceive nations longer, until are fulfilled the thousand years; and after these things he must be loosed a little time. [4] And I saw thrones, and they sat on them, and judgment was given to them, and the souls of those having been beheaded for the testimony of Jesus, and because of the word of God, and who not had worshiped the beast nor its image, and had not received the mark on their forehead, and on their hand; and they lived and reigned with Christ a thousand years. [5] But the rest did not live again until were fulfilled the thousand years. This is the first resurrection. [6] Blessed and holy (are) those having part in the first resurrection; the second death has no authority over these; but they will be priests to God and to Christ, and will reign with Him a thousand years. [7] And when the thousand years are fulfilled, Satan will be loosed out of his prison, [8] and he will go out to mislead the nations in the

four corners of the earth—
Gog and Magog—to assemble
them in war, of whom the
number (is) as the sand of
the sea. [9] And they went
up over the breadth of the
land, and encircled the camp
of the saints, and the beloved
city; and fire came down from
God out of Heaven, and
burned them up. [10] And
the Devil misleading them was
thrown into the Lake of Fire
and Brimstone, where (were)
the beast and the false prophet. And they will be tormented day and night forever (and)
ever. [11] And I saw a great

white throne, and Him sitting on it, of whom from
(His) face fled the earth and
the heaven. And a place was
not found for them. [12]
And I saw the dead, the small
and the great, standing before God. And books were
opened. And another book
was opened which is the
(Book) of Life. And the dead
were judged out of the things
having been written in the
books, according to their
works. [13] And the sea gave
up the dead in it, and death
and Hades gave up the dead
in them. And they were each
judged according to their
works. [14] And death and
Hades were thrown into the
Lake of Fire. This is the
second death. [15] And if
anyone was not found in the
Book of Life having been
written, he was thrown into
the Lake of Fire.

CHAPTER 21

[1] And I saw a new
heaven and a new earth; for
the first heaven and the first
earth passed away; and the
sea no longer is. [2] And
I, John, saw the holy city,
New Jerusalem, coming down
from God out of Heaven,
having been prepared as a
bride, having been adorned
for her Husband. [3] And I
heard a great voice out of
Heaven, saying, Behold, the

ἐν ταῖς τέσσαρσι γωνίαις τῆς γῆς, τὸν Γὼγ καὶ τὸν Μαγώγ,
in the      four      corners of the earth,      Gog and      Magog,
συναγαγεῖν αὐτοὺς εἰς πόλεμον· ὧν ὁ ἀριθμὸς ὡς ἡ ἄμμος
to assemble      them      in      war, of whom the number (is) as the sand

**9** τῆς θαλάσσης. καὶ ἀνέβησαν ἐπὶ τὸ πλάτος τῆς γῆς, καὶ
of the      sea.      And they went up over the      breadth of the land and
ἐκύκλωσαν τὴν παρεμβολὴν τῶν ἁγίων καὶ τὴν πόλιν τὴν
encircled      the      camp      of the      saints, and the      city
ἠγαπημένην· καὶ κατέβη πῦρ ἀπὸ τοῦ Θεοῦ ἐκ τοῦ οὐρανοῦ,
beloved,      and came down fire from      God out of      Heaven

**10** καὶ κατέφαγεν αὐτούς. καὶ ὁ διάβολος ὁ πλανῶν αὐτοὺς
and burned down them.      And the Devil      misleading      them
ἐβλήθη εἰς τὴν λίμνην τοῦ πυρὸς καὶ θείου, ὅπου τὸ θηρίον
was thrown into the Lake      of Fire and brimstone, where the beast
καὶ ὁ ψευδοπροφήτης· καὶ βασανισθήσονται ἡμέρας καὶ
and the false prophet (were); and the will be tormented      day      and
νυκτὸς εἰς τοὺς αἰῶνας τῶν αἰώνων.
night      to the      ages      of the      ages.

**11** Καὶ εἶδον θρόνον λευκὸν μέγαν, καὶ τὸν καθήμενον ἐπ᾿ αὐτοῦ
And I saw a throne      white      great, and the (One) sitting on      it,
οὗ ἀπὸ προσώπου ἔφυγεν ἡ γῆ καὶ ὁ οὐρανός, καὶ τόπος
of whom from (the) face fled the earth and the heaven;      and a place

**12** οὐχ εὑρέθη αὐτοῖς. καὶ εἶδον τοὺς νεκρούς, μικροὺς καὶ
not was found for them. And I saw      the      dead,      (the)small and
μεγάλους, ἑστῶτας ἐνώπιον τοῦ Θεοῦ, καὶ βιβλία ἠνεῴχθη-
great,      standing      before      God, and scrolls were opened.
σαν· καὶ βιβλίον ἄλλο ἠνεῴχθη, ὅ ἐστι τῆς ζωῆς· καὶ ἐκρί-
And Scroll another was opened, which is (the)(Scroll) of Life. And were
θησαν οἱ νεκροὶ ἐκ τῶν γεγραμμένων ἐν τοῖς βιβλίοις, κατὰ
judged the      dead out of those having been written in the scrolls, according to

**13** τὰ ἔργα αὐτῶν. καὶ ἔδωκεν ἡ θάλασσα τοὺς ἐν αὐτῇ νεκρούς,
the works of them. And gave the sea the in it dead,
καὶ ὁ θάνατος καὶ ὁ ᾅδης ἔδωκαν τοὺς ἐν αὐτοῖς νεκρούς· καὶ
and      death and Hades gave      the in them dead; and

**14** ἐκρίθησαν ἕκαστος κατὰ τὰ ἔργα αὐτῶν. καὶ ὁ θάνατος καὶ
they were judged each one according to their works. And      death      and
ὁ ᾅδης ἐβλήθησαν εἰς τὴν λίμνην τοῦ πυρός· οὗτός ἐστιν ὁ
Hades were thrown into the Lake      of Fire. This      is the

**15** δεύτερος θάνατος. καὶ εἴ τις οὐχ εὑρέθη ἐν τῇ βίβλῳ τῆς ζωῆς
second death. And if anyone not was found in the Scroll      of Life
γεγραμμένος, ἐβλήθη εἰς τὴν λίμνην τοῦ πυρός.
having been written, he was thrown into the Lake of Fire.

**CHAPTER 21**

**1** Καὶ εἶδον οὐρανὸν καινὸν καὶ γῆν καινήν· ὁ γὰρ πρῶτος
And I saw a heaven      new and an earth      new; the for      first
οὐρανὸς καὶ ἡ πρώτη γῆ παρῆλθε, καὶ ἡ θάλασσα οὐκ ἔστιν
heaven and the first earth went away, and the sea      not      is

**2** ἔτι. καὶ ἐγὼ Ἰωάννης εἶδον τὴν πόλιν τὴν ἁγίαν, Ἱερουσαλὴμ
still. And I      John,      saw the city      holy,      Jerusalem
καινήν, καταβαίνουσαν ἀπὸ τοῦ Θεοῦ ἐκ τοῦ οὐρανοῦ, ἡτοι-
New,      coming down      from      God out of      Heaven, having
μασμένην ὡς νύμφην κεκοσμημένην τῷ ἀνδρὶ αὐτῆς. καὶ
been prepared as a bride having been adorned for the Husband of her. And

**3** ἤκουσα φωνῆς μεγάλης ἐκ τοῦ οὐρανοῦ, λεγούσης, Ἰδού, ἡ
I heard a voice      great out of      Heaven,      saying,      Behold, the

tabernacle of God with men!
And He will tabernacle with
them, and they will be His
people; and God Himself will
be with them as their God.
[4] And God will wipe away
every tear from their eyes;
and death shall not be longer,
nor sorrow, nor clamor, nor
pain, will be any longer; for
the first things passed away
[5] And He sitting on the
throne said, Behold, I make
all things new. And He says
to me, Write, because these
words are true and faithful.
[6] And He said to me, It is
done. I am the Alpha and
the Omega, the Beginning and
the End. To him thirsting, I
will freely give of the fountain of the water of life.
[7] The (one) overcoming
will inherit all things, and I
will be God to him, and he
will be a son to Me. [8] But
(the) fearful, and unbelieving,
and hateful, and murderers,
and fornicators, and sorcerers,
and idolaters, and all the
lying ones, the part of them
(will be) in the Lake burning
with fire and brimstone,
which is (the) second death.
[9] And one of the seven
angels came to me, he having
the seven bowls being filled
(with) the seven last plagues,
and spoke with me, saying,
Come, I will show you the
bride, the wife of the Lamb.
[10] And he carried me in
Spirit onto a great and high
mountain, and showed me
the great city, holy Jerusalem,
coming down out of Heaven
from God, [11] having the
glory of God. And its light
(was) like a very precious
stone, as a jasper stone, being
clear as crystal. [12] and
having a great and high wall,
having twelve gates, and at
the gates twelve angels, and
names having been inscribed,
which is the twelve tribes
of the sons of Israel. [13]
From (the) east, three gates;
from (the) north, three gates;
from (the) south, three gates;
and from (the) west, three
gates.

σκηνὴ τοῦ Θεοῦ μετὰ τῶν ἀνθρώπων, καὶ σκηνώσει μετ'
tabernacle of God with        men!   And He will tabernacle with

αὐτῶν, καὶ αὐτοὶ λαοὶ αὐτοῦ ἔσονται, καὶ αὐτὸς ὁ Θεὸς ἔσται
them, and they peoples of Him will be, and Himself God will be

**4** μετ' αὐτῶν, Θεὸς αὐτῶν· καὶ ἐξαλείψει ὁ Θεὸς πᾶν δάκρυον
with them (the) God of them. And will wipe away God every tear

ἀπὸ τῶν ὀφθαλμῶν αὐτῶν, καὶ ὁ θάνατος οὐκ ἔσται ἔτι· οὔτε
from the eyes of them; and death not will be longer, nor

πένθος, οὔτε κραυγή, οὔτε πόνος οὐκ ἔσται ἔτι· ὅτι τὰ πρῶτα
mourning, nor outcry, nor pain not will be longer, for the things first

**5** ἀπῆλθον. καὶ εἶπεν ὁ καθήμενος ἐπὶ τοῦ θρόνου, Ἰδού,
went away. And said the (One) sitting on the throne, Behold,

καινὰ πάντα ποιῶ. καὶ λέγει μοι, Γράψον· ὅτι οὗτοι οἱ λόγοι
new all things I make. And He says to me, Write, because these words ·

**6** ἀληθινοὶ καὶ πιστοί εἰσι. καὶ εἶπέ μοι, Γέγονε. ἐγώ εἰμι τὸ
true and faithful are; and He said to me, It is done, I am the

Α καὶ τὸ Ω, ἡ ἀρχὴ καὶ τὸ τέλος. ἐγὼ τῷ διψῶντι δώσω ἐκ
Alpha and the Omega, the Head and the End. I to (the one) thirsting will give of

**7** τῆς πηγῆς τοῦ ὕδατος τῆς ζωῆς δωρεάν. ὁ νικῶν κληρονομή-
the fountain of the water of life freely. The (one) overcoming will in-

σει πάντα, καὶ ἔσομαι αὐτῷ Θεός, καὶ αὐτὸς ἔσται μοι ὁ υἱός.
herit all things, and I will be to him God, and he will be to Me the son.

**8** δειλοῖς δὲ καὶ ἀπίστοις καὶ ἐβδελυγμένοις καὶ φονεῦσι καὶ
to fearful But and unbelieving and abominable and murderers and

πόρνοις καὶ φαρμακεῦσι καὶ εἰδωλολάτραις, καὶ πᾶσι τοῖς
fornicators and sorcerers and idolaters and all the

ψευδέσι, τὸ μέρος αὐτῶν ἐν τῇ λίμνῃ τῇ καιομένῃ πυρὶ καὶ
lying ones, the part of them in the Lake burning with fire and

θείῳ, ὅ ἐστι δεύτερος θάνατος.
brimstone, which is (the) second death.

**9** Καὶ ἦλθε πρός με εἷς τῶν ἑπτὰ ἀγγέλων τῶν ἐχόντων τὰς
And came to me one of the seven angels, he having the

ἑπτὰ φιάλας τὰς γεμούσας τῶν ἑπτὰ πληγῶν τῶν ἐσχάτων,
seven bowls being filled of the seven plagues last,

καὶ ἐλάλησε μετ' ἐμοῦ, λέγων, Δεῦρο, δείξω σοι τὴν νύμφην
and spoke with me, saying, Come, I will show you the bride,

**10** τοῦ ἀρνίου τὴν γυναῖκα. καὶ ἀπήνεγκέ με ἐν Πνεύματι ἐπ'
of the Lamb the wife. And he carried me in Spirit onto

ὄρος μέγα καὶ ὑψηλόν, καὶ ἔδειξέ μοι τὴν πόλιν τὴν μεγάλην,
a mount great and high, and showed me the city great,

τὴν ἁγίαν Ἱερουσαλήμ, καταβαίνουσαν ἐκ τοῦ οὐρανοῦ
Holy Jerusalem, coming down out of Heaven

**11** ἀπὸ τοῦ Θεοῦ, ἔχουσαν τὴν δόξαν τοῦ Θεοῦ· καὶ ὁ φωστὴρ
from God, having the glory of God. And the lighting

αὐτῆς ὅμοιος λίθῳ τιμιωτάτῳ, ὡς λίθῳ ἰάσπιδι κρυσταλλί-
of it (was) like a stone very precious, as stone a jasper being clear as

**12** ζοντι· ἔχουσάν τε τεῖχος μέγα καὶ ὑψηλόν, ἔχουσαν πυλῶνας
crystal, having and wall a great and high, having gates

δώδεκα, καὶ ἐπὶ τοῖς πυλῶσιν ἀγγέλους δώδεκα, καὶ ὀνόματα
twelve, and at the gates angels twelve, and names

ἐπιγεγραμμένα, ἅ ἐστι τῶν δώδεκα φυλῶν τῶν υἱῶν Ἰσραήλ.
having been inscribed, which are of the twelve tribes of the sons of Israel.

**13** ἀπ' ἀνατολῆς, πυλῶνες τρεῖς· ἀπὸ βορρᾶ, πυλῶνες τρεῖς·
From (the) east, gates three; from (the) north, gates three;

ἀπὸ νότου, πυλῶνες τρεῖς· καὶ ἀπὸ δυσμῶν, πυλῶνες τρεῖς.
from (the) south, gates three; and from (the) west, gates three.

**14** καὶ τὸ τεῖχος τῆς πόλεως ἔχον θεμελίους δώδεκα, καὶ ἐν
And the wall of the city having foundations twelve, and in

**15** αὐτοῖς ὀνόματα τῶν δώδεκα ἀποστόλων τοῦ ἀρνίου. καὶ
them names of the twelve apostles of the Lamb. And

ὁ λαλῶν μετ᾽ ἐμοῦ εἶχε κάλαμον χρυσοῦν, ἵνα μετρήσῃ τὴν
he speaking with me had a reed of gold, that he may measure the

**16** πόλιν, καὶ τοὺς πυλῶνας αὐτῆς, καὶ τὸ τεῖχος αὐτῆς. καὶ
city, and the gates of it, and the wall of it. And

ἡ πόλις τετράγωνος κεῖται, καὶ τὸ μῆκος αὐτῆς τοσοῦτόν
the city four-cornered lies, and the leng of it so much

ἐστιν ὅσον καὶ τὸ πλάτος. καὶ ἐμέτρησε τὴν πόλιν τῷ
is as much as also the width. And he measured the city with the

καλάμῳ ἐπὶ σταδίων δώδεκα χιλιάδων· τὸ μῆκος καὶ τὸ
reed at stadia twelve thousands; the length and the

**17** πλάτος καὶ τὸ ὕψος αὐτῆς ἴσα ἐστί. καὶ ἐμέτρησε τὸ τεῖχος
width and the height of it equal are. And he measured the wall

αὐτῆς ἑκατὸν τεσσαρακοντατεσσάρων πηχῶν, μέτρον
of it, a hundred (and) forty-four cubits, a measure

**18** ἀνθρώπου, ὅ ἐστιν ἀγγέλου. καὶ ἦν ἡ ἐνδόμησις τοῦ τείχους
of a man, which is of an angel. And was the structure of the wall

αὐτῆς, ἴασπις· καὶ ἡ πόλις χρυσίον καθαρόν, ὁμοία ὑάλῳ
of it jasper; and the city (was) gold clean, like glass

**19** καθαρῷ. καὶ οἱ θεμέλιοι τοῦ τείχους τῆς πόλεως παντὶ λίθῳ
clean. And the foundations of the wall of the city with every stone

τιμίῳ κεκοσμημένοι. ὁ θεμέλιος ὁ πρῶτος, ἴασπις· ὁ δεύτερος,
precious was adorned; the foundation first, jasper; the second,

**20** σάπφειρος· ὁ τρίτος, χαλκηδών· ὁ τέταρτος, σμάραγδος· ὁ
sapphire; the third, chalcedony; the fourth, emerald; the

πέμπτος, σαρδόνυξ· ὁ ἕκτος, σάρδιος· ὁ ἕβδομος, χρυσόλιθος·
fifth, sardonyx; the sixth, sardius; the seventh, chrysolite;

ὁ ὄγδοος, βήρυλλος· ὁ ἔννατος, τοπάζιον· ὁ δέκατος,
the eighth, beryl; the ninth, topaz; the tenth,

χρυσόπρασος· ὁ ἑνδέκατος, ὑάκινθος· ὁ δωδέκατος, ἀμέ-
chrysoprase; the eleventh, hyacinth; the twelfth, ame-

**21** θυστος. καὶ οἱ δώδεκα πυλῶνες, δώδεκα μαργαρῖται· ἀνὰ
thyst. And the twelve gates (were) twelve pearls; respectively

εἷς ἕκαστος τῶν πυλώνων ἦν ἐξ ἑνὸς μαργαρίτου· καὶ ἡ
one each of the gates was of one pearl. And the

πλατεῖα τῆς πόλεως χρυσίον καθαρόν, ὡς ὕαλος διαφανής.
street of the city (was) of gold clean, as glass transparent.

**22** καὶ ναὸν οὐκ εἶδον ἐν αὐτῇ· ὁ γὰρ Κύριος ὁ Θεὸς ὁ παντο-
And a temple not I saw in it, the for Lord God

**23** κράτωρ ναὸς αὐτῆς ἐστί, καὶ τὸ ἀρνίον. καὶ ἡ πόλις οὐ
Almighty temple of it is, and the Lamb. And the city not

χρείαν ἔχει τοῦ ἡλίου, οὐδὲ τῆς σελήνης, ἵνα φαίνωσιν ἐν
need has of the sun, nor of the moon, that they might shine in

αὐτῇ· ἡ γὰρ δόξα τοῦ Θεοῦ ἐφώτισεν αὐτήν, καὶ ὁ λύχνος
it, the for glory of God enlightened it, and the lamp

**24** αὐτῆς τὸ ἀρνίον. καὶ τὰ ἔθνη τῶν σωζομένων ἐν τῷ φωτὶ
of it (is) the Lamb. And the nations of those saved in the light

αὐτῆς περιπατήσουσι· καὶ οἱ βασιλεῖς τῆς γῆς φέρουσι τὴν
of it will walk; and the kings of the earth bring the

**25** δόξαν καὶ τὴν τιμὴν αὐτῶν εἰς αὐτήν. καὶ οἱ πυλῶνες
glory and the honor of them into it. And the gates

**26** αὐτῆς οὐ μὴ κλεισθῶσιν ἡμέρας (νὺξ γὰρ οὐκ ἔσται ἐκεῖ) καὶ
of it not at all may be shut by day —night for not will be there— and

---

[14] And the wall of the city had twelve foundations, and in them (the) names of the twelve apostles of the Lamb. [15] And he speaking with me had a golden reed, that he may measure the city, and its gates, and its wall. [16] And the city lies square, even its length (is) as much as the width also is. And he measured the city with the reed at twelve thousand stadia; the length and the width and the height of it is equal. [17] And he measured its wall, a hundred (and) forty-four cubits, a measure of a man, which is of an angel. [18] And the coping of its wall (was) jasper; and the city (was) clean gold, like clean glass. [19] And the foundation of the wall of the city having been adorned with every precious stone: The first foundation, jasper; the second, sapphire; the third, chalcedony; the fourth, emerald; [20] the fifth, sardonyx; the sixth, sardius; the seventh, chrysolite; the eighth, beryl; the ninth, topaz; the tenth, chrysoprasus; the eleventh, hyacinth; the twelfth, amethyst. [21] And the twelve gates (were) twelve pearls; respectively each one of the gates was of one pearl. And the street of the city (was) clean gold, as transparent glass. [22] And I saw no temple in it, for (the) Lord God Almighty is its temple, and the Lamb. [23] And the city had no need of the sun, nor of the moon, that they might shine in it, for the glory of God enlightened it; and its lamp (is) the Lamb. [24] And the nations of those saved will walk in its light; and the kings of the earth bring their glory and honor into it. [25] And its gates not at all may be shut by day, for no night will be there. [26] And they will bring the glory and the

honor of the nations into it. [27] And not at all may enter into it all profaning, (or any) making an abomination or a lie; except those having been written in the Book of Life of the Lamb.

**27** οἴσουσι τὴν δόξαν καὶ τὴν τιμὴν τῶν ἐθνῶν εἰς αὐτήν· καὶ
they will bring the glory and the honor of the nations into it. And

οὐ μὴ εἰσέλθῃ εἰς αὐτὴν πᾶν κοινοῦν, καὶ ποιοῦν βδέλυγμα
not at all may enter into it all profaning, and (any) making an abomination

καὶ ψεῦδος· εἰ μὴ οἱ γεγραμμένοι ἐν τῷ βιβλίῳ τῆς ζωῆς τοῦ
and a lie, except those having been written in the Scroll of Life ot the

ἀρνίου.
Lamb.

## CHAPTER 22

[1] And he showed me a clean river of water of life, bright as crystal, coming forth out of the throne of God and of the Lamb. [2] In (the) midst of its street, and of the river, from here and from there, (was) a tree of life producing twelve fruits, by one month each yielding its fruit. And the leaves of the tree (were) for the healing of the nations.

[3] And every curse will no longer be. And the throne of God and the Lamb will be in it; and His slaves will serve Him; [4] and they will see His face; and His name on their foreheads. [5] And night will not be there; and they have no need of a lamp, and of the light of (the) sun, because (the) Lord God will shed light on them, and they shall reign forever (and) ever. [6] And he said to me, These words (are) faithful and true; and (the) Lord God of the holy prophets sent His angel to show His slaves what must happen quickly. [7] Behold, I am coming quickly. Blessed (is) the (one) keeping the words of the prophecy of this book. [8] And I, John, the (one) seeing and hearing these things; and when I heard and saw, I fell down to worship before the feet of the angel showing me these things. [9] And he says to me, See, stop! For I am a fellow-slave (with) you, and of your brothers the prophets, and of those keeping

**1** καὶ ἔδειξέ μοι καθαρὸν ποταμὸν ὕδατος ζωῆς, λαμ-
And he showed me a clean river of water of life,

πρὸν ὡς κρύσταλλον, ἐκπορευόμενον ἐκ τοῦ θρόνου τοῦ Θεοῦ
bright as crystal, coming forth out of the throne of God

**2** καὶ τοῦ ἀρνίου. ἐν μέσῳ τῆς πλατείας αὐτῆς, καὶ τοῦ
and of the Lamb. In (the) midst of the street of it, and of the

ποταμοῦ ἐντεῦθεν καὶ ἐντεῦθεν, ξύλον ζωῆς, ποιοῦν καρποὺς
river, from here and from there, a tree of life producing fruits

δώδεκα, κατὰ μῆνα ἕνα ἕκαστον ἀποδιδοῦν τὸν καρπὸν
twelve, according to month one each yielding the fruit.

αὐτοῦ· καὶ τὰ φύλλα τοῦ ξύλου εἰς θεραπείαν τῶν ἐθνῶν.
of it. And the leaves of the tree (will be) for healing of the nations·

**3** καὶ πᾶν κατανάθεμα οὐκ ἔσται ἔτι· καὶ ὁ θρόνος τοῦ Θεοῦ καὶ
And every curse not will be longer. And the throne of God and

τοῦ ἀρνίου ἐν αὐτῇ ἔσται· καὶ οἱ δοῦλοι αὐτοῦ λατρεύσουσιν
cf the Lamb in it will be, and the slaves of Him will do service

**4** αὐτῷ, καὶ ὄψονται τὸ πρόσωπον αὐτοῦ· καὶ τὸ ὄνομα
to Him, and they will see the face of Him, and the name

**5** αὐτοῦ ἐπὶ τῶν μετώπων αὐτῶν. καὶ νὺξ οὐκ ἔσται ἐκεῖ, καὶ
of Him (will be) on the foreheads of them. And night not will be there, and

χρείαν οὐκ ἔχουσι λύχνου καὶ φωτὸς ἡλίου, ὅτι Κύριος ὁ
need not they have of a lamp and a light of sun, because (the) Lord

Θεὸς φωτίζει αὐτούς· καὶ βασιλεύσουσιν εἰς τοὺς αἰῶνας τῶν
God will enlighten them, and they will reign to the ages of the

αἰώνων.
ages.

**6** Καὶ εἶπέ μοι, Οὗτοι οἱ λόγοι πιστοὶ καὶ ἀληθινοί· καὶ
And he said to me, These words (are) faithful and true, and

Κύριος ὁ Θεὸς τῶν ἁγίων προφητῶν ἀπέστειλε τὸν ἄγγελον
(the ) Lord God of the holy prophets sent the angel

αὐτοῦ δεῖξαι τοῖς δούλοις αὐτοῦ ἃ δεῖ γενέσθαι ἐν τάχει.
of Him to show the slaves of Him what must happen with speed.

**7** ἰδού, ἔρχομαι ταχύ. μακάριος ὁ τηρῶν τοὺς λόγους τῆς
Behold, I am coming quickly. Blessed the (one) keeping the words of the

προφητείας τοῦ βιβλίου τούτου.
prophecy of Scroll this.

**8** Καὶ ἐγὼ Ἰωάννης ὁ βλέπων ταῦτα καὶ ἀκούων. καὶ ὅτε
And I, John, the (one) seeing these things and hearing; and when

ἤκουσα καὶ ἔβλεψα, ἔπεσα προσκυνῆσαι ἔμπροσθεν τῶν
I heard and saw, I fell down to worship before the

**9** ποδῶν τοῦ ἀγγέλου τοῦ δεικνύοντός μοι ταῦτα. καὶ λέγει
feet of the angel showing me these things. And he says

μοι, Ὅρα μή· σύνδουλός σου γάρ εἰμι, καὶ τῶν ἀδελφῶν σου
to me, See, no! a fellow-slave of you For I am, and of the brothers of you,

τῶν προφητῶν, καὶ τῶν τηρούντων τοὺς λόγους τοῦ
the prophets, and of those keeping the words

the words of this book. Worship God. [10] And he says to me, Do not seal the words of this prophecy of this book, because the time is near. [11] He acting unjustly, let him still act unjustly; and the filthy, let (him) be filthy still; and the righteous, let (him) still (do) righteousness still; and the holy, let him still be sanctified. [12] And behold, I am coming quickly, and My reward (is) with Me, to give to each as his work is. [13] I am the Alpha and the Omega, the Beginning and the End, the First and the Last, [14] Blessed (are) those doing His commands, that their authority will be over the tree of life, and by the gates they may enter into the city [15] But outside (are) the dogs, and the sorcerers, and the fornicators, and the murderers, and the idolaters, and everyone loving and making a lie. [16] I, Jesus, sent My angel to testify to you these things over the churches. I am the Root and Offspring of David, the bright and Morning Star. [17] And the Spirit and the bride say, Come! And he hearing, let him say, Come! And he thirsting, let (him) come, and he wishing, let (him) take of the water of life freely. [18] For I testify together with everyone hearing the words of the prophecy of this book: If anyone adds to these things, God will add upon him the plagues having been written in this book; [19] and if anyone takes away from the words of (the) book of this prophecy, God will take away his part from (the) Book of Life, and out of the holy city, and of the things having been written in this book. [20] He testifying these things says, Yes, I am coming quickly. Amen. Yes, come, Lord Jesus. [21] The grace of our Lord Jesus Christ (be) with all of you. Amen.

βιβλίου τούτου· τῷ Θεῷ προσκύνησον.
Scroll   of this.        To God,   do worship.

10   Καὶ λέγει μοι, Μὴ σφραγίσῃς τοὺς λόγους τῆς προφητείας
And he says to me,      seal      the words of the   prophecy

11   τοῦ βιβλίου τούτου· ὅτι ὁ καιρὸς ἐγγύς ἐστιν. ὁ ἀδικῶν
Scroll   of this, because the time   near   is. He acting unjustly

ἀδικησάτω ἔτι· καὶ ὁ ῥυπῶν ῥυπωσάτω ἔτι· καὶ ὁ δίκαιος
let him act unjustly still; and the filthy, let be filthy still; and the righteous,

12   δικαιωθήτω ἔτι· καὶ ὁ ἅγιος ἁγιασ..ἤτω ἔτι. καὶ ἰδού,
righteousness (do) still; and the holy, let him be holy still. And behold,

ἔρχομαι ταχύ, καὶ ὁ μισθός μου μετ' ἐμοῦ, ἀποδοῦναι ἑκάστῳ
I am coming quickly, and My reward (is) with Me, to render to each

13   ὡς τὸ ἔργον αὐτοῦ ἔσται. ἐγώ εἰμι τὸ Α καὶ τὸ Ω, ἀρχὴ
as the work of him   is.   I   am the Alpha and the Omega the Head

14   καὶ τέλος, ὁ πρῶτος καὶ ὁ ἔσχατος. μακάριοι οἱ ποιουντες
and End, the First and the Last.   Blessed (are) those doing

τὰς ἐντολὰς αὐτοῦ. ἵνα ἔσται ἡ ἐξουσία αὐτῶν ἐπὶ τὸ ξύλον
the commands of Him, that will be the authority of them over the tree

τῆς ζωῆς, καὶ τοῖς πυλῶσιν εἰσέλθωσιν εἰς τὴν πόλιν.
of life, and by the gates they may enter into the city

15   ἔξω δὲ οἱ κύνες καὶ οἱ φαρμακοὶ καὶ οἱ πόρνοι καὶ οἱ φονεῖς
outside But the dogs and the sorcerers, and the fornicators and the murderers

καὶ οἱ εἰδωλολάτραι, καὶ πᾶς ὁ φιλῶν καὶ ποιῶν ψεῦδος.
and the idolaters, and everyone loving and making a lie.

16   Ἐγὼ Ἰησοῦς ἔπεμψα τὸν ἄγγελόν μου μαρτυρῆσαι
I, Jesus, sent the angel of Me to witness

ὑμῖν ταῦτα ἐπὶ ταῖς ἐκκλησίαις. ἐγώ εἰμι ἡ ῥίζα καὶ τὸ γένος
to you these things over the churches. I am the root and the offspring

τοῦ Δαβίδ, ὁ ἀστὴρ ὁ λαμπρὸς καὶ ὀρθρινός.
of David, the Star bright and morning.

17   Καὶ τὸ Πνεῦμα καὶ ἡ νύμφη λέγουσιν, Ἐλθέ. καὶ ὁ ἀκούων
And the Spirit and the bride say, Come! And he hearing,

εἰπάτω, Ἐλθέ. καὶ ὁ διψῶν ἐλθέτω· καὶ ὁ θέλων λαμβανέτω
let him say, Come! And he thirsting let come; and he willing, let him take

τὸ ὕδωρ ζωῆς δωρεάν.
of the water of life freely.

18   Συμμαρτυροῦμαι γὰρ παντὶ ἀκούοντι τοὺς λόγους τῆς
I testify together For everyone hearing the words of the

προφητείας τοῦ βιβλίου τούτου, Ἐάν τις ἐπιτιθῇ πρὸς
prophecy of Scroll this, If anyone add to

ταῦτα, ἐπιθήσει ὁ Θεὸς ἐπ' αὐτὸν τὰς πληγὰς τὰς γεγραμ-
these things, will add God upon him the plagues having been

19   μένας ἐν βιβλίῳ τούτῳ· καὶ ἐάν τις ἀφαιρῇ ἀπὸ τῶν λόγων
written in Scroll this; and if anyone take away from the words

βίβλου τῆς προφητείας ταύτης, ἀφαιρήσει ὁ Θεὸς τὸ μέρος
of (the) Scroll of prophecy this, will take away God the part

αὐτοῦ ἀπὸ βίβλου τῆς ζωῆς, καὶ ἐκ τῆς πόλεως τῆς ἁγίας,
of him from (the) Scroll of Life, and out of the city holy,

καὶ τῶν γεγραμμένων ἐν βιβλίῳ τούτῳ.
and of the things having been written in Scroll this.

20   Λέγει ὁ μαρτυρῶν ταῦτα, Ναί, ἔρχομαι ταχύ. ἀμήν. Ναί,
says The (One) testifying these things, Yes, I am coming quickly. Amen. Yes,

21   ἔρχου, Κύριε Ἰησοῦ. Ἡ χάρις τοῦ Κυρίου ἡμῶν Ἰησοῦ
come, Lord Jesus. The grace of the Lord of us Jesus

Χριστοῦ μετὰ πάντων ὑμῶν. ἀμήν.
Christ, (be) with all of you. Amen.

# THE MAJORITY TEXT NOTES
## AND HOW TO USE THEM

If the foregoing Received Text is modified by the following notes, it will then be in the closest possible agreement with the vast majority of all manuscripts.

These notes have purposely been kept very brief, yet clear. At first sight they may appear cryptic, but by observing the following rules they will be easy to use.

Certain variations are of no importance, and will not be noted: movable -ν and -ς in οὕτω-ς . Further, certain changes oc- cur frequently and involve the following proper names:

Ναζαρέθ ΤΟ -ρέτ — ΜΤ. 2.23, 4.13, 21.11, ΜΚ. 1.9, LU. 1.26, 2.4,39,51, 4.16, JN. 1.45,46, ACTS 10.38

'Ηλίας ΤΟ, 'Ηλ-, 'Ησαΐας ΤΟ 'Ησ- , 'Ιεριχω ΤΟ 'Ιερ- (which only involve the breathing).

Three levels of Majority support are shown:

Level 3 — 95-100% of all manuscripts support the change— these are unmarked, and most changes are of this type.

Level 2 — 80-94% of all manuscripts support the change— a very strong majority, marked with equals sign (=).

Level 1 — 61-79% of all manuscripts support the change— a dis- tinct majority, but not so strong, marked by a hyphen (-).

These are the important changes and are given in the first list called "MAJORITY CHANGES", with the support marks, when indicated, before the verse number. A second list, called "ALTERNATES", contains those readings where the evidence is about evenly divided (40-60% support): here we cannot be certain which reading represents the original—but it must be one of the two.

After the chapter and verse reference, the "key" word or words appear. These identify the location of the change. If these words occur more than once in the verse, the following number shows which one it is. (E.g. καὶ3 means that it is the third καί. )

After the "key" word(s) the changed reading is given. This is very brief. A dash (—) means that the "key" word(s) is/are to be omitted. A plus sign (+) means that the words shown are to be added immediately after the "key" word(s).

If there are words without a plus sign, then these words replace the "key" word(s) completely. (i.e., they are substituted for them.) If there are numbers given (or numbers and words), this indicates a change in word order (and words, if shown). First number the "key" words, then arrange them in the new order. (If numbers are omitted the corresponding words are to be omitted.) E.g.

  1    2    3
σημεῖα καὶ δυνάμεις    3-2-1    Read:    δυνάμεις καὶ σημεῖα

Quite often the change affects only a part of the word. In this case it is often clearest just to show the changed part of the word, and repre- sent the rest of the word with a hyphen. E.g.

προελθόντες    προσελ-    Read:    προσελθόντες
κατασστήσομεν   -σομεν              κατασστήσομεν

# THE MAJORITY TEXT NOTES
## AND HOW TO USE THEM
### (Continued)

Occasionally the changed reading is itself sometimes found one way and sometimes another. Usually this involves spelling. This is indicated by a slash (/) between the readings. E.g. λιμό/λιμὸ ; similarly, —-/καὶ would mean about half omit it and the other half read as shown.

In the book of the Revelation the number sign (#) indicates that the reading of the Received Text has very weak manuscript support. This situation is shown only when the majority support is Level 1 (-); it plainly says that the change has much stronger majority status than the Level 1 indicates, and that the Received Text reading cannot in any way be sustained.

In a few instances more full instructions are given, or there is some clarification of the nature of the change. For example, the change involves only the breathing (BREATH.), or the accent (ACCENT), or the subscript (SUBSCR.).

Sometimes where a long phrase or clause or verse is involved as a whole it appears as the first few words, plus three dots, then the last few words. (Often a count of the words affected is given to help.) This symbolism is sometimes used where two or more changes go together in one verse. See, for example, James 4.13.

## MAJORITY CHANGES

### MATTHEW

| MATTHEW | | |
|---|---|---|
| 1. 6 | Σολομῶντα | -μῶνα |
| 3. 8 | καρπὸν ἄξιον | καρποὺς ἀξίους |
| 11 | καὶ πυρί | — |
| 4.10 | ὕπαγε | + ὀπίσω μου |
| 18 | ὁ Ἰησοῦς | — |
| 5.23 | κἀκεῖ | καὶ ἐκεῖ |
| 27 | τοῖς ἀρχαίοις | — |
| 28 | αὐτῆς | αὐτήν |
| 44 | τοὺς μισοῦντας | τοῖς μισοῦσιν |
| 45 | ἐν | + τοῖς |
| 47 | ἀδελφούς | φίλους |
| 6.18 | ἐν τῷ φανερῷ | — |
| 24 | μαμμωνᾷ | μαμω- |
| 7. 2 | ἀντιμετρηθήσεται | μετρηθή- |
| 14 | ὅτι | τί |
| 8. 4 | ἀλλά | ἀλλ' |
| 5 | τῷ Ἰησοῦ | αὐτῷ |
| 8 | λόγον | λόγῳ |
| 13 | ἑκατοντάρχῳ | -χῃ |
| 15 | αὐτοῖς | αὐτῷ 2 |
| 25 | αὐτοῦ | αὐτῷ |
| -9.5 | | |
| 13 | ἀλλά | ἀλλ' |
| 17 | ἀμφότερα | -τεροι |
| 36 | ἐκλελυμένοι | ἐσκυλμένοι |
| 10. 8 | νεκροὺς ἐγείρετε | — |
| 25 | Βεελζεβούβ | -βούλ |
| 28 | οἰκιακούς | οἰκεια- |
| 28 | φοβεῖσθε | φοβήθητε |
| 28 | ἀποκτεινόντων | -τεννόντων |
| 11. 8 | βασιλέων | βασιλείων |
| 16 | παιδαρίοις | παιδίοις |
| 12. 6 | μεῖζον | μείζων |
| 8 | καί | — |
| 21 | ἐν | — |
| = 28 | ἐγὼ ἐν Πνεύματι Θεοῦ | 2-3-4-1 |
| 32 | ἄν 1 | ἐάν |
| 32 | τούτῳ τῷ | τῷ νῦν |
| 35 | τῆς καρδίας | — |
| 35 | τά | — |
| 42 | Σολομῶντος TWICE | -μῶνος |
| 13.14 | ἐπ' | — |

| MATTHEW | | |
|---|---|---|
| -13,15 | ἰάσομαι | -σωμαι |
| 24 | σπείραντι | -ροντι |
| 27 | τά | — |
| 28 | συλλέξωμεν | -ξομεν |
| 30 | τῷ | — |
| 33 | ἐνέκρυψεν | ἔκρυψεν |
| 40 | κατακαίεται | καίεται |
| 14.14 | αὐτοῖς | αὐτούς |
| 19 | καὶ 2 | — |
| 22 | αὐτοῦ | — |
| 15 | σου | σοι |
| 25 | προσεκύνει | -κύνησεν |
| 32 | ἡμέρας | ἡμέραι |
| 16.12 | ἀλλά | ἀλλ' |
| 28 | τῶν | — |
| -17. 2 | ἐστηκότων | ἑστῶτες |
| 2 | ἐγένετο | -νοντο |
| 9 | ἀπό | ἐκ |
| 12 | ἀλλά | ἀλλ' |
| 14 | αὐτῷ 2 | αὐτόν |
| 27 | ἀναβάντα | βαίνοντα |
| 18. 4 | ταπεινώσῃ | -σει |
| 6 | ἐπί | εἰς |
| 12,13 | ἐννενηκονταεννέα | ἐνενήκοντα ἐννέα |
| 19 | πάλιν | + ἀμήν |
| 28 | ὃ ὀφείλεις μοι | εἴ |
| 29 | πάντα | — |
| 30 | ἀλλά | ἀλλ' |
| 31 | αὐτῶν | ἑαυτῶν |
| 19. 9 | εἰ | ἤ |
| 19 | σου | σοι |
| 26 | ἐστι 2 | — |
| 20. 2 | συμφωνήσας δέ | καὶ συμφ. |
| 3 | τήν | — |
| 4 | κἀκείνοις | καὶ ἐκείνοις |
| 21 | εὐωνύμων | + σου |
| 22 | καί | — |
| 26 | ἔσται | ἔστω |
| -21. 1 | Βηθφαγή | Βηθσφαγή |
| 3 | ἀποστελεῖ | -στέλλει |
| 7 | ἐπεκάθισαν | -σεν |
| 14 | τυφλοὶ καὶ χωλοί | 3-2-1 |
| 22 | ἄν | ἐάν |

### MATTHEW

| MATTHEW | | |
|---|---|---|
| 21.41 | ἐκδόσεται | ἐκδόσει |
| 22. 7 | ἀποδώσας δέ | καί - 1 |
| 7 | βασιλεύς | + ἐκεῖνος |
| 37 | εἶπεν | ἔφη |
| = 37 | τῇ 1...τῇ 2 | —...— |
| 39 | αὐτῇ | αὕτη (Note) |
| 23. 3 | ἄν | ἐάν |
| 13,14 | REVERSE ORDER OF VERSES: 14 - 13, AND TRANSFER δέ AFTER οὐαί FROM OLD 13 TO NEW 13. | |
| 21 | κατοικοῦντι | -κήσαντι |
| 25 | ἀκρασίας | ἀδικίας |
| 36 | ὑμῖν | + ὅτι |
| 36 | ταῦτα πάντα | 2 - 1 |
| 37 | ἀποκτείνουσα | -τένουσα |
| 24. 2 | μή 2 | — |
| 17 | τι | τά |
| 20 | ἐν | — |
| 27 | καὶ 2 | — |
| 33 | πάντα ταῦτα | 2 - 1 |
| 36 | τῆς 2 | — |
| 25. 1 | αὐτῶν | αὐτῶν BREATH. |
| 3 | ἑαυτῶν | αὐτῶν |
| 4 | ἑαυτῶν TWICE | αὐτῶν BREATH. |
| 30 | ἐκβάλετε | -βάλετε |
| 44 | αὐτῷ | — |
| 26. 4 | κρατήσωσι δόλῳ | 2 - 1 |
| 17 | ἑτοιμάσωμέν | -σομεν |
| 26 | εὐλογήσας | εὐχαριστήσας |
| 33 | καί | — |
| 35 | ἀπαρνήσομαι | -σωμαι |
| 35 | οὕτως | + δέ |
| 38 | αὐτοῖς | + ὁ Ἰησοῦς |
| 39 | προελθών | προσελ- |
| 52 | ἀπολοῦνται | ἀποθανοῦνται |
| 59 | αὐτὸν θανατώσωσι | 2 - 1 |
| 70 | ἔμπροσθεν | + αὐτῶν |
| 71 | τοῖς | αὐτοῖς |
| 74 | καταναθεματίζειν | καταδεμα- |
| 27.33 | ὅς | ὅ |
| 35 | ἵνα...κλῆρον | — 19 WORDS |

### MATTHEW

| MATTHEW | | |
|---|---|---|
| 27.41 | πρεσβυτέρων | + καὶ Φαρισαίων |
| 42 | πιστεύσομεν | + ἐπ' |
| 44 | αὐτῷ 2 | αὐτόν |
| 45 | ἕνάτης | ἐνάτης |
| 46 | ἕνάτην | ἐνάτην |
| 46 | λαμά | λιμά/λειμά |
| 28. 9 | ὁ | — |
| 10 | κἀκεῖ | καὶ ἐκεῖ |
| 19 | οὖν | — |

### MARK

| MARK | | |
|---|---|---|
| 1. 6 | δέ | + ὁ |
| 16 | αὐτοῦ | + τοῦ Σίμωνος |
| 27 | αὐτοῦς | ἑαυτούς |
| 37 | ζητοῦσί σε | 2 - 1 |
| 36 | κἀκεῖ | καὶ ἐκεῖ |
| 2. 1 | πάλιν εἰσῆλθεν | 2 - 1 |
| 8 | οὕτως | αὐτοί |
| 9 | σοι | σου |
| 26 | τοῦ 2 | — |
| 3.12 | αὐτὸν φανερόν | 2 - 1 |
| 27 | οὐ δύναται οὐδείς | οὐδεὶς δύναται |
| 27 | διαρπάσει | -σῃ |
| 32 | σου 2 | + καὶ αἱ ἀδελ-φαί σου |
| 4. 4 | τοῦ οὐρανοῦ | — |
| 8 | ἐν 3 TIMES | ἐν BREATH. ACC. |
| 20 | ἐν 3 TIMES | ἐν BREATH. ACC. |
| 31 | κόκκῳ | κόκκον |
| 33 | ἠδύναντο | ἐδύ- |
| 5. 3 | μνημείοις | μνήμασι |
| 3 | ἠδύνατο | ἐδύ- |
| 11 | τὰ ὄρη | τῷ ὄρει |
| 16 | καὶ διηγήσαντο | 2 - δέ |
| 19 | ἐποίησε | πεποίηκε |
| 26 | ἑαυτῆς | αὐτῆς |
| 38 | καὶ 3 | — |
| 40 | ἅπαντας | πάντας |
| 6. 2 | ὅτι | — |
| 9 | ἐνδύσασθαι | -σησθαι |

**MARK**

```
6.15  ἤ                        ---            τῇ
  17  τῇ                       ---            -τορα
  27  σπεκουλάτωρα             -τορα          εὐθ-
  31  ὑπκαίρουν               εὐθ-            ---
  33  οἱ ὄχλοι                 ---            ---
  37  διακοσίων δηναρίων       2-1
  44  ὡσεί                     ---            -δὲν
  46  'Ιεριχώ                 'Ραββουνί
  51  'Ραββουνί               Βηθσφαγή     'Ιερ- BREATH.
-11. 1  Βηθσφαγή              -στέλλει
    3  ἀποστελεῖ              + ὁ            ---
   18  ἀποδέσουσιν            αἰτῆσθε
   22  ἀποκριθεὶς             καὶ ἐγὼ        ---
   24  αἰτεῖσθε               -τένοντες
   29  κἀγὼ
   32  ἐάν
12. 5  ἀποκτείνοντες          -τένοντες
   20  οὖν                    τοῦ
   23  οὖν                    τῆς
   26  τῆς                    πασῶν          πάντων
   28  πασῶν                  πασῶν          πάντων
   29  πασῶν                  θεός
   33  τῶν 2                  εἶπεν
   36  τῷ 1...τῷ 2            λέγει          λέγει...
   36  εἶπεν                  βαλλόντων
   43  βαλλόντων              σταθήσεσθε     -ωντων
13. 9  σταθήσεσθε             -εσθε          -ωντων
   21  πιστεύσητε             -σεται
   31  παρελεύσονται          ---
   32  καὶ τῆς                ἐν ἐμοί
14. 6  εἰς ἐμέ                ἔσχεν
    8  ἔσχεν                  + δὲ           ---
    9  ἀμήν                   ἐάν
    9  ἄν                     γενή-
   25  γεννήματος             + σὸ
   30  ὅτι                    -αιμωσ-
   31  ἀπαρνήσομαι            προσελ-
   33  τόν 2                  προσελ-
   41  προσελθών              + αὐτῷ
   45  λέγει                  -οδήσειν
   51  ἠκολούθει              τό
   60  τὸ                     καθήμενον ἐκ δεξιῶν  2-3-1
   62  καθήμενον ἐκ δεξιῶν    + ἕνεκεν
```

**MARK**

```
14.71  ὀμνύειν              ὀμνύναι
   72  τοῦ ῥήματος οὗ       τὸ ῥῆμα 8
15. 3  αὐτὸς δὲ οὐδὲν       ἀπεκρίνατο      4 WORDS
   18  βασιλεῦ              ὁ βασιλεὺς
   24  διεμερίζον           διαμερίζονται
   31  δέ                   ---
   32  πιστεύσωμεν          + αὐτῷ
   33  ἐνάτης               ἐνάτῳ
   34  λαμμα                λιμα
   34  λαμα                 ---
-16. 1  ἡ τοῦ               ---
    8  ταχὺ                 ---
   19  διὰ 1                -φρ
   20  βλάψει               ---
   20  ἀμήν                 ---
```

**LUKE**

```
= 1.10  τοῦ λαοῦ ἦν        3-1-2
   35  ἐκ σοῦ               ὑπέ-
   36  ὑγήρᾳ                γήρει
   44  ἐν ἀγαλλιάσει        τὸ βρέφος       3-4-1-2
2.12  τῇ                    ---
   20  ἐπέστρεψαν           ὑπέ-
   21  τὸ παιδίον           αὐτόν
   22  αὐτῆς                αὐτῶν
   25  Συμεών               Συμ-
   25  "Αγιον ἦν            2-1
   34  Συμεών               Συμ-
   39  αὐτῶν                ἑαυτῶν
3. 2  ἐπ'ἀρχιερέων          ἐπὶ ἀρχιερέως
      τοῦ                   ---
   19  Φιλίππου             εὐδ-
   22  ηὐδόκησα             ---
   23  'ΗΛΙ                 'ΗΛΙ BREATH.
   27  'Ιωαννᾶ              'Ιωανάν
   30  Συμεών               Συμ-
   31  Μενάμ                Ματτάν
   33  'Αράμ                + τοῦ 'Ιωράμ
   35  Σαρούχ               Σερούχ
   35  Φαλέκ                Φαλέγ
   35  'Εβέρ                'Εβέρ BREATH.
- 4. 4  ὁ                   ---
```

**LUKE**

```
= 4. 7  μου                 ---            ἐμοῦ
    7  πάντα                ---            πᾶσα
    8  γάρ                  ---
    9  δ                    ---
   11  ὅτι                  ---
   18  ἔνεκεν               εἵνεκεν
   18  εὐαγγελίζεσθαι       -λίσασθαι
   29  τῆς 2                ---
   35  τὸ 2                 ---
   38  ἦν                   ---
   42  ἐζήτουν              ἐπεζή-         2-1
5. 6  ἰχθύων πλῆθος         ---
    8  τοῦ                  ---
   19  διὰ 2                ---
   29  δ                    ---
   30  μετὰ                 ---
   36  ἐπίβλημα 2           ---
6. 7  αὐτόν                 ἀποκτεῖναι
    9  ἀπολέσαι             αὐτῷ
   10  οὕτω                 ---
   23  χαίρετε              χάρητε
   26  ὑμῖν                 ---
   26  πάντες               ---
   28  καὶ                  ---
   34  τοῦ                  ---
   37  μὴ 1                 καὶ μὴ
7. 2  ἤμελλε                ἔμε-
    7  ἀλλὰ                 ἀλλ'
    9  οὐδὲ                 οὔτε
   11  τῷ                   τῷ
   12  ἦν... ἦν             ---
   16  ἅπαντας              πάντας
   24  πρὸς τοὺς ὄχλους     τοῖς ὄχλοις
   31  εἶπε δὲ ὁ Κύριος     ---            4 WORDS
   34  τελωνῶν φίλος        2-1
= 8. 3  αὐτῷ                αὐτοῖς
    8  ἐπὶ                  εἰς
   18  ἄν... δ              ἄν
   32  παρεκάλουν           -κάλει
   33  εἰσῆλθεν             -θον
   34  ἀπελθόντες           ---
```

## LUKE

|  | | |
|---|---|---|
| 8.43 | εἰς ἰατρὸς | ἰατρὸς |
| 51 | εἰσελθὼν | ἐλθὼν |
| 51 | 'Ἰάκωβον καὶ 'Ἰωάννην | 3-2-1 |
| = 9. 1 | μαθητὰς αὐτοῦ | — |
| 5 | ἄν | ἐάν |
| 9 | ὁ | -όν |
| 10 | Βηθσαϊδά | — |
| 13 | δύο ἰχθύες | 2-1 |
| 22 | ἐγερθῆναι | ἀναστῆναι |
| 23 | καθ' ἡμέραν | — |
| = 24 | ἐστηκότων | ἐστώτων |
| 27 | γεύσονται | -σωνται |
| 28 | τόν | — |
| 33 | ὁ BEFORE Πέτρος | — |
| 33 | Μωσεῖ μίαν | 2-1 |
| = 38 | ἐπιβλέψον | ἐπιβλέψαι |
| 40 | ἐκβάλωσιν | -βάλωσιν |
| 41 | ὧδε τὸν υἱόν σου | 2-3-4-1 |
| 49 | τά | — |
| 62 | πρὸς αὐτὸν ὁ 'Ἰησοῦς | 3-4-1-2 |
| 10. 2 | ἐκβάλῃ | -βάλῃ |
| 6 | μέν | — |
| = 8 | ὁ δ' ἄν | ἄν |
| = 12 | δέ | — |
| 13 | Χοραζίν | Ἰορ- |
| = 19 | ἀδικήσει | -σῃ |
| 20 | μᾶλλον | — |
| 22 | πάντα | καὶ στραφεὶς πρὸς τοὺς μαθη- τὰς εἶπε, πάντα |
| 22 | παρεδόθη μοι | 2-1 |
| 36 | δοκεῖ σοι πλησίον | 3-1-2 |
| 40 | κατέλιπε | -λειπε |
| 11. 6 | μου | — |
| 8 | δώσων | ἤ |
| 11 | εἰ | ἤ |
| 13 | ἀγαθὰ δόματα | 2-1 |
| 26 | εἰσελθόντα | ἐλθόντα |
| 33 | κρυπτόν | -τὴν |
| 44 | οἱ 2 | — |

## LUKE

|  | | |
|---|---|---|
| 11.54 | καί | — |
| 12. 4 | ἀποκτεινόντων | -τενούντων |
| = 15 | αὐτοῦ 1 | αὐτῷ |
| 36 | ἀναλύσει | -σῃ |
| 56 | τοῦ οὐρανοῦ καὶ τῆς γῆς | 4-5-3-1-2 |
| - 58 | βάλῃ | βάλῃ |
| 59 | τό | τόν |
| 13. 6 | καρπὸν ζητῶν | 2-1 |
| 15 | 'Ὑποκριτά | -ταί |
| 20 | καί | — |
| 29 | ἀπὸ 2 | — |
| 34 | ἀποκτείνουσα | -τένουσα |
| 35 | ἀμὴν δὲ λέγω | λέγω δὲ |
| 14. 5 | ὄνος | υἱός |
| 10 | ἀνάπεσον | -σε |
| 15 | ἄρτον | ἄριστον |
| 26 | ἑαυτοῦ | αὐτοῦ |
| 27 | μου εἶναι | 2-1 |
| 28 | ὑμῶν, | + δ |
| 32 | αὐτοῦ πόρρω | εἰς |
| 15. 4,7 | ἐνενηκονταεννέα | ἐνενήκοντα ἐννέα |
| 20 | ἑαυτοῦ | αὐτῷ |
| 8 | γενεάν | + τήν |
| 15 | ἐστιν | — |
| 22 | τοῦ | — |
| 25 | ὅδε | ὧδε |
| 26 | ἐντεῦθεν | ἔνθεν |
| 17. 4 | ἐπί σε | Ἔχετε |
| 6 | εἴχετε | -σε |
| 9 | ἀνάπεσαι | — |
| 10 | ὠφείλομεν | δφ- |
| 24 | καί | — |
| 26 | τοῦ 1 | — |
| 34 | ᾖ 1 | ἤ |
| 35 | ἦ | — |
| 36 | δύο ἔσονται... | WHOLE VERSE |
| =18. 5 | ὑπωπιάζῃ | ὑποπ- |
| 7 | ποιήσει | -σῃ |

## LUKE

|  | | |
|---|---|---|
| 18. 9 | καὶ 1 | — |
| 14 | ἤ | + γάρ |
| 28 | δ | — |
| -19. 4 | δι' | — |
| 7 | ἅπαντες | πάντες |
| 23 | τήν | — |
| = 35 | ἐπιρρίψαντες | ἐπιρί- τερεῖς |
| 20. 1 | ἀρχιερεῖς | — |
| 5 | οὖν | — |
| 9 | τις | — |
| 19 | τὸν λαόν | — |
| 31 | αὐτήν | + ὡσαύτως |
| 31 | καὶ 3 | — |
| 35 | ἐκγαμίσκονται | -μίζονται |
| 21. 2 | καὶ τινα | 2-1 |
| 12 | ἀπάντων | πάντων |
| 16 | ἀδελφῶν καὶ συγγενῶν καὶ φίλων | 3-4-5-2-1 |
| 22 | πληρωθῆναι | πλησθῆναι |
| 34 | βαρυνθῶσιν | βαρηνθῶσιν |
| 36 | ταῦτα | — |
| -22. 4 | τοῖς 2 | — |
| 9 | ἑτοιμάσωμεν | -σομεν |
| 18 | γεννήματος | γενή- |
| 30 | ἐν τῇ βασιλείᾳ μου | —4 WORDS |
| 30 | καθέσεσθε | -σεσθε |
| 32 | ἐκλείπῃ | -λίπῃ |
| 34 | φωνήσει | -σῃ |
| 35 | οὐδενός | οὐδενὸς |
| 36 | πωλησάτω... ἀγορασάτω | -ήσει...-άσει παρενεγκεῖν |
| 42 | παρένεγκε | — |
| 45 | αὐτοῦ | αὐτούς |
| 47 | αὐτῶν | — |
| 60 | ὁ 3 BEFORE ἀλέκτωρ | — |
| 66 | τε | — |
| 66 | ἑαυτῶν | αὐτῶν |
| 23. 1 | ἤγαγεν | -γον |
| 8 | ἐξ ἱκανοῦ ἰδεῖν αὐτόν | 3-4-1-2 |
| 18 | τόν | — |
| 25 | αὐτόν | — |

## LUKE

|  | | |
|---|---|---|
| 23.26 | τοῦ 1 | — |
| 44 | ἐνάτης | ἐνάτης |
| 54 | καὶ 2 | — |
| 55 | καὶ 1 | — |
| 24. 4 | δύο ἄνδρες | 2-1 |
| 18 | ἐν 1 | — |

## JOHN

|  | | |
|---|---|---|
| = 1.28 | Βηθαβαρᾷ | Βηθανίᾳ |
| 39 | δέ | — |
| 41 | Μεσσίαν | Μεσσίαν |
| 41 | ὁ BEFORE Χριστός | — |
| 42 | δέ | — |
| 43 | ὁ 'Ἰησοῦς | — |
| 48 | ὁ | — |
| 2. 1,11 | Κανᾷ | Κανᾶ SUBSCR. |
| 17 | κατέφαγέ | καταφάγεται |
| 19 | ὁ | — |
| 22 | αὐτοῖς | + τοῖς |
| 23 | ἐν 1 | αὐτόν |
| 3. 2 | τὸν 'Ἰησοῦν | — |
| 5 | ὁ 1 | — |
| 10 | ὁ 1 | — |
| 23 | Σαλείμ | Σαλήμ |
| 25 | 'Ἰουδαίων | -δαίου |
| 28 | μοι | — |
| 4. 3 | πάλιν | — |
| 13 | ὁ 1 | — |
| 15 | ἔρχωμαι | -χομαι |
| 20 | τούτῳ τῷ ὄρει | 2-3-1 |
| 25 | Μεσσίας | Μεσσίας |
| 35 | τετράμηνόν | -ός |
| 37 | ἐστὶν 1 | + ὁ |
| 46 | ὁ 'Ἰησοῦς πάλιν | 3-1-2 |
| 47 | ἤμελλε | ἔμ- |
| 50 | αὐτῷ 2 | + ὁ |
| 5. 7 | βάλῃ | βάλῃ |
| 8 | ἀγαλλιασθῆναι | -λιασθῆναι |
| 6.15 | πάλιν | — |
| 24 | καὶ 1 | — |
| 29 | ὁ | — |
| 32 | Μωσῆς | Μωϋσῆς |
| 39 | ἐν | — |

## JOHN

| ref | word | variant |
|---|---|---|
| 6.44 | αὐτόν 2 | + ἐν |
| 45 | τοῦ 1 | --- |
| 45 | ἀκούσας | ἀκούων |
| 70 | ὁ 'Ιησοῦς | --- |
| 71 | ἤμελλεν | ἐμ- |
| 7.12 | δέ | + οὖν |
| 16 | ἀπεκρίθη | --- |
| 21 | ὁ | --- |
| 29 | δέ | --- |
| 32 | οἱ Φαρισαῖοι καὶ οἱ ἀρχιερεῖς ὑπηρέτας | ἀρχιερεῖς καὶ οἱ Φαρισαῖοι ὑπηρέτας 6-1-2-3-4-5 |
| 33 | αὐτοῖς | --- |
| 39 | ὁ | --- |
| 41 | δέ | --- |
| 8.3 | ἐν 1 | ἐπί |
| 4 | ἐπαυτοφώρῳ | ἐπ'αὐτοφώρῳ |
| 5 | Μωσῆς ἡμῖν | ἡμῶν Μωσῆς 2-1 |
| 6 | κατηγορεῖν | κατηγορίαν κατ' |
| 9 | ἐστῶσα | οὖσα |
| 10 | 'Η γυνή | --- |
| 11 | καί | + ἀπὸ τὸ νῦν |
| 12 | ὁ 'Ιησοῦς αὐτοῖς | 3-1-2 |
| 12 | περιπατήσει | -σῃ |
| 19 | δ 2 | + οὖν |
| 42 | εἶπεν | + τοῦ |
| 44 | ἐκ 1 | --- |
| 52 | γεύσεται | -σηται |
| 54 | ὑμῶν | ἡμῶν |
| 9.3 | ὁ | --- |
| 15 | ἐπὶ τοὺς ὀφθαλμούς μου | 4-1-2-3 |
| 20 | ἀπεκρίθησαν | + δέ |
| 21 | αὐτοῦ | ἑαυτοῦ |
| 28 | οὖν | --- |
| 25 | εἶπε | + οὖν |
| 36 | ὁ | πρωτα |
| =10.8 | πρὸ ἐμοῦ | --- |
| 22 | τοῖς | --- |
| 23 | τοῦ Σολομῶντος Σολομῶνος | Σολομῶντος |
| 11.5 | ἀλλ' | ἀλλά |
| 20 | ὁ | --- |

## JOHN

| ref | word | variant |
|---|---|---|
| 11.21 | ἤ | --- |
| 28 | λάθρα | -ρᾳ SUBSCR. |
| 32 | εἰς τοὺς πόδας αὐτοῦ | 4-1-2-3 |
| 51 | ὁ δ | --- |
| 12.2 | συνανακειμένων | ἀνακειμένων σύν |
| 6 | ἀλλά | ἀλλ' |
| 12 | ὁ 2 | --- |
| 13 | δ 2 | --- |
| 30 | ὁ | --- |
| 33 | ἤμελλεν | --- |
| 34 | ὅτι | --- |
| =13.25 | ἐκεῖνος | οὕτως |
| 31 | οὖν | --- |
| 37 | ὅτι | --- |
| 38 | φωνήσει | -σῃ |
| 14.20 | κἀγώ | καὶ ἐγώ |
| 22 | Κύριε, | + καί |
| 23 | ὁ | --- |
| 30 | τούτου | --- |
| 15.6 | εἰς | εἰ |
| 16.7 | γάρ | --- |
| 15 | λήψεται | λήμψεται |
| 16 | ἐγώ | --- |
| 25 | ὑμῖν | ἐμ- |
| 33 | ἔξετε | --- |
| 17.11 | οὕς | ᾦ |
| 20 | πιστευσόντων | -ευόντων |
| 18.3 | ὁ | + καί |
| 8 | ὁ | + ὁ |
| 15 | καί | τῇ |
| 20 | οὖν | --- |
| 25 | ἠρνήσατο | --- |
| 28 | πρωῒ | πρωτα |
| 19.6 | σταύρωσον 2 | + αὐτόν |
| 7 | υἱὸν τοῦ θεοῦ | θεοῦ υἱόν |
| 11 | ὁ δ 1 | --- |
| 12 | αὐτὸν 2 | --- |
| 17 | ἀπήγαγον | --- |
| 17 | τόν BEFORE λεγ. τόπον | --- |

## JOHN

| ref | word | variant |
|---|---|---|
| 19.20 | τῆς πόλεως ὁ τόπος | 3=4-1-2 |
| 27 | αὐτήν ὁ μαθητής | 2-3-1 |
| 28 | εἰδώς | ἰδών |
| 31 | ἐπὶ Παρασκευή, ἦν | PUT THIS AFTER σαββάτῳ |
| 34 | εὐθέως | εὐθέως |
| 35 | αὐτοῦ ἔστιν | 2-1 |
| 36 | συντριβήσεται | + ἀπ' |
| 38 | δ 1 | --- |
| 38 | ὁ | --- |
| 39 | ὡς | + ἐν |
| 40 | αὐτό | --- |
| 20.14 | ὁ | --- |
| 15 | αὐτὸν ἔθηκας | 2-1 |
| 20 | δ 1 | --- |
| 29 | Θωμᾶ | --- |
| 31 | δ 1 | --- |
| 21.3 | ἀνέβησ.. | ἐνέβ- |

## ACTS

| ref | word | variant |
|---|---|---|
| 1.4 | μετ'αὐτῶν | --- |
| 18 | τοῦ | --- |
| 24 | ἐκ τούτων τῶν δύο ὅν ἕνα ἐξελέξω | 5-7-1-2-3-4-6 |
| 2.7 | πάντες 1 | --- |
| 3.1 | ἐνάτην | ἐνάτην |
| 13 | ὑμεῖς | --- |
| 20 | προκεχειρισμένον | + μέν προκεχειρ-ισμένον |
| 20 | 'Ιησοῦν Χριστόν | --- |
| 21 | πάντων 2 | + τῶν |
| 22 | ὑμῶν 1 | ἡμῶν |
| 23 | ἐν | ἐάν |
| 24 | προκατήγγειλαν | κατήγγειλαν |
| 25 | Καί 2 | + ἐν |
| 4.2 | τὴν ἐκ | τῶν |
| 7 | τῷ | --- |
| 12 | ὑπὸ τὸν οὐρανόν | --- |
| 15 | συνέβαλον | -βαλον |

## ACTS

| ref | word | variant |
|---|---|---|
| 17 | ἀπειλησόμεθα | -σόμεθα |
| 21 | κολάζωνται | -σονται |
| 25 | τοῦ | --- |
| 32 | οὐδ' | οὐδέ |
| 32 | αὐτῶ | αὐτῶν |
| 36 | ὑπὸ | ἀπό |
| 5.3 | νοσφίσασθαι | + σε |
| 5 | δέ | + ὁ |
| 23 | Ἔξω | --- |
| 25 | λέγων | --- |
| 29 | δ | --- |
| 33 | ἀκούσαντες | ἀκούοντες |
| 36 | προσεκολλήθη | προσεκλίθη |
| 38 | αὔτη | --- |
| 41 | αὐτοῦ | τοῦ 'Ιησοῦ |
| 6.3 | καταστήσομεν | -σωμεν |
| 5 | πλήρη | πλήρης |
| 13 | τούτου | --- |
| 7.5 | αὐτῷ δοῦναι | 2-1 |
| 7 | δουλεύσωσι | -ουσι |
| 14 | αὐτοῦ 2 | --- |
| 16 | Σιχέμ 1.2 | Συ- |
| 16 | 'Εμμόρ | 'Εμμόρ |
| 20 | αὐτοῦ | --- |
| 21 | αὐτὸν 2 | --- |
| 22 | ἐν 2 | --- |
| 26 | δέ | τε |
| 31 | ἐθαύμασε | -μαζε |
| 36 | Αἰγύπτου | -τω |
| 37 | ὑμῶν 1 | ἡμῶν |
| 37 | αὐτοῦ ἀκούσεσθε | --- |
| 38 | λόγια | λόγον |
| 39 | ταῖς καρδίαις | τῇ -δίᾳ |
| 58 | αὐτῶν | --- |
| 8.1 | τε | δέ |
| 10 | πάντες | 2-1 |
| 12 | τοῦ 3 | --- |
| 16 | Κυρίου | Χριστοῦ |

**ACTS**

| | | |
|---|---|---|
| 8.28 | αὐτοῦ | + καί |
| 37 | εἶπε...Χριστόν | --WHOLE VERSE |
| 9. 5,6 | σκληρόν...αὐτόν...--20 WORDS | |
| | | THEN + Ἀλλά |
| | | ἈΛΛΑ |
| 8 | ἐννεοί | ἐννεός |
| 8 | δὲ 2 | τε |
| 13 | δ | -- |
| 17 | Ἰησοῦς | -- |
| 18 | παραχρῆμα | -- |
| 21 | ἐλήλυθει | ἐλήλυθεν |
| 26 | εἰς | ἐν |
| 28 | καὶ ἐκπορευόμενος | -- |
| 28 | εἰς | εἰς |
| 35 | Σάρωνα | Ἀσσάρωνα |
| 36 | Ταβιθά | Ταβηθά |
| 38 | δύο ἄνδρας | -- |
| 40 | Ταβιθά | Ταβηθά |
| -10. 3 | ἐννάτην | ἐννάτην |
| 5 | ὃς ἐπικαλεῖται | τὸν ἐπικαλού- |
| | Πέτρος | μενον Πέτρον |
| 6 | οὗτος λαλήσει σοι τί σε | -- |
| | δεῖ ποιεῖν | δεῖ ποιεῖν |
| 19 | ἐνθυμουμένου | διενθυ- |
| 19 | τρεῖς | -- |
| 21 | τοὺς ἀπεσταλμένους ἀπὸ τοῦ | -- |
| | Κορνηλίου πρὸς αὐτόν | -- |
| 23 | τῆς | -- |
| 25 | ἐγένετο | + τοῦ |
| 30 | ἐννάτην | ἐννάτην |
| 39 | ὃν | καί |
| 11.26 | αὐτὸν 1 | -- |
| 26 | ἐν 1 | -- |
| 29 | ηὐπορεῖτό | εὐπ- |
| - | | + αἱ |
| 12. 3 | ἦν | 2-1 |
| -22 | θεοῦ φωνή | θεοῦ φωνή |
| 23 | τήν | -- |
| 25 | ἐξ | εἰς (* |
| 13. 2 | τε | -- |
| 4 | τε | δέ |
| 11 | τοῦ | -- |
| 17 | Ἰσραήλ | -- |
| 19 | κατεκληροδότησεν | -ρονόμησεν |
| -18. 2 | διατεταχέναι | τεταχέναι |

(* To properly understand 12.25 a comma should be placed before εἰς and the comma removed after Ἰερουσαλήμ.

**ACTS**

| | | |
|---|---|---|
| 13.23 | ἤγειρε | ἤγαγε |
| 23 | σωτῆρα Ἰησοῦν | σωτηρίαν |
| 24 | παντὶ τῷ λαῷ | -- |
| 29 | ἅπαντα | πάντα |
| 41 | ἔργον ᾧ | ὅ |
| 43 | αὐτοῖς | τε |
| 44 | δέ | -- |
| 48 | ἔχαιρον | -ρεν |
| 14. 3 | καί 1 | -- |
| 8 | περιεπεπάτηκει | περιεπα- |
| 9 | ἤκουε | ἤκουσε |
| 10 | ὀρθός | -θῶς |
| 17 | ἡμῖν | ὑμῖν |
| 15. 2 | συζητήσεως | ζητήσεως |
| 11 | χάριτος | + τοῦ |
| 11 | Χριστοῦ | -- |
| 21 | Μωσῆς | Μωϋσῆς |
| 22 | τῷ | -- |
| 32 | δέ | -- |
| 34 | ἔδοξε δὲ τῷ Σίλᾳ ἐπιμεῖναι | -- |
| | αὐτοῦ | -- |
| 16.12 | κολωνία | -νεία |
| 12 | ταύτῃ | αὐτῇ OR αὐτῃ |
| 34 | ἠγαλλιάσατο | -λιᾶτο |
| 37 | ἡμᾶς 3 | -- |
| 40 | εἰς | πρός |
| 17. 2 | διελέγετο | -λέξατο |
| 5 | ζηλώσαντες δὲ | προσλαβόμενοι |
| | οἱ ἀπειθοῦν- | δὲ οἱ Ἰουδαῖ- |
| | τες Ἰουδαῖοι | οι οἱ ἀπειθοῦ- |
| | καὶ προσλαβό- | ντες |
| | μενοι | -- |
| 7 | πράττουσι | πράσσουσι |
| 10 | τῶν Ἰουδαίων | Ἰουδαίων ἀπῇεσαν 3-1-2 |
| 18 | δέ 1 | + καί |
| 18 | Στωϊκῶν | Στο- |
| 18 | αὐτοῖς | -- |
| 25 | καὶ τά | κατά |
| 26 | προτεταγμένους | προστετ- |
| 27 | κατ'οὐγε | καίγε |

**ACTS**

| | | |
|---|---|---|
| 18.17 | Ἔμελεν | Ἐμέλλεν |
| 19 | κἀκείνους | καὶ ἐκείνους |
| 19,16 | καταχριζέσθαι | -σαν |
| 27 | Ἀρτέμιδος ἱερόν | 2-1 |
| 27 | τε | δέ |
| 29 | ὅλη | + τῆς |
| 29 | τοῦ | -- |
| 33 | προβαλόντων | -βαλόντων |
| 34 | ἐπιγνόντων | -όντες |
| 36 | πράττειν | πράσσειν |
| 37 | θεάν | θεόν |
| 38 | πρός τινα λόγον | Ἔχουσιν 4-1-2-3 |
| 40 | οὗ | + οὐ |
| 40 | ἀποδοῦναι | δοῦναι |
| -20. 5 | προελθόντες | προσελ- |
| 6 | ἄχρις | ἄχρι |
| 7 | τοῦ | -- |
| 13 | ἦσαν 2 | ἦμεν |
| 13 | προελθόντες | προσελ- |
| 21. | Χριστόν | -- |
| 26 | διό | διότι |
| 28 | τοῦ 1 | + Κυρίου καί |
| 34 | δέ | -- |
| 35 | διδόναι μᾶλλον | -νέντες 2-1 |
| 21. 3 | ἀναφάναντες | ἦλθον |
| 8 | ἤλθομεν | -- |
| 8 | τοῦ | -- |
| 11 | τάς χεῖρας καὶ τοὺς πόδας | 4-5-3-1-2 |
| | τε | -- |
| 13 | δέ | -- |
| 15 | ἀποσκευασάμενοι | ἐπισκευ- |
| 20 | εἶπόν τε | εἰπόντες |
| 21 | Μωσέως | Μωϋσέως |
| 25 | τοιοῦτον | -το |
| 29 | προεωρακότες | ἑωρακότες |
| 33 | τότε | + δέ |
| 33 | ἐγγίσας | -- |
| 37 | τι | -- |
| 40 | προσεφώνησε | -φώνει |
| 22. 7 | νῦν | νυνί |
| 20 | καί 4(LAST καί) | -σά |
| 22 | καθῆκον | -κεν |

**ACTS**

| | | |
|---|---|---|
| -22.23 | κραυγαζόντων | κραζ- |
| 23. 5 | ὅτι | -- |
| - 7 | καὶ τῶν Σαδδουκαίων | -- |
| 10 | καταβάν | καταβῆναι καί |
| 16 | τὴν ἐνέδραν | τό ἐνέδρον |
| 29 | δέ | -- |
| 35 | τοῦ | -- |
| =24. 6-8 | καὶ κατά...ἐπί σε | 27 WORDS |
| 9 | συνέθεντο | συνέθεντο |
| 11 | ἤ | ᾗ |
| 13 | παραστῆσαι | + με |
| 16 | ἔχων | ἔχων |
| 19 | ἔδει | δεῖ |
| 20 | εἰ | -- |
| 24 | αὐτοῦ 1 | -- |
| 26 | δέ | -- |
| -25. 7 | αἰτιώματα | αἰτιάματα |
| 13 | ἀσπασόμενοι | -σάμενοι |
| 20 | εἰς 1 | -- |
| 26. 2 | μέλλων ἀπολογεῖσθαι | 3-4-1-2 |
| 3 | ἐθῶν | ἠθῶν |
| 7 | τῶν | -- |
| 17 | νῦν | τοῦ |
| 18 | καί 1 | ὑπο- |
| 18 | ἀπήγγελλον | ἀπαγγέλλων |
| 21 | με οἱ Ἰουδαῖοι | 2-3-1 |
| 22 | μαρτυρούμενος | -ρόμενος |
| 22 | Μωσῆς | Μωϋσῆς |
| 25 | ἀλλ' | ἀλλά |
| 26 | ἐστιν | ἔστιν |
| 27.10 | φόρτου | φορτίου |
| 11 | ἑκατοντάρχος | -τάρχης |
| 17 | σύρτιν | -την |
| 23 | τῇ νυκτὶ ταύτῃ | 3-1-2 |
| 33 | ἔμελλεν | ἤμ- |
| 38 | δέ | -- |
| 39 | δύναντο | δυνατόν |
| 42 | διαφύγοι | -γῃ |

## ACTS

| Ref | Reading | Variant |
|---|---|---|
| -28. 3 | ἐξελθοῦσα | διεξελ- |
| — | ἀνήχθημεν | ῆχθημεν |
| — 16 | στρατοπεδάρχ | -χῳ |
| — 26 | εἰπέ | εἰπόν |
| — 27 | ἰάσωμαι | -σομαι |

## ROMANS

| Ref | Reading | Variant |
|---|---|---|
| 1.13 | καρπόν τινα | 2-1 |
| 27 | ἄρσενες | ἄρρ- |
| 2. 5 | ἀποκαλύψεως | + καί |
| 4. 4 | τό | -- |
| 12 | ἐν τῇ ἀκροβυσ- τίᾳ πίστεως | τῇ πίστεως 4- τῆς -1-2-3 |
| 7. 6 | ἀποθανόντος | -ντες |
| 23 | με | + ἐν |
| 8.10 | δι' | διά |
| 11 | τοῦ ἐνοικοῦν- τος αὐτοῦ Πνεύματος | τό ἐνοικοῦν αὐτοῦ Πνεῦμα |
| 26 | προσευξόμεθα | -ξώμεθα |
| 36 | ἕνεκα | ἕνεκεν |
| 9. 3 | ηὐχόμην | εὐχ- |
| 11 | τοῦ θεοῦ πρόθεσις | 3-1-2 |
| 11 | θεοῦ | τοῦ θεοῦ |
| 10. 5 | Μωσῆ | Μωϋσῆ |
| 10. 5 | Μωσῆς | Μωϋσῆς |
| 19 | Μωσῆς | Μωϋσῆς |
| 11. 7 | τούτου | τοῦτο |
| 19 | οἱ | -- |
| 21 | φείσεται | -σεται |
| -12. 2 | συσχηματίζεσθε... μεταμορφοῦσθε | -σθαι...-σθαι -σθαι |
| 13. 1 | ἀπό | ὑπό |
| 9 | οὐ ψευδομαρτυρήσεις | -- |
| 9 | ἑαυτόν- 2 | σεαυτόν 2 |
| 14. 4 | φρονεῖ- 2 | + καί |
| 14 | ἀνέξηρεν | ἔξηρεν |
| 14 | ἑαυτοῦ | αὐτοῦ |
| 22 | σαυτόν | σεαυτόν |
| 15. 2 | γάρ | + διά |
| 7 | ἡμᾶς | ὑμᾶς |

## ROMANS

| Ref | Reading | Variant |
|---|---|---|
| 15. 8 | Ἰησοῦν Χριστόν | 2-1 |
| 14 | ἀλλήλους | ἄλλους |
| 17 | πρός | + τόν |
| -16. 3 | Πρίσκιλλαν | Πρίσχαν |
| 11 | Ἡροδίωνα | Ἡρῳδ- |
| 20 | ἀμήν | -- |
| 25-27 | MOVE THESE THREE VERSES TO END OF CHAPTER 14. | |
| 27 | Χριστοῦ | + ᾧ |
| 27 | αἰῶνας | + τῶν αἰῶνων |

## 1 CORINTHIANS

| Ref | Reading | Variant |
|---|---|---|
| 1.29 | αὐτοῦ | τοῦ θεοῦ |
| 3. 1 | λαλῆσαι ὑμῖν | 2-1 |
| = 2 | ἠδύνασθε | ἐδύν- |
| 11 | ὁ | -- |
| = 14 | ἐπικοδόμησε | ἐποικο- |
| = 5. 7 | οὖν | -- |
| | ἐτέθη | ἐτόθη |
| 11 | νυνί | νῦν |
| 13 | κρίνει | κρίνει ACCENT |
| 6. 5 | ἔστιν | ἐνί |
| = | ἐν | -- |
| 10 | κλέπται οὔτε πλεονέκται | 3-2-1 |
| 11 | ἡμῶν | ὑμῶν |
| 16 | ᾖ | -- |
| 7.24 | τῷ | τῷ |
| 28 | ὅτι | -- |
| 34 | μεμέρισται | μεμέρισται |
| 39 | δέ | + καί |
| 39 | αὐτῆς 2 | αὐτῆς 2 |
| = 8. 5 | τῆς | τῆς |
| = 9. 9 | Μωσῆς | Μωϋσῆς |
| 9 | Μωσῆν | Μωϋσῆν |
| 10. 7 | ὡς | ὥσπερ |
| 30 | δέ | -- |
| =11.15 | αὐτῇ 2 | αὐτῇ 2 |
| 18 | τῷ | τῷ |
| 27 | ἀναξίως | ἀναξίως |
| 27 | καί | + τοῦ Κυρίου |
| 12. 2 | ὅτι | + ὅτε |
| 21 | δέ | + ὁ |
| = 25 | σχίσμα | σχίσματα |

## 1 CORINTHIANS

| Ref | Reading | Variant |
|---|---|---|
| 13. 9 | οὐδέν | οὐδέν |
| 9 | γάρ | δέ |
| -14. 5 | διερμηνεύῃ | -εύει |
| 7 | δῷ | διδῷ |
| 10 | οὐδέν | + αὐτῶν |
| 26 | γενέσθω | γιν- |
| 33 | ἀλλά | ἀλλά |
| 37 | τοῦ | -- |
| 15. 2 | εἰκῇ | εἰκῇ SUBSCR. |
| 23 | οἱ | + τοῦ |
| 33 | χρήσθ' | χρηστά |
| 39 | σάρξ 3 | -- |
| 49 | φορέσομεν | -σωμεν |

## 2 CORINTHIANS

| Ref | Reading | Variant |
|---|---|---|
| 1. 5 | διά | + τοῦ |
| 6,7 | PUT καί ἡ ἐλπίς ἡμῶν BEFORE βεβαία ὑπέρ ὑμῶν εἴτε παρακαλούμεθα... | |
| 11 | ἡμῶν 2 | ὑμῶν |
| 15 | πρός ὑμᾶς ἐλθεῖν | 3-1-2- τό |
| 2. 1 | ἐλθεῖν ἐν λύπῃ πρός ὑμᾶς | 2-3-4-5-1 |
| 5 | ἀλλ' | ἀλλά |
| 17 | πολλοί | λοιποί |
| 3. 1 | ἤ | εἰ |
| 3 | χάρδιας | -δίαις |
| 6 | ἀποκτείνει | ἀποκτενεῖ |
| 10 | οὐδέ | οὐ |
| 13 | Μωσῆς | Μωϋ- |
| 15 | Μωσῆς | Μωϋ- |
| 4. 2 | ἀλλ' | ἀλλά |
| 5.21 | γινώμεθα | γεν- |
| 6.15 | Βελίαλ | Βελίαρ |
| -7.11 | ἀλλά | ἀλλά |
| | ἐν 1 | -- |
| 12 | ἡμῶν ὑπέρ ὑμῶν | 3-2-1 |
| 13 | ἐπί | + δέ |
| 13 | δέ | -- |
| 16 | οὖν | -- |
| = 8. 4 | δέξασθαι ἡμᾶς | -- |

## 2 CORINTHIANS

| Ref | Reading | Variant |
|---|---|---|
| 8.19 | ὑμῶν | ἡμῶν |
| 24 | καί 2 | -- |
| 9. 5 | ὥσπερ | ὡς |
| 10 | γεννήματα | γενή- |
| 11.16 | μικρόν τι κἀγώ | 3-1-2 |
| 25 | ἐρραβδίσθην | ἐραβ- |
| 31 | ἡμῶν | -- |
| 12.14 | ἀλλ' 1 | ἀλλά |
| 21 | ταπεινώσῃ | -σει |
| 13. 4 | καί 3 | -- |

## GALATIANS

| Ref | Reading | Variant |
|---|---|---|
| 1. 4 | ὑπέρ | περί |
| 17 | ἀλλ' | ἀλλά |
| 2. 2 | μή πως | μήπως |
| 3. 8 | εὐλογηθήσονται | Ἐνευλ- |
| 4.11 | μή πως | μήπως |
| 24 | αἱ | ἐτέχ- |
| 5. 7 | ἀνέκοψε | ἐνέχ- |
| = 6.13 | περιτετμημένοι | περιτεμνόμενοι |

## EPHESIANS

| Ref | Reading | Variant |
|---|---|---|
| 1.10 | τε | ἐπί |
| 10 | ἐν 2 | -- |
| 12 | τῆς | -- |
| 18 | διανοίας | χαρδίας |
| 20 | ἐκ | + τῶν |
| 23 | τοῦ | + τά |
| 2.21 | ἤ | -- |
| 3. 5 | ἐν 1 | -- |
| 8 | τῶν | -- |
| 9 | κοινωνία | οἰκονομία |
| 4. 6 | ὑμῖν | ἡμῖν |
| 14 | μεθοδείαν | -δίαν |
| 27 | μήτε | μηδέ |
| 32 | ὑμῖν | ἡμῖν |
| 5.21 | θεοῦ | Χριστοῦ |
| 23 | ὁ | 3-2-1 |
| | δέ | + δέ |
| 6. 8 | δέ | -- |
| 17 | δέξασθε | -σθαι |
| 19 | δοθείη | δοθῇ |
| 24 | END | ἀμήν |

## PHILIPPIANS

| | Ref | Text | Variant |
|---|---|---|---|
| = | 1. 6 | 'Ιησοῦ Χριστοῦ | 2-1 |
| | 7 | καί 1 | + ἐν |
| | 23 | γάρ | δέ |
| = | 2. 1 | τινα | τις |
| | 21 | τοῦ | ἀλλά |
| | 27 | ἀλλ' | λόπην |
| | 27 | λόπην | θεοῦ |
| = | 3. 8 | θεῷ | μέν οὖνγε |
| | 8 | μενοῦνγε | οὖπω |
| | 13 | οὐ | ναί |
| = | 4. 3 | καί 1 | --- |
| = | 23 | ἡμῶν | --- |

## COLOSSIANS

| | Ref | Text | Variant |
|---|---|---|---|
| = | 1. 2 | Κολοσσαῖς | Κολασ- |
| | 14 | διά τοῦ αἵματος αὐτοῦ | ἐπί |
| | 20 | ἐν | --- |
| = | 2. 4 | "Ος | τί τό |
| | 24 | μου 1 | τίς ὁ |
| | 27 | τίς ὁ | + ὑμᾶς |
| = | 2.13 | συνεζωοποίησε | ἡμῖν |
| | 16 | ᾖ | καί |
| | 17 | τοῦ | --- |
| | 20 | οὖν | --- |
| = | 3.12 | οἰκτιρμῶν | --- |
| | 2C | τό | ἐν |
| | 24 | ἀπολήφεσθε | λήφεσθε |
| = | 4.16 | Λαοδικέων | -καίων |

## 1 THESSALONIANS

| | Ref | Text | Variant |
|---|---|---|---|
| = | 1. 8 | καί 1 | + ἐν τῷ |
| | 10 | ἐκ 2 | + τῶν |
| = | 2. 2 | καί 1 | --- |
| | 6 | ἀπ' | ἀπό |
| | 8 | ἱμειρόμενοι | -ρόμενοι |
| | 11 | μαρτυρούμενοι | -ρόμενοι |
| | 14 | ταῦτα | τά αὐτά |
| | 19 | Χριστοῦ | --- |
| = | 3. 3 | τῷ | τό |

## 1 THESSALONIANS

| | Ref | Text | Variant |
|---|---|---|---|
| = | 3. 5 | μή πως | μήπως |
| | 8 | στήκητε | -κετε |
| = | 4. 1 | τό 1 | --- |
| = | 6 | προεείπαμεν | -ποιμεν |
| | 8 | ἡμᾶς | ὑμᾶς |
| = | 13 | θέλω | θέλομεν |
| = | 5.21 | πάντα | + δέ |

## 2 THESSALONIANS

| | Ref | Text | Variant |
|---|---|---|---|
| = | 1. 8 | Χριστοῦ | --- |
| | 10 | πιστεύουσιν | -εύσασιν |
| | 12 | Χριστοῦ | --- |
| = | 2. 4 | πᾶν τό | πάντα |
| | 3. 6 | παρελάβε | -βον |

## 1 TIMOTHY

| | Ref | Text | Variant |
|---|---|---|---|
| = | 1. 2 | 'Ιησοῦ Χριστοῦ | 2-1 |
| | 4 | οἰκοδομίαν | οἰκονομίαν |
| | 9 | πατραλῴαις... | πατρολ- μητρολ- |
| | 13 | ἀλλ' | ἀλλά |
| = | 3. 2 | νηφάλιον | -λεον |
| | 11 | νηφαλίους | -λέους |
| = | 5. 4 | καλόν καί | -κάλον |
| | 21 | πρόσκλισιν | -κλησιν |
| | 25 | δύναται | δύνανται |
| = | 6. 5 | παραδιατριβαί | διαπαρατρ- |
| | 12 | καί 1 | --- |
| | 17 | πλουσίως πάντα | 2-1 |
| | 20 | παρακαταθήκην | παραθήκην |

## 2 TIMOTHY

| | Ref | Text | Variant |
|---|---|---|---|
| = | 1.14 | παρακαταθήκην | παραθήκην |
| | 15 | Φύγελος | Φύγελλος |
| | 16 | ἐπησχύνθη | ἐπαισ- |
| = | 2.19 | Χριστοῦ | Κυρίου |
| | 3. 6 | τά | --- |

## TITUS

| | Ref | Text | Variant |
|---|---|---|---|
| - | 2. 2 | νηφαλίους | -λέους |
| | 8 | ὑμῶν | ἡμῶν |
| | 3. 8 | τῷ | --- |

## PHILEMON

| | Ref | Text | Variant |
|---|---|---|---|
| | 6 | ὑμῖν | ἡμῖν |
| | 7 | χαράν | χάριν |
| | 12 | ὦδε 'Εστί | τουτέστι |
| = | 17 | ἐμέ 1 | με |

## HEBREWS

| | Ref | Text | Variant |
|---|---|---|---|
| - | 1. 1 | ἐσχάτων | -του |
| - | 2. 1 | μή ποτε | μήποτε |
| | 7 | καί κατέστησας αὐτόν ἐπί τά ἔργα τῶν χειρῶν σου | --- |
| | 14 | τοῦτ'Εστί | τουτέστι |
| 3. | 1 | Χριστόν 'Ιησοῦν | 2-1 |
| | 2,5 | Μωσῆν | Μωΰ- |
| | 12 | μή ποτε | μήποτε |
| | 13 | τις ἐξ ὑμῶν | 2-3-1 |
| | 16 | Μωσέως | Μωΰ- |
| 4. | 1 | μή ποτε | μήποτε |
| | 2 | συγκεκραμένος | -μένος |
| | 15 | πεπειρασμένον | -ραμένον |
| 5. | 4 | ...ὁ | --- |
| 6. | 3 | ποιήσομεν | -σωμεν |
| | 10 | ἐνδείξασθε | ἐνεδεί- |
| | 5 | τοῦτ'Εστί | τουτέστι |
| 7. | 14 | Μωσῆς | Μωΰ- |
| 8. | 5 | Μωσῆς | Μωΰ- |
| | 6 | ποιήσῃς | -σεις |
| | 11 | πλησίον | πολίτην |
| 9. | 6 | διά παντός | διαπαντός |
| | 11 | τοῦτ'Εστί | τουτέστιν |
| | 17 | μή ποτε | μήποτε |
| | 28 | οὕτως | + καί |
| 10. | 1 | δύναται | -νανται |
| | 10 | ἐσμέν | + οἱ |

## HEBREWS

| | Ref | Text | Variant |
|---|---|---|---|
| | 10.10 | τοῦ 2 | --- |
| | 20 | τοῦτ'Εστί | τουτέστι |
| | 22 | λελουσμένοι | λελουσμένοι |
| | 28 | Μωσέως | Μωΰ- |
| | 34 | ἐν 1 | --- |
| = | 11. 4 | λαλεῖ | λαλεῖται |
| | 9 | τήν | --- |
| | 12 | ὦσεί | ὡς ἡ |
| | 13 | καί πεισθέντες | --- |
| | 16 | νυνί | νῦν |
| | 16 | τοῦτ'Εστί | τουτέστι |
| | 23,24 | Μωσῆς | Μωΰ- |
| | 26 | ἐν Αἰγύπτου | Αἰγύπτου |
| = | 12. 2 | ἐκάθισεν | κεκάθικεν |
| - | 7 | εἰ | εἰς |
| | 7 | ἐστιν υἱός | 2-1 |
| | 20 | ἤ βολίδι κατατοξευθήσεται | --- |
| | 21 | Μωσῆς | Μωΰ- |
| | 24 | κρείττονα | κρεῖττον |
| | 24 | τό | τόν |
| | 25 | τῆς | --- |
| | 28 | λατρεύωμεν | -ομεν |
| 13. | 5 | ἐγκαταλίπω | -λείπω |
| | 6 | φοβηθήσομαι | + . PUNCT. |
| | 9 | περιφέρεσθε | παραφερ- |
| | 15 | διά παντός | διαπαντός |
| | 15 | τοῦτ'Εστί | τουτέστι |

## JAMES

| | Ref | Text | Variant |
|---|---|---|---|
| | 1. 5 | μή | οὐχ |
| | 13 | τοῦ | --- |
| | 26 | ἀλλ | ἀλλά |
| | 27 | τῷ | --- |
| | 2. 5 | τούτου | -σεις ... |
| | 11 | μοιχεύσῃς ... φονεύσῃς | -σεις ... ἀνέλεος |
| | 13 | ἀνέλεως | --- |
| | 13 | καί | --- |
| | 13 | Ἔλεος 2 | Ἔλεον |

**JAMES**

| 2.18 | χωρίς | ἐκ |
|---|---|---|
| 3. 3 | ἰδού | ἴδε |
| 4. 2 | δέ | --- |
| 7 | ἀντίστητε | + δέ |
| 12 | σύ | + δέ |
| 13 | ἤ | καί |
| 13 | πορευσόμεθα... | -σώμεθα ... |
| | ποιήσομεν... | -σωμεν ... |
| | ἐμπορευσόμεθα... | -σώμεθα |
| | κερδήσομεν | -σωμεν |
| - | ἔστιν | ἔσται |
| 14 | δέ | + καί |
| 15 | ζήσομεν... | -σωμεν ... |
| | ποιήσομεν | -σωμεν |
| - | αὐτῷ | αὐτόν |
| 7 | ἄν | |
| 5. 7 | αὐτῷ | . ...σωμεν ... |
| 9 | καταχθῆτε | κριθῆτε |
| 10 | τῆς κακοπαθείας, ἀδελφοί | |
| | μου | 3-4-1-2 |
| 11 | εἴδετε | ἴδετε |
| 11 | ὁ Κύριος | |
| 12 | ὑπὸ κρίσιν | εἰς ὑπόκρισιν |

**1 PETER**

| 1. 7 | καί 2 | + εἰς |
|---|---|---|
| 12 | ἰδόντες | εἰδότες |
| 12 | ἡμῖν | ὑμῖν |
| 16 | γένεσθε | γί- |
| 17 | ἀπροσωπολήπτως | -λήμπτως |
| 2. 6 | διὸ καί | διότι |
| 12 | ἐν τοῖς ἔθνεσιν ἔχοντες | |
| | καλήν | 4-5-1-2-3 |
| 14 | μέν | |
| 17 | ἀγαπᾶτε | ἀγαπήσατε |
| 21 | ἡμῖν | ὑμῖν |
| 3. 1 | κερδηθήσωνται | -σονται |
| 5 | τόν | |
| 7 | ἐκκόπτεσθαι | ἐγκόπ- |
| 12 | οἱ | |
| 18 | θέλει | θέλοι |
| 18 | ἡμᾶς | ὑμᾶς |
| 18 | τῷ 2 | |

**1 PETER**

| 3.20 | ἅπαξ ἐξεδέχετο | ἀπεξεδέχετο |
|---|---|---|
| 20 | τοῦτ'ἔστιν | τουτέστιν |
| 21 | ᾦ | ὅ |
| 21 | καί ἡμᾶς ἀντίτυπον νῦν | |
| 4. 3 | ἡμῖν | ὑμῖν |
| 8 | ἧ | --- |
| 11 | ὡς | --- |
| 19 | ἑαυτῶν | αὐτῶν |
| 5. 3 | μηδ' | μηδέ |
| 8 | ὅτι | --- |
| 10 | ἡμᾶς | ὑμᾶς |
| 10 | στηρίξει, | -ξει, |
| | σθενώσαι | -σει, |
| | θεμελιώσαι | -σει |

**2 PETER**

| 1. 1 | Σίμων | Συμεών |
|---|---|---|
| 1 | ἡμῶν 2 | |
| 4 | μέγιστα ἡμῖν καί τίμια | 4-2-3-1 |
| | | 2-1 |
| 2. 2 | ἀπωλείας | ἀσελγείας |
| 3 | νυστάζει | -άξει |
| 5 | τετηρημένους | τηρουμένους |
| 5 | ἀλλ' | ἀλλά |
| 9 | πειρασμῶν | -μοῦ |
| 14 | πλεονεξίαις | -ξίας |
| 15 | τήν | --- |
| 18 | ἐν 1 | --- |
| 3. 2 | ἡμῶν | ὑμῶν |
| 3 | αὐτῶν ἐπιθυμίας | 2-1 |
| 7 | αὐτῷ | αὐτοῦ |

**1 JOHN**

| 1. 4 | ὑμῶν | ἡμῶν |
|---|---|---|
| 5 | αὕτη ἐστίν | 2-1 |
| 2.23 | ὁ ὁμολογῶν τόν υἱόν καί τόν | |
| | πατέρα ἔχει | ὑμᾶς |
| 3. 1 | ἡμᾶς | ὑμᾶς |
| 15 | αὐτῷ | ἑαυτῷ |

**1 JOHN**

| 3.16 | τοῦ θεοῦ | --- |
|---|---|---|
| 18 | μηδέ | + τῇ |
| 18 | ἀλλ' | + ἐν |
| 23 | ἡμῖν | -εται |
| 4. 2 | γινώσκετε | -εται |
| 3 | τόν | + μένει |
| 16 | αὐτῷ | ὑμῶν |
| -5. 4 | ἡμῶν | |
| 6 2 | | |
| 7,8 | ἐν τῷ οὐρανῷ ...ἐν τῇ γῇ | |
| | 25 WORDS | |
| 10 | ἑαυτῷ | αὐτῷ |
| 13 | ἔχετε αἰώνιον | 2-1 |
| 13 | εἰς τό ὄνομα τοῦ υἱοῦ | |
| | τοῦ θεοῦ | |
| 15 | ἄν | ἐάν |
| 20 | ἤ | --- |
| 21 | ἑαυτούς | ἑαυτά |

**2 JOHN**

| 3 | ὑμῶν | ἡμῶν |
|---|---|---|
| 12 | ἠβουλήθην | ἐβου- |

**3 JOHN**

| 7 | αὐτοῦ | --- |
|---|---|---|
| 11 | δέ | --- |

**JUDE**

| 12 | ὑμῖν | --- |
|---|---|---|
| 12 | περιφερόμεναι | παραφερ- |
| 13 | τόν | |
| 14 | μυριάσιν ἁγίαις | 2-1 |
| 15 | ἐξελέγξαι | ἐλέγξαι |
| 19 | ἑαυτούς | --- |
| 23 | τοῦ | --- |
| 24 | ὑμᾶς | αὐτούς |

**REVELATION**

=1. 2 τε — 
- 4 τοῦ — θεοῦ/--
- 5 ἐκ — 
- 6 βασιλεῖς καὶ — βασιλείαν
- 8 A — Ἄλφα
- 8 ἀρχὴ καὶ τέλος — 
- 8 ὁ Κύριος — Κύριος ὁ θεός
- 9 καὶ 1 — 
- 9 συγκοινωνός — κοινωνός
- 9 ἐν τῇ 2 — 
- 9 Ἰησοῦ Χριστῷ — ἐν Χριστῷ Ἰησοῦ
- 10 ὀπίσω μου φωνὴν 3-1-2
- 11 Ἐγώ εἰμι τὸ Α καὶ τὸ Ω, ὁ πρῶτος καὶ ὁ ἔσχατος καὶ — 13 WORDS
- 11 ταῖς ἐν Ἀσίᾳ — 
- 12 καὶ 1 + ἔχει
- 12 ἐλάλησε — ἐλάλει
- 17 μου — 
- 18 ᾅδου καὶ τοῦ θανάτου 4-2-3-1
- 19 γράψον + οὖν

=2. 1 Ἐφεσίνης — ἐν Ἐφέσῳ
- 2 ἐπείρασω — ἐπείρασας
- 2 φάσκοντας εἶναι ἀποστόλους — λέγοντας ἑαυτοὺς -3-2
- 3 καὶ 3 — 
- 3 κεκοπίακας — οὐκ ἐκοπίασας
- 3 οὐ κέκμηκας + μου
- 7 θεοῦ — ἐν Ἐμβρυκῃ
- 8 ἐκκλησίας Σμυρναίων — ἐν Σμύρνῃ ἐκκλησίας
- 9 πλούσιος δέ — ἀλλὰ -1
- 10 ἐξ ὑμῶν ὁ διάβολος 3-4-1-2
- 13 καὶ 4 — 
- 13 κατοικεῖ ὁ Σατανᾶς 2-3-1
- 14 ἐδίδαξε — ἐδίδαξε
- 15 ὃ μισῶ — ὁμοίως
- 17 ἔγνω — ἔγνω
- 19 διακονίαν καὶ τὴν πίστιν 4-2-3-1
- 19 καὶ 2 — 

**REVELATION**

-2.20 ὀλίγα — 
- 20 ἑᾶς — ἀφεῖς
- 20 γυναῖκα + σου
- 20 Ἰεζαβήλ — -βέλ
- 20 τὴν λέγουσαν — ἣ λέγει
- 20 διδάσκειν καὶ πλανᾷ τοὺς — καὶ διδάσκει καὶ πλανᾷ τοὺς
- 20 πλανᾶσθαι — 
- 20 εἰδωλόθυτα φαγεῖν 2-1
- 21 ἐκ τῆς πορνείας αὐτῆς, καὶ οὐ μετενόησεν — καὶ οὐ θέλει μετανοῆσαι - 1-2-3-4
- 22 ἐγώ — αὐτῆς
- 22 αὐτῶν — τοῖς
- 24 καὶ 2 — 
- 24 βάθη — Βαθέα
- 24 βαλῶ — βάλλω
- 27 συντρίβεται — συντριβήσεται

=3. 1 τό — 
- 2 μέλλει — Ἔμελλες
- 2 ἀποθανεῖν — ἀποβαλλεῖν
- 2 θεοῦ + μου
- 4 Ἔχεις ὀλίγα — ἀλλ' -2-1
- 4 καὶ 1 — 
- 5 ἐξομολογήσομαι — ὁμολογήσω
- 7 κλείει — κλείσει αὐτήν
- 7 καὶ κλείει — εἰ μὴ ὁ ἀνοίγων
- 8 ἀνοίγει — ἀνοίξει
- 9 ἐγώ — ἦν
- 9 ἐγώ — 
- 11 ἰδοὺ — 
- 14 ἐκκλησίας Λαοδικέων ὀδικέων — ἐν Λαοδικείᾳ ἐκκλησίας
- 15 εἴης — ζῆς
- 16 οὔτε BEFORE ψυχρός — οὔτε
- 16 ψυχρὸς οὔτε ζεστός 3-2-1
- 17 ὅτι 2 + ὁ
- 17 καὶ 4 + καὶ
- 20 θύραν, 2 — ἀνεῳγ-
- 3 καὶ ὁ καθήμενος ἦν — -δίῳ
- 3 σαρδίνῳ — 
- 3 καὶ 2 — 

**REVELATION**

-4. 4 εἴκοσι — 
- 4 καὶ 4 — 
- 4 ἔσχον — ἔσχον
- 5 βρονταὶ καὶ φωναὶ 3-2-1
- 5 θρόνου 2 + αὐτοῦ
- 5 τά — 
- 6 θρόνου 1 + ὡς
- 7 πετώμενῳ — πετο-
- 8 ἑαυτὸ — ἔχον
- 8 ἔχον — ἐν
- 8 γέμοντα — γέμουσιν
- 9 λέγοντα — λέγοντες
- 9 δώσουσι — δῶσι
- 10 προσκυνοῦσι — -κυνήσουσι
- 10 βάλλουσι — βαλοῦσι
- 11 Κύριε — ὁ Κύριος καὶ ἡμῶν ὁ θεὸς ἡμῶν ὁ ἅγιος

=5. 1 ὄπισθεν — ἔξωθεν + ἐν
- 2 κηρύσσοντα 2-1
- 3 ἐστιν ἄξιος — ἔστιν ἄξιος
- 3 ἠδύνατο — ἐδύν-
- 4 οὐδὲ 3 — οὔτε
- 4 πολλά — πολύ
- 4 καὶ ἀναγνῶναι — 
- 5 ὤν — 
- 6 λῦσαι — καὶ ἰδοὺ
- 6 καὶ ἰδού — ἅ
- 6 οἵ — ὅ
- 6 τοῦ θεοῦ πνεύματα — 
- 6 τά? ἀπεσταλμένα — ἀποστελλόμενα 3-1-2
- 7 τὸ βιβλίον — 
- 10 ἡμᾶς — αὐτούς
- 10 βασιλεύσομεν — -σουσιν
- 11 ἤκουσα + ὡς
- 11 κυκλόθεν — κύκλῳ
- 13 ἐν τῇ γῇ — ἐπὶ τῆς γῆς
- 13 πάντα — πάντας
- 13 αἰῶνων + ἀμήν
- 14 εἰκοσιτέσσαρες — -σον
- 14 ἔπεσαν — ἔπεσαν
- 14 ζῶντι εἰς τοὺς αἰῶνας τῶν αἰώνων — 

**REVELATION**

-6. 1 ὅτε — ὅτι
- 1 τῶν 1 + ἑπτά
- 1 φωνῆς + φωνῇ
- 1 βλέπε — ἴδε
- 2 αὐτῷ — αὐτόν
- 3 καὶ βλέπε — αὐτόν
- 4 αὐτῷ 1 — ἐκ
- 4 ἀπό — 
- 4 καὶ 3 — 
- 5 τρίτην σφραγῖδα 2- τὴν - 1
- 5 καὶ βλέπε — καὶ ἴδε/ --
- 5 αὐτῷ — αὐτόν
- 5 φωνὴν — 
- 7 λέγουσαν — λέγοντος
- 7 καὶ βλέπε — καὶ ἴδε/--
- 8 ἀκολουθεῖ — ἠκολούθει
- 8 αὐτοῖς — αὐτῷ
- 8 ἀποκτεῖναι ἐπὶ τὸ τέταρτον τῆς γῆς 2-3-4-5-6-1 + τοῦ ἀρνίου
- 9 μαρτυρίαν — 
- 10 ἔκραξαν — Ἔκραξαν
- 10 ὃ 3 — 
- 10 ἀπό — ἐκ
- 11 ἐδόθησαν — ἐδόθη
- 11 ἑκάστοις — αὐτοῖς
- 11 στολαὶ λευκαὶ — στολὴ λευκή
- 11 μικρόν — 
- 11 πληρώσονται — πληρώσωσι
- 11 ἀποκτείνεσθαι — -τενεσθαι
- 12 ἰδοὺ — 
- 12 ἐγένετο μέλας 2-1
- 13 ἔπεσαν — -σον
- 13 μεγάλου ἀνέμου 2-1
- 14 καὶ 1 + ὁ
- 14 ἑλισσόμενον — ἑλισσόμενος
- 15 πλούσιοι καὶ οἱ — 
- 15 χιλίαρχοι — 
- 15 δυνατοί — ἰσχυροί

-7. 1 ταῦτα — τοῦτο
- 4 ρμδ' — ἑκατὸν καὶ τεσσαράκοντα τέσσαρες
- 5-8 ἐσφραγισμένοι OMIT ALL EXCEPT THE FIRST AND THE LAST = ἑκατὸν καὶ τεσσαράκοντα τέσσαρες

## REVELATION

| Ref | Reading | Variant |
|---|---|---|
| -7.5 | 'Ρουβήν | -βίμ |
| - 9 | αὐτόν | ἐδών- |
| - 9 | ἠδύνατο | -κας |
| - 9 | φοίνικες | κράζουσι |
| - 10 | κράζοντες | τῷ θρόνῳ |
| - 10 | τοῦ θρόνου | εἰστήκεισαν |
| - 11 | ἑστήκεισαν | τά πρόσωπα |
| - 11 | πρόσωπον | εἶπον |
| - 14 | εἴρηκα | + μου |
| - 14 | Κύριε | οὐδ'οὐ |
| - 16 | οὐδέ 2 | ἀνά μέσον |
| - 17 | ἀνά μέσον | ζωῆς |
| - 17 | ζώσας | ἐκ |
| - 17 | ἀπό | |
| -8.3 | τό θυσιαστήριον 1 | |
| - 5 | τό | τόν |
| - 5 | αὐτό | αὐτόν |
| - 7 | μεμιγμένα | + ἐν |
| - 7 | γῆν | + καί τό τρί-τον τῆς γῆς κατεκάη |
| - 8 | πυρί | -- |
| - 8 | τῶν 2 | + τῶν |
| - 9 | πηγάς | + ὁ |
| - 11 | λέγεται | ἐγένετο |
| - 11 | γίνεται | + τῶν |
| - 11 | πολλοί | ἀετοῦ |
| - 13 | ἀγγέλου | πετο- |
| - 13 | πετομένου | καιομένης |
| -9.2 | μεγάλης | οὐ μή |
| - 6 | μόνους | |
| - 6 | οὐχ | |
| - 5 | ὁ θάνατος ἀπ'αὐτῶν | 3-4-1-2 |
| - 7 | ὅμοιοι χρυσῷ | χρυσοῦ |
| - 10 | ἦν | καί # |
| - 11 | καί 3 | |
| - 11 | καί 1 | Ἔχουσιν ἐπ'αὐ- \| Ἔχουσι βασι- |
| - 11 | Ἔχουσιν ἐπ'αὐτῶν βασιλέα τόν | λέα ἐπ'αὐτῶν |
| - 11 | 'Αβαδδών | 'Αβαδδών |
| - 11 | καί ἐν | ἐν δέ |

## REVELATION

| Ref | Reading | Variant |
|---|---|---|
| -9.12 | Ἔρχονται | -χεται |
| - 14 | ὅς εἶχε | ὁ ἔχων |
| - 15 | καί 2 | + τήν |
| - 16 | ἀριθμός | + τῶν |
| - 16 | δύο | |
| - 16 | καί 2 | ἀπό |
| - 18 | ὑπό | |
| - 18 | τριῶν | + πληγῶν |
| - 18 | ἐκ 2...ἐκ 3 | ... ::: ... |
| - 19 | αὐτῶν 1 | τῶν ἵππων |
| - 20 | αὐτῶν 2 | + τά |
| -10. 1 | ἄλλον | + ἡ |
| - 1 | καί 2 | + αὐτοῦ |
| - 1 | κεφαλῆς | βιβλίον # |
| - 2 | βιβλαρίδιον | τῆς θαλάσσης |
| - 2 | τήν θάλασσαν | τῆς γῆς |
| - 2 | τάς φωνάς ἑαυτῶν | -- |
| - 4 | μοι | αὐτά # |
| - 4 | ταῦτα | + τήν δεξιάν |
| - 5 | αὐτοῦ | οὐκέτι -2 |
| - 6 | οὐκ ἔσται ἔτι | ἀλλά |
| - 7 | ἀλλά | τούς δούλους αὐτοῦ |
| - 7 | τοῖς ἑαυτοῦ δούλοις | τούς -τας |
| - 7 | τοῖς προφήτας | βιβλαρίδιον |
| - 8 | βιβλαρίδιον | ἀνε- |
| - 8 | ἡνεῳγμένον | + τοῦ |
| - 8 | χειρί | βιβλαρίδιον |
| - 9 | βιβλαρίδιον | βιβλαρίδιον # |
| - 10 | βιβλαρίδιον | + ἐπί |
| - 11 | καί 2 | -- |
| -11. 1 | καί ὁ ἄγγελος εἱστήκει | Κυρίου |
| - 4 | θεοῦ | θέλει |
| - 5 | θέλῃ 1 | θέλει -1 |
| - 5 | αὐτοὺς θέλῃ 2 | οὕτως |
| - 5 | οὕτως 3 | |
| - 5 | βρέχῃ δετός ἐν ἡμέραις αὐτῶν τῆς προφητείας | 2-1- τάς ἡ-μέρας -6-7-5 |
| - 6 | γῆν | + ἐν |
| - 7 | πόλεμον μετ'αὐτῶν | 2-3-1 |

## REVELATION

| Ref | Reading | Variant |
|---|---|---|
| -11. 8 | πλατείας | + τῆς |
| - 8 | ἡμῶν | αὐτῶν |
| - 9 | βλέψουσιν | βλέπουσιν |
| - 9 | καί 5 | |
| - 9 | μνήματα | μνῆμα |
| - 10 | χαροῦσιν | χαίρουσιν |
| - 11 | ἐπ' | -σα |
| - 12 | ἤκουσαν | -σα |
| - 13 | ὥρᾳ | ἡμέρᾳ |
| - 14 | καί | |
| - 14 | ἰδού, ἡ οὐαί | 2-3-4-5-1 # |
| - 15 | 'Εγένοντο αἱ βασιλεῖα | 'Εγένετο ἡ βασιλεία |
| - 16 | καί 2 | -σου |
| - 16 | ἔπεσαν | |
| - 17 | καί ὁ ἐρχόμενος | -- |
| -12. 2 | κράζει | ἔκραξεν |
| - 3 | διαδήματα ἑπτά | 2-1 |
| - 5 | καί 3 | + πρός |
| - 6 | ἔχει | + ἐκεῖ |
| - 7 | ἐπολέμησαν κατά | πολεμῆσαι μετά |
| - 8 | οὔτε | οὐδέ |
| - 8 | αὐτῶν | αὐτῷ |
| - 9 | BEFORE Σατανᾶς | -- |
| - 10 | λέγουσαν ἐν τῷ οὐρανῷ | 2-3-4-1 ἐβλήθη |
| - 10 | κατεβλήθη | -- |
| - 12 | τοῖς κατοικοῦσι | |
| - 12 | τήν γῆν ... τήν θάλασσαν | τῇ γῇ ... τῇ θαλάσσῃ |
| - 14 | ὅπου τρέφεται | ὅπως τρέφεται |
| - 15 | ὀπίσω τῆς γυναικός ἐκ τοῦ στόματος αὐτοῦ | |
| - 15 | ταύτην | αὐτήν |
| - 17 | τοῦ 3 | |
| - 17 | Χριστοῦ | |
| -13. 1 | κεφαλάς ἑπτά καί κέρατα δέκα | 4-5-3-1-2 |
| - 1 | ὄνομα | ὀνόματα |

## REVELATION

| Ref | Reading | Variant |
|---|---|---|
| -13. 2 | δράκοντος | δράκου |
| - 3 | εἶδον | |
| - 3 | μίαν | + ἐκ |
| - 3 | ὡς | ὡσεί |
| - 4 | τόν δράκοντα | τῷ δράκοντι |
| - 4 | ἔδωκεν | + τήν |
| - 4 | τό θηρίον | τῷ θηρίῳ # |
| - 5 | βλασφημίας | -μιῶν # |
| - 5 | ἐξουσία | + πόλεμον |
| - 6 | καί 3 | |
| - 7 | πόλεμον ποιῆσαι | 2-1 |
| - 7 | φυλήν | + καί λαόν |
| - 8 | τά ὀνόματα | τό ὄνομα |
| - 8 | τῷ βιβλίῳ | τό βιβλίῳ |
| - 8 | ἀρνίου | + τοῦ |
| - 10 | αἰχμαλωσίαν συνάγει | -- |
| - 10 | εἰς | |
| - 12 | κατοικοῦντας | ἐν αὐτῇ |
| - 14 | ἔχει | εἶχε |
| - 15 | δοῦναι πνεῦμα | 2-1 |
| - 15 | ἄν | ἐάν |
| - 15 | τήν εἰκόνα | τῇ εἰκόνι |
| - 15 | ἵνα 2 | |
| - 16 | δώσῃ | δώσωσιν/δῶσιν |
| - 17 | ἤ 2 | |
| - 18 | τόν 1 | |
| -14. 1 | τεσσαράκοντατέσσαρες TWO WORDS | |
| - 1 | ὄνομα | + αὐτοῦ καί τό ὄνομα |
| - 2 | φωνήν 4 | ἡ φωνή ἦν |
| - 3 | ἤκουσα 2 | + ὡς |
| - 3 | τεσσαράκοντατέσσαρες TWO WORDS | |
| - 4 | οὗτοι 3 | + ὑπό 'Ιησοῦ |
| - 5 | δόλος | ψεῦδος |
| - 5 | ἐνώπιον τοῦ θρόνου τοῦ θεοῦ | |
| - 6 | ἄλλον | πετο- |
| - 6 | πετόμενον | καθημένους |
| - 6 | κατοικοῦντας | |

REVELATION

| -14. | 6 | καὶ 2 | + ἐπὶ |
|---|---|---|---|
| | 7 | λέγοντα | λέγων |
| | 8 | ἄγγελος | δεύτερος ἄγγελος # |
| | 8 | ἡ πόλις | --- |
| | 8 | ὅτι | + τὰ |
| | 8 | πάντα | --- |
| | 9 | τρίτος ἄγγελος | ἄλλος -2-1 |
| | 9 | τὸ θηρίον προσκυνεῖ | 3-1-2 |
| | 11 | ἀναβαίνει εἰς αἰῶνας αἰώνων | 2-3-4-1 |
| | 12 | ὧδε 1 | + ἡ |
| | 13 | ἀπ' ἄρτι | ἀπάρτι |
| | 14 | καθήμενος | καθήμενον |
| | | ὅμοιος | ὁμοίον |
| | 15 | μεγάλῃ φωνῇ | 2-1 |
| | 15 | σοι | --- |
| | 19 | τὴν μεγάλην | τὸν μέγαν |
| | 20 | ἔξω | ἔξωθεν |

| -15. | 3 | Μωϋσέως | Μωῦ- # |
|---|---|---|---|
| | 3 | ἁγίων | ἐθνῶν |
| | 4 | δοῦος | ἅγιος |
| | 5 | ἰδοῦ | --- |
| | 6 | ἄγγελοι | + οἱ / + οἱ ἦσαν |
| | 6 | ναοῦ, | --- |
| | 6 | καὶ 2 | --- |

| -16. | 1 | τὰς | + ἐπὶ |
|---|---|---|---|
| | 2 | εἰς | ἑπτὰ |
| | 2 | τῇ εἰκόνι αὐτοῦ προσκυνοῦντας | 4-1-2-3 |
| | 3 | Κύριε | --- |
| | 3 | καὶ 3 | --- |
| | 5 | ἑσόμενος | δοῦος |
| | 6 | γάρ | --- |
| | 7 | ἄλλου | --- |
| | 7 | ἐκ | --- |
| | 9 | ἐβλασφήμησαν | + ἄνθρωποι |
| | 12 | τὸν 3 | --- |
| | 13 | ὅμοια βατράχοις | ὡς βάτραχοι |
| | 14 | τῆς γῆς καὶ | --- |

REVELATION

| -16. | 18 | φωναὶ καὶ βρονταὶ καὶ ἀστραπαί | + καὶ οἱ / 5-4-3-2-1 # |
|---|---|---|---|
| | 18 | οὗτω | οὗτως |

| -17. | 1 | μοι | --- |
|---|---|---|---|
| | 2 | ἐκ τοῦ οἴνου τῆς πορνείας αὐτῆς οἱ κατοικοῦντες τὴν γῆν | 7-8-9-10-1-2-3-4-5-6 |
| | 4 | πορφόρᾳ | -ραν/-ρουν |
| | 4 | κοκκίνῳ | κόκκινον |
| | 4 | καὶ 3 | --- |
| | 8 | ἀκαθάρτητος | τὰ ἀκάθαρτα τῆς |
| | 8 | βλέποντες | βλεπόντων |
| | 8 | ὅ,τι | ὅτι |
| | 8 | καθ́περ ἐστὶν ἑπτὰ | 3-1-2 |
| | 9 | ὄρη εἰσὶν | |
| | 10 | καὶ 2 | --- |
| | 13 | ἑαυτῶν | αὐτῶν |
| | 13 | διαδιδόασιν | διδόασιν |
| | 16 | ἐπὶ | καὶ |
| | 17 | μίαν γνώμην | 2-1 |
| | 17 | τὰ ῥήματα | οἱ λόγοι |

| -18. | 2 | ἰσχυρᾷ | ἰσχυρῷ |
|---|---|---|---|
| | 2 | μεγάλῃ 1 | --- |
| | 3 | πέπωκε | πέπτωκαν |
| | 4 | ἵνα μὴ λάβητε ἐκ τῶν πληγῶν αὐτῆς | 4-5-6-7-1-2-3 |
| | 7 | λέγει | + ὅτι |
| | 8 | κρίνων | κρίνας |
| | 9 | κλαύσονται | -σουσιν |
| | 9 | αὐτήν | --- |
| | 9 | αὐτῇ | --- |
| | 10 | ἐν | --- |
| | 12 | πορφόρας | πορφύρου |
| | 14 | ἀπῆλθεν 2 | -ρου |
| | 14 | εὐφόρας | ἀπώλετο # |
| | 17 | πᾶς 2 | εὐρὺς # |
| | 17 | ὁ ὅμιλος | + ὁ |
| | 18 | ὁρῶντες | βλέποντες |
| | 19 | πενθοῦντες, | + καὶ |
| | 19 | ἔχοντες | + τὰ |
| | 20 | αὐτήν | αὐτῇ |

REVELATION

| -18. | 20 | ἅγιοι | + καὶ οἱ |
|---|---|---|---|
| | 24 | καὶ | αἵματα |

| -19. | 1 | ἤκουσα | + ὡς |
|---|---|---|---|
| | 1 | λέγοντος | λεγόντων |
| | 1 | καὶ ἡ τιμὴ | --- |
| | 1 | κυρίῳ τῷ Θεῷ | τοῦ Θεοῦ |
| | 2 | ἔφθειρε | διέφθειρε |
| | 4 | καὶ 2 | --- |
| | 5 | Θεῷ | + ἡμῶν |
| | 8 | καθαρὸν καὶ λαμπρὸν | 3-2-1 # |
| | 8 | ἐστι τῶν ἁγίων | 2-3-1 |
| | 10 | τοῦ 1 | --- |
| | 12 | ὡς | --- |
| | 12 | ἔχων | + ὀνόματα γεγραμμένα καὶ |
| | 14 | ἐφ' | ἐπὶ |
| | 14 | καὶ 2 | --- |
| | 15 | ῥομφαία | + δίστομος, |
| | 15 | πατάσσῃ | πατάξῃ |
| | 15 | καὶ 4 | --- |
| | 17 | πετωμένοις | πετο- |
| | 17 | συνάγεσθε | συνάχθητε |
| | 17 | τοῦ μεγάλου | τὸ μέγα τοῦ # |
| | 20 | μετὰ τούτου | μετ' αὐτοῦ |
| | 21 | ἐκπορευομένη | ἐξελθούσῃ |

| -20. | 1 | κλεῖδα | κλεῖν |
|---|---|---|---|
| | 2 | Σατανᾶς | + ὁ πλανῶν τὴν οἰκουμένην ὅλην |
| | 3 | αὐτὸν 2 | πλανᾷ |
| | 3 | πλανήσῃ | 3-1-2 |
| | 4 | τὰ ἔθνη ἔτι | + τοῦ |
| | 4 | μετὰ | καὶ οἱ |
| | 5 | οἱ δὲ | δεύτερος |
| | 8 | θάνατος ὁ δεύτερος | θάνατος |
| | 8 | δεύτερος | + τὸν |
| | 9 | ἀπὸ τοῦ Θεοῦ ἐκ τοῦ οὐρανοῦ | 4-5-6-1-2-3 |
| | 10 | ὅπου | + καὶ |
| | 11 | αὐτοῦ | αὐτόν |

REVELATION

| -20. | 12 | μικροὺς καὶ μεγάλους. | τοὺς -3-2- / τοὺς -1 |
|---|---|---|---|
| | 12 | Θεοῦ | θρόνου |
| | 12 | βιβλίον ἄλλο | 2-1 |
| | 13 | ἐν αὐτῇ νεκροὺς | 3- τοὺς -1-2 |
| | 13 | ἐν αὐτῇ νεκρός | 3- τοὺς -1-2 # |
| | 14 | δεύτερος θάνατος | 2- δ -1 # |
| | 14 | θάνατος | +, ἡ λίμνη τοῦ πυρός. |

| 21. | 2 | ἐγώ Ἰωάννης | --- |
|---|---|---|---|
| | 2 | εἶδον τὴν πόλιν τὴν ἁγίαν, Ἱερουσαλὴμ καινὴν | 2-3-4-5-6-7-1 |
| | 3 | λαὸς | λαός |
| | 3 | Θεὸς αὐτῶν | --- |
| | 4 | ὁ Θεὸς | # |
| | 5 | τοῦ θρόνου | τῷ θρόνῳ |
| | 6 | Γέγονε | -να |
| | 6 | εἰμὶ | --- |
| | 6 | Α | "Αλφα |
| | 7 | πάντα | ταῦτα |
| | 7 | ὁ 2 | --- |
| | 8 | δειλοῖς δὲ | τοῖς -2-1 |
| | 8 | ἀπίστοις | + καὶ ἁμαρτωλοῖς |
| | 8 | φαρμακεῦσι | φαρμακοῖς |
| | 8 | ἐστι | + ὁ |
| | 8 | δεύτερος θάνατος | 2- δ -1 |
| | 9 | πρὸς με | --- |
| | 9 | τὴν νύμφην τοῦ ἀρνίου τὴν γυναῖκα | 5-6-1-2-3-4 |
| | 11 | καὶ | --- |
| | 12 | ἔχουσαν τε | -σα --- |
| | 12 | ἔχουσαν 2 | -σα |
| | 13 | ἀπ' | ἀπὸ |
| | 13 | ἀνατολῆς | -λῶν |
| | 13 | τρεῖς, 1 | + καὶ |
| | 13 | τρεῖς, 2 | + καὶ |
| | 14 | ἐν αὐτοῖς | ἐπ' αὐτῶν |
| | 14 | αὐτοῖς | + δώδεκα |
| | 15 | εἶχε | + μέτρον |
| | 16 | τοσοῦτόν ἐστιν | --- |

# ALTERNATES

## REVELATION

| | | |
|---|---|---|
| = | 21.16 καὶ 5 | — |
| - | 16 σταδίων | -δίους |
| - | 17 τεσσαρακοντατεσσάρων | TWO WORDS |
| ‖ | 18 ὁμοία | ὅμοιον |
| ‖ | 20 ἔνατος | ἔννατος |
| ‖ | 20 ἀμέθυστος | ἀμέθυσος |
| ‖ | 21 θάλος | βελ- |
| ‖ | 21 διαυγής | διαυγῆς |
| ‖ | 23 ἐν | — |
| ‖ | 24 τὰ ἔθνη τῶν σωζομένων ἐν τῷ φωτὶ αὐτῆς περιπατή-σουσι. | 9-1-2- διὰ τοῦ φωτὸς αὐτῆς |
| ‖ | 24 τὴν δόξαν καὶ τὴν τιμήν αὐτῶν | αὐτῷ -2-3-5- τῶν ἐθνῶν # |
| ‖ | 27 κοινοῦν | κοινόν |
| - | 22.1 καθαρὸν ποταμὸν | 2-1 # |
| - | 2 ἕνα | — |
| ‖ | 2 ἀποδιδοῦν | -δοῦς |
| ‖ | 3 καταανάθεμα | κατάθεμα |
| ‖ | 5 φωτίζει | φωτιεῖ |
| ‖ | 6 ἁγίων | πνευμάτων τῶν |
| - | 8 βλέπων ταῦτα καὶ ἀκούων | 4-3-1-2 # |
| - | 8 ἔπεσα | -σον |
| - | 9 γάρ | — |
| ‖ | 11 ῥυπῶν ῥυπωσάτω | ῥυπαρὸς ῥυπα-ρευθήτω |
| ‖ | 11 δικαιωθήτω | δικαιοσύνην ποιησάτω |
| - | 12 καὶ 1 | — |
| ‖ | 13 εἰμί | — |
| ‖ | 15 δέ | — |
| - | 16 τοῦ | — |
| ‖ | 16 καὶ ὀρθρινός | ὁ πρωϊνός |
| ‖ | 17 Ἐλθέ...Ἐλθέ | Ἔρχου TWICE |
| ‖ | 17 ἐλθέτω | ἐρχέσθω |

| | | |
|---|---|---|
| = | 22.17 καὶ 5 | — |
| = | 17 λαμβανέτω | λαβέτω |
| = | 17 τό | — |
| - | 18 συμμαρτυροῦ-μαι γάρ | μαρτυρῶ ἐγώ |
| | 18 παντί | + τῷ |
| - | 18 ἐπιτιθῇ | ἐπιθῇ |
| | 18 πρός | ἐπ' |
| | 18 ταῦτα | αὐτά |
| | 18 ἐν | + τῷ |
| | 19 ἀφαιρῇ | ἀφελῇ |
| | 19 βιβλίου 1 | τοῦ βιβλίου |
| | 19 ἀφαιρήσει | ἀφελοῖ/ἀφελεῖ |
| | 19 βιβλίου 2 | τοῦ ξύλου |
| | 19 καὶ 3 | — |
| | 19 ἐν | + τῷ |
| = | 21 ἡμῶν | τῶν ἁγίων |
| = | 21 ὑμῶν | — |

Note: In addition to the above changes in the Revelation, a few others found in the "Alternates" section ought also to be considered Majority changes; those marked with the number sign. Where they are also marked with a plus sign (+), the basis for change is even stronger.

## MATTHEW

| | |
|---|---|
| 5.39 σου | — |
| 9.27 υἱέ | υἱός |
| 10.28 καὶ 2...καὶ 3 | + τήν, + τό |
| 11.16 ἀγοραῖς | ἑτέροις |
| 16 Βηθσαϊδά | -δάν |
| 23 ὑψωθεῖσα | -θῆ |
| 13.3 σπείρειν | σπεῖραι |
| 15.39 ἀνέβη | ἐνέβη |
| 19.5 πατέρα | + αὐτοῦ |
| 5 προσκολληθήσεται | κολληθήσεται |
| 21.30 δευτέρῳ | ἑτέρῳ |
| 33 τις | — |
| 22.9 ἄν | ἐάν |
| 23 οἱ | — |
| 24.2 πάντα ταῦτα | 2-1 |
| 26.11 πάντοτε γὰρ τοὺς πτωχοὺς | 3-4-2-1 |
| 15 κἀγώ | καὶ ἐγώ |
| 33 ἐγώ | + δέ |

## MARK

| | |
|---|---|
| 1.10 ὡσεί | ὡς |
| 2.4,9,11,12 κράββατον | κράβαττον |
| 9,11 ἔγειραι | -ρε |
| 3.5 ἀποκατεστάθη | ἀπεκ- |
| 4.30 ὁμοιώσωμεν | -ομεν |
| 37 ἐπέβαλλεν | -βαλεν |
| 6.16 ὅ | — |
| 8.7 παραθεῖναι | -θῆναι |
| 25 ἐνέβλεψε | ἀνέβ- |
| 26 τόν | — |
| 9.4,5 Μωσεῖ | -σῇ |
| 38 ὅ | — |
| 45 σοι | σε |
| 11.4 τόν | — |
| 12.26 Μωσέως | Μωϋσέως |
| 13.21 καί | — |
| 14.3 τό | τόν |
| 12 ἑτοιμάσωμεν | -ομεν |

## MARK

| | |
|---|---|
| 14.15 ἀνώγαιον | ἀνάγαιον |
| 68 οὐδέ | οὔτε |
| 15.42 προσάββατον | πρὸς σάββατον |

## LUKE

| | |
|---|---|
| 1.15 τοῦ | — |
| 3.26 Σεμεΐ | Σεμεεί |
| 34 Θάρα | Θάρρα |
| 6.18 ὑπό | ἀπό |
| 27 ἀλλ' | ἀλλά |
| 7.6 ὑπὸ τὴν στέγην μου | 4-1-2-3 |
| 37 ἁμαρτωλός | + καί |
| 8.3 Σουσάννα | Σωσάννα |
| 9.33 Μωσεῖ | -σῇ |
| 55-56 καὶ εἶπεν, Οὐκ...ἀλλὰ σῶσαι | 20 WORDS |
| 57 ἐν | ἐάν |
| 11.32 Νινευΐ | Νινεύεται |
| 14.24 δείπνου | + πολλοὶ γάρ εἰ-σιν κλητοὶ ὀλίγοι δὲ ἐκλεκτοί |
| 19.15 καὶ 2 | — |
| 29 Βηθφαγῆ | Βηθσφαγῆ |
| 20.32 ὕστερον | + δέ |
| 37 Μωσῆς | Μωϋσῆς |
| 22.12 ἀνώγεον | ἀνάγαιον |
| 42 γενέσθω | γιν- |
| 24.1 βαθέος | -θέως |
| 10 Μαρία 2 | + ἡ |

## JOHN

| | |
|---|---|
| 1.29 ὁ Ἰωάννης | ὡς |
| 32 ὡσεί | ὡς |
| 43 αὐτῷ | + ὁ Ἰησοῦς |
| 3.36 ὄψεται | + τήν |
| 5.1 ἦν | + ἡ |
| 14 τί σοι | 2-1 |
| 46 Μωσῇ | -σεῖ |
| 6.10 ἀνέπεσον | -σαν |
| 39 αὐτό | αὐτόν |
| 54 αὐτόν | + ἐν |
| 58 ζήσεται | ζήσει |
| 7.53 ἐπορεύθη | ἀπῆλθεν |

ALTERNATES

## JOHN

| | | |
|---|---|---|
| 8. 1 | Ἰησοῦς δέ | καί -1 |
| 2 | παρεγένετο | ἦλθεν |
| 3 | πρὸς αὐτόν | -- |
| 3 | ἐν 2 | + τῷ |
| 4 | λέγουσιν | εἶπον |
| 4 | αὕτη ἡ γυνή | ταύτην εὕρομεν |
| | κατελήφθη | ἐπ᾽ αὐτοφώρῳ |
| | μοιχευομένη | μοιχευομένην |
| 5 | λιθοβολεῖσθαι | λιθάζειν |
| 5 | λέγεις | + περὶ αὐτῆς |
| 6 | μὴ προσποιούμενος | -- |
| 7 | ἀνακύψας | ἀνέκυψε καί/ ἀναβλέψας |
| 7 | πρὸς αὐτούς | αὐτοῖς |
| 7 | τὸν λίθον ἐπ᾽ | λίθον βαλέτω |
| | αὐτὴ βαλέτω | ἐπ᾽ αὐτήν |
| 3 | καὶ ὑπὸ τῆς συνειδήσεως | |
| | ἐλεγχόμενοι | -- |
| 9 | Ἰησοῦς | -- |
| 10 | καὶ μηδένα | -- / εἶδεν |
| | θεασάμενος | αὐτὴν καί |
| | πλὴν τῆς | |
| | γυναικός | |
| 10 | ἐκεῖνοι | -- |
| 39 | ἐν | -- |
| 9.10 | ἀνεῴχθησάν | ἤνε- |
| 29 | Μωϋσῇ | -σεῖ |
| 12.16 | δ | -- |
| 40 | ἰάσομαι | -σομαι |
| 14. 3 | καὶ ἑτοιμάσω | ἑτοιμάσαι |
| 14 | αἰτήσητε | + με |
| 15.16 | δῷ | δώῃ |
| 17.24 | ἔδωκάς | δέδωκάς |
| 18.37 | δ 2 | -- |
| 19.14 | ὡς | ὡσεί |
| 26 | ἰδού | ἴδε |
| 20.11 | τὸ μνημεῖον | τῷ μνημείῳ |
| 21. 1 | μαθηταῖς | + αὐτοῦ |

## ACTS

| | | |
|---|---|---|
| 2.37 | ποιήσομεν | -σωμεν |
| 3. 6 | ἔγειραι | -ρε |
| 4.16 | ποιήσομεν | -σωμεν |
| 7.27 | ἡμᾶς | ἡμῶν |
| 43 | Ῥεμφάν | Ῥεφάν |
| 9.33 | κραββάτῳ | -του |
| 13. 6 | Βαριησοῦς | -σοῦν |
| 25 | δ | -- |
| 27 | ἐν | -- |
| 42 | ταῦτα | -- |
| 16.17 | ἡμῖν 1 | -- |
| 18. 3 | τὴν τέχνην | τῷ Σίλᾳ / τῇ τέχνῃ |
| 21.21 | Μωϋσέως | Μωϋσέος |
| 22.25 | προέτειναν | -νεν |
| 23.15 | αὐτόν καταγάγ | 2-1 |
| 20 | μέλλοντες | -οντα |
| 25.14 | διέτριβον | -βεν |
| 26. 7 | ἐκτενείᾳ | ἐκτενείᾳ |

## ROMANS

| | | |
|---|---|---|
| 3.10 | ὅτι | -- |
| 5.14 | Μωϋσέως | Μωϋ- |
| 6. 1 | ἐπιμένωμεν | -μένομεν |

## 1 CORINTHIANS

--

## 2 CORINTHIANS

| | | |
|---|---|---|
| 5.14 | εἰ | ἕνεκεν |
| 7.12 | εἵνεκεν... | ἕνεκεν / ἀνεὶ χ- |
| 11. 4 | ἠνείχεσθε | ἀνείχ- |

## GALATIANS

| | | |
|---|---|---|
| 2. 9 | ἡμεῖς | + μέν |
| 5. 4 | ἐξεπέσατε | -σετε |

## EPHESIANS

--

## PHILIPPIANS

--

## COLOSSIANS

| | | |
|---|---|---|
| 1. 6 | καρποφορούμενον, | + καὶ αὐξανό-μενον |

## 1 THESSALONIANS

| | | |
|---|---|---|
| 5.10 | γρηγορῶμεν | -ροῦμεν |
| 5.21 | δοκιμάζετε | -μάζοντες |

## 2 THESSALONIANS

--

## 1 TIMOTHY

--

## 2 TIMOTHY

--

## TITUS

--

## PHILEMON

--

## HEBREWS

--

## JAMES

--

## 1 PETER

--

## 2 PETER

--

## 1 JOHN

--

## 2 JOHN

--

## 3 JOHN

--

## JUDE

--

## ALTERNATES

## REVELATION

Because the evidence here is more detailed, it is possible to show that some readings have stronger support than others in this 50-50 range. Those with 55 to 60% support are marked with the plus (+) sign.

| | | | |
|---|---|---|---|
| + | 1. 4 | ἐστιν | |
| + | 5 | ἀγαπήσαντι | ἀγαπῶντι |
| | 14 | ὡς | ὡς |
| | 16 | αὐτοῦ χειρί | 2-1 |
| | 17 | ἐπέθηκε | ἔθηκε |
| | 17 | χεῖρα | χεῖρα |
| + | 18 | κλεῖς | κλεῖδας |
| + | 19 | γενέσθαι | γενέσθαι |
| + | 20 | ἑπτὰ λυχνίαι | 2- αἱ -1 |
| | 20 | ἃς εἶδες | |
| | 2. 3 | ἐβάστασας καί | |
| | | ὑπομονὴν ἔχεις | 3-4-2-1 |
| + | 5 | ἐκπέπτωκας | πέπτωκας |
| | 7 | μέσῳ τοῦ | |
| | | παραδείσου | τῷ παραδείσῳ |
| + | 9 | βλασφημίαν | + ἐκ |
| + | | | παθεῖν |
| + | 10 | πάσχειν | |
| + | 10 | ἰδού, | + δή |
| + | 10 | ἡμερῶν | ἡμέρας |
| | 13 | ἐν 2 | |
| | 14 | ἀλλ᾽ | ἀλλά |
| + | 14 | Ἰσραήλ | + καί |
| | 16 | μετανόησον | + οὖν |
| | 17 | φαγεῖν | |
| | 17 | ἀπό | |
| | 20 | ἀλλ᾽ | ἀλλά |
| | 3. 2 | ὅτι | καί |
| | 2 | στήριξον | -σον |
| ● | 3 | καὶ ἤκουσας, | |
| | | καὶ τήρει | γνῶθι |
| | 7 | κλεῖδα | κλεῖν |
| | 12 | μου 5 | |
| + | 18 | παρ᾽ ἐμοῦ χρυσίον | 3-1-2 |
| + | 18 | κολλόβριον | κολλύριον |
| | 18 | κολλόβριον | + ἵνα |
| | 18 | ἐγχρῖσον | ἐγχρῖσαι |
| + | 19 | ζήλωσον | ζήλευε |

ALTERNATES

**Panel 1 — REVELATION (chs. 4–7)**

| | REVELATION | ALTERNATE |
|---|---|---|
| | 4.1 λέγουσα | λέγων |
| | 2 καί 1 | --- |
| + | 2 τοῦ θρόνου | τόν θρόνου |
| | 3 ὅμοια | ὅμοιος |
| | 3 σμαραγδίνῳ | -ων |
| | 7 τό | --- |
| + | 7 ὡς ἄνθρωπος | ἀνθρώπου |
| | 7 ζῷον 4 | --- |
| | 8 καί 1 | + τά |
| | 8 ἑαυτό | + αὐτῶν |
| | 8 ἅγιος 3 TIMES | 9 TIMES |
| | 11 τά | --- |
| | 11 εἰσί | ἦσαν |
| + | 5.3 οὐρανῷ | + ἄνω |
| | 3 οὐδέ 1 | οὔτε |
| | 3 οὐδέ 2 | οὔτε |
| | 4 δυνατάς | ὁ ἀνοίγων |
| | 6 κιθάρας | -ραν |
| | 8 αἱ 2 | --- |
| | 12 καί 1 | + τόν |
| | 13 ἐστιν 1 | --- |
| | 13 ἅ | --- |
| + | 13 αὐτοῖς | αὐτοῖς· PUNCT |
| | 14 λέγοντα | λέγοντα |
| | 14 ἔλεγον | + τό |
| + | 6.2 καί εἶδον | ἐν 1 |
| | 4 πυρός | πυρρός |
| | 5 καί εἶδον | ἐν 2 |
| | 8 καί εἶδον | ἐν 3 |
| | 8 μετ'αὐτοῦ | αὐτῷ |
| | 10 φωνῇ μεγάλῃ | φωνήν μεγάλην |
| + | 11 αὐτοῖς 2 | καί |
| | 11 σελήνη | + ὅλη |
| | 13 βάλλει | βάλουσα |
| | 15 πᾶς 2 | --- |
| | 16 τοῦ θρόνου | τῷ θρόνῳ |
| | 7 πᾶν | τι |
| + | 7.4 ἐσφραγισμένοι | -μένων |
| | 8 ἐσφραγισμένοι | -μέναι(IAST.) |
| | 8 φωνές | -τας |
| | 9 περιβεβλημένοι | -μένους |
| | 9 θρόνου 1 | + αὐτοῦ |
| | 11 αὐτάς | --- |

**Panel 2 — REVELATION (chs. 7–11)**

| | REVELATION | ALTERNATE |
|---|---|---|
| + | 7.15 τοῦ θρόνου | τῷ θρόνῳ |
| | 17 ποιμανεῖ | ποιμαίνει |
| | 17 ὁδηγήσει | -σει |
| | 8.3 ὁδότ | |
| | 5 φωναί καί βρονταί 3-2-1 | |
| | 12 ἡ ἡμέρα μή φαίνῃ τό τρίτον | 5-6-7-3-4-1-2 |
| | 12 φαίνῃ | φάνῃ |
| | 13 τοῖς κατοικοῦσιν | τούς -κοῦντας |
| + | 9.2 καί ἤνοιξε τό φρέαρ τῆς ἀβύσσου | τῆς φρέαρ τῆς |
| + | 10 ἡ ἐξουσία αὐτῶν | ἐξουσίαν ἔχουσι τοῦ |
| | 12-13 οὐαί | οὐαί. NEW SENTENCE. PERIOD. μετά ταῦτα... |
| | 14 λέγουσαν | λέγοντος |
| + | 15 καί 2 | εἰς (WOULD PRECEDE τήν) |
| | 16 ἱππικοῦ | ἵππου |
| | 18 ἐκ 1 | ἀπό |
| | 19 ὄφεσιν | ὄφεων |
| + | 20 καί τά χαλκᾶ | --- |
| | 20 δύναται | -νανται |
| | 21 φαρμακειῶν | φαρμακῶν |
| | 10.2 εἶχεν | ἔχων |
| + | 6 ἐν 1 | --- |
| | 7 τελεσθῇ | ἐτελέσθη |
| | 9 δός | δοῦναί |
| | 11 λέγει | λέγουσι |
| | 11.1 "Ἔγειραι | -ρε |
| + | 6 τεσσαράκοντα | |
| | 6 ἐξουσίαν κλεῖσαι τόν οὐρανόν | 3-4-1-2 |
| | 6 πάσῃ πληγῇ, ὁσάκις ἐάν θελήσωσι | 3-4-5- ἐν -1-2 |
| | 8 τά πτώματα | τό πτῶμα |
| | 8 τά πτώματα | τό πτῶμα |
| | 10 πέμψουσιν | δώσουσιν |
| | 11 τάς | --- |
| | 11 ἔπεσεν | ἐπέπεσεν |
| | 12 φωνήν μεγάλην | φωνῆς μεγάλης |
| | 12 ...λέγουσαν | ...λεγούσης |
| | 13 καί 2 | --- |
| + | 16 ἐνώπλιον | + τοῦ θρόνου |

**Panel 3 — REVELATION (chs. 11–14)**

| | REVELATION | ALTERNATE |
|---|---|---|
| | 11.16 καθήμενοι | οἱ κάθηνται |
| | 19 ἠνοίγη | ἠνοίχθη |
| + | 19 αὐτοῦ | τοῦ Κυρίου |
| | 19 καί σεισμός | --- |
| | 12.3 μέγας πυρρός | 2-1 |
| | 3 πυρρός | πυρός |
| | 6 ἀπό | ὑπό |
| + | 6 τρέφωσιν | ἐκτρέφ- |
| | 8 ἴσχυσαν | -σεν |
| | 12 οἱ 1 | --- |
| +13. | 4 ὅς ἔδωκεν | τῷ δεδωκότι |
| | 4 ἐπρίν; 2 | + καί |
| | 4 δύναται | αὐτόν |
| | 8 αὐτῷ | αὐτόν |
| + | 12 ποιεῖ 2 | -ποιεῖ |
| | 13 ἵνα καί πῦρ ποιῇ καταβαίνειν ἐκ τοῦ οὐρανοῦ | 2-3-1-6-7- # 8- καταβαίνῃ # |
| | 13 εἰς | ἐπί |
| | 14 πλανᾷ | + τούς ἐμούς |
| | 14 ἔσφαξε | + ἀπό τῆς μαχαίρας |
| | 16 χάραγμα | χαράγματα |
| | 16 τῶν μετώπων | τό μέτωπον |
| | 17 δύνηται | δύναται |
| | 18 καί | + ἔστι |
| | 18 ἰδού | + τό |
| +14. | 1 αὐτοῦ 1 | + ἀριθμός |
| | 3 ἡδύνατο | ἐδύν- |
| | 4 οἱ | ἐάν |
| | 5 ἐν τῷ στόματι αὐτῶν οὐχ εὑρέθη | 5-6-1-2-3-4 |
| | 7 Θεόν | Κύριον |
| | 7 τῷ ποιήσαντι | αὐτόν τόν ποιήσαντα |
| | 8 "Ἔπεσεν ἔπεσε | OMIT ONE |
| | 12 μοι | --- |
| | 13 ναί, λέγει | λέγει ναί |
| | 15 τοῦ 2 | --- |
| | 18 ἐφώνησε | + ἐν |
| + | 18 ἤκμασαν αἱ σταφυλαί αὐτῆς ἤκμασεν ἡ | σταφυλή τῆς γῆς |

**Panel 4 — REVELATION (chs. 14–17)**

| | REVELATION | ALTERNATE |
|---|---|---|
| | 14.19 Ἔβαλεν | ἐξέβαλεν ---# |
| +15. | 2 ἐκ τοῦ χαράγματος αὐτοῦ | + τάς |
| | 2 Ἔχοντας | πάντες |
| | 4 πάντα τά ἔθνη | |
| | 8 ναός | + ἐκ τοῦ ναοῦ |
| | 8 ἡδύνατο | ἐδύν- |
| 16. | 1 ἐκ τοῦ ναοῦ | --- |
| | 1 καί 2 | --- |
| | 2 ἐπί | εἰς |
| | 3 ζῷα | --- |
| | 4 ἄγγελος | --- |
| | 5 ὁ 3 | --- |
| | 8 τούς ἀνθρώπους | ἐν πυρί 3-4-1-2 |
| | 10 ἄγγελος | --- |
| | 10 ἐμασῶντο | ἐμασῶντο |
| | 12 ἄγγελος | --- |
| | 12 ἀνατολῶν | -λῆς |
| | 13 τρία ἀκάθαρτα | 2-1 |
| | 14 δαιμόνων | δαιμονίων |
| | 16 'Αρμαγεδών | 'Αρμαγεδδών / Μαγεδών # |
| | 17 ἄγγελος | --- |
| | 17 εἰς | ἐπί |
| | 18 ἐγένετο | --- |
| 17. | 3 ὀνομάτων | ὀνόματα |
| | 4 χρυσῷ | χρυσῷ |
| | 4 χρυσοῦ ποτήριον | 2-1 |
| | 4 ἀνατολῶν | τῆς γῆς |
| | 6 ἐκ 1 | --- |
| | 7 σοί ἐρῶ | 2-1 |
| | 8 ἐπί τῆς γῆς | τήν γῆν |
| | 8 τά ὀνόματα | τό ὄνομα |
| | 10 τό θηρίον ὅ,τι ἦν | 3-4-5-1-2 |
| | 10 ἑπτά εἰσίν | -σιν |
| | 10 ἔπεσαν | -σαν |
| | 10 αὐτῶν δεῖ | 2-1 |
| | 13 ὅστος | οὗτος 2-1 |
| | 13 γνώμην ἔχουσι | 2-1 |
| + | 16 γυμνήν | + ποιήσουσιν αὐτήν |

ALTERNATES

REVELATION

| | | |
|---|---|---|
| +22.18 | ἐπιθήσει | —θῆσαι |
| 18 | ὁ θεὸς ἐπ'αὐτόν | 3-4-1-2 |
| 18 | τάς 1 | + ἑπτά |
| 20 | 'Ιησοῦ | + Χριστέ |

- - -

ALTERNATES

REVELATION

| | | |
|---|---|---|
| 20. 4 | αὐτῶν 1 | --- |
| 4 | Χριστοῦ | + τά |
| 5 | ἀνέζησαν ἕως | ἔζησαν ἄχρι # |
| 7 | ὅταν τελεσθῇ | μετά |
| 8 | ἀριθμός | + αὐτῶν |
| 9 | ἐκύκλωσαν | ἐκπόλεμησαν |
| 12 | ἠνεῴχθησαν | ἤνοιξαν |
| 15 | τῷ βιβλίῳ | τῷ βιβλίῳ |
| +21. 2 | ἀπὸ τοῦ θεοῦ ἐκ τοῦ | |
| | οὐρανοῦ | 4-5-6-1-2-3 |
| 3 | Ἔσται μετ' αὐτῶν | 2-3-1 |
| 4 | ἀπῆλθον | -θεν |
| 5 | καινὰ πάντα | 2-1 # |
| 5 | ἀληθινὸς καὶ πιστός | 3-2-1 |
| 6 | ἐγώ | --- |
| 7 | κληρονομήσει | δώσω αὐτῷ |
| 9 | τάς 2 | --- |
| 11 | κρυσταλλίζοντι | κρυσταλλ- |
| 12 | ἐστι | + ὀνόματα |
| 12 | τῶν 2 | # |
| 15 | καὶ τὸ τεῖχος αὐτῆς | --- |
| 16 | χιλιάδων | + δώδεκα |
| 17 | ἐμέτρησε | --- |
| 18 | δάλφ | θέλῳ |
| 19 | καί | --- |
| 20 | σάρδιος | σάρδιον |
| 26 | αὐτήν | + ἵνα εἰσέλθωσι |
| 22. 2 | ἐντεῦθεν 2 | ἐκεῖθεν |
| 2 | ἕκαστον ἀποδιδοῦν | 2-1 |
| 3 | Ἔτι | ἔχει |
| 5 | εἶπε | λέγει |
| 7 | ἰδού | καὶ ἰδού |
| 8 | καὶ ἐγώ | κἀγώ |
| 8 | δεικνύοντός | -νύοντος |
| 10 | ὅτι | --- |
| 10 | καιρός | + γάρ |
| 12 | αὐτοῦ Ἔσται | 2-1 |
| 13 | A | Ἄλφα |
| 13 | ἀρχὴ καὶ τέλος, ὁ πρῶτος | 4-5-6-7-8- |
| | καὶ ὁ ἔσχατος | ↑ -1-2- τό -3 |
| 15 | ὁ | + |

REVELATION

| | | |
|---|---|---|
| +17.17 | τελεσθῇ | -θῆσαι # |
| 18. 1 | καί 1 | --- |
| 2 | ἐν | + |
| 2 | "Ἔπεσεν Ἔπεσε | --- |
| 2 | τοῦ οἴνου τοῦ θυμοῦ | OMIT ONE |
| | | 3-4-1-2 |
| 4 | ἐξέλθετε | Ἔξελθε |
| 4 | ἐμνημόνευσεν | + αὐτῆς |
| 6 | ποτηρίῳ | + αὐτῆς |
| 8 | ἑαυτήν | αὐτήν |
| 8 | καί 1 | --- |
| 11 | κλαίουσι | κλαύσουσι |
| 11 | πενθοῦσιν | πενθήσουσιν |
| 11-12 | οὐκέτι. | οὐκέτι |
| | | PUNCT. |
| 12 | βύσσου | βυσσίνου |
| 13 | κτήνη, καὶ πρόβατα | 3-2-1 |
| 13 | ῥεδῶν | ῥαιδῶν |
| 16 | ἐν χρυσῷ | χρυσίῳ |
| 17 | τῶν πλοίων | τόπον |
| 19. 1 | καί 1 | --- |
| 1 | ὄχλου πολλοῦ μεγάλην | 3-1-2 # |
| 1 | δόξα καὶ ἡ τιμὴ καὶ ἡ | 7-2-3-1 # |
| | δύναμις | -κεν |
| 2 | τῆς | --- |
| 3 | εἴρηκαν | -κεν |
| 4 | Ἔπεσαν | -σον |
| 4 | τοῦ θρόνου | τῷ θρόνῳ |
| 5 | ἐκ | ἀπό |
| 6 | λέγοντας | -τες |
| 9 | εἰσι τοῦ θεοῦ | 2-3-1 |
| 10 | Ἔπεσον | -σα |
| 14 | σα | --- |
| 17 | ἕνα | --- |
| 18 | μικρῶν | + τε |
| 20 | καί 2 | + ὁ |
| 20 | τῷ | --- |
| 20. 2 | καί 4 | + ὁ |
| 3 | αὐτὸν λυθῆναι | 2-1 |
| 4 | τῷ θηρίῳ | τὸ θηρίον |
| 4 | οὔτε | οὐδέ |